Maloney's
ANTIQUES &
COLLECTIBLES
RESOURCE
DIRECTORY — 4th Edition

Maloney's
ANTIQUES &
COLLECTIBLES
RESOURCE
DIRECTORY — 4th Edition

David J. Maloney, Jr., ISA CAPP

ANTIQUE TRADER BOOKS
Dubuque, Iowa

ISBN: 0-930625-87-0

ISSN: 1083-8449

Published by Antique Trader Books
A division of Landmark Specialty Publications, Norfolk, Virginia 23510-2075

To order additional copies of this book, or to obtain a complete Antique Trader Books catalog, please call: 1-800-334-7165

This book is lovingly dedicated to my Father & Mother

Dave & Jane Maloney

They raised seven children during a military career that spanned over 30 years. Dad served in three wars, and Mom in one. They now enjoy their retirement in the mountains of Blue Ridge Summit, Pennsylvania.

They were "Depression" kids. With strong, traditional values, they raised their children to believe in God, to love their family, to serve their country, and to be considerate and caring of others, particularly those less fortunate. My brother Brian put it best as he, I and my sisters, Kathy, Leah, Karen, Lisa and Tara, honored Mom and Dad on the occasion of their 50th wedding anniversary:

We enjoy prosperity,
   Though you suffered the Depression.
We have our freedom,
   Because you fought for it.

We know how to behave —
   You taught us right from wrong.
We know what commitment is,
   Because your's never wavered.

CONTENTS

ABOUT THE AUTHOR

David J. Maloney, Jr., ISA CAPP is a nationally known appraiser, author, radio talk-show guest, lecturer, and host of the Public Television's series, *Collecting Across America*. His reputation is based on 30 years of practical experience, extensive academic and personal study, teaching and lecturing. As a graduate of the U.S. Coast Guard Academy, he earned his BS in Engineering and, later, his Masters in Management. Following his career in the Coast Guard, Maloney operated an antiques business for several years prior to founding Frederick Appraisal, Claims & Estate Services.

He is now a full-time professional personal property appraiser specializing in the valuation of antiques, collectibles, residential contents, vehicles, and business equipment for several functions including insurance, probate, business valuation, divorce, and charitable contribution. Maloney also provides appraisal consulting services to bank trust departments, personal representatives, accountants, lawyers, estate planners, insurance agents, and the moving industry. In addition, he advises his clients on the best options available for disposing of antiques and collectibles.

Maloney is a Certified Member of the International Society of Appraisers and is currently Vice President of the ISA. He teaches ISA courses in appraisal principles and practice across the country, and he has been awarded ISA's coveted Member of the Year Award and President's Award for his efforts in developing the new and highly-acclaimed ISA educational program.

In addition to appraisals, Maloney provides damage claims and inspection services for major van lines operating in the Maryland, Washington DC, Virginia, and West Virginia area. He has served as a member of the Board of Directors of the moving industry's Claims Prevention and Procedure Council. Maloney has written and spoken extensively on the role of an appraiser in the claims process, and he is a contributing author of the California Household Goods Carriers Claims Training & Reference Manual.

Maloney resides with his family in Frederick, Maryland.

FOREWORD

Some twenty-five years ago when I first became Editor of *The Antique Trader Weekly* there was no special source of information relating specifically to collecting clubs and organizations, appraisal groups, important museums, auction houses and specialists in the huge field of antiques and collectibles. Over the next few years I developed my own crude file of such information that was of some help in my work and in helping collectors and dealers who'd write or call for assistance. Happily, six years ago I was able to discard the cumbersome file and fine nearly everything I, or anyone else in the collecting field, could possible need in a single, comprehensive volume, *Maloney's Antiques & Collectibles Resource Directory.*

What a pleasure it has become to be able to pick up a single compact book and quickly find references to nearly every collecting specialty from A to Z. Each volume has increased in volume and scope and is ever changing and improving. With this edition the most current material is provided with the names, addresses, phone numbers and comment lines for a myriad of resources. The newest edition Mr. Maloney has compiled here also includes a special new bonus — the inclusion of numerous e-mail and Internet website addresses. Since "surfing the web" has become a great source of information and entertainment for people in all fields, it is natural that the antiques and collectibles field must also step into the computer age. I hope collectors will never lose the joy of meeting and gathering "face-to-face" at conventions, shows and auctions, but between times, meeting on the Internet will certainly keep all of us abreast of trends and other important data about our special collecting interests.

Although his core listing of 1,750 collecting clubs and over 1,000 periodicals serves as a basis for this reference, there is a great deal more information made available here. General major collecting categories are arranged alphabetically with large topics such as CERAMICS further subdivided into sub-specialties. Extensive references to notable experts, collectors, dealers, reference books, appraisers, auction services, and museums/libraries are all to be found in the following pages. As an added bonus, Mr. Maloney has also cross-referenced many category headings to allow the reader to see which other sections may also have pertinent information. I'm sure that having an extensive computer database to draw from helps with this work, but it's still a tremendous undertaking. We can all be grateful that David Maloney had the courage and forethought to begin this Directory and the willingness to continue to expand and improve it.

At the conclusion of the main text, this book provides additional bonus Appendices that are also invaluable to all collectors, dealers and researchers. Extensive listings of qualified appraisers, auction services, general interest periodicals, and repair services are all included and arranged in Zip Code order so you'll be able to check at a glance which of these services is available in your immediate area.

For me the crowning glory of this reference is the extensive and thorough Index at the end of the listings. Nothing is more maddening for me than to have a reference book in hand that has no proper Index of its contents. A Table of Contents is fine, but to really get at specific information quickly, an good index is an absolute necessity. Fortunately, *Maloney's Antiques & Collectibles Resource Directory* recognized this fact and offers a thorough index that saves you hours of flipping through pages.

So, for all you collectors, dealers, researchers, auctioneers, appraisers, adjusters, and museum professionals, *Antique Trader Books and Price Guides* is proud to present the newest edition of David Maloney's master work. You are certain to find it an indispensable tool of your trade and, as in our office, you'll likely find it to be one of your most frequently used references.

Once again, we all owe a debt of gratitude to Mr. Maloney for his service to all those who are involved in the wide world of collecting and studying the vast field of antiques and collectibles. Keep your copy of *Maloney's Antiques & Collectibles Resource Directory* close at hand. You'll never be sorry you did.

Kyle Husfloen, Editor
The Antique Trader Weekly
The Antique Trader Antiques &
          Collectibles Price Guide
August 1997

INTRODUCTION

Welcome to the 4th edition of *Maloney's Antiques & Collectibles Resource Directory*. This massive compilation contains over 15,750 resources to assist you in the location, study and authentication, replacement, repair, valuation, or buying and selling of over 2,900 categories of art, antiques, collectibles and other types of personal property.

Since its debut six years ago, this book has been hailed as the "...best one-volume research tool in print" by the *Gannett News Service* and has been listed as a Best Reference Book by the *Library Journal*. *Kipplinger's Personal Finance Magazine* refers to *Maloney's* as "...the industry bible..." This book is a unique and comprehensive, all-in-one resource for hard-to-find information about the personal property you own. And now with more than 2000 new listings (many now with e-mail and Internet addresses) in scores of new categories, the 4th edition of *Maloney's* is better than ever!

Maloney's Antiques & Collectibles Resource Directory is a pioneer in gathering and disseminating information about antiques-related resources to the public. The information contained within this edition is based on a verification mailing sent to several thousand former and new listees. (Please note that a listing should not be considered an endorsement, and no guarantee of satisfactory service is made. Comments I receive regarding service will be weighed, however, in considering those to be included in future editions.)

Specialized resources contained within *Maloney's* include buyers, collectors, dealers, experts, appraisers, periodicals, suppliers of parts, reproduction sources, reference book sellers, manufacturers/distributors/producers, clubs, societies and associations, museums and libraries, centers for specialized research, matching services, repair/restoration/conservation specialists, vendors to the trade, Internet resources, and mail-bid and gallery auctions. Many other miscellaneous services ranging from free-lance writers and antique buying trips to collector computer software and bottle cleaning kits are also included.

In addition to thousands of new and updated listings and scores of new categories, the 4th edition of *Maloney's* includes the following important features:

- A greatly expanded **cross-referencing system**. Readers are directed to other relevant categories which might contain information of interest. No other publication has ever cross-referenced antiques and collectibles to this degree.

- Four important **appendices**:
  1. Educated and Tested ISA Appraisers
  2. Auction Services
  3. General Interest Periodicals
  4. Repair Firms

- A redesigned and highly-detailed **index**.

- Nearly 2,000 listings with Internet **websites** and 3,000 with **e-mail** addresses.

- Have a collectible marked with a Patent date? Check out the *U.S. Patent Number/ Date Reference Table* on page 651 to approximate its age.

The goal of this book is to place as much information as possible at the user's fingertips to allow him or her to make decisions based on knowledge and fact. Veteran dealers and collectors are well aware that knowledge and information are the keys to success in the world of antiques and collectibles. Unfortunately, such informational resources are minimal is scope, widely scattered and often short-lived or frequently changing. Heretofore there was no organized method to capture, preserve, collate, and distribute collector resource information to efficiently keep the public accurately informed on a continuing basis. *Maloney's* is designed to overcome this shortfall through frequent updating and regular publication.

My personal experience as an appraiser demonstrates quite dramatically that most of the non-collecting public is unaware of the value of many of its own possessions. Even when people do realize that their collectible items are valuable and/or of interest to others, they are often at a loss as to how to set a price or find a buyer (should they choose to sell) or to locate information to learn more about their collectible.

This directory is an ideal source for locating potential buyers. Individual buyers are listed as are associated clubs and periodicals which are themselves excellent sources of information about potential buyers. Further, new research, repair techniques, theft and fraud alerts, reproductions, and an ever-changing value structure, coupled with the specialized nature of many periodicals makes serial publications and collectors' clubs more important than ever as the primary source of current and topical news in all fields of antiques and collectibles. The periodicals, trade publications and collector clubs/associations listed in *Maloney's* disseminate a wealth of timely information that is of great importance to the collector and researcher. In addition, the listed auction services (often specializing in a narrow area of collector interest) provide alternatives to selling to an individual.

For appraisers, dealers, estate liquidators, repairers, attorneys, claims adjusters, and other professionals, *Maloney's Antiques & Collectibles Resource Directory* is the unrivaled source of information to aid in the authentication and valuation of antiques and collectibles, or to help with the successful resolution of a loss or damage claim. Experts found among dealers, collectors, clubs and specialized periodicals offer an unparalleled source of expertise to help in confirming bona fide claims or in disproving fraudulent ones.

Of special interest to the moving, claims, and repair industries, *Maloney's* lists suppliers of such items as replacement crystals for chandeliers, furniture hardware, curved glass, tools, lamp parts, upholstery and caning supplies, clock parts, refinishing supplies and other obscure and hard-to-find items such as bed rail extenders and icebox hardware. The directory lists matching services for silver, crystal, dinnerware ("china"), conservation and repair supply sources, specialized repair services and, through the dealer listings, replacement sources for just about anything antique or collectible. Also listed are computer programs for collectors and sources of supplies for the collector and dealer such as bubble wrap, Mylar sleeves, acid-free storage containers, and display cases.

Two important resource categories have been added to this 4th edition of *Maloney's Antiques & Collectibles Resource Directory*:

ENDANGERED SPECIES

The first is ENDANGERED SPECIES which provides much-needed Federal and state contact information for your questions regarding the prohibition against possessing or trading in certain endangered/threatened species of flora or fauna, or the parts thereof. (An *endangered species* is any animal or plant in danger of extinction and a *threatened species* is any plant or animal likely to become extinct within the foreseeable future.)

More and more species of threatened and endangered animals continue to decline in numbers because of the destruction of their natural habitat and increased commercial exploitation. Modern transportation now makes it possible to provide exotic pets, pelts and other wildlife parts and products to a steadily growing worldwide market.

Know the Federal, state, and international laws before buying, selling, or possessing products from such animals as sea turtles, whales, walruses, polar bears, crocodiles, parrots and macaws, mounted birds, elephant ivory, migratory birds, bald eagles, furs from most larger spotted cats, or jewelry made from precious and semiprecious corals. Here is an overview of the relevant Federal Acts that pertain to ENDANGERED SPECIES:

Endangered Species Act — prohibits the import, export, sale or purchase, offer to sell or purchase, or possession of species or parts of species listed as endangered and most species listed as threatened. Note that exempt from this Act are species (except African elephant ivory) held in captivity or in a controlled environment on December 28, 1973 provided any subsequent holding or use was not in the course of a commercial activity. Also exempt are "antiques" more than 100 years old that have not been repaired or modified since December 28, 1973 with any part of a listed species. In addition, Alaska natives may take or import endangered or threatened species if such taking is primarily for subsistence purposes and is not done in a wasteful manner. Non-edible by-products of taken species may subsequently be sold in interstate commerce when made into authentic native articles of handicrafts and clothing.

Marine Mammal Protection Act — prohibits the import, taking, possession, transport, purchase or sale, or the offer to purchase or sell marine mammals and their parts and products. These include whales, walruses, narwhals, seals, sea lions, sea otters, and polar bears. While this Act does not apply to specimens taken before December 21, 1972 and for Alaskan natives.

Migratory Bird Treaty Act — prohibits the taking, possessing, import, export, sale, offer to sell, purchase, offer to purchase, barter, or offer for barter of any migratory bird, or any migratory bird part, nest, egg, or product.

Bale Eagle Protection Act — prohibits the taking ("taking" includes pursue, shoot, shoot at, poison, wound, kill, capture, collect, molest, or disturb), possession, transport, import or export, purchase, sale, or barter of the bald or golden eagles, dead or alive, their parts, nests or eggs. Exemptions may be made for Indian religious purposes. Possession and transportation is permitted without a Federal permit for bald eagles lawfully acquired before June 8, 1940 and for golden eagles lawfully acquired before October 24, 1962. However, the above may not be sold, purchased, traded, bartered, or otherwise commercialized.

African Elephant Conservation Act — prohibits the import of raw and worked African elephant ivory from all ivory producing and intermediary nations, and prohibits all exports from the U.S. of raw ivory from African elephants. Permits the noncommercial import of whole tusks from elephants that have been legally hunted in certain African countries. Antiques more than 100 years old are exempted.

Wild Bird Conservation Act — regulates or prohibits the import of many exotic bird species.

Lacey Act — prohibits the import of animal species that have been taken, possessed, transported, or sold in violation of foreign law. Many countries completely ban or strictly limit wildlife trade.

CITES (Convention on International Trade in Endangered Species of Wild Fauna and Flora) — a comprehensive international wildlife treaty signed by over 115 countries, including the United States, that regulates, and in many cases prohibits imports and exports of wild animal and plant species that are threatened by trade.

HERITAGE RESOURCES

The second new category to *Maloney's* that warrants mentioning is HERITAGE RESOURCES which provides contacts for questions relating to the preservation and protection of America's "antiquities" and "archeological resources." The later are defined as any material remains of past human life that are at least 100 years of age and that are on tribal lands or Federal lands, and they include, but are not limited to, pottery, basketry, bottles, weapon projectiles, tools, structures or portions of structures, pit houses, rock paintings and carvings, intaglios, graves, gun parts, Civil War belt buckles, pipes, shipwrecks and cargo, buttons, beads, human skeletal materials, as well as the sites themselves. Heritage resources also include places and items of ongoing historical, traditional, or cultural significance for a district, the nation, or a living culture.

More and more of our country's rich heritage is being destroyed or lost each year. Thousands of archaeological and historic sites have already been vandalized, looted or fallen into disrepair. Irreplaceable knowledge about America's historic and prehistoric past is being lost. Here is an overview of the relevant Federal Acts that pertain to HERITAGE RESOURCES:

Antiquities Act of 1906 — prohibits the appropriation, excavation, injury, or destruction of any historic or prehistoric ruin or monument, or any object of antiquity, situated on lands owned or controlled by the Government of the United States.

Archaeological Resources Protection Act — prohibits the attempted or actual damaging, looting or vandalizing of archaeological sites on Federal and Indian lands. Included is the prohibition against trafficking in archaeological resources acquired off public or Indian lands or interstate or international trafficking in these resources in violation of State or local law.

Native American Graves Protection & Repatriation Act — prohibits the sale, purchase, use for profit, or transportation for sale or profit, of Native American (Indian and Native Hawaiian) human remains without the right of possession, or of any defined Native American cultural items (funerary objects, objects placed with human remains, sacred objects, and items having an ongoing historical, traditional, or cultural importance central to the Native American group, i.e. cultural patrimony property) obtained in violation of the Act. The Act further provides for the return of such objects currently being held by museums or Federal agencies to lineal descendants of the Native American, to culturally affiliated Indian tribes, or to Native Hawaiian organizations. Museums which fail to comply with the provisions about collections are subject to civil penalties. "Museums" are defined as any institution, or state or local government agency (including any institution of higher learning) that receives federal funds and has possession of, or control over, Native American cultural items.

Alaska Historic Preservation Act — prohibits the appropriation, excavation, removal, injury or destruction of any historic, prehistoric or archaeological resources on state lands including tidal and submerged lands. This act also covers mammoth and mastodon ivory and prehistoric animal bone.

Abandoned Shipwreck Act — establishes the title of States in abandoned shipwrecks (including cargo) in or on State lands. The law or salvage and the law of finds does not apply to abandoned shipwrecks to which this Act applies.

Local Laws — All states, some municipalities, Native Alaska corporations, and tribal governments also have ordinances that protect archaeological sites on their lands.

Maloney's Antiques & Collectibles Resource Directory is published in book form every other year. However, we answer written and telephone inquiries between editions regarding information maintained in *Maloney's* database. We also answer questions from callers made during radio talk shows or received on CompuServe, and we disseminate information via the Internet at our website http://www.maloneysonline.com. So it's more important than ever that listees keep us informed of any changes to the information in this directory as soon as those changes occur.

We are always interested in correcting, updating and adding sources of information and in improving category nomenclature and structure. Please write or call (phone 301-695-8544, fax 301-695-6491 or e-mail dmaloney@ix.netcom.com) with your suggestions for changes. At the end of this Directory you will find a Listing Application & Change Form which you can submit at any time to either change your present listing or to add a new one. By the way, listings in *Maloney's Antiques & Collectibles Resource Directory* are free.

Maloney's is also available on **Art*fact***, a CD-ROM containing over a million antique, fine and decorative art auction sales results plus thousands of images. For more information about **Art*fact***, call 800-ART-FACT.

A special thanks to all those who are listed, and to our users for their feedback, suggestions, and overwhelming encouragement. We continue to strive for excellence in providing a thorough, accurate and all-encompassing antiques and collectibles resource directory. I encourage and welcome your comments and suggestions.

> David J. Maloney, Jr., ISA CAPP
> P.O. Box 2049
> Frederick, MD 21702-1049
> phone: 301-695-8544
> fax: 301-695-6491
> e-mail: dmaloney@ix.netcom.com
> Internet: http://www.maloneysonline.com

P.S. A special message to those listed in *Maloney's*:

You can now extend your marketing reach onto the Internet by joining *Maloney's On-line Resource Directory*. Every day, millions of consumers go on-line searching for antiques and collectibles and for related products, services and information — and you have what they are looking for:

- Where can they buy it?
- Who wants to buy what they're trying to sell?
- Who can repair it or supply parts for it?
- What club can they join?
- What periodical can they subscribe to?
- Who can appraise it?
- Who can auction it for them?
- Who are the experts?

Internet customers represent are a rapidly growing segment of the market. They'll find you more easily if you have a **bold** *Maloney's On-line Resource Directory* Internet listing or with a listing that is linked to your own website or to a *Maloney's* custom-designed website complete with graphics and all the information you want the world to know about the products or services you sell or buy—and you don't even need to own a computer. Contact me or visit us at http://www.maloneysonline.com for more information on how you can take advantage of this new and exciting opportunity.

USER'S GUIDE
Description of the General Listings

The main section of this book, the General Listings, contains more than 15,000 specific entries in over 2,900 subject categories arranged alphabetically by primary classification in CAPITAL LETTERS. Subclassifications appear where there are recognized subcategories in Upper and Lower case letters. Of particular importance is the extensive and comprehensive cross-referencing system which directs the user to related subject matter and which is unique to this publication. The following is a sample of headings and subheadings found in the General Listings:

ADVERTISING COLLECTIBLES
(see also BREWERIANA; BUTTONS, Pin-Back; COFFEE; GAS STATION COLLECTIBLES; GLASSES; LABELS; MAGAZINES, Covers & Tear Sheets; PAPER COLLECTIBLES; POCKET MIRRORS; TIN COLLECTIBLES)

Alka Seltzer
Beer & Soda

AIR LABELS

AIRLINE MEMORABILIA
(see, also AIRPLANES; AVIATION; AVIATION MEMORABILIA; LUGGAGE LABELS; STAMP COLLECTING, Air Mail Related; TOYS, Airplane Related; TRANSPORTATION COLLECTIBLES)

Baggage I.D. Labels
Models, desk
Pan-American Airways
Pilot Wings

Each entry contains as much of the following information as is applicable and available:
1) **PRIMARY CLASSIFICATION**
2) **Subclassification**
3) Entry Type (i.e. Dealer, Collector, Club, etc.; entries are in ZIP Code order)
4) Business, organization, club, or museum name
5) Contact's name
6) Periodical type and name
7) Address
8) Phone and fax numbers
9) E-mail address
10) Internet website
10) Descriptive comment

Primary Classifications and Subclassifications

Of critical importance was the establishment of a classification system which employs a well-defined system that is sensitive to nomenclature currently in vogue within the collecting community. A bi-level system of nomenclature which includes primary classifications and, where necessary, subclassifications, was adopted. Additional flexibility is afforded within either level by employing parenthetical terms such as **CERAMICS (AMERICAN)**, **Stoneware**, or **GLASS, Carnival (Post-1960)**.

Entry Type

The entry type heading identifies the listing as an appraiser, auction service, book seller, collector, collectors' club, dealer, expert, manufacturer/distributor/producer, matching service, miscellaneous service of special interest, museum or library, on-line (Internet) service, periodical, repair/restoration/conservation service, reproduction source, supplier or vendor. Entries are listed *alphabetically by type* and then in *ZIP Code order* for ease in locating services or specialists in your area. **Always check the comment sections to locate *collectors* or *experts* who might also buy and sell, supply parts, do repairs or provide other services relevant to the classification.**

- "Collectors" buy or trade primarily for their own enjoyment, with any profit motive being secondary.

- "Dealers" buy, sell, or trade. They may also be "Collectors", but dealers anticipate making a profit.

- "Experts" (while they may also be a "Collector" and/or "Dealer") are considered to be expert because they have lectured or written extensively on the subject, have authored books or articles, have curated exhibits or managed collections, have dealt extensively in the subject, appraise within a specialized field, have conducted lengthy studies on the subject, or otherwise have such a degree of experience that they are recognized within the trade as having an uncommonly high degree of knowledge about the subject.

- "Man./Dist./Prod." are businesses which either manufacturer, distribute or produce items such as modem collectibles or reproductions.

- "Suppliers" are sources of replacement parts or supplies. Included in this category are vendors who cater to the needs of collectors, dealers, repairers and restorers, conservators, etc.

- As a general rule, only "periodicals" (newsletters, magazines, newspapers, journals, etc.) issued more than once a year are included in this directory. Price guides and books about antiques and collectibles are not listed. Such reference sources are available through your local library or from the book sellers listed in this Directory under **BOOKS, Reference**. General interest periodicals appear in Appendix C. They also appear within the General Listings if they also focus on a particular specialty area. Periodicals, such as newsletters or magazines, issued by a club or society are listed with that club within its specialty area and are not also listed separately as a "Periodical." By the way, many fine club periodicals are available to members only, so you may wish to join in order to receive them.

Names, Addresses and Phone Numbers

Most listings name a contact, while a few wish to be listed only as an anonymous "Collector" or "Dealer". Also listed is the business and periodical name, address, phone and fax numbers. Requests not to list a street address and only phone numbers have been honored.

E-Mail Address

Three thousand entries in this edition of *Maloney's* are also accessible through electronic mail (e-mail) via computer. Those who are list an e-mail "address." With the growing popularity of electronic on-line computer services such as CompuServe, America On-Line, and Prodigy and most notably, the Internet, savvy antiques and collectibles enthusiasts are speeding down the "Information Super-Highway" to take advantage of information often found nowhere else.

Internet Website

Almost two thousand listings also feature an Internet website. With over 50 million users, the Internet offers an unparalleled opportunity for you to learn more about what you own and who shares your particular areas of interest worldwide! The Internet can also increase the world's awareness of you and improve your efforts to gain publicity for your group. The Internet may also prove a valuable way for you to market your antiques-and-collectibles related products and services.

Comment Line

Most entries include a comment line of amplifying information which users will find extremely valuable. Comment space was limited, so at times editorial license was taken to shorten or otherwise modify comments submitted by those listed.

Tips for Searching *Maloney's*

■ Sellers of new books focusing on antiques & collectibles are listed under **BOOKS, Reference.**

■ Repair, restoration and conservation services will be found 1) under the heading **REPAIR/RESTORATION/CONSERVATION,** 2) in the *Repair Firm* appendix, <u>or</u> 3) within their specialty classification listed in the General Listings under the entry type, *Repair Services*.

■ Objects made of fired clay (pottery, earthenware, stoneware, and porcelain) will be found under the primary classification of **CERAMICS,** which is further subdivided according to place of origin and type, e.g., **CERAMICS (AMERICAN ART POTTERY), Roseville Pottery Co.** By cross-reference, users are directed to such related areas as **COOKIE JARS, FAIRINGS** and **DINNERWARE** (a generic classification which contains most "china").

■ Matching services locate replacement pieces for dinnerware, glassware and flatware tableware services. Matching services will be found primarily under the categories **DINNERWARE; FLATWARE; GLASS, Elegant** and **GLASS, Crystal.**

■ Sports-related collectibles are listed alphabetically by sport subclassification under the primary classification of **SPORTS COLLECTIBLES.** By the way, **SPORTS COL-LECTIBLES** should not be confused with **SPORTING COLLECTIBLES.** (The latter includes items relating to the hunting sports such as decoys, hunting prints and paintings, sporting art, target shooting, duck game calls, etc.)

■ Contemporary collectibles, including limited editions, can be found under **COL-LECTIBLES (MODERN).**

■ Many supplies for the dealer and collector can be found under **ANTIQUES DEALERS & COLLECTORS, Supplies for.** Certain specific categories such as **STAMP COL-LECTING, Supplies for** and **COINS & CURRENCY, Supplies for** also list sources of supplies for those specialties.

■ Look in the Index under *Computer Programs for Antiques Dealers & Collectors* to find software programs for maintaining collections.

■ While many listings now include an Internet website, those listees who operate strictly on the Internet can be found listed within their specialty area under the entry type *On-line Services*.

■ The category **REPRODUCTION SOURCES** (sometimes catering only to the wholesale trade) lists businesses offering copies of antiques and collectibles — everything from R.S. Prussia porcelain and oak furniture to Diamond Dye lithographed tins and jukeboxes.

■ While appraisers, auction services, periodicals, and repair services that specialize are listed within the General Listings under their areas of expertise, the Appendices list others with a more general coverage:

— For a list of educated and trained ISA personal property appraisers (specialists as well as generalists), see Appendix A.
— For a list of general line auction services, see Appendix B.
— For a list of general interest periodicals, see Appendix C.
— For a list of talented repair firms, see Appendix D.

The Appendices

There are four appendices that you will find very useful:

■ Appendix A: Appraisers - Several hundred educated and tested members of the International Society of Appraisers listed in ZIP Code order.

■ Appendix B: Auction Services - General line auction services listed in ZIP Code order.

■ Appendix C: General Interest Periodicals - Periodicals of general interest to the antiques and collectibles trade listed in alphabetical order.

■ Appendix D: Repair Firms - Hundreds of repair firms that specialize in the repair and restoration of household goods listed in ZIP Code order. All firms are members of the moving industry's Claims Prevention & Procedure Council.

The Index

The Directory offers a detailed index to help you readily find both major and minor subject categories of interest. It features an exhaustive cross-reference system that will efficiently guide you to other categories of related interest.

Skim through the index - you'll be amazed at the diversity of items people collect. The index will also help you think of things you might own that may be valuable.

Can't locate information about an item? Try looking under related subjects. Our extensive cross-reference will usually guide you, but use your imagination. Many collectibles are crossovers, i.e. they have collector appeal in more than one field. For instance, an early 20th century calendar depicting bicyclists has appeal not only to paper collectors but also to bicycle enthusiasts.

Useful and Important Suggestions

■ When writing and requesting a reply from those listed, always send a long self-addressed and stamped envelope (LSASE) to help ensure and expedite a reply. Many collector clubs operate on a shoestring budget and require that a request for information be accompanied with an LSASE. Everyone will appreciate your courtesy. Include your phone number as well so the party can call you if they need additional information concerning your query. If you are selling, many would-be buyers are anxious to speak to you personally as soon as possible. They will often have specific questions to ask that can be best answered over the phone.

- When calling, DON'T CALL COLLECT unless otherwise directed (and very few do!); respect time zone differences; don't leave telephone or answering service messages unless you want the call returned collect. Suggest a time that the party should call back collect to ensure that you will be there. When calling about an item you own, be prepared. Have the item in hand (or good photographs of the item), along with notes on its dimensions, maker's mark, condition, signature, and any other identifying marks such as a patent number or date, model/serial number, etc.

- Don't send items without first notifying the receiving party and getting their permission. Items sent without permission can be considered "gifts" and do not need to be returned. When sending photographs, be sure that they are clear, close-up and in focus. Polaroids are seldom useful. Often, relatively flat objects such as small textiles, medals, ribbons, or paper items can be photocopied.

- When asking for help in identifying or authenticating an item, in addition to photos send complete descriptions including dimensions, maker's marks, materials, how long you've had it, how you acquired it, and its provenance (who owned it before you and for how long.)

- If selling, always state the price you would be willing to sell the item for. Most authorities agree that it's up to the seller to set the asking price although some dealers or buyers will help you. Unable to determine a fair price to ask? Your options are to seek comparable items in one of many price guide available today (booksellers are listed under **BOOKS, Reference**), or to retain the services of an expert, dealer or appraiser to assist you (look for appraisers within the general listings or in Appendix A, or call the International Society of Appraisers (see below) for a free referral.) By the way, the person you retain to do the appraisal should have no interest in purchasing the items you are selling.

- When you receive a reply from someone you've offered to sell an item to, make sure you respond promptly. If the party wants to buy the items you are offering, make sure you let him know of your final intentions to sell to him or otherwise. Don't keep him wondering whether or not you even received his reply. Often listees spend their valuable time and money in researching and/or corresponding with you. Make sure you are courteous and thoughtful in return.

- Be sensitive to the possible need for paying a few dollars when requesting catalogs, lists, samples or brochures. Always ask if there are charges for the service or product you are requesting, such as an appraisal or authentication.

- If an expert is not listed for your particular area of interest, try contacting a related collector's club or periodical. Often the club's contact or the periodical's editor or publisher are themselves experts. In any case, they are always excellent sources of information.

- Another excellent source when trying to locate an expert in your area is to call the International Society of Appraisers, a nonprofit organization and the largest association of personal property appraisers in North America. For a free, no-obligation referral to an appraiser in your area, call the ISA at 206-241-0359, e-mail at ISA_HQ@compuserve.com, or write the ISA at 16040 Christensen Rd., Ste. 320, Seattle, WA 98188. You can also check for an appraiser by going to the ISA's website at http://www.isa-appraisers.org.

- Finally, when looking for an expert, advice or service, don't forget to contact your own neighborhood resources. Museums, libraries, historical societies, and moving company claims departments (a great source for talented repairers) are just a few of the local sources to turn to when seeking advice. If you locate an unusual source, let us know about it, too. We'd love to include it in the next edition of this book. Don't forget to consult your local telephone Yellow Pages, too. Look under "Antique - Dealers," "Antiques - Repairing & Restoring," "Appraisers," "Furniture Repairing & Refinishing," "Jewelers," "Lamps," and "Moving & Storage" for local businesses which may also be able to help.

If you wish to be listed in a future edition of the *Resource Directory*, complete and return the form located at the end of this book. Remember, there is no charge for being listed in *Maloney's Antiques & Collectibles Resource Directory*.

GENERAL LISTINGS

007

(see CHARACTER COLLECTIBLES, Spy Memorabilia [James Bond]; TELEVISION SHOWS & MEMORA-BILIA, Private Eye)

1930s to 1960s

(see MODERNISM; POPULAR CULTURE; SOCIAL CAUSES)

20TH CENTURY

(see ART, Outsider; ART DECO; ELECTRICITY RELATED ITEMS, Appliances; MODERNISM; POPULAR CULTURE; SOCIAL CAUSES)

3-D PHOTOGRAPHICA

(see also CAMERAS & CAMERA EQUIPMENT; OPTICAL ITEMS; STEREO VIEWERS & STEREOVIEWS)

Collectors

Harry Poster
P.O. Box 1883
South Hackensack, NJ 07606-0483
phone: 201-794-9606
fax: 201-794-9553
e-mail: hposter@worldnet.att.net
Buying Tru-Vue rolls and viewers, View Master singles and three packs; wants Military, Cactus, Wildflowers, gold centers, Movie Pre-views ($50 ea.!); VM and Tru-Vue dealer displays, advertising, Novel View, and similar stereo slides.

Sheldon Aronowitz
487 Palmer Ave.
Teaneck, NJ 07666-3251
phone: 201-837-9508 or 800-982-7401
fax: 201-861-8648
Specializes in View-Master, Tru-Vue, Stori-Vue, Anaglyph, Lenticular, holograms, stereo cards, 3-D literature, 3-D cameras, 3-D views.

Kyle Spain
620 Brightside Lane
Pasadena, CA 91107-5342
phone: 818-449-9179
Collector wants to buy 3D/stereo slides (4"x1 5/6") made by amateur photographers from 1950s stereo cameras.

Chris Perry
Doctor 3D
7470 Church St., Ste. A
Yucca Valley, CA 92284-3248
phone: 760-365-0475
fax: 760-365-0495
Buys anything that is 3D: 3D cameras, projectors, viewers, Viewmaster, TRU-VUE, Realist slides, lenticular 3D pictures, holograms, novelviews, 3D filmstrips; 3D magazines that you view with 3D glasses or viewer; and any other 3D items.

Dealers

John Saddy
Jefferson Stereoptics
50 Foxborough Grove
London
Ontario N6K 4A8 Canada
phone: 519-641-4431
fax: 519-641-2899
e-mail: john.saddy.3d@sympatico.ca
Specializes in consignments for international phone and mail auctions; also buys and sells stereo photography and equipment.

Reel 3-D Enterprises, Inc.
P.O. Box 2368
Culver City, CA 90231-2368
phone: 310-837-2368
fax: 310-558-1653
Internet: http://www.3d-web.com/reel/reel3d.html
A catalog about 3-D photography and 3-D equipment collecting.

Dalia Miller
3-D from Dalia
P.O. Box 492
Corte Madera, CA 94976-0492
phone: 415-924-3356
fax: 415-924-6162
e-mail: dddalia@crl.com
Internet: http://www.3dstereo.com
Buys and sells 3-D supplies, equipment, stereo cameras, projectors, viewers, lenticulars, books, stereorama, View-Master reels and packets, Tru-Vue strips; great catalog.

Experts

Roger T. Nazeley
4921 Castor Ave.
Philadelphia, PA 19124-2411
phone: 215-535-9021 or 215-743-8999
fax: 215-288-8030
Buy, sell, trade View-Master reels and packets, Tru-Vue cards & film strips, look-a-like View-Masters, etc.; author of book on subject.

John Waldsmith
Antique Graphics
302 Granger Rd.
Medina, OH 44256-8434
phone: 216-239-1944
fax: 216-239-1944
Wants stereoscopic views, View-Master reels, photographica; conducts mail/phone auctions on regular basis; also direct sales; author of "Stereo

Views: An Illustrated History and Price Guide."

Periodicals

Dalia Miller
Magazine: Inside 3-D
P.O. Box 492
Corte Madera, CA 94976-0492
phone: 415-924-3356
fax: 415-924-6162
e-mail: dddalia@crl.com
Internet: http://www.3dstereo.com
Quarterly publication for 3D enthusiasts; information on stereo cameras, projectors, viewers, View-Master, Tru-Vue and other 20th century 3D.

View-Masters

Clubs/Associations

National Stereoscopic Association
Magazine: Stereo World
P.O. Box 14801
Columbus, OH 43214
phone: 614-263-4296
Internet: http://www.tisco.com/3d-web/nsa/nsa.htm
Members collect stereo views, stereoscopes, stereo cameras; View-Master reels, viewers, packets; all other 3-D collectibles; the glossy colorful magazine is published six timer per year.

Collectors

Jim Rohacs
9721 Lomond Dr.
Manassas, VA 22110-3104
phone: 703-369-5578
Wants to buy View-Masters and similar 3D items.

Howard & Jane Hazelcorn
6731 Ashley Ct.
Sarasota, FL 34241-9696
phone: 941-921-1815
Wants to buy early viewers and rare reels.

Bob Zeuschel
1638 Highland Valley Ctr.
Chesterfield, MO 63005
phone: 314-537-3145
Wants to buy View-Masters, Tru-Vue 3-D slide formats.

Kyle Spain
620 Brightside Lane
Pasadena, CA 91107-5342
phone: 818-449-9179
Collector wants to buy View-Master reels and packets; all types especially scenic, "Made in Belgium" reels, military training reels and medical reels.

Experts

Sheldon Aronowitz
487 Palmer Ave.
Teaneck, NJ 07666-3251
phone: 201-837-9508 or 800-982-7401
fax: 201-861-8648
Specializes in View-Master, Tru-Vue,

Stori-Vue, Anaglyph, Lenticular, holograms, stereo cards, 3-D literature, 3-D cameras, 3-D views.

Walter Sigg
3-D Entertainment
P.O. Box 208
Swartswood, NJ 07877-0208
Buys and sells View-Master, Tru-Vue, 3-D cameras, projectors, reels, and most 3-D items; also early non-cartoon single View-Master reels and the three reel packets, and reels and 3-D cameras by Sawyers and G.A.F.

John Waldsmith
Antique Graphics
302 Granger Rd.
Medina, OH 44256-8434
phone: 216-239-1944
fax: 216-239-1944
Wants stereoscopic views, View-Master reels, photographica; conducts mail/phone auctions on regular basis; also direct sales; author of "Stereo Views: An Illustrated History and Price Guide."

A.C. GILBERT

(see TOYS, Construction Sets [Erector]; TRAINS, Toy [American Flyer])

ABRAHAM LINCOLN

(see CIVIL WAR; PERSONALITIES [HISTORICAL], Abraham Lincoln)

ACCOUNT BOOKS

(see also PAPER COLLECTIBLES)

Collectors

Roy C. Kulp
P.O. Box 264
Hatfield, PA 19440-0264
phone: 215-362-0732
Wants to buy account books and day books by farmers, carpenters, blacksmiths, coffin & carriage makers, and weavers; also wants pre-1890 hand written travel diaries.

ACTING

(see PERFORMING ARTS)

ADDING MACHINES

(see also CALCULATORS; OFFICE EQUIPMENT; TYPEWRITERS)

Clubs/Associations

Darryl Rehr, Ed.
Early Typewriter Collectors Association
Magazine: ETCetera
2591 Military Ave.
Los Angeles, CA 90064-1933
phone: 310-477-5229
fax: 310-268-8420
e-mail: dcrehr@earthlink.net
Internet: http://www.earthlink.net/~dcrehr
An international club for collectors of old office equipment; provides contact

with worldwide network of over 500 members; free ads.

Collectors

Peter Frei
P.O. Box 500
Brimfield, MA 01010-0500
phone: 800-942-8968 or 413-245-4660
Wants old typewriters, adding machines, sewing machines, and old vacuum cleaners, etc.

Anthony Casillo
325 Nassau Blvd.
Garden City, NY 11530-5313
phone: 516-489-8300 or 516-742-4919
fax: 516-489-6501
e-mail: typebar@aol.com
Internet: http://www.members.aol.com/typebar/collectible/typewriter.htm
Wants to buy old and unusual pre-1920 adding machines.

Edward Stuart
P.O. Box 21114
Washington, DC 20009
phone: 202-332-6511
Wants old adding machines, key driven non-listing models only such as Comptometer or Burroughs Arithometer.

Arthur Cheslock
514 Paul St.
Baltimore, MD 21202
phone: 410-962-8580
fax: 410-752-8112
Wants pre-1945 calculators, adding machines and scientific instruments; also wants related literature.

Steve Leffel
Green Bay, WI 54302-3132
fax: 414-465-6505
Wants to buy adding machines and mechanical calculators.

Darryl Rehr
2591 Military Ave.
Los Angeles, CA 90064-1933
phone: 310-477-5229
fax: 310-268-8420
e-mail: dcrehr@earthlink.net
Internet: http://www.earthlink.net/~dcrehr/
Wants adding machines (machines that only add) of unusual and early designs; send SASE for free information packet.

ADIRONDACK

(see FURNITURE [ANTIQUE], Rustic)

ADS

Magazine

(see ADVERTISING COLLECTIBLES; MAGAZINES, Covers & Tear Sheets; PAPER COLLECTIBLES)

ADVERTISING COLLECTIBLES

(see also BREWERIANA; BUTTONS, Pin-Back; COFFEE; DINNERWARE, Advertising; GAS STATION COLLECTIBLES; GLASSES; LABELS; MAGAZINES, Covers & Tear Sheets; PAPER COLLECTIBLES; POCKET MIRRORS; POPULAR CULTURE; THERMOMETERS; TIN COLLECTIBLES; WATCH FOBS

Auction Services

Randy Inmann
James D. Julia Auctioneers Inc.
Rt. 201, Skowhegan Rd.
P.O. Box 830
Fairfield, ME 04937
phone: 207-453-7125
fax: 207-453-2502
Conducts specialized auctions of advertising and country store items; one of the leaders in the field; trade signs coin-operated items, gambling devices, syrup dispensers; uses nationally recognized experts to catalog specialty sales.

Howard Parzow
Howard B. Parzow, Auctioneers
P.O. Box 3464
Gaithersburg, MD 20885-3464
phone: 301-977-6741
fax: 301-208-8947
Conducts specialized auctions of country store, advertising, drug store, apothecary and medical related items, and Americana; advertises nationally.

Dave Beck
Beck Auctions
P.O. Box 435
Mediapolis, IA 52637-0435
phone: 319-394-3943
Conducts mail auctions of advertising watch fobs, mirrors, pin-back buttons, etc.; send stamp for illustrated auction catalog.

Buffalo Bay Antiques
11 E. Division St.
Buffalo, MN 55313
phone: 612-682-1825
Holds regular absentee advertising auctions.

Clubs/Associations

Ephemera Society of America Inc., The
Newsletter: Ephemera News
P.O. Box 95
Cazenovia, NY 13035-0095
phone: 315-655-2810
fax: 315-655-1078
The major organization for collectors and dealers of paper collectibles; focuses on the preservation and study of ephemera (short-lived printed matter); also publishes "The Ephemera Journal."

David Schnakenberg
Farm Machinery Advertising Collectors
10108 Tamarack Drive
Vienna, VA 22182-1843

David Hirsch
Antique Advertising Association of America
Newsletter: Past Times
P.O. Box 1121
Morton Grove, IL 60053
phone: 708-446-0904
Dedicated to collecting ALL forms of quality advertising: tobacco, coffee, whiskey, beer, candy, gum, clocks, country store, cabinets, etc.

Tin Container Collectors Association
Newsletter: Tin Type
P.O. Box 440101
Aurora, CO 80044

Collectors

Ludovic Kintgen
6 Rue De Longpont
Neuilly/Seine
France 92200
Buys, trades and collects advertising items.

April Rhodes
RR 1 Box 284-E
Sunbury, PA 17801-9618
Wants to buy sample advertising tins; prefers cosmetic and toiletry sample tins.

Barry
2300 Meadowlane Dr.
Easton, PA 18042
Beer, soda, whiskey, other advertising lithos: calendars, signs, trays, match holders.

Jerry A. Phelps
6013 Innes Trace Rd.
Louisville, KY 40222-6004
phone: 502-425-4765
Wants pre-1900 country store and advertising items: signs, broadsides, clocks, tins, bins, display cases, etc.

Mike & Shirley Sembric
3743 Willow Run
Westlake, OH 44155
phone: 216-734-2827
Specializes in country store advertising items.

Mark S. McNee
1009 Vassar Dr.
Kalamazoo, MI 49001-4483
phone: 616-343-8393
Wants to buy all forms of early advertising including signs, posters, tin containers, and store displays.

Tom Rutledge
3015 Bever Ave., SE
Cedar Rapids, IA 52403
phone: 319-399-1427
Wants country store advertising items, calendars, signs, broadsides, tins, posters for all types of products, especially ammunition, beer, whiskey, tobacco, and soft drink companies.

Mike Kranz
463 Stage Line Rd.
Hudson, WI 54016-7849
phone: 715-386-7333 or 715-386-9212
Wants to buy old store stock and store advertisements.

Steve Ketcham
P.O. Box 24114
Minneapolis, MN 55424-0114
phone: 612-920-4205
Seeking pre-1940 advertising signs, trays, mirrors, calendars, posters, etc. for all types of products, especially beer, whiskey, patent medicine, tobacco; send SASE with all inquiries.

Roger V. Baker
P.O. Box 620417
Redwood City, CA 94062-0417
phone: 369-851-7188
Wants signs, calendars, trays, etc. advertising firearms, ammunition, beer, whiskey, tobacco, and general store companies.

Dealers

Leila Dunbar
Dunbar's Gallery
76 Haven St.
Milford, MA 01757-3821
phone: 508-634-8697 or 508-634-8097
fax: 508-634-8698
Mail order Americana - no reproductions; buys, sells and specializes in vintage character and comic toys, banks, advertising, automobilia, and Halloween related items.

Rudy Franchi
Nostalgia Factory, The
336 Newbury St.
Boston, MA 02115-2703
phone: 617-236-8754 or 800-479-8754
e-mail: rf@nostalgia.com
Internet: http://www.nostalgia.com
Buys and sells all forms of old advertising, from Victorian trade cards to contemporary billboards; 25 years in business.

Robb Sequin
P.O. Box 1126
Dennis Port, MA 02639
phone: 508-760-2599
e-mail: rsequin@capecod.net
Internet: http://rsequin.com
Wants advertising signs with interesting subject matter either by company or graphically: signs, displays, products and calendars; no tear sheets, please.

Phelps Fullerton
Great Bay Trading Co.
281 Atlantic Ave.
North Hampton, NH 03862-2103
phone: 603-964-7093 or 603-964-9928
e-mail: pfullerton@aol.com
Buys and sells paper, tin, porcelain, and wood advertising signs, trays, tins, calendars, die-cuts, mirrors, display cases, country store items, etc. for all types of products.

Mary Ann Hahn
Second Hand Mary Ann's
HCR 65 Box 26
Boothbay Harbor, ME 04538-9703
phone: 207-633-2426
fax: 207-633-2426
Wants to buy old advertising die-cuts (cardboard signs with easels on back).

Louise Pennisi
Around the Kitchen
P.O. Box 840
Georgetown, CT 06829
phone: 203-438-2338 or 203-438-0671
e-mail: louise@aroundthekitchen.com
Internet: http://
www.aroundthekitchen.com
Buys and sells food and kitchen advertising, including kitchen appliance, recipe pamphlets, cookery booklets (Pillsbury, Baker's Chocolate, Jell-O, etc.), and collectible cookbooks (19th & 20th cent.); catalogs, searches, co. histories.

Marc Zydiak
Star Archives
P.O. Box 285
Westfield, NJ 07091-0285
phone: 908-654-6505

Alice Kasten
Alice's Advertising Antiques
131 Allenwood Rd.
Great Neck, NY 11023
phone: 516-466-8954
e-mail: alicek13@aol.com
Buys and sells advertising collectibles; thousands of trade cards, advertising blotters, pamphlets, etc. on database; can send list tailored to your wants.

Steve Colby
Off The Deep End
712 East St.
Frederick, MD 21701-5239
phone: 301-698-9006
e-mail: chilimon@offthedeepend.com
Antique to contemporary; also ephemera, 1950s home accessories, Playboy magazines, diner collectibles, pin-ups, nudes and Hula Girls (all types), used books.

Vic Kroll
Kroll's Kollectibles
3451 Nighthawk Ct.
Punta Gorda, FL 33950-6675
phone: 941-575-0303
e-mail: beer@sunline.net
Buys, sells, trades beer, whiskey, soda and tobacco advertising items.

Coshocton Art Works
P.O. Box 1146
Coshocton, OH 43812
Wants tin and celluloid advertising items.

Mike Schwimmer
Collectors Center
325 East Blodgett
Lake Bluff, IL 60044-2112
phone: 847-295-1901
Collector of cigar memorabilia;

dealer in all forms of vintage advertising; buys and sells.

Robert M. Levine
#2 Troll Court
Ballwin, MO 63011
phone: 314-394-4370
fax: 314-391-6618
Buys, sells, trades and collects advertising items with company logo; must be at least 25 years old.

Jim & Rita Hinton
Collector's Choice
P.O. Box 104284
Jefferson City, MO 65110-4284
phone: 573-636-7567

Kim & Mary Kokles
P.O. Box 495092
Garland, TX 75049
Buys and sells advertising; promotes national all-advertising show.

Stephen Hansrote
Griffin Trading Company
13663 Jupiter Rd., Ste. 406
Dallas, TX 75238
phone: 214-341-0660
fax: 214-341-0660
e-mail: griffintc@aol.com
Internet: http://www.members.aol.com/griffintc/website.htm
Buying and selling all types of American and European advertising such as displays, props, figures, paper goods, wood and metal signs.

John D. McKenna
McKenna Bros. Wholesale
801-803 W Cucharras St.
Colorado Springs, CO 80905
phone: 719-630-8732
Always buying, selling, trading antique signs, tins, trays, posters, and country store items; best prices paid for mint condition items.

Experts

Dennis O'Brien
Dennis & George Collectibles
3407 Lake Montebello Dr.
Baltimore, MD 21218
phone: 410-889-3964
With George Goehring runs collectibles mail order firm; collectors and dealers of upright pocket tobacco tins, advertising, etc.

Dawn E. Reno
3280 Shingler Terrace
Deltona, FL 32738-5351
phone: 904-532-1960
fax: 904-532-1960
e-mail: DawnReno@juno.com
Author of "Advertising Collectibles" (1993, Avon).

Craig & Donna Stifter
P.O. Box 6514
Naperville, IL 60540-6514
phone: 630-717-7949
Wants to buy older Coca-Cola, Pepsi-Cola, Dr. Pepper, Orange-Crush, Hire Root Beer and other brand soda memorabilia; writes columns for

several antiques periodicals; also interested in items pertaining to country (general) stores.

Museums/Libraries

Warsaw Collection of Business Americana
Smithsonian Institution
Washington, DC 20560
phone: 202-357-2414
Internet: http://www.si.edu/

National Museum of American History, Archives Center, Smithsonian Institution
14th & Constitution Ave. NW
Room C340, MRC 601
Washington, DC 20560
phone: 202-357-3270 or 202-357-1789
fax: 202-786-2453
Internet: http://www.si.edu/
Dedicated to advertising and American business ephemera from the late 1700s to 1980; also ethnic ephemera from 1890s to present.

Periodicals

Dennis M. Sater, Ed.
Newspaper: Paper & Advertising Collector (P.A.C.)
P.O. Box 500
Mount Joy, PA 17552-0500
phone: 717-653-4300 or 800-482-2886
fax: 717-653-6165

Newsletter: Tin Fax
205 Brolley Woods Dr.
Woodstock, GA 30188

Newspaper: Advertising Collectors Express, The
P.O. Box 221
Mayview, MO 64071-0221
phone: 816-584-6309
fax: 816-584-6259
Marketplace for advertising memorabilia: soft drinks, breweriana, gas, oil, automotive, tobacco, food and drug products; signs, trays, buttons, tins, thermometers, labels, trade cards, blotters, mirrors, calendars, clocks and more.

Repro. Sources

Country Lane, The
RD 1 Box 100 Ericsson Rd.
Kennedy, NY 14747
Carries reproduction advertising packages and tins.

A & P Items

Dealers

Syd E. Pitzer
Cherished Antiques & Collectibles
425 Old Bethel Church Rd.
Winchester, VA 22603-4050
phone: 703-667-4255

Alka Seltzer

Collectors

Darlene Shidler
58999 Lower Dr.
Goshen, IN 46528
phone: 219-533-6102
Wants Alka Seltzer and Miles Laboratories, Inc. (Elkhart, IN) items: bottles, boxes, toys, "Speedy" figures, advertising, etc.

Ammunition

Collectors

Bill Bramlett
P.O. Box 1105
Florence, SC 29503-1105
phone: 803-393-7390 or 803-665-3165
e-mail: bbramlett@pdn.net
Wants to buy 1890-1931 calendars, posters and signs advertising shotgun shells and cartridges from companies such as Peters, Austin, Remington, U.S. Cartridge Co., The Black Shells, Western.

Aunt Jemima

Collectors

Lynn Burkett
P.O. Box 671
Hillsdale, MI 49242
phone: 517-437-2149
Wants Aunt Jemima pancake advertising: recipe booklets, flyers, maps, paper masks, signs, posters, product containers, premium items, china, etc.

Beech-Nut

Collectors

Bruce A. Van Evera
94 Montgomery St.
Canajoharie, NY 13317-1213
phone: 518-673-3522
Wants to buy Beech-Nut Brand glass, tin or cardboard containers with excellent paper label intact: catsup, mustard, chili sauce, slice beef, ginger ale, sarsparilla, peanut butter, jams, K-rations, gum, biscuit tins, olive oil, etc.

Black & White Scotch

Collectors

Paul Stookey
Olde Towne Collectables
3436 Pointe Creek Ct. #202
Cape Coral, FL 34134
phone: 941-498-4502 or 941-498-6601
Wants to buy any "Black and White" Scotch advertising: signs, trays, bottles, back bar pieces, all black and white dogs, etc.

Camels

Clubs/Associations

Ron Schwinnew
Camel Joe & Friends
2205 Hess Dr.
Cresthill, IL 60435
Focuses on Camel Joe memorabilia.

Display Cases (Baranger)

Collectors

Frank Novak
7386 Beverly Blvd.
Los Angeles, CA 90036
phone: 213-683-1963
fax: 213-638-1312

Display Cases (Cast Iron)

Collectors

Rick Humphreys
214 Tuckahoe Cove
Memphis, TN 38117
phone: 901-761-9507
*Wants to buy unusual ice cream
dippers.*

Figures

(see also DOLLS, Advertising;
PHONOGRAPHS, Nipper)

Collectors

Roland Coover
1537 E. Strasburg Rd.
West Chester, PA 19380-6380
phone: 610-692-3112
*Wants to buy figures of trademark
characters such as Speedy Alka-
Seltzer, Mr. Clean, Reddy Kilowatt,
Quisp, Otto the Orkin Man, Raid Bug,
etc.*

Dealers

Marty Blank
P.O. Box 405
Flushing, NY 11365-0405
phone: 516-485-8071
e-mail: martyadver@aol.com
*Wants to buy Elsie, Campbell Kids,
Reddy Kilowatt, Coke, figural vinyl
advertising and Country Store items.*

Figures (Charlie Tuna)

Clubs/Associations

Cathy C. Runyan, Pres.
Charlie Tuna Collectors Club
7812 N.W. Hampton Rd.
Kansas City, MO 64152-4940
phone: 816-587-8687
fax: 816-587-8687

Experts

Cathy C. Runyan
Right Brain Publishing
7812 N.W. Hampton Rd.
Kansas City, MO 64152-4940
phone: 816-587-8687
fax: 816-587-8687
Collector, appraiser and specialist in

*Charlie Tuna memorabilia and
promotional items.*

Figures (Reddy Kilowatt)

Collectors

Carolyn T. Little
725 Esla Dr.
Chula Vista, CA 91910
e-mail: ladylight@prodigy.com
*Collects and specializes in light bulbs;
wants light bulbs with tips or unusual
light bulbs, Glow Lamps (neon) with
figurals inside, meters, sockets, bulbs
with figural or decorative filaments,
Edison, Westinghouse, Reddy
Kilowatt, etc.*

Experts

Warren Dotz
2999 Regent St., Ste. 300
Berkeley, CA 94705-2118
phone: 510-652-1159
fax: 510-540-0325
e-mail: wellipsis@aol.com
*Buys & specializes in advertising
character figural store displays,
banks, statuettes, and dolls;
cartoonish trademark characters
(Speedy Alka Seltzer, Reddy Kilowatt,
Elsie the Cow, etc.); author of
"Advertising Character Collectibles."*

Firearms Related

Collectors

Bill Bramlett
P.O. Box 1105
Florence, SC 29503-1105
phone: 803-393-7390 or 803-665-3165
e-mail: bbramlett@pdn.net
*Wants 1890-1931 firearms-related
advertising items such as calendars,
signs and posters that advertise
firearms, shotgun shells, gunpowders
from Remington, Marlin, Peters,
U.M.C., DuPont, Winchester, U.S.
Cartridge Co., Savage, etc.*

Gerber Baby

Experts

Joan Stryker Grubaugh
2342 Hoaglin Rd.
Van Wert, OH 45891
phone: 419-622-4411
fax: 419-622-3026
*Author of "Gerber Baby Dolls &
Advertising Collectibles."*

Grapette

Dealers

Don Hunter
16502 Barcelina
Friendswood, TX 77546-3304
phone: 713-482-4098
*Buys and sells Grapette items:
drinking glasses, poster signs, shirt
patches, shirt pins, pencils, clowns,
elephants; "Grapette Price Guide"
available for $29.95.*

Hormel

Museums/Libraries

First Century Museum
P.O. Box 800
Austin, MN 55912
phone: 507-437-5345
*Museum of the Hormel Company;
history, artifacts, advertisements,
SPAM history and exhibit.*

Johnson & Johnson

Collectors

Vi Leibecki
34 Westlawn Place
Palm Coast, FL 32164
phone: 904-446-9499
*Interested in all pre-1940 Johnson &
Johnson items.*

Lucky Strike

Collectors

John Van Alstyne
85 Brooks Ave.
Rochester, NY 14619-2453
*Wants to buy Lucky Strike items:
tobacco (including R.A. Patterson
brand) and cigarettes; any kind of
advertising or product item; American
Tobacco Co.; pre-1912 advertising or
products.*

Barnaby Conrad III
2101 Pacific Ave.
San Francisco, CA 94115
phone: 415-563-7418
*Wants Lucky Strike vintage displays,
ads, and related memorabilia.*

Monarch Food Products

Collectors

Bruce & Nada Ferris
3094 Oakes Dr.
Hayward, CA 94542-1234
phone: 510-581-5285
fax: 510-581-4469
e-mail: nada.ferris@kaiperm.org
*Wants Monarch food products items
from the 1920s: glass items with paper
labels, tins, Monarch cookbook, teenie
weenie popcorn, etc.; also Toledo, OH
advertising, Atlas, Woolson Spice &
Coffee, Toledo Biscuit, Buckey Beer.*

Nabisco Food Group

Clubs/Associations

Steve & Sandy Honican
Inner Seal Club
Newsletter: Inner Seal Club Bulletin
4585 Saron Dr.
Lexington, KY 40515
*A club dedicated to the collection and
discussion of antique and nostalgic
items carrying or relating to the
INNER SEAL trademark of the
Nabisco Foods Group.*

Phillip Morris

Collectors

Stuart Morrell
8925 Laureate Lane
Richmond, VA 23236-4406
Wants old Phillip Morris items.

Chuck Evarkiou
4223 Niagara Ave.
San Diego, CA 92107
phone: 619-222-8588
*Buys, sells, trades Phillip Morris
advertising, signs, promotions, etc.*

Piano Related

Collectors

Philip Jamison
17 Sharon Alley
West Chester, PA 19382
phone: 610-696-8449
fax: 610-696-8449
*Wants piano related material such as
advertising signs and posters,
catalogs, photographs of factory
interiors, piano trade publications,
etc.*

Janice E. Kelsh
633 Pennsylvania Ave.
Hagerstown, MD 21740-3769
phone: 301-797-7675
e-mail: kelshj@nihrrlib.ncrr.nih.gov
*Wants to buy piano advertising items;
also piano related trade cards and
postcards.*

Potteries Related

Collectors

Harvey Duke
577 Avenue Y
Brooklyn, NY 11235
*Wants catalogs, brochures, flyers and
other paper material from U.S.
potteries; also wants advertising
signs, dealer signs, ceramic Christmas
cards and calling cards, sample
plates, plant visit souvenirs, etc. from
U.S. potteries only.*

Roofing

Collectors

Troy Holck
1060 W. Santa Fe
Olathe, KS 66061
phone: 913-782-8136
*Wants to buy old roofing advertising
items: tin and porcelain signs, neon
signs, clocks, thermometers, figural
items, salesman's samples, cardboard
or counter display items, etc.*

Signs

Clubs/Associations

Robert C. English
Porcelain Advertising Collectors Club
P.O. Box 381
Marshfield Hills, MA 02051-0381
phone: 617-837-0111
Informal membership that acts as a clearinghouse for collectors & dealers interested in porcelain signs in all categories. e.g. country store & automobile products as well as directional and street signs; 1900-1950; call for more info.

Collectors

Alex Caiola
84 Seneca
Emerson, NJ 07630-1243
phone: 201-967-9540
Wants signs advertising soda, medicine, and tobacco.

Paul G. Engelke
23399 Rio Del Mar Dr.
Boca Raton, FL 33486-8504
phone: 407-338-3332
Wants to buy porcelain signs that advertise any type of merchandise: food, gas, oil, services, etc.

Michael Bruner
2615 Echo Lane
Ortonville, MI 48462
phone: 810-627-6351
Wants pre-1950 American or Canadian porcelain signs with good colors or graphics.

Richard Trautwein
437 Dawson St.
Sault Sainte Marie, MI 49783-2119
phone: 906-635-0356
Especially interested in porcelain advertising signs, neon clocks, and Coca Cola items.

Russell Barnes
P.O. Box 141994
Austin, TX 78714-1994
phone: 512-835-9510
fax: 512-835-1276
Wants to buy old, authentic, porcelain-on-metal advertising signs in good condition that are under 3' tall: signs such as gasoline, medicine, clothing, food, tobacco, beer, whiskey, soda water, lightning rods, etc.; please call collect.

Dealers

Robert C. English
P.O. Box 381
Marshfield Hills, MA 02051-0381
phone: 617-837-0111
Buys and sells porcelain signs including country store and automobile products as well as directional and street signs; 1900-1950.

Gary Darrow
Darrow's Fun Antiques
1101 1st Ave.
New York, NY 10021-8737
phone: 212-838-0730
fax: 212-838-3617
Buys & sells antique games, toys, ad signs, animated art, jukeboxes, slot machines, comic watches, bicycles & memorabilia of all types.

Walt Feiger
Walt's Antiques
2513 Nelson Rd.
Traverse City, MI 49686-8557
phone: 616-223-7386 or 616-223-4123
Wants to buy old porcelain or tin advertising signs.

Dave Beck
P.O. Box 435
Mediapolis, IA 52637-0435
phone: 319-394-3943
Buys all kinds of signs in any quantity; may be fairly new (but not reproductions) or 100 years old; tin, porcelain, cardboard, or paper; advertising soda, beer, tobacco, farm related items, or anything else.

Doug Clemence
Treasure Chest
436 North Chicago
Salina, KS 67401-2020
phone: 913-827-9371 or 913-825-4111
Buys, sells, trades old advertising signs.

Robert Newman
10809 Charnock Rd.
Los Angeles, CA 90034-6606
phone: 310-559-0539
Wants to buy neon and lighted clocks; also tin, cardboard and porcelain 1920s-1950s oil, auto, soft drink, bus and motorcycle advertising signs: Coca-Cola, Harley-Davidson, etc.; condition important; with graphics or pictures.

Experts

Bill Carlisle
P.O. Box 1146
Coshocton, OH 43812

Museums/Libraries

Museum of Transportation
15 Newton St.
Brookline, MA 02146
phone: 617-522-6140

Repro. Sources

Design Workshop
P.O. Box 236
West Barnstable, MA 02668

ANTIQUE-ALIKE
3147 Joppa Rd.
Cambridge, MD 21613-3640
Sells high quality copies of famous original cast iron banks, doorstops and tin advertising signs.

Attic Antiques, The
2301 Peach Orchard Rd.
Augusta, GA 30906
Sells reproduction paper and cardboard advertising signs.

New Century Galleries, Inc.
10613 Lorain Ave.
Cleveland, OH 44111
Sells reproduction paper and cardboard advertising signs.

Desperate Enterprises
P.O. Box 312
Wadsworth, OH 44281
phone: 216-334-1897
fax: 216-334-0153
Reproduces over 122 different nostalgia advertising signs on tin and over 725 nostalgia sepia toned 11"x14" photos.

Terri McCoy
AAA Sign Co.
354 S. State Line Rd.
Lowellville, OH 44436-9508
phone: 412-964-8394
fax: 412-964-1013
Manufactures and carries over 800 different reproduction (nostalgic) embossed tin sign designs; full color catalog $5; wholesale only, so send your business card and tax number.

4x1 Imports Inc.
5873 Day Rd.
Cincinnati, OH 45251
phone: 513-385-8185
fax: 513-385-8182
Over 250 signs in stock; painted on heavy die-cut metal stock; send $4 for catalog.

Meadow Breeze
2010 Wilmington Pk.
Cedarville, OH 45314

Spintops

Collectors

Glenn A. Scott
29 Upton Lane
Morrisville, PA 19067-2710
Wants to buy metal or celluloid spintops (half dollar size disk with wooden shaft) with advertising.

Sunshine Biscuit

Collectors

Liz & Dick Wilmes
38W567 Brindlewood Ave.
Elgin, IL 60123-7976
phone: 708-697-9679
fax: 708-742-1054
e-mail: Bblocks@cris.com
Wants to buy items produced by or for the Sunshine Biscuit Co. (or formally Loose-Wiles Company): display racks, containers, photos, trade cards, artwork, signs, toys, stationary, brochures, invoices, pins, calendars, etc.

Talcum Powder

Collectors

Millie Vaccarella
1955 Hythe St.
Roseville, MN 55113
phone: 612-631-2201
Wants to buy talcum powder tins, especially with babies or beautiful ladies.

Telephone & Telegraph

Experts

Michael Bruner
2615 Echo Lane
Ortonville, MI 48462
phone: 810-627-6351
Co-author with Bob Alexander of "A Collectors Guide to Telephone, Telegraph and Express Co. Advertising."

Tin Vienna Art Plates

Experts

Howard & Jane Hazelcorn
6731 Ashley Ct.
Sarasota, FL 34241-9696
phone: 941-921-1815
Authors of "Hazelcorn's Price Guide to Tin Vienna Art Plates"; tin advertising plates made from the 1890s to the 1950s. (Vienna Art is a trademark used by the H.D. Beach Co., OH.)

Tins

Dealers

Charles & Joan Rhoden
Rhoden's Antiques
605 N. Main
Georgetown, IL 61846-1439
phone: 217-662-8046 or 217-662-8440
fax: 217-662-8223
e-mail: jmrhoden@prairienet.org
Wants to buy pre-1960 lard tins and spice tins; send brand name and describe, include photo if possible.

Experts

David Zimmerman
6834 Newtonsville Rd.
Pleasant Plain, OH 45162
phone: 513-625-5188
Wants to buy advertising tin cans (smalls and samples): aspirins, condoms, needles, typewriter ribbons, medicines, etc. to publish "Encyclopedia of Advertising Tins, Vol. II"; send SASE plus 3 stamps for 20-page wants list with prices.

Trade Cards

(see also TRADING CARDS, Non-Sport)

Auction Services

Murray Cards (International) Ltd.
51 Watford Way
Hendon Central
London NW4 3JH, U.K.
phone: 0181-2025688
fax: 0181-2037578
e-mail: murraycards@ukbusiness.com
*Stocks and auctions trade cards; also
publishes "Cigarette Card Values" - a
catalog of cigarette and other trade
cards.*

Russell Mascieri
Victorian Images
3706 S. Acoma St.
Englewood, CO 80110
phone: 303-761-7906
e-mail: tccadc@aol.com
*Conducts specialized trade card mail
and telephone auctions.*

Clubs/Associations

Trade Card Collector's Association
Journal: Advertising Trade Card
Quarterly
3706 S. Acoma St.
Englewood, CO 80110
phone: 303-761-7906
e-mail: tccadc@aol.com

Collectors

Guy C. Weaver
302 South Newton St.
Pooler, GA 31322
phone: 912-748-6002
*Wants old trade cards, especially for
bottled products.*

Dealers

Jean Berg
P.O. Box 343
Granby, CT 06035
phone: 860-653-7982

Bill Mobley
P.O. Box 10
Schoharie, NY 12157

Stephen C. Jones
P.O. Box 267
Homer, NY 13077-0267
phone: 607-753-8822
*Wants pre-1910 advertising trade
cards illustrating products or services,
mechanical bank trade cards, Currier
& Ives trade cards, Victorian
scrapbooks, illustrated business
cards, cigar box sample labels and
sample books of labels.*

Karen Schechter
P.O. Box 563062
Dept. CIC
Charlotte, NC 28256-3072
*Buys and sells illustrator prints,
antique prints, Victorian paper
ephemera and postcards.*

Ron Schieber
1867 W. Market St.
Akron, OH 44313

Trade Cards (Tobacco)

(see also CIGARETTE COL-
LECTIBLES; SMOKING COL-
LECTIBLES)

Auction Services

Murray Cards (International) Ltd.
Newsletter: Cigarette Cards
51 Watford Way
Hendon Central
London NW4 3JH, U.K.
phone: 0181-2025688
fax: 0181-2037578
e-mail: murraycards@ukbusiness.com
*Stocks in excess of 20M cigarette &
trade cards; monthly specialist
auctions; publisher of card values &
books on card collecting.*

Collectors

Ron Stevenson
4920 Armoury St.
Niagara Falls
Ontario L2E 1T1 Canada
phone: 416-358-5497

William Nielsen
1379 Main St.
Brewster, MA 02631-1723
phone: 508-896-7389
*Wants U.S. tobacco related trade
cards.*

Charles Reuter
6 Joy Ave.
Mount Joy, PA 17552-1532
phone: 717-653-8505
*Collects cigarette silks and cigarette
trading cards.*

Paul Davis
308 Landsende Rd.
Devon, PA 19333
phone: 610-644-1216
*Wants insert and trade cards of
tobacco companies; also wants Liebig
and Au Bon Marche trade cards.*

Peter Gilleeny
36115-76 Rose Dr.
Fruitland Park, FL 34731
phone: 904-728-4819

Periodicals

David Stuckey
Magpie Publications
Magazine: Card Times
70 Winifred Lane
Aughton, Ormskirk
Lancashire L39 5DL, U.K.
phone: 0169 542 3470
fax: 0151 430 7836
*A monthly magazine focusing on trade
cards, cigarette silks and cards, also
trade cards of celebrities, politicians,
athletes, etc.; club activities, sales/
show calendars, ads.*

Typewriter Related

Collectors

Darryl Rehr
2591 Military Ave.
Los Angeles, CA 90064-1933
phone: 310-477-5229
fax: 310-268-8420
e-mail: dcrehr@earthlink.net
Internet: http://www.earthlink.net/
~dcrehr/
*Wants pre-1920 ads for typewriters
and office equipment; also trade
catalogs and business magazines, e.g.
"Business Man's Monthly."*

Woolson Spice Co.

Collectors

Bruce & Nada Ferris
3094 Oakes Dr.
Hayward, CA 94542-1234
phone: 510-581-5285
fax: 510-581-4469
e-mail: nada.ferris@kaiperm.org
*Wants Monarch food products items
from the 1920s: glass items with paper
labels, tins, Monarch cookbook, teenie
weenie popcorn, etc.; also Toledo, OH
advertising, Atlas, Woolson Spice &
Coffee, Toledo Biscuit, Buckey Beer.*

Experts

Randy Webb
42217 Cochran Mill Rd.
Leesburg, VA 20175
phone: 703-777-3600 or 540-668-6071
fax: 703-478-1160
e-mail: thewebbs3@aol.com
*Wants Wooson Spice Co. (Lion
Coffee) items: bags, cans, cards,
diecuts, premiums, store posters,
games, etc.; these materials needed
for entry into database and book on
everything Woolson Spice Co.*

AFRICAN AMERICANS

(see BLACK MEMORABILIA)

AGRICULTURE RELATED ITEMS

(see FARM COLLECTIBLES; FARM
MACHINERY; TOYS, Farm;
TRACTORS)

AIR LABELS

(see AIRLINE MEMORABILIA;
LUGGAGE LABELS)

AIRGUNS

(see also TOYS, BB Guns)

Clubs/Associations

Mike Ahuna, Sec.
Carolina Airgun Club
Newsletter: Carolina Airgun Club
Newsletter
5995 Renwood Dr.
Winston Salem, NC 27106
phone: 919-922-1031
fax: 919-922-1031
*The Club holds Target Matches, Field
Target Matches, and Silhouette
Matches the year round; Matches are
open to the public and Club members.*

Alan Waln
American Airgun Field Target
Association
Newsletter: AAFTA Newsletter
3050 Business Park Dr., Ste. B
Norcross, GA 30071-1452

Dealers

Mike Ahuna
Mike's Crosman Service
5995 Renwood Dr.
Winston Salem, NC 27106
phone: 919-922-1031
fax: 919-922-1031
*Buys and sells old and new airguns;
authorized Crosman airgun service
station, and is an authorized Beeman
5 Star Dealer.*

Periodicals

Newsletter: Airgun Letter, The
4614 Wodland Rd.
Ellicott City, MD 21042-6329
phone: 410-730-5496
fax: 410-730-9544
e-mail: staff@airgunletter.net
Internet: http://www.airgunletter.net
*A monthly newsletter for airgun users
and collectors.*

Barry Abel, Ed.
Newsletter: Airgun Ads
P.O. Box 33
Hamilton, MT 59840-0033
phone: 406-363-3805
fax: 406-363-4117
*Published monthly to enable
subscribers to buy and sell airguns of
all types, from Olympic match grade
to smooth bore, including parts,
accessories and literature.*

AIRLINE MEMORABILIA

(see also AIRPLANES; AIR
SICKNESS BAGS; AVIATION;
AVIATION MEMORABILIA;
LUGGAGE LABELS; STAMP
COLLECTING, Air Mail Related;
TOYS, Airplane Related; TRANS-
PORTATION COLLECTIBLES)

Clubs/Associations

Paul F. Collins
World Airline Historical Society
Magazine: Captain's Log
13739 Picarsa Dr.
Jacksonville, FL 32225
phone: 904-221-1446
Internet: http://www.aircruise.com/wahs/
*Members are interested in the
collecting of airline memorabilia and
in the study of airlines, airliners, kits,
models and related items.*

Louis Wendruck
Gay Airline Club, The
Magazine: Gay Airline Club Newsletter,
The
P.O. Box 69A04 - Dept. Mal
West Hollywood, CA 90069-0066
phone: 213-650-5112
e-mail: airlinet@hotmail.com
Internet: http://members.tripod.com
*A club for gay men interested in
meeting others who collect airline
memorabilia, travel or work in the
airline and travel industry; quarterly
magazine has ads for airline
collectibles wanted and for sale.*

Collectors

Charles C. Quarles
204 Reservation Dr.
Spindale, NC 28160-1534
phone: 704-286-2962 or 704-245-7803
fax: 704-286-3224
*Wants pilot and steward/ess wings,
hat badges, metal travel agency
display model airliners, etc. from
1930s to 1960s U.S. airlines.*

Randy Ridgely
447 Oglethorpe Ave.
Athens, GA 30606-2236
phone: 706-549-9264
*Wants railroad, steamship and airline
items.*

Bill Rosenbloom
1893 Worcester
Saint Paul, MN 55116-2614
phone: 612-699-2784
*Wants all older logoed airline items:
playing cards, schedules, posters,
kiddie wings, and all other logo-
marked items.*

Dick Wallin
P.O. Box 1784
Springfield, IL 62705-1784
phone: 217-498-9279
*Wants airline logo items: dishes,
glassware, playing cards, crew wings
and badges, silverplate pitchers,
creamers; also large travel agency
size plane models, chrome ashtrays
with plane models.*

Craig Morris
105 Silver Willow Ct.
Galt, CA 95632-2442
phone: 209-745-4539
*Wants to buy airline memorabilia:
1920-1960 airline postcards, time
tables, posters, paper ephemera, etc.;
will pay postage.*

Dealers

Bizarre Bazarre
130 1/4 East 65th St.
New York, NY 10021-7007
phone: 212-517-2100
fax: 212-517-2283
*Wants museum quality aviation
models, metal models of propelled
aircraft, airline and travel agent
display airplane models, factory and
industrial design models.*

Jeffrey D. Boutin
JB Airline Collectibles
705 White Bluff Ave.
Savannah, GA 31419-3140
phone: 912-920-9907
fax: 912-920-9906
e-mail: jefboutin@aol.com
*Wants to buy memorabilia from U.S.
airlines, past or present; postcards,
flight schedules/time tables,
glassware, dinnerware, flatware/
silverware, baggage tags, etc.,
especially Northeast, National,
Braniff.*

Just Plane Crazy
1224 N.W. 72nd Ave.
Miami, FL 33152-1238
*Buys/sells airline items: books,
calendars, magazines, models, shirts,
slides, etc.*

Mike Fleming
Mike Fleming Antiques & Aviation
   Collectibles
5221 N. Damen Ave.
Chicago, IL 60625-1318
phone: 312-561-8696
e-mail: faasale@aol.com
*Wants to buy commercial airlines
items, "anything with logos", travel
models, advertising, and old aviation
items; also Lindbergh items.*

Experts

Larry McLaughlin
17 Seventh Ave.
Smithtown, NY 11787-4508
phone: 516-265-9224
*Buys, collects and specializes in
airline items: travel agency models,
ashtrays, lighters, timetables, crew hat
badges, pins, wings, commercial or
military models, helmets, manuals;
also wants tin airplane toys.*

John R. Joiner
173 Green Tree Dr.
Newnan, GA 30265-2022
phone: 770-502-9565
*Wants pilot and flight attendant
wings, hat badges; also wants display
models, early signs, anniversary pins,
postcards, time tables, playing cards
from commercial airlines, pre-1970s;
no military items, please.*

Don Thomas
5134 Sugar Camp Rd.
Milford, OH 45150-9674
phone: 513-248-0485
fax: 513-248-0485
Buys, sells and specializes in airline

*memorabilia; author of "Nostalgia
Panamerican", "Poster Art of the
Airlines", "Lindbergh and Commer-
cial Aviation", "Nostalgia North
Americana", "Airline Artistry,"
"Nostalgia Artistica."*

Dick Wallin
P.O. Box 1784
Springfield, IL 62705-1784
phone: 217-498-9279
*Author of "Airline Collectibles
General Information"; he will try to
answer questions and provide
information on buying and selling of
specific items, or he will direct you to
someone who can.*

Periodicals

Magazine: Airliner
P.O. Box 521238
Miami, FL 33125
phone: 305-477-7163
fax: 305-599-1995

R.D. Roland
R.S. & T. Ry. Co.
Ad Paper: Main Line Journal, The
P.O. Box 121
Streamwood, IL 60107-0121
*A bi-monthly "ad" paper exclusively
for buying and selling railroad
collectibles as well as airline and
steamship memorabilia; subscribers
receive FREE ads.*

Magazine: Airways
P.O. Box 1109
Sandpoint, ID 83864
phone: 208-263-2098 or 800-440-5166
fax: 208-263-3313
e-mail: airways@rabd.nidlink.com
Internet: http://www.flightdata.com/
airways/airways.html
*International bi-monthly magazine
devoted to airlines and commercial
aircraft; a global review of
commercial flight; periodically
contains articles of interest to the
collector of airline memorabilia.*

Air Sickness Bags

Collectors

Dr. Walter Brinker
Niedernfeld 2
42477 Radevormwald
Germany
phone: 49-219540928
fax: 49-21956517
e-mail: walter.brinker@t-online.dc
*A collector with about 1100 air
sickness bags from 500 air lines.*

Baggage I.D. Labels

(see also LUGGAGE LABELS)

Experts

H. Van Dyk
7 Birchwood Ave.
Peabody, MA 01960
phone: 508-535-0353
*Author of "Catalog of Baggage I.D.
Labels, Vol. 1, U.S.A. & Canada" &*

*"..Vol. 2, Europe & Middle East";
buys airline baggage I.D. labels (for
travelers' name/address); 1st Class,
cabin baggage, crew, fragile, etc.; no
destination labels.*

Models

Experts

Bob Keller
Starline Hobbies
P.O. Box 38
Stanton, CA 90680-0038
phone: 714-826-5216
e-mail: prsdog@aol.com
Internet: http://pages.prodigy.com/prs7/
kitshow.html
*Especially wants to buy plastic model
kits; can provide professional
appraisals of collections.*

Models (Desk)

(see also TOYS, Airplane)

Collectors

Ira S. Kuperstein
22 Brush Hill Terrace
Butler, NJ 07405
phone: 201-283-2420 or 800-526-5177
fax: 201-283-2426
Wants to buy airplane display models.

David Ostrowski
5411 Masser Lane
Fairfax, VA 22032-3817
phone: 703-323-6674

Dealers

Steve & Sue Spatz
P.O. Box 541638
Merritt Island, FL 32954
phone: 407-452-4991
*Buys and sells airline/travel agent
promotional display models.*

Experts

Larry McLaughlin
17 Seventh Ave.
Smithtown, NY 11787-4508
phone: 516-265-9224
*Wants to buy airplane, rocket, missile
desk models: manufacturers' display
models, travel agency models,
commercial or military, etc.; has
written articles for aviation toy
magazines; staff editor for "Miniature
Aircraft Quarterly."*

Pilots Wings

(see also AVIATION MEMORA-
BILIA, Military Insignia)

Collectors

Michael Dusek
1058 Lupin Dr. #5
Salinas, CA 93906
phone: 408-757-2526
*Wants to buy military wings, civilian
wings, sterling silver wings; also*

wants China, Burma, or India bracelets related to aviation.

Playing Cards

Experts

Fred Chan
Top Flite Information
P.O. Box 2744
Sequim, WA 98382-2744
phone: 360-681-4671
fax: 360-681-4671
Author of "Airline Playing Cards" with supplements; buys, trades, and sells airline playing cards (decks and singles); organizes Airline Collectibles Shows in Seattle, WA; appraises airline playing card collections.

AIRPLANES

(see also AIRLINE MEMORABILIA; AVIATION; AVIATION MEMORABILIA; TOYS, Airplane Related)

Appraisers

Michael Bonventre
MJB Aviation
P.O. Box 1136
Seaford, NY 11783
phone: 516-328-0847
fax: 516-783-2536
e-mail: airdrv@aol.com
Airplane appraisal and consulting service: valuations, estates, bankruptcy, tax appeals, repossessions, matrimonial, insurance, corporate, condemnations, condition surveys.

National Aircraft Appraisers Association
P.O. Box 528
Hillsboro, MO 63050
phone: 314-285-4768

Auction Services

Jon Baddeley
Sotheby's
34-35 New Bond St.
London W1A 2AA, U.K.
phone: 0171-4938080 or 0171-4085205
fax: 0171-4085911
Conducts regular specialized auctions of vintage aircraft.

Clubs/Associations

Antique Aeroplane Association of Australia
Magazine: Rag & Tube
P.O. Box 1036
City Road P.O.
Victoria 3205 Australia
Australia's only dedicated old aeroplane magazine; published four times per year.

Popular Flying Association
Terminal Building, Shoreham Airport
Shoreham-by-Sea
W. Sussex BN43 5FF, U.K.
The United Kingdom's association for the construction of amateur-built

aircraft and vintage aircraft restoration.

L.E. Opdycke
World War I Aeroplanes, Inc.
15 Crescent Rd.
Poughkeepsie, NY 12601-4405
phone: 914-473-3679
A service organization devoted to those magnificent flying machines of 1900-1919 and 1920-1940; for builders, museums, restorers, historians, modelers and collectors; publishes the journals "WWI Aero" and "Skyways."

Great War Aeroplanes Association, The
Newsletter: Great Times, The
145 E. 14th St.
Indianapolis, IN 46202
Members share an interest in WWI aircraft.

Robert Taylor, Pres.
Antique Airplane Association, Inc.
Magazine: Antique Airplane News & Digest
Rte. 2 Box 172
Ottumwa, IA 52501
phone: 515-938-2773
The organization for antique and classic airplane owners, pilots and enthusiasts.

Dealers

Bob Von Willer
Exotic Aircraft Company
1718 North Marshall Ave.
El Cajon, CA 92020
phone: 619-562-7467
fax: 619-448-2110
e-mail: baron@skyguy.com
Internet: http://www.barnstormers.com/classify.html
Specializes in the marketing of antique aircraft, including warbirds; appraiser, dealer, expert, auctioneer, collector, and repair services offered.

Experts

Bob Von Willer
Exotic Aircraft Company
1718 North Marshall Ave.
El Cajon, CA 92020
phone: 619-562-7467
fax: 619-448-2110
e-mail: baron@skyguy.com
Internet: http://www.barnstormers.com/classify.html
Specializes in the marketing of antique aircraft, including warbirds; appraiser, dealer, expert, auctioneer, collector, and repair services offered.

Museums/Libraries

Piper Aviation Museum
One Piper Way
Lock Haven, PA 17745

Periodicals

L.E. Opdycke
World War I Aeroplanes, Inc.
Journal: WWI Aero
15 Crescent Rd.
Poughkeepsie, NY 12601-4405
phone: 914-473-3679
A quarterly magazine for collectors, restorers, replica builders, historians, and modelers focusing on 1900-1919 aircraft.

L.E. Opdycke
World War I Aeroplanes, Inc.
Journal: Skyways
15 Crescent Rd.
Poughkeepsie, NY 12601-4405
phone: 914-473-3679
A quarterly magazine for collectors, restorers, replica builders, historians, and modelers focusing on 1920-1940 aircraft.

Trader Publishing Company
Magazine: Aero Trader & Chopper Shopper
P.O. Box 9059
Clearwater, FL 34618-9059
phone: 813-712-0035 or 800-548-8889
fax: 813-712-0034
Internet: http://www.traderonline.com

TAP Publishing Co.
Newspaper: Trade-A-Plane
P.O. Box 509
Crossville, TN 38557
phone: 800-337-5263 or 615-484-5137
fax: 800-423-9030
Published three times each month; huge advertising newspaper containing everything to keep you flying: from antique airplanes to parts, electronics and related services.

Christina Gargano
Heartland Communications Group, Inc.
Magazine: Aviators Hot Line
1003 Central Ave.
Fort Dodge, IA 50501
phone: 800-247-2000
fax: 515-574-2233
Internet: http://www.hlipublishing.com
The national and international marketplace for active buyers and sellers of corporate and general aircraft, parts and service.

H.G. Frautschy
Experimental Aircraft Association
Magazine: Vintage Airplane
P.O. Box 3086
Oshkosh, WI 54903-3086
phone: 800-843-3612 or 414-426-6515
fax: 414-426-4873

H.G. Frautschy
Experimental Aircraft Association
Magazine: Sport Aviation
P.O. Box 3086
Oshkosh, WI 54903-3086
phone: 800-843-3612 or 414-426-6515
fax: 414-426-4873

H.G. Frautschy
Experimental Aircraft Association
Magazine: Sport Aerobatics
P.O. Box 3086
Oshkosh, WI 54903-3086
phone: 800-843-3612 or 414-426-6515
fax: 414-426-4873

Kathy Kingston
Intertec Publishing Corp.
Price Guide: Aircraft Bluebook - Price Digest
P.O. Box 12901
Overland Park, KS 66282
phone: 800-654-6776
Comprehensive quarterly index of the value of used fixed wing aircraft and helicopters; controlled availability; no vintage, antique, military, kit or experimental planes.

Steven D. Werner
Werner Publishing Corp.
Magazine: Plane & Pilot
12121 Wilshire Blvd., Ste. 1220
Los Angeles, CA 90025-1175
phone: 310-820-1500

Norman Ridker
Fancy Publications, Inc.
Magazine: Private Pilot
2401 Beverly Blvd.
Los Angeles, CA 90057
phone: 213-385-2222
fax: 213-385-8565

Joseph V. Mizrahi
Sentry Books, Inc.
Magazine: Airpower
10718 White Oak Ave.
Granada Hills, CA 91344
phone: 818-368-2012

Dave & Mary Lou Sclair
Northwest Flyer Inc.
Magazine: General Aviation News & Flyer
P.O. Box 39099
Tacoma, WA 98439-0099
phone: 206-471-9888
fax: 206-471-9911
e-mail: 73200.126@compuserve.com

Ford Tri-Motors

Dealers

Tim O'Callaghan
P.O. Box 512
Northville, MI 48167
phone: 248-449-2652
Wants to buy anything relating to Henry Ford or the Ford Motor Company; especially items relating to the Ford Tri-motor airplane of the 1920s and '30s; also pre-WWII aviation time tables and airplane & engine brochures.

Model

(see also KITS; MODELS)

Clubs/Associations

Larry Clark
Society of Antique Modelers
Newsletter: Sam Speaks
P.O. Box 528
Lucerne Valley, CA 92356
phone: 714-542-8294
e-mail: CWReich@aol.com
Internet: http://www.napanet.net/~nedn/
index.html
Focuses on the collecting, restoring and operating of free flight and R/C model model airplanes of vintage design; chapters worldwide.

Periodicals

Erika Daileda
Wise Owl Worldwide Publications
Magazine: Scale Aircraft Modeling
4314 West 238th St. - Dept. MACR
Torrance, CA 90505-4509
phone: 310-375-6258
fax: 310-375-0548
e-mail: wiseowl@sprintmail.com
A monthly English publication; gives details, historical facts, and photos on specific aircraft each month.

Model (Remote Control)

(see also MODELS, Aircraft [Flying])

Periodicals

Magazine: FlightSmith Radio Control Magazine
P.O. Box 59905
Chicago, IL 60659-0905
Bi-monthly publication for radio control flying; includes construction articles, beginner sections, product reviews.

Erika Daileda
Wise Owl Worldwide Publications
Magazine: Radio Control Scale Aircraft
4314 West 238th St. - Dept. MACR
Torrance, CA 90505-4509
phone: 310-375-6258
fax: 310-375-0548
e-mail: wiseowl@sprintmail.com
An English publication; how-to tips, engines building and repair, scale drawings, flying, buy/sell, ads for services and parts.

Magazine: R/C Modeler Magazine
P.O. Box 487
Sierra Madre, CA 91025
Complete R/C publication for the remote control enthusiast; construction, how-to's; equipment, contests, etc.

Sailplanes

Clubs/Associations

Robin Traves
Vintage Gliding Club
Magazine: VGC News
Rose View, Marden Rd.
Staplehurst
Kent TN12 0JG, U.K.
Members focus mainly on gliders designed during the 1930s, but includes some earlier and later; vintage gliders throughout the world, rallies, history.

J. Scott
Vintage Sailplane Association
Magazine: Bungee Cord
4310 River Bottom Dr.
Norcross, GA 30092
phone: 770-446-5533
e-mail: gnuse@alt.mindspring.com
Internet: http://www.iac.net/~feguy/VSA
Soaring enthusiasts who are keeping our gliding history and heritage alive by building, restoring, flying gliders from the past.

Collectors

J. Scott
4310 River Bottom Dr.
Norcross, GA 30092
phone: 540-882-5504
e-mail: Jscottvsa@aol.com
Private collector of rare and restorable gliders.

Waco

Clubs/Associations

Alan & Drina Abel
International Waco Association, The
Magazine: IWA Magazine
P.O. Box 665
Destin, FL 32540-0665
Maintains large file of air airplane history and photos; contributions of related material welcomed.

AIRSHIPS

(see also KITES; STAMP COLLECT-ING, Covers [Balloon Related])

Balloons

Clubs/Associations

Dr. A.D. Topping
Lighter-Than-Air Society
250 Saddle Horn Circle
Roswell, GA 30076

Collectors

Mark Walberg
P.O. Box 130
Sunbury, PA 17801
phone: 717-286-1617
fax: 717-286-9686
Wants anything with balloon subjects: letters, medals, drawings, fans, books, posters, prints, coins, etc.; 18th century to 19th century.

Alan Zimkus
Aerial Adventures, Inc.
1290 Creek Point Dr.
Rochester, MI 48307-1727
phone: 800-886-3766
fax: 810-650-3361
e-mail: azimkus@aol.com
Wants to buy items relating to early gas balloons: postcards, posters, memorabilia, books, medals, etc.

Dirigibles, Zeppelins, Blimps

Collectors

Hank Loescher
90 Scofield Rd.
Bridgeport, CT 06605-2953
phone: 203-368-4983
Wants zeppelin or dirigible related items: books, charts, photos, relics, souvenirs, fabric, personal items, info., etc.

Henry Heiman, III
P.O. Box 316
South Salem, NY 10590-0316
Specializes in Zeppelins, German flying boats.

Jason K. Phillips
130 Long Meadow Lane
State College, PA 16801
phone: 814-861-6533
e-mail: jkp107@psuvm.psu.edu
Wants to buy anything having to do with airships, zeppelins or dirigibles: books, china, flown items, photographs, postcards, artifacts, etc.

Frederick Lingenfelser
814 Byram St.
Reading, PA 19606-1446
Wants to buy pre-1945 Zeppelin items, must be passenger lines: post cards, letters, deck plans, books, tickets, brochures, dinnerware, souvenirs, models, menus, etc.

Charles M. Jacobs
P.O. Box 785
Kenton, OH 43326-0785
e-mail: zeppo@kenton.com

Alan Zimkus
Aerial Adventures, Inc.
1290 Creek Point Dr.
Rochester, MI 48307-1727
phone: 800-886-3766
fax: 810-650-3361
e-mail: azimkus@aol.com
Wants to buy items relating to dirigibles, zeppelins, and blimps: postcards, posters, memorabilia, books, medals, etc.

Dealers

Jody Stamp Studio Inc.
6001 Riverdale Ave.
Bronx, NY 10471-1615

Experts

Art Bink
Zeppelin
P.O. Box 2502
Cinnaminson, NJ 08077-5250
phone: 609-829-3959
Historian not dealer wants airship items: zeppelin, blimp, dirigible memorabilia; pieces, toys, photos, books, medals, china, etc.; no balloons.

Charles Ira Sachs
TransAtlantic Research
P.O. Box 8797
Studio City, CA 91618-8797
phone: 818-985-1345
fax: 818-985-1345
e-mail: transatlantic@juno.com
Buys/sells/specializes/lectures on ocean liner and zeppelin history & memorabilia from the high seas (i.e. none from coastal or river steamers) dating from 1840 to 1960s; posters, postcards and related material for collectors/museums.

Museums/Libraries

Art Bink
Navy Lakehurst Historical Society
P.O. Box 2502
Cinnaminson, NJ 08077-5250
phone: 609-829-3959

ALARM BOXES

Collectors

Tom Mills
30 Bay Path Rd.
Spencer, MA 01562-1602
phone: 508-885-9550
Wants fire alarm and police boxes especially ones with dates cast into them; seeks cast iron signs and street letter pickup boxes marked "U.S. MAIL"; best to write and send photos.

ALBUMS

(see also AUTOGRAPHS; CELLU-LOID ITEMS; PAPER COL-LECTIBLES; RECORDS)

Autograph

Dealers

M. McGovern
Home Grown
1012 Manoa Rd.
Wynnewood, PA 19096
phone: 610-649-6316
fax: 610-649-2369
Wants to buy 19th century "Friend-ship" Autograph Albums, female Americans only with multiple entries.

ALCOHOLICS ANONYMOUS ITEMS

Collectors

PREP
12 Crest Rd. E.
Rolling Hills, CA 90274
phone: 213-541-5256
fax: 213-541-0332
Wants Alcoholics Anonymous 1st edition books, with or without dust jackets and 2nd editions wit dust jackets; also wants literature from 1939 through 1975.

Dealers

Clark Phelps
Amusement Sales Co.
127 North Main St.
Midvale, UT 84047-2424
phone: 801-255-4731
Historian and book seller wants AA books, pamphlets, etc. before 1974.

Experts

Charles Bishop, Jr.
Bishop of Books, The
46 Eureka Ave.
Wheeling, WV 26003-1424
phone: 304-242-2937
Buy, sell, appraise books, magazines, posters, postcards, etc. relating to alcoholism or Alcoholics Anonymous.

ALMANACS

(see BOOKS)

ALUMINUM

Hammered

Book Sellers

Jo-D Books
81 Willard Terrace
Stamford, CT 06903-4927
phone: 203-322-0568
Books on Art Deco Chrome.

Clubs/Associations

Dannie Woodard
Hammered Aluminum Collectors Association
Newsletter: Aluminist, The
P.O. Box 1346
Weatherford, TX 76086
phone: 817-594-4680
Newsletter provides updated information on prices, patterns, ads and companies; group organized in 1990; 200 members.

Collectors

Danielle Lanier
Wendell August Collectors Guild
P.O. Box 107
Grove City, PA 16127-0107
phone: 800-386-6155

Mike Landis
P.O. Box 544
Akron, PA 17501
phone: 888-248-2291
Wants to buy hammered aluminum with the following marks: Arthur Armour, Palmer Smith, Cellini; also wants old Wendell August; call toll free or send picture and information.

Bonita Campbell, Ph.D.
P.O. Box 3151
Granada Hills, CA 91394
e-mail: hcspc003@csun.edu
Collector and researcher actively engaged in academic research of artisans, companies, marks, times of production, and other information pertinent to hammered aluminum;

also preparing research monographs as appropriate.

Dealers

John M. Rowley
Eye-Openers
HC 63, Box 356
South Acworth, NH 03607
phone: 603-835-2281 or 888-8OP-ENER
Buys and sells kitchen collectibles, gadgets, openers, and especially hammered aluminum.

Chuck Haley
Sherlock's
13926 Double Girth Ct.
Matthews, NC 28105
phone: 704-843-3433 or 704-847-5480
Dealing primarily in totally handwrought pieces, especially Wendell August and Arthur Armour, as well as Kensington.

Experts

Ed Gangawere
American Dream Collectibles
5128 Schultz Bridge Rd.
Zionsville, PA 18092-2542
phone: 215-679-2254
Buys, sells, collects hammered aluminum; National Hammered Aluminum Show held the last full weekend in October; call for location and time.

Dannie Woodard
P.O. Box 1346
Weatherford, TX 76086
phone: 817-594-4680
Co-author with Billie Wood of "Hammered Aluminum - Hand Wrought Collectibles."

Periodicals

Ed Gangawere
American Dream Collectibles
Newsletter: Continental Report, The
5128 Schultz Bridge Rd.
Zionsville, PA 18092-2542
phone: 215-679-2254
Published quarterly; focuses on all aspects of the Hammered Aluminum trade done by the Continental Company.

AMERICAN BANDSTAND

(see also MUSIC, Rock 'N' Roll)

Clubs/Associations

Dave Frees
American Bandstand 1950's Fan Club
Magazine: Bandstand Boogie
P.O. Box 131
Adamstown, PA 19501-0131
phone: 717-738-2513
Focuses on "American Bandstand" from the 1950s and 1980s; magazine published twice a year; sells "Dave's Collectables Catalog" (50s through 80s photos, magazines, etc.) for $1 - free to members.

Collectors

Lana Director
1 Gwizdak Court
Sayreville, NJ 08872
phone: 908-727-8647
Wants to buy pre-1964 American Bandstand, Teen-related magazines; also Ponytail, Dateline, and similar vinyl items.

AMERICAN INDIAN

(see also ARCHAEOLOGY; BASKETS; BEADS, Trade; BOOKS, Reference [American Indian]; CIGAR STORE COLLECTIBLES; EDGED WEAPONS; HERITAGE RESOURCES; INDIAN WARS; PREHISTORIC ARTIFACTS; TEXTILES, Blankets; WESTERN AMERICANA)

Appraisers

Maryann L'Heureux
Native American Arts Appraisals
P.O. Box 267
Hockessin, DE 19707-0267
phone: 302-234-3190 or 302-234-1358
fax: 302-234-3190
e-mail: maryann_lheureux@msn.com
Internet: http://www.concentric/net/ ~lheureaux/maryann.html
Senior member of the American Society of Appraisers, tested in North American Indian art and artifacts.

John C. Hill
Gallery of American Indian Art
6962 East First Ave., Ste. 104
Scottsdale, AZ 85251
phone: 602-946-2910
fax: 602-946-7410
Expert dealer and appraiser of old Southwestern Indian, and Indian beadwork.

Pierre Bovis
AZ-Tex Cowboy Trading Co., The
P.O. Box 13345
Tucson, AZ 85732-3345
phone: 520-318-9512
fax: 520-318-0023
Buy, sells, appraises cowboy memorabilia, primitive arts, American Indian arts, Napoleonic artifacts.

Gene Quintana
P.O. Box 533
Carmichael, CA 95609
phone: 916-485-8232
Collector and appraiser of American Indian basketry and blankets.

Auction Services

Linda Dyer
Skinner, Inc.
357 Main St.
Bolton, MA 01740-1104
phone: 508-779-6241 or 617-350-5400
fax: 508-779-5144
Established in 1964, Skinner Inc. is the fifth largest auction house in the US; has offices in Bolton and Boston, MA.

Willis Henry
Willis Henry Auctions, Inc.
22 Main St.
Marshfield, MA 02059
phone: 617-834-7774
fax: 617-826-3520
Specializes in the sale of American antiques of all kinds, particularly Shaker, American Indian and early American.

Sotheby's
1334 York Ave.
New York, NY 10021
phone: 212-606-7370 or 212-606-7000
Internet: http://www.sothebys.com
Over 70 collecting areas are featured at Sotheby's auctions including toys, dolls, porcelain, furniture, silver, art, books; exhibitions are free and everyone is welcome; for a free copy of "Sotheby's Newsletter", call 212-606-7245.

Garth's Auction, Inc.
2690 Stratford Rd.
P.O. Box 369
Delaware, OH 43015
phone: 614-362-4771 or 614-369-5085
fax: 614-363-0164

Old Barn Auction
10040 S.R. 224 West
Findlay, OH 45840
phone: 419-422-8531 or 419-384-3730
Conducts specialized auctions of American Indian items.

Doug Allard
Allard Indian Auctions
P.O. Box 460
Saint Ignatius, MT 59865
phone: 406-745-2951 or 800-821-3318
fax: 406-745-2961
Conducts auctions specializing in Indian items.

Preston E. Miller
Four Winds Indian Auction
P.O. Box 580
Saint Ignatius, MT 59865-0580
phone: 406-745-4336
Conducts mail/phone bid auctions of Indian collectibles: beadwork, old photos, stone relics, parfleches, weapons, pottery, trade beads, baskets, replicas, Navajo rugs, etc.; photo illustrated catalog $15.

Chuck Jackson
Dunning's Auction Service
755 Church Rd.
Elgin, IL 60123-9302
phone: 708-741-3483 or 800-462-2444
fax: 708-741-3589
Internet: http:///www.dunnings.com
Conducts semiannual Native American auctions.

Joy Luke
Joy Luke Auction Gallery
300 E. Grove St.
Bloomington, IL 61701-5232
phone: 309-828-5533
fax: 309-829-2266
Conducts periodic auctions specializing Indian items.

Butterfield & Butterfield
220 San Bruno Ave.
San Francisco, CA 94103-5018
phone: 415-861-7500
fax: 415-553-8678
Specialties include posters, toys, decorative arts, furniture, photography, etc.; the largest full service auction in the west.

Jack Sellner
Sellner Auctions
P.O. Box 308
Fremont, CA 94537-0308
Conducts annual auction of Indian items.

Clubs/Associations

Susan McGuire
Indian Arts & Crafts Association
Newsletter: IACA Newsletter
122 Laveta NE, Ste. B
Albuquerque, NM 87108-1613
phone: 505-265-9149 or 505-255-6032
To collect, promote, preserve, protect and enhance the understanding of authentic American Indian crafts and arts.

Collectors

Dr. Fred Cesana
49 E. Main St.
Plainville, CT 06062
phone: 203-747-2759
Wants pre-1880 Plains Indian weapons: tomahawks, knives, lances, clubs, rifles; also wants important beadwork.

Edwin Snyder
P.O. Box 156
Lancaster, KY 40444-0156
phone: 606-792-4816
Wants to buy baskets, totems and carvings.

Brian L. Ebosh
P.O. Box 261
Lagrange, OH 44050-0261
phone: 216-355-8118
Wants Indian and pioneer metal axes: pipe tomahawks, spike, spontoon, Missouri, and related items.

Jan Sorgenfrei
10040 S.R. 224 West
Findlay, OH 45840
phone: 419-422-8531 or 419-384-3730

Larry Jarvinen
313 Condon Rd.
Manistee, MI 49660
phone: 616-723-5063
Wants to buy American Indian trade beads, silver, axes, beadwork, brass kettles, etc.

Mike Kramer
P.O. Box 3257
Vallejo, CA 94590-0676
phone: 800-568-8883 or 800-446-6581
fax: 707-642-2456
Wants early American Indian items: model totems, trade totems, quality baskets.

Daniel Brown
P.O. Box 149
Davenport, CA 95017-0149
phone: 408-426-0134 or 800-492-6786
Wants to buy museum quality Indian relics: pre-1900 Plains Indian material including shirts, shields, weapons, beadwork, quillwork; large Pueblo pots, early Navajo blankets, saltillos, old Navajo jewelry, fine baskets, NW coast, etc.

Dealers

D.S. Ellis
RR 3
Dundas
Ontario L9H 5E3 Canada
phone: 519-756-9515
Wants to buy old Indian items: beadwork, pipes, wood or stone clubs, Eskimo artifacts, wooden masks, blankets, ivory, quillwork, etc.

Raheema Vasudevan
Chakra
8249 Shaughnessy St.
Vancouver
Brit. Col. V6P 3X9 Canada
phone: 604-325-5092
e-mail: chakra@marttnet.com
Internet: http://www.grantbc.com/chakra
Provides authentic, Southwestern native art and craft to collectors, interior designers, and retailers; collection consists of contemporary Navajo and Pueblo art and craft of exceptional quality.

Norman Hurst, ISA
Hurst Gallery
53 Mount Auburn St.
Cambridge, MA 02138
phone: 617-491-6888
fax: 617-661-0439
e-mail: hurst@world.std.com
Internet: http://world.std.com/~hurst/
Buys, sells, appraises, restores African, Oceanic, Native American, PreColumbian and Asian art.

David Summers
Native American Artifacts
45 West Parkway
Victor, NY 14564-1243
phone: 716-924-5167
Buys and sells North or South American Indian made or traded pieces or collections from either historic or prehistoric periods; wants to buy arrowheads and stone tools; send $5 for bi-annual catalog.

Von Hilliard
Indian Shop, The
Newsletter: Dig: The Archaeological Newsletter
P.O. Box 246
Independence, KY 41051-0246
phone: 606-428-2485
Publishes at least 4 large catalogs (50-80 pgs.) per year; send $5 for catalog.

Randy Sandler
Cincinnati Art Galleries
635 Main St.
Cincinnati, OH 45202
phone: 513-381-2128
fax: 513-381-7527

Conrad "Duke" Glodowski
White Deed Indian Traders
P.O. Box 506
Stevens Point, WI 54481-0506
phone: 715-344-9217
fax: 715-344-9217
Buys and sells Native American Indian arts and crafts; offers a search service for artifacts and contemporary North American crafts.

World City, Inc.
6935 James Ave. South
Minneapolis, MN 55423-2147
Buys and sells Indian items such as beaded items, pottery, Navajo rugs, quilled items, Kachinas, Northwest Coast items; both pre-historic and historic; send price wanted (unless unsure), description, photos, and SASE.

John Buxton
Shango Galleries
6717 Spring Valley
Dallas, TX 75240
phone: 972-239-4620 or 972-239-9943
fax: 972-239-9766
e-mail: jbuxton@arttrak.com
Internet: http://www.arttrak.com
Buys, sells, and appraises African, Precolumbian, Oceanic, and American Indian art.

Donna McMenamin
5001 Woodway #1002
Houston, TX 77056-1718
phone: 713-622-7252
fax: 713-780-9723
e-mail: DMcMenamin@msn.com
Internet: http://
www.donnamcmenamin.com
Buys and sells historical Native American baskets, pre-1900 beadwork, and Navajo rugs.

Christopher A. Jones
Squash Blossom, The
2531 W. Colorado Ave.
Colorado Springs, CO 80904
phone: 719-632-1899
Dealer/appraiser specializing in Southwestern Native American jewelry and art including pottery, weaving, Kachinas (both prehistoric and historic.)

Wayne & Kathryn Andros
White Dove Traders
P.O. Box 6572
Mesa, AZ 85216-6572
phone: 800-824-3606
Retailer and show promoter for contemporary Native American Indian arts and crafts.

John C. Hill
Gallery of American Indian Art
6962 East First Ave., Ste. 104
Scottsdale, AZ 85251
phone: 602-946-2910
fax: 602-946-7410
Wants to buy early Southwest Indian items including classic Navajo & Pueblo silver & turquoise, Indian blankets and other textiles, Kachina dolls, early pottery; also wants Plains and Northeast Indian beadwork, and fine Indian basketry.

Richard B. Troyanowski
Rich Relics
P.O. Box 432
Sandia Park, NM 87047-0432
phone: 505-281-2611 or 505-281-2329
Buys/sells prehistoric/historic Indian artifacts, cowboy, militaria, old world antiquities & coins, fossils & ethnographic collectibles.

Alexander Anthony, Jr.
Adobe Gallery
413 Romero NW
Albuquerque, NM 87104-1421
phone: 505-243-8485 or 800-821-5221
fax: 505-243-8403
Specializing in art of the Southwest Indian: historic Pueblo pottery, Navajo blankets and rugs, Hopi Kachina dolls and Navajo and Pueblo pawn jewelry.

Jeff Mark
P.O. Box 5178
Santa Monica, CA 90409-5178
phone: 800-666-9553 or 310-396-9767
fax: 310-396-2666
Wants to buy American Indian rugs, blankets, baskets, dolls, clothing, beadwork weapons, pots, historical memorabilia.

Barry Friedman
P.O. Box 55492
Valencia, CA 91385-0492
phone: 805-255-2365
e-mail: BaryF@fishnet.net

Jimmy Vitanza
Peregrine Galleries
508 Brinkerhoff Ave.
Santa Barbara, CA 93101-3441
phone: 805-963-3134
fax: 805-963-3134

Michael D. Higgins
American Indian Art
P.O. Box 60
Salinas, CA 93902-0060
Wants to buy American Indian items: Navajo rugs and blankets, Pueblo pottery, Kachina dolls, baskets,

jewelry, Plains Indian beadwork and
artifacts; also pre-Columbian.

John W. Barry
Indian Rock Arts
P.O. Box 583
Davis, CA 95617-0583
phone: 916-758-2561
*Wants California Indian baskets,
historic and modern pottery,
beadwork, Navajo rugs, stone items (if
documented), etc.*

Syd Bottomley, ISA
P.O. Box 1842
Nevada City, CA 95959
phone: 916-272-5400
fax: 916-272-2820
*Buys, collects, appraises and
specializes in American Indian art:
baskets, rugs, pottery, early California
paintings.*

Douglas Vincent
Far West Antiques
P.O. Box 371
Redmond, OR 97756
phone: 541-923-1847 or 541-923-2140
fax: 541-923-3874
e-mail: dgvince@ibm.net
Internet: http://
www.farwestantiques.com
*Buys, sells, trades in older Native
American items and Western
Americana inducing gambling
collectibles; also collects native
American beadwork, baskets, jewelry
and Kachina dolls.*

Experts

Gary L. Fogelman
RD 1 Box 240
Turbotville, PA 17772-9599
phone: 717-437-3698
*Specializes in and buys Indian
artifacts: single pieces or entire
collections; appraisals; author of "A
Projectile Point Typology for PA and
the Northeast" and "An Identification
and Price Guide for Indian Artifacts
of the Northeast."*

Dawn E. Reno
3280 Shingler Terrace
Deltona, FL 32738-5351
phone: 904-532-1960
fax: 904-532-1960
e-mail: DawnReno@juno.com
*Author of "Native American
Collectibles" (1994, Avon), and
"Today's Native American Artists"
(1995, Alliance).*

Terry L. Schafer
American Indian Art & Antiques
Rte. 2 Box 298
Marietta, OH 45750-9358
phone: 614-374-2807
e-mail: amindart@mcnet.marietta.edu
Internet: http://www.marietta.edu/
~amindart
*Wants old Indian items: baskets,
blankets, beadwork, Navajo rugs and
old pawn jewelry.*

Peter Eller
206 Dartmouth
Albuquerque, NM 87106
phone: 505-268-7437 or 505-344-7539
*Specializes in and appraises
American, Southwest, and "Western"
art; also Pueblo pottery, Navajo rugs
and other weavings, Spanish colonial
artifacts.*

Mary Elizabeth McDonald
620 Sierra Dr. SE
Albuquerque, NM 87108-3377
phone: 505-265-2842

Don Bennett
Don Bennett & Associates
P.O. Box 283
Agoura Hills, CA 91376-0283
phone: 818-991-5596
fax: 818-991-6866
*Collects, buys and sells; produces
shows on antique American Indian Art
and is a highly qualified appraiser of
American Indian Art.*

Misc. Services

Indian Arts & Crafts Board
U.S. Dept. Of The Interior
Room 4004 - MIB
Washington, DC 20240-0001
phone: 202-208-3773
*Write for a free "Source Directory"
book which lists Indian-owned arts &
crafts marketing firms throughout the
country.*

Museums/Libraries

Joe Liberkowski
Museum of Classical Antiquities &
Primitive Arts
P.O. Box 2161
Medford, NJ 08055-7161
*Wants African and American Indian
items; also pre-1940 Mexican and
South American Santos, Retablos, Ex
Votos, crucifixes, religious, historical
autographs/documents.*

Museum of the American Indian, Heye
Foundation
1 Bowling Green
New York, NY 10004
phone: 212-825-6700

U.S. Department of the Interior Museum,
The
18th & C Streets
Washington, DC 20240
phone: 202-343-3477

National Museum of Natural History
10th St. & Constitution Ave.
Washington, DC 20560
phone: 202-357-1300
Internet: http://www.si.edu/

Museum of the Cherokee Indian
P.O. Box 1599
Cherokee, NC 28719
phone: 704-497-3481
*Located on the Cherokee Indian
Reservation.*

Bryan W. Kwapil
Grand Rapids Public Museum
272 Pearl St. NW
Grand Rapids, MI 49504-5371
phone: 616-456-3977
fax: 616-456-3873
*Exhibits, publications and research
information relating to West
Michigan's Ottawa, Potawatomi, and
Chippewa people.*

Field Museum of Natural History
Roosevelt Rd. at Lake Shore Dr
Chicago, IL 60605
phone: 312-642-4600

Jerry P. Martin, Dir.
Indian Center Museum
650 North Seneca
Wichita, KS 67203
phone: 316-262-5221
*Dedicated to the preservation of
Native American Heritage; features a
wide range of exhibitions displaying
contemporary art as well as
traditional artifacts.*

Diana Pardue
Heard Museum, The
22 E. Monte Vista Rd.
Phoenix, AZ 85004
phone: 602-252-8848 or 602-252-8840
fax: 602-252-9757
Internet: http://www.heard.org
*Has over 32,000 works of art and
ethnographic objects including more
than 4,000 objects from the Fred
Harvey Company Fine Art Collection.*

Betty L. Cornelius
Colorado River Indian Tribes Museum
Rte. 1 Box 23-B
Parker, AZ 85344-9704
phone: 602-669-9211
fax: 602-669-5675

Dr. Anne I. Woosley, Dir.
Amerind Foundation, Inc., The
P.O. Box 400
Dragoon, AZ 85609
phone: 520-586-3003
fax: 520-586-4679
e-mail: amerind@theriver.com
*Archaeology and ethnology museum,
art gallery, and research library;
archaeological collections from the
Americas; ethnological material from
the SW, Mexico, Great Plains, Eastern
Woodlands, CA, Arctic.*

Jonathan Batkin
Wheelwright Museum of the American
Indian, The
Newsletter: Messenger, The
P.O. Box 5153
Santa Fe, NM 87502
phone: 505-982-4636

Favell Museum of Western Art & Indian
Artifacts
P.O. Box 165
Klamath Falls, OR 97601-0372
phone: 503-882-9996
fax: 541-882-9996

Josie De Falla, Dir.
Maryhill Museum of Art
35 Maryhill Museum Drive
Goldendale, WA 98620-4601
phone: 509-773-3733
fax: 509-773-6138
e-mail: MaryHill@gorge.net
*The extensive 5000 piece Native
American collection comprises rare
prehistoric rock carvings, baskets,
beadwork, and other objects which
are seen as both art and artifact.*

Periodicals

Gary L. Fogelman
Magazine: Indian-Artifact Magazine
RD 1 Box 240
Turbotville, PA 17772-9599
phone: 717-437-3698
*An easy reading quarterly focusing on
American Indian prehistory: artifacts,
tools, lifestyles, customs, archaeology,
book reviews.*

Magazine: Whispering Wind Magazine
8009 Wales St.
New Orleans, LA 70126-1952
phone: 504-246-3742
fax: 504-246-2876

American Indian Art, Inc.
Magazine: American Indian Art
Magazine
7314 E. Osborn Dr.
Scottsdale, AZ 85251-6418
phone: 602-994-5445
*Quarterly art journal devoted to
native American art from prehistoric
to modern; gorgeous photographs,
auction reports, reports on ethnographic and fine arts items, "Legal
Briefs" column.*

Martin Link, Pub.
Newspaper: Indian Trader, The
P.O. Box 1421
Gallup, NM 87305-1421
phone: 505-722-6694 or 800-748-1624
fax: 505-722-6696
e-mail: trader@cia-g.com
Internet: http://www.cia-g.com/~trader/
index.htm
*Focuses on old and new Indian art
and artifacts.*

Magazine: Indian Artist
P.O. Box 5465
Santa Fe, NM 87502-5465
phone: 505-982-1600 or 800-757-5278
fax: 505-983-0790
e-mail: 75467.1545@compuserve.com
*Focuses on contemporary Native
American art, music, literature, film,
photographs, theater, and dance;
quarterly four-color magazine.*

John M. Gogol
Magazine: American Indian Basketry
P.O. Box 66124
Portland, OR 97266
phone: 503-233-8131
*A magazine dedicated to Native
American Indian arts: basketry,
beadwork, pottery, baskets and
weaving, textiles, masks, jewelry, etc.*

Repair Services

Conrad "Duke" Glodowski
White Deed Indian Traders
P.O. Box 506
Stevens Point, WI 54481-0506
phone: 715-344-9217
fax: 715-344-9217
Specializes in the repair and conservation of American Indian artifacts.

Baskets

Dealers

Syd Bottomley, ISA
P.O. Box 1842
Nevada City, CA 95959
phone: 916-272-5400
fax: 916-272-2820
Buys, collects, appraises and specializes in American Indian art: baskets, rugs, pottery, early California paintings.

Experts

Barry Friedman
P.O. Box 55492
Valencia, CA 91385-0492
phone: 805-255-2365
e-mail: BaryF@fishnet.net
Wants to buy pre-1940 undamaged Indian baskets; please send good photo, dimensions and price; all letters answered!

Museums/Libraries

Diana Pardue
Heard Museum, The
22 E. Monte Vista Rd.
Phoenix, AZ 85004
phone: 602-252-8848 or 602-252-8840
fax: 602-252-9757
Internet: http://www.heard.org
Has over 32,000 works of art and ethnographic objects including more than 4,000 objects from the Fred Harvey Company Fine Art Collection; has an extensive collection of Native American baskets.

Eskimo & Northwest Coast

Auction Services

Seahawk Auctions
P.O. Box 1561
Aldergrove,
Brit. Columbia V4W 2V1 Canada
phone: 604-657-1147 or 604-657-2072
fax: 604-857-0575
e-mail: seahawk@uniserve.com
Internet: http://
www.seahawkauctions.com
Specializes in the sale of Northwest Indian items.

Collectors

Jerry Ford
818 Elaine Court
Alexandria, VA 22308-2035
phone: 703-360-3114
fax: 703-360-4427
Wants to buy Eskimo, Northwest Coast, Canadian, Greenland, Russian carvings; ivory, bone, stone, or wood.

Dealers

Jeffrey R. Myers
Jeffrey R. Myers, Primitive Arts
12 East 86th St.
New York, NY 10028-0506
phone: 212-472-0115
fax: 212-472-1665
Buys, sells, specializes and appraises pre-1915 NW masks, rattles, frontlets, bowls, textiles, boxes; pre-1915 Eskimo masks, carved boxes, bow drills, figural pieces, etc.

Arthur W. Erickson
Arthur E. Erickson, Inc.
1030 SW Taylor
Portland, OR 97205
phone: 503-227-4710
Buys and sells antique Native American and Eskimo arts with an emphasis on Columbian River items such as Wasco Sally bags, cork husk bags, Klicitat baskets and plateau figural and contour beadwork.

Lee
Northwest Tribal Art
1417 1st Ave.
Seattle, WA 98101
phone: 206-467-9330
fax: 206-624-6154
Carries a wide assortment of contemporary Native Eskimo and Pacific Northwest Coast Indian art, carvings, petrified walrus tusk, stone carvings, textiles, etc.

Richard A. Wood
Alaskan Heritage Bookshop
P.O. Box 22165
Juneau, AK 99802-2165
phone: 907-789-8450
fax: 907-789-8450
e-mail: akrare@alaska.net
Internet: http://www.alaska.net/~akrare
Buys and sells Northwest Coast antique Indian art objects including model boats, canoes, and kayaks, masks, baskets, handmade silver spoons, totem poles, Athabaskan beadwork, photographs.

Museums/Libraries

Samuel K. Fox Museum
P.O. Box 10021
Dillingham, AK 99576
phone: 907-842-5601

Carolyn Young
Sheldon Jackson Museum
104 College Dr.
Sitka, AK 99835-7657
phone: 907-747-8981
fax: 907-747-3004
Internet: http://ccl.alaska.edu/local/home.html
Focuses on Aleut, Athabaskan, and Northwest Coast Indians: Haida argillite carvings, Eskimo implements, ivory carvings, masks, skin clothing, baskets, kayaks, umiaks, totem poles, garments, ceremonial equipment, etc.

Totem Heritage Center
629 Dock St.
Ketchikan, AK 99901
phone: 907-225-5900

Grenfell Labrador Industries

Experts

Barry Friedman
P.O. Box 55492
Valencia, CA 91385-0492
phone: 805-255-2365
e-mail: BaryF@fishnet.net
Wants to buy any textile or purses labeled "Grenfell Labrador Industries." These always picture Northern scenes (polar bears, Eskimos, etc.); undamaged pieces only; send photo, dimensions, and price; all letters answered!

Repro. Sources

Grenfell Handicrafts
P.O. Box 290
St. Anthony
Newfoundland AOK 4S0 Canada
phone: 709-454-3576
Send for free catalog of new Grenfell mats currently for sale.

Kachina Dolls

Dealers

World City, Inc.
6935 James Ave. South
Minneapolis, MN 55423-2147
Buys and sells Indian items such as beaded items, pottery, Navajo rugs, quilled items, Kachinas, Northwest Coast items; both pre-historic and historic; send price wanted (unless unsure), description, photos, and SASE.

Christopher A. Jones
Squash Blossom, The
2531 W. Colorado Ave.
Colorado Springs, CO 80904
phone: 719-632-1899
Dealer/appraiser specializing in Southwestern Native American jewelry and art including pottery, weaving, Kachinas (both prehistoric and historic.)

John C. Hill
Gallery of American Indian Art
6962 East First Ave., Ste. 104
Scottsdale, AZ 85251
phone: 602-946-2910
fax: 602-946-7410
Wants to buy early Southwest Indian items including classic Navajo & Pueblo silver & turquoise, Indian blankets and other textiles, Kachina dolls, early pottery; also wants Plains and Northeast Indian beadwork, and fine Indian basketry.

Alexander Anthony, Jr.
Adobe Gallery
413 Romero NW
Albuquerque, NM 87104-1421
phone: 505-243-8485 or 800-821-5221
fax: 505-243-8403
Specializing in art of the Southwest Indian: historic Pueblo pottery, Navajo blankets and rugs, Hopi Kachina dolls and Navajo and Pueblo pawn jewelry.

Michael D. Higgins
American Indian Art
P.O. Box 60
Salinas, CA 93902-0060
Wants to buy American Indian items: Navajo rugs and blankets, Pueblo pottery, Kachina dolls, baskets, jewelry, Plains Indian beadwork and artifacts; also pre-Columbian.

Museums/Libraries

Diana Pardue
Heard Museum, The
22 E. Monte Vista Rd.
Phoenix, AZ 85004
phone: 602-252-8848 or 602-252-8840
fax: 602-252-9757
Internet: http://www.heard.org
Has over 32,000 works of art and ethnographic objects and one of the largest collections of Hopi Kachina dolls including 437 historic Kachina dolls from the Barry Goldwater Collection.

Navajo

Collectors

Andrew Nagen
P.O. Box 1306
Corrales, NM 87408
phone: 505-898-5058
Wants Navajo rugs and blankets; also Rio Grande, Pueblo, and Mexican textiles.

Dealers

Tyrone & Una Campbell
Una
7103 E. Main St.
Scottsdale, AZ 85251-4315
phone: 602-423-9160
Buys and sells antique American Indian weavings: Navajo, Pueblo and Hispanic weavings and folk art; specializes in appraising collections, consultations, and research of 19th & 20th C. Navajo weavings.

Ledge House Indian Craft Store
HC 71 Box 3
Tonalea, AZ 86044-9704
phone: 602-672-2366 or 602-672-2367
fax: 602-672-2345
Sells contemporary Indian crafts.

Experts

Gregg Leighton
Notah Dineh
345 West Main
Cortez, CO 81321
phone: 800-444-2024 or 303-565-9607
Internet: http://subee.com/nd/home.html
Buys and sells wide range of Navajo rugs, antique and contemporary; also carries large assortment of contemporary American Indian crafts and jewelry.

Barry Friedman
P.O. Box 55492
Valencia, CA 91385-0492
phone: 805-255-2365
e-mail: BaryF@fishnet.net
Wants to purchase pre-1940 Navajo rugs; send photo, condition, and price; undamaged items only; all letters answered!

Museums/Libraries

Navajo National Monument
HC 71 Box 3
Tonalea, AZ 86044-9704
phone: 602-672-2366 or 602-672-2367
fax: 602-672-2345
A national monument featuring the best preserved cliff dwellings in the SW; small museum and library (no checkout) for research (copier not available); prehistoric Pueblo and Navajo exhibits.

Pottery

Experts

John W. Barry
Indian Rock Arts
P.O. Box 583
Davis, CA 95617-0583
phone: 916-758-2561
Appraises Pueblo Indian pottery; author of "American Indian Pottery" (Books Americana), 1981 contributor to "Encyclopedia Native American in the 20th Century" (Garland Publishing) and "North American Artifacts" by Lar Hothem.

Museums/Libraries

Cherokee National Museum
P.O. Box 515
Tahlequah, OK 74465
phone: 918-456-6007

Diana Pardue
Heard Museum, The
22 E. Monte Vista Rd.
Phoenix, AZ 85004
phone: 602-252-8848 or 602-252-8840
fax: 602-252-9757
Internet: http://www.heard.org
Has over 32,000 works of art and ethnographic objects including an extensive collection of pottery, especially pieces made by Native American cultures in the Southwestern United States.

Institute of American Indian Arts
Museum
P.O. Box 20007
Santa Fe, NM 87504
phone: 509-988-6281

Repair Services

Andy Goldschmidt
Ceramicare
P.O. Box 1812
Corrales, NM 87048
phone: 505-898-2728
e-mail: agoldschmidt@waonline.com
Repairs and restores ceramic art; specializing in Native American Indian pottery - prehistoric, historic and contemporary.

Skookum Dolls

Dealers

William W. Wynn
2117 Hillcrest St.
Fort Worth, TX 76107-4329
phone: 817-763-8424
Wants to buy Skookum Indian dolls, beaded Zuni dolls, pre-1950 Plains Indian and Navajo rag dolls.

Experts

Linda Larouche
Linda Larouche Antiques & Collectibles
18 Polhemus Place
Brooklyn, NY 11215-2231
phone: 718-230-3830
e-mail: skookumgal@aol.com
Internet: http://www.skookumgal.com
Wants to buy Skookum Indian dolls in good condition; wants all sizes from 3" to 36".

Barry Friedman
P.O. Box 55492
Valencia, CA 91385-0492
phone: 805-255-2365
e-mail: BaryF@fishnet.net
Wants to buy undamaged Skookum Indian dolls over 12"; these dolls wear colorful Indian design blankets; send photo, size, and price; all letters answered!

Souvenirs

Experts

Abby Irons
D. Irons Antiques
RD 4 Box 101
Northampton, PA 18067-9232
phone: 610-262-9335

Souvenirs (Beadwork)

Experts

Marty & Mike Irons
D. Irons Antiques
RD 4 Box 101
Northampton, PA 18067-9232
phone: 610-262-9335

Tomahawks

Collectors

Michael Carrick
1230 Hoyt St. SE
Salem, OR 97302-2121
phone: 800-394-7797
fax: 888-395-7798
e-mail: carrick123@aol.com

Totems

Collectors

Edwin Snyder
P.O. Box 156
Lancaster, KY 40444-0156
phone: 606-792-4816
Wants to buy baskets, totems and carvings.

Dealers

John Cavanagh
Linda Larouche Antiques & Collectibles
18 Polhemus Place
Brooklyn, NY 11215-2231
phone: 718-230-3830
e-mail: jcav@metrografilk.com
Buys and sells well carved pre-1945 Pacific NW and Eskimo model totems in wood, bone or ivory; also wants ivory carved animals, fish, salt & peppers, etc.

AMMUNITION & EXPLOSIVE ORDNANCE

(see also ARMS & ARMOR; CANNONS; CIVIL WAR ARTIFACTS; FIREARMS; MILITARIA; TOYS, Cannons; TRENCH ART)

Auction Services

Dr. J.R. Crittenden Schmitt
Crittenden Schmitt Archives
Court House Station
P.O. Box 4253
Rockville, MD 20849-4253
phone: 301-946-2643
Only video auctions in the world of ordnance material: collector ammunition, bombs, grenades, mines; inert only, from all countries.

Clubs/Associations

Dr. J.R. Crittenden Schmitt
International Ammunition Association, Inc.
Magazine: International Ammunition Journal
Court House Station
P.O. Box 4253
Rockville, MD 20849-4253
phone: 301-946-2643

Experts

Dr. J.R. Crittenden Schmitt
Crittenden Schmitt Archives
Court House Station
P.O. Box 4253
Rockville, MD 20849-4253
phone: 301-946-2643
Family in business since 1849; full line of consulting expertise in all

areas of munitions: grenades, land mines, bombs, etc.

Periodicals

Magazine: Artilleryman, The
RR 1 Box 36
Tunbridge, VT 05077-9707
phone: 802-889-3500
fax: 802-889-5627
Published quarterly, the only magazine exclusively for the 1750-1898 artillery enthusiast: artillery history, unit profiles, shell collecting, etc.

Badges

Collectors

Dr. J.R. Crittenden Schmitt
Crittenden Schmitt Archives
Court House Station
P.O. Box 4253
Rockville, MD 20849-4253
phone: 301-946-2643
Wants only metal badges & pins relating to bomb squads, explosive ordnance disposal units, ammunition & weapons companies of the world.

Shell Casings

Collectors

Charles Eberhart
Lead Cannon, The
3616 Seward
Topeka, KS 66616-1652
phone: 913-235-1016
Wants to buy large brass military casings - the longer the better; also wants to buy decorated "Trench Art" shells.

AMUSEMENT PARK ITEMS

(see also CAROUSELS & CAROUSEL FIGURES; CARNIVAL ITEMS; COIN-OPERATED MACHINES, Arcade Games; ROLLER COASTERS; TARGETS, Shooting Gallery)

Auction Services

David A. Norton
Norton Auctioneers of Michigan, Inc.
Pearl at Monroe St.
Coldwater, MI 49036
phone: 517-279-9063
fax: 517-279-9191
Specializing in the auctioning of amusement rides, carousels, amusement parks, arcades, museums, etc.

Clubs/Associations

International Association of Amusement Parks & Attractions
1448 Duke St.
Alexandria, VA 22314
phone: 703-836-4800
fax: 703-836-4801
Internet: http://www.iaapa.org

Historic Amusement Foundation
Newsletter: HAF Times
4410 North Keystone Ave.
Indianapolis, IN 46205
phone: 317-841-7677

National Amusement Park Historical
 Association
Newsletter: National Amusement Park
 Historical News
P.O. Box 83
Mount Prospect, IL 60056
Internet: http://sgi.net/napha/

Collectors

Tom Keefe
P.O. Box 464
Tinley Park, IL 60477
*Wants signs, tickets, carousel horses,
tokens, photos, movies, letterheads,
ride manufacturer's catalogs, posters,
advertising items.*

Jim Abbate
1005 Hyde Park Lane
Naperville, IL 60565-1624
phone: 630-416-3543
*Wants roller coaster, carousel,
amusement park ephemera; photos,
brochures, stationery, ride manufacturers' catalogs, tickets, sheet music,
letterheads, matchbooks, signs,
advertisements, pamphlets, trade
cards, postcards, etc.*

Peter Dusza
385 Reed St.
Santa Clara, CA 95050-3104
phone: 408-988-8161 or 408-723-0722
fax: 408-988-2206
e-mail: pdusza@ix.netcom.com
*Wants to buy roller coaster souvenirs
and memorabilia: coffee cups,
drinking and shot glasses, pins,
patches, post cards, posters, and
buttons.*

Experts

Thomas G. Morris
Prize Publishers
P.O. Box 8307
Medford, OR 97504-0307
phone: 541-779-3164
*Specializing in carnival chalkware
figures; author of "The Carnival
Chalk Prize Vol. I and II"; will assist
with information or appraisals on the
subject.*

Museums/Libraries

Knoebels Amusement Park & Carousel
 Museum
P.O. Box 317, Rte. 487
Elysburg, PA 17824-0317
phone: 717-672-2572

Periodicals

Mark Wyatt, Ed.
Newspaper: Inside Track
P.O. Box 7956
Newark, DE 19714-7956
phone: 302-737-3667
fax: 302-368-8329
e-mail: mwyatt@magphone.com
*Monthly international amusement
park newspaper.*

Don Schockow
Rainbow Ridge Productions
VHS: Disney TV
P.O. Box 1064
Ojai, CA 93024-1064
phone: 805-640-8101
fax: 805-640-8101
e-mail: rrp@west.net
Internet: http://members.aol.com/
 dsneyanatv/index.html
*"Disneyana TV" is a quarterly VHS
television show covering everything
Disney; from behind the scenes to
future projects...it's all on Disneyana
TV.*

Coney Island

Collectors

Stanley Fried
195 Froehlich Farm Blvd.
Woodbury, NY 11797-2931
phone: 516-364-1112
fax: 516-625-4220
*Wants Coney Island related items such
as old postcards, souvenirs.*

ANCIENT COINS

(see COINS & CURRENCY, Coins
[Ancient])

ANGELS

Clubs/Associations

Jeanne Kehe
Angel Collector Club
Newsletter: Angels of the World
14 Parkview Ct.
Crystal Lake, IL 60012-3540
phone: 815-459-9259
*Members are collectors of any type of
angels; membership is limited to 225;
newsletter published 6 timer per year.*

Alberta Hedstrom
Angels Collectors' Club of America
Newsletter: Halo Everybody!
12225 South Patomac
Phoenix, AZ 85044
phone: 602-598-0458
e-mail: eadhedstrom@aol.com
*Over 3,500 members who collect
angels in any form.*

ANIMAL COLLECTIBLES

(see also ALLIGATOR BAGS;
ANIMAL TROPHIES; AQUARI-
UMS; DINOSAURS; ENDANGERED
SPECIES; FARM COLLECTIBLES;
FIGURINES, Mortens; INSECTS;
LICENSES, Animal; VETERINARY
MEDICINE ITEMS; WHALES &
DOLPHINS)

Dealers

Barbara Framke
"Just Animals"
15525 Fitzgerald
Livonia, MI 48154-1805
phone: 313-464-8493
*Buys and sells animal collectibles,
especially dog, cat and horse
figurines.*

Bears

(see SMOKEY THE BEAR ITEMS;
TEDDY BEARS)

Cats

(see also CERAMICS [AMERICAN],
Black Cats; HALLOWEEN
COLLECTIBLES)

Clubs/Associations

Marilyn Dipboye
Cat Collectors
Newsletter: Cat Talk
33161 Wendy Dr.
Sterling Heights, MI 48310-6473
phone: 810-264-0285
*For ailurophiles (cat lovers), this club
focuses on all types of cat collectibles;
offers catalog of extensive line of
antique/older cat collectibles for sale.*

Collectors

Jackie Durham
909 26th St. NW
Washington, DC 20037-2029
e-mail:
 durham@GameRoomAntiques.com
Internet: http://
 www.GameRoomAntiques.com
*Wants Chessie cat related items; also
wants Lou Wain cat items.*

Renae Giles
P.O. Box 6
Carver, MN 55315-0006
phone: 612-448-7046
e-mail: rgiles@beckman.com
*Advanced collector seeks all types of
cat collectibles, especially Goebel,
Hagen-Renaker, Josef Originals,
Lowell Davis, Border FIne Arts and
novelty salt and pepper shakers; also
trades.*

Dealers

Billie J. Parsons
431 Thomas Dr.
Webster, NY 14580
phone: 716-671-9388
*Specializes in canine, equine, and
feline collectibles: large dog figurines,*

*Western Hartlands, Kay Finch,
Hagen-Renaker, Breyer Horses.*

Barbara Framke
"Just Animals"
15525 Fitzgerald
Livonia, MI 48154-1805
phone: 313-464-8493
*Buys and sells all cat related items,
especially figurines and collector
plates, both current and secondary
market; current sale lists available for
SASE; if selling, please price and
describe items.*

Experts

Marbena "Jean" Fyke
132 North Montgomery, Ste. D-12
Walden, NY 12586
phone: 914-778-7327
*Author of "Collectible Cats," books I
and II (Collector's Books).*

Joyce & Judy
Krazy Cat Collectibles
8604 Second Ave. #235
Silver Spring, MD 20910
e-mail: KrazyCatCo@aol.com
*Specializing in unique and interesting
old cat items: toys, postcards,
advertising, jewelry, pictures, cookie
jars, sale & peppers, plates, vintage
clothing, figurines, etc.; will buy one
piece or entire collection.*

Marilyn Dipboye
33161 Wendy Dr.
Sterling Heights, MI 48310-6473
phone: 810-264-0285
*Wants antique cat memorabilia in all
collecting categories.*

Periodicals

Pamela Anger, Ed.
Newsletter: Midwestern Cat Society
68 Hawthorne Ave. E
Saint Paul, MN 55117-4607
phone: 612-489-7422

Cats (Goebel Figurines)

Experts

Linda Nothnagel
Rte. 3 Box 30
Shelbina, MO 63468-9406
phone: 573-588-4958 or 816-781-5291
*Wants out-of-production Goebel cat
figurines and Goebel cat related
items.*

Cats (Kliban)

Collectors

Sue Lucente
115 Marbeth Ave.
Carlisle, PA 17013-1626
phone: 717-249-9343
*Wants B. Kliban cat items: teapots,
candy dishes, pillows and sheets,
Christmas items, figurines, banks, salt
& pepper shakers, mugs, cookie jars,
cat feeders, framed pictures, book*

ends, T-shirts, stuffed animals, kitchen towels, etc.

Dogs

(see also LICENSES, Dog; TELEVISION SHOWS & MEMORABILIA, Lassie)

Clubs/Associations

Patty Shedlow, Ed.
Canine Collectors Club
Magazine: Canine Collectibles Quarterly
736 N. Western Ave., Ste. 314
Lake Forest, IL 60045
A publication devoted to the promotion, enjoyment and collecting of dog memorabilia. Information on a wide range of dog items, as well as a classified ad section to buy and sell.

Collectors

Jeffrey Jacobson
860 Graegin Place
Dyer, IN 46311-2215

Dealers

Billie J. Parsons
431 Thomas Dr.
Webster, NY 14580
phone: 716-671-9388
Specializes in canine, equine, and feline collectibles: large dog figurines, Western Hartlands, Kay Finch, Hagen-Renaker, Breyer Horses.

Denise Hamilton
899 Latta Brook Rd.
Elmira, NY 14901
phone: 607-732-2550
Buys dogs collectibles: figurines, old dog postcards, jewelry with dogs in it, etc.; Borzoi (Russian Wolfhound), greyhound, all Morten Studio and Erphila dogs and animals.

Meg Weitz
Tigger's Dog Stuff
601 Rockwood Rd.
Wilmington, DE 19802
phone: 302-762-8939
Buys and sells fine dog collectibles and prints.

Jo Ellen Arnold
Dog Lady, The
P.O. Box 2641
Springfield, VA 22152-0641
phone: 703-644-5201
fax: 703-644-5401
Specializes in fine canine collectibles.

Jane & John Carroll
2894 John Tyler Highway
Williamsburg, VA 23185-1335
phone: 757-258-9322
Buys and sells canine collectibles.

Mary Blacker
610 W. Siebenthaler Ave.
Dayton, OH 45405
phone: 513-278-6153
Antique & collectible dog figurines and art; Royal Doulton, Mortens

Studio, Rosenthal, Boehm, Kirmse, Dennis, Thorne, Eberhardt.

Barbara Framke
"Just Animals"
15525 Fitzgerald
Livonia, MI 48154-1805
phone: 313-464-8493
Buys and sells all dog related items, especially figurines and collector plates, both current and secondary market; current sale lists available for SASE; if selling, please price and describe items.

Sharlene Beckwith
Exclusively Dogs!
P.O. Box 1858
Upland, CA 91785-1858
phone: 909-946-1544
fax: 909-949-4796
Specializing in fine canine collectibles, especially Kay Finch dog figurines and any large or unusual Kay Finch animals, including cookie jars; also wants Kay Finch bronzes and dog jewelry.

Museums/Libraries

Roberta Vesley, Lib.
American Kennel Club, Inc. Library
51 Madison Ave.
New York, NY 10010
phone: 212-696-8254
fax: 212-696-8299
Research library open to the public; 17,000 volumes on dogs and related areas.

Dog Museum, The
1721 S. Mason Rd.
Saint Louis, MO 63131
phone: 314-821-3647
Commemorates every aspect of a dog's life; collection includes dog art and artifacts.

Dogs (Collies)

Collectors

Joan L. Neidhardt
428 Philadelphia Rd.
Joppa, MD 21085-3302
e-mail: ccolliespk@aol.com
Internet: http://www.members.aol.com/CCollieSpk
Wants to buy anything relating to Collies or to Lassie; old, new, unique; toys, figurines, character collectibles.

Debby Stratman
10851 Rosalie Dr.
Northglenn, CO 80233-3553
phone: 303-457-8665
Wants anything pertaining to Collie dogs, including paper, any condition considered; please write first.

Periodicals

Joan L. Neidhardt
Newsletter: COLLIEctively Speaking!
428 Philadelphia Rd.
Joppa, MD 21085-3302
e-mail: ccolliespk@aol.com
Internet: http://www.members.aol.com/CCollieSpk

Dogs (German Shepherds)

Collectors

Henry Heiman, III
P.O. Box 316
South Salem, NY 10590-0316
Wants to buy German Shepherd dog items.

Edythe Shepard
1334 E. Suncrest Dr.
Tucson, AZ 85706
Wants to buy items relating to Rin-Tin-Tin, Bullet, Mike (The Bionic Dog), Joe, Buddy (Seeing Eye Dog), Flame, Strongheart.

Dogs (Poodles)

Collectors

Elaine Butler
233 S. Kingston Ave.
Rockwood, TN 37854
phone: 423-354-0857
Wants 1950s poodle items: figurines with textured "spaghetti" look doing "people things", also wants other items from 1950s and 1960s featuring poodles.

Dogs (Scotties)

Clubs/Associations

David Bohlein
Wee Scots
Magazine: Scottie Sampler
P.O. Box 1597
Winchester, VA 22604-1597
A quarterly publication with historical data, current market prices, photos, ads, etc. for Scottie collectors and dealers.

Dealers

Van M. Jones
2847 Madison Rd.
Cincinnati, OH 45209
phone: 513-531-0244
Interested in all kinds of Scottie memorabilia, especially bronzes, porcelains, etchings & fine art, playing cards with Scottie motif.

Dogs (War Dogs)

Collectors

James Flurchick
395 Paramus Rd.
Paramus, NJ 07652
phone: 201-444-3403
Collects war dog militaria: equipment, postcards, insignia, back packs, awards, books, toys.

Flamingos

Collectors

Suzy Holleron
624 Morningside Dr.
San Antonio, TX 78209
phone: 210-826-6663
Known as the "Flamingo Lady;" collects everything with a flamingo motif.

Lynn Fry
P.O. Box 5495
Coos Bay, OR 97420
phone: 541-888-4177
Wants flamingo figurines, lamps, pictures, mirrors, etc.

Frogs

(see also FLOWER "FROGS")

Clubs/Associations

Ms. Merelaine Haskett, Ed.
Frog Pond, The
Newsletter: Ribbit Ribbit
P.O. Box 193
Beech Grove, IN 46107-0193
Newsletter has articles and buy/sell/trade ads; open to all who are interested in collecting frog related items.

Chicago Herpetological Society
Journal: Bulletin of the Chicago Herpetological Society
2001 North Clark St.
Chicago, IL 60614
phone: 312-281-1800 or 312-549-5199
Affiliated with the Chicago Academy of Sciences; focuses on the study of reptiles and amphibians; offers books about frogs and reptiles; 8 1/2" x 11" journal published monthly.

Dealers

Louise Mesa
"Frog Fantasies" Museum & Frogs Only Gift Shop
151 Spring St.
Eureka Springs, AR 72632
phone: 501-253-7227

Museums/Libraries

Louise Mesa
Frog Fantasies Museum, The
151 Spring St.
Eureka Springs, AR 72632
phone: 501-253-7227

Horse Related Items

(see also FARM COLLECTIBLES; HORSE-DRAWN VEHICLES; LEATHER; RIDING TOYS, Rocking Horses; SADDLES; SPORTS COLLECTIBLES, Polo; SPORTS COLLECTIBLES, Thoroughbred Racing; WESTERN AMERICANA)

Collectors

Bill Mackin
1137 Washington St.
Craig, CO 81625-1613
phone: 970-824-6717 or 970-824-6360
fax: 970-824-7175
e-mail: reust@nadja.com
Author of "Cowboy and Gunfighter Collectibles" with 1993-94 updated price guide; sells books for Old West collectors by mail and at shows; over 45 years collecting; wants nice gun leather and cowboy gear; appraises, consults, lectures.

Linda Paich
Bookends
P.O. Box 445
Los Olivos, CA 93441
phone: 805-688-3484
fax: 805-688-0307
Wants items relating to horses: postcards, books, statues, antique Western tack, etc.; antique and out-of-print on all types of horses and horse sport; buys and sells.

Dealers

Billie J. Parsons
431 Thomas Dr.
Webster, NY 14580
phone: 716-671-9388
Specializes in canine, equine, and feline collectibles: large dog figurines, Western Hartlands, Kay Finch, Hagen-Renaker, Breyer Horses.

Barbara Cole
October Farm
2609 Branch Rd.
Raleigh, NC 27610-9213
phone: 919-772-0482
fax: 919-779-6265
Buys and sells horse books and paper ephemera, especially relating to polo, carriages & driving, Morgan horses, American Saddlebred horses, and veterinary medicine; also old farm horse equipment and catalogs; mail order only.

Barbara Framke
"Just Animals"
15525 Fitzgerald
Livonia, MI 48154-1805
phone: 313-464-8493
Buys porcelain and ceramic horse figurines, especially by Hagen-Renaker, Beswick and Goebel; also wants horse related books; all items considered.

Museums/Libraries

Keith D. Bartz, Dir.
American Saddle Horse Museum Association
4093 Iron Works Pike
Lexington, KY 40511
phone: 606-259-2746
To learn about the American saddlebred horse, and to preserve and maintain artifacts pertinent to the history of the breed.

Bill Cooke, Dir.
International Museum of the Horse, Kentucky Horse Park
4089 Iron Works Pike
Lexington, KY 40511
phone: 606-233-4304
fax: 606-259-4212
e-mail: khp@mis.net
Internet: http://www.imh.org/

Horses (Draft)

Collectors

Jim Richendollar
508 W. Columbia Ave.
Belleville, MI 48111
phone: 313-699-3805
Wants draft (work horse like Clydesdales) horse memorabilia: books, magazines, photos, prints, paintings, sale catalogs, statues, figurines, etc.

Horses (Models)

Clubs/Associations

Stephanie Macejko
Breyer Collectors Club
Magazine: Just About Horses
14 Industrial Rd.
Pequannock, NJ 07440
phone: 201-694-5006
Offers information on model horse collecting and hobbying including customization, vintage models & horse model showing; no paid ads.

Sue P. Stewart
North American Model Horse Show Association
P.O. Box 50508
Denton, TX 76206

Sheryl Leisure
West Coast Model Horse Collectors Jamboree
Newsletter: Model Horse Trader, The
1000 W. Fourth St., #154
Ontario, CA 91762-2208
phone: 909-981-8096
fax: 909-590-0279
Convention end of August, monthly newsletter, information and appraisal service for collecting Breyer, Hartland, Hagen-Renaker, Beswick, North Light, Best, and other horse figurines.

Collectors

Chelle Fulk
1793 Ivy Oak Sq.
Rectortown, VA 20190-4723
phone: 703-471-1968 or 202-626-9773
fax: 202-626-9700
e-mail: anthem2@juno.com
Wants plastic horses, dogs, etc.: Breyer, Hartland, others; any size, condition, color.

Jessica Prior-Jennings
621 Pierson St.
Flint, MI 48503
phone: 810-239-6326
Wants Breyer and Hartland plastic

model horses, rider and animal models; will buy collections; also wants Hagen-Renaker, Designer's Workshop, or Beswick china horse figurines.

Dealers

Terri Mardis-Ivers
Terri's Toys & Nostalgia
419 S. First St.
Ponca City, OK 74601
phone: 405-762-8697
Specializes in Breyer and Hartland figures.

Black Horse Ranch
1024 Nobles Court
Minden, NV 89423
phone: 800-360-5BHR

Cascade Models
5310 136th Place SW
Edmonds, WA 98206
phone: 800-660-4080

Periodicals

Paula Hecker
Magazine: Hobby Horse News, The
2053 Dryehaven Dr.
Tallahassee, FL 32311-8656
phone: 904-562-8423
e-mail: thhn@aol.com
Bi-monthly magazine with hobby horse articles, shows, ads, etc.

Paula Beard
Magazine: TRR Pony Express
71 Aloha Circle
North Little Rock, AR 72120-1670
Bi-monthly magazine focusing on collecting and showing; feature articles on molds, brands, artists, model horse news, display, and buy/sell ads.

Sheryl Leisure
Newsletter: Model Horse Trader, The
143 Mercer Way
Upland, CA 91786
phone: 909-981-8096
Ads-only newsletter consisting of dealers' lists from across the country; not a reference or price guides; models identified only be model number; send $15, photos and LSASE for appraisals; checks payable to Sheryl Leisure.

Repair Services

Sue Thiessen
25115 Cemetery Rd.
Middleton, ID 83644-5103
phone: 208-585-3243
Specializing in restoring model horses, Roseville, and other pottery; also collector of Hagen Renaker horse and animal figurines.

Horses (Models/Breyer)

Dealers

Sue Coffee
Laysville Hardware
10 Saunders Hollow Rd.
Old Lyme, CT 06371-1126
phone: 860-434-5641
fax: 860-434-2653
e-mail: SueCoffee@aol.com
Buys and sells: present to discontinued; send SASE for list; wants Breyer from the 1950s and 1960s, especially woodgrains and decorators (gold, blue and dapple).

Arlene Bentley
Bentley Sales Company
642 Sandy Lane
Des Plaines, IL 60016
phone: 708-439-2049
Carries entire Breyer Model Horse line plus limited editions, discontinued and special run models.

Terry & Antina Richards
5838 Darlene Dr.
Rockford, IL 61109
Specialize in vintage Breyer horse models; please include SASE when writing.

Experts

Kimberly Grackowski
23046 Bagpipe Ct.
Lake Zurich, IL 60047
e-mail: springfvr@aol.com
Publishes a value guide of ALL Breyer models ever created; buys collections.

Kimberly Gackowski
23046 Bagpipe Ct.
Lake Zurich, IL 60047-7524
phone: 847-203-5809 or 847-827-1657
e-mail: SpringFvr@aol.com
Author of "Breyer Model Collector's Value Guide"; detailed descriptions and production years of regular models, special runs, lamps, night lights, music boxes; contains current market values, photos, etc.

Nancy Atkinson Young
268 Ross Court
Claremont, CA 91711-3139
e-mail: Atkinson@cgs.edu
Author of "Breyer Molds and Models," (available from author) the most comprehensive book available on Breyer model horses and other animals; does not do appraisals; please include SASE when writing.

Man./Prod./Dist.

Bentley Sales Co.
642 Sandy Lane
Des Plaines, IL 60016
phone: 708-439-2049
Contact for information on the new Breyer line.

Humane Society

Collectors

Wayne M. Besenty
9060 Hegel St.
Bellflower, CA 90706-4216
phone: 310-925-8574 or 310-595-5449
Collector of historical animal control and Humane Society items.

Mules

Collectors

Gene Hammerlun
1350 Cal Ct.
Gardnerville, NV 89410-6123
phone: 702-782-5945
Wants to buy anything related to mules: pictures, advertising, stories, etc.

Periodicals

Magazine: Western Mule Magazine
1780 West Elm
Lebanon, MO 65536
phone: 417-532-MULE
Pleasure, cutting, show and pack mules' training, health, trail riding, mule rodeos and more.

Owls

Experts

Donna Russell
RR 1 Box 990
Coquille, OR 97423-9752
phone: 503-396-2688

Pigs

Clubs/Associations

Gene Holt
Happy Pig Collectors Club, The
Newsletter: Happy Pig, The
P.O. Box 17
Oneida, IL 61467-0017
phone: 309-483-6192
e-mail: happypig@starcourier.com
For collectors of pigs items, so that they may gain more enjoyment from their hobby and mingle with others cursed with the same strange affliction; it's respectful to say "When I see a Pig, I think of you."

Collectors

Arlene McNaught
136 Edwards St.
Kewanee, IL 61443
phone: 309-853-4960

Gene Holt
P.O. Box 17
Oneida, IL 61467-0017
phone: 309-483-6192
e-mail: happypig@starcourier.com

Experts

Mary Hamburg
Tootsie's Antiques
20 Cedar Ave.
Danville, IL 61832-1525
phone: 217-446-2323 or 217-442-2725
Buys, sells, collects, and specializes in German china pig figurines; advisor to "Warman's Americana & Collectibles Price Guide."

Plastic Models

Collectors

Chelle Fulk
1793 Ivy Oak Sq.
Rectortown, VA 20190-4723
phone: 703-471-1968 or 202-626-9773
fax: 202-626-9700
e-mail: anthem2@juno.com
Wants plastic horses, dogs, cattle, wildlife, etc.; especially Breyer; any size, condition or color.

Possums

Collectors

Van Matre
15 S. Blaine
Hinsdale, IL 60521-4208
Wants possum-related items: vintage postcards, tins, games, children's books, anything featuring happy and healthy possums; all replies answered.

Reptiles

Clubs/Associations

Mark F. Miller
HERP-NET Electronic Bulletin Board
Newsletter: HERP-NET, INK
P.O. Box 52261
Philadelphia, PA 19115
phone: 215-464-3561
fax: 215-464-3561
e-mail: 70176.1153@compuserve.com
Club meets electronically via computer modem (dial 215-464-3562); members have interests in live reptiles and related art: stamps, postcards, books with reptile theme; operates free reptile book search service; buys reptile used books.

Experts

Mark F. Miller
P.O. Box 52261
Philadelphia, PA 19115
phone: 215-464-3561
fax: 215-464-3561
e-mail: 70176.1153@compuserve.com
Author of numerous articles regarding reptile care, reptile books, and collecting reptile literature, sculptures, prints, and postcards; past Editor or the "Bulletin of the Philadelphia Herpetology Society."

Tigers

Collectors

Sharon A. Mitchell
875 North Michigan, #3412
Chicago, IL 60611
phone: 312-787-3252 or 800-879-6948
fax: 312-266-7982
Tiger collector hungry to buy anything uncommon or unusual relating to this striped cat: toys, clothing, jewelry, circus, books, pictures, Black Sambo, ads, packaging, Tony & ESSO tigers, etc.; not interested in other cats.

ANIMAL TROPHIES

(see also ENDANGERED SPECIES; SKELETONS; SPORTING COLLECTIBLES)

Auction Services

Gerard Giguere
Giguere Auction Co.
P.O. Box 1272
Windham, ME 04062
phone: 207-892-3800
fax: 207-892-3800
Conducts sporting auctions: fishing, hunting, decoys, sporting art, taxidermy.

Dealers

Bob Hoffman
Moose River Lake & Lodge Store
69 Railroad St.
Barnet, VT 05891
phone: 802-633-4031 or 802-748-1581
Old taxidermy; deer, moose, elk, caribou antlers; skulls, folk art, prints, paintings and photos; snowshoes, pack baskets, creels, rustic & camp furnishings; by appointment.

Gene Harris
Art By God
50 Upper Alabama, Store No. 248
Underground Atlanta
Atlanta, GA 30303
phone: 404-577-7311 or 800-940-4449
fax: 305-573-9343
Mineral specimens, fossils, gems, sea shells, animal mounts, animal pelts, insects/butterflies, snail shells, skulls.

Edward Leep
American Natural Resources
128 N. Broad St.
Griffith, IN 46319-2219
phone: 219-922-6444
Sells mounts from around the world: full mounts, shoulder mounts, bear rugs, birds, etc.

David Boone
Boone's Trading Company
P.O. Box BB
Brinnon, WA 98320
phone: 360-796-4330 or 800-423-1945
fax: 360-796-4551
Buys and sells legal ivory, scrimshaw, furs and skulls: scrimshaw, netsuke, Eskimo artifacts, carvings, walrus, hippo, warthog, mammoth, jewelry, pistol grips, ivory beads, old trade beads, scrimshaw supplies and reproductions.

Experts

Gerard Giguere
Giguere Auction Co.
P.O. Box 1272
Windham, ME 04062
phone: 207-892-3800
fax: 207-892-3800
Conducts sporting auctions: fishing, hunting, decoys, sporting art, taxidermy; very knowledgeable about the regulations related to the sale of animal parts.

Museums/Libraries

Call of the Wild, The
850 S. Wisconsin Ave.
Gaylord, MI 49735
phone: 517-732-4336 or 517-732-4087

Suppliers

Van Dykes Supply Company
P.O. Box 278
Woonsocket, SD 57385-0278
phone: 800-558-1234 or 605-796-4425
fax: 605-796-4085
Issues large catalog of taxidermy supplies.

ANIMATION FILM ART

(see also AUDIO-VISUAL; CARTOON ART; CHARACTER COLLECTIBLES; SCIENCE FICTION)

Appraisers

Michael & Pamela Scoville, AAA
330 W. 45th St., Ste. 9D
New York, NY 10036-3864
phone: 212-765-3030
fax: 212-765-2727
Offers appraisal services for animation film art; certified member, Appraiser Association of America.

Melanie Smith
Seaside Gallery
P.O. Box 1
Nags Head, NC 27959
phone: 919-441-5418 or 800-828-2444
fax: 919-441-8563
e-mail: seaside@interpath.com
Accredited member of the International Society of Appraisers; specializes in fine art (paintings, graphics, sculpture) and animation art.

Auction Services

Howard Lowery
Lowery Auctions
3818 W. Magnolia Blvd.
Burbank, CA 91505
phone: 818-972-9080
Specializes in the auctioning of Disney animation art.

Clubs/Associations

Michael & Pamela Scoville
Animation Art Guild, Ltd.
Newsletter: Update, The
330 W. 45th St., Ste. 9D
New York, NY 10036-3864
phone: 212-765-3030
fax: 212-765-2727
Established in 1990; offers reliable, unbiased information; member services include book finders, auction hotline, appraisal services, flash advisories, art theft advisories, world's most comprehensive database on animation art values.

Nancy McClellan
Animation Art Collectors Club of Washington
2972 Yarling Ct.
Falls Church, VA 22042
phone: 703-876-0891 or 202-638-6411
Regional club interested in promotion and education of animation as an art form.

Dealers

Herb Barker
Barker Animation Art Galleries
1188 Highland Ave.
Cheshire, CT 06410-1624
phone: 800-227-5372 or 800-995-2357
fax: 203-699-1188
e-mail: fun@barkeranimation.com
Internet: http://www.BarkerAnimation.com

William Gunn
All American Collectibles, Inc.
24-04 Broadway
Fair Lawn, NJ 07410
phone: 201-797-2555 or 800-WOO-DY64
fax: 201-797-8668

Ari S. Goldman
355 E. 88th St.
New York, NY 10128-4904
Collector and dealer of fine animation art.

Cartoon Gallery
69-40 108th St.
Forest Hills, NY 11375
phone: 718-793-4714
fax: 718-793-4714
Buys and sells animation cels of your favorite cartoon characters from all of the major studios; limited edition and production cels.

Stu & Miriam Reisbord
Cartoon Carnival Gallery, The
2 Rabbit Run
Wallingford, PA 19086-6218
phone: 610-566-4343 or 610-566-1292
fax: 610-566-2727
e-mail: stureis@erols.com
Specializing in Disney vintage drawings, cels and backgrounds for over 20 years; also original pen & ink classic syndicated art.

Melanie Smith
Seaside Gallery
P.O. Box 1
Nags Head, NC 27959
phone: 919-441-5418 or 800-828-2444
fax: 919-441-8563
e-mail: seaside@interpath.com
Wants original oils, graphics, sculpture, and animation film art; also buys and sells old and new animation art.

Elvena Green
One-of-a-Kind Cartoon Art, Inc.
775 Livingstone Place
Decatur, GA 30030-3950
phone: 404-377-3333
fax: 404-377-6011

Taylor R. Robinson
3844 Oakbridge Lane
Dublin, OH 43017
phone: 614-799-0547 or 614-799-0541
fax: 614-799-0542
Buys, sells and trades fine animation art.

Dan & Mary Anne Ergezi
Art-Toons
P.O. Box 600
Northfield, OH 44067-0600
phone: 216-468-2655
fax: 216-468-2655
A family-owned business dedicated to give the public the enjoyment of owning animation art at affordable prices: Warner Bros., Walt Disney, commercials, MGM, super heroes, cult classics such as Heavy Metal, Wizards, Hanna Barbera.

Ron Silverstein
Silver Stone Gallery
2005 Palo Verde Ave., Ste. 205
Long Beach, CA 90815-3322
phone: 310-598-7600
fax: 310-598-7700
A private gallery for the discerning collector, specializing in buying & selling Disney Studio vintage animation art.

Joe Cesard
Sunday Funnies Inc.
20545 Plummer St.
Chatsworth, CA 91311
phone: 800-693-2369 or 818-341-9040
fax: 818-341-4850
World's largest distributor of animation and comic art featuring Betty Boop, Popeye, Archie, Fat Albert, Star Trek, Star Wars, Heckle & Jeckle, Cathy, Blondie, and many others.

Joseph Cesaro
Royal Animated Art, Inc.
20545 Plummer St.
Chatsworth, CA 91311-5110
phone: 818-341-9040
fax: 818-341-4850
Sells animated art: production cells, limited edition cels, and seri-cels; includes Archie, Fat Albert, Heckle & Jeckle, Blondie, Beetle Bailey, Star Trek, Star Wars, Lone Ranger, Lassie,

etc.; represents Filmation, Lucas Films, etc.

Museums/Libraries

Herb Barker
Barker Character, Comic & Cartoon Museum
1188 Highland Ave.
Cheshire, CT 06410-1624
phone: 800-227-5372 or 800-995-2357
fax: 203-699-1188
e-mail: fun@barkeranimation.com
Internet: http://www.BarkerAnimation.com
Features comic character collectibles, television collectibles, cartoon character collectibles, toys, and comic memorabilia.

Museum of Modern Art, The
11 W. 53rd. St.
New York, NY 10019
phone: 212-708-9889 or 800-447-6662

Baltimore Museum of Art, The
Art Museum Dr.
Baltimore, MD 21218
phone: 410-396-7101

David R. Smith
Walt Disney Archives
500 South Buena Vista St.
Burbank, CA 91521-1200
phone: 818-560-5424
Comprehensive Disney collection including complete U.S. and most foreign Disney comics; comics not available to researchers for preservation reasons, but much material is available by appointment.

Periodicals

Laughter Publications, Inc.
Magazine: Storyboard Magazine
80 Main St.
Nashua, NH 03060
phone: 603-883-9770
A bi-monthly high-quality magazine dedicated to animation art; feature articles and advertisements related to cel and merchandise collecting, the Disney motion pictures, and historical articles about the animators.

Newsletter: In Toon!
P.O. Box 487
White Plains, NY 10603
phone: 914-993-6218
The only publication devoted to collecting animation art; complete coverage of major auctions, features on the history of Limited Editions, interviews with animation personalities, columns on vintage cels and backgrounds, ads, etc.

Magazine: Animation Magazine
30101 Agoura Ct., Ste. 110
Agoura Hills, CA 91301-4301
phone: 800-996-TOON
fax: 818-991-3773
A bi-monthly magazine about the animation industry; animators, festivals, contests, fans, international animation, collecting animation art,

and ads for dealers selling animation art; also ads for animators and related services.

Directory: Animation Industry Directory
30101 Agoura Ct., Ste. 110
Agoura Hills, CA 91301-4301
phone: 800-996-TOON
fax: 818-991-3773
The most comprehensive reference guide to the people and companies active in the animation industry today.

Repair Services

Ron Stark, ISA
S/R Laboratories, Animation Art Conservation Center
Newsletter: Today
31200 Via Colinas, Ste. 210
Thousand Oaks, CA 91362-3939
phone: 818-991-9955
fax: 818-991-5418
e-mail: srlab@earthlink.net
Internet: http://www.srlabs.com
A conservation center for animation art cels; send for "Lab Notes", a series of helpful monographs on various aspects of animation art collecting.

ANTIQUES & COLLECTIBLES

(see also ANTIQUES DEALERS & COLLECTORS, Supplies For; ANTIQUES SHOP DIRECTORIES; ANTIQUES SHOW PROMOTERS; BOOKS, Reference [Antiques]; FLEA MARKET GUIDES; POPULAR CULTURE; PAWNBROKERS; TOURS/BUYING TRIPS)

Appraisers

(see also "APPRAISERS" Appendix in the back of this book for hundreds of educated, tested, and trained professional personal property appraisers - all credentialed members of the International Society of Appraisers.)

Rochelle Eisenberg, ASA
Art Directives, Inc.
P.O. Box 173
Ambler, PA 19002
phone: 215-646-0233
fax: 215-542-7015
Appraiser, consultant, writer, lecturer, author, advisor for Montgomery County newspapers, appeared on "Chubb Antiques Roadshow", instructor at Temple University.

Dewey W. Smith, ASA
Dewey W. Smith, ASA Antique Appraisals
2000 West Littletown Blvd.
Littleton, CO 80120-2070
phone: 303-347-1797
fax: 303-347-1549

Barbara Pickett, GCA, MCA, GGAC
Antique Rose, The
P.O. Box 771
Lakewood, CA 90714-0771
phone: 562-425-4149
fax: 562-425-4149
e-mail: bpfence@worldnet.att.net
*Personal property appraisals of
antiques, collectibles, estates,
insurance, probate, divorce, IRS.*

Nancy Alison Martin, ASA
Nancy Alison Martin & Associates
8 East Foothill Blvd., Ste. 201
Arcadia, CA 91006
phone: 818-445-0242
fax: 818-445-2046
*Appraises antique furniture, silver,
ceramics and glass, residential
contents.*

Clubs/Associations

Donna Carlson, Dir.
Art Dealers Association of America
Newsletter: ADAA Report
575 Madison Ave.
New York, NY 10022-2511
phone: 212-940-8590
fax: 212-940-7013
Internet: http://www.artdealers.org/
*Non-profit organization of nation's
lading dealers in fine art.*

Orva Heissenbuttel
American Antique Arts Association
Newsletter: A.A.A.A. Journal
P.O. Box 426
District Heights, MD 20747-0426
phone: 301-449-5372
*The AAAA is devoted to the
appreciation, study and preservation
of American antiques, architecture,
art, crafts and local history; the 14
chapters with 1000 members in MD,
N. VA, and DC invite membership of
any interested individual.*

Collectors' Society of America
P.O. Box 497
Clarkston, MI 48347-0497
*Monthly news and information about
your favorite collectibles.*

Young Collectors Club, The
Newsletter: Trading News, The
P.O. Box 5504
Coralville, IA 52241
*Sign up your collecting buddy-to-be
and he/she will receive a free
pamphlet of tips, a club ID card, a
fold-seal membership certificate, a
club pencil, and a subscription to the
newsletter.*

Clint Folin
Pack Rats of America
Newsletter: Rat's Nest
423 3rd St. NE
Glenwood, MN 56334
phone: 612-634-5577
Newsletter issued quarterly.

Lois R. Newton
Questers, The
8420 E. San Candido
Scottsdale, AZ 85258-2402
*Offers members a unique opportunity
to study and appreciate antiques; new
chapters are organized whenever
eight or more interested people apply
for a charter from the International
Organization.*

Victorian Homeowner's Association
Newsletter: Victorian Homeowner's
Association Newsletter
P.O. Box 846
Sutter Creek, CA 95685
phone: 209-267-0774
*For owners of Victorian homes; home
renovation, antiques and collecting
info.*

Experts

George E. Michael
P.O. Box 2087
Merrimack, NH 03054-2087
phone: 603-424-7400
fax: 603-424-7400
*Specialist in fine arts and antiques:
appraiser, expert witness, auctioneer,
writer, editor, consultant, lecturer and
instructor.*

Harry L. Rinker
Rinker Enterprises, Inc.
5093 Vera Cruz Rd.
Emmaus, PA 18049-9554
phone: 610-965-1122
fax: 610-965-1124
e-mail: rinkeron@fast.net
*Maintains research files, library
(books, periodicals, etc.), photos and
slides covering over 1500 antiques &
collectibles categories.*

Misc. Services

Bill Firla
Antique Researchers
P.O. Box 79
Waban, MA 02168-0001
phone: 617-449-1122
e-mail: antiqueres@aol.com
*Research detectives specializing in all
types of questions, problems, or issues
relating to collectibles, art, antiques;
identify artists, careers, craft persons,
hallmarks, initials, logos, trademarks,
provenance; does not buy or sell.*

Joan C. Browning
Papilion Lane Press
P.O. Box 436
Ronceverte, WV 24970-0436
phone: 304-645-6799
fax: 304-645-6799
*Features syndicate distributing
antiques/history features to
subscribing newspapers and
periodicals; publicist for history/
antiques entities on contract basis.*

Award Video & Film Distributors, Inc.
4441-B South Tamiami Trail
Sarasota, FL 34231
phone: 941-922-2472
fax: 941-922-2472
*Produces a series of videos; topics
include contemporary glass,
sculpture, painting, European glass,
American art glass, Lalique glass;
majolica, Rookwood pottery and
Venetian glass.*

Robert Reed, Ed.
Antique & Collectible News Service
P.O. Box 204
Knightstown, IN 46148-0204
phone: 765-345-7479
fax: 765-345-7479
e-mail: ACNS@aol.com
*Provides articles and book reviews to
publications around the US and
worldwide; more than 500 topics; lists
available.*

Judy L. Campbell
Attic Antiques
P.O. Box 27
Midland, MI 48640-0027
phone: 517-631-9263 or 517-631-4874
*Syndicated antiques columnist
specializing in answering readers'
questions regarding the history and
status of their antiques and
collectibles in today's market; also
refers readers to specialists, clubs and
other related resources.*

David Lisot
Advision, Inc.
3100 Arrowwood Lane
Boulder, CO 80303
phone: 303-444-2320 or 800-876-2320
*Advision specializes in producing and
distributing videotapes about coins
and collectibles; currently over 100
, video titles available.*

Museums/Libraries

Shelburne Museum, Inc.
P.O. Box 10
Shelburne, VT 05482-0010
phone: 802-985-3346 or 802-985-3344
fax: 802-985-2331
*37 historic structures and exhibit
buildings; diverse collection of
American folk, fine, decorative and
utilitarian art.*

Arthur H. Goetz, Dir.
Wicomico Country Free Library
P.O. Box 4148
Salisbury, MD 21803
phone: 410-749-3612
fax: 410-548-2968
*Offers a wide variety of antique and
collecting books and information
including identification and values,
contacts, etc.*

On-Line Services

Michael Almeida
DealerNet, Inc.
P.O. Box 2952
Woburn, MA 01888-1752
phone: 617-942-4626 or 617-944-6514
fax: 617-942-2626
e-mail: collectorweb@collectorweb.com
Internet: http://www.collectorweb.com
*Internet web based services for
collectors & dealers: page development & maintenance, management of
monthly sales/auctions, database
marketing, qualified buyers.*

Andy Kaufman
Real Time Antiques Market
P.O. Box 383
Manchester, NH 03105-0383
phone: 603-624-5600
e-mail: rtam@xensei.com
Internet: http://www.rtam.com
*An Internet site where buyers sign up
for categories and are instantly
notified the moment a dealer posts
them on the Internet; will design web
sites for dealers.*

Erik J. Wheeler
CollecTech Collector Online
P.O. Box 159
Burlington, VT 05402-0159
phone: 802-658-5411
e-mail: info@collectoronline.com
Internet: http://
www.collectoronline.com/
*Collector Online is a web site
dedicated to collectors and dealers;
buy and sell on the web.*

Jerry L. Pasco
Collectors' Clearinghouse, Inc.
P.O. Box 386
Somers, CT 06071-0386
phone: 860-763-5709
fax: 860-763-5709
e-mail: ctccl@aol.com
Internet: http://www.collectorsinc.com
*A listing service on the Internet; "For
Sale" and "Want" ads and
advertisements available.*

Collectors On-Line
44 West 77th St.
New York, NY 10024
Internet: http://www.collectors-on-
line.com
*An on-line leading fine arts, antiques
and collectibles database serving as a
central resource for information on,
and contact with, art dealers,
galleries, trade associations,
publications and shows.*

Susan Kopshc, Cust. Serv.
Internet Antique Shop, The
16 Heath Place
Garden City, NY 11530
e-mail: info@tias
Internet: http://www.tias.com/
*An on-line source of antiques and
collectibles.*

Kathy Kamnikar
Antique Networking
3132 Aulwood Ct.
Dublin, OH 43017-1707
phone: 614-889-9773 or 800-400-8674
fax: 614-889-9884
e-mail: antiqnet@ix.netcom.com
Internet: http://www.antiqnet.com
Internet on-line database that networks buyers and sellers of antiques locally, nationally, internationally; access information via PC and modem, or phone in to request staff to research items.

CompuServe Information Service
5000 Arlington Centre Blvd.
P.O. Box 20212
Columbus, OH 43220
phone: 800-848-8990 or 614-457-8650
Join the Collectibles Forum or Antiques Forum via computer modem: philatelists, numismatics and other collectors (sports, dolls, figurines, etc.); share pricing and trading information; also on-line buying and selling.

Randy Nauman
Collector's Super Mall Online
P.O. Box 1050
Dubuque, IA 52004-1050
phone: 800-482-3158 or 800-480-6169
fax: 800-531-0880
e-mail: webmaster@csmonline.com
Internet: http://www.csmonline.com
The largest on-line source of information and merchandise for collectors; classified ads, mall stores, directory listings, show and auction calendars, market news; for more information send e-mail or call.

American Collectors Network
525 South Old 81
Mc Pherson, KS 67460
phone: 316-241-7267
e-mail: lori@midusa.net
Internet: http://www.acollectorsnet.com
A great place to find what you want: glassware, paper items, sports memorabilia, military items, dolls, toys.

Stanley P. Wood
Internet Arts & Antiques
165 Highview Dr.
Lewisville, TX 75067
phone: 214-355-2495 or 800-894-7678
fax: 214-355-2812
e-mail: stan@wdsi.com
Internet: http://www.wdsi.com
An Internet site providing Internet store fronts for dealers.

Periodicals

David J. Maloney
Collector's Information Clearinghouse (CIC)
Directory: Maloney's Antiques & Collectibles Resource Dir.
P.O. Box 2049
Frederick, MD 21702-1049
phone: 301-695-8544
fax: 301-695-6491
e-mail: dmaloney@ix.netcom.com
Internet: http:// www.maloneysonline.com
Publishes major resource information source for collectors, sellers, claims adjusters, etc.: includes experts, buyers, clubs, periodicals, repairers, museums/libraries, matching services, dealers, etc.

Appraisers

(see the category APPRAISAL ASSOCIATIONS as well as the "APPRAISERS" Appendix and Appraisers listed under specific categories throughout this Directory.)

Auction Services

(see "AUCTION SERVICES" Appendix as well as Auction Services listed under specific categories throughout this Directory.)

Canadian

Auction Services

Erik J. Peters, ISA
Maynards Auctioneers
415 West 2nd Ave.
Vancouver
Brit. Columbia V5Y 1E3 Canada
phone: 604-876-6787 or 604-531-0166
fax: 604-876-2678
e-mail: Erik@Maynards.com
Internet: http://www.maynards.com
Quarterly auctions of Canadian, American & Western European fine art, antiques, silver, jewellery, china, glass, carpets and specialty collectables; Accredited Member of International Society of Appraisers.

Collectors

Colin R. Voorneveld, MD
27 Roncesvalles Ave., #408
Toronto
Ontario M6R 3B2 Canada
phone: 416-516-4751
e-mail: 72774.257@compuserve.com
Avid collector specializing in pre-1900 medical and pharmaceutical antiques; actively seeks medical instruments, spectacles, historic medicine, etc.

Misc. Services

Flora Hanst
Thesaurus
111 5th Ave.
New York, NY 10003
phone: 800-491-FIND
fax: 516-944-5278
Internet: http://thesaurus.co.uk
A pre-sale auction search service; a fee based service for subscribers to get advanced notice of upcoming items for sale at auctions around the world.

Periodicals

Paul Fiocca
Trajan Publishing Corp.
Magazine: Antique Showcase
103 Lakeshore Rd., Ste. 202
St. Catharines
Ontario L2N 2T6 Canada
phone: 905-646-7744
fax: 905-646-0995
e-mail: bret@trajan.com
Internet: http://www.vaxxine.com/trajan/
National magazine with diverse articles, show and auction reports, museum exhibits, book reviews, upcoming trends, etc.; also contains lots of display and classified ads for buyers of Canadian, US and European antiques; 9 times per year.

German

Auction Services

Jane Herz, US Rep.
Auction Team Koln
6731 Ashley Ct.
Sarasota, FL 34241-9696
phone: 941-925-0385
fax: 941-925-0487
Specializes in the sale of old office equipment, scientific instruments and devices, photographica, and old technology including toasters, typewriters, sewing machines, posters and lobby cards, tools telecommunications, etc.

Mexican

Dealers

El Paso Saddle Blanket Co.
601 N. Oregon
El Paso, TX 79901
Wants to buy old Mexican rugs, blankets, Sarahs; also old Navajo rugs and weavings, Tarahumara Indian art, Mexican ranch collectibles.

Experts

Gary L. Miller
Millchell
2112 Lipscomb
Ft. Worth, TX 76110-2047
phone: 817-923-3274
fax: 817-926-1970
Author of "Price Guide to Mexican Tourist Collectibles."

Periodicals

(see also "GENERAL INTEREST PERIODICALS" Appendix as well as Periodicals listed under specific categories throughout this Directory.)

Periodicals

Reed Reference Publishing
Directory: Official Museum Directory
121 Chanlon Rd.
New Providence, NJ 07974-1541
phone: 800-521-8110
Profiles more than 7,600 American institutions in 85 categories; aquariums, historic homes, museums, zoos; handy for those looking for information about specific types of antiques, fine art & collectibles; annual.

Repair Services

(see "REPAIR SERVICES" Appendix as well as Repair Services listed under REPAIR/RESTORATION/CONSERVATION and other specific categories throughout this Directory)

Reproductions

Clubs/Associations

Bill Mergenthal
American Antique Association
702 W. 76th St.
Davenport, IA 52806
phone: 800-473-7816 or 319-386-7866
A non-profit organization with the goal to stop the sale of unmarked reproductions; a consumer-oriented organization designed to help people who feel they may have purchased a reproduction.

Experts

Norman S. Young
Fake Publications
P.O. Box 766
Nassau, NY 12123-0766
e-mail: nsyoung@aol.com
Author of "Fabulous But Fake" (H/C book), the professional's guide to fake antiques; available from the author for $44.95.

Periodicals

Mark Chervenka
Newsletter: Antique & Collectors Reproduction News
P.O. Box 12130
Des Moines, IA 50312-9403
phone: 515-274-5886 or 800-227-5531
fax: 515-255-4530
Monthly newsletter showing differences between old originals &d new reproductions and fakes; 30-60 close-up photos of new and old side-by-side in each issue; all subjects; printed on glossy paper; annual index.; orders 800-227-5531.

Repro. Sources

Renovator's Supply
7577 Renovator's Old Mill
Millers Falls, MA 01349
phone: 413-659-2241
fax: 413-659-3796
Offers catalog of Victorian reproduction accessories, lighting, hardware, bath fixtures, and door, window and cabinet hardware.

Museum of Fine Arts, Boston -
Catalogue Sales Department
465 Huntington Ave.
P.O. Box 1044
Boston, MA 02120
phone: 800-225-5592
Internet: http://www.mfa.org
Not needed

Upper Deck, Ltd.
P.O. Box 1705
New Bedford, MA 02741
phone: 508-992-5424 or 508-992-3827
fax: 508-997-2123
Sells reproduction tin toys to the trade only.

G.R.'s Trading
Rte. 102 108 Chester Rd.
Derry, NH 03038
phone: 603-434-0220
fax: 603-425-2199
Sells repro. roll top desks, ice boxes, lamps, dolls, baskets, wicker, iron banks & toys, clocks, prints, pie safes, iron & brass beds, china cabinets, etc.

Sturbridge Yankee Workshop
90 Blueberry Rd.
Portland, ME 04102-1989
phone: 800-343-1144
fax: 207-774-2561

Artique Inc.
259 Godwin Ave.
Midland Park, NJ 07432-1808
phone: 201-444-8989
Repro. clay pipes, fraktur, advertising memorabilia, Christmas tree ornaments, pottery, flags, 19th century engravings, old maps, bells, sleigh bells, etc.

A.A. Importing Company, Inc.
30 Northfield Ave.
Raritan Center
Edison, NJ 08837
phone: 908-225-0770
Repro. Orientalia, porcelains, stoneware, cast iron banks and toys, simulated ivory, weathervanes, oak furniture; to the trade only.

Timeless Treasures
150 West 25th St.
New York, NY 10001
phone: 212-255-0340
fax: 212-255-6430
1000's of high-quality, framed and original oils, designer mirrors, decorative and functional bronze and marble art, Handel and Tiffany style lamps, handcarved or marquetry Furniture.

World Collectible Center
18 Vesey St.
New York, NY 10007
phone: 212-267-7100
Wholesale prices for reproduction collectibles: mammy cookie jar, Coca-Cola tip tray, KISS poster, gumball machines, Howdy Doody Western Set, etc.

Museum of Modern Art, The
11 W. 53rd. St.
New York, NY 10019
phone: 212-708-9889 or 800-447-6662

Metropolitan Museum of Art
Special Service Dept.
Middle Village, NY 11381
phone: 800-468-7386
Sells museum replicas.

Castle Antiques & Reproductions
515 Welwood Ave. & Rte. #6
Hawley, PA 18428
phone: 800-345-1667 or 717-226-8550
fax: 717-226-0454
They publish a full catalog of a large line of antique reproductions.

Fred & Dottie's Inc.
6711 Perkiomen Ave.
Birdsboro, PA 19508
phone: 610-582-1506
Reproduction ceramics, glass, cast iron; wholesale only.

Merritt's Antiques, Inc.
P.O. Box 277
Douglassville, PA 19518
phone: 610-689-9541 or 800-345-4101
fax: 610-689-4538
Internet: http://www.merritts.com
Carries a large line or reproduction clocks, ceramics, brass, dolls, furniture, glass, etc.

Winterthur Museum
Direct Mail Marketing Office
Winterthur, DE 19735-0001
phone: 800-448-3883
Internet: http://www.udel.edu/winterthur
Sells museum reproductions.

Avalon Forge
409 Gun Rd.
Baltimore, MD 21227
phone: 410-242-8431
Offers documented 18th century replicas for living history such as military goods, farm and home items.

Winterthur Museum Store, The
207 King Street
Old Town Alexandria, VA 22314
phone: 703-684-6092
fax: 703-684-6184
A select offering from Winterthur's elegant furnishings and decorative accessories collection.

Colonial Williamsburg
P.O. Box CH
Williamsburg, VA 23187
phone: 800-446-9240
Sell museum reproduction.

Kristina Neiman
Victorian Rapture Company
107 Saluda St.
Chester, SC 29706-1511
phone: 803-581-2703
e-mail: Kristina@victorianrapture.com
Internet: http://
www.victorianrapture.com
Custom makes high Victorian shades; 16" beaded fringe patterns & 85 frame choices to order; also covers old frames and supplier of reproduction Victorian lighting, jewelry (14K plated), bronzes, perfume bottles.

Ideal Imports, Inc.
20860 San Simeon Way, Apr. 405
Miami, FL 33179-1810
Sells new creations: bronzes, paintings, lamps, wood and more; special attention given to authentic patina.

IAC International
4001 Hiawatha Ave.
Minneapolis, MN 55406
phone: 612-724-7244
fax: 612-724-1238
Repro. Peanut jar and salt shakers, hen-on-a-nest, blue baby bottles, cast iron horse beer wagon and 5-car train, cast iron tractors, porcelain tea sets, and much more.

A.A. Importing Company, Inc.
7700 Hall St.
Saint Louis, MO 63147
phone: 800-325-0608 or 314-383-8800
fax: 314-383-2608
Repro. Orientalia, porcelains, stoneware, cast iron banks and toys, simulated ivory, weathervanes, oak furniture; to the trade only.

ReproCrafters, Inc.
11578 Industrial Park
Forney, TX 75126
phone: 800-654-8830 or 214-564-4441
fax: 214-552-9867
An import-direct warehouse carrying reproduction carousel horses, wicker doll carriages, bird cages, ship paintings, tricycles, sleds, etc.

Jim "Bud" Burton
Burton's Antiques & Antique
Reproductions
9333 Harwin Dr.
Houston, TX 77036
phone: 713-789-9333 or 713-977-5885
fax: 713-789-8181
Carries furniture and aluminum reproductions such as light poles, carousel horses, patio tables & chairs, etc.

A.A. Importing Company, Inc.
352 Shaw Rd.
South San Francisco, CA 94080
phone: 415-589-4422
Repro. Orientalia, porcelains, stoneware, cast iron banks and toys, simulated ivory, weathervanes, oak furniture; to the trade only.

ANTIQUES DEALERS & COLLECTORS

Clubs/Associations

Bob Warner
P.O. Box 442
Saxtons River, VT 05154
Specifically designed for antiques dealers across the country who are interested in improving their skills and who market their antiques in multi dealer centers, malls and other group shops.

National Antique & Art Dealers
Association of America
12 East 56th St.
New York, NY 10022
phone: 212-826-9707 or 212-319-0471
fax: 212-319-0471
Trade group represents art and antique dealers; sponsors antique and art exhibitions; promotes ethical trade practices among its members; free membership directory available.

Jim Tucker
Antiques & Collectibles Dealer
Association (ACDA)
Newsletter: ACDA News
P.O. Box 2782
Huntersville, NC 28070-2782
phone: 800-287-7127 or 704-948-3787
fax: 704-948-4296
e-mail: acda@ix.netcom.com
Provides a variety of services to dealers, such as insurance, merchant services, newsletter, seminars, travel and product discounts and more.

Jim Tucker
National Association of Collectors
Newsletter: NAC News
P.O. Box 2782
Huntersville, NC 28070-2782
phone: 800-287-7127 or 704-948-3787
fax: 704-948-4296
e-mail: acda@ix.netcom.com
Provides a variety of services to collectors, such as insurance programs, newsletter, biennial meeting, travel and product discounts and more.

Lester E. Sender
National Association of Dealers in
Antiques
23500 Mercantile Rd.
Cleveland, OH 44122-5914
phone: 216-595-1111
fax: 216-595-1111
Representing ethical antiques dealers nationally; also representing antique collectors in their "Collector Membership" category; write for details; pin, professional courtesies, Hdq. as a source of information, roster, current pricing.

Susan Feiger, Mem.
Associated Antique Dealers of America,
Inc.
2513 Nelson Rd.
Traverse City, MI 49684
Established in 1978 by a group of dedicated antique dealers united in their effort to foster and maintain the

honor and integrity of the profession; members pledge to conduct with integrity all business dealings, guarantee merchandise.

Periodicals

NU-Assets Press
Newsletter: Confidential Antique Market Letter
P.O. Box 47003
Indianapolis, IN 46247
phone: 317-887-3224
Monthly publication with in-depth articles for collectors and dealers: buying, selling, auctions, security, the Internet, etc.

Computer Programs For

Man./Prod./Dist.

Innovative Logic
Program: Artifax
38 Maple St.
Smith Falls
Ontario K7A 2A1 Canada
phone: 613-283-1345
Computerized collections database program.

Tom Bilotta
Carlisle Development Corp.
Program: Collector's Assistant
P.O. Box 291
Carlisle, MA 01741-0291
phone: 800-219-0257
e-mail: carlisle@aol.com
Internet: http://www.csmonline/carlisledc
Software for collectors and dealers; standard versions are available for over 40 collectibles categories: coins, currency, figurines, toys, autographs, sports cards, knives, military, etc.; custom versions available.

Joel Wilson, Pres.
Smalltown Software, Inc.
40 Moran St., Ste. 3
Newton, NJ 07860
phone: 201-948-0313
Developed with input from collectors and dealers the world over; systems are full-featured, versatile, and easy to use. Demonstration package available. Send for free information.

Serena Meyer
Program: Collector's Databank, The
163 Third Ave., Ste. 302
New York, NY 10003
phone: 212-674-9074
A computer-based tracking and inventory service for collectors; collection information is stored on a database created for the collector, from which reports and catalogs can be produced.

Russ Wood
Collector's Marketplace
Program: Intelligent Collector Software
RD 1 Box 213B
Montrose, PA 18801-9779
phone: 800-755-3123 or 717-278-4094
fax: 717-278-4377
e-mail: cmonline@epix.net
Internet: http://www.collectorsmarketplace.com

Michael Belofsky
MSdataBase Solutions
Program: Collectibles Database for Collectors
614 Warrenton Terrace NE
Leesburg, VA 22075-2465
phone: 800-407-4147 or 703-777-5660
fax: 703-777-5440
e-mail: msdbase@erols.com
Internet: http://www.collectorsoft.com
Windows: How many items to you own? How much have you spent? How much insured for? What items do you want? Includes on-line price guides for Prec. Mom., Hallmark Orns., Swarovski, D56, Tender Touches, Cher. Teddies, Disney Classics, others.

Michael Belofsky
MSdataBase Solutions
Program: Collectibles Database for Dealers
614 Warrenton Terrace NE
Leesburg, VA 22075-2465
phone: 800-407-4147 or 703-777-5660
fax: 703-777-5440
e-mail: msdbase@erols.com
Internet: http://www.collectorsoft.com
DOS: Keep track of inventory in stock, sold, sales tax, customers; print receipts, targeted mailings, price lists, inventory sheets, etc.; great for secondary market dealers! Refer to collector version for list of included price guides.

Linda Hiatt
Dimark Group
Program: Collectorpro 97
P.O. Box 2797
Murfreesboro, TN 37133-2797
phone: 615-896-7692 or 800-336-7692
e-mail: ibsinfo@edge.net
Internet: http://www.collectorpro.com
Software to catalog collections; keep track of item information, financial information, customer information and expense tracking; record sales and track sales tax; many reports and labels; stores and prints photos; WIN or WIN95 only.

Charles E. Crume
Charles Crume Software
P.O. Box 19940
Cincinnati, OH 45219-0940
phone: 513-471-0479
fax: 513-471-2590
e-mail: ccsmain@concentric.net
Internet: http://www.concentric.net/~ccsmain
IBM compatible program versions for malls, single dealers, collectors, consignment shops; optional modules

for auction houses; bar coding, credit card verification, extended inventory information, remote inventory entry, phone bids.

Fusion Software
Program: Value Vision
9337-B Katy Freeway, Ste. 444
Houston, TX 77024
phone: 800-856-8566 or 713-465-6363
fax: 713-465-9749
A personal inventory manager; Windows program to capture the contents of your home or office; quick, fun and easy; over 600 colorful icons to help you identify rooms and items; produces insurance claims form.

Bette Laswell
BDL Homeware
Program: BDL
2509 N. Campbell #328N
Tucson, AZ 85719-3304
phone: 602-298-4212 or 800-487-5206
fax: 520-885-1606
e-mail: scranton1@juno.com
Sells software for collectors and dealers; no computer skills required; inventories collections for insurance, keeps track of sales, does mailings, etc.; free catalog; also general bookkeeping software.

Third Rail
3377 Cimarron Dr.
Santa Ynez, CA 93460
phone: 805-688-7370
Sells computer inventory program for collectors; organize your collectibles; up to 225,000 items; for IBM PC/PCjr/XT/AT.

ArtStacks
57 Marguerite Ave.
Mill Valley, CA 94941
phone: 415-388-6917
fax: 415-389-6172
A collection management software program for Macintosh computers: purchase and appraisal information, images, framing information, edition information, provenance, exhibitions, bibliography, maintenance and restoration records, etc.

Lyons Computer
Program: Collection Organizer, The
346 Cernon St., Ste. C
Vacaville, CA 95688
phone: 800-799-3782

Steven Hudgik
PSG - HomeCraft Software
Program: HomeCraft
20676 SW Elk Horn Ct.
P.O. Box 974
Tualatin, OR 97062-0974
phone: 503-692-3732
fax: 503-692-0382
e-mail: homecraft@compuserve.com
Internet: http://www.homecraft.com
Publisher of computer software (Windows or DOS) for cataloging collections; features the ability to include pictures and sound as part of each entry; complete cataloging and

reporting flexibility allows you to catalog as you want.

Misc. Services

Stephen J. Abt, III
ArtFact, Inc.
Price Guide: ArtFact
1130 Ten Rod Rd., Ste. E104
North Kingstown, RI 02852-4158
phone: 401-295-2656 or 800-278-3228
fax: 401-295-2629
e-mail: sales@artfact.com
Internet: http://www.artfact.com
A computerized library recording auction sales of art and antiques; complete descriptions, prices realized, on-screen images.

Insurance

Misc. Services

International Collectors Insurance Agency
P.O. Box 6991
Warwick, RI 02887-6991
phone: 800-691-1114
Insures collections (mostly breakables - china, porcelain, glass, figurines, etc.); all risk coverage including accidental breakage.

Patty Rickey
RL&G Agency, Inc.
P.O. Box 426
Norwich, CT 06360
phone: 800-962-0431
Offers special protection policies for collectors.

American Collectors Insurance, Inc.
P.O. Box 8343
Cherry Hill, NJ 08002-0343
phone: 800-360-2277 or 609-779-7212
fax: 609-779-7289
Provides "agreed value" insurance protection to collectors of dolls, model trains, vintage toys, limited edition figurines, plates/steins, ornaments; "paper" collectibles (e.g. stamps) and coins ineligible; call for free quote.

W. Danforth Walker
APS Insurance Planer
P.O. Box 1200
Westminster, MD 21158
phone: 410-876-8833
fax: 410-876-9233
e-mail: dwalker@pipeline.com
Insurance for collectors: autographs, books, ceramics, clothing, comics, currency, dolls, figurines, movie memorabilia, paper ephemera, postcards, posters, records, stamps, stock certificates, Teddy bears, toys, trains, etc.

Jim Tucker
Village Insurance Agency
P.O. Box 2536
Chapel Hill, NC 27515
phone: 800-962-4611 or 919-968-4611
fax: 919-968-8991
Provides property and liability insurance to all dealers, mall owners, collectors, show promoters; programs

sponsored by the Antiques & Collectibles Dealer Association.

Mercy A. Komar, CIC
Insurance Center, The
P.O. Box 271
Warren, OH 44482-0271
phone: 330-394-6444 or 800-546-6444
fax: 330-393-8118
e-mail: insurancecenter@neonet.net
Internet: http://
www.insurancecenter.tywell.com
Specializing in insurance for dealers and collectors; member of Antiques & Collectibles Dealers Association and of the Society of Certified Insurance Counselors.

George Pelch, V.P.
Unirisc, Inc.
450 East 22nd St.
Lombard, IL 60148-6113
phone: 708-620-6562
fax: 708-932-8688
Provides fine arts insurance coverage for shops, galleries and collections; also coverage for shipping and storing.

Services For

Misc. Services

Dave Clark
National Collector Library
1331 Pleasant St.
Barre, MA 01005
phone: 508-355-6362
A nationwide clearinghouse and lifetime search service for collectors and collecting.

David & Becky Beane
Beane's Antiques & Photography
58 River Road
Benton, ME 04901
phone: 207-453-6790
e-mail: dbeane@mint.net
Internet: http://www.mint.net:80/
antiques/catalog/beane.html
A photography business specializing in illustrations of antiques for antiques publications, auctions, dealer advertisements and all relating photography; travels and covers the northern New England area.

Andrew Katz
Windham Antiques Research Service
P.O. Box 1212
Norwich, VT 05055-1212
phone: 802-649-5712
e-mail: windham@bmark.com
Internet: http://bmark.com/
windham.antiques
Specialty is research providing identification, documentation, historical and biographical background information pertaining to antiques, silver, ceramics and fine art for dealers, appraisers, and collectors.

Edward J. Pfeiffer
361 Lovely St.
Avon, CT 06001-4071
phone: 203-673-4120
fax: 203-676-9481
Publicity & public relations services for auctions, shows, dealers, museums; writing speeches, scripts, presentations.

Stanley & Bob Block
Block's Box
P.O. Box 51
Trumbull, CT 06611-0051
phone: 203-261-0057 or 203-926-8448
e-mail: BlocksChip@aol.com
Internet: http://pages.prodigy.com/
marbles/
Produce video tapes & catalogs for auctioneers and appraisers; full state-of-the-art video tape production facility.

Richard Michael Gramly, PhD
Great Lakes Artifact Repository
79 Perry St.
Buffalo, NY 14203-3037
phone: 716-849-0149
fax: 716-852-0093
Stores, sells, and conserves artifacts from all parts of the world in a secure, fireproof, climate-controlled working room and vault; examining room with drafting and photographic facilities; cataloguing of incoming collections, etc.

Harry L. Rinker
Institute for the Study of Antiques & Collectibles
5093 Vera Cruz Rd.
Emmaus, PA 18049-9554
phone: 610-965-1122
fax: 610-965-1124
e-mail: rinkeron@fast.net
Educational organization that offers seminars and workshops designed to improve business and object skills in the field of antiques and collectibles.

Donald L. Raleigh
Period Antiques Delivery Service, Inc.
P.O. Box 205
Millington, MD 21651
phone: 410-778-4357 or 800-962-1424
Specializes in the professional transportation of antiques and works of art.

Ashford Institute of Antiques
775 Gulf Shore Dr.
Destin, FL 32541
Offers a home study course for those wishing to start an antiques business.

Mary Antoine deJulio
Antoine & Associates
317 S. Wacouta Ave.
Prairie Du Chien, WI 53821
phone: 608-326-8225 or 608-326-6626
fax: 608-326-8225
Assistance in the care, management, protection, conservation, research, and documentation of American 18th and 19th century antiques.

Jim Crawford
Crawford Direct Marketing
5438 N 90th, Ste. 309
Omaha, NE 68134-1804
e-mail: crawcomm@sprynet.com
A direct marketing company specializing in the antiques and collectibles industry; offers imaginative ideas in mail and internet advertising.

Dr. Georgia Kemp Caraway
Texas Institute of Antiques & Collectibles
500 El Paseo
Denton, TX 76205-8502
phone: 817-056-5961 or 817-383-8809
fax: 817-383-8809
e-mail: tiac@cybergrill.com
Internet: http://www.dentonantiques.com
Texan Institute of Antiques & Collectibles offers a basic certificate in antiques brokerage to antique dealers and novices interested in learning about antiques & collectibles; hands-on training.

Supplies For

(see also ANTIQUES & COL-LECTIBLES; ANTIQUES DEALERS & COLLECTORS, Computer Programs For; AUCTION CATA-LOGS; BLACKLIGHTS [UV LAMPS]; GEMS & JEWELRY Suppliers; REPAIR/RESTORATION/CONSERVATION, Archival Supplies For; REPAIR/RESTORATION/CONSERVATION, Woodworking

Suppliers

Ken Sowman
13 Wynes Rd.
Barrie
Ontaria LN4 6T5 Canada
phone: 705-739-1087 or 705-739-0482
fax: 705-739-0482
e-mail: ksowman@netopia.net
Internet: http://www/
bconnex.net/~btracey\ken.html
All types of packaging supplies for 'collectibles, especially for paper collectibles and smalls; the main Canadian source for these items.

Arlington Industries
Dept. 182
Arlington, VT 05250
phone: 802-375-6139
fax: 802-375-9549
Sells sturdy, safe and crystal clear plateholders for museums, galleries and collectors.

Russell Norton
Photographic Antiques
P.O. Box 1070
New Haven, CT 06504-1070
phone: 203-562-7800
Carries 14 sizes of clear 2.5 mil polypropylene archival sleeves for photos and postcards up to 16" x 20".

Warren Abrams
Dealers Supply, Inc.
P.O. Box 717
Matawan, NJ 07747
phone: 908-583-3345 or 800-524-0576
fax: 908-591-8571
Carries table covers, aluminum show cases, canopies, lights, alarms, etc.

Collector's House
704 Ginesi Dr., Ste. 11A
Morganville, NJ 07751-1235
phone: 800-448-9298 or 908-972-6190
e-mail: collectorshouse@iof.com
Internet: http://www.cardmail.com/
collectors-house
Carries showcases, jewelry displays, velvet pads, trays, Riker mounts, butterfly boxes, table covers, plate stands, etc.; free catalog available.

Robbins Container Corp.
222 Conover St.
Brooklyn, NY 11231-1033
phone: 718-875-3204
fax: 718-797-3529
Carries corrugated mailers, cartons, boxes, stretch film, stackable cardboard bins, tote boxes, storage chests, strapping and sealing tape, foam, polystyrene chips, mailing envelopes, twine, bubble wrap, etc.

Source, The
P.O. Box 349
Brooklyn, NY 11235
Handmade jewelry displays and boxes, dinnerware displays, zip-lock bags, table covers, marking tags and labels, salesman cases, show cases, adhesives and more.

Mega-National Industries Inc.
P.O. Box 538
Round Lake, NY 12151-0538
phone: 518-899-6190 or 518-827-4443
Supplier of canopy tent units, and dealer display equipment; also archival quality protection polysleeves, archival rigids, semi-rigid sleeves for postcards, currency, stereoviews; archival pocket pages, backing boards, etc.

Bags Unlimited
7 Canal St.
Rochester, NY 14608-1910
phone: 800-767-2247 or 716-436-9006
fax: 716-328-8526
e-mail: bags@frontiernet.net
Internet: http://www.frontiernet.net/
~bags
Sells collector supplies: poly and paper sleeves, mailers, filler pads, album jackets, storage boxes, divider cards, etc.

Brodart
1609 Memorial Ave.
Williamsport, PA 17705
phone: 800-233-8959
fax: 800-283-6087
Internet: http://www.brodart.com
Carries clear protective covers for books; protect book dust jackets - they

may represent half or more of the value of a book.

SAFE Publications, Inc.
P.O. Box 263
Southampton, PA 18966-0263
phone: 215-357-9049
fax: 215-357-5202
Sells collecting systems for postcards, covers, documents, pins, medals, badges, stamps, coins, banknotes, telephone cards, etc.; crystal clear sleeves are PVC free.

Seidman Supply Co.
3366 Kensington Ave.
Philadelphia, PA 19134
phone: 215-423-8896
fax: 215-423-9242
Carries supplies for the sports card and memorabilia collector: ball cubes and holders; sorting trays, shoeboxes, acrylic card holders.

Mylan Enterprises
P.O. Box 971002
Boca Raton, FL 33497-1002
phone: 800-852-8119 or 561-852-0861
fax: 561-852-0862
e-mail: mylan @ix.netcom.com
Internet: http://members.tripod.com/
~mylan/padsbwbble.html
Carries a wide assortment of Wrapping Pads, Bubble Packs and Bubble Bags.

Demco
P.O. Box 7488
Madison, WI 53707
Carries clear protective covers for books; protect book dust jackets - they may represent half or more of the value of a book.

Kiefer Supply Co.
417 W. Stanton Ave.
Fergus Falls, MN 56537
phone: 800-435-2726
Forms, tags, tassels, pennants, stamps, showcase locks, rags, dealer signs, shopping bags, moving pads, banners, window lettering, etc.

Ronald Nootbaar
Roberts Colonial House, Inc.
570 W. 167th St.
South Holland, IL 60473
phone: 708-331-6233
fax: 708-331-0538
Sells plate hangers, plate stands, Plexiglass display cubes, quilted vinyl china cases, and over 1600 other items; send for catalog.

Maas International
1500 West 55th St.
La Grange, IL 60525
phone: 708-246-8581
fax: 708-246-8690
Sells Maas Polishing Creme, an amazing product that cleans, polishes and protects all metals: gold, pewter, dirigold, silver, aluminum, chrome, brass, dirilyte, Plexiglas, copper, stainless steel, enamel, and more.

Sandler Products, Inc.
2229 S. Halsted St.
Chicago, IL 60608
phone: 312-226-1414
Sells blue underpads - very useful for wrapping fragile items.

Boss Mfg. Co.
221 West First St.
Kewanne, IL 61443
phone: 800-447-4581
Carries a line of nylon tricot inspectors gloves for the safe handling of silver, glass, jewelry, etc.

Collectors Supply Company
8415 "G" St.
Omaha, NE 68127
phone: 402-597-3727
fax: 402-592-9015
Album pages, plastic bags, displays, price tags, aluminum and wood display cases, etc.

Collector's Care
4455 Torrance Blvd., #297
Torrance, CA 90503-4398
phone: 800-595-ACID or 805-497-7445
Supplies acid-free paper, boxes and related products for storing dolls, doll clothing, teddy bears, pressed flowers, wedding and christening gowns, quilts, needlepoint, heirlooms and linens.

Jones West Packaging Co.
P.O. Box 1084 - Dept. DL
Rohnert Park, CA 94927-1084
phone: 707-795-8552
Supplier of all sizes of ZIP CLOSE plastic bags and flat bags in small or large quantities; since 1981; credit cards accepted; catalog available.

Collector Items
P.O. Box 55511
Seattle, WA 98155
phone: 206-365-1188
fax: 206-367-1188
Sells nylon bubble bags.

Supplies For (Lighting)

Suppliers

Westgate Enterprises
2118 Wilshire Blvd., Ste. 612
Santa Monica, CA 90403-5784
phone: 310-477-5891
fax: 310-478-1954
e-mail: jw_mfa@lamg.com
Carries over 100 different full spectrum light bulbs and tubes; improved, glare-free, color corrected light bulbs that improve display lighting.

Supplies For (Safes)

Suppliers

Kingsberry Mfg. Corp.
715 W. Zavale
Crystal City, TX 78839
phone: 800-445-0763
Sells new safes for collectors.

Supplies For (Showcases)

Suppliers

Oodles of Stuff
29 Webster St.
Lynn, MA 01902
phone: 617-599-2332
Carries collector and jewelry items including cases, lighting, etc.

Megaworks
P.O. Box 341
East Hampton, CT 06424
phone: 860-267-7640
fax: 860-267-7641
Carries displays and aluminum show cases.

Dave Cohen
Dave Cohen & Associates
P.O. Box 868
Westwood, NJ 07675-0868
phone: 201-666-2222
fax: 201-666-2282
Supplier of glass display show cases for antiques shops, malls, co-ops, and private collectors.

Showcases by Lin Terry
1000 Airport Rd., #103
Lakewood, NJ 08701-5960
phone: 908-370-5252
fax: 908-370-4114
e-mail: linterry@aol.com
Sells handcrafted acrylic collectible display cases for trains, dolls, ships, sports memorabilia, comic books, magazines, wax boxes, figurines, etc.; many sizes; call or write for free catalog.

Monique Caron-Krug
Showcase Sales Gallery
P.O. Box 312
Otego, NY 13825
phone: 607-988-9173 or 800-246-2940
fax: 607-988-9173
e-mail: monique@norwich.net
Internet: http://www.csmonline.com/
showcase
Showcases, display cases and cabinets for a beautiful presentation of collectibles or shop merchandise; various styles and sizes.

National Showcase Company
724 York Rd.
Baltimore, MD 21204
phone: 800-628-2352 or 410-296-6556
fax: 410-296-5236
Distributes Allstate aluminum showcases.

Chris R. Jensen
Streamwood, Inc.
P.O. Box 1841
Easley, SC 29641-1841
phone: 864-859-2915
fax: 800-453-0398
e-mail: CJensen@mindspring.com
Internet: http://www.mindspring.com/
~cjensen/
Sells BoxWare display cases made from tough injection molded plastic, not cardboard; latched lids so no

more straight pins; replaceable glass or acrylic lenses.

Antique Mall Showcases
3039 W. Antioch Rd.
Springville, TN 38256
phone: 800-839-4928
Large capacity showcases, 40 watt fluorescent bulbs.

Bluegrass Case Company
272 Airport Rd.
P.O. Box 386
Stanton, KY 40380
phone: 606-663-9871 or 800-668-9871
fax: 606-663-6369
Sells black collector frames; also walnut, cherry or oak frames with locks.

Aluma-Case Co.
3655 Sherbrooke
Toledo, OH 43613
Distributes aluminum showcases, all sizes.

Coneaut Glass
200 East Main Rd.
Conneaut, OH 44030
phone: 216-593-6622
fax: 216-593-6015
Makes glass enclosures with oak bases for Barbie dolls, Ginny dolls, and Madam Alexander dolls.

Sales Dept.
Jamar Company
5015 State Rd.
Dept. MACR
Medina, OH 44256-8427
phone: 330-239-2889
fax: 330-239-2889
e-mail: jmdisplay@aol.com
Manufactures and sells a wide selection of acrylic display cases and cabinets.

Specialty Plastic Fabrications
972 Kahn Ave.
Hamilton, OH 45011-4458
phone: 800-582-9038 or 513-856-9475
Sells crystal clear acrylic display cases for dolls, antiques, toys, and other fine collectibles.

Collectible Displays, Inc.
9846 Crescent Park Dr.
West Chester, OH 45069
phone: 513-777-7784
fax: 513-777-7761
Solid wood lit display cabinets of the highest quality: hidden compartment under each shelf for wire storage, adjustable shelves, beveled glass, etc.

Douglas Hammetter
Creative Store Design, Inc.
3728 N Fratney St.
Milwaukee, WI 53212-1749
phone: 800-865-9595
fax: 414-963-4445
Sells upright display cases or trophy cases; full vision, glass cube displays, countertop showcases; delivery and setup available.

Crystal Showcase Design
315 Atwater St.
Saint Paul, MN 55117
phone: 612-489-5328
Makes specialized showcases.

Militaire Promotions
6427 W. Irving Park Rd., Ste. 160
Chicago, IL 60634-2437
phone: 312-777-0499
Sell J-mount display boxes; glass-top display boxes for small collectibles: jewelry, watches, buttons, badges, etc.; all sizes.

Garrett's
1264 East 2073 Rd.
Eudora, KS 66025
phone: 913-542-2339 or 800-447-7508
Sells black collector frames and aluminum or cherry sales/display/show cases.

Paul F. Gabel
Clear-View Display Cases
9251 Minnesota Ave.
Kansas City, KS 66112
phone: 913-299-8366
Manufactures clear plastic display cases with solid oak, cherry, or walnut bases; ideal for model tractors, cars, trucks, etc.

Michael A. Pratt, Sr.
Collector's Display Case Co.
Rte. 2 Box 73
687 "V" Road
Fremont, NE 68025
phone: 402-721-4765
fax: 402-721-4765
e-mail: mpratt@teknetwork.com
Internet: http://www.teknetwork.com/display
Manufactures unique inexpensive cases to display, organize, and protect small collectibles of all types including marbles; send SASE for more information.

ANTIQUES SHOP DIRECTORIES

(see also FLEA MARKETS, Directories)

Periodicals

Lisa Freeman
AntiqueSource, Inc.
Guide: Sloan's Green Guide to Antiquing in New England
P.O. Box 270
Belmont, VT 05730
phone: 802-259-3614
fax: 802-259-3615
e-mail: info@antiquesource.com
Internet: http://www.antiquesource.com
The definitive guide to antiques dealers and related services in the New England region (ME, NH, VT, RI, CT, MA, Eastern NY, Long Island); dealer inventory, hours of operation, detailed directions, services offered.

Michael P. Casey
Ultra Graphics
Guide: Antique Country
P.O. Box 649
Berryville, VA 22611
phone: 703-955-4412
Distributed free in the Tri-State area, Washington & Baltimore; subscriptions available for home delivery; includes pictures of items for sale, area map and an index of specialties for over 100 dealers in the VA, MD, WV, PA, DC area.

Southern Antiques
Guide: Southern Antiques Shop Guide
P.O. Drawer 1107
Decatur, GA 30031-1107
phone: 404-289-0054
fax: 404-286-9727
Lists the South's best antiques shops, hundreds of antiques shows, top auction houses, and special products and services.

Joan Bryant, Ed.
Antiques & Art Around Publishing, Inc.
Guide: Antiques & Art Around Florida
P.O. Box 2481
Fort Lauderdale, FL 33303-2481
phone: 954-768-9430 or 800-248-9430
fax: 954-768-0621
e-mail: aarf@shadow.com
Internet: http://www.aarf.com
Full color guide to Florida's antique shops; maps, shows, museums; feature articles on antiques and FL heritage.

Maude Gold Kiser
M & M Publishing
Guide: Treasure Hunters Guide to Middle-Tennessee, The
P.O. Box 40122
Nashville, TN 37204
Lists antiques shops, flea-markets, second-hand and junk stores within a 60-mile radius of Nashville, TN.

David & Kim Leggett
Rainy Day Publishing
Directory: Antique Atlas, The
1740 N. Germantown Pkwy, Ste. 18
Cordova, TN 38018
phone: 800-456-9326 or 901-755-5233
fax: 901-755-2529
A comprehensive guide to antiquing in America: over 15,000 shops and malls.

Judy Lloyd
FDS, Inc.
Directory: No Nonsense Antique Mall Directory
4 Brown Street
P.O. Box 188
Higginsport, OH 45131
phone: 937-375-3009
e-mail: mgcg1@aol.com
Internet: http://www.csmonline.com/nnamd.html
Directory of over 5,200 antique malls/multi-dealer antique shops in the US; alphabetically arranged by state/city; contains standardized listings of name, address, size, phone, hours and directions (when available); SASE for info.

Connie Swaim, Ed.
Mayhill Publications, Inc.
Guide: AntiqueWeek Antique Shop Directory
P.O. Box 90
Knightstown, IN 46148
phone: 317-345-5133 or 800-876-5133
fax: 800-695-8153
e-mail: antiquewk@aol.com
Internet: http://www.antiqueweek.com
AntiqueWeek Shop Guide is an annual directory that lists antique shops and malls; two editions are published: Eastern and Central.

Janice Reittinger
DJ's Publishing
Guide: Iowa's Complete Guide to Antique Shops & Malls
428 1st Ave. East
Dyersville, IA 52040
phone: 319-875-8640
Internet: http://www.collectoronline.com/guides/Iowa.html
Published every January; over 800 shops, shows, maps.

Terri Vopelak
CarPac Publishing Co.
Guide: Antiques Shops Directory
1800 W. D St.
P.O. Box 601
Vinton, IA 52349-0601
phone: 319-472-4763 or 319-472-4764
fax: 319-472-3117
Lists antiques shops in Illinois, Nebraska, Wisconsin, Kansas, Minnesota, Missouri, South Dakota, Texas and Iowa.

Irene Taylor
Moonlight Press
Guide: Taylor's Guide to Antique Shops in IL & So. WI
202 N. Brighton
Arlington Heights, IL 60004-6346
phone: 847-392-8438
fax: 847-392-8312
Internet: http://www.collectoronline.com/guides/taylors.html
Address and phone numbers of all known antique shops in northern Illinois and southern Wisconsin; includes antiques show dates; repair people; maps; published every April.

Jan Lindenberger
Guide: Antique Buyer's Guide
P.O. Box 7224
Colorado Springs, CO 80933
phone: 719-591-9558
fax: 719-591-9558
Covering the states of KS, OK, NM, CO, MO, NE and TX; addresses, ads, maps.

Guide: Arizona in Antiquing
P.O. Box 13412
Tucson, AZ 85732
phone: 520-323-0319
Comprehensive (135 pages) guide includes 500 shops, malls, shows, auctions, museums, buyers, appraisers, restoration, repair and much more; this is the book on where to buy and sell your treasures throughout Arizona.

Patricia F. Doering
Guide: Second Hand News
3120 41st St.
San Diego, CA 92105-4133
phone: 619-283-5245
fax: 800-243-8892
e-mail: secondhand@earthlink.net
Internet: http://www.bargainlink.com
A comprehensive 52 page 5"x8" guide to San Diego's thrift stores, rummage sales, swap meets, calendar of events, feature articles.

Bliss Cochran
Guide: Cochran's Collectors Guide to California
P.O. Box 750895
Petaluma, CA 94975-0895
phone: 707-769-9916 or 800-648-0526
fax: 707-769-0669
e-mail: cochran@sonic.net
This directory is a map book covering the entire state of California with an annual listing of antique shows; free at stores and shows; $5 by mail.

British

Periodicals

Carol Fisher
Carol Fisher Publishing
Guide: Touring British Antique Shops
P.O. Box 531
Melksham
Wiltshire SN12 8SL, U.K.
phone: 01225-700085
fax: 01225-790939
Annual paperback containing 60 illustrated guided tours of 3,500 antique shops in over 1400 towns and villages throughout Britain; compact and portable with 65 maps and full historic/tourist info enroute; $33.95 US airmail.

Canadian

Periodicals

Charlton Press, The
Guide: Charlton Collector's Guide to Ontario, The
2040 Yonge St., Ste. 208
Toronto
Ontario M4S 1Z9 Canada
phone: 800-442-6042 or 416-488-4653
fax: 800-442-1542
e-mail: chpress@pathway.com
Lists thousands of Ontario dealers, shows, flea markets, and more; complete with addresses and phone numbers.

ANTIQUES SHOW PROMOTERS

Clubs/Associations

Mitchell Sorenson, Ex. Dir.
Professional Show Manager's
  Association
P.O. Box 30
Bloomfield, CT 06002
phone: 203-243-3977
*Promotes a Code of Ethics for the
benefit of the consumer show industry
and to facilitate the exchange of
information among show managers of
consumer shows.*

Diana Bittel, Pres.
Antiques Council, The
P.O. Box 574
Southport, CT 06490
phone: 203-396-0192
fax: 203-396-0193
e-mail: pga@futuris.net
Internet: http://www.kiwi.futuris.net/ac/
  welcome.html
*An association of approximately 80
members across the nation who
manage antiques shows for charity
sponsors; members abide by code of
ethics; show schedule now includes
seven annual shows; founded in 1990.*

Misc. Services

Cathy Sykes
New England Antique Show Manage-
  ment
320 Pork Hill Rd.
Wolfeboro, NH 03894
phone: 603-569-9301
*Produces the Wolfeboro, NH Antiques
Fair and the Sandwich, NH New
England Antiques & Collectibles
Festival.*

ANTIQUITIES

(see also ARCHAEOLOGY; COINS
& CURRENCY, Coins [Ancient];
PRECOLUMBIAN; PREHISTORIC
ARTIFACTS)

Appraisers

Frederick P. Dose, Jr.
Frederick Dose Appraisals Ltd.
778 Pleasant Ave.
Highland Park, IL 60035-4613
phone: 847-433-1090 or 847-433-7870
*Appraises Egyptian, Greek, Roman,
etc. art for insurance, corporate,
private, and attorneys; references on
request; 6 year full-time as University
art historian.*

Auction Services

Greg Manning
Greg Manning Auctions, Inc.
775 Passaic Ave.
West Caldwell, NJ 07006
phone: 201-882-0004 or 800-221-0243
fax: 201-882-3499
*Since 1905, a leading auctioneer of
Americana, glass, stoneware, and
antiques.*

Christie's
502 Park Ave.
New York, NY 10022
phone: 212-546-1000
fax: 212-980-8163
Internet: http://www.sirius.com/
  ~christie/

Alex G. Malloy
Alex G. Malloy, Inc.
P.O. Box 38
South Salem, NY 10590-0038
phone: 203-438-0396 or 203-438-9652
fax: 203-438-6744
e-mail: alexmalloy@aol.com
Internet: http://www.members.aol.com/
  AlexMalloy/agmallory.htm
*Issues fixed price lists and mail bid
sales of ancient and medieval coinage,
and of ancient art and antiquities for
sale.*

Dealers

Allan Anawati
Medusa
10 Notre Dame East, Ste. 310
Montreal
Quebec H2Y 1B7 Canada
phone: 514-874-0337 or 514-876-1373
fax: 514-876-7998
e-mail: anawti@bam.net
Internet: http://www.anawati.com
*Dealing in Egyptian, Greek, Roman,
and Near Eastern antiquities for over
30 years.*

Allen G. Berman
Allen G. Berman Professional
  Numismatist
P.O. Box 605
Fairfield, CT 06430-0605
phone: 203-374-3032 or 203-374-6986
fax: 203-374-6986
e-mail: agberman@aol.com
*Medieval, Byzantine and European
seals including sealed documents,
lead seals to modern times, medieval
pilgrim badges; consultant to auction
houses on attribution of seals, oil
lamps and pottery; no New World or
Far Eastern handled.*

Alex G. Malloy
Alex G. Malloy, Inc.
P.O. Box 38
South Salem, NY 10590-0038
phone: 203-438-0396 or 203-438-9652
fax: 203-438-6744
e-mail: alexmalloy@aol.com
Internet: http://www.members.aol.com/
  AlexMalloy/agmallory.htm
*Issues fixed price lists and mail bid
sales of ancient and medieval coinage,
and of ancient art and antiquities for
sale.*

Frank J. Wagner
Classica Antiquities
P.O. Box 509
Syracuse, NY 13201-0509
phone: 315-687-0036 or 315-457-7249
e-mail: clasant@servtech.com
Internet: http://www.servtech.com/
  public/clasant/
*For over 30 years buying/selling
ancient and medieval Greek, Roman,
Egyptian, Near Eastern coins and
antiquities.*

Museums/Libraries

British Museum, The
Great Russell Street
London WC1B 3DG, U.K.
phone: 0171 636 1555
Internet: http://www.british-
  museum.ac.uk/
*Founded in 1753, world-famous
collections of antiquities from Egypt,
Western Asia, Greece and Rome.*

Abbe Museum
P.O. Box 286
Bar Harbor, ME 04609
phone: 207-288-3519

Periodicals

Emma Beatty
Aurora Publications Ltd.
Magazine: Minerva
14 Old Bond St.
London W1X 3BD, U.K.
phone: 44 171 495 2590
fax: 44 171 491 1595
Internet: http://www.desiderata.com
*The international review of ancient art
and archaeology; a bi-monthly
illustrated magazine focusing on
ancient art, antiquities, archaeology
and numismatic discoveries
worldwide.*

Bill Balinger
Newsletter: Prehistoric Antiquities &
  Archaeological News
P.O. Box 53
North Lewisburg, OH 43060
phone: 513-747-2225
*Quarterly newspaper about
archaeology and antiquities; articles,
ads, etc.*

Magazine: American Antiquities Journal
126 E. High St.
Springfield, OH 45502

Magazine: Celator, The
P.O. Box 123
Lodi, WI 53555-0123
phone: 608-592-4684
fax: 608-592-5084
e-mail: celator@aol.com
Internet: http://www.numisart.com/
  celator/
*A monthly magazine focusing on
antiquities and ancient coins; ads,
articles, auction reports, etc.*

Amphora

Experts

Robert Bowles
Newsletter: Amphora Market Report
600 Cherry St.
Lansing, MI 48933
Publishes "Amphora Market Report."

Egyptian

Dealers

Allan Anawati
Medusa
10 Notre Dame East, Ste. 310
Montreal
Quebec H2Y 1B7 Canada
phone: 514-874-0337 or 514-876-1373
fax: 514-876-7998
e-mail: anawti@bam.net
Internet: http://www.anawati.com
*Dealing in Egyptian, Greek, Roman,
and Near Eastern antiquities for over
30 years.*

David Markarian
Markarian Ancient Artifacts
P.O. Box 2476
Rancho Mirage, CA 92270
phone: 760-202-5000
Buys and sells Egyptian artifacts.

Greek & Roman

Dealers

Allan Anawati
Medusa
10 Notre Dame East, Ste. 310
Montreal
Quebec H2Y 1B7 Canada
phone: 514-874-0337 or 514-876-1373
fax: 514-876-7998
e-mail: anawti@bam.net
Internet: http://www.anawati.com
*Dealing in Egyptian, Greek, Roman,
and Near Eastern antiquities for over
30 years.*

Museums/Libraries

Ellen Reeder
Walters Art Gallery
600 N. Charles St.
Baltimore, MD 21201
phone: 410-547-9000

Toledo Museum of Art, The
2445 Monroe St.
P.O. Box 1013
Toledo, OH 43697
phone: 419-255-8000
*Internationally-recognized collection
of Greek vases, as well as glass,
paintings, and decorative arts.*

Medieval

Museums/Libraries

Dr. Gary Vikan
Walters Art Gallery
600 N. Charles St.
Baltimore, MD 21201
phone: 410-547-9000

Repro. Sources

Medieval Replicas
1925 Marber ave.
Long Beach, CA 90815-3111
phone: 310-431-0402
*Excellent quality weapons and armor;
write for free catalog.*

ANTLERS

(see ANIMAL TROPHIES; FURNITURE [ANTIQUE], Antler & Horn)

APOTHECARY ANTIQUES

(see MEDICAL, DENTAL & PHARMACEUTICAL)

APPLE PARERS

(see also KITCHEN COL-LECTIBLES)

Clubs/Associations

John D. Lambert
International Society for Apple Parer Enthusiasts
Newsletter: ISAPE Newsletter
17 E. High
Mount Vernon, OH 43050
phone: 614-892-2040 or 614-393-2598
Holds conventions; 12-page newsletter contains articles, old ads, patents and a buy/sell section; to date over 100 photos of different models have been presented.

Collectors

John D. Lambert
17 E. High
Mount Vernon, OH 43050
phone: 614-892-2040 or 614-393-2598
Pays top dollar for cast iron parers such as Bergner, Maxam, Browne, Brokaw's Climax, Thompson, Parker, Champion, Eureka, Nonpareil, Oriole, Yankee, Victor, Star, Selick's, Peerless.

Johnny Appleseed
8060 Sierra St.
Fair Oaks, CA 95628-7549
phone: 916-961-7174
Apple peelers wanted; give patent dates, model and description.

APPRAISAL ASSOCIATIONS

(see also "APPRAISERS" Appendix as well as Appraisers listed under specific categories throughout this Directory.)

Clubs/Associations

Canadian Association of Personal
  Property Appraisers
Newsletter: CAPPA News
2 Briar Place
Halifax
Nova Scotia B3M 2X2 Canada
phone: 902-443-5698
Membership consists of individuals covering all areas of personal property appraising, excluding vehicles of all types and heavy industrial equipment.

Victor Wiener, Ex. Dir.
Appraisers Association of America
Newsletter: Appraiser, The
386 Park Ave. S #2000
New York, NY 10016-8804
phone: 212-889-5404
fax: 212-889-5503
Oldest nonprofit association of personal property appraisers with approximately 1,000 members in more than 600 subspecialties in all areas of fine art, antiques, and insurance appraisals; membership directory available.

Deborah A. Sharpe
Appraisal Foundation, The
Newsletter: Foundation News
1029 Vermont Ave. NW, Ste. 900
Washington, DC 20005-3517
phone: 202-347-7722
fax: 202-347-7727
Internet: http://
  www.appraisalfoundation.org
Authorized by Congress as the source of appraisal standards and appraiser qualifications.

Rebecca L. Ewing
American Society of Appraisers
Journal: Valuation
P.O. Box 17265
Washington, DC 20041
phone: 703-478-2228 or 800-ASA-
  VALU
fax: 703-742-8471
e-mail: asainfo@apo.com
Internet: http://www.appraisers.org
"Valuation" is published twice a year; also publishes "Personal Property Journal" quarterly; contact ASA for subscription information.

James Jolliff
National Association of Jewelry
  Appraisers, The
Newsletter: Jewelry Appraiser, The
P.O. Box 6558
Annapolis, MD 21401-0558
phone: 301-261-8270 or 410-266-0744
Members perform gem and jewelry, silver flatware and holloware, and watch valuations exclusively; also watches and silver.

Christian Coleman, Ex. Dir.
International Society of Appraisers
Journal: ISA News Journal
16040 Christensen Rd., Ste. 320
Seattle, WA 98188
phone: 206-241-0359
fax: 206-241-0436
e-mail: ISA_HQ@compuserve.com
Internet: http://www.isa-appraisers.org
Largest association of professional personal property appraisers; over 1,200 members specializing in all areas of antiques & residential contents, gems & jewelry, fine art, machinery & equipment; free referrals; directory available.

Misc. Services

Stephen J. Abt, III
ArtFact, Inc.
Price Guide: ArtFact
1130 Ten Rod Rd., Ste. E104
North Kingstown, RI 02852-4158
phone: 401-295-2656 or 800-278-3228
fax: 401-295-2629
e-mail: sales@artfact.com
Internet: http://www.artfact.com
A computerized library recording auction sales of art and antiques; complete descriptions, prices realized, on-screen images.

William D. Hoefer, FGA, GG
Hoefers' Gemological Services
5016 Alan Ave., Ste. B4
San Jose, CA 95124-5741
phone: 408-264-0670
fax: 408-264-0725
Offers experts consultation and expert testimony to attorneys on personal property appraisal methodology, legal research, etc.

AQUARIUMS

Collectors

Gary Bagnall
3090 McMillan Rd.
San Luis Obispo, CA 93401
phone: 805-542-9988 or 805-782-0238
fax: 805-542-9295

Magazines

Dealers

Steve Stewart
Steve Stewart "Aquarium Literature"
P.O. Box 610118
Flushing, NY 11361-0118
phone: 718-352-2242
Wants freshwater aquarium literature: books, magazines, ephemera on tropical, gold, native fish; thousands of issues in stock, including various full sets; claims to have the largest assortment available.

Ornaments

Collectors

Darryl Rehr
P.O. Box 641824
Los Angeles, CA 90064-6824
phone: 310-477-5229
fax: 310-268-8420
e-mail: dcrehr@earthlink.net
Internet: http://www.earthlink.net/
  ~dcrehr/trans1.html
Wants attractive aquarium ornaments used in home aquariums: castles, sea creatures, divers, etc.

ARCHAEOLOGY

(see also AMERICAN INDIAN; ANTIQUITIES; HERITAGE RESOURCES; NATURAL HISTORY; FOSSILS; MINERALS; PREHISTORIC ARTIFACTS; TREASURE HUNTING)

Clubs/Associations

Archaeological Institute of America
Magazine: Archaeology
656 Beacon St.
Boston, MA 02215
phone: 617-353-9361
fax: 617-353-6550
e-mail: aia@bu.edu
Internet: http://
  www.csaws.brynmawr.edu:443/
  aia.html
Has phone numbers and addresses for all state archaeological departments; "Archaeology" is published bi-monthly; also publishes the "American Journal of Archaeology" quarterly; write for details.

Archeological Associates of Greenwich
33 Byram Dr.
Byram, CT 06830

Iris McGillivray, Mem.
Archeological Society of Maryland, Inc.
17 E. Branch Lane
Baltimore, MD 21202-2301
phone: 410-727-6417

Lee & Tracie Altman
Piedmont Archaeological Society
2438 Scott St.
Spartanburg, SC 29303
phone: 803-585-5764

Mark Clapp
Indiana Archaeological Society
RR 1 Box 74
New Richmond, IN 47967

Tommy W. Bryden
Illinois State Archaeological Society
Newsletter: Field Notes
2910 Vigal Rd.
Springfield, IL 62707-8970
phone: 217-529-8691
Collectors of prehistoric Native American and Pre Columbian artifacts: arrowheads, axes, pottery, inc.

Society for Historical Archaeology
P.O. Box 30446
Tucson, AZ 85751
phone: 520-886-8006
e-mail: sha@azstarnet.com
Internet: http://www.sha.org
For information on Public Education and Information Committee.

Collectors

Tommy W. Bryden
2910 Vigal Rd.
Springfield, IL 62707-8970
phone: 217-529-8691
Collector of prehistoric Native American artifacts such s arrowheads, axes, pottery.

Museums/Libraries

Kelsey Museum of Ancient & Medieval
  Archaeology
434 S. State St.
Ann Arbor, MI 48109
phone: 313-764-9304

Kampsville Archaeological Museum
P.O. Box 366
Kampsville, IL 62053
phone: 618-653-4316

Bade Institute of Biblical Archaeology
1798 Scenic Ave.
Berkeley, CA 94709
phone: 415-848-0529

Periodicals

Magazine: Ancient
82 Hythe Road
Brighton BN16JS, U.K.
Bi-monthly review of antiquity.

Emma Beatty
Aurora Publications Ltd.
Magazine: Minerva
14 Old Bond St.
London W1X 3BD, U.K.
phone: 44 171 495 2590
fax: 44 171 491 1595
Internet: http://www.desiderata.com
*The international review of ancient art
and archaeology; a bi-monthly
illustrated magazine focusing on
ancient art, antiquities, archaeology
and numismatic discoveries
worldwide.*

Magazine: Archaeology Monthly
135 William St.
New York, NY 10038

Magazine: Central States Archaeological
Journal
731 Thames Dr.
Schaumburg, IL 60193

ARCHITECTURAL ELEMENTS

(see also DOORKNOBS; FIREPLACE
ITEMS, Mantels; PLUMBING;
STAINED GLASS)

Auction Services

Julie Lewis
Great Gatsby's, The
5070 Peachtree Industrial Blvd
Atlanta, GA 30341
phone: 770-457-1917
fax: 770-457-7250
Internet: http://www.gatsbys.com
*Specializes in the sale of architectural
antiques.*

Dealers

Aardvark Antiques
475 1/2 Thames St.
Newport, RI 02840-6719
phone: 800-446-1052 or 401-849-7233
fax: 401-849-1591
e-mail: agrove181@aol.com
*Lighting, stained glass, statuary,
planters, sconces, pedestals,
fountains, fireplaces, gates, fences,
marble, iron, cast iron.*

Candi Soll
Architectural Antiques by Allan Soll
P.O. Box 307
Canaan, ME 04924-0307
phone: 207-474-5396
e-mail: solantiq@somtel.com
Internet: http://www.somtel.com/
solantiq
*Carries over 150 architectural c. 1900
stained and beveled glass windows;
also antique doors, mantles, lighting
fixtures, and other architectural items;
also wholesales antique furniture.*

United House Wrecking
535 Hope St.
Stamford, CT 06906-1316
phone: 203-348-5371
fax: 203-961-9472
Internet: http://www.united-
antiques.com
*Sells architectural elements; stained
and beveled glass, fireplace mantels
and accessories, brass & copper,
plumbing & lighting fixtures,
Victorian gingerbread, etc.*

Stephen G. Del Sordo
Principia Group
305 Oakley St.
Cambridge, MD 21613
phone: 410-228-8934
fax: 410-221-8061
e-mail: delsordo@shore.intercom.net
*A cultural resource management/
historic preservation firm that has
contracts to locate, provide,
authenticate artifacts for museums
and collectors; areas of expertise
include architecture, industry,
domestic, agriculture, and maritime.*

H. Weber Wilson
Oltz-Wilson Antiques
808 51st Avenue Plz. W
Bradenton, FL 34207-2819
phone: 800-508-0022
*Sells architectural antiques; garden
ornaments, vintage plumbing, quality
furniture, antique door hardware.*

Salvage One
1524 South Sangamon St.
Chicago, IL 60608
phone: 312-733-0098
fax: 312-733-6829
*Maintains large inventory of
American and European architectural
elements from the 18th through 20th
centuries.*

Architectural Antiques
403 Dawson St.
San Antonio, TX 78202
phone: 210-226-6863
Internet: http://www.ureweb.net/
architecturalantiques.htm
*Buys and sells architectural elements
including antique hardware, old pine
doors, mantles, porch spindles and
posts and brackets, old iron fencing,
etc.*

Museums/Libraries

Octagon, The; The Museum of the
American Architectural Foundation
1799 New York Ave., NW
Washington, DC 20006-5292
phone: 206-638-3221
fax: 202-879-7764

Periodicals

Victorian Homes
Directory: Victorian Homes Sourcebook
P.O. Box 61
Millers Falls, MA 01349
phone: 413-659-3785
fax: 413-659-3113
*Articles and ads on restoration
philosophy, moldings, wallpapers,
restoring old windows, kitchen
renovations; a complete directory of
products and services for the
Victorian Revival home market.*

Dovetale Publishers
Magazine: Old-House Journal, The
2 Main St.
Gloucester, MA 01930-5726
phone: 800-234-3797 or 508-283-3200
fax: 508-283-4629
*Monthly magazine focusing on the
repair of old houses; publishes "The
Old-House Journal Catalog"-
hundreds of sources for products &
services.*

Dovetale Publishers
Directory: Old-House Journal
Restoration Directory
2 Main St.
Gloucester, MA 01930-5726
phone: 800-234-3797 or 508-283-3200
fax: 508-283-4629
*Sourcebook listing companies large
and small which manufacture and sell
traditional hard-to-find items for the
old house owner: sinks, siding,
lumber, plumbing, stoves, etc.; also
call 800-931-2931.*

Ray Shepherd
Magazine: Traditional Building
69A 7th Ave.
Brooklyn, NY 11217-3618
phone: 718-636-0788
Internet: http://
www.traditionalbuilding.com
*Great source for products for
historical buildings.*

Magazine: Architectural Digest
5900 Wilshire Blvd.
Los Angeles, CA 90036
phone: 213-965-3700
*A monthly magazine of fine
architecture and interior design.*

Allan Mann
Allan Mann Communications
Newsletter: Historic Traveler, The
14519 Greenleaf St.
Sherman Oaks, CA 91403-3770
*A travel-oriented newsletter for
historic architecture buffs.*

Screen Doors

Collectors

Richard M. Bueschel
414 N. Prospect Manor Ave.
Mount Prospect, IL 60056-2046
phone: 847-253-0791
fax: 847-253-7919
e-mail: BuschlHist@aol.com
*Wants vintage screen doors with
unique designs; also wants photos,
photo postcards, advertising,
brochures, catalogs, etc. of old
wooden screen doors; send SASE if
requesting reply.*

Victorian Gingerbread

Suppliers

Vintage Wood Works
Highway 34 South
P.O. Drawer R, #2534
Quinlan, TX 75474
phone: 903-356-2158
fax: 903-356-3023
e-mail: mail@vintagewoodworks.com
Internet: http://
www.vintagewoodworks.com
*Sells solid wood gingerbread suitable
for Victorian homes: brackets, stair
parts, gazebo, newel posts, balusters,
moldings, gables, shelves, spandrels,
window cornices, etc.; send $2 for a
copy of their catalog of architectural
details.*

ARCHITECTURAL TOYS

(see TOYS, Construction Sets)

ARCHITECTURE & RELATED
ITEMS

(see also CATALOGS, Trade
[Homebuilding]; FRANK LLOYD
WRIGHT; HARDWARE; PLAN-
NING ITEMS)

Collectors

Herbert Mitchell
601 West 113th St., Apt. 8-H
New York, NY 10025
phone: 212-932-8667

Robert Des Marais
618 W. Foster Ave.
State College, PA 16801-3933
phone: 814-237-7141 or 814-237-7141
*Wants architect's, builder's and
carpenter's antique books; also
scientific instruments, old drawing
instruments, compasses, dividers,
protractors, drawing pens, architects
scales, old water color box sets, etc.*

ARCTIC EXPLORERS

Museums/Libraries

Bowdoin College, Peary-MacMillan
Arctic Museum
Hubbard Hall
Brunswick, ME 04011
phone: 207-725-3416

ARMS & ARMOR

(see also AMERICAN INDIAN, Tomahawks; EDGED WEAPONS; FIREARMS; KNIVES; MILITARIA; ORIENTALIA; POWDER HORNS; SWORDS)

Auction Services

Roy Butler
Wallis & Wallis
West Street Auction Galleries
Lewes
East Sussex BN7 2NJ, U.K.
phone: 01273-480208
fax: 01273-476562
Britain's specialist auctioneers of arms, armor, militaria and military orders.

Sotheby's
1334 York Ave.
New York, NY 10021
phone: 212-606-7370 or 212-606-7000
Internet: http://www.sothebys.com
Over 70 collecting areas are featured at Sotheby's auctions including toys, dolls, porcelain, furniture, silver, art, books; exhibitions are free and everyone is welcome; for a free copy of "Sotheby's Newsletter", call 212-606-7245.

Christie's
502 Park Ave.
New York, NY 10022
phone: 212-546-1000
fax: 212-980-8163
Internet: http://www.sirius.com/~christie/

Butterfield & Butterfield
220 San Bruno Ave.
San Francisco, CA 94103-5018
phone: 415-861-7500
fax: 415-553-8678

Collectors

David J. DeLaurant
1505 N. Lafayette
Fresno, CA 93728-1123
phone: 209-488-3229 or 209-233-1492
e-mail: dlaurant@sjvls.lib.ca.us
Serious student of pre-1914 military helmets & other body armor items from all nations; communicates with other body armor collectors via the "Body Armor Reporter", a quarterly newsletter; will identify armor free - send SASE.

Experts

Charles H. Clements, III
1741 Dallas St.
Aurora, CO 80010
phone: 303-364-0403
Appraises and specializes in arms & armor, hunting, gaming, military and leisure material for men, frontier, fur trade and Indian artifacts, etc.

Museums/Libraries

Higgins Armory Museum
100 Barber Ave.
Worcester, MA 01606
phone: 508-853-6015

Periodicals

David J. DeLaurant
Newsletter: Body Armor Reporter
1505 N. Lafayette
Fresno, CA 93728-1123
phone: 209-488-3229 or 209-233-1492
e-mail: dlaurant@sjvls.lib.ca.us
For the collector of pre-1914 military helmets & other body armor items from all nations.

Repro. Sources

Museum Replicas Limited
P.O. Box 840
Conyers, GA 30207
Sells authentic replica edged weapons, battle gear, period clothing; swords, daggers, axes, shields, helmets, tunics, etc.

Japanese

Collectors

Raymond Macy
P.O. Box 11
West Alexandria, OH 45381-0011
phone: 513-839-5721 or 513-839-5203
Wants Japanese swords, daggers, sword parts, matchlock guns, anything samurai.

Don Beck
P.O. Box 15305
Fort Wayne, IN 46885-5305
phone: 219-486-3010
Wants Japanese swords and sword items, guns, medals, daggers, head gear, from any war 1860 to 1945.

Japanese (Swords)

Clubs/Associations

Society for the Preservation of Japanese Art Swords, The
Journal: SPJAS Journal
NBTHK, 4-25-10, Yoyogi
Shibuya-Ku
Tokyo 151 Japan
Yearly dues are 19,500 yen; members receive a Japanese language journal four times per year.

Dr. T.C. Ford, Ed.
Japanese Sword Society of the United States, Inc.
Newsletter: Japanese Sword Society of U. S. Newsletter
P.O. Box 712
Breckenridge, TX 76024-0712
Internet: http://www.jssus.org/
Focuses on the study and preservation of Japanese swords.

Gloria Bill
Japanese Sword Society of Southern California
16241 Keats Circle
Westminster, CA 92683
e-mail: hurrasch@west.net
Internet: http://www.west.net/~kurrasch/jsssc.htm

Collectors

S.J. Moore
P.O. Box 524
Skaneateles, NY 13152-0524
phone: 315-685-8758
Buys and sells Japanese samurai swords and fittings: tsuba, menuki, fushi, kashira, kogai, kazuka, scabbards.

Robert Navrotski
1024 4th St.
Canonsburg, PA 15317-1910
phone: 412-745-4840
Wants to buy Samurai swords; free information and appraisal.

Greg Souchik
P.O. Box 161
Custer City, PA 16725-0161
phone: 814-362-2642
fax: 814-362-7356
e-mail: 104235.2430@compuserve.com
Wants to buy all WWII German and Japanese swords and daggers.

Mark Walberg
P.O. Box 130
Sunbury, PA 17801
phone: 717-286-1617
fax: 717-286-9686
Wants to buy Japanese swords, sword fittings, matchlock rifles, Samurai armor.

Ed Hicks
3805 Cumberland Rd.
Fayetteville, NC 28306-2439
phone: 910-425-7000
Wants Japanese swords and armor: daggers, bronzes, iron teapots, helmets, masks, lacquer, matchlock guns, Samurai relics, sword guards, sword fittings, metal work, tea ceremony artifacts and ceramics; free research on Samurai.

R.W. Lightner
P.O. Box 320042
Cocoa Beach, FL 32932-0042
phone: 407-783-0314 or 800-752-6135
Japanese swords and sword items; also guns, medals, daggers, head gear; member NBTHK, Tokyo.

K. Wiley
719 Baldwin SE
Grand Rapids, MI 49503-4470
phone: 616-451-8410
Wants Japanese swords, daggers, sword parts. Also German 3rd Reich daggers, swords, bayonets. References available.

Ron Hartmann
5907 Deerwood Dr.
Saint Louis, MO 63123-2707
phone: 314-577-2873 or 314-832-3477
Wants to buy Japanese swords, daggers, sword guards, and other parts; over 20 years experience; life member of Japanese Sword Society; always willing to help others realize fair price for their items; send photos and SASE with inquiries.

Dealers

Fred Coluzzi
Frederick's Swords
6919 Westview Dr.
Oak Forest, IL 60452-1566
phone: 708-687-3647
Buys and sells antique swords and daggers from all countries and all periods; issues 3 to 4 major catalogs per year: Japanese, US, German, Turkish, Moro, Indonesian, Philippine, Chinese.

Experts

Dale Garbutt
7 St. Paul St., Ste. 1400
Baltimore, MD 21202-1626
phone: 410-347-8710 or 410-358-1228
fax: 410-347-9475
Collects Japanese swords, sword fittings, matchlocks, and armor; member of the Japanese Sword Society of the U.S. and of The Society of Japanese Art Swords, Tokyo, Japan; will provide no-obligation evaluation by mail or in person.

Richard Fleming
P.O. Box 8394
Virginia Beach, VA 23450-8394
phone: 804-622-1343
fax: 804-463-3052
e-mail: rfleming@milcom-systems.com
Buys and specializes in Japanese swords; free translation of signed pieces; research, identification, evaluation performed and restoration services arranged; Gendaito Oshigata needed for future publication; literature bought.

Museums/Libraries

Museum of Fine Arts, Boston
465 Huntington Ave.
Boston, MA 02115-5523
phone: 617-267-9300
Internet: http://www.mfa.org/home.html
Home to more than 500 swords and thousands of sword fittings.

Miniature

Clubs/Associations

Don Beck
Miniature Arms Collectors/Makers Society
Newsletter: MAC/MS Newsletter
3329 Palm
Granite City, IL 62040

ARROWHEADS & POINTS

(see AMERICAN INDIAN;
ARCHAEOLOGY; PREHISTORIC
ARTIFACTS)

ART

(see also BRONZES; CARTOON
ART; CRAFTS; FOLK ART;
FRAMES; ILLUSTRATORS;
LAPIDARY; MEDALLIC SCULP-
TURES; ORIENTALIA; PERSON-
ALITIES [ARTISTS]; PRINTS;
REPAIR/RESTORATION/CONSER-
VATION, Art; SCULPTURES;
TATTOO; WESTERN ART &
CRAFTS)

Appraisers

Stephen van Cline, CAPP
van Cline & Davenport, Ltd.
792 Franklin Ave.
Franklin Lakes, NJ 07417-1343
*Specializes in paintings, watercolors,
drawings, bronze & marble sculpture;
appraisals, authentication, lectures,
expert testimony; minimum $25
charge; letter request only, SASE.*

Judith S. Jordan
Perrinart Associates
140 Scarborough Rd.
Briarcliff Manor, NY 10510-2006
phone: 914-762-1438 or 802-869-2784

Dr. Charles J. Semowich
242 Broadway
Rensselaer, NY 12144-2705
phone: 518-449-4756
*Appraiser of art, antiques and
decorative arts.*

Pamela E. Mayo, ISA
710 Washington St.
Sewickley, PA 15143-1845
phone: 412-749-0760
fax: 412-749-0760
*Fine art appraisals of American and
European art of the 18th to 20th
centuries; author of "Lue Osborne
and Corday Simmons" (exhibition
catalog), monograph on Doris
Spiegel; exhibition pamphlet on Bruce
Kimberling.*

Rochelle Eisenberg, ASA
Art Directives, Inc.
P.O. Box 173
Ambler, PA 19002
phone: 215-646-0233
fax: 215-542-7015
*Appraiser, consultant, writer, lecturer,
author, advisor for Montgomery
County newspapers, appeared on
"Chubb Antiques Roadshow",
instructor at Temple University.*

Randall C. Hunt
3503 Fulton St., NW
Washington, DC 20007
phone: 202-333-4035
fax: 202-333-1354
e-mail: 70673.3447@compuserve.com
Specializes in fine art.

Elen W. Shea, ISA
Antiques Critiques, Inc.
P.O. Box 34586
Bethesda, MD 20827
phone: 301-299-7314

Melanie Smith
Seaside Gallery
P.O. Box 1
Nags Head, NC 27959
phone: 919-441-5418 or 800-828-2444
fax: 919-441-8563
e-mail: seaside@interpath.com
*Accredited member of the Interna-
tional Society of Appraisers;
specializes in fine art (paintings,
graphics, sculpture) and animation
art.*

James Corcoran, ISA
Corcoran Fine Arts Limited, Inc.
2915 Fairfax Rd.
Cleveland, OH 44118-4015
phone: 216-397-0777
fax: 216-379-0222
Appraisals, consulting, private dealer.

Patricia M. Knight, ISA
Finetooth Comb Antiques Research &
    Appraisal Service
421 Ash Ave.
P.O. Box 1177
Ames, IA 50010-1177
phone: 515-292-9028
*Consultant and qualified appraiser of
19th century and early 20th century
oil paintings; also Oriental images on
paper.*

Frederick P. Dose, Jr.
Frederick Dose Appraisals Ltd.
778 Pleasant Ave.
Highland Park, IL 60035-4613
phone: 847-433-1090 or 847-433-7870
*Appraises US, British, Continental
paintings and furniture, prints,
porcelain, silver, decorative arts,
coins, antiquities; for corporate,
private, and attorneys; references on
request; 6 year full-time as University
art historian.*

Richard Casagrande, ISA
Casagrande Appraisals
8546 Broadway, Ste. 270-B
San Antonio, TX 78217
phone: 210-820-3535
fax: 210-820-3535
e-mail: 10441.545@compuserve.com
*Appraiser specializing in 19th century
American art; also the art of Texas
and the San Antonio region.*

Corrine Cain
Corinne Cain Ltd.
326 West Harmont Dr.
Phoenix, AZ 85021
phone: 602-906-1633
fax: 602-906-0677
e-mail: kogyo@primenet.com
*Appraises fine art and Native
American art.*

Diane Kruse, ISA CAPP
Art Appraisals of Tucson
HCR 1, Box 627
Tucson, AZ 85736-9712
phone: 520-822-1842 or 800-439-3901
fax: 520-822-1842
e-mail: 74250.1555@compuserve.com
*Appraises paintings, sculpture, prints,
watercolors, drawings; Certified
Appraiser of Personal Property.*

Kent Walter McDonald
Appraisal & Connoisseur Associates
620 Sierra Dr. SE
Albuquerque, NM 87108-3377
phone: 505-265-2842
*Appraisers, artists and brokers
serving the Southwest in painting,
prints and sculpture; also appraise
residential contents nationwide.*

Nicholas Fairrie, ISA
Fine Works of Art
2001 California St. #305
San Francisco, CA 94109
phone: 415-441-4146
fax: 415-441-1221
*Identification, authentication and
appraisal services; also functions in
advisory capacity to new collectors
and acts on their behalf to make new
acquisitions.*

Richard C. Frey, ISA
R.T.L.H. Enterprises
1275 East Ave.
Chico, CA 95926-1020
phone: 530-343-4528 or 800-567-7854
fax: 530-343-9380
e-mail: RFREY RTLH@aol.com
*Qualified appraiser of American and
European art, paintings, watercolors,
drawings, prints, sculpture, bronzes,
etc.; appraises for estates, arbitration,
and has testified as expert witness.*

Christian Coleman, Ex. Dir.
International Society of Appraisers
Journal: ISA News Journal
16040 Christensen Rd., Ste. 320
Seattle, WA 98188
phone: 206-241-0359
fax: 206-241-0436
e-mail: ISA_HQ@compuserve.com
Internet: http://www.isa-appraisers.org
*Largest association of professional
personal property appraisers;
members specialize in antiques &
residential contents, gems & jewelry,
fine art, and machinery & equipment;
call for appraiser nearest you.*

Auction Services

Colleen Fesko
Skinner, Inc.
357 Main St.
Bolton, MA 01740-1104
phone: 508-779-6241 or 617-350-5400
fax: 508-779-5144
*Established in 1964, Skinner Inc. is
the fifth largest auction house in the
US; has offices in Bolton and Boston,
MA.*

Philip C. Shute
Shute Auction Gallery
850 W. Chestnut St.
Brockton, MA 02401
phone: 508-588-0022 or 508-588-7833
fax: 508-559-6687
*Antique and custom furniture, art,
silver, glass and china, collectibles,
etc.*

Swann Galleries, Inc.
104 E. 25th St.
New York, NY 10010-2977
phone: 212-254-4710
fax: 212-979-1017
e-mail: SwannSales@aol.com
*Oldest/largest U.S. auctioneer
specializing in rare books, autographs
& manuscripts, Judaica, photographs,
and works of art on paper.*

Christie's East
219 E. 67th St.
New York, NY 10021
phone: 212-606-0400

Sotheby's
1334 York Ave.
New York, NY 10021
phone: 212-606-7370 or 212-606-7000
Internet: http://www.sothebys.com

Christie's
502 Park Ave.
New York, NY 10022
phone: 212-546-1000
fax: 212-980-8163
Internet: http://www.sirius.com/
    ~christie/

Louis Webre, Client Svc.
William Doyle Galleries
175 E. 87th St.
New York, NY 10128-2205
phone: 212-427-2730
fax: 212-369-0892
Internet: http://www.doylegalleries.com
*Holds over 30 auctions annually of
antique English, Continental and
American furniture, paintings,
decorations, jewelry, vintage and
couture clothing, collectible toys,
books and prints; specialty auctions of
Majolica, Lalique and wine.*

Megan Brown
Weschler's
905 E St. NW
Washington, DC 20004-2006
phone: 202-628-1281 or 800-331-1430
fax: 202-628-2366
*Conducts specialized auction sales of
art, paintings, prints and graphics.*

Frank Boos
Boos Gallery, Inc.
420 Enterprise Court
Bloomfield Hills, MI 48013
phone: 810-332-1500

Western Heritage Sale
1416 Ave. K
Plano, TX 75074
phone: 972-423-1500

Clubs/Associations

Archaeological Institute of America
Magazine: Archaeology
656 Beacon St.
Boston, MA 02215
phone: 617-353-9361
fax: 617-353-6550
e-mail: aia@bu.edu
Internet: http://
www.csaws.brynmawr.edu:443/
aia.html
*Has phone numbers and addresses for
all state archaeological departments;
"Archaeology" is published bi-
monthly; also publishes the
"American Journal of Archaeology"
quarterly; write for details.*

National Antique & Art Dealers
  Association of America
12 East 56th St.
New York, NY 10022
phone: 212-826-9707 or 212-319-0471
fax: 212-319-0471
*Trade group represents art and
antique dealers; sponsors antique and
art exhibitions; promotes ethical trade
practices among its members; free
membership directory available.*

Donna Carlson, Dir.
Art Dealers Association of America
575 Madison Ave.
New York, NY 10022-2511
phone: 212-940-8590
fax: 212-940-7013
Internet: http://www.artdealers.org/
*Non-profit organization of nation's
lading dealers in fine art.*

N. J. Fregin
American Society of Artists, Inc.
Newsletter: Art Lovers & Craft Fair
  Bulletin
P.O. Box 1326
Palatine, IL 60078
phone: 312-751-2500 or 847-991-4748
*National professional membership
organization; membership is juried,
with a crafts division - American
Artisans; presents shows, has lecture
and demonstration service; "ASA
Artisan" published quarterly for
members.*

Collectors

T.J. Ahlberg
1000 Irvine Blvd.
Tustin, CA 92680-3527
phone: 714-730-1000 or 714-654-1331
fax: 714-730-1752
*Wants anything by Edward Bohlin
(especially Ranger Buckle sets), Till
Goodan; all posters and pictorial
maps by Jo Mora: 101 Ranch, Wild
West Show/Buffalo Bill; also cowboy
and Indian bookends and books by Jo
Mora.*

Dealers

Henry B. Holt
125 Golden Hill
P.O. Box 699
Lee, MA 01238
phone: 413-243-3184
fax: 413-243-9918
*Buys and sells American art, oils or
watercolors; conservation, framing
and appraisals available; wants to
buy marines, still life, impressionist,
Hudson River, and folk art; member
Appraisers Association of America,
Inc.*

John Clement
John Clement Fine Art
36 Oakwood Ave.
Fitchburg, MA 01420-7421
phone: 508-345-5863
*Special interests include worldwide
master works of art, particularly
works on paper, including Japanese
woodblock prints; also fine paintings.*

Paul Lantagne
Paul Lantagne Fine Art
P.O. Box 3117
Westford, MA 01886
phone: 508-692-4961
*Appraiser and dealer of antiques and
American/European paintings.*

Tony Fusco
Fusco & Four, Associates
One Murdock Terrace
Brighton, MA 02135-2817
phone: 617-787-2637
fax: 617-782-4430
*Specializes in European and American
paintings from 1900-1950, with an
emphasis on Art Deco, WPA,
Modernist, Regionalists and American
Scene; will assist individuals and
organizations buying and selling
paintings and fine art.*

Sonnie Cucinotti
Spirits in the Attic
201 Msgr. O'Brien Hwy.
Cambridge, MA 02141
phone: 617-738-6054
*Buys and sells watercolors by listed
artists.*

Alyce Persky
Red Pines Farm
3513 Main St., Rt. 31
Coventry, CT 06238
phone: 203-742-0567
*Buys, sells, and appraises fine art;
also conserves and restores fine art
and frames for vendors and
individuals.*

Peter Falk
P. Hastings Falk, Inc.
859 Boston Post Rd.
Madison, CT 06443
phone: 203-245-2246 or 203-849-1655
fax: 203-245-5116
*Researches, writes and sells books
about artists listed in "Who's Who in
American Art"; also publishes/sells*

*art reference dictionaries and the "Art
Price Index International."*

Don Barese
Don Barese Fine Art & Antiques
47 Wakefield St.
Hamden, CT 06517-1328
phone: 203-281-7438
fax: 203-281-7438
*Buys and sells American & European
fine art, 19th and 20th century
paintings and prints.*

Graham Gallery
1014 Madison Ave.
New York, NY 10021
phone: 212-535-5767
*Specializes in 18th, 19th, and 20th
century art.*

Alexander Gallery
996 Madison Ave.
New York, NY 10021
phone: 212-472-1636
*Specializes in 18th, 19th, and 20th
century art.*

Arthur S. Liss
Marineart Gallery
151 East 83rd St/
Penthouse D
New York, NY 10028-1958
phone: 212-772-2737
fax: 212-861-4754
e-mail: info@marineart.com
Internet: http://www.marineart.com
*An art gallery specializing in fine 18th
and 19th century British and
American marine art; the gallery's
watercolor and painting exhibition
catalog is available on-line.*

Margaret McAuliffe
ARDAGH
P.O. Box 810
Carmel, NY 10512
phone: 914-225-1746 or 800-217-1746
*Buys and sells fine art: oils,
watercolors, prints, sculpture,
photographs.*

Sydney L. Germansky
Europa Master Gallery
16 A Lafayette Ave.
Suffern, NY 10901-5406
phone: 914-368-2707
Internet: http://members.qnn.com/europa

Robert B. Mayo
Gallery Mayo, Inc.
5705 Grove Ave.
Richmond, VA 23226-2345
phone: 804-288-2109
fax: 804-282-1374
*Buys and sells 19th through early 20th
century American art, with a specialty
in Southern and sporting art.*

Paul G. Hughes, ISA
Tudor House Galleries
1401 East Blvd.
Charlotte, NC 28203-5817
phone: 704-377-4748 or 704-332-4782
e-mail: 75027.474@compuserve.com
*Buys, sells and appraises 19th century
oil paintings and watercolors;*

*Accredited Member, International
Society of Appraisers.*

Stephen Dillon
S & S Dillon, Ltd.
P.O. Box 830
Depot Center
Clayton, GA 30525
Fine art expert.

James & Timothy Keny
Keny Galleries, Inc.
300 East Beck St.
Columbus, OH 43206
phone: 614-464-1228
fax: 614-464-1992
*Buys, sells, specializes in, and
appraises 19th, and 20th century art;
historic Ohio artists.*

Timothy Haines
1077 Celestial St.
Rookwood Bldg. #3, Ste. 400
Cincinnati, OH 45202-1629
phone: 513-871-0494
fax: 513-651-0860
e-mail: reyneh@aol.com
Internet: http://members.aol.com/
ReyneH
*Wants to buy 19th-20th century
American and European paintings,
watercolors and drawings by listed
artists.*

Bradley S. Vite
Bradley Vite Fine Arts
1600 West Beardsley Ave.
Elkhart, IN 46514-1800
phone: 219-293-1616
fax: 219-293-1616
*Buys, sells and appraises 19th and
20th century American and European
prints, paintings, watercolors, and
sculpture; especially interested in
Audubon prints and McKinney & Hall
prints.*

Sybil Tillman
Artco Inc.
3148 RFD Cuba Rd.
Lake Zurich, IL 60047-9606
phone: 847-438-8420
fax: 847-438-6464
*Specializing in fine art appraisals and
research; also buying and selling 19th
and 20th century, important and
contemporary American artists and
American Indian Art.*

Susan Larson, ISA
Susan Larson Fine Art
1150 Old Mill Dr.
Palatine, IL 60067
phone: 708-359-7799
fax: 708-359-7799
*Specialist in buying, selling and
appraising fine art including
paintings and prints; also consults
and advises on the development of
private and corporate fine art
collections.*

Farhad Radfar, ISA
MIR International Gallery, Inc.
P.O. Box 10678
Chicago, IL 60610
phone: 312-654-8510 or 773-477-2209
fax: 312-670-8182
e-mail: FRadfar@aol.com

Taylor Clark
Taylor Clark Gallery
2623 Government St.
Baton Rouge, LA 70806-5408
phone: 504-383-4929
fax: 504-383-3043
Specializes in 18th, 19th, and 20th century oil paintings, watercolors, and prints, especially all editions of Audubon prints.

Peter Eller
206 Dartmouth
Albuquerque, NM 87106
phone: 505-268-7437 or 505-344-7539
Specializes in and appraises American, Southwest, and "Western" art; also Pueblo pottery, Navajo rugs and other weavings, Spanish colonial artifacts.

De Ville Galleries
8751 Melrose Ave.
Los Angeles, CA 90069
phone: 213-652-0525
Specializes in 19th, and 20th century art.

Goldfield Galleries
8380 Melrose Ave.
West Hollywood, CA 90069-4522
phone: 213-651-1122
fax: 213-651-1168
Specializes in 19th and 20th century American Impressionist art, and California and Western art.

Christine Daniels
135 E. Shiloh Rd.
Santa Rosa, CA 95403-1254
phone: 707-838-6083
Buys and sells art: Maxfield Parrish, R. Atkinson Fix prints; also R. Atkinson oils, Louis Icart etchings, and early California oil paintings.

Richard C. Frey, ISA
R.T.L.H. Enterprises
1275 East Ave.
Chico, CA 95926-1020
phone: 530-343-4528 or 800-567-7854
fax: 530-343-9380
e-mail: RFREY RTLH@aol.com
Buys, sells and appraises fine art: paintings, watercolors, prints, drawings, sculpture, bronzes, etc.; American or European; Accredited Member of the International Society of Appraisers.

Experts

Joseph Ferrara
Fer-Duc Inc.
P.O. Box 1303
Newburgh, NY 12550
phone: 914-896-9492

Rosemary & Mike McKittrick
McKittrick Fine Arts
Price Guide: McKittrick's Art Price Guide
P.O. Box 461
Sewickley, PA 15143
phone: 412-741-0743
fax: 412-741-7802
Publishes an annual comprehensive listing of art auction sales results including over 50,000 works of art.

Myreen Moore
1404 Gates Ave.
Norfolk, VA 23507
phone: 804-623-7827
fax: 804-855-4312
Appraises, repairs, restores art, paintings, prints; twenty-five years experience as researcher/artist/writer; staff writer for "Mid-Atlantic Antiques Magazine"; listed in "Who's Who in American Art."

Bob Banks
Banks Fine Art
3316 Royal Lane
Dallas, TX 75229-5061
phone: 214-352-1811
fax: 214-352-6360
e-mail: artman2@ix.netcom.com
Internet: http://www.banksfineart.com
Buys, sells, auctions, appraises oil paintings and other 19th and 20th century fine art.

C. Van Northrup
Geolat & Associates
14110 Dallas Pkwy., #200
Dallas, TX 75240
phone: 972-239-9314
fax: 972-239-9313
American, European & Mexican fine art; modern paintings, drawings, watercolors; old & modern prints; modern sculpture.

Sally Tucker
Tucker Appraisal Associates
P.O. Box 13605
Houston, TX 77219
phone: 713-529-8878
Specializes in fine art, sculpture, paintings, watercolors, and drawings.

Alan Bamberger
Art Talk
2510 Bush St.
San Francisco, CA 94115-3002
phone: 415-931-7875
fax: 415-922-3580
e-mail: alanb@sirius.com
Internet: http://www.experts.com/bas.html
Author of "Buy Art Smart" and "Art For All"; syndicated columnist who answers questions about art; send SASE if you write and request a reply.

Misc. Services

Art Sales Index, Ltd.
Price Guide: Artquest Computer Service
1 Thames St.
Weybridge
Surrey KT13 8JG, U.K.
phone: 01932-856426
fax: 01932-842482
e-mail: asi@globalnet.co.uk
Internet: http://www.globalnet.co.uk/~asi
ARTQUEST on-line computer art database (also on CD-ROM) of art auction prices since 1970 (over 1.7 million records); also publishes the Annual Art Sales Index, Auction Prices of American Artists.

Lorraine Pierce-Hull
Pierce-Hull & Associates
P.O. Box 93
Carelton Place
Ontario K7C 3P3 Canada
phone: 613-257-2987
fax: 613-253-0949
e-mail: lphull@magi.com
Agent for Canadian artists; special events manager, fine arts appraiser.

Stephen J. Abt, III
ArtFact, Inc.
Price Guide: ArtFact
1130 Ten Rod Rd., Ste. E104
North Kingstown, RI 02852-4158
phone: 401-295-2656 or 800-278-3228
fax: 401-295-2629
e-mail: sales@artfact.com
Internet: http://www.artfact.com
A computerized library recording auction sales of art and antiques; complete descriptions, prices realized, on-screen images.

Peter Falk
Institute for Art Research & Documentation
170 Boston Post Rd., Box 150
Madison, CT 06443-2164
phone: 203-245-2246 or 203-849-1655
fax: 203-245-5116
Service bureau for museums, archives, and scholarly art reference publishers; compiles and transcribes original historical documents into database format.

Flora Hanft
Thesaurus
111 5th Ave.
New York, NY 10003
phone: 800-491-FIND
fax: 516-944-5278
Internet: http://thesaurus.co.uk
A pre-sale auction search service; a fee based service for subscribers to get advanced notice of upcoming items for sale at auctions around the world.

M. Barden Prisant
Telepraisal
P.O. Box 20686
New York, NY 10009-8973
phone: 212-614-9090 or 800-645-6002
fax: 212-780-9539
Computerized works of art data base search for art auctions and prices

realized; verbal or written reports on paintings, sculptures and prints.

OmniGuard Corporation
730 Fifth Ave.
New York, NY 10019
phone: 800-808-2882 or 212-727-8181
Uses a system of marks to authenticate, identify and register fine art.

Anna J. Kisluk
International Foundation for Art Research (IFAR)
Magazine: IFAR Reports
500 Fifth Ave., Ste 1234
New York, NY 10110
phone: 212-391-8791
fax: 212-391-8794
Clearinghouse for information on art theft, fraud, forgery; promotes recovery of stolen art & prevention of circulation of forged works; publishes Stolen Art Alert notices of art thefts and recoveries.

Nancy J. Little
International Foundation for Art Research (IFAR) Authentication Serv.
500 Fifth Ave., Ste 1234
New York, NY 10110
phone: 212-391-8791
fax: 212-391-8794
Offers a unique authentication service which examines works of art to assist in the resolution of questions of authenticity and attribution; for individuals, art dealers, museums, etc.

Anna J. Kisluk
Art Loss Register, The
500 Fifth Ave., Ste 1234
New York, NY 10110
phone: 212-391-8791
fax: 212-391-8794
A service to register lost art to assist in recovery.

National Gallery of Art
Dept. of Education Resources
6th & Constitution Ave. NW
Washington, DC 20565-0001
phone: 202-842-6273
FREE loan program of VHS, 16mm film, and slide/tape programs covering many facets of art and antiques. Send for free Extension Programs Catalogue.

Elly Friedman
Award Video & Film Distributors, Inc.
3520 Bayou Louise Ln.
Sarasota, FL 34242-1102
phone: 941-955-1818
fax: 941-346-2583
A distribution company handling quality art and collector videos including a Contemporary Art Series and a Collector Series.

Mayer-CD
Price Guide: Mayer's on CD
P.O. Box 758
Englewood, FL 34295-0758
phone: 888-MAY-ERCD
e-mail: mayercd@aol.com
Internet: http://www.artlibrary.com
*Fine art auction on CD-ROM; over
600,000 works of art sold at auction.*

ISIS Secure Registry System
257 Grant Ave.
San Francisco, CA 94108
phone: 415-788-8411 or 415-788-6008
*Uses advanced digital and forensic
technologies to identify and register
fine art to facilitate later identification
and recovery should it be stolen.*

Museums/Libraries

Musee du Louvre
75058 Paris Cedex 01 France
phone: (33-1) 40 20 50 50
Internet: http://mistral.culture.fr/louvre/
louvre/htm

Archives of American Art, Boston
87 Mount Vernon St.
Boston, MA 02108
phone: 617-565-8444
*Important source of biographical
material on American artists;
maintains records of paintings by
subject & artist; regional offices in
Boston, Detroit, New York, and San
Marino, CA.*

Museum of Art, Rhode Island School of
Design
224 Benefit St.
Providence, RI 02903-2711
phone: 401-454-6500
fax: 401-454-6556

Archives of American Art, New York
1285 Avenue of the Americas
New York, NY 10019
phone: 212-399-5015
*Important source of biographical
material on American artists;
maintains records of paintings by
subject & artist; regional offices in
Boston, Detroit, New York, and San
Marino, CA.*

Whitney Museum of American Art
945 Madison Ave. at 75th St.
New York, NY 10021
phone: 212-570-3676
Internet: http://www.echonyc.com/
~whitney/

William G. Stout, PR Off.
Frick Collection, The
1 East 70th St.
New York, NY 10021-4907
phone: 212-288-0700
fax: 212-628-4417
*Holds some of the best-known
paintings by the greatest European
artists, major works of sculpture
(finest groups of small Renaissance
bronzes in the world), superb 18th
century French furniture &*

porcelains, Limoges enamels, and
more.

Metropolitan Museum of Art
1000 Fifth Ave.
New York, NY 10028
phone: 212-879-5500
Internet: http://www.metmuseum.org/
*One of the largest and finest art
museums on the world; over 2 million
works of art spanning more than
5,000 years of world culture.*

Philadelphia Museum of Art
P.O. Box 7646
Philadelphia, PA 19101-7646
phone: 215-684-7860
Internet: http://pma.libertynet.org/

Pennsylvania Academy of Fine Arts
1301 Cherry St.
Philadelphia, PA 19102
phone: 215-972-7600

Holly Crider
National Museum of Women in the Arts
Magazine: Women in the Arts
1250 New York Ave. NW
Washington, DC 20005
phone: 202-783-5000
fax: 202-393-3235
Internet: http://www.nmwa.org/
*Brings recognition to the achieve-
ments of women artists of all periods
and nationalities by exhibiting,
preserving, acquiring, and researching art by women and by educating
the public concerning their
accomplishments.*

National Museum of American Art
Catalog: Smithsonian Art Index
8th & G Sts. N.W.
Washington, DC 20560
phone: 202-357-2504
*Identifies drawings, prints, paintings
and sculpture in Smithsonian divisions
but not part of the museum collection.*

National Museum of American Art
Catalog: Peter A. Juley & Son
Collection
8th & G Sts. N.W.
Washington, DC 20560
phone: 202-357-2504
*Over 127,000 photographic negatives
of art now lost, destroyed or altered.*

National Museum of American Art
Catalog: Slide & Photograph Archives
8th & G Sts. N.W.
Washington, DC 20560
phone: 202-357-2504
*Over 60,000 35mm color slides and
over 200,000 photographs and
negatives for visual documentation of
American art.*

National Museum of American Art
Catalog: Pre-1877 Art Exhibition
Catalogue Index
8th & G Sts. N.W.
Washington, DC 20560
phone: 202-357-2504
*A computerized index from over 700
rare catalogs of exhibitions held*

between 1790 and 1876; art unions,
fairs, museums, etc.

National Museum of American Art
Catalog: Permanent Collection Data
Base
8th & G Sts. N.W.
Washington, DC 20560
phone: 202-357-2504
*A computerized listing providing
information on the over 300,000
objects in the museum's permanent
collection.*

National Portrait Gallery, Archives of
American Art Headquarters
Journal: Archives of American Art
Journal
8th & F Streets N.W.
Washington, DC 20560-0001
phone: 202-357-2866
fax: 202-786-2565
Internet: http://www.si.edu/
*Important source of biographical
material on American artists;
maintains records of paintings by
subject & artist; regional offices in
Boston, Detroit, New York, and San
Marino, CA.*

Joaneath Spicer
Walters Art Gallery
600 N. Charles St.
Baltimore, MD 21201
phone: 410-547-9000
*Specializing in Renaissance/Baroque
paintings and sculpture.*

Chrysler Museum, Art Reference
Library, The
Olney Rd. & Mowbray Arch
Norfolk, VA 23510
phone: 804-622-1211

High Museum of Art, The
1280 Peachtree St.
Atlanta, GA 30309
phone: 404-848-4711
Internet: http://www.highorg/
museum.html

Toledo Museum of Art, The
2445 Monroe St.
P.O. Box 1013
Toledo, OH 43697
phone: 419-255-8000
*One of America's finest art collections
American and European paintings in
a building of exceptional beauty*

Archives of American Art, Detroit
Institute of Art
5200 Woodward Ave.
Detroit, MI 48202
phone: 313-226-7544
*Important source of biographical
material on American artists;
maintains records of paintings by
subject & artist; regional offices in
Boston, Detroit, New York, and San
Marino, CA.*

Milan R. Hugston, Librarian
Amon Carter Museum
3501 Camp Bowie Blvd.
Fort Worth, TX 76107-2695
phone: 817-738-1933
fax: 817-377-8523
Internet: http://www.cartermuseum.org
*Has large and distinguished collection
of paintings and sculpture by Frederic
Remington and Charles M. Russell.*

Los Angeles County Museum of Art
5905 Wilshire Blvd.
Los Angeles, CA 90036
phone: 213-857-60000
Internet: http://www.lacma.org

Art Institute of Chicago
111 S. Michigan Ave.
Chicago, IL c
phone: 312-443-0849
Internet: http://www.artic.edu/aic/
firstpage.html

On-Line Services

Florian Pfahler
Art Net Worldwide
145 East 57th St.
New York, NY 10022
phone: 212-497-9700 or 800-4AR-
TNET
fax: 212-497-9707
*An on-line index listing over
1,400,000 works of art by 170,000
artists that have been sold by over 500
auction houses since 1987;
descriptions, estimated prices, and bid
prices included; more than 400,000
illustrated; modem 800-278-6397.*

Diana Gabrielle Erdos
ArtNet Worldwide
145 East 57th St.
New York, NY 10022
phone: 800-427-8638 or 212-497-9704
e-mail: derdos@artnet.com
Internet: http://www.artnet.com
*Connects buyers with sellers, art
lovers with art experts; auction
results, auction previews, auction
research, galleries online, on-line
ArtNet Magazine.*

Periodicals

Magazine: Canadian Art
70 The Esplanade, 2nd Floor
Toronto
Ontario M5E 1R2 Canada
phone: 416-368-8854

Mercury Subscription Service
Newsletter: Modern Painters
2323 E-F Randolf Ave.
Avenel, NJ 07001
A quarterly journal of the fine arts.

Zachary P. Morfogen
Newsletter: Morgogen Associates
NEWS
P.O. Box 324
Mountain Lakes, NJ 07046
phone: 201-334-0675
fax: 201-334-7458
*Published quarterly for museums and
galleries, performing art institutions,*

corporate and foundation sponsors, art media; devote to previewing and promoting major museum and gallery exhibitions.

Newspaper: Art Newspaper, The
P.O. Box 3000
Denville, NJ 07834-9776
phone: 800-875-2997
Subscription office for "the international journal of art"; prints, paintings, antiques, sculpture; articles, reviews, schedule of events, museum and gallery exhibits, fairs; published ten times per year in England.

Reed Reference Publishing
Directory: Official Museum Directory
121 Chanlon Rd.
New Providence, NJ 07974-1541
phone: 800-521-8110
Profiles more than 7,600 American institutions in 85 categories; aquariums, historic homes, museums, zoos; handy for those looking for information about specific types of antiques, fine art & collectibles; annual.

Newsletter: Art/Antique Investment Report, The
99 Wall St.
New York, NY 10005
phone: 212-747-9500
Biweekly newsletter about the art market; for the art connoisseur, collector, curator and dealer; features interviews with prominent dealers, latest prices etc.

Magazine: Art & Auction
440 Park Ave. South
14th Floor
New York, NY 10016
phone: 800-777-8718 or 212-447-9555
e-mail: artauction@aol.com
Internet: http://www.artcity.com/
art&auction.html
Covers the international art markets, from antiquities to contemporary art; articles include pieces on artists or schools of art/furniture, analyses of trends in the market, auction reviews and previews, calendar of events, etc.

Art & Auction Magazine
Directory: International Directory for Collectors
440 Park Ave. South
14th Floor
New York, NY 10016
phone: 800-777-8718 or 212-447-9555
e-mail: artauction@aol.com
Internet: http://www.artcity.com/
art&auction.html
One issue per year of Art & Auction Magazine includes the Annual Directory of Galleries and Auction Houses International (including shows, art associations, fairs, art services, appraisers, conservators, etc.)

Newsletter: ARTnewsletter
48 West 38th St.
New York, NY 10018-6211
phone: 212-398-1690
fax: 212-819-0394
A biweekly international business report of the art market; has the latest news on auctions and trends in the art market.

Magazine: Art & Antiques
3 East 54th St.
New York, NY 10022-3108
phone: 212-752-5557 or 800-274-7594
Glossy magazine focusing on the fine and decorative arts and in antiques: colorful ads, articles, auction reports, etc.

Walter de Gruyter, Inc.
Magazine: International Journal of Cultural Property
200 Saw Mill River Rd.
Hawthorne, NY 10532-1525
phone: 914-747-0110
fax: 914-747-1326
e-mail: degruyter.ny@worldnet.att.net
Internet: http://www.degruyter.de
Addresses such issues as contested attributions, ethics of art historians and museum personnel, looting, national retention and protection, legal issues and evolving law regarding art.

Newington-Cropsey Foundation
Magazine: American Arts Quarterly, The
P.O. Box 326
Hastings On Hudson, NY 10706
Concentrates on figurative and classical works, with good color illustrations, and comments on art, architecture, and culture in general.

Haworth Press
Journal: Art Reference Services Quarterly
10 Alice St.
Binghamton, NY 13904-9981
phone: 800-342-9678 or 607-722-5857
fax: 800-895-0582
e-mail: getinfo@haworth.com
Internet: http://web:spectra.net/~haworth
Publication geared to art librarians focusing on reference services for art history, architecture, and the studio arts; legal resources for art, index to reviews of art reference titles, book reviews, etc.

Newsletter: Woman's Art Journal
1711 Harris Rd.
Laverock, PA 19118

Barbara Dougherty
Magazine: Art Calendar
P.O. Box 199
Upper Fairmount, MD 21867-0199
phone: 800-597-5988
fax: 410-651-5313
e-mail: barbdoug@dmv.com
A monthly magazine with artist and dealer interviews plus articles on art fraud, art scams, artist block, internships, shows, artist opportunities.

Barbara Dougherty
Directory: Annual Artists' Resource Directory
P.O. Box 199
Upper Fairmount, MD 21867-0199
phone: 800-597-5988
fax: 410-651-5313
e-mail: barbdoug@dmv.com
Annual containing art consultants, arts agencies and councils, college galleries, corporate collections, artwork insurers, etc.

Gale Research, Inc.
Directory: International Directory of Arts
835 Penobscot Bldg.
Detroit, MI 48226
phone: 313-961-2242 or 800-877-4253
fax: 313-961-6082
Art reference almanac: lists art museums, book publishers, artists, universities, schools, art and antique organizations, restorers, etc.

Magazine: New Art Examiner
1255 South Wabash, 4th Floor
Chicago, IL 60605
phone: 312-786-0200

Robert Spiel
Robert E. Spiel Associates
Newsletter: Art Intelligence Newsletter
549 West Randolph St., Ste. 425
Chicago, IL 60661-2208
phone: 312-258-0646
fax: 312-258-0815
Articles and commentary on art crimes; typical art fraud and their discovery; criminal techniques; former FBI Special Agent, Mr. Spiel dedicated most of his 20-year career to the recovery of stolen fine art and rare collectibles.

Tom Kellaway, Pub.
Magazine: American Art Review
P.O. Box 480500
Kansas City, MO 64148
phone: 913-451-8801
Bi-monthly magazine devoted to America's artistic heritage.

Fred B. Rothman & Co.
Newsletter: Critical Issues
10368 W. Centennial Rd.
Littleton, CO 80127
phone: 800-457-1986
fax: 303-978-1457
e-mail: orders@rothman.com
A bi-monthly newsletter presenting legal and business information about art and antiques.

Jo Ann Havens-Wright
Newsletter: American Art Collectors Newsletter
610 N. Delaware Ave.
Roswell, NM 88201-2135
phone: 505-623-8053
e-mail: johavens@rt66.com
Internet: http://www.rt66com/~johavens
Serves the needs and interest of collectors of American art and artists; works with collectible unpublished American artists.

Valerie Allan
Magazine: Apollo Magazine
P.O. Box 47
North Hollywood, CA 91603-0047
phone: 818-763-7673
fax: 818-753-9492
e-mail: apollousa@aol.com
The international magazine of art and antiques; an English monthly publication with detailed articles and glossy color photos.

Newsletter: Art Express
P.O. Box 10201
Newport Beach, CA 92660
A travel newsletter for dealers, collectors, curators and art travel connoisseurs; focuses on various cities worldwide where art events take place; exhibits, where to stay and eat.

African & Tribal

(see also SAFARI)

Clubs/Associations

Ramona Morris, Ex. Dir.
Antique Tribal Art Dealers Association, The
P.O. Box 620278
Woodside, CA 94062
phone: 415-851-8670
fax: 415-851-3508

Collectors

Marcia Hersey
P.O. Box 976
Ansonia Station
New York, NY 10023-0976
phone: 212-877-5328 or 212-874-3946
Specializes in primitive art: African, Indonesian, Himalayan, Pre-Columbian; wants to buy authentic old objects.

Richard McCoy
2719 Lakeview Ave.
St. Joseph, MI 49085
Wants African and South American artifacts: spears, masks, shields, arrows, weapons, skins, mounts, ivory, art, tools, body adornments.

Dealers

Norman Hurst, ISA
Hurst Gallery
53 Mount Auburn St.
Cambridge, MA 02138
phone: 617-491-6888
fax: 617-661-0439
e-mail: hurst@world.std.com
Internet: http://world.std.com/~hurst/
Buys, sells, appraises, restores African, Oceanic, Native American, PreColumbian and Asian art.

Phillip A. Alotta
Images Africaines
P.O. Box 8604
Saddle Brook, NJ 07663
phone: 201-797-3823 or 800-609-7565
Buys and sells African art.

Dominick Cardella
Artifactory
641 Indiana Ave. NW
Washington, DC 20004
phone: 202-393-2727
*Sells new and old African, Asian and
other foreign souvenir, arts and craft
items including carvings and textiles.*

Charles Jones
Charles Jones African Art
6716 Barren Inlet Rd.
Wilmington, NC 28405
phone: 910-686-0717
fax: 910-686-1313
e-mail: artafrica@aol.com

John Buxton
Shango Galleries
6717 Spring Valley
Dallas, TX 75240
phone: 972-239-4620 or 972-239-9943
fax: 972-239-9766
e-mail: jbuxton@arttrak.com
Internet: http://www.arttrak.com
*Buys, sells, and appraises African,
Precolumbian, Oceanic, and American
Indian art.*

Joel & Michael Malter
Joel L. Malter & Co., Inc.
17005 Ventura Blvd.
Encino, CA 91316-4128
phone: 818-784-7772 or 818-784-2181
fax: 818-784-4726

Experts

Scott Nelson
P.O. Box 6081
Santa Fe, NM 87502-6081
phone: 505-986-1176
*Wants authentic African, Oceanic, and
American Indian art and artifacts;
consultant to "Schroeder's Antiques
Price Guide."*

Museums/Libraries

African Art Museum of the S.M.A.
Fathers
23 Bliss Ave.
Tenafly, NJ 07670
phone: 201-567-0450

Joe Liberkowski
Museum of Classical Antiquities &
Primitive Arts
P.O. Box 2161
Medford, NJ 08055-7161
*Wants African and American Indian
items; also pre-1940 Mexican and
South American Santos, Retablos, Ex
Votos, crucifixes, religious, historical
autographs/documents.*

National Museum of African Art
Smithsonian Institution
950 Independence Ave.
Washington, DC 20560-0001
phone: 202-357-4600 or 202-357-2700
fax: 202-357-4879
*Museum's primary focus is collecting
& exhibiting the traditional arts of
Africa south of the Sahara; also
collects & exhibits the arts of other
African areas, including the arts of*

*northern Africa; also ancient and
contemporary arts.*

Periodicals

Jonathan Fogel, Ed.
Tribarts, Inc.
Magazine: Tribal Art Magazine
2261 Market St., #644
San Francisco, CA 94114
phone: 415-677-7917
fax: 415-431-8321
*The only magazine about the art,
ethnography, and culture of tribal and
ancient cultures around the world.*

Asian

(see also ART, Oriental; INDONESIA;
ORIENTALIA)

Book Sellers

Paragon Book Gallery, Inc.
1507 S Michigan Ave.
Chicago, IL 60605-2812
phone: 312-663-5155
fax: 312-663-5177
e-mail: paragon@paragonbook.com
Internet: http://webart.com/
paragonbook/
*Carries rare, out-of-print, and
scholarly books on Asia; specializes in
books on Asian arts and Asian
studies; new and out of print.*

Clubs/Associations

Harvey Sheppard, Sec.
Asia Society of Central Florida
Newsletter: ASCF Bulletin
P.O. Box 814
Winter Park, FL 32790
phone: 407-671-1173
*A non-profit cultural organization;
members interested in Asian art and
culture; monthly meetings held Sept.
to May with lectures and demonstrations on art of all Asian countries.*

Collectors

John Rudak
32 Princess Lane
North Stonington, CT 06359-1117
phone: 860-599-8489
*Wants Buddhist & Hindu art of SE
Asia; all representations desired;
interested in all Asian artistic
mediums including metalwork, wood
carvings, porcelain, pottery, works on
paper, etc.; special interest in
Buddhist art & artifacts.*

Dealers

Norman Hurst, ISA
Hurst Gallery
53 Mount Auburn St.
Cambridge, MA 02138
phone: 617-491-6888
fax: 617-661-0439
e-mail: hurst@world.std.com
Internet: http://world.std.com/~hurst/
*Buys, sells, appraises, restores
African, Oceanic, Native American,
PreColumbian and Asian art.*

Art of the Past
1242 Madison Ave.
New York, NY 10128-0515
phone: 212-860-7070
fax: 212-876-5373
*Specializing in paintings, sculptures,
textiles, Islamic and other works of art
from India, Tibet, Nepal, and
Southeast Asia.*

Sanuk
3618 Webster St.
San Francisco, CA 94123-1719
phone: 415-563-0270
fax: 415-563-1429
*Specializes in Asian Buddhist art,
early Chinese ceramics, furniture,
textiles and paintings.*

Experts

Pratapaditya Pal, Cur.
Los Angeles County Museum of Art
5905 Wilshire Blvd.
Los Angeles, CA 90036
phone: 213-857-60000
Internet: http://www.lacma.org
*Senior curator of Indian and
Southeast Asian Art; author of
"Tibetan Paintings"; specializes in
Indian and Himalayan arts; Tibetan
thankas, Hinduism and Buddhism.*

Museums/Libraries

Hiram Woodward
Walters Art Gallery
600 N. Charles St.
Baltimore, MD 21201
phone: 410-547-9000

Los Angeles County Museum of Art
5905 Wilshire Blvd.
Los Angeles, CA 90036
phone: 213-857-60000
Internet: http://www.lacma.org

Pacific Asia Museum
Newsletter: Pacific Asia Museum
Member Newsletter
46 N. Los Robles Ave.
Pasadena, CA 91101
phone: 818-449-2742
fax: 818-449-2754

Periodicals

Orientations Magazine Limited
Magazine: Orientations
200 Lockhart Road, 14th Floor
Hong Kong, Hong Kong
e-mail: info@orientations.com.hk
Internet: http://
www.orientations.com.hk/
*Brings readers informed articles on
all aspects of the arts of East Asia, the
Indian Subcontinent and Southeast
Asia; beautifully illustrated articles on
the ancient arts of painting,
calligraphy, bronzes, ceramics.*

HALI Publications, Ltd.
Magazine: HALI
Kingsgate House
Kingsgate Place
London NW6 4TA, U.K.
phone: 44 171 328 9341 or 44 171 328
1998
fax: 44 171 372 5924
e-mail: hali@centaur.co.uk
*"HALI" is the leading bi-monthly
international publication in the field
of carpet and textile art; an invaluable
encyclopedic source of information
with original research articles,
reviews of museum collections, etc.;
high color.*

Australia

Dealers

Ian Johnson
Harden, Johnson & Assoc.
93 Dorchester Ave.
Asheville, NC 28806-3524
phone: 704-254-2758
fax: 704-254-2758
*24 years experience in Australian,
New Zealand, South African paintings,
drawings, and watercolors from 1797
to present; also specializing in British,
Scottish, and Irish paintings from
1880-1950; daily contact with these
countries.*

Bad

Museums/Libraries

Museum of Bad Art
10 Vogel St.
Boston, MA 02123
phone: 617-325-8224 or 617-326-1463
e-mail: moba@world.std.com
Internet: http://glyphs.com/moba/
*Museum is located at 580 High Street,
Dedham MA 02026.*

Botanical

Museums/Libraries

James J. White
Hunt Institute for Botanical Documentation
Journal: Huntia
Carnegie Mellon University
Pittsburgh, PA 15213-3890
phone: 412-268-2434 or 412-268-2440
fax: 412-268-5677
e-mail: jw3u@andrew.cmu.edu
Internet: http://huntbot.andrew.cmu.edu/
HIBD/HuntInstitute.html
*Collection documents botanical
imagery from Renaissance onward;
center for research/documentation
into botanical science, history, art,
biography, bibliography; conducts
exhibitions of botanical art and
illustration; no appraisals.*

British

Auction Services

Ian Johnson
Harden, Johnson & Assoc.
93 Dorchester Ave.
Asheville, NC 28806-3524
phone: 704-254-2758
fax: 704-254-2758
*24 years experience in Australian,
New Zealand, South African paintings,
drawings, and watercolors from 1797
to present; also specializing in British,
Scottish, and Irish paintings from
1880-1950; daily contact with these
countries.*

Dealers

Ian Johnson
Harden, Johnson & Assoc.
93 Dorchester Ave.
Asheville, NC 28806-3524
phone: 704-254-2758
fax: 704-254-2758
*24 years experience in Australian,
New Zealand, South African paintings,
drawings, and watercolors from 1797
to present; also specializing in British,
Scottish, and Irish paintings from
1880-1950; daily contact with these
countries.*

Experts

Mark Samuels Lasner
1870 Wyoming Ave. NW, Apt. 101
Washington, DC 20009-1883
phone: 202-745-1927
e-mail: biblio@aol.com
*Wants to buy English literature and
art form the period 1850-1900;
especially association books,
manuscripts, letters, and original
drawings; co-author of two reference
books on this material.*

Museums/Libraries

Duncan Robinson, Dir.
Yale Center for British Art
P.O. Box 208280
New Haven, CT 06520-8280
phone: 203-432-2800 or 203-432-2850
fax: 203-432-9695
*Largest museum and research center
for British paintings, sculpture, prints,
drawings, and rare books outside
England; no decorative arts.*

Byzantine

Museums/Libraries

Dumbarton Oaks Research Library &
Collection
1703 32nd St. NW
Washington, DC 20007
phone: 202-342-3200

California

Appraisers

Richard C. Frey, ISA
R.T.L.H. Enterprises
1275 East Ave.
Chico, CA 95926-1020
phone: 530-343-4528 or 800-567-7854
fax: 530-343-9380
e-mail: RFREY RTLH@aol.com
*Qualified appraiser of American and
European art, paintings, watercolors,
drawings, prints, sculpture, bronzes,
etc.; appraises for estates, arbitration,
and has testified as expert witness.*

Auction Services

Angela Past
Butterfield & Butterfield
7601 Sunset Blvd.
Los Angeles, CA 90046-2714
phone: 213-850-7500
fax: 213-850-5843

John Moran
John Moran Auctioneers, Inc.
735 W. Woodbury Rd.
Altadena, CA 91001-5310

Dealers

Goldfield Galleries
8380 Melrose Ave.
West Hollywood, CA 90069-4522
phone: 213-651-1122
fax: 213-651-1168
*Specializes in 19th and 20th century
American Impressionist art, and
California and Western art.*

Marcia Osterkamp, ISA
327 Terrace Dr.
Brawley, CA 92227-3040
phone: 619-344-4810
fax: 619-344-4778
e-mail:
104672.3304@compuserve.comn
*Fine art appraiser; buys and sells
19th and 20th century American and
European paintings; also California
paintings.*

Ray Redfern
Redfern Galleries
1540 South Coast Hwy.
Laguna Beach, CA 92651
phone: 714-497-3356

Jimmy Vitanza
Peregrine Galleries
508 Brinkerhoff Ave.
Santa Barbara, CA 93101-3441
phone: 805-963-3134
fax: 805-963-3134

Paul Galli
873 Ticonderoga Dr.
Sunnyvale, CA 94087
phone: 408-730-4010
e-mail: paul.galli@lmco.com
*Buys and sells San Francisco abstract
expressionist art by John Saccard,
James Budd Dixon, Edward Corbett.*

Alfred C. Harrison, Jr.
Northpoint Gallery, The
250 Sutter St., 4th Floor
San Francisco, CA 94108
phone: 415-781-7550

Garzoli Gallery
930 B. St.
San Rafael, CA 94901
phone: 415-459-4321

Christine Daniels
135 E. Shiloh Rd.
Santa Rosa, CA 95403-1254
phone: 707-838-6083
*Buys and sells art: Maxfield Parrish,
R. Atkinson Fix prints; also R.
Atkinson oils, Louis Icart etchings,
and early California oil paintings.*

Syd Bottomley, ISA
P.O. Box 1842
Nevada City, CA 95959
phone: 916-272-5400
fax: 916-272-2820
*Buys, collects, appraises and
specializes in American Indian art:
baskets, rugs, pottery, early California
paintings.*

Museums/Libraries

Joan Irvine Smith
Irvine Museum, The
18881 Von Karman Ave., 12th Floor
Irvine, CA 92715
phone: 714-476-0294

Canvas Marks

Collectors

Alexander Katlan
Alexander Katlan Conservation Inc.
5638 Main St.
Flushing, NY 11355-5046
phone: 718-445-7458
*Interested in collecting American
canvas marks or maker's labels found
on the backs of paintings.*

Commercial Advertising

Man./Prod./Dist.

Craig Wolfe
Name That Toon Icons of Happiness
80 East Crescent Dr.
San Rafael, CA 94901-1658
phone: 415-456-3452 or 800-550-5202
fax: 415-456-9045
e-mail: nametoon@telis.org
*World's largest publisher of
commercial advertising/animation art;
framed and matted prints: Coca-Cola,
Anheuser-Busch, M&M/Mars,
Pillsbury, Hershey's, Campbell Soup,
Nabisco, Planter's, Life Savers, Oreo,
Ritz, etc.*

Contemporary

Auction Services

Christie's
502 Park Ave.
New York, NY 10022
phone: 212-546-1000
fax: 212-980-8163
Internet: http://www.sirius.com/
~christie/

Dealers

M. Knoedler & Company
19 East 70th St.
New York, NY 10021
phone: 212-794-0550
fax: 212-772-6932

Andre Emmerich Gallery
41 East 57th St.
New York, NY 10022
phone: 212-752-0124

Experts

Karen Holtzman
Holtzman & Gould
4201 Cathedral Ave. NW #707E
Washington, DC 20016
phone: 202-966-5877
Art consultant.

Museums/Libraries

Museum of Modern Art, The
11 W. 53rd. St.
New York, NY 10019
phone: 212-708-9889 or 800-447-6662

William Johnston
Walters Art Gallery
600 N. Charles St.
Baltimore, MD 21201
phone: 410-547-9000
*Specializing in the decorative arts and
modern paintings and sculpture.*

On-Line Services

Art Com Electronic Network (ACEN)
P.O. Box 193123
San Francisco, CA 94119-3123
phone: 415-431-7524
fax: 415-431-7841
*ACEN has the magazine, directories,
calendars, and an electronic art
gallery which are helpful resources
for people following new developments in contemporary art; trends,
studio openings, art materials,
censorship, etc.*

Periodicals

Magazine: Artforum International
P.O. Box 3000
Denville, NJ 07834-9950

Brant Art Publications
Magazine: Art in America
575 Broadway
New York, NY 10012
phone: 212-941-2800 or 800-925-8059
fax: 212-941-2897
*A full-color monthly magazine
focusing on contemporary art.*

Magazine: ARTnews
48 West 38th St.
New York, NY 10018-6211
phone: 212-398-1690
fax: 212-819-0394
A monthly magazine that reports on the contemporary art forms, personalities, issues, exhibitions, trends, and events that shape the international art world; subscriptions call 800-284-4625

Newspaper: West Art
P.O. Box 6868
Auburn, CA 95604-6868
phone: 916-885-0969
West Coast biweekly art publication; information and photographs of current West Coast fine art and craft exhibitions.

German

Collectors

Tony Vehr
4118 East Vernon Ave.
Phoenix, AZ 85008-2333
phone: 602-957-0653
fax: 602-957-1631
Wants to buy pen and ink sketches and prints by German artist Heinrich Kley.

Museums/Libraries

Busch-Reisinger Museum
32 Quincy St.
Cambridge, MA 02138
phone: 617-495-2317 or 617-495-9400
fax: 617-495-9936
Harvard University Art Museum's collection of Germanic art: masterpieces of Vienna Secession art, German Expressionism, 1920s abstraction, decorative arts and architectural drawings; also late Medieval, Renaissance, Baroque sculpture.

Haitian

Dealers

Le Jardin Cultured Art Gallery
225-09 Linden Blvd.
Jamaica, NY 11411
phone: 718-712-9377
fax: 718-528-1799

Bill Bollendorf
Galerie Macondo
406 S. Craig St.
Pittsburgh, PA 15213-3720
phone: 412-683-6486 or 412-661-1498
Devoted to informing collectors on trends in Haitian art, price trends, news of the Haitian art community and interviews with established and emerging artists.

Periodicals

Magazine: Hartian Art News
5440 N. Ocean Dr., Ste. 1506
West Palm Beach, FL 33404
Devoted to informing collectors on trends in Haitian art, price trends, news of the Haitian art community

and interviews with established and emerging artists.

Ireland

Dealers

Ian Johnson
Harden, Johnson & Assoc.
93 Dorchester Ave.
Asheville, NC 28806-3524
phone: 704-254-2758
fax: 704-254-2758
24 years experience in Australian, New Zealand, South African paintings, drawings, and watercolors from 1797 to present; also specializing in British, Scottish, and Irish paintings from 1880-1950; daily contact with these countries.

Islamic

Dealers

Mehmet Nabi Israfil
Fil Caravan Inc.
301 East 57th St.
New York, NY 10022
phone: 212-421-5972
fax: 212-421-5976
Established in 1976, Serves an international clientele in all aspects of Islamic Art including antiques, jewelry, textiles and fine Oriental rugs; has large selection of authentic Russian samovars.

Italian Renaissance

Museums/Libraries

Joan Norris
Isabella Stewart Gardner Museum
2 Palace Rd.
Boston, MA 02115-5807
phone: 617-566-1401
fax: 617-232-8039
e-mail: isgm@tiac.net
Internet: http://www.boston.com/gardner

Jewish

(see also JUDAICA)

Museums/Libraries

Center for Jewish Art
Journal: Jewish Art
P.O. Box 4262
Jerusalem 91042, Israel
phone: 972 02 6586605 or 972 02 658664
fax: 972 02 6586672
e-mail: cja@vms.huji.ac.il
An institution of the Hebrew University of Jerusalem dedicated to research, documentation, publication and education in the Field of Jewish art.

Marine

(see also NAUTICAL ANTIQUES)

Collectors

Kerry James McCaffrey
6 Senate Pl.
P.O. Box 6686
Jersey City, NJ 07306
Collector, expert.

Dealers

James & Ann Marenakos
Quester Gallery
77 Main St.
P.O. Box 446
Stonington, CT 06378
phone: 203-535-3860
fax: 203-535-3533
Buys, sells, consults on 19th & 20th century marine paintings, ships models, bronzes, campaign furniture, etc.

Rod & Becky Cardoza
West Sea Company
2495 Congress St.
San Diego, CA 92110-2820
phone: 619-296-5356
fax: 619-296-1097
Buys, sells all types of marine paintings, scrimshaw, ships' carvings, ship models, navigational and scientific instruments, sailor handcrafts, campaign furniture, hard hat diving, antique marine photography, nautical books, ceramics.

Experts

Sara Conklin
239 Sierra Pt. Rd.
Brisbane, CA 94005-1664
phone: 415-467-6249
fax: 415-467-6249
e-mail: 76363.536@compuserve.com
Managed the collections of the National Maritime Museum in San Francisco for ten years and is an expert in appraising marine fine art.

On-Line Services

Arthur S. Liss
Marineart Gallery
151 East 83rd St/
Penthouse D
New York, NY 10028-1958
phone: 212-772-2737
fax: 212-861-4754
e-mail: info@marineart.com
Internet: http://www.marineart.com
An on-line resource center for all manner of topics relating to marine art, including a link to The American Society of Marine Artists.

Periodicals

Robert R. McKenna, Ed.
Magazine: Nautical Collector
One Whale Oil Row
New London, CT 06320
phone: 860-444-0127
fax: 860-444-0129
e-mail: nautworld@aol.com
An authoritative bi-monthly magazine on the antiques, collectibles, art, artifacts, literature and memorabilia

associated with the seas, lakes and waterways.

New Zealand

Dealers

Ian Johnson
Harden, Johnson & Assoc.
93 Dorchester Ave.
Asheville, NC 28806-3524
phone: 704-254-2758
fax: 704-254-2758
24 years experience in Australian, New Zealand, South African paintings, drawings, and watercolors from 1797 to present; also specializing in British, Scottish, and Irish paintings from 1880-1950; daily contact with these countries.

Oceanic

Dealers

Norman Hurst, ISA
Hurst Gallery
53 Mount Auburn St.
Cambridge, MA 02138
phone: 617-491-6888
fax: 617-661-0439
e-mail: hurst@world.std.com
Internet: http://world.std.com/~hurst/
Buys, sells, appraises, restores African, Oceanic, Native American, PreColumbian and Asian art.

John Buxton
Shango Galleries
6717 Spring Valley
Dallas, TX 75240
phone: 972-239-4620 or 972-239-9943
fax: 972-239-9766
e-mail: jbuxton@arttrak.com
Internet: http://www.arttrak.com
Buys, sells, and appraises African, Precolumbian, Oceanic, and American Indian art.

Oriental

(see also ART, Asian; BRONZES, Oriental; CERAMICS [ORIENTAL]; COLLECTIBLES [MODERN], Sculptures [Japanese Themes]; ORIENTALIA; PRINTS, Woodblock [Japanese])

Auction Services

William P. Weschler
Weschler's
905 E St. NW
Washington, DC 20004-2006
phone: 202-628-1281 or 800-331-1430
fax: 202-628-2366
Conducts specialized auction sales of antique Oriental Art.

Experts

Dr. Daphne L. Rosenzweig
Rosenzweig Associates
P.O. Box 16187
Temple Terrace, FL 33617-6187
phone: 813-988-0880
fax: 813-989-8091
e-mail: rosetwig@aol.com
Consultant and appraiser dealing with Oriental Art; author of the books "Selected Works from the Fine Arts Group of Later Chinese Painting" and "The Appraisal of Oriental Art", and of Chinese jade catalogues.

Misc. Services

Arthur M. Sackler Gallery
Smithsonian Institution
1050 Independence Ave. SW
Washington, DC 20560
phone: 202-357-4880
Internet: http://www.si.edu/
Will authenticate your Japanese, Chinese, Near East and South & Southeast works of art; call for an appt.; limit 5 items/visit, 10 items/ year; may be able to work from good photographs.

Museums/Libraries

Freer Gallery of Art
Smithsonian Institution
12th & Jefferson Dr. SW
Washington, DC 20560
phone: 202-357-2104
Internet: http://www.si.edu/

Arthur M. Sackler Gallery
Smithsonian Institution
1050 Independence Ave. SW
Washington, DC 20560
phone: 202-357-4880
Internet: http://www.si.edu/

Periodicals

Jenny Marsh, Ex. Dir.
Magazine: Arts of Asia
1309 Kowloon Centre
29-39 Ashley Rd.
Kowloon, Hong Kong
A bi-monthly fully illustrated, scholarly magazine about the Oriental arts.

Wendy Holden, Editor
Newsletter: Newsletter, East Asian Art & Archaeology
Tappan Hall, Rm. 50
University of Michigan
Ann Arbor, MI 48109-1357
phone: 313-764-5555 or 313-936-2539
fax: 313-747-4121
e-mail: wholden@umich.edu
Published three times per year, NEAAA focuses on current exhibitions, symposia, newly published books, scholarly news, etc.

Repair Services

Janice & Dennis Dobson
Dobson Studios
810 N. Daniel St.
Arlington, VA 22201
phone: 703-243-7363
Conservator of Oriental screens, scrolls and wood block prints; repairs and conservation to other paper items as well.

Outsider

Auction Services

Steve Slotin
Slotin Folk Art Auction House
Newspaper: 20th Century Folk Art News
5967 Blackberry Lane
Buford, GA 30518
phone: 770-932-1000
fax: 770-932-0506
Internet: http://www.selftaught.com
Leading venue for self-taught, Outsider, Folk Art and Southern folk pottery; published newspaper twice each year chronicling important happenings in the field of 20th century folk art as the most popular feature, New, True & Blue Artists.

Clubs/Associations

Jeff Cory
In'Tuit: The Center of Intuitive and Outsider Art
Newsletter: In'Tuit Newsletter
1926 North Halstead St.
Chicago, IL 60614
phone: 3129297122
Committed to fostering and expanding the awareness of outsider, intuitive, and visionary art.

Dealers

Matt Lippa
Artisans
P.O. Box 256
Mentone, AL 35984-0256
phone: 205-634-4037
fax: 205-634-4037
e-mail: artisans@folkartisans.com
Internet: http://www.folkartisans.com
Buy and sell folk art, outsider art, fine art; Internet WWW site offers links to additional dealers; also offers non-profit clubs and museums with an outlet to post notices, press releases, calendar items, etc. at no charge.

Periodicals

Journal: Raw Vision
1202 Lexington Ave.
New York, NY 10028
A semiannual journal devoted outsider art (works ignored by the conventional art press).

Paintings

Appraisers

Charles B. Goldstein, ISA CAPP
Charles Barry International
8 Hardwicke Place
Rockville, MD 20850-3010
phone: 301-340-6775
fax: 301-340-1726
Buys, sells, and appraises 19th and 20th century, modern and contemporary American and European paintings; Certified Member, International Society of Appraisers; expert witness and trial consultant.

William Lavendusky, M.S., ISA
William Lavendusky, Fine Art
3345 So. Harvard, Bldg. 100
Tulsa, OK 74135
phone: 918-747-5336
fax: 918-742-3425
Dealer and appraiser of paintings and sculpture; specialist in 19th century French animal bronzes.

Dealers

Hirschl & Adler Galleries, Inc.
21 East 70th St.
New York, NY 10021
phone: 212-535-8810
fax: 212-772-7237

Don Treadway
2029 Madison Rd.
Cincinnati, OH 45208
phone: 513-321-6742 or 800-526-0491
fax: 513-871-7722
Internet: http://
www.treadwaygallery.com

Marcia Osterkamp, ISA
Poulsen Galleries, Inc.
327 Terrace Dr.
Brawley, CA 92227-3040
phone: 619-344-4810
fax: 619-344-4778
e-mail:
104672.3304@compuserve.comn
Fine art appraiser; buys and sells 19th and 20th century American and European paintings; also California paintings.

Jimmy Vitanza
Peregrine Galleries
508 Brinkerhoff Ave.
Santa Barbara, CA 93101-3441
phone: 805-963-3134
fax: 805-963-3134

Museums/Libraries

Barbara Buff
Museum of the City of New York
1220 5th Ave.
New York, NY 10029-5221
phone: 212-534-1672
fax: 212-534-5974
Special paintings and sculpture collections; access by appointment; research fee charged.

National Museum of American Art
Catalog: Inventory of Amer. Paintings Executed Before 1914
8th & G Sts. N.W.
Washington, DC 20560
phone: 202-357-2504
A computerized index of over 230,000 records of pre-1914 paintings in public and private collections; artist, location, subject, photo.

Paintings (Grandma Moses)

Museums/Libraries

Deborah Federhen, Cur.
Bennington Museum, The
W. Main St.
Bennington, VT 05201
phone: 802-447-1571
fax: 802-442-8305
Internet: http://www.benington.com/ museum
One of the finest regional art history museums in the country; works by Grandma Moses, American glass, VT furniture, Bennington pottery, the oldest Stars & Stripes in existence, the 1925 luxury touring car "The Wasp", and much more.

Paintings (Reverse on Glass)

Experts

Shirley R. Mace
Shadow Enterprises
P.O. Box 1602
Mesilla Park, NM 88047-1602
phone: 505-524-6717
fax: 505-523-0940
e-mail: shmace@nmsu.edu
Author of "History & Price Guide for Glass Silhouette Pictures" (1992); painted black on reverse of glass; sold in dimestores from the 1920s to 1950s; often with advertising and attached thermometers or calendars.

Peale Papers

Museums/Libraries

National Portrait Gallery
Catalog: Charles Wilson Peale Papers
8th & F Streets N.W.
Washington, DC 20560-0001
phone: 202-357-2866
fax: 202-786-2565
Internet: http://www.si.edu/
Specializing in documenting and cataloging all Peale family paintings and manuscripts.

Polynesia

Collectors

M.A. Blackburn
Wholesale Rug Outlet
2448 Lincoln Highway East
Lancaster, PA 17602
phone: 800-346-7847 or 717-295-9078
fax: 717-295-3494
e-mail: wrhawaii@epix.net
Internet: http://www.scmonline.com/
blackburn
Wants to buy over 50 year old art and artifacts from Polynesia; coral pounders, wood bowls, god figures, jewelry, personal adornment items, wood headrests, tapa cloth; from Tahiti, Cook Islands, New Zealand, Samoa, Fiji, Hawaii, etc.

Portraits

Misc. Services

Robert Stewart, Sr. Curator
4104 46th St. NW
Washington, DC 20016
phone: 202-357-2866
Will authenticate paintings and sculpture brought in for inspection; make an appointment first; may be able to work from good photographs.

Museums/Libraries

Linda Thrift, Keeper
National Portrait Gallery
Catalog: Catalog of American Portraits
8th & F Streets N.W.
Washington, DC 20560-0001
phone: 202-357-2578
fax: 202-786-2565
e-mail: capnpg@sivm.si.edu
Internet: http://www.npg.si.edu
Research database documenting more than 100,000 American portraits in public and private collections; offers on-line catalog on the INTERNET.

Portraits (Miniature)

Collectors

Sheldon Lerman
7505 Osler Dr.
Baltimore, MD 21204-7736
phone: 410-321-1514 or 410-828-5310
fax: 410-825-5710
Wants to buy American portrait miniatures on ivory.

Dealers

Dorothy Blitzer
Remembrance of Things Past
269 Bloomfield Ave.
Windsor, CT 06095
Buys, sells and collects portrait miniatures, especially those on ivory.

Experts

Lester E. Sender
Galerie Nouvelle
23500 Mercantile Rd.
Cleveland, OH 44122-5914
phone: 216-595-0000
fax: 216-595-1111
Buys and sells portrait miniatures on paper, ivory, canvas, porcelain or metal from the 17th century through 1930, American and Continental.

Prison Related

Dealers

Matt Lippa
Artisans
P.O. Box 256
Mentone, AL 35984-0256
phone: 205-634-4037
fax: 205-634-4037
e-mail: artisans@folkartisans.com
Internet: http://www.folkartisans.com
Buy and sell folk art, outsider art, fine art; Internet WWW site offers links to additional dealers; also offers non-profit clubs and museums with an outlet to post notices, press releases, calendar items, etc. at no charge.

Public

Experts

Joyce Pomeroy Schwartz
Works of Art for Public Spaces, Inc.
17 West 54th St.
New York, NY 10019
phone: 212-245-6468
fax: 212-333-3250
Specializes in large scale, outside or inside, public art: sculpture, fountains, landscape environment, murals, terra-cotta and stone reliefs, frescoes, etc.

Remington

Dealers

Fred Schulenburg
Museum Collections By Schulenburg, Inc.
P.O. Box 2369
Shelton, CT 06484
phone: 800-243-6229
Specializes in Remington bronzes and collector plates.

Museums/Libraries

Frederic Remington Art Museum
303 Washington St.
Ogdensburg, NY 13669
phone: 315-393-2425
fax: 315-393-4464
e-mail: broncho@northnet.org
Internet: http://www.northnet.org/
broncho
The only museum dedicated to the life and works of the renown artist of the Old West, Frederic Remington.

Rodin

Museums/Libraries

Rodin Museum, c/o Philadelphia
Museum Of Art
P.O. Box 7646
Philadelphia, PA 19101
phone: 215-763-8100

Josie De Falla, Dir.
Maryhill Museum of Art
35 Maryhill Museum Drive
Goldendale, WA 98620-4601
phone: 509-773-3733
fax: 509-773-6138
e-mail: MaryHill@gorge.net
The museum contains an internationally recognized collection of sculpture and drawings by the great French master Auguste Rodin.

Scotland

Dealers

Ian Johnson
Harden, Johnson & Assoc.
93 Dorchester Ave.
Asheville, NC 28806-3524
phone: 704-254-2758
fax: 704-254-2758
24 years experience in Australian, New Zealand, South African paintings, drawings, and watercolors from 1797 to present; also specializing in British, Scottish, and Irish paintings from 1880-1950; daily contact with these countries.

South Africa

Dealers

Ian Johnson
Harden, Johnson & Assoc.
93 Dorchester Ave.
Asheville, NC 28806-3524
phone: 704-254-2758
fax: 704-254-2758
24 years experience in Australian, New Zealand, South African paintings, drawings, and watercolors from 1797 to present; also specializing in British, Scottish, and Irish paintings from 1880-1950; daily contact with these countries.

Southern

Dealers

Robert B. Mayo
Gallery Mayo, Inc.
5705 Grove Ave.
Richmond, VA 23226-2345
phone: 804-288-2109
fax: 804-282-1374
Buys and sells 19th through early 20th century American art, with a specialty in Southern and sporting art.

Henry Barnet
516 Maverick Circle
Spartanburg, SC 29307-3707
phone: 864-579-2112
e-mail: 75347.322@compuserve.com
Buys, sells and appraises 18th

through 20th C. American art, specializing in Southern art, genre, sporting art; originals and prints.

Spanish

Museums/Libraries

Hispanic Society of America, The
613 W. 155th St.
New York, NY 10032
phone: 212-926-2234

Sporting

(see also ART, Wildlife; SPORTING COLLECTIBLES)

Collectors

Robert B. Mayo
Gallery Mayo, Inc.
5705 Grove Ave.
Richmond, VA 23226-2345
phone: 804-288-2109
fax: 804-282-1374
Wants American sporting art through the mid-20th century; author of "America, The Sporting View."

Dealers

James & Ann Marenakos
Quester Gallery
77 Main St.
P.O. Box 446
Stonington, CT 06378
phone: 203-535-3860
fax: 203-535-3533
Buys, sells, consults on 19th & 20th century sporting art and marine paintings.

Tony Laws
Woods & Water, Inc.
1019 McFarland Blvd.
Northport, AL 35476
phone: 205-333-1214
fax: 205-339-9573
Buys and sells sporting art: paintings, prints, drawings, classic firearms, rods & reels, sporting bronzes, wood carvings, advertising art, catalogs, brochures, books.

Robert Krause
Ravenwood Gallery
38745 Butternut Ridge Rd.
Elyria, OH 44035
phone: 216-458-4929
Wants to buy paintings, prints, etchings, calendars, and posters relating to hunting and fishing, birds, dogs, guns, ammunition and power companies; also duck and crow calls, decoys, sporting books, bamboo fly rods, rods, reels, etc.

Collectors Choice
10725 Equestrian Dr.
Santa Ana, CA 92705
phone: 714-730-2082
Buys and sells fine paintings, etchings and prints by artists such as Hagerbaumer, Maass, Reneson, Hardie, Schaldach, Bishop, Osthaus, Kouba, and others.

Frank J. Mikesh
1356 Walden Rd.
Walnut Creek, CA 94596-3158
phone: 510-934-9243
e-mail: natscibooks@netvista.net
Internet: http://www.netvista.net/
~natscibooks
Wildlife art, hunting, fishing, natural history.

Sports

(see also SPORTS COLLECTIBLES)

Museums/Libraries

University of New Haven National Art
Museum of Sport, Inc.
Newsletter: Museum of Sport Newsletter
300 Orange St.
West Haven, CT 06516
phone: 203-932-7197
Promotes sports art, e.g. paintings, sculptures, prints depicting fishing, track, boxing, racquet games, auto racing, baseball, etc.

Western

(see also WESTERN AMERICANA; WESTERN ART & CRAFTS)

Dealers

J.N. Bartfield Books, Inc.
30 West 57th St.
Third Floor
New York, NY 10019
phone: 212-245-8890
fax: 212-541-4860
Wants anything of American Historical interest, especially having to do with the West: paintings, bronzes, drawings, water colors; Cowboy and Indian, Western landscapes, Remington, Farny, Hansen, Krieghoff, Bierstadt, Homer, etc.

William L. King
Bozeman Trail Gallery
214 N. Main
Sheridan, WY 82801
phone: 307-672-3928 or 307-672-8318
fax: 307-672-2616
Wants 19th and early 20th cent. Western art, especially by Joe DeYong, E.W. Gollings, Hans Kleiber; also wants No. Plains Indian beadwork and related items, cowboy equipment, Colt Bisley's, mod. 1885 Remington pistols.

Museums/Libraries

M.J. VanDeventer
National Cowboy Hall of Fame &
Western Heritage Center
Magazine: Persimon Hill
1700 N.E. 63rd St.
Oklahoma City, OK 73111-7906
phone: 405-478-2250
fax: 405-478-4714
NCHA represents 17 western states; preserves the rich heritage of the Old West and the memory of those who contributed to it.

Periodicals

Duerr & Tierney, Inc.
Magazine: Art of the West
15612 Hwy. 7, Ste. 235
Hopkins, MN 55345-3551
phone: 612-935-5850
fax: 612-935-6546
Magazine featuring art of the West: cowboys, American landscapes, western wildlife, etc.

Wildlife

Dealers

Bob Dumaine
Sam Houston Philatelics
13310 Westheimer, Ste. 150
Houston, TX 77077-3506
phone: 281-493-6386 or 800-231-5926
fax: 281-496-1445
e-mail: rwhouduck@aol.com
Specializing in Wildlife Art, including originals, prints, sculptures, and gifts.

Periodicals

Pothole Publishing, Inc.
Magazine: Wildlife Art Magazine
P.O. Box 16246
Minneapolis, MN 55416
phone: 612-927-9056 or 800-626-0934
fax: 612-927-9353
Internet: http://www.wildlifeartmag.com
Largest magazine focusing on art relating to animals, birds, and art of the natural world; international in scope; full-color award-winning magazine; artists from around the world; painters, sculptors, wood carvers, etc.; bi-monthly.

ART DECO

(see also ARCHITECTURAL
ELEMENTS; CERAMICS; CLOCKS;
ELECTRICITY RELATED ITEMS,
Appliances; FRANKART; FURNI-
TURE [ANTIQUE]; GEMS &
JEWELRY; GLASS; MODERNISM;
RADIOS; SALOON & BAR
COLLECTIBLES, Cocktail Shakers)

Auction Services

Christie's East
219 E. 67th St.
New York, NY 10021
phone: 212-606-0400
Christie's East is well known in the collecting field for its Art Deco auctions.

Louis Webre, Client Svc.
William Doyle Galleries
175 E. 87th St.
New York, NY 10128-2205
phone: 212-427-2730
fax: 212-369-0892
Internet: http://www.doylegalleries.com
Conducts four annual "Belle Epoque" auctions featuring Art Deco.

Savoia's Auction Inc.
Rte. 23
South Cairo, NY 12482
phone: 518-622-8000
fax: 518-622-9453

Angela Past
Butterfield & Butterfield
7601 Sunset Blvd.
Los Angeles, CA 90046-2714
phone: 213-850-7500
fax: 213-850-5843
Two specialty auction each year.

Clubs/Associations

Twentieth Century Society, The
Journal: Journal, The
70 Cowcross St.
London EC1M 6DR, U.K.
phone: 0171-2503857
fax: 0171-2503022
e-mail: knewton.c$e.qd@gtnet.gov.uk
Internet: http://www.cms.livjm.ac.uk/
www/homepage/cmsknewt/c20.htm
Conservation and preservation group for post-1914 buildings; also concerned with visits, lectures and publications.

Canadian Art Deco Society
#302-884 Bute St.
Vancouver
Brit. Columbia V6E 1YA Canada
phone: 604-681-0505

Tony Fusco, Pres.
Art Deco Society of Boston
Newsletter: Motif
One Murdock Terrace
Brighton, MA 02135-2817
phone: 617-787-2637
fax: 617-782-4430
Purpose is to educate, and to preserve items and architecture relating to the Art Deco period.

Tony Fusco
International Coalition of Art Deco
Societies (ICADS)
Newsletter: ICADS Bulletin
One Murdock Terrace
Brighton, MA 02135-2817
phone: 617-787-2637
fax: 617-782-4430
Coalition of U.S. and international Art Deco Societies whose purpose is to educate and to preserve items and architecture relating to the Art Deco period; for free list of all Art Deco societies, please send SASE.

Art Deco Society of New York
Newsletter: Modernist
385 Fifth Ave., Ste. 501
New York, NY 10016
phone: 212-679-DECO
fax: 212-683-2662

Art Deco Society of Washington
Newsletter: Translux
P.O. Box 11090
Washington, DC 20008-0290
phone: 202-298-1100
Non-profit organization to foster public awareness and appreciation of the Art Deco period (1925-1950)

through volunteer actions to preserve the decorative, industrial, architectural, and cultural arts of that era.

Art Deco Society of South Carolina
856-A Liriope Lane
Mount Pleasant, SC 29464

George Neary
Miami Design Preservation League
Newsletter: Impressions
P.O. Box 190180
Miami Beach, FL 33119-0180
phone: 305-672-2014 or 305-672-1836
fax: 305-672-4319
Internet: http://infoguide.com/design/
main.htm
Non-profit Art Deco preservation society devoted to preserving, protecting and promoting the cultural, social, economic, environmental, and architectural integrity of the Miami Beach architectural district.

Sharon Koskoff
Art Deco Society of the Palm Beaches
Newsletter: Streamline
325 SW 29th Ave.
Delray Beach, FL 33444
phone: 407-276-9925
A non-profit organization dedicated to the preservation, education and awareness of Art Deco Architecture and design; custom Art Deco design services also available; newsletter published quarterly.

Cynthia Barta
Art Deco Society of Cleveland
P.O. Box 210134
Cleveland, OH 44121
phone: 216-382-3283

Art Deco Society of Northern Ohio
3439 West Brainard Rd., Ste. 260
Cleveland, OH 44122-4273
phone: 216-831-9110
fax: 216-292-7529

Detroit Area Art Deco Society
Newsletter: Modern, The
P.O. Box 1393
Royal Oak, MI 48068-1893
phone: 810-433-3700

Chicago Art Deco Society
Magazine: Chicago Art Deco Society
Magazine
400 Skokie #270
Northbrook, IL 60062-7902
phone: 847-291-4440
fax: 847-291-6677
Promotes the appreciation of the Art Deco era through publications and meetings.

Art Deco Society of Louisiana
P.O. Box 1326
Baton Rouge, LA 70821-6367
phone: 504-275-6367

Friends of Fair Park
P.O. Box 150246
Dallas, TX 75315
phone: 214-426-3400

Art Deco Society of Los Angeles
Newsletter: Exposition, The
P.O. Box 972
Hollywood, CA 90078
phone: 213-659-DECO

Art Deco Society of San Diego
P.O. Box 33762
San Diego, CA 92163

Art Deco Society of California
Magazine: Sophisticate, The
100 Bush St., Ste. 511
San Francisco, CA 94104-3908
phone: 415-982-DECO
Internet: http://www.wwpc.com/deco/
index.html
*Dedicated to the preservation of
California's Art Deco (1920s-1940s)
artistic expression heritage; also
publishes the newsletter "Streamlined
Times."*

Richard Unger
Sacramento Art Deco Society
Newsletter: Moderne Times Newsletter,
The
P.O. Box 162836
Sacramento, CA 95816-2836
phone: 916-736-1929
*Non-profit organization dedicated to
preserving all aspects of the Art Deco
period (1925-1945); monthly lectures
on architecture, design, jewelry,
music, art, etc.; offers walking tours;
educational and fun events.*

Collectors

Carl Ratner
550 Lamoka Ave.
Staten Island, NY 10312
e-mail: artdeco@bway.net
*Buy, sell, trade a wide range of Art
Deco items: Chase, Manning Bowman
and Revere chrome; clocks, cameras,
lighters, radios, telephones; Frankart;
lamps and lighting fixtures; kitchen
appliances; Roseville Futura pottery,
etc.*

Richard Trautwein
437 Dawson St.
Sault Sainte Marie, MI 49783-2119
phone: 906-635-0356
*Wants to buy quality Art Deco items in
glass, ceramics, sculpture, metalwork,
silver, jewelry, and rugs.*

John M. England, Jr.
P.O. Box 59136
Schaumburg, IL 60159-0136
phone: 708-823-5287
*Buys, sells, collects Art Deco items,
industrial design, Moderne
furnishings, radios, streamline.*

Dealers

Deco Deluxe
993 Lexington Ave.
New York, NY 10021
phone: 212-472-7222

Ron Savino
Times & Moments Antiques &
Collectibles
378 Atlantic Ave.
Brooklyn, NY 11217-1703
phone: 718-625-3145 or 718-497-4529
e-mail: moments@webtv.net
*With John Thomas Lee specializes in
Art Deco furniture, enamel-top kitchen
tables, waterfall furniture, especially
cedar chests.*

Joseph D. Cantara
Cantara/Galletti
61038 80th St.
Middle Village, NY 11379
phone: 718-651-9347 or 718-358-5923
*Buys, sells and specializes in art glass
and in Tiffany items such as lamps,
desk sets, glass and accessories; also
buys and sells Art Deco - especially
French & Austrian.*

Bob Aibel
Moderne Gallery
111 N. 3rd St.
Philadelphia, PA 19106-1903
phone: 215-923-8536
fax: 215-635-6962
e-mail: raibel@aol.com
*Wants to buy Art Deco items - glass,
ceramics, furniture, sculpture,
paintings, catalogs, etc.; specialty
areas include Ruba Rombic art glass
and Nakashima furniture.*

Bruce Marine
Cherub Antiques Gallery
2918 M. St. NW
Washington, DC 20007-3713
phone: 202-337-2224
fax: 202-337-2224
*Buys and sells Art Deco glass,
artwork, and metal wares.*

Ric Emmett
Modernism Gallery
1622 Ponce de Leon Blvd.
Miami, FL 33134-4012
phone: 305-442-8743
fax: 305-443-3074
*Wants to buy Deco and 1950s
furniture by Eames, Rhode, Nelson,
Frankl, Nakashima, Kagan, and other
designers; also wants lamps, pottery,
glass, bronzes, chrome and Mexican
silver.*

Connie Zeigler
Durwyn Smedley Antiques
853 Conner St.
Noblesville, IN 46060
phone: 317-776-0161
e-mail: smedley@iquest.net
Internet: http://www.smedley.com/
smedley
*Buys, sells, appraises all Art Deco
including furniture, pottery, lighting,
metalwork, textiles, glass, and other
decorative offerings.*

Jacques Caussin
First 1/2
12150 E. Outer Dr.
Detroit, MI 48224-2634
phone: 313-886-3443
fax: 313-886-1067
*Specializing in 1930s Industrial
Design: American chrome and metal
furnishings from Bel Geddes, Schoen,
and others.*

Steve Savitt
Josie's
545 Ridge Rd.
Wilmette, IL 60091-2439
phone: 847-256-7646
fax: 847-256-7004
*Specializes in Art Deco, 20th Century
Modern, art pottery, art glass and
jewelry; no reproductions.*

Anita Cochran
Anita's Antiques
2730 Virginia Pl.
Homewood, IL 60430-1135
phone: 708-957-2241
e-mail: lcoch37469@aol.com
*Buys and sells Art Deco; also
Depression glass and china; collects
Art Deco figurines.*

Frank Piccolo
Piccolo Pete's
13814 Ventura Blvd.
Sherman Oaks, CA 91423
phone: 818-990-5421
*First Art Deco establishment in Los
Angeles' San Fernando Valley; Art
Deco furniture, glassware, pottery,
jewelry, period lighting, etc.*

Experts

Tony Fusco
Fusco & Four, Associates
One Murdock Terrace
Brighton, MA 02135-2817
phone: 617-787-2637
fax: 617-782-4430
*Author of "The Confident Collector
Identification and Price Guide to Art
Deco"; offers appraisal and
brokerage services for 1909-1939 Art
Deco collectors; appraise and broker
fine Art Deco European and American
decorative arts.*

Ira & Miriam Raskin
Try To Remember
5120 Wilson Ln.
Bethesda, MD 20814-2436
phone: 301-652-1695
fax: 301-986-4528
e-mail: iraskin@aol.com
*Buys and sells functional nostalgia
from the 1920s to 1950s: radios,
clocks, watches, jewelry, books, etc.*

Museums/Libraries

Newark Museum, The
49 Washington St.
P.O. Box 540
Newark, NJ 07101-0540
phone: 201-596-6550

Cooper-Hewitt Museum National
   Museum of Design, Smithsonian
   Institution
2 East 91st St.
New York, NY 10128
phone: 212-860-6868

Frederick R. Brandt
Virginia Museum of Fine Arts
2800 Grove Ave.
Richmond, VA 23221-2466
phone: 804-367-0888
fax: 804-367-9393
*Fine arts museum covering the entire
range of history of art.*

Repro. Sources

Kenneth F. Kalbleish, Sr.
Sun Foundry
299 S. Lake St.
Burbank, CA 91502
phone: 818-841-7979 or 800-367-3479
Internet: http://home.earthlink.net/
~sunfoundry
*Manufactures bronze statues; send for
catalog of reproduction Art Deco
items.*

Chase Co. Brass & Copper

Clubs/Associations

Barry L. Van Hook
Chase Collectors Society
Newsletter: Art Deco Reflections
2149 West Jibsail Loop
Mesa, AZ 85202-5524
phone: 602-838-6971
*Dedicated to the collecting of the
products of the Chase Brass & Copper
Company. Publishes informative
newsletter, "Art Deco Reflections",
every other month.*

Lamps & Lighting

Dealers

Jack Beeler
Decorum
1400 Vallejo St.
San Francisco, CA 94109-2608
*Specializes in buying and selling
French and American Art Deco
lighting.*

Neon

Dealers

Dennis Clark
Off the Wall Antiques, Inc.
7325 Melrose Ave.
Los Angeles, CA 90046
phone: 213-930-1185
fax: 213-930-1595

ART MODERNE

(see MODERNISM)

ART NOUVEAU

(see also CERAMICS; FURNITURE
[ANTIQUE]; GEMS & JEWELRY;
GLASS)

Auction Services

Angela Past
Butterfield & Butterfield
7601 Sunset Blvd.
Los Angeles, CA 90046-2714
phone: 213-850-7500
fax: 213-850-5843
Two specialty auction each year.

Dealers

Joseph D. Cantara
Cantara/Galletti
61038 80th St.
Middle Village, NY 11379
phone: 718-651-9347 or 718-358-5923
*Buys, sells and specializes in art glass
and in Tiffany items such as lamps,
desk sets, glass and accessories; also
buys and sells Art Deco - especially
French & Austrian.*

Bruce Marine
Cherub Antiques Gallery
2918 M. St. NW
Washington, DC 20007-3713
phone: 202-337-2224
fax: 202-337-2224
*Buys and sells Art Nouveau glass,
artwork, and metal wares.*

Museums/Libraries

Frederick R. Brandt
Virginia Museum of Fine Arts
2800 Grove Ave.
Richmond, VA 23221-2466
phone: 804-367-0888
fax: 804-367-9393
*Fine arts museum covering the entire
range of history of art.*

ART POTTERY

(see CERAMICS [AMERICAN ART
POTTERY]; CERAMICS [EN-
GLISH], Art Pottery; CERAMICS
[CONTINENTAL], Art Pottery)

ART THEFT & FRAUD

Misc. Services

Anna J. Kisluk
International Foundation for Art
Research (IFAR)
Magazine: IFAR Reports
500 Fifth Ave., Ste 1234
New York, NY 10110
phone: 212-391-8791
fax: 212-391-8794
*Clearinghouse for information on art
theft, fraud, forgery; promotes
recovery of stolen art & prevention of
circulation of forged works; publishes
Stolen Art Alert notices of art thefts
and recoveries.*

Federal Trade Commission
6th St. & Pennsylvania Ave., Room 130
Washington, DC 20580
phone: 202-326-2222
*Has jurisdiction over art dealers; send
for free copy of a "Art Fraud"
brochure.*

ARTILLERY

(see CANNONS; MILITARIA;
AMMUNITION & EXPLOSIVE
ORDNANCE)

ARTS & CRAFTS

(see also ARCHITECTURAL
ELEMENTS, Arts & Crafts;
CERAMICS [AMERICAN]; FRANK
LLOYD WRIGHT; FURNITURE
[ANTIQUE], Stickley; COPPER
ITEMS, Stickley)

Auction Services

Garrett Sheahan
Skinner, Inc.
357 Main St.
Bolton, MA 01740-1104
phone: 508-779-6241 or 617-350-5400
fax: 508-779-5144
*Established in 1964, Skinner Inc. is
the fifth largest auction house in the
US; has offices in Bolton and Boston,
MA.*

David Rago
Rago's American Arts & Crafts Auction
17 Main St.
Lambertville, NJ 08530
phone: 609-397-9374
fax: 609-397-9377
e-mail: rago@ragoarts.com
Internet: http://www.ragoarts.com
*Specializing in the sale of American
art pottery and Arts and Crafts items.*

Don Treadway
Treadway Auctions
2029 Madison Rd.
Cincinnati, OH 45208
phone: 513-321-6742 or 800-526-0491
fax: 513-871-7722
Internet: http://
www.treadwaygallery.com
*Specializes in the sale of Arts and
Crafts pottery.*

Angela Past
Butterfield & Butterfield
7601 Sunset Blvd.
Los Angeles, CA 90046-2714
phone: 213-850-7500
fax: 213-850-5843
Two specialty auction each year.

Clubs/Associations

Jane Gram, Pres.
Foundation for the Study of the Arts &
Crafts Movement
Magazine: Craftsman Homeowner
Roycroft Campus
31 South Grove St.
East Aurora, NY 14052
phone: 716-652-3333 or 716-655-0562
*The foundation's mission is to study
and preserve the philosophical and
artistic legacy of the International
Arts & Crafts Movement; meetings,
seminars, appraisals, consultations,
discounts on china, furniture,
wallpaper, etc.*

Linda Hubbard Brady, Pres.
Roycrofters-At-Large Association
Newsletter: RALA Newsletter
P.O. Box 417
East Aurora, NY 14052
phone: 716-652-0213
*Studies the Arts & Crafts Movement
and fosters new crafts people at the
Roycroft Campus in East Aurora, NY;
lecture series, tours, sponsors a winter
and a summer crafts show.*

Collectors

Richard L. Sasicki
P.O. Box 3113
Glen Ellyn, IL 60138-3113
phone: 708-627-2630
e-mail: artwave@sprynet.com
*Wants to buy books, catalogs,
pamphlets, or any ephemera related to
American Art Pottery and Ceramics or
to the Arts & Crafts period.*

Bruce Richards
508 N. Belmont Ave.
Los Angeles, CA 90026-4124
phone: 213-413-4517
*Wants Roycroft, Karl Kipp, and The
Too Kay Shop handwrought copper
items in good condition with original
patina: letter openers, bookends,
candlesticks, desk sets, vasettes, vases,
trays, bowls.*

Dealers

Jim Messineo
JMW Gallery
144 Lincoln St.
Boston, MA 02111-2523
phone: 617-338-9097
fax: 617-338-7636
*Buys, sells and specializes along with
co-owner Mike Witt in the Arts &
Crafts movement, Mission furniture,
Lifetime, Limbert, Stickley; also
American Art Pottery from 1875 to
1950s: Grueby, Newcomb,
Marblehead, etc.*

John S. Zuk
106 Orchard St.
Belmont, MA 02178-2940
phone: 617-484-4800
fax: 617-864-3862
e-mail: jzuk@integral-inc.com
*Buys and sells metal work (Roycroft),
furniture (Stickley, Limbert), pottery
(Newcomb, Grueby, Rookwood) in the
Mission period.*

Rosalie & Aram Berberian
ARK Antiques
P.O. Box 3133
New Haven, CT 06515
phone: 203-387-3754
fax: 203-387-8671
*Wants American craftsman silver,
jewelry and metal of the first half of
the 20th century.*

David Rago
David Rago Arts & Crafts
17 Main St.
Lambertville, NJ 08530
phone: 609-397-9374
fax: 609-397-9377
e-mail: rago@ragoarts.com
Internet: http://www.ragoarts.com
*Wants American art pottery, and Arts
and Crafts items such as furniture and
metal items by Stickley, Rohlfs,
Wright, Roycroft, etc.*

Bruce A. Austin
c/o RIT/College Liberal Arts
92 Lomb Memorial Dr.
Rochester, NY 14623-5604
phone: 716-475-2879 or 716-387-9820
fax: 716-475-7732
e-mail: baagll@rit.edu
*Wants to buy L & JG Stickley, Stickley
Bros., Gustav Stickley, Limbert,
Roycroft, Rohlfs, Mission Oak
furniture, clocks, art pottery; also
hammered copper and lighting by
Roycroft, Dirk Van Erp, Jarvie,
Tiffany, Heintz, Albert Berry.*

Steve Traband
P.O. Box 7064
Saint Petersburg, FL 33734-7064
phone: 813-896-2308
*Buys and sells Mission style furniture:
Stickley, Roycroft, Limbert, Lifetime,
Rohlfs, F.L. Wright, etc.*

Don Treadway
2029 Madison Rd.
Cincinnati, OH 45208
phone: 513-321-6742 or 800-526-0491
fax: 513-871-7722
Internet: http://
www.treadwaygallery.com

Connie Zeigler
Durwyn Smedley Antiques
853 Conner St.
Noblesville, IN 46060
phone: 317-776-0161
e-mail: smedley@iquest.net
Internet: http://www.smedley.com/
smedley
*Buys, sells, appraises items from the
Arts & Crafts movement: marked and
unmarked furniture, art pottery, tile,
metalwork, textiles, books, fine art,
and other decorative accessories.*

John B. Marrella
Investments in Time
P.O. Box 611
Birmingham, MI 48012-0611
phone: 810-644-3100
fax: 810-644-2792

Ned & Ann Duke
Duke Gallery
625 S. Campbell Rd.
Royal Oak, MI 48067-4056
phone: 810-547-5511

John Toomey
John Toomey Gallery
818 North Blvd.
Oak Park, IL 60302
phone: 708-383-5234
fax: 708-383-4828
Conducts Arts and Crafts auctions in association with Don Treadway.

Experts

Rosalie & Aram Berberian
ARK Antiques
P.O. Box 3133
New Haven, CT 06515
phone: 203-387-3754
fax: 203-387-8671
Specializing in American Arts & Crafts Movement silver, jewelry and metal items.

Carole Hibel
John Hibel Antiques
185 Yerry Hill Rd.
Woodstock, NY 12498
phone: 914-679-2966 or 800-426-3357
fax: 914-679-3397
Author of "The Fulper Book," buying Fulper, Grueby, Marblehead, Teco, etc. pottery, Gustav Stickley, L & JG Stickley, Limberts, Roycroft, Van Erp furniture and lamps.

Fritz Gram
357 North Shore Rd.
Cuba, NY 14727-9227

Jim Graham
1407 S Street NW
Washington, DC 20009

Bruce Johnson
P.O. Box 8773
Asheville, NC 28814-8773
phone: 704-254-1912
fax: 704-254-1912
Writes furniture repair/refinishing column. Wrote price guide to arts and crafts movement items.

On-Line Services

Arts & Crfts Society
1209 W. Huron
Ann Arbor, MI 48103
phone: 313-665-4729
fax: 313-213-0045
e-mail: info@arts-crafts.com
Internet: http://www.arts-crafts.com/
Interactive electronic community dedicated to the philosophy and spirit of the original Arts & Crafts Movement of the late 19th and early 20th centuries.

Periodicals

David Rago
Journal: Style: 1900
17 Main St.
Lambertville, NJ 08530
phone: 609-397-9374
fax: 609-397-9377
e-mail: rago@ragoarts.com
Internet: http://www.ragoarts.com
The only periodical devoted entirely to the Arts & Crafts movement.

John Brinkmann
Magazine: American Bungalow
P.O. Box 756
Sierra Madre, CA 91204
phone: 818-355-3363
Focusing on Bungalow and Arts & Crafts architecture, design, how-to's, sources, interior and exterior decor, furniture, craftsmen, etc.

Furniture

Dealers

Douglass White
Classic Interiors & Antiques
2042 N Rio Grande Ave., Ste. E
Orlando, FL 32804-5644
phone: 407-839-0004
Wants to buy American Arts & Crafts period furniture.

Experts

Bruce Johnson
P.O. Box 8773
Asheville, NC 28814-8773
phone: 704-254-1912
fax: 704-254-1912
Writes furniture repair/refinishing column. Wrote price guide to arts and crafts movement items. Hosts annual Grove Park Inn Arts & Crafts Conference & Antiques Show, Asheville, NC.

Roycroft

(see also BOOKS, Roycroft)

Collectors

Richard Blacher
209 Plymouth Colony Rd.
Branford, CT 06405-4753
Wants Roycroft items: books, ephemera, etc.; please describe and price.

Gary Wood
733 Myrtle Rd.
North Brunswick, NJ 08902-2549
phone: 908-821-7633
Collector seeks single issues or bound volumes of all Roycroft magazines including "The Philistine," "Roycrofter," "The Fra," as well as books published by The Roycroft Press and craft items bearing the Roycroft cross-and-orb mark.

Francesca Gern
P.O. Box 2161
Hudson, OH 44236-0161
phone: 216-655-9325 or 888-RUM-RILL
fax: 216-655-9347
e-mail: rumrill2@aol.com
Wants to buy Roycroft desk sets, vases, sconces, candleholders, lamps, etc.

Experts

Fritz Gram
357 North Shore Rd.
Cuba, NY 14727-9227
Appraises and specializes in Roycroft items.

Charles F. Hamilton
P.O. Box 769
Tavares, FL 32778
Author of "Roycroft Collectibles."

Museums/Libraries

Elbert Hubbard Roycroft Museum
363 Oakwood Ave.
East Aurora, NY 14052-2319
phone: 716-652-4735 or 716-634-1231

Van Erp-Style Lamps

Repro. Sources

Jerry Cohen
Mission Oak Shop, The
123 Main St.
Putnam, CT 06260-1925
phone: 203-928-6662
fax: 203-928-1039
Makes hammered copper and mica light fixtures in the Arts & Crafts style of Dick Van Erp and Gustav Stickley.

William Morris

Clubs/Associations

Jean Johnson
William Morris Society of Canada, The
1942 Delaney Dr.
Mississaugua
Ontario L5J 3L1 Canada
phone: 416-973-4963
Exists to foster knowledge about the life, works and philosophy of the gifted and multi-faceted 19th century artist, author and craftsman William Morris (1834-1896.)

ASHTRAYS

Collectors

Betty Franks
1831 Penthley Ave.
Akron, OH 44312-1915
phone: 330-784-2869
Wants china or ceramic figural ashtrays with a big mouth or holes in nose, ears, or head for escaping smoke.

Periodicals

Chuck Thompson
Directory: Ashtray Collectors Directory and Source Book
10802 Greencreek Dr., Ste. 703
Houston, TX 77070-5367
For collectors of smokers' ashtrays; porcelain, glass, metal, brass, china, Bakelite, etc.

Casino

Experts

Art Anderson
P.O. Box 4103
Flint, MI 48504-0103
phone: 810-234-3400 or 810-659-4446
fax: 810-234-8656
Author of "Casinos and their Ashtrays."

ASTRONAUT MEMORABILIA

(see SPACE COLLECTIBLES)

ASTRONOMICAL ITEMS

(see also BOOKS, Astronomy; INSTRUMENTS & DEVICES, Scientific; SPACE COLLECTIBLES)

Comets

Experts

Stuart Schneider
P.O. Box 64
Teaneck, NJ 07666-0064
phone: 201-261-1983
Collector, writer wants items relating to Haley's comets; author of "Haley's Comet - Memories of 1910."

Meteorites

Collectors

Q. David Bowers
Bowers & Merena, Inc.
P.O. Box 1224
Wolfeboro, NH 03894
fax: 603-569-5319
Wants pre-1950 books, catalogs, and monographs describing meteorites, cataloging collections, offering specimens for sale.

Blaine Reed
P.O. Box 1183
Durango, CO 81302-1183
phone: 970-259-5326
fax: 970-254-5326
Buy, sell, trade all types of meteorites; free list; free identification on suspected meteorites for people who believe they may have found one.

Robert Haag
P.O. Box 27527
Tucson, AZ 85726
phone: 602-882-8804
fax: 601-743-7225

Dealers

Marvin Killgore
P.O. Box 95
Payson, AZ 85547
phone: 520-474-9515
fax: 520-474-2474

Experts

Randy D. Watson, M.D.
545 SE Oak, Ste. D
Hillsboro, OR 97123-4147
phone: 501-297-7424 or 503-640-1614
Advanced collector pays top dollar;

will buy any and all meteorites; also wants to buy meteorite books and pictures; says "I never met a meteorite I didn't like!"; has private museum of over 1500 microscopes and 200 meteorites.

Telescopes

Clubs/Associations

Walter H. Breyer, Sec.
Antique Telescope Society
Journal: Journal of the Antique Telescope Society
1275 Poplar Grove Lane
Cumming, GA 30131-7907
phone: 770-887-6359
e-mail: 71223.3430@compuserve.com
Members collect, study, restore, preserve and use antique telescopes & other early astronomical instruments, books, atlases, & related items; glossy stock journal published quarterly: technical, historical, restoration articles.

ATLANTIC CITY COLLECTIBLES

Dealers

M. McGovern
Home Grown
1012 Manoa Rd.
Wynnewood, PA 19096
phone: 610-649-6316
fax: 610-649-2369
Wants to buy dated ruby flash glass from Atlantic City.

ATLASES

(see also BOOKS; GLOBES; MAPS & CHARTS)

Collectors

Woodward
2425 University Blvd. W.
Jacksonville, FL 32217
phone: 904-733-7030
Wants to buy old atlases and maps.

Paul Mahoney
1746 Blake St.
Denver, CO 80202
phone: 303-296-7725
Wants atlases and folding pocket maps.

Dealers

Murray Hudson
Murray Hudson - Antiquarian Books & Maps
109 S. Church St.
P.O. Box 163
Halls, TN 38040-0163
phone: 901-836-9057 or 800-748-9946
fax: 901-836-9057
e-mail: mapman@usit.net
Internet: http://css.ecis.net/hudson
Buys/sells pre-1900 antique maps (especially pocket, wall, Civil War and railroad maps) & books with maps (e.g. atlases, travel guides, geographies, land surveys, etc.); esp. of S.E.

& S.W. US; also wants pre-1950 world globes.

Lahaina Printsellers, Ltd.
636 Luakini St.
Lahaina, HI 96761
phone: 808-667-7843
Wants to buy pre-1900 atlases.

AUCTION CATALOGS

Auction Services

Mid-Hudson Auction Galleries
One Idlewild Ave.
Cornwall On Hudson, NY 12520
phone: 214-534-7828

Doug Davies
Davies Auctions
P.O. Box 5542
Lafayette, IN 47903-5542
Specializes in antiques auctions.

Book Sellers

Andrew Rose
Catalog Kid
3 Seward Dr.
Asbury Park, NJ 07712-3724
phone: 800-258-2056
fax: 908-918-2546
e-mail: VanRose@injersey.com
Distributes post sale auction catalogs from Christie's, Sotheby's, Phillips, Bonhams, Hapsburg, etc. at remaindered prices; domestic and foreign sales.

Kathe Quinn
Auction Catalog, Co., The
503 Live Oak St.
Miami, AZ 85539-1226
phone: 520-473-4088 or 800-487-0428
fax: 520-473-4110
Sells most definitive, up-to-date reference in art, antiques & collectible market: Sotheby, Christie, Skinner post auction catalogs.

Misc. Services

Stanley & Bob Block
Block's Box
P.O. Box 51
Trumbull, CT 06611-0051
phone: 203-261-0057 or 203-926-8448
e-mail: BlocksChip@aol.com
Internet: http://pages.prodigy.com/marbles/
Produce video tapes & catalogs for auctioneers and appraisers; full state-of-the-art video tape production facility.

AUCTION SERVICES

(see "AUCTION SERVICES" Appendix as well as Auction Services listed under specific categories throughout this Directory.)

Periodicals

Newsmagazine: Auction World
417 W. Stanton
P.O. Box 745
Fergus Falls, NM 56537
phone: 218-739-4408
fax: 218-736-7474
The monthly magazine for professional auctioneers featuring news, feature stories and columns on auctions all over the U.S; also auctioneer supplies and services.

Government Contract

Manheim Auctions Government Services
1400 Lake Hearn Dr., NE
Atlanta, GA 30319
phone: 800-222-9885
Has a government contract to conduct government auctions of personal property including antiques, rare books, jewelry, collectibles, etc.; call to be placed on their mailing list

AUDIO EQUIPMENT

(see AUDIO-VISUAL)

AUDIO-VISUAL

(see also BROADCASTING; CAMERAS & CAMERA EQUIPMENT; FILMS; GAMES, Video Games; HI-FI EQUIPMENT; MOVIE MEMORABILIA; PHOTOGRAPHS; RADIO SHOWS, Old Time; RECORDS)

Appraisers

Steven Smolian
Smolian Sound Preservation Studios
1 Worman's Mill Court #4
Frederick, MD 21701
phone: 301-694-5134
fax: 301-694-5179
Record collections appraised for tax donation, estate & insurance loss purposes; all formats - 78s, 45s, LPs, cylinders, radio disks, etc.; rock, classical, country, old news broadcasts; over 20 years appraising major archives.

Experts

Dr. Steve Johnson
Behavioral Images, Inc.
Newsletter: Ten Thousands Words
302 Leland St., Ste. 101
Bloomington, IL 61701-5646
phone: 309-829-3931 or 800-988-6427
fax: 309-829-9677
e-mail: mediavalue@compuserve.com
Internet: http://ourworld.compuserve.com/homepages/mediavalue
Film, video, recordings, photographs, negatives; author of "Appraising Audio-visual Media; A Guide for Attorneys, Trust Officers, Insurance Professionals, & Archivists" (1993); $34.95 & $3 S&H; publishes newsletter ten times per year.

Misc. Services

Steven Smolian
Smolian Sound Preservation Studios
1 Worman's Mill Court #4
Frederick, MD 21701
phone: 301-694-5134
fax: 301-694-5179
Old recordings transferred from your squealing tapes, home discs, radio transcriptions, shellac records, etc. to tape and CD; uses a full range of professional equipment; over 30 years experience restoring audio for companies.

Tapes

Collectors

Jerry Menzies
4803 180th S.W. A108
Lynnwood, WA 98036
Buys or trades pre-recorded reel-to-reel tape.

Dealers

Tim Hunter
1668 Golddust
Sparks, NV 89436
phone: 702-626-5029
fax: 702-626-4423
e-mail: thunter8852@aol.com
Wants to buy pre-recorded reel-to-reel tapes: Rock, Pop, Country; clean tapes only, please.

Tapes (8-Track)

Periodicals

8-Tm Productions
Newsletter: 8-Track Mind
P.O. Box 90
Eastpointe, MI 48021-0900

AUTO RACING MEMORABILIA

(see also AUTOMOBILES; AUTOMOBILES, Racing; MODELS, Cars [Racing])

Clubs/Associations

Auto Racing Memories
P.O. Box 12226
Saint Petersburg, FL 33733

Collectors

Deek Scott
11169 Perry Hwy.
Wexford, PA 15090
phone: 412-935-3220
Wants to buy early auto racing programs, posters, Indy 500 memorabilia, board track items, etc.

George Koyt
8 Lenora Ave.
Morrisville, PA 19067-1206
phone: 215-295-4908
Wants all types of auto racing items: programs, postcards, books, toys, games, anything auto racing, A to Z, old/new, large or small; will buy one piece or entire collections.

Museums/Libraries

National Museum of Racing & Hall of
Fame
191 Union Ave.
Saratoga Springs, NY 12866
phone: 518-584-0400
fax: 518-584-4574

Don Naman, ExDir
International Motor Sports Hall of Fame
P.O. Box 1018
Talladega, AL 35160
phone: 205-362-5002 or 205-362-5003
fax: 205-362-3717
*Preserves the worldwide history of
motor sports; over $7M in racing
vehicles and memorabilia on display;
Hall of Fame.*

Indianapolis Motor Speedway Museum
4790 W. Sixteenth St.
Indianapolis, IN 46222

Drag

Clubs/Associations

Charles Gilmore
Eastern States Timing Association
Newsletter: ESTA Nostalgia News
P.O. Box 176
Lahaska, PA 18931
phone: 215-794-8611
*Promotes nostalgia drag racing shows
throughout the northeast; over 200
members interested in drag racing
restored or relics of pre-1972 drag
racing cars.*

National Drag Racing Association
P.O. Box 9438
Anaheim, CA 92802

Collectors

Mike & Cheryl Goyda
P.O. Box 192
East Petersburg, PA 17520-0192
phone: 717-569-7149
fax: 717-569-0909
e-mail: Goydagang@aol.com
*Wants to purchase drag racing
newspapers and magazines, handouts,
trophies, jackets, posters, programs,
etc.*

Museums/Libraries

Greg Capitano
Don Garlits Museum of Drag Racing
13700 SW 16th Ave.
Ocala, FL 34473
phone: 352-245-8661
fax: 352-245-6895
Internet: http://www.garlits,com
*Classic car and antique museum
encompasses 20,000 square feet of
displays, mostly auto related though
plenty of old "Americana" as well;
adjacent to the Auto Racing Hall of
Fame & Museum.*

Periodicals

Geoff Stunkard
Newsletter: Quarter Milestones
53 Milligan Ln.
Johnson City, TN 37601-9205

Indy 500

Clubs/Associations

John E. Blazier
National Indy 500 Collectors Club
Newsletter: Short Chute, The
10505 N. Delaware St.
Indianapolis, IN 46280-1353
phone: 317-848-4750
*Goal is to preserve the history of the
Indy 500 Mile Race; newsletter has
club notes, member spotlight, articles,
want, sell, trade, etc.*

Collectors

John E. Blazier
10505 N. Delaware St.
Indianapolis, IN 46280-1353
phone: 317-848-4750
*Founder of the National Indy 500
Collectors Club.*

Experts

Jack Mackenzie
6940 Wildridge Rd.
Indianapolis, IN 46256
Author of "Indy 500 Buyers Guide."

Museums/Libraries

Indianapolis Motor Speedway Hall of
Fame Museum
P.O. Box 24152
Speedway, IN 46224
phone: 317-248-6747

NASCAR

Clubs/Associations

National Racing Club, The
Newsletter: Inside Track
615 Hwy. A1A North, Ste. 105
Ponte Vedra Beach, FL 32082
phone: 888-722-3258 or 904-285-9409
fax: 904-285-5408
*For NASCAR enthusiasts: club
members get exclusive racing
collectibles, product discounts, special
member-only events.*

Collectors

John Adipotti
2728 Fifth St.
Monroeville, PA 15146
phone: 412-823-5095
fax: 412-856-3377

Dealers

Tom & Joanne Schwarz
3125 E. Main St.
Endicott, NY 13760
phone: 607-785-0707
fax: 607-785-0707
e-mail: nascartoys@aol.com

Brickel's Racing Collectibles
P.O. Box 205
Leesport, PA 19533
phone: 610-926-6719
fax: 610-926-6977
*Stock cars, sprints, late model dirt
cars, funny cars, top fuel dragsters,
Dually's, 1/18 racer toys, RCCA club
pieces, fan fueler items.*

Randy Kerschner
Randy Kershner's Racing Collectibles
871 Scenic Drive
Mohnton, PA 19540
phone: 610-777-5736
Glassware, ceramics, mail order.

Keith Moore
Last Lap Replicas
15 Park Ave.
Hagerstown, MD 21740
phone: 301-733-5019
*Specializes in NASCAR custom-built
models, banks and diecasts.*

A & L Racing Collectibles
13945 Statesville Blvd., #73
Cleveland, NC 27013
phone: 704-278-2122
fax: 704-278-2124
e-mail: krishers@salisbury.net

Luke Krisher
A & L Racing Collectibles
13945 Statesville Blvd., #73
Cleveland, NC 27013
phone: 704-278-2122
fax: 704-278-2124
e-mail: krishers@salisbury.net
Specializes in NASCAR trading cards.

John Williams
John's Wholesale Sports Collectibles
801 N. Salisbury St.
Lexington, NC 27292
phone: 910-476-9153 or 910-249-1622

Cathy's Racing Collectibles
1829 Old Watkins Rd.
Henderson, NC 27536
phone: 919-438-8614
fax: 919-438-9563
e-mail: CRCRacing@aol.com

JSI. Motorsports Collectibles
P.O. Box 1592
Anderson, SC 29622
phone: 864-231-9491
e-mail: jsi@carol.net
*Specializes in motorsports col-
lectibles: postcards, trading cards,
uniforms, programs.*

Strictly Racing
260 E. Semaran Blvd.
Casselberry, FL 32707
phone: 407-834-3743 or 800-898-3743
*NASCAR trading cards, die-cast,
memorabilia.*

White Rhino Racing Collectibles
7592 W. Farmington Blvd., Ste. 206
Memphis, TN 38138
phone: 901-753-4027
e-mail: wrracing@aol.com
*NASCAR diecast model cars and
trucks, funny cars, Ertl.*

Experts

Whit King
RPM Magazine
5610 Highway 29 S., Ste. 202
Harrisburg, NC 28075
phone: 704-455-1702
fax: 704-455-1707
e-mail: jwkmail@aol.com
*Editor-at-large of Tuff Stuff's "RPM"
magazine.*

Museums/Libraries

Hendrick Motorsports Museum & Gift
Shop
4400 Papa Joe Hendrick Blvd.
Harrisburg, NC 28075
phone: 704-455-0342
fax: 704-455-0341
*25 acre, 200,000 square foot racing
complex; display exhibits, souvenir
sales, race shop viewing.*

Jerry Cashman, Ex. Dir.
North Carolina Auto Racing Hall of
Fame
119 Knob Hill Rd.
Mooresville, NC 28115
phone: 704-663-5331
fax: 704-663-6949
Internet: http://www.racecityusa.com
*Features over 30 race cars dedicated
to al types of auto racing; racing
history films, Indy Simulator,
showcases of uniforms, helmets, and
photographs.*

Gloria Durant
Stock Car Hall of Fame Joe Weatherly
Museum
P.O. Box 500
Darlington, SC 29532
phone: 803-395-8821
*Has the largest collection of stock
cars in the world; fans can see the
pioneers who made the sport of
NASCAR what it is today; housed at
Darlington Raceway, NASCAR's
original Superspeedway.*

Periodicals

Christine Drury
Landmark Specialty Publications, Inc.
Magazine: Tuff Stuff's RPM
P.O. Box 1637
Glen Allen, VA 23060
phone: 804-266-0140 or 800-899-8833
fax: 804-264-4205
Internet: http://www.tuffstuffonline.com
*Monthly magazine focusing on
automobile racing collectibles
relating to NASCAR; articles, photos,
value guides, etc.*

Magazine: TRACE Magazine
P.O. Box 716
Kannapolis, NC 28082-0716
phone: 704-788-4660
fax: 704-786-3781
e-mail: racecollexch@prodigy.com
*The racing collector's exchange; race
fan guides, race schedules, collectibles ads.*

AUTOGRAPHS

(see also ALBUMS, Autograph;
BOOKS, Reference [Autographs];
HISTORICAL AMERICANA;
MANUSCRIPTS; PAPER COL-
LECTIBLES; PERSONALITIES;
PHOTOGRAPHS, Celebrity;
PLAYBOY ITEMS; SPORTS
COLLECTIBLES; PERFORMING
ARTS)

Appraisers

Brian Kathenes
Brian Kathenes Autographs &
Collectibles
Newsletter: Autograph Detective, The
P.O. Box 482
Hope, NJ 07844-0482
phone: 908-459-5225 or 800-323-5996
fax: 908-459-4899
e-mail: 76514.362@compuserve.com
*Full service autograph business;
buying, selling & appraising
autographs, rare books & historically
significant collectibles. Newsletter
published 6 times per year.*

Auction Services

Trevor Vennett-Smith
T. Vennett-Smith Chartered Auctioneer
11 Nottingham Rd.
Gotham
Nottingham NG11 OHE, U.K.
phone: 0115-9830541
fax: 0115-9830114
*Great Britain's leading professional
autograph auction house, specializing
in bi-monthly auctions of fine and
varied autographs.*

Stanley J. Richmond
Daniel F. Kelleher Company, Inc.
24 Farnsworth St., Ste. 605
Boston, MA 02210-1264
phone: 617-443-0033
fax: 617-443-0789
*U.S. and BNA stamps at auction; also
autographs and documents.*

Tom Beaber Jolie
Recollections Autographs
2-40 Bridge Ave.
Red Bank, NJ 07701
phone: 800-315-1776 or 908-747-3858
fax: 908-758-9730
*Full-time autograph dealers; holds bi-
monthly auctions and issues free
catalogs; publishers of "The Robot
That Helped to Make a President", the
definitive study of the John F.
Kennedy autograph.*

George Lowry
Swann Galleries, Inc.
104 E. 25th St.
New York, NY 10010-2977
phone: 212-254-4710
fax: 212-979-1017
e-mail: SwannSales@aol.com
*Oldest/largest U.S. auctioneer
specializing in rare books, autographs
& manuscripts, Judaica, photographs,
and works of art on paper.*

Chris Coover
Christie's
502 Park Ave.
New York, NY 10022
phone: 212-546-1000
fax: 212-980-8163
Internet: http://www.sirius.com/
~christie/

Robert H. Snyder
Cohasco, Inc.
P.O. Box 821
Yonkers, NY 10702-0821
phone: 914-476-8500
fax: 914-476-8573
*In business over 50 years, specializing
in paper collectibles, autographs,
documents, Americana, ephemera,
etc.; mail auction catalogs issued.*

Herman Darvick
Herman Darvick Autograph Auctions
P.O. Box 467
Rockville Centre, NY 11571
phone: 516-766-0289
fax: 516-766-7459
*Conducts six specialty auction
auctions per year; faxed and mail bids
accepted.*

Clubs/Associations

Urs Thoma
Swiss Autograph Collectors Association
Magazine: Swiss Autograph Magazine
Oberdorf 3
CH-8778
Schaenis, Switzerland

Douglas Wertman, Sec.
Universal Autograph Collectors Club
Magazine: Pen & Quill, The
P.O. Box 6181
Washington, DC 20044-6181
Internet: http://www.uacc.com
*The UACC has over 2000 members
worldwide; offers a bi-monthly
magazine with reports on facsimiles,
forgeries, authentication, auctions,
shows, celebrity addresses, etc.*

David R. Smith, Ex. Dir.
Manuscript Society, The
Magazine: Manuscripts
350 N. Niagara St.
Burbank, CA 91505-3648
Internet: http://www.manuscripts.org
*An organization of collectors, dealers,
librarians, archivists, scholars and
others interested in autographs and
manuscripts.*

Collectors

Stan Block
128 Cynthia Rd.
Newton, MA 02159
*Wants autographs, banners, leathers,
political pins, baseball cards, silks,
sports memorabilia.*

Ken Schwartz
79 Rte. 35
Eatontown, NJ 07724
phone: 908-542-1111
fax: 908-935-7467
e-mail: rmjd32a@prodigy.com
*Wants to buy autographs, documents,
or letters from famous people.*

Edward Bomsey
Edward N. Bomsey Autographs, Inc.
7317 Farr St.
Annandale, VA 22003
phone: 703-642-2040
fax: 703-642-2040
e-mail: enbainc@compuserve.com
Internet: http://www.abaa-booknet.com/
usa/bomsey/
*Wants letters, photographs, signatures
of personalities in politics, military,
science, history, music, arts, etc.*

Michael Reese II
P.O. Box 5704
South San Francisco, CA 94083-5704
phone: 415-641-5920
Internet: http://www.shutmymouth.com
*Wants autographs: early aviation
(1910-1939), letters, Presidents
letters, any Civil War (Union or
Confederate); also signed photos,
California Gold Rush period (1848-
1851).*

Dealers

Jerry Rubackin
Jerry's Cards & Collectibles
P.O. Box 1271
Framingham, MA 01701-0207
phone: 508-788-5197
fax: 508-788-5197
*Buys and sells WWII fighter aces
autographs and other WWII military
signatures; also want autographed
material by the crew of the Enola Gay
which dropped the first atomic bomb
on Hiroshima.*

Paul Longo
Paul Longo Americana
P.O. Box 5510
Gloucester, MA 01930-0007
phone: 508-525-2290
*Wants autographs of Presidents,
famous athletes, world famous
inventors, statesmen, actors and
actresses, etc.*

Mark Vardakis
P.O. Box 1430
Coventry, RI 02816
phone: 401-823-8440 or 800-342-0301
fax: 401-823-8861
Internet: http://
ourworld.compuserve.com/
homepages/markvautographs
*Buying and selling autographs:
presidents, authors, musicians,
celebrities, scientists, etc.; also
conducts autograph auctions.*

George & Julie Perron
Old Paperphiles, The
P.O. Box 135
Tiverton, RI 02878-0135
phone: 401-624-9420
fax: 401-624-4204
*Buys and sells paper collectibles:
books, autographs, sheet music,
postcards, photos, stereoviews,
documents, old letters; issues periodic
catalog of items for sale.*

George H. La Barre
La Barre Galleries
P.O. Box 746
Hollis, NH 03049
phone: 603-882-2411
*Major dealer and expert in auto-
graphs, and stocks and bonds.*

Bob Eaton
R & R Enterprises
3 Chestnut Dr.
Bedford, NH 03110
phone: 603-471-0808
fax: 603-471-2844
*Buys and sells photographs,
signatures, letters and documents
signed by famous personalities in all
fields: presidential, historical, sports,
music, film.*

University Archives
600 Summer St.
Stamford, CT 06901-1403
phone: 800-237-5692 or 203-975-9291
fax: 203-348-3560
*Buying and selling fine historical
autographs, manuscripts, documents,
autographed books and autographed
photographs of notable people
including U.S. presidents, Revolutionary and Civil War, literary, aviation,
science, art, and music.*

Marc Zydiak
Star Archives
P.O. Box 285
Westfield, NJ 07091-0285
phone: 908-654-6505

Tom Beaber Jolie
Recollections Autographs
2-40 Bridge Ave.
Red Bank, NJ 07701
phone: 800-315-1776 or 908-747-3858
fax: 908-758-9730
*Full-time autograph dealers; holds bi-
monthly auctions and issues free
catalogs; publishers of "The Robot
That Helped to Make a President", the
definitive study of the John F.
Kennedy autograph.*

Seth Kaller
M. Kaller & Assoc., Inc.
P.O. Box 173
Allenhurst, NJ 07711
phone: 908-774-0222
fax: 908-774-9401
*Buys and sells historical autographs
& documents: Civil War, Lincoln
items, U.S. Presidents, etc.*

Susan Levin Hoffman
North Shore Manuscript Company, Inc.
P.O. Box 458
Roslyn Heights, NY 11577
phone: 516-484-6828
fax: 516-625-3327
e-mail: nsmc@earthlink.net
Buys and sells historical manuscripts, documents, letters, signatures, and photos in the fields of politics, science, business, art, literature; specializing in Presidents and signers of the Declaration of Independence.

Jerry Docteur
Pages of History
P.O. Box 2840
Binghamton, NY 13902-2840
phone: 607-724-4943
fax: 607-724-4983
Wants presidential and other historical autographs and material; buys autographs in all fields; also wants Civil War letters and documents.

Robert Batchelder
1 West Butler Ave.
Ambler, PA 19002-5701
phone: 215-643-1430
fax: 215-643-6613
Wants autograph letters, manuscripts & documents (American & European in all fields): Presidents, historical, literary, musical, etc.; issues periodic catalogs of items for sale.

Catherine Barnes
Catherine Barnes Autographs
P.O. Box 30117
Philadelphia, PA 19103-8117
phone: 215-854-0175
fax: 215-854-0831
Wants autographs, letters, documents, etc. signed by historic individuals, e.g. Presidents, government, science, medicine, the arts, law, etc.

Mr. Carmen D. Valentino
Rare Books & Manuscripts
2956 Richmond St., Drawer 19
Philadelphia, PA 19134-5720
phone: 215-739-6056
Antiquarian bookseller specializing in rare books, manuscripts, documents, early newspapers, diaries, account books, ledgers, ephemera, broadsides; pre-WWI.

B.C. West, Jr.
Autos & Autos
P.O. Box 280
Elizabeth City, NC 27909
phone: 919-335-1117
Wants autographs of famous aviators, scientists, doctors, Presidents, etc.; author of "The Autograph Collector Checklist."

Al Wittnebert
Al Wittenbert Autographs, Inc.
P.O. Box 821297
South Florida, FL 33082-1297
phone: 954-437-5562
fax: 954-450-6585
e-mail: signhere@msn.com
Author of "Signature of the Stars"

(1989) and "The Study of Star Trek Autographs" (1994); dealer in all fields of autographs with over 30 years experience.

Cordelia & Tom Platt
2805 East Oakland Park Blvd., Ste. 380
Fort Lauderdale, FL 33306
phone: 954-564-2002
fax: 954-564-2002

Ed London
Autographs Incorporated
9408 NW 70 St.
Fort Lauderdale, FL 33321-3002
phone: 954-724-4294 or 954-724-4274
Buys and sells autographs; free giant super sale autograph catalog available upon request.

Joseph Rubinfine
American Historical Autographs
505 S. Flagler Dr., Ste. 1301
West Palm Beach, FL 33401-5923
phone: 561-659-7077
Advanced, experienced dealer; catalog of autograph and document offerings available for $3; focuses on 18th century autographs and documents.

Pieces of the Past
4521 PGA Blvd., #258
West Palm Beach, FL 33418

Stephen Koschal
P.O. Box 1581
Boynton Beach, FL 33425-1581
phone: 407-736-8409
fax: 407-736-5902
Buys, sells, and appraises autographs, signatures, letters, documents, books, signed photographs or anyone famous; former director UACC; catalogs issued; live auctions twice a year.

Richard Kohl
1840 N. Federal Highway
Boynton Beach, FL 33435
phone: 800-344-9103
fax: 407-364-8765
Internet: http://www.szgallery.com
Wants to buy autographs and historical documents: artists, authors, poets, entertainers, musicians/ composers, astronauts, explorers, inventors, aviators, presidents, political/foreign/military/religious leaders; also Americana.

W. Noble
1705 W Broad St.
Tampa, FL 33604-4637
phone: 813-930-6202
fax: 813-930-6202
Buys, sells and trades autographs in all fields; holds bi-monthly mail bid autograph auction; also sells celebrity address list.

Ramparts, Inc.
P.O. Box 9429
Dayton, OH 45409
phone: 800-463-1932
fax: 513-299-2151

Steve H. Nowlin
History Makers, Inc.
4040 E. 82nd St.
Indianapolis, IN 46250
phone: 800-424-9259 or 317-842-5828
fax: 317-842-5845
Internet: http://www.a1.com/history
Wants autographs of heroes, legends, superstars; any famous autographs from 1600 to present.

Linda Payne
Linda Payne Autographs
P.O. Box 081336
Racine, WI 53408-1336
phone: 414-663-7478
fax: 414-663-7525
e-mail: Pinda@aol.com
Wants all items signed by famous people; from 1 item to entire collections, especially good vintage items; catalog available.

William Butts
Main Street Fine Books & Manuscripts
206 N. Main St.
Galena, IL 61035-2244
phone: 815-777-3749
Open shop dealing in autographs and out-of-print books in most fields; specializing in all aspects of American history; boos and autograph catalogs issued regularly; member of A.B.A.A.

Robert A. LeGresley
P.O. Box 1199
Lawrence, KS 66044-8199
phone: 913-749-5458 or 913-843-0357
fax: 913-842-2203
Buys and sells autographs, specializing in historical, scientific, literary, musicians, composers, aviation, Civil War, entertainers, Papal and Saints, William Randolph Hearst.

Larry F. Vrzalik
Lone Star Autographs
P.O. Drawer 500
Kaufman, TX 75142
phone: 972-932-6050
fax: 972-932-7742

Tim Anderson
Autographs of America
P.O. Box 461
Provo, UT 84603-0461
Buy, sell, trade autographs: historical, Mormons, sports figures, etc.; specializing in movie stars of the 1930s, '40s and '50s.

Nate Sanders
Nate's Autographs Los Angeles
1015 Gayley Ave., Ste. 1168
Los Angeles, CA 90024
phone: 213-575-3851
fax: 213-575-4051
Buys and sells fine autographs; issues catalogs of autographs and manuscripts for sale; signed photographs, documents and letters from actors and actresses, U.S. presidents, musicians, etc.

Joseph Maddalena
Profiles in History
<u>Newsletter: Insider's Report</u>
345 North Maple Dr., Ste. 202
Beverly Hills, CA 90210
phone: 800-942-8856 or 310-859-7701
fax: 310-859-3842
Wants original letters, manuscripts, rare books of famous people. Cash paid. Serious inquiries only.

Myron Ross
Heroes & Legends
P.O. Box 1038
Agoura Hills, CA 91301-1038
phone: 818-991-5979
fax: 818-222-4571
e-mail: heroesross@aol.com
Wants character memorabilia, books, comic books, Fanzines, movie memorabilia, etc.; science fiction or fantasy, rock 'n roll, autographs.

Richard A. Basler
Colonnade of History
P.O. Box 4255
Irvine, CA 92716
phone: 714-551-2040
Buys/sells and takes items on consignment; leaders in autograph and manuscript hobby; issues extensive and well-researched quarterly catalogs.

Linda Murphy
Linda's Autographs
P.O. Box 1296
Sutherlin, OR 97479-1296
Autographs of famous people bought and sold.

Experts

Helen & George Sanders
Autograph House
2 Lake Dr.
P.O. Box 658
Enka, NC 28728-0658
phone: 704-667-9835
Co-authors with Ralph Roberts of "Collector's Guide to Autographs" (Wallace-Homestead, 1991); also other books; own one of the largest and extensive autograph collections; buys, sells, authenticates and appraises autographs.

Al Wittnebert
Al Wittenbert Autographs, Inc.
P.O. Box 821297
South Florida, FL 33082-1297
phone: 954-437-5562
fax: 954-450-6585
e-mail: signhere@msn.com
Author of "Signature of the Stars" (1989) and "The Study of Star Trek Autographs" (1994); dealer in all fields of autographs with over 30 years experience.

Misc. Services

Jim Romeo
Directory: Resource for Autograph
  Collectors
1008 Weeping Willow Dr.
Chesapeake, VA 23322-7701
  *Publishes a directory of resources for
  autograph collectors: dealers, clubs,
  associations, auction houses.*

Museums/Libraries

Pierpoint Morgan Library, The
29 E. 36th St.
New York, NY 10016
phone: 212-685-0008

New York Public Library, The
5th Ave. & 42nd St.
New York, NY 10018
phone: 212-930-0800

Periodicals

Christopher C. Jaeckel
Walter R. Benjamin Autographs, Inc.
Magazine: Collector, The
P.O. Box 255
Hunter, NY 12442-0255
phone: 518-263-4133
fax: 518-263-4134
e-mail: 72447.3642@compuserve.com

Jeffrey Morey
Newsletter: Autograph Review, The
305 Carlton Rd.
Syracuse, NY 13207-1530
phone: 315-474-3516
  *A bi-monthly 20-year publication for
  the serious collector; collector growth
  oriented: sports, military, actors'
  addresses, ads, mail-bid auctions,
  information and news. Courtesy
  sample $1 + LSASE.*

J.D. Bardwell
J.D. Bardwell Autographs

9131 College Parkway, Ste. 13B, Box
  101
Fort Myers, FL 33919-4827
phone: 813-481-5629
fax: 813-481-1487
e-mail: 75502.2126@cserve.com
  *Offers quality autographs at
  wholesale prices; issuing catalogs
  since 1986; specializes in autographs
  from those in the entertainment field;
  author of "In-Person Facsimile Guide
  of Celebrity Autographs."*

Newsletter: Autographs & Memorabilia
P.O. Box 224
Coffeyville, KS 67337
phone: 316-251-5308
  *A bi-monthly about movie and sports
  autographs and memorabilia.*

Classic Rarities & Co.

P.O. Drawer 29109
Lincoln, NE 68529
phone: 402-467-2948
fax: 402-467-3780

Marty Marsh
Marlan Group
Newspaper: Autograph Times
1125 W. Baseline Rd., #2-153-M
Mesa, AZ 85210-9501
phone: 602-777-8552 or 602-777-0842
fax: 602-777-0844
e-mail: MarlanPub@aol.com
  *News and information on all aspects
  of autograph collecting including
  historical, space, sports, entertainment and through the mail.*

Ev Phillips
Oddesy Publications
Magazine: Autograph Collector
510-A S. Corona Mall
Corona, CA 91720-1420
phone: 909-734-9636 or 800-395-1359
fax: 909-371-7139
Internet: http://
  www.autographcollector.com
  *A bi-monthly magazine covering all
  fields of autograph and historical
  document collecting: entertainment,
  sports, historical, etc.; for all ages;
  sample autographs, detailed articles,
  auctions, VIP addresses, ads, etc.*

Ev Phillips
Oddesy Publications
Magazine: Collecting
510-A S. Corona Mall
Corona, CA 91720-1420
phone: 909-734-9636 or 800-395-1359
fax: 909-371-7139
Internet: http://
  www.autographcollector.com
  *A monthly magazine focusing on
  collecting autographs, movie posters,
  movie memorabilia and props.*

Michael E. Johnson
Newsletter: Autograph Research
862 Thomas ave.
San Diego, CA 92109-3940
phone: 619-483-8632
  *Monthly newsletter presenting
  original research on autographs, their
  authenticity (fakes and authentics),
  pricing (trends and comparisons) and
  availability (autographs-by-mail,
  addresses, wholesale sources).*

Price Guide: Autograph Dealer's Price
  Guide
P.O. Box 1296
Sutherlin, OR 97479-1296
  *A comprehensive monthly report on
  the autograph market; values, auction
  results, ads.*

Astronaut

Dealers

Adam Harwood
Astronaut Autographs
1414 West Aries
Edmond, OK 73003-5826
phone: 405-359-7678
fax: 405-341-8405
e-mail: 75717.1061@compuserve.com
  *Over eight years experience buying
  and selling astronaut autographs; has
  worked with former astronauts and
  NASA employees to bring their*

collections to the space collectibles
market; writes space memorabilia
column for collectibles mag.

Periodicals

Michael E. Johnson
Newsletter: Space Autograph News
862 Thomas ave.
San Diego, CA 92109-3940
phone: 619-483-8632
  *The hobby's leading source of
  information on the subject of
  astronaut and cosmonaut autographs;
  describes who's who and why in the
  space program, describing prices for
  various autograph formats, fakes,
  sources, etc.*

Celebrity

Dealers

Jon Allan
Elmer's Nostalgia, Inc.
3 Putnam St.
Sanford, ME 04073-2024
phone: 207-324-2166

Doug Wirth
Hummerdude's
P.O. Box 4348
Dunellen, NJ 08812
phone: 908-424-9367
  *Buys and sells celebrity photos and
  autographs.*

Safka & Bareis Autographs
P.O. Box 886
Flushing, NY 11375
phone: 718-263-2276
  *Collections bought and sold;
  specializing in cinema, music, opera
  and ballet.*

Jim Weaver
405 Dunbar
Pittsburgh, PA 15235-5218
  *FREE AUTOGRAPHS! Over 1000
  personal addresses of celebrities who
  will usually send FREE, autographed
  photo. $10 for list; ask about other
  lists; also wants to buy vintage
  celebrity autographs, especially
  Universal horror stars and cast.*

Steven S. Raab
Steven S. Raab Autographs
P.O. Box 471
Ardmore, PA 19003
phone: 610-446-6193
fax: 610-446-4514
e-mail: raab@netaxs.com
Internet: http://www.izzy.com/~raab/
  autographs/
  *Specializes in vintage (pre-1970)
  entertainment autographs.*

Searle's Autographs
P.O. Box 9369
Asheville, NC 28815
  *Monthly catalog of celebrity
  autographs with emphasis on TV,
  movies, and theatre.*

Walk of Fame Autographs
P.O. Box 1026
Deland, FL 32721-1026
phone: 904-943-9500
fax: 904-943-4115
e-mail: autogrph@n-jcenter.com
Internet: http://www2.combase.com/
  ~walkoffame
  *Buys and sells celebrity autographs:
  Hollywood, TV, models, political,
  sports, music, celebrities.*

J.D. Bardwell
J.D. Bardwell Autographs
9131 College Parkway, Ste. 13B, Box
  101
Fort Myers, FL 33919-4827
phone: 813-481-5629
fax: 813-481-1487
e-mail: 75502.2126@cserve.com
  *Offers quality autographs at
  wholesale prices; issuing catalogs
  since 1986; specializes in autographs
  from those in the entertainment field;
  author of "In-Person Facsimile Guide
  of Celebrity Autographs."*

Steve Nowlin
Rare Find Gallery, A
4040 E. 82nd St.
Indianapolis, IN 46250
phone: 800-424-9259
fax: 317-842-5845
  *Buys and sells autographs of
  Hollywood movie stars.*

Merit Adventures
P.O. Box 66262
Houston, TX 77266-6262
phone: 713-680-0325
fax: 713-680-2233

Golden State Autographs
P.O. Box 14776
Albuquerque, NM 87191
phone: 505-293-7407

Mike Gould
Hollywood Legends
6621A Hollywood Blvd.
Los Angeles, CA 90028
phone: 213-962-7411
fax: 213-962-6742
  *Specializes in signed photographs of
  contemporary movie stars; also
  autographs of television stars.*

Phil Sears
24592 Via Carissa
Laguna Niguel, CA 92677-7039
phone: 714-643-1477
fax: 714-643-8376
  *Buys and sells 1930-1950 movie star
  autographs.*

Trudy Prescott
Star Struck International
2791 F. North Texas St., Ste. 112
Fairfield, CA 94533
phone: 707-426-4056
Internet: http://www.goodnet.com/
  photos/starintl.htm
  *Publishes an illustrated catalog of
  celebrity autographs, costumes and
  memorabilia.*

Thomas Burford
Celebrity Access
20 Sunnyside Ave., Ste. A241
Mill Valley, CA 94941-1928
phone: 415-389-8133
e-mail: AccessStar@aol.com
Internet: http://members.aol.com/
AccessStar
*Autograph dealers for over 2 decades,
specializing mostly in Hollywood;
publishes a celebrity address book
with over 7000 (mostly Hollywood)
celebrity addresses; members of
several organizations and are active
on TV and radio.*

Misc. Services

Cardiff Publishing Company
5173 Waring Rd.
San Diego, CA 92120
*Publishes annual directory of over
40,000 celebrity addresses.*

Periodicals

Michael E. Johnson
Newsletter: Celebrity Home Address
Newsletter
862 Thomas ave.
San Diego, CA 92109-3940
phone: 619-483-8632
*Bi-monthly source of information for
collecting celebrity autographs;
alphabetized lists of addresses,
advertising, addresses from diverse
sources.*

Hollywood Movie Archives
Directory: Celebrity Address Book
P.O. Box 1566
Apple Valley, CA 92307-0030
phone: 619-242-8569 or 800-596-2350
*Addresses for thousands of stars -
screen, stage, television, musicians,
singers, teenager, actors, industry
executives, ice skaters.*

Thomas Burford
Celebrity Access
Directory: Celebrity Access - The
Directory
20 Sunnyside Ave., Ste. A241
Mill Valley, CA 94941-1928
phone: 415-389-8133
e-mail: AccessStar@aol.com
Internet: http://members.aol.com/
AccessStar
*Autograph dealers for over 2 decades,
specializing mostly in Hollywood;
publishes a celebrity address book
with over 7000 (mostly Hollywood)
celebrity addresses; members of
several organizations and are active
on TV and radio.*

Music Related

Dealers

John & Jude Lubrano
J & J Lubrano, Music Antiquarians
8 George Street
Great Barrington, MA 01230
phone: 413-528-5799
fax: 413-528-4164
e-mail: lubrano@ben.net
Internet: http://www.abaa-booknet.com/
usa/lubrano/
*Buys and sells autograph manuscripts
from famous musicals and dance; rare
printed music and books about music,
musical autographs and manuscripts,
rare dance books 16th to 20th
centuries; established in 1977;
member ABAA, ILAB.*

J.B. Muns
Fine Arts Books & Musical Autographs
1162 Shattuck Ave.
Berkeley, CA 94707-2635
phone: 510-525-2420
fax: 510-525-1126
*Buys and sells musical autographs
(classical musicians, composers and
singers) as well as books on music.*

AUTOMATA

(see DOLLS, Automatons; MUSIC
BOXES)

AUTOMOBILES

(see also AUTOMOBILIA; BOOKS,
Reference [Automobiles]; BUSES;
KITS; MILITARIA, Vehicles;
MODELS, Cars; AUTO RACING
MEMORABILIA; TAXI RELATED
COLLECTIBLES; TOYS, Diecast;
TRACTORS & RELATED ITEMS;
TRAILERS & RV'S; TRUCKS;
VOLKSWAGEN RELATED ITEMS

Appraisers

James Wetzel
Hudson Valley Auto Appraisers, Inc.
118 North Plank Rd.
Newburgh, NY 12550
phone: 914-561-594
fax: 914-561-1745
e-mail: JWetzel218@msn.com
Internet: http://www.hvaa.com
*The source for vehicle appraising; in
business for over 30 years and
performed over 200,000 appraisals;
the internet source for appraising.*

Quentin Craft
P.O. Drawer 1139
Indiana, PA 15701
phone: 412-463-1530

Terry Shaw
Automotive Legal Service
P.O. Box 626
Dresher, PA 19025-0626
phone: 800-487-4947 or 215-659-4947
fax: 215-659-4947
*Government licensed appraisers for
all appreciable, collectible quality
vehicles; specialists in insurance
claims, restoration disputes, IRS*

*donations, estate & equity matters,
Lemon Law; qualified expert witness;
free information.*

Larry Batton
Auto Appraisal Group
RR 3 Box 184E
Charlottesville, VA 22903-9322
phone: 800-848-2886 or 804-295-1722
fax: 804-295-7918
*Nationwide appraisal service for all
classic and collectible type automobiles: prepurchase inspections,
insurance documentation, property
and divorce settlements, expert
witness testimony; also originality and
historical research.*

Marion Associates
4400 Washington St. W.
Charleston, WV 25313
phone: 304-744-1211

Arthur B. Shorts
New England Auto Appraisal Services,
Inc.
P.O. Box 664
Taylors, SC 29687-0664
phone: 803-297-3999 or 803-420-8844
fax: 804-297-3999
*Value appraisals for insurance claims
and coverage, IRS, estates, charitable
contributions and marital disputes;
also restoration, purchase and sale
consultant.*

Wayne Merritt
Merritt Appraisal Service
P.O. Box 664
Taylors, SC 29687-0664
phone: 803-297-3999 or 803-420-8844
fax: 804-297-3999
*Over 30 years experience in
appraising automobiles for insurance
claims and coverage.*

Dean Kruse
Kruse International
P.O. Box 190
Auburn, IN 46706
phone: 800-968-4444 or 219-925-5600
fax: 219-925-5467
Internet: http://
www.kruseinternational.com
Appraises all collector cars.

Mike Grippo
M & M Automobile Appraisers, Inc.
4349 W. N. Peotone Rd.
Beecher, IL 60401
phone: 708-258-6662
fax: 708-258-9675
*Special interest, collectible and
antique cars, machinery & equipment;
expert witness, marriage or business
dissolution, loan valuation and
insurance coverage; Associate
Member, International Society of
Appraisers.*

R.W. "Bob" Ryan
Auto Evaluators
5062 S. 108th St., Ste. 225
Omaha, NE 68137
phone: 402-681-2968
fax: 402-331-1638
Custom and classic auto appraiser;

*automotive legal consultant; court-
tested expert witness; mail appraisals
nationwide since 1983.*

Chris M. Zora
P.O. Box 9939
The Woodlands, TX 77386
phone: 713-362-8258
*Specializes in appraising special
interest automobiles; classics, street
rods, muscle cars.*

C. Erik Baltzar
Consulting Distributors
P.O. Box 1331
Palm Desert, CA 92261
phone: 619-346-1984
fax: 619-568-6354
Vehicle appraiser.

Dennis Mitosinka
Dennis Mitosinka's Classic Cars
619 E. Fourth St.
Santa Ana, CA 92701-4705
phone: 714-953-5303
fax: 714-953-1810
*Appraises all types of autos from 1900
to present; appraisals accepted by
FBI, IRS, FSLIC and insurance
companies; member of the Inter. Soc.
of Appraisers & the Antique
Appraisers of Amer.*

Auction Services

Kruse International
P.O. Box 190
Auburn, IN 46706
phone: 800-968-4444 or 219-925-5600
fax: 219-925-5467
Internet: http://
www.kruseinternational.com
*Specializes in auctioning antique,
classic and other special interest
automobiles, planes, motorcycles,
trucks, etc.*

Ken Lipton, ISA
Superior Auctions
P.O. Box 792427
San Antonio, TX 78279-2427
phone: 210-495-1319 or 210-697-0777
fax: 210-697-4217
Internet: http://www.saami.com
*Specializes in auction sales of classic
collector cars.*

Specialty Sales
4321 First St.
Pleasanton, CA 94566
phone: 510-484-2262 or 800-600-2262
fax: 510-426-8535
*Auctions antiques, classics, exotics;
largest indoor showroom; ships
overseas.*

Clubs/Associations

Southern Alberta Antique & Classic
Automobile Club
P.O. Box 1723
Lethbridge
Alberta T1J 4K4 Canada
phone: 403-345-4796
Internet: http://www.classicar.com/
clubs/saacac/saacac.htm

William Schmoll
Fifties Automobile Club of America
1114 Furman Dr.
Linwood, NJ 08221
phone: 609-927-4967
Purpose of the club is to encourage the restoration, preservation and use of historic, sports and racing cars.

William H. Smith, Ex. Dir.
Antique Automobile Club of America
Magazine: Antique Automobile
501 West Governor Rd.
P.O. Box 417
Hershey, PA 17033
phone: 717-534-1910
fax: 7175349101
e-mail: peterg@aaca.org
Internet: http://www.aaca.org
Dedicated to the history of the automobile; focuses on "antique" cars - (or by state registration a vehicle at least 25 years old); sponsors AACA tours, meets and discussions; regions and chapters across the U.S.

Nan Martin, Sec.
Society of Automotive Historians
Magazine: Automotive History Review
P.O. Box 339
Matamoras, PA 18336
phone: 317-852-0431
Interested in the preservation of historically valuable materials.

National Street Rod Association
4030 Park Ave.
Memphis, TN 38111
phone: 901-452-4030

National Muscle Car Association
3404 Democrat Rd.
Memphis, TN 38118
phone: 901-365-3779
fax: 901-366-1807
Internet: http://www.sojourn.com

William E. Donze, ExSec
Veteran Motor Car Club of America
Magazine: Bulb Horn
P.O. Box 360788
Strongsville, OH 44136-0014
phone: 216-238-2771
e-mail: vmcca@aol.com
Internet: http://web.buellreg.com/classic/vmcca.htm
A hobby club organized in 1938 to serve the needs of those interested in the preservation of collector vehicles and related memorabilia.

Jerry Flanary
Milestone Car Society
Magazine: Mile Post
P.O. Box 24612
Indianapolis, IN 46224
phone: 317-356-4246
Focuses on "milestone" cars; certain club-approved 1946-1974 cars which are gaining popularity with the passage of time.

James Garman
Historical Automobile Association
P.O. Box 10313
Fort Wayne, IN 46851-0313
phone: 219-837-7308

James J. Baxter
National Motorists Association
Newsletter: NMA News
6678 Pertzborn Rd.
Dane, WI 53529
phone: 608-849-6000
e-mail: nma@genie.geis.com
For the protection of the rights of motorists, enhancing personal mobility, encouraging rational traffic laws.

George Koehler
'48 'n Under, Inc.
708 Water St.
Sauk City, WI 53583
phone: 608-643-8146
For owners and enthusiasts of pre-1949 automobiles.

Classic Car Club of America
2300 East Devon Ave., Ste. 126
Des Plaines, IL 60018
phone: 708-390-0443
For owners of select cars from 1925 through 1948.

Henry Adamson
Vintage Sports Car Drivers Association
P.O. Box 490
Lake Forest, IL 60045
phone: 708-234-0303

Council of Vehicle Associations
10400 Roberts Rd.
Palos Hills, IL 60465
phone: 708-598-7070 or 800-227-7166
Special interest group representing all automotive enthusiasts regarding regulation and legislation potentially contrary to collector interest.

Mary Jean Flory
Contemporary Historical Vehicle Association
Magazine: Action Era Vehicle
P.O. Box 98
Tecumseh, KS 66542-0098
phone: 913-233-6715
For cars from 1928 through cars at least 20 years old.

Buddy Hoelzeman
Mid-America Old Time Automobile Association, The
Magazine: Antique Car Times
8 Jones Lane
Petit Jean Mountain
Morrilton, AR 72110
phone: 501-727-5427
Internet: http://www.classicar.com/clubs/motaa/motaa.htm
M.O.T.A.A. represents approximately 26 affiliated antique car clubs; "Antique Car Times" filled with articles featuring antique cars; recognizes cars manufactured through 1972.

Darryl Starbird
National Rod & Custom Car Hall of Fame
Magazine: Fun on Wheels
Rte. 3, No. 2 Star Kustom Ave.
Afton, OK 74331
phone: 918-257-4234
fax: 918-257-8224
Aims to establish rules for indoor specialty vehicle car shows; national events.

Sports Car Club of America, Inc.
9033 East Easter Pl.
Englewood, CO 80112
phone: 303-694-7222
Internet: http://www.na-motorcports.com/Organizations/SCCA/
Sanctions amateur and professional auto sports events throughout the U.S., and has done so for over 50 years.

World Organization of Automotive Hobbyists
P.O. Box 1331
Palm Desert, CA 92261-1331
phone: 619-568-6354
Representing automotive hobbyist interests vis-a-vis regulation and/or legislation.

Horseless Carriage Club of America
128 S. Cypress St., Ste. B
Orange, CA 92666-1314
phone: 714-538-4222
Internet: http://www.c_zone.net/dochemp/hcca1.html
Interested in brass-era touring cars.

Walt Skoczylas
Inliners International
Newsletter: 12 Port News, The
20045 SW Jaylee St.
Aloha, OR 97007-2864
phone: 503-642-9513
e-mail: Inliners@teleport.com
Internet: http://www.teleport.com/~inliners
For enthusiasts of all makes, models, years of stock, mild, or racing engines that are 4, 6, or 8 cylinders in-lines.

Dealers

Duffy Schamberger
Duffy's Collectible Cars
250 Classic Car Court S.W.
Cedar Rapids, IA 52404
phone: 319-364-7000
fax: 319-364-4036

Dennis Mitosinka
Dennis Mitosinka's Classic Cars
619 E. Fourth St.
Santa Ana, CA 92701-4705
phone: 714-953-5303
fax: 714-953-1810
Auto dealer in antique, classic and special interest cars.

Experts

Tad Burness
Auto Album
P.O. Box 247
Pacific Grove, CA 93950-0247
phone: 408-649-4864
Writes and illustrates syndicated "Auto Album" column for newspapers including "AntiqueWeek"; author of 23 books, most on transportation subjects.

Museums/Libraries

Sturbridge Auto Museum
P.O. Box 486
Sturbridge, MA 01566
phone: 617-867-2217

James A. Harwick, Cur.
Heritage Plantation Auto Museum
P.O. Box 566
Sandwich, MA 02563
phone: 617-888-3300

Greg Capitano
Don Garlits Auto Racing Hall of Fame & Museum
13700 SW 16th Ave.
Ocala, FL 34473
phone: 352-245-8661
fax: 352-245-6895
Internet: http://www.garlits,com
Classic car and antique museum encompasses 20,000 square feet of displays, mostly auto related though plenty of old "Americana" as well.

Dixie Gun Work's Old Car & Steam Engine Museum
P.O. Box 130
Union City, TN 38261
phone: 901-885-0561

Gilmore Classic Car Club Museum
6865 Hickory Rd.
Hickory Corners, MI 49060
phone: 616-671-5089
fax: 616-671-5843
Internet: http://www.classicar.com/MUSEUMS/GILMORE/GILMORE.HTM
Over 140 antique, classic and collector cars are displayed in six large historic Michigan barns; exhibits range from a 1899 Locomobile to a Cadillac styling concept car destined for the year 2002.

Gilmore - Classic Car Club of America Museum
6865 Hickory Rd.
Hickory Corners, MI 49060-9707
phone: 616-671-5089
fax: 616-671-5843

Duffy Schamberger
Duffy's Collectible Cars
250 Classic Car Court S.W.
Cedar Rapids, IA 52404
phone: 319-364-7000
fax: 319-364-4036
A car museum with 100 fully restored cars from the 1940s through 1960s; along with other memorabilia from the eras such as gas pumps, barber

poles, phone booths, wall murals, and a 1950s diner with neon signs.

Keith R. Gill
Museum of Science & Industry
57th St. & Lake Shore Dr.
Chicago, IL 60637
phone: 312-684-1414
fax: 312-684-5580

Antiques, Inc. Car Museum
P.O. Box 1887
Muskogee, OK 74402
phone: 918-687-4447

Hagan Stewart, Dir.
Imperial Palace Auto Collection
3535 Las Vegas Blvd., So.
Las Vegas, NV 89109
phone: 702-794-3174 or 702-731-3311
fax: 702-369-7430
Incredible collection of hundreds of classic cars: Dusenbergs, Cords, Auburns, etc.; also celebrity cars: Elvis, Marilyn Monroe, Steve McQueen, Al Capone, and presidential cars from Wilson to Nixon.

National Automobile Museum
10 Lake St. South
Reno, NV 89501-1558
phone: 702-333-9300
fax: 702-333-9309
A complete museum depicting the history of automobiles; TDD: 702-333-9307; automotive research service available through the mail.

On-Line Services

Lou Ann Hammond
Car-List
P.O. Box 460070
San Francisco, CA 94146-0070
phone: 916-823-6865
e-mail: lou@car-list.com
Internet: http://www.car-list.com
An on-line Internet service; Car-List is a used car locating service; you can also get a new car price quote; locate a car club from around the world, or list your car club for free.

Periodicals

John Hudson
CMM Publications
Magazine: Classic Motor Monthly
P.O. Box 129
Bolton
Lancashire BL3 4YQ, U.K.
phone: +44 1204 657212
fax: +44 1204 62479
e-mail:
    cmm_publication@compuserve.com
Internet: http://www.classicmotor.co.uk
One of the UK's leading publications for classic, vintage and veteran auto owners; each issue is packed with ads, events, news and much more; the on-line version reflects the character of the magazines.

Hemmings Motor News
Newsmagazine: Hemmings Motor News
P.O. Box 76
Bennington, VT 05201-0076
phone: 802-442-3101 or 800-227-4373
fax: 802-447-1561
Internet: http://www.hmn.com
Newsmagazine for antique and special interest auto enthusiasts; auctions, ads, services, insurance, restorations, etc.

David Brownell
Hemmings Motor News
Magazine: Special Interest Autos
P.O. Box 196
Bennington, VT 05201-0196
phone: 802-442-3101 or 800-227-4373
fax: 802-447-1561
e-mail: davehmn@sover.net
Internet: http://www.hmn.com
A bi-monthly magazine focusing on special interest vehicles.

Buzz Kanter, Pub.
TAM Communications, Inc.
Magazine: Rodder's Digest
6 Prowitt St.
Norwalk, CT 06855-1204
phone: 203-855-0008
fax: 203-852-9980
Internet: http://www.americaniron.com
Designed for the traditional street-rod enthusiast with a heavy emphasis on do-it-yourself building articles.

Jonathan A. Stein
Automobile Quarterly, Inc
Magazine: Automobile Quarterly
P.O. Box 348
Kutztown, PA 19530
phone: 610-683-3169
fax: 610-683-3287
Internet: http://www.autoquarterly.com
Hardbound magazine totally without advertising features in-depth articles on automotive history, nostalgia, art and much more for the serious auto collector and historian; packed with fine color and rare b&w photographs.

Price Guide: CPI Value Guide
P.O. Box 3190
Laurel, MD 20709-3190
phone: 301-317-4228
Published quarterly; covers more than 4,000 collectible and exotic cars and light trucks made since 1945; $22 per year.

Magazine: Car Collector Magazine
1241 Canton St.
Roswell, GA 30075
phone: 800-277-0175
Internet: http://www.carcollector.com

Magazine: Car Collector & Car Classics
8601 Dunwoody Pl., Ste. 144
Atlanta, GA 30350
A monthly glossy magazine with articles about classic, antique and special interest cars; also ads, parts sources and restoration services.

Tim Abbey
Trader Publishing Company
Magazine: Old Car Trader
P.O. Box 9059
Clearwater, FL 34618-9059
phone: 813-712-0035 or 800-548-8889
fax: 813-712-0034
Internet: http://www.traderonline.com

Kelly McKnight
DuPont Registry
Magazine: DuPont Registry
2325 Ulmerton Rd., Ste. 16
Clearwater, FL 34622
phone: 813-573-9339 or 800-233-1731
fax: 813-572-5523
Internet: http://
    www.dupontregistry.com/
A buyer's gallery of fine automobiles - classics, luxury, exotic, and muscle cars - plus worldwide auction coverage, drive tests, recommendations, profiles, book reviews.

Amos Press, Inc.
Magazine: Cars & Parts
P.O. Box 482
Sidney, OH 45365-0482
phone: 513-498-0803
fax: 513-498-0808
A monthly magazine for he collector of special interest & muscle cars; restoration, automotive history, how-to articles, show & auction coverage, etc.

Julie A. Ulrich, PR
Krause Publications
Newsmagazine: Old Cars
700 E. State St.
Iola, WI 54990-0001
phone: 715-445-2214
fax: 715-445-4087
e-mail: info@krause.com
Internet: http://www.krause.com
Weekly coverage of antique automobiles of all ages; auction reports, hobby events, car shows, swap meets, ads, club activities, etc.

Julie A. Ulrich, PR
Krause Publications
Magazine: Old Cars Price Guide
700 E. State St.
Iola, WI 54990-0001
phone: 715-445-2214
fax: 715-445-4087
e-mail: info@krause.com
Internet: http://www.krause.com
Bi-monthly lists current values in five grading categories for all American cars made from 1901-1989.

Deals on Wheels Publications
Magazine: Deals on Wheels
P.O. Box 205
Sioux Falls, SD 57101
phone: 605-338-7666 or 800-334-1886
fax: 605-338-5337
Internet: http://www.dealsonwheels.com
A comprehensive monthly listing with photo ads of cars for sale nationwide; also classified and display ads for the car enthusiast.

Deals on Wheels Publications
Magazine: Specialty Car Marketplace
P.O. Box 205
Sioux Falls, SD 57101
phone: 605-338-7666 or 800-334-1886
fax: 605-338-5337
Internet: http://www.dealsonwheels.com
Photo-ad magazine listing cars and trucks for sale.

Magazine: Special Car Journal
1730 Christopher Dr.
Deerfield, IL 60015
phone: 847-808-7620
fax: 847-808-7640
e-mail: editor@SpecialCar.com
Internet: http://www.specialcar.com

Magazine: Collectible Automobile
3841 W. Oakton St.
Skokie, IL 60076
phone: 312-676-3470

Magazine: Skinned Knuckles
175 May Ave.
Monrovia, CA 91016
The hobby's premier monthly auto restoration magazine.

Paisano Publications
Magazine: American Rodder
28210 Dorothy Dr.
Agoura Hills, CA 91301
phone: 818-889-8740
Focuses on latest trends and techniques in the field of street rodding.

Steve Ferguson, Ed.
National Automobile Dealers Association
Price Guide: N.A.D.A. Official Used Car Guide
P.O. Box 7800
Costa Mesa, CA 92628
phone: 800-966-6232
fax: 714-556-8715
e-mail: steve.ferguson@nadaguides.com
Internet: http://www.nadaguide.com
A series of value guides for domestic and foreign cars, trucks, vans, RV's, mobile homes, motorcycles, snowmobiles, and boats, small and large; also Heavy Duty Trucks and Aircraft Book, car clubs & organizations, museums.

Repair Services

Antique Vehicle Maintenance
57 Cannonball Rd.
Pompton Lakes, NJ 07442
phone: 201-616-6300

Martin Lum
Older Car Restoration
304 S. Main St.
P.O. Box 428
Mont Alto, PA 17237
phone: 717-749-3383 or 717-352-7701
fax: 717-749-3383
Manufactures and sells reproduction parts for antique cars; also chrome plating.

Realistic Auto Restorations, Inc.
2519 6th Ave. S.
Saint Petersburg, FL 33712-1640
phone: 813-327-5162 or 813-327-1877
Offers restoration services for antiques, classics, street rods, Corvettes and all sports cars; paint & body, upholstery, mechanics, woodwork, welding, wiring, stainless steel repair.

David Ten Brink
Beckley Auto Restoration Inc.
4405 S.W. Capital Ave.
Battle Creek, MI 49015
phone: 616-979-3013
fax: 616-979-1261
Offers complete classic and antique car restoration.

Dave Lewis
Dave Lewis Restorations
3825 South Second St.
Springfield, IL 62703
phone: 217-529-5290
Partial or complete show quality restorations; over 20 years experience.

Alfa Romeo

Clubs/Associations

Vintage Alfa Romeo International
900 North College
Fort Collins, CO 80521

Glenna Garret, Ex. Sec.
Alfa Romeo Owners Club
2468 Gum Tree Lane
Fallbrook, CA 92028
phone: 619-728-4875
fax: 619-723-2345

AMC

Clubs/Associations

AMC World Clubs
7963 Depew St.
Arvada, CO 80003-2527
phone: 303-428-8760

Darryl A. Salisbury, Pres.
American Motors Owners Association
Newsletter: American Motoring
6756 Cornell St.
Portage, MI c
phone: 619-323-0369
fax: 619-387-4806
e-mail: salisbury@wmich.edu
Internet: http://www.science/
  uwaterloo.co/~afleming/amo/
  amo.html
Founded in 1974 for AMC enthusiasts to distribute information pertaining to AMC cars and hobby; international convention and several regional meets around the world; for all AMC-built products from 1958 through 1988.

AMC Rambler

Clubs/Associations

Frank Wrenick
AMC Rambler Club
2645 Ashton Rd.
Cleveland, OH 44118
phone: 216-371-5946
Internet: http://www.classicar.com/
  rambler/rambler.htm

Aston Martin

Clubs/Associations

Aston Martin Owners Club, East
1A Hight Street
Sutton, Nr Ely
Cambridgeshire CB6 2RB, U.K.
phone: 01353-777353
fax: 01353-777648
e-mail: hgstaff@amoc.org
Internet: http://www.amoc.org/
  contracts.html

Auburn-Cord-Duesenberg

Clubs/Associations

Matt Bogart, Mem.
Auburn-Cord-Duesenberg Club
P.O. Box 18
Ringoes, NJ 08851
phone: 908-782-2806

Austin-Healey

Clubs/Associations

Edie Anderson
Austin-Healey Club of America, Inc.,
  The
Magazine: Chatter
603 East Euclid Ave.
Arlington Heights, IL 60004-5707
phone: 847-255-4069
fax: 847-590-5707
Internet: http://www.serve.com/AHCA/
For owners or those interested in Austin-Healey, Austin-Healey Sprite and other Healey marques; mission is to preserve the Austin-Healey and to maintain the highest standards by sharing technical and mechanical information.

Carroll Goldsworth
Austin-Healey Association
Newsletter: Healey Motor News
P.O. Box 28373
Santa Ana, CA 92799-8373
Dedicated to the enjoyment of a fine automobile.

Austin-Healey Club USA
Magazine: Austin-Healey Magazine
P.O. Box 6197
San Jose, CA 95150
phone: 888-4AHCUSA
fax: 510-484-2764
Internet: http://www.healey.org/
Established in 1970; members interested in the history, maintenance, restoration and enjoyment of all Austin-Healeys; ownership of an

Austin-Healey not required for membership.

Avanti

Clubs/Associations

Total Performance Avanti Club
1511 19th Ave.
West Bradenton, FL 34205

Avanti Owners Association International
P.O. Box 28788
Dallas, TX 75228-0788
phone: 972-709-6185
fax: 972-296-7920
e-mail: t44163@Rutadmin.rutgers.edu
Internet: http://www.classicar.com/
  clubs/aoai/aoaihome.htm

Bentley

Clubs/Associations

Bentley Drivers Club
16 Chearsley Rd.
Long Crendon, Aylesbury
Bucks HP18 9AW, U.K.
phone: 01844-208233
fax: 01844-208923

Bentley Drivers Club
2139 Torrey Pines Rd.
La Jolla, CA 92037

BMW

Clubs/Associations

Membership
BMW Car Club of America
2130 Mass. Ave.
Cambridge, MA 02140-9850
phone: 617-492-2500 or 800-878-9292
fax: 617-876-3424
e-mail: 102514.2477@compuserve.com
Internet: http://www.bmvcca.org/

BMW Automobile Club of America
P.O. Box 401
Los Angeles, CA 90078

BMW Vintage Club of America
P.O. Box S
San Rafael, CA 94913
phone: 415-897-0220
fax: 415-898-0831
For owners of 1929 through 1965 BMW automobiles.

British

Misc. Services

Karen Miller, Archivist
Jaguar Cars Inc.
555 MacArthur Blvd.
Mahwah, NJ 07430-2326
phone: 201-818-8144 or 914-221-0293
fax: 201-818-0281
A corporate archives offering individual vehicle research from original Jaguar Cars Ltd. build records; verify authenticity of Jaguar and Daimler (from 1960) automobiles.

Repair Services

Ed Miller
Reward Service, Inc.
172 Overhill Rd.
Stormville, NY 12582-5415
phone: 914-227-7647
fax: 914-221-0293
Appraisals, repair & restoration of classic British automobiles by an expert with more than 25 years experience in the field; own research library; family owned and operated, member International Society of Appraisers.

Bugatti

Clubs/Associations

American Bugatti Club
4484 Howe Hill Rd.
Camden, ME 04843
phone: 207-236-8288
fax: 207-236-0869

Collectors

Stanley King
260 Fifth Ave.
New York, NY 10001-6408
phone: 212-447-1880
fax: 212-447-0728
Wants to buy anything relating to the Bugatti automobile: car models, posters, auto parts, literature and sales brochures, etc.

Buick

Clubs/Associations

Val Ingram
Buick Club of America
Magazine: Bugle
P.O. Box 401927
Hesperia, CA 92340-1927
phone: 619-947-2485
fax: 619-947-2485
Internet: http://www.buickclub.org/
Over 10,000 members; "Bugle" published monthly; members share an interest in the cars made by the Buick Motor Division, their restoration, and preservation.

Cadillac

Clubs/Associations

Cadillac Convertible Owners of America
P.O. Box 269
Ossining, NY 10562

Jay Ann Edwards, Mem. Sec.
Cadillac-LaSalle Club, Inc.
Magazine: Self-Starter, The
P.O. Box 1916
Lenoir, NC 28645-1916
phone: 704-754-8146
fax: 704-754-8146
e-mail: CadLaSal@aol.com
Worldwide organization with 5000+ members; technical service, monthly magazine, annual issue, directory, and annual meet held in various parts of the U.S.

Wray Tibbs
Cadillac Drivers Club
Newsletter: Leland Letters, The
5825 Vista Ave.
Sacramento, CA 95824
phone: 916-421-3193
Keep your Cadillac on the road forever!

Checker

Clubs/Associations

Roy Dickinson, Ed.
Checker Car Club of America
Newsletter: CCCA Newsletter
10350 W. Alabama Ave.
Sun City, AZ 85351-3544
phone: 602-974-4987
fax: 602-974-4987
Internet: http://www.classicar.com/
  checker/checher.htm
For the preservation and enjoyment of Checker automobiles from 1922-1982.

Chevrolet

Clubs/Associations

Garnett Rogers
National Association of Chevrolet Owners
Newsletter: Chevy Capers
P.O. Box 9879
Bowling Green, KY 42102
phone: 502-737-6022 or 800-801-7329
e-mail: ccabg@ekx.infi.net

Classic Chevy Club International
P.O. Box 607188
Orlando, FL 32860
phone: 407-880-1505 or 800-456-1957
fax: 407-299-3341
108 chapters; and '55 to '57 Chevrolet, including Corvette and pickup.

National Chevy Association
Newsletter: Partsline
947 Arcade
Saint Paul, MN 55106-3850
phone: 612-778-9522
fax: 612-778-9686
'54-'54 Chevrolet specialists.

Dennis Fink
Vintage Chevrolet Club of America
P.O. Box 5387
Orange, CA 92613-5387
phone: 714-633-1310
Internet: http://www.classicar.com/
  clubs/vcclub/cccaclub.htm

Periodicals

Magazine: Corvette & Chevy Trader
P.O. Box 9059
Clearwater, FL 34618-9059
phone: 813-712-0035 or 800-548-8889
fax: 813-712-0034
Internet: http://www.traderonline.com

Chevrolet Camaro

Clubs/Associations

Bob Clifford
International Camaro Club, Inc.
Magazine: In The Fast Lane
2001 Pittson Ave.
Scranton, PA 18505-3233
phone: 717-585-4082
Club for all Camaro owners, from the 1967 Classic Collectibles to the present; bi-monthly magazine has technical tips, trim tag ID, classifieds; newsletter is an award winning publication for all Camaro fans!

U.S. Camaro Club
P.O. Box 608167
Orlando, FL 32860
phone: 407-880-1967 or 800-CAMAROS
fax: 407-880-1972

Repair Services

Camaro Specialties
112 Elm St.
East Aurora, NY 14052
phone: 716-652-7086
fax: 716-652-2279
Parts and restorations for '66-'72 FM muscle cars; Camaro and Firebird specialists.

Chevrolet Chevelle

Clubs/Associations

Mark Meekins
National Chevelle Owners Association
Newsletter: Chevelle Report, The
7343-J West Friendly Ave.
Greensboro, NC 27410
phone: 910-854-8935
Focus on interest is on 1964-1987 Chevelle and El Camino; monthly color magazine featuring members' cars, tech tips, factory photos, production information, parts sources, classified ads, chapter club news; over 6,000 members.

Chevrolet Corvair

Clubs/Associations

Harry Jensen
Corvair Society of America
P.O. Box 607
Lemont, IL 60439-0607
phone: 708-257-6530
fax: 708-257-5540

Chevrolet Corvette

Clubs/Associations

Mary Showalter
National Corvette Owners Association
Newsletter: For Vettes Only
900 So. Washington St., Ste. G-13
Falls Church, VA 22046-4020
phone: 703-533-7222
fax: 703-533-1153
Dedicated to the concept of uniting all Corvette enthusiasts with a common goal, i.e. that of encouraging and increasing the Corvette enjoyment among all members.

Garnett Rogers
Corvette Club of America
Newsletter: Corvette Capers
P.O. Box 9879
Bowling Green, KY 42102
phone: 502-737-6022 or 800-801-7329
e-mail: ccabg@ekx.infi.net

Gary Mortimer
National Corvette Restorers Society
6291 Day Road
Cincinnati, OH 45252-1334
phone: 513-395-8526
fax: 513-385-8554
Internet: http://www.ncrs.org
For people interested in 1953 through 1982 Corvettes; 32 chapters.

Nancy Sable
National Council of Corvette Clubs, Inc.
P.O. Box 5032
Lafayette, IN 47903-5032
phone: 800-245-VETT or 716-637-4029
fax: 716-637-2211
Internet: http://www.classicar.com/
  clubs/NCCCBLUE/
  NCCCBLUE.HTM
Founded in 1960; non-profit, all volunteer national organization of more that 280 member clubs that sponsor more than 1000 competitive events each year; Concours, wheel-to-wheel drags, autocrosses, rallies, economy runs.

Western States Corvette Council
2321 Falling Water Court
Santa Clara, CA 95054

Periodicals

Dobbs Publishing Group
Magazine: Corvette Fever
3816 Industry Blvd.
Lakeland, FL 33811
phone: 941-644-0449 or 815-734-6026
e-mail: dobbs@gate.net
Internet: http://www.d-p-g.com/
For enthusiasts who take the love of their automobile seriously; do-it-yourself technical articles, beautiful color features, advice from top Corvette industry experts, interesting news and events listings.

Dobbs Publishing Group
Magazine: Corvette Marketplace
3816 Industry Blvd.
Lakeland, FL 33811
phone: 941-644-0449 or 815-734-6026
e-mail: dobbs@gate.net
Internet: http://www.d-p-g.com/
A Corvette classified magazine that provides the opportunity to sell Corvettes and Corvette parts, services and literature on both the Internet and newsstands across the U.S.

Magazine: Corvette & Chevy Trader
P.O. Box 9059
Clearwater, FL 34618-9059
phone: 813-712-0035 or 800-548-8889
fax: 813-712-0034
Internet: http://www.traderonline.com

Chevrolet Impala

Clubs/Associations

Dennis Naasz
National Impala Association
Magazine: National Impala Association Magazine
P.O. Box 968
Spearfish, SD 57783-0968
phone: 605-642-5864
fax: 605-642-5868
Dedicated to the preservation of all full-size Chevrolets from 1958 through 1969; bi-monthly magazine.

Chevrolet Monte Carlo

Clubs/Associations

National Monte Carlo Owners Association
P.O. Box 187
Independence, KY 41051
phone: 606-491-2378

Chevrolet Nova

Clubs/Associations

National Nostalgic Nova
P.O. Box 2344
York, PA 17405
phone: 717-252-4192
fax: 717-252-1666

Chrysler

Clubs/Associations

Ray Montgomery
Chrysler Products Owners Club, Inc.
806 Winhall Way
Silver Spring, MD 20904
phone: 301-622-2962

Wendy McKenney
National Hemi Owners Association
P.O. Box 171
Reese, MI 48757-9574
phone: 517-868-4921
For enthusiasts of hemi-engined Chrysler products.

Richard Bowman
Walter P. Chrysler Club, Inc.
Newsletter: W.P.C. News
P.O. Box 3504
Kalamazoo, MI 49003-3504
phone: 616-375-5535
fax: 616-375-5535
Internet: http://www.pacificcoast.net/
  ~viwpc/
Dedicated to the preservation, restoration, enjoyment of Chrysler products: Plymouth, Dodge, DeSoto, Chrysler, Imperial, Jeep, Eagle, and related vehicles including antecedents Maxwell and Chalmers Motor Cars.

Eleanor Riehl
Chrysler 300 Club International, Inc.
Magazine: Club News
4900 Jonesville Rd.
Jonesville, MI 49250-9439
phone: 517-849-2783
fax: 517-849-7445
e-mail: mayerd@hartwick.edu
Internet: http://www.classicar.com/
clubs/chrysler/300club.htm
*Of particular interest to owners of
Chrysler 300 letter series automobiles.*

Periodicals

Dobbs Publishing Group
Magazine: Mopar Muscle
3816 Industry Blvd.
Lakeland, FL 33811
phone: 941-644-0449 or 815-734-6026
e-mail: dobbs@gate.net
Internet: http://www.d-p-g.com/
*Covers all aspects of interest to
Chrysler-oriented performance car
enthusiasts; articles ranging from
concours-restored cars to all-out Pro
Street modifieds to street rods, drag
cars, even Chrysler-powered race
boats!*

Citroen

Clubs/Associations

Citroen Car Club
8180 Miramar Rd.
San Diego, CA 92126
phone: 619-566-2860
fax: 619-566-2432

Periodicals

Michael Cox, Ed.
Magazine: Citroen Quarterly
P.O. Box 30
Boston, MA 02113-0001
phone: 617-742-6604
e-mail: citq@aol.com
*The "Citroen Quarterly" contains
technical information, Citroen history
and events; also publishes "Citroen
Quarterly Archives"; sponsors and
organizes the "Citroen Quarterly"
Rendezvous on Fathers Day weekend
in Northfield, MA.*

Datsun Roadster

Clubs/Associations

Datsun Roadster Association
P.O. Box 60997
Pasadena, CA 91116
phone: 619-591-9818 or 909-391-3083

Datsun/Nissan Z Cars

Clubs/Associations

Datsun "Z" Club, Inc.
P.O. Box 24-176
Royal Oak
Auckland 1030 New Zealand, GA
phone: 64-9-636-5443
fax: 64-9-636-5443

DeLorean

Clubs/Associations

John Truscott, Mem.
DeLorean Owners' Association
Magazine: DeLorean World
879 Randolph Rd.
Santa Barbara, CA 93111-1030
phone: 805-964-5296
e-mail: delorean@impulse.net
Internet: http://www.delorean-
owners.org

DeSoto

Clubs/Associations

Steve Thursby, Sec.
National DeSoto Club, Inc.
Magazine: DeSoto Adventures
4873 Summerford Dr.
Atlanta, GA 30338
e-mail: desoto@flash.net
Internet: http://www.desoto.org/
join.html
*Purpose of the club is to promote the
restoration, preservation and
enjoyment of the DeSoto automobile;
non-profit corporation with
international membership.*

Walter O'Kelly
DeSoto Club of America
105 East 96th
Kansas City, MO 64114
phone: 816-421-6006
*Get information about DeSotos,
restoration and locating parts.*

Dodge

Clubs/Associations

Shelby Dodge Automobile Club
755 East 500 South
Bountiful, UT 84010
phone: 801-292-9374
*Committed to preserving the history of
Shelby-built and inspired Dodge-
powered automobiles.*

Edsel

Clubs/Associations

Judy Zegers
International Edsel Club
P.O. Box 371
Sully, IA 50251-0371
phone: 515-594-4284

Edsel Owners Club, Inc.
4713 Queal Dr.
Shawnee Mission, KS 66203

Edsel Owners Club, Inc.
4713 Queal Dr.
Shawnee Mission, KS 66203

Collectors

Judy Zegers
P.O. Box 371
Sully, IA 50251-0371
phone: 515-594-4284

Electric

Clubs/Associations

Frank Didik
Electric Car Owners Club
167 Concord St.
Brooklyn, NY 11201
phone: 718-797-4311
fax: 718-596-4852
e-mail: adc@dorsai.org

Electric Automobile Association
Newsletter: Current Events
2710 Snt. Giles Lane
Mountain View, CA 94040
phone: 800-537-2882 or 510-685-7580
Internet: http://www.calweb.com/
~tonyc/eaa/locations.html

Ferrari

Clubs/Associations

Ferrari Club of America, Inc.
3186 Alton Rd.
Atlanta, GA 30341
phone: 800-328-0444

Ferrari Owners Club
1708 Seabright Ave.
Long Beach, CA 90813
phone: 213-432-9607
fax: \

Fiat

Clubs/Associations

Santo Bimbo
Fiat Club of America, Inc.
11 Linden Circle
Somerville, MA 02143-0192
phone: 617-776-8576

Ford

Clubs/Associations

Barbara Lemaster
Performance Ford Club of America, Inc.
Magazine: Ford Enthusiast Magazine,
The
13155 U.S. Route 23
Ashville, OH 43103
phone: 614-983-2273
fax: 614-983-9691
*For all Ford-powered vehicle
enthusiasts; hosts car shows, swap
meets, and cruise-ins; magazine
published bi-monthly.*

Toby & Sandy Gorny
Crown Victoria Association
Newsletter: FoMoCo Times
P.O. Box 6
Bryan, OH 43506
phone: 419-636-2475
fax: 419-636-8449
*For owners of all 1954 through 1956
Fords.*

Mike McCarville
'49,50,51 Ford-Mercury Association
P.O. Box 30647
Oklahoma City, OK 73140-3647
phone: 405-737-6021

Dan Wittern
Early Ford V-8 Club of America
Newsletter: V-8 Times
P.O. Box 2122
San Leandro, CA 94577
phone: 619-283-8117
*For 1932 through 1953 V-8 FOrd,
Mercury, Lincoln owners.*

Museums/Libraries

Towe Ford Museum
2200 Front St.
Sacramento, CA 95818
phone: 916-442-6802
fax: 916-442-2646
*The world's most complete antique
Ford museum.*

Periodicals

Dobbs Publishing Group
Magazine: Ford Marketplace
3816 Industry Blvd.
Lakeland, FL 33811
phone: 941-644-0449 or 815-734-6026
e-mail: dobbs@gate.net
Internet: http://www.d-p-g.com/
*Buy and sell Ford cars, parts, and
services.*

Dobbs Publishing Group
Magazine: Super Ford Magazine
3816 Industry Blvd.
Lakeland, FL 33811
phone: 941-644-0449 or 815-734-6026
e-mail: dobbs@gate.net
Internet: http://www.d-p-g.com/
The only monthly all-Ford magazine.

Magazine: Ford & Mustang Trader
P.O. Box 9059
Clearwater, FL 34618-9059
phone: 813-712-0035 or 800-548-8889
fax: 813-712-0034
Internet: http://www.traderonline.com

Ford Econoline

Clubs/Associations

Jay Long
Econo Club
15039 Costela St.
San Leandro, CA 94579-1524
*For owners of 1961-1967 Econoline
and Falcon vans and pickups.*

Ford Escort

Clubs/Associations

Marc Rossi
Ford Escort Club
107 S West Street #278
Alexandria, VA 22314-2891
e-mail: 76427.1127@compuserve.com

Ford Fairlane

Clubs/Associations

Mike Mieth
Fairlane Club of America
Magazine: Fairlaner, The
2116 Manville Rd.
Muncie, IN 47302-4854
phone: 765-282-4308
Internet: http://www.classiccar.com/
clubs/fairlane/fairlane.htm
*For owners of '62 through '75
Fairlanes and Torinos; impressive
colorful "Fairlaner" published six
times per year: restoration tips, how-
to's, ads, color photos.*

Ford Falcon

Clubs/Associations

Jim Throgmorton
Falcon Club of America
Newsletter: Falcon, The
P.O. Box 113
Jacksonville, AR 72078-0113
phone: 501-982-9721
Internet: http://www.falconclub.com/
*For owners of 1960 through 1970 1/2
Falcons.*

Ford Galaxie

Clubs/Associations

Mike Reynolds
Ford Galaxie Club of America
Newsletter: Galaxie Gazette
883 South Basin Rd.
Colville, WA 99114-9577
phone: 509-684-8132
Internet: http://www.galaxieclub.com/
*For owners of 1959 through 1975
Ford Galaxies.*

Ford Model A

Clubs/Associations

Model "A" Restorers Club
Magazine: Model "A" News, The
24800 Michigan Ave.
Dearborn, MI 48124-1713
phone: 313-278-1455
fax: 313-278-2624
*To encourage members to acquire,
preserve, restore, exhibit and make
use of Model A Fords (1928-1931);
many regional chapters; articles,
event reviews, lots of ads for parts,
supplies, and services.*

Jerry Wilhelm
Model A Ford Club of America
Magazine: Restorer, The
250 S. Cypress
La Habra, CA 90631-5515
phone: 310-697-2712 or 310-697-2737
fax: 310-690-7452
Internet: http://www.mafca.com
*Over 15,000 members; dedicated to
the restoration and preservation of the
1928-1931 Model A Ford.*

Ford Model T

Clubs/Associations

Howard Gustavson
Model T Ford Club International
Magazine: Model-T Times
P.O. Box 438315
Chicago, IL 60643-8315
phone: 773-233-2989
e-mail:
HGPiewagon@mcs.comustav@aol.com
Internet: http://www.xnet.com/~karens/
modelt.html
*Dedicated to the preservation and
enjoyment of the 1909 to 1927 Model
T Ford automobile.*

Barbara Klehfoth
Model T Ford Club of America
Magazine: Vintage Ford
P.O. Box 743936
Dallas, TX 75374-3936
phone: 972-783-7531
e-mail: gus@airmail.net
Internet: http://www.MTFCA.com

Ford Mustang

Clubs/Associations

Mustang Club of America, Inc.
Magazine: Mustang Times
3588 Highway 138, Ste. 365
Stockbridge, GA 30281
phone: 770-477-1965
fax: 770-477-1965
e-mail: mustang@mustang.org
Internet: http://www.mustang.org/
*An association for the Ford Mustang
and Shelby collector, restorer and
enthusiast.*

Paul McLaughlin
Mustang Owners Club International
Newsletter: Pony Express
2720 Tennessee N.E.
Albuquerque, NM 87110
phone: 505-296-2554
Internet: http://classicar.com/clubs/
mustang/mustang.htm
For all Mustang enthusiasts.

Vintage Mustang Owners Association
P.O. Box 5772
San Jose, CA 95150-5772
e-mail: webmaster@vntg-mustang.com
Internet: http://www.vntg-mustang.com/
*Members interested in 1964 o 1977
Ford Mustangs.*

Museums/Libraries

Mustang Museum
432 Lakeshore St.
Jasper, GA 30143
Internet: http://www.mustang.org/
museum.html

Periodicals

Dobbs Publishing Group
Magazine: Mustang Monthly
3816 Industry Blvd.
Lakeland, FL 33811
phone: 941-644-0449 or 815-734-6026
e-mail: dobbs@gate.net
Internet: http://www.d-p-g.com/
*Dedicated to the entire scope of
Mustang production: repair,
restoration, how-to's, performance
modifications, etc.*

Magazine: Ford & Mustang Trader
P.O. Box 9059
Clearwater, FL 34618-9059
phone: 813-712-0035 or 800-548-8889
fax: 813-712-0034
Internet: http://www.traderonline.com

Repair Services

Joe Palmere
Garden State Mustang
160 Horseneck Rd.
Fairfield, NJ 07004-2328
phone: 201-227-0364
fax: 201-227-0282
*Specializes in restoration and general
service/repairs of Ford Mustangs and
Mustang II's; also supply parts: new,
used, repro, and NOS for same.*

Ford Ranchero

Clubs/Associations

Gene Makrancy
Ranchero Club
Newsletter: Ranchero Courier
1339 Beverly Rd.
Port Vue, PA 15133
e-mail: Ranchero@gnn.com
*For all Ranchero and Courier
enthusiasts.*

Ford Thunderbird

Clubs/Associations

Kenneth Leaman
International Thunderbird Club
Magazine: Script
8 Stag Trail
Fairfield, NJ 07004
e-mail: rlsdc@csrling.net
Internet: http://www.tbird.org/itc/
*For those interested in all
Thunderbirds from 1955 to present.*

Robert J. Gadra, Pres.
Vintage Thunderbird Club International
Magazine: Thunderbird Scoop
P.O. Box 2250
Dearborn, MI 48123-2250
phone: 716-674-7251
e-mail: alantast@radkis.net
Internet: http://www.classicar.com/
clubs.vintbird/vintbird.htm
*Focuses on vintage Thunderbirds,
1958 to present.*

John Draxler
Thunderbirds of America
P.O. Box 2766
Cedar Rapids, IA 52406
phone: 712-884-6546

Don Kimrey
Heartland Vintage Thunderbird Club of
America
P.O. Box 18113
Kansas City, MO 64133
Internet: http://www.classicar.com/
clubs/hvtcoa/hvtchome.htm
*For owners of 1958 to 1969
Thunderbirds.*

Marjorie Price
Classic Thunderbird Club International
Newsletter: Early Bird
P.O. Box 4148
Santa Fe Springs, CA 90670-1148
phone: 562-945-6836
Internet: http://www.tbird.org/ctci/
*For owners and enthusiasts of 1955
through 1957 T-Birds; 110 local
chapters.*

Hupmobile

Clubs/Associations

Steve Christie
Hupmobile Club
158 Pond Rd.
North Franklin, CT 06254
phone: 860-642-6997

Collectors

L. Robert Hurwitz
P.O. Box 243
Syracuse, NY 13215-0243
phone: 315-468-4281
*Wants to buy 1909-1941 Hupmobile
related items, literature, dealer
giveaways and related collectibles
such as factory badges, stickpins,
fobs, lapel pins, signs, postcards,
trohpies, toys, banners, signs, clocks,
etc.*

Italian

Clubs/Associations

John DeBoer
Italian Car Registry
3305 Valley Vista Rd.
Walnut Creek, CA 94598-3943
phone: 510-458-1163
*Research association devoted to the
study of the Italian automobile
industry; directory includes
information on more than 15,000
limited production automobiles; SASE
for details.*

Jaguar

Clubs/Associations

Jerry Parkhill, Membr.
Jaguar Clubs of North America
9685 McLeod Rd., RR #2
Chilliwack
Brit. Col. V2P 6H4 Canada
phone: 604-794-3652
fax: 604-794-3654
International organization of Jaguar enthusiasts; over 5000 members; sponsors car shows, Concours D'Elegance, rallies and slaloms.

Jack Ribill
Classic Jaguar Association
2860 West Victoria Dr.
Alpine, CA 91901
phone: 619-445-3152

Experts

Karen Miller, Archivist
Jaguar Cars Inc.
555 MacArthur Blvd.
Mahwah, NJ 07430-2326
phone: 201-818-8144 or 914-221-0293
fax: 201-818-0281
Research service; maintains facility housing an extensive photographic collection, technical library, service & parts bulletins, technical bulletins, owner, parts and service manuals, advertising, and paint & upholstery information.

Jeep

Clubs/Associations

Willys/Kaiser/AMC Jeep Club
1511 19th Ave. West
Bradenton, FL 34205
For 1946 through 1987 Jeeps.

Periodicals

Dobbs Publishing Group
Magazine: Jp Magazine
3816 Industry Blvd.
Lakeland, FL 33811
phone: 941-644-0449 or 815-734-6026
e-mail: dobbs@gate.net
Internet: http://www.d-p-g.com/
The only all-Jeep periodical about Jeeps and the Jeep lifestyle (no Broncos, Samurais, Explorers, Hummers, Blazers, Scouts, just Jeeps); bi-monthly covering from the first military models to the current TJ Wranglers, Cherokees, etc.

Kit Built

Clubs/Associations

Vintage Kit & Custom Club
RR 1, Box 185
Jacksonville, IL 62650

Lamborghini

Clubs/Associations

Jim Kaminski
Lamborghini Owners Club
Newsletter: LOC Newsletter
P.O. Box 7214
Saint Petersburg, FL 33734
Organized in 1978; members in 15 countries; tech tips, services sources, parts information, collectibles, and meeting information.

Lincoln

Clubs/Associations

Jim Griffin
Lincoln Owners Club
22 Spring St.
Cary, IL 60013
phone: 715-356-3039

Becky D'Ambrosia
Lincoln & Continental Owners' Club
Newsletter: Continental Comments
P.O. Box 157
Boring, OR 97009
phone: 503-658-3119
fax: 503-658-6119
Dedicated to the preservation and restoration of all Lincolns, Lincoln Continentals and Continentals; ownership of a car is not required for membership.

Becky & Steve D'Ambrosia
Lincoln & Continental Owners Club
Magazine: Continental Comments
P.O. Box 157
Boring, OR 97009-0157
phone: 503-658-3119
fax: 503-658-6119
International club dedicated to the preservation and restoration of all Lincolns, Lincoln Continentals, and Continentals; three national meets every year; magazine published 7 times per year.

Locomobile

Clubs/Associations

Norm Buckhart
Locomobile Society of America
3165 California St.
San Francisco, CA 94115-2412
phone: 415-563-1771

Lotus

Clubs/Associations

Mark Winston
Lotus, Ltd.
P.O. Box L
College Park, MD 20741-3010
phone: 301-982-4054
fax: 301-982-4054

Maserati

Clubs/Associations

Harvey Goldberg
Maserati Club of America
Newsletter: Il Tridente
945 Middle Country Rd.
Selden, NY 11784
phone: 516-736-1200
fax: 516-736-1200
A nationwide, non-profit member-run club for Maserati enthusiasts; holds major events from Maine to Florida.

Maserati Owners Club of North America
14220 Saddlebow Ct.
Reno, NV 89511

Maserati Club International
P.O. Box 772
Mercer Island, WA 98040
phone: 206-455-4707 or 206-455-4449
fax: 206-646-5458
Internet: http://maserati.worldwide.net

Mazda

Clubs/Associations

Mazda Club
P.O. Box 11238
Chicago, IL 60611
phone: 312-769-6262
fax: 312-769-6262
e-mail: tnwb52A@prodigy.com
Internet: http://pages.prodigy.com/IL/franko/mazdaclub.html

Mercedez-Benz

Clubs/Associations

Ron Farrar
Mercedez-Benz Club of America
Magazine: Star, The
1907 Leleray St.
Colorado Springs, CO 80909
phone: 800-637-2360 or 716-633-6427
fax: 716-633-9283
Internet: http://www.mbca.org/

Mercury

Clubs/Associations

Jerry Robbin
International Mercury Owners Association
Newsletter: Quicksilver
6445 West Grand Ave.
Chicago, IL 60635-3410
phone: 773-622-6445 or 773-622-3602
Internet: http://www.classicar.com/clubs/INTMERC/INTMERC.HTM
Open to all Mercury owners (regardless of year or make) and Mercury enthusiasts alike; over 700 members.

Mike McCarville
'49,50,51 Ford-Mercury Association
P.O. Box 30647
Oklahoma City, OK 73140-3647
phone: 405-737-6021

Mercury Comet

Clubs/Associations

Comet Enthusiasts Group
5878 Hobe Lane
Saint Paul, MN 55110

Mercury Cougar

Clubs/Associations

John W. Baumann
Cougar Club of America
Magazine: At the Sign of the Cat
0-4211 North 120th Ave.
Holland, MI 49424
phone: 616-396-0390
fax: 616-396-0366
Dedicated to the preservation of 1967 through 1973 Mercury Cougars.

MG

Clubs/Associations

MG Car Club Ltd., The
P.O. Box 251
Abingdon
Oxfordshire OX14 1FF, U.K.
phone: 01235-555552
fax: 01235-533755
e-mail: carclub@mgcars.org.uk
Internet: http://www.mgcars.org.uk/mgcc/
U.S. chapters and clubs.

Sarah Owen
MG Owners Club, The
Magazine: Enjoying MG
Octagon House
Swavesey
Cambridge CB4 SQ2, U.K.
phone: 0044 1954 231125
fax: 0044 1954 232106
e-mail: mginfo@mgownersclub.com.uk
Internet: http://www.mgownersclub.com.uk
Largest single marque car club in the world offering advice, spares, events, camaraderie, accessories, insurance, rallies: everything for the MG owner.

Lou Merchant
MG Car Club of America
137 Keller-Smithfield North
Keller, TX 76248-3717
phone: 817-431-9322

MG A Series

Clubs/Associations

Jonathan A. Stein
A Coupe Group
7450 Valley View Lane
Reading, PA 19606
phone: 610-779-9710
fax: 610-779-9710
An informal registry for MGA coupes, offering free information and assistance.

MG B Series

Clubs/Associations

Harold W. Roeth
North American MGB Register
2 County Route 2
Berne, NY 12023-4211
phone: 800-626-4271
e-mail: hroldlbt@ix.netcom.com
Internet: http://mermbers.aol.com/
namgarusa/mg.htm

Frank Ochal
American MGB Association
P.O. Box 11401
Chicago, IL 60611-0401
phone: 800-723-MGMG or 773-878-
5055
fax: 773-769-3240
e-mail: amgba@aol.com
Internet: http://www.british-cars.org.uk/

Miniature

Clubs/Associations

Microcar & Minicar Club
Magazine: Minutia
P.O. Box 43137
Montclair, NJ 07043
*For the preservation and restoration
of small cars usually under 1,000cc;
foreign and domestic; national and
regional meets.*

Marc Delmont
MicroCar Club
6675 South Sherman St.
Littleton, CO 80121
phone: 303-798-8589

Muscle Cars

Periodicals

Dobbs Publishing Group
Magazine: Muscle Car Review
3816 Industry Blvd.
Lakeland, FL 33811
phone: 941-644-0449 or 815-734-6026
e-mail: dobbs@gate.net
Internet: http://www.d-p-g.com/
*Bi-monthly magazine dedicated to the
American muscle car.*

Nash

Clubs/Associations

Nash Car Club of America
1-N-274 Prarie
Glen Ellyn, IL 60137

Collectors

Bob Walker
2428 Level Ave.
Anaheim, CA 92804
phone: 714-821-4507
*Wants Nash automobiles and Nash
1902-1957 memorabilia: dealer signs,
desk accessories, giveaways,
promotional items, keychains, dealer
films, sales literature.*

Oldsmobile

Clubs/Associations

Charles Degges
National Antique Oldsmobile Club
Magazine: Runabouts to Rockets
11730 Moffitt Lane
Manassas, VA 22111-3312
phone: 800-565-OLDS
1897 through 1965 Oldsmobiles only.

Penny Casteele
Oldsmobile Club of America, Inc.
Newsletter: Journey With Olds
P.O. Box 80318
Lansing, MI 48908-0318
phone: 517-321-8825
fax: 517-321-8770
*For owners and enthusiasts of all
Oldsmobile products.*

Opel

Clubs/Associations

Opel Association of North America
P.O. Box 9638
Richmond, VA 23228
phone: 804-262-3511
Internet: http://www.opel-na.com/

Opel Motorsport Club
5161 Gelding Circle
Huntington Beach, CA 92649

Opel Drivers Club of America
P.O. Box 385
Pebble Beach, CA 93953

Packard

Clubs/Associations

Packard Automobile Classics, Inc.
Magazine: Cormorant News Bulletin
P.O. Box 28788
Dallas, TX 75228-0788
phone: 972-709-6185 or 800-527-3452
fax: 972-296-7920
Internet: http://www.ptd.net/~athene/
*Worldwide club for fans of the
Packard automobile; monthly
newsletter and quarterly magazine;
national meet for all members.*

Carol Mauck
Packards International
Magazine: Packards International
Magazine
302 French St.
Santa Ana, CA 92701-4845
phone: 714-541-8431
Internet: http://www.classicar.com/
clubs/PACKINTL/PACKINTL.HTM
*Dedicated to the preservation and
driving of the Packard auto; technical
information, source of parts, free
classified ads for members.*

Periodicals

R-Mac Publications
Magazine: Packard Motor Car Magazine
Rt. 3, Box 425
Jasper, FL 32052
Internet: http://www.packardcar.com/
Packar6.htm
*Bi-monthly magazine dedicated to the
Packard company and to the Packard
brothers who established the Packard
Motor Company.*

Pantera

Clubs/Associations

Pantera Owners Club of America
1048 Camino Del Cerritos
San Dimas, CA 91773-4466
phone: 818-966-08890
e-mail: poca1@aol.com
Internet: http://www.horizon.com/
personnel/ingate/poca.html

Linda & David Adler
Pantera International Car Club
18586 Main St., Ste. 100
Huntington Beach, CA 92648-1720
phone: 714-848-6674
fax: 714-843-5851
Internet: http://www.panteracars.com/

Pierce-Arrow

Clubs/Associations

Bernard J. Weis
Pierce-Arrow Society, Inc.
Magazine: Arrow, The
135 Edgerton St.
Rochester, NY 14607-2945
Internet: http://users.why.net/morris/
*Provides technical and historical
information on all Pierce vehicles
through "The Arrow" magazine, the
"Service Bulletin" (technical bulletin)
and "The Emporium" (current events
and advertising newsletter.)*

Collectors

Lee Pattison
6 Christview Dr.
Cuba, NY 14727-1202
phone: 716-968-2458
*Wants Pierce-Arrow car items, parts
and literature.*

Plymouth

Clubs/Associations

Plymouth Owners Club, Inc.
Magazine: Plymouth Bulletin
P.O. Box 416
Cavalier, ND 58220-0416
Internet: http://www.classicar.com/
clubs/plymouth/home.htm
*Recognizes all 4, 6 & V8 powered
Plymouth cars, Plymouth trucks and
Fargo commercial vehicles built from
1928 through cars over 25 years of
age.*

Plymouth Barracuda

Clubs/Associations

Plymouth Barracuda/Cuda Owners Club
4825 Indian Trail Rd.
Northampton, PA 18067

Police & Sheriff

Clubs/Associations

Sgt. James Post
Police Car Owners of America
Rte. 6, Box 345B
Eureka Springs, AR 72632
phone: 501-253-4948
fax: 501-253-4949
Internet: http://www.policeguide.com

Pontiac Fiero

Clubs/Associations

Huff
Fiero Owners Club of America
Magazine: Fiero Owner
2165 S. DuPont Dr., Ste. 1
Anaheim, CA 92806
phone: 714-978-3132
fax: 714-978-3059
e-mail: fiero@fieroowners.com
Internet: http://www.fieroowners.com/
*The only Fiero network resource;
informational data, historical info,
restorative facts and modification
upgrades; magazine has articles, car
parts for sale.*

Pontiac Firebird

Clubs/Associations

Tom Scherer
National Firebird Club
P.O. Box 11238
Chicago, IL 60611-0238
phone: 773-769-6262
fax: 773-769-3240
e-mail: firebirdclub@prodidgy.com
Internet: http://classicar.com/clubs/
hatfireb/hatfireb.htm
*For all Firebirds including the Trans
AM Formula and Firehawk.*

Pontiac GTO

Clubs/Associations

GTO Association of America
1321 Seventh St., #210
Santa Monica, CA 90401
phone: 800-GTO-1964

Porche

Clubs/Associations

Porche Club of America
Newsletter: Porche Panorama
P.O. Box 30100
Alexandria, VA 22310-8100
phone: 703-992-9300
Internet: http://www.pca.org

Preservation

Clubs/Associations

Auto Restorers Club
P.O. Box 138
Eagle Lake, MN 56024

Elaine Jordan
International Society for Vehicle
   Preservation
Magazine: Restoration Magazine
P.O. Box 50046
Tucson, AZ 85703
phone: 520-622-2201
fax: 520-792-8501
e-mail: isvp@aztexcorp.com
Internet: http://www.aztexcorp.com/root/
   isvp.html
*For appreciation, preservation,
restoration of self-propelled vehicles;
how-to help in restoring, sourcing of
materials.*

Professional

Clubs/Associations

Beverly Ruff, Mem.
Professional Car Society
Magazine: Professional Car, The
P.O. Box 9636
Columbus, OH 43209
phone: 614-237-2350
e-mail: blruff@freenet.columbus.oh.us
Internet: http://www.professionalcar.org/
*For all interested in the preservation
of hearses, flower cars, ambulances,
limousines, and service cars.*

Racing

Clubs/Associations

Antique Auto Racing Association
P.O. Box 486
Fairview, NC 28730

Sportscar Vintage Racing Association
P.O. Box 489
Charleston, SC 29402
phone: 803-723-7872
fax: 803-723-7372
Internet: http://www.classicar.com/
   clubs/svra/svra.htm

George Elliott
International Hot Rod Association
Highway 11 E.
Bristol, TN 37620
phone: 423-764-1164
*A sanctioning organization for drag
strips and racing events throughout
N.A. and Europe; 70 member tracks;
produces Snap-on Tools Drag Racing
Series of professional and sportsman
drag racing.*

Thomas Saal
National Auto Racing Historical Society
Magazine: Auto Racing History
1488 West Clifton Blvd.
Lakewood, OH 44107-3309
phone: 216-521-3588
*Shares resources among members,
assisting publishing and advertising
efforts; provides documentation.*

Historic Stock Car Racing Group
5418 Reeve Rd.
Mazomanie, WI 53560
phone: 800-677-6171
Internet: http://www.ntrslts.com/
   hscrg.htm

Mike Giel
Asphalt Drag Racing Association
Newsletter: Draggins' Tale
P.O. Box 1890
Saint Paul, MN 55101
phone: 612-639-1928
*Car shows, mystery runs, cruises,
regional events.*

Vintage Auto Racing Association
3426 N. Knoll Dr.
Los Angeles, CA 90068
phone: 213-874-9135 or 800-280-VARA
e-mail: vara@directnet.com
Internet: http://www.directnet.com/
   ~vara/

Nostalgia Drag Racing Association
P.O. Box 9438
Anaheim, CA 92802
phone: 714-539-NDRA

Steve Earle
Historic Motor Sports Association
P.O. Box 489
Buellton, CA 93427-0489
phone: 805-686-9292

Collectors

Megan Collins
2925 Denison Ave.
San Pedro, CA 90731
phone: 310-833-6757

Renault

Clubs/Associations

Renault Owners Club of America
Newsletter: Renault Report, The
1380 156th Ave. NE, Ste. 204
Bellevue, WA 98007
phone: 206-882-0952

REO

Clubs/Associations

REO Club of America
P.O. Box 336
Rumson, NJ 07760

Periodicals

Ray Wood
Newsletter: Reo Echo
20 Arbor Rd.
South Burlington, VT 05403-5743

Rolls-Royce

Clubs/Associations

Rolls-Royce Owners' Club
Magazine: Flying Lady, The
191 Hempt Rd.
Mechanicsburg, PA 17055
phone: 717-697-4671

Silver Ghost Association
1700 East Iron
P.O. Box 737
Salina, KS 67401
phone: 913-827-9331

Collectors

Glyn Morris
1730 Christopher Dr.
Deerfield, IL 60015-3912
phone: 847-945-9603
fax: 847-945-9636
e-mail: belmont@wwa.com
Internet: http://www.SpecialCar.com
*Wants any paper items relating to
Rolls-Royce and Bentley: books,
manuals, photos, etc.*

Rover

Clubs/Associations

Rover Owners Club of North America
P.O. Box 43005
Tucson, AZ 85719

SAAB

Clubs/Associations

SAAB Club of North America
Magazine: Nines
2416 London Rd., #900
Duluth, MN 55812-2221
phone: 218-724-1336
e-mail: 71151.1354@compuserve.com
*Magazine contains valuable
information for owners of all SAAB
cars; from 2-stroke through
Turbomobiles - tech tips, SAAB news,
history, service bulletins, classified
ads, and business ads.*

Shelby

Clubs/Associations

Rick Kopec
Shelby American Automobile Club
Magazine: Shelby American, The
P.O. Box 788
Sharon, CT 06069-0788
phone: 203-364-0449
fax: 860-364-0769
e-mail: saac@li.com
Internet: http://www.saac.com

Shelby Owners of America, Inc.
P.O. Box 1429
Great Bend, KS 67530
*Annual convention; bi-monthly
newsletter.*

Station Wagons

Clubs/Associations

Ken McDaniel
American Station Wagon Owners
   Association
Newsletter: Wagon Roundup
6110 Bethesda Way
Indianapolis, IN 46254
phone: 317-291-0321
*Dedicated to the preservation of
American-built station wagons.*

Steam

Clubs/Associations

Steam Automobile Club of America
1227 West Voorhees
Danville, IL 61832
phone: 217-442-0268
Internet: http://www.classicar.com/
   clubs/STEAM/STEAM.HTM
*Encourages the preservation of steam
cars and the design of modern ones.*

Studebaker

Clubs/Associations

Studebaker Drivers Club
Magazine: Turning Wheels
P.O. Box 28788
Dallas, TX 75228-0788
phone: 214-709-6185 or 800-527-3452
fax: 214-296-7920
Internet: http://www.carport.com/
   carport/sdc/index.htm

Sheldon Harrison
Antique Studebaker Club
Magazine: Antique Studebaker Review
P.O. Box 28845
Dallas, TX 75228-0845
phone: 972-709-6185 or 800-527-3452
fax: 972-296-7920
For pre-1946 Studebakers.

Stutz

Clubs/Associations

William Greer
Stutz Club
Magazine: Stutz News
7400 Lantern Rd.
Indianapolis, IN 46256-2120
phone: 317-849-3443

Subaru

Clubs/Associations

Ed Parsil
Subaru 360 Drivers' Club
Newsletter: Quarterly Newsletter
1421 North Grady Ave.
Tucson, AZ 85715-5013
phone: 502-290-6492
*All-volunteer association of owners/
drivers of 2-cylinder Subarus.*

Sunbeam

Clubs/Associations

Doug Ferrell
Midwest Sunbeam Club
3701 NW Eric Dr.
Topeka, KS 66618
phone: 913-286-2987

Sunbeam Owners Group of San Diego
2250 Rosecrans
San Diego, CA 92106
phone: 619-223-0496

Triumph

Clubs/Associations

Triumph International Owners Club
229 Lowland St.
Holliston, MA 01746
phone: 508-429-4221
fax: 508-429-6213
Internet: http://www.classicar.com/
clubs/TRIUMPH/TRIUMPH.HTM

Dennis Riley
Vintage Triumph Register
Magazine: Vintage Triumph Magazine
15218 W Warren Ave.
Dearborn, MI 48126-1356
phone: 404-475-1088
Internet: http://www.vtr.org/
*Focuses on vintage Triumphs; also
publishes "The English Channel"
newsletter.*

Tucker

Clubs/Associations

William E. Pommering
Tucker Automobile Club of America
Newsletter: Tucker Topics
311 West 18th St.
Tifton, GA 31794-3446
phone: 619-562-9644
fax: 619-573-0196
e-mail: TuckerClub@aol.com

Volkswagen

Clubs/Associations

Vintage Volkswagen Club of America -
Eastern Division
Magazine: VWCA News
5705 Gordon Dr.
Harrisburg, PA 17112
phone: 717-540-9972

Vintage Volkswagen Club of America
5705 Gordon Dr.
Harrisburg, PA 17112
e-mail: vvwca@primenet.com
Internet: http://www.cris.com/~Vvwca/
new.htm

Volkswagen Club of America
P.O. Box 154, Dept. MAC
North Aurora, IL 60542-0154
phone: 708-896-2803

Vintage Volkswagen Club of America -
Western Division
P.O. Box 4108
Mountain View, CA 94040

Collectors

Volksgallery
P.O. Box 517
Crompond, NY 10517
*Wants Volkswagen-related memora-
bilia: advertising, brochures,
accessories, pictures, toys, etc.*

Frank Koinsky
290 Third Ave. Extension
Rensselaer, NY 12144
phone: 518-465-0477
Wants anything to do with

*Volkswagens: toys, models, literature,
memorabilia.*

Volvo

Clubs/Associations

Gretchen Adams
Volvo Club of America
Magazine: Rolling
P.O. Box 16
Afton, NY 13730-0016
phone: 607-639-2279
fax: 607-639-2279
e-mail: rollingmag@aol.com
Internet: http://www.vcoa.org

Willys

Clubs/Associations

Gordon Lyndahl
Willys Club
Magazine: Willys World
795 North Evans St.
Pottstown, PA 19464
phone: 610-326-2907
*For help in the restoration of Willys
cars, trucks, and Jeeps from 1933
through 1963.*

Woodies

Clubs/Associations

John Lee
National Woodie Club
Newsletter: Woodie Times
P.O. Box 6134
Lincoln, NE 68506-0134
phone: 402-488-0990
*For restorers and owners of wood-
bodied cars; advice, ads, information.*

AUTOMOBILIA

(see also FARM MACHINERY;
FORD MOTOR COMPANY ITEMS;
GAS STATION COLLECTIBLES;
LICENSE PLATES; LICENSES,
Driver; MODELS; MOTORCYCLES;
MOTOR SCOOTERS; TOYS, Cars;
TRANSPORTATION COL-
LECTIBLES)

Auction Services

Kruse International
P.O. Box 190
Auburn, IN 46706
phone: 800-968-4444 or 219-925-5600
fax: 219-925-5467
Internet: http://
www.kruseinternational.com

Clubs/Associations

David K. Bausch
Automobile Objects D'Art Club
Newsletter: Automobile Objects of Art
Newsletter
252 N. 7th St.
Allentown, PA 18102-4024
phone: 610-432-3355
fax: 610-820-9368
*A club for collectors interested in
early automobile history as shown
through art and objects of art.*

Collectors

Dave Ogden
P.O. Box 223
Northbrook, IL 60062-0223
phone: 847-564-2893
fax: 847-564-2893
e-mail: musical@flash.net
*Wants to buy early automobile lights,
horns, radiator caps, and accessories.*

Mike Diafera
605 Samoset Lane
Schaumburg, IL 60193
phone: 708-980-6869
*Wants to buy automobile memora-
bilia: oil cans, grease tins, dealership
signs, etc.*

Dealers

Leila Dunbar
Dunbar's Gallery
76 Haven St.
Milford, MA 01757-3821
phone: 508-634-8697 or 508-634-8097
fax: 508-634-8698
*Mail order Americana - no reproduc-
tions; buys, sells and specializes in
vintage character and comic toys,
banks, advertising, automobilia, and
Halloween related items.*

Robert H. Snyder
P.O. Box 821
Yonkers, NY 10702-0821
phone: 914-476-8500
fax: 914-476-8573
*Wants automobile literature,
materials, periodicals, artifacts &
collectibles of all kinds relating to
autos, trucks, motorcycles, etc.;
collections assembled for institutions
& specialists; also Duryea, Napier/
Edge, pre-war Japanese.*

Ron & Deb Ladley
1850 Valley Forge Rd.
Lansdale, PA 19446
phone: 610-584-1665
*Wants pre-1970 auto, truck and
motorcycle literature, ephemera,
catalogs, brochures, manuals, signs,
dealership items, etc.; any age.*

Experts

Jim & Nancy Schaut
Aquarius Antiques
P.O. Box 10781
Glendale, AZ 85318-0781
phone: 602-878-4293
e-mail: nschaut@aztec.asu.edu
*Buys, sells; publishes a quarterly
automobilia catalog: gas station
maps, dealer signs, automobile
literature, oil company items, service
station giveaways, etc.; authors of
"American Automobilia", illustrated
history & price guide.*

Museums/Libraries

Museum of Transportation
15 Newton St.
Brookline, MA 02146
phone: 617-522-6140

William E. Swigart, Jr.
Swigart Museum
Rte. 22 E
Huntingdon, PA 16652
phone: 814-643-0885 or 814-643-2024
fax: 814-643-2857
*Cars, toys, lights, license plates,
emblems, bicycles, clothing, and much
more.*

Periodicals

Eric Killorin
Hyatt Research Corp.
Magazine: Mobilia Magazine
P.O. Box 575
Middlebury, VT 05753-0575
phone: 800-967-8068 or 802-388-3071
fax: 802-388-2215
e-mail: mobilia@aol.com
Internet: http://www.mobilia.com
*Monthly magazine focusing on
automobile collectibles: petroliana,
toys, books, car art, models, pedal
cars, sculpture; market outlook, price
guides, news, auction reports,
restoration hints, buy/sell ads.*

Eric Killorin
Hyatt Research Corp.
Directory: Mobilia Sourcebook
P.O. Box 575
Middlebury, VT 05753-0575
phone: 800-967-8068 or 802-388-3071
fax: 802-388-2215
e-mail: mobilia@aol.com
Internet: http://www.mobilia.com
A directory of automobile specialist.

Newsletter: Automobilia News
P.O. Box 3528
Glendale, AZ 85311

Sue Elliott, Pub.
Full Throttle Enterprises
Magazine: Car Toys
7950 Deering Ave.
Canoga Park, CA 91304
phone: 818-887-0550
*Monthly magazine covers model cars
of all types, sizes, materials, and
vintage; also covers automobilia from
automotive art and racing collectibles
to pedal cars, porcelain signs, neon
clocks, apparel, literature, gas pumps,
etc.*

Bugatti Related

Clubs/Associations

Andy Martin
Miniature Bugattistes Association
Newsletter: MBA Newsletter
4008 24th Ave. S.
Minneapolis, MN 55406-3024
*Member collect Bugatti related items
and miniatures.*

Buick Related

Collectors

Alvin Heckard
RD 1 Box 88
Lewistown, PA 17044-9801
phone: 717-248-7071 or 717-248-2816
Wants pre-1965 Buick promotional items: paperweights, desk sets, ash trays, key chains, promotional models, matchbooks, awards, literature, etc.

Flower Vases

Collectors

Dulce Holt
504 Broadway
Chesterton, IN 46304-2320
phone: 219-926-2838 or 219-926-4170
Wants to buy 1900-1930 flower vases (with or without metal attaching brackets) from old cars; also wants related information.

Roger Olszewski
1509 Lamplighter Lane
Fort Worth, TX 76134
phone: 817-293-3013
Wants to buy all types, sizes and colors of automobile flower vases that were used in vintage cars.

Hood Ornaments

Collectors

Sy & Ronnie Margolis
17853 Santiago Blvd., #170-210
Villa Park, CA 92861
phone: 714-974-5938
fax: 714-921-0731
Wants pre-WWII hood ornaments/ mascots; also wants related signs, brochures, catalogs.

Dealers

Mike Z. Kleba
P.O. Box 70
Mallorytown
Ontario K0E 1R0 Canada
phone: 613-923-5934
Wants to buy hood ornaments from old cars; good or broken; metal or glass; one piece or many; roosters, eagles, aeroplanes, flying man and lady, Superman, Uncle Sam, devil, Indian head, etc.

Hubcaps

Clubs/Associations

Dennis Kuhn
Hubcap Collectors Club
Newsletter: Hubcapper
P.O. Box 54
Buckley, MI 49620
phone: 616-269-3555
Focus on the older threaded hubcaps.

Dealers

Hubcaps
2825 Selzer
Evansville, IN 47712-3884
Buys and sells; thousands available from 1949 through 1982.

Instruments

Repair Services

John Wolf & Co.
4550 Wood St.
Willoughby, OH 44094

Literature

Collectors

Peter Tilp
B & T Publications
P.O. Box 580
Summit, NJ 07901-0580
Wants to buy automobile showroom catalogues for 1925-1048 classic cars.

Walter Miller
6710 Brooklawn Pkwy.
Syracuse, NY 13211-2104
phone: 315-432-8282
fax: 315-432-8256
Buys 1900-1975 automobile sales brochures, repair manuals, parts catalogs, showroom items or any other related literature.

J.B. Hoffert
P.O. Box 801
Reading, PA 19607
phone: 610-777-0105
Wants automotive sales brochures and manuals.

Bob Olds
364 Vinewood Ave.
Tallmadge, OH 44278
phone: 216-633-5938
Wants to buy auto, truck, motorcycle, bicycle sales and dealer literature, owner's manuals, shop manuals, and any related memorabilia or scale model cars.

Jay Ketelle
Jay Ketelle Collectibles, Inc.
3721 Farwell
Amarillo, TX 79109
phone: 806-355-3456
Wants to buy automobile literature.

Ralph Dunwoodie
5935 Calico
Sun Valley, NV 89433-6910
phone: 702-673-3811
Wants truck, car and motorcycle magazines, literature and catalogs from 1895 to 1942.

S.E. Penning
1242 S. Mountain St.
Visalia, CA 93277-4264
Automobile, truck dealers showroom brochures wanted 1900 - 1970; also factory service, owner's manuals; wants advertising/promotional items

of all kinds from auto companies and dealers.

Dealers

Bob Johnson
Bob Johnson's Auto Literature
21 Blandin Ave.
Framingham, MA 01701-7072
phone: 508-872-9173 or 800-334-0688
fax: 508-626-0991
e-mail: 102433.100@compuserve.com
Internet: http://www.classicar.com/ vendors/bobautl/home
Automobile literature wanted: brochures, manuals; sales, service & parts books; dealer items, etc.

Rob & Sharon McLellan
McLellan's Automotive History
9111 Longstaff Dr.
Houston, TX 77031-2711
phone: 713-772-3285
fax: 713-772-3287
Buys and sells books, sales literature, art, programs, magazines and memorabilia on sport, luxury, classic, antique and racing cars; quarterly catalogs of items for sale; publishes catalog 6 timer per year.

W.R. Sewell
Model Auto
P.O. Box 79253
Houston, TX 77279-9253
phone: 713-468-4461
fax: 713-468-4461
e-mail: modelaut@ix.netcom.com
Buys and trades all makes of auto sales literature: dealer albums, promotional model cars and old model car kits, shop manuals.

Model A Advertising

Dealers

Jim Thomas
8165 Glenmill Ct.
Cincinnati, OH 45249
phone: 513-489-7430
Wants 1928-1931 Ford Model "A" car and truck advertising, sales literature, posters, dealer items, memorabilia; buy/sell/trade.

Plaques (Car Club)

Collectors

Malcolm Andrus
420 Jackson Dr.
Vidor, TX 77662
phone: 409-769-4607 or 717-248-2816
Wants old car club plaques.

Spark Plugs

Clubs/Associations

Jeff Bartheld
Spark Plug Collectors of America
Magazine: Ignitor, The
14018 NE 85th St.
Elk River, MN 55330-6818
phone: 612-441-7059
Dedicated to the promotion of spark plug collecting and research, and the

preservation of spark plug history; the magazine is published quarterly; also publishes the "Hot Sheet" newsletter.

Collectors

Robert J. Harrington
6 Village Rd.
Milford, CT 06460
phone: 203-878-8013
Wants to buy old and unusual spark plugs.

Charles Langley
7370 East 500 South
Kokomo, IN 46902
phone: 317-628-7579
Wants to buy antique brand name spark plugs; also wants related catalogs and charts, and auto magazines from 1900 to 1925.

Don McKinsey
P.O. Box 94
Wilkinson, IN 48186
Buying spark plugs; needs old NOS obsolete plugs; prefers Champion, AC, Splitdorf, Mosler, but will consider others; also old spark plug catalogs and advertising items; send LSASE for 6-page list covering over 800 spark plugs wanted.

Jeff Bartheld
14018 NE 85th St.
Elk River, MN 55330-6818
phone: 612-441-7059

Experts

Cornelius Bergbower
P.O. Box 144
Bluford, IL 62814-0144
phone: 618-732-6195
Author of "Spark Collector's Guide", available from the author - Vol I $11 ppd., Vol. II $14 ppd.; also wants to buy spark plugs with odd names and shapes, especially plugs with priming cups, gadgets, etc.

Studebaker Related

Collectors

Paul Straughn
4111 Carnation Dr.
Arlington, TX 76016
phone: 817-572-2817
Wants Studebaker related memorabilia, 1852-1966: car/truck/horse-drawn items: literature, photographs, catalogs, signs, sheet music, stock certificates, pins, badges, promotional and dealership items, models, china, banners, etc.

AVIATION

(see also AIRLINE MEMORABILIA; AIRPLANES; AIRSHIPS; AVIATION MEMORABILIA; BOOKS, Reference [Aviation]; MILITARIA; PERSONALITIES [FAMOUS], Charles A. Lindbergh; STAMP COLLECTING, Air Mail Related; TOYS, Airplane Related)

Clubs/Associations

Popular Flying Association
Magazine: Popular Flying
Term. Bldg., Shoreham Airport
Shoreman-by-Sea
Sussex BN43 4FF, U.K.
The United Kingdom Association of amateur-built and vintage aircraft restoration.

Canadian Aviation Historical Society
P.O. Box 224, Station A
Willowdale
Ontario M2N 5S8 Canada

Maine Aviation Historical Society
Newsletter: MAHS Newsletter
101 Monroe Ave.
Westbrook, ME 04092-4020

Florida Aviation Historical Society
Newsletter: FAHS Newsletter
P.O. Box 127
Indian Rocks Beach, FL 34635
From the state where naval aviation, commercial aviation and space travel began.

Florida Aviation Historical Society
P.O. Box 127
Indian Rocks Beach, FL 34635

American Aviation Historical Society
Magazine: AAHS Journal
2333 Otis St.
Santa Ana, CA 92704-3846
phone: 714-549-4818
Internet: http://
www.industrial.artworks.com/AAHS/
Provides source of factual historical data compiled by leading historians; quarterly newsletter and journal contain articles on personalities, unit histories, machines, aviation history, buy and sell ads, etc.

Collectors

Alan C. King
P.O. Box 86
Radnor, OH 43066-0086
Wants aviation related repair manuals, magazines, handbooks, etc.

Experts

Frank Strnad
Aero Collectables
P.O. Box 240
Northport, NY 11768-0240
phone: 516-261-0140
Wants to buy aviation books and magazines (Aero Digest, Popular Aviation, MAN), erection and maintenance manuals, engine manuals, factory brochures and drawings, instruments, models, name plates, photos, memorabilia, etc.

Jon Aldrich
Pine Mountain Lake Airport
P.O. Box 706
Groveland, CA 95321-0706
phone: 209-962-6121
fax: 209-962-6121
Long time dealer in vintage aeronautical memorabilia, both civil

and military; wants to buy aviation autographs, books, war relics, pilot memorabilia, airplane parts, aero nostalgia; please send price and description; appraisal.

Museums/Libraries

Byron Reynolds
Reynolds Aviation Museum
4110 - 57 St.
Wetaskiwin
Alberta T9A 2B6 Canada
phone: 403-352-5201 or 403-526-6201
fax: 403-352-4666

National Aviation Museum
P.O. Box 9724 Ottowa Terminal
Ottowa
Ontario K1G 5A3 Canada
phone: 613-993-2010

New England Air Museum of the
Connecticut Aeronautical Historical
Assoc.
Bradley International Airport
Windsor Locks, CT 06096
phone: 203-623-3305

Mid Atlantic Air Museum
P.O. Box 9381
Reading, PA 19605
phone: 610-372-7333

National Air & Space Museum
6th St. & Independence Ave. SW
Washington, DC 20560
phone: 202-357-2700
Internet: http://www.si.edu/

Alan & Drina Abel
Aviation Heritage Research Center
Newsletter: Drina's Hanger Flyer
P.O. Box 665
Destin, FL 32540-0665
Maintains large file of air airplane history and photos as well as a small museum; contributions of related material welcome.

Ron Twellman, Coll. Mngr.
Experimental Aircraft Association
Aviation Foundation, Inc.
P.O. Box 3065
Oshkosh, WI 54093-3065
phone: 414-426-4800 or 414-426-5917
fax: 414-426-6174
e-mail: museum@caa.org
Collection of over 90 vintage airplanes.

Keith R. Gill
Museum of Science & Industry
57th St. & Lake Shore Dr.
Chicago, IL 60637
phone: 312-684-1414
fax: 312-684-5580

Planes of Fame Air Museum
HCR 34 Box B
Williams, AZ 86046
phone: 520-635-1000

Periodicals

Magazine: FlyPast
P.O. Box 100
Stamford
Lincs PE9 1XQ, U.K.
phone: 01780 755131
fax: 01780 757261
e-mail: flypast@keymags.demon.co.uk
Internet: http://www.keymags.co.uk/
flypast/
Britain's top selling aviation monthly.returned

J. Mac McClellan
Hachette Filipacchi Magazines, Inc.
Magazine: Flying Magazine
500 West Putnam Ave.
Greenwich, CT 06830
phone: 203-622-2700
fax: 203-622-2725

Rozonna Kinlen
Magazine: Flying Review
P.O. box 9191
Albuquerque, NM 87119
phone: 505-836-4646 or 505-842-4184
fax: 505-842-4405

Magazine: Small Air Forces Observer
27965 Berwick Dr.
Carmel, CA 93923
Aviation history, aircraft markings.

Nick Veronico
Magazine: In Flight Aviation News
P.O. Box 620447
Woodside, CA 94062
phone: 415-364-8110
fax: 415-364-1359
A 120 page newspaper devoted to aviation & aviation history; editors will answer questions about memorabilia and refer sellers to buyers.

·Art

Dealers

Jerry Beach
Aeronautical Classics & Fine Arts
1305 King Street
Alexandria, VA 22314
phone: 703-548-7122
fax: 703-548-6414
Fine aviation prints, paintings, memorabilia, books, desk models, propellers, gifts, etc.

Aviation Arts
533 South Coast Hwy.
Laguna Beach, CA 92651
Offers new aviation related art of interest to collectors.

Stephen Remington
AviationArt
2555 Robert Fowler Way, #A
Reid-Hillview Airport
San Jose, CA 95148-1011
phone: 408-259-3366
fax: 408-259-4223
e-mail: 72245.747@compuserve.com
Original aviation art, limited edition prints, bronze sculptures, display models, display models, aeronautical

collectibles, aviation books, model airplane exhibits, museum.

Military

Clubs/Associations

Air-Britain
5 Bradley Rd.
London SE19 3NT, U.K.

Dealers

Bob Von Willer
Exotic Aircraft Company
1718 North Marshall Ave.
El Cajon, CA 92020
phone: 619-562-7467
fax: 619-448-2110
e-mail: baron@skyguy.com
Internet: http://www.barnstormers.com/
classify.html
Specializes in the marketing of antique aircraft, including warbirds; appraiser, dealer, expert, auctioneer, collector, and repair services offered.

Museums/Libraries

AMPHA Warbirds Museum
Allaire Airport
1717 St. Hwy. S., Bldg 2
Farmingdale, NJ 07727

U.S. Army Aviation Museum
P.O. Box 610
Fort Rucker, AL 36362
phone: 205-255-4507

Richard L. Uppstrom, Dir.
U.S. Air Force Museum
Wright-Patterson A.F.B., OH 45433-
6518
phone: 513-255-3286
fax: 513-255-3910
World's largest aviation museum with 10 1/2 acres of aircraft and other exhibits under roof.

Yankee Air Force
P.O. Box 590
Belleville, MI 48112
phone: 313-483-4030

Combat Air Museum
P.O. Box 19142
Topeka, KS 66619
phone: 913-862-3303

Laird Doctor, Dir.
Cavanaugh Flight Museum
4572 Claire Chennault
Dallas, TX 75248
phone: 972-380-8800 or 800-206-3953
Historic warbirds, trainers, fighters, jets and other aircraft chronicle heroes, battles and technological advances from WWI to present.

Col. J. Ward Boyce, Ret.
American Fighter Aces Museum
Foundation
Magazine: American Fighter Aces
   Bulletin
4636 Fighter Aces Dr.
Mesa, AZ 85205-2502
phone: 602-854-7170
fax: 602-830-9463
   *Friends of the American Fighter Aces
   formed to provide funding support to
   American Fighter Ace Museum
   Foundation. Open to all interested in
   American Fighter Aces and fighter
   aircraft.*

Periodicals

Quadrant Subscription Services
Magazine: Aeroplane Monthly
P.O. Box 272, Oakfield House
Perrymount Rd., Haywards Heath
West Sussex RH16 3FS, U.K.
   *Articles on the veterans of WWI, the
   Spitfires, Hurricanes, Heinkels and
   Messerschmitts of WWII; preserva-
   tion, competition, photos, etc.*

Magazine: Classic Wings Downunder
P.O. Box 534
Blenheim
New Zealand
   *The only journal dedicated exclusively
   to vintage and warbird aeroplanes in
   Australia and New Zealand; high
   quality publication packed with in-
   depth articles, news and superb
   photographs.*

Warbirds Worldwide International, Inc.
Magazine: Warbirds Worldwide
P.O. Box 99
Mansfield
Notts NG19 9GU, U.K.
phone: 1623 845556
   *A quarterly journal for serious vintage
   airplane enthusiasts: worldwide news
   reports on fighters, bombers and
   vintage jets, pilot reports, features on
   museums and high quality photographic coverage of aircraft being
   rebuilt.*

H.G. Frautschy
Experimental Aircraft Association
Magazine: Warbirds Magazine
P.O. Box 3086
Oshkosh, WI 54903-3086
phone: 800-843-3612 or 414-426-6515
fax: 414-426-4873

Magazine: Air Wars
8931 Kittyhawk Ave.
Los Angeles, CA 90045-4128
   *Focuses on the restoration of classic
   (1919-1939) fighter planes; how-to
   articles and photos, museum articles,
   plans for models, etc.*

Erika Daileda
Wise Owl Worldwide Publications
Magazine: Windsock
4314 West 238th St. - Dept. MACR
Torrance, CA 90505-4509
phone: 310-375-6258
fax: 310-375-0548
e-mail: wiseowl@sprintmail.com
   *A bi-monthly English publication; the
   journal for WWI aeroplane
   enthusiasts and modelers.*

Challenge Publications, Inc.
Magazine: Air Classics
7950 Deering Ave.
Canoga Park, CA 91304
phone: 818-887-0550
fax: 818-884-1343
e-mail: warbirdmag@aol.com

Races & Meets

Clubs/Associations

Herman Schaub, Sec.
Society of Air Racing Historians
168 Marian Lane
Berea, OH 44017-1566
phone: 216-234-2301
Internet: http://www.airrace.com
   *Dedicated to preserving air racing
   history from 1909 to the present.*

Collectors

Pete Kramer
P.O. Box 52
Glen Ellyn, IL 60138-0052
phone: 630-627-4051
   *Wants to buy 1909-1939 aviation meet
   and air race programs, posters,
   tickets, autographed photos, and
   souvenirs.*

AVIATION MEMORABILIA

(see also AIRLINE MEMORABILIA;
AIRPLANES; AVIATION; BADGES;
MILITARIA; MINIATURES,
Airplanes; STAMP COLLECTING,
Air Mail Related; TOYS, Airplane
Related)

Auction Services

Joe Gertler, Jr.
Raceway Engineering
P.O. Box 366
Guntersville, AL 35976-0367
   *$2.5M aviation collection; profes-
   sional aviation museum consultant;
   conducts auctions of major aviation
   collections; I.R.S. appraisals; has
   50,000 unit aviation reference library;
   sells to museums & collectors; WWI a
   specialty; lectures.*

Dealers

Dixie Aviation Collectibles
P.O. Box 302
Holmdel, NJ 07733-0302
phone: 908-946-8528
fax: 908-332-1068

Frank Cea
Barnstormer Enterprises & Auctions
P.O. Box 260331
Jamaica, NY 11426-0331
phone: 516-741-3694 or 516-727-6191
fax: 516-877-0646
   *Buys and sells aviation and model
   aircraft items; memorabilia, photos,
   magazines, brochures, artifacts,
   books, model kits, model motors, race
   cars, catalogs, built planes, airline
   models and ephemera.*

Peter NeNevai
20th C. Aviation Collectibles
HC63 Box 5
Duchesne, UT 84021
   *Have available artifacts, equipment,
   aircraft pieces, books, manuals,
   periodicals, timetables, toys,
   postcards, etc. relating to most
   aspects of 20th century aviation
   history; sells, trades; illustrated list
   for $1.*

Experts

Herb Jacobs
P.O. Box 1286
Mattituck, NY 11952
phone: 516-298-4135
fax: 516-298-4181
   *Buys, sells, appraises and specializes
   in aviation memorabilia.*

Russ Huff
P.O. Box 17276
Sarasota, FL 34276-0276
phone: 941-923-3600
e-mail: russhuff@ix.netcom.com
   *Buys, sells and specializes in military
   aviation qualification badges of the
   world; also other aviation memorabilia.*

Joe Gertler, Jr.
Raceway Engineering
P.O. Box 366
Guntersville, AL 35976-0367
   *$2.5M aviation collection; profes-
   sional aviation museum consultant;
   conducts auctions of major aviation
   collections; I.R.S. appraisals; has
   50,000 unit aviation reference library;
   sells to museums & collectors; WWI a
   specialty; lectures.*

Museums/Libraries

Southern Museum of Flight
4343 N. 73rd St.
Birmingham, AL 35026
phone: 205-833-8226

Joe Gertler, Jr.
Raceway Collection, The
P.O. Box 366
Guntersville, AL 35976-0367
   *$2.5M aviation collection; profes-
   sional aviation museum consultant;
   conducts auctions of major aviation
   collections; I.R.S. appraisals; has
   50,000 unit aviation reference library;
   sells to museums & collectors; WWI a
   specialty; lectures.*

Stephen Remington
Newsletter: News & Views
2555 Robert Fowler Way, #A
Reid-Hillview Airport
San Jose, CA 95148-1011
phone: 408-259-3366
fax: 408-259-4223
e-mail: 72245.747@compuserve.com
   *Associated with aviation for over 40
   years; has his own art gallery and
   museum of aircraft recognition items;
   art gallery with originals and prints,
   aviation memorabilia; always buying
   pre-1950 aviation memorabilia.*

Military

Clubs/Associations

Jan Jaobs
F-4 Phantom II Society
Magazine: Smoke Trails
P.O. Box 900174
San Diego, CA 92190-0174
phone: 619-689-9227
fax: 619-578-8839
e-mail: f14ro@aol.com
Internet: http://www.f4phantom.org
   *Focuses on the F-4 Phantom II;
   "Smoke Trails" is published
   quarterly.*

Collectors

Charles Donald
P.O. Box 822
Union City, NJ 07087-0822
phone: 201-330-9619
   *Wants WWI squadron memorial
   volumes and squadron histories 1914
   to 1918, aviation-related photos from
   1920s to 1940s, photo albums, log
   books, groups of negatives; only
   wants to buy negative collections, not
   individual negatives.*

David Ostrowski
5411 Masser Lane
Fairfax, VA 22032-3817
phone: 703-323-6674
   *Wants to buy military and civilian
   aircraft models, ID/recognition
   aircraft models, photos/negatives/
   slides of military and civilian aircraft.*

Dennis Gordon
1246 N Ave.
Missoula, MT 59801-6602
phone: 406-549-6280
   *Wants World War I (c. 1914-1918)
   aviation items and American
   Volunteer items: U.S. and foreign;
   pilot log books, I.D. cards, books,
   photos, aircraft instruments, souvenir
   items, insignia, helmets, uniforms,
   medals, documents.*

Dealers

Bob McKowen
215 S. Ace. C
Washington, IA 52353
phone: 319-653-5776
   *Specializes in WWII aircraft cockpit
   instruments.*

Robert Chad LeBeau
Aviation Artifacts, Inc.
1213 Sandstone Dr.
Saint Charles, MO 63304-6830
phone: 314-441-2706
fax: 314-447-4071
*Buys flight gear: flight helmets,
oxygen masks, parachutes, ejection
seats, aircraft parts, instruments.*

James E. Garcia
9 Atumnwood Ct.
Edgewood, NM 87015
*Buys and sells vintage helmets,
goggles, maps, pilot wrist watches,
clocks, flight manuals, and other
aviation items.*

Lee Herron
Aviators World
1434 Flightline #13
Mojave, CA 93501-1666
phone: 805-824-2424
fax: 805-824-2723
e-mail: herron@hughes.net
*Buys and sells plane and pilot
collectibles from all eras: air combat,
military, civil, space; issues detailed
illustrated catalog of items for sale
four times each year.*

Experts

Jeff Mark
P.O. Box 5178
Santa Monica, CA 90409-5178
phone: 800-666-9553 or 310-396-9767
fax: 310-396-2666
*Wants to buy Air Force and 1900-
1970 aviation related items including
flying jackets, airplane parts, silver
wings, medals, memorabilia, patches,
helmets, goggles, etc.; wants U.S.,
German, Japanese, or British.*

Military Insignia

(see also AIRLINE MEMORABILIA,
Pilots Wings; MILITARIA; BADGES)

Collectors

Robert Missero
4 Kakiat Lane
Spring Valley, NY 10977-2009
phone: 914-425-0013
*Wants all types of WWII sterling silver
U.S. Army Air Force wings; 1", 2", 3";
also wing bracelets.*

Experts

Russ Huff
P.O. Box 17276
Sarasota, FL 34276-0276
phone: 941-923-3600
e-mail: russhuff@ix.netcom.com
*Buys, sells and specializes in military
aviation qualification badges of the
world; also other aviation memorabilia.*

Propellers

Dealers

Philip Wallick
Vintage Aeroplane Propellers
P.O. Box 3699
Chico, CA 95927
phone: 916-877-0352
*Buys and sells wooden airplane
propellers; original or reconditioned;
also offers for sale high quality
vintage reproduction propellers for
wall decoration and display; write or
call for color brochure.*

AVON COLLECTIBLES

(see also BOTTLES, Perfume &
Scent; CALIFORNIA PERFUME
COMPANY)

Clubs/Associations

Connie Clark, Pres.
National Association of Avon
Collectors, Inc.
Newsletter: Avon Times
P.O. Box 7006
Kansas City, MO 64113-0006
phone: 816-822-2347
*A national association of Avon
collectors; promotes the hobby of
Avon collecting; many members clubs
throughout the U.S. and Canada;
newslettter has buy/sell ads, upcoming
shows schedules.*

Dealers

Dwight & Vera Young
P.O. Box 9868
Kansas City, MO 64134-0868
phone: 816-537-8223
Buys and sell Avon collectibles.

Experts

Bud Hastin
Hastin Books
P.O. Box 9868
Kansas City, MO 64134-0868
phone: 954-566-0691
*Author of "Bud Hastin's Avon
Collectibles Price Guide."*

Periodicals

Dwight & Vera Young
Avon Times
Newsletter: Avon Times
P.O. Box 9868
Kansas City, MO 64134-0868
phone: 816-537-8223
*A monthly newsletter with interna-
tional circulation that contains
articles, ads, photos, history,
convention and show news; buy and
sell ads from around the world;
devoted strictly to the hobby of Avon
collecting.*

AWARDS

(see MEDALS, ORDERS &
DECORATIONS)

Here are some tips when contacting someone listed in this book:

When requesting information about a particular item, include a description (material, dimensions, maker's mark, model number, etc.) and a photo, sketch, or photocopy of the item in question. ■

Always ask if there are charges for samples or for the services requested. ■

When writing, please be sure to include a Large (#10 business size) Self-Addressed and Stamped Envelope (LSASE) if requesting a reply or the return of photographs. ■

Never call collect unless otherwise directed. When calling, be considerate of time zone differences and always ask if the party you are calling has time to talk. When leaving an answering machine message, always instruct the party to call you back collect. ■

BABY CARRIAGES

(see CHILDREN'S THINGS; PERAMBULATORS)

BADGES

(see also AVIATION MEMORA-BILIA; FRATERNAL ORGANIZA-TION ITEMS; MEDALS, ORDERS & DECORATIONS; LAW ENFORCE-MENT MEMORABILIA; MILITARIA; AMMUNITION & EXPLOSIVE ORDNANCE, Badges; PATCHES; PINS; SOCIAL CAUSES; TAXI; VETERAN ITEMS)

Collectors

R. MacVicar
P.O. Box 337
Houghton Lake, MI 48629
Wants to buy country club and taxi badges.

Chauffeurs

Collectors

Albert Velocci
62 Cherrywood Dr.
Hillside Manor, NY 11040
Wants to buy chauffeur badges, especially early and undated badges.

George A. Coupe
1243 1st St. S.E.
Washington, DC 20003
phone: 202-554-1000 or 800-368-5466
fax: 202-863-0775
Wants to buy chauffeur badges; one or whole collections.

Howard Share
4349 La Vale Ct.
Clemmons, NC 27012-9009
phone: 910-766-6579
e-mail: denarnc@aol.com
Wants to buy chauffeur or driver license badges, especially from Southern states and Hawaii; will also trade.

Trent Culp
P.O. Box 550
Misenheimer, NC 28109-0550
phone: 704-279-6242
Collects chauffeurs' badges from all states and all years, especially badges from the Southern states.

Jerome Schaeper, Jr.
705 Philadelphia St.
Covington, KY 41011-1252
phone: 606-581-3729
Collects and appraises city or state issued driving badges, early Southern badges especially wanted.

Mike O'Brien
215 Meadowlark
Sandwich, IL 60548
Wants to buy chauffeur's badges from all states and cities: licensed, registered, conditional, professional, taxi driver, chauffeur, etc.

Dealers

Walt Feiger
Walt's Antiques
2513 Nelson Rd.
Traverse City, MI 49686-8557
phone: 616-223-7386 or 616-223-4123
Wants to buy Michigan chauffeur badges.

Experts

Dr. Edward H. Miles
888 Eighth Ave.
New York, NY 10019-5704
phone: 212-765-2660
Editor/publisher "Chauffeurs Badges & Transportation Related Badges of the World" Vol. I N.Y. State & City Badges, Vol. II New England City & State Badges. There is a price guide.

John Connors
3811 Grantley Rd.
Toledo, OH 43613-4218
Author of "Price Guide to American & Canadian Chauffeur Badges."

Employee

Collectors

Gary Wood
733 Myrtle Rd.
North Brunswick, NJ 08902-2549
phone: 908-821-7633
Collector seeking "plant badges" with photos; these are pinback buttons worn by employees; often included a photo of the employee for identification; used primarily 1930s through 1960s; pays $5 to $50 each depending on condition.

Douglas W. Tietze
4909 Harter Rd.
Slatington, PA 18080
Collects 1920s to 1950s employee badges: oval, round, square; brass, copper, plated steel, plastic; many contain a photograph of the employee.

Federal

Experts

Ken W. Lucas, Sr.
3052 Bel Pre Rd., Apt. 101
Silver Spring, MD 20906-2415
phone: 301-871-0877
Author of "Federal Law Enforcement Badges"; Agriculture, Commerce, Defense, Energy, Health & Human Services, Interior, Park Police, Fish & Wildlife, Indian, Justice, U.S. Marshals, FBI, DEA, Labor, CIA, Postal, Customs, etc.

BAGS

(see AIRLINE MEMORABILIA, Airline Sickness Bags; FEED & GRAIN BAGS; PURSES)

BAKELITE

(see GEMS & JEWELRY, Vintage & Costume; PLASTIC COL-LECTIBLES)

BALLS

Agitator

Collectors

Fred Meadows
Crew Chief, Auto Fac., American Airlines
3707 North Harbor Dr.
San Diego, CA 92101
phone: 619-231-5483
Collects the little agitator balls found inside aerosol cans.

BANANA COLLECTIBLES

Clubs/Associations

L. Ken Bannister, T.B.
International Banana Club
Newsletter: Woddis Newsletter
2524 N. El Molino Ave.
Altadena, CA 91001-2318
phone: 818-798-2272
e-mail: bananasTB@aol.com
Internet: http://www.banana-club.com
A "fun" humorous club founded in 1972; purpose is to keep people smiling and exercising their sense of humor each day.

Museums/Libraries

L. Ken Bannister, T.B.
Banana Museum
2524 N. El Molino Ave.
Altadena, CA 91001-2318
phone: 818-798-2272
e-mail: bananasTB@aol.com
Internet: http://www.banana-club.com
More than 17,000 items on display; opened by prearranged appointment only; featured on national TV and magazines.

Stickers

Periodicals

George Griffin
Newsletter: Banana Label Times
P.O. Box 159
Old Town, FL 32680-0159
phone: 904-542-3447
fax: 904-542-3447
Published quarterly: for collectors of banana stickers by Chiquita, DelMonte, Dole, Turbana, Fielder, Banacol, Sunisa, etc.

BAND ORGANS

(see MUSICAL INSTRUMENTS, Mechanical [Band Organs])

BANKING

(see also COINS & CURRENCY; CREDIT CARDS & CHARGE ITEMS; MONEYCARDS; PAPER COLLECTIBLES; SCRIP; STAMP COLLECTING, Revenue & Tax Stamps; TELEPHONE CARDS; TOKENS; WOODEN MONEY)

Museums/Libraries

Wells Fargo Bank History Museum
420 Montgomery St.
San Francisco, CA 94163
phone: 415-396-2619

Bank Checks

Clubs/Associations

Coleman Leifer, Sec.
American Society of Check Collectors
Journal: Check Collector, The
P.O. Box 577
Garrett Park, MD 20896-0577
e-mail: cal493@aol.com
Founded in 1969, ASCC is open to collectors of all types of fiscal paper: engravings, revenue stamps on checks; over 400 members; journal published quarterly.

Collectors

Gary Ronk
6247 Cove Rd.
Roanoke, VA 24019-1715
phone: 540-562-2368
Wants to buy pre-1900 bank checks, especially those that are illustrated with vignettes or have imprinted revenue stamps.

Lee Poleske
P.O. Box 871
Seward, AK 99664-0871
Wants pre-1900 bank checks, drafts, and bills of exchange; please send photocopy or sample with price.

Dealers

Douglas McDonald
Gypsyfoot Enterprises, Inc.
P.O. Box 5833
Helena, MT 59604-5833
phone: 406-449-8076
fax: 406-443-8514
Buys, sells and collects old pre-1902 bank checks, drafts, exchanges, money orders, warrants, etc.; please send photocopies for offer.

Warren Anderson
America West Archives
P.O. Box 100
Cedar City, UT 84721-0100
phone: 801-586-9497 or 801-586-7323
Buys and sells pre-1910 issued bank checks and other financial papers from the Western U.S.; catalogs issued; author of "Owning Western History."

Experts

Rodney Battles
P.O. Box 54101
Hurst, TX 76054-4101
Author of "Introduction to Check Collecting."

Periodicals

Julie A. Ulrich, PR
Krause Publications
Newspaper: Bank Note Reporter
700 E. State St.
Iola, WI 54990-0001
phone: 715-445-2214
fax: 715-445-4087
e-mail: info@krause.com
Internet: http://www.krause.com
Monthly news source and marketplace for collectors of U.S. and world paper money, notes, checks and related fiscal paper.

BANKS

(see also BANKING; LOCKS; SOUVENIR & COMMEMORATIVE ITEMS, Buildings; STOCKS & BONDS; TOYS)

Auction Services

Sam Haney
Haney Auction Co.
2686 Green St.
Eden, NY 14057
phone: 716-992-3300
Specializes in the auctioning of toys and banks.

Henry/Pierce Auctioneers
1525 S. Arcadian Dr.
New Berlin, WI 53151
phone: 414-797-7933

Mike Henry
Henry/Pierce Auctioneers
1456 Carson Court
Homewood, IL 60430-4013
phone: 708-799-1732 or 414-797-7933
Appraises and auctions still and mechanical banks.

Collectors

Bob Brady
1375 Harrisburg Pike
Lancaster, PA 17601
phone: 717-569-7408
Wants to buy mechanical and still banks.

George A. Coupe
1243 1st St. S.E.
Washington, DC 20003
phone: 202-554-1000 or 800-368-5466
fax: 202-863-0775
Collector looking for old cast iron or tin mechanical banks or toys; will buy one or whole collection; call toll free 24 hours.

Jim Conley
2758 Coventry Lane
Canton, OH 44708-1320
phone: 330-477-7725 or 330-499-9283
fax: 330-879-2950
Very interested in buying mechanical

and still banks; OK for sellers to call collect.

Jim Rocheleau
1137 Cadieux
Grosse Point, MI 48230
phone: 313-885-7805
Wants mechanical and still banks.

Mike Henry
1456 Carson Court
Homewood, IL 60430-4013
phone: 708-799-1732 or 414-797-7933
Mechanical and still banks wanted.

Dealers

Jackie Durham
909 26th St. NW
Washington, DC 20037-2029
e-mail:
durham@GameRoomAntiques.com
Internet: http://
www.GameRoomAntiques.com
Buys and sells mechanical and still banks; send SASE for list.

David A. Hull
Small Town Coins & Collectibles
7498 E. Davison Rd.
Davison, MI 48423-2014
phone: 810-658-1992
fax: 810-658-2977
e-mail: towncoin@concentric.net
Internet: http://www.concentric.net/
~towncoin
Buys and sells still and mechanical cast iron banks.

Norman Bowers
1916 Cleveland St.
Evanston, IL 60202-1910
phone: 708-866-7165 or 708-333-7880
fax: 708-333-9561
Buys, sells, trades, and appraises old still and mechanical banks.

Clive Devenish
Whitney Antiques
P.O. Box 907
Orinda, CA 94563
phone: 510-254-8383
Wants to buy old penny banks; still and mechanical.

Experts

Robert L. McCumber
201 Carriage Dr.
Glastonbury, CT 06033
phone: 203-633-4984
Author of several books about toy banks covering repros and fakes, mechanical and still banks, Chein banks, registering banks, building banks, iron safe banks, penny banks, and more.

Sy Schreckinger
P.O. Box 104
East Rockaway, NY 11518-0104
phone: 516-536-4154
Buy/sell mechanical and still banks: cast iron, tin, wood or lead; also wooden bank shipping boxes, bank trade cards, catalogs, etc.; also wants

old photos of children with banks and toys.

Charles Reynolds
Reynolds Toys
2836 Monroe St.
Falls Church, VA 22042-2007
phone: 703-533-1322
Specializes in mechanical and still banks.

Ross Hermann
c/o AntiqueWeek
P.O. Box 90
Knightstown, IN 46148
phone: 317-345-5133 or 800-876-5133
fax: 800-695-8153
e-mail: antiquewk@aol.com
Internet: http://www.antiqueweek.com
Writes column about mechanical and still banks for "AntiqueWeek", will answer questions, but a SASE must be enclosed if photos are to be returned.

Earnest & Ida Long
Long's Americana
P.O. Box 90
Mokelumne Hill, CA 95245
phone: 209-286-1348
Specializes in toys, banks, games and other children's items; publishes "Dictionary of Toys, Vol I & II" and "Penny Lane."

Repair Services

Sy Schreckinger
P.O. Box 104
East Rockaway, NY 11518-0104
phone: 516-536-4154
Offers professional, museum quality repair, restoration and cleaning of iron and tin mechanical and still banks.

Repro. Sources

ANTIQUE-ALIKE
3147 Joppa Rd.
Cambridge, MD 21613-3640
Sells high quality copies of famous original cast iron banks, doorstops and tin advertising signs.

Glass

Collectors

John Honl
P.O. Box 1201
Kailua Kona, HI 96745-1201
phone: 808-325-9905
Wants to buy glass bottle banks including Galaxy Spaceman, Snowcrest seal clown and penguin, administration building, Jumbo peanut butter elephant, Guttuso rabbit, Jocko monkey (prepared mustard), etc.

Periodicals

Newsletter: Glass Bank Collector
P.O. Box 155
Poland, NY 13431-0155
Issued three times per year: articles

about glass banks and glass container banks.

Mechanical

Clubs/Associations

Rick Mihlhiem, Sec.
Mechanical Bank Collectors of America
Newsletter: Mechanical Banker
P.O. Box 128
Allegan, MI 49010-0128
phone: 616-673-4509

Dealers

Bill Bertoia
1881-G Spring Rd.
Vineland, NJ 08630
phone: 609-692-1881
fax: 609-692-8697

Bryan Kittelberger
Kittelberger Galleries
82 1/2 E. Main St.
Webster, NY 14580
phone: 716-265-1230

Stephen Steckbeck
200 W. Superior St.
Fort Wayne, IN 46802
phone: 219-625-3537
Buys, sells and appraises old mechanical banks.

Experts

Mark Suozzi
P.O. Box 102
Ashfield, MA 01330
phone: 413-628-3241
Antique penny banks, 1 cent arcade machines, advertising signs, folk art, and wind-up clockwork toys.

Leon M. Weiss
Gemini Antiques Ltd.
12 E. 76th St.
New York, NY 10021
phone: 212-734-3681

James S. Maxwell, Jr.
P.O. Box 367
Lampeter, PA 17537
phone: 717-464-5573
Advisor to "Warman's Antiques & Collectibles Price Guide."

Dr. Greg Zemenick
Dr. "Z"
1350 Kirts, Ste. 160
Troy, MI 48084-4830
phone: 248-642-8129 or 248-244-9430
fax: 248-244-9495
e-mail: DrZzeezz@aol.com
Internet: http://www.drzzeezzi.com
Buys, sells, brokers and specializes in mechanical banks, any condition or completeness; wooden or cardboard packing boxes; trade cards, catalogs; also bell toys; member ATCA, MBCA, SBCA and others.

Repro. Sources

Charles Reynolds
Reynolds Toys
2836 Monroe St.
Falls Church, VA 22042-2007
phone: 703-533-1322
*Offers limited editions of new original
penny banks, of sand-cast aluminum;
political, holiday and event themes;
over 100 editions produced from
1970-1990.*

Oil Can (Miniature)

Collectors

Peter Capell
1838 West Grace St.
Chicago, IL 60613-2724
phone: 773-871-8735
*Wants tin or tin with paper label
miniature oil can banks produced as
promotional giveaways for gasoline
and motor oil dealers.*

Registering

Collectors

Goerge P. Juergens
35 Farrah Dr.
Elkton, MD 21921
phone: 410-398-5041
*Wants to buy Uncle Sam, Add-o-Bank
and other registering banks.*

Experts

Robert L. McCumber
201 Carriage Dr.
Glastonbury, CT 06033
phone: 203-633-4984
*Author of "Registering Banks";
registering banks (e.g. pocket tube
banks) show amount as coins are
deposit.*

Rocket/Space

Collectors

Anthony Glab
4154 Falls Rd.
Baltimore, MD 21211-1644
phone: 410-235-1777
fax: 410-889-1937
e-mail: glab@aol.com
*Wants to buy rocket/space banks in
mint condition by Astro Mfg.*

Safe Shaped

Collectors

Larry Egelhoff
4175 Millersville Rd.
Indianapolis, IN 46205-2966
phone: 317-846-7228

Still

Clubs/Associations

Larry Egelhoff, Mem.
Still Bank Collectors Club of America
Newsletter: Penny Bank Post
4175 Millersville Rd.
Indianapolis, IN 46205-2966
phone: 317-846-7228
*To stimulate knowledge of, interest in,
and the collection of antique and
contemporary still banks and, further,
within the limits of friendly rivalry, to
assist members in adding to and
enhancing the value of their
collections.*

Collectors

Harry Ward
153 Scott Ave.
Bloomsburg, PA 17815-1020
phone: 717-784-3946

Tom Kellogg
6125 Rockdale Lane
Sylvania, OH 43560-3644
phone: 419-885-5562
fax: 419-261-1988
e-mail: ironbanks@aol.com
*Wants to buy still banks in the form of
buildings; also wants other forms of
still and mechanical banks.*

Dealers

Mike Henry
1456 Carson Court
Homewood, IL 60430-4013
phone: 708-799-1732 or 414-797-7933
Buys and sells still banks.

Experts

Leon M. Weiss
Gemini Antiques Ltd.
12 E. 76th St.
New York, NY 10021
phone: 212-734-3681

Repro. Sources

Charles Reynolds
Reynolds Toys
2836 Monroe St.
Falls Church, VA 22042-2007
phone: 703-533-1322
*Offers limited editions of new original
still banks of sand-cast aluminum;
political, holiday, and event themes;
flyer on request.*

Still (Ceramic)

Dealers

Carol Silagyi
C.S. Antiques & Jewelry
P.O. Box 151
Wyckoff, NJ 07430
phone: 201-934-6528
*Has collection of over 400 figural
ceramic banks; wants to buy cartoon,
Disney, ABC, Leeds, McCoy,
Japanese, etc.*

BANKS (MODERN)

(see also TOYS, Diecast)

Dealers

Donald Amnott
Small Wheels of America
34 Huckleberry Lane
Southington, CT 06489
phone: 800-258-7776
fax: 860-621-8885
*Diecast cars, trucks, planes and
blimps by Ertl, First Gear, Spec-Cast,
PEM; oil company tankers by Hess,
Texaco, Servco and many others.*

Rocky's Contemporary Mechanical
Banks
1 Rydal Place
Montclair, NJ 070423
phone: 201-746-9584
*Buys, sells, trades contemporary
mechanical banks produced from the
1950s and thereafter: banks by
Capron, Book of Knowledge,
Richard's, John Wright, Reynolds,
Wilton, and older Taiwan.*

Kathy & Walter Easterbrook
Eastco Banks & Collectibles
P.O. Box 412
Hancock, NY 13783-0412
phone: 607-467-3040
*Diecast banks and toys: Ertl, Spec-
Cast, First Gear, plastic gas station
promotions.*

Art & Judy Turner
Homestead Collectibles
P.O. Box 173
Mill Hall, PA 17751
phone: 717-726-3597
*Specializing in diecast metal banks
and airplane banks; over 3,200
different banks in stock; send $1 for
price list.*

Toy Collector Club of America
P.O. Box 302
Dyersville, IA 52040
phone: 800-452-3303 or 319-875-7444
*Give collectors the opportunity to
purchase diecast metal banks;
newsletter lists what is available for
purchase and discounts on products.*

Darryl & Georgia Schulz
Georgia's Replica of Yesterday
6945 S 155th W Ave.
Sapulpa, OK 74066
phone: 918-224-2259
*Specializes in die cast collectibles and
banks; Ertl, JLE, Spec-Cast, First
Gear.*

Experts

Richard L. Heuser
Heuser Publishing Div. of Heuser
Enterprises
508 Clapson Rd.
P.O. Box 300
West Winfield, NY 13491-0300
phone: 315-822-4804
fax: 315-822-4804
e-mail: toybanks@concentric.net
Internet: http://www.concentric.net/
~toybanks
*Buys, collects, appraises and
specializes in modern collectible toy
banks and diecast toys.*

Periodicals

Richard L. Heuser
Heuser Publishing Div. of Heuser
Enterprises
Price Guide: Heuser's Price Guide to
Official Collectible Banks
508 Clapson Rd.
P.O. Box 300
West Winfield, NY 13491-0300
phone: 315-822-4804
fax: 315-822-4804
e-mail: toybanks@concentric.net
Internet: http://www.concentric.net/
~toybanks
*Quarterly price guide features Ertl,
First Gear, Liberty Classics, Spec
Cast, Action Racing Collectibles,
Gearbox, Crown Premium/Vees
Collectibles, DG Productions and
others; listed by name, no., quantity,
color, year made and value.*

Richard L. Heuser
Heuser Publishing Div. of Heuser
Enterprises
Newsletter: Heuser's Quarterly
Collectible Diecast Newsletter
508 Clapson Rd.
P.O. Box 300
West Winfield, NY 13491-0300
phone: 315-822-4804
fax: 315-822-4804
e-mail: toybanks@concentric.net
Internet: http://www.concentric.net/
~toybanks
*Focuses on modern diecast collectible
banks and custom imprinted replicas;
new issues; articles of interest to
collectors; listing of dealers and
manufacturers; listing of upcoming
toy shows.*

BAR COLLECTIBLES

(see SALOON & BAR COL-
LECTIBLES)

BARBED WIRE

(see also FENCE COLLECTIBLES)

Clubs/Associations

Dan & Nancy Sowle
New Mexico Barbed Wire Collectors
  Association
Newsletter: Wire Barb & Nail
P.O. Box 102
Stanley, NM 87056-0102
phone: 505-832-4339

John & Eva Tye
California Barbed Wire Collectors
  Association
Newsletter: CBWCA Newsletter
7336 Earhart Ave.
Hesperia, CA 92345
phone: 619-948-0710

John Mantz
American Barbed Wire Collectors
  Society
Newsletter: Wire Collector News
1023 Baldwin Rd.
Bakersfield, CA 93304-4203
phone: 805-397-9572
fax: 805-831-3491
  *The only national association for
  collectors of barbed wire and
  associated fencing tools.*

Collectors

Bill Prain
129 West Homewood Ct.
Genoa, IL 60135-1134
phone: 815-784-2663
  *Collects, trades barbed wire and
  barbed wire related items.*

Experts

Charles & Rosie Dalton
1322 Lark
Lewisville, TX 75067-7606
phone: 972-317-7999
  *Buys, sells, collects and auctions
  barbed wire; authors of "Pocket Book
  of Wires", publishers of "The Barbed
  Wire Collector" newsletter.*

John Mantz
1023 Baldwin Rd.
Bakersfield, CA 93304-4203
phone: 805-397-9572
fax: 805-831-3491

Museums/Libraries

Director
Barbed Wire Museum
P.O. Box 716
La Crosse, KS 67548-0716
phone: 913-222-9900
  *Exhibit includes thousands examples
  of barbed wire plus related tools.*

M.J. VanDeventer
National Cowboy Hall of Fame &
  Western Heritage Center
Magazine: Persimon Hill
1700 N.E. 63rd St.
Oklahoma City, OK 73111-7906
phone: 405-478-2250
fax: 405-478-4714
  *NCHA represents 17 western states;
  preserves the rich heritage of the Old
  West and the memory of those who
  contributed to it.*

Delbert Trew, Dir.
Historical Museum of Barbed Wire &
  Related Fencing Tools
Magazine: Barbed Wire Collector
100 Kingsley St.
P.O. Box 290
Mclean, TX 79057-0290
phone: 806-779-2225 or 806-779-3164
  *Also known as The Devil's Rope
  Museum, has the largest barbed wire
  collection in the world; largest library
  on barbed wire; stocks and publishes
  books on barbed wire.*

BARBER SHOP COLLECTIBLES

(see also BEAUTY SHOP COL-
LECTIBLES; BOTTLES, Barber;
HAIR WORK; SHAVING COL-
LECTIBLES)

Auction Services

James Hagenbuch
Glass Works Auctions
P.O. Box 180
East Greenville, PA 18041
phone: 215-679-5849
fax: 215-679-3068
  *Specializes in the auction of historical
  flasks, fruit jars, barber bottles, food
  and milk bottles, sodas, poisons,
  whiskeys, medicines, inks, bitters,
  target & range balls, scent bottles,
  shaving mugs, blown & pressed glass,
  etc.*

Tony Nard
Nard Auctions
U.S. Rte. 220
Milan, PA 18831
phone: 717-888-9404
fax: 717-888-7723
e-mail: tonynardAclarityconnect.com
  *Conducts specialized auctions of
  occupational shaving mugs, barber
  bottles, razors, country store and
  advertising items, etc.*

Clubs/Associations

Penny Nader
National Shaving Mug Collectors
  Association
Newsletter: Barber Shop Collectibles
  Newsletter
320 S. Glenwood St.
Allentown, PA 18104-6529
phone: 610-437-2534
fax: 610-770-1818
  *Mission is to stimulate the study of
  shaving mugs, razors, barber bottles,
  and all related barbering items.*

Collectors

Burton Handelsman
18 Hotel Dr.
White Plains, NY 10605-3531
phone: 914-428-4480
fax: 914-428-2145
  *Wants to buy shaving mugs,
  personalized barber bottles decorated
  with glass labels, barber shop photos
  and related catalogs.*

Mike Griffin
11 Walton Ave.
White Plains, NY 10606-3212
phone: 914-949-7041
  *Buys early shaving mugs, occupa-
  tional shaving mugs, barber bottles,
  signs, old barber photos; editor of the
  "National Shaving Mug Collectors
  Association Newsletter."*

Bill Campesi
P.O. Box 140
Merrick, NY 11566-0140
phone: 516-546-9630
  *Collector of straight razors, especially
  fancy handles; also wants related
  trade catalogs, advertising, show
  cases, postcards, etc.*

D. Perkins
2317 N. Kessler Blvd.
Indianapolis, IN 46222
phone: 317-638-4519
  *Wants fancy backbars, mugs, cabinets,
  shaving mugs with names and scenes,
  handpainted barber bottles, shave
  paper, vases, signs, shop photos,
  wooden chairs, salesman sample
  chairs, and child chairs, etc.*

Dealers

Chris Jones
Barber Shop Museum, The
1959 Rte. 33, Ste. A
Trenton, NJ 08690-1713
phone: 609-261-4258
fax: 609-261-4258
  *Buys and sells anything Barber Shop
  related; wants signs, tools, backbar
  items, bleeding/cupping and leeching
  utensils, furniture.*

Sigmund Wohl
Razor's Edge, The
P.O. Box 429
Bronxville, NY 10708-0429
phone: 914-476-5939
fax: 914-376-4160
e-mail: swohl@compuserve.com
  *Buys and sells barber and shaving
  collectibles, fancy and unusual razors,
  and related advertising.*

Mike & Mary Sparks
Antiquities, Ltd.
765 Oak Hollow Lane
Lewisville, TX 75067
phone: 972-317-1279 or 972-490-4085
e-mail: msparks1@airmail.net
Internet: http://www.unlimited-ltd.com
  *Buys and sells barber and shaving
  related items, especially shaving
  mugs, barber bottles, fancy straight
  and early safety razors, and barber
  shop furnishings.*

Experts

Chris Jones
Barber Shop Museum, The
1959 Rte. 33, Ste. A
Trenton, NJ 08690-1713
phone: 609-261-4258
fax: 609-261-4258
  *Educational lectures, slide presenta-
  tions, stage and movie prop rentals;
  also does appraisals of barber shop
  and shaving antiques.*

Museums/Libraries

Chris Jones
Barber Shop Museum, The
1959 Rte. 33, Ste. A
Trenton, NJ 08690-1713
phone: 609-261-4258
fax: 609-261-4258
  *Over 3000 items of barbering/shaving
  history documenting the subject from
  the stone age to present; highlights
  include complete, working 1896
  barber shop; tours available by
  appointment only.*

Edwin Jeffers
Barber Museum, The
2 1/2 S. High St.
Canal Winchester, OH 43110
phone: 614-833-9931
  *Collection includes straight razors,
  shaving mugs, barber poles, wooden
  chairs, bloodletting tools, etc.*

Barber Poles

Book Sellers

Robert Marvy
William Marvy Company
1540 St. Clair Ave.
Saint Paul, MN 55105-2344
phone: 612-698-0726 or 800-874-2651
fax: 612-698-4048
  *Manufactures barber poles and
  replacement parts: domes, motors,
  glass and paper cylinders, etc.; also
  sells barber shop books.*

Collectors

John & Joanna Kille
1319 Farley Court South
Arnold, MD 21012
phone: 410-757-8118
  *Buys early wooden and porcelain
  barber poles and chairs; also wants
  unusual barber signs and advertising.*

Suppliers

Robert Marvy
William Marvy Company
1540 St. Clair Ave.
Saint Paul, MN 55105-2344
phone: 612-698-0726 or 800-874-2651
fax: 612-698-4048
  *Manufactures barber poles and
  replacement parts: domes, motors,
  glass and paper cylinders, etc.; also
  sells barber shop books.*

Furnishings

Collectors

Joel Scheckner
15 Glendale Dr.
Englishtown, NJ 07726
phone: 908-462-3827
Wants to buy barbershop contents: wooden barber chairs, child's chairs, salesman samples, barber poles, mug racks, shoeshine stands, backbars, etc.

Shaving Mugs

Clubs/Associations

Penny Nader
National Shaving Mug Collectors Association
Newsletter: Barber Shop Collectibles Newsletter
320 S. Glenwood St.
Allentown, PA 18104-6529
phone: 610-437-2534
fax: 610-770-1818
Mission is to stimulate the study of shaving mugs, razors, barber bottles, and all related barbering items.

Collectors

Lester Dequaine
155 Brewster St.
Bridgeport, CT 06605-3149
phone: 203-335-6833
Wants to buy shaving mugs in figural shapes or animals, humans, birds; also shaving brushes with handles in figural shapes; also early safety razors, mechanical blade sharpeners, razor blade banks, and related advertisements.

Mike Griffin
11 Walton Ave.
White Plains, NY 10606-3212
phone: 914-949-7041
Buys early shaving mugs, occupational shaving mugs, barber bottles, signs, old barber photos; editor of the "National Shaving Mug Collectors Association Newsletter."

Robert Fortin
5334 Strawflower Dr.
Syracuse, NY 13212-1243
Buys and sells barber shop collectibles: occupational shaving mugs, wooden barber poles, child's barber chair, salesman barber chair, good barber signs.

Ralph Nix
P.O. Box 655
Red Bay, AL 35582-0655
phone: 205-356-2997
Wants old, personalized shaving mugs including Occupational and Fraternal mugs.

Morris Pickerell, Jr.
103 South Crawford
Tompkinsville, KY 42167
phone: 800-826-4499
Wants to buy occupational, fraternal, and decorative shaving mugs.

Richard Hebel
233 Dietrich Crescent Dr.
Lawrenceburg, IN 47025
phone: 317-848-2977

Dealers

Joseph Albanese
70 Loretta Dr.
Torrington, CT 06790
phone: 860-482-1854
Buys, sells, collects and appraises barber bottles and shaving mugs: occupational, fraternal, and photographical; also wants to buy interior and exterior photographs of barber shops.

Experts

Burton Handelsman
18 Hotel Dr.
White Plains, NY 10605-3531
phone: 914-428-4480
fax: 914-428-2145
Buys and sells occupational shaving mugs and personalized barber bottles; author of the "Shaving Mugs" section in the Time-Life "Encyclopedia of Collectibles" series.

Chris Machmer
P.O. Box 222
Annville, PA 17003
Major collector specializing in occupational shaving mugs.

Museums/Libraries

Atwater Kent Museum - the History Museum of Philadelphia
15 S. 7th St.
Philadelphia, PA 19143
phone: 215-922-3031

Lightner Museum
P.O. Box 334
Saint Augustine, FL 32085
phone: 904-824-2874

BAROMETERS

(see also INSTRUMENTS & DEVICES, Scientific)

Collectors

Paul H. Hayashi, PE
18 Tarabrook Dr.
Orinda, CA 94563-3121
phone: 510-254-5074 or 510-253-1038
fax: 510-253-0592
Wants to buy old stick barometers.

Dealers

Jill & Chuck Probst
Charles Edwin Antiques
P.O. Box 1340
Louisa, VA 23093-1340
phone: 540-967-0416
fax: 540-967-0416
e-mail: cei@charles-edwin.com
Internet: http://www.charles-edwin.com
Buys, sells, repairs mercury barometers only.

Experts

Jill & Chuck Probst
Charles Edwin Antiques
P.O. Box 1340
Louisa, VA 23093-1340
phone: 540-967-0416
fax: 540-967-0416
e-mail: cei@charles-edwin.com
Internet: http://www.charles-edwin.com
Buys, sells, repairs mercury barometers only.

John Forster
Barometer Fair
P.O. Box 25502
Sarasota, FL 34277
phone: 941-923-6136
fax: 941-923-6136
e-mail: barometer@glimmer.com
Buys, sells, restores all antique barometers; also deals in antique maps, globes, compasses, telescopes and other scientific instruments.

Repair Services

Jill & Chuck Probst
Charles Edwin Antiques
P.O. Box 1340
Louisa, VA 23093-1340
phone: 540-967-0416
fax: 540-967-0416
e-mail: cei@charles-edwin.com
Internet: http://www.charles-edwin.com
Buys, sells, repairs mercury barometers only.

Bob Elsner
Heights Antiques
29 Clubhouse Ln.
Boynton Beach, FL 33436
phone: 561-736-1362
fax: 561-737-2382
Buys, sells, appraises and repairs barometers; antique and reproduction.

BARS

(see BREWERIANA)

BARWARE

(see SALOON & BAR COLLECTIBLES)

BASEBALL CAPS

(see CAPS)

BASKETS

(see also AMERICAN INDIAN; KITCHEN COLLECTIBLES; REPAIR/RESTORATION/CONSERVATION, Cane & Basketry)

Museums/Libraries

Old Salem, Inc.
Salem Station
Drawer F
Winston-Salem, NC 27108
phone: 919-723-3688

Repro. Sources

Stephen Zeh
Stephen Zeh, Basketmaker
Newsletter: News From the Basket Shop
P.O. Box 381
Temple, ME 04984-0381
phone: 207-778-2351
fax: 207-778-6439
e-mail: 71334.3627@compuserve.com
Handcrafted brown ash splint baskets in the tradition of Maine woodsmen, Shakers, and the Native American basket makers; catalog $2.

Davis Lewis Basketry
RD 2 Box 684
Bedford, PA 15522

Darryl & Karen Arawjo
P.O. Box 477
Bushkill, PA 18324-0477
phone: 717-588-6957
Reproduction of Nantucket, Shaker and Appalachian baskets in hand-split white oak; brochure available.

Beth Peterson
Splintworks
P.O. Box 858
Cave Junction, OR 97523

Longaberger

Auction Services

Greg Michael
Craft & Michael Auctioneers
P.O. Box 7
Camden, IN 46917-0007
phone: 219-686-2615 or 219-967-4442
fax: 219-686-9100
Conducts periodical basket auctions.

BATHING BEAUTIES

Nudies & Naughties

(see also EROTICA; FIGURINES, Lady)

Collectors

Dave Harris
1206- 1101 Bay St.
Toronto
Ontario M5S 2W8 Canada
phone: 416-972-6331

Lori Landgrebe
2331 E. Main St.
Decatur, IL 62521-2263
phone: 217-423-2254
Wants German bathing beauties.

BATHROOM FIXTURES

(see PLUMBING)

BATTERSEA ENAMEL BOXES

(see BOXES, Enamel [Battersea]; ENAMELS)

BAUHAUS

(see MODERNISM)

BEADS

(see also AMERICAN INDIAN; GEMS & JEWELRY; PURSES)

Clubs/Associations

Beadesigner International, The New
  England Area Bead Society
135 Aspinwall Ave.
Brookline, MA 02146
phone: 617-499-9432
e-mail: beadesigner@geocities.com
Internet: http://www.geocities.com/
  SoHo/3542/

Peter Francis, Jr
Center for Bead Research
Newsletter: Margaretologist
4 Essex St.
Lake Placid, NY 12946-1236
phone: 518-523-1794
fax: 518-523-0197
e-mail: pfgr@northnet.org
Internet: http://www.thebeadsite.com
  *International leader in the field of
  bead research; publications,
  workshops, lectures, tours, website;
  all devoted to all kinds of beads.*

Bead Society of Greater Washington
P.O. Box 70036
Bethesda, MD 20813-0036
phone: 202-462-8933 or 301-656-9255
  *Monthly meetings featuring slide-
  illustrated lectures, how-to workshops
  about beads and related topics;
  newsletter five times a year with
  articles on bead research, travel,
  collecting, bead bazaars, bead books
  for sale, etc.*

Naomi Rubin
Chicago Midwest Bead Society
Newsletter: Chicago Midwest Bead
  Society
1020 Davis St.
Evanston, IL 60201-3610
phone: 708-328-4040
  *Focuses on glass, organic and metal
  beads and beadwork from ancient to
  contemporary; workshops, speakers,
  bazaar.*

Lestger A. Ross
Society of Bead Researchers
Journal: Bead
56489 El Dorado Dr.
Yucca Valley, CA 92284-4230
phone: 714-792-1497

Paula Althoff, Mem.
Northern California Bead Society
Newsletter: Northern California Bead
  Society Bulletin
1650 Lower Grand Ave.
Piedmont, CA 94611
phone: 510-655-5332
  *Dedicated to the study of beads;
  meetings have lecture slide presentations; members wear beads pertaining
  to the announced meeting topic; major
  annual sale open to the public.*

Alice Scherer
Center for the Study of Beadwork
Newsletter: Notes From a Beadworker's
  Journal
P.O. Box 13719
Portland, OR 97213-0719
phone: 503-248-1848
fax: 503-248-1011
  *Purpose is to gather and disseminate
  information on beadwork; maintains a
  study collection, library, articles file,
  and slide bank; quarterly newsletter.*

Dealers

Mary Roody
Lauren Enterprises, Ltd.
12 North Third St.
St. Charles, IL 60174
phone: 708-513-7306 or 708-584-3899
  *An international bead bazaar;
  specializing in rare beads, pendants,
  textiles and Oriental antiques.*

Naomi Rubin
Originals Gallery of Antique Jewelry &
  Beads
1020 Davis St.
Evanston, IL 60201-3610
phone: 708-328-4040
  *Buys and sells a wide selection of
  beads and components for designing
  and collecting; also design and repair
  of beaded jewelry.*

Ari Imports
8 South Michigan Ave., Ste. 2008
Chicago, IL 60603
phone: 312-332-1988
  Bead importer and distributor.

Christina Blessing
Lost Cities
3395 South Jones #204
Las Vegas, NV 89102
phone: 800-525-3053
  Sells old unusual beads.

Simma Chester
Chester Bead
205 Camino Alto, Ste. 130
Mill Valley, CA 94941
phone: 415-381-3934
  Beads, supplies, jewelry.

Museums/Libraries

Museum of the American Indian, Heye
  Foundation
1 Bowling Green
New York, NY 10004
phone: 212-825-6700

Corning Museum of Glass, The
One Museum Way
Corning, NY 14830-2253
phone: 607-937-5371
fax: 607-937-3352
  *Over 24,000 glass objects, innovative
  exhibits, videos, models; glass history,
  archaeology, and early manufacturing.*

Bead Museum, The
140 South Montezuma
Prescott, AZ 86301
phone: 602-445-2431

Periodicals

Martin Rubin
Newsletter: Old Jewelry News
P.O. Box 272
Evanston, IL 60204
phone: 708-328-6336
  *Publication filled mainly with
  classified ads for old jewelry and
  beads; also classifieds for supplies,
  tools, displays, books, literature, and
  services such as custom design,
  appraisals, repair, advertising,
  photography, etc.*

Suppliers

Gampel Supply Corp.
11 West 37th St.
New York, NY 10018
phone: 212-398-9222
fax: 212-575-0931

Barry
Berger Specialty Company
413 E 8th St.
Los Angeles, CA 90014-2301
phone: 213-627-8785
fax: 213-680-9743
e-mail: Bergers@earthlink.net
  Mail order OK.

Trade

Experts

Gary L. Fogelman
RD 1 Box 240
Turbotville, PA 17772-9599
phone: 717-437-3698
  *Author of "Glass Trade Beads in the
  Northeast and Including Aboriginal
  Bead Industries."*

BEAM BOTTLES

(see BOTTLES, Special Edition
[Beam])

BEAUTY SHOP COLLECTIBLES

(see also HAIR WORK)

Collectors

Collector
P.O. Box 3193
Wallington, NJ 07057
  *Wants barber shop or hair dressers
  collectibles: trade magazines or texts,
  old barber or beauty shop tools or
  furniture; also any photos or material
  on bobbed hair fad of the 1920s.*

Museums/Libraries

Max Factor Museum
1666 North Highland Ave.
Los Angeles, CA 90028
phone: 213-463-6668
  *Filed with artifacts and movie
  memorabilia: a beauty calibrator,
  makeup from the 1920s to 1960s,
  vintage Max Factor ads, etc.*

BEEKEEPING MEMORABILIA

Collectors

John O. Burgess
10738 Harley Rd.
Lorton, VA 22079-3908
  *Wants to buy beekeeping memorabilia
  especially glass honey containers.*

BEER CAN OPENERS

(see CAN OPENERS)

BEER CANS

(see also BREWERIANA)

Clubs/Associations

John Fisher
Capitol City Chapter of the Beer Can
  Collectors of America
Newsletter: Capitol City News
P.O. Box 1526
Prince Frederick, MD 20678
  *If you collect beer cans and
  breweriana, or simple enjoy good
  tasting beer, this club is for you;
  serving Washington DC, Virginia,
  Maryland, and beyond.*

Craig Myers
Gambrinus Chapter of the Beer Can
  Collectors of America
985 Maebelle Way
Westerville, OH 43081-1273
phone: 614-890-0835
  Sponsors annual breweriana show.

Don Hicks, Pres.
Beer Can Collectors of America
Newsletter: Beer Can Collectors News
747 Merus Court
Fenton, MO 63026-2092
phone: 314-343-6486
fax: 314-343-6486
  *Also publishes the "BCCA Want Ad
  Bulletin" newsletter.*

Collectors

Steve Gordon
3821 Queen Mary Dr.
Olney, MD 20832-2103
phone: 301-774-7651 or 301-439-4116
fax: 301-439-7296
e-mail: gono@aol.com
  *Wants to buy pre-1970s U.S. cans,
  especially 12 ounce conetops and flat
  tops; will answer any letter or call
  promptly; also will consider other
  beer-related items.*

Dick Caughey
1410 Brookside Dr.
Memphis, TN 38138
phone: 901-754-4609
  *Wants to buy cone top soda and beer
  cans.*

John Conrad
3245 N. 650 East
Churubusco, IN 46723
phone: 219-693-3507 or 219-693-2464
  *Old beer cans & advertisements; also
  1 qt. old metal oil cans.*

Dealers

AAACRC
P.O. Box 8061
Saddle Brook, NJ 07662-8061
Buys, trades and sells beer cans, complete sets; bottom opened; will sell or trade for silver coins. 12 oz size only, US.

Museums/Libraries

Museum of Beverage Containers & Advertising, The
192 Ridgecrest Dr.
Goodlettsville, TN 37072
phone: 615-859-5236
fax: 615-859-5238
The largest collection of soda and beer cans in the world; buy, sell, trade beer & soda advertising items; also cleans rust from old beer cans.

Suppliers

Soda Mart - Can World
192 Ridgecrest Dr.
Goodlettsville, TN 37072
phone: 615-859-5236
fax: 615-859-5238
Sells breweriana books; also cleans and de-rusts on cans, and sells supplies for the beer can collector.

BEER RELATED COL-
LECTIBLES

(see BEER CANS; BREWERIANA; STEINS)

BEER STEINS

(see STEINS)

BELIEVE IT OR NOT! COL-
LECTIBLES

(see RIPLEY'S BELIEVE IT OR NOT!)

BELLS

Clubs/Associations

American Bell Association International, Inc.
Magazine: Bell Tower, The
P.O. Box 19443
Indianapolis, IN 46219-0443
phone: 210-674-1814
e-mail: jfforman@loop.com
Internet: http://
www.collectoronline.com/club-ABA.html
Purpose is primarily education in the field of bells; the bi-monthly publication is filled with bell related articles.

Collectors

George A. Coupe
1243 1st St. S.E.
Washington, DC 20003
phone: 202-554-1000 or 800-368-5466
fax: 202-863-0775
Wants unusual bells, tap bells, figural, but no bells with handles.

Bells
207 Irwin St.
Brooklyn, MI 49230
phone: 517-592-9030
fax: 517-592-4511
Wants bronze or brass bells from 9" to huge.

Don Hicks
747 Merus Court
Fenton, MO 63026-2092
phone: 314-343-6486
fax: 314-343-6486

Kay Weaver
7210 Bellbrook Dr.
San Antonio, TX 78227-1002
phone: 210-674-1814

Dealers

Don Mathews
3215 Garner Ave.
Ames, IA 50010-4225
phone: 515-232-0938
Wants to buy old metal bells, figural and figurine bells, door bells, books on bells, "Bell" brand product advertising, bell-shaped memorabilia; send photo and price.

Experts

Dorothy Malone Anthony
World of Bells
802 S. Eddy
Fort Scott, KS 66701-2536
phone: 316-223-3404
Over 200 bells in color in each of the 11 books published to date in the "World of Bells" book series; flyer on request.

Museums/Libraries

Iva Mae Long
Bell Haven
Rte. 4 Box 54
Tarentum, PA 15084
One of the largest collections with over 30,000 bells.

Tap

Collectors

T.C. Scott
8511 Cathedral Forest Dr.
Fairfax Station, VA 22039
phone: 703-548-5454 or 800-368-5466
fax: 703-549-3439
Collector wants to buy ornate "tap" bells that were used on counters in hotels, etc.; brass, silver, unusual; will buy single piece or whole collection.

BELT BUCKLES

(see also CLOTHING & ACCESSO-RIES, Vintage; CUFF LINKS)

Clubs/Associations

Bob Bracken
Buckle Buddies International
3208 Jackson Dr.
Holiday, FL 34691-3335

Dealers

High Desert Belt Buckles
P.O. Box 267
Mojave, CA 93502
Wants to buy old belt buckles; send asking price and photocopy or pencil rubbing of front and back.

Experts

Bob Bracken
3208 Jackson Dr.
Holiday, FL 34691-3335
President of Buckle Buddies Int.; appraises, buys, sells, reproduces belt buckles; former staff writer for Buckle Buddies Magazine.

John Deere

Clubs/Associations

John Cooklin
International Association of John Deere Buckle Collectors
2120 22 1/2 Ave.
Rock Island, IL 61201
phone: 309-786-9747

BERMUDA COLLECTIBLES

Collectors

Ernest M. Roberts
5 Corsa St.
Huntington Station, NY 11746-6607
e-mail: roberer@mail.northgrum.com
Wants pre-1950 postcards, covers, hotel stationery, maps, prints, old books, photographs, and other paper ephemera relating to Bermuda; old plates, mugs, cups, silver spoons and all tourist trinkets from Bermuda.

BIBLES

(see also BOOKS)

Collectors

Burke O. Long
16 McLellan St.
Brunswick, ME 04011
phone: 207-725-8920
e-mail: blong@polar.bowdoin.edu
Wants old advertising using Bible scenes, quotes, or themes: paper, postcards, trade cards, signs, celluloids, tin, etc.

Museums/Libraries

American Bible Society
Magazine: Record
1865 Broadway
New York, NY 10023-7503
phone: 212-408-1325
fax: 212-408-1546
Internet: http://www.americanbible.org
Collection of nearly 50,000 bibles, testaments, and scripture portions in approximately 2,000 languages, dating from the 15th cent.

BICYCLES & RELATED MEMO-
RABILIA

(see also RIDING TOYS)

Auction Services

Michael Fallon
Copake Country Auction
P.O. Box H
Copake, NY 12516
phone: 518-329-1142
fax: 518-329-3369
Conducts auctions specializing in the sale of classic bicycles.

Bill Feasel
Bill's Classic Cyclery
2080 Lublin Dr.
Reynoldsburg, OH 43068
Conducts auctions specializing in the sale of classic bicycles, tricycles, wagons and toy pedal vehicles.

Clubs/Associations

Mary Peoples
Wheelmen, The
Magazine: Wheelmen Magazine, The
55 Bucknell Ave.
Trenton, NJ 08619-2059
phone: 609-587-6487
A club with about 800 members dedicated to the enjoyment and preservation of our bicycle heritage.

Executive Director
League of American Bicyclists
Magazine: Bicycle USA
190 West Ostend St., Ste. 120
Baltimore, MD 21230-3755
phone: 410-539-3399
Internet: http://www.bikeleague.org
Bicycle advocacy, bicycle safety promotion, schedules bike events; many antique bike collectors as well as replica builders; newsletter has frequent articles about antique bikes.

Robert B. Balcomb, Past-Pres.
International Veteran Cycle Association
Newsletter: Veteran Cyclist, The
248 Highland Dr.
Findlay, OH 45840-1207
phone: 419-423-2760
International umbrella organization for national clubs of bicycle collectors, historians, enthusiasts; promotes the heritage of the bicycle; focuses on pre-WWI bicycles.

Ron Klaus
Classic Bicycle & Whizzer Club of
America
Newsletter: CBWCA Newsletter
35769 Simon Dr.
Clinton Township, MI 48035
phone: 810-791-5594
*This organization is dedicated to the
preservation, restoration and
enjoyment of special-interest bicycles
and Whizzer Motor Bikes; monthly
newsletter.*

John McDonald, Sec.
Cascade Classic Cycle Club
Newsletter: West-Coaster
7935 SE Market St.
Portland, OR 97215-3655
phone: 503-775-2688
*A club devoted to riding and restoring
classic bicycles; offers members
seminars, technical trips and tours;
newsletter published bi-monthly.*

Collectors

Richard Roy
P.O. Box 280
Branchville, NJ 07826
*Wants old pre-1900 bicycles, tricycles
and related items.*

Wayne R. Batten
RFD 3 #259 Jackson Rd.
Berlin, NJ 08009
phone: 609-767-5994
*Serious collector interested in buying
antique bicycles, related memorabilia,
or related items pertaining to antique
bicycles: advertisements, tools, parts,
clocks, trophies, steins, figurines,
photos, lights, etc.*

Don Peoples
55 Bucknell Ave.
Trenton, NJ 08619-2059
phone: 609-587-6487
*Wants antique pre-1900 highwheel
bicycles and related items such as
bells, cyclometers, lamps, etc.*

John Lannis
P.O. Box 5600
Pittsburgh, PA 15207-0600
phone: 412-461-5099
*Wants bicycles or related literature
1860-1880.*

Art Bransky
1840 Siegfriedale Rd.
Breinigsville, PA 18031-2246
phone: 610-285-6180
*Wants 1930-1960 Deluxe balloon tire
bicycles; also any delivery bicycle or
tricycle or bicycle sidecars.*

Ron Klaus
35769 Simon Dr.
Clinton Township, MI 48035
phone: 810-791-5594

Dealers

Village Schwinn Shop
606 New Road
Somers Point, NJ 08244
phone: 609-927-3775

Bill Feasel
Bill's Classic Cyclery
2080 Lublin Dr.
Reynoldsburg, OH 43068
*Buys/sells antique and classic
bicycles, pedal cars, motorbikes and
motorcycles; mail order catalog of
parts, decals, etc.*

Experts

Jerry Peters
Chestnut Hollow, Ltd.
6060 Bordman Rd.
P.O. Box 6
Almont, MI 48003
phone: 810-798-3158
*Largest collector of classic bicycles in
the US with over 1000; free museum/
showroom with 300 of rarest and
finest bicycles; issues catalog of parts
and accessories for sale ($6); offers
free bicycle identification service.*

Leon Dixon
P.O. Box 28242
Santa Ana, CA 92799-8242
phone: 714-647-1949
e-mail: Oldbicycle@aol.com
Internet: http://members.aol.com/
oldbicycle/index.html
*Wants old deluxe, streamlined (1920-
1965) bicycles, bicycle literature,
memorabilia, catalogs, parts, etc.;
curator of the National Bicycle
History Archive; makes personal
appearances with slide shows, old
movies etc. on bicycles.*

Museums/Libraries

Carl & Clarice Burgwardt
Burgwardt Bicycle Museum
3943 N. Buffalo Rd.
Orchard Park, NY 14127-1841
phone: 716-662-3853 or 716-662-7882
fax: 716-662-4594
e-mail: BicycleMus@aol.com
Internet: http://members.aol.com/
bicyclemus/Bike_Museum/
PedHist.htm
*Contains a sizable collection of
bicycles and related items such as
carbide & kerosene lamps, photographs, advertising & nearly 100
antique steins; will help with research
or appraisals.*

Jerry Peters
Chestnut Hollow, Ltd.
6060 Bordman Rd.
P.O. Box 6
Almont, MI 48003
phone: 810-798-3158
*Largest collector of classic bicycles in
the US with over 1000; free museum/
showroom with 300 of rarest and
finest bicycles; issues catalog of parts
and accessories for sale ($6); offers
free bicycle identification service.*

Leon Dixon, Curator
National Bicycle History Archive
P.O. Box 28242
Santa Ana, CA 92799-8242
phone: 714-647-1949
e-mail: Oldbicycle@aol.com
Internet: http://members.aol.com/
oldbicycle/index.html
*NBHA performs research on old
bicycles and bicycle history; archive
includes in excess of 30,000 original
catalogs, movies, photos, advertisements, books, etc.; each research
based on fee which varies according
to services needed.*

Periodicals

Newsletter: Selector, The
25 E. Fifth Rd.
Oswego, NY 13126
phone: 315-593-2253

John Lannis
Magazine: National Antique & Classic
Bicycle
P.O. Box 5600
Pittsburgh, PA 15207-0600
phone: 412-461-5099
*A monthly publication for buying and
selling antique and classic bicycles.*

Arjay Communications, Inc.
Directory: North Amer. Dir. of Vintage
Bicycle Collectors
325 West Hornbeam Dr.
Longwood, FL 32779-2532
phone: 407-862-0031
e-mail: thecabe@aol.com
*Listing phone numbers and addresses
of people in the hobby.*

Arjay Communications, Inc.
Newsletter: Classic & Antique Bicycle
Exchange
325 West Hornbeam Dr.
Longwood, FL 32779-2532
phone: 407-862-0031
e-mail: thecabe@aol.com

Newsletter: Newsletter by John
5546 Northland Rd.
Indianapolis, IN 46208-2065
phone: 317-297-4755

Magazine: Antique/Classic Bicycle
News
P.O. Box 1049
Ann Arbor, MI 48106
phone: 312-404-8443
fax: 312-404-8443
*The "Voice for the Hobby" bi-
monthly; information on companies,
reprints from catalogs, ads, and event
notices.*

Steve Culver
Newsletter: Classic Bike News
5046 East Wilson Rd.
Clio, MI 48420-9712
phone: 810-687-3528
fax: 810-687-7636
e-mail: artronic@aol.com
*News, history, restoration tips, photo
classifieds and much more.*

Newsletter: Bicycle Trader, The
P.O. Box 3324
Ashland, OR 97520
e-mail: biketrde@mind.net

Repro. Sources

Art Bransky
1840 Siegfriedale Rd.
Breinigsville, PA 18031-2246
phone: 610-285-6180
*Makes repro. parts for Schwinn,
Roadmaster & Ross cycle trucks:
baskets, brackets, store name plates,
kickstands, fender clips.*

Suppliers

Larry Busch
Memory Lane Classics
12551 Jefferson St.
Perrysburg, OH 43551
phone: 419-874-4501
*Publishes a catalog of old and
reproduction parts for sale; also
published the "Bicycle Blue Book"
which lists current prices for vintage
bikes.*

Golden Era Bikes
26448 Rialto
Madison Heights, MI 48071
phone: 810-546-0842
*Carries a wide variety of reproduction
parts for vintage bicycles.*

Maple Island Sales
RR 1, Box 155
Hollandale, MN 56045
phone: 507-889-0842
*Carries a wide variety of reproduction
parts for vintage bicycles.*

Bikes-R-Us
P.O. Box 5065
Bossier City, LA 71171-5065
*Supplier of parts for vintage bicycles;
fully illustrated 60 page catalog for
$7.50.*

License Plates

Collectors

James C. Case
10189 Crane Rd.
Lindley, NY 14858-9719
phone: 607-524-6606
*Wants pre-1920 sidepath tags (early
bike licenses) from all states but
especially New York.*

Roy Klotz
3251 Lenape Dr.
Dresher, PA 19025
phone: 215-884-0808
*Wants bicycle license plates; any
town, any year.*

BILLIARD RELATED ITEMS

Collectors

Tim Lawrence
2489 Bexford Place
Columbus, OH 43209-1710
phone: 614-235-9472
Wants to buy billiard and pool tables,

magazines, books, ivory balls, catalogs, art, old prints, billiard cigarette cards and postcards, antique cues and cue racks, and all other billiard related collectibles; pool table expert.

Maccoun
77 Beale #2313
San Francisco, CA 94106
phone: 415-973-2954
Wants to buy billiard memorabilia from Brunswick, Balke, Collender: catalogs, etc.

Dealers

Ed Lanza
Ed Lanza Billiard Co.
209 W. Evesham Ave.
Magnolia, NJ 08049
phone: 609-346-0384
Antique billiard and pool table accessories.

Paul Giammatteo
Yesteryear Billiards
509 Woodlawn Ave.
Newark, DE 19711-5537
phone: 302-453-8788 or 302-453-8823
fax: 281-251-5993
Dealer and appraiser of antique pool and billiard tables, pool room accessories: cues, chairs, lights, catalogs, trade catalogs, books, ephemera, and related memorabilia; also does restoration of old pool tables.

Dilworth Billiards
300 East Tremont
Charlotte, NC 28203
Wants pool tables, cues and accessories.

Mark Stellinga
416 Sierra Trail
Coralville, IA 52241-1124
phone: 319-354-7287
fax: 319-354-7287
Buys, sells, trades Victorian tables, cue and ball racks, lights, ivory balls, and related collectibles and accessories.

Steven Sawyer
Billiard Warehouse
103 Hardaman Ave.
South Saint Paul, MN 55075
phone: 800-422-7665 or 612-455-1150
fax: 612-455-1150
Wants pool and billiard items: old catalogs, books, posters, letterhead, racks, balls, cues, or anything billiard related.

Al Schwinghammer
Antique Billiard Tables & Accessories
3735 18th St. South
Saint Cloud, MN 56301
phone: 320-259-0294
e-mail: schwing@gte.net
Internet: http://home1.gte.net/schwing/index.htm
Featuring the finest in antique billiards restorations; 19th century

Brunswick tables and rare accessories; buy, sell, trade.

Alan Conway
1696 W. Morton Ave.
Porterville, CA 93257
phone: 209-782-0505
Wants to buy pre-1970 custom pool, billiard, and snooker cues with decoration or inlay; also wants pre-1930 pool tables with decoration or carving, and decorated cue and ball racks.

Dan M. Jacobson
P.O. Box 277101
Sacramento, CA 95827-7101
Wants to buy pool hall, billiard, snooker, and related advertising material.

Experts

Ken Hash
Classic Billiards
4302 Chapel Rd.
Perry Hall, MD 21128-9714
phone: 410-256-0765 or 410-882-7665
Buys, sells, appraises and specializes in antique pool tables or related items; also offers repair/restoration/conservation services.

Periodicals

Magazine: Pool & Billiard Magazine
1701 Bloomingdale Rd.
Glendale Heights, IL 60139-2130

Repair Services

Time After Time
5 Padanaran Rd.
Danbury, CT 06811
phone: 203-743-2801
Wants pool tables, cues and accessories; buys, sells and restores.

Brunswick

Collectors

Dave Wicker
Antique Billiard Center
400 S. Church St.
Monroe, NC 28112
phone: 704-289-4302
Wants Brunswick billiard items from 1845 to 1930: billiard table catalogs, posters, trade cards, lion's head pool tables (Monarchs), and any old paper memorabilia.

BILLIKENS

Collectors

Ronnie Kaplan
209 Harvard St.
Brookline, MA 02146
phone: 617-964-0619
Wants billikens or any information about them.

Judy Knauer
1224 Spring Valley Lane
West Chester, PA 19380-5112
phone: 610-431-3477
e-mail: winkjk@voicenet.com
Wants items that feature a Billiken on them; anything from postcards to dolls and flatware; not interested in carved ivory, gemstones, or novelties from Alaska. Billiken - The God of Good Luck or The God of Things As They Ought To Be.

Belva Green, Ed.
3748 Sunray Dr.
Holiday, FL 34691-3239
phone: 813-942-7354 or 708-549-9970
fax: 708-549-9935
Collecting anything Billikens, Royal Order of Jesters (ROJ): jewelry, figurines (ivory or other material), toys; old or new; query with SASE.

BINOCULARS

(see also OPTICAL ITEMS)

Collectors

Edward Stuart
P.O. Box 21114
Washington, DC 20009
phone: 202-332-6511
Wants old binoculars, American or European, prism type only.

Experts

William M. Beacom
Quality Binoculars
2423 Jackson St.
Sioux City, IA 51104-3548
phone: 712-255-3412
fax: 712-255-0844
Wants binoculars of all types, foreign and domestic; can identify and appraise; also does repairs on some models or will buy any and all for parts.

BIRD CAGES

Repro. Sources

Guemes Arts & Crafts
P.O. Box 3700
Edinburg, TX 78540

J.K. Reed
Victorian Fantasies
1805 SE Union Ave.
Portland, OR 97214

BIRD DECOYS

(see DECOYS, Waterfowl)

BIRD HOUSES

Dealers

Susie Fisk Stern
Birdnest of Ridgefield
2 Big Shop Lane
Ridgefield, CT 06877
phone: 203-431-9889
Buys and sells antique bird houses as well as new ones (some of which are crafted to look old) in hundreds of

styles; welcomes inquiries; will ship merchandise nationwide; always buying old bird houses.

BIRD'S-EYE-MAPLE

Collectors

Norwood H. Keeney, III
P.O. Box 1026
Georges Mills, NH 03751-1026
phone: 603-763-9157
e-mail: keeney@kear.tds.net
Wants items made from bird's-eye-maple, any period; also wants information about this wood and its use; photos encouraged.

BIRTH RELATED ITEMS

(see also PERSONALITIES [Famous], Dionne Quintuplets)

Museums/Libraries

"Miss Helen" Kirk
Multiple Birth Museum
P.O. Box 254
Galveston, TX 77553-0254
phone: 409-762-4792
Interested in anything related to any multiple births.

BISCUIT BARRELS/JARS/TINS

Collectors

Catherine Saunders-Watson
P.O. Box 302
Greenville, NH 03048-0302
phone: 603-878-2171
fax: 603-878-2171
e-mail: gollyqueen@aol.com

Trudie & Les Anderson
Anderson Antiques & Gifts
5224 Sue Marie Lane
Houston, TX 77091
phone: 713-697-1858
Compiling complete history of the biscuit barrel/jar and cracker jars; seeking research material and ephemera; buys and collects Victorian and early 20th century biscuit and cracker barrels/jars.

BISQUE

(see CERAMICS [AMERICAN PRODUCTION ARTWARE], American Bisque Company)

BLACK MEMORABILIA

(see also CHARACTER COLLECTIBLES, Uncle Remus; CIVIL WAR ARTIFACTS; COLLECTIBLES [MODERN], Black Related; DOLLS, Black; MOVIE MEMORABILIA, Movie Posters [Black]; POLITICALLY INCORRECT COLLECTIBLES; SLAVERY ITEMS; SOCIAL CAUSES)

Appraisers

Virgil J. Mayberry
V.J.M. Unlimited, Inc.
559 22nd Ave.
Rock Island, IL 61201-4129
phone: 309-786-6595
fax: 309-786-2114
Appraises one item or complete collections for insurance companies, individuals, and museums; over 30 years experience with black memorabilia; deals only in black memorabilia.

Auction Services

Mike Kranz
Krantz Black Memorabilia Phone Auctions
463 Stage Line Rd.
Hudson, WI 54016-7849
phone: 715-386-7333 or 715-386-9212
Specializes in phone bid auctions of black memorabilia.

Clubs/Associations

Editor
Black Memorabilia Collector's Association
Newsletter: Collecting Our Culture
2482 Devoe Terrace
Bronx, NY 10468
phone: 212-946-1281
Provides information and promotes activities that encourage the collecting, preservation and documentation of black memorabilia.

Collectors

Jan Thalberg
23 Mountain View Dr.
Weston, CT 06883-1317
phone: 203-227-8175
Wants early rag dolls, greeting cards, sewing items, children's books, kitchen items, Aunt Jemima items, playing cards, games & puzzles, canes, perfume bottles, mini bronzes, candy containers; photocopy helpful; please send SASE.

Constance Brendel
P.O. Box 8226
Jersey City, NJ 07308
phone: 201-451-7653
Wants to buy African American early quality photos, historical, military, occupations, Western, children.

Ed Natale, Jr.
P.O. Box 222
Wyckoff, NJ 07481
phone: 201-848-8485
fax: 201-891-4252
Wants to buy black memorabilia: insulting, exaggerated features; figurines, paper, signs; photos helpful.

Lillian Bartok
341 W. 24th St.
New York, NY 10111
phone: 212-255-1059

Dr. E. Maynard
RD 7 Box 370
Monroe, NY 10950
phone: 914-783-1552
Wants black American books and memorabilia: history, biography, fiction, non-fiction.

Richard R. Newman
83 Chauncey St.
Brooklyn, NY 11233
Wants to buy/trade smoking items, toys, figurines, jewelry.

Gene Peters
'Tiques
P.O. Box 3267
Farmingdale, NY 11735-0679
phone: 516-842-9549
Wants documents, pictures, articles and artifacts relating to African-American life from the 19th century through the Civil Rights movement.

Judy Posner
4195 South Tamiami Trail, Ste. 183
Venice, FL 34293-5112
phone: 941-497-7149
fax: 941-493-8085
e-mail: Judyandjef@aol.com
Internet: http://www.tias.com/stores/jpc
Wants black Mammy and Chef cookie jars, salt & pepper shakers and kitchen items.

David L. Hartline
P.O. Box 775
Columbus, OH 43085
Wants 1860-1950 medals, badges and awards given to Black soldiers; also wants military uniforms from Black regiments; prefers if inscribed; all letters answered; 30 years experience.

Margaret Betts
P.O. Box 21790
Detroit, MI 48221

Mike Kranz
463 Stage Line Rd.
Hudson, WI 54016-7849
phone: 715-386-7333 or 715-386-9212
Wants Black memorabilia: cookie jars, string holders, toys, salt & peppers, linens, advertising, etc.

John Hamilton
100 Military Rd.
Newport, MN 55055
phone: 612-458-3939
Wants to buy black collectibles: quality cookie jars, salt and peppers, humidors, toys, string holders, figures, advertising; wants one piece or entire collection.

Esther Roman
6087 Glen Harbor Drive
San Jose, CA 95123-4321
phone: 408-227-1162
Wants to buy Black memorabilia.

Dealers

Catherine Saunders-Watson
P.O. Box 302
Greenville, NH 03048-0302
phone: 603-878-2171
fax: 603-878-2171
e-mail: gollyqueen@aol.com
Wants golliwoggs and other black items: china, humidors, tins, books, toys, games, puzzles, banks, Aunt Jemima, linens, advertising, jewelry, etc.

Leslie Fleuranges
Mahogany Curio Collection
85 Maple St.
Teaneck, NJ 07666
phone: 201-836-7234
Specializing in black porcelain collectibles.

Mitch Kaidy
Born Yesterday Antiques
921 Crittenden Rd.
Rochester, NY 14623
phone: 716-424-4746
Wants black documents, photos, publications on black migration to the North and life in Northern cities 1920s to 1930s; also wants slavery items and items relating to the 1960s Civil Rights movement.

Malinda Saunders
That Certain Place
1401 University Blvd.
Hyattsville, MD 20783
phone: 301-445-2495
Specializing in black memorabilia and in the promotion of black memorabilia shows.

Mark E. Mitchell
African-American History
3002 Winter Pine Ct.
Fairfax, VA 22031-1125
phone: 703-591-3150
fax: 703-385-3152
Buying and selling African-American letters, documents, prints, etc.

Arnold F. Winfield
Winfield Associates
P.O. Box 181
North Chicago, IL 60064-0181
phone: 847-475-8049
Buys and sells black exonumia including tokens, medals and other unusual collectibles.

Bindy Bitterman
Eureka! Antiques
705 W. Washington
Evanston, IL 60202-2214
phone: 847-869-9090
Wants to buy black memorabilia; everything from kitsch to historical; a small shop - they send no lists but write detailed individual letters; SASEs get first attention.

Experts

Gloria & Joe Canada
Canadian Antiques
10812 Southall Dr.
Largo, MD 20772
phone: 301-350-0982
Collector seeking advanced items of Black Americana: porcelains, dolls, bisque, advertising, art, etc.

Dawn E. Reno
3280 Shingler Terrace
Deltona, FL 32738-5351
phone: 904-532-1960
fax: 904-532-1960
e-mail: DawnReno@juno.com
Author of "Encyclopedia of Black Collectibles" (1995, Chilton).

Steven D. Lewis
Lewis & Blalock Collection of Black Memorabilia
P.O. Box 88679
Indianapolis, IN 46208-0679
phone: 317-927-7190
fax: 317-927-7190
Exhibitions and lectures relating to black memorabilia; also wants to buy black memorabilia; does workshops on how to start and build a valuable collection of black memorabilia; Black Memorabilia Hall of Fame 1990.

Jan Lindenberger
P.O. Box 7224
Colorado Springs, CO 80933
phone: 719-591-9558
fax: 719-591-9558
Buys and sells black memorabilia; author of "Black Memorabilia for the Kitchen - Information and Price Guide" and "Black Memorabilia Around the House - Information & Price Guide" (Schiffer Pub., 1993).

Misc. Services

UNICA Shows Unlimited
5406 9th St. NW
Washington, DC 20011
phone: 202-726-8931 or 301-445-2495

Steven D. Lewis
Lewis & Blalock Collection of Black Memorabilia
P.O. Box 88679
Indianapolis, IN 46208-0679
phone: 317-927-7190
fax: 317-927-7190
The Lewis & Blalock Collection was established in 1981 and is housed in Wash., DC; call for further information on lectures and exhibits; Black Memorabilia Hall of Fame 1990.

Esther Roman
6087 Glen Harbor Drive
San Jose, CA 95123-4321
phone: 408-227-1162
Exhibitions and lectures relating to Black memorabilia; workshops on how to start and build a Black collection.

Museums/Libraries

Dr. John E. Fleming, Dir.
National Afro-American Museum &
  Culture Center
P.O. Box 578
Wilberforce, OH 45384-0578
phone: 937-376-4944
fax: 937-376-2007
e-mail: naamcc@erinet.com
Internet: http://winslo.ohio.gov/ohsww/
  places/afroam/index.html
  *Mission is to educate the public about
  African American heritage and culture
  from the African origins to the present
  by collecting, preserving, and
  interpreting material evidence of the
  Black experience.*

Museum of African American History
315 E. Warren St.
Detroit, MI 48201
phone: 313-494-5800
fax: 313-494-5855
Internet: http://www.detnews.com/maah/

Great Plains Black Museum
2213 Lake St.
Omaha, NE 68110
phone: 402-345-2212
  *One of 120 American museums
  belonging to the African American
  Museum Association.*

Periodicals

JAK Productions
Directory: Black Mail Order Directory
30 Limerick Dr.
Albany, NY 12204-1742
  *Listing of black mail order directories,
  marketers, etc.*

Virgil J. Mayberry
V.J.M. Unlimited, Inc.
Newsletter: Blackin'
559 22nd Ave.
Rock Island, IL 61201-4129
phone: 309-786-6595
fax: 309-786-2114
  *Designed to inform subscribers of the
  different black memorabilia items
  being bought and sold.*

Esther Roman
Newsletter: Lookin Back At Black
6087 Glen Harbor Drive
San Jose, CA 95123-4321
phone: 408-227-1162
  *Newsletter published four times a year
  promotes black collecting and sharing
  of information; send SASE for info.*

Postcards (Dance Related)

Collectors

William G. Sommer, MD
9 W. 10th St.
New York, NY 10011-8748
phone: 212-260-0999
  *Wants post cards depicting African-
  American dancing, e.g. Cake Walk,
  Jitterbug; also Waltz, Tango, etc. &
  dance items in other media.*

Sheet Music (Dance Related)

Collectors

William G. Sommer, MD
9 W. 10th St.
New York, NY 10011-8748
phone: 212-260-0999
  *Wants sheet music depicting African-
  American dancing, e.g. Cake Walk,
  Jitterbug; also Waltz, Tango, etc. &
  dance items in other media.*

BLACK POWDER RIFLES

(see FIREARMS, Rifles [Single Shot])

BLACKLIGHTS (UV LAMPS)

Dealers

Rick Morris
Rick's Black Lights & Art Glass
194 Stonefield Circle
Macon, GA 31206
phone: 912-781-5119
e-mail: southern@mindspring.com
Internet: http://www.mindspring.com/
  ~southern1/blacklig.htm
  *Detect fakes and reproductions in cut
  glass, cast iron, paper products,
  pattern glass, vaseline glass, art glass
  and more.*

Man./Prod./Dist.

UVP Inc.
2066 W 11th St.
Upland, CA 91786-3509
phone: 909-946-3197 or 800-452-6788
fax: 909-946-3597
Internet: http://www.uvp.com
  *Suppliers of all styles of high quality
  ultraviolet lamps (blacklights.)*

Misc. Services

Mark Chervenka
Antique & Collectors Reproduction
  News
P.O. Box 12130
Des Moines, IA 50312-9403
phone: 515-274-5886 or 800-227-5531
fax: 515-255-4530
  *Sells pocket size to professional size
  models of readmission lights, invisible
  marking pens, etc.; publishes "Black
  Light for Antiques & Collectibles" 84
  pg. book of tests for damages/repairs,
  fakes, reproductions on glass, china,
  paper.*

BLACKSMITHING ITEMS

(see also KNIVES; TOOLS)

Collectors

Richard L. Weiss
RD 2 Box 641
Breinigsville, PA 18031
phone: 610-285-4122
  *Wants rare and unusual blacksmithing
  tools, literature, advertising signs and
  related items.*

Museums/Libraries

Eugene I. Morris, Dir.
New England Fire & History Museum
Newsletter: Siren Soundings
1439 Main St. (Rte. 6A)
Brewster, MA 02631
phone: 508-896-5711 or 508-945-9413
  *Mr. Morris appraises and has written
  many articles relating to fire fighting,
  apothecary and blacksmithing
  material.*

BLIMPS

(see AIRSHIPS)

BLOTTERS

(see also INKWELLS &
INKSTANDS; PAPER COL-
LECTIBLES; PENS)

Collectors

Homer Neel
4213 Westridge Dr.
North Little Rock, AR 72116
  *Wants old advertising ink blotters: all
  subjects, must be in mint condition.*

Pat Patrick
501 Crawford #302
Houston, TX 77002
phone: 713-546-3244
  *Wants to buy advertising ink blotters,
  especially monkeys; pre-1940 of
  special interest; will consider any that
  are in excellent condition; please send
  photo.*

BLUE JEANS

(see CLOTHING & ACCESSORIES,
Denim)

BLUE RIDGE

(see CERAMICS [AMERICAN
DINNERWARE], Southern Potteries/
Blue Ridge)

BOATS

(see also OUTBOARD MOTORS;
MODELS, Boats; NAUTICAL
ANTIQUES; STEAMBOAT
COLLECTIBLES; TOYS, Boats &
Outboards)

Auction Services

David A. Norton
Norton Auctioneers of Michigan, Inc.
Pearl at Monroe St.
Coldwater, MI 49036
phone: 517-279-9063
fax: 517-279-9191
  *Conducts specialized auctions for
  antique, classic and collectible boats.*

Clubs/Associations

Antique & Classic Boat Society
Newsletter: Rusty Rudder
715 Mary St.
Clayton, NY 13624
phone: 315-686-BOAT

Century Boat Club
P.O. Box 761
Manistee, MI 49660

Collectors

C.E. Berry
13375 Havelock Trail
Apple Valley, MN 55124
  *Wants to buy boat catalogs and
  related literature; also factory items
  for any wooden boat from the 1890s to
  1960s: Hacker, Garwood, Chris-
  Craft, Century, and others.*

James King
1178 Chillem Dr.
Batavia, IL 60510-3309
phone: 630-879-2263
  *Wants to buy mahogany boats;
  inboard launches, runabouts, racers.
  Chris-Craft, Garwood, Greavette,
  Century, Streblow, etc.*

Experts

Wilson W. Wright
217 South Adams St.
Tallahassee, FL 32301-1720
phone: 904-224-5169
fax: 904-224-1033
Internet: http://www.nettally.com/
  wnright
  Specializes in antique boats.

Museums/Libraries

Herreshoff Maritime Museum
P.O. Box 450
Bristol, RI 02809-0450
phone: 401-253-5000

Maine Maritime Museum
Journal: Rumb Line, The
243 Washington St.
Bath, ME 04530
phone: 207-443-1316
fax: 207-443-1665
e-mail: maritime@bathmaine.com
Internet: http://www.bathmaine.com
  *The repository and exhibition space
  for the premier collection of objects
  illustrating Maine's maritime
  heritage.*

Adirondack Museum, The
Rte. 30
P.O. Box 99
Blue Mountain Lake, NY 12812
phone: 518-352-7311
  *Sponsors wooden boat regatta to
  learn about the rich heritage of boats
  in the region; has an extensive boat
  collection.*

Antique Boat Museum
750 Mary St.
Clayton, NY 13624
phone: 315-686-4104
  *General focus in on freshwater boats
  and engines: 150 antique and classic
  boats, 300 engines and related
  objects; conducts annual boat auction.*

Pete Lesher, Cur.
Chesapeake Bay Maritime Museum
Magazine: Water Gauge, The
P.O. Box 636
Saint Michaels, MD 21663-0636
phone: 410-745-2916
fax: 410-745-6088
Internet: http://www.cbmm.org
*A major regional maritime museum
with a 5200 volume research library;
collections include 10,000 objects,
9.000 photos, 1,200 ships' plans, 72
linear feet of manuscripts; decoys,
oystering, lighthouses, charts,
nautical, tools.*

Periodicals

Bob Hicks
Magazine: Messing About In Boats
29 Burley St.
Wenham, MA 01984
phone: 508-774-0906
*Great biweekly magazine about
interesting boats & people who
design, build, restore and/or use them
- sail, oar, antique, steam, etc.*

Magazine: WoodenBoat
P.O. Box 78
Brooklin, ME 04616
phone: 207-359-4651 or 800-877-5284
fax: 207-359-8920
Internet: http://www.woodenboat.com
*A glossy bi-monthly magazine for
wooden boat owners, builders, and
designers; construction plans and
techniques; calendar of events, ads,
navigation, wood and other boat
building supplies, etc.*

Trader Publishing Company
Magazine: Yacht Trader
P.O. Box 9059
Clearwater, FL 34618-9059
phone: 813-712-0035 or 800-548-8889
fax: 813-712-0034
Internet: http://www.traderonline.com

Steve Ferguson, Ed.
National Automobile Dealers Association
Price Guide: N.A.D.A. Official Used Car
Guide
P.O. Box 7800
Costa Mesa, CA 92628
phone: 800-966-6232
fax: 714-556-8715
e-mail: steve.ferguson@nadaguides.com
Internet: http://www.nadaguide.com
*A series of value guides for domestic
and foreign cars, trucks, vans, RV's,
mobile homes, motorcycles,
snowmobiles, and boats, small and
large; also Heavy Duty Trucks and
Aircraft Book, car clubs & organizations, museums.*

Directory: Mahogany Dreams
P.O. Box 1081
Lodi, CA 95241-1081
*Directory and resource guide to firms
and individuals specializing in parts
and services for the repair and
restoration of antique/classic ·
mahogany runabouts and cruisers.*

Canoes

Clubs/Associations

P. Christopher Merigold, Pres.
Wooden Canoe Heritage Association,
Ltd.
Magazine: Wooden Canoe
P.O. Box 226
Blue Mountain Lake, NY 12812
phone: 803-643-3800
*Non-profit association dedicated to
preserving, studying, building,
restoring and using wooden and birch
bark canoes; articles and ads for
supplies, restorers, parts, gatherings,
etc.; chapters across the U.S. and
Canada.*

Misc. Services

David Gidmark
Box 26
Maniwaki
Quebec J9E 3B3 Canada
*Offers course on birch bark canoe
building.*

Periodicals

Magazine: Kanawa
1029 Hyde Park Rd., Ste. 5
London
Ontario N0M 1Z0 Canada
phone: 519-473-2109 or 519-641-1261
fax: 519-473-6560
*The "Voice of Paddling in Canada",
72-page full color magazine covering
everything you need to know about
canoeing.*

Magazine: Canoe Magazine
P.O. Box 3146
Kirkland, WA 98083
phone: 206-827-6363

Repair Services

West Coast Canoe Company
P.O. Box 143
Campbell River
British Col. V9w 5A7 Canada
phone: 604-287-7348
*Wooden canoe restoration and
repairs.*

Northwoods Canoe Co.
RFD 3 Box 118-A2
Dover Foxcroft, ME 04426
*Restores classic boats and builds
custom boats.*

McGreivey's Canoe Shop
1379 Old State Rd.
Cato, NY 13033
phone: 315-626-6635
*Restorers of classic canoes and guide
boats.*

Gilbert Cramer
Wooden Canoe Shop, Inc.
03583 RD 13
Bryan, OH 43506-9804
phone: 419-636-1689
*Repairs and restorations of wood/
canvas canoes and boats; buys and
sells unrestored canoes and sells
restored canoes.*

Chris Crafts

Clubs/Associations

Wilson W. Wright, Ex.Dir.
Chris Craft Antique Boat Club, Inc.
Newsletter: Brass Bell
217 South Adams St.
Tallahassee, FL 32301-1720
phone: 904-224-5169
fax: 904-224-1033
Internet: http://www.nettally.com/
wnright
*Assists members with collecting,
restoring, maintaining vintage Chris
Crafts; quarterly newsletter has
antique boat show calendar, articles,
how-to hints, ads, restorers/boat
works, model builders, marine
instrument repairs, etc.*

Engines

Collectors

James King
1178 Chillem Dr.
Batavia, IL 60510-3309
phone: 630-879-2263
*Wants to buy old inboard marine
engines, one to twelve cylinders.
Marinized aero engines, racing
engines. Scripps, Kermath, Hisso,
Packard, etc.*

Model

Clubs/Associations

John Snow
U.S. Vintage Model Yacht Group
Newsletter: Vintage Model Yacht
Newsletter
78 East Orchard St.
Marblehead, MA 01945
phone: 617-631-4203 or 617-639-0779
Internet: http://www.swcp.com/usvmyg
*Devoted to the preservation and
sailing of older wooden model
sailboats (pond boats) and to the
study of the history of model yachting
in North America; library of old
model yachting, periodicals, articles
and design plans available.*

Dealers

J. Tobin
Antique & Classic Boats
12 Carstead Dr.
Slingerlands, NY 12159
phone: 518-439-0477
fax: 518-439-0477
*Buys and sells pond boats - late 19th
and early 20th century sail boats
designed to be sailed on ponds.*

Steam

Clubs/Associations

International Steamboat Society
Journal: Steamboating
Rte. 1 Box 262
Middlebourne, WV 26149-9748
phone: 304-386-4434
fax: 304-386-4868

Tug

Clubs/Associations

Tugboat Enthusiasts Society of the
Americas
Magazine: Tug Bitts
308 Quince St.
Mount Pleasant, SC 29464-3420
phone: 803-881-1173
*Published quarterly; covers steamboat
& inland river history; packed with
news, photos, articles on all types of
tow boats, tugboats (harbor, ocean,
military) and work boat salvage,
restoration and history; a must for
tugboat enthusiasts.*

BONES

(see ANIMAL TROPHIES;
FURNITURE [ANTIQUE], Antler &
Horn; ODDITIES & THE MORBID;
SKELETONS)

BOOK ARTS

(see also BOOKS, Repair Services for;
PRINTING EQUIPMENT)

Experts

Floyd Pearce
Pterodactyl Press
Main St.
Cumberland, IA 50843
phone: 712-744-2244
*Expert in the old-fashioned way of
printing: typesetting, bookbinding,
marbling paper, etc.*

Museums/Libraries

University of California, Special
Collections Department
P.O. Box 5900
Riverside, CA 92517
phone: 714-787-3233 or 714-784-7324
fax: 714-787-3285
*Collection of material on the Book
Arts, especially book binding,
papermaking, fine presses, forgeries,
etc.*

BOOKLETS

(see PAPER COLLECTIBLES)

BOOKMARKS

(see also PAPER CLIPS;
STEVENGRAPHS)

Clubs/Associations

Richard W. Kelly
Antique Bookmark Collector's
  Association
2224 Cherokee
Saint Louis, MO 63118

Collectors

Joan L. Huegel
1002 West 25th St.
Erie, PA 16502-2427

Experts

Dr. Judith Ackerman
P.O. Box 354
West Long Branch, NJ 07764-0354
phone: 908-531-3624
e-mail: 75107.3410@compuserve.com
  *Researching and writing about all
  aspects of bookmarks, including all
  materials, periods and styles.*

Periodicals

Joan L. Huegel
Newsletter: Bookmark Collector
1002 West 25th St.
Erie, PA 16502-2427
  *A friendly, informative newsletter for
  all collectors; for those wanting only
  antique as well as those who collect
  new and modern bookmarks, too;
  published quarterly.*

Notched

Collectors

John T. Ogle
P.O. Box 252
Ocean Springs, MS 39566-0252
  *Wants to buy paper clips and notched
  bookmarks: antique, foreign, plastic,
  novelty, advertising; also wants early
  paper clip advertising.*

BOOKPLATES

Clubs/Associations

Mr. G.P. Smith, Mem.
Bookplate Society
Journal: Bookplate Society Newsletter
Stancroft
125 Brampton Rd., Carlisle
Cumbria CA3 9AP, U.K.
  *Write for details; membership
  includes journal and newsletter, free
  book and bookplates.*

Audrey Spencer Arellanes, Ed.
American Society of Bookplate
  Collectors & Designers
Newsletter: Bookplates in the News
605 N. Stoneman Ave., No. F
Alhambra, CA 91801-1406
phone: 818-570-9404
  *Quarterly newsletter features articles
  on contemporary bookplate artists &
  collectors, news of exhibitions,
  competitions, literature.*

Collectors

Lewis Jaffe
1919 Chestnut St., Apt. 1117
Philadelphia, PA 19103-3418
phone: 215-568-9253
fax: 215-568-6768

Dealers

James Wilson
22 Castle St.
Berkhamsted
Hertfordshire HP4 2DW, U.K.
phone: 01442-873396
  *Largest dealer in England for
  bookplates and books about
  bookplates.*

Thomas G. Boss Fine Books
355 Boylston St.
Boston, MA 02116-3313
phone: 617-427-1880
fax: 617-536-7072
  *Carries the largest stock of bookplates
  in the U.S.; Art Deco, Art Nouveau,
  Arts & Crafts; also fine bindings.*

BOOKS

(see also ACCOUNT BOOKS;
AUTOGRAPH BOOKS; ATLASES;
AUCTION CATALOGS; BIBLES;
BOOK ARTS; COMIC BOOKS;
COOKBOOKS; DIARIES; HYM-
NALS; ILLUSTRATORS; MAPS &
CHARTS; MYSTERY/DETECTIVE
ITEMS; PAPER COLLECTIBLES;
PERSONALITIES [LITERARY];
SCIENCE FICTION)

Appraisers

Lee Temares
50 Heights Rd.
Manhasset, NY 11030-1413
phone: 516-627-8688 or 516-627-2647
fax: 516-627-7822
  *Buys children's series books; must
  have dust jackets if they originally had
  them; also wants Limited Editions
  Club and Heritage Press books, but
  must be in very good condition and in
  fine boxes; appraises all books except
  law & medicine.*

Kevin T. Ransom
Kevin T. Ransom Bookseller
P.O. Box 176
Amherst, NY 14226
phone: 716-839-1510
  First editions and rare books.

Auction Services

Richard Oinonen
Oinonen's Book Auctions
P.O. Box 470
Sunderland, MA 01375

Richard & Mary Sykes
New Hampshire Book Auctions
P.O. Box 460
Weare, NH 03281
phone: 603-529-7432
  *Specializes in the auction of books,
  maps, prints and ephemera.*

Swann Galleries, Inc.
104 E. 25th St.
New York, NY 10010-2977
phone: 212-254-4710
fax: 212-979-1017
e-mail: SwannSales@aol.com
  *Oldest/largest U.S. auctioneer
  specializing in rare books, autographs
  & manuscripts, Judaica, photographs,
  and works of art on paper.*

Lynn Martin
Freeman/Fine Arts of Philadelphia
1808 Chestnut St.
Philadelphia, PA 19103
phone: 215-563-9275 or 215-563-9453
fax: 215-563-8236
  *America's oldest auction house:
  Continental, English and American
  furniture, paintings, silver and
  decorative arts; Oriental rugs, rare
  books, fine jewelry, Orientalia.*

Dale Sorenson
Waverly Auctions, Inc.
4931 Cordell Ave.
Bethesda, MD 20814-2508
phone: 301-951-8883
fax: 301-718-8375
e-mail: wavauc@clark.net
  *Specializes in the auction of graphic
  art, books, paper, atlases, prints,
  postcards, autographs, and other
  paper ephemera.*

Chris Bready
Baltimore Book Co., Inc.
2114 N. Charles St.
Baltimore, MD 21218
phone: 410-659-0550
  *Buys and auctions books, prints,
  paintings, autographs, photographs,
  and ephemera.*

Stephen Neil Greengard
California Book Auction Galleries
220 San Bruno Ave.
San Francisco, CA 94103-5018
phone: 415-861-7500
fax: 415-553-8678

George K. Fox
Pacific Book Auction Galleries
133 Kearny St., 4th Floor
San Francisco, CA 94108-4805
phone: 415-989-2665
fax: 415-989-1664
e-mail: pba@slip.net
Internet: http://www.nbn.com/pba
  *Conducts numerous auctions each
  year of rare books, manuscripts,
  maps, autographs, historical material,
  early photography, prints, and fine
  literary property.*

Clubs/Associations

Antiquarian Booksellers Association of
  America
Newsletter: ABAA Newsletter
50 Rockefeller Plaza
New York, NY 10020-1605
phone: 212-757-9395
fax: 212-459-0307
e-mail: abaa@panix.com
Internet: http://www.abaa-booknet.com/
  booknet1.html
  *A non-profit association; publishes a
  membership directory and a
  newsletter.*

Lee Temares
Long Island Antiquarian Book Dealers
  Association
Newsletter: LIABDA Newsletter
P.O. Box 622
Plandome, NY 11030
phone: 576-627-8688 or 576-368-4858
fax: 576-627-7822

Lee Harrer
Florida Bibliophile Society
Newsletter: FBL Newsletter
P.O. Box 3887
Saint Petersburg, FL 33731-3887
phone: 813-536-4029
  Newsletter is published monthly.

Collectors

Joseph W. Toti, Esq.
4719 Easthill Dr., SW
Roanoke, VA 24018
  *Collects primarily signed first edition
  books; however, also a collector of all
  genre of books.*

Ivan Gilbert, MD
A.A. Miran Art & Books
921 Eastwind Dr., Ste. 104
Westerville, OH 43081
  *Buys and sells books, catalogs,
  medical books, art, photography,
  Americana, modern 1st editions, and
  erotica.*

Tom Rutledge
3015 Bever Ave., SE
Cedar Rapids, IA 52403
phone: 319-399-1427
  *Wants rare & antiquarian books,
  manuscripts, autographs, first
  editions, children's books, fore-edge
  painted books, illustrated books,
  Modern Library books, pop-ups, Asian
  art, and collectible paperbacks.*

Dealers

Steve Finer
Steve Finer Rare Books
P.O. Box 758
Greenfield, MA 01302
phone: 413-773-5811

Thomas G. Boss Fine Books
355 Boylston St.
Boston, MA 02116-3313
phone: 617-427-1880
fax: 617-536-7072
  *Fine printing, fine binding and
  illustration, especially in the 1890-*

1946 period; also bookplates, drawings, posters, and prints.

Karen & Jim Weyant
Scribe's Perch, The
58 Ayrault St.
Middletown, RI 02840
phone: 401-849-8839
fax: 401-848-5608
e-mail: karen@scribesperch.com
Internet: http://www.scribesperch.com
Dealers in out-of-print and collectible books; specializing in Americana, military history, nautical, literature; has searchable database on web site.

George & Julie Perron
Old Paperphiles, The
P.O. Box 135
Tiverton, RI 02878-0135
phone: 401-624-9420
fax: 401-624-4204
Buys and sells paper collectibles: books, autographs, sheet music, postcards, photos, stereoviews, documents, old letters; issues periodic catalog of items for sale.

Tuttle Antiquarian Books
28 South Main St.
Rutland, VT 05701
phone: 802-773-8229
e-mail: tuttbook@interloc.com
Internet: http://www.abaa-booknet.com/usa/tuttle
General second-hand bookshop specializing in Americana, Orientalia, genealogy; welcomes quotations and inquiries concerning miniature books, genealogies, and family histories.

Bel Canto Books
P.O. Box 55
Metuchen, NJ 08840-0055
phone: 732-548-7371
Wants books about music and dance.

J.N. Bartfield Books, Inc.
30 West 57th St.
Third Floor
New York, NY 10019
phone: 212-245-8890
fax: 212-541-4860
Wants to buy fine books: Americana, atlases, Canadiana, color plate books, fore-edge painting, fine leather bindings, rare books, first editions, sporting books, autographs, manuscripts, original diaries and journals.

Bibi Mohamed
Imperial Fine Books, Inc.
790 Madison Ave. Ste. 200
New York, NY 10021
phone: 212-861-6620
fax: 212-249-0333
Fine books bought and sold; sets, fine and decorative bindings, first editions, fore-edge paintings, children's & illustrated books, etc.; issues catalogs; bookbinding.

Argosy Book Store
116 East 59th St.
New York, NY 10022
phone: 212-753-4455
Carries rare books in all subject areas.

Diana Rudy
Book Look
P.O. Box 450
Warwick, NY 10990
phone: 800-223-0540
fax: 914-651-1233
e-mail: sales@booklook.com
Internet: http://www.booklook.com
Largest out-of-print book search service in the U.S.; any book located.

Dan Weaver
Daniel T. Weaver, Bookseller
21 Bunn St.
Amsterdam, NY 12010-3505
phone: 518-842-3498
Buys and sells used and out-of-print books in almost all subject areas, but especially Protestant religion, children's books and books for home schoolers; also offers search service.

George S. MacManus Co.
1317 Irving St.
Philadelphia, PA 19107
phone: 215-735-4456

Carmen D. Valentino
Rare Books & Manuscripts
2956 Richmond St., Drawer 19
Philadelphia, PA 19134-5720
phone: 215-739-6056
Antiquarian bookseller specializing in rare books, manuscripts, documents, early newspapers, diaries, account books, ledgers, ephemera, broadsides; pre-WWI.

Howard Weetall
Antiquarian Bookworm, The
7315 Wisconsin Ave.
Bethesda, MD 20814-3202
phone: 301-656-3779
e-mail: weetal@erols.com
Buying and selling out-of-print books since 1968; Americana, Civil War, non-fiction, natural History; interested in purchasing good quality books, maps, and prints.

Stan Modjesky
Book Miser, Inc.
906 Fell St.
Baltimore, MD 21231-3504
phone: 410-276-9880
fax: 410-276-1405
e-mail: 71660.3355@compuserve.com
Dealer in used, rare and new books; specializes in maritime/nautical, history, MD history, music, religion, and Americana books; Interloc participants; Bibliofind participants.

Bookpress, Ltd., The
P.O. Box KP
Williamsburg, VA 23187
phone: 804-229-1260
fax: 804-229-0498
A rare book service buying and selling fine books, old maps and prints.

Judge of Mysteries (J.O.M.) Books
4719 Easthill Dr.
Roanoke, VA 24018-2841
Buys and sells all sorts of books; offers periodic catalog listing items for sale.

Jim Reed
Reed Books
P.O. Box 55893
Birmingham, AL 35255
phone: 205-326-4460
fax: 205-326-4468
e-mail: 73252.1706@compuserve.com
Reed Books is a specialized, international book search company that finds old out-of-print books and magazines.

Joe Davidson
Aaron's Archives
5185 Windfall Rd.
Medina, OH 44256-8703
phone: 330-723-7172
Wants to buy pre-1895 books containing color plates, etchings, engravings plus pre-1600 Medieval books and manuscripts.

William Butts
Main Street Fine Books & Manuscripts
206 N. Main St.
Galena, IL 61035-2244
phone: 815-777-3749
Open shop dealing in autographs and out-of-print books in most fields; specializing in all aspects of American history; boos and autograph catalogs issued regularly; member of A.B.A.A.

Bob & Beverlee Reimers
Peddler's Wagon
P.O. Box 109
Lamar, MO 64759-0109
phone: 417-682-3734
Buys and sells books on quilting, needlework, children's illustrated books, Little Golden books, and series books; mail order only.

Barbara Ruppert
Alcott Books
5909 Darnell
Houston, TX 77074-7719
phone: 713-774-2202
e-mail: bruppert@webtv.net
Wants to buy books: Dick and Jane Readers, first edition mysteries with dust jackets, signed editions, early first editions of Stephen King, books illustrated by Maxfield Parrish, OZ books.

Barrie D. Watson
Barrie D. Watson Bookseller
P.O. Box 38
Beulah, CO 81023
phone: 719-485-3136 or 800-785-3136
fax: 719-485-3838

Barbara Gelink
OTENTO Book Search
4756 Terrace Dr.
San Diego, CA 92116-2514
phone: 619-281-8962
Book finder for out-of-print books; places ads in national book magazines and has realized a 50% success rate; charges $2 per title to locate book which usually takes 2-3 months; specializes in cookbooks, children's books, and bibles.

Jean Parmer
Parmer Books
7644 Forrestal Rd.
San Diego, CA 92120-2203
phone: 619-287-0693
fax: 619-287-6135
e-mail: parmerbook@aol.com
Polar, Arctic, Antarctic, voyages, sail, Pacific, exploration.

Richard Gilbo
Richard Gilbo - Bookseller
P.O. Box 12
Carpinteria, CA 93014-0012
phone: 805-684-2892
Specializes in books about food and drink, cats; also specializes in literature.

Thorn Books
P.O. Box 1244
Moorpark, CA 93020
phone: 805-529-3647

Brick Row Book Shop
49 Geary St. #235
San Francisco, CA 94108-5705
phone: 415-398-0414
fax: 415-398-0435
e-mail: crichton@brickrow.com
Internet: http://www.brickrow.com
Specializes in first editions of English and American literature, especially of the 18th and 19th centuries; over 8,000 titles in stock; want lists accepted; buys fine and rare books.

Alan Bamberger
2510 Bush St.
San Francisco, CA 94115-3002
phone: 415-931-7875
fax: 415-922-3580
e-mail: alanb@sirius.com
Internet: http://www.experts.com/bas.html
Buys and sells rare, out-of-print and collectible reference books on the fine and decorative arts.

J.B. Muns
Fine Arts Books & Musical Autographs
1162 Shattuck Ave.
Berkeley, CA 94707-2635
phone: 510-525-2420
fax: 510-525-1126
Buys and sells books: art, architecture, dance, photography; member

ABAA, Manuscript Society, UACC, PADA; serving libraries, the public and other dealers since 1964; by appointment only.

Great Northwest Book Store
1234 SW Stark
Portland, OR 97205-2310
phone: 503-223-8098

Wessel & Lieberman
121 First Ave. S.
Seattle, WA 98104
phone: 206-682-3545

Experts

Pat & Allen Ahearn
Quill & Brush
P.O. Box 5365
Rockville, MD 20853-5365
phone: 301-460-3700
fax: 301-871-5425
Author of "Book Collecting, A Comprehensive Guide", "Collected Books, The Guide to Values" and "Author Price Guides."

Douglas O'Dell
Chapel Hill Rare Books
143 W. Franklin St., Ste. 310
Chapel Hill, NC 27516
phone: 919-929-8351
Fine rare books in all fields, first editions in literature and Americana; inscribe copies, bindings, travels, etc.; author on books.

Robert & Arne Hayman
Robert G. Hayman Antiquarian Books
575 West St.
Carey, OH 43316-1421
e-mail: BAHayman@aol.com
Writes "Antiquarian Books" column for AntiqueWeek newspaper; will respond to queries but only if a SASE is included with the request.

Ray Walsh
Curious Book Shop
307 E. Grand River
East Lansing, MI 48823-4324
phone: 517-332-0112
Dealer/expert; owner of three book shops in Michigan; hosts radio call-in show about books and paper collectibles; writes columns; send a SASE for reply when writing.

Museums/Libraries

Library of Congress
10 First St. SE
Washington, DC 20540
phone: 202-707-5000

Consortium of Popular Culture Collections
Popular Culture Library
Bowling Green State University
Bowling Green, OH 43403-0001
phone: 419-372-2450
fax: 419-372-7996
Consortium composed of Bowling Green State U., Kent State U., Michigan State U., and Ohio State U.; the largest academic library

collections of primary research material in comic art, popular fiction, popular music, performing arts.

Toledo Museum of Art, The
2445 Monroe St.
P.O. Box 1013
Toledo, OH 43697
phone: 419-255-8000
Internationally-recognized collection of artist-illustrated books, as well as paintings, decorative arts, graphic arts, and glass.

On-Line Services

Michael Carnell
Data by Design
P.O. Box 31994
Charleston, SC 29417
phone: 803-556-0562
Runs "The Book Board", a computer/modem bulletin board system for book collectors and dealers; pricing; place ads, events, fairs, signings, collectors' programs, etc.

Richard M. Weatherford
Interloc, Inc.
P.O. Box 5
Southworth, WA 98386-0005
phone: 360-871-3617
fax: 360-871-5626
e-mail: weatherf@Interloc.com
Internet: http://www.interloc.com
The electronic marketplace for books; reach more buyers and sellers; select from 2+ million titles offered by booksellers worldwide; book searching; appraisal offerings.

Periodicals

D. Leab
Price Guide: American Book Prices Current
P.O. Box 1236
Washington Depot, CT 06793
phone: 212-737-2715
fax: 203-868-0080
ABPC is an annual volume listing over 35,000 prices of books, serials, autographs & manuscripts, broadsides, and maps from actual auction sales in U.S. and abroad; the standard reference work in the field.

Magazine: AB Bookman's Weekly
P.O. Box AB
Clifton, NJ 07015
phone: 201-772-0020
fax: 201-772-9281
e-mail: abbookman@aol.com
Internet: http://www.abaa-booknet.com/booknet1.html
Weekly magazine for the book collecting world; excellent guide to out-of-print and rare books.

John C. Huckans, Ed.
Magazine: Book Source Monthly
2007 Syosset Dr.
P.O. Box 567
Cazenovia, NY 13035-0567
phone: 315-655-8499
fax: 315-655-8499
Book Source Monthly serves both

members of the antiquarian book trade and private collectors; books, paper ephemera; contains book fair calendar, book auction calendar, specialists' directories, catalogs received, open shop guide.

Ruth E. Robinson
Ruth E. Robinson Books
Directory: Buy Books Where, Buy Books Where
Rte. 7 Box 162A
Morgantown, WV 26505
An annual directory listing people who sell and buy specialties.

Newsletter: Bookseller
P.O. Box 8183
Ann Arbor, MI 48107-8183
phone: 313-930-0450
fax: 313-930-0450
Covers out-of-print, rare and used books; published 24 times per year; oversized newsletter filled with names of book searchers, dealers, and collectors in search of specific books; books wanted and book for sale ads; free sample copy.

Doug Watson
Magazine: Paper Collectors' Marketplace
470 Main St.
P.O. Box 128
Scandinavia, WI 54977-0128
phone: 715-467-2379
fax: 715-467-2243
e-mail: pcmpaper@gglbbs.com
Internet: http://www.tias.com/pubs/pcm
Monthly magazine for collectors of autographs, paperbacks, postcards, advertising, photographica, magazines; all types of paper ephemera.

Charles Amery
Newsletter: Rare Book Bulletin
P.O. Box 201
Peoria, IL 61650-0201
A bi-monthly newsletter focusing on books: paperback, hardback, book reviews, coming events, antique & collectible books, buy/sell/trade ads, etc.

Magazine: Firsts: The Book Collector's Magazine
P.O. Box 65166
Tucson, AZ 85728-5166
phone: 520-529-1355
fax: 520-529-5847
The monthly magazine for book collectors: surveys of various collecting areas, checklists of authors' published works, retail prices for collectible books, keys to identification.

Liza Karp
Magazine: Biblio Magazine
845 Wilamette St.
Eugene, OR 97401
phone: 800-840-3810 or 541-345-3800
fax: 541-302-9872
e-mail: csell@bibliomag.com
Internet: http://www.bibliomag.com

Repair Services

Don E. Sanders
Don E. Sanders Bookbinder
1116 Pinion Dr.
Austin, TX 78748
phone: 512-282-4774
20 years experience; custom binding & cases, restoration and repair.

Peregrine Arts Bookbindery
P.O. Box 1691
Santa Fe, NM 87504
phone: 505-982-0490
Book repair, marbling.

Gary D. Muir
Muir's Book Repair
1617 Willis St.
Redding, CA 96001
phone: 916-241-1948
Repair/restore any and all types of books, bibles, cookbooks, newspapers and magazines; also other historical documents; chewed-up by dog, moisture or water damage, fire damage, lost spine, lost front or back, loose or torn pages.

Astronomy

Book Sellers

Lee & Peggy Price
Knollwood Books
P.O. Box 197
Oregon, WI 53575-0197
phone: 608-835-8861
fax: 608-835-8421
e-mail: books@tdsnet.com
Issues quarterly catalogs; buys and sells out-of-print books on astronomy, meteorology, and space exploration; also books about microscopes, old scientific instruments, optics, and related areas.

Aviation Related

Collectors

Paul Davis
308 Landsende Rd.
Devon, PA 19333
phone: 610-644-1216
Wants books on general aviation and military aviation history, airplanes, etc.

Big Little

Clubs/Associations

Larry Lowery
Big Little Book Collectors Club of America
Newsletter: Big Little Times
P.O. Box 1242
Danville, CA 94526-8242
phone: 510-837-2086
Club provides a conduit among collectors and dealers interested in Big Little Books and similar books; publishes research and other information pertaining to Big Little Books; bi-monthly newsletter.

■

Experts

Ken Mitchell
710 Conacher Dr.
Willowdale
Ontario M2M 3N6 Canada
phone: 416-222-5808
Buys and sells comic character collectibles (comic books, Sunday funnies, "Big Little Books", etc.) and other nostalgic paper including music (Pop) magazines and books from 1890 through 1960s.

Ron Donnelly
Saturday Heroes
P.O. Box 7047
Panama City, FL 32413-0047
phone: 904-234-7944
fax: 904-233-9316
Buys and sells Big Little Books; advisor to "Schroeder's Price Guide."

Larry Lowery
P.O. Box 1242
Danville, CA 94526-8242
phone: 510-837-2086
Author of "The Collector's Guide to Big Little and Similar Books."

Boys'

Collectors

Joseph A. Ruttar
3116 Teesdale
Philadelphia, PA 19152-4514
Wants boys' series books: Andy Blake, Trigger Berg, Hal Keen, Conquest of U.S., Sam Steele, Boy Fortune Hunters, Jack Race, Jack Straw, Dave Porter (no Special Edition), Square Dollar Boys, Boys of Liberty.

British

Experts

Mark Samuels Lasner
1870 Wyoming Ave. NW, Apt. 101
Washington, DC 20009-1883
phone: 202-745-1927
e-mail: biblio@aol.com
Wants to buy English literature and art form the period 1850-1900; especially association books, manuscripts, letters, and original drawings; co-author of two reference books on this material.

Children's

(see also BOOKS, Pop-up & Movable)

Collectors

Alan Levine
P.O. Box 1577
Bloomfield, NJ 07003
phone: 201-743-5288

Mary Young
P.O. Box 9244
Dayton, OH 45409-9244
Wants to buy children's school readers (primarily first and second grade readers) from the 1920s to 1960s, 1930-1960s coloring and punch-out books, and girls' series books, storybooks by Platt and Munk, Whitman, Beckley Cardy Co.

Joel Birenbaum
2765 Shellingham Dr.
Lisle, IL 60532-4245
phone: 708-637-8530
e-mail: jbirenbaum@lucent.com
Buying better out-of-print illustrated children's books, preferably first editions in very good condition; illustrators wanted include Charles Robinson, Willy Pogany, Arthur Rackham, Johnny Gruelle, B.P. Gutmann, Ralph Stedman, etc.

Margery Wilder
1409 1st St.
Port Townsend, WA 98368-3078
Wants Tasha, Tudor, Maurice Sendak and various other charming illustrated books.

Dealers

Marion F. Adler
P.O. Box 627
Stockbridge, MA 01262
phone: 413-298-3559
Specializing in out-of-print children's books.

Ten Eyck Books
P.O. Box 84
Southborough, MA 01772
phone: 508-481-3517
Specializing in out-of-print children's books.

Debbi Manley
P.O. Box 370
Bogota, NJ 07603
Wants to buy vintage children's books: juvenile series, pop-ups, mechanicals, color illustrated, cookbooks, black children's, anything Dick & Jane; authors/illustrators Maud Hart Lovelace, Tasha Tudor, Maud Humphrey, etc.

Helen & Marc Younger
Alphe-Bet Books
218 Waters Edge
Valley Cottage, NY 10989
phone: 914-268-7410
fax: 914-268-5942
Buys and sells children's and illustrated books.

Lee Temares
50 Heights Rd.
Manhasset, NY 11030-1413
phone: 516-627-8688 or 516-627-2647
fax: 516-627-7822
Buys children's series books; must have dust jackets if they came originally had them; also wants Limited Editions Club and Heritage Press, but must be very good condition and in fine boxes; appraises all books except law & medicine.

Jo Ann Reisler
360 Glyndon St., NE
Vienna, VA 22180-3537
phone: 703-938-2967
fax: 703-938-9057
e-mail: Reisler@clark.net
Internet: http://www.clark.net/pug/ Reisler
Wants to buy fine and unusual children's and illustrated books.

Bill & Jane McCullam
Catermole Books
9880 Fairmount Rd.
Newbury, OH 44065
phone: 216-338-3253
Specializes in 20th century children's non-series fiction; offers a 1,500-book catalog of items for sale.

Cattermole
9880 Fairmont Rd.
Newbury, OH 44065
phone: 216-338-3253
Specializes in buying and selling 20th century children's books.

Helmar & Dorothy Kern
Marvelous Books
P.O. Box 1510
Ballwin, MO 63022-1510
phone: 314-458-3301
fax: 314-273-5452
e-mail: marvlous@interlog.com
Buy/sell quality children's books and illustrated books; search service available; catalogs issued $5; want list available; friendly service for 20 years.

Ruppert Books
5909 Darnell
Houston, TX 77074-7719
phone: 713-774-2202
fax: 713-774-2202
e-mail: bruppert@webtv.net
Wants books: Nancy Drew, Hardy Boys, Dana Girls, Judy Bolton, Tom Swift, Rick Brant, Little Black Sambo, Raggedy Ann, Dick and Jane Readers, OZ, all children's series books in fine conditions, with dust jackets, illustrated.

James Keeline
Prince & the Pauper Collectible Children's Books
3201 Adams St.
San Diego, CA 92116-1654
phone: 619-283-4380
fax: 619-283-4666
e-mail: keeline@cerf.net
Largest book store specializing exclusively in children's books; 50,000 out-of-print and collectibles children's books; maintains active, long-term search service and research library related to children's books.

Dorothy G. Cook
Dorothy G. Cook - Antiquarian Children's Books
80 Hollins Dr.
Santa Cruz, CA 95060
phone: 408-426-1119
Sells movables and pop-ups; also rare children's books and ephemera.

Experts

E. Lee Baumgarten
718 1/2 W. John St.
Martinsburg, WV 25401-2204
phone: 304-267-2711
Compiler of "Price Guide & Bibliographic Checklist for Children's Illustrated Books - 1880-1960"; write or call anytime for free information; separate, related printing available featuring Library of Congress call numbers.

Joyce Magee
7219 Auld Rd.
Bradford, OH 45308
phone: 513-447-7134
Advisor to "Warman's Antiques & Collectibles Price Guide."

Martha Rasmussen
P.O. Box 1488
Ames, IA 50010-1488
phone: 515-292-9309
e-mail: mart515@aol.com
Collector and publisher of "Martha's KidLit" newsletter.

James Keeline
Prince & the Pauper Collectible Children's Books
3201 Adams St.
San Diego, CA 92116-1654
phone: 619-283-4380
fax: 619-283-4666
e-mail: keeline@cerf.net
Specializes in children's books: Dick & Jane textbooks, Little GOlden Books, L.M. Montgomery, Jules Verne, Hardy Boys series, Nancy Drew Series, Tom Swift series, Clive Cussler (modern author), and others.

Museums/Libraries

American Antiquarian Society
185 Salisbury St.
Worcester, MA 01609
phone: 508-755-5221

Free Library of Philadelphia
1901 Vine St.
Philadelphia, PA 19103
phone: 215-686-5370 or 215-686-5416

Lucile Clarke Memorial Children's Library
Central Michigan University
Mount Pleasant, MI 48859
phone: 517-774-3197

Periodicals

Rebecca Grayson
Newspaper: Gold Mine Review, The
P.O. Box 209
Hershey, PA 17033-0209
phone: 717-533-3039
e-mail: sunnybrook.msn.com
*For collectors of all children's
illustrated books from 1900-1970, e.g.
those published by the Golden Book
Company.*

Martha Rasmussen
Newsletter: Martha's KidLit Newsletter
P.O. Box 1488
Ames, IA 50010-1488
phone: 515-292-9309
e-mail: mart515@aol.com
*Your guide to out-of-print antiquarian
children's books; ads, reviews,
articles about favorite books and
authors or illustrators, want lists.*

Clothing & Accessories

Book Sellers

Fred Struthers
Fred Struthers Books
P.O. Box 2706
Fort Bragg, CA 95437-2706
phone: 707-964-8662
e-mail: fsbks@mcn.org
*An important source to collectors and
researchers for hard-to-find and out-
of-print books on costume, textiles,
tailoring; caries period sewing and
etiquette books and periodicals;
publishes two catalogs per year for
$2.50.*

Dictionaries

Collectors

Edwin A. Miles
2645 Alta Glen Dr.
Birmingham, AL 35243-4509
phone: 205-967-2504
*Wants pre-1865 English-language
dictionaries (including medical,
scientific, technological, legal,
musical, fine arts, agricultural,
commercial, etc.); also works of slang,
Americanisms, and lexicography.*

Etiquette

Collectors

Maret Webb
4118 East Vernon Ave.
Phoenix, AZ 85008-2333
phone: 602-957-0653
fax: 602-957-1631
*Wants vintage etiquette books, pre-
1875, pretty bindings, gilded edges,
"deportment", "decorum", manners.*

First Editions

Collectors

Maria E. Raymond
Plow & Pen, Inc.
P.O. Box 251
Robbins, CA 95676-0251
phone: 916-735-6596
fax: 916-735-6112
e-mail: 73113.1362@compuserve.com
*Wants first editions only: Atwood,
Sarton, Plath, Sexton, Duras, Walker,
Hurston.*

Dealers

Ron Lieberman
Family Album, The
RD 1 Box 42
Glen Rock, PA 17327-9707
phone: 717-235-2134
fax: 717-235-8765
e-mail: ronbiblio@delphi.com
*Buys and sells fine books in all fields,
specializing in American and
European first editions; advisor to
"Warman's Antiques & Collectibles
Price Guide."*

Pat & Allen Ahearn
Quill & Brush
P.O. Box 5365
Rockville, MD 20853-5365
phone: 301-460-3700
fax: 301-871-5425
*Book dealer specializing in 19th &
20th century first editions.*

Fishing

Dealers

Steve & Susan Starrantino
Armchair Angler
P.O. Box 755
Hillburn, NY 10931-0755
*Sells out-of-print fishing books and
related material.*

Flip

(see BOOKS, Pop-Ups & Movable
[Flip])

Fore-Edge Painted

Experts

Ron Lieberman
Family Album, The
RD 1 Box 42
Glen Rock, PA 17327-9707
phone: 717-235-2134
fax: 717-235-8765
e-mail: ronbiblio@delphi.com
*Buys and sells fine books in all fields,
specializing in American and
European first editions; advisor to
"Warman's Antiques & Collectibles
Price Guide."*

German

Collectors

R.L. Rice
612 E. Front St.
Bloomington, IL 61701
*Wants oversized illustrated language
books and handwritten diaries in
German including Bibles, children's,
fashion, art; also wants art books and
magazines 1830s -1920s.*

Horatio Alger, Jr.

(see also PERSONALITIES
[LITERARY], Horatio Alger, Jr.)

Collectors

George Owens
23 Kiowa Lane
Palmyra, VA 22963
phone: 804-589-3373
e-mail: caddowens@juno.com
*Wants Horatio Alger, Jr. books; state
title, publisher, condition and price.*

Illustrated

(see also ILLUSTRATORS)

Dealers

Jo Ann Reisler
360 Glyndon St., NE
Vienna, VA 22180-3537
phone: 703-938-2967
fax: 703-938-9057
e-mail: Reisler@clark.net
Internet: http://www.clark.net/pug/
Reisler
*Wants to buy fine and unusual
children's and illustrated books.*

Joseph L. Mashburn
Colonial House
P.O. Box 609 - M
Enka, NC 28728-0609
phone: 704-667-1427
fax: 704-667-1111
e-mail: jmashb@aol.com
Internet: http://www.postcard-
books.com
*Wants large gift books with
illustrations by Harrison Fisher,
Coles Phillips, Clarence Underwood,
Henry Hutt, Howard C. Christy,
Charles Gibson, Pogany, Dulac, Erte.*

Periodicals

Denis C. Jackson, Ed.
Newsletter: Illustrator Collector's News,
The
P.O. Box 1958
Sequim, WA 98382-1958
phone: 360-683-2559
fax: 360-683-2559
e-mail: ticn@olypen.com
Internet: http://www.olypen.com/ticn/
*A monthly publication for collectors of
magazines, books and other paper
illustrations; free classifieds for
subscribers; send LSASE for free
information guide offer.*

Jules Verne

Clubs/Associations

Betty Harless
North American Jules Verne Society
4310 Springwood Trail
Indianapolis, IN 46208
phone: 317-291-5598
*Members interested in items related to
Jules Verne: books, comics, stamps,
movies, and other memorabilia.*

Collectors

Dana V. Eales
2447 Delta Dr.
Uniontown, OH 44685-8117
phone: 216-699-5341
e-mail: ealesd@newreach.net
*Collects French, English and
American translations of Jules Verne
novels; primarily early editions but
also little known or unusual titles.*

Dealers

James Keeline
Prince & the Pauper Collectible
Children's Books
3201 Adams St.
San Diego, CA 92116-1654
phone: 619-283-4380
fax: 619-283-4666
e-mail: keeline@cerf.net
*Largest book store specializing
exclusively in children's books;
50,000 out-of-print and collectibles
children's books; maintains active,
long-term search service and research
library related to children's books.*

Juvenile Series

Clubs/Associations

Horatio Alger Society
Newsletter: Newsboy, The
P.O. Box 70361
Richmond, VA 23255
e-mail: alger-l@listserv.wuacc.edu
Internet: http://www.wuacc.edu/sobu/
broach/algerres.html
*To further the philosophy of Horatio
Alger, Jr. and to encourage the spirit
of Strive & Succeed.*

Collectors

Mike DeBaptiste
4402 Prasse Rd.
Cleveland, OH 44121
phone: 216-381-8092
*Wants Nancy Drew books in dust
jackets; also similar series books such
as Hardy Boys, Tom Swift, Judy
Bolton, Rick Brant, etc.*

Victoria Broadhurst
5009 Queen Victoria Rd.
Woodland Hills, CA 91364-4757
phone: 818-883-3127
fax: 818-887-3739
e-mail: mrscdrew@aol.com
*Wants to buy Nancy Drew and Hardy
Boys books in dust jackets.*

Dealers

Gary Nerman
Nerman's Books & Collectibles
721 Osborne St. South
Winnipeg
Manitoba R2K 0V7 Canada
phone: 204-475-1050 or 204-255-2196
fax: 204-947-0753
e-mail: nerman@escape.ca
Publishes a highly informative catalog; always interested in buying children and juvenile books.

James Keeline
Prince & the Pauper Collectible
  Children's Books
3201 Adams St.
San Diego, CA 92116-1654
phone: 619-283-4380
fax: 619-283-4666
e-mail: keeline@cerf.net
Largest book store specializing exclusively in children's books; 50,000 out-of-print and collectibles children's books; maintains active, long-term search service and research library related to children's books.

Experts

Virginia & David Brown
RR 1, Box 73
Machias, ME 04654-9711
phone: 207-255-4223
e-mail: cybertiques@nemaine.com
Internet: http://www.nemaine.com/cybertiques

Periodicals

Virginia & David Brown
Newsletter: Authorized Edition
  Newsletter, The
RR 1, Box 73
Machias, ME 04654-9711
phone: 207-255-4223
e-mail: cybertiques@nemaine.com
Internet: http://www.nemaine.com/cybertiques
Covers all aspects of collecting, caring for and enjoying the Whitman Publishing Company's juvenile books.

Gil O'Gara
Yellowback Press
Magazine: Yellowback Library
P.O. Box 36172
Des Moines, IA 50315-0310
phone: 515-287-0404
Focuses on juvenile series books and dime novels; largest circulation in the hobby.

Fred Woodworth, Pub.
Magazine: Mystery & Adventure Series
  Review
P.O. Box 3488
Tucson, AZ 85722-3488
Quarterly magazine devoted to collecting and preserving c. 1925-1965 series-books, e.g. Hardy Boys, Ken Holt & Rick Brant.

Kate Emburg
Society of Phantom Friends, The
Newsletter: Whispered Watchword, The
P.O. Box 1437
North Highlands, CA 95660-1437
phone: 916-331-7435
e-mail: dolladopt@aol.com
A club for readers and collectors of girls' juvenile fiction from 1900 to present, including but not limited to Nancy Drew, Judy Bolton, Trixie Belden, and Beany Malone; books bought and sold; please send SASE with inquiries.

Law Reference

Collectors

Clint Miller
1604 N. Harrison St.
Little Rock, AR 72207-5322
phone: 501-664-8424 or 501-682-7466
Wants to buy books on legal reasoning, legal writing, jurisprudence, criminal law, American constitutional law and legal questions.

Dealers

Luke Pavone, VP
National Law Resource, Inc.
328 S. Jefferson
Chicago, IL 60661-5605
phone: 800-279-7799 or 800-886-1800
fax: 312-382-0323
e-mail: lawstuff@aol.com
Book dealer of up-to-date, excellent quality, pre-owned law books; carries inventories of all Federal, National, Regional and state sets; also tax libraries, labor law libraries, GPO titles, bound legal periodicals, ultrafiche.

Little Golden Books

Clubs/Associations

Steve Santi
Golden Book Club
Newsletter: Pokey Gazette, The
19626 Ricardo Ave.
Hayward, CA 94541
phone: 510-481-2586
A newsletter for Little Golden Book collectors.

Collectors

Ilene Kayne
1308 S. Charles St.
Baltimore, MD 21230-4219
phone: 410-685-3923
Wants Little Golden Books; especially those with dust jackets or in a foreign language.

Gloria Flager
5966 Barcelona Dr. S.E.
Salem, OR 97301
Wants certain Little Golden Books to complete collection; write for want list; also has duplicates for sale.

Dealers

James Keeline
Prince & the Pauper Collectible
  Children's Books
3201 Adams St.
San Diego, CA 92116-1654
phone: 619-283-4380
fax: 619-283-4666
e-mail: keeline@cerf.net
Largest book store specializing exclusively in children's books; 50,000 out-of-print and collectibles children's books; maintains active, long-term search service and research library related to children's books.

Experts

Steve Santi
19626 Ricardo Ave.
Hayward, CA 94541
phone: 510-481-2586
Buys and sells Little Golden Books by Books Americana; author of "Collecting Little Golden Books."

Periodicals

Rebecca Greason
Newspaper: Gold Mine Review, The
P.O. Box 209
Hershey, PA 17033-0209
phone: 717-533-3039
e-mail: sunnybrook.msn.com
For collectors of all children's illustrated books from 1900-1970, e.g. those published by the Golden Book Company.

Metaphysics

Dealers

Dennis E. Whelan
Samadhi Metaphysical Literature
P.O. Box 170
Lakeview, AR 72642
phone: 501-431-8830
Collector and seller of metaphysical books/magazines: esoterica, mysticism, yoga, astrology, Tibet, Egypt, Atlantis, herbalism, UFO, tarot, crystal balls, the unexplained, etc.; SASE plus $1 for annual catalog; free search service.

Meteorology

Book Sellers

Lee & Peggy Price
Knollwood Books
P.O. Box 197
Oregon, WI 53575-0197
phone: 608-835-8861
fax: 608-835-8421
e-mail: books@tdsnet.com
Issues quarterly catalogs; buys and sells out-of-print books on astronomy, meteorology, and space exploration; also books about microscopes, old scientific instruments, optics, and related areas.

Military History

(see also MILITARY HISTORY)

Dealers

Paul Hunt
Book Castle, Inc.
P.O. Box 10907
Burbank, CA 91510-0907
phone: 818-409-9761 or 818-845-6467
fax: 818-845-0460
Buys and sells books, specialty: back issue magazines, and military and history.

Miniature

Experts

Ron Lieberman
Family Album, The
RD 1 Box 42
Glen Rock, PA 17327-9707
phone: 717-235-2134
fax: 717-235-8765
e-mail: ronbiblio@delphi.com

Modern Library

Periodicals

A. Oestreich
Newsletter: Modern Library Collector,
  The
340 Warren Ave.
Cincinnati, OH 45220-1135
For collectors of "Modern Library" and "Viking Portable" books; published twice a year.

Mountaineering

Book Sellers

Chessler Books
P.O. Box 399
Kittredge, CO 80457
phone: 800-654-8502 or 303-670-0093
fax: 303-670-9727
Extensive selection of books on mountaineering, rock climbing, exploration, guidebooks.

Movable

(see BOOKS, Children's; BOOKS, Pop-Up & Movable)

Movie & TV Related

Dealers

Paul Hunt
Book Castle, Inc.
P.O. Box 10907
Burbank, CA 91510-0907
phone: 818-409-9761 or 818-845-6467
fax: 818-845-0460
Buys and sells books, specialty: back issue magazines, and military and history.

Mystery

Collectors

Beverley Furlow-Cleary
1555 N. Arcadia Ave.
Tucson, AZ 85712-4010
phone: 502-323-1709
e-mail: beverleyf@aol.com
*Buys, sells, and appraises collectible
mystery/detective items: books,
vintage clothing and hats.*

Dealers

Peggy Ell
Peggy's Paper
218 Gratton
Burlington, IA 52601
phone: 319-752-7670
*Buys and sells mystery magazines
such as Alfred Hitchcock and Ellery
Queen mystery magazines; also wants
hardback mystery books.*

New York

Collectors

James L. Sedore, Jr. CPA
431 McGrath Blvd.
Fishkill, NY 12524-2831
phone: 914-831-8535 or 831-297-1111
fax: 914-297-1432
*Wants to buy books on New York
State; Dutchess City, NY; Hudson
Valley, NY; also of Indians of the
Hudson River Valley; also wants
American history books and books
about the American Revolution.*

Paperback

(see also MAGAZINES, Pulp)

Clubs/Associations

Paul Duncan
British Association of Paperback
Collectors
17 Tregullan Rd.
Conventry CV7 9NG, U.K.
*International club interested in
vintage paperback books.*

Dealers

Nancy Mancing
Buck Creek Books, Ltd.
838 Main St.
Lafayette, IN 47901
phone: 317-742-6618
*Publishes a free catalog of vintage
paperbacks; also sells hardback
books.*

Experts

Ray Walsh
Curious Book Shop
307 E. Grand River
East Lansing, MI 48823-4324
phone: 517-332-0112
*Dealer/expert; owner of three book
shops in Michigan; hosts radio call-in
show about books and paper
collectibles; writes columns; send a
SASE for reply when writing.*

Periodicals

Howard Hopkins, Ed.
Magazine: Golden Perils
5 Milliken Mills Rd.
Scarboro, ME 04074
*A tri-annual magazine focusing on
serials and pulp magazines.*

Gary Lovisi
Gryphon Publications
Magazine: Paperback Parade
P.O. Box 209
Brooklyn, NY 11228-0209
phone: 718-646-6126
*A magazine for paperback readers
and collectors; news, articles, lists,
interviews; a hobby publication full of
news and info about paperbacks;
issues are 100+ pages with color
covers; $7 each, subscriptions $35/
year.*

R.C. Holland
Magazine: Books Are Everything!
302 Martin Drive
Richmond, KY 40475
phone: 606-624-9176
fax: 606-623-9354
A quarterly magazine.

Journal: Dime Novel Round-Up
P.O. Box 226
Dundas, MN 55019
*A magazine devoted to the collecting,
preservation and literature of the old-
time dime and nickel novels and
popular story papers.*

Tom Johnson
Magazine: Echoes
504 E. Morris St.
Seymour, TX 76380
*Focuses on dime novels and pulp
magazines; sample copy of "Echoes"
$3.60.*

Pocket

Collectors

Bruce Axler
Ansonia Station
P.O. Box 1288
New York, NY 10023-1288
phone: 212-362-4429
fax: 212-579-1274
*Wants to buy pocket books from the
19th century (1800s) that people
carried which were loaded with
information, e.g. dictionaries,
almanacs, encyclopedias, reckoners;
no fiction, religious, poetry, foreign,
speeches, or bio.*

Pop-Up & Movable

(see also BOOKS, Children's)

Clubs/Associations

Ann Montanaro
Movable Book Society
Newsletter: Movable Stationery
P.O. Box 11645
New Brunswick, NJ 08906-1645
phone: 908-247-6071 or 908-445-5896
fax: 908-846-7928
e-mail: montanar@rci.rutgers.edu
Internet: http://www.rci.rutgers.edu/
~montanar/
*Forum for collectors of pop-up and
movable books to share collecting
resources, research, and questions
about individual titles.*

Collectors

Ann Montanaro
P.O. Box 11645
New Brunswick, NJ 08906-1645
phone: 908-247-6071 or 908-445-5896
fax: 908-846-7928
e-mail: montanar@rci.rutgers.edu
Internet: http://www.rci.rutgers.edu/
~montanar/
*Wants to buy pop-up and movable
books.*

Margery Wilder
1409 1st St.
Port Townsend, WA 98368-3078
*Collecting pop-up, mechanical, fold-
out, unusual children's books.*

Dealers

A. Dalrymple
1791 Graefield
Birmingham, MI 48009
*Always wants to buy pop-ups and
movable books.*

Mr. Books
2814 W Bell Rd., Ste. 1495
Phoenix, AZ 85023-7532
*Issues catalog of pop-up books for
sale.*

Dorothy G. Cook
Dorothy G. Cook - Antiquarian
Children's Books
80 Hollins Dr.
Santa Cruz, CA 95060
phone: 408-426-1119
*Sells movables and pop-ups; also rare
children's books and ephemera.*

Pop-Up & Movable (Flip)

Collectors

Robin Klein
801 Welington St.
Baltimore, MD 21211
e-mail: eajqrobin@ube.ubalt.edu
*Interested in contacting other
collectors of flip books.*

Jeff Jurich
1220 Hudson St.
Denver, CO 80220

Railroad

Experts

Jim Younger
4628 Old Dragon Path
Ellicott City, MD 21042-5970
phone: 410-964-1949
e-mail: jmyr@erols.com
*Buys, sells, trades out-of-print
railroad-themed fiction (novels, short
stories, juveniles, poetry, dime novels,
paperbacks, etc.) and true stories
(autobiographies, biographies,
reminiscences of or by railroaders, c.
1830-1990.*

Reference (American Indian)

Book Sellers

Lar Hothem
Hothem House
P.O. Box 458
Lancaster, OH 43130-0458
phone: 614-653-9030
*Buys and sells Indian related books
covering archaeology, artifacts,
earthworks, U.S. prehistory.*

Reference (Antiques)

Book Sellers

John Ives
John Ives Antiquarian Books
5 Normanhurst Dr.
Twickenham
Middlesex TW1 1NA, U.K.
phone: 0181-8926265
fax: 0181-7443944
*Supplies specialist reference books on
antiques and collecting to customers
all over the world; send for free
catalog.*

Dave McGee
Diversity Antiques & Collectibles
Incorporated
P.O. Box 31275
Halifax
Nova Scotia B3K 5Y5 Canada
phone: 902-425-5331
*Carries selected American, English
and Canadian titles; also Canadian
stockist for publications of the
Torquay Pottery Collectors' Society,*

Charlton Press, The
Guide: Charlton Collector's Guide to
Ontario, The
2040 Yonge St., Ste. 208
Toronto
Ontario M4S 1Z9 Canada
phone: 800-442-6042 or 416-488-4653
fax: 800-442-1542
e-mail: chpress@pathway.com
*Specializes in books on Royal
Doulton, Beswick, Chintz, Wade,
Coalport, Royal Worcester, coins,
paper money, country store
collectibles.*

Grace Miller Dickinson
Miller's Daughter, The
21 Poplar Hill Rd.
West Whately, MA 01039
phone: 413-665-4464
fax: 413-665-4464
*Essential reference books on the
decorative arts, antiques and
collectibles; appearing at selected
shows; also by mail order and from
the shop.*

A-Book & Company
54 Redstone Hill
Lancaster, MA 01523-1858
phone: 800-47A-BOOK or 508-365-
6456
*Send for free catalog; over 1,700 titles
in stock.*

Joslin Hall Rare Books
P.O. Box 516
Concord, MA 01742
phone: 508-371-3101
fax: 508-371-6445
Internet: http://www.joslinhall.com
*Specialists in rare books on the
decorative arts and American fine art.*

John Hart
John Hart - Wellesley Antiques & Books
P.O. Box 620268
Newton, MA 02162-0268
phone: 800-867-7019 or 617-964-6979
fax: 617-243-0202
e-mail: welbooks@tiac.net
Internet: http://www.antiqnet.com/
wellesley
*New reference books on antiques and
collectibles; over 1200 titles, mail
order and shows, catalog available;
Arts & Crafts Movement and 20th
Century Design a specialty.*

F. Russack Antiques & Books
20 Beach Plain Rd.
Danville, NH 03819
phone: 603-642-7718
fax: 603-642-7718
*Specializes in out-of-print books about
decorative arts, folk art, Americana.*

Greg Johnson
Books About Antiques
168 New Milford Tpke.
P.O. Box 2358
New Preston, CT 06777
phone: 860-868-1611
fax: 860-868-1620

Gregory Morson
Apollo Books
Gracie Station
P.O. Box 339
New York, NY 10028
phone: 212-289-3981 or 800-431-5003
*Issues catalog of books on art
reference, antiques & collectibles; Art
Sales Index, Mayer's International
Auction Records, ADEC, Leonard's
Auction Index, Gordon's Print Price
Annual, Davenport's, etc.*

Timothy Trace Booksellers
144 Red Mill Rd.
Cortdandt Manor, NY 10566
phone: 914-528-4074
*Sells out-of-print books about
furniture and the decorative arts:
ceramics, silver, jewelry, metalwork,
textiles, rugs and carpets, wallpaper,
clocks and watches, China Trade,
glass, folk art, and art reference.*

Christie's Publications
21-44 44th Ave.
Long Island City, NY 11101
phone: 718-784-1480

Richard & Eileen Dubrow
Richard & Eileen Dubrow Antiques &
Books
P.O. Box 128
Flushing, NY 11361-0128
phone: 718-767-9758
fax: 718-767-8172
*Sells books (out of print and current)
about 19th C. furniture and about
furniture and decorative arts.*

Art Books Services
P.O. Box 360
Hughsonville, NY 12537-0360
phone: 800-247-9955 or 914-297-0003
fax: 914-297-0068
e-mail: info@artbk.com
Internet: http://www.antiquecc.comm
*Carries the best books and price
guides on the fine and decorative arts;
also on architecture and garden
design; retail sales; Mayer's on CD,
Gordon's, art books, price guides,
furniture, glass, textiles, metalwork,
ceramics*

Antique Collectors' Club, Ltd.
91 Market St. Industrial Park
Wappingers' Falls, NY 12590
phone: 914-297-0003 or 800-252-5231
fax: 914-297-0068
e-mail: sales@antiquec.com
Internet: http://www.antiquec.com
*Offers only the highest quality
standard reference works on antiques,
art, gardening and architecture;
wholesale sales only.*

Doris Motta
ArtBooks
P.O. Box 713
Cooperstown, NY 13326-0745
e-mail: artbooksdm@aol.com
*Books and catalogs on fine and
decorative arts.*

Whitehouse-Books.com
90 W. Market St.
Corning, NY 14830-2527
phone: 607-936-8536 or 800-935-8536
fax: 607-936-2465
e-mail: elizabeth@whitehouse-
books.com
Internet: http://www.whitehouse-
books.com
*Sells books about glass, ceramics,
silver, furniture, jewelry, etc.*

William Blystone
Blystone Books
2132 Delaware Ave.
Pittsburgh, PA 15218-1811
phone: 412-371-3511
*Sells in print & out of print
collectibles books by mail; specialty
areas are dolls, toys and train books;
looking for new book sources.*

Betty Johnston
Reference Rack, Inc., The
P.O. Box 445
Orefield, PA 18069-0445
phone: 800-722-7279 or 610-395-0004
fax: 610-706-0229
Internet: http://www.referencerack.com
*New reference books on antiques, art
and collectibles; issues one free
catalog per year.*

Schiffer Publishing, Ltd.
77 Lower Valley Rd.
Atglen, PA 19310-9717
phone: 610-593-1777
fax: 610-593-2002
e-mail: schifferbk@aol.com
*Carries a line of high quality books
focusing on antiques and collectibles.*

Winterthur Museum Bookstore
Winterthur, DE 19735-0001
phone: 800-448-3883
Internet: http://www.udel.edu/winterthur

Random House Inc./House of
    Collectibles
400 Hahn Rd.
Westminster, MD 21157
phone: 800-733-3000

Crown Publishers, Inc.
c/o Random House
400 Hahn Rd.
Westminster, MD 21157
phone: 212-572-2537
*Offers books about antiques and
collectibles.*

Carl Mikalauskas
Country Lane Books
P.O. Box 656
Braddock Heights, MD 21714-0656
phone: 800-769-5961 or 301-371-6284
e-mail: clane@fred.net
Internet: http://www.countrylane.com
*Carries price guides and reference
books on antiques, collectibles, art,
toys, trains, glass, pottery, tools, etc.;
call for free catalog.*

Book Savers
2706 Elsmore St.
Fairfax, VA 22031-1409
*International wholesale distributor of
books on antiques and collectibles.*

Perry Franks
Collector's Companion
P.O. Box 935
Mechanicsville, VA 23111-0935
phone: 804-321-9212
e-mail: bookscc@aol.com
*Offering over 3,600 different new and
out-of-print reference/price guides
dealing with antiques and collectibles;
exhibits at many VA, DC, and North*

*Carolina shows; limited book displays
at selected VA antique malls; mail
order available.*

B.J. Hicks
Homebiz Books & More
2919 Mistwood Forest Dr.
Chester, VA 23831-7043
*Offers antique and collectible
reference books; also buys bottle
books.*

Harold Haskins
Southeastern Library Service
P.O. Box 44
Gainesville, FL 32602-0044
phone: 904-466-4789
*Sells wholesale to booksellers and
libraries; bi-monthly catalogs.*

Gerry Haskins
Haskins House
P.O. Box 44
Gainesville, FL 32602-0044
phone: 904-466-4789

Bill Schroeder
Collector Books
P.O. Box 3009
Paducah, KY 42002-3009
phone: 800-626-5420 or 502-898-6211
fax: 502-898-8890
*Publishers of books on antique and
collectibles; specializes in full color
value guides; since 1970.*

Karen Nester
Green Gate Books
P.O. Box 934
Lima, OH 45802-0934
phone: 419-222-3816 or 800-228-3816
fax: 419-227-3816
*Offers large wholesale, retail
selection of books on antiques,
collectibles and crafts.*

L-W Book Sales
P.O. Box 69
Gas City, IN 46933-0069
phone: 800-777-6450
Wholesale and retail book sales.

Nancy Johnson
Library, The
P.O. Box 37
Des Moines, IA 50301-0037
phone: 515-262-6714
fax: 515-263-8116
*Reference books on antiques,
collectibles and the decorative arts;
including foreign and private presses;
over 6000 titles in stock; sells at
antiques shows in Midwest and West
and by mail order.*

Mark Chervenka
P.O. Box 12130
Des Moines, IA 50312-9403
phone: 515-274-5886 or 800-227-5531
fax: 515-255-4530
*Buys and sells used reference books
on antiques.*

Antique Trader Books
P.O. Box 1050
Dubuque, IA 52004-1050
phone: 800-334-7165
fax: 800-531-0880
Internet: http://www.csmonline.com
Offers best selling price guides and reference books on nearly every antique and collectible category imaginable; quality purchase discounts available; send or call for free catalog.

Julie A. Ulrich, PR
Krause Publications
700 E. State St.
Iola, WI 54990-0001
phone: 715-445-2214
fax: 715-445-4087
e-mail: info@krause.com
Internet: http://www.krause.com

Charles & Joan Rhoden
"MEMORIES" Book Sales
605 N. Main
Georgetown, IL 61846-1439
phone: 217-662-8046 or 217-662-8440
fax: 217-662-8223
e-mail: jmrhoden@prairienet.org
Carries over 1200 new books on antiques and collectibles; send for free catalog; wholesale and retail; mail order and open shop.

Enid & Len Waska
Bookworm, The
P.O. Box 90063
Houston, TX 77290-0063
phone: 281-583-7448
e-mail: bookworm@blkbox.com
Internet: http://www.houstonet.com/bookworm
Specializing in price guides and reference books on antiques and collectibles; over 1900 titles available.

Sam's Books
7875 SE 13th Ave.
Portland, OR 97202-6307
phone: 503-232-3755
Large selection of collectors' reference books - new, used and out-of-print; buys and sells.

Richard J. Perry
Collectors Press, Inc.
P.O. Box 230986
Portland, OR 97281-0986
phone: 503-684-3030 or 888-680-3030
fax: 503-684-3777
e-mail: perr@teleport.com
Publishes books on nostalgia, art, and collecting; always looking for new book submissions and /or ideas.

J.R.'s Collector Reference Books
934 SW 8th St.
Newport, OR 97365-5135
phone: 800-726-5086
Wholesale mail order source for newly published antiques and collectibles reference books.

Bristol Antiques & Books
310 W. Holly St.
Bellingham, WA 98225
phone: 360-733-7809
e-mail: egelder@nas.com

Herzinger & Co.
2821 N.E. 65th Ave.
Vancouver, WA 98661-6817
phone: 360-737-7998 or 800-428-2670
fax: 800-285-1502
Sells reference books on antiques, collectibles, dolls, and art.

Collectors

Karen S. Rabe, ISA CAPP
Asset Appraisals
P.O. Box 21
Lake Forest, IL 60045
phone: 847-604-8770
fax: 847-356-2124
e-mail: krabe@compuserve.com
Wants to buy out-of-print books about the fine arts and decorative arts, furniture, glass, ceramics, and silver.

Reference (Architecture)

Dealers

Arcade Books
P.O.Box 5176
FDR Station
New York, NY 10150-5176
phone: 212-724-5371

Reference (Art)

Book Sellers

Currier Fine Art, Inc.
Price Guide: Currier Price Guides
241 Main St.
Stoneham, MA 02180
phone: 800-344-0760 or 617-438-6178
fax: 617-438-6321
Publisher of four art and print price guides including guides to American artists at auction, European artists at auction, American & European prints at auction, and Currier & Ives prints.

Arthur Fraumeni
New England Gallery
367 Gov. Wentworth Hwy.
Wolfeboro, NH 03894-4616
phone: 603-569-3501 or 305-733-9237
fax: 603-569-3501
List of art reference books and art price guides available; also sells the Zelco battery-operated blacklight.

Peter Falk
Sound View Press
859 Boston Post Rd.
Madison, CT 06443
phone: 203-245-2246 or 203-849-1655
fax: 203-245-5116
Researches, writes and sells books about artists listed in "Who's Who in American Art"; also publishes/sells art reference dictionaries and the "Art Price Index International."

Museum Gallery Book Shop
360 Mine Hill Rd.
fairfield, CT 06530
phone: 203-259-7114
Sells and art reference books; publishes catalog of current offerings.

Dealer's Choice Books
P.O. Box 710
Land O Lakes, FL 34639-0710
phone: 813-996-6599 or 800-238-8288
fax: 813-996-5226
e-mail: booksales@art-amer.com
Sells art reference books (new only), e.g. Hislop's "Art Sales Index", "Who Was Who in American Art", "Signatures of American Artists", "Davenport's Art Price Guide", "Benezit", "Meyer's", Falk's "Print Price Index", etc.

Collectors

Karen S. Rabe, ISA CAPP
Asset Appraisals
P.O. Box 21
Lake Forest, IL 60045
phone: 847-604-8770
fax: 847-356-2124
e-mail: krabe@compuserve.com
Wants to buy out-of-print books about the fine arts and decorative arts, furniture, glass, ceramics, and silver.

Reference (Art, Asian)

Book Sellers

Rare Oriental Book Co.
P.O. Box 1599
Aptos, CA 95001-1599
phone: 408-689-0203
fax: 408-689-0204
e-mail: jgs@rareorient.coom
Internet: http://www.rareorientbooks.com
`Sells old, rare choice books on Japan, Korea, China, Tibet, S.E. Asia, Philippines, Indonesia, Siam, Malaya, Singapore, Cambodia, Laos, Burma, Vietnam, Mongolia, New Guinea, Bali, etc.*

Reference (Autographs)

Book Sellers

Brian Kathenes
Brian Kathenes Autographs & Collectibles
P.O. Box 482
Hope, NJ 07844-0482
phone: 908-459-5225 or 800-323-5996
fax: 908-459-4899
e-mail: 76514.362@compuserve.com

Reference (Automobiles)

Book Sellers

Eric Waiter Associates
369 Springfield Ave.
P.O. Box 188
Berkeley Heights, NJ 07922
phone: 908-665-7811 or 908-665-7812
fax: 908-665-7814
Internet: http://www.eracars.com
Carries large selection of automobile related books, magazines and videos; over 1500 titles on a wide variety of subjects; catalog sent free on request.

Classic Motorbooks
P.O. Box 1
Osceola, WI 54020
phone: 800-826-6600
fax: 715-294-4448
The best selections of books and video tapes about special interest cars, tractors, trucks, motorcycles, racing, restoration, street rods, etc.

Dennis Mitosinka
Dennis Mitosinka's Classic Cars
619 E. Fourth St.
Santa Ana, CA 92701-4705
phone: 714-953-5303
fax: 714-953-1810
Over 400 titles of car-related out-of-print books including large selection of Clymer books, Indy 500 Year Books, Salt Flat Racing.

Reference (Aviation)

Book Sellers

Alan & Drina Abel
Aviation Heritage Books
P.O. Box 665
Destin, FL 32540-0665
Publishes and distributes books about aviation.

Zenith Books
P.O. Box One
Osceola, WI 54020
phone: 800-826-6600
fax: 715-294-4448
e-mail: mbibks@win.bright.net
World's best selection of aviation, modeling, radio control model aircraft, and military books and videos.

Historic Aviation
1401 Kings Wood Rd.
Eagan, MN 55122
phone: 800-225-5575

Reference (Breweriana)

Book Sellers

Soda Mart - Can World
192 Ridgecrest Dr.
Goodlettsville, TN 37072
phone: 615-859-5236
fax: 615-859-5238
Sells breweriana books; also cleans and de-rusts on cans, and sells supplies for the beer can collector.

Reference (Cameras)

Book Sellers

Centennial Photo
11595 State Route 70
Grantsburg, WI 54840
phone: 715-689-2153
fax: 715-689-2277
Publisher of "McKeown's Price Guide to Antique & Classic Cameras", the world's leading camera reference work; over 9,000 different models with values; heavily illustrated; send for details on latest edition; dealer inquiries invited.

Jim McKeown
Centennial Photo Service
11595 State Route 70
Grantsburg, WI 54840
phone: 715-689-2153
fax: 715-689-2277
Publisher and seller of books relating to collectible cameras.

William P. Carroll
ACR Books
P.O. Box 4294
Whittier, CA 90607-4294
phone: 562-693-8421
fax: 562-945-6011
Antique and classic cameras for sale; offers new and used books on kaleidoscopes, cameras and the history of photography.

Reference (Ceramics)

Book Sellers

John-Peter J. Hayden, Jr.
Hayden & Fandetta
Radio City Station
P.O. Box 1549
New York, NY 10101-1549
phone: 212-582-2505 or 212-581-8520
Foremost source for rare, obscure, and old books on the decorative arts specializing in pottery and porcelain.

David Richardson
Antique Publications
P.O. Box 553
Marietta, OH 45750-0553
phone: 800-533-3433 or 614-373-6146
fax: 614-373-6917
e-mail: 76710.2337@compuserve.com
Offers a wide selection of books about pottery and glass.

Reference (Civil War)

Book Sellers

Nancy Dearing Rossbacher
North South Trader
P.O. Drawer 631
Orange, VA 22960-0370
phone: 540-67C-1VIL
fax: 540-672-7283
e-mail: nstcw@msn.com
Carries extensive inventory of hardbound and softbound books for Civil War historians, enthusiasts and collectors.

First Corps Books
42 Eastgrove Ct.
Columbia, SC 29212-2404
phone: 803-781-2709
Carries hundreds of Civil War books, both new and out-of-print.

Theodore P. Savas
SAVAS Publishing Company
1475 S. Bascom Ave., Ste. 204
Campbell, CA 95008-0629
phone: 408-879-9039 or 800-848-6585
fax: 408-879-9327
e-mail: mhbooks@aol.com
Publisher of Civil War books.

Reference (Clocks)

Book Sellers

Heart of America Press
P.O. Box 9808
Kansas City, MO 64134
phone: 816-761-0080
fax: 816-763-9382
Issues catalog of horological books and literature.

Loren Scanlon
Scanlon American Reprints Co.
P.O. Box 379
Modesto, CA 95353-0379
phone: 209-667-2906 or 800-854-8639
e-mail: dlscanlon@aol.com
Large selection of watch and clock books and price guides - over 800 titles.

Reference (Coin-Operated)

Book Sellers

Joseph S. Jancuska
TAJ Distributing
619 Miller St.
Luzerne, PA 18709-1307
phone: 717-287-3478
Carries a large supply of books and literature related to coin-operated machines.

Ken Durham
909 26th St. NW
Washington, DC 20037-2029
e-mail:
durham@GameRoomAntiques.com
Internet: http://
www.GameRoomAntiques.com
Sells large selection of books and service manuals on same; send SASE for information.

Eric D. Hatchell, Pub.
P.O. Box 315
Clifton, VA 22024-0315
phone: 703-968-9665
fax: 703-968-9667

Richard M. Bueschel
414 N. Prospect Manor Ave.
Mount Prospect, IL 60056-2046
phone: 847-253-0791
fax: 847-253-7919
e-mail: BuschlHist@aol.com
Authors and sells numerous books on coin-operated items: slot machines,

scales, pinball games, arcade sports games, trade stimulators, etc.

Russell's Antiques
2404 W. 111th St.
Chicago, IL 60655
phone: 312-233-3205
Sells books and literature related to coin-operated machines.

Hoflin Publishing Ltd.
4401 Zephyr St.
Wheat Ridge, CO 80033-3259
phone: 303-420-2222 or 800-352-5678
Internet: http://www.hoflin.com/
CoinSlot.html
Books, old catalog reprints, posters, service manuals, etc. on antique coin-operated machines.

Rosanna Harris
5815 W. 52nd Ave.
Denver, CO 80212-7503
phone: 303-431-9266
fax: 303-431-6978
e-mail: rbltd@cris.com
Internet: http://ww.concentric.net/
royalbell/
Carries selection of books and service manuals relating to slot machines.

Peter Movsesian
Coin-Op Classics Series
17844 Toiyabe St.
Fountain Valley, CA 92708
phone: 714-756-8746
fax: 714-963-1718
e-mail: http://www.coin-op-classics.com
Publishes books on vintage coin-operated machines; books include photos, history, original service manuals, schematics, etc.; all books include price guides.

Reference (Coins)

Book Sellers

Q. David Bowers
Bowers & Merena, Inc.
P.O. Box 1224
Wolfeboro, NH 03894
fax: 603-569-5319
Sells books relating to all areas of the US coin business and hobby; gold, silver, tokens, and all other areas of numismatics including exonumia; member International Association of Professional Numismatists.

George Frederick Kolbe
Fine Numismatic Books
P.O. Drawer 3100
Crestline, CA 92325-3100
phone: 909-338-6527
fax: 909-338-6980
e-mail: 72763.640@aompuserve.com
Sells numismatic literature.

Reference (Dolls)

Book Sellers

F. Russack Antiques & Books
20 Beach Plain Rd.
Danville, NH 03819
phone: 603-642-7718
fax: 603-642-7718

Hobby House Press, Inc.
One Corporate Drive
Grantsville, MD 21536
phone: 301-895-3792 or 800-554-1447
fax: 301-895-5029
e-mail: hobbyhouse@aol.com
Specializes on books dealing with Dolls, Teddy Bears, Paper Dolls, Vintage Clothing.

Reference (Exonumia)

Book Sellers

Rich Hartzog
World Exonumia
P.O. Box 4143 BSB
Rockford, IL 61110-0643
phone: 815-226-0771
fax: 815-397-7662
Carries a large selection of titles relating to tokens, medals, and exonumia.

Reference (Farm Toys)

Book Sellers

Shawn Van Meeuwen
Diamond Enterprises & Book Publishers
P.O. Box 537
Alexandria Bay, NY 13607-0537
phone: 613-475-1771 or 800-481-1353
fax: 613-475-1748
e-mail: diamond@intranet.cq
Internet: http://www.yesteryeartoys.com
Offers a complete line of hobby and toy publications; specialty in hobby steam and farm toys including antique tractor books.

Reference (Firearms)

Book Sellers

INFO-ARM
Newsletter: INFO-ARM Newsletter
P.O. Box 1262
Champlain, NY 12919
Specializing in books on handguns, rifles, shotguns, ammunition, edged weapons, etc.

Ray Riling Arms Books Co.
P.O. Box 18925
Philadelphia, PA 19119
Carries every gun book in print.

Bill Williams
Guncraft Sports Inc.
10737 Dutchtown Rd.
Knoxville, TN 37932-3208
phone: 423-966-4545
fax: 423-966-4500
e-mail: findit@guncraft.com
Internet: http://www.usit.net/hp/guncraft
Serving the shooting public since 1947; a multi-faceted supplier of guns,

accessories, appraisal services, training, gunsmithing, gun related books.

Reference (Gems/Jewelry)

Book Sellers

Stuart M. Matlins
Gemstone Press
P.O. Box 237
Woodstock, VT 05091-0237
phone: 802-457-4000 or 800-962-4544
fax: 802-457-4004
International source for books and other items designed to help people in the gem trade and consumers learn more about gems & jewelry.

Gemological Institute of America
Bookstore
5355 Armada Dr.
Carlsbad, CA 92008
phone: 800-421-7250
Internet: http://www.gia.org

Reference (Glass)

Book Sellers

David Richardson
Antique Publications
P.O. Box 553
Marietta, OH 45750-0553
phone: 800-533-3433 or 614-373-6146
fax: 614-373-6917
e-mail: 76710.2337@compuserve.com
Offers a wide selection of books about pottery and glass.

Nordic Art Glass Inc.
P.O. Box 2247
Colorado Springs, CO 80901
A great source for reference books on Scandinavian art glass.

Reference (Japanese Items)

Book Sellers

Theresa Yoneyama
Ginza, "Things Japanese"
1721 Connecticut Ave., NW
Washington, DC 20009-1108
phone: 202-331-7991
Carries a wide assortment of Japan related books in English: art, crafts, history, fiction, tea ceremony, Zen, cooking, martial arts, poetry, some graphic novels, origami, architecture, interior design, fengshui/geomancy, tapes, etc.

Alan D. Meaux
Ronin Art Productions
P.O. Box 1271
Oak Harbor, WA 98277-1271
phone: 360-675-8429 or 360-678-8787
Specializes in rare and hard to find books in English and Japanese dealing with Japanese arms and armor and related subjects.

Reference (Japanese Prints)

Book Sellers

G. C. Uhlenbeck
Ukiyo-E Books B.V./Anthro Books
Breestraat 113a
23211 CL Leiden
The Netherlands
phone: (071) 514 35 52/512 44 59
fax: (071) 514 14 88/512 38 55
e-mail: ukiyoe@xs4all.nl

Reference (Jukeboxes)

Book Sellers

Michael F. Baute
221 Yesler Way
Seattle, WA 98104-2622
phone: 206-233-9460
fax: 206-233-9871
e-mail: alwaysjuke@aol.com
Sells books about jukeboxes, jukebox service manuals and records.

Reference (Knives)

Book Sellers

Knife World Books
P.O. Box 3395
Knoxville, TN 37927-3395
phone: 615-397-1955 or 800-828-7751
fax: 615-397-1969
Specializes in books about knives.

Louise Weyer
Weyer International - Book Division
2740 Nebraska Ave.
Toledo, OH 43607
phone: 419-534-2020 or 800-448-8424
fax: 419-534-2697
Specializes in books about knives.

Reference (Militaria)

Book Sellers

Military Bookman, The
29 East 93rd St.
New York, NY 10128
phone: 212-348-1280
Deals exclusively in military, naval and aviation history o/p books, with related pictorial items; by mail or on site; catalogs available.

Antheil Booksellers
2177 Isabelle Court
Bellmore, NY 11710-1599
phone: 516-826-2094
fax: 516-826-3101
Specializes in naval, maritime, military and aviation books, both new and used; many books from Germany, Great Britain, Japan, and Australia; business done exclusively by mail; 48-page catalog subscription $6 for four catalogs.

Terry Hannon
Phoenix Militaria, Inc. Military
  Bookstore
116 Lyons Rd.
Mertztown, PA 19539-9801
phone: 610-682-1010 or 800-446-0909
fax: 610-682-1066
Internet: http://
  www.phoenixmilitaria.com
Sells a wide variety of military-related books and publications.

Nautical & Aviation Publishing Co.
8 West Madison St.
Baltimore, MD 21201
phone: 410-659-0220
fax: 410-539-8832
Carries naval, aviation and Civil War military books; many titles are primary sources, i.e. memoirs, biographies, etc.

Military Book Club, The
P.O. Box 6325
Indianapolis, IN 46206-6325
phone: 317-541-8920
Focuses on books about wars, strategies, battles and weapons; extensive back list and reference material useful to collectors.

Zenith Books
P.O. Box One
Osceola, WI 54020
phone: 800-826-6600
fax: 715-294-4448
e-mail: mbibks@win.bright.net
World's best selection of aviation, modeling, radio control model aircraft, and military books and videos.

Reference (Music)

Book Sellers

Linda Osborne
Jellyroll Productions
P.O. Box 255
Port Townsend, WA 98368
phone: 360-385-1200
fax: 360-385-6572
Specializes in books relating to the hobby of music & music memorabilia collecting; artists, titles, price guides, etc.

Reference (Natural History)

Book Sellers

Donald E. Hahn
Natural History Books
P.O. Box 1004
Cottonwood, AZ 86326-1004
phone: 520-634-5016 or 520-634-1217
fax: 520-634-1217
Offers technical publications about earth, biological sciences, and meteorites.

Reference (Nautical)

Book Sellers

Bob Glick
Columbia Trading Company
1 Barnstable Rd.
Hyannis, MA 02601
phone: 508-778-2929
fax: 508-778-2922
e-mail: nautical@capecod.net
Internet: http://www.by-the-sea.com/
  nautical/
Issues 6 catalogs a year each offering 600 nautical, boating, and naval books, magazines and ephemera for sale.

Reference (Orientalia)

Book Sellers

Paragon Book Gallery, Inc.
1507 S Michigan Ave.
Chicago, IL 60605-2812
phone: 312-663-5155
fax: 312-663-5177
e-mail: paragon@paragonbook.com
Internet: http://webart.com/
  paragonbook/
Carries rare, out-of-print, and scholarly books on Asia; specializes in books on Asian arts and Asian studies; new and out of print.

Jerrold G. Stanoff
Rare Oriental Book Co.
P.O. Box 1599
Aptos, CA 95001-1599
phone: 408-689-0203
fax: 408-689-0204
e-mail: jgs@rareorient.coom
Internet: http://
  www.rareorientbooks.com
Sells old, rare choice books on Japan, Korea, China, Tibet, S.E. Asia, Philippines, Indonesia, Siam, Malaya, Singapore, Cambodia, Laos, Burma, Vietnam, Mongolia, New Guinea, Bali, etc.

Reference (Paperweights)

Book Sellers

Paul H. Dunlop
Dunlop Collection, The
P.O. Box 6269
Statesville, NC 28687
phone: 800-227-1996 or 704-871-2626
fax: 704-871-2329
"Paperweights of the 19th & 20th Centuries," (Paul Jokelson & Gerald Ingold); "Old Glass Paperweights of Southern New Jersey," (Clarence Newell), "The Jokelson Collection of Antique Cameo Incrustation," (Paul H. Dunlop).

Lawrence H. Selman
L.H. Selman, Ltd.
761 Chestnut St.
Santa Cruz, CA 95060-3751
phone: 800-538-0766 or 408-427-1177
fax: 408-427-0111
e-mail: lselman@got.net
Internet: http://www.paperweight.com
Carries over 50 books about

paperweights.

Reference (Phonographs)

Book Sellers

Allen Koenigsberg
502 E. 17th St.
Brooklyn, NY 11226-6606
phone: 718-941-6835
fax: 718-941-1408
Carries the most complete list of phonograph related books, catalogs, manuals, discographies, posters and magazines; "The Antique Phonograph Monthly" available for $15 per volume, or sample for $3 in stamps.

Reference (Postcards)

Book Sellers

Dr. James Lewis Lowe, Dir.
Deltiologists of America
Magazine: Postcard Classics
P.O. Box 8
Norwood, PA 19074
phone: 610-485-8572
International postcard society for collectors, dealers, librarians, and archivist; offers several postcard related books for sale.

Reference (Quilts)

Book Sellers

Kris Driessen
Hickory Hill Antique Quilts
P.O. Box 273
Esperance, NY 12066
phone: 518-875-6299
fax: 518-875-9141
e-mail: oldquilt@albany.net
Internet: http://
   www.HickoryHillQuilts.com
Offers antique quilt tops, blocks by catalog; also offers vintage and reproduction fabrics, as well as restoration supplies and Quilt Heritage reference books.

Reference (Railroads)

Book Sellers

Richard C. Barrett
Railroad Research Publications
3400 Ridge Rd. West, Ste. 5-266
Rochester, NY 14626-3458
phone: 716-227-6903
Publishes and sells books on railroad collectibles and railroad history; send SASE for catalog.

Reference (Records)

Book Sellers

Linda Osborne
Jellyroll Productions
P.O. Box 255
Port Townsend, WA 98368
phone: 360-385-1200
fax: 360-385-6572
Offers an assortment of publications for the record collector.

Reference (Reptile/Amphibians)

Book Sellers

Mark F. Miller
HERP-NET Electronic Bulletin Board
Newsletter: HERP-NET, INK
P.O. Box 52261
Philadelphia, PA 19115
phone: 215-464-3561
fax: 215-464-3561
e-mail: 70176.1153@compuserve.com
Club meets electronically via computer modem (dial 215-464-3562); members have interests in live reptiles and related art: stamps, postcards, and books with reptile theme; operates free reptile book search service; sells reptile books.

Reference (Space Collectibles)

Book Sellers

Richard H. Jackson
Missile, Space or Rocket Used Books
P.O. Box 93
Mount Vernon, VA 22121-0093
phone: 703-360-7677
fax: 703-360-2886
e-mail: spacebooks@csgi.com
Internet: http://www.nss.org/space/
   books.html
Buys and sells used books about missile, space or rockets; mail order; quarterly price lists.

Reference (Stamps)

Book Sellers

Leonard H. Hartmann
Philatelic Bibliophile
P.O. Box 36006
Louisville, KY 40233-6006
fax: 502-459-8538
e-mail: pbbooks@ibm.net
Internet: http://www.pbbooks.com
Sells new books (no annual catalogs such as Scott's, S.G., Minkus, Yvert) stocked from over 100 publishers plus used stamp books; does not drop ship; check out website.

Newspaper: Linn's Stamp News
P.O. Box 29
Sidney, OH 45365-0029
phone: 937-498-0801
fax: 800-340-9501
e-mail: linns@linns.com
Internet: http://www.linns.com
World's largest stamp marketplace with up-to-the-minute hobby news, reports on topics from trends in values, special interest collections to under-collected stamps; well-respected in the hobby; indispensable for the stamp collector.

Reference (Teddy Bears)

Book Sellers

Hobby House Press, Inc.
One Corporate Drive
Grantsville, MD 21536
phone: 301-895-3792 or 800-554-1447
fax: 301-895-5029
e-mail: hobbyhouse@aol.com
Specializes on books dealing with Dolls, Teddy Bears, Paper Dolls, Vintage Clothing.

Reference (Tiles)

Book Sellers

Chris Blanchett
Buckland Books
Holly Tree House
18 Woodlands Rd, Littlehampton
West Sussex BN17 5PP, U.K.
phone: 01903 717648
fax: 01903 717648
A mail-order service selling new and secondhand books about tiles and associated subjects such as architecture, majolica, delftware and art pottery; publishes six monthly book lists.

Joseph Taylor
Tile Heritage Foundation
P.O. Box 1850
Healdsburg, CA 95448
phone: 707-431-8453
fax: 707-431-8455
Offers a large line of books about tile: terra cotta, foreign, decorated tiles, Delftware, English medieval, Victorian tiles, etc.

Reference (Tools)

Book Sellers

Emil S. Pollak
Astragal Press, The
P.O. Box 239
Mendham, NJ 07945-0239
phone: 201-543-3045
fax: 201-543-3044
Publishes and distributes books on early tools, trades, and technology including books on woodworking tools, scientific instruments, architecture, wood turning, machinists' tools, and reprints of early trade catalogs.

Bob & Maxine Finch
Glen Moor Press
1864 Glen Moore Dr.
Lakewood, CO 80215-3038
phone: 303-232-1932
fax: 303-232-8826
e-mail: rffinch@aol.com

Ron Barlow
Windmill Publishing Co.
2147 Windmill View Rd.
El Cajon, CA 92020-1353
phone: 619-448-5390
Author of "The Antique Tool Collector's Guide to Value" (Windmill

Publishing Co.); the most widely distributed price guide on old tools.

Reference (Toys)

Book Sellers

F. Russack Antiques & Books
20 Beach Plain Rd.
Danville, NH 03819
phone: 603-642-7718
fax: 603-642-7718

Joseph E. Freed
Freedom Publishing Co., Inc.
6209 Sandy Forks Rd.
Raleigh, NC 27624-9534
phone: 919-847-7365
fax: 919-847-3822

Patricia Mullins
P.E.I. International
6001 Johns Rd., Ste. 148
Tampa, FL 33634
phone: 813-855-4213
Publishers and distributors of reference books about rocking horses, toy soldiers, penny toys, dolls, teddy bears, war toys, and all types of other toys.

Reference (Vintage Clothing)

Book Sellers

Hobby House Press, Inc.
One Corporate Drive
Grantsville, MD 21536
phone: 301-895-3792 or 800-554-1447
fax: 301-895-5029
e-mail: hobbyhouse@aol.com
Specializes on books dealing with Dolls, Teddy Bears, Paper Dolls, Vintage Clothing.

Wooden Porch Books
Rte. 1 Box 262
Middlebourne, WV 26149-9748
phone: 304-386-4434
fax: 304-386-4868
6 catalogs per year listing approximately 2400 out-of-print books and magazines on the fiber arts and kindred subjects.

Fred Struthers
R.L. Shep Publications
P.O. Box 2706
Fort Bragg, CA 95437
phone: 707-964-8662
fax: 707-964-8662
e-mail: fsbks@mcn.org
Reprints of Victorian and Edwardian costume books stressing patterns, instructions, embroidery, etc.; women and men; practical manuals; also Civil War books about women's activities.

Reference (Watches)

Book Sellers

Heart of America Press
P.O. Box 9808
Kansas City, MO 64134
phone: 816-761-0080
fax: 816-763-9382
Issues catalog of horological books and literature.

Reference (Western Americana)

Book Sellers

Early West, The
P.O. Box 9292
College Station, TX 77842
phone: 800-245-5841
fax: 409-764-7758
Sells, buys and trades non-fiction books on the old west: outlaws, lawmen, towns, areas.

Bill Mackin
1137 Washington St.
Craig, CO 81625-1613
phone: 970-824-6717 or 970-824-6360
fax: 970-824-7175
e-mail: reust@nadja.com
Sells books and reprinted catalogs for Old West and cowboy collectors; over 50 titles including his own "Cowboy and Gunfighter Collectibles" with updated prices; $25 plus $3 postage.

Kenneth Asher
Maverick Distributors
P.O. Drawer 7289
Bend, OR 97708
phone: 503-382-2728
fax: 503-382-8444
e-mail: kenasher@teleport.com
Internet: http://www.bookquest.com
Sells Western Americana books: Indian art & artifacts, bottles, cowboy & horse collectibles, fruit jars, railroad, logging, fur trade, history, etc.

Roycroft

Collectors

Gary Wood
733 Myrtle Rd.
North Brunswick, NJ 08902-2549
phone: 908-821-7633
Collector seeks single issues or bound volumes of all Roycroft magazines including "The Philistine," "Roycrofter," "The Fra," as well as books published by The Roycroft Press and craft items bearing the Roycroft cross-and-orb mark.

Dealers

David B. Ogle
Antiquarian Archive, The
379 State St.
Los Altos, CA 94022-2816
phone: 415-949-1593
e-mail: archive@batnet.com
Specialist in Western Americana, railroadiana, nautical & maritime, military history & memoirs, books of the Roycroft printing shop.

Scientific

Book Sellers

Lee & Peggy Price
Knollwood Books
P.O. Box 197
Oregon, WI 53575-0197
phone: 608-835-8861
fax: 608-835-8421
e-mail: books@tdsnet.com
Issues quarterly catalogs; buys and sells out-of-print books on astronomy, meteorology, and space exploration; also books about microscopes, old scientific instruments, optics, and related areas.

Sports

Collectors

John Buonaguidi
540 Reeside Ave.
Monterey, CA 93940-1828
phone: 408-655-2363
Wants 19th century non-fiction books about baseball, football, or boxing.

BORGHESE

Collectors

David Elder
306 South Chapman St.
Greensboro, NC 27403
Wants Borghese decorative boxes, lamps, pictures, plaques, figurines, bookends, etc.; usually made from plaster and painted gold, green, maroon, etc., sometimes with pictures of flowers pasted on; black felt bottom with paper label.

BOTTLE CAPS

(see also BOTTLES, Milk; BREWERIANA; DAIRY COLLECTIBLES; SOFT DRINK COLLECTIBLES)

Crown

Clubs/Associations

John Vetter
Crown Collectors Society International
Newsletter: Crown Cappers Exchange
4300 San Juan Dr.
Fairfax, VA 22030-5351
phone: 703-591-3060
A collector's organization dedicated to helping those interested in collecting and working to preserve the rich colorful history of the bottle crown closure as used for beer, soda, mineral water, etc. bottles.

Collectors

Barry Oremland
1260 Washington St.
Walpole, MA 02081
phone: 508-688-9086 or 617-864-0161
fax: 617-864-4422
Collects, trades, buys, sells crown caps of all types; all origins, and all reasonable conditions; also wants crown industry material, reseal caps, signs, pictures, articles, letters, etc. depicting or mentioning crown caps.

David Friedman
11129 Barman Ave.
Culver City, CA 90230
phone: 310-837-3089
Runs the ABA Crown Cap Exchange.

Dealers

C.A. Leppek
1016 S. Washington St.
Denver, CO 80209-4318
phone: 303-744-8385
e-mail: redraven75@aol.com
Buys, sells and trades crowns (bottle caps); vintages, nationalities of all types - beers, sodas, waters, oddball. Will buy loners, groups or entire collections.

Milk

(see also POGS)

Collectors

Jerry Jerard
402 Western Ave.
Brattleboro, VT 05301-2538
phone: 802-254-5815

Dealers

Carole Schauer
Carole's Collectibles
P.O. Box 232
Elcho, WI 54428-0232
phone: 715-275-5200
Buys and sells milk bottle caps and small dairy items.

Experts

Dan Ryan
45 Sunnyside Ave.
Putnam, CT 06260-1830
phone: 860-928-5014
Writes "Covering Caps" column for "The Milk Route", newsletter of The National Association of Milk Bottle Collectors.

BOTTLE OPENERS

Figural

(see also BREWERIANA; CAN OPENERS; CORKSCREWS)

Clubs/Associations

Nancy Robb
Figural Bottle Opener Collectors Club
Newsletter: Opener, The
3 Avenue A
Latrobe, PA 15650
phone: 412-539-1048
Formed to promote interest in and knowledge about figural bottle openers.

John Stanley
Just for Openers
Newsletter: Just for Openers Newsletter
P.O. Box 64
Chapel Hill, NC 27514
phone: 919-419-1546 or 919-966-5794
Just for Openers is a club for bottle and corkscrew collectors; quarterly newsletter.

Collectors

John Stanley
P.O. Box 64
Chapel Hill, NC 27514
phone: 919-419-1546 or 919-966-5794
Wants any bottle opener or corkscrew from the Southeast U.S.; also wants to buy any beer advertising items.

Kelly C. Devlin
Rte. 1 Box 93
Wahoo, NE 68066
phone: 402-443-4305
Wants to buy figural bottle openers.

Experts

Charles Reynolds
Reynolds Toys
2836 Monroe St.
Falls Church, VA 22042-2007
phone: 703-533-1322
An advanced collector paying top dollar for openers, e.g. wall mount boy winking, Amish Man, Skull, Coyote, Bear, Eagle, Standing College Figures, etc.

Phyllis Eisenach
3759 SW Whispering Sound Dr.
Palm City, FL 34990-7735
phone: 561-223-8275
Interested in figural (three-dimensional) bottle openers; 16 years collecting; member of the Figural Bottle Opener Collectors Club; prefers iron or other metal openers.

Repro. Sources

Charles Reynolds
Reynolds Toys
2836 Monroe St.
Falls Church, VA 22042-2007
phone: 703-533-1322
Offers limited editions of new original figural bottle openers of sand-cast aluminum; flyer on request.

BOTTLES

(see also BOTTLE CAPS; DAIRY COLLECTIBLES; FRUIT JARS; INFANT FEEDERS; INKWELLS & INKSTANDS; INSULATORS; SALOON & BAR COLLECTIBLES; SODA FOUNTAIN COLLECTIBLES; SOFT DRINK COLLECTIBLES; TREASURE HUNTING)

Auction Services

A.R. Blakeman
B.B.R. Auctions
P.O. Box 310
Richmond
Surrey TW9 1FS, U.K.
England's leading specialists and auction house for antique bottles, pot lids and related advertising material.

James A. Megura
Skinner, Inc.
357 Main St.
Bolton, MA 01740-1104
phone: 508-779-6241 or 617-350-5400
fax: 508-779-5144
Established in 1964, Skinner Inc. is the fifth largest auction house in the US; has offices in Bolton and Boston, MA.

Norman C. Heckler
Norman C. Heckler & Company
79 Bradford Corner Rd.
Woodstock Valley, CT 06282-2002
phone: 860-974-1634
fax: 860-974-2003
Specializes in the sale of early glass and bottles; Heckler & Co. sold a single bottle for $66,000 at auction in 1993.

James Hagenbuch
Glass Works Auctions
P.O. Box 180
East Greenville, PA 18041
phone: 215-679-5849
fax: 215-679-3068
Specializes in the auction of historical flasks, fruit jars, barber bottles, food and milk bottles, sodas, poisons, whiskeys, medicines, inks, bitters, target & range balls, scent bottles, shaving mugs, blown & pressed glass, etc.

Pacific Glass Auctions
1507 21st St., Ste. 203
Sacramento, CA 95814
phone: 916-443-3296 or 916-443-3210
Internet: http://www.pacglass.com

Clubs/Associations

Philip R. Donovan, Jr.
New England Antique Bottle Club
Newsletter: NEABC News
120 Commonwealth Rd.
Lynn, MA 01904-2052
Membership throughout New England; meets 2nd Sunday of each month (except July & August) in Kennebunk, ME; newsletter published 10 times per year; for club information pack or bottle related questions please send SASE.

Yankee Bottle Club
P.O. Box 702
Keene, NH 03431

Somers Antique Bottle Club
P.O. Box 373
Somers, CT 06071

Joe Maggi
North Jersey Antique Bottle Collectors Association
117 Lincoln Pl.
Waldwick, NJ 07463-2114
phone: 201-445-9079

Jersey Shore Bottle Club
P.O. Box 995
Toms River, NJ 08754-0649

Kim Bloomer
Hudson Valley Antique Bottle Club
6 Columbus Ave.
Cornwall On Hudson, NY 12520

Bob Dicker, Pres.
Empire State Bottle Collectors Association
Newsletter: ESBCA Newsletter
22 Paris Rd.
New Hartford, NY 13413

Genessee Valley Bottle Collectors Association
P.O. Box 7528
Rochester, NY 14615

Engvard Johnson
Pittsburgh Antique Bottle Club
RD 3 Box 280
Indiana, PA 15701
phone: 412-465-8287

Pennsylvania Bottle Collector's Association
Newsletter: Dirty Bottle, The
251 Eastland Ave.
York, PA 17402-1105
phone: 717-854-4965
Members collect or are interested in antique bottles and are from various states with the majority of members from the York-Lancaster-Harrisburg area.

Forks of the Delaware Bottle Collectors Association
P.O. Box 693
Easton, PA 18042

Bill Baumgardner
Delmarva Antique Bottle Club
57 Lakewood Dr.
Lewes, DE 19958

Baltimore Antique Bottle Club
Newsletter: Baltimore Bottle Digger
P.O. Box 36061
Townson, MD 21286-6061
phone: 301-997-1999
Monthly meetings include displays, selling/trading and speaker programs about bottles & related items: jugs, fruit jars, etc.

Mike Jordan
Potomac Bottle Club
Newsletter: Potomac Pontil, The
8411 Porter Ln.
Alexandria, VA 22308-2140
phone: 703-360-8181
Club serves the metropolitan Washington, D.C. area; provides a monthly meeting with educational programs, library, public speakers, annual bottle show, and other services

of interest to collectors of antique bottles and jars.

Frank Kowalski
Apple Valley Bottle Collectors Club
3015 Northwestern Pike
Winchester, VA 22603-3825
phone: 540-877-1093
Members are interested antique bottles: bitters, whiskeys, beers, mineral waters, White House vinegars, milks, medicines, cures, Depression glassware, local pottery, postcards and milk glass.

C.G. Richardson
Historical Bottle Diggers of Virginia, The
Newsletter: HBDV Newsletter
1176 South Dogwood Dr.
Harrisonburg, VA 22801
phone: 703-434-1506
Member of National Federation of Historical Bottle Collectors; newsletter published bi-monthly.

Richmond Area Bottle Collectors
2801 Battery Ave.
Richmond, VA 23228

Fred Taylor
Southeastern Antique Bottle Club
143 Scatterfoot Dr.
Peachtree City, GA 30269-1853

M-T Bottle Collectors Association, Inc.
Newsletter: Diggers Dispatch
P.O. Box 1581
De Land, FL 32721
Sponsors an annual bottle show usually in March.

J. Carl Sturm, Pres.
Federation of Historical Bottle Collectors, Inc.
Magazine: Bottles & Extras
88 Sweetbriar Branch
Longwood, FL 32750-2783
phone: 407-332-7689
e-mail: glassman@qnet.com
Internet: http://www.av.qnet.com/~glassman
"Bottles & Extras" contains articles, pictures, letters, show dates, and show and auction reports in the field of antique bottles, insulators, fruit jars and associated items; check website for list of scores of clubs by region.

Ed Herrold
Sarasota-Manatee Antique Bottle Collectors Association
P.O. Box 3105
Sarasota, FL 34230-3105
phone: 813-923-6550
Networking for education and pleasure of antique bottle, insulator, and fruit jar collectors; only interested in 19th century and earlier; no Jim Beam bottles or Avon bottles.

Nancy Pennington
Middle Tennessee Bottle & Collector's Club
Newsletter: MTBCC Newsletter
1750 Keyes Rd.
Greenbrier, TN 37073
phone: 615-643-0290
fax: 615-643-0290
e-mail: npenn2405@aol.com

Bruce Webb
East Tennessee Bottle & Collectibles Society
Newsletter: Bottle Digger, The
4521 Jones Rd.
Knoxville, TN 37918-7722
phone: 615-687-0846
Newsletter published bi-monthly; club hosts annual Bottle Collectibles Show & Sale 2nd Saturday in June at Knoxville Convention Center, Knoxville, TN; largest show of its kind in the country.

Norman & Junne Barnett
Midwest Antique Fruit Jar & Bottle Club
Newsletter: Midwest Glass Chatter, The
P.O. Box 38
Flat Rock, IN 47234
phone: 812-587-5560
Sponsors two fruit and bottle shows each year in Indianapolis.

Shaun Kotlarsky
Huron Valley Antique Bottle & Insulator Club
2475 West Walton Blvd.
Waterford, MI 48329-4435
phone: 810-673-1650

Antique Bottle Club of Northern Illinois
P.O. Box 571
Lake Geneva, WI 53147

John E. Panek
First Chicago Bottle Club
Newsletter: Midwest Bottle News, The
P.O. Box A3382
Chicago, IL 60690
phone: 708-945-5493
Organization of antique bottle and stoneware collectors who research, educate, buy and sell at monthly meetings, annual shows, and annual auctions.

Gulf Coast Bottle & Jar Club
P.O. Box 1754
Pasadena, TX 77501

Dottie Daugherty
Las Vegas Antique Bottle & Collectibles Club
Newsletter: Punkin Seed, The
3901 E. Stewart #16
Las Vegas, NV 89110-3152
phone: 702-452-1263
Members promote the hobby of collecting, researching, displaying and trading of antique bottles and collectibles; sponsors an annual collectibles show and sale in February of each year.

Willy Young
Antique Bottle & Collectibles Club
P.O. Box 1061
Verdi, NV 89439
phone: 702-746-0922

San Bernardino County Historical Bottle
   & Collectible Club
P.O. Box 6759
San Bernardino, CA 92412

San Jose Antique Bottle Collectors
   Association
P.O. Box 5432
San Jose, CA 95159

Collectors

Leo A. Bedard
39 Chestnut St., Apt. 102
Ludlow, MA 01056-3462
phone: 413-583-5746
   *Collects antique bottles, specializing
   in embossed, strapsided, and coffin
   flasks.*

Philip R. Donovan, Jr.
120 Commonwealth Rd.
Lynn, MA 01904-2052
   *Collect/buy/trade 1870s to 1920s
   bottles: medicine, soda, milk; will buy
   collections of dug bottles of all types;
   purchases labeled embossed 1800s-
   1910s medicines, sodas, beers, foods,
   etc. for personal collection; also digs.*

Douglas Anderson
112 S. Commerce St.
Centreville, MD 21617-1116
phone: 410-758-3278

Dan Argentati
61342 Creekview Dr.
South Lyon, MI 48178
phone: 810-437-6104
   *Collector of antique bottles,
   specializing in bitters bottles and any
   bottles from Michigan cities.*

Mark S. McNee
1009 Vassar Dr.
Kalamazoo, MI 49001-4483
phone: 616-343-8393
   *Wants to buy early American bottles
   of all types including bitters, poisons,
   historical flasks, and medicines.*

Steve Ketcham
P.O. Box 24114
Minneapolis, MN 55424-0114
phone: 612-920-4205
   *Buying pre-1900 American bottles
   with embossed or paper labels:
   especially flasks, bitters, cures,
   figurals, barber bottles, etc.; please
   send SASE with inquiries; $1 plus
   SASE for illustrated bottle dating
   pamphlet.*

John Panek
1790 Hickory Knoll
Deerfield, IL 60015
   *Specialists in historical flasks, bitters,
   sodas and Chicago bottles and
   stoneware.*

Barbara A. Harms
14521 Atlantic Ave.
Riverdale, IL 60627
phone: 708-841-4068

Ed Krol
Krol's Rock City and Mobile Park
Star Rte. 2 Box 15A
Derning, NM 88030
phone: 505-546-4368
   *Hutchinson sodas, embossed &
   painted milks, inks, Coca Colas, cures,
   hairs, seltzer, beers, baby bottles,
   whiskeys, druggist, etc.*

Kitty & Russell Umbraco
P.O. Box 5331
Richmond, CA 94805-0331
phone: 510-235-1656
   *Wants to buy Western bottles,
   especially Nevada, San Francisco and
   related advertising.*

John Goetz
P.O. Box 1570
Cedar Ridge, CA 95924
phone: 916-272-4644
   *Buying pre-1920 embossed glass
   bottles: bitters, fifths, flasks, mineral
   water, beer, California bottles.*

Scott Grandstaff
P.O. Box 409
Happy Camp, CA 96039
phone: 916-493-2032

Dealers

Mike Sheridan
30 Brabant Rd.
Cheadle Hulme, Cheadle
Cheshire SK8 7AU, U.K.
phone: 0161-4860927
   *English dealer/collector seeks old
   English bottles now resident in the
   US: stenciled Scots/Irish whiskeys,
   pontiled medicine, including
   Turlingtons, old stoneware bottles,
   highly pictorial and colorful old
   labels of all types.*

Frank Kowalski
Polish Barn Antiques, The
3015 Northwestern Pike
Winchester, VA 22603-3825
phone: 540-877-1093
   *Interested in antique bottles: bitters,
   whiskeys, beers, mineral waters, White
   House vinegars, milks, medicines,
   cures, Depression glassware, local
   pottery, postcards and milk glass.*

Don Dzuro
Antique of Copley
1442 St. Michaels Ave.
Akron, OH 44320
phone: 330-867-8024
   *Buys, sells and trades bottles, jars and
   pottery; author of "Ohio Bottles."*

Experts

Mike Jordan
Jordan Antiques & Research Co.
8411 Porter Ln.
Alexandria, VA 22308-2140
phone: 703-360-8181
   *Buy, sells, appraises and specializes
   in rare, early American bottles.*

Jamie Houdeshell
16255 Normandy South
Perrysburg, OH 43551
phone: 419-872-1966
   *Buys, sells, appraises and specializes
   in antique bottles and early American
   glass.*

Misc. Services

Wayne Lowry
Jar Doctor
2105 East-250 South
Lebanon, IN 46052
phone: 317-482-4033
   *Manufacturers a bottle and jar
   cleaning system.*

Museums/Libraries

A.R. Blakeman
National Bottle Museum
P.O. Box 310
Richmond
Surrey TW9 1FS, U.K.
   *Specialist museum covering all areas
   of bottles: wines, medicines, inks,
   brewery, etc.*

Charles McDonald
Old Bottle Museum
4 Friendship Dr.
Salem, NJ 08079
phone: 609-935-5631

Jan Rutland, Dir.
National Bottle Museum
Newsletter: Bottle Muse, The
76 Milton Ave.
Ballston Spa, NY 12020-1405
phone: 518-885-7589
   *Open year round; exhibits, videos and
   library deal with the history and
   beauty of 18th and 19th century
   bottles manufactured with hand tools
   and lung power; artifacts represent an
   industry and way of life that has
   vanished.*

Hawaii Bottle Museum
Newsletter: Hawaii Bottle Museum
News
P.O. Box 25152
Honolulu, HI 96825
phone: 808-395-4671

Periodicals

A.R. Blakeman
B.B.R. Publishing
Magazine: British Bottle Review
P.O. Box 310
Richmond
Surrey TW9 1FS, U.K.
   *The world's longest continuous
   running publication covering the
   multitudinous areas of antique bottles;*

*including world news; published
quarterly.*

Magazine: Antique Bottle Collecting
Magazine
4 Lower Clifton Hill
Clifton
Bristol B58, U.K.

Mike Sheridan
Magazine: Bottles & Bygones
30 Brabant Rd.
Cheadle Hulme, Cheadle
Cheshire SK8 7AU, U.K.
phone: 0161-4860927
   *Magazine loaded with articles and
   photos about glass and stoneware
   bottles and related items; published
   quarterly; Britain's most informative
   bottle magazine; company histories,
   new discoveries, digging articles;
   great source for info!*

Magazine: Canadian Bottle & Stoneware
Collector
P.O. Box 310
Ontario L1C 3L1 Canada
phone: 705-277-3704
   *More in-depth articles on more topics
   than any other bottle magazine in the
   world; black glass, fruit jars, ginger
   jars, sodas, insulators, etc.*

James Hagenbuch
Magazine: Antique Bottle & Glass
Collector
P.O. Box 180
East Greenville, PA 18041
phone: 215-679-5849
fax: 215-679-3068
   *A monthly magazine for the glass and
   bottle collector.*

Barber

(see also BARBER SHOP COL-
LECTIBLES)

Collectors

George A. Coupe
1243 1st St. S.E.
Washington, DC 20003
phone: 202-554-1000 or 800-368-5466
fax: 202-863-0775
   *Wants barber bottles; must be in good
   condition.*

Bitters

Experts

Robert Daly
10341 Jewell Lake Ct.
Fenton, MI 48430-2418
phone: 810-629-4934
e-mail: ldaly1@aol.com

Periodicals

Greg Price
Newsletter: Bitters Report, The
P.O. Box 1253
Bunnell, FL 32110-1253
phone: 904-437-2807
   *A newsletter for bitters bottle
   enthusiasts.*

Bubble Bath

Collectors

Pete Nowicki
1531 39th Ave.
San Francisco, CA 94122-3015
phone: 415-566-7506
Collects plastic Soaky and Purex containers which came in the shape of figures such as Donald Duck, Batman, Mr. Magoo; were filled with soap to get kids clean; when empty they became a new toy.

Ginger Beer

Collectors

Keith Roloson
6220 Carriage Ct.
Cumming, GA 30130-9111
phone: 770-781-5021 or 770-750-6429
e-mail: kroloson@ems.att.com
Internet: http://www.insulators.com
Wants to buy American, Canadian, South African, Australian, and other stone ginger beer bottles with pictorials.

Experts

Sven Stau
240 Know Ave.
Buffalo, NY 14224-1250
phone: 716-825-5448
fax: 716-822-3120
Author of "The Illustrated Stone Ginger Beer"; wants to buy pottery ginger beer bottles and related paper items.

Historical Flasks

Experts

John Crary
P.O. Box 417
Canton, NY 13617
Author of "Guide to the Value of Historical Flasks."

Robert Daly
10341 Jewell Lake Ct.
Fenton, MI 48430-2418
phone: 810-629-4934
e-mail: ldaly1@aol.com

Japanese

Collectors

Al Sparacino
743 La Huerta Way
San Diego, CA 92154
phone: 619-690-3632
Wants Japanese figural sake, wine, liquor bottles: House of Koshu, Kikukawa, Kamotsuru, Kikkoman, Sasaiti Shuzo, Okura Shuzu, etc.

Japanese/German Giveaway

Collectors

Paul Stookey
3436 Pointe Creek Ct. #202
Cape Coral, FL 34134
phone: 941-498-4502 or 941-498-6601
Wants Japanese and German giveaway bottles - "nippers."

Milk

(see also BOTTLE CAPS, Milk; DAIRY COLLECTIBLES)

Clubs/Associations

Thomas Gallagher
National Association of Milk Bottle Collectors, Inc.
Newsletter: Milk Route, The
4 Ox Bow Rd.
Westport, CT 06880-2602
phone: 203-227-5244
fax: 203-227-2206
Internet: http:// www.collectoronline.com/club-NAMBC-wp.html
Focuses on milk and dairy history and related memorabilia; membership includes the newsletter and directory of members; newsletter has articles, ads, show dates, information exchange, patents, events, etc.

Collectors

Jerry Jerard
402 Western Ave.
Brattleboro, VT 05301-2538
phone: 802-254-5815

Gus Dueben
10215 117th Dr.
Largo, FL 33773-2336

Dealers

O. B. Lund
13009 So. 42nd St.
Phoenix, AZ 85044
phone: 602-893-3567

Experts

Thomas Gallagher
4 Ox Bow Rd.
Westport, CT 06880-2602
phone: 203-227-5244
fax: 203-227-2206
Internet: http:// www.collectoronline.com/club-NAMBC-wp.html

Tony Knipp
P.O. Box 105
Blooming Grove, NY 10914-0105
phone: 914-496-6841 or 914-938-4580
Internet: http:// www.collectoronline.com/

Robert Bickel
7545 US Highway 522 S
Mc Veytown, PA 17051-7450
Wants milk bottles from Mifflin Co., PA (McVeytown, Lewistown, Milroy, Reedsville, Burnham, McClure,
Belleville, Allensville, Granville, Matawana, Newton); also wants beer cans from PA breweries and stoneware marked "Lewistown".

Ralph Riovo
686 Franklin St.
Alburtis, PA 18011-9578
phone: 610-966-2536
Buying and selling milk and dairy items for 18 years; wants milk bottles with Hopalong Cassidy, Annie Oakley, Disney characters, etc.

John Tutton
Early American Workshop
1967 Ridgeway Rd.
Front Royal, VA 22630-8652
phone: 703-635-7058 or 703-635-6141
Involved in milk bottles for 23 years; covering collecting, buying and selling; lecturer and author of three books on milk bottles; author of "Udderly Beautiful", updated in 1997.

Milk (Figural)

Collectors

Ed & Carol Clemens
65 Hickory Ave.
Bergenfield, NJ 07621
phone: 201-384-9236
Collects "Baby Top" and "Cop for Creams" figural milk bottles.

Miniature

Collectors

Lee Weiss
5626 Corning Ave.
Los Angeles, CA 90056-1305
phone: 213-294-3231 or 310-534-4943
Wants miniature bottles such as whiskey, beer, liquor and pop containers.

Harry Ford
54 Village Circle
Manhattan Beach, CA 90266-7222

Fred Hawley
1311 Montero Ave.
Burlingame, CA 94010
phone: 415-342-7085
Collector of miniature liquor bottles wants minis with labels from pre-prohibition through the 1950s; especially interested in 1930s minis from California.

Dealers

Flask, The
12194 Ventura Blvd.
Studio City, CA 91604
phone: 818-761-5373
Carries large selection of minis.

Periodicals

David Spaid
Briscoe Publications
Magazine: Miniature Bottle Collector, The
P.O. Box 2161
Palos Verdes Peninsula, CA 90274-8161
phone: 310-534-4943
fax: 310-534-8437
For collectors of modern or old miniature bottles; published six times per year.

Miniature Beer & Soda

Dealers

Alexander Mullin
Miscellanea
331 North Lehigh Circle
Swarthmore, PA 19081
phone: 610-328-7381
e-mail: amullin@itrc.dciu.kiz.pa.us
Wants American and foreign MINIATURE beer bottles (3"-6" high), 1880-1960; bottles may be embossed; most will have paper, decal, or foil labels; labels must be in good condition; small breweries bring premium; describe, especially label.

Miniature Liquor

Auction Services

Albert Rieland
Mini-Bottle Auction Club
Nording 16A
064832 Babenhausen, Germany
Bi-monthly auctions; 1600 to 2500 bottles in each issue.

Frank Callan
Mini-Bottle International
52 Betty's Lane
P.O. Box 777
Brewster, MA 02631
phone: 508-896-6491
fax: 508-896-6491
Specializes in the auction of mini liquor bottles & figurals from all over the world; quarterly auction catalog has 800-1000 items.

Clubs/Associations

Mini Bottle Club, The
Newsletter: Mini Bottle Club Newsletter
47 Burradon Rd.
Burradon
Northumberland NE23 7NF U.K.
Large bi-monthly newsletter with latest information on old & new miniatures as well as members' buy/sell ads, feature articles, and bottle outlets; primarily scotch whisky but also gins, cognacs, rums, vodkas, liquors, and ceramics.

Western New York Miniature Liquor Bottle Club
P.O. Box 182
Cheektowaga, NY 14225-0182
phone: 716-683-8939

Norm Luber
Del-Val Miniature Bottle Club
Newsletter: It's A Small World
57104 Del Aire Landing Rd.
Philadelphia, PA 19114
Members show and exchange information on miniature liquor bottles; club meets every other month; two shows every year.

Paul M. Murray
Great Lakes Miniature Bottle Club
Newsletter: GLMBC Newsletter
19745 Woodmont
Harper Woods, MI 48225-1873
phone: 313-882-8917
Club is devoted to collecting miniature liquor bottles and related items such as giveaways and mini beers; all are welcome.

Harry Ford, Treas.
Lilliputian Bottle Club, The
: Gulliver's Gazette
54 Village Circle
Manhattan Beach, CA 90266-7222
215 member club is 20 years old and very active; meets monthly, sponsors a mini-bottle show and sale each October.

Collectors

Dr. Dana Cable
8605 Pinecliff Dr.
Frederick, MD 21701
phone: 301-694-9297
fax: 301-694-3539
e-mail: dadacable@msn.com
Buys and sells miniature liquor bottles; interested in purchase of individual bottles; send description and price.

Paul Stookey
3436 Pointe Creek Ct. #202
Cape Coral, FL 34134
phone: 941-498-4502 or 941-498-6601
Buys, sells, trades miniature whiskey jugs and older miniature whiskey bottles.

Bill Costas
Roscoes Restaurant
22746 Roscoe Blvd.
West Hills, CA 91304
phone: 818-883-5597
1000s of mini's on display.

Thomas F. Nagelin, Sr.
13271 Clinton St.
Garden Grove, CA 92643
phone: 714-638-3041 or 714-554-8000
fax: 714-554-1798
Wants miniature liquor bottles; 1930s and 1940s; has collection of over 11,000 minis.

John Goetz
P.O. Box 1570
Cedar Ridge, CA 95924
phone: 916-272-4644
Buy/sell ceramic & glass figural mini bottles: dancers, pigs, drunks, Santas, octopus and other whimsical figures; sorry, no Beam types.

Perfume & Scent

(see also AVON COLLECTIBLES; PERFUME LAMPS)

Auction Services

Randy Monsen
Cocktails & Laughter Antiques
P.O. Box 529
Vienna, VA 22183-0529
phone: 703-938-2129
Cataloged auctions of perfume bottles: commercial, Czechoslovakian, Lalique, Baccarat, Victorian, Crown Top, Fractices, miniatures.

Clubs/Associations

Jeannine Malien
Parfum Plus Collections
1590 Louis-Carrier, Ste. 502
Montreal
Quebec H4N 2Z1 Canada

Randy Monsen, Mem.
International Perfume Bottle Association
Newsletter: Perfume Bottle Quarterly
P.O. Box 529
Vienna, VA 22183-0529
phone: 703-938-2129
Informative quarterly newsletter, annual meeting, membership directory, special programs for members.

Anne Conrad
International Perfume Bottle Association, Lone Star Chapter
481 Cottonwood Pl.
Mc Kinney, TX 75069
phone: 214-542-8987

Collectors

Vallerie Roberts Shutterly
Victorian Touch
P.O. Box 4
Micanopy, FL 32667
phone: 352-466-4022
fax: 351-591-2872
Wants to buy ornate jeweled perfume bottles and powder jars: colored glass bottles covered with fancy brass filigree and jewels; especially cut-to-clear in pinks and roses with jeweled ornamentation; marked Czechoslovakia.

Donna G. Sims
P.O. Box 187
Galena, OH 43021-0187
phone: 614-965-5693
Editor of the "Perfume Bottle Quarterly," the quarterly publication of the International Perfume Bottle Association.

Jeane Parris
Sugarplums, etc.
2022 E. Charleston Blvd.
Las Vegas, NV 89104-2018
phone: 702-385-6059
fax: 702-388-1202

Carol Kahn
3519 Wycliff Dr.
Modesto, CA 95355

Dealers

Ken Leach
Gallery #47
1050 2nd Ave.
New York, NY 10022
phone: 800-942-0550 or 212-888-0165
fax: 212-355-4403
Buys and sells commercial and Czechoslovakian perfume bottles.

Randy Monsen
Cocktails & Laughter Antiques
P.O. Box 529
Vienna, VA 22183-0529
phone: 703-938-2129
Wants all kinds, especially with original labels: by Guerlain, Coty, Nina Ricci, Dior, Corday, Lalique, etc.

Experts

Christie Mayer Lefkowith
FDR Station
P.O. Box 5200
New York, NY 10150-5200
phone: 212-838-2932 or 212-758-8550
fax: 212-688-9313
e-mail: mayerlef@panix.com
Internet: http://www.panix.com/~mayerlef/
Buys all sizes of commercial perfume bottles, preferably with boxes: Lalique, Baccarat, and others from 1850 to 1960; author of "The Art of Perfume, Discovering and Collecting Perfume Bottles."

Madeleine France
Madeleine France Antiques
P.O. Box 15555
Fort Lauderdale, FL 33318-5555
phone: 305-584-0009 or 305-921-0022
fax: 305-584-0014
Wants perfume bottles and boudoir items: Lalique, Baccarat, Viard, St. Louis, Moser, Sterling Scents, Steuben, DeVilbiss, Victorian laydowns, etc.

Mary Hallier
P.O. Box 34
Swanton, OH 43558
Specializes in DeVilbiss atomizers, or "perfumizers."

Emily Hart Killian
1211 E. Front St., Ste. 131
Traverse City, MI 49684-2928
phone: 616-946-7144
Author of "Perfume Bottles Remembered"; available from the author for $16 plus $2 S&H.

Periodicals

Christie Mayer Lefkowith
Newsletter: Phillips Perfume Presentations
FDR Station
P.O. Box 5200
New York, NY 10150-5200
phone: 212-838-2932 or 212-758-8550
fax: 212-688-9313
e-mail: mayerlef@panix.com
Internet: http://www.panix.com/~mayerlef/
A bi-annual review of specialty perfume bottle auctions at Phillips International Auctions.

Repair Services

Oldies but Goodies
P.O. Box 217
Hankins, NY 12741-0217
phone: 914-887-5272
fax: 914-887-5272
Will custom fit their atomizer perfume parts onto your bottle or top; send SASE for information.

Shari Hopper
Paradise & Co.
2902 Neal Rd.
Paradise, CA 95969-6169
phone: 916-872-5020
fax: 916-872-5022
e-mail: paradise@sunset.net
Replacement parts for atomizers: cords, balls, tassels; metal sprayer tops and collars; glass siphon tubing and daubers; also repairs, restoration and conservation available for perfume bottles.

Suppliers

Shari Hopper
Paradise & Co.
2902 Neal Rd.
Paradise, CA 95969-6169
phone: 916-872-5020
fax: 916-872-5022
e-mail: paradise@sunset.net
Replacement parts for atomizers: cords, balls, tassels; metal sprayer tops and collars; glass siphon tubing and daubers; also repairs, restoration and conservation available for perfume bottles.

Perfume & Scent (Miniature)

Clubs/Associations

Melinda Churchfield
Miniature Perfume Bottle Collectors
Newsletter: Mini-Scents
28227 Paseo El Siena
Laguna Niguel, CA 92677-4500
phone: 714-364-9510
For collectors of miniature perfume bottles; newsletter includes what's new, history of perfume houses, different versions and a color center page.

Collectors

Arielle Hart
1123 North Flores St., #21
West Hollywood, CA 90069
phone: 213-654-0277
fax: 213-656-7477
Collector of commercial perfume bottles; would enjoy hearing from anyone who would like to sell or trade; or anyone who would just like to chat about perfumes.

Melinda Churchfield
28227 Paseo El Siena
Laguna Niguel, CA 92677-4500
phone: 714-364-9510

Poison

Collectors

Mary Riggin
Rt. 617
Marionville, VA 23408-9999
phone: 757-442-2179
fax: 757-442-5391
Collector wants to buy old poison bottles.

Experts

Noel Cook
Mr. Poison
6601 Woodbine Rd.
Woodbine, MD 21797
phone: 410-781-7013
Buys trades, and sells embossed poison bottles from anywhere in the world; willing to help any new poison bottle collector.

Puzzle

Collectors

Alvin Schenk
5728 Pimlico Rd.
Baltimore, MD 21209
phone: 410-367-4371
Collects puzzle bottles - small, handcarved curiosities placed in bottles with small openings.

Soda

(see also SODA FOUNTAIN COLLECTIBLES; SOFT DRINK COLLECTIBLES)

Experts

Paul & Karen Bates
Interactive Publishers
192 Ridgecrest Dr.
Goodlettsville, TN 37072
phone: 615-859-5236
fax: 615-859-5238
Publishes always-current price updates to earlier soda bottle books.

Ron Fowler
P.O. Box 45251
Seattle, WA 98145-0251
Author of "Ice-Cold Soda Pop 5¢", "Washington Sodas:, The Bottler's Helper", and "An Introduction to Collecting Soda Pop Bottles."

Special Edition

Dealers

Roy M. Willis
Heartland of Kentucky Decanters & Steins
P.O. Box 428
Lebanon Junction, KY 40150
phone: 502-833-2827
Hundreds of whiskey decanters by Jim Beam, Wild Turkey, Ski Country, McCormick and others; also beer steins, domestic or foreign; call ONLY 9-5 eastern time.

Special Edition (Beam)

Clubs/Associations

Angelo J. Triantafellow
Cape Codders Jim Beam Bottle & Specialties Club
80 Lincoln Rd.
Rockland, MA 02370

Jim Beam Bottle & Specialties Club
2015 Burlington Ave.
Kewanee, IL 61443-8348

Special Edition (Ski Country)

Clubs/Associations

National Ski Country Bottle Club
Newsletter: Ski Country Collector, The
1224 Washington Ave.
Golden, CO 80401
phone: 303-279-3373
Designed as a source of information on collector decanters, old and new; newsletter features articles about a broad range of decanters with an emphasis on decanters by Ski Country.

Western Whiskey

Clubs/Associations

John Goetz
49'er Historical Bottle Club
P.O. Box 1570
Cedar Ridge, CA 95924
phone: 916-272-4644
Always glad to provide information on West coast bottles or on club membership.

Experts

R.E. Barnett
P.O. Box 109
Lakeview, OR 97630
phone: 503-947-2415
Author of "Western Whiskey Bottles."

BOW HUNTING

(see SPORTING COLLECTIBLES, Archery)

BOXES

(see also ADVERTISING COLLECTIBLES; BATTERSEA ENAMEL BOXES; CEREAL BOXES; CIGAR BANDS, BOXES & LABELS; ENAMELS; ORIENTALIA; PLASTIC COLLECTIBLES, Celluloid; RUSSIAN ITEMS; SMOKING COLLECTIBLES, Snuff Boxes; STAMP BOXES)

Collectors

Betty Bird
107 Ida St.
Mount Shasta, CA 96067-2629
phone: 916-926-4331 or 916-926-2231
Wants any type of figural or unusual boxes and containers: enamels, glass, porcelain, metal; also small scent containers.

Dealers

Sally Kaltman
Sallea Antiques
66 Elm St.
New Canaan, CT 06840
phone: 203-972-1050
Buys, sells and specializes in distinctive antique boxes; all shapes, styles, materials and sizes.

Experts

Janice & Richard Vogel
4720 SE Fort King St.
Ocala, FL 34470-1501
phone: 352-694-5776
fax: 352-694-7330
Authors of "Victorian Trinket Boxes," a handbook with price guide for the porcelain trinket box collector.

Candy

Collectors

Lynn Goldfinger
P.O. Box 4962
Burlingame, CA 94011-4962
phone: 415-342-7829
fax: 415-343-3269
e-mail: goldie1943@aol.com
Wants to buy Victorian cardboard candy boxes; all styles and sizes with artwork on the box.

Enamel

Dealers

Bob Smith
Cameron & Smith Ltd.
P.O. Box 637
Vero Beach, FL 32961-0637
phone: 800-472-9862
Buys and sells enamel boxes: Halcyon Days, Staffordshire, Crummles, Bilston, Battersea, etc.; limited editions wanted; specializing in retired limited editions Beatrix Potter enamels and any Royalty enamels; also Holiday boxes.

Enamel (Battersea)

Dealers

John Harrigan
1900 Hennepin
Minneapolis, MN 55403-3160
phone: 612-872-0226
fax: 612-872-0224
Prefers to buy motto boxes, but will consider others.

Experts

Mel & Barbara Alpern
14 Carter Rd.
West Orange, NJ 07052
phone: 201-731-9427
Advisor to "Warman's Antiques & Collectibles Price Guide."

Seed

Collectors

Lynn Anderson
15500 S.E. Royer Rd.
Clackamas, OR 97015
phone: 503-658-3607
Wants seed boxes; must have colorful paper labels on the inside.

BOY SCOUT MEMORABILIA

(see also CAMPING EQUIPMENT; GIRL SCOUT MEMORABILIA; LONE SCOUT MEMORABILIA; STAMP COLLECTING, Boy Scouting)

Book Sellers

Doug Bearce
Scouting Collectables
P.O. Box 4742
Salem, OR 97302-8742
phone: 503-399-9872
fax: 503-399-0559
Publishes and sells books on collecting Boy Scout items.

Clubs/Associations

Paul Sciera
Western New York Traders Association
15 Kellybrook Ct.
West Seneca, NY 14224
phone: 716-675-6313

Glen T. Wright
International Badgers Club
Magazine: Badgers Club Magazine
2903 W Woodbine Dr.
Maryville, TN 37801
Members interested in collecting Scout and Guide badges of the entire world.

Nate Mercurio, Ed.
Illinois Traders Association
Newsletter: ITA Newsletter
1639 W Hudson Ave.
Chicago, IL 60641
phone: 213-664-9433

Billie Lee
National Scouting Collectors Society
Newsletter: Scouting Collectors
Quarterly
806 E. Scott St.
Tuscola, IL 61953-1726
phone: 217-253-3243

American Scouting Traders Association,
Inc.
Newsletter: American STAR, The
P.O. Box 210013
San Francisco, CA 94121
phone: 714-641-4845
e-mail: doug3toe@aol.com
Internet: http://www.scouter.org/asta/
*ASTA members share an interest in the
collecting and trading of Scouting
memorabilia; for Scouts and Scouters
only.*

Collectors

Norm Sapolnick
P.O. Box 5
Hillside, NJ 07205-0005
phone: 908-687-3920 or 908-964-5800
fax: 908-687-6300

Bruce White
3 Woodfern Ave.
Trenton, NJ 08628
phone: 609-882-5584
*Wants Boy Scouts of America patches,
pins, literature, WWW items,
jamboree, etc.*

Mike Wroblewski
5526 E. County Rd. 100 N.
Greensburg, IN 47240-8805
phone: 812-663-9403 or 812-934-7001
e-mail: bwrob00@mail.gpbx.net
*Wants all Boy Scout related
memorabilia: books, pictures, OA
items, uniforms, patches, equipment,
unusual items, etc.; special interest in
all Indiana related Scouting items.*

Dr. Larry Ruehlen, Sr.
21124 Hoffman St.
Saint Clair Shores, MI 48082-1517
*Wants Scout rings, square merit
badges and ranks, Air Scout items,
Eagle items, OA vigil items.*

Robert N. Hightower
Rt. 11 Box 469
Palestine, TX 75801
phone: 903-723-0418
*Buys Boy Scout items: patches, pins,
books, uniforms, medals, equipment,
etc.*

John C. Williams
P.O. Box 23374
Waco, TX 76702-3374
phone: 817-772-1106
*Wants to buy Boy Scout patches:
Order of the Arrow (WWW), Philmont,
High Adventure, Jamboree; also
wants other Boy Scout related
memorabilia.*

Doug Bearce
P.O. Box 4742
Salem, OR 97302-8742
phone: 503-399-9872
fax: 503-399-0559
*Wants Boy Scout items: books,
uniforms, patches, pins, OA items,
Jamboree, etc.*

Dealers

James W. Clough
Scout Collectors Shop
9 Elmwood Dr.
South Glens Falls, NY 12803-5454
phone: 518-793-4037
*Wants Boy Scout items; sashes,
medals, pins, patches, uniforms, etc.*

Richard Shields
Carolina Trader, The
P.O. Box 769
Monroe, NC 28112-0769
phone: 704-282-1339 or 704-289-1604
e-mail: carotrader@trellis.net
Internet: http://www.trellisnet/carotrader
*Buys anything associated with the Boy
Scouts of America; author of "Patrol
Yell - History of the Patrol Medallions
of the BSA"; publishes large catalog
of BSA items for sale.*

Roland Sayers
Boy Scout Collectors Swap Meet
P.O. Box 629
Brevard, NC 28712-0629
phone: 704-883-9562

Chris R. Jensen
Streamwood, Inc.
P.O. Box 1841
Easley, SC 29641-1841
phone: 864-859-2915
fax: 800-453-0398
e-mail: CJensen@mindspring.com
Internet: http://www.mindspring.com/
~cjensen/
*Wants Boy Scout memorabilia: pre-
1936 handbooks, Order of the Arrow
(WWW), merit badges, jamboree,
medals, patches, insignia, uniforms;
publishes extensive catalog four/five
times a year; 40-page tabloid paper;
send for free sample.*

Experts

Chris R. Jensen
Streamwood, Inc.
P.O. Box 1841
Easley, SC 29641-1841
phone: 864-859-2915
fax: 800-453-0398
e-mail: CJensen@mindspring.com
Internet: http://www.mindspring.com/
~cjensen/
*30 years experience as dealer/
collector/appraiser; largest sale list of
exclusive Scouting items in the world;
largest inventory of Scout collecting
guide books available anywhere;
author of 7 Scout collecting books and
price guides.*

Fran & Cal Holden
P.O. Box 264 - M264
Doylestown, OH 44230-0264
phone: 800-663-2793
*Wants old or unusual pins, badges,
medals; from O/A, Jamboree, Senior
Scouts; also uniforms, games, official
literature, postcards, etc.; offers
subscription sales lists to collectors of
Boy Scout literature.*

Jack O'Brian
Memory Tree
P.O. Box 9462
Madison, WI 53715
phone: 414-261-6641
fax: 414-261-9461
*Buys and sells Eagle Scout and Air
Scout medals and ribbons, enamel
pins, Lone Scout, posters, banks, tins,
toys, watch fobs; will help identify and
date items if inquiries are accompanied by a SASE.*

Jim & Bea Stevenson
Stevensons, The
316 Sage Lane
Euless, TX 76039-7906
phone: 817-354-8903
fax: 817-354-9382
e-mail: the_stevensons@msn.com
*Wants Boy Scout handbooks, paper
items, Jamboree items, uniforms,
insignia, Sea Scouts, Skippers, Order
of the Arrow, etc.; issues 10 catalogs
per year for $10/yr.*

Museums/Libraries

Dr. Edward Rowan, Ed.
Lawrence L. Lee Scout Museum & Max
I. Silber Scouting Library
Magazine: Scout Memorabilia
P.O. Box 1121
Manchester, NH 03105-1121
phone: 603-627-1492 or 603-669-8919
fax: 603-625-2467
Internet: http://
www.scoutingmuseum.org
*Home to one of the finest collections
of Boy Scout memorabilia; "Scout
Memorabilia" has insert listing sales,
auctions, ads, etc.*

Susan K. Crawford
Murray State University National
Museum of the Boy Scouts of
America
Murray, KY 42071
phone: 502-762-3383

Mrs. Ralph Zitelman
Zitelman Scout Museum
1818 Wisteria Rd.
Rockford, IL 61107-2348
phone: 815-962-3999
*Worldwide Scouting: patches, books,
uniforms & equipment including Boy
and Girl Scouts, Brownies, Explorers,
Scoutmasters, etc.*

Periodicals

Dr. Edward Rowan, Ed.
Lawrence L. Lee Scout Museum & Max
I. Silber Scouting Library
Magazine: Scout Memorabilia
P.O. Box 1121
Manchester, NH 03105-1121
phone: 603-627-1492 or 603-669-8919
fax: 603-625-2467
Internet: http://
www.scoutingmuseum.org
*Home to one of the finest collections
of Boy Scout memorabilia; "Scout
Memorabilia" has insert listing sales,
auctions, ads, etc.*

Ken Wiltz
Magazine: Fleur-de-Lis
5 Dawes Ct. - Dept. CIC
Novato, CA 94947-4406
phone: 415-892-5977
fax: 415-892-5977
e-mail: kenwiltx@juno.com
*An international scouting memora-
bilia magazine now read in 30
countries.*

Camps

Periodicals

David Minnihan
Newsletter: Camp Patch Collector, The
P.O. Box 210013
San Francisco, CA 94121
phone: 714-641-4845
e-mail: doug3toe@aol.com
Internet: http://www.scouter.org/asta/
*Newsletter dealing with history and
memorabilia of Boy Scout Camps.*

Neckerchief Slides

Collectors

John Koppen
12705 N.W. Puddy Gulch Rd.
Yamhill, OR 97148

Order Of The Arrow

Collectors

Greg Souchik
P.O. Box 161
Custer City, PA 16725-0161
phone: 814-362-2642
fax: 814-362-7356
e-mail: 104235.2430@compuserve.com
*Wants to buy "Order of the Arrow"
embroidered patches; may have
"W.W.W.", "Lodge", or "O.A." on
them; will pay up to $1000 for some
patches; send photos or photocopies.*

Seals

Clubs/Associations

Murray Fried
World Scout Sealers
Newsletter: World Scout Sealers
Quarterly
509-11 Margaret Ave.
Kitchener
Ontario N2H 6M4 Canada
phone: 519-745-7947
*Members buy, sell and trade Scout
seals, decals and other Boy Scout
memorabilia; publishes an 8-page
newsletter twice a year.*

BRASS ITEMS

(see also BELLS;
CANDLEHOLDERS; FIREPLACE
ITEMS; GARDEN HOSE NOZZLES;
INSTRUMENTS & DEVICES;
LAMPS & LIGHTING; MEDICAL,
DENTAL & PHARMACEUTICAL;
REPAIR/RESTORATION/CONSER-
VATION, Metal Items; TRENCH
ART)

Repair Services

Don L. Reedy
Brass & Copper Polishing Shop
13 South Carroll St.
Frederick, MD 21701-5606
phone: 301-663-4240 or 301-662-5503
fax: 301-663-3478
e-mail: shineit4u@aol.com
*Repairs and polishes or lacquers
brass and copper items.*

Repro. Sources

Becky Ballew
Virginia Metalcrafters
1010 East Main St.
Waynesboro, VA 22980
phone: 540-949-9400 or 800-368-1002
*Makes and sells andirons, fireplace
tools and fenders, chandeliers,
candlesticks, sconces, garden
sculpture.*

BREWERIANA

(see also ADVERTISING COL-
LECTIBLES; BEER CANS;
BOTTLES; BOTTLE CAPS; BOTTLE
OPENERS; COLLECTIBLES
[MODERN], Steins; CORKSCREWS;
GLASSES, Drinking; NEON; PAPER
COLLECTIBLES; PROHIBITION
ITEMS; SALOON & BAR COL-
LECTIBLES; STEINS)

Appraisers

Judy Owen, ISA
Antique Appraisers - Grand Traverse
10332 Stoneybeach Pointe
Traverse City, MI 49686
phone: 616-946-2534
fax: 616-946-2573
*Collects, specializes in, and appraises
breweriana: Strohs, Goebels, all
Michigan breweries, pre-prohibition
trays and signs, etched glasses, bottle-
shaped openers, etc.*

Auction Services

Pete Kroll
Glasses, Mugs & Steins Auction
P.O. Box 207
Sun Prairie, WI 53590-0207
phone: 608-837-4818
fax: 608-825-4205
*Produces a semi-annual mail auction
featuring collectible advertising
glasses, mugs & steins: beer, soda,
cartoon, Disney, root beer, Budweiser,
whiskey shot glasses, whiskey
pitchers, etc.*

Lynn Geyer
Lynn Geyer Advertising Auctions
300 Trail Ridge
Silver City, NM 88061-6071
phone: 505-538-2341
fax: 505-388-9000
*Conducts semi-annual mail/phone bid
specialized auctions on all aspects of
breweriana and soda-pop; also
contemporary steins, mugs & drinking
glasses; advertising trays, advertising
signs, tap knobs.*

Clubs/Associations

John Stanley
East Coast Breweriana Association
Newsletter: Keg, The
P.O. Box 64
Chapel Hill, NC 27514
phone: 919-419-1546 or 919-966-5794
*The oldest breweriana collectors
organization; serving collectors of all
types of brewery advertising;
emphasis on Eastern US; write and
request a membership application.*

Keith Ajayan
Beer Can & Breweriana Collectors of
America, Mile High Chapter
414 Wright St. #107
Lakewood, CO 80228
phone: 303-763-5811
e-mail: beerstuff@aol.com

Stan Galloway, Ex. Dir.
American Breweriana Association, Inc.
Journal: American Breweriana Journal
P.O. Box 11157
Pueblo, CO 81001-0157
phone: 719-544-9267
e-mail: breweriana@aol.com
*Association of brewery historians and
collectors of beer advertising and
collectibles; offers seven free
exchange services for collectors,
Lending Library, and annual meeting
for members to buy/sell/trade
breweriana; 3,300 members.*

Collectors

Ed Natale, Jr.
P.O. Box 222
Wyckoff, NJ 07481
phone: 201-848-8485
fax: 201-891-4252
*Wants to buy beer trays with brewery
scenes, women, dogs, children; foam
scrapers, NJ & NYC brewery items,
painted label bottles, punch-top and
spout-top cans, signs; photos helpful.*

Steve Ketcham
P.O. Box 24114
Minneapolis, MN 55424-0114
phone: 612-920-4205
*Wants pre-prohibition brewery
memorabilia: calendars, publications,
brewery signs, trays, glasses, posters,
pocket mirrors, steins, etc.; please
send SASE with inquiries.*

Dale Schmidt
610 Howell Prairie Rd. SE
Salem, OR 97301-9097
phone: 503-364-0499
fax: 503-585-3071
*Wants anything pre-Prohibition that is
related to beer and/or breweries.*

Dealers

Bob Miller
P.O. Box 640245
Flushing, NY 11364
phone: 718-776-7409
*Wants old (pre-Prohibition up to
1940s) American beer advertising
items such as match safes, trays,
signs, corkscrews, unusual bottle
openers, paperweights, signs, etched
glassware, etc.*

Paul Jarmusz
Vintage Original Fruit Crate Labels
2845 D St. N.E.
Salem, OR 97301-1600
phone: 503-371-0868
fax: 503-371-0868
e-mail: mjz@teleport.com
*Buys and sells old can labels, beer
labels, soda labels; unused stock
found from breweries, old packing
houses, canneries, produce
businesses.*

Experts

Lynn Geyer
300 Trail Ridge
Silver City, NM 88061-6071
phone: 505-538-2341
fax: 505-388-9000
*Specializes in all aspects of
breweriana and soda-pop; also
contemporary steins, mugs & drinking
glasses; advertising trays, advertising
signs, tap knobs.*

Museums/Libraries

American Museum of Brewing History
& Arts
I-75 at the Buttermilk Pike Exit
Ft. Mitchell, KY 41017
phone: 606-341-2802
*World's largest collection of
breweriana: tens of thousands of
labels, coasters, bottles, cans, match
boxes, signs, foam scrapers, etc.*

Periodicals

Michael Allison
Magazine: All About Beer
1627 Marion Ave.
Durham, NC 27705-5808
phone: 800-977-2337
fax: 919-490-0865
e-mail: allabtbeer@aol.com
Internet: http://www.allaboutbeer.com
*For fifteen years the voice of beer
lovers.*

Sandra L. Powers
Bosak Publishing Co.
Magazine: Suds 'N Stuff
4764 Galicia Way
Oceanside, CA 92056
phone: 619-724-4447
*Bi-monthly beer publication; articles,
history, memorabilia, ads, etc.*

Advertising

Clubs/Associations

Robert E. Jaeger
National Association of Breweriana
Advertising
Newsletter: Breweriana Collector, The
2343 Met-To-Wee Lane
Milwaukee, WI 53226-1612
phone: 414-257-0158
*Focuses on anything with the word
"Beer" or "Brewery" on it;
encourage the collection, preservation
and study of American brewery
advertising on a national level;
membership directory and annual
convention; 4 newsletters per year.*

Collectors

David Donovan
129 S. Linwood Ave.
Baltimore, MD 21224
phone: 410-276-7577
*Interested in all types of advertising
from any Baltimore brewery.*

Robert E. Jaeger
2343 Met-To-Wee Lane
Milwaukee, WI 53226-1612
phone: 414-257-0158
*Wants any advertising item with the
word "Beer" or "Brewery" on it.*

Back Bar Statues

Dealers

Bill Taylor
405 Holmes Dr. NW
Vienna, VA 22180
phone: 703-255-3887
Buys and sells back bar beer statues.

Experts

George Baley
310 Grandview Ave.
Kalamazoo, MI 49001-3609
phone: 616-382-4833
Author of "Back Bar Breweriana."

Coasters

Collectors

George Barone
94 Ridgeview Place
Cheshire, CT 06410
e-mail: geobaron@ix.netcom.com
Author of "Coasters of New England."

Ken Kositzke
1623 N. Linwood Ave.
Appleton, WI 54914
Runs the ABA Coaster Exchange.

Scott deMasi
5443 Dove Foreste Ln.
Humble, TX 77346-1224
phone: 281-852-0077
e-mail: demasi@flash.net

Dealers

Vic Kroll
Kroll's Kollectibles
3451 Nighthawk Ct.
Punta Gorda, FL 33950-6675
phone: 941-575-0303
e-mail: beer@sunline.net
Buys, sells, trades U.S. brewery coasters, postcards, letterheads, tokens, stock certificates and other advertising items.

Hamm's Beer

Collectors

Chris Ventzke
1837 Park Blvd.
Fargo, ND 58103
phone: 701-293-1547
Looking for Hamm's Beer signs, point of sale displays, neon signs, pre-prohibition items.

Pete Nowicki
1531 39th Ave.
San Francisco, CA 94122-3015
phone: 415-566-7506
Collector desires to obtain older Hamm's Beer advertising: glasses, signs, neons, etc.; the older the better.

Heienken

Collectors

Peter van Otterloo
Libanonstraat 12
Delft 2622 HS The Netherlands
phone: 015-2564580
e-mail: 106254.3013@compuserve.com
Collects all kind of items of Heienken beer, especially pre-1950 glasses and mugs from all countries of the world.

Historian

Experts

James D. Robertson
Tycho's Nose Antiques
57 Heights Terrace
Fair Haven, NJ 07704
phone: 908-741-7770 or 908-747-3251
Wine and beer historian and collector interested in breweriana.

Labels

Collectors

Pat Wheeler
4330 W 152nd St.
Cleveland, OH 44135-1367
e-mail: abalabex@aol.com
Internet: http://members.aol.com/abalabex/labex.htm
Coordinates the ABA Label Exchange program.

Dealers

Nelson V. Rich, III
12479 Windcliff
Davisburg, MI 48350

Adrian Angleton
1303 Main
South Roxana, IL 62087
phone: 618-254-0401

Napkins

Collectors

Jeff Coolaw
5132 Round Rock Drive
El Paso, TX 79924
Runs the ABA Napkin Exchange.

Openers

(see also BOTTLE OPENERS)

Collectors

Lawrence Biehl
448 Crandon
Calumet City, IL 60449
e-mail: l-biehl@gorst.edu
Wants to buy beer can, bottle or cork openers that have name of brewery on them.

Trays

Collectors

Floyd Buck
P.O. Box 9
Wolcott, VT 05680
Wants to buy beer trays.

BREYER HORSE MODELS

(see ANIMAL COLLECTIBLES, Horses [Models/Breyer])

BRICKS

Clubs/Associations

Ken Jones
International Brick Collectors Association
Journal: International Brick Collectors Association Journal
100 Manor Dr.
Columbia, MO 65203
phone: 573-445-7171
Organization trades bricks at swap meets.

Collectors

Barb Brownlee
80 E. 106th Terrace
Kansas City, MO 64114

Ken Jones
100 Manor Dr.
Columbia, MO 65203
phone: 573-445-7171

Museums/Libraries

Museum of Ancient Brick, The General Shale Corp.
3211 North Roan St.
Johnson City, TN 37601
phone: 615-282-4661

BRIDAL COLLECTIBLES

Experts

Ann C. Bergin
P.O. Box 105
Amherst, NH 03031-0105
fax: 508-649-6807
e-mail: PFBergin@aol.com

Periodicals

Ann C. Bergin
Newsletter: Bridal Collector's Roster
P.O. Box 105
Amherst, NH 03031-0105
fax: 508-649-6807
e-mail: PFBergin@aol.com
Wants wedding and bride related pictorial books, dolls, music boxes, etc.; also first communions, Christenings, "rites" of passage.

Cake Toppers

Collectors

Jeff Dykes
6 Wildwood Terrace
Glen Ridge, NJ 07028
phone: 201-748-4990 or 973-748-4990
Wants to buy German bisque and spun sugar wedding cake tops from 1890s to 1940s; especially wants military groom pieces; all must be in excellent condition; also look for bride/groom photo mirrors from 1910-1930s.

Experts

Cathy Cook
10 E. 13th St., #2D
New York, NY 10003-4467
e-mail: cook710@aol.com
Collector always looking for

historical information on bride-and-groom cake toppers; also wants to buy vintage toppers.

BRIDGE

(see also PLAYING CARDS)

Dealers

Bill Sachen
Wankegan Bridge Center
927 Grand Ave.
Waukegan, IL 60085
phone: 847-662-7294
Buys and sells items relating to bridge and other indoor games as well as playing cards; many books in foreign languages.

Periodicals

Magazine: Bridge Buff's Bulletin
927 Grand Ave.
Waukegan, IL 60085
phone: 847-662-7294
A quarterly publication for collectors of bridge books and periodicals.

BROADCASTING

(see also AUDIO-VISUAL; FILMS; MOVIE MEMORABILIA; RADIO SHOWS, Old Time; RADIOS; TELEVISION SHOWS & MEMORA-BILIA; TELEVISIONS; TELE-GRAPH ITEMS)

Experts

Mike Adams
112 Crescent Ct.
Scotts Valley, CA 95066-2815
phone: 408-924-4545
fax: 408-924-4543
e-mail: mhadams@sdsuvm1.susu.edu
Specialty area is radio and broadcast history; produced "Radio Collector" series for PBS TV; writes for "Antique Radio Classified."

Military

Collectors

Bob Putnam
9140 Conversation Way
Springfield, VA 22153
phone: 703-644-9711
Serious collector wants all items, transcripts, pictures, etc. concerning military broadcasters who served in WWII, Korea and Vietnam as well as in all other military campaigns.

BROADSIDES

(see PAPER COLLECTIBLES; POSTERS)

BRONZES

(see also ART; COLLECTIBLES [MODERN], Sculptures; ORIENTALIA; SCULPTURE)

Appraisers

Stephen van Cline, CAPP
van Cline & Davenport, Ltd.
792 Franklin Ave.
Franklin Lakes, NJ 07417-1343
Specializes in paintings, watercolors, drawings, bronze & marble sculpture; appraisals, authentication, lectures, expert testimony; minimum charge $25; letter request only, SASE.

Faber Donoughe
201 W. 89th St.
New York, NY 10024
phone: 212-873-5882
A recognized appraiser of bronze sculptures.

Jerry Bengis, ISA
9860 SW 122nd St.
Miami, FL 33176-4928
phone: 305-232-1143
fax: 305-251-1450
Fine art appraiser specializing in prints (especially Salvador Dali), graphics (Miro, Chagall, Picasso, Warhol), etchings, engravings, prints, bronzes.

William Lavendusky, M.S., ISA
William Lavendusky, Fine Art
3345 So. Harvard, Bldg. 100
Tulsa, OK 74135
phone: 918-747-5336
fax: 918-742-3425
Dealer and appraiser of paintings and sculpture; specialist in 19th century French animal bronzes.

Dealers

Cameron Shay
James Graham & Sons
1014 Madison Ave. at 78th St.
New York, NY 10021
phone: 212-535-5767
fax: 212-794-2454
Specializes in fine bronze sculptures: Akeley, Baryre, Bonheur, Bugatti, Carpeaux, Remington, Russell, St. Gaudens, etc.

Repair Services

Cavalier Arts
One Landmark Square
Stamford, CT 06901
phone: 203-325-8444
Bronze sculpture restorations; master restorer of bronzes for over 20 years; patina, welding, mold making, casting; miniature to monumental size bronzes; also appraisals.

Repro. Sources

Ideal Imports, Inc.
20860 San Simeon Way, Apr. 405
Miami, FL 33179-1810
Sells new creations: bronzes, paintings, lamps, wood and more; special attention given to authentic patina.

Bronze Works, Inc.
P.O. Box 11529
Chattanooga, TN 37401
phone: 615-855-0468
Reproduction bronze Art Nouveau sculptures of females, lamps, animals, Indians.

Jim Solk
Jim Solk Co., Inc.
4073 Glencoe Ave.
Marina Del Rey, CA 90292
phone: 310-448-4433 or 800-835-3600
fax: 310-448-4435
e-mail: solk@ix.netcom.com
Internet: http://www.solk.com
Extensive selection of reproduction bronzes after famous artists.

Deborah Lopez
Everything Metal Imaginable, Inc.
401 E. Cypress
Visalia, CA 93277-2834
phone: 209-732-8126 or 800-777-8126
fax: 209-732-5961
Internet: http://www.emiartbronze.com
Buy foundry direct bronze sculptures by Remington, Russell, Mene, Bonhuer; over 300 quality "lost wax" bronze reproductions; send $10 for 56 page full-color catalog.

Remington

Repro. Sources

Manny Shaool
Manny's Oriental Rugs
72 W. Washington St.
Hagerstown, MD 21740
phone: 301-797-7434
Importer of Oriental ivory, porcelain, reverse paintings, rugs; also Remington recast bronzes, clocks, lacquered furniture.

Darrell Coker
Henry Bonnard Bronze Co. & Associates
1490 S US Highway 17-92
Longwood, FL 32750-6543
phone: 407-339-9103 or 800-521-3179
fax: 407-332-0531
Offers large selection of Frederic Remington bronzes; call or write for color catalog.

Vienna

Dealers

Joe Zobel
P & S Antiques
P.O. Box 741
Crompond, NY 10517
phone: 914-528-7209
Deals in fine quality 19th and early 20th century cold painted Austrian bronze figures.

BROTHER JUNIPER

Collectors

John Ferry
36 West Nyack Rd.
Nanuet, NY 10954
phone: 914-627-2163
Wants Brother Juniper figurines, bookends, ashtrays, etc.

BROWNIES

(see ELVES; ILLUSTRATORS, Palmer Cox)

BUBBLE GUM & CANDY WRAPPERS

Collectors

David Welch
P.O. Box 714
Murphysboro, IL 62966-0714
phone: 618-687-2282
fax: 618-684-2243
e-mail: PexDude1@aol.com
Wants pre 1970 chewing gum items: Wrigleys, Beechnut, Adams, Clarks, etc.; wrappers, packages, advertising (no magazine ads), displays, boxes, etc.; especially wants gum/candy items with cartoon, TV, movie character tie-ins.

Carl Lepiane
104 Karina Ct.
San Jose, CA 95131
phone: 408-436-1727 or 408-356-8474
Wants old chewing gum: pre-1950s tins, full boxes, packs, sticks, or wrappers; also gum cases, store displays and advertising.

BUBBLE GUM CARDS

(see also TRADING CARDS, Non-Sport)

Collectors

Charles Reuter
6 Joy Ave.
Mount Joy, PA 17552-1532
phone: 717-653-8505
Wants to buy gum and candy cards.

BUCKLES

(see BELT BUCKLES; CLOTHING & ACCESSORIES, Vintage)

BUGGIES

(see HORSE-DRAWN VEHICLES, Carriages)

BUILDERS ITEMS

(see ARCHITECTURE & RELATED ITEMS)

BUILDING BLOCKS

(see TOYS, Construction Sets)

BUILDING REPLICAS

(see SOUVENIR & COMMEMORA-TIVE ITEMS, Buildings)

BULB VASES

Dealers

Alan M. Goffman
Alan M. Goffman Gallery
264 East 78th St.
New York, NY 10021-2021
phone: 212-517-8192
fax: 212-517-8193
e-mail: goffman@interport.net
Internet: http://www.artnet.com
Buys and sells bulb vases (hyacinth vases) of handblown glass enjoyed for their sculptural qualities; a hyacinth bulb is placed in the top "cup" section and the vase is filled with water to cover the bottom of the bulb.

BUMPER STICKERS

Radio Station

Collectors

Doreen Lynn Hansen
2311 Morris Thomas Rd.
Duluth, MN 55811
phone: 218-628-3462
Collector/trader of bumper stickers from AM/FM radio stations in the USA, Canada and Mexico; will trade other promo items for stickers.

BURLESQUE

(see STRIPTEASE)

BURMA SHAVE COLLECTIBLES

Collectors

Steve Soelberg
29126 Laro Dr.
Agoura Hills, CA 91301-1635
phone: 818-889-9909
Burma Shave collectibles bought and sold, especially road signs; write with complete description and price; sorry, no list available; world's largest Burma Shave collector.

BURNT WOOD COLLECTIBLES

(see PYROGRAPHY ITEMS)

BUS LINE COLLECTIBLES

(see also TRANSPORTATION COLLECTIBLES)

Collectors

Charles Wotring
Royal Coach
911 Conley Dr.
Mechanicsburg, PA 17055
Wants to buy bus-related memorabilia from models to paper ephemera; also sells promotional bus banks.

Greyhound

Collectors

Tim Shipp
5039 Wildflower Ct. #D
Indianapolis, IN 46254
phone: 317-290-8473
Wants to buy Greyhound Bus memorabilia; toy busses, pins, pictures and related Greyhound lines items; please send list with detailed description and cost.

BUSES

Clubs/Associations

Bernard Drovillard
Bus History Association
Magazine: Bus Industry Magazine
965 McEwan
Windsor
Ontario N9B 2G1 Canada
phone: 519-977-0664
Founded to preserve and record data, information and other materials related to the bus industry in North America and worldwide.

Motor Bus Society
Magazine: Motor Coach Age
P.O. Box 251
Paramus, NJ 07653
Internet: http://motorbussociety.org/
Publishes "Motor Coach Age" which emphasizes history and "Motor Coach Today" which provides fresh coverage of ever-changing bus fleets from charter operators to transit to over-the-road companies.

Robert B. Redden, Sr.
International Bus Collectors Club
Newsletter: IBCC Newsletter
1518 "C" Trailee Dr.
Charleston, SC 29407-4144
phone: 803-571-2489
e-mail: nitebus@worldnet.att.net
The definitive bus club in the U.S.; work as consultants to the movie industry and media; produces the only American line of bus models; 20+ original video productions available; send for catalog.

Collectors

Eugene R. Farha
P.O. Box 633
Cedar Grove, WV 25039-0633
phone: 304-340-3308 or 304-595-2296
fax: 304-340-3315
Wants Greyhound and Trailways memorabilia: 10-yr. and 20-yr. service watch, years-of-service pins, match covers, Greyhound Bus Depot sign with dog; also wants Trailways items and Greyhound data, Greyhound ring.

BUSINESS CARD HOLDERS

Collectors

Stephen Seltzer
7912 Georgia Ave.
Silver Spring, MD 20910-4837
phone: 301-565-2444 or 301-565-3339
fax: 301-565-2228
e-mail: eseltzer@aol.com
Wants to buy business cards and wallets - any material.

BUSINESS CARDS

(see also PAPER COLLECTIBLES)

Clubs/Associations

Avery N. Pitzak
American Business Card Club
Newsletter: Card Talk
P.O. Box 460297
Aurora, CO 80046-0297
phone: 303-690-6496
The American Business Card Club is a unique resource for business people and collectors alike; please provide SASE with inquiries.

Collectors

Stephen Seltzer
7912 Georgia Ave.
Silver Spring, MD 20910-4837
phone: 301-565-2444 or 301-565-3339
fax: 301-565-2228
e-mail: eseltzer@aol.com
Wants to buy unusual business cards.

Jack Gurner
116 Dupuy St.
Water Valley, MS 38965-2901
phone: 601-473-1154
e-mail: jgurner@watervalley.net
Wants to buy OLD business cards; also wants some trade cards related to photographers and newspapers; main interest is in illustrated, odd or unusual.

Experts

Avery N. Pitzak
P.O. Box 460297
Aurora, CO 80046-0297
phone: 303-690-6496
Author of "Make Your Business Cards INCREDIBLE EFFECTIVE!"

BUTTER PATS

Clubs/Associations

Alice Black
Butter Pats International Collectors Club
Newsletter: BPICC Newsletter
38 Acton St.
Maynard, MA 01754
phone: 508-897-2434
For collectors of porcelain and other 3 inch butter pats; newsletter, buy, sell, trade, research, appraisals.

Collectors

Fred & Lila Schrader
2025 Highway 199
Crescent City, CA 95531
phone: 707-458-3525

Experts

Alice Black
38 Acton St.
Maynard, MA 01754
phone: 508-897-2434
Author of "The Joy of Collecting: Butter Pats and Miniature Plates."

Periodicals

Newsletter: Butter Pat Collectors' Notebook
5955 S.W. 179th Ave.
Beaverton, OR 97007

BUTTON COVERS

(see CLOTHING & ACCESSORIES, Vintage; CUFF LINKS)

BUTTONHOOKS

Clubs/Associations

Buttonhook Society, The
Newsletter: Boutonneur, The
2 Romney Place
Maidstone
Kent ME15 6LE, U.K.
To promote interest and research in the history, origins, uses and the collecting of buttonhooks; newsletters, exhibitions; new American point of contact: Priscilla Stoffel, Box 287, White Marsh, MD 21162-0287.

Collectors

Paul Moorehead
2 Romney Place
Maidstone
Kent ME15 6LE, U.K.
Seeks unusual buttonhooks singles or in sets.

Richard Mathes
P.O. Box 1408
Springfield, OH 45501-1408
Wants all types of buttonhooks to add to substantial collection; boot/shoe hooks, glove hooks, loop buttoners, or collar buttoners.

Dealers

Priscilla Washed
Victorian Lady, The
102 South Main St.
P.O. Box 424
Waxhaw, NC 28173-0424
phone: 704-843-4467 or 800-786-1886
A Victorian specialty store featuring 19th century ladies decorative & fashion accessories; buys and sells purses; also sewing and needlework tools, vintage fashion, Victoriana, and combs; mail order; catalog $5.

BUTTONS

(see also CUFF LINKS; SEWING ITEMS & GO-WITHS)

Appraisers

Lisa Schulz
1317 Lynndale Rd.
Madison, WI 53711-3316
phone: 608-271-4566
fax: 608-271-4566
e-mail: 70137.3556@compuserve.com
Collectible clothing buttons appraised, bought and sold; also sells button collecting products (mounting cards and wire, storage envelopes); catalog on request; e-mail on CompuServe at 70137,3556 or on America On Line at ButtonLdy.

Clubs/Associations

Pioneer Button Club
102 Frederick St.
Oshawa
Ontario L1G 2B3 Canada

Frances Howell
Buckeye State Button Society
251 Pfeiffer Ave.
Akron, OH 44312-1354

Lois Pool, Sec.
National Button Society
Newsletter: National Button Bulletin
2733 Juno Place, Apt. 4
Akron, OH 44313-4137
phone: 330-864-3296
Over 4000 members worldwide; focuses on preserving buttons and learning button history; one national show each year.

Dr. Georgia Kemp Caraway
Denton Button Club
500 El Paseo
Denton, TX 76205-8502
phone: 817-056-5961 or 817-383-8809
fax: 817-383-8809
e-mail: tiac@cybergrill.com
Internet: http://www.dentonantiques.com

Button Club, The
Newsletter: Button Club Newsletter
P.O. Box 2274
Seal Beach, CA 90740
phone: 310-431-5671
Bi-monthly newsletter.

Collectors

Warren K. Tice
W. Tice & Company
8 Orchard Terrace
Essex Junction, VT 05452-3501
phone: 802-878-3835
e-mail: wtice@vbimail.champlain.edu
Wants to purchase decorative ladies buttons.

A. Barth
1120 Laurelwood Dr.
Mc Lean, VA 22102-1519
phone: 703-734-0306
Wants fine quality 19th century buttons of all materials and sizes.

Dealers

Gail Busche
Archangel Antiques
334 East Ninth St.
New York, NY 10003-7924
phone: 212-260-9313
Buying antique buttons, cuff links, eye glasses, and vintage lighters; always seeking fine examples such as enamel Deco and Art Nouveau.

Kevin & Marilyn Kinne
Grist Books & Stuff
P.O. Box 91375
East Ridge, TN 37412-6375

Gwen Daniel
18 Belleau Lake Ct.
O Fallon, MO 63366-3144
phone: 314-978-3190
e-mail: gdaniel@mail.win.org
Buys and sells old interesting sewing buttons and related items.

Bill Nelson
Newsletter: Bill Nelson Newsletter, The
P.O. Box 41630
Tucson, AZ 85717-1630
phone: 520-629-0868 or 800-368-8434
fax: 520-629-0387
Monthly newsletter with news, tips, and sources; for collectors of Olympic, Sports, Disney, Coca Cola pins; large selection in stock; established in 1985.

Jude Allen
Vintage Collection
356 Main St.
Half Moon Bay, CA 94019
phone: 415-712-0366
fax: 415-654-0842
Buys and sells linen and lace; also old yardage, buttons, quilts, sewing implements, sewing machines and miniature sewing machines.

Georgia Fox
Foxes' Den Antiques
P.O. Box 846
Sutter Creek, CA 95685
phone: 209-267-0774
Wants antique clothing buttons: porcelain, metal, gilt and Satsuma buttons with pictures, fables, buildings, and heads of famous people.

Experts

Diana Epstein
Tender Buttons
143 East 62nd St.
New York, NY 10021
phone: 212-758-7004 or 212-980-3540
fax: 212-319-8474
Has the largest collection of antique buttons in America for both the collector and the wholesale dealers; author of "A Collector's Guide to Buttons" and co-author with Millicent Safro of "Buttons."

Millicent Safro
Tender Buttons
143 East 62nd St.
New York, NY 10021
phone: 212-758-7004 or 212-980-3540
fax: 212-319-8474
Has the largest collection of antique buttons in America for both the collector and the wholesale dealers; co-author with Diana Epstein of "Buttons."

Lois Pool
2733 Juno Place, Apt. 4
Akron, OH 44313-4137
phone: 330-864-3296

Man./Prod./Dist.

Donald B. Petersen
Waterbury Companies, Inc.
P.O. Box 1812
Waterbury, CT 06722
phone: 203-596-0800
fax: 203-574-1040
Manufacturer of metal buttons for uniforms and fashion garments since 1812; oldest continuous producer of metal buttons in the US.

Museums/Libraries

Gay Nineties Button & Doll Museum
Rte. 4 Box 420
Eureka Springs, AR 72632
phone: 501-253-9321

Suppliers

Lisa Schulz
1317 Lynndale Rd.
Madison, WI 53711-3316
phone: 608-271-4566
fax: 608-271-4566
e-mail: 70137.3556@compuserve.com
Collectible clothing buttons appraised, bought and sold; also sells button collecting products (mounting cards and wire, storage envelopes); catalog on request; e-mail on CompuServe at 70137,3556 or on America On Line at ButtonLdy.

Military (American)

Collectors

Warren K. Tice
W. Tice & Company
8 Orchard Terrace
Essex Junction, VT 05452-3501
phone: 802-878-3835
e-mail: wtice@vbimail.champlain.edu
Wants to purchase U.S. Military, Confederate, and high quality decorative buttons; also wants to buy military antiques.

Experts

William L. Leigh III
P.O. Box 145
Fairfax, VA 20159
phone: 703-779-8723 or 540-338-7367
fax: 703-385-2876
Buys and specializes in 1770-1900 U.S. military buttons, especially in

Civil War Confederate States Army and Navy buttons.

Bob French
Military Buttons
P.O. Box 79
Fairfax, VA 22030-0079
phone: 703-369-0031
fax: 703-369-0031
Noted expert in American Military Buttons 1776-1865; buys and sells all types of American uniform and historical buttons; written appraisals available.

Daniel J. Binder
927 20th St.
Rockford, IL 61104-3508
phone: 815-226-9056 or 815-654-2501
Wants 1812-1865 U.S. military buttons, especially Confederate States, Southern State seals, and Southern military school buttons.

Pin-Back

(see also PINS; POLITICAL COLLECTIBLES)

Collectors

Bob Cereghino
6400 Baltimore National Pike, Ste. 170A-319
Baltimore, MD 21228-3914
phone: 410-766-7593
Wants advertising, entertainment and political pin-back buttons.

Millie Vaccarella
1955 Hythe St.
Roseville, MN 55113
phone: 612-631-2201
Wants to buy pin-back buttons: advertising, sports, movie stars, etc.; interested in single items or large collections.

Scott Weiss
316 25th St.
Santa Monica, CA 90402-2522
phone: 310-395-4318
fax: 310-395-9686
Wants to buy TV and movie pinback buttons, pins, badges, and ribbons; promotional, licensed, product tie-ins, prop or cast and crew; wants from all years.

Experts

Ted Hake
Hake's Americana & Collectibles Auction
P.O. Box 1444
York, PA 17405-1444
phone: 717-848-1333
Always purchasing items for mail-bid auctions of Disneyana, historical Americana, toys, premiums, political items, character and other collectibles; author of "Price Guide to Collectible Pin-Back Buttons."

Pin-Back (Advertising)

Dealers

Dave Beck
P.O. Box 435
Mediapolis, IA 52637-0435
phone: 319-394-3943
Buys and sells advertising watch fobs, mirrors and pin-backs; send stamp for illustrated mail auction catalog.

Pin-Back (Character/Comic)

Collectors

Walter Koenig
P.O. Box 4395
North Hollywood, CA 91617-0395
Wants to buy comic (strip kind) pin-back buttons 1890s-1960s; no pep cereal buttons.

Transportation Employees'

Experts

Donald P. Van Court
41 Hillcrest Rd.
Madison, NJ 07940-2559
phone: 732-377-2676
Author of books illustrating the monograms, sets of initials, trade marks and designs on buttons; historical notes on companies (land, sea and air) for which button designs were created.

BUYING TRIPS

(see TOURS/BUYING TRIPS)

CABINET CARDS

(see PHOTOGRAPHS)

CALCULATORS

(see also ADDING MACHINES; COMPUTERS; OFFICE EQUIPMENT; SLIDE RULES; TYPEWRITERS)

Clubs/Associations

Guy Ball
International Association of Calculator Collectors
Newsletter: International Calculator Collector, The
P.O. Box 345
Tustin, CA 92781-0345
phone: 714-730-6140
fax: 714-730-6140
e-mail: mrcalc@usa.net
Internet: http://geocities.com/siliconvalley/park/7227
Informative quarterly newsletter about collecting calculators from the "golden years" (1971-1978); send SASE for more information.

Collectors

Erez Kaplan
20A Harkafot St.
Kefar Shemaryahu
Israel 46910
phone: 972-9-584552
e-mail: 100274.1423@compuserve.com
Internet: http://www.webcom.com/calc/
Interested in collecting mechanical calculating machines (non-electrical) dating from 1642 through 1965.

Peter Frei
P.O. Box 500
Brimfield, MA 01010-0500
phone: 800-942-8968 or 413-245-4660

Arthur Cheslock
514 Paul St.
Baltimore, MD 21202
phone: 410-962-8580
fax: 410-752-8112
Wants pre-1945 calculators, adding machines and scientific instruments; also wants related literature.

Dale R. Beeks
Perceptions Scientifica
P.O. Box 117
Mount Vernon, IA 52314
phone: 800-880-5178 or 319-895-0506
Wants to buy pre-1960 pocket-sized adders and slide rules; also any in unusual forms.

Bruce Flamm
P.O. Box 70513
Riverside, CA 92513-0513
fax: 909-353-5625
e-mail: bruce.flamm@kp.org
Wants pocket or hand-held calculators.

Robert Otnes
2160 Middlefield Rd.
Palo Alto, CA 94301-4022
phone: 415-324-1821
A leading collector of calculating machines and slide rules.

Robert De Cesaris
7429 Bree Ann Ct.
Citrus Heights, CA 95610-2455
phone: 916-356-5769
Very serious collector of mechanical calculators, early adders, and slide rules; seeking lever-set (Marchant, Brunsviga, Odhner, etc.), Arithometers, small adders (Calcumeter, Webb, Stephenson, etc.), Curta calculators, and others.

Dealers

Joe Pfeiffer
Zapper Technologies
P.O. Box 253
Sandy, UT 84091-0253
phone: 801-571-5453
e-mail: 72622.127@compuserve.com
Buy, sell, trade early portable and pocket L.E.D. calculators: Summit, NCE, PRA, Hewlett Packard and other "lighted" display electronic calculators.

Experts

Darryl Rehr
2591 Military Ave.
Los Angeles, CA 90064-1933
phone: 310-477-5229
fax: 310-268-8420
e-mail: dcrehr@earthlink.net
Internet: http://www.earthlink.net/~dcrehr/
Wants early calculators (they subtract, multiply, divide and add) such as the "Comptometer", "Curta", and "Millionaire."

Guy Ball
P.O. Box 345
Tustin, CA 92781-0345
phone: 714-730-6140
fax: 714-730-6140
e-mail: mrcalc@usa.net
Internet: http://geocities.com/siliconvalley/park/7227
Recognized authority on early, electronic, pocket calculators; co-author of "Collector's Guide to Pocket Calculators" (1997); producer of "Collecting Calculators" video; send SASE with requests for rarity and/or pricing information.

Hewlett-Packard

Collectors

Craig Finseth
1343 LaFond
Saint Paul, MN 55104-2437
phone: 612-644-4027
Maintains database of HP calculators, their backgrounds, and their features.

Novelty

Collectors

Janice Goings-Flamm
P.O. Box 70513
Riverside, CA 92513-0513
fax: 909-353-5625
e-mail: bruce.flamm@kp.org
Wants to buy novelty calculators, i.e. those with odd shapes.

CALENDAR PLATES

Collectors

Jane M. Cummings
37943 Wright St.
Willoughby, OH 44094-5851
phone: 216-946-2174
Wants any '20s, '30s & '40s or earlier calendar plates, especially the unusual or pre-1906.

Dealers

Alan Gumtow
Odd Things
710 N. Lake Shore Drive
Barrington, IL 60010-1277
phone: 708-526-5319
Buys and sells 1880-1933 calendar plates with or without store, town or person on it, old giveaways.

Periodicals

Alan Gumtow
Newsletter: Calendar, The
710 N. Lake Shore Drive
Barrington, IL 60010-1277
phone: 708-526-5319
A quarterly newsletter for collectors and dealers of old calendar plates from 1880-1949.

CALENDARS

(see also ADVERTISING COLLECTIBLES; ILLUSTRATORS; PAPER COLLECTIBLES)

Clubs/Associations

Larry L. Krug
Calendar Collector Society
18222 Flower Hill Way, #299
Gaithersburg, MD 20879-5300
phone: 301-926-8663
fax: 301-926-7648
e-mail: ccs@collectors.org
Internet: http://www.collectors.org/ccs

Collectors

Larry L. Krug
Americana Resources, Inc.
18222 Flower Hill Way, #299
Gaithersburg, MD 20879-5300
phone: 301-926-8663
fax: 301-926-7648
e-mail: ccs@collectors.org
Internet: http://www.collectors.org/ccs

Dealers

Robb Sequin
P.O. Box 1126
Dennis Port, MA 02639
phone: 508-760-2599
e-mail: rsequin@capecod.net
Internet: http://rsequin.com
Strong buyer of calendars dating from 1900 to 1970 relating to advertising, pin-ups, celebrities, commercial artists; condition and interesting subject matter are important; quantities wanted too.

Mary Ann Hahn
Second Hand Mary Ann's
HCR 65 Box 26
Boothbay Harbor, ME 04538-9703
phone: 207-633-2426
fax: 207-633-2426
Wants to buy calendars of all kinds and categories: pin-up, scenics, hunting & fishing, children's illustrators, advertising, auto, Coca-Cola.

Firearms Related

Collectors

Bill Bramlett
P.O. Box 1105
Florence, SC 29503-1105
phone: 803-393-7390 or 803-665-3165
e-mail: bbramlett@pdn.net
Wants to buy 1897-1927 calendars, posters and signs advertising shotgun shells and cartridges from companies such as Peters, Austin Cartridge Co., Remington-UMC, Selby shells, Union Metallic Cartridge Co., Western, Winchester.

CALIFORNIA PERFUME COMPANY

(see also AVON COLLECTIBLES; BOTTLES, Perfume & Scent)

Collectors

Patrick Brady
210 Fulton St.
Elmira, NY 14904-1215
phone: 607-732-2894
Wants CPC paper, tins, bottles, anything.

Experts

Dick Pardini
3107 N. El Dorado St., Dept. MACRD
Stockton, CA 95204-3412
phone: 209-466-5550
Wants certain CPC items (1886 to 1929), must have "EUREKA" trade

marks; no AVON please; will help with CPC prices and identification; enclose LSASE for information; LSASE NOT necessary when offering items for sale.

CALLIGRAPHY

(see also INKWELLS & INKSTANDS; PENS)

Clubs/Associations

New Orleans Lettering Arts Association
49 E. 96th St. #14-D
New York, NY 10128
phone: 212-410-9273

Greater Cincinnati Calligrapher's guild
P.O. Box 429345
Cincinnati, OH 45242-9345

Wisconsin Calligraphers' Guild
P.O. Box 55120
Madison, WI 53705

Misc. Services

Sally Boric Wilson
Lettering Arts
104 S. Main St.
Morrisville, PA 19067
phone: 215-493-8916
Offers calligraphy services.

CALLING CARDS

(see BUSINESS CARDS)

CALLIOPES

(see CAROUSELS & CAROUSEL FIGURES; MUSICAL INSTRU-MENTS, Mechanical [Band Organs])

CALLS

(see SPORTING COLLECTIBLES, Game Calls)

CAMERAS & CAMERA EQUIP-MENT

(see also BOOKS, Reference [Cameras]; 3-D PHOTOGRAPHICA; MAGIC LANTERNS; PHOTO-GRAPHS; PHOTOGRAPHY; SPY EQUIPMENT; STEREO VIEWERS & STEREOVIEWS; TOYS, Optical)

Appraisers

David L. Studebaker
10421 Delwood Dr. S.W.
Tacoma, WA 98498-4321
phone: 206-582-4878
Specializes in classic old cameras, colored cameras, subminiatures, stanhopes, old images, and photographs and daguerreotypes.

Auction Services

Michael Pritchard
Christie's South Kensington, Ltd.
85 Old Brompton Rd.
London SW7 3LD, U.K.
phone: 0171 581 7611 or 0171 321 3279
fax: 0171 321 3321
e-mail:
mpritchard@cix.compulink.co.uk
An international auction house specializing in the sale of rare and collectible cameras, photographic equipment and optical toys.

Bryan W. Ginns
2109 Cty. Rte. 21
Valatie, NY 12184-6001
phone: 518-392-5805
fax: 518-392-7925
e-mail: the3dman@aol.com
Conducts mail sales specializing in optical items such as cameras, magic lantern slide projectors, stereographica, polyorama pantoptiques, praxinoscopes, zeotropes, kinoras, coin-operated mutoscopes, etc.

Clubs/Associations

Michael Pritchard, Editor
Photographic Collectors Club of Great
   Britain
Magazine: Photographica World
5 Station Industrial Estate
Prudhoe
Northumberland NE42 6NP U.K
phone: (+44) 0117 9831839
e-mail:
mpritchard@cix.compulink.co.uk
Internet: http://www.nmsi.ac.uk/nmpft/pccgb.htm
Club aims to promote the study and collection of photographic equipment and images by publications, meetings, auctions and shows; covers cameras, lenses, photographers, optical toys, stereoscopes, magic lanterns, and related areas.

Rolf Eipper, Pres.
Western Canada Photographic Historical
   Association
P.O. Box 78082, 2606 Commercial
   Drive
Vancouver
British Colum. V5N 5W1 Canada
phone: 604-254-6778
fax: 604-254-6778

Delaware Valley Photographic
   Collectors Association
P.O. Box 5074
Delanco, NJ 08075

William J. Tangredi, Sec.
Camera & Memorabilia Enthusiasts
   Regional Association (C.A.M.E.R.A.)
15 Turner Ln.
Loudonville, NY 12211

Pennsylvania Photographic Historical
   Society, Inc.
P.O. Box 862
Beaver Falls, PA 15010
phone: 412-843-5688

John Durand
Ohio Camera Collectors Society, The
Newsletter: Developments, The
   Members Memo
P.O. Box 282
Columbus, OH 43216-0282
phone: 614-885-3224
Focuses on cameras, camera equipment, images and photographic history; holds annual show, sale, auction, guest speakers on Memorial Day weekend; various members have considerable camera expertise about cameras and makers; annual auction.

William S. Nehez, Mem. Ch.
Photographic Historical Society of the
   Western Reserve
Newsletter: Collector, The
P.O. Box 25663
Cleveland, OH 44125
phone: 216-662-9008
To further advance the collection and preservation of historical photo-graphic material; for those with an interest in photography and photographic equipment; bi-monthly newsletter; holds annual Photo-graphic Flea Market.

Bill Bond, Pres.
Tri-State Photographic Collectors
   Society
8910 Cherry
Blue Ash, OH 45242
phone: 513-891-5266
Collectors of cameras and various photographic equipment, prints, books and anything related to photography.

Michigan Photographic Historical
   Society
Newsletter: Photogram, The
P.O. Box 2278
Birmingham, MI 48012-2278
phone: 313-882-1113 or 810-549-6026

Chicago Photographic Collectors
   Society
Newsletter: CPCS Newsletter
P.O. Box 303
Grayslake, IL 60030
phone: 312-262-5979
A non-profit organization in its 25th year; over 200 U.S. and foreign members; sponsors two trade shows a year in the Chicago area; "CPCS Newsletter" is published monthly; also publishes the journal "By Daylight".

Club Daguerr-Darrah
2562 Victoria
Wichita, KS 67216
phone: 316-265-0393

Photographic Collectors of Houston
1201 McDuffie #104
Houston, TX 77019

Dr. Stu Cole
American Society of Camera Collectors
7415 Reseda Blvd.
Reseda, CA 91335
phone: 818-345-2660
An educational society dedicated to

the restoration and preservation of all types of photographica.

David Silver
Bay Area Photographica Association
Newsletter: BAPA News
2538 34th Ave.
San Francisco, CA 94116-2801
phone: 415-664-6498 or 415-681-4356
e-mail: silver@well.com
A collectors' group specializing in cameras, photographs and related materials; members buy, sell and trade collectibles as well as share information on the field of photo-history.

David L. Studebaker
Puget Sound Photographic Collectors
   Society
Newsletter: Bellows
10421 Delwood Dr. S.W.
Tacoma, WA 98498-4321
phone: 206-582-4878
Dedicated to the collection and preservation of historical photographica; holds monthly meetings, sponsors annual camera show, publishes monthly newsletter.

Collectors

Dan Colucci
82 Brick Kiln Rd.
Chelmsford, MA 01824
phone: 617-790-4915
e-mail: DColucci@aol.com
Internet: http://members.aol.com/
   dcolucci/index.html

Norman D. Leckert
P.O. Box 363
Bethel, VT 05032
phone: 802-234-5657 or 800-717-2021
fax: 802-234-6104
Wants to buy old cameras, lenses and accessories.

Harry Poster
P.O. Box 1883
South Hackensack, NJ 07606-0483
phone: 201-794-9606
fax: 201-794-9553
e-mail: hposter@worldnet.att.net
Buying stereoscopic cameras, viewers, and projectors; wants anything 3D; Stereo Realist, Stereo Kodak, Wollensack, etc.; 2-lens viewers & projectors; dealer displays, books, catalogs; also Nikon, Canon, Leica cameras.

Pearl Dearkin
Kingrade Optics, Ltd.
P.O. Box 2405
Morristown, NJ 07960-2405
Wants old, odd, very large or very small cameras; or with three of more lenses; no Kodaks or Polaroids; also camera books and catalogs.

Fred Spira
158-17 Riverside Dr.
Flushing, NY 11357-1341
phone: 718-767-6761 or 718-767-5297
Private collector buys early (Daguerreian, wet-plate), color,

detective and other rare and unusual cameras and camera accessories; single items or entire collections; also pre-1900 photographic images and photo albums.

Bob Coyle
1006 Lincoln
Dubuque, IA 52001
phone: 319-588-9464
Wants to buy collectible cameras; please send price and description.

Dave Gorski
244 Cutler
Waukesha, WI 53186-4943
phone: 414-542-3069
fax: 414-542-9730
e-mail: camera19@mail.idt.net
Internet: http:// www.collectoronline.com/wb-cameras.html
Wants to buy stereo cameras, wood cameras with two or more lenses, folding or box cameras, any multi-lens camera, 1920s movie cameras or projectors; also cameras by Canon, Nikon, Leica, Zeiss, Voightlander, Alpa, Ernemann.

Marv B. Chait
P.O. Box 1979
Chicago, IL 60645
phone: 312-262-5979

Richard Ogden
P.O. Box 210
Chapman, NE 68827
phone: 308-986-2247
fax: 308-986-2247
e-mail: exoticam@kdsi.net
Wants exotic cameras: machine gun training, aerials, military, medical, concealed, special purpose, subminiature cameras, beverage can shaped cameras and others that are odd or unusual.

Jim Kopke
P.O. Box 4310
Dillon, CO 80435-4310
Wants to buy old, odd and unique cameras and related equipment.

Mike Kramer
P.O. Box 3257
Vallejo, CA 94590-0676
phone: 800-568-8883 or 800-446-6581
fax: 707-642-2456
Collector wants to buy pre-1960 range-finder cameras such as Nikon, Canon, Leica, Zeiss plus all stereo, subminiature and colored cameras.

Dealers

John S. Craig
P.O. Box 1637
Torrington, CT 06790
phone: 860-496-9791
fax: 860-496-0664
e-mail: jscraig1@snet.net
Buys and sells antique and collectible photographica: cameras, daguerreotypes, stereos, literature.

Allen & Hilary Weiner
80 Central Park West
New York, NY 10023-5204
phone: 212-787-8357 or 212-496-6502
e-mail: amwcamera@msn.com
Well-established and respected dealers who are always interested in buying entire collections or fine individual items.

Konny Lang, Pres.
Atlantic Camera Repair
276 Higbie Lane
West Islip, NY 11795-2822
phone: 516-587-7959
fax: 516-587-7750
Buys and sells cameras and photographic equipment.

Bryan W. Ginns
2109 Cty. Rte. 21
Valatie, NY 12184-6001
phone: 518-392-5805
fax: 518-392-7925
e-mail: the3dman@aol.com
Wants large collections of stereo views, old cameras, daguerreotypes, magic lanterns, optical toys; anything relating to photographics.

Jim O'Neil
Fredonia Camera
60 West Main St.
Fredonia, NY 14063
phone: 716-679-4582 or 800-786-6861
e-mail: 74250.2007@compuserve.com
Buying Leica, Nikon, Minox, Super Ikonta, Unhof, Stereo Realist, Rolleiflex, Contarex, Hasselblad, Retina, Voigtlander, Plaubel, and many others.

Herb
Camera Man, The
1614 Bethlehem Pike
Flourtown, PA 19031-2026
phone: 215-233-4025 or 800-396-0506
fax: 215-233-4025
Wants to buy Leica, Zeiss, Nikon, Minox, wood cameras, toy cameras, miniatures, stereo, German cameras: Hasselblad, Rolleiflex, Alpa, etc.

Robert L. Johnson
North Georgia Graphics
P.O. Box 309
Chickamauga, GA 30707-0309
phone: 706-375-4326
e-mail: oldgoat@voy.net
Specializing in large-format (view and studio) cameras, panoramic and banquet cameras and enlargers, lenses, accessories, books on photography history, collectible cameras.

Eric Mehl
Columbus Camera Group, Inc.
55 East Blake Ave.
Columbus, OH 43202
phone: 614-267-0686
fax: 614-267-5526
Buys and sells all photographic equipment new and old; Nikon, Stereo, Rollei, Linhof, Zeiss; appraises

estates; also buy current equipment as well as photos and darkrooms.

T.K. Treadwell
4201 Nagle Rd.
Bryan, TX 77801-3938
phone: 409-846-0209
e-mail: 71222.1571@compuserve.com

Brian P. Wolfe
BPW Limited Photographic
4351 S. Sepulveda Blvd.
Culver City, CA 90230-4715
phone: 310-397-5576
fax: 310-391-6478
e-mail: Brian@bpwltd
Internet: http://www.bpwltd.com
Buys, sells, trades, restores, rents photographic equipment.

William P. Carroll
ACR Books
P.O. Box 4294
Whittier, CA 90607-4294
phone: 562-693-8421
fax: 562-945-6011
Antique and classic cameras for sale; offers new and used books on kaleidoscopes, cameras and the history of photography.

Experts

Fred Waterman
1704 Valencia Dr.
Rockford, IL 61108
Buys and specializes in novel cameras with unusual devices or appearances; also in camera accessories such as meters, exposure guides, darkroom equipment, etc.

William P. Carroll
ACR Books
P.O. Box 4294
Whittier, CA 90607-4294
phone: 562-693-8421
fax: 562-945-6011
Buys, specializes in early shutters, small format roll-film cameras, mechanically complex cameras (built-in motor drives or other unusual features); also wants camera look-alikes (flasks, compacts, etc.)

Mike & Gladys Kessler
25749 Anchor Circle
San Juan Capistrano, CA 92675
phone: 717-661-3320
Buys and specializes in unusual 1880-1890s disguised or detective cameras; also Simon Wing cameras.

Museums/Libraries

Jack Naylor
Cameras & Images International, Inc.
P.O. Box 23
Waltham Station
Boston, MA 02254
phone: 617-277-0207 or 617-277-7878
A private museum with photographic exhibitions for collectors and historians; pre-photography, the first photograph, wet and dry plate, roll film, research library.

Fleetwood Museum, The
614 Greenbrook Rd.
North Plainfield, NJ 07063
phone: 908-757-5507
Exhibits a collection of vintage cameras and images; maintains a photo-techniques and photo-history library.

On-Line Services

Dan Colucci
Internet Directory of Camera Collectors
82 Brick Kiln Rd.
Chelmsford, MA 01824
phone: 617-790-4915
e-mail: DColucci@aol.com
Internet: http://members.aol.com/ dcolucci/index.html
An Internet directory of camera collectors; this is a free on-line subscription e-mail list of serious camera collectors; 110 members from around the world.

Periodicals

Neil Smith
Magazine: Photographic Trader
P.O. Box 95
Carina
Qld 4152 Australia
phone: 0167 3843 2319 or 0167 398 3801
fax: 0167 3842 0135
e-mail: neil@phototrader.com.au
Australia's marketplace for photographic equipment and collectors news.

Paolo Namias, Ed.
Zoom America, Inc.
Magazine: Classic Camera
P.O. Box 1270
New York, NY 10156
phone: 800-535-6745
fax: 212-888-8407
Very nice, glossy quarterly magazine printed in both Italian and English; feature articles and original research on cameras worldwide.

Magazine: Shutterbug
P.O. Box F
Titusville, FL 32781
phone: 407-268-5010
fax: 407-267-7216
Geared to the advanced to professional photographer; articles about new/old equip. & access., collectibles and new products; many ads.

Repair Services

Konny Lang, Pres.
Atlantic Camera Repair
276 Higbie Lane
West Islip, NY 11795-2822
phone: 516-587-7959
fax: 516-587-7750
Repairs cameras, studio equipment, 35mm SLRs, video and movie cameras, VCRs, meters, graphic art lenses, projectors, electronic strobes, surveillance equipment, underwater

cameras; also modifies or restores cameras including antique.

Cliff Ratcliff
Cameratek
1780 N. Market St.
Frederick, MD 21701
phone: 301-695-9733
Professional repair service; also buy, sell, trade, used cameras.

Ken Ruth
Photography on Bald Mountain
113 Bald Mountain
Davenport, CA 95017-0113
phone: 408-423-4465
Repairs all older and classic cameras; parts fabrication, modifications, adaptations.

Kodak

Clubs/Associations

Dr. George Layne
International Kodak Historical Society
P.O. Box 21
Flourtown, PA 19301

Leica

Clubs/Associations

Leica Historical Society of America
Journal: Viewfinder, The
7611 Dornoch Lane
Dallas, TX 75248-2327
phone: 972-386-4005
An international group of photographers, collectors, enthusiasts and historians dedicated to the use of the Leica system and the preservation of its heritage.

Movie

(see also MOVIE PROJECTORS)

Clubs/Associations

Adrian J. Levesque, Jr.
Movie Machine Society, The
Newsletter: Sixteen Frames
42 Deerhaven Dr.
Nashua, NH 03060
phone: 603-889-4056
Devoted to the exchange of information among those interested in the technical history of all kinds of apparatus designed to create a moving image, from Arriflexes to Zoopraxiscopes.

Collectors

David Hale
17 West Broad St.
Hazleton, PA 18201
phone: 717-459-7049
Wants hand crank movie cameras and hand crank movie projectors from the 1940s through 1960s; any condition.

Edward Stuart
P.O. Box 21114
Washington, DC 20009
phone: 202-332-6511
Wants pre-1952 Bell & Howell movie

projectors (those with brown wrinkle finish), 8mm or 16mm, silent only; also B&H mod. 130 sound.

Gregory J. Vonderheide
29032 Rivergate Run
Zephyrhills, FL 33543-6544
phone: 813-907-9291
fax: 813-949-9252
e-mail: GVondl@aol.com
Wants to buy wind-up movie cameras; all mm, prefer pre-1940; must be working.

Michael Zaiontz
1946 Gentilly Blvd.
New Orleans, LA 70119
phone: 504-566-6090
Wants to buy 3-strip film, lens, projection equipment, manuals, theatre blueprints, etc.

Wes Lambert
1568 Dapple Ave.
Camarillo, CA 93010
phone: 805-482-5331
Early cine collector wants to buy pre-1923, hand-crank, 35, 28 & 17 1/2 mm, motion picture cameras; will correspond with other cine collectors.

Dealers

International Cinema Equipment
Company, Inc.
100 NE 39th St.
Miami, FL 33137
phone: 305-573-7339
fax: 305-573-8101
Sells pre-owned, rebuilt, refurbished, and secondhand professional cinema equipment.

Randy Donley
Donley's Wild West Town & Museum
8512 S. Union Rd.
Union, IL 60180-9661
phone: 815-923-9000
fax: 815-923-2253
Wants pre-1930 34mm hand-crank movie projectors and cameras.

Experts

Alan Kattelle
50 Old Country Rd.
Hudson, MA 01749-3026
e-mail: alankatt@aol.com
Wants unusual amateur movie cameras & projectors: Devry 16 Deluxe, Pathe KOK Projector, and Victor Cine cameras & projectors.

Periodicals

Linda Kellbach
Antique Trader Publications, Inc.
Newspaper: Big Reel
P.O. Box 1050
Dubuque, IA 52004-1050
phone: 800-334-7165 or 800-482-4155
fax: 800-531-0880
e-mail: 76143.72@compuserve.com
Internet: http://www.csmonline.com
A monthly tabloid for movie and television memorabilia collectors and

fans: ads, news, current & nostalgic feature articles, obits, etc.

Nikon

Clubs/Associations

Robert J. Rotoloni
Nikon Historical Society
Magazine: Nikon Journal, The
P.O. Box 3213
Hammond, IN 46321-0213
phone: 708-895-5319
fax: 708-865-9663
Internet: http://ww.nikonhs.org
Focuses on the history of Nikon cameras; magazine contains articles and ads for the Nikon collector.

Collectors

Harry Poster
P.O. Box 1883
South Hackensack, NJ 07606-0483
phone: 201-794-9606
fax: 201-794-9553
e-mail: hposter@worldnet.att.net
Paying $500 - $5,000 for early Nikons, Nikon accessories, plus Canon and Leica cameras.

Experts

Robert J. Rotoloni
P.O. Box 3213
Hammond, IN 46321-0213
phone: 708-895-5319
fax: 708-865-9663
Internet: http://ww.nikonhs.org
Author of "The Nikon..An Illustrated History of the Nikon Camera", founder of the Nikon Historical Society.

Russian

Clubs/Associations

Vitaliy Marchenko
Ukraine Camera Collectors
4-b, Zaporozhskaya Str., Flat 23
Saporozhye 330002, Ukraine
fax: 061-234-5142
Members collect Soviet cameras, consult on Soviet cameras, sell Soviet and other collectible cameras; also publishes a book and a catalog on Russian and Soviet cameras (in English.)

Stereo Cameras

(see also STEREOVIEWERS & STEREOGRAPHS)

Experts

George Kirkman
P.O. Box 24468
Los Angeles, CA 90024
phone: 213-208-6148
Buys and specializes in early stereo cameras (1900-1940.)

Subminiature

(see also SPY EQUIPMENT)

Collectors

Dave Gorski
244 Cutler
Waukesha, WI 53186-4943
phone: 414-542-3069
fax: 414-542-9730
e-mail: camera19@mail.idt.net
Internet: http://
www.collectoronline.com/wb-cameras.html
Wants to buy cameras disguised in hats, binoculars, canes, guns, lighters, purses, pens or watches; or just very tiny cameras.

Zeiss

Clubs/Associations

Zeiss Historica Society
Journal: Zeiss Historica Society Journal
300 Waxwing Drive
Cranbury, NJ 08512
phone: 540-981-1036
e-mail: msmall@roanoke.infi.net
Internet: http://www.netins.net/
showcase/crye/zi-hist.htm
Dedicated to the study & exchange of information on the history of Carl Zeiss Optical Co. and Zeiss-Ikon, its people and products (cameras, accessories, and optical equipment of all types) from 1846 to present; semi-annual journal.

CAMPBELL SOUP COL-LECTIBLES

Clubs/Associations

David R. Young
Campbell Soup Collectors Club
Newsletter: Soup Collector, The
414 Country Lane Ct.
Wauconda, IL 60084
phone: 708-487-4917
Networking; quarterly newsletter features articles and classified ads; write for more information.

Experts

Mary Jane Lamphier
Quilted Keepsakes & Unique Dolls
Exhibit
577 Main St.
Arlington, IA 50606-9712
phone: 319-633-5885
Specializes in Campbell's Soup Kids; please include a SASE if requesting a reply or the return of photos.

Museums/Libraries

Campbell Museum, The
Campbell Soup Comany World
Headquarters
Camden, NJ 08101
phone: 609-342-6440
fax: 609-342-6439
Collection of over 300 soup utensils, tureens and bowls.

Periodicals

Barbara Kline
Newsletter: Campbell's Soup Link
311 Cambridge Dr.
Dimondale, MI 48821-9775
phone: 517-646-6831
For collectors of Campbell Soup memorabilia.

CAMPING EQUIPMENT

(see also BOY SCOUT MEMORABILIA; SPORTING COLLECTIBLES; TRAILERS & RV'S)

Coleman

Clubs/Associations

Ernest L. Hiatt
International Coleman Collector's Network, The
Newsletter: Coleman Collector, The
3404 West 450 North
Rochester, IN 46975-8370
phone: 219-223-3232
fax: 219-223-2842
For collectors of any Coleman products such as lamps, lanterns, irons, camp stoves and other pressurized liquid fuel appliances; also literature, old repair manuals, sales samples.

Collectors

Levi Esh
Rt. 2, Kesslet Rd.
Millersburg, PA 17061

Bud Michael
P.O. Box 1236
Lincolnton, NC 28093-1236
phone: 704-735-8643
e-mail: bud@vnet.net

Ernest L. Hiatt
3404 West 450 North
Rochester, IN 46975-8370
phone: 219-223-3232
fax: 219-223-2842
Wants to buy Coleman items; also wants parts and catalogs.

Jim Adkins
808 Turner Rd.
Independence, MO 64056
phone: 816-796-9205

Experts

Carl R. Tucker
3715 Riveria N.W.
Massillon, OH 44546
Author of "Coleman Collector's Guide."

Man./Prod./Dist.

Coleman Company, The
P.O. Box 1762
Wichita, KS 67201
phone: 316-261-3211
Manufacturer of quality sporting and camping equipment.

Museums/Libraries

Ernest L. Hiatt
3404 West 450 North
Rochester, IN 46975-8370
phone: 219-223-3232
fax: 219-223-2842
Museum of personal collection of Coleman products.

CAN OPENERS

Collectors

Stan Dickinson
307 1/2 B.E. Lake St.
Petoskey, MI 49770
phone: 616-347-1022

Richard M. Bueschel
414 N. Prospect Manor Ave.
Mount Prospect, IL 60056-2046
phone: 847-253-0791
fax: 847-253-7919
e-mail: BuschlHist@aol.com
Wants cast iron can openers that cut metal, c. 1850-1930; any size, shape or form; also images, photos, advertising of can openers in use.

Joe Young
P.O. Box 587
Elgin, IL 60121-0587
phone: 847-695-0108 or 847-254-8208
fax: 847-695-1679
e-mail: istamp2@msn.com
Wants to buy unusual can openers; also interested in combination tools with can openers; all correspondence answered.

CAN-CAN

Collectors

Taylor Warren
P.O. Box 1802
Williamsburg, VA 23187-1802
Wants stills and clippings of can-can dancers; wants girls wearing skirts, especially Las Vegas can-can programs and can-can items from the movies.

CANAL COLLECTIBLES

Clubs/Associations

Charles W. Derr, Sec.
American Canal Society, Inc.
Newsletter: American Canals
117 Main St.
Freemansburg, PA 18017
Focuses on the preservation, restoration, interpretation and use of the historic navigational canals of the Americas.

Collectors

Harry L. Rinker
5093 Vera Cruz Rd.
Emmaus, PA 18049-9554
phone: 610-965-1122
fax: 610-965-1124
e-mail: rinkeron@fast.net
Seeks artifacts, books, paper ephemera and commemorative objects associated with America's mule-drawn canal era.

Museums/Libraries

Erie Canal Museum
Newsletter: Canal Packet, The
318 Erie Blvd.
Syracuse, NY 13202
phone: 315-471-0593

Canal Society of New York State, Inc.
311 Montgomery St.
Syracuse, NY 13202
phone: 315-428-1862

Canal Museum & Hugh Moore Park
P.O. Box 877
Easton, PA 18044-0877
phone: 610-559-6613
Internet: http://www.canals.org

Cape Cod Canal

Collectors

N.H. Webber
126 Westfield St.
Dedham, MA 02026
phone: 617-326-5329
Wants to buy items related to the Cape Cod Canal: postcards, photos, souvenirs, china, pamphlets, log books, schedules, maps.

Panama Canal

Collectors

Frederick Lingenfelser
814 Byram St.
Reading, PA 19606-1446
Collecting anything related to the construction of the Panama Canal, 1870-1914, the French or American effort: maps, letters, photographs, books, autographs, diaries, etc.

Dealers

C&H Stamps
P.O. Box 324
Syracuse, NY 13209-0324
Buys and sells collectibles related to the Panama Canal or its construction including photos, books, maps, stamps; postcards, souvenirs, etc.; always interested in buying anything Canal Zone or Panama Canal related; please describe.

CANCELLATIONS
Postal

(see STAMP COLLECTING, Cancels)

CANDY

(see also BOXES, Candy; BUBBLE GUM & CANDY WRAPPERS; MOLDS, Candy; PEZ)

Museums/Libraries

Michelle Havrilla
Candy Americana Museum, The
48 N. Broad St.
Lititz, PA 17543
phone: 717-626-0967
Collection of the making of candy: antique novelty candy containers, cocoa tins, chocolate molds.

CANDY BARS

(see BUBBLE GUM & CANDY WRAPPERS; CANDY)

CANDY CONTAINERS

(see also BUBBLE GUM & CANDY WRAPPERS; CANDY; PEZ)

Clubs/Associations

Candy Container Collectors of America
Newsletter: Candy Gram, The
P.O. Box 352
Chelmsford, MA 01824-0352

Collectors

Ross Hartsough
aTaVa collectibles
98 Bryn Mawr Rd.
Winnipeg
Manitoba R3T 3P5 Canada
phone: 204-269-1022
Wants glass and plastic figural candy containers, especially PEZ containers.

Douglas Dezso
864 Paterson Ave.
Maywood, NJ 07607
phone: 201-845-7707

Terry Whitmeyer
88 Woodbine Dr.
Hershey, PA 17033-2668
phone: 717-533-3716

Kit Carter Weilage
506 Briar Hill Rd.
Louisville, KY 40206
phone: 502-561-5030
Buys and sells Christmas collectibles, specializing in German-made Santa candy containers.

Dealers

Vincent G. Krug
Childhood Memories, Inc.
7120 Little River Tkp.
Annandale, VA 22003
phone: 703-750-0841
Wants uncommon glass, tin, and papier-mache candy containers.

Paul W. Schofield
Lion's Den Antiques
7988 Bethel Burley Rd. SE
Port Orchard, WA 98366
phone: 360-876-3364
fax: 360-876-5421
Buys, sells, appraises, and specializes in old Santas, candy containers, Halloween, Easter, Christmas, Easter, Dresden, figural lights.

Museums/Libraries

Cambridge Glass Museum, The
812 Jefferson Ave.
Cambridge, OH 43725
phone: 614-432-3045
*Over 5000 pieces of Cambridge glass
on display; also 100 pieces of
Cambridge Art Pottery; private
museum.*

Jars

Collectors

Tom "The Jar Man"
421 De La Vina
Santa Barbara, CA 93101
phone: 805-966-3076
*Wants pedestal candy jars, any size or
condition.*

CANES & WALKING STICKS

(see also PIPES; POLITICAL
COLLECTIBLES; UMBRELLAS)

Auction Services

Nancy & Henry Taron
Tradewinds Auctions
63 Main St.
Essex, MA 01929
phone: 508-526-4085 or 508-768-3327
fax: 508-526-4085
*Conducts all-cane auctions twice a
year.*

Henry & nancy Taron
Tradewinds Antiques & Auctions
Box 249
Manchester, MA 01944-0239
phone: 508-768-3327 or 508-526-4085
fax: 508-526-4085
*Conducts at lease two all antique cane
auction each year.*

Collectors

Bruce Thalberg
23 Mountain View Dr.
Weston, CT 06883-1317
phone: 203-227-8175
*Wants to buy canes: carved wood,
ivory and bone figural handles and
knobs, container and gadget canes;
handles without shafts are acceptable;
photocopy helpful; please send SASE.*

Barry Koffman
1 Vincent St.
Binghamton, NY 13905
phone: 607-723-5167
Specializes in carved folk art canes.

R.W. Carlson
7718 Georgetown Pike
Mc Lean, VA 22102
*Wants to buy unusual walking sticks,
especially "gadget" canes or heavily
carved or personalized sticks.*

Cecil Curtis
4051 E. Olive Rd. #231
Pensacola, FL 32514
phone: 904-477-3995
Wants to buy canes and walking

sticks, and any and all related
information.

Arnold Scher
Beaver Bros. Antiques
1637 Market St.
San Francisco, CA 94103-1217
phone: 415-863-4344
fax: 415-863-4399
*Wants dual purpose, container,
weapon, gadget, fancy carved ivory,
gold or silver canes; also wants
carved folk art canes.*

Dealers

Nancy & Henry Taron
Tradewinds Antiques
63 Main St.
Essex, MA 01929
phone: 508-526-4085 or 508-768-3327
fax: 508-526-4085

Henry & nancy Taron
Tradewinds Antiques & Auctions
Box 249
Manchester, MA 01944-0239
phone: 508-768-3327 or 508-526-4085
fax: 508-526-4085
*Buys, sells, appraises and specializes
in walking sticks: carved ivory, folk
art, nautical, gadget, etc., also
Victorian style cane stands; conducts
at lease two all antique cane auction
each year.*

Brian J. Kiracofe
Newport Scrimshander, The
14 Bowen's Wharf
Newport, RI 02840
phone: 401-849-5680 or 800-653-5234
fax: 401-849-9306
e-mail: newportscrimshaw@juno.com
*Carries an extensive collection of
canes and walking sticks; mostly ivory
handles.*

Kim Robertson
Robertsons
6365 Greenhill Rd.
New Hope, PA 18938
phone: 215-297-5068
fax: 215-297-5669
*Buys and sells walking sticks,
especially quality decorative, ivory,
system and defense walking sticks.*

C.B. Grissom
Cane Man, The
2180 Stephens Lane
Lexington, KY 40504-3020
phone: 606-277-7665
*Wants to buy antique canes, walking
sticks, umbrella handles; karat gold,
sterling, ivory, V.I.P., container,
watch.*

Keeil's Antiques
325 Royal St.
New Orleans, LA 70130
phone: 504-522-4552
fax: 504-522-8754
*Specializes in walking and "system"
sticks: shaving knife & brush, sewing
kits, animal sticks, flask sticks, sword
and dagger sticks, camera and opium*

pipe sticks, gaming and writing canes,
etc.

Experts

George H. Meyer
100 West Long Lake Rd., Ste. 100
Bloomfield hills, MI 48304
*Author of "American Folk Art Canes -
Personal Sculpture."*

Museums/Libraries

Essex Institute
132 Essex St.
Salem, MA 01970
phone: 508-744-3390

Curator
Fairfield Historical Society
636 Old Post Rd.
Fairfield, CT 06430-6647
phone: 203-259-1598
fax: 203-255-2716

Remington Gun Museum
P.O. Box 179
Ilion, NY 13357-0179
phone: 315-895-3350
fax: 315-895-3237
*Affiliated with the Remington Arms
Company, Inc.*

Stacey Swigart, Cur.
Valley Forge Historical Society, The
P.O. Box 122
Valley Forge, PA 19481-0122
phone: 610-783-0535 or 610-783-0448
fax: 610-783-0448

Periodicals

Linda L. Beeman
Newsletter: Cane Collector's Chronicle,
The
2515 Fourth Ave. #405
Seattle, WA 98121-1461
phone: 206-441-4459
fax: 206-441-4459
e-mail: lbeeman507@aol.com
*A quarterly newsletter for the
collector of antique walking sticks:
articles, ads, photographs, auction
results, book reviews, Q&A, etc.*

Political

Collectors

Jim Gifford
P.O. Box 51
Bath, OH 44210
*Specializes in collecting canes that
have a political theme or motif.*

CANNING JARS

(see BOTTLES; FRUIT JARS; JELLY
CONTAINERS)

CANNONS

(see also ARMS & ARMOR; CIVIL
WAR ARTIFACTS; FIREWORKS
MEMORABILIA; MILITARIA:
AMMUNITION & EXPLOSIVE
ORDNANCE; TOYS, Cannons;
TOYS, Cap)

Collectors

Charles G. Kratz, Jr.
17821 Golfview
Homewood, IL 60430-1210
phone: 708-799-8478 or 312-951-0336
*Wants old muzzle loading military
cannons (only full-size, authentic type)
in any condition; also want U.S.
artillery clothing and equipment such
wooden artillery carriages and
ammunition chests.*

Starter

Man./Prod./Dist.

Robert B. George
R.B.G. Cannons
20 Amber Trail
Madison, CT 06443-2037
phone: 203-245-1216
*Cannon manufacturers for over 35
years; most cannons are scale
reproductions, meticulously finished
with special attention to details; used
as starting cannons and trophies;
units fire black powder or 10 ga. black
powder shells.*

CANS

(see ADVERTISING COL-
LECTIBLES; BEER CANS;
BREWERIANA; OYSTER RELATED
COLLECTIBLES; SOFT DRINK
COLLECTIBLES, Soft Drink Cans)

CANTON

(see CERAMICS [ORIENTAL],
Chinese Export Porcelain)

CAP PISTOLS

(see TOYS, Cap Guns)

CAPODIMONTE

(see also COLLECTIBLES [MOD-
ERN], Flowers [Capodimonte])

Dealers

James R. Highfield
Diamond Jim's
1601 Lincolnway East
South Bend, IN 46613
phone: 219-288-0300
*Wants old crown N cherub style
capodimonte to purchase; please sent
picture and price; also need pictures
and information for upcoming book.*

CAPS

(see BOTTLE CAPS)

Clubs/Associations

Gene Dittman
National Cap Association
Newsletter: NCPA Newsletter
2503 Co. Hwy G
Emerald, WI 54012-8127
phone: 715-269-7407
*Members collect baseball-style caps
with logos on them; quarterly*

newsletter, members receive annual cap printed with the year and different logo.

CARDS

(see also ADVERTISING COL-LECTIBLES, Trade Cards; BUBBLE GUM CARDS; CHRISTMAS COLLECTIBLES, Christmas Cards; CREDIT CARDS & CHARGE ITEMS; HOLIDAY COLLECTIBLES; GAMES, Cards; PLAYING CARDS; SPORTS COLLECTIBLES; TRADING CARDS, Non-Sport)

Greeting

Periodicals

Milton Kristt
Magazine: Greetings Magazine
309 Fifth Ave.
New York, NY 10016
phone: 212-679-6677
fax: 212-679-6374
Monthly magazine published for all those interested in greeting cards and gifts at the retail buying level.

Tarot

Collectors

Rochard Cornwell
701 Sheridan Ave.
Findlay, OH 45840
Wants pre-1970 tarot cards; send any available information.

CARNEGIE HALL ITEMS

Collectors

Gino Francesconi
Carnegie Hall Corporation
881 Seventh Ave.
New York, NY 10019
phone: 212-903-9629
Wants house programs, stagebills, photographs of building, posters of events, other early memorabilia.

CARNIVAL ITEMS

(see also AMUSEMENT PARK ITEMS; CAROUSELS & CAROU-SEL FIGURES)

Collectors

David Gaylin
P.O. Box 9686
Rosedale, MD 21237
phone: 410-665-6295
Always seeking carnival-related advertising, posters, promotional items, literature, ride manufacturers' literature, games, etc.

Chalkware

Experts

Cathy Cook
10 E. 13th St., #2D
New York, NY 10003-4467
e-mail: cook710@aol.com
Interested in historical information

about carnival chalkware and carnivals in general.

Thomas G. Morris
Prize Publishers
P.O. Box 8307
Medford, OR 97504-0307
phone: 541-779-3164
Buys, sells and specializes in carnival chalkware figures; author of "The Carnival Chalk Prize" Vol. I and Vol. II; will assist with information or appraisals on the subject; SASE for info.

Repro. Sources

Peg McCormack
Folkwerks
1760 Elbow Lane
Allentown, PA 18103-9639
phone: 610-398-3328
fax: 610-398-3328
e-mail: folkwerks@aol.com
Sculpts original pieces in earth clay; a mold is made, each piece is cast, handpainted, signed, dated, and numbered.

CAROUSELS & CAROUSEL FIGURES

(see also AMUSEMENT PARK ITEMS; CARNIVAL ITEMS; COLLECTIBLES [MODERN], Carousels; FOLK ART; MUSICAL BOXES; MUSICAL INSTRUMENTS, Mechanical [Band Organs])

Appraisers

Ken Weaver
Weavers Antiques
7 Cooks Glen Road
Spring City, PA 19475-3303
phone: 610-469-6331
fax: 610-469-6845
e-mail: BarbMGR@aol.com
Auctions, buys, sells, restores and appraises carousel figures.

Mary Jenkins
3845 Telegraph Rd.
Elkton, MD 21921-2442
phone: 410-392-4289
fax: 410-392-6129
e-mail: mjenkins@netgsi.com
Internet: http://www.carousel.org/acs.html
Collects, appraises and specializes in carousels and carousel art; Executive Secretary of the American Carousel Society.

Auction Services

Arlan Ettinger
Guernsey's Auction
136 East 73rd St.
New York, NY 10021-4208
phone: 212-794-2280
fax: 212-744-3638
Specializes in the sale of carousel figures.

Bob Kissel
Robert R. Kissel Company
8001 E Lee Hill Rd.
Madison, IN 47250-8746
Dealer of carousel horses; carousel auctions.

David A. Norton
Norton Auctioneers of Michigan, Inc.
Pearl at Monroe St.
Coldwater, MI 49036
phone: 517-279-9063
fax: 517-279-9191
Specializing in the auctioning of amusement rides, carousels, amusement parks, arcades, museums, etc.

Jim Aten
7626 S.W. Hood
Portland, OR 97219
phone: 503-452-2383

Clubs/Associations

Mary Jenkins, Ex. Sec.
American Carousel Society
Newsletter: Rounding Board, The
3845 Telegraph Rd.
Elkton, MD 21921-2442
phone: 410-392-4289
fax: 410-392-6129
e-mail: mjenkins@netgsi.com
Internet: http://www.carousel.org/acs.html
The goal of the ACS is to preserve operating carousels and carousel art; please send SASE for information.

National Carnival Association
P.O. Box 4165
Salisbury, NC 28145-4165
phone: 704-636-0841
fax: 704-636-1051

Edward F. Gallenstein
National Wood Carvers Association
Newsletter: Chip Chats
7424 Miami Ave.
Cincinnati, OH 45243
phone: 513-561-0627 or 513-561-9051
NWCA's aims are to promote woodcarving and fellowship among members; encourage exhibitions; list tool and wood suppliers, and find markets for those who sell their work - in short, anything that aids the carver and/or whittler.

Terry Blake, ExSec.
National Carousel Association
Magazine: Merry-Go-Roundup
P.O. Box 4333
Evansville, IN 47724-0333
phone: 812-428-3675
Internet: http://www.carousel.org/nca.html
Primary goal is to protect existing wooden operating carousels; please send SASE for information.

Colorado Carousel Society
P.O. Box 66
Stratton, CO 80836

Grace K. Miller
Washington Antique Carousel Society
1901 South Adams
Tacoma, WA 98405

Collectors

Tommy Sciortino
1904 W. Waters Ave.
Tampa, FL 33604-1006
phone: 813-248-5387
fax: 813-247-6369
Restores antique carousels; buys and sells whole carousels, horses, chariots, parts, etc.

Dealers

Bruce Zubee
Amusement Arts
15 Jerome Ave.
Burlington, CT 06013-2407
phone: 203-675-7653
fax: 203-675-7653
Wants to buy any old wooden carousel horses or menagerie figures in any condition; also buying band organs, carousel scenery panels and rounding boards, etc.; sales, purchases, museum quality restorations, worldwide service.

John Wester
Just Carousel Animals
157 Murray Ave.
Piscataway, NJ 08854-3141

Ken Weaver
Weavers Antiques
7 Cooks Glen Road
Spring City, PA 19475-3303
phone: 610-469-6331
fax: 610-469-6845
e-mail: BarbMGR@aol.com
Auctions, buys, sells, restores and appraises carousel figures.

Phil & Molly Rader
Rader's Horse House
2277 Ogden Rd.
Wilmington, OH 45177
phone: 513-382-3266 or 513-865-4498
Buys, sells and trades carousel horses; also creates original carousel and equestrian paintings, prints and T-shirt apparel.

Bob Kissel
Robert R. Kissel Company
8001 E Lee Hill Rd.
Madison, IN 47250-8746
Dealer of carousel horses; carousel auctions.

Don Snider
Merry-Go-Art
2606 Jefferson
Joplin, MO 64804
phone: 417-624-7281
Buys and sells carousel figures, and video tapes of antique carousels.

John & June Reely
Flying Tails
1209 Indiana Ave.
South Pasadena, CA 91030-3611
phone: 213-256-8657
Send 2 stamp SASE for catalog: carousel figures hair tails and stands, etc.

Experts

William Manns
P.O. Box 6459
Santa Fe, NM 87502-6459
phone: 505-995-0102
fax: 505-995-0103
Author of "Painted Ponies, American Carousel Art." Send photo and request for information about your carving and its authenticity.

Marianne Stevens
Wooden Horse, The
920 W. Mescalero
Roswell, NM 88201
phone: 505-622-7397
Buys, sells, trades, brokers, and appraises carousel figures.

Misc. Services

Tommy Sciortino
American Carousel & Novelty
1904 W. Waters Ave.
Tampa, FL 33604-1006
phone: 813-248-5387
fax: 813-247-6369
Experienced in relocation, setup and dismantling of carousels.

Museums/Libraries

Heritage Plantation of Sandwich
P.O. Box 566
Sandwich, MA 02563
phone: 617-888-3300

Louise L. DeMars
New England Carousel Museum, Inc.
95 Riverside Ave.
Bristol, CT 06010
phone: 203-585-5411
Internet: http://www.carousel.org/
museums.html

Herschell Carousel Factory Museum
Newsletter: Carousel Newsletter
180 Thompson St.
P.O. Box 672
North Tonawanda, NY 14120-0672
phone: 716-693-1885 or 716-693-7972
fax: 716-693-1885
Internet: http://www.carousel.org/
museums.html
Allen Herschell wooden carousel c. 1916 (wood), a metal children's carousel c. 1946, and original Allan Herschell factory site; exhibit on history of Herschell Co., carousels, amusement rides, and band organs.

Carousel World Museum
Rtes. 202 and 263
Lahaska, PA 18931
phone: 215-794-8960
Internet: http://www.carousel.org/
museums.html

Rachel C. Pratt, Dir.
Merry-Go-Round Museum
W. Washington & Jackson Sts.
P.O. Box 718
Sandusky, OH 44870-0718
phone: 419-626-6111 or 419-627-5412
fax: 419-626-1297
Features a working carousel, and master carver Gustav Dentzel's 19th century carving shop; restoration services for carousel animals & band organs.

Indianapolis Children's Museum
3010 North Meridian
P.O. Box 3000
Indianapolis, IN 46206

American Carousel Museum
665 Beach St.
San Francisco, CA 94109
phone: 415-928-0550

Carol Perron
International Museum of Carousel Art
P.O. Box 797
Hood River, OR 97031
phone: 503-387-2979
Historical museum dedicated to preserving the carousel.

Periodicals

Walter Loucks
Magazine: Carousel News & Trader, The
87 Park Ave. West, Ste. 206
Mansfield, OH 44902
phone: 419-529-4999
fax: 419-529-2321
Internet: http://www.carousel.net/trader/
index.htm
Monthly magazine serving the carousel enthusiast since 1985; color photos, ads, stories, auctions, restoring, events, etc.

Walter Loucks
Directory: Carousel News & Trader
Carousel Buyer's Guide
87 Park Ave. West, Ste. 206
Mansfield, OH 44902
phone: 419-529-4999
fax: 419-529-2321
Internet: http://www.carousel.net/trader/
index.htm
Lists carousel-related services and items for sale: dealers, auctioneers, restorers, appraisers, reproductions, tails, stands, jewelry, artists, books, carvers, music, supplies, etc.

William Manns
Zon International Publishing
Directory: Carousel Shopper
P.O. Box 6459
Santa Fe, NM 87502-6459
phone: 505-995-0102
fax: 505-995-0103
A carousel resource directory: suppliers, museums, carousel events, shows, restorers, auctions, reproductions, cards, posters, etc.

Phyllis Carlson Brown
Newsletter: Carousel Collecting & Crafting
3755 Avocado Blvd., Ste. 164
La Mesa, CA 91941-7301
phone: 602-842-4000
fax: 602-842-2664
A monthly newsletter with news, views, and how-to's.

Repair Services

William R. Finkenstein
R & F Designs, Inc.
95 Riverside Ave.
Bristol, CT 06010
phone: 203-585-5411
Internet: http://www.carousel.org/
museums.html
Considered the best carousel restoration firm, examples: New Orleans, City Park, Derby Ride, Playland, Rye, NY.

Marsha A. Schloesser
Carousel Workshop, The
218 High St.
De Land, FL 32720
phone: 904-738-4229
Dealer and lecturer; buys, sells, restores carousel figures.

Carousel Magic!
P.O. Box 1466
Mansfield, OH 44901-1466
phone: 419-526-4009
fax: 419-526-4561
e-mail: carmagic@richnet.net
Highest quality custom made full size carousels, individual animals, restorations, carving classes and carving kits.

Craig Swanson
Midwest Carousel Organization
1952 Lake Drive
Independence, MO 64055-1863
phone: 816-833-3573
Internet: http://www.finest1.com/hand/
World famous woodcarver, professional animal restorations; also buys, sells, and trades.

Pegi Sanders
Sanders Carousel Company
7119 E. Shea Blvd., 106-424
Scottsdale, AZ 85254
phone: 606-948-3268
Complete, basket cases to final paint.

Bill Hughes
Hughes Carousel Restoration
10325 Dougherty Ave.
Morgan Hill, CA 95037-9241
phone: 408-778-5077
Museum quality restorations.

Repro. Sources

William R. Finkenstein
Carvers Inc.
95 Riverside Ave.
Bristol, CT 06010
phone: 203-585-5411
Internet: http://www.carousel.org/
museums.html
Specializing in carving carousel figures in an existing or new design.

Elizabeth Gimblett
Horses Galore
12819 Chapman Hwy.
Seymour, TN 37865
phone: 615-453-2195
Hand painted, fiberglass, aluminum, plastic, wood figures.

Joe & Susan Leonard
Custom Woodworking Studio
SR 88, Box 12107
Garrettsville, OH 44231
phone: 216-527-2307
Specializing in restoring and carving carousel figures.

Tom Gardiner
Carousel Carvings
332 El Camono Rd.
Carmel Valley, CA 93924-9651
Handcarved and handpainted animals.

Vince Martinico
Wild Horse, A
923 Lincoln Way
Auburn, CA 95603
phone: 916-823-7870
Handcarved Dentzels and Mullers.

Suppliers

Sally Craig
Nostalgia
336 W. High St.
Elizabethtown, PA 17022
phone: 717-367-4616
Reins, stirrups, jewels, tails, twisted brass; send SASE for list.

Peter Millar
Quill, Hair & Ferrule, Ltd.
P.O. Box 23927
Columbia, SC 29224-3927
phone: 800-421-7961 or 803-788-4499
fax: 803-736-4731
Professional restoration supplies: Japan & oil colors, brushes, abalone & mother-of-pearl, aluminum, copper, composition, gold leaf, burnishing tools, imported gold sizes, non-tarnish iridescent & metallic pigments, etc.

George Faircloth
Faircloth Carousel Restoration Studios
4633 Coolidge St.
Concord, CA 94521-1347
phone: 415-682-PONY
Eyes, tails, stands, restoration guide, materials.

Miniature

Clubs/Associations

Jerry Defenderfer
Miniature Carousel Builders, Inc.
2746 Warmspring Rd.
Chambersburg, PA 17201
phone: 717-375-4256

Patrick Wentzel
Carousel Modelers & Miniatures
Association
Magazine: Horse Tales
2310 Highland Ave.
Parkersburg, WV 26101-2920
phone: 304-428-3544
*Formed in 1986 for those interested in
the building miniature carousels and
related items.*

Collectors

Patrick Wentzel
2310 Highland Ave.
Parkersburg, WV 26101-2920
phone: 304-428-3544
*Wants to buy carousel, carnival,
amusement park, and circus items
including photographs, miniature
carvings, books, and related articles.*

Suppliers

Simone Gagne
Miniature Carousel Components
8 N. Munroe Terrace
Boston, MA 02122-2508
phone: 617-265-2243
*Carousel mechanisms, roped rods,
crankshafts, details.*

Patrick Wentzel
2310 Highland Ave.
Parkersburg, WV 26101-2920
phone: 304-428-3544
*Sells scale wood carving kits in 1", 1
1/2", and 2" scales; over 50 different
kits available.*

Albert Krueger
Merry-Go-Rounds
19771 Lexington Lane
Huntington Beach, CA 92646
phone: 714-963-2676
*Miniature kits, five sizes, scale,
operating.*

CARPENTER ITEMS

(see ARCHITECTURE & RELATED
ITEMS)

CARPET SWEEPERS

(see VACUUM CLEANERS)

CARRIAGES

(see HORSE-DRAWN VEHICLES,
Carriages)

CARS

(see AUTOMOBILES;
AUTOMOBILIA; AUTO RACING
MEMORABILIA; KITS;
MILITARIA, Vehicles; MODELS,
Cars; TOYS, Diecast; TRAILERS &
RV'S)

CARTE-DE-VISITES

(see CIVIL WAR ARTIFACTS,
Photographs; PHOTOGRAPHS)

CARTOON ART

(see also ANIMATION FILM ART;
CHARACTER COLLECTIBLES;
COMIC BOOKS; COMIC STRIPS,
Sunday Newspaper; POLITICAL
COLLECTIBLES, Nast Cartoons;
POPULAR CULTURE; POSTERS,
Cartoon; SCIENCE FICTION)

Clubs/Associations

Marge D. Devine
National Cartoonists Society
Magazine: Cartoonist, The
14 Tibet Dr.
Carmel, NY 10512-9771
*National club interested in profes-
sional cartooning.*

Collectors

Tim Isaacson
1002 Clinton
Oak Park, IL 60304-1824
phone: 708-383-5646
*Wants to buy original comic art:
comic book covers and pages, Sunday
and daily comic strip art; Dick Tracy,
Prince Valiant, The Phantom, Little
Orphan Annie, etc.*

Bill Bush
P.O. Box 61868
Houston, TX 77208-1868
*Wants to buy original cartoons and
comic art by Caniff, Baker, Eisner,
Interlandi, Kaufman, Kremps, Lichty,
Machamer, Priscilla, Rayon, Ross,
Ben Roth, Shermund, Simms
Campbell, Troop, Wenzel, Wood, and
Wolfe.*

Dealers

Bill & Joanne Bruegman
Toy Scouts, Inc.
137 Casterton Ave.
Akron, OH 44303-1543
phone: 330-836-0668
fax: 330-869-8668
e-mail: toyscout@newreach.net
Internet: http://www.csmonline.com/
toyscouts/
*Wants to buy original artwork from
comic books, especially super hero;
artists such as Jack Kirby, Steve
Ditko, Will Eisner, John Comita.*

Robert A. LeGresley
P.O. Box 1199
Lawrence, KS 66044-8199
phone: 913-749-5458 or 913-843-0357
fax: 913-842-2203
Buys and sells original comic art.

Cartoon Museum, The
814 Mission St.
San Francisco, CA 94103
phone: 415-227-8666
*Buys and sells original cartoon art of
all types; also "spin offs": books,
collectibles, comic books, magazines,
etc.; a private museum with original
art for more than 2,500 cartoons of all
kinds, especially comic art.*

Experts

Frederick P. Dose, Jr.
Frederick Dose Appraisals Ltd.
778 Pleasant Ave.
Highland Park, IL 60035-4613
phone: 847-433-1090 or 847-433-7870
*Has verified and valued over 60,000
original gag and political cartoons for
the Cartoon Museum of Ohio State
University, plus 5,000 Chester Gould
Dick Tracy and Gravies strips.*

Misc. Services

News America Syndicate
3145 Killarney Ln.
Costa Mesa, CA 92626-2610
A major comic strip syndicator.

Museums/Libraries

Nancy McClellan, Dir.
National Gallery for Caricature &
Cartoon Art
P.O. Box 40308
Washington, DC 20016-0308
phone: 202-638-6411

Curator
Cartoon Research Library, University of
Ohio
023L Wexner
27 West 17 Avenue Mall
Columbus, OH 43210-1393
phone: 614-292-0538
fax: 614-292-6184
e-mail: cartoons@osu.edu
Internet: http://www.lib.ohio-state.edu
*Houses more than 200,000 original
cartoons including editorial cartoons,
comic strips, sports cartoons,
magazine cartoons, and comic book
art; several hundred cartoonists are
represented including Milton Caniff
and Walt Kelly.*

Consortium of Popular Culture
Collections
Popular Culture Library
Bowling Green State University
Bowling Green, OH 43403-0001
phone: 419-372-2450
fax: 419-372-7996
*Consortium composed of Bowling
Green State U., Kent State U.,
Michigan State U., and Ohio State U.;
the largest academic library
collections of primary research*

*material in comic art, popular fiction,
popular music, performing arts.*

Molly Kiely
Cartoon Art Museum of California
Newsletter: Cartoon Times
814 Mission St., 2nd Floor
San Francisco, CA 94103
phone: 415-546-3922 or 415-CAR-
TOON
fax: 415-243-8666
*Broad collection of original daily and
Sunday comic strip art, editorial and
political cartoons, animation cels,
magazine panels, comic book pages
and covers, and toy-related items.*

San Francisco Academy of Comic Art
2850 Ulloa
San Francisco, CA 94116-2223
phone: 415-681-1737
fax: 415-681-1737
*Millions of newspaper strips, bound
files, major dailies from 1890-1960,
pulps, all science fiction, crime fiction,
film history, children's books, comic
books; excellent copies made of all
graphic material; dup material for
trade.*

Comics

Collectors

John S. Fawcett
P.O. Box 1156
Waldoboro, ME 04572-1156
phone: 207-832-7398
*Wants to buy original comic art:
wants original Krazy Kat by George
Herriman, original Lone Ranger art
and pulp cover paintings of Lone
Ranger; also Pogo originals by Walt
Kelly.*

Milton Caniff

Collectors

Tyler Hess
63 Madison Ave.
Mount Holly, NJ 08060
phone: 609-267-8598
*Wants to buy original Caniff art of
any nature.*

Bill Bush
P.O. Box 61868
Houston, TX 77208-1868
*Wants to buy Milton Caniff sketches,
color guides and proofs, letters,
photos, audios, VHS videos and other
ephemera.*

Periodicals

Carl Horak
Journal: Canifffites Journal
1319 108 Avenue SW
Calgary
Alberta T2W 0C6 Canada
phone: 403-252-0878
*Members focus on the works of Milton
Caniff - original art or Sunday comic
strips: Terry and the Pirates, Steve
Canyon, etc.; newsletter published 4
times a year.*

Posters

Collectors

Mark Wilson
P.O. Box 340
Castle Rock, WA 98611
phone: 206-274-9163
Wants to buy all 1910-1970 original release cartoon posters, especially from the years 1928-1941; also wants pre-1945 cartoon pressbooks, lobby cards & 8x10 stills from Fleisher, Disney, Warner Bros.

Walt Kelly

Experts

Steve Thompson
6908 Wentworth Ave. South
Minneapolis, MN 55423-2363
phone: 612-869-6320
Internationally-known bibliographer and biographer of Walt Kelly and "Pogo"; active collector of unusual and esoteric Kellyana.

CARTS

(see RIDING TOYS)

CASH REGISTERS

Collectors

Lt. Col. B.A. Gill (Ret.)
P.O. Box 3811
Clifton Park, NY 12065
phone: 513-371-6035
Brass or wood in any condition; also literature, ads, sales brochures.

Hayne Dominick
562 Gammon Rd.
Kingsport, TN 37663-4119
phone: 423-323-9579
Buying early and unusual cash registers; specializing in National Cash Register, related memorabilia & advertising; sales, repairs and restorations.

Lewis
18915 Los Palominos Dr.
Yorba Linda, CA 92886-2649
phone: 714-970-8390
Wants to buy cash registers and related items, especially small wooden, figural, ornate, unusual machines.

Dealers

Bill Heuring
Hickory Bend Antiques & Collectibles
2995 Drake Hill Rd.
Jasper, NY 14855-9715
phone: 607-792-3343
fax: 607-792-3309
Cash registers bought and sold; professional restoration and repair; also sells parts.

Experts

Sam Robins
Play It Again Sam's, Inc.
5310 W. Devon
Chicago, IL 60646
phone: 312-763-1771
Buys, sells, trades machines; has extensive register parts inventory; also offers a full restoration service for cash registers.

John Gillman
18381 Linden St.
Fountain Valley, CA 92708
phone: 714-962-4002
Buys, sells, repairs and completely restores NCR cash registers for customers throughout the U.S.

Henry Bartsch
Antique Registers
P.O. Box 444
Rockaway Beach, OR 97136-0444
phone: 503-355-2932
Author of "Antique Cash Registers 1880-1920"; offers antique cash register sales and service.

CASINO COLLECTIBLES

(see ASHTRAYS, Casino; GAMBLING COLLECTIBLES; MATCHCOVERS, Casino)

CAST IRON ITEMS

(see also BANKS; FARM COLLECTIBLES, Cast Iron Seats; FIREPLACE ITEMS; GARDEN FURNITURE; KITCHEN COLLECTIBLES; METAL ITEMS; PAPERWEIGHTS, Cast Iron; STOVES; TARGETS; TOYS; WATER SPRINKLERS; WINDMILL COLLECTIBLES, Weights)

Clubs/Associations

Jim Bell
Cast Iron Collectors, Southern Regional Chapter
P.O. Box 355
Swainsboro, GA 30401
phone: 912-237-7815

Collectors

Dave Johnson
113 Hix Ave.
Rye, NY 10580
phone: 914-967-4809
Wants cast iron match safes, string holders, muffin pans, etc.

Craig Dinner
P.O. Box 4399
Long Island City, NY 11104-0399
phone: 718-729-3850 or 802-365-7181

Joan Baldini
3007 Plum St.
Erie, PA 16508
phone: 814-868-1316 or 814-459-2503
Collects Erie related cast iron items.

Dealers

Sonnie Cucinotti
Spirits in the Attic
201 Msgr. O'Brien Hwy.
Cambridge, MA 02141
phone: 617-738-6054
Wants to buy cast and and wrought iron decorative and utilitarian items.

John & Nancy Smith
American Sampler
P.O. Box 371
Barnesville, MD 20838-0371
phone: 301-972-6250
Wants cast iron doorstops, figural bottle openers, doorknockers, paperweights, etc, banks, doorstops, etc.

Dan & Sally Mosholder
13020 W. Carlisle Rd.
Frazeysburg, OH 43822-9706
phone: 614-828-3023
Buys and sells all kinds of cast iron items.

Louis Picek
Main Street Antiques and Art
110 West Main
P.O. Box 340
West Branch, IA 52358-0340
phone: 319-643-2065
Buys and sells figural iron of all types; offers a monthly list of items for sale.

J.M. Ellwood
Irontiques
7077 E. Main #4
Scottsdale, AZ 85251-4325
phone: 602-947-6220 or 602-947-9679
Wants trivets, match holders, irons, banks, children's stoves and irons, advertising items, cigar cutters, cap exploders, figural bottle openers, miners candlesticks.

Experts

Craig Dinner
P.O. Box 4399
Long Island City, NY 11104-0399
phone: 718-729-3850 or 802-365-7181
Wants cast iron doorstops, figural bottle openers, doorknockers, paperweights, lawn sprinklers, shooting gallery targets, architectural items, etc.

Richard Tucker
Argyle Antiques
P.O. Box 262
Argyle, TX 76226-0262
phone: 817-464-3752
fax: 817-464-7293
e-mail: millwt@pop.intex.net

Periodicals

Steve Stephens
Newsletter: Cast Iron Cookware News
28 Angela Ave.
San Anselmo, CA 94960
phone: 415-453-7790
A 6-issue-per-volume (about 40 pages) newsletter (one volume every 1-2 years); illustrated and packed with detailed information focusing on cast iron kitchen cookware (including Griswold.)

Repair Services

Ken Kohut
Metal Works
30 Olive St.
Danbury, CT 06810
Repairs, reproductions, and custom work; blacksmithing, welding, painting, sand blasting, chemical stripping.

Rocco V. DeAngelo
RD 1 Box 187R
Cherry Valley, NY 13320
phone: 607-264-3607
Quality restoration of antique cast iron; sandblasting, painting, repair, fabrication of parts; garden furniture, urns, fences installed, handwrought iron, brass & iron beds, etc.

Repro. Sources

Ian Eddy
Ian Eddy Blacksmith
RFD 1 Box 975
Putney, VT 05346

Charles W. Euston
Woodbury Blacksmith & Forge
P.O. Box 278
Woodbury, CT 06798

Darold Rinedollar
Darold Rinedollar Blacksmith
P.O. Box 365
Clarksville, MO 63336

Griswold

Clubs/Associations

David G. Smith
Griswold & Cast Iron Cookware Association
P.O. Drawer B
Perrysburg, NY 14129-0301
phone: 716-532-5154
e-mail: DGSpanman@aol.com
Internet: http://www.C1web.com/panman
Dedicated to the promotion and education of its members in cast iron kitchen collectibles; 650+ members nationwide; annual swap meet and meeting.

Collectors

Sally Swanson
3302 West 11th St.
Erie, PA 16505-3710
phone: 814-838-1866
Wants to buy cast iron items made by the Griswold Manufacturing Co.

Larry Foxx
400 Creek Rd.
Carlisle, PA 17013-9645
phone: 717-243-9231
Interested in collecting cast iron, aluminum, tin and other items made

by the Griswold Manufacturing Co., Erie, PA.

Experts

David G. Smith
Pan Man, The
P.O. Drawer B
Perrysburg, NY 14129-0301
phone: 716-532-5154
e-mail: DGSpanman@aol.com
Internet: http://www.C1web.com/panman
Cast iron collector specializing in cast iron muffin pans; has over 250 different patterns and/or variations; buys, sells and trades cast iron cookware; author of "The Book of Griswold & Wagner."

Periodicals

David G. Smith, Ed.
Newsletter: Kettles 'n Cookware
P.O. Drawer B
Perrysburg, NY 14129-0301
phone: 716-532-5154
e-mail: DGSpanman@aol.com
Internet: http://www.C1web.com/panman
Focuses on cast iron, aluminum, tin and other items made by the Griswold and other manufacturers.

Wagner

Collectors

Thomas Todson
678 Sagewood Rd.
Chaparral, NM 88021-7417
phone: 505-522-6074
Authors of "Griswold Cast Collectibles" a history and value guide.

CASTOR SETS

Collectors

Juanita Wilkins
Bird of Paradise
430 S. Cole St.
Lima, OH 45805-3367
Wants art glass or colored pattern glass shakers, cruets, syrup pitchers, and castor sets.

CATALOGS

(see also ADVERTISING COL-LECTIBLES; HARDWARE; MACHINERY & EQUIPMENT, Catalogs; MAGAZINES; PAPER COLLECTIBLES; PLUMBING)

Christmas

Dealers

Christmas Catalog Collector, The
175 East Delaware, #7403
Chicago, IL 60611-1731
phone: 800-879-6948 or 312-337-3123
fax: 312-266-7982
Seeks toy and Christmas catalogs and flyers from Sears, Wards, all retailers, wholesalers and manufacturers; also buying toy magazines and general

merchandise catalogs if containing many toys.

Mail Order

Dealers

Judy Hesson
Hesson Collectables
1261 S. Lloyd
Lombard, IL 60148-4234
phone: 630-627-3298
fax: 630-627-3298
Buys & sells mail order catalogs: Sears, Montgomery Ward, Penny, Aldens, Spiegel: 1900-1990; also other catalogs; send $4 for list of 2000 for sale.

Trade

(see also ADVERTISING COL-LECTIBLES; MACHINERY & EQUIPMENT, Catalogs; MAGA-ZINES)

Collectors

Richard M. Bueschel
414 N. Prospect Manor Ave.
Mount Prospect, IL 60056-2046
phone: 847-253-0791
fax: 847-253-7919
e-mail: BuschlHist@aol.com
Wants 1850-1950 trade catalogs of amusement rides, coin machines & other products for use in saloons, diners, restaurants, hotels.

Dealers

Steve Finer
P.O. Box 758
Greenfield, MA 01302
phone: 413-773-5811

Joseph F. Loccisano
Historic Photographs & Paper Americana
2264 Nicholson Square Dr.
Lancaster, PA 17601-3966
phone: 717-560-7750
Wants to buy pre-1915 catalogs (hardcover or softcover) illustrating hardware specialties, tinware, occupational supplies, photographic apparatus, architectural supplies, toys, etc.

Kenneth Schneringer
271 Sabrina Ct.
Woodstock, GA 30188-4228
phone: 404-926-9383
Offers lists of trade catalogs for sale.

Judy Hesson
Hesson Collectables
1261 S. Lloyd
Lombard, IL 60148-4234
phone: 630-627-3298
fax: 630-627-3298
Buys and sells trade catalogs: sports, fashion, hardware, architectural, wholesale, retail; send $4 for list of 900 for sale.

Robert D. Verhines
1705 Longwood Dr., Apt. 202
Sycamore, IL 60178-2743
phone: 815-899-3121
Buys and sells trade catalogs, e.g. Sears, Wards, Penny's, Alden, Spiegel, etc.; especially wants Christmas issues.

Trade (Furniture)

Museums/Libraries

Christian G. Carron
Grand Rapids Public Museum
272 Pearl St. NW
Grand Rapids, MI 49504-5371
phone: 616-456-3977
fax: 616-456-3873
Large collection of 20th century furniture and furniture manufacturing trade catalogs.

Trade (Homebuilding)

Collectors

Jerry L. Wilson
1002 E. Main St.
P.O. Box 220
Cherryvale, KS 67335-0220
phone: 316-336-2495 or 316-336-2176
fax: 316-336-2177
Wants to buy millwork or sash & door company catalogs from the 1800s to 1920; also wants any other building related catalogs such as stained glass, paint, general hardware, metal ceilings, etc. from the same era.

Trade (Kitchen Collectibles)

Collectors

Reid Cooper
5458 Complex St., #401
San Diego, CA 92123
phone: 619-469-3966 or 619-569-6716
fax: 619-569-6793
Advanced collector/researcher wants to buy pre-1920 trade catalogs of kitchen implements, gadgets, eggbeaters, etc.; also interested in old advertising, billheads, and trade cards that relate to same; send price, sample photocopy.

Trade (Medical)

Museums/Libraries

Michael Rhode, Archiv.
National Museum of Health & Medicine
Bldg. 54
Walter Reed Medical Center
Washington, DC 20306
phone: 202-576-2438 or 202-576-0401
fax: 202-576-2164
Federal government museum archives that collects catalog material related to the history of medicine, especially military medicine.

Trade (Woodworking)

Collectors

John Treggiari
Salem, MA 01970-1225
phone: 508-744-2897
fax: 508-744-5572
e-mail: micrometer@juno.com
Serious collector wants to buy tool catalogs: woodworking, machinist, drafting, and hardware store catalogs showing tools are all needed, but should have been published prior to 1920.

Repro. Sources

Harold Barker
3108 Klinger Rd.
Ada, OH 45810
phone: 419-634-7328
Specializes in the sale of high quality photocopies of old catalogs and manuals, especially in the field of woodworking.

CAVE RELATED ITEMS

Collectors

Jack Speece
711 East Atlantic Ave.
Altoona, PA 16602-5405
phone: 814-946-3155 or 814-342-0470
fax: 814-342-5660
Wants items pertaining to caves, caverns, speleo history and folklore.

Bert Ashbrook
Cave Investigation and Exploration
1257 Lehigh Parkway South
Allentown, PA 18103-3875
phone: 610-797-3981
Collects books, ephemera, antiques, and memorabilia related to caves, commercial caverns, wild caves, cave history, and cave science.

Anthony Glab
4154 Falls Rd.
Baltimore, MD 21211-1644
phone: 410-235-1777
fax: 410-889-1937
e-mail: glab@aol.com
Wants to buy cave memorabilia such as paperweights, signs, souvenirs, etc.

Gordon Smith
P.O. Box 217
Marengo, IN 47140-0217
phone: 812-945-5721
Wants items pertaining to caves and caverns: books, pamphlets, brochures, photos, souvenir plates and spoons, stereo views, sheet music, etc.

CELEBRITIES

(see AUTOGRAPHS; MOVIE MEMORABILIA; PERSONALITIES; PHOTOGRAPHS; TELEVISION SHOWS & MEMORA-BILIA)

CELLULOID ITEMS

(see also ALBUMS)

Auction Services

Kurt R. Krueger
Krueger Auctions
160 N. Washington St.
Iola, WI 54945
phone: 715-445-3845
fax: 715-445-4100

Clubs/Associations

Victorian Era Celluloid Collectors
Association
P.O. Box 470
Alpharetta, GA 30239-0470
Club for collectors of Victorian celluloid covered boxes, photo albums, tri-fold mirrors and other Victorian celluloid covered items; send SASE for info.

Collectors

John Andreae
P.O. Box 156
Granger, IN 46530
phone: 219-272-2337
fax: 219-271-1146
Wants celluloid advertising pieces: pocket mirrors, pinback buttons, bookmarks and blotters; anything that is made of celluloid and that has advertising on it.

Andra Behrendt
P.O. Box 7236
Westchester, IL 60154-7236
phone: 708-345-8593
e-mail: andra@lady-a.com
Internet: http://www.lady-a.com
Collects decorative Celluloid glove, collar, trinket, dresser set boxes and celluloid autograph albums; must be in mint condition; also wants 1895-1910 catalogs that advertise these items.

Sherry & Mike Miller
303 Holiday Dr. #130
Tuscola, IL 61953-2118
phone: 217-253-4991
e-mail: miller@tuscola.net
Wants to buy Victorian era boxes which held collars/cuffs, gloves, neckties, shaving sets, etc.; also photograph albums and autograph albums; must have lithograph prints of scenes or people; all covered in thin layer of clear Celluloid.

Dealers

Judith Rubin
This Time Around Antiques
6294 Clay Pipe Ct.
Manassas, VA 20120-5621
Wants to buy Victorian (1895-1910) celluloid boxes (collar/cuff, vanity, etc.), photo albums, autograph albums, 3-way shaving mirrors; excellent condition only; contents not necessary in boxes or albums; no ivorine, or French ivory.

Andra Behrendt
Lady A Antiques
P.O. Box 7236
Westchester, IL 60154-7236
phone: 708-345-8593
e-mail: andra@lady-a.com
Internet: http://www.lady-a.com
Buys, sells and collects decorative Celluloid glove, collar, trinket, dresser set boxes and celluloid autograph and photograph albums; must be in mint condition; also wants 1893-1910 catalogs that advertise these items.

Experts

Julie Robinson
P.O. Box 744
Davidsville, PA 15928
phone: 814-479-2212
Identification of natural and synthetic moldable materials: Gutta Percha, Vulcanite, Horn, Tortoise shell, Ivory imitations, Celluloid, Casine, bakelite, Beetleware, Acrylic, Acetate, and early poly plastics; written extensively.

CELS

(see ANIMATION FILM ART; AUDIO-VISUAL)

CERAMICS

(see also ADVERTISING COL-LECTIBLES, Potteries Related; CALENDAR PLATES; COL-LECTIBLES [MODERN]; COOKIE JARS; DINNERWARE; FAIRINGS; FIGURINES; POT LIDS; PRECOLUMBIAN; REPAIR/RESTORATION/CONSERVATION; RAILROAD COLLECTIBLES, China; SHOES; STEINS

Appraisers

Karen J. Russo, G.G., ISA
Karen Jocelyn, Inc.
792 Partridge Dr.
P.O. Box 6795
Bridgewater, NJ 08807
phone: 908-806-6706 or 908-526-8440
fax: 908-526-8348
Specializing in 19th and 20th century ceramics; has constant contact with metropolitan area galleries that specialize in this area; appraisal, photography, market research.

Patricia M. Knight, ISA
Finetooth Comb Antiques Research & Appraisal Service
421 Ash Ave.
P.O. Box 1177
Ames, IA 50010-1177
phone: 515-292-9028
Consultant and qualified appraiser of ceramics of Oriental, European, English and American origin or style, including "American Satsuma."

Linda H. Richard, ISA
Cajun Collection
3609 Oak Hill
Bryan, TX 77802-4622
phone: 409-846-3558 or 817-774-8608
Buys, sells and appraises pottery, porcelain, art pottery.

Auction Services

Angela Past
Butterfield & Butterfield
7601 Sunset Blvd.
Los Angeles, CA 90046-2714
phone: 213-850-7500
fax: 213-850-5843

Clubs/Associations

Ontario Clay & Glass Association, The
Magazine: Fusion Magazine
140 Yorkville Ave.
Toronto
Ontario M5R 1C2 Canada
phone: 416-504-9899
Focuses on contemporary potters and techniques.

Susan Gray Detweiler
American Ceramic Circle
Journal: American Ceramic Circle
Journal
419 Gate Lane
Philadelphia, PA 19119
e-mail: 71712.1437@compuserve.com
Founded in 1970, a nonprofit organization that promotes scholarship and research in the history, use, and preservation of ceramics of all kinds, periods, and origins.

San Francisco Ceramic Circle
P.O. Box 15163
San Francisco, CA 94115
Monthly lectures and meetings; affiliated with the Fine Arts Museum of San Francisco.

Dealers

Paul G. Hughes, ISA
Tudor House Galleries
1401 East Blvd.
Charlotte, NC 28203-5817
phone: 704-377-4748 or 704-332-4782
e-mail: 75027.474@compuserve.com
Buys, sells and appraises 18th and 19th century ceramics; Accredited Member, International Society of Appraisers.

Marilyn Stellberg
Heritage Antiques
P.O. Box 844
Bellville, TX 77418-0844
Wants pre-1880 English or American porcelain, pottery or stoneware, etc. of any type; also offers antiques research by mail.

Antique Appraisal & Estate Sale Service - K. Bailey
P.O. Box 75191
Seattle, WA 98125-5345
phone: 206-746-2777
fax: 206-365-0633
Specializes in 18th and 19th century porcelain, plaques, enamels.

Experts

Dr. Dorothy I. Godfrey-Smith
TOSL Research Laboratory
Department of Earth Sciences
Dalhousie University
Halifax, N.S. B3H 3J5 Canada
phone: 902-494-1451 or 902-494-2358
fax: 902-494-6889
e-mail: digs@is.dal.ca
Internet: http://www.is.dal.ca/~digs/t-intro.htm
Offers an analytical service using thermoluminescence to analyze ceramic artifacts and art objects; used by museums, art galleries, private collectors and estate appraisers wishing to ensure authenticity of ceramic objects.

Elinor Racine, ISA
175 Bessborough Drive
Toronto
Ontario M4G 3J8 Canada
phone: 416-483-8675
fax: 416-440-2809
e-mail: 75317.2331@compuserve.com
Specialist in contemporary ceramics: appraiser, collector, author.

Susan & Jim Harran
World of Ceramics, The
208 Hemlock Dr.
Neptune, NJ 07753
Authors of "World of Ceramics" column.

Mary Bang
5200 Duggan Plaza
Edina, MN 55439
phone: 612-941-4754
Specializes in American and European pottery and porcelain.

Susan & Al Bagdade
Country Peasants, The
3136 Elder Ct.
Northbrook, IL 60062-5832
phone: 847-498-1468
fax: 847-392-5848
e-mail: ADBSDB@aol.com

Misc. Services

Shirley Vickers
Shirley Vickers School of China Repair
P.O. Box 688
Pine, AZ 85544-0688
phone: 520-476-3703
fax: 520-476-3703
Will buy damaged pottery of any kind; also cookie jars (must have value over $50); call or fax or write with descriptions of damage and price.

Museums/Libraries

George Gardiner Museum of Ceramic
    Art
111 Queen's Park
Toronto
Ontario M5S 2C6 Canada
phone: 416-586-8000

Miss Dorothy Lee Jones, Dir.
Jones Museum of Glass & Ceramics,
    The
Douglas Mountain Rd.
East Sebago, ME 04029
phone: 207-787-3370 or 207-787-2800
    *Unique museum, over 8500 examples
    of glass & ceramics ranging from
    ancient to modern; large holdings of
    Chinese Export & Oriental wares,
    Wedgwood, Spode, and other 19th C.
    English potters; 20th C. American art
    pottery; European porcelain.*

National Museum of American History
14th & Constitution Ave. NW
Washington, DC 20560
phone: 202-357-2700
Internet: http://www.si.edu/

Periodicals

Lladro USA
Newsletter: Lladro Antique News
1 Lladro Dr.
Moonachie, NJ 07074
phone: 201-807-1177 or 800-634-9088
fax: 201-807-1168
    *Focuses on the current secondary
    market values of Lladro's 3,000 hard-
    paste porcelain figurines produced
    since 1941; also covers history of
    hard-paste porcelain (1000 AD to
    present) such as Meissen, Sevres,
    Nymphenburg, etc.*

Professional Publications
Magazine: Ceramics Monthly
1609 Northwest Blvd.
Box 12448
Columbus, OH 43212
phone: 614-488-4561
    *A trade publication for ceramic artists
    and art education institutions; a
    glossy, quality magazine!*

Scott Publications
Magazine: Ceramics Magazine
30595 Eight Mile
Livonia, MI 48152-1761
phone: 800-458-8237 or 810-477-6650
fax: 810-477-6795
e-mail: 104137.1254@compuserve.com
    *Published monthly, informing
    contemporary ceramists with projects
    and profiles of trends and artists;
    special section issues feature articles
    on a specific trend, technique, or
    theme.*

Scott Publications
Magazine: Ceramic Arts & Crafts
30595 Eight Mile
Livonia, MI 48152-1761
phone: 800-458-8237 or 810-477-6650
fax: 810-477-6795
e-mail: 104137.1254@compuserve.com
    The "Bible" for the ceramic hobbyist

*since 1955; each monthly issue filled
with projects and patterns, celebrity
clips, new products, show listings,
industry news, shoppers guides, book
reviews, ads and classifieds.*

Newspaper: Pottery Collectors Express
P.O. Box 221
Mayview, MO 64071-0221
phone: 816-584-6309
fax: 816-584-6259
    *Marketplace for pottery of every type
    and description; free ads; monthly
    publication.*

Newsletter: Pottery Today
P.O. Box 221
Mayview, MO 64071-0221
phone: 816-584-6309
fax: 816-584-6259
    *Keeps collector and dealer up to date
    with the latest news concerning
    pottery, china, porcelain, ceramics:
    news, auction reports, show reports,
    book reviews, current market prices.*

Belleek

Clubs/Associations

Belleek Collectors' Society, The, c/o
    Reed & Barton Co.
Newsletter: Belleek Collector, The
144 W. Britannia St.
Taunton, MA 02780
phone: 508-824-6611 or 800-822-1824
fax: 508-822-7269
    Carries Irish Belleek.

Experts

Miriam & Aaron Levine
881 Whalley Ave.
New Haven, CT 06515
phone: 203-389-5440

Jack Mulhern
3212 Winterset Dr.
Dayton, OH 45440-3630
phone: 937-426-2592
    Specializes in Irish Belleek.

Mary Bang
5200 Duggan Plaza
Edina, MN 55439
phone: 612-941-4754
    *Collects and lectures on Irish and
    American Belleek.*

Kathleen Mitchell
Old Pump Antiques
P.O. Box 774
San Bruno, CA 94066-0774
phone: 415-588-9514 or 415-588-4894
fax: 415-875-7556
    *Buys, sells, appraises and specializes
    in 18th and 19th century porcelain
    including black mark Irish Belleek,
    Dresden, and Meissen; also
    specializes in Irish Belleek stoneware.*

Museums/Libraries

Mark Twyford
Museum of Ceramics at East Liverpool
400 E. 5th St.
East Liverpool, OH 43920-3134
phone: 216-386-6001
    *Detailed exhibit of the local ceramic
    industry; "The East Liverpool, Ohio
    Pottery District: Identification of
    Manufacturers & Marks" by Wm.
    Gates, Jr. and Dana Ormerod can be
    obtained by contacting the museum.*

Belleek (American)

Appraisers

Peggy Sebek, ISA, AAA
Century Appraisals, Inc.
3255 Glencairn Rd.
Shaker Heights, OH 44122-3407
phone: 216-991-2356 or 318-232-5100
    *Specializes in and appraises American
    Belleek; also residential contents,
    Victorian furniture, and silver.*

Blue & White Pottery

Clubs/Associations

Howard Gardner
Blue & White Pottery Club
Newsletter: Blue & White Pottery Club
    Newsletter
224 12th St. NW
Cedar Rapids, IA 52405
phone: 319-362-8116
    *For collectors of blue and white
    stoneware, blue and white
    spongeware, and related blue
    stoneware.*

Experts

Gregg Ellington
Upper Loft Antiques
47 Columbus St.
Wilmington, OH 45177
phone: 513-382-4311
    *Buys, sells, trades and collects
    graniteware and American ceramics
    including mochaware, yellowware,
    spongeware, etc.*

Blue Willow

(see CERAMICS, Willow Pattern)

Chalkware

Collectors

Dave Harris
1206- 1101 Bay St.
Toronto
Ontario M5S 2W8 Canada
phone: 416-972-6331
    *Wants chalkware or plaster items, e.g.
    statuettes, figurines, ashtrays,
    figurals, etc., but no carnival
    chalkware please.*

Chintz

(see also CERAMICS [ENGLISH],
Royal Winton)

Clubs/Associations

Chintz Connection
Newsletter: Chintz Connection
    Newsletter
P.O. Box 222
Riverdale, MD 20738-0222

Jane Fehrenbacher
Chintz Chums
600 Columbia St.
Pasadena, CA 91105
phone: 818-441-2490
fax: 818-441-4122

Linda Eberle
Chintz China Collector, The
Newsletter: Chintz Collector, The
P.O. Box 6126
Folsom, CA 95630
phone: 916-985-6762
fax: 916-457-1447
    *An international club for collectors of
    chintz china; newsletter has news,
    buy/sell ads.*

Collectors

Bruce E. Thulin
P.O. Box 121
Ellsworth, ME 04605
phone: 207-667-5225
e-mail: thulin@acadia.net
    *Wants chintz ceramics with all over
    decoration: Royal Winton, Shelley,
    Lord Nelson, James Kent, Crown
    Ducal, Midwinter; teapots, plates,
    stacking teapots, cups, etc.*

Dealers

Joyce Settel
Joyce Settel Ltd.
P.O. Box 94
Quogue, NY 11959
phone: 516-653-5670 or 516-288-0431
    *Specializes in English porcelain,
    Chintz, Royal Winton, James Kent,
    Lord Nelson, Crown Ducal.*

Dianne Howerton
Royal Pair Antiques, The
12707 Hillcrest Dr.
Longmont, CO 80501-1162
phone: 303-772-2760 or 303-772-2309
e-mail: dwh65@juno.com
    *Buys and sells English semi-porcelain
    chintzware in Royal Winton, Lord
    Nelson, James Kent, Midwinter,
    Myott, Crown Ducal, Ridgeway,
    Shelley, Wood & Sons and Empire
    Porcelain Co. patterns.*

Experts

Susan Scott
882 Queen Street West
Toronto
Ontario M6J 1G3 Canada
phone: 416-657-8278
fax: 416-658-4675
e-mail: scottca@ibm.net
    *Specializing in chintz ceramics,
    especially by Royal Winton, Crown
    Ducal, James, Kent, Elijah Cotton; co-
    author with Linda Eberle of*

"Charlton Standard Catalogue of Chintz, 2nd Edition."

Linda Eberle
P.O. Box 6126
Folsom, CA 95630
phone: 916-985-6762
fax: 916-457-1447
Co-author with Susan Scott of "Charlton Standard Catalogue of Chintz, 2nd Edition."

Flow Blue

Clubs/Associations

Sorita Wussow
Flow Blue International Collectors Club
Newsletter: Blue Berry Notes
11560 West 95th St., #297
Shawnee Mission, KS 66214
phone: 913-469-6517

Collectors

Larie Hensley
28 Irene St.
Brooksville, FL 34601

Christine Stucko
2774 East Main St., Ste. 136
Saint Charles, IL 60174

Dealers

Pot O Gold Antiques
P.O. Box 124
Allenwood, NJ 08720-0124
phone: 908-528-6648 or 908-528-6648
fax: 908-528-6648
e-mail:
PotOGoldAntiques@worldnet.att.net

Carl McCann
Troy & Black, Inc.
P.O. Box 228
Red Creek, NY 13143-0228
phone: 315-754-8115
Buys and sells high quality flow blue, Staffordshire figurines, American painted furniture, stoneware, redware, coverlets, samplers, and other American textiles, folk art, etc.

Louise M. Loehr
Louise's Old Things
163 W. Main St.
P.O. Box 208
Kutztown, PA 19530-0208
phone: 610-683-8370
Co-author of "Willow Pattern China." Specializing in willow, flow blue, and early children's china. Wants one piece or collections.

Pam & Ralph Krainik
Seven Gables Antiques
P.O. Box 204
Baraboo, WI 53913

Experts

Sunny Lenzer
1345 Sierra Linda Dr.
Escondido, CA 92025
Buys and sells flow blue; also.offers seminars on flow blue.

Gaudy

Clubs/Associations

Gaudy Collector's Society
P.O. Box 274
Gates Mills, OH 44040
phone: 216-449-0653
Members interested in Gaudy Welsh, Gaudy Ironstone, and Gaudy Dutch china.

Experts

John D. Querry
RD 2 Box 137B
Martinsburg, PA 16662
phone: 814-793-3185
Specializes in Gaudy Dutch; advisor to "Warman's Antiques & Collectibles Price Guide."

Handpainted

Clubs/Associations

World Organization of China Painters, The
Magazine: China Painter, The
2641 N.W. 10th St.
Oklahoma City, OK 73107-5407
phone: 405-521-1237
fax: 405-521-1265
Organization with 7000 members; museum dedicated to handpainted china; seminars, courses, library.

Museums/Libraries

World Organization of China Painters, The
Magazine: China Painter, The
2641 N.W. 10th St.
Oklahoma City, OK 73107-5407
phone: 405-521-1237
fax: 405-521-1265
Museum houses examples of handpainted porcelain from all over the U.S. and from several foreign countries.

Head Vase Planters

Clubs/Associations

Maddy Gordon
Head Vase Convention
Newsletter: Head Hunters Newsletter
P.O. Box 83H
Scarsdale, NY 10583-8583
phone: 914-472-0200

Collectors

Dan Morphy
1555 N. Reading Rd.
Stevens, PA 17578
phone: 717-335-2907
fax: 717-336-0044
Top dollar paid for Disney, Marilyn Monroe, unusual lady head vases.

Dealers

Diane Leach
201 Filors La.
Stony Point, NY 10980-2641
phone: 914-942-2074
fax: 914-942-2320
e-mail: cupplate@aol.com
Wants to buy Betty Lou Nichols head vases, figurines and planters; also any head vases 7" or larger; call collect.

Millie Miller
1027 Emory Lane
Indianapolis, IN 46241
phone: 317-241-4123
Buys, sells, or trades head vases.

Lois & Ralph Behm
Lois' Collectibles of Antique Market III
413 W. Main St.
Saint Charles, IL 60174-1815
phone: 630-377-5599 or 847-831-5997
Buys and sells lady head vases; will buy entire collections.

Jennifer Sykes
Jennifer Sykes Antiques
9018 Balboa Blvd. #595
Northridge, CA 91325-2610
phone: 818-993-1916
fax: 818-993-7612
e-mail: Veeda10@aol.com
Buys, sells Lady Head vases, especially those over 7" tall; also buying Head Vases by Betty Lou Nichols.

Peggy Cole
134 E. Laveta
Orange, CA 92666-1908
phone: 714-997-7379
Wants to buy ladies head vases, especially Jackie Kennedy, Carmen Miranda, and any Ceramic Arts Studio ladies head vases.

Experts

Mike Posgay
P.O. Box 93022
Brampton
Ontario LGY 4V8 Canada
phone: 905-453-9074
Specializes in head-vase planters; co-author with Ian Warner of "Head Vases Identification and Values."

Ironstone (Mason's)

Clubs/Associations

Susan Hirshman
Mason's Ironstone Collectors' Club
Newsletter: MICC Newsletter
542 Seskeyon Blvd.
Medford, OR 97504-7628

Ironstone (Tea Leaf)

Clubs/Associations

Eleanor Washburn, Mem.
Tea Leaf Club International
Newsletter: Tea Leaf Readings
324 Powderhorn Dr.
Houghton Lake, MI 48629
phone: 517-366-4709
Purpose is to inform membership about Tea Leaf Ironstone and its copper lustre variants.

Collectors

Dick Brackin
15565 Willow Creek Rd.
Athens, OH 45701
Purpose is to inform membership about Tea Leaf Ironstone and its copper lustre variants.

Chris Weinbrenner
2216 B Avenue NE
Cedar Rapids, IA 52402

Experts

Julie Rich
411 Kinross Dr.
Newark, DE 19711-1535
phone: 302-456-5769
fax: 302-454-8538
e-mail: RRich411@aol.com
Buys, sells, collects and specializes in Tea Leaf & White Ironstone; writes and lectures on American ironstone, especially Tea Leaf.

Dale Abrams
960 Bryden Rd.
Columbus, OH 43205-1809
phone: 614-258-5258
fax: 614-258-6663
e-mail: 70003.2061@compuserve.com
Internet: http://
ourworld.compuserve.com/
homepages/da
Buys and sells quality Tea Leaf and Teaberry ironstone china and other white ironstone decorated with copper lustre motifs.

William Durham
Hospice House Antiques
9633 Beaver Valley Rd.
Belvidere, IL 61008
phone: 815-547-5128

Ironstone (White)

Clubs/Associations

Jim & Mara Kerr
White Ironstone China Association, Inc.
Newsletter: White Ironstone Notes
RD 1 Box 23
Howes Cave, NY 12092-9703
phone: 518-296-8052

Collectors

Ernie & Bev Dieringer
Dieringer's Antiques
P.O. Box 536
Redding Ridge, CT 06876
fax: 203-938-8378
e-mail: dieringer@aol.com
*Editors of "White Ironstone Notes,"
newsletter for The White Ironstone
China Association, Inc.; send e-mail
for membership information; ask
about the web site under construction.*

Experts

Jean Wetherbee
P.O. Box 856
Hillsborough, NH 03244
phone: 603-464-5462 or 603-464-6747
*Author of "A Look at White
Ironstone."*

Julie Rich
411 Kinross Dr.
Newark, DE 19711-1535
phone: 302-456-5769
fax: 302-454-8538
e-mail: RRich411@aol.com
*Buys, sells, collects and specializes in
Tea Leaf & White Ironstone; writes
and lectures on American ironstone,
especially Tea Leaf.*

Dale Abrams
960 Bryden Rd.
Columbus, OH 43205-1809
phone: 614-258-5258
fax: 614-258-6663
e-mail: 70003.2061@compuserve.com
Internet: http://
ourworld.compuserve.com/
homepages/da
*Buys and sells quality Tea Leaf and
white ironstone china.*

William Durham
Hospice House Antiques
9633 Beaver Valley Rd.
Belvidere, IL 61008
phone: 815-547-5128

Jugs (Face)

Dealers

Singleton Bailey
4125 Main St.
P.O. Box 95
Loris, SC 29569-0095
phone: 803-756-7495 or 803-756-4021
fax: 803-756-9124
e-mail: dsbailey@sccoast.net
Specializes in Southern Folk pottery.

Jugs (Molded)

Experts

Kathy Hughes
Tudor House Galleries
1401 East Blvd.
Charlotte, NC 28203-5817
phone: 704-377-4748 or 704-332-4782
e-mail: 75027.474@compuserve.com
*Specializes in 19th century relief-
molded jugs (pitchers); author of "A*

*Collector's Guide to 19th Century
Jugs" Vol. I and Vol. II.*

Lefton

Clubs/Associations

Loretta DeLozier
National Society of Lefton Collectors
Newsletter: Lefton Collector
1101 Polk St.
Bedford, IA 50833-9107
phone: 712-523-2289
e-mail: leftonlady@aol.com
*Members are interested in dinnerware
and figurines made by Lefton.*

Collectors

Loretta DeLozier
1101 Polk St.
Bedford, IA 50833-9107
phone: 712-523-2289
e-mail: leftonlady@aol.com
*Wants to buy Lefton porcelain
dinnerware and figurines.*

Majolica

Auction Services

Louis Webre, Client Svc.
William Doyle Galleries
175 E. 87th St.
New York, NY 10128-2205
phone: 212-427-2730
fax: 212-369-0892
Internet: http://www.doylegalleries.com
*Holds over 30 auctions annually of
antique English, Continental and
American furniture, paintings,
decorations, jewelry, vintage and
couture clothing, collectible toys,
books and prints; specialty auctions of
Majolica, Lalique and wine.*

Michael G. Strawser
Strawers Auctions
P.O. Box 332
Wolcottville, IN 46795-0332
phone: 219-854-2859 or 219-854-2235
fax: 219-854-3979
*Specializing in Majolica auctions in
the U.S.*

Clubs/Associations

Majolica International Society
Newsletter: Majolica International
Society Newsletter
1275 First Ave., Ste. 103
New York, NY 10021-5601
fax: 212-744-1124
*Conventions held in April/May each
year with international speakers and
show/sale; members are collectors,
dealers, experts.*

Collectors

Michael G. Strawser
P.O. Box 332
Wolcottville, IN 46795-0332
phone: 219-854-2859 or 219-854-2235
fax: 219-854-3979

Dealers

Hardy Hudson
Our Antiques Market
5453 Lake Howell Rd.
Winter Park, FL 32792-1033
phone: 407-657-2100 or 407-788-3908
*Buys and sells and specializes in
majolica by Minton, George Jones,
Hold Croft, Wedgwood, Fielding,
Copeland, Etruscan, James Carr;
majolica oyster plates.*

Majolica Wares, Inc.
2314 Guthrie Ave., N.W.
Cleveland, TN 37311
phone: 615-339-3975
*Collects originals in order to make
reproductions; buys and sells antique
Victorian majolica upon availability
and request.*

Experts

Nicholas Dawes
67 East 11th St.
New York, NY 10003
phone: 212-473-5111
fax: 212-353-3845
*Buys, sells and specializes in
Victorian majolica; author of
"Majolica" (Crown Publishers,
1989).*

Linda Ketterling
Linda Ketterling Antiques
Toledo, OH 43606-1207
phone: 419-536-5531
*Buys and sells English and American
majolica, good condition; unusual
pieces particularly desired.*

Brenda Wilson
2720 N. 45th Road
Manton, MI 49663
phone: 616-824-3043
fax: 616-824-9357
*.Will answer collectors questions to
help identify majolica; please include
SASE for reply.*

Repro. Sources

Majolica Wares, Inc.
2314 Guthrie Ave., N.W.
Cleveland, TN 37311
phone: 615-339-3975
*Produces high-quality American-made
majolica reproductions.*

Mexican

Experts

Crystal Payton
3020 S. National, #340
Springfield, MO 65804-4247
phone: 417-886-7124
fax: 417-889-3345
*Buys, sells and specializes in Mexican
tourist pottery made from 1920 to
1960; writes articles.*

Military Related

Collectors

Rex Stark
P.O. Box 1029
Gardner, MA 01440
phone: 508-630-3237
*Wants to buy china with American
political and military portraits or
scenes; Liverpool, lustreware, parian
ware, Staffordshire, etc.*

Mochaware

Experts

Gregg Ellington
Upper Loft Antiques
47 Columbus St.
Wilmington, OH 45177
phone: 513-382-4311
*Buys, sells, trades and collects
graniteware and American ceramics
including mochaware, yellowware,
spongeware, etc.*

Picasso Editions

Appraisers

Stephen van Cline, CAPP
van Cline & Davenport, Ltd.
792 Franklin Ave.
Franklin Lakes, NJ 07417-1343
*Minimum charge $25; letter request
only, SASE.*

Collectors

Albert Merola
Universal Fine Objects, Inc.
26 Bayberry Ave.
Provincetown, MA 02657-1212
phone: 508-487-4424
fax: 508-487-4743
*Fine art dealer in prints, paintings,
and ceramic; primary interest is
Picasso ceramic editions.*

Political Related

Collectors

Rex Stark
P.O. Box 1029
Gardner, MA 01440
phone: 508-630-3237
*Wants to buy china with American
political and military portraits or
scenes; Liverpool, lustreware, parian
ware, Staffordshire, etc.*

Redware

Dealers

Richard Hume
American Stoneware Collectors
P.O. Box 281
Bay Head, NJ 08742
phone: 732-899-8707 or 732-295-9285
*Collects, appraises, buys, sells,
auctions American decorated
stoneware: jugs, crocks, etc.; also
Southern pottery, American redware,
folk pots, etc.; conducts auctions twice
a year.*

Carl McCann
Troy & Black, Inc.
P.O. Box 228
Red Creek, NY 13143-0228
phone: 315-754-8115
*Buys and sells high quality flow blue,
Staffordshire figurines, American
painted furniture, stoneware, redware,
coverlets, samplers, and other
American textiles, folk art, etc.*

Repro. Sources

Stephen Nutt
Steve Nutt, Potter
25 Ellicott Place
Staten Island, NY 10301
phone: 718-273-6815
e-mail: yankeered@aol.com
*Reproductions of 19th century Mid-
Atlantic and New England redware
plates; also designs and make
seasonal, holiday and thematic plates;
send $2 for catalog and sample
newsletter.*

Carolyn Nygren Curran
CNC Pottery
8 Pershing Rd.
Glen Falls, NY 12804

James Nyeste
RD #3
Seven Valleys, PA 17360
phone: 717-428-3314
*Makes figural redware sculptures:
animals and figures in the Pennsylvania and Shenandoah Valley traditions.*

C. Ned Foltz
Foltz Pottery
225 N. Peartown Rd.
Reinholds, PA 17569

Lester Breininger
Breininger Pottery
476 S. Church St.
Robesonia, PA 19551
phone: 610-693-5344

Souvenir & Commemorative

(see also SOUVENIR & COMMEMO-
RATIVE ITEMS)

Collectors

Gary Leveille
P.O. Box 562
Great Barrington, MA 01230-0562
phone: 413-528-5490

David Sloane
4 Edgehill Terrace
Hamden, CT 06517
phone: 203-624-4206

Dealers

Tom & Barbara Tripp
P.O. Box 366
Peterborough, NH 03458
phone: 603-924-6106
e-mail: tripptom@aol.com
*Wants to buy antique souvenir china
from New England towns.*

Periodicals

Gary Leveille
Newsletter: Antique Souvenir Collector
P.O. Box 562
Great Barrington, MA 01230-0562
phone: 413-528-5490
*The nationwide marketplace for
antique souvenirs of all kinds:
souvenir china, spoons, photos, glass,
postcards - anything souvenir.*

Spongeware

Experts

Gregg Ellington
Upper Loft Antiques
47 Columbus St.
Wilmington, OH 45177
phone: 513-382-4311
*Buys, sells, trades and collects
graniteware and American ceramics
including mochaware, yellowware,
spongeware, etc.*

Repro. Sources

Carolyn Nygren Curran
CNC Pottery
8 Pershing Rd.
Glen Falls, NY 12804

Studio Pottery

Experts

Jim Messineo
JMW Gallery
144 Lincoln St.
Boston, MA 02111-2523
phone: 617-338-9097
fax: 617-338-7636
*Buys, sells and specializes along with
co-owner Mike Witt in the Arts &
Crafts movement, Mission furniture,
Lifetime, Limbert, Stickley; also
American Art Pottery from 1875 to
1950s: Grueby, Newcomb,
Marblehead, etc.*

Terra Cotta

Clubs/Associations

Susan Tunick
Friends of Terra Cotta
771 West End Avemue, #10E
New York, NY 10025
Internet: http://www.preserve.org/fotc/
*Formed to promote and educate and
research architectural terra cotta and
related ceramic materials.*

Texas

Collectors

James E. Kattner
P.O. Box 11132
Spring, TX 77391
phone: 281-986-6916 or 281-376-4826
*Wants to buy Texas whiskey jugs
which display the merchant's name
and town; some may display saloon
name and town; especially want Texas
jugs, but will pay equally well for same*

*from other Southern and Western
states.*

Russell Barnes
P.O. Box 141994
Austin, TX 78714-1994
phone: 512-835-9510
fax: 512-835-1276
*Wants to buy Texas pottery, jugs,
crocks, and related items.*

Wedgwood

Experts

Leslie V. Canavan
Alexis Antiques
22 Cloverleaf Lane
Ballwin, MO 63011-4001
phone: 314-391-1603
fax: 800-769-5109
e-mail: antiques@iwc.com
Internet: http://www.iwc.com/antiques
*Appraiser, dealer, collector
specializing in Wedgwood products of
all types and eras; china matching,
giftware; college, commemorative &
historical plates; appraisals.*

Willow Pattern

Clubs/Associations

Jeff Siptak
Willow Society of Tennessee
Newsletter: Willow Bridge, The
P.O. Box 41312
Nashville, TN 37204
phone: 615-383-7855
fax: 615-269-7123
e-mail: WillowWare@aol.com
*For collectors interested in Willow
pattern china and collectibles; open to
all; bi-monthly newsletter covers
meeting news, recent finds, current
prices, and other related stories.*

Marge LaLonde
Ohio Willow Society
4820 Center Rd., Rte 83
Avon, OH 44011

International Willow Collectors
P.O. Box 13382
Arlington, TX 76094-0382
*Members interested in collecting and
studying of ceramics and other
materials decorated with the willow
pattern.*

Mary Lina Berndt
Willow Society of North Texas
P.O. Box 13382
Arlington, TX 76094-0382

Collectors

Nancy Blaney
933 12th Ave., Apt. 107
Huntington, WV 25701-3450

Sandra Leonard
Rt. 2
Boaz, KY 42027
phone: 502-856-3442

Al Little
151 Highway 173
Antioch, IL 60002
phone: 847-395-7752
fax: 847-395-7703
*Buy, sells and trades Blue Willow
china.*

Dealers

Louise M. Loehr
Louise's Old Things
163 W. Main St.
P.O. Box 208
Kutztown, PA 19530-0208
phone: 610-683-8370
*Co-author of "Willow Pattern China."
Specializing in willow, flow blue, and
early children's china. Wants one
piece or collections.*

Experts

Connie Rogers
1733 Chase St.
Cincinnati, OH 45223-2057
phone: 513-541-2013
e-mail: Con1733@aol.com
*Editor of "American Willow Report"
7/87 through 5/90; consultant to "The
Official Price Guide to Pottery and
Porcelain"; author of "Willow Ware
Made in the USA," (1996), available
from author.*

Periodicals

Mary Lina Berndt, Pub.
Newsletter: Willow Word, The
P.O. Box 13382
Arlington, TX 76094-0382
*A newsletter addressing all aspects of
"Blue Willow", the world's most
popular china pattern; its 200 year
history, the "Willow Legend", current
sources for both old and new
willowware; a forum for questions,
gossip, convention news.*

Yellowware

Collectors

Bill Carroll
RR 1, Box 62
Hope, ND 58046-9760
phone: 701-945-2416
fax: 701-945-2772
e-mail: BillND299@aol.com
Internet: http://
www.collectoronline.com/booth-
74.html
Wants to buy yellowware!

Experts

Gregg Ellington
Upper Loft Antiques
47 Columbus St.
Wilmington, OH 45177
phone: 513-382-4311
*Buys, sells, trades and collects
graniteware and American ceramics
including mochaware, yellowware,
spongeware, etc.*

CERAMICS (AMERICAN)

Clubs/Associations

Wisconsin Pottery Association
P.O. Box 1171
Madison, WI 53701

Dealers

Naomi's
1817 Polk St.
San Francisco, CA 94109
phone: 415-775-1207
Buys/sells American dinnerware: Hall, Bauer, Tepco, Wallace, Coors, Autumn Leaf, Russel Wright, American Modern, Iroquois, etc.

Experts

Harvey Duke
577 Avenue Y
Brooklyn, NY 11235
Author of "Price Guide to Pottery and Porcelain"; covering 90 collectible American potteries with 22,000 items priced; $21.95 ppd.; specializes in Ohio and West Virginia dinnerware made from the 1890s to 1950s.

Lorrie Kitchen
3905 Torrance Dr.
Toledo, OH 43612
phone: 419-478-3815
Specializing in American dinnerware such as Hall China, Fiesta, Blue Ridge and Shawnee.

Dan Tucker
3905 Torrance Dr.
Toledo, OH 43612
phone: 419-478-3815
Specializing in Hall china, Fiesta, Blue Ridge, Shawnee.

Susan & Al Bagdade
Country Peasants, The
3136 Elder Ct.
Northbrook, IL 60062-5832
phone: 847-498-1468
fax: 847-392-5848
e-mail: ADBSDB@aol.com
Author of "Warman's American Pottery & Porcelain" (Wallace-Homestead).

Museums/Libraries

Everson Museum of Art of Syracuse & Onondaga County
401 Harrison St.
Syracuse, NY 13202
phone: 315-474-6064

Mark Twyford
Museum of Ceramics at East Liverpool
400 E. 5th St.
East Liverpool, OH 43920-3134
phone: 216-386-6001
Detailed exhibit of the local ceramic industry; "The East Liverpool, Ohio Pottery District: Identification of Manufacturers & Marks" by Wm. Gates, Jr. and Dana Ormerod can be obtained by contacting the museum.

Scio Pottery Museum
38250 Crimm Rd.
P.O. Box 565
Scio, OH 43988
phone: 614-945-3111

Periodicals

Teri Steele, Ed.
Depression Glass Daze, Inc.
Newspaper: Daze, The
275 State Rd.
P.O. Box 57
Otisville, MI 48463-0057
phone: 810-631-4593
fax: 810-631-4567
A monthly newspaper catering to the dealers and collectors of glass, china and pottery from the 1920s and 1930s.

Art Deco

Museums/Libraries

Victoria F. Peltz
Cowan Pottery Museum at the Rocky River Public Library
1600 Hampton Rd.
Rocky River, OH 44116-2699
phone: 216-333-7610
Features a collection of over 700 pieces by the artists of the Cowan Pottery Studio of Lakewood and Rocky River, Ohio, 1912-1932.

Cranbrook Academy of Art Museum
P.O. Box 801
Bloomfield Hills, MI 48013
phone: 810-645-3323

Bennington

(see also CERAMICS [AMERICAN], Stoneware)

Experts

Gregg Ellington
Upper Loft Antiques
47 Columbus St.
Wilmington, OH 45177
phone: 513-382-4311
Buys, sells, trades and collects graniteware and American ceramics including mochaware, yellowware, spongeware, etc.

Museums/Libraries

Deborah Federhen, Cur.
Bennington Museum, The
W. Main St.
Bennington, VT 05201
phone: 802-447-1571
fax: 802-442-8305
Internet: http://www.benington.com/museum
One of the finest regional art history museums in the country; works by Grandma Moses, American glass, VT furniture, Bennington pottery, the oldest Stars & Stripes in existence, the 1925 luxury touring car "The Wasp", and much more.

George Ohr

Experts

Dr. Eugene Hecht
Adelphi University Physics Department
Adelphi University
Garden City, NY 11530
e-mail: genehecht@aol.com
Is available by mail to help authenticate George Ohr pottery; send SASE with inquiry; this is not an appraisal service.

Marty Shack
P.O. Box 25
Bellmore, NY 11710-0025
Is available by mail to help authenticate George Ohr pottery; send SASE with inquiry; this is not an appraisal service.

Illinois

Clubs/Associations

Eva Mounce
Foundation for Historical Research of Illinois Potteries
2108 Church St.
Streator, IL 61364-3831
phone: 815-672-2827
Purpose of the Foundation is to research and document the history of the Illinois pottery industry, c. 1830-1930.

David A. McGuire
Collectors of Illinois Pottery & Stoneware
Newsletter: Collectors of Ill. Pottery & Stoneware Newsletter
1527 East Converse St.
Springfield, IL 62702
phone: 217-544-9048 or 217-523-0592
An organization for persons interested .in collecting Illinois pottery; quarterly newsletter features photos and information.

Collectors

David A. McGuire
1527 East Converse St.
Springfield, IL 62702
phone: 217-544-9048 or 217-523-0592
Paying top dollar for early salt glaze or unusual Illinois pottery.

Lewistown Pottery

Collectors

Scott Armstrong
RD 4 Box 115
Lewistown, PA 17044-9364
phone: 717-248-5285
Wants pieces marked Lewistown Pottery.

Limoges

Experts

Mrs. Raymonde Limoges
Raymonde Limoges
P.O. Box 73263
Puyallup, WA 98373-0263
phone: 253-845-3889
fax: 253-845-3889
e-mail: r.limoges@worldnet.att.net
Specializes in American Limoges china made in Sebring Ohio (1900-1955); mostly dinnerware; author of "American Limoges - A Collector's Guide."

Pennsylvania German

Museums/Libraries

James McMahon
Hershey Museum
170 W. Hersheypark Dr.
Hershey, PA 17033
phone: 717-534-3439
fax: 717-534-8940
Focused collection of objects detailing the town of Hershey, its community, Founder, and the various industries which bear his name; regional PA German heritage, and native American material culture.

Russel Wright Designs

(see also RUSSEL WRIGHT)

Dealers

Robert & Nancy Perzel
Popkorn Antiques
4 Mine St.
P.O. Box 1057
Flemington, NJ 08822-1057
phone: 908-782-9631

Experts

Ann M. Kerr
P.O. Box 437
Sidney, OH 45365
phone: 513-492-6369
fax: 513-492-6369
Wants Russel Wright dinnerware, stainless, chrome; Bauer art ware, etc.; author of "Collector's Encyclopedia of Russell Wright Designs", updated with 1993 prices; $21.95 ppd. from author.

Southern Folk Pottery

Auction Services

Billy Ray & Susan Hussey
Southern Folk Pottery Collectors Society
Newsletter: SFPCS Newsletter
1828 N. Howard Mill Rd.
Robbins, NC 27325-7477
phone: 910-464-3961
fax: 910-464-2530
Formed for the purpose of educating and continuing the role of the self-taught Southern folk potter of the 18th and 19th centuries and today; holds two absentee auctions per year.

Steve Slotin
Slotin Folk Art Auction House
Newspaper: 20th Century Folk Art News
5967 Blackberry Lane
Buford, GA 30518
phone: 770-932-1000
fax: 770-932-0506
Internet: http://www.selftaught.com
Leading venue for self-taught, Outsider, Folk Art and Southern folk pottery; published newspaper twice each year chronicling important happenings in the field of 20th century folk art as the most popular feature, New, True & Blue Artists.

Clubs/Associations

Billy Ray & Susan Hussey
Southern Folk Pottery Collectors Society
Newsletter: SFPCS Newsletter
1828 N. Howard Mill Rd.
Robbins, NC 27325-7477
phone: 910-464-3961
fax: 910-464-2530
Formed for the purpose of educating and continuing the role of the self-taught Southern folk potter of the 18th and 19th centuries and today; holds two absentee auctions per year.

Experts

Roy Thompson
19 Hubbard Run
Glastonbury, CT 06033-2323
phone: 203-633-3121
Author of "Face Jugs, Chickens and Other Whimseys."

Museums/Libraries

Billy Ray & Susan Hussey
Southern Folk Pottery Collectors Society
 Shop/Museum
Newsletter: SFPCS Newsletter
1828 N. Howard Mill Rd.
Robbins, NC 27325-7477
phone: 910-464-3961
fax: 910-464-2530
Formed for the purpose of educating and continuing the role of the self-taught Southern folk potter of the 18th and 19th centuries and today; holds two absentee auctions per year.

Stoneware

Auction Services

Marlin G. Denlinger
P.O. Box 975
Morrisville, VT 05661-0975
phone: 802-888-2774

Richard Hume
American Stoneware Collectors
P.O. Box 281
Bay Head, NJ 08742
phone: 732-899-8707 or 732-295-9285
Collects, appraises, buys, sells, auctions American decorated stoneware: jugs, crocks, etc.; also Southern pottery, American redware, folk pots, etc.; conducts auctions twice a year in April and October.

Vicki & Bruce Waasdorp
Antiques & Americana
Newsletter: Stoneware
10931 Main St.
P.O. Box 434
Clarence, NY 14031
phone: 716-759-2361
fax: 716-759-2397
Provides a mail and phone bid auction service for both collectors and dealers of Decorated American Stoneware; also appraisals, category history, and pertinent information on request; newsletter has post-sale auction prices.

Wayne Arthur
Arthur Auctioneering
RD 2 Box 155
Hughesville, PA 17737
phone: 717-584-3697
Conducts specialized sales of decorated stoneware.

Clubs/Associations

American Stoneware Collectors Society
Newsletter: ASCC Newsletter
P.O. Box 281
Bay Head, NJ 08742
phone: 732-899-8707 or 732-295-9285
A growing society of stoneware collectors; call or write for more information.

Mike Pell
American Stoneware Association
208 Cresent Ct.
Mars, PA 16066-3308

Collectors

Alex Caiola
84 Seneca
Emerson, NJ 07630-1243
phone: 201-967-9540
Wants marked stoneware jugs, crocks, bottles.

Ivy & Geoff Bean
8200 Mountain Laurel Ln.
Gaithersburg, MD 20879-1558
phone: 301-963-7469
Wants blue decorated American stoneware: crocks, jugs, jars, etc.; specific interest is in Western Pennsylvania region; buys, sells, trades all regions and areas.

Ed McDermott
1415 McKendree
Kevil, KY 42053
phone: 502-488-3420
Wants stencil or scratch advertising stoneware from pre-1920 grocery and whiskey firms; especially wants whiskey jugs from small towns located in Southern and Western states.

Don Johnson
5110 S. Greensboro Pike
Knightstown, IN 46148-9596
phone: 317-345-5758
e-mail: djohnson@comsys.net
Buys, sells and collects all types of Indiana stoneware and pottery.

Steve Ketcham
P.O. Box 24114
Minneapolis, MN 55424-0114
phone: 612-920-4205
Primarily interested in crocks, jugs, etc. which carry name of product or advertising such as liquor dealers, medicines, etc.; especially wants Red Wing stoneware; please send SASE with all inquiries.

James E. Kattner
P.O. Box 11132
Spring, TX 77391
phone: 281-986-6916 or 281-376-4826
Wants to buy Texas whiskey jugs which display the merchant's name and town; some may display saloon name and town; especially want Texas just, but will pay equally well for same from other Southern and Western states.

Bruce & Nada Ferris
3094 Oakes Dr.
Hayward, CA 94542-1234
phone: 510-581-5285
fax: 510-581-4469
e-mail: nada.ferris@kaiperm.org
Wants mini advertising jugs, advertising 7" spongeband pitcher, advertising spongeware bowls, dometop stoneware jars; Ferris jugs from NY; any dated or holiday mini advertising jugs.

Scott Grandstaff
P.O. Box 409
Happy Camp, CA 96039
phone: 916-493-2032

Dealers

Richard Hume
American Stoneware Collectors
P.O. Box 281
Bay Head, NJ 08742
phone: 732-899-8707 or 732-295-9285
Collects, appraises, buys, sells, auctions American decorated stoneware: jugs, crocks, etc.; also Southern pottery, American redware, folk pots, etc.; conducts auctions twice a year.

Greg Walsh
32 River View Lane
P.O. Box 747
Potsdam, NY 13676
phone: 315-265-9111 or 800-371-9286
fax: 315-265-9222
Stoneware dealer since 1979 wants to buy blue decorated stoneware of exceptional quality; also appraises.

Anthony & Barb Zipp
Anthony & Barbara Zipp Antiques
P.O. Box 725
Riderwood, MD 21139-0725
phone: 410-337-5090
Buys and sells quality, 19th century, blue decorated stoneware.

Barry Friedman
P.O. Box 55492
Valencia, CA 91385-0492
phone: 805-255-2365
e-mail: BaryF@fishnet.net
Seeking stoneware bottles with maker's names; no unmarked bottles; also American only, please.

Experts

Vicki & Bruce Waasdorp
Antiques & Americana
10931 Main St.
P.O. Box 434
Clarence, NY 14031
phone: 716-759-2361
fax: 716-759-2397
Provides a mail and phone bid auction service for both collectors and dealers of Decorated American Stoneware; also buys, sells, appraisals, category history, and pertinent information on request.

Museums/Libraries

Mark Twyford
Museum of Ceramics at East Liverpool
400 E. 5th St.
East Liverpool, OH 43920-3134
phone: 216-386-6001
Detailed exhibit of the local ceramic industry; "The East Liverpool, Ohio Pottery District: Identification of Manufacturers & Marks" by Wm. Gates, Jr. and Dana Ormerod can be obtained by contacting the museum.

Repro. Sources

Salmon Falls Stoneware
P.O. Box 452
Dover, NH 03820-0452

Eldreth Pottery
4351 Forge Rd.
Nottingham, PA 19362

Georgia Folk Pottery
2579 W. Fontainebleau Ct.
Doraville, GA 30360

Three Rivers Pottery Productions
P.O. Box 462
Coshocton, OH 43812

Bastine Pottery
RR 3 Box 111
Noblesville, IN 46060

Rowe Pottery Works
404 England St.
Cambridge, WI 53523
phone: 608-764-5435 or 800-356-5003
fax: 608-423-4273
Produces authentic reproductions of 19th century salt-glaze stoneware plates, figurines, miniatures and steins; also wrought iron.

Stoneware (Red Wing Pottery)

Clubs/Associations

Doug Podpeskar
Red Wing Collectors Society, Inc.
<u>Newsletter: Red Wing Collectors
Newsletter</u>
624 Jones St.
Eveleth, MN 55734-1631
phone: 218-744-4854

Collectors

Peter M. Naysmith
Mounted Rte. Box 444
Two Harbors, MN 55616
phone: 218-834-4770
*Collector of Red Wing stoneware
always looking for advertising pieces
including moonshine jugs; will pay up
to $50 for stoneware (jugs preferred)
with advertising on the side and the
name of the pottery on the bottom.*

Ken & Dee Dee Gorgan
P.O. Box 184
Galesburg, IL 61402-0184
phone: 414-625-3090

Charles Casad
801 Tyler Ct.
Monticello, IL 61856-2246
phone: 217-762-2303
*Wants Red Wing crocks, beehive jugs,
shoulder jugs, water coolers,
commemorative pieces, Red Wing
advertising pieces and any other
unusual Red Wing pieces; mint or
near-mint only, please.*

CERAMICS (AMERICAN ART POTTERY)

Appraisers

Tony McCormak
McCormack & Company
P.O. Box 49093
Atlanta, GA 30320
phone: 941-952-1244
*Collector, dealer, expert, appraiser
specializing in American art pottery;
always buying Rookwood, Grueby,
Newcomb College, Teco, Marblehead,
Overbeck; dated Van Briggle, George
Ohr, Weller & Roseville pottery;
member ISA.*

Auction Services

Louise Luther
Skinner, Inc.
357 Main St.
Bolton, MA 01740-1104
phone: 508-779-6241 or 617-350-5400
fax: 508-779-5144
*Established in 1964, Skinner Inc. is
the fifth largest auction house in the
US; has offices in Bolton and Boston,
MA.*

Mike Clum
Mike Clum, Inc.
P.O. Box 2
Rushville, OH 43150
phone: 614-536-9220
*Conducts periodic auctions
specializing in American art pottery.*

Riley Humler
Cincinnati Art Galleries
635 Main St.
Cincinnati, OH 45202
phone: 513-381-2128
fax: 513-381-7527
*Conducts specialty auctions of
American art pottery including
Rookwood, Van Briggle, Newcomb,
Grueby, etc.*

Don Treadway
Treadway Auctions
2029 Madison Rd.
Cincinnati, OH 45208
phone: 513-321-6742 or 800-526-0491
fax: 513-871-7722
Internet: http://
www.treadwaygallery.com
*Specializes in the sale of Arts and
Crafts pottery.*

Jon Crisman, ISA
Jackson's Auctioneers & Appraisers
2229 Lincoln St.
Cedar Falls, IA 50613
phone: 319-277-2256
fax: 319-277-1252
e-mail: jacksons@jacksonsauction.com
Internet: http://
www.jacksonsauction.com
*Conducts specialty auctions of art
pottery including Rookwood, Van
Briggle, Roseville, Weller, Grueby,
Teco, etc.*

Clubs/Associations

Pat Sallaz
Pottery Lovers Reunion
<u>Newsletter: Pottery Lovers Newsletter</u>
4969 Hudson Dr.
Stow, OH 44224
*Publishes a quarterly newsletter
describing activities and plans for the
upcoming Pottery Lovers Reunion and
show.*

Gordon Hoppe
Minnesota Art Pottery Association
10120 32nd Ave.
Minneapolis, MN 55441

Jean Oberkirsch, Sec.
American Art Pottery Association
<u>Magazine: Journal of the AAPA</u>
P.O. Box 525
Cedar Hill, MO 63016

Jack Kilgore
Southwest Art Pottery Association
345 Main St.
Rosebud, TX 76570

Collectors

Bruce E. Thulin
P.O. Box 121
Ellsworth, ME 04605
phone: 207-667-5225
e-mail: thulin@acadia.net
*Wants to buy pottery signed Grand
Feu Pottery, Flame, Losanti, Pauleo,
etc.*

Bob Hut
P.O. Box 1495
New York, NY 10163
phone: 800-321-7687
*Wants to buy dated Van Briggle,
artist-signed Rookwood, decorated
Marblehead and Grueby; also any and
all unusual pre-1930 high quality
American and French Art Nouveau
and Art Deco pottery (no Roseville,
Fulper, Hull, McCoy).*

Richard L. Sasicki
P.O. Box 3113
Glen Ellyn, IL 60138-3113
phone: 708-627-2630
e-mail: artwave@sprynet.com
*Wants to buy Van Briggle, Pine Ridge,
Broadmoor, Coors Pottery, Teco,
Grueby, Fulper, Newcomb, Arts &
Crafts style and other American Art
pottery; author of "The Collector's
Encyclopedia of Van Briggle Art
Pottery."*

Dealers

John Keaveny
222 Fitchburg Rd.
Ashburnham, MA 01430
phone: 508-827-6809
*Wants to buy Roseville, Weller,
Rookwood, and other art potteries.*

Jim Messineo
JMW Gallery
144 Lincoln St.
Boston, MA 02111-2523
phone: 617-338-9097
fax: 617-338-7636

Patti's Past Perfect Pottery
P.O. Box 1226
Westport, MA 02790
phone: 508-679-5910

Marvin McKee
65 Chase Rd.
Bangor, ME 04401-2633
phone: 207-945-3450
e-mail: mmckee@agate.net
*Buys and sells American art pottery,
especially Roseville.*

Edward E. Stump
6 High St.
Mullica Hill, NJ 08062-9540
phone: 609-478-4488
*Wants Roseville and Weller art
pottery.*

David Rago
David Rago Arts & Crafts
17 Main St.
Lambertville, NJ 08530
phone: 609-397-9374
fax: 609-397-9377
e-mail: rago@ragoarts.com
Internet: http://www.ragoarts.com
*Wants American art pottery, and Arts
and Crafts items such as furniture and
metal items by Stickley, Rohlfs,
Wright, Roycroft, etc.*

Bob Berman
441 S. Jackson St.
Media, PA 19063-3715
phone: 610-566-1516
*Wants to buy American art pottery by
Teco, Rookwood, George Ohr, Van
Briggle, Cowan, Newcomb College,
Fulper, Grueby, etc.*

Martin Kramer
313 Arch St., Ste. 203
Philadelphia, PA 19106-1810
phone: 215-592-0103
fax: 215-592-0103
*Wants to buy American art pottery:
Rookwood, Fulper, Roseville, Weller,
Cowan, UND, Van Briggle, SEG,
Pewabic, Niloak, Marblehead,
Hampshire, Grueby, Newcomb Art
Pottery; also anything by The
Cleveland School ceramic artists.*

Gerald Shultz
Antique Gallery, The
8523 Germantown Ave.
Philadelphia, PA 19118-3316
phone: 215-248-1700
fax: 215-247-8411
*Boch, Pilkington, B. Moore, Martin
Bros., Moorecroft, DeMorgan,
Amphora, Wedgwood, Crimson, B.
Leach, Doulton, Rambervillers, T.
Deck, T. Doat, Clarice Cliff, S.
Cooper, Carltonware.*

Caren Fine
11603 Gowrie Ct.
Potomac, MD 20854-3623
phone: 301-299-2116 or 301-299-6886
*Wants art pottery: Rookwood,
Newcomb College, Van Briggle,
Grueby, Teco, Roseville, Marblehead,
SEG, Paul Revere, North Dakota
School, Overbeck, Tiffany, Robineau,
Redlands, Arequipa, Cowan, etc.*

Tony McCormak
McCormack & Company
P.O. Box 49093
Atlanta, GA 30320
phone: 941-952-1244
*Collector, dealer, expert, appraiser
specializing in American art pottery;
always buying Rookwood, Grueby,
Newcomb College, Teco, Marblehead,
Overbeck; dated Van Briggle, George
Ohr, Weller & Roseville pottery;
member ISA.*

Hardy Hudson
Our Antiques Market
5453 Lake Howell Rd.
Winter Park, FL 32792-1033
phone: 407-657-2100 or 407-788-3908
Buys and sells Grueby, Newcomb, Ohr, Weller animals/birds/garden ornaments, Roseville, Teco, Cowan figurals, Overbeck, S.E.G., Marblehead, Fulper, Arequipa, Owens, Clifton, Avon, Niloak Swirl, Kay Finch, Dedham, Rookwood.

Steve Traband
P.O. Box 7064
Saint Petersburg, FL 33734-7064
phone: 813-896-2308
Buys and sells American Art Pottery: Rookwood, Grueby, Newcomb, Teco, Marblehead, Fulper, Dedham, Hampshire, S.E.G.-O.B.K., early Van Briggle, etc.

Tina & Mark Richey
Spotted Horse Collectibles
12141 Couch Mill Rd.
Knoxville, TN 37932-1102
e-mail: shcollect@aol.com
Internet: http://members.aol.com/ shcollect/homepage.html
Collectors and dealers of American Art Pottery including Rookwood, Fulper, Niloak, Missionware, Cowan, Van Briggle, Weller.

Betty Powell
Pottery Place, The
P.O. Box 571
Columbus, OH 43085-0571
fax: 614-885-1962
Buys and sells American art pottery, specializing in Rookwood, Roseville, Arts & Crafts style.

Riley Humler
Cincinnati Art Galleries
635 Main St.
Cincinnati, OH 45202
phone: 513-381-2128
fax: 513-381-7527
Rookwood is their specialty; also want Van Briggle, Newcomb, Grueby, etc.

Don Treadway
2029 Madison Rd.
Cincinnati, OH 45208
phone: 513-321-6742 or 800-526-0491
fax: 513-871-7722
Internet: http:// www.treadwaygallery.com

Connie Zeigler
Durwyn Smedley Antiques
853 Conner St.
Noblesville, IN 46060
phone: 317-776-0161
e-mail: smedley@iquest.net
Internet: http://www.smedley.com/ smedley
Buys, sells and appraises American art pottery.

Sue Morse
Emma's Trunk
1701 Orange Tree Lane
Redlands, CA 92374-2857
phone: 909-798-7865 or 909-864-8445
fax: 909-798-7386
Wants to buy Clemison, Roseville, Weller, Hull, Bauer; marked pieces only; please call, write or fax for specifics on pricing.

Barry & Donna Williams
300 San Antonio Rd.
Santa Barbara, CA 93110-1316
phone: 805-964-4820
Special interest in Walrath, Newcomb, and Rhead pottery.

Bill Warmboe
1003 California Dr.
Burlingame, CA 94010
phone: 415-579-7908
Buys and sells art pottery: Catalina Island, Bauer, Roseville, Batchelder, Rookwood, Arequipa, Van Briggle, Fiesta, Weller, Teco, Rhead, Robertson, McCoy, Newcomb College, California Faience, Peters & Reed, Vernon Kilns.

Experts

Joseph Ferrara
Fer-Duc Inc.
P.O. Box 1303
Newburgh, NY 12550
phone: 914-896-9492
Specializing in American art pottery: Ohr, Rookwood, Zanesville, etc.

Gerard Schultz
Antique Gallery, The
8523 Germantown Ave.
Philadelphia, PA 19118
phone: 215-248-1700
fax: 215-247-8411
Buys, sells, and specializes in Weller, Sicard, Roseville, Fulper, Cowan, Matt Morgan, Rookwood, Grueby, Pillin, California - all American art pottery.

Norman Haas
264 Clizbe Rd.
Quincy, MI 49082-9504
phone: 517-639-8537
Owns and manages the APEC (American Pottery, Earthenware & China) Show and Sale held annually in Springfield, IL in late summer.

Harold Nichols
Nichols Art Pottery
2419 Knapp
Ames, IA 50010
Specializes in American art pottery: Roseville, Weller, McCoy etc.

Museums/Libraries

Everson Museum of Art of Syracuse & Onondaga County
401 Harrison St.
Syracuse, NY 13202
phone: 315-474-6064

Zanesville Art Center
620 Military Rd.
Zanesville, OH 43701
phone: 614-452-0741

Cincinnati Art Museum
Eden Park
Cincinnati, OH 45202
phone: 513-721-5204

Newcomb College Art Gallery
1229 Broadway
New Orleans, LA 70118
phone: 504-865-5327

American Art Clay Co.

Experts

Virginia Heiss
7777 N. Alton Ave.
Indianapolis, IN 46268-7901
phone: 317-875-6797
Specializes in pottery made by the American Art Clay Co., Indianapolis, IN.

Clewell Pottery

Museums/Libraries

Dennis R. Boden, Ex. Dir
Jesse Besser Museum
491 Johnson St.
Alpena, MI 49707
phone: 517-356-2202
fax: 517-356-3133
e-mail: jbmuseum@northland.lib.mi.us
Owns a large and important collection of Clewell Pottery.

Cowan Pottery Co.

Collectors

Laura Walker
3907 North Blvd.
Tampa, FL 33603
phone: 813-229-6332
Wants to buy Cowan Pottery nude female figurals and flower frogs; also wants unusual Cowan pieces, especially those signed by the artist.

Ann M. Kerr
P.O. Box 437
Sidney, OH 45365
phone: 513-492-6369
fax: 513-492-6369
Wants Cowan figural items done by Guy Cowan, Gregory, Schrekengast, Winter, etc.

Experts

Timothy & Jamie Saloff
P.O. Box 339
Edinboro, PA 16412
phone: 814-734-5189
fax: 814-734-7162
e-mail: jlsaloff@erie.net
Authors of "The Collectors Encyclopedia of Cowan Pottery."

Mark Bassett
1235 Fifth
Nevada, IA 50201-1517
phone: 515-382-3103
Author of "Cowan Pottery" (Schiffer, 1996); also interested in studio pottery by R. Guy Cowan and his associates including Arthur Baggs, Paul Bogatay, Thelma Frazier, Edris Echardt, Waylande Gregory, Russell Barnett Aitken, and others.

Museums/Libraries

Cowan Pottery Museum, Rocky River Public Library
1600 Hampton Rd.
Rocky River, OH 44116
phone: 216-333-7610

Victoria F. Peltz
Cowan Pottery Museum at the Rocky River Public Library
Journal: Cowan Pottery Journal
1600 Hampton Rd.
Rocky River, OH 44116-2699
phone: 216-333-7610
Features a collection of over 700 pieces by the artists of the Cowan Pottery Studio of Lakewood and Rocky River, Ohio, 1912-1932.

Dedham Pottery Co.

Clubs/Associations

Jim Kaufman
Dedham Pottery Collectors Society
Newsletter: Dedham Pottery Collectors Society Newsletter
248 Highland St.
Dedham, MA 02026-5833
phone: 800-283-8070 or 617-329-8070
fax: 617-329-9538
Devoted to the history and study of Dedham and Chelsea Keramic Art Works pottery; published by Jim Kaufman, curator for Dedham pottery at the Dedham Historical Society, Dedham, MA; quarterly newsletter.

Collectors

Jane Lee
P.O. Box 134
Monmouth Junction, NJ 08852-0134
phone: 201-429-1531
Wants to buy Dedham dinnerware and service pieces produced in the late 1800s and early 1900s in Massachusetts; "Bunny" items preferred.

Experts

Jim Kaufman
248 Highland St.
Dedham, MA 02026-5833
phone: 800-283-8070 or 617-329-8070
fax: 617-329-9538
Wants to buy Dedham pottery and Chelsea Keramic Art Works pottery and related papers or other historical information; all calls are welcome.

Museums/Libraries

Jim Kaufman
Dedham Historical Society
P.O. Box 215
Dedham, MA 02027-0215
phone: 617-326-1385
fax: 617-326-5762
e-mail: dhs@dedham.com
Internet: http://www.c9.com/dhs.htm
The Society's museum displays the largest public collection of Dedham pottery as well as Chelsea Keramic Art Works pottery.

Repro. Sources

Potting Shed Inc., The
P.O. Box 1287
Concord, MA 10742
phone: 508-369-1382 or 800-722-2487
fax: 508-369-1416
Hand made Dedham reproduction pottery; each piece signed by the artist.

Fulper Pottery Co.

Collectors

Terry Seger
880 Foxcreek Ln.
Cincinnati, OH 45233-1462
Wants to buy Stickley Brothers copper; also large examples of Fulper pottery.

Dealers

Robert & Nancy Perzel
Popkorn Antiques
4 Mine St.
P.O. Box 1057
Flemington, NJ 08822-1057
phone: 908-782-9631

Experts

Douglass White
Classic Interiors & Antiques
2042 N Rio Grande Ave., Ste. E
Orlando, FL 32804-5644
phone: 407-839-0004

Man./Prod./Dist.

Fulper Tile
P.O. Box 373
Morrisville, PA 19067
phone: 215-736-8512
For information on current production.

Gonder Pottery

Clubs/Associations

Jim & Carol Boshears
Gonder Collectors Club
Newsletter: Gonder Collector
917 Hurl Drive
Pittsburgh, PA 15236-3636
phone: 412-655-1380

Collectors

Jim & Carol Boshears
917 Hurl Drive
Pittsburgh, PA 15236-3636
phone: 412-655-1380

Ron Hoopes
P.O. Box 4263
North Myrtle Beach, SC 29597

Experts

Ron Hoppes
P.O. Box 21
Crooksville, OH 43731

John & Marilyn McCormick
6400 Payne St.
Shawnee Mission, KS 66226
Buys and sells; consultant to "The Official Price Guide to Pottery and Porcelain."

Houghton/Dalton

Experts

Jim & Mira Houdeshell
JMJ Antiques
1801 N. Main St.
Findlay, OH 45840-3815
phone: 419-423-2895 or 419-424-4551
fax: 419-424-6974
Author of "Houghton and Dalton Pottery."

Newcomb College

Dealers

David Rago
David Rago Arts & Crafts
17 Main St.
Lambertville, NJ 08530
phone: 609-397-9374
fax: 609-397-9377
e-mail: rago@ragoarts.com
Internet: http://www.ragoarts.com
Wants American art pottery, and Arts and Crafts items such as furniture and metal items by Stickley, Rohlfs, Wright, Roycroft, etc.

Cliff Catania
David Chase Gallery
234 Griffen St.
Phoenixville, PA 19460-4419
Buy and sell Newcomb pottery; special interest in early, high-glaze pieces.

Caren Fine
11603 Gowrie Ct.
Potomac, MD 20854-3623
phone: 301-299-2116 or 301-299-6886
Wants to buy all decorated pieces, vases, plaques, lamps, jardiniers; special interest in large pieces, even if not perfect.

North Dakota

Clubs/Associations

Sandy Short, Mem. Ch.
North Dakota Pottery Collectors Society
Newsletter: North Dakota Pottery Collectors Society Newsletter
P.O. Box 14
Beach, ND 58621-0014
phone: 701-872-3236
Focuses on North Dakota potteries, e.g. Rosemeade (Wahpeton Pottery Co.), WPA, Dakota, UND School of Mines.

Collectors

Bill Carroll
RR 1, Box 62
Hope, ND 58046-9760
phone: 701-945-2416
fax: 701-945-2772
e-mail: BillND299@aol.com
Internet: http://www.collectoronline.com/booth-74.html
Wants to buy North Dakota art pottery: Rosemeade, ND School of Mines, Dickota, 3 Tribes; please send info and asking price.

Owens Pottery Co.

Experts

Frank L. Hahn
P.O. Box 934
Lima, OH 45802-0934
phone: 419-225-3816 or 419-222-3816
fax: 419-227-3816
Expert and avid collector of J.B. Owens Pottery of Zanesville, OH; also buys, sells and appraises; has published a book on Owens Pottery.

Jeanette & Marvin Stoftt
45 12th St.
Tell City, IN 47586
phone: 812-547-5707
Co-managers along with Kristy & Rick McKibben of the Pottery Lovers AMerican Art Pottery Show and Sale and co-authors of "Owens Pottery Unearthed."

Kristy & Rick McKibben
45 12th St.
Tell City, IN 47586
phone: 812-547-5707
Co-managers along with Jeanette & Marvin Stoftt of the Pottery Lovers AMerican Art Pottery Show and Sale and co-authors of "Owens Pottery Unearthed."

Pisgah Forest

Collectors

Roland Sayers
P.O. Box 629
Brevard, NC 28712-0629
phone: 704-883-9562
Wants to buy Pisgah Forest and Nonconnah Pottery, most are dated;

also wants Pisgah Forest cameo pieces with designs.

Red Wing

Experts

Ron Linde
500 South Water Street
Northfield, MN 55057
Collects and consultant to "The Official Price Guide to Pottery and Porcelain."

Ray Reiss
2144 North Leavitt
Chicago, IL 60647
phone: 312-384-3245 or 800-355-2324
fax: 312-384-3252
Author of "Red Wing Art Pottery"; interested in buying Red Wing art pottery (including pottery made for RumRill), classic American pottery from the 1930s through 1960s.

Rookwood Pottery Co.

Auction Services

Don Treadway
Treadway Auctions
2029 Madison Rd.
Cincinnati, OH 45208
phone: 513-321-6742 or 800-526-0491
fax: 513-871-7722
Internet: http://www.treadwaygallery.com
Specializes in the sale of Arts and Crafts pottery.

Collectors

Bob Hut
P.O. Box 1495
New York, NY 10163
phone: 800-321-7687
Wants to buy Rookwood pottery, artist signed by Schmidt, Valentine, Daly, Toohey, Horsfall, McDonald, Laurence, Nichols, Wilcox, Storer, Wareham, Hurley, Shirayamadani, Artus Van Briggle, Conant, Robineau.

Frank L. Hahn
P.O. Box 934
Lima, OH 45802-0934
phone: 419-225-3816 or 419-222-3816
fax: 419-227-3816
Collector of Rookwood paperweights.

Experts

Mary E. Mecklenborg
Special Things Antiques
5701 Cheviot Rd.
Cincinnati, OH 45247-7007
phone: 513-741-9127 or 513-598-1275
Buys, sells and specializes in Ohio art pottery, especially Rookwood.

Man./Prod./Dist.

Art Townley
Rookwood Pottery Co.
10696 Hewitt Rd.
Brooklyn, MI 49230-9760
phone: 517-592-2169
Company makes new pottery.

Roseville Pottery Co.

Clubs/Associations

Jack & Nancy Bomm
Roseville's of the Past Pottery Club
Newsletter: Roseville Connection
P.O. Box 656
Clarcona, FL 32710-0656
phone: 407-294-3980
fax: 407-294-7836
e-mail: rosepast@worldnet.att.net
For Roseville pottery collectors, dealers, and enthusiasts; bi-monthly newsletter contains articles, buy/sell/ trade ads, commentary, collector profiles, etc.; complete information on all aspects of Roseville Pottery.

Collectors

Todd P. Violette
P.O. Box 2594
Waterville, ME 04901-2594
phone: 207-873-8898
Wants Roseville Pottery pieces: vases, umbrella stands, pedestals.

John Overton
3601 Connecticut Ave. NW, Ste. 609
Washington, DC 20008
phone: 202-244-2609

Jack & Nancy Bomm
P.O. Box 656
Clarcona, FL 32710-0656
phone: 407-294-3980
fax: 407-294-7836
e-mail: rosepast@worldnet.att.net

Dealers

Marvin McKee
65 Chase Rd.
Bangor, ME 04401-2633
phone: 207-945-3450
e-mail: mmckee@agate.net
Buys and sells American art pottery, especially Roseville.

Ruman
292 Pershing Ave.
Leechburg, PA 15656
phone: 412-845-7275

Randy Monsen
P.O. Box 529
Vienna, VA 22183-0529
phone: 703-938-2129

Mary E. Mecklenborg
Special Things Antiques
5701 Cheviot Rd.
Cincinnati, OH 45247-7007
phone: 513-741-9127 or 513-598-1275
Buys, sells and specializes in Ohio art pottery, especially Rookwood.

Andrew E. Thomas
Chasing the Clay
4681 North 84th Way
Scottsdale, AZ 85251-1864
phone: 602-947-5693
fax: 602-994-4382
Buys, sells, trades all patterns of Roseville pottery from Apple Blossom to Zephyr Lily; any condition from mint to severely damaged.

Experts

Tom Rago
716 Silver Court
Hamilton Square, NJ 08690
Buys and sells; consultant to "The Official Price Guide to Pottery and Porcelain."

Gordon Hoppe
10120 32nd Ave.
Minneapolis, MN 55441
Buys and sells; consultant to "The Official Price Guide to Pottery and Porcelain."

John W. Humphries
P.O. Box 965
Los Molinos, CA 96055
Author of "A Price Guide to Roseville Pottery by the Numbers."

San Jose Pottery

Experts

Susan Frost
806 Rosedale Terrace
Austin, TX 78704-3159
phone: 512-447-2575 or 512-447-0407
e-mail: Reuter@io.com
Researches and collects San Jose Pottery, San Jose Mission Crafts, Mexican Arts & Crafts, Inc., and other related San Antonio pottery and tiles.

Van Briggle Pottery Co.

Dealers

Gary Lickver
P.O. Box 1778
San Marcos, CA 92079
phone: 760-761-0868
Buys, sells, collects 1901-1940 Van Briggle art pottery; at most quality indoor antique shows in California.

Experts

Richard L. Sasicki
P.O. Box 3113
Glen Ellyn, IL 60138-3113
phone: 708-627-2630
e-mail: artwave@sprynet.com
Author of "The Collector's Encyclopedia of Van Briggle Art Pottery."

Scott Nelson
P.O. Box 6081
Santa Fe, NM 87502-6081
phone: 505-986-1176
Wants early and dated Van Briggle, decorated North Dakota, Hylong, and any fine pottery, damage OK if priced accordingly; consultant to "The Official Price Guide to Pottery and

Porcelain," author of book on Van Briggle.

Man./Prod./Dist.

Van Briggle Pottery Co.
600 S. 21st St.
Colorado Springs, CO 80901
phone: 719-633-7729 or 719-633-4080
fax: 719-633-7720
In continuous operation since 1899. Free tour through production facility. Showroom for retail sales of beautiful pottery figurines and tiles.

Weller Pottery Co.

Dealers

Mary E. Mecklenborg
Special Things Antiques
5701 Cheviot Rd.
Cincinnati, OH 45247-7007
phone: 513-741-9127 or 513-598-1275
Buys, sells and specializes in Ohio art pottery, especially Rookwood.

Experts

Ann Gilbert McDonald
P.O. Box 7321
Arlington, VA 22207
Author of "All About Weller."

CERAMICS (AMERICAN DINNERWARE)

(see also DINNERWARE)

Collectors

Dave Folckemer
RD2 Box 394
Hollidaysburg, PA 16648-9200
phone: 814-696-0301

Dealers

Carolyn Brooks
Neat Stuff
7808 Scotia Dr.
Dallas, TX 75248-3115
phone: 972-404-1951
fax: 972-404-1870
Specializes in Franciscan handpainted dinnerware, Fiestaware, Coors Rosebud.

Joanne Jasper
28005 Balkins Dr.
Agoura Hills, CA 91301-1801
phone: 818-597-0234
fax: 818-597-9503
e-mail: 73653.2626@compuserve.com
Author of "The Collectors Encyclopedia of Homer Laughlin China" (Collector Books); autographed copies available; buys and sells Home Laughlin Decorated china and turn of the century American china.

Experts

Harvey Duke
577 Avenue Y
Brooklyn, NY 11235
Author of "Price Guide to Pottery and Porcelain"; covering 90 collectible American potteries with 22,000 items

priced; $21.95 ppd.; specializes in Ohio and West Virginia dinnerware made from the 1890s to 1950s.

Blair Ceramics

Collectors

Lori Hinterleiter
P.O. Box 9394
Arlington, VA 22219
phone: 703-522-2150
e-mail: lhinterl@aol.com
Wants to buy Blair Ceramics in all patterns.

Buffalo Pottery Co.

Collectors

Thomas Knopke
1430 E. Brookdale Place
Fullerton, CA 92631
phone: 714-526-1749

Fred & Lila Schrader
2025 Highway 199
Crescent City, CA 95531
phone: 707-458-3525
Wants to buy Buffalo pottery: Deldare, Blue Willow, jugs and pitchers, game and fish sets.

Experts

Phillip M. Sullivan
P.O. Box 69
South Orleans, MA 02662
Collector and consultant to "The Official Price Guide to Pottery and Porcelain."

Vi & Si Altman
Vi & Si's Antiques
8970 Main St.
Clarence, NY 14031
phone: 716-634-4488
Buys, sells, appraises and specializes in all ceramic items marked Buffalo Pottery Co. and Buffalo China; authors of "The Book of Buffalo Pottery" $30.50 ppd.

Man./Prod./Dist.

Buffalo China, Inc.
658 Bailey Ave.
Buffalo, NY 14206
phone: 716-824-8515 or 800-828-7033

Buffalo Pottery Co. (Deldare)

Collectors

Jerome P. Puma
78 Brinton St.
Buffalo, NY 14214-1175
phone: 716-838-5674

John & Joanna Kille
1319 Farley Court South
Arnold, MD 21012
phone: 410-757-8118
Wants to buy Emerald Deldare; also wants Dr. Syntax items, especially wants "Dr. Syntax Returns Home" humidor.

Coors Porcelain Co.

Collectors

Ed Bour
6110 W Pleasant Ridge Rd., #4771
Arlington, TX 76016
Wants Coors Pottery items: vases, Rosebud, Rockmount, Thermoporcelain, etc.

Jo Ellen Winther
8449 W. 75th Way
Arvada, CO 80005-4533
phone: 800-872-2345 or 303-421-2371
fax: 303-431-5350

Experts

Robert Schneider
3808 Carr Pl. N.
Seattle, WA 98103-8126
phone: 206-632-1144
Author of "Coors Rosebud Pottery"; general knowledge of all Coors Pottery and thermo-porcelain including Rosebud, Rockmount, Mello-Tone, Coorado and Art Vases.

Periodicals

Robert Schneider
Newsletter: Coors Pottery Newsletter
3808 Carr Pl. N.
Seattle, WA 98103-8126
phone: 206-632-1144

Gladding-McBean/Franciscan

Clubs/Associations

Franciscan Collectors Club
Newsletter: Franciscan Newsletter
8412 5th Ave. NE
Seattle, WA 98115
fax: 206-362-5520
e-mail: gmcbl@aol.com

Dealers

Alan Phair
Alan's Antiques
P.O. Box 30373
Long Beach, CA 90853-0373
phone: 310-438-9395
fax: 310-434-8746
Buys pieces marked "Catalina Pottery" made by Gladding-McBean; shells and some pieces marked with blue ink stamp "MADE IN U.S.A."; G.M.B., Franciscan and Catalina Pottery advertising items and price lists; also Franciscan dinnerware.

Experts

Marv Fogleman
1914 West Carriage Dr.
Santa Ana, CA 92704
Buys and sells; consultant to "The Official Price Guide to Pottery and Porcelain."

James Elliott
7345 35th Ave. NE
Seattle, WA 98115
Buys and sells; consultant to "The

Official Price Guide to Pottery and Porcelain."

Matching Services

Delleen Enge
Franciscan Matching
323 E. Matilija, Ste. 112
Ojai, CA 93023-2775
Specializing in mail order sales of Franciscan (trade name used by Gladding McBean and Co.) china, earthenware, and stoneware; large inventory in stock; author of "Franciscan Ware" and "Embossed and Handpainted Franciscan."

Gorham

Man./Prod./Dist.

Gorham, Inc.
100 Lenox Dr.
Lawrenceville, NJ 08648
phone: 609-896-2800 or 800-635-3669
Sterling and stainless steel flatware, sterling and silverplated hollowware; fine china, crystal stemware, giftware and dolls; a division of Lenox Brands.

Hall China Co.

Clubs/Associations

Virginia Lee
Hall Collector's Club
Newsletter: Hall China Collector's Club Newsletter
P.O. Box 360488
Cleveland, OH 44136
phone: 330-220-7456
Association commissions Hall China to produce unique, limited edition items in the Autumn Leaf, Silhouette, Red Poppy, crocus and other patterns; newsletter published yearly; 2000+ members; send SASE for free information.

Experts

Elizabeth Boyce
38 Carlotia Dr.
Jeffersonville, IN 47130-5278
phone: 812-282-8697
Buys and sells; collecting Hall China for over 24 years; consultant to "The Official Price Guide to Pottery and Porcelain."

Jane & Don Warner-Smith
RR1, Box 94B
Farmersville, IL 62533
Buys and sells; consultant to "The Official Price Guide to Pottery and Porcelain."

Hall China Co./Autumn Leaf

Clubs/Associations

Tom Whipple
National Autumn Leaf Collectors Club
62200 E 236 Rd.
Wyandotte, OK 74370-2925

Dealers

Virginia Lee
China Specialties, Inc.
P.O. Box 361280
Strongsville, OH 44136
phone: 330-220-7456
Specializes in the Autumn Leaf pattern.

Experts

Harvey Duke
577 Avenue Y
Brooklyn, NY 11235
Author of "Superior Quality Hall China" and "Hall 2", the authoritative books on the Hall China Company; each is $16.95 ppd.; Price Update is $8.50 ppd.

Margaret & Kenn Whitmyer
P.O. Box 30806
Gahanna, OH 43230
Author of "The Collector's Guide to Hall China."

Ben Moulton
300 West York Dr.
Terre Haute, IN 47802
phone: 812-234-3870
Specializes in Hall China: refrigerator ware, kitchenware, dinnerware, novelties, tea pots, etc.

Shirley Easley
120 West Dowell Rd.
Mc Henry, IL 60050
Buys and sells; consultant to "The Official Price Guide to Pottery and Porcelain."

Jo Cunningham
535 E. Normal
Springfield, MO 65807-1659
phone: 417-831-1320
,Author of "The Autumn Leaf Story," ."The Collectors' Encyclopedia of American Dinnerware," and "The Best of Collectible Dinnerware."

Man./Prod./Dist.

Hall China Company, The
2356 Elizabeth Ave.
East Liverpool, OH 43920
phone: 216-385-2900
Maker of Hall China since 1903.

Homer Laughlin China Co.

Dealers

Edward E. Stump
6 High St.
Mullica Hill, NJ 08062-9540
phone: 609-478-4488
Specializes in Homer Laughlin China Company's Fiesta, Harlequin and Riviera patterns; buying and selling.

Experts

Michael Haas
Rte. 46E Box 106
Buttzville, NJ 07829
phone: 908-453-2918
Buys and sells; consultant to "The

Official Price Guide to Pottery and Porcelain."

Joanne Jasper
28005 Balkins Dr.
Agoura Hills, CA 91301-1801
phone: 818-597-0234
fax: 818-597-9503
e-mail: 73653.2626@compuserve.com
Author of "The Collectors Encyclopedia of Homer Laughlin China" (Collector Books); autographed copies available; buys and sells Home Laughlin Decorated china and turn of the century American china.

Man./Prod./Dist.

Homer Laughlin Co., The
6th & Harrison Sts.
Newell, WV 26050
phone: 304-387-1300 or 800-452-4462
fax: 304-387-0593
Vitrified china and ironstone dinnerware.

Periodicals

Richard Racheter, Ed.
Newsletter: Laughlin Eagle, The
1270 63rd Terrace So.
Saint Petersburg, FL 33705-5842
phone: 813-867-3982
fax: 813-867-3982
Published quarterly.

Homer Laughlin/Fiesta

Auction Services

Ronald E. Kay
P.O. Box 15383
Machesney Park, IL 61115-5383
phone: 815-282-3104 or 815-282-2585
fax: 815-282-3179
Conducts annual Fiesta auction.

Clubs/Associations

Virginia Lee
Fiesta Collectors Club
Newsletter: Fiesta Collectors Quarterly
P.O. Box 471
Valley City, OH 44280
phone: 330-220-7456
The original association for Fiesta Collectors, now in its fourth year; newsletter dedicated to Fiesta, Harlequin Riviera and other 1930s to 1970s solid-glazed dinnerware from the Newell/East Liverpool region; buy and sell ads.

Ronald E. Kay, Pres.
Fiesta Club of America, Inc.
Newsletter: Fiesta Club of America Newsletter
P.O. Box 15383
Machesney Park, IL 61115-5383
phone: 815-282-3104 or 815-282-2585
fax: 815-282-3179
Club objective is to promote Fiesta while having fun; club meetings, newsletter; annual convention; send LSASE for sample newsletter.

Dealers

Helene Guarnaccia
52 Coach Lane
Fairfield, CT 06430
phone: 203-374-6034

Gus Gustafson
Buttzville Center
Rte. 46E Box 106
Buttzville, NJ 07829-9999
phone: 908-453-2918
Buys and sells, specializes in Homer Laughlin China Company's Fiesta pattern; consultant to "The Official Price Guide to Pottery and Porcelain."

Robert & Nancy Perzel
4 Mine St.
P.O. Box 1057
Flemington, NJ 08822-1057
phone: 908-782-9631

Liz Kramar
Kramar's Kollectible Korner
P.O. Box 30
Elk Mills, MD 21920-0030
phone: 410-398-0105
e-mail: kram5688@dpnet.net

Chester Sturm
Fiesta Antiques
P.O. Box 1325
Harpers Ferry, WV 25425
phone: 304-535-2456
Specializing in American art pottery.

Mick & Lorna Chase
Fiesta Plus
380 Hawkins Crawford Rd.
Cookeville, TN 38501
phone: 615-372-8333
Buys and sells Fiesta, Franciscan USA, Metlox, Lu Ray, Vernon Kilns, Harlequin, Riviera, Kitchen Kraft; ships anywhere; ironclad money back guarantee; credit cards welcome.

Virginia Lee
China Specialties, Inc.
P.O. Box 361280
Strongsville, OH 44136
phone: 330-220-7456
Buys and sells Fiesta, all colors and all pieces; carries full line of new Fiesta as well.

Experts

Dennis Bialek
RD 4, Box 43
Hudson, NY 12534
Buys and sells; consultant to "The Official Price Guide to Pottery and Porcelain."

Ronald E. Kay
P.O. Box 15383
Machesney Park, IL 61115-5383
phone: 815-282-3104 or 815-282-2585
fax: 815-282-3179
Has written price guide for the club and has traveled throughout the US giving appraisals of vintage Fiesta.

Repair Services

Fiestoration
4011 Butterfield Trail
Fayetteville, AR 72701
Specializing in the invisible restoration of all sizes of chips in FiestaWare.

Iroquois China Co.

Experts

Paul Beedenbender
1203 East Paris St.
Tampa, FL 33604
Collects and consultant to "The Official Price Guide to Pottery and Porcelain."

Metlox Potteries

Experts

Carl Gibbs, Jr.
P.O. Box 131584
Houston, TX 77219-1584
phone: 713-521-9661
Author of "Collector's Encyclopedia of Metlox Potteries"; autographed copies for $24.95 plus $3 postage.

Marv Fogleman
1914 West Carriage Dr.
Santa Ana, CA 92704
Buys and sells; consultant to "The Official Price Guide to Pottery and Porcelain."

Pennsbury Pottery Co.

Collectors

Mark Supnick
2771 Oakbrook Manor
Fort Lauderdale, FL 33332
phone: 305-389-3911
Author of "Shawnee Pottery", and "Collecting Hull's Little Red Riding Hood."

Experts

Joe Simone
6 Duchess Lane
Dayton, NJ 08810
Buys and sells; consultant to "The Official Price Guide to Pottery and Porcelain."

Pfaltzgraff Pottery Co.

Experts

David Zeiger
P.O. Box 105
Spring Grove, PA 17362
phone: 717-632-5912
Buys and sells anything "Pfaltzgraff": Salt, Albany, and Bristle glazed stoneware Art Pottery, dinner ware patterns, old brochures and catalogs, etc.; consultant to "The Official Price Guide to Pottery and Porcelain."

Dave Walsh
Pfaltzgraff Co., The
140 East Market
York, PA 17401
phone: 717-848-5500
fax: 717-846-1133
e-mail: David.Walshsuspfz.com
Begun in 1811 in York, PA, Pfaltzgraff manufactured cobalt-decorated salt-glazed stoneware, Bristol-glazed ware, blue sponge, yellowware, Art Pottery, kitchen and ovenware, etc.; today a leading manufacturer of ceramic dinnerware.

Matching Services

David Zeiger
P.O. Box 105
Spring Grove, PA 17362
phone: 717-632-5912
Matching and/or replacements for old and new Pfaltzgraff dinner ware patterns; also others upon request.

Pickard

Auction Services

Joy Luke
Joy Luke Auction Gallery
300 E. Grove St.
Bloomington, IL 61701-5232
phone: 309-828-5533
fax: 309-829-2266
Conducts periodic auctions specializing in the sale of toys, banks, trains and dolls.

Clubs/Associations

Jackie Pope
Pickard Collectors Club
Newsletter: Pickard Collectors Club Newsletter
300 E. Grove St.
Bloomington, IL 61701-5232
phone: 309-828-5533
fax: 309-829-2266
Organized to advance the knowledge of collectors and dealers about this fine porcelain hand decorated in America.

Collectors

Glenda Ridgway
P.O. Box 231
Anna, IL 62906
Charter member, Pickard Collectors Club.

Dealers

Milt Steinfeld
P.O. Box 457
Westfield, NJ 07090
phone: 908-233-0950
fax: 908-233-0950
Mail order dealer in R.S. Prussia, Pickard, Victorian silverplate, Royal Bayreuth, Wallace Nutting, Cordey and Art Glass.

Veronica Wexler
Wit's End Antiques & Collectibles
840 Blossom Dr.
Santa Clara, CA 95050-5115
phone: 408-261-9742 or 408-984-2423
e-mail: rwexler@rivendell.com
Buys and sells hand painted Pickard China.

Experts

Alan Reed
Firstlight, Inc.
723 N. Linden Ave.
Oak Park, IL 60302
phone: 708-383-1817
fax: 708-383-9256
e-mail: areed@juno.com
Author of the "Collector's Encyclopedia of Pickard China"; lists Pickard and all major Chicago china decorators.

Man./Prod./Dist.

Pickard China Co.
782 Corona Ave.
Antioch, IL 60002-1574
phone: 708-395-3800
fax: 708-395-3827
Fine china dinnerware and giftware; limited edition plates.

Porcelier

Clubs/Associations

Shirley Hall
Porcelier Collectors Club
Newsletter: Porcelier Paper, The
21 Tamarac Swamp Rd.
Wallingford, CT 06492-5529
phone: 203-265-5791
For collectors of Porcelier dinnerware, service pieces and all-ceramic small electrical kitchen appliances; bi-monthly newsletter features information and pictures of patterns, new finds, and research; free ads for members.

Collectors

Shirley Hall
21 Tamarac Swamp Rd.
Wallingford, CT 06492-5529
phone: 203-265-5791
Collectors of Porcelier china, coffee pots, teapots, service pieces and all-ceramic small electrical kitchen appliances.

Red Wing

Experts

Monna Erickson
1712 Harrison Court
Northfield, MN 55057
Collects and consultant to "The Official Price Guide to Pottery and Porcelain"; specializing in Red Wing hand-painted dinnerware.

Mary Bang
5200 Duggan Plaza
Edina, MN 55439
phone: 612-941-4754
Collects and consultant to "The Official Price Guide to Pottery and Porcelain"; specializing in Red Wing hand-painted dinnerware.

Reed & Barton

Man./Prod./Dist.

Reed & Barton
144 W. Britannia St.
Taunton, MA 02780
phone: 508-824-6611 or 800-822-1824
fax: 508-822-7269
Produces china, crystal, silver, silverplate, and stainless flatware, collectible plates, bells, dolls, ornaments and accessories.

Royal China Co./Currier & Ives

Clubs/Associations

Dave Folckemer
Currier & Ives Dinnerware Collectors Club
Newsletter: Collectors' Newsletter
RD2 Box 394
Hollidaysburg, PA 16648-9200
phone: 814-696-0301
For collectors of Currier & Ives dinnerware by the Royal China Co. of Sebring, OH.

Collectors

Dave Folckemer
RD2 Box 394
Hollidaysburg, PA 16648-9200
phone: 814-696-0301

Eldon R. "Bud" Aupperle
29470 Saxon Rd.
Toulon, IL 61483
phone: 309-896-3331

Experts

Jack & Treva Hamlin
RR 4 Box 150, Kaiser St.
Proctorville, OH 45669

Betsey Edmondson
Betsey's Collectibles
1404 Sylan Dr.
Plano, TX 75074
Buys and sells; consultant to "The Official Price Guide to Pottery and Porcelain."

Southern Potteries/Blue Ridge

Clubs/Associations

Wanda Hashe
Blue Ridge Collectors Club
208 Harris St.
Erwin, TN 37650
phone: 423-743-9337

Collectors

Linda Weeks
22 Stevens Ave.
Meredith, NH 03253-5855
phone: 603-279-3357
Wants to buy Blue Ridge - Homer Laughlin dishes.

Don & Susan Burkett
233 East Wesley Rd.
Atlanta, GA 30305
Your Southern Potteries and Blue Ridge ideas, questions and pictures are always welcome; please include a SASE if requesting a reply; consultant to "The Official Price Guide to Pottery and Porcelain."

Dealers

Diana E. Bullock
Bullock Antiques
P.O. Box 5427
Somerset, NJ 08875
phone: 908-846-1368
Buys and sells Blue Ridge/Southern Pottery dinnerware and Stangl dinnerware.

Mary & Ray Farley
B R Barn, The
1379 West Commerce
Lewisburg, TN 37091
phone: 615-359-2906

Experts

Norma Lilly
144 Highland Dr.
Blountville, TN 37617-5404
phone: 615-323-5247
Wants Blue Ridge china made by Southern Potteries, Inc.; any unusual form or pattern.

Susan Moore
493 Gatewood Lane
Grayslake, IL 60030-3732
Collects and consultant to "The Official Price Guide to Pottery and Porcelain."

Periodicals

Bryan & Kim Snyder
Magazine: Blue Ridge Beacon Magazine
P.O. Box 629
Mountain City, GA 30562-0629
phone: 800-851-6481
e-mail: bksnyder@acme-brain.com
16 pages in full color; includes articles on collecting Blue Ridge, rare and unusual Blue Ridge, interesting Erwin history, interviews with Southern Potteries employees, old photographs and advertisements, new patterns, classifieds, etc.

Norma Lilly
Newsletter: National Blue Ridge Newsletter
144 Highland Dr.
Blountville, TN 37617-5404
phone: 615-323-5247
10 pre-punched pages; Q&A up-date, articles, new patterns, readers

comment section; published bi-monthly.

Stangl Pottery Co.

(see also CERAMICS [AMERICAN FIGURES], Stangl Pottery Co.)

Dealers

Diana E. Bullock
Bullock Antiques
P.O. Box 5427
Somerset, NJ 08875
phone: 908-846-1368
Buys and sells Blue Ridge/Southern Pottery dinnerware and Stangl dinnerware.

Experts

Robert & Nancy Perzel
Popkorn Antiques
4 Mine St.
P.O. Box 1057
Flemington, NJ 08822-1057
phone: 908-782-9631
Offers a Stangl Pottery dinner matching service; also Stangl birds and Artware; consultant to "The Official Price Guide to Pottery and Porcelain," "Schroeder's," and "Warman's."

Taylor, Smith & Taylor/LuRay

Collectors

Joe Zacharias
1233 Moultrie Ct.
Raleigh, NC 27615-6032
phone: 919-848-6966
e-mail: IBUYLURAY2@aol.com
Wants LuRay PASTELS: chocolate/straight-sided A/D pots, sugars, creamers; blue/green, 7" mini-plates; blue handleless sugar; yellow flat-spout teapot, 5 1/2" and 6 3/4" mixing bowls; grey 8" plates, 36's bowls, grill plates, eggcups.

Dealers

Edward E. Stump
6 High St.
Mullica Hill, NJ 08062-9540
phone: 609-478-4488
Specializes in Taylor, Smith and Taylor Company's LuRay Pastels line.

Experts

Ray & Virginia Cramble
Antiques From Memory Lane
7340 Memory Lane Lane NE
Minneapolis, MN 55432-3217
Buys, sells, collects and appraises almost all Abingdon and rare LuRay.

Vernon Kilns Co.

Collectors

Bill Stern
361 North Orange Dr.
Los Angeles, CA 90036

Dealers

Judi & Dave Thompson
1668 Melissa Way
Anaheim, CA 92802

Experts

Harold Mathews
24 Church St.
Honeoye, NY 14471
Consultant to "The Official Price Guide to Pottery and Porcelain."

Maxine Nelson
7657 E. Hazelwood St.
Scottsdale, AZ 85251-1510
Author of "Collectible Vernon Kilns."

Bess Christensen
1313 East Locust Ave.
Lompoc, CA 93436-7442
Consultant to "The Official Price Guide to Pottery and Porcelain."

Periodicals

Newsletter: Vernon Views
P.O. Box 945
Scottsdale, AZ 85252
The newsletter for collectors of Vernon Kilns pottery; recent finds, free ads, interesting articles.

Wallace China Co.

Experts

Marv Fogleman
1914 West Carriage Dr.
Santa Ana, CA 92704
Buys and sells; consultant to "The Official Price Guide to Pottery and Porcelain."

Warwick China Co.

Experts

Donald C. Hoffmann, Sr.
1291 N. Elmwood Dr.
Aurora, IL 60506
phone: 708-859-3435
Author of "Why Not Warwick," "Warwick A to W"; also advisor to Schroeder's Price Guide.

Matching Services

Ackerman Antiques
100 Colonial Way Circle
Columbus, OH 43235-5611

Watt Pottery Co.

Clubs/Associations

Dennis Thompson, Dir.
Watt Pottery Collectors
Newsletter: Spoutings
P.O. Box 26067
Cleveland, OH 44126-0067
phone: 216-235-8548
e-mail: dthomp@stratos.net
Internet: http://www.execpc.com/~wmhill/
Publishes original research on the Watt Pottery, its history and wares; provides identification of wares

produced under trade names used by Watt and other potteries; national conventions in Cooksville, OH, home of Watt pottery.

Wendy Stinocher
Watt Collectors Association
Newsletter: Watt News
P.O. Box 1995
Iowa City, IA 52244-1995
phone: 319-338-9181
A non-profit educational organization dedicated to the study and preservation of this unique segment of the pottery world.

Experts

Dennis Thompson, Dir.
P.O. Box 26067
Cleveland, OH 44126-0067
phone: 216-235-8548
e-mail: dthomp@stratos.net
Internet: http://www.execpc.com/
~wmhill/
Author of "Watt Pottery, a Collectors Reference with Price Guide" (Schiffer, 1994); 240 pages; 800 color photos; $43ppd from author; consultant to "The Official Price Guide to Pottery and Porcelain."

Dave & Sue Morris
3388 Merlin Rd., Ste. 351
Grants Pass, OR 97526
phone: 541-955-8411
e-mail: smorris@cdsnet.net
Buys and sells Watt pottery; authors of "Watt Pottery - An Identification and Value Guide"; available from authors for $22 ppd.

CERAMICS (AMERICAN FIGURES)
Ceramic Arts Studio

Clubs/Associations

Jim Petzold
Ceramic Arts Studio Collectors
  Association
Newsletter: CAS Collector
P.O. Box 46
Madison, WI 53701-0046
phone: 608-241-9138
fax: 608-241-8770
e-mail: ceramics@execpc.com
Provides accurate information on authentic Ceramic Arts Studio (Madison, WI) works; stories and memories of the Studio and the collecting experience; "Inventory Record & Price Guide" lists 800+ works, $12 ppd.

Collectors

Tim Holthaus
P.O. Box 46
Madison, WI 53701-0046
phone: 608-241-9138
fax: 608-241-8770
e-mail: ceramics@execpc.com
Co-editor with of "CAS Collector"; wants to buy all Ceramic Arts Studio & Royal Copley creations including

shakers, figurines, dolls, lamps, and metal art.

Dealers

Jim Petzold
P.O. Box 46
Madison, WI 53701-0046
phone: 608-241-9138
fax: 608-241-8770
e-mail: ceramics@execpc.com
Co-editor with of "CAS Collector"; wants to buy all Ceramic Arts Studio & Royal Copley creations including shakers, figurines, dolls, lamps, and metal art.

Experts

Gunther Schmidt
818 Rte. 518
Skillman, NJ 08558-2614

Florence

Clubs/Associations

Beth Dunigan
Florence Collectors Club
Newsletter: Florence Collectors Club
  Newsletter
P.O. Box 122
Richland, WA 99352-0122
phone: 909-683-1485 or 509-943-0971
e-mail: pdunigan@aol.com

Dealers

Mike & Bev
637 E. Main St.
Cottage Grove, OR 97424
phone: 541-942-3664

Experts

Sue & Jerry Kline
913 East End Ct.
Gatlinburg, TN 37738
Buys and sells; consultant to "The Official Price Guide to Pottery and Porcelain."

Jeanne Fredericks
12364 Downey Ave.
Downey, CA 90242-3556
phone: 562-861-4781
Collector and consultant to "The Official Price Guide to Pottery and Porcelain."

Rita Bee
6960 Abel Stearns Ave.
Riverside, CA 92509
phone: 909-683-1485
e-mail: BeAntique@aol.com

Kay Finch

Dealers

Sharlene Beckwith
Exclusively Dogs!
P.O. Box 1858
Upland, CA 91785-1858
phone: 909-946-1544
fax: 909-949-4796
Specializing in fine canine collectibles, especially fine porcelains

(Rosenthal, Boehm, etc.), Kay Finch dog figurines and any large or unusual Kay Finch animals, including cookie jars; also wants Kay Finch bronzes and dog jewelry.

Experts

Frances Finch Webb
1589 Gretel Lane
Mountain View, CA 94040-3704
phone: 415-968-0739
Author of "The New Kay Finch Field Identification Guide," available from author; keeper of FINCH archival and historic records; research consultant for other authors on Kay Finch.

Stangl Pottery Co.

(see also CERAMICS [AMERICAN DINNERWARE], Stangl Pottery Co.)

Clubs/Associations

Robert Runge, Pres.
Stangl/Fulper Club
Newsletter: Stangl/Fulper Club
  Newsletter
P.O. Box 538
Flemington, NJ 08822
phone: 908-995-2696
Promotes Stangl/Fulper pottery, dinnerware, birds, animals.

Collectors

Jim Davidson
P.O. Box 419
Ringoes, NJ 08551
phone: 609-397-8984

Dealers

Jim Davidson
P.O. Box 419
Ringoes, NJ 08551
phone: 609-397-8984
Stangl birds collector will pay top prices.

Liz Kramar
Kramar's Kollectible Korner
P.O. Box 30
Elk Mills, MD 21920-0030
phone: 410-398-0105
e-mail: kram5688@dpnet.net
Wants to buy Stangl birds.

Experts

Harvey Duke
577 Avenue Y
Brooklyn, NY 11235
Author of "Stangl Pottery", the most comprehensive and authoritative price and identification guide on Stangl; $22.45 ppd.

CERAMICS (AMERICAN PRODUCTION ARTWARE)

(see also COOKIE JARS)

Dealers

Susan & Mark Wiskow
5214 F Diamond Heights #302
San Francisco, CA 94131
phone: 415-587-9133
fax: 415-239-5148
Buys and sells American-made pottery and glass figurines from the period 1920 to 1950.

Abingdon

Clubs/Associations

Elaine Westover
Abingdon Pottery Club
Newsletter: Abingdon Pottery Collectors
  Newsletter
210 Knox Hwy. 5
Abingdon, IL 61410
Sponsors annual show and flea market on the 3rd Saturday in August of every year.

Collectors

Don King
7474 Jason Ave. NE
Monticello, MN 55362-3000
phone: 612-295-8405
Wants Abingdon Pottery decorated pieces, tableware, salesman samples, cookie jars.

Penny Vaughan
212 South Fourth
Monmouth, IL 61462
phone: 309-734-2337

Dealers

Barbara Nyboer
Some Where in Time Antiques
3655 Quadrille
Holt, MI 48842-9723
phone: 517-699-8372 or 517-337-4988
fax: 517-694-5650
Buys and sells Abingdon pottery.

Experts

Ray & Virginia Cramble
Antiques From Memory Lane
7340 Memory Lane Lane NE
Minneapolis, MN 55432-3217
Buys, sells, collects and appraises almost all Abingdon and rare LuRay.

Robert Rush
210 North Main St.
Abingdon, IL 61410
Collects and consultant to "The Official Price Guide to Pottery and Porcelain."

Elaine Westover
210 Knox Hwy. 5
Abingdon, IL 61410
Collects and consultant to "The Official Price Guide to Pottery and Porcelain."

American Bisque Company

Experts

Joyce Roerig
RR 2 Box 504
Walterboro, SC 29488-9278
phone: 803-538-2487
Buys and sells; consultant to "Official Price Guide to Pottery & Porcelain"; founded in 1919, American Bisque Company produced florist ware, kitchenware, and cookie jars.

Lawrence Koons
18 Walnut, #3
Belpre, OH 45714-2429
phone: 614-423-3393 or 614-423-5478
fax: 614-423-9638

Arkansas Potteries

Clubs/Associations

David Gifford
Arkansas Pottery Collectors Society
P.O. Box 7617
Little Rock, AR 72217
phone: 501-225-0225
Will answer questions about Arkansas pottery such as Camark, Niloak and Ouchita pottery; please include LSASE with questions.

Brush-McCoy Pottery

Experts

Martha & Steve Sanford
230 Harrison Ave.
Campbell, CA 95008
phone: 408-978-8408
Authors of "The Guide to Brush-McCoy Pottery."

California Potteries

(see also CERAMICS [AMERICAN PRODUCTION ARTWARE], Catalina Island Pottery, CERAMICS [AMERICAN PRODUCTION ARTWARE], Sascha Brastoff)

Experts

Jack Chipman
P.O. Box 1079
Venice, CA 90291-1079
phone: 310-396-5320
e-mail: chipman396@aol.com
Buys and sells; consultant to "The Official Price Guide to Pottery and Porcelain", and "Collector's Encyclopedia of California Pottery."

Steve Soukup
California Crazed
P.O. Box 7662
Van Nuys, CA 91406-7662
phone: 818-787-5990 or 818-781-9262
Buys and sells California pottery and tiles: Bauer, Catalina, Batchelder, Pacific Pottery, Romanelli, Vernon Kilns, Metlox, Meyers, Poxon, Padre, California Rainbow, Tropico Pottery, GMB, Brayton, etc.

Susan Cox
c/o Main Street Antique Mall
237 E. Main
El Cajon, CA 92020-3911
phone: 619-447-0811

Periodicals

Verlangieri Gallery
Newsletter: California Pottery Trader, The
P.O. Box 844
Cambria, CA 93428-0844
phone: 805-927-4428
fax: 805-927-4428
e-mail: verlangieri@thegrid.net
Internet: http://www.thebook.com/verlangieri
Features dealer ads, pottery news, pottery show coverage, and books on California pottery.

California Potteries (Bauer)

Collectors

James L. Harmon
P.O. Box 25
Banks, OR 97106
phone: 503-324-7041
Wants to buy Bauer; Bauer ringware wanted in all colors; top dollar paid for black; bowls especially wanted.

Experts

Jack Chipman
P.O. Box 1079
Venice, CA 90291-1079
phone: 310-396-5320
e-mail: chipman396@aol.com
Buys and sells; consultant to "The Official Price Guide to Pottery and Porcelain", author of "Collector's Guide to Bauer Pottery" (1997).

Camark Pottery Co.

Experts

Doris & Burdell Hall
B & B Antiques
P.O. Box 1501
Fairfield Bay, AR 72088
phone: 501-884-6571 or 309-263-2988
Buys and sells; consultant to "The Official Price Guide to Pottery and Porcelain."

David Gifford
P.O. Box 7617
Little Rock, AR 72217
phone: 501-225-0225
Buys and sells; consultant to "The Official Price Guide to Pottery and Porcelain."

Cardinal China Co.

Collectors

Trish Claar
2621 Manor Court
Owings, MD 20736-9145
phone: 301-855-6531
Collector and consultant to "The Official Price Guide to Pottery and Porcelain."

Catalina Island Pottery

Collectors

Steven Hoefs
P.O. Box 1024
Avalon, CA 90704
phone: 310-510-2623
Wants to buy Catalina Island Pottery.

Walter Sanford
321 Redondo Ave.
Long Beach, CA 90814-2652
phone: 310-434-7253
fax: 310-434-6353
Buy, sells and specializes in ceramics produced by the Catalina Island Pottery from 1927 through 1937.

Dealers

Alan Phair
Alan's Antiques
P.O. Box 30373
Long Beach, CA 90853-0373
phone: 310-438-9395
fax: 310-434-8746
Buys pieces marked "Catalina Pottery" made by Gladding-McBean; shells and some pieces marked with blue ink stamp "MADE IN U.S.A."; G.M.B., Franciscan and Catalina Pottery advertising items and price lists; also Franciscan dinnerware.

Cliftwood

Experts

Doris & Burdell Hall
B & B Antiques
P.O. Box 1501
Fairfield Bay, AR 72088
phone: 501-884-6571 or 309-263-2988
Buys and sells; specializing in Morton potteries including Cliftwood Art Potteries Inc (Midwest Potteries Inc.), and American dinnerware.

Frankoma Pottery Co.

Clubs/Associations

Nancy Littrell
Frankoma Family Collectors Association
Journal: Pot & Puma Journal
P.O. Box 32571
Oklahoma City, OK 73123-0771
phone: 405-722-2941 or 918-224-6610
fax: 405-728-3332
e-mail: ffca4nancy@aol.com
A national non-profit organization dedicated to the appreciation, preservation and promotion of Frankoma Pottery as a collectible; quarterly journal and Trader; annual show and auction; complete resource for the dedicated collector.

Collectors

Nancy Littrell
P.O. Box 32571
Oklahoma City, OK 73123-0771
phone: 405-722-2941 or 918-224-6610
fax: 405-728-3332
e-mail: ffca4nancy@aol.com
Major collector of Frankoma.

Donna Frank
1300 Luker Lane
Sapulpa, OK 74066-6024
phone: 918-224-6610
fax: 918-224-6610
e-mail: FFCA4Donna@aol.com
Author of "Clay in the Master's Hands," a history of Frankoma founder and artist John Frank, his family and Frankoma Pottery; a must for all Frankoma collectors; details evolution of ceramics in American Southwest.

Dealers

Aaron's
P.O. Box 1303
Bethany, OK 73008
Wants to buy Frankoma pottery: early vases, statues of ladies, horses, dogs, buffalo, dealer signs.

Experts

Tom & Phyllis Bess
14535 East 13th St.
Tulsa, OK 74108
phone: 918-437-7776
Buys and sells; authors of "Frankoma Treasurers" with price guide; $22 postpaid; consultant to "The Official Price Guide to Pottery and Porcelain."

Susan Cox
c/o Main Street Antique Mall
237 E. Main
El Cajon, CA 92020-3911
phone: 619-447-0811
Author of "The Collectors Guide to Frankoma, Book 2," "How to Successfully Own a Booth in a Mart"; columnist for "The Antique Trader Weekly" and "The Collector."

Man./Prod./Dist.

Frankoma Pottery, Inc.
2400 Frankoma Rd.
P.O. Box 789
Sapulpa, OK 74067
phone: 918-224-5511 or 800-331-3650
fax: 918-227-3117
Earthenware dinnerware, serving accessories, floral containers.

Haeger/Royal Haeger

Experts

Lee Garmon
1529 Whittier St.
Springfield, IL 62704
phone: 217-789-9574
Specializes in Royal Haeger and Royal Hickman American ceramics.

Man./Prod./Dist.

Haeger Potteries
7 Maiden Lane
Dundee, IL 60118
phone: 312-426-3441

Harker

Experts

Neva Colbert
69565 Crescent Rd.
Saint Clairsville, OH 43950-9350
phone: 614-695-2355
e-mail: colbert@1st.net
*Author of "The Collector's Guide to
Harker Pottery"; writes and
distributes "The Harker Arrow", a
newsletter about cameoware and
other Harker pottery; also is a
contributor to "American Country
Collectibles" magazine.*

Periodicals

Neva Colbert
Newsletter: Harker Arrow, The
69565 Crescent Rd.
Saint Clairsville, OH 43950-9350
phone: 614-695-2355
e-mail: colbert@1st.net

Harlequin

Collectors

Jim Stewart
807 Twin Pine
St. Louis, MO 63122
phone: 314-821-9913
*Wants to buy Harlequin ceramic
animal figurines; also any unusual
Harlequin items.*

Hull Pottery

Clubs/Associations

Hull Pottery Association
4 Hilltop Rd.
Council Bluffs, IA 51503

Experts

Joan Gray Hull
1376 Nevada S.W.
Huron, SD 57350-3135
phone: 605-352-1685
*Author of "Hull - The Heavenly
Pottery", an alphabetized, numerical,
pictorial, pocket size price guide; all
newly revised 5th edition with updated
prices; advisor to "Warman's
Antiques & Collectibles Price Guide",
$24 ppd.*

Brenda Roberts
Country Side Antiques
RR 2 Hwy 65 South
Marshall, MO 65340-9802
phone: 816-886-8888
*Author of "The Collector's Encyclope-
dia of Hull Pottery", "Roberts'
Ultimate Encyclopedia of Hull
Pottery" and "The Companion Guide
to Roberts' Ultimate Encyclopedia of
Hull Pottery."*

Periodicals

Joe & Betty Yonis
Newsletter: Hull Pottery Newsletter
11023 Tunnell Hill NE
New Lexington, OH 43764
phone: 614-982-6763
*Monthly newsletter directed to Hull
Pottery collectors; designed to bring
collectors the most up-to-date
information on the subject and an
outlet to meet other collectors and
share collecting interests and
experiences.*

Dan & Kimberly Pfaff
Newsletter: Hull Pottery News, The
466 Foreston Place
Saint Louis, MO 63119-3927
phone: 314-963-1087
*A monthly newsletter for collectors of
Hull Pottery; each issue contains
classifieds, upcoming events, articles
and stories about other collectors and
their special pieces.*

Hull Pottery/Red Riding Hood

Experts

Mark Supnick
2771 Oakbrook Manor
Fort Lauderdale, FL 33332
phone: 305-389-3911
*Author of "Shawnee Pottery", and
"Collecting Hull's Little Red Riding
Hood."*

Mike Zimpfer
Antiquity Collectibles
3714 Lexington Rd.
Michigan City, IN 46360
phone: 219-879-0409
fax: 219-874-7296
*Buying Hull pottery especially
Bowknot, Red Riding Hood, all
baskets and large vases, advertising
materials; also Fiesta Ware.*

Twins Antiques & Collectibles, The
Highway 242
Wayne City, IL 62895
*Buys and sells; consultant to "The
Official Price Guide to Pottery and
Porcelain."*

McCoy Pottery Co.

Collectors

Geri Strebel
P.O. Box 277
East Moriches, NY 11940
*Wants McCoy Pottery items: vases,
planters, baskets, etc.*

Dealers

Ruth Weeks
Borrowed Time
Uniontown Rd.
Phillipsburg, NJ 08865
phone: 908-859-0097
*Wants to buy McCoy pottery from the
1930s and 1940s; prefers decorative
vases in matte glazes and animal*

*figures and planters, especially
animal-form pitchers.*

Experts

Joanne Lindberg
79 Lexington Dr.
Metuchen, NJ 08840
*Buys and sells; consultant to "The
Official Price Guide to Pottery and
Porcelain."*

Chiquita Prestwood
120 Echo Dr.
Lenoir, NC 28645
*Buys and sells; consultant to "The
Official Price Guide to Pottery and
Porcelain."*

Craig Nissen
P.O. Box 223
Grafton, WI 53024-0223
e-mail: mccoyen@aol.com
*Co-author with Bob & Margaret
Hanson of "McCoy Pottery
Collectors' Reference & Value
Guide."*

Jean Bushnell
3081 Rock Creek Dr.
Broomfield, CO 80020
phone: 303-469-8309
*Editor of "The NM Express" McCoy
newsletter.*

Periodicals

Jean Bushnell, Ed.
Newsletter: NM Express, The
3081 Rock Creek Dr.
Broomfield, CO 80020
phone: 303-469-8309
*Lighthearted, fun to read bulletin
directed at McCoy and Brush McCoy
pottery enthusiasts; informative and
fact-filled articles and warm human
interest stories concerning collectors;
large buy/sell ad section.*

Morton Potteries

Experts

Doris & Burdell Hall
B & B Antiques
P.O. Box 1501
Fairfield Bay, AR 72088
phone: 501-884-6571 or 309-263-2988
*Buys and sells; specializing in Morton
pottery and American dinnerware;
author of "Morton's Potteries: 99
Years."*

Muncie Pottery Co.

Collectors

Barbara Norman
P.O. Box 251382
West Bloomfield, MI 48325-1382
phone: 248-855-7766
fax: 248-855-5224
e-mail: bnorman7282@aol.com
*Wants to buy Ruba Rombic, red or
cased pieces of Phoenix or Consolidated Art Glass, Catalonian, and
Muncie Ruba Rombic pottery.*

Paul Galli
873 Ticonderoga Dr.
Sunnyvale, CA 94087
phone: 408-730-4010
e-mail: paul.galli@lmco.com
*Wants to buy or trade Muncie Pottery,
Ruba Rombic line.*

Experts

Virginia Heiss
7777 N. Alton Ave.
Indianapolis, IN 46268-7901
phone: 317-875-6797
*Specializes in pottery made by the
Muncie Clay Products Co., of Muncie,
IN.*

Jack D. Wilson
P.O. Box 81974
Chicago, IL 60681-0974
phone: 773-282-9553
e-mail: jdwilson1@earthlink.com
Internet: http://home.earthlink.net/
~jdwilson1/
*See website for information on this
company.*

Nemadji Tile & Pottery Co.

Clubs/Associations

Michelle Lee
Nemadji Collectors
Newsletter: Left Hand Gazette
4310 Old Co. Rd. 8
Moose Lake, MN 55767-8157
phone: 218-485-8173
e-mail: nemadji@cp.duluth.mn.us
*Nemadji is made in Moose Lake, MN;
newsletter published quarterly; free
sample newsletter with SASE.*

Collectors

Michelle Lee
4310 Old Co. Rd. 8
Moose Lake, MN 55767-8157
phone: 218-485-8173
e-mail: nemadji@cp.duluth.mn.us
*Specializes in Nemadjy pottery,
"Indian" pottery, and tiles.*

V. Chermishnok
726 Beech St.
Redwood City, CA 94063
phone: 415-368-3070

Niloak Pottery

Experts

Doris & Burdell Hall
P.O. Box 1501
Fairfield Bay, AR 72088
phone: 501-884-6571 or 309-263-2988
*Buys and sells; consultant to "The
Official Price Guide to Pottery and
Porcelain."*

David Gifford
P.O. Box 7617
Little Rock, AR 72217
phone: 501-225-0225
*Author of "Collector's Encyclopedia
of Niloak Pottery."*

Pewabic Pottery

Man./Prod./Dist.

Pewabic Pottery
10125 East Jeferson
Detroit, MI 48214
phone: 313-823-0954

Purinton

Experts

Jamie Johnson
228 Egbert Hall
Clarion, PA 16214
phone: 800-820-5087

Lori Hinterleiter
P.O. Box 9394
Arlington, VA 22219
phone: 703-522-2150
e-mail: lhinterl@aol.com
Specializes and always seeking rare and unusual pieces of Purinton Pottery, especially signed pieces, souvenir items, kiddie ware, and the following patterns: Pennsylvania Dutch, Chartreuse, Peasant Garden, Petals, Cactus, Ribb.

Dave & Sue Morris
3388 Merlin Rd., Ste. 351
Grants Pass, OR 97526
phone: 541-955-8411
e-mail: smorris@cdsnet.net
Buys and sells Purinton pottery; author of "Purinton Pottery - An Identification and Value Guide" available from author for $27.95.

Periodicals

Lori Hinterleiter
Newsletter: Purinton Pastimes
P.O. Box 9394
Arlington, VA 22219
phone: 703-522-2150
e-mail: lhinterl@aol.com
Published quarterly, devoted solely to Purinton Pottery; research, historical articles, photos, recent finds, auction updates and prices, and free classified ads; annual convention.

Ransburg

Experts

Jo Lauderdale
2014 Richmond Rd.
Decatur, IL 62521
Collects and consultant to "The Official Price Guide to Pottery and Porcelain."

Regal China Corp.

Experts

Judy Posner
4195 South Tamiami Trail, Ste. 183
Venice, FL 34293-5112
phone: 941-497-7149
fax: 941-493-8085
e-mail: Judyandjef@aol.com
Internet: http://www.tias.com/stores/jpc
Collects and consultant to "

Official Price Guide to Pottery and Porcelain."

Rumrill Pottery Co.

Clubs/Associations

Francesca Malone-Gern
Rumrill Society, The
Newsletter: Rumrill Society Newsletter, The
P.O. Box 2161
Hudson, OH 44236-0161
phone: 216-655-9325 or 888-RUM-RILL
fax: 216-655-9347
e-mail: rumrill2@aol.com
Quarterly newsletter discusses RumRill art pottery and post Redwing RumRill art pottery.

Experts

Francesca Gern
P.O. Box 2161
Hudson, OH 44236-0161
phone: 216-655-9325 or 888-RUM-RILL
fax: 216-655-9347
e-mail: rumrill2@aol.com
Expert and avid collector of Rumrill pottery; also buys and sells and appraises; publisher of The Rumrill Society Newsletter.

Mike Zaeske
1796 North 9th St.
Kalamazoo, MI 49099
Collects and consultant to "The Official Price Guide to Pottery and Porcelain."

Ron Linde
500 South Water Street
Northfield, MN 55057
Collects and consultant to "The Official Price Guide to Pottery and Porcelain."

Sascha Brastoff

Experts

De Wayne Bethany
256 S. Robertson Blvd., Ste. 109
Beverly Hills, CA 90211
Co-author with Bill Seay (assisted by Steve Conti) of the "Collector's Encyclopedia of Sascha Brastoff."

Shawnee Pottery Co.

Clubs/Associations

Pamela D. Curran
Shawnee Pottery Collectors Club
Newsletter: Exclusively Shawnee
P.O. Box 713
New Smyrna Beach, FL 32170-0713
phone: 904-760-6600
fax: 904-760-5004
A club for Shawnee Pottery (made in Zanesville until 1961) collectors and enthusiasts; send LSASE for information. Monthly newsletter with plenty of pictures, letters, buy/sell

classifieds, and new discoveries; chartered 1990.

Collectors

Pamela D. Curran
P.O. Box 713
New Smyrna Beach, FL 32170-0713
phone: 904-760-6600
fax: 904-760-5004
Buys, collects, and specializes in Shawnee Pottery; interested in purchasing all Shawnee Pottery including cookie jars, Valencia, salt & pepper shakers, miniatures, lamps, and most gold-trimmed planters.

Experts

Pamela D. Curran
P.O. Box 713
New Smyrna Beach, FL 32170-0713
phone: 904-760-6600
fax: 904-760-5004
Author of "Shawnee Pottery, The Full Encyclopedia"; publishes the Shawnee newsletter, "Exclusively Shawnee."

Mark Supnick
2771 Oakbrook Manor
Fort Lauderdale, FL 33332
phone: 305-389-3911
Author of "Shawnee Pottery", and "Collecting Hull's Little Red Riding Hood."

Bev & Jim Mangus
5147 Broadway NE
Louisville, OH 44641
Collects and consultant to "The Official Price Guide to Pottery and Porcelain."

Duane & Janice Vanderbilt
4040 Westover Dr.
Indianapolis, IN 46268
·*Collects and consultant to "The Official Price Guide to Pottery and Porcelain."*

Spaulding China/Royal Copley

Collectors

Barbara Burke
4028 Palo Alto Ct.
Orlando, FL 32817-3803

Experts

Joe Devine
1411 3rd St.
Council Bluffs, IA 51503
Collects and consultant to "The Official Price Guide to Pottery and Porcelain."

Jim Petzold
P.O. Box 46
Madison, WI 53701-0046
phone: 608-241-9138
fax: 608-241-8770
e-mail: ceramics@execpc.com
Co-editor with of "CAS Collector"; wants to buy all Ceramic Arts Studio & Royal Copley creations including

shakers, figurines, dolls, lamps, and metal art.

Periodicals

Dan Benton
Newsletter: Copley Courier, The
1639 N. Catalina St.
Burbank, CA 91505-1605
phone: 818-848-6541
Internet: http://www.csmonline.com/booth59.html
For collectors of Royal Copley china which was made by the Spaulding China of Sebring, OH (1942-1957); Spaulding also made the Royal Windsor and the Spaulding patterns; published bi-monthly.

Stanford Pottery

Experts

Kathy Kimball
140 Linnell Rd.
Grand Marais, MN 55604
Collects and consultant to "The Official Price Guide to Pottery and Porcelain."

Tamac Pottery

Experts

Tom & Phyllis Bess
14535 East 13th St.
Tulsa, OK 74108
phone: 918-437-7776
Buys and sells; consultant to "The Official Price Guide to Pottery and Porcelain."

Treasure Craft Pottery

Experts

Joyce Roerig
RR 2 Box 504
Walterboro, SC 29488-9278
phone: 803-538-2487
Buys and sells; consultant to "Official Price Guide to Pottery & Porcelain."

Twin Winton

Experts

Joyce Roerig
RR 2 Box 504
Walterboro, SC 29488-9278
phone: 803-538-2487
Buys and sells; consultant to "Official Price Guide to Pottery & Porcelain."

Uhl Pottery Co.

Clubs/Associations

Don Schwartz
Uhl Collectors Society, Inc.
Newsletter: Uhl Collectors Society Newsletter
P.O. Box 1081
Michigan City, MI 46361-8281
phone: 219-872-2308
Purpose is the preservation and sharing of information relating to the production of Uhl pottery; production

dates back to 1849 and ran through the mid-1940s when the company ceased operation.

Collectors

Tom & Donna Uebelhor
233 E. Timberlin Lane
Jasper, IN 47546
phone: 812-482-9575

Joseph Erbacher
P.O. Box 98
St. Anthony, IN 47565-0098
phone: 812-326-2777
President of Uhl Collectors Society; membership info sent on request; annual convention.

Dave & Donna Swick
506 Martin St.
Newton, IL 62448
phone: 618-783-3455

Dealers

Don Schwartz
P.O. Box 1081
Michigan City, MI 46361-8281
phone: 219-872-2308

Experts

Tim Hodges
1378 West Andrew Lane
Jasper, IN 47546
Consultant to "The Official Price Guide to Pottery and Porcelain."

Wahpeton Pottery Co./ Rosemeade

Experts

Irene J. Harms
2316 West 18th St.
Sioux Falls, SD 57104
Co-author with Shirley L. Sampson of "Beautiful Rosemeade."

CERAMICS (CONTINENTAL)

(see also DINNERWARE)

Auction Services

Christie's
502 Park Ave.
New York, NY 10022
phone: 212-546-1000
fax: 212-980-8163
Internet: http://www.sirius.com/ ~christie/

Collectors

John Coates
324 Woodland Dr.
Stevens Point, WI 54481
phone: 715-341-6113
Especially interested in Boch Feres/ Keramis Belgium art pottery depicting animals or birds, and those pieces with strong Art Deco design.

Dealers

Gerald Shultz
Antique Gallery, The
8523 Germantown Ave.
Philadelphia, PA 19118-3316
phone: 215-248-1700
fax: 215-247-8411
18th century Sevres, Coalport, Worcester, Meissen, Bow, Chelsea.

Farhad Radfar, ISA
MIR International Gallery, Inc.
P.O. Box 10678
Chicago, IL 60610
phone: 312-654-8510 or 773-477-2209
fax: 312-670-8182
e-mail: FRadfar@aol.com
Specializing in Meissen, KPM and Vienna porcelain.

Experts

Gerard Schultz
Antique Gallery, The
8523 Germantown Ave.
Philadelphia, PA 19118
phone: 215-248-1700
fax: 215-247-8411
Buys, sells and specializes in 18th century Delft, Sevres, Meissen, Longwy, Galle, Massier, Quimper, Doat, Boch, etc.

Susan & Al Bagdade
Country Peasants, The
3136 Elder Ct.
Northbrook, IL 60062-5832
phone: 847-498-1468
fax: 847-392-5848
e-mail: ADBSDB@aol.com
Author of "Warman's English & Continental Pottery & Porcelain" (Wallace-Homestead); advisor to "Warman's Antiques & Collectibles Price Guide."

Museums/Libraries

Wadsworth Atheneum
600 Main St.
Hartford, CT 06103
phone: 860-278-2670
fax: 860-527-0803
Featured displays include the Harold & Wendy Newman Collection of Veilleuses, the J. Pierpont Morgan Collection of Meissen Porcelain, and other diverse examples of fine European ceramics.

Amphora

Collectors

John Cobabe
800 South Pacific Hwy., Ste. 8-301
Redondo Beach, CA 90277
phone: 310-316-2982
Wants to buy Amphora; send photo, size and price.

Experts

Les & Irene Cohen
P.O. Box 17001
Pittsburgh, PA 15235-0001
phone: 412-793-0222 or 412-795-3030
Buys, collects and specializes in Austrian Amphora art pottery.

Jack Gunsaulus
Gray's Gallery
583 W. Ann Arbor Trail
Plymouth, MI 48170-1627
phone: 313-455-2373
Buys and sells Teplitz-Turn art pottery, e.g. items made by the Amphora Porcelain Works and Alexandra Works.

Art Pottery

Dealers

Alain Fournier
La Verrerie D'Art
P.O. Box 757
Bowie, MD 20718-0757
phone: 301-464-3251
Buys, sells, specializes in European art pottery from the Art Nouveau and Art Deco eras; C. Catteau, Dage, Amphora, early Sarraguemine, Czech, Austrian, French, Belgian.

Conta & Boehme

Experts

Janice & Richard Vogel
4720 SE Fort King St.
Ocala, FL 34470-1501
phone: 352-694-5776
fax: 352-694-7330

Czechoslovakian

Clubs/Associations

Kathy Foster
Czechoslovakian Collectors Guild International
Newsletter: CCGI Newsletter
P.O. Box 901395
Kansas City, MO 64190-1395
phone: 816-891-9115
fax: 816-891-0988
e-mail: ccgi@corp.pkgsvc.com
For collectors of anything Czechoslovakian and Bohemian: glass, pottery, art.

Collectors

Burt Smith
1103 Commonwealth Ave.
Boston, MA 02215
Wants large unusual pieces of Czech porcelain with dime-size round label marked "Made in Czechoslovakia"; figurals of birds, animals, people; also wants pitchers, urns, vases.

Mike & Cheryl Goyda
P.O. Box 192
East Petersburg, PA 17520-0192
phone: 717-569-7149
fax: 717-569-0909
e-mail: Goydagang@aol.com
Wants to buy Czech pottery.

Danish

Dealers

Phil Anderson
Anderson & Associates
2147 W. Farwell
Chicago, IL 60645-4900
phone: 773-338-1758
fax: 773-338-1758
Buys and sells porcelain figurines and vases from the Denmark, especially Royal Copenhagen, Bing & Grondahl, and Dahl Jensen; also collects Scandinavian wood carvings especially those signed Trygg and/or Gunnarsson.

French

Experts

Martin Spickler, PhD
Tova's Treasures
11410 Strand Dr., #207
Rockville, MD 20852
phone: 301-984-5954
Specializes in English, French, Meissen, Wedgwood, and Oriental ceramics.

Haviland

(see also CERAMICS [CONTINENTAL], Limoges; DINNERWARE, Haviland)

Clubs/Associations

Susan Carter, Mem.
Haviland Collectors Internationale Foundation
Newsletter: HCIF Newsletter
P.O. Box 802462
Santa Clarita, CA 91380-2462
phone: 805-297-0132
An organization dedicated to the study and promotion of porcelain and pottery made by the Haviland companies of France and America; newsletter published quarterly.

Dealers

Grace Graves
219 N. Milwaukee St.
Milwaukee, WI 53202-5818
phone: 414-291-9111
fax: 414-291-9018
e-mail: hmsgraves@aol.com

Experts

Dee & Maurice Hooks
Dee's China Shop
P.O. Box 142
Lawrenceville, IL 62439-0142
phone: 618-943-2741

Dick & Dona Schleiger
1626 Crestview Rd.
Redlands, CA 92374
*Author of several Haviland pattern
books; developers of "Schleiger"
numbers for Haviland identification.*

Herend

Dealers

Frank Juhasz
Diamond & Gem Trading USA, Co.
P.O. Box 1266
Sugar Land, TX 77487-1266
phone: 800-843-7363 or 713-908-5962
fax: 713-980-5964
*Specializes in Herend and Zsolnay
porcelain; carries the largest
inventory of Herend in the U.S.; buys,
sells and appraises Herend and
Zsolnay.*

Hutschenreuther

Experts

Jack Gunsaulus
Gray's Gallery
583 W. Ann Arbor Trail
Plymouth, MI 48170-1627
phone: 313-455-2373

Italian

Dealers

Shaw
P.O. Box 5096
Southfield, MI 48086
*Wants to buy Italian ceramics:
Gamboni, Fantoni, Melotti, Gratti,
Melandri, Campi, Ginori, Garaboldi,
Mazzotti, Albisola, Fabbari, Tasca,
Fontana, Patrinini, Arte Della
Ceramica, etc.*

KPM

Man./Prod./Dist.

KPM (Royal Porcelain Manufacturer)
Wegley Str. #1
W-1000
Berlin 12 Germany

Limoges

Dealers

Susan Leite
44 Glenwood Rd.
Brewster, MA 02631-2202
phone: 508-385-4905
*Wants to buy undamaged Limoges
items.*

Massier

Collectors

John Cobabe
800 South Pacific Hwy., Ste. 8-301
Redondo Beach, CA 90277
phone: 310-316-2982

Meissen

Dealers

Martin & Helene Schwalberg
Meissen Shop, The
329 Worth Ave.
Palm Beach, FL 33480-6012
phone: 561-832-2504
fax: 561-833-4171
*Devoted exclusively to antique
Meissen porcelain.*

Experts

Martin Spickler, PhD
Tova's Treasures
11410 Strand Dr., #207
Rockville, MD 20852
phone: 301-984-5954
*Specializes in English, French,
Meissen, Wedgwood, and Oriental
ceramics.*

Mimi Levine
Mimi & Steve Levine Antiques, Inc.
6205 Marilyn Drive
Alexandria, VA 22310
phone: 703-971-3941
e-mail: mimilev@erols.com
*Buys and sells pre-1900 English,
American, and German porcelains
and English pottery: Meissen,
Wedgwood, Worcester, Minton, and
other excellent companies; also
appraises and lectures.*

Mottahedeh

Man./Prod./Dist.

Mottahedeh & Co.
225 Fifth Ave.
New York, NY 10010
phone: 212-685-3050
fax: 212-889-9483
*Porcelain, pottery, glassware,
brassware; antique reproductions,
metal and wood and ceramics; china
dinnerware.*

Old Ivory

Clubs/Associations

John Harms
Old Ivory Porcelain Society
P.O. Box 326
Osage, IA 50461
phone: 515-732-3872

Periodicals

Pat Fitzwater
Newsletter: Old Ivory Newsletter
P.O. Box 1004
Wilsonville, OR 97070-1004
phone: 503-655-1420
fax: 503-655-1420
*Focuses on the Old Ivory (Silesia)
patterns of porcelain dinnerware
produced in Germany during the late
1800s by the Ohme factory; send a
LSASE for a sample copy.*

Portuguese

Dealers

Tucha Gift Shop, Inc.
110 Ferry St.
Newark, NJ 07105
phone: 201-589-3681 or 201-589-6672
fax: 201-589-8284
*Carries a large line of contemporary
items made in Portugal, especially
handpainted ceramics.*

Quimper

Dealers

Charles & Marianne Wilson
Thistle hill B&B Inn
5541 Sperryvile Pike
Boston, VA 22713
phone: 540-987-9142

Betty & John Lucas
Shop on Main, The
15 W. Friend St.
Columbiana, OH 44408
phone: 216-482-0111

Experts

Sandra Bondhus
P.O. Box 100
Unionville, CT 06085
phone: 203-678-1808
*Author of "Quimper Pottery";
specializes in 19th & 20th century
Quimper of fine artistic merit; always
buying and selling Quimper.*

Noelle B. Beatty
Old Quimper Pottery
3438 34th Place, NW
Washington, DC 20016-3136
phone: 202-537-0855
fax: 202-537-1609
e-mail: qw-nb-beatty@msn.com
Internet: http://www.nsws.com/quimper/
*Buys, sells, specializes in Quimper;
wide variety of 19th and 20th century
Quimper for sale; will answer
collectors' questions about old
Quimper.*

Joan Datesman
105 Market St.
Annapolis, MD 21401
phone: 410-268-6233
fax: 410-268-3061
*Author of "Collecting Quimper;
Quimper Collections"; trips to France
maintains large 1860-1930 inventory;
rustic to elaborate designs.*

Susan & Al Bagdade
Country Peasants, The
3136 Elder Ct.
Northbrook, IL 60062-5832
phone: 847-498-1468
fax: 847-392-5848
e-mail: ADBSDB@aol.com
*Buys and sells Quimper pottery,
especially unusual pieces: figures and
early decorative examples; authors,
lecturers, staff writers.*

Man./Prod./Dist.

Quimper Faience
Newsletter: Le Monde de Quimper
141 Water St.
Stonington, CT 06378
phone: 860-535-1712
fax: 860-535-3509
*The American branch of the French
Quimper factory; retail mail order
available.*

R.S. Prussia

Clubs/Associations

Frances Coy
International Association of R. S.
Prussia Collectors Inc.
Newsletter: IARSPC Newsletter
212 Wooded Falls Rd.
Louisville, KY 40243

Dealers

Ward Stewart
Stewart's Antiques
1000 Coolidge
Lafayette, LA 70503-2336
phone: 318-232-2957

Veronica Wexler
Wit's End Antiques & Collectibles
840 Blossom Dr.
Santa Clara, CA 95050-5115
phone: 408-261-9742 or 408-984-2423
e-mail: rwexler@rivendell.com
*Buys and sells R.S. Prussia, marked
and unmarked.*

Experts

Milt Steinfeld
P.O. Box 457
Westfield, NJ 07090
phone: 908-233-0950
fax: 908-233-0950

Juanita Wilkins
Bird of Paradise
430 S. Cole St.
Lima, OH 45805-3367

Dee & Maurice Hooks
Dee's China Shop
P.O. Box 142
Lawrenceville, IL 62439-0142
phone: 618-943-2741
*Has been buying and selling R.S.
Prussia for 20 years.*

Rosenthal

Man./Prod./Dist.

Rosenthal USA Limited
355 Michele Pl.
Carlstadt, NJ 07072-2304
*Glassware, giftware, flatware,
dinnerware, china and stoneware,
stemware, silverplate, stainless steel,
figurines, ceramic, glass, wood
serving accessories.*

Royal Bayreuth

Clubs/Associations

Howard & Sarah Wade
Royal Bayreuth International Collectors'
Society
Newsletter: RBICS Newsletter
P.O. Box 325
Orrville, OH 44667-0325
phone: 330-682-8551
fax: 330-682-3655
e-mail: ukdolls@aol.com
*Bi-monthly newsletter with informa-
tion on members' collections, new
finds, price trends across the country
and classified ads.*

Judith White
Royal Bayreuth Collectors' Club
926 Essex Circle
Kalamazoo, MI 49008
phone: 616-343-6066

Collectors

Eric Sidman
Eric's Antiques
381 Elliot St.
Newton, MA 02164
phone: 617-331-3744 or 401-333-3008
*Wants old blue mark Royal Bayreuth
items; all figurals but especially Santa
Claus, Tiger, Squirrel, Rabbit, etc.;
Rose Tapestry items, Sunbonnets,
Snow Babies, Beach Babies; any
unusual or rare items; will pay for
photos; prompt reply.*

Howard & Sarah Wade
P.O. Box 325
Orrville, OH 44667-0325
phone: 330-682-8551
fax: 330-682-3655
e-mail: ukdolls@aol.com

Juanita Wilkins
Bird of Paradise
430 S. Cole St.
Lima, OH 45805-3367

Experts

Mary McCaslin
272 Canterbury Dr.
Danville, IN 46122
phone: 317-745-6330
*Author of "Royal Bayreuth: A
Collector's Guide."*

Dee & Maurice Hooks
Dee's China Shop
P.O. Box 142
Lawrenceville, IL 62439-0142
phone: 618-943-2741

Royal Copenhagen

Dealers

Pat Owen
Viking Import House, Inc.
690 NE 13th St.
Ft. Lauderdale, FL 33304-1110
phone: 305-763-3388 or 800-327-2297
fax: 305-462-2317
*Operates the VIDEX, a buy/sell
service for any and all Royal*

Copenhagen and Bing & Grondahl
collectibles.

Man./Prod./Dist.

Steen Nottelman, Cur.
Royal Copenhagen Ltd.
45 Smallegrade
DK2000 Frederiksberg
Denmark

Josephine Dillon
Royal Copenhagen/Bing & Grondahl
Co.
27 Holland Ave.
White Plains, NY 10603-3317
phone: 914-428-8222 or 800-431-1992
fax: 914-428-8251
*Royal Copenhagen, Bing & Grondahl,
Holmegaard, and Georg Jensen are
the best of Scandinavian collectibles;
manufactures dinnerware, cobalt blue
underglaze collector plates, figurines,
bells, dolls, ornaments and gift
accessories.*

Royal Copenhagen/Flora Danica

Dealers

Jeff E. Purtell
P.O. Box 28
Amherst, NH 03031-0028
phone: 603-673-4331 or 800-973-4331
fax: 603-673-1525
*Specializes in Royal Copenhagen
Flora Danica.*

Scandinavian

Dealers

Anita L. Grashof
Gallerie Ani'tiques
Stage House Village
Park & Front Streets
Scotch Plains, NJ 07076
phone: 908-322-4600 or 201-377-3032
fax: 201-765-9565
*Buys, sells, appraises Swedish art
pottery such as Argenta by Kage,
Gustavsberg, Rorstrand; also Finnish
Arabia pottery.*

Schlegelmilch

(see CERAMICS [CONTINENTAL],
R.S. Prussia)

Sitzendorf

Man./Prod./Dist.

Sitzendorfer Porzellanmanufaktur
Hautstr. 26, 07429
Sitzendorfe, Germany

Teplitz-Turn

Experts

Les & Irene Cohen
P.O. Box 17001
Pittsburgh, PA 15235-0001
phone: 412-793-0222 or 412-795-3030
Buys, collects and specializes in

Teplitz-Turn art pottery such as
Amphora Porcelain Works, Alexandra
Works, Heliosine Ware, "PD" marked
Teplitz.

Jack Gunsaulus
Gray's Gallery
583 W. Ann Arbor Trail
Plymouth, MI 48170-1627
phone: 313-455-2373
*Buys and sells Teplitz-Turn art
pottery, e.g. items made by the
Amphora Porcelain Works and
Alexandra Works.*

Villeroy & Boch

Collectors

Steve Elliott
1600 Tennessee St.
Vallejo, CA 94590
phone: 707-552-8400 or 707-642-1949
fax: 707-552-0881
*Wants antique Villeroy & Boch
Mettlach items.*

Man./Prod./Dist.

Villeroy & Boch Co.
41 Madison Ave.
New York, NY 10010
phone: 212-683-1747
fax: 212-481-0283
Imported dinnerware, glassware.

Museums/Libraries

Villeroy & Boch Keramik Museum
Mettlach
Schloss Ziegelberg
D-6642
Mettlach, Germany

Zsolnay

Collectors

Les & Irene Cohen
P.O. Box 17001
Pittsburgh, PA 15235-0001
phone: 412-793-0222 or 412-795-3030
*Buys and collects Zsolnay art pottery,
vases preferred.*

John Cobabe
800 South Pacific Hwy., Ste. 8-301
Redondo Beach, CA 90277
phone: 310-316-2982

Dealers

Federico Santi
Zsolnay Store, The
152 Spring St.
Newport, RI 02840-6806
phone: 401-841-5060
fax: 401-848-0953
e-mail: zsolnay@drawrm.com
Internet: http://www.drawrm.com
*Buys and sells Hungarian Zsolnay and
Eastern European pottery; interested
in Zsolnay, Amphora, Turin-Tepliz art
pottery; send photos and price; can
buy from photo.*

Frank Juhasz
Diamond & Gem Trading USA, Co.
P.O. Box 1266
Sugar Land, TX 77487-1266
phone: 800-843-7363 or 713-908-5962
fax: 713-980-5964
*Specializes in Herend and Zsolnay
porcelain; carries the largest
inventory of Herend in the U.S.; buys,
sells and appraises Herend and
Zsolnay.*

Experts

Laszlo Gyugyi
P.O. Box 17329
Pittsburgh, PA 15235
phone: 412-256-2300 or 412-731-1753
fax: 412-256-2223
*Collector wants to buy quality Zsolnay
pieces from the Art Nouveau period
and from the preceding classical
periods; quality more important than
price; send photo and/or description;
all letters answered; information
seekers welcome.*

Misc. Services

American Hungarian Foundation, The
300 Somerset St.
New Brunswick, NJ 08901
phone: 201-846-5777
*Held exhibit of art pottery from the
factory of Vilmos Zsolnay in Pecs,
Hungary.*

CERAMICS (ENGLISH)

Mimi Levine
Mimi & Steve Levine Antiques, Inc.
6205 Marilyn Drive
Alexandria, VA 22310
phone: 703-971-3941
e-mail: mimilev@erols.com
*Buys and sells pre-1900 English,
American, and German porcelains
and English pottery: Meissen,
Wedgwood, Worcester, Minton, and
other excellent companies; also
appraises and lectures.*

(see also DINNERWARE)

Auction Services

W. Buckley
Potteries Antique Center Auctions
271 Waterloo Road
Cobridge, Stoke on Trent
Staffordshire ST6 3HR, U.K.
phone: 01782-201455
fax: 01782-201518
*Conducts three specialized British
pottery auctions each year.*

Stuart Slavid
Skinner, Inc.
357 Main St.
Bolton, MA 01740-1104
phone: 508-779-6241 or 617-350-5400
fax: 508-779-5144
*Established in 1964, Skinner Inc. is
the fifth largest auction house in the*

US; has offices in Bolton and Boston, MA.

Clubs/Associations

Dr. Keith McLeod
Wedgwood International Seminar
Newsletter: WIS Proceedings
22 DeSavry Crescent
Toronto
Ontario M4S 2L2 Canada, TX
phone: 416-978-7011
fax: 416-489-4089
e-mail: k.mcleod@utoronto.ca
An educational association sharing the latest information in the field of English ceramics; also publishes the "Annual Proceedings"; also lectures and annual seminars; annual conference.

Dealers

W. Buckley
Potteries Antique Center Auctions
271 Waterloo Road
Cobridge, Stoke on Trent
Staffordshire ST6 3HR, U.K.
phone: 01782-201455
fax: 01782-201518
Antique store with large stocks of British pottery from the 19th and 20th centuries.

Wynn A. Sayman
Wynn A. Sayman, Inc.
Old Fields
Richmond, MA 01254
phone: 413-698-2272
fax: 413-698-3282
e-mail: wynnsayman@compuserve.com
Specializes in English pottery and porcelain of the 18th and early 19th century: salt-glaze, redware, tortoise shell wares, creamware, pearlware and Staffordshire bocage figures; some Chelsea, Bow, Worcester, and Derby; by appointment.

Eric H. Granberg
Deja Vue Antiques
16 George St., #9
Attleboro, MA 02703
phone: 508-226-1816 or 508-222-9905
Buys and sells English travel commemoratives, Wedgwood, Queensware, Staffordshire, etc.

Leo Kaplan
Leo Kaplan, Ltd.
967 Madison Ave.
New York, NY 10021
phone: 212-249-6766 or 212-249-7574
Specializes in early English pottery and porcelain.

Dennis Lockard
2 Hats Collectibles
P.O. Box 1192
Clarksville, VA 23927
Specializes in 20th century English dinnerware.

L.B. Belsley
Anglia Antiques
c/o Antique Center of Texas
1001 W. Loop North, #442
Houston, TX 77055
phone: 713-496-1114
fax: 713-496-1019
Specializes in Wedgwood, English Royal commemoratives, and other English ceramics.

Experts

Susan Scott
882 Queen Street West
Toronto
Ontario M6J 1G3 Canada
phone: 416-657-8278
fax: 416-658-4675
e-mail: scottca@ibm.net
Specializes in 20th century English ceramics.

Stuart Slavid
86 Johnson Dr.
Marlborough, MA 01752-1438
phone: 508-485-5993
Specializes in Wedgwood, Staffordshire, and Royal Worcester.

David & Linda Arman
P.O. Box 39
Portsmouth, RI 02871-0039
phone: 401-841-8403
fax: 401-841-8403
Internet: http://
www.oaklandpublications.com

Gerard Schultz
Antique Gallery, The
8523 Germantown Ave.
Philadelphia, PA 19118
phone: 215-248-1700
fax: 215-247-8411
Buys, sells and specializes in English ceramics: Coalport, Worcester, Bow, Chelsea, Davenport, Doulton.

Martin Spickler, PhD
Tova's Treasures
11410 Strand Dr., #207
Rockville, MD 20852
phone: 301-984-5954
Specializes in English, French, Meissen, Wedgwood, and Oriental ceramics.

E. Jefferson Hynds
1317 Cranbrook Dr.
Saginaw, MI 48603-5470
Interested in English transferware of the 18th and 19th centuries. Most interested in acquiring the wares of Spode and Copeland, particularly the 18th century blue and white Spode. Also collect antique Adams jasperware.

Susan & Al Bagdade
Country Peasants, The
3136 Elder Ct.
Northbrook, IL 60062-5832
phone: 847-498-1468
fax: 847-392-5848
e-mail: ADBSDB@aol.com
Author of "Warman's English & Continental Pottery & Porcelain"

(Wallace-Homestead); advisor to "Warman's Antiques & Collectibles Price Guide."

Periodicals

David & Linda Arman
Magazine: China & Glass Quarterly
P.O. Box 39
Portsmouth, RI 02871-0039
phone: 401-841-8403
fax: 401-841-8403
Internet: http://
www.oaklandpublications.com
Deals with the fields of English ceramics 1750-1865 (Historical Staffordshire, Pratt Ware, Lustre, Figures, transferware) and Early American glass 1750-1880 (blown three mold, freeblown, pattern molded, pressed, paperweights.)

ABC Plates

Clubs/Associations

Dr. Joan M. George
ABC Collectors' Circle
Newsletter: ABC Collectors' Circle Newsletter
67 Stevens Ave.
Old Bridge, NJ 08857-2244
phone: 908-679-8924
fax: 908-679-6102
e-mail: drjgeorge@nac.net
Collectors of educational plates and mugs in china, tin and glass; many collect only those with alphabet displayed; most prefer 19th century items; buy, sell, trade through quarterly newsletter.

Applied Sprig Wares

Experts

Stephanie M. Schnatz
17 Tallow Ct.
Baltimore, MD 21244-2516
phone: 410-944-0819
Buying applied sprig ware (called Chelsea or Grandmother's Ware); willing to buy any motif in lavender on white china, or white motifs/ decorations on lavender china: jugs, foot bath, soup tureen, miniatures, toast rack, creamers, etc.

Art Pottery

Experts

Gerard Schultz
Antique Gallery, The
8523 Germantown Ave.
Philadelphia, PA 19118
phone: 215-248-1700
fax: 215-247-8411
Buys, sells and specializes in Bernard Moore, Doulton, Pilkington, Clarice Cliff, Susie Cooper, Moorcroft, Roole, Minton, Carlton Ware.

Carlton Ware

Clubs/Associations

Helen & Keith Martin
Carlton Ware International
Newsletter: Carlton Times
P.O. Box 161
Sevenoaks
Kent Tn15 6GA, U.K.
Leading Carlton Ware club.

Dealers

Helen & Keith Martin
P.O. Box 161
Sevenoaks
Kent Tn15 6GA, U.K.
World's leading Carlton Ware specialists.

Clarice Cliff

Clubs/Associations

Leonard R. Griffin
Clarice Cliff Collector's Club
Fantasque House
Tennis Drive, The Park
Nottingham NG7 1AE, U.K.

Collectors

Darryl Rehr
2591 Military Ave.
Los Angeles, CA 90064-1933
phone: 310-477-5229
fax: 310-268-8420
e-mail: dcrehr@earthlink.net
Internet: http://www.earthlink.net/
~dcrehr/
Wants handpainted "Bizarre-Ware" only; many patterns including "Fantasque", "Cruise Ware" and others; please send photos.

Experts

Susan Scott
882 Queen Street West
Toronto
Ontario M6J 1G3 Canada
phone: 416-657-8278
fax: 416-658-4675
e-mail: scottca@ibm.net

Carole A. Berk
8020 Norfolk Ave.
Bethesda, MD 20814-2504
phone: 800-382-2413

Doulton

(see also CERAMICS [ENGLISH], Royal Doulton; COLLECTIBLES [MODERN], Royal Doulton)

Collectors

James Hardie
P.O. Box 661
Saint Charles, IL 60174
phone: 708-584-0019
The bi-monthly MADCAP newsletter is devoted to serious Doulton collectors, with an active buy, sell and trade section.

Dealers

Tom & Annette Power
Collector, The
9 Church St.
London NW8 8DEE, U.K.
phone: 0171-7064586
fax: 0171-7062948
e-mail: collector@globalnet.co.uk
*Specializing in discontinued Doulton:
character jugs, figurines, seriesware,
Kingsware, Bunnykins, Flambe,
stoneware, etc.*

Yesterdays, Inc.
P.O. Box 296
New City, NY 10956
phone: 800-Tob-yJug or 914-634-8456
*Send LSASE for brochure; buys single
pieces or entire collections; will
arrange to come to your house to
inspect/pack collections; after 7:00
pm call 800-Toby Mug or 914-634-
8456.*

Rita Leiter
Mainly Doulton
40 Chestnut Hill
North Hills, NY 11576
phone: 516-365-1836
*Buys and sells discontinued jugs,
whiskey pieces, series ware, etc.*

Yesterdays South, Inc.
P.O. Box 161083
Miami, FL 33116-1083
phone: 800-368-5866 or 305-251-1988
fax: 305-254-5977
*Send SASE for list of almost 1000
Doultons and Lladros for sale.*

Betty J. Weir
Doulton Divvy Service
P.O. Box 2434
Joliet, IL 60434
phone: 815-725-7348
fax: 815-725-7388
*Maintains a list of both For Sale and
Wanted to Buy Doulton and Royal
Doulton items; will contact the parties
when a match is found; for all
Doulton figurines, character jugs,
animals, series ware, dinnerware,
advertising, etc.*

Periodicals

Betty J. Weir, Co-Ed.
Magazine: Doulton Divvy
P.O. Box 2434
Joliet, IL 60434
phone: 815-725-7348
fax: 815-725-7388
*A quarterly magazine focusing on
Doulton and Royal Doulton figurines,
character jugs and Toby jugs; also
older Doulton, brown stoneware, art
pottery, seriesware, commemoratives,
etc.; asking prices, ads, Q&A, articles,
etc.*

Goss China/Crested Ware

Clubs/Associations

Alisa Schofield, Sec.
Goss Collectors Club
Magazine: Goss Hawks, The
4 Khasiaberry
Walnut Tree
Milton Keynes MK7 7DP, U.K.
phone: +44 0181 491 4035
fax: +44 0181 262 9713
e-mail:
    frank@gosscrestedchina.demon.co.uk
Internet: http://
    www.gosscrestedchina.demon.co.uk/
    Club.html
*Worldwide membership with regional
meetings held in England.*

Mike Wallington
Crested Circle
75 Cannon Grove
Fetcham, Leatherhead
Surrey KT22 9LP, U.K.
phone: 01372-376612

Lynda & Nicholas Pine
Goss & Crested China Club
62 Murray Road
Waterlooville P08 9JL, U.K.
phone: 01705 597440

Collectors

Jeanne Goss Spaulding
1325 West Ave.
Hilton, NY 14468
phone: 716-392-2706
*Only wants pieces marked "W.H.
Goss"; pictorials, parian busts,
cottages, monuments, and animals
preferred.*

Minton

Museums/Libraries

Minton Museum
Minton House, London Road
Stoke-on-Trent
Staffordshire ST4 7QD, U.K.

Moorcroft

Collectors

Poole
P.O. Box 692
Mill City, OR 97360

Dealers

John Harrigan
1900 Hennepin
Minneapolis, MN 55403-3160
phone: 612-872-0226
fax: 612-872-0224
Please write with pictures of items.

Museums/Libraries

Moorcroft Museum
Sandbach Road
Burslem
Stoke-on-Trent ST2 2DQ, U.K.

Rabbitware

Collectors

William F. Oliver, Jr.
P.O. Box 886
Fernandina Beach, FL 32035-0886
phone: 904-261-5328
*Wants to buy rabbitware - a colorful
Staffordshire ceramic; comes in four
patterns: Virginia Rose, Single Rose,
Adams Rose and Bullseye, with rabbits
around the rim or in the center;
usually in form of plates, platters,
mugs, chargers.*

Royal Doulton

(see also CERAMICS [ENGLISH],
Doulton; COLLECTIBLES
[MODERN], Royal Doulton)

Dealers

Jean-Paul Iannantuoni
P.O. Box 563062
Dept. CIC
Charlotte, NC 28256-3072
*Buys and sells Doulton and Royal
Doulton character jugs, figurines and
series ware. Send $2 for current price
list.*

Sal Castillo
Pascoe & Company
101 Alameria Ave.
Coral Gables, FL 33134
phone: 800-872-0195 or 305-445-3229
e-mail: pascoe@vmsmiami.com
Internet: http://www.vmsmiami.com/
    pascoe
*Buying Royal Doulton figurines,
character jugs, and coaching ware;
carries large inventory for sale.*

Stan Worrey
Colonial House Antiques
182 Front St.
Berea, OH 44017
phone: 216-826-4169 or 800-344-9299
fax: 216-826-0839
*Specializes in old and new Royal
Doulton figurines and character jugs.*

John Harrigan
1900 Hennepin
Minneapolis, MN 55403-3160
phone: 612-872-0226
fax: 612-872-0224
*Interested in Toby jugs; please write
with pictures of items.*

Wellington & Co.
2394 Leeward Circle
Westlake Village, CA 91361
phone: 805-379-3066
Wants old Royal Doulton mugs.

Carol Payne
Carol's Antique Gallery
14455 Big Basin Way
Saratoga, ÇA 95070-6008
phone: 408-867-7055
*Wants to buy animal figurines; will
also consider lady figurines, series
ware (teapots, or plates with scenes,*

*etc.), stoneware, Toby jugs, teapots
and cups.*

Man./Prod./Dist.

Customer Service
Royal Doulton USA Inc.
701 Cottontail Lane
Somerset, NJ 08873
phone: 908-356-7880 or 800-682-4462
fax: 908-764-4974
*China, dinnerware; cups and saucers,
figurines, crystal giftware and
stemware.*

Periodicals

A.R. Blakeman
B.B.R. Publishing
Magazine: Collecting Doulton
P.O. Box 310
Richmond
Surrey TW9 1FS, U.K.
*Leading magazine for the coverage of
all aspects of Royal Doulton pottery:
character jugs, figurines, advertising
items, etc.; published bi-month:ly.*

Royal Winton

Clubs/Associations

Jane Fehrenbacher
Royal Winton International Collectors
Club
Newsletter: RWICC Newsletter
600 Columbia St.
Pasadena, CA 91105
phone: 818-441-2490
fax: 818-441-4122
*Based in England, this club focuses on
chintz, cottage, luster and other wares
made by Grimwade Brothers and
Royal WInton from 1886 until the
1960s; club newsletter six timer per
year.*

Man./Prod./Dist.

Royal Winton, Unit 1, Lompark Estate
Chadwick Street, Longton
Stoke on Trent
Staffordshire ST3 1PJ, U.K.
phone: 01782 598811
fax: 01782 342737

Seacombe

Collectors

Peter Blundell
P.O. Box 6
Vernon
B.C. V1T 6M1 Canada
phone: 250-542-4540
*English-born collector, born where
this pottery existed in the 1850s near
Liverpool; has researched extensively
this poor quality pottery that was
made wharfside for export to the US,
Canada, West Indies, Australia.*

Shelley Potteries

Clubs/Associations

Shelley Group
Newsletter: Shelley Group Newsletter
12 Lilleshall Rd.
Clayton, Newcastle-Under-Lyme
Staffordshire ST5 3BX, U.K.

Anji Davis
National Shelley China Club
5585 NW 164th Ave.
Portland, OR 97229-8915
phone: 503-452-9761

Experts

Phyllis Osjecki
Phyllis'
P.O. Box 792
Canyonville, OR 97417
phone: 541-839-4135 or 541-839-6151
Buys, sells, and appraises Shelley china.

Spode

Dealers

Carol Payne
Carol's Antique Gallery
14455 Big Basin Way
Saratoga, CA 95070-6008
phone: 408-867-7055
Wants to purchase any pre-1950 Spode; one item or sets; must be in perfect condition; especially likes the "Mayfair" pattern.

Man./Prod./Dist.

Spode
Historical Consultant
Stoke-on-Trent
U.K. ST4 1BX
e-mail: spode@spode.co.uk
Internet: http://www.spode.co.uk
Will answer questions about Spode and Copeland factory wares.

Museums/Libraries

Curator
Spode Museum
Historical Consultant
Stoke-on-Trent
U.K. ST4 1BX
e-mail: spode@spode.co.uk
Internet: http://www.spode.co.uk

Staffordshire

Appraisers

Stephen van Cline, CAPP
van Cline & Davenport, Ltd.
792 Franklin Ave.
Franklin Lakes, NJ 07417-1343
Specializes in English Staffordshire & Wedgwood ceramics; appraisals, authentication, lectures, expert testimony; minimum charge $25; letter request only, SASE.

Auction Services

Joseph Arman
Collector's Sales & Services
P.O. Box 39
Portsmouth, RI 02871-0039
phone: 401-841-8403
fax: 401-841-8403
Internet: http://www.oaklandpublications.com
Specialize in mail-bid auctions for historical Staffordshire, Quimper, American glass, paperweights, bottles, etc.

Dealers

Anita L. Grashof
Gallerie Ani'tiques
Stage House Village
Park & Front Streets
Scotch Plains, NJ 07076
phone: 908-322-4600 or 201-377-3032
fax: 201-765-9565
Buys, sells and appraises 19th century English figurines and dogs; royalty, theater, naval and army, sports and miscellaneous groups; also all animals and breeds of dogs in pairs.

Carl McCann
Troy & Black, Inc.
P.O. Box 228
Red Creek, NY 13143-0228
phone: 315-754-8115
Buys and sells high quality flow blue, Staffordshire figurines, American painted furniture, stoneware, redware, coverlets, samplers, and other American textiles, folk art, etc.

Dennis Lockard
2 Hats Collectibles
P.O. Box 1192
Clarksville, VA 23927

J. Wagner
Bygones
P.O. Box 1558
North Bend, OR 97459-0090
phone: 541-756-7111
Buyers of English Staffordshire transferware, old blue and colors; specializes in the Adams potteries.

Experts

Adele Kenny
c/o Schiffer Publishing, Ltd.
77 Lower Valley Road
Atglen, PA 19310
phone: 908-889-7223
Author of "Staffordshire Spaniels: A collector's Guide to History and Values" (Schiffer); wants to buy and trade all types of Staffordshire figures 1740-1900.

Staffordshire (Historical)

Dealers

William & Teresa Kurau
P.O. Box 457
Lampeter, PA 17537
phone: 717-464-0731
Wants dark blue and lighter colors; Arms of the States by Mayer; Erie

Canal and Liverpool pitchers; list of items for sale available.

Roger Powers
P.O. Box 424
Riderwood, MD 21139
phone: 410-821-6788

Staffordshire (Romantic)

Experts

Mark Brown
Seekers Antiques
P.O. Box 10083
Columbus, OH 43201
phone: 614-291-2203
Advisor to "Warman's Antiques & Collectibles Price Guide."

Tim Sublette
Seekers Antiques
P.O. Box 10083
Columbus, OH 43201
phone: 614-291-2203
Advisor to "Warman's Antiques & Collectibles Price Guide."

Susie Cooper China Ltd.

Clubs/Associations

Susie Cooper Collectors Group
Newsletter: Susie Cooper Collectors Group Newsletter
P.O. Box 7436
London N12 7QF, U.K.
An international organization for collectors of Susie Cooper ceramics; quarterly newsletter with news, buy/sell ads, auctions, etc.; please send SASE with inquiries.

Collectors

Darryl Rehr
2591 Military Ave.
Los Angeles, CA 90064-1933
phone: 310-477-5229
fax: 310-268-8420
e-mail: dcrehr@earthlink.net
Internet: http://www.earthlink.net/~dcrehr/
Wants Art Deco style patterns and shapes; please send photo and SASE for guaranteed reply.

Experts

Susan Scott
882 Queen Street West
Toronto
Ontario M6J 1G3 Canada
phone: 416-657-8278
fax: 416-658-4675
e-mail: scottca@ibm.net

Torquay

Clubs/Associations

Shirley Everett, Mem.
Torquay Pottery Collectors Society
23 Holland Ave.
Cheam, Sutton
Surrey SM2 6HW. U.K.
phone: 0121 355 4152
e-mail: tpcs@macatala.demon.co.uk
Internet: http://www.macatala.demon.co.uk

Mary Jo O'Connor, Sec.
North American Torquay Society
Magazine: Torquay Collector, The
12 Stanton
Madison, CT 06443
phone: 203-732-4107
For the enhancement of knowledge and enjoyment of Torquay pottery; magazine offers articles, ads, convention news; magazine published quarterly; send LSASE for membership form.

Collectors

Joseph Brewer
P.O. Box 397
Dalton, GA 30722

Gerry & Jerry Kline
604 Orchard View Dr.
Maumee, OH 43537
phone: 419-893-1226

Experts

Cynthia Holt
c/o Rumbo
8738 1/2 Hunting Drive
San Gabriel, CA 91775-1265
phone: 818-286-6223
Collector and expert in Torquay pottery from all the major firms (Aller Vale, Longpark, Watcombe, etc.); especially wants pottery with scrolls, scenes, figurals; also exceptional motto-ware, especially "Kerswell Daisy."

Wade

Clubs/Associations

Wade Watch
8199 Pierson Ct.
Arvada, CO 80005
phone: 303-421-9655
fax: 303-721-0317

Dealers

Patty Keenan
Keenan Antiques
P.O. Box 111
Dover, PA 17315
phone: 717-292-4820
fax: 717-292-4664
Dealer in commissioned Christmas ornaments from Wade; major dealer in English/Irish Wade.

Liz Kramar
Kramar's Kollectible Korner
P.O. Box 30
Elk Mills, MD 21920-0030
phone: 410-398-0105
e-mail: kram5688@dpnet.net
Wants to buy English/Irish Wade.

Experts

Ian Warner
POS-NER Associates
P.O. Box 93022
Brampton
Ontario LGY 4V8 Canada
phone: 905-453-9074
Co-author with Mike Posgay of "The World of Wade," "The World of Wade Book 2," and "Wade Price Trends First Edition."

Wedgwood

Appraisers

Stephen van Cline, CAPP
van Cline & Davenport, Ltd.
792 Franklin Ave.
Franklin Lakes, NJ 07417-1343
Specializes in English Staffordshire & Wedgwood ceramics; appraisals, authentication, lectures, expert testimony; minimum charge $25; letter request only, SASE.

Clubs/Associations

Wedgwood Society
The Roman Villa
Rockbourne, Fordingbridge
Hants SP6 3PG, U.K.

Ronald F. Frazier
Wedgwood Society of Boston, Inc.
Newsletter: WSB Newsletter
132 Middle St.
Braintree, MA 02184-4841
phone: 617-843-5091
e-mail: r-m-s-frazier@worldnet.att.net
Internet: http://angelfire.com/ma/wsb
Publishes regular newsletter with in-depth articles on Wedgwood; holds regular meetings with speakers on Wedgwood.

Wedgwood Society of New York
Magazine: ARS Ceramica
5 Dogwood Ct.
Glen Head, NY 11545-2740
phone: 516-626-3427
fax: 516-626-3430
An annual publication with in-depth articles about Wedgwood and other English ceramics, ads and auctions; also publishes a bi-monthly newsletter.

Collectors

Stuart Slavid
86 Johnson Dr.
Marlborough, MA 01752-1438
phone: 508-485-5993
Wants to buy old Wedgwood; one piece or entire collections.

B. Stern
56 Center St.
Clinton, NJ 08809
Wants to buy yellow, pink, lilac or other unusual colors of Wedgwood.

Bernard Starr
5 Dogwood Ct.
Glen Head, NY 11545-2740
phone: 516-626-3427
fax: 516-626-3430
Specializes in Wedgwood and other English ceramics.

Dealers

Benton Rosen
Mansion House, Inc.
9 Kenilworth Way
Pawtucket, RI 02860
phone: 401-722-2927 or 508-759-4303
Wants to buy Wedgwood transfer print decorated commemorative items.

Howard Lewis
Howard Lewis Antiques
P.O. Box 5911
Wilmington, DE 19808-0911
phone: 302-731-5597
Buying and selling 18th, 19th and collectible 20th century Wedgwood: Jasper, Basalt, Caneware, Rosso Antico, Drabware, etc.; also wants non-Wedgwood porcelain and china of all types.

Collector's Wedgwood
P.O. Box 462
Newbury Park, CA 91319-0462
Specializes in antique and collectors' Jasper, Fairyland, Creamware, Basalts, Dry Bodies, Majolica; all shapes; no dinnerware, please; send SASE for list.

Experts

Ronald F. Frazier
132 Middle St.
Braintree, MA 02184-4841
phone: 617-843-5091
e-mail: r-m-s-frazier@worldnet.att.net
Internet: http://angelfire.com/ma/wsb
Collects and lectures on Wedgwood; freelance writer/contributor for periodicals' member of most major Wedgwood collector organizations.

Miriam & Aaron Levin
881 Whalley Ave.
New Haven, CT 06515
phone: 203-389-5440

Leslie V. Canavan
Alexis Antiques
22 Cloverleaf Lane
Ballwin, MO 63011-4001
phone: 314-391-1603
fax: 800-769-5109
e-mail: antiques@iwc.com
Internet: http://www.iwc.com/antiques
Appraiser, dealer, collector specializing in Wedgwood products of all types and eras; china matching, giftware; college, commemorative & historical plates; appraisals.

Man./Prod./Dist.

Waterford Wedgwood USA Inc.
P.O. Box 1276
Wall, NJ 07719
phone: 908-938-5800
fax: 908-938-6915
Bone china and earthenware.

Museums/Libraries

Wedgwood Visitor Center & Museum
Barlaston
Stoke-on-Trent
U.K. ST12 9ES
phone: 01782-204218

Bryding Adams
Birmingham Museum of Art
2000 8th Ave. N.
Birmingham, AL 35203-2278
phone: 205-254-2565
fax: 205-254-2714

CERAMICS (ORIENTAL)

(see also DINNERWARE; ORIENTALIA)

Appraisers

Stephen van Cline, CAPP
van Cline & Davenport, Ltd.
792 Franklin Ave.
Franklin Lakes, NJ 07417-1343
Specializes in Japanese and Chinese porcelains; minimum charge $25; letter request only, SASE.

Experts

Martin Spickler, PhD
Tova's Treasures
11410 Strand Dr., #207
Rockville, MD 20852
phone: 301-984-5954
Specializes in English, French, Meissen, Wedgwood, and Oriental ceramics.

Chinese Export Porcelain

Appraisers

Patricia M. Knight, ISA
Finetooth Comb Antiques Research & Appraisal Service
421 Ash Ave.
P.O. Box 1177
Ames, IA 50010-1177
phone: 515-292-9028
Consultant and qualified appraiser and lecturer on Chinese export porcelains.

Experts

Stuart Slavid
86 Johnson Dr.
Marlborough, MA 01752-1438
phone: 508-485-5993

Hobart D. Van Deusen
28 The Green
Watertown, CT 06795-2118
phone: 860-945-3456
Wants to buy rare & unusual forms of blue & white Canton; willing to assist

others in identifying and pricing their Canton.

Elinor Gordon
P.O. Box 211
Villanova, PA 19085
phone: 610-525-0981

Museums/Libraries

Peabody Museum of Salem
East India Square
Salem, MA 01970
phone: 617-745-9500

Dr. Dana D. Ricciardi
Captain Robert Bennet Forbes House
215 Adams St.
Milton, MA 02186-4215
phone: 617-696-1815
A Boston China trade merchant's country mansion; 19th century furnishings, American and Chinese export porcelain, prints, paintings, furniture; also Abraham Lincoln memorabilia.

Geisha Girl Porcelain

Experts

E. Litts
P.O. Box 394
Morris Plains, NJ 07950-0394
phone: 201-361-4087
Author of "The Collector's Encyclopedia of Geisha Girl Porcelain."

Mikasa

Man./Prod./Dist.

Mikasa
1 Mikasa Dr.
Secaucus, NJ 07096
phone: 201-867-9210 or 800-833-4681
fax: 201-867-0457
Dinnerware, crystal giftware, flatware, linens; call for location of nearest Mikasa factory store.

Matching Services

Mikasa Factory Store
595 Revell Highway
Annapolis, MD 21401
phone: 410-757-8400
Over 300 patterns of Mikasa dinnerware; also glassware, flatware and gift items.

Cleo Kapilla
CK's China Trace
P.O. Box 5297
Ocala, FL 34478-5297
phone: 352-622-4077
A matching service for thousands of fine & casual discontinued pieces of Mikasa dinnerware; buys, sells, locates.

Mikasa Factory Store
Pacific Edge Outlet Center
312 Fashion Way
Burlington, WA 98233
phone: 206-757-7400
Over 300 patterns of Mikasa

dinnerware; also glassware, flatware and gift items.

Nippon

Auction Services

Jon Crisman, ISA
Jackson's Auctioneers & Appraisers
2229 Lincoln St.
Cedar Falls, IA 50613
phone: 319-277-2256
fax: 319-277-1252
e-mail: jacksons@jacksonsauction.com
Internet: http://
www.jacksonsauction.com
Specializes in Nippon.

Clubs/Associations

Janice C. Eldridge
New England Nippon Collectors Club
64 Burt Rd.
Springfield, MA 01118
phone: 413-783-4629
Regional chapter of the International Nippon Collectors' Club.

Tim Trapani
Long Island Nippon Collectors Club
145 Andover Pl.
West Hempstead, NY 11552-1603
phone: 516-292-8355 or 718-464-9009
fax: 718-464-8448
Members study, trade, and discuss Nippon and Noritake; regional chapter of the international Nippon Collectors' Club.

Walt Maytan
Upstate New York Nippon Collectors' Club
122 Laurel Ave.
Herkimer, NY 13350
Regional chapter of the International Nippon Collectors' Club.

George Avezzano
MD-PA Nippon Collectors' Club
1016 Erwin Dr.
Joppa, MD 21085
Regional chapter of the International Nippon Collectors' Club.

Anne Dickinson
Sunshine State Nippon Collectors' Club
P.O. Box 425
Frostproof, FL 33843
phone: 941-635-4866
Regional chapter of the International Nippon Collectors' Club.

Kathy Wojciechowski
Lakes & Plains Nippon Collectors Club
4305 W. Beecher Rd.
P.O. Box 230
Peotone, IL 60468-0230
phone: 708-258-6105
fax: 708-258-6105
Please include a LSASE when requesting a reply; regional chapter of the International Nippon Collectors' Club.

Leola Harman
Ark-La-Tex Nippon Club
6800 Arapaho Rd., #1057
Dallas, TX 75248
Regional chapter of the International Nippon Collectors' Club.

Debra Tuttle
International Nippon Collectors Club
Magazine: INCC Journal
112 Ascot Dr.
Southlake, TX 76092-5117
phone: 817-481-4129 or 972-242-2160
fax: 972-466-0532
Fun club specializing in Nippon porcelain; annual convention with seminars, in-room selling, auction, etc.; focusing now on education regarding danger of reproduction items; INCC Journal 3 times a year; INCC Newsletter 3 times a year.

Collectors

Stephen Costa
145 Londonderry Rd.
Windham, NH 03087

Tim Trapani
145 Andover Pl.
West Hempstead, NY 11552-1603
phone: 516-292-8355 or 718-464-9009
fax: 718-464-8448
Wants to buy Art Deco Noritake, especially women and men figurals; no dinnerware, please.

Debra Tuttle
112 Ascot Dr.
Southlake, TX 76092-5117
phone: 817-481-4129 or 972-242-2160
fax: 972-466-0532

Dealers

Janice C. Eldridge
64 Burt Rd.
Springfield, MA 01118
phone: 413-783-4629
Wants to buy Nippon - moriage, coralene, high quality vases, urns, etc..

Susan Leite
44 Glenwood Rd.
Brewster, MA 02631-2202
phone: 508-385-4905
Wants to buy undamaged Nippon items.

Mark Griffin
1417 Steele St.
Fort Myers, FL 33901
phone: 800-726-1489
e-mail: nippononly@nippononly.com
Internet: http://www.nippononly.com
Buys quality Nippon: chocolate & tea sets, molded, portraits, wall plaques, coralene, urns, jugs, moriage, figural, Deco Noritake.

Deborah Smallwood
Seller of Dreams
P.O. Box 428
Powell, OH 43065
phone: 614-436-8393
Buys and sells all types of quality Nippon.

James Walker
5481 US 50 W.
Hillsboro, OH 45133
phone: 513-393-5264
Buys and sells Nippon.

Ward Stewart
Stewart's Antiques
1000 Coolidge
Lafayette, LA 70503-2336
phone: 318-232-2957

Experts

Wilf Pegg
c/o Infinity
744 Dundas St. East
Toronto
Ontario M5A 2C3 Canada
Advanced collector specializing in early "blown-out" or relief-molded Nippon (1891-1921); features animals, birds and humans in relief.

Kathy Wojciechowski
Quality Nippon
4305 W. Beecher Rd.
P.O. Box 230
Peotone, IL 60468-0230
phone: 708-258-6105
fax: 708-258-6105
Pays top dollar for high quality undamaged Nippon: large vases, urns, portraits, moriage, coralene, tapestry, dresser sets, dolls, etc.; author of "The Wonderful World of Nippon Porcelain (1891-1921)", appraiser, lecturer on Nippon.

Noritake

Clubs/Associations

Tim Trapani
Noritake Collectors' Society
Newsletter: Noritake News
145 Andover Pl.
West Hempstead, NY 11552-1603
phone: 516-292-8355 or 718-464-9009
fax: 718-464-8448
Art Deco, 1920s through 1940s Noritake Lustreware, excluding dinnerware; quarterly newsletter, holds annual convention.

Dealers

Gloria Munsell
Allenwood Americana Antiques
P.O. Box 116
Allenwood, PA 17810-0116
phone: 717-538-1440
Wants the Azalea pattern & scenic Noritake (Trees-in-The Meadow) china; largest dealer of these patterns in the country; over 20 years experience; always buying & selling.

Vance Etzler
Rocking Chair Treasures
111 South Carroll St.
Frederick, MD 21701
phone: 301-695-9304

Mark Griffin
1417 Steele St.
Fort Myers, FL 33901
phone: 800-726-1489
e-mail: nippononly@nippononly.com
Internet: http://www.nippononly.com
Wants to buy Noritake Art Deco men and women, also figural and Deco floral decors.

Experts

David H. Spain
1237 Federal Ave. East
Seattle, WA 98102-4329
phone: 206-323-8102
fax: 206-328-8264
e-mail: dspain@u.washington.edu
Editor of "Noritake News," the official publication of the Noritake Collectors Society.

David Spain
1237 Federal Ave. E
Seattle, WA 98102-4329
phone: 206-323-8102
fax: 206-328-8264
e-mail: dspain@u.washington.edu

David Spain
1237 Federal Ave. E
Seattle, WA 98102-4329
phone: 206-323-8102
fax: 206-328-8264
e-mail: dspain@u.washington.edu
Publishes and lectures on Art Deco, 1920s through 1940s Noritake Lustreware, excluding dinnerware.

Phoenix Bird Pattern

Clubs/Associations

Joan Oates
Phoenix Bird Collectors of America
Newsletter: Phoenix Bird Discoveries
5912 Kingsfield
West Bloomfield, MI 48322
phone: 616-435-8353
Members interested in ceramics decorated in the blue-and-white Phoenix Bird pattern and variants; advisor to "Warman's Antiques & Collectibles Price Guide," "Schroeder's Price Guide," and to "Garage Sale & Flea Market Annual."

Collectors

Dalen Whitt
Rte. 6 - Unus Road
Lewisburg, WV 24901
phone: 304-497-2425
Wants to buy rare items in Phoenix Bird China (spots on breast of bird); also Jadite kitchenware by McKee, Noritake HOWO China, and Delphite kitchenware.

Dealers

Florence B. Albright
16 Main St. E, Ste. 300
Rochester, NY 14614-1803
Advanced collector and dealer of Flying Turkey, Flying Dragon and other related patterns of Phoenix Bird China.

Carleton L. Cotting
1441 Crowell Rd.
Vienna, VA 22182-1512
phone: 703-759-5646
Collects, buys and sells Phoenix Bird pattern china.

Experts

Joan Oates
5912 Kingsfield
West Bloomfield, MI 48322
phone: 616-435-8353
Collector, historian, consultant; also author of "Phoenix Bird Chinaware" Books I, II, III and IV; available from the author.

Satsuma

Dealers

Joseph Belperio
1303 Hawthorne Ct.
Sewell, NJ 08080
phone: 609-256-0791
Specializes in fine quality Japanese Satsuma and cloisonne.

Bill Eberhardt
Harry A. Eberhardt & Son
2010 Walnut St.
Philadelphia, PA 19103-5608
phone: 215-568-4144
Specializes in Japanese cloisonne and fine Satsuma.

CEREAL BOXES

(see also PAPER COLLECTIBLES; PREMIUMS, Cereal Boxes)

Auction Services

Jack O'Brian
Memory Tree
P.O. Box 9462
Madison, WI 53715
phone: 414-261-6641
fax: 414-261-9461
Conducts specialty mail auctions of cereal boxes and backs, and character premium rings.

Clubs/Associations

Kevin Meisner
Sugar-Charged Cereal Collectors
Magazine: Freakie Magnet, The
5400 Cheshire Meadows Way
Fairfax, VA 22032-3216
phone: 703-527-3485
e-mail: slid-erkev@aol.com
High-quality magazine for cereal box and cereal box prize collectors; articles, photos, artwork featuring cereals from 1960s to present; buy/ sell cereal boxes, prizes, cereal art.

Collectors

Scott Bruce
P.O. Box 481
Cambridge, MA 02140-0004
phone: 617-492-5004
e-mail: scottbruce@flake.com
Internet: http://www.flake.com
Buy, sell, trade cereal prizes, displays and boxes from 1950s to 1970s; especially interested in character material such as Quisp, Quake, monsters and personalities.

John S. Fawcett
P.O. Box 1156
Waldoboro, ME 04572-1156
phone: 207-832-7398
Wants all boxes showing Disney, cowboys, radio premiums, Bugs Bunny; top dollar for a Kix Atomic Bomb Ring Cereal Box.

Steve Roden
P.O. Box 36B16
Los Angeles, CA 90036-1154
phone: 213-933-3158
fax: 213-933-3158
Wants to buy cereal boxes, back panels and premiums; also trading cards, bubble gum items, and radio premiums.

Dan Goodsell
P.O. Box 342
Culver City, CA 90232
phone: 310-815-0465
Interested in all 1950s to 1970s kid's food packaging and premiums such as cereal boxes.

Experts

David Welch
P.O. Box 714
Murphysboro, IL 62966-0714
phone: 618-687-2282
fax: 618-684-2243
e-mail: PexDude1@aol.com
Wants pre-1975 food or household product boxes showing TV, movie, cartoon, sports, or comic characters or premium offers, especially super heroes; up to $1500 for 1940s-1950s Batman or Superman.

Oats

Collectors

Mike Boggs
2075 Beaver Valley Rd.
Beaver Creek, OH 45385-9521
phone: 937-426-2171
Wants pre-1965 oat boxes; either round or rectangular; Rolled Oats or Quick Oats; such brands as Kamo, Friends, Purity, etc.; any oat boxes with pictures or early artwork.

CHARACTER COLLECTIBLES

(see also COMIC BOOKS; COMIC COLL.; COMIC STRIPS; COWBOY HEROES; DISNEY COLLECTIBLES; FAN CLUBS; MOVIE MEMORABILIA; POPULAR CULTURE; PREMIUMS; SCHMOO MEMORABILIA; SPACE COLLECTIBLES; TELEVISION SHOWS & MEMORABILIA; TOYS, Character; WATCHES, Character/ Comic

Collectors

Joedi Johnson
P.O. Box 565
Billings, MT 59101-0656
phone: 406-248-4875
fax: 407-248-4875
Purchasing promotional advertising characters and figures: plaster and composition store displays (Jockey Underwear, Simplicity, Paul Parrot Shoes, Buster Brown), plastic and vinyl figures, cereal boxes and premiums.

Lee H. Mitchell
175 E. Delaware, #8210
Chicago, IL 60611-1732
phone: 800-869-7869 or 312-337-3123
fax: 312-266-7982
Voracious collector always buying various character collectibles like Hoppy, Roy, Gene, Superman, Green Hornet, Bruce Lee, Captain Midnight, Captain Video, Buck Rogers, Howdy, Bilko, etc.; happy to hear from dealers and collectors.

Sharon A. Mitchell
875 North Michigan, #3412
Chicago, IL 60611
phone: 312-787-3252 or 800-879-6948
fax: 312-266-7982
Ardent collector seeking character toys and collectibles relating to famous adventure, comic, cowboy, TV, movie stars and super heroes; also buys collections.

Warren Dotz
2999 Regent St., Ste. 300
Berkeley, CA 94705-2118
phone: 510-652-1159
fax: 510-540-0325
e-mail: wellipsis@aol.com
Wants to buy advertising trademark character figures in the form of store displays, banks, statuettes, premiums and dolls; characters include Speedy Alka-Seltzer, PEP Boys, Reddy Kilowatt, Mido Watch Robot, Elsie the Cow, etc.

Dealers

Dave Haveles
Extensive Search Service
51 Squaw Rock
Danielson, CT 06239
phone: 860-774-1203
fax: 860-774-7137
Catalogs of special mailings available for $3 per category; bona-fide dealers are eligible to receive special

wholesale character and toy collectibles catalog; obtains large quantities and pass savings on to dealers.

Gary Lundquist
Oasis of Quality
336 Shamrock Rd.
Saint Augustine, FL 32086-6560
phone: 904-797-9745
Beatles pinback buttons, Hopalong Cassidy badge, Marilyn Monroe ring; also reproduction Batman, KISS, Lone Ranger, Popeye, Casper, Tom Mix, Shirley Temple related collectibles.

Experts

John Marshall
P.O. Box 340
Rancocas, NJ 08073-0340
phone: 609-267-6903
Buys, sells, collects and specializes in character collectibles, e.g. Mickey Mouse watches.

Doug & Pat Wengel
P.O. Box 305
Skillman, NJ 08558-0305
phone: 609-466-2461
fax: 609-466-8911
Buys, sells and specializes in vintage character collectibles, especially those with early images of Disney characters Mickey, Minnie, Horace and Clarabelle.

Judith Katz-Schwartz
Twin Brooks Antiques & Collectibles
P.O. Box 6572
New York, NY 10128-0006
phone: 212-876-3512
fax: 212-876-3512
e-mail: twinb@tiac.net
Internet: http://www.tiac.net/users/twinb
Buys, sells, appraises vintage character items, especially early Disneyana, Popeye, Betty Boop, Felix, G.I Joe, Charlie McCarthy, Howdy Dowdy, etc.

Mary Jane Lamphier
Quilted Keepsakes & Unique Dolls Exhibit
577 Main St.
Arlington, IA 50606-9712
phone: 319-633-5885
Buys, sells and trades advertising dolls and characters such as Jolly Green Giant, the Ronald McDonald collection, Campbell Soup Kids, etc.; author of "Zany Characters of the Ad World" (Collector Books, 1995).

Warren Dotz
2999 Regent St., Ste. 300
Berkeley, CA 94705-2118
phone: 510-652-1159
fax: 510-540-0325
e-mail: wellipsis@aol.com
Buys & specializes in advertising character figural store displays, banks, statuettes, and dolls; cartoonish trademark characters (Speedy Alka Seltzer, Reddy Kilowatt,

Elsie the Cow, etc.); author of "Advertising Character Collectibles."

Museums/Libraries

Herb Barker
Barker Character, Comic & Cartoon
Museum
1188 Highland Ave.
Cheshire, CT 06410-1624
phone: 800-227-5372 or 800-995-2357
fax: 203-699-1188
e-mail: fun@barkeranimation.com
Internet: http://
www.BarkerAnimation.com
Features comic character collectibles, television collectibles, cartoon character collectibles, toys, and comic memorabilia.

Periodicals

John Koenig
Antique Trader Publications, Inc.
Newspaper: Toy Trader
922 Churchill St., Ste. #1
Waupaca, WI 54981
phone: 715-258-7525 or 800-768-9225
fax: 715-258-8707
e-mail: jkoenig@add-inc.com
Internet: http://www.csmonline.com
Monthly newspaper with information on how to buy, sell and trade all types of toys; market trends, the latest prices, "how-to" columns, listings of toy clubs and upcoming toy shows and auctions; also full of buy and sell ads.

101 Dalmatians

Collectors

Kyla Covington
14 Elm St.
Saraland, AL 36571
phone: 205-679-0049
Collects anything to do with the movie "101 Dalmatians."

Alf

Clubs/Associations

Thomas Cannavo
ALFmeisters - ALF Collector Fan Club
25 Arizona Ave.
Jackson, NJ 08527-2134
phone: 908-364-0104

Collectors

Thomas Cannavo
25 Arizona Ave.
Jackson, NJ 08527-2134
phone: 908-364-0104
Buys, sells, trades anything ALF.

Scott Brodnax
225 Church
Clover, SC 29710
phone: 803-222-1066
Wants to buy Alf related toys, books, paper items, fan club items, and NBC material, etc. Fellow ALF collectors please write.

Val Bendel
4072 Tumbleweed Trail
Loves Park, IL 61111

Alice In Wonderland

Clubs/Associations

Ellie Luchinsky
Lewis Carroll Society of North America
Newsletter: Knights Letter, The
18 Fitzharding Place
Owings Mills, MD 21117
phone: 410-356-5110
Internet: http://www.students.uiuc/edu/
~jbirenba/carroll.html
Many members also collect books and other Lewis Carroll related materials.

Joel Birenbaum
Alice in Wonderland Collectors Network
Newsletter: Alice in Wonderland
Collectors Network Newsletter
2765 Shellingham Dr.
Lisle, IL 60532-4245
phone: 708-637-8530
e-mail: jbirenbaum@lucent.com
An organization of collectors, buyers and sellers of Alice In Wonderland and Lewis Carroll items.

Collectors

Alice Berkey
127 Alleyne Dr.
Pittsburgh, PA 15215-1401
phone: 412-782-2686
Wants old Alice in Wonderland items: Alice dolls, toys, figurines, books (especially translations into foreign languages), etc.; anything Alice! Complete and original only, please.

Joel Birenbaum
2765 Shellingham Dr.
Lisle, IL 60532-4245
phone: 708-637-8530
e-mail: jbirenbaum@lucent.com

Betty Boop

Clubs/Associations

Barbara West
Betty Boop Fan Club, The
Newsletter: Betty Boop Fan Club
Newsletter
6025 Fullerton Ave., Apt. 2
Buena Park, CA 90621-2345
phone: 714-994-1948
Publishes places to find Betty Boop items, special stories about members, pictures for members to use, stories about Betty's past and old "Boopabelia"; newsletter published quarterly.

Dealers

Gina Forlano
390 Ridgeview Rd.
Orange, CT 06477
phone: 203-795-0070
Buying, collecting and selling Betty Boop for over 12 years.

Barbara West
6025 Fullerton Ave., Apt. 2
Buena Park, CA 90621-2345
phone: 714-994-1948
Buys and sells "Betty Boop"-a-bilia, both new and old; will buy collections or will sell collections on consignment; send LSASE for latest catalog.

Man./Prod./Dist.

Connie Bingaman
810 Courtland Dr.
Ballwin, MO 63021-6730
phone: 314-391-6651
fax: 314-230-9559
e-mail: mr356@aol.com
Sells many new different Betty Boop collectible items; send SASE for list.

California Raisins

Collectors

George & Pam Curran
P.O. Box 713
New Smyrna Beach, FL 32170-0713
phone: 904-760-6600
fax: 904-760-5004
Advanced collector looking for PVC characters and any of the related California Raisins products; prefers mint in box, but will consider rarity of item; also welcomes calls from dealers and other collectors who want to "talk Raisins."

Ken Alexander
415 Morgan St.
Elgin, IL 60123-7537
phone: 847-931-0174
Wants to buy items relating to the California Raisins.

Experts

Larry DeAngelo
516 King Arthur Dr.
Virginia Beach, VA 23464-2236
phone: 804-424-1691
Wants to buy or trade California Raisin figurines: surfboards, tambourines, Mom, AC, Graduates, Leonard and Cecil; buys old store stock and closeouts.

Cartoon & Comic

(see also ANIMATION FILM ART; COMIC BOOKS; COMIC STRIPS, Sunday Newspaper; POLITICAL COLLECTIBLES, Nast Cartoons; POSTERS, Cartoon; SCIENCE FICTION)

Collectors

Mel Birnkrant
P.O. Box 254
Beacon, NY 12508
phone: 914-831-6237
fax: 914-831-8012
Artist and avid collector; creator of the popular "Baby Face" dolls; would enjoy hearing from anyone with early comic collectibles to offer.

Dealers

Cartoon Museum, The
Newsletter: Cartoon Times
814 Mission St.
San Francisco, CA 94103
phone: 415-227-8666
Buys and sells original cartoon art of all types; also "spin offs": books, collectibles, comic books, magazines, etc.; a private museum with original art for more than 2,500 cartoons of all kinds, especially comic art.

Experts

Norm Vigue
62 Bailey St.
Stoughton, MA 02072
phone: 617-344-5441
Wants to buy character collectibles: ceramic figures, banks, movie sheets, tin toys, dolls - Rocky & Bullwinkle, Tom & Jerry, Dick Tracy, Flintstones, Roy Rogers, Howdy Doody, Buck Rogers, Superman, Warner Bros., Terry Toons, etc.

Repro. Sources

Warner Bros. Collections
4000 Warner Blvd.
Burbank, CA 91522
Send for catalog of Looney Tunes memorabilia.

Dagwood-Blondie

Clubs/Associations

Dagwood-Blondie Fan Club
541 El Paso
Jacksonville, TX 75766
phone: 903-586-1355

Davy Crockett

Collectors

Gary Pimenta
64 Lakeside Dr.
Tiverton, RI 02878-3111
Wants to buy Davy Crockett, The Alamo, and Zorro character collectibles including toys, banks, magazines, comic books, trading cards, records, etc.

Dick Tracy

Clubs/Associations

Dick Tracy Fan Club
Magazine: Dick Tracy Fan Club
Magazine
P.O. Box 632
Manitou Springs, CO 80829-0632
phone: 719-685-9086
e-mail:
dick.tracy.magazine@worldnet.att.net
Published quarterly.

Experts

Larry Doucet
2351 Sultana Dr.
Yorktown Heights, NY 10598-3706
phone: 914-245-1320
fax: 914-739-9094
Buys, sells, appraises, Dick Tracy; co-author of "The Authorized Guide to Dick Tracy Collectibles"; will appraise Dick Tracy collectibles and memorabilia free of charge; wants to buy anything from premiums and toys to ephemera and art.

Felix The Cat

Collectors

Jason Schmidt
3567 Benton St., #500
Santa Clara, CA 95051
phone: 408-248-5741
fax: 408-248-5551
e-mail: ses2485741@aol.com
Wants to buy Felix the Cat items from the 1920s through the 1960s: furniture, toys, games, cells, postcards.

Flintstones

Collectors

Troy Holck
1060 W. Santa Fe
Olathe, KS 66061
phone: 913-782-8136

Garfield

Clubs/Associations

Denise Karl
Garfield Connection, The
Newsletter: Garfield Connection Newsletter
2 Lyons Rd.
Armonk, NY 10504-2224
phone: 914-273-3575
e-mail: garfconect@aol.com

David Abrams
Garfield Collectors Society
Newsletter: Garfield Collectors Society Newsletter
7744 Foster Ridge Rd.
Memphis, TN 38138-7036
phone: 901-753-1026
A club for serious Garfield collectors; the newsletter serves as the only source of information about Garfield events and collecting NEW and OLD Garfield products.

Dealers

Denise Karl
2 Lyons Rd.
Armonk, NY 10504-2224
phone: 914-273-3575
e-mail: garfconect@aol.com
Buys, sells, trades Garfield collectibles; entire collections wanted.

Carolyn Berens
Collection Connection, The
P.O. Box 18552
Hamilton, OH 45018
phone: 513-851-9217
Has hundreds of Garfield items in stock.

Hanna-Barbera

Collectors

John Krupienski
5200 Hilltop Dr.
P.O. Box AA6
Brookhaven, PA 19015-1200
phone: 610-874-3003
Collector specializing in Hanna-Barbera character collectibles: Flintstones, Jetsons, Huckleberry Hound, Pixie and Dixie, Quick Draw McGraw, Yogi Bear and Top Cat.

Howdy Doody

Clubs/Associations

Doodyville Historical Society
8 Hunt Court
Flemington, NJ 08822
phone: 908-782-1159

Jeff Judson
Howdy Doody Memorabilia Collectors Club
Newsletter: Howdy Doody Times
8 Hunt Court
Flemington, NJ 08822-3349
phone: 908-782-1159
fax: 908-782-0188
e-mail: jjudson@postoffice.ptd.net
Members are interested in anything related to Howdy Doody - old or new; also known as the Doodyville Historical Society.

Collectors

Chris Swain
74 Ranney Corder Rd.
Ashfield, MA 01330
phone: 413-628-3213
Wants Howdy Doody memorabilia.

Christmas Catalog Collector, The
175 East Delaware, #7403
Chicago, IL 60611-1731
phone: 800-879-6948 or 312-337-3123
fax: 312-266-7982
Major and enthusiastic collector wants more Howdy Doody toys and other Howdy items; also wants all pre-1985 toy/Christmas catalogs.

Experts

Jack Koch
P.O. Box 428
Morrisville, PA 19067
e-mail: jackk87289@aol.com
Author of "Howdy Doody Collector's Reference and Trivia Guide."

Humpty Dumpty

Collectors

Dee Sharp
P.O. Box 315
Clifton, VA 20124
phone: 703-968-5816
Wants old Humpty Dumpty related items: paper, wooden, metal, figurines, etc.

Jigglers

Collectors

Debra Sellitti
23 Miller Rd.
Farmingdale, NY 11735
phone: 516-249-1332
Wants jigglers, thick rubbery critters marked "RDF"; some sat, some hung; with ribbon marked "Untouchables" Russberry.

Greg Whitaker
2535 Marsh Lane, #506
Carrollton, TX 75006
phone: 972-418-9442
Wants to buy "jigglers", rubbery creatures from the 1960s.

Little Orphan Annie

Periodicals

Jon Merrill
Newsletter: Annie People
517 North Fenwick St.
Allentown, PA 18103

Mutt & Jeff

Collectors

Larry Whitefield
P.O. Box 1330
Duvall, WA 98019
phone: 206-788-1523
Wants to buy Mutt & Jeff figurines, dolls, and comic books.

Mystery Science Theater 3000

Clubs/Associations

MST3K Information Club
P.O. Box 5325
Hopkins, MN 55343
e-mail: juliewa@aol.com
Interested in the low-budget cable show featuring Tom Servo, Mike Nelson, and Crow T. Robot.

Peanuts Characters

Clubs/Associations

Andrea C. Podley
Peanuts Collector Club, Inc.
Newsletter: Peanuts Collector Club Newsletter
539 Sudden Valley
Bellingham, WA 98226-4811
phone: 360-733-5209
fax: 360-733-5239
e-mail: acp@nas.com
Internet: http://www.dcn.davis.ca.us/~bang/peanuts
A privately-owned club dedicated to the art & memorabilia associated with "Peanuts" and with its creator, Charles M. Schulz; also interested in memorabilia associated with the related characters in the "Peanuts" strip.

Experts

Freddi Margolin
12 Lawrence Lane
Bay Shore, NY 11706
phone: 516-666-6861
fax: 516-665-7986
e-mail: snupius@li.net
Wants to buy Snoopy/Peanuts character items; especially wants older wooden music musicals, ephemera, old catalogs from 1967 through the 70s showing Peanuts items.

Andrea C. Podley
539 Sudden Valley
Bellingham, WA 98226-4811
phone: 360-733-5209
fax: 360-733-5239
e-mail: acp@nas.com
Internet: http://www.dcn.davis.ca.us/~bang/peanuts
Co-author with Freddi Margolin of "The Official Price Guide to Peanuts Collectibles."

Pee-Wee Herman

Collectors

Barry Mann-Pee-Wee-Man
10602 Denell Circle
Austin, TX 78753
Wants anything to do with Pee-Wee Herman.

Pink Panther

Collectors

Cheryl Dickinson
P.O. Box 36
Montague, MA 01351
phone: 413-367-9389
Wants all Pink Panther collectibles: toys, ceramics, books, and ephemera; U.S. or foreign.

Pogo

Clubs/Associations

Steve Thompson
Pogo Fan Club
Magazine: Fort Mudge Most, The
6908 Wentworth Ave. South
Minneapolis, MN 55423-2363
phone: 612-869-6320
International club explores all aspects of Walt Kelly's career; magazine reprints scarce and unpublished Kellyana, ads, letters, strip; magazine published bi-monthly.

Dealers

Dave Haveles
Extensive Search Service
51 Squaw Rock
Danielson, CT 06239
phone: 860-774-1203
fax: 860-774-7137
Catalogs of special mailings available for $3 per category; bona-fide dealers are eligible to receive special wholesale character and toy collectibles catalog; obtains large quantities and pass savings on to dealers.

Experts

Steve Thompson
6908 Wentworth Ave. South
Minneapolis, MN 55423-2363
phone: 612-869-6320
Author of "The Walt Kelly Collector's Guide: A Bibliography and Price Guide."

Popeye

Clubs/Associations

Official Popeye Fan Club
Newsletter: Popeye Fan Club Newsletter
1001 State St.
Chester, IL 62233
phone: 618-826-4567
fax: 618-826-3322
e-mail: ace1@midwest.net
Internet: http://www.midwest.net/orgs/ace1/
Specializes in Popeye related collectibles; quarterly newsletter.

Collectors

Fred Grandinetti
FG Productions
96 Edenfield Ave.
East Watertown, MA 02172

Pat Norberg
1135 W. 18th Ave.
Eugene, OR 97402
phone: 541-345-9409
Collects Popeye the Sailor Man toys, art and other related collectibles.

Dealers

Spinach Can Collectibles
1001 State St.
Chester, IL 62233
phone: 618-826-4567
fax: 618-826-3322
e-mail: ace1@midwest.net
Internet: http://www.midwest.net/orgs/ace1/

Punch & Judy

Dealers

Jonathan & Lisa Reynolds
Dramatis Personae - Booksellers
P.O. Box 1070
Sheffield, MA 01257-1070
phone: 413-229-7735
fax: 413-229-7735
e-mail: dramatisp@ad.com
Wants to buy pre-1890 Punch and Judy books, prints, ephemera, puppets, pottery, memorabilia, etc.

Red Riding Hood

Clubs/Associations

Ann C. Bergin
Red Riding Hood!
Newsletter: Red Riding Hood Network
P.O. Box 105
Amherst, NH 03031-0105
fax: 508-649-6807
e-mail: PFBergin@aol.com
For collectors of (Little) Red Riding Hood.

Road Runner

Collectors

Rik
P.O. Box 681045
Indianapolis, IN 46268
phone: 317-290-9274
Wants Road Runner related toys, books, puzzles, games, lunch boxes and drinking glasses.

Robin Hood

Periodicals

J.M. Pellerin
Robin of Sherwood
Newsletter: Friends
P.O. Box 837
West Upton, MA 01587
phone: 508-529-6665
A quarterly focusing on Robin Hood, medieval interests.

Rocky & Bullwinkle

Dealers

Dudley Do-Right Emporium
8218 Sunset Blvd.
Los Angeles, CA 90046
Filled with T-shirts, keychains, charms, pictures, Wossammatta U sweatshirts, and many other types of merchandise, all related to the Jay Ward characters; mail order also.

Periodicals

Gary David
Newsletter: Frostbite Falls Far-Flung Flier
P.O. Box 39
Macedonia, OH 44056-0039
phone: 216-467-1074
Focuses on Rocky & Bullwinkle and Jay Ward cartoons.

Sherlock Holmes

(see also BOOKS, Mystery; MAGAZINES, Mystery; MYSTERY/DETECTIVE ITEMS; PIPES; SMOKING COLLECTIBLES)

Collectors

Rev. Sherlock S. Holmes, D.D.
P.O. Box 3
Worcester, MA 01613-0003
phone: 508-754-9907
e-mail: SherlockHolmes@writeme.com
Internet: http://members.aol.com/sherlocksh/home.html
Collects Sherlockiana and Victorian period household books and items; also wants wax seal seals.

Robert C. Hess
559 Potter Blvd.
Brightwaters, NY 11718-1615
phone: 516-665-8365
Wants Sherlock Holmes/Sir Arthur Conan Doyle items: figurines, sculpture, statuary, dolls, original artwork, illustrations, etc.

Jerry Margolin
10007 SW Quail Post Rd.
Portland, OR 97219-6368
phone: 503-293-7274
Wants to buy and and all things relating to Sherlock Holmes.

Dealers

Chuck Haley
Sherlock's
13926 Double Girth Ct.
Matthews, NC 28105
phone: 704-843-3433 or 704-847-5480
Interested on all things Sherlockian.

Smurf

Clubs/Associations

Suzanne Lipschitz
Smurf Collectors Club International
Newsletter: Smurf Collectors Newsletter
24 Cabot Rd. West - Dept. M
Massapequa, NY 11758-8025
phone: 516-799-3221
Focuses on Smurf memorabilia from 56 countries; quarterly newsletter; send SASE for more information.

Collectors

Kerry Culhane
129 58th St.
West New York, NJ 07093-2713
Wants to buy and Smurf or related items.

S. Lund
24CH Cabot Rd. W.
Massapequa, NY 11758
phone: 516-799-3221
Wants European items only; post cards, metal cars, books, figurines; must have "Peyo" (creator's name) license mark.

Dealers

Colleen Lewis
Buffalo Road Hobby
10120 Main St.
Clarence, NY 14031-2049
phone: 716-759-7541
fax: 716-759-7462
e-mail: pcc@toyline.com
Internet: http://www.toyline.com/pcc
Carries complete line of Smurfs, including figures, supers, playsets, super playsets, cottages, castle, displays, key chains, mugs, jewelry, toys, etc.; $3 for catalog; collections sought to buy.

Periodicals

Alan G. Rennard
Newsletter: Smurfing Times
3 Indian Lane
Burlington, NJ 08016-5123
phone: 609-386-8186
fax: 609-386-8186
Dedicated to creating a worldwide Smurf collectors network.

Snoopy

(see CHARACTER COLLECTIBLES, Peanuts Characters)

Soupy Sales

Collectors

Bob Averill
1942 W. Market St.
Pottsville, PA 17901-2043
phone: 800-637-6484 or 717-628-3084
Wants Soupy Sales collectibles: board games, dolls, pencil cases, cards, pencils, pens, cereal boxes, books, clothing, anything Soupy.

Spy Memorabilia

Clubs/Associations

Charles Helfenstein
Secret Agent Fan Club
Newsletter: Spies
P.O. Box 476
Frederick, MD 21705-0476
phone: 301-695-4367
e-mail: ohmss@erols.com
Spies, 007, Avengers, Mission Impossible, Man from U.N.C.L.E.

Dealers

Spy Guise
261 Central Ave.
P.O. Box 205
Jersey City, NJ 07307
Buys, sells, trades; world's largest dealer of spy memorabilia: James

Bond 007, Our Man Flint, Man From U.N.C.L.E., I Spy, Avengers; toys, games, novelties, records, lobby cards, posters from around the world.

Spy Memorabilia (James Bond)

Clubs/Associations

Graham Rye
James Bond 007 Fan Club & Archive, The
Magazine: 007 Magazine
P.O. Box 007
Addlestone
Surrey KT15 1DY, U.K.
phone: 01483-756007
fax: 01483-756007
Focuses on James Bond; publishes "007 Magazine" (glossy, professionally produced, many never-before-seen photographs) and "007 Extra" newsletter (James Bond news worldwide) three times each year.

James Bond Fan Club
Newsletter: Bondage
P.O. Box 414
Bronxville, NY 10708

Collectors

Gary Pimenta
64 Lakeside Dr.
Tiverton, RI 02878-3111
Wants to buy James Bond 007 related toys, clothes, posters, records, magazines, books, etc.; also wants first edition books by Ian Fleming (with dust jackets.)

Tarzan

(see also PERSONALITIES [LITERARY], Edgar Rice Burroughs)

Collectors

Jim Gerlach
2206 Greenbrier Dr.
Irving, TX 75060
phone: 972-790-0922

Three Stooges

Clubs/Associations

Gary Lassin
Three Stooges Fan Club
Newsletter: Three Stooges Journal
P.O. Box 747
Gwynedd Valley, PA 19437-0747
phone: 215-654-9466
fax: 215-368-3595

Collectors

Frank R. Levine
393 Charles St.
Malden, MA 02148-6318
phone: 617-321-0639
Wants 3 Stooges memorabilia.

John Krupienski
5200 Hilltop Dr.
P.O. Box AA6
Brookhaven, PA 19015-1200
phone: 610-874-3003

Gary Lassin
P.O. Box 747
Gwynedd Valley, PA 19437-0747
phone: 215-654-9466
fax: 215-368-3595
Wants 3 Stooges memorabilia; toys, games, posters, stills, anything.

Jan Benham
2457 Raymond SE
Grand Rapids, MI 49507-3923
phone: 616-247-0072
e-mail: jabenham@post.grcc.cc.mi.us
Wants candid, out-of-character photos of Moe Howard "The Three Stooges" fame.

Harry S. Ross
P.O. Box 72
Skokie, IL 60076-0072
phone: 847-432-4820
fax: 847-432-4820
Wants to buy Three Stooges toys, games, original movie posters, props, autographs, autographs, and more!

Neil J. Teizeira
P.O. Box 20812
Piedmont, CA 94620
phone: 510-658-9938
Wants anything related to The Three Stooges: posters, lobby cards, toys, memorabilia, promotional items.

Neal Austinson
P.O. Box 1691
Windsor, CA 95492-1691
phone: 707-837-9685
Wants to buy Three Stooges 1930s ceramic head hand puppets, toys, etc.

Man./Prod./Dist.

David Blaise
Soitenly Stooges, Inc.
P.O. Box 72
Skokie, IL 60076-0072
phone: 800-378-6643
fax: 800-329-8735
Catalog of new Three Stooges gifts - dolls, books, videos, posters, T-shirts, watches, ties, magnets, comics, photos, clocks, etc.; send for quarterly "Soitenly Stooges" catalog.

Uncle Remus

Museums/Libraries

Uncle Remus Museum
P.O. Box 3184
Highway 441 S.
Eatonton, GA 31024
phone: 706-485-6856
Collection of items related to Joel Chandler Harris, author of the fables of Br'er Rabbit and Br'er Fox.

Uncle Wiggily

Collectors

Martin McCaw
1124 School Ave.
Walla Walla, WA 99362
phone: 800-451-9755
Wants to buy Uncle Wiggly items including puzzles, books, Sunday comics, candy tins, cloth dolls (Nurse Jane, too), animal cracker box, all dishes, advertising items, etc.; call toll free about anything Uncle Wiggily.

Underdog

Clubs/Associations

Don Martinec
Underdog Collectors Club
8856 Ridge Rd. NE
Kinsman, OH 44428
phone: 216-876-6727
National club interested in the Underdog cartoon series.

Yellow Kid

Clubs/Associations

Richard Olson
R. F. Outcault Society
Newsletter: R. F. Outcault Reader, The
103 Doubloon Dr.
Slidell, LA 70461-2715
phone: 504-641-5173 or 504-280-6778
fax: 504-280-6049
e-mail: olson32@ibm.net
Members collect the art and history of Richard F. Outcault, creator of The Yellow Kid, Buster Brown, and Poor Li'l Mose.

Collectors

William Nielsen
1379 Main St.
Brewster, MA 02631-1723
phone: 508-896-7389
Wants Yellow Kid items.

Craig Koste
2187 State Route 22B
Morrisonville, NY 12962-3423
phone: 518-643-8173
Serious collector buying or trading for all Yellow Kid items.

Richard Olson
103 Doubloon Dr.
Slidell, LA 70461-2715
phone: 504-641-5173 or 504-280-6778
fax: 504-280-6049
e-mail: olson32@ibm.net
Wants all Yellow Kid items including pin-backs, gum cards, toys, ads, magazines, comic supplements, etc.

CHARACTER JUGS

(see CERAMICS [ENGLISH], Royal Doulton; COLLECTIBLES [MODERN], Toby Jugs)

CHARGE CARDS

(see CREDIT CARDS & CHARGE ITEMS)

CHARLIE TUNA

(see ADVERTISING COLLECTIBLES, Figures [Charlie Tuna])

CHARMS

(see also PLASTIC COLLECTIBLES)

Clubs/Associations

Maureen McCaffrey
Bubble-Gum Charm Collector's Club
Newsletter: Charmed I'm Sure!
24 Seafoam St.
Staten Island, NY 10306
phone: 718-979-8496
fax: 718-351-8832

Plastic

Collectors

David Brandt
2600 Knollwood Ct., Apt. 27
Cameron Park, CA 95682-8980
phone: 916-677-4376
Wants celluloid (plastic) charms from the 1930s-40s: Disney, Popeye, Betty Boop, Kewpie, Mobil, Schmoo, etc.

Poole
P.O. Box 692
Mill City, OR 97360
Wants older plastic charms.

CHARTS

(see MAPS & CHARTS)

CHATELAINES

Collectors

Verity
P.O. Box 2316
Newport Beach, CA 92659-1316
Wants to buy chatelaines (items hanging by chains attached to a hook, worn at the waist); complete or individual pieces.

CHECKS

(see BANKING, Bank Checks; COINS & CURRENCY)

CHESS SETS

(see also GAMES)

Appraisers

Jeffrey Litwin, ISA
Litwin Antiques
P.O. Box 5865
Trenton, NJ 08638-0865
phone: 609-275-1427 or 609-275-0996
fax: 609-275-1427
e-mail: jsl58@ix.netcom.com
Buys, sells and appraises chess sets, chess books, chess art and chess ephemera. Please send description and/or photo of items for sale;

Accredited Member of the international Society of Appraisers.

Clubs/Associations

Dr. Thomas Thomsen
Chess Collectors International
Newsletter: Chess Collector, The
P.O. Box 166
Commack, NY 11725-0166
phone: 516-543-1330
fax: 516-543-7901
International membership interested in collecting chess sets, chess stamps, chess books, chess art, and other chess related items; meetings held biennially in the even numbered years.

Collectors

Jim Stephens
10906 Watermill Ct.
Oakton, VA 22124-1024
phone: 703-620-2031
Wants chess sets and related books, pictures, catalogs, etc.; fabricates decorated chess sets from molds.

David Warther II
David Warther Carving Museum
2561 Crestview Dr. NW
Dover, OH 44622-7405
phone: 330-852-3455 or 330-343-1868
Collects quality antique chess sets; greatest interest is in wood or ivory sets of European or Indian origin.

Dennis Horwitz
P.O. Box 301
Topanga, CA 90290-0301
phone: 310-455-4002
Collects antique or unusual chess sets, especially figural sets based on themes; describe condition and composition of set; height of pawn and king; date, location and price of purchase; board or box; include SASE and photo for reply.

Ned Munger, Ph.D.
1201 East California
Pasadena, CA 91125-0001
phone: 818-395-3634
fax: 818-795-1547
e-mail: munger@hss.caltech.edu
Wants ethnic, historic, or geographic theme chess sets; no boards.

Experts

Floyd Sarisohn
P.O. Box 166
Commack, NY 11725-0166
phone: 516-543-1330
fax: 516-543-7901

Museums/Libraries

Bernice & Floyd Sarisohn
Long Island Chess Museum
P.O. Box 166
Commack, NY 11725-0166
phone: 516-543-1330
fax: 516-543-7901
Private museum of over 750 chess sets and related art and collectibles; viewing by appointment only.

Josie De Falla, Dir.
Maryhill Museum of Art
35 Maryhill Museum Drive
Goldendale, WA 98620-4601
phone: 509-773-3733
fax: 509-773-6138
e-mail: MaryHill@gorge.net
Collection contains over 200 antique and unusual sets from around the world.

CHILDREN'S THINGS

(see also BOOKS; DOLLS; DOLL HOUSES & FURNISHINGS; DR. SEUSS ITEMS; HANDKERCHIEFS, Children's; MINIATURES; PERAMBULATORS; RIDING TOYS; TOYS)

Auction Services

Jim & Shari McMasters
McMasters Doll Auctions
P.O. Box 1755
Cambridge, OH 43725-6755
phone: 800-842-3526 or 614-432-4419
fax: 614-432-3191
Specializes in auctioning antique and collectible dolls and doll related items such as teddy bears, children's dishes, toys, children's books, etc.

Clubs/Associations

Linda Martin
Children's Things Collectors Society
Newsletter: CTCS Newsletter
P.O. Box 983
Durant, IA 52747

Collectors

Mary Young
P.O. Box 9244
Dayton, OH 45409-9244
Wants to buy children's tin tea sets from Ohio Art and Wolverine, school readers (primarily first and second grade readers) from the 1920s to 1960s, 1930-1960s coloring and punch-out books.

Dealers

Marjorie Jeffreys
Going to Pieces
P.O. Box 390
Cibolo, TX 78108
phone: 210-659-2458
Buys and sells old games, toys, blocks and children's dishes and children's baking items.

Alphabet Plates

Collectors

Walter Lozoski
17430 Ballinger Way NE
Seattle, WA 98155-5515
Wants children's alphabet (A.B.C.) plates.

Baby Rattles

Collectors

Marcia Hersey
P.O. Box 976
Ansonia Station
New York, NY 10023-0976
phone: 212-877-5328 or 212-874-3946
Wants to buy baby rattles: gold, silver, wood, celluloid, plastic, etc.

Dealers

Jennifer Sykes
Jennifer Sykes Antiques
9018 Balboa Blvd. #595
Northridge, CA 91325-2610
phone: 818-993-1916
fax: 818-993-7612
e-mail: Veeda10@aol.com
Wants to buy Bakelite crib toys, pre-1970 sterling/celluloid/tin antique baby rattles, boudoir dolls.

Cups

Collectors

Deborah Gillham
47 Midline Ct.
Gaithersburg, MD 20878-1996
phone: 301-977-5727
e-mail: dgillham@erols.com
Internet: http://www.his.com/~Judy/reamer.html
Wants whimsical children's cups with whistles or figurals on handles or with writing and child illustrations on cup.

Dishes

Clubs/Associations

Shelley Smith
Toy Dish Collectors Club
Newsletter: Tiny Times, The
P.O. Box 159
Bethlehem, CT 06751-0159
phone: 203-266-7496
fax: 203-266-7343
Internet: http://www.members.aol.com/toydish
Collectors are interested in children's dishes, furniture, glass, toy kitchen and stores.

Collectors

Mary Young
P.O. Box 9244
Dayton, OH 45409-9244
Wants to buy children's tin tea sets from Ohio Art and Wolverine.

Doris M. Diabo
19953 Great Oaks Circle S.
Clinton Township, MI 48036-2440
phone: 810-463-5651
Wants to buy children's tea sets, especially Majolica; also R.S. Prussia, Wedgwood, Royal Doulton, Royal Rudolstadt, and other quality makers; send photocopy of pattern & markings with price, # of pieces, condition and SASE.

F.J. Steffen
9705 Mill Creek Dr.
Eden Prairie, MN 55347
phone: 612-944-1041
Wants to buy children's dishes, furniture, kitchen and shops, etc.

Dealers

Shelley Smith
P.O. Box 159
Bethlehem, CT 06751-0159
phone: 203-266-7496
fax: 203-266-7343
Internet: http://www.members.aol.com/toydish
Buys and sells toys, miniatures, Steiff, children's collectibles, and country smalls.

Abbie Kelly
P.O. Box 351
Camillus, NY 13031-0351
phone: 315-487-7451
e-mail: toydish@aol.com
Internet: http://members.aol.com/toydish
Buys and sells doll dishes, toy glass, toy tea sets, doll furniture.

Anna Green
P.O. Box 92
Effort, PA 18330-0092
phone: 717-992-4566
Wants to buy children's dishes in pressed glass, Akro Agate, and depression glass; also china, tin litho, sets or individual pieces.

Louise M. Loehr
Louise's Old Things
163 W. Main St.
P.O. Box 208
Kutztown, PA 19530-0208
phone: 610-683-8370
Co-author of "Willow Pattern China." Specializing in willow, flow blue, and early children's china. Wants one piece or collections.

Experts

Cathy Cook
10 E. 13th St., #2D
New York, NY 10003-4467
e-mail: cook710@aol.com
Always looking for tin litho dishes by Ohio Art, Chein Wolverine, etc.

Margaret & Kenn Whitmyer
P.O. Box 30806
Gahanna, OH 43230
Author of "Collector's Encyclopedia of Children's Dishes."

Lorraine Punchard
8201 Pleasant Ave. So.
Minneapolis, MN 55420-2264
phone: 612-888-1079
fax: 612-888-8527
Author of "Playtime Kitchen Items and Table Accessories" (1993), "Playtime Pottery & Porcelain from the United Kingdom and the U.S." (1996), and "Playtime Pottery & Porcelain from Europe and Asia" (1996).

Handkerchiefs

Collectors

J.J. Murphy
920 Emerald St.
Madison, WI 53715-1614
phone: 608-257-3855
fax: 608-257-3730
Collector seeks 19th century printed children's kerchiefs and bandannas; special interest in moralistic, religious, instructional and black related examples (e.g. Uncle Tom's Cabin); condition important; serious sellers only, please.

CHINA

(see CERAMICS; DINNERWARE)

CHINESE ITEMS

(see FURNITURE [ANTIQUE], Chinese; ORIENTALIA)

CHIPS

(see GAMBLING COLLECTIBLES, Gambling Chips & Gaming Tokens)

CHRISTMAS COLLECTIBLES

(see also CATALOGS, Christmas; COLLECTIBLES [MODERN], Ornaments; COLLECTIBLES [MODERN], Christmas; ELVES; HOLIDAY COLLECTIBLES; LIGHT BULBS)

Auction Services

Robert J. Connelly, ASA
Bob & Sallie Connelly Auctions
666 Chenango St.
Binghamton, NY 13901-2015
phone: 607-722-9593 or 607-722-3555
fax: 607-722-1266
Conducts specialty Christmas sales.

Clubs/Associations

Robert Dalluge
Golden Glow of Christmas Past
Newsletter: Golden Glow of Christmas Past
6401 Winsdale St.
Minneapolis, MN 55427-4250
phone: 612-544-8933
Network of Christmas antique collectors focusing on 1870-1950; annual convention.

Collectors

Bob Merck
44 Newtown Turnpike
Weston, CT 06883-2118
Wants pre-1940 figural glass or paper ornaments; Santa Claus figures, Santa blocks & games, figural glass light bulbs (need not work.)

Linda L. Vines
P.O. Box 43721
Montclair, NJ 07043
phone: 973-748-4990 or 201-748-4990
Wants to buy 1880-1940 German

Santas, candy containers, glass and paper ornaments, early Christmas books, Snow Babies.

Greg Spatafore
103 Wilgate Rd.
Owings Mills, MD 21117-3325
phone: 800-866-5739 or 410-848-9295
Wants to buy old Christmas lighted decorations: bubble lights, candelabras, matchless stars, lighted plaques, unusual bulbs, etc.

Cindy Chipps
4027 Brooks Hill Rd.
Brooks, KY 40109-5002
phone: 502-955-9238
fax: 502-957-5027
e-mail: holauction@aol.com
Internet: http://members.aol.com/holauction/index.html
Wants figural light bulbs, Matchless Wonder Stars; also other Christmas items, electrical or mechanical.

Coleen Detzel
28 Lacresta Dr.
Florence, KY 41042-9663
phone: 606-282-0456
Wants older blown glass ornaments, older Santas; also any Christmas related items from the 1940s and 1950s.

J. W. & Treva Courter
3935 Kelley Rd.
Kevil, KY 42053-9431
phone: 502-488-2116
fax: 502-488-2116
e-mail: brtknight@aol.com
Internet: http://www.aladdinknights.org
Wants German Christmas glass figural ornaments, old Father Christmas and matchless Wonder Stars.

Mac Databae
3470 E. Pershing Rd.
Lincoln, NE 68502-4835
Wants to buy old Santas, Christmas figural light bulbs, ornaments, candy containers, etc.

Susan Murphy
29668 Orinda Rd.
San Juan Capistrano, CA 92675-1211
phone: 714-364-4333
Wants to buy pre 1940s Christmas collectibles: Santa Claus, all ornaments, nativity sets, animals, celluloid toys, candy containers, etc.; please enclose SASE.

Sally Kimmel
1471 Lark Lane
Concord, CA 94521
phone: 510-676-2857
Wants to buy elves, Santas, snowmen, angels, reindeer, toy soldiers, etc.; ornaments and decorations made out of plastic, paper cardboard, etc. made during the 1930s to 1970s; also wants Nativity scenes, sets and mangers.

Dealers

Bettie Petzoldt
178 Woolen Mill Rd.
New Park, PA 17352
phone: 717-382-1416
Internet: http://www.mindyourbusiness.com
Collect/buy/sell early Christmas ornaments: glass, diecut, Dresden, cotton, snow babies, lights, Santas; free monthly illustrated sales list available.

Kit Carter
Ticker Talker Toys
506 Briar Hill Rd.
Louisville, KY 40206
phone: 502-561-5030
Specializes in pre-1920 Christmas collectibles, especially papier-mache candy containers.

Jenny Tarrant
4 Gardenview Dr.
Saint Peters, MO 63376-3507
phone: 314-397-1763
Wants German Santas, bisque Santas, celluloid Santas, and Santa candy containers.

Mary Lou Holt
12510 Jackson
Grandview, MO 64030

Connie Reece
Von Reece & Daughters
440 Bunny Run
Austin, TX 78746
Sells and promotes shows for collectors of Christmas collectibles: ornaments, figurines, plates and bells, limited editions, etc.

Paul W. Schofield
Lion's Den Antiques
7988 Bethel Burley Rd. SE
Port Orchard, WA 98366
phone: 360-876-3364
fax: 360-876-5421
Buys, sells, appraises, and specializes in old Santas, candy containers, Halloween, Easter, Christmas, Easter, Dresden, figural lights.

Experts

Lissa & Richard Smith
3 Baldtop Heights
Danville, PA 17821
phone: 717-275-7796
Advisor to "Warman's Antiques & Collectibles Price Guide", authors of "Christmas Collectibles."

Margaret & Kenn Whitmyer
P.O. Box 30806
Gahanna, OH 43230
Author of "Christmas Collectibles."

Dave Eppelheimer
47 Union Ave., SE
Grand Rapids, MI 49503
phone: 616-459-0474

Periodicals

Rita B. Bocher, Pub.
Newsletter: Creche Herald
117 Crosshill Rd.
Wynnewood, PA 19096-3511
phone: 610-649-7520
e-mail: crecher@op.net
Internet: http://www.op.net/~crecher
Christmas events, art, collections, products; creche competitions, exchange for trading, selling, buying creches, figurines; send #10 SASE for free sample.

Janie Schmidt
I Love Christmas
Newsletter: I Love Christmas
P.O. Box 5708
Coralville, IA 52241
phone: 319-337-8270
A 100% all-Christmas newsletter with Christmas related reader-written stories, poetry, recipes, ads, articles on collecting; readers invited to share their collections and stories; send $2 for a 6-page sample.

Christmas Cards (Celebrity)

Experts

William J. Flechner
700 E. Macoupin St.
Staunton, IL 62088
phone: 618-635-2712
Specializes in celebrity-related Christmas cards, i.e. cards sent by musicians such as Elvis, Rudy Vallee, pianist Roger Williams, Pat Boon, Johnny Cash, etc.

Creches

Clubs/Associations

Dr. George F. Drake, Pres.
International Creche Festival Association
1421 Cornwall Ave., #B
Bellingham, WA 98225
phone: 360-734-9757
fax: 360-734-9830
e-mail: gdrake@creche.org
Internet: http://www.creche.org/creche/
Folk art nativity sets of the world; annual international contest brings creches from over 30 countries.

Collectors

Rita B. Bocher, Pub.
117 Crosshill Rd.
Wynnewood, PA 19096-3511
phone: 610-649-7520
e-mail: crecher@op.net
Internet: http://www.op.net/~crecher

Periodicals

Rita B. Bocher, Pub.
Newsletter: Creche Herald
117 Crosshill Rd.
Wynnewood, PA 19096-3511
phone: 610-649-7520
e-mail: crecher@op.net
Internet: http://www.op.net/~crecher
Christmas events, art, collections,

products; creche competitions, exchange for trading, selling, buying creches, figurines; send #10 SASE for free sample.

Feather Trees

Repro. Sources

Karen Shields
Twins Feather Trees & Holiday
Collectibles
1543 Pullan Ave.
Cincinnati, OH 45223-2164
phone: 513-681-9357
Limited productions of quality reproductions of feather trees and other Christmas items; Santa figures, Putz animals, fences; also Easter and Halloween; offers antique feather repair and restoration.

Mail Order Catalogs

Dealers

Judy Hesson
Hesson Collectables
1261 S. Lloyd
Lombard, IL 60148-4234
phone: 630-627-3298
fax: 630-627-3298
Buys & sells Christmas mail order catalogs: Sears, Montgomery Ward, Penny, Aldens, Spiegel: 1900-1990; also other catalogs; send $4 for list of 900 for sale.

Mexican

Dealers

Ed Barry
Shop, The
116 E. Palace Ave.
Santa Fe, NM 87501-2011
phone: 505-983-4823 or 800-525-5764

Santa Claus

Collectors

Douglas M. Singleton
P.O. Box 416
Westmoreland, NY 13490-0416
phone: 315-336-7792
Wants to buy Santa Clause pin back buttons from Department stores, banks, advertising products, etc.; also wants Santa pocket mirrors, whistles, spinners, etc.

Martha Tucker
21 Briar Hollow #803
Houston, TX 77027
phone: 713-877-1133
Has an extensive collection of over 2,500 Santas.

CHRONOMETERS

(see CLOCKS, Marine Chronometers)

CIGAR BANDS, BOXES & LABELS

(see also CIGAR STORE COLLECTIBLES; LABELS; PAPER COLLECTIBLES; SMOKING COLLECTIBLES; TOBACCO COLLECTIBLES)

Clubs/Associations

Cigar Label Collectors International
Newsletter: Stone Press
P.O. Box 66
Sharon Center, OH 44274-0066
For individuals who collect stone lithograph images that were designed to decorate cigar boxes; quarterly newsletter loaded with information on new discoveries, historical information, sales and auctions, plus ads for members.

International Seal, Label & Cigar Band Society
Newsletter: Inter. Seal, Label & Cigar Band Soc. Bulletin
8915 E. Bellevue St.
Tucson, AZ 85715
phone: 602-296-1048
Interested in hotel, cigar box, beer, fruit crate, etc. labels; also matchcovers, charity stamps, Christmas seals, sugar packets, etc.

Collectors

David & Barbara Freiberg
Cerebro
P.O. Box 327
East Prospect, PA 17317-0327
phone: 717-252-2400 or 800-69L-ABEL
fax: 717-252-3685
Wants cigar box, cigar bands, old advertising labels: fire cracker labels, baggage labels, US cigarette cards, sample books of labels.

Jerry L. Striker
P.O. Box 10755
Lancaster, PA 17605-0755
phone: 717-291-6614
fax: 717-391-2562
Internet: http://www.redrose.net/wildsoft/cigar.htm
Wants to buy antique lithographed cigar box labels and cigar boxes.

Joseph Hruby
1511 Lyndhurst Rd.
Lyndhurst, OH 44124
phone: 216-449-0977
Wants old cigar band collections in good condition.

James Mount
730 Tall Oaks Ave.
Lima, OH 45805
phone: 419-227-2320

Margo Toth
Up Down Tobacco Shop
1550 N. Wells St.
Chicago, IL 60610
phone: 312-337-8505

Dr. Tony Hyman
Treasure Hunt Publications
P.O. Box 3028
Pismo Beach, CA 93448-3028
phone: 805-773-6777 or 805-733-0117
fax: 805-773-8436
e-mail: thyman@tobacciana.com
Internet: http://www.tobacciana.com
Collector, expert, author; wants pre-1920 cigar box labels, cans & all else related to cigar making, selling or smoking such as photos and historical ephemera; author of "Handbook of Cigar Boxes" and many articles on tobacco collectibles.

Dealers

David M. Beach
Paper Americana
P.O. Box 2026
Goldenrod, FL 32733-2026
phone: 407-657-7403
fax: 407-657-6382
Wants to buy old cigar box labels.

Joe Davidson
Aaron's Archives
5185 Windfall Rd.
Medina, OH 44256-8703
phone: 330-723-7172
Buys and sells rare cigar labels.

Silas W. Bass
788 Cuchillo St.
Oceanside, CA 92057
phone: 619-726-9937
Wants to buy cigar labels.

Experts

Stephen C. Jones
P.O. Box 267
Homer, NY 13077-0267
phone: 607-753-8822
Buy, sells, collects and specializes in cigar box labels; cigar box sample books, sample labels & proofs; also wants pre-1900 trade cards, cigarette cards, business cards, billheads, letterheads illustrating products sold; no cigar bands.

Joe & Sue Davidson
Aaron's Archives
5185 Windfall Rd.
Medina, OH 44256-8703
phone: 330-723-7172
Author and expert specializing in stone lithography especially cigar box labels; author of "The Art of the Cigar Label," "Smoker's Art."

Dr. Tony Hyman
Treasure Hunt Publications
P.O. Box 3028
Pismo Beach, CA 93448-3028
phone: 805-773-6777 or 805-733-0117
fax: 805-773-8436
e-mail: thyman@tobacciana.com
Internet: http://www.tobacciana.com
Collector, expert, author; wants pre-1920 cigar box labels, cans & all else related to cigar making, selling or smoking such as photos and historical ephemera; author of "Handbook of

Cigar Boxes" and many articles on tobacco collectibles.

Periodicals

Ed Barnes
Newsletter: Cigar Label Gazette, The
P.O. Box 3
Lake Forest, CA 92630-0003
phone: 714-457-0737
fax: 714-457-0680
e-mail: edbarnes@primenet.com
Internet: http://www.primenet.com/~edbarnes
A bi-monthly newsletter specializing in collecting cigar label art; lists and reviews cigar label auctions; articles, terminology, book reviews, advertisements.

CIGAR STORE COLLECTIBLES

(see also CIGAR BANDS, BOXES & LABELS; SMOKING COLLECTIBLES; TOBACCO COLLECTIBLES)

Collectors

Dr. Greg Zemenick
Dr. "Z"
1350 Kirts, Ste. 160
Troy, MI 48084-4830
phone: 248-642-8129 or 248-244-9430
fax: 248-244-9495
e-mail: DrZzeezz@aol.com
Internet: http://www.drzzeezzi.com
Wants cigar store items: Indians, figures, cigar cutters, lighters, photos, blinking eye clocks, cast iron items: anything cigar store.

Mike Schwimmer
325 East Blodgett
Lake Bluff, IL 60044-2112
phone: 847-295-1901
Collector of cigar memorabilia; dealer in all forms of vintage advertising; buys and sells.

Russell Barnes
P.O. Box 141994
Austin, TX 78714-1994
phone: 512-835-9510
fax: 512-835-1276
Wants to buy pre-1910 cigar store Indians and other figures; wood or metal; also wants original pictures of cigar store Indians; willing to travel; please call collect; pays finders fees.

Museums/Libraries

New York Public Library, Arents Collections, The
5th Ave. & 42nd St.
New York, NY 10018
phone: 212-930-0800

Cigar Cutters

Collectors

Howie Gross
407 Lincoln Rd.
Miami Beach, FL 33139
phone: 305-534-4757
fax: 305-538-5504
Wants to buy cigar cutters: desk, pocket, figural, counter advertising.

Experts

William J. Ennis
12220 14th Dr. S.E.
Everett, WA 98208-5929
phone: 425-337-5068
Collects any type of cigar cutter; has written several articles about cigar cutters and has done a complete USA patent search on cigar cutters.

CIGARETTE COLLECTIBLES

(see also ADVERTISING COL-
LECTIBLES, Trade Cards [Tobacco];
ADVERTISING COLLECTIBLES,
Lucky Strike; ADVERTISING
COLLECTIBLES, Philip Morris;
LIGHTERS; MATCHCOVERS;
MATCHBOXES & LABELS;
MATCH SAFES; SMOKING
COLLECTIBLES; TOBACCO
COLLECTIBLES

Collectors

Betty Bird
107 Ida St.
Mount Shasta, CA 96067-2629
phone: 916-926-4331 or 916-926-2231
Buy and sell smokers' sets, cigarette cases, match safes, etc.

Cards

(see ADVERTISING COL-
LECTIBLES, Trade Cards [Tobacco])

Cigarette Boxes

Collectors

David Frankel
P.O. Box 41
Kinckerbocker Station
New York, NY 10002-0041
phone: 212-473-5321
Wants to buy cigarette boxes that have a gimmick.

Dealers

Lenore Monleon
33 Fifth Ave.
New York, NY 10003
phone: 212-475-7871 or 212-229-0958
Wants enamel and sterling match safes and cigarette boxes.

Packs

Clubs/Associations

Richard Elliott
Cigarette Pack Collectors' Association
Newsletter: Brandstand
61 Searle St.
Georgetown, MA 01833-2213
phone: 508-352-7377
e-mail: cigpack@aol.com
Internet: http://members.aol.com/
cigpakc
For those interested in cigarette packs, tins, boxes and related advertising items; especially obsolete U.S. brands.

Collectors

Richard Elliott
61 Searle St.
Georgetown, MA 01833-2213
phone: 508-352-7377
e-mail: cigpack@aol.com
Internet: http://members.aol.com/
cigpakc

David Brame
5405 Vicksburg Lane
Durham, NC 27712

Roll-Your-Own Papers

Collectors

Paul Scheuer
6753 Humbolt Ave.
Minneapolis, MN 55430-1533
phone: 612-561-7321
Internet: http://www.underthebridge.com
Collects Roll-Your-Own cigarette paper packets and related memora-bilia; also wants old pipe cleaner containers.

Silks

Collectors

William Nielsen
1379 Main St.
Brewster, MA 02631-1723
phone: 508-896-7389
Wants U.S. cigarette silks, leathers, and inserts.

Charles Reuter
6 Joy Ave.
Mount Joy, PA 17552-1532
phone: 717-653-8505
Collects cigarette silks and cigarette trading cards.

Stands

Collectors

Lawrence Hartnell
P.O. Box 352
Collingwood
Ontario L9Y 3Z7 Canada
Wants footed cigarette holders (stands) (1920-1935) shaped like wine glasses; some have the foot rolled up to serve as an ashtray.

CIGARS

(see SMOKING COLLECTIBLES)

CIPHER MACHINES

(see SPY EQUIPMENT)

CIRCUS COLLECTIBLES

(see also CIRCUS EQUIPMENT,
Miniature Models of; CLOWN
COLLECTIBLES; PERFORMING
ARTS)

Auction Services

Kurt R. Krueger
Krueger Auctions
160 N. Washington St.
Iola, WI 54945
phone: 715-445-3845
fax: 715-445-4100
Conducts periodic specialized auctions of circus and Wild West Show memorabilia.

Clubs/Associations

Gordon Taylor
Circus Fans Association of America
Magazine: White Tops, The
1544 Piedmont Ave. ME, Ste. 41
Atlanta, GA 30324
phone: 404-872-8680
e-mail: b_taylor@mindspring.com
Focuses on circus history, current acts and activities, reviews of books about the circus, circus bands, etc.

Dale C. Haynes, Sec.
Circus Historical Society
3477 Vienna Court
Westerville, OH 43081

Collectors

Al Mordas
66 Surrey Dr.
Bristol, CT 06010

Irvin C. Mohler
P.O. Box 59710
Potomac, MD 20859-9710
phone: 301-762-8272

Tommy Sciortino
1904 W. Waters Ave.
Tampa, FL 33604-1006
phone: 813-248-5387
fax: 813-247-6369
Circus equipment and memorabilia, carousels, amusement devices, coin-ops; no circus toys.

Museums/Libraries

P.T. Barnum Museum
820 Main St.
Bridgeport, CT 06604
phone: 203-576-7320

John & Mable Ringling Museum of Art
5401 Bayshore Rd.
Sarasota, FL 34243
phone: 941-359-5700
fax: 941-359-5745
e-mail: ringling@concentric.net

Circus City Festival Museum
154 North Broadway
Peru, IN 46970-2234
phone: 765-472-3918

Fred Dahlinger, Dir.
Circus World Museum, Robert L.
   Parkinson Library & Research Center
426 Water St.
Baraboo, WI 53913-2560
phone: 608-356-8341
fax: 608-356-1800
Maintains the largest publicly accessible collection of circus ephemera and documentation in the world.

Emmett Kelly Historical Museum
202 E. Main
Sedan, KS 67361-1629
phone: 316-725-3470

Periodicals

Don Marcks
Newsletter: Circus Report
525 Oak St.
El Cerrito, CA 94530-3699
phone: 510-525-3332
A weekly newsletter devoted to the circus.

Ricketts Circus

Collectors

Bill Ricketts
P.O. Box 9605
Asheville, NC 28805-0605
phone: 704-669-2205 or 704-669-2668
fax: 704-669-2205
Wants to buy any posters, newspaper ads, etc. which advertise the Ricketts Circus (first circus in the US - Phila., PA.)

CIRCUS EQUIPMENT
Miniature Models Of

Clubs/Associations

Sally Conover Weitlauf
Circus Model Builders International
Newsletter: Little Circus Wagon
347 Lonsdale Ave.
Dayton, OH 45419-3249
phone: 513-299-0515
For builders and collectors of miniature models of circus equipment.

CIVIL RIGHTS

(see BLACK MEMORABILIA;
PAPER COLLECTIBLES; POLITI-
CAL COLLECTIBLES; SLAVERY
ITEMS; SOCIAL CAUSES)

CIVIL WAR ARTIFACTS

(see also AMMUNITION &
EXPLOSIVE ORDNANCE; BLACK
MEMORABILIA; BOOKS, Reference
[Civil War]; CIVIL WAR HISTORY;
MEDICAL, DENTAL & PHARMA-
CEUTICAL, Civil War; MILITARIA;
PERSONALITIES [HISTORICAL],
Abraham Lincoln)

Auction Services

Kurt R. Krueger
Krueger Auctions
160 N. Washington St.
Iola, WI 54945
phone: 715-445-3845
fax: 715-445-4100

Clubs/Associations

Joe Bilardello
Company H 119th NY Volunteers
  Historical Association, Inc.
Newsletter: Hempstead Volunteer, The
P.O. Box 184
Manorville, NY 11949-0184
phone: 516-874-3044
*Focuses on photos, letters, posses-
sions, records of the original 119th
N.Y. Civil War soldiers, 11th and later
20th Corps.*

Collectors

Warren K. Tice
W. Tice & Company
8 Orchard Terrace
Essex Junction, VT 05452-3501
phone: 802-878-3835
e-mail: wtice@vbimail.champlain.edu
*Wants to purchase U.S. Military,
Confederate, and high quality
decorative buttons; also wants to buy
military antiques.*

Gene Peters
'Tiques
P.O. Box 3267
Farmingdale, NY 11735-0679
phone: 516-842-9549
*Wants documents, pictures, articles
and artifacts relating to the African/
Americans during the Civil War.*

Julie Brighenti
RD 2 Box 61
Belle Vernon, PA 15012-9802
phone: 412-929-7311
*Wants to buy Civil War memorabilia:
swords, belt buckles, medals,
regimental books, etc.*

Gil Barrett
8322 Sperry Court
Laurel, MD 20723-1184
phone: 301-498-1412
*Wants Civil War photos and
memorabilia particularly Maryland
Union, 6th and 8th Mass. Infantry,
and Boston Light Artillery.*

Barry Smith
1707 Brookcliff Dr.
Greensboro, NC 27408-2504
phone: 919-288-4375
fax: 919-282-6784
*Wants Union or Confederate Civil
War memorabilia: letters, documents,
autographs, photos, etc.*

Garl Fugitt
2430 Canterbury Chase
Murfreesboro, TN 37129
phone: 615-893-7762
Wants to buy Union and Confederate

*Civil War items: buckles, buttons,
carte de visites, etc.*

James Mejdrich
128 N. Knollwood Dr.
Wheaton, IL 60187
*Wants Civil War photos, letters,
diaries, and personal items.*

Karl Sundstrom
2512 2nd Ave.
North Riverside, IL 60546
phone: 708-447-8673
*Wants to buy all Civil War items
including photographs, Corps or unit
badges, paper, books, weapons,
personal items, letters, flags, cloth,
etc.*

Jim Kopke
P.O. Box 4310
Dillon, CO 80435-4310
*Wants to buy Civil War arms,
uniforms, paper items, artifacts,
pictures, etc.*

Dealers

Bedford & Janet Hayes
Gunsight Antiques
P.O. Box 687
Standish, ME 04084-0687
phone: 207-839-3825
*Specializing in quality items of the
Civil War era; especially wants
significant items belonging to Civil
War soldiers from Maine.*

Anna Pansini
P.O. Box 5031
South Hackensack, NJ 07606-4231
phone: 201-296-0419
*Buying and selling various Civil War
items including books, pamphlets,
postcards, prints, audio cassettes,
currency, postage stamps, videos, and
commemorative medals; send SASE
for price list/catalog.*

Charles G. Moore
Charles G. Moore Americana Ltd.
32 E. 57th St.
New York, NY 10022
phone: 212-751-1900

Mike & Rose Klinepeter
Blue & Gray Relic Shop
HCR 81 Box 75
Big Cove Tannery, PA 17212-9603
phone: 717-294-3326
*Original and reproductions mail
order lists available; send 2 stamps
for original and $1 for reproduction
list.*

Howard A. Hoffman
Military Americana
97 Johnson Rd.
Bangor, PA 18013-9274
phone: 610-588-8853
fax: 610-588-2815

Brian & Maria Green
Brian Michael Green
P.O. Box 1816
Kernersville, NC 27285-1816
phone: 910-993-5100
fax: 910-993-1801
Internet: http://
ww.eastnc2.coastalnet.com/militaria/
bmginc.html
*Buy & sell Confederate States and
Union autographs, letters and
documents, especially military
related; also photos, CDV's and other
memorabilia.*

R. Douglas Sanders
McGowan Book Company
39 Kimberly Dr.
Durham, NC 27707
phone: 919-403-1503 or 800-449-8406
fax: 919-403-1706
e-mail: mcgowan@vnet.net
Internet: http://
www.mcgowanbooks.com
*Wants to buy Civil War books,
autographs, documents and
memorabilia.*

Jerry R. Robbins
P.O. Box 1349
Hampstead, NC 28443
phone: 800-686-0222
*Wants to buy Civil Way and other
types of militaria: old swords, flags,
uniforms, hats, old daggers and
knives, Bowie knives, German, US,
Japanese, pistols, Winchester rifle,
Civil War guns; also wants Civil War
dug items.*

Will Gorges
Will Gorges Civil War Items
2100 Trent Blvd.
New Bern, NC 28560-5326
phone: 919-636-3039 or 919-514-5548
fax: 919-637-1862
e-mail: rebel!@abaco.coastalnet.com
Internet: http://www.collectorsnet.com
*Full time dealer buys, sells, collects
and appraises authentic Civil War
artifacts: firearms, accoutrements,
edged weapons, dug items, documents,
uniforms, coins, etc.; catalog
available.*

Earby S. Markham
Ye Old Post Office Antiques & Militaria
P.O. Box 9
17070 Scenic Highway 98
Point Clear, AL 36564
phone: 334-928-0108

Larry W. Hicklen
Yesteryear Civil War Relics
3511 Old Nashville Highway
Murfreesboro, TN 37129-3094
phone: 615-893-3470
*Send $5/yr. for five mail order lists of
artifacts for sale; buys & sells CW
muskets, pistols, sabers, buckles,
buttons, letters, etc.*

Paul & Linda Gibson
Gibson's Civil War Newspapers
303 Sequoyah Dr.
Blountville, TN 37617
phone: 615-323-2427
fax: 615-968-7797
*Buys and sells Civil War era (1861-
1865) newspapers as well as Civil
War related letters, diaries, flags,
uniforms, photos; CSA bonds,
currency and interim deposit slips;
slavery items.*

William Butts
Main Street Fine Books & Manuscripts
206 N. Main St.
Galena, IL 61035-2244
phone: 815-777-3749
*Open shop dealing in autographs and
out-of-print books in most fields;
specializing in all aspects of American
history; boos and autograph catalogs
issued regularly; member of A.B.A.A.*

Alex Peck
Antique Scientifica
P.O. Box 710
Charleston, IL 61920
phone: 217-348-1009
*Wants uniforms, insignia, guns,
swords, diaries, photos, Corps
badges, Bowie knives, medical
instruments, hats, medals, belt plates,
tokens, autographs, Lincoln items.*

Experts

Ken & Jean Owings
Americana & Bookbinding
P.O. Box 389
Whitman, MA 02382
phone: 617-447-7850
fax: 617-447-3435
*Civil War, Colonial American
documents, books, autographs and
related collectibles.*

Richard Friz
P.O. Box 472
Peterborough, NH 03458
phone: 603-563-8155
*Author of "Official Price Guide to
Civil War Collectibles."*

Mike Woshner
2306 Spokane Ave.
Pittsburgh, PA 15210-4414
phone: 412-884-9299
e-mail: mwoshner@bellaatlantic.net
*Collects India-rubber and gutta-
percha military and civilian artifacts;
conducts patent research, publishes
articles, displays artifacts and delivers
presentations.*

Dale & Debra Anderson
Dale C. Anderson Co.
4 W. Confederate Ave.
Gettysburg, PA 17325
phone: 717-334-1031
*Sells, appraises guns, swords,
uniforms, headgear, relics, personal
items, more; all offered in bi-monthly
catalog ($12/yr); covers all periods
1775-1945; US & foreign; emphasis*

on Civil War/Indian Wars period; over 30 years experience.

Courtney Wilson
American Military Antiques
8398 Court Ave.
Ellicott City, MD 21043-4514
phone: 410-465-6827
Military antiques 1700-1900: appraiser, consultant, broker, dealer; arms, uniforms, equipment, memorabilia - especially Civil War.

Craig Wofford
2101 Harrison Ave.
Orlando, FL 32804-5467
phone: 407-872-7425
Collects, appraises and specializes in Civil War memorabilia, Union or Confederate: photographs, letters, documents, diaries, uniforms, canteens, etc.; 25 years experience; free appraisals with SASE; references available.

Museums/Libraries

Grand Army of the Republic Memorial Museum & Library
4278 Griscom St.
Philadelphia, PA 19124-3954
phone: 215-673-1688 or 215-289-6484
e-mail: garmuslib@aol.com
Internet: http://libertynet.org/~gencap/gar.html
Civil War Museum & Library; artifacts, personal memorabilia, paintings, G.A.R. & S.U.V.C.W. records; open first Sunday or by appt.

Museum of the Confederacy, The
1201 East Clay St.
Richmond, VA 23219
phone: 804-649-1861
One of the largest and most comprehensive collections of Confederate art, artifacts, and memorabilia.

Will Gorges, Dir.
New Bern Civil War Museum
301 Metcalf St.
Trent Woods, NC 28562-5687
phone: 919-633-2818 or 919-636-3039
fax: 919-637-1862
e-mail: rebel!@abaco.coastalnet.com
Houses one of the finest in-depth private collections of Civil War memorabilia and weapons in the U.S. and open to the public; brochure available.

Dr. B.D. Patterson
Confederate Research Center
P.O. Box 619
Hillsboro, TX 76645
phone: 817-582-2555
Large collection of Civil War artifacts; museum provides information about Confederate soldiers & capsule histories of Confederate regiments.

Periodicals

Cutter & Locke, Inc.
Newspaper: Civil War Book Exchange & Collector's Newspaper
4 Water St.
P.O. Box C
Arlington, MA 02174

Magazine: Artilleryman, The
RR 1 Box 36
Tunbridge, VT 05077-9707
phone: 802-889-3500
fax: 802-889-5627
Published quarterly, the only magazine exclusively for the 1750-1898 artillery enthusiast: artillery history, unit profiles, shell collecting, etc.

Linda Kellbach
Antique Trader Publications, Inc.
Newspaper: Military Trader
P.O. Box 1050
Dubuque, IA 52004-1050
phone: 800-334-7165 or 800-482-4155
fax: 800-531-0880
e-mail: 76143.72@compuserve.com
Internet: http://www.csmonline.com
Monthly publication focusing on military collectibles: articles, collecting, interviews with dealers, military toy column, book reviews, collectibles for sale, espionage.

Confederate

Experts

Lewis Leigh, Jr.
P.O. Box 4327
Leesburg, VA 20177
phone: 703-771-3081
fax: 703-771-1432
Wants to buy Confederate uniforms, swords, buttons, weapons, belts, soldiers' letters & diaries, hats and related items.

Confederate Bonds

Experts

Jule Dews
Stoneridge Institute
7703 Baltimore National Pike
Frederick, MD 21702-3557
phone: 301-473-8287
Author/publisher of "Windows of Confederate Finance - CSA Bearer Bonds;" $16 ppd.

Confederate Swords

Collectors

Steve Hess
P.O. Box 3476
De Land, FL 32720-3476
phone: 904-736-1067 or 904-254-1809

Currency

Dealers

Cy Phillips, Jr.
S C Coin & Stamp Co. Inc.
P.O. Drawer 661180
Arcadia, CA 91066-1180
phone: 818-445-8277 or 800-367-0779
fax: 818-445-8278
Wants Confederate stamps, Civil War tokens, medals, currency, encased postage, etc.

Medical

Museums/Libraries

Burton K. Kummerow, Ex.Dir.
National Museum of Civil War Medicine
P.O. Box 470
Frederick, MD 21705-0470
phone: 301-695-1864
fax: 301-695-6823
Contains the Gordon Dammann Collection of thousands of items including the only surviving CW surgeon's tent, medical chests, uniforms, stretchers, medical instruments, swords, books and personal effects.

Paper Items

Collectors

Jack Donahue
P.O. Box 610123
Bayside, NY 11361
phone: 718-225-0446 or 800-248-4592
fax: 718-225-4067
Wants Civil War autographs, letters, diaries, arms; also daguerreotypes, ambrotypes, tintypes, carte-de-visites; North and South.

Dealers

Bob & Pat Bartosz
P.O. Box 226
Wenonah, NJ 08090-0226
phone: 609-468-0866
Wants Civil War paper items, e.g. letters, diaries, bank checks, fire department items, early baseball, slave papers. Author of "The Civil War Letter of George R. White 19th Mass. Vol."

Photographs

Collectors

Peter Falk
P. Hastings Falk, Inc.
859 Boston Post Rd.
Madison, CT 06443
phone: 203-245-2246 or 203-849-1655
fax: 203-245-5116
Wants important vintage Civil War photographs, especially of notable figures such as Abraham Lincoln, Grant, Lee, etc.

Tom Molocea
P.O. Box 100
North Lima, OH 44452-0100
Wants to buy vintage Civil War

photographs in any format; will buy single image or entire collection.

Dealers

Henry Deeks
P.O. Box 2260
Acton, MA 01720
phone: 508-263-1861
Buys and sells Civil War images, photographs and CDV's; issues a sales catalog twice a year.

Van Nitz
Fields of Glory
55 York St.
Gettysburg, PA 17325
phone: 717-337-2837
Buys and sells Civil War images.

Swords

Repro. Sources

Sudha Gupta
Legendary Arms, Inc.
P.O. Box 479
Three Bridges, NJ 08887-0479
phone: 800-528-2767 or 908-788-7330
fax: 908-788-8522
Offers line of reproduction knives and swords; Civil War swords include CSA Artillery, M1850 US Staff & Field, M1850 US Foot Officer, M1860 US Cavalry, CSA Foot Officer, CSA NCO, etc.

Tokens

Clubs/Associations

Dale Cade
Civil War Token Society
Journal: Civil War Token Journal
26548 Mazur Dr.
Rancho Palos Verdes, CA 90274
phone: 310-378-4182
Purpose is to promote the study of Civil War tokens along educational, historic and scientific lines.

Veterans

(see VETERAN ITEMS, Civil War)

CIVIL WAR HISTORY

(see also CIVIL WAR ARTIFACTS)

Clubs/Associations

Civil War Society, The
Magazine: Civil War Magazine
P.O. Box 770
Berryville, VA 22611
phone: 800-247-6253 or 703-955-1176
fax: 703-955-1297
e-mail: cwmag@mnsinc.com
An international organization of Civil War enthusiasts; publishes full-color "Civil War" magazine bi-monthly.

Glenn Wiche
Chicago Civil War Round Table, The
Newsletter: Civil War Roundtable
Newsletter
410 S. Michigan Ave., Ste. 1402
Chicago, IL 60605-1402
*The nation's leading organization
dedicated to the study of Civil War
history.*

Jerry L. Russell
Heritagepac
P.O. Box 7388
Little Rock, AR 72217-
phone: 501-225-3996
Internet: http://www.civilwarbuff.org
*The nation's leading battlefield
preservation organization.*

Jerry L. Russell, NatCh.
Civil War Round Table Associates
Newsletter: Civil War Round Table
Digest
P.O. Box 7388
Little Rock, AR 72217-
phone: 501-225-3996
Internet: http://www.civilwarbuff.org
*The nation's leading battlefield
preservation organization.*

Jerry L. Russell
Confederate Historical Institute, The
Newsletter: CHI Dispatch
P.O. Box 7388
Little Rock, AR 72217-
phone: 501-225-3996
Internet: http://www.civilwarbuff.org
*The only organization devoted to the
study of the history of The Confeder-
ate States of America.*

Dr. Stephen Engle
Society of Civil War Historians, The
Newsletter: SCWH Newsletter
P.O. Box 7388
Little Rock, AR 72217-
phone: 501-225-3996
Internet: http://www.civilwarbuff.org
*The only organization for the teachers
of Civil War history; Dr. Engle can be
e-mailed at engle@acc.fau.edu.*

Misc. Services

National Archives & Records
Administration
7th & Pennsylvania Ave. NW
Washington, DC 20408
*For locating military records of Civil
War veterans.*

Veterans Administration, Director of
National Cemetery System
818 Vermont Ave. NW
Washington, DC 20420
*Contact to find out where a Civil War
ancestor was buried during or after
the Civil War.*

Marie Varrelman Melchiori, CGRS,
CGL
121 Tapawingo Rd. SW
Vienna, VA 22180-5964
phone: 703-938-8103
fax: 703-938-7279
e-mail: mvmcgrs@juno.com
Certified Genealogical Record

*Specialist in Civil War research; will
help identify owners of historical
items; will assist members of the legal
profession locate missing heirs.*

On-Line Services

George H. Hoemann
American Civil War Homepage, The
719 Luttrell
Knoxville, TN 37920
phone: 423-974-5917
fax: 423-546-3182
e-mail: hoemann@utk.edu
*Gathers together in one place
hypertext links to the most useful
identified electronic files about the
American Civil War.*

Periodicals

Newspaper: Civil War News, The
RR 1 Box 36
Tunbridge, VT 05077-9707
phone: 802-889-3500
fax: 802-889-5627
*A current events newspaper published
ten times per year for people with an
active interest in Civil War history.*

Anna Pansini
Distant Frontier Press
Newsletter: Mail Call
P.O. Box 5031
South Hackensack, NJ 07606-4231
phone: 201-296-0419
*Published six times per year, each
issue is filled with excerpts from
letters, stories, diaries, journals, and
poems written to, by or about Civil
War soldiers.*

Dave Gallagher
Newspaper: Civil War Courier, The
2503 Delaware Ave.
Buffalo, NY 14216
phone: 716-873-2594 or 800-418-1861
fax: 716-873-0809
e-mail: galprint@local.net
*A bi-monthly newspaper containing
classified ads, articles, events,
calendar, book reviews, reenactors,
and goods/services for Civil War
buffs.*

Cowles Magazines, Inc.
Magazine: Civil War Times Illustrated
741 Miller Dr. SE, Ste. D2
Harrisburg, PA 20175
phone: 703-771-9400 or 800-829-3340
fax: 703-779-8345
Internet: http://www.thehistorynet.com
*A bi-monthly magazine focusing on
the historical aspects of the great
conflict; a general interest magazine
examining all aspects of the Civil War
era, including personalities, battles,
travel, art, artifacts and politics; bi-
monthly.*

Cowles Magazines, Inc.
Magazine: America's Civil War
741 Miller Dr. SE, Ste. D2
Harrisburg, PA 20175
phone: 703-771-9400 or 800-829-3340
fax: 703-779-8345
Internet: http://www.thehistorynet.com
*A bi-monthly magazine with colorful
articles on Civil War battles,
personalities, units; also ads for Civil
War related products, prints, books,
models, etc.*

Nancy Dearing Rossbacher
Magazine: North South Trader's Civil
War Magazine
P.O. Drawer 631
Orange, VA 22960-0370
phone: 540-67C-IVIL
fax: 540-672-7283
e-mail: nstcw@msn.com
*Bi-monthly magazine for Civil War
relic hunters, collectors, reenactors &
historians.*

Steve Davis
Newsletter: Grave Matters
1163 Warrenhall Lane
Atlanta, GA 30319
*A newsletter for Civil War buffs who
carry their hobby to the ultimate dead
end!*

Journal: Journal of Confederate History
P.O. Box 2071
Harrogate, TN 37752-0901
*A serial book; scholarly articles about
Confederate history: battles, the
homefront, women in the war, secret
agents, the Navy etc.*

Magazine: Blue & Gray Magazine
P.O. Box 28685
Columbus, OH 43228
phone: 800-248-4592
Internet: http://www.mmnewsstand.com/
`BlueGray.index.html
*A bi-monthly full-color magazine
focusing on the Civil War.*

Magazine: Confederate Veteran
8506 Braesdale
Houston, TX 77071
*Includes scholarly articles about the
battles, leaders and soldiers of the
War Between the States; images,
Southern heritage, etc. MAIL
RETURNED.*

Theodore P. Savas
Regimental Studies, Inc.
Journal: Civil War Regiments
1475 S. Bascom Ave., Ste. 204
Campbell, CA 95008-0629
phone: 408-879-9039 or 800-848-6585
fax: 408-879-9327
e-mail: mhbooks@aol.com
*A quarterly journal of the American
Civil War; book reviews, The
Preservation Report and The
Regimental Bookshelf, unit-related
articles.*

Cavalry

Experts

Nick Nichols
Heartland House
Old Blue Ridge Turnpike
Rochelle, VA 22738
phone: 703-672-9267
fax: 703-672-9267
*Over 20 years of intensive research
&scholarship on Civil War history;
special emphasis on cavalry themes;
extensive background in material
culture, tactics, etc.; references
provided on request; buys & collects
cavalry-related items.*

Misc. Services

Nick Nichols
1st Reg't. Virginia Cavalry, CSA
Old Blue Ridge Turnpike
Rochelle, VA 22738
phone: 703-672-9267
fax: 703-672-9267
*Nationwide non-profit equestrian
living history organization with an
emphasis on authenticity/education;
established in 1970; interpretive
historians, not reenactors; available
for presentations, demonstrations, etc.*

Repro. Sources

Nick Nichols
Heartland House
Old Blue Ridge Turnpike
Rochelle, VA 22738
phone: 703-672-9267
fax: 703-672-9267
*Museum-quality replica items for
collectors & interpreters; exclusive
line of Confederate central government issue horse furniture &
accoutrements; also carries reference
materials, patterns, etc.; conservation;
consultations; catalog $4.*

Reenactors

(see also LIVING HISTORY)

Periodicals

Magazine: Harness Shop News, The
347 Elk Rd.
Sylva, NC 28779
phone: 704-586-8938
fax: 704-586-8938
*Original McClellans, sources for
military hardware, accoutrements,
and reproductions; professional
leather workers, saddle makers,
saddle & shoe repairmen, holster
manufacturers, harness makers, boot
makers; ads, calendar of events.*

Jeff H. Grzelak
Department of the South
Newspaper: Hilton Head Dispatch
7214 Laurel Hill Rd.
Orlando, FL 32818-5233
phone: 407-295-7510
*Carries the latest information on all
Southeastern Civil War events: shows,*

reenactments, book fairs; for historians, reenactors, buffs in S.E.

Newspaper: Camp Chase Gazette
P.O. Box 707
Marietta, OH 45750
phone: 614-373-1865
For 17 years the voice of the Civil War reenactor: recruiting, events, equipment, etc.

Magazine: Civil War Lady, The
622 3rd Ave. S.W.
Pipestone, MN 56164
phone: 507-825-3182
The best Civil War bi-monthly reenacting magazine for women: fashion news & articles, research, reenacting tips, child rearing, ads, etc.

Patrick Publishing
Magazine: Reenactor's Journal
P.O. Box 1864
Varna, IL 61375
phone: 309-463-2123
fax: 309-463-2188
A concise, to-the-point monthly magazine for reenactors of the War Between the States; for military or civilian reenactor.

Newspaper: Yesteryears Chronicle
P.O. Box 132
Sullivan, IL 61951
phone: 217-728-7128
The leading interpretive historical publication for period fashion and living: recipes, fashion, poems, needlework, activities, etc.

Suppliers

Regimental Quartermaster, The
P.O. Box 553
Hatboro, PA 19040
phone: 215-672-6891
fax: 215-672-9020
Civil War reproduction Muskets, Revolvers, Swords, Uniforms, Leather Goods, Buckles, Buttons, Accouterments, Accessories, etc.; send $2 for list.

Staley's Sundries
710 Caroline St.
Fredericksburg, VA 22401
phone: 703-373-8349
Carries American Revolution and Civil War era gifts, flags, music, costumes, accessories, costume patterns, accouterments, etc.

CIVILIAN CONSERVATION CORPS ITEMS

Clubs/Associations

Association of Civilian Conservation Corps Alumni
P.O. Box 16429
Saint Louis, MO 63125
A group of over 10,000 members founded in 1977.

Collectors

Jake Eckenrode
310 Wallace Rd.
Bellefonte, PA 16823
phone: 814-355-8769
Wants CCC items from the 1930s.

Robert A. Fratkin
2322 20th St. NW
Washington, DC 20009
phone: 202-483-0274 or 800-336-0156
fax: 202-332-8538
e-mail: coxfrd@erols.com

Larry Jarvinen
313 Condon Rd.
Manistee, MI 49660
phone: 616-723-5063
Wants CCC or WPA marked items and early forestry or conservation related items.

J. Izatt
1002 E. Cherry St.
Le Roy, IL 61752
phone: 309-962-9454
Wants to buy CCC items from the 1920s-1930s.

Thomas W. Pooler
P.O. Box 1861
Grass Valley, CA 95945-1861
phone: 916-268-1338
Wants all CCC material: medals, flags, rings, tokens, insignia (especially numbered company patches - will pay $25 for each numbered Unit sleeve patch.) Send description AND price.

Dealers

Ken Kipp
Allenwood Americana Antiques
P.O. Box 116
Allenwood, PA 17810-0116
phone: 717-538-1440
Established dealer with over 20 years experience; always buying and selling.

CLOCKS

(see also ART DECO; BOOKS, Reference [Clocks]; INSTRUMENTS & DEVICES, Scientific; NAUTICAL ANTIQUES, Marine Chronometers; NEON, Clocks; WATCHES)

Appraisers

Robert J. Connelly, ASA
Bob & Sallie Connelly Auctions
666 Chenango St.
Binghamton, NY 13901-2015
phone: 607-722-9593 or 607-722-3555
fax: 607-722-1266
Appraisers and brokers of American & European clocks.

Walter A. Dayett
Dayett's Clock Repair & Appraisals
75 Study Rd.
Littlestown, PA 17340-9746
phone: 717-359-4850
fax: 717-359-4850
e-mail: dayett@juno.com
Specializes in antique and contempo-

rary clock repair, primarily weight and spring driven movements; also specializes in clock appraisals.

Martha Tips
7012 Blackwood Dr.
Dallas, TX 75231-5706
phone: 214-348-0075 or 214-349-0095
fax: 214-349-0095
Author of "Tips on Identifying and Appraising Clocks"; appraisals furnished on a fee-basis.

Auction Services

George Horan
Jones & Horan Auction Team
453 Mast Rd.
Goffstown, NH 03045
phone: 603-625-5314

Robert Schmitt
R.O. Schmidt Fine Arts
P.O. Box 1941
Salem, NH 03079
phone: 603-893-5915
fax: 603-893-9777
e-mail: roschmit@worldnet.att.net
Two antique auctions per year.

Clubs/Associations

Mrs. P.V.. Hossbach
Antiquarian Horological Society, The
Magazine: Antiquarian Horology
"New Howe", High Street
Ticehurst
East Sussex TN5 7AL, U.K.
phone: 01580-200155
fax: 01580-201323
Internet: http:// ourworld.compuserve.com/ homepages/ahsoc/
The world's leading organization in this field; the Society's aim is to serve all those interested in antique clocks, watches and other time-measuring instruments; publishes the quarterly journal, books, and monographs.

British Watch & Clock Collectors Association
5 Cathedral Lane
Truro
Cornwall TR1 2SQ U.K.
phone: +44 01872 41953
Geared mainly to the collector, but also solicits membership from restorers and repairers.

British Horological Institute
Upton Hall, Upton
Heark
Notts. NG23 5TE, U.K.
phone: (01636) 813795
fax: (01636) 812258
e-mail: clocks@bhi.co.uk
Internet: http://www.bhi.co.uk/
Education is a major part of the BHI; strong ties with institutions offering horological training; members have access to museum collection for study; membership open to anyone with an interest in timekeeping.

Thomas J. Bartels, ExDir
National Association of Watch & Clock Collectors, Inc.
Magazine: Bulletin of the NAWCC
514 Poplar St.
Columbia, PA 17512-2130
phone: 717-684-8261
fax: 717-684-0878
e-mail: patti@nawcc.org
Internet: http://www.nawcc.org
The NAWCC is a non-profit and scientific association founded in 1943 and now serving the horological interests of 38,000 members worldwide.

American Watchmakers-Clockmakers Institute
Magazine: Horological Times
701 Enterprise Dr.
Harrison, OH 45030-1696
e-mail: awi-info@awi-net.org
Internet: http://www.awi-net.org
For those interested in horology as a profession or avocation; monthly technical magazine, technical bulletins, training, public relations, networking.

Doug Cowan
British Horology
110 Central Terrace
Cincinnati, OH 45215

Les McAlister
National 400-Day Clock Chapter
1369 Manuka Dr.
O Fallon, MO 63366

Delle Morrow
Las Vegas Timekeepers
P.O. Box 12265
Las Vegas, NV 89112
phone: 702-471-6500
A regional chapter of the National Association of Watch & Clock Collectors.

Collectors

Jerry Boxenhorn
Clock Exchange, The
2045 Legion St.
South Bellmore, NY 11710
phone: 516-221-7077 or 718-429-6251
fax: 718-429-6251
Wants to buy one clock or entire collections; also movements, parts, and all clock related items; especially wants Ansonia statue clocks, Ansonia Royal Bonn clocks, French bronze clocks, and any animated or unusual clocks.

John B. Marrella
Investments in Time
P.O. Box 611
Birmingham, MI 48012-0611
phone: 810-644-3100
fax: 810-644-2792
Wants to buy miniature enamel clocks, repeaters, annular, industrial motifs.

Larry Spilkin
P.O. Box 5039
Southfield, MI 48086-5039
phone: 810-642-3722
Wants Lawson, Herman-Miller, Howard-Miller clocks.

Jim Rocheleau
1137 Cadieux
Grosse Point, MI 48230
phone: 313-885-7805
Wants cast iron blinking eye clocks, plus all others.

Paul H. Hayashi, PE
18 Tarabrook Dr.
Orinda, CA 94563-3121
phone: 510-254-5074 or 510-253-1038
fax: 510-253-0592
Wants to buy precision wall regulators with different escapments.

Dealers

Robert C. Cheney
Robert C. Cheney Fine Antique Clocks
RFD 1 Box 158B
Brimfield, MA 01010
phone: 413-245-7017
Since 1900 the Cheney clock makers have provided consulting services, restoration, appraisals, and sales of fine antique clocks; by appointment.

John & Barbara Delaney
435 Main St.
Route 119
Townsend, MA 01474
phone: 508-597-2231
Largest selection of American tall case clocks in the country.

Bob Frishman
Bell-Time Clocks
53 Poor St.
Andover, MA 01810-2501
phone: 508-475-5001
Buys and sells clocks of all styles, ages, sizes and nationalities; also repairs and restores clocks.

Larson's Clock Shop
P.O. Box 144
Westminster, VT 05158
Issues large catalog of clocks for sale.

Meurs Renehan
234 Long Hill Rd.
Guilford, CT 06437-1871

Ed Kazemekas
35 Riverview Circle
Wolcott, CT 06716
phone: 203-879-1814

Charles F. Breuel
P.O. Box 261
Glenmont, NY 12077
phone: 518-439-6717
Specializing in American time pieces.

Bruce A. Austin
c/o RIT/College Liberal Arts
92 Lomb Memorial Dr.
Rochester, NY 14623-5604
phone: 716-475-2879 or 716-387-9820
fax: 716-475-7732
e-mail: baagll@rit.edu
Buying American clocks manufactured between 1800 - 1915; especially interested in wall regulators.

Old Timers Antique Clocks
P.O. Box 392
Camp Hill, PA 17001-0392
phone: 717-761-1908
fax: 717-767-7446
Wants to buy antique clocks; must be at least 100 years old, no reproductions, electrics, cuckoos, or grandfather clocks; if selling, seller must send clear photos and asking for each clock.

Patrick Managan
P.M. Clock & Watch Company
497 English Rd.
Bath, PA 18014
phone: 610-837-7326

Gordon S. Converse
Gordon S. Converse & Co.
503 W. Lancaster Ave.
Strafford, PA 19087
phone: 610-964-7632 or 800-789-1001
fax: 610-964-1181
Internet: http://www.pond.com/~gsc
Specializes in fine antique clocks including American, French, English, porcelain, banjo, Vienna regulators, ships clocks, skeleton clocks, mantel and tallcase; high quality color catalog issued periodically.

Jill & Chuck Probst
Charles Edwin Antiques
P.O. Box 1340
Louisa, VA 23093-1340
phone: 540-967-0416
fax: 540-967-0416
e-mail: cei@charles-edwin.com
Internet: http://www.charles-edwin.com

Mark Peer
Mark of Time
24 South Lemon Ave.
Sarasota, FL 34236-5721
phone: 800-277-5275 or 941-955-3211
fax: 941-951-6524
Buys and sells antique clocks and entire clock collections.

David Pendley
Pendley's Clock Repair
6804 Cochise Dr.
Knoxville, TN 37918-5253
phone: 423-922-1892
Repairs, restores, buys, sells old vintage antique clocks, member NAWCC.

C.L. Horton
201 Culpepper Rd.
Lexington, KY 40502
phone: 606-255-0287 or 606-266-4532
fax: 606-255-2162
Issues large catalog of clocks for sale.

Judith Rubin
Eureka! Antiques
705 W. Washington
Evanston, IL 60202-2214
phone: 847-869-9090
Specializes in old neon, back-lit, advertising and novelty clocks; also wall and mantel key-wind clocks.

Experts

Eric Chandlee Wilson
16 Bondsville Rd.
Thorndale, PA 19372
phone: 610-383-5597
Tallcase clock dealer specializing in Chester County, PA clocks and an expert on clocks by the Chandlee's.

Julian Gibbard
P.O. Box 1092
Harpers Ferry, WV 25425
phone: 304-725-2035
Specialist in long case clocks.

Joe Cohen
4250 Galt Ocean Dr., Apt. 9A
Oakland Park, FL 33308
phone: 954-561-2234
Specializing in 17th, 18th, and 19th century clocks and watches.

Museums/Libraries

Nancy Connelly
American Clock & Watch Museum
Journal: Timepiece Journal
100 Maple St.
Bristol, CT 06010-5034
phone: 203-583-6070
Preserves the history of American horology, especially Connecticut and Bristol's role; large displays of clocks & watches.

Patricia Tomes, Cur.
National Association of Watch & Clock Collectors Museum, Inc., The
514 Poplar St.
Columbia, PA 17512-2130
phone: 717-684-8261
fax: 717-684-0878
e-mail: patti@nawcc.org
Internet: http://www.nawcc.org
The Watch & Clock Museum of the NAWCC strives to illustrate the history of timekeeping from the 1600's to the present with a collection of more than 8000 horological items.

National Museum of American History
14th & Constitution Ave. NW
Washington, DC 20560
phone: 202-357-2700
Internet: http://www.si.edu/

K. Klimesh
Bily Clock Exhibit/Antonin Dvorak Exhibit
323 Main St.
P.O. Box 258
Spillville, IA 52168-0258
phone: 319-562-3569 or 319-562-3457
fax: 319-562-4373
One-of-a-kind exhibit displaying clocks by the two Bily brothers; historical and educational display of

handcarved clocks; housed in the building famous composer Antonin Dvorak lived in during his stay in 1893.

Dorothy Mastricola
Time Museum, The
7801 E. State St.
P.O. Box 5285
Rockford, IL 61125-0285
phone: 815-398-6000
fax: 815-398-4700
Has an extensive collection of time-measuring devices from all parts of the world dating from ancient instruments to the atomic clock.

Old Clock Museum
929 E. Preston St.
Pharr, TX 78577
phone: 512-787-1923

Periodicals

Nexus Special Interests
Magazine: Clocks
Nexus House, Boundary Way
Hemel
Hempstead HP2 7ST, U.K.
phone: 01442-66551 or 01312 295550
fax: 01442-66998
The international monthly magazine for clock enthusiasts; feature articles on clock history and restoration from all over the world; horological news and views; clock questions and answers.

Magazine: Watch & Clock Review
2403 Champa St.
Denver, CO 80205-2621
phone: 303-296-1600
fax: 303-295-2159
Monthly magazine primarily for new and vintage watch and clock retailers; features articles on watches, clocks and shops; also ads for buyers, sellers, and restorers.

Erika Daileda
Wise Owl Worldwide Publications
Magazine: Clocks
4314 West 238th St. - Dept. MACR
Torrance, CA 90505-4509
phone: 310-375-6258
fax: 310-375-0548
e-mail: wiseowl@sprintmail.com
A monthly English publication; the international monthly magazine for clock enthusiasts; feature articles on clock history and restoration from all over the world; horological news and views; clock questions and answers; great photos!

Repair Services

Burt Dial Company
P.O. Box 774
Raymond, NH 03077
phone: 603-895-2879
Specializes in reverse painting on glass for clock tablets and doors, and in the restoring of clock dials.

Garrett Moore
Garrett's Clock Sales & Repair
24 Main St.
Clinton, NJ 08809
phone: 908-735-0496
Buys, sells and restores clocks - new and old.

Philip M. Poniz
European Watch & Casemakers, Ltd.
P.O. Box 1314
Highland Park, NJ 08904-1314
phone: 908-777-0111
Restoration of watches, clocks, and music boxes; museum experience; can make any part and restore any watch; clients include Sotheby's, Cartier, collectors in USA, Asia and Europe; appraises, researches, lectures on watch making, fakes.

Walter A. Dayett
Dayett's Clock Repair & Appraisals
75 Study Rd.
Littlestown, PA 17340-9746
phone: 717-359-4850
fax: 717-359-4850
e-mail: dayett@juno.com
Specializes in antique and contemporary clock repair, primarily weight and spring driven movements; also specializes in clock appraisals.

Charles Miller
Miller's Clock Shop
1721 Stanton St.
York, PA 17404-5330
phone: 717-843-0363
Repairs and restores clocks; member NAWCC, AWI.

Old Clockworks, The
Rockville, MD 20853-1416
phone: 301-924-6741
Restoration and repair of antique and fine timepieces.

Joel Vernick
Antique Clock Repair
10807 Kenilworth Ave.
P.O. Box 81
Garrett Park, MD 20896-0081
phone: 301-933-0654 or 301-933-4689
fax: 301-933-4689
e-mail: J.Vernick@erols.com
Over 30 years experience in clock repair.

Harvey Flemister
512 Highgate Terrace
Silver Spring, MD 20904-6314
phone: 301-622-3686
Many years experience in the repair, service and restoration of antique clocks.

Lee M. Flemister
Old Clockworks, The
10201 Kings Arms Tavern Court
Ellicott City, MD 21042
phone: 301-854-5514
Restoration of fine clocks, cases, dials, and glass tablets.

John Stephens
Clock Doc
429 St. Johns St.
Havre De Grace, MD 21078-2818
phone: 410-939-3334
Area's largest selection of antique clocks; also offers on-site repair facility.

Kenzie Smith
N. Kenzie Smith & Sons, Inc.
3836 Jefferson Pike
Jefferson, MD 21755
phone: 301-473-4095
Repairs and restores all mechanical clocks and watches; references upon request.

David Pendley
Pendley's Clock Repair
6804 Cochise Dr.
Knoxville, TN 37918-5253
phone: 423-922-1892
Repairs, restores, buys, sells old vintage antique clocks, member NAWCC.

Billy E. Young
Young's Ole Clock & Music Box Shop
3511 Rio Grande Circle
Dallas, TX 75233
phone: 214-331-8265
Buys, sells and restores.

Repro. Sources

Tec Specialties
705 San Fernando Dr. SE
Smyrna, GA 30080-1437
Makes replacement clock dials, decals, backboard labels and calendar strips for antique clocks; also carries supplies for the hobbyist; free catalog upon request; mail order only; wholesale prices to everyone; ships worldwide.

Suppliers

Mason & Sullivan Co. Classics in the Making
586 Higgins Crowell Rd.
West Yarmouth, MA 02673
Mail order source for quality kits; boats, guitars, steam engines, kaleidoscopes, instruments, etc.; also supplies.

Rick Dunnuck, VP
S. LaRose, Inc.
3223 Yanceyville St.
P.O. Box 21208
Greensboro, NC 27420-1208
phone: 910-621-1936
fax: 910-621-0706
e-mail: slarose@worldnet.att.net
Internet: http://www.slarose.com
Supplier of clock and watch parts.

Butterworth
1715 Pearlview Ct.
Muscatine, IA 52761
phone: 319-263-7659 or 800-258-5418
Sells clock movements.

KLOCKIT
P.O. Box 636
Lake Geneva, WI 53147
phone: 800-556-2548
Mail order source for clock movements, hands, faces, hardware, music boxes, barometers, parts, tools, etc.

American Clockmaker, The
P.O. Box 326
Clintonville, WI 54929
phone: 715-823-5101
Mail order source for clock movements, kits, parts and supplies; including shelf, grandfather and German cuckoo clocks.

Turncraft Clock Imports Co.
P.O. Box 100
Mound, MN 55364
phone: 800-544-1711 or 612-471-9573
fax: 612-471-8579
Mail order source of fine clock movements, kits, parts and supplies.

Southwest Clock Supply
P.O. Box 394
Carthage, MO 64836-0394
phone: 417-358-1865 or 800-654-8629
fax: 417-358-7446

Time Savers
P.O. Box 12700
Scottsdale, AZ 85267-2700
phone: 602-483-3711 or 800-552-1520
fax: 800-522-1522
Sells new clock parts, tools, books and kits.

Otto Frei - Jules Borel
P.O. Box 796
Oakland, CA 94604
phone: 415-832-0355
Carries complete line of clock parts.

Anniversary (400-Day)

Repair Services

Mike Murray
Mike's Clock Clinic
1326 Stanford Street
Santa Monica, CA 90404-2502
phone: 310-828-6707
fax: 310-828-7381
e-mail: z4murray@webcom.com
Internet: http://www.webcom.com/z4murray/
Specializing in the repair and dating of Atmos, 400 day (anniversary), and plug-in electric clocks.

Art

Clubs/Associations

Arlyn J. Rath
Horological Art
113 Hayes St.
Garden City, NY 11530
A specialty chapter within the National Association of Watch & Clock Collectors, Inc.; focuses on clocks, watches and time keeping devices in art, i.e. art incorporating

clock themes but having no movements.

Art Deco

Dealers

John Sakas
P.O. Box 4124
South Hackensack, NJ 07606-4124
phone: 201-794-0437
fax: 201-794-8359
e-mail: John@Radioclaze.com
Specializing in Catalin, Deco, mirror radios; also in Art Deco clocks.

Experts

Ira Raskin
Try To Remember
5120 Wilson Ln.
Bethesda, MD 20814-2436
phone: 301-652-1695
fax: 301-986-4528
e-mail: iraskin@aol.com
Buys and sells Art Deco radios and clocks of the 1920s to 1950s; also repairs electric clocks.

Character/Comic

Collectors

David Welch
P.O. Box 714
Murphysboro, IL 62966-0714
phone: 618-687-2282
fax: 618-684-2243
e-mail: PexDude1@aol.com
Wants pre-1980 watches/clocks relating to sports, TV, cartoon, comic, movie characters with original boxes ONLY; also wants empty boxes; no political, please.

Experts

Howard S. Brenner
106 Woodgate Terrace
Rochester, NY 14625-1735
phone: 716-482-3641
fax: 716-288-3122
e-mail: grvd25a@prodigy.com
Specializes in mint/boxed examples of comic watches; author of "Collecting Comic Character Clock & Watches."

Cuckoo

Collectors

Steve Elliott
1600 Tennessee St.
Vallejo, CA 94590
phone: 707-552-8400 or 707-642-1949
fax: 707-552-0881
Wants to buy carved wooden cuckoo clocks.

Dials

Repair Services

Dorothy Briggs
410 Ethan Allen Ave.
Takoma Park, MD 20912
phone: 301-270-4166
Specializes in the restoration of

painted clock dials as well as reverse painting on glass.

Dial House, The
2287 Buchanan Highway
Dallas, GA 30132-5712
phone: 770-445-2877
fax: 770-443-5426
Antique clock dials only; preserved, restored or replaced; call or write before shipping.

Suppliers

E-Z Way Chemical
P.O. Box 525
Burlington, WA 98233
Sells "Silverplater", a 99.987% real silver solution that cleans and recoats a metal surface with silver.

Electric

Clubs/Associations

Martin Swetsky, Pres.
Electric Horology Society, Chapter 78
NAWCC
Journal: Electric Horology Society Journal
2443 E. 26th St.
Brooklyn, NY 11235
A specialty chapter within the National Association of Watch & Clock Collectors, Inc.; purpose is to inform members of the various types of battery/electrical clocks from the earliest inception to present.

Elmer G. Crum, FNAWCC
Midwest Electric Horology Group
18220 Oak Way Dr.
Hudson, FL 34667-6333
phone: 813-868-0181
A specialty chapter within the National Association of Watch & Clock Collectors, Inc.; purpose is to inform members of the various types of battery/electrical clocks from the earliest inception to present.

Ron Wronski
Western Electrics
1410 Gopher Canyon Rd.
Vista, CA 92084
A specialty chapter within the National Association of Watch & Clock Collectors, Inc.; purpose is to inform members of the various types of battery/electrical clocks from the earliest inception to present.

Experts

Elmer G. Crum, FNAWCC
18220 Oak Way Dr.
Hudson, FL 34667-6333
phone: 813-868-0181
Collects, repairs, appraises and specializes in early battery and electric clocks; from time of their inception to present including watches; lectures on electric horology; a Fellow of the NAWCC.

Mike Murray
Mike's Clock Clinic
1326 Stanford Street
Santa Monica, CA 90404-2502
phone: 310-828-6707
fax: 310-828-7381
e-mail: z4murray@webcom.com
Internet: http://www.webcom.com/z4murray/
Specializing in the repair and dating of Atmos, 400 day (anniversary), and plug-in electric clocks.

Repair Services

Mike Murray
Mike's Clock Clinic
1326 Stanford Street
Santa Monica, CA 90404-2502
phone: 310-828-6707
fax: 310-828-7381
e-mail: z4murray@webcom.com
Internet: http://www.webcom.com/z4murray/
Specializing in the repair and dating of Atmos, 400 day (anniversary), and plug-in electric clocks.

Electric (Atmos)

Experts

Mike Murray
Mike's Clock Clinic
1326 Stanford Street
Santa Monica, CA 90404-2502
phone: 310-828-6707
fax: 310-828-7381
e-mail: z4murray@webcom.com
Internet: http://www.webcom.com/z4murray/
Specializing in the repair and dating of Atmos, 400 day (anniversary), and plug-in electric clocks.

European

Experts

Frank Vitale
Brielle Galleries
707 Union Ave.
Brielle, NJ 08730
phone: 908-528-9300
Foremost collector and dealer of 17th, 18th, and 19th century European clocks.

European (French)

Dealers

Robert Beaver
Classic Touch Antiques
P.O. Box 27
Newport, RI 02840-0001
phone: 401-849-1717 or 401-849-9870
Buys and sells all types of French clocks, including clock movements, cases, etc.

Military

Clubs/Associations

William R. Bricker
Society of Military Horologists
4 Hull Cove
Jamestown, RI 02835
A specialty chapter within the National Association of Watch & Clock Collectors, Inc.; focuses on time keeping devices as applied to military use.

Novelty Animated

Collectors

Carole Kaifer
P.O. Box 232
Bethania, NC 27010-0232
phone: 910-924-9672
Novelty clocks are spring-powered and pendulum operated from 1930s to 1950s; wants to buy clocks by Lux, Keebler, Westclox, Columbia Time, Oswald, and Mi-Ken.

Experts

Sam & Anna Samuelian
P.O. Box 504
Edgemont, PA 19028-0504
phone: 610-566-7248
fax: 610-566-7285
Buys, sells, restores novelty electric animated clocks; leading buyers and sellers with largest collection in the world from 1920s-1980s; can reproduce parts; book in the offing.

Tower

Clubs/Associations

Alton A. Dubois, Pres.
Tower Clock
67 Peggy Ann Rd.
Queensbury, NY 12804
A specialty chapter within the National Association of Watch & Clock Collectors, Inc.; focusing on tower clocks.

Willard

Museums/Libraries

Willard House & Clock Museum, Inc.
P.O. Box 156
Grafton, MA 01519
phone: 617-839-3500
Largest known collection of Willard clocks and memorabilia.

CLOISONNE

(see also ORIENTALIA)

Clubs/Associations

Cloisonne Collectors Club
Newsletter: Cloison, The
P.O. Box 96
Rockport, MA 01966
Focuses on different types of enameling such as cloisonne, plique a jour and miniature enamel paintings.

Dealers

Alan R. Glazer
36 College Ave. #B3
Somerville, MA 02144
phone: 617-776-4475
Buys, sells and specializes in Chinese and Japanese cloisonne and other enamels; wants pre-1930 (and preferably pre-1898) "smalls" such as boxes, multi-piece sets, vases, bowls; minor flaws acceptable, but no pieces with major damage.

Joseph Belperio
1303 Hawthorne Ct.
Sewell, NJ 08080
phone: 609-256-0791
Specializes in fine quality Japanese Satsuma and cloisonne.

Bill Eberhardt
Harry A. Eberhardt & Son
2010 Walnut St.
Philadelphia, PA 19103-5608
phone: 215-568-4144
Specializes in Japanese cloisonne and fine Satsuma.

Experts

Stephen Fisher
P.O. Box 26178
Baltimore, MD 21210
phone: 410-435-1957
e-mail: williaman@erols.com
Collector of 23 years seeks superb examples of Japanese cloisonne and offers advice and assistance to beginning and intermediate collectors.

Museums/Libraries

George Walter Vincent Smith Art Museum
220 State St.
Springfield, MA 01103-1703
phone: 413-263-6800
fax: 413-263-6814
Internet: http://www.spfldlibmus.org/home.htm
Recognized collections of American paintings; Orientalia including Japanese arms & armor, screens, lacquers, textiles and ceramics; Islamic rugs; and the largest collection of Chinese cloisonne in the western world

CLOTHES HANGERS

Collectors

Roger & Cheryl Brinker
3140-B West Tilghman St., #165
Allentown, PA 18104
Collects unusual 1890s to 1940s wire clothes hangers.

CLOTHES SPRINKLERS

Collectors

Craig Dinner
P.O. Box 4399
Long Island City, NY 11104-0399
phone: 718-729-3850 or 802-365-7181
Wants to buy ceramic laundry sprinkler bottles.

Al Little
151 Highway 173
Antioch, IL 60002
phone: 847-395-7752
fax: 847-395-7703
Buy, sells and trades laundry sprinkle bottles.

Loretta Anderson
1208 Lakeshore Dr.
Rockwall, TX 75087-4222
phone: 972-771-9636 or 972-771-8100
e-mail: lainrkwltx@aol.com
Wants to buy ceramic figural clothes sprinkler bottles.

Dealers

Carol Silagyi
C.S. Antiques & Jewelry
P.O. Box 151
Wyckoff, NJ 07430
phone: 201-934-6528
Wants figural ceramic clothes sprinklers; Cardinal, American bisques, Japanese, etc.

Estelle Sharp
ESCO Enterprises, Inc.
441 E. River Oaks Dr.
Baton Rouge, LA 70815-4063
phone: 504-924-5089
fax: 504-924-5089
Buys and sells clothes sprinklers.

CLOTHING & ACCESSORIES

(see also ALLIGATOR BAGS;
BUTTONS; BUTTON HOOKS;
CLOTHES HANGERS; CLOTHES
SPRINKLERS; COMPACTS;
COMBS & HAIR ACCESSORIES;
CUFF LINKS; DRESSER ITEMS;
LIVING HISTORY; LUGGAGE;
PURSES; REPAIR/RESTORATION/
CONSERVATION, Textiles;
SEWING ITEMS & GO-WITHS;
TEXTILES

Dealers

Joyce & Judy
Krazy Cat Collectibles
8604 Second Ave. #235
Silver Spring, MD 20910
phone: 301-309-2513
e-mail: KrazyCatCo@aol.com
Buys and sells exceptional quality vintage ladies accessories and jewelry: Lucite purses, vintage beaded bags, enamel compacts, etc.

Periodicals

Magazine: Ornament
P.O. Box 2349
San Marcos, CA 92079-2349
phone: 800-888-8950 or 619-599-0222
A quarterly magazine focusing on craft and art items of personal adornment in any media or form: fiber, glass, metal, historic/ethnic ornament; ethnographic and tribal jewelry; also reviews of museum exhibits and publications.

1960s

Collectors

Steve Hannan
141 East Central St.
Natick, MA 01760-3625
Wants to buy 1960s leather clothing, mini-skirts, micro-skirts, and hotpants; no suede, please.

Boots

Collectors

D. Seagraves
111 Cleveland Rd. #78
Pleasant Hill, CA 94523
phone: 510-934-4848
Wants to buy 1950s women's rubber boots.

Collars & Cuffs

(see CUFF LINKS)

Denim

Dealers

Mark Luers
Tatters
2928 Lyndale Ave. South
Minneapolis, MN 55408
phone: 612-823-5285
fax: 612-823-6887

Experienced Denim
P.O. Box 239
Fayetteville, AR 72702-0239
phone: 501-444-7541 or 800-336-4694
fax: 501-521-8331
e-mail: exdeni19@intellinet.com
Wants '30s-'50s Levis, denim wear of all types, '40s-'50s gabardine shirts & jackets, Hawaiian and bowling shirts; also vintage fabrics, textiles, bedspreads, tablecloths with Western or Mexican theme; vintage mens wear, casual clothing.

Blue Denim Clothing Co.
3213 Jeannie Ln.
Muskogee, OK 74403
phone: 918-683-1589
Wants to buy vintage Levis, Lee, Wrangler: jeans, jackets, men's 501 Blue Jeans, vintage workwear advertising, pre-1960 sweatshirts, vintage Air Jordans and pre-1980 Nike shoes, Buddy Lee Dolls, banners, denim shirts, etc.

Jay Fraterigo
Velvet Pelvis, The
531 Haight St.
San Francisco, CA 94117
phone: 415-864-7034

David Bailey
Bailey's Antiques & Thrift
517 Kapahulu Ave.
Honolulu, HI 96815-3854
phone: 808-734-7628
Buys and appraises pre-1960 Levis, pre-1960 Aloha Shirts, and Hawaiiana; pre-1960 Levis have a capital "E", hence "Big E" on small red tag at side of left breast pocket (jackets) and right rear pocket (pants).

Danny Eskenazi
Jack Hammer Ltd.
1909 First Ave.
Seattle, WA 98101-1010
phone: 800-289-5017 or 206-441-1865
fax: 206-932-1449
e-mail: k7ss@mcimail.com
Wants to buy vintage denim, examples of early denim clothing, jeans, jackets, overalls, and denim advertising signs; especially wants "Levi" brand.

Larry McKaugham
Heller's Far West Clothing
1000 Lenora, Ste. 116
Seattle, WA 98121
phone: 206-233-9014 or 800-328-5384
Wants to buy 1930s and 1940s denim buckleback pants, vintage running and basketball shoes from 1970s and 1980s.

Husky Boy Vintage
4441 S. Meridian, Ste. 471
Puyallup, WA 98373-5959
phone: 800-HUS-KYBO or 206-472-6341
Internet: http://www.huskyboy.com
Wants to buy Nike Air Jordan 1985-1991 and 1970s-1980s Nike shoes and sportswear; also buying vintage denim workwear, i.e. Levi's, Lee, etc. and vintage military flight jackets.

Experts

Jeff Mark
P.O. Box 5178
Santa Monica, CA 90409-5178
phone: 800-666-9553 or 310-396-9767
fax: 310-396-2666
America's largest buyer of and leading authority on Levi & Lee brand old blue jeans, jackets, and advertising display materials; especially wants older (pre-1970) button-fly jeans.

Museums/Libraries

Levi Strauss & Co. Museum
250 Valencia St.
San Francisco, CA 94103
phone: 415-565-9153
Open by appointment; located in the oldest factory.

Hats

Collectors

Daniell Ware
1199 S. Main Rd.
Vineland, NJ 08360
phone: 609-794-8300
fax: 609-794-8300
Long time collector wants to buy millinery items: hat stands, hat blocks, signs, trade cards, ladies hats, hat boxes, beaded and mesh purses from 1800s to 1940s.

Dealers

Janine Smith
Hats by Janine
87367 Green Hill Rd.
Eugene, OR 97402-9170
Buys and sells hats; large selection from 1900-1960; also restores vintage hats and makes reproductions of period hats.

Museums/Libraries

Colonial Williamsburg Millinery Shop
P.O. Box C
Williamsburg, VA 23185
phone: 804-229-1000

Repro. Sources

Mike & Pat Stevens
P.O. Box 2
Myersville, MD 21773
Specialize in the manufacture of turn-of-the-century hats and bonnets; also parasols, feathers, related items and supplies.

Suppliers

Manny's Millinery
26 W. 38th St.
New York, NY 10018-6227
phone: 212-840-2235 or 212-840-2236
Sells hatmaking supplies in small quantities for refurbishing old ones or making new hats.

Lingerie

Museums/Libraries

Frederick's of Hollywood Lingerie
Museum & Celebrity Lingerie Hall of Fame
66087 Hollywood Blvd.
Los Angeles, CA 90028
phone: 213-466-8506
Contains famous underfashions beginning with lingerie and bras from 1946.

Mannequins

Collectors

Gwen Daniel
18 Belleau Lake Ct.
O Fallon, MO 63366-3144
phone: 314-978-3190
e-mail: gdaniel@mail.win.org
Wants Victorian through 1950s mannequins; heads only or full

mannequins; send photos first if possible.

Suppliers

Goldsmith, Inc.
10-09 43rd Ave.
Long Island City, NY 11101
Sells Victorian and Edwardian mannequins.

Neckties

Experts

Dr. Ron Spark
P.O. Box 43414
Tucson, AZ 85733-3414
phone: 520-323-8714
fax: 520-324-5341
Author of "Fit-To-Be-Tied" (Abbeville, 1988) specializes in 1940s neckties; inquiries always invited.

Parasols

Repair Services

Abbie Orem
265 N. Union St.
Russianville, IN 46979-9602
phone: 765-883-5108
Recovers parasols; call first to discuss the project.

Patterns

Book Sellers

Fred Struthers
R.L. Shep Publications
P.O. Box 2706
Fort Bragg, CA 95437
phone: 707-964-8662
fax: 707-964-8662
e-mail: fsbks@mcn.org
Publishes reprints of dressmaking/ tailoring manuals and needlework books.

Collectors

Joy Emery
84 Estelle Dr.
West Kingston, RI 02892
Devoted collector who is compiling a complete database of tissue patterns.

Dealers

Nancy Garcelon
Antique & Otherwise
10 Hastings Ave.
Millbury, MA 01527
phone: 508-754-2267
Buys and sells used books on costume, sewing, knitting, crochet; vintage patterns and pattern catalogs; send for free list.

Bette S. Feinstein
Hard-to-Find Needlework Books
96 Roundwood Rd.
Newton, MA 02164-1217
phone: 617-969-0942
fax: 617-969-0942
e-mail: feinstein@umbsky.cc.umb.edu
Internet: http://www.ambook.org/ bookstore/needlework
Buys and sells vintage fashion magazines, old and new books on many types of needlework.

Saundra Ros Altman
Past Patterns
P.O. Box 2446
Richmond, IN 47375-2446
phone: 317-962-3333
Carries a large selection of copies of sewing patterns from 1900 to 1950 in original sizes.

Shoes

Museums/Libraries

Center for the History of Foot Care and Foot Wear
Pennsylvania College of Podiatric Medicine
8th & Race Streets
Philadelphia, PA 19107
phone: 215-629-0300
Collection contains over 700 examples of shoes, dating back to Egyptian burial sandals c. 2000 B.C.

Shoes (Oversize)

Clubs/Associations

Danny Eskenazi, Pres.
Society for Preservation of Oversize Footwear (SPOOF)
1909 First Ave.
Seattle, WA 98101-1010
phone: 800-289-5017 or 206-441-1865
fax: 206-932-1449
e-mail: k7ss@mcimail.com
Wants to buy big display shoes.

Suspender Buckles

Experts

Robert James Lloyd
158 Brookside Blvd.
Newark, DE 19711
Collects and studies suspenders and garter belts.

T-shirts

Collectors

Rich Cacioppo
44 Brookside Terrace
North Caldwell, NJ 07006
phone: 201-364-1765
fax: 201-364-1766
Interested in the history of imprinted T-shirts.

Ties

Collectors

Al Guerra
636 Tulip Ave.
Stewart Manor, NY 11001-3755
Collector of rare ties; specializes in 1940s-1950s hand-painted men's neckties; also other vintage, souvenir/ commemorative ties such as political, World's Fair, fraternal, advertising, pin-up, and cowboy/western. Include SASE for reply.

Vintage

(see also ALLIGATOR BAGS; BUTTONS; BUTTON HOOKS; COMPACTS; COMBS & HAIR ACCESSORIES; CUFF LINKS; DRESSER ITEMS; LIVING HISTORY; LUGGAGE; PURSES; REPAIR/RESTORATION/CONSER-VATION, Textiles; SEWING ITEMS & GO-WITHS; TEXTILES)

Appraisers

Kathleen Flynn
Carriage House Antiques
4212 Gallatin St.
Hyattsville, MD 20781-2049
phone: 301-779-3696
Always buying vintage fashions, accessories and jewelry; prefers Victorian though 1950s; especially wants antique purses, compacts, silver smalls, and costume jewelry.

Auction Services

Louis Webre, Client Svc.
William Doyle Galleries
175 E. 87th St.
New York, NY 10128-2205
phone: 212-427-2730
fax: 212-369-0892
Internet: http://www.doylegalleries.com
Holds over 30 auctions annually of antique English, Continental and American furniture, paintings, decorations, jewelry, vintage and couture clothing, collectible toys, books and prints; specialty auctions of Majolica, Lalique and wine.

Robert J. Connelly, ASA
Bob & Sallie Connelly Auctions
666 Chenango St.
Binghamton, NY 13901-2015
phone: 607-722-9593 or 607-722-3555
fax: 607-722-1266
Conducts specialty vintage clothing and fabric auctions.

Clubs/Associations

Pat Poppy
Costume Society, The
Journal: Costume
21 Oak Rd.
Woolston
Southampton S019 9BQ, U.K.
phone: 01202 622115
Formed to promote the study and preservation of significant examples of costume history and development;

publishes an illustrated journal and newsletters; organizes an annual symposium; visits collections; study days.

Costume Society of America, The
Newsletter: Dress
P.O. Box 73
Earleville, MD 21919-0073
phone: 410-275-2329 or 419-372-2026
fax: 410-275-8936
e-mail: cunningham.190@postbox.acs.ohio-state.edu
Internet: http://www.hec.ohio-state.edu/ cts.research/dress.htm
Dedicated to advancing the global understanding of all aspects of dress and appearance; also published the journal "Dress."

Textile & Costume Guild, c/o Fullerton Museum Center
Newsletter: Textures
301 North Pomona Ave.
Fullerton, CA 92632
phone: 714-738-6545
Guild meets 2nd Sat. of the month Sept.-June; extensive costume collection; women's and mens from 1820s to the present.

Federation of Vintage Fashion
Newsletter: Federation of Vintage Fashion Newsletter
401 Dan Gabriel
Vallejo, CA 94590
Sponsors vintage fashion exhibitions and other regional activities; the newsletter is published quarterly.

Collectors

Lydia M. Jackson-Fryer
608 Winans Way
Baltimore, MD 21229-1430
phone: 410-233-3317
Wants to buy vintage clothing female size 18 or plus size; also male 44 regular.

Lynda Anne Long
Antiquity Perfection, The
RD 1 Box 1903
Middletown, VA 22645
phone: 703-869-7680
Wants vintage clothing: dresses, suits and accessories from the 1900 through 1950.

Dealers

Judith LeFavour
Vintage, Etc.
1796 Massachusetts Ave.
Cambridge, MA 02140
phone: 617-497-1516
Carries women's hats and dresses from the teens to the 1950s; specializes in formal wear.

Fay Knicely
Antique Apparel
P.O. Box 1
Acworth, NH 03601-0001
phone: 603-835-2295
Over 25 years buying and selling a

wide range of antique and vintage clothing, accessories, and related goods; unheated shop open by chance or appointment.

Nancy Haugh
Victorian Whites
7 Winterbrook Ct.
York, ME 03909
phone: 207-363-8111

Judith A. Young
Yesterday's Threads
206 Meadow St.
Branford, CT 06405-3634
phone: 203-481-6452
Buys and sells women's, men's and childrens' clothing and accessories from mid-1800s through 1960s; call for information about upcoming vintage clothing shows.

Pahaka September
Pahaka
19 Fox Hill
Upper Saddle River, NJ 07458-1314
phone: 201-327-1464
Buys and sells women's, men's and children's clothing 1880-1950s; also jewelry, hats, shoes, and patterns; by appointment or mail order; sorry, no catalog.

Sid Warshafsky
240 Overlook Rd.
Woodstock, NY 12498
phone: 914-246-9363
Wants to buy vintage clothing, jewelry, hats, accessories: Christian Dior, Chanel, Yves St. Laurant, Gucci, Hermes bags, Louis Vuitton, Pucci, Fortuny, Halston, etc.; veils, collars, umbrellas, curtains, shawls.

Meredith Fiel
RD 2 Box 159
Corinth, NY 12822
phone: 518-696-4896
Wants to buy antique clothing from 1920-1940s; also wants good costume jewelry.

Carol Canty-Moyse
Collage Antiques
7 North Court St.
Frederick, MD 21701-5413
phone: 301-694-0513 or 301-831-6314
Wants pre-1950 vintage clothing, accessories, and jewelry; vintage bridal gowns, silk shawls, beaded and mesh purses, fine wearable vintage apparel, antique jewelry.

Priscilla Washed
Victorian Lady, The
102 South Main St.
P.O. Box 424
Waxhaw, NC 28173-0424
phone: 704-843-4467 or 800-786-1886
A Victorian specialty store featuring 19th century ladies decorative & fashion accessories; buys and sells purses; also sewing and needlework tools, vintage fashion, Victoriana, and combs; mail order; catalog $5.

Suzanne Silance
Scarlett Magnolia's Vintage Apparel, Textiles & Gifts
361 Congress Parkway
Mansfield, GA 30255
phone: 770-682-8999 or 888-999-9985
Buying and selling quality vintage apparel and textiles; selling through Buckhead Design Center, 2133 Piedmont Rd., Atlanta, GA 30324 (404-872-0751).

Joanne Haug
Reflections of the Past
26758 Lake Rd.
Bay Village, OH 44140
phone: 216-835-6924

Gayle Wilson
Gayle's Vintage Clothing & Accessories
3742 Kellogg Ave.
c/o Ferguson Antiques Mall
Cincinnati, OH 45226
phone: 513-321-7341 or 513-271-3722
Buys and sells vintage clothing; men's, women's, children's, wedding gowns; also costume jewelry;

Julia Mahern
Modern Times
5363 N. College Ave.
Indianapolis, IN 46220
phone: 317-253-8108
Women's and men's vintage clothing and jewelry from the early 1940s to the early 1970s.

Patricia O'Brien
Flapper Alley Ltd.
1518 North Farwell Ave.
Milwaukee, WI 53202
phone: 414-276-6252 or 414-332-3618
Wants to buy antique clothing and textiles from the 1920s and earlier; also fancy beaded bags; appraisal services available.

Carrie Homann
Carrie's Vintage Clothing
204 N. Neil
Champaign, IL 61820
phone: 217-352-3231
A complete range of 20th century stock through the 1970s.

Carol F. Obradovits
Caris Corp.
105 W. 69th Terrace
Kansas City, MO 64113-2537
phone: 816-361-1173
fax: 816-822-7502
Buys and sells women's, childrens' and men's clothing and accessories from the period 1890-1950; mail order only.

Diane McGee
Diane McGee Estate Clothing Company
5225 Jackson
Omaha, NE 68106-1331
phone: 402-551-0727
Mail order only; complete line from 1850s to 1960s.

Sarah Fox
Somewhere in Time
103 Newcastle Dr.
Lafayette, LA 70503
phone: 318-235-1081 or 318-984-9863
Wants buttons, belt buckles, ornamental sew-on or clamp-on handbag frames, Art Nouveau or Art Deco jewelry; offers clothes 1850-1960.

Janene Fawcett
Vintage Clothing
1301 Pomona St.
Crockett, CA 94525
phone: 510-787-7274

Jules Kliot
Lacis
3163 Adeline St.
Berkeley, CA 94703-2401
phone: 510-843-7178
fax: 510-843-5018
Antique & historic textiles, lace from the 16th century, vintage garments and accessories; sells books and supplies for costume, lace and embroidery; also offers repairs and conservation services.

Reed Wetter
Moon Zooom
813 Pacific Ave.
Santa Cruz, CA 95060-4433
phone: 408-423-8500 or 408-287-5876
fax: 408-423-8500
e-mail: calkid@aol.com
Internet: http://www.antiqueinfo.com/moonzooom/mz.htm

Experts

Irene M. Spaulding
1487 Old North Main St.
Laconia, NH 03246-2684
Specialist in antique purses and vintage clothing.

Evelyn Siefert Kennedy
Evelyn of Sewtique
391 Long Hill Rd.
P.O. Box 1293
Groton, CT 06340-1293
phone: 860-445-7320 or 860-464-2001
fax: 860-445-1448
e-mail: sewtique@aol.com
Internet: http://www.members/aol.com/sewtique/home.htm
Specialist in restoration, preservation & conservation of apparel and textiles; full service by mail/phone or appt.; appraises textiles, laces, tapestries, etc.; removes spots & stains; teaches textile appraisal & restoration workshops.

Elizabeth S. Brown
45 Whippoorwill Way
Belle Mead, NJ 08502
phone: 908-359-3395
fax: 908-874-7590
Lecturer, appraiser & costume consultant on various aspects of clothing collecting & conservation; uses own collection for lectures; also buys after inspection.

Jack Frascatore
Time Warp Custom & Vintage Attire
24 Jay St., Ste. 222
Schenectady, NY 12305
phone: 518-347-1126
fax: 518-347-1126
e-mail: timewarp@global2000.net
Internet: http://www.members.global2000.net/~timewarp
Buys/sells/appraises vintage clothing, jewelry, accessories; reproduces vintage and historical clothing for museums, reenactment, theater, ballroom dancing, etc.; also restores, repairs and alters clothing, textiles and costume jewelry.

Roseann Ettinger
Remember When
2 E. Broad St.
Hazleton, PA 18201-6530
phone: 717-454-8465 or 717-450-5542
Author of "50's Popular Fashions."

Diane McGee
5225 Jackson
Omaha, NE 68106-1331
phone: 402-551-0727
Author of "A Passion for Fashion: Antique, Collectible, & Retro Clothes 1850-1950"; 200 pgs., over 190 photos; send $24.95 + $2 UPS.

Frances Grimble
Lavolta Press
20 Meadowbrook Dr.
San Francisco, CA 94132
phone: 415-566-6259
e-mail: lavolta@beste.com
Lavolta Press has published "After a Fashion," "The Edwardian Modiste," and "The Voice of Fashion"; Frances Grimble collects pre-1930 clothing, books and magazines with clothing patterns, and books and mags with dance instruction.

Kristina Harris
904 N. 65th St.
Springfield, OR 97478-7021
phone: 545-174-66810
Internet: http://victoriana.com/shops.html
Lectures on collectible clothing and historical fashion; columnist for internationally distributed magazine; author of eight books on the subject, including "Vintage & Edwardian Fashions For Women: 1840-1919."

Terry McCormick
2009 23rd Ave. W, Apt 2
Seattle, WA 99899-4145
phone: 206-545-2945
Gives workshops on vintage clothing and hats.

Misc. Services

Danny Eskenazi
Jack Hammer Ltd.
1909 First Ave.
Seattle, WA 98101-1010
phone: 800-289-5017 or 206-441-1865
fax: 206-932-1449
e-mail: k7ss@mcimail.com
*Has extensive collection of 1920s-
1970s clothing available for rental to
designers, films, etc.*

Museums/Libraries

Museum of Costume
Assembly Rooms
Bennett St., Batt
Somerset BA1 2QH, U.K.
phone: 0122-5477752 or 0122-5477754
fax: 0122-5444793
e-mail:
    costume_enquiries@bathnes.gov.uk
*The museum's collection includes all
aspects of fashion from the 16th
century to the present - handmade,
ready-to-wear and designer.*

Museum of Fine Arts, Boston
465 Huntington Ave.
Boston, MA 02115-5523
phone: 617-267-9300
Internet: http://www.mfa.org/home.html

Museum of Art, Rhode Island School of
    Design
224 Benefit St.
Providence, RI 02903-2711
phone: 401-454-6500
fax: 401-454-6556

Wadsworth Atheneum
600 Main St.
Hartford, CT 06103
phone: 860-278-2670
fax: 860-527-0803
*Regularly changing themed
exhibitions display and interpret
selections from an extensive collection
of historic costumes and textiles.*

Fashion Institute of Technology, Edward
    C. Blum Design Laboratory
227 West 27th St.
New York, NY 10001
phone: 212-760-7970

Metropolitan Museum of Art, The
    Costume Institute
1000 Fifth Ave.
New York, NY 10028
phone: 212-879-5500
Internet: http://www.metmuseum.org/

Phyllis Magidson
Museum of the City of New York
1220 5th Ave.
New York, NY 10029-5221
phone: 212-534-1672
fax: 212-534-5974
*Specializes in street and theatrical
costumes; access by appointment;
research fee charged.*

Museums at Stony Brook, The
Newsletter: News & Events
Rte. 25A Box 1208
Stony Brook, NY 11790-1931
phone: 516-751-0066
fax: 516-751-0353
*Large collection of American Art,
decoys, horse-drawn vehicles,
costumes, and miniature period
rooms; museum shop.*

Anne R. Fabbri, Dir.
Philadelphia College of Textiles &
    Science, The Goldey Paley Design
    Center
4200 Henry Ave.
Philadelphia, PA 19144
phone: 215-951-2860

National Museum of American History
14th & Constitution Ave. NW
Washington, DC 20560
phone: 202-357-2700
Internet: http://www.si.edu/

Colleen Callahan
Valentine Museum
1015 East Clay
Richmond, VA 23219
phone: 804-649-0711
fax: 804-643-3510
e-mail: valmus@mindspring.com
Internet: http://
    www.valentinemuseum.com
*Largest costume and textile collection
in the South.*

Western Reserve Historical Society
10825 East Blvd.
Cleveland, OH 44106-1703
phone: 216-721-5722
fax: 216-721-0645
Internet: http://www.wrhs.org
*Oldest cultural institution in
Cleveland, with a research/
genealogical library, costume wing,
auto & aviation museum and restored
mansion under one roof; special
interest area in costume and textiles.*

Indianapolis Museum of Art, Indiana
    Fashion Design Collection
1200 W. 38th St.
Indianapolis, IN 46208
phone: 317-923-1331

Detroit Historical Museum
5401 Woodward Ave.
Detroit, MI 48202
phone: 313-833-1805

Chicago Historical Society
Clark St. at North Ave.
Chicago, IL 60614
phone: 312-642-4600

Missouri Historical Society
P.O. Box 11940
Saint Louis, MO 63112-0040
phone: 314-746-4527
fax: 314-746-4548

Patti McClain
Museum of Vintage Fashion, Inc.
10 Lacassie Court
Lafayette, CA 94549
phone: 510-944-1896 or 510-938-3810
*Research center, historical and
vintage clothing (1736-1980), library.*

Periodicals

Molly Turner
Molly's Vintage Promotions
Newsletter: Vintage Gazette, The
194 Amity St.
Amherst, MA 01002-2201
phone: 413-549-6446
e-mail: merrylees@aol.com
*Quarterly newsletter focusing on
vintage clothing.*

Newsletter: Glass Slipper, The
653 S. Orange Ave.
Sarasota, FL 34236-7503

Magazine: Lady's Gallery
P.O. Box 40443
Bay Village, OH 44140-0443
phone: 800-622-5676
e-mail: lady@bright.net
Internet: http://www.victoriana.com/
    lady.html
*A bi-monthly magazine focusing on
Victorian wedding dresses and their
contemporary counterparts, children's
fashions, vintage compacts, mesh
purses, Victorian wedding rings, and
other features.*

Jacqueline Horning
Newsletter: Lill's Vintage Clothing
    Newsletter
19 Jamestown Dr.
Cincinnati, OH 45241-1435
phone: 513-779-3708
*Written for collectors and dealers of
vintage clothing; bi-monthly.*

Kristina Harris, Editor
Newsletter: Vintage Connection, The
904 N. 65th St.
Springfield, OR 97478-7021
phone: 545-174-66810
Internet: http://victoriana.com/
    shops.html
*For collectors of vintage and antique
fashions; covers specific areas of the
19th and 20th centuries; reproductions, sources, and dealers; also offers
a number of related book titles.*

Repair Services

Jack Frascatore
Time Warp Custom & Vintage Attire
24 Jay St., Ste. 222
Schenectady, NY 12305
phone: 518-347-1126
fax: 518-347-1126
e-mail: timewarp@global2000.net
Internet: http://
    www.members.global2000.net/
    ~timewarp
*Buys/sells/appraises vintage clothing,
jewelry, accessories; reproduces
vintage and historical clothing for
museums, reenactment, theater,
ballroom dancing, etc.; also restores,*

*repairs and alters clothing, textiles
and costume jewelry.*

Alicia Repairs Textiles
New Orleans, LA 70118-3957
phone: 504-862-9956
*All textile repair: clothing, costume,
beaded bags, Native American, quilts,
lace, embroidery, tapestry, needlepoint, rugs including reweave and
repiling of ORientals, Aubussons,
hooked, kilim.*

Mountain Shadow Studio
P.O. Box 619
Nederland, CO 80466

Repro. Sources

Barbara Amster
Nineteenth Century Mercantile
No. 2 North Main St.
South Yarmouth, MA 02664
phone: 508-398-1888
*Ready-made period clothing and
patterns c. 1803-1899; also fashion
accessories such as shoes, hats,
gloves, parasols, jewelry and hoops;
for men, women and children; no mail
order.*

Jack Frascatore
Time Warp Custom & Vintage Attire
24 Jay St., Ste. 222
Schenectady, NY 12305
phone: 518-347-1126
fax: 518-347-1126
e-mail: timewarp@global2000.net
Internet: http://
    www.members.global2000.net/
    ~timewarp
*Buys/sells/appraises vintage clothing,
jewelry, accessories; reproduces
vintage and historical clothing for
museums, reenactment, theater,
ballroom dancing, etc.; also restores,
repairs and alters clothing, textiles
and costume jewelry.*

Mike & Pat Stevens
P.O. Box 2
Myersville, MD 21773

Kathi Reynolds
Creative Clothes
330 N. Church St.
Thurmont, MD 21788-1640
phone: 301-695-5340
*Makes all styles of period costume for
men, women, and children, especially
18th and 19th centuries.*

Saundra Ros Altman
Past Patterns
P.O. Box 2446
Richmond, IN 47375-2446
phone: 317-962-3333
*Sells clothing patterns from the years
1830-1949 in woman's sizes 8-20;
also men and children's patterns
available; free information.*

Heidi Marsh
Heidi Marsh Patterns
3494 N Valley Rd.
Greenville, CA 95947-9604
Men's, women's, and children's

patterns from the Civil War era; many taken from Godey's Lady Book diagrams and patterns; catalog $3.

Suppliers

Greenburg & Hammer
24 W. 57th St.
New York, NY 10019
phone: 800-955-5135
fax: 212-765-8475
Supplier of mounting and displaying products for clothing: silk thread, hangers, ready-made torsos, steamers, Kraft wrapping paper.

Cherish
P.O. Box 941
New York, NY 10024-0941
phone: 212-724-1748
Carries Orvus and other conservation supplies for the storage, cleaning and displaying of vintage textiles and clothing.

Baltimore Display
1900 Bayard St.
Baltimore, MD 21230
phone: 800-638-3764 or 410-685-3393
fax: 410-685-6877
A clothing store supply company selling display cases, racks, etc.; also sells "poly forms" for the display of vintage clothing.

Vintage (Black)

Museums/Libraries

Lois K. Alexander, Dir.
Black Fashion Museum, The
155 W. 126th St.
New York, NY 10027
phone: 212-666-1320
A textile and vintage fashion research center for students and collectors of costume history, art and design.

Joyce Bailey, Dir.
Black Fashion Museum, The
2007 Vermont Ave. NW
Washington, DC 20001-4029
phone: 202-667-0744 or 301-577-7949
A textile and vintage fashion research center for students and collectors of costume history, art and design; an extension of The Black Fashion Museum of New York.

Wearable Art

Appraisers

Sally A. Ambrose
P.O. Box 536
11156 North Rd.
Leavenworth, WA 98826-9512
phone: 509-548-7472
fax: 509-548-0240
e-mail: 104734.701@compuserve.com
Specializes in the appraising of antique and contemporary American quilted textiles, as well as contemporary wearable art. Wearable art is not always quilted but may exhibit surface design in a variety of art media and embellishment.

CLOWN COLLECTIBLES

(see also CIRCUS COLLECTIBLES; COLLECTIBLES [MODERN], Figurines [Emmett Kelly, Jr.])

Emmett Kelly

Collectors

N.W. Neill, Jr.
P.O. Box 38
Ennice, NC 28623-0038
phone: 910-657-8152
fax: 910-657-8084
Wants to buy Emmett Kelly SR/JR pieces, dolls, Circus items, books, photos; anything related to Emmett Kelly Senior or Junior.

Museums/Libraries

Emmett Kelly Historical Museum
202 E. Main
Sedan, KS 67361-1629
phone: 316-725-3470

COAST GUARD

(see also NAUTICAL ANTIQUES; NAUTICAL ANTIQUES, Light-houses)

Collectors

Bob Glick
Columbia Trading Company
1 Barnstable Rd.
Hyannis, MA 02601
phone: 508-778-2929
fax: 508-778-2922
e-mail: nautical@capecod.net
Internet: http://www.by-the-sea.com/nautical/

J. Carol Duncan
Keeper's Lighthouse Establishment
1027 Garden St.
Santa Barbara, CA 93101
phone: 805-963-9129 or 805-965-1174
fax: 805-962-5054
Wants to buy Coast Guard items; also wants to buy lighthouse artifacts and antiques: lamps, lanterns, oil cans, maps, photographs, lighthouse keeper items, lighthouse ephemera, Fresnel lens (whole or in parts).

Dealers

James W. Claflin
Kenrick A. Claflin & Son
30 Hudson St.
Northborough, MA 01532
phone: 508-869-6955
Collectors and dealers in fine nautical antiques; specializing in U.S. Lighthouse Service, U.S. Lifesaving Service, U.S. Revenue Cutter Service, U.S. Coast Guard.

Adin Otto
253 Bonnybrook Rd.
Carlisle Barracks, PA 17013
Wants to buy U.S. Lifesaving Service, Lighthouse Service, Revenue Cutter Service, and Coast Guard items:

photographs, uniforms, china, annual reports, etc.

Museums/Libraries

Robert Nason Davis, Cur.
Shore Village Museum
104 Limerock St.
Rockland, ME 04841-2945
phone: 207-594-0311 or 207-236-3206
fax: 207-594-9481
Internet: http://www.tiac.net/users/buster/shorevillage
Largest collection of lighthouse and Coast Guard artifacts in the U.S.; navigation instruments, ship models, scrimshaw, lighthouse models, and 5,000 lighthouse postcards from around the world; also lighthouses, Civil War, navigation, GAR.

U.S. Coast Guard Museum
U.S. Coast Guard Academy
15 Mohegan Ave.
New London, CT 06320-4195
phone: 203-444-8511
History of the U.S. Coast Guard including the Lifesaving Service.

U.S. Life-Saving Service

Clubs/Associations

U.S. Life-Saving Service Heritage Association, The
P.O. Box 75
Caledonia, MI 49316-0075
Internet: http://www.maine.com/lights/lssha.htm
Quarterly magazine on the Life-Saving Service and the Coast Guard, historic preservation activities, station tours, learn about shipwrecks, rescues and maritime history.

Dealers

James W. Claflin
Kenrick A. Claflin & Son
30 Hudson St.
Northborough, MA 01532
phone: 508-869-6955
Collectors and dealers in fine nautical antiques; specializing in U.S. Lighthouse Service, U.S. Lifesaving Service, U.S. Revenue Cutter Service, U.S. Coast Guard.

Jacques Noel Jacobsen, Jr.
60 Manor Rd.
Staten Island, NY 10310-2698
phone: 718-981-0973
Buys and sells U.S. Lifesaving Service, U.S. Lighthouse Service, and lighthouse artifacts, photographs, books and ephemera; American military antiques 1840-1940 large illustrated catalog, 3 issues for $12 ($15 overseas).

U.S. Lighthouse Service

Collectors

Timothy Harrison
P.O. Box 1690
Wells, ME 04090
phone: 800-758-1444 or 207-646-0515
fax: 207-646-0516
e-mail: lhdigest@biddeford.com
Internet: http://www.lhdigest.com
Wants to buy memorabilia from U.S. Lighthouse Service (USLHS) or U.S. Lighthouse Establishment (USLHE): badges, flags, dinnerware, buttons, uniforms, old photographs of keepers and their families, postcards, newspaper stories.

Dealers

James W. Claflin
Kenrick A. Claflin & Son
30 Hudson St.
Northborough, MA 01532
phone: 508-869-6955
Collectors and dealers in fine nautical antiques; specializing in U.S. Lighthouse Service, U.S. Lifesaving Service, U.S. Revenue Cutter Service, U.S. Coast Guard.

U.S. Revenue Cutter Service

Dealers

James W. Claflin
Kenrick A. Claflin & Son
30 Hudson St.
Northborough, MA 01532
phone: 508-869-6955
Collectors and dealers in fine nautical antiques; specializing in U.S. Lighthouse Service, U.S. Lifesaving Service, U.S. Revenue Cutter Service, U.S. Coast Guard.

COAT OF ARMS

(see also BOOKS, Heraldry)

Clubs/Associations

Genealogical & Heraldic Institute of America
111 Columbia Heights
Brooklyn, NY 11201

COCA-COLA COLLECTIBLES

(see SOFT DRINK COLLECTIBLES, Coca-Cola)

CODE MACHINES

(see SPY EQUIPMENT)

COFFEE

(see also ELECTRICITY RELATED ITEMS, Appliances (Coffee Pots))

Collectors

Bill Park
12312 Starlight Lane
Bowie, MD 20715-2138
phone: 301-464-1608
Wants to buy coffee containers of all

types (condition important), but prefers 1-lb. screw-top and sample sizes; also wants other types of coffee memorabilia.

Nancy Pennington
1750 Keyes Rd.
Greenbrier, TN 37073
phone: 615-643-0290
fax: 615-643-0290
e-mail: npenn2405@aol.com
Wants coffee related collectibles such as coffee jars.

Arbuckles Bros. Coffee Co.

Collectors

Al Kruse
2536 Teslin St.
Juneau, AK 99801
phone: 907-789-1817
Wants to buy memorabilia relating to Arbuckles Bros. Coffee Company.

Experts

Greg Q. ArBuckle
Arbuckles' Coffee Museum
97 16th Ave. SW
Cedar Rapids, IA 52404-5948
phone: 319-363-1242
fax: 319-365-5115
Wants to buy memorabilia relating to Arbuckles Bros. Coffee Company.

Museums/Libraries

Greg Q. ArBuckle
Arbuckles' Coffee Museum
97 16th Ave. SW
Cedar Rapids, IA 52404-5948
phone: 319-363-1242
fax: 319-365-5115
Large displayed collection of Arbuckles Bros. Co. products: coffee tins, spice tins, tea tins, trade cards, company documents, billings, letters, covers, bottles, banners, signs, counter displays, magazine ads.

Mills

Clubs/Associations

John White
Association of Coffee Mill Enthusiasts
Newsletter: Grinder Finder
5941 Wilkerson Rd.
Rex, GA 30273
phone: 770-474-0509

Collectors

Terry Friend
839 Glendale Rd.
Galax, VA 24333
phone: 703-236-9027

Joe MacMillian
657 Old Mountain Rd.
Marietta, GA 30064-1339
phone: 404-427-6434

John White
5941 Wilkerson Rd.
Rex, GA 30273
phone: 770-474-0509

Repro. Sources

Cumberland General Store
#1 Highway 68
Crossville, TN 38555
phone: 615-484-8481
fax: 615-456-1211

Tins

Collectors

Hugh Pinney
1387 Madison
Santa Clara, CA 95050-4758
phone: 408-241-5417
Buys keywind coffee tins which are mint or near mint and free of rust or cancer, must have right tops! Also wants certain unopened keywind tins.

Dealers

Tim Schweighart
1123 Santa Luisa Dr.
Solana Beach, CA 92075-1614
phone: 619-481-8315
fax: 619-481-5699
Collector, appraiser, and dealer of coffee tins.

COFFINS

(see FUNERAL ITEMS)

COIN-OPERATED MACHINES

(see also AMUSEMENT PARK ITEMS; BOOKS, Reference [Coin-Operated]; GAMES, Punchboards; POPULAR CULTURE; REPAIR/RESTORATION/CONSERVATION, Metal Items; SCALES; SOFT DRINK COLLECTIBLES, Soda Machines)

Auction Services

Bill Hughes
United States Amusement Auctions
P.O. Box 4819
Louisville, KY 40204
phone: 502-451-1263
Specialized auctions of video games, slot machines, juke boxes, arcade games, collectibles, trade stimulators, etc.

Collectors

Andy Rudoff
P.O. Box 111
Oceanport, NJ 07757-0111
phone: 908-542-3712
fax: 908-542-3712
Wants pre-1945 coin operated machines: arcade machines, vending, slots, trade stimulators, and games; send description and price; photos very helpful.

Joe Iozzia
P.O. Box 1005
Pomona, NJ 08240-1005
phone: 609-652-8504
Buys coin-operated slot machines, trade stimulators, and early arcade machines.

Richard O. Gates
P.O. Box 187
Chesterfield, VA 23832-0187
phone: 804-748-0382 or 804-794-5146
fax: 804-748-6349
Wants coin-operated machines including jukeboxes, pinballs, trade stimulators, slot machines, old gumball machines, Coca-Cola, Pepsi, R.C., Dr. Pepper machines and any signs or literature related to any of the above.

Lucky Riley
901 Lynne Ave.
Napoleon, OH 43545-1217

Mike Gorski
1770 Dover Rd.
Westlake, OH 44145
phone: 216-871-6071
Slot machines, old penny arcade machines; Wurlitzer 78 RPM jukeboxes, odd vending machines; Regina musical boxes, old coin-operated machines.

Frank Demayo
2424 Goshen Rd.
Fort Wayne, IN 46808
phone: 219-489-0053 or 800-258-8243
Wants coin-operated slot, gum, card, dice machines.

Richard McCoy
2719 Lakeview Ave.
St. Joseph, MI 49085
Wants slot machines, trade stimula-·tors, gumball machines, pinball machines, arcade games, etc.

Richard Trautwein
437 Dawson St.
Sault Sainte Marie, MI 49783-2119
phone: 906-635-0356
Wants to buy coin-op machines such as slot machines, scales, gumball and other vending machines; also wants arcade games such as strength tester games and games of skill, etc.

Dave Ogden
P.O. Box 223
Northbrook, IL 60062-0223
phone: 847-564-2893
fax: 847-564-2893
e-mail: musical@flash.net
Wants to buy early coin-operated machines, gambling and slot machines.

Bob McNally
Antique Coin-Operated Machines
P.O. Box 232414
Encinitas, CA 92023-2414
phone: 619-431-5907

John Anderson
15500 S.E. Royer Rd.
Clackamas, OR 97015
phone: 503-658-3607
Wants slot machines or other coin-operated machines.

Dealers

John S. Zuk
106 Orchard St.
Belmont, MA 02178-2940
phone: 617-484-4800
fax: 617-864-3862
e-mail: jzuk@integral-inc.com
Buys, sells and repairs slot machines, jukeboxes, arcade machines, gumballs, neon clocks, etc.

Gary Darrow
Darrow's Fun Antiques
1101 1st Ave.
New York, NY 10021-8737
phone: 212-838-0730
fax: 212-838-3617
Buys & sells antique games, toys, ad signs, animated art, jukeboxes, slot machines, comic watches, bicycles & memorabilia of all types.

Ken Durham
909 26th St. NW
Washington, DC 20037-2029
e-mail: durham@GameRoomAntiques.com
Internet: http://www.GameRoomAntiques.com
Buy/sell/trade countertop coin-operated machines: trade stimulators, vending machines, arcade machines, punchboards; also sells large selection of books and service manuals on same; send $2 for list.

Harold Daniel
Quicksilver Oddities Antique Coin-Ops & Collectibles
2500 E. Grann Blanc Rd.
Grand Blanc, MI 48439
phone: 810-750-9543 or 810-694-0787
Wants slot machines 25 yrs. old or older; also antique coin-operated gaming devices, trade stimulators, vending machines, arcade games, and items with sports themes.

Ted & Betty Salveson
Coin Machine Trader
P.O. Box 602
Huron, SD 57350-0602
phone: 605-352-3870 or 605-352-6460
fax: 605-352-7590
Buys, sells and repairs various types of coin-operated machines: slots, pinball, jukeboxes, gumballs, arcade games, etc.

Dennis Clark
Off the Wall Antiques, Inc.
7325 Melrose Ave.
Los Angeles, CA 90046
phone: 213-930-1185
fax: 213-930-1595

Harold Adler
MANtiques
14572 Deervale
Sherman Oaks, CA 91403-4611
phone: 818-990-2461
*Buys, trades, sells, restores pre-1940
coin-operated vending machines:
games of skill, chance, 3 reel, dice,
etc., counter models; parts and
repairs available on many old type
coin-operated vending machines; buys
broken machines.*

Wild Bill's Casino
2318 N.W. Vaughn St.
Portland, OR 97210
phone: 503-658-3607
*Buys, sells, trades, repairs, restores
vintage amusement machines.*

Experts

Bill Nesnay
P.O. Box 167
Matawan, NJ 07747-0167
phone: 908-583-2590 or 201-714-2293
fax: 201-714-2345
*Specializes in and wants to buy
baseball related coin-op machines:
gumball, pinball, arcade, vending,
and trade stimulators; please no calls
after 10 pm EST.*

Bob Levy
Unique One, The
2802 Centre St.
Merchantville, NJ 08109-5304
phone: 609-663-2554
*Buys and sells coin-operated
machines including slot machines and
arcade games; advisor to "Warman's
Antiques & Collectibles Price Guide."*

Joseph S. Jancuska
619 Miller St.
Luzerne, PA 18709-1307
phone: 717-287-3478
*Buys, sells, repairs and appraises slot
machines, trade stimulators, gum &
nut machines & other coin-operated
machines.*

Richard M. Bueschel
414 N. Prospect Manor Ave.
Mount Prospect, IL 60056-2046
phone: 847-253-0791
fax: 847-253-7919
e-mail: BuschlHist@aol.com
*Author of "Collector's Guide to
Vintage Coin Machines" (Schiffer,
1995), "Lemons, Cherries and Bell-
Fruit-Gum" (Royal Bell Books, 1995),
"Coin-Ops On Location"
(Wovelmarque, 1993).*

Bill Enes
8520 Lewis Dr.
Shawnee Mission, KS 66227-3277
phone: 913-441-1492 or 913-441-1502
fax: 913-441-1502
*Author of "Silent Salesmen - an
Encyclopedia of Collectible Gum,
Candy & Nut Machines."*

Museums/Libraries

Marvin Yagoda
Marvin's Marvelous Mechanical
Museum
31005 Orchard Rd.
Farmington, MI 48334
phone: 313-626-5020

On-Line Services

Ken Durham
GameRoomAntiques
909 26th St. NW
Washington, DC 20037-2029
e-mail:
durham@GameRoomAntiques.com
Internet: http://
www.GameRoomAntiques.com
*A World Wide Web site dedicated to
game room collecting: pinball
machines, juke boxes, Coke machines,
etc.; monthly feature articles, book
reviews, links to other game room
resources.*

Periodicals

Magazine: Coin Slot International
P.O. Box 57, Daltry St.
Oldham
Manchester OL1 4BB, U.K.
*The U.K.'s premier weekly magazine
for the coin-op industry.*

Magazine: Gameroom Magazine
P.O. Box 41
Keyport, NJ 07735-0041
phone: 908-739-1955
fax: 908-739-2834
e-mail:
coinop@gameroommagazine.com
*A great source of information for the
collector and dealer of jukeboxes,
pinballs, Coke machines and other
gameroom collectibles.*

Ted & Betty Salveson
Coin Machine Trader
Newsletter: Coin Machine Trader
P.O. Box 602
Huron, SD 57350-0602
phone: 605-352-3870 or 605-352-6460
fax: 605-352-7590
*A monthly newsletter featuring
articles on various types of coin-op.
machines: slots, pinball, jukeboxes,
gumballs, arcade games, etc.; lots of
ads for parts and services.*

Ted & Betty Salveson
Coin Machine Trader
Magazine: Salveson's Coin Machine
Trader
P.O. Box 602
Huron, SD 57350-0602
phone: 605-352-3870 or 605-352-6460
fax: 605-352-7590
*Monthly magazine focusing on pinball
machines, slot machines, and other
coin-operated machines; news, ads,
parts, services, machine descriptions,
auction results, early advertisements
reproduced.*

Hoflin Publishing Ltd.
Magazine: Coin Slot, The
4401 Zephyr St.
Wheat Ridge, CO 80033-3259
phone: 303-420-2222 or 800-352-5678
Internet: http://www.hoflin.com/
CoinSlot.html
*Focuses on antique vending machines,
slot machines, pinball machines,
arcade games, coin-operated musical
instruments, etc.*

Rosanna Harris
Newspaper: Coin Drop International
5815 W. 52nd Ave.
Denver, CO 80212-7503
phone: 303-431-9266
fax: 303-431-6978
e-mail: rbltd@cris.com
Internet: http://ww.concentric.net/
royalbell/
*A bi-monthly publication with a major
focus on vintage slot machines,
jukeboxes, pinball machines, arcade
machines, scales, coin operated music,
shows, etc.*

Mead Publishing Co.
Magazine: Loose Change
1551 South Commerce St.
Las Vegas, NV 89102-2703
phone: 702-387-8750
fax: 702-366-1599
*A monthly magazine with articles on
coin-operated gaming machines, and
gambling and related subjects;
contemporary and antique.*

Peter Movsesian
Magazine: Coin-Op Classics
17844 Toiyabe St.
Fountain Valley, CA 92708
phone: 714-756-8746
fax: 714-963-1718
e-mail: http://www.coin-op-classics.com
*Published bi-monthly; leading
magazine bridging all vintage coin-op
machines: slots, vending, jukeboxes,
pinballs, arcade, counter games, and
scales; full color, profusely
illustrated, articles by leading names
in the hobby.*

Repair Services

Gary Taplin
Penny Arcade Restorations
28 Southfield Ave.
Stamford, CT 06902
phone: 203-357-1913
*Restores all kinds of coin-operated
machines: mechanical, electro-
mechanical, pneumatics, part
fabrication, cabinetry refinishing,
marbleizing, graphics, marquees,
papier mache, glass, carving,
castings, polishing, plating.*

Joseph S. Jancuska
619 Miller St.
Luzerne, PA 18709-1307
phone: 717-287-3478
*Buys, sells, repairs and appraises slot
machines, trade stimulators, gum &
nut machines & other coin-operated
machines.*

Repro. Sources

Mechanical Antiques & Amusements
Co.
R.R. 7 Bateman Circle
Barrington, IL 60010
phone: 847-381-1234
*Sells recreations of coin-operated
machines such as Grandmother
Predictions.*

Suppliers

Rick Frink
2977 Eager
Howell, MI 48843-6711
*Supplies reelstrips, pay cards, decals,
instruction sheets, and mint wrappers
for antique slot machines and some
trade stimulators; send 7 1st class
postage stamps for catalog; also buys
and repairs antique machines.*

Advertising

Experts

Richard M. Bueschel
414 N. Prospect Manor Ave.
Mount Prospect, IL 60056-2046
phone: 847-253-0791
fax: 847-253-7919
e-mail: BuschlHist@aol.com
*Wants photos of coin machines
(vending, scales, jukeboxes, arcade,
slot machines), advertising, literature,
catalogs, etc.; send SASE if requesting
a reply.*

Arcade Games

Dealers

TNT Amusements
1310 Industrial Blvd.
Southampton, PA 18966
phone: 215-953-1188
fax: 215-953-8535
*Specializes in buying, selling,
restoring quality arcade video games,
pinball machines, jukeboxes.*

Gumball Machines

Collectors

Don L. Reedy
13 South Carroll St.
Frederick, MD 21701-5606
phone: 301-663-4240 or 301-662-5503
fax: 301-663-3478
e-mail: shineit4u@aol.com
*Buying pre-1940 cast iron or
porcelain gumball and peanut vending
machines and parts.*

Dealers

Rich Brinkos
Antique Gumball Machines
948 Clyde Lane
Philadelphia, PA 19128-1136
phone: 215-482-1429 or 215-482-9099
*Sells, restores, repairs and services
gumball and peanut machines; globes,
parts, vending products, stands;*

anything required to make a fully authentic period vending machine.

Repair Services

Rich Brinkos
Antique Gumball Machines
948 Clyde Lane
Philadelphia, PA 19128-1136
phone: 215-482-1429 or 215-482-9099
Sells, restores, repairs and services gumball and peanut machines; globes, parts, vending products, stands; anything required to make a fully authentic period vending machine.

Jukeboxes

(see also BOOKS, Reference [Jukeboxes])

Collectors

Joe Weber
604 Centre St.
Ashland, PA 17921-1332
phone: 717-875-4787 or 717-875-4401
Wants early Capehart & Wurlitzer jukeboxes which play 78 rpm records; will arrange pickup; all letters answered; will offer advise.

Mike Gorski
1770 Dover Rd.
Westlake, OH 44145
phone: 216-871-6071
Slot machines, old penny arcade machines; Wurlitzer 78 RPM jukeboxes, odd vending machines;Regina musical boxes, old coin-operated machines.

Roark Vane
6839 Havenside Dr.
Sacramento, CA 95831-2168
phone: 916-392-3864
e-mail: neonclock@aol.com
Wants to buy Wurlitzer, Rock-Ola or other 1929-1948 jukeboxes; also wants jukebox related accessories or related advertising items.

Dealers

John T. Johnston
6742 Fifth Ave.
Brooklyn, NY 11220-5418
phone: 718-833-8455
fax: 718-833-0560
Buys, sells, rents, trades and repairs slot and jukeboxes; wants to buy old jukeboxes, slot machines, vending, arcade, old gambling items, neons, cash registers, music boxes, phonographs, syrup dispensers.

TNT Amusements
1310 Industrial Blvd.
Southampton, PA 18966
phone: 215-953-1188
fax: 215-953-8535
Specializes in buying, selling, restoring quality arcade video games, pinball machines, jukeboxes.

Lloyd Thoburn
Lloyd's Jukeboxes
11804 Greybirch Place
Reston, VA 20191
phone: 703-620-3850
Buys jukeboxes in any condition; free phone appraisal of wholesale values; has over 300 jukeboxes in stock.

David Reed
Jukebox Central
841 West Main St.
Lorain, OH 44052-9763
phone: 216-428-6666
Buys, sells, collects and repairs jukeboxes and other coin-op equipment; also sells jukebox accessory equipment and parts.

Experts

Rick Botts
2545 SE 60th Ct.
Des Moines, IA 50317-5049
phone: 515-265-8324
fax: 515-265-1980

Ted Salveson
Coin Machine Trader
P.O. Box 602
Huron, SD 57350-0602
phone: 605-352-3870 or 605-352-6460
fax: 605-352-7590
Author of "Juke Boxes, What Every Collector Needs to Know," and "Introduction to Coin Operated Amusement Games."

Frank Zygmunt
Zygmunt & Associates (Jukeboxes)
Illinois Antique Slot Machine Co.
P.O. Box 542
Westmont, IL 60559-0542
phone: 630-985-2742 or 630-971-1015
fax: 630-985-5151
Buys and sells slot machines and jukeboxes; 150-200 slot machines & Wurlitzer jukeboxes in stock; also Wurlitzer One More Time distributor; also interested in music boxes, nickelodeons, and Coke machines.

Periodicals

Ken Durham
Newspaper: Antique Amusements Slot Machine & Jukebox Gazette
909 26th St. NW
Washington, DC 20037-2029
e-mail:
durham@GameRoomAntiques.com
Internet: http://
www.GameRoomAntiques.com
Semi-annual newspaper focusing on slot machines and jukeboxes; lots of ads, articles, shows, auctions; send SASE for info.

Rick Botts
Magazine: Jukebox Collector
2545 SE 60th Ct.
Des Moines, IA 50317-5049
phone: 515-265-8324
fax: 515-265-1980
A monthly magazine with large classified ad department, reprinted

articles, repair information, shows, auctions, etc.

Michael F. Baute
Newspaper: Always Jukin'
221 Yesler Way
Seattle, WA 98104-2622
phone: 206-233-9460
fax: 206-233-9871
e-mail: alwaysjuke@aol.com
Largest circulation monthly jukebox publication; photos, show reports, ads, new products, restoring guides, etc.

Repair Services

Chance Tess
Pinball Wizard Sales & Service
39425 Atkinson Dr.
Sterling Heights, MI 48313-5018
phone: 810-978-0393
Restores '50s and '60s Seeburg & Wurlitzer juke boxes.

David Headley
DH Distributors
P.O. Box 48623
Wichita, KS 67201-8623
phone: 316-684-0050
fax: 316-684-0050
Repairs and restores jukeboxes; chassis and cabinet restorations.

Repro. Sources

Edward Cadmus
Nostalgic Music Company
58 Union Ave.
New Providence, NJ 07974
phone: 908-464-5538
Sells the Antique Apparatus line of reproduction jukeboxes and speakers; specializing in 45 and CD jukeboxes.

Jukeboxes (Film)

Experts

Fred Bingaman
810 Courtland Dr.
Ballwin, MO 63021-6730
phone: 314-391-6651
fax: 314-230-9559
e-mail: mr356@aol.com
Wants audio visual (film) jukeboxes (scopitones), and related advertising items, films, spare parts, etc.

Periodicals

Fred Bingaman
Newsletter: Scopitone Newsletter, The
810 Courtland Dr.
Ballwin, MO 63021-6730
phone: 314-391-6651
fax: 314-230-9559
e-mail: mr356@aol.com

Pinball Machines

Collectors

Joe Iozzia
P.O. Box 1005
Pomona, NJ 08240-1005
phone: 609-652-8504
Buys, sells, trades vintage pinball machines.

Bill Cowles
Vintage Pinballs
4255 Green Ave.
Los Alamitos, CA 90706
phone: 562-594-6489

Dealers

Steve Young
Pinball Resource, The
8 Commerce St.
Poughkeepsie, NY 12603
phone: 914-223-5613
fax: 914-223-7365
e-mail: pbresource@aol.com
Source for maintenance manuals, schematics, replacement parts and supplies to restore and maintain vintage pinball machines; manufacturer of replacement parts; sells pinball books and price guides.

TNT Amusements
1310 Industrial Blvd.
Southampton, PA 18966
phone: 215-953-1188
fax: 215-953-8535
Specializes in buying, selling, restoring quality arcade video games, pinball machines, jukeboxes.

Chance Tess
Pinball Wizard Sales & Service
39425 Atkinson Dr.
Sterling Heights, MI 48313-5018
phone: 810-978-0393
Pinball machine expert; buys, sells, trades and restores all makes and models of pinball machines; also repairs '50s and '60s Seeburg & Wurlitzer juke boxes.

Experts

Gordon A. Hasse, Jr.
Silverball Amusements
140 East 95th St., 6-D
New York, NY 10128-1722
phone: 212-885-3619 or 212-996-3825
Expert & collector of pinball machines with access to most of the country's collectors; fair value for properly graded Gottlieb & Williams wood-rail pinball machines 1948-1958; seeks quantity purchases but will buy one.

Ted Salveson
Coin Machine Trader
P.O. Box 602
Huron, SD 57350-0602
phone: 605-352-3870 or 605-352-6460
fax: 605-352-7590
Specializes in all types of pinball machines from Bingo type to Flipper, electrical mechanical and solid state; 50 years experience; author of

"Introduction to Coin Operated Amusement Games."

Richard M. Bueschel
414 N. Prospect Manor Ave.
Mount Prospect, IL 60056-2046
phone: 847-253-0791
fax: 847-253-7919
e-mail: BuschlHist@aol.com
Author of "Pinball 1"; wants pinball related photos showing games in use, photo post cards, sales literature, advertising, manuals, operator reminiscences, etc.; send SASE if requesting a reply.

Periodicals

Jim Schelberg, Ed.
Journal: pinGame journal
31937 Olde Franklin Dr.
Farmington, MI 48334-1731
phone: 810-626-5203
fax: 810-626-5203
e-mail: jim@pingamejournal.com
Focuses on old as well as new pinball machines; articles on game development, repair and play; lots of buy and sell ads.

Kelly Altemueller
Magazine: Pinhead Classified
1945 "N" St., Ste. 111
Newman, CA 95360
phone: 209-862-2609
e-mail: pinchick@aol.com
Contains classifieds, display ads, and other editorial content pertaining only to pinball machines.

Repair Services

Steve Engel
Mayfair Amusement Company
60-41 Woodbine St.
Flushing, NY 11385-3234
phone: 718-417-5050
Repair or replace most Bally and Williams circuit boards.

Don Bryant
Bryant Antique Players
4819 Stallcup
Mesquite, TX 75150-1143
phone: 972-270-0135
fax: 972-613-1627
e-mail: aplayr@airmail.net
Sales, service and rebuilding of player pianos, pump organs, reproducing & coin-operated instruments, pin balls, & game room equipment; since 1975.

Bill Cowles
Vintage Pinballs
4255 Green Ave.
Los Alamitos, CA 90706
phone: 562-594-6489
Restores the old-style vintage pinball machines.

Suppliers

Steve Engel
Mayfair Amusement Company
60-41 Woodbine St.
Flushing, NY 11385-3234
phone: 718-417-5050
Source for over 6,000 backglasses in stock.

Tim Nabours
Nabours Novelty Inc.
320 Hwy. 55 West
P.O. Box 204
Maple Lake, MN 55358
phone: 800-657-4657 or 612-963-5953
fax: 612-963-5953
Parts for Foosball and Pinball machines: rubber rings, coils, flipper rings, rebound rubbers, plastic pins, etc.; for Atari, Bally, Chicago Coin, Gottlieb, Game Plan, Williams, Stern, etc.; also carries complete pinballs and jukeboxes.

Scales

Dealers

Bill & Jan Berning
135 W. Main St.
Genoa, IL 60135-1101
phone: 815-784-3134
Buys, sell, repair, restore, collect, trade and operate coin-operated scales and most other scales; also sells original and reproduction parts; free parts and repair diagram with LSASE.

Repair Services

Bill & Jan Berning
135 W. Main St.
Genoa, IL 60135-1101
phone: 815-784-3134
Buys, sell, repair, restore, collect, trade and operate coin-operated scales and most other scales; also sells original and reproduction parts; free parts and repair diagram with LSASE.

Slot Machines

Clubs/Associations

John Jerseffy, Pres
Colorado Antique Slot Collectors
1420 S. Ivy Way
Denver, CO 80224
Publishes a bi-monthly newsletter and sponsors an annual antique slot machine and jukebox show and sale.

Collectors

Martin Roenigk
Mechantiques
26 Barton Hill
East Hampton, CT 06424-1138
phone: 800-671-6333
fax: 860-267-1120
e-mail: mroenigk@aol.com
Internet: http://www.mechantiques.com
Slot machines and other coin-operated

machines; also Wurlitzer 78 rpm jukeboxes.

Mike Gorski
1770 Dover Rd.
Westlake, OH 44145
phone: 216-871-6071
Slot machines, old penny arcade machines; Wurlitzer 78 RPM jukeboxes, odd vending machines;Regina musical boxes, old coin-operated machines.

Scott Fawcett
3835 Birch St.
Newport Beach, CA 92660-2616
phone: 714-756-8677 or 714-968-5000
Collector wants to buy unusual slot machines including Watling Rol-A-Top and other slot machines in tall floor model console stands; also wants Silver Dollar slot machines including Fey.

Fred & Marjie Ryan
Slot Closet
P.O. Box 83135
Portland, OR 97203
phone: 503-286-3597 or 503-235-2279
Wants slot machines and related literature and advertisements.

Dealers

John T. Johnston
6742 Fifth Ave.
Brooklyn, NY 11220-5418
phone: 718-833-8455
fax: 718-833-0560
Buys, sells, rents, trades and repairs slot and jukeboxes; wants to buy old jukeboxes, slot machines, vending, arcade, old gambling items, neons, cash registers, music boxes, phonographs, syrup dispensers.

Alan D. Sax
Nationwide Amusement/Slot Machine Brokers, Inc.
3239 R.F.D.
Lake Zurich, IL 60047
phone: 847-438-5900

Hans Havlicek
Jennings Junction
4418 N. Elston
Chicago, IL 60630
phone: 312-736-6624
fax: 312-736-4390
Specializes in rebuilt and restored Jennings slot machines; replacement plastic for Sun Chiefs, console cabinets available, repro payout cards available separately, most all machines and parts; Jennings parts catalog available.

Tom Kolbrener
St. Louis Slot Machine Company
9400 Manchester Rd.
Saint Louis, MO 63119-1428
phone: 314-961-4612
$3 for 32 page color catalog of fully-restored antique slot machines for sale.

Vintage Slots
3379 Industrial Rd.
Las Vegas, NV 89109
phone: 800-228-SLOT or 702-369-2323
Buys, sells and trades slot machines.

Experts

Bob Levy
Unique One, The
2802 Centre St.
Merchantville, NJ 08109-5304
phone: 609-663-2554
Buys and sells coin-operated machines including slot machines and arcade games; advisor to "Warman's Antiques & Collectibles Price Guide."

Richard Reddock
914 Isle Ct.
Bellmore, NY 11710-1545
phone: 516-826-2032 or 800-223-PNUT
e-mail: pnutfanclb@aol.com
Buys, sells, restores slot machines; author of "Price Guide to Antique Slot Machines."

Richard M. Bueschel
414 N. Prospect Manor Ave.
Mount Prospect, IL 60056-2046
phone: 847-253-0791
fax: 847-253-7919
e-mail: BuschlHist@aol.com
Wants slot machine photos showing games in use, photo post cards, sales literature, advertising, manuals, operator reminiscences, etc.; send SASE if requesting a reply.

Frank Zygmunt
Zygmunt & Associates (Jukeboxes)
Illinois Antique Slot Machine Co.
P.O. Box 542
Westmont, IL 60559-0542
phone: 630-985-2742 or 630-971-1015
fax: 630-985-5151
Buys and sells slot machines and jukeboxes; 150-200 slot machines & Wurlitzer jukeboxes in stock; also Wurlitzer One More Time distributor; also interested in music boxes, nickelodeons, and Coke machines.

Clark Phelps
Amusement Sales Co.
127 North Main St.
Midvale, UT 84047-2424
phone: 801-255-4731

Marshall Fey
Liberty Belle Saloon Saloon & Restaurant
4250 South Virginia St.
Reno, NV 89502-6011
phone: 702-825-1776
Collector of antique slot machines for 38 years; author of "Slot Machines - A Pictorial History of the First 100 Years," $29.95 ppd.

Museums/Libraries

Marshall Fey
Liberty Belle Saloon & Slot Machine
  Collection
4250 South Virginia St.
Reno, NV 89502-6011
phone: 702-825-1776
  *Nations largest display of antique slot
  machines; also other antiques; free
  admission.*

Periodicals

Ken Durham
Newspaper: Antique Amusements Slot
  Machine & Jukebox Gazette
909 26th St. NW
Washington, DC 20037-2029
e-mail:
  durham@GameRoomAntiques.com
Internet: http://
  www.GameRoomAntiques.com
  *Semi-annual newspaper focusing on
  slot machines and jukeboxes; lots of
  ads, articles, shows, auctions; send
  SASE for info.*

Repair Services

David Claxton
2952 Lynn Ave.
Billings, MT 59102-6640
phone: 406-656-0949
  *Buys, sells and trades slot machines;
  specializes in the repair of Mills,
  Jennings, and Pace slot machines.*

Bill Whelan
Slot Dynasty Restorations
P.O. Box 617
Daly City, CA 94017-2332
phone: 415-756-1189
  *Specializes in the repair of slot
  machines as well as all other types of
  coin-operated gaming machines such
  as trade stimulators and arcade
  games; also buys/sells/trades coin-
  operated gaming machines.*

Suppliers

Tom Krahl
Antique Slot Machine Part Co.
140 N. Western Ave.
Carpentersville, IL 60110
phone: 847-428-8476
fax: 847-428-4471
  *Publishes a catalog of reproduction
  slot machine parts; also repairs.*

Bernie Berten
9420 S. Trumbull Ave.
Evergreen Park, IL 60642-2224
phone: 708-499-0688
fax: 708-499-5797
  *Carries just about every spring
  needed by coin machines; also
  castings for antique slot machines.*

Bill Whelan
Slot Dynasty Restorations
P.O. Box 617
Daly City, CA 94017-2332
phone: 415-756-1189
  Sells reel strips and award &

*instruction cards for trade stimulators
(counter model gambling machines.)*

Vending Machines

(see also SOFT DRINK COL-
LECTIBLES, Soda Machines)

Collectors

Don L. Reedy
13 South Carroll St.
Frederick, MD 21701-5606
phone: 301-663-4240 or 301-662-5503
fax: 301-663-3478
e-mail: shineit4u@aol.com
  *Buy, sell, trade gumball and peanut
  machines; also Coca-Cola advertising.*

Mike Gorski
1770 Dover Rd.
Westlake, OH 44145
phone: 216-871-6071
  *Slot machines, old penny arcade
  machines; Wurlitzer 78 RPM
  jukeboxes, odd vending machines;
  Regina musical boxes, coin-operated
  machines.*

Steve Perry
593 Lavina
Hemet, CA 92544
phone: 909-658-4620
  *Wants to buy old gum, peanut, and
  candy machines; even if incomplete or
  not working.*

Dealers

Rich Brinkos
Antique Gumball Machines
948 Clyde Lane
Philadelphia, PA 19128-1136
phone: 215-482-1429 or 215-482-9099
  *Sells, restores, repairs and services
  gumball and peanut machines; globes,
  parts, vending products, stands;
  anything required to make a fully
  authentic period vending machine.*

Experts

Bill Enes
8520 Lewis Dr.
Shawnee Mission, KS 66227-3277
phone: 913-441-1492 or 913-441-1502
fax: 913-441-1502
  *Author of "Silent Salesmen -
  Encyclopedia of Collectible Gum,
  Candy, and Nut Machines"; buys and
  sells.*

Periodicals

Newsletter: Around the Vending Wheel
5417 Castana Ave.
Lakewood, CA 90712
  *A monthly newsletter dedicated to
  vending machines such as gumballs,
  peanuts, candy, cigarettes, condoms,
  Coke, Pepsi, 7-Up and other pop
  machines.*

Repair Services

Rich Brinkos
Antique Gumball Machines
948 Clyde Lane
Philadelphia, PA 19128-1136
phone: 215-482-1429 or 215-482-9099
  *Sells, restores, repairs and services
  gumball and peanut machines; globes,
  parts, vending products, stands;
  anything required to make a fully
  authentic period vending machine.*

Suppliers

Gary Kothera
Antique Vender Supply
15465 Kinsman Rd.
P.O. Box 411
Middlefield, OH 44062
phone: 216-632-0423

COINS & CURRENCY

(see also ANTIQUITIES; BANKING,
Bank Checks; BOOKS, Reference
[Coins]; CIVIL WAR ARTIFACTS,
Currency; CREDIT CARDS &
CHARGE ITEMS; ELONGATED
COINS; GOLD; MACERATED
CURRENCY ITEMS; SILVER;
STOCKS & BONDS; TOKENS;
WOODEN MONEY)

Appraisers

Dr. Spencer Peck
P.O. Box 526
Oldwick, NJ 08858-0526
phone: 908-236-2880
  *One of only nine accredited
  appraisers of rare coins, currency,
  tokens and medals for IRS, estate,
  insurance, trust, liquidation and
  equitable distribution purposes in the
  U.S.*

Charles R. Hoskins
International Numismatic Society
P.O. Box 2091
Aston, PA 19014
phone: 610-494-2880
fax: 610-494-2270
  *Specializes in and appraises rare
  coins and currency.*

Thomas J. Terpilak
Metro Gem Consultants
7315 Wisconsin Ave.
Bethesda, MD 20814-3202
phone: 301-654-0838 or 301-654-8678
Internet: http://lan2wan.com/mgc
  *Professional numismatist and
  numismatic appraiser.*

John L. Frank
John Frank Rare Coins
725 South Adams, Ste. 21
Birmingham, MI 48009-6916
phone: 248-644-8818
fax: 248-258-5058
  *Buys, sells, appraises rare coin &
  currency collections; liquidates for
  maximum value; certified in rare coin
  grading by Adelphi University
  Institute of Numismatics & Philatelic*

*Studies; constructs rare coin
portfolios; guest speaker.*

Joseph J. Pojmonski, ISA
P.O. Box 1232
Dolan Springs, AZ 86441-1232
phone: 602-767-4774 or 602-767-4107
fax: 602-767-3900
  *Buys, sells, specializes in, and
  appraises U.S. coins; professionally
  trained and tested auctioneer and
  appraiser; member International
  Society of Appraises, and National
  Auctioneers Association.*

Auction Services

Spink & Son, Ltd.
King St.
St. James's
London SW1Y 6QS, U.K.
  *Auctioneers and dealers of coins
  (ancient to present), medals, orders,
  tokens, decorations and other
  numismatic items.*

Q. David Bowers
Bowers & Merena, Inc.
P.O. Box 1224
Wolfeboro, NH 03894
fax: 603-569-5319
  *Specializes in coin auctions; member
  International Association of
  Professional Numismatists.*

Lawrence Stack
Stack's Coin Galleries
123 West 57th St.
New York, NY 10019-2280
phone: 212-582-2580
fax: 212-245-5018
Internet: http://www.stacks.com
  Specializes in coin auctions.

Christie's
502 Park Ave.
New York, NY 10022
phone: 212-546-1000
fax: 212-980-8163
Internet: http://www.sirius.com/
  ~christie/

John D. Compton
J.D. Compton Auctioneering
13833 Rockdale Rd.
Clear Spring, MD 21722
phone: 301-582-0727 or 800-662-8284
fax: 301-582-6114
  *Specializes in the auction sale of U.S.
  coins and currency; call toll-free in
  the U.S. 1-800-66-AUCTION.*

Kurt R. Krueger
Krueger Auctions
160 N. Washington St.
Iola, WI 54945
phone: 715-445-3845
fax: 715-445-4100
  *Specializing in the mail-bid auction of
  tokens, advertising, brewery items,
  Western Americana, postcards,
  World's Fair & Expo., autographs,
  sports, coins & currency, pinbacks,
  military memorabilia, automotive,
  Disneyana, etc.*

Clubs/Associations

Jean-Paul Divo, Sec.
International Association of Professional
Numismatists
Lowenstrasse, 65
Zurich CH-8001 Switzerland
Internet: http://coin-universe.com/org/
iapa/
*Object is to develop a healthy and
prosperous numismatic trade
conducted according to the highest
ethical standards; membership limited
to firms or departments of commercial
institutions; all sales by members are
fully guaranteed.*

Canadian Numismatic Association
P.O. Box 226
Barrie
Ontario L4M 4T2 Canada

Benjamin Phillips
Young Numismatists of America
Newsletter: Young Numismatists Digest
8 Iroquois Trail
Monsey, NY 10952-4293
Internet: http://www.coin-universe.com/
org/young/
*Only nationwide club dedicated
specifically to young numismatists.*

David J. Davis
John Reich Collectors Society
Journal: John Reich Journal
P.O. Box 205
Ypsilanti, MI 48197
phone: 313-845-3866
*The purpose of the JRCS is to
encourage the study of numismatics,
particularly US gold and silver coins
minted before 1838.*

Boyd Mattox
Fremont Coin Club, Inc.
2064 E. 3rd St.
Fremont, NE 68025
phone: 402-721-0269

George Van Trump, Jr.
Jefferson County Coin Club
Newsletter: JCCC Newsletter
6837 Murray Lane
Annandale, VA 22003

Robert J. Leuver, ExDir
American Numismatic Association
Magazine: Numismatist, The
818 N. Cascade Ave.
Colorado Springs, CO 80903-3279
phone: 719-632-2646 or 800-367-9723
fax: 719-632-2646
Internet: http://www.money.org
*Worldwide assoc. of collectors of
coins, paper money, medals, tokens;
over 30,000 members; offers collector
services/benefits; web site lists
hundreds of coin and related clubs
worldwide arranged by specialty or by
state and country.*

Paul L. Koppenhauer
Professional Numismatists Guild
P.O. Box 430
Van Nuys, CA 91408
phone: 818-781-1764
fax: 818-781-0107
Internet: http://www.coin-universe.com/
png/
*Send for free copy of "The Pleasure of
Coin Collecting." Founded in 1955,
the P.N.G. has more than 300
members in 35 states. Directory lists
professional member numismatists
who possess knowledge, responsibil-
ity, and integrity.*

San Bernardino County Coin Club
P.O. Box 295
Patton, CA 92369-0295
phone: 909-864-7617
*Program speakers, auctions, short
general meeting; meets monthly at the
San Bernadino County Museum in
Redlands, CA; a fun time!*

Rick Webster, Treas.
Pacific Coast Numismatic Society
1941 Jones St.
San Francisco, CA 94133

Collectors

Frederick Lingenfelser
814 Byram St.
Reading, PA 19606-1446
*Wants pre-1950 coin auction catalogs,
books, price lists, photographic plates
of coins, and signed letters from coin
dealers of yesteryear; also wants to
buy any undamaged U.S. coins dated
before 1816.*

John & Nancy Wilson
Wilson's Syngraphics
P.O. Box 27185
Milwaukee, WI 53227-0185
phone: 414-545-8636
fax: 414-554-8894
*Wants any pre-1934 paper money
issued in the U.S.; also wants any pre-
1930 postcards depicting banks.*

Dealers

Q. David Bowers
Bowers & Merena, Inc.
Magazine: Rare Coin Review
P.O. Box 1224
Wolfeboro, NH 03894
fax: 603-569-5319
*Buys and sells U.S. coins and
currency; publishes Rare Coin Review
bi-monthly, includes articles, price
lists, coins for sale; member
International Association of
Professional Numismatists.*

Allen G. Berman
Allen G. Berman Professional
Numismatist
P.O. Box 605
Fairfield, CT 06430-0605
phone: 203-374-3032 or 203-374-6986
fax: 203-374-6986
e-mail: agberman@aol.com
*Buying, selling and appraising
foreign, ancient, medieval and rare*

*U.S. coins since 1973; extensively
published; consultant to auction
houses; will consider purchase of
items too early of esoteric for smaller
"main line" dealers.*

Jim Fehr
Ellesmere Numismatics
Newsletter: Winning Edge, The
P.O. Box 402
Brookfield, CT 06804-0402
phone: 203-794-1232 or 800-426-3343
*Buys and sells PCGS and NGC
certified U.S. coins; also publishes
"The Winning Edge" every three
weeks (call for free copy) which
contains current market information
as well as a listing of certified coins
for sale.*

Arthur & Ira Friedberg
Coin & Currency Institute, Inc.
P.O. Box 1057
Clifton, NJ 07014
phone: 201-471-1441
fax: 201-471-1062
*Member International Association of
Professional Numismatists.*

Richard & Sara Margolis
P.O. Box 2054
Teaneck, NJ 07666
phone: 201-848-9379
fax: 201-847-0134
*Foreign coins, medals, tokens,
patterns; member International
Association of Professional
Numismatists.*

Henry Christensen
Henry Christensen, Inc.
P.O. Box 1732
Madison, NJ 07940
phone: 201-822-2242
*Member International Association of
Professional Numismatists.*

Nathan Sonnheim
Private Collectors Group
Cherry Hill, NJ 08002-1562
phone: 609-667-3796
*Buys coins and paper money,
American and foreign; calls welcome.*

Gene Yotka
H.F.Y. Rare Coin
2100 Hwy. 35
Sea Girt, NJ 08750
phone: 908-974-8855

Harvey Stack
Stack's Coin Galleries
123 West 57th St.
New York, NY 10019-2280
phone: 212-582-2580
fax: 212-245-5018
Internet: http://www.stacks.com
*United States, European, ancient,
medieval coins; member International
Association of Professional
Numismatists.*

Wade Hinderling
P.O. Box 606
Manhasset, NY 11030
phone: 516-365-3729
Buys and sells coins of the US and

*France; member International
Association of Professional
Numismatists.*

William S. Panitch
William S. Panitch, Inc.
P.O. Box 12845, 855 Central Ave. Ste.
103
Albany, NY 12212-2845
phone: 518-489-4400
fax: 518-489-2776
e-mail: wsprd@aol.com
*Buys and sells U.S. and foreign coins,
commemorative and award medals,
paper money, etc.; also lectures and
appraises.*

Steven Schor
P.O. Box 811
Liberty, NY 12754-0811
phone: 914-292-3304
e-mail: eddiedee@zelacom.com
*Buy, sell, trade all coins, tokens,
medals and currency; wants better
numismatic items for inclusion in
brochure.*

C.E. Bullowa
Coinhunter
1616 Walnut St., Ste. 2112
Philadelphia, PA 19103-5364
phone: 215-735-5517
fax: 215-735-5517
*Buys and sells U.S., ancient and
foreign coins and books; appraisals;
member International Association of
Professional Numismatists.*

Guy Whidden
Guy Whidden Numismatist
7504 Rockwood Rd.
Frederick, MD 21702-3648
phone: 301-473-8375
*Specializes in coin identification and
values; many years of experience.*

Mark E. Mitchell
3002 Winter Pine Ct.
Fairfax, VA 22031-1125
phone: 703-591-3150
fax: 703-385-3152
*Buying coin collections and
accumulations.*

Ron Gordon
San Juan Precious Metals Corp.
4818 San Juan Ave.
Jacksonville, FL 32210-3232
phone: 904-387-3466
fax: 904-387-5166
*Buys and sells all US and foreign
coins and currency.*

Ed Kuszmar
Florida Currency & Coins
P.O. Box 4049
Boca Raton, FL 33429
phone: 561-995-7985
fax: 561-995-7983
e-mail: EdKuszmar@aol.com
*Interested in coins, currency, paper
Americana, ephemera, and 1893
Columbia Exposition items.*

William Skelton
Highland's Vault
P.O. Box 55448
Birmingham, AL 35205
phone: 205-939-1178 or 205-939-3166
Wants to buy coins and paper money.

Kent Froseth
K.M. Froseth, Inc.
P.O. Box 23116
Minneapolis, MN 55423-0116
phone: 612-831-9550 or 800-648-7662
fax: 612-835-3903
US, foreign gold and silver coins; member Professional Numismatists Guild, International Association Professional Numismatists; also life member of ANA and CNA.

E. Milas
Rare Coin Company of America, Inc.
6262 South Rte. 83
Willowbrook, IL 60514
phone: 708-654-2580
fax: 708-654-3556
U.S., foreign type coins and paper money; member International Association of Professional Numismatists.

Harlan Berk
Harlan J. Berk, Ltd.
31 North Clark St.
Chicago, IL 60602
phone: 312-609-0016
fax: 312-609-1309
Buys and sells all coins 700 BC to present; classical antiquities; member International Association of Professional Numismatists.

John G. Ross
55 West Monroe St., Ste. 1070
Chicago, IL 60603
phone: 312-236-4088
U.S. coins, coins of the world; member International Association of Professional Numismatists.

Dr. R.A. Hiett
Maple City Coin
P.O. Drawer 47
Monmouth, IL 61462-0047
phone: 309-734-3212
fax: 309-734-8083
Buys and sells all coins and numismatic items; also knives, Indian artifacts, fishing lures, old pens, and many other miscellaneous items.

Blanchard & Co.
P.O. Box 61740
New Orleans, LA 70161-1740
phone: 800-880-4653
fax: 504-837-4884
Internet: http//
www.blanchardonline.com
Dealers in rare coins and precious metals.

Darwin S. Marshall
MHG Services
1520 Grand
Texarkana, AR 71854-4452
phone: 501-773-2128
fax: 501-772-3703
e-mail: marshall@slink.net
Internet: http://www.tmdweb.com/mhg-darwin
Buys, sells, collects, auctions, and specializes in US and foreign coins.

Klaus J. Degler
Rocky Mountain Coin Exchange, Inc.
538 S. Broadway
Denver, CO 80209-4002
phone: 303-777-2491 or 307-777-4653
fax: 303-733-4946
e-mail: rmcoin@aol.com
Appraises, buys, sells, collects and specializes in coins and currency.

John J. Ford, Jr.
P.O. Box 10317
Phoenix, AZ 85064
phone: 602-957-6443
fax: 602-957-1861
Collects and deals; U.S. colonial coins, US silver, gold medals; member International Association of Professional Numismatists; also specializes in counterfeit coins scales and detectors.

Ira Goldberg
Superior Stamp & Coin
9478 West Olympic Blvd.
Beverly Hills, CA 90212-4299
phone: 310-203-9855
fax: 310-203-0496
US coins and currency, foreign and ancient coins; member Professional Numismatist Guild.

Cy Phillips, Jr.
S C Coin & Stamp Co. Inc.
P.O. Drawer 661180
Arcadia, CA 91066-1180
phone: 818-445-8277 or 800-367-0779
fax: 818-445-8278
Tokens, medals, coins, currency, badges, expo. and fair items, scrap gold and silver.

Teller Numismatic Enterprises
16027 Ventura Blvd., Suit 606
Encino, CA 91436
phone: 818-783-8545
fax: 818-783-9083
e-mail: awwwa@earthlink.net
Internet: http://www.tellercoins.com
Gold and silver coins of the World; specialist in Russia, China, 19th Century Oriental coins, and choice foreign paper money; member International Association of Professional Numismatists.

Neil Osina
Best Variety Sports Cards & Coins
358 W. Foothill Blvd.
Glendora, CA 91740-3327
phone: 818-914-2273
fax: 818-914-6624
Wants to buy coins from the period 1792 through 1885; Life Member of

all major associations; over 34 years experience.

Karl Stephens
Karl Stephens, Inc.
P.O. Box 458
Temple City, CA 91780-0458
phone: 818-445-8154
fax: 818-447-6591
Foreign coins, medals, tokens, eastern Europe, US type and copper coins; member International Association of Professional Numismatists.

Richard Ponterio
Ponterio & Associates, Inc.
1818 Robinson Ave.
San Diego, CA 92103
phone: 800-854-2888 or 612-299-0400
fax: 619-299-6952
Coins, medals and banknotes of Mexico and Latin America, World paper money, gold coins and crowns, Ancient coins; member International Association of Professional Numismatists.

Howard Markham
Howard Markham Professional Numismatist
5225 Canyon Crest Dr., Bldg 200, Ste. 254
Riverside, CA 92507
phone: 909-686-2122 or 800-953-3027
Buys all U.S. coins, gold coins, collections and accumulations; nationally recognized numismatist; will pay top dollar for rare coins; will travel to buy larger collections.

Freeman Craig
P.O. Box 4176
San Rafael, CA 94913-4176
phone: 415-883-5336
fax: 415-382-1008
e-mail: raccoonnet@earthlink.net
Expert in Latin American coinage in gold, silver and minor metals from 1536-1950 including medals; member International Association of Professional Numismatists.

James F. Elmen
World-Wide Coins of California
P.O. Box 3684
Santa Rosa, CA 95492
phone: 707-527-1007
fax: 707-527-1204
World coins and medals 1500 to present; member International Association of Professional Numismatists.

Dick Wagner
Tipsico Coin LLC
P.O. Box 1128
North Bend, OR 97459-0306
phone: 541-756-7111
Appraises, sells and buys all U.S. and world coins via a 44 page catalog; coin albums and supplies, plus gold and silver bullion are also offered; specialties include Morgan and Peace dollars, Lincoln and Indian cents.

Experts

Allen G. Berman
Allen G. Berman Professional Numismatist
P.O. Box 605
Fairfield, CT 06430-0605
phone: 203-374-3032 or 203-374-6986
fax: 203-374-6986
e-mail: agberman@aol.com
Co-author of "Warman's Coins & Currency" (1997 Wallace-Home-stead), author/editor of numerous books & articles on early coinage; leading authority on coins of Middle Ages and Papacy; recognized authority by periodicals & auction houses.

Scott A. Travers
Scott Travers Rare Coin Galleries, Inc.
P.O. Box 171
F.D.R. Station
New York, NY 10150-1711
phone: 212-535-9135
e-mail: travers@inch.com
Internet: http://www.inch.com/~travers/travers3.htm
Author of "How to Make Money in Coins Right Now."

Milton Mitchell
3401 Hallaton Ct.
Silver Spring, MD 20906
phone: 301-598-7959

Klaus J. Depler
Rocky Mountain Coin Exchange, Inc.
538 S. Broadway
Denver, CO 80209-4002
phone: 303-777-2491 or 307-777-4653
fax: 303-733-4946
e-mail: rmcoin@aol.com
Professional Numismatist Guild, American Numismatic Assoc., Inter. Society of Appraisers, Industry Council for Tangible Assets, CO-WY Numismatic Assoc., consultant to the American Numismatic Assoc., V.P. Colorado Coin Dealers Assoc.

Man./Prod./Dist.

Kennedy Mint, Inc., The
12102 Pearl Rd.
Strongsville, OH 44136-3398
phone: 800-442-6468
Sells individual and proof sets of early and new commemorative U.S. coins; write for catalog - in addition to coins and coin sets for sale, it contains tools and storage devices for coin collectors.

Misc. Services

Numismatic Guaranty Corporation of America (NGC)
P.O. Box 1776
Parsippany, NJ 07054
phone: 201-984-6222
Grades coins and issues a guarantee of authenticity.

Charles R. Hoskins
International Numismatic Society
Newsletter: Numorum
P.O. Box 2091
Aston, PA 19014
phone: 610-494-2880
fax: 610-494-2270
The INS offers authentication and grading of rare coins and paper money to the public for a nominal fee.

ANACS
P.O. Box 182141
Columbus, OH 43218-2141
phone: 800-888-1861
fax: 614-791-9103
Grades coins and issues a guarantee of authenticity.

Professional Coin Grading Service (PCGS)
P.O. Box 9458
Newport Beach, CA 92658-9458
phone: 800-447-8848
Grades coins and issues a guarantee of authenticity.

Museums/Libraries

Bank of Canada Currency Museum
245 Sparks St.
Ottawa
Ontario K1A 0G9 Canada
phone: 613-782-8914
Eight galleries trace the history of money from barter to modern currency, with emphasis on Canada's monetary history; impressive coin and paper money exhibits.

Newark Museum, The
49 Washington St.
P.O. Box 540
Newark, NJ 07101-0540
phone: 201-596-6550
Numismatics is a specialty area.

Mr. Leslie A. Elam, Dir.
American Numismatic Society, The
Newsletter: American Numismatic Society Newsletter, The
Broadway at 155th St.
New York, NY 10003
phone: 212-234-3130
Internet: http://www.coin-universe.com/org/armenian/
Has a major collection of American coins in addition to major and important collections of ancient, Latin American, Islamic, European, and other material; also publishes "American Journal of Numismatics" and "Numismatic Literature."

National Museum of American History, National Numismatic Collection
14th & Constitution Ave. NW
Washington, DC 20560
phone: 202-357-2700
Internet: http://www.si.edu/
The Hall of Monetary History and Medallic Art exhibits an amazing number of U.S. and foreign coins, tokens, medals, and paper money from earliest times to the present; the finest coin collection in the world.

Money Museum, Federal Reserve Bank of Richmond
701 East Byrd St.
Richmond, VA 23219
phone: 804-697-8108
fax: 804-697-8123
Internet: http://www.rich.frb.org
Primitive monies, ancient coins, Colonial money, U.S. coins and paper money, Confederate currency, and U.S. commemorative coins are on display.

Robert J. Leuver, ExDir
Museum of the American Numismatic Association
818 N. Cascade Ave.
Colorado Springs, CO 80903-3279
phone: 719-632-2646 or 800-367-9723
fax: 719-632-2646
Internet: http://www.money.org
A museum collection 400,000 items including American, ancient, Latin American, Islamic, European, and other coins; largest numismatic circulating library with books and A/V material free to members.

Old Mint Museum
5th & Mission Sts.
San Francisco, CA 94103
phone: 415-744-6830
Collection of coins, numismatic items, and mining equipment and related items.

On-Line Services

L.D. Mitchell, Pres.
NumisNet
P.O. Box 902317
Palmdale, CA 93590-2317
24-hr. computer bulletin board service on 301-498-8205 for numismatic collectors; electronic messaging/programs for 2 dozen specialties.

Periodicals

Trajan Publishing Corporation
Newspaper: Canadian Coin News
103 Lakeshore Rd., Ste. 202
St. Catharines
Ontario L2N 2T6 Canada
phone: 905-646-7744
fax: 905-646-0995
e-mail: bret@trajan.com
Internet: http://www.vaxxine.com/trajan/
All the news on Canadian coin collecting.

Trajan Publishing Corp.
Magazine: Les Monnaies
103 Lakeshore Rd., Ste. 202
St. Catharines
Ontario L2N 2T6 Canada
phone: 905-646-7744
fax: 905-646-0995
e-mail: bret@trajan.com
Internet: http://www.vaxxine.com/trajan/
North America's only French language periodical on the subject of coins, medals and paper money.

Susan
Newsletter: Restrike, The
RFD 1 Box 530
Winthrop, ME 04364-9764
Buy, sell, trade with other collectors nationwide; published monthly.

Newsletter: Silver News, The
1112 16th St. NW, Ste. 240
Washington, DC 20036
phone: 202-835-0185

Newsletter: Silver & Gold Report
P.O. Box 109665
West Palm Beach, FL 33410
phone: 800-289-9222 or 561-627-3300
fax: 561-625-6685
e-mail: sgr@weissinc.com
Internet: http://www.wessinc.com
Financial advice newsletter in precious medals, and gold & silver bullion and coins.

Leenie Folsom
Newspaper: Coin World
P.O. Box 150
Sidney, OH 45365
phone: 800-253-4555
fax: 937-498-0812
e-mail: lfolsom@amospress.com
Internet: http://www.csmonline.com/coinworld
The weekly newspaper for the entire numismatic field; articles, ads, paper money, foreign and ancient coins, auctions, value guides, grading, etc.; the world's largest weekly stamp newspaper and marketplace.

Julie A. Ulrich, PR
Krause Publications
Magazine: Coin Prices
700 E. State St.
Iola, WI 54990-0001
phone: 715-445-2214
fax: 715-445-4087
e-mail: info@krause.com
Internet: http://www.krause.com
Provides complete current market prices for U.S. coins; values listed for up to 12 grades of preservation; frequently updated pricings; bi-monthly.

Julie A. Ulrich, PR
Krause Publications
Magazine: Coins
700 E. State St.
Iola, WI 54990-0001
phone: 715-445-2214
fax: 715-445-4087
e-mail: info@krause.com
Internet: http://www.krause.com
Leading monthly newsstand magazine provides in-depth features on U.S. coins with color photos; collector columns, articles, values, ads; the complete magazine for collectors.

Julie A. Ulrich, PR
Krause Publications
Newspaper: Numismatic News
700 E. State St.
Iola, WI 54990-0001
phone: 715-445-2214
fax: 715-445-4087
e-mail: info@krause.com
Internet: http://www.krause.com
A weekly guide to the coin collecting hobby serving active collectors of U.S. coins with timely news; values, ads, calendar.

Julie A. Ulrich, PR
Krause Publications
Newsmagazine: World Coin News
700 E. State St.
Iola, WI 54990-0001
phone: 715-445-2214
fax: 715-445-4087
e-mail: info@krause.com
Internet: http://www.krause.com
Monthly guide serving world coin collectors; news, historical features, huge ad section, coin values, show calendar.

Dennis R. Barker
CDN Publications
Newsletter: Certified Coin Dealer Newsletter (The "Bluesheet")
P.O. Box 7939
Torrance, CA 90504
phone: 310-515-7369
fax: 310-515-7534
e-mail: greysheet@msn.com
Internet: http://www.greysheet.com
A weekly report on the certified coin market; unbiased wholesale information on rare coins for the coin hobby and business.

CDN Publications
Newsletter: Coin Dealer Newsletter, The (The "Greysheet")
P.O. Box 7939
Torrance, CA 90504
phone: 310-515-7369
fax: 310-515-7534
e-mail: greysheet@msn.com
Internet: http://www.greysheet.com
A weekly report on the certified coin market; unbiased wholesale information on rare coins for the coin hobby and business.

CDN Publications
Newsletter: Currency Dealer Newsletter, The (The "Greensheet")
P.O. Box 7939
Torrance, CA 90504
phone: 310-515-7369
fax: 310-515-7534
e-mail: greysheet@msn.com
Internet: http://www.greysheet.com
A monthly newsletter reporting on the currency market.

Newsletter: Consultant's Certified Coin Report
P.O. Box 8277
Fountain Valley, CA 92728
phone: 714-662-0237

James Miller Publications
Magazine: COINage
4880 Market St.
Ventura, CA 93003
phone: 805-644-3824

Newsletter: Dines Letter, The
P.O. Box 22
Belvedere Tiburon, CA 94920-0022

Repro. Sources

Ron Landis
Gallery Mint Museum
Newsletter: Gallery Mint Report
P.O. Box 706
Eureka Springs, AR 72632
phone: 501-253-5055
*A mint and museum; reproductions of
early American coins and commemorative medals, hobo nickels and tokens
for collectors; preserves numismatic
arts and coin-making techniques.*

Coin Errors

Collectors

Robert E. Weisblut
11109 Nicholas Dr.
Silver Spring, MD 20902-3532
phone: 301-649-4002
*Buys coins that display errors caused
during the manufacturing process.*

George Van Trump, Jr.
6837 Murray Lane
Annandale, VA 22003

Dealers

Neil Osina
Best Variety Sports Cards & Coins
358 W. Foothill Blvd.
Glendora, CA 91740-3327
phone: 818-914-2273
fax: 818-914-6624
*Wants to buy coin errors; Life
Member of all major associations;
over 34 years experience.*

Periodicals

Arnold Margolis
Magazine: Error Trends Coin Magazine
P.O. Box 158
Oceanside, NY 11572-0158
phone: 516-764-8063
*A monthly magazine focusing on coin
errors.*

Coins (Ancient)

(see also ANTIQUITIES)

Auction Services

Alex G. Malloy
Alex G. Malloy, Inc.
P.O. Box 38
South Salem, NY 10590-0038
phone: 203-438-0396 or 203-438-9652
fax: 203-438-6744
e-mail: alexmalloy@aol.com
Internet: http://www.members.aol.com/
AlexMalloy/agmallory.htm
*Issues fixed price lists and mail bid
sales of ancient and medieval coinage,*

*and of ancient art and antiquities for
sale; co-author of "Warman's Coins
& Currency" (1994 Wallace-
Homestead).*

Classic Numismatic Group, Inc.
P.O. Box 479
Lancaster, PA 17608-0479
phone: 717-786-4013
*Specializes in the auction sale of
classical coins: Greek, Roman,
Byzantine, Medieval, British, foreign,
etc.*

Clubs/Associations

Ancient Coin Club
P.O. Box 227
Canoga Park, CA 91305

Ancient Numismatic Society
8713 Caminto Abrazo
La Jolla, CA 92037

Dealers

Jan Blamberg
Stack's Coin Galleries
123 West 57th St.
New York, NY 10019-2280
phone: 212-582-2580
fax: 212-245-5018
Internet: http://www.stacks.com
*Buys and sells European, ancient,
medieval coins; member International
Association of Professional
Numismatists.*

Alex G. Malloy
Alex G. Malloy, Inc.
P.O. Box 38
South Salem, NY 10590-0038
phone: 203-438-0396 or 203-438-9652
fax: 203-438-6744
e-mail: alexmalloy@aol.com
Internet: http://www.members.aol.com/
AlexMalloy/agmallory.htm
*Issues fixed price lists and mail bid
sales of ancient and medieval coinage,
and of ancient art and antiquities for
sale; co-author of "Warman's Coins
& Currency" (1994 Wallace-
Homestead).*

David Hendin
P.O. Box 805
Nyack, NY 10960

Frank J. Wagner
Classica Antiquities
P.O. Box 509
Syracuse, NY 13201-0509
phone: 315-687-0036 or 315-457-7249
e-mail: clasant@servtech.com
Internet: http://www.servtech.com/
public/clasant/
*For over 30 years buying/selling
ancient and medieval Greek, Roman,
Egyptian, Near Eastern coins and
antiquities.*

Edward J. Waddell, Jr.
Edward J. Waddell, Ltd.
444 N. Frederick Ave., Ste. 316
Gaithersburg, MD 20877
phone: 301-990-7446
fax: 301-990-3712
*Greek, Roman, Byzantine and
Medieval coins, antiquities and
numismatic literature; member
International Association of
Professional Numismatists.*

Carl & Jon Subak
Subak Inc.
22 West Monroe St.
Room 1506
Chicago, IL 60603
phone: 312-346-0609 or 312-346-0673
fax: 312-346-0150
*Roman, Byzantine, medieval coins;
member International Association of
Professional Numismatists.*

Joel & Michael Malter
Joel L. Malter & Co., Inc.
17005 Ventura Blvd.
Encino, CA 91316-4128
phone: 818-784-7772 or 818-784-2181
fax: 818-784-4726
*Buys and sells ancient and medieval
coins, classical antiquities,
numismatic books and literature;
member International Association of
Professional Numismatists.*

Frank L. Kovacs
P.O. Box 25300
San Mateo, CA 94402
phone: 415-574-2028
fax: 415-574-1995
*Buys and sells ancient and Byzantine
coins and antiquities; member
International Association of
Professional Numismatists.*

Periodicals

Magazine: Celator, The
P.O. Box 123
Lodi, WI 53555-0123
phone: 608-592-4684
fax: 608-592-5084
e-mail: celator@aol.com
Internet: http://www.numisart.com/
celator/
*A monthly magazine focusing on
antiquities and ancient coins; ads,
articles, auction reports, etc.*

Coins (Copper)

Clubs/Associations

Early American Coppers
Newsletter: Penny-Wise
1468 Timberlane Dr.
Saint Joseph, MI 49085
*Interested in early American copper
coinage.*

Coins (Encased)

(see also GOOD LUCK)

Auction Services

Bob Slawsky
P.O. Box 864
Windermere, FL 34786-0864
phone: 407-352-7807
fax: 407-352-BIDS
e-mail: WWGD54A@prodigy.com
*Buys, sells, auctions tokens, medals,
badges, small advertising items,
political, World's Fair, Olympic items,
encased coins, etc.*

Collectors

R. Wells
5 Elm
Trenton, NJ 08611-2501
*Wants encased coins; good luck,
advertising, etc.; describe item, date
on coin, price.*

Coins (World Proof)

Clubs/Associations

Gail P. Gray, Sec.
World Proof Numismatic Association
Newsletter: Proof Collectors Corner
P.O. Box 4094
Pittsburgh, PA 15201-0094
phone: 412-782-4477
fax: 412-782-0227
*WPNA is dedicated to the collector of
proof and BU coinage; purpose is to
bring forth the latest news on new
coin issues, medals and books, etc.;
special Master Price List is mailed out
to all members containing over 1,000
proof coins.*

Dealers

Edward J. Moschetti
Treasures of the World
P.O. Box 4094
Pittsburgh, PA 15201-0094
phone: 412-782-4477
fax: 412-782-0227
*Medals in silver and gold proof
condition; offering the Rarities Mint
issues, plus Batman, Bugs Bunny, etc.*

Coins (World)

Collectors

S.E. Penning
1242 S. Mountain St.
Visalia, CA 93277-4264
*Buying pre-1950 foreign coins from
all countries; will also buy gold and
silver coins of any age.*

Commemorative Coins

Clubs/Associations

Cindy Mohon, Sec.
Society for U.S. Commemorative Coins
14252 Culver #490
Irvine, CA 92714
*Members dedicated to sharing the
knowledge and enjoyment of
collecting U.S. commemorative coins.*

Croatian

Clubs/Associations

Croatian Philatelic Society, Numismatic
Dept.
Newsletter: Trumpeter, The
R.R. 1, Box 729-F
Rockville, IN 47872
*Focuses on the history of the stamps
and numismatic items of all the Baltic
states, past and present.*

Double Dies

Clubs/Associations

Gary Wagnon
Society of Doubled Die Collectors of
America
Newsletter: Double Talk
16611 60th St. N
Loxahatchee, FL 33470-3309
*Club devoted strictly to the study and
advancement of the doubled die
hobby.*

Medieval

(see ANTIQUITIES; COINS &
CURRENCY, Coins [Ancient])

Paper Money

Auction Services

R.M. Smythe & Company
26 Broadway, Ste. 271
New York, NY 10004-1701
phone: 212-943-1880 or 800-622-1880
fax: 212-908-4047
*Conducts auctions of Colonial
currency, Confederate currency,
federal essay notes, proof vignettes,
fractional and obsolete currency,
stocks, bonds, coins and autographs.*

Clubs/Associations

Canadian Paper Money Society
P.O. Box 465
West Hill
Ontario M1E 2P0 Canada

Arthur C. Matz
Latin American Paper Money Society
Newsletter: LANSA
3304 Milford Mill Rd.
Baltimore, MD 21244-2041
phone: 410-655-3109
*A booklet issued three times a year for
those interested in Latin American and
Iberia paper money.*

Professional Currency Dealers
Association
P.O. Box 573
Milwaukee, WI 53201
*This organization is just for dealers,
but send a SASE for a free list of
respectable dealers; also send 59
cents for the booklet "How to Collect
Paper Money."*

Milan Alusic, GenSec
International Bank Note Society
Journal: International Bank Note Society
Journal
P.O. Box 1642
Racine, WI 53401
phone: 414-554-6255
*Members interested in worldwide
bank notes and paper currencies;
journal published quarterly with
articles, ads, etc.*

Bob Cochran
Society of Paper Money Collectors
Journal: Paper Money
P.O. Box 1085
Florissant, MO 63031-0085
*Interested in all aspects of collecting
paper currency; welcomes opportunity
to help non-collectors, but PLEASE
send SASE for reply.*

Collectors

Bob Cochran
P.O. Box 1085
Florissant, MO 63031-0085
*Collector of U.S. paper money; also
banking history.*

Dealers

William Barrett
P.O. Box 9
Victoria Station
Montreal H3Z 2V4 Canada
phone: 514-937-4131
fax: 514-937-8075
*Specialist in British, French,
Portuguese, Spanish and Danish
colonies; Chinese foreign banks, all
proof and specimen notes.*

Jim Sciuto
GoldTek
P.O. Box 128
Methuen, MA 01844
phone: 508-374-2254 or 603-645-4717
fax: 508-373-1088
Internet: http://www.pm-connect.com/
sciuto/
*Wants old paper money: gold
certificates, silver certificates, errors,
star notes, red seals, etc.*

Denly's of Boston
P.O. Box 1010
Boston, MA 02205
phone: 617-482-8477
fax: 617-357-8163
*Buys and sells national currency,
banknotes, fractional and Colonial
currency.*

William S. Panitch
William S. Panitch, Inc.
P.O. Box 12845, 855 Central Ave. Ste.
103
Albany, NY 12212-2845
phone: 518-489-4400
fax: 518-489-2776
e-mail: wsprd@aol.com
*Buys and sells U.S. and foreign coins,
commemorative and award medals,
paper money, etc.; also lectures and
appraises.*

Art Leister
Commercial Coin Co.
1611 Market St.
P.O. Box 607
Camp Hill, PA 17001-0607
phone: 717-737-8981 or 717-761-8264
Buys and sells national banknotes.

Tom Knebl, Inc.
P.O. Box 3689
Carson City, NV 89702-3689
*Wants all world bank notes; also U.S.
large size notes and military currency;
U.S. fractional currency; Colonial
currency, etc.*

Brigg's Coin & Currency
P.O. Box 1514
Riverside, CA 92506
phone: 714-781-3121 or 714-781-3123
*Buys and sells national banknotes,
Confederate currency, obsolete notes,
type notes, etc.*

Experts

Ken D. Tanaka
Nova Online, Inc.
P.O. Box 231028
Portland, OR 97281-1028
phone: 503-671-0761
fax: 503-671-9561
e-mail: chipmunk@teleport.com
*Specialist in all forms of paper money;
offering evaluations and appraisals;
also buys and sells paper money.*

Periodicals

Token Publishing, Ltd.
Magazine: Coin News
P.O. Box 14
Honiton
Devon EX14 9YP, U.K.
*A monthly English publication
focusing on coins and paper money.*

Julie A. Ulrich, PR
Krause Publications
Newspaper: Bank Note Reporter
700 E. State St.
Iola, WI 54990-0001
phone: 715-445-2214
fax: 715-445-4087
e-mail: info@krause.com
Internet: http://www.krause.com
*Monthly news source and marketplace
for collectors of U.S. and world paper
money, notes, checks and related
fiscal paper.*

Paper Money (World)

Dealers

Yasha Beresiner
InterCol Gallery
43 Templars Crescent
London N3 3QR, U.K.
phone: 018—34-2207
fax: 018—34-9539
e-mail: 100447.3341@compuserve.com
*Buys and sells world banknotes,
playing cards and maps.*

Steve Eyer
P.O. Box 123 -MA
Mount Zion, IL 62549-0321
phone: 217-864-4321
fax: 217-864-3021
*Buys and sells world coins and world
banknotes.*

Gary Snover
P.O. Box 9696
San Bernardino, CA 92427-0696
phone: 909-883-5849
fax: 909-886-6874
e-mail: snover@ix.netcom.com
*Buys and sells world banknotes; send
for free catalog; active buyer of all
world paper money.*

Experts

Neil Shafer
P.O. Box 17138
Milwaukee, WI 53217
phone: 414-352-5962
e-mail: nelsshaf@aol.com
*Editor of "Standard Catalog of World
Paper Money."*

Play Money

Clubs/Associations

Jack Phillips
American Play Money Society
2044 Pine Lake Trail, NW
Arab, AL 35016

Souvenir Cards

Clubs/Associations

Souvenir Card Collectors Society
Journal: Souvenir Card Journal
P.O. Box 4155
Tulsa, OK 74159-0155
phone: 918-664-6724
e-mail: dmarr5569@aol.com
*Souvenir cards are 8 1/2" x 11" cards
with engraved reproductions of
philatelic or numismatic designs from
original plates.*

Supplies For

Suppliers

Lighthouse Publications
P.O. Box 705
Hackensack, NJ 07602-0705
phone: 201-342-1513
fax: 201-342-7142
*Carries full line of products for the
coin and stamp collector: albums,
binders, blank pages, magnifiers,
tongs, UV lamps.*

Brooklyn Gallery Coin & Stamp
8725 Fourth Ave.
P.O. Box 146
Brooklyn, NY 11209-0146
phone: 718-745-5701
fax: 718-745-2775
Send $1.50 for 104 page catalog.

Linder Publications, Inc.
P.O. Box 5056
Syracuse, NY 13220
phone: 315-437-0463 or 800-654-0324
fax: 315-437-4832
Sells collector's accessories for stamps, coins, telephone cards, postcards: ring binders, blank album pages, UV lamps, magnifiers, stamp tongs, clear pocket pages, protective covers, coin holders, etc.

Topical

Clubs/Associations

Dennis G. Rainey
Topical Numismatics Society
3708 Nipomo Ave.
Long Beach, CA 90808
phone: 213-429-4153
Focuses on coins and bank notes that are based on themes or topics such as transportation, birds, plants, sports events, etc.

COLLAR BUTTONS & PINS

(see CLOTHING & ACCESSORIES, Vintage; CUFF LINKS)

COLLECTIBLES

(see ANTIQUES & COLLECTIBLES; COLLECTIBLES [MODERN])

COLLECTIBLES (MODERN)

(see also ANIMATION FILM ART; DOLLS; ENESCO; FIGURINES; MINIATURES, Sculptures; STEIFF)

Clubs/Associations

Cowboy Collector Society, The, c/o Shade Tree Creations, Inc.
6210 NW 124th Place
Gainesville, FL 32606-1071
phone: 800-327-6923
fax: 904-462-1799
e-mail: BVernon@afn.com

Hunter Haines
Collectibles & Platemakers Guild
P.O. Box 1474
Northbrook, IL 60065

Susan Elliott, Ex. Dir.
National Association of Limited Edition Dealers
5235 Monticello Ave.
Dallas, TX 75206-6035
phone: 214-826-2002
e-mail: naled@collectibles.net
Internet: http://www.naled.com

Dealers

Bob Dorman
New England Collectibles Exchange
Newsletter: New England Collectibles Exchange Newsletter
201 Pine Ave.
North Adams, MA 01247-4640
phone: 413-663-3643
fax: 413-663-5140
e-mail: nece@collictiblesbroker.com
Internet: http://www.collectiblesbroker.com
Monthly newsletters for collectors; list, buy, sell or trade limited editions and retired pieces; ads free for active members: Cherished Teddies, Anri, Cat's Meow, Dept. 56, Shelia's, Hummel, Disney Classics, Tom Clark, Boyds Bears, etc.

Linda's Originals & The Yankee Craftsmen
230 Rt. 6A
Brewster, MA 02631
phone: 800-385-4758
All God's Children, Armani, Annalee Dolls, Byers Choice, Cat's Meow, Cherished Teddies, Dept. 56, Harbour Lights, Hummel, Krystonia, Lilliput Lane, Shelia's, Steinbeck, and more.

Maurice Nasser Co.
New London Shopping Center
New London, CT 06320
phone: 203-443-6523 or 800-243-0895

Elissa Cohen ISA CAPP, GG
Suburban Jewelers
126 East Front St.
Plainfield, NJ 07060-1202
phone: 908-756-1774
Authorized dealer of Lladro, Hummel, Precious Moments, Swarovski, All God's Children, Sarah's Attic, G. Armani, Miss Martha, Ebony Visions, Tom Clark, and other modern collectibles; buys, sells, trades.

Joan Lewis
Lewis/Welch Collectors Exchange
12 Legion Dr.
Valhalla, NY 10595-2012
phone: 914-948-4655
fax: 914-948-4367
State of the art computer database of wanted to sell and wanted to buy listings for Lladro, Swarovski, and Armani.

Sy Schreck
Gift Gallery, The
19 Vermont St.
Melville, NY 11747-1619
phone: 516-627-6500
Deals in collectibles: Precious Moments, Dept. 56 cottages, Hummels, plates, Boehm, Swarovski, Krystonia, David Winter, Anri, etc.

Magdalena Interiors
3235 Chestnut St. NW
Washington, DC 20015
phone: 202-966-8755

Tiara Gifts
1675 Rockville Pike
Rockville, MD 20852-1619
phone: 301-949-0210 or 800-457-9911
Lladro, Waterford, Swarovski, David Winter, Chilmark, Hummels, Goebel miniatures, Sarah's Attic, Tom Clark, Armani, Dept. 56, Boehm, Connoisseur, Herend, EKJ.

Happy Clown, The
911 W. 7th St.
Frederick, MD 21701
phone: 301-695-8874
Specializes in the sale of Tom Clark Gnomes, Emmett Kelly Junior Clowns, Memories of Yesterday, Precious Moments, and Hummels.

Donny Biggs
Biggs Collectibles
5517 Lakeside Ave.
Richmond, VA 23228
phone: 804-266-7744 or 800-637-0704
fax: 804-266-7775
Carries lots of limited edition dolls (Ashton Drake dealer of the year); also Chilmark, Hummel, David Winter, Lladro, Jan Hagara, Lowell Davis, Maud Humphrey, Swarovski, etc.

Collectible Exchange, Inc.
P.O. Box 429
New Middletown, OH 44442
phone: 800-752-3208
fax: 330-542-9644
Offers a brokerage service; buy or sell your retired, limited edition collectibles: Anri, Cybis, Lowell Davis, Jan Hagara, Gartlan, Duncan Royale, Ispanky, Lladro, Swarovski, Emmett Kelly, Jr., Hummel, etc.

Collectibles etc., Inc.
1127 Cass St.
La Crosse, WI 54601
phone: 800-558-5594
Specializes in old and new Precious Moments figurines, old and new collector plates, Ashton Drake and Perillo dolls, accessories; Georgetown Collection, Hamilton Collection; plates - Bradford Exchange, P.B. Moss, Perillo, Hibel, etc.

Tom Hayes
Collectibles Showcase
Newsletter: Collectibles Showcase Newsletter
1047 Burnsville Center
Burnsville, MN 55306
phone: 612-892-0552 or 800-723-4072
fax: 612-892-1596
Largest collectibles store in U.S.; located in the Mall of America; thousands of collectibles; many lines discounted 20% or more including Lladro, David Winter, Lilliput Lane, Waterford; also Precious Moments, Hummel, Dept. 56.

British Collectibles
917 Chicago Ave.
Evanston, IL 60202
phone: 800-634-0431 or 847-570-4867
fax: 847-570-4871
Produces Toby Jugs designed by Francis Salmon and Kevin Pearson; carries a wide assortment of modern collectibles, focusing on British.

Sue Reeves
Eloise's Gifts & Antiques
722 South Goliad
Rockwall, TX 75087-3936
phone: 972-771-6371 or 800-771-6371
fax: 972-771-6371
Carries Cairn, All Gods, Armani, L. Davis, Dept. 56, Duncan Royale, EKJ, Hummel, Hagara, Sarahs, D. Winter, Lilliput Lane, Wee Forest, plates, Cat's Meow, Swarovski, ENESCO,, Byers, Lizzie High, Dreamsicles, Cherished Teddies, etc.

OHI Collectibles & Gifts
Newsletter: OHI Exchange
1050 IH 35E., Ste. 400
New Braunfels, TX 78130
phone: 210-629-1191 or 800-627-1600
fax: 210-629-0153
Acts as broker to match buyers and sellers of all limited edition collectibles such as collector plates, figurines, bells, ornaments, dolls, etc.; Dept. 56, David Winter, Lowell Davis, Hummel, Duncan Royale, etc.

Genevra Fox
Fox's Gifts & Collectables
7030 5th Ave.
Scottsdale, AZ 85251
phone: 602-947-0560 or 800-592-2555
Specializes in modern collectibles by Ted DeGrazia, Cat's Meow, J. Hagara, Dept. 56, and Bradford plates.

Eva Flynn
Eva Flynn Collectibles
P.O. Box 1011
Carlsborg, WA 98324-1011
phone: 360-683-7725
Specializes in B&G/RC Christmas plates; search service for back issues for most major collectibles including Disney, Raggedy Ann, Peanuts, Rockwell, Hummels, Royal Doulton, doll plates, Ferrandiz, Veneto Flair, Rosenthal; send SASE.

Experts

Peggy Veltri
Collectors' Information Bureau
Newsletter: C.I.B. Report & Showcase, The
5065 Shoreline Rd., Ste. 200
Barrington, IL 60010-1700
phone: 847-842-2200
fax: 847-842-2205
CIB provides collectors with the most accurate and up-to-date information on limited edition plates, figurines, bells, graphics, ornaments, and dolls; publishes an annual "Collectibles

Price Guide" and a quarterly newsletter.

Man./Prod./Dist.

Lance Corporation
321 Central St.
Hudson, MA 01749
phone: 508-568-1401
fax: 508-568-8741
Producers of collectible figurines, plates, Christmas ornaments; line include Chilmark limited edition collectibles, Hudson Pewter, Sebastian Miniatures, and c.p. smithshire Shirelings.

American Artists
66 Poppasquash Rd.
Bristol, RI 02809
phone: 800-828-0086 or 401-254-1191
fax: 401-254-8881
Manufactures and distributes limited edition plates, figurines and prints by artists such as Fred Stone, Donald Zolan and Susan Leigh.

Anna-Perenna, Inc.
35 River St.
New Rochelle, NY 10801
phone: 914-633-3777 or 800-627-2550
fax: 914-633-8727
Manufactures and publishes limited edition figurines, sculpture and plates by artists such as P. Buckley Moss.

Customer Service
Reco International Corp.
Newsletter: Sandra Kuck Newsletter
P.O. Box 951
Port Washington, NY 11050-0244
phone: 516-767-2400 or 800-221-5356
fax: 516-767-2409
Distributor of collector plates, bells, Christmas ornaments, dolls, figurines and graphics based in designs by noted artists such as John McClelland and Sandra Kuck, and Jody Beresma.

Ebeling & Reuss
33 Court St.
P.O. Box 1289
Allentown, PA 18105-1289
phone: 610-776-7102
fax: 610-776-7102
A major importer of fine giftware and collectibles: Goebel annual collectible bells, eggs, ornaments, Domex beer steins, Gerz steins, Duchess China collectible china and figurines from Europe.

U. S. Historical Society
25 E. Main St.
Richmond, VA 23219
phone: 804-648-4736
fax: 804-648-0002
Direct mail marketer of plates, figurines, dolls and Christmas ornaments in stained glass, pewter, porcelain and other materials.

Tamara Armstrong
Fenton Art Glass Company, The
700 Elizabeth St.
Williamstown, WV 26187-1028
phone: 304-375-6122 or 800-249-4527
fax: 304-375-6459
Manufactures collectible plates, figurines and bells.

J.H. Boone's Inc.
624A Matthews-Mint Hill Rd.
Matthews, NC 28105-2797
phone: 704-847-0404
fax: 704-847-0428
Produces figurines designed by Neil Rose (Old West), Paul Carrico, Gary Rose, Tom Snyder, and Bill Atkinson; also prints by Edward Curtis and Gary Rose, and Southwest Indian artifacts.

Flambro Imports, Inc.
P.O. Box 93507
Atlanta, GA 30377-0507
phone: 800-355-2582 or 404-352-1381
fax: 404-352-2150
e-mail: collsoc@flambro.com
Internet: http://signaturecoll.com
Importer of collectible clowns (Emmett Kelly, Jr.) and circus-related items, plates, ornaments, figurines and miniatures.

Hamilton Collection, The
P.O. Box 44051
Jacksonville, FL 32232-4051
phone: 904-723-6000 or 800-228-2945
fax: 904-725-8997
Formerly The Hamilton Mint, produces collectible plates, figurines and dolls.

Pat Owen
Viking Import House, Inc.
Newsletter: Viking Newsletter
690 NE 13th St.
Ft. Lauderdale, FL 33304-1110
phone: 305-763-3388 or 800-327-2297
fax: 305-462-2317
Distributes prints, plates, figurines, bells, dolls, ornaments, etc. for most manufacturers of limited edition collectibles; Bing & Grondahl, Royal Copenhagen, Kaiser, Hamilton Collection, Wedgwood, etc.

American Greetings Corp.
10500 American Rd.
Cleveland, OH 44144
phone: 216-252-7300 or 216-252-4944
fax: 216-252-6979
World's largest manufacturer of greeting cards and social expression products, gift wrap and accessories, Christmas ornaments, collector plates, etc.; licenses Holly Hobbie, Ziggy, Strawberry Shortcake, and the Care Bears.

Midwest Importers of Cannon Falls, Inc.
P.O. Box 20
Cannon Falls, MN 55009-0020
phone: 507-263-4261 or 800-377-3335
Imports and wholesales unique gifts from around the world - bells, paperweights, dolls, ornaments, figurines, German nutcrackers, etc.

ENESCO Corp.
225 Windsor Dr.
Itasca, IL 60143
phone: 630-875-5300 or 800-436-3726
fax: 630-875-5359
Giftware company produces/designs fine gifts & collectibles: figurines, musicals, waterballs, etc. by Precious Moments and others.

Hollywood Limited Editions, Inc.
6990 Central Park Ave.
Lincolnwood, IL 60645
phone: 708-673-3250 or 800-323-1413
fax: 708-673-4037
Distributes an extensive line of collector plates, figurines, bells, ornaments and accessories.

Dave Grossman Creations
1608 N. Warson Rd.
Saint Louis, MO 63132
phone: 314-423-5600
fax: 314-423-7620
Producer of collectible plates, ornaments and figurines including Rockwell, Gone With the Wind, Wizard of Oz, and Emmett Kelly, Sr.

Robert M. Ready
World of Products
1410 Oak Tree Drive
Houston, TX 77055-4316
Colorful catalog full of modern collectibles, knickknacks, curios: figurines, lit cottages, night lights, miniature furniture, carousel horses, frames, wall decor, music boxes, brass and wood sculptures, music boxes, "Mandarin" ivory.

Carlos & Minerva Estevez
CREART U.S.A., Inc./Estevez Creations
209 E. Ben White Blvd., #103
Austin, TX 78740-7372
phone: 512-707-2699 or 800-343-1505
fax: 512-707-9918
e-mail: 73024.2001@compuserve.com
Produces limited edition, extraordinarily realistic wildlife and animal figurines from bonded marble.

Heirloom Editions
25100-B South Normandie Ave.
Harbor City, CA 90710
phone: 310-539-5587
fax: 310-539-8891
Manufacturer of porcelain bells and thimbles; also produces Viennese Bronze bands and novelties; imports collectible Staffordshire Fine Ceramic teapots.

Michael McCarthy
Character Collectibles
10861 Business Drive
Fontana, CA 92337
phone: 909-822-9999
fax: 909-823-6666
Manufacturers of Barkley Crossing, Hippity Hollow, Mooseberry Farms, Red Hats of Courage, and Celestial

Guardians limited edition collectible figurines.

Giftstar
630 A Airpark Rd.
Napa, CA 94558
phone: 800-835-0181 or 707-226-2323
fax: 707-226-6464
Produce collectibles: snowglobes, Brian Baker building wall hangings, etc.

Willitts Designs
1129 Industrial Ave.
Petaluma, CA 94975
phone: 800-358-9184 or 707-778-7211
fax: 707-769-0304
Produces The American Carousel limited edition collections by Tobin Fraley; also other collectibles including plates, figurines, etc.

Matching Services

Hans J. Schindhelm
8 John Walsh Blvd., Ste. 412
Peekskill, NY 10566-5330
phone: 914-734-8410
fax: 914-734-8410
e-mail: siegmar@aol.com
Offers exchange service for limited edition collectibles; free listings and appraisals for listed items.

Misc. Services

Pam Danziger
Unity Marketing
Newsletter: Collectibles Business
206 E. Church St.
Stevens, PA 17578
phone: 717-336-1600
fax: 717-336-1601
e-mail: unity_marketing@msn.net
Specializes in tracking the contemporary collectibles marketplace and in publishing market research studies.

Periodicals

Tom Power
Magazine: Collector, The
9 Church St.
London NW8 8DEE, U.K.
phone: 0171-7064586
fax: 0171-7062948
e-mail: collector@globalnet.co.uk
55 page collectibles magazine published twice a year; lots of articles and items for sale; specialist dealer in modern collectibles such as Doulton, Beswick, David Winter, Lilliput Lane; call 800-514-8176, ext. 3328.

Joan M. Pursley, Ed.
Magazine: Collector Editions
170 Fifth Ave. - 12th Floor
New York, NY 10010
phone: 212-989-8700 or 800-347-6969
fax: 212-645-8976
A biweekly consumer magazine covering contemporary collector plates, figurines, prints and glass objects; companies, artists, etc.

Geyer-McAllister Publications, Inc.
Magazine: Gifts & Decorative
    Accessories
51 Madison Ave.
New York, NY 10010-1603
phone: 212-689-4411
fax: 212-683-7929
    *Trade magazine for new gifts,
    decorative accessories, collectibles,
    stationery, gift baskets, and tabletop
    wares; buyer's resource directory
    guide available with subscription.*

Pam Danziger
Unity Marketing
Newsletter: Collectibles Business
206 E. Church St.
Stevens, PA 17578
phone: 717-336-1600
fax: 717-336-1601
e-mail: unity_marketing@msn.net
    *Specializes in tracking the contempo-
    rary collectibles marketplace and in
    publishing market research studies.*

Cherie Souhrada, Pub.
Collectors News Co.
Magazine: Collectors News
P.O. Box 156
Grundy Center, IA 50638-0156
phone: 319-824-6981 or 800-352-8039
fax: 319-824-3414
e-mail: collectors@collectors-news.com
Internet: http://collectors-news.com
    *The monthly publication for antiquers
    & collectors; complete show & sale
    calendar, articles, expert advice,
    values, etc.; a special emphasis is
    always given to contemporary limited
    edition collectibles: what's new,
    artists, events.*

Julie A. Ulrich, PR
Krause Publications
Magazine: Collector's mart magazine
700 E. State St.
Iola, WI 54990-0001
phone: 715-445-2214
fax: 715-445-4087
e-mail: info@krause.com
Internet: http://www.krause.com
    *Bi-monthly magazine for limited
    edition art and collectibles:
    classifieds, articles, dealers ads, club
    notices, etc.*

Peggy Veltri
Collectors' Information Bureau
Directory: Directory to Secondary
    Market Retailers
5065 Shoreline Rd., Ste. 200
Barrington, IL 60010-1700
phone: 847-842-2200
fax: 847-842-2205
    *Lists scores of dealers and exchanges
    to assist in liquidating, buying,
    locating, or trading your contempo-
    rary limited edition artwork: prints,
    figurines, plates, bells, ornaments, etc.*

Newsletter: International Collectible
    Showcase
One Westminster Place
Lake Forest, IL 60045
    *A quarterly newsletter about modern
    collectibles.*

Rosie Wells
Rosie Wells Enterprises, Inc.
Magazine: Collectors' Bulletin
22341 E. Wells Rd.
Canton, IL 61520
phone: 309-668-2565 or 800-445-8745
fax: 800-337-6743
e-mail: Rosie@RosieWells.com
Internet: http://www.RosieWells.com
    *Articles about today's collectibles:
    Lowell Davis, Anri, Dept. 56, Precious
    Moments, Cherished Teddies,
    Hallmark ornaments, Jan Hagara,
    Maud Humphrey, David Winter and
    more.*

Rosie Wells
Rosie Wells Enterprises, Inc.
Newsletter: Weekly Collectors' Gazette
22341 E. Wells Rd.
Canton, IL 61520
phone: 309-668-2565 or 800-445-8745
fax: 800-337-6743
e-mail: Rosie@RosieWells.com
Internet: http://www.RosieWells.com
    *News bits for Hallmark, Disney
    Classics, Disney Collectibles,
    Dreamsicles, Cherished Teddies,
    McDonald's, Barbie, Hot Wheels,
    Dept. 56, Snowbabies, Precious
    Moments, Memories of Yesterday,
    Steiff, Longaberger baskets, etc.*

Magazine: Treasure Trunk
P.O. Box 13554
Arlington, TX 76094
phone: 817-461-9400
    *Monthly magazine focusing on
    modern collectibles, limited editions.*

Bessie Pease Gutmann

(see also PRINTS, Bessie Pease
Gutmann)

Clubs/Associations

Gutmann Collectors Club
1353 Elm Ave.
Lancaster, PA 17604-4743
    *Focuses on the works of Bessie Pease
    Gutmann.*

Dealers

Edward J. Meschi
129 Pinyard Rd.
Monroeville, NJ 08343-1870
phone: 609-358-7293
fax: 609-358-7293
    *Buying paintings, calendars, original
    works of art.*

Bing & Grondahl

Dealers

Pat Owen
Viking Import House, Inc.
690 NE 13th St.
Ft. Lauderdale, FL 33304-1110
phone: 305-763-3388 or 800-327-2297
fax: 305-462-2317
    *Operates the VIDEX, a buy/sell
    service for any and all Royal
    Copenhagen and Bing & Grondahl
    collectibles.*

Man./Prod./Dist.

Josephine Dillon
Royal Copenhagen/Bing & Grondahl
    Co.
27 Holland Ave.
White Plains, NY 10603-3317
phone: 914-428-8222 or 800-431-1992
fax: 914-428-8251
    *Royal Copenhagen, Bing & Grondahl,
    Holmegaard, and Georg Jensen are
    the best of Scandinavian collectibles;
    manufactures dinnerware, cobalt blue
    underglaze collector plates, figurines,
    bells, dolls, ornaments and gift
    accessories.*

Black Related

Dealers

Karl J. Graham
Graham Collection, The
1800 Belmont Rd. NW
Washington, DC 20009
phone: 202-232-0911
    *Comprehensive collection of quality
    new Black collectibles: Giuseppe
    Armani, Duncan Royale, All God's
    Children, Positive Image Collection,
    John Sandridge, Daddy Long Legs,
    Black Legends, Enesco, LuvLife,
    Norman Hughes, and more.*

Buildings (Brandywine)

Clubs/Associations

Truman Whiting
Brandywine Neighborhood Association
104 Greene Dr.
Yorktown, VA 23692-4800
phone: 800-336-5031 or 757-898-5031
fax: 757-898-6895
e-mail: heartbwine@aol.com
    A company sponsored collectors club.

Man./Prod./Dist.

Truman Whiting
Brandywine Woodcrafts Inc.
104 Greene Dr.
Yorktown, VA 23692-4800
phone: 800-336-5031 or 757-898-5031
fax: 757-898-6895
e-mail: heartbwine@aol.com
    *Manufactures three types of miniature
    collectible houses and accessories in
    hand painted cast resin and full color
    prints on wood; all buildings can be
    personalizes with your choice of name
    on sign.*

Buildings (Brian Baker)

Clubs/Associations

Brian Baker's Deja Vu Collectors' Club
Newsletter: Brian's Backyard
630 A Airpark Rd.
Napa, CA 94558
phone: 800-835-0181 or 707-226-2323
fax: 707-226-6464
    *A club for collector's of Brian Baker's
    architectually-inspired wall
    sculptures.*

Man./Prod./Dist.

Giftstar
630 A Airpark Rd.
Napa, CA 94558
phone: 800-835-0181 or 707-226-2323
fax: 707-226-6464
    *Produces Brian Baker's
    architectually-inspired wall
    sculptures.*

Buildings (Cat's Meow)

Clubs/Associations

Cat's Meow Collectors Club
Newsletter: Village Mews, The
2163 Great Trails Dr.
Wooster, OH 44691-3738
phone: 330-264-1377
fax: 330-263-0219
    *For collectors of the Cat's Meow
    Village, a product line of two-
    dimensional miniature historical
    buildings and accessories.*

Man./Prod./Dist.

F.J. Designs, Inc./The Cat's Meow
2163 Great Trails Dr.
Wooster, OH 44691-3738
phone: 330-264-1377
fax: 330-263-0219
    *Manufacturer of the Cat's Meow
    Village, a product line of two-
    dimensional miniature historical
    buildings and accessories.*

Buildings (My Friends & Me)

Man./Prod./Dist.

My Friends & Me
P.O. Box 2274
Hudson, OH 44236
phone: 216-650-6157
    *4" to 6" hand-cast reproductions of
    historic homes.*

Buildings (R.R. Creations)

Man./Prod./Dist.

R.R. Creations
P.O. Box 8707
Pratt, KS 67124
phone: 800-779-3610
    *Makes two-dimensional miniature
    homes, lighthouses and buildings.*

Buildings (Shelia's)

Clubs/Associations

Shelia's Collectors Society
Newsletter: Our House
P.O. Box 31028
Charleston, SC 29417
phone: 803-766-0485 or 800-227-6564
fax: 803-556-0040
    *Miniature handpainted two-
    dimensional houses made of wood.*

Man./Prod./Dist.

Shelia's Collectibles
P.O. Box 31028
Charleston, SC 29417
phone: 803-766-0485 or 800-227-6564
fax: 803-556-0040
*Miniature handpainted two-
dimensional houses made of wood.*

Buildings (Town Square)

Man./Prod./Dist.

Cavanaugh Group International
1000 Holcomb Woods Pkwy., #440-B
Roswell, GA 30078
phone: 800-895-8100 or 800-850-BEAR
*Manufacturer of high-quality
porcelain buildings.*

Christmas

Clubs/Associations

Cavanaugh's Coca-Cola Christmas
  Collectors' Society
P.O. Box 420157
Atlanta, GA 30342
phone: 800-653-1221
*Sells modern Coca-Cola collectibles
with a Christmas theme.*

Old World Christmas Collectors' Club
Newsletter: Old World Christmas Star
Gazette
P.O. Box 8000
Spokane, WA 99203-0030
phone: 800-962-7669 or 509-534-9000
fax: 509-534-9098
*Club members can purchase exclusive
German holiday collectibles made of
wood or glass.*

Man./Prod./Dist.

Kurt S. Adler
Kurt S. Adler, Inc.
1107 Broadway
New York, NY 10010
phone: 212-924-0900 or 800-243-9627
fax: 212-807-0575
*The nations leading importer,
designer and supplier of Christmas
ornaments, decorations and
accessories.*

Great American Taylor Collectibles
  Corp.
P.O. Box 428
Aberdeen, NC 28315
Manufacturer of old world Santas.

Knobstone Studio
RR 3 Box 168A
Scottsburg, IN 47170
phone: 812-752-7022
fax: 812-752-5222
*Produces collectible old world Santas;
each face is an original (not molded
or cast), bodies are soft sculpture.*

Old World Christmas Collectors' Club
P.O. Box 8000
Spokane, WA 99203-0030
phone: 800-962-7669 or 509-534-9000
fax: 509-534-9098
Distributes high-quality, collectible

*Christmas collectibles and decora-
tions.*

Christmas (Clothtique)

Clubs/Associations

Santa Claus Network
Newsletter: Santa Claus Network
Newsletter
6 Perry Drive
Foxboro, MA 02035-1051
phone: 508-543-6667
fax: 508-543-4255
*Members receive free Possible
Dreams Clothique (stiffened cloth)
Santa and more.*

Possible Dreams Limited
6 Perry Drive
Foxboro, MA 02035-1051
phone: 508-543-6667
fax: 508-543-4255
*Manufacturer of the Clothique (uses a
centuries-old method of stiffening
cloth) line of collectible Christmas
ornaments and figurines such as
angels and Santa Claus.*

Clarissa Johnson

Man./Prod./Dist.

Clarissa Johnson
Clarissa's Creations
18111 Meyers
Detroit, MI 48235
phone: 313-341-7762
*Produces original Afro American
artwork: prints, collector plates, and
note and greeting cards designed by
Clarissa Johnson.*

Clowns (Ron Lee)

Clubs/Associations

Ron Lee's Greatest Clown Collector's
  Club
Newsletter: Collectible News From Ron
Lee
330 Carousel Parkway
Henderson, NV 89014
phone: 800-829-3928 or 702=434-1700
fax: 702-434-4310
*For collectors of Ron Lee's fine white
metal or pewter figurines with 24-
karat gold plating and hand painting;
on hand-cut onyx bases with gold
beading.*

Man./Prod./Dist.

Ron Lee's World of Clowns
330 Carousel Parkway
Henderson, NV 89014
phone: 800-829-3928 or 702=434-1700
fax: 702-434-4310
*Manufacturer and sculpture of clown
and circus-theme collectibles; fine
white metal or pewter figurines with
24-karat gold plating and hand
painting; on hand-cut onyx bases with
gold beading.*

Computer Programs For

Man./Prod./Dist.

Russ Wood
Collector's Marketplace
Program: Intelligent Collector Software
RD 1 Box 213B
Montrose, PA 18801-9779
phone: 800-755-3123 or 717-278-4094
fax: 717-278-4377
e-mail: cmonline@epix.net
Internet: http://
www.collectorsmarketplace.com
*Lists secondary market products,
mainly Dept. 56; also David Winter,
Lilliput Lane, Swarovski, Lladro,
Precious Moments, Barbie, Disney
Classics, Harbour Lights, Radko, and
others; developer of Windows
software for collectors.*

Michael Belofsky
MSdataBase Solutions
Program: Collectibles Database for
Collectors
614 Warrenton Terrace NE
Leesburg, VA 22075-2465
phone: 800-407-4147 or 703-777-5660
fax: 703-777-5440
e-mail: msdbase@erols.com
Internet: http://www.collectorsoft.com
*Windows: How many items to you
own? How much have you spent? How
much insured for? What items do you
want? Includes on-line price guides
for Prec. Mom., Hallmark Orns.,
Swarovski, D56, Tender Touches,
Cher. Teddies, Disney Classics,
others.*

Cottages

Man./Prod./Dist.

Department 56, Inc.
Magazine: Quarterly
P.O. Box 44056
Eden Prairie, MN 55344-1056
phone: 800-548-8696
fax: 612-943-4500
Internet: http://www.department56.com
*Produces "Snow Village", "Dickens'
Village" and other lighted houses and
accessories.*

Cottages (David Winter)

Clubs/Associations

Ann Hamlet
Cottage Exchange, The
Newsletter: Cottage Times, The
45 The Avenue
Leighton Bromswold
Cambridgeshire PE18 0SH UK
phone: 01480-891304
fax: 01480-891895
e-mail: 100111.3240@compuserve.com
*The only U.K. club for David Winter
Collectors; all retired David Winter
pieces available; write for a price list
and any other details regarding your
favorite collectible.*

Enesco David Winter Cottages
  Collectors Guild
Magazine: Cottage Country
225 Windsor Dr.
Itasca, IL 60143
phone: 630-875-5300 or 800-436-3726
fax: 630-875-5359
*For David Winter Cottage collectors;
membership includes "Cottage
Country" magazine plus the "Squeek"
& "Studio News" newsletters,
members-only pieces, complimentary
gift from David Winter.*

Dealers

Paul Fruchey
1802 Lamar Lane
Napoleon, OH 43545
phone: 419-592-0024
*Specialists in retired David Winter
Cottages.*

Stan Worrey
Colonial House Antiques
182 Front St.
Berea, OH 44017
phone: 216-826-4169 or 800-344-9299
fax: 216-826-0839
Specializes in David Winter cottages.

Experts

Bette Page
Front Parlor, The
300 Cemetery Rd.
Oakland, IL 61943
phone: 217-346-3533 or 800-346-5996
fax: 217-346-3533
e-mail: frntprlr@advant.com
*Writes monthly column about David
Winter cottages for the "Collectors'
Bulletin."*

Cottages (Forma Vitrum)

Man./Prod./Dist.

Woody Smith
Forma Vitrum
Newsletter: Vitreville Voice
P.O. Box 517
Cornelius, NC 28031
phone: 704-896-9963 or 800-596-9963
fax: 704-892-5438
e-mail: formavit@aol.com
*Manufacturer of collectible lit glass
cottages handcrafted by artist Bill
Job.*

Cottages (Fraser Int'l.)

Man./Prod./Dist.

Fraser International
5990 N. Belt East, Unit 606
Humble, TX 77396
phone: 305-370-9204
fax: 305-370-9255
*Produces handcrafted miniature
cottages.*

Cottages (Hawthorne)

Man./Prod./Dist.

Hawthorne Architectural Register
9210 N. Maryland Ave.
Niles, IL 60714
phone: 708-966-0070 or 800-772-4277
A leading marketer of highly detailed architectural miniatures with an emphasis on sculptures inspired by traditional architecture.

Cottages (Hopkins Shop)

Man./Prod./Dist.

Hopkins Shop
Hwy. 52 S & Resinwood Drive
Moncks Corner, SC 29461
phone: 803-761-7626
fax: 803-761-7634
Create the Village Lights, a series of lighted English and turn-of-the-century American style cottages.

Cottages (Landmarks)

Man./Prod./Dist.

Landmarks Co.
4997 Bent Oak Dr.
Acworth, GA 30101
phone: 404-590-9621
Creates highly detailed, exact replicas of famous properties - stately mansions, plantation homes, magnificent churches and grand palaces in cold-cast porcelain.

Cottages (Lefton)

Clubs/Associations

Lefton Collectors' Service Bureau
P.O. Box 09178
Chicago, IL 60609-9970
phone: 800-938-1800 or 800-628-8492
fax: 312-254-4545
Serves as an information center and assists collectors in pursuit of "Colonial Village" buildings and accessories produced by the George Zoltan Lefton Co.; a company sponsored club.

Man./Prod./Dist.

George Zoltan Lefton Co.
P.O. Box 09178
Chicago, IL 60609-9970
phone: 800-938-1800 or 800-628-8492
fax: 312-254-4545
Manufacturer of "Colonial Village" buildings and accessories.

Cottages (Lemax)

Man./Prod./Dist.

Lemax, Inc.
25 Pequot Way
Canton, MA 02021-2354
phone: 800-665-3629 or 617-821-4555
fax: 617-821-4455
Produces the Lemax Dickensvale Collectible line of fine handcrafted

porcelain cathedrals, quaint cottages, and accessories.

Cottages (Pleasantville)

Clubs/Associations

Mary Lee Graham
Pleasantville 1893 Historical Preservation Society, c/o Flambro
Newsletter: Pleasantville Gazette
P.O. Box 93507
Atlanta, GA 30377-0507
phone: 800-355-2582 or 404-352-1381
fax: 404-352-2150
e-mail: collsoc@flambro.com
Internet: http://signaturecoll.com
Bisque porcelain village figurines by Joan Berg Victor; sponsored by Flambro, Inc; gazette, Pleasantville Gazette lighted building, lapel pin, and retailer listing.

Cottages (Windy Meadows)

Clubs/Associations

Jan Richardson
Windy Meadows Pottery Collector Club, c/o Windy Meadows Pottery
1036 Valley Rd.
Knoxville, MD 21758
phone: 301-834-8857 or 800-527-6274
fax: 301-663-0612
Specializes in the original hand-constructed stoneware Windy Meadows candlehouses & cottages designed by Jan Richardson. A company-sponsored club.

Crystal

Man./Prod./Dist.

Crystallite
963 Transport Way
Petaluma, CA 94954
phone: 800-999-9856 or 707-765-0500
fax: 707-765-0600
Distributes Austrian crystal figurines by Charles Castelli and cold-cast porcelain fantasy figurines by Mark Newman and Randy Bowen.

Crystal (Beadazzled)

Man./Prod./Dist.

Beadazzled Crystal, Inc.
P.O. Box 2638
Berkeley, CA 94702-0638
phone: 510-527-5796
Dedicated to bringing the customer state-of-the-art design, quality materials and classic crafting in all crystal figurine creations.

Crystal (Crystal Reflection)

Man./Prod./Dist.

Crystal Reflection
150 Park Lane
Brisbane, CA 94005-1312
phone: 415-468-2520
fax: 415-468-2554
A leader in the design and production

of 32% Austrian lead crystal collectibles.

Crystal (Crystal World)

Man./Prod./Dist.

Crystal World Co., The
3 Borinski Dr., Unit B
Lincoln Park, NJ 07035
phone: 201-633-0707 or 800-445-4251
fax: 201-633-0102
Offers Austrian crystal figurines, paperweights, bells & prisms.

Crystal (Iris Arc)

Clubs/Associations

Joelene Bowen
Iris Arc Crystal Collectors Society
Newsletter: Illuminations
114 East Haley St.
Santa Barbara, CA 93101-2347
phone: 805-963-3661 or 800-392-7546
fax: 805-965-2458
For collectors of Iris Arc full lead crystal collectibles including cottages, ornaments, figurines, miniatures, etc.

Man./Prod./Dist.

Joelene Bowen
Iris Arc Crystal
114 East Haley St.
Santa Barbara, CA 93101-2347
phone: 805-963-3661 or 800-392-7546
fax: 805-965-2458
Designs and manufactures full lead crystal collectibles including cottages, ornaments, figurines, miniatures, etc.

Crystal (Silver Deer)

Clubs/Associations

Silver Deer's Crystal Zoo Collectors' Club
Newsletter: Facets
P.O. Box 17250
Boulder, CO 80308
phone: 303-449-6771 or 800-729-3337
fax: 303-449-0653
A manufacturer-sponsored club offering members-only figurines, special club activities and promotions, and a quarterly newsletter with information about designers, product retirements and upcoming events.

Man./Prod./Dist.

Brian Danziger
Silver Deer, Ltd.
P.O. Box 17250
Boulder, CO 80308
phone: 303-449-6771 or 800-729-3337
fax: 303-449-0653
Designs, manufactures and distributes limited edition crystal figurines, cold-cast handcrafted and handpainted animal figurines, and other giftware.

Crystal (Swarovski)

Clubs/Associations

Swarovski Collectors Society, c/o Swarovski America, Ltd.
Newsletter: Swarovski Collector
2 Slater Rd.
Cranston, RI 02920
phone: 800-556-6478 or 800-426-3088
fax: 401-463-8459
Focuses on Austrian Swarovski crystal figurines and giftware. Sponsored by Swarovski America, Ltd.

Dealers

Robin Yaw
Crystal Connection, The
Newsletter: Crystal News
8510 N. Knoxville Ave., Ste. 218
Peoria, IL 61615-2034
phone: 309-692-2221
fax: 309-692-2221
e-mail:
crystalconnection@worldnet.att.net
Internet: http://www.crystal.org
A comprehensive listing service for collectors worldwide interested in buying, selling, trading retired Swarovski crystal on the secondary market; free listings, registration, search, courier delivery and appraisal services; member ISA.

Ben Swan
Golden Swan Collectibles
895 Lincoln Way
Auburn, CA 95603
phone: 916-823-7926 or 800-231-9055
fax: 916-823-1945
Offers a "search and find" and a listing service to collectors, buyers and sellers of Lladro figurines; also for Swarovski, Walt Disney Classics, and Disneyana Convention figurines.

Experts

Jane Warner, ISA
7613 W. Frederick-Garland Rd.
Englewood, OH 45322-9621
phone: 513-698-4508
fax: 513-698-4508
e-mail: wnsx06a@prodigy.com
Appraises and specializes in Swarovski crystal; author of "Warner's Blue Ribbon Book on Swarovski Silver Crystal."

Robin Yaw
Crystal Connection, The
8510 N. Knoxville Ave., Ste. 218
Peoria, IL 61615-2034
phone: 309-692-2221
fax: 309-692-2221
e-mail:
crystalconnection@worldnet.att.net
Internet: http://www.crystal.org
Buy, sell, trade appraises retired Swarovski crystal on the secondary market; free listings, registration, search, courier delivery and appraisal services; Accredited Member ISA, member BBB.

Jimer Devries
9740 Campo Road, Ste. 134
Spring Valley, CA 91977-1415
phone: 619-462-2333
fax: 619-462-5517
e-mail: jimer@swanseekers.com
Internet: http://www.swanseekers.com
A long-time Swarovski collector; knowledgeable about manufacturing variations and values of current and retired Swarovski Silver Crystal including items not available at retail in USA.

Man./Prod./Dist.

Swarovski America Ltd.
2 Slater Rd.
Cranston, RI 02920
phone: 800-556-6478 or 800-426-3088
fax: 401-463-8459

Matching Services

Jimer Devries
Swan Seekers Network
9740 Campo Road, Ste. 134
Spring Valley, CA 91977-1415
phone: 619-462-2333
fax: 619-462-5517
e-mail: jimer@swanseekers.com
Internet: http://www.swanseekers.com
Dedicated strictly to the Swarovski secondary market. Buy, sell, trade or information about retired and current Swarovski Silver Crystal for collectors in USA and 38 other countries.

Periodicals

Dean A. Genth
Newsletter: Crystal Report, The
1322 N. Barron St.
Eaton, OH 45320-1016
phone: 937-456-4151
fax: 937-456-7851
e-mail: dean@millershallmark.com
Internet: http://
www.millershallmark.com
The international forum for collectors of retired Swarovski silver crystal: histories, secondary market reports and prices, information on variations, collector questions and answers, classified ads.

Jimer Devries
Newsletter: Swan Seekers News
9740 Campo Road, Ste. 134
Spring Valley, CA 91977-1415
phone: 619-462-2333
fax: 619-462-5517
e-mail: jimer@swanseekers.com
Internet: http://www.swanseekers.com
Dedicated to the Swarovski secondary market; published three times per year; provides information about retired Swarovski crystal pieces: articles on connoisseurship, Q&A, collector profiles, sales, prices, wanted list.

Danbury Mint

Man./Prod./Dist.

Danbury Mint, The
47 Richards Ave.
Norwalk, CT 06857
phone: 203-853-2000 or 800-243-4664
A direct mail marketer of collector plates. Also produces miniatures, dolls, figurines and other collectibles.

Dept. 56

Clubs/Associations

Joe Ehrlich
Windy City 56ers
1078 Warren Ln.
Vernon Hills, IL 60061-3218
Organizer of Dept. 56 National Collector Clubs Convention.

Collectors

Sue Coffee
10 Saunders Hollow Rd.
Old Lyme, CT 06371-1126
phone: 860-434-5641
fax: 860-434-2653
e-mail: SueCoffee@aol.com
Buys and sells retired Dept. 56 snowbabies.

Dealers

Ken & Jamie Boucher
Northeast Collectors Exchange
145 W 5th St.
Bloomsburg, PA 17815-2119
phone: 800-231-6364 or 717-784-4377
A brokerage and listing service for retired collectibles; specializes in Dept. 56 Villages, Snowbabies and accessories.

Becky Carter
Becky Carter, Inc.
9605 Red Bird Lane
Alpharetta, GA 30202-7101
phone: 404-475-8138
Specializes in Department 56: all villages, accessories, ornaments, snowglobes; also offers a full-service collectibles exchange for Department 56 items.

Partridge Christmas Shop, The
105 Riverwalk
New Orleans, LA 70130
phone: 504-566-0149
Sells Heritage Village, Snow Village, Disney Parks Village.

Experts

Peter & Jeanne George
757 Park Ave.
Cranston, RI 02910-2137
phone: 401-467-9343
fax: 401-467-9359
e-mail: d56er@aol.com
Internet: http://
www.villagechronicle.com
Publishers of "The Village Chronicle."

Linda Harlan
303 Murfreesboro Rd.
Nashville, TN 37210-2834
phone: 800-388-2556 or 615-832-0564
fax: 615-244-1553
Collector specializing in Dept. 56 ceramic cottages and other Dept. 56 collectibles.

Man./Prod./Dist.

Department 56, Inc.
Magazine: Quarterly
P.O. Box 44056
Eden Prairie, MN 55344-1056
phone: 800-548-8696
fax: 612-943-4500
Internet: http://www.department56.com
Produces "Snow Village", "Dickens' Village" and other lighted houses and accessories.

Matching Services

Linda C. Ross
Best Collectibles
P.O. Box 152
Morganton, GA 30560-0152
phone: 706-838-5920
e-mail: bestcoll@mail.tds.net
A matching service for several types of contemporary collectibles: Byers' Choice, Dept. 56, Hallmark, Lefton, Walt Disney Classics and others.

Lynda W. Blakenship
Dickens' Exchange, Inc.
Magazine: Dickens' Exchange
5150 Highway 22, Ste. C-9
Metaire, LA 70471-2515
phone: 514-845-1954
fax: 514-845-1873
Offers an exchange service to match buyer and seller of Dept. 56 ceramic cottages.

Periodicals

Peter & Jeanne George
Magazine: Village Chronicle, The
757 Park Ave.
Cranston, RI 02910-2137
phone: 401-467-9343
fax: 401-467-9359
e-mail: d56er@aol.com
Internet: http://
www.villagechronicle.com
A bi-monthly publication created expressly for collectors of Department 56 Villages & Snowbabies; includes the latest news, tips, information, display ideas, and secondary market articles. "All the news that's LIT to print!".

Linda Harlan
Newsletter: Snowflake News
303 Murfreesboro Rd.
Nashville, TN 37210-2834
phone: 800-388-2556 or 615-832-0564
fax: 615-244-1553
A newsletter for Dept. 56 collectors: published bi-monthly, photos, club activities, upcoming activities, collector profiles.

Roger L. Bain
Newsletter: Village Press Newsletter, The
P.O. Box 556
Rockford, IL 61105-0556
phone: 815-965-0901 or 815-965-5656
e-mail: Dept56News@aol.com
Oldest publication for Department 56 collectors; news and views, exclusive investigative reports, brokerage and insurance services.

Lynda W. Blakenship
Dickens' Exchange, Inc.
Magazine: Dickens' Exchange
5150 Highway 22, Ste. C-9
Metaire, LA 70471-2515
phone: 514-845-1954
fax: 514-845-1873
A magazine for collectors of "Dept. 56" items: Dickens, Alpine, New England, Snow Village & Snowbabies; ads, articles, prices.

Palu & Mirta Burns
Newsletter: Vintages Classified
P.O. Box 34166
Granada Hills, CA 91344-9166
phone: 818-368-6765
fax: 818-360-6612
A monthly newsletter with buy and sell ads, articles, regional club news, photos of new releases.

Dolls

(see also DOLLS)

Auction Services

Nancy Farley
Auctions by Nancy
505 Trelawney Lane
Apex, NC 27502
phone: 919-362-7235
Conducts auction sales of collectible dolls.

Book Sellers

Scott Publications
30595 Eight Mile
Livonia, MI 48152-1761
phone: 800-458-8237 or 810-477-6650
fax: 810-477-6795
e-mail: 104137.1254@compuserve.com
Issues free catalog of books offering an array of information on ceramics, china painting, doll crafting, doll collecting, and miniatures.

Clubs/Associations

Jeanne Niswonger
Modern Doll Club
Journal: Modern Doll Club Journal
P.O. Box 338
Oakdale, CA 95361-0338
A corresponding club for doll collectors; members receive illustrated journal featuring research articles, doll stories, craft ideas for dolls, patterns, paper dolls, photos, etc.

Dealers

Laura Dorrer
Lavender n' Lace
110 West 25th St.
New York, NY 10001
phone: 212-924-5230 or 516-681-4124
Buys and sells one-of-a-kind artist dolls, limited editions dolls and antique dolls; also one-of-a-kind artist bears, and vintage and collectible bears.

Alisa Bernaresh
Alisa's Dolls
#3 Arapaho Ct.
Suffern, NY 10901
phone: 914-368-2509
Strictly a mail order business; Alisa is considered an expert in both contemporary and older dolls.

Sharon Greenfield
Sharon's Dolls
Rte. 1, Box 235-R
Martinsburg, WV 25401
phone: 304-267-4882
Specializes in original artist and limited edition dolls.

Doll Market, The
4215 Highpoint Rd.
Greensboro, NC 27407
phone: 910-632-4600 or 800-432-DOLL
fax: 910-632-4466
Carries limited edition and collector dolls from scores of artists.

Jean's Dolls
616 12th St.
West Columbia, SC 29169
phone: 803-791-7421 or 803-799-1382
Sells wide range of contemporary artists dolls.

Littlest Princess Doll Shoppe, The
6365 Spalding Dr.
Norcross, GA 30092
phone: 770-446-8909
fax: 770-446-7103
Disney, Gunzel, limited editions, Alexander, Zook, Barbie, Annalee, Gotz, Royal, Susan Wakeen.

Celia's & Susan's Dolls & Collectibles
800 East Hallandale Beach Blvd.
Hallandale, FL 33009
phone: 954-458-0661
fax: 954-458-5609
Barbie, Lee Middleton, Susan Wakeen, Effanbee, Connie Walser Derek, Robin Woods, Madame Alexander, Gotz, R. John Wright, Julie Good-Kruger, Georgetown, Turner, Gunzel, Wendy Lawton, Fayzah Spanos, Zook, Himstedt, Steiff, etc.

Beckett's Doll House
646 High Street
Columbus, OH 43085-4106
phone: 614-848-9636
Madame Alexander, Annette Himstedt, Barbie, Effanbee, Pfaltzgraff, Ginny.

Lots of Dolls
215 Garfield Ave.
Milford, OH 45150
phone: 513-248-2151 or 800-755-6402
Sells older and contemporary artists dolls; Barbies, Robin Wood, Ashton Drake, Annalees, Steiff, Alexanders, Wendy Lawton, Annette Himstedt, Hartman, etc.

Man./Prod./Dist.

Dollmakers Originals International, Inc.
1230 Pottstown Pike
Glenmoore, PA 19343
phone: 610-458-0277
fax: 610-458-7488
Manufactures, imports, and distributes some of the finest quality dolls in the industry.

C.V. Gambina, Inc.
2005 Gentilly Blvd.
New Orleans, LA 70119
phone: 504-947-0626
fax: 504-947-7542
Manufactures porcelain, rag and vinyl dolls designed by C.V. Gambina and Joel Eguigure.

Periodicals

Brian Savage
Fun Publications
Newspaper: Master Collector
12513 Birchfalls Dr.
Raleigh, NC 27614-9675
phone: 800-772-6673 or 919-847-5263
e-mail: bsavage@mastercollector.com
Internet: http://
www.mastercollector.com
Ads-only newspaper; dolls (antique and modern collectible), toys, banks, models, cars, Matchbox, monsters, puzzles, political, toy trains, etc.; subscribers receive free 30 word ad each month; published monthly; reaches 20,000.

Newsletter: Doll Collectors' Market Report
P.O. Box 128
Headland, AL 36345-0128
A bi-monthly market analysis report of surveyed prices for collectible & vinyl modern dolls.

Beth Schwartz, Ed.
House of White Birches
Magazine: Doll World
306 East Parr Rd.
Berne, IN 46711
phone: 219-589-8741 or 800-829-5865
fax: 219-589-8093
A bi-monthly magazine which covers many aspects of dolls and doll collecting: articles on doll history, patterns, interviews with doll artists, how-to articles, doll ID, etc.

Scott Publications
Magazine: Doll Crafter
30595 Eight Mile
Livonia, MI 48152-1761
phone: 800-458-8237 or 810-477-6650
fax: 810-477-6795
e-mail: 104137.1254@compuserve.com
Most complete magazine for creating and collecting beautiful dolls; filled with beautiful color photos of antique reproduction and modern dolls; informative articles by experts on how-to-make, collect, costume and sculpt dolls.

Scott Publications
Magazine: Contemporary Doll Collector
30595 Eight Mile
Livonia, MI 48152-1761
phone: 800-458-8237 or 810-477-6650
fax: 810-477-6795
e-mail: 104137.1254@compuserve.com
Award-winning magazine covers the vast doll market for doll lovers; how-to collect, where to buy, restoring your dolls and display ideas; published monthly; breathtaking color photos of dolls; large color pullout; original paper doll.

Scott Publications
Magazine: Ceramic Arts & Crafts
30595 Eight Mile
Livonia, MI 48152-1761
phone: 800-458-8237 or 810-477-6650
fax: 810-477-6795
e-mail: 104137.1254@compuserve.com
The "Bible" for the ceramic hobbyist since 1955; each monthly issue filled with projects and patterns, celebrity clips, new products, show listings, industry news, shoppers guides, book reviews, ads and classifieds.

Scott Publications
Magazine: Ceramics Magazine
30595 Eight Mile
Livonia, MI 48152-1761
phone: 800-458-8237 or 810-477-6650
fax: 810-477-6795
e-mail: 104137.1254@compuserve.com
Published monthly, informing contemporary ceramists with projects and profiles of trends and artists; special section issues feature articles on a specific trend, technique, or theme.

Jones Publishing, Inc.
Magazine: Dollmaking
P.O. Box 5000
Iola, WI 54945
phone: 715-445-5000
fax: 715-445-4053
e-mail: jonespub@gglbbs.com
A bi-monthly magazine of dollmaking projects and plans; beautifully and lavishly illustrated.

Jones Publishing, Inc.
Magazine: Doll Artisan
P.O. Box 5000
Iola, WI 54945
phone: 715-445-5000
fax: 715-445-4053
e-mail: jonespub@gglbbs.com
A bi-monthly publication of reproduction porcelain dollmaking, projects, and plans illustrated with photos of antique and reproduction dolls.

Dolls (Annette Himstedt)

Clubs/Associations

Annette Himstedt Collector Club
333 Continental Blvd., M1-0114
El Segundo, CA 90245
Original artist dolls by Annette Himstedt.

Dolls (Ashton-Drake)

Man./Prod./Dist.

Ashton-Drake Galleries, The
9200 Maryland Ave.
Niles, IL 60648-1397
phone: 847-581-8057
Direct mail marketer of dolls by various designers such as Yolando Bello, Dianna Effner, Cindy M. McClure, and Kathy Hippensteel.

Dolls (Attic Babies)

Clubs/Associations

Attic Babies Collectors Club
P.O. Box 912
Drumright, OK 74030
phone: 918-352-4414

Man./Prod./Dist.

Attic Babies
P.O. Box 912
Drumright, OK 74030
phone: 918-352-4414
Manufacturer of Attic Babies dolls.

Dolls (Bradley)

Clubs/Associations

Joanna Harstein
Bradley's Collectibles Doll Club
Newsletter: Bradley Doll Club Newsletter
1400 North Spring St.
Los Angeles, CA 90014
phone: 213-221-4162
fax: 213-221-8272
Focuses on the collectible dolls issued by Bradley Collectibles. A manufacturer-sponsored club.

Dolls (Daddy's Long Legs)

Clubs/Associations

Daddy's Long Legs Collector's Club
Newsletter: Daddy's Long Legs Newsletter
300 Bank St.
Southlake, TX 76092-9972
phone: 817-488-4644
A club sponsored by the manufacturer, KVC, Inc.

Man./Prod./Dist.

KVC, Inc.
300 Bank St.
Southlake, TX 76092-9972
phone: 817-488-4644
Produces Daddy's Long Legs dolls.

Dolls (Dynasty)

Man./Prod./Dist.

Stanley & Irene Wahlberg
Cardinal, Inc./Dynasty Doll Collection
P.O. Box 99
Port Reading, NJ 07064
phone: 908-636-6160
Imports the Dynasty Doll collection and Concord miniatures.

Dynasty Doll Collection
P.O. Box 99
Port Reading, NJ 07064
phone: 908-636-6160
Produces high quality porcelain dolls.

Dolls (Elke's Originals)

Man./Prod./Dist.

Elke's Originals, Ltd.
9525 SW 155th Ave.
Beaverton, OR 97007-5999
Specializes in the production of limited edition porcelain dolls by artist Elke Hutchens.

Dolls (Ellenbrooke)

Man./Prod./Dist.

Ellenbrooke Dolls, Inc.
1450 Marcy Loop
Grants Pass, OR 97527
Specializes in the production of limited edition dolls by artist Connie Wasler-Derek.

Dolls (Frederica Kasabasic)

Man./Prod./Dist.

Frederica Dolls of Fine Art
4501 West Highland Rd.
Milford, MI 48380
phone: 800-421-DOLL or 248-887-9575
fax: 248-887-9575
Produces dolls in the highest quality vinyl and porcelain.

Dolls (Georgetown Collection)

Man./Prod./Dist.

Georgetown Collection, Inc.
866 Spring St.
Westbrook, ME 04092
phone: 800-626-3330
fax: 207-775-6457
A direct mail marketer of heirloom quality collectibles, including porcelain dolls and figurines.

Dolls (Good-Kruger)

Man./Prod./Dist.

Good-Kruger Dolls
1842 William Pen Way, Ste. A
Lancaster, PA 17601
phone: 717-399-3602
fax: 717-399-3021
Manufactures dolls designed by Julie Good-Kruger.

Dolls (Jan Goodyear)

Man./Prod./Dist.

Doll Workshop, The
3560 Aurora Rd.
Melbourne, FL 32934
phone: 407-242-2678
Manufactures limited edition dolls by Jan Goodyear.

Dolls (Jerri)

Clubs/Associations

Jim McCloud
Jerri Collector's Society
Newsletter: Jerri Collector's Society
P.O. Box 561748
Charlotte, NC 28256
phone: 800-248-2188
Collectors are interested in dolls by Jerri. Sponsored by Dolls by Jerri.

Man./Prod./Dist.

Dolls by Jerri
P.O. Box 561748
Charlotte, NC 28256
phone: 800-248-2188
Produces limited edition imaginative all-porcelain dolls.

Dolls (Lee Middleton)

Clubs/Associations

Lee Middleton Collectors Club
Newsletter: Lee's Dolls Today
1301 Washington Blvd.
Belpre, OH 45714
phone: 614-423-1717
fax: 614-423-5983
For collectors of original porcelain and vinyl dolls designed by artist and sculptor, Lee Middleton.

Man./Prod./Dist.

Lee Middleton Original Dolls, Inc.
1301 Washington Blvd.
Belpre, OH 45714
phone: 614-423-1717
fax: 614-423-5983
The sole manufacturer and producer of original porcelain and vinyl dolls designed by artist and sculptor, Lee Middleton.

Dolls (Lenox)

Man./Prod./Dist.

Lenox Collections/Gorham
P.O. Box 519
Langhorne, PA 19047-0519
phone: 215-750-6900 or 800-225-1779
fax: 215-750-7362
Producers of the Lenox Collection/ Gorham line of collectible porcelain dolls.

Lexington Hall Ltd., c/o The Wimbledon Collection
P.O. Box 21948
Lexington, KY 40522-1948
phone: 606-277-8531 or 606-277-8532
fax: 606-277-9231
The Wimbledon Collection, more widely known as Lexington Hall Dolls, produces high-quality porcelain dolls.

Dolls (Lizzie High)

Clubs/Associations

Lizzie High Society
Newsletter: Lizzie High Notebook
220 North Main St.
Sellersville, PA 18960
phone: 215-453-8200 or 800-76D-OLLS
Wooden folk art dolls by husband and wife Peter Wisber and Barbara Kafka Wisber.

Man./Prod./Dist.

Ladie & Friends
220 North Main St.
Sellersville, PA 18960
phone: 215-453-8200 or 800-76D-OLLS
Producers of the Lizzie High doll collection.

Dolls (Lois Jeanne)

Man./Prod./Dist.

Lois Jeanne Dolls, Inc.
537 Shearer St.
North Wales, PA 19454
phone: 215-699-9298
Produces a limited edition line of pressed felt dolls.

Dolls (Madame Alexander)

Clubs/Associations

Tanya McWhorter, Pres.
Madame Alexander Doll Club
Newsletter: Review
P.O. Box 330
Mundeline, IL 60060
phone: 708-949-9200 or 512-241-3105
fax: 708-949-9201
Members receive the "Madame Alexander Shopper" which is devoted to buying and selling Madame Alexander dolls and accessories.

Collectors

Elaine DeVylder
2 Weed Circle
Stamford, CT 06902-4414

Leah Sargent
74 The Oaks
Roslyn, NY 11576
phone: 800-421-9912 or 516-621-7517

Experts

Barbara Jo McKeon
B.J. Dolls & Gifts
P.O. Box 1481-6
Brockton, MA 02403
phone: 508-586-1279
Buys and sell dolls and other limited edition collectibles; specializes in rare and hard-to-find Madame Alexander collector dolls.

Man./Prod./Dist.

Alexander Doll Company, Inc.
615 West 131 St.
New York, NY 10027
phone: 212-283-5900
Manufactures, produces and/or distributes Madame Alexander dolls.

Dolls (Marie Osmond)

Clubs/Associations

L.L. Knickerbocker
Marie Osmond International Collector Club
3005 Comercia
Rancho Santa Margarita, CA 92688
phone: 800-779-5335

Dolls (Naber)

Periodicals

Newsletter: Naber Kids News report
8915 S. Suncoast Blvd.
Homosassa, FL 34446
Monthly newsletter containing information for doll collectors and enthusiasts alike; focuses on Naber dolls.

Dolls (Phyllis Parkins)

Clubs/Associations

Phyllis Parkins
Phyllis' Collectors Club
Newsletter: PCC Newsletter
Rte. 4 Box 503
Rolla, MO 65401-9300
phone: 314-364-7849 or 800-874-7120
fax: 314-364-2448
Focuses on the Phyllis Parkins' collectible dolls, treetop angels, and a line of Victorian jewelry and frames. Sponsored by The Collectables, Inc.

Man./Prod./Dist.

Collectables, The
Rte. 4 Box 503
Rolla, MO 65401-9300
phone: 314-364-7849 or 800-874-7120
fax: 314-364-2448
Produces Phyllis Parkins' collectible dolls, treetop angels, and a line of Victorian jewelry and frames.

Dolls (Prestige)

Man./Prod./Dist.

Prestige Dolls
P.O. Box 1081
Gresham, OR 97030
phone: 503-667-1008
Produces limited edition happy-face dolls based on the designs of Caroline Kandt-Lloyd.

Dolls (Robin Holland)

Man./Prod./Dist.

Starshine Dolls
1724 Hull St.
Ft. Collins, CO 80526
phone: 303-225-1654
Manufactures limited edition Native American dolls in vinyl and porcelain designed by artist Robin Holland.

Dolls (Robin Woods)

Collectors

Elaine DeVylder
2 Weed Circle
Stamford, CT 06902-4414
Wants cloth or vinyl "Robin Woods" dolls; also Madame Alexander dolls.

Dolls (Seymour Mann)

Clubs/Associations

Seymour Mann Collectible Doll Club
230 Fifth Ave., Ste. 1500
New York, NY 10001
phone: 212-683-7262
For collectors of the Seymour Mann Signature Collection of collectible dolls.

Man./Prod./Dist.

Seymour Mann, Inc.
225 Fifth Ave., Rm. 102
New York, NY 10010
phone: 212-683-7262
Produces the Seymour Mann Signature Collection of collectible dolls, as well as a cat musical collection featuring cats in whimsical settings accompanied by popular tunes; also unique collectible teapots.

Dolls (Susan Wakeen)

Man./Prod./Dist.

Susan Wakeen Doll Company, Inc.
P.O. Box 1321
Litchfield, CT 06759-1321
Manufactures collectible vinyl and porcelain dolls designed by Susan Wakeen.

Dolls (Terri Lee)

Periodicals

Mt. Healthy Promotions
Newsletter: TL Love of a Lifetime
SR 110 Box 05432
Minster, OH 45865-9404
phone: 419-628-3405
A bi-monthly newsletter about the Terri Lee Family Dolls.

Dolls (Victoria Impex)

Man./Prod./Dist.

Victoria Impex Corporation
2250 Galaxy Ct., Ste. E
Concord, CA 94520-4926
Produce porcelain dolls, clowns and pierrots.

Dolls (Virginia Turner)

Man./Prod./Dist.

Turner Dolls, Inc.
P.O. Box 36
Heltonville, IN 47436
phone: 812-834-6692
Designs and distributes modern collectible dolls by artist Virginia Turner.

Dolls (Wendy Lawton)

Clubs/Associations

Lawton Collectors Guild
Newsletter: Lawton Collectors Guild Newsletter
P.O. Box 969
Turlock, CA 95381-0969
phone: 209-632-3655
fax: 209-632-6788
Original artist dolls by artist Wendy Lawton.

Man./Prod./Dist.

Lawton Doll Company
548 North First
Turlock, CA 95380-3804
phone: 209-632-3655
fax: 209-632-6788
Original artist dolls by artist Wendy Lawton.

Dolls (Wimbledon)

Man./Prod./Dist.

Wimbledon Collection
P.O. Box 21948
Lexington, KY 40522-1948
phone: 606-277-8531
fax: 606-277-9231

Dolls (Xavier Roberts)

(see DOLLS, Cabbage Patch Kids)

Dolls (Zook)

Man./Prod./Dist.

Debbie O'Neal
Johannes Zook Originals
1519 S. Badour Rd.
Midland, MI 48640
phone: 517-835-9388
Limited edition collectible vinyl dolls, 22" tall, which are sculpted after real children.

Donald Zolan

Collectors

Jo Hancock
Jo' Antiques & Collectibles
621 S. Main St.
Nashville, AR 71852-2707
Sells Donald Zolan items, also Lenox collectibles, Cybis figurines, Pickard, Royal Bonn, and Art Glass by Moser, Loetz, Webb, etc.

Duncan Royale

Clubs/Associations

Duncan Royale Collectors Club
Newsletter: Royale Courier
1141 South Acacia Ave.
Fulerton, CA 92631
phone: 714-879-1360
fax: 714-879-4611
Focuses on the collectible figurines, graphics and plates issued by Duncan Royale. Sponsored by Duncan Royale Co.

Man./Prod./Dist.

Duncan Royale Co.
1141 South Acacia Ave.
Fulerton, CA 92631
phone: 714-879-1360
fax: 714-879-4611
Produces collectible figurines, graphics, ornaments, and plates.

Eggs

Man./Prod./Dist.

eggspressions!
1635 Deadwood Ave.
Rapid City, SD 57702-0353
phone: 800-551-9138 or 605-342-4268
Manufacturer of decorated porcelain eggs containing jewels, cute bunnies, foliage or other decorations.

Figurines

Dealers

Robert Goins
Replacements Ltd.
P.O. Box 26029
Greensboro, NC 27420
phone: 800-737-5223 or 800-REP-LACE
fax: 910-697-3100
e-mail: replaceltd@aol.com
Internet: http://www.imall.com/stores/replacements
Carries post-1960 limited edition figurines in addition to china, crystal and flatware (obsolete, active and inactive.)

Stan Worrey
Colonial House Antiques
182 Front St.
Berea, OH 44017
phone: 216-826-4169 or 800-344-9299
fax: 216-826-0839
Specializes in old Royal Doultons, Hummels, David Winter & Lilliput Lane Cottages; mails catalogs three times a year.

Emily's Hallmark & Collectibles
14855 Clayton Rd.
Chesterfield, MO 63017
phone: 314-391-8755 or 800-726-0440
fax: 314-391-8755
Internet: http://www.collectibles.net/naled/emilys
Sell modern figurines: Precious Moments, Armani, Lladro, Walt Disney Classics and Enchanted Places, Harbour Lights, Swarovski, David Winter cottages, Dept. 56, Cherished Teddies, etc.

Man./Prod./Dist.

H & G Studios
5660 Corporate Way
West Palm Beach, FL 33407
phone: 561-615-9900 or 800-777-1333
fax: 561-615-8400
Produces collectible plates, figurines, dolls and graphics by leading artists; exclusive distributor of M.I. Hummel music boxes in North America.

Anne Cutter
Hadley Companies, The
11001 Hampshire Ave. South
Bloomington, MN 55438
phone: 612-943-8478
fax: 612-943-8098
Producer of hand-carved decoys and a major publisher of limited edition art including plates and prints.

David Grossman Creations, Inc.
1608 North Warson Rd.
Olivette, MO 63132
phone: 314-423-5600
fax: 314-423-7620
Creates and markets metal sculptures and other collectible art.

Donna Lamb
United Design Corp.
P.O. Box 1200
Noble, OK 73068-1200
phone: 800-727-4883 or 405-872-3468
fax: 405-360-4442
e-mail: dl4ude@aol.com
A producer of figurines by sculptors Donna Kennicutt, Suzan Bradford, Larry Miller, Ken Memoli and Penni Jo Jonas; publishes "PenniBear Post" newsletter twice a year and "The Legend of Santa Claus" newsletter once a year.

Periodicals

Cowles Magazines, Inc.
Magazine: Figurines & Collectibles
741 Miller Dr. SE, Ste. D2
Harrisburg, PA 20175
phone: 703-771-9400 or 800-829-3340
fax: 703-779-8345
Internet: http://www.thehistorynet.com
A vehicle for both the advertiser and the reader with a vehicle to sell and buy figurines; covers porcelain, resin, crystal, and pewter figurines - both new and old; secondary market information.

Figurines (Alaska Porcelain)

Clubs/Associations

Alaska Porcelain Collector's Society
Newsletter: Alaska Porcelain Review
P.O. Box 1550
Soldotna, AK 99669
phone: 907-262-5626
Focuses on figurines, dolls, bells, and Christmas ornaments manufactured by the Alaska Porcelain Studios, Inc.

Man./Prod./Dist.

Alaska Porcelain Studios, Inc.
P.O. Box 1550
Soldotna, AK 99669
phone: 907-262-5626
Manufactures, produces and/or distributes figurines, dolls, bells, and Christmas ornaments.

Figurines (All God's Children)

Clubs/Associations

Kathy Martin, Dir.
All God's Children Collector's Club
Magazine: All God's Children
  Collector's Edition
P.O. Box 5038
Gadsden, AL 35905-0038
phone: 205-492-0221
Focuses on All God's Children figurines; offers members personal checklist and the opportunity to purchase members-only figurines.

Man./Prod./Dist.

Miss Martha Originals, Inc.
P.O. Box 5038
Glencoe, AL 35905
phone: 205-492-0221
Manufacturer of nostalgic figurines cast from original sculptures by Martha Holocombe.

Figurines (Andrea by Sadek)

Collectors

A. Grisham
11101 Anderson, Ste. 203
Little Rock, AR 72212
phone: 501-868-1020

Figurines (Anri)

Clubs/Associations

Vicki Farris
ANRI Collectors Society
Newsletter: ANRI Collector Society
  Newsletter
P.O. Box 380760
Duncanville, TX 75138-0760
phone: 800-730-2674 or 972-283-8378
fax: 972-283-3522
e-mail: anriwood@aol.com
Internet: http://www.anri.com
Caters to collector; information on new products, exclusive figures for purchase, limited research on old pieces.

Collectors

Philly
1401 Brentwood Dr.
Harrison, AR 72601
phone: 501-743-2040
fax: 501-743-2120
Wants to buy handcarved wooden sculptures: corkstoppers, bar sets, cigarette boxes, book ends, cork-screws, openers, pourers, napkin rings, figurines, letter openers, spoons, forks, key and spoon racks, pipe racks, nutcrackers, etc.

Man./Prod./Dist.

Vicki Farris
ANRI U.S.
P.O. Box 380760
Duncanville, TX 75138-0760
phone: 800-730-2674 or 972-283-8378
fax: 972-283-3522
e-mail: anriwood@aol.com
Internet: http://www.anri.com
Import and distribution of high-end collectible ANRI wooden hand carved maple figurines; emphasis on Nativity sets and religious items, also animals, children, and chess sets.

Figurines (Armani)

Clubs/Associations

Giuseppe Armani Society
Magazine: Giuseppe Armani Review
300 Mac Lane
Keasbey, NJ 08832
phone: 908-417-0330 or 800-327-6264
fax: 908-417-0031
For fans and collectors of the cold cast porcelain figurines of master sculptor Giuseppe Armani.

Dealers

A.D. & Pat Clay
Clemons-Eicken Fine European Imports
6166 N. Scottsdale Rd., #204
Paradise Valley, AZ 85253
phone: 602-998-9042 or 800-250-5423
fax: 602-998-3755
Carries Lladro, Armani, Boehm, Lalique, Cybis.

Experts

Sid Perkins
Roberta's Place
4972 North Pine Rd.
Fort Lauderdale, FL 33351

Herb Miller
Miller Import Co.
14027 Memorial Dr.
Houston, TX 77079

Figurines (Bridal)

Man./Prod./Dist.

Today's Creations, Inc.
167 Main St.
Lodi, NJ 07644
phone: 800-5TO-DAYS
Manufacturer of hand-painted 8" high bridal figurines.

Figurines (Bunny Toes)

Man./Prod./Dist.

Pacific Rim Import Corp.
5930 Fourth Ave. S.
Seattle, WA 98108
phone: 800-425-5932
fax: 206-767-9179
Manufacturers of resin molded "Bunny Toes" figurines.

Figurines (Byers)

Clubs/Associations

Caroler Chronicle, The
P.O. Box 158
Chalfont, PA 18914
phone: 215-822-6700
fax: 215-822-3847
For collectors of Byers caroling figurines.

Dealers

Linda's Originals & The Yankee
  Craftsmen
230 Rt. 6A
Brewster, MA 02631
phone: 800-385-4758
Buy and sell new and old Byers Choice Carolers dolls.

Man./Prod./Dist.

Byers' Choice Ltd.
P.O. Box 158
Chalfont, PA 18914
phone: 215-822-6700
fax: 215-822-3847
Manufacturer of caroling figurines reminiscent of the 19th century.

Matching Services

Linda C. Ross
Best Collectibles
P.O. Box 152
Morganton, GA 30560-0152
phone: 706-838-5920
e-mail: bestcoll@mail.tds.net
A matching service for several types of contemporary collectibles: Byers'

Choice, Dept. 56, Hallmark, Lefton, Walt Disney Classics and others.

Museums/Libraries

Byers' Choice Museum
Wayside Country Store
1015 Boston Post Rd.
Marlboro, MA 01752
phone: 508-481-3458

Figurines (Cairn)

Clubs/Associations

Cairn Collector Society, The
Newsletter: Cairn Collector Society
  Newsletter
P.O. Box 400
Davidson, NC 28036
phone: 704-892-5859
Internet: http://www.cairnstudio.com
Focuses on collectible figurines such as Dr. Tom Clark's Gnomes issued by Cairn Studio Ltd. Sponsored by Cairn Studio, Ltd.

Man./Prod./Dist.

Cairn Studio Ltd.
P.O. Box 400
Davidson, NC 28036
phone: 704-892-5859
Internet: http://www.cairnstudio.com
Manufactures gnomes and other character figurines by artist Dr. Tom Clark.

Museums/Libraries

Tom Clark Museum
P.O. Box 400
Davidson, NC 28036
phone: 704-892-5859
Internet: http://www.cairnstudio.com
Large collection of sculptures by noted artist, Dr. Tom Clark.

Figurines (Carousels by PJ)

Clubs/Associations

Jim Hennon
PJ's Carousel Collectors Club
Newsletter: PJ's Carousel Collectors
  Club Newsletter
P.O. Box 355
Newbern, VA 24126
phone: 703-674-4300
fax: 703-674-2356
Focuses on the miniature replica carousel animals from the turn of the century. Sponsored by PJ's, Inc.

Figurines (Carousels)

Dealers

Melody in Motion by Waco Products
  Corp.
P.O. Box 898]
Pine Brook, NJ 07058-0898
phone: 201-882-1820
Buys and sells retired Waco carousel figurines: Santas, Clowns, Madames, Willies.

Man./Prod./Dist.

Cape Collectibles
210 Old Dairy Rd., #A
Wilmington, NC 28405-3770
phone: 800-262-5447 or 910-452-7544
fax: 910-452-7721
Produces the Original Bedford Falls Village buildings and accessories; also the first copyrighted carousel horse collection in the world.

Suppliers

Simone Gagne
Miniature Carousel Components
8 N. Munroe Terrace
Boston, MA 02122-2508
phone: 617-265-2243
Sells miniature carousel components such as roped solid brass rods with ball finials, complete drive mechanisms; send LSASE for free information and brochure.

Figurines (Cherished Teddies)

Clubs/Associations

Enesco Cherished Teddies Collectors Club
P.O. Box 99
Itasca, IL 60143-0099
phone: 630-875-5300 or 800-436-3726
fax: 630-875-5359
For collectors of Cherished Teddies resin figurines.

Figurines (Clay Art)

Man./Prod./Dist.

Clay Art
239 Utah Ave.
South San Francisco, CA 94080
phone: 415-244-4970 or 800-252-9555
fax: 415-244-4979
Specializes in collectible giftware and tabletop accessories; handcrafted ceramic masks, salt & peppers, cookie jars, creamers & sugars, mugs, plates, and more designed with a unique and whimsical nature.

Figurines (Constance Guerra)

Man./Prod./Dist.

Constance Collection Collectors Club, The
Rte. 1 Box 538
P.O. Box 250
Midland, VA 22728
phone: 703-788-4500
fax: 703-788-4100
Produces figurines, ornaments and miniatures from crushed pecan wood resin designed by Constance Angela Guerra.

Figurines (Disney)

Clubs/Associations

Walt Disney Collectors Society, The
Magazine: Sketches
500 South Buena Vista St.
Burbank, CA 91521-8028
phone: 818-567-5500 or 800-932-5749
For Disney collectors around the world; members get free animation sculpture, quarterly magazine, opportunity to buy "member only" figurines, and advance notice of new releases.

Dealers

Ben Swan
Golden Swan Collectibles
895 Lincoln Way
Auburn, CA 95603
phone: 916-823-7926 or 800-231-9055
fax: 916-823-1945
Offers a "search and find" and a listing service to collectors, buyers and sellers of Lladro figurines; also for Swarovski, Walt Disney Classics, and Disneyana Convention figurines.

Figurines (Dreamsicles)

Clubs/Associations

James Farrell
Dreamsicles Collectors' Club
Newsletter: ClubHouse
1120 California Ave.
Corona, CA 91719-3324
phone: 800-437-5818 or 909-371-3025
fax: 909-371-0674
A company-sponsored club for collectors of Dreamsicles collectible cherubs and animals; also sells Bumpkins and Ivy & Innocence figurines.

Man./Prod./Dist.

Cast Art Industries, Inc.
1120 California Ave.
Corona, CA 91719-3324
phone: 800-437-5818 or 909-371-3025
fax: 909-371-0674

Figurines (Emmett Kelly, Jr.)

(see also CLOWN COLLECTIBLES)

Clubs/Associations

Mary Lee Graham
Emmett Kelly, Jr. Collectors' Society, c/o Flambro
Journal: EK Journal
P.O. Box 93507
Atlanta, GA 30377-0507
phone: 800-355-2582 or 404-352-1381
fax: 404-352-2150
e-mail: collsoc@flambro.com
Internet: http://signaturecoll.com
Focuses on the Emmett Kelly, Jr. clown figurines. Sponsored by Flambro Imports, Inc.; journal, binder, pin, "members only" plaque; enrollment includes member's plaque,
newsletter, lapel pin, registry, member's-only redemption coupon.

Emmett's Friends, c/o Frankenmuth Gallery
568 South Main St.
Frankenmuth, MI 48734
Focuses on the clown figurines issued by Flambro Imports, Inc.

Collectors

N.W. Neill, Jr.
P.O. Box 38
Ennice, NC 28623-0038
phone: 910-657-8152
fax: 910-657-8084
Wants anything related to Emmett Kelly, Jr. or Emmett Kelly, Sr.: advertising, postcards, Flambro pieces, dolls, etc.

Dealers

Happy Clown, The
911 W. 7th St.
Frederick, MD 21701
phone: 301-695-8874
Specializes in the sale of Tom Clark Gnomes, Emmett Kelly Junior Clowns, Memories of Yesterday, Precious Moments, and Hummels.

Periodicals

Shane Rhyne
Cumberland Communications
Magazine: Collections
P.O. Box 333
Tazewell, TN 37879
phone: 615-626-8250
fax: 615-626-8253
A quarterly collectibles magazine containing the "Emmett Kelly, Jr. Collectors Edition" supplement/value guide.

Figurines (Enchanted Kingdom)

Clubs/Associations

Enchanted Kingdom Collector's Club
Newsletter: Enchanted Times
347 W. Sierra Madre Blvd.
Sierra Madre, CA 91024
phone: 818-355-1813
fax: 818-355-1982
e-mail: vcarolina@Charleston.net
For fantasy and castle enthusiasts.

Figurines (Fontanini)

Clubs/Associations

Fontanini Collectors' Club
Newsletter: Fontanini Collector
555 Lawrence Ave.
Rosell, IL 60172-1599
phone: 708-529-3000 or 800-729-7662
fax: 708-529-1121
For collectors of Fontanini nativity sets and plates; sponsored by Roman, Inc.

Man./Prod./Dist.

Roman, Inc.
555 Lawrence Ave.
Rosell, IL 60172-1599
phone: 708-529-3000 or 800-729-7662
fax: 708-529-1121
Produces figurines, plates, lithographs, bells, dolls, music boxes, etc. Exclusive importer of Fontanini nativity sets and plates.

Figurines (Gail Laura)

Man./Prod./Dist.

Gail Laura Collectables, Inc.
105 Mimosa Rd.
Bristol, TN 37620-4526
phone: 615-968-7713
Produces figurines based on the designs of artist Gail Laura.

Figurines (Goebel)

Clubs/Associations

Goebel Networkers
P.O. Box 396
Lemoyne, PA 17043

Dealers

Lois & Ralph Behm
Lois' Collectibles of Antique Market III
413 W. Main St.
Saint Charles, IL 60174-1815
phone: 630-377-5599 or 847-831-5997
Buys and sells Goebel figurines (no Hummels); will buy entire collections.

Experts

Matthew L. Szynkiewicz
Gobel King, The
1725 Pine Ridge Way E #F
Palm Harbor, FL 34684-2113
phone: 813-784-8719 or 813-535-2022
fax: 813-536-9707
Largest Goebel collection in nation; buys, sells, trades nationwide; 20 years collecting and accumulating information for future, comprehensive book; would like chance to purchase or photograph unusual items for book.

Man./Prod./Dist.

Customer Service
Goebel United States
P.O. Box 10
Pennington, NJ 08534-0010
phone: 609-737-8700 or 800-366-4632
fax: 609-737-8685
Distributors of Goebel and other figurines.

Figurines (Goebel-Miniatures)

Clubs/Associations

Jacci Bednar
Club Olszewski, Inc.
Newsletter: Small Talk
P.O. Box 29067
Parma, OH 44129-0067
fax: 216-433-7071
A fan club for Robert Olszewski with

the primary purpose of sharing personal information on this talented artist & his miniatures.

Experts

Dick Hunt
Hunt's Collectibles
595 Jackson Ave.
Satellite Beach, FL 32937-2929
phone: 407-777-1313
fax: 407-777-1362
e-mail: huntcoll@aol.com
Internet: http://www.miniature.com
Specializes in buying and selling Goebel Miniatures by Robert Olszewski; also author of "The Goebel Miniatures of Robert Olszewski."

Man./Prod./Dist.

Goebel Miniatures
P.O. Box 10
Pennington, NJ 08534-0010
phone: 609-737-8700 or 800-366-4632
fax: 609-737-8685
Produces fine handpainted limited edition Goebel miniature figurines.

Figurines (Great American)

Clubs/Associations

Great American Collector's Guild
Newsletter: Big Bear Tracks
P.O. Box 428
Aberdeen, NC 28315
phone: 910-944-7447
Wood carving reproductions of Old World Santas, teddy bears, and houses; made of resin.

Figurines (Janco Studio)

Man./Prod./Dist.

Bert Anderson
Janco Studio
P.O. Box 30012
Lincoln, NE 68503
phone: 402-435-1430 or 800-490-1430
Produce very detailed figurines and Christmas ornaments.

Figurines (June McKenna)

Dealers

Brenda Higgins
Handmaiden, The
P.O. Box 392
Fiskdale, MA 01518
phone: 508-347-7757
Specializes in buying and selling works by artist June McKenna.

Man./Prod./Dist.

June McKenna Collectibles, Inc.
P.O. Box 1540
Ashland, VA 23005
phone: 804-798-2024
Designs, manufactures and distributes three dimensional highly detailed limited edition figurines including Black Folk Art Figurines and

Christmas/Santa Figurines designed by June McKenna.

Figurines (Krystonia)

Clubs/Associations

Krystonia Collectors Club
Newsletter: Phargol Horn
125 W. Ellsworth Rd.
Ann Arbor, MI 48108-2203
phone: 313-663-1885 or 313-663-1989
fax: 313-663-2343
Focuses on the collectible Krystonia dragons, wizards, and storybooks. Sponsored by Precious Art/Panton, Inc.; "members' only" pieces available.

Man./Prod./Dist.

Precious Art/Panton Inter.
125 W. Ellsworth Rd.
Ann Arbor, MI 48108-2203
phone: 313-663-1885 or 313-663-1989
fax: 313-663-2343
Manufacturer of make-believe collectible Krystonia dragons, wizards, and storybooks.

Figurines (Lighthouses)

Clubs/Associations

Harbour Lights Collectors' Society
8130 La Mesa Blvd.
La Mesa, CA 91941
phone: 800-365-1219 or 619-579-1820
fax: 619-579-1911
For collectors of Harbour Lights Hydrostone lighthouses.

Man./Prod./Dist.

Cheryl Spencer Collin Studio
24 River Rd.
Eliot, ME 03903
phone: 207-439-6016
fax: 207-439-5787
Produces exquisite lighthouse recreations of incredible detail.

Harbour Lights
8130 La Mesa Blvd.
La Mesa, CA 91941
phone: 800-365-1219 or 619-579-1820
fax: 619-579-1911
Manufacturer of Hydrostone lighthouses.

Figurines (Lilliput Lane)

Clubs/Associations

Enesco Lilliput Lane Collectors' Club
225 Windsor Dr.
Itasca, IL 60143
phone: 630-875-5300 or 800-436-3726
fax: 630-875-5359
For collectors of Lilliput Lane miniature cottages.

Experts

Annette Power
9 Church St.
London NW8 8DEE, U.K.
phone: 0171-7064586
fax: 0171-7062948
e-mail: collector@globalnet.co.uk
Author of "The Collector's Handbook of Lilliput Lane Cottages."

Man./Prod./Dist.

ENESCO Corp.
225 Windsor Dr.
Itasca, IL 60143
phone: 630-875-5300 or 800-436-3726
fax: 630-875-5359

Figurines (Little Cheesers)

Clubs/Associations

Little Cheesers Collectors' Club
Newsletter: Cheeserville Gazette, The
908 Niagara Falls Blvd.
North Tonawanda, NY 14120-2016
phone: 800-724-5902
fax: 416-851-6669
For collectors of the endearing mice line of figurines known as Little Cheesers. A GANZ Co. sponsored club.

Man./Prod./Dist.

GANZ Co.
908 Niagara Falls Blvd.
North Tonawanda, NY 14120-2016
phone: 800-724-5902
fax: 416-851-6669
Manufacturer of the line of mice figurines knows as Little Cheesers.

Figurines (Margaret Furlong)

Man./Prod./Dist.

Margaret Furlong Designs
210 State St.
Salem, OR 97301-3444
phone: 503-363-6004
fax: 503-371-0676
Produces white-on-white porcelain angels, shell stars, hearts, snowflakes, wreaths, picture frames, and miniature chairs.

Figurines (Maruri)

Man./Prod./Dist.

Maruri USA
7541 Woodman Place
Van Nuys, CA 91405-1545
phone: 818-780-0704 or 800-562-7874
fax: 818-780-9871
Producer and distributor of high quality porcelain plates and figurines.

Figurines (Maud Humphrey)

Clubs/Associations

Barbara Schrage
Maud Humphrey Bogart Collectors' Club
Newsletter: Victorian Times
225 Windsor Dr.
Itasca, IL 60143
phone: 630-875-5300 or 800-436-3726
fax: 630-875-5359
Members receive symbol of membership figurine, quarterly newsletter, membership card, members' only offering, collection registry, catalog.

Figurines (Memories Of Yesdy')

Clubs/Associations

Enesco Memories of Yesterday Collectors' Society
Newsletter: Sharing Memories...
225 Windsor Dr.
Itasca, IL 60143
phone: 630-875-5300 or 800-436-3726
fax: 630-875-5359
Members receive symbol of membership figurine, club newsletter, membership card, members' only offering, club binder.

Experts

Debbie & Allen Eulert
Eulert Enterprises
2814 Spring Dr.
Vandalia, IL 62471-3811
phone: 618-283-9151
Writes "Allen's Views of Memories of Yesterday" column for "Collectors' Bulletin."

Periodicals

Laryl Berry, Pub.
Berry Enterprises, Inc.
Newsletter: MOY Connection, The
3906 W. Ina Rd. #200-227
Tucson, AZ 85741-2295
phone: 602-744-1456
fax: 602-744-8989
For collectors of Memories of Yesterday figurines and other collectibles designed by Mabel Lucie Attwell; articles and classified listings for secondary market buying and selling.

Figurines (Michael Garman)

Man./Prod./Dist.

Michael Garman Productions, Inc.
2418 West Colorado Ave.
Colorado Springs, CO 80904
phone: 800-874-7144 or 719-471-1600
Internet: http://www.chest.com/garman/index.html
Manufactures three-dimensional sculptures of people who have shaped America: cowboys, aviators, soldiers, policemen, wino, heroes, etc.

Figurines (Myth & Magic)

Clubs/Associations

Myth & Magic Collectors Club
Newsletter: Methtintdour Times
P.O. Box 431729
Houston, TX 77243-1729
phone: 713-462-0076
*For collectors of Olde English pewter
figurines, each of which incorporates
a piece of Swarovski Crystal.*

Man./Prod./Dist.

Fantasy Creations
P.O. Box 431729
Houston, TX 77243-1729
phone: 713-462-0076
*For collectors of Myth & Magic
pewter figurines, each of which
incorporates a piece of Swarovski
Crystal.*

Figurines (Patchville)

Man./Prod./Dist.

MCK Gifts, Inc.
P.O. Box 621848
Littleton, CO 80162-1848
phone: 303-979-1715
fax: 303-979-6838
*Produces the world of Patchville -
individually cast and delicately
handpainted whimsical, lop-eared
bunnie figurines.*

Figurines (PenDelfin)

Clubs/Associations

PenDelfin Family Circle
Newsletter: PenDelfin Times, The
Atlanta Gift Mart
230 Spring St. MW, Ste. 1238
Atlanta, GA 30303-1063
phone: 800-263-4491 or 404-523-3380
*For collectors of PenDelfin miniature
stoneware handpainted Rabbit Family
members backdrop cottages, shops
and landmarks.*

Man./Prod./Dist.

PenDelfin Sales Inc.
Atlanta Gift Mart
230 Spring St. MW, Ste. 1238
Atlanta, GA 30303-1063
phone: 800-263-4491 or 404-523-3380
*Manufacturer of PenDelfin miniature
stoneware handpainted Rabbit Family
members backdrop cottages, shops
and landmarks.*

Figurines (Pocket Dragons)

Clubs/Associations

Pocket Dragons & Friends Collectors
Club, c/o Flambro
Newsletter: Pocket Dragon Gazette
P.O. Box 93507
Atlanta, GA 30377-0507
phone: 800-355-2582 or 404-352-1381
fax: 404-352-2150
e-mail: collsoc@flambro.com
Internet: http://signaturecoll.com
*Members get Membership card,
newsletter, lapel pin, exclusive
members-only figurines, club-
sponsored events.*

Figurines (Red Mill)

Clubs/Associations

Karen S. McClung
Red Mill Collectors Society
Newsletter: RMCS Newsletter
One Hunters Ridge
Summersville, WV 26651-1774
phone: 304-872-5237
fax: 304-872-5234
*A manufacturer-sponsored club for
collectors of Red Mill figurines made
from crushed pecan shells.*

Man./Prod./Dist.

Karen S. McClung
Red Mill Mfg., Inc.
1023 Arbuckle Rd.
Summersville, WV 26651-1747
phone: 304-872-5231
fax: 304-872-5234
*Manufactures Red Mill figurines made
from crushed pecan shells.*

Figurines (Ron Lee)

Man./Prod./Dist.

Ron Lee's World of Clowns
330 Carousel Parkway
Henderson, NV 89014
phone: 800-829-3928 or 702=434-1700
fax: 702-434-4310

Figurines (Sarah Schultz)

Clubs/Associations

Forever Friends Collectors Club
Magazine: From the Heart
126 1/2 W. Broad
P.O. Box 448
Chesaning, MI 48616
phone: 517-845-3990 or 800-437-4363
fax: 517-845-3477

Man./Prod./Dist.

Sarah's Attic
126 1/2 W. Broad
P.O. Box 448
Chesaning, MI 48616
phone: 517-845-3990 or 800-437-4363
fax: 517-845-3477
*Manufactures collectible figurines
designed by Sarah Schultz; "From the
Heart" magazine is published twice a
year; also publishes "The Forever
Friends Club Newsletter" quarterly.*

Figurines (Sebastian)

Clubs/Associations

Cyndi McNally
Sebastian Miniatures Collectors Society,
c/o The Lance Corp.
Newsletter: Sebastian Miniatures
Collectors Society News
321 Central St.
Hudson, MA 01749
phone: 508-568-1401
fax: 508-568-8741
*Focuses on the Sebastian collectible
figurines. Sponsored by the Lance
Corp.; members receive free
miniature, annual value guide; also
distributes the "Sebastian Exchange
Quarterly" newsletter for secondary
market information.*

Dealers

Jim Waite
Blossom Shop Collectibles
112 No. Main
Farmer City, IL 61842-1424
phone: 309-928-3222 or 800-842-2593
*Buys and sells old and new Sebastian
miniatures by P.W. and "Woody"
Baston, private issues, commercial &
Marblehead, MA.; sponsors Midwest
Sebastian fair which includes an
auction of hard-to-find pieces.*

Museums/Libraries

Official Sebastian Miniatures Museum,
The
Stacy's Gifts & Collectibles
The Mall at Walpole
East Walpole, MA 02032
phone: 508-688-4212

Periodicals

Paul J. Sebastian
Price Guide: Sebastian Exchange
2072 Pine Dr.
Lancaster, PA 17601
phone: 717-394-3874
*Issues three newsletters each year
covering the secondary market; also
publishes annual Sebastian "Value
Register Handbook."*

Figurines (Second Nature)

Man./Prod./Dist.

Second Nature Design
110 S. Southgate Dr., #C-4
Chandler, AZ 85226
phone: 602-961-3963 or 800-939-3963
fax: 602-961-4178
*Creates affordable wildlife collectible
figurines.*

Figurines (Shade Tree)

Clubs/Associations

Rick Warner
Shade Tree Cowboy Collector Society
Newsletter: Cowboy Times
6210 NW 124th Place
Gainesville, FL 32606-1071
phone: 800-327-6923
fax: 904-462-1799
e-mail: BVernon@afn.com
*For collectors of Bill Vernon's
humorous cowboy figurines; wildlife
images which seem to "evolve" from
twisted pieces of driftwood.*

Man./Prod./Dist.

Rick Warner
Shade Tree Creations
6210 NW 124th Place
Gainesville, FL 32606-1071
phone: 800-327-6923
fax: 904-462-1799
e-mail: BVernon@afn.com
*Creators of sculptures designed by
artists including Bill Vernon: dragons,
Road kill, Shade Tree Cowboys,
Treeples, Mini Nuts, The Series of
Evolution.*

Figurines (Silver Deer)

Clubs/Associations

Silver Deer's Ark Collectors' Club
Newsletter: Peaceable Kingdom, The
P.O. Box 17250
Boulder, CO 80308
phone: 303-449-6771 or 800-729-3337
fax: 303-449-0653
*A manufacturer-sponsored club for
collectors of cold-cast figurines;
special club activities/promotions,
members-only figurines, and a
quarterly newsletter with information
about designers, product retirements
and upcoming events.*

Man./Prod./Dist.

Brian Danziger
Silver Deer, Ltd.
P.O. Box 17250
Boulder, CO 80308
phone: 303-449-6771 or 800-729-3337
fax: 303-449-0653
*Designs, manufactures and distributes
limited edition crystal figurines, cold-
cast handcrafted and handpainted
animal figurines, and other giftware.*

Figurines (VickiLane)

Clubs/Associations

VickiLane Collectors Club
3233 NE Cadet Ave.
Portland, OR 97220
phone: 800-456-4259
fax: 503-747-1957
*Focuses on collectible figurines
designed by Vicki Anderson and
others at VivkiLane.*

Figurines (Wee Forest Folk)

Clubs/Associations

Betty Jo Royster, Pres.
Wee Forest Folk Collector's Club
Newsletter: Folktales
511 Clayton Rd.
Durham, NC 27703
phone: 919-596-6456
Club provides information about Wee Forest Folk figurines, past and present; helps locate figurines from 1978 to present.

Collectors

Jeanne Fredericks
12364 Downey Ave.
Downey, CA 90242-3556
phone: 562-861-4781
Collector wants older, retired Wee Forest Folk figurines created by the Peterson family.

Dealers

Creative Hands
342 R.P. Coffin Rd.
Long Grove, IL 60047
phone: 708-634-0545 or 708-459-1922
Specializes in the endearing miniature figurines sculpted by Annette Peterson of Wee Forest Folk.

Periodicals

Kathy Ethington
Newsletter: California Critters
1082 N. Oak Canyon Way
Brea, CA 92621
phone: 714-671-2954
A bi-monthly publication for Wee Forest Folk collectors.

Figurines (Wizards & Dragons)

Clubs/Associations

Mary Lee Graham
Wizards & Dragons Collectors Club, c/o Flambro
Newsletter: Land of Legend
P.O. Box 93507
Atlanta, GA 30377-0507
phone: 800-355-2582 or 404-352-1381
fax: 404-352-2150
e-mail: collsoc@flambro.com
Internet: http://signaturecoll.com
Figurines of amazingly detailed dragons and wizards with splendid coloring and stones; designed by international artist Hap Henriskson.

Flowers (Capodimonte)

Man./Prod./Dist.

Napoleon
P.O. Box 860
Oaks, PA 19456-0860
phone: 610-666-1650
fax: 610-666-1379
Produces capodimonte flowers with the crown/"N" mark.

Folk Art

Man./Prod./Dist.

Vaillancourt Folk Art
145 Armsby Rd.
Sutton, MA 01590
phone: 508-865-9183
fax: 508-865-4140
Creates limited edition chalkware replicas cast from antique chocolate molds and ice cream forms.

Franklin Mint

Clubs/Associations

Franklin Mint Collectors Society
Newsletter: Franklin Mint Almanac, The
Franklin Center
Franklin Center, PA 19091-0001
phone: 800-523-7622 or 610-459-6480
fax: 610-459-6880
Focuses on the quality jewelry, crystal, collectibles, and sculpture issued by The Franklin Mint which sponsors the Society.

Collectors

Jim Crane
15 Clemson Ct.
Newark, DE 19711-4301
phone: 302-738-6031
Wants Franklin Mint items, books and ads.

Dealers

AAACRC
P.O. Box 8061
Saddle Brook, NJ 07662-8061
Wants silver coins, complete sets or single piece from Franklin Mint or any other mint.

Man./Prod./Dist.

Customer Service
Franklin Mint, The
Franklin Center
Franklin Center, PA 19091-0001
phone: 800-523-7622 or 610-459-6480
fax: 610-459-6880
Designs, manufactures and markets collectibles including jewelry, sculpture, dolls, figurines, bells, ornaments, arms replicas, etc.

Gregory Perillo

Clubs/Associations

Liz Morsi, Dir.
Artaffects Perillo Collectors Club
Newsletter: Drumbeats
P.O. Box 40
Staten Island, NY 10307
phone: 718-948-6767
fax: 718-967-4521
Focuses on the Native American collectibles designed by Gregory Perillo. Sponsored by ArtAffects, Inc.

Holly Hobbie

Clubs/Associations

Helen McCale
Holly Hobbie Collectibles of America
Newsletter: Holly Hobbie Collectibles of America Newsletter
P.O. Box 397
Butler, MO 64730
phone: 816-679-3690
Formed for the preservation and appreciation of Holly Hobbie memorabilia; the bi-monthly newsletter has articles, information, buy/sell/trade ads; holds annual convention for Holly Hobbie collectors; send SASE to join.

Collectors

Mary Winfrey
3202 Kilgrennan Ct.
Herndon, VA 22071
phone: 703-435-3788
Wants to buy pre-1990 adult luncheon and dinner sets, fabric, playing cards, adult tea sets, bicentennial glasses, Holly Hobbie porcelain dolls, music boxes, figurines, sterling silver plates, and Christmas tree ornaments.

Helen McCale
P.O. Box 397
Butler, MO 64730
phone: 816-679-3690

Man./Prod./Dist.

Sue Holiday
American Greetings Corp.
10500 American Rd.
Cleveland, OH 44144
phone: 216-252-7300 or 216-252-4944
fax: 216-252-6979
American Greetings produced Holly Hobbie items - including figurines, plates, bells, etc. - from 1974 through 1986. Items were reintroduced through the Summit Corp. in 1990-91; the "Summit" figurines have also now been retired.

Jan Hagara

Clubs/Associations

Jan Hagara Collectors' Club, c/o Royal Orleans
Newsletter: Official Jan Hagara Collectors' Club Newsletter
40114 Industrial Park
Georgetown, TX 78626-4704
phone: 512-863-9499
fax: 512-869-2093
For collectors of Hagara prints, figurines, porcelain dolls, miniatures. Sponsored by Jan Hagara Collectables, Inc.

Dealers

Mary Sower
Card Cupboard, The
116 W. Main St.
Coldwater, OH 45828
phone: 419-678-2417
Maintains a price list for Jan Hagara

collectibles; will try to find any retired Jan Hagara item for customers.

Barbara Burks
Burks
1770 Burks Ave., Rt. 16
Springfield, MO 65807
Specializes in retired Jan Hagara collectibles.

Man./Prod./Dist.

B & J Company, The
P.O. Box 67
Georgetown, TX 78627
phone: 512-863-8318 or 800-722-3996
fax: 512-863-0833
Produces and distributes prints, porcelain dolls, cards and collector plates by Jan Hagara.

Lenox

Man./Prod./Dist.

Lenox Collections
P.O. Box 519
Langhorne, PA 19047-0519
phone: 215-750-6900 or 800-225-1779
fax: 215-750-7362
Direct mail marketing division of Lenox Corp. selling doll, ornament, figurines and giftware collectibles issued by Lenox.

Lithophanes

Man./Prod./Dist.

David N. Failing
Schmidt-Failing, Ltd.
10579 Miller Rd.
Utica, NY 13502-7005
phone: 315-724-1139 or 800-498-5866
fax: 315-724-0496
David Failing is the only American artist skilled in the creation of original porcelain lithophanes; all are signed, numbered & limited.

Lowell Davis

Clubs/Associations

Lowell Davis Farm Club, c/o Schmid, Inc.
Newsletter: Lowell Davis Farm Club Gazette
P.O. Box 636
Carthage, MO 64836
phone: 617-961-3000 or 800-343-7902
Focuses on the collectible plates and figurines designed by artist Lowell Davis. Sponsored by Schmid Co.

Experts

Rosie Wells
22341 E. Wells Rd.
Canton, IL 61520
phone: 309-668-2565 or 800-445-8745
fax: 800-337-6743
e-mail: Rosie@RosieWells.com
Internet: http://www.RosieWells.com
Author of "Lowell Davis Collectibles - The Official Secondary Market Price Guide."

Music Boxes

Man./Prod./Dist.

Splendid Music Box Co.
225 Fifth Ave.
New York, NY 10010
phone: 212-532-9304
fax: 212-532-9334
Imports over 1000 types of music boxes from all over the world.

H & G Studios
5660 Corporate Way
West Palm Beach, FL 33407
phone: 561-615-9100 or 800-777-1333
fax: 561-615-8400
Sells Italian-made, wooden music boxes; containing images of exclusive original art; have Swiss Reuge musical movements.

Norman Rockwell

(see also ILLUSTRATORS, Norman Rockwell)

Experts

Mary Moline
2155 Promontory Point Ln.
Gold River, CA 95670-7274
phone: 916-638-6788
World authority on original Norman Rockwell art; author of "Norman Rockwell Collectibles Values Guide," "Norman Rockwell Encyclopedia" as well as sixty other books on the subject.

Nutcrackers

Clubs/Associations

Steinbach/KSA Collectible Nutcracker Club
1107 Broadway
New York, NY 10010
phone: 212-924-0900 or 800-243-9627
fax: 212-807-0575

Ornaments

(see also CHRISTMAS COL-LECTIBLES; HOLIDAY COL-LECTIBLES)

Clubs/Associations

New England Ornament Collectors Club
1231 East Main St.
Meriden, CT 06450
phone: 800-524-6123

Treasury of Christmas Ornaments Collectors' Club
P.O. Box 277
Itasca, IL 60143-0277
phone: 708-875-5404
fax: 708-875-5359

Collectors

Maret Webb
4118 East Vernon Ave.
Phoenix, AZ 85008-2333
phone: 602-957-0653
fax: 602-957-1631
Wants Biederman brass ornaments;

also will buy or trade for sterling ornaments by Wallace, Reed & Barton, Gorham, Swarovski and others; also wants to buy Swarovski ornaments.

Dealers

Ornament Retailer, The
1231 East Main St.
Meriden, CT 06450
phone: 800-524-6123
Offers Enesco ornaments, Carlton Heirloom ornaments, Precious Moments Bisque ornaments, Troll ornaments.

Alice Korman
Alice's Past & Presents Replacements
P.O. Box 465
Merrick, NY 11566-0465
phone: 516-379-1352
fax: 516-379-7302
Specializes in Lenox, Gorham, Towle and other Christmas ornaments.

Man./Prod./Dist.

Kirk Stieff Co. Outlet Store
800 Wyman Park Dr.
Baltimore, MD 21211
phone: 410-338-6080 or 800-531-7946
fax: 410-338-6097
Sterling, silverplate, stainless steel and pewter flatware, sterling and silverplate hollowware; pewter, jewelry; a division of Lenox Brands.

Periodicals

Rosie Wells
Rosie Wells Enterprises, Inc.
Magazine: Ornament Collector, The
22341 E. Wells Rd.
Canton, IL 61520
phone: 309-668-2565 or 800-445-8745
fax: 800-337-6743
e-mail: Rosie@RosieWells.com
Internet: http://www.RosieWells.com
The magazine specializing in Ornament Collector news, especially in Hallmark, Enesco, Carlton ornaments; ads, articles, photos, etc.; many classified ads from collectors.

Ornaments (Buccellati)

Man./Prod./Dist.

Buccellati, Inc.
46 East 57th St.
New York, NY 10022
phone: 212-308-2900
fax: 212-750-1323
Produces hundreds of entirely handmade ornaments annually using classical and baroque influences, gold, silver, precious and semi-precious stones

Ornaments (Carlton Cards)

Man./Prod./Dist.

Carlton Cards
10500 American Rd.
Cleveland, OH 44144
phone: 216-252-7300 or 216-252-4944
fax: 216-252-6979
Offers many ornaments including Jim Hensen's Muppets and lighted ornaments.

Ornaments (Cazenovia Abroad)

Man./Prod./Dist.

Glen Trush
Cazenovia Abroad, Ltd.
67 Albany St.
Cazenovia, NY 13035-1219
phone: 315-655-3433
fax: 315-655-4249
Offers a collection of over 50 full-size ornaments and almost as many miniature ornaments; also offers limited edition carousel figurines.

Ornaments (Christopher Radko)

Clubs/Associations

Christopher Radko Starlight Family of Collectors
Newsletter: Starlight
P.O. Box 745
Ardsley, NY 10502
phone: 800-717-2356

Experts

David Williams
Williams Nursery & The Gift House
524 Springfield Ave.
Westfield, NJ 07090
phone: 888-88R-ADKO or 908-232-4076
fax: 908-232-0079
e-mail: williamsnursery@compuserve.com
Internet: http://www.radkoshop.com
A Christopher Radko Rising Star store; large selection of Radko ornaments; visit website for live ornament chat, bulletin board, and current inventory.

Man./Prod./Dist.

Christopher Radko
P.O. Box 745
Ardsley, NY 10502
phone: 800-717-2356
Carries mouth blown Christmas ornaments and accessories for the home.

Ornaments (Danforth)

Man./Prod./Dist.

Danforth Pewterers
P.O. Box 828
Middlebury, VT 05753
phone: 802-388-8666
fax: 802-388-0099
Specializes in Christmas ornaments; also original Danforth Pewter hollowware.

Ornaments (Enesco)

Clubs/Associations

Enesco Treasury of Christmas Ornaments Collectors' Club
Newsletter: Treasury Trimmings
P.O. Box 277
Itasca, IL 60143-0277
phone: 630-875-5300 or 800-436-3726
fax: 630-875-5359
Members receive symbol of membership ornament, membership card, club newsletter, subscription to Treasury Trimmings, collector's guide, list of dealers.

Ornaments (Hallmark)

Clubs/Associations

California Ornament Collectors Club
Newsletter: California Ornament Collectors Newsletter
6 Ness Place
Marietta, OH 45750
phone: 614-373-3114
A club for collectors of Hallmark Christmas ornaments; the original and the largest such club for Hallmark collectors.

Hallmark Collectors Club Connection
P.O. Box 110
Fenton, MI 48430

Nancy M. Soddy
Central Wisconsin Ornament Collectors Club
401 Novak St.
Mosinee, WI 54455-2030
phone: 715-693-4135
Members interested primarily in collecting Hallmark Christmas ornaments; some members have other areas of interest as well.

Hallmark Keepsake Ornament Collectors Club
Newsletter: Collector's Courier
P.O. Box 412734
Kansas City, MO 64141-2734
phone: 816-274-4000 or 800-425-5627
fax: 816-274-5061
Focuses on Hallmark Ornaments made of wood, acrylic, bone china, porcelain. A manufacturer-sponsored club.

Dealers

Kathy Parrott
Christmas in Vermont
51 Jalbert Rd.
Barre, VT 05641
phone: 802-479-2024
e-mail: katparrott@aol.com
Specializes in mail order Hallmark Christmas ornaments, Kiddie Car classics, Merry Christmas and other Hallmark collectibles; serving collectors worldwide since 1988; catalog 4 times per year, send $3 for copy.

Experts

Rosie Wells
22341 E. Wells Rd.
Canton, IL 61520
phone: 309-668-2565 or 800-445-8745
fax: 800-337-6743
e-mail: Rosie@RosieWells.com
Internet: http://www.RosieWells.com
Author of "Secondary Market Price Guide for Hallmark Ornaments and Merry Miniatures."

Man./Prod./Dist.

Hallmark Cards, Inc.
Consumer Affairs #216
P.O. Box 419034
Kansas City, MO 64108
phone: 800-425-5627
Producer of Christmas ornaments and figurines.

Museums/Libraries

Jess Prudencio & David Hamrick
Hallmark Ornament Museum
c/o The Party Shop
3418 Lake City Hwy.
Warsaw, IN 46580
phone: 219-267-8787
Displays over 2,800 Hallmark ornaments - one of every design produced since Hallmark debuted its line of Keepsake Ornaments in 1973.

Hallmark Visitors Center
P.O. Box 419580
Kansas City, MO 64141
phone: 816-274-5672 or 800-425-5627
Internet: http://www.hallmark.com

Periodicals

Joan Ketterer
Carousel Collectibles
Newsletter: Twelve Months of Christmas
P.O. Box 97172
Pittsburgh, PA 15229
phone: 412-367-2352
A biweekly newsletter for new and long-time Hallmark collectors.

Newsletter: Hallmarkers
P.O. Box 97172
Pittsburgh, PA 15229
phone: 412-367-2352
For Hallmark collectors.

Ornaments (Silver)

Clubs/Associations

Hand & Hammer Collectors Club
Newsletter: Silver Tidings
2610 Morse Lane
Woodbridge, VA 22192
phone: 703-491-4866 or 800-SIL-VERY
fax: 703-491-2031
Focuses on the sterling silver collectibles designed by Chip deMatteo. Sponsored by Hand & Hammer, Co.

Collectors

Betty Overtons
200 Avenida Santa Margarita
San Clemente, CA 92672
phone: 714-498-5330 or 714-498-4027
fax: 714-498-5330
Wants sterling and silverplated Christmas ornaments which have been made by many silver companies since 1970.

Dealers

Peg Zurkowski
Becker Brooks Antiques
Chevy Chase, MD 20815-3029
phone: 301-588-8558
Specializing in out-of-production sterling ornaments.

Nan Horn
Circa Antiques
549 Spring Rd.
Elmhurst, IL 60126
phone: 708-834-4088

Experts

Peggy & Arthur Hart
Ornament Collector, The
101 E. Holly Ave., Ste. 2
Sterling, VA 20164
phone: 703-444-6155
fax: 703-421-9386
Co-authors with Don and Lea Galyean of "All That Glitters", an illustrated book about sterling silver ornaments; also author of "Sterling Ornaments"; introduced first Peggy Hart sterling ornament "The Heart of Christmas" in 1992.

Man./Prod./Dist.

Hand & Hammer Silversmiths
Newsletter: Silver Tidings
2610 Morse Lane
Woodbridge, VA 22192
phone: 703-491-4866 or 800-SIL-VERY
fax: 703-491-2031
Manufacturer of sterling silver Christmas ornaments.

P. Buckley Moss

Clubs/Associations

P. Buckley Moss Society
Newsletter: Sentinel
601 Shenandoah Village Dr., Box 1C
Waynesboro, VA 22980
phone: 703-943-5678
fax: 703-949-8408
Focuses on the collectible figurines, plates and graphics designed by P. Buckley Moss. Sponsored by The Moss Portfolio.

Man./Prod./Dist.

Moss Portfolio, The
1 Poplar Grove Ln.
Mathews, VA 23109
Publisher and distributor of watercolors, original prints, offset lithographs, plates, dolls, and figurines by P. Buckley Moss.

Penni Anne Cross

Man./Prod./Dist.

Cross Gallery, Inc.
P.O. Box 4181
Jackson, WY 83001-4181
phone: 307-733-2200
fax: 307-733-1414
Offers plates, figurines, dolls, Christmas ornaments, and graphics designed by Penni Anne Cross.

Pickard

Man./Prod./Dist.

Pickard China Co.
782 Corona Ave.
Antioch, IL 60002-1574
phone: 708-395-3800
fax: 708-395-3827
In addition to dinnerware, manufactures collectible plates, bells, ornaments, steins and bowls.

Plates

(see also PLATES)

Clubs/Associations

Hunter Haines
Collectibles & Platemakers Guild
P.O. Box 1474
Northbrook, IL 60065

Marjorie M. Rosenberg, Pr.
International Plate Collectors Guild
Newsletter: Platter Platter
P.O. Box 487
Artesia, CA 90702-0487
phone: 213-924-6335
A monthly newsletter for plate collectors.

Dealers

Bradford Exchange Trading Center, The
9333 N. Milwaukee Ave.
Niles, IL 60714
phone: 312-966-2770 or 800-323-5577
e-mail: custrv@bradex.com
Internet: http://www.bradex.com
A brokerage service to match secondary market buyers and sellers of collector plates that are no longer in production.

Experts

Ross Ernst
Collectors Plates
7308 Izard
Omaha, NE 68114-3237
phone: 402-391-3469
Buys and sells Bradford plates, Royal Copenhagen (RC), Bing & Grondahl (B/G), P. Buckley Moss plates, Perillo, M.I. Hummel, Duncan Royale, Lilliput Lane, Hamilton Dolls, Ashton Drake Dolls, and old estate RC & B/G plates.

Man./Prod./Dist.

Lance J. Klass, Pres.
Porterfield's
12 Chestnut Pasture Rd.
Concord, NH 03301
phone: 603-228-1864
fax: 603-228-1888
e-mail: clientservices@www.porterfields.com
Internet: http://www.porterfields.com
Porterfield's, Fine Art in Limited Editions, specializes in producing the fine limited edition porcelain mini plates on early childhood by award-winning artist Rob Anders.

Jerry Miley
Eklund's, Ltd.
1701 West St. Germain St.
Saint Cloud, MN 56301
phone: 612-252-3942
fax: 612-252-9397
Producers of limited edition collector plates and prints by artist Derk Hansen.

Bradford Exchange, The
9333 N. Milwaukee Ave.
Niles, IL 60714
phone: 312-966-2770 or 800-323-5577
e-mail: custrv@bradex.com
Internet: http://www.bradex.com
Pioneered direct mail marketing of collector plates and created an organized secondary market trading exchange for collector plates.

Matching Services

Robert Goins
Replacements Ltd.
P.O. Box 26029
Greensboro, NC 27420
phone: 800-737-5223 or 800-REP-
LACE
fax: 910-697-3100
e-mail: replaceltd@aol.com
Internet: http://www.imall.com/stores/
replacements
*Carries collector plates in addition to
china, crystal and flatware (obsolete,
active and inactive.)*

Museums/Libraries

Bradford Museum of Collector's Plates,
The
9333 N. Milwaukee Ave.
Niles, IL 60714
phone: 312-966-2770 or 800-323-5577
e-mail: custrv@bradex.com
Internet: http://www.bradex.com

Plates (Bareuther)

Man./Prod./Dist.

WARA Intercontinental Co.
20101 West 8 Mile Rd.
Detroit, MI 48219
phone: 313-535-9110
fax: 313-535-9112
*Sole importer and distributor of
Bareuther cobalt blue collector plates
and bells.*

Plates (Rockwell)

Clubs/Associations

Michael J.P. Collins, Pres.
Rockwell Society of America
Newsletter: Rockwell Society of
America Newsletter
P.O. Box 705
Ardsley, NY 10502-0705
phone: 914-631-3171
*Founded in 1974 and dedicated to the
appreciation of America's most
famous artist, Norman Rockwell;
specializing in original paintings,
drawings, collectibles, e.g. Saturday
Evening Post covers/magazines,
illustrated books, etc.*

Prayer Ladies

Experts

April M. Tvorak
P.O. Box 94
Warren Center, PA 18851
phone: 717-395-3775
*Wants to buy Mother-in-the-Kitchen
(Prayer Ladies) ceramic figurines and
accessories; imported in the 1960s by
ENESCO; typically decorated with a
motif of an older woman with hair in
bun, head bowed, hands in prayer,
and prayer on apron.*

Steve Johnson
4003 Jefferson St.
Sioux City, IA 51108
Collector and consultant to "The

*Official Price Guide to Pottery and
Porcelain."*

Juarine Woolridge
418 Country Lane
Mount Vernon, MO 65712-1906
*Collector and consultant to "The
Official Price Guide to Pottery and
Porcelain."*

Precious Moments

Appraisers

Rosie Wells
Limited Edition Appraisers
22341 E. Wells Rd.
Canton, IL 61520
phone: 309-668-2565 or 800-445-8745
fax: 800-337-6743
e-mail: Rosie@RosieWells.com
Internet: http://www.RosieWells.com
*Specializes in the appraisal of
Precious Moments porcelain bisque
collectibles.*

Clubs/Associations

Enesco Precious Moments Collectors'
Club
Newsletter: Goodnewsletter
P.O. Box 99
Itasca, IL 60143-0099
phone: 630-875-5300 or 800-436-3726
fax: 630-875-5359
*Members receive symbol of
membership figurine, quarterly
newsletter, membership card,
members' only offerings, gift registry,
club binder, annual local chapter
national convention, Orient tour.*

Enesco Precious Moments Birthday
Club
Newsletter: Good News Parade
P.O. Box 689
Itasca, IL 60143-0689
phone: 630-875-5300 or 800-436-3726
fax: 630-875-5359
*For young collectors; this category of
Precious Moments figurines feature
animals and circus themes; members
receive symbol of membership
figurine, club newsletter, membership
certificate, members' only offerings,
birthday card.*

Rosie Wells
Precious Moments Collectors
Magazine: Precious Collectibles
22341 E. Wells Rd.
Canton, IL 61520
phone: 309-668-2565 or 800-445-8745
fax: 800-337-6743
e-mail: Rosie@RosieWells.com
Internet: http://www.RosieWells.com
*A glossy magazine with ads, articles,
collector interviews, etc.; published
exclusively for Precious Moments
collectors; keeps track of numerous
area Precious Moments collector
clubs throughout the country.*

Dealers

Limited Edition, The
2170 Sunrise Highway
Merrick, NY 11566
phone: 516-623-4400 or 800-645-2864
*Specializes in suspended and retired
Precious Moments figurines.*

Experts

Rosie Wells
22341 E. Wells Rd.
Canton, IL 61520
phone: 309-668-2565 or 800-445-8745
fax: 800-337-6743
e-mail: Rosie@RosieWells.com
Internet: http://www.RosieWells.com
*Author of "Secondary Market Price
Guide for Precious Moments";
specializing in Precious Moments
bisque collection, dolls, pewter, etc.
since 1983; offers appraisals of
Precious Moments porcelain bisque
collectibles.*

Misc. Services

Sandy Forgach
Collectibles etc., Inc. Match Service
1127 Cass St.
La Crosse, WI 54601
phone: 800-558-5594
*A specialized service matching buyers
and sellers of older Precious
Moments.*

Rosie Wells Enterprises, Inc.
22341 E. Wells Rd.
Canton, IL 61520
phone: 309-668-2565 or 800-445-8745
fax: 800-337-6743
e-mail: Rosie@RosieWells.com
Internet: http://www.RosieWells.com
*Rosie's Instant Hot Top Line has news
flashes & hot tips for Precious
Moments collectors; message changes
Thursdays at noon; call 900-740-
7575; $2/min.*

Precious Moments (Musicals)

Clubs/Associations

Enesco Musical Society
Newsletter: Musical Notes
225 Windsor Dr.
Itasca, IL 60143
phone: 630-875-5300 or 800-436-3726
fax: 630-875-5359
*For collectors of Enesco's musical
collectibles; members receive color
calendar, quarterly newsletter,
membership certificate, members' only
offering.*

Prints

(see also PRINTS)

Dealers

Tom & Rosemarie Prendergast
Pelican Art Galleries & Framers
One Nasturtium Ave.
Glenwood, NJ 07418
phone: 201-764-7149 or 561-283-6813
fax: 561-283-6813
*Focuses on the collectible conserva-
tion prints, Duck Prints, equine prints,
sport prints autographed by artist and
player, and signed & numbered
limited prints; deals with the
secondary market*

Man./Prod./Dist.

Greenwich Workshop, Inc.
1 Greenwich Place
Shelton, CT 06484-4618
*Publishes aviation, Western, and
fantasy art in limited edition print
form.*

Periodicals

Magazine: InformArt
204 Playhouse Corner
Southbury, CT 06488
phone: 203-262-9220 or 800-906-9600
fax: 203-262-9225
e-mail: peggyc@trib.com
*A quarterly magazine focusing on
modern limited edition prints (signed
& numbered); ads, articles, new
releases, secondary market values.*

Magazine: Art Business News
270 Madison Ave.
New York, NY 10016-0601
*Focuses on the contemporary
photoreproduction print market, but
includes timely information on tax
changes and laws, as well as analysis
of markets.*

Magazine: Decor
330 N. Fourth St.
Saint Louis, MO 63102
phone: 314-421-5445
*Aimed at the frame shop/gallery
owner; lots of articles about how to
increase sales, gallery floor plans,
advertising; occasionally covers some
new trend in print making; also
published annual Sources issues.*

Prints (Adolf Sehring)

Man./Prod./Dist.

American Artist Portfolio, Inc.
9625 Tetley Dr.
Somerset, VA 22972
phone: 800-842-4445 or 703-672-0286
*Founded in 1988 to publish and
market the works of realist artist Adolf
Sehring.*

Prints (Barbara Hails)

Man./Prod./Dist.

Hails Fine Art
18319 Georgia Ave.
Olney, MD 20832-1435
phone: 301-774-6249 or 800-451-6411
Produces limited edition fine prints

based on the pastels and oils of artist
Barbara Hails; recently introduced
canvas lithographs of her distinctive
art.

Prints (Diane Graebner)

Clubs/Associations

Diane Graebner Collector's Club
Newsletter: Diane Graebner Collector's
  Club Newsletter
P.O. Box 174
Millersburg, OH 44654
phone: 800-626-4306 or 216-867-7942
*Limited edition, paper prints depicting
the Amish lifestyle.*

Man./Prod./Dist.

Diane & Ted Graebner
Lynn's Prints
P.O. Box 353
Millersburg, OH 44654
phone: 330-674-6664 or 330-674-6755
fax: 330-674-6664
*Producer of limited edition prints by
Diane Graebner which depict Amish
living.*

Prints (Fred Stone)

Man./Prod./Dist.

American Artists
66 Poppasquash Rd.
Bristol, RI 02809
phone: 800-828-0086 or 401-254-1191
fax: 401-254-8881

Prints (Irene Spencer)

Man./Prod./Dist.

Irene Spencer
Irene Spencer, Inc.
1202 Star View Dr.
Vista, CA 92084
phone: 619-727-0847 or 617-727-0092
*Produces and publishes the
lithographs and plates of artist Irene
Spencer.*

Prints (Jody Bergsma)

Man./Prod./Dist.

Jody Bergsma Galleries
1344 King St.
Bellingham, WA 98226-6224
phone: 206-733-1101
fax: 206-647-2758
e-mail: bergsma@pacificrim.net
Internet: http://olympic.pacificrim.net/
  bergsma/
*Publishes and markets the works of
artist Jody Bergsma.*

Prints (Marty Bell)

Clubs/Associations

Marty Bell Collector's Society
Newsletter: Sounds of Bells, The
9550 Owensmouth Ave.
Chatsworth, CA 91311-4801
phone: 818-700-0754 or 800-637-4537
fax: 818-709-7668
*Focuses on the collectible prints of
English thatched, tiled and slate roof
cottages by Marty Bell.*

Man./Prod./Dist.

Marty Bell Fine Art, Inc.
9550 Owensmouth Ave.
Chatsworth, CA 91311-4801
phone: 818-700-0754 or 800-637-4537
fax: 818-709-7668
*Publishes limited edition lithographs
from the original paintings of Marty
Bell.*

Prints (Thomas Kinkade)

Clubs/Associations

Thomas Kinkade Collectors' Society, c/o
  Lightpost Publishing
Newsletter: Thomas Kinkade Collectors'
  Society Newsletter
P.O. Box 90267
San Jose, CA 95109
phone: 800-366-3733
fax: 408-287-1169
*Canvas lithographs and luminous
archival paper prints.*

Man./Prod./Dist.

Lightpost Publishing
Ten Almaden Blvd., 9th Floor
San Jose, CA 95113
phone: 408-279-4777
fax: 408-947-4677
*Widely known in the limited edition
print field for its publishing of fine art
prints by artist Thomas Kinkade.*

Reed & Barton

Man./Prod./Dist.

Reed & Barton
144 W. Britannia St.
Taunton, MA 02780
phone: 508-824-6611 or 800-822-1824
fax: 508-822-7269
*Produces china, crystal, silver,
silverplate, and stainless flatware,
collectible plates, bells, dolls,
ornaments and accessories.*

Royal Copenhagen

Man./Prod./Dist.

Josephine Dillon
Royal Copenhagen/Bing & Grondahl
  Co.
27 Holland Ave.
White Plains, NY 10603-3317
phone: 914-428-8222 or 800-431-1992
fax: 914-428-8251
*Royal Copenhagen, Bing & Grondahl,
Holmegaard, and Georg Jensen are*

*the best of Scandinavian collectibles;
manufactures dinnerware, cobalt blue
underglaze collector plates, figurines,
bells, dolls, ornaments and gift
accessories.*

Royal Doulton

(see also CERAMICS [ENGLISH],
Doulton; CERAMICS [ENGLISH],
Royal Doulton)

Clubs/Associations

Patricia O'Brien, Manager
Royal Doulton International Collectors
  Club
Magazine: Gallery
850 Progress Ave.
Scarborough
Ontario M1H 3C4 Canada
phone: 416-431-4202 or 800-268-4040
fax: 416-431-0089
*Focuses on the Royal Doulton
collectibles; members entitled to
purchase "member only" figurines or
character and Toby jugs; advance
notice of introductions and withdrawals; a newsletter has free buy/sell ads
for members.*

Elizabeth Mayer
Royal Doulton International Collectors
  Club
Magazine: Gallery
Minton House, London Road
Stoke-on-Trent
Staffordshire ST4 7QD, U.K.
*Focuses on the Royal Doulton
collectibles; members entitled to
purchase "member only" figurines or
charter and Toby jugs; advance notice
of introductions and withdrawals; a
newsletter has free buy/sell ads for
members.*

Royal Doulton International Collectors
  Club
Magazine: Gallery
701 Cottontail Lane
Somerset, NJ 08873
phone: 908-356-7880 or 800-682-4462
fax: 908-764-4974
*Focuses on the Royal Doulton
collectibles; members entitled to
purchase "member only" figurines or
character and Toby jugs; advance
notice of introductions and withdrawals; a newsletter has free buy/sell ads
for members.*

Dealers

Arlene & Barry
Recollections
3823 Oceanside Rd. East
Oceanside, NY 11572
phone: 516-678-4652

Matching Services

Regina Negrotti
Tablescapes
49 Elkton Ave.
P.O. Box 3165
Cheshire, CT 06410
phone: 800-801-4084

Royal Worcester

Dealers

Gwendolyn R. Reasoner
Re Vann Galleries
1501 Boardwalk at NY Ave.
Atlantic City, NJ 08401-7012
phone: 609-345-7474 or 800-821-4278
fax: 318-762-3534
*Largest Boehm dealer in the U.S.;
specializes in the Boehm secondary
market; also Cybis, Royal Worcester,
Erte; also appraises.*

Man./Prod./Dist.

Royal Worcester Limited
Severn St.
Worcester WR1 2NE, U.K.
Plates, figurines.

Russian

Man./Prod./Dist.

Marina's Russian Collection
507 North Wolf Rd.
Wheeling, IL 60090
phone: 708-808-0994
fax: 708-808-0997
*Distributes Russian matryoshka
(nesting dolls) and lacquered boxes.*

Sculptures (Cain)

Clubs/Associations

Mike Kemp
Cain Studios Collectors Guild
Newsletter: Rick Cain Studios'
  Collectors Guild News
619 S. Main St.
Gainesville, FL 32601
phone: 800-535-3949
fax: 904-377-7038
*A club for fans of artist Rick Cain;
members receive free membership
sculpture, redemption coupons,
members-only sculptures, and more.*

Sculptures (Chilmark)

Clubs/Associations

Jim Swiezynski, Dir.
Chilmark Gallery, c/o The Lance Corp.
Newsletter: Chilmark Report
321 Central St.
Hudson, MA 01749
phone: 508-568-1401
fax: 508-568-8741
*Focuses on Chilmark pewter
sculptures. Sponsored by the Lance
Corp. The "Chilmark Report"
reports on new editions and artist
appearances. "The Observer" keeps*

collectors up-to-date on secondary
markets and values.

Repair Services

CRC Workshop
16 Drumlin Hill
Grofton, MA 01450
phone: 508-448-5252
*Specializes in the complete restoration
of Chilmark pewters made by the
Lance Corp.; extremely knowledgeable about Lance materials, processes
and techniques.*

Sculptures (CPSmithshire)

Clubs/Associations

Pangaean Society, The, c/o The Lance
Corp.
Newsletter: Shirespeak
321 Central St.
Hudson, MA 01749
phone: 508-568-1401
fax: 508-568-8741
*Focuses on Cindy Smity's collection of
Shireling Figurines.*

Sculptures (Don Polland)

Clubs/Associations

Polland Collectors Society, c/o Polland
Studios
Newsletter: Collectors Review
P.O. Box 2468
Prescott, AZ 86302
phone: 520-778-1900
fax: 520-778-4034
*Focuses on Don Polland's pewter
sculpture collectible figurines.
Sponsored by Polland Studios.*

Man./Prod./Dist.

Donald J. Polland
Polland Studios
P.O. Box 2468
Prescott, AZ 86302
phone: 520-778-1900
fax: 520-778-4034
*Focuses on Don Polland's pewter
sculpture collectible figurines.
Sponsored by Polland Studios (Gerard
Corp.)*

Sculptures (Japanese Themes)

Man./Prod./Dist.

Alan D. Meaux
Ronin Art Productions
P.O. Box 1271
Oak Harbor, WA 98277-1271
phone: 360-675-8429 or 360-678-8787
*Seller of limited edition bronze
sculptures of Japanese samurai and
related subjects by sculptor Alan D.
Meaux.*

Sculptures (Kronberg)

Clubs/Associations

Kronberg Collectors' Guild
3150 State Line Rd.
North Bend, OH 45052
phone: 513-353-3390
*For collectors of Kronberg miniature
bronze statuary.*

Sculptures (LEGENDS)

Clubs/Associations

Starlite Collectors Society
2665-D Park Center Dr.
Simi Valley, CA 93065
phone: 800-726-9660 or 805-520-9660
fax: 805-520-9670
*Collectors of art sculptures in mixed
media such as bronze, fine pewter and
24 karat gold vermeil made by
Legends. A manufacturer-sponsored
collector's club.*

Man./Prod./Dist.

LEGENDS
2665-D Park Center Dr.
Simi Valley, CA 93065
phone: 800-726-9660 or 805-520-9660
fax: 805-520-9670
*Producers of art sculptures in mixed
media such as bronze, fine pewter and
24 karat gold vermeil.*

Sculptures (Mark Hopkins)

Clubs/Associations

L. Susan Fife
Mark Hopkins Bronze Guild
Newsletter: Bronzeworks
21 Shorter Industrial Blvd.
Rome, GA 30165-1838
phone: 800-678-6564 or 706-235-8773
fax: 706-235-2814
*Focuses on bronze castings by Mark
Hopkins.*

Man./Prod./Dist.

Russell Bower
Mark Hopkins Bronze Guild
21 Shorter Industrial Blvd.
Rome, GA 30165-1838
phone: 800-678-6564 or 706-235-8773
fax: 706-235-2814
*Produces and sells fine bronze
sculptures.*

Sculptures (Rawcliffe)

Man./Prod./Dist.

Rawcliffe Corp.
155 Public St.
Providence, RI 02903
phone: 401-331-1645 or 800-343-1811
*Manufactures giftware and
collectibles in fine pewter.*

Sculptures (Remington)

Man./Prod./Dist.

Fred Schulenburg
Museum Collections By Schulenburg,
Inc.
P.O. Box 2369
Shelton, CT 06484
phone: 800-243-6229
*Manufactures plates and bronzes.
Official reproducer of Frederic
Remington design bronze sculptures.*

Sculptures (Sandcast)

Clubs/Associations

Steve Yaptangco
Sandcast Collectors Guild
Newsletter: Paw Press
P.O. Box 910079
San Diego, CA 92191-0079
phone: 619-695-9611 or 800-722-3316
fax: 619-695-0615
*For collectors of animal sculptures
noted for their lifelike appearance and
designed by artist Sandra A. Brue;
annual members-only piece not
available to the general public.*

Man./Prod./Dist.

Steve Yaptangco
Sandcast, Inc.
P.O. Box 910079
San Diego, CA 92191-0079
phone: 619-695-9611 or 800-722-3316
fax: 619-695-0615
*Manufacturer of handcast and
handpainted animal sculptures noted
for their lifelike appearance and
designed by artist Sandra A. Brue;
Paw Press published semiannually.*

Sculptures (Tom Clark)

Man./Prod./Dist.

Cairn Studio Ltd.
P.O. Box 400
Davidson, NC 28036
phone: 704-892-5859
Internet: http://www.cairnstudio.com
*Manufactures gnomes and other
character figurines by artist Dr. Tom
Clark.*

Skippy

Clubs/Associations

Skippy Collectors Club, c/o Skippy, Inc.
Newsletter: Skippy Newsletter
7716 Lafayette Forest Dr., Apt P2
Annandale, VA 22003-6346
*Focuses on the Skippy print and doll
collectibles. Sponsored by Skippy,
Inc.*

Spangler's Realm

Man./Prod./Dist.

Spangler's Realm Collectors Club, c/o
Realms, Inc.
11733 Lackland Rd.
Maryland Heights, MO 63146
phone: 314-991-0793
fax: 314-991-0958
*Focuses on the Spangler's Realm line
of figurines, bells, ornaments and
prints. Sponsored by Realms, Inc.*

Sports Related

(see also SPORTS COLLECTIBLES)

Dealers

Morgan Co., The
6301 Highbanks Rd.
Mascoutah, IL 62258
phone: 618-566-7568 or 800-422-4510
fax: 618-566-7518
*Specializes in limited edition figurines
and plates; Gartlan USA, Sports
Impressions, etc.*

Man./Prod./Dist.

Mark Bloomquist
S. A. M. Inc.
P.O. Box 77
Palo Alto, CA 94301
phone: 800-483-2643 or 415-369-0190
*Manufactures sports related ceramic
bobbing head dolls.*

Sports Related (Gartlan)

Clubs/Associations

Bob Martin
Collectors' League
Newsletter: Collectors' Quarterly
575 Hwy. 73 North
West Berlin, NJ 08091-9289
phone: 609-753-9229
fax: 609-753-9280
e-mail: info@www.gartlanusa.com
Internet: http://www.gartlanusa.com
*Focuses on the Gartlan sports and
entertainment collectibles; sponsored
by Gartlan USA.*

Man./Prod./Dist.

Gartlan USA
575 Hwy. 73 North
West Berlin, NJ 08091-9289
phone: 609-753-9229
fax: 609-753-9280
e-mail: info@www.gartlanusa.com
Internet: http://www.gartlanusa.com
*Produces sports and entertainment
collectibles including plates, figurines,
graphics, ornaments, and baseballs.*

Sports Related (Sports Imp.)

Man./Prod./Dist.

ENESCO Corp.
225 Windsor Dr.
Itasca, IL 60143
phone: 630-875-5300 or 800-436-3726
fax: 630-875-5359
Distributor of Sports Impressions.

Sports Related (Start. Lineup)

Dealers

All-Star Sports Cards
P.O. Box 351
Syracuse, NY 13211
phone: 315-454-8700

Midwest Sports Collectibles
1027 Shayler Rd.
Cincinnati, OH 45245
phone: 513-752-4939
fax: 513-752-8960

Minnesota Connection, The
17773 Kenwood Trail
Lakeville, MN 55044
phone: 612-892-0406
fax: 612-892-7445
Large dealer in Kenner's Starting Lineup figures.

Golden Glove Sportscards & Lineups
3025 Eagandale Place, Apt. 340
Saint Paul, MN 55121-1236
phone: 612-452-4868
fax: 612-452-1311

D & J Collectibles
4256 W. 131st St.
Savage, MN 55378
phone: 612-882-9373
fax: 612-895-1084

Man./Prod./Dist.

Kenner
615 Elsinore Place
Cincinnati, OH 45202
phone: 513-579-4000 or 800-327-8264
Manufacturer of Staring Lineup sports figures.

Periodicals

Christine Drury
Landmark Specialty Publications, Inc.
Magazine: Tuff Stuff's Guide to Starting Lineup
P.O. Box 1637
Glen Allen, VA 23060
phone: 804-266-0140 or 800-899-8833
fax: 804-264-4205
Internet: http://www.tuffstuffonline.com
For collectors of Kenner's Starting Lineup line of 4" tall sports figures; published quarterly.

Steins

(see also GLASSES, Drinking)

Clubs/Associations

Joyce M. Reyhons, Pres.
Advertising Cup & Mug Collectors of America
Newsletter: Cupletter, The
P.O. Box 680
Solon, IA 52333
phone: 319-644-3636
For collectors of special custom-made ceramic or plastic mugs, cups, and steins from advertisers, fund raisers, shows, conventions, or promotions; quarterly newsletter; send $2 plus LSASE for sample.

Anheuser-Busch Collectors Club
2700 South Broadway
Saint Louis, MO 63118
phone: 313-577-7465 or 800-305-2582
fax: 314-577-9656
For collectors of Anheuser-Busch steins and related collectibles.

Dealers

Sam & Samantha May
Sam's Steins & Collectibles
2207 Lincoln Highway East
Lancaster, PA 17602-1111
phone: 717-394-6404
fax: 717-394-6427
e-mail: SamsSteins@msn.com
For the collector of mugs and steins: Anheuser Busch, Strohs, Coors, Miller, Hamm's, Pabst, Yuengling, etc.; also German steins, Cavanaugh Coca-Cola bear figurines; send two 32 cent stamps for list.

Sam & Samantha May
Sam's Steins & Collectibles
2207 Lincoln Highway East
Lancaster, PA 17602-1111
phone: 717-394-6404
fax: 717-394-6427
e-mail: SamsSteins@msn.com
Carries over 900 different steins at discount pricing; also carries Ertl truck banks and other brewery collectibles; 20-page catalog of U.S. brewery steins issued quarterly.

Bob Lamson
Bob Lamson Beer Steins, Inc.
509 N. 22nd St.
Allentown, PA 18104-4305
phone: 610-435-8611 or 800-435-8611

Roy M. Willis
Heartland of Kentucky Decanters & Steins
P.O. Box 428
Lebanon Junction, KY 40150
phone: 502-833-2827
Hundreds of whiskey decanters by Jim Beam, Wild Turkey, Ski Country, McCormick and others; also beer steins, domestic or foreign; call ONLY 9-5 eastern time.

Bill Cress
P.O. Box 989
Alton, IL 62002-0989
phone: 618-466-3513
Buys and sells all of the new and lots

of the old steins; quarterly lists of modern steins and mugs for sale.

Doug & Natalie Marks
Flash Collectibles
560 N. Moorpark Rd., Ste. 287
Thousand Oaks, CA 91360-3703
phone: 805-499-9222
fax: 805-374-4160
Buys and sells contemporary beer steins by mail order; specializes in American beer brands, Budweiser, Miller, Coors, Hamms, Pabst, Old Style, etc.

Man./Prod./Dist.

C.U.I., Inc./Carolina Connections/Dram Tree
1502 North 23rd St.
Wilmington, ND 28405
phone: 919-251-1110
fax: 919-251-3587
Manufactures collectible steins of high quality.

M. Cornell Importers, Inc.
1462 18th St.
St. Paul, MN 55112
phone: 612-633-8690
fax: 612-636-3568
Focuses on importing hundreds of new conventional, miniature, character, and special-interest German steins each year; constantly introducing new artists, molds, color combinations, handles and lids.

Anheuser-Busch, Inc.
2700 South Broadway
Saint Louis, MO 63118
phone: 313-577-7465 or 800-305-2582
fax: 314-577-9656
Creates collector steins and plates of character and celebration, with classic and contemporary themes and styles.

OHI Collectibles & Gifts
1050 IH 35E., Ste. 400
New Braunfels, TX 78130
phone: 210-629-1191 or 800-627-1600
fax: 210-629-0153
OHI offers exclusive limited edition steins and mugs for the discerning collector.

Ted DeGrazia

Man./Prod./Dist.

Artists of the World
2915 N. 67th Place
Scottsdale, AZ 85251
phone: 602-946-6361
fax: 602-941-8918
Produces collector plates, figurines, ornaments and miniatures based on the work of Ted DeGrazia.

Toby Jugs

Periodicals

RBT Antiques
Newsletter: Tobies to Tinies
1035 Lupine Dr.
Sunnyvale, CA 94086-8733
phone: 408-733-4755
Newsletter for Toby and Character Jug collectors.

Toby Jugs (Kevin Francis)

Clubs/Associations

Kevin Francis Toby Jug Collectors Guild
917 Chicago Ave.
Evanston, IL 60202
phone: 800-634-0431 or 847-570-4867
fax: 847-570-4871
Produces Toby Jugs designed by Francis Salmon and Kevin Pearson.

COLLEGE COLLECTIBLES

Collectors

Beisner
P.O. Box 580613
Minneapolis, MN 55458
Wants to buy college yearbooks from Kansas colleges; also wants to buy histories of college social sororities and fraternities; describe and price.

Experts

Kevin McCandless
P.O. Box 435
Champaign, IL 61824-0435
phone: 217-367-4466

Humor Magazines

Collectors

Michael Gessel
P.O. Box 748
Arlington, VA 22216-0748
phone: 703-542-0462
Wants magazines (bound or individual copies); also posters and anthologies.

Pins

Collectors

Beisner
P.O. Box 580613
Minneapolis, MN 55458
Wants to buy college social sorority and fraternity pins as well as other sorority or fraternity jewelry; send sketch or photocopy, and price.

COMBS & HAIR ACCESSORIES

(see also BARBER SHOP COLLECTIBLES; BEAUTY SHOP COLLECTIBLES; CLOTHING & ACCESSORIES, Vintage; DRESSER ITEMS, Hatpins & Hatpin Holders; GEMS & JEWELRY; SHAVING COLLECTIBLES)

Clubs/Associations

Belva Green, Ed.
Antique Comb Collectors Club
    International
Newsletter: Antique Comb Collector
3748 Sunray Dr.
Holiday, FL 34691-3239
phone: 813-942-7354 or 708-549-9970
fax: 708-549-9935
*Organization dedicated to sharing
research and information about
antique and ornamental accessories
for the hair from any culture; offers
research, networking, networking, bi-
annual convention.*

Collectors

Mary Bachman
4901 Grandview
Ypsilanti, MI 48197-3762
phone: 313-434-2045

Glenn L. Beall
32981 N. River Rd.
Libertyville, IL 60048-4259
phone: 847-549-9970
fax: 847-549-9935

Betty Miller
5285 Marble Dr.
Gold Junction, AZ 85219
phone: 602-983-4655

Dealers

Priscilla Washed
Victorian Lady, The
102 South Main St.
P.O. Box 424
Waxhaw, NC 28173-0424
phone: 704-843-4467 or 800-786-1886
*A Victorian specialty store featuring
19th century ladies decorative &
fashion accessories; buys and sells
purses; also sewing and needlework
tools, vintage fashion, Victoriana, and
combs; mail order; catalog $5.*

Experts

Belva Green
3748 Sunray Dr.
Holiday, FL 34691-3239
phone: 813-942-7354 or 708-549-9970
fax: 708-549-9935
*Collector, historian, researcher,
lecturer on combs, jewelry and
accessories for the hair; editor for
Antique Comb Collector Club
International newsletter; manuscripts
welcome; query with SASE.*

Museums/Libraries

David Wilson
Leominster Historical Society, Field
    School Museum
17 School St.
Leominster, MA 01453
phone: 508-534-5375
*One of the best comb collections in the
U.S.*

Miller's Museum of Antique Combs
P.O. Box 316
Homer, AK 99603
phone: 907-235-8819
*The entire museum is dedicated to
combs and headdress.*

COMIC ART

(see CARTOON ART)

COMIC BOOKS

(see also CARTOON ART;
CHARACTER COLLECTIBLES;
COMIC ART; COMIC COL-
LECTIBLES; COWBOY HEROES;
DISNEY COLLECTIBLES; FAN
CLUBS; PREMIUMS; SCIENCE
FICTION; SUPER HEROES;
TRADING CARDS, Non-Sport)

Clubs/Associations

Lawrence Doro
American Comics Exchange
351-T Baldwin Rd.
Hempstead, NY 11550
phone: 516-481-0528
Please send SASE for information.

William Fink
Philadelphia Comic Book Collectors
    Club
2235 W. Ontario St.
Philadelphia, PA 19134
*Focuses on comic books and non-
sports cards.*

Collectors

Gary Pimenta
64 Lakeside Dr.
Tiverton, RI 02878-3111
*Wants to buy comic books based on
TV shows and theatrical movies.*

Peter Tilp
B & T Publications
P.O. Box 580
Summit, NJ 07901-0580
Wants to buy pre-1960 comic books.

Charles Reuter
6 Joy Ave.
Mount Joy, PA 17552-1532
phone: 717-653-8505

Steve A. Geppi
Diamond Comic Distributors
1966 Greenspring Dr., Ste. 300
Lutherville Timonium, MD 21093-4161
*Golden Age, DC's, Timelys, Marvels,
all 10 cent and 12 cent comics pre-
1968; also baseball cards or related
items.*

Dealers

Philip M. Levine & Sons
P.O. Box 246
Three Bridges, NJ 08887
phone: 908-788-0532
fax: 908-788-1028
*Buys and sells comic books, TV
Guides, magazines, etc.*

Metropolis Collectibles
873 Broadway, Ste. 201
New York, NY 10003
phone: 212-627-9691 or 800-229-6387
fax: 212-627-5947
*Buys and sells vintage movie posters
and comic books; free appraisals;
finders fees paid.*

Greg Bazaz
M&M Comics & Cards
150A Main St.
Nyack, NY 10960-3002
*Advisor to Alex Malloy's "Comic
Values Annual."*

ComicLink
P.O. Box 630299
Flushing, NY 11363-0299
phone: 718-423-9801
e-mail: comiclink@worldnet.att.net
Internet: http://www.comiclink.com

Richard Semowich
56 John Smith Rd.
Binghamton, NY 13901
phone: 607-648-4025
*Wants old comic books from 1933 to
1970; buying any size collection;
contact for the best price.*

Jon Warren
American Collectibles Exchange
P.O. Box 2512
Chattanooga, TN 37409
phone: 423-265-5515 or 800-880-4289
fax: 423-265-5506
e-mail: jonrwarren@aol.com
*Wants comics, also wants cartoon art,
Disney, Big Little Books, Pulp
Magazines, Baseball and Non-Sport
Cards.*

Bill & Joanne Bruegman
Toy Scouts, Inc.
137 Casterton Ave.
Akron, OH 44303-1543
phone: 330-836-0668
fax: 330-869-8668
e-mail: toyscout@newreach.net
Internet: http://www.csmonline.com/
    toyscouts/
*Wants to buy 1935-1965 super hero,
horror, etc. 10 cent and 12 cent
comics.*

Carl Bonasera
Al-American Comic Shops, Ltd.
3514 W. 95th St.
Evergreen Park, IL 60642
phone: 708-425-7555
Internet: http://www.comics2000.com/
    allamerican
*Advisor to Alex Malloy's "Comic
Values Annual"; specializes in 1950s-
1990s comic books, magazines,
science fiction digests and pulps.*

Bruce Mohrhard
Mo's Comics
4530 Gravois
Saint Louis, MO 63116
phone: 314-353-9500

Clint's Bookstore
3943 Main St.
Kansas City, MO 64111
phone: 816-561-2848
*The place to find old, new and obscure
comic books from the Golden Age to
present.*

Le Roy Young
Kwality Comics
1111 Massachusetts
Lawrence, KS 66044
*Advisor to Alex Malloy's "Comic
Values Annual."*

Comics Unlimited
P.O. Box 1414
Oklahoma City, OK 73101
phone: 405-236-5303
Wants pre-1965 comic books.

Stan Gold
As Time Goes By
7042 Dartbrook Dr.
Dallas, TX 75240
phone: 972-239-8621 or 214-352-2765
fax: 972-239-9632
e-mail: record@unicomp.net
Internet: http://www.astimegoesby.com/
    atgb
*Wants to buy Golden Age, Silver Age,
1940s and 1950s horror/humor/war
comic books, TV related and Western
comics; also wants vintage comic
related puzzles, books, records and
toys.*

Dennis Schamp
Comic Gallery, The
4224 Balboa Ave.
San Diego, CA 92117
*Advisor to Alex Malloy's "Comic
Values Annual."*

Experts

Ken Mitchell
710 Conacher Dr.
Willowdale
Ontario M2M 3N6 Canada
phone: 416-222-5808
*Buys and sells comic character
collectibles (comic books, Sunday
funnies, "Big Little Books", etc.) and
other nostalgic paper including music
(Pop) magazines and books from 1890
through 1960s.*

Jerry Weist
897 Union St.
Brooklyn, NY 11215-1401

Robert Overstreet
Overstreet Publications Inc.
11729 Mayfair Field Dr.
Lutherville Timonium, MD 21093-7011

Ernst Gerber
Gerber Publishing
P.O. Box 906
Minden, NV 89423
phone: 702-883-4100
*Author of "The Photo-Journal Guide
to Comic Books."*

Museums/Libraries

David R. Smith
Walt Disney Archives
500 South Buena Vista St.
Burbank, CA 91521-1200
phone: 818-560-5424
Comprehensive Disney collection including complete U.S. and most foreign Disney comics; comics not available to researchers for preservation reasons, but much material is available by appointment.

Periodicals

Ken Mitchell
Newsletter: Comic Buyers Guide
710 Conacher Dr.
Willowdale
Ontario M2M 3N6 Canada
phone: 416-222-5808
A weekly publication.

Fictioneer Books, Ltd.
Magazine: Comics Interview
234 Fifth Ave.
New York, NY 10001
High-quality monthly magazine that interviews today's top talents, yesterday's legendary greats, and all the other people involved in every aspect of comics.

Newsletter: Wizard: The Guide To Comics
151 Wells Ave.
Congers, NY 10920-2064

Gary M. Carter
Overstreet Publications Inc.
Magazine: Overstreet's Comic Book Marketplace
1996 Greenspring Dr., Ste. 405
Lutherville Timonium, MD 21093-4117
Monthly comic book price guide; values, latest hot titles, regional market reports, fully illustrated; full color, 130-150 pgs.

Gary M. Carter
Overstreet Publications Inc.
Magazine: Overstreet's Advanced Collector
1996 Greenspring Dr., Ste. 405
Lutherville Timonium, MD 21093-4117
Quarterly magazine the specifically focuses on Golden Age & Silver Age comic books & collectibles.

Jon Warren
American Collectibles Exchange
Magazine: Comics Source
P.O. Box 2512
Chattanooga, TN 37409
phone: 423-265-5515 or 800-880-4289
fax: 423-265-5506
e-mail: jonrwarren@aol.com
A monthly comics magazine about collecting, learning, reminiscing, buying, selling, trading, visiting, and sharing stories.

Julie A. Ulrich, PR
Krause Publications
Newspaper: Comics Buyer's Guide
700 E. State St.
Iola, WI 54990-0001
phone: 715-445-2214
fax: 715-445-4087
e-mail: info@krause.com
Internet: http://www.krause.com
Only weekly newspaper serving comic fans, collectors & the entire comics industry; articles on comics of the past & present, news, columns by top writers, comics show calendar, monthly price guide supplements on comics & trading cards.

Julie A. Ulrich, PR
Krause Publications
Magazine: Comics Retailer
700 E. State St.
Iola, WI 54990-0001
phone: 715-445-2214
fax: 715-445-4087
e-mail: info@krause.com
Internet: http://www.krause.com
Contains business-related editorial to help retailers become more profitable; covers comics, games, video, books, toys, trading cars; columns written by retailers and business experts.

Dana Gabbard
Magazine: Duckburg Times
3010 Wilshire Blvd. #362
Los Angeles, CA 90010-1146
phone: 213-388-2364
Focuses on comics based on Walt Disney characters.

Gary Carter, Ed.
Newsletter: Comic Book Market Place
P.O. Box 180900
Coronado, CA 92178-0900

Magazine: Comics Journal, The
7563 Lake City Way
Seattle, WA 98115
phone: 206-524-1967
Monthly magazine for the comic book industry: news, interviews, comic reviews, etc.

Repair Services

Kelley Miles Essoe
Collector's Restoration Service
P.O. Box 110409
Big Bear Lake, CA 92315
phone: 909-866-7226
Professional, expedient, top-of-the-line restoration at reasonable cost; references available.

Archie

Periodicals

Mary Smith
Magazine: Archie Fan Magazine
185 Ashland St.
Holliston, MA 01746
phone: 508-429-4674
Interested in Archie comics; all titles; people behind the books; also penpals.

Fawcett

Clubs/Associations

P.S. Hamerlinck
Fawcett Collectors of America
P.O. Box 24751
Minneapolis, MN 55424-0751
e-mail: WaltGrogan@aol.com
Internet: http://shazam.imginc.com/fca/
For collectors of Fawcett comics and Magazine Enterprise comics.

Magazine Enterprise

Clubs/Associations

P.S. Hamerlinck
Fawcett Collectors of America
P.O. Box 24751
Minneapolis, MN 55424-0751
e-mail: WaltGrogan@aol.com
Internet: http://shazam.imginc.com/fca/
For collectors of Fawcett comics and Magazine Enterprise comics.

Super Heroes

Dealers

Tom Burkert
Adventure Ink
97 Woodmere Rd.
Stamford, CT 06905
phone: 914-741-2510
Interested in super hero comic books.

Western

Experts

Robert Phillips
1703 North Aster Place
Broken Arrow, OK 74012
phone: 918-254-8205
fax: 918-252-9362
e-mail: rawhidebob@aol.com
Has studied and collected Western comics and Western comic art for years; has written many articles on the subject and is currently writing a reference book to be published.

COMIC COLLECTIBLES

(see also CARTOON ART; CHARACTER COLLECTIBLES; COMIC ART; COMIC BOOKS; COWBOY HEROES; DISNEY COLLECTIBLES; FAN CLUBS; PREMIUMS; SCIENCE FICTION; SUPER HEROES)

COMIC STRIPS

Sunday Newspaper

(see also CARTOON ART; CHARACTER COLLECTIBLES; ELVES)

Collectors

Claude Held
P.O. Box 515
Cheektowaga, NY 14225
Wants to buy pre-1970 Sunday comic sections; also pulp magazines before

1950, and pre-1950 E.R. Burroughs books with dust jackets.

Experts

Ken Mitchell
710 Conacher Dr.
Willowdale
Ontario M2M 3N6 Canada
phone: 416-222-5808
Buys and sells comic character collectibles (comic books, Sunday funnies, "Big Little Books", etc.) and other nostalgic paper including music (Pop) magazines and books from 1890 through 1960s.

David Begin
4901 Cabrillo Pt.
Byron, CA 94514-9476
Buys and sells Sunday newspaper comics from 1890-1980s.

Museums/Libraries

San Francisco Academy of Comic Art
2850 Ulloa
San Francisco, CA 94116-2223
phone: 415-681-1737
fax: 415-681-1737
Millions of newspaper strips, bound files, major dailies from 1890-1960, pulps, all science fiction, crime fiction, film history, children's books, comic books; excellent copies made of all graphic material; dup material for trade.

Periodicals

Tom Heintjes
Magazine: Hogan's Alley
P.O. Box 47684
Atlanta, GA 30362-0684
phone: 770-458-2624
fax: 215-957-6503
e-mail: heintjes@mindspring.com
Contains coverage of comic strips, comic books, animation, political cartooning, gag cartooning, illustration, children's books, and more.

COMMEMORATIVE ITEMS

(see ROYALTY COLLECTIBLES; SOUVENIR & COMMEMORATIVE ITEMS)

COMMUNISM

(see SOCIAL CAUSES)

COMPACT DISCS

(see also RECORDS)

Dealers

Princeton Record Exchange
20 S. Tulane St.
Princeton, NJ 08542
phone: 609-921-0881
Internet: http://www.prex.com
Buys and sells new and used CDs, LPs, and tapes: rock, jazz, alternative,

imports, oldies, shows, new releases, soundtracks, classical, opera, etc.

Record Setter, The
742 Rt. 18 N.
East Brunswick, NJ 08816
phone: 908-257-3888
fax: 908-257-2366
Specializing in new and used CDs and out-of-print albums.

Paul C. Mawhinney
Record-Rama Sound Archives
4981 McKnight Rd.
Pittsburgh, PA 15237-3407
phone: 412-367-7330 or 800-445-2357
fax: 412-367-7388
e-mail: recrama@musicmaster.com
Internet: http://www.musicmaster.com
Carries over 2,500,000 vinyl sound recordings and over 200,000 compact discs; orders only number 1-800-4-45-CD-LP.

Wax Trax
1225 N. 5th St.
Stroudsburg, PA 18360
phone: 717-421-3320
fax: 717-420-1006
Records, cassettes, compact discs; buys record collections; specializes in out-of-print records.

Golden Gallery
P.O. Box 267
Strausstown, PA 19559
phone: 717-933-5361
fax: 717-933-8817
Deals only in CDs, no vinyl; specializing in domestic and import oldies CDs, music of the 50s, 60s, and 70s.

Mike Hawkinson
Disc Collector
P.O. Box 4000
Parker, CO 80134
phone: 303-841-3000
fax: 303-840-9373
Specializing in oldies from the '50s to '70s; one of the world's largest selections.

Experts

Paul Bergquist
6406 W. Olympic Blvd.
Los Angeles, CA 90048
Co-author with Jerry Osborne of "The Official Price Guide to Compact Discs" (House of Collectibles, 1994).

Jerry Osborne
P.O. Box 255
Port Townsend, WA 98368
phone: 360-385-1200
fax: 360-385-6572
e-mail: jpo@olympus.net
Internet: http://www.olympus.net/personal/jpo
Co-author with Paul Bergquist of "The Official Price Guide to Compact Discs" (House of Collectibles, 1994).

Periodicals

Henry Rael
Newspaper: ICE
P.O. Box 3043-A
Santa Monica, CA 90408-3043
phone: 310-829-1291
fax: 310-829-2979
Internet: http://www.icemagazine.com/ice
ICE provides collectors and enthusiasts a monthly dose of unrivaled CD coverage: release schedules, first word on new albums, upcoming box sets, reissues, and industry news; published monthly.

COMPACTS

(see also CLOTHING & ACCESSORIES, Vintage; DRESSER ITEMS; PURSES)

Clubs/Associations

British Compact Collector's Society
P.O. Box 131
Working
Surrey GU24 9YR, U.K.

Roselyn Gerson
Compact Collectors Club
Newsletter: Powder Puff
P.O. Box 40
Lynbrook, NY 11563-0040
phone: 516-593-8746
fax: 516-593-0611
An international club whose members collect compacts, vanities, necessaires, etc.; newsletter contains articles, buy/sell ads, etc.

Collectors

Sherry & Mike Miller
303 Holiday Dr. #130
Tuscola, IL 61953-2118
phone: 217-253-4991
e-mail: miller@tuscola.net
Wants ladies powder compacts in shape of objects (figural compacts), e.g. shaped like a bird, a guitar, or a padlock; many made from 1920s through early 1960s by companies like Volupte, Zell, and Elgin.

Lori Landgrebe
2331 E. Main St.
Decatur, IL 62521-2263
phone: 217-423-2254
Wants to buy ladies' compacts and compact purses; buying any colorful, Art Deco, enamel novelty and figural compacts; must be in good to mint condition.

Susan Murphy
29668 Orinda Rd.
San Juan Capistrano, CA 92675-1211
phone: 714-364-4333
Wants to buy older powder compacts and anything with a compact in it or a part of it such as purses, lighters; please enclose SASE.

Dealers

Susan Murphy
29668 Orinda Rd.
San Juan Capistrano, CA 92675-1211
phone: 714-364-4333
Buys and sells ladies powder compacts, any and all that are in good to mint condition.

Experts

Roselyn Gerson
P.O. Box 100
Malverne, NY 11565
phone: 516-593-8746
fax: 516-593-0611
Wants unusual gadget compacts: cane/compact, hatpin/compact, gun/compact; also compact advertising; author of "Ladies' Compacts of the 19th & 20th Centuries", a fully-illustrated identification & value guide.

Roseann Ettinger
Remember When
2 E. Broad St.
Hazleton, PA 18201-6530
phone: 717-454-8465 or 717-450-5542
Author of "Compacts and Smoking Accessories."

Repair Services

Anton Laub Glass Corp.
1873 Second Ave.
New York, NY 10029-7453
phone: 212-734-4270 or 718-430-1901
Installation, beveling and resilvering of glass mirrors including the especially thin mirrors required for compacts.

Daniel De Tagle
de Tagle Goldsmith Shop
14400 Union Ave.
San Jose, CA 95124-2815
phone: 408-377-7000
Jeweler who repairs and replaces missing twist closures, hinges and frames on various articles including compacts; also goldsmith and manufacturer of custom and fine gold jewelry.

COMPUTERS

(see also ANTIQUES DEALERS & COLLECTORS, Computer Programs For; CALCULATORS; SLIDE RULES)

Clubs/Associations

David Greelish
Historical Computer Society
Newsletter: Historically Brewed
3649 Herschel St.
Jacksonville, FL 32205-9060
e-mail: historical@aol.com

Computer History Association of California
Newsletter: Analytical Engine, The
4159-C El Camino Way
Palo Alto, CA 94306-4010
phone: 415-856-9915
fax: 415-856-9914
e-mail: engine@chac.org
Internet: http://www.chac.org/
Focuses on the history of computers and the computer industry in California.

Collectors

Harold Layer, AV/ITV
San Francisco State University
1600 Holloway Ave.
San Francisco, CA 94132-1722
phone: 415-338-2637
e-mail: hlayer@sfsu.edu
Interested in pre-1977 computers.

Dealers

Steve Spevak
P.O. Box 3173
Winchester, VA 22604-2373
phone: 540-877-2561 or 540-665-7375
fax: 540-877-2561
Wants to buy bulk quantities of old computer circuit boards, telephone equipment circuit boards, boards from main frame computers preferred; also wants to buy bulk quantities of old vacuum tubes from old amplifiers, etc.

Experts

Thomas F. Haddock
P.O. Box 2626
Ann Arbor, MI 48106
Author of "A Collector's Guide to Personal Computers and Pocket Calculators: A Historical, Rarity, and Value Guide" (Books Americana, 1993).

Museums/Libraries

Steve Plotkin
Real World Computer Museum
Dougherty Blvd. at Rte. 1
Glen Mills, PA 19342
phone: 610-358-3245
fax: 610-358-0268
e-mail: steve_plotkin@phila.usconnect.com
A regional computer museum dedicated to preserving and displaying computing and allied technologies, storage devices, semiconductor technology, computer art; seeking old computers and electronic relics, devices and related memorabilia.

Gwen & Gordon Bell
American Computer Museum
234 East Babcock St.
Bozeman, MT 59715
phone: 406-587-7545
fax: 406-587-9620
Internet: http://www.compustory.com
Comprehensive display of calculation devices spanning 4,000 years of

history; from slide rules to micro chips.

Jim & Marie Petroff
Computer Museum of America at Coleman College
7380 Parkway Dr.
La Mesa, CA 91942
phone: 619-465-8226
Showcases computers from the 1950s punch-card processors and "ancient" video games like Pac-Man.

San Francisco Computer Museum
110 McAllister, Ste. 409
P.O. Box 420914
San Francisco, CA 94142-0914
phone: 415-703-8362
fax: 415-703-8359
Internet: http://www.fog.com/sfcm/index.html

CONDOM TINS

(see PROPHYLACTICS, Tins)

CONJURING

(see MAGICIANS PARAPHERNALIA)

CONSERVATION

(see also REPAIR/RESTORATION/CONSERVATION)

Museums/Libraries

American Association of State & Local History
Newsletter: History News Dispatch
530 Church St., Ste. 600
Nashville, TN 37219-2325
phone: 615-255-2971
fax: 615-255-2979
Supplies technical leaflets on such things as proper lighting techniques for collectors & small museums; write for list of leaflets and books on similar subjects that are offered for sale; the "Dispatch" monthly, "History News" bi-monthly.

CONSERVATORS

(see REPAIR/RESTORATION/CONSERVATION)

CONSTRUCTION EQUIPMENT

(see INDUSTRY RELATED ITEMS; MACHINERY & EQUIPMENT)

COOKBOOKS

(see also BOOKS; COOKIES & COOKIE SHAPING; FOOD COLLECTIBLES; MENUS; RECIPES)

Clubs/Associations

Bob & Jo Ellen Allen
Cook Book Collectors Club of America, Inc.
Newsletter: Cook Book Gossip
P.O. Box 56
Saint James, MO 65559-0056
phone: 314-265-8296
Focuses on cookbooks & advertising cook books and recipe publications by many companies such as Jell-O, Pillsbury, Betty Crocker, etc.

Collectors

Steve Armstrong
P.O. Box 1409
Florence, AL 35631-1409
Wants pre-1950 soft bound cookbooks, booklets, advertising recipe publications such as baking powder, JELL-O, flour, etc.; send complete description and price.

Sue Erwin
P.O. Box 32369
San Jose, CA 95152-2369
phone: 408-258-8657

Dealers

Louise Pennisi
Around the Kitchen
P.O. Box 840
Georgetown, CT 06829
phone: 203-438-2338 or 203-438-0671
e-mail: louise@aroundthekitchen.com
Internet: http://www.aroundthekitchen.com
Buying and selling collectible cookbooks (19th & 20th century), cookery booklets (Pillsbury, Baker's Chocolate, Jell-O, etc.), antique kitchen instruction & recipe pamphlets; issues catalogs of items for sale.

Mary Barile
Heritage Publications
P.O. Box 335
Arkville, NY 12406
phone: 914-586-3810
fax: 914-586-2797
Offers out-of-print and rare cookbooks; also "Cookbooks Worth Collecting", an illustrated history and guide with prices to the world of American cookbooks; for collectors, dealers, sellers, etc.; send SASE for information.

Betty Gabbert
Cookbooks 'N Things
HCR 33 Box 58
Compton, AR 72624
phone: 501-420-3418
Issues periodic catalog of contemporary cookbooks for sale.

Janet Jarvits
Janet Jarvits, Bookseller
P.O. Box 11327
Burbank, CA 91510-1327
phone: 818-848-4630
fax: 818-848-6357
e-mail: cookbkjj@interloc.com
Sells out-of-print cookbooks, books on

wine and beverages, and related magazines, ephemera, etc.; issues periodic catalogs listing items for sale; want list is available upon request; mail order.

Barbara Gelink
OTENTO Book Search
Newsletter: Old Cookbook News & Views
4756 Terrace Dr.
San Diego, CA 92116-2514
phone: 619-281-8962
Specialist in out-of-print cookbooks; also a book finder for out-of-print cookbooks; places ads in national book magazines and has realized a 50% success rate; charges $2 per title to locate book which usually takes 2-3 months.

Dick Perier
Dick Perier - Books
P.O. Box 1
Vancouver, WA 98666-0001
phone: 306-696-2033

Experts

Bob & Jo Ellen Allen
231 E. James Blvd.
P.O. Box 85
Saint James, MO 65559-0085
phone: 314-265-8296
Wants cookbooks & advertising cook books and recipe publications by many companies such as Jell-O, Pillsbury, Betty Crocker, etc.; author of "A Guide to Collecting Cookbooks - A Value Guide."

Museums/Libraries

Schlesinger Library at Radcliffe College
10 Garden St.
Cambridge, MA 02138-3630
phone: 617-495-8647
50,000 volumes including repository of cookbooks and manuscript materials including many charity cookbooks; also women's history and psychology.

Culinary Institute of America, Katherine Angell Library
Rte. 9
Hyde Park, NY 12538
phone: 914-452-9600
Large cookbook collection including many hard-to-find modern cookbooks and videos.

Library of Congress, Rare Books & Special Collections Division
First & Independence Aves. SE
Washington, DC 20540-4860
phone: 202-707-4144
fax: 202-707-4142
e-mail: rbsc@loc.gov
Houses the Katherine Bitting and Elizabeth Pennell collections of gastronomy and culinary publications including the musical cookbook in which recipes may be sung.

Home Economics Library, Ohio State University
Campbell Hall
1787 Neil Ave.
Columbus, OH 43210
Wide selection of cookbooks, old and new.

Periodicals

Newsletter: Cook Book
P.O. Box 88
Steuben, ME 04680
A newsletter subtitled "The Food Book Review for Cooks Who Read"; great source about cookbooks.

Sue Erwin
Newspaper: Cookbook Collectors' Exchange
P.O. Box 32369
San Jose, CA 95152-2369
phone: 408-258-8657
Lists cookbooks for sale or trade; voluntarily assist in locating items; non-commercial ads are free to collectors; articles, etc.

COOKIE JARS

(see also CERAMICS [AMERICAN PRODUCTION ARTWARE])

Auction Services

Lawrence Koons
Cookie Jar Mail Order Auctions
18 Walnut, #3
Belpre, OH 45714-2429
phone: 614-423-3393 or 614-423-5478
fax: 614-423-9638
Conducts special catalog auctions of cookie jars 6 times each year; catalog $3; consignments accepted.

Clubs/Associations

Olga Andreau
Cookie Jar Club
P.O. Box 451005
Miami, FL 33245-1005

Collectors

John Krupienski
5200 Hilltop Dr.
P.O. Box AA6
Brookhaven, PA 19015-1200
phone: 610-874-3003
Wants to buy character shaped cookie jars.

Ellen Supnick
2771 Oakbrook Manor
Fort Lauderdale, FL 33332
phone: 305-389-3911
Wants to buy figural cookie jars.

Peggy Vaught
Neardark
P.O. Box 32
Mendon, OH 45862
phone: 419-795-3404
e-mail: neardark@bright.net
Wants to buy cookie jars.

Darryl Rehr
2591 Military Ave.
Los Angeles, CA 90064-1933
phone: 310-477-5229
fax: 310-268-8420
e-mail: dcrehr@earthlink.net
Internet: http://www.earthlink.net/
~dcrehr/
*Buys interesting pre-1960 figural
cookie jars: Pearl China Chef,
Abington Witch and many, many
others.*

Loretta Hamburg
P.O. Box 1305
Woodland Hills, CA 91365-1305
phone: 818-346-1269
fax: 818-346-0215
*Wants to buy character, figural, and
advertising cookie jars of all types.*

Carl & Gari McCallum
918 Rosewood
Wasco, CA 93280
phone: 805-758-5630
*Buy, sell, trade cookie jars; collects
all types but prefers figural and
advertising jars.*

Dealers

Carol Silagyi
C.S. Antiques & Jewelry
P.O. Box 151
Wyckoff, NJ 07430
phone: 201-934-6528
*Buys and sells cartoon, Storybook, etc.
cookie jars by Abingdon, Brush,
McCoy, RRP, Shawnee, Regal, etc.;
also collects head/faces cookie jars -
over 200 in collection.*

Martin C. Sobin
Ye Olde Cookie Jar Trader
91 Fox Hollow Rd.
Sparta, NJ 07871-1107
phone: 201-729-9492
*Wants to buy figural cookie jars in
very good or better condition,
especially interested in cookie jars
made by Abingdon, Brush, and
Shawnee.*

Mark McMahon
Cookie Jars, Etc.
110 West 25th St., 8th Floor
New York, NY 1000107401
phone: 212-633-1923
fax: 212-924-8535
e-mail: peter@peterandmark.com
*Buy, sell, trade cookie jars, banks, salt
& peppers and PEZ.*

Mel Cohen
Cooki-Jar
P.O. Box 700
Pomona, NY 10970-0700
phone: 914-354-8707
Serious cookie jar collector.

Judy Posner
4195 South Tamiami Trail, Ste. 183
Venice, FL 34293-5112
phone: 941-497-7149
fax: 941-493-8085
e-mail: Judyandjef@aol.com
Internet: http://www.tias.com/stores/jpc
*Wants FIGURAL cookie jars: comic
characters, Disney, Black Mammys,
Chefs, Butlers, etc.; send for
illustrated want list.*

Jean & Bill Correll
Great Jars by Jean
1615 N Street
Bedford, IN 47421
phone: 812-279-2549

Lois & Ralph Behm
Lois' Collectibles of Antique Market III
413 W. Main St.
Saint Charles, IL 60174-1815
phone: 630-377-5599 or 847-831-5997
*Buys and sells cookie jars; will buy
entire collections.*

Mercedes DiRenzo
Jazz'e Junque
3831 N. Lincoln
Chicago, IL 60613
phone: 773-472-1500
fax: 773-472-1552
*Buys and sells vintage and new cookie
jars.*

Loretta Anderson
Pastimes Collectibles
1208 Lakeshore Dr.
Rockwall, TX 75087-4222
phone: 972-771-9636 or 972-771-8100
e-mail: lainrkwltx@aol.com
*Buys and sells figural and character
cookie jars, salt & pepper shakers,
character banks, teapots; call or write
with description and price.*

Experts

Fred & Joyce Roerig
RR 2 Box 504
Walterboro, SC 29488-9278
phone: 803-538-2487
*Buys/sells/collects cookie jars; 20+
years experience; wants figural cookie
jars not in books: Metlox, Twin
Winton Jars & accessories, black
Americana, ND School of Mines
Mammy; author of "The Collector's
Encyclopedia of Cookie Jars."*

Mike Schneider
206 Wenner St.
Wellington, OH 44090
*Author of "The Complete Cookie Jar
Book" (Schiffer Publishing, 1991.)*

Harold Nichols
Nichols Art Pottery
2419 Knapp
Ames, IA 50010
*Specializes in American art pottery:
Roseville, Weller, McCoy etc.*

Ermagene Westfall
RR 1 Box 222
Richmond, MO 64085
Author of "An Illustrated Value Guide

*to Cookie Jars" and "An Illustrated
Value Guide to Cookie Jars - Book
II," 8 1/2" x 11"; with history, dates of
companies, over 1000 cookie jars plus
full color pictures; send SASE with all
inquiries.*

Museums/Libraries

Lucille Bromberek
Cookie Jar Museum, The
23 Stephen St.
Lemont, IL 60439
phone: 630-257-5012
*Only Cookie Jar Museum in the
world; over 2000 jars from U.S. and
all over the world; also buys and sells.*

Periodicals

Joyce Roerig
Newsletter: Cookie Jarrin'
RR 2 Box 504
Walterboro, SC 29488-9278
phone: 803-538-2487
*A bi-monthly newsletter with new
information, current pricing, exciting
discoveries, lots of photos; carefully
researched for accuracy providing
collectors and dealers with an
unequaled professional quality
newsletter.*

Newsletter: Crazed Over Cookie Jars
P.O. Box 254
Savanna, IL 61074

Newspaper: Cookie Jar Collectors
Express
P.O. Box 221
Mayview, MO 64071-0221
phone: 816-584-6309
fax: 816-584-6259
*Marketplace for cookie jars; free ads;
monthly publication.*

COOKIES & COOKIE SHAPING

. (see also COOKBOOKS; COOKIE
JARS; KITCHEN COLLECTIBLES)

Clubs/Associations

Ruth Capper
Cookie Cutter Collectors Club
Newsletter: Cookie Crumbs
1167 Teal Rd. S.W.
Dellroy, OH 44620-9704
phone: 216-735-2839 or 202-966-0869
*Focusing on cookie cutters, boards
and rollers.*

Collectors

Joyce Moorhouse
2763 310th St.
Cannon Falls, MN 55009

Priscilla Hinners
2711 Jaynia Place
Lemon Grove, CA 91945-1319
phone: 619-265-1046
e-mail: mhinners@aol.com
*Wants cookie/cake boards, cookie
molds, multiple cutters, springerle,
rollers.*

Dealers

Bob & Kaaren Grossman
B & K Kitchen Primitives & Collectibles
354 Rte. 206
Chester, NJ 07930
phone: 908-879-7935
*Specializes in pre-1900 cookie cutters
and will mail-order all over the
country.*

Experts

Phyllis S. Wetherill
Cookies
9610 Greenview Lane
Manassas, VA 20109-3320
phone: 202-966-0869
*Buys/collects cookie shaping items
and anything related to cookies:
cutters, molds, presses, irons,
photographs, postcards, ads, etc.*

Periodicals

Rosemary Henry
Newsletter: Cookies
9610 Greenview Lane
Manassas, VA 20109-3320
phone: 202-966-0869
*In its 21st year, "Cookies" contains
historical information about the
shaping of cookies: new and old
cutters, molds, irons, presses, etc.; bi-
monthly.*

Milli Simerl
Newsletter: Around Ohio
508 N. Clinton
Defiance, OH 43512
phone: 419-784-1545
*Newsletter contains new cutter
sources, old cutter research, area and
national events, Q & A column.*

Repro. Sources

Robert & Sylvia Gerlack
P.O. Box 213
Emmaus, PA 18049

Gooseberry Patch
P.O. Box 634
Delaware, OH 43015

COPPER ITEMS

(see also ARTS & CRAFTS, Roycroft)

Repro. Sources

Kurt Sterhl
Orpheus Coppersmith
52 Clematis Rd.
Agawam, MA 01001

John Kopas
Copper Antiquities
P.O. Box 153
Cummaquid, MA 02637

Steve Kayne
Kayne & Son Custom Forged Hardware
100 Daniel Ridge Rd.
Candler, NC 28715
phone: 704-667-8868 or 704-665-1988
fax: 704-665-8303
*Steel, brass, bronze reproductions of
locks, pulls, thumb latches, furniture*

& interior/exterior hardware, fireplace tools & accessories, lighting, kitchen utensils, etc.; also does repairs, restoration & conservation; $5 for two catalogs.

Stickley

Collectors

Terry Seger
880 Foxcreek Ln.
Cincinnati, OH 45233-1462
Wants to buy Stickley Brothers copper; also large examples of Fulper pottery.

CORKPULLERS

(see CORKSCREWS)

CORKSCREWS

(see also BOTTLE OPENERS, Figural; WINES & WINE RELATED ITEMS)

Clubs/Associations

Donald A. Bull
International Correspondence of
  Corkscrew Addicts
20 Fairway Dr.
Stamford, CT 06903-1422
phone: 203-968-1925
e-mail: corkskrue@aol.com
Internet: http://members.aol.com/
  corkskrue/icca.htm
Membership limited to 50; members interested in corkscrews as well as wine paraphernalia such as decanters, wine strainers, funnels, etc.

Milt Becker
Canadian Corkscrew Collectors Club
Newsletter: Quarterly Worm, The
P.O. Box 5295
Englewood, NJ 07631
phone: 201-567-1500
fax: 201-493-0685
e-mail: clarethous@aol.com
Worldwide membership; write for application form.

John Stanley
Just for Openers
Newsletter: Just for Openers Newsletter
P.O. Box 64
Chapel Hill, NC 27514
phone: 919-419-1546 or 919-966-5794
Just for Openers is a club for bottle and corkscrew collectors; quarterly newsletter.

Collectors

Mike Gordon
57 Bundy Lane
Storrs, CT 06268
phone: 860-429-3834
fax: 860-429-3834
Wants to buy any old or unusual corkscrew; please photocopy.

Milt Becker
P.O. Box 5295
Englewood, NJ 07631
phone: 201-567-1500
fax: 201-493-0685
e-mail: clarethous@aol.com
Wants any corkscrew or corkpuller; buys single items or entire collections; send photocopy of item and price.

Joe Young
P.O. Box 587
Elgin, IL 60121-0587
phone: 847-695-0108 or 847-254-8208
fax: 847-695-1679
e-mail: istamp2@msn.com
Wants to buy unusual corkscrews; also interested in combination tools with corkscrews; all correspondence answered.

Aaron Corenman
P.O. Box 747
Los Altos, CA 94023
phone: 415-948-6174

Dealers

Paul P. Luchsinger
1126 Wishart St.
Hermitage, PA 16148-4410
phone: 412-346-2331
fax: 412-246-2331
Buys, sells, collects old and unusual corkscrews as well as other wine related items.

Experts

Donald A. Bull
20 Fairway Dr.
Stamford, CT 06903-1422
phone: 203-968-1925
e-mail: corkskrue@aol.com
Internet: http://members.aol.com/
  corkskrue/icca.htm
Buys corkscrews or anything picturing corkscrews; author of "A Price Guide to Beer Advertising Openers and Corkscrews."

Mark Barlow
Winetiques
3107A Medlock Bridge Rd.
Norcross, GA 30071-1423
phone: 770-449-7610
fax: 770-449-1839
Buys, sells and specializes in corkscrews and all wine related items; from basic to unique patents.

Roger V. Baker
Baker's Lady Luck Emporium
P.O. Box 620417
Redwood City, CA 94062-0417
phone: 369-851-7188
Specializing in saloon collectibles: gambling, bar bottles, shaving mugs, razors, Bowie knives, daggers, barber items, match safes.

CORN COLLECTIBLES

(see also SACKS)

Clubs/Associations

E. Eloise Alton, Ed.
Corn Items Collectors Association Inc.
Newsletter: Bang Board, The
613 N. Long St.
Shelbyville, IL 62565-1544
phone: 217-774-5002
Association collecting and studying anything having to do with corn, i.e. inventions, corn collectibles, etc.; large format newsletter with lots of pictures and articles.

Corn Shellers

Collectors

Robert Rauhauser
RR 2 Box 766
Thomasville, PA 17364-9622
Wants corn shellers: handheld, table mounted, box mounted; any unusual corn shellers; also popcorn shellers.

Don Monnier
P.O. Box 772
Sidney, OH 45365
phone: 513-492-1420
Wants hand held iron or primitive handmade style corn shellers.

Jim Moffet
P.O. Box 200
Modesto, IL 62667-0200
phone: 217-439-7358
Wants all styles of hand-held ear corn shellers.

CORONATION MEMORABILIA

(see POSTCARDS, Royalty Related; ROYALTY COLLECTIBLES, British)

COSTUME JEWELRY

(see GEMS & JEWELRY, Vintage & Costume)

COSTUMES

(see CLOTHING & ACCESSORIES, Vintage; MOVIE MEMORABILIA; SCIENCE FICTION, Costuming)

COUNTERFEIT DETECTING ITEMS

Collectors

Donald Gorlick
P.O. Box 24541
Seattle, WA 98124-0541
phone: 206-824-0508
Wants counterfeit currency detectors, coin testers, scales, scanners, grids, books, reporters, recorders, magnifiers, Detectographs, etc.

COUNTRY STORE COL-LECTIBLES

(see ADVERTISING COL-LECTIBLES; BOTTLES; CIGAR BANDS, BOXES & LABELS; FARM COLLECTIBLES; LABELS; STRING HOLDERS; TIN CONTAINERS)

COVERED BRIDGES

Clubs/Associations

Russell J. Holmes
Theodore Burr Covered Bridge Society
  of Pennsylvania, Inc.
Magazine: Wooden Covered Spans
P.O. Box 2382
Lancaster, PA 17606
phone: 717-428-1006
Society is committed to saving and preserving covered bridges; monthly meeting held for collectors of bridge related material; also publishes the newsletter "Pennsylvania Crossings."

Collectors

Marie Ward
2461 E High St., #A-7
Pottstown, PA 19464-3111
phone: 610-970-6299
Wants items relating to covered bridges.

COVERLETS

(see also FOLK ART; REPAIR/ RESTORATION/CONSERVATION, Textiles; TEXTILES)

Clubs/Associations

Barbara Frisbie
Colonial Coverlet Guild of America
Newsletter: CCGA Newsletter
5617 Blackstone
La Grange, IL 60525-3420
phone: 708-352-3812
Members are interested in coverlets or antique textiles, their preservation and in the present revival of weaving.

Dealers

Carl McCann
Troy & Black, Inc.
P.O. Box 228
Red Creek, NY 13143-0228
phone: 315-754-8115
Buys and sells high quality flow blue, Staffordshire figurines, American painted furniture, stoneware, redware, coverlets, samplers, and other American textiles, folk art, etc.

Misc. Services

University of Maryland Historic Textile
  Data Base
Dept. of Theater
0202 Tawee
College Park, MD 20742
Compiling coverlet information from museums, researchers, and collectors.

Barbara Luck
Abby Aldrich Rockefeller Folk Art
  Center
P.O. Box 1776
Williamsburg, VA 23187
Will assist in identifying an unknown coverlet weaver.

Museums/Libraries

Museum of American Textile History
491 Dutton St.
Lowell, MA 01854
phone: 508-441-0400
fax: 508-441-1412
Outstanding collection of textiles and textile making machinery and equipment; tools, machines, prints, photographs, business records, industry periodicals, textiles, swatches, sample books, trade catalogs, etc.

Repro. Sources

David C. Kline
Family Heir-Loom Weavers
775 Meadowview Dr.
Red Lion, PA 17356-8608
phone: 717-246-2431 or 717-246-2431
fax: 717-246-2431
e-mail:
FamilyHeirloom@mindspring.com
Makers of fancy jacquard coverlets, ingrain carpets & other historic textiles; send $4.00 for brochure.

Goodwin Weavers
P.O. Box 408
Blowing Rock, NC 28605

COW COLLECTIBLES

(see also DAIRY COLLECTIBLES; ELSIE THE BORDEN COW ITEMS)

Clubs/Associations

Cow Observers Worldwide
240 Wahl Ave.
Evans City, PA 16033
e-mail: peiffer@chapel.fcasd.edu

Man./Prod./Dist.

Carol J. Peiffer, Pub.
Cowtree Collector
240 Wahl Ave.
Evans City, PA 16033-1053
phone: 412-538-5038
e-mail: peiffer@chapel.fcasd.edu
Distributor of original cow art and matted reproductions of humorous cow art; these "visual puns" include "Americow Graffiti," "A Line of Bull," "The Darkside of the MOO," "Beautiful Creamer," "Blue MOO" and more.

Periodicals

Carol J. Peiffer, Pub.
Cowtree Collector
Newsletter: MOOsletter, the
240 Wahl Ave.
Evans City, PA 16033-1053
phone: 412-538-5038
e-mail: peiffer@chapel.fcasd.edu
Quarterly newsletter with cow talk, cartoons, mail order sources for whatever has been produced using the cow theme ("COWllectibles"): stories on collectors, cow and dairy information, from the serious to the UDDERLY ridiculous.

Carol J. Peiffer, Pub.
Cowtree Collector
Directory: Cow Buying Guide
240 Wahl Ave.
Evans City, PA 16033-1053
phone: 412-538-5038
e-mail: peiffer@chapel.fcasd.edu
This directory contains the names, addresses and phone numbers of more than 300 individuals, companies, corporations and associations who buy and sell cow-related merchandise or who provide information on cows or the dairy industry.

COWBOY HEROES

(see also CHARACTER COLLECTIBLES; COMIC BOOKS, Super Heroes; MOVIE MEMORABILIA, Westerns; POPULAR CULTURE; PREMIUMS; TELEVISION SHOWS & MEMORABILIA, Westerns; WESTERN AMERICANA)

Clubs/Associations

Norman Kietzer
Westerns & Serials Fan Club
Magazine: Westerns & Serials
Rte. 1 Box 103
Vernon Center, MN 56090-9744
phone: 507-549-3677
fax: 507-549-3788
A club for collectors as well as non-collectors interested in westerns and serials of the silver screen; also interested in related memorabilia.

Collectors

Jim Babchak
313 East 85 #4B
New York, NY 10028
phone: 212-861-1356
Wants to buy old cowboy stuff including cowboy boots, shirts, horsehair bridles, spurs, chaps, children's costumes from the 1940s and 1950s, anything Roy Rogers, Hopalong Cassidy or Gene Autry.

Lee H. Mitchell
175 E. Delaware, #8210
Chicago, IL 60611-1732
phone: 800-869-7869 or 312-337-3123
fax: 312-266-7982
Lover of Hoppy, Roy Rogers, Gene Autry, etc. seriously wants to buy cowboy hero collectibles or collections; welcomes hearing from dealers and other collectors.

Phil Ellis
P.O. Box 11042
Santa Rosa, CA 95406
phone: 707-544-6050
Wants Hopalong Cassidy, Roy Rogers, Gene Autry; comic toys, Disneyana, radio premiums, TV Westerns, etc.

Dealers

Barry Friedman
P.O. Box 55492
Valencia, CA 91385-0492
phone: 805-255-2365
e-mail: BaryF@fishnet.net
Buys blankets and bedspreads with cowboy or Indian designs.

Jim & Shirley's Antiques
146 N. Glassell St.
Orange, CA 92866
phone: 714-639-9662 or 562-598-1914
Specializes in Hopalong Cassidy, and Roy Rogers and Dale Evans memorabilia.

Experts

Mario De Marco
152 Maple St.
West Boylston, MA 01583-1825
phone: 508-835-4085
Author and publisher of books on Charles Starrett, George "Gabby" Hayes, Tom Mix, Horse Bits and B Westerns, John Wayne, Don Barry, Tex Ritter and Fred Scott, Sagebrush heroes, William "Hoppy" Boyd, and others.

Ron Donnelly
Saturday Heroes
P.O. Box 7047
Panama City, FL 32413-0047
phone: 904-234-7944
fax: 904-233-9316
Specializes in Hopalong Cassidy and other Cowboy Heroes; owns the original tools and dies that made the foil faces for the Arvin "Hopalong Cassidy" radio; advisor to "Schroeder's Price Guide."

Periodicals

John Koenig
Antique Trader Publications, Inc.
Newspaper: Toy Trader
922 Churchill St., Ste. #1
Waupaca, WI 54981
phone: 715-258-7525 or 800-768-9225
fax: 715-258-8707
e-mail: jkoenig@add-inc.com
Internet: http://www.csmonline.com
Monthly newspaper with information on how to buy, sell and trade all types of toys; market trends, the latest prices, "how-to" columns, listings of toy clubs and upcoming toy shows and auctions; also full of buy and sell ads.

Joe Caro
Newsletter: Cowboy Collector Newsletter, The
P.O. Box 7486
Long Beach, CA 90807
phone: 310-428-6972
Articles on Hopalong Cassidy, Gene Autry, Roy Rogers, The Lone Ranger, etc.

Buck Jones

Clubs/Associations

Joe Silva
Buck Jones Western Corral
Newsletter: Buck Jones Western Corral Newsletter
301 Alta Lane
Brookings, OR 97415-9670
phone: 503-469-1969

Gene Autry

Clubs/Associations

Alf Hill
Gene Autry International Fan Club
Newsletter: Gene Autry International Fan Club Bulletin
20 Cranleigh Gardens
Stoke Bishop
Bristol BS9 1HD, U.K.

Rosemarie Addison
Gene Autry Fan Club
4322 Heidelberg Ave.
Saint Louis, MO 63123-6812

Museums/Libraries

Elvin Sweeten
Gene Autry Museum
Newspaper: Gene Autry Star Telegram
P.O. Box 67
Gene Autry, OK 73436
phone: 405-389-5335 or 405-294-3047
fax: 405-389-5139
Museum of Gene Autry memorabilia including photos, posters, etc.; also local memorabilia; the newspaper is an annual to promote the community & the man; very big with collectors world over; includes photos & stories relating to both.

Gene Autry Western Heritage Museum
Magazine: Spur
4700 Western Heritage Way
Los Angeles, CA 90027-1462
phone: 213-667-2000
fax: 213-660-5721
Collects items relating to the American West, including Western film memorabilia.

Hopalong Cassidy

Clubs/Associations

John Spencer, Pres.
Friends of Hopalong Cassidy International Fan Club
Newsletter: Hoppy Talk
4613 Araby Church Rd.
Frederick, MD 21701-7791
phone: 301-663-6539
Club organized to establish a museum in Cambridge, OH (boyhood home of William Boyd); newsletter contains, articles, buy/sell ads, etc.; newsletter published quarterly.

Collectors

Chris Swain
74 Ranney Corder Rd.
Ashfield, MA 01330
phone: 413-628-3213
Wants items relating to Hopalong Cassidy.

Harry L. Rinker
5093 Vera Cruz Rd.
Emmaus, PA 18049-9554
phone: 610-965-1122
fax: 610-965-1124
e-mail: rinkeron@fast.net
Seeking Hopalong Cassidy memorabilia.

Ron Pieczkowski
1707 Orange Hill Dr.
Brandon, FL 33510-2632
phone: 813-685-2338
Wants to buy Hopalong Cassidy collectibles; single items or entire collections.

Laura Bates
6310 Friendship Dr.
New Concord, OH 43762-9708
phone: 614-826-4850
Editor of "Hoppy Talk", the newsletter of the Friends of Hopalong Cassidy International Fan Club.

Dealers

Howard R. Cherry
1301 N. 11th St.
Cambridge, OH 43725
phone: 614-432-5700 or 614-432-3454
Wants to buy Cowboy memorabilia: Roy Rogers, Gene Autry, Hopalong Cassidy.

Experts

Joe Caro
P.O. Box 7486
Long Beach, CA 90807
phone: 310-428-6972
Author of "Collectors Guide to Hopalong Cassidy Memorabilia."

Jimmy Wakely

Clubs/Associations

Hubert Martin
Jimmy Wakely Saddle Pals
Newsletter: Jimmy Wakely Saddle Pals Bulletin
Cherokee Foothills
Scenic Highway 11
Gaffney, SC 29340

Lone Ranger

Clubs/Associations

John Samorajczyk
Lone Ranger Fan Club
Newsletter: Pictorial Scrapbook
19205 Seneca Ridge Court
Gaithersburg, MD 20879-3135

Collectors

John S. Fawcett
P.O. Box 1156
Waldoboro, ME 04572-1156
phone: 207-832-7398
Wants to buy 1930s to 1950s Lone Ranger items; wants everything.

Karl L. Rommel
1377 Cloverleaf Rd.
Lansing, MI 48906
phone: 517-484-7865
Wants all 1933-1955 "Lone Ranger" memorabilia.

Dealers

Terry & Kay Klepey
P.O. Box 553
Forks, WA 98331-0553
phone: 360-327-3726 or 360-374-5717
Buys, sells and collects Lone Ranger and related items: comics, toys, books, dolls, etc.; also interested in other 1950s Westerns.

Periodicals

Terry & Kay Klepey
Silver Bullet, The
Newsletter: Silver Bullet
P.O. Box 553
Forks, WA 98331-0553
phone: 360-327-3726 or 360-374-5717
A quarterly newsletter for Lone Ranger enthusiasts and collectors; publishing for over 38 issues since 1988.

Red Ryder

Collectors

Gabby Talkington
4703 Upland Dr.
Richmond, CA 94803-3227
phone: 510-223-1142
fax: 510-233-3388
e-mail: oldlures@aol.com
Wants Red Ryder games, books, guns, puzzles, etc. for private collection.

Robert Fuller

Clubs/Associations

Janette Anderson
Robert Fuller Fan Club
Newsletter: Laramie Trail, The
407 West Rosemary Lane
Falls Church, VA 22046-3847
fax: 703-358-5402
The official fan club for western star, Robert Fuller.

Roy Rogers & Dale Evans

Clubs/Associations

Nancy Horsley, ExSec
Roy Rogers - Dale Evans Collectors Association
Newsletter: RRDECA Newsletter
P.O. Box 1166
Portsmouth, OH 45662-1166
phone: 614-353-0900 or 614-353-4002
Organized as a part of the Portsmouth Area Community Exhibits which maintains the Roy Rogers Hometown Exhibit in Portsmouth, Roy's boyhood hometown.

Collectors

Laura Lee Gwaltney
3104 East 5th St.
Anderson, IN 46012
phone: 317-642-6318
Especially interested in Western paper items, but also collects anything to do with Roy Rogers & his family.

Don Mabbitt
P.O. Box 114
Sheldon, IL 60966
phone: 815-429-3671
Wants to buy Roy Rogers and Dale Evans collectibles: cap guns, toys, and other memorabilia.

Janey Miller
1822 Chelle Ct.
Jefferson City, MO 65101-6003
phone: 573-635-5171
e-mail: millczy4rr@aol.com
Collects all memorabilia related to Roy Rogers and Dale Evans: audio, video, paper, toys, etc.

Experts

Robert Phillips
1703 North Aster Place
Broken Arrow, OK 74012
phone: 918-254-8205
fax: 918-252-9362
e-mail: rawhidebob@aol.com
Has conducted pioneering research with Roy Rogers comics, has collected Roy Rogers memorabilia for over 30 years, conducted extensive research into the careers of Roy Rogers and Dale Evans; authored/edited book on subject.

Museums/Libraries

Roy Rogers Hometown Exhibit, c/o Chamber of Commerce
P.O. Box 509
Portsmouth, OH 45662
phone: 614-353-1116

Roy Rogers & Dale Evans Museum
15650 Seneca Rd.
Victorville, CA 92392
phone: 619-243-4547

Tom Mix

Book Sellers

Paul E. Mix
PM Publications
Newsletter: Western Legends
P.O. Box 180182
Austin, TX 78718-0182
phone: 512-836-8005
Sells Tom Mix related booklets and photo catalogs; also collects, buys and sells Tom Mix memorabilia.

Clubs/Associations

John Samorajczyk
Tom Mix Fan Club
Newsletter: Tom Mix Fan Club Newsletter
19205 Seneca Ridge Court
Gaithersburg, MD 20879-3135
Membership includes four issues of the club newsletter.

Experts

Mario De Marco
152 Maple St.
West Boylston, MA 01583-1825
phone: 508-835-4085
Author of "Photostory of The Screen's Greatest Cowboy - Tom Mix"; one of the very early publications on Tom Mix, soft cover, 100+ pages, loaded with rare photos and bio of Tom and some of the other associated stars; $10.50 ppd.

M.G. "Bud" Norris
1324 N. Hague Ave.
Columbus, OH 3204-2108
phone: 614-274-4646
Buys Tom Mix memorabilia; author of "The Tom Mix Book"; publicity director of the International Tom Mix Festival; consultant to the Tom Mix Museum, Dewey, OK.

Museums/Libraries

Tom Mix Museum
721 North Delaware
Dewey, OK 74029
phone: 918-534-1555

Periodicals

Paul E. Mix
PM Publications
Newsletter: Western Legends
P.O. Box 180182
Austin, TX 78718-0182
phone: 512-836-8005
An quarterly newsletter focusing primarily on Tom Mix.

COWBOY/COWGIRL COLLECTIBLES

(see COWBOY HEROES; WESTERN AMERICANA)

CRACKER JACK TOYS

Clubs/Associations

Larry White
Cracker Jack Collectors Association
Newsletter: Prize Insider, The
108 Central St.
Rowley, MA 01969
phone: 508-948-8187
A nonprofit association dedicated to the collector of Cracker Jack and related memorabilia; share knowledge and correspondence; membership includes newsletter and membership card; holds annual convention.

Collectors

Larry White
108 Central St.
Rowley, MA 01969
phone: 508-948-8187

Ann Brogley
P.O. Box 16033
Philadelphia, PA 19114-0033
phone: 215-824-4698
fax: 215-824-4698
Wants to buy Cracker Jack items; one item or entire collections; all letters answered.

Ann Brogley
P.O. Box 16033
Philadelphia, PA 19114-0033
phone: 215-824-4698 or 215-824-2350
fax: 215-824-4698
e-mail: mostprod@erols.com
President of Cracker Jack Collectors Association.

Wes Johnson
106 Bauer Ave.
Louisville, KY 40207-2559
Advanced collector wants tin, cast metal, plastic toy prizes, old paper items; also ANGELUS Marshmallows, CHECKERS Confection items.

Edwin Snyder
P.O. Box 156
Lancaster, KY 40444-0156
phone: 606-792-4816
Wants to buy Cracker Jack, Checkers Confections, Chums, and related items, prizes and advertising.

Barry Brandon
651 Linda Ln.
Bonner Springs, KS 66012-1809
phone: 913-441-8663
Wants Cracker Jack prizes: tin, cast metal, plastic and paper; also collects Angelus, Checkers, Reliable Confections.

Experts

Ron Toth, Jr.
72 Charles St.
Rochester, NH 03867-3413
phone: 603-335-2062
Collects and specializes in Cracker Jack memorabilia.

Museums/Libraries

Columbus Science Museum
280 East Broad St.
Columbus, OH 43215

CRAFTS

(see also ART; GEMS & JEWELRY)

Clubs/Associations

American Craft Association
21 South Eltings Corner Rd.
Highland, NY 12528
phone: 800-724-0859 or 914-863-6100
fax: 914-883-6130
An association offering trade and professional services to craft persons and craft retailers.

Fred Bair, Jr.
Society of Workers in Early Arts & Trades
Newsletter: Sweat Rag, The
606 Lake Lena Blvd.
Auburndale, FL 33823-2937
phone: 941-967-3262
fax: 941-967-3262
Members are largely those who do public demonstrations of early crafts, but membership is open to anyone; exchange knowledge of practices in crafts; promotes the finding, making and exchange of tools; annual directory.

Misc. Services

Linda Gibbs
Victorian - An Era of the Past
10380 Miranda Ave.
Buena Park, CA 90620
phone: 714-827-6488
Offers classes in the lost Victorian crafts; hearts, flowers, a touch of lace create old fashioned delights, one-of-a-kind items that will become your heirloom keepsakes; send SASE for info.

Museums/Libraries

American Craft Museum
40 West 53rd St.
New York, NY 10019
phone: 212-956-6047

On-Line Services

CraftWEB, c/o Opportunity Network
3701 Heary Blvd., #325
San Francisco, CA 94118
e-mail: kmcmahon@craftweb.com
Internet: http://www.craftweb.com
On-line resource for artisans who make unique, quality, handcrafted fine craft art: craftspeople, craft organizations, etc.; basketry, ceramics, glass, textiles, woodworking.

Periodicals

American Craft Council
Magazine: American Craft
72 Spring St.
New York, NY 10012-4019
phone: 212-274-0630
fax: 212-274-0650
Non-profit educational organization founded in 1943; offers juried craft fairs, maintains special library of 20th century crafts; offers seminars and services to professional crafts people; membership open to all.

Magazine: Crafts Report, The
P.O. Box 1992
Wilmington, DE 19899-1992
phone: 302-656-2209
e-mail: subscribe@assocgraphics.com
Internet: http://www.craftsreport.com
The business journal for the crafts industry.

Magazine: Ornament
P.O. Box 2349
San Marcos, CA 92079-2349
phone: 800-888-8950 or 619-599-0222
A quarterly magazine focusing on craft and art items of personal adornment in any media or form: fiber, glass, metal, historic/ethnic ornament; ethnographic and tribal jewelry; also reviews of museum exhibits and publications.

Glass

(see also GLASS; STAINED GLASS)

Periodicals

Magazine: Glass Line
120 S. Kroeger St.
Anaheim, CA 92805-4011
phone: 714-520-0121
fax: 714-520-4370
e-mail: editor@hotglass.com
Internet: http://www.hotglass.com/
Bi-monthly; glass working information, supplies, etc.; the number one publication for the hot glass artists; beads, hobby, glass art, sculptures, supplies, equipment, collectors.

Jewelry

Appraisers

Daloma Armentrout
Armentrout-Hawken Appraisal Associates
P.O. Box 160906
Austin, TX 78716-0906
phone: 512-288-1507
fax: 512-328-9411
Expert specializing in the appraisal of fine contemporary art jewelry and art metals crafts; author of "Art Jewelry & Metals - Makers, Markets, Meaning"; also collection consultant, and educator.

Metal

Clubs/Associations

Society of North American Goldsmiths
Journal: Metalsmith
5009 Londonderry Dr.
Tampa, FL 33647-9910
phone: 813-977-5326
fax: 813-977-8462
e-mail: rmitchel@cftnet.com
Internet: http://www.craftweb.com/org/snag/snag.html
An association for jewelers and metal artisans; quarterly magazine devoted to the development and appreciation for the craft of fine metalsmithing: jewelry, decorative art, etc.

CRANBERRY INDUSTRY ITEMS

Collectors

Peter K. Meier
P.O. Box 184
Halifax, MA 02338
phone: 617-293-3218
Wants to buy cranberry scoops and related items; paper goods, tools and implements related to the cranberry growing industry.

CREDIT CARDS & CHARGE ITEMS

(see also BANKING; CIVIL WAR ARTIFACTS, Currency; COINS & CURRENCY; MONEYCARDS; TELEPHONE CARDS; WOODEN MONEY)

Clubs/Associations

Bill Wieland, Pres.
American Credit Card Collectors Society
Newsletter: ACCCS Newsletter
P.O. Box 2465
Midland, MI 48640
phone: 517-839-2026
fax: 517-839-2026
e-mail: tmcgrath@proaxis.com
Internet: http://www.proaxis.com/~tmcgrath/acccs.htm

Collectors

Robert A. Hendel
1385 York Ave. #16B
New York, NY 10021
phone: 212-772-9070 or 212-450-4733
fax: 212-450-5521
Wants to buy all types of plastic or paper cards; also wants metal charge plates; will pay premium for American Express and Diners Club cards; ship cards for appraisal and offer.

Gary Olsen
505 S. Royal Ave.
Front Royal, VA 22630
phone: 703-635-7157 or 703-635-7158
fax: 703-635-1818
e-mail: hpfrigko@interloc.com
Collecting since 1960s; will pay $1 each plus postage for any age, quantity or condition of expired credit cards; plastic, paper, metal.

Jerry Ballard
P.O. Box 1992
Midlothian, VA 23112-1992
phone: 804-744-7700
fax: 804-744-6600
Wants credit cards and charge coins; will pay $1 to $5 for each pre-1985 card; send photocopy or cards.

Ron Kempner
P.O. Box 981
Wilmette, IL 60091
phone: 708-869-6757
Wants to buy credit cards, charge plates; paper or plastic; AMX, Diners, Carte Blanche most desirable.

T.L. Helgeson
Credit Card Collector, The
1645 W. Valencia Rd. Box 432
Tucson, AZ 85746
phone: 602-294-6865
fax: 602-573-1509
*Wants to buy all types of credit and
charge items: paper, plastic, metal,
and celluloid from the late 1800s to
1990s; expired/closed account items
only; send photocopy and description
of what you have.*

Experts

Lin Overholt
P.O. Box 8481
Saint Petersburg, FL 33738-8481
phone: 813-393-5397
e-mail: axvisamc@aol.com
Internet: http://members.aol.com/
AXVISAMC/index.html
*Author of "Standard Catalog of
International Credit Cards."*

Periodicals

Lin Overholt
Newsletter: Credit Cards & Phone Cards
News
P.O. Box 8481
Saint Petersburg, FL 33738-8481
phone: 813-393-5397
e-mail: axvisamc@aol.com
Internet: http://members.aol.com/
AXVISAMC/index.html
*Quarterly publication for collectors of
telephone tokens/cards, charge coins,
charge plates, credit cards.*

Magazine: Moneycard Collector
P.O. Box 783
Sidney, OH 45365
phone: 513-498-0879 or 800-221-3148

CRESTED WARE

(see CERAMICS [ENGLISH], Goss
Pottery Co./Crested Ware)

CRIME

(see LAW ENFORCEMENT
MEMORABILIA; MYSTERY/
DETECTIVE ITEMS; OUTLAWS &
LAWMEN; PERSONALITIES
[CRIMINALS])

CRUCIFIXES

(see RELIGIOUS COLLECTIBLES,
Crosses)

CRUETS

(see also GLASS, Pattern; GLASS,
Art)

Experts

Elaine Ezell
Cruets, Cruets, Cruets
P.O. Box 1609
Pasadena, MD 21122-1609
phone: 410-255-6777 or 410-551-4101
*Advanced collector and co-author
with George Newhouse of "Cruets,*

*Cruets, Cruets" (Vol I $29.95 and Vol
II $32.95 from author); buys/sells art
glass and colored Victorian cruets.*

CRUISE SHIP ITEMS

(see OCEAN LINER COL-
LECTIBLES)

CRYPTOGRAPHIC DEVICES

(see SPY EQUIPMENT)

CRYSTAL BALLS

(see UFO'S & UNEXPLAINED
PHENOMENA)

CUBAN COLLECTIBLES

Collectors

Miquel A. De Dios
P.O. Box 8155
Union City, NJ 07087-1855
*Wants to buy Cuba-related col-
lectibles and memorabilia; send
description and price.*

Dealers

Ayer Books
15921 SW 85th St.
Miami, FL 33193-3077
*Wants books, Cuban authors,
magazines, movie posters that mention
Cubans, Cuban memorabilia.*

Museums/Libraries

Museo Historica Cubano
3131 Coral Way
Miami, FL 33145
phone: 305-567-313
fax: 305-567-1416

CUFF LINKS

(see also BELT BUCKLES;
CLOTHING & ACCESSORIES,
Vintage; GEMS & JEWELRY; TIE
BARS, CLIPS & TACKS)

Clubs/Associations

Eugene R. Klompus
National Cuff Link Society
Newsletter: Link, The
P.O. Box 346
Prospect Heights, IL 60070-0346
phone: 847-816-0035
fax: 847-816-0035
*For collectors of cuff links, tie bars,
tie tacks, collar buttons, collar pins,
shirt studs, stick pins, money clips,
vintage collars/cuffs, belt buckles, and
button covers; members get 6 free cuff
link appraisals per year.*

Collectors

Claude Jeanloz
Yield House Industries, Inc.
P.O. Box 2525
Conway, NH 03818
phone: 603-447-8500 or 413-659-3109
fax: 603-447-1717
Wants all types of cull links for cuff

*link museum: cuff links, cuff buttons,
cuff jewelry, and cuff link memorabilia.*

James S. McCormick
476 Windswept Dr.
Asheville, NC 28801
phone: 704-253-2660 or 704-254-0071
e-mail: 75362.1253@compuserve.com

Dealers

Gail Busche
Archangel Antiques
334 East Ninth St.
New York, NY 10003-7924
phone: 212-260-9313
*Buying antique buttons, cuff links, eye
glasses, and vintage lighters; always
seeking fine examples such as enamel
Deco and Art Nouveau.*

Experts

Eugene R. Klompus
P.O. Box 346
Prospect Heights, IL 60070-0346
phone: 847-816-0035
fax: 847-816-0035
*Buys, sells, collects, appraises cuff
links; writes articles for collectors'
publications; author of "Collectors
Guide to Cuff Link Collecting"; expert
spokesperson on cuff links and related
miscellaneous jewelry.*

Howard L. Bell, Jr.
P.O. Box 11695
Kansas City, MO 64138-0195
phone: 816-756-3888
*Buys, sells, collects, appraises Cuff
Jewelry: cuff links & buttons,
bachelor's buttons, button covers, silk
knots; author of "Cuff Jewelry; A
Historical Account for Collector and
Dealer"; writes articles and speaks on
the topic.*

Museums/Libraries

Cuff Link Museum
P.O. Box 2525
Conway, NH 03818
phone: 603-447-8500 or 413-659-3109
fax: 603-447-1717

CUP PLATES

(see also GLASS)

Clubs/Associations

Ernets Remondini, Mem.
Pairpoint Cup Plate Collectors of
America
Magazine: Thistle
P.O. Box 890052
East Weymouth, MA 02189-0001
phone: 617-335-2716
*An organization for collectors of cup
plates; "Thistle" published twice a
year; also publishes the "Mini-
Thistle" bi-monthly newsletter.*

Experts

John E. Bilane
2065 Morris Ave., Apt. 109
Union, NJ 07083-6015
phone: 908-686-3060
*Buys and sells antique glass cup
plates.*

CURRENCY

(see COINS & CURRENCY)

CUTLERY

(see DIAMOND EDGE; KEEN
KUTTER; KNIVES)

**Here are some tips
when contacting
someone listed in this
book:**

**When requesting
information about a
particular item, include a
description (material,
dimensions, maker's
mark, model number,
etc.) and a photo, sketch,
or photocopy of the item
in question. ■**

**Always ask if there are
charges for samples or
for the services
requested. ■**

**When writing, please be
sure to include a Large
(#10 business size)
Self-Addressed and
Stamped Envelope
(LSASE) if requesting a
reply or the return of
photographs. ■**

**Never call collect unless
otherwise directed.
When calling, be
considerate of time zone
differences and always
ask if the party you are
calling has time to talk.
When leaving an
answering machine
message, always instruct
the party to call you
back collect. ■**

DAGUERREOTYPES

(see PHOTOGRAPHS)

DAIRY COLLECTIBLES

(see also BOTTLE CAPS, Milk; BOTTLES, Milk; COW COL-LECTIBLES; DAIRY QUEEN MEMORABILIA; ELSIE THE BORDEN COW ITEMS; FARM COLLECTIBLES; KITCHEN COLLECTIBLES)

Clubs/Associations

Thomas Gallagher
National Association of Milk Bottle Collectors, Inc.
Newsletter: Milk Route, The
4 Ox Bow Rd.
Westport, CT 06880-2602
phone: 203-227-5244
fax: 203-227-2206
Internet: http://
www.collectoronline.com/club-NAMBC-wp.html
Focuses on milk and dairy history and related memorabilia; membership includes the newsletter and directory of members; newsletter has articles, ads, show dates, information exchange, patents, events, etc.

Collectors

Stephen Foster
94 Knobb Hill Rd.
Milford, CT 06460-7245
phone: 203-877-5802
Wants to buy milk bottles and "udder" dairy items.

Sam A. Stephens
319 Juniper St.
Warminster, PA 18974-4720
phone: 215-672-4814 or 215-443-4173
Collector of advertising items relating to cream separators and the dairy industry,

Nancy Pennington
1750 Keyes Rd.
Greenbrier, TN 37073
phone: 615-643-0290
fax: 615-643-0290
e-mail: npenn2405@aol.com
Wants to buy dairy items such as milk bottles, advertising, cow pitchers, and ice cream items.

Dealers

Ridgecrest Farm
43 Ridgecrest Dr.
Wilton, ME 04294
phone: 207-645-2443
Your "Maine" connection for dairy

collectibles, milk bottles; buys and sells; send SASE for latest catalog of offerings; from Nov. 1 through April 30 contact at 22201 Scenic Ridge Ct., Mt. Dora, FL 32575 (352-735-3831).

Ralph Riovo
686 Franklin St.
Alburtis, PA 18011-9578
phone: 610-966-2536
Adlactilist and dealer in milk and dairy memorabilia; wants milk bottles, dairy advertising and related memorabilia.

Experts

Thomas Gallagher
4 Ox Bow Rd.
Westport, CT 06880-2602
phone: 203-227-5244
fax: 203-227-2206
Internet: http://
www.collectoronline.com/club-NAMBC-wp.html

Tony Knipp
P.O. Box 105
Blooming Grove, NY 10914-0105
phone: 914-496-6841 or 914-938-4580
Internet: http://
www.collectoronline.com/

Leigh Giarde
LG Enterprises
P.O. Box 2243
Redlands, CA 92373-0741
phone: 909-792-8681
fax: 909-792-8681
e-mail: vikinghus@cpl.net
Mail order sales and purchases of milk bottles and go-withs; author of "Glass Milk Bottles: Their Makers and Marks."

Museums/Libraries

New York State Historical Association and The Farmers' Museum, Inc., The
P.O. Box 800
Cooperstown, NY 13326
phone: 607-547-2593 or 607-547-2533

Periodicals

Lenga Dairy Collectibles
Newsletter: Udder Collectibles, The
HC 73 Box 1
Smithville Flats, NY 13841-9502
Focuses on dairy collectibles such as milk bottles, cow facts and more.

Cream Separators

Clubs/Associations

Dr. Paul Dettloff, Sec.
Cream Separator Association
Newsletter: Cream Separator & Dairy News
Rt. 3 Box 189
Arcadia, WI 54612
phone: 608-323-7470
For those interested in cream separators and other dairy items; newsletter contains articles, free ads for subscribers, photos, etc.

Collectors

Sam A. Stephens
319 Juniper St.
Warminster, PA 18974-4720
phone: 215-672-4814 or 215-443-4173
Collector of advertising items relating to cream separators and the dairy industry,

Dave Ogle
954 W. Monroe
Jackson, MI 49202-2036
phone: 517-688-4561
Wants to buy DeLaval, Sharples, or other cream separator advertising: calendars, signs, trays, match holders, fobs, etc.

Larry Schrof
25971 E. 1200 St.
Geneseo, IL 61254
phone: 309-441-5055
Wants DeLaval or other cream separator advertising.

Dealers

Bill Heuring
Hickory Bend Antiques & Collectibles
2995 Drake Hill Rd.
Jasper, NY 14855-9715
phone: 607-792-3343
fax: 607-792-3309
Cream separators and related dairy collectibles bought and sold.

Creamers

Collectors

Toni & Michael Fusco
2629 Oneida St.
Utica, NY 13501
phone: 315-724-8773

Dealers

Ken Clee
P.O. Box 11412
Philadelphia, PA 19111-0412
phone: 215-722-1979
Wants to buy dairy creamers with names printed on creamers; will buy one or an entire collection.

Periodicals

Lloyd Bindscheattle
Newsletter: Creamers
P.O. Box 11
Lake Villa, IL 60046-0011
Collector and expert on dairy creamers; "Creamers" is a quarterly, 16 page newsletter dealing with glass, advertising, individual, dairy, coffee creamers; free ads.

Dairy Case Tags

Collectors

Betty R. Foley
129 Meadow Valley Rd., Trlr. 11
Ephrata, PA 17522-1843
Wants porcelain dairy tags; these were attached to old wooden milk

crates to advertise the names of the dairies; usually 1 1/2" x 5."

Isaly Dairy Company

Collectors

Brian A. Butko
2640 Sunset Dr.
West Mifflin, PA 15122-3565
Collects 1910-1980 souvenirs from this regional chain best known for their Klondike bars, chipped ham, and skyscraper cones: milk cartons, signs, china, calendars, menus, etc.; no bottles, please.

DAIRY QUEEN MEMORABILIA

Collectors

Charles Cook
Rte. 23 Box 1481
Butler, NJ 07405
phone: 201-838-3043
Wants Dairy Queen memorabilia from the 1940s to 1950s: signs, containers, premiums, advertisements, cups, etc.

DANCE MEMORABILIA

(see STRIPTEASE; PERFORMING ARTS)

DATE NAILS

Clubs/Associations

Jerry Waits
Texas Date Nail Collectors Association
Newsletter: Nailer News
501 W. Horton
Brenham, TX 77833-2357
phone: 409-830-1495
Date nails are 1" to 2" long; dime-size heads are marked with number on top to show the year installed; driven into railroad ties, telephone poles, or other wood products; shows the year put in service; collect by years or sets.

Collectors

Dick Gartin
619 Adams
Duncanville, TX 75137
phone: 972-296-8742

Jerry Waits
501 W. Horton
Brenham, TX 77833-2357
phone: 409-830-1495

DAY BOOKS

(see ACCOUNT BOOKS; PAPER COLLECTIBLES)

DEALERS

(see ANTIQUES DEALERS & COLLECTORS)

DECANTERS

Special Edition Whiskey

(see BOTTLES, Special Edition)

DECORATED OBJECTS

(see FOLK ART; FURNITURE [ANTIQUE], Painted)

DECORATIVE ARTS

(see also "APPRAISERS" Appendix as well as Appraisers listed under specific categories throughout this Directory.)

Clubs/Associations

Gerald Ward, Pres.
Museum of Fine Arts, Boston
Newsletter: Decorative Arts Society Newsletter
465 Huntington Ave.
Boston, MA 02115-5523
phone: 617-267-9300
Internet: http://www.mfa.org/home.html

American Decorative Arts Forum
c/o M.H. deYoung Museum
Golden Gate Park
San Francisco, CA 94118
phone: 415-431-6930
A nonprofit organization that seeks to encourage the study, understanding, end enjoyment of American decorative arts.

Museums/Libraries

Victoria & Albert Museum
Cromwell Rd.
London SW7 2RL, U.K.
phone: +44 171 938 8500
Internet: http://www.vam.ac.uk/
The V&A is Britain's national museum of art and design; houses many of the world's greatest decorative art treasures from priceless Oriental carpets to Italian sculpture.

Deborah Waters
Museum of the City of New York
1220 5th Ave.
New York, NY 10029-5221
phone: 212-534-1672
fax: 212-534-5974
Access by appointment; research fee charged.

Daughters of the American Revolution Museum
1776 D St. NW
Washington, DC 20006-5303
phone: 202-879-3254 or 202-879-3241
fax: 202-628-0820
e-mail: museum@dar.org

National Museum of American History Branch Library
Smithsonian Institution
Washington, DC 20560
phone: 202-357-2414
Internet: http://www.si.edu/
Books/journals/trade catalogs on material culture, decorative arts, domestic & community life, applied science, engineering, technology.

Paula Hooper
Museum of Early Southern Decorative Arts
Journal: Journal of the Early Southern Decorative Arts
P.O. Box 10310
Winston Salem, NC 27108-0310
phone: 910-721-7360 or 888-653-7253
fax: 910-721-7367
Internet: http://www.mesda.org
Focuses on Southern decorative arts; has Research Center, Catalog of Early Southern Decorative Arts, and Index of Southern Artists.

Periodicals

Decorative Arts Trust
Newsletter: Decorative Arts Trust Newsletter
106 Bainbridge St.
Philadelphia, PA 19147-2402
phone: 215-627-2859
fax: 215-925-1144
Study and preservation of American decorative arts; features private collections, museums, restorations, and preservation; Spring and Fall symposiums each year held at various, rich historic sites throughout the US; a non-profit group.

Paula Hooper
Museum of Early Southern Decorative Arts
Journal: Journal of the Early Southern Decorative Arts
P.O. Box 10310
Winston Salem, NC 27108-0310
phone: 910-721-7360 or 888-653-7253
fax: 910-721-7367
Internet: http://www.mesda.org
Focuses on Southern decorative arts; has Research Center, Catalog of Early Southern Decorative Arts, and Index of Southern Artists.

DECOYS

(see also ART, Wildlife; FISHING COLLECTIBLES; FOLK ART; SPORTING COLLECTIBLES)

Book Sellers

Dean Dashner
Hunting Rig
349 S. Green Bay Rd.
Neenah, WI 54956
phone: 414-725-4421
e-mail: dashners@tcccom.net
Internet: http://www2.tcccom.net/~dashners
Buys and sells decoys, duck calls, Ducks Unlimited Pinbacks, sporting books, old sporting magazines.

Misc. Services

Richard C. Motzer
Dick's Duck Den
2878 Saddleback
Cincinnati, OH 45244-3915
phone: 513-231-5953
Sells contemporary decoy carvings; also gives carving instructions.

Periodicals

Robert Woollens
R.W. Publishing
Magazine: Sporting Collector's Monthly
P.O. Box 305
Camden Wyoming, DE 19934-0305
phone: 302-678-0113
fax: 302-734-3707
A monthly with hundreds of buy, sell and trade ads; fish and waterfowl decoys, hunting equipment, fishing gear, loading tools, wildlife art, decorative wildlife & fish carvings, and related books, catalogs, magazines, etc.

Canadian

Experts

Bernie Gates
P.O. Box 653
Smiths Falls
Ontario K7A 5B8 Canada
phone: 613-283-1168
fax: 613-283-1345
e-mail: uppercanadian@recorder.ca
Author of "Ontario Decoys III"; $23.95 Canadian.

Factory

Experts

Henry Fleckenstein
P.O. Box 577
Cambridge, MD 21613
phone: 410-221-0076
Author of "American Factory Decoys," "Decoys of the Mid-Atlantic Region," "Southern Decoys of Virginia & the Carolinas," "Shorebird Decoys," and "New Jersey Decoys."

Fish

Clubs/Associations

Frank R. Baron, Sec.
Great Lakes Fish Decoy Collectors & Carvers Association
35824 West Chicago
Livonia, MI 48150-2522
phone: 313-427-7768
Regular meetings and newsletter; long range goal is to establish a permanent display of spearfishing artifacts.

John E. Shoffner
American Fish Decoy Association
Newsletter: American Fish Decoy Forum, The
624 Merritt St.
Fife Lake, MI 49633-9142
phone: 616-879-3912
3 year old association is the largest fish decoy collectors association with approx. 160 members; newsletter has color photos.

Collectors

R.C. Egan
c/o Meade Johnson Co.
2404 Penn Ave.
Evansville, IN 47708
Wants to buy wooden ice fishing decoys and wooden painted bobbers.

Dealers

Ronald J. Fritz
5221 Camberlea Ave.
Zephyrhills, FL 33541
phone: 813-788-2312
Buying and selling old working fish decoys by carvers from Michigan, New York as well as from other areas.

Frank R. Baron
Great Lakes Ice Decoys
35824 West Chicago
Livonia, MI 48150-2522
phone: 313-427-7768
Buys, sells, trades fish decoys; quarterly list of decoys for sale; author of "Bud Stewart, Michigan's Legendary Lure Maker."

John E. Shoffner
624 Merritt St.
Fife Lake, MI 49633-9142
phone: 616-879-3912
Issues 6 lists a year with approx. 600 fish decoys and antique fishing tackle items for sale.

Art Kimball
North Haven Antiques
P6790 Wildcat Drive
P.O. Box 252
Boulder Junction, WI 54512
phone: 715-385-2862
Periodic lists with photos of investment grade guaranteed authentic older fish decoys for sale; has written and published four available books on fish decoys.

John Cook
Peace Antiques
HC 3 Box 13A
Remer, MN 56672-9602
phone: 218-566-2793
Has specialized in buying and selling fish and duck decoys for 20 years.

Experts

Ronald J. Fritz
5221 Camberlea Ave.
Zephyrhills, FL 33541
phone: 813-788-2312
Specialist in the fish decoy carvings of Michigan carvers Peterson, Nelson, Ramey, Hulbert & Bruning; author of book on subject.

Man./Prod./Dist.

Mikko
Mikko's Bait Shop
P.O. Box 100
Osakis, MN 56360-0100
phone: 612-859-3536 or 800-252-1186
Wholesale fish decoys to dealers only.

Waterfowl

Auction Services

Ted Harmon
Decoys Unlimited
2320 Main St.
West Barnstable, MA 02668
phone: 508-362-2766

Frank M. Schmidt
Guyette & Schmidt, Inc.
P.O. Box 522
West Farmington, ME 04992
phone: 207-778-6256 or 207-625-8055
fax: 207-778-6501
The world's largest decoy auction firm; please note that an alternate fax number is 207-625-4742.

Clubs/Associations

Ted Harmon
New England Decoy Collectors Association
2320 Main St.
West Barnstable, MA 02668
phone: 508-362-2766

Ohio Decoy Collectors & Carvers Association
P.O. Box 499
Richfield, OH 44286
Focuses on both vintage and contemporary decoys and their makers.

Dick Brust
Minnesota Decoy Collectors Association
P.O. Box 385333
Minneapolis, MN 55438-5333
phone: 612-636-7700
A support group to the MN Decoy Foundation, specializing in MN waterfowl decoys.

Herb Desch
Midwest Decoy Collectors Association
3006 Fox Glen Dr.
Saint Charles, IL 60174-8809
phone: 630-377-2743

Collectors

Sheldon Lerman
7505 Osler Dr.
Baltimore, MD 21204-7736
phone: 410-321-1514 or 410-828-5310
fax: 410-825-5710
Wants to buy old decoys.

David A. Galliher
2500 W. Berwyn Rd.
Muncie, IN 47304-5113
phone: 317-289-2233 or 317-284-6668
fax: 317-289-2376
Wants to buy antique or old decoys from the Midwest area, especially by the carver Charles Perdew (deceased) from Henry, IL; publishing a book on Charles Perdew; 295 pgs, 400 illustrations, color, museum quality printing and binding.

Dealers

Russ & Karen Goldberger
RJK Antiques
P.O. Box 2033
Hampton, NH 03843-2033
phone: 603-926-1770
fax: 603-929-4267
e-mail: rjduck@nh.ultranet.com
Internet: http://www.maineantiquedigest.com/adimg/decoys.htm
Specializes in quality working decoys, folk art, and American furniture and accessories in their original painted surfaces.

Lisa Trayer
Brickerville Antiques & Decoys
117 E. 28th Div. Hwy (Rte. 322)
Lititz, PA 17543
phone: 717-627-2466
Specializes in old factory and working decoys; also sporting antiques related to hunting and fishing; buy/sell/trade old decoys, creels, fishing tackle, eel traps, gigs, old advertising, salesman sample decoys, shell boxes, shorebirds.

Andrea J. Shreiner
Initialed Duck Antiques & Collectibles
3812 Hamilton Ave.
Baltimore, MD 21206-3505
Buys, sells and collects waterfowl decoys.

John Cook
Peace Antiques
HC 3 Box 13A
Remer, MN 56672-9602
phone: 218-566-2793
Has specialized in buying and selling fish and duck decoys for 20 years.

Museums/Libraries

Peabody Museum of Salem
East India Square
Salem, MA 01970
phone: 617-745-9500

Heritage Plantation of Sandwich
P.O. Box 566
Sandwich, MA 02563
phone: 617-888-3300
Contains an outstanding exhibit of decoys by carvers including Elmer Crowell and his memorabilia.

Shelburne Museum, Inc.
P.O. Box 10
Shelburne, VT 05482-0010
phone: 802-985-3346 or 802-985-3344
fax: 802-985-2331
37 historic structures and exhibit buildings; diverse collection of American folk, fine, decorative and utilitarian art.

Museums at Stony Brook, The
Newsletter: News & Events
Rte. 25A Box 1208
Stony Brook, NY 11790-1931
phone: 516-751-0066
fax: 516-751-0353
Large collection of American Art, decoys, horse-drawn vehicles, costumes, and miniature period rooms; museum shop.

Karen Marshall, Dir.
Havre de Grace Decoy Museum
Magazine: Canvasback, The
Giles & Market Sts.
P.O. Box A
Havre De Grace, MD 21078
phone: 410-939-3739
fax: 410-939-3775

Pete Lesher, Cur.
Chesapeake Bay Maritime Museum
Magazine: Water Gauge, The
P.O. Box 636
Saint Michaels, MD 21663-0636
phone: 410-745-2916
fax: 410-745-6088
Internet: http://www.cbmm.org
A major regional maritime museum with a 5200 volume research library; collections include 10,000 objects, 9,000 photos, 1,200 ships' plans, 72 linear feet of manuscripts; decoys, oystering, lighthouses, charts, nautical, tools.

Doug Johnson
Ward Museum of Wildfowl Art (Ward Foundation)
Magazine: Wildfowl Art
P.O. Box 3416
Salisbury, MD 21802
phone: 410-742-4988
fax: 410-742-3107
Conducts seminars on carving and painting decoys; the "Decoy Express" service offers up-to-the-minute information via your fax machine about available carvings.

Refuge Waterfowl Museum
Maddox Blvd.
P.O. Box 272
Chincoteague, VA 23336
phone: 804-336-5800

Periodicals

Cathy Hart
Stackpole Publishing
Magazine: Wildfowl Carving & Collecting
500 Vaughn St.
Harrisburg, PA 17110-2220
phone: 717-234-5091
fax: 717-234-1359
Quarterly magazine devoted exclusively to bird carving; complete "how-to" and reference information for professional and amateur carvers alike; ads, articles, competition photos, special annual "Competition" issue.

Joe Engers
Decoy Magazine
Magazine: Decoy Magazine
P.O. Box 277
Burtonsville, MD 20866-0277
phone: 301-890-0262
Internet: http://www.dbqinc.com/decoy
Only bi-monthly magazine serving the decoy collecting market; classifieds, calendar, auction news, carver profiles, full color.

Magazine: Decoy Hunter Magazine
901 North 9th
Clinton, IN 47842
phone: 317-832-2525

Hillcrest Publications
Magazine: North American Decoys
P.O. Box 246
Spanish Fork, UT 84660

Repro. Sources

Richard Morgan
Painted Bird, The
770 Rte. 47
Woodbury, CT 06798

Duane Sylor
49 Horner Rd.
Angelica, NY 14709
phone: 716-466-7700
Make and sells handcarved carved and painted duck and shorebird decoys; copies of original working decoys.

Frank O'Brien
Frank O'Brien Decoys
P.O. Box 522
Bryn Athyn, PA 19009

Back Bay Decoys
684 Princess Anne Rd.
Virginia Beach, VA 23457

James Long
356 Devonwood Ct.
Taylors, SC 29687-4205

Tidewater Shorebirds
2818 Lancelot Dr.
Baton Rouge, LA 70816

Waterfowl (Mason)

Experts

Russ Goldberger
P.O. Box 2033
Hampton, NH 03843-2033
phone: 603-926-1770
fax: 603-929-4267
e-mail: rjduck@nh.ultranet.com
Internet: http://www.maineantiquedigest.com/adimg/decoys.htm
Specializes in quality working decoys, folk art, and American furniture and accessories in their original painted surfaces; co-author with Alan G. Haid of "Mason Decoys, A Complete Pictorial Guide."

DENTAL

(see MEDICAL, DENTAL & PHARMACEUTICAL, Dental)

DESERT STORM

Collectors

Carl F. Pflanzer
73 Cloverhill Dr.
Flanders, NJ 07836
e-mail: carl@ewacars.com
Internet: http://www.ewacars.com
Wants Desert Storm memorabilia: Marx Playsets, trading cards, games, propaganda, etc.

DETECTIVE ITEMS

(see BOOKS, Mystery; CHARACTER COLLECTIBLES, Sherlock Holmes; MAGAZINES, Mystery; MYSTERY/ DETECTIVE ITEMS)

DIAMOND EDGE (SHAPLEIGH HARDWARE)

(see also HARDWARE; KEEN KUTTER [SIMMONS HARDWARE]; KNIVES; TOOLS; WINCHESTER COLLECTIBLES)

Auction Services

Bob Simmons
Simmons & Company Auctioneers
Rte. 1 Box 186
Richmond, MO 64085-9760
phone: 816-776-2936
fax: 816-470-5016
e-mail:
simmons_auction@raycounty.com
Internet: http://www.raycounty.com/ simmons.html
Conducts annual specialty auctions of Winchester, Keen Kutter (E.C. Simmons Hardware) and Diamond Edge (Shapleigh Hardware) collectibles; has a well-established reputation for expertise and high quality merchandise.

Experts

Bob Simmons
Rte. 1 Box 186
Richmond, MO 64085-9760
phone: 816-776-2936
fax: 816-470-5016
e-mail:
simmons_auction@raycounty.com
Internet: http://www.raycounty.com/ simmons.html
Collects and specializes in Diamond Edge (Shapleigh Hardware) items especially advertising, catalogs, store signs and displays, promotions, sporting goods, and household items made for this St. Louis firm from the late 1800s to 1940.

Periodicals

Tom Basore
Hardware Companies Kollectors' Club
Newsletter: Winchester Keen Kutter Diamond Edge Chronicles
715 West 20th Ave.
Hutchinson, KS 67502
phone: 316-665-3613 or 816-776-2936
fax: 816-470-5016
e-mail: webmaster@raycounty.com
Internet: http://www.raycounty.com/ simmons.html
A non-profit organization to serve as an interactive information distribution center for collectors of Keen Kutter, Diamond Edge, Winchester Store (non-gun), Simmons & Shapleigh and other hardware store brands.

DIARIES

Collectors

Roy C. Kulp
P.O. Box 264
Hatfield, PA 19440-0264
phone: 215-362-0732
Wants to buy account books and day books by farmers, carpenters, blacksmiths, coffin & carriage makers, and weavers; also wants pre-1890 hand written travel diaries.

DICE

(see also GAMBLING COLLECTIBLES)

Collectors

Bill Whelan
P.O. Box 617
Daly City, CA 94017-2332
phone: 415-756-1189
Wants to buy dice with casino or location imprints; also color variations, shapes and sizes; any type of dice.

DIECUTS

(see PAPER COLLECTIBLES)

DIME NOVELS

(see BOOKS, Paperback)

DIMESTORE SOLDIERS

(see SOLDIERS, Toy)

DINERS & RELATED ITEMS

(see also RESTAURANT COLLECTIBLES)

Collectors

Daniel Zilka
110 Benevolent St.
Providence, RI 02906
phone: 410-331-8575 or 410-461-7932
fax: 401-351-0127
Wants to buy diner photographs, postcards, matchbook covers, diner magazines, diner stools, coffee urns, vintage restaurant equipment.

Brian A. Butko
2640 Sunset Dr.
West Mifflin, PA 15122-3565
Wants only souvenir items from factory-built diners which typically look like wooden or stainless steel train cars; roadside diners were especially popular with automobile tourists from 1920 to 1970.

Larry Spilkin
P.O. Box 5039
Southfield, MI 48086-5039
phone: 810-642-3722
Wants postcards and matchbook covers of drive-ins, diners, cafes, gas stations and 1930s-1950s motels, restaurant/bar, cabins and Art Deco streamline hotels.

Man./Prod./Dist.

William Scott Cheverie
Deco Echoes Diner Co.
P.O. Box 2321
Mashpee, MA 02649-8321
phone: 508-428-2324
fax: 508-428-0077
True 1950s reproduction diners, all steel construction, delivered fully equipped and ready for operation, many plans to choose from.

Museums/Libraries

Daniel Zilka
American Diner Museum
110 Benevolent St.
Providence, RI 02906
phone: 410-331-8575 or 410-461-7932
fax: 401-351-0127
A museum showcasing numerous manufacturers and various aspects of the diner industry; extensive photograph and artifact collection and reference library; wants photos and other items relating to diner history.

Periodicals

Coffee Cup Publications
Magazine: Roadside
11 Homer St.
Worcester, MA 01602
phone: 508-791-1838
e-mail: roadsider@aol.com
A quarterly journal for the diner owner; the only publication devoted to the appreciation and preservation of the American Diner.

Repair Services

Daniel Zilka
110 Benevolent St.
Providence, RI 02906
phone: 410-331-8575 or 410-461-7932
fax: 401-351-0127
Performs restoration work on historic diners.

Steve Harwin
Diversified Diners
2043 Random Rd. #302
Cleveland, OH 44106
phone: 216-229-4003
fax: 216-229-4005
Buys, sells and restores diners and related items; restoration consultant.

Suppliers

Bill Raymer
Restoration Resources
31 Thayer St.
Roxbury, MA 02118
phone: 617-542-3033
Supplies vintage parts for diners: stools, jukeboxes, etc.

DINNERWARE

(see also CERAMICS; CERAMICS [AMERICAN DINNERWARE]; CERAMICS [CONTINENTAL]; CERAMICS [ENGLISH]; CERAMICS [ORIENTAL]; FLATWARE; GLASS, Elegant; GLASS, Crystal; MODERNISM; REPAIR/RESTORATION/CONSERVATION; TABLEWARE)

Matching Services

William Ashley Ltd.
50 Bloor Street West
Toronto
Ontario M4W 3L8 Canada
phone: 416-964-2900 or 800-268-1122
Discontinued pattern service specializing in English china and crystal manufacturers.

Old China Patterns Ltd.
1560 Brimley Rd.
Scarborough
Ontario M1P 3G9 Canada
phone: 800-663-4533 or 416-299-8880
fax: 416-299-4721
e-mail: ocp@chinapatterns.com
Canada's largest matching service; buys and sells internationally; since 1966; specializing in English & American china and crystal; charter member International Association of Dinnerware Matchers.

Tom & Annette Power
Tablewhere?
9 Church St.
London NW8 8DEE, U.K.
phone: 0171-7064586
fax: 0171-7062948
e-mail: collector@globalnet.co.uk
Specializing in discontinued tableware of most British manufacturers from 1900 to the present day; worldwide mail order service; VISA/MC/AMEX.

Lina Shanfield
Bargain Shanfields-Meyers
188 Ouellette Ave.
Windsor
Ontario N9A 1A4 Canada
phone: 519-253-6098 or 313-961-8435
fax: 519-253-3355
Royal Doulton, Lenox, Minton, Aynsley, Denby, Mikasa, Dansk, Spode, Noritake, Rosenthal, Royal

Albert, Wedgwood, Royal Crown, Derby, Bernardaud, Herend, and more.

Pat's Patterns China Matching
P.O. Box 95024
Newton, MA 02195-0024
phone: 617-969-6058 or 800-807-6058
Huge inventory of discontinued china from all the major manufacturers; specializing in Lenox and English makers; fancy service plates, complete dinner services; always buying china.

Ross Simmons
#9 Ross Simmons Dr.
Cranston, RI 02920-4476
phone: 800-556-7376
Sells new, active patterns of Royal Doulton, Minton, Wedgwood, Noritake, Villeroy & Boch, Royal Worcester, Lenox, etc.

China By Pattern International Matching Service
P.O. Box 129
Farmington, CT 06034-0129
phone: 203-678-7079
Send SASE to locate/match Castleton, Lenox, Spode, Doulton, Worcester, Minton, Coalport, Franciscan, Rosenthal, Syracuse, Wedgwood, Haviland, Noritake, Johnson Bros., etc.

Regina Negrotti
Tablescapes
49 Elkton Ave.
P.O. Box 3165
Cheshire, CT 06410
phone: 800-801-4084
A small, personal matching service with a constantly changing inventory; want lists are kept; send photocopy or photo when unsure of pattern name; specializes in Lenox.

Silver & China Exchange
P.O. Box 4601
Dept. MA
Stamford, CT 06907-0601
phone: 203-322-5963
Specializing in Lenox/Oxford china; over 250 different patterns in stock.

Paul & Pearl Hoffman
China Brokers, Ltd.
11 Westgate Ct.
Colts Neck, NJ 07722
phone: 908-866-6613 or 800-867-6613
Over 40,000 dinnerware patterns in stock; obsolete, inactive, active.

Alice Korman
Alice's Past & Presents Replacements
P.O. Box 465
Merrick, NY 11566-0465
phone: 516-379-1352
fax: 516-379-7302
Matching and locating service for Wedgwood, Adams, Coalport, Derby, Franciscan, Gorham, Lenox, Metlox, Mikasa, Minton, Noritake, Royal Doulton and others.

Pattern Finders, A
P.O. Box 206
Port Jefferson Station, NY 11776-0206
phone: 516-928-5158 or 800-216-2446
fax: 516-928-5170
e-mail: apattern@aol.com
Adams, Arabia, Aynsley, Castleton, Coalport, Denby, Enoch, Franciscan, Gorham, Haviland, Johnson Brothers, Lenox, Mikasa, Minton, Noritake, Oxford, Rosenthal, Royal Doulton, Royal Worcester, Spode, Syracuse, Wedgwood.

Sophia Papapanu
Sophia's China & Crystal
141 Sedgwick Rd.
Syracuse, NY 13203-1136
phone: 315-472-6834
Discontinued china and crystal patterns; over 16 years service; American, English, and other manufacturers; mail order or by special appointment; please send SASE with requests for information.

Constance Stolz
China Match & Crystal Match
72 Longacre Rd.
Rochester, NY 14621-1019
phone: 716-338-3781
e-mail: chinamat@frontiernet.net
Replacements of discontinued china and stoneware; Fitz & Floyd, Royal Doulton, Royal Worcester, Spode, Wedgwood; buy and sell.

Dick & Rosemarie Lewis
Dining Antiques
#6 Market Plaza
Reinholds, PA 17569
phone: 888-346-4642
Specializes in matching Syracuse china, 9,000 pieces and 80 patterns in stock.

Cee Cee China
3904 Parsons Rd.
Chevy Chase, MD 20815
phone: 301-654-7308 or 800-619-6226
e-mail: ccchina@aol.com
Buys, sells and locates; specializing in Lenox, Oxford, and Syracuse only.

China Matching, Inc.
420 Belle Grove Rd.
Middletown, VA 22645
phone: 540-869-1261
Discontinued china & crystal; Castleton, Haviland, Lenox and Wedgwood china; Fostoria & Lenox crystal.

Mildred G. Brumback
China & Crystal Matching, Inc.
420 Belle Grove Rd.
Dept. M
Middletown, VA 22645
phone: 703-869-1261
Send requests with SASE; specializes in Lenox and Castleton.

Van Ness China Company
1124 Fairway Dr.
Waynesboro, VA 22980
phone: 703-942-2827
Discontinued English bone china:

Aynsley, Coalport, Minton, Royal Dounton, Royal Worcester, Spode, Wedgwood.

Harry Weitkemper
China Finders
1-B South Holy Ave.
Highland Springs, VA 23075
phone: 888-244-6239 or 804-328-2897
Buys and sells Castleton, Lenox, Doulton, Franciscan, Haviland, Spode, Wedgwood, Shelley, Minton, Noritake, Adams, Metlox, Vernon Kilns, and most major manufacturers.

Thurber's
2256C Dabeny Rd.
Richmond, VA 23230
phone: 804-278-9080 or 800-848-7237
Carries only active patterns.

Randy Foster
Replacements Ltd.
P.O. Box 26029
Greensboro, NC 27420
phone: 800-737-5223 or 800-REP-LACE
fax: 910-697-3100
e-mail: replaceltd@aol.com
Internet: http://www.imall.com/stores/replacements
China, crystal and flatware (obsolete, active and inactive.)

D & J Locations
1601 E. Canal St.
Tarboro, NC 27886
phone: 919-823-5333 or 800-818-5565
Discontinued china: Gorham, Haviland, Lenox, Metlox, Mikasa, Minton, Noritake, Pickard, Royal Doulton, Spode, Wedgwood, and other major brands; buys, sells, locates.

China Cabinet, The
214 Hillside Dr.
P.O. Box 426
Clearwater, SC 29822
phone: 803-593-9655
Features a number of Metlox Potteries patterns.

J.B. & ME
3576 Clairmont Rd.
Atlanta, GA 30319-3626
phone: 404-634-1194

China & Crystal Matchers, Inc.
2379 John Glenn Dr., Ste. #108-M
Atlanta, GA 30341-1901
phone: 770-455-1162
fax: 770-452-8616
All manufacturers; buys, sells, locates; member of the International Association of Dinnerware Matchers.

Tableware Matching Unlimited
P.O. Box 0628
Winter Park, FL 32790
phone: 407-275-9835
fax: 407-382-7996
Buys and sells; 30,000+ patterns in American, English & Japanese china and crystal.

Atlantic Silver & China
7405 N.W. 57th St.
Tamarac, FL 33319
phone: 800-288-6665 or 954-720-4559
fax: 954-720-4577
Inactive Lenox, Noritake, Rosenthal, Royal Doulton, Wedgwood.

Paul Church
Replacement Service, A
1415 Michigan Ave.
Saint Cloud, FL 34769
phone: 407-957-1719 or 800-222-7357
Buys, sells, locates Lenox, Oxford, Temperware, Castleton, Franciscan fine china and earthenware.

Jewel Box
P.O. Box 145
Albertville, AL 35950
phone: 205-878-3301

Mary Ann Lowery
Crystal Corner, Inc., The
P.O. Box 756
Boaz, AL 35957
phone: 205-593-6169
fax: 205-593-6560
e-mail: ccorner@stargate.imatrex.com
Royal Doulton, Fitz & Floyd, Gorham, Noritake, Mikasa, Haviland, etc.

Bruce & Donna Johnston
Abby's Attic
28107 Eugene E. Ladner Rd.
Perkinston, MS 39573
phone: 601-255-2799
Buys, sells, locates Dansk, Franciscan, Gorham, Lenox, Noritake and others.

Allan & Cathy Griggs
Chinamates
1673 Lakecrest Dr.
Sullivan, IN 47882-9585
phone: 800-726-0345 or 812-268-6411
fax: 812-268-6411
e-mail: chinamates@viaduct.custom.net
Stocks, locates discontinued patterns only of china & crystal; Franciscan, Fostoria, Gorham, Haviland, Lenox, Minton, Oxford, Castleton, Adams, Johnson Brothers, Pickard, Royal Doulton, Wedgwood, etc.; member Fostoria Glass Soc. of Am.

Barron's
P.O. Box 994
Novi, MI 48376
phone: 800-538-6340
Carries only active patterns.

Heritage China of Iowa
P.O. Box 49
Palo, IA 52324
phone: 319-227-7781 or 319-227-7781
Buys and sells discontinued china: Dansk, Denby, Franciscan, Haviland, Homer Laughlin, Mikasa, Minton, Noritake, Royal Doulton, Sango, Wedgwood, Japanese patterns, etc.

Clintsman International
20855 Watertown Rd.
Waukesha, WI 53186-1873
phone: 414-798-0440 or 800-781-8900
fax: 414-798-8879
*All manufacturers: Adams, Denby,
Gorham, Johnson Brothers, Lenox,
Metlox, Mikasa, Noritake, Royal
Doulton, Spode, Syracuse, Wedgwood,
and others; buys and sells.*

Jacquelynn Ives
Jacquelynn's China Matching Service
219 N. Milwaukee St.
Milwaukee, WI 53202-5818
phone: 414-272-8880 or 800-482-8287
fax: 414-272-0361
*English/American exclusively;
discontinued Coalport, Castleton,
Franciscan, Lenox, Minton, Spode,
Royal Doulton, Wedgwood,
Flintridge/Gorham, Royal Crown
Derby, Royal Worcester, Pickard,
Royal Winton, Royal Albert, etc.*

China & Crystal Replacements
P.O. Box 187
Excelsior, MN 55331
phone: 612-474-6418
*Discontinued and active china,
dinnerware and crystal bought and
sold.*

Audrey Rickard
China Trade Ltd.
2133 Birchwood Ave.
Wilmette, IL 60091-2305
phone: 708-256-7414 or 800-295-4200
fax: 708-256-5952
e-mail: Trick2@juno.com
*Specializing in major manufacturers
of discontinued china; also 18th and
19th century porcelain.*

Heirloom Completions
C-1620 Venice St.
Granite City, IL 62040
phone: 618-931-4333
*Adams, Castleton, Corning,
Franciscan, Haviland, Johnson,
Lenox, Meakin, Metlox, Mikasa,
Minton, Noritake, Rosenthal, Sango,
Spode, Syracuse, Wedgwood plus 785
more manufacturers;*

Don's Antiques - Heirloom Completions
Division
1620-D Venice St.
Granite City, IL 62040-2355
phone: 618-931-4333
*Castleton, Doulton, Franciscan,
Haviland, Japan, Johnson, Lenox,
Meakin, Metlox, Mikasa, Minton,
Noritake, Rosenthal, Sango, Spode,
Wedgwood.*

China Replacements
P.O. Box 508
High Ridge, MO 63049
phone: 800-562-2655
*Buys, sells, and locates all major
brands of china; Lenox/Oxford, Royal
Doulton, Royal Worcester/Spode,
Denby, Castleton, Syracuse,
Franciscan, Wedgwood, Noritake,
Mikasa and many others.*

Arlene Mauer
International Association of Dinnerware
Matchers
P.O. Box 656
High Ridge, MO 63049-0656
*IADM is a group of independent
dinnerware matchers (china, crystal,
and flatware) in the US & Canada
organized to promote honesty and
integrity within the profession;
publishes a directory of members.*

Dining Elegance, Ltd.
P.O. Box 4203
Saint Louis, MO 63163
phone: 314-865-1408
*American Lenox/Oxford; most English
manufacturers; French & American
Haviland; French Ceralene-Raynaud;
listing of patterns in stock sent upon
request; $1.*

Jacqueline Healey
Heirloom Crystal & China
P.O. Box 149
Mount Vernon, MO 65712
phone: 417-466-3818 or 800-927-6471
*Buys, sells, takes consignments,
stocks, locates regionally unavailable
and discontinued patterns of fine and
casual china; most manufacturers;
extensive Mikasa resources.*

Betty Stachurski
Betty's Crystal & China
P.O. Box 433
Lawrence, KS 66044-0433
phone: 913-842-8054
*Aynsley, Castleton, Denby,
Franciscan, Gorham, Adams,
Midwinter, Coalport, Lenox, Oxford,
Temperware, Royal Doulton, Minton,
Royal Worcester, Spode, Royal Crown
Derby, Metlox, Mikasa, Noritake and
others.*

Peggy Endicott
Bygone China Match
1225 W. 34th North
Wichita, KS 67204-4236
phone: 316-838-6010
fax: 316-838-6010
e-mail: byeonchina@aol.com
*Large inventory of discontinued
patterns in Dansk, Denby, Fitz/Floyd,
Franciscan, Gorham, Haviland,
Lenox, Metlox, Mikasa, Noritake,
Royal Doulton, Sango china/pottery.*

Barbara Coleman
Finders Keepers China Lady
1537 Metairie Rd.
Metairie, LA 70005-3938
phone: 504-455-1530
fax: 504-885-2512
*Stock or locate Doulton, Lenox/
Oxford, Minton, Noritake, Pickard,
Spode, Wedgwood; also other china
and crystal.*

Jo Hancock
Jo' Antiques & Collectibles
621 S. Main St.
Nashville, AR 71852-2707
*China and crystal matching; Lenox
and other fine brands.*

Locators, Inc.
2217 Cottondale Lane
Little Rock, AR 72202-2018
phone: 501-663-1114 or 800-367-9690
*Carries out-of-production (discontin-
ued) china and crystal, and
discontinued as well as active sterling
flatware patterns.*

Advisory Replacement Service
901 W. Walnut Hill Ln., 5A-9
Irving, TX 75038
*A china replacement service: Lenox,
Royal Doulton, Rosenthal, Royal
Copenhagen, Noritake, Mikasa,
Haviland, Hutschenreuther, Spode,
Royal Worcester, Villory & Boch,
Wedgwood, Gorham, Pickard.*

China Teacup
418 Texas Ave.
Mart, TX 76664
phone: 972-254-1713
*All major brands: Castleton, Denby,
Franciscan, Lenox, Gorham, Mikasa,
Royal Doulton, Noritake, Spode,
Syracuse, Wedgwood, etc.; buys and
sells.*

David Lackey Antiques & China
Matching
2311 Westheimer
Houston, TX 77098-1317
phone: 713-942-7171
*Buys and sells major brands: Lenox,
Castleton, Wedgwood, Noritake,
Franciscan, Haviland, Spode, Royal
Doulton.*

Mrs. Davie Lou Solka, Pres.
Dollars Mdsg. Co.
501 Bermuda
Corpus Christi, TX 78411
phone: 512-852-5815
*Buy/sell inactive patterns of china by
Caselton, Flintridge, Franciscan,
Haviland, Lenox, Oxford and
Syracuse.*

Larry & Anne McDonald
A & A Dinnerware Locators
P.O. Box 50222
Austin, TX 78763-0222
phone: 512-264-1054 or 888-898-4202
fax: 512-264-2727
e-mail: 73612.470@compuserve.com
*Locate/match discontinued china,
earthenware, etc.; all major
manufacturers: American, European,
Japanese: Castleton, Adams, Doulton,
Franciscan, Gorham, Lenox, Metlox,
Mikasa, Noritake, Spode, Worcester;
primarily mail order.*

Olympus Cove Antiques & China
Matching
179 E. 300 St.
Salt Lake City, UT 84111
phone: 800-284-8046
*Buys and sells discontinued china:
Syracuse, Spode, Lenox, Franciscan,
Castleton, Haviland, and much more.*

Sara's China Closet
7749 E. Luke Lane
Scottsdale, AZ 85250
phone: 602-946-9145
*Discontinued china patterns from
most major English and American
Manufacturers.*

Beverly Hills Pattern Matching Service
270 N. Canon Drive, #1419
Beverly Hills, CA 90210
phone: 800-443-1122
fax: 818-707-0425
*Discontinued patterns of china:
Gorham, Lenox, Pickard, Royal
Doulton, Minton, Royal Worcester-
Spode, Sango.*

Carol Ulrey
Unique Antiques
P.O. Box 15815
San Diego, CA 92175-5815
phone: 619-281-8650
fax: 619-282-8407
e-mail: curley@webcc.net
*Specializing in china matching:
Haviland, old French and American;
also Lenox china and crystal.*

Joanne Cone Matching Service
34 Silverwood
Irvine, CA 92714-2845
phone: 714-551-3173
e-mail: jochina@aol.com
*Buys, sells, locates all major
manufacturers (Mikasa specialist):
Mikasa, Castleton, Denby,
Franciscan, Johnson, Lenox, Metlox,
Noritake, Royal Doulton, Spode,
Syracuse, Wedgwood, etc.*

China Traders Replacement Service
P.O. Box 1920
Simi Valley, CA 93062
phone: 805-578-3800 or 800-638-9955
fax: 805-578-3803
e-mail: sales@chinatraders.com
Internet: http://www.chinatraders.com
*Totally computerized discontinued
china matching service; all major
patterns; large inventory; friendly and
knowledgeable staff.*

Past & Present
14851 Avenue 360
Visalia, CA 93292
phone: 415-258-1775 or 209-798-0029
fax: 209-798-1415
*Formal and casual: Castleton,
Community, Denby, Doulton,
Flintridge, Franciscan, Gorham, Hall,
Haviland, Johnson Bros., Lenox,
Mason's, Metlox, Mikasa, Noritake,
Redwing, Rosenthal, Spode, Syracuse,
Wedgwood, etc.*

Silver Lane Antiques
P.O. Box 322
San Leandro, CA 94577-0032
phone: 510-483-0632
*Buys and sells discontinued patterns
by major American and English china
and earthenware companies; Lenox,
Spode, Minton, Franciscan, Syracuse,
Wedgwood, Royal Copenhagen,*

*Doulton, Ceralene, American
Haviland, Rosenthal, Castleton, etc.*

White's Collectables & Fine China, Etc.
616 E. First
P.O. Box 680
Newberg, OR 97132
phone: 503-538-7421
*Discontinued china: Castleton, Denby,
Lenox, Oxford, Royal Doulton, Royal
Worcester, Franciscan, Syracuse,
Spode, Minton, and Wedgwood; also
current patterns of major manufactur-
ers.*

Michael Lundsey
Laguna Vintage Pottery
609 Second Ave.
Seattle, WA 98104
phone: 206-682-6162
*Specializes in American made
dinnerware only: Bauer, Franciscan,
Hall, Heath, Metlox, Russel Wright,
Red Wing, Vernon, Winfield.*

Warren & Betty Roundhill
Patterns Unlimited International
Dept. CIC
P.O. Box 15238
Seattle, WA 98115-0238
phone: 206-523-9710
fax: 206-524-1252
*Buy and sell china from England,
France and USA; also appraises
discontinued tableware patterns of all
china, silver and glass.*

Periodicals

Cleo Kapilla
Joyful Ventures
Directory: Directory of Discontinued
Tableware Services
P.O. Box 4995
Ocala, FL 34478-4995
phone: 352-622-4077 or 352-622-4914
*Publishes biennial directory listing
over 50 matching services that sell
and search for discontinued tableware
items - china, crystal, and flatware.*

Susan Ranta
Ranta Publishing
Directory: Set Your Table
13419 Van Buren St., NE
Anoka, MN 553046959
phone: 612-754-6483 or 800-600-2172
fax: 612-754-6483
e-mail: sranta@setyourtable.com
Internet: http://www.setyourtable.com
*Annual international directory of
antique dealers and matching services
for discontinued dinnerware, flatware,
hollowware and glassware for the
table; also repair, restoration sources
on Internet; check out website for
great information!*

Advertising

Collectors

Bruce Fernie
121 Newbury St.
Boston, MA 02116
phone: 617-859-8593
fax: 617-859-0043
*Wants china, porcelain, dinnerware,
and silverplated hotelware decorated
with hotel, restaurant, cruise line,
club, corporate, steamship, railroad,
and diner custom logos, crests, names,
and designs.*

British

Matching Services

China Registry, THe
682 St. James St.
London
Ontario N5Y 3PB Canada
phone: 519-439-6268
*Deals specifically in discontinued
British dinnerware.*

Danish

Matching Services

Saxe Floral
2402 N.E. 65th
Seattle, WA 98115
phone: 206-523-4415
*Specializing in antique, discontinued,
and new Danish makers including
Royal Copenhagen, Bing & Grondahl,
and Georg Jensen.*

European

Matching Services

Joan Nackman
China Matching Service
56 Meadowbrook
Ballwin, MO 63011
phone: 314-227-3444
*Buys, sells, locates discontinued
china, specializing in Bavarian,
German, Czechoslovakian, Austrian
dinnerware; Heinrich, Villeroy &
Boch, Hutschenreuther, Johann
Haviland, Tirschenreuth; most
European Chinas; also stocks Lenox
china.*

Haviland

(see also CERAMICS [CONTINEN-
TAL], Haviland)

Appraisers

Virginia Cannon, ISA
China House, The
801 W. Eldorado
Decatur, IL 62522
phone: 217-428-7212 or 217-864-2938
fax: 217-864-4852
*Matches, specializes in, and appraises
French & American; carries large
selection of Haviland patterns for sale
by mail order or from the shop; also
most other major brands.*

Matching Services

Sailor's Wife, The
RR 3 Box 137
Gorham, ME 04038-9418
phone: 207-929-3009
*Specializing in old French Haviland;
matching service for Haviland & Co.,
Theodore Haviland and C.F.H.
backmarks; some American Haviland;
send Schleiger number or photocopy
for identification.*

China By Pattern International Matching
Service
P.O. Box 129
Farmington, CT 06034-0129
phone: 203-678-7079
*Send SASE to locate/match American
and French Haviland dinnerware
china as well as Johann Haviland
(Bavaria); no charge to list or search
for wanted items.*

Jan Fenger
Presence of the Past
488 Main St.
Old Saybrook, CT 06475-2530
phone: 860-388-9021
fax: 860-388-2025
*Haviland, Noritake; send Schleiger
number or sample saucer with SASE.*

Linda Kinnett
Kinnett Antiques
110 Lake Terrace Ct.
Hendersonville, TN 37075-5101
phone: 615-824-5987
*A Haviland matching service with
hundreds of patterns in stock; member
of A.A.D.A.; in business for over 30
years.*

Walker's Haviland Matching Service
P.O. Box 357
Athens, OH 45701
phone: 614-593-5631
*Buys and sells French or American
patterns of Haviland.*

Scott's Haviland Matching Service
1911 Leland Ave.
Des Moines, IA 50315-4952
phone: 800-952-7857 or 515-285-2739
fax: 515-285-0744
e-mail: scottshaviland@worldnet.att.net
Internet: http://
www.havilandchinabyscotts.com
*Specializing in French, American,
Bavarian, Charles Field, (Johann)
Haviland; buy, sell, and identify; send
Schleiger number or photocopy of
front and of backstamp; enclose
LSASE please.*

Scott's Haviland Matching Service
1911 Leland Ave.
Des Moines, IA 50315-4952
phone: 800-952-7857 or 515-285-2739
fax: 515-285-0744
e-mail: scottshaviland@worldnet.att.net
Internet: http://
www.havilandchinabyscotts.com
*Stocks, matches, and locates French
Haviland, French or American
Theodore Haviland; sets available;*
*send Schleiger identification, photo
and backmarks.*

Scott's Haviland Matching Service
1911 Leland Ave.
Des Moines, IA 50315-4952
phone: 800-952-7857 or 515-285-2739
fax: 515-285-0744
e-mail: scottshaviland@worldnet.att.net
Internet: http://
www.havilandchinabyscotts.com
*Carries French, American, Charles
Field and Johann (Bavarian)
Haviland.*

Grace Graves
Haviland Matching Service, Ltd.
219 N. Milwaukee St.
Milwaukee, WI 53202-5818
phone: 414-291-9111
fax: 414-291-9018
e-mail: hmsgraves@aol.com
*Specialists in identifying and locating
French & American Haviland
patterns; use Schleiger number or
send photocopy for pattern identification.*

Old Toll Gate Antiques
209 3rd Ave. W
Milan, IL 61264-2443
phone: 309-787-2392
*French and American Haviland; send
Schleiger number or photocopy of
front and back.*

Mary Jane Jurgens
50 DuClaire Rd.
Decatur, IL 62521-5527
phone: 217-423-8303
*Buys, sells, matches, and appraises
dinnerware with a specialty in
Haviland.*

Virginia Cannon, ISA
China House, The
801 W. Eldorado
Decatur, IL 62522
phone: 217-428-7212 or 217-864-2938
fax: 217-864-4852
*Matches, specializes in, and appraises
French & American; carries large
selection of Haviland patterns for sale
by mail order or from the shop; also
most other major brands.*

Kick L. Tex
Ann's Antiques
P.O. Box 7196
Springfield, IL 62791-7196
phone: 217-652-3862 or 217-546-4048
*Appraises, matches and locates
French Haviland; sells Haviland by
mail; no charge for listing or
searching; send pattern number or
picture of saucer for identification.*

Herbert Crosson
Crosson Antiques
835 N. 3rd Ave.
Minneapolis, KS 67467
phone: 913-392-2810
Specializes in Haviland china.

Joanne Copeland
Sweet Nothings
5533 S. 20th St.
Lincoln, NE 68512
phone: 402-420-1620

Nora Travis
Haviland China Replacements
P.O. Box 6008-161
Cerritos, CA 90701
phone: 714-521-9283
fax: 714-521-9283
*Specializing in French and American
Haviland; will identify and locate
your pattern if possible; large
inventory; send Schleiger number or
photocopy of your pattern; author of
"Haviland China - Age of Elegance"
(Schiffer.)*

Carol Ulrey
Unique Antiques
P.O. Box 15815
San Diego, CA 92175-5815
phone: 619-281-8650
fax: 619-282-8407
e-mail: curley@webcc.net
*Specializing in china matching:
Haviland, old French and American;
also Lenox china and crystal.*

Carol Williams
Lillian Johnson Antiques
405 Third St.
P.O. Box 1207
San Juan Bautista, CA 95045
phone: 408-623-4381
fax: 408-623-4381
*Well-established French and
American Haviland matching service;
pattern predominantly from the WWI
era; buys, sells, appraises.*

Auld Lang Syne
6311 Delta Ct.
Magalia, CA 95954-9535
*Over 30,000 patterns of Haviland;
send photocopy of front and back,
color and description plus SASE and
$7.50 for identification.*

Misc. Services

Frances M. Jepson
Jepson Haviland China
P.O. Box 295
Chinese Camp, CA 95309-0295
phone: 209-984-4432
*Experienced, identification only. Send
photocopy of front and back of plate,
color and description plus $7.50 and
SASE; will refund if cannot identify;
appraisals $75.*

Johnson Bros.

Matching Services

Mary J. Finegan
Marfine Antiques
P.O. Box 3618
Boone, NC 28607
phone: 704-262-3441
*Johnson Brothers dinnerware
exclusively.*

J.B. & ME
3576 Clairmont Rd.
Atlanta, GA 30319-3626
phone: 404-634-1194
*Tremendous stock of Johnson
Brothers dinnerware available for
additions or replacements; want lists
maintained; handles exclusively
Johnson Brothers.*

Lenox

Man./Prod./Dist.

Lenox China Shop
53 Commerce Dr.
Cranberry, NJ 08512
phone: 609-395-8054 or 800-367-7467
*Retail showroom selling open stock on
current stemware, dinnerware, and
giftware patterns.*

Lenox China & Crystal Consumer
Service
100 Lenox Dr.
Lawrenceville, NJ 08648
phone: 609-896-2800 or 800-635-3669
*Offers Matching Services List of
dealers who offer replacements for
current of discontinued Lenox items;
also gives insurance estimates.*

Matching Services

Regina Negrotti
Tablescapes
49 Elkton Ave.
P.O. Box 3165
Cheshire, CT 06410
phone: 800-801-4084
*A small, personal matching service
with a constantly changing inventory;
want lists are kept; send photocopy or
photo when unsure of pattern name;
specializes in Lenox.*

Lenox China Chasers
Tilton Rd.
Pomona, NJ 08240
phone: 800-423-8946
*Sells from remaining stocks of
discontinued patterns of Lenox
dinnerware; normally does not carry
anything over a few years old.*

Allan & Cathy Griggs
Chinamates
1673 Lakecrest Dr.
Sullivan, IN 47882-9585
phone: 800-726-0345 or 812-268-6411
fax: 812-268-6411
e-mail: chinamates@viaduct.custom.net
*Stocks and located discontinued Lenox
patterns; also Oxford; no giftware;
call or write; SASE; mail order only.*

Carol Ulrey
Unique Antiques
P.O. Box 15815
San Diego, CA 92175-5815
phone: 619-281-8650
fax: 619-282-8407
e-mail: curley@webcc.net
*Specializing in china matching:
Haviland, old French and American;
also Lenox china and crystal.*

Lesley Hall
Lesley's Lenox
24438 SE 46th Place
Los Altos, CA 98029
phone: 206-391-2330 or 800-553-6693
fax: 206-391-3383
*Lenox only; extensive inventory of
discontinued Lenox Fine China and
Lenox casual chinas; mail or phone
inquiries welcomed.*

Noritake

Matching Services

Noritake Co., Inc.
75 Seaview Dr.
Secaucus, NJ 07094
phone: 201-319-0600
fax: 201-319-1962
*Japanese and Irish dinnerware,
crystal, china and crystal giftware.*

Peggy Roush
Peggy's Matching Service, Ltd.
P.O. Box 476
Ocala, FL 32678-0476
phone: 352-629-3954
*Deals exclusively in discontinued
Noritake fine and casual china; over
1000 patterns in current inventory;
buys and sells.*

R.L. Watson
Matchers, The
181 Belle Meade
Memphis, TN 38117-3017
phone: 901-683-1337
fax: 901-682-9491
*Noritake specialists; also Lenox,
Royal Doulton, American Haviland,
Oxford, Wedgwood, Franciscan, and
other major factories; best to phone.*

Ms. China
P.O. Box 229
Monterey, CA 93942
phone: 800-688-6807 or 408-655-9984
fax: 408-655-0198
*Noritake only; pre-war and newly
discontinued china identification and
matching service.*

Rosenthal

Matching Services

Mary Zawaski
Vintage Patterns Unlimited
3571 Crestnoll Dr.
Cincinnati, OH 45211-1813
phone: 513-622-2543
*Former Rosenthal representative
dealing exclusively in Rosenthal; send
photo of cup and dinner plate; mail
order only.*

Wedgwood

Matching Services

Vintage Patterns IV
9303 McKinney Rd.
Loveland, OH 45140
phone: 513-489-6247
*Wedgwood specialists; also Adams,
Coalport; buys and sells; send SASE.*

Allan & Cathy Griggs
Chinamates
1673 Lakecrest Dr.
Sullivan, IN 47882-9585
phone: 800-726-0345 or 812-268-6411
fax: 812-268-6411
e-mail: chinamates@viaduct.custom.net
*Stocks and locates Wed wood china
and crystal; no giftware; call or write;
SASE; mail order only.*

Wedgwood China Cupboard, ABC
740 N. Honey Creek Pkwy.
Wauwatosa, WI 53213
phone: 414-259-1025
*Wedgwood, Adams, Coalport,
Midwinter; discontinued patterns
bought and sold; large collection of
Wedgwood in stock.*

Gloria Voss Beyer
Beyer's Wedgwood China Cupboard
740 Honey Creek Parkway
Milwaukee, WI 53213
phone: 800-893-WWCC
*Discontinued Wedgwood, Coalport,
Midwinter, and Adams.*

DINOSAURS

Clubs/Associations

Mike Fredericks
Prehistoric Times, The
Newsletter: Prehistoric Times, The
145 Bayline Circle
Folsom, CA 95630-8077
phone: 916-985-7986 or 916-985-2481
fax: 916-985-2481
e-mail: pretimes@aol.com
*The Prehistoric Times is a fanzine
dedicated to dinosaur collectors and
enthusiasts, including info on all
manner of collectibles and other items
of interest for Dinophiles everywhere;
48+ pages; bi-monthly; nothing like
it!*

Collectors

April Rhodes
RR 1 Box 284-E
Sunbury, PA 17801-9618
*Wants to buy anything dinosaur:
advertising premiums, old books,
games, etc.*

DIPPERS

(see SODA FOUNTAIN COL-
LECTIBLES)

DIRECTORIES

(see ANTIQUES SHOP DIRECTO-
RIES; FLEA MARKETS, Directories;
TOURS/BUYING TRIPS)

DIRIGIBLES

(see AIRSHIPS)

DIRILYTE FLATWARE

(see FLATWARE)

DISCONTINUED TABLEWARE PATTERNS

(see FLATWARE; DINNERWARE; GLASS, Elegant; GLASS, Crystal)

DISNEY COLLECTIBLES

(see also CHARACTER COL-
LECTIBLES; COLLECTIBLES
[MODERN]; POPULAR CULTURE;
POSTCARDS, Disney)

Appraisers

Robert G. Jason-Ickes
2115 9th Ave. SW, #A4
Olympia, WA 98502
phone: 360-705-1861
*Specializes in pre-1950 Disney
collectibles; also lectures.*

Clubs/Associations

Robert Crooker
Mouse Club East
Newsletter: Mouse Club East Newsletter
P.O. Box 3195
Wakefield, MA 01880-0774
phone: 617-246-3876
fax: 617-245-4511
*Interested in Disney related
collectibles.*

Disneyana Dreamers of San Diego
County
Newsletter: Disneyana Dreamers of San
Diego County Newsletter
P.O. Box 106
Escondido, CA 92033
phone: 619-747-2990
Monthly newsletter.

Louis Boish
National Fantasy Fan Club for
Disneyana Collectors & Enthusiasts
Journal: Fantasyline Express
P.O. Box 19212
Irvine, CA 92713-9212
phone: 714-731-4705
e-mail: info@nffc.org
Internet: http://www.nffc.org
*To preserve the legacy of Walt Disney
through collecting and preserving of
Disney memorabilia, research and
sharing of information; a monthly
newsletter.*

Golden Gate Disney Club
P.O. Box 547
San Lorenzo, CA 94580

Kate Klein
Imagination Guild
Newsletter: ImaginEars
P.O. Box 907
Boulder Creek, CA 95006-0907
phone: 408-335-2755
fax: 408-335-0800
e-mail: disney@cruzio.com
*For the beginner and advanced
collector or for the Disney enthusiast;
no pictures or ads, just news on
collectibles and where to find them;
also shows and information on the
Parks and Studio; monthly newsletter.*

Kim & Julie McEuen
Mouse Club, The
Newsletter: Mouse Club, The
2056 Cirone Way
San Jose, CA 95124
phone: 408-377-2590
fax: 408-379-6903
*A club with a bi-monthly newsletter
devoted to articles about Disneyana
collecting; sponsors semi-annual
show and sale of strictly Disneyana.*

Collectors

John S. Fawcett
P.O. Box 1156
Waldoboro, ME 04572-1156
phone: 207-832-7398
*Collects 1930s comic character items,
Post Toasties Disney cereal boxes &
other old Disneyana.*

Bob Havey
P.O. Box 183
North Sullivan, ME 04664-0183
phone: 207-422-3083
fax: 207-422-3430
*Disney collector buys all nice 1930s/
40s items; excellent prices paid.*

Charles Sanna
P.O. Box 27
Brooklyn, NY 11231
phone: 800-252-6261 or 718-448-7528
fax: 718-625-2895
*Wants to buy all types of early Disney
and comic collectibles.*

Linda Trew Ahlfield
Divine Inc.
513 Fawn Ct.
Fayetteville, NC 28303
phone: 910-868-3894
*Wants to buy pre-1970 Mickey Mouse
memorabilia.*

Jim Conley
2758 Coventry Lane
Canton, OH 44708-1320
phone: 330-477-7725 or 330-499-9283
fax: 330-879-2950
Very interested in early Disney.

Dealers

Robert Crooker
Mouse Man Ink, The
P.O. Box 3195
Wakefield, MA 01880-0774
phone: 617-246-3876
fax: 617-245-4511
*Buys and sells, specializing in pre-
1941 Disney; large catalog available
for $1.*

Jane & John Carroll
2894 John Tyler Highway
Williamsburg, VA 23185-1335
phone: 757-258-9322
Buys and sells Disneyana.

Dan Goodsell
Tick Tock Toys
P.O. Box 342
Culver City, CA 90232
phone: 310-815-0465
Wants to buy vintage (1950s and

*1960s) Disneyland memorabilia
especially guide books, maps,
souvenirs, toys, model kits, brochures,
etc.*

Experts

Doug & Pat Wengel
P.O. Box 305
Skillman, NJ 08558-0305
phone: 609-466-2461
fax: 609-466-8911
*Buys, sells and specializes in vintage
character collectibles, especially those
with early images of Disney
characters Mickey, Minnie, Horace
and Clarabelle; offers matching
service for Disney china dishes -
Japanese, Bavarian, Paragon.*

Ted Hake
Hake's Americana & Collectibles
Auction
P.O. Box 1444
York, PA 17405-1444
phone: 717-848-1333
*Always purchasing items for 8 mail-
bid auctions per year covering
hundreds of categories including toys,
character collectibles, Disney, cowboy
heroes, premiums, television,
politicals, pin-back buttons,
advertising and more.*

Ron Donnelly
Saturday Heroes
P.O. Box 7047
Panama City, FL 32413-0047
phone: 904-234-7944
fax: 904-233-9316

Joel J. Cohen, ISA
Cohen Books & Collectibles
P.O. Box 810310
Boca Raton, FL 33481-0310
phone: 561-487-7888
fax: 561-487-3117
e-mail: cohendisney@prodigy.com
Internet: http://www.bbai.onramp.net/
bbai.cohen.htm
*Walt Disney specialist and collector;
will find what you want; buys, sells,
appraises Disneyana from Mickey
Mouse to Snow White to Pocahontas;
vintage as well as limited edition
items, animation art, books, figurines,
toys, etc.*

Tom Tumbusch
Tomart Publications
3300 Encrete Lane
Dayton, OH 45439-1944
phone: 513-294-2250
fax: 513-294-1024
*Buys Disneyana items; author of
"Tomart's Illustrated Disneyana
Catalog and Price Guide" series
depicting 20,000 items in color.*

Museums/Libraries

David R. Smith
Walt Disney Archives
500 South Buena Vista St.
Burbank, CA 91521-1200
phone: 818-560-5424
Comprehensive Disney collection

*including complete U.S. and most
foreign Disney comics; comics not
available to researchers for
preservation reasons, but much
material is available by appointment.*

Periodicals

Laughter Publications, Inc.
Magazine: Storyboard Magazine
80 Main St.
Nashua, NH 03060
phone: 603-883-9770
*A bi-monthly high-quality magazine
dedicated to animation art; feature
articles and advertisements related to
cel and merchandise collecting, the
Disney motion pictures, and historical
articles about the animators.*

Tom Tumbusch
Tomart Publications
Magazine: Tomart's Disneyana Digest
3300 Encrete Lane
Dayton, OH 45439-1944
phone: 513-294-2250
fax: 513-294-1024
Published quarterly.

John Koenig
Antique Trader Publications, Inc.
Newspaper: Toy Trader
922 Churchill St., Ste. #1
Waupaca, WI 54981
phone: 715-258-7525 or 800-768-9225
fax: 715-258-8707
e-mail: jkoenig@add-inc.com
Internet: http://www.csmonline.com
*Monthly newspaper with information
on how to buy, sell and trade all types
of toys; market trends, the latest
prices, "how-to" columns, listings of
toy clubs and upcoming toy shows and
auctions; also full of buy and sell ads.*

Don Schockow
Rainbow Ridge Productions
VHS: Disney TV
P.O. Box 1064
Ojai, CA 93024-1064
phone: 805-640-8101
fax: 805-640-8101
e-mail: rrp@west.net
Internet: http://members.aol.com/
dsneyanatv/index.html
*"Disneyana TV" is a quarterly VHS
television show covering everything
Disney; from behind the scenes to
future projects...it's all on Disneyana
TV.*

Ceramics

Dealers

Judy Posner
4195 South Tamiami Trail, Ste. 183
Venice, FL 34293-5112
phone: 941-497-7149
fax: 941-493-8085
e-mail: Judyandjef@aol.com
Internet: http://www.tias.com/stores/jpc
*Wants Disney bisque figures, Disney
dinnerware, character cookie jars &
shakers; send $1 for catalog; send for
wants list.*

Disneyland Souvenirs

Collectors

Dean Mancina
P.O. Box 2274
Seal Beach, CA 90740
phone: 310-431-5671

DIVING EQUIPMENT

(see NAUTICAL ANTIQUES, Diving)

DIXIE CUP LIDS

Collectors

Leonard Schneir
184 Sixth Ave.
New York, NY 10013
phone: 212-966-4357
Wants one or an entire collection.

DOCUMENTS

(see AUTOGRAPHS; BOOKS;
PAPER COLLECTIBLES; MANU-
SCRIPTS)

DOILIES

(see TEXTILES, Needlework)

DOLL HOUSES & FURNISHINGS

(see also CHILDREN'S THINGS;
DOLLS; MINIATURES)

Appraisers

Judy Owen, ISA
Antique Appraisers - Grand Traverse
10332 Stoneybeach Pointe
Traverse City, MI 49686
phone: 616-946-2534
fax: 616-946-2573
*Specializing in doll houses and
miniatures.*

Clubs/Associations

Shelley Smith
Toy Dish Collectors Club
Newsletter: Tiny Times, The
P.O. Box 159
Bethlehem, CT 06751-0159
phone: 203-266-7496
fax: 203-266-7343
Internet: http://www.members.aol.com/
toydish
*Collectors are interested in children's
dishes, furniture, glass, toy kitchen
and stores.*

Sharon Unger
Dollhouse & Miniature Collectors
Newsletter: Dollhouse & Miniature
Collectors Quarterly
P.O. Box 16
Bellaire, MI 49615
phone: 616-377-7397
e-mail: dmcg@collector.org
*Purpose is to promote commercial and
handmade dollhouses considered
antique & collectible (not contempo-
rary pieces).*

Collectors

Sharon Wilkins
1105 Burnham St.
Cocoa, FL 32922-6838
e-mail: bugs20@.comm
*Wants to buy 1940s and 1950s doll
houses.*

Jerry A. Phelps
6013 Innes Trace Rd.
Louisville, KY 40222-6004
phone: 502-425-4765
*Wants to buy old dollhouses with
paper lithography on wood; also
wants early clockwork toys.*

Peggy Ell
218 Gratton
Burlington, IA 52601
phone: 319-752-7670
*Collects commercial doll houses: tin,
masonite, fiberboard, cardboard,
paper, and any other material.*

R.L. Rice
612 E. Front St.
Bloomington, IL 61701
*Wants to buy metal doll house
furniture; one piece or an entire set;
please state brand and price.*

Dealers

Ann Mechan
P.O. Box 6686
Portsmouth, NH 03802
phone: 603-433-5650

Robert Dankanics
Dollhouse Factory, The
P.O. Box 456
Lebanon, NJ 08833-0456
phone: 908-236-6404
fax: 908-236-7899
Wants old dollhouses and miniatures.

Abbie Kelly
P.O. Box 351
Camillus, NY 13031-0351
phone: 315-487-7451
e-mail: toydish@aol.com
Internet: http://members.aol.com/toydish
*Wants to buy German kitchens and
stores, doll dishes, doll accessories.*

Experts

Marian Schmuhl
7 Revolutionary Ridge Rd.
Bedford, MA 01730
phone: 617-275-2156 or 508-477-4520
*Specializes in dolls and doll house
furnishings from the 1950s.*

Museums/Libraries

Essex Institute
132 Essex St.
Salem, MA 01970
phone: 508-744-3390

Strong Museum, The
1 Manhattan Square
Rochester, NY 14607
phone: 716-263-2700

Washington Dolls' House & Toy
Museum
5236 44th St. NW
Washington, DC 20015
phone: 202-244-0024

Wrecker's Museum
322 Duval St.
Key West, FL 33040
phone: 305-294-9502

Art Institute of Chicago, Thorne
Miniature Rooms
111 S. Michigan Ave.
Chicago, IL c
phone: 312-443-0849
Internet: http://www.artic.edu/aic/
firstpage.html

Periodicals

June Stowe, Ed.
Magazine: International Dolls' House
News
P.O. Box 79
Southampton S09 7EZ, U.K.
*In publication for over 25 years;
specialist magazine devoted to doll
houses and miniatures both old and
new.*

Magazine: Doll Castle News
P.O. Box 247
Washington, NJ 07882
phone: 201-689-6513 or 201-689-7042
fax: 908-689-6320
*A magazine focusing on dolls,
miniatures, doll houses and related
items; ads, paper doll section,
needlework, patterns, etc.*

Scott Publications
Magazine: Miniature Collector
30595 Eight Mile
Livonia, MI 48152-1761
phone: 800-458-8237 or 810-477-6650
fax: 810-477-6795
e-mail: 104137.1254@compuserve.com
*An international bi-monthly
publication devoted exclusively to
contemporary and antique scale
miniatures: artists, manufacturers,
retailers, collectors, room settings,
etc.*

Plastic

Collectors

Bobbie Segal
415 Julian Woods Lane
P.O. Box 39
Julian, PA 16844
phone: 814-355-2542
*Wants plastic dollhouse furniture from
the 1940s through the 1960s; by
Renwal, Ideal, etc.*

Dealers

Judy Mosholder
186 Pine Springs Camp Road
Boswell, PA 15531-2421
phone: 814-629-9277
*Buys and sells dollhouses and plastic
dollhouse furniture, especially*

*Renwal, Ideal, and Marx; send LSASE
for list of items for sale.*

DOLLS

(see also AMERICAN INDIAN,
Skookum Dolls; AMER. INDIAN,
Kachina Dolls; BOOKS, Reference
[Dolls]; CHARACTER COL-
LECTIBLES; CHILDREN'S
THINGS; COLLECTIBLES
[MODERN], Dolls; ELVES; DOLL
HOUSES & FURNISHINGS; STEIFF;
TEDDY BEARS; TOYS, Action
Figures; TROLLS

Appraisers

Darlene Joy Gengelbach
Darlene's Joys
4785 St. Paul Blvd.
Rochester, NY 14617
phone: 716-544-6997
fax: 716-266-4623
*Doll appraisals, lectures, research,
consultant, restoration, conservation;
private or museums; presently
working for two museums.*

Stuart Holbrook
Theriault's Auction
P.O. Box 151
Annapolis, MD 21404-0151
phone: 410-224-3655 or 800-638-0422
fax: 410-224-2515
e-mail: webmaster@theriaults
Internet: http://www.talongrp.com/
theriaults
*Chief appraiser and buyer for one of
the nation's largest doll auction
houses; one doll or entire collection
can be appraised.*

Cary Raesner, Ed.
House of White Birches
Magazine: Doll Collector's Price Guide
306 East Parr Rd.
Berne, IN 46711
phone: 219-589-8741 or 800-829-5865
fax: 219-589-8093
*Offers free doll appraisals to
subscribers.*

R. Rebecca Moncrief, ISA
2007 Sea Cove Ct.
Houston, TX 77058-4228
phone: 713-333-3672
fax: 713-333-0201
e-mail: becky@ufdc.org
Specializes in antique dolls.

Barbara De Feo
Janara Antique Dolls
P.O. Box 662
Bonita, CA 91908-0662
phone: 619-482-8575
*Appraisals and conservation of
antique dolls; buys and sells at shows
or by mail order; will buy one doll or
entire collection; member National
Antique Doll Dealer's Association,
and UFDC; has written articles for
"Antique Doll World."*

Julie J. Scott, ISA
Plumed Horse, The
P.O. Box 904
Bellevue, WA 98009
phone: 206-453-9822
*Buys, consigns, sells, and appraises
toys and dolls.*

Norene Ott
Antique & Collectible Doll Appraisal of
  Seattle
P.O. Box 46134
Seattle, WA 98146-0134
phone: 206-246-2290 or 206-244-8007
fax: 206-244-8007

Auction Services

Jon Baddeley
Sotheby's
34-35 New Bond St.
London W1A 2AA, U.K.
phone: 0171-4938080 or 0171-4085205
fax: 0171-4085911
*Conducts specialty auctions of
tinplate toys, diecasts, trains, antique
dolls, teddy bears, automata.*

Mildred Ewing
Skinner, Inc.
357 Main St.
Bolton, MA 01740-1104
phone: 508-779-6241 or 617-350-5400
fax: 508-779-5144
*Established in 1964, Skinner Inc. is
the fifth largest auction house in the
US; has offices in Bolton and Boston,
MA.*

Withington, Inc.
RD 2 Box 440
Hillsboro, NH 03244
phone: 603-464-3232

Randy Inman
James D. Julia Auctioneers Inc.
Rt. 201, Skowhegan Rd.
P.O. Box 830
Fairfield, ME 04937
phone: 207-453-7125
fax: 207-453-2502
*Conducts specialized auctions of toys
and doll items and are one of the
leaders in this field in North America.*

Stuart Holbrook
Theriault's Auction
P.O. Box 151
Annapolis, MD 21404-0151
phone: 410-224-3655 or 800-638-0422
fax: 410-224-2515
e-mail: webmaster@theriaults
Internet: http://www.talongrp.com/
  theriaults
*One of the oldest and perhaps largest
doll auction houses in America; will
send "Doll Information Guide"
pamphlet upon request and LSASE;
doll auction color catalogs are $154
for 10 issues per year; holds over 50
doll auctions per year.*

Dorothy Hunt
Sweetbriar
P.O. Box 37
Earleville, MD 21919-0037
phone: 410-275-2094
*Auctions dolls and doll costumes; also
offers doll seminars and appraisals.*

Ann Hays
Kenneth S. Hays & Associates, Inc.
120 S Spring St.
Louisville, KY 40206-1953
phone: 502-584-4297
fax: 502-585-5896
e-mail: auctionctr@ntr.net
Internet: http://www.ntr.net/~auctionctr
Conducts specialty doll auctions.

David M. Cobb
Cobb's Doll Auction
1909 Harrison Rd. N.
Johnstown, OH 43031-9539
phone: 614-964-0444
*Conducts quarterly antique doll,
automata, bears, etc. auctions; send
$22 for catalog; send address for
advance notice flyer.*

Jim & Shari McMasters
McMasters Doll Auctions
P.O. Box 1755
Cambridge, OH 43725-6755
phone: 800-842-3526 or 614-432-4419
fax: 614-432-3191
*Specializes in auctioning antique and
collectible dolls and doll related items
such as teddy bears, Barbie dolls and
accessories, children's dishes, toys,
children's books, etc.*

Korin Dunning Helsdon
Dunning's Auction Service
755 Church Rd.
Elgin, IL 60123-9302
phone: 708-741-3483 or 800-462-2444
fax: 708-741-3589
Internet: http:///www.dunnings.com

Barbara Frasher
Frasher's Doll Auction
Rte. 1 Box 142
Oak Grove, MO 64075
phone: 816-625-3786
fax: 816-625-6079
Conducts doll specialty auctions.

Clubs/Associations

Sara Patterson
National Organization of Miniaturists &
  Dollers
Newsletter: NOMAD Dolletter
1300 Schroder
Normal, IL 61761
*Stories, articles, illustrations,
patterns, and how-to information.*

United Federation of Doll Clubs
Newsletter: Doll News
10920 N. Ambassador Dr.
Kansas City, MO 64153
phone: 816-891-7040 or 816-891-8417
fax: 816-891-8360
e-mail: ufdc@aol.com
Internet: http://www.ufdc.org
Contact to locate a club in your area.

West Phoenix Doll Club
7154 N. 58th Dr.
Glendale, AZ 85301
phone: 602-931-1579

Collectors

Linda L. Vines
P.O. Box 43721
Montclair, NJ 07043
phone: 973-748-4990 or 201-748-4990
*Wants to buy antique bisque head
dolls in excellent condition; also doll
clothes and accessories.*

Kate Emburg
P.O. Box 1437
North Highlands, CA 95660-1437
phone: 916-331-7435
e-mail: dolladopt@aol.com
*Collector especially interested in
Madame Alexander, hard plastic and
composition dolls.*

Marci Van Ausdall
P.O. Box 946
Quincy, CA 95971
phone: 916-283-2770
e-mail: dreams@psln.com
*Wants to buy all original, excellent
condition and mint-in-box fashion
dolls and clothing from the 1950s-
1960s such as Ideal Toni, Shirley
Temple, Sweet Sue, Revelons,
American Character Toni.*

Dealers

Judith Armistead
Doll Works, The
P.O. Box 195
Lynnfield, MA 01940
phone: 617-334-5577
*Interested in buying bisque,
composition, cloth, snow babies, half
dolls, and early cartoon characters.*

Eileen Mosteller
Dollworks
62-C Franklin St., #107
Westerly, RI 02891-3123
phone: 401-596-4674
*Buys/sells mint & mint-in-box 1930-
1970 dolls, especially rare cloth,
composition & hard plastic Madame
Alexanders plus fabulous Ginnys,
Jills, Mary Hoyers, Arranbees,
Effanbees, Style Shows, Shirley
Temples, Revelons, etc.; $2 for list.*

Linda Dalenberg
Timeless Pieces
246 West Main St.
Hillsboro, NH 03244
phone: 603-464-5621
fax: 603-464-6747
*Wants to buy antique dolls, doll beds,
doll clothes, and doll accessories.*

Liz Olimpio
Aladdin Antiques
Governor's Rd.
Sanbornville, NH 03872
phone: 603-522-8503
fax: 603-522-8933
*Buy, sells, repairs antique dolls and
antique clothing.*

Debra Gulea
Debra's Dolls
P.O. Box 705
Mullica Hill, NJ 08062
phone: 609-478-9778 or 609-694-2007
*Antique dolls bought and sold; doll
furniture, clothing; doll houses, and
accessories also available; member of
UFDC and NADDA; send for photo
doll list.*

Debra's Dolls
P.O. Box 705
Mullica Hill, NJ 08062
phone: 609-478-9778 or 609-694-2007

Sherri & Jack Dempsey
1009 East 38th St.
P.O. Box 10037
New York, NY 10037
phone: 814-825-6381
*Specializes in antique dolls and Marx
toys; also doll restorations.*

Roberta's Doll House
140 Caryl Ave.
Yonkers, NY 10705
phone: 800-569-9739 or 914-968-3033
fax: 914-968-4172

Bonnie J. Cook
P.O. Box 134
East Greenbush, NY 12061
phone: 518-477-7272
*Wants to buy American and European
antique dolls.*

Jacquie Henry
Antique Treasures & Toys
2240 Academy St.
P.O. Box 17
Walworth, NY 14568-0017
phone: 315-986-1424
e-mail: JHenry5792@aol.com
*Buys and sells antique German and
French bisque dolls, and mint
condition 1950s hard plastic dolls in
original clothes such as Toni,
Arranbee, Madame Alexander,
Ginnys, Gingers, and Nancy Ann
Storybooks.*

Nikki Kvitka
Nikel Enterprises, Inc.
4536 Custer Dr.
Harrisburg, PA 17110
phone: 717-236-7148
fax: 717-236-6807

Dawn Herlocher
Dawn's Dolls
Maple Ave.
Mackeyville, PA 17750
phone: 717-726-6458
*Specializing in fine quality Japanese
Satsuma and cloisonne.*

Joyce & Judy
Krazy Cat Collectibles
8604 Second Ave. #235
Silver Spring, MD 20910
phone: 301-309-2513
e-mail: KrazyCatCo@aol.com
*Buys and sells dolls: antique bisque,
composition, vinyl, pre-1972 Barbie,
modern artist dolls, Campbell Kids,
Liddle Kiddles, Glamour dolls like
Miss Revlon; also wants clothing and
accessories.*

Walter LaValley
Bachelor II Dolls & Bears
247 S. Van Dorn St.
Wheaton Plaza
Alexandria, VA 22304
phone: 703-823-BEAR
fax: 703-823-1787
Specializes in dolls and bears.

Julia Melton
Melton's Antique Dolls
4201 Indian River Rd.
Chesapeake, VA 23325-3005
phone: 757-420-9226
fax: 757-420-1462
e-mail: BMelton156@aol.com

Robert Zacher
Heirloom Doll Shoppe/Hospital/
    Museum
416 E. Broadway
Waukesha, WI 53186
phone: 414-544-4739

Valerie LaBreche
Enchanted World Doll Museum
615 North Main
Mitchell, SD 57301-1945
phone: 605-996-9896
fax: 605-996-0210
*Buys and sells antique and collectible
dolls and accessory items; specializes
in 1800 to early 1900s bisque and
china dolls.*

David & Brenda Greener
7313 Wind Chime
Fort Worth, TX 76133
phone: 817-292-0909
*Buys, sells and appraises dolls;
former doll show promoter.*

Turn of the Century Antiques
1475 S. Broadway
Denver, CO 80210
phone: 303-722-8700 or 303-778-7077

Gert :Leonard
E & G Antiques
P.O. Box 296
San Dimas, CA 91773
phone: 909-599-2723

Donna Purkey
P.O. Box 2871
Anaheim, CA 92804-0871
phone: 714-828-5909
*Wants to buy older Barbie dolls and
accessories; also wants special limited
edition dolls such as Holidays,
Mackies, porcelain, etc.*

Carmel Doll Shop
P.O. Box 7198
Carmel, CA 93921
phone: 408-373-5131
fax: 408-655-5755

Gloria McCarty
Doll Cellar, The
23337 46th Ave., S.W.
Seattle, WA 98116
phone: 206-938-4446
*Buys, sells, collects, appraises and
repairs dolls.*

Experts

Judith Izen
P.O. Box 623
Lexington, MA 02173
e-mail: jizenres@aol.com
*A noted doll historian who has
compiled histories of several
American doll companies including
Ideal, Vogue, Eegee, Deluxe Reading,
Mattel.*

Patricia Snyder
My Dear Dolly
P.O. Box 303
Sparta, NJ 07871-0303
phone: 201-729-8087
e-mail: dolly@intercall.com
Internet: http://www.mydeardolly.com
*Wants old dolls, bodies, parts, doll
clothing, accessories, doll dishes,
snowbabies; publishes monthly list of
dolls for sale; also appraises*

Mary Gorham
Gems of the Doll World
9399 Shelly Lane
Cincinnati, OH 45242-7607
*Writes "Gems of the Doll World"
column about dolls. Send SASE along
with drawing of mold marks and
photographs for identification of your
antique, not modern, dolls.*

Carol Sumpter
Cardan's Doll Shop
3808 Loughborough
Saint Louis, MO 63116
phone: 314-351-7955
*Buys, sells, collects, specializes in,
and appraises dolls.*

Don & Vella Painter
Doll Restoration
23483 Shephard Rd.
Clatskanie, OR 97016
phone: 888-763-5122 or 503-728-3503
e-mail: homestead@aone.com
Internet: http://www.webdolls.com/OR/
    Homestead_Collectibles
*Buys, sells, appraises, collects and
repairs dolls: antiques, compositions,
pull string and battery operated
talkers, mechanical, toys, vinyl; also
reroots hair.*

JoAnn Morgan
Morgan's Collectibles
831 SE 170th Dr.
Portland, OR 97233
Writes column about antique dolls and

teddy bears for the "National Doll &
Teddy Bear Collector" newspaper.

Michele Karl
P.O. Box 6543
Lynnwood, WA 98036
phone: 206-744-0983
*Focuses on 20th century composition
dolls: Barbie, Schoenhuts, Alexenders,
Cameo Doll Co., Ideal Toy Co.,
Effanbee, character dolls.*

Misc. Services

Dwaine E. Gipe
Dollogist
1406 Sycamore Rd.
Montoursville, PA 17754
phone: 717-323-9604
*Teaches four-day doll restoration
seminar; brochure available; also
sells step-by-step video covering use
of modern restoration materials
including air brush, sources provided,
tools used, tricks.*

JoAnn Mathias
G & M Doll Restoration Seminar
6204 Ocean Front Ave.
Virginia Beach, VA 23451
phone: 757-428-1609
e-mail: 73121.1505@compuserve.com
*Offers four-day hands-on doll
restoration seminars; write or call for
brochure.*

RoseAnn L. Donahoo
"My Dolls System"
P.O. Box 2288
Winter Park, FL 32790
phone: 406-332-0954
*"My Dolls System" is a working
system for organizing, coding, and
protecting a private doll collection;
for non-commercial use; no high-tech
or special skills needed; 70 lb. weight
paper, instructions, special forms.*

Linda Holderbaum
Doll Detective, The
107 North 32nd
Battle Creek, MI 49015
phone: 616-963-6291
*Lectures, appraise, organizes
exhibitions; restoration and
conservation work formerly a museum
curator.*

Museums/Libraries

Bethnel Green Museum of Childhood
Cambridge Heath Rd.
London E2 9PA, U.K.
phone: 081-980-3204
fax: 081-980-4759
*National collection of dolls, toys,
games, puppets, and children's
costumes.*

Eleanor E. Thompson, Dir.
Wenham Museum
132 Main St.
Wenham, MA 01984-1520
phone: 508-468-2377
*Largest permanent display of toy
soldiers in the U.S.; collection
includes pre-war Britains, large and*

small scale Heyde, composition
figures and more; also model train
room with operating layouts.

Yesteryears Museum
<u>Newsletter: Yesteryears Museum News</u>
P.O. Box 609
Sandwich, MA 02563
phone: 617-888-1711

Doll Museum, The
520 Thames St.
Newport, RI 02840-6711
phone: 401-849-0405
fax: 401-849-0405
*Featuring a fine collection of antique
and modern dolls; museum toy shop
carries antiques, collectibles, etc.;
offers repairs and appraisals.*

Curator
Fairfield Historical Society
636 Old Post Rd.
Fairfield, CT 06430-6647
phone: 203-259-1598
fax: 203-255-2716

Doll Castle Doll Museum
P.O. Box 247
Washington, NJ 07882
phone: 201-689-6513 or 201-689-7042
fax: 908-689-6320
*Houses hundreds of dolls and related
items collected by the staff of "Doll
Castle News."*

Sheila Clark
Museum of the City of New York
1220 5th Ave.
New York, NY 10029-5221
phone: 212-534-1672
fax: 212-534-5974
*Access by appointment; research fee
charged.*

Aunt Len's Doll House, Inc.
6 Hamilton Terrace
New York, NY 10031
phone: 212-926-4172

Town of Yorktown Museum
1974 Commerce St.
Yorktown Heights, NY 10598
phone: 914-962-2811

Linda Greenfield
Victorian Doll Museum & Chili Doll
    Hospital
4332 Buffalo Rd.
North Chili, NY 14514-1206
phone: 716-247-0130
*A wonderland exhibiting over 2000
identified dolls from mid-1800s to
present; puppet show, toy circus, doll
houses, paper dolls, etc.*

Strong Museum, The
1 Manhattan Square
Rochester, NY 14607
phone: 716-263-2700

Marjorie Darrah
Mary Merritt Doll Museum, The
843 Benjamin Hwy.
Douglassville, PA 19518
phone: 610-385-3809
fax: 610-689-4538
Dolls on display range from a 17th

century bone doll to French wax mini-manequins, bisque dolls, and Jumeaus.

Washington Dolls' House & Toy Museum
5236 44th St. NW
Washington, DC 20015
phone: 202-244-0024

National Museum of American History
14th & Constitution Ave. NW
Washington, DC 20560
phone: 202-357-2700
Internet: http://www.si.edu/

Edwina Gill
Mary Miller Doll Museum
1523 Glynn Ave.
Brunswick, GA 31520
phone: 912-267-7569
3,000 dolls, doll houses, miniatures from 90 countries; dolls dating from 1850 to present.

Ellen E. Mauer
Milan Historical Museum, Inc.
Newsletter: New Milan Ledger
P.O. Box 308
Milan, OH 44846
phone: 419-499-2968
fax: 419-499-9004
A seven-building complex 500 yards from the birthplace of Thomas A. Edison; restored home, carriage shed, blacksmith shop, general store, collections from the 19th century.

Children's Museum/Detroit Public Schools
67 East Kirby
Detroit, MI 48202
phone: 313-494-1210

Valerie LaBreche
Enchanted World Doll Museum
615 North Main
Mitchell, SD 57301-1945
phone: 605-996-9896
fax: 605-996-0210
4000 antique & collectible dolls set in 400 unique displays; gift shop features dolls, doll books, paper dolls, doll accessories, and Dept. 56, Dickens and Snow Babies.

House of a Thousand Dolls
P.O. Box 136
Loma, MT 59460-0136
phone: 406-739-4338

Eugene Field House & Toy Museum
Newsletter: Field Notes
634 So. Broadway St.
Saint Louis, MO 63102
phone: 314-421-4689
Birthplace and childhood home of Eugene Field, the children's poet; large collection of antique toys always on display.

Sandi Russell
Toy & Miniature Museum of Kansas City
5235 Oak St.
Kansas City, MO 64112-2877
phone: 816-333-2055 or 816-333-9328
fax: 816-333-2055
Museum housed in an elegant mansion features collections of miniatures, antique dolls' houses and antique toys.

Prairie Museum of Art & History
P.O. Box 465
Colby, KS 67701
phone: 913-462-6972

Gay Nineties Button & Doll Museum
Rte. 4 Box 420
Eureka Springs, AR 72632
phone: 501-253-9321

Eliza Cruce Hall Doll Museum
320 E. Street, N.W.
Ardmore, OK 73401
phone: 405-223-8290
fax: 405-223-2033

Francis & Clara Franks
Franks Antique Doll Museum
410 N. Grove St.
Marshall, TX 75670-3243
phone: 903-935-3065 or 903-935-3070

Hobby City Doll & Toy Museum
1238 South Beach Blvd.
Anaheim, CA 92804
phone: 714-527-2323

Periodicals

Directory: Doll Castle News Doll Directory, The
P.O. Box 247
Washington, NJ 07882
phone: 201-689-6513 or 201-689-7042
fax: 908-689-6320
Lists classified ads for hundreds of sources of interest to the doll collector.

Magazine: Doll Castle News
P.O. Box 247
Washington, NJ 07882
phone: 201-689-6513 or 201-689-7042
fax: 908-689-6320
A magazine focusing on dolls, miniatures, doll houses and related items; ads, paper doll section, needlework, patterns, etc.

Stephanie Finnegan, Ed.
Magazine: Dolls - The Collectors Magazine
170 Fifth Ave. - 12th Floor
New York, NY 10010
phone: 212-989-8700 or 800-347-6969
fax: 212-645-8976
Full-color magazine covering antique and contemporary collector dolls and the artists that designed them; auction reports, current prices, museum collections.

Newsletter: Costume Quarterly for Doll Collectors
118-01 Sutter Ave.
Jamaica, NY 11420-2407

Donna Kaonis, Ed.
Magazine: Antique Doll World
225 Main St., Ste. 300
Northport, NY 11768-1737
phone: 516-261-8337 or 800-828-1429
fax: 516-261-8235
Internet: http://www.tias.com/mags/IC/AntiqueDollWorld/
Articles about antique dolls, vintage teddy bears, dolls' houses and miniatures; articles by leading doll experts, visits to major collections, coverage of shows and auctions; published bi-monthly.

Cowles Magazines, Inc.
Magazine: Doll Reader
741 Miller Dr. SE, Ste. D2
Harrisburg, PA 20175
phone: 703-771-9400 or 800-829-3340
fax: 703-779-8345
Internet: http://www.thehistorynet.com
Gives both the beginning & advanced collector information on antique, collectible and modern dolls; current collecting trends, popular manufacturers and artists, new product releases, events calendar, display ideas.

Sharon Moran
Newsletter: Dollmasters, The
P.O. Box 151
Annapolis, MD 21404-0151
phone: 410-224-3655 or 800-638-0422
fax: 410-224-2515
e-mail: webmaster@theriaults
Internet: http://www.talongrp.com/theriaults
"The Dollmasters" is published quarterly and contains articles about doll market news as well as recent auction reports and doll related products and accessories.

Brian Savage
Fun Publications
Newspaper: Master Collector
12513 Birchfalls Dr.
Raleigh, NC 27614-9675
phone: 800-772-6673 or 919-847-5263
e-mail: bsavage@mastercollector.com
Internet: http://www.mastercollector.com
Ads-only newspaper; dolls (antique and modern collectible), toys, banks, models, cars, Matchbox, monsters, puzzles, political, toy trains, etc.; subscribers receive free 30 word ad each month; published monthly; reaches 20,000.

Martha Pullen Co.
Magazine: Sew Beautiful Magazine
518 Madison St.
Huntsville, AL 35801
phone: 800-547-4176
fax: 205-533-9630
Internet: http://www.marthapullenco.com
The magazine about heirloom sewing,

primarily children's clothing but also includes patterns for dolls.

Cary Raesner, Ed.
House of White Birches
Magazine: Doll Collector's Price Guide
306 East Parr Rd.
Berne, IN 46711
phone: 219-589-8741 or 800-829-5865
fax: 219-589-8093
A quarterly magazine that focuses on antique and collectible dolls, identification, fakes, auction results, ads, investing, teddy bears, etc.

Beth Schwartz, Ed.
House of White Birches
Magazine: Doll World
306 East Parr Rd.
Berne, IN 46711
phone: 219-589-8741 or 800-829-5865
fax: 219-589-8093
A bi-monthly magazine which covers many aspects of dolls and doll collecting: articles on doll history, patterns, interviews with doll artists, how-to articles, doll ID, etc.

Magazine: Antique & Collectible Dolls
218 W. Woodin Blvd.
Dallas, TX 75224
phone: 214-943-2107
A monthly magazine with ads and articles about dolls, auctions, and shows.

Sandra Hood, Gen. Mngr.
Newspaper: Antique & Collectables
P.O. Box 13560
El Cajon, CA 92022
phone: 619-593-2925 or 619-593-2933
fax: 619-442-4043
The largest monthly newspaper in Southern California covering the antiques & collectibles industry with focus sections on Nevada and Arizona; 72+ pages; events and show section, feature articles; columns, ads.

Rose Morgan, Ed.
Penultimate Press
Newspaper: National Doll & Teddy Bear Collector
P.O. Box 4032
Portland, OR 97208-4032
fax: 503-234-6170
e-mail: oleprospector@worldaccessnet.com
Internet: http://www.worldaccessnet.com/~goldbug/kewpies.htm
A monthly newspaper for doll, Kewpie and teddy bear collectors, dealers and artists.

Repair Services

Doll Lady Hospital, The
94 Pent Rd.
Branford, CT 06405-4013
Repair all types of dolls; supplier of parts and reproduction service; costume work; all work done by appointment only; 21 years experience.

Mary Flanagan
Mary's Doll Hospital
75 Main St.
Chester, NJ 07930
phone: 908-879-4101 or 201-366-9485
*Dolls and bears bought, sold and
repaired.*

Linda Greenfield
Victorian Doll Museum & Chili Doll
Hospital
4332 Buffalo Rd.
North Chili, NY 14514-1206
phone: 716-247-0130
*Recognized expert in doll restoration;
repairs all types of dolls; restringing,
leather body repair, replacement of
cloth bodies.*

Dwaine E. Gipe
Dollogist
1406 Sycamore Rd.
Montoursville, PA 17754
phone: 717-323-9604
*Can solve most doll problems: paper
mache, bisque, composition;
conservation, restoration; reset eyes,
wigs, missing parts, recoloring.*

JoAnn Mathias
Beach Doll Hospital
6204 Ocean Front Ave.
Virginia Beach, VA 23451
phone: 757-428-1609
e-mail: 73121.1505@compuserve.com
*All types of doll repair, specializing in
bisque and composition dolls.*

Doll Heaven
502 Broadway
New Haven, IN 46774-1404
phone: 219-493-6428
*Doll restoration & repair; specializ-
ing in broken bisque and composition
dolls; modern, antique, collector
dolls; all materials.*

Mary Gates
Doll Doctor, The
P.O. Box 334
Pontiac, IL 61764-0334
phone: 815-842-3442
*Doll repairs; specializes in
composition work; work shown in
museums and sold in antique shops;
also does custom dressing of old dolls
using her own designs.*

Darla Waters
Doll Restoration
1115 Bear Ave.
Idaho Falls, ID 83402
phone: 208-522-4255
*Antique and bisque doll restoration;
reconstruct broken parts, repaint,
refurbish old wigs, reset eyes, redress;
specializes in basket cases.*

Don & Vella Painter
Doll Restoration
23483 Shephard Rd.
Clatskanie, OR 97016
phone: 888-763-5122 or 503-728-3503
e-mail: homestead@aone.com
Internet: http://www.webdolls.com/OR/
Homestead_Collectibles
Buys, sells, appraises, collects and

*repairs dolls: antiques, compositions,
pull string and battery operated
talkers, mechanical, toys, vinyl; also
reroots hair.*

Louise Crino
Heidi's Doll Repair
269 E. Main St.
Hillsboro, OR 97123
phone: 503-649-5808

Gloria McCarty
Doll Cellar, The
23337 46th Ave., S.W.
Seattle, WA 98116
phone: 206-938-4446
*Buys, sells, specializes in, and
appraises dolls; also sells doll-related
books.*

Repro. Sources

Lynne Robuccio
Linen Bonnet, The
29 Lantern Ln.
Leominster, MA 01453

Nancy Castendyk
Penny Wooden Doll, The
16 Hall Rd.
Sturbridge, MA 01566

Suzanne Berg
1264 Estate Dr.
West Chester, PA 19380

Judy Tasch
Judy Tasch Original Dolls
3208 Clearview
Austin, TX 78703

Suppliers

Ron Lipstein
Dollspart Supply Co.
8000 Cooper Ave., Bldg. 28
Flushing, NY 11385-7734
phone: 718-326-4500 or 800-336-3655
fax: 718-326-4971
*Sells full range of doll books and
parts: eyes, wigs, bodies, clothing,
tools, etc.*

Banner Doll Supply Inc.
P.O. Box 32
Mechanicsburg, PA 17055
phone: 717-766-1503 or 800-637-8305
*Bodies, displays, eyes & eyelashes,
footwear, hats, molds, paints,
patterns, reference books, wigs.*

Pacific International Corp.
4438 E. Lake Mead Blvd.
Las Vegas, NV 89115
phone: 702-452-2133
fax: 702-647-3170
*Specializes in high quality glass eyes,
wigs, eye lashes, doll stands, human
hair and mohair wigs, molds,
patterns, etc.*

Advertising

(see also ADVERTISING COL-
LECTIBLES, Figures)

Experts

Mary Jane Lamphier
Quilted Keepsakes & Unique Dolls
Exhibit
577 Main St.
Arlington, IA 50606-9712
phone: 319-633-5885
*Buys, sells and trades advertising
dolls and characters such as Jolly
Green Giant, the Ronald McDonald
collection, Campbell Soup Kids, etc.;
author of "Zany Characters of the Ad
World" (Collector Books, 1995).*

Joleen A. Robinson
812 Fox Chase Ct.
Lawrence, KS 66049
*Wants advertising dolls (trademark or
promotional dolls): Dough Boy, Green
Giant, Aunt Jemima, etc.*

Annalee

Clubs/Associations

Townsend Thorndike, Dir.
Annalee Doll Society
Magazine: Collector, The
P.O. Box 1137
Meredith, NH 03253-1137
phone: 800-433-6557 or 603-279-3333
fax: 603-279-6659
*A collectors club sponsored by the
Annalee Doll Co.; conducts annual
Annalee doll auction; sells Annalees
dolls on consignment.*

Collectors

Lois Sauchelli
105 Canvas Ct.
Manahawkin, NJ 08050-1609
phone: 609-698-1502
*Wants to buy Annalee dolls; write or
phone.*

Lorraine Orsenigo
2774 Ocean Ave.
Lake Ronkonkoma, NY 11779
phone: 516-467-5674
*Wants to buy older Annalee dolls,
frogs, monkeys, foxes, Christmas
ornaments, bunnies, mice, pre-1980
catalogs, anything Annalee.*

Margie Motzer
2878 Saddleback
Cincinnati, OH 45244-3915
phone: 513-231-5953
*Buys, sells, trades Annalee Dolls and
or catalogs; whole collections or
individual pieces; send SASE for
special price list.*

Dealers

Annalee Antique & Collectible Doll
Shoppe
Newsletter: Collector, The
P.O. Box 1137
Meredith, NH 03253-1137
phone: 800-433-6557 or 603-279-3333
fax: 603-279-6659
*A company-sponsored shop; the
monthly newsletter lists the Annalee
dolls currently for sale; appraisals of
Annalee dolls are available for $5 per*

*doll; also offers restoration and
repair services for Annalee dolls.*

Sue Coffee
Laysville Hardware
10 Saunders Hollow Rd.
Old Lyme, CT 06371-1126
phone: 860-434-5641
fax: 860-434-2653
e-mail: SueCoffee@aol.com
*Buys, sells, collects, appraises; send
SASE with $1.01 postage for
discontinued list; specializes in 1950s
and 1960s Annalee dolls; send
description, condition, photo and
telephone number or call with the doll
in front of you.*

Experts

Richard Rogers
15 Owen Dr.
Mahopac, NY 10541
phone: 914-621-3702
*Buys Annalee dolls, all kinds and all
years; especially wants 1950s to
1960s.*

Man./Prod./Dist.

Annalee Mobilitee Dolls, Inc.
P.O. Box 1137
Meredith, NH 03253-1137
phone: 800-433-6557 or 603-279-3333
fax: 603-279-6659
*Creates, produces and distributes
posable felt dolls of distinction which
contain wire armatures for flexibility
and repositioning.*

Museums/Libraries

Annalee Doll Museum
P.O. Box 1137
Meredith, NH 03253-1137
phone: 800-433-6557 or 603-279-3333
fax: 603-279-6659

Periodicals

Newsletter: Chatter Box News
22 Ryan St.
West Islip, NY 11795-3429
*A newsletter that specializes in
Annalee Dolls: secondary market ads
and retail prices; swap, trade, and buy
ads; articles, raffles, etc.*

Automatons

Dealers

Cindy Oakes
34025 W. 6 Mile
Livonia, MI 48152
phone: 313-591-3252
*Wants bisque automatons or bisque
dolls on music boxes; any condition;
1890-1900s.*

Barbie

Auction Services

Jim & Shari McMasters
McMasters Doll Auctions
P.O. Box 1755
Cambridge, OH 43725-6755
phone: 800-842-3526 or 614-432-4419
fax: 614-432-3191
Specializes in auctioning antique and collectible dolls and doll related items such as teddy bears, Barbie dolls and accessories, children's dishes, toys, children's books, etc.

Ann Walcher
Ann Christina's Remember When
   Collectibles & Auctions
5465 Rowland Rd.
Minnetonka, MN 55343-4398
Buy, sells, trades, consigns, auctions Barbie and family items.

Christensen Auctions
1226 W. Fifth St.
Santa Ana, CA 92703
phone: 714-647-0294
fax: 714-647-0418
Specializing in Barbie dolls, clothing and accessories; one item or an entire collection.

Clubs/Associations

Dean Lillibridge
Barbie Collectors of New England
Newsletter: Barbie O.N.E.
575 Pleasant St.
Holyoke, MA 01040

Dora Lerch
Barbie Doll Collectors Club International
Newsletter: Barbie Newsletter
P.O. Box 586
White Plains, NY 10603-0586
phone: 914-362-4657
fax: 914-362-3258
e-mail: bdcci@juno.com
Ads, upcoming shows, show reports, identification tips, convention news, etc.

World of Collectibles - Collector Club
   International
P.O. Box 245
Garnerville, NY 10923
phone: 914-362-4657 or 914-362-3258
fax: 914-362-3258
e-mail: bdcci@juno.com
Over 200 members; annual convention.

Amy Reed
Barbie Lover's Club
399 Winfield Rd.
Rochester, NY 14622
phone: 716-266-4965
e-mail: amyblc@worldnet.att.net

Barbie
617 W. San Jose Ave.
Clovis, CA 93612-2384

Collectors

Keri Jones
420 Winthrop St.
Taunton, MA 02780-2157
Wants to buy vintage Barbie dolls and clothing from the 1960s to early 1970s; send description and price.

David & Becky Beane
Beane's Antiques & Photography
58 River Road
Benton, ME 04901
phone: 207-453-6790
e-mail: dbeane@mint.net
Internet: http://www.mint.net:80/
   antiques/catalog/beane.html
Collector of pre-1970 Barbie dolls, fashions and accessories; call or write with descriptions and prices.

Monica Castillo
310 - 70th Street Apt. 1E
Guttenberg, NJ 07093
phone: 201-861-2666

Irene Davis
27036 Withams Rd.
Oak Hall, VA 23416
phone: 804-824-5524
Wants dolls from 1959 to 1965; also clothes, cars and other Barbie related items; send photos for offer.

Dan Stapleton
8237 Banyan Blvd.
Orlando, FL 32819
phone: 407-345-1132
Wants to buy mint condition (not removed from box), Holiday Barbies.

Margie Schultz
P.O. Box 9371
Cincinnati, OH 45209
Wants to buy 1959-1972 Barbie dolls, clothes, cases, and houses.

Tim Gordon
1750 W. Kent
Missoula, MT 59801-5508
phone: 406-728-1812
e-mail: stacey1165@aol.com
Wants singles, collections, accessories, clothing, related dolls; offers appraisal services.

Tammy Rodrick
1509 N. 300th St.
Sumner, IL 62466-2117
Wants to buy Barbie dolls and other dolls, new or old; also wants old toys, especially toy dishes and child-size appliances.

Lois Burger
2323 Lincoln
Beatrice, NE 68310-3306
phone: 402-228-2797
Wants pre-1966 Barbie clothes, accessories, Ken, Midge, Skipper & their clothes; also anything Barbie related such as comics, cars.

Marcie Melillo
P.O. Box 27705
Denver, CO 80227
phone: 303-933-0233
fax: 303-932-0468
e-mail: BugsHead@aol.com
Always buying Barbie and family dolls, clothes, etc.; author of "The Ultimate Barbie Doll Book," contact for signed copies.

Dealers

Bobbi Stavros
730 Boston Rd.
Billerica, MA 01821-5337
phone: 508-667-1187 or 617-273-0293
Buys and sells Barbie dolls.

Lisa Scherzer
54 Gates Court
Matawan, NJ 07747-9716
phone: 908-290-1407
fax: 908-290-0636
Specializing in Barbie.

Marl B. Davidson
Marl & Barbie
10301 Braden Run
Bradenton, FL 34202-1744
phone: 914-751-6275
fax: 941-751-5463
Always buying Barbies; issues catalogs listing items for sale including Barbies from 1959 through present including fashions and accessories, especially hard-to-find Barbie items; send $7.50 for sample catalog.

Faye Leach
Faye's Dolls of Yesterday
434 Newman Ave.
Newport, KY 41075
phone: 606-781-1038
Specializing in Barbie.

Paul David
Newsletter: Paul David Exclusively
   Barbie
610 Blackwater Rd.
Chillicothe, OH 45601-9004
phone: 614-642-2747
fax: 614-642-2755
Carries all the latest Barbies and old stock and accessories; newsletter is 40 pages, hundreds of Barbies listed for sale, articles, news, what's new, limited editions, special editions, values, updated prices, gossip, etc.

Cindy Oakes
34025 W. 6 Mile
Livonia, MI 48152
phone: 313-591-3252
Buying 1960s and 1970s Barbie and Friends dolls, and clothing, Holiday Barbie and Special Editions; will purchase entire collections; paying up to $1000 for #1 Barbie.

Diamonds & Dolls by Miss Alice
511 St. Louis
Springfield, MO 65806
phone: 417-868-8111
Buys, sells, trades Barbies.

Anne Henderson
Anne's Dolls, Marvins Toys
13629 Victory
Van Nuys, CA 91401-1735
phone: 818-785-1177
Wants to buy Barbie and family dolls, clothes, etc.; also other dolls as well as Disney, wind-up, and battery-operated toys.

Experts

Jane Sarashon-Kahn
355 Friendship Dr.
Paoli, PA 19301-1206
phone: 610-296-5085
fax: 610-296-8278
e-mail: 72560.2517@compuserve.com
Author of "Contemporary Barbie 1980 to Present."

Joe Blitman
5163 Franklin Ave.
Los Angeles, CA 90027
phone: 213-953-6490
fax: 213-953-0888
Publisher of "Oh, You Beautiful Doll" Barbie videotape.

Museums/Libraries

Evelyn Burkhalter
Barbie Hall of Fame
460 Waverly St.
Palo Alto, CA 94301
phone: 415-326-5841
Collection has over 16 thousand Barbie dolls and related friends and accessories.

Periodicals

Newsletter: Barbie Fashions
387 Park Avenue South
New York, NY 10016

Brian Savage
Fun Publications
Newspaper: Master Collector
12513 Birchfalls Dr.
Raleigh, NC 27614-9675
phone: 800-772-6673 or 919-847-5263
e-mail: bsavage@mastercollector.com
Internet: http://
   www.mastercollector.com
Ads-only newspaper; dolls (antique and modern collectible), toys, banks, models, cars, Matchbox, monsters, puzzles, political, toy trains, etc.; subscribers receive free 30 word ad each month; published monthly; reaches 20,000.

Jacqueline Horning
Journal: Barbie Talks Some More
19 Jamestown Dr.
Cincinnati, OH 45241-1435
phone: 513-779-3708
A 65-page journal with 13 years of vital information for the Barbie collector; the author is a dealer/collector herself; $12.95 ppd.

Barbie Bazaar, Inc.
Magazine: Barbie Bazaar
5617 6th Ave.
Kenosha, WI 53140-4101
phone: 414-658-1004
fax: 414-658-0433

Barbara & Dan Miller
Magazine: Miller's Barbie Collector
P.O. Box 8722
Spokane, WA 99203-0722
phone: 509-747-0139
fax: 509-455-6115
A bi-monthly exclusively-Barbie publication with in-depth articles, full color photography, directory of clubs and events, prices, ads, etc.; call subscriptions to 800-874-5201.

Betsy McCall

Experts

David & Marci Van Ausdall
P.O. Box 946
Quincy, CA 95971
phone: 916-283-2770
e-mail: dreams@psln.com
Buys, sells, appraises, specializes in Betsy McCall of all sizes as well as clothing and related merchandise (toys, paperdolls, etc.); one item or collection.

Periodicals

David & Marci Van Ausdall
Betsy's Fan Club
Newsletter: Betsy's Fan Club Newsletter
P.O. Box 946
Quincy, CA 95971
phone: 916-283-2770
e-mail: dreams@psln.com

Black

(see also BLACK MEMORABILIA)

Dealers

Erlene Reed
Afro-American Doll Gallery
1794 Verbena St., NW
Washington, DC 20012
phone: 202-829-7170
Wants Black-related dolls, plates, banks, door stops, folk art, etc.

Periodicals

Laverne Hall
VELB Associates
Newsletter: Doll-E-Gram
P.O. Box 1212
Bellevue, WA 98009-1212
phone: 206-643-4154
The newsletter of the black doll collector.

Bobbing Head

(see also SPORTS COLLECTIBLES, Baseball)

Collectors

Chip Norris
P.O. Box 235
Leonardtown, MD 20650
phone: 301-475-2951

Daniel G. Miller, Sr.
P.O. Box 578
Churchville, MD 21028-0578
phone: 410-676-1813
Wants to buy Baltimore Oriole bobbin' head dolls; also other vintage Baltimore/Oriole memorabilia; will correspond with other collectors with same interests.

Dale Jenkins
1647 Elbur Ave.
Lakewood, OH 44107
phone: 216-226-7349

Experts

Tim Hunter
1668 Golddust
Sparks, NV 89436
phone: 702-626-5029
fax: 702-626-4423
e-mail: thunter8852@aol.com
Buys, sells and specializes in sports and advertising bobbing head dolls; author of "The Bobbing Head Price Guide."

Man./Prod./Dist.

Mark Bloomquist
S. A. M. Inc.
P.O. Box 77
Palo Alto, CA 94301
phone: 800-483-2643 or 415-369-0190
Manufactures ceramic bobbing head dolls.

Buddy Lee

Collectors

Marc Mapelli
28545 Felix Valdez B-2
Temecula, CA 92590
phone: 909-694-8113
Wants to buy Buddy Lee dolls, any outfit; also wants individual clothes or hats.

Betsy Stubbs
28545 Felix Valdez B-2
Temecula, CA 92590
phone: 909-694-8113
Wants to buy Buddy Lee dolls, any outfit, from the 1950s.

Cabbage Patch Kids

Clubs/Associations

Cabbage Patch Kids Clubs
1027 Newport Ave.
Pawtucket, RI 02862
phone: 401-727-5507
For collectors of Hasbro collectible Cabbage Patch Kids Dolls.

Julie Edwards
Cabbage Patch Kids Collectors Club
Newsletter: Limited Edition
P.O. Box 714
Cleveland, GA 30528
phone: 706-865-2171
fax: 706-865-5862
Focuses on the Cabbage Patch Kids and Little People soft-sculpture collectibles by Xavier Roberts. Sponsored by Original Appalachian Artworks, Inc.

Man./Prod./Dist.

Original Appalachian Artworks, Inc.
P.O. Box 714
Cleveland, GA 30528
phone: 706-865-2171
fax: 706-865-5862
Manufacturer of Cabbage Patch Kids dolls.

Chatty Cathy

(see also TOYS, Talking [Pullstring])

Clubs/Associations

Lisa Eisenstein
Chatty Cathy Collector's Club
Newsletter: Chatty News
P.O. Box 140
Readington, NJ 08870-0140
e-mail: chatty@eclipse.net
Internet: http://www.ttinet/chattycathy
For collectors of Chatty Cathy; share and learn all about Mattel's 1960s line of talking dolls; send SASE for information; quarterly club newsletter since 1989.

Collectors

Lisa Eisenstein
P.O. Box 140
Readington, NJ 08870-0140
e-mail: chatty@eclipse.net
Internet: http://www.ttinet/chattycathy
Wants Chatty Cathy items: clothes, case, accessories; books and all other related items.

Marci Van Ausdall
P.O. Box 946
Quincy, CA 95971
phone: 916-283-2770
e-mail: dreams@psln.com
Wants to buy all original, excellent condition Chatty Family dolls, clothing, accessories, paper dolls, etc.

Repair Services

Kathy Lewis
Chatty Cathy's Haven
187 N. Marcello Ave.
Thousand Oaks, CA 91360
phone: 805-499-7932
Repairs, buys and sells pullstring talkers.

Cloth

Periodicals

Judy Beswick
Magazine: Cloth Doll Magazine, The
P.O. Box 2167
Lake Oswego, OR 97035
phone: 503-244-3539 or 800-695-7005
fax: 503-244-2370
A quarterly magazine on cloth/fabric dolls: how-to articles, artist profiles, collector information, sources of supplies, book reviews, patterns, etc.

Clothing

Clubs/Associations

Doll Costumer's Guild
7112 W. Grovers Ave.
Glendale, AZ 85308

Man./Prod./Dist.

Sheryl Garacia
11 N. Beverly Ave.
Youngstown, OH 44515-2930
phone: 216-792-0549
Makes gorgeous, reasonably-priced reproduction doll clothes; also all newer doll clothing; brochure $3.

Misc. Services

Alma Bucid
Royal-T Cleaners
17942 Magnolia
Fountain Valley, CA 92708
phone: 714-963-6110
Offers an special cleaning service for doll clothing; personal inspection to determine best method of cleaning (dry or wet) based on age, stains and overall condition; calls client to discuss stains, age and cost; do not sent doll.

Dawn

Experts

Joedi Johnson
P.O. Box 565
Billings, MT 59101-0656
phone: 406-248-4875
fax: 407-248-4875
Buying all Dawn collections, dolls, fashions and accessories; looking for additional material for second printing of her Dawn price and guidebook; especially interested in international items, promotions, store displays.

Ginny

Clubs/Associations

Ginny Doll Club
1 Corporate Dr.
Grantsville, MD 21536
phone: 800-554-1447
Club sponsored by the manufacturer, Vogue Doll Co.

Ginny Doll Club
Newsletter: Ginny Doll Club News
P.O. Box 338
Oakdale, CA 95361-0338
Focuses on Ginny dolls and club news.

Experts

Jeanne Niswonger
P.O. Box 338
Oakdale, CA 95361-0338
Author of "That Doll, Ginny."

Golliwoggs

Collectors

Beth B. Savino
P.O. Box 798
Holland, OH 43528-0798
phone: 419-473-9801 or 800-862-8697
fax: 419-473-3947
e-mail: toystore@toynet.com
Internet: http://www.toynet.com
Golliwoggs are black characters dolls based on a series of British children's books originating in 1895 and written by American authoress Florence Upton.

Dealers

Catherine Saunders-Watson
P.O. Box 302
Greenville, NH 03048-0302
phone: 603-878-2171
fax: 603-878-2171
e-mail: gollyqueen@aol.com
Wants golliwoggs and other black items: china, humidors, tins, books, toys, games, puzzles, banks, Aunt Jemima, linens, advertising, jewelry, etc.

Half

Collectors

Sharon Wilkins
1105 Burnham St.
Cocoa, FL 32922-6838
e-mail: bugs20@.comm
Wants half dolls; porcelain half dolls decorated a lady's dresser in the '20s and '30s.

Iaulanda's

Experts

Jamie Saloff
P.O. Box 339
Edinboro, PA 16412
phone: 814-734-5189
fax: 814-734-7162
e-mail: jlsaloff@erie.net
Daughter of the Iaulanda Turner Downey, creator of Iaulanda's Storyteller Dolls (high quality, handcrafted felt dolls made in the 1960s-'70s for the Christmas tree.)

Ideal

Clubs/Associations

Judith Izen
Ideal Toy Co. Collector's Club
Newsletter: Ideal Toy Co. Collectors Club Newsletter
P.O. Box 623
Lexington, MA 02173
e-mail: jizenres@aol.com

Collectors

Elizabeth Arnold
205 Penns Lane
Malvern, PA 19355
phone: 610-647-8468
Wants to buy Saucey Walker dolls by Ideal.

Kewpie

(see also ROSE O'NEILL COLLECTIBLES)

Clubs/Associations

Mary Lou Ratcliff
International Rose O'Neill Club
P.O. Box 668
Branson, MO 65616

Collectors

Jeff Dykes
6 Wildwood Terrace
Glen Ridge, NJ 07028
phone: 201-748-4990 or 973-748-4990
Wants to buy German bisque Kewpies - the "action" pieces such as Kewpie gardener, Kewpie with dog, Kewpie soldier; must be in excellent original condition; also wants Kewpies made of celluloids and Kewpie tea sets.

Kitty Watson
201 Dena Dr.
Guthrie, OK 73044-9043
phone: 405-282-2287
Wants to buy Kewpies, Scootles, and Rose O'Neill items, preferably "action" bisque, and metal pieces, signed.

Periodicals

Rose Morgan, Ed.
Penultimate Press
Newspaper: National Doll & Teddy Bear Collector
P.O. Box 4032
Portland, OR 97208-4032
fax: 503-234-6170
e-mail: oleprospector@worldaccessnet.com
Internet: http://www.worldaccessnet.com/~goldbug/kewpies.htm
A monthly newspaper for doll, Kewpie and teddy bear collectors, dealers and artists.

Rose Morgan, Ed.
Penultimate Press
Newsletter: Traveler
P.O. Box 4032
Portland, OR 97208-4032
fax: 503-234-6170
e-mail: oleprospector@worldaccessnet.com
Internet: http://www.worldaccessnet.com/~goldbug/kewpies.htm
The only colored, illustrated monthly newsletter devoted entirely to the world of Kewpies and other Rose O'Neil related items; documents prices realized from auction and private sales.

Liddle Kiddles

Clubs/Associations

Heidi Neufield
Little Kiddle Club - East Coast
16 Weathervane Way
Marlboro, NJ 07746-1693
fax: 908-617-1104
e-mail: Heididdle@aol.com

Laura Miller
Liddle Kiddles Klub
Newsletter: Liddle Kiddles Klub Newsletter
3639 Fourth Ave.
La Crescenta, CA 91214-2441
A bi-monthly newsletter all about Liddle Kiddles (dolls by Mattel 1966-1971); classifieds; send SASE for more information or $3 for sample newsletter.

Collectors

Jill Salerno
245 Sunnyridge Ave., Unit #41
Fairfield, CT 06430-4646
phone: 203-332-1469
Wants to buy Liddle Kiddles by Mattel; old stock, mint on card, or childhood collections.

Linda Strumski
74 Pierpont RD E-7
Waterbury, CT 06705-3847
phone: 203-757-8103
e-mail: JSmicro633@aol.com
Collector wants to buy Liddle Kiddles dolls, accessories, cases, and related paper items.

Joedi Johnson
P.O. Box 565
Billings, MT 59101-0656
phone: 406-248-4875
fax: 407-248-4875
Buying Kiddle collections, especially coloring books, riddle books, puzzles, vinyl wallet, magic slate and paper dolls; also buying Mattel Upsy Downsy dolls, accessories and books.

Dealers

Lisa Slote
P.O. Box 2024
Port Washington, NY 11050
phone: 516-767-1638
Wants all dolls and related items; send $2 for extensive catalog.

Dawn Parrish
9931 Gaynor Ave.
Granada Hills, CA 91343-1604

Sharon Rialto
Rialto Movie Art
81 1/2 S. Washington St.
Seattle, WA 98104
phone: 206-622-5099

Experts

Paris Langford
Kollecting Kiddles
415 Dodge Ave.
Jefferson, LA 70121-3311
phone: 504-733-0676 or 504-733-0676
e-mail: bbean415@aol.com
Buy, sell, trade Liddle Kiddles by Mattel and other small dolls from 60s to 70s; send SASE for current list of offerings; author of "Liddle Kiddles Identification and Value Guide," (Collector Books, 1995).

Nancy Ann Storybook

Collectors

Elaine M. Pardee
3613 Merano Way
Santa Rosa, CA 95843-5538

Nisbet

Clubs/Associations

Howard & Sarah Wade
Peggy Nisbet International Collectors' Society
Newsletter: PNICS Newsletter
P.O. Box 325
Orrville, OH 44667-0325
phone: 330-682-8551
fax: 330-682-3655
e-mail: ukdolls@aol.com
Clearinghouse for information about Peggy Nisbet portrait and costume dolls and Nisbet bears from Britain, both primary and secondary markets.

Man./Prod./Dist.

Howard & Sarah Wade
Nisbet Dolls & Bears
P.O. Box 325
Orrville, OH 44667-0325
phone: 330-682-8551
fax: 330-682-3655
e-mail: ukdolls@aol.com
U.S. distributor for Peggy Nisbet dolls and Nisbet bears from Britain.

Paper

(see also PAPER COLLECTIBLES)

Clubs/Associations

Jenny R. Taliadoros
Original Paper Doll Artists Guild, The
Magazine: OPDAG News
P.O. Box 14
Kingfield, ME 04947-0014
phone: 207-265-2500
fax: 207-265-2500
e-mail: opdag@somtel.com
Internet: http://www.mint.net/opag
An organization of paper doll enthusiasts to promote the PD hobby; magazine has PD news, how-to's, paper dolls, artist features, etc.

Virginia A. Crossley
Paper Doll Queens & Kings of Metro Detroit
685 Canyon Rd.
Rochester, MI 48306
phone: 810-651-3203

Collectors

Mary Keiller
1206 W. 10th St.
Erie, PA 16502
Wants to buy pre-1970 paper dolls either cut or uncut.

Loretta Willis
808 Lee Ave.
Tifton, GA 31794-4134
Deals with many paper doll and doll collectors who collect PD's as a hobby; wants PD movie stars, nostalgia, new & old for collection.

R. H. Stevens
R. H. Stevens Antiques
17838 South East Hwy. 452
Umatilla, FL 32784
Paper dolls wanted: cut or uncut; send $1 for list.

Shirley Hedge
Rte. 2 Box 52
Princeton, IN 47670-9601
phone: 812-385-4080
Wants any paper dolls printed in the "Chicago Tribune" - comics or otherwise; advertising paper dolls, antique sets, book, boxed or packaged sets printed prior to 1950; pre-1935 magazine sets; any sets from children's magazines.

Lynne Hough
1603 Kenilworth Pl
Aurora, IL 60506-5376
Wants to buy all types of paper dolls.

Sharon Rogers
1813 Junius
Fort Worth, TX 76103
Wants pre-1970 paper dolls, cut or uncut, sorted or unsorted; celebrities, antique, advertising, etc.; please describe & price.

Dealers

Carolyn Thompson
P.O. Box 157
Orleans, MA 02653
phone: 508-896-6748

Gepetto's Doll House
U.S. Hwy. 441
P.O. Box 524
Cherokee, NC 28719

Barbara Gilland
Fond Memories
105 Darcee Court
Lawrenceville, GA 30245-7404
phone: 770-963-0324
Vintage paper dolls, reproduction paper dolls, contemporary artist paper dolls, newest paper dolls, many other paper items.

Judy M. Johnson
Judy's Place
P.O. Box 176
Skandia, MI 49885-0176
phone: 906-942-7865
fax: 906-942-7865
e-mail: Judysplc@aol.com
Internet: http://www.mint.net/opdag
Author/artist artist buys, sells, collects and designs paper dolls and PD books; wants paper dolls, especially original art and unique or comic paper dolls; send 2 first class stamps for catalog.

Peggy Ell
Peggy's Paper
218 Gratton
Burlington, IA 52601
phone: 319-752-7670
Buys and sells paper dolls, cut or uncut; send double-stamped LSASE for most recent list of paper dolls for sale.

Johana Gast Anderton
6408 North Flora
Gladstone, MO 64118
phone: 816-468-0558
Specializes in original & antique paper dolls and other paper collectibles, antique dolls and teddy bears, original doll clothes; lecturer, author; LSASE for information.

Loraine Burdick
Journal: Celebrity Doll Journal
413 10th Ave. Ct. NE
Puyallup, WA 98372-2948
Celebrity Doll Journal features research on collectibles and creators; also offers sales list of paper dolls.

Experts

Marta Krebs
13628 Middlevale Lane
Silver Spring, MD 20906-2123
phone: 301-460-1068
Buys and sells paper dolls; publisher of former "Paper Doll Update" newsletter - back issues available; author of "Royalty of Paper Dolls," "Advertising Paper Dolls," and several Dover books.

Mary Young
P.O. Box 9244
Dayton, OH 45409-9244
Buys, sells and specializes in paper dolls; puts together a for-sale list of paper dolls twice a year; welcomes

questions; author of "Paper Dolls & Their Artists," "Magazine Paper Dolls" with price guide, and other books.

Emma Terry
P.O. Box 807
Vivian, LA 71082-0807
phone: 318-375-4768
Publisher of the bi-monthly "Paper Doll News" newsletter.

Denis C. Jackson
P.O. Box 1958
Sequim, WA 98382-1958
phone: 360-683-2559
fax: 360-683-2559
e-mail: ticn@olypen.com
Internet: http://www.olypen.com/ticn/
Author of "The Price & Identification Guide to Old Magazine Paperdolls", 3rd Edition; with a strong focus on the golden age of paper, 'teens through the 1960s; send LSASE for information.

Man./Prod./Dist.

Charlotte Whatley
Brain Maps
224 Fishback Ave.
Fort Collins, CO 80521
phone: 303-493-4485
Designs and markets contemporary line of paper dolls.

Periodicals

Jenny Bloomfield
Newsletter: Paper Doll Circle
5 Jackson Mews
Immingham, NR. Grimsby
S Humbs DN40 2HQ, U.K.
Paper doll newsletter for enthusiasts worldwide; free sample issue on request.

Arlene Del Fava
Newsletter: Now & Then
67-40 Yellowstone Blvd.
Flushing, NY 11375-2614
Newsletter published three times a year; covers some new but mostly nostalgic paper dolls and their times; about 30 pages.

Loretta Willis
Newsletter: Loretta's Place Paper Doll Newsletter
808 Lee Ave.
Tifton, GA 31794-4134
Focuses on original artists' paper dolls and features artists work and paper dolls in each issue; also old paper dolls; 4 issues ("in color" paper doll on front page) per year for $15.

Loretta Willis
Newsletter: Yesterday's Paper Dolls
808 Lee Ave.
Tifton, GA 31794-4134
Identification guide newsletter that illustrates, identifies, and prices old nostalgic paper dolls; 4 issues per year for $12.

Mary Longo
Newsletter: Paper Doll & Doll Diary
P.O. Box 12146
Lake Park, FL 33403
Bi-monthly publication for people who collect, make, and play with paper dolls; publishing over 10 years; news of paper dolls old and new, paper doll gossip, sources, reviews, reader opinions; sample $3.

Marilyn Henry
Magazine: Paperdoll Review
P.O. Box 584
Princeton, IN 47670-0584
phone: 812-423-5334 or 812-385-4080
Co-editors are Marilyn Henry and Shirley Hedge; published quarterly; a paper doll printed in color in each issue; lots of paper doll photos, and articles about paper dolls and related items; send LSASE for subscription information.

Janie Varsolona
Newsletter: Midwest Paper Dolls & Toys Quarterly
P.O. Box 131
Galesburg, KS 66740
phone: 316-763-2247 or 316-763-2561
A 32-page quarterly newsletter of interest to collectors of paper dolls; also buys, sells, collects and conducts specialty PD auctions.

Emma Terry
Newsletter: Paper Doll News
P.O. Box 807
Vivian, LA 71082-0807
phone: 318-375-4768
A bi-monthly newsletter sharing news of the paper doll world; review paper dolls and share all known information regarding paper dolls; promote paper doll artists and share addresses in every issue of "Paper Doll News".

Nan Moorehead
Newsletter: Golden Paper Doll & Toy Opportunities
P.O. Box 252
Golden, CO 80402-0252
Concentrates on antique and collectible paper dolls.

Sharon Hill
Newsletter: Cornerstones
2216 S. Autumn Ln.
Diamond Bar, CA 91789

Beverly Wethington
Newsletter: Northern Lights Paperdoll News
P.O. Box 871189
Wasilla, AK 99687-1189
phone: 907-745-4334

Repro. Sources

Kathi Reynolds
Creative Clothes
330 N. Church St.
Thurmont, MD 21788-1640
phone: 301-695-5340
Creates authentically 1660-1760 period costumed paper dolls.

Parts

Collectors

Dorothy Grinewitlki
2424 Shoreham Highland Dr.
St. Joseph, MI 49085
Wants bisque dolls, heads or parts; also complete dolls.

Pincushion

Experts

Susan Endo
P.O. Box 4051
Covina, CA 91723
phone: 818-339-6352
Author of "A Price Guide to Pincushion Dolls" and "2nd Price Guide to Pincushion Dolls"; both available from the author; always buying and selling quality pincushion dolls; send LSASE for current list with colored photo.

Raggedy Ann & Andy

Dealers

Gwen Daniel
18 Belleau Lake Ct.
O Fallon, MO 63366-3144
phone: 314-978-3190
e-mail: gdaniel@mail.win.org
Wants Raggedy Ann & Andy's, books and related items; also teddy bears, Lulu & Tubby, Nancy & Sluggo, Howdy Doody and Barbie.

Periodicals

Barbara Barth
Newsletter: Rags
P.O. Box 823
Atlanta, GA 30301
A quarterly newsletter devoted to the creations of Johnny Gruelle; ads, articles, photos, etc. for Raggedy Ann and other cloth dolls.

Strawberry Shortcake

Clubs/Associations

Peggy Jimenez
Strawberry Shortcake Collectors' Club
Newsletter: Berry-Bits
1409 72nd St.
North Bergen, NJ 07047-3827
phone: 201-868-7334

Vogue

Collectors

Victoria Broadhurst
5009 Queen Victoria Rd.
Woodland Hills, CA 91364-4757
phone: 818-883-3127
fax: 818-887-3739
e-mail: mrscdrew@aol.com
Wants to buy Vogue dolls and accessories.

Experts

Judith Izen
P.O. Box 623
Lexington, MA 02173
e-mail: jizenres@aol.com
Co-author with Carol Stover of "Vogue Dolls" (1997); covers all Vogue dolls including Ginny, Jill, Ginnette, Li'l Imp, Baby Dear, Toddles, Jeff, Jan, etc.

DOLPHINS

(see WHALES)

DOOR PUSH PLATES

Collectors

Betty R. Foley
129 Meadow Valley Rd., Trlr. 11
Ephrata, PA 17522-1843
Wants porcelain door push (or pull) plates with advertising; attached to old wooden porch doors; Red Rose Tea, Chesterfields, etc.

DOORBELLS

Collectors

Doorbells
P.O. Box 91395
Los Angeles, CA 90009
Wants to buy all mechanical types of door bells, one or many; send description and price.

DOORKNOBS

(see also HARDWARE; LOCKS)

Book Sellers

Maudie L. Eastwood
Antique Doorknob Publishing Company
17300 135th Ave. NW, #103
Woodinville, WA 98072
phone: 206-483-5848
Books about doorknobs and other builders' hardware.

Clubs/Associations

Loretta & Raymond Nemec, Ed.
Antique Doorknob Collectors of America, The
Newsletter: Doorknob Collector, The
P.O. Box 126
Eola, IL 60519-0126
phone: 630-357-2381
fax: 630-357-2391
A club for doorknob and related hardware collectors and enthusiasts; conventions, seminars, banquets, trading sessions.

Collectors

Richard C. Hubbard
162 Poplar Ave.
Hackensack, NJ 07601
phone: 201-342-1274
Wants to buy old doorknobs; historical, figural or emblematic knobs; please describe and price.

Charles W. Wardell
P.O. Box 195
Trinity, NC 27370-0195
phone: 910-434-1145
Wants ornate doorknobs, escutcheon plates, store door handles, push plates, door knockers, doorbells, mail slots, etc.; 1870-1920.

Loretta & Raymond Nemec
P.O. Box 126
Eola, IL 60519-0126
phone: 630-357-2381
fax: 630-357-2391

Dealers

H. Weber Wilson
Oltz-Wilson Antiques
808 51st Avenue Plz. W
Bradenton, FL 34207-2819
phone: 800-508-0022
Buys and sells vintage door hardware, especially doorknobs; also wants vintage plumbing items.

Experts

Maudie L. Eastwood
Antique Doorknob Publishing Company
17300 135th Ave. NW, #103
Woodinville, WA 98072
phone: 206-483-5848
Researcher, expert, collector and consultant specializing in antique builders hardware and author of books on early American door and other builders hardware.

DOORSTOPS

(see also CAST IRON ITEMS)

Clubs/Associations

Jeanne Bertoia
Doorstop Collectors of America
1881-G Spring Rd.
Vineland, NJ 08630
phone: 609-692-1881
fax: 609-692-8697

Collectors

Bill Price
Paperweight Potentate of Pittsburgh, The
P.O. Box 82501
Pittsburgh, PA 15218-0501
phone: 412-351-5297
fax: 412-271-4329
e-mail: paperwghts@aol.com
Internet: http://www.collectoronline.com/collect/wb-paperweights.html
Wants to buy glass doorstops advertising businesses or with people's portraits; also wants glass paperweights advertising businesses or with people's portraits.

Dealers

John & Nancy Smith
American Sampler
P.O. Box 371
Barnesville, MD 20838-0371
phone: 301-972-6250
Wants cast iron doorstops, figural

bottle openers, doorknockers, paperweights, etc, banks, doorstops, etc.

Experts

Jeanne Bertoia
1881-G Spring Rd.
Vineland, NJ 08630
phone: 609-692-1881
fax: 609-692-8697
Collector and dealer of cast iron figural doorstops; wants to buy painted cast iron doorstops; author of "Doorstop Identification & Values."

Craig Dinner
P.O. Box 4399
Long Island City, NY 11104-0399
phone: 718-729-3850 or 802-365-7181
Advisor to "Warman's Antiques & Collectibles Price Guide."

Repro. Sources

Yield House
P.O. Box 2525
Conway, NH 03818-2525

ANTIQUE-ALIKE
3147 Joppa Rd.
Cambridge, MD 21613-3640
Sells high quality copies of famous original cast iron banks, doorstops and tin advertising signs.

007

(see Chapter "A", page 2)

DR. SEUSS COLLECTIBLES

Collectors

Michael Gessel
P.O. Box 748
Arlington, VA 22216-0748
phone: 703-542-0462
Wants Dr. Seuss books, pamphlets, posters, advertising, ephemera, original illustrations, anything related to Dr. Seuss.

Daniel Hirsch
P.O. Box 5096
Chapel Hill, NC 27514
phone: 919-542-1816
fax: 919-542-1817
e-mail: rhirsch@interserv.com
Wants Dr. Seuss posters, books, dolls, etc.

DRAMA

(see PERFORMING ARTS)

DRAWINGS

(see also ART; PRINTS)

Misc. Services

Wendy Reaves, Cur.
National Portrait Gallery
Prints & Drawings
8th & F Streets N.W.
Washington, DC 20560
phone: 202-357-1356 or 202-357-1633
Internet: http://www.si.edu/
Will authenticate prints & drawings brought in for inspection; make an appointment first; may be able to work from good photographs.

DRESSER ITEMS

(see also BUTTON HOOKS;
CLOTHING & ACCESSORIES,
Vintage; COMPACTS; COMBS &
HAIR ACCESSORIES)

Collectors

K. Hartman
7459 Shawnee Rd.
North Tonawanda, NY 14120
phone: 716-693-4143
Wants to buy Victorian, Art Nouveau, and Art Deco dresser dolls, powder boxes, dresser trays, pin trays, hatpin holders, hair receivers, and other dresser items of china, pottery, glass, or metal.

Hatpins & Hatpin Holders

Clubs/Associations

Lillian Schoephoerster
International Club for Collectors of
  Hatpins & Hatpin Holders
Newsletter: Points
1013 Medhurst Rd.
Columbus, OH 43220
phone: 614-451-7368
For collectors of hat pins and hatpin holders; also publishes an annual 32 page Pictorial Journal.

Virginia J. Woodbury
American Hatpin Society
Newsletter: American Hatpin Society
  Newsletter
20 Monticello Dr.
Rolling Hills Estates, CA 90274-4249
phone: 310-326-2196
e-mail: hatpnginia@aol.com
Internet: http://
  www.collectiononline.com/AHS/
A society for hatpin & hatpin holder collectors and enthusiasts; meetings held quarterly; newsletter published quarterly.

Dealers

Gail & John Dunn
P.O. Box 234
Waterville, OH 43566
phone: 419-878-9515
Buys and sells vintage purses and hatpins.

Diane Richardson
Gold Hatpin, The
P.O. Box 993
Oak Park, IL 60303-0993
phone: 708-848-3247 or 708-445-0610
Wants all types hatpins & holders: Satsuma, vanity, enameled, figural, fancy & the unusual; no repros.

Deena M. Zachritz, Dir.
Rocking Chair Emporium Showcase
  Antique Mall
123 N Glassell
Orange, CA 92666
phone: 714-633-5206
fax: 714-633-5726
Authority on women's hatpins, hatpin holders and related ephemera (1890-1920). Buys, sells, trades one piece or entire collection.

Experts

Lillian Baker
1013 Medhurst Rd.
Columbus, OH 43220
phone: 614-451-7368
Specializes in high fashion costume jewelry, hatpins, hatpin holders, miniatures; author of books on hatpins & holders; founder of the Inter. Club for Collectors of Hatpin & Hatpin Holders; author of books about hatpins.

Collector
P.O. Box 93
Canoga Park, CA 91305
Buys, sells, collects, specializes in, and appraises hatpins and hatpin holders; wants to buy very ornate Victorian hatpins; also free standing or wall-type hatpin holders.

Repro. Sources

Hatpins
P.O. Box 24606
Philadelphia, PA 19111
phone: 610-372-3887
Sells reproduction hat pins.

DRIVE-IN THEATERS

Collectors

Brian A. Butko
2640 Sunset Dr.
West Mifflin, PA 15122-3565
Wants items relating to Drive-In theaters: toys, flyers, photos, articles, and souvenirs such as postcards and ashtrays.

DRUM & BUGLE CORPS

Collectors

L.R. Hogan
36457 N. 83
Lake Villa, IL 60046
phone: 708-356-2875
Wants Drum & Bugle Corps records, tapes, videos and memorabilia.

DUCK CALLS

(see SPORTING COLLECTIBLES,
Game Calls)

DUCK DECOYS

(see DECOYS, Waterfowl)

DUMMY BOARDS

Repro. Sources

Boardwalk Originals
P.O. Box 358
Bristol, IN 46507

Here are some tips when contacting someone listed in this book:

When requesting information about a particular item, include a description (material, dimensions, maker's mark, model number, etc.) and a photo, sketch, or photocopy of the item in question. ■

Always ask if there are charges for samples or for the services requested. ■

When writing, please be sure to include a Large (#10 business size) Self-Addressed and Stamped Envelope (LSASE) if requesting a reply or the return of photographs. ■

Never call collect unless otherwise directed. When calling, be considerate of time zone differences and always ask if the party you are calling has time to talk. When leaving an answering machine message, always instruct the party to call you back collect. ■

EASTER COLLECTIBLES

(see HOLIDAY COLLECTIBLES; RUSSIAN ITEMS, Faberge)

ECCLESIASTICAL ITEMS

(see RELIGIOUS COLLECTIBLES)

EDGED WEAPONS

(see also ARMS & ARMOR; AMERICAN INDIAN; SWORDS; KNIVES; MILITARIA)

Auction Services

Ronnie Roberts, ISA
Dixie Sporting Collectibles
1206 Rama Rd.
Charlotte, NC 28211-4345
phone: 704-364-2900 or 704-364-3382
fax: 704-364-2322
e-mail: gun1898@aol.com
Internet: http://www.sportauction.com

Collectors

Brian Wojtowicz
Antique Exchange, The
9 Kettle Creek Rd.
Toms River, NJ 08753
phone: 908-255-9277 or 800-927-8463
Private collector wants to buy Japanese swords and daggers, German swords and daggers, European swords and daggers; also wants Japanese sword guards, related awards and documents, medals and photos, etc.

Brian L. Ebosh
P.O. Box 261
Lagrange, OH 44050-0261
phone: 216-355-8118
Wants Indian and pioneer metal axes: pipe tomahawks, spike, spontoon, Missouri, and related items.

John S. Fischer
10950 W. Pico Blvd.
Los Angeles, CA 90064-2115
Wants British and American edged weapons from WWI and WWII; no bayonets, please; state description, price and phone number.

Dealers

David L. Hartline
P.O. Box 775
Columbus, OH 43085
Buys and sells edged weapons; has large library and over 30 years experience; specialty is pre-1920 Bowie knives; has had many articles published on edge weapons; answers

every letter; does appraisals and will authenticate.

Experts

Ron G. Hickox
M.R.A. Co.
P.O. Box 360006
Tampa, FL 33673-0006
phone: 813-899-1776
fax: 813-744-5678
e-mail: rhickox@ix.netcom.com
Specializing in military edged weapons from all countries; author of "Collectors Guide to Ames U.S. Contract Edged Weapons 1832-1906" and "U.S. Military Edged Weapons of the Second Seminole War, 1816-1842."

German

Collectors

Greg Souchik
P.O. Box 161
Custer City, PA 16725-0161
phone: 814-362-2642
fax: 814-362-7356
e-mail: 104235.2430@compuserve.com
Wants to buy all WWII German and Japanese swords and daggers.

Dealers

Thomas T. Wittmann
Thomas T. Whittmann, Antique
  Militaria
P.O. Box 350
Moorestown, NJ 08057
phone: 609-866-8733 or 609-231-0323
fax: 609-235-4954
e-mail: TWittm350@aol.com
Internet: http://members.aol.com/
  TWittm350/
Buys and sells edged weapons: daggers, swords and certain bayonets; specializing in German 3rd Reich or Imperial period weapons; author of "Exploring the Dress Daggers of the German Army," Vol. 1 and other books.

Experts

Thomas T. Wittmann
Thomas T. Whittmann, Antique
  Militaria
P.O. Box 350
Moorestown, NJ 08057
phone: 609-866-8733 or 609-231-0323
fax: 609-235-4954
e-mail: TWittm350@aol.com
Internet: http://members.aol.com/
  TWittm350/
Buys and sells edged weapons: daggers, swords and certain bayonets; specializing in German 3rd Reich or Imperial period weapons; author of "Exploring the Dress Daggers of the German Army," Vol. 1 and other books.

LTC(Ret) Thomas Johnson
312 Butler Road, Bldg. 403
Fredericksburg, VA 22405-2514
phone: 800-851-2665 or 540-373-9150
fax: 540-373-0087
e-mail: ww2daggers@aol.com
Internet: http://www.ww2daggers.com
Wants to buy German War booty; specific interest is in edged weapons (dress swords, daggers, bayonets); author of several books about Imperial and 3rd Reich German edged weapons.

EDUCATIONAL TOYS

(see TOYS, Construction Sets)

EGGCUPS

Clubs/Associations

Dr. Joan M. George
Eggcup Collectors Club
Newsletter: Eggcup Collectors' Corner
67 Stevens Ave.
Old Bridge, NJ 08857-2244
phone: 908-679-8924
fax: 908-679-6102
e-mail: drjgeorge@nac.net
A quarterly newsletter for eggcup collectors; buy, sell, trade ads; share information, review books, meetings of collectors arranged.

Collectors

Sharon A. Mitchell
875 North Michigan, #3412
Chicago, IL 60611
phone: 312-787-3252 or 800-879-6948
fax: 312-266-7982
Ardent collector wants more figural and character eggcups, especially ones showing heads, bodies, or images of people or animals.

Periodicals

Audrey Diamond
Newsletter: Eggcup World
Flat 5, Cherry Court
Cherry Close Parkstone, Poole
Dorset BH14 OLJ, U.K.

EIFFEL TOWER

(see SOUVENIR & COMMEMORA-TIVE ITEMS, Buildings [Eiffel Tower])

ELECTRICITY RELATED ITEMS

(see also AUDIO-VISUAL; CLOCKS, Electric; COIN-OPERATED MACHINES; FANS, Mechanical; INSULATORS; KITCHEN COLLECTIBLES; LAMPS & LIGHTING; LIGHT BULBS; MODERNISM; RADIOS; TELE-GRAPH ITEMS; TELEVISIONS; TOASTERS, Electric; VACUUM CLEANERS; WASHING MA-CHINES)

Clubs/Associations

Harry Goldman
Tesla Coil Builders' Association
Newsletter: TCBA News
3 Amy Lane
Queensbury, NY 12804
phone: 518-792-1003
TCBA is a clearinghouse on the history of electricity, wireless, electrotherapy, etc.; acts as consultants for high voltage historical equipment.

Collectors

Harvey Greenspan
15 Chatham Circle
Brookline, MA 02146
phone: 617-566-4191
Wants early electric motors, generators, dynamos and other pre-1900 electrical/mechanical instruments for science, industry, business.

Dealers

Jim & Felicia Kreuzer
New Wireless Pioneers
P.O. Box 398
Elma, NY 14059
phone: 716-681-3186
fax: 716-681-4540
Buys and sells 1850-1950 books, catalogs, magazines, autographs, and other literature dealing with early radio, wireless, pre-1940 television, medical, x-ray and electricity.

Ye Ole Electric Store
504 W. 6th St.
Beaumont, CA 92223
phone: 909-849-7539
For the collector, experimenter, hobbyist: tesla coils, old electrical therapy devices, small appliances, test instruments, radio and tech books, neon signs, old motors, fans, meters, tubes, trains, etc.

Hank Andreoni
Ye Olde Electric Store
250-D South Lyon Ave.
Hemet, CA 92543
phone: 909-849-7539
For the collector, experimenter, hobbyist, researcher: tech. books, electronic surplus, fans, neon signs, old motors, small appliances, test instruments, trains, tubes, radios, meters, old electrical therapy devices, Tesla coils, etc.

Museums/Libraries

George D. Tselos, Archivist
Edison National Historic Site
Main St. at Lakeside Ave.
West Orange, NJ 07052
phone: 201-736-5050
fax: 201-736-8496
A museum with exhibits in all fields of Edison's contributions.

National Museum of American History
14th & Constitution Ave. NW
Washington, DC 20560
phone: 202-357-2700
Internet: http://www.si.edu/
The most extensive research facility in the U.S. for electric relics; trade catalogs, electric razors, refrigerators, TV's, radios, etc.

Edison Winter Home & Museum
2350 McGregor Blvd.
Fort Myers, FL 33901
phone: 813-334-3614
Contains Edison-related displays: appliances, early bulbs, and scientific equipment.

Laurence J. Russell, Curator
Thomas Edison Birthplace Museum
P.O. Box 451
Milan, OH 44846-0451
phone: 419-499-2135
fax: 419-499-3241
e-mail: edison@accnorwalk.com
Internet: http://www.edisonbp.org
An Edison exhibit featuring phonographs, lamps, fans, photos, and other items related to Thomas Edison.

Bakken, The
3537 Zenith Ave. South
Minneapolis, MN 55416
phone: 612-927-6508
Collects medical electricity items (no violet rays needed); have 2000 artifacts; 10,000 books.

Masden Electric Museum
3251 E. Washington Blvd.
Los Angeles, CA 90023

Appliances

Clubs/Associations

Jackie Shedden
Old Appliance Club
Newsletter: Old Road Home, The
P.O. Box 65
Ventura, CA 93002
phone: 805-643-3532
fax: 805-643-3532
e-mail: jes@west.net
An organization for dealers, owners, restorers, users and fans of American appliances; accent is placed on mostly antique and classic ranges 1920s-1950s, Monitor-top refrigerators; builds thermostats, applies new porcelain, restores.

Collectors

Daniel Zilka
110 Benevolent St.
Providence, RI 02906
phone: 410-331-8575 or 410-461-7932
fax: 401-351-0127
Wants to buy older coffee pots, percolators, waffle irons, mixers, vaculator coffee makers; performs restorations; seeking manufacturers' promotional material and brochures.

Dennis Thompson, Dir.
P.O. Box 26067
Cleveland, OH 44126-0067
phone: 216-235-8548
e-mail: dthomp@stratos.net
Internet: http://www.execpc.com/~wmhill/
Collects and researches early electric mixers, especially those with depression glass bottom jars; collection is on-line at website.

Dealers

Jim Barker
Toaster Master
P.O. Box 41
Bethlehem, PA 18016
phone: 610-439-0751

Experts

K. M. Scotty Mitchell
Millchell
2112 Lipscomb
Ft. Worth, TX 76110-2047
phone: 817-923-3274
fax: 817-926-1970
Collector of small electrical kitchen appliances (1893-1940): toaster, waffle irons, coffee makers and specialty items, etc.

Gary L. Miller
Millchell
2112 Lipscomb
Ft. Worth, TX 76110-2047
phone: 817-923-3274
fax: 817-926-1970
Collector of small electrical kitchen appliances (1893-1940): toaster, waffle irons, coffee makers and specialty items, etc.

Repair Services

William Randle
William Randle Restorations
2706 Deerford St.
Lakewood, CA 90712
phone: 310-422-2424
Antique electrical and mechanical restoration and repair; buys, sells and repairs old electrical kitchen appliances; has vintage parts in stock; also has ten different varieties of new cloth covered power cord; rewiring, fabricating.

Appliances (Coffee Pots)

Collectors

Carole Lundy
3 Long Lane
Hummelstown, PA 17036-9545
phone: 717-566-6016
Wants to buy porcelain coffee pots made by Hall, Westinghouse, Robeson Rochester, and Porcelier.

Appliances (Porcelier)

Clubs/Associations

Shirley Hall
Porcelier Collectors Club
Newsletter: Porcelier Paper, The
21 Tamarac Swamp Rd.
Wallingford, CT 06492-5529
phone: 203-265-5791
For collectors of Porcelier dinnerware, service pieces and all-ceramic small electrical kitchen appliances; bi-monthly newsletter features information and pictures of patterns, new finds, and research; free ads for members.

Collectors

Carole Lundy
3 Long Lane
Hummelstown, PA 17036-9545
phone: 717-566-6016
Wants to buy Porcelier brand electric coffee pots, toasters, waffle irons, sandwich grills, and related items.

General Electric

Collectors

V. Mitchell
P.O. Box 795
Douglasville, GA 30133
Wants to buy General Electric logoed items: older items preferred; water bottles, salt shakers, trays, neon signs; send description and price.

Power Utilities Items

Collectors

Tommy Bolack
P.O. Box 2059
Farmington, NM 87499
phone: 503-325-7873
Wants any early watthour meter: GE, Thompson, Edison-Chemical, Semco, Duncan, Fort Wayne, Sangamo, prepay meters of any type; also any other early or foreign types.

Museums/Libraries

Dayton Power & Light Company Museum
P.O. Box 1247-Courthouse Sq.
Dayton, OH 45401
phone: 513-224-6428
Over 1000 electrical and non-electrical appliances and historical artifacts pertaining to the gas & electric utility industry.

Rocky Beach Dam, Gallery of Electricity
P.O. Box 1231
Wenatchee, WA 98801-1231
phone: 509-663-8121
The museum features communications and power relics.

ELEPHANT COLLECTIBLES

Clubs/Associations

Richard W. Massiglia
National Elephant Collectors Society, The
380 Medford St.
Somerville, MA 02145-3810
phone: 617-625-4067
For information send LSASE plus $1.

Collectors

Rosita Williams
2221 Shorefield Dr., Apt. 412
Takoma Park, MD 20912-1850
phone: 301-946-5356
e-mail: arentfox@mcimail.com

Experts

Richard W. Massiglia
380 Medford St.
Somerville, MA 02145-3810
phone: 617-625-4067

Periodicals

Joan L. Huegel
Newsletter: Jumbo Jargon
1002 West 25th St.
Erie, PA 16502-2427
Quarterly publication; free ad for subcribers; articles, meet other collectors, "from the expert" column, classified ads, etc.; available only by subscription.

ELONGATED COINS

Clubs/Associations

Howard C. Sharkey
Elongated Collectors, The
Newsletter: TEC News
203 S. Gladiolus St.
Momence, IL 60954-1709
phone: 815-472-4967
Focuses on elongated coins but includes all denominations plus tokens and foreign coins rolled under extreme pressure through steel rollers forming custom designed oblong souvenirs commemorating people, places, things, and events.

Collectors

Doug Fairbanks, Sr.
5937 Beadle Dr.
Jamesville, NY 13078-9534
phone: 315-469-4682
Wants to buy "Oldie" elongated coins (rolled-out pennies, etc.) from 1893 to 1965; please write, describe and price.

C. Meccarello
Elongated Coin Museum
1572 Bowmans Trail
Lakeland, FL 33809-5006
phone: 941-859-7194 or 941-859-7194
Buys, sells, collects OPA tokens, Bank postcard, elongated coins.

Dealers

Rich Hartzog
World Exonumia
P.O. Box 4143 BSB
Rockford, IL 61110-0643
phone: 815-226-0771
fax: 815-397-7662
Wants any elongated coins, tokens, medals, exonumia: badges, buttons, World's Fair items, political items, banners, etc.

ELSIE THE BORDEN COW ITEMS

(see also COW COLLECTIBLES; DAIRY COLLECTIBLES)

Collectors

Susan Schwartz
291 E. 4th Street
Brooklyn, NY 11218
Wants Elsie the Cow novelties.

Richard Reddock
914 Isle Ct.
Bellmore, NY 11710-1545
phone: 516-826-2032 or 800-223-PNUT
e-mail: pnutfanclb@aol.com
Wants to buy all Elsie Cow items: clocks, signs, rubber Elsie doll, papier mache Elsie head, letter opener, drinking glasses.

Tim Greener
5791 Blossom Lake Dr.
Seminole, FL 33772-7405
phone: 813-398-1518
Wants anything (except magazine ads) advertising Elsie the Cow or her family: clocks, signs, pins, watches, salt and pepper shakers, cookie jars, etc.

Robb Johnson
1155 Crescent Lake Rd.
Waterford Township, MI 48327
phone: 810-673-2804
Wants to buy Borden items.

Ron Selcke
P.O. Box 237
Bloomingdale, IL 60108-0237
phone: 630-543-4848
Wants Elsie games, cookbooks, comic books, cups, glasses, Christmas cards, books, pictures, blotters, postcards, clocks, signs, neon signs, Borden Milk bottles and creamers, Borden Milk postcards, Borden Condensed Milk trade cards.

Dealers

Marty Blank
P.O. Box 405
Flushing, NY 11365-0405
phone: 516-485-8071
e-mail: martyadver@aol.com
Wants to buy Elsie, Campbell Kids, Reddy Kilowatt, Coke, figural vinyl advertising and Country Store items.

ELVES

Collectors

Walter Dworkin
8 Rugby Rd.
Westbury, NY 11590
phone: 516-334-4674
Collects Pixieware - those oh-so-cute ceramic containers for condiments, liquor, hor d'oeuvres, salt and pepper, and oil and vinegar bade by the Holt-Howard company of Stamford, CT from 1958 to the early 1960s.

Sally Kimmel
1471 Lark Lane
Concord, CA 94521
phone: 510-676-2857
Elf lover wants to buy elves and pixies: Christmas tree, wall, hanging, table decorations and ornaments and any other holiday (Easter, Valentines Day, St. Patrick's Day, etc.) elves, pixies, fairies and leprechauns - anything with elves!

EMBALMING ITEMS

(see FUNERAL ITEMS)

EMBROIDERY

(see MILITARIA, Silk Embroideries; TEXTILES)

ENAMELS

(see also BATTERSEA ENAMEL BOXES; BOXES; CLOISONNE; GLASS; METAL ITEMS; RUSSIAN ITEMS)

Clubs/Associations

Tom Ellis, Ed.
Enamelist Society, The
Magazine: Glass on Metal
P.O. Box 310
Newport, KY 41072
phone: 609-291-3800
fax: 606-291-1849
e-mail: klinedl@ucbeh.san.uc.edu
Over 1300 members worldwide with interests in all aspects of enameling - glass on metal; the magazine is published 5 times per year plus 2 bulletins; conventions, exhibitions.

ENDANGERED SPECIES

(see also ANIMAL COLLECTIBLES; ANIMAL TROPHIES; IVORY; NAUTICAL ANTIQUES; SCRIMSHAW; SPORTING COLLECTIBLES)

Misc. Services

World Wildlife Fund
1250 24th Street, NW
Washington, DC 20037
Check with TRAFFIC USA regarding regulations for importing and exporting wildlife or wildlife products; TRAFFIC USA is the wildlife trade monitoring program of the World Wildlife Fund.

Canadian

Misc. Services

Canadian Wildlife Service Headquarters, CITES Administrator
351 St. Joseph Blvd., 3rd Floor
Place Vincent Massey, Hull
Quebec K1A 0H3 Canada
phone: 819-953-1411
fax: 819-994-4065
Canadian HQ contact for inquiries regarding CITES (the Convention on International Trade in Endangered Species of Wild Fauna & Flora); an international agreement that protects endangered and threatened species of animals & plants.

Canadian Wildlife Service, Pacific & Yukon Region
P.O. Box 340
Delta
B. C. V4K 3Y3 Canada
phone: 604-946-8643
fax: 604-946-8359
Regional Canadian contact for inquiries regarding CITES (the Convention on International Trade in Endangered Species of Wild Fauna & Flora); an international agreement that protects endangered and threatened species of animals & plants

Canadian Wildlife Service, Western & Northern Region
115 Perimeter Road
Saskatoon
Saskatchewan S7N 0X4 Canada
phone: 306-975-4290
fax: 306-975-4089
Regional Canadian contact for inquiries regarding CITES (the Convention on International Trade in Endangered Species of Wild Fauna & Flora); an international agreement that protects endangered and threatened species of animals & plants

Canadian Wildlife Service, Ontario Region
70 Fountain St. E
Guelph
Ontario N1H 3N6 Canada
phone: 519-766-1661
fax: 519-766-1750
Regional Canadian contact for inquiries regarding CITES (the Convention on International Trade in Endangered Species of Wild Fauna & Flora); an international agreement that protects endangered and threatened species of animals & plants

Canadian Wildlife Service, Atlantic Region
P.O. Box 1590
Sackville
New Brunswick E0A 3C0 Canada
phone: 506-364-5044
fax: 506-364-5062
Regional Canadian contact for inquiries regarding CITES (the Convention on International Trade in Endangered Species of Wild Fauna & Flora); an international agreement that protects endangered and threatened species of animals & plants

Canadian Wildlife Service, Quebec Region
C.P. 10100
Ste-Foy
Quebec G1V 4H5 Canada
phone: 418-649-6122
fax: 418-649-6475
Regional Canadian contact for inquiries regarding CITES (the Convention on International Trade in Endangered Species of Wild Fauna & Flora); an international agreement that protects endangered and threatened species of animals & plants

National Marine Fisheries Ser.

Misc. Services

Special Agent in Charge
NOAA/NMFS Office of Enforcement, Northeast Region
1 Blackburn Drive, Room 206
Gloucester, MA 01930
phone: 508-281-9213
fax: 508-281-9317
National Oceanic & Administration/ National Marine Fisheries Service enforcement office, Northeast Region; call to join the NOAA Fisheries Enforcement PARTNERS program to help find solutions to marine resource problems.

National Marine Fisheries Service, Office of Protected Resources (F/PR)
1335 East-West Highway
Silver Spring, MD 20910
phone: 301-713-2332
Contact for current information on endangered marine life (whales, fish, dolphins); for most other flora and fauna contact U.S. Fish & Wildlife Service; point of contact for issues relating to the Endangered Species Act.

Nat. Marine Fisheries Serv., Asst. Administrator for Fisheries, c/o Permit Div.
Office of Protected Resources & Habitat Prog.
1335 East-West Hwy., Rm 7324
Silver Spring, MD 20910
phone: 301-713-2289
Contact for permits and inquiries regarding The Marine Mammal Protection Act for all whales, dolphins, seals, and sea lions (i.e. marine mammals other than polar bears, manatees, otters, walruses and dungongs.)

Chief
NOAA/NMFS Office of Enforcement,
Headquarters
8484 Georgia Ave., Ste. 415
Silver Spring, MD 20910
phone: 301-417-2300
fax: 301-427-2055
*National Oceanic & Administration/
National Marine Fisheries Service
Office of Enforcement, Headquarters;
call to join the NOAA Fisheries
Enforcement PARTNERS program to
help find solutions to marine resource
problems.*

Special Agent in Charge
NOAA/NMFS Office of Enforcement,
Southeast Region
9721 Executive Center Drive, Room 130
Saint Petersburg, FL 33702
phone: 813-570-5344
fax: 813-570-5343
*National Oceanic & Administration/
National Marine Fisheries Service
enforcement office, Southeast Region;
call to join the NOAA Fisheries
Enforcement PARTNERS program to
help find solutions to marine resource
problems.*

Special Agent in Charge
NOAA/NMFS Office of Enforcement,
Southwest Region
501 W. Ocean Boulevard, Ste. 4400-A
Long Beach, CA 90802
phone: 562-980-4050
fax: 562-980-4058
*National Oceanic & Administration/
National Marine Fisheries Service
enforcement office, Southwest Region;
call to join the NOAA Fisheries
Enforcement PARTNERS program to
help find solutions to marine resource
problems.*

Special Agent in Charge
NOAA/NMFS Office of Enforcement,
Northwest Region
7600 Sand Point Way NE
Seattle, WA 98115
phone: 206-526-6133
fax: 206-526-6528
*National Oceanic & Administration/
National Marine Fisheries Service
enforcement office, Northwest Region;
call to join the NOAA Fisheries
Enforcement PARTNERS program to
help find solutions to marine resource
problems.*

Special Agent in Charge
NOAA/NMFS Office of Enforcement,
Alaska Region
P.O. Box 21767
Juneau, AK 99802
phone: 907-586-7225
fax: 907-586-7200
*National Oceanic & Administration/
National Marine Fisheries Service
enforcement office, Alaska Region;
call to join the NOAA Fisheries
Enforcement PARTNERS program to
help find solutions to marine resource
problems.*

State Conservation Agencies

Misc. Services

Commissioner
Department of Conservation & Cultural
Affairs
P.O. Box 4340
Charlotte Amalie
St Thomas, VI 00801
*Each state has its own wildlife laws
which may differ from Federal laws.
Check with state and local authorities
for restrictions on ownership or
commercial transactions of protected
wildlife.*

Secretary
Department of Natural Resources
P.O. Box 58887
San Juan, PR 00906
phone: 809-722-1429
*Each state has its own wildlife laws
which may differ from Federal laws.
Check with state and local authorities
for restrictions on ownership or
commercial transactions of protected
wildlife.*

Natural Heritage & Endangered Species
Program, Division of Fisheries &
Wildlife
100 Cambridge Street
Boston, MA 02202
phone: 617-727-3151
*Each state has its own wildlife laws
which may differ from Federal laws.
Check with state and local authorities
for restrictions on ownership or
commercial transactions of protected
wildlife.*

Chief
Division of Fish & Wildlife
Government Center
Wakefield, RI 02879
phone: 401-789-3094
*Each state has its own wildlife laws
which may differ from Federal laws.
Check with state and local authorities
for restrictions on ownership or
commercial transactions of protected
wildlife.*

Director
Fish & Game Department
34 Bridge St.
Concord, NH 03301
phone: 603-271-3421
*Each state has its own wildlife laws
which may differ from Federal laws.
Check with state and local authorities
for restrictions on ownership or
commercial transactions of protected
wildlife.*

Commissioner
Department of Inland Fisheries &
Wildlife
284 State St.
Augusta, ME 04333
phone: 207-289-2766
*Each state has its own wildlife laws
which may differ from Federal laws.
Check with state and local authorities
for restrictions on ownership or*

commercial transactions of protected
wildlife.

Commissioner
Fish & Game Department
State Office Building
Montpelier, VT 05602
phone: 802-479-3242
*Each state has its own wildlife laws
which may differ from Federal laws.
Check with state and local authorities
for restrictions on ownership or
commercial transactions of protected
wildlife.*

Deputy Commissioner
Department of Environmental
Protection, Preservation & Conservation Division
State Office Building
165 Capitol Building
Hartford, CT 06106
phone: 203-566-4522
*Each state has its own wildlife laws
which may differ from Federal laws.
Check with state and local authorities
for restrictions on ownership or
commercial transactions of protected
wildlife.*

Director
Division of Fish, Game & Wildlife
CN 400
Trenton, NJ 08625
phone: 609-292-9400
*Each state has its own wildlife laws
which may differ from Federal laws.
Check with state and local authorities
for restrictions on ownership or
commercial transactions of protected
wildlife.*

Director
Division of Fish & Wildlife, Department
of Environmental Conservation
50 Wolf Road
Albany, NY 12233
phone: 518-457-3400
*Each state has its own wildlife laws
which may differ from Federal laws.
Check with state and local authorities
for restrictions on ownership or
commercial transactions of protected
wildlife.*

Executive Director
Fish Commission
P.O. Box 1673
Harrisburg, PA 17105
phone: 717-657-4515
*Each state has its own wildlife laws
which may differ from Federal laws.
Check with state and local authorities
for restrictions on ownership or
commercial transactions of protected
wildlife.*

Executive Director
Game Commission
2001 Elmerton Ave.
Harrisburg, PA 17110-9797
phone: 717-787-3033
*Each state has its own wildlife laws
which may differ from Federal laws.
Check with state and local authorities
for restrictions on ownership or*

commercial transactions of protected
wildlife.

Director
Division of Fish & Wildlife
Richardson & Robbins Building
P.O. Box 1401
Dover, DE 19903
phone: 904-488-1554
*Each state has its own wildlife laws
which may differ from Federal laws.
Check with state and local authorities
for restrictions on ownership or
commercial transactions of protected
wildlife.*

Director
Department of Natural Resources,
Maryland Forest, Park & Wildlife
Tawes State Office Building
Annapolis, MD 21401
phone: 301-269-3776
*Each state has its own wildlife laws
which may differ from Federal laws.
Check with state and local authorities
for restrictions on ownership or
commercial transactions of protected
wildlife.*

Executive Director
Commission of Game & Inland Fisheries
4010 W. Broad Street
P.O. Box 11104
Richmond, VA 23230
phone: 804-367-1000
*Each state has its own wildlife laws
which may differ from Federal laws.
Check with state and local authorities
for restrictions on ownership or
commercial transactions of protected
wildlife.*

Director
Department of Natural Resources
1800 Washington Street, East
Charleston, WV 25305
phone: 304-348-2754
*Each state has its own wildlife laws
which may differ from Federal laws.
Check with state and local authorities
for restrictions on ownership or
commercial transactions of protected
wildlife.*

Executive Director
Wildlife Resources Commission
Archdale Building
512 N. Salisbury Street
Raleigh, NC 27611
phone: 919-733-3391
*Each state has its own wildlife laws
which may differ from Federal laws.
Check with state and local authorities
for restrictions on ownership or
commercial transactions of protected
wildlife.*

Executive Director
Wildlife & Marine Resources
Bldg. D, Dutch Plaza
P.O. Box 167
Columbia, SC 29202
phone: 803-734-3888
*Each state has its own wildlife laws
which may differ from Federal laws.
Check with state and local authorities
for restrictions on ownership or*

commercial transactions of protected wildlife.

Director
Department of Natural Resources, Game & Fish Division
270 Washington Street, SW
Atlanta, GA 30334
phone: 404-656-3523
Each state has its own wildlife laws which may differ from Federal laws. Check with state and local authorities for restrictions on ownership or commercial transactions of protected wildlife.

Director
Game & Fresh Water Fish Commission
620 South Meridian
Tallahassee, FL 32301
phone: 904-488-1960
Each state has its own wildlife laws which may differ from Federal laws. Check with state and local authorities for restrictions on ownership or commercial transactions of protected wildlife.

Department of Natural Resources
100 8th Ave. SE
Saint Petersburg, FL 33701
phone: 904-488-1554
Each state has its own wildlife laws which may differ from Federal laws. Check with state and local authorities for restrictions on ownership or commercial transactions of protected wildlife.

Director
Division of Game & Fish, Department of Conservation & Natural Resources
64 N. Union St.
Montgomery, AL 36130
phone: 205-242-3467
Each state has its own wildlife laws which may differ from Federal laws. Check with state and local authorities for restrictions on ownership or commercial transactions of protected wildlife.

Ch. of Law Enforcement
Wildlife Resource Agency
Ellington Agricultural Center
P.O. Box 40747
Nashville, TN 37204
phone: 615-360-0581
Each state has its own wildlife laws which may differ from Federal laws. Check with state and local authorities for restrictions on ownership or commercial transactions of protected wildlife.

Director of Wildlife Conservation, Game & Fish Commission
Southport Mall
P.O. Box 451
Jackson, MS 39205
phone: 601-961-5311
Each state has its own wildlife laws which may differ from Federal laws. Check with state and local authorities for restrictions on ownership or

commercial transactions of protected wildlife.

Commissioner
Department of Fish & Wildlife Resources
Capitol Plaza Tower
Frankfort, KY 40601
phone: 502-564-3400
Each state has its own wildlife laws which may differ from Federal laws. Check with state and local authorities for restrictions on ownership or commercial transactions of protected wildlife.

Director
Department of Natural Resources
Fountain Square D-3
Columbus, OH 43224
phone: 614-265-6877
Each state has its own wildlife laws which may differ from Federal laws. Check with state and local authorities for restrictions on ownership or commercial transactions of protected wildlife.

Director
Division of Fish & Wildlife, Department of Natural Resources
607 State Office Building
Indianapolis, IN 46204
phone: 317-232-4080
Each state has its own wildlife laws which may differ from Federal laws. Check with state and local authorities for restrictions on ownership or commercial transactions of protected wildlife.

Director
Department of Natural Resources, Wildlife Division, Permit Specialist
P.O. Box 30028
Lansing, MI 48909
phone: 517-373-1263
Each state has its own wildlife laws which may differ from Federal laws. Check with state and local authorities for restrictions on ownership or commercial transactions of protected wildlife.

Director
State Conservation Commission
Wallace State Office Building
300 Fourth Street
Des Moines, IA 50319-0034
phone: 515-281-5145
Each state has its own wildlife laws which may differ from Federal laws. Check with state and local authorities for restrictions on ownership or commercial transactions of protected wildlife.

Secretary
Department of Natural Resources
P.O. Box 7921
Madison, WI 53707
phone: 608-226-7012
Each state has its own wildlife laws which may differ from Federal laws. Check with state and local authorities for restrictions on ownership or

commercial transactions of protected wildlife.

Director
Department of Natural Resources, Wildlife Division
Box 20
500 Lafayette Rd.
Saint Paul, MN 55146
phone: 612-296-3344
Each state has its own wildlife laws which may differ from Federal laws. Check with state and local authorities for restrictions on ownership or commercial transactions of protected wildlife.

Secretary
Department of Game, Fish & Parks
Sigurd Anderson Building
Pierre, SD 57501
phone: 605-773-3485
Each state has its own wildlife laws which may differ from Federal laws. Check with state and local authorities for restrictions on ownership or commercial transactions of protected wildlife.

Director
Game & Fish Department
2121 Lovett Ave.
Bismarck, ND 58505
phone: 701-224-2180
Each state has its own wildlife laws which may differ from Federal laws. Check with state and local authorities for restrictions on ownership or commercial transactions of protected wildlife.

Director
Fish & Game Department
1420 East Sixth
Helena, MT 59601
phone: 406-444-2452
Each state has its own wildlife laws which may differ from Federal laws. Check with state and local authorities for restrictions on ownership or commercial transactions of protected wildlife.

Director
Department of Conservation
524 South Second St.
Springfield, IL 62706
phone: 217-782-6302
Each state has its own wildlife laws which may differ from Federal laws. Check with state and local authorities for restrictions on ownership or commercial transactions of protected wildlife.

Director
Department of Conservation
P.O. Box 180
Jefferson City, MO 65102-0180
phone: 314-751-4115
Each state has its own wildlife laws which may differ from Federal laws. Check with state and local authorities for restrictions on ownership or commercial transactions of protected wildlife.

Assistgant Secretary
Department of Wildlife & Parks, Operations Office
Route 2, Box 54A
Pratt, KS 67124
phone: 316-672-5911
Each state has its own wildlife laws which may differ from Federal laws. Check with state and local authorities for restrictions on ownership or commercial transactions of protected wildlife.

Director
Game & Parks Commission
2200 N. 33rd St.
P.O. Box 30370
Lincoln, NE 68503
phone: 402-464-0641
Each state has its own wildlife laws which may differ from Federal laws. Check with state and local authorities for restrictions on ownership or commercial transactions of protected wildlife.

Director
Department of Wildlife & Fisheries, Ecological Studies Section
P.O. box 98000
Baton Rouge, LA 70898-9000
phone: 504-765-2806
Each state has its own wildlife laws which may differ from Federal laws. Check with state and local authorities for restrictions on ownership or commercial transactions of protected wildlife.

Director
Department of Fish & Game
#2 Natural Resources Drive
Little Rock, AR 72205
phone: 501-223-6300
Each state has its own wildlife laws which may differ from Federal laws. Check with state and local authorities for restrictions on ownership or commercial transactions of protected wildlife.

Director
Department of Wildlife Conservation
1801 N. Lincoln
P.O. Box 53465
Oklahoma City, OK 73152
phone: 405-521-3851
Each state has its own wildlife laws which may differ from Federal laws. Check with state and local authorities for restrictions on ownership or commercial transactions of protected wildlife.

Executive Director
Parks & Wildlife Department
4200 Smith School Rd.
Austin, TX 78744
phone: 512-389-4864
Each state has its own wildlife laws which may differ from Federal laws. Check with state and local authorities for restrictions on ownership or commercial transactions of protected wildlife.

Division of Wildlife
6060 Broadway
Denver, CO 80216
phone: 303-297-1192
*Each state has its own wildlife laws
which may differ from Federal laws.
Check with state and local authorities
for restrictions on ownership or
commercial transactions of protected
wildlife.*

Director
Game & Fish Division
Cheyenne, WY 82002
phone: 307-777-4500
*Each state has its own wildlife laws
which may differ from Federal laws.
Check with state and local authorities
for restrictions on ownership or
commercial transactions of protected
wildlife.*

Commissioner
Fish & Game Department
600 South Walnut Street
P.O. Box 25
Boise, ID 83707
phone: 208-334-3736
*Each state has its own wildlife laws
which may differ from Federal laws.
Check with state and local authorities
for restrictions on ownership or
commercial transactions of protected
wildlife.*

Director
Division of Wildlife Resources
1596 West North Temple
Salt Lake City, UT 84116
phone: 801-538-4700
*Each state has its own wildlife laws
which may differ from Federal laws.
Check with state and local authorities
for restrictions on ownership or
commercial transactions of protected
wildlife.*

Director
Game & Fish Department, Nogame
Branch
2222 West Greenway Rd.
Phoenix, AZ 85023
phone: 602-942-3000
*Each state has its own wildlife laws
which may differ from Federal laws.
Check with state and local authorities
for restrictions on ownership or
commercial transactions of protected
wildlife.*

Director
Director of Game & Fish
Village building
Santa Fe, NM 87503
phone: 505-827-7899
*Each state has its own wildlife laws
which may differ from Federal laws.
Check with state and local authorities
for restrictions on ownership or
commercial transactions of protected
wildlife.*

Director
Department of Wildlife
P.O. Box 10678
Reno, NV 89520
phone: 702-789-0500
*Each state has its own wildlife laws
which may differ from Federal laws.
Check with state and local authorities
for restrictions on ownership or
commercial transactions of protected
wildlife.*

Director
Department of Fish & Game
1416 Ninth St.
Sacramento, CA 95814
phone: 916-445-3531
*Each state has its own wildlife laws
which may differ from Federal laws.
Check with state and local authorities
for restrictions on ownership or
commercial transactions of protected
wildlife.*

Governor of American Samoa
Pago Pago, Tutila, AS 96799
*Each state has its own wildlife laws
which may differ from Federal laws.
Check with state and local authorities
for restrictions on ownership or
commercial transactions of protected
wildlife.*

Director
Division of Fish & Game, Department of
Land & Natural Resources
1151 Punchbowl Street
Honolulu, HI 96813
phone: 808-548-4002 or 808-548-2861
*Each state has its own wildlife laws
which may differ from Federal laws.
Check with state and local authorities
for restrictions on ownership or
commercial transactions of protected
wildlife.*

Chief
Aquatic & Wildlife Resources
Agana, GU 96910
*Each state has its own wildlife laws
which may differ from Federal laws.
Check with state and local authorities
for restrictions on ownership or
commercial transactions of protected
wildlife.*

Director
Fish & Wildlife Department
P.O. Box 59
Portland, OR 97208
phone: 503-229-5551
*Each state has its own wildlife laws
which may differ from Federal laws.
Check with state and local authorities
for restrictions on ownership or
commercial transactions of protected
wildlife.*

Director
Department of Game
600 North Capitol Way
Olympia, WA 98504
phone: 206-753-1707
*Each state has its own wildlife laws
which may differ from Federal laws.
Check with state and local authorities
for restrictions on ownership or*

*commercial transactions of protected
wildlife.*

Commissioner
Department of Fish & Game
P.O. Box 3-2000
Juneau, AK 99802
phone: 907-465-4190
*Each state has its own wildlife laws
which may differ from Federal laws.
Check with state and local authorities
for restrictions on ownership or
commercial transactions of protected
wildlife.*

U.S. Fish & Wildlife Service

Misc. Services

Regional Director
U.S. Fish & Wildlife Service, Region 5
One Gateway Center, Ste. 700
Newton, MA 02158
phone: 617-968-5100
*Regional U.S. Fish & Wildlife Service
contact for inquiries regarding laws
pertaining to endangered and
threatened species of wild fauna and
wild flora; covers CT, DE, DC, ME,
MD, MA, NH, NJ, NY, PA, RI. VT, VA,
WV.*

U.S. Fish & Wildlife Service, Asst.
Regional Director, Law Enforcement
P.O. Box 129
New Town Branch
Newton, MA 02258
phone: 617-965-2298 or 617-965-5100
*Contact for permit applications and
inquiries about The Migratory Bird
Treaty Act (covers any migratory bird,
any part, nest, egg, or product made
from a migratory bird, part, nest, or
egg.)*

U.S. Fish & Wildlife Service, Asst.
Regional Director, Law Enforcement
P.O. Box 129
New Town Branch
Newton, MA 02258
phone: 617-965-2298 or 617-965-5100
*Contact for permit applications and
inquiries about The Bald Eagle
Protection Act - protects bald
(Haliaeetus leucocephalus) and
golden (Aquilachrysaetos) eagles, live
or dead, their parts, nests or eggs.*

U.S. Fish & Wildlife Service, Office of
Endangered Species
4401 N. Fairfax Dr.
Arlington, VA 22203
phone: 703-358-2171
*Contact for current information on
endangered flora and fauna species,
other than marine (in which case
contact National Marine Fisheries
Service); point of contact for issues
relating to the Endangered Species
Act and the Lacey Act.*

U.S. Fish & Wildlife Service, Office of
Management Authority
4401 N. Fairfax Drive, Room 430
Arlington, VA 22203
phone: 703-358-2104
Contact for permits and inquiries

*regarding The Convention on
International Trade in Endangered
Species of Wild Fauna & Flora
(CITES).*

U.S. Fish & Wildlife Service, Office of
Management Authority
4401 N. Fairfax Drive, Room 430
Arlington, VA 22203
phone: 703-358-2104
*Contact for permits and inquiries
regarding The African Elephant
Conservation Act (forbids the import
of raw and worked African elephant
ivory from all ivory producing and
intermediary nations, and all African
ivory exports from the U.S.)*

U.S. Fish & Wildlife Service, Office of
Management Authority
4401 N. Fairfax Drive, Room 430
Arlington, VA 22203
phone: 703-358-2104
*Contact for permits and inquiries
regarding The Marine Mammal
Protection Act (only for certain
marine animals, specifically polar
bears, manatees, otters, walruses and
dungongs.)*

U.S. Fish & Wildlife Service, Division
of Law Enforcement
P.O. Box 3247
Arlington, VA 22203-3247
phone: 703-358-1949
*Check with the U.S. Fish & Wildlife
Service about regulations for
importing and exporting wildlife or
wildlife products.*

Regional Director
U.S. Fish & Wildlife Service, Region 4
75 Spring Street, SW, Rm. 1200
Atlanta, GA 30303
phone: 404-331-3588
*Regional U.S. Fish & Wildlife Service
contact for inquiries regarding laws
pertaining to endangered and
threatened species of wild fauna and
wild flora; covers AL, AR, FL, GA,
KY, LA, MS, NC, SC, TN, Puerto Rico,
U.S. Virgin Islands.*

Regional Director
U.S. Fish & Wildlife Service, Region 3
P.O. Box 45
Twin Cities, MN 55111
phone: 612-725-3563
*Regional U.S. Fish & Wildlife Service
contact for inquiries regarding laws
pertaining to endangered and
threatened species of wild fauna and
wild flora; covers IL, IN, IA, MI, MN,
MO, OH, WI.*

Regional Director
U.S. Fish & Wildlife Service, Region 6
P.O. Box 25486
Denver Federal Bldg.
Denver, CO 80225
phone: 303-236-7920
*Regional U.S. Fish & Wildlife Service
contact for inquiries regarding laws
pertaining to endangered and
threatened species of wild fauna and*

wild flora; covers CO, KS, MT, NE, ND, SD, UT, WY.

Regional Director
U.S. Fish & Wildlife Service, Region 2
P.O. Box 1306
Albuquerque, NM 87103
phone: 505-766-2321
Regional U.S. Fish & Wildlife Service contact for inquiries regarding laws pertaining to endangered and threatened species of wild fauna and wild flora; covers AZ, NM, OK, TX.

Regional Director
U.S. Fish & Wildlife Service, Region 1
911 N.E. 11th Ave.
Portland, OR 97232-4181
phone: 503-231-2234
Regional U.S. Fish & Wildlife Service contact for inquiries regarding laws pertaining to endangered and threatened species of wild fauna and wild flora; covers CA, HI, ID, NV, OR, WA, American Samoa, Marinas Islands, Guam.

Regional Director
U.S. Fish & Wildlife Service, Region 7
1100 E. Tudor Rd.
Anchorage, AK 99503
phone: 907-786-3542
Regional U.S. Fish & Wildlife Service contact for inquiries regarding laws pertaining to endangered and threatened species of wild fauna and wild flora; covers Alaska.

ENESCO

(see also COLLECTIBLES [MOD-ERN]; COLLECTIBLES [MODERN], Ornaments [Enesco])

Experts

Steve Johnson
4003 Jefferson St.
Sioux City, IA 51108
Consultant to "The Official Price Guide to Pottery and Porcelain."

Juarine Woolridge
418 Country Lane
Mount Vernon, MO 65712-1906
Consultant to "The Official Price Guide to Pottery and Porcelain."

ENGINES

(see also BOATS, Engines; FARM MACHINERY; LAWN MOWERS; MAYTAG; MODELS; STEAM-OPERATED, Models & Equipment; TRACTORS; WASHING MACHINES)

Collectors

Tom Copper
Tom's Small Engines
1416 Ralapen St.
Roxboro, NC 27573-4232
phone: 910-599-6908
e-mail: tcopper@roxboro.net
Internet: http://bbs.roxboro.net/tcopper/index.htm
Collector of Maytag, Briggs &

Stratton and other engines; repairs, rebuilds, and restores most small engines; locates parts and/or related supplies and services.

Ed & Karen Laginess
2211 W. Sigler Rd.
Carleton, MI 48117-9581
phone: 313-654-9269
fax: 313-241-9403
Wants to buy unusual flywheel engines and old spark plugs.

Experts

Charles Chiarchiaro
Owls Head Transportation Museum
Rte. 73 Box 277
Owls Head, ME 04854
phone: 207-594-4418
fax: 207-594-4410
e-mail: ohtmuseum@aol.com
Mr. Chiarchiaro is an expert in pre-1910 internal combustion and steam engines, and related technologies.

Museums/Libraries

Rod Groenewold
Antique Gas & Steam Engine Museum, Inc.
Newsletter: Ignitor
2040 Santa Fe Ave.
Vista, CA 92083-1534
phone: 619-941-1791 or 800-587-2286
fax: 619-941-0690
40-acre living history museum focused on the period (1840-1950). Collections include historic agricultural and industrial equipment. Reference library on-site. Biennial Threshing Bee and Antique Engine Shows.

Periodicals

Erika Daileda
Wise Owl Worldwide Publications
Magazine: Model Engineers' Workshop
4314 West 238th St. - Dept. MACR
Torrance, CA 90505-4509
phone: 310-375-6258
fax: 310-375-0548
e-mail: wiseowl@sprintmail.com
A bi-monthly English publication; helps the amateur machinist get the most from his tools and equipment in the home engineering workshop.

Gasoline

Book Sellers

Alan C. King
King's Books
P.O. Box 86
Radnor, OH 43066-0086
Carries tractor and gas engine manuals.

Clubs/Associations

Mary Jane Holtzleiter, Sec.
Tri-State Gas Engine & Tractor Association, Inc.
11815 E. 850 S. 27
Hartford City, IN 47348
phone: 317-348-3597

Emilie & Wayne Williamson
Antique Steam & Gas Engine Club, Inc.
5199 Lee Acres Dr.
Boonville, IN 47601
phone: 812-925-7666

Charley Stark
Early Day Gas Engine & Tractor Association, Inc.
Newsletter: National, The
Rte. 2 Box 167A
Republic, MO 65738
phone: 417-732-7136
e-mail: edgeta@ave.net
Internet: http://www.ave.net/~edgeta/index.html
A national organization with 90 regional "Branches" interested in early gas engines and tractors.

Periodicals

Stemgas Publishing Co.
Magazine: Gas Engine Magazine
P.O. Box 328
Lancaster, PA 17608-0328
phone: 717-392-0733
fax: 717-392-1341
Internet: http://www.sitematrix.com/stemgas/
G.E.M. is the leading magazine for antique tractor and gas engine collectors; articles, ads, auctions, models, Maytag gas engines, restoration tips, histories, auctions, suppliers, parts, etc.; published monthly.

Suppliers

Bill Starkey
Starbolt Engine Supplies
3403 Buckeystown Pike
Adamstown, MD 21710
phone: 301-874-2821 or 301-694-6840
Sells parts for old gas engines; mail order only; open evenings until 9 p.m.

Simpson Motors
3708 S. Amherst Hwy.
Madison Heights, VA 24572
phone: 804-929-4468
New and used Maytag engine parts, restoration supplies, engines, etc.; rebuild, restore, supply parts for early gasoline engines that powered early washing machines; no appliance parts; makes parts not otherwise available.

Steam

Clubs/Associations

Conrad Milster
International Stationary Steam Engine Society
Newsletter: ISSES Bulletin
178 Emerson Place
Brooklyn, NY 11205-3803
phone: 718-857-9524 or 718-636-3694
Members interested in the history, documentation and preservation of stationary steam engines throughout the world; publishes a quarterly "Bulletin" and an annual "Journal."

Frances Zollars
Tri-State Historical Steam Engine Association
RD 2 Box 173A
Monongahela, PA 15063
phone: 412-483-5144 or 412-348-8210

Collectors

Bruce Cynar
10023 St. Clair's Retreat
Fort Wayne, IN 46825
phone: 219-489-5004
Wants steam engines (small but not toys), steam whistles, and steam gauges.

Museums/Libraries

Dixie Gun Work's Old Car & Steam Engine Museum
P.O. Box 130
Union City, TN 38261
phone: 901-885-0561

EPHEMERA

(see ADVERTISING COL-LECTIBLES; PAPER COL-LECTIBLES)

EQUIPMENT

(see MACHINERY & EQUIPMENT)

ERECTOR SETS

(see TOYS, Construction Sets [Erector])

EROTICA

(see also BATHING BEAUTIES, Nudies & Naughties; PIN-UP ART; PLAYBOY ITEMS; STRIPTEASE)

Auction Services

Robert Bessette
Green Dragon Arts
P.O. Box 588
Burlington, VT 05402-0588
phone: 802-862-1930
Conducts auctions specializing in the sale of early erotica from 18th century to present; also underground adult comics and men's girlie magazines.

Gail Wolpin, ISA
Phoebus Auction Gallery
14-16 E. Mellen St.
Hampton, VA 23663
phone: 757-722-9210
fax: 757-723-2280
e-mail: bwelch@phoebusauction.com
Internet: http://www.phoebusauction.com
Conducts auctions of antiques, collectibles, estates, furniture, decorative and fine arts, etc.

Collectors

Ivan Gilbert, MD
A.A. Miran Art & Books
921 Eastwind Dr., Ste. 104
Westerville, OH 43081

Bizarre Lady
P.O. Box 1252
Dayton, OH 45401
Wants to buy old erotica.

Mitch O'Connell
6425 N. Newgard
Chicago, IL 60626
*Wants oddball and offbeat sexy and
sexist kitsch and tasteless; artwork,
gag gifts, figurines, postcards, photos,
magazines, etc.*

Hasco Enterprises
P.O. Box 857
Wynne, AR 72396-0857
*Wants erotica, semi-nude: real photos
featuring sexy lingerie, men
magazines showing sexy women.*

Dealers

Edward Swain
P.O. Box 7420
Wayne, PA 19087
phone: 610-688-2882
*Erotic fine art: American, European,
Asian; bought and sold.*

Edward Swain
Edward Swain Erotic Fine Art
P.O. Box 7420
Wayne, PA 19087-7420
phone: 610-688-2882
fax: 610-688-2882
*Buys and sells all types of erotic fine
art and artifacts: American paintings,
drawings, prints, sculpture and
photos; European and Asian artists of
the 18th-20th C.; no catalogs at this
time but photos of specific items upon
request.*

Miss Naomi Antiques & Erotica
Box 1421
Lutz, FL 33549-1421
phone: 813-949-3412
fax: 813-949-3148
*Wants erotic art, all mediums, for wall
or display.*

ESTATE JEWELRY

(see GEMS & JEWELRY)

EXIT GLOBES

Collectors

Michael Bruner
2615 Echo Lane
Ortonville, MI 48462
phone: 810-627-6351
*Wants exit globes in all style, shapes
and colors.*

EXONUMIA

(see COINS; BADGES; BOOKS,
Reference [Exonumia]; FRATERNAL
ORGANIZATION ITEMS; MEDALS,
ORDERS & DECORATIONS;
POLITICAL COLLECTIBLES;
TOKENS; VETERAN ITEMS)

EXPOSITIONS

(see WORLD'S FAIRS & EXPOSI-
TIONS)

EYE RELATED ITEMS

(see also MEDICAL, DENTAL &
PHARMACEUTICAL; OPTICAL
ITEMS)

Eyecups

Collectors

W.T. Atkinson
P.O. Box 10402
Wilmington, NC 28405-3792
Wants to buy unusual eyecups.

Ken Jermac
215 Westridge Ct.
Chapin, SC 29036
phone: 803-345-9780
*Buys and trades eyecups and eye
related items.*

Dealers

Doris K. Bagwell, R.N.
Bagwell Antiques
5607 Concord Dr.
Jackson, MS 39211-4239
phone: 601-956-3508
*Wants to buy eye wash baths (eye
cups).*

Eyeglasses

Appraisers

J. William Rosenthal, MD, ISA
3434 Prytania St., Ste. 250
New Orleans, LA 70115-3551
phone: 504-891-1988 or 504-947-3332
fax: 504-947-2593
*Buys, sells, specializes in and
appraises visual aids; author of
"Spectacles and Other Visual Aids: A
History and Guide to Collecting."*

Collectors

Charles Letocha
444 Rathton Rd.
York, PA 17403
phone: 717-846-0428
fax: 717-854-9728
*Wants to buy antique spectacles,
opthalmoscopes, spectacle catalogs,
trade cards, etc.*

W.H. Marshall
P.O. Box 1023
Melrose, FL 32666-1023
*Wants to buy eye related antiques,
optic trade signs, advertising,
memorabilia, rare glasses, etc.*

D & L
P.O. Box 1411
Cuyahoga Falls, OH 44224
*Wants to buy pre-1935 eyeglasses of
all kinds and quantities; send photos
and/or descriptions.*

John Boggs
P.O. Box 66833
Seattle, WA 98166-0833
*Wants to buy eyeglasses from the
1960s or older including unused
frames and especially round lens wire
rim; minimum seven.*

Dealers

Gail Busche
Archangel Antiques
334 East Ninth St.
New York, NY 10003-7924
phone: 212-260-9313
*Buying antique buttons, cuff links, eye
glasses, and vintage lighters; always
seeking fine examples such as enamel
Deco and Art Nouveau.*

Museums/Libraries

Optometry Museum, The
338 W. Tenth Ave.
Columbus, OH 43210
phone: 614-292-2788
*Large collection of eyeglasses once
owned by famous people; also
spectacle styles on display as well as
related items.*

**Here are some tips
when contacting
someone listed in this
book:**

**When requesting
information about a
particular item, include a
description (material,
dimensions, maker's
mark, model number,
etc.) and a photo, sketch,
or photocopy of the item
in question.** ■

**Always ask if there are
charges for samples or
for the services
requested.** ■

**When writing, please be
sure to include a Large
(#10 business size)
Self-Addressed and
Stamped Envelope
(LSASE) if requesting a
reply or the return of
photographs.** ■

**Never call collect unless
otherwise directed.
When calling, be
considerate of time zone
differences and always
ask if the party you are
calling has time to talk.
When leaving an
answering machine
message, always instruct
the party to call you
back collect.** ■

FAIRIES

(see ELVES; TOOTH FAIRY)

FAIRINGS

Experts

Mel & Barbara Alpern
14 Carter Rd.
West Orange, NJ 07052
phone: 201-731-9427
Advisor to "Warman's Antiques & Collectibles Price Guide."

Janice & Richard Vogel
4720 SE Fort King St.
Ocala, FL 34470-1501
phone: 352-694-5776
fax: 352-694-7330

FAIRS

(see WORLD'S FAIRS & EXPOSITIONS)

FAIRY LAMPS

(see LAMPS & LIGHTING, Miniature; NIGHT LIGHTS)

FAN CLUBS

(see also COMIC BOOKS; CHARACTER COLLECTIBLES; MOVIE MEMORABILIA; PERSONALITIES; SCIENCE FICTION; TELEVISION SHOWS & MEMORABILIA; SPORTS COLLECTIBLES)

Clubs/Associations

Bridget Wilkinson
Fans Across the World
Newsletter: Fans Across the World Newsletter
17 Monosa, 29 Avenue Rd.
Tottenham
London N15 5JF, U.K.
International club interested in promotion contact between fandoms.

Tenata Lima
International Collectors Friends Club
Magazine: Radical Collectors
Nossa Sra. Copacabana J089 Apt. 1101
P.O. Box 44028
Rio De Jan. 22062-970 Brazil
International club of fans and fan clubs.

Linda Kay
National Association of Fan Clubs
Newsletter: Fan Club Monitor
P.O. Box 7487
Burbank, CA 91510-7487
phone: 818-763-3280
fax: 818-752-4848
e-mail: lknafc@aol.com
An international organization dedicated to promoting fan clubs from around the world in all fields of entertainment; has directory of over 2,000 fan clubs.

Periodicals

Harry Hopkins, Pub.
FANDATA Publications
Directory: FANDOM Directory
7761 Asterella Ct.
Springfield, VA 22152-3133
phone: 703-913-5575 or 888-FAN-DATA
fax: 703-913-5575
e-mail: fandata@aol.com
Internet: http://members.aol.com/fandata
Fandom Directory (R) lists over 20,000 fans, collectors, dealers, stores, clubs, and conventions worldwide: science fiction, TV shows, Star Trek, etc.; now in its 17th annual edition; your listing published free of charge upon request.

J.A. Bateman
Directory: Fan Resource Directory
P.O. Box 159008
Nashville, TN 37215
phone: 615-333-3282
An annual guide to helping fans find anything and everything needed for fannish projects - electronic parts, costume findings, fanzines, clubs, etc.; quarterly updates.

Hollywood Movie Archives
Directory: Fan Club Directory
P.O. Box 1566
Apple Valley, CA 92307-0030
phone: 619-242-8569 or 800-596-2350
How to start a fan club, where to join, movie associations, movie & TV fan clubs, authorized country music fan clubs, where to write movie & TV stars, teens, soap stars, rock and rap stars; where to write for stars' autographs.

FANS

Collectors

Lowell J. Wagner
Sunni-hill Farm Antiques
Waconia, MN 55387-9562
phone: 612-544-4543 or 612-442-4036
fax: 612-544-9283
Wants to buy hot air fans; also full size hot air engines, models and toys; may be known as Stirling engines.

Dealers

Phil Massie
Wind Wizards, The
1924 Hilton Ave.
Dover, PA 17315-3834
phone: 717-764-2359
Wants antique electric fans with brass blades, related advertising and ephemera, especially metal signs, books and publications on electricity and pre-1900 electrical lighting.

Hand

Clubs/Associations

Mrs. J.D. Milligan
Fan Circle International
Magazine: Fans
Cronk-Y-Voddy, Rectory Rd.
Coltishall
Norwich NR12 7HF, U.K.
A worldwide society to promote the interest and knowledge in all aspects of fan collecting.

Colin Johnson
Fan Association of North America
Journal: FANA Quarterly
6138 Deacon Dr.
Windermere, FL 34786-8936
phone: 610-799-2072
Promotes fans as art objects and historical artifacts; supports fan research; guides members and non-members in fan collecting; encourages fan exhibits; has active grants program; holds annual conferences with lectures and displays.

East Bay Fan Guild
Newsletter: East Bay Fan Guile Newsletter
P.O. Box 1054
El Cerrito, CA 94530

Collectors

Gretchen Walberg
P.O. Box 101
Sunbury, PA 17801-0101
phone: 717-286-6225
fax: 717-286-6229
e-mail: info@fancards.com
Wants hand fans with depictions: American historical, ballooning, printed or painted, World's Fair, etc.

Dorothy Fowler
201 Palmetto Court W.
Saint Simons Island, GA 31522

Cynthia Fendel
Dallas, TX 75287
e-mail: Fancollec@aol.com
Wants to buy fans: folding, advertising, commemorative, novelty, etc.; send photo or photocopy and price; Fan Association of North America (FANA) representative on CompuServe.

Experts

Mary S. Frazier, Cur.
132 Middle St.
Braintree, MA 02184-4841
phone: 617-843-5091
e-mail: r-m-s-frazier@worldnet.att.net
Internet: http://angelfire.com/ma/wsb
Wrote only book on American hand fans; lectures extensively; author of "Hunt and Allen Fans."

Wendy Blue
2118 Van Buren Dr.
Whitehall, PA 18052
phone: 610-799-2072
Wants to buy any type of good quality hand fan: fashion accessories (ivory, tortoise, folding, cockade, etc.); advertising, historical, World's Fair & Expositions souvenirs; good graphics & condition; send photo & description & SASE.

Grace R. Grayson
2133 Pine Knoll Dr. #16
Walnut Creek, CA 94595-2187
phone: 510-256-0949
A FAN-atic! Collects antique and contemporary fans; European, Oriental, ethnic, etc.; also fan related advertising and literature; lecturer, writer.

Museums/Libraries

Mary S. Frazier, Cur.
Braintree Historical Society
31 Tenny Rd.
Braintree, MA 02184
phone: 617-848-1640
Collection of approximately 400 hand fans; primarily American.

Colonial Williamsburg
P.O. Box C
Williamsburg, VA 23185
phone: 804-229-1000
Specializes in early American furniture and the decorative arts.

John & Mable Ringling Museum of Art
5401 Bayshore Rd.
Sarasota, FL 34243
phone: 941-359-5700
fax: 941-359-5745
e-mail: ringling@concentric.net
Holds collection of over 150 fans.

Repair Services

T. W. DeLeo
Cereus, Inc.
31 Brook Lane
Cortlandt Manor, NY 10566
phone: 914-737-3769 or 914-739-0754
fax: 914-737-4333
Specializes in the conservation of hand fans: folding, pleated, brise, fixed; European or Oriental.

Mechanical

(see also ELECTRICITY RELATED ITEMS)

Clubs/Associations

Nancy J. Tausssig
American Fan Collectors Association
Newsletter: Fan Collector Newsletter, The
P.O. Box 5473
Sarasota, FL 34277-5473
phone: 941-388-5513
fax: 941-388-2053
e-mail: sandersant@aol.com
Interested in water powered, steam, electric, and other types of mechanical fans; the AFCA sponsors an annual convention and publishes its newsletter for 400 members.

Collectors

Kevin Shail
30 Old Middle Rd.
Brookfield, CT 06804
phone: 203-775-7017
Interested in old mechanical fans, especially non-electric fans such as those driven by hot-air (kerosene), water power, or wind-ups.

Rick Padron
1005 E. Idlewild Ave.
Tampa, FL 33604-6831
phone: 813-238-8535 or 800-320-FANS
Serious collector wants to buy pre-1920 fans.

Hilly Griffin
P.O. Box 877
Grenada, MS 38901
phone: 601-675-8270 or 601-226-3032
fax: 601-226-3439
Wants odd or unusual looking fans.

Michael Breedlove
P.O. Box 804
South Bend, IN 46624-0804
phone: 219-272-1231 or 800-858-3267

Jim Daggs
617 Main Street
Ackley, IA 50601
phone: 515-847-2623
fax: 515-847-3588
Author of "A Scrapbook of Fans" (1997).

Steve Cunningham
3200 Ashland Dr.
Bedford, TX 76021-6502
phone: 817-267-9851 or 800-991-0165
fax: 817-991-0166
e-mail: cunning@cyberramp.net
Buying antique electric table fans with brass blades and brass cages; also very old ornate ceiling fans (paddle type); especially interested in very old antique electric motors; also wants books and catalogs on these items.

Mike Roberts
4416 Foxfire Way
Fort Worth, TX 76123-6704
phone: 817-294-2133
Wants to buy unusual fans; also motors, parts, toys, or anything fan related.

Mike Roberts
4416 Foxfire Way
Fort Worth, TX 76133-6704
phone: 817-294-2133
Wants to buy any odd, unusual fan in any condition; also wants motors, parts, toys and anything fan related.

Roger Anthony
23214 Whispering Willow Dr.
Spring, TX 77373-6232
phone: 281-353-4576
Wants to buy pre-1912 antique mechanical fans; electrical fans with brass guard and brass blades; battery powered and bipolar (exposed coil) fans; unusual oscillators (flaps, gyro & vane fans, etc.); water powered and wind-up fans.

Dealers

Normand Mainville
Machine Age
354 Congress St.
Boston, MA 02210
phone: 617-482-0048

Donald E. Taussig
Sanders' Antique Mall
22 N. Lemon Ave.
Sarasota, FL 34236-5711
phone: 941-366-0400
fax: 941-388-2053
e-mail: sandersant@aol.com
Buys, sells, restores ceiling and desk fans pre-1900 through 1940s: electric, hot-air, water-powered, etc.

Experts

Howard Hazelcorn
6731 Ashley Ct.
Sarasota, FL 34241-9696
phone: 941-921-1815
Specializes in early (1889-1905) battery type electric fans.

Scott MacClymonds
Classic Fans & Lighting
10525 Airline Dr.
Houston, TX 77037
phone: 713-448-4739 or 713-697-0069
fax: 713-448-0189
Wants to buy unusual pre-1939 electric, water, kerosene power fans with ornate castings, brass blades and cages, fancy ornamentation, unusual mechanisms, ceiling or desk.

Kurt House
Fan Man, The
218 Country Wood
San Antonio, TX 78216-1607
phone: 210-490-2433
fax: 210-490-3433
Author of "Antique Mechanical Fans"; repairs, sells/buys, antique mechanical fans including electrical, fuel-driven, etc.; specializes in the restoration of antique fans and the manufacturing of fans and fan parts; wants fan information.

Museums/Libraries

Olde Fan Museum, The
1914 Abrams Parkway
Dallas, TX 75214
phone: 214-826-7700
Over 600 mechanical fans of all sizes are on display.

Repair Services

Bud Stasa
A-One Electric Company
1032 East Harry
Wichita, KS 67211
phone: 316-267-5646
Antique fan restorations: motor winding, speed coils, armatures, rewiring, polishing, plating, cage and blade repair or reconstruction, bronze bearings, bead blasting, etc.

Sidney Lamb
1501 Kesser Dr.
Plano, TX 75025
phone: 972-517-4526
Motor rewinding; old motors and choke coils rewound.

FANTASY

(see HORROR; SCIENCE FICTION)

FARM COLLECTIBLES

(see also CORN COLLECTIBLES; ENGINES; FARM MACHINERY; ANIMAL COLLECTIBLES, Horses; SACKS; TOYS, Diecast; TOYS, Farm; WATCH FOBS, Farm Related; TRACTORS; WEANERS, Calf & Cow; WINDMILL COLLECTIBLES)

Collectors

Phyllis Moffet
P.O. Box 200
Modesto, IL 62667-0200
phone: 217-439-7358
Interested in buying farm items such as handheld corn shellers, horse hay forks, etc.

Gary Van Hoozer, Ed.
812 N. 3rd St.
Tarkio, MO 64491-1101
phone: 816-736-4528
Collects and specializes in farm toys.

Dealers

Stephen G. Del Sordo
Principia Group
305 Oakley St.
Cambridge, MD 21613
phone: 410-228-8934
fax: 410-221-8061
e-mail: delsordo@shore.intercom.net
A cultural resource management/ historic preservation firm that has contracts to locate, provide, authenticate artifacts for museums and collectors; areas of expertise include architecture, industry, domestic, agriculture, and maritime.

Experts

Philip C. Whitney
303 Fisher Rd.
Fitchburg, MA 01420-1548
phone: 508-342-1350
Specializes in farm tools.

Museums/Libraries

Esther Munroe Smith, Lib.
Billings Farm & Museum
P.O. Box 489
Woodstock, VT 05091
phone: 802-457-2355
Museum of farm life & technology of the late 19th century; darying, haying, general store, ice cutting, apple orchard, etc.

New York State Historical Association and The Farmers' Museum, Inc., The
P.O. Box 800
Cooperstown, NY 13326
phone: 607-547-2593 or 607-547-2533

Landis Valley Farm Museum
2451 Kissel Hill Rd.
Lancaster, PA 17601
phone: 717-569-0401

Carroll County Farm Museum
500 S. Center St.
Westminster, MD 21157-5615
phone: 410-848-7775 or 410-876-2667
fax: 410-876-8544
Internet: http://www.carr.lib.md.us/carroll/carroll.htm
Focuses on Victoriana in rural America.

Ron & Lois Smith
Neverrest Farm Family Museum
1911 Harper Rd.
Mason, MI 48854-9260
phone: 517-676-9391
Located on a working farm and open on a "by chance" or by appointment.

David Huey
Living History Farms
2600 N.W. 111th St.
Urbandale, IA 50322
phone: 515-278-2400 or 515-278-5286
fax: 515-278-9808
A 600-acre, open-air museum specializing in the past 300 years of Midwest agriculture; interpreters in period clothing work out of authentic buildings with historically accurate tools and machinery to recreate routines of early farmers.

W. Vernon, Dir.
National Agricultural Center & Hall of Fame
630 Hall of Fame Dr.
Bonner Springs, KS 66012
phone: 913-721-1075 or 913-721-3355
fax: 913-721-1075
Collection of a wide range of farming and farm family related items: plows, tools, implements, art, dishes, schoolhouse items, etc.

Periodicals

Newspaper: Country Wagon Journal,
The
600 Otterhold Rd.
P.O. Box 331
West Milford, NJ 07480
*Produced by folks who enjoy country
values and like to work the soil;
enjoyable articles and earthy tips.*

Richard Van Vleck
Greybird Publishing
Newsletter: Scientific, Medical &
Mechanical Antiques
P.O. Box 412
Taneytown, MD 21787
phone: 301-447-2680
e-mail: smma@fred.net
Internet: http://www.bestware.net/smma/
*For collectors, dealers and
researchers; recent articles include
reaper knife grinders, grain cradles,
early cow milkers, hand corn shellers
and rope machines; free ads for
subscribers.*

Gary Van Hoozer, Ed.
Magazine: Farm Antiques News
812 N. 3rd St.
Tarkio, MO 64491-1101
phone: 816-736-4528
*For collectors, restorers, traders of all
types/sizes of old (pre-1950) farm
items: tractors, horse & other
machinery, toys, etc.*

Repro. Sources

McLanahan Country
217 Rockwell Rd.
Wilmington, NC 28405

Cast Iron Seats

Clubs/Associations

John D. Friedly, Editor
Cast Iron Seat Collectors Association
Newsletter: CISCA Newsletter
P.O. Box 14
Ionia, MO 65335
phone: 816-285-3451
*Club for collectors of cast iron seats
from farm implements and machinery;
newsletter contains articles, notices of
meets and shows, auction sale results,
collector profiles.*

Collectors

Williams
P.O. Box 17
Rockville, MO 64780
phone: 816-598-2595
*Wants to buy implement seats, die cut
or embossed.*

Haying Tools

Collectors

Robert Rauhauser
RR 2 Box 766
Thomasville, PA 17364-9622
*Buys haying tools (forks, carriers &
knives), corn items (shellers, planter*

lids, etc.), hog oilers, wrenches, horse
mower tool box lids, etc.

Hog Oilers

Collectors

Robert Rauhauser
RR 2 Box 766
Thomasville, PA 17364-9622
*Author of "Good-Bye Mr. Louse - Hog
Oiler Patents 1903 to 1995."*

Literature

Collectors

Clarence L. Goodburn
101 W. Main
Madelia, MN 56062-1439
phone: 507-642-3281
fax: 507-642-3281
*Wants to buy sales literature,
calendars, magazines, hardback
books, etc. about farm tractors and
equipment, crawler tractors, heavy
construction and mining equipment,
and trucks.*

David Yates
321 West Church St.
Genoa, IL 60135
phone: 815-784-3369
*Wants to buy farm sales literature, all
brands.*

FARM MACHINERY

(see also AUTOMOBILIA;
ENGINES; FARM COLLECTIBLES;
HORSE-DRAWN VEHICLES;
MACHINERY & EQUIPMENT;
STEAM-OPERATED, Models &
Equipment; TOYS, Farm; TRAC-
TORS)

Auction Services

Blaine Renzel
Renzel Auctions
P.O. Box 222
Emigsville, PA 17318
phone: 717-764-6412
*Specializes in the sale of old and new
farm machinery and equipment.*

Iron Horse Auction Co.
519 South Hancock St.
P.O. Box 1267
Rockingham, NC 28379
phone: 919-997-2248
fax: 919-895-1530
*Conducts auctions specializing in the
sale of antique steam engines, tractors
and farm related items.*

Bill Dean
Waverly Sale Co.
P.O. Box 355
Waverly, IA 50677
phone: 319-352-3177
*Specializes in the sale of old and new
farm machinery and equipment.*

Clubs/Associations

Susan Knaub
Early American Steam Engine & Old
Equipment Society
P.O. Box 652
Red Lion, PA 17356
phone: 717-244-2912
*Interested in old steam and gas
powered equipment, especially
engines, tractors and other farm
machinery.*

David Semmel
Antique Engine, Tractor & Toy Club,
Inc.
Newsletter: AETTC Newsletter
5731 Paradise Rd.
Slatington, PA 18080-4028
phone: 610-767-4768
*Organized in 1986 with over 500
members; dedicated to preservation
and enjoyment of old time farm
engines, tractors and related toys;
newsletter three times per year.*

David Schnakenberg
Farm Machinery Advertising Collectors
10108 Tamarack Drive
Vienna, VA 22182-1843

Misc. Services

Austin Farms Salvage
Rte. 4 Box 241
Butler, MO 64730
phone: 816-679-4080
fax: 816-679-6488
*Send $20 for a directory listing
names, addresses, phone numbers of
800 used agri-parts yards; for new
used and antique farm equipment.*

Museums/Libraries

Ontario Agricultural Museum
P.O. Box 38
Milton
Ontario L9T 2Y3 Canada

Bucks County Historical Society
Newsletter: Penny Lots
84 S. Pine St.
Doylestown, PA 18901-4930
phone: 215-345-0210
fax: 215-230-0823
Internet: http://www.libertynet.org:80/
~bchs
*Operates three Nat. Historical
Landmarks; Mercer Museum has over
50,000 tools of Early American
trades/crafts; Spruance Library has
research material on trades & crafts;
Fonthill Museum is a concrete castle
laden with tiles & treasures.*

Jim Stafslien
Makoti Threshers Museum
P.O. Box 94
Makoti, ND 58756
phone: 701-726-5693 or 701-726-5622
*Show each year first full weekend in
October; come see antique machines
run.*

W. Vernon, Dir.
National Agricultural Center & Hall of
Fame
630 Hall of Fame Dr.
Bonner Springs, KS 66012
phone: 913-721-1075 or 913-721-3355
fax: 913-721-1075
*Collection of a wide range of farming
and farm family related items: plows,
tools, implements, art, dishes,
schoolhouse items, etc.*

Periodicals

Suzanne Wright
Kelsey Publishing Ltd.
Magazine: Stationary Engine
Kelsey House, 77 High St.
Beckenham
Kent BR3 1AN, U.K.
phone: 0181-6583531
fax: 0181-6508035
*A 40-page illustrated monthly
magazine dealing with all types of gas
engines, history, information, news
and views, classified, "Helpline",
identification assistance, restorations,
readers' offers.*

Suzanne Wright
Kelsey Publishing Ltd.
Magazine: Farm & Horticultural
Equipment Collector
Kelsey House, 77 High St.
Beckenham
Kent BR3 1AN, U.K.
phone: 0181-6583531
fax: 0181-6508035
*A 16-page bi-monthly illustrated
magazine solely devoted to farm
equipment and implement collecting;
packed with information, pictures;
plus articles covering barn machinery,
sawing machinery, garden machinery,
hand tools, etc.*

Gerald Lestz
Stemgas Publishing Co.
Magazine: Iron Men Album, The
P.O. Box 328
Lancaster, PA 17608-0328
phone: 717-392-0733
fax: 717-392-1341
Internet: http://www.sitematrix.com/
stemgas/
*Published six times per year; carries
articles, ads, auctions for steam
traction machinery: tractors,
threshers, steam engines, etc.*

Stemgas Publishing Co.
Directory: Steam & Gas Engine Show
Directory
P.O. Box 328
Lancaster, PA 17608-0328
phone: 717-392-0733
fax: 717-392-1341
Internet: http://www.sitematrix.com/
stemgas/
*The annual show directory guides old-
time farming enthusiasts to over 900
shows in the U.S. and Canada; $8
postpaid.*

Stemgas Publishing Co.
Directory: Farm Museum Directory
P.O. Box 328
Lancaster, PA 17608-0328
phone: 717-392-0733
fax: 717-392-1341
Internet: http://www.sitematrix.com/
  stemgas/
  *Over 200 listings, ads and pictures of
  farm museums and exhibits in 40
  states and Canada; published in
  cooperation with The Association of
  Living Historical Farm and
  Agricultural Museums (ALHFAM).*

Christina Gargano
Heartland Communications Group, Inc.
Magazine: Farmers Hot Line &
  Manufacturer's Editions
1003 Central Ave.
Fort Dodge, IA 50501
phone: 800-247-2000
fax: 515-574-2233
Internet: http://www.hlipublishing.com
  *REgional and state editions are edited
  for buyers and sellers of farm
  equipment.*

Christina Gargano
Heartland Communications Group, Inc.
Magazine: Farmers Hot Line Parts
  Edition
1003 Central Ave.
Fort Dodge, IA 50501
phone: 800-247-2000
fax: 515-574-2233
Internet: http://www.hlipublishing.com
  *Directory for the largest selection and
  the best prices of new, used, rebuilt
  parts and attachments.*

Christina Gargano
Heartland Communications Group, Inc.
Magazine: Hot Line Farm Equipment
  Guide
1003 Central Ave.
Fort Dodge, IA 50501
phone: 800-247-2000
fax: 515-574-2233
Internet: http://www.hlipublishing.com
  *The only monthly locating and pricing
  guide for farm equipment.*

Shawn Rogers
Magazine: Rusty Iron Monthly
P.O. Box 342
Sandwich, IL 60548
phone: 815-496-9267
  *Focuses on the old iron marketplace:
  early gas and steam engines, tractors
  and related equipment.*

Kurt Aumann, Editor
Magazine: Belt Pulley, The
P.O. Box 83
Nokomis, IL 62075
phone: 217-594-2825
  *Features farm machinery, all makes
  and models, 1900-1950; antique
  tractors, farm machinery and
  equipment; bi-monthly.*

Gary Van Hoozer, Ed.
Magazine: Farm Antiques News
812 N. 3rd St.
Tarkio, MO 64491-1101
phone: 816-736-4528
  *For collectors, restorers, traders of all
  types/sizes of old (pre-1950) farm
  items: tractors, horse & other
  machinery, toys, etc.*

International Harvester

Clubs/Associations

Allen Dummler, Mem. Sec.
International Harvester Collectors
Newsletter: Harvester Highlights
310 Busse Hwy., Ste. 250
Park Ridge, IL 60068-3251
phone: 847-823-8612
fax: 847-683-0207
e-mail: ihcclub@aol.com
  *An association of International
  Harvester equipment and memorabilia
  collectors and enthusiasts; sanctions
  regional chapters.*

Salesman Samples

Collectors

Allan Hoover
2133 14th St.
Peru, IL 61354-1670
phone: 815-223-1159 or 815-223-1160
fax: 815-223-1499
  *Wants samples of walking plows, hay
  mowers, hay rakes, balers, cultivators,
  binders, reapers, windmills, silos,
  pitch forks, etc.*

FASHION

(see CLOTHING & ACCESSORIES)

FAST FOOD COLLECTIBLES

(see also FOOD COLLECTIBLES;
GLASSES, Drinking; PREMIUMS;
RESTAURANT COLLECTIBLES)

Clubs/Associations

Jeff Escue
Fast Food Toy Club of Northern Illinois
164 Larchmont Ln.
Bloomingdale, IL 60108
phone: 708-307-7320
  *Buying fast food toys and related
  collectibles, i.e. boxes toys are given
  out in, every company's toys wanted
  from ARBYs to WHITE CASTLE;
  include SASE with inquiries; all
  letters answered.*

Dealers

William M. Poe
POE-pourri
220 Dominica Circle E.
Niceville, FL 32578-4085
phone: 904-897-4163
fax: 904-987-2606
e-mail: McPoes@aol.com
  *Buys, sells, and trades; specializes in
  McDonald's; buys old McDonald's
  collections and collections of PEZ and
  Smurfs; publishes 80-page catalog of*

*All fast Food Toys; $3 refundable with
first order.*

Richard Eymann
2619 E. Lynne Ln.
Phoenix, AZ 85040-4724
phone: 602-243-7064
e-mail: richarde@getnet.com
  *Buy, sell, trade fast food toys; most
  restaurants; some foreign toys; send
  SASE for list.*

Experts

Ken Clee
P.O. Box 11412
Philadelphia, PA 19111-0412
phone: 215-722-1979
  *Author of "Tomart's Price Guide to
  Kids Meal Collectibles."*

David Stone
2773 Curtis Way
Sacramento, CA 95818
phone: 916-451-0243

Periodicals

Nigel Thomas
Newsletter: Collecting Fast Food &
  Advertising Premiums
9 Ellacombe Rd.
Longwell Green
Bristol BS15 6BQ, U.K.
  *Published six times each year; covers
  British and mainland Europe
  promotions (no US), fast food and
  advertising premiums: McDonald's,
  Burger King, Pizza Hut, Kelloggs and
  many others.*

Newsletter: Fast Food Collectors
  Express, The
P.O. Box 221
Mayview, MO 64071-0221
phone: 816-584-6309
fax: 816-584-6259

Kentucky Fried Chicken

Museums/Libraries

Colonel Harland Sanders Museum
1441 Gardiner Lane
Louisville, KY 40232-2070
phone: 502-456-8607

McDonald's

Auction Services

John & Eleanor Larsen
523 3rd St.
Colusa, CA 95932-2716
phone: 916-458-4769
e-mail: elmcd@colusanet.com
  *A major McDonald's collector; also
  small mom-and-pop McDonald's
  specialty auction from time to time;
  looking for things with the old McD
  slash logo, McDonald's cigarette
  lighters and unusual or regional McD
  cups and glasses.*

Clubs/Associations

Bill & Pat Poe
Sunshine Chapter, McDonald's
  Collectors Club
Newsletter: Sunshine Express
220 Dominica Circle E.
Niceville, FL 32578-4085
phone: 904-897-4163
fax: 904-987-2606
e-mail: McPoes@aol.com
  *Membership is open to all; send SASE
  for membership form.*

Jeanne Bruce
Music City McDonald's Collectors Club
11 Burton Hills Blvd #256
Nashville, TN 37215-6103

Linda Gegorski, Sec.
McDonald's Collectors Club
Newsletter: McDonald's Collectors Club
  News
424 White Rd.
Fremont, OH 43420-1539
phone: 419-334-6377
  *For collectors of McDonald's
  memorabilia: Happy Meal toys and
  boxes, advertising, ephemera,
  glassware, pins, garments, etc.,
  quarterly newsletter.*

Ann Jackson
Metro St. Louis MacDonald's Collectors
  Club
4009 S. Park Dr.
Belleville, IL 62226-5346
phone: 618-234-2370

Collectors

Linda Gegorski
424 White Rd.
Fremont, OH 43420-1539
phone: 419-334-6377

Robert Brown
897 N. Kingwood Ct.
Holland, MI 49424
phone: 616-399-1256

Tenna Greenberg
5400 Waterbury Rd.
Des Moines, IA 50312
phone: 515-279-0741

Pat Longeran
P.O. Box 2262
Melrose Park, IL 60164
  *Major collector of McDonald's
  memorabilia.*

David Tuttle
329 Callan Ave.
Evanston, IL 60202
phone: 708-475-8676

Barbara Saitta
5407 W. Berenice Ave.
Chicago, IL 60641
phone: 312-736-3298

Meredith Williams
P.O. Box 633
Joplin, MO 64802-0633
phone: 417-624-2518 or 417-781-3855
  *Wants to buy McDonald's items:
  buttons, postcards, displays, old*

uniforms, kids clothes, Happy Meal boxes, toys, annual reports, old and rare comic books, signs, etc.

Dealers

Ron Abler
Certified McNut, The
5516 Maplefield Place
Alexandria, VA 22310-1891
phone: 703-971-9590 or 703-971-3524
e-mail: 73770.2110@compuserve.com
Buys/sells/trades McDonald's Happy Meal translites, point-of-purchase displays, cartons, and other items; specializes in MIP (mint in package) items; also interested in other fast food items; send LSASE for free buy/ sell/trade list.

Experts

Terry & Joyce Losonsky
Ski Publishing
7506 Summer Leave Lane
Columbia, MD 21046-2455
Authors of "Collectors Guide to McDonald's Happy Meal Boxes and Premiums"; available from author for $7 plus $2 postage.

Matt Welch
P.O. Box 30444
Tucson, AZ 85751
phone: 602-886-0505
fax: 602-722-3607
Wants to buy any unusual items from McDonald's restaurants: uniforms, glasses, paper items, souvenirs, pins & buttons, regional items, reports, books, displays, signage, items not made available to the public.

John & Eleanor Larsen
523 3rd St.
Colusa, CA 95932-2716
phone: 916-458-4769
e-mail: elmcd@colusanet.com
A major McDonald's collector; also small mom-and-pop McDonald's specialty auction from time to time; looking for things with the old McD slash logo, McDonald's cigarette lighters and unusual or regional McD cups and glasses.

Misc. Services

Laura Kleiner
McDonald's Archives
2010 E. Higgins Rd.
Elk Grove Village, IL 60007-2504
phone: 708-952-2348
Publishes "Happy Meal History"; offers a list of past promotions available for $5, updated quarterly.

Museums/Libraries

McDonald's Museum #1 Store, The
400 Lee St.
Des Plaines, IL 60016
phone: 708-297-5022
The first McDonald's; limited openings; across the street is an active

McDonald's restaurant with lots of memorabilia.

McDonald's World Corporate Headquarters, The Ray Crock Museum
McDonald's Plaza
Oak Brook, IL 60521

Periodicals

Meredith Williams
Newsletter: Collecting Tips Newsletter
P.O. Box 633
Joplin, MO 64802-0633
phone: 417-624-2518 or 417-781-3855
A monthly newsletter filled with up-to-date information about old and new McDonald's restaurant collectibles; also buy, sell and trade ads; send two stamps plus SASE for sample copy.

McDonald's (Happy Meal Toys)

Dealers

Jim Christoffel
409 Maple
Elburn, IL 60119
phone: 708-365-2914
Buys and sells McDonald's Happy Meal Toys.

Experts

Ron Abler
Certified McNut, The
5516 Maplefield Place
Alexandria, VA 22310-1891
phone: 703-971-9590 or 703-971-3524
e-mail: 73770.2110@compuserve.com
Publishes the "Pocket Guide to Happy Meat Toys 1975-1994", a loose-leaf pocket-sized checklist of all U.S. Happy Meal toys; updated annually.

Meredith Williams
P.O. Box 633
Joplin, MO 64802-0633
phone: 417-624-2518 or 417-781-3855
Author of "Tomart's Price Guide to McDonald's Happy Meal Collectibles - List - Pictures - Prices - All Happy Meals 1977-1995," $30.95 ppd. from the author.

McDonald's (Pins)

Clubs/Associations

Michael Fountaine
McDonald's International Pin Club
Newsletter: MIPC Newsletter
3587 Oak Ridge Dr.
Slatington, PA 18080-3247
phone: 800-647-2746 or 610-767-3988
fax: 610-767-7831
For collectors of McDonald's lapel pins; newsletter published two times per year; catalog of over 500 McDonald's pins for sale; sponsors shows to meet other collectors.

FASTENERS

Collectors

Mel Kirsner
726 Deal Ct.
San Diego, CA 92109
phone: 619-488-9805
Wants fasteners, bolts, nuts, washers or screw related items, pre-1950 only: advertising displays, promotional items, wooden boxes, metal tins, signs, catalogs, etc.

FEED SACKS

(see also TEXTILES; QUILTS)

Clubs/Associations

Jane Clark Stapel
Feedsack Club, The
Newsletter: Switches & Swatches
25 S Starr Ave., Apt. 16
Pittsburgh, PA 15202-3424
phone: 412-766-3996
e-mail: baglady111@aol.com
Members buy, sell, trade and exhibit feedsacks which are used to make quilts, vests, baby quilts, doll quilts, miniatures, clothing and for decorating.

Dealers

Sandra Sorgenfrie
R 2, Box 103
Winnebago, MN 56098
phone: 507-866-4688
Buys and sells feedsacks: flowers, stripes, plaids, doubles, triples.

Experts

Ron Bennett
R1 1870 Strong Rd.
Victor, NY 14564
phone: 716-657-7505
Collector of all kinds of fabric bags; sells original feed sack prints; charm packs of 36 all different prewashed and ironed cut to 6" x 6" swatches for $16 ppd.; also vests made of original feed and seed bags with logos, animals, etc.

Jane Clark Stapel
25 S Starr Ave., Apt. 16
Pittsburgh, PA 15202-3424
phone: 412-766-3996
e-mail: baglady111@aol.com
Specializes, lectures on feedsacks and their use in quilts, clothing and as decoration.

Repro. Sources

Lamb & Lanterns
902 N Walnut St.
Dover, OH 44622

Creative Signs
5640 S 92nd St.
Hales Corners, WI 53130

FENCE COLLECTIBLES

(see also BARBED WIRE)

Posts

Museums/Libraries

Post Rock Museum, The
202 West 1st St.
La Crosse, KS 67548
phone: 913-222-2719
Documents the quarrying and use of limestone for fence posts and buildings in the Midwest.

FIESTA

(see CERAMICS [AMERICAN DINNERWARE], Homer Laughlin/ Fiesta)

FIGURINES

(see also ANIMAL COLLECTIBLES; BATHING BEAUTIES; Nudies & Naughties; CERAMICS; COLLECTIBLES [MODERN]; REPAIR/ RESTORATION/CONSERVATION; TOYS, Action Figures; TOYS, Playsets)

Collectors

Warren C. Galbus
756 Kerry Dr.
Winona, MN 55987-2119
phone: 507-452-1135
fax: 507-452-1135
Collector of figurines by Wallace Berrie, Sillisculpts and Supersculpts, @C&W Berrie Co., 1966; wants all colors and sizes including miniatures 1974-1976; also American Greetings and Paulas from the same time period.

Matching Services

Advisory Replacement Service
901 W. Walnut Hill Ln., 5A-9
Irving, TX 75038
A replacement service for porcelain figurines: Swarovski, Sadek, Lladro, Lalique, Boehm, Hummel, Royal Doulton, etc.

Boehm

Appraisers

Stephen van Cline, CAPP
van Cline & Davenport, Ltd.
792 Franklin Ave.
Franklin Lakes, NJ 07417-1343
Minimum charge $25; letter request only, SASE.

Clubs/Associations

Boehm Porcelain Society, The
Magazine: Boehm Guild Advisory, The
P.O. Box 5051
Trenton, NJ 08638
phone: 609-392-2207 or 800-257-9410
fax: 609-392-1437
A Boehm manufacturer-sponsored club.

Collectors

Leon Reimert
121 Highland Dr.
Coatesville, PA 19320-1709
phone: 610-383-6969
Wants to buy Boehm porcelain dogs, horses, colts, and other animal figurines.

Dealers

Gwendolyn R. Reasoner
Re Vann Galleries
1501 Boardwalk at NY Ave.
Atlantic City, NJ 08401-7012
phone: 609-345-7474 or 800-821-4278
fax: 318-762-3534
Largest Boehm dealer in the U.S.; specializes in the Boehm secondary market; also Cybis, Royal Worcester, Erte; also appraises.

Benjamin Gallery
1303 Pennsylvania Ave.
Hagerstown, MD 21742
phone: 301-797-4775
Carries large selection of Boehm porcelain figurines.

Carol Marren
Kenneth R Gallery
2709 E. Commercial
Fort Lauderdale, FL 33308-4112
phone: 305-938-9700
fax: 305-938-0082
e-mail: kennethR6@aol.com
Specializing in fine porcelain sculptures, antiquarian prints and paintings; also contemporary art and crystal; dealers in Boehm, Cybis, Doughty, Lindner, and Connoisseur.

Pat Clay
Clemons-Eicken
6166 N. Scottsdale Rd. #204
Scottsdale, AZ 85253
phone: 602-998-9042 or 800-250-5423
fax: 602-998-3255
Boehm, Lladro, Cybis, Armani; Lalique, Swarovski; also a Disney full line dealer.

A.D. & Pat Clay
Clemons-Eicken Fine European Imports
6166 N. Scottsdale Rd., #204
Paradise Valley, AZ 85253
phone: 602-998-9042 or 800-250-5423
fax: 602-998-3755
Carries Lladro, Armani, Boehm, Lalique, Cybis.

Man./Prod./Dist.

Boehm Porcelain, Inc.
25 Fairfax St.
Trenton, NJ 08638
phone: 609-392-2207 or 800-257-9410
fax: 609-392-1437
Handcrafted porcelain art objects.

Borsato

Clubs/Associations

Borsato Collectors Club
2421 West Pratt Blvd., Ste. 307
World's largest database on Italian porcelain and artist, Antonio Borsato; newsletter, appraisal, largest Borsato library in the world.

Bossons

Clubs/Associations

Dr. Robert E. Davis, ExDir
International Bossons Collectors
Society, Inc.
Newsletter: Bossons Briefs
21 John Maddox Dr.
Rome, GA 30165-1413
phone: 770-684-1922
fax: 770-684-0300
Bossons character heads or figurines.

Collectors

Bruce Bleier
73 Riverdale Rd.
Valley Stream, NY 11581
phone: 516-791-4353
e-mail: bellovaman@aol.com
Buys and sells BOSSONS artware including faces, animals and plaques.

Andy Jackson
501 Falcon Lane
West Chester, PA 19382-5716
phone: 610-692-0269 or 610-272-7900
Wants all Bossons artware: face masks, dogs, animals and plaques; will buy, sell or trade.

Dealers

Donald M. Hardisty
Don's Collectibles
3020 E. Majestic Ridge
Las Cruces, NM 88001-4639
phone: 505-522-3721
fax: 505-522-7909
Specializes in buying, selling and restoring Bossons and Hummel figurines and Artware; orders only call 800-267-7667.

Experts

Dr. Robert E. Davis
International Bossons
21 John Maddox Dr.
Rome, GA 30165-1413
phone: 770-684-1922
fax: 770-684-0300
Author of "The Imagical World of Bossons" and "The Imagical World of Bossons - Book II."

Man./Prod./Dist.

Andrew D. Darvas, Inc.
2165 Dwight Way
Berkeley, CA 94704
phone: 510-843-7838
fax: 510-843-1815
A major importer of Bossons Character Wall Masks from England.

Cybis

Dealers

Gwendolyn R. Reasoner
Re Vann Galleries
1501 Boardwalk at NY Ave.
Atlantic City, NJ 08401-7012
phone: 609-345-7474 or 800-821-4278
fax: 318-762-3534
Largest Boehm dealer in the U.S.; specializes in the Boehm secondary market; also Cybis, Royal Worcester, Erte; also appraises.

Carol Marren
Kenneth R Gallery
2709 E. Commercial
Fort Lauderdale, FL 33308-4112
phone: 305-938-9700
fax: 305-938-0082
e-mail: kennethR6@aol.com
Specializing in fine porcelain sculptures, antiquarian prints and paintings; also contemporary art and crystal; dealers in Boehm, Cybis, Doughty, Lindner, and Connoisseur.

A.D. & Pat Clay
Clemons-Eicken Fine European Imports
6166 N. Scottsdale Rd., #204
Paradise Valley, AZ 85253
phone: 602-998-9042 or 800-250-5423
fax: 602-998-3755
Carries Lladro, Armani, Boehm, Lalique, Cybis.

Pat Clay
Clemons-Eicken
6166 N. Scottsdale Rd. #204
Scottsdale, AZ 85253
phone: 602-998-9042 or 800-250-5423
fax: 602-998-3255
Boehm, Lladro, Cybis, Armani; Lalique, Swarovski; also a Disney full line dealer.

Man./Prod./Dist.

Cybis Porcelains
65 Norman Ave.
Trenton, NJ 08618-3003
phone: 609-392-6074
Creates fine porcelain sculptures; contact for purchasing or appraising limited or open edition figurines; also offers authentic Cybis restorations.

Doughty

Dealers

Carol Marren
Kenneth R Gallery
2709 E. Commercial
Fort Lauderdale, FL 33308-4112
phone: 305-938-9700
fax: 305-938-0082
e-mail: kennethR6@aol.com
Specializing in fine porcelain sculptures, antiquarian prints and paintings; also contemporary art and crystal; dealers in Boehm, Cybis, Doughty, Lindner, and Connoisseur.

Hartland

Collectors

Steve McPherson
RR 2 Box 139-A
La Belle, MO 63447
phone: 816-462-3994
Wants to buy statues by Hartland Plastics: western, baseball, football, religious.

Experts

Patrick Flynn
Minnie Memories
50 Eginton Rd.
Mankato, MN 56001-2607
phone: 507-387-6864
Author of "Bobbin Head Dolls/ Hartland Statues."

Hummel

(see also COLLECTIBLES [MODERN], Figurines [Goebel])

Auction Services

Cindy Isennock
Isennock Auctions & Appraisals, Inc.
4203 Norrisville Rd.
White Hall, MD 21161-9306
phone: 410-557-8052
fax: 410-692-6449
Sells and appraises Hummel figurines.

Clubs/Associations

M.I. Hummel Club
Newsletter: Insights
Goebel Plaza, Rte. 31
P.O. Box 11
Pennington, NJ 08534-0011
phone: 609-737-8777 or 800-666-2582
fax: 609-737-1545
e-mail: feedback@mihummel.com
Internet: http://
www.mihummelclub.com/
Oldest collectors club of its kind; members receive information on Hummel figurines, plates & bells history & artistry.

Dorothy Dous, Pres.
Hummel Collector's Club, Inc.
Newsletter: Hummel Collector's Club Quarterly
P.O. Box 257
Morrisville, PA 19067-8257
phone: 215-493-6705 or 215-493-6204
fax: 215-321-7367
Specializing in M.I. Hummel items; fact-filled newsletter includes new releases, discontinued and older figurines, sale items and monthly figurine giveaway; also conducts monthly mail auctions of 1200-1600 items.

Tampa Area M.I. Hummel Club
P.O. Box 3
Lutz, FL 33549
phone: 813-855-5680 or 813-932-2263

Larry L. Jensen
Mountaineers, The
1524 S. Tucson St.
Aurora, CO 80012
phone: 303-751-3782

Dealers

Don & Beth Woodworth
Dustables, Inc.
6558 Fourth Section Rd. #170
Brockport, NY 14420-2472
phone: 800-560-6996
fax: 716-494-1617
e-mail: service@dustables.com
*Buys and sells M.I. Hummel figurines
by mail order; checks, money orders,
major credit cards accepted; free
price list available upon request.*

Cindy Oakes
34025 W. 6 Mile
Livonia, MI 48152
phone: 313-591-3252
*Wants complete set of Hummel plates;
also Hummel figurines from crown
mark to present.*

Larry L. Jensen
1524 S. Tucson St.
Aurora, CO 80012
phone: 303-751-3782
*Buys, sells, trades Hummel figurines;
selling secondary market figurines at
half price.*

Donald M. Hardisty
Don's Collectibles
3020 E. Majestic Ridge
Las Cruces, NM 88001-4639
phone: 505-522-3721
fax: 505-522-7909
*Specializes in buying, selling and
restoring Bossons and Hummel
figurines and Artware; orders only
call 800-267-7667.*

Experts

Dorothy Dous
P.O. Box 257
Morrisville, PA 19067-8257
phone: 215-493-6705 or 215-493-6204
fax: 215-321-7367
*Buys, sells, collects, appraises,
auctions and specializes in Hummels;
runs the Hummel Collector's Club.*

Carl Luckey
1973 Lingerlost Trail
Country Road 471
Killen, AL 35645
fax: 205-757-5803
e-mail: cluckey@mail.hiwaay.net
*Mail contact only, please; send SASE
for replier; author of books on
Hummels, decoys, antique American
fishing tackle, and depression glass.*

Dean A. Genth
Miller's Gift Gallery
1322 N. Barron St.
Eaton, OH 45320-1016
phone: 937-456-4151
fax: 937-456-7851
e-mail: dean@millershallmark.com
Internet: http://
www.millershallmark.com
*Offers replacements and loss claim
analysis; author of the "Price Guide
to M.I. Hummel."*

Man./Prod./Dist.

Schmid, Inc.
P.O. Box 636
Carthage, MO 64836
phone: 617-961-3000 or 800-343-7902
*Distributor of collectibles including
Hummel and Lowell Davis figurines,
woodcarvings by Anri, Walt Disney,
Beatrix Potter, etc.*

Museums/Libraries

Doreen Schaeffer
Hummel Museum, The
199 Main Plaza
P.O. Box 311100
New Braunfels, TX 78131-1100
phone: 800-456-HUMM or 210-625-
5636
fax: 210-625-5966
*Exhibits the world's largest collection
of original drawings by M.I. Hummel;
figurines and other Hummel items for
sale in gift shop.*

Repair Services

Dona Danzinger
Clay Works, The
4058 S. Main St.
P.O. Box 352
Exmore, VA 23350
phone: 757-414-0567
*Crazing corrections - trademarked in
1995; this is a kiln-fired process for
the Hummels which eliminates
crazing; call for free information
sheet.*

Hummel Look-Alikes

Collectors

Joan Oates
5912 Kingsfield
West Bloomfield, MI 48322
phone: 616-435-8353
*Interested in child-like, Hummel look-
alikes "Designed by Erich Stauffer",
made in Japan and imported by
Arnart Imports, NY; these 4 1/2" to
10" figurines resemble Hummels, but
are not; wants to compare style
numbers, info with others.*

Kaiser

Man./Prod./Dist.

Don Thompson
Kaiser Porcelain Co.
R.R. #3
Shelburne
Ontario L0N 1S0 Canada
phone: 705-466-2246
fax: 705-466-3542
e-mail: kaiser@bconnex.net
Internet: http://www.kaiser-porc.com
*Porcelain dinnerware and bone china;
artificial flowers, vases, figurines and
wallplates, giftware and collectibles.*

Kaiser Porcelain (US) Inc.
2045 Niagara Falls Blvd.
Units 11 & 12
Niagara Falls, NY 14304
phone: 716-297-2331
fax: 716-297-2749
*Porcelain dinnerware and bone china;
artificial flowers, vases, figurines and
wallplates.*

Lady

(see also BATHING BEAUTIES,
Nudies & Naughties)

Collectors

Ann M. Kerr
P.O. Box 437
Sidney, OH 45365
phone: 513-492-6369
fax: 513-492-6369
*Always looking for fine quality lady
figurines; must be signed and in
perfect condition.*

Lefton

Clubs/Associations

Loretta DeLozier
National Society of Lefton Collectors
Newsletter: Lefton Collector
1101 Polk St.
Bedford, IA 50833-9107
phone: 712-523-2289
e-mail: leftonlady@aol.com
*Members are interested in dinnerware
and figurines made by Lefton.*

Lladro

Clubs/Associations

Lladro Collectors Society
Magazine: Expressions
1 Lladro Dr.
Moonachie, NJ 07074
phone: 201-807-1177 or 800-634-9088
fax: 201-807-1168
*Focuses on the collectible Lladro
figurines. Sponsored by Lladro Co.*

Dealers

Joan Lewis
Work of Art, A
Magazine: Work of Art, A
12 Legion Dr.
Valhalla, NY 10595-2012
phone: 914-948-4655
fax: 914-948-4367
*Buys and sells retired Lladro
figurines; the magazine focuses on the
secondary market Lladro prices with
auction prices and articles about the
care, display and history of Lladro
figurines.*

Yesterdays South, Inc.
P.O. Box 161083
Miami, FL 33116-1083
phone: 800-368-5866 or 305-251-1988
fax: 305-254-5977
*Send SASE for list of almost 1000
Doultons and Lladros for sale.*

Janet Gale Hammer
Retired Collection, A
550 Harbor Cove Circle
Longboat Key, FL 34228-3544
phone: 941-387-0102 or 800-332-8594
fax: 941-383-8865
e-mail: LladroLady@aol.com
Internet: http://www.hkproducts.com/
lladro-lady
*Secondary market dealer specializing
in Lladro.*

A.D. & Pat Clay
Clemons-Eicken Fine European Imports
6166 N. Scottsdale Rd., #204
Paradise Valley, AZ 85253
phone: 602-998-9042 or 800-250-5423
fax: 602-998-3755
*Carries Lladro, Armani, Boehm,
Lalique, Cybis.*

Ben Swan
Golden Swan Collectibles
895 Lincoln Way
Auburn, CA 95603
phone: 916-823-7926 or 800-231-9055
fax: 916-823-1945
*Offers a "search and find" and a
listing service to collectors, buyers
and sellers of Lladro figurines; also
for Swarovski, Walt Disney Classics,
and Disneyana Convention figurines.*

Man./Prod./Dist.

Lladro USA
1 Lladro Dr.
Moonachie, NJ 07074
phone: 201-807-1177 or 800-634-9088
fax: 201-807-1168
*Manufactures and distributes quality
handcrafted porcelains from Valencia,
Spain. Place orders through 1-800-
937-3524.*

Museums/Libraries

Lladro Museum & Galleries
43 West 57th St.
New York, NY 10019
phone: 212-838-9356
*A manufacturer-sponsored museum
and retail outlet.*

Periodicals

Lladro USA
Newsletter: Lladro Antique News
1 Lladro Dr.
Moonachie, NJ 07074
phone: 201-807-1177 or 800-634-9088
fax: 201-807-1168
*Focuses on the current secondary
market values of Lladro's 3,000 hard-
paste porcelain figurines produced
since 1941; also covers history of
hard-paste porcelain (1000 AD to
present) such as Meissen, Sevres,
Nymphenburg, etc.*

Monks

Collectors

Joseph
P.O. Box 32145
Oklahoma City, OK 73123
*Wants monk-shaped character
figurines.*

Mortens

Collectors

Gene Roberts
1500 Gilbert Rd.
Kennesaw, GA 30144
phone: 404-422-4143
*Interested in buying anything
Mortens: dogs, cats, livestock,
wildlife, horses, bookends, head
studies, plaques, people, birds; also
wants Mortens catalogs, history, any
information.*

Dealers

Denise Hamilton
899 Latta Brook Rd.
Elmira, NY 14901
phone: 607-732-2550
*Buys dogs collectibles: figurines, old
dog postcards, jewelry with dogs in it,
etc.; Borzoi (Russian Wolfhound),
greyhound, all Morten Studio and
Erphila dogs and animals.*

Pen Delfin

Collectors

George Sparacio
P.O. Box 791
Malaga, NJ 08328-0791
phone: 609-694-4167
fax: 609-694-4536
*Wants to buy pre-1975 retired Pen
Delfin figurines; will buy one or entire
collection; quality items only; will
answer all correspondence.*

Royal Doulton

(see CERAMICS [ENGLISH],
Doulton; CERAMICS [ENGLISH],
Royal Doulton; COLLECTIBLES
[MODERN], Royal Doulton)

FILMS

(see also AUDIO-VISUAL;
CAMERAS & CAMERA EQUIP-
MENT; MOVIE MEMORABILIA)

Appraisers

Larry Urbanski
Urbanski Film & Video
P.O. Box 438
Orland Park, IL 60462-0438
phone: 708-460-9082
fax: 708-460-9099
e-mail: larryu@moviecraft.com
*Film collection appraisals (8mm,
16mm, 35mm) for legal purposes and/
or insurance claims; 30 years
experience; member of AMIA
(Association of Moving Image
Archivists).*

Dr. Steve Johnson
Behavioral Images, Inc.
Newsletter: Ten Thousands Words
302 Leland St., Ste. 101
Bloomington, IL 61701-5646
phone: 309-829-3931 or 800-988-6427
fax: 309-829-9677
e-mail: mediavalue@compuserve.com
Internet: http://
ourworld.compuserve.com/
homepages/mediavalue
*Film, video, recordings, photographs,
negatives; author of "Appraising
Audio-visual Media; A Guide for
Attorneys, Trust Officers, Insurance
Professionals, & Archivists" (1993);
$34.95 & $3 S&H; publishes
newsletter ten times per year.*

Clubs/Associations

Vintage Film Club, The
Magazine: Flickers: The Collector's
Guide to Vintage Film
11 Norton Rd.
Knowle
Bristol BS4 2EZ, U.K.
*For those interested in vintage films,
projectors, film books and magazines,
and related items; magazine published
three times per year with articles,
display ads, and a large free
classifieds marketplace insert for club
members.*

Association of Moving Image
Archivists, Nat. Ctr. for Film & Video
Preservation
P.O. Box 27999
2021 N. Western Ave.
Los Angeles, CA 90027

Dealers

Kathy & Bill Lozowski
K & B Film & Collectibles
50 32nd St.
Copiague, NY 11726
phone: 516-842-3446
Also sells commercials on 16mm film.

Larry Urbanski
Urbanski Film & Video
P.O. Box 438
Orland Park, IL 60462-0438
phone: 708-460-9082
fax: 708-460-9099
e-mail: larryu@moviecraft.com
*16mm film exchange and sales;
specializing in cartoons, educational
features, TV shows, and shorts;
projectors and equipment available;
16mm and 35mm; also buys and
trades film; send two stamps for
catalog.*

Repair Services

Sockets International
4454 Coldwater Canyon Ave., Ste. #303
Studio City, CA 91604
phone: 818-508-0464
*Certified Tomakote agent; Tomakote
keeps all film stock soft and pliable so
there is no eventual drying-to-
brittleness; contains a powerful anti-
static agent to reduces friction during
projection and acts to repel dirt.*

Newsreels

Collectors

Castle Newsreels
P.O. Box 295 CI
Cliffside Park, NJ 07010-0295
phone: 201-956-8342
*Wants Castle newsreels, 8mm or
16mm, sound or silent, complete
editions, send lists; also any 1933
newsreel, 8 mm of 200/400 ft.; also
1927-1932 "Our Gang" comedies.*

Videos

Man./Prod./Dist.

Larry Urbanski
Moviecraft Inc.
P.O. Box 438
Orland Park, IL 60462-0438
phone: 708-460-9082
fax: 708-460-9099
e-mail: larryu@moviecraft.com
*Offers a nostalgic/historical line of
home videos including TV shows,
World Fair, automotive, rare
cartoons, classics, unique contemporary releases, war newsreels and
propaganda, special interest subjects,
and feature films.*

Periodicals

Newspaper: VideoMania
P.O. Box 47
Princeton, WI 54968
*Bi-monthly newspaper for video
collectors.*

Magazine: Video Movie Collector
P.O. Box 62067
Minneapolis, MN 55426
phone: 612-924-6099
fax: 612-929-0522
*The monthly publication for collectors
of movies on video tape or disc: up-to-
the-minute news and information for
the movie on video collector; listings
of hard-to-find titles, articles, reviews,
etc.*

FINANCIAL PAPER

(see BANKING; CIVIL WAR
ARTIFACTS, Confederate Bonds;
COINS & CURRENCY, Paper
Money; PAPER COLLECTIBLES;
SCRIP; STOCKS & BONDS)

FIRE FIGHTING MEMORABILIA

Auction Services

Chuck Deluca
Maritime Auctions
P.O. Box 322
York, ME 03909
phone: 207-363-4247
fax: 207-363-1416
e-mail: maritim2@ix.netcom.com
Internet: http://www.maritiques.com
*Author of "Firehouse Memorabilia - A
Collector's Reference"; two cataloged
auctions per year in April and August.*

Clubs/Associations

David Cerull
Fire Collectors Club
P.O. Box 992
Milwaukee, WI 53201-0992
Collectors of Fire Service medals.

International Fire Photographers
Association
P.O. Box 8337
Rolling Meadows, IL 60008

Hall of Flame
6101 East Van Buren St.
Phoenix, AZ 85008
phone: 602-275-3473

Collectors

Bob Arnold
12 Stone St.
Belleville
Ontario K8P 1Z9 Canada

M. Gimley
P.O. Box 244
Oakland, NJ 07436-0244
*Wants items from the 1800s to 1920s:
gold & silver badges, buckets, engine
lights, helmets, lanterns, tintypes,
statues of firemen, etc.*

Ralph Jennings
301 Fort Washington Ave.
Fort Washington, PA 19034-1542
phone: 215-646-7178
*Interested in fire fighting and fire
insurance related collectibles.*

Jeb S. Fuller
9 Durey Ct.
Cartersville, GA 30120
phone: 404-984-1282
*Wants to buy firehouse items:
postcards, ads or photographs
featuring firemen or fire trucks, old
fire trucks, extinguishers, trumpets,
badges, alarms, helmets, etc.*

David Cerull
P.O. Box 992
Milwaukee, WI 53201-0992
Wants Fire Service medals from any country; send detailed description, rubbing or photocopy along with price.

Marvin Karsten
6217 Crystal Dr.
Alta Loma, CA 91701-3411
phone: 909-987-5084
Wants to buy firehouse memorabilia: American fire helmets, wood cased fire alarm bells, street boxes, speaking trumpets, Gamewell equipment, fire insurance advertising, fire toys, fire lanterns.

Stan Zukowski
1867 Ellard Place
Concord, CA 94521
phone: 510-687-6426
Wants fire department antiques: fire alarm boxes, wood cased fire station bells, desk bells, keys, books, catalogs, parts; anything fire alarm related in any condition; also wants helmets, lanterns, trumpets, glass grenades, etc.

Dealers

Robert H. Harper
Cary Station Antiques
22 Spring St.
Cary, IL 60013
phone: 708-639-7434
Wants helmets, trumpets, presentation badges, painted leather buckets, lamps, parade hats, alarm equipment, etc.

Experts

H. Thomas & Pat Laun
Little Century
215 Paul Ave.
Syracuse, NY 13206-3220
phone: 315-437-4156 or 315-654-3244
Buys and sells fire related antiques and collectibles, any number; supplies and manufactures parts for firematic items; also repairs; call 315-437-4156 in the winter, and 315-654-3244 in summer.

Germaine Broussard
8280 Greensboro Drive #200
Mc Lean, VA 22102-3807
phone: 703-556-8183 or 800-336-0156
fax: 703-356-6492
e-mail: coxfdr@erols.com
Buys, sells, appraises fire department memorabilia; one piece or collection; early ribbons are a specialty; will answer questions for new collectors; former firefighter and paramedic.

Museums/Libraries

Eugene I. Morris, Dir.
New England Fire & History Museum
Newsletter: Siren Soundings
1439 Main St. (Rte. 6A)
Brewster, MA 02631
phone: 508-896-5711 or 508-945-9413
One of the world's most varied collections of antique fire engines; 35 historic fire engines; Mr. Morris appraises and has written many articles relating to fire fighting, apothecary and blacksmithing material.

New York City Fire Museum, The
Newsletter: Burning Issues
278 Spring St.
New York, NY 10013-1405
phone: 212-691-1303
fax: 212-924-0403
Focuses on fire related art and artifacts from the mid-18th century to present.

American Museum of Fire Fighting
P.O. Box 413
Corton Falls, NY 10519
phone: 518-828-7695
The mailing address is as noted above, but located on Harry Howard Ave., Hudson, NY.

Fire Museum of Maryland
1301 York Rd.
Lutherville, MD 21093
phone: 410-321-7500

Jerry Pajak, Sec.
Toledo Firefighting Museum, Inc.
Newsletter: Hook & Letter, The
918 W. Sylvania Ave.
Toledo, OH 43612
phone: 419-478-3473
Comprehensive collection of fire fighting antiques and 2000 volume library.

Oklahoma Firefighters Museum
2716 NE 50th St.
Oklahoma City, OK 73100
phone: 405-424-3440

San Francisco Fire Department
Memorial Museum
260 Golden Gate Ave.
San Francisco, CA 94102
phone: 415-861-8000

Repair Services

H. Thomas & Pat Laun
Little Century
215 Paul Ave.
Syracuse, NY 13206-3220
phone: 315-437-4156 or 315-654-3244
Repairs fire fighting antiques and collectibles; wood and metal parts fabricated.

Apparatus

(see also TRUCKS, Emergency)

Clubs/Associations

Marvin Cohen
Society for the Preservation & Appreciation of Motor Fire Apparatus in America
P.O. Box 2005
Syracuse, NY 13220
phone: 914-343-4219

William A. Conn
Great Lakes International Antique Fire Apparatus Association
P.O. Box 2519
Detroit, MI 48231
phone: 810-684-1521

Antique Fire Apparatus Club of America
5420 South Kedvale Ave.
Chicago, IL 60632
phone: 312-585-1301

Collectors

Bob Ward
2461 E High St., #A-7
Pottstown, PA 19464-3111
phone: 610-970-6299

Periodicals

Magazine: Fire Apparatus Journal
P.O. Box 141295
Staten Island, NY 10314-1295
phone: 718-448-5009
fax: 718-981-2359
e-mail: fireappjnl@aol.com
Focuses on all sorts of fire fighting apparatus: trucks, boats; also related modeling.

Fire Alarm Telegraphy

Collectors

Gary Carino
805 W. 3rd St.
Duluth, MN 55806-2201
phone: 218-722-6565
fax: 218-878-0488
Wants wood cased gongs by Gamewell or Moses G. Crane.

Experts

Steven Scher
3010 Grand Concourse
Bronx, NY 10458-1504
Wants to buy antique fire alarm gongs and telegraph items; advises other collectors about same; author of magazine articles and contributor to a book on fire alarm telegraphy; also historical advisor to the NYC Fire Museum.

Grenades

Collectors

Jerry Pajak
4457 285th St.
Toledo, OH 43611-1912
phone: 419-726-4325
Wants turn-of-the-century fire fighting hand grenade fire extinguisher bottles (empty or full) which were originally sealed with a cork or with cement.

Larry Meyer
4001 Elmwood
Berwyn, IL 60402-4146
phone: 708-749-1564

FIRE INSURANCE RELATED COLLECTIBLES

(see also INSURANCE COLLECTIBLES)

Collectors

Ralph Jennings
301 Fort Washington Ave.
Fort Washington, PA 19034-1542
phone: 215-646-7178
Interested in fire fighting and fire insurance related collectibles.

Glenn Hartley, Sr.
2859 Marlin Dr.
Chamblee, GA 30341-5119
phone: 770-451-2651
Buys and sells at area fire musters and apparatus shows.

Museums/Libraries

Glenn Hartley, Sr.
Smokey's Fire Museum
2859 Marlin Dr.
Chamblee, GA 30341-5119
phone: 770-451-2651

Fire Marks

Clubs/Associations

Glenn Hartley, Sr.
Fire Mark Circle of the Americas, The
Newsletter: Fire Mark Circle of the Americas Newsletter, The
2859 Marlin Dr.
Chamblee, GA 30341-5119
phone: 770-451-2651
Contains club news, auction prices, and articles about fire marks; also publishes the "FMCA Journal"; published addendum and booklets on fire marks and automobile insurance tags; also "Signs of Insurance", a book on insurance co. signs.

FIREARMS

(see also ADVERTISING COLLECTIBLES, Firearms Related; AIRGUNS; ARMS & ARMOR; BOOKS, Ref. [Firearms]; CIVIL WAR ARTIFACTS; MILITARIA; AMMUNITION & EXPLOSIVE ORDNANCE; POWDER HORNS; SPORTING COLLECTIBLES; TARGET SHOOTING MEMORABILIA; TOYS, BB Guns; TRAPSHOOTING

Appraisers

Robert A. Dewar
Robert A. Dewar & Assoc.
512 Canal St.
New Smyrna Beach, FL 32168
phone: 904-428-3331
Dealer and appraiser in both antique and modern firearms.

Joseph G. Balshone, GG, ISA
463 East Town St.
Columbus, OH 43215-4796
phone: 800-209-4367 or 614-224-2404
fax: 614-224-5630
e-mail: jbalshone@compuserve.com
*Specializing in appraising post-1800
firearms.*

Paul Jurgens
50 DuClaire Rd.
Decatur, IL 62521-5527
phone: 217-423-8303
Specializes in appraising firearms.

Auction Services

Karen Harvey
William Harvey Gun Auctions
P.O. Box 280
Cataumet, MA 02534
phone: 508-563-2550 or 508-548-0660
Internet: http://
www.firearmsauctions.com

Randy Inman
James D. Julia Auctioneers Inc.
Rt. 201, Skowhegan Rd.
P.O. Box 830
Fairfield, ME 04937
phone: 207-453-7125
fax: 207-453-2502
*One of the leading firearms
auctioneers in North America.*

Ronnie Roberts, ISA
Dixie Sporting Collectibles
1206 Rama Rd.
Charlotte, NC 28211-4345
phone: 704-364-2900 or 704-364-3382
fax: 704-364-2322
e-mail: gun1898@aol.com
Internet: http://www.sportauction.com

Chuck Jackson
Dunning's Auction Service
755 Church Rd.
Elgin, IL 60123-9302
phone: 708-741-3483 or 800-462-2444
fax: 708-741-3589
Internet: http:///www.dunnings.com

Rock Island Auction Co.
1050 36th Ave.
Moline, IL 61265
phone: 309-797-1500

Clubs/Associations

Jack Ackerman
New York State Arms Collectors
  Association
24 South Mountain Terrace
Binghamton, NY 13902-3128
phone: 607-723-5668

Potomac Arms & Collectors Association
P.O. Box 1812
Wheaton, MD 20915
phone: 301-949-5008

Attn: Membership
National Rifle Association
Magazine: American Rifleman
11250 Waples Mill Rd.
Fairfax, VA 22030
phone: 800-NRA-3888
Internet: http://www.nra.org/
  welcome.html

Collectors

Harry Bittle
904 N 2nd St.
Harrisburg, PA 17102
Wants to buy antique firearms.

Jim Kopke
P.O. Box 4310
Dillon, CO 80435-4310
Wants to buy antique firearms.

Dealers

New England Arms Co.
P.O. Box 278
Kittery Point, ME 03905
phone: 207-439-0593
fax: 207-439-6726
*Largest display of modern and antique
sporting arms on the East Coast:
Purdey, Boss, Woodward, Holland &
Holland, Sauer, Merkel, Browning,
Dumoulin, Ferlib, Fabbri, Piotti,
Rizzini, Arrazabalaga, Arrieta, etc.*

Greg Souchik
TMP Co.
P.O. Box 161
Custer City, PA 16725-0161
phone: 814-362-2642
fax: 814-362-7356
e-mail: 104235.2430@compuserve.com
*Buys all broken and old firearms
including parts.*

William A. Kelley, Jr.
Gun Center, The
5831 Buckeystown Pike
Frederick, MD 21701
phone: 301-694-6887
*A full service gun store offering
special order services, gunsmithing,
and firearms appraisals; buy, sell,
trade, consignment.*

Dave Condon
David Condon, Inc.
P.O. Box 7
Middleburg, VA 22117
phone: 703-687-5642 or 703-689-1363
Antique firearms bought and sold.

Bill Williams
Guncraft Sports Inc.
10737 Dutchtown Rd.
Knoxville, TN 37932-3208
phone: 423-966-4545
fax: 423-966-4500
e-mail: findit@guncraft.com
Internet: http://www.usit.net/hp/guncraft
*Serving the shooting public since
1947; a multi-faceted supplier of guns,
accessories, appraisal services,
training, gunsmithing, gun related
books.*

Dixie Gun Work's Old Car & Steam
  Engine Museum
P.O. Box 130
Union City, TN 38261
phone: 901-885-0561
*Specializes in the sale of black powder
rifles.*

Douglas R. Carlson
Antique American Firearms
P.O. Box 71035
Des Moines, IA 50325
phone: 515-224-6552
*Wants antique American revolvers
and derringers 1848-1898; offers
antique firearms catalogs every 12
weeks; hundreds of items per issue.*

Dean Williams
Antique & Collector Firearms
RR 7157
Spirit Lake, IA 51360
phone: 712-336-5634
*Buys and sells, especially Colts,
Remingtons, Winchesters, Smith &
Wessons, flintlocks and derringer;
offers quarterly antique firearms.*

Randy Donley
Donley's Wild West Town & Museum
8512 S. Union Rd.
Union, IL 60180-9661
phone: 815-923-9000
fax: 815-923-2253
*Buys, sells and collects antique
firearms of all sorts.*

Collectors Gun Shop
140 S Seminary St.
Galesburg, IL 61401-4805
phone: 309-342-5800
*Wants antique firearms, Civil War
carbines and muskets, Colts,
European muskets, Derringers,
Winchester, etc.*

Michael Wamsher
17732 W. 67th St.
Shawnee Mission, KS 66217
phone: 913-631-0686
Specializes in military firearms.

Experts

Courtney Wilson
American Military Antiques
8398 Court Ave.
Ellicott City, MD 21043-4514
phone: 410-465-6827
*Wants to buy collectible and antique
firearms; all periods.*

Norm Flayderman
P.O. Box 2446
Ft. Lauderdale, FL 33303
phone: 305-761-8855
*Offers annual catalog of antique arms
for sale.*

Bill Williams
Guncraft Sports Inc.
10737 Dutchtown Rd.
Knoxville, TN 37932-3208
phone: 423-966-4545
fax: 423-966-4500
e-mail: findit@guncraft.com
Internet: http://www.usit.net/hp/guncraft
*Serving the shooting public since
1947; a multi-faceted supplier of guns,
accessories, appraisal services,
training, gunsmithing, gun related
books.*

Robert H. Balderson
2830 Arden Way, #110
Sacramento, CA 95825
phone: 916-484-7906
fax: 916-484-7906
*Specializes and appraises firearms,
Western Americana, and Native
American weapons; author of
"Official Price Guide to Antique and
Modern Firearms."*

Man./Prod./Dist.

Smith & Wesson
2100 Roosevelt Ave.
Springfield, MA 01104
phone: 800-331-0852
Internet: http://www.smith-wesson.com

Greg Souchik
Allegheny Arsenal, Inc.
P.O. Box 161
Custer City, PA 16725-0161
phone: 814-362-2642
fax: 814-362-7356
e-mail: 104235.2430@compuserve.com
*Manufacturers of Guardian Gun Care
products: gun wipe, lubricant,
corrosive ammo neutralizer, and metal
finishing products, gun blue and
Parkerizing kits.*

Museums/Libraries

Springfield Armory National Historic
  Park
1 Armory Square
Springfield, MA 01105-1204
phone: 413-734-8551

Roberto M. Rodriguez
American Precision Museum Association, Inc.
P.O. Box 679
Windsor, VT 05089
phone: 802-674-5781
fax: 802-674-2524
e-mail: 103362.1676@compuserve.com
Internet: http://
  ourworld.compuserve.com/
  homepages/Precision_Museum
*Collections include examples of all of
the guns manufactured in the museum
building over its long history as an
armory; examples include Sharpes,
Jennings, Palmer, Ball, Robbins &
Lawrence, Enfield, and L.G.Y.*

Bruce M. Moseley, Cur.
Fort Ticonderoga Museum
Newsletter: Bulletin of the Fort
Ticonderoga Museum
P.O. Box 390
Ticonderoga, NY 12883
phone: 518-585-2821
fax: 518-585-2210
*10,000 volume research library
specializing in 19th century military
history and the history of the
Champlain Valley; museum depicts
history of the area and the campaigns
during the 7 Year War and the
Revolutionary War.*

Randy Donley
Donley's Wild West Town & Museum
8512 S. Union Rd.
Union, IL 60180-9661
phone: 815-923-9000
fax: 815-923-2253

Herman's House of Guns
P.O. Box 191
Dorris, CA 96023
phone: 916-397-2611

Periodicals

Andrew Mowbray, Pub.
Magazine: Man at Arms
11250 Waples Mill Rd.
Fairfax, VA 22030
phone: 800-NRA-3888
Internet: http://www.nra.org/
welcome.html
*"Man at Arms" is the official arms
collecting periodical of the NRA. A
non-shooting magazine focusing on
collectible firearms, arms and armor.*

Magazine: Guns & Ammo
437 Madison Ave., 28th Floor
New York, NY 10022
phone: 212-935-9150 or 800-800-2666

Magazine: Arms Collecting
P.O. Box 70
Alexandria Bay, NY 13607-0070
phone: 613-393-2980
*Reaches collectors, museums and
librarians in 35 countries.*

Joseph P. Tartado, Ed.
Newspaper: Gun Week
P.O. Box 488
Buffalo, NY 14209-0488
phone: 716-885-6408
fax: 716-884-4471
*Covers all aspects of the shooting
sport: new products, hunting
regulations, gun legislation, shows
and collecting.*

Magazine: Gun News Digest
P.O. Box 488
Buffalo, NY 14209-0488
phone: 716-885-6408
fax: 716-884-4471
*Quarterly magazine; in-depth
coverage of important issues that
effect gun owners.*

: Women & Guns
P.O. Box 488
Buffalo, NY 14209-0488
phone: 716-885-6408
fax: 716-884-4471
*The only magazine of its kind; written
and edited by women for women.*

Dave Mullin
Magazine: Gun Dealers Network
Magazine
120 Franklin Ave., Ste. 195
Scranton, PA 18503
phone: 717-941-9740
fax: 717-346-6236
Two issues per month.

Richard Cecilio
Wildcat Enterprises, Inc.
Journal: Wildcat Collectors Journal
15158 N.E. 6 Ave.
Miami, FL 33162-5034
phone: 305-945-3228
*Featuring classified ads to buy/sell/
trade guns, knives, medals and related
militaria; gun shows, auctions, other
events; subscribers get FREE 40 word
ad.*

Richard Binger
Stott's Creek Armory, Inc.
Calendar: Stott's Creek Calendar - "The
Gun Show Bible"
Rte. 1 Box 70
Morgantown, IN 46160-9619
phone: 317-878-5489
*This schedule calendar lists antique
gun and knife shows in the US plus
many in Canada and England; each
schedule or calendar lists shows for 8
months; published three times a year
so they overlap by 3 months each to
keep current.*

Magazine: Double Gun Journal, The
5014 Rockery School Rd.
East Jordan, MI 49727-9636
phone: 616-536-7439
*The world's only periodical dedicated
to double barrel shotguns and rifles.*

Julie A. Ulrich, PR
Krause Publications
Newsmagazine: Gun List
700 E. State St.
Iola, WI 54990-0001
phone: 715-445-2214
fax: 715-445-4087
e-mail: info@krause.com
Internet: http://www.krause.com
*Ad newspaper for buying/selling
collectible firearms, parts &
accessories; gunsmithing services;
reloading supplies; archery and
knives; over 50,000 alphabetized guns
in each issue.*

Julie A. Ulrich, PR
Krause Publications
Magazine: Gun Show Calendar
700 E. State St.
Iola, WI 54990-0001
phone: 715-445-2214
fax: 715-445-4087
e-mail: info@krause.com
Internet: http://www.krause.com
Largest listing of gun shows

*available; lists shows throughout the
U.S. and Canada; listings updated
quarterly.*

World-Wide Gun Report, Inc.
Magazine: Gun Report, The
P.O. Box 38
Aledo, IL 61231-0038
phone: 309-582-5311 or 309-582-5312
fax: 309-582-5555
*The monthly magazine serving the
antique gun collector and dealer for
over 40 years.*

Magazine: Machine Gun News
P.O. Box 459
Lake Hamilton, AR 71951
phone: 501-525-7541
Internet: http://
www.machinegunnews.com
*A monthly magazine providing a
centralized source of information
about automatic weapons for the
shooting and collecting public.*

Repro. Sources

Daniel Winkler
P.O. Box 255
Boone, NC 28607

William J. Cooey
248 Van Horn Rd.
Milton, FL 32570

Log Cabin Shop
P.O. Box 275
Lodi, OH 44254

Colt

Clubs/Associations

Karen Green, Sec.
Colt Collectors Association
25000 Highland Way
Los Gatos, CA 95030
phone: 408-353-COLT
fax: 408-353-3613

Collectors

John S. Fischer
Coltania
10950 W. Pico Blvd.
Los Angeles, CA 90064-2115
*Buys and sells Colt factory items:
original catalogs, pamphlets,
advertising & promotional, books,
posters: anything Colt, his factory or
guns.*

Experts

John T. Ogle
P.O. Box 252
Ocean Springs, MS 39566-0252
*Collects memorabilia of the Colt
Firearms Companies; author of
Krause "Price Guide to Colt
COmpany Collectibles" (1998).*

Connecticut Arms & Mfg. Co.

Collectors

Edward Clark
P.O. Box 1812
Wheaton, MD 20915
phone: 301-949-5008
*Collecting and researching Hammond
Bulldog single shot pistols manufac-
tured by the Connecticut Arms & Mfg.
Co. from 1863 to 1868.*

Garand (M1)

Clubs/Associations

Garand Collectors Association
P.O. Box 181
Richmond, KY 40475
*For collectors of M1 and M14 rifles
made by John Garand originally in
the 1950s.*

Periodicals

Anthony Pucci, Jr.
Orion 7 Enterprises, Inc.
Newsletter: Garand Times
P.O. Box 1592
Rocky Point, NY 11778
phone: 516-744-5842
fax: 516-821-8446
e-mail: orion7@p6.net
Internet: http://www.p6.net/~orion7
*For the M1 collector, enthusiast, and
shooter.*

G.S. Publications
Newsletter: Garand Strand Report, The
P.O. Box 34005
Houston, TX 77234-4005

German

Clubs/Associations

Chris Cox
Karabiner Collector's Network
Newsletter: KCN Newsletter
P.O. Box 5773
High Point, NC 27262
phone: 910-884-5566
*Network for collectors of German
militaria; German rifles and snipers,
pistols and holsters, Mausers, German
medals and badges, helmets and
uniforms, books, photographs,
cartridges and ammo, field gear,
edged weapons, etc.*

Dealers

Tom Heller
Heller Arms, Ltd.
P.O. Box 398
Saint Charles, MO 63302-0398
phone: 314-447-3006
*German pistols bought, sold, and
appraised; Luger, Walther, Mauser;
carries parts for most German pistols,
plus original factory magazines and
accessories for most pistols.*

Gunsmithing

Dealers

Richard Binger
Stott's Creek Armory, Inc.
Rte. 1 Box 70
Morgantown, IN 46160-9619
phone: 317-878-5489
Antique only; buys, sells and collects flintlocks and cartridge rifles and muskets.

Repair Services

Laurence R. Mock
P.O. Box 105
Eliot, ME 03903-0105
phone: 207-439-2436
Fine antique guns restored, repaired, cleaned, appraised; wood repaired/ replaced & color matched, metalwork in iron, steel, silver, brass, wire inlay, engraving; over 30 years experience.

William Kennedy
Kennedy Firearms
10 No. Market St.
Muncy, PA 17756
phone: 717-546-6695
Muzzleloading gunsmith specializing in the restoration and recreation of black powder rifles; manufactures replacement metal parts, stocks and forearms for muskets, Sharps, Maynard & Gallager.

William A. Kelley, Jr.
Gun Center, The
5831 Buckeystown Pike
Frederick, MD 21701
phone: 301-694-6887
Offers a full line of gunsmithing services: repair, hot blueing, custom metal and stock work, etc.

Ron E. Dilliott
Dilliott Gunsmithing, Inc.
655 Scarlett Rd.
Dandridge, TN 37725-6005
phone: 423-397-9204
Repair and restoration of antique firearms; make obsolete parts; metal and wood refinishing; 30 years experience.

Richard Binger
Stott's Creek Armory, Inc.
Rte. 1 Box 70
Morgantown, IN 46160-9619
phone: 317-878-5489
Buys and sells muzzle loaders and cartridge rifles and muskets; specializing in gunsmithing and restoration.

Japanese Matchlocks

Collectors

Mark Fletcher
1611 Chesapeake Ave.
Hampton, VA 23661
phone: 804-244-1442
Collects Japanese matchlock and Japanese percussion firearms; also antique guns with Japanese markings.

Raymond Macy
P.O. Box 11
West Alexandria, OH 45381-0011
phone: 513-839-5721 or 513-839-5203
Wants Japanese swords, daggers, sword parts, matchlock guns, anything samurai.

Experts

Alan D. Meaux
Ronin Art Productions
P.O. Box 1271
Oak Harbor, WA 98277-1271
phone: 360-675-8429 or 360-678-8787
Evaluates, appraises and collects Japanese matchlocks, flint strikers and other samurai arms and armor.

Machine Guns

Dealers

J. Curtis Earl
5512 North Sixth St.
Phoenix, AZ 85102-1309
phone: 802-264-3166 or 208-336-9330
A knowledgeable dealer of machine guns. Issues catalogs that are of interest to the beginning collector and to the advanced collector. 28 years in business listing a vast inventory of Title-II items; illustrated brochure $6 ppd.

Mannlicher

Clubs/Associations

Thomas Seefeldt, Sec.
Mannlicher Collectors Association
Newsletter: Mannlicher Collector, The
P.O. Box 1455
Kalispell, MT 59903
phone: 406-257-6721
For collectors of the Continental firearms by Mannlicher.

Mossberg

Clubs/Associations

National Mossberg Collectors Association
Newsletter: NMCA News
P.O. Box 487
Festus, MO 63028-0487
phone: 314-937-6401
For the collector or sporting enthusiast interested in Mossberg firearms, optics, and history; special assistance given to members in locating obsolete parts and accessories; newsletter published bi-monthly.

Collectors

Art Snyder
110 White Oak Dr.
Butler, PA 16001-3446
phone: 412-287-0278
Buys, sells, trades all pre-1950 Mossberg firearms, especially hammerless pump action rifles and smooth bore Targo guns; also wants any related accessories or literature.

Victor Havlin
P.O. Box 487
Festus, MO 63028
phone: 314-937-6401

Pistols

Clubs/Associations

National Automatic Pistol Collectors Association
Newsletter: Auto Mag
P.O. Box 15738
Saint Louis, MO 63163
phone: 314-638-6505 or 314-481-4344
For the automatic hand gun enthusiast.

Remington

Museums/Libraries

Remington Firearms Museum
P.O. Box 179
Ilion, NY 13357-0179
phone: 315-895-3350
fax: 315-895-3237
Affiliated with the Remington Arms Company, Inc.

Rifles

Experts

Richard Binger
Stott's Creek Armory, Inc.
Rte. 1 Box 70
Morgantown, IN 46160-9619
phone: 317-878-5489
Specialist in antique firearms; Life Member NRA, American Single Shot Rifle Assn., National Muzzle Loading Rifle Assn., Ohio Gun Collectors Assn.

Rifles (Single Shot)

Clubs/Associations

Gary Staup
American Single Shot Rifle Association
709 Carolyn Dr.
Delphos, OH 45833-1316
phone: 419-692-3866
Organization dedicated to the shooting and collecting of single shot rifles from the turn of the century Schuetzen, benchrest, and long range traditions.

Periodicals

Magazine: Single Shot Exchange, The
P.O. Box 1055
York, SC 29745-1055
phone: 803-628-5326
fax: 803-628-5326
e-mail: singleshotex@earthlink.net
Internet: http://www.earthlink.net/ singleshotex/webdocs/
The magazine for black powder cartridge, silhouette, and Schuetzen shooters and antique gun collectors; monthly buy-sell-trade publication includes historical articles, collector's information, product reviews, match schedules, and more.

Winchester

Clubs/Associations

Richard A. Berg
Winchester Arms Collectors Association, Inc., The
Journal: Winchester Arms Journal, The
P.O. Box 6754
Great Falls, MT 59406-6754
phone: 406-771-8948
fax: 406-771-0601
Anything and everything for the collectors of Winchester firearms, ammunition, sporting goods, hardware items, posters, and anything else made by Winchester.

Dealers

LeRoy Merz
Rt. 1, Nirschi Addition #3
Fergus Falls, MN 56537
phone: 218-739-3255
Wants to buy fine antique Winchesters.

Doug Clemence
Treasure Chest
436 North Chicago
Salina, KS 67401-2020
phone: 913-827-9371 or 913-825-4111
Buys, sells, trades Winchester related items.

Museums/Libraries

Shozo Kagoshima, Dir. of Mkt.
Winchester Mystery House, Historic Firearms Museum
525 South Winchester Blvd.
San Jose, CA 95128
phone: 408-247-2000
fax: 408-247-2090
Internet: http://ca.living.net/trav/unique/ carwh.htm
Medium size display of firearms through the ages.

FIRECRACKERS

(see FIREWORKS MEMORABILIA)

FIREPLACE ITEMS

Dealers

Hearthstone, The
P.O. Box 517
Corona Del Mar, CA 92625-0517
Wants to buy old fireplace items: andirons, fire tools, fenders, etc.

Chimney Sweep

Collectors

Homestead Chimney Sweep
P.O. Box 5182
Clinton, NJ 08809
phone: 908-730-8319
fax: 908-537-7642
Wants chimney sweep items including toys, dolls, pictures, jewelry, figurines, etc.

Firebacks

Repro. Sources

Kurt Sterhl
Orpheus Coppersmith
52 Clematis Rd.
Agawam, MA 01001

Patricia Euston
New England Firebacks
P.O. Box 268
161 Main St. South
Woodbury, CT 06798
phone: 203-263-5737
*Makes and sells reproduction solid
cast iron firebacks.*

Wendy Stoughton
Country Iron Foundry
800 Laurel Oak Dr., Ste. 200
Dept. MAC97
Naples, FL 34108
phone: 941-513-1400
fax: 941-513-0969
*Firebacks are decorative cast iron
plates that protect the rear wall of the
fireplace from heat damage; call for
catalog of firebacks and andirons.*

Fireboards

Repro. Sources

Hope Angier
Sheepscot Stenciling
RFD 1 Box 613
Wiscasset, ME 04578-9734
phone: 207-586-5692

Country Hand
P.O. Box 212
West Terre Haute, IN 47885

Mantels

Dealers

Park Pigott
Mantels of Yesteryear
70 W. Tennessee Ave.
P.O. Box 908
Mc Caysville, GA 30555
phone: 706-492-5534
fax: 706-492-3758

Repro. Sources

Williams Cabinetry
P.O. Box 39
North Sullivan, ME 04664

Tools

Repro. Sources

Lemee's Fireplace Equipment
815 Bedford St.
Bridgewater, MA 02324-3007
phone: 508-697-2672

Charles R. Messner
Colonial Lighting & Tinware Reproductions
316 Franklin St.
Denver, PA 17517-1240
phone: 717-336-6295 or 717-336-0424
*Makes Early American tinware:
cookie cutters, coffee pots, wall*

*sconces, chandeliers (electric and
non-electric), post lights.*

Virginia Metalcrafters
1010 East Main St.
Waynesboro, VA 22980
phone: 540-949-9400 or 800-368-1002
*Makes and sells andirons, fireplace
tools and fenders, chandeliers,
candlesticks, sconces, garden
sculpture.*

Steve Kayne
Kayne & Son Custom Forged Hardware
100 Daniel Ridge Rd.
Candler, NC 28715
phone: 704-667-8868 or 704-665-1988
fax: 704-665-8303
*Fireplace tools, cranes, oven doors,
enclosures, andirons, kitchen utensils,
etc.; also does repairs, restoration &
conservation; $5 for two catalogs.*

Ronald Potts
Chiswell Forge
2255 Manchester Rd.
North Lawrence, OH 44666

FIREWORKS MEMORABILIA

(see also TOYS, Cannons; TOYS, Cap
Guns)

Collectors

Brian J. Zompanti
P.O. Box 3193
New Britain, CT 06050-3193
phone: 203-223-8872 or 203-225-5137
*Wants to buy old firecracker packs,
boxes, catalogs, labels, etc.*

Stuart Schneider
P.O. Box 64
Teaneck, NJ 07666-0064
phone: 201-261-1983
*Wants old firecracker pack labels
from the turn of the century to the
1950s.*

Barry Zecker
Collectors Exchange, Inc.
P.O. Box 217
Martinsville, NJ 08836-0217
phone: 908-253-3400
*Wants firecracker packs, fireworks
catalogs; boxes for Sparklers, caps,
salutes, torpedoes; also price lists,
flyers, salesman's samples, photos of
old fireworks plants and employees;
happy to appraise items you have; 42
years exper.*

R.J. Scheurer
1 Milburn Rd., RD #3
Goshen, NY 10924
phone: 914-294-7093
*Wants fireworks, 1850-1967 4th of
July memorabilia, firecracker labels,
packs, posters and catalogs.*

Rick Fuith
5429 N. Linder
Chicago, IL 60630
phone: 312-775-6792
*Wants firecracker labels, packs,
catalogs, anything on fireworks.*

Bill Scales
130 Fordham Circle
Pueblo, CO 81005-1649
phone: 719-561-0603
*Especially wants old firecracker
packs, labels, catalogs, etc.*

Experts

Karen Lea Rose
4420 Wisconsin Ave.
Tampa, FL 33616-1031
phone: 813-839-6245
*Wants old packs of fireworks or old
firecracker catalogs.*

Hal Kantrud
Newsletter: Phoenix, The
Rt. 7 Box 52
Jamestown, ND 58401
phone: 701-252-5639
e-mail: Hal.Kantrud@daktelco.com
*Wants old firecracker packs and
labels plus other fireworks related
items; published quarterly newsletter.*

Museums/Libraries

Al Castellano, Jr.
Firework City, Inc.
1444 W. 18th St.
P.O. Box 548
Rochester, IN 46975-0548
phone: 219-223-1616
fax: 219-223-3666
*Extensive collection; looking for old
fireworks packs, labels, catalogs,
price lists, posters, salesman samples,
pictures or anything 4th of July; will
trade any of the above for live
fireworks; donated items will bear
donor's name.*

FISHING COLLECTIBLES

(see also AQUARIUMS; BOOKS,
Reference [Fishing]; DECOYS, Fish;
SPORTING COLLECTIBLES)

Auction Services

Withington, Inc.
RD 2 Box 440
Hillsboro, NH 03244
phone: 603-464-3232

Bob Lang
Lang's Auction
31R Turtle Cove
Raymond, ME 04071
phone: 207-655-4265
fax: 207-655-4265

Ronnie Roberts, ISA
Dixie Sporting Collectibles
1206 Rama Rd.
Charlotte, NC 28211-4345
phone: 704-364-2900 or 704-364-3382
fax: 704-364-2322
e-mail: gun1898@aol.com
Internet: http://www.sportauction.com

Lindy Egan
Lures Etc.
4052 Sequoia Ave.
Grove City, OH 43123
phone: 614-871-3162

Clubs/Associations

Florida Antique Tackle Collectors, Inc.
P.O. Box 420703
Kissimmee, FL 34742-0703

Raymond & Barb Carver
National Fishing Lure Collectors Club
Newsletter: NFLCC Gazette
22325 B Drive South
Marshall, MI 49068-9722
phone: 616-781-5668
*3500 members; fosters awareness of
fishing tackle collecting as a hobby;
assists members in identification,
location and valuing fishing tackle,
etc.; 26 pg. newsletter published
quarterly; also publishes NFLCC full
color magazine.*

Collectors

Paul Webber
P.O. Box K
Stockton, NJ 08559-0350
phone: 609-397-8727

Don Bailen
6 Carol Ave.
Fredonia, NY 14063
phone: 716-679-7292
*Collects old metal lures stamped
"Haskell," "Chapman," "Comstock,"
and most other lures stamped with
pre-1920 patent dates.*

Sam G. Husselman
474 Johnston Dr.
Bethlehem, PA 18017-1815
phone: 610-866-7984
e-mail: husselman@enter.net
Internet: http://www.enter.net/
~husselman/sam.html
*Very familiar with the identification
and pricing of most antique fishing
lures and other fishing collectibles;
his web page has original research
and information on the Heddon Crazy
Crawler and 210 lures, two of his
specialties.*

Philip W. Hartman
1 South Alley
P.O. Box 263
New Market, MD 21774
phone: 301-865-5651
fax: 301-865-0518
e-mail: ritam@erols.com
Internet: http://www.newmarketmd.com/
grange.htm
*Buys lures, reels (including German
silver reels), tackle, bobbers, etc.;
wrote the first article, "Fishing Pike
Floats & Bobbers" in "Antique
Angler" (Aug. 1985); expert on
bobbers.*

David A. Gladwell
P.O. Box 238
Bedford, VA 24523-0238
phone: 540-586-1488 or 540-586-9575
*Wants old fishing tackle, especially
lures or plugs, and advertisements.*

Brian Shillito
5501 65th Ave. North
Pinellas Park, FL 33781
phone: 813-541-7540
*Wants pre-1950 fishing lures and
tackle.*

Lindy Egan
4052 Sequoia Ave.
Grove City, OH 43123
phone: 614-871-3162
*Wants to buy most anything having to
do with fishing.*

Rich Treml
P.O. Box 1791
Dearborn, MI 48121

Raymond L. Carver
22325 B Drive South
Marshall, MI 49068-9722
phone: 616-781-5668
*Author of "Bud Stewart - Michigan's
Legendary Lure Maker."*

Richard McCoy
2719 Lakeview Ave.
St. Joseph, MI 49085
*Wants to buy all kinds of fishing
tackle: sinkers, bobbers, plugs, lures,
poles, reels, tackle boxes.*

James Anderson
P.O. Box 120704
New Brighton, MN 55112
phone: 612-484-3198
*Wants old fishing related items: lures,
reels, posters, calendars, pins,
envelopes, bobbers, etc.*

Tome Yanke
400 Longfellow Lane
Columbia, MO 65201

Eric Fuchslocher
8050 Ventura Cyn Ave.
Panorama City, CA 91402
phone: 818-994-1492
*Wants to buy old wooden fishing
lures.*

George S. Lawson, Jr.
P.O. Box 796
Capitola, CA 95010-0796
phone: 408-476-6475
e-mail: fishnstuff@aol.com
*Collector of quality split bamboo fly
rods, all types of reels, old wooden
lures, vintage tackle catalogs, creels
and pre-1940 fishing licenses; author
of "Lawson's Price Guide to Old
Fishing Reels."*

Dealers

Martin J. Keane
Classic Rods & Tackle, Inc.
P.O. Box 288
Ashley Falls, MA 01222
phone: 413-229-7988
*Buys and sells antique rods, reels, and
exotic accessories; high grade rods
and reels bought and appraised.*

Bob Greenbaum
Bob & Shirley's Antiques
6151 Beverly Hills Rd.
Coopersburg, PA 18036
phone: 610-282-4881
*Wants all items related to the sport of
fishing.*

Neil Ghingold
Neil Ghingold Antiques
1230-32 Broad St.
Augusta, GA 30901-1116
phone: 706-722-3483
Wants to buy fishing collectibles.

John E. Shoffner
624 Merritt St.
Fife Lake, MI 49633-9142
phone: 616-879-3912
*Issues 6 lists a year with approx. 600
fish decoys and antique fishing tackle
items for sale.*

Experts

Gary Wood
Fishing Lure and Angling Collector
733 Myrtle Rd.
North Brunswick, NJ 08902-2549
phone: 908-821-7633
*Buying and appraising old fishing
lures, reels, floats, and related
advertising; feel free to call and chat;
"If it's got a hook, I'll take a look!"*

Ed & Carolyn Corwin
P.O. Box 1119
Hastings, FL 32145
phone: 904-692-2037
fax: 904-692-2037
*Buys, sells and appraises; general
information no charge; send SASE
with request; include photos or
photocopies if possible (lures can be
photocopied); specializes in pre-1940
reels, creels, lures, tackle catalogs.*

Robert Whitaker
2810 E. Desert Cove Ave.
Phoenix, AZ 85028-2620
phone: 602-992-7304
fax: 602-493-5598

Rick Edmisten
P.O. Box 686
North Hollywood, CA 91603-0686
phone: 818-763-9406
fax: 818-763-5974
*Wants to buy pre-1940 wooden lures,
quality reels, catalogs, some high
grade rods, tackle boxes, art prints,
etc.; collect calls O.K.; offers free
appraisal of any and all fishing tackle
from photos sent if SASE included.*

Gabby Talkington
4703 Upland Dr.
Richmond, CA 94803-3227
phone: 510-223-1142
fax: 510-233-3388
e-mail: oldlures@aol.com
*Longtime buyer/seller of vintage
fishing tackle: wood fishing lures,
reels, rods, advertising and catalogs;
sale list available; free appraisals; life*

*member National Fishing Lures
Collectors Club.*

Richard Streater
P.O. Box 393
Mercer Island, WA 98040-0393
phone: 206-232-9060
fax: 206-232-9060
*Collector of antique fishing lures and
tackle; author of "Streater's
Reference Catalogue of Old Fishing
Lures", available from the author;
fishing gadgetry a specialty.*

Museums/Libraries

American Museum of Fly Fishing
Magazine: American Fly Fisher, The
P.O. Box 42
Manchester, VT 05254
phone: 802-362-3300
*Non-profit educational institution
dedicated to preserving the rich
history of fly fishing and American
angling; over 1,500 rods, 800 reels,
40,000 flies, 2,500 books, manuscripts, photos, etc.*

Ted Dzialo
National Fresh Water Fishing Hall of
Fame
Newsletter: Splash, The
One Fame Dr.
P.O. Box 33
Hayward, WI 54843-0033
phone: 715-634-4440
fax: 715-634-4440
*Custodian of historical sport fishing
artifacts; world record qualifier;
clearinghouse for contemporary &
historical fishing facts.*

Periodicals

Abenaki Publishers
Magazine: American Angler
P.O. Box 4100
Bennington, VT 05201-4100
phone: 802-446-1518
*Contains periodic articles about
vintage fishing collectibles.*

Joseph A. Arches
Newsletter: Fisherman's Trader, The
P.O. Box 203
Gillette, NJ 07933-0203
phone: 908-647-9356
fax: 908-647-9356
e-mail: joeftrdr@aol.com
*A bi-monthly publication which
includes articles on new, used, and
antique fishing tackle and equipment;
over 130 classified ads, many of which
list antique fishing lures and
equipment for sale.*

Magazine: Fishing Collectibles
Magazine
2005 Tree House Lane
Plano, TX 75023
phone: 972-867-5980
*The magazine for anyone interested in
fishing or fishing collectibles; covers
all aspects of fishing collectibles
including art, advertising, books,*

*decoys, lures, paraphernalia, rods,
reels, etc.; free appraisals.*

Fly Fishing

Experts

Chuck Allen
Sporting Adventure
919 Baltimore Pike
Ellicott City, MD 21043
phone: 410-465-1112
*Buys and sells high quality fly fishing
equipment and other sporting gear;
takes collectible equipment on
consignment to sell.*

Periodicals

Abenaki Publishers
Magazine: Saltwater Fly Fishing
P.O. Box 4100
Bennington, VT 05201-4100
phone: 802-446-1518
*Bonefish, tarpon, permit, redfish,
snook, stripers, blues; destinations,
flats, rigging/knots, techniques, skills,
flies, casting, conservation, new
products.*

Fly Fishing (Flies)

Experts

David Klausmeyer
New England Angler, The
P.O. Box 105
Steuben, ME 04680-0105
phone: 207-546-2018

Ice Fishing Spears

Experts

Marcel L. Salive, Ph.D.
1483 Dunster Lane
Potomac, MD 20854-6107
phone: 301-762-1909
e-mail: msalive@erols.com
*Author of "Ice Fishing Spears"
(MarJac Publishing).*

Reels

Clubs/Associations

Arne Soland, Mem.
Old Reel Collectors Association
Newsletter: Old Reel Collectors
Association Newsletter
849 NE 70th Ave.
Portland, OR 97213
phone: 503-253-1741
e-mail: spurr@kingfisher.com
Internet: http://www.gorp.com/cl_angle/
canecoun/orca.htm
*Purpose is the further the knowledge
about reels used in fishing from 1800
through 1970.*

Collectors

Royal E. Fox
64 Colifield
Staten Island, NY 10302
Wants spinning reels; working or not;

parts, boxes, literature, brochures, manuals.

Michael Nogay
3501 Riverview Dr.
P.O. Box 2540
Weirton, WV 26062

Reels (Fly Fishing)

Experts

Jim Brown
97 Franklin St.
Stamford, CT 06901-1309
phone: 203-324-5441
Specializes in collecting American fly reels and fly rod lures; author of "Fishing Reel Patents of the U.S., 1838 - 1940" (1985) and "A Treasury of Reels" (1990).

Rods (Bamboo)

Collectors

Lee Pattison
6 Christview Dr.
Cuba, NY 14727-1202
phone: 716-968-2458
Wants old and new fishing tackle, large ocean reels, old wood tackle boxes, fishing books, tackle catalogs.

Udwary
629 Spencer Circle
Spartanburg, SC 29307-2507
Wants to buy bamboo fly rods, pre-1965, 7', 7 1/2', 8' sizes; Edwards, Leonard, Thomas, High-Grade Granger, Hardy, Heddon, Phillipson; OK if in need of repair, but must be priced accordingly.

Experts

David Klausmeyer
P.O. Box 105
Steuben, ME 04680-0105
phone: 207-546-2018
Buys and sells quality bamboo fly rods; also manufacturers bamboo rods and provides expert appraisal services for quality bamboo fly rods.

FLAGS & FLAG RELATED COLLECTIBLES

(see also MILITARIA)

Clubs/Associations

Scot Guenter
North American Vexillological Association
Newsletter: NAVA News
1977 N. Olden Ave., Ste. 225
Trenton, NJ 08618-2193
Dedicated to the promotion of vexillogy, the scientific & scholarly study of flag history and symbolism; publishes bi-monthly newsletter and annual "Raven" journal, annual meetings, publishes booklets, undertakes special projects.

Collectors

Jon Radel
3806 Candlelight Ct.
Alexandria, VA 22310-2248
e-mail: jon@radel.com
Internet: http://www.radel.com/
Collects flags, flag books, and other printed matted concerning flags, including postcards; older foreign and local flags, foreign publications of special interest. No common or 20th cent. U.S. flags or flag items, please.

Mark Sutton
2035 St. Andrews Circle
Carmel, IN 46032-9547
phone: 317-844-5648
Buys/trades old cloth American flags with 47 or less than 45 stars; wants original flags from 6" to HUGE; also unusual star patterns.

Dealers

James J. Ferrigan III
Flag Store, The
520 Broadway
Sonoma, CA 95476
phone: 707-996-8140 or 888-GET-FLAG
fax: 707-996-8171
e-mail: flags@vom.com
Internet: http://www.3000.com/flags
Dealer, expert, vendor, manufacturer.

Experts

Robert Banks
Stars & Stripes
18901 Gold Mine Court
Brookeville, MD 20833-2711
phone: 301-774-7850
Seeking antique American flags with 43 stars or less; also wants unique or uncommon examples of any period.

Man./Prod./Dist.

Carrot-Top Industries, Inc.
328 Elizabeth Brady Rd.
P.O. Box 820
Hillsborough, NC 27278
phone: 800-628-3524 or 919-732-6200
Sells new flags and related hardware: US, states and territories, international, flagpoles, mounting hardware, parade accessories, NASCAR, special interest flags, historical and military flags, globes, pennants, custom designed flags.

Military

Experts

Ben K. Weed
Colours, The
P.O. Box 4643
Stockton, CA 95204
e-mail: B.K.Weed@worldnet.att.net
Internet: http://www.collectoronline.com/collect/wb-old-flags.html
Largest private collector of worldwide military flags; buys flags, parts and photos.

FLASHLIGHTS

Clubs/Associations

Bill Utley
Flashlight Collectors of America
Newsletter: Flashlight Newsletter
P.O. Box 4095
Tustin, CA 92681-4095
phone: 714-730-1252
fax: 714-505-4067
e-mail: flashlights@worldnet.att.net
Eight page flashlight newsletter printed quarterly: articles of flashlight history, great finds, questions & answers, classified ads, old flashlight catalog reprints.

Collectors

John Treggiari
Salem, MA 01970-1225
phone: 508-744-2897
fax: 508-744-5572
e-mail: micrometer@juno.com
Serious collector wants to buy old flashlights and related manufacturer catalogs and displays; flashlights need not be working; especially wants with patent dates prior to 1930; old flashlight batteries also purchased.

Stuart Schneider
P.O. Box 64
Teaneck, NJ 07666-0064
phone: 201-261-1983
Buys odd and unusual or early flashlights and flashlight advertising; author of "Collecting Flashlights."

Kent Myers
P.O. Box 4074
Cave Creek, AZ 85331
phone: 602-488-1616
Flashlight collector wants to buy pre-1920 flashlights, related literature, etc.; please send photo and price.

Bill Utley
P.O. Box 4095
Tustin, CA 92681-4095
phone: 714-730-1252
fax: 714-505-4067
e-mail: flashlights@worldnet.att.net
Collector/historian wants old flashlights, flashlight advertising, flashlight catalogs and other flashlight related items; interested in almost any portable object containing a dry cell battery and a light bulb.

Dealers

Shaw
P.O. Box 5096
Southfield, MI 48086
Wants to buy 1920s-1960s vintage flash lights: brass, chrome, enamel, etc.

FLATWARE

(see also SILVER; SILVERPLATE; TABLEWARE)

Matching Services

Paul & Pearl Hoffman
China Brokers, Ltd.
11 Westgate Ct.
Colts Neck, NJ 07722
phone: 908-866-6613 or 800-867-6613

Wilma Saxton, Inc.
37 Celementon Rd. Box 395
Berlin, NJ 08009
phone: 609-767-8640 or 800-267-8029
fax: 609-768-7795
Matching service for sterling, silverplate, stainless, pewter, dirilyte; flatware and hollowware; also repairs and replating; write for free price list in your pattern.

Alice Korman
Alice's Past & Presents Replacements
P.O. Box 465
Merrick, NY 11566-0465
phone: 516-379-1352
fax: 516-379-7302
Matching and locating service for stainless and silverplate flatware; most manufacturers.

Tony Garfield
Yudin & Associates
P.O. Box 1980
Boothwyn, PA 19061
phone: 610-859-9698
fax: 610-859-0142
Community, Gorham, Holmes & Edwards, National, Oneida, 1847 Rogers, Wallace, silverplate.

Cecil F. Skillin
111 Caribbean Rd.
Naples, FL 33963-2795
phone: 813-597-3676
fax: 813-597-3676
Matching service for all types of flatware except sterling silver: carries silverplate, sterling II, stainless, Dirilyte, and pewter flatware.

Mary Ann Lowery
Crystal Corner, Inc., The
P.O. Box 756
Boaz, AL 35957
phone: 205-593-6169
fax: 205-593-6560
e-mail: ccorner@stargate.imatrex.com
Specializes in stainless and silverplate flatware.

Sterling & Collectables
P.O. Box 1665
Mansfield, OH 44901
phone: 800-537-5783
Sterling, silverplate, stainless, dirilyte; all manufacturers; current and discontinued.

Dona Miller
Ann Arbor Dinnerware Exchange
P.O. Box 6054
Ann Arbor, MI 48106-6054
phone: 313-663-9883
fax: 313-663-5766
e-mail: aadinex@aadinex.com
Internet: http://www.aadinex.com
A matching service for stainless, silverplate and sterling; sells Oneida

products at discount; WWW homepage contains a frequently updated flatware item identification guide available free of charge.

Barron's
P.O. Box 994
Novi, MI 48376
phone: 800-538-6340
  Matches stainless, silverplate, and sterling flatware.

Clintsman International
20855 Watertown Rd.
Waukesha, WI 53186-1873
phone: 414-798-0440 or 800-781-8900
fax: 414-798-8879
  Stocks all manufacturers of discontinued patterns for sterling silver, silverplate, and stainless steel flatware.

Don's Antiques - Heirloom Completions Division
1620-D Venice St.
Granite City, IL 62040-2355
phone: 618-931-4333
  Dirilyte, Sterling, Silverplate, Stainless.

China Replacements
P.O. Box 508
High Ridge, MO 63049
phone: 800-562-2655
  Matches all major brands of sterling, silverplate, and stainless.

Betty Stachurski
Betty's Crystal & China
P.O. Box 433
Lawrence, KS 66044-0433
phone: 913-842-8054
  Stainless, silverplate and sterling: 1881 Rogers, 1847 Rogers Bros., Alvin, Christofle, Community, COntinental, Dansk, Fine Arts, Frank Smith, Fraser, Gorham, Harmony House, Heritage, International, Kirk-Stieff, Reed & Barton, etc.

Advisory Replacement Service
901 W. Walnut Hill Ln., 5A-9
Irving, TX 75038
  A replacement service for stainless, silverplate, and sterling silver flatware: Reed & Barton, Gorham, Oneida, Buccellati, etc.

Joanne Cone Matching Service
34 Silverwood
Irvine, CA 92714-2845
phone: 714-551-3173
e-mail: jochina@aol.com
  All manufacturers; stainless, silverplate and sterling silver; Oneida specialist, Fraser, Gense, Gorham, International, Lauffer, Mikasa, National, Noritake, Oxford Hall, Reed & Barton, Roberts, Towle, Wallace, etc.

Past & Present
14851 Avenue 360
Visalia, CA 93292
phone: 415-258-1775 or 209-798-0029
fax: 209-798-1415
  Silverplate, sterling, stainless,

Dirilyte; by Alvin, Easterling, Frank Smith, Fraser, Gorham, International, Jensen, Kirk, Lunt, Manchester, Oneida, Reed & Barton, Steiff, Tiffany, Towle, Wallace, Westmoreland, etc.

Sterling Shop, The
P.O. Box 595
Silverton, OR 97381-0595
phone: 503-873-6315
  Sterling and silverplate flatware matching service.

Grace Ann Kupferschmid
Matchmaker of Iowa
109 Discovery Bay St.
Sequim, WA 98382-9327
phone: 360-683-7517
  Major brands of discontinued stainless, pewter, gold electroplated including Lunt, Wallace-International, Gorham, Oneida, Reed & Barton, Towle (including Lauffer, Supreme Cutlery), Fraser, Mikasa.

Aames' Nationwide Network for Stainless, Silverplate, Sterling
P.O. Box 88840
Steil, WA 98388
phone: 206-984-0701

Mrs. Kay's Sterling, Stainless & Silverplate
Dept. MA-693
P.O. Box 99211
Tacoma, WA 98499-0211
phone: 206-582-4636
  Matching service for DISCONTINUED FLATWARE only; Dirilyte, stainless, silverplate, and sterling; takes trade-in's; does insurance appraisals; nation-wide network of pickers, suppliers.

Suppliers

Dennis Blaine
Cutlery Specialties
22 Morris Lane
Great Neck, NY 11024-1707
phone: 516-829-5899 or 516-773-0071
fax: 516-773-8076
e-mail: Dennis13@aol.com
  Preservation products for flatware: waxes, polishes, cleaners, glues, epoxies, adhesives, chamois, buffs, putty.

Silverplate

Matching Services

Michael Kucharski
Vintage Silver
33 LeMay Court
Williamsville, NY 14221-3628
phone: 716-631-0419
fax: 716-433-2850
e-mail: mikekuch@localnet.com
  Buys and sells; specializes in matching 1890-1950 silverplated flatware; 20,000 pieces in stock; 100s of patterns.

John Benetti
Silver Scotty
420 Ashwood Rd.
Darlington, PA 16115
phone: 412-827-2188
fax: 412-827-2811

Silver Girls
168 Riverview Rd. SW
Eatonton, GA 31024-6836
phone: 912-968-5225
fax: 912-968-5225
  Silverplated flatware; all major manufacturers of discontinued/collectible patterns.

Phil & Angela Dreis
Antique Cupboard
3712 N. 92 St.
Milwaukee, WI 53222
phone: 800-637-4583
fax: 414-464-1616
  Over 900 sterling and 1000 plated patterns in stock; buys and sells current and obsolete patterns and rare and unusual pieces; largest inventory in the Midwest.

Helen Lawler
Helen Lawler's Silverplate Matching Service
5400 East County Rd. #2
Blytheville, AR 72315
phone: 573-720-8502
  Large inventory of silverplated flatware; call or write for your pattern listing with prices; antique and recently discontinued patterns.

Kinzie's Silverplate Matching
P.O. Box 522
Turlock, CA 95381
phone: 209-634-4880
  Silverplated flatware, some sterling; send photocopy or tracing of place setting, pattern name and backstamp; want lists maintained.

Sterling Silver

Matching Services

Silver Lady Antiques
Echo Bridge Mall
381 Elliot St.
Newton, MA 02164
phone: 617-243-0900 or 617-784-9184
fax: 617-784-0628
  Tiffany, Jensen, Gorham, Kirk flatware and holloware.

Ross Simmons
#9 Ross Simmons Dr.
Cranston, RI 02920-4476
phone: 800-556-7376
  Sells new, active patterns for Gorham, Reed & Barton, Wallace, Towle, Lunt, Kirk-Stieff, International.

Regina Negrotti
Tablescapes
49 Elkton Ave.
P.O. Box 3165
Cheshire, CT 06410
phone: 800-801-4084
  A small, personal matching service with a constantly changing inventory;

want lists are kept; send photocopy or photo when unsure of pattern name.

Silver & China Exchange
P.O. Box 4601
Dept. MA
Stamford, CT 06907-0601
phone: 203-322-5963
  Sterling flatware only; no stainless or silverplate; computerized search service available.

R.S. Goldberg
67 Beverly Rd.
Hawthorne, NJ 07506-3201
phone: 800-252-6655 or 201-427-6555
  Hundreds of patterns in stock; always buying and selling.

Nathan Horowicz
Nathan Horowicz Antiques
1050 2nd Ave., Gallery 82
New York, NY 10022
phone: 800-214-6320 or 212-755-6320
fax: 212-755-6438
  Large assortment of flatware, tea sets, holloware; Tiffany, Georg Jensen; all American and European manufacturers.

Pattern Finders, A
P.O. Box 206
Port Jefferson Station, NY 11776-0206
phone: 516-928-5158 or 800-216-2446
fax: 516-928-5170
e-mail: apattern@aol.com

Martin Spickler, PhD
Tova's Treasures
11410 Strand Dr., #207
Rockville, MD 20852
phone: 301-984-5954
  A specialized matching matching service for American sterling silver patterns.

Thurber's
2256C Dabeny Rd.
Richmond, VA 23230
phone: 804-278-9080 or 800-848-7237
  Carries only active patterns.

Joe Batista
Replacements Ltd.
P.O. Box 26029
Greensboro, NC 27420
phone: 800-737-5223 or 800-REP-LACE
fax: 910-697-3100
e-mail: replaceltd@aol.com
Internet: http://www.imall.com/stores/replacements
  China, crystal and flatware (obsolete, active and inactive.)

Beverly H. Bremer
Beverly Bremer Silver Shop
3164 Peachtree Rd. NE
Atlanta, GA 30305
phone: 404-261-4009
fax: 404-261-5742
  Appraises, buys, sells and matches sterling silver flatware, new and antique sterling silver holloware & giftware; send for inventory of your sterling pattern or send photocopy of

your pattern; no SASE required; answers all inquiries.

Atlantic Silver & China
7405 N.W. 57th St.
Tamarac, FL 33319
phone: 800-288-6665 or 954-720-4559
fax: 954-720-4577
Inactive and active sterling silver flatware and hollowware; buys and sells.

Silver Queen
730 N. Ind. Rocks Rd.
Belleair Bluffs, FL 33770
phone: 800-262-3134 or 813-581-6827
High quality, estate and new flatware; call or write for inventory list of your pattern; also buys sterling silver flatware.

Antique Silver House, The
8976 Seminole Blvd.
Largo, FL 34642
phone: 813-392-7250 or 800-SIL-VER5

Debra Bonner
Colonial Silver Shoppe
20 Gaylan Court
Montgomery, AL 36109
phone: 800-675-4837 or 334-272-7282
Gorham, Wallace, International, Towle, Kirk-Stieff, Lunt.

Tim & Nancy Young
Alcove Antiques
9825 Concord Rd.
Brentwood, TN 37027
phone: 615-776-5152
fax: 615-776-3039

Carol Lewis
Sterling & Collectables, Inc.
P.O. Box 1665
Mansfield, OH 44901
phone: 800-537-5783 or 419-756-8800
fax: 419-756-2990
A matching service for discontinued and current sterling tableware, both flatware and hollowware; also carries current and back years of sterling and crystal Christmas ornaments.

Benjamin Randolph
Eden Sterling
7672 Montgomery Rd.
Cincinnati, OH 45236
phone: 800-385-3336 or 513-792-9345

Phil & Angela Dreis
Antique Cupboard
3712 N. 92 St.
Milwaukee, WI 53222
phone: 800-637-4583
fax: 414-464-1616
Over 900 sterling and 1000 plated patterns in stock; buys and sells current and obsolete patterns and rare and unusual pieces; largest inventory in the Midwest.

Ted Rickard
Silver Service
Wilmette, IL 60091
phone: 708-256-5900
fax: 708-256-5952
e-mail: trick2@juno.com
Specializing in matching discontinued American and English sterling silver flatware; also locates antique sterling silver flatware.

Audrey Rickard
China Trade Ltd.
2133 Birchwood Ave.
Wilmette, IL 60091-2305
phone: 708-256-7414 or 800-295-4200
fax: 708-256-5952
e-mail: Trick2@juno.com
Discontinued and antique sterling patterns: Gorham, Reed & Barton, Towle, Kirk Stieff, International, Tiffany, WAllace, Lunt, Dominick & Haff, Durgin, Alvin, Whiting, Tuttle, etc.

Dining Elegance, Ltd.
P.O. Box 4203
Saint Louis, MO 63163
phone: 314-865-1408
Sterling silver - full sets only.

MidweSterling
4311 NE Vivion Rd.
Kansas City, MO 64119-2838
phone: 816-454-1990
fax: 816-454-1605
Largest sterling flatware inventory in the country; buys/sells sterling; also polishes, repairs, reblades knives; big buyer of sterling silver flatware and hollowware.

Madeleine Guice Nicoladis
Melange Sterling
5419 Magazine St.
New Orleans, LA 70115
phone: 800-513-3991 or 504-899-4796
fax: 504-899-4796
Specializes in active, inactive, and obsolete American, British and Continental sterling flatware.

Helen & Duncan Cox
As You Like It Silver Shop
3025 Magazine St.
New Orleans, LA 70115-2232
phone: 800-828-2311 or 504-897-6915
fax: 504-895-4149
e-mail: ayliss@cris.com
Internet: http://www.cris.com/~ayliss/
Large inventory of active and inactive patterns; also tea services, goblets, mint juleps, etc.

Locators, Inc.
2217 Cottondale Lane
Little Rock, AR 72202-2018
phone: 501-663-1114 or 800-367-9690
Carries out-of-production (discontinued) china and crystal, and discontinued as well as active sterling flatware patterns.

Betty's Sterling Silver Matching Service
200 Avenida Santa Margarita
San Clemente, CA 92672
phone: 714-498-5330 or 714-498-4027
fax: 714-498-5330
Active, inactive, and obsolete sterling silver patterns; all manufacturers; send want lists and photocopy; also sterling silver holloware and sterling silver ornaments from 1970 to present.

Silver Lane Antiques
P.O. Box 322
San Leandro, CA 94577-0032
phone: 510-483-0632
American sterling flatware in complete sets or by the piece; tea services, trays, etc. also available; specializing in unique pieces for advanced collectors.

Brenda Clayton
Silver Thistle
14314 SW Allen Blvd. #217
Beaverton, OR 97005
phone: 503-235-3749
Rogers, International, Gorham, Holmes and Edwards, and others; send SASE with pattern, manufacturer or photocopy for identification.

Repair Services

MidweSterling
4311 NE Vivion Rd.
Kansas City, MO 64119-2838
phone: 816-454-1990
fax: 816-454-1605
Expert knife reblading, silverware repair, polishing, full-time silversmiths on staff; also sells loose knife blades.

FLEA MARKETS

(see also ANTIQUES SHOP DIRECTORIES; TOURS/BUYING TRIPS)

Periodicals

Lawrence Koons
Newspaper: Worldwide Auction Results
18 Walnut, #3
Belpre, OH 45714-2429
phone: 614-423-3393 or 614-423-5478
fax: 614-423-9638
Monthly tabloid featuring worldwide press releases from auction companies; price realized; for buyers and sellers; sample copy $2.

Suppliers

Lawrence Koons
18 Walnut, #3
Belpre, OH 45714-2429
phone: 614-423-3393 or 614-423-5478
fax: 614-423-9638

Directories

Periodicals

House of Collectibles
Guide: Official Directory to U.S. Flea Markets
201 East 50th St.
New York, NY 10022-7703
phone: 212-572-8796
e-mail: 71732.1726@compuserve.com
Internet: http://www.randomhouse.com1
Covers about 500 markets; provides quality information about each.

Dorothy & Charles Clark
Clark's Publications
Guide: Clark's Flea Market U.S.A.
419 Garcon Point Rd.
Milton, FL 32583
phone: 904-623-0794
A national flea market directory issued quarterly; over 2,000 flea markets and swap meets listed; subscription.

Jim Goodridge
Goodridge Guides
Guide: Official Flea Market Directory
P.O. Box 510085
Saint Louis, MO 63129
phone: 314-296-0989
e-mail: jimgoodridge@delphi.com
Covers all 50 states; contains over 3,500 separate listings of flea markets across North America.

Directories (Foreign)

Periodicals

Peter Manston
Travel Keys
Guide: Manston's Flea Market Guides
P.O. Box 160691
Sacramento, CA 95816-0691
phone: 916-452-5200
Publishes a series of Flea Market Guides, for Britain, France and Germany; $9.95 plus $4.00 shipping; accepts credit card orders.

FLICKERS

Dealers

Joe Statkus
84 State Rd.
Eliot, ME 03903
phone: 207-439-7429
Carries a wide selection of flicker rings and specializes in hard-to-find flickers.

Gary Kraut
Alphaville
226 W. Houston St.
New York, NY 10014-4846
phone: 212-675-6850
fax: 212-741-2609
e-mail: alphavil@mindspring.com
Internet: http://www.alphaville.com
Sells ring, button, pin, key chain flickers; flickers are those specially coated dimestore images mounted on cardboard backings that "moved" or shifted scenes as if animated when

moved or viewed from a different angle.

FLOORCLOTHS

Repro. Sources

Sharon & Roger Mason
Olde Virginia Floorcloth & Trading Co.
4408 Faigle Rd.
Portsmouth, VA 23703-4815
phone: 804-564-0600
  Painted canvas floorcloths created in 18th cent. style; 100% cotton canvas heavily primed, decorated with oils, varnished; supplies.

Angie Nelson
Homeplace Collection
1882 Kennedy Farm Rd. N
Thomasville, NC 27360-8335
phone: 910-472-6396
fax: 910-472-6396
  Offers handpainted canvas floorcloths, and tabletop accessories (place mats, table runners, coasters/ trivets.)

FLOWER "FROGS"

Collectors

William G. Sommer, MD
9 W. 10th St.
New York, NY 10011-8748
phone: 212-260-0999
  Wants ceramic figural flower "frogs": dancing ladies or nudes American (Cowan, Fulper, Rookwood) or European (Germany, England.)

Susan Cox
c/o Main Street Antique Mall
237 E. Main
El Cajon, CA 92020-3911
phone: 619-447-0811
  Wants American pottery flower frogs.

FOBS

(see WATCH FOBS)

FOLK ART

Richard Trump
Folk Art Association of the Southwest
3993 Old Santa Fe Trail
Santa Fe, NM 87501
phone: 505-984-8680

(see also BOTTLES, Puzzle; CAROUSELS & CAROUSEL FIGURES; CIGAR STORE COLLECTIBLES; COVERLETS; DECOYS; ANIMAL COL-LECTIBLES, Eagles; FRAKTURS; POPULAR CULTURE; QUILTS; RUGS, Hooked; SAMPLERS; SCRIMSHAW; SILHOUETTES; TRAMP ART)

Auction Services

Steve Slotin
Slotin Folk Art Auction House
Newspaper: 20th Century Folk Art News
5967 Blackberry Lane
Buford, GA 30518
phone: 770-932-1000
fax: 770-932-0506
Internet: http://www.selftaught.com
  Leading venue for self-taught, Outsider, Folk Art and Southern folk pottery; published newspaper twice each year chronicling important happenings in the field of 20th century folk art as the most popular feature, New, True & Blue Artists.

Clubs/Associations

Robin H. Wyllie
Nova Scotia Folk Art Festival Society
Newsletter: Nova Scotia Folk Art News
East LaHave, R.R. 3
Bridgewater
Nova Scotia B4V-2W2 Canada
phone: 902-766-4382

North Carolina Folk Art Society
141 Norwood Ave.
Asheville, NC 28804

Bill Rose
Deep South Society, Art & Pleasure Club
3500 St. Charles Ave., #204
New Orleans, LA 70115

Mel Penner
American Folk Art Society
597 Chippendale Ave.
Simi Valley, CA 93065
  For those interested in carousel art, quilts, weathervanes, and other historical and contemporary folk art.

Collectors

Michael J. Hennigan
20816 E. Eleven Mile
Saint Clair Shores, MI 48081
phone: 313-822-9730 or 810-445-4847
fax: 313-821-2766
  Wants Canadian folk art, muffler figures, tin man figure, bottle cap figures.

Dealers

Russ & Karen Goldberger
RJK Antiques
P.O. Box 2033
Hampton, NH 03843-2033
phone: 603-926-1770
fax: 603-929-4267
e-mail: rjduck@nh.ultranet.com
Internet: http:// www.maineantiquedigest.com/adimg/ decoys.htm
  Specializes in quality working decoys, folk art, and American furniture and accessories in their original painted surfaces.

Gary Guyette
Gary Guyette Antiques
P.O. Box 522
West Farmington, ME 04992
phone: 207-778-6256 or 207-625-8055
fax: 207-778-6501

Marguerite Riordan
Marguerite Riordan Antiques
8 Pearl St.
Stonington, CT 06378
phone: 203-535-2511 or 203-535-3431
fax: 203-535-3431
  Specializes in Folk Art, American furniture, paintings and decorative accessories; by appointment.

Peter H. Tillou Fine Arts
Prospect St.
Litchfield, CT 06759
phone: 203-567-5706

American Hurrah Antiques
766 Madison Ave.
New York, NY 10021
phone: 212-535-1930

Muleskinner Antiques
10626 Main St.
Clarence, NY 14031
  Buys and sells redware, antique lighting, fold art, game boards, primitives, weathervanes, early glass, decoys, trade signs, etc.

Edwin Hild
Old Hope Antiques, Inc.
Rte. 202 Box 209
New Hope, PA 18938
phone: 215-862-5055

M. Finkel & Daughter
936 Pine St.
Philadelphia, PA 19107
phone: 215-627-7797
fax: 215-627-8199

John C. Newcomer
John C. Newcomer & Assoc.
P.O. Box 130
Funkstown, MD 21734
phone: 301-790-1327

Joe Adams
America, Oh Yes!
P.O. Box 3075
Hilton Head, SC 29928
phone: 803-785-7100
fax: 803-671-9107
  Wants Folk Art paintings, carvings, quilts, crafts by Southern artisans (contemporary and antique.)

Donald E. Taussig
Sanders' Antique Mall
22 N. Lemon Ave.
Sarasota, FL 34236-5711
phone: 941-366-0400
fax: 941-388-2053
e-mail: sandersant@aol.com
  Buys and sells decoys, antique lighting, trade signs, decorative accessories.

Matt Lippa
Artisans
P.O. Box 256
Mentone, AL 35984-0256
phone: 205-634-4037
fax: 205-634-4037
e-mail: artisans@folkartisans.com
Internet: http://www.folkartisans.com
  Buy and sell folk art, outsider art, fine art; Internet WWW site offers links to additional dealers; also offers non-profit clubs and museums with an outlet to post notices, press releases, calendar items, etc. at no charge.

Louis Picek
Main Street Antiques and Art
110 West Main
P.O. Box 340
West Branch, IA 52358-0340
phone: 319-643-2065
  Buys and sells folk art; offers a monthly list of items for sale.

Frank & Barbara Pollack
1214 Green Bay Rd.
Highland Park, IL 60035-4011
phone: 708-433-2213 or 708-433-2295
fax: 312-372-8343
Internet: http:// www.maineantiquedigest.com/adimg/ pollack.htm
  Buys and sells American primitives: paintings, furniture, toleware, folk art, textiles, etc.

Experts

David A. Schorsch
David A. Schorsch Inc.
30 East 76th St.
New York, NY 10021
phone: 212-439-6100
fax: 212-439-6170

Helaine Fendelman
Helaine Fendelman & Assoc.
1248 Post Rd.
Scarsdale, NY 10583-2153
phone: 914-725-0292
fax: 914-472-2266
e-mail: HFendelman@aol.com
  Appraises and liquidates estates; author of the "Official Identification and Price Guide to American Folk Art."

Museums/Libraries

Robert D. Farwell, Dir.
Fruitlands Museums, Inc.
102 Prospect Hill Rd.
Harvard, MA 01451
phone: 508-456-3924
  A 19th century American art and history museum complex.

Museum of Fine Arts, Boston
465 Huntington Ave.
Boston, MA 02115-5523
phone: 617-267-9300
Internet: http://www.mfa.org/home.html

Yale University Art Gallery, Garvan
Collection
P.O. Box 2006 Yale Station
New Haven, CT 06520
phone: 203-432-0600

Museum of American Folk Art
61 West 62nd St.
New York, NY 10023
phone: 212-977-7170
e-mail: info@folkartmuse.org
Internet: http://www.folkartmuse.org/
*Dedicated to exploring the diversity of
American culture as expressed
through folk art.*

New-York Historical Society, The
Two West 77th St.
New York, NY 10024
phone: 212-873-3400
fax: 212-874-8706
e-mail: nyhs@interport.net
Internet: http://www.nyhistory.org
*An unparalleled resource for the study
and appreciation of American art,
history, and culture.*

Albany Institute of History & Art
125 Washington Ave.
Albany, NY 12210
phone: 518-463-4478

New York State Historical Association
and The Farmers' Museum, Inc., The
P.O. Box 800
Cooperstown, NY 13326
phone: 607-547-2593 or 607-547-2533

Landis Valley Farm Museum
2451 Kissel Hill Rd.
Lancaster, PA 17601
phone: 717-569-0401

Bucks County Historical Society
Newsletter: Penny Lots
84 S. Pine St.
Doylestown, PA 18901-4930
phone: 215-345-0210
fax: 215-230-0823
Internet: http://www.libertynet.org:80/
~bchs
*Operates three Nat. Historical
Landmarks; Mercer Museum has over
50,000 tools of Early American
trades/crafts; Spruance Library has
research material on trades & crafts;
Fonthill Museum is a concrete castle
laden with tiles & treasures.*

Pennsylvania Academy of Fine Arts
1301 Cherry St.
Philadelphia, PA 19102
phone: 215-972-7600

Dick Rominiecki
Historical Society of Pennsylvania
Magazine: Pennsylvania Magazine of
History & Biography
1300 Locust St.
Philadelphia, PA 19107
phone: 215-732-6200
e-mail: hsppr@aol.com
Internet: http://www.libertynet.org/
~pahist
*Largest independent center for
research in Pennsylvania; over 15
million archival documents, books,*

*maps, prints, drawings, photographs
and genealogical records.*

Daughters of the American Revolution
Museum
1776 D St. NW
Washington, DC 20006-5303
phone: 202-879-3254 or 202-879-3241
fax: 202-628-0820
e-mail: museum@dar.org

National Museum of American History
14th & Constitution Ave. NW
Washington, DC 20560
phone: 202-357-2700
Internet: http://www.si.edu/

Abby Aldrich Rockefeller Folk Art
Center
P.O. Box C
Williamsburg, VA 23185
phone: 804-229-1000

Paula Hooper
Museum of Early Southern Decorative
Arts
Journal: Journal of the Early Southern
Decorative Arts
P.O. Box 10310
Winston Salem, NC 27108-0310
phone: 910-721-7360 or 888-653-7253
fax: 910-721-7367
Internet: http://www.mesda.org
*Focuses on Southern decorative arts;
has Research Center, Catalog of Early
Southern Decorative Arts, and Index
of Southern Artists.*

David Warren
Bayou Bend Collection & Gardens, The
P.O. Box 6826
Houston, TX 77265-6826
phone: 713-639-7750
fax: 713-639-7770
*One of the nation's premier American
decorative arts collections, housed in
the former residence of Houston
philanthropist Miss Ima Hogg;
collection includes over 4,800 works
of American art: furniture, textiles,
paintings, etc.*

Museum of International Folk Art
P.O. Box 2087
Santa Fe, NM 87504
phone: 505-827-8350

On-Line Services

Matt Lippa
Artisans
P.O. Box 256
Mentone, AL 35984-0256
phone: 205-634-4037
fax: 205-634-4037
e-mail: artisans@folkartisans.com
Internet: http://www.folkartisans.com
*Buy and sell folk art, outsider art, fine
art; Internet WWW site offers links to
additional dealers; also offers non-
profit clubs and museums with an
outlet to post notices, press releases,
calendar items, etc. at no charge.*

Periodicals

Museum of American Folk Art
Magazine: Folk Art
61 West 62nd St.
New York, NY 10023
phone: 212-977-7170
e-mail: info@folkartmuse.org
Internet: http://www.folkartmuse.org/

Repro. Sources

Mulberry Magic
P.O. Box 62
Ruckersville, VA 22968

Folk Art Emporium
3591 Forest Haven Lane
Chesapeake, VA 23321

Carvings

Repro. Sources

Vaughn Rawson
Whimsical Whittler, The
1745 W. Columbia Rd.
Mason, MI 48854-9259
phone: 517-676-4846
*Specializes in reproduction folk art
carvings.*

Contemporary

Clubs/Associations

Ann Oppenhimer
Folk Art Society of America
Newsletter: Folk Art Messenger
P.O. Box 17041
Richmond, VA 23226-7041
phone: 804-285-4532 or 800-527-3655
fax: 804-285-4532
e-mail: fasa@folkart.org
Internet: http://www.folkart.org
*Non-profit organization formed to
discover, study, promote, preserve,
exhibit, and document contemporary
folk art, folk artists, and folk
environments; newsletter published
quarterly.*

Museums/Libraries

Joan M. Bendetti, Lib.
Craft & Folk Art Museum
5800 Wilshire Blvd.
Los Angeles, CA 90036-4500
phone: 213-934-9684 or 213-937-5544
fax: 213-937-5576
*Specializing in contemporary craft,
design, folk art: clay, fiber, wood,
glass, paper, costume, dolls, masks,
etc.; artist's registry.*

Periodicals

Florence Laffal, Ed.
Gallery Press
Newsletter: Folk Art Finder
One River
Essex, CT 06426
phone: 860-767-0313
*FAF is devoted to news and
information on contemporary folk art;
calendar, feature stories, readers*

*exchange, new artists, ads, etc.;
published quarterly.*

Mexican

Experts

Donna McMenamin
5001 Woodway #1002
Houston, TX 77056-1718
phone: 713-622-7252
fax: 713-780-9723
e-mail: DMcMenamin@msn.com
Internet: http://
www.donnamcmenamin.com
*Author of "Popular Arts of Mexico
1850-1950"; buys and sells.*

Paintings

Repro. Sources

Diane Ulmer Pedersen
15 Avery Rd.
Holden, MA 01520-1235
phone: 508-829-7258
*Specializes in reproduction style folk
art paintings: still lives on checkerboard, landscapes, scenes with (or w/
o) scripture, children, portraits; all
works are original compositions.*

Terence J. Graham
P.O. Box 19
Zieglerville, PA 19492
*Specializes in reproduction folk art
paintings.*

Scherenschnitte

Repro. Sources

Pamela Dalton
RD 2 Box 266A
Ghent, NY 12075
*Specializes in reproduction decorative
paper cutting.*

Faye & Bernie DuPlessis
Traditional Papercutting
101 Blue Rock Rd.
Edgewood Hills, DE 19809
*Specializes in reproduction decorative
paper cutting.*

Melissa Pottenger
Sabbath Toys
11800 Jason Ave.
Concord Twp., OH 44077
*Specializes in reproduction decorative
paper cutting.*

Tree Toys, Inc.
P.O. Box 492
Hinsdale, IL 60521
*Specializes in reproduction decorative
paper cutting.*

Stoneware

Dealers

Richard Hume
P.O. Box 281
Bay Head, NJ 08742
phone: 732-899-8707 or 732-295-9285

Theorems

Repro. Sources

Hope Angier
Sheepscot Stenciling
RFD 1 Box 613
Wiscasset, ME 04578-9734
phone: 207-586-5692

Terence J. Graham
P.O. Box 19
Zieglerville, PA 19492

Jean Smith
343 Cliffview Dr.
Columbus, OH 43230-2905

Tinware

Museums/Libraries

Cooper-Hewitt Museum National
    Museum of Design, Smithsonian
    Institution
2 East 91st St.
New York, NY 10128
phone: 212-860-6868

Weathervanes

Museums/Libraries

Heritage Plantation of Sandwich
P.O. Box 566
Sandwich, MA 02563
phone: 617-888-3300

Repro. Sources

Lemee's Fireplace Equipment
815 Bedford St.
Bridgewater, MA 02324-3007
phone: 508-697-2672

Salt & Chestnut Weathervanes
P.O. Box 41
West Barnstable, MA 02668
phone: 508-362-6085
    *A unique shop specializing in
    American-made weathervanes -
    antique, new and custom-designed.*

Brian Chabot
Cape Cod Cupula
78 State Rd., Rte. 6
North Dartmouth, MA 02747-2991
phone: 508-994-2119
fax: 508-997-2511
    *Sells reproduction weathervanes and
    custom-made copulas.*

Copper House, The
RR 1 Box 4
Epsom, NH 03234-9101
phone: 603-736-9798
fax: 603-736-9798
    *Handmade copper reproduction
    lighting fixtures and weathervanes.
    No imports. Catalog $3 deducted
    from purchase.*

Country Cupulas
Main St.
East Conway, ME 04037

Town & Country
Main St.
East Conway, ME 04037

Terence J. Graham
P.O. Box 19
Zieglerville, PA 19492

Unfinished Business
P.O. Box 246
Wingate, NC 28174

Antique Hardware Store, The
1C Mathews Dr.
Hilton Head Island, SC 29926-3701

American Folklore
330 W. Pleasant
Freeport, IL 61032

Whirligigs

Repro. Sources

Bill Muehling
440 Yemmerdall Rd.
Lititz, PA 17543

Len Norman
Whirligig Creations
5726 North Mobile
Chicago, IL 60646-6124
phone: 312-792-1380

FOOD COLLECTIBLES

(see also BANANA COLLECTIBLES;
CEREAL BOXES; COFFEE;
COOKBOOKS; COOKIES &
COOKIE SHAPING; FAST FOOD
COLLECTIBLES; GROCERY
STORE ITEMS; MENUS; NUT
RELATED COLLECTIBLES;
POPCORN ITEMS; PREMIUMS,
Cereal Box; RECIPES; RESTAU-
RANT COLLECTIBLES)

Dealers

Louise Pennisi
Around the Kitchen
P.O. Box 840
Georgetown, CT 06829
phone: 203-438-2338 or 203-438-0671
e-mail: louise@aroundthekitchen.com
Internet: http://
    www:aroundthekitchen.com
    *Buying and selling collectible
    cookbooks (19th & 20th century),
    cookery booklets (Pillsbury, Baker's
    Chocolate, Jell-O, etc.), antique
    kitchen instruction & recipe
    pamphlets; issues catalogs of items for
    sale.*

Fake Food

Man./Prod./Dist.

Fake Food
P.O. Box 184
Telford, PA 18969
phone: 215-679-6152
fax: 215-679-3975
    *The first food-art product line of this
    kind in the country; pies, miniature
    fake food products, etc.*

Ketchup

Collectors

Ralph Finch
20135 Evergreen Meadows
Southfield, MI 48076-4222
phone: 248-358-4763 or 800-678-6400
fax: 313-222-2451
    *Wants antique material relating to
    ketchup.*

Mustard

Clubs/Associations

Mount Horeb Mustard Museum
109 E. Main St.
Mount Horeb, WI 53572
phone: 608-437-3986

FORD MOTOR COMPANY ITEMS

Collectors

Cliff Moebius
484 Winthrop St.
Westbury, NY 11590
phone: 516-333-3797
fax: 516-333-1712
    *Wants Ford Motor Co. and Henry
    Ford memorabilia: joke books,
    postcards, books, photos, Christmas
    cards, records, sheet music, script
    pens, pins, china, silverware, menus,
    sales literature, etc.*

Dealers

Tim O'Callaghan
P.O. Box 512
Northville, MI 48167
phone: 248-449-2652
    *Buys, sells, trades all Ford Motor
    Company memorabilia: postcards,
    books, pins, badges, etc.; SASE for list
    of Ford items for sale.*

FOSSILS

(see also ARCHAEOLOGY;
MINERALS; NATURAL HISTORY;
PREHISTORIC ARTIFACTS;
SKELETONS)

Clubs/Associations

Bone Valley Fossil Society, Inc.
2704 Dixie Rd.
Lakeland, FL 33801

Mid-American Paleontology Society
4800 Sunset Dr. SW
Cedar Rapids, IA 52404

Collectors

Scott Young
P.O. Box 8452
Port Saint Lucie, FL 34985-8452
phone: 407-878-5634
    *Buys, sells, trades vertebrate fossils
    from around the world.*

Dealers

Two Guys Fossils
1087 Plymouth St.
East Bridgewater, MA 02333-2131
phone: 800-FOS-SILS
fax: 508-378-7081
e-mail: app@twoguysfossils.com
Internet: http://www.twoguysfossils.com
    Insects in amber, dinosaurs.

Gene Harris
Art By God
50 Upper Alabama, Store No. 248
Underground Atlanta
Atlanta, GA 30303
phone: 404-577-7311 or 800-940-4449
fax: 305-573-9343
    *Mineral specimens, fossils, gems, sea
    shells, animal mounts, animal pelts,
    insects/butterflies, snail shells, skulls.*

J.F. Ray
P.O. Box 1364
Ocala, FL 32678-1364
    *Catalog sales of fossils; supplies
    museums, shops, schools; since 1962.*

Eric S. Kendrew
Fossil Store, The
4436 Tevalo Dr.
Valrico, FL 33594-7343
phone: 813-681-4330
e-mail: iceage@gte.net
    *Buy, sell, trade for fossils worldwide;
    prepare fossils; gives lectures;
    supplies schools and museums with
    fossils; expert underwater and land
    excavations; written articles on
    fossils; featured in many magazines
    and newspaper articles.*

John & Karen Mediz
Copper City Rock Shop
566 Ash St.
Globe, AZ 85501
phone: 520-425-7885 or 520-425-4506
fax: 520-425-4506
    *Buys and sells mining artifacts; also
    wants to buy minerals and fossils,
    especially old collections.*

Richard B. Troyanowski
Rich Relics
P.O. Box 432
Sandia Park, NM 87047-0432
phone: 505-281-2611 or 505-281-2329
    *Buys/sells prehistoric/historic Indian
    artifacts, cowboy, militaria, old world
    antiquities & coins, fossils &
    ethnographic collectibles.*

Museums/Libraries

Fick Fossil & History Museum
700 W. 3rd St.
Oakley, KS 67748
phone: 913-672-4839

On-Line Services

Rockhound's Information Page
14407 Big Basin Way, Ste. B
Saratoga, CA 95070
phone: 408-868-9700
fax: 408-868-0314
e-mail: rockhounds-
owner@infodyn.com
Internet: http://www.rahul.net/infodyn/
rockhounds/
*Great website for rockhound
information: shops and galleries;
images and pictures; books, articles
and other publications; general earth
science information; paleontology-
related sites; collecting sites and
trips; clubs & societies.*

Canadian Rockhound
e-mail: dfs846@mail.ussk.ca
Internet: http://pangea.usask.co/~dfs846/
rockhound/home.html
*An on-line magazine providing
interesting and educational stories on
rock, fossil and mineral collecting, the
art of lapidary, gems and faceting,
and on the earth sciences as well.*

Periodicals

Cindy Valerio
Magazine: Lapidary Journal
P.O. Box 1100
Devon, PA 19333-0905
phone: 610-293-1112 or 800-676-4336
fax: 610-293-1717
*Serves gem cutters, mineral/fossil
collectors, jewelry, jewelry arts, rock
enthusiasts; published monthly; also
has a book & video sales department.*

FOUNTAIN PENS

(see PENS)

FOURTH OF JULY ITEMS

(see FIREWORKS MEMORABILIA;
HOLIDAY COLLECTIBLES)

FRAKTURS

(see also FOLK ART; STATE
RELATED COLLECTIBLES,
Pennsylvania German Heritage)

Book Sellers

Russell D. Earnest
P.O. Box 1007
East Berlin, PA 17316-0507
Sells books on fraktur.

Dealers

Russell D. Earnest
P.O. Box 1007
East Berlin, PA 17316-0507
*Buys and sells fraktur including
printed fraktur, birth and baptism
certificates, bookplates, fraktur-like
watercolors, or other decorated
manuscripts; send photo or clear
photocopy; describe and state price.*

Experts

Ron Lieberman
Family Album, The
RD 1 Box 42
Glen Rock, PA 17327-9707
phone: 717-235-2134
fax: 717-235-8765
e-mail: ronbiblio@delphi.com
*Buys, sells and appraises German
Americana: fraktur, books, manu-
scripts, artwork, etc.*

Pstr. Frederick Weiser
55 Kohler School Rd.
New Oxford, PA 17350-9201
phone: 717-624-4106

Museums/Libraries

Free Library of Philadelphia
1901 Vine St.
Philadelphia, PA 19103
phone: 215-686-5370 or 215-686-5416
*The Henry S. Borneman collection of
Pennsylvania German Fraktur.*

Repro. Sources

Sally Greene Bunce
4826 Mays Ave.
Reading, PA 19606

Pine Cone Primitives
P.O. Box 682
Troutman, NC 28166

Cecil Cox
Primitives 'n Paper
4932 Baylor Dr.
Charlotte, NC 28210

Harwell Graphics
P.O. Box 8
Napoleon, IN 47034

FRAMES

(see also REPAIR/RESTORATION/
CONSERVATION, Gilding)

Clubs/Associations

International Institute for Frame Study
P.O. Box 50130
Washington, DC 20091
phone: 202-342-2067
e-mail: iifs@iifs.org
Internet: http://www.iifs.com
*Established in 1992 as the first public
archive devoted exclusively to the
history of picture frames; archive has
hundreds of photographs, drawings,
out-of-print books, auction and frame
makers' catalogs, articles, videos, etc.*

Dealers

John Baker
50 Granite St.
Foxboro, MA 02035
phone: 508-543-4626
Wants to buy ornate gilt frames.

Eli Wilner
Eli Wilner & Co.
1525 York Ave.
New York, NY 10028
phone: 212-744-6521
fax: 212-628-0264
*Sells, buys and restores fine 19th and
20th century frames.*

Carol Payne
Carol's Antique Gallery
14455 Big Basin Way
Saratoga, CA 95070-6008
phone: 408-867-7055
*Wants to buy stand-up frames of
wood, silver, brass, ivory, enamel,
etc.; send photocopy of front and back
of frame plus description for a cash
offer.*

Experts

William Adair
Gold Leaf Studios, Inc.
443 I Street NW
Washington, DC 20091
phone: 202-638-4660
fax: 202-347-4569
e-mail: bill@goldleafstudios.com
Internet: http://
www.goldleafstudions.com

Repair Services

Susan B. Jackson
Harvard Art
49 Littleton County Rd.
Harvard, MA 01451-1729
phone: 508-456-9050
*Restoration and conservation of
period frames and other gilded
objects; touch-up, consolidation,
gilding and toning to match the
existing surface.*

Alexandra Hadik
Gilder's Studio, The
34 Jarves St.
Sandwich, MA 02563-2039
phone: 508-833-0782
*Custom gold leaf framing and
conservation.*

R. Wayne Reynolds
R. Wayne Reynolds, Inc.
3618 Falls Rd.
Baltimore, MD 21211
phone: 410-467-1800 or 410-467-1890
*Specializes in the application of gold
leaf; complete restoration services for
gilded art objects, including furniture,
frames, and mirrors.*

Paul J. Buco
Fine Arts Services, Inc.
127 N. Front St.
Wilmington, NC 28401-3904
phone: 910-251-8859
*Restoration of frames including oil
and water gilding, recasting and
replacement of lost ornament.*

Duane Mitch
Mercury Furniture Service
302 Sycamore St.
West Chicago, IL 60185-3150
phone: 708-293-7207
fax: 708-653-2485
*A complete picture frame workshop
with in-house repair facilities
including the ability to fabricate
custom moldings, or to replace or
restore existing frame moldings.*

Repro. Sources

Motyka Art & Frame
103 Chestnut St.
Central Falls, RI 02863
phone: 401-726-8786
*High quality period reproduction
frames, hand carved and gilded in
22K gold or metal leaf.*

Tabletop Photo

Collectors

Mary Ellen Colquhonn
610 Sabal Luke Dr., #202
Longwood, FL 32779
phone: 407-786-5871
*Collects miniature photo frames;
prefers jeweled or enamel but
interested in all.*

FRANK LLOYD WRIGHT

(see also ARCHITECTURE &
RELATED ITEMS; ARTS &
CRAFTS)

Collectors

Jerry A. McCoy
800 Thayer Ave.
Silver Spring, MD 20910-4504
phone: 301-565-2519
fax: 301-565-0780
*Wants anything related to architect
Frank Lloyd Wright: autographs,
books, furniture, drawings, etc.*

Dealers

Michael FitzSimmons
Michael FitzSimmons Decorative Arts
311 West Superior St.
Chicago, IL 60610
phone: 312-787-6343
fax: 312-787-0496
*Specializing in 20th century
architecture and decorative arts
especially Frank Lloyd Wright and the
Prairie School of design; also Gustav
Stickley and others.*

J.B. Muns
Fine Arts Books & Musical Autographs
1162 Shattuck Ave.
Berkeley, CA 94707-2635
phone: 510-525-2420
fax: 510-525-1126
*Specializes in Frank Lloyd Wright;
catalogs issued since 1964; by
appointment only.*

Museums/Libraries

National Center for the Study of Frank
  Lloyd Wright
P.O. Box 444
Ann Arbor, MI 48106
phone: 313-995-4504

FRANKART

(see also ART DECO)

Collectors

Adrienne Leff
1550 S Dixie Hwy. #210
Miami, FL 33146-3034
phone: 305-667-4214
fax: 305-668-2592
  *Buys, sells, trades and collects
  Frankart lamps, ashtrays, bookends
  and candlestick holders.*

Jeff Leegood
DecoLectibles
P.O. Box 596553
Dallas, TX 75359-6653
phone: 214-824-7917
fax: 214-824-7917
  *Buys all types of Frankart: nude
  figures, animals, etc.; Frankart made
  lamps, bookends, ashtrays, etc.; items
  were made in the '20s & '30s and are
  of cast metal; most pieces are marked;
  also buys other similar Art Deco
  figures.*

Dealers

David Negley
438 W. 47th St., #1A
New York, NY 10036-2330
phone: 212-459-8954
  Buys and sells all Frankart items

Experts

Walter Glenn
Geode, Ltd.
3393 Peachtree Rd.
Atlanta, GA 30326-1109
phone: 404-261-9346
  *Buys and sells Frankart, Inc. items;
  also advisor to collectors, dealers,
  auction houses, etc.*

FRATERNAL ORGANIZATION ITEMS

(see also BADGES; VETERAN
ITEMS; SOCIAL CAUSES)

Collectors

James Berkel
684 Ironwood Cir.
Venice, FL 34292-2237
  *Wants Union and lodge badges 7"
  long with fringe on bottom; also wants
  any Improved Order of the Red Man
  badges or pins.*

American Legion

Collectors

Bob Bowen
13516 Kingsman Rd.
Woodbridge, VA 22193
phone: 703-590-3945
  *Buy American Legion convention
  badges or related Legion memorabilia.*

Elks

Collectors

F.E.I.
P.O. Box 1187
Poplar Bluff, MO 63901
phone: 314-686-1926
fax: 314-686-1926
  *Wants Elks Lodge memorabilia;
  BPOE badges, tankards, steins,
  souvenir plates, programs, jewelry,
  etc.*

Knights Of Columbus

Museums/Libraries

Mary Lou Cummings, Cur.
Knights of Columbus Headquarters
  Museum
One Columbus Plaza
New Haven, CT 06510-3326
phone: 203-772-2130
fax: 203-777-0114
Internet: http://www.kofc-supreme-
  council.org
  *Museum and archives revealing the
  history, formation and activities of the
  K. of C. as an international, Catholic,
  service-oriented, fraternal organiza-
  tion with insurance benefits.*

Lions

Collectors

Frank Johnson
73 West Johnston St.
Washington, NJ 07882-1332
  *Wants Lions Club pins and other
  memorabilia.*

Tom Owen
P.O. Box 435
Marshfield, MO 65706-0435
phone: 417-468-2791
  Wants to buy Lion's Club pins.

Masonic

Collectors

Dave
315 So. 4th St.
P.O. Box 522
Manhattan, KS 66502-0502
phone: 913-776-1433
  *Wants Masonic/Shriners jewelry,
  coins, tokens, books, paper items,
  memorabilia, anything Masonic
  needed for collection.*

Experts

Stanley W. Johnson
P.O. Box 462
Auburn, MA 01501-0462
phone: 508-799-6300
  *Specializes in the material culture of
  Freemasons including the obscure,
  cryptic, esoteric, enigmatic and genre;
  also Blue Lodge, Scottish Rite, York
  Rite, Royal Arch, Knights Templar,
  Shrine; member Museum Of Our
  National Heritage.*

George B. Spielman
1604 Rohrersville Rd.
Knoxville, MD 21758-1128
  Author of "Masonic Collectables."

Museums/Libraries

Thomas W. Leavitt, Dir.
Museum of our National Heritage
33 Marrett Rd.
P.O. Box 519
Lexington, MA 02173-0519
phone: 617-861-6559
fax: 617-861-9846
  *Research library specializing in the
  history of Freemasonry and related
  fraternal organizations in the U.S.*

Iowa Masonic Library & Museum
P.O. Box 279
Cedar Rapids, IA 52406-0279
phone: 319-365-1438
fax: 319-365-1439
e-mail: Grand_Lodge_IA@msn.com

Masonic Grand Lodge Library &
  Museum of Texas
P.O. Box 446
Waco, TX 76703
phone: 817-753-7395

Odd Fellows

Collectors

Greg Spiess
230 E. Washington St.
Joliet, IL 60433-1006
phone: 815-722-5639
fax: 815-722-0171
e-mail: spiessantq@aol.com
  *Wants to buy Odd Fellows items:
  steins, badges, medals, pins, ritual
  prints, coffins, banners, ark of
  covenants, flags, pedestals, heart in
  hand items, carvings with symbolism,
  supply catalogs.*

Museums/Libraries

Odd Fellows Historical Society
2055 Center Ave.
Payepte, ID 83661
phone: 208-459-2091
  *Mailing address is as noted above.
  Museum is located in Caldwell, ID.*

FREAKS

(see MORBID & ODD ITEMS)

FRENCH FOREIGN LEGION

Collectors

David Stevens
Playboy Magazine
680 North Lake Shore Dr.
Chicago, IL 60611
phone: 312-751-8000
  *Wants to buy French Foreign Legion
  ephemera.*

FRETWORK

Collectors

Rick Ralston
99-969 Iwaena St.
Aiea, HI 96701-3249
phone: 800-486-9794
fax: 808-486-1276
  *Wants to buy fretwork models; trains,
  buses, boats, etc.*

FRUIT JARS

(see also BOTTLES; JELLY
CONTAINERS; INSULATORS)

Clubs/Associations

J. Carl Sturm, Pres.
Federation of Historical Bottle
  Collectors, Inc.
Magazine: Bottles & Extras
88 Sweetbriar Branch
Longwood, FL 32750-2783
phone: 407-332-7689
e-mail: glassman@qnet.com
Internet: http://www.av.qnet.com/
  ~glassman
  *"Bottles & Extras" contains articles,
  pictures, letters, show dates, and show
  and auction reports in the field of
  antique bottles, insulators, fruit jars
  and associated items; check website
  for list of scores of clubs by region.*

Norman & Junne Barnett
Midwest Antique Fruit Jar & Bottle Club
Newsletter: Midwest Glass Chatter, The
P.O. Box 38
Flat Rock, IN 47234
phone: 812-587-5560
  *Sponsors two fruit and bottle shows
  each year in Indianapolis.*

Mason Bright
Ball Collectors Club
Newsletter: Ball Collectors Club
  Newsletter
22203 Doncaster
Riverview, MI 48192-8257
phone: 313-283-5965 or 313-242-3430
fax: 313-242-3436
e-mail: balljars@cheerful.com
  *Focuses on collecting Ball fruit jars
  and GO-WITHS; newsletter includes
  information on Ball jars; lists jars for
  sale by members.*

Collectors

Richard Dalton
30 Primrose Lane
Brick, NJ 08724
phone: 908-458-7650
Collects, buys, sells, trades old fruit jars or canning jars.

Art Snyder
110 White Oak Dr.
Butler, PA 16001-3446
phone: 412-287-0278
Buys/sells/trades all types of fruit jars especially Ball jars, odd closures, pint sizes, midgets and highly whittled quart size examples.

Collector
P.O. Box 71
Wallburg, NC 27373
Wants old fruit jars. One or a collection.

Claude Bellar
1750 Keyes Road
Greenbrier, TN 37073
phone: 615-643-0290
fax: 615-643-0290
e-mail: cbellar@aol.com

Harry Fisher
Rte. 1 Box 197
Owensville, MO 65066
phone: 314-437-4227
Wants Globe, Lightning, Masons amber, Millville Atmospherics and Improveds, Princess, Perfections, The Darling, Royal Amber, etc.; any unusual jars, please describe and price.

Scott Grandstaff
P.O. Box 409
Happy Camp, CA 96039
phone: 916-493-2032

Experts

John Hathaway
Hathaway's Antiques
3 Mills Rd.
Bryant Pond, ME 04219
phone: 207-665-2124
Buys and sells fruit jars; hundreds of rare jars to inexpensive jars in all categories.

Dick Roller
364 Gregory Ave.
West Orange, NJ 07052-3743
Author of "Standard Fruit Jar Reference."

Mike Jordan
Jordan Antiques & Research Co.
8411 Porter Ln.
Alexandria, VA 22308-2140
phone: 703-360-8181
Buy, sells, appraises and specializes in rare, early American fruit jars; specializing in odd closures and colors.

Mason Bright
22203 Doncaster
Riverview, MI 48192-8257
phone: 313-283-5965 or 313-242-3430
fax: 313-242-3436
e-mail: balljars@cheerful.com
Specialist and collector of BALL fruit jars; wants jars, letterheads, advertising items, GO-WITHS; has largest collection in the U.S.

Doug Leybourne
P.O. Box 5417
Muskegon, MI 49445-0417
phone: 616-744-2003
Author of "Red Book No. 8: The Collector's Guide to Old Fruit Jars," a price guide of over 5000 known jars; available from the author for $30 ppd.; also author of "The Fruit Jar Works," a 2-vol. encyclopedia, the set for $59 ppd.

Alice Creswick
0-8525 Kenowa SW
Grand Rapids, MI 49504
phone: 616-453-9565
Author of "Red Book No. 6: The Collector's Guide to Old Fruit Jars"; also sells books about old canning jars.

Jerry McCann
5003 West Berwin
Chicago, IL 60630
phone: 312-777-0443
Wants to buy unusual fruit jars.

Alex Kerr
4709 Forman Ave.
N. Hollywood, CA 91602
phone: 818-762-6320

Periodicals

Dick Roller
Newsletter: Fruit Jar Newsletter
364 Gregory Ave.
West Orange, NJ 07052-3743
Covers new finds, glass factory histories, jar news in general plus want ads, for-sale page and show dates.

FUNERAL ITEMS

(see also MORBID & ODD ITEMS)

Collectors

Rich Hartzog
World Exonumia
P.O. Box 4143 BSB
Rockford, IL 61110-0643
phone: 815-226-0771
fax: 815-397-7662
Wants items showing or issued by funeral parlors; tokens, badges, medals, ribbons, and other small collectibles.

Caskets

Collectors

Steve DeGenaro
P.O. Box 5662
Youngstown, OH 44504-0662
phone: 216-757-7735

FURNITURE (ANTIQUE)

(see also ARTS & CRAFTS; ART DECO; ART NOUVEAU; GARDEN FURNITURE; MODERNISM; ORIENTALIA; REPAIR/RESTORA-TION/CONSERVATION, Furniture; SHAKER ITEMS; WALLACE NUTTING; WICKER; see also "REPAIR SERVICES" Appendix)

Appraisers

Steve Elliott, ASA
493 Simsbury Rd.
Bloomfield, CT 06002-1512
phone: 860-243-1646
Appraiser, expert witness, lecturer, writer, author of articles in "Maine Antique Digest": "The Faking of Antique Furniture," and "Historical Cabinetmaking Construction."

Stephen van Cline, CAPP
van Cline & Davenport, Ltd.
792 Franklin Ave.
Franklin Lakes, NJ 07417-1343
Specializes in 18th & early 19th cent. furniture & accessories; appraisals, authentication, lectures, expert testimony; minimum charge $25; letter request only, SASE.

Rochelle Eisenberg, ASA
Art Directives, Inc.
P.O. Box 173
Ambler, PA 19002
phone: 215-646-0233
fax: 215-542-7015
Appraiser, consultant, writer, lecturer, author, advisor for Montgomery County newspapers, appeared on "Chubb Antiques Roadshow", instructor at Temple University.

Dealers

Peter Eaton 18 Century Furniture
39 State St.
P.O. Box 632
Newburyport, MA 01950
phone: 508-465-2754

Russ & Karen Goldberger
P.O. Box 2033
Hampton, NH 03843-2033
phone: 603-926-1770
fax: 603-929-4267
e-mail: rjduck@nh.ultranet.com
Internet: http://www.maineantiquedigest.com/adimg/decoys.htm
Specializes in quality working decoys, folk art, and American furniture and accessories in their original painted surfaces.

R. Jorgensen Antiques
502 Post Road
Wells, ME 04090
phone: 207-646-9444
fax: 207-646-4954
Family business on historical property selling 18th and 19th C. American, British and Continental period antique furniture and accessories; also fireplace equipment and clocks.

Cooper
Main Street Antiques at the Farmington Lodge
185 Main St.
Farmington, CT 06032
phone: 860-677-5423 or 860-674-1035
fax: 860-677-5423
e-mail: cyncooper@imagine.com

Nathan Liverant & Son
168 South Main St.
P.O. Box 103
Colchester, CT 06415
phone: 203-537-2409 or 203-537-2060

Wayne Pratt & Company
346 Main Street South
Woodbury, CT 06798
phone: 203-263-5676
fax: 203-266-4766
Internet: http://www.litchfield.com/antiques/waynprat.html
Fine American 18th and 19th century furniture with an emphasis on original condition and patina; also a selection of fine line-for-line handmade copies of authentic antiques.

James B. Grievo Fine American Antiques
RR 5 Box 52
Califon, NJ 07830
phone: 908-439-2147

Leigh Keno
Leigh Keno American Antiques
980 Madison Ave. at 76th St.
New York, NY 10021
phone: 212-734-2381
fax: 212-734-0707
Specializes in fine American antique furniture.

John Keith Russell Antiques, Inc.
Spring St.
South Salem, NY 10590
phone: 914-763-8144 or 203-537-2060
fax: 914-763-3553

Philip Bradley
Philip H. Bradley Co.
Rte. 30
Downingtown, PA 19335
phone: 610-269-0427 or 610-269-8173
Specializes in fine American antique furniture.

H.L. Chalfant Antiques
1352 Paoli Pike
West Chester, PA 19380-6263
phone: 610-696-1862
Specializes in American antique furniture.

Richard & Lois Maimberg
Boyertown Antiques
1283 Weisstown Rd.
Boyertown, PA 19512
phone: 610-367-2452

G.K.S. Bush, Inc.
2828 Pennsylvania Ave. NW
Washington, DC 20007
phone: 202-965-0653
fax: 202-342-6560
*Specializes in fine American antique
furniture.*

John C. Newcomer
John C. Newcomer & Assoc.
P.O. Box 130
Funkstown, MD 21734
phone: 301-790-1327

Bob O'Dell
Era of Elegance Antiques
Kennerly Rd.
Irmo, SC 29063
phone: 803-345-1689
*Buys and sells period antiques from
1830-1890; by appointment; East
coast only.*

Deborah Smallwood
Seller of Dreams
P.O. Box 428
Powell, OH 43065
phone: 614-436-8393
*Specializes in Victorian furniture, but
also carries primitive and
handpainted furniture; restoration
and refinishing available.*

Experts

Steve Elliott, ASA
493 Simsbury Rd.
Bloomfield, CT 06002-1512
phone: 860-243-1646
*Reaccredited Senior Member of the
American Society of Appraisers,
Personal Property, Furniture
designation; author of articles in
"Maine Antique Digest": "The Faking
of Antique Furniture," and "Historical Cabinetmaking Construction."*

Suzy McLennan Anderson
Heritage Antiques, Inc.
65 East Main St.
Holmdel, NJ 07733-2310
phone: 908-946-8801
fax: 908-946-1036
*Authentication service offered for pre-
1840 American furniture; also buys
and sells.*

Robert F. Weinhagen, Jr.
221 Cameron St.
Alexandria, VA 22314-3203
phone: 703-549-2560
*Author of "Assume Nothing: A
Manual For Buyers of American and
English Antique Furniture"*

J. Robert Boykin, III
Boykin Appraisals, Inc.
P.O. Box 7440
Wilson, NC 27895
phone: 919-237-1700
fax: 919-237-2314
*Specializing in American & English
antique furniture, decorative arts, and
appreciable residential contents.*

Museums/Libraries

Society for the Preservation of New
England Antiquities, The
141 Cambridge Street
Boston, MA 02114
phone: 617-227-3956
fax: 617-227-9204
*A museum of cultural history that
preserves, interprets, and collects
buildings, landscapes, and objects
reflecting New England life from the
17th century to present.*

Museum of Art, Rhode Island School of
Design
224 Benefit St.
Providence, RI 02903-2711
phone: 401-454-6500
fax: 401-454-6556

Deborah Federhen, Cur.
Bennington Museum, The
W. Main St.
Bennington, VT 05201
phone: 802-447-1571
fax: 802-442-8305
Internet: http://www.benington.com/
museum
*One of the finest regional art history
museums in the country; works by
Grandma Moses, American glass, VT
furniture, Bennington pottery, the
oldest Stars & Stripes in existence, the
1925 luxury touring car "The Wasp",
and much more.*

Winterthur Museum
Winterthur, DE 19735-0001
phone: 800-448-3883
Internet: http://www.udel.edu/winterthur

Colonial Williamsburg
P.O. Box C
Williamsburg, VA 23185
phone: 804-229-1000
*Specializes in early American
furniture and the decorative arts.*

Bernice Bienenstock Furniture Library
1009 North Main St.
High Point, NC 27262
phone: 919-883-4011
*Comprehensive library covering
furniture design, styles, periods,
motifs, production, history, etc.*

Henry Ford Museum
P.O. Box 1970
Dearborn, MI 48120
Internet: http://hfm.umd.umich.edu

Edison Institute
20900 Oakwood Blvd.
Dearborn, MI 48121

Repro. Sources

Virginia Dowd Oberlin
Antique Catalog, The
207 N. Bowman Ave.
Merion Station, PA 19066
phone: 610-668-1138
*Catalog source for fine quality
handcarved walnut and mahogany
reproduction Federal-style furniture.*

Mack S. Headley & Sons
Rt. 1 Box 1245 Senseny Rd.
Berryville, VA 22611-9705
phone: 703-955-2022
*Fine, handcrafted reproduction
furniture; also antique restorations.*

American Antique Reproductions, Inc.
P.O. Box 72846
Chattanooga, TN 37407-5846
phone: 800-221-1988 or 423-867-1988
fax: 423-867-1788
e-mail: AmerAntRep@worldnet.att.net
*Wholesale only: handcrafted
American oak furniture and mahogany
reproduction furniture from
Indonesia; also reproduction leaded
glass table lamps, and reproduction
American made ice cream table and
chair sets, signs, prints, posters.*

Antler & Horn

Collectors

J.A. Higgins
5017 Walnut
Kansas City, MO 64112-2758
phone: 816-931-4095
Wants to buy old horn furniture.

Experts

Alan Rogers
1012 Shady Dr.
Gladstone, MO 64188
phone: 816-436-9008
*Has studied and collected Texas cattle
horns, horn furniture, and related
items for over 20 years; wants to buy
old steer horns over 7' long, but not
horns wrapped in tooled leather.*

Beds

Dealers

Mendes Antiques
Rte. 44
52 Blanding Rd.
Rehoboth, MA 02769
phone: 508-336-7381
*Specializing in antique four-poster
beds, all sizes.*

Beds (Brass)

Repair Services

Bedpost, The
32 S. High St.
East Bajor, PA 18013
phone: 610-588-4667
*Manufactures brass and iron beds;
also repairs antique brass beds and
provides parts.*

Belter

Dealers

Richard & Eileen Dubrow
Richard & Eileen Dubrow Antiques &
Books
P.O. Box 128
Flushing, NY 11361-0128
phone: 718-767-9758
fax: 718-767-8172
*Specializing in 19th century American
cabinet maker furniture and
decorative arts; will identify pieces as
to maker by photo; also sells books
(out of print and current) about 19th
C. furniture and about furniture and
decorative arts.*

British

Experts

David P. Lindquist
Whitehall at the Villa
1213 E. Franklin St.
Chapel Hill, NC 27514-3307
phone: 919-942-3179 or 919-933-3305
fax: 919-942-3179
*Author of "The Official Price Guide to
Antiques & Collectibles: English &
Continental Furniture - With Prices";
co-author with Caroline Warren of
"English and Continental Furniture -
With Prices."*

Chairs (Folding)

Collectors

Richard M. Bueschel
414 N. Prospect Manor Ave.
Mount Prospect, IL 60056-2046
phone: 847-253-0791
fax: 847-253-7919
e-mail: BuschlHist@aol.com
*Wants old folding wooden chairs with
advertising backs; also wants photos,
advertising, brochures, and catalogs
of wooden folding chairs; send SASE
if requesting reply.*

Chinese

Dealers

Evelyn's Antique Chinese Furniture, Inc.
381 Hayes St.
San Francisco, CA 94102-2440
phone: 415-255-1815
*Offers a large inventory of Classic
Chinese furniture and works of art
from the Ming & Qing Dynasties.*

Shen's Gallery
1368 Pacific Ave.
Santa Cruz, CA 95060
phone: 408-425-0525
*Offers fine Oriental furniture and
antiques; also ancient Chinese
ceramics, carvings and statuary.*

Colonial Revival

Experts

David P. Lindquist
Whitehall at the Villa
1213 E. Franklin St.
Chapel Hill, NC 27514-3307
phone: 919-942-3179 or 919-933-3305
fax: 919-942-3179
Co-author with Caroline Warren of "Colonial Revival Furniture - With Prices."

Man./Prod./Dist.

Henkle-Harris Furniture Company
P.O. Box 2170
Winchester, VA 22604

Bassett Furniture Industries, Inc.
P.O. Box 626
Bassett, VA 24055

Sligh Furniture Company
201 W. Washington Ave.
Zeeland, MI 49464

Kindel Furniture Company
P.O. Box 2047
Grand Rapids, MI 49501

Baker Furniture Company
1661 Monroe Ave. NW
Grand Rapids, MI 49505

Museums/Libraries

Judith Smith, PR
Reynolds House Museum of American Art
P.O. Box 11765
Winston Salem, NC 27116
phone: 910-725-5325
fax: 910-721-0991
e-mail: reynolds@ols.net
Internet: http://www.reynoldshouse.org
Magnificent former home of Richard J. Reynolds, founder of the R. J. Reynolds Tobacco Company; houses the finest fine art collection in the area.

International Home Furnishings Center
210 East Commerce St.
High Point, NC 27260

Bernice Bienenstock Furniture Library
1009 North Main St.
High Point, NC 27262
phone: 919-883-4011
Comprehensive library covering furniture design, styles, periods, motifs, production, history, etc.

Grand Rapids Public Library
60 Library Plaza, Northeast
Grand Rapids, MI 49503

Public Museum of Grand Rapids
272 Pearl St. NW
Grand Rapids, MI 49504-5371
phone: 616-456-3977
fax: 616-456-3873
Focus is on furniture made in the Grand Rapids area; exhibits, publications and research information relating to all styles of 19th and 20th century furniture manufactured in Grand Rapids.

Baker Furniture Library
1661 Monroe Ave. NW
Grand Rapids, MI 49505

Continental

Experts

David P. Lindquist
Whitehall at the Villa
1213 E. Franklin St.
Chapel Hill, NC 27514-3307
phone: 919-942-3179 or 919-933-3305
fax: 919-942-3179
Author of "The Official Price Guide to Antiques & Collectibles: English & Continental Furniture - With Prices"; co-author with Caroline Warren of "English and Continental Furniture - With Prices."

French

Dealers

Nancy Kramer
Sparrows
4115 Howard Ave.
Kensington, MD 20895-2417
phone: 301-530-0175
fax: 301-530-0189
e-mail: NSKramer@aol.com
Internet: http://www.sparrows.com
Specializes in 19th and early 20th century French antique furniture and decorative arts.

Shelley & David Stevens
Orion Antique Importers, Inc.
1435 Slocum St.
Dallas, TX 75207
phone: 214-748-1177
fax: 214-748-1491
Offers fine quality French furniture, chandeliers, mirrors, paintings, and architecturals; also in-house restoration facilities.

Horn

(see FURNITURE [ANTIQUE], Adirondack; FURNITURE [ANTIQUE], Antler & Horn; WESTERN AMERICANA)

Kitchen Cabinets

Dealers

Uncle Tom's Antique Hoosier Cabinets & Parts
5680 W. McNeely St.
Ellettsville, IN 47429-9411
phone: 812-876-5060 or 800-892-5695
fax: 812-876-5045
e-mail: tomscab@ix.netcom.com
Internet: http://www.in.net/milestone/uncletoms
Selling top quality oak Hoosier cabinets and cupboards; also originally cabinet glassware, flour bins, cabinet accessories, etc.; parts catalog $1.

Experts

Rick Zirpoli
Hoosier Emporium, The
HC 1 Box 1826
Milanville, PA 18443
phone: 717-729-7080
Buys/sells kitchen cabinets; the most extensive line of parts & supplies; authority on Hoosier and Hoosier-type kitchen cabinets.

Phyllis & Phil Kennedy
Phyllis Kennedy Hardware
9256 Holyoke Court
Indianapolis, IN 46268-1237
phone: 317-873-1316
fax: 317-873-8662
Author of "Hoosier Cabinets."

Suppliers

Phyllis & Phil Kennedy
Phyllis Kennedy Hardware
9256 Holyoke Court
Indianapolis, IN 46268-1237
phone: 317-873-1316
fax: 317-873-8662
Author of "Hoosier Cabinets;" stocks parts for Hoosier cabinets including flour sifters, cardboard door charts, metal tags, sugar bins, etc.; send for catalog.

Muff's Antiques
135 S. Glassell St.
Orange, CA 92866
phone: 714-997-0243
fax: 714-997-1601
Internet: http://www.tias.com/amdir/SpecTrunks.html
Mail order source for kitchen cabinet hardware (Hoosiers) including hinges, labels, canisters, castors, and rolls; also 25 sizes of lids for jars, and salt & pepper canisters from Hoosier & Depression items; catalog $5.

Oak

Museums/Libraries

Christian G. Carron
Public Museum of Grand Rapids
272 Pearl St. NW
Grand Rapids, MI 49504-5371
phone: 616-456-3977
fax: 616-456-3873
Focus is on furniture made in the Grand Rapids area; exhibits, publications and research information relating to all styles of 19th and 20th century furniture manufactured in Grand Rapids.

Patented

Experts

Glenn McAndrews
402 E. Warren St.
Lebanon, OH 45036
phone: 513-932-5448

Pie Safes

Experts

Dennis & Louise Paustenbach
65 Roan Place
Woodside, CA 94062
Authors of a book about pie safes.

Rustic

Dealers

Bert Savage
Rte. 126 Box 11
Center Strafford, NH 03815
phone: 603-269-7411
Wants to buy rustic furniture: Adirondack, Indiana Hickory, twig, birch bark, root, burl.

Chris Guille
256 Osbrook Pt.
Pawcatuck, CT 06379
phone: 203-599-1244
fax: 203-536-1267
e-mail: cwguille@aol.com
Wants quality Adirondack furniture and accessories: Old Hickory, Rittenhouse, birch bark, rustic lamps, coat racks, mirrors, Black Forest carved bears and clocks, miniature canoes, pond boats, camp signs, art and advertising.

Ralph Kylloe
Kylloe Antiques
P.O. Box 669
Lake George, NY 12845-0669
Specializes in buying and selling antiques for the cabin; old hickory, Adirondack, root, twig, antler furnishings, and rustic accessories; also creels, snowshoes, skis, sailboats, fishing nets, camp signs, birch bark frames, canoes, etc.

Bob Berman
441 S. Jackson St.
Media, PA 19063-3715
phone: 610-566-1516

Michael T. Meadows
Meadows House Antiques
919 Stiles St.
Baltimore, MD 21202-4426
phone: 410-837-5427
Buys and sells Adirondack and other rustic furniture and accessories.

Museums/Libraries

Adirondack Museum, The
Rte. 30
P.O. Box 99
Blue Mountain Lake, NY 12812
phone: 518-352-7311

Soap Hollow

Museums/Libraries

Julie Robinson
Conemaugh Township Area Historical
Society
100-104 South Main St.
P.O. Box 307
Davidsville, PA 15928
phone: 814-479-2211 or 814-479-2067
*Historical information on the
furniture makers of Soap Hollow;
lecture frequently on furniture style,
hallmarks and stencils of the unique
Mennonite craftsmen.*

Stickley

Dealers

Dennis Lucier
1034 Mammoth Rd.
Dracut, MA 01826
phone: 508-957-0143
*Buys and sells Gustav, L & JG
Stickley mission oak furniture.*

Jerry Cohen
Mission Oak Shop, The
123 Main St.
Putnam, CT 06260-1925
phone: 203-928-6662
fax: 203-928-1039
*Original antique Stickley and other
Mission style furniture makers; over
4,000 square feet furniture on display.*

Bob Berman
441 S. Jackson St.
Media, PA 19063-3715
phone: 610-566-1516

Caren Fine
11603 Gowrie Ct.
Potomac, MD 20854-3623
phone: 301-299-2116 or 301-299-6886
*Wants to buy Arts & Crafts items such
as furniture and copper lamps by
Stickley, Dirk Van Erp, Roycroft,
Limbert, Harden, Rohlfs, Wright;
pottery, paintings, Spratling silver.*

Museums/Libraries

Craftsman Farms Foundation, Inc.
2352 Rt. 10-W, Box 5
Morris Plains, NJ 07950
phone: 201-540-1165
fax: 201-540-1167
*Runs Stickley's National Landmark
family home in Parsippany, NJ;
sponsors Stickley exhibits and related
catalogs.*

Repro. Sources

L. & J.G. Stickley, Inc.
P.O. Box 480
Manlius, NY 13104-0480
phone: 315-682-5500
fax: 315-682-6306

Twig

(see FURNITURE [ANTIQUE],
Adirondack)

Victorian

Auction Services

Pettigrew Auction Company
1645 South Tejon St.
Colorado Springs, CO 80906
phone: 719-633-7963
fax: 719-633-5035

Museums/Libraries

Newark Museum, Ballantine House
49 Washington St.
P.O. Box 540
Newark, NJ 07101-0540
phone: 201-596-6550

Henry Duffy, Curator
Lyndhurst
635 S. Broadway
Tarrytown, NY 10591-6401
phone: 914-631-4481
fax: 914-631-5634
*Furniture, paintings, decorative arts,
library, archive; Gothic Revival
mansion on 67 acre European-style
park; tours, special events, catering
for parties, gallery.*

Wallace Nutting

Museums/Libraries

Wadsworth Atheneum
600 Main St.
Hartford, CT 06103
phone: 860-278-2670
fax: 860-527-0803
*The collection of Wallace Nutting 17th
century American furniture, the
largest of its kind, includes a wide
array of "Pilgrim-Century"
housewares and tools; also has two
fully-restored period rooms.*

Windsors

Repro. Sources

Sharon & Roger Mason
Olde Virginia Floorcloth & Trading Co.
4408 Faigle Rd.
Portsmouth, VA 23703-4815
phone: 804-564-0600
*Makes a line of handcrafted
reproduction 18th century style
Windsor chairs and settees.*

Wooton Desks

Clubs/Associations

Richard & Eileen Dubrow
Wooton Desk Owners Society, Inc.
Newsletter: Wooton Desk Owners
  Society Newsletter, The
P.O. Box 128
Flushing, NY 11361-0128
phone: 718-767-9758
fax: 718-767-8172
*Archival records, authentication, and
sales of Wooton desks.*

FURS

Dealers

Farhad Radfar, ISA
MIR International Gallery, Inc.
P.O. Box 10678
Chicago, IL 60610
phone: 312-654-8510 or 773-477-2209
fax: 312-670-8182
e-mail: FRadfar@aol.com

Misc. Services

Richard A. Newman
Newman Fur Appraisers & Consultants,
  Inc.
350 Gashion Ave.
New York, NY 10001-5013
phone: 212-564-4733
fax: 212-564-4735
*Fur appraiser, consultant, all phases
of the fur industry; damage claim
consultant.*

Museums/Libraries

Charles E. Hanson, Jr., Dir.
Museum of the Fur Trade
Magazine: MFT Quarterly
6321 Highway 20
Chadron, NE 69337-9501
phone: 308-432-3843
*Dedicated to the study of the American
fur trade from colonial times to the
present; furs, traps, trade guns, trade
goods, Indians; not involved with
present day trapping.*

Here are some tips when contacting someone listed in this book:

When requesting information about a particular item, include a description (material, dimensions, maker's mark, model number, etc.) and a photo, sketch, or photocopy of the item in question. ■

Always ask if there are charges for samples or for the services requested. ■

When writing, please be sure to include a Large (#10 business size) Self-Addressed and Stamped Envelope (LSASE) if requesting a reply or the return of photographs. ■

Never call collect unless otherwise directed. When calling, be considerate of time zone differences and always ask if the party you are calling has time to talk. When leaving an answering machine message, always instruct the party to call you back collect. ■

G-MAN

(see LAW ENFORCEMENT MEMORABILIA, FBI)

G.A.R. MEMORABILIA

(see VETERAN ITEMS, Civil War)

G.I. JOE

(see TOYS, Action Figures [G.I. Joe])

GAMBLING COLLECTIBLES

(see also COIN-OPERATED MACHINES, Slot Machines; DICE; MATCHCOVERS, Casino; PLAYING CARDS; SALOON & BAR COLLECTIBLES; TOKENS)

Collectors

Robert Eisenstadt
P.O. Box 020767-Y
Brooklyn, NY 11202
phone: 718-625-3553
fax: 718-522-1087
e-mail: chipe@ix.netcom.com
Collects and buys all kinds of gambling chips (casino, ivory, mother of pearl, clay poker chips, etc. but no light plastic chips); also wants gambling-related items such as equipment, books, catalogs, playing cards, etc.

John A. Greget
John A. Greget - Magic Lists
2631 E Claire Dr.
Phoenix, AZ 85032-4932
Buys and appraises gambling books or equipment.

Kitty & Russell Umbraco
P.O. Box 5331
Richmond, CA 94805-0331
phone: 510-235-1656
Wants to buy gambling collectibles including Faro, playing cards, etc.

Dealers

Larry Lubliner
Re-Finders
25303 Rutledge Crossing
Farmington Hills, MI 48335-1350
phone: 810-426-0066
e-mail: joker1854@aol.com
Buys and sells gambling items including playing cards, poker chips, Faro, poker, roulette, dice; also wants related advertising items, sales catalogs, and books.

Gambling Chips & Gaming Tokens

Clubs/Associations

Archie A. Black, Pres.
Casino Chips & Gaming Tokens Collectors Club
Magazine: Casino Chips & Token News
P.O. Box 63
Brick, NJ 08723-0063
Collectors of casino chips and gaming tokens; ANA affiliation, yearly convention in Las Vegas, 100+ page quarterly newsletter; over 1600 members.

Collectors

Charles Tomarchio
P.O. Box 8386
Turnersville, NJ 08012

Archie A. Black
P.O. Box 63
Brick, NJ 08723-0063

Robert Eisenstadt
P.O. Box 020767-Y
Brooklyn, NY 11202
phone: 718-625-3553
fax: 718-522-1087
e-mail: chipe@ix.netcom.com
Collects and buys all kinds of gambling chips (casino, ivory, mother of pearl, clay poker chips, etc. but no light plastic chips); also wants gambling-related items such as equipment, books, catalogs, playing cards, etc.

Nate Pincus
P.O. Box 693
Havertown, PA 19083-0693
phone: 610-642-6093
fax: 610-642-3641
e-mail: JGJM82A@prodigy.com
Collector of casino chips from all areas; buy, sell, trade.

John Benedict
P.O. Drawer 1423
Loxahatchee, FL 33470
phone: 561-798-2520
fax: 561-798-2520
e-mail: benedict@webtv.net
Internet: http://www.netmar.com/~creator/benedict/
Wants old casino chips and ivory poker chips.

Dave Brattain
P.O. Box 335
Zionsville, IN 46077
phone: 317-769-3257
Wants to buy old or unique gambling chips and sets, U.S. or foreign; premium paid for ivories.

Janice O'Neal
P.O. Box 706
Howell, MI 48844
phone: 517-548-3886

Tom Dirnberger
8493 142nd St. West
Apple Valley, MN 55124

Michael Skelton
112 Simmons St.
Coppell, TX 75019

Charles T. Rodgers
P.O. Box 4572
Lakewood, CA 90711

Marv Weaver
1673 Heatherwood Dr.
Pittsburg, CA 94565
phone: 510-432-6469

Dealers

Bob Mera
Gaming Emporium, The
3011 Boardwalk
Atlantic City, NJ 08401-6203
phone: 800-354-3075
Gambling books, tapes and casino related equipment and supplies.

New York Chip Connection
2950 Hempstead Turnpike
Levittown, NY 11756
phone: 800-NYC-HIPS

Wilcox Enterprises
P.O. Box 395
Carthage, IL 62321-0395
Buys and sells chips, tokens, cards, matches and dice from river boats, Indian reservations, Deadwood, Colorado.

Tom Arestad
P.O. Box 1931
Lake Oswego, OR 97035

Experts

Michael Knapp
P.O. Box 340345
Columbus, OH 43234
phone: 614-451-0006
e-mail: chip99a@prodigy.com
Buys, collects and specializes in poker chips.

Dale Seymour
11170 Mora Dr.
Los Altos, CA 94024-6536
phone: 415-948-0948
fax: 415-941-3695
Wants old poker chips; ivory, clay, or casino; no paper, plain or plastic chips wanted. Author of book on same.

GAME ROOM AMUSEMENTS

(see COIN-OPERATED MACHINES)

GAMEBOARDS

Repro. Sources

Barbara Wagaman
Ridge Hollow Folk Art
14 Ridge Dr.
Lititz, PA 17543

Robin Lankford
Folk Hearts
15005 Howe Rd.
Portland, MI 48875

Barbara Strickland
Folk Hearts
728 Hawthorne
El Cajon, CA 92020

GAMES

(see also BILLIARD RELATED ITEMS; BRIDGE; CHESS SETS; DICE; FRISBEES; GAMBLING COLLECTIBLES; GAMEBOARDS; MARBLES; PAPER COLLECTIBLES; PLAYING CARDS; PUZZLES; TOYS)

Appraisers

Lee Dennis
447 Park Ave., Apt. 12
Keene, NH 03431-6506
phone: 603-358-0060
Author of "Warman's Antique American Games, 1840 - 1940"; republished in 1991 with updated prices.

Auction Services

Withington, Inc.
RD 2 Box 440
Hillsboro, NH 03244
phone: 603-464-3232

Clubs/Associations

American Game Collectors Association
Newsletter: Game Times
49 Brooks Ave.
Lewiston, ME 04240-5901
phone: 215-674-1072
Internet: http://www.agca.com/~rfinn/agca.htm
Focuses on board and card games as well as puzzles, playing cards, tops, yo-yos, and action games; also publishes "Game Researchers' Notes" - reports on member's research.

Robert R. Grew
Antique Toy Collectors of America, Inc., The
Newsletter: Toy Chest
c/o Carter, Ledyard & Milburn
Two Wall St. - 13th Floor
New York, NY 10005
phone: 212-238-8803
fax: 212-732-3232
An organization focusing on antique toys and games; since membership is by invitation only for established collectors, there is a waiting list; bi-monthly newsletter available only to members.

H.M. Levy, Pres.
Gamers Alliance
Newsletter: Gamers Alliance Report
P.O. Box 197 -CIC
East Meadow, NY 11554-0197
e-mail: gamers@pipeline.com
Members receive quarterly reports with news, views and reviews on games plus FREE out-of-print catalogs, FREE research service, and more; send SASE for more information; also buys games - one or one thousand.

Collectors

Mary Lou Alpert
Green Hill Game Farm
RFD 1 Box 93
Yorktown, NY 10598
phone: 914-245-1401

Joe Angiolilo
P.O. Box 44
Dresher, PA 19025

Dealers

Maurice & Laya Jakubowicz
L'affiche Francaise
Le Plateau - Bazincourt
B.P. 42
21740 Gisors, France
phone: 332-32555476
fax: 332-32271012
Large collection of "saussine" board games from 1880-1940; catalog sent on request.

Robert DeCenzo
18 Barber Rd.
Framingham, MA 01701
phone: 508-879-8541
Buys and sells games; dealer and mail order.

Wizard of Os
57 Lakeshore Dr.
Marlborough, MA 01752
phone: 508-481-1087

Paul Fink
Fun & Games
P.O. Box 488
Kent, CT 06757-0488
phone: 860-927-4001
Buys and sells Victorian games, comic and cartoon games, TV & nostalgia games; dealer and mail order.

Gary Darrow
Darrow's Fun Antiques
1101 1st Ave.
New York, NY 10021-8737
phone: 212-838-0730
fax: 212-838-3617
Buys & sells antique games, toys, ad signs, animated art, jukeboxes, slot machines, comic watches, bicycles & memorabilia of all types.

Of Dice & Men
161 Belmont St.
Carbondale, PA 18407
phone: 717-282-3503

John & Mildred Spear
8336 Millman St.
Philadelphia, PA 19118-3925

Marjorie Jeffreys
Going to Pieces
P.O. Box 390
Cibolo, TX 78108
phone: 210-659-2458
Buys and sells old games, toys, blocks and children's dishes and children's baking items.

Experts

Lee Dennis
447 Park Ave., Apt. 12
Keene, NH 03431-6506
phone: 603-358-0060
Author of "Warman's Antique American Games, 1840 - 1940"; former curator-owner of the country's largest collection of board games; continues to offer slide film presentation about games to clubs/ associations/Historical Societies.

Pat McFarland
P.O. Box 161
Averill Park, NY 12018-0161
phone: 518-674-8390
Buyer of American board games 1800s to 1940s; McLoughlin, Bliss, Ives, Doan, early Parker and Bradley; also wants game catalogs and ephemera; pre-1936 Monopoly; player related Baseball; The Landlord's Game; related information.

Bob Cereghino
6400 Baltimore National Pike, Ste. 170A-319
Baltimore, MD 21228-3914
phone: 410-766-7593

Earnest & Ida Long
Long's Americana
P.O. Box 90
Mokelumne Hill, CA 95245
phone: 209-286-1348
Specializes in toys, banks, games and other children's items; publishes "Dictionary of Toys, Vol I & II" and "Penny Lane."

Museums/Libraries

University of Waterloo Museum & Archive of Games
Waterloo
Ontario N2L 3G1 Canada
phone: 519-888-4424 or 519-885-4567
fax: 519-746-6776
2000 references: books, journals, reports, patent information, scholarly studies, and other printed materials concerning games and playing behavior; also many photos, color slides, advertisements, catalogs, and rules about games.

Museum & Archive of Games
University of Waterloo
BMH Room 1016
Ontario N2L 3G1 Canada
phone: 519-888-4424

Essex Institute
132 Essex St.
Salem, MA 01970
phone: 508-744-3390

Washington Dolls' House & Toy Museum
5236 44th St. NW
Washington, DC 20015
phone: 202-244-0024

Board

Clubs/Associations

American Game Collectors Association
Newsletter: Game Times
49 Brooks Ave.
Lewiston, ME 04240-5901
phone: 215-674-1072
Internet: http://www.agca.com/~rfinn/agca.htm
Focuses on board and card games as well as puzzles, playing cards, tops, yo-yos, and action games; also publishes "Game Researchers' Notes" - reports on member's research.

Collectors

Bill Smith
56 Locust St.
East Douglas, MA 01516-2440
phone: 508-476-2015
Wants all board games; any age or theme.

Bernard Newman
2004 Delancy Place
Philadelphia, PA 19103
phone: 800-523-3256
Wants pre-1930 board games, especially by McLoughlin, Parker, Bliss, Ives; must be in excellent condition with excellent graphics.

Dealers

Debra Krim
P.O. Box 2273
Peabody, MA 01960-7273
phone: 508-535-3140
fax: 508-535-7522
e-mail: dlkrim@star.net
Internet: http://www.old_toys.com
Wants boxed & board games from 1843 to 1970: McLoughlin, Ives, Bliss and other companies; baseball and TV games; cartoon strip games.

Paul Fink
Fun & Games
P.O. Box 488
Kent, CT 06757-0488
phone: 860-927-4001
Buys and sells Victorian games, comic and cartoon games, TV & nostalgia games; dealer and mail order.

Bill & Joanne Bruegman
Toy Scouts, Inc.
137 Casterton Ave.
Akron, OH 44303-1543
phone: 330-836-0668
fax: 330-869-8668
e-mail: toyscout@newreach.net
Internet: http://www.csmonline.com/toyscouts/

Jeff Lowe
Jeff Lowe's ExtranaGAMEza
5005 Tamara Lane
West Des Moines, IA 50265-6912
phone: 515-267-8765
e-mail: gamesguy1@aol.com
Internet: http://www.ewtech.com/games
Collector and dealer with catalog of

over 2500 games available for nominal postage charge.

Experts

Lee Dennis
447 Park Ave., Apt. 12
Keene, NH 03431-6506
phone: 603-358-0060
Author of "Warman's Antique American Games, 1840 - 1940"; former curator-owner of the country's largest collection of board games; continues to offer slide film presentation about games to clubs/ associations/Historical Societies.

Bruce Whitehill
Big Game Hunter, The
620 Park Ave. #202
Rochester, NY 14607
phone: 716-442-8998
Buys/sells/collects; one of the world's foremost authorities on American games; author of "Games: American Games & Their Makers, 1822-1992, With Values" (Wallace-Homestead, 1992); book available from author for $23.00 ppd.

Rick Polizzi
4602 Morse Ave.
Sherman Oaks, CA 91423-3326
Co-author with Fred Shaeffer of "Spin Again: Board Games From the Fifties and Sixties."

Board (TV Show Related)

Experts

Norm Vigue
62 Bailey St.
Stoughton, MA 02072
phone: 617-344-5441
Author of "Name of the Game." Buys & sells board games from TV cartoons, comedies, westerns, adventure, comic strip, detective, etc.

Card

Experts

Lee Dennis
447 Park Ave., Apt. 12
Keene, NH 03431-6506
phone: 603-358-0060
Author of "Warman's Antique American Games, 1840 - 1940"; former curator-owner of the country's largest collection of board games; continues to offer slide film presentation about games to clubs/ associations/Historical Societies.

Bruce Whitehill
Big Game Hunter, The
620 Park Ave. #202
Rochester, NY 14607
phone: 716-442-8998
Buys/sells/collects; one of the world's foremost authorities on American games; author of "Games: American Games & Their Makers, 1822-1992, With Values" (Wallace-Homestead,

1992); book available from author for $23.00 ppd.

Checkers

Collectors

Henry A. Justice
30 Thomas Ct.
Stockbridge, GA 30281-2900
phone: 770-389-8527
Wants checkers: plastic, wood, etc.; loose, boxed, sets, with or without board.

Checker Book World
3520 Hillcrest, Apt. 4
Dubuque, IA 52002
Wants to buy old checker sets, books and memorabilia.

Experts

Don Deweber
John Caldwell-Irving Windt Library of
Checkers
3520 Hillcrest, Apt. 4
Dubuque, IA 52002
Wants to buy old checker sets, checker books, and other checker memorabilia.

Museums/Libraries

International Checkers Hall of Fame
P.O. Box A
220 Lynn Ray Rd.
Petal, MS 39465
phone: 601-582-7090
Hosts international checkers competitions

Cribbage Boards

Clubs/Associations

Bette L. Bemis
Cribbage Board Collectors Society
Newsletter: Members of the Board
P.O. Box 170
Carolina, RI 02812-0170
phone: 401-364-7241
For collectors of cribbage boards.

Collectors

Bette L. Beamis
P.O. Box 170
Carolina, RI 02812-0170
phone: 401-364-7241

Al Tenebaum
3095 N. Course Dr., #401
Pompano Beach, FL 33069

Mah Jongg

Collectors

Allan Weitz
12 Van Every Cr.
Kirkland
Quebec H9J 2P5 Canada, CA
phone: 514-697-3276
Wishing to share mah jongg information; buys, sells, trades old Chinese sets; will travel.

Punchboards

(see also COIN-OPERATED MACHINES; PAPER COLLECTIBLES)

Dealers

Ken Durham
909 26th St. NW
Washington, DC 20037-2029
e-mail:
durham@GameRoomAntiques.com
Internet: http://
www.GameRoomAntiques.com
Buys and sells punchboards with gambling, sport, pin-up and other colorful decorations; send $2 for illustrated list; also buys in quantity.

Clark Phelps
Amusement Sales Co.
127 North Main St.
Midvale, UT 84047-2424
phone: 801-255-4731
Wants to buy punchboards.

Skill & Action

Experts

Bruce Whitehill
Big Game Hunter, The
620 Park Ave. #202
Rochester, NY 14607
phone: 716-442-8998
Buys/sells/collects skill & action games: Mouse Trap, Operation, spinner games, Pick-Up Sticks (Jack Straws), Tiddley Winks, marble games, ball games, table top billiards/croquet/pinball (bagatelle), Twister, Hungry Hippo, etc.

Video Games

Collectors

Frank Polosky
Video Games
P.O. Box 9542
Pittsburgh, PA 15223-0542
Wants to buy video games: Sega, Apple, Atari, Commodore 64, Vic 20, Odyssey, Bally Astrocade, ColecoVision; also wants related books and magazines; wants all 8 bit games: Mappy, Space Cavern, Apollo, Sewer Sam; write before sending.

GANGSTER RELATED COL-LECTIBLES

(see LAW ENFORCEMENT MEMORABILIA; PERSONALITIES [CRIMINAL]; PROHIBITION ITEMS)

GARBAGE RELATED

Collectors

Carolyn Petrus
205 E. Beaver Ave., Ste. 201
State College, PA 16801
phone: 814-238-2060 or 814-234-0678
fax: 814-238-7123
Wants to buy garbage related items:

antique toy garbage trucks, war effort recycling posters, trash related art, photographs, memory art, paintings of dumps, collection services, recycling; very good condition, only, please.

Toy Trucks

Collectors

A.J. Perez
5408 North Diversey
Milwaukee, WI 53217
Wants to buy garbage trucks of all sizes and condition.

GARDEN FURNITURE

Furniture & Ornaments

(see also CAST IRON ITEMS)

Dealers

New England Garden Ornaments
38 East Brookfield Rd.
North Brookfield, MA 01535-0235
phone: 508-867-4474
fax: 508-867-8409
Internet: http://
www.negardenornaments.com
Carries old and new garden architecture and ornamentation: sundials, statuary, planters, urns, wrought iron, pedestals, birdbaths, etc.

Experts

Elizabeth Schumacher
Garden Accents
947 Longview Rd.
Gulph Mills, PA 19406
phone: 610-525-3287 or 610-825-5525
fax: 610-825-1958
Buys and sells best assortment of antique garden accessories: urns, planters, statuary, benches, fountains; bronze, iron, lead, etc.

Margaret Lindquist
Whitehall at the Villa
1213 E. Franklin St.
Chapel Hill, NC 27514-3307
phone: 919-942-3179 or 919-933-3305
fax: 919-942-3179
Author of "The Official Price Guide to Garden Furniture and Accessories."

Repro. Sources

Nathan's Forge
3476 Uniontown Rd.
Uniontown, MD 21158

John C. Allen, Jr.
Robinson Iron
P.O. Box 1119
Alexander City, AL 35010
phone: 205-329-8486
Makes reproduction furniture and fountains; catalog $5.

Country Is...Country Castings
P.O. Box 824
Jacksonville, AL 36265

GARDEN HOSE NOZZLES

(see WATER SPRINKLERS)

GAS STATION COLLECTIBLES

(see also AUTOMOBILIA; GAUGES; HIGHWAY COLLECTIBLES; LICENSE PLATES; TOYS, Gas Station Related; TRAILERS & RV'S)

Clubs/Associations

Jerry Keyser
International Petroliana Collectors
Association
Magazine: Check the Oil!
P.O. Box 937
Powell, OH 43065-0937
phone: 614-848-5038 or 800-228-6224
fax: 614-436-4760
Internet: http://home.stlnet.com/
~jimpotts/cto.htm
Pumps, oil cans, signs, oil bottles, pens, pump globes; anything to do with the petroleum industry of days gone by.

John Logsdon
Iowa Gas Swap Meet
2417 Linda Dr.
Des Moines, IA 50322-5200
phone: 515-251-8811
An organization dedicated to the collecting of all oil, gas, petroleum and auto advertising including signs, globes, pumps, cans, bottles, and related memorabilia. The annual convention held each August is the largest of its kind.

Collectors

Ted Appleby
29 Baptiste Rd.
South Baptiste
AB T9S 1R7 Canada
phone: 403-675-5371
fax: 403-675-5205
Buy, sell, trade Canadian quart oil cans, gas pumps, globes and signs, clocks, thermometers, etc. from tire companies, farm implement dealers, automobile companies, etc.; Canadian oil can appraiser; author of "Oil Cans of Canada."

Ed Natale, Jr.
P.O. Box 222
Wyckoff, NJ 07481
phone: 201-848-8485
fax: 201-891-4252
Wants to buy gas station and petroliana signs, uniform pins and badges, oil cans, pre-WWII road maps; photos helpful.

Larry Spilkin
P.O. Box 5039
Southfield, MI 48086-5039
phone: 810-642-3722
Wants postcards and matchbook covers of drive-ins, diners, cafes, gas stations and 1930s-1950s motels, restaurant/bar, cabins and Art Deco streamline hotels.

Peter Capell
1838 West Grace St.
Chicago, IL 60613-2724
phone: 773-871-8735
*Collects gasoline company/service
station items: pump globes, giveaways
such as banks, thermometers, salt &
pepper shaker sets in the shape of gas
pumps.*

Bill Allard
1801 Fernside
Tacoma, WA 98465-1310
phone: 253-565-2545
e-mail: liber1@msn.com

Ace Feek
P.O. Box 1358
Chelan, WA 98816
phone: 509-682-5345
*Wants to buy oil company and service
station cap badges: Mobile, Union
Oil, Mohawk Gasoline, Texaco, Shell,
Union 76, etc.*

Experts

Mark Anderton
Collectors Auction Services
P.O. Box 13732
Seneca, PA 16346
phone: 814-677-6070
fax: 814-677-6166
*Co-author with Sherry Mullen of "Gas
Station Collectibles" (Wallace-
Homestead, 1994).*

Wayne Henderson
20 Worley Rd.
Marshall, NC 28753
phone: 704-649-2716
*World's largest collection of
historical material concerning service
stations and oil company collectibles;
co-author of "Gasoline Pump
Globes", the new comprehensive
catalog of known gas pump globes
with complete company histories.*

Scott Anderson
Time Passages, Ltd.
P.O. Box 65596
West Des Moines, IA 50265-0596
phone: 515-279-0194
*Author of "Check the Oil" (Wallace-
Homestead).*

Periodicals

Scott Benjamin
Newsletter: Petroleum Collectibles
  Monthly
411 Forest St.
Lagrange, OH 44050
phone: 216-355-6608
Internet: http://home.stlnet.com/
  ~jimpotts/pcm.htm
*Research on all phases of gasoline
marketing; world's largest collection
of historical material concerning
service stations and oil company
collectibles: cans, signs, paper, toys,
gas pumps, globes, large ad section.*

Clark Miller
Newsletter: WOCCO
36100 Chardon Rd.
Willoughby, OH 44094-8302
phone: 216-946-2640

Frontier

Collectors

Jim Hollabaugh
3800 Congress Parkway
P.O. Box 460
Richfield, OH 44286-0460
phone: 216-659-3888 or 800-662-6344
fax: 216-659-9410
*Wants to buy Shell & Frontier
petroliana: containers, globes, signs,
toys, promotional items, shell pocket
watches with fobs; specializes in Shell
and Frontier.*

Gulf Oil

Collectors

Charles Roach
3212 Tudor
Oklahoma City, OK 73122-1346
phone: 405-942-4520
*Wants to buy Gulf Oil gas station
collectibles: maps, signs, cans,
giveaways, ads, paper items,
letterheads; only Gulf Oil items,
please.*

Lubrication Devices

Collectors

Robert Larson
3517 Vernal Ct.
Merced, CA 95340-0689
phone: 209-723-7828
*Wants to buy oil cans (push the
bottom type) and other lubrication
devices such as grease guns,
lubricators, grease cups and fittings.*

Pumps & Globes

Collectors

Gary Hildman
3240 Sevier Rd.
Marcellus, NY 13108-9624
phone: 315-673-2535
fax: 315-673-2412
*Wants gasoline pump globes and
related items: inserts, glass and metal
bodies; also wants porcelain, tin, and
neon signs.*

Bob Fousek
2436 Fairview Rd.
Grantsville, MD 21536
phone: 301-245-4277
*Wants complete globes or parts; also
gas advertising, tins, etc.*

Kent Blaine
505 N. Mission Rd.
Winona, MS 38967-9534
phone: 601-624-2947 or 601-283-3524
*Wants gas station items through
1950s; especially brass padlocks with
oil company logos, e.g. Texaco, Pan*

*Am, Crown, etc.; also wants 15" single
globe lens.*

Scott Benjamin
411 Forest St.
Lagrange, OH 44050
phone: 216-355-6608
Internet: http://home.stlnet.com/
  ~jimpotts/pcm.htm
*Wants gasoline globes, inserts, etched
globes, aviation, Benzol and others.*

Dealers

Walt Feiger
Walt's Antiques
2513 Nelson Rd.
Traverse City, MI 49686-8557
phone: 616-223-7386 or 616-223-4123
*Buys and sells gas pumps, globes,
signs, auto memorabilia, and slot
machines.*

Repro. Sources

Benkin & Co.
14 E. Main
Tripp City, OH 45371
phone: 513-667-5975
*Handmade antique-style gas pumps,
wide selection of colors, 35 oil
company globes to chose from; sold in
kits or completely finished; write for
flyer.*

Suppliers

Ted Appleby
29 Baptiste Rd.
South Baptiste
AB T9S 1R7 Canada
phone: 403-675-5371
fax: 403-675-5205
*Restoration parts, supplies for vintage
gas pumps; Canada's largest selection
of Canadian globes, decals; castings,
glass, I.D. tags, brass nozzles, hose,
etc. for Gilbert 7 Barker and
Clearvision single and 20 gallon twin;
catalog $4.*

Scott Anderson
Time Passages, Ltd.
P.O. Box 65596
West Des Moines, IA 50265-0596
phone: 515-279-0194
*Supplies restoration parts and
supplies for vintage gasoline pumps.*

Gasoline Pump Parts
P.O. Box 771
Burton, TX 77835
*Supplies restoration parts and
supplies for vintage gasoline pumps.*

Road Maps

Collectors

Peter Sidlow
5895 Duneville St.
Las Vegas, NV 89118
phone: 702-873-1818
fax: 702-248-4288
*Wants early road maps; oil company
or other issues; prefers colorful
graphics.*

Experts

Doug Yorke
7 Conover Lane
Rumson, NJ 07760
e-mail: Yorke_D@ix.netcom.com
*Co-author with John Margolies of
"Hitting the Road."*

Shell

Collectors

Jim Hollabaugh
3800 Congress Parkway
P.O. Box 460
Richfield, OH 44286-0460
phone: 216-659-3888 or 800-662-6344
fax: 216-659-9410
*Wants to buy Shell & Frontier
petroliana: containers, globes, signs,
toys, promotional items, shell pocket
watches with fobs; specializes in Shell
and Frontier.*

Texaco

Collectors

Richard Eaves
9838 Rustic Gate
La Porte, TX 77571
phone: 713-470-2191
*Wants Texaco toys, literature,
memorabilia.*

GAUGES

(see also GAS STATION COL-
LECTIBLES; INSTRUMENTS &
DEVICES)

Collectors

Barry L. David
c/o D.M. Goodsell
91 E 200 S.
Newton, UT 84327

Jarvis
P.O. Box 2245
Lynnwood, WA 98036-8636
*Wants tire pressure gauges having car
names or other advertising on them.*

Experts

Brian Lerohl
29048 486th Ave.
Fairview, SD 57027
phone: 605-987-5378
*Collector and historian of fluid
pressure gauges, especially Bourdon
tube and diaphragm type steam
gauges.*

Repair Services

West Virginia Railroad Co.
839 South Conkling St.
Baltimore, MD 21224
phone: 301-522-0079
Repairs and restores all gauges.

Suppliers

E-Z Way Chemical
P.O. Box 525
Burlington, WA 98233
Sells "Silverplater", a 99.987% real silver solution that cleans and recoats a metal surface with silver.

GAVELS

Collectors

Bill Retskin
P.O. Box 18481
Asheville, NC 28814-0481
phone: 704-254-4487
fax: 704-254-1066
e-mail: matchclub@circle.net
Internet: http://www.matchcovers.com
Wants to buy gavels: auctioneers', judicial, ceremonial, toy, giant, traditional size, miniature; prefers wood; please no mallets, meat tenderizers, or hammers.

GEMS & JEWELRY

(see also AMERICAN INDIAN, Jewelry; BEADS; BOOKS, Reference [Gems/Jewelry]; CHATELAINES; COMBS & HAIR ACCESSORIES; COMPACTS; CRAFTS; CUFF LINKS; GOLD; DRESSER ITEMS, Hatpins & Hatpin Holders; IVORY; JADE; LAPIDARY; MINERALS; WATCHES)

Appraisers

Martin D. Haske, GG, ISA
Adamas Gemological Laboratory
P.O. Box 470828
Brookline Village, MA 02147-0828
phone: 617-232-5508
fax: 617-232-5508

Judith Fineblit Anderson, GG, ISA
CAPP
Bijoux Extraordinaire, Ltd.
P.O. Box 1424
Manchester, NH 03105-1424
phone: 603-624-8672
e-mail: judi@bijoux.mv.com
Internet: http://www.bel-cg.com
Appraises diamonds, colored gems, antique & period jewelry, and contemporary designer jewelry for insurance, estate, divorce, charitable donation, damage reports, expert witness testimony.

Jo Anne M. Whitteaker,ISA CAPP, GG
Independent Gemological Lab
Appraisers & Consultants
23 W. Westfield Ave.
P.O. Box 4086
Roselle Park, NJ 07204-2252
phone: 908-241-8800 or 908-298-0121
e-mail: polygon.net@3580
Professional gemological examinations, grading, appraisals, fraudulent claims investigations, expert witness; appraisals for casualty loss, insurance replacement, liquidation, damage, equitable distribution, donation, estate, etc.

Karen J. Russo, G.G., ISA
Karen Jocelyn, Inc.
792 Partridge Dr.
P.O. Box 6795
Bridgewater, NJ 08807
phone: 908-806-6706 or 908-526-8440
fax: 908-526-8348
Provides a full range of appraisal and consultation services for studio/art jewelry, antique/estate jewelry, mineral specimens, and collector gemstones; market research, identification, photography, provenance research, portable services.

Jerry Ehrenwald, GG, ISA
International Gemological Institute
579 5th Ave.
New York, NY 10017-1917
phone: 212-398-1700 or 212-398-1701
fax: 212-869-8047
e-mail: igi@interport.net
Internet: http://www.igi-usa.com
Devoted to identification, authentication and valuation of gems and jewelry from an unbiased point of view; no buying or selling.

Paul Cassarino ISA, GG
Gem Lab, The
4098 W. Henrietta Rd.
Rochester, NY 14623-5222
phone: 716-359-3900
fax: 716-359-8932
e-mail: 102073.2774@compuserve.com

Pennye Jones-Napier, FGA
1415 Shepherd St. NW
Washington, DC 20036-5409
phone: 202-393-2747 or 202-291-5575
fax: 202-291-5345
e-mail: pennye@ziplink.net
Appraiser specializing in Studio/Design jewelers, and contemporary and antique jewelry targeting the 19th and 20th centuries; also offers consultation services to auction houses worldwide.

Dan James, GG
Antique Jewelry Specialists
4212 Gallatin St.
Hyattsville, MD 20781-2049
phone: 301-779-3696
Graduate gemologist, appraiser, specialist in antique jewelry, diamonds and colored gemstones; Georgian to modern; gemological lab on premises for appraisals and evaluations; by appointment only.

Thomas J. Terpilak, GG, ASA
Metro Gem Consultants
7315 Wisconsin Ave.
Bethesda, MD 20814-3202
phone: 301-654-0838 or 301-654-8678
Internet: http://lan2wan.com/mgc
Gemological consultant and professional jewelry appraiser.

James Jolliff
National Association of Jewelry Appraisers, The
Newsletter: Jewelry Appraiser, The
P.O. Box 6558
Annapolis, MD 21401-0558
phone: 301-261-8270 or 410-266-0744
Members perform gem and jewelry, silver flatware and hollowware, and watch valuations exclusively; also watches and silver.

James Jolliff
P.O. Box 6558
Annapolis, MD 21401-0558
phone: 301-261-8270 or 410-266-0744
Appraises antique to contemporary gems and jewelry, silver flatware and hollowware, and watches exclusively.

Joette Humphrey, GG
Shelley's Auction Gallery
429 N. Main St.
Hendersonville, NC 28792-4903
phone: 704-698-8485 or 704-692-3615
fax: 704-693-4305
Buy, consign and auction antiques and collectibles with a heavy emphasis on antique jewelry and diamonds.

Rose & Lornie Mueller, ISA, GG
Lithos Jewelry
344 Corey Ave.
Saint Petersburg, FL 33706
phone: 813-367-9010
fax: 813-367-9011
High-end jewelry dealer; trained and accredited appraisers.

Joseph G. Balshone, GG, ISA
Columbus Gemological Laboratories, Inc.
463 East Town St.
Columbus, OH 43215-4796
phone: 800-209-4367 or 614-224-2404
fax: 614-224-5630
e-mail: jbalshone@compuserve.com
Specializing in appraising gems & jewelry, post-1800 firearms, and vintage and modern writing instruments and accessories.

Pamela L. Hickman, ISA, GG
International Diamond & Gold Design
4026 E 82nd St.
Indianapolis, IN 46250-4209
phone: 317-578-4653
fax: 317-578-9335
Specializes in gems, jewelry, diamonds, colored stones, gold, platinum, pearls, and estate and custom jewelry.

Katherine Vandygriff, GG,ISA CAPP
Katherine's
605 Sunset Dr.
Muscatine, IA 52761-2778
phone: 319-263-6008 or 319-263-1050
fax: 319-263-1050
e-mail: Katherine@muscanet.com
Professional, independent gems & jewelry appraiser.

Daniel M. Balboni, ISA, GG
Gemological Appraisal Consultant
8200 Pat Booker Rd.
San Antonio, TX 78233
phone: 210-653-6552
fax: 210-653-1072
Graduate Gemologist, appraisals, consultant, expert witness; appraisals for casualty loss, insurance, replacement, equitable distribution, liquidation, estate, etc.

Anne Hawken, GG, ASA
Anne Hawken Gems
P.O. Box 160906
Austin, TX 78716-0906
phone: 512-288-1507
fax: 512-328-9411
Buys, sells, brokers, and appraises fine and collectible gemstones; also collection consultant, expert witness, educator; Accredited Senior Appraiser (ASA), AGA-Certified Gem Laboratory.

Sharon Wakefield
Northwest Gemological Lab
P.O. Box 8243
Boise, ID 83707-2243
phone: 208-362-3938
fax: 208-362-2889
e-mail: sharon@gem-science.com
Internet: http://www.gem-science.com/Index.htm
Noted expert, appraiser, lecturer and author specializing in the appraisal of diamonds, gems and jewelry.

Larry Phillips, GG, ISA
Phillips & Associates
2430 Juan Tabo NE, Ste. 275
Albuquerque, NM 87112
phone: 505-299-7999
Master Gemologist Appraiser.

Barbara Pickett, GCA, MCA, GGAC
Antique Rose, The
P.O. Box 771
Lakewood, CA 90714-0771
phone: 562-425-4149
fax: 562-425-4149
e-mail: bpfence@worldnet.att.net

Christian Coleman, Ex. Dir.
International Society of Appraisers
Journal: ISA News Journal
16040 Christensen Rd., Ste. 320
Seattle, WA 98188
phone: 206-241-0359
fax: 206-241-0436
e-mail: ISA_HQ@compuserve.com
Internet: http://www.isa-appraisers.org
Largest association of professional personal property appraisers; members specialize in antiques & residential contents, gems & jewelry, fine art, and machinery & equipment; call for appraiser nearest you.

Auction Services

Gloria Lieberman
Skinner, Inc.
357 Main St.
Bolton, MA 01740-1104
phone: 508-779-6241 or 617-350-5400
fax: 508-779-5144
Established in 1964, Skinner Inc. is the fifth largest auction house in the US; has offices in Bolton and Boston, MA.

Peter J. Shemonsky
Grogan & Company Auctioneers
22 Harris St.
Dedham, MA 02026-1835
phone: 617-437-9550 or 617-569-1502
fax: 617-437-0513

Sotheby's
1334 York Ave.
New York, NY 10021
phone: 212-606-7370 or 212-606-7000
Internet: http://www.sothebys.com
Over 70 collecting areas are featured at Sotheby's auctions including toys, dolls, porcelain, furniture, silver, art, books; exhibitions are free and everyone is welcome; for a free copy of "Sotheby's Newsletter", call 212-606-7245.

John S. Weschler
Weschler's
905 E St. NW
Washington, DC 20004-2006
phone: 202-628-1281 or 800-331-1430
fax: 202-628-2366
Specializes in the auction sale of jewelry, coins, and watches.

Joette Humphrey, GG
Shelley's Auction Gallery
429 N. Main St.
Hendersonville, NC 28792-4903
phone: 704-698-8485 or 704-692-3615
fax: 704-693-4305
Buy, consign and auction antiques and collectibles with a heavy emphasis on antique jewelry and diamonds.

William Milne
Dunning's Auction Service
755 Church Rd.
Elgin, IL 60123-9302
phone: 708-741-3483 or 800-462-2444
fax: 708-741-3589
Internet: http:///www.dunnings.com

Clubs/Associations

Canadian Jewellers Association
Newsletter: Jewellry World
20 Eglinton Ave. W., Ste. 1203
Toronto
Ontario M4R 1K8 Canada
phone: 416-480-1424
fax: 416-480-2342
e-mail: cjaa@cyor.ca
Internet: http://ppcimage.worldgate.com/cja/2nd_floor/cja.html

W. Knight, Ed.
Canadian Gemmological Association
Magazine: Canadian Gemmologist, The
1767 Avenue Rd.
North York
Ontario M5M 3Y8 Canada
phone: 416-785-0962
fax: 416-785-9043
A non-profit educational institution which teaches gemmology; magazine published quarterly.

Gemmological Association of Great Britain
27 Greville St., 1st Floor
London EC1N 8SU, U.K.
phone: (171) 404-3334
fax: (171) 404-8843
Offers correspondence and in-residence classes in gemology.

Canadian Institute of Gemmology
Newsletter: Gemmology Canada
P.O. Box 57010
Vancouver
Brit. Col., V5K 5G6 Canada
phone: 604-530-8569
Internet: http//www.deepcove.com/cig/

Manufacturing Jewelers & Silversmiths of America, Inc.
Magazine: American Jewelry Manufacturer
One State St., 6th Floor
Providence, RI 02908
phone: 401-274-3840 or 800-444-6572
e-mail: mjsa@internetMCI.com
Internet: http://mjsa.polygon.net/
A national trade association for the jewelry manufacturing industry; for jewelry manufacturers, goldsmiths and silversmiths, casters, refiners, electroplaters, gemstone dealers, findings manufacturers, suppliers, sales reps.

International Colored Gemstone Association
3 East 48th St., 5th Floor
New York, NY 10017
phone: 212-688-8452
fax: 212-688-9006
e-mail: ica@gemstone.org
Internet: http://www.gemstone.org/
Represents the intentional gemstone industry; working to increase the understanding, appreciation of colored gemstones worldwide; website with great information for the public on stone identification and grading; members are trade only.

Jerry Goldfarb, Ex. Dir.
Society of Antique & Estate Jewelry, Ltd.
570 Seventh Ave., Ste. 1900
New York, NY 10018
phone: 212-354-0520
fax: 212-730-0403
An international organization dedicated to creating greater understanding of this special class of precious objects through education, networking, news dissemination and promotion of special events.

Joyce Jonas
American Society of Jewelry History
Journal: Journal of the ASJH
215 East 80th St.
New York, NY 10022-0531
phone: 212-535-2479
Promotes education and appreciation of antique jewelry, crossing all periods from ancient to present; quarterly newsletter informs members of related lectures, exhibitions, and book reviews.

C.R. Beesley, Pres.
Accredited Gemologists Association
Journal: Cornerstone
580 Fifth Ave., Ste. 706
New York, NY 10036
phone: 212-704-0727 or 615-966-0580
fax: 615-966-0583
Professional association of gemstone experts, quality grading laboratories, appraisers, and dealers; all professional members are advanced, degree-holding gemologists, subscribing to a strong code of ethics and professional practice.

Jewelry Information Center
19 West 44th St., 9th Floor
New York, NY 10036
phone: 800-459-0130 or 212-398-2319
fax: 212-398-2324
e-mail: jic@polygon.net
Internet: http://jic.polygon.net/index.html
Founded in 1946 to provide public relations for the entire jewelry industry; provides consumers with information about fine jewelry, how to buy, how to care for it, its history, and new product trends.

Jewelers of America, Inc.
1185 Avenue of the Americas
New York, NY 10036
phone: 800-223-0673 or 212-768-8777
fax: 212-768-8087
Internet: http://jewelers.org/
A national association of retail jewelers; part of their mission is to provide consumers with information and education about fine jewelry; website offers information on how to select a jeweler, consumer news, test your jewelry knowledge.

Lucille Tempesta
Vintage Fashion & Costume Jewelry Club
Newsletter: VFCJ Newsletter
P.O. Box 265
Glen Oaks, NY 11004-0265
phone: 718-939-3095
fax: 718-939-7988

Society of North American Goldsmiths
Journal: Metalsmith
5009 Londonderry Dr.
Tampa, FL 33647-9910
phone: 813-977-5326
fax: 813-977-8462
e-mail: rmitchel@cftnet.com
Internet: http://www.craftweb.com/org/snag/snag.html
An association for jewelers and metal artisans; quarterly magazine devoted to the development and appreciation for the craft of fine metalsmithing: jewelry, decorative art, etc.

Thomas P. Dorman, Ex. Dir.
American Gem Society
8881 West Saraha Ave.
Las Vegas, NV 89117
phone: 702-255-6500
fax: 702-255-7420
e-mail: agstom@aol.com
Internet: http://www.ags.org/
Founded in 1934 to protect consumers in their purchases of fine jewelry.

Gemological Institute of America
Journal: Gems & Gemology
5355 Armada Dr.
Carlsbad, CA 92008
phone: 800-421-7250
Internet: http://www.gia.org

Dealers

Judith Fineblit Anderson, GG, ISA CAPP
Bijoux Extraordinaire, Ltd.
P.O. Box 1424
Manchester, NH 03105-1424
phone: 603-624-8672
e-mail: judi@bijoux.mv.com
Internet: http://www.bel-cg.com
Buys, sells, brokers fine quality antique and estate jewelry, contemporary designer jewelry, diamonds and colored gemstones; also custom design and restorations of antique jewelry; appraisal services; lecturer on jewelry.

Elissa Cohen ISA CAPP, GG
Suburban Jewelers
126 East Front St.
Plainfield, NJ 07060-1202
phone: 908-756-1774
Dealer and appraiser of modern and period jewelry, GIA Graduate Gemologist, Certified Member of the ISA, appraiser of diamonds, gemstones, pearls, jewelry.

S.J. Moore
P.O. Box 524
Skaneateles, NY 13152-0524
phone: 315-685-8758
Buys and sells fine jewelry and diamonds, ruby, sapphire, emeralds.

Dan James, GG
Antique Jewelry Specialists
4212 Gallatin St.
Hyattsville, MD 20781-2049
phone: 301-779-3696
Buys and sells diamonds and colored stone jewelry, antique to 1940s; including platinum, enameled and costume jewelry.

Kenneth M. Glass
Glyndon Jewelry
4880 Butler Rd.
Glyndon, MD 21071
phone: 410-526-4112
fax: 410-526-0344
Manufacturer and wholesaler of 10K, 14K, 18K and platinum vintage style earrings, pendants, rings, brooches,

etc. with genuine stones; also restore and repair and will make models from your merchandise; to the trade only.

Tony Laughter
Perry's at SouthPark
SouthPark Mall
Charlotte, NC 28211
phone: 704-364-1391
Deals in fine, antique and estate jewelry; Accredited Member of the International Society of Appraisers.

Ed London
Parke Lloyds International, Inc.
9408 NW 70 St.
Fort Lauderdale, FL 33321-3002
phone: 954-724-4294 or 954-724-4274
Wants to buy old jewelry.

Anne Foster
1913 Hyde St.
San Francisco, CA 94109
phone: 415-776-8865
Wants Bakelite jewelry, bracelets, pins, necklaces, earrings, rings, etc.

Ray L. Elsey
Associate Jewelers Inc.
534 SW Third Ave.
Portland, OR 97204
phone: 800-224-8086
fax: 503-226-6787
e-mail: raylc@tradeshop.com
Internet: http://www.tradeshop.com/master/lobby.html
A union professional fine jewelry tradeshop, designing, building and servicing fine jewelry since 1974; refined working drawings, custom wax carving, special order manufacturing, platinum manufacturing, Celtic design bands.

Experts

Judith Fineblit Anderson, GG, ISA CAPP
Bijoux Extraordinaire, Ltd.
P.O. Box 1424
Manchester, NH 03105-1424
phone: 603-624-8672
e-mail: judi@bijoux.mv.com
Internet: http://www.bel-cg.com
Buys, sells, brokers fine quality antique and estate jewelry, contemporary designer jewelry, diamonds and colored gemstones; also custom design and restorations; offers extensive consulting and appraisal services; lecturer on jewelry.

Patti J. Geolat, FGA, GG
Geolat & Associates
14110 Dallas Pkwy., #200
Dallas, TX 75240
phone: 972-239-9314
fax: 972-239-9313
Specializes in gemology and gemstones; jewelry (antique and modern), diamonds.

William D. Hoefer, FGA, GG
Hoefers' Gemological Services
5016 Alan Ave., Ste. B4
San Jose, CA 95124-5741
phone: 408-264-0670
fax: 408-264-0725
Specializes in the appraisal of gemstones, diamonds, and contemporary jewelry; also offers expert testimony for attorneys, court, etc.

Misc. Services

Jewelers Vigalance Committee
401 East 34th St., Ste. N13A
New York, NY 10016-8578
Internet: http://www.gis.net/~adamas/jvc.html
Has published "Recommended Minimum Guidelines for Insurance Replacement Cost Estimate Documentation foe Jewelers," see this website for the guidelines in full.

Rapaport Diamond Report RapNet
15 West 47th St.
New York, NY 10036
phone: 212-354-0575
fax: 212-840-0243
Internet: http://www.diamonds.com/
Lings together all aspects of the jewelry industry to form an electronic community; a secured site for members of the trade only; provides instant access to diamond price data as well as continuously updated news; a fee service.

Howard Rubin
GemDialogue Systems, Inc.
P.O. Box 7683
Rego Park, NY 11374-7683
phone: 718-997-0231
fax: 718-997-9057
GemDialogue is a gemstone descriptive system for colored stones and fancy colored diamonds; it gives you visual comparison points for over 60,000 colors; a grading system is also included.

On-Line Services

Polygon, The Jewelry Industry WebCenter
First Bank Center, #201
P.O. Box 4806
Dillon, CO 80435
phone: 800-221-4435 or 970-468-1245
fax: 970-468-1247
e-mail: sales@polygon.net
Internet: http://www.polygon.net/
World's largest cluster of website-based on-line services for the jewelry industry; operated within a password-protected environment for trade-only communication; the public can find a local jeweler, and get tips for buying jewelry.

Ray L. Elsey
Gemology & Lapidary Pages, c/o
   Associate Jewelers Inc.
534 SW Third Ave.
Portland, OR 97204
phone: 800-224-8086
fax: 503-226-6787
e-mail: raylc@tradeshop.com
Internet: http://www.tradeshop.com/master/lobby.html
Great website for consumer information about gemstones; judging cut, color, clarity, carat; how gemstones are classified; gem substitutes; grading; caring for your gemstones; ccheck out the jewelry Hall of Shame.

Periodicals

Carol Besler, Ed.
Magazine: Canadian Jeweller
1448 Lawrence Ave. E., Ste. 302
Toronto
Ontario M4A 2V6 Canada
phone: 416-755-5199
fax: 416-755-9123
e-mail: style@stylecom.on.ca
Internet: http://canadianjeweller.worldgate.com
A bi-monthly glossy magazine focusing on gems, jewelry and timepieces; trade shows, business news, products and services.

Magazine: American Jewelry Manufacturer
One State St.
Providence, RI 02908-5035
phone: 401-274-3840
fax: 401-274-0265
e-mail: 102262.223@aompuserve.com
Internet: http://www.mjsa.polygon.net
A monthly glossy trade publication; industry articles, ads for jewelry manufacturing goods and services.

Magazine: National Jeweler
1 Penn Plaza
New York, NY 10019
phone: 212-615-2380 or 800-250-2430
Internet: http://www.national-jeweler.com/
The most popular jewelry industry resource; up-to-the-minute news twice a month.

Magazine: Rapaport Diamond Report
15 West 47th St.
New York, NY 10036
phone: 212-354-0575
fax: 212-840-0243
A weekly report of world wide activity relating to diamonds, colored stones and jewelry; price performances, cash asking prices, precious metal prices, actual transaction prices for diamonds and diamond jewelry, etc.

PTN Publishing Co.
Magazine: Modern Jeweler
455 Broad Hollow Rd., Ste. 21
Melville, NY 11747
phone: 516-845-2700
Monthly trade magazine for the jewelry industry.

Jewelers' Circular-Keystone
Magazine: Jewelers' Circular-Keystone Magazine
201 King of Prussia Rd.
Wayne, PA 19089-0001
phone: 610-964-4480
fax: 610-964-4481
Internet: http://www.chilton.net/jck/
A monthly trade magazine focusing on new and antique gems, jewelry, and watches.

Cindy Valerio
Magazine: Colored Stone
P.O. Box 1100
Devon, PA 19333-0905
phone: 610-293-1112 or 800-676-4336
fax: 610-293-1717
The international reporter of the gemstone trade; features also include The Annual Buyers Guide, The Fall Show Guide, and the Tucson Show Guide - a guide to the largest US gemstone show held annually in Arizona; also book & video sales.

Magazine: Colored Stone Magazine
P.O. Box 1100
Devon, PA 19333-0905
phone: 610-293-1112 or 800-676-4336
fax: 610-293-1717

Gemworld International, Inc.
Magazine: Guide, The
630 Dundee Rd., Ste. 235
Northbrook, IL 60062
phone: 708-654-0555
fax: 708-564-0557
Quarterly price guides and related information on gems.

Martin Rubin
Newsletter: Old Jewelry News
P.O. Box 272
Evanston, IL 60204
phone: 708-328-6336
Publication filled mainly with classified ads for old jewelry and beads; also classifieds for supplies, tools, displays, books, literature, and services such as custom design, appraisals, repair, advertising, photography, etc.

Magazine: Gems & Gemology
P.O. Box 2110
Santa Monica, CA 90407-9985
phone: 310-829-2991 or 800-421-7250
fax: 310-453-4478

Magazine: Ornament
P.O. Box 2349
San Marcos, CA 92079-2349
phone: 800-888-8950 or 619-599-0222
A quarterly magazine focusing on craft and art items of personal adornment in any media or form: fiber, glass, metal, historic/ethnic ornament; ethnographic and tribal jewelry; also reviews of museum exhibits and publications.

Magazine: JQ Magazine
585 Fifth Street West
Sonoma, CA 95476-6800
phone: 707-938-1082

Repair Services

Richard P. Hegeman
Hegeman & Co.
361 S. Main St.
Providence, RI 02903-2912
phone: 401-831-6812
Cutters of all precious/semi-precious stones; specializing in the repair & restoration of all types of jewelry (antique and contemporary); gemstone replacements and repairs.

Pat Morse
Edelstein & Morse Antique Jewelry Repair
Rt 4A Box 425
Bar Mills, ME 04004
phone: 207-929-4034
e-mail: Edelmorse@mix-net.net
Specializes in the fine repair and restoration of antique jewelry, holloware and small objects of art including gold, platinum, silver, gemstones, diamonds.

Antiques Restoration by Julian
110 West 25th St., #208
New York, NY 10001
phone: 212-647-0305 or 201-791-7875
Gold, silver and any metal subjects; lamps and small sculptures; jewelry and costume jewelry; gold and silver plating.

Ray L. Elsey
Associate Jewelers Inc.
534 SW Third Ave.
Portland, OR 97204
phone: 800-224-8086
fax: 503-226-6787
e-mail: raylc@tradeshop.com
Internet: http://www.tradeshop.com/master/lobby.html
A union professional fine jewelry tradeshop, designing, building and servicing fine jewelry since 1974; does remanufacturings and restorations; specializes in platinum.

Gilbertson & Co.
800 SW Morrison, 2nd Floor
Portland, OR 97205
phone: 503-274-2802

Suppliers

Prized Posessions
P.O. Box 1147
Fresno, CA 93715
e-mail: jack@gemworld.com
Internet: http://www.gemworld.com
Provides opals, gemstones, collector stones, synthetics, cabbing and faceting rough, lapidary equipment and supplies, appraisals, etc.; extensive website.

Diamonds

Dealers

Rose Proler
Rose Proler, Inc.
5433 Westheimer, Ste. 1105
Houston, TX 77056
phone: 713-627-3098 or 800-627-3098
fax: 713-627-0504
Specializes in rough and polished diamonds.

Periodicals

Rapaport Diamond Report
15 West 47th St.
New York, NY 10036
phone: 212-354-0575
fax: 212-840-0243
Internet: http://www.diamonds.com/
Can subscribe to a monthly or to a weekly price report; these reports are considered the primary source of diamond price information by the jewelry trade.

Joseph W. Tenhagen
Newsletter: Diamond Value Index
36 NE 1st St., #419
Miami, FL 33132
phone: 305-374-2411

Hair

(see HAIR WORK)

Opals

Experts

Paul B. Donning
Majestic Gems & Carvings
P.O. Box 1348
Estes Park, CO 80517
phone: 800-468-0324 or 970-586-2411
fax: 970-586-0996
Importer of rough opal; cutter and designer; author of three books on opals: "Opal Identification and Value", "Opal Adventures", and "Opal Cutting Made Easy."

Periodicals

Majestic Press, Inc.
Magazine: Opal Market News
P.O. Box 2265
Estes Park, CO 80517
phone: 800-468-0324

Pearls

Periodicals

Richard Torrey, Editor
Pearl World - The International Pearling Journal
5501 N 7th Ave., Ste. 331
Phoenix, AZ 85021-1700
phone: 602-246-1586
fax: 602-246-1688
Covers whatever is happening in the pearling industry: statistics, market developments, auctions, interviews with cultivators and importers,

coverage of major trade fairs, educational materials, history of pearling, etc.

Pearls (Majorican)

Man./Prod./Dist.

Majorica
366 5th Ave., Ste. 507
New York, NY 10001
phone: 800-223-7560
Distributor of Majorican simulated pearls; also sold through fine department stores such as Nieman-Marcus.

Pearls (Mikimoto)

Man./Prod./Dist.

Mikimoto America
730 Fifth Ave.
New York, NY 10036
phone: 212-586-7153

Stick Pins

Collectors

Elynore "Pet" Kerins
82 Briarwood
Terre Haute, IN 47803-1770
phone: 812-877-1264
Serious stickpin collector with over 2700 in many categories: cameos, pearls, enamel, mourning, carved, dogs, cats, other animals, advertising, political and patriotic, colored stones, diamonds, etc.

Experts

Elynore "Pet" Kerins
82 Briarwood
Terre Haute, IN 47803-1770
phone: 812-877-1264
Co-author with Jack Kerins of "Collecting Antique Stickpins - Identification & Value Guide."

Supplies For

(see ANTIQUES DEALERS & COLLECTORS, Supplies For; BLACKLIGHTS [UV LAMPS])

Suppliers

26th St. Supply House
P.O. Box 680
Bellmore, NY 11710
phone: 800-605-2626
fax: 516-781-7831
Loupes, illuminated magnifiers, gold & silver testing kits, diamond testers, electronic metal testers, scales of all kinds, black lights, Riker mounts, etc.

Kassoy
16 Midland Ave.
Hicksville, NY 11801
phone: 800-452-7769
fax: 516-942-0402
Internet: http://www.kassoy.com
Mail order source for tools, supplies and instruments for the jewelry trade:

diamond testers, gold testers, loupes, gauges, diamond scales, gold scales, colorimeters, magnifiers, polishing equipment, watch repair tools, etc.

Robert Gitnick
R & D Supply Co.
1310 Apple Ave.
Silver Spring, MD 20910
phone: 301-588-7296
fax: 301-495-7312
Phone or mail order for jewelry tools and supplies: loupes, diamond testers, tweezers, gold test equipment, black lights, diamond measuring gauges, etc.

Indiana Jewelers Supply Inc.
31 E. Georgia, #202
Indianapolis, IN 46204-3621
phone: 317-632-6346 or 800-382-9973
Supplier of jewelers tools and equipment, and watch parts.

Swest Inc.
11090 North Stemmons Freeway
P.O. Box 59389
Dallas, TX 75229-1389
phone: 972-247-7744 or 800-527-5057
fax: 800-441-5162
Internet: http://www.swest.com
Mail order source for tools, supplies and instruments for the jewelry trade; for Eastern orders call Atlanta 800-241-5738: diamond testers, loupes, scales, gold testing kits, etc.

David D. Harleston
Lathrop's
6704 Ferris St.
Bellaire, TX 77401
phone: 713-665-2699
fax: 713-665-0214
Jeweler supplies and findings; loupes, scales, test kits.

Vintage & Costume

Clubs/Associations

Lucille Tempesta
Vintage Fashion & Costume Jewelry Club
Newsletter: VFCJ Newsletter
P.O. Box 265
Glen Oaks, NY 11004-0265
phone: 718-939-3095
fax: 718-939-7988

Pandora L. Farnum, Ed.
Leaping Frog Antique Jewelry & Collectible Club
Newsletter: LFAJCC Newsletter
4841 Martin Luther King Blvd.
Sacramento, CA 95820-4932
phone: 916-451-2022
Articles of interest regarding antique and collectibles jewelry and other collectible items such as hats, furs, smoking items, compacts, purses and more; annual convention.

Collectors

Doris M. Diabo
19953 Great Oaks Circle S.
Clinton Township, MI 48036-2440
phone: 810-463-5651
Wants to buy butterfly pins (brooches) - designer names or not - especially those flashy with colored rhinestones; send photocopies, price, condition, SASE.

Patti Vahary
Curious Cat, The
41 Crosby Dr.
Battle Creek, MI 49014
phone: 616-965-0943
Buys estate jewelry, especially costume signed work and 1800s style jewelry; also interested in Art Deco and jewelry from the 1920s through 1940s.

Daniel Brown
P.O. Box 149
Davenport, CA 95017-0149
phone: 408-426-0134 or 800-492-6786
Wants to buy old jewelry from A to Z; fine antique Victorian and Art Nouveau gold to Edwardian and Art Deco platinum; especially with fine colored stones; Taxco silver, especially Spratling, Aquilar, Davis, etc., pre-1940 Navajo pieces.

Dealers

Elisha Morgan
Elisha Morgan & Associates
5 The Green
Woodstock, VT 05091
phone: 800-444-4367 or 802-457-5700
fax: 802-457-2529
Dealer and purchaser of fine estate jewelry, gemstones, and vintage watches.

Shirley Mariaschin
Jewelry Just For You
110 West 25th St.
New York, NY 10001
phone: 212-989-3414
Buys and sells Victorian, Art Nouveau, Arts & Crafts jewelry.

Leigh Nacht
Bernard Nacht & Co., Inc.
589 Fifth Ave., Ste. 910
New York, NY 10017-1923
phone: 212-371-8100 or 800-348-3419
fax: 212-371-8284
e-mail: leigh5@mail.idt.net
Buys and sells antique, estate and period jewelry and objects as well as diamonds and gemstones.

Kurt E. Knab, G.G.
P.O. Box 31
Camp Hill, PA 17011
phone: 717-766-9302
Buys/sells modern, antique and estate jewelry; especially wants antique jewelry, diamonds, colored stones, Russian objects.

Ronald Talley
Talley Jewelry, Inc.
Village Sq. Shopping Center
P.O. Box 245
Waldorf, MD 20604
phone: 301-645-5144 or 301-870-9593
Buys, sells, appraises, repairs, and restores jewelry.

Carol & Eugene Rooney, GG
Victorian Manor
P.O. Box 285
New Market, MD 21774
phone: 301-865-3083
Buys and sells antique and estate jewelry; repairs, restores, re-enameling, remounting, restring, and custom design jewelry.

Barbara Kinney Renfrow
Glitz & Nostalgia
2335 Federal Dr., D-3
Dyersburg, TN 38024-1945
phone: 901-286-2675 or 901-382-3534
Buys and collects old Art Deco, Victorian and Art Nouveau costume jewelry (mostly if signed); also sterling silver jewelry, Victorian hair jewelry; also wants old, ornate, small buttons.

Patricia A. Witt, GG, CGA, ISA
Way-Fil Jewelry
1123 West Main St.
Tupelo, MS 38801-3453
phone: 601-844-2427
fax: 601-840-4791
e-mail: pattiwit@ebicom.net
Manufacturer, appraisals, repairs, buy/sell, consignments, estate disposal.

Candace Silvasy
Silvasy & Tangeman Antiques
P.O. Box 6796
Cincinnati, OH 45206-0796
phone: 513-281-2827 or 513-312-2817
fax: 513-569-2602
International dealers; deals privately and in trade shows and antique fairs.

Barbara Nyboer
Some Where in Time Antiques
3655 Quadrille
Holt, MI 48842-9723
phone: 517-699-8372 or 517-337-4988
fax: 517-694-5650
Buys and sells antique and collectible jewelry, especially Victorian and hair jewelry, colored stones.

Jerry Forrest, GG, ISA CAPP
Jewelry Forest, The
9100 N. Central Expy., Ste. 185
Dallas, TX 75231-5901
phone: 214-368-5352 or 800-368-5376
Custom jewelers and gemologists, AGS Accredited Gem Laboratory, Accredited Member, ISA.

Lynn Muller
Harlequin Antiques
242 Almond Dr.
Lake Jackson, TX 77566
phone: 409-849-8834 or 409-297-0410
Dealer and collector specializing in all eras of vintage costume jewelry;

especially interested in signed Bakelite cameos; also wants compacts, vanity bags, ladies accessories; over 30 years experience buying and selling.

Patsy Comer
Patsy Comer Antiques & Jewelry
7249 Reseda Blvd.
Reseda, CA 91335-3046
phone: 818-345-1631
fax: 818-385-7477
Buys and sells costume and fine jewelry from all eras including designer; also costume jewelry, gold and sterling; 1960s memorabilia such as peace signs, designer costume and 1960s and 70s jewelry; sells to the trade, does mail order

Eve Lickver
P.O. Box 1778
San Marcos, CA 92079
phone: 760-761-0868
Buys and sells carved and figural Bakelite jewelry; also wants signed costume jewelry of 1920s through 1950s including sterling, copper, enamel.

Susan Murphy
29668 Orinda Rd.
San Juan Capistrano, CA 92675-1211
phone: 714-364-4333
Wants to buy pre-1950 costume jewelry; please enclose SASE.

Veronica Wexler
Wit's End Antiques & Collectibles
840 Blossom Dr.
Santa Clara, CA 95050-5115
phone: 408-261-9742 or 408-984-2423
e-mail: rwexler@rivendell.com
Buys and sells signed, vintage jewelry (Eisenberg, Weiss, Trifari, Hobe, Haskell, etc.), particularly with colored gemstones.

Betty Bird
Memory Lane Antiques
107 Ida St.
Mount Shasta, CA 96067-2629
phone: 916-926-4331 or 916-926-2231
Buys and sells antique and collectible jewelry; prefers Victorian through 1950 especially signed pieces.

Experts

Peter J. Shemonsky
Grogan & Company Auctioneers
22 Harris St.
Dedham, MA 02026-1835
phone: 617-437-9550 or 617-569-1502
fax: 617-437-0513

Peter J. Theriault, FGA, GG
Northeast Gemlab, Inc.
58 Bayview St.
Camden, ME 04843-2242
phone: 207-236-3933
fax: 207-236-3933
e-mail: gemlab@midcoast.com
Independent gems and jewelry appraiser; publishes "The Art & Antique Service Directory", the "Redbook"; writes gemology column

for "Maine Antique Digest" and "Antiques West."

Judith Katz-Schwartz
Twin Brooks Antiques & Collectibles
P.O. Box 6572
New York, NY 10128-0006
phone: 212-876-3512
fax: 212-876-3512
e-mail: twinb@tiac.net
Internet: http://www.tiac.net/users/twinb
Buys, sells, appraisers signed and unsigned pieces of costume jewelry: brooches & pins, bracelets, earrings, rings, rhinestone jewelry, dress clips, Bakelite, sets, etc.

Gail B. Levine, GG
Timeless, Inc.
P.O. Box 7683
Rego Park, NY 11374-7683
phone: 718-897-7305
fax: 718-997-9057
e-mail: 76766.614@compuserve.com
Graduate Gemologist, appraiser, lecturer, editor of "Auction Market Resource For Gems & Jewelry", a semi-annual jewelry price, condition, quality report.

Jack Frascatore
Time Warp Custom & Vintage Attire
24 Jay St., Ste. 222
Schenectady, NY 12305
phone: 518-347-1126
fax: 518-347-1126
e-mail: timewarp@global2000.net
Internet: http://www.members.global2000.net/~timewarp
Buys/sells/appraises vintage clothing, jewelry, accessories; reproduces vintage and historical clothing for museums, reenactment, theater, ballroom dancing, etc.; also restores, repairs and alters clothing, textiles and costume jewelry.

Roseann Ettinger
Remember When
2 E. Broad St.
Hazleton, PA 18201-6530
phone: 717-454-8465 or 717-450-5542
Author of "Popular Jewelry 1840-1940," and "Forties and Fifties Popular Jewelry."

Arthur Guy Kaplan
P.O. Box 1942
Baltimore, MD 21203
phone: 410-752-2090 or 410-664-8350
fax: 410-783-2723
Author of "The Official Price Guide to Antique Jewelry."

Elaine Luartes, GG
Athena Antiques
100 Beta Dr.
Franklin, TN 37064-3912
phone: 615-377-3442
Specializes in antique and estate jewelry; Board of Advisors, Warman's; wants jewelry emphasizing craftsmanship and design.

Lillian Baker
1013 Medhurst Rd.
Columbus, OH 43220
phone: 614-451-7368
Specializes in high fashion costume jewelry, hatpins and hatpin holders, and miniatures; author of "20th Century Fashionable Plastic Jewelry" and other books on collectible, Art Deco, and Art Nouveau jewelry.

Christie Romero
Center for Jewelry Studies
P.O. Box 424
Anaheim, CA 92815-0424
phone: 714-778-1828
fax: 714-778-3432
e-mail: CR4jewelry@aol.com
One of America's leading scholars on antique & vintage jewelry; author of "Warman's Jewelry - An Identification & Price Guide to 19th & 20th Century Fine & Costume Jewelry" (1995); host of video "Hidden Treasures"; lecturer, consultant.

Periodicals

Gail B. Levine, GG
Timeless, Inc.
Magazine: Auction Market Resource for Gems & Jewelry
P.O. Box 7683
Rego Park, NY 11374-7683
phone: 718-897-7305
fax: 718-997-9057
e-mail: 76766.614@compuserve.com
A semi-annual publication providing data for a wide range of jewelry items including antique through contemporary, diamonds and colored stones; detailed text with photographs; offers research services to track fads, trends, etc.

GENEALOGY

(see also IMMIGRATION)

Misc. Services

Marie Varrelman Melchiori, CGRS
121 Tapawingo Rd. SW
Vienna, VA 22180-5964
phone: 703-938-8103
fax: 703-938-7279
e-mail: mvmcgrs@juno.com
Certified Genealogical Record Specialist in Civil War research; will help identify owners of historical items; will assist members of the legal profession locate missing heirs.

Rea Clodfelter Whicker
90 N. 500 E.
Kaysville, UT 84037
phone: 801-544-9447
Genealogical research in world's largest resource library; 26 years experience; references furnished upon request.

Family History Library, Genealogical Society of Utah
25 North West Temple St.
Salt Lake City, UT 84150
fax: 801-240-1584
e-mail: fhl@byu.edu

Museums/Libraries

Western Reserve Historical Society
10825 East Blvd.
Cleveland, OH 44106-1703
phone: 216-721-5722
fax: 216-721-0645
Internet: http://www.wrhs.org
Oldest cultural institution in Cleveland, with a research/genealogical library, costume wing, auto & aviation museum and restored mansion under one roof; special interest area in genealogical research.

Periodicals

Magazine: Heritage Quest
P.O. Box 329
Bountiful, UT 84011
phone: 800-760-2455
e-mail: sales@agll.com
Internet: http://www.heritagequest.com
America's leading magazine for genealogists and family historians; published bi-monthly.

Newsletter: Ancestry Newsletter
P.O. Box 476
Salt Lake City, UT 84110
Published bi-monthly.

GERMAN ITEMS

(see ANTIQUES & COLLECTIBLES, German; MILITARIA; NAZI ITEMS; SWORDS, Nazi)

GILBERT

(see TOYS, Construction Sets; TRAINS, Toy [American Flyer])

GIRL SCOUT MEMORABILIA

(see also BOY SCOUT MEMORABILIA)

Collectors

Phyllis Palm
P.O. Box 5272
Hamden, CT 06518-0272
phone: 203-288-9190
Wants to buy old Girl Scout uniforms, insignia, dolls, etc.

D. Nordlinger Stern
385 Bayview Dr. NE
Saint Petersburg, FL 33704-2430
phone: 813-894-4000
fax: 813-894-1040
e-mail: dnordstern@aol.com
Wants girl scout memorabilia; please send list of items and prices.

Jerry King
8429 Katy Freeway
Houston, TX 77024
phone: 713-465-2500
Wants Girl Scout memorabilia: pre-

1960 catalogs, postcards, magazines, handbooks, 1912-1920 uniforms, equipment, etc.; do not send items without prior arrangements.

Dealers

Jack O'Brian
Memory Tree
P.O. Box 9462
Madison, WI 53715
phone: 414-261-6641
fax: 414-261-9461
Heavy buyer of brown and gray uniforms, cloth badges, medals with ribbons, early Brownie, Golden Eaglet, dolls, cookie (candy) containers, prof. badges; will help identify and date if inquiries are accompanied by a SASE.

Experts

Judy Kirsch
Girl Scouts of the U.S.A., c/o National Equipment Service
420 Fifth Ave.
New York, NY 10018-2702
phone: 212-852-8000
Authority on Girl Scout items.

Fran & Cal Holden
P.O. Box 264 - M264
Doylestown, OH 44230-0264
phone: 800-663-2793
Wants old or unusual pins, badges, medals; from Brownies, Senior Scouts, Roundups, Adult insignia, Councils, official literature, etc.; offers subscription sales list to collectors of Girl Scout memorabilia.

Museums/Libraries

Mrs. Ralph Zitelman
Zitelman Scout Museum
1818 Wisteria Rd.
Rockford, IL 61107-2348
phone: 815-962-3999
Worldwide Scouting: patches, books, uniforms & equipment including Boy and Girl Scouts, Brownies, Explorers, Scoutmasters, etc.

GLASS

(see also BOOKS, Reference [Glass]; BULB VASES; CUP PLATES; CRAFTS, Glass; ENAMELS; GLASS KNIVES; GLASSES; KITCHEN COLLECTIBLES; POWDER JARS; REPAIR/RESTORATION/CONSERVATION, Glass; SALOON & BAR COLLECTIBLES; TABLEWARE)

Auction Services

James A. Megura
Skinner, Inc.
357 Main St.
Bolton, MA 01740-1104
phone: 508-779-6241 or 617-350-5400
fax: 508-779-5144
Established in 1964, Skinner Inc. is the fifth largest auction house in the US; has offices in Bolton and Boston, MA.

Ed Swann
James D. Julia Auctioneers Inc.
Rt. 201, Skowhegan Rd.
P.O. Box 830
Fairfield, ME 04937
phone: 207-453-7125
fax: 207-453-2502
Conducts specialized auctions of all types of quality glassware including Tiffany, Galle, Royal Flemish, fine quality cut glass, Victorian glass and early glassware; uses nationally recognized experts to catalog sales.

William A. Fox
Fox Auctions, Inc.
P.O. Box 4026
Farmingdale, NY 11735
phone: 516-454-7857
fax: 516-454-7857

James Hagenbuch
Glass Works Auctions
P.O. Box 180
East Greenville, PA 18041
phone: 215-679-5849
fax: 215-679-3068
Specializes in the auction of bottles, flasks, barber bottles, jars, bitters bottles, scent bottles, shaving mugs, and related go-withs.

Gene Harris Antique Auction Center, Inc.
203 South 18th Ave.
P.O. Box 476
Marshalltown, IA 50158
phone: 515-752-0600 or 800-862-6674
fax: 515-753-0226
Internet: http://www.csmonline.com/harris/
Specialized auctions of flint glass, Sandwich, Pittsburgh; also ceramics such as transferware, lustre, historical Staffordshire, etc.

Pacific Glass Auctions
1507 21st St., Ste. 203
Sacramento, CA 95814
phone: 916-443-3296 or 916-443-3210
Internet: http://www.pacglass.com

Book Sellers

Robert Eaton
Eaton's Glass Books on the Web
P.O. Box 1081
Derry, NH 03038-1081
e-mail: reaton@concentric.net
Internet: http://www.concentric.net/~Reaton/booklist.htm
Sells glass books via the Internet.

Clubs/Associations

Glass Research Society of New Jersey
1501 Glasstown Rd.
Millville, NJ 08332-1566
phone: 609-825-6800 or 800-998-4552

Nancy Sheriff, Mem.
National Early American Glass Club, The, Ltd.
Newsletter: Glass Shards
P.O. Box 8489
Silver Spring, MD 20907-8489
An international organization devoted

to the study and appreciation of glass from antiquity to present; the semi-annual newsletter of the NEAGC covers glass exhibits, chapter activities, etc.; also publishes the Glass Club Bulletin.

Bill Donalson
Tallahassee Glass & Antiques Club
Newsletter: TGAC Newsletter
3808 Forsythe Way
Tallahassee, FL 32308-2532
phone: 904-893-9794
Collectors of glass, china, pottery, silver and tools.

Glass Collectors Club of Toledo
6122 Cross Trails Rd.
Sylvania, OH 43560-1714

Greater Chicago Glass Collectors' Club
Newsletter: Glass Club Bulletin
339 Selborne Road
Riverside, IL 60546-1624
phone: 708-442-1624

Houston Glass Club
5338 Creekbend Dr.
Houston, TX 77096
phone: 713-729-4267

Collectors

Stanford C. Steppa
9820 Glenolden Dr.
Potomac, MD 20854
phone: 301-299-5040
Advanced collector of items marked R. Lalique: cire perdue, vases, mascots, perfumes, metals, etc.; one piece or entire collection.

Dealers

Bud Marchant
Lil Bud Antiques
142 Main St.
Yarmouth Port, MA 02675
phone: 508-362-8984

George Kamm
24 Townsend Ct.
Lancaster, PA 17603-6797
phone: 717-872-7858
fax: 717-872-7858
Buys and sells antique and contemporary glass paperweights; paperweight appraisals; bi-monthly color brochure for $5/yr.; sample upon request.

Barbara M. Lessig, ISA CAPP
Pleasant Valley Antiques
21000 Georgia Ave.
Brookeville, MD 20833-1138
phone: 301-924-2293
fax: 301-570-1625
e-mail: jlessig@mail2.lmi.org
Specialist in appraising and selling all types of glassware.

Stephen G. Del Sordo
Principia Group
305 Oakley St.
Cambridge, MD 21613
phone: 410-228-8934
fax: 410-221-8061
e-mail: delsordo@shore.intercom.net
A cultural resource management/

historic preservation firm that has contracts to locate, provide, authenticate artifacts for museums and collectors; areas of expertise include architecture, industry, domestic, agriculture, and maritime.

Jim & Barbara Payne
Liberty Ridge Antiques
9634 St. Rt. 12 West
Findlay, OH 45840
phone: 419-422-7920
Specializes in buying and selling antique glassware, especially Findlay, Fostoria, Tiffin.

Experts

Dianne Greg
10413 Gary Rd.
Potomac, MD 20854
phone: 301-299-6456

Man./Prod./Dist.

Joe Rice
House of Glass, Inc., The
7900 E State Road 28
Elwood, IN 46036-8449
phone: 317-552-6841
fax: 317-552-6854
Makes paperweights all signed by owner, Joe Rice; also makes all sorts of other solid glass: ashtrays, pears, ringholders, etc.

Museums/Libraries

Currier Gallery of Art, The
192 Orange St.
Manchester, NH 03104
phone: 603-669-6144

Miss Dorothy Lee Jones, Dir.
Jones Museum of Glass & Ceramics, The
Douglas Mountain Rd.
East Sebago, ME 04029
phone: 207-787-3370 or 207-787-2800
Unique museum, over 8500 examples of glass & ceramics ranging from ancient to modern; large holdings of Early American lacy and pressed glass, paperweights; also 20th C. tablewares and studio art glass, fluid lamps, cut glass, etc.

Deborah Federhen, Cur.
Bennington Museum, The
W. Main St.
Bennington, VT 05201
phone: 802-447-1571
fax: 802-442-8305
Internet: http://www.benington.com/museum
One of the finest regional art history museums in the country; works by Grandma Moses, American glass, VT furniture, Bennington pottery, the oldest Stars & Stripes in existence, the 1925 luxury touring car "The Wasp", and much more.

Museum of American Glass at Wheaton Village
1501 Glasstown Rd.
Millville, NJ 08332-1566
phone: 609-825-6800 or 800-998-4552
Covers all types of American glass: Stiegel, Amelung, flasks, pressed, art glass, art nouveau, paperweights, lamps & lighting, cut glass, 20th century art glass, reproductions, pre-studio movement, contemporary studio glass, etc.

Corning Museum of Glass, The
Journal: Journal of Glass Studies
One Museum Way
Corning, NY 14830-2253
phone: 607-937-5371
fax: 607-937-3352
Over 24,000 glass objects, innovative exhibits, videos, models; glass history, archaeology, and early manufacturing.

Chrysler Museum, The
Olney Rd. & Mowbray Arch
Norfolk, VA 23510
phone: 804-622-1211
Fine collection of early to 20th century glass; also ancient to modern artifacts from all over the world.

Toledo Museum of Art, The
2445 Monroe St.
P.O. Box 1013
Toledo, OH 43697
phone: 419-255-8000
Internationally-recognized collections of glass, paintings, and decorative and graphic arts.

Glass Museum, The
309 S. Franklin
Dunkirk, IN 47336-1209
phone: 765-768-6809 or 765-768-6872
fax: 765-768-6872
e-mail: dunklibr@spynet.com

Jan Smith, Curator
Bergstrom-Mahler Museum
165 N. Park Ave.
Neenah, WI 54956
phone: 414-751-4658 or 414-751-4672
Extensive collection of glass paperweights, Bohemian Glass and Victorian Art Glass.

Historical Glass Museum Foundation
1157 N. Orange
P.O. Box 921
Redlands, CA 92373
phone: 714-797-1528
A breathtaking display of American glassware.

Periodicals

James Hagenbuch
Magazine: Antique Bottle & Glass Collector
P.O. Box 180
East Greenville, PA 18041
phone: 215-679-5849
fax: 215-679-3068
A monthly magazine for the glass and bottle collector.

David Richardson
Antique Publications
Magazine: Glass Collector's Digest
P.O. Box 553
Marietta, OH 45750-0553
phone: 800-533-3433 or 614-373-6146
fax: 614-373-6917
e-mail: 76710.2337@compuserve.com
A bi-monthly magazine focusing on the glass collecting specialties; articles and ads feature lots of color photography.

Teri Steele, Ed.
Depression Glass Daze, Inc.
Newspaper: Daze, The
275 State Rd.
P.O. Box 57
Otisville, MI 48463-0057
phone: 810-631-4593
fax: 810-631-4567
A monthly newspaper catering to the dealers and collectors of glass, china and pottery from the 1920s and 1930s.

Ruth Grizel, Ed.
Newspaper: Glass Post, The
P.O. Box 205
Oakdale, IA 52319-0205
phone: 319-626-3216
fax: 319-626-3216
Monthly 18-20 page newsletter featuring classified ads for selling glass, collectibles like plates, china, pottery, dolls, etc.; subscription cost includes cost of ads for one year; all ads free to subscribers.

Akro Agate/Westite

Clubs/Associations

Roger Hardy
Akro Agate Collector's Club, Inc.
Newsletter: Clarksburg Crow
10 Bailey St.
Clarksburg, WV 26301-2524
phone: 304-624-4523 or 304-624-7600
Focuses on Akro marbles, children's dishes and general line items.

Collectors

Albert Morin
668 Robbins Ave. #23
Dracut, MA 01826
phone: 508-454-7907
Wants either Akro Agate or Westite items.

Experts

Roger Hardy
Log Cabin Antiques
10 Bailey St.
Clarksburg, WV 26301-2524
phone: 304-624-4523 or 304-624-7600
Author of "The Complete Line of Akro Agate, With Prices."

Anchor Hocking (Fire King)

Experts

April M. Tvorak
P.O. Box 94
Warren Center, PA 18851
phone: 717-395-3775
Author of "History and Price Guide to Fire-King," "Fire-King II", and "Fire-King '95," "Fire-King 5th Ed.-97 Values," "Fire-King Fever, 95-96 Values" updated values; please include a SASE with all correspondence.

Garry Kilgo
P.O. Box 473
Addison, AL 35540
phone: 205-462-3122 or 205-462-3544
Co-author with Dale Kilgo, and Jerry and Gail Wilkins of "A Collectors Guide to Anchor Hockings Fire King Glassware."

Ancient

Collectors

Earl Jacobs
21540 West Eleven Mile Rd.
Southfield, MI 48076-3876
Interested in ancient glass - from its most early types through blown glass, cast, cone form and Islamic; interested in scholarship, acquisition, disposition and publication.

Animals

Experts

Lee Garmon
1529 Whittier St.
Springfield, IL 62704
phone: 217-789-9574
Co-author with Dick Spencer of "Glass Animals & Figure Flower Frogs of the Depression Era."

Periodicals

Ruth Grizel
Newsletter: Glass Animal Bulletin, The
P.O. Box 143
North Liberty, IA 52317-0143
phone: 319-626-2807
fax: 319-626-2807
Full color monthly magazine featuring glass animal figurines and covered animal dishes of all kinds; free classified ads to subscribers.

Art

(see also LAMPS & LIGHTING, Tiffany/Handel/Pairpoint; TIFFANY ITEMS)

Appraisers

Stephen van Cline, CAPP
van Cline & Davenport, Ltd.
792 Franklin Ave.
Franklin Lakes, NJ 07417-1343
Minimum charge $25; letter request only, SASE.

Auction Services

Louise Luther
Skinner, Inc.
357 Main St.
Bolton, MA 01740-1104
phone: 508-779-6241 or 617-350-5400
fax: 508-779-5144
Established in 1964, Skinner Inc. is the fifth largest auction house in the US; has offices in Bolton and Boston, MA.

Early Auction Co.
123 Main St.
Milford, OH 45150
phone: 513-831-4833
fax: 513-831-1441

James L. Jackson, ISA
Jackson's Auctioneers & Appraisers
2229 Lincoln St.
Cedar Falls, IA 50613
phone: 319-277-2256
fax: 319-277-1252
e-mail: jacksons@jacksonsauction.com
Internet: http://www.jacksonsauction.com
Conducts specialty auctions of Victorian, Art Nouveau and Art Deco glass, leaded and reverse painted lamps, etc.

Jon Crisman, ISA
Jackson's Auctioneers & Appraisers
2229 Lincoln St.
Cedar Falls, IA 50613
phone: 319-277-2256
fax: 319-277-1252
e-mail: jacksons@jacksonsauction.com
Internet: http://www.jacksonsauction.com
Specializes in art glass.

Joy Luke
Joy Luke Auction Gallery
300 E. Grove St.
Bloomington, IL 61701-5232
phone: 309-828-5533
fax: 309-829-2266
Conducts auctions specializing in fine art glass.

Clubs/Associations

Henry Tyler
13 Bellevue Dr.
Saint Petersburg, FL 33706-1201
Interested in Mount Washington, Crown Milano, Web art glass, English cameo.

Reyne Hogan
Art Glass Discussion Group
2507 Observatory Ave.
Cincinnati, OH 45208-1212
phone: 513-321-5141 or 713-913-7289
e-mail: reyne@tias.com
Internet: http://www.tias.com/RHA
Collectors talk about book reviews, auction information, reproduction information, buying and selling; no dues; e-mail access essential.

Collectors

John O. Burgess
10738 Harley Rd.
Lorton, VA 22079-3908
Wants to buy Burmese art glass from any source or time period.

Dealers

Valerie Sevene
Val's New & Used
70 South Winooski Ave., Ste. 126
Burlington, VT 05401
phone: 802-685-6891 or 802-658-2572
fax: 802-658-6891
e-mail: sevene@together.net
Wants to buy Murano and other art glass.

Lenore Monleon
33 Fifth Ave.
New York, NY 10003
phone: 212-475-7871 or 212-229-0958
Wants Galle, Lalique, silver overlay, Art Deco, Art Nouveau.

Joseph D. Cantara
Cantara/Galletti
61038 80th St.
Middle Village, NY 11379
phone: 718-651-9347 or 718-358-5923
Buys, sells and specializes in art glass and in Tiffany items such as lamps, desk sets, glass and accessories; also buys and sells Art Deco - especially French & Austrian.

Dottie Freeman
P.O. Box 429
Chester Heights, PA 19017
phone: 610-459-5265 or 717-336-6622

Gerald Shultz
Antique Gallery, The
8523 Germantown Ave.
Philadelphia, PA 19118-3316
phone: 215-248-1700
fax: 215-247-8411
Galle, Daum, Moser, Lalique, Legras, Durand, Tiffany, Venetian, Quezal, Bohemian, Steuben.

Jim & Grace Greenwald, ISA
Greenwald Antiques
925 Walnut St.
Royersford, PA 19468
phone: 610-948-9391 or 610-948-1308

Alain Fournier
La Verrerie D'Art
P.O. Box 757
Bowie, MD 20718-0757
phone: 301-464-3251
Buys, sells and specializes in European art glass of the Art nouveau and Art Deco eras (1880-1940); Schneider, Daum, Muller Fres., Loetz, D'Avesn.

Caren Fine
11603 Gowrie Ct.
Potomac, MD 20854-3623
phone: 301-299-2116 or 301-299-6886
Wants glass and lamps by Renee Lalique, Tiffany, Galle, Handel, Quezal; also wants Italian glass.

L. Michael Boak
Initialed Duck Antiques & Collectibles
3812 Hamilton Ave.
Baltimore, MD 21206-3505
Buys, sells and collects Steuben, Mt. Washington, Webb, Libbey, Venetian, Stevens & Williams, Hobbs & Brockunier; wants American, English and Continental art glass.

Reyne Hogan
2507 Observatory Ave.
Cincinnati, OH 45208-1212
phone: 513-321-5141 or 713-913-7289
e-mail: reyne@tias.com
Internet: http://www.tias.com/RHA
Buys and sells Tiffany glass, lamps, bronze, jewelry and windows; also buys art glass of the same period.

John B. Marrella
Investments in Time
P.O. Box 611
Birmingham, MI 48012-0611
phone: 810-644-3100
fax: 810-644-2792
Specializes in Lalique, Steuben, Galle, and Daum.

Fred Wishine
Wishful Things Art Glass & Antiques
207 E. Buffalo St.
Milwaukee, WI 53202
phone: 414-765-1117
fax: 414-765-0785
e-mail: luvglass@mail.execpc.com
Internet: http://bmark.com/wishfulthings.antiques
Specializing in art glass from Victorian to contemporary; everything is unconditionally guaranteed.

Veronica Wexler
Wit's End Antiques & Collectibles
840 Blossom Dr.
Santa Clara, CA 95050-5115
phone: 408-261-9742 or 408-984-2423
e-mail: rwexler@rivendell.com
Buys and sells enameled Victorian art glass (Moser, Webb, Mt. Washington, etc.), Daum, Schneider, etc.

Steve Hetherington
Glasstiques
P.O. Box 6177
Vacaville, CA 95696-6177
phone: 707-451-3688
e-mail: glasstiques@msn.com
Internet: http://www.bmark.com/glasstiques
Wants to buy art glass: Rose Amber, Peachblow, Napoli, Crown Milano, Colonial Ware, Royal Flemish, Burmese, Lava, M.O.P., Verona, Alexandrite, Silveria, Agata, Pink Slag, Holly Amber, Amberina, Plated Amberina; also fairy lamps.

Antique Appraisal & Estate Sale Service - K. Bailey
P.O. Box 75191
Seattle, WA 98125-5345
phone: 206-746-2777
fax: 206-365-0633
Specializing in fine Art Glass; Tiffany,

Steuben, Lalique, Moser, Webb, Galle, Daum, etc..

Experts

Louis O. St. Aubin, Jr.
Brookside Antiques "Art Glass Gallery"
44 North Water St.
New Bedford, MA 02740
phone: 508-993-4944
Museum consultant, expert, established in 1964, author of "Pairpoint Lamps. A Collectors Guide"; nationally known authority, lecturer, appraiser, auction house consultant; founder of the New Bedford Glass Museum.

Scott Roland
Glimmer Glass Antiques
P.O. Box 262
Schenevus, NY 12155-0262
phone: 607-638-9543
Buys, sells, specializes in and appraises Victorian glass, art glass, milk glass, water pitchers and tumblers, etc.

Clarence Maier
Burmese Cruet, The
P.O. Box 432
Montgomeryville, PA 18936-0432
phone: 215-855-5388
Specializes in Burmese, Crown Milano, and Royal Flemish art glass; advisor to "Warman's Antiques & Collectibles Price Guide" and to "Schroeder's Price Guide."

Mildred & Ralph Lechner
P.O. Box 554
Mechanicsville, VA 23111-0554
phone: 804-737-3347
Feature writers on antique glassware for "AntiqueWeek"; authors of "The World of Salt Shakers," Vols. 1 & 2 ; Victorian art and pattern glass reproduction identification experts; collectors of art and pattern glass salt & pepper shakers.

Robin & June Greenwald
June Greenwald Antiques, Inc.
3096 Mayfield Rd.
Cleveland, OH 44118
phone: 216-932-5535
Nationally recognized art glass dealers.

Museums/Libraries

Wadsworth Atheneum
600 Main St.
Hartford, CT 06103
phone: 860-278-2670
fax: 860-527-0803
Collection of decorative art glass includes examples ranging from Roman times to Victorian America.

Ellen E. Mauer
Milan Historical Museum, Inc.
Newsletter: New Milan Ledger
P.O. Box 308
Milan, OH 44846
phone: 419-499-2968
fax: 419-499-9004
A seven-building complex 500 yards from the birthplace of Thomas A. Edison; restored home, carriage shed, blacksmith shop, general store, collections from the 19th century.

Art (1950s)

Collectors

Dennis Boyd
P.O. Box 14642
Richmond, VA 23221-0642
phone: 804-560-0753
Wants 1950s art glass by Venini, Sarpaneva, Tapio Wirkkala, Kosta, Orrefors, Kaj Franck, Nutajari-Notsjo, Flysfors, Leerdam, Toso, Barovier, Seguso; any Italian or Scandinavian art glass (signed or unsigned.)

Art (Austrian)

Dealers

Eric's Antiques
381 Elliot St.
Newton Upper Falls, MA 02164
phone: 617-332-3744
Specializes in fine Austrian art glass.

Baccarat

(see also PAPERWEIGHTS)

Man./Prod./Dist.

Chantal Sironneau
Baccarat Inc.
36 Mayfield Ave.
Edison, NJ 08837-3821
Only Baccarat store in the U.S.; Baccarat also sold through Bailey, Banks & Biddle stores; French full lead crystal, glassware, giftware and accessories; will research and identify items.

Black

Collectors

Marge Dozier
1835 Southeast Dr.
Point Pleasant, NJ 08742
phone: 908-8928441
Wants black (black amethyst) glass items.

Experts

Marlena Toohey
c/o Antique Publications
P.O. Box 553
Marietta, OH 45750-0553
phone: 800-533-3433 or 614-373-6146
fax: 614-373-6917
e-mail: 76710.2337@compuserve.com
Author of "A Collector's Guide to Black Glass."

Blenko

Museums/Libraries

Richard Blenko
Blenko Glass Visitor Center Museum
  and Wholesale Outlet
Newsletter: Antique Notes
P.O. Box 67
Milton, WV 25541-0067
phone: 304-743-9081
fax: 304-743-0547
e-mail: warhol2@aol.com
Museum and outlet for nationally known blown glassware; also stained glass studio.

Bohemian

Collectors

Tom Price
10122 Windward Way N.
Jacksonville, FL 32256
phone: 904-646-9162 or 904-646-9357
e-mail: merprice3@aol.com
Wants to buy Bohemian glass; especially interested in glass made by Rossler.

Tom Bradshaw
325 Carol Dr.
Ventura, CA 93003-1710
Wants to buy antique Bohemian decorated drinking glasses, vases, decanters, beakers, goblets, wine glasses, etc. that are engraved, cut, painted, gilded, overlay, etc.; colored or clear glass.

Experts

Bob Truitt
5120 White Flint Dr.
Kensington, MD 20895-1037
phone: 301-929-2539
Author of "Collectible Bohemian Glass 1880-1940."

Boyd's Crystal Art

Dealers

Rick Morris
Rick's Black Lights & Art Glass
194 Stonefield Circle
Macon, GA 31206
phone: 912-781-5119
e-mail: southern@mindspring.com
Internet: http://www.mindspring.com/
  ~southern1/blacklig.htm

Darrell Crim
Jody & Darrell's Glass Collectibles
P.O. Box 180833
Arlington, TX 76096-0833
phone: 817-467-5483

Man./Prod./Dist.

Boyd's Crystal Art
Newsletter: Boyd's Crystal Art Glass
  Newsletter
1203 Morton Ave.
P.O. Box 127
Cambridge, OH 43725
phone: 614-439-2077
fax: 614-432-1827
e-mail: 73250.2104@compuserve.com
Manufacturers many collectible glass items in a wide array of colors.

Periodicals

Jody Best
Newsletter: Jody & Darrell's Glass
  Collectibles Newsletter
P.O. Box 180833
Arlington, TX 76096-0833
phone: 817-467-5483
Published bi-monthly, focuses on Boyd's Crystal Art Glass and other contemporary glass collectibles; subscription includes an exclusive figurine produced by Boyd's Art Glass; articles, secondary market price information, classified ads.

Cambridge

Clubs/Associations

Charles A. Upton
National Cambridge Collectors, Inc.
Newsletter: Cambridge Crystal Ball
P.O. Box 416
Cambridge, OH 43725-0416
phone: 614-432-4245 or 614-432-6794
fax: 614-432-4245
Preserves and studies the products of the Cambridge Glass Co., Cambridge, OH; please send a SASE when requesting information.

Collectors

Susan Leite
44 Glenwood Rd.
Brewster, MA 02631-2202
phone: 508-385-4905
Wants to buy Cambridge Etch #520 in pink.

Museums/Libraries

Cambridge Glass Museum, The
812 Jefferson Ave.
Cambridge, OH 43725
phone: 614-432-3045
Over 5000 pieces of Cambridge glass on display; also 100 pieces of Cambridge Art Pottery; private museum.

Charles A. Upton
Museum of the National Cambridge
    Collectors, Inc.
P.O. Box 416
Cambridge, OH 43725-0416
phone: 614-432-4245 or 614-432-6794
fax: 614-432-4245
*Preserves and studies the products of
the Cambridge Glass Co., Cambridge,
OH.*

Periodicals

Linda Land
Newsletter: Camark Newsletter
1529 Kempton Court
Longmont, CO 80501
phone: 303-772-0076

Candlewick

Clubs/Associations

Virginia R. Scott
National Candlewick Collector's Club,
    The
Newsletter: Candlewick Collector
    Newsletter, The
275 Milledge Terrace
Athens, GA 30606-4937
phone: 706-548-5966
*The newsletter is devoted to the
Candlewick pattern, collectors, finds,
prices, questions answered, look-
alikes and repros. discussed.*

Cliff McCaslin
National Imperial Glass Collectors
    Society
Newsletter: Glasszette
P.O. Box 534
Bellaire, OH 43906
phone: 816-436-7719
fax: 816-436-6955
e-mail: rocliff@unicom.net
*Members interested in the history and
glassware produced by the Imperial
Glass Corp.; conducts an annual
convention offering seminars, show
and sale, and "members only"
auction; establishing an Imperial
museum.*

Lucille R. Geisler, Treas/Mem
Michiana Association of Candlewick
    Collectors
Newsletter: Spyglass
17370 Battles Rd.
South Bend, IN 46614
phone: 219-291-9245

Collectors

Lucille R. Geisler
17370 Battles Rd.
South Bend, IN 46614
phone: 219-291-9245

Dealers

Kathy Burch
221 N. Maple
Ithaca, MI 48847-1025
phone: 517-875-3138
*Buys and sells unusual pieces of
Candlewick glass including colored
pieces.*

Penny Drucker
Mother Drucker's
P.O. Box 50261
Irvine, CA 92619-0261
phone: 888-637-8253 or 714-551-5529
fax: 714-551-2116
e-mail: motherdruc@aol.com
*Always changing inventory of color,
cut, rare and common pieces; send
LSASE for list.*

Experts

Virginia R. Scott
275 Milledge Terrace
Athens, GA 30606-4937
phone: 706-548-5966
*Author of "The Collector's Guide to
Imperial Candlewick"; a very
complete book illustrating almost
every known Candlewick pattern
piece, including colors, variations,
cuttings; has look-alike and
reproduction appendix.*

Mary M. Wetzel-Tomalka
17370 Battles Rd.
South Bend, IN 46614
phone: 219-291-9245
*Author of "Candlewick - The Jewel of
Imperial."*

Juanita Williams
P.O. Box 1624
Jacksonville, OR 97530
e-mail: alan@wsfire.com

Matching Services

Ackerman Antiques
100 Colonial Way Circle
Columbus, OH 43235-5611

Carnival

Auction Services

Tom Burns
Burns Auction Service
109 East Steuben St.
Bath, NY 14810
phone: 607-776-7942
*Sells Victorian and art glass, Nippon,
Noritake, lamps, carnival glass.*

Cooper & Albrecht Auctions
202 South Mill St.
Clio, MI 48420

Seeck Auctions
17736 280th St.
Mason City, IA 50401-9096

Mickey Reichel Auction Service
516 3rd St.
Boonville, MO 65233

Woody Auction Company
P.O. Box 618
Douglass, KS 67039
phone: 316-746-2694
fax: 316-746-2145

Clubs/Associations

Carol Cressman, Sec.
Canadian Carnival Glass Association
Newsletter: CCAA Newsletter
107 Montcalm Dr.
Kitchener
Ontario N2B 2R4 Canada
*Meetings are held every six weeks in
the southwestern area of Ontario;
holds annual convention; newsletter
published every six weeks with
articles, auction reports, sales, shows,
etc.*

Eva Backer
New England Carnival Glass Club
12 Sherwood Rd.
W Hartford, CT 06117-2738

Mary Sharp
Keystone Carnival Glass Club
719 W. Brubaker Valley Rd.
Lititz, PA 17543
phone: 717-626-5521

Barbara Hobbs
Tampa Bay Carnival Glass Club
Newsletter: Tampa Bay Carnival Glass
    Club Newsletter
5501 101st Ave. N
Pinellas Park, FL 33782-3311
phone: 813-541-6164
e-mail: wfhbbm@aol.com
*Non-profit group, meetings,
conventions, auctions, shows, monthly
newsletter.*

Cliff McCaslin
National Imperial Glass Collectors
    Society
Newsletter: Glasszette
P.O. Box 534
Bellaire, OH 43906
phone: 816-436-7719
fax: 816-436-6955
e-mail: rocliff@unicom.net
*Members interested in the history and
glassware produced by the Imperial
Glass Corp.; conducts an annual
convention offering seminars, show
and sale, and "members only"
auction; establishing an Imperial
museum.*

Larry Yung
American Carnival Glass Association
Newsletter: American Carnival Glass
    News
9621 Springwater
Miamisburg, OH 45342
*Learn about highly collectible
carnival glass; news, conventions;
send SASE for full color brochure.*

Lee Markley, Sec.
International Carnival Glass Association
Newsletter: Town Pump, The
P.O. Box 306
Mentone, IN 46539-0306
phone: 219-353-7678
*Promotes interest in collecting old
Carnival Glass; holds annual
convention featuring displays,
seminars and banquet.*

Clubs/Associations

Ellen Hemm, Sec.
Lincoln Land Carnival Glass Club
N 951 Highway 27
Conrath, WI 54731
phone: 715-532-5816

Karen Skinner
Gateway Carnival Glass Club
108 Riverwoods Cove
East Alton, IL 62024
phone: 618-259-1373

C. Lucille Britt
Heart of America Carnival Glass
    Association
Newsletter: HOACGA Bulletin
3048 Tamarak Dr.
Manhattan, KS 66502
phone: 913-539-1933
*Focuses on old carnival glass;
members share information; monthly
newsletter contains articles about
OLD carnival glass, club meeting
dates and secretary reports; members
can advertise free of charge.*

Paula Thompson
Texas Carnival Glass Club
260 Shoreline
Azle, TX 76020
phone: 817-238-9163

Diane Fry, Sec.
San Diego Carnival Glass Club
5395 Middleton Rd.
San Diego, CA 92019
phone: 619-272-1663

Marie McGee
San Joaquin Carnival Glass Club
3906 E. Acacia Ave.
Fresno, CA 93726
phone: 209-222-0796

Mary Christian
Northern California Carnival Glass Club
4324 Raiders Way
Modesto, CA 95355
phone: 209-521-9062

Jerry Reynolds
Pacific Northwest Carnival Glass Club
1305 N. Highlands Parkway, B-6
Tacoma, WA 98406
phone: 206-759-2263

Collectors

Eva Backer
12 Sherwood Rd.
W Hartford, CT 06117-2738

Dick Hatscher
142 Walnut Hill Rd.
Bethel, CT 06801
phone: 203-743-1468
*Wants to buy Carnival glass, any
color or amount.*

John O. Burgess
10738 Harley Rd.
Lorton, VA 22079-3908
Wants pre-1950 US carnival glass.

Barbara Hobbs
5501 101st Ave. N
Pinellas Park, FL 33782-3311
phone: 813-541-6164
e-mail: wfhbbm@aol.com
*Collects only old carnival glass,
carnival glass hatpins, carnival glass
bottles.*

Larry Yung
9621 Springwater
Miamisburg, OH 45342

Cliff McCaslin
Rocliff Communications
8422 N. Park Ct.
Kansas City, MO 64155
phone: 816-436-7719
fax: 816-436-6955
e-mail: rocliff@unicom.net
*Wants to buy several manufacturers of
carnival glass, stretch and art
glassware patterns including
Northwood, Dugan-Diamond,
Millersburg.*

Cliff McCaslin
Rocliff Communications
8422 N. Park Ct.
Kansas City, MO 64155
phone: 816-436-7719
fax: 816-436-6955
e-mail: rocliff@unicom.net
*Specializes in Northwood carnival
glass.*

Dealers

W. J. Warren
38 Mosher Dr.
Tonawanda, NY 14150-5218
phone: 716-692-2886
*Buys and sells; wants all colors of
carnival glass; one piece or a
collection.*

Charles & Marianne Wilson
Thistle hill B&B Inn
5541 Sperryvile Pike
Boston, VA 22713
phone: 540-987-9142

C. Lucille Britt
3048 Tamarak Dr.
Manhattan, KS 66502
phone: 913-539-1933
*Buyer and seller of old carnival glass;
active member of the Heart of
American Carnival Glass Association.*

Gary Lickver
P.O. Box 1778
San Marcos, CA 92079
phone: 760-761-0868
*California's largest carnival glass
dealer and collector; consistently at
most quality indoor antique shows in
California; wants to buy one piece or
entire collections.*

Experts

Helen Greguire
Helen's Antiques
103 Trimmer Rd.
Hilton, NY 14468-9305
phone: 716-392-2704
*Author of "Carnival Lighting",
focusing on carnival glass used in
lighting such as Gone With The Wind
lamps, electric and kerosene lamp
shades, chandeliers, etc.; the book is
out of print but copies are still
available from the author.*

Donald Grizzle
Sanctified Cross-Eyed Bear, The
P.O. Box 1296
Huntsville, AL 35807-1296
phone: 205-534-9076
*Published the most extensive sales
references available for carnival
glass: reports on over 30,000 actual
sales during the past five years;
clarifies upward and downward price
trends.*

Tom & Sharon Mordini
36 North Mernitz Ave.
Freeport, IL 61032
phone: 815-235-4407
fax: 815-232-3911
e-mail: tmordini@mwci.net
*Publishes annual list of 5,000 carnival
glass auction prices.*

Kitty & Russell Umbraco
P.O. Box 5331
Richmond, CA 94805-0331
phone: 510-235-1656
*Buys and sells; author of "Iridescent
Stretch Glass."*

Museums/Libraries

Tamara Armstrong
Fenton Art Glass Company, The
700 Elizabeth St.
Williamstown, WV 26187-1028
phone: 304-375-6122 or 800-249-4527
fax: 304-375-6459
*Large attractive display of early
Fenton and Upper Ohio Valley glass.*

Carnival (Post-1960)

Clubs/Associations

Wilma Thurston
Collectible Carnival Glass Association
Newsletter: CCGA Newsletter
2360 N. Old S.R. 9
Columbus, IN 47203-9430
phone: 812-546-5724
e-mail: johnval@facets.net
Internet: http://www.facets.net/facets/
freeserv-edu/ccg/
*For collectors of newer carnival glass
made after 1960; quarterly newsletter
has articles about carnival glass, and
for sale and want ads; annual
convention with sale and seminars.*

Collectors

Annette Bosselman
3101 Brentwood Circle
Grand Island, NE 68801

Annetta Bosselman
3101 Brentwood Circle
Grand Island, NE 68801-7217
phone: 308-382-6384

Dealers

Wilma Thurston
2360 N. Old S.R. 9
Columbus, IN 47203-9430
phone: 812-546-5724
e-mail: johnval@facets.net
Internet: http://www.facets.net/facets/
freeserv-edu/ccg/

Coin

Collectors

Robert E. Bender
515 West Cedar
Zionsville, IN 46077-1305
Wants to buy U.S. coin glass.

Experts

Tim Timmerman
11655 S.W. Allen Blvd. #31
Beaverton, OR 97005-4850
phone: 503-646-8300
*Author of "U.S. Coin Glass" (dated
1892); 70 page book includes pictures
and descriptions of 88 pieces and also
a section on reproductions; available
from author for $20.*

Commemorative Historical

Collectors

Forrest Gesswein
9514 Powderhorn Lane
Baltimore, MD 21234
phone: 410-668-7890
*Collects American glass that
commemorates people, places and
events in our Nations history.*

Consolidated

Clubs/Associations

Mark Lawyer
Phoenix & Consolidated Glass
Collectors' Club
Newsletter: Phoenix & Consolidated
Collectors News & Views
P.O. Box 3847
Edmond, OK 73083-3847
phone: 405-341-0020
e-mail: mcdd@aol.com
Internet: http://
www.collectoronline.com/club-
PCGCC-wp.html
*For collectors/dealers of art glass
produced by Phoenix Glass Co. of
Monaca, PA and Consolidated Lamp
& Shade Co. of Coraopolis, PA; bi-
monthly newsletter - market trends,
repro. alerts, buy/sell ads, price
reports, articles.*

Collectors

Kevin & Barbara Kiley
23 Harvard Terrace
West Orange, NJ 07052
phone: 210-736-2997
*Wants to buy Ruba Rombic, red &
black Consolidated, Imperial &
Fenton freehand.*

Barbara Norman
P.O. Box 251382
West Bloomfield, MI 48325-1382
phone: 248-855-7766
fax: 248-855-5224
e-mail: bnorman7282@aol.com
*Wants to buy Ruba Rombic, red or
cased pieces of Phoenix or Consolidated Art Glass, Catalonian, and
Muncie Ruba Rombic.*

Experts

Jack D. Wilson
P.O. Box 81974
Chicago, IL 60681-0974
phone: 773-282-9553
e-mail: jdwilson1@earthlink.com
Internet: http://home.earthlink.net/
~jdwilson1/
*Author of "Phoenix & Consolidated
Art Glass: 1926-1980"; features in-
depth research, 48 color pages
illustrating over 750 items; available
from author for $34.95 + $2.50
postage; wants original Consolidated
catalogs & company literature.*

Consolidated (Ruba Rombic)

Collectors

Paul Galli
873 Ticonderoga Dr.
Sunnyvale, CA 94087
phone: 408-730-4010
e-mail: paul.galli@lmco.com
*Wants to buy Consolidated's Ruba
Rombic pattern glass.*

Experts

Jack D. Wilson
P.O. Box 81974
Chicago, IL 60681-0974
phone: 773-282-9553
e-mail: jdwilson1@earthlink.com
Internet: http://home.earthlink.net/
~jdwilson1/
*Wants to buy examples of the Ruba
Rombic pattern of art glass made by
the Consolidated Lamp & Glass Co. of
Coraopolis, PA; author of "Phoenix
& Consolidated Art Glass: 1926-
1980"; advisor to Schroeder's.*

Crackle

Clubs/Associations

Stan & Arlene Weitman
Collectors of Crackle Glass
Newsletter: Crackle Glass Club
Newsletter
P.O. Box 1186
Massapequa, NY 11758
phone: 516-799-2619
fax: 516-797-3039
e-mail: scrackle@htp.net

Cranberry

Clubs/Associations

Pilgrim Glass Cranberry Collector's
Club
P.O. Box 395
Ceredo, WV 25507
phone: 304-453-3553
*A company-sponsored club; free
Pilgrim Glass catalog, free "cut"
Hummingbird & Fuchsia Cranberry
bud vase, advance notice of new
offerings.*

Cranberry Opalescent

Collectors

Larry Nellans
15065 McGregor Blvd., Ste. #107
Fort Myers, FL 33908-1902
phone: 813-481-6665
fax: 813-481-7391
*Advanced collector of cranberry
opalescent Victorian glass; will pay
highest prices for rare cranberry
opalescent barber bottles, water
pitchers, table sets, oil lamps, etc.*

Crystal

(see also GLASS, Elegant; LAMPS &
LIGHTING, Chandeliers)

Matching Services

Old China Patterns Ltd.
1560 Brimley Rd.
Scarborough
Ontario M1P 3G9 Canada
phone: 800-663-4533 or 416-299-8880
fax: 416-299-4721
e-mail: ocp@chinapatterns.com
*Canada's largest matching service;
buys and sells internationally; since
1966; specializing in English &
American china and crystal; charter
member International Association of
Dinnerware Matchers.*

China By Pattern International Matching
Service
P.O. Box 129
Farmington, CT 06034-0129
phone: 203-678-7079
*Locate and match all manufacturers
of stemware and crystal; send SASE
with manufacturer, size and shape
wanted, quantity, and photocopy if
available: Fostoria, Cambridge,
Lenox, Waterford, etc.*

Regina Negrotti
Tablescapes
49 Elkton Ave.
P.O. Box 3165
Cheshire, CT 06410
phone: 800-801-4084
*A small, personal matching service
with a constantly changing inventory;
want lists are kept; send photocopy or
photo when unsure of pattern name;
specializes in Lenox.*

Paul & Pearl Hoffman
China Brokers, Ltd.
11 Westgate Ct.
Colts Neck, NJ 07722
phone: 908-866-6613 or 800-867-6613

Alice Korman
Alice's Past & Presents Replacements
P.O. Box 465
Merrick, NY 11566-0465
phone: 516-379-1352
fax: 516-379-7302
*Matching and locating service for
Gorham, Wedgwood, Lenox, Mikasa,
Noritake, and others.*

Pattern Finders, A
P.O. Box 206
Port Jefferson Station, NY 11776-0206
phone: 516-928-5158 or 800-216-2446
fax: 516-928-5170
e-mail: apattern@aol.com
*All major brands of dinnerware and
crystal stocked in huge inventory;
locating service for hard to find
patterns; Rosenthal specialists.*

Sophia Papapanu
Sophia's China & Crystal
141 Sedgwick St.
Syracuse, NY 13203-1136
phone: 315-472-6834
*Discontinued china and crystal
patterns; over 16 years service;
American, English, and other
manufacturers; mail order or by
special appointment; please send
SASE with requests for information.*

Constance Stolz
China Match & Crystal Match
72 Longacre Rd.
Rochester, NY 14621-1019
phone: 716-338-3781
e-mail: chinamat@frontiernet.net
*Replacements of discontinued glass
and crystal stemware; Fostoria,
Gorham, Lenox, Noritake, Mikasa,
Royal Doulton; buy and sell.*

China Matching, Inc.
420 Belle Grove Rd.
Middletown, VA 22645
phone: 540-869-1261
*Discontinued china & crystal;
Castleton, Haviland, Lenox and
Wedgwood china; Fostoria & Lenox
crystal.*

Mildred G. Brumback
China & Crystal Matching, Inc.
420 Belle Grove Rd.
Dept. M
Middletown, VA 22645
phone: 703-869-1261
Specializes in Fostoria and Lenox.

Thurber's
2256C Dabeny Rd.
Richmond, VA 23230
phone: 804-278-9080 or 800-848-7237
Carries only active patterns.

David Thompson
Replacements Ltd.
P.O. Box 26029
Greensboro, NC 27420
phone: 800-737-5223 or 800-REP-
LACE
fax: 910-697-3100
e-mail: replaceltd@aol.com
Internet: http://www.imall.com/stores/
replacements
*China, crystal and flatware (obsolete,
active and inactive.)*

D & J Locations
1601 E. Canal St.
Tarboro, NC 27886
phone: 919-823-5333 or 800-818-5565
*Discontinued crystal: Fostoria,
Franciscan, Gorham, Imperial, Lenox,
Lotus, Mikasa, Noritake, Seneca,
Tiffin, Wedgwood, and other major
brands; buys, sells, locates.*

China Cabinet, The
214 Hillside Dr.
P.O. Box 426
Clearwater, SC 29822
phone: 803-593-9655
*Matches fine & casual crystal;
Cambridge, Franciscan, Fostoria,
Galway, Glastonbury, Gorham,
Imperial, Lenox, Lotus, Mikasa,
Noritake, Royal Doulton, Seneca,
Tiffin, Towle, etc.*

China & Crystal Matchers, Inc.
2379 John Glenn Dr., Ste. #108-M
Atlanta, GA 30341-1901
phone: 770-455-1162
fax: 770-452-8616
*All manufacturers; buys, sells,
locates; member of the International
Association of Dinnerware Matchers.*

Paul Church
Replacement Service, A
1415 Michigan Ave.
Saint Cloud, FL 34769
phone: 407-957-1719 or 800-222-7357
*Buys, sells and locates Fostoria and
Lenox crystal.*

Mary Ann Lowery
Crystal Corner, Inc., The
P.O. Box 756
Boaz, AL 35957
phone: 205-593-6169
fax: 205-593-6560
e-mail: ccorner@stargate.imatrex.com
*Fostoria, Tiffin, Mikasa, Lenox,
Imperial, Gorham, Franciscan, etc.*

Allan & Cathy Griggs
Chinamates
1673 Lakecrest Dr.
Sullivan, IN 47882-9585
phone: 800-726-0345 or 812-268-6411
fax: 812-268-6411
e-mail: chinamates@viaduct.custom.net
*Stocks and locates discontinued
patterns only of china and crystal;
Franciscan, Fostoria, Gorham, Lenox,
Tiffin, Waterford crystal, Wedgwood,
etc.; member Fostoria Glass Society of
American.*

Barron's
P.O. Box 994
Novi, MI 48376
phone: 800-538-6340

Heritage China of Iowa
P.O. Box 49
Palo, IA 52324
phone: 319-227-7781 or 319-227-7781
*Crystal by Fostoria, Heisey, Imperial,
Candlewick, Lenox, Noritake, Sasaki.*

Clintsman International
20855 Watertown Rd.
Waukesha, WI 53186-1873
phone: 414-798-0440 or 800-781-8900
fax: 414-798-8879
*All manufacturers: Atlantis, Fostoria,
Galway, Gorham, Imperial, Kosta,
Lenox, Lotus, Mikasa, Noritake,
Stuart, Tiffin, Waterford, Wedgwood,
and others; buys and sells.*

Gloria Voss Beyer
Beyer's Wedgwood China Cupboard
740 Honey Creek Parkway
Milwaukee, WI 53213
phone: 800-893-WWCC
*Specializes in discontinued patterns of
Wedgwood crystal.*

Crystal Connection
8661 West Midland Dr.
Greendale, WI 53219-1038
phone: 414-425-1321
*Crystal matching service specializing
in Lenox and Fostoria.*

China & Crystal Replacements
P.O. Box 187
Excelsior, MN 55331
phone: 612-474-6418
*Discontinued and active china,
dinnerware and crystal bought and
sold.*

Heirloom Completions
C-1620 Venice St.
Granite City, IL 62040
phone: 618-931-4333
*Anchor, Atlas, Cambridge, Duncan,
Federal, Fenton, Fostoria, Heisey,
Imperial, Indiana, Jeanette Macbeth,
Smith, Tiffin, Westmoreland,
Depression, Elegant, Carnival,
Opalescent glass patterns, stems,
place, serving pieces.*

China Replacements
P.O. Box 508
High Ridge, MO 63049
phone: 800-562-2655
Matches Lenox, Fostoria, Tiffin,

Cambridge, Gorham, Lotus, Stuart, Noritake, Mikasa, and many others.

Dining Elegance, Ltd.
P.O. Box 4203
Saint Louis, MO 63163
phone: 314-865-1408
List of patterns in stock available upon request; $1.

Jacqueline Healey
Heirloom Crystal & China
P.O. Box 149
Mount Vernon, MO 65712
phone: 417-466-3818 or 800-927-6471
Discontinued patterns of fine and casual crystal by most manufacturers; current and discontinued Mikasa; search file maintained; buys, trades, locates.

Betty Stachurski
Betty's Crystal & China
P.O. Box 433
Lawrence, KS 66044-0433
phone: 913-842-8054
Atlantis, Bryce, Cambridge, Dansk, Denby, Duncan & Miller, Fostoria, Glastonbury/Lotus, Heisey, Josair, Lenox, Mikasa, Noritake, Royal Doulton, Tiffin, Wedgwood, and others.

Peggy Endicott
Bygone China Match
1225 W. 34th North
Wichita, KS 67204-4236
phone: 316-838-6010
fax: 316-838-6010
e-mail: byeonchina@aol.com
Stock and locates Fostoria, Gorham, Lenox, Mikasa, and Tiffin crystal.

Barbara Coleman
Finders Keepers China Lady
1537 Metairie Rd.
Metairie, LA 70005-3938
phone: 504-455-1530
fax: 504-885-2512
Stock or locate Doulton, Lenox/ Oxford, Minton, Noritake, Pickard, Spode, Wedgwood; also other china and crystal.

Locators, Inc.
2217 Cottondale Lane
Little Rock, AR 72202-2018
phone: 501-663-1114 or 800-367-9690
Carries out-of-production (discontinued) china and crystal, and discontinued as well as active sterling flatware patterns.

Advisory Replacement Service
901 W. Walnut Hill Ln., 5A-9
Irving, TX 75038
A replacement service for crystal: Waterford, Baccarat, Orrefors, Mikasa, Gorham, Lenox, Ceska, St. Louis, Galway, Wedgwood, etc.

David Lackey Antiques & China
  Matching
2311 Westheimer
Houston, TX 77098-1317
phone: 713-942-7171
Buy and sell most major brands:

Fostoria, Lenox, Tiffin, Waterford, Stuart, baccarat, etc.

Larry & Anne McDonald
A & A Dinnerware Locators
P.O. Box 50222
Austin, TX 78763-0222
phone: 512-264-1054 or 888-898-4202
fax: 512-264-2727
e-mail: 73612.470@compuserve.com
Locate/match discontinued crystal patterns; all major manufacturers: American, European, Japanese; primarily mail order.

Glass Urn, The
456 West Main St.
Mesa, AZ 85201-6523
phone: 602-833-2702 or 602-838-5936
Specializing in discontinued American made glass: Cambridge, Fostoria, Heisey, Tiffin, etc.; from 1890s to 1970s; open shop or mail order.

Past & Present
14851 Avenue 360
Visalia, CA 93292
phone: 415-258-1775 or 209-798-0029
fax: 209-798-1415
Baccarat, Cambridge, Denby, Duncan & Miller, Fostoria, Franciscan, Gorham, Heisey, Imperial, Lalique, Lenox, Mikasa, Nancy Prentiss, Noritake, Orrefors, Sasaki, Tiffin, Towle, Val St. Lambert, Waterford, etc.

Silver Lane Antiques
P.O. Box 322
San Leandro, CA 94577-0032
phone: 510-483-0632
Discontinued crystal available by most major manufacturers.

White's Collectables & Fine China, Etc.
616 E. First
P.O. Box 680
Newberg, OR 97132
phone: 503-538-7421
Discontinued crystal: Lenox, Fostoria, Cambridge, Gorham, Tiffin, and Kausak; also current patterns from major manufacturers.

Curved

(see also REPAIR/RESTORATION/ CONSERVATION, Glass)

Suppliers

Hudson Glass
219 North Division St.
Peekskill, NY 10566-2716
phone: 800-431-2964 or 914-737-2124
fax: 914-737-4447
Sells bent glass for china cabinets; convex picture frame glass; also carries restoration/old house glass in stock; sells stained glass tools and supplies (no stained glass repair); stained glass supply catalog available for $3.

B.J.'s Custom Curve Glass Co.
49 South Monroe St.
Monroe, MI 48161
phone: 313-241-4629

B & L Antiqurie, Inc.
P.O. Box 453
Lexington, MI 48450-0453
phone: 800-840-1110 or 810-359-8623
fax: 810-359-7498
Bent glass, convex portrait glass, antique flat glass, beveled mirror shapes, domes, and other specialty glass products for over 30 years.

M.D. King
403 E. Montgomery
Knoxville, IA 50138
phone: 515-842-6394
Curved glass for china cabinets; all sizes; will ship.

George J. Hoffer
Hoffer Glass
P.O. Box 1756
Appleton, WI 54913-1756
phone: 414-731-8101
Curved glass for china cabinets; send width, length and a radius template; will quote picked up or shipped UPS.

Central Glass Products
405 West Hamon Ave.
Pocola, OK 74902
phone: 918-436-2401

Patrick McCluskey
PECO Glass Bending
P.O. Box 777
Smithville, TX 78957
phone: 512-237-3600
Bends glass for antique china cabinets and similar items.

Cut

Clubs/Associations

Kathy Emerson
American Cut Glass Association
Newsletter: Hobstar, The
P.O. Box 482
Ramona, CA 92065-0482
phone: 768-789-2715
fax: 768-789-7112
Focuses on the Brilliant Period (1880-1915) of American glass.

Collectors

Mike & Lynda Carrigan
RR2 Box 128
New Freedom, PA 17349
phone: 717-235-7159
Collects Brilliant Period cut glass.

Charles Blanton
118 Magothy Bridge Rd.
Severna Park, MD 21146-1221
phone: 410-647-2841
Advanced collector wants one piece or entire collection.

Dealers

Frank W. Larned
Bagwells Flowers & Antiques, Inc.
312 S. Peninsula Dr.
Daytona Beach, FL 32118
phone: 904-252-7687
Specializes in American Brilliant Period cut glass.

Randeen Cummings, ISA CAPP
Cummings & Associates
P.O. Box 5484
Eugene, OR 97405
phone: 503-345-5856 or 503-484-4604
fax: 503-345-8192
Specializes appraising residential contents, in the sale of estates, and in the buying and selling cut glass, especially from the American Brilliant period.

Experts

Joan & Dick Randles
From the Cutter's Wheel Antiques
P.O. Box 285
Webster, NY 14580-0285
phone: 716-671-3760
Specializes, buys and sells American Brilliant period cut glass and engraved glass; members ACGA; eves and weekends best time to call.

Chet Cassel
910 Pheasant Run
Newark, DE 19711
phone: 302-737-3819
Buys, sells (retail/wholesale) and collects examples of fine cut glass.

Bill & Louise Boggess
4016 Martin Dr.
San Mateo, CA 94403-3623
phone: 415-345-5230
Authors of "Identifying American Brilliant Cut Glass" "Collecting American Brilliant Cut Glass," and "Reflection on American Brilliant Cut Glass."

Martha Louise Swan
3930 SE 162nd Ave., Unit 61
Portland, OR 97236-7006
phone: 503-669-8697
Author of "American Cut & Engraved Glass: The Brilliant Period in Historical Perspective (1876-1916)", revised, updated price guide, available from author.

Misc. Services

Dean & Sharon DeOgny
Sentimental Journey Antiques
121 S. Washington Ave., Ste. 810
Minneapolis, MN 55401
phone: 612-332-3270
fax: 612-630-9496
e-mail: ddeogny@usinternet.com
Internet: http://www.antiquenet.com/ sentimentaljourney
Produces a series of videos about cut glass: signatures, assembly line cutting, details of cutting, pattern names, why stoppers are not

interchangeable, figured blanks, what to do with broken pieces, etc.

Museums/Libraries

High Museum of Art, The
1280 Peachtree St.
Atlanta, GA 30309
phone: 404-848-4711
Internet: http://www.highorg/
museum.html

Lightner Museum
P.O. Box 334
Saint Augustine, FL 32085
phone: 904-824-2874

Czechoslovakian

Appraisers

Peggy Sebek, ISA, AAA
Century Appraisals, Inc.
3255 Glencairn Rd.
Shaker Heights, OH 44122-3407
phone: 216-991-2356 or 318-232-5100

Clubs/Associations

Kathy Foster
Czechoslovakian Collectors Guild
International
Newsletter: CCGI Newsletter
P.O. Box 901395
Kansas City, MO 64190-1395
phone: 816-891-9115
fax: 816-891-0988
e-mail: ccgi@corp.pkgsvc.com
For collectors of anything Czechoslo-vakian and Bohemian: glass, pottery, art.

Dealers

Gillian Hine
Gillian Hine Antiques
858 W. Armitage, Box 241
Chicago, IL 60614
phone: 312-281-4186
Buys and sells Czech and German glass and pottery.

Experts

Charles & Barbara Plummer
11417 Sherrie Lane
Silver Spring, MD 20902

Joseph Mattis
Black Swan
P.O. Box 925
Spencer, WV 25276

Polly Enloe, ISA
Century Antiques & Appraisals, Inc.
212 Miller St.
Lafayette, LA 70503
phone: 318-232-5100
Specializes in and appraises Czechoslovakian glass.

Museums/Libraries

Bob Truitt
Friends of the Glass Museum at Novy
Bor
5120 White Flint Dr.
Kensington, MD 20895-1037
phone: 301-929-2539
Organizes symposiums and other research and educational functions focusing on the glassware produced or decorated in the Novy Bor region of Czechoslovakian; supports the Glass Museum at Novy Bor, Czechoslovakia.

Periodicals

Ludbila Halkovovo
Efekt Co. Ltd.
Magazine: New Glass Review
Bardounova 2140
149 00 Praha 4
Prague, Czechoslovakia
Brief, well illustrated articles in English covering all aspects of Czechoslovakian and Slovak glass; production glass, art glass, plus artists; Bohemian glass, novelties, new trends & technologies; also china & ceramics.

Dalzell-Viking

Man./Prod./Dist.

Dalzell-Viking Glass
P.O. Box 459
New Martinsville, WV 26155
phone: 304-455-2900
fax: 304-455-5984
Has outlet store adjacent to factory; also in Cambridge, OH.

Degenhart

Clubs/Associations

Friends of Degenhart
Newsletter: Heartbeat
65323 Highland Hills Rd.
P.O. Box 186
Cambridge, OH 43725-0186
phone: 614-432-2626
Open to all Degenhart collectors and supporters; free museum admission, 5% discount on most purchases, newsletter, annual "Gathering."

Museums/Libraries

Degenhart Paperweight & Glass
Museum, Inc.
65323 Highland Hills Rd.
P.O. Box 186
Cambridge, OH 43725-0186
phone: 614-432-2626
History of glass in the Ohio valley; video, exhibits, research library, gift shop.

Depression

Clubs/Associations

Edith Hacking
Canadian Depression Glass Club
Newsletter: CDGC Newsletter
1026 Forestwood Dr.
Mississauga
Ontario L5C 1GB Canada
The newsletter is published monthly.

W. Lee
North Jersey Dee Geer's
82 High St.
Butler, NJ 07405

Gerald Manitone
Depression Glass Club of Greater
Rochester
Newsletter: Bits & Pieces
P.O. Box 10362
Rochester, NY 14610
phone: 716-288-4290

Depression Glass Club of North East
Florida
2604 Jolly Rd.
Jacksonville, FL 32207

Millie Downey
Land of Sunshine Depression Glass Club
Newsletter: LSDGC Newsletter
P.O. Box 560275
Orlando, FL 32856-0275
phone: 407-298-3355 or 407-855-5502
Purpose of the club is to preserve the history of Depression glass and to encourage new collectors and familiarize the public with glassware of the era.

Frank Stasy
Clearwater Depression Glass Club
10038 62nd Terrace North
Saint Petersburg, FL 33708

Ruth Gullis, Membr.
Western Reserve Depression Glass Club
8669 Courtland Dr.
Strongsville, OH 44136
phone: 216-398-1540

J. Ryan
Buckeye Dee Geer's
2501 Campbell St.
Sandusky, OH 44870

Jeff Settell
Iowa Depression Glass Association
Newsletter: ISGA Newsletter
5871 Vista Dr., Apt. 725
West Des Moines, IA 50266
phone: 515-223-9364

20-30-40 Society, Inc.
Newsletter: Society Page, The
P.O. Box 856
La Grange, IL 60525-0856
phone: 708-354-1448
Formed in 1972; devoted to collecting and learning about Depression-era glassware; annual glass show every March.

Jim Garrison
National Depression Glass Association,
The
Newsletter: News & Views
P.O. Box 8264
Wichita, KS 67209-0264
phone: 918-272-6414
A central organization for depression glass collectors; sponsors an annual show and sale in July.

Gary Greenawalt
Greater Tulsa Depression Era Glass Club
P.O. Box 470763
Tulsa, OK 74147-0763
e-mail: garyg74112@aol.com

A. Nicholson
Big "D" Pression Glass Club
10 Winding Creek Trail
Garland, TX 75043

Collectors

Anita Wood
1412 Alamosa
Odessa, TX 79763
phone: 915-337-1297

Dealers

Susan Leite
44 Glenwood Rd.
Brewster, MA 02631-2202
phone: 508-385-4905
Wants to buy all pink, green and jadite (creamy green) depression glass; must be undamaged.

Jay Adams
245 Lakeview Ave., Ste. 208
Clifton, NJ 07011
phone: 201-365-5970
Specializing in Depression era glass and china: also wants to buy elegant glass such as Cambridge, Tiffin, Fostoria and others; send SASE with wants; will search and keep want list on file; best to call 6-11 EST; mail order only.

Robert & Nancy Perzel
Popkorn Antiques
4 Mine St.
P.O. Box 1057
Flemington, NJ 08822-1057
phone: 908-782-9631

Gerald Manitone
P.O. Box 10362
Rochester, NY 14610
phone: 716-288-4290
Buys, sells, and collects Depression glass.

Millie Downey
Millie's Glass & China
P.O. Box 560275
Orlando, FL 32856-0275
phone: 407-298-3355 or 407-855-5502
Wants to buy Depression glass; collects many patterns.

Mary Faria
Izmar's Antique Designs
P.O. Box 32321
San Jose, CA 95152-2321
phone: 408-258-0413
Buying and selling transparent pink, apple green, mayfair blue depression glass for over 15 years; specializing in Cambridge "keyhole" and "open lace work" patterns; also kitchen glass, soda fountain, vanity and perfume glass items.

Experts

Gene Florence
P.O. Box 22186
Lexington, KY 40522-2186
phone: 606-266-4615 or 352-742-3380
Internet: http://www.geneflorence.com
Author of several books about Depression glass.

Margaret & Kenn Whitmyer
P.O. Box 30806
Gahanna, OH 43230
Specializing in Depression era bedroom and bathroom glassware. Author of "Bedroom & Bathroom Glassware of the Depression Years."

Nadine Pankow
P.O. Box 207
Willow Springs, IL 60480

Kay Larsson
20825 102nd Ave., SE
Kent, WA 98031

Periodicals

Teri Steele, Ed.
Depression Glass Daze, Inc.
Newspaper: Daze, The
275 State Rd.
P.O. Box 57
Otisville, MI 48463-0057
phone: 810-631-4593
fax: 810-631-4567
A monthly newspaper catering to the dealers and collectors of glass, china and pottery from the 1920s and 1930s.

Domes

Man./Prod./Dist.

Glass Dome Co., The
62 Priory Rd.
Tonbridge
Kent TN9 2BL, U.K.
phone: 01732-367181
fax: 01732-360830

Suppliers

B & L Antiqurie, Inc.
P.O. Box 453
Lexington, MI 48450-0453
phone: 800-840-1110 or 810-359-8623
fax: 810-359-7498
Bent glass, convex portrait glass, antique flat glass, beveled mirror shapes, domes, and other specialty glass products for over 30 years.

Duncan & Miller

Clubs/Associations

National Duncan Glass Society
Journal: National Duncan Glass Journal
525 Jefferson Ave.
P.O. Box 965
Washington, PA 15301
phone: 412-225-9950
Focuses on the glassware produced by the Duncan & Miller Glass Co.

Collectors

Cliff McCaslin
Rocliff Communications
8422 N. Park Ct.
Kansas City, MO 64155
phone: 816-436-7719
fax: 816-436-6955
e-mail: rocliff@unicom.net
Wants to buy Duncan and Duncan-Miller glass; all patterns.

Museums/Libraries

Duncan Miller Glass Museum
525 Jefferson Ave.
P.O. Box 965
Washington, PA 15301
phone: 412-225-9950
Museum has over 1400 pieces of Duncan glass in five display rooms; annual show and sale in July.

Durand

Dealers

Edward J. Meschi
129 Pinyard Rd.
Monroeville, NJ 08343-1870
phone: 609-358-7293
fax: 609-358-7293
Buys and sells Durand art glass; wants original sales catalogs for Durand Art Glass which operated under the name of Vineland Flint Glass Co. in the 1920s.

Early American

Auction Services

Norman C. Heckler
Norman C. Heckler & Company
79 Bradford Corner Rd.
Woodstock Valley, CT 06282-2002
phone: 860-974-1634
fax: 860-974-2003
Specializes in the sale of early glass and bottles; Heckler & Co. sold a single bottle for $66,000 at auction in 1993.

Clubs/Associations

Walter B. Moore
Early American Glass Traders
RD 5 Box 638
Milford, DE 19963-9805
phone: 302-422-0932
Association of collectors of early American pressed glass who are interested in improving their collections by trading or selling their duplicates amongst themselves.

Experts

Jamie Houdeshell
16255 Normandy South
Perrysburg, OH 43551
phone: 419-872-1966
Buys, sells, appraises and specializes in antique bottles and early American glass.

Museums/Libraries

Sandwich Glass Museum
Newsletter: Cullet, The
129 Main St.
P.O. Box 103
Sandwich, MA 02563
phone: 508-888-0251
The museum preserves and displays the glass manufactured in Sandwich 1825-1907.

Miss Dorothy Lee Jones, Dir.
Jones Museum of Glass & Ceramics, The
Douglas Mountain Rd.
East Sebago, ME 04029
phone: 207-787-3370 or 207-787-2800
Unique museum, over 8500 examples of glass & ceramics ranging from ancient to modern; large holdings of Early American lacy and pressed glass, paperweights; also 20th C. tablewares and studio art glass, fluid lamps, cut glass, etc.

Periodicals

David & Linda Arman
Magazine: China & Glass Quarterly
P.O. Box 39
Portsmouth, RI 02871-0039
phone: 401-841-8403
fax: 401-841-8403
Internet: http://www.oaklandpublications.com
Deals with the fields of English ceramics 1750-1865 (Historical Staffordshire, Pratt Ware, Lustre, Figures, transferware) and Early American glass 1750-1880 (blown three mold, freeblown, pattern molded, pressed, paperweights.)

Repro. Sources

Ebenezer Averill Co., The
P.O. Box 156
Milford, NH 03055

Art Reed
Sweetwater Glass
RD 1 Box 88
De Lancey, NY 13752

Elegant

(see also GLASS, Cambridge; GLASS, Crystal; GLASS, Duncan & Miller; GLASS, Fostoria; GLASS, Heisey; GLASS, Imperial; GLASS, Tiffin)

Dealers

Jay Adams
245 Lakeview Ave., Ste. 208
Clifton, NJ 07011
phone: 201-365-5970
Specializing in Depression era glass and china: wants to buy elegant glass such as Cambridge, Tiffin, Fostoria and others; send SASE with wants; will search and keep want list on file; best to call 6-11 EST.; mail order only.

Allan & Cathy Griggs
Chinamates
1673 Lakecrest Dr.
Sullivan, IN 47882-9585
phone: 800-726-0345 or 812-268-6411
fax: 812-268-6411
e-mail: chinamates@viaduct.custom.net
Stocks and locates Cambridge, Fostoria, Gorham, Lenox, Wedgwood crystal; send wants; SASE; mail order only; members of Fostoria Glass Society of America.

Experts

Genevieve Belson
Junk General Store, The
Trade Mart - Booth 10
2121 Sam Houston Tollway
Houston, TX 77043
phone: 713-437-9421 or 713-467-2506
Specializes in 20th century glassware; Fostoria, Cambridge, Tiffin, Depression era, etc.

Matching Services

China By Pattern International Matching Service
P.O. Box 129
Farmington, CT 06034-0129
phone: 203-678-7079
Locating crystal & glassware: Fostoria, Cambridge, etc.

Florence & Jay Solito
Solito
54 Old Stafford Rd.
Tolland, CT 06084
phone: 203-872-3294
Tiffin, Morgantown, Imperial, Fostoria, Depression glass, Cambridge, and other elegant glassware.

Fran Jay
Fran Jay's Glass
10 Church St.
Lambertville, NJ 08530-2102
phone: 609-397-1571
e-mail: glasjay@mail.idt.net
Internet: http://www.GlassShow.com
Cambridge, Depression glass, Fenton, Fostoria, Heisey, and other elegant glass companies; daily hours, also mail order.

Harry Weitkemper
China Finders
1-B South Holy Ave.
Highland Springs, VA 23075
phone: 888-244-6239 or 804-328-2897
*Candlewick, Fostoria, Cambridge,
Tiffin, Libby, etc.*

Jerry Gallagher
Red Horse Inn Antiques
420 1st Ave. N.W.
Plainview, MN 55964-1213
phone: 507-534-3511
e-mail: morgantown@aol.com
*Specializes in matching glass by
Cambridge, Fostoria, Morgantown,
Heisey, Tiffin, Duncan and Fry; no
European glass companies in stock.*

Joanne Copeland
Sweet Nothings
5533 S. 20th St.
Lincoln, NE 68512
phone: 402-420-1620
*Specializes in Heisey, Tiffin, Fostoria,
Cambridge, Hawkes.*

Milbra's Crystal Matching
P.O. Box 784
Cleburne, TX 76033-0784
phone: 817-645-6066 or 817-294-9837
*Crystal matching: Fostoria, Tiffin,
Lenox & others; buy and sell; requests
kept on file; send SASE for reply.*

Mrs. Davie Lou Solka, Pres.
Ettelman's Discontinued China &
Crystal
501 Bermuda
Corpus Christi, TX 78411
phone: 512-852-5815
*Buys/sells inactive patterns of elegant
glassware by Cambridge, Duncan,
Fostoria, Heisey, Lenox and Tiffin.*

Michael Krumme
P.O. Box 5542 - Dept. CIC
Santa Monica, CA 90409-5542
phone: 213-936-4214
e-mail: mkrumme@pacbell.net
*Send detailed want list; searches for
Cambridge, Heisey, Fostoria,
Duncan-Miller, New Martinsville,
Fenton, Tiffin, Imperial, Morgantown,
and Paden City Glass; specializes in
obscure and less-collected etched
patterns.*

Periodicals

Teri Steele, Ed.
Depression Glass Daze, Inc.
Newspaper: Daze, The
275 State Rd.
P.O. Box 57
Otisville, MI 48463-0057
phone: 810-631-4593
fax: 810-631-4567
*A monthly newspaper catering to the
dealers and collectors of glass, china
and pottery from the 1920s and 1930s.*

European

Auction Services

Ron Fox
Ron Fox Auctions
P.O. Box 2030
Brentwood, NY 11717-0997
phone: 516-231-0633
fax: 516-952-7719
*Conducts periodic auctions of
European glass.*

Dealers

Ron Fox
P.O. Box 2030
Brentwood, NY 11717-0997
phone: 516-231-0633
fax: 516-952-7719
*Wants old European glass:
transparent or opaque enamel, wheel
cut, engraved, overlay, iridescent, etc.*

Fenton

Clubs/Associations

Fenton Art Glass Collectors of America,
Inc.
Newsletter: Butterfly Net, The
P.O. Box 384
Williamstown, WV 26187
phone: 304-375-6196
fax: 304-375-4679
e-mail: dnielsen@csinet.net
Internet: http://
www.collectoronline.com/club-
FAGCA.html
*FAGCA is a non-profit educational
corporation dedicated to learning
about Fenton art glass.*

Richard Staats
National Fenton Glass Society
Newsletter: Fenton Flyer, The
P.O. Box 4008
Marietta, OH 45750-7008
phone: 614-374-3345 or 614-374-6902
e-mail: nfgs@ee.net
Internet: http://ww.axces.com/nfgs/
nfgsd.htm

Jackie Shirley
Pacific Northwest Fenton Association
Newsletter: Fenton Nor'Wester
8225 Kilchis River rd.
Tillamook, OR 97141-9279
phone: 503-842-4815

Collectors

John O. Burgess
10738 Harley Rd.
Lorton, VA 22079-3908
Wants pre-1970 Fenton art glass.

Dealers

Fenton Showcase Dealer
P.O. Box 3602
Allentown, PA 18106
phone: 610-432-1158
*Full line of Fenton art glass, old and
new.*

Judy Herman
Marshall Lynn Enterprises
705 East Bay Dr., #266
Largo, FL 33770
phone: 813-585-4184

Experts

Ferill J. Rice
302 Pheasant Run
Kaukauna, WI 54130-1802
phone: 414-788-4123 or 414-766-9176
*Advisor to "Warman's Antiques &
Collectibles Price Guide."*

Man./Prod./Dist.

Ann Stull
Fenton Art Glass Company Gift Store
420 Caroline Ave.
Williamstown, WV 26187
phone: 304-375-7772
fax: 304-375-6459
*Retail outlet for replacement pieces
still in stock; also many discontinued
items still available for purchase;
knowledge of old Fenton glass.*

Tamara Armstrong
Fenton Art Glass Company, The
Newsletter: Glass Messenger
700 Elizabeth St.
Williamstown, WV 26187-1028
phone: 304-375-6122 or 800-249-4527
fax: 304-375-6459
*Manufacturer of unique art glass such
as Burmese and Rosalene; currently
manufactures plates, figurines, bells,
ornaments and a "Connoisseur
Collection."*

Periodicals

Ferill J. Rice
Newsletter: Butterfly Net
302 Pheasant Run
Kaukauna, WI 54130-1802
phone: 414-788-4123 or 414-766-9176
Published six times per year.

Findlay

Clubs/Associations

Marilyn Jackson
Collectors of Findlay Glass
Newsletter: Melting Pot
P.O. Box 256
Findlay, OH 45839-0256
phone: 419-424-0332
*Club for members to share informa-
tion about Findlay Glass and the
current activity in the marketplace;
quarterly newsletter.*

Dealers

Jennifer Payne
Gifts In Time
540 S. Main St.
Findlay, OH 45840
phone: 419-422-7227
fax: 419-422-3824
Buys and sells Findlay pattern glass.

Fire-King

Clubs/Associations

Fire-King Collectors Club
1406 E. 14th St.
Des Moines, IA 50316
phone: 515-265-6667

Flowers

Museums/Libraries

Botanical Museum of Harvard
University, The Blaschka Collection
24 Oxford St.
Cambridge, MA 02138
phone: 617-495-2326
*Lifelike handcrafted glass replicas of
plants and flowers.*

Fostoria

Clubs/Associations

Clifford Bucy
Fostoria Glass Society of America, The
Newsletter: Facets of Fostoria
P.O. Box 826
Moundsville, WV 26041-0826
phone: 304-845-9188 or 304-845-2170

Fostoria Glass Association
109 N. Main St.
Fostoria, OH 44830

Theresa Ujfalusi
Fostoria Glass Collectors
Newsletter: Fostoria Reflections
P.O. Box 1625
Orange, CA 92668
phone: 714-770-4088
*A nonprofit organization dedicated to
the study and preservation of Fostoria
glass as well as all American
handmade glassware.*

Dealers

Allan & Cathy Griggs
Chinamates
1673 Lakecrest Dr.
Sullivan, IN 47882-9585
phone: 800-726-0345 or 812-268-6411
fax: 812-268-6411
e-mail: chinamates@viaduct.custom.net
*Stock and locate Fostoria glassware;
mail order only; call or write; SASE;
send wants; member of Fostoria Glass
Society of America.*

Matching Services

China By Pattern International Matching
Service
P.O. Box 129
Farmington, CT 06034-0129
phone: 203-678-7079
*Send SASE to locate/match Fostoria
and other stemware and crystal
pieces. No charge to list/search for
wanted items. Send quantity, shape,
photocopy, size, etc.*

Charlotte Krauch
Charlotte's Glass Reflections
1516 Florida Blvd.
Bradenton, FL 34207
phone: 800-221-2953 or 813-756-1940
Specializes in Fostoria glassware; all discontinued patterns; locating service; send wants; SASE for reply.

Fostoria Registry
1060 Crestline Dr.
Crete, NE 68333
phone: 402-826-2622
Matching service for Fostoria from 1940 to 1982; locating service for items in stock; SASE required for reply.

Aames' Nationwide Network for Fostoria
P.O. Box 88840
Steil, WA 98388
phone: 206-984-0701
Specializing in "Colony" and "American" patterns; buys, sells and appraises.

Museums/Libraries

Clifford Bucy
Fostoria Glass Museum
P.O. Box 826
Moundsville, WV 26041-0826
phone: 304-845-9188 or 304-845-2170

Fry

Clubs/Associations

H.C. Fry Glass Society
P.O. Box 41
Beaver, PA 15009

Gay Fad Studios

Experts

Donna McGrady
154 Peters Ave.
Lancaster, OH 43130
phone: 614-653-0376
Collects and specializes in glassware decorated from 1945-1964 by the Gay Fad Studios of Lancaster, Ohio; Gay Fad was known for applying fanciful decorations to plain glass tumblers.

Goofus

Experts

John Martin Davis, Jr.
2705 Swiss Ave.
Dallas, TX 75204
phone: 214-823-9367
Writing a book about goofus glass.

Periodicals

Leon Travis
Travis Antiques
Newsletter: Goofus Glass Gazette
9 Lindenwood Ct.
Sterling, VA 20165
phone: 703-430-7314
Quarterly newsletter for goofus

collectors; educational articles, free classifieds with subscription.

Gorham

Man./Prod./Dist.

Gorham, Inc.
100 Lenox Dr.
Lawrenceville, NJ 08648
phone: 609-896-2800 or 800-635-3669
Sterling and stainless steel flatware, sterling and silverplated holloware; fine china, crystal stemware, giftware and dolls; a division of Lenox Brands.

Greentown

Clubs/Associations

Annette LaRowe
National Greentown Glass Association
Newsletter: National Greentown Glass Association Newsletter
P.O. Box 8264
Greentown, IN 46936
phone: 765-628-2093
Annual meetings are held 2nd Saturday in June at the National Greentown Glass Museum, Greentown, IN.

Collectors

LeAnne Milliser
19596 Glendale Ave.
South Bend, IN 46637-1814
phone: 219-272-1184

Dealers

Jerry Garrett
Jerry's Antiques & Postcards
1807 West Madison St.
Kokomo, IN 46901-1829
phone: 765-457-5256
Buys and sells Greentown glass as well as chocolate glass made by other National Company factories.

Experts

Jim & Mira Houdeshell
JMJ Antiques
1801 N. Main St.
Findlay, OH 45840-3815
phone: 419-423-2895 or 419-424-4551
fax: 419-424-6974

Museums/Libraries

Greentown Glass Museum
112 N. Meridian
P.O. Box 161
Greentown, IN 46936-0161
phone: 765-628-6206
An exhibit from the old Indiana Tumbler & Goblet Co. (1894-1903.)

Grand Rapids Public Museum
272 Pearl St. NW
Grand Rapids, MI 49504-5371
phone: 616-456-3977
fax: 616-456-3873

Hazel-Atlas

Collectors

Kenneth G. Sloan
5707 S. Kenwood
Chicago, IL 60637-1718
phone: 773-752-4247
Wants to buy Hazel-Atlas company catalogs, re-use containers and packers, especially tumblers.

Heisey

Clubs/Associations

Bay State Heisey Collectors Club
354 Washington St.
East Walpole, MA 02032-1132
phone: 508-660-2979

"Butch" Jones
National Capital Heisey Collectors
Newsletter: Heisey Herald
P.O. Box 23
Clinton, MD 20735
phone: 301-505-0041
Purpose is to study and preserve Heisey glassware; meetings held second Monday of each month except July and August; programs on Heisey patterns, pieces, colors, etc.

Molly Kaspar
Heisey Collectors of America
Newsletter: Heisey News, The
169 W. Church St.
Newark, OH 43055
phone: 614-345-2932
fax: 614-345-9638
Every production color and pattern is on display in the King House, built in 1831.

Collectors

Cliff McCaslin
Rocliff Communications
8422 N. Park Ct.
Kansas City, MO 64155
phone: 816-436-7719
fax: 816-436-6955
e-mail: rocliff@unicom.net
Wants to buy glassware by Heisey.

Cliff McCaslin
Rocliff Communications
8422 N. Park Ct.
Kansas City, MO 64155
phone: 816-436-7719
fax: 816-436-6955
e-mail: rocliff@unicom.net

Dealers

Ward Stewart
Stewart's Antiques
1000 Coolidge
Lafayette, LA 70503-2336
phone: 318-232-2957

Robert Henicksman
Classic Glass
916 Q St.
Sacramento, CA 95814
phone: 916-448-0840
Buys and sells all patterns of Heisey

glass; also maintains want lists and will search for customer needs.

Museums/Libraries

Katherine McCracken, Curator
National Heisey Glass Museum, The
169 W. Church St.
Newark, OH 43055
phone: 614-345-2932
fax: 614-345-9638
Owned and operated by Heisey Collectors of America; hundreds of patterns of glass made by A.H. Heisey & Co. 1895-1957 on display.

Periodicals

Ralph & Sandra McKelvey
Heisey Publications
Newsletter: Newscaster, The
P.O. Box 102
Plymouth, OH 44865
phone: 419-935-0338
A quarterly newsletter on identification and research.

Imperial

Clubs/Associations

Cliff McCaslin
National Imperial Glass Collectors Society
Newsletter: Glasszette
P.O. Box 534
Bellaire, OH 43906
phone: 816-436-7719
fax: 816-436-6955
e-mail: rocliff@unicom.net
Members interested in the history and glassware produced by the Imperial Glass Corp.; conducts an annual convention offering seminars, show and sale, and "members only" auction.

Collectors

Kathy Doub
5359 Iron Pen Place
Columbia, MD 21044-1811
phone: 410-995-1254

Cliff McCaslin
Rocliff Communications
8422 N. Park Ct.
Kansas City, MO 64155
phone: 816-436-7719
fax: 816-436-6955
e-mail: rocliff@unicom.net

Dealers

Cliff McCaslin
Rocliff Communications
8422 N. Park Ct.
Kansas City, MO 64155
phone: 816-436-7719
fax: 816-436-6955
e-mail: rocliff@unicom.net
Wants to buy all patterns of Imperial glass.

Penny Drucker
Mother Drucker's
P.O. Box 50261
Irvine, CA 92619-0261
phone: 888-637-8253 or 714-551-5529
fax: 714-551-2116
e-mail: motherdruc@aol.com
Always changing inventory of color, cut, rare and common pieces; send LSASE for list.

Experts

Myrna & Bob Garrison
Collector's Loot
3816 Hastings Dr.
Arlington, TX 76013-1900
phone: 817-275-6342
fax: 817-275-6342
e-mail: 73074.3655@compuserve.com
Authors of "Imperial Cape Cod Tradition to Treasure", 2nd Edition, $16.45 ppd. plus $1.16 tax for TX residents; and of "Imperial's Boudoir, Etcetera", 1996, $29.95 ppd. plus #2.09 for TX residents; available from authors.

Misc. Services

Cliff McCaslin
Rocliff Communications
8422 N. Park Ct.
Kansas City, MO 64155
phone: 816-436-7719
fax: 816-436-6955
e-mail: rocliff@unicom.net
Offers videotapes on popular glassware patterns of the Depression era, Imperial Candlewick, Imperial Slag, Imperial Cape Cod.

Italian

(see also MODERNISM)

Dealers

Vetri Italian Glass
P.O. Box 191
Fort Lee, NJ 07024
phone: 201-969-0373
fax: 201-969-0373
Carries a large selection of Italian glass; also sells books on Italian glass.

David Huffman
P.O. Box 26151
Charlotte, NC 28221-6151
phone: 800-327-9654 or 704-598-7720
e-mail: batant@ix.netcom.com
Wants to buy Italian glass.

Kenneth P. Lesko
Kenneth Paul Lesko 20th Century
   Decorative Arts
P.O. Box 16099
Rocky River, OH 44116-0099
phone: 216-356-0275
fax: 216-331-1280
e-mail: kplesko@aol.com
Internet: http://members.aol.com/
   kplesko/kplesko.html
Specialist in Italian glass 1920-1970; wants to buy Venini, Matinuzzi, Scarpa, Seguso, Barovier, Cenedese,

A. Toso/Dino Martens, MVM Cappelin, CVM, Avem, Salir, Nason, Fratelli Toso, Salviati, Vistosi, A. Barbini.

Ara Tavitian
Retro Gallery
524 1/2 N. La Brea Ave.
Los Angeles, CA 90036-2016
phone: 213-936-5261
fax: 213-936-5262
Art glass from the 1940s through the 1960s; specializing in Italian and Scandinavian glass.

Experts

Howard Lockwood
P.O. Box 191
Fort Lee, NJ 07024-0191
phone: 201-692-9780
fax: 201-692-9780
Buys, sells and specializes in Venini and other Italian glass.

Dan Ripley
Dan Ripley Antiques
644 E. 52nd St.
Indianapolis, IN 46205
phone: 317-920-1435
fax: 317-920-1436
e-mail: dnripley@netride.com
A most experienced dealer; specializes in Italian and Scandinavian glass and ceramics; thousands of pieces sold privately and at auction; guest speaker at International Society of Appraisers' convention.

Periodicals

Howard Lockwood
Newsletter: VETRI: Italian Glass News
P.O. Box 191
Fort Lee, NJ 07024-0191
phone: 201-692-9780
fax: 201-692-9780
Quarterly newsletter for the collector, museum curator, and dealer in 20th century Italian glass.

Kosta Boda

Man./Prod./Dist.

Kosta Boda USA Ltd. (Div. of Orrefors)
140 Bradford Dr.
Berlin, NJ 08009
phone: 609-768-5400
fax: 609-768-9726
Swedish full lead crystal glassware, giftware and accessories.

Lalique

Auction Services

Louis Webre, Client Svc.
William Doyle Galleries
175 E. 87th St.
New York, NY 10128-2205
phone: 212-427-2730
fax: 212-369-0892
Internet: http://www.doylegalleries.com
Holds over 30 auctions annually of antique English, Continental and American furniture, paintings, decorations, jewelry, vintage and

couture clothing, collectible toys, books and prints; specialty auctions of Majolica, Lalique and wine.

Clubs/Associations

Lalique Collectors Society
Magazine: Lalique
400 Veterans Blvd.
Carlstadt, NJ 07072
phone: 800-274-7825
fax: 201-939-4492
Focuses on the collectibles issued by Lalique. A Jacques Jugeat Co. marketer-sponsored club.

Collectors

Jeff Myers
P.O. Box 26151
Charlotte, NC 28221-6151
phone: 800-327-9654 or 704-598-7720
e-mail: batant@ix.netcom.com
Wants to buy R. LALIQUE glass; also wants Galle, Daum and Tiffany glass.

Dealers

David Huffman
P.O. Box 26151
Charlotte, NC 28221-6151
phone: 800-327-9654 or 704-598-7720
e-mail: batant@ix.netcom.com
Wants to buy R. LALIQUE glass; also wants Loetz, Daum, and Italian glass.

A.D. & Pat Clay
Clemons-Eicken Fine European Imports
6166 N. Scottsdale Rd., #204
Paradise Valley, AZ 85253
phone: 602-998-9042 or 800-250-5423
fax: 602-998-3755
Carries Lladro, Armani, Boehm, Lalique, Cybis.

Experts

Nicholas Dawes
67 East 11th St.
New York, NY 10003
phone: 212-473-5111
fax: 212-353-3845
Buys, sells and specializes in pre-war works by Rene Lalique; author of "Lalique Glass" (Crown Publishers, 1986).

Carole Hibel
John Hibel Antiques
185 Yerry Hill Rd.
Woodstock, NY 12498
phone: 914-679-2966 or 800-426-3357
fax: 914-679-3397
Wants to buy R. Lalique art glass.

Randy Monsen
Cocktails & Laughter Antiques
P.O. Box 529
Vienna, VA 22183-0529
phone: 703-938-2129
Wants vases and perfumes by Lalique; prefers pre-1940 pieces by Rene Lalique but will consider later pieces.

Man./Prod./Dist.

Jugeat Co., Jacques
400 Veterans Blvd.
Carlstadt, NJ 07072
phone: 201-939-4199
French porcelain, crystal, stemware, dinnerware and giftwares; distributor of Lalique porcelain, crystal, jewelry, silk scarves, and "parfum" in U.S. (crystal patterns are never discontinued.)

Lenox

Man./Prod./Dist.

Lenox China & Crystal Consumer
   Service
100 Lenox Dr.
Lawrenceville, NJ 08648
phone: 609-896-2800 or 800-635-3669
Offers Matching Services List of dealers who offer replacements for current of discontinued Lenox items; also gives insurance estimates.

Lenox Shop
P.O. Box 1115
Mt. Pleasant, PA 15666
phone: 800-842-3681
Factory where crystal is made. Call to place custom orders for inactive pattern replacements.

Matching Services

Carol Ulrey
Unique Antiques
P.O. Box 15815
San Diego, CA 92175-5815
phone: 619-281-8650
fax: 619-282-8407
e-mail: curley@webcc.net
Specializing in china matching: Haviland, old French and American; also Lenox china and crystal.

Lesley Hall
Lesley's Lenox
24438 SE 46th Place
Los Altos, CA 98029
phone: 206-391-2330 or 800-553-6693
fax: 206-391-3383
Lenox only; specializing in discontinued patterns of Lenox elegant stemware, casual crystal and barware; brochure available; founding member of Haviland Collectors International Foundation.

Libbey

Man./Prod./Dist.

Libbey Glass, Div. of Owens-Illinois
One Seagate
Toledo, OH 43666
phone: 419-247-5000
fax: 419-727-2433

Mary Gregory

Experts

Bob Truitt
5120 White Flint Dr.
Kensington, MD 20895-1037
phone: 301-929-2539
*Author of "Mary Gregory Glass-
ware."*

Milk

Clubs/Associations

Helen Storey
National Milk Glass Collectors Society
Newsletter: Opaque News
46 Almond Dr.
Hershey, PA 17033-1759
phone: 717-534-8585
*Dedicated to the study, collection and
preservation of milk glass items.*

Collectors

June & Stan Sohl
P.O. Box 2291
Salina, KS 67402
phone: 913-823-1320 or 913-823-6627

Arlene Johnson
1113 Birchwood Dr.
Garland, TX 75043

Experts

Barbara Joyce Kaye
P.O. Box 20346
Cherokee Station
New York, NY 10021-0065
*Author of "White Gold: A Primer for
Previously Unlisted Milk Glass, Book
1" (out of print) and "White Gold: A
Primer for Previously Unlisted Milk
Glass, Book II."*

April M. Tvorak
P.O. Box 94
Warren Center, PA 18851
phone: 717-395-3775
*Buys and sells pink milk glass
including Jeanette, Cambridge,
Fenton, Westmoreland, etc.*

Myrna & Bob Garrison
Collector's Loot
3816 Hastings Dr.
Arlington, TX 76013-1900
phone: 817-275-6342
fax: 817-275-6342
e-mail: 73074.3655@compuserve.com
*Authors of "Imperial's Vintage Milk
Glass", 1992; available from the
authors for $18.70 ppd. plus $1.32 tax
for TX residents.*

Phyllis Osjecki
Phyllis'
P.O. Box 792
Canyonville, OR 97417
phone: 541-839-4135 or 541-839-6151
Buys, sells, and appraises milk glass.

Museums/Libraries

Houston Antique Museum, The
201 High St.
Chattanooga, TN 37403
phone: 615-267-7176

Moser

Experts

Gary Baldwin
Touch of Glass, A
P.O. Box 213
Simpsonville, MD 21150-0213
phone: 410-997-8425 or 410-765-2439
*Buys, sells and collects European
enameled glass; co-author with Lee
Carno of "Moser - Artistry in Glass."*

Man./Prod./Dist.

Bohemia-Moser
110 00 Praha 1, NA
Prikope 12
Czechoslovakia
The Moser factory.

Mount Washington

Clubs/Associations

Mount Washington Art Glass Society
Magazine: Mount Washington Art Glass
Newsletter, The
P.O. Box 24094
Fort Worth, TX 76124-1094
phone: 817-457-3246 or 817-457-9315
fax: 817-451-9357
*A national society dedicated to the
appreciation, preservation and study
of the art glass wares made by the
Mount Washington Glass Co. from
1870 to 1900.*

Collectors

Henry Tyler
13 Bellevue Dr.
Saint Petersburg, FL 33706-1201

Phillip T. Egelston
P.O. Box 748
Jonesboro, IL 62952-0748
phone: 618-833-2862
*Consultant, broker, author, expert;
founding editor "The Mount
Washington Art Glass Review"; has
written a book on Mother-of-pearl
satin glass featuring 40 patterns plus
information on decoration, reproduction, rarity.*

Northwood

Experts

Claudia A. Minick
Light Up My Life Antiques
RD 4 Box 307
Blairsville, PA 15717-8942
phone: 412-459-7539
*Specializes in glassware from the
Northwood/Dugan/Diamond Glass
Co. of Indiana, PA including carnival
glass, custard glass, art glass, cut
glass, hand-painted glass, milk glass,*

silver deposit glass, and depression
glass.

Old Morgantown

Clubs/Associations

Old Morgantown Glass Collectors'
Guild
Newsletter: Topics
P.O. Box 894
Morgantown, WV 26507-0894
phone: 304-292-9400
*Dedicated to the education of
members and the preservation of Old
Morgantown glass through the
establishment of a museum in
Morgantown, WV.*

Jerry Gallagher
Morgantown Collectors of America, Inc.
Newsletter: Morgantown Newscaster,
The
420 1st Ave. N.W.
Plainview, MN 55964-1213
phone: 507-534-3511
e-mail: morgantown@aol.com
*The M.C.A. goals are to research and
preserve the history of The Old
Morgantown Glass Company, West
Virginia.*

Orrefors

Man./Prod./Dist.

Orrefors, Inc.
140 Bradford Dr.
Berlin, NJ 08009
phone: 609-768-5400
fax: 609-768-9726
*Crystal stemware and giftware, bar
accessories, Christmas ornaments,
and art glass.*

Paden City

Experts

Michael Krumme
P.O. Box 5542 - Dept. CIC
Santa Monica, CA 90409-5542
phone: 213-936-4214
e-mail: mkrumme@pacbell.net
*Author/researcher seeks any printed
information regarding the Paden City
Glass Mfg. Co. of Paden City, WV;
1916-1952 catalogs, trade journal
ads, previously published articles;
please price & describe; no Paden
City Pottery Co., please.*

Pairpoint

Man./Prod./Dist.

Valerie Kelly
Pairpoint Glass Works
851 Sandwich Rd.
P.O. Box 515
Sagamore, MA 02561
phone: 508-888-2344 or 800-899-0953
fax: 508-888-3537
*Blowing room open to visitors;
catalog $2 (refundable.)*

Pattern

Clubs/Associations

Bill & Jo Reidenbach
Early American Pattern Glass Society
P.O. Box 340023
Columbus, OH 43234-0023
phone: 207-695-3909 or 614-885-0853
Devoted solely to pattern glass.

Dealers

Bill & Elaine Henderson
EAPG Inc.
1220 Monroe, NE
Albuquerque, NM 87110
phone: 505-268-0819
fax: 505-266-7204
e-mail: ElaineEAPG@aol.com
*Pattern matching service exclusively
for early American pattern glass
tableware, 1850-1910; sellers may list
their inventory in a computer
database at no charge; free computer
searches for collectors.*

Experts

Dori Miles
Pattern Glass Historian
B20
Crown Point, NY 12928
phone: 518-597-3432
*Buys, sells, appraises, collects,
specializes in pattern glass; over
13,000 pieces in stock; lid and base
matching service; want lists wanted;
former pattern glass editor for
Warman's; contributing editor for
Glass Collectors Digest.*

John & Alice Ahfeld
2634 Royal Rd.
Lancaster, PA 17603
phone: 717-397-7313
*Advisor to "Warman's Antiques &
Collectibles Price Guide."*

Mike Anderton
6619 52 St. NE
Marysville, WA 98270
phone: 206-334-1902
*Advisor to "Warman's Antiques &
Collectibles Price Guide."*

Periodicals

David Richardson
Antique Publications
Magazine: Glass Collector's Digest
P.O. Box 553
Marietta, OH 45750-0553
phone: 800-533-3433 or 614-373-6146
fax: 614-373-6917
e-mail: 76710.2337@compuserve.com
*A bi-monthly magazine focusing on
the glass collecting specialties;
articles and ads feature lots of color
photography.*

Pattern (Moon & Star)

Clubs/Associations

Linda & George Breeze
Moon & Star Collectors Club
Newsletter: Moon & Star Club News
4207 Fox Creek
Mount Vernon, IL 62864
phone: 618-244-3567

Phoenix

Clubs/Associations

Mark Lawyer
Phoenix & Consolidated Glass
  Collectors' Club
Newsletter: Phoenix & Consolidated
  Collectors News & Views
P.O. Box 3847
Edmond, OK 73083-3847
phone: 405-341-0020
e-mail: mcdd@aol.com
Internet: http://
  www.collectoronline.com/club-
  PCGCC-wp.html
  *For collectors/dealers of art glass
  produced by Phoenix Glass Co. of
  Monaca, PA and Consolidated Lamp
  & Shade Co. of Coraopolis, PA; bi-
  monthly newsletter - market trends,
  repro. alerts, buy/sell ads, price
  reports, articles.*

Collectors

Kathy Hansen
1621 Princess Ave.
Pittsburgh, PA 15216-3738
phone: 412-561-3379
  *Wants to buy Phoenix glass: vases,
  bowls, boxes, oil lamps, light shades,
  Reuben Line, Vollenden Ware,
  catalogs, ads, photos, postcards;
  compiling history of the Phoenix Glass
  Co. from 1880 to present; seeks others
  interested in Phoenix.*

Barbara Norman
P.O. Box 251382
West Bloomfield, MI 48325-1382
phone: 248-855-7766
fax: 248-855-5224
e-mail: bnorman7282@aol.com
  *Wants to buy Ruba Rombic, red or
  cased pieces of Phoenix or Consolidated Art Glass, Catalonian, and
  Muncie Ruba Rombic.*

Mark Lawyer
P.O. Box 3847
Edmond, OK 73083-3847
phone: 405-341-0020
e-mail: mcdd@aol.com
Internet: http://
  www.collectoronline.com/club-
  PCGCC-wp.html

Scott Montroy
P.O. Box 182082
Arlington, TX 76096-2082
phone: 817-467-0537
e-mail: connix@flash.net
Internet: http://www.flash.net/~connix
  Editor of the "Phoenix & Consoli-

dated Glass Collectors News &
Views" bi-monthly newsletter.

Dealers

Susan Frost
806 Rosedale Terrace
Austin, TX 78704-3159
phone: 512-447-2575 or 512-447-0407
e-mail: Reuter@io.com
  *Buys and sells Phoenix & Consoli-
  dated glass.*

Experts

Kathy Hansen
1621 Princess Ave.
Pittsburgh, PA 15216-3738
phone: 412-561-3379
  *Wants to buy Phoenix glass: vases,
  bowls, boxes, oil lamps, light shades,
  Reuben Line, Vollenden Ware,
  catalogs, ads, photos, postcards;
  compiling history of the Phoenix Glass
  Co. from 1880 to present; seeks others
  interested in Phoenix.*

Jack D. Wilson
P.O. Box 81974
Chicago, IL 60681-0974
phone: 773-282-9553
e-mail: jdwilson1@earthlink.com
Internet: http://home.earthlink.net/
  ~jdwilson1/
  *Author of "Phoenix & Consolidated
  Art Glass: 1926-1980"; features in-
  depth research, 48 color pages
  illustrating over 750 items; available
  from author for $34.95 + $2.50
  postage; wants original Phoenix
  catalogs & company literature.*

Pilgrim

Clubs/Associations

Pilgrim Cameo/Art Glass Club
Newsletter: PAGC Notebook
P.O. Box 395
Ceredo, WV 25507
phone: 304-453-3553
  Focuses on Pilgrim cameo/art glass.

Pilgrim Cranberry Glass Collectors Club
Newsletter: PCGCC Newsletter
P.O. Box 395
Ceredo, WV 25507
phone: 304-453-3553
  *For those interested in Pilgrim
  cranberry glass.*

Post-WWII

Clubs/Associations

April M. Tvorak
Postwar Glass & Other Oddities Club
Newsletter: 50's Flea!!!, The
P.O. Box 94
Warren Center, PA 18851
phone: 717-395-3775
  *Members interested in 1940s-1970s
  glass and other items; the yearly
  covers any kitchen glass subject from
  1940-1970; free for members; please
  include SASE with all correspondence.*

Matching Services

April M. Tvorak
P.O. Box 94
Warren Center, PA 18851
phone: 717-395-3775
  *Buys, sells, matches any glassware
  from 1940-1970; please include SASE
  with all correspondence.*

Pressed

Museums/Libraries

Schminck Memorial Museum
128 South E St.
Lakeview, OR 97630-1721
phone: 503-947-3134
  *Large collection of American pressed
  glass, 1830-1920.*

Reed & Barton

Man./Prod./Dist.

Reed & Barton
144 W. Britannia St.
Taunton, MA 02780
phone: 508-824-6611 or 800-822-1824
fax: 508-822-7269
  *Produces china, crystal, silver,
  silverplate, and stainless flatware,
  collectible plates, bells, dolls,
  ornaments and accessories.*

Riverside

Experts

Cliff Gorham
Heartlights
P.O. Box 2962
Springfield, MO 65801
phone: 800-833-2007
fax: 417-473-6466
  *Author of "Riverside Glasswork of
  Wellsburg, WV 1879-1907," available
  from author for $35 ppd.; focuses on
  Riverside bar accessories, vases,
  bowls, decorative objects, presenta-
  tion awards.*

Rose Bowls

Clubs/Associations

Johanna & Sean Billings
Rose Bowl Collectors Club
Newsletter: Rose Bowl Collectors Club
  Newsletter
111 Delps Rd.
Danielsville, PA 18038
phone: 610-760-0953 or 717-333-4561
fax: 610-760-8780
e-mail: bankie@concentric.net
Internet: http://www.facets.net/facets/
  freeserv-edu/rosebowl/
  *Free sample newsletter; club helps
  collectors identify and appreciate both
  old and new rose bowls; newsletter
  buy and sell ads free to members.*

Collectors

Johanna & Sean Billings
111 Delps Rd.
Danielsville, PA 18038
phone: 610-760-0953 or 717-333-4561
fax: 610-760-8780
e-mail: bankie@concentric.net
Internet: http://www.facets.net/facets/
  freeserv-edu/rosebowl/
  *Author of several articles on rose
  bowls.*

Sandwich

Museums/Libraries

Sandwich Glass Museum
Journal: Acorn, The
129 Main St.
P.O. Box 103
Sandwich, MA 02563
phone: 508-888-0251
  *The museum contains and studies
  glass associated with the Sandwich
  Factory era.*

Scandinavian Art

Dealers

Anita L. Grashof
Gallerie Ani'tiques
Stage House Village
Park & Front Streets
Scotch Plains, NJ 07076
phone: 908-322-4600 or 201-377-3032
fax: 201-765-9565
  *Buys, sells, appraises Swedish
  (Orrefors, Kosta, glass by Gate, Hald,
  Lindstand) and Finish (Karhula,
  Littala, glass by Wirkkala, Sarpaneva)
  art glass; also Finnish (Tittala,
  Karhula, Wirkkala, Sarpaneva).*

Shoes

Clubs/Associations

Earlene Freeman
Miniature Shoe Collectors Club
P.O. Box 2390
Apple Valley, CA 92308-0045
phone: 760-868-5814 or 909-624-2402

Experts

Libby Yalom
Shoe Lady, The
P.O. Box 7146
Hyattsville, MD 20787-7146
phone: 301-422-2026
fax: 301-422-0713
e-mail: libbyshoes@aol.com
  *Wants to buy glass and china slippers,
  shoes and boots; author of "Shoes of
  Glass" (Antique Publications.)*

Silver Overlay

Collectors

Milan
P.O. Box 971002
Boca Raton, FL 33497-1002
phone: 800-852-8119 or 561-852-0861
fax: 561-852-0862
e-mail: mylan @ix.netcom.com
Internet: http://members.tripod.com/
~mylan/padsbwbble.html
*Wants to buy silver overlay vases,
perfumes, decanters - beautifully
decorated and mint.*

Souvenir & Commemorative

(see also SOUVENIR & COMMEMO-
RATIVE ITEMS)

Periodicals

Gary Leveille
Newsletter: Antique Souvenir Collector
P.O. Box 562
Great Barrington, MA 01230-0562
phone: 413-528-5490
*The nationwide marketplace for
antique souvenirs of all kinds:
souvenir china, spoons, photos, glass,
postcards - anything souvenir.*

St. Louis

(see PAPERWEIGHTS)

Steuben

Dealers

Jeff E. Purtell
P.O. Box 28
Amherst, NH 03031-0028
phone: 603-673-4331 or 800-973-4331
fax: 603-673-1525
*Buys and sells Steuben animals,
exhibition pieces, etc.*

Experts

Stephen Milne
Stephen Milne Collection
45 Tudor City Place, Ste. 210
New York, NY 10017-7615
phone: 212-687-4420 or 800-322-7337
fax: 212-687-4420
e-mail: cardrstubn@aol.com
*Buys and sells the finest Carder
Steuben; the Stephen Milne Collection
has been praised by the Smithsonian
Inst., and acclaimed in publications
such as the NY Times, San Francisco
Business Times, House Beautiful, and
on national TV.*

Man./Prod./Dist.

Steuben Glass
715 Fifth Ave.
New York, NY 10022
phone: 212-752-1441
*Bar accessories, vases, bowls, lead
crystal, decorative objects, presentation awards.*

Museums/Libraries

Robert F. Rockwell, III
Rockwell Museum, The
111 Cedar St.
Corning, NY 14830
phone: 607-937-5386
fax: 607-974-4536
e-mail: rmuseum@stny.1run.com
Internet: http://www.stny.1run.com/
RockwellMuseum
*Largest public exhibition (2,000+
examples) of Frederick Carder's
Steuben Glass, 1903-1932, and
Carder's later glass sculpture; also
permanent exhibitions of Western art,
firearms, Native American artifacts,
antique toys.*

Stretch

Clubs/Associations

Stretch Glass Society
Newsletter: SGS Newsletter
P.O. Box 573
Hampshire, IL 60140
*For collectors of iridescent stretch
glass made by such companies as
Fenton, Imperial and Northwood;
annual convention late April;
newsletter contains articles submitted
by membership; line drawings of
shapes by company.*

Collectors

John Madeley
7720 Deer Rd.
Woodridge, IL 60517
phone: 708-985-7201
Wants to buy iridescent stretch glass.

Dealers

William Crowl
1500 Avery St.
Parkersburg, WV 26101
phone: 304-422-5042
*Buys and sells unusual shapes and
colors of stretch glass; one piece or
entire collection.*

Experts

Kitty & Russell Umbraco
P.O. Box 5331
Richmond, CA 94805-0331
phone: 510-235-1656
*Buys and sells; author of "Iridescent
Stretch Glass."*

Studio (Contemporary)

Dealers

Sarah Hansen
Glass Gallery
4720 Hampden
Bethesda, MD 20814-2910
phone: 301-657-3478
fax: 301-657-3478
Internet: http://www.artresources.com/
the.glass.gallery.html
*Retails one-of-a-kind contemporary
glass sculptures and wall pieces;
emphasizes glass as an art form.*

Periodicals

Uta Klotz, Ed.
Kunsthandwerk & Design
Magazine: Neu Glaz (New Glass)
Rudolf - Diesel - Str. 5-7
Frechen 50226 Germany
phone: +49 2234 1866 21
fax: +49 2234 1866 90
*Many well illustrated bilingual
articles on contemporary European as
well as U.S. studio glass; reports
worldwide.*

Sulphides-Cameos In Glass

Museums/Libraries

Alex Vance, ExDir
Bergstrom-Mahler Museum
165 N. Park Ave.
Neenah, WI 54956
phone: 414-751-4658 or 414-751-4672

Tiffin

Clubs/Associations

Ruth Hemminger, Pres.
Tiffin Glass Collectors' Club
Newsletter: Tiffin Glassmasters
P.O. Box 554
Tiffin, OH 44883-0554
phone: 419-447-5505
Internet: http://www.wavefront.com/
~eag/club.html
*Established in 1985 to study and
preserve the fine glassware produced
from 1892-1984 by the Tiffin Glass
Company, Tiffin, OH; holds glass
shows and fund raisers to benefit the
Tiffin Glass Museum; monthly
meetings in Tiffin.*

Collectors

Cliff McCaslin
Rocliff Communications
8422 N. Park Ct.
Kansas City, MO 64155
phone: 816-436-7719
fax: 816-436-6955
e-mail: rocliff@unicom.net
*Collects all patterns of Tiffin
glassware (US Glass Company -
Factory R).*

Cliff McCaslin
Rocliff Communications
8422 N. Park Ct.
Kansas City, MO 64155
phone: 816-436-7719
fax: 816-436-6955
e-mail: rocliff@unicom.net

Toy

(see CHILDREN'S THINGS)

Vaseline

Clubs/Associations

Jerry Chambers
Vaseline Glass Collectors
Newsletter: Vaseline Glass Networking
Newsletter
2163 Pomona Place
Fairfield, CA 94533
phone: 707-425-6166

Verlys

Experts

R. Rosenberg
P.O. Box 554
Hicksville, NY 11802-0554
phone: 516-669-5321
fax: 516-333-4149
*Wants to buy Verlys, also Val St.
Lambert and Baccarat.*

Carole & Wayne McPeek
McPeek Antiques & Books
1211 Pembroke Rd.
Newark, OH 43055-1627
phone: 614-344-7846
*Authors of "Verlys of America
Decorative Art, 1935-1951" (1992);
advisor to "Warman's Antiques &
Collectibles Price Guide"; author of
"Verlys of France" (1993).*

Waterford

Man./Prod./Dist.

Waterford Wedgwood USA Inc.
P.O. Box 1276
Wall, NJ 07719
phone: 908-938-5800
fax: 908-938-6915
Crystal stemware.

Wave Crest

Appraisers

Peggy Sebek, ISA, AAA
Century Appraisals, Inc.
3255 Glencairn Rd.
Shaker Heights, OH 44122-3407
phone: 216-991-2356 or 318-232-5100

Clubs/Associations

Linda Johnson, Sec.
Wave Crest Collectors Club
P.O. Box 2722
Meriden, CT 06450
phone: 203-237-4733

Dealers

Ward Stewart
Stewart's Antiques
1000 Coolidge
Lafayette, LA 70503-2336
phone: 318-232-2957

Lyn Livingston, ISA CAPP
Remember When Antiques &
  Collectibles
P.O. Box 42224
Oklahoma City, OK 73132-3224
phone: 405-722-7034 or 405-721-1475
fax: 405-722-5754
e-mail: 76235.1441@compuserve.com
  *Desires exchange of ideas, identifica-
  tion tips and impressions on C.F.
  Monroe glass with other collectors;
  also buys and sells.*

Westmoreland

Clubs/Associations

Steve Jensen
Westmoreland Glass Society
Newsletter: Westmoreland Glass Society
  Newsletter
P.O. Box 2883
Iowa City, IA 52244-2883
phone: 319-337-9647
  *Sponsors annual Westmoreland Glass
  convention, auction and souvenir
  limited edition items.*

Collectors

Daniel Sperry
P.O. Box 949
Denville, NJ 07834-0949
  *Wants to buy Westmoreland glass,
  especially Ruby Stain; also wants
  Westmoreland catalogs.*

Jim Fisher
513 Fifth Ave.
Coralville, IA 52241
phone: 319-354-5011

Kathryn Hickey
P.O. Box 322
Oxford Junction, IA 52323

Dealers

Cynthia Pergantides
MediaSpecialists Westmoreland Gallery
  On-Line
28 Revell Ave.
Northampton, MA 01060
phone: 413-586-7571 or 413-584-1034
fax: 413-584-1034
e-mail: milkglass@mediaspec.com
Internet: http://www.mediaspec.com/
  GNET/wmoreland
  *Buys, sells, specializes in
  Westmoreland glass; checkout the on-
  line catalog.*

Betty J. Viecelli
Viecelli Antiques & Collectibles
615 Gaskill Ave.
Jeannette, PA 15644
phone: 412-863-3677 or 412-527-2222

Experts

Ruth Grizel
P.O. Box 143
North Liberty, IA 52317-0143
phone: 319-626-2807
fax: 319-626-2807
  *Author of two books about
  Westmoreland Glass.*

Museums/Libraries

Phillip Rosso
Westmoreland Glass Museum
1815 Trimble Ave.
Port Vue, PA 15133
phone: 412-678-7352
  *Over 4,000 pieces on display; original
  photos, tools, molds, etc.; also
  wholesales glass.*

Periodicals

Ruth Grizel, Ed.
Newsletter: Original Westmoreland
  Collectors Newsletter, The
P.O. Box 143
North Liberty, IA 52317-0143
phone: 319-626-2807
fax: 319-626-2807
  *Full color monthly publication for
  Westmoreland glass collectors and
  dealers; features classified section,
  plus articles and photos; sponsors
  yearly glass convention; over 1,400
  subscribers worldwide.*

Wheaton

Clubs/Associations

Lois Clark
Classic Wheaton Club
Newsletter: Classic Wheaton Club
  Newsletter
c/o Creative WHeaton Collectibles
P.O. Box 59
Downingtown, PA 19335
phone: 610-692-4474

Whimsies

Clubs/Associations

Lon Knickerbocker
Whimsey Club, The
Newsletter: Whimsical Notions
20 William St.
Dansville, NY 14337
phone: 716-335-6506
  *For collectors of hand blown glass
  whimsies such as ink pens, smoke
  bells, flip flops, witch balls, canes,
  rolling pins, etc.*

Collectors

Chris Davis
522 Woodhill
Newark, NY 14513
phone: 315-331-4078 or 716-652-7752
  *Founder of The Whimsey Club;
  interested in hand blown glass
  whimsies such as smoke bells, flip
  flops, witch balls, canes, rolling pins,
  etc.*

Jeff & Mary Waterhouse
4544 Cairo Dr.
Whitehall, PA 18052

Experts

Joyce Blake
1220 Stolle Rd.
Elma, NY 14059
phone: 716-652-7752
  *Advisor to "Warman's Antiques &
  Collectibles Price Guide."*

Whimsies (Pens)

(see also PENS)

Experts

Lon & Trina Knickerbocker
20 William St.
Dansville, NY 14437
phone: 716-335-6506
  *Collects glass ink pens; advisor to
  "Warman's Antiques & Collectibles
  Price Guide."*

Witches Balls

Collectors

Sylvia Hopkins
39 Highland St.
Dedham, MA 02026

GLASS (MODERN)

Clubs/Associations

Penny Berk, Ex. Dir.
Glass Art Society
Journal: Glass Art Society Journal
1305 4th Ave. #711
Seattle, WA 98101-2401
phone: 206-382-1305
fax: 206-382-2630
e-mail: glassartsoc@earthlink.net
Internet: http://www.best.com/~gas
  *An international organization to
  encourage excellence and to advance
  the appreciation, understanding and
  development of the glass arts.*

GLASS EYES

Collectors

Donald Gorlick
P.O. Box 24541
Seattle, WA 98124-0541
phone: 206-824-0508
  *Wants human glass eyes, either left or
  right, colors and size unimportant,
  just human eyes.*

GLASS KNIVES

Collectors

Brenda Macomber
RD 3 Box 201-K
Delta, PA 17314-9588
phone: 717-456-6116
  *Wants Depression-era glass knives,
  daggers, and butter spreaders.*

Wilbur Peterson
711 Kelly Dr.
Lebanon, TN 37087
phone: 615-444-4303

Doug Heaton
8723 Artesia Blvd.
Bellflower, CA 90706
  *Wants to buy glass knives; give price
  and description; all letters answered.*

Adrienne S. Escoe
4448 Ironwood Ave.
Seal Beach, CA 90740-2926
phone: 562-430-6479 or 562-598-1585
e-mail: escoebliss@earthlink.net
  *Wants to buy rare glass knives (used
  for fruit and cake, given away at
  World's Fairs and Expositions as
  souvenirs) especially forest green,
  amber and rare crystal.*

Michele Rosewitz
P.O. Box 3843
San Bernardino, CA 92413
phone: 909-862-8534
  *Wants to buy glass knives; especially
  ribbed handle knives, opal, forest
  green, amber, cobalt, and ruby colors;
  please describe and price.*

GLASSES

(see also BREWERIANA; EYE
RELATED ITEMS, Eyeglasses; FAST
FOOD COLLECTIBLES; SPORTS
COLLECTIBLES, Thoroughbred
Racing; STEINS; SWANKYSWIGS)

Dealers

Gail Busche
Archangel Antiques
334 East Ninth St.
New York, NY 10003-7924
phone: 212-260-9313
  *Buying antique buttons, cuff links, eye
  glasses, and vintage lighters; always
  seeking fine examples such as enamel
  Deco and Art Nouveau.*

Drinking

Auction Services

Pete Kroll
Glasses, Mugs & Steins Auction
P.O. Box 207
Sun Prairie, WI 53590-0207
phone: 608-837-4818
fax: 608-825-4205
  *Produces a semi-annual mail auction
  featuring collectible advertising
  glasses, mugs & steins: beer, soda,
  cartoon, Disney, root beer, Budweiser,
  whiskey shot glasses, whiskey
  pitchers, etc.*

Tom Hoder
Tom Hoder Collectables
444 S. Cherry
Itasca, IL 60143-2109
phone: 708-773-2635
  *Conducts mail-bid auctions of
  cartoon, character, and horse racing
  drinking glasses three times each year
  (15th of January, April, and October.)*

Clubs/Associations

Mark E. Chase
Promotional Glass Collectors Association
3991 Bethel Rd.
New Wilmington, PA 16142
phone: 412-946-2838
fax: 412-946-9012
e-mail: cgn@glassnews.com
Internet: http://www.glassnews.com
Association of promotional drinking glass collectors - cartoon, character, sports, soft drink, root beer, advertising, Disney, etc.; regional and national meetings; buy, sell, trade.

Collectors

Matt Maloney
390 S. Broadway
Lindenhurst, NY 11757

Tim Russell
245 East St., Apt. 101
Honeoye Falls, NY 14472-1235

Steve Zehr
P.O. Box 74
Fogelsville, PA 18051

Carl Sehnert
4595 Limestone Lane
Memphis, TN 38141-7870
phone: 901-794-8723

Ed Dunwoody
3055 Handview Dr.
Rochester, MI 48306
phone: 810-362-1750 or 810-659-9322

Tom Hoder
444 S. Cherry
Itasca, IL 60143-2109
phone: 708-773-2635
Specializing in cartoon, character and horse racing drinking glasses.

Carol Markowski
3141 W. Platte Ave.
Colorado Springs, CO 80904
phone: 719-633-7399
Wants to buy drinking glasses with cartoon figures on them: Pepsi, Coke, fast food logos, early Disney, sports, etc.

Jim Pojmonski, ISA
P.O. Box 1232
Dolan Springs, AZ 86441-1232
phone: 602-767-4774 or 602-767-4107
fax: 602-767-3900

Les & Bev Chapman
P.O. Box 638
Lindsay, CA 93247
Major collector of drinking glasses.

Dealers

Dale & Debbie Morrison
1810 Ferry St.
Easton, PA 18042
phone: 610-250-0242
Wants to buy cartoon, super heroes, sports drinking glasses.

Jimmy Driver
Glasses Galore
934 Greenbriar Dr.
Harrisonburg, VA 22801
phone: 540-434-5193
e-mail: glasgalore@aol.com
Wants to buy character and promotional drinking glasses: Pepsi, Coke, fast food, sports, Peanut Butter, and other food products.

Jay Honan
4349 Robertson Rd.
Stuart, FL 34997
phone: 407-286-8845
Buys, sells and trades cartoon and character drinking glasses.

Pat & Larry Aikins
Lunch Box Connection
Rt. 5, Box 5174
Athens, TX 75751
phone: 903-675-3765

Experts

Michael J. Kelly
108 Poplar Forest Dr.
P.O. Box 308
Slippery Rock, PA 16057
phone: 412-946-2838 or 412-794-2540
fax: 412-946-9012
e-mail: cgn@glassnews.com
Internet: http://www.glassnews.com
Buys and sells cartoon, sports, and fast-food drinking glasses: Disney, super heroes from '30s to present; author of books on same.

Mark E. Chase
3991 Bethel Rd.
New Wilmington, PA 16142
phone: 412-946-2838
fax: 412-946-9012
e-mail: cgn@glassnews.com
Internet: http://www.glassnews.com
Author of "Drinking Glass Collectibles," and "Contemporary Fast-Food & Drinking Glass Collectibles," co-editor of "Collector Glass News"; wants to buy cartoon, sports and fast-food drinking glasses from the '30s to the present.

Pete Kroll
Glasses, Mugs & Steins Auction
P.O. Box 207
Sun Prairie, WI 53590-0207
phone: 608-837-4818
fax: 608-825-4205
Buys and sells collectible advertising glasses, mugs, & steins.

Hazel Marie Weatherman
Weatherman Glass Books
Rte. 7 Box 7540
Ozark, MO 65721
phone: 417-581-7812
Author of "The Decorated Tumbler."

Lynn Geyer
Lynn Geyer Advertising Auctions
300 Trail Ridge
Silver City, NM 88061-6071
phone: 505-538-2341
fax: 505-388-9000
Conducts semi-annual mail/phone bid

specialized auctions on all aspects of breweriana and soda-pop; also contemporary steins, mugs & drinking glasses.*

Periodicals

Michael J. Kelly
Newsletter: Collector Glass News
108 Poplar Forest Dr.
P.O. Box 308
Slippery Rock, PA 16057
phone: 412-946-2838 or 412-794-2540
fax: 412-946-9012
e-mail: cgn@glassnews.com
Internet: http://www.glassnews.com
Information for the collector of cartoon, fast food, sports and promotional glassware; each issue features articles, classified ads, new issues, and an auction; co-author with Mark Chase of "Collectible Drinking Glasses."

Dave & Kathy Nader
Newsletter: Root Beer Float
P.O. Box 571
Lake Geneva, WI 53147

Shot

Auction Services

Lawrence Powers
Shot Glass Exchange
P.O. Box 219
Western Springs, IL 60558-0219
phone: 708-246-1559
fax: 708-246-1559
Created in 1989 to provide an open national market for buyers and sellers of whiskey tumblers and shot glasses via the semi-annual mail-bid auction; color photos and bid tab provided for each catalog; sells books on shot glasses.

Clubs/Associations

Mark Pickvet
Shot Glass Club of America, The
Newsletter: Shot of News
5071 Watson Dr.
Flint, MI 48506
Members collect shot glasses; the newsletter is published monthly and contains articles about new and old shot glasses, where to obtain them, membership directories, etc.

Collectors

Carl F. Pflanzer
73 Cloverhill Dr.
Flanders, NJ 07836
e-mail: carl@ewacars.com
Internet: http://www.ewacars.com
Wants to buy shot glasses, advertising spirits glasses, and foreign shot glasses.

Experts

Mark Pickvet
5071 Watson Dr.
Flint, MI 48506
Author of "Shot Glasses: An American Tradition" (Antique Publications.)

Spirit (Advertising)

Collectors

Carl F. Pflanzer
73 Cloverhill Dr.
Flanders, NJ 07836
e-mail: carl@ewacars.com
Internet: http://www.ewacars.com
Wants to buy shot glasses, advertising spirits glasses, and foreign shot glasses.

GLIDERS

(see AIRPLANES, Sailplanes)

GLOBES

(see also ATLASES; EXIT GLOBES; GAS STATION COLLECTIBLES, Pumps & Globes; INSTRUMENTS & DEVICES; MAPS & CHARTS)

Dealers

George D. Glazer
28 East 72nd St. at Madison Ave.
New York, NY 10021
phone: 212-535-5706
fax: 212-988-3992
e-mail: worldglobe@aol.com
Buys and sells terrestrial and celestial globes, orreries, armillary spheres, maps, etc.

John Forster
Barometer Fair
P.O. Box 25502
Sarasota, FL 34277
phone: 941-923-6136
fax: 941-923-6136
e-mail: barometer@glimmer.com
Buys, sells, restores all antique barometers; also deals in antique maps, globes, compasses, telescopes and other scientific instruments.

Murray Hudson
Murray Hudson - Antiquarian Books & Maps
109 S. Church St.
P.O. Box 163
Halls, TN 38040-0163
phone: 901-836-9057 or 800-748-9946
fax: 901-836-9057
e-mail: mapman@usit.net
Internet: http://css.ecis.net/hudson
Buys/sells pre-1900 antique maps (especially pocket, wall, Civil War and railroad maps) & books with maps (e.g. atlases, travel guides, geographies, land surveys, etc.); esp. of S.E. & S.W. US; also wants pre-1950 world globes.

GO-KARTS

(see also SOAP BOX DERBY)

Clubs/Associations

Kart Expo International
P.O. Box 101
Wheaton, IL 60189
phone: 708-653-7368
fax: 708-653-2637
*Conducts annual Kart Expo
International.*

GOLD

(see also COINS & CURRENCY;
GEMS & JEWELRY)

Dealers

Blanchard & Co.
P.O. Box 61740
New Orleans, LA 70161-1740
phone: 800-880-4653
fax: 504-837-4884
Internet: http//
www.blanchardonline.com
*Dealers in rare coins and precious
metals.*

Judy Brown
P.O. Box 5368
Frazier Park, CA 93222
phone: 805-242-5411
*Mail order only dealer of gold and
silver smalls: boxes, chatelaines,
match safes, sewing items, Victorian
or earlier frames and silverplate
items; long time dealer.*

Periodicals

M. Murenbeeld & Associates
Newsletter: Gold Monitor
P.O. Box 6187, Depot #1
Victoria
Brit. Columbia V8P 5L5 Canada
phone: 604-477-7579

Newsletter: Gold & Money
P.O. Box 4634
Greenwich, CT 06830
phone: 203-661-5474
*A commentary on precious metals and
monetary matters.*

Newsletter: Gold News, The
1112 16th St. NW, Ste. 240
Washington, DC 20036
phone: 202-835-0185

Newsletter: Silver & Gold Report
P.O. Box 109665
West Palm Beach, FL 33410
phone: 800-289-9222 or 561-627-3300
fax: 561-625-6685
e-mail: sgr@weissinc.com
Internet: http://www.wessinc.com
*Financial advice newsletter in
precious medals, and gold & silver
bullion and coins.*

Newsletter: Moneypower
1304 Edgewood Ave.
Ann Arbor, MI 48103-5522
phone: 612-537-8096
*Consumer periodical on buying and
selling gold.*

Scrap

Dealers

Jim Sciuto
GoldTek
P.O. Box 128
Methuen, MA 01844
phone: 508-374-2254 or 603-645-4717
fax: 508-373-1088
Internet: http://www.pm-connect.com/
sciuto/
*Buys scrap gold and silver: class
rings, wedding bands, gold coins, gold
watches, gold plated circuit boards,
gold solder, gold wire, gold teeth;
also scrap sterling silver flatware,
coins, bars, silver flake, silver anodes,
etc.*

Greg Walsh
32 River View Lane
P.O. Box 747
Potsdam, NY 13676
phone: 315-265-9111 or 800-371-9286
fax: 315-265-9222
*Wants to buy gold and silver rings,
coins, estate jewelry, pocket watches,
diamonds, sterling silver items, scrap
gold, broken or damaged jewelry,
dental gold, etc.; 24-hour turn
around; ship on approval or call for
quote; since 1979.*

Michael A. Merrill
Michael A. Merrill, Inc.
Crestar Bank Building
2045 York Rd.
Timonium, MD 21093
phone: 410-453-9400
e-mail: merrill@home.com
Internet: http://members.home.net/
merrill/
*Buying precious metals from the
public, dealers since 1974; buys scrap
gold, diamonds, old gold, dental gold,
school rings, gold & silver numismatic
coins, sterling silver (Kirk & Steiff),
Franklin Mint, platinum, palladium,
exotics.*

Cy Phillips, Jr.
S C Coin & Stamp Co. Inc.
P.O. Drawer 661180
Arcadia, CA 91066-1180
phone: 818-445-8277 or 800-367-0779
fax: 818-445-8278
*Tokens, medals, coins, currency,
badges, expo. and fair items, scrap
gold and silver.*

GOLD LEAF

(see REPAIR/RESTORATION/
CONSERVATION, Gilding)

GOLD RUSH MEMORABILIA

Collectors

Chester Jaffee
P.O. Box 5369
Berkeley, CA 94705
*Wants items relating to the California
Gold Rush 1848-1858.*

Dealers

Cy Phillips, Jr.
S C Coin & Stamp Co. Inc.
P.O. Drawer 661180
Arcadia, CA 91066-1180
phone: 818-445-8277 or 800-367-0779
fax: 818-445-8278
*Wants gold rush items; also historical
trail items; old west town tokens.*

Museums/Libraries

Yukon Archives
Box 2703
Whitehorse
Yukon Territory Y1A 2C6 Canada
phone: 403-667-5321 or 800-661-0408
fax: 403-667-4253
*Responsible for acquiring, preserving,
displaying documentary sources
related to the Yukon including the
Klondike gold rush; 100,000 photos,
12,000 maps, newspapers, 1,600
hours of sound recordings, etc.*

Dawson City Museum
Box 303
Dawson City
Yukon Territory Y0B 1G0 Canada
phone: 403-993-5291
fax: 403-993-5839
*Maintains an extensive collection of
records and photographs and
provides research services; has over
7,000 photos.*

Klondike Gold Rush National Historical
Park
117 S. Main
Seattle, WA 98104
phone: 206-442-7220

GOOD LUCK ITEMS

(see also COINS & CURRENCY,
Coins [Encased])

Collectors

J.A. Higgins
5017 Walnut
Kansas City, MO 64112-2758
phone: 816-931-4095
*Wants items with "Good Luck" on
them.*

GRANITEWARE

(see also KITCHEN COL-
LECTIBLES)

Clubs/Associations

Dan Allers
National Graniteware Society
Newsletter: National Graniteware News
P.O. Box 10013
Cedar Rapids, IA 52410-0013
phone: 319-393-0252
*For collectors to share information
about graniteware.*

Collectors

Patricia Peltz
24815 Shoshone Dr.
Murrieta, CA 92562-5825
Wants blue graniteware.

Dealers

Rita Mueller
Grange Hall Antiques
1 South Alley
P.O. Box 263
New Market, MD 21774
phone: 301-865-5651
fax: 301-865-0518
e-mail: ritam@erols.com
Internet: http://www.newmarketmd.com/
grange.htm
*Quality Steiff animals from 1950s
through 1980s; always buying one
piece or entire collection: teddy bears,
Schuco, Hermann, Steiff; also fine
country graniteware from Germany
available; mail orders and layaways.*

Bob Techav
Techav's Antiques
220 6th St.
De Witt, IA 52742
phone: 319-659-8365
*Buys and sells graniteware; all types
and all colors.*

Experts

Helen Greguire
Helen's Antiques
103 Trimmer Rd.
Hilton, NY 14468-9305
phone: 716-392-2704
*Author of "The Collector's Encyclope-
dia of Granite Ware."*

Gregg Ellington
Upper Loft Antiques
47 Columbus St.
Wilmington, OH 45177
phone: 513-382-4311
*Buys, sells, trades and collects
graniteware and American ceramics
including mochaware, yellowware,
spongeware, etc.*

Pamela & Allan Luttig
Blue Boar Antiques
P.O. Box 423
Grand Ledge, MI 48837

Gary & Lorraine Boggio
North Wind Antiques
420 E. High St.
Hennepin, IL 61327
phone: 815-925-7264
*Buy, sell and specializes in
graniteware.*

Repro. Sources

Faith Mountain Country Fare
P.O. Box 199
Sperryville, VA 22740

French

Dealers

David T. Pikul
Chuctanunda Antique Company, The
1 Fourth Ave.
Amsterdam, NY 12010-3803
phone: 518-843-3983
fax: 518-843-3983
*Sells French and European enameled
ware: coffee pots, canisters, utensil
racks, etc.; colorful and highly
decorative; free color brochure
available.*

GRAVESTONES

Clubs/Associations

Caylah Pafenbach, Admn.
Association for Gravestone Studies
Newsletter: AGS Quarterly
278 Main St., Ste. 207
Greenfield, MA 01301-3230
phone: 413-772-0836
e-mail: ags@berkshire.net
Internet: http://www.berkshire.net/ags
*The AGS offers information and
restoration referrals for gravestones;
NOTE: Respect gravestones; they are
sacred and not collectible!*

GREETING CARDS

(see CARDS, Greeting; HOLIDAY
COLLECTIBLES; PAPER COL-
LECTIBLES; POSTCARDS;
VALENTINES)

GROCERY STORE ITEMS

(see CEREAL BOXES; FOOD
COLLECTIBLES; PREMIUMS,
Cereal Box)

GUIDES

(see ANTIQUE SHOP DIRECTO-
RIES; FLEA MARKET GUIDES;
TOURS/BUYING TRIPS)

GUINNESS WORLD RECORDS

Museums/Libraries

Guiness World of Records Museum
2780 Las Vegas Blvd., South
Las Vegas, NV 89109
phone: 702-792-3766
*This unique museum brings the
Guiness Book of World Records to
three-dimensional life via life-sized
replicas, computerized databanks and
color videos.*

GUITARS

(see MUSICAL INSTRUMENTS,
String [Guitars])

GUM

(see BUBBLE GUM CARDS;
BUBBLE GUM & CANDY
WRAPPERS; TRADING CARDS,
Non-Sport)

GUMBALL MACHINES

(see COIN-OPERATED MACHINES,
Vending Machines)

GUNFIGHTERS

(see WESTERN AMERICANA)

GUNS

(see ADVERTISING, Firearms
Related; AIRGUNS; ARMS &
ARMOR; CIVIL WAR ARTIFACTS;
FIREARMS; MILITARIA; TOYS, BB
Guns; TOYS, Cap Guns;
TRAPSHOOTING; WESTERN
AMERICANA)

Here are some tips when contacting someone listed in this book:

When requesting information about a particular item, include a description (material, dimensions, maker's mark, model number, etc.) and a photo, sketch, or photocopy of the item in question. ■

Always ask if there are charges for samples or for the services requested. ■

When writing, please be sure to include a Large (#10 business size) Self-Addressed and Stamped Envelope (LSASE) if requesting a reply or the return of photographs. ■

Never call collect unless otherwise directed. When calling, be considerate of time zone differences and always ask if the party you are calling has time to talk. When leaving an answering machine message, always instruct the party to call you back collect. ■

HAIR ACCESSORIES

(see BARBER SHOP COL-
LECTIBLES; BEAUTY SHOP
COLLECTIBLES; CLOTHING &
ACCESSORIES, Vintage; COMBS &
HAIR ACCESSORIES; DRESSER
ITEMS, Hatpins & Hatpin Holders;
GEMS & JEWELRY; SHAVING
COLLECTIBLES)

HAIR WORK

(see also BARBER SHOP COL-
LECTIBLES; BEAUTY SHOP
COLLECTIBLES; SHAVING
COLLECTIBLES)

Clubs/Associations

Ruth Gordon
Hair Art International
Newsletter: H.A.I.R. Line
24629 Cherry St.
Dearborn, MI 48124-3103
phone: 313-277-2479
*H.A.I.R. is an acronym for Hair Art
International Restorers, a society
interested in hair art: collectors, hair
workers, and others interested in the
art of making beautiful things out of
human and animal hair.*

Collectors

Jerry Denzler
P.O. Box 127
Marengo, IA 52301-0127
phone: 319-642-3528 or 319-642-7777
*Wants to buy human hair jewelry and
other items made of hair or with hair
such as framed mourning wreaths,
postcards, buttons, purses; also wants
samples of tablework and equipment
used in weaving hair.*

Dealers

Vince Tartaglione
T-Graphix
P.O. Box 2116
Patterson, NJ 07509-2116
phone: 201-450-8948
*Buys hair and hair related items:
video, photographs, books, ads,
labels, haircutting; long hair or no
hair; Rapunzel, Sutherland Sisters;
also buys braids, ponytails.*

Experts

Ruth Gordon
Cherished Memories
24629 Cherry St.
Dearborn, MI 48124-3103
phone: 313-277-2479
*Practices the art of Victorian
hairweaving to create jewelry;*
*reproduces hairweaving catalog of
pins, earrings, watchfobs, shadow-
boxes, bell jars, etc.; lectures,
magazine articles.*

Wreaths

Museums/Libraries

Leila Cohoon
Leila's Hair Museum
815 West 23rd St.
Independence, MO 64055
phone: 816-252-HAIR
*An interesting display of various items
made from human hair and dating
back to the 1800s; over 150 wreathes
and 500 pieces of hair jewelry.*

HALLMARK

(see COLLECTIBLES [MODERN],
Ornaments [Hallmark])

HALLOWEEN COLLECTIBLES

(see also ANIMAL COLLECTIBLES,
Cats; HOLIDAY COLLECTIBLES;
WITCHES)

Collectors

Mark Bergin
P.O. Box 3073
Peterborough, NH 03458-3073
phone: 603-924-2079
fax: 603-924-2022
*Wants Jack-o'-lanterns, candy
containers, nodders, any figures, die-
cuts, crepe paper, noise makers,
postcards, anything Halloween.*

Linda L. Vines
P.O. Box 43721
Montclair, NJ 07043
phone: 973-748-4990 or 201-748-4990
*Wants to buy pre-1950 decorations
including candy containers, jack-o'-
lanterns, witches, black cats,
skeletons.*

Tom Rutledge
3015 Bever Ave., SE
Cedar Rapids, IA 52403
phone: 319-399-1427
*Wants only pre-1950 Halloween
collectibles including decorations,
postcards, candy containers, lanterns,
invitations, papier-mache items,
plaster of Paris items, etc.*

Dawn Kroma
P.O. Box 143
Brookfield, IL 60513-0143
phone: 708-387-0334 or 708-387-0334
fax: 708-387-0334
e-mail: NooNews@aol.com

David Welch
P.O. Box 714
Murphysboro, IL 62966-0714
phone: 618-687-2282
fax: 618-684-2243
e-mail: PexDude1@aol.com
*Wants Don Post rubber monster
masks (sold through Famous Monster
magazines only); also '50s-'60s
monster, TV, movie, comic, and*
*cartoon costumes; must be in original
boxes; $500 for Captain Action.*

Gwen Daniel
18 Belleau Lake Ct.
O Fallon, MO 63366-3144
phone: 314-978-3190
e-mail: gdaniel@mail.win.org

Casper
3470 E. Pershing Rd.
Lincoln, NE 68502-4835
Wants early Halloween items.

Dealers

Leila Dunbar
Dunbar's Gallery
76 Haven St.
Milford, MA 01757-3821
phone: 508-634-8697 or 508-634-8097
fax: 508-634-8698
*Mail order Americana - no reproduc-
tions; buys, sells and specializes in
vintage character and comic toys,
banks, advertising, automobilia, and
Halloween related items.*

Hugh Alan Luch Collections, The
P.O. Box 111
Wenonah, NJ 08090
phone: 609-464-9751
*Buys and sells illustrator and holiday
collectibles with emphasis on Maxfield
Parrish and Halloween.*

Jenny Tarrant
4 Gardenview Dr.
Saint Peters, MO 63376-3507
phone: 314-397-1763
*Wants Halloween items, papier-mache
candy containers, Jack O'Lanterns,
Halloween party books, party
decorations and favors, Halloween
postcards.*

Paul W. Schofield
Lion's Den Antiques
7988 Bethel Burley Rd. SE
Port Orchard, WA 98366
phone: 360-876-3364
fax: 360-876-5421
*Buys, sells, appraises, and specializes
in old Santas, candy containers,
Halloween, Easter, Christmas, Easter,
Dresden, figural lights.*

Experts

Chris Russell
Halloween Queen
P.O. Box 499
Winchester, NH 03470-0499
phone: 603-239-8875
fax: 603-239-8875
*Author of "Halloween - An American
Holiday" (Schiffer).*

Stuart Schneider
Hudson Valley Graphics
Newsletter: Pens
P.O. Box 64
Teaneck, NJ 07666-0064
phone: 201-261-1983
*Wants to buy Halloween decorations
from the turn-of-the-century to 1960,
especially trick-or-treat bags, party*
*invitations, and Dennisons products;
author of "Halloween in America."*

Periodicals

Chris Russell
Halloween Queen
Newsletter: Trick or Treat Trader, The
P.O. Box 499
Winchester, NH 03470-0499
phone: 603-239-8875
fax: 603-239-8875
*For the collector of Halloween related
memorabilia; published quarterly;
almost 14 years old.*

Dawn Kroma
Kromazone Media
Newsletter: BooNews
P.O. Box 143
Brookfield, IL 60513-0143
phone: 708-387-0334 or 708-387-0334
fax: 708-387-0334
e-mail: NooNews@aol.com
*Quarterly, full color subscription
based newsletter for Halloween
enthusiasts; provides information and
networking regarding old and modern
Halloween collectibles, reproductions,
history, photos, interviews, events,
shows, etc.*

HANDBAGS

(see PURSES)

HANDS

Wooden

Collectors

Donald Gorlick
P.O. Box 24541
Seattle, WA 98124-0541
phone: 206-824-0508
*Wants wooden hands with articulated
fingers; may be a glove stretcher mold
for sizing gloves; wooden with fingers
and thumb that move.*

HARDWARE

(see also ARCHITECTURAL
ELEMENTS; ARCHITECTURE &
RELATED ITEMS; CATALOGS,
Trade; DIAMOND EDGE; DOOR-
KNOBS; FASTENERS; KEEN
KUTTER [SIMMONS HARDWARE];
PLUMBING; REPAIR/RESTORA-
TION/CONSERVATION, Woodwork-
ing; TOOLS; WINCHESTER
COLLECTIBLES)

Appraisers

Rilla Simmons, CAGA
Simmons & Company Auctioneers
Rte. 1 Box 186
Richmond, MO 64085-9760
phone: 816-776-2936
fax: 816-470-5016
e-mail:
simmons_auction@raycounty.com
Internet: http://www.raycounty.com/
simmons.html
Appraises Keen Kutter (Simmons

Hardware), Diamond Edge (Shapleigh Hardware), Winchester tools.

Auction Services

H. Weber Wilson
Web Wilson's Antique Hardware
  Auction
808 51st Avenue Plz. W
Bradenton, FL 34207-2819
phone: 800-508-0022
  Conducts two phone/fax auctions per year of quality builders' hardware including door knobs, bells, shutter pulls, plates, etc.

Experts

H. Weber Wilson
Web Wilson's Antique Hardware
  Auction
808 51st Avenue Plz. W
Bradenton, FL 34207-2819
phone: 800-508-0022

Ron Barlow
Windmill Publishing Co.
2147 Windmill View Rd.
El Cajon, CA 92020-1353
phone: 619-448-5390
  Author of "Victorian Houseware, Hardware, Kitchenware - A Price Guide."

Periodicals

Tom Basore
Hardware Companies Kollectors' Club
Newsletter: Winchester Keen Kutter
  Diamond Edge Chronicles
715 West 20th Ave.
Hutchinson, KS 67502
phone: 316-665-3613 or 816-776-2936
fax: 816-470-5016
e-mail: webmaster@raycounty.com
Internet: http://www.raycounty.com/
  simmons.html
  A non-profit organization to serve as an interactive information distribution center for collectors of Keen Kutter, Diamond Edge, Winchester Store (non-gun), Simmons & Shapleigh and other hardware store brands.

Suppliers

Muff's Antiques
135 S. Glassell St.
Orange, CA 92866
phone: 714-997-0243
fax: 714-997-1601
Internet: http://www.tias.com/amdir/
  SpecTrunks.html
  Has thousands of pieces of hardware in stock both new and old for restoration of furniture and homes from antique to modern: door plates, locks/keys, knobs, light fixtures, electric and oil lamps; catalog $5.

HEALTH & BEAUTY
Devices To Restore

Collectors

Olg Lindan
1404 Dorsh Rd.
Cleveland, OH 44121-3840
phone: 216-382-7113
  Wants old electrotherapeutic and controversial healing devices and related literature; also wants medical, scientific instruments.

HEBRAICA

(see JUDAICA)

HERALDRY

(see BOOKS, Heraldry; COAT OF ARMS)

HERITAGE RESOURCES

(see also AMERICAN INDIAN; ARCHAEOLOGY; PREHISTORIC ARTIFACTS)

Clubs/Associations

National Conference of State Historic
  Preservation Offices
Hall of States, Suite 342
444 North Capitol Street, NW
Washington, DC 20001-1512

National Institute for the Conservation
  of Cultural Property
3299 K St. NW, Ste. 602
Washington, DC 20007
phone: 800-422-4612 or 202-625-1495
fax: 202-625-1485
Internet: nttp://www.nic.org/
  Provides national leadership to promote * facilitate the conservation and preservation of the nation's heritage, including works of art, anthropological artifacts, documents, historic objects, architecture and natural science specimens.

Center for Archaeology in the Public
  Interest
Magazine: Public Archaeology Review
Department of Anthropology
425 University Blvd., IUPUI
Indianapolis, IN 46202-5140

Misc. Services

Repatriation Coordin'tr
American Indian Ritual Object
  Repatriation Foundation
463 East 57th St.
New York, NY 10022-3003
phone: 212-980-9441
fax: 212-421-2746
e-mail: RepatFdn@aol.com
Internet: http://
  www.repatriationfoundation.org
  A non-federally funded intercultural partnership committed to assisting in the return of ceremonial material to American Indian Nations and to educating the public about the importance of repatriation.

Licensing Officer
National Trust for Historic Preservation
Magazine: Preservation
1785 Massachusetts Ave., NW
Washington, DC 20036
phone: 202-588-6000
fax: 202-588-6292
Internet: http://www.nationaltrust.com
  Licenses some of America's leading home furnishings, decorative arts, giftware and collectibles manufacturers to reproduce objects related to Nat. Trust sites, and American history & culture; educates public about historic preservation.

Naval Historical Center, Office of the
  Senior Historian
Washington Navy Yard
901 M Street SE
Washington, DC 20374-5060
phone: 202-433-7229 or 202-433-7230
fax: 202-433-3593
  Department of Navy ship and aircraft wrecks remain government property; questions and information concerning historic U.S. Navy aircraft and shipwrecks should be addressed to the Naval Historical Center.

Museums/Libraries

National Museum of Natural History,
  Anthropology Department
Smithsonian Institution
Washington, DC 20560
  Contact about "Anthro Notes", a bulletin for teachers.

National Park Service

Misc. Services

National Park Service, Mid-Atlantic
  Regional Office
2nd & Chestnut Streets, Room 251
Philadelphia, PA 19106
  Technical assistance, publications, training, Secretary of the Interior's Report on Federal Archeology, National Archeological Database (NADB), Listing of Education in Archeology Projects (LEAP), Regional Office Programs.

Department of Consulting Archaeologist, Archaeology & Ethnography
  Program
National Park Service, DOI
P.O. Box 37127, Mail Stop 2275
Washington, DC 20013-7127
phone: 202-343-4101
fax: 202-523-1547
e-mail: DCA@nps.gov
Internet: http://www.cr.nps.gov/aad/
  Contact for information about general public education and outreach activities in archaeology programs and projects.

National Register of Historic Places,
  National Register, History &
  Education
National Park Service, DOI
P.O. Box 37127, Mail Stop 2280
Washington, DC 20013-7127
phone: 202-343-9500
fax: 202-343-1836
e-mail: nr_reference@nps.gov
Internet: http://www.cr.nps.gov/nr/
  nrhome.html
  For information on the National Register of Historic Places and "Teaching With Historic Places."

National Park Service, Headquarters,
  Archeological Assistance Division
P.O. Box 37127
Washington, DC 20013-7127
Internet: http://www.cr.nps.gov/aad/
  Technical assistance, publications, training, Secretary of the Interior's Report on Federal Archeology, National Archeological Database (NADB), Listing of Education in Archeology Projects (LEAP), Regional Office Programs.

Richard Waldbauer
National Park Service, DOI, Archeology
  & Ethnography Program
P.O. Box 37127
Mail Stop NC2275, Ste. 210
Washington, DC 20013-7127
phone: 202-343-4113
fax: 202-523-1547
e-mail: richard_waldbauer@nps.gov
  Can convey information concerning the federal archaeological program from a land management perspective.

David Tarler
National Park Service, DOI, Archeology
  & Ethnography Program
P.O. Box 37127
Mail Stop NC2275, Ste. 210
Washington, DC 20013-7127
phone: 202-343-1108
fax: 202-523-1547
e-mail: david_tarler@nps.gov
  Can convey information concerning both criminal and civil federal law relating to heritage resources from both a lawyer's and archeologist's perspective.

Tim McKeown
National Park Service, DOI, Archeology
  & Ethnography Program, NAGRPA
  Team Leader
P.O. Box 37127
Mail Stop NC2275, Ste. 340
Washington, DC 20013-7127
phone: 202-343-1142
fax: 202-523-1547
e-mail: tim_mckeown@nps.gov
  Can convey information concerning Native American human remains, funerary objects, sacred objects, and objects of cultural patrimony as defined by the Native American Graves Protection & Repatriation Act (NAGPRA).

National Park Service, Southeast
Regional Office
75 Spring St., SW
Atlanta, GA 30303
*Technical assistance, publications,
training, Secretary of the Interior's
Report on Federal Archeology,
National Archeological Database
(NADB), Listing of Education in
Archeology Projects (LEAP), Regional
Office Programs.*

National Park Service, Rocky Mountain
Regional Office
12795 West Alameda Parkway
P.O. Box 25287
Denver, CO 80225-0287
*Technical assistance, publications,
training, Secretary of the Interior's
Report on Federal Archeology,
National Archeological Database
(NADB), Listing of Education in
Archeology Projects (LEAP), Regional
Office Programs.*

National Park Service, Western Regional
Office
600 Harrison St., Ste. 600
San Francisco, CA 94107-1372
*Technical assistance, publications,
training, Secretary of the Interior's
Report on Federal Archeology,
National Archeological Database
(NADB), Listing of Education in
Archeology Projects (LEAP), Regional
Office Programs.*

National Park Service, Alaska Regional
Office
2525 Gambell Street
Anchorage, AK 99503
*Technical assistance, publications,
training, Secretary of the Interior's
Report on Federal Archeology,
National Archeological Database
(NADB), Listing of Education in
Archeology Projects (LEAP), Regional
Office Programs.*

State Archaeologists

Misc. Services

Senior Archaeologist, Dept. of Planning
& Natural Resources, Div. of
Archaeology
Nisky Center, Suite 231
St Thomas, VI 00802
phone: 809-774-3320
fax: 809-775-5706
*Provides information on laws,
procedures, current research,
education programs, and other
aspects of archaeology for this state
or possession.*

State Historic Preservation Office
La Fortaleza
P.O. Box 82
San Juan, PR 00901
phone: 809-721-3737
fax: 809-723-0957
*Provides information on laws,
procedures, current research,
education programs, and other*

*aspects of archaeology for this state
or possession.*

State Archaeologist, D-SHPO,
Massachusetts Historical Commission
220 Morrissey Blvd.
Dorchester, MA 02125
phone: 617-727-8470
fax: 617-727-5128
*Provides information on laws,
procedures, current research,
education programs, and other
aspects of archaeology for this state
or possession.*

Principal/State Archaeologist, Historic
Preservation Commission
Old State House
150 Benefit St.
Providence, RI 02903
phone: 401-277-2678
fax: 401-277-2968
*Provides information on laws,
procedures, current research,
education programs, and other
aspects of archaeology for this state
or possession.*

State Archaeologist, Division of
Historical Resources
Walker Building
P.O. Box 2043
Concord, NH 03302-2043
phone: 603-271-3483
fax: 603-271-3558
*Provides information on laws,
procedures, current research,
education programs, and other
aspects of archaeology for this state
or possession.*

Archaeologist, Maine Historic
Preservation Commission
55 Capitol St.
State House Station 65
Augusta, ME 04333
phone: 207-287-2132
fax: 207-287-2335
*Provides information on laws,
procedures, current research,
education programs, and other
aspects of archaeology for this state
or possession.*

State Archaeologist, Division for
Historic Preservation
135 State St., Drawer 33
Montpelier, VT 05633-1201
phone: 802-828-3226
fax: 802-828-3206
*Provides information on laws,
procedures, current research,
education programs, and other
aspects of archaeology for this state
or possession.*

State Archaeologist, State Museum of
Natural History
U-23 University of Connecticut
Storrs Mansfield, CT 06269-3023
phone: 860-486-5248
fax: 860-486-4460
*Provides information on laws,
procedures, current research,
education programs, and other*

*aspects of archaeology for this state
or possession.*

State Archaeologist, New Jersey State
Museum
205 W. State St., CN 530
Trenton, NJ 08625
phone: 609-292-8594
fax: 609-599-4098
*Provides information on laws,
procedures, current research,
education programs, and other
aspects of archaeology for this state
or possession.*

Archaeologist, New York State Museum
3122 Cultural Education Center, Rm.
3124
Empire State Plaza
Albany, NY 12224
phone: 518-486-2015
*Provides information on laws,
procedures, current research,
education programs, and other
aspects of archaeology for this state
or possession.*

Chief, Division of Archaeology &
Protection
P.O. Box 1026
Harrisburg, PA 17120-1026
phone: 717-738-9926
fax: 717-783-1073
*Provides information on laws,
procedures, current research,
education programs, and other
aspects of archaeology for this state
or possession.*

State of Delaware, Department of State,
Division of Historical/Cultural Affairs
15 The Green
Dover, DE 19901-3611
phone: 302-736-5685
fax: 302-739-6711
*Provides information on laws,
,procedures, current research,
education programs, and other
aspects of archaeology for this state
or possession.*

Archaeologist, Historic Preservation
· Office
614 H Street, NW - Rm. 305
Washington, DC 20001
phone: 202-727-7360
fax: 202-727-7211
*Provides information on laws,
procedures, current research,
education programs, and other
aspects of archaeology for this state
or possession.*

Office of Archaeology, Division of
Historical/Cultural Programs
100 Community Place
Crownsville, MD 21032-2032
phone: 410-514-7600
fax: 410-987-4071
*Provides information on laws,
procedures, current research,
education programs, and other
aspects of archaeology for this state
or possession.*

State Archaeologist, Department of
Historic Resources
221 Governors St.
Richmond, VA 23219
phone: 804-786-3134
fax: 804-225-4261
*Provides information on laws,
procedures, current research,
education programs, and other
aspects of archaeology for this state
or possession.*

Senior Archaeologist, West Virginia
Division of Culture/History
The Cultural Center
1900 Kanowha Blvd. East
Charleston, WV 25305-0300
phone: 304-580-220
fax: 304-558-2779
*Provides information on laws,
procedures, current research,
education programs, and other
aspects of archaeology for this state
or possession.*

State Archaeologist
109 E. Jones St.
Raleigh, NC 27601-2807
phone: 919-733-7342
fax: 919-715-2671
*Provides information on laws,
procedures, current research,
education programs, and other
aspects of archaeology for this state
or possession.*

Director/State Archaeologist, SC
Institute of Archaeology/Anthropol-
ogy
University of South Carolina
1321 Pendleton St.
Columbia, SC 29201-0071
phone: 803-777-8170
fax: 803-254-1338
*Provides information on laws,
procedures, current research,
education programs, and other
aspects of archaeology for this state
or possession.*

State Archaeologist
Martha Munro, Rm. 308
West Georgia College
Carrollton, GA 30118
phone: 404-836-6455 or 404-836-6767
*Provides information on laws,
procedures, current research,
education programs, and other
aspects of archaeology for this state
or possession.*

State Archaeologist, Division of
Historical Resources
500 S. Bronough St.
Tallahassee, FL 32399-0250
phone: 904-487-2299
fax: 904-488-3353
*Provides information on laws,
procedures, current research,
education programs, and other
aspects of archaeology for this state
or possession.*

Chief, Archaeological Services Division,
Alabama Historical Commission
468 S. Perry St.
Montgomery, AL 36130
phone: 334-242-3184
fax: 334-240-3477
Internet: http://www.lib.uconn.edu/
NASA/
*Provides information on laws,
procedures, current research,
education programs, and other
aspects of archaeology for this state
or possession.*

State Archeologist, Dept. of Environment & Conservation, Div. of
Archaeology
5103 Edmonson Pike
Nashville, TN 37211-5129
phone: 615-741-1588
fax: 615-741-7329
*Provides information on laws,
procedures, current research,
education programs, and other
aspects of archaeology for this state
or possession.*

Chief, Department of Archives &
History
P.O. Box 571
Jackson, MS 39205
phone: 601-359-6940
fax: 601-359-6955
*Provides information on laws,
procedures, current research,
education programs, and other
aspects of archaeology for this state
or possession.*

State Archaeologist, Department of
Anthropology
University of Kentucky
Lexington, KY 40506-0024
phone: 606-258-5735
*Provides information on laws,
procedures, current research,
education programs, and other
aspects of archaeology for this state
or possession.*

Deputy SHPO, Ohio Historic Preservation Office, Ohio Historical Society
1982 Velma Ave.
Columbus, OH 43211
phone: 614-297-2470
fax: 614-297-2546
*Provides information on laws,
procedures, current research,
education programs, and other
aspects of archaeology for this state
or possession.*

Department of Natural Resources,
Division of Historic Preservation/
Archaeology
402 W. Washington, Rm. W274
Indianapolis, IN 46204
phone: 317-232-1646
fax: 317-232-8036
*Provides information on laws,
procedures, current research,
education programs, and other
aspects of archaeology for this state
or possession.*

John R. Halsey
State Archaeologist, Michigan Historical
Center
717 W. Allegan St.
Lansing, MI 48918
phone: 517-373-6358
fax: 517-373-0851
*Provides information on laws,
procedures, current research,
education programs, and other
aspects of archaeology for this state
or possession.*

State Archaeologist, University of Iowa
305 Eastlawn
Iowa City, IA 52242
phone: 319-335-2389
fax: 319-335-2776
*Provides information on laws,
procedures, current research,
education programs, and other
aspects of archaeology for this state
or possession.*

Archaeologist, State Historical Society
of Wisconsin
816 State St.
Madison, WI 53706
phone: 608-264-6500
fax: 608-264-6404
*Provides information on laws,
procedures, current research,
education programs, and other
aspects of archaeology for this state
or possession.*

State Archaeologist
Fort Snelling History Center
Saint Paul, MN 55111
phone: 612-725-2411
fax: 612-725-2429
*Provides information on laws,
procedures, current research,
education programs, and other
aspects of archaeology for this state
or possession.*

State Archaeologist, State Archaeological Research Center
2425 E. St. Charles St.
P.O. Box 1257
Rapid City, SD 57709-1257
phone: 605-394-1936
fax: 605-394-1941
*Provides information on laws,
procedures, current research,
education programs, and other
aspects of archaeology for this state
or possession.*

Chief Archaeologist, State Historical
Society of ND, Arch. & Hist. Pres.
Div.
North Dakota Heritage Center
612 E. Boulevard Ave.
Bismarck, ND 58505-0830
phone: 701-328-2672
fax: 701-328-3710
*Provides information on laws,
procedures, current research,
education programs, and other
aspects of archaeology for this state
or possession.*

State Archaeologists, Montana Historical
Society
1410 8th Ave.
P.O. Box 20102
Helena, MT 59620
phone: 406-444-7715
fax: 406-444-6575
*Provides information on laws,
procedures, current research,
education programs, and other
aspects of archaeology for this state
or possession.*

State Archaeologist, Preservation
Services Div., IL Historic Preservation
Agency
500 East Madison St.
Springfield, IL 62701
phone: 217-785-4999
fax: 217-782-8161
*Provides information on laws,
procedures, current research,
education programs, and other
aspects of archaeology for this state
or possession.*

Senior Archaeologist, Historic
Preservation Program
P.O. Box 176
Jefferson City, MO 65102
phone: 314-751-7958
fax: 314-526-2852
*Provides information on laws,
procedures, current research,
education programs, and other
aspects of archaeology for this state
or possession.*

State Archaeologist
120 W. Tenth
Topeka, KS 66612
phone: 913-296-4781
fax: 913-296-1005
*Provides information on laws,
procedures, current research,
education programs, and other
aspects of archaeology for this state
or possession.*

Curator of Anthropology, State
Historical Society
1500 R. St.
P.O. Box 82554
Lincoln, NE 68501
phone: 402-471-4787
fax: 402-471-3100
*Provides information on laws,
procedures, current research,
education programs, and other
aspects of archaeology for this state
or possession.*

State Archaeologist, Division of
Archaeology
Capitol Annex Building
P.O. Box 44247
Baton Rouge, LA 70804
phone: 504-342-8170
fax: 504-342-8173
*Provides information on laws,
procedures, current research,
education programs, and other
aspects of archaeology for this state
or possession.*

State Archaeologist, Arkansas
Archeological Survey
P.O. Box 1249
Fayetteville, AR 72702-1249
phone: 501-575-3556
fax: 501-575-5453
*Provides information on laws,
procedures, current research,
education programs, and other
aspects of archaeology for this state
or possession.*

State Archaeologist, University of
Oklahoma, Oklahoma Archaeology
Survey
111 East Chesapeake, Rm. 102
Norman, OK 73019
phone: 405-325-7211
fax: 405-325-7604
*Provides information on laws,
procedures, current research,
education programs, and other
aspects of archaeology for this state
or possession.*

State Archaeologist, Texan Historical
Commission
Box 12276, Capitol Station
Austin, TX 78711
phone: 512-463-8882
fax: 512-463-2530
*Provides information on laws,
procedures, current research,
education programs, and other
aspects of archaeology for this state
or possession.*

State Archaeologist, Colorado Historical
Society
1300 Broadway
Denver, CO 80203
phone: 303-886-2736
fax: 303-866-4464
*Provides information on laws,
procedures, current research,
education programs, and other
aspects of archaeology for this state
or possession.*

State Archaeologist, Department of
Anthropology
Box 3413
University Station
Laramie, WY 82071
phone: 307-766-5301
fax: 307-766-4052
*Provides information on laws,
procedures, current research,
education programs, and other
aspects of archaeology for this state
or possession.*

State Archaeologist
210 Main St.
Boise, ID 83703
phone: 208-334-3847
fax: 208-334-2775
*Provides information on laws,
procedures, current research,
education programs, and other
aspects of archaeology for this state
or possession.*

State Archaeologist, Division of State
History
310 Rio Grande
Salt Lake City, UT 84101
phone: 801-533-3527
fax: 801-533-3503
*Provides information on laws,
procedures, current research,
education programs, and other
aspects of archaeology for this state
or possession.*

Curator of Archaeology, Arizona State
Museum
University of Arizona
Tucson, AZ 85721
phone: 520-621-2556
fax: 520-621-2976
e-mail: archaeo@ccit.arizona.edu
*Provides information on laws,
procedures, current research,
education programs, and other
aspects of archaeology for this state
or possession.*

State Archaeologist, Historic Preservation Division
Villa Rivera Bldg.
228 E. Palace Ave.
Santa Fe, NM 87503
phone: 505-827-6320
fax: 505-827-6338
*Provides information on laws,
procedures, current research,
education programs, and other
aspects of archaeology for this state
or possession.*

State Historic Preservation Office
100 Stewart Street
Capitol Complex
Carson City, NV 89710
phone: 702-687-6362
*Provides information on laws,
procedures, current research,
education programs, and other
aspects of archaeology for this state
or possession.*

Office of Historic Preservation
P.O. Box 942896
Cotati, CA 94926-0001
phone: 916-653-6624
fax: 916-653-9824
*Provides information on laws,
procedures, current research,
education programs, and other
aspects of archaeology for this state
or possession.*

Head Archaeologist, State Historic
Preservation Division
33 S King Street, 6th Floor
Honolulu, HI 96813
phone: 808-587-0012
fax: 808-587-0018
*Provides information on laws,
procedures, current research,
education programs, and other
aspects of archaeology for this state
or possession.*

Department of Parks & Recreation
Building 13-8 Tiyan
P.O. Box 2950
Agana, GU 96910
phone: 671-475-6290
fax: 671-477-2822
*Provides information on laws,
procedures, current research,
education programs, and other
aspects of archaeology for this state
or possession.*

Archaeologist, Historic Preservation
Office, State Parks & Recreation
1115 Commercial St., NE
Salem, OR 97310-1001
phone: 503-378-5001
fax: 503-378-6447
*Provides information on laws,
procedures, current research,
education programs, and other
aspects of archaeology for this state
or possession.*

State Archaeologist, Dept. of Community, Trade & Economic Development
111 W. 21st Ave. SW, KL-11
P.O. Box 48343
Olympia, WA 98504-8343
phone: 206-753-4405
fax: 206-586-0250
*Provides information on laws,
procedures, current research,
education programs, and other
aspects of archaeology for this state
or possession.*

State Archaeologist
State of Alaska Office of History &
Archaeology
3601 C Street, #1278
Anchorage, AK 99503-5921
phone: 907-269-8721 or 907-269-8727
fax: 907-269-8908
e-mail: oha@alaska.net
Internet: http://www.lib.uconn.edu/
NASA/
*Provides information on laws,
procedures, current research,
education programs, and other
aspects of archaeology for this state
or possession.*

HI-FI EQUIPMENT

(see also AUDIO-VISUAL;
PHONOGRAPHS; RADIOS;
RECORDS)

Collectors

Jeffrey Viola
784 Eltone Rd.
Jackson, NJ 08527
phone: 201-928-0666
*Wants to buy old tubes and tube-type
Hi-fi & stereo equipment by such
manufacturers as Marantz, Mcintosh,
Fisher, Dynaco, Eico, Harman
Kardon, Heathkit, Acrosound,
Western Electric, Altec Lansing,
Fairchild, others; no Japanese
equipment.*

Summer McDaniel
One Edgewood Place
North Brunswick, NJ 08902
phone: 908-249-3738
*Wants to buy 1940s-1960s audio
equipment; theater or home hi-fidelity
amplifiers, speakers, horns, tube
collections, microphones, etc.*

Sonny Goldson
1413 Magnolia Lane
Midwest City, OK 73110
phone: 405-737-3312
fax: 405-737-3355
*Wants commercial tube hi-fi sound
equipment: speakers, horns, and
tubes; McIntosh, Altec, Jensen,
Marantz, Heath, Dynaco, James
Lansing, Western Electric, Fisher,
Scott, Eico, Electrovoice, Tannoy,
RCA, etc.*

Maury Corb
12325 Ashcroft
Houston, TX 77035
phone: 713-728-4343
fax: 713-723-1301
*Wants to buy old, new or used
electronics and sound equipment:
speakers, amps, turntables, horns,
misc. by Western Electric, RCA,
McIntosh, Altec, Jensen, Marantz, Ev,
Dynaco, JBL, etc.*

HIGHWAY COLLECTIBLES

(see also AUTOMOBILIA; GAS
STATION COLLECTIBLES; HOTEL
COLLECTIBLES; DINERS &
RELATED ITEMS; SOUVENIR &
COMMEMORATIVE ITEMS;
TRAILERS & RV'S)

Clubs/Associations

Dr. Thomas J. Snyder
2-Lane America
Newsletter: 2-Lane America Newsletter
P.O. Drawer 5323
Oxnard, CA 93030
phone: 805-485-9923
*Organization focusing on protecting
and promoting Rt. 66 (The Mother
Road) and other U.S. roads; also
collecting items relating thereto.*

Decals

Dealers

Richard Schneider
Lost Highway Art Co.
P.O. Box 164
Bedford Hills, NY 10507-1064
phone: 914-234-6016
fax: 914-234-2761
*Buys and sells souvenir water-dip
decals: states, parks, cities,
attractions, etc., wants singles or
collections or inventories.*

Repro. Sources

Richard Schneider
Lost Highway Art Co.
P.O. Box 164
Bedford Hills, NY 10507-1064
phone: 914-234-6016
fax: 914-234-2761
*Large variety of vintage travel images
available for graphic artists or
reproduced on mugs, magnets and t-
shirts.*

Lincoln Highway

Collectors

Brian A. Butko
2640 Sunset Dr.
West Mifflin, PA 15122-3565
*Collects souvenirs of what was the
first auto road in the U.S. to cross the
country; interested in Lincoln
Highway ephemera such as books,
pennants, and materials from early
businesses along the route only.*

Pennsylvania Turnpike Related

Collectors

Edward Foley
129 Meadow Valley Rd., Trlr. 11
Ephrata, PA 17522-1843
*Wants PA Turnpike souvenirs from
1940 to 1960; no postcards or maps,
please; all responses answered
promptly.*

Route 66 Items

Clubs/Associations

Laura & Jeff Meyer
Route 66 Association of Illinois
P.O. Box 8262
Rolling Meadows, IL 60008-8262
phone: 847-392-0860 or 847-577-2501
*Organization focusing on protecting
and promoting Rt. 66 (The Mother
Road) and collecting items relating
thereto.*

Signs & Traffic Devices

Periodicals

Jeff Francis
Newsletter: Signpost
P.O. Box 41381
Saint Petersburg, FL 33743
phone: 813-343-4316
*An association focusing on the
research and preservation of traffic
devices, markers and signs.*

HIPPIE ITEMS

(see SOCIAL CAUSES)

HISTORICAL AMERICANA

(see also AUTOGRAPHS; GLASS,
Commemorative; IMMIGRATION;
MANUSCRIPTS; MILITARIA;
PAPER COLLECTIBLES; POLITI-
CAL COLLECTIBLES; SOCIAL
CAUSES; VETERAN ITEMS)

Auction Services

Rex Stark
Rex Stark Americana
P.O. Box 1029
Gardner, MA 01440
phone: 508-630-3237
Conducts mail auctions of quality historical Americana: political, early military, advertising, sports, etc.

East Coast Books
P.O. Box 849
Wells, ME 04090
phone: 207-646-3584
fax: 207-646-0416
Specializes in mail-bid auctions of historically significant autographs, manuscripts and letters, art works on paper.

Remember When Antiquities
P.O. Box 1829
Wells, ME 04090-1829
Wants autographs, books, historical ephemera, sports memorabilia for consignment auctions; free quarterly auction catalogs.

Donald Ackerman
Provenance Galleries, Inc.
P.O. Box 3487
Wallington, NJ 07057-1621
phone: 201-779-8785
Conducts periodic mail catalog auctions featuring historical Americana such as political items, early photography, autographs, Civil War, broadsides, etc.

David Frent
Frent Auctions
P.O. Box 455
Oakhurst, NJ 07755
phone: 201-922-0768
Specializes in mail-bid auctions of political items and historical Americana.

Gary Garland
Swann Galleries, Inc.
104 E. 25th St.
New York, NY 10010-2977
phone: 212-254-4710
fax: 212-979-1017
e-mail: SwannSales@aol.com
Oldest/largest U.S. auctioneer specializing in rare books, autographs & manuscripts, Judaica, photographs, and works of art on paper.

Robert H. Snyder
Cohasco, Inc.
P.O. Box 821
Yonkers, NY 10702-0821
phone: 914-476-8500
fax: 914-476-8573
Mail bid auctions of paper and Americana: medallic art, Civil War, presidential ephemera and letters, music, old newspapers, prints, maps, political, financial, aviation, Judaica, legal, Lincolniana, personalities, royalty, sports, etc.

William A. Fox
Fox Auctions, Inc.
P.O. Box 4026
Farmingdale, NY 11735
phone: 516-454-7857
fax: 516-454-7857
Specializes in the sale of Americana, ephemera, and U.S. and foreign stamps and covers.

Eric Caren
HCA Historical Collectibles Auction
3 Neptune Rd.
Poughkeepsie, NY 12601
phone: 914-462-1230
fax: 914-248-6439

Ted Hake
Hake's Americana & Collectibles Auction
P.O. Box 1444
York, PA 17405-1444
phone: 717-848-1333
Always purchasing items for 8 mail-bid auctions per year covering hundreds of categories including toys, character collectibles, Disney, cowboy heroes, premiums, television, politicals, pin-back buttons, advertising and more.

Robert Coup
Historicana
P.O. Box 348
Leola, PA 17540-0348
phone: 717-656-7780
Specializes in mail-bid auctions of character collectibles, Disneyana, political items & historical Americana; sample catalog $2.

C. Wesley Cowan
747 Park Ave.
Terrace Park, OH 45174
phone: 513-248-8122
fax: 513-248-2566
Sells historical Americana: photographic images, political items, manuscripts, autographs, etc.

Al Anderson
Anderson Auction
P.O. Box 644
Troy, OH 45373
phone: 513-339-0850
Specializes in mail-bid auctions of political items and historical Americana.

Tom Slater
Political Gallery, The
5335 N Tacoma Ave., Ste. 24
Indianapolis, IN 46220-3648
phone: 317-257-0863
fax: 317-254-9167
Specializing in mail-bid auctions of Disneyana, historical Americana, toys, political items, and other collectibles.

U.I. "Chick" Harris
Harris Auctions
P.O. Box 20614
Saint Louis, MO 63139-0614
phone: 314-352-8623
Collector/specialist in all types of political Americana; conducts specialized mail-auctions of political and historical Americana.

Collectors

Sheldon Lerman
7505 Osler Dr.
Baltimore, MD 21204-7736
phone: 410-321-1514 or 410-828-5310
fax: 410-825-5710
Wants to buy historical documents, Presidential and historical signatures.

Mike Farmer
1406 Bigelow Ave. NW
Olympia, WA 98506-4417
phone: 360-352-7189
fax: 360-352-7189
Wants to buy pre-1930 stocks & bonds, land grants, graphic bill heads, broadsides, posters, maps, business letters, Civil War, American Indian, cancelled checks, Alaska, any old interesting paper; send copy or call; prompt reply.

Dealers

Rex Stark
Rex Stark Americana
P.O. Box 1029
Gardner, MA 01440
phone: 508-630-3237
Buys & sells historical Americana; wants 1770-1870 Amer. historical pottery; offers catalog of historical/political Americana for sale.

University Archives
600 Summer St.
Stamford, CT 06901-1403
phone: 800-237-5692 or 203-975-9291
fax: 203-348-3560
Buying and selling fine historical autographs, manuscripts, documents, autographed books and autographed photographs of notable people including U.S. presidents, Revolutionary and Civil War, literary, aviation, science, art, and music.

Peter Hlinka
Peter Hlinka Historical Americana
P.O. Box 310
New York, NY 10028-0017
phone: 718-409-6407
Buys, sells, and appraises historical Americana; publishes a large catalog of militaria, military insignia, war relics, related books, and other historical Americana; also foreign.

Charles Zeder
Zeder's Antiques
6755 Coralite St. #D
Long Beach, CA 90808-4725
phone: 562-421-0881
Deals in 19th century ephemera, Civil War items, stock certificates, bonds, fruit box labels, 19th century advertising.

Steve Schmale
Out West
2231 Creekside Rd.
Santa Rosa, CA 95405-8022
phone: 707-838-1859 or 707-575-5406
e-mail: outweststv@aol.com
Buys and sells better vintage postcards since 1976; approval service; strong in Western states views; always buying better cards and real photos; also wants railroad paper, stereoviews, photos, brochures, trade cards; member IFPD.

HITCHING POSTS

Collectors

Bob Maclin
1436 Lakewood
Lexington, KY 40502
phone: 606-269-4450
Interested in corresponding with others who are interested in hitching posts.

HOBBY HORSES

(see RIDING TOYS, Rocking Horses)

HOBBY TOYS

(see TOYS, Construction Sets)

HOBO COLLECTIBLES

(see also TRAMP ART)

Clubs/Associations

Buzz Potter
National Hobo Association
Newsletter: Hobo Times
P.O. Box 706
Nisswa, MN 56468
Hobo tails, hobo calendar of events, hobo poetry, news and notes; sponsors hobo gatherings.

Hobo Alumni Association of America
World Way Center
P.O. Box 90430
Los Angeles, CA 90009
phone: 310-645-1500
For anyone who has experienced the thrill of riding, watching or hearing America's freight trains (need not be a hobo); preserves and memorializes this vital part of Americana through fellowship, folkfests and social gatherings.

HOLIDAY COLLECTIBLES

(see also CHRISTMAS COLLECTIBLES; COLLECTIBLES [MODERN], Ornaments; ELVES; HALLOWEEN COLLECTIBLES; VALENTINES; ST. PATRICK)

Auction Services

Cindy Chipps
Holiday Auction, The
4027 Brooks Hill Rd.
Brooks, KY 40109-5002
phone: 502-955-9238
fax: 502-957-5027
e-mail: holauction@aol.com
Internet: http://members.aol.com/
holauction/index.html
*Holds bi-monthly mail auction of a
wide variety of holiday items from the
common to the very rare; send for free
catalog.*

Collectors

Ann C. Bergin
P.O. Box 105
Amherst, NH 03031-0105
fax: 508-649-6807
e-mail: PFBergin@aol.com
*Wants items relating to holidays, and
ceremonies of life (Christenings,
baptisms, weddings, confirmations,
graduations, birthdays, etc.)*

Linda L. Vines
P.O. Box 43721
Montclair, NJ 07043
phone: 973-748-4990 or 201-748-4990
*Wants to buy pre-1950 holiday
decoration including German
Christmas, Halloween, Easter and
patriotic candy containers, pumpkins,
and Santas.*

Trish Claar
2621 Manor Court
Owings, MD 20736-9145
phone: 301-855-6531
*Wants 1950s and 1960s Holiday
collectibles, especially Christmas.*

Kit Carter Weilage
506 Briar Hill Rd.
Louisville, KY 40206
phone: 502-561-5030
*Buys and sells Christmas collectibles,
specializing in German-made Santa
candy containers.*

Dealers

Chris Savino
P.O. Box 419
Breesport, NY 14816-0419
phone: 607-739-3106
fax: 607-739-3106
*Wants Holiday items including
Christmas, Halloween, Easter; Santas,
papier mache items such as
ornaments, party favors, decorations,
candy containers; tin toys, devils,
skulls, witches; items made in
Germany, Japan or USA.*

Bettie Petzoldt
178 Woolen Mill Rd.
New Park, PA 17352
phone: 717-382-1416
Internet: http://
www.mindyourbusiness.com
*Wants pre-1940 Christmas items:
unusual, collectible (figural)*

*Christmas ornaments, snow babies,
lights, Santas; other holiday items too.*

Jenny Tarrant
Holly-Daze
4 Gardenview Dr.
Saint Peters, MO 63376-3507
phone: 314-397-1763
*Wants German Santas, Halloween
candy containers, Jack O'Lanterns,
German rabbits, and George
Washington composition candy
containers.*

Experts

Lissa & Richard Smith
3 Baldtop Heights
Danville, PA 17821
phone: 717-275-7796
*Advisor to "Warman's Antiques &
Collectibles Price Guide", authors of
"Christmas Collectibles."*

Easter

Dealers

Paul W. Schofield
Lion's Den Antiques
7988 Bethel Burley Rd. SE
Port Orchard, WA 98366
phone: 360-876-3364
fax: 360-876-5421
*Buys, sells, appraises, and specializes
in old Santas, candy containers,
Halloween, Easter, Christmas, Easter,
Dresden, figural lights.*

HOLLOWWARE

(see SILVER; SILVERPLATE)

HOLLYWOOD POSTERS

(see MOVIE MEMORABILIA, Movie
Posters; PHOTOGRAPHS, Celebrity)

HOLOGRAMS

Man./Prod./Dist.

Excalibur
P.O. Box 14478
Philadelphia, PA 19115
phone: 215-342-6913
*Promo cards, non-sports and adult
trading cards.*

NeoVisions Productions
P.O. Box 74277
Los Angeles, CA 90004
phone: 213-387-0461
fax: 213-387-0461
*Holograms for home and industry:
Star Wars, Star Trek, Deep Space
Nine, Next Generation, Aliens, MAD,
Jurassic Park, dozens of collectible
licensed holographic items: pens,
pencils, badges, bookmarks,
keychains, stickers, etc.*

HOLSTERS

(see TOYS, Cap Guns; WESTERN
AMERICANA)

HOLT HOWARD

Collectors

Trish Claar
2621 Manor Court
Owings, MD 20736-9145
phone: 301-855-6531
*Holt Howard items are usually
ceramic, always whimsical.*

HOMESPUN

(see TEXTILES)

HOOSIER CABINETS

(see FURNITURE [ANTIQUE],
Kitchen Cabinets)

HORNS & WHISTLES

(see also NAUTICAL ANTIQUES;
SPORTING COLLECTIBLES, Game
Calls; STEAM-OPERATED, Models
& Equipment)

Clubs/Associations

Harry D. Barry
Air Horn & Steam Whistle Enthusiasts
Newsletter: Horn & Whistle
275 Windswept Dr.
North East, PA 16428
phone: 814-725-8150
*Purpose is to preserve, increase, and
disseminate knowledge concerning
horns, whistles, sirens, and bells in
industrial, marine, transportation,
signaling, and warning applications.*

James C. Fitch
Call & Whistle Collectors Association
Newsletter: Whistle Notes
2839 E. 26th Place
Tulsa, OK 74114-4309
phone: 918-747-3202
e-mail: jchesterf@aol.com
*Club for collectors of game calls,
antique whistles, bo's'n pipes, flutes,
bird calls, advertising whistles, toy
whistles, and folk art whistles.*

Collectors

Lin Chapman
58 Blakeslee Rd.
Wallingford, CT 06492

Harry D. Barry
275 Windswept Dr.
North East, PA 16428
phone: 814-725-8150
*Collects steam whistles and horns
which were and are used on
locomotives, ships, factories, boilers,
etc.*

Sirens

Collectors

Bill Cary
1104 Clinton St.
Rome, NY 13440-2516
phone: 315-336-7623
Wants to buy hand-cranked sirens;

*working or not working, parts,
brackets, etc.*

HORROR

(see also MOVIE MEMORABILIA;
SCIENCE FICTION)

Collectors

Rich Zelachowski
220 Centre Ave.
Secaucus, NJ 07094
phone: 201-319-9339
e-mail: richz@tiac.net
*Wants to buy horror collectibles: toys,
games, props, models, autographs,
books, magazines, posters, robots,
records, etc.*

Dracula

Clubs/Associations

Velvet Vampyre Society, The
P.O. Box 68
Keighley
West Yorkshire BD2 6R, U.K.

Dr. M. Jeanne Youngson
Count Dracula Fan Club
Journal: Dracula News
29 Washington Square West
New York, NY 10011-9180
phone: 212-982-6754
*Club keeps members of the CDFC up
on everything happening in the world
of the undead; also publishes other
newsletters.*

Museums/Libraries

Dr. M. Jeanne Youngson
Count Dracula Permanent Collection of
Vampire Memorabilia
29 Washington Square West
New York, NY 10011-9180
phone: 212-982-6754
*Figurines, posters, games, pulps,
autographed photos of Lugosi,
Hamilton Deane, Karloff, Langella,
Kinski, Price, Cushing, Lanchester,
etc., original art, early playbills; also
Frankenstein and Wolfman
memorabilia.*

Frankenstein

Museums/Libraries

Dr. M. Jeanne Youngson
Count Dracula Permanent Collection of
Vampire Memorabilia
29 Washington Square West
New York, NY 10011-9180
phone: 212-982-6754
*Figurines, posters, games, pulps,
autographed photos of Lugosi,
Hamilton Deane, Karloff, Langella,
Kinski, Price, Cushing, Lanchester,
etc., original art, early playbills; also
Frankenstein and Wolfman
memorabilia.*

Wolfman

Museums/Libraries

Dr. M. Jeanne Youngson
Count Dracula Permanent Collection of
Vampire Memorabilia
29 Washington Square West
New York, NY 10011-9180
phone: 212-982-6754
*Figurines, posters, games, pulps,
autographed photos of Lugosi,
Hamilton Deane, Karloff, Langella,
Kinski, Price, Cushing, Lanchester,
etc., original art, early playbills; also
Frankenstein and Wolfman
memorabilia.*

HORSE-DRAWN VEHICLES

(see also FARM COLLECTIBLES;
FARM MACHINERY; ANIMAL
COLLECTIBLES, Horses)

Auction Services

Paul Martin, Jr.
Martin Auctioneers, Inc.
14 S. Holland Rd.
P.O. Box 477
Intercourse, PA 17534-0477
phone: 717-768-8108
fax: 717-768-7714
*Specializes in the sale of horse drawn
carriages, buggies, hitch wagons, tack
and other horse-related items; buys
and sells through private transactions
and public auction; will buy complete
collections or single pieces.*

Carrollton Sleigh & Wagon Auction
P.O. Box 323
Carrollton, OH 44615
phone: 800-452-8452
e-mail: garner@imperium.net
*Conducts auctions of horse-drawn
carriages, buggies, hitch wagons, tack
and other horse-related items.*

Shipshewana Annual Mid-West Carriage
Auction
P.O. Box 185
Shipshewana, IN 46565
*Conducts an annual (May/June)
auction of horse-drawn vehicles and
related items.*

Sweeney's Horse & Carriage Sale
P.O. Box 67
Waukon, IA 52172

Dealers

Don Sawyer
West Newbury Wagon Works
40 Bachelor St.
West Newbury, MA 01985
phone: 508-346-4724 or 508-363-2983
fax: 508-346-4841
*Buys, sells, trades horse-drawn
carriages, wagons, fire vehicles; also
repairs, restores lamps and vehicles;
offers a search services for missing
parts.*

Horse-Drawn Carriages
P.O. Box 1392
Santa Rosa, CA 95402-1392
*Wants horse-drawn wagons, fifth
wheel wagons, light delivery wagons,
stagecoaches, etc.*

Periodicals

Magazine: Driving Digest Magazine
P.O. Box 467
Brooklyn, CT 06234
*A magazine for horsemen interested in
competitive driving of a single horse,
pairs and four-in-hands.*

Draft Horse Journal, Inc.
Magazine: Draft Horse Journal
P.O. Box 670
Waverly, IA 50677
phone: 319-352-4046
fax: 319-352-2232
Internet: http://www.horseshoes.com
*A trade magazine of the Draft Horse
and Mule Industry; present day uses
along with historical material; horses,
mules, and equipment advertised.*

Repair Services

Don Sawyer
West Newbury Wagon Works
40 Bachelor St.
West Newbury, MA 01985
phone: 508-346-4724 or 508-363-2983
fax: 508-346-4841
*Buys, sells, trades horse-drawn
carriages, wagons, fire vehicles; also
repairs, restores lamps and vehicles;
offers a search services for missing
parts.*

Repro. Sources

Cumberland General Store
#1 Highway 68
Crossville, TN 38555
phone: 615-484-8481
fax: 615-456-1211

Carriages

Auction Services

Paul Martin, Jr.
Martin Auctioneers, Inc.
14 S. Holland Rd.
P.O. Box 477
Intercourse, PA 17534-0477
phone: 717-768-8108
fax: 717-768-7714
*Specializes in the sale of horse drawn
carriages, buggies, hitch wagons, tack
and other horse-related items; buys
and sells through private transactions
and public auction; will buy complete
collections or single pieces.*

Clubs/Associations

Mrs. Jenny Dillon, Sec.
British Driving Society, The
Newsletter: British Driving Society
  Newsletter
27 Dugard Place
Barford
Warwick CV35 8DX, U.K.
Focuses on carriage driving and

horse training.

Carriage Association of America
Journal: Carriage Journal, The
177 Pointers-Auburn Rd.
Salem, NJ 08079
phone: 609-935-1616
fax: 609-935-4955
e-mail: caa177@aol.com
Internet: http://www.horsecountry.com/
  ~horsec/carriage/index.html
*To foster knowledge, collecting,
restoring, driving and research of
horse-drawn vehicles.*

American Driving Society
Newsletter: Whip, The
P.O. Box 160
Metamora, MI 48455
phone: 810-664-8666
fax: 810-664-2405
e-mail: AmDrivSo@aol.com
Internet: http://www.equisearch.com/
  ads.ads_toc.html
*Promotes the sport of carriage driving
and horse training for sport and
pleasure; articles, ads, competitions,
carriage maintenance.*

Collectors

Carriage Collector, The
P.O. Box 71
Blue Ball, PA 17506-0071
phone: 717-768-8306
fax: 717-768-7714
*Wants to buy horse drawn coaches,
carriages and sleighs; also carriage
lamps, books, stable fixtures,
miniature goat wagons and any item
pertaining to the horse.*

Museums/Libraries

Museums at Stony Brook, The
Newsletter: News & Events
Rte. 25A Box 1208
Stony Brook, NY 11790-1931
phone: 516-751-0066
fax: 516-751-0353
*Large collection of American Art,
decoys, horse-drawn vehicles,
costumes, and miniature period
rooms; museum shop.*

Susan Green
Carriage Museum of America
P.O. Box 417
Bird In Hand, PA 17505
phone: 717-656-7019
*A research library that serves as a
source for historically accurate
technical information on horse-drawn
vehicles and related subjects.*

Rose Hill Manor
1611 N. Market St.
Frederick, MD 21701
phone: 301-694-1650

Periodicals

Magazine: Driving West
P.O. Box 1137
Atascadero, CA 93423-1137
phone: 805-462-9378 or 805-466-2814
fax: 805-461-3842
e-mail: dwemail@thegrid.net
*A monthly publication serving all
driving enthusiasts; send for one free
sample.*

Repair Services

Ivan Burkholder
Woodlyn Coach Co.
4410 TR 628
Millersburg, OH 44654
phone: 216-674-9124
*Specializes in the repair and complete
restoration of horse drawn carriages,
buggies and wagons; also builds new
hitch wagons.*

Alvin Raber
A & D Buggy Shop
4682 Rte. 5 TR 628
Millersburg, OH 44654
phone: 614-599-6131
*Specializes in the repair and
restoration of horse drawn carriages
and buggies.*

Suppliers

Ivan Burkholder
Woodlyn Coach Co.
4410 TR 628
Millersburg, OH 44654
phone: 216-674-9124
*Carries buggy restoration and supply
parts; send for catalog.*

Plank & Sons
RR 2 Box C-23AA
Arthur, IL 61911
phone: 217-543-3307
*Carries buggy restoration and supply
parts.*

Conestoga Wagons

Clubs/Associations

Joan Browning, Sec.
American Wagon Association
P.O. Box 436
Ronceverte, WV 24970
phone: 304-645-6799
*Members interested in the history and
preservation of the Conestoga wagon.*

HOTEL COLLECTIBLES

(see also HIGHWAY COL-
LECTIBLES; NIGHTCLUB
MEMORABILIA; SOUVENIR &
COMMEMORATIVE ITEMS;
TRAILERS & RV'S)

Collectors

Steve Rushmore
372 Willis Ave.
Mineola, NY 11501
phone: 516-248-8828
Wants hotel key tags; also hotel .

*memorabilia; old or new; must show
name of hotel.*

Larry Spilkin
P.O. Box 5039
Southfield, MI 48086-5039
phone: 810-642-3722
  *Wants postcards and matchbook
  covers of drive-ins, diners, cafes, gas
  stations and 1930s-1950s motels,
  restaurant/bar, cabins and Art Deco
  streamline hotels.*

Tourist Cabins

Collectors

Brian A. Butko
2640 Sunset Dr.
West Mifflin, PA 15122-3565
  *Wants to buy books, brochures, guides
  and souvenirs from tourist courts that
  had individual cabins; no postcards
  please.*

HOUSEWARES

  (see ELECTRICITY RELATED
  ITEMS, Appliances; CLOTHES
  HANGERS; KITCHEN COL-
  LECTIBLES)

HUMIDORS

  (see SMOKING COLLECTIBLES)

HUMMELS

  (see COLLECTIBLES [MODERN],
  Figurines [Goebel]; FIGURINES,
  Hummel)

HUNTING

  (see ANIMAL TROPHIES;
  LICENSES, Hunting & Fishing;
  SPORTING COLLECTIBLES;
  TRAPS)

HYMNALS

  (see also BOOKS; SHEET MUSIC)

Collectors

Christian Williams
8 Elm Rd.
Scarsdale, NY 10583
phone: 914-723-8739
  *Wants to buy old hymnals; prefers
  Victorian era with picture on cover;
  also small Sunday school books; send
  title, date, condition and price; all
  offers considered.*

294

Here are some tips when contacting someone listed in this book:

When requesting information about a particular item, include a description (material, dimensions, maker's mark, model number, etc.) and a photo, sketch, or photocopy of the item in question. ■

Always ask if there are charges for samples or for the services requested. ■

When writing, please be sure to include a Large (#10 business size) Self-Addressed and Stamped Envelope (LSASE) if requesting a reply or the return of photographs. ■

Never call collect unless otherwise directed. When calling, be considerate of time zone differences and always ask if the party you are calling has time to talk. When leaving an answering machine message, always instruct the party to call you back collect. ■

ICE CREAM MEMORABILIA

(see ICE INDUSTRY; MOLDS, Ice Cream; SODA FOUNTAIN COLLECTIBLES)

ICE INDUSTRY

Collectors

T.J. Lucia
2145 Wilbraham Rd.
Springfield, MA 01129-1806
Wants to buy ice business memora-bilia: ice cards, advertising, ice tools, ice picks with ice company names, photos, etc.; send asking price and description.

Joe Pedro
9 Whitcomb Ave.
Ayer, MA 01432-1627
phone: 508-772-2971
Wants ice memorabilia: signs, paper, tokens, photos, badges, watches, fobs, tools, delivery bags, picks, axes; anything to do with the ice business.

Experts

Philip C. Whitney
Whitney Historic Programs
303 Fisher Rd.
Fitchburg, MA 01420-1548
phone: 508-342-1350
Specializes in demonstrating the art of antique ice harvesting and the matching of buyers and sellers of ice harvesting equipment; owner of the largest mobile collection of ice harvesting equipment in the country.

Museums/Libraries

Ice House Museum
303 Franklin Street
Cedar Falls, IA 50613
phone: 319-277-8817 or 319-266-5149

ICONS

(see also RUSSIAN ITEMS)

Dealers

James L. Jackson, ISA
Jackson's Sacred Heart
2229 Lincoln St.
Cedar Falls, IA 50613
phone: 319-277-2256
fax: 319-277-1252
e-mail: jacksons@jacksonsauction.com
Internet: http://
www.jacksonsauction.com
Specializing in quality 17th, 18th and 19th century Russian icons and related items; quarterly full color catalog offering Russian icons and related items.

Experts

Tad Sviderskis
Icon-Painting Conservation & Restoration Company, The
730 Fifth Ave., 9th Floor
New York, NY 10019-4105
phone: 800-510-9799
fax: 717-698-8192
e-mail: sviders@aol.com
First and only company in N.A. specializing in professional methods for treatment, conservation and restoration of 14th to 19th century Russian, Greek, Byzantine icons; also provides appraisal service, authentication, lecturing.

James L. Jackson, ISA
Jackson's Sacred Heart
2229 Lincoln St.
Cedar Falls, IA 50613
phone: 319-277-2256
fax: 319-277-1252
e-mail: jacksons@jacksonsauction.com
Internet: http://
www.jacksonsauction.com
Has written and lectured widely on Russian icons, and has traveled extensively throughout Russia and the former Soviet Union studying Russian icons.

Museums/Libraries

Dr. Gary Vikan
Walters Art Gallery
600 N. Charles St.
Baltimore, MD 21201
phone: 410-547-9000

Repair Services

Tad Sviderskis
Icon-Painting Conservation & Restoration Company, The
730 Fifth Ave., 9th Floor
New York, NY 10019-4105
phone: 800-510-9799
fax: 717-698-8192
e-mail: sviders@aol.com
Specializing in professional conservation and restoration treatment of ancient icon painting; consolidation of paint layer, grounding, size cleavage, cleaning of grime and deteriorated varnish; employs scientific methodology.

Boris Paskvan
Awesome Metal Restorations, Inc.
4233-G Howard Ave.
Kensington, MD 20895
phone: 301-897-3266
fax: 310-942-6532
European expert restores gold, gilt, bronze, silver, silver plating, icons, metal accessories, sculptures, etc. for museums, homes, insurance.

ILLUSTRATORS

(see also ART; BOOKS, Illustrated; MAGAZINES; PAPER COL-LECTIBLES, Illustrated; PERSON-ALITIES [ARTISTS]; PIN-UP ART; PRINTS)

Auction Services

Illustration House
96 Spring St., 7th Floor
New York, NY 10012-3923

Collectors

Charles Martignette
P.O. Box 293
Hallandale, FL 33008
phone: 305-454-3474
American illustration art historian wants to buy original illustration artwork: original paintings and drawings, magazine front-cover art, magazine story illustrations, advertising art; please send photos, dimensions, price.

Tim Isaacson
1002 Clinton
Oak Park, IL 60304-1824
phone: 708-383-5646
Wants to buy original illustrator art: paintings & interior illustrations used for magazine covers, paperback books, pulp magazines, The Shadow, comic book art pages, daily & Sunday comic strip funnies, science fiction, detective, etc.

Wendy Hoffman
Wendy Hoffman Gallery
8305 Rosewood
Shawnee Mission, KS 66207-1742
phone: 913-649-1717
e-mail: wendysart@aol.com
Wants to buy art by illustrators Fox, Parrish, Gutmann, Humphrey; Esquire magazines with Vargas gatefolds; pin-up calendars/prints by Elvgren, Moran, Mozert and Armstrong; sporting calendars/prints by Goodwin, Stick, etc.

Dealers

American Illustrations Gallery
18 East 77th St.
New York, NY 10021
phone: 212-744-5190
fax: 212-744-0128
Specializes in works by American illustrators.

Alan M. Goffman
Alan M. Goffman Gallery
264 East 78th St.
New York, NY 10021-2021
phone: 212-517-8192
fax: 212-517-8193
e-mail: goffman@interport.net
Internet: http://www.artnet.com
Specializing in paintings, watercolors and drawings from the "Golden Age" of American illustration 1880-1940.

Matt Iarocci
Matt's
P.O. Box 290H
Scarsdale, NY 10583-8790
phone: 914-472-6361
Buys and sells original illustrator art; done for magazine covers, stories, pulps, ads, calendars, posters, comics, etc.; subjects include Western, adventure, fashion, pin-up, horror, sports, movies, travel.

Jo Ann Reisler
360 Glyndon St., NE
Vienna, VA 22180-3537
phone: 703-938-2967
fax: 703-938-9057
e-mail: Reisler@clark.net
Internet: http://www.clark.net/pug/Reisler
Wants to buy original illustrator art.

Museums/Libraries

Society of Illustrators Museum of American Illustration
128 E. 63rd. St.
New York, NY 10021
phone: 212-838-2560

Periodicals

Joan Jenkins
Newsletter: Calendar Art Collectors' Newsletter
45 Brown's Lane
Old Lyme, CT 06371
phone: 203-434-1852
Illustrated articles about Parrish, Fox, Thompson, VanNortwick, Garratt, Whitroy, Grossman, Icart-type, Gutmann, Becker, Fangel, Kenyon, Hibel, "Cupid" prints, Pressler, Eggleston, Leyendecker, Phillips, Indian Maiden prints.

Doug Watson
Magazine: Paper Collectors' Market-place
470 Main St.
P.O. Box 128
Scandinavia, WI 54977-0128
phone: 715-467-2379
fax: 715-467-2243
e-mail: pcmpaper@gglbbs.com
Internet: http://www.tias.com/pubs/pcm
Monthly magazine for collectors of autographs, paperbacks, postcards, advertising, photographica, magazines; all types of paper ephemera.

Denis C. Jackson, Ed.
Newsletter: Illustrator Collector's News, The
P.O. Box 1958
Sequim, WA 98382-1958
phone: 360-683-2559
fax: 360-683-2559
e-mail: ticn@olypen.com
Internet: http://www.olypen.com/ticn
A bi-monthly publication for collectors of magazines and other paper illustrations; free classifieds for subscribers; send LSASE for information; old prints, calendars.

Arthur Szyk

Clubs/Associations

George W. Gooche
Arthur Szyk Society, Inc.
Newsletter: Arthur Szyk Newsletter
1294 Sao Paula Ave.
Placentia, CA 92670
phone: 714-993-4969
fax: 714-993-4593
e-mail: 73504.176@compuserve.com
Arthur Szyk (1894-1951, artist, miniaturist, illuminator, illustrator) is regarded as the greatest miniature painter and illustrator of his times; newsletter published six timer per year.

Bessie Pease Gutmann

Collectors

George & Janice Parola
43 Oakfield Ave.
Freeport, NY 11520-1935
phone: 516-868-8439
fax: 516-379-1534
Wants Bessie Pease Gutmann prints, magazine covers, postcards, calendars, etc.

Warren Wissemann
521 South Dyre Ave.
West Islip, NY 11795
phone: 516-587-7633
Wants prints by Bessie Pease Gutmann, Eda Doench, Bessie Collins Pease, and Meta Grimball.

Eleanor Popelka
530 S. Chicot Ave.
West Islip, NY 11795-4206
phone: 516-587-8260
e-mail: popedel@msn.com
Collector of prints, postcards, magazine covers, books and calendars illustrated by Bessie Pease Gutmann, Meta Grimball, and Eda Doench; no reproductions, please.

Jim & Sharon Eckert
P.O. Box 62
Anchor, IL 61720-0062
phone: 309-723-4241
e-mail: jreckert@aol.com
Wants Wallace Nutting, Bessie Pease Gutmann prints.

Coles Phillips

Experts

Denis C. Jackson
P.O. Box 1958
Sequim, WA 98382-1958
phone: 360-683-2559
fax: 360-683-2559
e-mail: ticn@olypen.com
Internet: http://www.olypen.com/ticn/
Covered magazines from 1900 to 1926; author of "The Price & ID Guide to Coles Phillips", 2nd Edition; send LSASE for information.

Eloise Wilkin

Experts

Joanne Arnold
1040 S. Kenilworth
Oak Park, IL 60304-1915
Wants items illustrated by Eloise Wilkin: pre-1960 children's books posters, paper dolls, puzzles, advertisements, etc. Wants dolls designed by Eloise Wilkin; Baby Dear, Baby & Bobby Dear One, Baby & Bobby Too Dear; by Vogue Inc.

Fern Bisel Peat

Experts

David W. Peat
1225 Carroll White
Indianapolis, IN 46219-3907
phone: 317-357-6895
Wants books, tin toys, other metal or paper children's items from 1927-1947 illustrated by my aunt, Fern Bisel Peat.

Grace Drayton

Experts

G.L. Wine
649 Bayview Dr.
Akron, OH 44319-1502
Researcher who specializes in the life and art of Campbell Kids' creator, Grace G. Drayton.

Harrison Fisher

(see also POSTCARDS)

Clubs/Associations

Deena M. Zachritz, Dir.
Harrison Fisher Society, The
Newsletter: Harrison Fisher Society Newsletter
123 N Glassell
Orange, CA 92666
phone: 714-633-5206
fax: 714-633-5726
The Society gathers and researches references and works by or about Harrison Fisher.

Dealers

Naomi Welch
309 Playa Blvd.
La Selva Beach, CA 95076-1737
phone: 408-685-2655
e-mail: naomiwelch@sprintmail.com
Buys and sells Harrison Fisher illustrated art books, magazines, magazine covers, posters, postcards, prints, calendars, playing cards, sheet music, programs; wants anything related to Fisher.

J.C. & F.X. Leyendecker

Experts

Denis C. Jackson
P.O. Box 1958
Sequim, WA 98382-1958
phone: 360-683-2559
fax: 360-683-2559
e-mail: ticn@olypen.com
Internet: http://www.olypen.com/ticn/
Specializes in illustrators from 1890s through 1950s; author of "The Price Guide to JC & FX Leyendecker" 2nd edition; send LSASE for information.

Joan Walsh Anglund

Experts

Ann C. Bergin
P.O. Box 105
Amherst, NH 03031-0105
fax: 508-649-6807
e-mail: PFBergin@aol.com

Periodicals

Ann C. Bergin
Newsletter: Joan Walsh Anglund Collectors News
P.O. Box 105
Amherst, NH 03031-0105
fax: 508-649-6807
e-mail: PFBergin@aol.com
An annual newsletter containing information on children's book illustrator Joan Walsh Anglund; free buy, sell ad for subscribers.

Kate Greenaway

Clubs/Associations

Dr. James Lewis Lowe, Dir.
Kate Greenaway Society
P.O. Box 8
Norwood, PA 19074
phone: 610-485-8572

Maxfield Parrish

Collectors

John Crawford
3442 Manor Hill
Cincinnati, OH 45220
phone: 513-221-6050
Wants Maxfield Parrish illustrations, especially magazine items.

John Buonaguidi
540 Reeside Ave.
Monterey, CA 93940-1828
phone: 408-655-2363
Wants to buy Maxfield Parrish collectibles including calendars, posters, books, advertising items, paintings, prints, etc. - anything Parrish!

Dealers

John S. Zuk
106 Orchard St.
Belmont, MA 02178-2940
phone: 617-484-4800
fax: 617-864-3862
e-mail: jzuk@integral-inc.com
Buys and sells Maxfield Parrish prints, books, and originals (pen & ink, watercolor, etc.); premium paid for Edison Mazda calendars, lamp testers, etc.

Hugh Alan Luch Collections, The
P.O. Box 111
Wenonah, NJ 08090
phone: 609-464-9751
Buys and sells illustrator and holiday collectibles with emphasis on Maxfield Parrish and Halloween.

Edward J. Meschi
129 Pinyard Rd.
Monroeville, NJ 08343-1870
phone: 609-358-7293
fax: 609-358-7293
Buys and sells Maxfield Parrish prints and paintings.

Richard Strell
Parrish to the Max
908 Merrick Rd.
Baldwin, NY 11510
phone: 516-825-8077
Specializing in Maxfield Parrish prints and collectibles.

Ruman
292 Pershing Ave.
Leechburg, PA 15656
phone: 412-845-7275

Barb & Dan Fromer
Fromer's Antiques
P.O. Box 224
New Market, MD 21774-0224
phone: 301-831-6712
Buys and sells Maxfield Parrish prints.

John Walkowiak
3452 Humbolt Ave. S.
Minneapolis, MN 55408
phone: 612-824-0785
Maxfield Parrish prints, books, calendars, advertising, reference items, posters, and other items bought and sold.

William T. Byrne
1625 Broadway, Ste. 2450
Denver, CO 80202-4624
phone: 303-744-9403
Seeking mint condition Maxfield Parrish calendars, prints, posters, books, letters, originals, playing cards, games, puzzles, signs, novelty and ad items.

Experts

Bill Holland
William Holland Fine Arts
1708 E. Lancaster Ave.
Paoli, PA 19301-1553
phone: 610-648-0369
fax: 610-647-4448
*Buys and sells Parrish art prints,
calendars, posters, advertising items,
books, and magazine covers; author of
"The Collectible Maxfield Parrish",
$60 ppd.*

John Goodspeed Stuart
Parrish House, The
1740 Marion St.
Denver, CO 80218-1121
phone: 303-831-0055
fax: 303-831-4901
e-mail: jgstuart@aol.com
Internet: http://www.parrish-house.com
*Buys, sells, appraises and specializes
in Maxfield Parrish prints, books, etc.;
send for free price list; author of
"Young Maxfield Parrish" and "The
Art of MAxfield Parrish."*

Denis C. Jackson
P.O. Box 1958
Sequim, WA 98382-1958
phone: 360-683-2559
fax: 360-683-2559
e-mail: ticn@olypen.com
Internet: http://www.olypen.com/ticn/
*Maxfield Parrish prints, calendars,
books, magazines; author of "The
Price and Identification Guide to
Maxfield Parrish" 9th edition; send
LSASE for information.*

Misc. Services

Laurence S. Cutler
Maxfield Parrish Family Trust, The
P.O. Box 687
Holderness, NH 03245-0687
phone: 603-968-3067
fax: 603-968-3068
e-mail: artasap@aol.com
*Dedicated to keeping the work of
Maxfield Parrish before the public
eye; licenses the right to use images
produced by Maxfield Parrish.*

Norman Rockwell

(see also COLLECTIBLES [MOD-
ERN], Norman Rockwell)

Clubs/Associations

Michael J.P. Collins, Pres.
Rockwell Society of America
P.O. Box 705
Ardsley, NY 10502-0705
phone: 914-631-3171
*Founded in 1974 and dedicated to the
appreciation of America's most
famous artist, Norman Rockwell;
specializing in original paintings,
drawings, collectibles, e.g. Saturday
Evening Post covers/magazines,
illustrated books, etc.*

Experts

Denis C. Jackson
P.O. Box 1958
Sequim, WA 98382-1958
phone: 360-683-2559
fax: 360-683-2559
e-mail: ticn@olypen.com
Internet: http://www.olypen.com/ticn/
*Magazines and paper items from 1914
to present; author of "The Price
Guide to Norman Rockwell", 3rd
edition; send LSASE for information.*

Museums/Libraries

Norman Rockwell Museum at
Stockbridge, The
Route 183
Stockbridge, MA 01262
phone: 413-298-4100

Marshall Stoltz
Norman Rockwell Museum
601 Walnut St.
Philadelphia, PA 19106-3310
phone: 215-922-4345
*American's largest exhibit of the
history and works of Norman
Rockwell; complete collection of
Norman Rockwell "Saturday Evening
Post" covers.*

Joyce Devore
Museum of Norman Rockwell Art
227 S. Park
Reedsburg, WI 53959-1945
phone: 608-524-2123
Private museum with gift shop.

Palmer Cox

Experts

Wayne Morgan
69 Main Street East
Grimsbyg
Ontario L3M 1N5 Canada
phone: 905-945-5754
fax: 905-945-5754
*Interested in all aspects of life and
work of Palmer Cox (1840-1924) -
children's author most famous for The
Brownies; can advise or assess
collections; author of several articles
on Cox's contributions to modern
culture.*

R. Atkinson Fox

Clubs/Associations

Pat Gibson, Sec.
R. Atkinson Fox Society
Newsletter: Fox Tales
38280 Guava Dr.
Newark, CA 94560
phone: 408-287-1863

Collectors

Frances L. Woodworth
P.O. Box 358
Janesville, IA 50647
phone: 319-987-2168

Sharon Gergen
8141 Main
Kansas City, MO 64114-2401
phone: 816-361-7539
e-mail: fcum65a@prodigy.com

Sherri Fountain
1511 W. 4th Ave.
Hutchinson, KS 67501
phone: 316-663-4293

Pat Gibson
38280 Guava Dr.
Newark, CA 94560
phone: 510-792-0586
*Always looking for any R.A. Fox
prints, calendars, oils, postcards, and
anything with his work on it.*

Dealers

Edward J. Meschi
129 Pinyard Rd.
Monroeville, NJ 08343-1870
phone: 609-358-7293
fax: 609-358-7293
Buying oil paintings.

Experts

Rita Mortenson
727 North Spring
Independence, MO 64050
*R. Atkinson Fox (1860-1927) was a
Canadian artist. Rita Mortenson is
author of "R. Atkinson Fox: His Life
and Work" (Vol. I & II.); SASE
required for reply.*

Tasha Tudor

Experts

E. Hollebaugh
1234 Larke Ave.
Rogers City, MI 49779
*Tasha Tudor is best known for her
illustrations in children's books.*

IMMIGRATION

Collectors

Kathy Sheeran
P.O. Box 520251
Miami, FL 33152-0251
*Wants photos, documents and
passports from pre-1950 immigrants
to the US; also wants buttons and
ribbons from immigrant groups
(A.O.H., Sons of Italy, etc.); also Ellis
Island and anti-immigrant items.*

IMPLEMENT SEATS

(see FARM COLLECTIBLES, Cast
Iron Seats)

INAUGURATION ITEMS

(see PERSONALITIES [HISTORI-
CAL]; POLITICAL COLLECTIBLES;
WHITE HOUSE MEMORABILIA)

INDIA

(see ART, Asian)

INDIAN ITEMS

(see AMERICAN INDIAN)

INDIAN WARS ITEMS

(see also AMERICAN INDIAN;
MILITARIA; MILITARY HISTORY)

Clubs/Associations

Jerry L. Russell, NatCh.
Order of the Indian Wars, The
Newsletter: Order of the Indian Wars
Communique
P.O. Box 7388
Little Rock, AR 72217-
phone: 501-225-3996
Internet: http://www.civilwarbuff.org
*The only national organization
devoted to the study & preservation of
Indian Wars history.*

Collectors

Thomas W. Pooler
P.O. Box 1861
Grass Valley, CA 95945-1861
phone: 916-268-1338
*Wants to buy INDIAN WARS medals
and insignia; also wants National and
United Indian War Veterans medals,
convention ribbons, pins, flags,
photos, etc.*

INDONESIA

(see ART, Asian; ORIENTALIA)

Dealers

Lobsang Aye
Mandala Gallery
110 West 25th St.
New York, NY 10001
phone: 212-989-1829
*Specializes in Far Eastern art and
artifacts from Tibet, Southeast Asia,
India, China, Japan.*

Borneo

Experts

Michael G. Price
P.O. Box 468
Michigan Center, MI 49254
phone: 517-764-4517
e-mail: mgprice@sojourn.com
*Wants Philippine picture postcards,
photos, magazines, books, maps; also
wants items from nearby islands such
as Borneo.*

Philippines

Collectors

Roy Stephens
201 West Shore Rd.
Great Neck, NY 11024-1638
phone: 516-829-8827
fax: 718-281-2055
*Wants Indonesian and Philippine art:
paintings, wood carvings, inlaid
chests, batik, textiles, brass, krises,*

betel nut boxes, swords and other
weapons.

Experts

Michael G. Price
P.O. Box 468
Michigan Center, MI 49254
phone: 517-764-4517
e-mail: mgprice@sojourn.com
*Wants Philippine picture postcards,
photos, magazines, books, maps; also
wants items from nearby islands such
as Borneo.*

INDUSTRIAL DESIGN

(see MODERNISM)

INDUSTRY RELATED ITEMS

(see also BEEKEEPING MEMORA-
BILIA; CONSTRUCTION EQUIP-
MENT; CRANBERRY INDUSTRY;
FARM MACHINERY; FASTENERS;
ICE INDUSTRY; LOGGING;
MACHINERY & EQUIPMENT;
MILLING; MINING; MODERNISM;
SCRIP; SOCIAL CAUSES; TOOLS;
WHISKEY INDUSTRY ITEMS)

Appraisers

Robert L. Johnson
Whistles in the Woods Museum Services
P.O. Box 309
Chickamauga, GA 30707-0309
phone: 706-375-4326
e-mail: oldgoat@voy.net
*Consultants specializing in 1750 -
early 20th century historic machinery;
power-generation, tools, machines,
scientific & technical instruments,
mining, milling, transportation,
logging & lumbering, steam engines,
etc.*

Clubs/Associations

Elton W. Hall, Ex. Dir.
Early American Industries Association,
The
Newsletter: Shavings, The
167 Bakersville Rd.
South Dartmouth, MA 02748
phone: 508-993-4198
Internet: http://
ourworld.compuserve.com/
homepages/Old_Tools/about.htm
*Interested in old tools, implements,
utensils, vehicles, "Whatsits"; and to
discover, identify and preserve same;
also publishes the magazine
"Chronicle."*

Museums/Libraries

Keith R. Gill
Museum of Science & Industry
57th St. & Lake Shore Dr.
Chicago, IL 60637
phone: 312-684-1414
fax: 312-684-5580
*Archives contains documents &
photos of the 1893 Columbian
Exposition.*

INFANT FEEDERS

(see also BOTTLES)

Clubs/Associations

Jo Ann Todd
American Collectors of Infant Feeders
Newsletter: Keeping Abreast
5161 West 59th St.
Indianapolis, IN 46254-1107
phone: 317-291-5850
*Founded in 1973 for those interested
in feeding infants and the devices used
therefore: nursers, baby bottles,
infant/invalid feeders; book, "A Guide
to American Nursing Bottles" is now
available.*

Collectors

Jo Ann Todd
5161 West 59th St.
Indianapolis, IN 46254-1107
phone: 317-291-5850
*Wants infant/invalid feeders; nursers,
baby bottles, etc.; made of horn,
wood, pewter, silver, glass, plastic or
pottery.*

Man./Prod./Dist.

Playtex Family Products, Inc.
215 College Rd.
Paramus, NJ 07652
*Provides order forms for collectible
baby bottles.*

INK BLOTTERS

(see BLOTTERS; INKWELLS &
INKSTANDS; PAPER COL-
LECTIBLES; PENS)

INKWELLS & INKSTANDS

(see also BOTTLES; BLOTTERS;
CALLIGRAPHY; PAPER COL-
LECTIBLES; PENCILS; PENS)

Clubs/Associations

Vince McGraw
Society of Inkwell Collectors, The
Newsletter: Stained Finger, The
5136 Thomas Ave. So.
Minneapolis, MN 55410-2241
phone: 612-922-2792
fax: 612-920-7835
e-mail: soic@concentric.net
*Features articles about inkwells, pens
and writing accessories; has catalog
offering books about inkwells, and
replacement inserts, quills, rocker
blotters. etc.; newsletter published
quarterly.*

St. Louis Inkwell Collectors Society
P.O. Box 29396
St. Louis, MO 63126

Collectors

Robert Kwalwasser
168 Camp Fatima Rd.
Renfrew, PA 16053-9104
phone: 412-789-7766
Wants to buy traveling inkwells.

Lew Poggiali
7421 Pakepark Dr.
West Chester, OH 45069

Elaine Hinkle Crittenden
Calligraphy Heaven
14902 Preston Rd., Ste. 216
Dallas, TX 75240-9103
phone: 972-934-1055
fax: 972-934-1055
*Buys inkwells and related items such
as blotters, desk sets, dip pen points,
etc.*

John E. Kochenburger
1304 Robertson St.
Fort Collins, CO 80524-4258
phone: 304-484-0274
*Collects a variety of inkstands,
inkwells, ink bottles and "go-withs";
also buys and sells.*

Dealers

Gerard Schultz
Antique Gallery, The
8523 Germantown Ave.
Philadelphia, PA 19118
phone: 215-248-1700
fax: 215-247-8411
*Buys and sells inkwells: ceramic,
brass, glass, traveling, figural.*

Sam Fiorella
Pendemonium
15231 Larkspur Lane
Dumfries, VA 22026-1075
phone: 703-670-8549
fax: 703-670-3785
e-mail: sam@pendemonium.com
Internet: http://www.pendemonium.com
*Buys and sells fountain pens, inkwells,
ink bottles, pen stands, blotters, pen
catalogs, magazine covers and
advertisements; write for current
"Writing Collectibles" catalog, it's
FREE!*

Bill Thompson
502 Woodhaven Rd.
Centerville, GA 31028-1327
*Buys and sells anything related to
writing; inkwells, rocker blotters,
letter openers, lap desks, etc.*

Sandra I. Van Tine
Lora's Memory Lane
13133 N. Caroline St.
Chillicothe, IL 61523-9115
phone: 309-579-3040
fax: 309-579-2696
e-mail: lorasink@aol.com
*Buys and sells inkwells, inkstands, and
ink related items.*

Carol Payne
Carol's Antique Gallery
14455 Big Basin Way
Saratoga, CA 95070-6008
phone: 408-867-7055
*Wants to buy inks of any material;
sometimes considers broken ones for
parts; also wants desk items like letter
racks, wax seals, blotters, pens, pen
stands, pen wipers, etc.*

Experts

Veldon Badders
692 Martin Rd.
Hamlin, NY 14464-9744
phone: 716-964-3360
*Author of "Collector's Guide to
Inkwells."*

Ray & Bev Jaegers
P.O. Box 29396
Saint Louis, MO 63126-0396
e-mail: USPsiSquad@aol.com
Experts and historians.

INSECTS

Museums/Libraries

University of California, Berkeley, Essig
  Museum of Entomology
311 Wellman Hall
Berkeley, CA 94720
phone: 415-642-4779

Butterflies

Museums/Libraries

Treasure of El Camino Real
P.O. Box 1047
Atascadero, CA 93423
phone: 805-466-0142
*The Victor Clemence butterfly
collection.*

Cockroaches

Museums/Libraries

Michael Bohdan
Combat Cockroach Hall of Fame, The
  Pest Shop Inc.
2231-B West Fifteenth St.
Plano, TX 75075
phone: 972-519-0355
*Come see dressed up cockroaches like
Roach Pero or Liberoachi!*

Ticks

Museums/Libraries

U.S. National Tick Collection, Institute
  of Anthropodology and Parasitology
Georgia Southern University
Landrum, Box 8056
Statesboro, GA 30460
phone: 912-681-5564
*Collection of over one million ticks -
the smallest fits on the head of a pin,
the largest is the size of a quarter;
history of each includes location
collected and the "host" organism.*

INSTRUMENTS & DEVICES

(see also ARCHITECTURE &
RELATED ITEMS; ASTRONOMI-
CAL ITEMS; BAROMETERS;
GAUGES; GLOBES; MEDICAL,
DENTAL & PHARMACEUTICAL;
MICROSCOPES; NAUTICAL
ANTIQUES; OFFICE EQUIPMENT;
SCALES; SLIDE RULES; SPY
EQUIPMENT; SURVEYING
INSTRUMENTS; THERMOMETERS

Compasses

Dealers

David S. Bennett
Bennett Antiques
15800 26th Ave. N.
Minneapolis, MN 55447-1940
Wants to buy military compasses, pocket variety of WWI, WWII and earlier; pocket compasses in wooden boxes; old sport compasses; Boy Scout and Girl Scout pocket compasses; also pocket transits.

Scientific

Auction Services

Jon Baddeley
Sotheby's
34-35 New Bond St.
London W1A 2AA, U.K.
phone: 0171-4938080 or 0171-4085205
fax: 0171-4085911
Conducts regular auctions of scientific instruments.

Sotheby's
1334 York Ave.
New York, NY 10021
phone: 212-606-7370 or 212-606-7000
Internet: http://www.sothebys.com
Over 70 collecting areas are featured at Sotheby's auctions including toys, dolls, porcelain, furniture, silver, art, books; exhibitions are free and everyone is welcome; for a free copy of "Sotheby's Newsletter", call 212-606-7245.

Clubs/Associations

Howard Dawes
Scientific Instrument Society
P.O. Box 15, Pershore
Worcestershire WR10 2RD U.K.
A British organization that travels extensively; quarterly journal with polished articles.

Zeiss Historica Society
Journal: Zeiss Historica Society Journal
300 Waxwing Drive
Cranbury, NJ 08512
phone: 540-981-1036
e-mail: msmall@roanoke.infi.net
Internet: http://www.netins.net/showcase/crye/zi-hist.htm
Dedicated to the study & exchange of information on the history of Carl Zeiss Optical Co. and Zeiss-Ikon, its people and products (cameras, accessories, and optical equipment of all types) from 1846 to present; semi-annual journal.

Dr. Sam Koslov
Maryland Microscopical & Scientific Instrument Society
8621 Polk St.
McLean, VA 22102
phone: 703-893-9102
Focuses on instruments and devices: medical, surveying, photographic, microscopical, navigational, horological, astronomical, etc.

Collectors

Thomas B. Perera
11 Squire Hill Rd.
Caldwell, NJ 07006-4718
phone: 201-226-9185
e-mail: pererat@alpha.montclair.edu
Internet: http://www.chss.montclair.edu/~pererat/telegraph.html
Wants to buy early scientific instruments; has been collecting for over 40 years.

Dr. Allan Wissner
P.O. Box 102
Ardsley, NY 10502-0102
phone: 914-693-4628
e-mail: wissnea@war.wyeth.com
Wants microscopes, medical, scientific instruments: Zentmayer, Grunow, Bullock, McAllister, Gundlack, McIntosh, Tolles, Queen, Pike.

Paul Ferraglio
3332 W. Lake Rd.
Canandaigua, NY 14424-2441
phone: 716-394-7663
fax: 716-394-5424
e-mail: p4alyo@aol.com
Buys old scientific instruments: microscopes, surveying instruments, mineralogical & other optical instruments in any condition; also books & catalogs; also wants parts.

W. Feely
1172 Lindsay La.
Jenkintown, PA 19046-1839
phone: 215-884-5640
fax: 215-884-8660
Wants unusual drafting and navigation equipment, coast artillery manuals and memorabilia.

Dr. Sam Koslov
8621 Polk St.
McLean, VA 22102
phone: 703-893-9102
Wants to buy medical, surveying, photographic, microscopical, navigational, horological, astronomical, etc. instruments & devices.

Jon Lewin
622 Raleigh Ave., Apt. 3
Norfolk, VA 23507-2034
phone: 757-625-6732
Wants to buy floor-standing electro-medical machines, electro-static generators, leyden jars, oddly-shaped vacuum tubes or x-ray tubes, hand-operated vacuum pumps, glass-legged tables and stools, glass-handled rods, astronomical models.

John M. Shannon
7319 West Cedar Circle
Lakewood, CO 80226-2019
phone: 303-232-1534
e-mail: rovers@aol.com
Wants to buy assay balances (wood and glass encased with small pans) - both laboratory and portable; also wants brass scientific instruments.

Paul H. Hayashi, PE
18 Tarabrook Dr.
Orinda, CA 94563-3121
phone: 510-254-5074 or 510-253-1038
fax: 510-253-0592
Buys old scientific instruments: surveying, microscopes, barometers, calculators, drafting sets, chronometers, navigational devices, etc.

Robert De Cesaris
7429 Bree Ann Ct.
Citrus Heights, CA 95610-2455
phone: 916-356-5769
Serious collector of slide rules, early mechanical adders and calculators; special interests include circular, cylindrical or other unusual slide rules and lever set calculators right up to the Curta calculator.

Dealers

David L. Isabelle
MediaSpecialies
28 Revell Ave.
Northampton, MA 01060
phone: 413-586-7571 or 413-584-1034
fax: 413-584-1034
e-mail: instrumentation@mediaspec.com
Internet: http://www.mediaspec.com/GNET/mediaspecialties
Specializing in medical, scientific, optical, cameras, images, and cinema.

David & Yola Coffeen
Tesseract
P.O. Box 151
Hastings On Hudson, NY 10706-0151
phone: 914-478-2594
fax: 914-478-5473
Issues a series of well illustrated catalogs of early scientific instruments: astronomy, microscopy, sundials, surveying, calculation, computation, adding, navigation, etc.; always interested in buying single items of collections.

James & Norvell Kennedy
James Kennedy Antiques, Ltd.
905 W. Main St.
Durham, NC 27701-2054
phone: 919-682-1040 or 800-236-1868
fax: 919-683-9633
Specialist in scientific and medical instruments and prints; also nautical instruments.

John Forster
Barometer Fair
P.O. Box 25502
Sarasota, FL 34277
phone: 941-923-6136
fax: 941-923-6136
e-mail: barometer@glimmer.com
Buys, sells, restores all antique barometers; also deals in antique maps, globes, compasses, telescopes and other scientific instruments.

Alex Peck
Antique Scientifica
P.O. Box 710
Charleston, IL 61920
phone: 217-348-1009
Wants to buy early microscopes,

telescopes, telegraphs, globes, electrical, patent models, surveying instruments, scales, nautical, demonstration items.

Al & Bobbie Roberts
Rational Past, The
221 Oceano Dr.
Los Angeles, CA 90049
phone: 310-476-6277
fax: 310-476-6278
e-mail: rational-past@mindspring.com
Organizer of West Coast Scientific & Technical Antique and Collectible Shows (Los Angeles in the winter and San Francisco are in late summer.)

Gemmary, The
P.O. Box 816
Redondo Beach, CA 90277
phone: 310-372-6149 or 310-372-5969
fax: 310-372-5969
Antique scientific instruments: 18th & 19th C. mathematical, philosophical, optical instruments, microscopes, telescopes, globes, orreries, sundials, compasses, surveying, navigating, drawing, medical, laboratory.

Rod & Becky Cardoza
West Sea Company
2495 Congress St.
San Diego, CA 92110-2820
phone: 619-296-5356
fax: 619-296-1097
Buys, sells all types of marine paintings, scrimshaw, ships' carvings, ship models, navigational and scientific instruments, sailor handcrafts, campaign furniture, hard hat diving, antique marine photography, nautical books, ceramics.

Lynn Harding
Antique Instruments of the Professions and Sciences
103 West Aliso St.
Ojai, CA 93023-2603
phone: 805-646-0204
fax: 805-646-0204
Specializes in buying and selling antique scientific and technological instruments: orreries, steam, calculating, optics, electrical, golfing, tennis, medical, microscopes, scales & weights, measuring, books, tools, drafting, surveying.

Experts

Thomas B. Perera
11 Squire Hill Rd.
Caldwell, NJ 07006-4718
phone: 201-226-9185
e-mail: pererat@alpha.montclair.edu
Internet: http://www.chss.montclair.edu/~pererat/telegraph.html
Maintains internet telegraph and scientific instrument museum and collector's guide.

Dale R. Beeks
Perceptions Scientifica
P.O. Box 117
Mount Vernon, IA 52314
phone: 800-880-5178 or 319-895-0506
Buys fine microscopes; old scientific,

surveying, technical, medical and precision instruments; pre-1900 typewriters, calculating devices, medical items & quackery.

Museums/Libraries

National Museum of American History
  Branch Library
Smithsonian Institution
Washington, DC 20560
phone: 202-357-2414
Internet: http://www.si.edu/
Books/journals/trade catalogs on material culture, decorative arts, domestic & community life, applied science, engineering, technology.

Periodicals

David & Yola Coffeen
Tesseract
Journal: Rittenhouse
P.O. Box 151
Hastings On Hudson, NY 10706-0151
phone: 914-478-2594
fax: 914-478-5473
A quarterly periodical to facilitate communication among collectors, curators & historians of scientific instruments; provides a forum for information about instruments made and/or sold in America.

Richard Van Vleck
Greybird Publishing
Newsletter: Scientific, Medical &
  Mechanical Antiques
P.O. Box 412
Taneytown, MD 21787
phone: 301-447-2680
e-mail: smma@fred.net
Internet: http://www.bestware.net/smma/
A bi-monthly newsletter about scientific, medical and mechanical devices; microscopy, surveying, scales, navigation, surgical, quackery, steam, electrical, agriculture, astronomy, calculators, etc.; ads, auction reports, article.

Sundials

Collectors

Cal Frye
125 E. Oak St.
Kent, OH 44240-3825
phone: 330-678-7006
fax: 330-678-7006
e-mail: cj_frye@bigfoot.com
Internet: http://Phoenix.kent.edu/~cfrye
Wants oddball slide rules: circular, cylindrical, special-purpose, or big (classroom-sized); also wants pocket/ portable sundials.

INSULATORS

(see also BOTTLES)

Appraisers

John McDougald
5N941 Ravine Dr.
Saint Charles, IL 60175-8272
phone: 630-513-1544
fax: 630-513-8278
e-mail: mcd@crownjewelsofthewire.com
Internet: http://
  crownjewelsofthewire.com
Buys, sells, appraises glass insulators.

Clubs/Associations

Doug MacGillvary
Yankee Polecat Insulator Club, The
Newsletter: YPIC Newsletter
79 New Bolton Rd.
Manchester, CT 06040
phone: 203-649-0477
Oldest continuing insulator club in the country; members throughout New England and surrounding areas; annual show, swap meets.

Kevin Lawless, Sec.
Capital District Insulator Club
Newsletter: Pilgrim Hat, The
41 Crestwood Dr.
Schenectady, NY 12306-3433
phone: 518-355-5688 or 518-356-0300
fax: 518-356-1947
Club for collectors of antique electrical insulators; membership based in Northeast U.S.; annual show; regular club swaps and meetings.

Ken Wehr
Chesapeake Bay Insulator Club
10 Ridge Rd.
Catonsville, MD 21228
phone: 410-747-7126
Members are collectors of glass and ceramic electrical insulators.

Keith Roloson
Dixie-Jewels Insulator Club
Newsletter: DJIC Newsletter
6220 Carriage Ct.
Cumming, GA 30130-9111
phone: 770-781-5021 or 770-750-6429
e-mail: kroloson@ems.att.com
Internet: http://www.insulators.com
Newsletter published quarterly; complimentary back issue available upon request.

J. Carl Sturm, Pres.
Federation of Historical Bottle
  Collectors, Inc.
Magazine: Bottles & Extras
88 Sweetbriar Branch
Longwood, FL 32750-2783
phone: 407-332-7689
e-mail: glassman@qnet.com
Internet: http://www.av.qnet.com/
  ~glassman
"Bottles & Extras" contains articles, pictures, letters, show dates, and show and auction reports in the field of antique bottles, insulators, fruit jars and associated items; check website for list of scores of clubs by region.

Central Florida Insulator Collectors Club
Newsletter: CFICC Newsletter
707 N.E. 113th St.
Miami, FL 33161

Joe J. Beres, Mem.
National Insulator Association
Newsletter: Drip Point
1315 Old Mill Path
Broadview Heights, OH 44147-3276
phone: 216-526-3478
e-mail: jjjb@aol.com
An organization for those interested in collecting electrical insulators and other artifacts connected with related industries.

Francis Bixler
National Trails Insulator Club
408 Arlington Rd.
Brookville, OH 45309
phone: 513-833-2577

Paul Ickes
Missouri Valley Insulator Club
52 Lakewood Lane
Council Bluffs, IA 51502
phone: 712-366-3434

Rick Soller
Greater Chicago Insulator Club
Newsletter: GCIC Newsletter
34273 Homestead Rd.
Gurnee, IL 60031-4206
phone: 847-855-9136 or 847-543-2958
fax: 847-548-3383
e-mail: rick-soller@clc.cc.il.us
Hosts shows, swap meets and hunts.

Carolyn Merritt
O.K. Insulator Club
Rte. 2 Box 27
Carnegie, OK 73015
phone: 405-654-1770

Elton Gish
Lone Star Insulator Club
Newsletter: Lone Star Lines
P.O. Box 1317
Buna, TX 77612-1317
phone: 409-994-5662 or 409-989-7161
fax: 409-989-7407
e-mail: giahen@sat.net
Internet: http://www.insulators.com
Meets monthly on the 3rd Friday in Houston, TX; educational programs offered at each meeting.

Bob Ryckman
Triple Ridge Insulator Club
2120 S. Vaughn Way
Aurora, CO 80014-1375
phone: 303-696-6172

Tom Katonak
Enchantment Insulator Club
1024 Camino de Lucia
Corrales, NM 87048-8314
phone: 505-898-5592
Internet: http://www.insulators.com
Specialty area includes telegraph, telephone, and power insulators; glass and porcelain; experts in identification and evaluation.

Ron Norton
Central/Southern Counties Insulator
  Club
234 N. 5th St.
Port Hueneme, CA 93041
phone: 805-488-7445

Jack Foote
North-Cal Insulator Club
2551 Verna Way
Sacramento, CA 95821
phone: 916-489-9413

Collectors

Dario Dimare
1 Elda Rd.
Framingham, MA 01701-4335
phone: 508-877-4444 or 508-877-0958
fax: 508-877-4474
Buys, sells, appraises glass insulators; one piece or entire collection; wants threadless and good colored glass such as cobalt blue, purple, yellow, citron, 7-Up green, and amber; also wants pre-1900 telegraph maps, books and catalogs.

John DeSousa
5 Brownstone Rd.
East Granby, CT 06026-9705
phone: 203-658-0353

Dick Bowman
1253 LaBaron Circle
Webster, NY 14580-9529
phone: 716-872-4015
Wants to buy quality insulators, especially threadless insulators.

Allen Klapaska
6242 Glen Arm Rd.
Hydes, MD 21082
phone: 410-592-6416

John Hunsaker
7651 Wesley Rd.
Manassas, VA 22110-3321
phone: 703-361-5996

Jim Meyer
3310 State Rd. 40
Ormond Beach, FL 32174-2537
phone: 904-677-0530
fax: 904-673-9883
Wants to buy better insulators.

Mark Reutebuch
3125 Redwing Ln.
Rapid City, SD 57701
phone: 605-393-9707
Buys, sells, trades glass and wooden insulators.

Ross Baird
P.O. Box 937
Fort Worth, TX 76101
phone: 817-236-5580
Wants to buy glass insulators embossed Boston Bottle Works, Cal. Elec. Works, Emminger, Seilers, Harloe, Chester, E.C.M. & Co. (color), Combination Safety.

Ross Thompson
1212 West Camino Desierto
Tucson, AZ 85704
phone: 602-297-5898
Wants to buy quality insulators,
especially threadless insulators.

Dwayne Anthony
1066 Scenic Drive
San Bernardino, CA 92408-1818
phone: 909-888-6417

Dealers

Doug MacGillvary
79 New Bolton Rd.
Manchester, CT 06040
phone: 203-649-0477
Glass & porcelain insulators,
collections or singles bought/sold/
traded; a reputation built on twenty
years of honest dealing.

Experts

Bill & Jill Meier
103 Canterbury Ct.
Carlisle, MA 01741-1860
phone: 508-369-0208
e-mail: meier@insulators.com
Internet: http://www.insulators.com
Specialists in Hemingray, H.G. Co.
and DEC 19 1871 insulators and
other Hemingray items such as water
bottles and H.G. Co. fruit jars;
looking to expand collection;
interested in sharing knowledge with
others.

Kevin Lawless
41 Crestwood Dr.
Schenectady, NY 12306-3433
phone: 518-355-5688 or 518-356-0300
fax: 518-356-1947
Buys and sells all types of antique
insulators; glass, porcelain,
threadless, foreign, colored, rare,
common, singles or collections.

Keith Roloson
6220 Carriage Ct.
Cumming, GA 30130-9111
phone: 770-781-5021 or 770-750-6429
e-mail: kroloson@ems.att.com
Internet: http://www.insulators.com
Interested in all glass and porcelain
insulators; seeks Southeastern
threadless-pinhole styles; specializes
in radio antenna "strain" insulators,
early (1860-1890) telegraph styles;
also offers free appraisals.

Len. L. Linscott
3557 Nicklaus Dr.
Titusville, FL 32780-5356
phone: 407-267-9170
Wants "eared" glass electrical
insulators; especially CD#250-
CD#270; also those with rare colors
of embossing errors; sells book solely
devoted to insulators; willing to assist
the novice collector with insulator
information & ID.

Michael Bruner
2615 Echo Lane
Ortonville, MI 48462
phone: 810-627-6351
Wants rare or unusual style
insulators; single or entire collec-
tions; also wants related telephone/
telegraph items such as signs,
catalogs.

John & Carol McDougald
5N941 Ravine Dr.
Saint Charles, IL 60175-8272
phone: 630-513-1544
fax: 630-513-8278
e-mail: mcd@crownjewelsofthewire.com
Internet: http://
crownjewelsofthewire.com
Buys, sells, trades insulators &
telephone related items & lightning
rod balls and weathervanes; authors
of "Insulators-A History and Guide to
North Amer. Glass Pintype Insulators,
Vol. 1 & 2"; $68.50 both vols. &
current price guide.

Elton Gish
P.O. Box 1317
Buna, TX 77612-1317
phone: 409-994-5662 or 409-989-7161
fax: 409-989-7407
e-mail: giahen@sat.net
Internet: http://www.insulators.com
Wants 1890-1930 unipart or multipart
porcelain insulators; author of
"Multipart Porcelain Insulators,"
"Biography of Fred M. Locke - The
Father of Porcelain Insulators",
"Value Guide for Porcelain
Insulator."

Michael G. Guthrie
1209 West Menlo
Fresno, CA 93711-1477
phone: 209-435-6127
e-mail: mgg17@cvip.fresno.com
Internet: http://www.insulators.com
Author of "A Handbook for the
Recognition & Identification of Fake,
Altered and Repaired Insulators";
Treasurer for the National Insulator
Association.

Paul Keating
1705 S. 41st St.
Tacoma, WA 98405-1610
phone: 206-474-9659
Author of an "Milholland Price
Guide", an insulator price guide;
published about every two years;
currently $15 ppd., 159 pages, with
historical notes, full descriptions, and
average mint price.

Periodicals

Magazine: Canadian Insulator Magazine
Mayne Island
B.C. V0N 2J0 Canada

John McDougald
Magazine: Crown Jewels of the Wire
5N941 Ravine Dr.
Saint Charles, IL 60175-8272
phone: 630-513-1544
fax: 630-513-8278
e-mail: mcd@crownjewelsofthewire.com
Internet: http://
crownjewelsofthewire.com
76-page monthly magazine of
insulator and telephone history; glass,
porcelain; foreign columns; classified
ads, show dates, etc.

Patti Norton
Newsletter: Rainbow Riders Trading
Post
P.O. Box 1423
Port Hueneme, CA 93044
phone: 805-488-7445
e-mail: rrtp@ix.netcom.com
Internet: http://www.netcom.com/~rrtp/
main.html
Ads, stories, interesting articles; no
sales of insulators, just trading
allowed.

Foreign

Experts

Marilyn Albers
14715 Oak Bend Dr.
Houston, TX 77079-6418
phone: 281-497-4146 or 281-497-3320
fax: 281-497-3957
e-mail: marilynAFI@aol.com
Co-author of "Glass Insulators From
Outside North America," "Worldwide
Porcelain Insulators," "Price Guide
for Glass Insulators from Outside
North America" (1996); specialist in
foreign insulators.

INSURANCE MEMORABILIA

(see also FIRE INSURANCE
RELATED COLLECTIBLES)

Collectors

Byron Gregerson
P.O. Box 951
Modesto, CA 95353-0951
phone: 209-523-3300
fax: 209-523-3399
Collector wants pre-1930 auto and
fire (no life insurance items, please)
insurance memorabilia especially
advertising signs: reverse-painting-
on-glass, tin & lithography.

State Farm

Collectors

Ken Jones
100 Manor Dr.
Columbia, MO 65203
phone: 573-445-7171

INVALID FEEDERS

(see also BOTTLES; INFANT
FEEDERS)

Collectors

Ken Odiorne
Rte. 2 Box 22
Bertram, TX 78605
phone: 512-355-2542
Wants invalid feeders: "cup", "boat"
or "Aladdin's" lamp shapes; no plain
white in "cup" or "boat" shapes
unless unusual shape or mark.

IRONS

Pressing

(see also KITCHEN COL-
LECTIBLES; WATER SPRIN-
KLERS; TRIVETS)

Clubs/Associations

Lynette Conrad
Midwest Sad Iron Collectors Club
Newsletter: Pressing News
24 Nob Hill Dr.
Saint Louis, MO 63138-1458
phone: 314-741-4171
Quarterly newsletter, membership
directory, annual meeting.

Club of the Friends of Ancient
Smoothing Irons
P.O. Box 215
Carlsbad, CA 92008
phone: 619-729-1740

Collectors

William "Buck" Carson
936 Dove Island Rd.
Newton, NJ 07860
phone: 201-383-4894

Jerry Jankowski
754 34th Pl.
West Des Moines, IA 50265

Beverly Hillner
811 First Ave.
Vinton, IA 52349

Paul & Lynette Conrad
24 Nob Hill Dr.
Saint Louis, MO 63138-1458
phone: 314-741-4171

Jay Poirier
5964 S. Lee Way
Littleton, CO 80127
phone: 303-973-4255
Wants mint or near mint gasoline,
kerosene, or alcohol fueled pressing
irons; also wants parts.

Dealers

Carole Meeker
Box 169 Kelly St.
Rhinecliff, NY 12574
phone: 914-876-7818
Wants to buy rare and unusual small
patented mechanical antiques, early
American technology and occupa-
tional-related photography,
advertising and catalogs.

Experts

David & Sue Irons
D. Irons Antiques
RD 4 Box 101
Northampton, PA 18067-9232
phone: 610-262-9335
Buys and sells; issues semi-annual catalog of irons for sale; advisor to "Warman's Antiques & Collectibles Price Guide"; published "Irons by Irons" (106 pgs. $43.45 ppd.) and "Pressing Iron Patents" (70 pgs. $21 ppd.).

Periodicals

Carol & Jimmy Walker
Magazine: Iron Talk
P.O. Box 68
Waelder, TX 78959-0068
phone: 512-665-7166 or 800-532-IRON
fax: 512-665-7166
e-mail: jimmy@irontalk.com
Internet: http://www.irontalk.com
Know today's prices, markets, trends, collectors' articles on gasoline irons, box irons, sad irons, fluters, little irons, heaters, sprinkle bottles and more.

ISRAEL

(see JUDAICA)

IVER JOHNSON ARMS & CYCLE WORKS

Experts

Charles W. Best
11523 Pine Valley Dr.
Franktown, CO 80116-8708
phone: 303-660-2318
Advanced collector and historian for Iver Johnson Arms & Cycle Works of Fitchburg, MA; interested in any Iver Johnson product including guns, tools, bicycles, motorcycles, signs, advertising and memorabilia.

IVORY

(see also ENDANGERED SPECIES; GEMS & JEWELRY; NAUTICAL ANTIQUES; NETSUKE; ORIENTALIA; SCRIMSHAW)

Clubs/Associations

Robert E. Weisblut
International Ivory Society
Newsletter: International Ivory Society Newsletter
11109 Nicholas Dr.
Silver Spring, MD 20902-3532
phone: 301-649-4002
Provides a basis for people interested in ivory to network worldwide and learn to identify ivory and its history, care, and current pricing.

Dealers

Brian J. Kiracofe
Newport Scrimshander, The
14 Bowen's Wharf
Newport, RI 02840
phone: 401-849-5680 or 800-653-5234
fax: 401-849-9306
e-mail: newportscrimshaw@juno.com
Carries an extensive collection of European and Far Eastern carved ivory antiques.

David Boone
Boone's Trading Company
P.O. Box BB
Brinnon, WA 98320
phone: 360-796-4330 or 800-423-1945
fax: 360-796-4551
Buys and sells legal ivory, scrimshaw, furs and skulls: scrimshaw, netsuke, Eskimo artifacts, carvings, walrus, hippo, warthog, mammoth, jewelry, pistol grips, ivory beads, old trade beads, scrimshaw supplies and reproductions.

Experts

Ed Tripp
Collector's World
139 Main St.
Cooperstown, NY 13326
phone: 607-547-5509
fax: 607-547-5483

Robert E. Weisblut
11109 Nicholas Dr.
Silver Spring, MD 20902-3532
phone: 301-649-4002
Wants to buy books about ivory: care, identification, collections, the ivory trade, etc.

David Warther II
David Warther Carving Museum
2561 Crestview Dr. NW
Dover, OH 44622-7405
phone: 330-852-3455 or 330-343-1868
Purchases pre-ban (pre-1989) elephant tusks for ongoing ivory carving art project; only wants tusks from African elephants and they must predate 1989; (purchases only); authority on tusks and related laws.

Museums/Libraries

David Warther II
David Warther Carving Museum
2561 Crestview Dr. NW
Dover, OH 44622-7405
phone: 330-852-3455 or 330-343-1868
Purchases pre-ban (pre-1989) elephant tusks for ongoing ivory carving art project; only wants tusks from African elephants and they must predate 1989; (purchases only).

Periodicals

Joan L. Cervi
Newsletter: Netsuke & Ivory Carving Newsletter-Video
3203 Adams Way
Ambler, PA 19002-3741
phone: 215-628-2026
fax: 215-628-2026
A wholesaler who offers VHS videos and a monthly newsletter about imported netsuke, ivory carvings and other Orientalia.

Repair Services

David Warther II
David Warther Carving Museum
2561 Crestview Dr. NW
Dover, OH 44622-7405
phone: 330-852-3455 or 330-343-1868
Restores wood and ivory carvings and turnings; specialty is in small objects in ivory: chess sets, finials, small turned items, insulators, handles, and finials of ivory or sterling hollowware.

John Edward Cunningham
1525 E. Berkley
Springfield, MO 65804-3203
phone: 417-889-7702
Ivory, highly detailed and handcarved; genuine ivory replacement parts for Art Deco and Japanese figurines; also ivory and mother-of-pearl inlays; will travel for large restorations.

Here are some tips when contacting someone listed in this book:

When requesting information about a particular item, include a description (material, dimensions, maker's mark, model number, etc.) and a photo, sketch, or photocopy of the item in question. ■

Always ask if there are charges for samples or for the services requested. ■

When writing, please be sure to include a Large (#10 business size) Self-Addressed and Stamped Envelope (LSASE) if requesting a reply or the return of photographs. ■

Never call collect unless otherwise directed. When calling, be considerate of time zone differences and always ask if the party you are calling has time to talk. When leaving an answering machine message, always instruct the party to call you back <u>collect</u>. ■

JACQULET

(see PRINTS, Woodblock [Jacoulet])

JADE

(see also GEMS & JEWELRY; ORIENTALIA)

Periodicals

Friends of Jade
Journal: Bulletin of the Friends of Jade
5004 Ensign St.
San Diego, CA 92117
fax: 619-581-1511
The "Bulletin" is an annual comprehensive source of of jade information.

JAMES BOND

(see CHARACTER COLLECTIBLES, Spy Memorabilia [James Bond])

JAPANESE ITEMS

(see ART, Oriental; ARMS & ARMOR, Japanese; BOOKS, Reference [Japanese Items]; FIREARMS, Japanese Matchlocks; OCCUPIED JAPAN; MILITARIA; ORIENTALIA, Japanese Items; PRINTS, Woodblock [Japanese])

JARS

(see BOTTLES; BISCUIT BARRELS/ JARS/TINS; CANDY CONTAINERS, Jars; FRUIT JARS; JELLY CONTAINERS; TOBACCO COLLECTIBLES, Jars)

JELL-O MEMORABILIA

Collectors

Roberta Deal
P.O. Box 17
Mecklenburg, NY 14863

Lee Davis
4150 Old Orchard Rd.
York, PA 17402-3319
phone: 717-757-7267
Collects only pre-1912 JELL-O recipe books.

Ron Schieber
1867 W. Market St.
Akron, OH 44313

Experts

Bob Allen
231 E. James Blvd.
P.O. Box 85
Saint James, MO 65559-0085
phone: 314-265-8296

JELLY CONTAINERS

(see also FRUIT JARS)

Clubs/Associations

Art Snyder, Treas.
Jelly Jammers
Newsletter: Jelly Jammers' Journal
110 White Oak Dr.
Butler, PA 16001-3446
phone: 412-287-0278
Jelly Jammers focuses on collecting jelly jars, glasses, molds, cups, mugs and samples or miniatures, and on the education of its members.

Collectors

Art Snyder
110 White Oak Dr.
Butler, PA 16001-3446
phone: 412-287-0278
Buys/sells/trades all types of jelly glasses, jars, molds and cups, especially patented examples; also wants all related material.

Margaret Shaw
6086 W Boggstown Rd.
Boggstown, IN 46110-9731
phone: 317-835-7121
e-mail: emshaw@in.net

Janice Andres
1951 St. Rd. 28 East
Lafayette, IN 47905

Experts

Barbara Bowditch
1173 Peck Rd.
Hilton, NY 14468
Author of "American Jelly Glasses: A Collector's Notebook."

JEWELRY

(see ART DECO; GEMS & JEWELRY)

JOHNSON SMITH CO.

Collectors

Stan Timm
Uniquely Racine
6001 Leeward Lane
Racine, WI 53402-9783
phone: 414-639-2304 or 414-639-3312
e-mail: mtimm@aol.com
Wants to buy Johnson Smith Co. catalogs and items sold by the company; writing book about the company and would be interested in any anecdotes, stories or experiences with the company and its products.

JUDAICA

(see also ART, Jewish; STAMP COLLECTING, Holly Land; TEXTILES, Needlework [Judaic])

Auction Services

Sotheby's
1334 York Ave.
New York, NY 10021
phone: 212-606-7370 or 212-606-7000
Internet: http://www.sothebys.com
Over 70 collecting areas are featured at Sotheby's auctions including toys, dolls, porcelain, furniture, silver, art, books; exhibitions are free and everyone is welcome; for a free copy of "Sotheby's Newsletter", call 212-606-7245.

Clubs/Associations

Israel I. Bick, Pres.
Judaica Collectors Society
Newsletter: Judaica Collectors Society Newsletter
P.O. Box 854
Van Nuys, CA 91408-0854
phone: 818-997-6496
fax: 818-988-4337
e-mail: iibick@aol.com
Internet: http://www.4free.com/bick
Dealing with and promoting the knowledge of all things related to Judaica and the state of Israel.

Collectors

David Frankel
P.O. Box 41
Kinckerbocker Station
New York, NY 10002-0041
phone: 212-473-5321
Wants to buy old Hebrew books, Jewish religious articles, charity boxes, menorahs, etc.

Peter H. Schweitzer
5 East 22nd St., Apt. 21A
New York, NY 10010
phone: 212-677-6939
Wants Jewish photos, signs, advertising, letterhead, business-related, anti-Semitic, family documents, books, tins, bottles, cookbooks, postcards, ephemera, Judaica, chatchkelas, etc.

Judaix Art
P.O. Box 248
Monsey, NY 10952
Wants pre-1950 Judaica: menorahs, illustrated books, boxes, children's items, posters.

Stanley Fried
195 Froehlich Farm Blvd.
Woodbury, NY 11797-2931
phone: 516-364-1112
fax: 516-625-4220

Mark Tanenbaum
824 Poplar St.
Erie, PA 16502
phone: 814-452-2567 or 814-459-3437
Private collector wants Jewish items: books, Hebrew writings, religious artifacts & household items, sterling wine cups, Torahs, spice boxes, furniture, maps, jewelry, paintings, photos, wedding contracts, folk art, etc.

Dealers

Alan Scop
Menorah Antiques, Ltd.
1318 Avenue J.
Brooklyn, NY 11230-3635
phone: 718-692-3683
fax: 718-692-0084
Buys and sells Judaica: postcards, posters, prints, photos, menorahs, spice boxes, kiddush cups, esrog boxes, Holocaust memorabilia.

Gary Niederkorn
Gary Niederkorn Silver
Newspaper: Silver Edition
2005 Locust St.
Philadelphia, PA 19103-5606
phone: 215-567-2606
fax: 215-567-2606
Specializes in 19th and 20th cent. silver novelties, jewelry napkin rings, Judaica, picture frames, etc.; also Tiffany, Jensen, Mexican.

Israel I. Bick
Bick International
P.O. Box 854
Van Nuys, CA 91408-0854
phone: 818-997-6496
fax: 818-988-4337
e-mail: iibick@aol.com
Internet: http://www.4free.com/bick
Wants to buy Jewish postcards, Hollywood memorabilia, stamps, coins, documents, currency, photos, bonds, religious articles, everything from the 1933-1945 Holocaust era.

Historicana
1200 Edgehill Dr., Ste. D
Burlingame, CA 94010
phone: 415-343-9578
Wants to buy Jewish rare books, manuscripts, documents, works by Arthur Szyk.

Experts

Lael Bower
507 Michigan Ave.
Grayling, MI 49738
phone: 517-348-6984 or 810-378-5785
Wants to buy Christian and Judaic collectibles; co-author with Penny Forstner of "Guide to Collecting Christian and Judaic Artifacts."

Arthur M. Feldman
1815 St. Johns Ave.
Highland Park, IL 60035-3215
phone: 847-432-8858
fax: 847-266-1199
e-mail: ars.dura@aol.com
Buys, sells and specializes in Judaica; former Director, Jewish Museum of Chicago; former Curator at Smithsonian; former Visiting Curator at the Victoria & Albert Museum.

Museums/Libraries

Sylvia Herskowitz
Yeshiva University Museum
2520 Amsterdam Ave.
New York, NY 10033
phone: 212-960-5390
Exhibits and programs relating to Jewish themes, featuring fine and decorative art, textiles and costumes, photography, manuscripts, contemporary crafts and sculpture.

Jewish Museum, The
1109 5th Ave.
New York, NY 10128
phone: 212-423-3200 or 212-423-3271
fax: 212-423-3232

National Museum of American Jewish History
55 N. 5th St.
Philadelphia, PA 19106
phone: 215-923-3811

Ori Z. Soltes
B'nai B'rith Klutznick Museum
1640 Rhode Island Ave. NW
Washington, DC 20036-3278
phone: 202-857-6583
fax: 202-857-1099
e-mail: osoltes@bnaibrith.org
The only museum in Washington, DC offering the sweep of Jewish culture and history; exhibits and programs on ethnography, history, and art which examines the contributions of Jewish culture to human civilization.

Judaic Museum
6125 Montrose Rd.
Rockville, MD 20852
phone: 301-881-0100

Spertus Museum of the Spertus Institute of Jewish Studies
618 S. Michigan Ave.
Chicago, IL 60605
phone: 312-922-9012
Contains the most comprehensive Judaic collection in the Midwest.

Morton B. Weiss Museum of Judaica
1100 Hyde Park Blvd.
Chicago, IL 60615
phone: 312-924-1234

Plotkin Judaica Museum of Greater Phoenix
3310 No. 10th Ave.
Phoenix, AZ 85013
phone: 602-264-4428

Judah L. Magnes Memorial Museum
2911 Russell St.
Berkeley, CA 94705
phone: 415-849-2710
Third largest Jewish museum in the U.S.; permanent collections, changing exhibitions, library, archives, educational and outreach programs.

JUGS

(see CERAMICS, Jugs; CERAMICS, Stoneware; SALOON & BAR COLLECTIBLES, Whiskey Pitchers;)

KALEIDOSCOPES

(see also OPTICAL TOYS)

Clubs/Associations

Cozy Baker
Brewster Society
Newsletter: Brewster Society Newsletter
9020 McDonald Dr., #B
Bethesda, MD 20817-1940
phone: 301-365-1855
fax: 301-365-2284
Sponsors an annual kaleidoscope convention.

Collectors

Martin Roenigk
Mechantiques
26 Barton Hill
East Hampton, CT 06424-1138
phone: 800-671-6333
fax: 860-267-1120
e-mail: mroenigk@aol.com
Internet: http://www.mechantiques.com
Buys and repairs high quality kaleidoscopes from the 1800s made of wood, leather, brass by Bush, Brewster, Bate, Carpenter, etc.

Coleen Detzel
28 Lacresta Dr.
Florence, KY 41042-9663
phone: 606-282-0456
Wants to buy quality kaleidoscopes, especially unusual and older pieces.

Dealers

Lucille Malitz
Lucid Antiques
P.O. Box KH
Scarsdale, NY 10583
phone: 914-636-7825 or 914-636-5171

William P. Carroll
ACR Books
P.O. Box 4294
Whittier, CA 90607-4294
phone: 562-693-8421
fax: 562-945-6011
Buys, sells and collects modern, top quality kaleidoscopes and, at times, antique kaleidoscopes.

Eric Sinizer
Light Opera Retail Gallery
174 Grant Ave.
San Francisco, CA 94108-5405
phone: 415-956-9866
fax: 415-956-5624

Experts

Cozy Baker
9020 McDonald Dr., #B
Bethesda, MD 20817-1940
phone: 301-365-1855
fax: 301-365-2284

KEEN KUTTER (SIMMONS HARDWARE)

(see also DIAMOND EDGE; HARDWARE; KNIVES; TOOLS; WINCHESTER COLLECTIBLES)

Auction Services

Bob Simmons
Simmons & Company Auctioneers
Rte. 1 Box 186
Richmond, MO 64085-9760
phone: 816-776-2936
fax: 816-470-5016
e-mail:
    simmons_auction@raycounty.com
Internet: http://www.raycounty.com/
    simmons.html
Conducts annual specialty auctions of Winchester, Keen Kutter (E.C. Simmons Hardware) and Diamond Edge (Shapleigh Hardware) collectibles; has a well-established reputation for expertise and high quality merchandise.

Collectors

Frank Miller
960 Kirkwood Lane
La Habra, CA 90631
phone: 714-870-5902
Wants Keen Kutter memorabilia.

Experts

Jerry & Elaine Heuring
RR 1, Box 1110
Scott City, MO 63780
phone: 573-264-3947
e-mail: jheuring@igateway.net
Authors of "Keen Kutter Collectibles: An Illustrated Price Guide."

Bob Simmons
Rte. 1 Box 186
Richmond, MO 64085-9760
phone: 816-776-2936
fax: 816-470-5016
e-mail:
    simmons_auction@raycounty.com
Internet: http://www.raycounty.com/
    simmons.html
Collects and specializes in Keen Kutter (E.C. Simmons Hardware) items especially advertising items and unusual items (household, sporting goods, catalogs, signs) made for this St. Louis firm from the late 1800s to 1940.

Periodicals

Tom Basore
Hardware Companies Kollectors' Club
Newsletter: Winchester Keen Kutter Diamond Edge Chronicles
715 West 20th Ave.
Hutchinson, KS 67502
phone: 316-665-3613 or 816-776-2936
fax: 816-470-5016
e-mail: webmaster@raycounty.com
Internet: http://www.raycounty.com/
    simmons.html
A non-profit organization to serve as an interactive information distribution center for collectors of Keen Kutter, Diamond Edge, Winchester Store (non-gun), Simmons & Shapleigh and other hardware store brands.

KENTUCKY DERBY

(see SPORTS COLLECTIBLES, Thoroughbred Racing)

KEY CHAINS

Clubs/Associations

Dr. Edward H. Miles
License Plate Key Chain & Mini License Plate Collectors
Newsletter: Key Chain News
888 Eighth Ave.
New York, NY 10019-5704
phone: 212-765-2660
Focuses on miniature Disabled American Veterans key chains, chauffeurs' badges, gum cards featuring license plates, windshield stickers, mini license plates.

Collectors

John Vahary, Jr.
41 Crosby Dr.
Battle Creek, MI 49014
phone: 616-965-0943
Collects key chains in any form, shape or color, especially those with advertising.

KEY FOBS

Collectors

Key Sentry
P.O. Box 10108
Naples, FL 33941
Wants to buy brass key tags (returns lost keys by mail.)

KEYS

(see also KEY CHAINS; KEY FOBS; LOCKS; RESTRAINT DEVICES; SAFES)

Clubs/Associations

Bob Heilemann
West Coast Lock Collectors
Newsletter: West Coast Lock Collectors Newsletter
1427 Lincoln Blvd.
Santa Monica, CA 90401-2732
phone: 310-454-7295 or 310-230-3004
Call evenings; no collect calls, please.

Collectors

Joseph Biunno
129 West 29th St.
New York, NY 10001
phone: 212-629-5630
fax: 212-268-4577
Wants furniture locks and keys; barrel, skeleton, door, drawer, old or new; also wants escutcheons in all styles and sizes.

Bruce Axler
Ansonia Station
P.O. Box 1288
New York, NY 10023-1288
phone: 212-362-4429
fax: 212-579-1274
Wants pocket items, i.e. items/gadgets designed to fit in the pocket: tools,

knives, lighters, compacts, folding cups, items which look like a pocket watch but are not, calculators, leather items, matchsafes, candle safes, travel items.

KITCHEN COLLECTIBLES

(see also APPLE PARERS; CAST IRON ITEMS; CASTOR SETS; CATALOGS; CERAMICS; COOKIES & COOKIE SHAPING; COOKIE JARS; DAIRY COLLECTIBLES; ELECTRICITY RELATED ITEMS, Appliances; GRANITEWARE; IRONS; MOLDS; PIE BIRDS; RANGES; SPOONS; STOVES; STRING HOLDERS)

Clubs/Associations

Carol Bohn
Kollectors of Old Kitchen Stuff
501 Market St.
Mifflinburg, PA 17844

Collectors

Trish Claar
2621 Manor Court
Owings, MD 20736-9145
phone: 301-855-6531
Wants 1950s and 1960s kitchen collectibles, gadgets and furniture.

Phyllis Moffet
P.O. Box 200
Modesto, IL 62667-0200
phone: 217-439-7358
Interested in buying old kitchen items: egg beaters, nutmeg grinders, apple parers, etc.

Reid Cooper
Mixer Mania
5458 Complex St., #401
San Diego, CA 92123
phone: 619-469-3966 or 619-569-6716
fax: 619-569-6793
Kitchen collector seeking to purchase tin advertising egg separators or tea strainers in good or better condition; also wants to buy other tin or iron kitchen implements with advertising; please describe fully and price.

Dealers

Bob & Kaaren Grossman
B & K Kitchen Primitives & Collectibles
354 Rte. 206
Chester, NJ 07930
phone: 908-879-7935
Specializing in tin, copper, Japanned ware and mechanicals for household, hotel and bakery use.

Jerry Harmyk
Kitschen
380 Bleecker St.
New York, NY 10014
phone: 212-727-0430
Buys and sells kitchen collectibles from the 1920s through 1970s.

Carole Meeker
Box 169 Kelly St.
Rhinecliff, NY 12574
phone: 914-876-7818
Wants to buy rare and unusual small patented mechanical antiques, early American technology and occupational-related photography, advertising and catalogs.

Stephen G. Del Sordo
Principia Group
305 Oakley St.
Cambridge, MD 21613
phone: 410-228-8934
fax: 410-221-8061
e-mail: delsordo@shore.intercom.net
A cultural resource management/ historic preservation firm that has contracts to locate, provide, authenticate artifacts for museums and collectors; areas of expertise include architecture, industry, domestic, agriculture, and maritime.

Nancy C. Lord
Rags to Riches
3382 S. McCall Rd.
Englewood, FL 34224
phone: 941-473-0300 or 941-474-9432

Tom Lawson
Buckeye Appliance
714 W. Fremont
Stockton, CA 95203-2702
phone: 209-464-9643
Specializes in the sales, parts and restoration of antique gas stoves; also sells kitchen collectibles, Hoosiers, 1950s chrome dinettes, and porcelain-top tables.

Experts

Teri & Joe Dziadul
6 South George Washington Rd.
Enfield, CT 06082
Buy, sell and specialize in kitchen and hearth antiques.

Repro. Sources

Applecore Creations
P.O. Box 29696
Columbus, OH 43229
Carries reproduction kitchen utensils.

Ronald Potts
Chiswell Forge
2255 Manchester Rd.
North Lawrence, OH 44666
Carries reproduction kitchen utensils.

Howard's Country Store
4307 Gotfredson Rd.
Plymouth, MI 48170
Carries reproduction kitchen utensils.

Brooms

Repro. Sources

Kenelm Winslow III
252 Clover Hill Rd.
Newburg, PA 17240

Bill Case
Mellow Mountain Broom Co.
3190 Raulerson Rd. E
Saint Augustine, FL 32092

Ogle's Broom Shop
808 Crest View Dr.
Gatlinburg, TN 37738

Butter Churns

Repro. Sources

Zimmerman Handcrafts
254 East Main St.
Leola, PA 17540

Coffee Grinders

Collectors

Stu Johnson
710 Taylor Ave. #B
Alameda, CA 94501
phone: 510-523-1089
Wants to buy cast iron, double wheel coffee grinders in all sizes; no electric.

Egg Separators

Collectors

Don Thornton
1345 Poplar Ave.
Sunnyvale, CA 94087-3770
phone: 408-737-0434
fax: 408-737-0191
e-mail: offbeatbks@aol.com
Wants old tin or aluminum egg separators, with advertising.

Egg Timers

Collectors

Lance V. Kuntzman
21 Perry
South Dartmouth, MA 02748-1803
phone: 508-994-5934
Wants to buy unusual or figural egg timers with sand glass attached.

Pat klein
P.O. Box 262
East Berlin, CT 06023
phone: 860-828-3973

Jeannie Greenfield
310 Parker Rd.
Stoneboro, PA 16153-2810
phone: 412-376-2584
Wants figural egg timers; any condition.

Eggbeaters

Collectors

Craig Dinner
P.O. Box 4399
Long Island City, NY 11104-0399
phone: 718-729-3850 or 802-365-7181
Wants early or unusual egg beaters.

Dana & Darlene DeMore
4645 Laurel Ridge Dr.
Harrisburg, PA 17110-3446
phone: 717-545-7320
Wants to buy old eggbeaters; one or entire collection.

Clay Tontz
4043 Nora
Covina, CA 91722
phone: 818-338-99767

Reid Cooper
5458 Complex St., #401
San Diego, CA 92123
phone: 619-469-3966 or 619-569-6716
fax: 619-569-6793
Advanced collector/researcher buying pre-1920 U.S. made eggbeaters, mayonnaise mixers, cream whips and stoneware beater bowls in top working order and/or condition; no electrics, plastic, or stainless; send price, photo or sketch.

Experts

Don Thornton
1345 Poplar Ave.
Sunnyvale, CA 94087-3770
phone: 408-737-0434
fax: 408-737-0191
e-mail: offbeatbks@aol.com
Wants old eggbeaters and related memorabilia and paper items, especially old catalogs; author of "Beat This, The Eggbeater Chronicles," (1994) and "The Eggbeater Book," (1983).

Flour Sifters

Collectors

Dana & Darlene DeMore
4645 Laurel Ridge Dr.
Harrisburg, PA 17110-3446
phone: 717-545-7320
Wants to buy mechanical flour sifters.

John Latovich
1455 Pulaski Ave.
Shamokin, PA 17872
Collector always looking for unusual and rare mechanical flour sifters, advertisements and related information.

Ice Shavers

Collectors

Don Thornton
1345 Poplar Ave.
Sunnyvale, CA 94087-3770
phone: 408-737-0434
fax: 408-737-0191
e-mail: offbeatbks@aol.com
Wants old ice shavers, cast iron planes and bowls.

Ironing Boards

Repro. Sources

John & Naomi Olivera
201 Crest Dr.
Havelock, NC 28532
Specializes in making wooden ironing boards.

Mixers

Collectors

Norman Hagey
Mr. Sunbeam
19672 Steavens Creek #424
Cupertino, CA 95014-2485
phone: 408-973-8129
Wants to buy old Sunbeam mixers: complete mixers, attachments, bowls, toasters, and information on model numbers and types; books, pamphlets.

Nutmeg Grinders

Collectors

Dana & Darlene DeMore
4645 Laurel Ridge Dr.
Harrisburg, PA 17110-3446
phone: 717-545-7320
Wants to buy mechanical nutmeg grinders.

Pie Crimpers/Jaggers

Collectors

Priscilla Hinners
2711 Jaynia Place
Lemon Grove, CA 91945-1319
phone: 619-265-1046
e-mail: mhinners@aol.com
Wants all types of pie crimpers (jaggers): ceramic, ivory, metal, unusual wooden, etc.

Pot Scrubbers

Collectors

Don Thornton
1345 Poplar Ave.
Sunnyvale, CA 94087-3770
phone: 408-737-0434
fax: 408-737-0191
e-mail: offbeatbks@aol.com
Wants old pot scrubbers - the ugly chain-mail variety.

Reamers

Clubs/Associations

Deborah Gilham
National Reamer Collectors Association (NRCA)
Newsletter: NRCA Quarterly Review
47 Midline Ct.
Gaithersburg, MD 20878-1996
phone: 301-977-5727
e-mail: reamers@erols.com
Internet: http://www.his.com/~judy/reamer.html
A non-profit organization with over 350 members devoted to promoting citrus and juice reamer and squeezer collecting; interested in reamers of all

materials - porcelain, glass, wood, metal, etc.

Loretta Harrington, Sec.
Mid-American Reamer Collectors
Newsletter: Juicy Journal
P.O. Box 48
Stanford, IN 47463
phone: 812-825-2152
Club is an affiliate of the National Reamers Collectors Association; membership in the NRCA is required for Regional Club membership.

Jim Pulliam
Southwest Reamer Collectors Association
1925 Ashley Dr.
Edmond, OK 73034
phone: 405-340-8710
Club is an affiliate of the National Reamers Collectors Association; membership in the NRCA is required for Regional Club membership.

Terry McDuffee
Western Regional Reamer Collectors Association
1478 W. Cypress Ave.
Redlands, CA 92373
phone: 714-739-9534
Club is an affiliate of the National Reamers Collectors Association; membership in the NRCA is required for Regional Club membership.

Collectors

Bobbie & Alan Bryson
1 St. Eleanoras Ln.
Tuckahoe, NY 10707-1307
phone: 914-779-1405
e-mail: napkindoll@aol.com
Wants figural reamers.

Deborah Gillham
47 Midline Ct.
Gaithersburg, MD 20878-1996
phone: 301-977-5727
e-mail: dgillham@erols.com
Internet: http://www.his.com/~Judy/reamer.html
Membership chairman for the National Reamer Collectors Association.

Betty Franks
1831 Penthley Ave.
Akron, OH 44312-1915
phone: 330-784-2869
Wants old and unusual glass, china or pottery reamers; domestic or foreign, especially figurals.

Ray Maxwell
222 Cooper Ave.
Elgin, IL 60120-2128
phone: 708-695-6284
Collects all reamers; especially interested in glass reamers from the Depression era.

Terry McDuffee
1478 W. Cypress Ave.
Redlands, CA 92373
phone: 714-739-9534
Buys and sells reamers, juicers and

kitchen glassware; rare and unusual items wanted; please price and describe.

Dealers

John & Peggy Hoy
Monrovia West Antique Mall
925 West Foothill Blvd.
Monrovia, CA 91016-1915
phone: 818-355-5081
Avid collectors and dealers specializing in reamers, jadite.

Experts

Dee Long
112 S. Center
Lacon, IL 61540-1306
phone: 309-246-8996 or 309-246-5278
e-mail: merle.long@juno.com

Ed & Mary Walker
13550 Addison St.
Sherman Oaks, CA 91423
phone: 714-793-9534
Authors of three volumes about reamers.

Rolling Pins

Collectors

Priscilla Hinners
2711 Jaynia Place
Lemon Grove, CA 91945-1319
phone: 619-265-1046
e-mail: mhinners@aol.com
Wants all types of rolling pins: Nailsea, Meissen, Harker, ceramic, glass, stoneware, advertising, metal, unusual wooden, springerle, and other types of rollers.

Rugbeaters

Collectors

Bill Carroll
RR 1, Box 62
Hope, ND 58046-9760
phone: 701-945-2416
fax: 701-945-2772
e-mail: BillND299@aol.com
Internet: http://www.collectoronline.com/booth-74.html
Collects rug beaters and related items such as catalogs and samples.

Sausage Stuffers

Collectors

Dale Schmidt
610 Howell Prairie Rd. SE
Salem, OR 97301-9097
phone: 503-364-0499
fax: 503-585-3071
Wants all types; complete or parts.

Spoons (Wooden)

Repro. Sources

Richard McCollum
White Forest Spoons
P.O. Box 687
Bryn Athyn, PA 19009

Kentucky Hills Industries
P.O. Box 186
Pine Knot, KY 42635

Wire Ware

Repro. Sources

Mathews Wire
654 West Morrison
Frankfort, IN 46041-1670
phone: 800-826-9650
fax: 317-659-1059
Wholesale supplier of wire reproductions; egg baskets, display racks, etc.; also reproduction toys and advertising signs.

KITES

Clubs/Associations

American Kitefliers Association
Newsletter: Kiting
352 Hungerford Dr.
Rockville, MD 20850-4117
phone: 800-252-2550
e-mail: aka@aka.kite.org
Internet: http://aka.kite.org/
Non-profit volunteer organization of 4500 kitefliers in 29 countries; educates the public in the art, history, technology, and practice of building and flying kites; directory includes member/merchants nationwide.

S.F. Cody Kite Society
1082 Bethesda St.
Eugene, OR 97402
phone: 503-689-8175
Members have a strong interest in the history of kites and of the designs of Samuel Franklin Cody.

Collectors

Tim Hunter
1668 Golddust
Sparks, NV 89436
phone: 702-626-5029
fax: 702-626-4423
e-mail: thunter8852@aol.com
Wants to buy all types of 1950s-1960s paper kites.

Experts

Valerie Govig
P.O. Box 446
Randallstown, MD 21133-0446
phone: 410-922-1212
fax: 410-922-4262
e-mail: kitelines@compuserve.com
Editor of "Kite Lines Magazine."

Man./Prod./Dist.

Andrew Gelinas
Burlesque Kites
18 W. 3rd. St.
Bethlehem, PA 18015-1222
phone: 610-867-3313 or 610-867-1665
fax: 610-867-4999
Specializes in handmade parachuting Teddy Bears and other fine parafauna; also sells parafauna supplies, 'chutes, releases, etc.; also imports "hand-painted" art on silk that flies - 30" to 10' birds, insects, dragons, pandas, etc.

Museums/Libraries

Japan Kite Museum
1-12-10 Nihonbashi
Chuo-ku
Tokyo, 103, Japan

Periodicals

Valerie Govig, Ed.
Magazine: Kite Lines Magazine
P.O. Box 446
Randallstown, MD 21133-0446
phone: 410-922-1212
fax: 410-922-4262
e-mail: kitelines@compuserve.com
A quarterly publication with articles, ads, etc. relating to kites, kite making, kite history and kite flying; also sells a large line of books relating to kites; will help make connections with kite buyers and sellers.

Suppliers

High Fly Kite, Co.
P.O. Box 2146
Haddonfield, NJ 08033
phone: 609-429-6260
fax: 609-429-0142
Mail order kite specialists; kites, lines, reels and handles, kite building supplies and parts, etc.

World of Kites
525 S. Washington
Royal Oak, MI 48067
phone: 810-398-5900
fax: 609-429-0142
The kite flier's pro shop: kites, lines, reels and handles, accessories; Oriental, sportsman's, custom, stunters and fighters.

KITS

(see also MODELS)

Clubs/Associations

Gordy Dutt
International Figure Kit Club
Magazine: KitBuilders Magazine
P.O. Box 201
Sharon Center, OH 44274-0201
phone: 330-239-1657
fax: 330-239-2991
e-mail: Gordys_kitbuilders@juno.com
Internet: http://www.gremlins.com/
kitbuilders
Published four times a year, this magazine deals mostly with plastic,

vinyl, and resin figure or Sci/Fi type model kits from the 1950s to present.

Dealers

Gordy Dutt
Gordy's
P.O. Box 201
Sharon Center, OH 44274-0201
phone: 330-239-1657
fax: 330-239-2991
e-mail: Gordys_kitbuilders@juno.com
Internet: http://www.gremlins.com/
kitbuilders
Buys and sells plastic, vinyl, and resin figure or Sci/Fi type model kits from the 1950s to present; also toys from the late '50s to the early '70s.

Trader Rick's Collectible Toy Cars
P.O. Box 161
Newark, IL 60541
phone: 815-695-9484
Wants to buy toy cars and model cars; also built or unbuilt car kits.

John F. Green
John F. Green, Inc.
P.O. Box 92517
Riverside, CA 92517
phone: 909-684-5300 or 800-807-4759
fax: 909-684-8819
e-mail: jfgreen@msn.com
Internet: http://www.recylcer.com/com/
jfgreenmodelkits/
Sells, buys, trades plastic model kits from and of science fiction, TV, figures, space movies, etc.; old and new; send for free sales catalog.

Experts

Terry J. Webb
P.O. Box 30885
Columbus, OH 43230
phone: 614-882-2125
fax: 614-882-6012
Internationally renowned expert on the Garage Kit hobby; author of "Reverence of the Garage Kit That Ate My Wallet."

Gordy Dutt
Gordy's
P.O. Box 201
Sharon Center, OH 44274-0201
phone: 330-239-1657
fax: 330-239-2991
e-mail: Gordys_kitbuilders@juno.com
Internet: http://www.gremlins.com/
kitbuilders

Periodicals

Terry J. Webb
Amazing Publications & Communications Inc.
Magazine: Amazing Figure Modeler
P.O. Box 30885
Columbus, OH 43230
phone: 614-882-2125
fax: 614-882-6012
A quarterly magazine that focuses on the international garage and model kit market.

Newsletter: Garage, The
330 Merriman Rd.
Akron, OH 44303-1552
Focuses on vinyl and resin-poured kit modeling: classic horror figures, sci-fi monsters, movie stars, classical beauties; new and exciting kits being produced each year.

Magazine: Modeler's Resource, The
1141 Holly Ave.
Clovis, CA 93611-6210
Bi-monthly magazine with up-to-date information on what's new in the vehicular and figure kit market.

Plastic

Clubs/Associations

Fred Horky
International Plastic Modelers Society
USA
Journal: IPMS/USA Modelers Journal
P.O. Box 6138
Warner Robins, GA 31095-6138
phone: 912-922-7132 or 912-452-3744
fax: 912-452-3744
Journal includes review of new kits and accessories, scratch-building, convention articles, IPMS news, etc.

John W. Burns
Society for the Preservation & Encouragement of Scale Model Kit Collecting
Magazine: Kit Collectors Clearinghouse
3213 Hardy Dr.
Edmond, OK 73013-5319
phone: 405-341-4640
e-mail: cheersjwb@aol.com
A bi-monthly magazine for kit collectors; buy and sell ads, re-issue notices, information on new kits, vacuum-formed and resin kits, etc.

Bob Keller
Kit Collectors International
P.O. Box 38
Stanton, CA 90680-0038
phone: 714-826-5216
e-mail: prsdog@aol.com
Internet: http://pages.prodigy.com/prs7/
kitshow.html
Sponsors the "Kit Collectors Exposition & Sale" three times each year. The world's largest model kit collectors swap meet and show; buys and sells collections.

Collectors

Wally Krocsko
P.O. Box 307
Atlasburg, PA 15004-0307
phone: 412-947-5671
Buys, sells, trades plastic model kits; must enclose a LSASE to get a reply to buy/sell/trade inquiries; please call evenings.

John Krupienski
5200 Hilltop Dr.
P.O. Box AA6
Brookhaven, PA 19015-1200
phone: 610-874-3003

Jim Crane
15 Clemson Ct.
Newark, DE 19711-4301
phone: 302-738-6031
Wants Aurora, Revell, Monogram plastic kits; built or unbuilt; any condition; wants figures, planes, boats and catalogs.

Experts

John W. Burns
3213 Hardy Dr.
Edmond, OK 73013-5319
phone: 405-341-4640
e-mail: cheersjwb@aol.com
Author of "Collectors Value Guide for Scale Model Plastic Kits," and "In Plastic: WWII Aircraft Kits"; willing to buy unbuilt plastic model kits of all subjects.

Plastic (Aurora)

Dealers

Rocky Sorrentino
Art 'N' Things
133 S. Andersen Ave.
Fairview, NJ 07022
phone: 201-943-2288
Buys and sells original Aurora figure model kits, reproduction boxes and battery-operated clocks.

Experts

Bill & Joanne Bruegman
Toy Scouts, Inc.
137 Casterton Ave.
Akron, OH 44303-1543
phone: 330-836-0668
fax: 330-869-8668
e-mail: toyscout@newreach.net
Internet: http://www.csmonline.com/
toyscouts/
Author of "Aurora History and Price Guide."

David Welch
P.O. Box 714
Murphysboro, IL 62966-0714
phone: 618-687-2282
fax: 618-684-2243
e-mail: PexDude1@aol.com
Specializing in Aurora figure kits; buying any pre-1977 TV, science fiction, comic, movie, monster related kits; must have original boxes unless factory promos; contributor to "O'Brien's Collecting Toys" and Tomart's "Garage Sale Gold."

KKK

(see KU KLUX KLAN COLLECTIBLES; POLITICALLY INCORRECT COLLECTIBLES)

KNIFE RESTS

Collectors

Beverly Ales
4046 Graham St.
Pleasanton, CA 94566-5619
phone: 510-846-5297

Periodicals

Beverly Ales
Newsletter: Knife Rests of Yesterday &
Today
4046 Graham St.
Pleasanton, CA 94566-5619
phone: 510-846-5297

KNIVES

(see also ARMS & ARMOR;
BLACKSMITHING ITEMS; BOOKS,
Reference [Knives]; DIAMOND
EDGE; EDGED WEAPONS; KEEN
KUTTER; KNIFE RESTS)

Clubs/Associations

Murray White
Canadian Knife Collectors Club
1200 Shamir Cr.
Mississaugua
Ontario L9T 5B4 Canada
phone: 905-275-8320
fax: 905-275-0492
e-mail: murphy@octonline.com
Internet: http://home.interhop.net/
~bleblanc/ckcc/ckcc.htm

John R. Freeman, Sec./Treas,
Canadian Knifemakers Guild
160 Concession St.
Cambridge
Ontario N1R 2H7 Canada
e-mail: freeman@golden.net
Internet: http://home.interhop.net/
~bleblanc/ckg/guild.htm

Cindy Taylor
Northeast Cutlery Collectors Association
P.O. Box 624
Mansfield, MA 02048
phone: 508-226-5157

Ruth Trout, Sec.
Allegheny Mountain Knife Collectors
Association
P.O. Box 23
Hunker, PA 15639
phone: 412-925-2713

Keystone Blade Association
P.O. Box 46
Lewisburg, PA 17837
phone: 717-523-3211

Susquehanna Knife Collectors
Association
839 Beaver Lane
Reading, PA 19606

Glenn Smit
Chesapeake Bay Knife Club
627 Cindy Court
Aberdeen, MD 21001
phone: 410-272-2959

Ernie Cook
Northern Virginia Knife Collectors
P.O. Box 501
Falls Church, VA 22040
phone: 703-790-1960

Shenandoah Valley Knife Collectors
P.O. Box 843
Harrisonburg, VA 22801

John Riddle
Old Dominion Knife Collectors
4236 Lakeridge Circle
Troutville, VA 24175-2540
phone: 703-977-0242

Mason Dixon Knife Club
P.O. Box 2726
Martinsburg, WV 25401-5526

Tar Heel Cutlery Club
2730 Tudor Rd.
Winston Salem, NC 27106
phone: 910-725-1016

Gene Abernathy
North Carolina Cutlery Club
113 Powell Dr.
Fuquay Varina, NC 27526
phone: 919-552-9075

Jim Goes
Dare Blade Collectors' Society
3938 Pineway Dr.
Kitty Hawk, NC 27949-4303
phone: 919-261-1149
  *Interested in all knives, from ancient
  native American stone artifacts to
  historic military blades & modern
  custom made knives.*

Palmetto Cutlery Club
P.O. Box 1356
Greer, SC 29652
phone: 803-877-0303

Chattachoochee Cutlery Club
P.O. Box 568
Tucker, GA 30085

Jimmy Green
Three Rivers Knife Club
783 NE Jones Mill Rd.
Rome, GA 30165-9075
phone: 706-235-0581 or 706-234-2540

Deep South Knife Collectors
P.O. Box 9001
Pensacola, FL 32513-9001
phone: 904-477-2202
fax: 904-477-2202
e-mail: dskc@cheney.net
Internet: http://home.cheney.net/~feldor/
  index.html

Mitch Weiss
Art Knife Collector's Association
2211 Lee Rd.
Winter Park, FL 32789
phone: 407-740-8778
fax: 407-740-8283
e-mail: mitch@artknife.com
Internet: http://artknife.com/

Louie Prothman
Florida Knife Collectors Association
5321 Holden Rd.
Cocoa, FL 32927
phone: 407-636-1876

Gator Cutlery Club
P.O. Box 41201
Saint Petersburg, FL 33743
phone: 941-746-0435

Fort Myers Knife Club
P.O. Box 1274
Fort Myers, FL 33902

Ann Piper
Riverland Knife Collectors Club
P.O. Box 1298
Dunnellon, FL 34430-1298
phone: 352-489-8138

Gary G. Nichols
Heart of Dixie Cutlery Club
4141 Camp Coleman
Trussville, AL 35173-2818
phone: 205-655-7789

Wheeler Basin Knife Club
P.O. Box 346
Hartselle, AL 35640

Fight'n Rooster Cutlery Club
Newsletter: FRCC Newsletter
P.O. Box 936
Lebanon, TN 37087
phone: 615-444-8070

Soddy Daisy knife Collectors
  Association Club
P.O. Box 1224
Soddy Daisy, TN 37379
phone: 615-842-2663

National Knife Collectors Association
Magazine: National Knife Magazine
P.O. Box 21070
Chattanooga, TN 37421
phone: 800-548-3907
  *Each month receive "National Knife
  Magazine" (focuses mainly on new
  knives but also carries some articles
  about old knives); free admission to
  NKCA sanctioned shows; annual club
  knife.*

American Blade Collectors Association
P.O. Box 22007
Chattanooga, TN 37422
phone: 615-894-0339
fax: 615-892-7254
  *Membership includes annual club
  knife offer, annual commemorative
  Blade Show and Cutlery fair knife.*

North East Tennessee Knife Club
P.O. Box 562
Kingsport, TN 37660

Memphis Knife Collectors
1439 Elmgrove Rd.
Burlison, TN 38015
phone: 901-476-3834

Kentucky Cutlery Association
4914 Bluebird Ave.
Louisville, KY 40213
phone: 502-267-9456

Central Kentucky Knife Club
P.O. Box 55049
Lexington, KY 40555

Mahoning Valley Knife Collectors
1900 McCloskey
Columbiana, OH 44408

Western Reserve Cutlery Association
P.O. Box 355
Dover, OH 44622

James Webb
Johnny Appleseed Knife Collectors
668 Lenox Ave.
Mansfield, OH 44906
phone: 419-747-7551

Fort City Knife Collectors Club
P.O. Box 31396
Cincinnati, OH 45231-0396

Ed Etchason
Indiana Knife Collectors
P.O. Box 101
Fountaintown, IN 46130-0101
phone: 317-835-7487

Patrick Donovan
Wolverine Knife Collectors Club
Newsletter: Wolverine Knife Collectors
  Newsletter
P.O. Box 52
Belleville, MI 48112-0052
phone: 810-247-5883
  *Michigan's largest knife collectors
  club; members are expert in most knife
  collecting categories; annual show is
  one of the largest in the Midwest;
  affiliated with the National Knife
  Collectors Association.*

Mack McDonald
Marble Plus Knife Club
P.O. Box 228
Gladstone, MI 49837
phone: 906-428-1075

Hawkeye Knife Collectors Club
800 Knob Hill Dr.
Des Moines, IA 50317-7810
phone: 515-266-4976

Bob Schrap
Badger Knife Club, Inc.
Newsletter: Badger Knife Club
  Newsletter
P.O. Box 511
Elm Grove, WI 53122-0511
phone: 414-479-9765 or 515-771-6472
fax: 414-784-2996
e-mail: RSchrap@aol.com
  *Club for all knife collectors; custom,
  factory, military, antique knives; for
  knife collectors, makers and dealers.*

North Star Blade Collectors
P.O. Box 20523
Bloomington, MN 55420

Professional Knifemakers Association,
  Inc.,
P.O. Box 5716
Helena, MT 59604-5716
phone: 406-458-6552

Jim McNally
American Edge Collectors Association
Newsletter: AECA Newsletter
P.O. Box 2565
Country Club Hills, IL 60478-8565
phone: 630-759-0749

L. Lutz
Soy Knife Collectors
P.O. Box 532
Warrensburg, IL 62573

Larry Hancock
Jefferson County Custom Knife Club
Rt. 8
Mount Vernon, IL 62864
phone: 618-242-4514

Gateway Area Knife Club
310 Andrews Trail
Saint Peters, MO 63376

Kansas Knife Collectors Association
P.O. Box 1125
Wichita, KS 67201
phone: 316-838-0540

Ft. Smith Knife Club
3907 Kenner Chapel Road
Rudy, AR 72952
phone: 501-474-4474

Mike Ramsey, Sec.
Sooner Knife Collectors Club
1813 SW 30th St.
Moore, OK 73160
phone: 405-799-8698

Mike Moeskau
Gulf Coast Knife Club
P.O. Box 265
Pasadena, TX 77501-0265
phone: 713-479-3072

Richard White, Sec.
Rocky Mountain Blade Collectors
P.O. Box 115
Louisville, CO 80227
phone: 303-450-7164

Joseph G. Cordova
American Blacksmith Society
P.O. Box 977
Peralta, NM 87042-0977
phone: 505-869-3912
fax: 505-869-2509
e-mail: abs@rt66.com
Internet: http://www.web2.com/abs
An international society composed of knifemakers who use the forging method to make the blade and of collectors who appreciate the forged blade.

Joseph G. Cordova
American Bladesmith Society
P.O. Box 977
Peralta, NM 87042-0977
phone: 505-869-3912
fax: 505-869-2509
e-mail: abs@rt66.com
Internet: http://www.web2.com/cordo
For knifemakers and knife enthusiasts.

Lowell Shelhart
Southern California Blades Knife
  Collectors Club
P.O. Box 1140
Lomita, CA 90717
phone: 310-530-8412

Bay Area Knife Collectors Association
P.O. Box 223
Fremont, CA 94537
phone: 415-683-9122

Oregon Knife Collectors
P.O. Box 2091
Eugene, OR 97402
phone: 503-484-5564

Collectors

Bruce Axler
Ansonia Station
P.O. Box 1288
New York, NY 10023-1288
phone: 212-362-4429
fax: 212-579-1274
Wants pocket items, i.e. items/gadgets designed to fit in the pocket: tools, knives, lighters, compacts, folding cups, items which look like a pocket watch but are not, calculators, leather items, matchsafes, candle safes, travel items.

Kenneth D. Smith
55 Howard Ave.
Staten Island, NY 10301-4404
Wants to buy Fairbairn-Sykes fighting knives with personalized Wilkinson blades.

Bill Campesi
P.O. Box 140
Merrick, NY 11566-0140
phone: 516-546-9630
Buy, sell, trade all cutlery and related advertising: catalogs, postcards, cutlery display items; pocket, sheath, Bowie knives.

Gerald A. Shaw
1928 Causton Bluff Rd.
Savannah, GA 31404-1310
phone: 912-232-0771
Wants knives by Remington, Boker, Winchester, CASE, Russell, Western, Ka-Bar, etc.; also wants razors, knife books, daggers, hunting knives, pocket knives, etc.

Guy Manwaring
P.O. Box 361
Tecumseh, MI 49286-0361
phone: 517-423-4466
fax: 517-423-4466
Collects knives: pocket, Bowie, hunting, American switchblades, etc.; also wants old magazine ads for knives or Keen Kutter hardware, cardboard pocket knife boxes, countertop displays, postcards, catalogs, any cutlery items.

A.L. Hunt
P.O. Box 711
Excelsior Springs, MO 64024
phone: 816-637-8464
Wants to buy military knives & bayonets from WI, WWII, Korea, Vietnam: Special Forces stilettos & bolos, Seals dive knives, USMC recon knives & KA Bars, presentation knives, trench knives, M-4s, M-6s, bayonets, Randalls, EKS.

Dealers

Bob Albrecht
Bob's Antiques & Curios
P.O. Box 108
Collinsville, CT 06022
phone: 860-747-0009
e-mail: hugybear@esslink.com
Wants Connecticut made folding knives, especially Ebenizer Wing, Southington Cutlery (Empire, Winsted, etc.) and Northfield; also collect other folding knives.

Dennis Blake
Cutlery Specialties
22 Morris Lane
Great Neck, NY 11024-1707
phone: 516-829-5899 or 516-773-0071
fax: 516-773-8076
e-mail: Dennis13@aol.com
Buys, sells, trades, designs knives and other related cutlery items.

Tom Clark
Blue Ridge Knives
Rt. 6 Box 185 Adwolfe Rd.
Marion, VA 24354-9351
phone: 540-783-6143
fax: 540-783-9298
e-mail: blueridgeknives@symweb.com
Will purchase entire knife collections or by the piece; interested in antique, commemorative, custom hardware, or entire business inventories; immediate payment; also wholesales current factory knives.

Parkers' Knife Collector Service
6715 Heritage Business Court
P.O. Box 23522
Chattanooga, TN 37422
phone: 800-247-0599 or 615-892-0448
Distributes all kinds of knives including Winchester, antique Case, Remington, Club knives, Marbles, Fightn' Rooster, New German knives, antique knives, Bulldog Brand Pit Bull collector knives, prototypes, etc.

J. Bruce Voyles
Heritage Antique Knives
P.O. Box 22007
Chattanooga, TN 37422
phone: 615-894-8319
fax: 615-892-7254
e-mail: jbruce77@aol.com
Buys, sells, collects, appraises and specializes in all kinds of knives including store closing inventories, Bowie knives, old pocket knives, antique, current, commemorative, advertising; also store displays, knife memorabilia, etc.

Parkers' Knife Collector Service
P.O. Box 23522
Chattanooga, TN 37422
phone: 800-247-0599 or 423-892-0448
Buy and sell knives; carries discontinued Case Classics, standard production Case knives, Bulldog brand knives, Swiss Army knives; issues catalogs throughout the year.

Roger Worley
P.O. Box 5128
Boise, ID 83705-0128
phone: 208-343-6476 or 208-344-4625
fax: 208-344-5583
Send SASE for large monthly listing of antique knives for sale or trade.

Experts

J. Bruce Voyles
P.O. Box 22007
Chattanooga, TN 37422
phone: 615-894-8319
fax: 615-892-7254
e-mail: jbruce77@aol.com
Former publisher of "Blade Magazine" and "Edges, The Journal of American Knife Collecting"; author of 16 books on knives including price guides; edits the Knives entry of the "World Book Encyclopedia"; member Cutlery Hall of Fame.

Charles H. Price
c/o Knife World
P.O. Box 3395
Knoxville, TN 37927-3395
phone: 615-397-1955
fax: 615-397-1969
Author of "The Official Price Guide to Collector Knives."

Jim Weyer
2740 Nebraska Ave.
Toledo, OH 43607
phone: 419-534-2020 or 800-448-8424
fax: 419-534-2697
Author of the "Knives: Points of Interest" book series which focuses on custom made knives.

Charles D. Stapp
7037 Haynes Rd.
Georgetown, IN 47122-8610
phone: 812-923-3483
Wants pre-1965 folding and non-folding knives; free appraisals; provide photocopy or tracing and send with SASE.

Alex Peck
Antique Scientifica
P.O. Box 710
Charleston, IL 61920
phone: 217-348-1009
Collects early Bowie knives, American or English, especially with a motto and Civil War era; also California knives, knives by Rose, Goulding, Schively, Bell, Rees.

Charles H. Clements, III
1741 Dallas St.
Aurora, CO 80010
phone: 303-364-0403
Appraises and specializes in arms & armor, hunting, gaming, military and leisure material for men, frontier, fur-trade and Indian artifacts, etc.

Bernard Levine
P.O. Box 2404
Eugene, OR 97402-0124
phone: 541-484-0294
Identification and appraisal, museum consultation, expert witness, research,

writing; author of "Levine's Guide to Knives and Their Values."

Museums/Libraries

National Knife Collectors Museum
7201 Shallowford Rd.
Chattanooga, TN 37421
phone: 615-892-5007
Collection includes over 20,000 knives from the Bronze Age to present.

Periodicals

Richard Cecilio
Wildcat Enterprises, Inc.
Journal: Wildcat Collectors Journal
15158 N.E. 6 Ave.
Miami, FL 33162-5034
phone: 305-945-3228
Featuring classified ads to buy/sell/ trade guns, knives, medals and related militaria; gun shows, auctions, other events; subscribers get FREE 40 word ad.

Newspaper: Knife World
P.O. Box 3395
Knoxville, TN 37927-3395
phone: 615-397-1955 or 800-828-7751
fax: 615-397-1969
A monthly newspaper with ads, shows, knife makers, knife artistry, knife making supplies, knife books, articles of interest to collectors and knife historians; has knife identification and value columns.

Julie A. Ulrich, PR
Krause Publications
Magazine: Blade
700 E. State St.
Iola, WI 54990-0001
phone: 715-445-2214
fax: 715-445-4087
e-mail: info@krause.com
Internet: http://www.krause.com
A monthly magazine focusing on all aspects of knives, razors, pocket knives, knife making, care, sharpening, etc.

Julie A. Ulrich, PR
Krause Publications
Magazine: Blade Trade
700 E. State St.
Iola, WI 54990-0001
phone: 715-445-2214
fax: 715-445-4087
e-mail: info@krause.com
Internet: http://www.krause.com
Directed at the retailer who sells cutlery; provides important tips and product knowledge on how to sell cutlery; full range of cutlery is covered.

Repair Services

Garry L. Wackerhagen
2910 McNutt Ave.
Maryville, TN 37801
phone: 615-977-WACK
Knife repair and restorations; reasonable rates.

Wendell Carson's Knife Exchange
1041 CR 59
New Albany, MS 38652
Factory authorized knife repair center; Case, KaBar, Queen, Bulldog, LL Bean, and others.

Suppliers

Texas Knifemakers Supply
P.O. Box 79402
Houston, TX 77279
phone: 713-461-8632
An extensive selection of micarta, steel, pakkawood, exotic woods, brass, books, stag horn, bone handle fasteners, rod tubing, ox horn, belt sanders, belts, buffing wheels, rouge, epoxy, heat treating ovens, custom sheaths.

Bowie

Clubs/Associations

Paul L. Holmer
Antique Bowie Knife Association
Newsletter: Antique Bowie Journal
Buley Library, S. Ct. State U
501 Crescent St.
New Haven, CT 06515-1330
phone: 203-392-5746 or 203-248-6318
fax: 203-392-5740
e-mail: holmer@scsud.ctstateu.edu
The ABKA exists to serve collectors and students of antique Bowie-type knives; the Journal is published four times per year and an annual meeting features a board to authenticate members' knives.

Collectors

David Wallach
P.O. Box 150285
San Rafael, CA 94915
phone: 415-883-3242
Editor of the "Antique Bowie Journal."

Dealers

David L. Hartline
P.O. Box 775
Columbus, OH 43085
Buys and sells edged weapons; has large library and over 30 years experience; specialty is pre-1920 Bowie knives; has had many articles published on edge weapons; answers every letter; does appraisals and will authenticate.

Experts

Paul L. Holmer
P.O. Box 6091
Hamden, CT 06517-0091
phone: 203-392-5746
fax: 203-392-5740
e-mail: holmer@scsud.cstateu.edu
Always interested in talking with collectors or students and sharing information; has special interest in knives (e.g. Bowie, folding dirks, silver-mounted American daggers)

made in the northeastern states during the 19th century.

Buck

Clubs/Associations

W. Murray Andrews
Buck Collectors Club
P.O. Box 3
Enon, OH 45323-0003
phone: 937-767-7613
fax: 937-767-1773
For collectors of both fixed blade and folding pocket knives produced by Buck Knives, Inc. and their founders; former newsletter editor and has written for some periodicals pertaining to Buck knives.

Case

Collectors

Tony Foster
5926 Willard Dr.
Charleston, SC 29406
phone: 803-554-7090
Wants to buy case pocketknives, especially 10 Dot and older.

Frank Miller
960 Kirkwood Ln.
LaHabra, CA 90631
phone: 714-870-5902
Wants CASE knives in mint condition: Doctors, Peanuts, Toothpicks, Melon Tasters, Flyfishermen and Appaloosa; also CASE memorabilia.

Military

Clubs/Associations

Military Knife & Bayonet Club
Newsletter: Military Blade Journal, The
1142 West Grace St.
Richmond, VA 23220
An international fraternity of collectors, annual limited edition club knife, quarterly newsletter, expert Advisory Board, official club museum and gift shop.

Collectors

Rickie Marquette
P.O. Box 343133
Homestead, FL 33034-0133
phone: 305-246-5431 or 305-245-2323
fax: 305-245-9295
Wants to buy military fighting knives, especially John Ek, Scagel, Randall, and Gerber knives; also Special Forces, S.O.G. knives, presentation pieces, and edged weapons in general.

Miniature

Clubs/Associations

Gary Bradburn
Miniature Knifemakers' Society
1714 Park Place
Wichita, KS 67203
phone: 316-269-4273
Promotes the collecting and making of miniature knives.

Collectors

Jim
6831 Colton Blvd.
Piedmont, CA 94611-1347
phone: 510-339-1147
Wants quality old miniature (1" or less) folding knives.

Pocket

Collectors

Steve Deer
1503 Albin Pond
Greencastle, IN 46135
phone: 317-653-9437
Wants tricky openers; also picture handled carnival or punchboard knives.

Dealers

Harrell Braddock, Jr.
1412 Los Colinos
Graham, TX 76450-4447
phone: 940-549-2607
Buys and sells all pocket knives, any condition, any number; send SASE for list of knives for sale.

Periodicals

Magazine: Edges
P.O. Box 22007
Chattanooga, TN 37422
phone: 615-894-0339
fax: 615-892-7254
The bi-monthly journal of American knife collecting: antique & contemporary pocket knives & folders, collector profiles, club info.

Repair Services

Ken Lukes
405 E. Wakeham Ave.
Santa Ana, CA 92701
phone: 714-542-8553
Any pocket knife restored.

Randall

Clubs/Associations

Randall Knife Society of America
Newsletter: Randall Knife Society Newsletter
P.O. Box 539
Roseland, FL 32957
Internet: http://www.ipartners.com/rks
Formed with the approval of the Randall Made Knives, Orlando, FL; over 1700 members; newsletter on old and new knives, military Randall's, Randall history, latest shop news, ads, etc.

Sheaths

Suppliers

Bob Schrap
Custom Leather Knife Sheath Co.
7024 W. Wells St.
Milwaukee, WI 53213
phone: 414-771-6472 or 414-784-0863
fax: 414-784-2996
e-mail: RSchrap@aol.com
Maker of custom leather knife sheaths.

Switchblade/Automatic

Collectors

Sheldon
P.O. Box 1775
Warren, MI 48089
*Long time collector wants to buy
vintage and antique switchblades;
American, Italian, or foreign; working
or broken.*

Periodicals

Newsletter: Automatic Knife Resource
  Guide & Newsletter
2269 Chestnut Street, Ste. 212
San Francisco, CA 94123
phone: 415-664-2105
*Issued quarterly; photos, in-depth
articles, maintenance and repair tips,
latest trends, resources of ALL kinds
of automatic knives, free classified ads
and more.*

KU KLUX KLAN COLLECTIBLES

(see also POLITICALLY INCOR-
RECT COLLECTIBLES; SOCIAL
CAUSES)

Collectors

Steve DeGenaro
P.O. Box 5662
Youngstown, OH 44504-0662
phone: 216-757-7735

Roger Henry
RR 1 Box 192
Smithshire, IL 61478-9801
*Wants KKK books and other KKK
items.*

Dealers

Roy Winfield
Winfield Historical
P.O. Box 305 - WOB
West Orange, NJ 07052-0305
phone: 201-672-2236

Historical Collections
P.O. Box 42
Waynesboro, PA 17268-0042
phone: 717-762-3068
Wants KKK material and items.

Experts

Michael Y. Graham
Chicago's Roaring 20's
33133 N Oplaine Rd.
Gurnee, IL 60031-3445
phone: 708-263-6285
*Klan material from 1920 to 1933 and
focusing on 1928 Smith/Hoover
election.*

Here are some tips when contacting someone listed in this book:

When requesting information about a particular item, include a description (material, dimensions, maker's mark, model number, etc.) and a photo, sketch, or photocopy of the item in question. ■

Always ask if there are charges for samples or for the services requested. ■

When writing, please be sure to include a Large (#10 business size) Self-Addressed and Stamped Envelope (LSASE) if requesting a reply or the return of photographs. ■

Never call collect unless otherwise directed. When calling, be considerate of time zone differences and always ask if the party you are calling has time to talk. When leaving an answering machine message, always instruct the party to call you back <u>collect</u>. ■

LABELS

(see also ADVERTISING COL-
LECTIBLES; AIRLINE MEMORA-
BILIA; BANANA COLLECTIBLES,
Stickers; BREWERIANA, Labels;
CIGAR BANDS, BOXES &
LABELS; LUGGAGE LABELS;
MATCHBOXES & LABELS; PAPER
COLLECTIBLES)

Clubs/Associations

Joe Davidson
American Antique Graphics Society
5185 Windfall Rd.
Medina, OH 44256-8703
phone: 330-723-7172
*Members interested in graphic arts
prints: from medieval, natural history
to cigar labels, can labels, fruit labels.*

Dealers

David & Barbara Freiberg
Cerebro
P.O. Box 327
East Prospect, PA 17317-0327
phone: 717-252-2400 or 800-69L-ABEL
fax: 717-252-3685
*Wants cigar labels, pictorial cigar
bands, fruit crate labels, firecracker
labels, can labels, and other
graphically pleasing labels.*

Paul Jarmusz
Vintage Original Fruit Crate Labels
2845 D St. N.E.
Salem, OR 97301-1600
phone: 503-371-0868
fax: 503-371-0868
e-mail: mjz@teleport.com
*Buys and sells fruit crate or vegetable
crate labels, old can labels, beer
labels, soda labels, medical labels,
cosmetic labels, etc.; unused stock
found from old packing houses,
canneries, produce businesses.*

Bread Package Ends

Experts

Don Shelley
P.O. Box 11
Bozrah, CT 06334-0011
phone: 203-887-6163
*Bread labels and albums - Howdy
Doody, spaceman, movie stars,
Hoppy, Autry, Cisco Kid, Rough
Rider, Lone Ranger, sports, Disney,
etc.; co-author with Christopher
Benjamin of "Bread End Labels
Illustrated Price Guide," $18 ppd.*

Christopher Benjamin
P.O. Box 4020
Saint Augustine, FL 32085-4020
fax: 904-826-1600
*Author of "Bread End Labels,
Illustrated Price Guide."*

Fruit Crate

Clubs/Associations

Jerry Chicone
Florida Citrus Label Collectors
Association
P.O. Box 547636
Orlando, FL 32854-7636
phone: 407-841-3815
fax: 407-290-2717

Noel Gilbert, Sec.
Citrus Label Society, The
Newsletter: Citrus Peal
131 Miramonte Dr.
Fullerton, CA 92635
phone: 714-871-2864
*Members concentrate on the collection
of citrus fruit crate labels and on the
history of the citrus fruit industry.*

Carole Crim
Fruit Crate Label Society
Journal: Box End, The
Rt 2, Box 695
Chelan, WA 98816
phone: 509-682-5879
fax: 509-682-5879
*Newsletter published six times per
year; the club for collectors of fruit
crate labels; to promote
agrilithography.*

Collectors

Michael Urban
2029 N. Mitchell St.
Phoenix, AZ 85006-2126
phone: 602-252-8615
Buys early citrus labels.

Dealers

Gerry Haskins
Haskins House
P.O. Box 44
Gainesville, FL 32602-0044
phone: 904-466-4789

Jerry & Rocky Hensley
P.O. Box 86
Burbank, WA 99323
phone: 509-544-9513
*Wants to buy fruit crate labels: apple,
pear, orange, lemon, cherry, peach,
apricot, grape and tomato.*

Experts

Lloyd Crim
Rt 2, Box 695
Chelan, WA 98816
phone: 509-682-5879
fax: 509-682-5879
*Buys, sells, appraises, and specializes
in fruit crate labels and the history of
apple growing and processing.*

Produce

Periodicals

K.H. Foster, Ed.
Newsletter: Please Stop Snickering
4113 Paint Rock Dr.
Austin, TX 78731-1320
phone: 512-346-8253
e-mail: john.foster@camel.com
*Bi-monthly newsletter for produce
seal (label) collectors; banana seals,
asparagus hangtags, apple stickers,
broccoli aprons, tissue wrappers, and
any kind of fruit or vegetable
identification.*

LABOR UNION ITEMS

(see BADGES; MINING RELATED
ITEMS; PINS; POLITICAL
COLLECTIBLES; SOCIAL CAUSES,
Labor Unions)

LADY HEAD VASES

(see CERAMICS, Head Vase Planters)

LAMPS & LIGHTING

(see also ART DECO; CAMPING
EQUIPMENT, Coleman; FLASH-
LIGHTS; LIGHT BULBS; MINING
RELATED ITEMS, Lamps; NIGHT
LIGHTS; PERFUME LAMPS;
RAILROAD COLLECTIBLES, Signal
Lamps; REPAIR/RESTORATION/
CONSERVATION, Lamps &
Lighting)

Auction Services

Ed Swann
James D. Julia Auctioneers Inc.
Rt. 201, Skowhegan Rd.
P.O. Box 830
Fairfield, ME 04937
phone: 207-453-7125
fax: 207-453-2502
*Conducts specialized auctions of fine
glass and lamps of all types including
miniature lamps, early lighting
devices, fluid lamps, art glass such as
Tiffany, Handel, Pairpoint, etc.*

Clubs/Associations

Jack Germa
Historical Lighting Society of Canada
Newsletter: HLS Newsletter
P.O. Box 561, Postal Station R
Toronto
Ontario M4G 4E1 Canada
phone: 416-724-0703 or 905-824-4117
*A social club organized by Catherine
Thuro on 1981; primary interest is
kerosene lamps and lighting from
1850 to the 1930s; two meetings per
year.*

Historical Lighting Club
89 Parsonage Lane
Bishops Stortford
Hert., CM23 5BA, U.K.

Hugh F. Hicks, Cur.
Incandescent Lamp Collectors
Association, The, c/o Museum of
Lighting
717 Washington Place
Baltimore, MD 21201-5235
phone: 410-752-8586 or 410-837-1705

Marianne Nolan
Rushlight Club Inc., The
Journal: Rushlight, The
8312 Vera Dr.
Brecksville, OH 44141-2203
*One of the oldest organizations
focusing on early lighting including
lighting devices and fuels; also
publishes the "Flickerings"
newsletter.*

Collectors

Peter Blundell
P.O. Box 6
Vernon
B.C. V1T 6M1 Canada
phone: 250-542-4540
*Involved in research since 1969; a
founding member of the Historical
Lighting Society of Canada; primarily
interested in North American kerosene
lighting.*

Bruce Axler
Ansonia Station
P.O. Box 1288
New York, NY 10023-1288
phone: 212-362-4429
fax: 212-579-1274
*Wants to buy pocket, portable, and
travel lighting devices and fire
appliances: cap lighters, pocket
lamps, folding candlesticks,
matchsafes, candle safes, lamps in
cases.*

Anthony Glab
4154 Falls Rd.
Baltimore, MD 21211-1644
phone: 410-235-1777
fax: 410-889-1937
e-mail: glab@aol.com
*Wants CARBIDE miners and bicycle
lamps; no railroad lanterns.*

Lynn Goldfinger
P.O. Box 4962
Burlingame, CA 94011-4962
phone: 415-342-7829
fax: 415-343-3269
e-mail: goldie1943@aol.com
*Wants whimsical lamps from the
1940s through 1960s: moss lamps,
spinners, anything unusual.*

Dealers

Don & Doreen Jewell
Spring House Antiques
RR 6
Barrie
Ontari L4M 5P5 Canada
phone: 705-722-3950
Wants to buy early lighting.

Dan Johnson
#7 Rte. 28
Orleans, MA 02653
phone: 508-255-8513
*Carries hundreds of restored antique
lamps and lighting fixtures.*

Federico Santi
Drawing Room of Newport, The
152 Spring St.
Newport, RI 02840-6806
phone: 401-841-5060
fax: 401-848-0953
e-mail: zsolnay@drawrm.com
Internet: http://www.drawrm.com
*Buys and sells high style 19th century
gas lighting and gas shades.*

Judy Oppert
Victorian Lighting, Inc.
29 York St.
P.O. Box 1067
Kennebunk, ME 04043-1067
phone: 207-985-6868
*Buys and sells antique lighting, 1840-
1930; gas, kerosene and early electric,
chandeliers, wall sconces, table
lamps, floor lamps and outdoor
lighting; fixtures and shades.*

JoAnne Fuerst
Pine Bough
Main Street
P.O. Box 46
Northeast Harbor, ME 04662-0046
phone: 207-276-5079
*Quarter century as scholar, dealer,
author, with broad knowledge of pre-
1875 lighting devices.*

Ray Christensen
Metzger's Lamps & Lighting
15 South Main St.
W Hartford, CT 06107
phone: 860-232-1843
fax: 860-232-5267
e-mail: rayp10@aol.com
*Buys and sells 1880-1930 antique
lamps and lighting.*

Trudy Chatlos
Chester Antique Center
32 Grove St.
P.O. Box 253
Chester, NJ 07930
phone: 908-879-4331
fax: 908-766-0386
*Carries large selection of quality
period lighting, hanging fixtures, table
and floor lamps; wants to buy
unrestored period fixtures.*

Hugo A. Ramirez, Pres.
Hugo Ltd.
233 East 59th St.
New York, NY 10022-1425
phone: 212-750-6877 or 212-288-8444
fax: 212-750-7346
*A leading authority on 19th cent.
lighting; restorer and supplier to U.S.
Senate, Treasury Dept., Nantucket
Hist. Soc., Gracie Mansion NYC,
Metropolitan Museum NYC; restores
and conserves to factory original
finish all by hand.*

Peter B. Gregory
Gatehouse, The
P.O. Box 195
Morris, NY 13808
phone: 607-263-5855 or 607-263-5746
*Wants to buy early lighting, kerosene
lamps.*

Fred Neece, Jr.
1307 Hadtner St.
Williamsport, PA 17701-3707
phone: 717-323-4679
fax: 717-323-5293
*Wants to buy candle, kerosene, and
gas lamps, lighting fixtures,
chandeliers, pieces, parts, shades, etc.*

Marco Astrologo
SPQR Lamps & Lighting Unlimited
8200 Cadwalader Ave.
Elkins Park, FL 19027
phone: 215-782-8288
Buys and sells art glass lamps.

Stephen G. Del Sordo
Principia Group
305 Oakley St.
Cambridge, MD 21613
phone: 410-228-8934
fax: 410-221-8061
e-mail: delsordo@shore.intercom.net
*A cultural resource management/
historic preservation firm that has
contracts to locate, provide,
authenticate artifacts for museums
and collectors; areas of expertise
include architecture, industry,
domestic, agriculture, and maritime.*

Carleton L. Cotting
1441 Crowell Rd.
Vienna, VA 22182-1512
phone: 703-759-5646
*Collects, buys and sells oil lamps -
miniature and full size.*

Richard Dudley
A-Bit-of-Antiquity
1412 Forest Lane
Woodbridge, VA 22191-3024
phone: 703-491-2878
e-mail: dudleyre@erols.com
*Huge inventory of table, piano,
student, hanging, bracket and banquet
lights; many new and old parts for oil
lamps; buys and sells.*

David & Phyllis Helphenstine
David's Brass Works
P.O. Box 111
Washington, KY 41096
phone: 606-759-7423
*Buys, sells, repairs lamps of all sorts;
custom lamp repair, rewire, polish,
lacquered, complete antique lamp
restoration, glass lampshades, hand
painted and artist signed shades,
custom shades.*

Tom & Linda Millman
231 S. Main St.
Bethel, OH 45106-1327
phone: 513-734-6884
fax: 513-734-6884
*Wants to buy early metal and colored
glass kerosene lamps; figural glass
electric lamps; parts for kerosene*

*lamps; original shades for both
kerosene and electric; send
description and price.*

Bohnet Electric Co.
2918 N. Grand River Ave.
Lansing, MI 48906-3808
phone: 517-482-2654
*Stained glass lighting, antique
lighting, fabric and fringed lamp
shades, table and floor lamps,
hanging lamps, crystal lighting,
crystal prisms, ceiling fans; also lamp
repairing and parts, lighting
glassware, glass fringe.*

Karl Kester
Karlucci Studios
1255 Lincoln Ave.
Saint Paul, MN 55105
phone: 612-690-2975
e-mail: karlucci@gte.net
Internet: http://home1.gte.net./karlucci/
index.htm
*Buys, sells, restores antique lighting;
this homepage gives information
about the history of lighting and
architectural styles in the US;
regularly updated listing with pictures
of fixtures and lamps for purchase on-
line.*

Scott MacClymonds
Classic Fans & Lighting
10525 Airline Dr.
Houston, TX 77037
phone: 713-448-4739 or 713-697-0069
fax: 713-448-0189
*Wants to buy art glass lighting,
especially by Quezal.*

Michael Dalio
Light Years Antiques & Restorations
8006 Grandview Ave.
Arvada, CO 80002-2404
phone: 303-422-4379
*Extensive inventory of antique,
reproduction lighting fixtures, parts,
shades, etc. consisting of floor, table,
and desk lamps also chandeliers, wall
sconces, exterior lighting & street
lights; also does custom plating and
appraisals.*

John D. McKenna
McKenna Bros. Wholesale
801-803 W Cucharras St.
Colorado Springs, CO 80905
phone: 719-630-8732
*Buys, sells and trades gas, fluid and
electric lighting devices 1850-1930.*

Greg Davidson
Greg Davidson Antiques
1307 First Ave.
Seattle, WA 98101-2002
phone: 206-625-0406
*Carries an outstanding selection of
original Victorian chandeliers, wall
sconces and other lighting devices;
gas, electric, kerosene, Tiffany,
Handel, Pairpoint, etc.*

Experts

Michael Dalio
Light Years Antiques & Restorations
8006 Grandview Ave.
Arvada, CO 80002-2404
phone: 303-422-4379
*Restores, designs, builds, fabricates
lighting fixtures: Denver Mint, Stanley
Hotel, Scottish Rites Temple, Love Oil
Company; provides lighting fixtures
for movies, commercials and plays;
consultant.*

Periodicals

Tom Barnard
Newsletter: Light Revival
35 West Elm Ave.
Quincy, MA 02170-2423
phone: 617-773-3255
*Quarterly newsletter for collectors
and dealers of medium-priced lamps
with a focus on late 19th and early
20th century lighting.*

Repair Services

Richard Dermody
Brass n' Bounty
68 Front St.
Marblehead, MA 01945-3275
phone: 617-631-3864 or 617-631-6204
*Restores brass chandeliers, sconces,
floor and table lamps; also refinishes
metal, rewires.*

Don L. Reedy
Brass & Copper Polishing Shop, The
13 South Carroll St.
Frederick, MD 21701-5606
phone: 301-663-4240 or 301-662-5503
fax: 301-663-3478
e-mail: shineit4u@aol.com
*Repairs and polishes brass and
copper items.*

Don L. Reedy
Brass & Copper Polishing Shop, The
13 South Carroll St.
Frederick, MD 21701-5606
phone: 301-663-4240 or 301-662-5503
fax: 301-663-3478
e-mail: shineit4u@aol.com
*Repair and restore antique lighting;
1000s or antique and new lamp parts
and supplies in stock; replacement
glass shades and chimneys.*

Robert Daly
Robert Daly's Historic Lighting
Restoration Sales & Service
10341 Jewell Lake Ct.
Fenton, MI 48430-2418
phone: 810-629-4934
e-mail: ldaly1@aol.com
*Veteran restorer wants to buy lamps
and light fixtures from the early 1800s
to the early 1940s; old iron, brass, tin
electric, gas or kerosene fixtures.*

Repro. Sources

Renovator's Supply
7577 Renovator's Old Mill
Millers Falls, MA 01349
phone: 413-659-2241
fax: 413-659-3796
Offers catalog of Victorian reproduction accessories, lighting, hardware, bath fixtures, and door, window and cabinet hardware.

Barbara Amster
Nineteenth Century Mercantile
No. 2 North Main St.
South Yarmouth, MA 02664
phone: 508-398-1888
Carries Gone-With-The-Wind lamps; hanging parlor, kitchen and library lamps; banquet lamps, kerosene lamps, replacement ball shades, dome shades, gas shades; all lamps can be kerosene or electrified; no mail order.

Copper House, The
RR 1 Box 4
Epsom, NH 03234-9101
phone: 603-736-9798
fax: 603-736-9798
Handmade copper reproduction lighting fixtures and weathervanes. No imports. Catalog $3 deducted from purchase.

Ray Christensen
Metzger's Lamps & Lighting
15 South Main St.
W Hartford, CT 06107
phone: 860-232-1843
fax: 860-232-5267
e-mail: rayp10@aol.com
Has huge stock of reproduction lighting and parts plus catalog orders.

Hugh C. Pribell
Early Lighting Specialties
24219 West Main St.
Columbus, NJ 08022-1917
phone: 609-298-9125
Reproduction early lighting burners and cut glass shades: camphene fluid burners, whale oil burners, Noyes 1855 patent lamp extinguishers for camphene fluid burners, brass fluid burner with coronets, betty lamps, other brass burners.

John Blowers
Olde Mill House Shoppe
105 Strasburg Pike
Lancaster, PA 17602
phone: 717-299-0678
fax: 717-299-5822
Dealer in reproduction colonial and country indoor and outdoor lighting.

Jack Cunningham
American Period Lighting
3004 Columbia Ave.
Lancaster, PA 17603-4001
phone: 717-392-5649
fax: 717-392-3557
Sells complete line of reproduction period style lighting fixtures; also offers restoration of antiques lamps and lighting fixtures.

Cumberland General Store
#1 Highway 68
Crossville, TN 38555
phone: 615-484-8481
fax: 615-456-1211
Aladdin, Dietz; send $4 for catalog.

Bill Wiebold
Pewter Reproduction Works
5950 Park Rd. #3
Madeira, OH 45243
phone: 513-831-2815
Makes replicas of pewter oil lamps, bull's-eye lamps, candlesticks, baby bottles, and funnels; complete with antique patina, nicks, dents, bends; all reproductions permanently marked as such.

Suppliers

Lamp Glass
P.O. Box 791
Cambridge, MA 02140
phone: 617-497-0770
fax: 617-497-2074
e-mail: lampglas@tiac.net
Internet: http://www.tiac.net/users/lampglas
A unique retail store specializing in replacement glass lamp shades; over one hundred in stock: Gone-With-The-Wind globes, student shades, chimneys, hurricanes, banker's shades, cased glass, prisms, glass shades, sconce glass, etc.

Ray Christensen
Metzger's Lamps & Lighting
15 South Main St.
W Hartford, CT 06107
phone: 860-232-1843
fax: 860-232-5267
e-mail: rayp10@aol.com
Sells and manufactures parts for new and old lamps.

Aladdin

Clubs/Associations

J. W. Courter
Aladdin Knights, The
Newsletter: Mystic Light, The
3935 Kelley Rd.
Kevil, KY 42053-9431
phone: 502-488-2116
fax: 502-488-2116
e-mail: brtknight@aol.com
Internet: http://www.aladdinknights.org
Purpose is to preserve Aladdin kerosene and electric lamps and Aladdin advertising history and memorabilia; sponsors annual national lamp and lighting show.

Collectors

Richard Melcher
1206 Okanogan St.
Wenatchee, WA 98807
phone: 509-662-0386
Wants to buy Aladdin lamps or lamp parts.

Dealers

Jim & Sheri Van Es
222 W. Washington St.
Charles Town, WV 25414
phone: 304-725-1673 or 703-435-9045
e-mail: wdnshu@aol.com
Buys, sells, and repairs Aladdin lamps, glass and parts.

Experts

J. W. Courter
3935 Kelley Rd.
Kevil, KY 42053-9431
phone: 502-488-2116
fax: 502-488-2116
e-mail: brtknight@aol.com
Internet: http://www.aladdinknights.org
Wants Aladdin and "angle" lamps; author of "Aladdin Collectors Manual & Price Guide #14 Kerosene Mantle Lamps."

Repair Services

Richard Dudley
A-Bit-of-Antiquity
1412 Forest Lane
Woodbridge, VA 22191-3024
phone: 703-491-2878
e-mail: dudleyre@erols.com
Expert restoration, repair, deplating & polishing of gas and electric lamps; specializing in oil lighting; carries old parts & shades; also buys and sells old lamps and lamp parts.

Suppliers

Bruce B. Phillips
Phillips Lamp Shades Ltd.
172 Main St.
Toronto
Ontario M4E 2W1 Canada
phone: 416-691-7372
fax: 416-691-7360
Parts & expert repairs for Aladdin lamps; wicks, chimneys, mantles, holders, decorated glass shades, electric adapters; parts catalog $5; dealing in lighting since 1925.

Angle

Collectors

G. Millman
231 S. Main St.
Bethel, OH 45106-1327
phone: 513-734-6884
fax: 513-734-6884
Wants to buy wall-mounted cast-metal angle lamps (glass desired, but not necessary); also old angle chimneys and elbows; send description and price.

Experts

J. W. Courter
3935 Kelley Rd.
Kevil, KY 42053-9431
phone: 502-488-2116
fax: 502-488-2116
e-mail: brtknight@aol.com
Internet: http://www.aladdinknights.org
Wants Aladdin and "angle" lamps; author of "Aladdin Collectors Manual & Price Guide #15 Kerosene Mantle Lamps."

Bellova

Collectors

Bruce Bleier
73 Riverdale Rd.
Valley Stream, NY 11581
phone: 516-791-4353
e-mail: bellovaman@aol.com
Buys and sells Bellova lamps.

Candlesticks

Collectors

William G. Hodges
Ridgefield, Inc.
12509 Patterson Ave.
Richmond, VA 23233-6414
phone: 703-768-6562

Dealers

Bruce A. Sikora
P.O. Box 163
Bay Shore, NY 11706
phone: 516-665-0665
fax: 516-665-0634
Buys, sells, and specializes in 15th through 18th century lighting.

Lois A. Temple
Temple & Co.
110 Bittersweet N.E.
Ada, MI 49301
phone: 616-676-3659 or 616-776-2515
fax: 616-752-2500
Interested in antique wooden candlesticks and candle stands, including wooden pieces with petal, glass, or ceramic components.

Carol Payne
Carol's Antique Gallery
14455 Big Basin Way
Saratoga, CA 95070-6008
phone: 408-867-7055
Wants clear or colored glass, silver, silverplated, pottery and porcelain candlesticks; will consider brass and wooden ones; send photo and list any markings and measurements; pairs or singles.

Betty Bird
107 Ida St.
Mount Shasta, CA 96067-2629
phone: 916-926-4331 or 916-926-2231
Wants to buy brass candlesticks, silver, bronze, pewter candleholders; also wants glass candleholders, fairy lamps and miniature lamps of all sorts.

Carriage

Collectors

Larry Sluiter
4186 East Lamm Rd.
Freeport, IL 61032
phone: 815-235-1249
Wants coachman driven and carriage

lamps in pairs; also wants horse-drawn carriages.

Chandeliers

Experts

Rick Charpie
Crystal Clear Chandelier Care
9602 W. 156th St.
Overland Park, KS 66221-9709
phone: 913-681-6700 or 800-373-7804
fax: 913-897-7608
Crystal & glass chandeliers a specialty: repair/cleaning/restoration, electrification of gas or candle devices, replacement of parts & prisms, buys whole or broken chandeliers and old trade catalogs, chandelier consultant, etc.

Suppliers

Lighting Designs
1500 Rockville Pike
Rockville, MD 20852
phone: 301-468-7300
Carries large selection of crystal chandeliers and parts for same.

Emeralite

Collectors

Bruce Bleier
73 Riverdale Rd.
Valley Stream, NY 11581
phone: 516-791-4353
e-mail: bellovaman@aol.com
Buys and sells Emeralite and Bellova lamps.

Jerry Propst
P.O. Box 45
Janesville, WI 53547-0045
phone: 608-752-2816
fax: 608-752-7691
Buys and sells Emeralite, Amrolite and Bellova shades and lamp bases; also literature on same; when writing, please include a LSASE if requesting a reply.

Gas

Experts

Dan Mattausch
Cortelyou House
260 Maryland Ave., NE
Washington, DC 20002
phone: 202-544-4415
fax: 202-544-4415
e-mail: NMattausch@technautics.com
Researching and collecting gaslight burners, igniters, galleries, and mantles; also any related new-old-stock, packaging, catalogs, or advertising; wants anything that comes off a gaslight fixture when it is electrified.

Kerosene

Museums/Libraries

George L. Sherwood, Curator
Winchester Center Kerosene Lamp
  Museum & Lighting Emporium
100 Old Waterbury Turnpike
Winchester Center, CT 06094
phone: 860-379-2612
fax: 860-738-4446

Lanterns

Dealers

Dennis Kuhl
A-n-D Antiques
4052 Altura Drive
Oceanside, CA 92056-4315
phone: 760-941-6816
Wants to buy pre-1940 lanterns.

Experts

Anthony Hobson
238 Schoolhouse Rd.
Ghent, NY 12075-4028
phone: 518-392-3732
fax: 518-392-3742
Specializes in and appraises railroad, marine, fire, carriage, farm, and other lanterns; author of "Lanterns That Lit Our World."

Lava Lamps

Suppliers

Lava-Simplex Internationale
2321 N. Keystone
Chicago, IL 60639-3709
phone: 312-342-5700
Call to locate nearest dealer in new Lava Lamps or to order replacement globes.

Miniature

Clubs/Associations

Bob Culver
Night Light Club
Newsletter: Night Light Newsletter
38619 Wakefield Ct.
Northville, MI 48167-9060
phone: 248-473-8575
e-mail: rculver107@aol.com
The goal of Night Light is to further the hobby of collecting miniature oil lamps; newsletter published quarterly.

Dealers

Betty Bird
107 Ida St.
Mount Shasta, CA 96067-2629
phone: 916-926-4331 or 916-926-2231
Wants fairy lamps and miniature lamps of all sorts.

Motion

Collectors

Amy Kanis
5000 W. 96th St.
Indianapolis, IN 46268
phone: 317-873-2727
Wants 1930s-60s revolving lamps, i.e. plastic or glass w/light bulb-heat propelled inner cylinder; all applications desired.

Rich & Jean Glendinning
P.O. Box 19188
Oakland, CA 94619-0188
phone: 510-635-0712
Wants to buy motion lamps with scenes in motion, Econolite, Goodman, etc.

Dealers

Jim Whitaker
P.O. Box 475
Lynnwood, WA 98046
phone: 800-774-6910
Buys and sells motion (revolving) lamps.

Experts

Sam & Anna Samuelian
P.O. Box 504
Edgemont, PA 19028-0504
phone: 610-566-7248
fax: 610-566-7285
Buys, sells, restores motion lamps: Econolite, L.A. Goodman, Scene-In-Action, Roto-Vue, etc.; leading buyers and sellers with largest collection in the world from 1920s-1980s; can reproduce parts; book in the offing.

Bill & Linda Montgomery
P.O. Box 68572
Oak Grove, OR 97268
phone: 503-652-2992
Authors of "Montgomery's Animated Motion Lamps: A Price Guide" (L-W Book Sales, 1991).

Neon

(see also NEON)

Collectors

Len Davidson
2140 Mount Vernon St.
Philadelphia, PA 19130-3134
phone: 215-232-0478
fax: 215-232-0478
Wants to buy antique neon signs.

Stephen Seltzer
7912 Georgia Ave.
Silver Spring, MD 20910-4837
phone: 301-565-2444 or 301-565-3339
fax: 301-565-2228
e-mail: eseltzer@aol.com
Wants to buy neon signs - new and antique - working or not.

Dealers

Dennis Clark
Off the Wall Antiques, Inc.
7325 Melrose Ave.
Los Angeles, CA 90046
phone: 213-930-1185
fax: 213-930-1595
Wants to buy figural neon signs; die cut and animated preferred; porcelain or painted; send photos.

Museums/Libraries

Len Davidson
Neon Museum of Philadelphia
2140 Mount Vernon St.
Philadelphia, PA 19130-3134
phone: 215-232-0478
fax: 215-232-0478
Museum restores & displays antique neon signs.

Museum of Neon Art
704 Traction Ave.
Los Angeles, CA 90013
phone: 213-617-1580

Periodicals

Newsletter: Neon News
P.O. Box 668
Volcano, HI 96785
fax: 808-967-7648
A quarterly newsletter for neon enthusiasts and craftsmen; covers historic restoration and design issues as well as offering classified ads to subscribers.

Repair Services

Volcano Neon
P.O. Box 668
Volcano, HI 96785
fax: 808-967-7648
Specializes in restoring and repairing historic neon signs for clients around the world; also makes accurate reproductions, and designs custom neon signs, lighting, art, and gifts.

Shades

Dealers

Deborah Smallwood
Seller of Dreams
P.O. Box 428
Powell, OH 43065
phone: 614-436-8393
Custom makes all types of lamp shades; specializes in Victorian shades; lamp rewiring also available.

Man./Prod./Dist.

Claudia A. Minick
Light Up My Life Antiques
RD 4 Box 307
Blairsville, PA 15717-8942
phone: 412-459-7539
Replacement shades on your frame or mine; shade restorations; lamps rewired and repaired.

Kristina Krause
Victorian Rapture Company
107 Saluda St.
Chester, SC 29706-1511
phone: 803-581-2703
e-mail: Kristina@victorianrapture.com
Internet: http://
www.victorianrapture.com
*Custom makes high Victorian shades;
16" beaded fringe patterns & 85
frame choices to order; also covers
old frames and supplier of reproduction Victorian lighting, jewelry (14K
plated), bronzes, perfume bottles.*

Faith Kovach
201 W. Alyea St.
P.O. Box 522
Hebron, IN 46341-0522
phone: 219-996-2924
*Makes Victorian lamp shades made
with silk, satin lace and fringes.*

Dorothy Primo
Lampshades of Antique
P.O. Box 2
Medford, OR 97501-0001
phone: 503-826-9737
*Manufactures and sells 96 styles of
cloth and fringed replacement
Victorian lamp shades; also will
recover your frame; catalog $4.*

Daniel Primo
Lampshades of Antique
P.O. Box 1507
Medford, OR 97501-0112
phone: 541-826-9737
fax: 541-826-1086
*Designers, manufacturers, vendor or
elegant lampshades for restaurants,
hotels, movies, casinos, antiques,
lighting stores; extensive selection of
fabrics, laces & trim; also repairs and
restores.*

Repair Services

Daniel Primo
Lampshades of Antique
P.O. Box 1507
Medford, OR 97501-0112
phone: 541-826-9737
fax: 541-826-1086
*Designers, manufacturers, vendor or
elegant lampshades for restaurants,
hotels, movies, casinos, antiques,
lighting stores; extensive selection of
fabrics, laces & trim; also repairs and
restores.*

Tiffany/Handel/Pairpoint

Collectors

Harvey Weinstein
22 Halifax Dr.
Morganville, NJ 07751
phone: 201-536-4467 or 800-321-0204
*Wants lamps and glass by Tiffany,
Galle, Daum Nancy, Handel, Lotz,
Pairpoint, Lalique, etc.*

Alan Grodsky
642 Franklin Ave.
Garden City, NY 11530-5729
phone: 800-431-8256 or 800-835-0008
*Buys, sells Pairpoint puffies and
painted scenic lamps; also Tiffany and
Handel painted lamps and accessories.*

Mark Kaplan
135 W. Penn St.
Long Beach, NY 11561-4040
phone: 800-626-1752
*Wants Pairpoint puffies, painted
scenes; also Handel painted lamps
and accessories.*

Robert Ogorek
6400 Davidson Rd.
Burton, MI 48509
phone: 810-743-5358
Serious collector of Tiffany lamps.

Dr. Neil Superfon
2121 W. Indian School Rd.
Phoenix, AZ 85015
phone: 602-277-1449 or 800-258-0216
fax: 602-263-8523
*Wants Handel, Galle, Pairpoint,
Tiffany lamps and glass.*

Dealers

Joseph D. Cantara
Cantara/Galletti
61038 80th St.
Middle Village, NY 11379
phone: 718-651-9347 or 718-358-5923
*Buys, sells and specializes in art glass
and in Tiffany items such as lamps,
desk sets, glass and accessories; also
buys and sells Art Deco - especially
French & Austrian.*

Plantation Galleries, Inc.
2685 SW 17th Ave.
Coconut Grove, FL 33133
phone: 305-854-4651 or 305-673-1431
fax: 305-854-0023
*Specializes in the buying and selling
of art glass lamp shades.*

Experts

Sheila & Edward Malakoff
276 Princeton Dr.
River Edge, NJ 07661-1031
phone: 201-487-1989
fax: 201-489-0179
Authors of "Pairpoint Lamps."

Carole Hibel
John Hibel Antiques
185 Yerry Hill Rd.
Woodstock, NY 12498
phone: 914-679-2966 or 800-426-3357
fax: 914-679-3397
*Buys, sells, collects, appraises in
Handel lamps; author of "Handel
Lamps - Painted Shades & Glass-
ware."*

Carl Heck
Carl Heck Decorative Antiques
P.O. Box 8416
Aspen, CO 81612-8416
phone: 970-925-8011
fax: 970-925-8100
*Specializes in lamps by Tiffany,
Pairpoint, Handel, Galle, etc.*

Museums/Libraries

Edward Malakoff
Pairpoint Lamp Museum
276 Princeton Dr.
River Edge, NJ 07661-1031
phone: 201-487-1989
fax: 201-489-0179
Author of "Pairpoint Lamps."

Repair Services

Joan Meyer
104 Colwyn Lane
Bala Cynwyd, PA 19004
phone: 610-664-3174
*Repairs Tiffany lamps; expert
craftsmanship, only uses Tiffany glass,
damaged shades purchased.*

Repro. Sources

Dale Tiffany, Inc.
6 Willow St.
Moonachie, NJ 07074
phone: 201-473-1900
fax: 201-507-1842
*Sells brand new solid bronze Tiffany
replica lamp bases; 30 different
Tiffany bases available including urn
turtleback, four-sided turtleback,
lion's paw, snake base, and roots
telescope.*

Asher Shahar
3146 J.P. Curcie Dr., Bldg. 3-A
Hallandale, FL 33009
phone: 305-981-7440
fax: 305-981-7440
*Sells 2, 3, 12, and 18 light Lily Lamps
and many other Tiffany reproductions.*

LANDMARK REPLICAS

(see SOUVENIR & COMMEMORA-
TIVE ITEMS, Buildings)

LANTERNS

(see LAMPS & LIGHTING; MINING
RELATED ITEMS, Lamps;
RAILROAD COLLECTIBLES, Signal
Lamps)

LAPIDARY

(see also GEMS & JEWELRY;
MINERALS)

Clubs/Associations

Rollin' Rock Club
Magazine: Rollin' Rock Club Newsletter
15 Kennington Dr.
Warrington, FL 32507-1099
phone: 904-455-6424
*Interest is in lapidary: cutting,
shaping and polishing of stones.*

Ute Mountain Gem & Mineral Society
P.O. Box 385
Cortez, CO 81321

Dealers

Susan McCune, ISA
GemFacets
20649 Keswick St.
Winnetka, CA 91306-2028
phone: 818-348-6701
fax: 818-348-6701
*Active in the lapidary arts field;
represents lapidary artists.*

Dad's Rock Shop
112 E. Cherry Ave.
P.O. Box 169
Arroyo Grande, CA 93421
phone: 805-489-2470 or 800-844-DADS
*Dealers in geodes, fossils, lapidary
equipment and supplies, rock carving
material, rockhound books.*

Misc. Services

William Holland School of Lapidary
Arts
P.O. Box 980
Young Harris, GA 30582
phone: 706-379-2126
Internet: http://www.eng.clemson.edu
Offers classes in the lapidary arts.

Museums/Libraries

Lizzadro Museum of Lapidary Art
220 Cottage Hill Ave.
Elmhurst, IL 60126-3351
phone: 312-833-1616
*Large collection of hard stone
carvings (especially Chinese jade
carvings), rocks, minerals, and a
unique gift shop.*

On-Line Services

Canadian Rockhound
e-mail: dfs846@mail.ussk.ca
Internet: http://pangea.usask.co/~dfs846/
rockhound/home.html
*An on-line magazine providing
interesting and educational stories on
rock, fossil and mineral collecting, the
art of lapidary, gems and faceting,
and on the earth sciences as well.*

Thoms W. Corson
Rockhound's Information Page, c/o
Information Dynamics
14407 Big Basin Way, Ste. B
Saratoga, CA 95070
phone: 408-868-9700
fax: 408-868-0314
e-mail: rockhounds-
owner@infodyn.com
Internet: http://www.rahul.net/infodyn/
rockhounds/
*Great website for rockhound
information: shops and galleries;
images and pictures; books, articles
and other publications; general earth
science information; paleontology-
related sites; collecting sites and
trips; clubs & societies.*

Periodicals

Cindy Valerio
Magazine: Lapidary Journal
P.O. Box 1100
Devon, PA 19333-0905
phone: 610-293-1112 or 800-676-4336
fax: 610-293-1717
Serves gem cutters, mineral/fossil collectors, jewelry, jewelry arts, rock enthusiasts; published monthly; also has a book & video sales department; extensive directory of dealers and clubs.

Repair Services

Richard P. Hegeman
Hegeman & Co.
361 S. Main St.
Providence, RI 02903-2912
phone: 401-831-6812
Cutters of all precious/semi-precious stones; specializing in the repair & restoration of all types of jewelry (antique and contemporary); gemstone replacements and repairs.

LARKIN SOAP COMPANY

Collectors

Jerome P. Puma
78 Brinton St.
Buffalo, NY 14214-1175
phone: 716-838-5674
Would like any items pertaining to the Larkin Soap Co. of Buffalo, NY: catalogs, calendars, other paper items and Larkin items; also any item dealing with the Larkin administration building designed by Frank Lloyd Wright.

LAW ENFORCEMENT MEMORA-BILIA

(see also BADGES; OUTLAWS & LAWMEN; RESTRAINT DEVICES; WESTERN AMERICANA)

Experts

Lt. Talbert Kanigher, Ret.
Tal's Nostalgia
P.O. Box 6294
Burbank, CA 91505-6294
phone: 818-848-6469
Collecting for over 30 years; interested in anything pertaining to outlaws, lawmen, police, gangsters, murderers.

FBI

Collectors

Dick Guttler
P.O. Box 2114
Garden City, NY 11531-9998
phone: 516-935-7218
fax: 516-935-7218
Wants G-Man, Melvin Purvis, Gangbusters, books, badges, toys, collectibles.

Barry O'Neill
6500 Ridge Rd.
Mount Airy, MD 21771
phone: 301-829-2050
Wants G-Man, Melvin Purvis, FBI collectibles.

Police & Sheriff

Collectors

Hervey P. Cote
P.O. Box 2053
Westford, MA 01886-5053
phone: 508-692-2161
Collector of police memorabilia including badges, uniforms, hats, Bobby helmets, etc.; especially interested in older badges and memorabilia from MA and New England.

Bob Fischer
P.O. Box 9763
Baldwin, MD 21013
Wants to buy old police badges.

Daryl Weseloh
P.O. Box 606
Delavan, IL 61734-0606
phone: 309-244-8277
fax: 309-244-8437
Wants to buy all sorts of police uniform articles, equipment, police toys, badges, shoulder patches, etc.

Walt Gist
4190 Juniper Creek Rd.
Reno, NV 89509
phone: 702-747-2888
Wants to buy law enforcement memorabilia including paper, photos, badges, etc.; has over 39 years experiencing collecting.

Donald G. Robinson
United States Marshals Posse
P.O. Box 590487
San Francisco, CA 94159
phone: 415-386-1565
fax: 415-386-2316
Wants to buy police and sheriff memorabilia.

Dealers

Baird Co.
P.O. Box 7240
Moreno Valley, CA 92303-7240
phone: 909-943-4180
fax: 909-943-8491
e-mail: bedoya2@aol.com
Internet: http://www.bairdco.com
Publishes lists of law enforcement memorabilia available; also conducts specialty mail auctions of same.

Experts

Gene Matzke
Gene's Badges & Emblems
2345 S. 28th
Milwaukee, WI 53215-2925
phone: 414-383-8995
fax: 414-645-8288
Wants police/fire/sheriffs & related law enforcement badges; also old

cabinet police photos, handcuffs, leg irons and related items.

George E. Virgines
P.O. Box 13761
Albuquerque, NM 87192-3761
phone: 505-292-3853
Consultant, historian and author of "Badges of Law and Order" and "Police Collectibles Pictorial Guide"; collector of lawmen badges.

Museums/Libraries

New York City Police Academy Museum
235 E. 20th St.
New York, NY 10003
phone: 212-477-9753

Suffolk County Police Department Museum
30 Yaphank Ave.
Yaphank, NY 11980
phone: 516-345-6011

Jim Gordon
American Police Hall of Fame & Museum
Magazine: Chief of Police and Police Times
3801 Biscayne Blvd.
Miami, FL 33137
phone: 305-573-0202
fax: 305-573-9819
Over 11,000 items on display; equipment, uniforms, firearms, etc. from the 1700s; wants anything related to law enforcement.

Florence Panson, Dir.
American Police Center & Museum
1717 S. State St.
Chicago, IL 60616
phone: 312-431-0005
fax: 312-939-1122
An educational museum with over 10,000 sq. ft. of exhibits and viewing; guided tours are available; free parking; wheelchair accessible.

Sgt. James Post
Last Precinct Police Museum, The
Rte. 6, Box 345B
Eureka Springs, AR 72632
phone: 501-253-4948
fax: 501-253-4949
Internet: http://www.policeguide.com
Over 150 years of law enforcement history, movie memorabilia, police toys, advertising, badges, weapons, uniforms; also four decades of police cars and motorcycles.

Periodicals

Newsletter: Police Collectors News
RR 1 Box 14
Baldwin, WI 54002

Prison Related

Collectors

Larry Franklin
3238 Hutchison Ave.
Los Angeles, CA 90034
phone: 310-559-4461
Collects all American manufactured handcuffs, non-medical restraints in any form: handcuffs, leg irons, Oregon boots, manacles, slave irons, thumb cuffs, etc.; also wants toys or patent models of same.

Museums/Libraries

San Quentin Prison Museum
Building 106, Delores Way
P.O. Box 205
San Quentin, CA 94964
phone: 415-454-1460

LAWMEN

(see LAW ENFORCEMENT MEMORABILIA, Police & Sheriff; OUTLAWS & LAWMEN; WESTERN AMERICANA)

LAWN FURNITURE & ORNA-MENTS

(see GARDEN FURNITURE, Furniture & Ornaments)

LEAD SOLDIERS

(see SOLDIER, Toy)

LEADED WINDOWS

(see STAINED GLASS)

LEATHER

(see also ANIMAL COLLECTIBLES, Horses; ANIMAL COLLECTIBLES, Mules; KNIVES, Sheaths; LUGGAGE; OUTLAWS & LAWMEN; PURSES; SADDLES; SPORTS COLLECTIBLES, Equipment; TRUNKS)

Clubs/Associations

Saddle, Harness & Allied Trades Association
Newsletter: Harness Shop News, The
347 Elk Rd.
Sylva, NC 28779
phone: 704-586-6389
fax: 704-586-8938
Members are makers of saddles, chaps, harnesses, whips, holsters; carving & tooling, luggage repair, sewing machine maintenance.

Collectors

Bill Mackin
1137 Washington St.
Craig, CO 81625-1613
phone: 970-824-6717 or 970-824-6360
fax: 970-824-7175
e-mail: reust@nadja.com
Wants pre-1940s cowboy and tack items: guns, cartridge belts, chaps,

law badges, neckerchiefs, brands and brand books, spurs, knives, quirts, cowboy boots, hats, neckerchiefs, vests, cuffs, gauntlets, gun and saddle catalogs, etc.

Periodicals

Magazine: Harness Shop News, The
347 Elk Rd.
Sylva, NC 28779
phone: 704-586-8938
fax: 704-586-8938
Professional leather workers, saddle makers, shoe and saddle repairmen, holster manufacturers, harness makers, boot makers; ads, calendar of events.

Magazine: Leather Crafters & Saddlers Journal, The
331 Annette Court
Rhinelander, WI 54501

Newsletter: DNN Newsletter
P.O. Box 820
Los Lunas, NM 87031
phone: 505-865-5282

Repair Services

Bruce Hamilton
R. Bruce Hamilton, Furniture Restoration
P.O. Box 815
West Newbury, MA 01985
phone: 508-363-2638
fax: 508-363-2638
Repairs and replaces leather and cloth table tops; brochure available; 20th year.

Maria Pukownik
Fine Art & Paper Conservation
1045 Orrtanna Rd.
Orrtanna, PA 17353
phone: 717-337-0668
Surface cleaning, softening of cockled and distorted leather, stabilizing and flattening, calligraphy, conservation of wax seals and other materials.

Gary Martin
Martin Leather Furniture Restoration
P.O. Box 535
Manassas, VA 22110
phone: 703-369-7914 or 800-553-3872
fax: 703-369-7914
Cleans, repairs, refinishes, colors leather furniture, auto leather, etc.

Suppliers

Wickett & Craig of American
120 Copper Rd.
Curwensville, PA 16833
phone: 800-TAN-NERY
Leather supplier.

Smucker's Harness Shop
2014 Main St.
Narvon, PA 17555
phone: 717-445-5956
fax: 717-445-7752

Bill Confer
Hereford Bi-Products, Inc.
P.O. Box 2257
Hereford, TX 79045
phone: 800-858-4384
American made rawhide for saddle & tree makers, braiders and craftsmen.

Charles L. Hardtke, Inc.
11040 Argal Ct.
El Paso, TX 79935
phone: 915-590-0088
Specializing in fine leathers from around the world: kangaroo, calf, cowhide, water buffalo, kid & goat, ostrich, alligator, pangolin, stringray, snake skins, etc.

Charles H. Clements, III
Charles Clements Leathercraft
1741 Dallas St.
Aurora, CO 80010
phone: 303-364-0403
Makes cases, luggage, specialty items for Rodeo, Circus, Safari, Fashion/ Commercial, Advertising/Cinema, etc.

R. Stephen Dorsey
Pecard
P.O. Box 263
Eugene, OR 97440
Sells the very best antique leather preservative - moisturizes, preserves, colorless, softens, odorless, long lasting, safe; 6 oz. sample tube $9.50 ppd.

LETTER OPENERS

Experts

Diane Levin
880 North Lake Shore Dr. #3C
Chicago, IL 60611-1701
phone: 312-337-4913
Buys and sells old, vintage letter openers; please include a SASE if requesting a reply; wants old letter openers, especially celluloid figurals; no advertising; seeks contact with other collectors as there is no club or newsletter.

LETTERHEADS

(see PAPER COLLECTIBLES, Billheads)

LETTERING ARTS

(see CALLIGRAPHY)

LETTERS (FAMILY)

(see MANUSCRIPTS; PAPER COLLECTIBLES)

LEVIS

(see CLOTHING & ACCESSORIES, Denim)

LICENSE PLATE ATTACH-MENTS

Automobile

Collectors

Edward Foley
129 Meadow Valley Rd., Trlr. 11
Ephrata, PA 17522-1843
Wants cast or steel license plate attachments (bolts to top of a plate): cities, beaches, tourist meccas, oil company, porcelain, etc.

LICENSE PLATES

(see also AUTOMOBILIA; BICYCLES & RELATED MEMORA-BILIA; GAS STATION COL-LECTIBLES; LICENSE PLATE ATTACHMENTS)

Collectors

Trent Culp
P.O. Box 550
Misenheimer, NC 28109-0550
phone: 704-279-6242
Collects license plates from all states: porcelain, early tin, motorcycle, Presidential Inauguration, early Alaskan & Hawaiian, etc.

Dealers

Dwayne Spark
Nostalgia Plus
8441 Sublaines
Anjou
Quebec H1K 2C1 Canada
phone: 514-352-6892
fax: 514-352-1856
e-mail: dspark@montrealnet.ca
Wants to buy current passenger license plates and commemorative from US States and Canadian Provinces; prefers to buy in lots of 50 or more plates.

Drew Steitz
PL8S Magazine
P.O. Box 222
East Texas, PA 18046-0222
phone: 610-791-7979
fax: 610-791-7979
e-mail: pl8seditor@aol.com
Internet: http://www.pl8s.com
Collects, buys, sells and trades all types of license plates: porcelain, leather, U.S. or Canada, foreign, errors, blanks, tests, political, low number, motorcycle, movie props or prototypes, etc.

Jeff Francis
P.O. Box 41381
Saint Petersburg, FL 33743
phone: 813-343-4316

Chuck Batey
1115 Theresa St.
Stuart, FL 34996
phone: 407-283-1881 or 407-283-5335
Internet: http://auto4world.com/parts/ chuck-batey.htm
Buys and sells license plates from 1925 to 1994

Walt Feiger
Walt's Antiques
2513 Nelson Rd.
Traverse City, MI 49686-8557
phone: 616-223-7386 or 616-223-4123
Wants all kinds of older Michigan license plates.

On-Line Services

P.A. Rothfuss
International License Plate Collector's BBS
4901 Butterfield Trail NW
Albuquerque, NM 87120-2856
phone: 508-898-6356
e-mail: rothfuss@apsicc.aps.edu
A BBS for buying and selling license plates.

Periodicals

Stephen Tuday
Newsletter: Plate Trader, The
21 Ridge Run SE, Apt. D
Marietta, GA 30067
phone: 404-421-0864
A monthly newsletter dedicated to the promotion of the hobby by encouraging the trading of plates instead of buying them; subscribers are entitled to FREE advertising every month.

Automobile

Clubs/Associations

Gary Brent Kincade
Automobile License Plate Collectors Association, Inc.
Newsletter: ALPCA Newsletter
P.O. Box 7
Horner, WV 26372
phone: 304-842-3773
A non-profit organization to promote interest in the collecting of motor vehicle license plates and to share information among members.

Dealers

Conrad Hughson
Self Help Services
P.O. Box 399
Brattleboro, VT 05302-0941
phone: 802-387-4223
Collector of U.S. and Canadian license plates since 1952; will buy entire collections of early plates; many duplicates; appraisal service available; consignment sales of license plates and related collectibles; since 1952.

Experts

Chuck Crisler
P.O. Box 114
Ponchatoula, LA 70454-0114
Author of "License Plates Values."

Periodicals

Bob Bittner
Newsletter: Island Plate Chronicle
30 Edwardel Rd.
Needham, MA 02192
Quarterly color newsletter focusing on island license plates.

Drew Steitz
Magazine: PL8S - The License Plate Collector's Hobby Paper
P.O. Box 222
East Texas, PA 18046-0222
phone: 610-791-7979
fax: 610-791-7979
e-mail: pl8seditor@aol.com
Internet: http://www.pl8s.com
A bi-monthly hobby magazine dedicated to the license plate collecting hobby; license plate photos, puzzles, cartoons, giveaways, games, ads, and lots more.

Automobile (Delaware)

Collectors

Dave Lincoln
P.O. Box 331
Yorklyn, DE 19736-0331
phone: 610-444-4144
Collector seeks Delaware plates of all types, variety, and vintage for comprehensive display and forthcoming book. Largest DELA-WARE collection extant; finders fees paid; references available; information requests are welcome.

Automobile (Porcelain)

Collectors

Tom Mills
30 Bay Path Rd.
Spencer, MA 01562-1602
phone: 508-885-9550
Wants to buy porcelain license plates and signs; best to write and send photos first.

Stephen S. Uss
60 Homecrest Ave.
Yonkers, NY 10703
phone: 914-423-0442
Wants early porcelain, leather and tin auto or motorcycle license plates; also chauffeurs badges and dashboard registration discs.

Dave Lincoln
P.O. Box 331
Yorklyn, DE 19736-0331
phone: 610-444-4144
Active hobbyist interested in expired plates from anywhere; any type, any number, any vintage; 30 years collecting; sells or swaps extras; collecting and researching PORCE-LAIN-ENAMEL plates - information wanted; postage costs refunded.

Jim Crilly
8261 141st St. N.
Seminole, FL 34646-2835
phone: 813-393-7295
Collects state and city porcelain

license plates; also wants 1940 B.F. Goodrich license plate key chain tags from AZ, AR, NV, NM, and SC; have mint 39 NM and SC will trade for 40 NM and SC.

Carl Malsahn
3351 Elder Rd.
Carp Lake, MI 49718-9774
Porcelain license plates any state, Michigan plates before 1945.

Government

Experts

Jake Eckenrode
310 Wallace Rd.
Bellefonte, PA 16823
phone: 814-355-8769
Wants old U.S. Government license plates from any agency including old Civilian Conservation Corps (CCC) signs, and Pennsylvania licenses (vehicle, hunting, fishing, dog); author of "Collector's Guide to Pennsylvania Licenses."

Miniature

Clubs/Associations

Dr. Edward H. Miles
License Plate Key Chain & Mini License Plate Collectors
Newsletter: Key Chain News
888 Eighth Ave.
New York, NY 10019-5704
phone: 212-765-2660
Focuses on miniature Disabled American Veterans key chains, chauffeurs' badges, gum cards featuring license plates, windshield stickers, mini license plates.

Collectors

Virginia Young
15463 McNeill Rd.
Sterling, NY 13156-4212
phone: 315-947-5840 or 315-947-5782
fax: 315-947-6905
Wants DAV and BFG miniature license keychain tags; also gum and cereal plates depicting license plates; all years, all state; especially looking for older, Western or Southern states, or a 1943 round DAV tag.

Edward Foley
129 Meadow Valley Rd., Trlr. 11
Ephrata, PA 17522-1843
Wants B.F. Goodrich keychain license plates from all states, 1939 - 1942; many painted brass with B.F. Goodrich on back; 1 3/4" x 3/4."

LICENSES

(see also AUTOMOBILIA; LICENSE PLATES)

Animal

Clubs/Associations

William Bone
International Society of Animal License Collectors
Newsletter: Paw Prints
928 SR 2206
Clinton, KY 42031-8412
phone: 502-653-6060
e-mail: tagman@ibm.net
Animal license collectors united for the exchange of hobby material; annual convention in various areas of the U.S.

Collectors

Trudy & Marty Doll
38 Carrolls Tract Rd.
Fairfield, PA 17320
Wants any and all kinds of animal licenses, primarily dog.

Experts

Karen Lea Rose
4420 Wisconsin Ave.
Tampa, FL 33616-1031
phone: 813-839-6245
Collects paper or metal animal licenses; tags or certificates.

William Bone
928 SR 2206
Clinton, KY 42031-8412
phone: 502-653-6060
e-mail: tagman@ibm.net
Has published a book on pre-1900 animal license tags.

Dog

Collectors

James C. Case
10189 Crane Rd.
Lindley, NY 14858-9719
phone: 607-524-6606
Wants log licenses and dog tags dated before 1920; especially interested in pre-1917 tags from New York state.

Jerome Schaeper, Jr.
705 Philadelphia St.
Covington, KY 41011-1252
phone: 606-581-3729
Collects and appraises early dog (canine) license tags, especially pre-1920, from any state or country.

Driver

Collectors

Albert Velocci
62 Cherrywood Dr.
Hillside Manor, NY 11040
Wants to buy divers licenses and vehicle registrations; also wants any early automobile related paper.

Driver (PA Licensed Operator)

Collectors

Edward Foley
129 Meadow Valley Rd., Trlr. 11
Ephrata, PA 17522-1843
Wants PA Licensed Operator badges 1910-1929. The 1910 is keystone shape, 1911-1928 oval, 1929 is round; also special Licensed Driver.

Hunting & Fishing

Collectors

James C. Case
10189 Crane Rd.
Lindley, NY 14858-9719
phone: 607-524-6606
Wants hunting, fishing, trapping licenses and license buttons as well as guide badges from all states (mainly pre-1945.)

Ron Brownawell
331 Old State Rd.
Shermans Dale, PA 170907
phone: 717-582-2088
Wants hunting and fishing licenses: especially PA related; also pin-back type licenses from all states and Canada.

Howard Share
4349 La Vale Ct.
Clemmons, NC 27012-9009
phone: 910-766-6579
e-mail: denarnc@aol.com
Wants to buy state hunting and fishing licenses, especially from the Southern states and Hawaii; will also trade.

Dealers

Walt Feiger
Walt's Antiques
2513 Nelson Rd.
Traverse City, MI 49686-8557
phone: 616-223-7386 or 616-223-4123
Buys old Michigan hunting or fishing licenses.

Frank's Antiques
7242 Heil Ave.
Huntington Beach, CA 92647
phone: 714-847-0707
fax: 717-843-5645
e-mail: franks@franksupply.com
Internet: http://www.franksupply.com
Wants hunting, fishing, trapping license buttons, any state; also Ducks Unlimited buttons; gun company or fishing tackle company buttons, posters.

Experts

Jake Eckenrode
310 Wallace Rd.
Bellefonte, PA 16823
phone: 814-355-8769
Wants old U.S. Government license plates from any agency including old Civilian Conservation Corps (CCC) signs, and Pennsylvania licenses (vehicle, hunting, fishing, dog); author

of "Collector's Guide to Pennsylvania
Licenses."

Robert F. Miller
RR 1 Box 67
Ulysses, PA 16948-9717
phone: 814-435-2140
*Collects and appraises; author of "A
Guide to Collecting Pennsylvania
Hunting and Fishing Licenses", 1992
edition; $10 plus $2 P&H; also
collects PA Game Commission items.*

LIDS

(see also POT LIDS)

Suppliers

Charles Bodiker
Lid Lady, The
7790 East Ross Rd.
New Carlisle, OH 45344-9624
phone: 513-845-1266
*Carries replacement lids for ceramic,
glass, metal, and plastic vessels and
containers.*

LIGHT BULBS

(see also CHRISTMAS COL-
LECTIBLES; LAMPS & LIGHTING)

Collectors

Rob M. Simon
245 N. Stewart
Lombard, IL 60148
phone: 708-620-4770
*Wants to buy pre-1900 light bulbs and
anything pertaining to light bulbs.*

Experts

Carolyn T. Little
725 Esla Dr.
Chula Vista, CA 91910
e-mail: ladylight@prodigy.com
*Collects and specializes in light bulbs;
wants light bulbs with tips or unusual
light bulbs, Glow Lamps (neon) with
figurals inside, meters, sockets, bulbs
with figural or decorative filaments,
Edison, Westinghouse, Reddy
Kilowatt, etc.*

Museums/Libraries

Hugh F. Hicks, Cur.
Mount Vernon Museum of Incandescent
Lighting
717 Washington Place
Baltimore, MD 21201-5235
phone: 410-752-8586 or 410-837-1705
*Museum with display of electric light
bulbs depicting the entire industry
which spans 110 years.*

Carolyn T. Little
Light Bulb Museum
1655 Morena Blvd.
San Diego, CA 92110
phone: 619-276-1500
e-mail: ladylight@prodigy.com

Glow Lights

Clubs/Associations

Cindy Chipps
Glowlight Collectors Club
4027 Brooks Hill Rd.
Brooks, KY 40109-5002
phone: 502-955-9238
fax: 502-957-5027
e-mail: holauction@aol.com
Internet: http://members.aol.com/
holauction/index.html
*A club for beginners to advanced
collectors dedicated to collecting
Glow Lights and related items.*

Experts

Cindy Chipps
4027 Brooks Hill Rd.
Brooks, KY 40109-5002
phone: 502-955-9238
fax: 502-957-5027
e-mail: holauction@aol.com
Internet: http://members.aol.com/
holauction/index.html
*Buys/sells Glow Lights; made by
Aerolux, Birdseye, Luxram and others;
also wants advertising for same;
author of book on Glow Lights.*

LIGHTERS

(see also CIGARETTE COL-
LECTIBLES; SMOKING COL-
LECTIBLES)

Clubs/Associations

Pocket Lighter Preservation Guild &
Historical Society, Inc.
Newsletter: Flint & Flame
380 Brooks Dr., Ste. 209A
Hazelwood, MO 63042
phone: 314-731-2411
*An organization to help promote,
maintain and preserve interest in the
hobby of lighter collecting; newsletter
published bi-monthly.*

Judith Sanders, Ed.
International Lighter Collectors
Newsletter: On The Lighter Side
P.O. Box 536
Quitman, TX 75783-0536
phone: 903-763-2795
fax: 903-763-4953
*Members collect cigar & cigarette
lighters & research lighter history; bi-
monthly newsletter; send SASE for
information.*

Collectors

Barry D. Hoffman
393 Commonwealth Ave.
Boston, MA 02115
phone: 617-267-9000 or 617-326-3333
fax: 617-266-6666
*Wants to buy Ronson, Zippo and
Dunhill cigarette lighters; also offers
free appraisal service.*

Wes & Elaine Hart
963 Westhaven St.
Columbus, OH 43228
phone: 614-870-7141
*Wants to buy "trench" lighters and
other vintage or unique lighters; also
pre-1960 Zippo pocket lighters with
advertising, and Zippo table lighters.*

John B. Marrella
Investments in Time
P.O. Box 611
Birmingham, MI 48012-0611
phone: 810-644-3100
fax: 810-644-2792
*Buying Dunhill and Cartier lighters
with or without enamel or watches.*

John E. Shoffner
624 Merritt St.
Fife Lake, MI 49633-9142
phone: 616-879-3912

Karen L. Cairo
Cairo Lighters
P.O. Box 1054
Addison, IL 60101
phone: 708-543-9120
fax: 708-834-4051
*Wants to buy cigar and cigarette
lighters made in U.S. or in Europe:
pocket or table models, figural,
complicated mechanisms, case and
lighter sets, solid gold lighters with
watches, advertising displays, etc.*

Leonard Shafer
3202 West Magnolia Blvd.
Burbank, CA 91505-2905
phone: 818-846-5655
*Wants to buy Ronson, Zippo and
Dunhill cigarette lighters.*

Dealers

Peter Stanton
57 Earle St.
Central Falls, RI 02863
phone: 401-725-0055
Wants Ronson, Dunhill, Zippo.

Richard Weinstein
Authorized Repair Service
30 W. 57th St.
New York, NY 10019
phone: 212-541-5618
fax: 212-586-1296
*Wants to buy unusual pocket and table
model cigarette lighters: cigarette
case and light combinations, figurals,
watch lighters, etc.; Dunhill, Evans,
Ronson, Zippo, etc.*

Shaw
P.O. Box 5096
Southfield, MI 48086
*Wants to buy table model cigarette
lighters: Dunhill, Ronson, Evans,
Thorens, etc.*

Ron Bash
P.O. Box 888271
Grand Rapids, MI 49588-8271
*Buys, sells and trades cigarette
lighters: Zippo, Ronson, Dunhill,
Evans, Trench.*

Experts

Ira Pilossof
Vintage Lighters, Inc.
P.O. Box 1325
Fair Lawn, NJ 07410-8325
phone: 201-797-6595 or 888-454-4483
fax: 201-797-8642
*Avid collector, dealer and specialist in
cigarette lighters; wants to buy any
unusual lighter from the 1880s-1940s,
especially Dunhill lighters; also with
lighters watches and any related
memorabilia.*

Jack Seiderman
1631 N.W. 114 Ave.
Hollywood, FL 33026-2539
phone: 305-438-0928
fax: 305-438-0928
*Buys, sells, & collects collectible
lighters, accessories, advertising,
catalogs, books, brochures,
instruction sheets, etc.; author of
"Lighter Encyclopedia" (soon to be
published).*

Jeff Mogilner
Racine & Laramie, Ltd.
2737 San Diego Ave.
San Diego, CA 92110-2731
phone: 619-291-7833
fax: 619-297-6653
e-mail: alexracine@aol.com
*Wants to buy antique & unusual
lighters: Ronson (LVA, AMW, Art
Metal Works), Dunhill, Zippo; U.S.
Navy ships, air squadrons, US Marine
lighters; also repairs lighters*

Ronson

Collectors

Frank Briola
P.O. Box 44022
Pittsburgh, PA 15205-0222
phone: 412-937-8787 or 800-372-6509
Wants to buy Zippo lighters.

Experts

Urban K. Cummings
P.O. Box 1482
Palo Alto, CA 94302
*Author of "Ronson: The World's
Greatest Lighter" (Bird Dog Books,
1993).*

LIGHTING

(see LAMPS & LIGHTING)

LIGHTNING BALLS & RODS

(see LIGHTNING PROTECTION
COLLECTIBLES)

LIGHTNING PROTECTION COLLECTIBLES

Auction Services

Russell Barnes
P.O. Box 141994
Austin, TX 78714-1994
phone: 512-835-9510
fax: 512-835-1276
Conducts periodic auction sales of lightning rod collectibles; recently published "Lightning Rod Collectibles Price Guide," available from the author for $32.95 ppd.

Collectors

John Gephart
1 Firestone Ct.
Fairfield, OH 45014
phone: 513-858-3368
Lightning rods, balls, arrows, vanes, all related catalogs, paper and advertising.

Phil Steiner
15832 So. C.R. 900 W
Wanatah, IN 46390
phone: 219-733-2713
Wants to buy anything roof related including lightning rod balls, glass roof trim and pendants, and wind directionals.

Mike Sovereign
1S777 Westview
Lombard, IL 60148
Wants lightning rod items including balls, arrows, vanes, advertising, paper, etc.

Experts

Michael Bruner
2615 Echo Lane
Ortonville, MI 48462
phone: 810-627-6351
Wants lightning rod balls, catalogs, installation tags, rods, braces, etc.; co-author of "The Complete Book of Lightning Rod Balls."

Rod Krupka
2615 Echo Lane
Ortonville, MI 48462
phone: 810-627-6351
Buys, sells lightning rod balls, weathervanes, related catalogs and ads; co-author of "The Complete Book of Lightning Rod Balls."

Russell Barnes
P.O. Box 141994
Austin, TX 78714-1994
phone: 512-835-9510
fax: 512-835-1276
Author of the "Lightning Rod Collectibles Price Guide," available from the author for $32.95 ppd.

Periodicals

Rod Krupka
Newsletter: Crown Point, The
2615 Echo Lane
Ortonville, MI 48462
phone: 810-627-6351
Devoted to the history of lightning protection and the collecting of related items.

LIMITED EDITION COLLECTIBLES

(see COLLECTIBLES [MODERN])

LINCOLN

(see PERSONALITIES [HISTORICAL], Abraham Lincoln)

LINENS

(see TEXTILES, Lace & Linens)

LITERATURE

(see also AUTOGRAPHS; BOOKS; MANUSCRIPTS; PERSONALITIES [LITERARY])

Victorian

Experts

Mark Samuels Lasner
1870 Wyoming Ave. NW, Apt. 101
Washington, DC 20009-1883
phone: 202-745-1927
e-mail: biblio@aol.com
Wants to buy English literature and art form the period 1850-1900; especially association books, manuscripts, letters, and original drawings; co-author of two reference books on this material.

LITHOPHANES

(see also COLLECTIBLES [MODERN], Lithophanes)

Collectors

Donald Gorlick
P.O. Box 24541
Seattle, WA 98124-0541
phone: 206-824-0508
Wants "Berlin transparencies": looks like bisque but when turned to light it has a picture in it; in tea sets, lamp shades, beer steins.

Dealers

Lucille Malitz
Lucid Antiques
P.O. Box KH
Scarsdale, NY 10583
phone: 914-636-7825 or 914-636-5171

LIVING HISTORY

(see also CIVIL WAR HISTORY, Reenactors; CLOTHING & ACCESSORIES; MILITARY HISTORY)

Clubs/Associations

Darrell K. English
Living History Association
Newspaper: Living Historian
P.O. Box 1389
Wilmington, VT 05363
phone: 802-464-5569 or 413-339-3960
One of the largest group of reenactors in the country; members dress up according to the era, and act our battles, home life, balls, etc.; catalog of merchandise, lectures, school programs, teaches workshops, etc.; quarterly magazine.

Periodicals

Magazine: Artilleryman, The
RR 1 Box 36
Tunbridge, VT 05077-9707
phone: 802-889-3500
fax: 802-889-5627
Published quarterly, the only magazine exclusively for the 1750-1898 artillery enthusiast: artillery history, unit profiles, shell collecting, etc.

Magazine: Au Chant de L'Alouette
P.O. Box 3
Bristol, VT 05443-0003
Fills the void of French colonial information and news; covers history, sites and events for the 18th century French reenactor.

Magazine: Smoke & Fire News
P.O. Box 166
Grand Rapids, OH 43522-0166
phone: 419-832-0303
e-mail: dmeyers@smoke-fire.com
Internet: http://www.smoke-fire.com
Contains national listings of living history events; emphasis on the 18th century and Rendezvous period primarily in the Midwest; good coverage on War of 1812 era; numerous ads, classifieds, reenacting articles.

Magazine: Backwoodsman Magazine
P.O. Box 627
Westcliffe, CO 81252
Covers muzzleloading, primitive weapons, how-to projects, history and more.

Suppliers

Collector's Armoury
3000 South Eads St.
Arlington, VA 22202
phone: 800-544-3456 or 703-684-6111
fax: 703-683-5486
Offers museum quality reproductions: Civil War swords, knives, pistols and field gear; non-firing Western pistols, rifles and collectibles; medieval, Samurai and military swords; historic miniature Gatling guns and cannons.

Ron Eberhart
Western Trading Post
P.O. Box 9070
Denver, CO 80209-0070
phone: 303-777-7750
fax: 303-698-1387
A complete Indian craft supply store; has everything from beads and buckskins to tipis and tomahawks,

LOBBY CARDS

(see MOVIE MEMORABILIA; PAPER COLLECTIBLES)

LOCKS

(see also BANKS; DOORKNOBS; HARDWARE; KEYS; RESTRAINT DEVICES; SAFES)

Clubs/Associations

Charles Chandler
American Lock Collectors Association
Newsletter: American Lock Collectors Association Newsletter
36076 Grennada
Livonia, MI 48154-5278
phone: 313-522-0920
fax: 313-522-0920
Club newsletter reports on coming lock shows, also articles on locks, keys, handcuffs; prices, unusual items, historical information.

Bob Heilemann
West Coast Lock Collectors
Newsletter: West Coast Lock Collectors Newsletter
1427 Lincoln Blvd.
Santa Monica, CA 90401-2732
phone: 310-454-7295 or 310-230-3004
Call evenings; no collect calls, please.

Bob Heilemann
Key Collectors International
Newsletter: Padlock Quarterly
1427 Lincoln Blvd.
Santa Monica, CA 90401-2732
phone: 310-454-7295 or 310-230-3004

Collectors

Alene Saap
400 Calaf St., Ste. 80
San Juan, PR 00918-1314
phone: 787-758-5606 or 787-782-0020
Wants antique or unusual padlocks with key.

Richard C. Hubbard
162 Poplar Ave.
Hackensack, NJ 07601
phone: 201-342-1274
Interested in old US key or combination padlocks, embossed RR locks, figural shapes and unusual mechanisms or early patent dates.

Joseph Biunno
129 West 29th St.
New York, NY 10001
phone: 212-629-5630
fax: 212-268-4577
Wants furniture locks and keys; barrel, skeleton, door, drawer, old or

new; also wants escutcheons in all styles and sizes.

Al Cahill
13 Loudon Dr., Apt. 4
Fishkill, NY 12524-1816
Wants to buy old and unusual padlocks; also wants brass figural doorknobs.

Tom Gallian
P.O. Box 545
906 West Broad
Dunn, NC 28334
phone: 919-892-9104
Serious collector wants collectible padlocks.

Lane Clark
540 2nd Ln. NE
Fairfield, MT 59436-9326
Wants to buy unusual combination locks, especially letter combos; editor of "West Coast Lock Collectors" newsletter.

Franklin Arnall
Collector, The
P.O. Box 253
Claremont, CA 91711-0253
phone: 909-621-2461
Wants to buy antique padlocks: brass railroad and express, odd miniatures, any unusual cast iron of brass; any quantity.

Daniel C. Zolezzi
2211 Froude St.
San Diego, CA 92107
phone: 619-223-7440
Wants to buy old padlocks, keys and locks.

Dealers

Joseph & Pamela Tanner
Wheeler-Tanner ESCAPES
3024 E. 35th Ave.
Spokane, WA 99223
phone: 509-448-8457
fax: 509-448-8457
Wants padlocks of all sizes and shapes; figural, combination, round pancake types, railroad, Winchester, Wells Fargo, Express Co's., etc.

Experts

Bob Heilemann
1427 Lincoln Blvd.
Santa Monica, CA 90401-2732
phone: 310-454-7295 or 310-230-3004
Collector and historian of antique padlocks; also repairs and restores padlocks; call evenings; no collect calls, please.

Museums/Libraries

Thomas Hennessy, Cur.
Lock Museum of America
Newsletter: Lock Museum of America Newsletter
130 Main St.
P.O. Box 104
Terryville, CT 06786
phone: 203-589-6359
fax: 203-589-6359

Repair Services

Muff's Antiques
135 S. Glassell St.
Orange, CA 92866
phone: 714-997-0243
fax: 714-997-1601
Internet: http://www.tias.com/amdir/SpecTrunks.html
Specializes in the repairing and rekeying of antique locks.

LODGE BADGES

(see FRATERNAL ORGANIZATION ITEMS)

LOGGING RELATED ITEMS

(see also SCRIP)

Auction Services

Mike Levy
3895 Mack Rd.
Saginaw, MI 48601
Conducts mail bids of lumber or logging items.

Museums/Libraries

Ashland Logging Museum, Inc.
P.O. Box 348
Ashland, ME 04732
phone: 207-435-3281

Hoo-Hoo International Forestry Museum
P.O. Box 118
Gurdon, AR 71743
phone: 501-353-4554

LONE SCOUT MEMORABILIA

Collectors

Fran & Cal Holden
P.O. Box 264 - M264
Doylestown, OH 44230-0264
phone: 800-663-2793
Wants to buy Lone Scout (1915-1925) memorabilia (sometimes marked "LSA"): old pins, badges, medals, uniforms, literature, etc.

LOOMS

(see COVERLETS; SPINNING WHEELS)

LORGNETTES

(see EYE RELATED ITEMS, Eyeglasses)

LOTTERY TICKETS

Instant (Used)

Clubs/Associations

Bill Pasquino
Lottery Collectors Society
Newsletter: Lottery Collectors Newsletter
1824 Lyndon Ave.
Lancaster, PA 17602-4711
phone: 717-393-0843
Unites lottery collectors and provides services such as newsletters, ticket catalog, and trading roster.

Collectors

Bill Pasquino
1824 Lyndon Ave.
Lancaster, PA 17602-4711
phone: 717-393-0843
Wants losing instant lottery tickets; instant rub off lottery tickets from the 1970s and early 1980s.

Karen Lea Rose
4420 Wisconsin Ave.
Tampa, FL 33616-1031
phone: 813-839-6245
Wants to buy used instant (throwaway, scratched) lottery tickets and 19th century paper tickets.

Periodicals

Karen Lea Rose
Newsletter: Lotologist, The
4420 Wisconsin Ave.
Tampa, FL 33616-1031
phone: 813-839-6245

LUGGAGE

(see also ALLIGATOR BAGS; CLOTHING & ACCESSORIES, Vintage; LEATHER; TRUNKS)

Louis Vuitton

Collectors

Brian J. Vazquez
25 Comstock Hill Rd.
Norwalk, CT 06850
phone: 203-846-3767
Wants to buy Louis Vuitton trunks and luggage.

Duane S. Bietz
Les Meilleurs
6461 S.E. Thornburn
Portland, OR 97215-1378
phone: 503-238-6888
fax: 503-233-1602
e-mail: dbietz@aol.com
Collects and sells Louis Vuitton items: hard luggage and trucks, specialty pieces, cosmetic cases, shoe cases, collar cases, liquor trunks of cases.

LUGGAGE LABELS

(see also AIRLINE MEMORABILIA, Baggage I.D. Labels; PAPER COLLECTIBLES)

Collectors

Hal Turin
P.O. Box 663
San Dimas, CA 91733
Has one of the largest collections of airline labels.

LUMBERING

(see LOGGING RELATED ITEMS)

LUNCH BOXES

Clubs/Associations

Brian Mullins
Step Into The Ring
Newsletter: Ring Results
829 Jackson St. Ext.
Sandusky, OH 44870

Collectors

Peter Reginato
60 Green St.
New York, NY 10012
phone: 212-925-9787
Wants lunch boxes from 1950s through 1970s.

David Reed
841 West Main St.
Lorain, OH 44052-9763
phone: 216-428-6666
Wants Jetsons, Lost in Space, Westerns, TV Shows, Space: metal and vinyl.

Andy Galbus
Pak-Rat
900 8th St. NW
Kasson, MN 55944-1079
e-mail: lhpakrat@polaristel.net
Wants to buy lunch boxes.

Fred & Jan Carlson
P.O. Box 2
Hillsboro, OR 97123-0002
phone: 503-648-8477
Wants to buy lunch pails and thermoses.

Tom Hattrup
P.O. Box 246
Moxee, WA 98936
phone: 509-457-4027
Wants to buy lunch boxes; Toppie the Elephant, NHL, Our Friends, and others.

Dealers

Gary Sohmers
Wex Rex Collectibles
P.O. Box 702
Hudson, MA 01749
phone: 508-568-0856
fax: 508-562-1196

Mark Walters
Ricky Smith Toys
6159 N 9th Ave.
Pensacola, FL 32504-8204
phone: 904-857-1343
fax: 904-477-8508

Terri Ivers
Terri's Toys & Nostalgia
419 South First St.
Ponca City, OK 74601
phone: 405-762-8697

Experts

Bill Henry
Box-O-Rama
104 Davidson Lane
Oak Ridge, TN 37830-7705
phone: 615-483-0769
fax: 615-482-1581
   Buys, sells, and trades lunch boxes;
   promoter of Box-O-Rama, the only
   show devoted exclusively to Lunch
   Boxes; show is usually on the second
   weekend in August and includes a sale
   and auction.

Pat & Larry Aikins
Lunch Box Connection
Rt. 5, Box 5174
Athens, TX 75751
phone: 903-675-3765
   Author of "Pictorial Price Guide to
   Vinyl & Plastic Lunch Boxes" and
   "Pictorial Price Guide to Metal Lunch
   Boxes" (L-W Book Sales); wants to
   buy lunch boxes, thermos bottles:
   metals, soft vinyls, promotional, odd
   shaped plastics boxes.

Museums/Libraries

Allen Woodall
Lunch Box Museum
1236 Broadway
Columbus, GA 31901
phone: 800-445-4106

Periodicals

Magazine: Paileontologist's Retort
P.O. Box 3255
Burbank, CA 91508
phone: 818-846-1342
   A bi-monthly magazine for lunch box
   enthusiasts.

LURAY

   (see CERAMICS [AMERICAN
   DINNERWARE], Taylor, Smith &
   Taylor/LuRay)

LURES

   (see FISHING COLLECTIBLES)

Here are some tips when contacting someone listed in this book:

When requesting information about a particular item, include a description (material, dimensions, maker's mark, model number, etc.) and a photo, sketch, or photocopy of the item in question. ■

Always ask if there are charges for samples or for the services requested. ■

When writing, please be sure to include a Large (#10 business size) Self-Addressed and Stamped Envelope (LSASE) if requesting a reply or the return of photographs. ■

Never call collect unless otherwise directed. When calling, be considerate of time zone differences and always ask if the party you are calling has time to talk. When leaving an answering machine message, always instruct the party to call you back collect. ■

MACERATED CURRENCY ITEMS

Collectors

Bertram M. Cohen
Great American Co.
169 Marlborough St.
Boston, MA 02116-1830
phone: 617-247-4754
fax: 617-247-9093
e-mail: marblebert@aol.com
Wants items made from macerated U.S. money 1880-1940, original advertisements for macerated currency items, and any magazine articles regarding macerated money.

Donald Gorlick
P.O. Box 24541
Seattle, WA 98124-0541
phone: 206-824-0508
Wants macerated currency - items made up of ground-up money pulp; usually souvenir items, statues, plates, animals; often with a tag.

MACHINE AGE

(see MODERNISM)

MACHINERY & EQUIPMENT

(see also AIRPLANES; CONSTRUCTION EQUIPMENT; FARM MACHINERY; INDUSTRY RELATED ITEMS; LAWN MOWERS; TOOLS; WASHING MACHINES)

Appraisers

Association of Machinery & Equipment
Appraisers (AMEA)
1110 Spring St.
Silver Spring, MD 20910
phone: 301-587-9335
fax: 301-588-7830
e-mail: amea@his.com
Internet: http://www.amea.org
Association of machinery and equipment appraisers; publishes directory of appraisers who are used machinery dealers and/or auctioneers actively involved in the used machinery marketplace.

Christian Coleman, Ex. Dir.
International Society of Appraisers
Journal: ISA News Journal
16040 Christensen Rd., Ste. 320
Seattle, WA 98188
phone: 206-241-0359
fax: 206-241-0436
e-mail: ISA_HQ@compuserve.com
Internet: http://www.isa-appraisers.org
Largest association of professional personal property appraisers; members specialize in antiques &

residential contents, gems & jewelry, fine art, and machinery & equipment; call for appraiser nearest you.

Auction Services

Ken Lipton, ISA
Superior Auctions
P.O. Box 792427
San Antonio, TX 78279-2427
phone: 210-495-1319 or 210-697-0777
fax: 210-697-4217
Internet: http://www.saami.com
Specializes in the auction sale machinery and equipment, oil rigs, classic cars.

Museums/Libraries

Roberto M. Rodriguez
American Precision Museum Association, Inc.
Newsletter: Tools & Technology
P.O. Box 679
Windsor, VT 05089
phone: 802-674-5781
fax: 802-674-2524
e-mail: 103362.1676@compuserve.com
Internet: http://ourworld.compuserve.com/homepages/Precision_Museum
Housed in the original Robbins & Lawrence Armory and Machine Shop, the museum features the largest collection of historic precision machine tools in the nation.

Periodicals

National Auto Research Division
Magazine: Black Book Official Auction Report
P.O. Box 758
Gainesville, GA 30501
phone: 404-532-4111 or 800-554-1026
Monthly publication including values for all sorts of machinery.

Randall Publishing Co.
Magazine: Equipment World
3200 Rice Mine Road, N.E.
Tuscaloosa, AL 35406
phone: 205-349-2990
fax: 205-750-8070
e-mail: 73264.377@compuserve.com
Monthly magazine with articles about new equipment on the market

Randall Publishing Co.
Magazine: Top Bid
3200 Rice Mine Road, N.E.
Tuscaloosa, AL 35406
phone: 205-349-2990
fax: 205-750-8070
e-mail: 73264.377@compuserve.com
Monthly auction report listing machinery & equipment prices realized as well as an upcoming auction schedule.

Christina Gargano
Heartland Communications Group, Inc.
Magazine: Contractors Hot Line Equipment Guide
1003 Central Ave.
Fort Dodge, IA 50501
phone: 800-247-2000
fax: 515-574-2233
Internet: http://www.hlipublishing.com
Lists construction equipment manufacturer's addresses, basic equipment specs., original selling prices, current market values; published annually; information source for buyers, sellers, dealers, auctioneers, appraisers.

Christina Gargano
Heartland Communications Group, Inc.
Magazine: Hot Line's Parts Connection
1003 Central Ave.
Fort Dodge, IA 50501
phone: 800-247-2000
fax: 515-574-2233
Internet: http://www.hlipublishing.com
Directory for the largest selection and best prices of new, used, rebuilt parts and attachments for construction equipment.

Christina Gargano
Heartland Communications Group, Inc.
Magazine: Industrial Machine Trade
1003 Central Ave.
Fort Dodge, IA 50501
phone: 800-247-2000
fax: 515-574-2233
Internet: http://www.hlipublishing.com
The only weekly nationwide publication that links active buyers and sellers of new and used industrial machinery.

Christina Gargano
Heartland Communications Group, Inc.
Magazine: Contractors Hot Line
1003 Central Ave.
Fort Dodge, IA 50501
phone: 800-247-2000
fax: 515-574-2233
Internet: http://www.hlipublishing.com
The vital link between heavy equipment buyers and sellers for over 30 years.

Christina Gargano
Heartland Communications Group, Inc.
Magazine: Mine & Quarry Hot Line
1003 Central Ave.
Fort Dodge, IA 50501
phone: 800-247-2000
fax: 515-574-2233
Internet: http://www.hlipublishing.com
Offers the buyers and sellers of aggregate equipment a direct way to reach thousands of highly qualified customers in their specific industry.

Magazine: Machinery Trader Marketbook
P.O. Box 85670
Lincoln, NE 68501
phone: 800-247-4898 or 402-479-2144
fax: 402-479-2108
Internet: http://www.machinerytrader.com
A free monthly magazine: M&E ads,

auction results, retail prices, rental equipment prices, industry software contractors, Internet web sites; very useful in the appraisal of equipment.

Dataquest Incorporated
Magazine: Green Guide
1290 Ridder Park Dr.
San Jose, CA 95131-2398
phone: 800-227-8444 or 408-437-8001
fax: 408-434-6795
Professionally researched market values on construction equipment; average resale values to 20 years old; 3,000 equipment models, all types; original and current prices, serial numbers for years of manufacture, basic specs.

Dataquest Incorporated
Magazine: Serial Number Guide
1290 Ridder Park Dr.
San Jose, CA 95131-2398
phone: 800-227-8444 or 408-437-8001
fax: 408-434-6795
Lists year of manufacture by maker and model.

Catalogs

(see also CATALOGS, Trade)

Collectors

Marvin McKinley
1652 Rte. 9
Ashland, OH 44805
Wants old sales catalogs and manuals for machinery, steam engines, gas engines, windmills, farm machinery, buggies, sleighs, etc.

Dealers

Eldon Bryant
Broken Kettle Book Service
702 East Madison St.
Fairfield, IA 52556
Wants old sales catalogs and manuals for machinery, steam engines, gas engines, windmills, farm machinery, buggies, sleighs, etc.

Construction

Auction Services

Walter Vilsmeier
Vilsmeier Auction Company, Inc.
Rt. 309
Montgomeryville, PA 18936
phone: 215-699-5833
Specializes in the sale of used machinery and equipment; tractor crawlers, loader backhoes, air compressors, graders, etc.

Forke Brothers
P.O. Box 21960
Lincoln, NE 68542-1960
Specializes in the sale of used machinery and equipment; tractor crawlers, loader backhoes, air compressors, graders, etc.

Road Making

Clubs/Associations

D.J. Crampton, Mem.
Road Roller Association
6 Norwood Close
Mackworth
Derby DE3 4GA, U.K.
e-mail: dean@drayner.demon.co.uk
Internet: http://
www.drayner.demon.co.uk/rrapp.html
*Caters specifically to those interested
in the science of road making and
road repair and in the associated
equipment involved with these
operations.*

Collectors

C.P. Freeman
Oron, 11 Avenue Road
Chelmsford
Essex CM2 9TY, U.K.
*Interested in road making and road
repair equipment.*

Woodworking

Experts

Mr. Dana Martin Batory
402 E. Bucyrus St.
Crestline, OH 44827-1506
*Wants catalogs, photographs,
advertising, manuals, reminiscences,
etc. pertaining to woodworking
machinery and/or their manufacturers.*

MAGAZINES

(see also AQUARIUMS, Magazines;
BOOKS; COLLEGE COL-
LECTIBLES, Humor Magazines;
ILLUSTRATORS; MYSTERY/
DETECTIVE ITEMS; PAPER
COLLECTIBLES; SPORTING
COLLECTIBLES, Magazines;
TELEVISION SHOWS & MEMORA-
BILIA, TV Guide)

Collectors

Bob Havey
P.O. Box 183
North Sullivan, ME 04664-0183
phone: 207-422-3083
fax: 207-422-3430
*Wants many magazines from the
1800s to 1950: Movie Magazine,
Vogue, Pictorial Review, Esquire,
Good Housekeeping, McCall's, etc.*

Gary Olsen
505 S. Royal Ave.
Front Royal, VA 22630
phone: 703-635-7157 or 703-635-7158
fax: 703-635-1818
e-mail: hpfrigko@interloc.com
*Wants pre-1970 Life, Look, Colliers,
Post, etc. especially with WWI and/or
WWII stories and articles.*

Dealers

Ken Mitchell
710 Conacher Dr.
Willowdale
Ontario M2M 3N6 Canada
phone: 416-222-5808
*Appraises, collects, buys and sells
1890 to 1970s comic books,
newspapers, comic strips, "Big Little"
books, popular music/jazz books/
magazines/tapes; pulp magazines,
original comic art, radio and cereal
premiums.*

Ron Lee
101 Middlesex Tpke., Ste. 6-219
Burlington, MA 01803
phone: 508-663-2001
fax: 508-670-2412
*Wants to buy magazines and
paperbacks: Playboy, Penthouse,
Club, monster, horror, movie, TV,
detective, True Story, science fiction,
etc.*

Back Number Wilkins
P.O. Box 247
Danvers, MA 01923-0447
phone: 508-531-5058
*Buys and sell old magazines; over
1,200,000 back issue magazines
dating from 1850; thousands of titles;
mail order only.*

Charles Zayic
Magazine Man, The
P.O. Box 57
Ellsworth, ME 04605-0057
phone: 207-667-7342
*Wants old magazines from the teens
and 1920s; especially Ladie's Home
Journal, Pictorial Review, Woman's
Home Companion, McCall's,
Delineator, Modern Priscilla, and
Needlecraft.*

Stan Gold
As Time Goes By
7042 Dartbrook Dr.
Dallas, TX 75240
phone: 972-239-8621 or 214-352-2765
fax: 972-239-9632
e-mail: record@unicomp.net
Internet: http://www.astimegoesby.com/
atgb
*Wants to buy Life 1936-1972, Post,
Time, Playboy 1953-1965, Sports
Illustrated 1954-1970s, TV Guides
1947-1970s, vintage movie magazines,
aviation, men's adventure, automotive, sports, pin-up magazines 1920s
to 1960s, world's fair pre 1940.*

Experts

Denis C. Jackson
P.O. Box 1958
Sequim, WA 98382-1958
phone: 360-683-2559
fax: 360-683-2559
e-mail: ticn@olypen.com
Internet: http://www.olypen.com/ticn/
*Buys, sells, collects and specializes in
OLD magazines; author of "The
Masters Price & Identification Guide*

*to Old Magazines" 3nd edition 1995;
send LSASE for information.*

Periodicals

Doug Watson
Magazine: Paper Collectors' Marketplace
470 Main St.
P.O. Box 128
Scandinavia, WI 54977-0128
phone: 715-467-2379
fax: 715-467-2243
e-mail: pcmpaper@gglbbs.com
Internet: http://www.tias.com/pubs/pcm
*Monthly magazine for collectors of
autographs, paperbacks, postcards,
advertising, photographica,
magazines; all types of paper
ephemera.*

Denis C. Jackson, Ed.
Newsletter: Illustrator Collector's News,
The
P.O. Box 1958
Sequim, WA 98382-1958
phone: 360-683-2559
fax: 360-683-2559
e-mail: ticn@olypen.com
Internet: http://www.olypen.com/ticn/
*A monthly publication for collectors of
magazines and other paper
illustrations; free classifieds for
subscribers; send LSASE for
information; free magazines guide
offer.*

Automotive

Dealers

Dave Allen
Imperial Palace Auto Collection
3535 Las Vegas Blvd., So.
Las Vegas, NV 89109
phone: 702-731-3311
*Buys and sells out-of-print motorcycle
and automotive magazines: "Hot
Rod," "Motor Trend," "Speed Age,"
"Road Track," also all half-size
magazines.*

Black Mask

Collectors

Frank Vogel
60 Cindy Cove
Gulfport, MS 39503
*Wants Black Mask magazines 1933 to
1940; describe and price.*

Covers & Tear Sheets

Dealers

Mary Ann Hahn
Second Hand Mary Ann's
HCR 65 Box 26
Boothbay Harbor, ME 04538-9703
phone: 207-633-2426
fax: 207-633-2426
*Buys and sells magazine covers and
tear sheets of any advertisement or
illustration.*

Charles Zayic
Magazine Man, The
P.O. Box 57
Ellsworth, ME 04605-0057
phone: 207-667-7342
*Buys and sells vintage magazines ads,
11"x14", full page color originals,
mixed subjects, 1920s, 1930s, 1940s
and 1950s; send SASE for list.*

Experts

Susan Nicholson
Greater Chicago Productions
P.O. Box 595
Lisle, IL 60532
phone: 630-964-5240
*Buys and sells rare and unusual
postcards, Victorian valentines,
periodicals, advertising trade cards,
etc.*

Life

Dealers

Dwayne Spark
Nostalgia Plus
8441 Sublaines
Anjou
Quebec H1K 2C1 Canada
phone: 514-352-6892
fax: 514-352-1856
e-mail: dspark@montrealnet.ca
*Wants to buy Life magazines from
1970 and earlier in small or large
quantities.*

Charles Zayic
Magazine Man, The
P.O. Box 57
Ellsworth, ME 04605-0057
phone: 207-667-7342
*Buys and sells Life magazines 1936
through 1972; maintains active
inventory of over 5,000 copies for
sale, send SASE for list.*

Experts

Denis C. Jackson
P.O. Box 1958
Sequim, WA 98382-1958
phone: 360-683-2559
fax: 360-683-2559
e-mail: ticn@olypen.com
Internet: http://www.olypen.com/ticn/
*Author of "Life Magazines", major
illustrators from 1898 to 1930s.*

MAD

Auction Services

Michael Lerner
32862 Springside Lane
Solon, OH 44139-2067
phone: 216-349-3776
Buys and sells MAD memorabilia.

Collectors

Jim McClane
232 Butternut Dr.
Wayne, NJ 07470
phone: 201-616-1538
*Wants to buy MAD magazines and
related memorabilia; anything to do*

with MAD or with Alfred E. Newman: post cards, records, jewelry, games, dolls, etc.

Roland Coover
1537 E. Strasburg Rd.
West Chester, PA 19380-6380
phone: 610-692-3112
Wants anything related to MAD magazine or Alfred E. Neuman: jewelry, presidential campaign kits, Halloween costume, clothing, straight jacket, postcards, toys, etc.; no paperbacks or magazines, please.

Casey Nicholson
415 Vancleave Ave.
Ocean Springs, MS 39564
phone: 601-872-8864 or 601-872-4280

Gary Kritzberg
P.O. Box 47
Yorkville, IL 60560
phone: 708-553-7653
Wants MAD Magazine collectibles: magazines, comics, toys, shirts, records, hardback books, jewelry, pins, buttons, etc.

Experts

Michael Lerner
32862 Springside Lane
Solon, OH 44139-2067
phone: 216-349-3776
Buys and sells MAD memorabilia.

Men's

(see also PLAYBOY ITEMS)

Men's (Girlie)

Experts

Denis C. Jackson
P.O. Box 1958
Sequim, WA 98382-1958
phone: 360-683-2559
fax: 360-683-2559
e-mail: ticn@olypen.com
Internet: http://www.olypen.com/ticn/
Author of "The Price & Identification Guide to Men's (Girlie) Magazines", 4th edition; also issues 6 sale catalogs/year of magazines for sale; $3 per catalog; send LSASE for information.

Men's (Playboy)

Dealers

Passaic Books
594 Main St.
Passaic, NJ 07055
Sells a price guide devoted strictly to "Playboy" magazines; $10.95 postpaid.

Clint's Bookstore
3943 Main St.
Kansas City, MO 64111
phone: 816-561-2848
One of the largest national dealers in back issues of Playboy.

Experts

Douglas L. Tracy
Centerfold Shop, The
1220 23rd St., Ste. 2-M
San Diego, CA 92102-1960
phone: 619-235-6010
fax: 619-235-8005
Specializing in Playboy magazines from the 1950s, since 1968; mail order only; $8 for 20 page catalog; internationally recommended by Playboy Enter., Inc.

Denis C. Jackson
P.O. Box 1958
Sequim, WA 98382-1958
phone: 360-683-2559
fax: 360-683-2559
e-mail: ticn@olypen.com
Internet: http://www.olypen.com/ticn/
Author of "The Price & Identification Guide to Playboy Magazines", 1995 2nd Edition; send LSASE for information.

Monster

Collectors

Steve Dolnick
P.O. Box 69
East Meadow, NY 11554-0069
phone: 516-486-5085
fax: 516-458-5085
Buys, sells and trades monster magazines: wants Famous Monsters, Vampirella, Monsters Parade, World Famous Creatures, Little Shoppe of Horrors, and other monster magazines and fanzines.

Motorcycle

Dealers

Dave Allen
Imperial Palace Auto Collection
3535 Las Vegas Blvd., So.
Las Vegas, NV 89109
phone: 702-731-3311
Buys and sells out-of-print motorcycle and automotive magazines: "Hot Rod," "Motor Trend," "Speed Age," "Road Track," also all half-size magazines.

Movie

(see also MOVIE MEMORABILIA)

Dealers

Pauline Harry
11493 Spring Hill Blvd.
Brooksville, FL 34609

Mary Wagner
419 W. King St.
Aberdeen, WA 98520

Experts

Denis C. Jackson
P.O. Box 1958
Sequim, WA 98382-1958
phone: 360-683-2559
fax: 360-683-2559
e-mail: ticn@olypen.com
Internet: http://www.olypen.com/ticn/
Author of "The Old Movie, Television, Soap Opera, Radio Magazines Price & Identification Guide", 1st edition, 1994, 1914 through 1994.

Periodicals

Ray Stewart
Magazine: Magazines of the Movies
45 Killybawn Rd., Saintfield
Ballynahinch, Co Down
N. Ireland BT24 7JP U.K.
Published each May; informs collectors of all screen periodicals available today; aimed at film/TV magazine collectors; professionally printed publication with illustrations of magazine covers, reviews, etc.

Mystery

Collectors

Jack Deveny
6805 Cheyenne Trail
Edina, MN 55439-1158
phone: 612-941-2457
Wants Spider, Shadow, Doc Savage, Spicy, Detective, Mystery, Horror, Terror, etc.

Dealers

Peggy Ell
Peggy's Paper
218 Gratton
Burlington, IA 52601
phone: 319-752-7670
Buys and sells mystery magazines such as Alfred Hitchcock and Ellery Queen mystery magazines; also wants hardback mystery books.

Experts

Alan Betrock
Shake Books
449 12 St.
Brooklyn, NY 11215-5167
phone: 718-499-6941
Author of "Unseen America - The Greatest Cult Exploitation Magazines 1950-1966," "Illustrated Price Guide to Cult Magazines, 1945-1969," and "Hitsville: The Greatest Rock 'n Roll Magazines, 1954-1968."

National Geographic

Collectors

William Barr
6341 Werk Rd.
Cincinnati, OH 45248-2924
phone: 513-451-6174
Buys and sells pre-1916 National Geographic Magazines, maps, publications.

Dealers

B. Spiker
245 New Rd.
Southampton, PA 18966
phone: 215-364-8471
Buys and sells; free search.

Jeanne K. Bauxbaum
Baxbaum Geographics
P.O. Box 3746
Wilmington, DE 19807
phone: 302-994-2663
Buys and sells National Geographic from 1888-1920 only.

Don Smith
Don Smith's National Geographic Magazines
3930 Rankin St.
Louisville, KY 40214-1748
phone: 502-366-7504
Wants magazines from 1888; buying and selling; author of "National Geographic Magazines (1888-1996) For Collectors" price guide booklet.

Office Related

Collectors

Darryl Rehr
2591 Military Ave.
Los Angeles, CA 90064-1933
phone: 310-477-5229
fax: 310-268-8420
e-mail: dcrehr@earthlink.net
Internet: http://www.earthlink.net/~dcrehr/
Wants pre-1920 magazines & articles relating to old office equipment: "System", "Business Man's Monthly", "Phonographic World", etc.

Puck & Judge

Collectors

Bob Putnam
9140 Conversation Way
Springfield, VA 22153
phone: 703-644-9711
Wants to buy "Puck" and "Judge" periodicals, especially political cartoons pages, dating from 1876'to 1910; whole issues preferred; also wants to buy cartoons by Thomas Nast (1840-1902.)

Dealers

Mary Ann Hahn
Second Hand Mary Ann's
HCR 65 Box 26
Boothbay Harbor, ME 04538-9703
phone: 207-633-2426
fax: 207-633-2426
Buys "Puck & Judge" periodicals as well as Brown Book, The Truth, Verdict & Vim prior to 1910.

Pulp

(see also BOOKS, Paperback; SCIENCE FICTION/FANTAST/HORROR)

Clubs/Associations

Ron Hanna
Secret Society of the Sanctum, The
Newsletter: Secret Sanctum
10811 Columbus Ave., #13
Mission Hills, CA 91345
e-mail: RHanna@gnn.com
*Focuses on pulp characters such as
The Shadow, Doc Savage, The SPider,
Tarzan, The Phantom, and more.*

Collectors

Jack Deveny
6805 Cheyenne Trail
Edina, MN 55439-1158
phone: 612-941-2457
*Wants Spider, Shadow, Doc Savage,
Spicy, Detective, Mystery, Horror,
Terror, etc.*

Doug Ellis
6942 N. Oleander
Chicago, IL 60631-1132
phone: 773-763-8763 or 773-269-8069
e-mail: pulpvlt@ix.netcom.com
*Wants to buy all pulp magazines,
especially adventure genre pulps,
pulps published by Clayton, and
"spicy" pulps; also issues sale
catalogs from time to time.*

Dealers

Jerry Peters
Chestnut Hollow, Ltd.
6060 Bordman Rd.
P.O. Box 6
Almont, MI 48003
phone: 810-798-3158
*Wants pulp magazines from the 1900s
to 1950s: The Shadow, Doc Savage,
weird tales, amazing stories,
astounding, astonishing, planet
stories, The Spider, spicy detective,
thrilling wonder stories, detective
stories, G-man, adventure.*

Experts

Ray Walsh
Curious Book Shop
307 E. Grand River
East Lansing, MI 48823-4324
phone: 517-332-0112
*Dealer/expert; owner of three book
shops in Michigan; hosts radio call-in
show about books and paper
collectibles; writes columns; send a
SASE for reply when writing.*

Museums/Libraries

San Francisco Academy of Comic Art
2850 Ulloa
San Francisco, CA 94116-2223
phone: 415-681-1737
fax: 415-681-1737
*Millions of newspaper strips, bound
files, major dailies from 1890-1960,
pulps, all science fiction, crime fiction,
film history, children's books, comic
books; excellent copies made of all
graphic material; dup material for
trade.*

Periodicals

Newsletter: Pulp & Paperback Market
Newsletter
5813 York Ave.
Edina, MN 55410
phone: 612-922-9144

Doug Ellis
Tattered Pages Press
Magazine: Pulp Vault
6942 N. Oleander
Chicago, IL 60631-1132
phone: 773-763-8763 or 773-269-8069
e-mail: pulpvlt@ix.netcom.com
*Irregularly published magazine
devoted to pulps; approx. 128 pgs, 8
1/2x11, perfect-binding; reprints
fiction stories from pulps; articles
about the pulps; recollections of the
pulp era; priced per issue; no
subscriptions.*

Tom Johnson
Magazine: Echoes
504 E. Morris St.
Seymour, TX 76380
*Focuses on dime novels and pulp
magazines; sample copy of "Echoes"
$3.60.*

Pulp (Doc Savage)

Periodicals

Howard Wright
Green Eagle Publications
Newsletter: Bronze Gazette, The
2900 Standiford Ave., #136
Modesto, CA 95350-0167

Radio & Wireless

(see also TELEGRAPH ITEMS)

Collectors

Paul Thompson
315 Larkspur Dr.
Santa Maria, CA 93455-1625
phone: 805-934-2778
*Wants radio and wireless magazines
before 1940.*

Scandal/Cult/R 'N' R

Experts

Alan Betrock
Shake Books
449 12 St.
Brooklyn, NY 11215-5167
phone: 718-499-6941
*Author of "Unseen America - The
Greatest Cult Exploitation Magazines
1950-1966," "Illustrated Price Guide
to Cult Magazines, 1945-1969," and
"Hitsville: The Greatest Rock 'n Roll
Magazines, 1954-1968."*

Toy

Collectors

Christmas Catalog Collector, The
175 East Delaware, #7403
Chicago, IL 60611-1731
phone: 800-879-6948 or 312-337-3123
fax: 312-266-7982
*Collector eager to buy pre-1970 back
copies of toy industry magazines such
as "Playthings" and "Toys and
Novelties;" also wants toy and
Christmas catalogs.*

Trade

Collectors

Richard M. Bueschel
414 N. Prospect Manor Ave.
Mount Prospect, IL 60056-2046
phone: 847-253-0791
fax: 847-253-7919
e-mail: BuschlHist@aol.com
*Wants trade magazines, e.g. saloons
(Bar & Buffet, 1899-1910), drug
stores (American Druggist) and coin
machines (Coin Machine Journal,
Automatic Age, others.)*

TV Guide

Dealers

Philip M. Levine & Sons
P.O. Box 246
Three Bridges, NJ 08887
phone: 908-788-0532
fax: 908-788-1028
*Buys and sells comic books, TV
Guides, magazines, etc.*

MAGIC LANTERNS & SLIDES

(see also CAMERAS & CAMERA
EQUIPMENT; OPTICAL ITEMS;
TOYS, Optical)

Clubs/Associations

Jack Judson, Jr.
Magic Lantern Society of the U. S. &
Canada
Magazine: Magic Lantern Gazette
1419 Austin Hwy.
San Antonio, TX 78209
phone: 210-805-0011
fax: 210-822-1226

Collectors

Daniel Gerber
6115 Shady Oak Lane
Bethesda, MD 20817
phone: 301-229-2702
*Wants to buy magic lanterns and
optical toys.*

Sherry L. Werdon
400 N. Washington
Lowell, MI 49331-1465
phone: 616-897-9580
*Wants unusual magic lanterns or
color magic lantern slides; also round
extra large slides and wooden
viewers, pantoscope, etc.*

Jack Judson, Jr.
1419 Austin Hwy.
San Antonio, TX 78209
phone: 210-805-0011
fax: 210-822-1226
*Wants to buy magic lanterns and
slides.*

Dealers

Bryan W. Ginns
2109 Cty. Rte. 21
Valatie, NY 12184-6001
phone: 518-392-5805
fax: 518-392-7925
e-mail: the3dman@aol.com
*Wants large collections of stereo
views, old cameras, daguerreotypes,
magic lanterns, optical toys; anything
relating to photographics.*

Ronald Krueger
R.W. Krueger's
P.O. Box 741
Oak Park, IL 60303-0741
phone: 708-788-8235
*Collects glass slides used to advertise
movies (coming attraction slides);
also wants song slides.*

Experts

Jack Judson, Jr.
1419 Austin Hwy.
San Antonio, TX 78209
phone: 210-805-0011
fax: 210-822-1226
*Has extensive knowledge, collection/
museum, and research facilities
focusing on the magic lantern and
other optical devices.*

Museums/Libraries

Jack Judson, Jr.
Magic Lantern Castle Museum
1419 Austin Hwy.
San Antonio, TX 78209
phone: 210-805-0011
fax: 210-822-1226
*Open by appointment; one man's
collection of optical projection devices
and items relating to the science of
optics and optical projection.*

MAGICIANS PARAPHERNALIA

(see also MORBID & ODD ITEMS;
PERFORMING ARTS; POSTERS;
RESTRAINT DEVICES; WITCHES)

Clubs/Associations

Edward Hill
New England Magic Collectors
Association
3 Chandler St.
North Providence, RI 02911-2210
phone: 401-231-1215
*Association of serious collectors of
magic who reside in the New England
area; three meetings/year; all
collectors welcome as guests.*

David Meyer
Magic Collector's Association
Magazine: Magicol
P.O. Box 511
Glenwood, IL 60425-0511
For collectors of all kinds of magic related memorabilia; magazine published quarterly.

Collectors

Joseph Gargano
P.O. Box 170
Lake Hiawatha, NJ 07034
phone: 201-538-2501
Wants to buy original, old pre-1940 posters and lithographs of magicians; please state condition and price.

Ken Trombly
1825 K St. NW, #901
Washington, DC 20006
phone: 800-673-8158 or 202-887-5000
fax: 202-457-0343
e-mail: trombly@erols.com
Wants magic posters, Mysto Magic sets, magic books and Houdini items; also wants broadsides and old photos of magicians; will pay top dollar or will trade from his collection.

Dan Stapleton
8237 Banyan Blvd.
Orlando, FL 32819
phone: 407-345-1132
Collector only, not a dealer; wants to buy old magic kits (pre-1965), magic lithographs and posters (pre-1950).

Ron Allesi
P.O. Box 54922
Cincinnati, OH 45254-0922
Wants to buy magic sets, apparatus, books and toys.

LaVerne Anderson
944 35th St.
Des Moines, IA 50312-3102
phone: 515-274-4443 or 515-274-9196
fax: 515-274-9196
Wants old magic books and magic tricks.

Andy Gross
P.O. Box 6134
Beverly Hills, CA 90212-1134
phone: 310-820-3308 or 310-285-8815
fax: 310-768-1097
e-mail: apedoll69@aol.com
Wants old magic tricks, kits, books, posters.

Michael Jaffe
P.O. Box 61484
Vancouver, WA 98666-1484
phone: 360-695-6161 or 800-782-6770
fax: 360-695-1616
e-mail: mjaffe@gstis.net
Wants to buy magic, magicians, escape artists, ventriloquists, jugglers; also related photo cards, advertising cards.

Dealers

Frank Herman
710 Anchor Way
Carlsbad, CA 92008
phone: 619-434-2254
Buys and sells magician related items: autographs, posters, programs, Mysto Magic sets, toys; also mentalists, escape artists, ventriloquists, fire eaters, spiritualists; plus all related books and apparatus; all offering lists answered.

Experts

Mario Carrandi
Mario Carrandi Inc. Antiquarian Magic
& Collectibles
122 Monroe Ave.
Belle Mead, NJ 08502-4608
phone: 908-874-0630
fax: 908-874-4892
Buys, sells, appraises and specialize in all categories of magic; one of the oldest and largest dealer in the field.

Herb Jacobs
P.O. Box 1286
Mattituck, NY 11952
phone: 516-298-4135
fax: 516-298-4181
Buys, sells, appraises and specializes in magic and conjuring memorabilia.

John A. Greget
John A. Greget - Magic Lists
2631 E Claire Dr.
Phoenix, AZ 85032-4932
Buys and appraises magic books, posters, magazines, ephemera, equipment, etc.; singles or collection.

Museums/Libraries

Houdini Magical Hall of Fame
Niagara Falls
Ontario L2E 6V6 Canada

Elaine Lund
American Museum of Magic
107 E. Michigan
P.O. Box 5
Marshall, MI 49068
phone: 616-781-7666 or 616-781-7674
Museum with holdings of approximately 250,000 items, all on magic.

Periodicals

Stan Allen
Magazine: Magic, An Independent
Magazine for Magicians
7380 South Eastern #124-179
Las Vegas, NV 89123
phone: 702-798-0099

Phil Temple
Newsletter: Magic Set Collector's
Newsletter
P.O. Box 561
Novato, CA 94949
phone: 415-897-5130
fax: 415-897-5130
A bi-monthly newsletter.

Houdini

Collectors

Sidney Radner
1050 Northampton St.
Holyoke, MA 01040-1321
phone: 413-532-6009 or 413-533-3000
fax: 413-536-9634
Wants items related to Houdini: posters, playbills, books, ephemera, etc.; honorary curator of the Houdini Historical Center.

Kevin Connolly
257 E Woodland Rd.
New Milford, NJ 07646-2321
Wants anything Houdini or about magic: books, posters, autographs, tricks, tokens, sets, apparatus, etc.

Ken Trombly
1825 K St. NW, #901
Washington, DC 20006
phone: 800-673-8158 or 202-887-5000
fax: 202-457-0343
e-mail: trombly@erols.com
Wants magic posters, Mysto Magic sets, magic books and Houdini items; also wants broadsides and old photos of magicians; will pay top dollar or will trade from his collection.

Arthur Moses
4205 Wildring Dr. E
Fort Worth, TX 76109-4717
Wants to buy Houdini and related items: books, articles, posters, photos, autographs, personal effects, programs, pamphlets, playbills, scrapbooks, letters, lobby cards, films, etc.

Dealers

Michael Griffin
International Handcuff Exchange
356 W. Powell Rd.
Powell, OH 43065-9650
phone: 614-846-0585
Buys/sells Houdini memorabilia and old collectible magic; also handcuffs, leg irons, etc.; list of items for sale available.

Joseph & Pamela Tanner
Wheeler-Tanner ESCAPES
3024 E. 35th Ave.
Spokane, WA 99223
phone: 509-448-8457
fax: 509-448-8457
Wants Houdini & other escape artist items: autographs, posters, letters, postcards, books, photos, playbills, equipment, etc.

Museums/Libraries

Curator
Houdini Historical Center
330 East College Ave.
Appleton, WI 54911-5715
phone: 414-733-8445

MAGNETS

Refrigerator Door

Collectors

Karen Lea Rose
4420 Wisconsin Ave.
Tampa, FL 33616-1031
phone: 813-839-6245
Collector wants to trade for refrigerator door-type magnets that ADVERTISE a company, business or product.

MAILBOXES

Collectors

Charles W. Wardell
P.O. Box 195
Trinity, NC 27370-0195
phone: 910-434-1145
Wants 1870-1940 cast iron mailboxes; these boxes were fancy in design and served on homes and shops; usually with many coats of paint.

MANUALS & INSTRUCTION BOOKLETS

(see PAPER COLLECTIBLES)

MANUSCRIPTS

(see also AUTOGRAPHS; BOOKS; HISTORICAL AMERICANA; PAPER COLLECTIBLES)

Clubs/Associations

David R. Smith, Ex. Dir.
Manuscript Society, The
Magazine: Manuscripts
350 N. Niagara St.
Burbank, CA 91505-3648
Internet: http://www.manuscripts.org
An organization of collectors, dealers, librarians, archivists, scholars and others interested in autographs and manuscripts.

Dealers

George & Julie Perron
Old Paperphiles, The
P.O. Box 135
Tiverton, RI 02878-0135
phone: 401-624-9420
fax: 401-624-4204
Buys and sells paper collectibles: books, autographs, sheet music, postcards, photos, stereoviews, documents, old letters; issues periodic catalog of items for sale.

University Archives
600 Summer St.
Stamford, CT 06901-1403
phone: 800-237-5692 or 203-975-9291
fax: 203-348-3560
Buying and selling fine historical autographs, manuscripts, documents, autographed books and autographed photographs of notable people including U.S. presidents, Revolutionary and Civil War, literary, aviation, science, art, and music.

Gary J. Zimet
Moments in Time, Inc.
5 Cardinal Dr.
Washingtonville, NY 10992
phone: 914-497-7373
fax: 914-496-6367
Wants to buy rare letters and manuscripts: Washington, Adams, Jefferson, Lincoln, M.L. King, Malcolm X, Churchill, Disney, Ruth, Lee, Grant, Custer, etc.

Carmen D. Valentino
Rare Books & Manuscripts
2956 Richmond St., Drawer 19
Philadelphia, PA 19134-5720
phone: 215-739-6056
Antiquarian bookseller specializing in rare books, manuscripts, documents, early newspapers, diaries, account books, ledgers, ephemera, broadsides; pre-WWI.

Pennsylvania

Experts

Ron Lieberman
Family Album, The
RD 1 Box 42
Glen Rock, PA 17327-9707
phone: 717-235-2134
fax: 717-235-8765
e-mail: ronbiblio@delphi.com
Buys, sells, appraises all Pennsylvania related books, manuscripts, artwork, etc.

MAPS & CHARTS

(see also ATLASES; GAS STATION COLLECTIBLES, Road Maps; GLOBES; NAUTICAL ANTIQUES, Maps & Charts; PAPER COLLECTIBLES; PRINTS; STAMP COLLECTING, Maps & Charts; TRAILERS & RV'S)

Auction Services

Paulus Swain
Interactive Auction of Rare Maps & Atlases
Hofstraat 19
5664 HS Geldrop
Netherlands
e-mail: paulus@swaen.com
Internet: http://www.swaen.com
Conducts interactive map auctions on the Internet.

James E. Hess
P.O. Box 412
Lititz, PA 17543-0412
phone: 717-626-5002
fax: 717-626-8858
e-mail: heritage@carto.com
Internet: http://www.carto.com

Book Sellers

Kimmel Publications
P.O. Box 12
Amherst, MA 01004-0012
phone: 413-256-8900
fax: 413-256-6291
e-mail: navigateur@aol.com
Publisher of the "Antique Map Price

Record & Handbook"; news, comments, recommended references, book reviews, collectors' considerations, glossary of terms, directory of dealers, price listing, title and geographical index, etc.

Clubs/Associations

Jenny Harvey
International Map Collectors Society
27 Lanford Rd.
Putney
London SW15 1AQ, U.K.
e-mail: jeh@harvey27.demon.co.uk

Siegfried Feller
Cartomania
8 Amherst Rd.
Pelham, MA 01002-9746
phone: 413-253-3115
Purpose is to provide and exchange information and news by/from/for collectors of maps in various formats.

Chicago Map Society, The
Newsletter: Mapline
60 West Walton St.
Chicago, IL 60610
phone: 312-943-9090
Oldest map society in North America.

Dealers

Yasha Beresiner
InterCol Gallery
43 Templars Crescent
London N3 3QR, U.K.
phone: 018—34-2207
fax: 018—34-9539
e-mail: 100447.3341@compuserve.com
Buys and sells world banknotes, playing cards and maps.

Siegfried Feller
Cartomania
8 Amherst Rd.
Pelham, MA 01002-9746
phone: 413-253-3115
Buys and sells maps and map related memorabilia.

Amherst Antiquarian Maps
P.O. Box 12
Amherst, MA 01004-0012
phone: 413-256-8900
fax: 413-256-6291
e-mail: navigateur@aol.com
General stock of antique maps and charts.

Reg Lombard
Lombard Antiquarian Maps & Prints
P.O. Box 281
Cape Elizabeth, ME 04107
phone: 207-799-1889
fax: 207-799-9593
e-mail: lamr@cybertours.com
Internet: http://www.cybertours.com/
~lamp
Specializes in fine maps, charts, rare botanical, natural history and architectural prints; also maps, prints, and books relating to Napoleon I.

G.B. Manasek, Inc.
P.O. Box 1204
Norwich, VT 05055
phone: 802-649-1722
fax: 802-649-2256
e-mail: manasekinc@aol.com
Buys maps and atlases from almost any region; also star maps, city plans and sea charts; folding (pocket), wall and roller maps of states, countries, continents and the world; offers appraisals on a fee-for-services basis.

Charles Neuschafer
New World Maps, Inc.
Apple Hill Road
Bennington, VT 05201-9544
phone: 802-442-2846
e-mail: CharlieNeu@aol.com
Internet: http://www.pages.prodigy.com/
maproom
Buys and sells antique and collectible maps and charts; author of a column on map collecting in "Paper Collectors' Marketplace."

Latitudes
P.O. Box 66
Essex, CT 06426-0066
phone: 203-767-3001 or 203-526-2100
Dealer/collector buys and sells unusual format maps (folding, strip, ribbon of rivers, canals), wall maps (CT & MA counties & entire US), harbor charts (USCS, Blunt, Eldridge, New England), coast pilot books, Nantucket, Block Island.

Lynn Vigeant
Maps of Antiquity
P.O. Box 160 Midland Ave.
Montclair, NJ 07042
phone: 973-744-4364
Buys and sells historical decorative antique maps primarily from the 19th century; catalogs issued.

Lynn Vigeant
Maps of Antiquity
160 Midland Ave.
Montclair, NJ 07042
phone: 201-744-4364
Buys and sells historical, decorative maps, 19th century and earlier.

George D. Glazer
28 East 72nd St. at Madison Ave.
New York, NY 10021
phone: 212-535-5706
fax: 212-988-3992
e-mail: worldglobe@aol.com
Buys and sells terrestrial and celestial globes, orreries, armillary spheres, maps, etc.

High Ridge Books, Inc.
P.O. Box 286
Rye, NY 10580
phone: 914-967-3332
fax: 914-967-6056
Wants to buy 19th century American cartography; atlases, wall maps, sea charts, pocket maps.

James E. Hess
P.O. Box 412
Lititz, PA 17543-0412
phone: 717-626-5002
fax: 717-626-8858
e-mail: heritage@carto.com
Internet: http://www.carto.com
One of the largest map and atlas dealers in the world; buys, sells, collects, appraises.

Heritage Antique Maps
551 Christopher Ln.
Doylestown, PA 18901-3127
phone: 215-340-9662
fax: 215-340-9662
Interested in purchasing maps.

Christopher W. Lane
Philadelphia Print Shop, Ltd., The
8441 Germantown Ave.
Philadelphia, PA 19118
phone: 215-242-4750
fax: 215-242-6977
e-mail: PhilaPrint@PhilaPrintShop.com
Buys, sells, appraises prints, maps, related rare books and atlases; also bookstore of reference books related to antique prints and maps; also paper conservation and restoration, museum quality framing.

Judith Blakely
Old Print Gallery, The
1220 31st St. NW
Washington, DC 20007-3422
phone: 202-965-1818
fax: 202-965-1869
Wants antique maps: American or foreign, 16th to 19th centuries.

Luke & Patricia Vavra
Cartographic Arts
P.O. Box 2202
Petersburg, VA 23804-1502
phone: 804-861-6770
fax: 804-861-3021
e-mail: carto@dogstar.com
Internet: http://www.dogstar.com/carto
Buys and sells only antique maps and charts; no reproductions.

John Forster
Barometer Fair
P.O. Box 25502
Sarasota, FL 34277
phone: 941-923-6136
fax: 941-923-6136
e-mail: barometer@glimmer.com
Buys, sells, restores all antique barometers; also deals in antique maps, globes, compasses, telescopes and other scientific instruments.

Murray Hudson
Murray Hudson - Antiquarian Books & Maps
109 S. Church St.
P.O. Box 163
Halls, TN 38040-0163
phone: 901-836-9057 or 800-748-9946
fax: 901-836-9057
e-mail: mapman@usit.net
Internet: http://css.ecis.net/hudson
Buys/sells pre-1900 antique maps (especially pocket, wall, Civil War and railroad maps) & books with maps

(e.g. atlases, travel guides, geographies, land surveys, etc.); esp. of S.E. & S.W. US; also wants pre-1950 world globes.

Mary & George Ritzlin
George Ritzlin Maps & Books
469 Roger Williams Ave.
Highland Park, IL 60035-4704
phone: 847-433-2627
fax: 847-433-6389
Buys and sells antique maps and atlases 1500-1900; cartographic references; books on early travel and exploration; pre-WWII Baedekers; illuminated medieval manuscripts; natural history prints.

Experts

David C. Jolly
1310 N Mitchell Ave.
Arlington Heights, IL 60004-4650
Author of "Antique Maps, Sea Charts, City Views, Celestial Charts & Battle Plans Price Record & Handbook", out-of-print.

Museums/Libraries

James E. Hess
Heritage Map Museum
P.O. Box 412
Lititz, PA 17543-0412
phone: 717-626-5002
fax: 717-626-8858
e-mail: heritage@carto.com
Internet: http://www.carto.com
The only museum in the world dedicated to the 15th through 19th century original maps.

Periodicals

Frank Watkins Design
Magazine: Map Collector, The
Clement House, 23 High Street
Tring
Hertfordshire HP23 5AH, U.K.
phone: (0)1442 827 997
fax: (0)1442 891 850
e-mail: fwdesign@kbnet.co.uk
Internet: http://www.kbnet.co.uk/fwdesign/fw.pages/fw0022.html
A quarterly publication devoted to antique maps.

Patrick M. O'Brien
Compass, The
Newsletter: Antique Map & Print Quarterly
P.O. Box 254
West Simsbury, CT 06092
phone: 860-651-5962
This free newsletter is designed to stimulate interest in the collection of antique maps and prints; articles, shows & exhibition schedules, map and chart values, free ads as space permits; write for information about a free subscription.

Jennifer Lindsey, Ed.
Magazine: Mercator's World
845 Williamette St.
Eugene, OR 97401-2918
phone: 541-345-3800 or 800-840-3810
fax: 541-302-9872
e-mail: jlindsey@asterpub.com
Internet: http://www.mercatormag.com
A magazine of maps, atlases, globes and charts; articles cover maps and charts from antiquity to present including profiles of cartographers and explorers who made and followed the maps.

Folding

Collectors

Paul Mahoney
1746 Blake St.
Denver, CO 80202
phone: 303-296-7725
Wants atlases and folding pocket maps.

Map Related Memorabilia

Clubs/Associations

Siegfried Feller
Association of Map Memorabilia Collectors
Newsletter: Cartomania
8 Amherst Rd.
Pelham, MA 01002-9746
phone: 413-253-3115
For collectors & lovers of maps: on postcards, stamps/envelopes, postmarks/cancels, labels, fabrics, trays/plates, etc.

MARBLES

Auction Services

Robert S. Block
Block's Box
P.O. Box 51
Trumbull, CT 06611-0051
phone: 203-261-0057 or 203-926-8448
e-mail: BlocksChip@aol.com
Internet: http://pages.prodigy.com/marbles/
Conducts mail-bid and Internet auctions of marbles received from collectors, dealers, estates, museums and others.

Lloyd & Chris Huffer
Gold Medal Videos
Star Route
Damascus, PA 18415
phone: 717-224-4012
Conducts twice-yearly auctions by video.

Danny & Gretchen Turner
Running Rabbit Video Auctions
P.O. Box 701
Waverly, TN 37185-0701
phone: 615-296-3600
fax: 615-296-1732
e-mail: marbles@worldnet.att.net
Internet: http://www.runningrabbit.com
Conducts marble mail auctions using VHS video tape/catalog or full color catalog. Quality marbles are shown

on well-detailed 2 hr. tape. Excellent educational tool!

Clubs/Associations

Canadian Marble Collectors Association
10B Murdock St.
Georgetown
Ontario L7G 3L6 Canada

Beverly Brule
Marble Collectors Unlimited
Newsletter: Marble Mart/Newsletter
P.O. Box 206
Northborough, MA 01532-0206
phone: 508-393-2923
The newsletter is published for and by members of MCU; contains items of interest such as meets, auctions, member buy/sell/trade ads, etc.

Stanley Block
Marble Collectors Society of America
Newsletter: Marble Mania
P.O. Box 222
Trumbull, CT 06611-0222
phone: 203-261-3223
Established to gather and disseminate information and to perform services to further the hobby of marbles and marble collecting.

Jim Ridpath
National Marble Club of America
Newsletter: National Marble Club of America Newsletter
440 Eaton Rd.
Drexel Hill, PA 19026-1205
phone: 610-622-4444
To keep marble collectors informed, to encourage children to once again play the game, and to advise members on all aspects of marbles.

Roger Dowdy
Blue Ridge Marble Club
Newsletter: Marble Circle News
3410 Plymouth Pl.
Lynchburg, VA 24503-1301
phone: 804-384-7359
For collectors, dealers, and shooters.

Cape Fear Marble Club
121-A Columbus Cr.
Wilmington, NC 28403

Betty Barnard
Buckeye Marble Collectors Club
Newsletter: BMC Newsletter
437 Meadowbrook Dr.
Newark, OH 43055
phone: 614-366-7002
Active club sponsoring annual convention in Columbus, OH; newsletter contains articles, buy/sell ads, calendar of events, etc.

Tulsa Marble Collectors
5635 S. Quebec
Tulsa, OK 74135

Southern California Marble Collectors Society
P.O. Box 6913
San Pedro, CA 90734

Sea-Tac Marble Collectors Club
Newsletter: Marble Monitor
P.O. Box 793
Monroe, WA 98272
phone: 360-794-5266

Collectors

Beverly Brule
P.O. Box 206
Northborough, MA 01532-0206
phone: 508-393-2923
Buy/sell/trade marbles and marble related items.

David & Becky Beane
Beane's Antiques & Photography
58 River Road
Benton, ME 04901
phone: 207-453-6790
e-mail: dbeane@mint.net
Internet: http://www.mint.net:80/antiques/catalog/beane.html
Buys, sells and trades marbles; will travel for collections.

Jack Whistance
288 Rte. 28
Kingston, NY 12401
phone: 914-338-4397
Wants old handmade marbles: swirls, onion skins, Lutz, slags, opaques, micas, sulphides, etc.; also wants pre-1940's machine made marbles.

Edwin Snyder
P.O. Box 156
Lancaster, KY 40444-0156
phone: 606-792-4816
Akro agate and other old marbles in original boxes/packages; also machine made: Oxbloods, Bricks, Lemonades, Cork Screws, Guineas, Large Slags; also antique handmade marbles

Collector
1021 East Wylie St.
Bloomington, IN 47401
Wants to buy old sulphide or swirl marbles.

Yvonne Marie Holmberg
7229 Pine Island Dr., NE
Bradley, MI 49311-9534
phone: 616-784-1715
Wants to buy all pre-1940 glass marbles except sulphides; pays current market value.

Lynn Christian
1114 Wilson Ave.
Ames, IA 50010-5570
phone: 515-232-2222
Wants old figural sulfides, swirls, etc.; also prizes from marble tournaments and contests.

Bill Tinkcom
2406 West Madison
Sioux Falls, SD 57104
phone: 605-331-5740
Wants to buy all kinds of marbles and marble type items such as marble games and old time marble boxes or bags.

Dealers

Bertram M. Cohen
Great American Co.
169 Marlborough St.
Boston, MA 02116-1830
phone: 617-247-4754
fax: 617-247-9093
e-mail: marblebert@aol.com
*Marbles bought and sold, especially
"art glass" marbles; also wants
postcards showing children playing
with marbles; organizes the Northeast
Marble Meet in October of each year
(Columbus Day weekend).*

Bill Sweet
P.O. Box 4736
Rumford, RI 02916-0736
phone: 401-434-4548
*Marble dealer, collector and
appraiser.*

Jerry Biern
Rare Marbles, etc.
65 Crest Drive
Cranston, RI 02921
phone: 401-826-3933
*Buys and sells rare, antique marbles;
free appraisals backed with data from
previous sales.*

Ardyth & John Stimson
What Goes Around
P.O. Box 513
Glen Ridge, NJ 07028-0513
e-mail: ajs@viconet.com
*Buys, sells, collects machine-made or
antique marbles; will trade, buy or
sell.*

Charles Eson
Hawkeye Collectibles
128 Western Ave.
Altamont, NY 12009
phone: 578-861-6256
*Buys and sells antique and machine
made collectible marbles; also sells
plastic display cases for marbles and
other collectibles.*

Gloria Munsell
Allenwood Americana Antiques
P.O. Box 116
Allenwood, PA 17810-0116
phone: 717-538-1440
*Buying and selling marbles and
marble games, etc.*

Elliot Pincus
Elliot's Marbles
P.O. Box C
Jenkintown, PA 19046
phone: 215-886-7421

Wayne E. Sanders
2202 Livingston St.
Jefferson City, MO 65109-0850
phone: 314-636-7515
*Buys, sells and collect antique
handmade marbles and collectible
machine-made marbles; no
contemporary marbles; looking for
single ribbon cores, clouds and
unusual or colored figure sulphides;
send $1 for list of marbles for sale.*

Experts

Stanley & Bob Block
Block's Box
P.O. Box 51
Trumbull, CT 06611-0051
phone: 203-261-0057 or 203-926-8448
e-mail: BlocksChip@aol.com
Internet: http://pages.prodigy.com/
marbles/
*Buys, sells, and specializes in
marbles; experts on identification and
valuation of marbles; offers 18-page
list of marbles currently available;
send LSASE with 52 cents postage.*

Jeff Carskadden
Muskingum Valley Archaeology Survey
24 South 6th St.
Zanesville, OH 43701
*Author of "Chinas: Hand Painted
Marbles of the Late 19th Century."*

Cathy C. Runyan
Marble Lady, The
7812 N.W. Hampton Rd.
Kansas City, MO 64152-4940
phone: 816-587-8687
fax: 816-587-8687
*Author of "Knuckles Down - A Fun
Guide to Marble Play"; helps people
identify & value their marbles; also
teaches, demonstrates & lectures
about marbles and marble playing;
interested in handmades, machine
made, and marble memorabilia.*

Michael A. Pratt, Sr.
Marble Emporium, The
Rte. 2 Box 73
687 "V" Road
Fremont, NE 68025
phone: 402-721-4765
fax: 402-721-4765
e-mail: mpratt@teknetwork.com
Internet: http://www.teknetwork.com/
display
Buys, sells, and appraises marbles.

Larry Castle
Castle Fair
P.O. Box 1857
Ogden, UT 84403
phone: 801-393-8131
*Advanced collector and nationally
recognized expert with over 10 years
experience with marbles; buys,
appraises and repairs marbles.*

Repair Services

Larry Castle
Castle Fair
P.O. Box 1857
Ogden, UT 84403
phone: 801-393-8131
*Restores and regrinds glass marbles;
over ten years experience and more
that 6000 marbles restored.*

Suppliers

Michael A. Pratt, Sr.
Marble Emporium, The
Rte. 2 Box 73
687 "V" Road
Fremont, NE 68025
phone: 402-721-4765
fax: 402-721-4765
e-mail: mpratt@teknetwork.com
Internet: http://www.teknetwork.com/
display
*Manufactures unique inexpensive
cases to display, organize, and protect
small collectibles of all types
including marbles; send SASE for
more information.*

MARDI GRAS ITEMS

Collectors

Michael Reese II
P.O. Box 5704
South San Francisco, CA 94083-5704
phone: 415-641-5920
Internet: http://www.shutmymouth.com
*Wants anything relating to New
Orleans ad Mardi Gras: invitations,
medals, call out gifts, etc.*

New Orleans

Collectors

Marilyn & Celeste Bordelon
1750 St. Charles Ave., Ste. 303
New Orleans, LA 70130
phone: 504-596-6550
*Wants to buy pre-1950 New Orleans
Mardi Gras items: ball invitations,
dance cards, admit, newspaper print
of floats, carnival bulletins, programs,
pendants, pins, buttons, favors,
postcards, medal or rhinestone
badges.*

Experts

Arthur Hardy
Arthur Hardy Enterprises, Inc.
602 Metairie Rd., Ste. C
Metairie, LA 70005-4009
phone: 504-838-6111
fax: 504-838-0100
*Buys, collects and specializes in
Mardi Gras memorabilia such as ball
invitations, post cards, carnival
bulletins (parade papers), photos,
illustrated feature articles, brochures,
etc.*

Museums/Libraries

Mardi Gras World
P.O. Box 6307
New Orleans, LA 70174
phone: 504-362-8211

Periodicals

Arthur Hardy
Arthur Hardy Enterprises, Inc.
Magazine: Arthur Hardy's Mardi Gras
Guide
602 Metairie Rd., Ste. C
Metairie, LA 70005-4009
phone: 504-838-6111
fax: 504-838-0100
*Published annually on December
31st: Mardi Gras history, stories
about collectibles, interviews, parade
routes, etc.*

Arthur Hardy
Arthur Hardy Enterprises, Inc.
Newsletter: Arthur Hardy's Carnival
Times Newsletter
602 Metairie Rd., Ste. C
Metairie, LA 70005-4009
phone: 504-838-6111
fax: 504-838-0100

MARINE ARTIFACTS

(see NAUTICAL ANTIQUES)

MARINE CORPS ITEMS

Collectors

Dick Weisler
53-07 213th St.
Flushing, NY 11364-1823
phone: 718-428-9829 or 718-626-7110
fax: 718-726-2011
*Wants recruiting posters, sheet music,
belt buckles, cigarette lighters, steins,
trucks, toy soldiers, documents, trench
art, etc.*

Stan Clark
915 Fairview Ave.
Gettysburg, PA 17325-2905
phone: 717-337-1728
fax: 717-337-0581
*Wants Marine Corps items: books
(unit histories, memoirs, campaigns,
etc.), postcards, tapestries, recruiting,
letters, documents, embroideries,
prints, photographs, scrap books, toy
soldiers, etc.*

Bruce Updegrove
RD 5 Box 546
Boyertown, PA 19512
phone: 610-369-1798

LtCol J.K. Williams, USMC (Ret'd.)
6025 Makely Dr.
Fairfax Station, VA 22039-1324
phone: 703-250-8421 or 202-371-8880
fax: 202-371-8258
e-mail: bva@bva.org
*Wants U.S. Marine Corps WWI-era
recruiting posters, photos, bus/trolley
cards, tin signs, brochures,
advertisements, etc.*

Harold Dylhoff
23511 Paulson's Rd.
Gobles, MI 49055-9605
phone: 616-628-4051
*Wants to buy letters and postal history
from U.S. Marine Corp (WWI through
WWII), including postmarks from
bases, camps and other locations;*

send photocopies and LSASE for reply.

MARIONETTES

(see PUPPETS)

MARITIME ANTIQUES

(see NAUTICAL ANTIQUES)

MASCOTS

(see AUTOMOBILIA, Hood Ornaments)

MATCH SAFES

(see also CIGARETTE COL-LECTIBLES; CIGAR STORE COLLECTIBLES; LIGHTERS; MATCHBOXES & LABELS; MATCHCOVERS; TOBACCO COLLECTIBLES)

Collectors

George Sparacio
P.O. Box 791
Malaga, NJ 08328-0791
phone: 609-694-4167
fax: 609-694-4536
Buys, sells and trades pocket match safes; especially interested in fancy, figural and unusual match safes; also interested in pre-1915 match safe related catalogs, advertisements and ephemera; will answer all correspondence.

Dealers

Lenore Monleon
33 Fifth Ave.
New York, NY 10003
phone: 212-475-7871 or 212-229-0958
Wants enamel and sterling match safes and cigarette boxes.

MATCHBOOKS

(see MATCHCOVERS)

MATCHBOX

(see MATCHBOXES; MODELS; TOYS, Diecast [Matchbox])

MATCHBOXES

Clubs/Associations

Leslie M. Good
New Moon Matchbox & Label Club
Newsletter: New Moon News
425 East 51st St.
New York, NY 10022
Newsletter is published 5 times per year.

MATCHCOVERS

(see also PAPER COLLECTIBLES)

Auction Services

Dave Hampton
16425 Dam Rd. #31
Clearlake, CA 95422-9787

Clubs/Associations

Morris Pasternack
Trans-Canada Matchcover Club
151 Cooperage Cres.
Richmond Hill
Ontario L4C 9K8 Canada

Ellen Gutting, Membr.
Liberty Bell Matchcover Club
Newsletter: Liberty Bell Crier
5001 Albridge Way
Mount Laurel, NJ 08054-2652
phone: 609-231-4602
Members are interested in the collecting of matchcovers & matchboxes; hosts annual national convention; holds shows, auctions, bi-monthly meetings with displays and trading.

Bill Retskin
American Matchcover Collecting Club, The
Journal: Front Striker Bulletin, The
P.O. Box 18481
Asheville, NC 28814-0481
phone: 704-254-4487
fax: 704-254-1066
e-mail: matchclub@circle.net
Internet: http://www.matchcovers.com
Devoted to the study and collecting of older matchcovers; the publication includes a matchcover mail auction and covers history and current status of the matchbook industry as well as the matchcover collecting hobby.

Don Gingrich
Tri-State Cardinal Matchcover Club
5720 Pleasant Ave.
Fairfield, OH 45014-3543

John C. Williams, Librarian
Rathkamp Matchcover Society
Newsletter: RMS Bulletin
1359 Surrey Rd., Dept. CH
Vandalia, OH 45377-1646
phone: 937-890-8684
e-mail: rmsed@psyber.com
Internet: http://www.psyber.com/~rmsed

Evelyn Ramlow
Badger State Matchcover Club
N9032 E Miramar Dr.
East Troy, WI 53120-2312
phone: 414-363-2961
e-mail: Evelyn5@ix.netcom.com

Bob Cigrang
Windy City Matchcover Club
Newsletter: Windy City Matchcover News
622 N. Russel St.
Mount Prospect, IL 60056-2028

Nancy Bailey
Angelus Matchcover Club
12707 Montague St.
Pacoima, CA 91331-4138

Emily Hiller, Treas.
Long Beach Matchcover Club
Newsletter: Matchcover Beachcomber
2501 West Sunflower, H-5
Santa Ana, CA 92704-7503
phone: 714-540-8220
fax: 714-252-5265

Loren Moore
Sierra-Diablo Matchcover CLub
4067 Palm Ave.
Sacramento, CA 95842
phone: 916-348-1085

Collectors

Joe DeGennaro
309 East 87th St., Apt. 6E
New York, NY 10128
phone: 212-876-1730 or 212-975-4108
fax: 212-975-8424
e-mail: jtdegennaro@cbs.com
Internet: http://www.psyber.com/~rmsed

Mike Landis
P.O. Box 544
Akron, PA 17501
phone: 888-248-2291
Buys and sells matchcovers; full books and especially feature matches; call toll free.

Marie Harbison
6048 N. Water St.
Philadelphia, PA 19120
phone: 215-424-5218
Members are interested in the collecting of matchcovers & matchboxes; hosts annual national convention; holds shows, auctions, bi-monthly meetings with displays and trading.

John C. Williams
1359 Surrey Rd., Dept. CH
Vandalia, OH 45377-1646
phone: 937-890-8684
e-mail: rmsed@psyber.com
Internet: http://www.psyber.com/~rmsed

Calvin J. Meider
P.O. Box 170
Excelsior, MN 55331-0170
phone: 612-926-2142

Dean Hodgon
2920 E. 77th St.
Tulsa, OK 74136-8723

Neil Hospers
4000 Edgehill Rd.
Fort Worth, TX 76116
phone: 817-738-8181

Jo Wilding
25 Huntsman's Horn
The Woodlands, TX 77380-0938

Dave Hampton
16425 Dam Rd. #31
Clearlake, CA 95422-9787

Mike Prero
12659 Eckard Way
Auburn, CA 95603
e-mail: rmsed@psyber.com

Experts

Wray Martin
221 Upper Paradise
Hamilton
Ontario L9C 5C1 Canada
phone: 416-383-0454

Bill Retskin
P.O. Box 18481
Asheville, NC 28814-0481
phone: 704-254-4487
fax: 704-254-1066
e-mail: matchclub@circle.net
Internet: http://www.matchcovers.com
Author of "The Matchcover Resource Book and Price Guide," and "The Matchcover Collectors Price Guide - 1st Edition."

Periodicals

Michael Zaun
Newsletter: Match Hunter, The
755 Zamia Ave.
Boulder, CO 80304-4317
phone: 303-449-8547
20-page quarterly newsletter; letters, ads, articles about matchcovers and collections, games, etc.

Dave Hampton
Newsletter: Matchcover Classified
16425 Dam Rd. #31
Clearlake, CA 95422-9787
Newsletter devoted to buy/sell/trade ads.

Casino

Clubs/Associations

Richard D. Hagerman
Casino Matchcover Collectors Club
Newsletter: Gambling Gazette
5001 Albridge Way
Mount Laurel, NJ 08054-2652
phone: 609-231-4602
Members are dedicated to the collection of all casino and gaming establishment matchbooks and matchboxes which are displayed and traded at regular meetings throughout the US and Canada; monthly newsletter.

Collectors

Richard D. Hagerman
5001 Albridge Way
Mount Laurel, NJ 08054-2652
phone: 609-231-4602
Buys older matchcovers from Atlantic City hotels, restaurants; and Atlantic City businesses other than casinos.

MATCHING SERVICES

(see DINNERWARE; FLATWARE; GLASS, Elegant; GLASS, Crystal)

MAYTAG

(see also WASHING MACHINES)

Clubs/Associations

Mark A. Shulaw
Maytag Collectors Club Eastern
   Division
452 County Road 33
Bluffton, OH 45817-9601
phone: 419-358-7076
   *A chapter of the national Maytag
   Collectors Club; dedicated to the
   preservation and restoration of all
   types of Maytag items, anything built
   by Maytag.*

Nate & Charlene Stoller
Maytag Collectors Club
Newsletter: Maytag Collectors Club
   Newsletter
960 Reynolds Dr.
Ripon, CA 95366
phone: 209-956-5244 or 209-529-5300
e-mail: multimotor@aol.com
   *Over 250 members nationwide
   collecting all types of Maytag items;
   lots of ads for Maytag engines, meat
   grinders, washers, new and used
   parts, gaskets, replacement decals,
   etc.*

Collectors

Tom Copper
Tom's Small Engines
1416 Ralapen St.
Roxboro, NC 27573-4232
phone: 910-599-6908
e-mail: tcopper@roxboro.net
Internet: http://bbs.roxboro.net/tcopper/
   index.htm
   *Collector of Maytag, Briggs &
   Stratton and other engines; repairs,
   rebuilds, and restores most small
   engines; locates parts and/or related
   supplies and services.*

Les Parker
1513 Hanover St.
Raleigh, NC 27608
phone: 919-828-1221

Mark A. Shulaw
452 County Road 33
Bluffton, OH 45817-9601
phone: 419-358-7076
   *Buying anything Maytag: cans,
   engines, washer accessories,
   literature, tools, new old stock and
   used engine parts, promotional items,
   almost anything that is Maytag; will
   answer questions; please send SASE
   with inquiries.*

Larry Benton
P.O. Box 336
Monroe, IA 50170
phone: 515-259-2322

Man./Prod./Dist.

Orville Butler, Hist.
Maytag Company Archives
1 Dependability Sq.
Newton, IA 50208
phone: 515-792-7000
   *Private company archives include
   paper artifacts, production records,*

*old catalogs; will help identify or date
your Maytag machine.*

Museums/Libraries

Hans J. Brosig, Dir.
Maytag Exhibit, Jasper County
   Historical Museum
1700 South 15th Ave. West
P.O. Box 834
Newton, IA 50208-0834
phone: 515-792-9118
   *A museum about Jasper County, Iowa;
   contains a large artifact collection of
   the Maytag Company: washing
   machines, seed cleaners, ironers,
   dryers, advertising & promotional
   items.*

Suppliers

Simpson Motors
3708 S. Amherst Hwy.
Madison Heights, VA 24572
phone: 804-929-4468
   *New and used Maytag engine parts,
   restoration supplies, engines, etc.;
   rebuild, restore, supply parts for early
   gasoline engines that powered early
   washing machines; no appliance
   parts; makes parts not otherwise
   available.*

MEDALLIC SCULPTURES

   (see also MEDALS, ORDERS &
   DECORATIONS; SCULPTURES)

Auction Services

Bob Slawsky
P.O. Box 864
Windermere, FL 34786-0864
phone: 407-352-7807
fax: 407-352-BIDS
e-mail: WWGD54A@prodigy.com
   *Buys, sells, auctions tokens, medals,
   badges, small advertising items,
   political, World's Fair, Olympic items,
   encased coins, etc.*

Clubs/Associations

American Medallic Sculpture
   Association
Newsletter: Members Exchange
172 North Plank Rd.
Newburgh, NY 12550
e-mail: amsa@queenbee.net
Internet: http://amsa.queenbee.net/
   *A group of sculptors, collectors,
   suppliers, producers and scholars
   interested in high relief medallic
   sculptures; annual exhibitions;
   newsletter published bi-monthly,
   "Medallic Sculpture" magazine
   published annually.*

MEDALS

   (see BADGES; COINS & CUR-
   RENCY; MEDALS, ORDERS &
   DECORATIONS; MILITARIA;
   RELIGIOUS COLLECTIBLES;
   TOKENS; VETERAN ITEMS)

MEDALS, ORDERS & DECORA-
TIONS

   (see also HISTORICAL AMERI-
   CANA; MEDALLIC SCULPTURES;
   VETERAN ITEMS; MILITARIA;
   MILITARIA, Russian; TOKENS)

Auction Services

Roy Butler
Wallis & Wallis
West Street Auction Galleries
Lewes
East Sussex BN7 2NJ, U.K.
phone: 01273-480208
fax: 01273-476562
   *Britain's specialist auctioneers of
   arms, armor, militaria and military
   orders.*

Spink & Son, Ltd.
King St.
St. James's
London SW1Y 6QS, U.K.
   *Auctioneers and dealers of coins
   (ancient to present), medals, orders,
   tokens, decorations and other
   numismatic items.*

David M. Gale
C & D Gale
2404 Berwyn Rd.
Wilmington, DE 19810-3525
phone: 302-478-0872 or 302-478-6866
e-mail: cdgale@dol.net
   *Conducts mail bid auctions of medals,
   tokens, religious items, trade checks,
   miscellaneous items, Civil War tokens
   and other exonumia; issues fixed-price
   exonumia catalogs.*

Jeffrey B. Floyd
Floyd, Johnson & Paine, Inc.
P.O. Box 9791
Alexandria, VA 22304-0469
phone: 703-461-9582
fax: 703-461-3059
   *Conducts three sales per year of
   orders, medals and decorations.*

Floyd, Johnson & Paine, Inc.
6427 W. Irving Park Rd., Ste. 160
Chicago, IL 60634-2437
phone: 312-777-0499

Clubs/Associations

Cameron Ward, CSMMI
Canadian Society of Military Medals &
   Insignia
1 King St.
Dundas
Ontario L9H 1B7 Canada
phone: 905-627-1815 or 905-547-8293

Mr. Leslie A. Elam, Dir.
American Numismatic Society, The
Newsletter: American Numismatic
   Society Newsletter, The
Broadway at 155th St.
New York, NY 10003
phone: 212-234-3130
Internet: http://www.coin-universe.com/
   org/armenian/
   *Has a major collection of American
   coins in addition to major and
   important collections of ancient, Latin*

*American, Islamic, European, and
other material; also publishes
"American Journal of Numismatics"
and "Numismatic Literature."*

David E. Schenkman, PR
Token & Medal Society
Journal: Token & Medal Society Journal
P.O. Box 366
Bryantown, MD 20617-0366
phone: 301-274-3441
   *Promotes and stimulates "exonumia",
   the study of non-government issue
   tokens and medals; an organization of
   collectors and researchers of tokens,
   medals and related items.*

Robert J. Leuver, ExDir
American Numismatic Association
Magazine: Numismatist, The
818 N. Cascade Ave.
Colorado Springs, CO 80903-3279
phone: 719-632-2646 or 800-367-9723
fax: 719-632-2646
Internet: http://www.money.org
   *Worldwide assoc. of collectors of
   coins, paper money, medals and
   tokens; over 30,000 members; offers
   collector services and benefits.*

Collectors

Stanley Steinberg
P.O. Box 512
Malden, MA 02148-0004
   *Wants tokens and all engraved awards
   and medals: military, political,
   merchant advertising, agriculture,
   schools & colleges, historical, city
   and town, associations, expositions,
   lifesaving awards, etc.*

Howard Averbach
1919 Delaware Ave.
Pittsburgh, PA 15218-1801
phone: 412-441-6904
   *Wants to buy quality U.S. Military
   campaign medals and decorations; no
   reproductions.*

Rickie Marquette
P.O. Box 343133
Homestead, FL 33034-0133
phone: 305-246-5431 or 305-245-2323
fax: 305-245-9295
   *Wants to buy American medals and
   orders, especially named and/or
   numbered pieces, valor awards, and
   Southern Crosses of Honor.*

Jerome Schaeper, Jr.
705 Philadelphia St.
Covington, KY 41011-1252
phone: 606-581-3729
   *Collects, appraises United Confeder-
   ate reunion badges, WWI homecoming
   medals and Civil War dog tags.*

Alan Harrow
2292 Chelan Dr.
Los Angeles, CA 90068-2621
phone: 213-874-3474
   *Primarily interested in military
   campaign and gallantry medals of
   most countries, especially US and
   Great Britain, as well as related*

documents; also wants civilian medals for heroism.

Dealers

Michael Rice
Michael Rice Collectibles
P.O. Box 286
Saanichton
B.C. V8M 2C5 Canada
phone: 250-652-9412
e-mail: mrice@pacificcoast.net
Wants pre-1946 medals and badges from all English speaking countries; military (except US), fraternal, sports, academic, memberships, etc.; approvals or photocopies welcome; will make offer; send 2 stamps to ensure reply.

Peter Hlinka
Peter Hlinka Historical Americana
P.O. Box 310
New York, NY 10028-0017
phone: 718-409-6407
Buys, sells, and appraises historical Americana; publishes a large catalog of militaria, war medals, military insignia, war relics, related books, and other historical Americana; also foreign.

Steve Johnson
Steve Johnson Medals & Militaria
P.O. Box 4706
Aurora, IL 60507
phone: 708-851-0744
fax: 708-851-0866
Large dealer; issues 3 to 4 catalogs per year.

Dan Farek
P.O. Box 1212
Bellaire, TX 77402-1212
phone: 713-666-2629
fax: 713-666-2629
Dealer in military medals of the world; issues list of items for sale for $8/yr.; sample list $1.

Cy Phillips, Jr.
S C Coin & Stamp Co. Inc.
P.O. Drawer 661180
Arcadia, CA 91066-1180
phone: 818-445-8277 or 800-367-0779
fax: 818-445-8278
Tokens, medals, coins, currency, badges, expo. and fair items, scrap gold and silver.

Ackley Unlimited
P.O. Box 82144
Portland, OR 97282-0144
phone: 503-659-4681
Buys, sells, trades orders, decorations and medals.

Experts

Jeffrey B. Floyd
P.O. Box 9791
Alexandria, VA 22304-0469
phone: 703-461-9582
fax: 703-461-3059
Buys, sells, trades, specializes in all military medals & decorations; specializing in Imperial German,

British and American awards; all periods.

S. Vernon
P.O. Box 890280
Temecula, CA 92589-0280
phone: 909-698-1646
fax: 909-698-7091
e-mail: svernon@aol.com
Author of "Vernon's Collectors' Guide to Medals & Decorations" III edition; catalog of Orders, Medals & Decorations available for a subscription fee.

Museums/Libraries

Robert J. Leuver, ExDir
Museum of the American Numismatic Association
Magazine: Numismatist, The
818 N. Cascade Ave.
Colorado Springs, CO 80903-3279
phone: 719-632-2646 or 800-367-9723
fax: 719-632-2646
Internet: http://www.money.org
A museum collection including 400,000 items; collection includes medals, orders and decorations from all countries and time periods.

John Langton, Jr.
Military Medal Museum & Research Center
448 N. San Pedro St.
San Jose, CA 95110-2232
phone: 408-298-1100
Send for free "History of the U.S.S. Washington" of WWII fame.

Periodicals

Token Publishing, Ltd.
Magazine: Medal News
P.O. Box 14
Honiton
Devon EX14 9YP, U.K.
A monthly English publication focusing on military history, medals, and badge collecting.

Medal of Honor

Clubs/Associations

Congressional Medal of Honor Society, The
40 Patriots Point Rd.
Mount Pleasant, SC 29464
phone: 803-884-8662
Internet: http://www.awod.com/gallery/probono/cmhs/

Museums/Libraries

National Medal of Honor Museum of Military History
400 Georgia Ave.
Chattanooga, TN 37403
phone: 423-267-1737
Internet: http://bertha/chattanooga.net/honor/museuminfo.htm

MEDICAL, DENTAL & PHARMACEUTICAL

(see also BOOKS, Medical & Dental; CIVIL WAR ARTIFACTS, Medical; EYE RELATED ITEMS; HEALTH & BEAUTY; INSTRUMENTS & DEVICES, Scientific; OPTICAL ITEMS; STAMP COLLECTING, Medical; VETERINARY MEDICINE ITEMS)

Clubs/Associations

Wellcome Institute for the History of Medicine
183 Euston Rd.
London NW1 2BE, U.K.
phone: +44 171 11 8888
fax: +44 171 611 8545
e-mail: library@wellcome.ac.uk
Internet: http://www.wellcome.ac.uk

Dr. M. Donald Blaufox, MD, Phd
Medical Collectors Association
Newsletter: Medical Collectors Newsletter
Montefiore Medical Park
1695A Eastchester Rd.
Bronx, NY 10461
phone: 718-405-8545
fax: 718-824-0625
The association meets once a year and issues its newsletter semi-annually.

Dr. Sam Koslov
Maryland Microscopical & Scientific Instrument Society
8621 Polk St.
McLean, VA 22102
phone: 703-893-9102
Focuses on instruments and devices; medical, surveying, photographic, microscopical, navigational, horological, astronomical, etc.

Collectors

Colin R. Voorneveld, MD
27 Roncesvalles Ave., #408
Toronto
Ontario M6R 3B2 Canada
phone: 416-516-4751
e-mail: 72774.257@compuserve.com
Avid collector specializing in pre-1900 medical and pharmaceutical antiques; actively seeks medical instruments, spectacles, historic medicine, etc.

Mike Gordon
57 Bundy Lane
Storrs, CT 06268
phone: 860-429-3834
fax: 860-429-3834
Wants to buy pre-WWII medical and dental items: diagnostic, surgical, bloodletting instruments, tooth extractors, opthalmic devices, obstetric forceps, hearing aids, phrenological heads and quack items.

Norman B. Meadow
225 E. 64th St.
New York, NY 10021
phone: 212-628-0032
Wants pre-1900 medical and surgical instruments or medical books; all

specialties: eye, obstetrics, surgery, ear, dental, etc.; one instrument or an operating room full.

Dr. Allan Wissner
P.O. Box 102
Ardsley, NY 10502-0102
phone: 914-693-4628
e-mail: wissnea@war.wyeth.com
Wants microscopes, medical, scientific instruments: Zentmayer, Grunow, Bullock, McAllister, Gundlack, McIntosh, Tolles, Queen, Pike.

Richard Van Vleck
Greybird Publishing
P.O. Box 412
Taneytown, MD 21787
phone: 301-447-2680
e-mail: smma@fred.net
Internet: http://www.bestware.net/smma/
Wants medical and scientific antiques of all sorts; especially microscopes, eye-related instruments, laboratory and demo devices.

Jon Lewin
622 Raleigh Ave., Apt. 3
Norfolk, VA 23507-2034
phone: 757-625-6732
Buying medical & scientific items: bleeding instruments, wood/bone-handled surgical tools, phrenology heads, electric or violet ray quack boxes, electric belts, microscopes, 19th C. medical books, eye-massagers, ear trumpets, etc.

Dr. J. Gimesh
P.O. Box 53788
Fayetteville, NC 28305-3788
phone: 919-484-2219
Buys and sells medical, dental, apothecary items, spectacles, books, etc.

Jerry A. Phelps
6013 Innes Trace Rd.
Louisville, KY 40222-6004
phone: 502-425-4765
Wants pre-1900 medical and apothecary antiques, especially colored pontiled medicine bottles, bleeding items, leeching jars; also pre-1900 country store items and advertising items.

Atled Delta, Ph.D.
2911 N.W. 122nd, Ste. 262
Oklahoma City, OK 73120-1900
phone: 405-751-0859
Wants to buy any medical or sick room device having a black, hard rubber nozzle/tip that penetrates any body orifice such as rubber douche syringes (bag or bulb).

Andrew E. Thomas
4681 North 84th Way
Scottsdale, AZ 85251-1864
phone: 602-947-5693
fax: 602-994-4382
Buying apothecary antiques and drug store collectibles; show globes, drug jars, drug mills, mortars and pestles, balances and scales, displays, pill

tiles, labels and label cabinets; specialty is show globes.

Dealers

Ruth & C. Keith Wilbur, M.D.
Doctor's Bag, The
397 Prospect St.
Northampton, MA 01060-2089
phone: 413-584-1440
Buys, sells, appraises apothecary, medical, dental, surgical, optical & quack instruments, equipment, advertising, books, etc.; catalogs available 3 to 4 times a year; author of "Antique Medical Instruments."

Lucille Malitz
Lucid Antiques
P.O. Box KH
Scarsdale, NY 10583
phone: 914-636-7825 or 914-636-5171

Eric P. Kane
285 Sills Rd., Bldg #7
Patchogue, NY 11772
phone: 516-475-2144
fax: 516-475-1588
Wants to buy medical antiques from the Civil War and earlier: medical instruments, cased sets, especially marked "USA Hospital/Medical Dept.", medical texts, and associated materials such as medicine bottles, tins, etc.

Rod Harmic
Harmic's Antique Gallery
550 Rose Dale Lane
Dover, DE 19904
phone: 302-736-1174 or 302-736-1266
e-mail: rodney.harmic@dol.net
Internet: http://www.harmic.com
Wants to buy medical antiques.

James & Norvell Kennedy
James Kennedy Antiques, Ltd.
905 W. Main St.
Durham, NC 27701-2054
phone: 919-682-1040 or 800-236-1868
fax: 919-683-9633
Specialist in scientific and medical instruments and prints; also nautical instruments.

Doris K. Bagwell, R.N.
Bagwell Antiques
5607 Concord Dr.
Jackson, MS 39211-4239
phone: 601-956-3508
Buys and sells any medical related items: surgical, instruments, supplies, books, etc.

Al & Bobbie Roberts
Rational Past, The
221 Oceano Dr.
Los Angeles, CA 90049
phone: 310-476-6277
fax: 310-476-6278
e-mail: rational-past@mindspring.com
Organizer of West Coast Scientific & Technical Antique and Collectible Shows (Los Angeles in the winter and San Francisco are in late summer.)

Experts

L.C. & C.G. Richardson
Mortar & Pestle Antiques
1176 South Dogwood Dr.
Harrisonburg, VA 22801
phone: 703-434-1506
Buys, sells and specializes in medical and pharmaceutical antiques; authors of "A Book on Apothecary Antiques and Collectibles" (Old Fort Press.)

Paul Wherry
Pharmatiques
20 West North St.
Columbus, OH 43085-4133
phone: 614-885-1322
Collects and appraises pharmacy antiques.

Dale R. Beeks
Perceptions Scientifica
P.O. Box 117
Mount Vernon, IA 52314
phone: 800-880-5178 or 319-895-0506
Buys fine microscopes; old scientific, surveying, technical, medical and precision instruments; pre-1900 typewriters, calculating devices, medical items & quackery.

Dr. Robert E. Kravetz, M.D.
6707 N. 19th Ave.
Phoenix, AZ 85015-1104
phone: 602-242-2555
Medical museum curator, collector and historian; deals mainly with 18th and 19th century medical & pharmaceutical antiques.

Museums/Libraries

Mutter Museum, The
19 South 22nd St.
Philadelphia, PA 19103
phone: 215-563-3737
Collection consists of antique medical instruments, rare anatomical specimens, and medical curiosities: the Soap Lady, Balloon Man, anatomical Hall of Fame, latex eyeballs, swallowed objects including ammunition.

Adrianne Noe, Curator
National Museum of Health & Medicine
Bldg. 54
Walter Reed Medical Center
Washington, DC 20306
phone: 202-576-2438 or 202-576-0401
fax: 202-576-2164
Historical collections containing over 1100 artifacts documenting the history of medicine; actively seeking medical instruments.

Hugh Mercer Apothecary Shop
1200 Charles St.
Fredericksburg, VA 22401
phone: 703-373-3362

Country Doctor Museum, The
P.O. Box 34
Bailey, NC 27807
phone: 919-235-4165

McDowell House & Apothecary Shop
125 S. Second St.
Danville, KY 40422-1801
phone: 606-236-2804
Has an outstanding apothecary shop museum.

Transylvania Museum
300 N. Broadway
Lexington, KY 40508-1797
phone: 606-233-8228

James M. Edmonson, PhD
Dittrick Museum of Medical History
11000 Euclid Ave.
Cleveland, OH 44106-1714
phone: 216-368-3648
fax: 216-368-6421
e-mail: jme3@po.cwru.edu
Internet: http://www.cwru.edu/cwru/chsl/hist_div.htm
Collection of 75,000 artifacts: medical history, diagnostic instruments, microscopes, surgical and obstetric instruments, etc.

Bakken, The
3537 Zenith Ave. South
Minneapolis, MN 55416
phone: 612-927-6508
Collects medical electricity items (no violet rays needed); have 2000 artifacts; 10,000 books.

International Museum of Surgical Science
1524 North Lake Shore Dr.
Chicago, IL 60610
phone: 312-642-6502

Dr. Robert E. Kravetz, M.D.
Medical Museum
6025 N. 20th Ave.
Phoenix, AZ 85015
phone: 602-249-0212

Periodicals

Richard Van Vleck
Greybird Publishing
Newsletter: Scientific, Medical & Mechanical Antiques
P.O. Box 412
Taneytown, MD 21787
phone: 301-447-2680
e-mail: smma@fred.net
Internet: http://www.bestware.net/smma/
For collectors, dealers, researchers; recent articles include formaldehyde disinfectors, galvanic spectacles and electric dumbbells; free ads for subscribers.

Civil War

Dealers

Alex Peck
Antique Scientifica
P.O. Box 710
Charleston, IL 61920
phone: 217-348-1009
Wants surgical and bloodletting instruments, any Civil War (and pre-1890) medical gear, USA Hosp. Dept., etc.; anything Civil War.

Dental

Collectors

William Winburn, Jr.
1502 Showalter Rd.
Grafton, VA 23692
phone: 804-898-8246
fax: 804-898-6689
Dental instruments especially extracting; also contents of old dental offices.

Ralph Nix
P.O. Box 655
Red Bay, AL 35582-0655
phone: 205-356-2997
Wants dental antiques such as fancy wooden dental cabinets, four-leg dental chairs, wood or ivory handled instruments, foot engines, etc.

Peter Chu, DDS
5470 Folkestone Dr.
Dayton, OH 45459
phone: 513-435-6849
Dental cabinets, instruments and catalogs.

Dr. Barry Janov
2454 Depmster St., Ste. 416
Des Plaines, IL 60016-5320
Collector of early dental tools and related memorabilia.

Ken DuVal, DDS
P.O. Box 9074
Rancho Santa Fe, CA 92067

Museums/Libraries

National Museum of Dentistry
666 W. Baltimore St.
Baltimore, MD 21201-1586
phone: 410-706-8314
fax: 410-706-3028
e-mail: b25001@dental3.ab.umd.edu
Poster art advertising dentists or dental products, pre-1950 dentist's directories (e.g. Polk's, Beecher's), trade catalogs, etc.

Macaulay Museum of Dental History,
Medical University of South Carolina
171 Ashley Ave.
Charleston, SC 29425-0001
phone: 803-792-2288
Collection made up of six thousand artifacts and books.

Dr. John Harris Dental Museum
1370 Dublin Dr.
Columbus, OH 43215
phone: 614-486-2700
Mailing address is as above, but located in Bainbridge, OH.

Museum of Dentistry
295 S. Flower St.
Orange, CA 92668
phone: 714-634-8944
fax: 714-978-2686

Drug Store

Appraisers

Jim McMahon
James L. McMahon & Sons
635 Gilbert Hwy.
Fairfield, CT 06430-1646
phone: 203-226-3430
Buys, sells, collects, and appraises antique apothecary (pharmacy) and medical items.

Clubs/Associations

American Institute for the History of Pharmacy
University of Wisconsin
425 North Charter St.
Madison, WI 53703

Collectors

Mart James
487 Oak Ridge Rd.
Dyersburg, TN 38024-6511
phone: 901-286-2025
Wants to buy label-under-glass apothecary bottles, show globes, porcelain and show jars, medicine advertising, drug store window display pieces, etc.

Andrew E. Thomas
4681 North 84th Way
Scottsdale, AZ 85251-1864
phone: 602-947-5693
fax: 602-994-4382
Buying apothecary antiques and drug store collectibles; show globes, drug jars, drug mills, mortars and pestles, balances and scales, displays, pill tiles, labels and label cabinets; specialty is show globes.

Dealers

Jim McMahon
James L. McMahon & Sons
635 Gilbert Hwy.
Fairfield, CT 06430-1646
phone: 203-226-3430
Buys, sells, collects, and appraises antique apothecary (pharmacy) and medical items.

Experts

Patricia McDaniel
P.O. Box 357
Dublin, IN 47335
phone: 317-478-4809
Author of "Drugstore Collectibles" (Wallace-Homestead).

Museums/Libraries

Eugene I. Morris, Dir.
New England Fire & History Museum
Newsletter: Siren Soundings
1439 Main St. (Rte. 6A)
Brewster, MA 02631
phone: 508-896-5711 or 508-945-9413
"The Schmidt Apothecary Shop" contains the largest collection of pharmaceutical bottles, original medicines and prescriptions; library contains many volumes dealing with pharmaceutical history.

Periodicals

Newsletter: Drug Store Collector, The
3851 Gable Lane Dr., #513
Indianapolis, IN 46208

Hearing Aids

Collectors

Jon Kolger
6906 Meade Dr.
Colleyville, TX 76034-6416
phone: 817-329-5262
Wants to buy all sorts of primitive hearing-aid devices such as conversation tubes, ear trumpets, early battery-powered hearing-aids, etc.

Patent Medicines

Collectors

Mark S. McNee
Nostrums & Quackery
1009 Vassar Dr.
Kalamazoo, MI 49001-4483
phone: 616-343-8393
Collector for 20 years wants pre-1910 patent medicine bottles, tins, packages, and pills; also wants to buy advertising items and contents of old drug stores.

Harold Dylhoff
23511 Paulson's Rd.
Gobles, MI 49055-9605
phone: 616-628-4051
Wants to buy Hadacol patent medicine memorabilia, almanacs, flyers, Captain Hadacol comics, Col. LeBlanc items; send photocopies and LSASE for reply.

Dan Cowman
43 Shallow Pond Place
Spring, TX 77381-3224
phone: 713-367-2935
fax: 713-292-0637
Wants to buy any items relating to patent medicines: almanacs, trade cards, billheads, labeled bottles, boxes, packages, tins, plasters, advertising, druggist trade catalogs, tin and paper patent medicine advertising signs, etc.

Repro. Sources

Barbara Amster
Nineteenth Century Mercantile
No. 2 North Main St.
South Yarmouth, MA 02664
phone: 508-398-1888
Carries large selection of 100+ year old remedies thought to be out of production: liniments, salves, ointments, syrups, balms; no mail order.

Phrenology Busts

Collectors

Jon Lewin
622 Raleigh Ave., Apt. 3
Norfolk, VA 23507-2034
phone: 757-625-6732
Wants to buy phrenology heads, instruments or machines for measuring the head, fortune telling hands marked with zones, and related books, signs, etc.

Donald Gorlick
P.O. Box 24541
Seattle, WA 98124-0541
phone: 206-824-0508
Wants to buy phrenology busts showing zones.

Quackery

(see also HEALTH & BEAUTY, Devices to Restore)

Collectors

Jon Lewin
622 Raleigh Ave., Apt. 3
Norfolk, VA 23507-2034
phone: 757-625-6732
Wants to buy "electric" or "violet ray" quack boxes, "electric" belts, "electric" medals, "electric" brushes, big floor standing electrostatic gen., etc.; also wants books, advertisements, and other items relating to medical quackery.

O. Lindan
1404 Dorsh Rd.
Cleveland, OH 44121-3840
phone: 216-382-7113
Wants old electrotherapeutic and controversial healing devices and related literature; also wants medical, scientific instruments.

Ed Keller
1205 Imperial Dr.
Pittsburg, KS 66762-6123
Wants quack medical devices, cure-all devices, and old electrotherapeutic gadgets which shock, spark, buzz, light up or remain silent; no violet-rays, please; please send name, brief description and price.

Museums/Libraries

O. Lindan
Lindan Hist. Coll. of Electrotherapeutic & Controversial Medical Devices, The
1404 Dorsh Rd.
Cleveland, OH 44121-3840
phone: 216-382-7113
Focuses on old electrotherapeutic and controversial healing devices and related literature.

Robert W. McCoy, Dir.
Museum of Questionable Medical Devices
219 S.E. Main St.
Minneapolis, MN 55414-2149
phone: 612-545-1113 or 612-379-4046
fax: 612-540-9999
e-mail: quack@mtn.org
Internet: http://www.mtn.org/quack
Nation's largest display of quack devices, from the AMA, FDA, St. Louis Science Center, Bakken Library and the National Council Against Health Fraud; publishes copies of old posters & advertising brochures dealing with medical quackery.

National Museum of Medical Quackery, The
3839 Lindell Boulevard
Saint Louis, MO 63108

Diablo Valley College Museum
Golf Club Rd.
Pleasant Hill, CA 94523
phone: 415-685-1230

Stethoscopes

Collectors

Chris Papadopoulos, MD
1107 Chaterleigh Circle
Baltimore, MD 21286-1755
phone: 410-825-9157
Wants antique and unusual stethoscopes; please send photos and price.

MEDICINE RELATED ITEMS

(see MEDICAL, DENTAL & PHARMACEUTICAL)

MEMORY ART

(see GARBAGE RELATED)

MENUS

(see also COOKBOOKS; PAPER COLLECTIBLES; RESTAURANT COLLECTIBLES)

Collectors

John Bantock
2531 E. Milmar Dr.
Sarasota, FL 34237-7255
Buys and sells menus.

Museums/Libraries

Strong Museum, The
1 Manhattan Square
Rochester, NY 14607
phone: 716-263-2700
Has a small collection of 100 menus dating back to the 1840s; fully cataloged on a computer database.

Cornell School of Hotel Administration
Library
Cornell University
Ithaca, NY 14853
phone: 607-255-3673
*Over 10,000 menus from the 1850s
through the 1940s.*

National Restaurant Association
1200 17th St. NW
Washington, DC 20036
phone: 202-331-5960
*Computer cataloged collection of
thousands of menus from the 1930s to
present.*

MERMAIDS

Collectors

Stephanie M. Schnatz
17 Tallow Ct.
Baltimore, MD 21244-2516
phone: 410-944-0819
*Wants to buy any old articles with
mermaids or merpeople on them:
silver, porcelain, paper, metal, linens,
jewelry, etc.; either three dimensional
or two dimensional as on maps.*

Jennifer Sykes
9018 Balboa Blvd. #595
Northridge, CA 91325-2610
phone: 818-993-1916
fax: 818-993-7612
e-mail: Veeda10@aol.com
*Wants to buy mermaid items: wall
plaques, figurines.*

METAL DETECTING

(see TREASURE HUNTING)

METAL ITEMS

(see also ALUMINUM, Hammered;
BRASS ITEMS; BRONZES; CAST
IRON ITEMS; CHROME; GOLD,
Scrap; PLATINUM, Scrap; SILVER,
Scrap; REPAIR/RESTORATION/
CONSERVATION, Metal Items)

Museums/Libraries

Judy Wallace
National Ornamental Metal Museum
Newsletter: Museum News
374 Metal Museum Drive
Memphis, TN 38106
phone: 901-774-6380
fax: 901-774-6382
*Conservation and restoration services
available to the public and private
sector; changing exhibits of historic
and contemporary metalwork, classes,
metalsmithing demonstrations.*

Repro. Sources

Steve Kayne
Kayne & Son Custom Forged Hardware
100 Daniel Ridge Rd.
Candler, NC 28715
phone: 704-667-8868 or 704-665-1988
fax: 704-665-8303
*Steel, brass, bronze reproductions of
locks, pulls, hinges, thumb latches,
furniture & interior/exterior*

*hardware, fireplace tools &
accessories, military accoutrements,
etc.; also does repairs, restoration; $5
for two catalogs.*

Heintz Art Metal

Collectors

David Surgan
328 Flatbush Ave., Ste. 123
Brooklyn, NY 11238-4302
phone: 718-638-3768
*Avid collector of Heintz Art Metal
Shop items including vases, bowls,
lighting, boxes, bookends, picture
frames, etc.*

METALSMITHS

(see CRAFTS; METAL ITEMS;
REPAIR/RESTORATION/CONSER-
VATION, Metal Items)

METEORITE COLLECTIBLES

(see ASTRONOMICAL ITEMS,
Meteorites)

METTLACH

(see STEINS)

MICROSCOPES

(see also INSTRUMENTS &
DEVICES, Scientific; OPTICAL
ITEMS)

Clubs/Associations

Fritz Schulze
Historical Microscopical Society of
Canada
RR #2
Priceville
Ontario NOC 1K0 Canada
phone: 519-369-2855
fax: 519-369-2855

Manuel del Cerro, MD
Microscope Historical Society
14 Tall Acres Dr.
Pittsford, NY 14534
*Interested in the antique microscopes,
parts, and history.*

Dr. Sam Koslov
Maryland Microscopical & Scientific
Instrument Society
8621 Polk St.
McLean, VA 22102
phone: 703-893-9102
*Focuses on instruments and devices;
medical, surveying, photographic,
microscopical, navigational,
horological, astronomical, etc.*

David Hirsch, Treas.
Los Angeles Microscope Society, The
11815 Indianapolis St.
Los Angeles, CA 90066
*One of the largest and most active
societies in the U.S.*

Collectors

G.P.O., Inc.
P.O. Box 472
Mantua, NJ 08051
fax: 609-468-9288
*Wants pre 1900 microscopes,
microscope slides and slide-making
equipment.*

Paul Ferraglio
3332 W. Lake Rd.
Canandaigua, NY 14424-2441
phone: 716-394-7663
fax: 716-394-5424
e-mail: p4alyo@aol.com
*Wants to buy antique brass
microscopes, scientific and surveying
instruments in any condition; also
wants related books and catalogs;
also wants parts.*

Richard Van Vleck
Greybird Publishing
P.O. Box 412
Taneytown, MD 21787
phone: 301-447-2680
e-mail: smma@fred.net
Internet: http://www.bestware.net/smma/
*Seeking pre-1900 American
microscopes by Zentmayer, Tolles,
Gundlach, McIntosh, McAllister,
Bulloch, Grunow, Spencer, Baush &
Lomb and others.*

Paul H. Hayashi, PE
18 Tarabrook Dr.
Orinda, CA 94563-3121
phone: 510-254-5074 or 510-253-1038
fax: 510-253-0592
Wants to buy pre-1900 microscopes.

Dealers

Ruth & C. Keith Wilbur, M.D.
Doctor's Bag, The
397 Prospect St.
Northampton, MA 01060-2089
phone: 413-584-1440
*Buys, sells, appraises microscopes,
apothecary, medical, dental, surgical,
optical & quack instruments,
equipment, advertising, books, etc.;
catalogs available 3 to 4 times a year;
author of "Antique Medical
Instruments."*

Experts

Dale R. Beeks
Perceptions Scientifica
P.O. Box 117
Mount Vernon, IA 52314
phone: 800-880-5178 or 319-895-0506

Randy D. Watson, M.D.
545 SE Oak, Ste. D
Hillsboro, OR 97123-4147
phone: 501-297-7424 or 503-640-1614
*Advanced collector wants all
microscopes; antique and toy; also
wants related books; says "I never met
a microscope I didn't like!"; has
private museum of over 1500
microscopes and 200 meteorites.*

Museums/Libraries

Adrianne Noe, Curator
National Museum of Health & Medicine,
Billings Microscope Collection
Bldg. 54
Walter Reed Medical Center
Washington, DC 20306
phone: 202-576-2438 or 202-576-0401
fax: 202-576-2164
*Approx. 1000 microscopes and 700
accessories; documents histological
techniques by the inclusion of
microtomes, accessories &
microslides.*

MILITARIA

(see also ARMS & ARMOR;
AVIATION; BADGES; CANNONS;
CIVIL WAR; FIREARMS; FLAGS;
FRENCH FOREIGN LEGION;
INDIAN WARS; KNIVES; MEDALS,
ORDERS & DECORATIONS;
MILITARY HISTORY; NAZI
ITEMS; AMMUNITION; POSTERS;
SWORDS; TRENCH ART;
VETERAN ITEMS; VIETNAM
ITEMS)

Appraisers

Carl A. Robin, ISA, ASA
Military Heritage Services
P.O. Box 30244
Raleigh, NC 27622-0244
phone: 919-787-0206
fax: 919-782-1718
*Provides documented appraisals,
appraisal reviews, litigation support,
and authentication of U.S. antique
arms, uniforms, accoutrements,
insignia and medals.*

Auction Services

Roy Butler
Wallis & Wallis
West Street Auction Galleries
Lewes
East Sussex BN7 2NJ, U.K.
phone: 01273-480208
fax: 01273-476562
*Britain's specialist auctioneers of
arms, armor, militaria and military
orders.*

Kelley's
553 Main St.
Woburn, MA 01801
phone: 617-935-3389 or 617-272-9167
*Conducts several auctions per year of
militaria from the Revolution to
present day.*

Anthony B. Lawson
Anthony B. Lawson, Inc.
P.O. Box 7051
Oakland, NJ 07436
phone: 201-337-5584 or 800-BID-2WIN
*Auction sales of historical antiques,
militaria, orders & medals: edged
weapons, American militaria, helmets,
flags, uniforms, edged weapons, arms
& armor; also sells art, collectibles
and autographs from all nations, all
periods.*

Raymond J. Zyla
Mohawk Arms Inc.
P.O. Box 399
Utica, NY 13503-0399
phone: 315-724-1234
fax: 315-724-5003
Internet: http://www.militaryrelics.com
*Three auctions per year: original
historical militaria, personality items,
daggers, swords, medals, award
documents, uniforms, headgear, art
items, presentation pieces, etc.*

Stephen Flood, Pres.
AAG, International Militaria Mail
Auction
1226-B Sans Souci Parkway
Wilkes Barre, PA 18702-1230
phone: 717-822-5300 or 717-822-5300
fax: 717-822-9992
*Specializing in mail-bid auctions of
militaria from Revolutionary War to
Vietnam with emphasis on WWII,
guns, Nazi, Japanese swords; all
countries; 3 catalogs with over 7,000
items for $35.*

Roger S. Steffen
Roger S. Steffen Historical Militaria
P.O. Box 280
Newport, KY 41076
phone: 606-431-4499
*Conducts periodic mail bid militaria
auctions: firearms, military art, rare
books, medals, uniforms, photos, etc.*

Manion's Auction House
P.O. Box 12214
Kansas City, KS 66112-0214
phone: 913-299-6692
fax: 913-299-6792
e-mail: manions@qni.com
Internet: http://www.manions.com
*The largest auction service in the U.S.
handling military related antiques and
items from U.S., Germany, Japan & all
other countries.*

Clubs/Associations

Rickie Marquette
Militaria Collectors Society of Florida
Newsletter: Frontal Dispatch, The
P.O. Box 343133
Homestead, FL 33034-0133
phone: 305-246-5431 or 305-245-2323
fax: 305-245-9295
*Purpose is to promote the knowledge,
study and preservation of military
relics, and to support militaria
collectors in the pursuit of their
hobby; meets monthly; promotes
shows; buy, sell, trade.*

American Society of Military History
Los Angeles Patriotic Hall
1816 S. Figueroa
Los Angeles, CA 90015
phone: 213-746-1776
*Society of men and women dedicated
to developing programs to perpetuate
and maintain the great American
military heritage.*

Great War Society, The
P.O. Box 4585
Palo Alto, CA 94309

Collectors

Darrell K. English
P.O. Box 1389
Wilmington, VT 05363
phone: 802-464-5569 or 413-339-3960
*Wants to buy any and all militaria:
Revolution through WWII; U.S. and
foreign; medals, uniforms, insignia,
headgear, edged weapons.*

Warren K. Tice
W. Tice & Company
8 Orchard Terrace
Essex Junction, VT 05452-3501
phone: 802-878-3835
e-mail: wtice@vbimail.champlain.edu
*Wants to purchase U.S. Military,
Confederate, and high quality
decorative buttons; also wants to buy
military antiques.*

Kenneth D. Smith
55 Howard Ave.
Staten Island, NY 10301-4404
*Wants to buy WWII OSS memorabilia,
relics and documents; also buys
espionage items, cryptographic and
code/cipher machines, devices, books
and manuals; any era, any nation.*

Gene Christian
3849 Bailey Ave.
Bronx, NY 10463-2503
phone: 718-548-0243
*Wants Foreign Legion, Devils Isl.;
Shanghai, Tientsin Volunteer Corps -
police - fire; China (Marines, 15th
Inf., gunboats, White Russians, Fr.
Forces, Warlords, P.A.A. China
Clipper, Imperial Chinese headdress;
animal rescue, truant off.*

Jason K. Phillips
130 Long Meadow Lane
State College, PA 16801
phone: 814-861-6533
e-mail: jkp107@psuvm.psu.edu
*Wants to buy militaria: bayonets,
swords, books, paper items, medals,
etc.*

Charles Dubsky
686 North Dupont Blvd. #328
Milford, DE 19963
phone: 302-422-7766
fax: 302-424-1928
e-mail: CCC@bdsnet.com

Pat Olson
4533 Rutledge Ave.
Minneapolis, MN 55436
phone: 612-927-0560
*Wants military war souvenirs from all
countries and all periods: daggers,
swords, uniforms, helmets, flags,
papers, badges, wings, patches,
medals, squadron insignia.*

Charles G. Kratz, Jr.
17821 Golfview
Homewood, IL 60430-1210
phone: 708-799-8478 or 312-951-0336
*Wants old military cannons (only full-
size, authentic type) in any condition;
also want U.S. artillery clothing and
equipment such wooden artillery
carriages and ammunition chests.*

Vladimir M. Kolesik
4028 Bedford Ave.
Independence, MO 64055
phone: 816-373-3934
*Organizes the Military Association
Show.*

Ron L. Willis
2110 Fox Ave.
Moore, OK 73160-4217
phone: 405-793-9604 or 405-521-3484
*Wants U.S. Navy - any period -
patches, wings, uniforms, books,
documents, edged weapons, photos,
plaques, flags, etc.*

Ed Royse
P.O. Box 33489
Fort Sill, OK 73752-1258
phone: 405-357-8000
fax: 405-875-2063
e-mail: shared@juno.com
*Wants to buy US military collectibles,
US Army firearms, swords, knives and
accoutrements from Civil War to
present; also wants US WWI and
WWII posters, patriotic, recruiting,
Red Cross, propaganda.*

Jim Kopke
P.O. Box 4310
Dillon, CO 80435-4310
*Wants to buy nearly anything from the
Civil War through the Indian Wars.*

David J. DeLaurant
1505 N. Lafayette
Fresno, CA 93728-1123
phone: 209-488-3229 or 209-233-1492
e-mail: dlaurant@sjvls.lib.ca.us
*Serious student of pre-1914 military
helmets & other body armor items
from all nations; communicates with
other body armor collectors via the
"Body Armor Reporter", a quarterly
newsletter; will identify armor free -
send SASE.*

Dealers

Geoff Pollard
Geoff Pollard Militaria
P.O. Box 89
Lytham St. Annes
Lancashire FY8 3UQ, U.K.
phone: 01253 721070
*Specializes in German and WWII
memorabilia.*

Blue Cape Antiques
620 Great Rd., Rte. 119
Littleton, MA 01460
phone: 508-486-4709
*Wants to buy military collectibles; US,
German, Japanese.*

Morgan's Books
RR 1 Box 1275
Jay, ME 04239
phone: 207-897-4078
*Buys and sells militaria books, paper
and ephemera: WWI, WWII, Civil
War, GAR and other veteran related
items from all eras, etc.*

Military Specialties, Inc.
2543 Berlin Tnpk.
Newington, CT 06111
phone: 860-666-4275
fax: 860-666-1939
*Buys and sells WWI and WWII British
military combat clothing and
equipment; WWI to present U.S.
military combat clothing and
equipment; and WWII Japanese
military collectibles.*

Jacques Noel Jacobsen, Jr.
60 Manor Rd.
Staten Island, NY 10310-2698
phone: 718-981-0973
*American military antiques 1840-1940
large illustrated catalog, 3 issues for
$12 ($15 overseas).*

Eric P. Kane
285 Sills Rd., Bldg #7
Patchogue, NY 11772
phone: 516-475-2144
fax: 516-475-1588
*Wants to buy Civil War and earlier
antique guns and militaria, uniforms,
photographs; also wants books on
guns.*

Raymond J. Zyla
Mohawk Arms Inc.
P.O. Box 399
Utica, NY 13503-0399
phone: 315-724-1234
fax: 315-724-5003
Internet: http://www.militaryrelics.com

Kathleen Miller
Kat's Militaria
906 Chambers Ridge
York, PA 17402
phone: 717-840-4156
*Buying anything military, from Roman
Empire to Desert Storm; buy small
items like dog tags or large items like
tanks; buying and selling for over 30
years; free phone estimates, but prefer
to work from photos.*

Ken Kipp
Allenwood Americana Antiques
P.O. Box 116
Allenwood, PA 17810-0116
phone: 717-538-1440
*Established militaria dealer and
Veteran with over 20 years experi-
ence; especially interested in WWI
and WWII memorabilia; buys and
sells.*

Terry Hannon, Pres.
Phoenix Militaria, Inc.
P.O. Box 245
Lyon Station, PA 19536-9986
phone: 610-682-1010 or 800-446-0909
fax: 610-682-1066
Internet: http://
  www.phoenixmilitaria.com
Buys/sells general militaria; also sells militaria collecting books & periodicals.

Mike Schoenberger
1221 US Highway A1A S
Saint Augustine, FL 32084-5421
phone: 904-461-0273

Ron Gordon
San Juan Precious Metals Corp.
4818 San Juan Ave.
Jacksonville, FL 32210-3232
phone: 904-387-3466
fax: 904-387-5166
Wants German, US, Japanese, Vietnam military items: helmets, flags, uniforms, badges, swords, coins, daggers, etc.

Donald E. Taussig
Sanders' Antique Mall
22 N. Lemon Ave.
Sarasota, FL 34236-5711
phone: 941-366-0400
fax: 941-388-2053
e-mail: sandersant@aol.com
Buys and sells military related swords, medals.

William Skelton
Highland's Vault
P.O. Box 55448
Birmingham, AL 35205
phone: 205-939-1178 or 205-939-3166
Wants to buy all military collectibles from Civil War through WWII.

Steffen's Historical Militaria
14 Mornan Rd.
Newport, KY 41076-9723
phone: 606-431-4499
Antique firearms, accouterments, swords, helmets, orders, medals; Revolutionary War, Civil War, WWI, WWII, Korean War, Vietnam War; American, Imperial German and Third Reich, British, French, Russian.

John W. Poling
John W. Poling: Military & Political Collectibles
5998 South Ridgeview Rd.
Anderson, IN 46013-9774
phone: 765-778-2714
Mail order dealer in military collectibles (helmets, uniforms, medals, war souvenirs); issues periodic catalog of items for sale; send $2 for latest catalog; most prices in catalog well below current retail.

Barrett Behnke
Barrett's Toys and Collectibles
136 Chestnut
Wyandotte, MI 48192
phone: 313-282-6754 or 313-282-3072
Buys and sells U.S. militaria from the

Civil War to present; also general military items of all countries.

Hayes Otoupalik
14000 Highway 93 N.
Missoula, MT 59802
phone: 406-549-4817
Wants to buy all American military items from 1845 to 1945: Civil War, Indian and Spanish American Wars, blue wool uniforms and caps, WWI doughboy uniforms and helmets, WWII flyers jackets, paratrooper uniforms, patch collections, etc.

Randy Donley
Donley's Wild West Town & Museum
8512 S. Union Rd.
Union, IL 60180-9661
phone: 815-923-9000
fax: 815-923-2253
Buys and sells souvenirs and relics from all wars: uniforms, helmets, medals, weapons, guns, swords, etc.

Warren Anderson
America West Archives
P.O. Box 100
Cedar City, UT 84721-0100
phone: 801-586-9497 or 801-586-7323
Buys and sells pre-1900 U.S. military documents, letters, autographs, photos, especially interested in Civil War, Indian Wars, and military documents from the Western U.S.; author of "Owning Western History."

Stewart's Military Antiques
108 W. Main St.
Mesa, AZ 85201
phone: 602-834-4004
Buys and sells helmets, medals, insignia, uniforms, photos, swords, and other military collectibles from 1860 to 1945.

Robert C. Thomas, Jr.
1926 W. Trask Ave.
Santa Ana, CA 92706-1363
phone: 714-971-2258
fax: 714-971-1531
e-mail: milathomas@aol.com
Buys and sells military collectibles; collects WWII U.S. Airborne related items.

Experts

Dale & Debra Anderson
Dale C. Anderson Co.
4 W. Confederate Ave.
Gettysburg, PA 17325
phone: 717-334-1031
Sells, appraises guns, swords, uniforms, headgear, relics, personal items, more; all offered in bi-monthly catalog ($12/yr); covers all periods 1775-1945; US & foreign; emphasis on Civil War/Indian Wars period; over 30 years experience.

Stephen Flood, Pres.
AAG, International Militaria Mail Auction
1226-B Sans Souci Parkway
Wilkes Barre, PA 18702-1230
phone: 717-822-5300 or 717-822-5300
fax: 717-822-9992
Buys and sells militaria from Revolutionary War to Vietnam with emphasis on WWII; all countries; issues a catalog every six months.

Richard Hovis
Timeframes Inc.
P.O. Box 3679
Washington, DC 20007-0179
phone: 202-333-7849
fax: 202-333-0938
Buys, trades, sells, consults, appraises, and specializes in original and authentic militaria, especially on 1776-1950 U.S. Navy uniforms, photographs, paper and memorabilia.

Courtney Wilson
American Military Antiques
8398 Court Ave.
Ellicott City, MD 21043-4514
phone: 410-465-6827
Military antiques 1700-1900: appraiser, consultant, broker, dealer; arms, uniforms, equipment, memorabilia - especially Civil War.

Robert Fisch
c/o Greenberg Publishing Co.
7566 Main St.
Sykesville, MD 21784
phone: 410-795-7447
Author of "Field Equipment of the Infantry: 1914 - 1945."

Sheperd Paine
6427 W. Irving Park Rd., Ste. 160
Chicago, IL 60634-2437
phone: 312-777-0499
Wants British, French and German pre-1914 uniforms, helmets, swords; familiar with military items from most countries & periods.

David C. Williams
Lost Cause Relics
2237 Brookhollow Dr.
Abilene, TX 79605-5507
phone: 915-692-1858
Collector and dealer in U.S. medals and medal groupings of all periods; also military photography, documents, uniforms, aviation items, etc.

Museums/Libraries

Greg Souchik
Allegheny Arms & Armor Museum, Inc.
P.O. Box 161
Custer City, PA 16725-0161
phone: 814-362-2642
fax: 814-362-7356
e-mail: 104235.2430@compuserve.com
Firearms, cannons, all types of historical military material.

George W. Marinos
Battlefield Military Museum
900 Baltimore Pike
P.O. Box 3192
Gettysburg, PA 17325-0192
phone: 717-334-6568
Wants war relics - U.S., German, any country and any war; guns, swords, medals, helmets, belts, buckles, flags, etc.

U.S. Marine Corps Museum/Library
Marine Corps Historical Center
Washington Navy Yard
Washington, DC 20374
phone: 202-433-3534

Navy Museum, The
Bldg. 76
901 M St. SE
Washington, DC 20374-5060
phone: 212-433-4882
fax: 202-433-8200
e-mail: nsssi@navtap.navy.mil

Director
U.S. Army Transportation Museum
Bldg. 300, Besson Hall, ATTN: ATZF-PTM
Fort Eustis, VA 23604
phone: 804-878-1115
Collects, exhibits and interprets the history of U.S. Army transportation activities from the Revolutionary War to present.

Parris Island Museum, The
Marine Corps Recruit Depot
Parris Island, SC 29905
phone: 803-525-2951

National Infantry Museum
U.S. Army Infantry School
Fort Benning, GA 31905
phone: 706-545-2958 or 706-545-6762
fax: 706-545-5158

Richard L. Uppstrom, Dir.
U.S. Air Force Museum
Wright-Patterson A.F.B., OH 45433-6518
phone: 513-255-3286
fax: 513-255-3910
World's largest aviation museum with 10 1/2 acres of aircraft and other exhibits under roof.

Museum of the Soldier
P.O. Box 518
Portland, IN 47371

Randy Donley
Donley's Wild West Town & Museum
8512 S. Union Rd.
Union, IL 60180-9661
phone: 815-923-9000
fax: 815-923-2253
Large display of souvenirs and relics from all wars: uniforms, helmets, medals, weapons, guns, swords, etc.

Liberty Memorial Museum, The
100 West 26th St.
Kansas City, MO 64108
phone: 816-221-1918

On-Line Services

Steve baker
Antique Militaria & Collectibles
  Network
106 Osprey Ct.
Morehead City, NC 28557
phone: 919-393-7821
e-mail: ddesign@collectorsnet.com
Internet: http://www.collectorsnet.com
*A network dedicated to militaria
dealers of all eras; put your list on-
line for as little as $21.50 per month
and advertise to over 12,000 visitors
per day.*

Chris Arnold
Military Collectors' Exchange, The
P.O. Box 1129
Jacksonville, AR 72078
phone: 501-988-2565
e-mail: chris@aristotle.net
Internet: http://www.tmcx.com
*TMCX is designed to assist both
beginner and advanced collectors of
militaria; feature articles, free ads,
international advertisers; webmaster,
Chris Arnold, is a recognized expert
on U.S. steel combat helmets.*

Periodicals

Imperial War Museum
Magazine: Imperial War Museum
  Review
Mail Order Department
Duxford
Cambridge CB2 4QR, U.K.
*A richly illustrated journal from the
UK's museum of 20th century conflict;
covering war history and art; primary
source material covering documents,
films, posters, photographs;
invaluable for the historian, student or
teacher.*

Magazine: Militaria Magazine
P.O. Box 2925
Framingham, MA 01701
*US address for a French monthly
magazine in English featuring pristine
examples of existing memorabilia,
supported with historical photos.*

RZM Imports
Magazine: After The Battle
P.O. Box 2925
Framingham, MA 01701
*English quarterly magazine focusing
on WWII.*

Terry Hannon, Ed.
Phoenix Militaria, Inc.
Directory: American Militaria
  Sourcebook & Directory
P.O. Box 245
Lyon Station, PA 19536-9986
phone: 610-682-1010 or 800-446-0909
fax: 610-682-1066
Internet: http://
  www.phoenixmilitaria.com
*A complete listing of militaria dealers,
service companies and organizations.*

Cowles Magazines, Inc.
Magazine: Military History
741 Miller Dr. SE, Ste. D2
Harrisburg, PA 20175
phone: 703-771-9400 or 800-829-3340
fax: 703-779-8345
Internet: http://www.thehistorynet.com
*A guide through history focusing on
armed conflicts; incisive accounts of
land, naval and air warfare in world
history from ancient to modern times;
published bi-monthly.*

Cowles Magazines, Inc.
Magazine: World War II
741 Miller Dr. SE, Ste. D2
Harrisburg, PA 20175
phone: 703-771-9400 or 800-829-3340
fax: 703-779-8345
Internet: http://www.thehistorynet.com
*A bi-monthly magazine; the ultimate
authority on WWII: weapons,
personalities, tactics.*

War of 1812 Consortium, The Star
Spangled Banner Flag House & 1812
Museum
Magazine: Journal of the War of 1812 &
  the Era 1800 to 1840
844 E. Pratt St.
Baltimore, MD 21202
e-mail: cgeorge@phnet.sph.jhu.edu
Internet: http://www.jagunet.com/MC/
  1812.html
*For those interested in the early years
of our history.*

Richard Cecilio
Wildcat Enterprises, Inc.
Journal: Wildcat Collectors Journal
15158 N.E. 6 Ave.
Miami, FL 33162-5034
phone: 305-945-3228
*Featuring classified ads to buy/sell/
trade guns, knives, medals and related
militaria; gun shows, auctions, other
events; subscribers get FREE 40 word
ad.*

Linda Kellbach
Antique Trader Publications, Inc.
Newspaper: Military Trader
P.O. Box 1050
Dubuque, IA 52004-1050
phone: 800-334-7165 or 800-482-4155
fax: 800-531-0880
e-mail: 76143.72@compuserve.com
Internet: http://www.csmonline.com
*Monthly publication focusing on
military collectibles: articles,
collecting, interviews with dealers,
military toy column, book reviews,
collectibles for sale, espionage.*

Newsmagazine: Military
1901 Royal Oaks Dr., #190
Sacramento, CA 95815-3817
phone: 800-366-9192
*Monthly newsmagazine with articles,
ads, etc.; many articles on military
aviation.*

Repro. Sources

Collector's Armoury
3000 South Eads St.
Arlington, VA 22202
phone: 800-544-3456 or 703-684-6111
fax: 703-683-5486
*Offers museum quality reproductions:
Civil War swords, knives, pistols and
field gear; non-firing Western pistols,
rifles and collectibles; medieval,
Samurai and military swords; historic
miniature Gatling guns and cannons.*

Anti-Axis

Collectors

Ken Fleck
496 2nd St.
Highspire, PA 17034-1505
phone: 717-939-8441
fax: 717-939-0064
*Wants to buy WWII Anti-Axis items
depicting anti-Hitler, anti-Mussolini,
anti-Tojo, etc. sentiments: toys, games,
coin-ops, banks, ashtrays, paper,
textiles, etc.*

Martin Jacobs
P.O. Box 22026
San Francisco, CA 94122-0026
phone: 415-661-7552
*Collector seeks WWII memorabilia
from the Homefront 1941-1945; will
purchase any size collection; wants
victory pins, Cinderella stickers and
stamps, envelope art, war propaganda, Anti-Axis art, matchcovers,
postcards, etc.*

British

Clubs/Associations

Publicity Officer
Military Heraldry Society
37 Wolsey Close
Southall
Middlesex UB2 4NQ, U.K.
*Formed in 1951 for collectors of cloth
formation signs: shoulder sleeve
insignia, shoulder titles, regimental
and unit flashes, etc.*

Publicity Officer
Crown Imperial Society
37 Wolsey Close
Southall
Middlesex UB2 4NQ, U.K.
*Formed in 1973 to study the history,
traditions and regalia of the forces of
the crown and other insignia.*

Publicity Officer
Indian Military Historical Society
37 Wolsey Close
Southall
Middlesex UB2 4NQ, U.K.
*Formed in 1983 to bring together
those interested in the military history
of the Indian Subcontinent.*

Experts

Brian Whitely
British Regalia Imports
P.O. Box 50473
Nashville, TN 37205
phone: 615-321-4027
fax: 615-321-3854
*Wants to buy British and Scottish
regimental insignia and accessories:
cap badges, rank badges, uniform
buttons, patches, wings, garrison
belts, berets, blazer crests, ties,
officers' swagger canes, swords, flags,
medals, maps, etc.*

German

Clubs/Associations

J.J Daub
Imperial German Military Collectors
Association
Journal: Kaiserzeit
82 Atlantic St.
Keyport, NJ 07735-1857
phone: 908-739-1799 or 816-455-3214
*Military collectors and historians with
a wide range of interests in all aspects
of the Imperial German military (pre-
1919).*

Chris Cox
Karabiner Collector's Network
Newsletter: KCN Newsletter
P.O. Box 5773
High Point, NC 27262
phone: 910-884-5566
*Network for collectors of German
militaria; German rifles and snipers,
pistols and holsters, Mausers, German
medals and badges, helmets and
uniforms, books, photographs,
cartridges and ammo, field gear,
edged weapons, etc.*

Collectors

John Telesmanich
P.O. Box 62
White Plains, NY 10604-0062
phone: 914-949-5519
*Wants WWII or earlier German
daggers, swords, medals, uniforms,
helmets, flags, books, documents,
patches, belt buckles, postcards, etc.*

Dealers

Military Specialties, Inc.
2543 Berlin Tnpk.
Newington, CT 06111
phone: 860-666-4275
fax: 860-666-1939
*Buys and sells German military
souvenirs from WWII: helmets, hats,
uniforms, swords, daggers, knives,
medals, patches, insignia, firearms,
etc.*

Albert Steckler
Military Collectibles
674 Hampton Ave.
Southampton, PA 18966
phone: 215-357-4107
*Wants to buy original German helmets
from both WWI and WWII; also wants
to buy German holsters, daggers,*

swords, medals, and uniforms from both wars.

Gus Villarreal
7300 Glen Hart
San Antonio, TX 78239
phone: 210-656-4597
Specializing in Waffen SS, army panzer, arm, army tropical & Luftwaffe, headgear items, helmets, visors, overseas caps & M43 caps, SS totenkopf collar tabs, cufftitles & uniforms, SS helmets, etc.

Experts

Richard J. Kimmel
P.O. Box 19
Bayville, NJ 08721-1412
phone: 908-269-8738
e-mail: richkimm@aol.com
Author of "The Phenomenon of Third Reich Badge Collecting: From the Hocus Bogus to True Genuine."

Periodicals

John Harrell
Journal: Regimental Quarterly
P.O. Box 793
Frederick, MD 21705
phone: 301-694-7344
fax: 301-694-7345
Quarterly booklet focusing on Imperial German regimental steins and historical material as it relates to regimental steins.

Repro. Sources

Richard & John Holt
4 Marion St.
Nesconset, NY 11767
Offers fully illustrated catalog of over 100 WWII German reproduction badges.

German (East)

Clubs/Associations

Lee Stewart
Society of East German Militaria Collectors
Magazine: SEGMC Magazine
P.O. Box 2153
Reston, VA 20195-0153
phone: 703-715-0683
Source for information on history, uniforms, and insignia of former East German forces; quarterly newsletter.

Insignia

Clubs/Associations

George Duell, Jr.
American Society of Military Insignia Collectors
Journal: Trading Post
526 Lafayette Ave.
Palmerton, PA 18071-1621
fax: 610-826-5067
Dedicated to the collection and preservation of U.S. military cloth and metal insignia; newsletter available only to members and contains members' buy/sell ads; approximately

3000 members; send for application and dues information.

Chute & Dagger
P.O. Box 7201
Arlington, VA 22207-7201
Parachute and Special Force insignia collectors.

Collectors

Hank McGonagle
26 Broad St.
Newburyport, MA 01950-2103
phone: 508-462-2354
Wants to buy medals and cloth shoulder insignia; all nations and eras.

Paul Belschner
11303 Woodson Ave.
Kensington, MD 20895-1431
Buys and trades military shoulder insignia (patches).

Don Sexton
400 Flamingo Circle
Greeneville, TN 37743-6126
phone: 423-639-4725
fax: 423-639-3960
President of the American Society of Military Insignia Collectors.

Dealers

H.J. Saunders
5025 Tamiami Trail East
Naples, FL 34113-4126
phone: 941-775-2100 or 800-442-3133
fax: 941-774-3323
e-mail: hjs1usmi@naples.net
Internet: http://www.naples.net/clubs/zmilins.htm
America's largest retail insignia company; issues large catalog of new and old insignia; shoulder patches, aviation wings, National Guard, Special Forces, squadron patches, ribbons, medals, military awards, etc.

Aeroemblem
P.O. Box 6206
Witchita Falls, TX 76311-6206
Thousands of U.S. Air Force insignia in stock for the collector.

McGrogan's Military Patches
P.O. Box 502
Orofino, ID 83544-0502
1000s of submarine, ship, Navy, Marine, Air Force, Army and Air Borne patches in stock.

Experts

Mario De Marco
152 Maple St.
West Boylston, MA 01583-1825
phone: 508-835-4085
Have book on Naval ships and aircraft, insignias and history; also Naval and Marine; price $9 each ppd.

David C. Williams
Lost Cause Relics
2237 Brookhollow Dr.
Abilene, TX 79605-5507
phone: 915-692-1858
Collector and dealer in U.S. medals and medal groupings of all periods; also military photography, documents, uniforms, aviation items, etc.

Insignia (British)

Experts

Ian Kelly
Major Ian G. Kelly (Militaria)
P.O. Box 18
South District Office
Manchester M14 6BB, U.K.
e-mail: 101360.2131@compuserve.com
Buys and sells original post WWII British military and police badges; send 2 international postal response coupons for free catalog: caps and collar insignia, trade and proficiency badges, shoulder titles, etc.

Italian

Clubs/Associations

Association of Militaria Italian Collectors International
P.O. Box 14402
Huntsville, AL 35815

Japanese

(see ARMS & ARMOR; FIREARMS, Japanese Matchlocks; ORIENTALIA, Japanese Items)

Manuals

Dealers

George Kastner
Daddy Warbooks
P.O. Box 6397
Los Osos, CA 93412-6397
phone: 805-528-1614
Wants to buy military books and manuals from 1900-1965.

Medals

(see also MEDALS, ORDERS & DECORATIONS)

Clubs/Associations

John E. Lelle, Sec.
Orders & Medals Society of America
Newsletter: Medal Collector, The
P.O. Box 484
Glassboro, NJ 08028-0484
Internet: http://www.coin-universe.com/org/medals/
Interested in collecting and studying military and civil orders, decorations and medals of all countries.

Collectors

W.D. Grissom, Sr.
Grissom's
P.O. Box 12001 - #216
Chula Vista, CA 91912
phone: 619-267-7839
fax: 619-267-7839
Buys and sells U.S. and foreign medals, old and new; for the beginner and intermediate collector; send $1 for lists.

Nuclear

Collectors

Danial Saks
Ground Zero
365 Hill St.
San Francisco, CA 94114
phone: 415-826-8337
Wants items related to nuclear warfare and testing: Manhattan Project, Pacific Tests, Nevada Tests, WWII.

Museums/Libraries

National Atomic Museum, Kirtland Air Force Base
P.O. Box 5400
Albuquerque, NM 87115
phone: 505-845-6670
Exhibits cover the complete history of U.S. nuclear development.

Russian

(see also RUSSIAN ITEMS)

Dealers

Igor Moiseyev
Atlantic Crossroads, Inc.
P.O. Box 290715
Brooklyn, NY 11229-5904
phone: 718-332-5889
fax: 718-332-5904
Sells 1918-1980s Russian military and civilian decorations, documented award groups, WWII and 1950s uniforms and field gear, historical documents, reference books, military badges and insignia; offers appraisals, research, translations.

Silk Embroideries

Collectors

Howard Averbach
1919 Delaware Ave.
Pittsburgh, PA 15218-1801
phone: 412-441-6904
Wants to buy patriotic/military silk embroideries purchased as souvenirs by U.S. soldiers and sailors in the Orient; embroidered ships, flags, eagles, mottoes; wallhangings only; no pillowcases or clothing.

Spanish-American War

Collectors

Morris Pickerell, Jr.
103 South Crawford
Tompkinsville, KY 42167
phone: 800-826-4499
Wants to buy anything relating to Admiral George Dewey and the Spanish-American War.

Submarine Related

Collectors

Ken Blazier
2937 Elda St.
Duarte, CA 91010-1431
Wants WWII submarine memorabilia.

U-Boats

Clubs/Associations

Harry Cooper
Sharkhunters International Inc.
Magazine: KTB Magazine (Kriegs Tag Buch)
P.O. Box 1539
Hernando, FL 34442
phone: 352-637-2917 or 904-637-2917
fax: 352-637-6289
Internet: http://uboat.europe.is/about/sharks.htm
Locates and preserves the history of the German and Italian U-Boat forces; recognized leading authority on the subject; Sharkhunters is the largest research center in the Western hemisphere on German U-Boat history.

Museums/Libraries

Keith R. Gill
Museum of Science & Industry
57th St. & Lake Shore Dr.
Chicago, IL 60637
phone: 312-684-1414
fax: 312-684-5580

Uniforms

Clubs/Associations

Company of Military Historians
Newsletter: Military Collector & Historian
North Main St.
Westbrook, CT 06498
phone: 203-399-9460

Gil Sanow, Ed.
Association of American Military Uniform Collectors
Newsletter: Footlocker
P.O. Box 1876
Elyria, OH 44036-1876
phone: 216-365-5321
fax: 216-322-1868
Members are interested in improving their personal collections and in sharing information, ideas and knowledge about U.S. military uniforms.

Louis Wendruck
Military & Police Uniform Association
Magazine: Military & Police Uniform Association Newsletter
P.O. Box 69A04 - Dept. Mal
West Hollywood, CA 90069-0066
phone: 213-650-5112
e-mail: airlinet@hotmail.com
Internet: http://members.tripod.com
A club for men into the uniform lifestyle including military, police, WWII, SS and boots; magazine has photos, stories, buy/sell ads.

Collectors

Joe Weber
604 Centre St.
Ashland, PA 17921-1332
phone: 717-875-4787 or 717-875-4401
Wants to buy Victorian, WWI (especially aviation), and WWII (especially CBI theater-made uniforms); all countries (US, Britain, German, France, Russia.)

Dealers

Experienced Denim
P.O. Box 239
Fayetteville, AR 72702-0239
phone: 501-444-7541 or 800-336-4694
fax: 501-521-8331
e-mail: exdeni19@intellinet.com
Wants to buy vintage fatigue wear, denim wear, khaki pants, nylon flight jackets, tanker boots, etc.

Vehicles

Clubs/Associations

S. Sebring
Red Ball Military Transport
400 Ave. C
Stroudsburg, PA 18360

Joe McClain
Indiana Chapter of the Military Vehicle Preservation Association
2330 Crystal St.
Anderson, IN 46012-1726
phone: 765-649-8265
fax: 765-642-0262

Leo Jankowski
Midwest Military Vehicle Association
Newsletter: MMVA Newsletter
P.O. Box 37596
Milwaukee, WI 53237-0596
phone: 414-483-3787

Kay Willard
Military Vehicle Preservation Association
Newsletter: Army Motors & Supply Line
P.O. Box 520378
Independence, MO 64052-0378
phone: 816-737-5111
fax: 816-737-5423
e-mail: mvpa-hq@mupa.org
Internet: http://www.mvpa.org
Since 1976, an international organization dedicated to the preservation of military transport from trucks to tanks.

Museums/Libraries

Joe McClain
Historical Military Armour Museum
2330 Crystal St.
Anderson, IN 46012-1726
phone: 765-649-8265
fax: 765-642-0262
One of the most complete collections of Light U.S. Tanks; plus a dozen prototypes of various vehicles; 30,000 sq. ft. of displays; collection has armored vehicles from WWI through Desert Storm.

Periodicals

Magazine: Military Vehicles
12-Q1 Indianhead
Morristown, NJ 07960
phone: 973-285-0716
fax: 973-534-5934
e-mail: mvehicle@aol.com
Internet: http://members.aol.com/mvehicle/home.htm
A bi-monthly magazine for military vehicle (wheeled & tracked) enthusiasts.

Repair Services

John A. Headley, Jr.
Doncar Equipment Co.
P.O. Box 133
Flanders, NJ 07836
phone: 201-927-0940
Restores military vehicles.

Suppliers

Daniel Janquitto
Canvas Beach Works
P.O. Box 137
Island Heights, NJ 08732
phone: 908-929-3168
Provides parts for WWII military vehicles such as Jeeps.

Peter Bella Jeep Parts
242 D Silas Carter Rd.
Manorville, NY 11949

Vehicles (Armored)

Museums/Libraries

Bill Gasser
American Armoured Foundation
2383 5th Ave.
Ronkonkoma, NY 11779
phone: 516-588-0033
Museum of armored vehicles, weapons and militaria dedicated in the honor of all veterans.

Gary Dever
Patton Museum of Cavalry & Armor
P.O. Box 208
Fort Knox, KY 40121-0208
phone: 502-624-3812
fax: 502-624-6968
Established to preserve historical materials relating to Cavalry and Armor and to make these properties available for public use.

American Military Museum
Whittier Narrows Rec. Area
1918 North Rosemead Blvd.
El Monte, CA 91732
phone: 818-442-1776
Maintained by the American Society of Military History; contains the largest collection of tanks and military vehicles in the U.S.

WWI Items

Book Sellers

Battery Press, The
P.O. Box 198885
Nashville, TN 37219
phone: 615-298-1401
Carries books about WWI.

Collectors

Randy Trawnik
800 5th Ave. #514
Fort Worth, TX 76104
phone: 214-941-2445
Wants WWI German spiked helmets, uniforms, etc. Any condition.

Experts

Dale & Debra Anderson
Dale C. Anderson Co.
4 W. Confederate Ave.
Gettysburg, PA 17325
phone: 717-334-1031
Sells, appraises guns, swords, uniforms, headgear, relics, personal items, more; all offered in bi-monthly catalog ($12/yr); covers all periods 1775-1945; US & foreign; emphasis on Civil War/Indian Wars period; over 30 years experience.

WWI Items (Posters)

(see also POSTERS)

Collectors

Ken Khuans
155 Harbor Dr. #4812
Chicago, IL 60601-7378
phone: 312-642-0554
Collector wants WWI posters; also books relating to WWI posters.

Dealers

Maurice & Laya Jakubowicz
L'affiche Francaise
Le Plateau - Bazincourt
B.P. 42
21740 Gisors, France
phone: 332-32555476
fax: 332-32271012
Buys and sells posters, mainly French, some foreign; catalog sent on request.

Experts

George Theofiles
Miscellaneous Man
P.O. Box 1776
New Freedom, PA 17349-0191
phone: 717-235-4766
fax: 717-235-2853
Collects, buys and sells; since 1970

offering catalogs of rare posters and early advertising and ephemera on hundreds of subjects; descriptive flyer available; author of "American Posters of World War I".

WWII Items

Collectors

Richard Harrow
8523 210 St.
Jamaica, NY 11427
phone: 718-740-1088
Wants any item relating to WWII: allied forces, anti-fascist propaganda, Jewish Holocaust, soldier benevolent aid, etc.

Daniel Lee
P.O. Box 1142
Brentwood, TN 37024-1142
phone: 615-370-3220
Wants to buy German and Japanese war relics: daggers, documents, flags, guns, headgear, medals, optics, swords, uniforms, etc.

Harry Fisher
Rte. 1 Box 197
Owensville, MO 65066
phone: 314-437-4227
Wants WWII items: books, magazines, unit records (especially 8th Air Force memorabilia), etc.; please describe and price.

Dealers

Jerry Rubackin
Jerry's Cards & Collectibles
P.O. Box 1271
Framingham, MA 01701-0207
phone: 508-788-5197
fax: 508-788-5197
Buys and sells WWII fighter aces autographs and other WWII military signatures; also want autographed material by the crew of the Enola Gay which dropped the first atomic bomb on Hiroshima.

Anthony Jessen
Jessen's Relics, Inc.
P.O. Box 9523
Birmingham, AL 35220
phone: 205-681-6382
fax: 205-680-9171
Specializing in German WWII relics, some US and other nations, 400 to 500 German insignia each catalog: medals, badges, pins, buckles, flags, cloth insignia, visor hats, helmets and uniforms, field gear, edged weapons; catalog $10.

Don Gillis
WWII Productions
4750 S. Padre Island Dr.
Corpus Christi, TX 78411
phone: 512-854-3541
e-mail: wwii@trip.net
Internet: http:// www.historicalmilitaria.com
Buys, sells, collects WWII militaria.

Wolfe-Hardin
6490 Bixby Hill Rd.
Long Beach, CA 90815
phone: 310-596-6610
fax: 310-596-0086
Buys and sells top quality items; especially interested in SS Allach, china documents, regimental embroidery, trumpet banners, poletops, streamers, gorgets, cased medals, orders and decorations, edged weapons, headgear, etc.

Experts

Dale & Debra Anderson
Dale C. Anderson Co.
4 W. Confederate Ave.
Gettysburg, PA 17325
phone: 717-334-1031
Sells, appraises guns, swords, uniforms, headgear, relics, personal items, more; all offered in bi-monthly catalog ($12/yr); covers all periods 1775-1945; US & foreign; emphasis on Civil War/Indian Wars period; over 30 years experience.

Periodicals

Magazine: WWII Military Journal
P.O. Box 28906
San Diego, CA 92198-0906
phone: 619-451-8688
fax: 619-451-8699
For anyone interested in the history of WWII; declassified reports, photos, information for collectors, exciting articles, and much more.

WWII Items (Homefront)

Collectors

Martin Jacobs
P.O. Box 22026
San Francisco, CA 94122-0026
phone: 415-661-7552
Collector seeks WWII memorabilia from the Homefront 1941-1945; will purchase any size collection; wants victory pins, Cinderella stickers and stamps, envelope art, war propaganda, Anti-Axis art, matchcovers, postcards, etc.

Periodicals

Magazine: 1940's Today
P.O. Box 2006
Baltimore, MD 21284

WWII Items (Paratroop)

Collectors

Ed Hicks
3805 Cumberland Rd.
Fayetteville, NC 28306-2439
phone: 910-425-7000
Airborne collector/historian wants to buy WWII Paratroop and Elite militaria: jump jackets, pants, boots, M1C helmets, A-2 leather jackets, fighting and jump knives, T-5 parachutes, unit histories, all related equipment.

WWII Items (Photographs)

Collectors

Scott A. Swanson
50 Gloucester St.
Boston, MA 02115-3141
phone: 617-536-8013
Wants photos of American, European soldiers, sailors; all fronts, all branches; albums, single snapshots, photos taken by soldiers rather than official or press; no printed cards or reproductions; also German and P.O.W.

WWII Items (Posters)

(see also POSTERS)

Collectors

John Stachmus
RR 1 Box 110
Homer, IL 61849
phone: 217-896-2859
Collector wants WWII posters.

Dealers

Maurice & Laya Jakubowicz
L'affiche Francaise
Le Plateau - Bazincourt
B.P. 42
21740 Gisors, France
phone: 332-32555476
fax: 332-32271012
Buys and sells posters, mainly French, some foreign; catalog sent on request.

Jim Meehan
Meehan Military Collectibles
P.O. Box 477
New York, NY 10028-0018
phone: 212-734-5683
fax: 212-535-4249
e-mail: meehan@interport.net
Internet: http://www.posterfair.com/mm/ storefront.htm

Experts

George Theofiles
Miscellaneous Man
P.O. Box 1776
New Freedom, PA 17349-0191
phone: 717-235-4766
fax: 717-235-2853

MILITARY HISTORY

(see also AVIATION, Military; AVIATION MEMORABILIA; BOOKS, Collector [Militaria]; CIVIL WAR HISTORY; INDIAN WARS; LIVING HISTORY; MARINE CORPS ITEMS; MILITARIA; SOLDIERS, Toy; VIETNAM ITEMS)

Clubs/Associations

Company of Military Historians
Newsletter: Military Collector & Historian
North Main St.
Westbrook, CT 06498
phone: 203-399-9460

Collectors

Earle
520 Grant
Hinsdale, IL 60521
Wants Division histories of the WWI American Expeditionary Forces, 1917-1919; also handwritten diaries or journals.

Museums/Libraries

Stephen T.C. Seams
Massachusetts National Guard Military Museum & Archives
Worcester Armory
44 Salisbury St.
Worcester, MA 01609
phone: 508-797-0334 or 508-757-2410
Military history museum and archive related to the history of the Massachusetts National Guard from 1638 to present.

Commonwealth of Massachusetts Military Division History, Research Museum
143 Speen St.
Natick, MA 01760-2599
phone: 508-651-1776

Bruce M. Moseley, Cur.
Fort Ticonderoga Museum
Newsletter: Bulletin of the Fort Ticonderoga Museum
P.O. Box 390
Ticonderoga, NY 12883
phone: 518-585-2821
fax: 518-585-2210
10,000 volume research library specializing in 19th century military history and the history of the Champlain Valley; museum depicts history of the area and the campaigns during the 7 Year War and the Revolutionary War.

Virginia War Museum
9285 Warwick Blvd.
Newport News, VA 23607
phone: 757-247-8523 or 757-247-8522
fax: 757-247-8627
Museum interprets U.S. military history from 1775 to present; featuring over 60,000 artifacts.

Periodicals

Magazine: Artilleryman, The
RR 1 Box 36
Tunbridge, VT 05077-9707
phone: 802-889-3500
fax: 802-889-5627
Published quarterly, the only magazine exclusively for the 1750-1898 artillery enthusiast: artillery history, unit profiles, shell collecting, etc.

Robert Cowley, Ed.
MHQ Inc.
Magazine: MHQ: The Quarterly Journal of Military History
29 W. 38 St.
New York, NY 10018
phone: 212-398-1550
fax: 212-840-6790
A quarterly magazine containing a

wide variety of articles on military history.

Erika Daileda
Wise Owl Worldwide Publications
Magazine: Regiment
4314 West 238th St. - Dept. MACR
Torrance, CA 90505-4509
phone: 310-375-6258
fax: 310-375-0548
e-mail: wiseowl@sprintmail.com
A bi-monthly English publication; regimental or unit histories presented through pictorial records; weapons, vehicles, accoutrements, uniforms, medals and decorations, equipment, etc.; photographs, colored illustrations; model soldiers.

Erika Daileda
Wise Owl Worldwide Publications
Magazine: Military Illustrated
4314 West 238th St. - Dept. MACR
Torrance, CA 90505-4509
phone: 310-375-6258
fax: 310-375-0548
e-mail: wiseowl@sprintmail.com
A monthly English publication; all periods of military history from ancient to WWII; in-depth research, rare photos, specially commissioned artwork make this magazine one of the finest reference sources for collectors and enthusiasts.

Meredith Vezina
Heritage Press
Magazine: Traditions: Military History Jrnl. of the Pacific
102 West 6th Ave.
Escondido, CA 92025
phone: 800-277-1977 or 760-735-9313
fax: 760-432-9043
Focuses on the military heritage of the San Diego, CA area; articles, in-depth interviews, profiles focusing on San Diego's military history.

Cavalry

Museums/Libraries

Patricia S. Bright
U.S. Cavalry Association & Museum
Journal: Cavalry Journal
P.O. Box 2325
Fort Riley, KS 66442-0325
phone: 913-784-5759
fax: 913-784-5797
e-mail: cavalry@flinthills.com
Internet: http://www.wtvl.com/cavalry/
Collects, preserves and displays the uniforms, weapons and equipment used by cavalry soldiers from the Revolutionary War through WWII.

Periodicals

Nick Nichols
Magazine: Cavalry!
Old Blue Ridge Turnpike
Rochelle, VA 22738
phone: 703-672-9267
fax: 703-672-9267
A quarterly journal devoted exclusively to the in-depth and

accurate portrayal of the 19th century horse soldier.

Unit Histories

Collectors

Bill Baumann
P.O. Box 319
Esperance, NY 12066-0319
phone: 518-875-6753
Collects military unit history books from all American wars (i.e. Civil War, Spanish American War, WWI, WWII, Korea, Vietnam); also wants unit photos, holiday menus, albums, posthumous decorations; specializes in black militaria.

Museums/Libraries

U.S. Military History Institute
22 Ashburn Drive
Carlisle Barracks
Carlisle, PA 17013-5008
phone: 717-245-3611
Specialized library to research military history including unit histories.

U.S. Army Library
The Pentagon
Room 1A518
Washington, DC 20310
Specialized library to research military unit histories.

U.S. Army Center of Military History, Museum Branch
20 Massachusetts Ave. NW
Washington, DC 20314
phone: 202-272-0310
Specialized library to research military unit histories.

U.S. Marine Corps Museum/Library
Marine Corps Historical Center
Washington Navy Yard
Washington, DC 20374
phone: 202-433-3534
Specialized library to research military unit histories.

Library of Congress
10 First St. SE
Washington, DC 20540
phone: 202-707-5000
Specialized library to research military unit histories.

U.S. Army Military Police Corps Regimental Museum
Bldg. 3182
Fort McClellan, AL 36205
phone: 205-848-3522 or 205-848-3050
Gift shop provides military police memorabilia on site and by mail order.

Jerry G. Burgess, Dir.
Women's Army Corps Museum
Newsletter: WAC Newsletter
USAMP CS/TC & FM
Fort McClellan, AL 36205-5000
phone: 205-848-3512 or 205-848-5559
fax: 205-848-7323
e-mail: jerry_burgess@prodigy.com
Cannot buy, sell or appraise items;

can only provide information to collectors and researchers.

MILLING

(see also SACKS)

Appraisers

Robert L. Johnson
Whistles in the Woods Museum Services
P.O. Box 309
Chickamauga, GA 30707-0309
phone: 706-375-4326
e-mail: oldgoat@voy.net
Consultants specializing in 1750 - early 20th century historic machinery; power-generation, tools, machines, scientific & technical instruments, mining, milling, transportation, logging & lumbering, steam engines, etc.

Book Sellers

Sidney Halma
Mill Book Store
P.O. Box 1055
Newton, NC 28658
phone: 704-465-0383
Internet: http://www.spoom.org
Sells books relating to milling; many reprints.

Clubs/Associations

Sidney Halma
Society for the Preservation of Old Mills (SPOOM)
Magazine: Old Mill News
P.O. Box 1055
Newton, NC 28658
phone: 704-465-0383
Internet: http://www.spoom.org
Organization focuses on the milling industry: mills, millwrights, equipment, techniques; ads, mills for sale, millwrights, stones, etc.; in existence for over 20 years; over 2000 members.

Museums/Libraries

Hanford Mills Museum
P.O. Box 99
East Meredith, NY 13757
phone: 607-278-5744
fax: 607-278-5840

Bobbins & Spools

Man./Prod./Dist.

Dirk & Ann Poole
Ma's Bobbin Works, Inc.
P.O. Box 667
Newcastle, ME 04553-0667
phone: 207-563-1210 or 800-782-8581
fax: 207-633-2313
Manufactures a wide assortment of items (candle holders, lamps, etc.) from old textile mill bobbins.

Repro. Sources

David W. Harris
Joel S. Perkins & Son, Inc.
P.O. Box 299
South Strafford, VT 05070-0076
phone: 802-889-3260
fax: 802-889-3316
Textile mill supplies, bobbins, spools, shuttle, mill memorabilia.

MINERALS

(see also FOSSILS; GEMS & JEWELRY; GOLD; LAPIDARY; MINING RELATED ITEMS; NATURAL HISTORY; SAND)

Clubs/Associations

Mineralogical Society of America
Magazine: American Mineralogist
1015 Eighteenth St. NW, Ste. 601
Washington, DC 20036
phone: 202-775-4344
fax: 202-775-0018
e-mail: j_a_speer@minsocam.org
Internet: http://www.geology.smith.edu/msa.html
Members are interested in mineralogy, crystallography, and petrology; promotes, through education and research, the understanding and application of mineralogy by industry, universities, government and the public.

Dr. Rodney Burroughs
Fluorescent Mineral Society
Newsletter: UV Waves
P.O. Box 572694
Tarzana, CA 91357-2694
e-mail: 71543.3343@compuserve.com
Over 400 members worldwide specialize in the collection and study of fluorescent minerals.

Collectors

Stephen Seltzer
7912 Georgia Ave.
Silver Spring, MD 20910-4837
phone: 301-565-2444 or 301-565-3339
fax: 301-565-2228
e-mail: eseltzer@aol.com
Wants to buy specimen size minerals and fossils for display.

Gary E. Fleck
P.O. Box 2886
Hot Springs National Park, AR 71914
phone: 501-623-4098
fax: 501-623-4098
Wants to buy mineral collections, natural rock crystals, cutting rough rock.

Dealers

Let Tolonen
Keweenaw Agate Shop
P.O. Box 20
Copper Harbor, MI 49918
phone: 906-289-4491

Jayne Horak
Crystal Springs Mining & Jewelry
P.O. Box 40
Royal, AR 71968
phone: 501-991-3557
fax: 501-991-3281

Joe Pfeiffer
XTAL Publishing
P.O. Box 253
Sandy, UT 84091-0253
phone: 801-571-5453
e-mail: 72622.127@compuserve.com
*Buy, sell, trade books on mining,
geology, mineralogy; USGS
publications, rockhound books, any
old geology literature and paper or
memorabilia related to mining and
minerals; publisher of "A System of
Mineral Collecting."*

John & Karen Mediz
Copper City Rock Shop
566 Ash St.
Globe, AZ 85501
phone: 520-425-7885 or 520-425-4506
fax: 520-425-4506
*Buys and sells mining artifacts; also
wants to buy minerals and fossils,
especially old collections.*

Tome & Sue Robertson
Robertson's Rock Works
1785 Tumalo Dr. SE
Salem, OR 97301
phone: 503-363-9678
fax: 503-364-3750

Experts

Dr. Abraham Rosenzweig
Rosenzweig Associates
P.O. Box 16187
Temple Terrace, FL 33617-6187
phone: 813-988-0880
fax: 813-989-8091
e-mail: rosetwig@aol.com
*Consultant specializing in mineralogy
and gemology.*

Museums/Libraries

Mineralogical Museum of Harvard
  University
24 Oxford St.
Cambridge, MA 02138
phone: 617-495-2326

Pennsylvania State University Earth &
  Mineral Sciences Museum & Art
  Gallery
Streidle Bldg. On Pollack Rd.
State College, PA 16802
phone: 814-865-6427
e-mail: sicree@geosc.psu.edu
*Displays of minerals, materials,
gemstones, and art work related to
mining; displays of old lamps and
other mining artifacts.*

Rebecca Lamb
Colburn Gem & Mineral Museum
Newsletter: Touchstone
P.O. Box 1617
Asheville, NC 28802
phone: 704-254-7162
fax: 704-251-5652
Internet: http://www.main.nc.us/colburn
*Features gems and minerals from
North Carolina and around the world.*

Arizona Mining Museum
Mineral Bldg.
State Fairgrounds
Phoenix, AZ 85007
phone: 602-255-3791

On-Line Services

Rockhound's Information Page
14407 Big Basin Way, Ste. B
Saratoga, CA 95070
phone: 408-868-9700
fax: 408-868-0314
e-mail: rockhounds-
owner@infodyn.com
Internet: http://www.rahul.net/infodyn/
  rockhounds/
*Great website for rockhound
information: shops and galleries;
images and pictures; books, articles
and other publications; general earth
science information; paleontology-
related sites; collecting sites and
trips; clubs & societies.*

Canadian Rockhound
e-mail: dfs846@mail.ussk.ca
Internet: http://pangea.usask.co/~dfs846/
  rockhound/home.html
*An on-line magazine providing
interesting and educational stories on
rock, fossil and mineral collecting, the
art of lapidary, gems and faceting,
and on the earth sciences as well.*

Smithsonian Gem & Mineral Collection,
  National Museum of Natural History
10th St. & constitution Ave.
Washington, DC 20560
phone: 202-357-1300
*A Smithsonian website with a great
selection of mineral specimen images
with descriptions.*

Periodicals

Heldref Publications
Magazine: Rocks & Minerals
1319 18th St., NW
Washington, DC 20036-1802
phone: 800-365-9753 or 202-396-6267
fax: 202-296-5149
*America's oldest popular magazine
about minerals; bi-monthly;
mineralogy, geology, and paleontology.*

James Miller Publications
Magazine: Rock & Gem
4880 Market St.
Ventura, CA 93003
phone: 805-644-3824
A monthly magazine.

MINIATURES

(see also ART, Portraits [Miniature];
BOOKS, Miniature; BOTTLES,
Miniature; BOTTLES, Puzzle;
CHILDREN'S THINGS; DOLL
HOUSES & FURNISHINGS; IRONS,
Pressing [Miniature]; MODELS, Cars;
PIANOS, Miniature; TRUCKS,
Miniature)

Appraisers

Judy Owen, ISA
Antique Appraisers - Grand Traverse
10332 Stoneybeach Pointe
Traverse City, MI 49686
phone: 616-946-2534
fax: 616-946-2573
*Specializing in doll houses and
miniatures.*

Clubs/Associations

John Purcell
National Association of Miniature
  Enthusiasts
Magazine: Miniature Gazette
P.O. Box 69
Carmel, IN 46032
phone: 317-571-8094
*N.A.M.E. serves the miniature
collector and builder; the monthly
magazine contains articles, ads,
dealer listings, etc.*

Sara Benz
Miniature Industry Association of
  America
Newsletter: MIAA Member News
2770 Jacquelyn Dr.
Madison, WI 53711
phone: 608-273-1131
fax: 608-273-1131

Collectors

Betty Bird
107 Ida St.
Mount Shasta, CA 96067-2629
phone: 916-926-4331 or 916-926-2231
*Wants to buy tiny toys, doll house
items, and salesman's samples.*

Experts

Lillian Baker
1013 Medhurst Rd.
Columbus, OH 43220
phone: 614-451-7368
*Author of "Creative and Collectible
Miniatures."*

Misc. Services

Kay Fisher
College of Miniature Knowledge
13757 Upper Cow Creek Rd.
Azalea, OR 97410
phone: 503-837-3743
*Organizes instructional classes in
miniature craftsmanship.*

Museums/Libraries

Museums at Stony Brook, The
Newsletter: News & Events
Rte. 25A Box 1208
Stony Brook, NY 11790-1931
phone: 516-751-0066
fax: 516-751-0353
*Large collection of American Art,
decoys, horse-drawn vehicles,
costumes, and miniature period
rooms; museum shop.*

Toy & Miniature Museum of Delaware
P.O. Box 4053
Wilmington, DE 19807
phone: 302-427-8697

Washington Dolls' House & Toy
  Museum
5236 44th St. NW
Washington, DC 20015
phone: 202-244-0024

Art Institute of Chicago, Thorne
  Miniature Rooms
111 S. Michigan Ave.
Chicago, IL c
phone: 312-443-0849
Internet: http://www.artic.edu/aic/
  firstpage.html

Sandi Russell
Toy & Miniature Museum of Kansas
  City
5235 Oak St.
Kansas City, MO 64112-2877
phone: 816-333-2055 or 816-333-9328
fax: 816-333-2055
*Museum housed in an elegant mansion
features collections of miniatures,
antique dolls' houses and antique
toys.*

Carole & Barry Kay Museum of
  Miniatures
5900 Wilshire Blvd.
Los Angeles, CA 90036
phone: 213-937-6464
Internet: http://museumofminiatures.com

Periodicals

June Stowe, Ed.
Magazine: International Dolls' House
  News
P.O. Box 79
Southampton S09 7EZ, U.K.
*In publication for over 25 years;
specialist magazine devoted to doll
houses and miniatures both old and
new.*

Magazine: Doll Castle News
P.O. Box 247
Washington, NJ 07882
phone: 201-689-6513 or 201-689-7042
fax: 908-689-6320
*A magazine focusing on dolls,
miniatures, doll houses and related
items; ads, paper doll section,
needlework, patterns, etc.*

Scott Publications
Magazine: Miniature Collector
30595 Eight Mile
Livonia, MI 48152-1761
phone: 800-458-8237 or 810-477-6650
fax: 810-477-6795
e-mail: 104137.1254@compuserve.com
*An international bi-monthly glossy
publication devoted exclusively to
contemporary and antique scale
miniatures: artists, manufacturers,
retailers, suppliers, collectors, room
settings, etc.*

Sybil Harp
Kalmbach Publishing Co.
Magazine: Nutshell News
P.O. Box 1612
Waukesha, WI 53187-1612
phone: 414-796-8776 or 800-533-6644
fax: 414-796-1383
e-mail: customerservice@kalmbach.com
*Monthly magazine with techniques,
how-to's, projects, plans, collections,
artists profiles, reviews of miniature
shows, extensive calendar of events,
etc.*

Repro. Sources

Duane Sylor
49 Horner Rd.
Angelica, NY 14709
phone: 716-466-7700
*Makes & sells authentically crafted 1/
2 scale traditionally painted furniture
accurately copying Early American
examples; great for dolls, teddies, tots.*

Little House of Miniatures
615 Sycamore St.
Waterloo, IA 50703-4725
phone: 319-233-6585
*Complete mail-order source for
dollhouse miniatures: wallpaper,
carpet, electric wiring, building
supplies, etc.*

Airplanes

(see also AVIATION MEMORA-
BILIA; TOYS, Airplane Related)

Clubs/Associations

Robert A. Blaney, Sec.
International Miniature Aircraft
Association, Inc.
3380 14 Parkview Rd.
Long Valley, NJ 07853

MINING RELATED ITEMS

(see also INDUSTRY RELATED
ITEMS; MINERALS; SCRIP;
SOCIAL CAUSES; STOCKS &
BONDS, Mining Related)

Appraisers

Robert L. Johnson
Whistles in the Woods Museum Services
P.O. Box 309
Chickamauga, GA 30707-0309
phone: 706-375-4326
e-mail: oldgoat@voy.net
*Consultants specializing in 1750 -
early 20th century historic machinery;*

*power-generation, tools, machines,
scientific & technical instruments,
mining, milling, transportation,
logging & lumbering, steam engines,
etc.*

Collectors

David C. Crawford
1308 Halsted Rd.
Rockford, IL 61103
phone: 815-637-6720
*Wants to buy all mining items: oil,
safety, and carbide lamps; blasting
cap tins, photos, postcards; United
Mine Workers of America, Western
Federation of Miners, and local union
ribbons, banners, and patches.*

John M. Shannon
7319 West Cedar Circle
Lakewood, CO 80226-2019
phone: 303-232-1534
e-mail: rovers@aol.com
*Wants to buy mining memorabilia
including assay balances (wood and
glass encased with small pans) - both
laboratory and portable; also wants
brass scientific instruments.*

Dealers

Leo Stambaugh
Powder Cache Antiques
P.O. Box 779
Georgetown, CO 80444-0779
phone: 800-651-2848 or 303-569-2109
*Wants to buy mining books, catalogs,
photos, equipment, maps; anything
mining related and pre-1930,
especially from Colorado.*

Warren Anderson
America West Archives
P.O. Box 100
Cedar City, UT 84721-0100
phone: 801-586-9497 or 801-586-7323
*Buys and sells pre-1920 mining
related documents including letters,
maps, photos, checks, stock
certificates, prospectuses, etc.; author
of "Owning Western History."*

John & Karen Mediz
Copper City Rock Shop
566 Ash St.
Globe, AZ 85501
phone: 520-425-7885 or 520-425-4506
fax: 520-425-4506
*Buys and sells mining artifacts; also
wants to buy minerals and fossils,
especially old collections.*

Museums/Libraries

Pennsylvania State University Earth &
Mineral Sciences Museum & Art
Gallery
Streidle Bldg. On Pollack Rd.
State College, PA 16802
phone: 814-865-6427
e-mail: sicree@geosc.psu.edu
*Displays of minerals, materials,
gemstones, and art work related to
mining; displays of old lamps and
other mining artifacts.*

Matchless Mine Museum
414 W. 7th St.
Leadville, CO 80461
phone: 719-486-0371

Bisbee Mining & Historical Museum
P.O. Box 14
Bisbee, AZ 85603
phone: 602-432-7071

Old Mint Museum
5th & Mission Sts.
San Francisco, CA 94103
phone: 415-744-6830
*Collection of coins, numismatic items,
and mining equipment and related
items.*

Periodicals

Jim Van Fleat
Magazine: Eureka
222 Market St.
Mifflinburg, PA 17844
phone: 717-966-3308

Ted Bobrink
Newsletter: Mining Artifact Collector,
The
34612 Avenue B
Yucaipa, CA 92399-4185

Coal Mining

Collectors

William Blake
506 Driftwood Dr. Lot A
Charleston, WV 25306-6306
phone: 304-925-3780
*Coal mine items wanted; all
categories: carbide lights, safety
lamps, oil wicks, etc.*

Museums/Libraries

Museum of Anthracite Mining
Pine & 17th St.
Ashland, PA 17921
phone: 717-875-4708

Colorado

Collectors

George Foott
6683 S. Yukon Way
Littleton, CO 80123-3071
phone: 303-979-8688
*Wants to buy early Western mining
memorabilia (especially Colorado):
photographs, maps, promotional
pamphlets, books, mining directories,
miners' candleholders; also wants Old
West cattle brand books, saddle
catalogs, cowboy items.*

Lamps

(see also LAMPS & LIGHTING)

Clubs/Associations

Henry A. Pohs
Old Mine Lamp Collectors Society of
America
Newsletter: Underground Lamp Post,
The
4537 Quitman St.
Denver, CO 80212-2535
phone: 303-455-3922
*Focuses on old non-electric mining
lamps and related items.*

Collectors

Brian Williamson
4690 Springgate Dr.
Powder Springs, GA 30073
phone: 404-439-7003
*Buys, sells, restores and specializes in
older carbide mining lamps, especially
those made by Justrite, Baldwin,
Autolite, etc.; also interested in lamp
parts and in British mining lamps.*

John W. Coons
9757 S. Isabel Ct.
Littleton, CO 80126
phone: 303-791-6496
*Wants to buy mining lamps,
candlestick holders, carbide lamps.*

Experts

Henry A. Pohs
4537 Quitman St.
Denver, CO 80212-2535
phone: 303-455-3922
*Mine lighting historian; buys, sells,
trades old non-electric mining lamps
and related items; author of two books
on the subject.*

MIRRORS

(see POCKET MIRRORS; REPAIR/
RESTORATION/CONSERVATION,
Mirrors)

MISSILES

(see ROCKETS; SPACE COL-
LECTIBLES)

MISSION STYLE

(see ARTS & CRAFTS; COPPER
ITEMS, Stickley; FURNITURE
[ANTIQUE], Stickley)

MIXERS

(see KITCHEN COLLECTIBLES,
Eggbeaters; KITCHEN COL-
LECTIBLES, Mixers)

MOBILE HOMES

(see TRAILERS & RV'S)

MODEL KITS

(see KITS)

MODELS

(see also AIRLINE MEMORABILIA, Models [Desk]; AIRPLANES, Model; KITS; MILITARY HISTORY; NAUTICAL ANTIQUES, Models; SOLDIERS, Toy; STEAM-OPERATED; TOYS, Diecast; TOYS, Hess Trucks; TRAINS)

Dealers

Toys for Collectors
P.O. Box 1406
North Attleboro, MA 02763
phone: 508-695-0588 or 508-695-6966
If you collect models of cars, trucks, fire trucks, construction equipment, cranes, buses, race cars, NASCARS, etc. this is the source for better quality 1/43 scale models as well as 1/50, 1/18 and 1/14 scale models.

Colleen Lewis
Buffalo Road Hobby
10120 Main St.
Clarence, NY 14031-2049
phone: 716-759-7541
fax: 716-759-7462
e-mail: pcc@toyline.com
Internet: http://www.toyline.com/pcc
Dealer, collector, appraiser, distributor of construction scale models; also diecast scale model military vehicles, aircraft, ships, soldiers; also replacement parts for old models.

Museums/Libraries

Paul Cardwell, Jr.
Hippogriff
1127 Cedar
Bonham, TX 75418
phone: 903-583-3218
A private library (not located at this address) of over 9,000 model periodicals and books; send $1 and SASE for listings on a given subject; covers all model subjects including static and operating; copies of drawings made for small fee.

Periodicals

Raymond G. Strutt
Newspaper: Collectors Gazette
18 Calvert Close
West Park Heights, Uckfield
East Sussex TN22 2BZ, U.K.
phone: +44 (0) 1825 768776
fax: +44 (0) 1825 760600
e-mail: cliente@icn.co.uk
Internet: http://www.icn.co.uk/cg.html
Published 10 times per year for toy and model collectors worldwide; covers tinplate toys, obsolete and modern diecast cars (Corgi, Dinky, Matchbox, EFE, Lledo, Days Gone, etc.) and models, trains, airplanes, ships, dolls, etc.

Robert Thomason
Newspaper: American Modeler
P.O. Box 1446
Raleigh, NC 27602-1446
phone: 919-662-9334
fax: 919-662-9334
e-mail: agencyfoto@aol.com
Bi-monthly publication of scale modeling news and features; construction, collections, competition events, news from model manufacturers, products and services section, clubs, upcoming events, museum collections, etc.

Bob Hayden, Ed.
Magazine: FineScale Modeler
P.O. Box 1612
Waukesha, WI 53187-1612
phone: 414-796-8776
fax: 414-796-1383
e-mail: rhayden@finescale.com
Internet: http://www.finescale.com
For those interested in the scaled-down universe including aircraft, military vehicles, ships, cars or dioramas; how-to tips and techniques, new project ideas and step-by-step instructions that make modeling more fun.

Paul Cardwell, Jr.
Hippogriff Publications
Directory: Index to Model Publications
1127 Cedar
Bonham, TX 75418
phone: 903-583-3218
Publishes an annual index to model publications.

Suppliers

Ernie Weinberg
Superior Aircraft Materials
12020 Centralia Ave. #G
Hawaiian Gardens, CA 90716-1064
phone: 562-865-3220
fax: 562-860-0327
e-mail: balsa@ix.netcom.com
Specializes in supplying wood materials (balsa, spruce, plywood) for the model builder.

Aircraft

Collectors

Charles Martignette
P.O. Box 293
Hallandale, FL 33008
phone: 305-454-3474
Wants to buy travel agency and airport counter displays of model airplanes; please send length, width, height and asking price along with photographs.

Periodicals

Erika Daileda
Wise Owl Worldwide Publications
Magazine: Aeromodeller
4314 West 238th St. - Dept. MACR
Torrance, CA 90505-4509
phone: 310-375-6258
fax: 310-375-0548
e-mail: wiseowl@sprintmail.com
Great Britain's favorite model aircraft magazine; a monthly featuring reviews, plans and news from the world of aircraft modeling and flight.

Erika Daileda
Wise Owl Worldwide Publications
Magazine: Plastic Kit Constructor
4314 West 238th St. - Dept. MACR
Torrance, CA 90505-4509
phone: 310-375-6258
fax: 310-375-0548
e-mail: wiseowl@sprintmail.com
A U.K. quarterly magazine for plastic model aircraft modelers.

Aircraft (Flying)

(see also AIRPLANES, Model [Remote Control])

Periodicals

Ron Firth
PAMAG Publications Ltd.
Magazine: Flying Model Designer & Constructor
3 Lowfield Court
Sark Road, Heeley
Sheffield S2 4HG, U.K.
phone: 0114 255 0641
e-mail: ronald.firth@ukonline.co.uk
A quarterly magazine for flying model aircraft modelers.

Cars

(see also AUTOMOBILIA; KITS; NASCAR; TOYS, Cars; TOYS, Diecast; TOYS, Hess Trucks)

Clubs/Associations

Ben Lawson
Northland Toy Club
Newsletter: Northland News
8 N. Gate Dr.
Albany, NY 12203-5102
Focuses on all kinds of model vehicles.

Ray Denney
Model Car Collectors Association
Journal: Model Car Collectors Association Journal
5113 Sugar Loaf Dr. SW
Roanoke, VA 24018
phone: 703-744-8109
Dedicated to the promotion & enjoyment of the model car hobby; a bi-monthly journal features kit reviews, how-to's, free member ads.

Peter H. Foss
Michigan Model Car Collectors
Newsletter: MMCC Newsletter
33290 W. 14 Mile Rd. #454
West Bloomfield, MI 48322-3549
phone: 810-682-0272
fax: 810-682-5782
A regional chapter of The Toy Car Collectors Club.

Automotive Modelers Society
Newspaper: Scale Wheels
806 S. Ripley
Neosho, MO 64850
Club for builders & collectors of scale vehicles; annual convention, membership roster, local club affiliates, bi-monthly newsletter.

Tucson Miniature Auto Club
Newsletter: Tucson Miniature Auto Club
1111 E. Limberlost Dr., #164
Tucson, AZ 85719-1062
phone: 602-293-3178 or 800-484-1097

Jay Olins
Precision Die Cast Car Collectors Club
Newsletter: PDCCCC Newsletter
P.O. Box 2480
Huntington Beach, CA 92647
phone: 213-500-4355
e-mail: jay@via.net
Internet: http://www.gennera.com/diecast
For collectors of Danbury Mint and Franklin Mint models and all other precision die cast models; published bi-monthly newsletter with photos and reviews of new models, classifieds, etc.

Bill Goddard
1/87th Scale Vehicle & Equipment Club, The
P.O. Box 382
Brentwood, CA 94513-0382
Covers intermodal, modern truck, vintage vehicles and equipment, military, logging, carnival, emergency, construction, bus and coach, maintenance and automobiles, all in 1/87th scale.

Collectors

Ken Katz
354 Townline Rd.
Commack, NY 11725-1423
phone: 516-462-5808
fax: 516-499-0366
Internet: http://www.kennyskars.com
Wants models of automotive vehicles: plastic, friction, built or unbuilt kits, promotional models.

Dealers

MODELAUTO
P.O. Box SM2
Leeds LS25 5XA, U.K.
phone: 0113-2686685
fax: 01977-681991
e-mail: hotline@modelauto.co.uk
Internet: http://www.modelauto.co.uk
Worldwide mail order specializing in 1:43 and 1:50 scales, but other models stocked as well; see

advertisement in "Model Auto Review."

Dean Klein
Distinctive Die-Cast Inc.
P.O. Box 656
Tallman, NY 10982
phone: 914-357-3382
Specializing in Dinky and Corgi diecast toys.

Tailfin Productions
2014 Green Juniper Ln.
Brandon, FL 33511
phone: 813-684-3785
Buys and sells model car kits from the 1950s to present; promos, original auto art, and relate items.

Trader Rick's Collectible Toy Cars
P.O. Box 161
Newark, IL 60541
phone: 815-695-9484
Wants to buy toy cars and model cars; also built or unbuilt car kits.

Man./Prod./Dist.

Miniature Cars USA, Inc.
369 Springfield Ave.
P.O. Box 188
Berkeley Heights, NJ 07922
phone: 908-665-7811 or 908-665-7812
fax: 908-665-7814
Internet: http://www.eracars.com
Carries North America's largest inventory of scale model automobiles - over 90,000 in stock from 350 manufacturers including many rare and hard-to-find pieces.

Misc. Services

Edward Soltis
68 Spruce St.
Stratford, CT 06497-7903
Will quote price for building any kit; 1/25th plastic kits, 1/43 and 1/25 diecasts, etc.; ask for pictures; many satisfied customers.

Periodicals

Magazine: Model Auto Review
P.O. Box SM2
Leeds LS25 5XA, U.K.
phone: 0113-2686685
fax: 01977-681991
e-mail: hotline@modelauto.co.uk
Internet: http://www.modelauto.co.uk
MAR is a bi-monthly glossy magazine with many color and b/w photos; covering model cars, trucks, buses, military vehicles.

Magazine: Model Collector
Link House, Dingwall Avenue
Croydon
Surrey CR9 2TA, U.K.
phone: 0181 686 2599
A glossy monthly English with detailed articles about old and new model cars, buses, trucks, motorcycles, trains, etc.; new releases; lots of advertisements.

Bill Reed
Magazine: Diecast Digest
P.O. Box 12510
Knoxville, TN 37912-0510
phone: 615-922-1091
fax: 615-922-1614
A monthly magazine focusing on diecast model cars including NASCAR and Formula 1; articles, advertising, models.

Model Collectors Warehouse
Magazine: Model Collectors Digest
P.O. Box 8943
Waukegan, IL 60079-8943
Focuses primarily on model cars.

Jeff Atkinson
Newsletter: Traders Horn
1903 Schoettler Valley Rd.
Chesterfield, MO 63017-5203
phone: 314-532-3871
The oldest, largest bi-monthly periodical dedicated to the sales, trading of diecast toy vehicles, promotional models, model kits; obsolete, rare, current automotive & other transportation miniatures and related memorabilia; all scales.

Dennis Doty
MCJ Associates
Magazine: Model Car Journal
P.O. Box 154135
Irving, TX 75015-4135
phone: 972-790-5346
fax: 972-790-5346
Complete coverage of the model car hobby; kits, diecast, promos, resin models, histories, events list, ads, how-to's; since 1974.

Cars (Dinky)

Clubs/Associations

Jerry Fralick
Dinky Toy Club of America
Newsletter: DTCA Newsletter
P.O. Box 11
Highland, MD 20777
phone: 301-854-2217
fax: 301-854-2217
For Dinky collectors.

Cars (Spon-On)

Clubs/Associations

Bruce Sterling
Spon-On Collectors Club
185 West Houston St.
New York, NY 10014

Engines

Clubs/Associations

Danny Bynum
Gas Toy Collector's Association
P.O. Box 440181
Houston, TX 77244-0818
phone: 713-531-5711

Collectors

Joe Balsam
#4 Pickwick Hills Dr.
Huntington Station, NY 11746-1241
phone: 516-271-3267
Wants to buy pre-1955 model airplane, car, and boat engines; also wants model race cars and other related items.

Danny Bynum
P.O. Box 440181
Houston, TX 77244-0818
phone: 713-531-5711
Wants to buy old model engines, Cox Thimble Drone Cars, airplanes, boats, old gas powered toy cars.

Bill Bickel
3121 W. Cavedale Dr.
Phoenix, AZ 85027-7637
phone: 602-582-0211
Wants to buy or trade for old model plane engines and gas powered race cars; also wants gas powered planes and cars that were originally sold as ready-to-run toys; incomplete or damaged items and parts also wanted.

Periodicals

Robert A. Washburn, Ed.
Magazine: Strictly I.C.
24920 43th Ave. S.
Kent, WA 98032
fax: 206-946-5253
A bi-monthly periodical of information promoting the design and construction of internal combustion miniature model engines in the home shop.

Trucks & Equipment (Winross)

Clubs/Associations

Winross Collectors Club of America
Newsletter: Winross Collectors Club of America Newsletter
18 W. Main St.
P.O. Box 444
Mount Joy, PA 17552-0444
phone: 717-653-7327
fax: 717-653-1247
The purpose of this organization is to share and preserve the common interest of dedication to the collection and preservation of 1/64-inch scale Winross trucks; monthly newsletter.

Man./Prod./Dist.

Winross
Newsletter: Collector Series
P.O. Box 38
Palmyra, NY 14522-0038
phone: 800-227-2060 or 315-998-6306
fax: 315-986-3849
Internet: http://www.winross.com

MODERNISM

(see also ART, Outsider; ART DECO; CERAMICS [AMERICAN], Russel Wright Designs; ELECTRICITY RELATED ITEMS, Appliances; GLASS, Italian; POPULAR CULTURE; SOCIAL CAUSES)

Auction Services

David Rago
17 Main St.
Lambertville, NJ 08530
phone: 609-397-9374
fax: 609-397-9377
e-mail: rago@ragoarts.com
Internet: http://www.ragoarts.com
Specializing in the sale of 20th century decorative and applied arts from 1920 to present.

Don Treadway
Treadway Gallery
2029 Madison Rd.
Cincinnati, OH 45208
phone: 513-321-6742 or 800-526-0491
fax: 513-871-7722
Internet: http://www.treadwaygallery.com
Special auction sales of 1950s/Modern design.

L.A. Modern Auctions
P.O. Box 462006
Los Angeles, CA 90046
phone: 213-845-9456

Collectors

John M. England, Jr.
P.O. Box 59136
Schaumburg, IL 60159-0136
phone: 708-823-5287
Buys, collects, and sells machine age design, Art Deco and Moderne furnishings, radios.

Dealers

Dennis Bradbury
Deco Reflections
44 Market St.
Amesbury, MA 01913-2424
phone: 508-388-6250
fax: 508-388-6250
Specializing in items from the 20th century: Chase chrome, Manhattan glass, kitchen appliances, toasters, blenders, lamps & lighting, clocks, dinnerware, furniture, and costume jewelry.

Normand Mainville
Machine Age
354 Congress St.
Boston, MA 02210
phone: 617-482-0048
Buys and sells vintage modern furniture and decorative arts from the '30s to the '50s: desks, chairs, lamps, vases, ceramics, radios, telephones, ashtrays, sofas, clocks, fans, irons, mirrors, toys, globes, toasters, blenders, etc.

City Barn Antiques
362 Atlantic Ave.
Brooklyn, NY 11217
phone: 718-855-8566
Buys and sells mid-century modern furniture, lighting and accessories: Herman Miller, Knoll, Conanc Ball, Heywood-Wakefield, Widdicomb, John Stuart, Simmons, Chase, Frankart.

Catch It All
159 N. 3rd St.
Philadelphia, PA 19106
phone: 215-627-0299

Suite Lorain
7105 Lorain Ave.
Cleveland, OH 44102
phone: 216-281-1959
*Specializes in Deco to 1950s: vintage
fabric, kitchen kitsch, ceramics and
glass, lighting, Herman Miller,
Heywood-Wakefield, Eames, Saarinen,
Herman Miller, clocks, televisions,
radios.*

Steve Hachen
2109 Luray Ave.
Cincinnati, OH 45206-2630
phone: 513-221-1959
*Wants 1950s accessories and designer
furniture by Herman Miller, Charles
Eames, George Nelson, Knoll, Harry
Bertoia, Russell Wright, Eero
Saarinen, Isamu Noguchi.*

Don Treadway
Treadway Gallery
2029 Madison Rd.
Cincinnati, OH 45208
phone: 513-321-6742 or 800-526-0491
fax: 513-871-7722
Internet: http://
www.treadwaygallery.com
*Wants to buy mid-20th century
"modern design" furniture and
decorative arts by designers Charles
and Ray Eames, Kem Weber, Gio
Ponti, George Nakashima, Isamu
Noguchi, George Nelson, Herman
Miller, Lloyd Manufacture, Troy, etc.*

Lee Hay
Weird & Wonderful
P.O. Box 14898
Cincinnati, OH 45250-0898
phone: 513-621-6034
fax: 513-621-6448
e-mail: heywood@sprintmail.com
*Wants to buy Peter Max, 1960's
protest items, books on 1930-1970
designers; strange one-of-a-kind items
from the 1930s through the 1970s.*

Connie Zeigler
Durwyn Smedley Antiques
853 Conner St.
Noblesville, IN 46060
phone: 317-776-0161
e-mail: smedley@iquest.net
Internet: http://www.smedley.com/
smedley
*Buys, sells and appraises upscale Mid
20th Century Modern designs
including furniture, pottery, lighting,
metalwork, textiles, fine art, and other
decorative items.*

Steve Savitt
Josie's
545 Ridge Rd.
Wilmette, IL 60091-2439
phone: 847-256-7646
fax: 847-256-7004
Specializes in Art Deco, 20th Century

*Modern, art pottery, art glass and
jewelry; no reproductions.*

Zig Zag
3419 North Lincoln Ave.
Chicago, IL 60657
phone: 312-525-1060
*Buys, sells, and rents Art Deco and
Moderne furnishings, Bakelite jewelry,
industrial design, radios, purses, etc.*

Urban Artifacts
2928 N. Lincoln
Chicago, IL 60657-4109
phone: 773-404-1008
*Buys and sells vintage modern
furniture and decorative arts from the
'40s to the '70s.*

20th Century Classics
3017-B Routh St.
Dallas, TX 75201
phone: 214-880-0020
fax: 214-351-6208
*Wants 20th century collectibles:
Knoll, H. Miller, Juhl, Artlo, Noguchi,
Venini, etc.*

Citi Modern
2928 Main St.
Dallas, TX 75226
phone: 214-651-9200
*Buys and sells 1950s and 1960s
modern, futurist, Heywood-Wakefield,
microphones, lighting, Bakelite,
industrial design.*

Aqua
1415 S. Congress
Austin, TX 78704-2434
phone: 512-916-8800
fax: 512-916-8800
*Herman Miller, ethnic, 20th century
modern, architectural.*

Frank Novak
7386 Beverly Blvd.
Los Angeles, CA 90036
phone: 213-683-1963
fax: 213-638-1312

David Skelley
Boomerang
3795 Park Blvd.
San Diego, CA 92103
phone: 619-295-1953
*Buys and sells 20th century modern
design items; top quality Knoll,
Herman-Miller; American and
European.*

Jet Age
250 Oak St.
San Francisco, CA 94102
phone: 415-864-1950
*Buys and sells classic modern
furnishings from the 1930s to 1960s;
Art Deco, '30s and '40s modern,
Eames, Nelson, Noguchi, Saarinen,
Bertoia, Aalto, Herman-Miller, Knoll,
etc.*

Peter & Deborah Keresztury
Deco to 50s
1217 Waterview Dr.
Mill Valley, CA 94941-3412
Wants to buy furniture, accessories,

*rugs, art, fabric, jewelry, and
decorative objects of the 20th century.*

Wrinkled Bohemia
1125 Pike
Seattle, WA 98101
phone: 206-464-0850
*Buys and sells mid-20th century
furniture, dishware, and decorative
arts by Russell Wright, Eva Zeisel,
Charles and Ray Eames, Ken Weber,
Noguchi, George Nelson, Herman
Miller, Knoll Associates, Paul
McCobb, Heywood-Wakefield, etc.*

Biff Brayman
Laguna
5828 Roosevelt Way
Seattle, WA 98105
*Specializes in 20th century dinner-
ware.*

Experts

Jan Lindenberger
P.O. Box 7224
Colorado Springs, CO 80933
phone: 719-591-9558
fax: 719-591-9558
*Buys and sells '50s and '60s
memorabilia; author of "'50s-'60s
Memorabilia - Information & Price
Guide" (Schiffer Pub., 1993).*

Steve Cabella
Modern "i", The
500 Red Hill Ave.
San Anselmo, CA 94960-2409
phone: 415-456-3960
*Collecting modern furniture, products
and design facts for over 20 years;
specialize in the work of Ray and
Charles Eames; also always buying
50s modernist craft jewelry and
ceramics; settle estates of artists,
architects, designers.*

Museums/Libraries

Annabel Hanson
Walter Gropius House, Society for the
Preservation of New England
Antiquities
68 Baker Bridge Rd.
Lincoln, MA 01773
phone: 617-259-8098 or 617-227-3957
fax: 617-227-9204
*Designed and lived in by architect
Walter Gropius (founder of the
German design school known as
Bauhaus), SPNEA's Gropius House is
open to the public; house tours run
regularly; admission charged.*

Periodicals

Scott Cheverie
Deco Echoes Publications
Magazine: Echoes Magazine
P.O. Box 2321
Mashpee, MA 02649-8321
phone: 508-428-2324 or 800-695-5768
fax: 508-428-0077
e-mail: hey@deco-echoes.com
Internet: http://www.deco-echoes.com
*Glossy, elegantly designed quarterly
dedicated to the styles & designs of*

*the mid-20th C.; emphasis on 1920s-
1960s eras including Art Deco,
Streamline Moderne, Biomorphic
'50s, Abstract '60s styles and
movements from kitsch to high-end.*

Heywood-Wakefield

Dealers

Lee Hay
Weird & Wonderful
P.O. Box 14898
Cincinnati, OH 45250-0898
phone: 513-621-6034
fax: 513-621-6448
e-mail: heywood@sprintmail.com
*Wants to buy Heywood-Wakefield
advertising pieces, catalogs, and
furniture.*

Cadillac Jack
2820 Gilroy St.
Los Angeles, CA 90039
phone: 800-775-5078
*Featuring the largest selection of
Heywood-Wakefield furniture in the
country; total restoration available;
buy, sell, trade.*

Experts

Lee Stanley
Antique Store, An
1450 W. Webster Ave.
Chicago, IL 60614-3050
phone: 773-935-6060
fax: 773-871-6660
*Buys, sells, appraises Heywood-
Wakefield furniture and original
catalogs, signs, advertising, etc.; also
wants Dunbar and Widdicomb
furniture catalogs, brochures, etc.*

Peter Max

Collectors

Bill Triola
1114 E. Mt. Hope Ave.
Lansing, MI 48910
phone: 517-332-1203 or 517-331-7387
fax: 517-484-3480

Dealers

Lee Hay
Weird & Wonderful
P.O. Box 14898
Cincinnati, OH 45250-0898
phone: 513-621-6034
fax: 513-621-6448
e-mail: heywood@sprintmail.com
Wants to buy Peter Max memorabilia.

MOLDS

(see also KITCHEN COL-
LECTIBLES)

Butter

Collectors

Priscilla Hinners
2711 Jaynia Place
Lemon Grove, CA 91945-1319
phone: 619-265-1046
e-mail: mhinners@aol.com
Wants butter molds, stamps, multiple prints, rollers.

Dealers

Carleton L. Cotting
1441 Crowell Rd.
Vienna, VA 22182-1512
phone: 703-759-5646
Collects, buys and sells butter molds and stamps.

Repro. Sources

M & M Enterprises
P.O. Box 185
Atkins, VA 24311
Sells 1/2 lb. round reproduction wooden butter molds with either a starburst or a cow design.

M & M Enterprises
P.O. Box 185
Atkins, VA 24311

Holcraft
P.O. Box 792
Davis, CA 95616

Candy

Collectors

Priscilla Hinners
2711 Jaynia Place
Lemon Grove, CA 91945-1319
phone: 619-265-1046
e-mail: mhinners@aol.com
Wants candy molds, chocolate, maple sugar, rollers, etc.

Museums/Libraries

Wilbur's Americana Candy Museum
48 N. Broad St.
Lititz, PA 17543-1026
phone: 717-626-3249

Chocolate

Collectors

Shirley Baumann
21090 Floyd Ave.
Iowa Falls, IA 50126
Wants any two-piece mold.

Experts

Lorry & Bruce Hanes
Dad's Follies
40 Kingston Ct.
Gibsonville, NC 27249-3353
phone: 910-449-0494
fax: 910-449-9670
Buys, sells, and specializes in ice cream molds; carries large inventory of tin and pewter chocolate and ice cream molds.

Ice Cream

Experts

Lorry & Bruce Hanes
Dad's Follies
40 Kingston Ct.
Gibsonville, NC 27249-3353
phone: 910-449-0494
fax: 910-449-9670
Buys, sells, and specializes in ice cream molds; carries large inventory of tin and pewter chocolate and ice cream molds.

Allan Mellis
Mr. Ice Cream
1115 W. Montana
Chicago, IL 60614-2220
phone: 773-327-9123
fax: 773-327-9456
e-mail: mellis@enteract.com
Wants postcards, pewter molds, ice cream trays, and ice cream-related watch fobs, magazines, valentines, buttons, ice cream and soda fountain real photo postcards, trade cards, pre-1920 ephemera, and supply catalogs.

MONEY

(see BANKING; CIVIL WAR ARTIFACTS, Currency; COINS & CURRENCY; CREDIT CARDS & CHARGE ITEMS; MONEYCARDS; TELEPHONE CARDS; WOODEN MONEY)

MONEY CLIPS

(see CUFF LINKS)

MONEYCARDS

(see also BANKING; CIVIL WAR ARTIFACTS, Currency; COINS & CURRENCY; CREDIT CARDS & CHARGE ITEMS; TELEPHONE CARDS; WOODEN MONEY)

Periodicals

Amos Press, Inc.
Magazine: Moneycard
911 Vandemark Rd.
Sidney, OH 45365
phone: 513-498-0879
fax: 513-498-0876
e-mail: mchurch@eri.com
Internet: http://hmt.com/moneycard/index.html

MONSTER COLLECTIBLES

(see CHARACTER COLLECTIBLES; COMIC BOOKS; HORROR; SCIENCE FICTION; TELEVISION SHOWS & MEMORABILIA; MOVIE MEMORABILIA; TOYS, Monsters; UFO'S & UNEXPLAINED PHENOMENA)

MONUMENT REPLICAS

(see SOUVENIR & COMMEMORA-TIVE ITEMS, Buildings)

MORBID & ODD ITEMS

(see also CIRCUS COLLECTIBLES; FUNERAL ITEMS; SCIENCE FICTION; RIPLEY'S BELIEVE IT OR NOT!; SKELETONS; SHRUNKEN HEADS; UFO'S & UNEXPLAINED PHENOMENA)

Museums/Libraries

Mutter Museum, The
19 South 22nd St.
Philadelphia, PA 19103
phone: 215-563-3737
Collection consists of antique medical instruments, rare anatomical specimens, and medical curiosities: the Soap Lady, Balloon Man, anatomical Hall of Fame, latex eyeballs, swallowed objects including ammunition.

Harvey Lee Boswell
Palace of Wonders Museum
P.O. Box 446
Elm City, NC 27822-0446
Wants to buy anything strange, odd and unusual: Tibetan items, 2-headed calf, shrunken head, mummy, skeleton, tombstones, antique funeral items, mounted reptiles/fish/animals, circus & carnival sideshow items, jungle weapons, etc.

MORMON ITEMS

Dealers

Neil Burnett
P.O. Box 1
Provo, UT 84603
phone: 801-373-1111
Wants old Mormon books, old pamphlets, histories, etc.

Warren Anderson
America West Archives
P.O. Box 100
Cedar City, UT 84721-0100
phone: 801-586-9497 or 801-586-7323
Buying and selling documents, letters, autographs and other types of printed ephemera related to Mormonism; author of "Owning Western History."

MOTOR SCOOTERS

(see also MOTORCYCLES)

Collectors

Howard Murrill
826 DeWitt Dr.
Lenoir City, TN 37772-5514
phone: 423-986-3042
e-mail: hmurrill@ix.netcom.com
Wants unrestored motor scooters and parts, especially Cushman, Silver Pigeon, Vespa, Powell, Autoglide, Salsbury, Fuji Rabbit, Zun Dap, Doodlebug; must be 30 years old or older; also need cycle license plates, Cushman signs.

Cushman

Clubs/Associations

Tom O'Hara, Sec.
Cushman Club of America
Magazine: Cushman Club of America Member Magazine
P.O. Box 661
Union Springs, AL 36089-0661
phone: 205-738-3874
Dedicated to the preservation and restoration of Cushman Motor Scooters.

MOTORCYCLES

(see also AUTOMOBILIA; MAGAZINES, Motorcycle; MOTOR SCOOTERS)

Auction Services

Jerry Wood
J. Wood Co. Auctioneers
P.O. Box 852
Searsport, ME 04974
phone: 207-548-2113 or 901-795-8895
fax: 207-548-2100

Clubs/Associations

Long Island Classic Motorcycle Club of New York
18 Burnett St.
Southampton, NY 11968

American Motorcycle Association
P.O. Box 6114
Westerville, OH 43081
phone: 614-891-2425
Has over 200,000 members.

Dick Winger, Mem.
Antique Motorcycle Club of America
Magazine: Antique Motorcycle, The
P.O. Box 300
Sweetser, IN 46987-0300
phone: 317-384-5421
fax: 317-384-7002
A club of 6000 members worldwide dedicated to the preservation, restoration and enjoyment of antique motorcycles; have approximately 8-10 shows and swap meets, and road rides around the country each year.

Women on Wheels
Magazine: WOW Magazine
P.O. Box 546
Sparta, WI 54656-9546
phone: 800-322-1969 or 608-269-0241
fax: 608-269-0231
e-mail: wowmag@centuryinter.net
Internet: http://cpdmp.arme.cornell.edu/WOW/WOW-off.html
Has over 65 chapters in the US and Canada; over 1500 members.

Collectors

Ken Kiczynski
1075 W. Chestnut St.
Union, NJ 07083-6767
phone: 908-688-9475
Wants to buy old motorcycles, motorcycle toys, parts, literature, memorabilia, anything motorcycle.

Ed Natale, Jr.
P.O. Box 222
Wyckoff, NJ 07481
phone: 201-848-8485
fax: 201-891-4252
*Wants motorcycle related item: club/
gang items such as photos, pins; also
oil cans, tools, literature, advertising,
clothing, pre-1970s license plates,
trinkets, etc.; photos helpful.*

Kevin Flanagan
P.O. Box 503
Rockaway, NJ 07866
phone: 201-328-3027
*Wants to buy motorcycles, parts,
literature, memorabilia, motorcycle
toys, pre-1950, motorcycle watch fobs
and stick pins.*

Wayne R. Batten
RFD 3 #259 Jackson Rd.
Berlin, NJ 08009
phone: 609-767-5994
*Serious collector interested in buying
antique motorcycles, related
memorabilia, or related items
pertaining to motorcycles: parts,
tools, basket cases, trophies, toys,
photos, advertisement, accessories;
one item or collection.*

Herb Glass
RD 1 Box 506A
Pine Bush, NY 12566-9778
phone: 914-361-3657
*Wants to buy antique American pre-
1920 motorcycles, motorcycle
literature and motorcycle advertising
items: factory sales catalogs, manuals,
magazines, pins, fobs, trophies,
medals, etc.*

Bob "Sprocket" Eckardt
P.O. Box 172
Gansevoort, NY 12866-0172
phone: 518-584-2405
*Buys motorcycle memorabilia:
literature, posters, toys, trophies,
medals, fobs, pennants, programs,
photos, jerseys, F.A.M., AMA, Gypsy
tour items, advertising items, clocks,
signs, showroom items; anything to do
with motorcycles.*

Jack C. Bishop
RD 1 Box 439
Montgomery, PA 17752-9733
phone: 717-547-2578
*A collector of pre-1970 European and
antique American motorcycles,
clothing, pins, literature, and
advertising.*

Richard L. Weiss
RD 2 Box 641
Breinigsville, PA 18031
phone: 610-285-4122
*Specialized wants: Smith, Briggs &
Stratton, Merkel, Steffy motor wheels;
Whizzer & pre-1940 American
motorcycles; whole or parts.*

Dealers

Chris Savino
P.O. Box 419
Breesport, NY 14816-0419
phone: 607-739-3106
fax: 607-739-3106
*Dealer and collector wants to buy
motorcycle literature, pins, awards,
motorcycles, clothing, toys, shop
signs, old parts inventory, motorcycle
license plates, dealer plates; anything
motorcycle!*

David Gaylin
Motor Cycle Days
P.O. Box 9686
Rosedale, MD 21237
phone: 410-665-6295
*Author of "Triumph Motorcycles in
America," (1993) and "Triumph
Motorcycle Restoration Guide,"
(1997); always seeking original
motorcycle literature, art, especially
from British and Japanese makers;
also wants motorcycle movie posters.*

Clarke's Classic Cycles
4908 SW 36th Ct.
Hollywood, FL 33023-6939
*Buys and sells British and American
classic motorcycles and scooters.*

Gainsville Cycle
2509 Linebaugh Rd.
Xenia, OH 45385-9512
*Buys and sells modern and classic
motorcycles including German,
Italian, British and Japanese.*

Mick Stamm
Antique & Vintage Motorcycles
3401 S. 1st
Abilene, TX 79605-1708
phone: 915-676-8788
*American motorcycles, parts,
advertising items, Harley/Indian
dealer items, signs, clocks, mirrors,
original boxed parts, oil/paint cans,
clothing, toys, jewelry, ash trays,
literature, pins, awards, ribbons, fobs,
license plates.*

Museums/Libraries

Motorcycle Heritage Museum
P.O. Box 6114
Westerville, OH 43081
phone: 614-891-2425
*Museum belongs to the American
Motorcycle Association.*

Rocky Mountain Motorcycle Museum &
Hall of Fame
308 E. Arvada
Colorado Springs, CO 80906-1439
phone: 719-633-5392
*A non-profit Colorado corporation
dedicated to the preservation of early
American motorcycling and the
pioneers of the sport.*

Periodicals

Magazine: Candian Biker Magazine
P.O. Box 4122
Victoria
Brit. Col. V8X 2X4 Canada
phone: 604-384-0333
Internet: http://www.islandnet.com/
~canbike/canbike.html

Buzz Kanter, Pub.
TAM Communications, Inc.
Magazine: Old Bike Journal
6 Prowitt St.
Norwalk, CT 06855-1204
phone: 203-855-0008
fax: 203-852-9980
Internet: http://www.americaniron.com
*For collectors and others interested in
older motorcycles; the best seller in its
field throughout North America;
average of 700-1000 classified ads
per issue; 17 issues per year.*

Buzz Kanter, Pub.
TAM Communications, Inc.
Magazine: American Iron Magazine
6 Prowitt St.
Norwalk, CT 06855-1204
phone: 203-855-0008
fax: 203-852-9980
Internet: http://www.americaniron.com
*For collectors and others interested in
American motorcycles, specifically
Harleys and Indians.*

Luis Hernandez
Magazine: Motorcycle Shopper
Magazine
1353 Herndon Ave.
Deltona, FL 32725-9046
phone: 407-860-1989 or 800-982-4599
fax: 407-574-1014
e-mail: 74047.624@compuserve.com
*A comprehensive buy-sell-trade
monthly magazine distributed
worldwide; covers all brands of
motorcycles and all aspects of the
sport and hobby.*

Magazine: Walneck's Classic Cycle
Trader
P.O. Box 9059
Clearwater, FL 34618-9059
phone: 813-712-0035 or 800-548-8889
fax: 813-712-0034
Internet: http://www.traderonline.com
*Buy, sell, trade; color photos, road
tests, bikes and parts; published
monthly.*

Steve Ferguson, Ed.
National Automobile Dealers Association
Price Guide: N.A.D.A. Official Used Car
Guide
P.O. Box 7800
Costa Mesa, CA 92628
phone: 800-966-6232
fax: 714-556-8715
e-mail: steve.ferguson@nadaguides.com
Internet: http://www.nadaguide.com
*A series of value guides for domestic
and foreign cars, trucks, vans, RV's,
mobile homes, motorcycles,
snowmobiles, and boats, small and
large; also Heavy Duty Trucks and*

*Aircraft Book, car clubs & organiza-
tions, museums.*

Magazine: Rider
2575 Vista Del Mar Dr.
Ventura, CA 93001
phone: 805-667-4100 or 800-926-0484
Covers all motorcycles.

Repair Services

Antique Motorcycle Restoration
14611 N. Nebraska Ave.
Tampa, FL 33613
phone: 813-972-9297
e-mail: 74047.624@compuserve.com
*Complete ground-up restoration;
painting, sheet metal repair, sand
blasting, engine repair, transmission
repair, welding.*

Don Doody
North West Classic Motorcycles
P.O. Box 774
Lynden, WA 98264-0774
fax: 604-530-5077
*Sells and repairs antique Harley and
Indian motorcycles.*

BMW

Clubs/Associations

Vintage BMW Motorcycle Owners, Ltd.
P.O. Box 67
Exeter, NH 03833
phone: 603-772-9799

British

Clubs/Associations

British Iron Association of Connecticut
Newsletter: British Iron Association of
Connecticut Newsletter
P.O. Box 610
Canton, CT 06019

British (Triumph)

Clubs/Associations

John W. Healy
Triumph International Owners Club/
British Motorcycle Association
Newsletter: TIOC/BMA Newsletter
P.O. Box 6676
Holliston, MA 01746-6676
phone: 508-429-4221
fax: 508-429-6213
*Dedicated to the riding, restoration
and racing of Triumph motorcycles;
3,000 members; annual rally in
various parts of the US; newsletter
includes rallies, ads, classifieds, and
varying social and technical articles.*

European

Collectors

Jack C. Bishop
RD 1 Box 439
Montgomery, PA 17752-9733
phone: 717-547-2578
*A collector of pre-1970 European and
antique American motorcycles,*

clothing, pins, literature, and advertising.

Harley-Davidson

Clubs/Associations

Greg & Judy Duray
Competition Network for Harleys
P.O. Box 95881
Hoffman Estates, IL 60195
phone: 708-884-6033

Periodicals

Buzz Kanter, Pub.
TAM Communications, Inc.
Magazine: Thunder Alley
6 Prowitt St.
Norwalk, CT 06855-1204
phone: 203-855-0008
fax: 203-852-9980
Internet: http://www.americaniron.com
Every issue packed with articles which offer everything from hands-on technical explanations, complete with clear photos and diagrams, to profiles and reviews of the parts and people that make up the go-fast Harley world.

Magazine: American Rider
2575 Vista Del Mar Dr.
Ventura, CA 93001
phone: 805-667-4100 or 800-926-0484
A quarterly magazine for the Harley-Davidson enthusiast; historical profiles, technical information, racing coverage, club news, road tests, product evaluations, etc.

Indian

Clubs/Associations

Don Doody
Laughing Indian Riders
Newsletter: Laughing Indian Riders Newsletter
P.O. Box 774
Lynden, WA 98264-0774
fax: 604-530-5077

Museums/Libraries

Charles Manthos, Dir.
Indian Motocycle Museum & Hall of Fame
33 Hendee St.
P.O. Box 90003 Mason Sq. Sta.
Springfield, MA 01139-3003
phone: 413-737-2624

Periodicals

Buzz Kanter, Pub.
TAM Communications, Inc.
Magazine: Indian Motorcycle Illustrated
6 Prowitt St.
Norwalk, CT 06855-1204
phone: 203-855-0008
fax: 203-852-9980
Internet: http://www.americaniron.com
Special interest magazine dedicated to Indian motorcycles, once the most popular motorcycle in the world.

Japanese

Clubs/Associations

Ron Burton
Vintage Japanese Motorcycle Club
Newsletter: Vintage Japanese Motorcycle Club Newsletter
24 Cathy Street
Merrimack, NH 03054-2840
phone: 603-429-2436
fax: 603-424-5589
e-mail: ronvjmc@aol.com
Welcomes collectors, riders, restorers, and racers of vintage Japanese motorcycles; 18 year old club; 800+ members; make contact with others involved in all aspects of vintage and classic Japanese motorcycles.

Don Brown
Classic Japanese Motorcycle Club
Newsletter: Classic Japanese Motorcycle Club Newsletter
3139 Hawkcrest Circle
San Jose, CA 95139
phone: 408-225-3274
fax: 408-629-8850
Dedicated to having fun with pre-1984 Japanese motorcycles; newsletter has information, technical help, and the largest Japanese motorcycle want ad section; free want ads!

Collectors

Ron Burton
24 Cathy Street
Merrimack, NH 03054-2840
phone: 603-429-2436
fax: 603-424-5589
e-mail: ronvjmc@aol.com
Buys/sells/trades/collects vintage and collectible Japanese motorcycles and associated brochures, dealer catalogs, owner's manuals, parts manuals, maintenance manuals, banners, posters, toys, models, parts, accessories, and memorabilia.

Literature

Collectors

S.E. Penning
1242 S. Mountain St.
Visalia, CA 93277-4264
Wants to buy pre-1965 motorcycle dealers' sales brochures, and all other motorcycle advertising and promotional items.

Moto Guzzi

Clubs/Associations

Frank Wedge, Dir.
Moto Guzzi National Owners Club
801 State St.
Larned, KS 67550-2540
Focuses on the collection and restoration of Moto Guzzi motorcycles and related items.

Collectors

Bernard L. Mei
P.O. Box 90
Mazon, IL 60444-0090
Collects, rides and exchanges information with other collectors of Moto Guzzi motorcycles.

Bob Mounce
2108 Church St.
Streator, IL 61364-3831
phone: 815-672-2827
Collects, rides and exchanges information with other collectors of Moto Guzzi motorcycles.

Sidecars

Periodicals

Jim Dodson, Ed.
Magazine: Hack'd
P.O. Box 813
Buckhannon, WV 26201-0813
phone: 304-472-6146
fax: 304-472-7027
Internet: http://www.sidecar.com/HACKD/
The magazine for and about sidecarists.

Suzuki

Clubs/Associations

International Suzuki Owners Club
Newsletter: International Suzuki Owners Club Newsletter
P.O. Box 262613
Houston, TX 77207

Whizzer

Clubs/Associations

Ron Klaus
Classic Bicycle & Whizzer Club of America
Newsletter: CBWCA Newsletter
35769 Simon Dr.
Clinton Township, MI 48035
phone: 810-791-5594
This organization is dedicated to the preservation, restoration and enjoyment of special-interest bicycles and Whizzer Motor Bikes; monthly newsletter.

Collectors

Ron Klaus
35769 Simon Dr.
Clinton Township, MI 48035
phone: 810-791-5594

Don Hooper
9645 Sylvia Ave.
Northridge, CA 91324-1756
phone: 818-772-1721
fax: 818-772-4647
Wants to buy Whizzer bikes, parts, tanks, accessories, literature, etc.

MOTTOES (PICTURE POEMS)

Clubs/Associations

Howard & Sarah Wade
Mad About Mottoes
Newsletter: Mad About Mottoes Newsletter
P.O. Box 325
Orrville, OH 44667-0325
phone: 330-682-8551
fax: 330-682-3655
e-mail: ukdolls@aol.com

Collectors

Howard & Sarah Wade
P.O. Box 325
Orrville, OH 44667-0325
phone: 330-682-8551
fax: 330-682-3655
e-mail: ukdolls@aol.com
Has extensive collection of mottoes and picture poems by Buzza, P.F. Volland, Cincinnati Art Publishers, Mottograph, Buckbee-Grehn, and Gibson.

MOUNTS

(see ANIMAL TROPHIES)

MOVIE MEMORABILIA

(see also AUDIO-VISUAL; AUTOGRAPHS; BROADCASTING; COWBOY HEROES; DISNEY COLLECTIBLES; FAN CLUBS; FILMS; HORROR; MAGAZINES, Movie; PERSONALITIES [MOVIE STARS]; PHOTOGRAPHS, Celebrity; SCIENCE FICTION; STUNTMEN; TELEVISION SHOWS & MEMORABILIA

Appraisers

John Kisch
Separate Cinema
P.O. Box 114
Hyde Park, NY 12538-0114
phone: 914-452-1998
fax: 914-454-7131
e-mail: johnkisck@aol.com
Appraises movie memorabilia of all kinds.

Auction Services

Miles Barton
Sotheby's
34-35 New Bond St.
London W1A 2AA, U.K.
phone: 0171-4938080 or 0171-4085205
fax: 0171-4085911
Conducts regular auctions of movie memorabilia.

Alexandra Peters
Phillips Fine Art & Auctioneers
406 East 79th St.
New York, NY 10022
phone: 212-570-4830
fax: 212-570-2207
Solicits items for sale in their London office; specializes in the sale of jewelry, paintings, prints, silver,

coins, stamps, toys (especially lead soldiers), and movie memorabilia.

Heather Holmberg
Holmberg Auctions
171 Pier Ave., #124
Santa Monica, CA 90405
phone: 213-654-6306
fax: 213-650-7503
e-mail: heather@collectible.com
Internet: http://www.collectible.com
Specializes in the auctioning of motion picture and entertainment memorabilia.

Butterfield & Butterfield
220 San Bruno Ave.
San Francisco, CA 94103-5018
phone: 415-861-7500
fax: 415-553-8678
Specialties include posters, toys, decorative arts, furniture, photography, etc.; the largest full service auction in the west.

Book Sellers

Hollywood Movie Archives
P.O. Box 1566
Apple Valley, CA 92307-0030
phone: 619-242-8569 or 800-596-2350
Sells hard-to-find movie information for the collector & movie buff; star's birthdays and addresses, fan club directories, old theaters, where stars are buried, where to find movie memorabilia, movie star stamps, etc.; brochure available.

Collectors

Bob Havey
P.O. Box 183
North Sullivan, ME 04664-0183
phone: 207-422-3083
fax: 207-422-3430
Wants to buy 1930s-1940s posters, lobby cards, advertising, magazines; anything movie related.

Van Polla
16-64 155 St.
Whitestone, NY 11357
phone: 718-746-0911 or 212-527-6516
Wants to buy Hollywood memorabilia: posters, lobby cards, photos, sheet music, magazines, animation art, TV & radio items, etc.

Bill Simmons
8955 NW 19th St.
Coral Springs, FL 33071-6109
phone: 954-340-0734
Wants all movie memorabilia, autographs, posters, photos; especial wants anything on Chuck Connors including baseball and basketball items.

Scott Weiss
316 25th St.
Santa Monica, CA 90402-2522
phone: 310-395-4318
fax: 310-395-9686
Wants to buy movie and TV promotional and advertising specialty gift items such as pin-back buttons,

badges (plastic, metal, cardboard, laminated), cloisonne pins, cloth usher ribbons, paperweights, tokens, snow domes, ashtrays, etc.

Dealers

Bill Day
Bill Day Movie Memorabilia
643 Pleasant St.
P.O. Box 344
Canton, MA 02021
phone: 617-828-4386
Wants posters, magazines, autographs, silent & talkies.

Jon Allan
Elmer's Nostalgia, Inc.
3 Putnam St.
Sanford, ME 04073-2024
phone: 207-324-2166

Dennis & Mary Luby
Casey's Collectible Corner
HCR 30 Box 30
No. Blenheim, NY 12131
phone: 607-588-6464
Buys and sells collectible toys: comic characters, TV shows and personalities; also space and monster toys, sports collectibles, etc.

Mitch Kaidy
Born Yesterday Antiques
921 Crittenden Rd.
Rochester, NY 14623
phone: 716-424-4746
Wants movie memorabilia paper collectibles.

John Kachmar
Techno-Fantasy Traders
779 Carissa Dr.
West Palm Beach, FL 33411-3412
phone: 407-798-5978
fax: 407-798-5978
e-mail: kachmar@aol.com

Sandra McGovern
Global Music Enterprises
488 Archer Lane
Kissimmee, FL 34746
phone: 800-869-5251 or 407-396-4176
Mail order business selling vintage sheet music and movie/movie star memorabilia; will put you on her wants list; when requesting lists, send LSASE for each list.

Cinema Collectors
1507 Wilcox Ave.
Los Angeles, CA 90028
phone: 213-461-6516

Larry Edmunds Book Shop
6644 Hollywood Blvd.
Los Angeles, CA 90028-6219
phone: 213-463-3273
fax: 213-463-4245
Sells movie memorabilia, stills, posters, books and TV and movie scripts.

Book City Collectibles
6627 Hollywood Blvd.
Los Angeles, CA 90028-6285
phone: 213-466-0120 or 213-962-7411
fax: 213-962-6742
Sells movie memorabilia, books and TV and movie scripts.

Myron Ross
Heroes & Legends
P.O. Box 1038
Agoura Hills, CA 91301-1038
phone: 818-991-5979
fax: 818-222-4571
e-mail: heroesross@aol.com
Wants character memorabilia, books, comic books, Fanzines, movie memorabilia, etc.; science fiction or fantasy, rock 'n roll, autographs.

Eddie Brandt's Saturday Matinee
6310 Colfax Ave.
North Hollywood, CA 91602
phone: 818-506-4242
A great source for stills, posters, and lobby cards.

Chris Perry
Doctor 3D
7470 Church St., Ste. A
Yucca Valley, CA 92284-3248
phone: 760-365-0475
fax: 760-365-0495
Buys glass slides that were used in movie theaters; prefers pre-1940 slides but buys slides from all eras; these slides measure 4"x3 1/4"; also buys all 3D movie memorabilia (says "3D" or "3-Dimension" on it).

Sylvia Bongiovanni
P.O. Box 5025
Fullerton, CA 92635-0025
Buys and sells movie and TV memorabilia: books, magazines, lobby cards, etc.

J. Dyson
P.O. Box 10013
Fullerton, CA 92838
Sells movie and TV memorabilia by mail order; sends a list upon request; provide name of star or show you are interested in; enclose SASE.

Loraine Burdick
Quest-Eridon Books
413 10th Ave. Ct. NE
Puyallup, WA 98372-2948
Buys/sells movie magazines, theater advertising, memorabilia, stills, clippings on specific stars by request, Shirley Temple, pre-1960.

Experts

Richard C. De Thuin
875 West End Ave., Apt. 11F
New York, NY 10025-4954
e-mail: Rdethuin@aol.com
Welcomes written inquiries; please keep inquiries to a max of two items and include both condition and a photograph; SASE required for reply which will be dictated by volume of mail received; please be patient.

Richard Alan Davis
Bijou Dream
9500 Old Georgetown Rd.
Bethesda, MD 20814-1724
phone: 301-530-5904
fax: 301-530-8532
Wants to buy photographs of movie stars.

Richard L. Wilson
Norma's Jeans
3511 Turner Lane
Chevy Chase, MD 20815-3213
phone: 301-652-4644
fax: 301-907-0216
Buys, sells, collects and appraises entertainment costumes, props, promo items; also belongings of famous people, historical relics and artifacts; issues periodic catalog of celebrity items for sale.

Museums/Libraries

Library & Museum of the Performing Arts, Shelby Cullom Davis Museum
111 Amsterdam Ave.
New York, NY 10023
phone: 212-870-1613

Arielle Greenberg
American Museum of the Moving Image
35 Avenue at 36 Street
Long Island City, NY 11106
phone: 718-784-4520 or 718-784-0077
fax: 718-784-4681
The only museum in the US devoted to the art, history, technology of film, television, video, interactive media; collection includes costumes, dolls, movie posters, magazines, TV sets, movie cameras, and other items of film & TV history.

Debbie Reynolds Hollywood Hotel/ Casino/Movie Museum
305 Convention Center Drive
Las Vegas, Nevada, 89109
phone: 702-734-0711 or 800-633-1777
Internet: http://www.lasvegashost.com/ lvh_t1.htm
Largest private collection of movie memorabilia in the world; 3,000 costumes, 36,000 square feet of props and furniture.

American Film Institute, The
2021 N. Western Ave.
Los Angeles, CA 90027
phone: 213-856-7600

Max Factor Museum
1666 North Highland Ave.
Los Angeles, CA 90028
phone: 213-463-6668
Filed with artifacts and movie memorabilia: a beauty calibrator, makeup from the 1920s to 1960s, vintage Max Factor ads, etc.

Periodicals

George A. Carpinone, Ed.
Magazine: Celebrity Collector Magazine
P.O. Box 1115
Boston, MA 02117-1115
phone: 617-426-7724
fax: 617-426-7724
Interviews with classic movie stars, TV stars, and fan club presidents; exploration of Hollywood memorabilia collecting and collection care; contributions by readers; classified ads; beautifully designed as a collectible on glossy paper.

Newspaper: Nostalgia World
P.O. Box 231
North Haven, CT 06473

Magazine: Chiller Theatre
P.O. Box 23
Rutherford, NJ 07070

Magazine: Cineaste
P.O. Box 2242
New York, NY 10009-8917
phone: 212-982-1241
fax: 212-982-1241
Internet: http://www.lib/berkeley.edu/MRC/CineasteMenu.html
A quarterly magazine on the art and politics of the cinema; interviews, articles, and reviews of films, videos and books; funded by the New York State Council on the Arts.

George Reed
Magazine: Movie Advertising Collector
P.O. Box 28587
Philadelphia, PA 19149-0587
phone: 215-725-3003
A bi-monthly magazine focusing on movie advertising material: posters, lobby cards, magazines, pressbooks, glass slides, souvenir programs, heralds, stills, books, premiums, etc.

Magazine: Movie Club Magazine
12 Moray Court
Baltimore, MD 21236

Jon Warren
American Collectibles Exchange
Magazine: Collecting Hollywood Magazine
P.O. Box 2512
Chattanooga, TN 37409
phone: 423-265-5515 or 800-880-4289
fax: 423-265-5506
e-mail: jonrwarren@aol.com
Articles and stories for film fans and memorabilia collectors.

Magazine: American Movie Classics
P.O. Box 2065
Marion, OH 43305

Brian A. Bukantis
Newspaper: Movie Collector's World
17230 13 Mile Rd.
Roseville, MI 48066-1916
phone: 810-774-4311
fax: 810-774-5450
e-mail: mcwarena@aol.com
Internet: http://www.csmonline.com
Largest leading biweekly movie memorabilia collecting publication

existing; posters, stills, videos, etc. offered in each issue; over 525 consecutive biweekly issues published.

Linda Kellbach
Antique Trader Publications, Inc.
Newspaper: Big Reel
P.O. Box 1050
Dubuque, IA 52004-1050
phone: 800-334-7165 or 800-482-4155
fax: 800-531-0880
e-mail: 76143.72@compuserve.com
Internet: http://www.csmonline.com
A monthly tabloid for movie and television memorabilia collectors and fans: ads, news, current & nostalgic feature articles, obits, etc.

Bob King
Classic Images
Newspaper: Classic Images
P.O. Box 809
Muscatine, IA 52761
phone: 319-263-2331
fax: 319-262-8042
e-mail: classicimages@classicimages.com
Internet: http://www.classicimages.com
Monthly tabloid featuring articles and advertisements directed at film buffs; classic screen biographies, filmographies, interviews, and historical articles on the film industry.

Bob King
Classic Images
Magazine: Films of the Golden Age
P.O. Box 809
Muscatine, IA 52761
phone: 319-263-2331
fax: 319-262-8042
e-mail: classicimages@classicimages.com
Internet: http://www.classicimages.com
For classic movie buffs; beautifully produced stories and art will take you back to Hollywood's Golden Age; 100 pages in each issue; published quarterly.

Doug Watson
Magazine: Paper Collectors' Marketplace
470 Main St.
P.O. Box 128
Scandinavia, WI 54977-0128
phone: 715-467-2379
fax: 715-467-2243
e-mail: pcmpaper@gglbbs.com
Internet: http://www.tias.com/pubs/pcm
Monthly magazine for collectors of autographs, paperbacks, postcards, advertising, photographica, magazines; all types of paper ephemera.

Joe Bob Briggs
Joe Bob Briggs Museum of American Culture
Newsletter: We Are The Weird
P.O. Box 2002
Dallas, TX 75221-9702
fax: 214-368-2310
A biweekly newsletter with movie reviews, short satire, humor, commentary, innovative cartoonists.

Jordan Young
Moonstone Press
Newsletter: Past Times
7308-H Filmore Dr.
Buena Park, CA 90620
phone: 714-956-2246
A quarterly newsletter covering music, movies, and radio programs from the 1920s, '30s, and '40s.

Jordan Young
Moonstone Press
Directory: Nostalgia Entertainment Sourcebook
7308-H Filmore Dr.
Buena Park, CA 90620
phone: 714-956-2246
Complete resource guide to classic movies, vintage radio, old time music, and theater: programs, sheet music, equipment, where to replace and repair, where to rent or buy old movies, theater posters.

Ev Phillips
Oddesy Publications
Magazine: Collecting
510-A S. Corona Mall
Corona, CA 91720-1420
phone: 909-734-9636 or 800-395-1359
fax: 909-371-7139
Internet: http://www.autographcollector.com
A monthly magazine focusing on collecting autographs, movie posters, movie memorabilia and props.

George Lucas

Clubs/Associations

Dan Madsen
Lucasfilm Fan Club
Newsletter: Lucasfilm Fan Club Newsletter
P.O. Box 111000
Aurora, CO 80042
phone: 303-341-1813 or 800-878-3326
Internet: http://www.sestran.com/~accaaa/swi.html
Quarterly newsletter.

Gone With The Wind

(see also PERSONALITIES [LITERARY], Margaret Mitchell)

Clubs/Associations

Vivien Leigh Fan Club
5 Highpoint Rd.
Perkasie, PA 18944

Collectors

Robert Buchanan
277 W. 22nd St.
New York, NY 10011-2755
phone: 212-989-3917
Wants any GWTW items; also any Vivien Leigh and Clark Gable.

June Crawford
Katie Scarlett's Place
55 E. Patrick St.
Frederick, MD 21701
phone: 301-662-3111

John Wiley, Ed.
1347 Greenmoss Dr.
Richmond, VA 23225-4112
phone: 804-330-5484
Wants to buy early copies of the novel in dust jackets and limited editions (US and foreign); Margaret Mitchell items (personal effects, business cards, etc.), movie & stage version items (programs, scarves, novelties, scripts, etc.)

Herb Bridges
P.O. Box 192
Sharpsburg, GA 30277-0192
phone: 404-253-4934
Seeks the many GWTW movie tie-in items which were produced in the 1940s: figurines, dolls, games, jewelry, perfume bottles, powder boxes, book ends, candy boxes, handkerchiefs, stationary boxes; also GWTW posters, programs, banners.

Kenneth Nix
307 Rosewood Dr.
Dublin, GA 31021-4133
phone: 912-275-0281 or 912-272-4335
fax: 912-272-4972
Especially wants merchandising tie-ins associated with both the book and film versions of GWTW. "Scarlett's Chocolates" candy box, neckties, scarves, handkerchiefs, puzzles, games, etc.; publisher of "Gone With The Wind Marketplace."

Barb Kieffer
P.O. Box 43406
Cincinnati, OH 45243
phone: 513-530-5633
Wants to buy Gone With The Wind collectibles, especially cast iron bookends and magazines featuring Scarlett and Rhet.

Dealers

Command Center
506 E. Alexander St.
Plant City, FL 33566
phone: 813-752-7700
Buying and selling GWTW; has over 1,000 items.

Museums/Libraries

Road to Tara Museum
659 Peachtree St.
Atlanta, GA 30308
phone: 404-897-1939
fax: 404-875-1411
Memorabilia from around the world has been collected and offered in over 6,000 square feet of displays, artwork and artifacts that are of interest to the serious historian as well as the curious traveler.

Periodicals

John Wiley, Ed.
Newsletter: Scarlett Letter, The
1347 Greenmoss Dr.
Richmond, VA 23225-4112
phone: 804-330-5484
Published quarterly; honors both

book and film; keeps collectors up-to-date on all aspects of GWTW; articles, auction results, ads, etc.

Kenneth Nix
Newsletter: Gone With The Wind Marketplace
307 Rosewood Dr.
Dublin, GA 31021-4133
phone: 912-275-0281 or 912-272-4335
fax: 912-272-4972
Publication sent to subscribers in U.S., Canada, England, Australia, and Romania keeping them up-to-date on all the latest GWTW-related collectibles on the market; also offers FREE classifieds.

Horror Films & Literature

(see HORROR; SCIENCE FICTION)

Indiana Jones

Dealers

Cindy Oakes
34025 W. 6 Mile
Livonia, MI 48152
phone: 313-591-3252
Wants Indiana Jones dolls, figurines, playsets, etc.

Movie Posters

Auction Services

Morris Everett, Jr.
Last Moving Picture Company, The
2044 Euclid Ave.
Cleveland, OH 44115
phone: 216-781-1821 or 216-579-9995
fax: 216-579-9172

Howard Lowery
Lowery Auctions
3818 W. Magnolia Blvd.
Burbank, CA 91505
phone: 818-972-9080

Collectors

Sam Sarowitz
241 Centre St., Suite 5F
New York, NY 10013-3224
phone: 212-226-2207
fax: 212-226-2102
e-mail: sam@posteritati.com
Wants movie posters, lobby cards; 1900-1970s; small or large collections bought; immediate cash available; call, fax or write.

Ed Royse
P.O. Box 33489
Fort Sill, OK 73752-1258
phone: 405-357-8000
fax: 405-875-2063
e-mail: shared@juno.com
Wants to buy movie posters, B Westerns, any Audie Murphy of John Wayne movie posters.

Gene Arnold
2234 South Blvd.
Houston, TX 77098-5225
phone: 713-524-9000 or 800-557-1880
Wants any old movie posters or 11" x 14" lobby cards.

Dealers

Hollywood Canteen, The
1516 Danforth Ave.
Toronto
Ontario M4J 1N4 Canada
phone: 416-461-1704
Buys and sells movie posters and movie books.

Rudy Franchi
Nostalgia Factory, The
336 Newbury St.
Boston, MA 02115-2703
phone: 617-236-8754 or 800-479-8754
e-mail: rf@nostalgia.com
Internet: http://www.nostalgia.com
Always buying all forms of movie advertising from 1900 to present; posters, lobby cards, stills, press books, press kits, inserts, etc.

Q. David Bowers
Bowers & Merena, Inc.
P.O. Box 1224
Wolfeboro, NH 03894
fax: 603-569-5319
Wants American film posters from 1895-1915.

Alan Levine
P.O. Box 1577
Bloomfield, NJ 07003
phone: 201-743-5288
Buys and sells movie posters and lobby cards.

Marc Zydiak
Star Archives
P.O. Box 285
Westfield, NJ 07091-0285
phone: 908-654-6505

Poster World
9 Bolton Place
Fair Lawn, NJ 07410
phone: 201-791-1073
Specializing in movie posters from 1940 through 1970.

Metropolis Collectibles
873 Broadway, Ste. 201
New York, NY 10003
phone: 212-627-9691 or 800-229-6387
fax: 212-627-5947
Buys and sells vintage movie posters and comic books; free appraisals; finders fees paid.

Jerry Ohlinger
Jerry Ohlinger's Movie Material Store, Inc.
242 W. 14th St.
New York, NY 10011-7206
phone: 212-989-0869
fax: 212-989-1660
Buys and sells motion picture photos and posters from 1920 to present; also TV photos; research services available; free lists available;

complete lists of 100,000 black & white photos or of 100,000 color photos are $4 each.

Joe Burtis
Motion Picture Arts Gallery
133 E. 58th St.
New York, NY 10022
phone: 212-223-1009
Buys and sells posters, lobby cards, etc.

Todd Richard Feiertag
Poster City
3 Henry St.
P.O. Box 94
Orangeburg, NY 10962-0094
phone: 914-359-0177 or 800-272-3323
Buys and sells movie posters; entire collections purchased; free appraisals; will travel anywhere.

John Hazelton
235 Horton Highway
Mineola, NY 11501
phone: 800-224-6394

George Theofiles
Miscellaneous Man
P.O. Box 1776
New Freedom, PA 17349-0191
phone: 717-235-4766
fax: 717-235-2853
Collects, buys and sells vintage film posters; since 1970 offering catalogs of rare posters and early advertising and ephemera on hundreds of subjects. Descriptive flyer available.

Morris Everett, Jr.
Last Moving Picture Company, The
2044 Euclid Ave.
Cleveland, OH 44115
phone: 216-781-1821 or 216-579-9995
fax: 216-579-9172

Marty Davis
Vintage Film Posters
15875 Van Aken Blvd., Ste. 304C
Cleveland, OH 44120-5384
phone: 216-751-8888
fax: 216-751-8885
Buys and sells movie posters, all sizes and periods; also related movie memorabilia; specialist in silent era, especially Chaplin, Keaton and Lloyd.

Celebrity Graphics
P.O. Box 385
Flushing, MI 48433-0385
phone: 810-659-8751
Wants movie posters, lobby cards, any vintage, any quantity.

Dwight M. Cleveland
P.O. Box 10922
Chicago, IL 60610-0922
phone: 773-525-9152
fax: 773-525-2969
Buys, sells and collects movie posters, lobby cards, 1-sheets, 3-sheets, window cards, glass slides, studio annuals, motion picture heralds, etc.; highest prices paid.

Bruce Hershenson
P.O. Box 874
West Plains, MO 65775-0874
phone: 417-256-9616
fax: 417-256-0686
Wants high quality original posters from major pre-1940 Hollywood films.

Hollywood Movie Posters
6727 Hollywood Blvd.
Los Angeles, CA 90028
phone: 213-463-1792

Experts

Ron Donnelly
Saturday Heroes
P.O. Box 7047
Panama City, FL 32413-0047
phone: 904-234-7944
fax: 904-233-9316
Buys and sells 1900s and 1950s movie posters; also collects Gone With The Wind.

Jon Warren
American Collectibles Exchange
P.O. Box 2512
Chattanooga, TN 37409
phone: 423-265-5515 or 800-880-4289
fax: 423-265-5506
e-mail: jonrwarren@aol.com
Author of "Warren's Movie Poster Price Guide."

Cinemonde - Movie Poster Center
1932-J Polk St.
San Francisco, CA 94109-3006
phone: 415-776-9988 or 615-742-3048
fax: 415-776-1424
Buys, sells, specializes in movie posters.

Periodicals

John Kisch
Price Guide: Movie Poster Price Database
P.O. Box 114
Hyde Park, NY 12538-0114
phone: 914-452-1998
fax: 914-454-7131
e-mail: johnkisck@aol.com
An annual price guide.

Jon Warren
American Collectibles Exchange
Newsletter: Movie Poster Update, The
P.O. Box 2512
Chattanooga, TN 37409
phone: 423-265-5515 or 800-880-4289
fax: 423-265-5506
e-mail: jonrwarren@aol.com

Repro. Sources

Moviead Corp.
475 Ramblewood Dr.
Pompano Beach, FL 33071
Full color poster reproductions in one sheet sizes, 27" x 41".

Movie Posters (Black)

Dealers

John Kisch
Separate Cinema
P.O. Box 114
Hyde Park, NY 12538-0114
phone: 914-452-1998
fax: 914-454-7131
e-mail: johnkisck@aol.com
*Buys, sells and collects black movie
posters; publishes "Movie Poster
Price Data Base" twice a year with
prices, dealers, and lists.*

Movie Posters (Silent Movies)

Dealers

Ronald Krueger
R.W. Krueger's
P.O. Box 741
Oak Park, IL 60303-0741
phone: 708-788-8235
*Buys, sells, and trades silent movie
related posters, stills, portraits,
magazines, glass slides, etc.;
especially wants Mary Miles Minter
and Valentino.*

Oscars

Collectors

Jon Warren
P.O. Box 2512
Chattanooga, TN 37409
phone: 423-265-5515 or 800-880-4289
fax: 423-265-5506
e-mail: jonrwarren@aol.com
*Wants to buy Oscars; from insignifi-
cant technical award to major aware.*

Scripts

Collectors

Grayson D. Cook
Grayson D. Cook, Bookseller
367 W. Ave. 42
Los Angeles, CA 90065
phone: 213-227-8899
*Wants to buy screenplays and movie
scripts; prefers original studio
production copies; will consider
agency copies or photocopies; please
send description (title, writer, and
draft).*

Dealers

California Script
8033 Sunset Blvd.
Hollywood, CA 90046
phone: 213-460-2535

Serials

Periodicals

Linda S. Downey
World of Yesterday, The
Journal: Cliffhanger
104 Chestnut Wood Drive
Waynesville, NC 28786
phone: 704-648-5647
Periodic journal focusing on serials.

Silent Films

Experts

Richard Alan Davis
Bijou Dream
9500 Old Georgetown Rd.
Bethesda, MD 20814-1724
phone: 301-530-5904
fax: 301-530-8532
*Wants silent movie items: posters,
lobby cards, programs, stills, Star
Garment Co. hangers with head/
shoulder of movie stars.*

Periodicals

Gene Vazzana
Newsletter: Silent Film Monthly, The
700 5th St., Apt. 12
Oakmont, PA 15139-1568
*Devoted to the silent film era;
contains articles and reviews of silent
films and the men and women who
made them - recounted in thoughtful,
interesting articles by writers who
know their subject.*

Star Wars

Clubs/Associations

Martin Thurn
Newsletter: Star Wars Collector, The
20982 Homecrest Ct.
Ashburn, VA 22011-4015
e-mail: thurn@cis.ohio-state.edu
Internet: http://www.cis.ohio-state.edu/
~thurn/swc
*The only bi-monthly publication by
Star Wars collectors, for Star Wars
collectors of all ages; all about
collecting anything and everything
related to Star Wars.*

Official Star Wars Fan Club
Magazine: Star Wars Insider
P.O. Box 111000
Aurora, CO 80042
phone: 303-341-1813 or 800-878-3326
Internet: http://www.sestran.com/
~accaaa/swi.html
*Publishes full-color magazine and
official catalog, "The Jawa Trader."*

Collectors

David Welch
P.O. Box 714
Murphysboro, IL 62966-0714
phone: 618-687-2282
fax: 618-684-2243
e-mail: PexDude1@aol.com
*Wants complete items with original
packaging only; especially interested
in Kenner Action Figure related items;
paying over $1000 for rarer items; no
books, records or comics, please.*

Dealers

Cindy Oakes
34025 W. 6 Mile
Livonia, MI 48152
phone: 313-591-3252
*Wants Star Wars figures, jewelry,
vehicles, autographs.*

Toys from the Attic
20165 N. 67th Ave., Ste 122A
Glendale, AZ 85308
phone: 602-547-2564
fax: 602-938-0925
Wants to buy old Star Wars toys.

Brian Rachfal
P.O. Box 7772
San Jose, CA 95150-3766
phone: 408-298-9070 or 408-629-3980
*Wants to buy Star Wars action figures
and related items.*

Experts

L.I. Kyro
6030 Magnolia
Saint Louis, MO 63139
e-mail: llkmtfbwy@aol.com
*Expert, collector, historian, authority
on Star Wars.*

Star Wars (Art)

Experts

William Plumb
5646 Terrace Drive
Rocklin, CA 95765
phone: 916-632-3267
Internet: http://
www.origartgallry_starwars.com
*Collects all Star Wars original art:
drawings, sketches, paintings; plans
on opening a museum of original Star
Wars art.*

Steven Spielberg

Clubs/Associations

Dan Archer
Spielberg Film Society
Newsletter: Spielberg Film Society
Newsletter
P.O. Box 13712
Tucson, AZ 85732
*International club interested in Steven
Spielberg and all aspects of film
making.*

The Godfather

Collectors

Lynn Goldfinger
P.O. Box 4962
Burlingame, CA 94011-4962
phone: 415-342-7829
fax: 415-343-3269
e-mail: goldie1943@aol.com
*Wants to buy unusual and hard-to-find
The Godfather (I and II) and related
actor memorabilia: promo items,
photos, costumes, props, etc.*

Trade Publications

Collectors

George Reed
P.O. Box 28587
Philadelphia, PA 19149-0587
phone: 215-725-3003
*Wants illustrated movie advertising
trade books, coming attraction folios,
pamphlets, etc., in color or black and*

*white; also exhibitors/trade magazines
and publications, pressbooks and
souvenir programs, and related
material.*

VHS Recordings

Periodicals

Don Stewart
Newsletter: Poorman's VHS Movie
Collectors Newsletter
902 East Country Gables
Phoenix, AZ 85022

Westerns

(see also COWBOY HEROES)

Clubs/Associations

Alan Dobrey
Western Film Appreciation Club of
Alberta
Newsletter: Western Film Appreciation
Society Bulletin
9826 1171A Ave.
Edmonton
Alberta Canada
phone: 403-456-3769
*Dedicated to keeping the Western
films of yesteryear (1930s to 1950s)
alive through the screening and
promoting of these films; holds
monthly meetings; open to the public.*

Eric G. Lilley, Pres.
Boys Hollywood
2 Holly Close, Crookham Park
Crookhan Common, Thatcham
Berkshire RG19 8QZ, U.K.
phone: 01635-869694
*Focuses on the great Hollywood
Western film stars of the 1930s to
1950s: Roy Rogers, Gene Autry,
William Boyd.*

Barrie Hanfling
Westerns - N.Z. Chapter
Magazine: Westerns
79 Tiroroa Ave.
Te Atatu South
Auckland 1008 New Zealand
*Publishes bi-monthly magazine on old
Westerns, both "A" and "B".*

Milo Holt
Old Time Western Film Club
Newsletter: Old Time Western Film
Newsletter
P.O. Box 142
Siler City, NC 27344-0142
phone: 919-737-3460
*Interested in promoting the showing of
old westerns and in the collecting of
memorabilia relating thereto; meets
every other month for Western film
festival; 500 on mailing list.*

Western Film Preservation Society, Inc.,
Raleigh Chapter
Newsletter: Western Film Preservation
Society Newsletter
1012 Vance St.
Raleigh, NC 27608

Mark Houston
Tennessee Western Film Club
398 Piney Flats Rd.
Piney Flats, TN 37686
phone: 615-538-8019

Bobby Copeland
Riders of the Silver Screen Club
Newsletter: Riders Newsletter
104 Henley Rd.
Oak Ridge, TN 37830

Norman Kietzer
Westerns & Serials Fan Club
Magazine: Westerns & Serials
Rte. 1 Box 103
Vernon Center, MN 56090-9744
phone: 507-549-3677
fax: 507-549-3788
A club for collectors as well as non-collectors interested in westerns and serials of the silver screen; also interested in related memorabilia.

Dealers

Jerry Ohlinger
Jerry Ohlinger's Movie Material Store, Inc.
242 W. 14th St.
New York, NY 10011-7206
phone: 212-989-0869
fax: 212-989-1660
Buys and sells motion picture photos and posters from 1920 to present; also TV photos; research services available; free lists available; complete lists of 100,000 black & white photos or of 100,000 color photos are $4 each.

Museums/Libraries

Big Slims Western Museum
61 Park Ave.
Rutherford, NJ 07070

Periodicals

Colin Momber
Magazine: Wrangler's Roost
23 Sabrina Way
Bristol BS9 1ST, U.K.
phone: 0117-9684776
A 32-page periodical published three times per year; longest running fanzine in the western field; printed on gloss paper and is directed at enthusiasts of the old "B" Western movies.

Janette & Bob Anderson
Magazine: Trail Dust
407 West Rosemary Lane
Falls Church, VA 22046-3847
fax: 703-358-5402
Glossy magazine devoted to both television and feature-length westerns.

Linda S. Downey
World of Yesterday, The
Journal: Under Western Skies
104 Chestnut Wood Drive
Waynesville, NC 28786
phone: 704-648-5647
Focuses on the old west of the Silver Screen & TV.

Westerns (Italian)

Periodicals

Tom Betts
Newsletter: Westerns...All' Italiana!
P.O. Box 25042
Anaheim, CA 92825-5042
Quarterly newsletter focusing on Italian Westerns.

MOVIE PROJECTORS

(see CAMERAS & CAMERA EQUIPMENT, Movie; FILMS; MAGIC LANTERNS)

MOVING & STORAGE ASSOCIATIONS

(see also REPAIR/RESTORATION/CONSERVATION)

Clubs/Associations

Estelle Tredway
National Moving & Storage Association
Newspaper: M & S Times
11150 Main St.
Fairfax, VA 22030-5066
phone: 703-934-9111
fax: 703-934-9712
NMSA provides educational and certification programs for the moving & storage industry; worldwide members are providers of goods & services of use to moving & storage agents & warehousemen; also publishes "Direction" monthly journal.

Chuck Naylor, Ex. Dir.
Claims Prevention & Procedure Council
Newsletter: CPPC Newsletter
P.O. Box 1367
Englewood, FL 34295-1367
phone: 941-473-CPPC
fax: 941-473-2775
A moving industry related organization of repairmen, van lines, appraisers, insurance companies, lawyers and claims adjusters.

MOXIE

(see SOFT DRINK COLLECTIBLES, Moxie)

MR. PEANUT

(see PLANTERS PEANUTS ITEMS)

MUGS

(see BARBER SHOP COLLECTIBLES, Shaving Mugs; COLLECTIBLES [MODERN], Steins; GLASSES, Drinking; STEINS)

MUSIC

(see also AUTOGRAPHS, Music Related; BOOKS, Reference [Music]; DRUM & BUGLE CORPS; MUSIC BOXES; MUSICAL INSTRUMENTS; PERFORMING ARTS; PERSONALITIES [MUSICIANS]; PHONOGRAPHS; PIANO ROLLS; ROCK 'N' ROLL COLLECTIBLES; RECORDS; SHEET MUSIC; TICKETS)

Clubs/Associations

James Henderson
Sonneck Society for American Music & Music in America
Newsletter: Sonneck Society Bulletin
P.O. Box 476
Canton, MA 02021-0476
phone: 617-828-8450
fax: 617-828-8915
e-mail: acadsvc@aol.com
Promotes the dissemination of accurate information on all aspects of American music and music in America; also publishes "American Music", a quarterly journal addressing music in America.

James Henderson
Music Library Association
Magazine: Notes
P.O. Box 487
Canton, MA 02021-0487
phone: 617-828-8450
fax: 617-828-8915
e-mail: acadsvc@aol.com
For music scholars, teachers, performers, librarians: scholarly articles, reviews, CR reviews, music publishers' information; also ads for records, scores, books, journals and other services.

Dealers

Leland Stein
Roundup Records
Newsletter: Record Roundup
1 Camp St.
Cambridge, MA 02140-1194
phone: 617-661-6308 or 800-443-4727
fax: 617-868-8769
e-mail: rupinfo@rounder.com
Mail order CDs, LPs, cassettes; specializing in hard to find blues, country, R&B, Rock 'N' Roll, jazz, bluegrass, etc.; "Record Roundup" is a bi-monthly catalog/newsletter.

Periodicals

Julie A. Ulrich, PR
Krause Publications
Magazine: Goldmine
700 E. State St.
Iola, WI 54990-0001
phone: 715-445-2214
fax: 715-445-4087
e-mail: info@krause.com
Internet: http://www.krause.com
A biweekly magazine containing articles, ads about records & recording artists from 1940s to present; the record & CD marketplace.

1960s

Dealers

Charles F. Rosenay
Liverpool Productions
P.O. Box 1008
Los Angeles, CA 90066-1088
phone: 310-391-0778
fax: 301-390-7475
e-mail: gds1964@aol.co,
Buys and sells '60s music and memorabilia relating to the Beatles, British Invasion, Monkees and Beach Boys.

Big Band

Collectors

John L. Mickolas
172 Liberty St.
Trenton, NJ 08611-2631
phone: 609-530-5568 or 609-599-9672
Wants Glenn Miller, Bunny Berigan, autographs, recordings, photos, sheet music, magazines, films, anything related.

Mark Rosenblum
10776 Blackley St.
Temple City, CA 91780-3501
phone: 818-453-8890
Wants big band memorabilia: concert posters, programs, advertising, magazines, ballroom tickets pertaining to Miller, Goodman, Dorsey, James, Ellington, etc.

Country

Museums/Libraries

Country Music Hall of Fame & Museum, Country Music Foundation
4 Music Square, East
Nashville, TN 37203
phone: 615-255-2245

Periodicals

Disc Collector Publications
Newsletter: Disc Collector
P.O. Box 315
Cheswold, DE 19936
phone: 302-674-3632
Focuses on bluegrass and old time country music.

Cowboy

Periodicals

Mary Rogers, Pub.
Magazine: Song of the West
136 Pearl St.
Fort Collins, CO 80521-2424
phone: 303-484-3209
Historical and contemporary magazine on cowboy and Western music; articles, artist features, album reviews, events, ads.

Cowboy (Bob Wills)

Experts

Robert Phillips
1703 North Aster Place
Broken Arrow, OK 74012
phone: 918-254-8205
fax: 918-252-9362
e-mail: rawhidebob@aol.com
Researched heavily the life, career and music of The Father of Western Swing Music, Bob Wills; collects Bob Wills music and memorabilia.

Dixieland & Ragtime

Dealers

Don Hoffman
P.O. Box 4231
Salinas, CA 93912-4231
phone: 408-449-7311
Wants to buy blues, jazz, ragtime, minstrel, Dixieland related items: posters, tickets, programs, autographs, videos, broadsides, antique photos, souvenirs, ephemera, memorabilia, books, booklets, souvenirs; describe and price, please.

Periodicals

Richard Zimmerman, Ed.
Maple Leaf Club
Newsletter: Rag Times, The
15522 Ricky Ct.
Grass Valley, CA 95949-6672
A bi-monthly newsletter with everything about ragtime - past and present; since 1967.

Jazz & Blues

Clubs/Associations

Joe Lang
New Jersey Jazz Society
187 Watchung Ave.
Chatham, NJ 07928
phone: 201-635-2761 or 201-635-2713
Mission is to promote and preserve interest in jazz; many members are collectors of jazz related music and records.

American Federation of Jazz Societies, Inc.
2787 Del Monte St.
W. Sacramento, CA 95691
phone: 916-372-5277
fax: 916-372-3479
Serving jazz societies, individuals, musicians, and the music industry.

Collectors

Stanley King
260 Fifth Ave.
New York, NY 10001-6408
phone: 212-447-1880
fax: 212-447-0728
Wants to jazz band and jazz musician memorabilia: photos, posters, advertisements, postcards, contracts, letters, etc.

Chuck Moore
P.O. Box 280
Gladstone, OR 97027
phone: 503-654-9994
fax: 503-656-7603
Wants Jazz LP's, singles, 78's; also older books, magazines, sheet music on jazz.

Dealers

Gary Alderman
G's Jazz
P.O. Box 9164
Madison, WI 53715-0164
phone: 608-274-3527
fax: 608-277-1999
Wants to buy jazz LP's, jazz literature, jazz photos, autographs, etc.

Don Hoffman
P.O. Box 4231
Salinas, CA 93912-4231
phone: 408-449-7311
Wants to buy blues, jazz, ragtime, minstrel, Dixieland related items: posters, tickets, programs, autographs, videos, broadsides, antique photos, souvenirs, ephemera, memorabilia, books, booklets, souvenirs; describe and price, please.

Rock 'N' Roll

(see also AMERICAN BANDSTAND)

Auction Services

Stephen Maycock
Sotheby's
34-35 New Bond St.
London W1A 2AA, U.K.
phone: 0171-4938080 or 0171-4085205
fax: 0171-4085911
Conducts regular auctions of Rock 'N Roll memorabilia.

Clubs/Associations

Dave Frees
American Bandstand 1950's Fan Club
Magazine: Bandstand Boogie
P.O. Box 131
Adamstown, PA 19501-0131
phone: 717-738-2513
Focuses on "American Bandstand" from the 1950s and 1980s; magazine published twice a year; sells "Dave's Collectables Catalog" (50s through 80s photos, magazines, etc.) for $1 - free to members.

Experts

Jean Blankenship
P.O. Box 7274
Pasadena, TX 77508-7274
phone: 713-266-6311
Buys, sells, and specializes in Elvis records, magazines, photos, posters, books, cards, and other non-record memorabilia; also Buddy Holly, and Fifties and Sixties Rock 'n Roll; since 1956; lists mailed every other month.

Museums/Libraries

Rock and Roll Hall of Fame and Museum
One Key Plaza
Cleveland, OH 44114
phone: 800-493-ROLL

Periodicals

Gene Bondy
Magazine: Rock & Roll Radio Archives
677 - 49th St.
Brooklyn, NY 11220
Bi-monthly publication devoted to music radio of around thirty years ago.

Newsletter: Tune Talk
P.O. Box 851
Marshalltown, IA 50158
50s rock 'n' roll newsletter on music, records, artists.

MUSIC BOXES

(see also DOLLS, Automatons; MUSICAL INSTRUMENTS, Mechanical)

Clubs/Associations

Alan Wyatt
Musical Box Society of Great Britain
P.O. Box 299
Waterbeach
Cambridge CB4 4PJ, U.K.

Beatrice Robertson
Musical Box Society International
Magazine: Journal of Mechanical Music
12140 Anchor Lane SW
Moore Haven, FL 33471
phone: 941-675-5828
e-mail: brobertsn@aol.com
Internet: http://www.mbsi.org
Members collect, study, preserve all types of instruments that mechanically produce music: musical boxes, orchestrions, band organs, player pianos, musical clocks, automata, etc.; "News Bulletin" contains Mart for buying & selling.

Collectors

Martin Roenigk
Mechantiques
26 Barton Hill
East Hampton, CT 06424-1138
phone: 800-671-6333
fax: 860-267-1120
e-mail: mroenigk@aol.com
Internet: http://www.mechantiques.com
Wants all types of mechanical music instruments: music boxes, player organs, coin pianos, singing birds, Wurlitzer 78 rpm jukeboxes, etc.

John W. Hess
244 Bernaski Rd.
Amsterdam, NY 12010
phone: 518-843-6117
Wants to buy Vogue picture disc records, horn phonographs, music boxes, roller organs; also wants parts, empty cabinets, horns; any condition, any material.

Jackie Durham
909 26th St. NW
Washington, DC 20037-2029
e-mail: durham@GameRoomAntiques.com
Internet: http://www.GameRoomAntiques.com
Wants coin-operated music boxes and bird boxes, especially with vending.

Jim Brady
2725 E. 56th St.
Indianapolis, IN 46220
phone: 317-259-4307
Music boxes wanted; any type or condition; also jukeboxes.

Frank Rider
1062 Alber St.
Wabash, IN 46992-1003
phone: 219-563-5030

Angelo Rulli
887 Orange Ave. East
Saint Paul, MN 55106-2051
phone: 612-774-2590
fax: 612-772-2464

Dave Ogden
P.O. Box 223
Northbrook, IL 60062-0223
phone: 847-564-2893
fax: 847-564-2893
e-mail: musical@flash.net
Wants disc and cylinder music boxes; Regina; also monkey organs and any self playing musical instruments.

Ralph Schack
P.O. Box 58806
Los Angeles, CA 90058-0806
phone: 310-377-5240
fax: 310-377-5240
Buys and sells cylinder and disc music boxes, musical snuff boxes, automata, musical clocks, nickelodeons, monkey organs, orchestrions, player grand pianos, violin machines.

Dealers

Rita Ford Music Boxes
19 E 65th St.
New York, NY 10021
phone: 212-535-6717
fax: 212-772-0992
Buys, sells, repairs antique music boxes.

R.C. Bornand
Bornand Music Box Company
801 Zinnia Ln.
Fort Lauderdale, FL 33317
phone: 954-791-3837

Doug Negus
Phonograph Phanatic
215 Mason St.
Sutherland, IA 51058-7606
phone: 712-446-2270 or 712-446-3746
e-mail: negus@nwidt.com
Music boxes, phonographs, cylinder records, pianos, NO piano rolls, older mechanical musical instruments, pre-1930; any parts or repairables wanted.

Experts

William H. Edgerton
P.O. Box 88
Darien, CT 06820-0588
phone: 203-655-0566
fax: 203-655-8066
Buys, sells, repairs pianos and rolls, musical boxes, player organs, nickelodeons, and automata.

Nancy Fratti
P.O. Box 210
Whitehall, NY 12887-0210
phone: 518-282-9770
fax: 518-282-9800
Specializes in, buys, sells and restores antique cylinder and disc musical boxes, restoration supplies; restoration school, books, discs, recordings of automatic musical instruments; catalog available for $5.

Ken Danckaert
231 Kennedy Ct.
Severna Park, MD 21146-3039
phone: 410-544-0260
e-mail: ken@weasel.acs.umbc.edu
Internet: http://www.kend@lemur.org
Collects, buys, sells, appraises, and repairs music boxes, phonographs, and organettes; in business since 1972; an expert who gives lectures, presentations and videos.

David & Carol Beck
75 Waters Edge Lane
Newnan, GA 30263-3579
phone: 404-304-9066
Specializes in cylinder and disc music boxes; offers quality repair of cylinder and disc music boxes.

Marty Persky
6514 N. Trumball
Chicago, IL 60645-3835
phone: 847-675-6114
fax: 847-675-6160
Specializes in disc and cylinder music boxes.

Christian Eric
Antique Music Box Restoration
1825 Placentia Ave.
Costa Mesa, CA 92627-3565
phone: 714-548-1542
fax: 714-631-9996
Specialists in antique musical boxes, emphasis on early cylinder, miniature and sur plateau mechanisms; author on subject.

Museums/Libraries

Lockwood-Matthews Mansion Museum
295 West Ave.
Norwalk, CT 06850
phone: 203-838-1434

Musical Museum, The
P.O. Box 901
Deansboro, NY 13328
phone: 315-841-8774

Museum of Musical Instruments, The
Schubert Club
75 W. 5th St.
Saint Paul, MN 55102
phone: 612-292-3267

Repair Services

Donald Tendrup
7 Ashland Ct.
Holtsville, NY 11742
phone: 516-758-4755
Music box repairs; over 30 years experience; complete machine shop on premises; cylinder repining, main springs, governor work, comb work, gear work, etc.

Chester Ramsay
Chet Ramsay Antiques
2460 Strasburg Rd.
Coatesville, PA 19320-4339
phone: 610-384-0514
Wants all types of pre-1912 music boxes; buy, sell and repair; also wants parts.

George Paladics
1840 Colonial Dr.
Green Cove Springs, FL 32043-8004
European craftsman repairs or restores antique music boxes; capable of making necessary parts.

Emerson E. Whitacre
Mechanical Music Man
7550 President Court
Dayton, OH 45414-3671
phone: 513-898-6044 or 513-898-0865
Repairs, adjusts and cleans disc music boxes, cylinder music boxes, antique phonographs, etc.

Jim Brady
2725 East 56th St.
Indianapolis, IN 46220
phone: 317-259-4307 or 317-849-1469
Buys, sells and restores automatic musical instruments: music boxes; tooth replacement, comb dampening, governor work, cylinder repining, new gears, sound board restoration, case refinishing, tuning, inlay repair, etc.

Mechanical Musicologist
420 W. State St.
Belle Plaine, MN 56011
phone: 612-873-6704
Repairs all types of music boxes.

K.R. Powers
K.R. Powers Antique Music Boxes
28 Alton Circle
Rogers, AR 72756-9251
phone: 501-263-2643
Disc and cylinder music box restoration, sales and repairs.

Billy E. Young
Young's Ole Clock & Music Box Shop
3511 Rio Grande Circle
Dallas, TX 75233
phone: 214-331-8265
Buys, sells and restores.

Christian Eric
Antique Music Box Restoration
1825 Placentia Ave.
Costa Mesa, CA 92627-3565
phone: 714-548-1542
fax: 714-631-9996
Specialists in antique musical boxes, emphasis on early cylinder, miniature and sur plateau mechanisms; fine precision restoration; all facets of restoration personally undertaken in house.

Birds & Bird Boxes (Singing)

Experts

Angelo Rulli
887 Orange Ave. East
Saint Paul, MN 55106-2051
phone: 612-774-2590
fax: 612-772-2464
Specializes in singing birds, bird boxes, whistlers.

Cylinder

Experts

Alan Bies
357 N. Oak Post Rd.
Houston, TX 77008
phone: 713-686-5669
Specializes in cylinder music boxes.

Steve Boehck
357 N. Oak Post Rd.
Houston, TX 77008
phone: 713-686-5669
Specializes in cylinder music boxes.

David Wells
P.O. Box 280368
Lakewood, CO 80228
phone: 303-985-4481
Specializes in cylinder music boxes.

Larry Karp
2557 Perkins Ln.
Seattle, WA 98199
phone: 206-284-9203
Specializes in cylinder music boxes.

Disc

Experts

Coulson Conn
432 Old Forge Rd.
Media, PA 19063-5511
phone: 610-459-0367
Specializes in disc music boxes.

Susan & Al Choffnes
Collector's World, Inc.
2 High Terrace
Bannockburn, IL 60015-1585
phone: 708-948-1472
fax: 708-948-1486
Buys, sells and specializes in disc music boxes: Regina, large German glass front upright music boxes, table models, console models, Stella, Mira; also cylinder music boxes, mechanical organs and pianos.

Barry Johnson
1305 Hoover St.
Menlo Park, CA 94025-4218
phone: 415-964-0685
Specializes in disc music boxes.

MUSICAL INSTRUMENTS

(see also CAROUSELS & CAROUSEL FIGURES; DRUM & BUGLE CORPS; MUSIC; MUSIC BOXES)

Auction Services

Graham Wells
Sotheby's
34-35 New Bond St.
London W1A 2AA, U.K.
phone: 0171-4938080 or 0171-4085205
fax: 0171-4085911
Conducts regular auctions of vintage musical instruments.

Kerry Keane
Skinner, Inc.
357 Main St.
Bolton, MA 01740-1104
phone: 508-779-6241 or 617-350-5400
fax: 508-779-5144
Established in 1964, Skinner Inc. is the fifth largest auction house in the US; has offices in Bolton and Boston, MA.

Christie's
502 Park Ave.
New York, NY 10022
phone: 212-546-1000
fax: 212-980-8163
Internet: http://www.sirius.com/
~christie/

Clubs/Associations

Jeannine E. Abel, Sec.
American Musical Instrument Society
Newsletter: Newsletter & Journal of the AMIS
RD 3 Box 205-B
Franklin, PA 16323-9319
phone: 814-374-4119
fax: 814-374-4563
Inter. organization founded to promote the study of the history, design and use of musical instruments; all periods and cultures; also publishes the "Journal of the AMIS".

Dealers

William D. Voiers
William D. Voiers Fine Musical Instruments
P.O. Box 23
North Egremont, MA 01252
phone: 413-528-3321 or 800-788-3521
fax: 413-528-5801
Dealer, collector, appraiser of the violin family of instruments: violins, violas, cellos, bows, banjos, ukuleles, guitars and mandolins; electric or acoustic; also saxes, brasses, drums, percussion; also buys, sells, collects and trades.

Dominic S. Cucinotti
Dominic's Music
169 Msgr. O'Brien Hwy.
Cambridge, MA 02141
phone: 617-491-8051 or 617-661-0367
fax: 617-661-0367
*Buys, sells, and repairs musical
instruments.*

Guitars Unlimited
151 Morehouse St.
Bridgeport, CT 06605
phone: 203-221-0040
fax: 203-366-6416
*Wants to buy musical instruments
such as guitars, amps, saxophones,
violins, mandolins, banjos; also wants
related catalogs, signs, clocks, etc.*

John G. McAuliffe
ARDAGH Vintage Musical Instruments
P.O. Box 810
Carmel, NY 10512
phone: 914-225-1746 or 800-217-1746
*Buys, sells, collects, appraises buy
fine violins, violas, cellos, bows,
guitars, banjos, mandolins, ukes,
harps, concertinas, wood flutes, ivory
flutes, glass flutes, silver flutes by
Powell, Haynes, Badger, etc.*

Louis J. Porsi, Jr.
King Louie Music
115 Marbeteh Ave.
Carlisle, PA 17013-1626
phone: 717-258-1177
Internet: http://members.aol.com/
kingloumus/index.htm
*Vintage musical instruments including
drums, guitars and basses, microphones, amplifiers, etc.; also wants
instrument catalogs, banners,
advertising pieces, salesman promos
and dealer items.*

Frederick W. Oster
Vintage Instruments
1529 Pine St.
Philadelphia, PA 19102-4623
phone: 215-545-1100
fax: 215-735-3634
e-mail: vintageFO@aol.com
*Dealer, appraiser, consultant; rare &
antique musical instruments;
specializing in violins, violas, cellos,
bows; American fretted instruments -
guitars, mandolins, banjos; antique
wind instruments, etc.; SASE for reply.*

Mickie Zekley
Lark in the Morning
P.O. Box 1176
Mendocino, CA 95460
phone: 707-964-5569
fax: 707-964-1979
e-mail: larkinam@larkinam.com
Internet: http://www.larkinam.com

Experts

Sid Glickman
Antique Musical Instrument Service
43 Butterwood E.
Irvington, NY 10533-2336
phone: 914-591-5371
fax: 914-591-5371
Buys and sells all types of musical

*instruments, especially antique and
ethnic; availability lists to collectors;
send SASE for copy; free estimates to
dealers and collectors; also answers
questions about musical instruments.*

Frederick W. Oster
Vintage Instruments
1529 Pine St.
Philadelphia, PA 19102-4623
phone: 215-545-1100
fax: 215-735-3634
e-mail: vintageFO@aol.com
*Dealer, appraiser, consultant; rare &
antique musical instruments;
specializing in violins, violas, cellos,
bows; American fretted instruments -
guitars, mandolins, banjos; antique
wind instruments, etc.; SASE for reply.*

Museums/Libraries

Yale University Collection of Musical
Instruments
P.O. Box 2117
New Haven, CT 06520
phone: 203-436-4935

Musical Museum, The
P.O. Box 901
Deansboro, NY 13328
phone: 315-841-8774

University of Michigan, Stearns
Collection of Musical Instruments
Newsletter: Stearns Newsletter, The
School Of Music
Ann Arbor, MI 48109-2085
phone: 313-763-4389
*A collection of over 2000 musical
instruments from around the world.*

Periodicals

Joel M. Cowan
Magazine: Concertina & Squeezebox
P.O. Box 6706
Ithaca, NY 14851
*The quarterly magazine for free reed
aficionados; if you can squeeze it, this
magazine covers it: concertinas,
accordions, squeezeboxes.*

Christina Gargano
Heartland Communications Group, Inc.
Magazine: Midwest Musicians Hot Line
1003 Central Ave.
Fort Dodge, IA 50501
phone: 800-247-2000
fax: 515-574-2233
Internet: http://www.hlipublishing.com
*The monthly buy, sell and trade
magazine by performing musicians for
performing musicians in the Midwest.*

Newsletter: Jerry's Musical Newsletter
4624 West Woodland Rd.
Minneapolis, MN 55424
phone: 612-926-7775

David Lusterman, Pub.
String Letter Press, The
Price Guide: Musical Instrument
Auction Price Guide
P.O. Box 767
San Anselmo, CA 94979-0767
phone: 415-485-6946 or 800-827-6837
fax: 415-485-0831
*Lists values for musical instruments
that are sold at auction; string
instruments, wind instruments, pianos,
etc.*

Repair Services

Frederick W. Oster
Vintage Instruments
1529 Pine St.
Philadelphia, PA 19102-4623
phone: 215-545-1100
fax: 215-735-3634
e-mail: vintageFO@aol.com
*Dealer, appraiser, consultant; rare &
antique musical instruments;
specializing in violins, violas, cellos,
bows; American fretted instruments -
guitars, mandolins, banjos; antique
wind instruments, etc.; SASE for reply.*

Accordions

Collectors

Fran Barnes
25 Fifth Ave. 9B
New York, NY 10003-4310
phone: 212-505-2720
*Wants images and figurines of small
guys playing the accordion or squeeze
box.*

Jared Snyder
511 Carpenter Lane
Philadelphia, PA 19119-3402
phone: 215-842-0896
e-mail: amedee@delphi.com
*Wants anything accordion related:
photographs, illustrations, postcards,
etc. with emphasis on button
accordions and exotic locales.*

Drums

Dealers

Ned Ingberman
Vintage Drum Center
2243 Ivory Dr.
Libertyville, IA 52567
phone: 800-729-3111 or 515-693-3611
fax: 515-693-3101
*Wants to buy pre-1980 drums, and
cymbals; also wants drum catalogs.*

Experts

Dan Paul
3049 W. 71st St.
Indianapolis, IN 46268-2241
phone: 317-293-5057 or 317-842-6165
fax: 317-842-6165
*Collects drums and related memora-
bilia including catalogs and
magazines.*

Harmonicas

Collectors

Alan G. Bates
495 Dogwood Dr.
Hockessin, DE 19707-9358
phone: 302-239-4296
e-mail: harmonicas@compuserve.com
*Seeking many makes and models,
especially with bells or trumpets
attached, three or more in one mount,
etc.; also wants harmonica catalogs,
advertising, display stands, records
and music.*

Horns

Dealers

Charles Fail Music, Inc.
4710G Ecton Dr.
Marietta, GA 30066-1095
phone: 404-591-0645 or 404-926-3960
fax: 404-591-9893
e-mail: cfail@mindspring.com
Internet: http://www.charlesfail.com
*Wants to buy saxophones, any age or
condition; also wants to buy old brass
and woodwind band instruments.*

Play-It-Again, Bob
1235 W. Murray Dr.
Springfield, MO 65810
phone: 800-755-8289
*Wants saxophones, double French
horns, old Cornets, and other antique
brass and reed instruments; also
wants trumpets, trombones, clarinets,
oboes, bassoons, English horns, etc.*

Horns (Brass)

Collectors

Jim Kopke
P.O. Box 4310
Dillon, CO 80435-4310
*Wants to buy antique and unusual
horns, other instruments, and related
items.*

Dealers

David Reed
841 West Main St.
Lorain, OH 44052-9763
phone: 216-428-6666
*Buys, sells and collects saxophones
and band instruments: silver plated or
brass; any condition; also wants
parts, early sax sales brochures, etc.*

Robb Stewart
Robb Stewart Brass Instruments
140 E. Santa Clara St., #18
Arcadia, CA 91006-3204
phone: 818-447-1904
fax: 818-447-1904
*Will buy all brass instruments,
especially pre-1880 and high quality
later instruments; also wants
interesting woodwinds; offers
restoration, repair and conservation
of brass instruments; send for free
price guide and sale list.*

Museums/Libraries

Franz X. Streitwieser
Streitwieser Foundation Trumpet
Museum
Newsletter: Sound the Trumpet, Blow
the Horn
880 Vaughan Rd.
Pottstown, PA 19465-8022
phone: 610-327-1351
fax: 610-970-9752
*A major collection over 750 brass
instruments; also prints, recordings,
books, figurines, sheet music, etc.;
seeking additions including old brass
instruments, band photos, uniforms
and recordings.*

Mechanical

Clubs/Associations

Australian Collectors of Mechanical
Musical Instruments
4 Lobellia St.
Chatswood, N.S.W. 2067
Australia

Jurgen Hocker
Society of Friends of Mechanical
Musical Instruments
Heiligenstock 46
D 5060 Bergisch
Gladbach, Germany

Beatrice Robertson
Musical Box Society International
Magazine: Journal of Mechanical Music
12140 Anchor Lane SW
Moore Haven, FL 33471
phone: 941-675-5828
e-mail: brobertsn@aol.com
Internet: http://www.mbsi.org
*Members collect, study, preserve all
types of instruments that mechanically
produce music: musical boxes,
orchestrions, band organs, player
pianos, musical clocks, automata, etc.;
"News Bulletin" contains Mart for
buying & selling.*

Collectors

Frank Rider
1062 Alber St.
Wabash, IN 46992-1003
phone: 219-563-5030

Angelo Rulli
887 Orange Ave. East
Saint Paul, MN 55106-2051
phone: 612-774-2590
fax: 612-772-2464

Dealers

John S. Zuk
106 Orchard St.
Belmont, MA 02178-2940
phone: 617-484-4800
fax: 617-864-3862
e-mail: jzuk@integral-inc.com
*Buys, sells and repairs musical boxes,
phonographs, and related mechanical
music machines.*

Danilo Konvalinka
Musical Wonder House Museum, The
18 High St.
P.O. Box 604
Wiscasset, ME 04578-0604
phone: 207-882-7163 or 800-336-3725
e-mail:
musicbox@musicalwonderhouse.com
Internet: http://
www.musicalwonderhouse.com/
*Buys & sells music boxes, wind-up
phonographs, player pianos & rolls,
cylinder records, complete or parts;
full repair services: combwork,
gearwork, spring repairs.*

Wayne Edmonston
2177 Bishop Estates Rd.
Jacksonville, FL 32259-3019
phone: 904-287-5996
fax: 904-287-4131
*Wants to buy music boxes of all types,
player grand pianos, coin-operated
machines, Wurlitzer 78 rpm jukeboxes,
nickelodeons and orchestrions, violin
machines, monkey and band organs,
and other automatic musical
machines.*

Doug Negus
Phonograph Phanatic
215 Mason St.
Sutherland, IA 51058-7606
phone: 712-446-2270 or 712-446-3746
e-mail: negus@nwidt.com
*Music boxes, phonographs, cylinder
records, pianos, NO piano rolls, older
mechanical musical instruments, pre-
1930; any parts or repairables
wanted.*

Experts

William H. Edgerton
P.O. Box 88
Darien, CT 06820-0588
phone: 203-655-0566
fax: 203-655-8066
*Buys, sells, repairs pianos and rolls,
musical boxes, player organs,
nickelodeons, and automata.*

Marty Persky
6514 N. Trumball
Chicago, IL 60645-3835
phone: 847-675-6114
fax: 847-675-6160
*Specializes in automatic musical
instruments.*

Museums/Libraries

Danilo Konvalinka
Musical Wonder House Museum, The
18 High St.
P.O. Box 604
Wiscasset, ME 04578-0604
phone: 207-882-7163 or 800-336-3725
e-mail:
musicbox@musicalwonderhouse.com
Internet: http://
www.musicalwonderhouse.com/
*America's unique Music Museum in
an 1852 sea captain's mansion;
antique music boxes, player pianos,
wind-up phonographs; restored pieces
in rooms furnished with antiques of
the period; founded 1963; instruments
bought, sold, repaired.*

Smithsonian Institution
Division of Musical History
Washington, DC 20560
Internet: http://www.si.edu/

Neil Ratliff
Music Library
Hornbrake 3210
College Park, MD 20742

Marvin Yagoda
Marvin's Marvelous Mechanical
Museum
31005 Orchard Rd.
Farmington, MI 48334
phone: 313-626-5020

Repair Services

Danilo Konvalinka
Musical Wonder House Museum, The
18 High St.
P.O. Box 604
Wiscasset, ME 04578-0604
phone: 207-882-7163 or 800-336-3725
e-mail:
musicbox@musicalwonderhouse.com
Internet: http://
www.musicalwonderhouse.com/
*Buys & sells music boxes, wind-up
phonographs, player pianos & rolls,
cylinder records, complete or parts;
full repair services: combwork,
gearwork, spring repairs.*

Mechanical (Band Organs)

(see also CAROUSELS & CAROU-
SEL FIGURES; MUSICAL
INSTRUMENTS, Organs)

Clubs/Associations

Ken Smith
American Band Organ Association
3766 Mann Rd.
Blacklick, OH 43004
*Members interested building, re-
building, and playing band,
fairground, and monkey organs.*

Dealers

Alan S. Erb, P.E. (M.E.)
Erb Engineering
2318 Tahiti St.
Hayward, CA 94545-3436
phone: 510-783-5068
fax: 510-783-5068
Internet: http://www.quikpage.com/E/
erbc
*Expert buys, sells, restores, repairs
organs and parts; offers the finest
pipework including reed pipes; also
makes custom made organs and
calliopes to any customer specification (commercial use, home use, etc.)*

Experts

Mike Kitner
P.O. Box 555
Carlisle, PA 17013
phone: 717-249-3851
Specializes in band organs.

Jerry Biasella
286 W. 14th Pl.
Chicago Heights, IL 60411
phone: 708-756-3307
Specializes in band organs.

Art Reblitz
Reblite Restorations Inc.
P.O. Box 7392
Colorado Springs, CO 80933
*Specializes in the restoration of
orchestrions and band organs; also
music arranging for these instruments.*

Repair Services

Art Reblitz
Reblite Restorations Inc.
P.O. Box 7392
Colorado Springs, CO 80933
*Specializes in the restoration of
orchestrions and band organs; also
music arranging for these instruments.*

Alan S. Erb, P.E. (M.E.)
Erb Engineering
2318 Tahiti St.
Hayward, CA 94545-3436
phone: 510-783-5068
fax: 510-783-5068
Internet: http://www.quikpage.com/E/
erbc
*Expert buys, sells, restores, repairs
organs and parts; offers the finest
pipework including reed pipes; also
makes custom made organs and
calliopes to any customer specification (commercial use, home use, etc.)*

Repro. Sources

Stinson Organ Co.
4691 Co. Rd. 91
Bellefontaine, OH 43311
phone: 515-593-5709
Makes new band organs.

Organs

(see also MUSIC BOXES; MUSICAL
INSTRUMENTS, Mechanical [Band
Organs])

Clubs/Associations

J.L.M. Van Dinteren
Netherlands Mechanical Organ Society
(KDV)
Postbus 147
6160 AC Geleen
Netherlands

Arthur H. Sanders
Reed Organ Society, Inc. - The Musical
Museum
Magazine: Reed Organ Society Bulletin
P.O. Box 901
Deansboro, NY 13328
phone: 315-841-8774
*Focuses to all aspects of reed organs:
music, construction, historical value,
repair, etc.*

Dealers

Gary Besteman
Pump & Pipe Shop, The
7698 Kraft Ave.
Caledonia, MI 49316-9402
phone: 616-891-8743
Specializes in the restoration, buying and selling of reed organs; also buys parts.

Don Bryant
Bryant Antique Players
4819 Stallcup
Mesquite, TX 75150-1143
phone: 972-270-0135
fax: 972-613-1627
e-mail: aplayr@airmail.net
Sales, service and rebuilding of player pianos, pump organs, reproducing & coin-operated instruments, pin balls, & game room equipment; since 1975

Experts

Ken Danckaert
231 Kennedy Ct.
Severna Park, MD 21146-3039
phone: 410-544-0260
e-mail: ken@weasel.acs.umbc.edu
Internet: http://www.kend@lemur.org
Collects, buys, sells, appraises, and repairs music boxes, phonographs, and organettes; in business since 1972; an expert who gives lectures, presentations and videos.

Periodicals

Fred Pelton
Newsletter: Great Lakes Reed Organ Newsletter, The
3517 Mill Race
Caledonia, MI 49316
phone: 616-698-2112
Articles, restoration tips.

Repair Services

Gary Besteman
Pump & Pipe Shop, The
7698 Kraft Ave.
Caledonia, MI 49316-9402
phone: 616-891-8743
Specializes in the restoration, buying and selling of reed organs; also buys parts.

Pianos

(see also PIANOS, Miniature)

Museums/Libraries

Roland Loest, Cur.
Museum of the American Piano, The
211 West 58th St.
New York, NY 10019
phone: 212-246-4646
Collection of about 25 primarily American pianos spanning a period from the late 1700s to 1940s; also related tools, machines.

Periodicals

David Lusterman, Pub.
String Letter Press, The
Magazine: Piano & Keyboard
P.O. Box 767
San Anselmo, CA 94979-0767
phone: 415-485-6946 or 800-827-6837
fax: 415-485-0831
A bi-monthly magazine of interviews, memories, insights, practical knowledge, music to play, piano history, legend & lore; for piano teachers, beginning through advanced students, educators, musicologists, amateur piano players.

Pianos (Player)

(see also PIANO ROLLS)

Clubs/Associations

Everson Whittle, Sec.
North West Player Piano Association, The
Journal: NWPPA Journal
47 Raikes Road, Preston
Lancashire PR1 5EQ, U.K.
phone: 01772 792795
Association dealing in all aspects of Mechanical Music, repair of instruments, and interest in the hobby.

Nederlandse Pianola Vereniging (Dutch Pianola Association)
Eikendreef 24
5342 HR OSS
The Netherlands

Frances Broadway
Player Piano Group
36 Snyder Rd.
Stoke Newington
London N16 7UF, U.K.

Michael A. Barnhart, Mem.
Automatic Musical Instrument Collectors Association (AMICA)
Magazine: AMICA News Bulletin
919 Lantern Glow Trail
Dayton, OH 45431-2915
phone: 513-254-5580
Purpose is to foster preservation and appreciation of instruments and recordings of roll-actuated instruments, especially piano type.

Dealers

David M. Hall, Sr.
P.O. Box 161
Uxbridge, MA 01569
phone: 508-278-2874
Player piano sales and service since 1959; pickup and deliver on the East Coast with own trucks.

Don Bryant
Bryant Antique Players
4819 Stallcup
Mesquite, TX 75150-1143
phone: 972-270-0135
fax: 972-613-1627
e-mail: aplayr@airmail.net
Sales, service and rebuilding of player pianos, pump organs, reproducing &

coin-operated instruments, pin balls, & game room equipment; since 1975.

Museums/Libraries

International Piano Archives at Maryland, Neil Ratliff Music Library
Hornbrake 3210
College Park, MD 20742

Repair Services

Beatrice Bryant
Bryant Stove Works & Music Inc.
RR 2 Rich Rd.
P.O. Box 2048
Thorndike, ME 04986
phone: 207-568-3665
Restores player pianos.

Jeff Morgan
833 S. Front St.
Allentown, PA 18103-3384
phone: 610-797-3381
fax: 610-797-3381
Consultant, expert who specializes in the repair, restoration and technical history of reproducing pianos.

Mel Septon
9045 N. Karlov Ave.
Skokie, IL 60076
phone: 708-679-3455
Specializes in the repair of reproducing pianos.

W. Gilstrap
Player Action Rebuilding
1374 E. Chestnut St.
Canton, IL 61520-2365
Rebuilds all makes of player pianos actions: Gulbransen, Schulz, Standard, etc.; packing crate supplied for stacks.

Bill Singleton
1101 South Kingshighway
Saint Louis, MO 63110
Specializes in the repair of reproducing pianos.

Craig Brougher
Brougher Restorations
3500 Claremont
Independence, MO 64052
phone: 816-254-1693
Complete restoration facilities for reproducers, orchestrions and fine grand pianos; also case and veneer repairs.

Alan S. Erb, P.E. (M.E.)
Erb Engineering
2318 Tahiti St.
Hayward, CA 94545-3436
phone: 510-783-5068
fax: 510-783-5068
Internet: http://www.quikpage.com/E/erbc
Expert buys, sells, restores, repairs organs and parts; offers the finest pipework including reed pipes; also makes custom made organs and calliopes to any customer specification (commercial use, home use, etc.)

Suppliers

Player Piano Co., Inc.
704 East Douglas
Wichita, KS 67202-3506
phone: 316-263-3241 or 316-263-1714
Complete line of player piano restoration supplies, service manuals, music rolls; catalog if mailed free upon request.

Picks

Collectors

Tony Weathers
4043 McKinley Dr.
Lithonia, GA 30058
phone: 404-979-0241
Buys, sells, trades guitar picks; any musical swag.

String

Collectors

Richard Schwartz
24550 Hawthorne Dr.
Cleveland, OH 44122-2314
phone: 216-464-0183
Wants to buy older violins, violas, cellos, basses, bows, etc.; also wants books and catalogs about string instruments.

Ann Pertoney
2344-D Oakley Ave.
Chicago, IL 60608

Dealers

Jim Bollman
Music Emporium, Inc., The
165 Massachusetts Ave.
Lexington, MA 02173-4039
phone: 617-860-0049
fax: 617-860-0051
Wants old guitars, ukuleles, banjos, mandolins, concertinas, wooden flutes or other stringed instruments in any condition.

Stanley M. Jay
Mandolin Brothers, Ltd.
Newsletter: Vintage News, The
629 Forest Ave.
Staten Island, NY 10310-2515
phone: 718-981-3226 or 718-981-8585
fax: 718-816-4416
e-mail: mandolin@ix.netcom.com
Internet: http://www.mandoweb.com
Wants to buy guitars, banjos & mandolins by fine American brands: Gibson, C.F. Martin, National, Dobro, D'Angelico, Fender, Gretsch, Rickenbacker, Paramount, Vega, B&D, Epiphone, Stromberg, S.S. Stewart; free telephone appraisals.

R.D. Kress
503 W. Lakeshore Dr. #503A1
Port Clinton, OH 43452-9324
Wants violas, cellos, violins, string basses.

Stan Werbin
Elderly Instruments
P.O. Box 14210
Lansing, MI 48901-4210
phone: 517-372-7890 or 517-372-7880
fax: 517-372-5155
e-mail: swerbin@elderly.com
Internet: http://www.elderly.com
Specializes in American made fretted stringed instruments including guitars, banjos, mandolins: by Martin, Gibson, Vega, B&D, D'Angelico, Stromberg, Maurer, Fender, etc.

Experts

David E. Schenkman
Turtle Hill Banjo Co.
P.O. Box 265
Bryantown, MD 20617-0265
phone: 301-274-3441
Buying vintage stringed instruments: banjos, guitars, mandolins, and ukuleles; especially wants instruments made by Gibson, Martin, Fairbanks, B & D, Bacon, Vega, Paramount, Weymann, etc.

Fritz Reuter
Fritz Reuter & Sons, Inc.
3917 W. Touhy Ave.
Chicago, IL 60645-1027
phone: 708-677-7255 or 708-677-7257
fax: 708-677-7256
Internet: http://www.fritz-reuter.com
Specializes in string instruments (violins, violas, cellos, bows); also repairs and restores string instruments.

Periodicals

Mary Van Clay
Magazine: Strings
P.O. Box 767
San Anselmo, CA 94979-0767
phone: 415-485-6946 or 800-827-6837
fax: 415-485-0831
The bi-monthly magazine for players and makers of bowed instruments; articles, profiles, instrument making and repair, music schools, ads; also publishes annual auction Price Guide and annual Resource Guide.

Repro. Sources

John & Ann Rawdon
Dulcimers by JR
10068 Stonecreek Rd.
Newcomerstown, OH 43832
phone: 614-498-7753
Builders of fine quality lap and hammered dulcimers; price lists upon request; some wholesale, ask for details.

String (Guitars)

Appraisers

Steve Underwood, ISA
Appraisals & Consulting by F. Steven Underwood
2516 Larwood Dr.
Charleston, WV 25302-4318
phone: 304-345-4089
Independent, professional appraisals of electric and acoustic guitars, banjos, mandolins, etc. for insurance, estate valuation, tax, legal, and other matters; Member, International Society of Appraisers; does not appraise violins.

Paul Johnson
Gruhn Guitars, Inc.
400 Broadway
Nashville, TN 37203-3931
phone: 615-256-2033
fax: 615-255-2021
e-mail: gruhn@gruhn.com
Internet: http://ww.gruhn.com/
Buys, sells, appraises, and specializes in American vintage or custom-made fretted instruments; issues monthly catalog of over 1500 vintage guitars, mandolins and banjos.

Collectors

K. Wiley
719 Baldwin SE
Grand Rapids, MI 49503-4470
phone: 616-451-8410
Wants American-made stringed musical instruments, particularly electric guitars; also wants amps and recording equipment.

Sonny Goldson
1413 Magnolia Lane
Midwest City, OK 73110
phone: 405-737-3312
fax: 405-737-3355
Wants to buy old guitars, amplifiers and effects: Gibson, Fender, VOX, Gretsch, Ricken Backer, Mosrite, Silvertone, Guico, Harmony, Martin, Epiphone, National, Valco.

Dealers

Southworth Guitars
7854 Old Georgetown Rd.
Bethesda, MD 20814
phone: 301-718-1667
fax: 301-718-0391

American Vintage, Inc.
8375 Leesburg Pike, Ste. 333
Vienna, VA 22182
phone: 703-759-4113
fax: 703-749-7978

East Coast Guitars
8 Oak Grove Pl.
Dublin, VA 24084-2533

Guitar Emporium
1610 Bardstown Rd.
Louisville, KY 40205
phone: 502-459-4153
fax: 502-454-3661

Gordy's Music
23525 Woodward Ave.
Ferndale, MI 48220
phone: 810-546-7447
fax: 810-546-5249

Stan Werbin
Elderly Instruments
P.O. Box 14210
Lansing, MI 48901-4210
phone: 517-372-7890 or 517-372-7880
fax: 517-372-5155
e-mail: swerbin@elderly.com
Internet: http://www.elderly.com
Specializes in American made fretted stringed instruments including guitars, banjos, mandolins: by Martin, Gibson, Vega, B&D, D'Angelico, Stromberg, Maurer, Fender, etc.

Guitarville
19258 15th NE
Seattle, WA 98155
phone: 206-363-8188
fax: 206-363-0478
e-mail: 102101.2517@compuserve.com

Experts

Mike Longworth
Longworth Enterprises
P.O. Box 202
Nazareth, PA 18064
phone: 610-759-4440
fax: 610-759-2340
Historian, Martin Guitar Co.; curator (ret.) of Martin Museum; author of "Martin Guitars, A History"; offers appraisals and authoritative letters on Martin instruments.

George Gruhn
Gruhn Guitars, Inc.
400 Broadway
Nashville, TN 37203-3931
phone: 615-256-2033
fax: 615-255-2021
e-mail: gruhn@gruhn.com
Internet: http://www.gruhn.com/
Buys, sells, appraises, and specializes in American vintage or custom-made fretted instruments; issues monthly catalog of over 1500 vintage guitars, mandolins and banjos.

Steve Evans
Jacksonville Guitar Center
1105 Burman Dr.
Jacksonville, AR 72076-4386
phone: 501-982-4933
Buys, collects and specializes in vintage guitars; has collection of over 100 cowboy guitars.

Museums/Libraries

Steve Evans
Jacksonville Guitar Center
1105 Burman Dr.
Jacksonville, AR 72076-4386
phone: 501-982-4933
Large collection of vintage guitars on permanent display; includes over 100 cowboy guitars, c. 1930s-1950s, made with painted cowboy scenes showing Gene Autry, Roy Rogers, Buck Jones and others.

Periodicals

Jim & Larry Acunto
Magazine: 20th Century Guitar
135 Oser Ave.
Hauppauge, NY 11788
phone: 516-273-1674
fax: 516-434-9057
A bi-monthly magazine covering the vintage guitar market; up-to-date reports on technical information, guitar prices, shows, photo classifieds, as well as interesting, off-beat interviews with celebrity musicians who collect.

Magazine: Bluegrass Unlimited
P.O. Box 111
Broad Run, VA 22014
phone: 540-349-8181 or 800-258-4727
fax: 540-341-0011
Bluegrass Festival calendar, artist interviews, personal appearance calendar, some articles about vintage guitars.

Vintage Guitar Inc.
Magazine: Vintage Guitar Magazine
P.O. Box 7301
Bismarck, ND 58507
phone: 701-255-1197
fax: 701-255-0250
e-mail: vintage@vguitar.com
Internet: http://www.vguitar.com
Guitar related articles, ads, parts, supplies, books, music, used and new guitars for sale, amps, price guides, guitar factories, repairs, interviews, guitar cases.

Vintage Guitar Inc.
Magazine: VG Classics
P.O. Box 7301
Bismarck, ND 58507
phone: 701-255-1197
fax: 701-255-0250
e-mail: vintage@vguitar.com
Internet: http://www.vguitar.com
A quarterly glossy magazine dedicated to vintage guitars and other stringed instruments; also publishes "The Official Vintage Guitar Magazine Instrument Price Guide."

Magazine: Guitar Player
600 Harrison St.
San Francisco, CA 94107
phone: 415-655-4308
Monthly glossy magazine serving the guitar playing community; some articles about collectible vintage guitars.

Magazine: Acoustic Guitar
P.O. Box 767
San Anselmo, CA 94979-0767
phone: 415-485-6946 or 800-827-6837
fax: 415-485-0831
The magazine acoustic guitars.

Suppliers

C.F. Martin Guitar Co.
P.O. Box 202
Nazareth, PA 18064
phone: 610-759-4440
fax: 610-759-2340
*Offers Woodworker's Guitar Makers
Connection for Woodworkers &
Luthiers; tools, materials, parts for
the fretted instrument maker; factory
tours M-F; Guitar Makers Connection
catalog $2 ppd.*

String (Violins)

Collectors

Ron Midgett
15 Lovefield St.
Easthampton, MA 01027
phone: 413-527-8033 or 800-207-2400
*Wants violins, violas, cellos;
American or European.*

Dealers

William D. Voiers
William D. Voiers Fine Musical
Instruments
P.O. Box 23
North Egremont, MA 01252
phone: 413-528-3321 or 800-788-3521
fax: 413-528-5801
*Dealer, collector, appraiser of the
violin family of instruments: violins,
violas, cellos, bows, banjos, ukuleles,
guitars and mandolins; electric or
acoustic; also saxes, brasses, drums,
percussion; also buys, sells, collects
and trades.*

Robert Portukalian
Providence Violin Shop
1279 North Main St.
Providence, RI 02904
phone: 401-521-5145
*Wants quality handcrafted or factory-
made violins.*

Peter Zaret
Peter Zaret Violins
861 W 46th St.
Norfolk, VA 23508-2009
phone: 800-222-2998 or 804-423-3336
fax: 804-423-3340
e-mail: zaret@exis.net
*Sells all sizes of new and old violins
including violins made in China and
Eastern Europe; also deals in violas,
cellos and their bows; instruments &
bows by contemporary luthier also
available; expert repairs & bow
rehairing.*

John Montgomery
John Montgomery, Inc.
509 Hillsborough St.
Raleigh, NC 27603-1729
phone: 919-821-4459
fax: 919-821-4459
*Dealer in the violin family of
instruments; violin maker and
restorer.*

Al Stancel
Casa Del Sol Violins, Ltd.
4302 East 62nd St.
Indianapolis, IN 46220-4568
phone: 800-423-0236 or 317-257-9923
*Buys, sells, and restores old violins;
also makes and sells new violins;
especially wants French bows and
Italian violins.*

Experts

William L. Monical
William L. Monical, Inc., Dealers &
Restorers of Fine Violins
288 Richmond Terrace
Staten Island, NY 10301-1512
phone: 718-816-7878 or 718-816-7176
fax: 718-816-7711
*Specializes in bowed string
instruments of modern & Baroque
violin and viola da gamba families:
sales, restoration, appraisals, cases.*

Periodicals

Magazine: Strad, The
P.O. Box 363
Avenel, NJ 07001-0363
phone: 800-688-6247
*A monthly English magazine with
auction results, orchestral news,
master classes, and educational
developments; performers, great
teachers, master luthiers, leading
critics.*

MYSTERY/DETECTIVE ITEMS

(see also BOOKS, Mystery;
CAMERAS & CAMERA EQUIP-
MENT, Subminiature; CHARACTER
COLLECTIBLES, Sherlock Holmes;
CHARACTER COLLECTIBLES, Spy
Memorabilia; MAGAZINES, Mystery;
SPY EQUIPMENT)

Collectors

Beverley Furlow-Cleary
1555 N. Arcadia Ave.
Tucson, AZ 85712-4010
phone: 502-323-1709
e-mail: beverleyf@aol.com
*Buys, sells, and appraises collectible
mystery/detective items: books,
vintage clothing and hats.*

MYSTICAL ARTS

(see UFO'S & UNEXPLAINED
PHENOMENA)

Here are some tips when contacting someone listed in this book:

When requesting information about a particular item, include a description (material, dimensions, maker's mark, model number, etc.) and a photo, sketch, or photocopy of the item in question. ■

Always ask if there are charges for samples or for the services requested. ■

When writing, please be sure to include a Large (#10 business size) Self-Addressed and Stamped Envelope (LSASE) if requesting a reply or the return of photographs. ■

Never call collect unless otherwise directed. When calling, be considerate of time zone differences and always ask if the party you are calling has time to talk. When leaving an answering machine message, always instruct the party to call you back collect. ■

NAPKIN DOLLS

Collectors

Bobbie & Alan Bryson
1 St. Eleanoras Ln.
Tuckahoe, NY 10707-1307
phone: 914-779-1405
e-mail: napkindoll@aol.com

NAPKIN RINGS

Figural

Collectors

Steve Aaronson
P.O. Box 7522
Northridge, CA 91327
phone: 818-368-6052
*Wants to buy American silverplate
figural napkin rings; old only.*

Maria E. Raymond
Plow & Pen, Inc.
P.O. Box 251
Robbins, CA 95676-0251
phone: 916-735-6596
fax: 916-735-6112
e-mail: 73113.1362@compuserve.com
*Interested in buying Meriden
Company napkin rings only.*

Dealers

Sandra Whitson
Van Anda's Antiques
P.O. Box 272
Lititz, PA 17543-0272
phone: 717-626-4978
fax: 717-626-7625
*Buys and sells fine quality Victorian
figural napkin rings; co-author of
"Figural Napkin Rings" (1996), a
collector's identification and value
guide.*

NASA

(see SPACE COLLECTIBLES)

NATIVE AMERICAN ARTS

(see AMERICAN INDIAN)

NATURAL HISTORY

(see also ANIMAL COLLECTIBLES;
ASTRONOMICAL ITEMS; BOOKS,
Reference [Natural History]; CAVE
RELATED ITEMS; FOSSILS;
HERITAGE RESOURCES;
LAPIDARY; MINERALS)

Book Sellers

Frank J. Mikesh
1356 Walden Rd.
Walnut Creek, CA 94596-3158
phone: 510-934-9243
e-mail: natscibooks@netvista.net
Internet: http://www.netvista.net/
~natscibooks

NAUTICAL ANTIQUES

(see also ART, Marine; BOATS;
COAST GUARD; DIVING
EQUIPMENT; INSTRUMENTS &
DEVICES; MAPS & CHARTS;
IVORY; OCEAN LINER MEMORA-
BILIA; OUTBOARD MOTORS;
SCRIMSHAW; SEASHELLS;
SHIPPING; SHIP RELATED;
STEAMBOAT COLLECTIBLES;
TITANIC MEMORABILIA;
WHALES & DOLPHINS; WHALING)

Auction Services

Chuck Deluca
Maritime Auctions
P.O. Box 322
York, ME 03909
phone: 207-363-4247
fax: 207-363-1416
e-mail: maritim2@ix.netcom.com
Internet: http://www.maritiques.com
*Three catalog auctions per year in
March, July and October.*

Clubs/Associations

Nautical Research Guild
Journal: Nautical Research Journal
62 Marlboro St.
Newburyport, MA 01950-3134
phone: 508-462-6970
Internet: http://www.naut-Res-Guild.org
*Focuses on the story of the ship, the
technologies of marine transportation,
the shipwrights and sailors.*

National Maritime Historical Society
Magazine: Sea History
P.O. Box 68
Peekskill, NY 10566-9934
phone: 914-737-7378
e-mail: seahistory@aol.com
Internet: http://www.marineart.com/
nmhs/
*Preservation (full-rigger ship,
brigantine, schooner, tug boat),
education to heighten the maritime
awareness of young Americans across
the country, and publication of the
magazines "Sea History" and the
monthly newsletter "Gazette."*

Harry D. Barry
Air Horn & Steam Whistle Enthusiasts
Newsletter: Horn & Whistle
275 Windswept Dr.
North East, PA 16428
phone: 814-725-8150
*Purpose is to preserve, increase, and
disseminate knowledge concerning
horns, whistles, sirens, and bells in
industrial, marine, transportation,
signaling, and warning applications.*

Collectors

Bob Glick
Columbia Trading Company
1 Barnstable Rd.
Hyannis, MA 02601
phone: 508-778-2929
fax: 508-778-2922
e-mail: nautical@capecod.net
Internet: http://www.by-the-sea.com/
nautical/
*Wants to buy all marine items; items
relating to lighthouses, Coast Guard,
naval, yachting, marine architecture,
marine engineering, boating, sailing,
marine engines, outboard motors,
boat building, ship building, etc.*

Stephen Seltzer
7912 Georgia Ave.
Silver Spring, MD 20910-4837
phone: 301-565-2444 or 301-565-3339
fax: 301-565-2228
e-mail: eseltzer@aol.com
*Wants to buy authentic brass items
salvaged form ships.*

Dealers

Bernhard W. Sound
Jonesport Nautical Art & Antiques
20 Everett St.
Fitchburg, MA 01420-5504
phone: 508-537-1413 or 207-497-5655
fax: 508-537-1413
e-mail: bsund@NauticalAntiques.com
Internet: http://
www.NauticalAntiques.com
*Specializes in nautical art, nautical
antiques, and nautical reproductions:
compasses, binnacles, charts, and
other items of interest.*

James W. Claflin
Kenrick A. Claflin & Son
30 Hudson St.
Northborough, MA 01532
phone: 508-869-6955
*Collectors and dealers in fine nautical
antiques; specializing in U.S.
Lighthouse Service, U.S. Lifesaving
Service, U.S. Revenue Cutter Service,
U.S. Coast Guard.*

Richard Dermody
Brass n' Bounty
68 Front St.
Marblehead, MA 01945-3275
phone: 617-631-3864 or 617-631-6204
*Buys and sells navigation instruments,
telescopes, binnacles, compasses,
sextants, clocks, barometers; also
yachting items.*

Andrew Jacobson
Andrew Jacobson Marine Antiques
P.O. Box 2155
South Hamilton, MA 01982-0155
phone: 508-468-6276
*Fine marine artifacts, paintings,
models, half-hulls, antique scrimshaw,
navigational instruments, photography, out-of-print books, manuscript
material.*

John F. Rinaldi
Nautical Antiques
P.O. Box 765
Kennebunkport, ME 04046-0765
phone: 207-967-3218
fax: 207-967-2918
*Buys and sells marine antiques,
antique scrimshaw, paintings, naval
items; fully illustrated catalog for $5.*

John T. Newton
Marine Antiques
Rte. 1 Drawer D
Wiscasset, ME 04578
phone: 207-882-7203
*Buys and sells nautical antiques such
as ship carvings, instruments, half
models, etc.*

James & Ann Marenakos
Quester Gallery
77 Main St.
P.O. Box 446
Stonington, CT 06378
phone: 203-535-3860
fax: 203-535-3533
*Buys, sells, consults on 19th & 20th
century marine paintings, ships
models, bronzes, campaign furniture,
etc.*

J. Tobin
Antique & Classic Boats
12 Carstead Dr.
Slingerlands, NY 12159
phone: 518-439-0477
fax: 518-439-0477

Robert Shourot
Coastal Diving Operations
10297 Rainbow Rd.
Carrollton, VA 23314-4109
phone: 757-826-3945
fax: 757-826-7879
*Specialty is nautical artifacts and
diving antiques including pumps,
helmets, bells, steam gauges, engine
telegraphs, portholes, lights, etc.*

Daniel Alex Haase
Haase's Nautical Antiques & Furnishings
6150 Virginia Beach Blvd.
Norfolk, VA 23502
phone: 804-461-2465 or 804-461-6150
*Makers of resin-covered hatch cover
tables; buys and sells nautical
antiques: brass lights, ship's wheels,
sextants, etc.; also specializes in
restoring nautical antiques.*

James & Norvell Kennedy
James Kennedy Antiques, Ltd.
905 W. Main St.
Durham, NC 27701-2054
phone: 919-682-1040 or 800-236-1868
fax: 919-683-9633
*Specialist in scientific and medical
instruments and prints; also nautical
instruments.*

Raymond & Lyn Newman
Martifacts, Inc.
P.O. Box 8604
Jacksonville, FL 32239-0604
phone: 904-645-0150
fax: 904-645-0150
Buys/sells authentic brass and/or wood nautical items salvaged from ships: lights, compasses, clocks, bells, hatch covers, sextants, etc.

John McSwain
Marine Antiques & Maritime Artifacts
4155 Hwy. 11
Deland, FL 32724-9745
phone: 904-734-8786
fax: 904-738-5629
e-mail: mcswain1@mindspring.com
Specializes in deep sea diving, gauges, antique outboard motors 1900-1955, boating equipment and accessories.

Jack P. Berten
Antiques of Merit
2400 SW 30th Ave.
Hallandale, FL 33009
phone: 305-456-1657 or 305-763-3223
fax: 305-767-3528
Specializes in 18th, 19th and early 20th century marine antiques.

Marc J. Cohen
P.O. Box 220153
Hollywood, FL 33022-0153
phone: 954-565-9754
Buys, sells and collects antique "hard hat" diving gear: helmets, hoses, shoes, knives, weights, belts, dresses, pumps, tools, catalogs, books, pictures, and other related "hard hat" diving equipment items.

Donald E. Taussig
Sanders' Antique Mall
22 N. Lemon Ave.
Sarasota, FL 34236-5711
phone: 941-366-0400
fax: 941-388-2053
e-mail: sandersant@aol.com
Buys and sells ship models, helmets, instruments, maps, clocks, bells, etc.

Gordon Stanley
Maritime Gallery
P.O. Box 40
Fulton, TX 78358-0040
phone: 512-729-4026
Specializes in 1800s to 1900s maritime artifacts; shows at high quality antique shows.

Al & Bobbie Roberts
Rational Past, The
221 Oceano Dr.
Los Angeles, CA 90049
phone: 310-476-6277
fax: 310-476-6278
e-mail: rational-past@mindspring.com
Organizer of West Coast Scientific & Technical Antique and Collectible Shows (Los Angeles in the winter and San Francisco are in late summer.)

Rod & Becky Cardoza
West Sea Company
2495 Congress St.
San Diego, CA 92110-2820
phone: 619-296-5356
fax: 619-296-1097
Buys, sells all types of marine paintings, scrimshaw, ships' carvings, ship models, navigational and scientific instruments, sailor handcrafts, campaign furniture, hard hat diving, antique marine photography, nautical books, ceramics.

Kenneth Brown
Franks Fisherman
366 Jefferson St.
San Francisco, CA 94133
phone: 415-775-1165
fax: 415-776-6549
e-mail: franksfish@earthlink.net
Fine selection of authentic nautical antiques including diving helmets, scrimshaw and whaling artifacts, ship models and scientific instruments; buys, sells, consignments, rentals; located two blocks from SF Maritime Museum.

Fred Von Wiegen
Ship Store Galleries
P.O. Box 1058
Kapaa, HI 96746-1058
phone: 808-822-4999
Buys and sells 18th and 19th century shipboard items: old maps and charts, models, scrimshaw; particularly Pacific vessels and South Sea items.

James W. Coulson
Cuttysark of Bellevue
10235 Main St.
Bellevue, WA 98004-6121
phone: 206-453-1265
fax: 206-451-8779
Buys and sells a general line of marine items: flags, marine antiques, models, clocks, etc.

A. Rex Bennett
Anchor Antiques Co.
5129 No. Pearl St.
Tacoma, WA 98407
phone: 206-752-1134
Specializes in diver's helmets and old oil lamps.

Experts

Sara Conklin
239 Sierra Pt. Rd.
Brisbane, CA 94005-1664
phone: 415-467-6249
fax: 415-467-6249
e-mail: 76363.536@compuserve.com
Appraises maritime items and collections: ship models, scrimshaw, navigational instruments, figurehead carvings, marine art, paper & ephemera archival collections, telescopes, shipwrecks, diving equip., ocean liner memorabilia, whaling.

Museums/Libraries

Peabody Museum of Salem
Magazine: American Neptune
East India Square
Salem, MA 01970
phone: 617-745-9500

Kittery Historical & Naval Museum
Rogers Road
P.O. Box 453
Kittery, ME 03904
phone: 207-439-3080
Shipwright's tools, whaling gear, scrimshaw, navigation instruments, ship models (including shadow boxes and builders' half hulls), submarines, Portsmouth Naval Shipyard material.

Mystic Seaport Museum
75 Greenmanville Ave.
P.O. Box 6000
Mystic, CT 06355-0990
phone: 203-572-0711 or 203-572-5317
e-mail: info@mysticseaport.org
Internet: http://www.mysticseaport.org
General focus is 19th century seafaring America: scrimshaw, figureheads, instruments, maritime art, carvings, etc.

U.S. Naval Academy Museum
Naval Academy, MD 21402
phone: 410-293-1000
Focuses on the heritage of the U.S. Navy; ship models, paintings, prints, flags, uniforms, swords, medals, sculptures, rare books, photographs, instruments and gear, personal memorabilia.

Pete Lesher, Cur.
Chesapeake Bay Maritime Museum
Magazine: Water Gauge, The
P.O. Box 636
Saint Michaels, MD 21663-0636
phone: 410-745-2916
fax: 410-745-6088
Internet: http://www.cbmm.org
A major regional maritime museum with a 5200 volume research library; collections include 10,000 objects, 9.000 photos, 1,200 ships' plans, 72 linear feet of manuscripts; decoys, oystering, lighthouses, charts, nautical, tools.

Mariners' Museum, The
100 Museum Dr.
Newport News, VA 23606
phone: 804-595-0368
Internet: http://www.mariner.org

Leon Lyons
9-C King St.
Saint Augustine, FL 32084-4451
phone: 904-825-0184 or 904-825-4504
fax: 904-824-9588
A private museum; main focus is on deep sea diving equipment, including books, photos, toys, etc.; world's largest collection; general interest in maritime artifacts and instruments.

Keith R. Gill
Museum of Science & Industry
57th St. & Lake Shore Dr.
Chicago, IL 60637
phone: 312-684-1414
fax: 312-684-5580

Maritime Museum of Monterey
5 Custom House Plaza
Monterey, CA 93940-2430
phone: 408-375-9259
fax: 408-665-3054

Lynn Cullivan
San Francisco Maritime National
   Historical Park
Bldg. E, Fort Mason Center
San Francisco, CA 94123
phone: 415-556-3002
fax: 415-556-1624

On-Line Services

Bill Momsen
Nautical Brass Online
P.O. Box 3966
Fort Myers, FL 33918-3966
e-mail: nbrass@peganet.com
Internet: http://members.aol.com/nbrass/ezine.htm
Provides free on-line information about nautical antiques.

Periodicals

Robert R. McKenna, Ed.
Magazine: Nautical Collector
One Whale Oil Row
New London, CT 06320
phone: 860-444-0127
fax: 860-444-0129
e-mail: nautworld@aol.com
An authoritative bi-monthly magazine on the antiques, collectibles, art, artifacts, literature and memorabilia associated with the seas, lakes and waterways.

Repair Services

Richard Dermody
Brass n' Bounty
68 Front St.
Marblehead, MA 01945-3275
phone: 617-631-3864 or 617-631-6204
Repairs nautical instruments such as compasses, sextants, telescopes; polishes and lacquers marine hardware and lights.

Frank (Buddy) Pollock
shorevillagemaritimerestorations
45 Lawn Ave.
Rockland, ME 04841
phone: 207-596-2962
Restoration/cleaning of classical lighthouse lenses; restoration of all maritime artifacts; glass and brass a specialty; all antique electronics; from polishing to complete restoration; volunteer restorer for Shore Village Museum, ME.

New York Nautical Instrument &
Service Corp.
140 West Broadway
New York, NY 10013
phone: 212-962-4522
fax: 212-406-8420
*Repairs nautical instruments such as
sextants, barometers, marine clocks,
compasses, etc.*

Diving

Clubs/Associations

Nick Baker, Sec.
Historical Diving Society
Magazine: Underwater Contractor
Magazine
23 Brompton Drive
Brierley Hill
West Midlands DY5 3N7, U.K.
phone: (44) 1384 896079
fax: (44) 1384 896079
e-mail: 101463.726@compuserve.com
Internet: http://www.resort-guide.co.uk/
subsea/hds/
*Dedicated to the preservation, study
and promotion of our diving heritage;
enables individuals, organizations and
divers interested in the historical
aspect of diving to make academic,
social and practical contacts on a
national level.*

Dealers

Leon Lyons
Helmets of the Deep
9 King St.
Saint Augustine, FL 32084-4451
phone: 904-825-0184 or 704-825-4504
*Collects all types and material of deep
sea diving equipment; wrote and
published the book "Helmets of the
Deep", available from author.*

Diving Helmets

Collectors

Dan Cramer
P.O. Box 447
Swartz Creek, MI 48473
phone: 810-635-4957
*Wants deep sea diving helmets and
related items.*

L.D.
P.O. Box 60063
Phoenix, AZ 85082
*Wants to buy deep sea diving helmets,
especially U.S. Navy Mark V.*

Dealers

Larry Pitman
Pioneer Peddler Antiques
5424 Bryan Station Rd.
Paris, KY 40361
phone: 606-299-5022
fax: 606-299-4522
Wants diving helmets.

Repair Services

Diving Equipment & Supply Co.
240 N. Milwaukee St.
Milwaukee, WI 53202
phone: 414-272-2371
*Old helmets repaired and recondi-
tioned; in business since 1937.*

Figureheads & Ships Carvings

Experts

Sara Conklin
239 Sierra Pt. Rd.
Brisbane, CA 94005-1664
phone: 415-467-6249
fax: 415-467-6249
e-mail: 76363.536@compuserve.com
*Managed the collections of the
National Maritime Museum in San
Francisco for ten years and is an
expert in appraising figureheads and
other ship carvings such as
trailboards, sternboards, beakboards,
and billetheads.*

Fishing Floats

Collectors

John Honl
P.O. Box 1201
Kailua Kona, HI 96745-1201
phone: 808-325-9905
*Buys and trades glass fishing floats;
looking to buy floats with embossing;
also wants odd shapes and colors.*

Stu Farnsworth
P.O. Box 847
Wilsonville, OR 97070
*Has written articles about glass
fishing floats for the "Antique Trader
Weekly."*

Experts

Stu Farnsworth
P.O. Box 847
Wilsonville, OR 97070-0847
phone: 513-393-9115
*Wants to buy glass fishing floats;
unusual colors such as pink, lavender,
purple, black, cobalt blue, red,
orange, etc.; also wants rolling pin
floats with writing on side, European
floats with embossed markings or
characters; no repros.*

Lighthouses

Clubs/Associations

Lighthouse Preservation Society, The
4 Middle Street
Newburyport, MA 01950
phone: 508-499-0011 or 800-727-
BEAM
fax: 508-499-0026
Internet: http://www.maine.com/lights/
lps.htm

Timothy Harrison
New England Lighthouse Foundation
P.O. Box 1690
Wells, ME 04090
phone: 800-758-1444 or 207-646-0515
fax: 207-646-0516
e-mail: lhdigest@biddeford.com
Internet: http://www.lhdigest.com
*Mission is to act as an agency to
encourage Historic Preservation, to
foster and support local lighthouse
initiatives, and to improve public
awareness and appreciation of and
access to all of New England's
lighthouses.*

United States Lighthouse Society
Magazine: Keeper's Log
244 Kearney St., 5th Floor
San Francisco, CA 94108
phone: 415-362-7255 or 415-362-7464
Internet: http://www.maine.com/lights/
uslhs.htm
*Nonprofit historical/educational
society; maintains comprehensive
library and archives on lighthouse
matters, conducts regional and
foreign lighthouse tours, conducts
research, hosts photography contests,
has state chapters.*

Collectors

Bob Glick
Columbia Trading Company
1 Barnstable Rd.
Hyannis, MA 02601
phone: 508-778-2929
fax: 508-778-2922
e-mail: nautical@capecod.net
Internet: http://www.by-the-sea.com/
nautical/
*Wants to buy items relating to
lighthouses.*

Timothy Harrison
P.O. Box 1690
Wells, ME 04090
phone: 800-758-1444 or 207-646-0515
fax: 207-646-0516
e-mail: lhdigest@biddeford.com
Internet: http://www.lhdigest.com
*Wants to buy memorabilia from U.S.
Lighthouse Service (USLHS) or U.S.
Lighthouse Establishment (USLHE):
badges, flags, dinnerware, buttons,
uniforms, old photographs of keepers
and their families, postcards,
newspaper stories.*

J. Carol Duncan
Keeper's Lighthouse Establishment
1027 Garden St.
Santa Barbara, CA 93101
phone: 805-963-9129 or 805-965-1174
fax: 805-962-5054
*Wants to buy lighthouse artifacts and
antiques: lamps, lanterns, oil cans,
maps, photographs, lighthouse keeper
items, lighthouse ephemera, Fresnel
lens (whole or in parts); also wants to
buy Coast Guard items.*

Man./Prod./Dist.

Lighthouse Depot
P.O. Box 427
Wells, ME 04090-0427
phone: 800-758-1444
fax: 207-646-0516
*Issues catalog containing new items
having the lighthouse motif: clocks,
lamps, figurines, clothing, lighthouse
replicas, prints, steins, jewelry boxes,
glassware, watches, candles, key fobs,
snow globes, etc.*

Museums/Libraries

Pete Lesher, Cur.
Chesapeake Bay Maritime Museum
Magazine: Water Gauge, The
P.O. Box 636
Saint Michaels, MD 21663-0636
phone: 410-745-2916
fax: 410-745-6088
Internet: http://www.cbmm.org
*A major regional maritime museum
with a 5200 volume research library;
collections include 10,000 objects,
9,000 photos, 1,200 ships' plans, 72
linear feet of manuscripts; decoys,
oystering, lighthouses, charts,
nautical, tools.*

Periodicals

Timothy Harrison
Newspaper: Lighthouse Digest
P.O. Box 1690
Wells, ME 04090
phone: 800-758-1444 or 207-646-0515
fax: 207-646-0516
e-mail: lhdigest@biddeford.com
Internet: http://www.lhdigest.com
*America's only monthly Lighthouse
newspaper; issues catalog of a large
selection of contemporary lighthouse
collectibles.*

Repair Services

Frank (Buddy) Pollock
shorevillagemaritimerestorations
45 Lawn Ave.
Rockland, ME 04841
phone: 207-596-2962
*Restoration/cleaning of classical
lighthouse lenses; restoration of all
maritime artifacts; glass and brass a
specialty; all antique electronics; from
polishing to complete restoration;
volunteer restorer for Shore Village
Museum, ME.*

Maps & Charts

Dealers

W.J. Auburn
Chartifacts
P.O. Box 8954
Richmond, VA 23225-0654
phone: 804-272-7120
*Buys and sells U.S. Coast Survey
maps, charts, sketches, recons;
primarily 1850-1871, both original
lithographs and selected reprints;
issues 1) East Coast, ME to GA, and*

2) Gulf and West Coasts, FL to WA catalogs.

Marine Chronometers

Dealers

Larry D. Harnden, Jr.
Marine Antiques & Timepieces
23632 Highway 99, Ste. #433
Edmonds, WA 98026
phone: 206-774-8159
fax: 206-775-2940
Specializes in Elgin and Hamilton marine chronometers, military timepieces and parts; also other antique and modern marine instruments.

Experts

James P. Connor
J.P. Connor & Co.
P.O. Box 305
Devon, PA 19333-0305
phone: 610-644-1474
fax: 610-993-0760
Specialist in antique and modern marine chronometers, deck watches, ship's clocks and sextants; buys and sells, appraisals, evaluating, dating; catalog available.

Repair Services

Philip M. Poniz
European Watch & Casemakers, Ltd.
P.O. Box 1314
Highland Park, NJ 08904-1314
phone: 908-777-0111
Restoration of watches, clocks, and music boxes; museum experience; can make any part and restore any watch; clients include Sotheby's, Cartier, collectors in USA, Asia and Europe; appraises, researches, restores chronometers.

P. Howard
4220 Virginia Beach Blvd.
Virginia Beach, VA 23452
phone: 804-481-7633
Sells marine chronometers (send SASE for list); also repairs and restores; buys chronometers, working or not.

Merchant Marine

Collectors

Ian A. Millar
1806 Bantry Trail
Kernersville, NC 27284
Wants memorabilia of the WWI Merchant Marine (U.S. or England): pins, badges, caps, uniforms, medals, awards, photos, etc.; send price.

Museums/Libraries

Harvey Lee Boswell
Palace of Wonders Museum
P.O. Box 446
Elm City, NC 27822-0446
Wants Merchant Marine and U.S. Maritime Service items: flags, uniforms, photos, medals, etc.

Models (Ship)

Dealers

Arrangements Inc., Marine Div.
P.O. Box 126
Mount Kisco, NY 10549-0126
phone: 914-238-1300
Buys, sells, custom builds, appraises, and restores ship models.

Experts

R. Michael Wall
American Marine Model Gallery, Inc.
12 Derby Square
Salem, MA 01970-3704
phone: 508-745-5777
fax: 508-745-5778
e-mail: wall@shipmodel.com
Internet: http://www.shipmodel.com
Buys, sells, appraises and specializes in model ships; representing the finest work of internationally acclaimed model makers; all models fully documented; 92 pg. illustrated catalog $10.

Sara Conklin
239 Sierra Pt. Rd.
Brisbane, CA 94005-1664
phone: 415-467-6249
fax: 415-467-6249
e-mail: 76363.536@compuserve.com
Managed the collections of the National Maritime Museum in San Francisco for ten years & is an expert in appraising ship models, ships-in-bottles, marine art, scrimshaw, figureheads, paper ephemera, instruments, whaling, diving equipment.

Periodicals

Jeffrey A. Phillips
Magazine: Model Ship Builder
P.O. Box 128
Cedarburg, WI 53012-0128
phone: 414-377-7888
fax: 414-377-7888
e-mail: modelship@aol.com
A bi-monthly magazine covering all aspects of building museum-quality model ships including also book, product, and museum reviews.

Repair Services

R. Michael Wall
American Marine Model Gallery, Inc.
12 Derby Square
Salem, MA 01970-3704
phone: 508-745-5777
fax: 508-745-5778
e-mail: wall@shipmodel.com
Internet: http://www.shipmodel.com
Offers complete professional restoration services, custom models, cases, appraisals.

Al August
44 Cambridge Dr.
Mashpee, MA 02649-2219
phone: 508-477-4169
Ship model repair; also buys wood ship models old or new in any condition; total or partial wrecks, hulls, kits; will give repair or restoration quotes from good photos; also will buy and sell through photos.

Shipwrecks

Experts

Sara Conklin
239 Sierra Pt. Rd.
Brisbane, CA 94005-1664
phone: 415-467-6249
fax: 415-467-6249
e-mail: 76363.536@compuserve.com
Managed the collections of the National Maritime Museum in San Francisco for ten years and is an expert in appraising shipwreck material such as vessel fragments and related objects.

Telescopes

Dealers

Daniel J. Vaughn
Spyglass, The
618 Main St.
Chatham, MA 02633
phone: 508-945-9686
Buys, sells, repairs and restores telescopes (especially mounted scopes); world's largest dealer.

NAZI ITEMS

(see also EDGED WEAPONS; MILITARIA; SWORDS, Nazi)

Collectors

J. Burnet
P.O. Box 1472
Massapequa, NY 11758-0908
Wants to buy WWII Nazi relics: flags, helmets, badges, etc.; also wants Adolf Hitler memorabilia: postcards, cigarette cards and albums, silverware, etc.; anything pertaining to Hitler.

Roy Capino
4309 Feldspar Rd.
Middletown, MD 21769
phone: 301-371-6497 or 301-662-2131
Wants to buy all WWII, German and Nazi items: guns, badges, uniforms, edged weapons, American, Japanese, British, Italian, etc.

K. Wiley
719 Baldwin SE
Grand Rapids, MI 49503-4470
phone: 616-451-8410
Wants Japanese swords, daggers, sword parts. Also German 3rd Reich daggers, swords, bayonets. References available.

Dealers

Brent's Military Antiques
P.O. Box 9255
Greensboro, NC 27429-0255
phone: 910-288-5061
e-mail: bsmith1181@aol.com
Wants WWII Nazi military items: swords, daggers, helmets, medals, hats, uniforms, autographs, etc.

Dr. R.A. Hiett
Maple City Coin
P.O. Drawer 47
Monmouth, IL 61462-0047
phone: 309-734-3212
fax: 309-734-8083
Wants any Nazi or SS related items.

Repro. Sources

Hutchinson House
P.O. Box 41021
Chicago, IL 60641-0021
Sells large selection of reproduction Nazi medals and badges; also war mementos from other countries; illustrated catalog $1.

Siegfried Line
P.O. Box 156203
Fort Worth, TX 76155-1203
Nazi regalia reproductions from Europe; over 200 new items.

NEEDLEWORK

(see TEXTILES)

NEON

(see also BREWERIANA; COIN-OPERATED MACHINES; LAMPS & LIGHTING, Neon)

Collectors

Roark Vane
6839 Havenside Dr.
Sacramento, CA 95831-2168
phone: 916-392-3864
e-mail: neonclock@aol.com
Wants to buy vintage neon clocks, small advertising neon signs, neon light bulbs, or other unusual illuminated advertising signs; also signs with "bubble tubes" - glass tubes or letters are filled with a liquid that "bubbles."

Periodicals

Magazine: Gameroom Magazine
P.O. Box 41
Keyport, NJ 07735-0041
phone: 908-739-1955
fax: 908-739-2834
e-mail: coinop@gameroommagazine.com
A great source of information for the collector and dealer of jukeboxes, pinballs, Coke machines and other gameroom collectibles.

Clocks

Collectors

Van Stueart
2240 Hwy 27 N
Nashville, AR 71852
phone: 870-845-4864
Buys and trades all types of advertising neon clocks; also wants Cleveland type neon thermometers.

Dealers

Wayne Woodrum
Wayne's Neon Clocks
10955 Lower Valley Pk.
Medway, OH 45341
phone: 513-849-6727
fax: 513-849-6658
Old, new, parts.

David A. Dyer
Neon Clock
246 Third Ave.
New Lenox, IL 60451
phone: 815-485-5573
fax: 815-485-0483
Old neon clocks bought and sold.

Robert Newman
10809 Charnock Rd.
Los Angeles, CA 90034-6606
phone: 310-559-0539
Wants to buy neon and lighted clocks, with or without advertising.

Repair Services

Tom Arrington
Neon Specialties
P.O. Box 2292
Chapel Hill, NC 27515-2292
phone: 919-932-5747
fax: 919-932-1782
Reproduction and restoration of vintage neon clocks.

NETSUKE

(see also ORIENTALIA)

Clubs/Associations

Netsuke Kenkyukai Society
Journal: Netsuke Kenkyukai Study Journal
P.O. Box 471686
San Francisco, CA 94147-1686
e-mail: yukiyama@hooked.net
Internet: http://www.hooked.net/users/ yukiyama/
Over 600 members in 25 countries; celebrates 20th anniversary in 1995.

Dealers

Alan R. Glazer
36 College Ave. #B3
Somerville, MA 02144
phone: 617-776-4475
Buys, sells and specializes in Chinese and Japanese cloisonne and other enamels; wants pre-1930 (and preferably pre-1898) "smalls" such as boxes, multi-piece sets, vases, bowls; minor flaws acceptable, but no pieces with major damage.

Bill Egleston
509 Brentwood Rd.
Marshalltown, IA 50158
phone: 800-798-4579
fax: 515-752-4570
Specializing in mail order sale of Oriental art, jade, cloisonne, netsuke, etc.; send for catalog.

Periodicals

Joan L. Cervi
Newsletter: Netsuke & Ivory Carving Newsletter-Video
3203 Adams Way
Ambler, PA 19002-3741
phone: 215-628-2026
fax: 215-628-2026
A wholesaler who offers VHS videos and a monthly newsletter about imported netsuke, ivory carvings and other Orientalia.

NEWSBOY ITEMS

Clubs/Associations

Mark Peters
Newspaper Memorabilia Collectors Network
Newsletter: NMCN Newsletter
504 Boynton Ave.
Berkeley, CA 94707-1704
phone: 510-525-7972
fax: 510-525-7972
e-mail: hawkerlore@aol.com
For collectors of items relating to newspaper promotion and circulation, and newsboy items.

Collectors

Mark Peters
504 Boynton Ave.
Berkeley, CA 94707-1704
phone: 510-525-7972
fax: 510-525-7972
e-mail: hawkerlore@aol.com
Wants to buy newsboy memorabilia including badges, buttons, ephemera, figurines, photos, books, etc.; anything related to newsboys.

Experts

Tony Lee
P.O. Box 134
Monmouth Junction, NJ 08852-0134
phone: 201-429-1531
Collector and dealer of badges and other credentials issued to newsboys, as well as the buttons, ribbons, aprons and hats they wore to advertise the newspapers they sold.

NEWSPAPERS

(see also COMIC STRIPS, Sunday Newspaper; PAPER COL-
LECTIBLES; NEWSBOY ITEMS)

Auction Services

Bob Raynor
Historical Collectible Auctions
P.O. Box 975
Burlington, NC 27215
phone: 910-570-2803
fax: 910-570-2748
e-mail: bobnews@aol.com
Buys, sells historic newspapers from 1760 through 1945; also conducts periodic mail/phone bid auctions of old collectible newspapers.

Clubs/Associations

Rick Brown
Newspaper Collectors Society of America
Magazine: Collectible Newspapers
6031 Winterset
Lansing, MI 48911
phone: 517-887-1255 or 517-887-8027
e-mail: rickb10507@aol.com
Internet: http://www.historybuff.com
Send #10 SASE and $1.50 for a 24 page primer (with extensive value guide) about old and historic newspapers; quarterly magazine for libraries, institutions, historical societies, and journalism buffs as well as for newspaper collectors.

Collectors

Gene Peters
'Tiques
P.O. Box 3267
Farmingdale, NY 11735-0679
phone: 516-842-9549
Wants 18th and 19th C. newspapers and articles documenting the African-American experience.

B. J. Hughes
P.O. Box 979
Watertown, NY 13601-0797

Joe Weber
604 Centre St.
Ashland, PA 17921-1332
phone: 717-875-4787 or 717-875-4401
Wants to buy pre-1890 newspapers, especially those discussing important events; also papers from Pennsylvania; will advise others.

Rick Brown
6031 Winterset
Lansing, MI 48911
phone: 517-887-1255 or 517-887-8027
e-mail: rickb10507@aol.com
Internet: http://www.historybuff.com
Collects, appraises and specializes in old newspapers.

Dealers

Eric Caren
Caren Archives, The
P.O. Box 185
Lincolndale, NY 10540-0185
phone: 914-248-8038
fax: 914-248-6439
Buys and sells Americana, Western, rare Newspapers.

Timothy Hughes
Timothy Hughes Rare & Early Newspapers
P.O. Box 3636
Williamsport, PA 17701-8636
phone: 717-326-1045
fax: 717-326-7606
Buys and sells old newspapers; Colonial era through 1915; catalog of offerings upon request.

Bob Morris
706 Pawnee St.
Bethlehem, PA 18015-1432
phone: 610-865-9052
Wants to purchase bound volumes of newspapers; Colonial to 1900; also wants Harpers's.

Steve Goldman
P.O. Box 359
Parkton, MD 21120
phone: 410-357-8204
Buys and sells historical newspapers, large or small quantities, bound volumes, single issues; from 18th, 19th, or 20th centuries.

Mark E. Mitchell
Original Historic Newspapers, Letters & Documents
3002 Winter Pine Ct.
Fairfax, VA 22031-1125
phone: 703-591-3150
fax: 703-385-3152
Buys and sells 1620-1885 original high quality newspapers and periodicals; including Amer. Rev., Civil War, Harper's Weekly.

Bob Raynor
Vintage Cover Story
P.O. Box 975
Burlington, NC 27215
phone: 910-570-2803
fax: 910-570-2748
e-mail: bobnews@aol.com
Buys, sells historic newspapers from 1760 through 1945; also conducts periodic mail/phone bid auctions of old collectible newspapers.

Fort Hamilton Press
312 Ross Ave.
Rossville, OH 45013
Buys and sells old newspapers; sells American front pages, many mounted, 1774-1993; also ephemera, scrapbooks, 1876-1910.

Experts

Jim Lyons
P.O. Box 580
Los Altos, CA 94023
phone: 415-948-5666
Specializes in rare newspapers. Author of "Collecting American Newspapers."

On-Line Services

Rick Brown
History Buff's Home Page/Online
6031 Winterset
Lansing, MI 48911
phone: 517-887-1255 or 517-887-8027
e-mail: rickb10507@aol.com
Internet: http://www.historybuff.com
On-line magazine with over 600 files of information about old and historic newspapers; files include price guide, collector primer, reprint guide and much more.

NICKELODEONS

(see CAROUSELS & CAROUSEL FIGURES; MUSICAL INSTRUMENTS, Mechanical [Band Organs])

NIGHT LIGHTS

(see also LAMPS & LIGHTING, Miniature)

Collectors

George A. Coupe
1243 1st St. S.E.
Washington, DC 20003
phone: 202-554-1000 or 800-368-5466
fax: 202-863-0775
Wants to buy fairy lamps.

Bob Ruf
4201 Palomino
Reno, NV 89509-2939
fax: 702-747-2675
Wants to buy fairy lamps.

NIGHTCLUB MEMORABILIA

Collectors

Bruce Fernie
121 Newbury St.
Boston, MA 02116
phone: 617-859-8593
fax: 617-859-0043
Wants nightclub and high life memorabilia, '20s-'50s; ashtrays, china, barware, tablephotos, matches, menus, ads, glassware, etc; anything from the Stork Club, El Morocco, The Copa, etc.

T. M.
1015 S. Cedar Rd.
Minneapolis, MN 55405
phone: 612-374-1162
Wants to buy memorabilia from American nightclubs that featured entertainment and/or gambling, 1930-1960.

1930s to 1960s

(see Chapter "A", page 2)

NIPPER

(see PHONOGRAPHS, Nipper)

NIPPON

(see also CERAMICS [ORIENTAL], Nippon)

NORMAN ROCKWELL

(see ILLUSTRATORS, Norman Rockwell; COLLECTIBLES [MODERN], Norman Rockwell)

NUMISMATICS

(see COINS & CURRENCY; MEDALS, ORDERS & DECORATIONS; SOUVENIR CARDS; TOKENS)

NURSES

(see also RED CROSS)

Collectors

Brunswick
P.O. Box 9729
Baltimore, MD 21286-9729
Wants books illustrating baby and child care, home nursing, basic nursing treatments and procedures, sick care, home health, nursing school manuals and films, etc.; prefer 1900-1970, especially photo-illustrated; also foreign.

NUT RELATED COLLECTIBLES

(see also COLLECTIBLES [Modern], Nutcrackers)

Museums/Libraries

Elizabeth Tashjian
Nut Museum, The
303 Ferry Rd.
Old Lyme, CT 06371
phone: 203-434-7616
Focuses on the hard-shell fruit.

Nutcrackers

Collectors

Claudia J. Davis
East 4400 English Point Rd.
Hayden, ID 83835
phone: 208-772-6801
fax: 208-772-5311
World's largest nutcracker collection; bronze, iron, ivory, brass, porcelain, wood.

NUTS & BOLTS

(see FASTENERS)

OCCUPIED GERMANY

Clubs/Associations

Larry L. Krug
Occupied Germany Collectors Club
18222 Flower Hill Way, #299
Gaithersburg, MD 20879-5300
phone: 301-926-8663
fax: 301-926-7648
e-mail: ccs@collectors.org
Internet: http://www.collectors.org/ccs
Collectors of items produced in Germany following World War II and marked "U.S. Zone," "British Zone," or "French Zone."

Collectors

Larry L. Krug
Americana Resources, Inc.
18222 Flower Hill Way, #299
Gaithersburg, MD 20879-5300
phone: 301-926-8663
fax: 301-926-7648
e-mail: ccs@collectors.org
Internet: http://www.collectors.org/ccs

OCCUPIED JAPAN

Clubs/Associations

Florence Archambault
Occupied Japan Club, The
Newsletter: Upside Down World of an O.J. Collector, The
29 Freeborn St.
Newport, RI 02840-1821
phone: 401-846-9024
Focuses on Japanese-made items marked "Occupied Japan"; newsletter includes free buy/sell ads, up-to-date price information, lots of photos, and more; newsletter published bi-monthly; send SASE for more information.

Collectors

Margaret Bolbat
8714 Alicia St.
Philadelphia, PA 19115-4103
phone: 215-671-1766
Advanced collector looking for quality bisque and porcelain, large bisque birds, American children, objects with Mioj Hokutosha mark, books pamphlets, maps or paper marked "Printed in Occupied Japan.

Linda Trew Ahlfield
Divine Inc.
513 Fawn Ct.
Fayetteville, NC 28303
phone: 910-868-3894
Wants figurines only: Pizies, shelf sitters, ethnic figurines, mermaids and dancers; no cups, plates, fans or metal items.

Bernard G. Toll
Toll Antiques
9195 Collins Ave., Apt. 4A
Miami, FL 33154-3103
phone: 305-865-0093
Buys and sells Occupied Japan: toys, celluloid, tin, novelties, etc.

Dealers

Stephanie Seguin
Occupied Attic, The
1 Gleneagles Blvd.
Ballston Lake, NY 12019
phone: 518-899-5030
e-mail: Occupied-Attic@usa.com
Buys and sells Occupied Japan items; also a member of the OJ Club; deals mostly with unusual items, e.g. sewing machines, rugs, dinnerware sets, tea sets, toys, large figurines and bisque; deals in US and in Japan.

Experts

Florence Archambault
29 Freeborn St.
Newport, RI 02840-1821
phone: 401-846-9024

OCEAN LINER COLLECTIBLES

(see also DINNERWARE, Advertising; NAUTICAL ANTIQUES; SHIPPING; SHIP RELATED; STEAMBOAT COLLECTIBLES; TITANIC MEMORABILIA; TRANSPORTATION COLLECTIBLES)

Clubs/Associations

Sue Ewen
Steamship Historical Society of America, Inc.
Magazine: Steamboat Bill
300 Ray Dr., Ste. #4
Providence, RI 02906
phone: 401-274-0805
For those interested in maritime history; publishes high quality quarterly magazine; has photo bank of thousands of negatives of powered vessels, national and regional meetings.

Walter Shields
Steamship Historical Society of America, Inc., Suncoast Chapter
P.O. Box 67064
Saint Petersburg, FL 33736-7064
phone: 813-367-7600

Charles Ira Sachs
Oceanic Navigation Research Society, Inc.
Journal: Ship To Shore
P.O. Box 8797
Studio City, CA 91618-8797
phone: 818-985-1345
fax: 818-985-1345
e-mail: transatlantic@juno.com
Studies the history of ocean liner travel with a focus on the transatlantic service from 1840 to present; quarterly journal focuses on a topic or ship using rare illustrations and memorabilia to highlight this romantic era of travel.

Collectors

Ken Schultz
P.O. Box M753
Hoboken, NJ 07030
phone: 201-656-0966
fax: 201-418-8640
Wants all items relating to ocean liners: brochures, deck plans, souvenirs, postcards, models, menus, etc.

Frederick Lingenfelser
814 Byram St.
Reading, PA 19606-1446
Wants to buy pre-1945 ocean liner collectibles: post cards, letters, ship blue prints, deck plans, books, tickets, brochures, dinnerware, souvenirs, models, menus, etc.; especially wants Titanic items.

Dave Cooper
2900 Faulkland Rd.
Wilmington, DE 19808-2514
phone: 302-999-9940
Collects White Star Line china, silver, souvenirs (no paper, please).

Randy Ridgely
447 Oglethorpe Ave.
Athens, GA 30606-2236
phone: 706-549-9264
Wants railroad, steamship and airline items.

Robert L. Loewenthal
10161 SW 1st Court
Fort Lauderdale, FL 33324-2226
phone: 954-474-4246
fax: 954-382-1213
e-mail: bobship@wcu.campus.mci.net
Wants to buy ocean liner memorabilia: postcards, china, silver, deck plans, models, posters, books, paper, etc.

New Steamship Consultants
P.O. Box 30088
Mesa, AZ 85275-0088
phone: 602-924-4334
e-mail: ships@pobox.com
Wants ocean liner deck plans, brochures, menus, etc.; world's largest buyers of all ships and lines; quote or send on approval.

Bill Gardner
P.O. Box 1031
Desert Hot Springs, CA 92240-0914
phone: 619-329-8300
Wants old liner cabin plans, view booklets, etc. that promote ship travel.

Dave Lathom
P.O. Box 5053
Bellingham, WA 98227-5053
phone: 360-676-0715
Wants to buy U.S. and Canadian steamship china and memorabilia, especially Pacific Coast, Northwest, and Great Lakes and river operations.

E.S. Radcliffe
3732 Colonial Lane SE
Port Orchard, WA 98366-1846
phone: 206-876-8615
Wants pre-1940 ocean liner related items: brochures, labels, cards, tableware, books, souvenirs and all paper items.

Dealers

Richard C. Faber, Jr.
230 E. 15th St.
New York, NY 10003
phone: 212-228-7353
fax: 212-477-9392
Wants booklets, china, deck plans, models, souvenirs, posters, etc. from Lusitania, Titanic, Normandie, Queen Mary, Andrea Doria, etc.

George Theofiles
Miscellaneous Man
P.O. Box 1776
New Freedom, PA 17349-0191
phone: 717-235-4766
fax: 717-235-2853
Issues catalog of ocean liner collectibles for sale.

David Rhinehart
ShipShape
1041 Tuscany Place
Winter Park, FL 32789-1017
phone: 407-644-2892
fax: 407-644-1833
e-mail: shipshape@shipshape.com
Internet: http://www.shipshape.com
Buy, sell ocean liner (cruise ship) china, silver, models, deck plans, souvenirs, ephemera.

Robert L. Loewenthal
10161 SW 1st Court
Fort Lauderdale, FL 33324-2226
phone: 954-474-4246
fax: 954-382-1213
e-mail: bobship@wcu.campus.mci.net
Wants ocean line memorabilia: postcards, china, books, pictures, silverplate, posters, deck plans, models, etc.

Experts

Charles Ira Sachs
TransAtlantic Research
P.O. Box 8797
Studio City, CA 91618-8797
phone: 818-985-1345
fax: 818-985-1345
e-mail: transatlantic@juno.com
Buys/sells/specializes/lectures on ocean liner and zeppelin history & memorabilia from the high seas (i.e. none from coastal or river steamers) dating from 1840 to 1960s; posters, postcards and related material for collectors/museums.

Sara Conklin
239 Sierra Pt. Rd.
Brisbane, CA 94005-1664
phone: 415-467-6249
fax: 415-467-6249
e-mail: 76363.536@compuserve.com
Managed the collections of the National Maritime Museum in San Francisco for ten years and is an expert in appraising Titanic and other ocean liner objects and related paper ephemera and archival collections.

Museums/Libraries

South Street Seaport Museum, The
207 Front St.
New York, NY 10038
phone: 212-732-5168

Periodicals

R.D. Roland
R.S. & T. Ry. Co.
Ad Paper: Main Line Journal, The
P.O. Box 121
Streamwood, IL 60107-0121
A bi-monthly "ad" paper exclusively

for buying and selling railroad collectibles as well as airline and steamship memorabilia; subscribers receive FREE ads.

ODDITIES

(see MORBID & ODD ITEMS; GUINNESS WORLD RECORDS; RIPLEY'S BELIEVE IT OR NOT)

OFFICE EQUIPMENT

(see also ADDING MACHINES; CALCULATORS; CLOCKS, Time; INSTRUMENTS & DEVICES; PAPER CLIPS; PENCIL SHARPENERS; PENS; PENCILS; TYPEWRITERS)

Clubs/Associations

Internationales Forum Historische Burowelt
Magazine: Historische Burowelt
P.O. Box 50 11.19
D-50971 Koln
Germany
phone: 941-925-0385
fax: 941-925-0487
Quarterly magazine in German for members of the I.F.H.B. only; in non-German speaking countries with English summaries only.

Darryl Rehr, Ed.
Early Typewriter Collectors Association
Magazine: ETCetera
2591 Military Ave.
Los Angeles, CA 90064-1933
phone: 310-477-5229
fax: 310-268-8420
e-mail: dcrehr@earthlink.net
Internet: http://www.earthlink.net/~dcrehr/
An international club for collectors of old office equipment; provides contact with worldwide network of over 500 members; free ads.

Collectors

William Feigin
Dualoy, Inc.
45 W. 34th St., Ste. 405
New York, NY 10001-3008
phone: 212-736-3360
fax: 212-594-8327
Wants very old check writers, check perforators, staplers in working condition.

Uwe H. Breker
6731 Ashley Ct.
Sarasota, FL 34241-9696
phone: 941-925-0385
fax: 941-925-0487
Wants to buy office equipment, typewriters, calculators, pre-1900 printing presses and equipment, adding machines, pencil sharpeners, office literature and magazines.

Bob Titus
P.O. Box 265
Pomeroy, OH 45769-0265
phone: 614-992-5052
Wants to buy early typewriters (Hammond, Peoples, World, etc.); also wants early adding machines by Burroughs and Comptometer.

Don Bryant
Bryant Office Machine Repairs
4819 Stallcup
Mesquite, TX 75150-1143
phone: 972-270-0135
fax: 972-613-1627
e-mail: aplayr@airmail.net
Collector since 1956.

Larry Wilhelm
P.O. Box 1922
Wichita Falls, TX 76307-1922
Wants to buy old calculators, adding machines or devices, typewriters, check writers, etc.

Dealers

William Feigin
Dualoy, Inc.
45 W. 34th St., Ste. 405
New York, NY 10001-3008
phone: 212-736-3360
fax: 212-594-8327
Buys and sells very old check writers, check perforators, staplers in working condition.

Carole Meeker
Box 169 Kelly St.
Rhinecliff, NY 12574
phone: 914-876-7818
Wants to buy rare and unusual small patented mechanical antiques, early American technology and occupational-related photography, advertising and catalogs.

Experts

Trent Condellone, Esq.
P.O. Box 2741
Springfield, MO 65801-2741
phone: 417-865-3902 or 417-866-5081
fax: 417-868-8274
e-mail: TCondellone@worldnet.att.net
Buys, collects and specializes in adding machines, calculating devices, teletypes, clipless stand machines, and any advertising pieces, manuals, parts, tools, etc. relating to the above.

Museums/Libraries

Todd Holmes
National Office Equipment Historical Museum
12411 Wornall Rd.
Kansas City, MO 64145

OIL COMPANY MEMORABILIA

(see GAS STATION COLLECTIBLES)

OIL DRILLING COLLECTIBLES

Museums/Libraries

Hill City Oil Museum
821 West Main St.
Hill City, KS 67642-1937
phone: 913-674-5621

OLD SLEEPY EYE

Clubs/Associations

Jim Martin
Old Sleepy Eye Collectors Club of
America
Newsletter: Sleepy Eye Newsletter
P.O. Box 12
Monmouth, IL 61462-0012
phone: 309-734-2703

OLYMPIC GAMES COL-
LECTIBLES

(see also PINS; SPORTS COL-
LECTIBLES; STAMP COLLECT-
ING, Sports Related)

Collectors

Harvey & Sandy Dolin
Harvey Dolin & Co.
5 Beekman St.
New York, NY 10038-2206
phone: 212-267-0216
Wants to buy Olympic items.

G. Johnson
P.O. Box 52976
Atlanta, GA 30355
phone: 404-261-5065
*Wants to buy old Olympics memora-
bilia.*

Jim Greensfelder
5825 Squire Hill Ct.
Cincinnati, OH 45241-6021
phone: 513-489-6750
fax: 513-489-6757
e-mail: medal_man@fuse.net
*Wants to buy, sell or trade Olympic
pins, medals, torches, automobile
items, clothing, banners, uniforms,
badges, mugs, steins, anything.*

Jim Clark
6100 Walnut Street
Kansas City, MO 64113-2236
phone: 816-361-4311
*Wants anything related to the
Olympics: pins, dolls, coins, toys,
mascots, displays, and anything
marked with the Olympic rings.*

Alan Polsky
4086 Hayvenhurst Dr.
Encino, CA 91436-3645
e-mail: olyarp@aol.com
*Wants any original Olympic Games
memorabilia including medallions,
badges worn by athletes, press and
officials, programs, pins, torches, etc.*

John & Virginia Torney
P.O. Box 2387
Huntington Beach, CA 92647-0387
phone: 714-840-7778
*Olympic Games memorabilia wanted;
all years; winter and summer games;*

*wants medals, badges, torches, pins,
flags, diplomas, documents, programs,
uniforms, etc.*

Dealers

Ray Smith
P.O. Box 254
Elizabeth, NJ 07207-0254
phone: 908-354-5224
fax: 908-352-1576
*Buys and sells Olympic memorabilia:
posters, pins, medals, ephemera, wire
photos, programs, cigarette cards,
uniforms, autographs, tickets, etc.*

Pins & Buttons

Clubs/Associations

Don Bigsby
Olympic Pin Collector's Club
1386 5th St.
Schenectady, NY 12303
phone: 518-355-9445
*The largest pin trading club in North
America.*

Rowan Fay
International Pin Collectors Club
Newsletter: IPCC Newsletter
602 Chenango St.
Binghamton, NY 13901-2029
phone: 607-724-4583 or 607-723-7421
fax: 607-723-3687
*Interested in all sorts of pins:
Olympic, Coca Cola, sports, Desert
Storm, media, etc.*

Collectors

Don Bigsby
1386 5th St.
Schenectady, NY 12303
phone: 518-355-9445

Dealers

Rowan Fay
602 Chenango St.
Binghamton, NY 13901-2029
phone: 607-724-4583 or 607-723-7421
fax: 607-723-3687
*Buys and sells Olympic memorabilia
and pins.*

Bill Nelson
Newsletter: Bill Nelson Newsletter, The
P.O. Box 41630
Tucson, AZ 85717-1630
phone: 520-629-0868 or 800-368-8434
fax: 520-629-0387
*Monthly newsletter with news, tips,
and sources of where to write for free
pins and buttons; world's largest
retailer of Olympic items; established
in 1985.*

OPENERS

(see BOTTLE OPENERS; CAN
OPENERS; CORKSCREWS)

OPTICAL ITEMS

(see also BINOCULARS; CAMERAS
& CAMERA EQUIPMENT; EYE
RELATED ITEMS; INSTRUMENTS
& DEVICES; KALEIDOSCOPES;
MEDICAL, DENTAL & PHARMA-
CEUTICAL; MAGIC LANTERNS &
SLIDES; MICROSCOPES;
STANHOPES; STEREO VIEWERS &
STEREOVIEWS; 3-D
PHOTOGRAPHICA; TOYS, Optical)

Appraisers

J. William Rosenthal, MD, ISA
3434 Prytania St., Ste. 250
New Orleans, LA 70115-3551
phone: 504-891-1988 or 504-947-3332
fax: 504-947-2593
*Buys, sells, specializes in and
appraises visual aids; author of
"Spectacles and Other Visual Aids: A
History and Guide to Collecting."*

Auction Services

Bryan W. Ginns
2109 Cty. Rte. 21
Valatie, NY 12184-6001
phone: 518-392-5805
fax: 518-392-7925
e-mail: the3dman@aol.com
*Conducts mail sales specializing in
optical items such as cameras, magic
lantern slide projectors,
stereographica, polyorama
pantoptiques, praxinoscopes,
zeotropes, kinoras, coin-operated
mutoscopes, etc.*

Clubs/Associations

J. William Rosenthal, MD, ISA
Ocular Heritage Society
3434 Prytania St., Ste. 250
New Orleans, LA 70115-3551
phone: 504-891-1988 or 504-947-3332
fax: 504-947-2593
Annual meetings, sale, lectures.

Collectors

Valda J. Tull
467 West Market St.
York, PA 17404

Jon Lewin
622 Raleigh Ave., Apt. 3
Norfolk, VA 23507-2034
phone: 757-625-6732
*Wants to buy eye-massagers (looks
like binoculars with rubber bulb
intended to squirt air at eyes),
collections of old eye glasses (with
telescoping ear pieces, no nose pads),
microscopes, kaleidoscopes, and
anything optical and exotic.*

Maret Webb
4118 East Vernon Ave.
Phoenix, AZ 85008-2333
phone: 602-957-0653
fax: 602-957-1631
*Wants to buy antique spyglasses,
telescopes, microscopes.*

Dealers

Ruth & C. Keith Wilbur, M.D.
Doctor's Bag, The
397 Prospect St.
Northampton, MA 01060-2089
phone: 413-584-1440
*Buys, sells, appraises apothecary,
medical, dental, surgical, optical &
quack instruments, equipment,
advertising, books, etc.; catalogs
available 3 to 4 times a year; author
of "Antique Medical Instruments."*

Al & Bobbie Roberts
Rational Past, The
221 Oceano Dr.
Los Angeles, CA 90049
phone: 310-476-6277
fax: 310-476-6278
e-mail: rational-past@mindspring.com
*Organizer of West Coast Scientific &
Technical Antique and Collectible
Shows (Los Angeles in the winter and
San Francisco are in late summer.)*

ORDNANCE

(see AMMUNITION & EXPLOSIVE
ORDNANCE)

ORIENTALIA

(see also ARMS & ARMOR; ART,
Asian; ART, Oriental; BRONZES;
CERAMICS [ORIENTAL];
CLOISONNE; FURNITURE
[ANTIQUE], Chinese; INDONESIA;
IVORY; JADE; NETSUKE; PRINTS,
Woodblock [Japanese]; SILVER,
Chinese; SNUFF BOTTLES)

Appraisers

Elisabeth Weikert Douglas
China Coast Oriental Art Appraisal
Services
11266 Taylor Draper Lane, Apt. 2024
Austin, TX 78759-3972
phone: 512-288-3043
fax: 512-345-8420
e-mail: wiew@texas.net
*Active in the field of Asian art and
antiques for over 20 years; owned and
operated antiques export service in
Bangkok, Thailand; owned and
operated Oriental art and antiques
shop in Washington DC.*

Scott Singer, ISA
411 W. Galer St.
Seattle, WA 98119
phone: 206-285-0394
fax: 206-283-5264
*Specializes in Asian art, furniture,
porcelain, pottery, ceramics.*

Auction Services

Stuart Slavid
Skinner, Inc.
357 Main St.
Bolton, MA 01740-1104
phone: 508-779-6241 or 617-350-5400
fax: 508-779-5144
*Established in 1964, Skinner Inc. is
the fifth largest auction house in the*

US; has offices in Bolton and Boston, MA.

John H. Schofield
Eldred's
P.O. Box 796
East Dennis, MA 02641-0796
phone: 508-385-3116
fax: 508-385-7201
Internet: http://capecod.net/eldreds
Specialists with annual week-long series of auction dedicated to Orientalia for over 25 years.

Sotheby's
1334 York Ave.
New York, NY 10021
phone: 212-606-7370 or 212-606-7000
Internet: http://www.sothebys.com
Over 70 collecting areas are featured at Sotheby's auctions including toys, dolls, porcelain, furniture, silver, art, books; exhibitions are free and everyone is welcome; for a free copy of "Sotheby's Newsletter", call 212-606-7245.

Christie's
502 Park Ave.
New York, NY 10022
phone: 212-546-1000
fax: 212-980-8163
Internet: http://www.sirius.com/
~christie/

Lynn Martin
Freeman/Fine Arts of Philadelphia
1808 Chestnut St.
Philadelphia, PA 19103
phone: 215-563-9275 or 215-563-9453
fax: 215-563-8236
America's oldest auction house: Continental, English and American furniture, paintings, silver and decorative arts; Oriental rugs, rare books, fine jewelry, Orientalia.

Butterfield & Butterfield
220 San Bruno Ave.
San Francisco, CA 94103-5018
phone: 415-861-7500
fax: 415-553-8678
Specialties include posters, toys, decorative arts, furniture, photography, etc.; the largest full service auction in the west.

McClain Auctions
825 Halekauwila St.
Honolulu, HI 96813-5315
phone: 808-538-7227 or 808-596-3900
fax: 808-545-7007
e-mail: auctions@worldnet.att.net

Clubs/Associations

Oriental Art Society of Chicago
P.O. Box 59863
Chicago, IL 60659-0863

Collectors

Marty Webster
2756 Kimberly
Ann Arbor, MI 48104
phone: 313-665-2030
Wants oriental antiques: Chinese, Japanese, and Korean.

Dealers

Alan R. Glazer
36 College Ave. #B3
Somerville, MA 02144
phone: 617-776-4475
Buys, sells and specializes in Chinese and Japanese cloisonne and other enamels; wants pre-1930 (and preferably pre-1898) "smalls" such as boxes, multi-piece sets, vases, bowls; minor flaws acceptable, but no pieces with major damage.

Lobsang Aye
Mandala Gallery
110 West 25th St.
New York, NY 10001
phone: 212-989-1829
Specializes in Far Eastern art and artifacts from Tibet, Southeast Asia, India, China, Japan.

Sandra Andracht
P.O. Box 94
Flushing, NY 11363-0094
phone: 718-229-6593
Buys and sells Oriental antiques.

Bob Miller
P.O. Box 640245
Flushing, NY 11364
phone: 718-776-7409
Buys and sells antique Chinese, Korean, and Japanese items; included are ceramics, hardstone, snuff bottles, woodblock prints, ivory carvings, metalware, weapons, lacquer, inro, ojimes, bronzes, silver, jewelry, and Japanese cloisonne.

Susan Akins
Oriental Antiques by Susan Akins
3740 Howard Ave.
Kensington, MD 20895-3347
phone: 301-946-4609
All Asian countries: China, Japan, Indonesia, S.E. Asia, India, etc.; specializing in fine porcelains, furniture, ivories, carvings, hangings, ancient artifacts.

Sharon & Arno Ziesnitz
7835 Painted Daisy Dr.
Springfield, VA 22152
phone: 703-451-1033
fax: 703-569-4221
Lecturers, authors, consultants want fine works of art: netsuke, inro, ojime, sword accessories, cloisonne, Satsuma, ivory and wood carvings, Chinese snuff bottles, Japanese traveling shrines, and Japanese metalworks.

Byla Simon Kunis
Oriental Treasures Antiques
159 W. Kenzie St.
Chicago, IL 60610-4514
phone: 773-761-2907 or 312-527-0533
Specializes in Chinese and Japanese antiques: textiles, ivory, jade, lacquer, metal; also appraises.

Experts

Patricia M. Grove
PMG Antique Appraisal Research
3 Ober St.
Beverly, MA 01915-4639
phone: 508-927-2979
Collects, researches and appraises decorative and fine arts of the China, Japan, India and Russia export trades, 17th through mid-19th centuries: paintings, silver, ivory, tortoise carvings, furniture, fans, lacquer.

Sandra Andracht
P.O. Box 94
Flushing, NY 11363-0094
phone: 718-229-6593
Author of "Oriental Antiques Art - An Identification and Value Guide", (Wallace-Homestead.)

Dr. Daphne L. Rosenzweig
Rosenzweig Associates
P.O. Box 16187
Temple Terrace, FL 33617-6187
phone: 813-988-0880
fax: 813-989-8091
e-mail: rosetwig@aol.com
Consultant and appraiser dealing with Oriental Art; author of "Selected Works from the Fine Arts Group of Later Chinese Painting"; specializes in Chinese art, and Japanese prints and ceramics.

Richard R. Silverman
838 N. Doheny Dr. #1102
West Hollywood, CA 90069-4851
phone: 310-271-1896 or 310-273-3838
fax: 310-273-3843
Specializes in Japanese prints and ceramics; netsuke and inro; also Thai, Burmese, Indian and Nepalese items; call 12:00 noon to 12:00 midnight PST.

Museums/Libraries

George Walter Vincent Smith Art Museum
220 State St.
Springfield, MA 01103-1703
phone: 413-263-6800
fax: 413-263-6814
Internet: http://www.spfldlibmus.org/home.htm
Recognized collections of American paintings; Orientalia including Japanese arms & armor, screens, lacquers, textiles and ceramics; Islamic rugs; and the largest collection of Chinese cloisonne in the western world

Arthur M. Sackler Gallery
Smithsonian Institution
1050 Independence Ave. SW
Washington, DC 20560
phone: 202-357-4880
Internet: http://www.si.edu/
The Chinese Dept. will authenticate your Chinese works of art; call to make an appointment; limit 5 items per visit, 10 items per year; may be able to work from good photographs.

Art Institute of Chicago
111 S. Michigan Ave.
Chicago, IL c
phone: 312-443-0849
Internet: http://www.artic.edu/aic/firstpage.html
Galleries of Chinese, Japanese, and Korean art contain 20,000 works covering nearly 5,000 years representing a variety of media from China, Japan, Korea, Southeast Asia, India, and the Near and Middle East.

Pacific Asia Museum
Newsletter: Pacific Asia Museum Member Newsletter
46 N. Los Robles Ave.
Pasadena, CA 91101
phone: 818-449-2742
fax: 818-449-2754

Asian Art Museum of San Francisco, The Avery Brundage Collection
Golden Gate Park
San Francisco, CA 94118-4598
phone: 415-379-8800
e-mail: info@asianart.org
Internet: http://www.asianart.org

Periodicals

Sandra Andracht
Journal: Orientalia Journal
P.O. Box 94
Flushing, NY 11363-0094
phone: 718-229-6593
A bi-monthly newsletter about all types of Chinese and Japanese art; areas covered include pottery, porcelain, wood, metal, paintings, prints, textiles, netsuke, Satsuma, Chinese & S.E. Asian bronzes, Oriental rugs, cloisonne, etc.

Repro. Sources

Joan L. Cervi
Arts of Asia
3203 Adams Way
Ambler, PA 19002-3741
phone: 215-628-2026
fax: 215-628-2026
Importer of statues, netsuke, snuff bottles, etc., etc., wholesale prices; annual catalog with updates $5; annual video $5.

Peking Arts
12141 Nebel St.
Rockville, MD 20852
phone: 301-258-8117
Sells (new) ceramics, carved stone, lacquered screens, furniture, embroidery, etc.

Manny Shaool
Manny's Oriental Rugs
72 W. Washington St.
Hagerstown, MD 21740
phone: 301-797-7434
Importer of Oriental ivory, porcelain, reverse paintings, rugs; also Remington recast bronzes, clocks, lacquered furniture.

Chinese Antiques & Art
9615 Las Tunas Dr.
Temple City, CA 91780
phone: 818-286-8696 or 818-286-8698
Carries porcelain, bronze, lacquer ware, jade, cloisonne, antique furniture, ivory, antique clocks, carvings and much more.

Chinese Items

Dealers

Jadestone Gallery
10922 N.E. St. Johns Rd.
Vancouver, WA 98686
phone: 206-573-2580 or 800-854-JADE
fax: 206-573-4834
Specializes in Chinese art and antiquities: Neolithic, tomb sculptures, pottery and porcelain, fine jade and other carvings.

Misc. Services

Arthur M. Sackler Gallery
Smithsonian Institution
1050 Independence Ave. SW
Washington, DC 20560
phone: 202-357-4880
Internet: http://www.si.edu/
The Chinese Dept. will authenticate your Chinese works of art; call to make an appointment; limit 5 items per visit, 10 items per year; may be able to work from good photographs.

Japanese Items

(see also ARMS & ARMOR, Japanese; BOOKS, Reference [Japanese Items]; FIREARMS, Japanese Matchlocks; OCCUPIED JAPAN; PRINTS, Woodblock [Japanese])

Auction Services

John H. Schofield
Eldred's
P.O. Box 796
East Dennis, MA 02641-0796
phone: 508-385-3116
fax: 508-385-7201
Internet: http://capecod.net/eldreds
Specialists with annual week-long series of auction dedicated to Orientalia for over 25 years.

Dealers

Denis Szeszler
Antique Oriental Art
P.O. Box 714
New York, NY 10028-0044
phone: 212-427-4682
fax: 212-860-4426
Specializes in antique netsuke and

related works of art: inro and other sagemono, pipe cases, yatate, okimono, etc.; buys and sells; researches and appraises.*

Theresa Yoneyama
Ginza, "Things Japanese"
1721 Connecticut Ave., NW
Washington, DC 20009-1108
phone: 202-331-7991
Specialty gift store 95% Japanese imports/collectibles/decorative accessories: fine china, sake sets, tea sets, kimono & happi coats, futons/ frames, bonsai/ikebana, origami, toys, dolls/cases, shoji screens & lamps, prints, lanterns, etc.

McMullen's Japanese Antiques - Kottoya
146 N. Robertson Blvd.
Los Angeles, CA 90048
phone: 213-652-9492
Specializes in tansu, folk arts, lacquer, kimono, porcelain, ceramics, obi, netsuke, ojime, large wooden carvings, doors and architectural items, etc.

Imari, Inc.
40 Filbert Ave.
Sausalito, CA 94965
phone: 415-332-0245
fax: 415-332-3621
Specializes in Japanese antiques and screens.

Experts

Dr. Daphne L. Rosenzweig
Rosenzweig Associates
P.O. Box 16187
Temple Terrace, FL 33617-6187
phone: 813-988-0880
fax: 813-989-8091
e-mail: rosetwig@aol.com
Consultant and appraiser dealing with Oriental Art; author of "Selected Works from the Fine Arts Group of Later Chinese Painting"; specializes in Chinese art, and Japanese prints and ceramics.

Alan D. Meaux
Ronin Art Productions
P.O. Box 1271
Oak Harbor, WA 98277-1271
phone: 360-675-8429 or 360-678-8787
Evaluates, appraises and collects clothing, swords, armor and other weapons of the samurai and from WWII.

Misc. Services

Barbara Brooks
Arthur M. Sackler Gallery
Smithsonian Institution
1050 Independence Ave. SW
Washington, DC 20560
phone: 202-357-4880
Internet: http://www.si.edu/
The Japanese Dept. will authenticate your Japanese works of art; call to make an appointment; limit 5 items

per visit, 10 items per year; may be able to work from good photographs.*

Museums/Libraries

Morikami Museum & Japanese Gardens
4000 Morikami Park Rd.
Delray Beach, FL 33446
phone: 407-495-0233
Focuses on Japanese folk crafts and utilitarian objects of everyday use; also contains a comprehensive Japanese textile collection.

Lacquer

Experts

Janet Francine Cobert
Fine Art of Asia
P.O. Box 2976
Beverly Hills, CA 90213
phone: 310-470-2176
fax: 818-986-5584
e-mail: asianart@interserv.com
Specializes in and appraises Oriental lacquer.

Repair Services

Janet Francine Cobert
Fine Art of Asia
P.O. Box 2976
Beverly Hills, CA 90213
phone: 310-470-2176
fax: 818-986-5584
e-mail: asianart@interserv.com
Restores Oriental lacquer and ceramic wares.

Near East Items

Misc. Services

Arthur M. Sackler Gallery
Smithsonian Institution
1050 Independence Ave. SW
Washington, DC 20560
phone: 202-357-4880
Internet: http://www.si.edu/
The Near East Dept. will authenticate your Near East works of art; call to make an appointment; limit 5 items per visit, 10 items per year; may be able to work from good photographs.

South & Southeast Asia

Collectors

John Rudak
32 Princess Lane
North Stonington, CT 06359-1117
phone: 860-599-8489
Wants Buddhist and Hindu art of Southeast Asia; all representations desired.

Dealers

Art of the Past
1242 Madison Ave.
New York, NY 10128-0515
phone: 212-860-7070
fax: 212-876-5373
Specializing in paintings, sculptures, textiles, Islamic and other works of art

from India, Tibet, Nepal, and Southeast Asia.*

Misc. Services

Arthur M. Sackler Gallery
Smithsonian Institution
1050 Independence Ave. SW
Washington, DC 20560
phone: 202-357-4880
Internet: http://www.si.edu/
The South & Southeast Dept. will authenticate your South & Southeast Asian works of art; call to make an appointment; limit 5 items/visit, 10 items/year; may be able to work from good photographs.

OSBORNES IVOREX

Collectors

Andy Jackson
501 Falcon Lane
West Chester, PA 19382-5716
phone: 610-692-0269 or 610-272-7900
Wants wall plaques, figurines, calendars and advertising brochures; will buy, sell or trade.

OUTBOARD MOTORS

(see also BOATS; NAUTICAL ANTIQUES; TOYS, Boats & Outboards)

Clubs/Associations

Antique Outboard Motor Club
P.O. Box 09293
Milwaukee, WI 53209

Collectors

Bob Glick
Columbia Trading Company
1 Barnstable Rd.
Hyannis, MA 02601
phone: 508-778-2929
fax: 508-778-2922
e-mail: nautical@capecod.net
Internet: http://www.by-the-sea.com/ nautical/
Buys old and antique outboard motors.

Richard Mussehl
Antique Outboard Motor Man
320 W. 20th St.
Erie, PA 16502
phone: 800-354-6089
Wants old rowboat motors by Waterman, Clarke, Amphion, etc.

Dealers

John McSwain
Marine Antiques & Maritime Artifacts
4155 Hwy. 11
Deland, FL 32724-9745
phone: 904-734-8786
fax: 904-738-5629
e-mail: mcswain1@mindspring.com
Specializes in deep sea diving, gauges, antique outboard motors 1900-1955, boating equipment and accessories.

Walter Pawlikowski
Superior Antiques
4022 E 2nd St.
Superior, WI 54880-4209
phone: 715-398-3665
*Buys, collects antique outboards,
marine engines, and antique boat
equipment or related fishing
equipment, boat models and outboard
toys literature on pre-1940 items;
offers free appraisals on antique
outboards; historical writer.*

Experts

Walter Pawlikowski
Superior Antiques
4022 E 2nd St.
Superior, WI 54880-4209
phone: 715-398-3665
*Buys, collects antique outboards,
marine engines, and antique boat
equipment or related fishing
equipment, boat models and outboard
toys literature on pre-1940 items;
offers free appraisals on antique
outboards; historical writer.*

OUTDOOR COLLECTIBLES

(see ANIMAL TROPHIES; ART,
Sporting; CAMPING EQUIPMENT;
DECOYS; FISHING COL-
LECTIBLES; LICENSES, Hunting &
Fishing; SPORTING COL-
LECTIBLES; TARGET SHOOTING
MEMORABILIA; TRAP SHOOT-
ING; TRAPS)

OUTHOUSES

Collectors

David Norwood
638 Newport Rd.
Bristol, PA 19007
phone: 215-781-1873
*Wants outhouse related items:
postcards, banks, books, articles,
miniatures, almost anything.*

J. W. Courter
3935 Kelley Rd.
Kevil, KY 42053-9431
phone: 502-488-2116
fax: 502-488-2116
e-mail: brtknight@aol.com
Internet: http://www.aladdinknights.org
*Wants items relating to outhouses:
post cards, books, old photographs,
plans, catalogs, models, etc.*

Experts

Ron Barlow
Windmill Publishing Co.
2147 Windmill View Rd.
El Cajon, CA 92020-1353
phone: 619-448-5390
*Author of "The Vanishing American
Outhouse, A History of Country
Plumbing."*

OUTLAWS & LAWMEN

(see also LAW ENFORCEMENT
MEMORABILIA, Police & Sheriff;
WESTERN AMERICANA)

Clubs/Associations

Hank Clark
National Association for Outlaw &
Lawman History
Newsletter: NOLA Newsletter &
Quarterly
P.O. Box 812
Waterford, CA 95386-0812
phone: 209-874-2640
*Members interested in Western outlaw
and lawmen history and artifacts;
sponsors annual Rendezvous.*

Collectors

Bill Mackin
1137 Washington St.
Craig, CO 81625-1613
phone: 970-824-6717 or 970-824-6360
fax: 970-824-7175
e-mail: reust@nadja.com
*Author of "Cowboy and Gunfighter
Collectibles" with 1993-94 updated
price guide; sells books for Old West
collectors by mail and at shows; over
45 years collecting; wants nice gun
leather and cowboy gear; appraises,
consults, lectures.*

OVENS

(see RANGES)

OYSTER RELATED COL-
LECTIBLES

Clubs/Associations

Andrea H. Sullivan
Oyster Plate & Collectibles Society
International
Newsletter: OPCS Newsletter
P.O. Box 632
Brigantine, NJ 08203-0632
phone: 609-226-3989 or 215-342-6450

Collectors

Donald C. Bell
89 Canoe Brook Rd.
Trumbull, CT 06611
phone: 203-268-7380
*Wants old oyster cans, bottles, boxes,
barrels, advertising and related items;
no oyster plates, please.*

Robert & Helene Blom
P.O. Box 19
Cedarbrook, NJ 08018
*Wants oyster tins, bottles, crocks,
wood boxes, and any other items
relating to oysters or to the oyster
industry.*

Sheldon Katz
211 Roanoke Ave.
Riverhead, NY 11901-2778
phone: 516-369-1100

Carlton G. Riggin
Rt. 617
Marionville, VA 23408-9999
phone: 757-442-2179
fax: 757-442-5391
*Wants to buy old oyster cans and
containers, oyster advertising,
envelopes and letterheads, postcards,*

*trade cards, and other oyster related
items.*

Dealers

Vivian & James Karsnitz
1428 Jerry Lane
Manheim, PA 17545-9353
phone: 717-665-4202
*Buys and sells oyster cans, advertising
and related items; authors of "Oyster
Plates" and "Oyster Cans" (Schiffer,
1993.)*

Oscar Schabb
P.O. Box 1377
Brooklandville, MD 21022-1377
phone: 410-486-2436
fax: 410-486-0653
*Buys, sells, trades and collects old
oyster cans and memorabilia; also
wants 1# peanut butter pails, pocket
tobacco tins, coffee tins with good
graphics.*

OZ

(see WIZARD OF OZ)

Here are some tips when contacting someone listed in this book:

When requesting information about a particular item, include a description (material, dimensions, maker's mark, model number, etc.) and a photo, sketch, or photocopy of the item in question. ■

Always ask if there are charges for samples or for the services requested. ■

When writing, please be sure to include a Large (#10 business size) Self-Addressed and Stamped Envelope (LSASE) if requesting a reply or the return of photographs. ■

Never call collect unless otherwise directed. When calling, be considerate of time zone differences and always ask if the party you are calling has time to talk. When leaving an answering machine message, always instruct the party to call you back collect. ■

PADLOCKS

(see LOCKS)

PAINT CANS

Collectors

Irene Davis
27036 Withams Rd.
Oak Hall, VA 23416
phone: 804-824-5524
*Wants to buy old paint cans, paint
advertising displays, or retail items;
send photos for offer.*

PAINTINGS

(see ART)

PAMPHLETS

(see PAPER COLLECTIBLES)

PAPER CLIPS

Collectors

John T. Ogle
P.O. Box 252
Ocean Springs, MS 39566-0252
*Wants to buy paper clips and notched
bookmarks: antique, foreign, plastic,
novelty, advertising; also wants early
paper clip advertising.*

PAPER COLLECTIBLES

(see also ADVERTISING COL-
LECTIBLES; AUTOGRAPHS;
BLOTTERS; BOOKS; BUSINESS
CARDS; CALENDARS; CARDS;
CATALOGS; HISTORICAL
AMERICANA; MAPS & CHARTS;
MAGAZINES; NEWSPAPERS;
POSTCARDS; POSTERS; REPAIR/
RESTORATION/CONSERVATION,
Paper Items; SHE

Auction Services

Russell Mascieri
Victorian Images
3706 S. Acoma St.
Englewood, CO 80110
phone: 303-761-7906
e-mail: tccadc@aol.com

Robert H. Snyder
Cohasco, Inc.
P.O. Box 821
Yonkers, NY 10702-0821
phone: 914-476-8500
fax: 914-476-8573
*In business over 50 years, specializing
in paper collectibles, autographs,
documents, Americana, ephemera,
etc.; mail auction catalogs issued.*

Dale Sorenson
Waverly Auctions, Inc.
4931 Cordell Ave.
Bethesda, MD 20814-2508
phone: 301-951-8883
fax: 301-718-8375
e-mail: wavauc@clark.net
*Specializes in the auction of graphic
art, books, paper, atlases, prints,
postcards, autographs, and other
paper ephemera.*

Harold Trainor
P.O. Box 13055
Fort Pierce, FL 34979
phone: 407-878-7376
fax: 407-878-3676
*Conducts mail bid auctions of tokens,
medals, pins, paper items, World's
Fair and Exposition, beer & whiskey
items, celluloid mirrors, political, fire
department, Centennial items,
automobilia, railroadiana, airline
collectibles.*

Joseph Millard
Grandma's Trunk
P.O. Box 404
Northport, MI 49670
phone: 616-386-5351
e-mail: maxfield@traverse.com
Internet: http://www.antiquepaper.com
*Trade cards, rewards of merit,
valentines, etc.*

Kurt R. Krueger
Krueger Auctions
160 N. Washington St.
Iola, WI 54945
phone: 715-445-3845
fax: 715-445-4100
*Specializing in the mail-bid auction of
paper collectibles: stocks & bonds,
advertising, books, letters, manuscripts, children's books, prints,
photographs, historical Americana,
posters, etc.*

Dunning's Auction Service
755 Church Rd.
Elgin, IL 60123-9302
phone: 708-741-3483 or 800-462-2444
fax: 708-741-3589
Internet: http:///www.dunnings.com
*Premier mid-American auction firm
selling antiques, fine art, jewelry,
American Indian art, and real estate.*

Clubs/Associations

Ephemera Society of Canada, The
Newsletter: Ephemera Canada
36 Macauley Dr.
Thornhill
Ontario L3T 5S5 Canada
phone: 416-492-5958
fax: 416-492-5958
*Dedicated to the preservation, study
and display of Canada's printed
heritage.*

Ephemera Society of England, The
Journal: Ephemerist, The
12 Fitzroy Square
London W1P 5HQ, U.K.

Ephemera Society of England, The
12 Fitzroy Square
London W1P 5HQ, U.K.

Wolaskowitz Frederick
Ephemera Society of Austria, The
Journal: Ephemera Journal
Baumlegarten 5
A-6973
Hochst, Austria EUROPE
phone: 0043 5578 76903
*Members collect mostly coffee cream
lids (peel offs) and lids from hone,
lemon, jam, marmalade containers;
also collect packaging items and
advertising collectibles and promotion
items from food and drink; want
contact with US collectors.*

Ephemera Society of Australia, The
345 Highett St.
Richmond
Victoria 3121 Australia

Ephemera Society of America Inc., The
Newsletter: Ephemera News
P.O. Box 95
Cazenovia, NY 13035-0095
phone: 315-655-2810
fax: 315-655-1078
*The major organization for collectors
and dealers of paper collectibles;
focuses on the preservation and study
of ephemera (short-lived printed
matter); also publishes "The
Ephemera Journal."*

Collectors

Tom Rutledge
3015 Bever Ave., SE
Cedar Rapids, IA 52403
phone: 319-399-1427
*Wants rare and antiquarian books,
paper, manuscripts, documents,
calendars, postcards, valentines, trade
cards, maps, atlases, autographs,
railroadiana, cook books, posters,
rewards of merit, and children's
books.*

James E. Kattner
P.O. Box 11132
Spring, TX 77391
phone: 281-986-6916 or 281-376-4826
*Wants to buy Texas saloon letter-
heads, envelopes, advertising cards,
photographs, and other saloon paper
collectibles; also wants same from
pre-1919 Texas liquor dealers.*

Mike Farmer
1406 Bigelow Ave. NW
Olympia, WA 98506-4417
phone: 360-352-7189
fax: 360-352-7189
*Wants to buy pre-1930 stocks &
bonds, land grants, graphic bill heads,
broadsides, posters, maps, business
letters, Civil War, American Indian,
cancelled checks, Alaska, any old
interesting paper; send copy or call;
prompt reply.*

Dealers

Ken Sowman
13 Wynes Rd.
Barrie
Ontario LN4 6T5 Canada
phone: 705-739-1087 or 705-739-0482
fax: 705-739-0482
e-mail: ksowman@netopia.net
Internet: http://www/
bconnex.net\~btracey/ken.html
*Deals in all kinds of paper col-
lectibles; any subject, any age.*

Jerry Rubackin
Jerry's Cards & Collectibles
P.O. Box 1271
Framingham, MA 01701-0207
phone: 508-788-5197
fax: 508-788-5197
*Buys and sells WWII fighter aces
autographs and other WWII military
signatures; also want autographed
material by the crew of the Enola Gay
which dropped the first atomic bomb
on Hiroshima.*

George & Julie Perron
Old Paperphiles, The
P.O. Box 135
Tiverton, RI 02878-0135
phone: 401-624-9420
fax: 401-624-4204
*Buys and sells paper collectibles:
books, autographs, sheet music,
postcards, photos, stereoviews,
documents, old letters; issues periodic
catalog of items for sale.*

Deborah Lavoie
Deborah Leavoie Fine Books & Paper
Treasures
P.O. Box 117
New Boston, NH 03070-0117
phone: 603-487-2369 or 800-337-2369
fax: 603-487-2333
e-mail: rare@worldnet.att.net
Internet: http://abebooks.com/home/
RARE/
*Buys/sells rare and antiquarian books,
paper, ephemera, documents,
catalogs, newspapers, postcards,
trade cards, diaries, ledgers, atlases,
maps, etc.; also offers shrinkwrapping
services for dealers, collectors, or
auctioneers.*

Old Paper Archive, The
122 West 25th St.
New York, NY 10001-7401
phone: 212-645-3983
*Specializing in antique prints, ads,
books, movie posters, sports,
postcards, photographica, magazines.*

Stephen Cohen
Cohen's Collectibles
110 West 25th St., Room 305
New York, NY 10001-7401
phone: 212-675-5300
*Photographs, autographs, steamship,
airline, World's Fair, travel, black
heritage, Judaica, sheet music, film
memorabilia, postcards, trade
catalogs; only open shop for
ephemera in Manhattan.*

Judith Katz-Schwartz
Twin Brooks Antiques & Collectibles
P.O. Box 6572
New York, NY 10128-0006
phone: 212-876-3512
fax: 212-876-3512
e-mail: twinb@tiac.net
Internet: http://www.tiac.net/users/twinb
Buys, sells, appraises postcards, photos, old magazines, valentines, advertising fans, cookbooks and pamphlets, 39 World's Fair, advertising trade cards, blotters, die cuts, calendars, etc.

George Theofiles
Miscellaneous Man
P.O. Box 1776
New Freedom, PA 17349-0191
phone: 717-235-4766
fax: 717-235-2853
Issues periodic catalog of paper items for sale including labels, poster stamp, etc.

Ridgley G. Hill
Beaver Tree Ephemera
5039 Ijamsville Rd.
Ijamsville, MD 21754
phone: 301-865-0335
Buys and sells paper Americana, specializing in western travel, railroad, land promotion, bird's-eye views, trade catalogs, trade cards; will also consider all other categories of collectible paper ephemera.

Richard & Mark Sikes
1213 Saggus Rd.
Lincolnton, GA 30817-9667
Wants comics, bubble gum cards, radio premiums, sports items, advertising items, political items, posters, old magazines, etc.

306 Main St.
Eau Claire, WI 54701
phone: 715-832-2494
e-mail: mgallery@edp.net
Wants large folio pre-1920 books, scrap albums, quantities of pre-1940 magazines, old prints, miscellaneous paper items.

Bindy Bitterman
Eureka! Antiques
705 W. Washington
Evanston, IL 60202-2214
phone: 847-869-9090
Specializes buying and selling early paper advertising, catalogs, calendars, etc.; a small shop - they send no lists but write detailed individual letters; SASEs get first attention.

Susan Nicholson
Past & Present
P.O. Box 595
Lisle, IL 60532
phone: 630-964-5240
Buys and sells rare and unusual postcards, Victorian valentines, periodicals, advertising trade cards, etc.

Yesterday's Paper
31815 Camino Capistrano, Ste. 11
San Juan Capistrano, CA 92675
phone: 714-248-0945 or 714-583-9838
fax: 714-583-1899
Buys and sells anything made of old paper: books, maps, prints, comics, catalogs, posters, newspapers, documents, Disneyana, magazines, etc.

Ada Fitzsimmons
Paper Pile
P.O. Box 337
San Anselmo, CA 94979-0337
phone: 415-454-5552
fax: 415-454-2947
Shop and mail order dealer of all kinds of paper items and ephemera; specialties are postcards, magazines, advertising trade cards, valentines, poster stamps and stickers, sheet music, advertising, handmade/primitive paper items, etc.

Tom Osjecki
Phyllis' Philatelics
P.O. Box 792
Canyonville, OR 97417
phone: 541-839-4135 or 541-839-6151
Buys, sells and specializes in postcards, paper Americana, stamps and covers; over 25,000 covers and postcards listed by state or topic.

R.A. Knott
Papereneur, The
P.O. Box 819
Concrete, WA 98237
phone: 360-853-8228
e-mail: raknott@sos.net
Offers a unique selection of paper ephemera, historical documents, and collectibles.

Experts

A. David Rutstein
As Time Goes by Ephemera & Nostalgia Shop
P.O. Box 73
Great Barrington, MA 01230-0073
phone: 413-528-3002
Buys and sells paper collectibles and ephemera, especially WWI posters, Victorian scrapbooks, sheet music, baseball, ethnic, non-sports trading cards, etc.; has spoken extensively on WWI propaganda and on sheet music.

Norman E. Martinus
Nostalgia Gallery, Inc.
3501 N Croatan Hwy.
Kill Devil Hills, NC 27948-8350
phone: 919-441-1881 or 919-261-2002
Co-author with Harry Rinker of "Warman's Paper" (Wallace-Homestead, 1994); wants to buy pre-1940 surfing paper, Wright Bros., paper related to spiders, US Coast Guard Stations in N.C.

Ray Walsh
Curious Book Shop
307 E. Grand River
East Lansing, MI 48823-4324
phone: 517-332-0112
Dealer/expert; owner of three book shops in Michigan; hosts radio call-in show about books and paper collectibles; writes columns; send a SASE for reply when writing.

Ken Prag
Ken Prag Paper Americana
P.O. Box 14817
San Francisco, CA 94114-0817
phone: 415-586-9386
Eager to buy old stocks and bonds, quality picture postcards, western stereoviews, old timetables and brochures, etc.

Misc. Services

Deborah Lavoie
Deborah Leavoie Fine Books & Paper Treasures
P.O. Box 117
New Boston, NH 03070-0117
phone: 603-487-2369 or 800-337-2369
fax: 603-487-2333
e-mail: rare@worldnet.att.net
Internet: http://abebooks.com/home/RARE/
Offers shrinkwrapping services for dealers, collectors, or auctioneers for display and protection; shrinkwraps prints, ephemera and paper of all shapes and sizes on white foam board or on cardboard.

Museums/Libraries

Crane Museum
30 South St.
Dalton, MA 01226
phone: 413-648-2600
Operated by the Crane Paper Company.

Periodicals

Magazine: Intercard's Magazine
Via Valfre, 4-10121
Torino, Italy
Covers advertising, movie posters, postcards, calendars, political and historical documents, autographs, and all paper collectibles.

Dennis M. Sater, Ed.
Newspaper: Paper & Advertising Collector (P.A.C.)
P.O. Box 500
Mount Joy, PA 17552-0500
phone: 717-653-4300 or 800-482-2886
fax: 717-653-6165

Doug Watson
Magazine: Paper Collectors' Marketplace
470 Main St.
P.O. Box 128
Scandinavia, WI 54977-0128
phone: 715-467-2379
fax: 715-467-2243
e-mail: pcmpaper@gglbbs.com
Internet: http://www.tias.com/pubs/pcm
Monthly magazine for collectors of autographs, paperbacks, postcards, advertising, photographica, magazines; all types of paper ephemera.

Ada Fitzsimmons, Ed.
Paper Pile Press
Magazine: Paper Pile Quarterly
P.O. Box 337
San Anselmo, CA 94979-0337
phone: 415-454-5552
fax: 415-454-2947
A quarterly magazine with many ads for both buyer and seller; also contains feature articles about collectibles, book reviews, auction reviews, show/auction calendar.

Repro. Sources

Antiquity Reprints
P.O. Box 370
Rockville Centre, NY 11571

Arcade Cards

Clubs/Associations

R.J. Schulhof
Arcade Collectors International
Newsletter: Penny Arcade
3621 Silver Spur Lane
Acton, CA 93510-1268
phone: 805-269-2841
fax: 805-269-2854
Ads, news, research, price lists, check list of arcade cards, especially Exhibit Supply Co. & Nutoscope Co.

Experts

R.J. Schulhof
3621 Silver Spur Lane
Acton, CA 93510-1268
phone: 805-269-2841
fax: 805-269-2854
Advisor to "Warman's Paper" (Wallace-Homestead, 1994).

Billheads

Dealers

Joseph F. Loccisano
Historic Photographs & Paper Americana
2264 Nicholson Square Dr.
Lancaster, PA 17601-3966
phone: 717-560-7750
Wants to buy billheads and business letterheads (1850s - 1920s) that graphically show products, buildings, logos, etc.

Canadian

Dealers

Michael Rice
Michael Rice Collectibles
P.O. Box 286
Saanichton
B.C. V8M 2C5 Canada
phone: 250-652-9412
e-mail: mrice@pacificcoast.net
*Wants pre-1940 Canadian and
English picture postcards, and other
pre-1940 Canadian interesting paper
memorabilia; stock certificates,
photographs, steamship souvenirs,
posters, autographs; all queries
answered.*

Certificates

Repro. Sources

Sally Green Bunce
4826 Mays Ave.
Reading, PA 19606

Mark Sutton
Victorian Certificates
2035 St. Andrews Circle
Carmel, IN 46032-9547
phone: 317-844-5648
*Reproduces Victorian-era certificates;
add your own photos & calligraphy;
commemorate weddings, anniversa-
ries, births or baptisms.*

Harwell Graphics
P.O. Box 8
Napoleon, IN 47034

Dance Cards

Dealers

Federico Santi
Drawing Room of Newport, The
152 Spring St.
Newport, RI 02840-6806
phone: 401-841-5060
fax: 401-848-0953
e-mail: zsolnay@drawrm.com
Internet: http://www.drawrm.com
*Buys, sells, and collects late 19th
century and early 20th century dance
cards; prefers fancy examples; can
buy from photo or photocopy.*

Historical

Auction Services

Remember When Antiquities
P.O. Box 1829
Wells, ME 04090-1829
*Wants autographs, books, historical
ephemera, sports memorabilia for
consignment auctions; free quarterly
auction catalogs.*

Collectors

Gary Ronk
6247 Cove Rd.
Roanoke, VA 24019-1715
phone: 540-562-2368
Wants to buy early deeds, indentures,

*land grants, etc., especially those that
have revenue stamps or seals.*

Illustrated

Periodicals

Denis C. Jackson, Ed.
Newsletter: Illustrator Collector's News,
The
P.O. Box 1958
Sequim, WA 98382-1958
phone: 360-683-2559
fax: 360-683-2559
e-mail: ticn@olypen.com
Internet: http://www.olypen.com/ticn/
*A bi-monthly for collectors and
dealers of old art prints, calendars,
books, magazines, pin-ups, posters
and original artwork and old paper
relating to illustrators 1800s-1990s.*

Radio Related

(see also RADIOS)

Dealers

Jim & Felicia Kreuzer
New Wireless Pioneers
P.O. Box 398
Elma, NY 14059
phone: 716-681-3186
fax: 716-681-4540
*Buys and sells 1850-1950 books,
catalogs, magazines and other
literature dealing with early radio,
wireless, x-ray and electricity.*

Southern

Dealers

Henry Barnet
516 Maverick Circle
Spartanburg, SC 29307-3707
phone: 864-579-2112
e-mail: 75347.322@compuserve.com
*Buys, sells, appraises paper, photos,
documents, maps, autographs, and
prints associated with The Old South
or New South.*

Western

(see also WESTERN AMERICANA)

Auction Services

Warren Anderson
America West Archives
P.O. Box 100
Cedar City, UT 84721-0100
phone: 801-586-9497 or 801-586-7323
*Buys and sells paper Americana
associated with the Western US: old
documents, letters, photos, stocks,
maps, autographs, prints, etc.; author
of "Owning Western History."*

PAPERDOLLS

(see DOLLS, Paper)

PAPERWEIGHTS

(see also GLASS)

Auction Services

Lawrence H. Selman
L.H. Selman, Ltd.
761 Chestnut St.
Santa Cruz, CA 95060-3751
phone: 800-538-0766 or 408-427-1177
fax: 408-427-0111
e-mail: lselman@got.net
Internet: http://www.paperweight.com
*Conducts periodic auctions of fine
paperweights.*

Clubs/Associations

Cambridge Paperweight Circle
Newsletter: CPC Newsletter
34 Huxley Rd.
Welling
Kent DA16 2EW, U.K.
*The only paperweight club in the U.K.
with members worldwide; newsletter
covers paperweight activity, auctions,
and new books.*

Michel-Pierre Grenier
Montreal Paperweight Collectors
3275 Sherbrooke St. East, #2
Montreal
Quebec H1W 1C3 Canada
phone: 514-523-9580

Phyllis Helfand
Ontario Paperweight Collectors
16 Tanburn Place
Don Mills
Ontario M3A 1X5 Canada
phone: 416-447-4659

Peter Pommerencke
Paperweight Club of Deutchland
Postfach 1733
D-82145 Planegg
Germany

Margaret Hunt, Pres.
New England Paperweight Collectors
168 Oxbow Rd.
Wayland, MA 01778
phone: 508-358-7612
*NEPCA holds meetings to provide
members the opportunity to learn
more about paperweights by offering
educational programs and to
purchase paperweights from dealers.*

Andrew Dohan
Delaware Valley Chapter, Paperweight
Collectors Association
Newsletter: DVC-PCA Newsletter
49 East Lancaster Ave.
East Frazer, PA 19355-2120
phone: 610-647-3310 or 610-688-8718
fax: 610-647-3318
e-mail: Dohan@juno.com
*Full program meetings four times a
year; color photography quarterly
newsletter.*

James Lefever
Paperweight Collectors Association, Inc.
Newsletter: Paperweight Collector's
Bulletin
P.O. Box 1263
Beltsville, MD 20704
phone: 410-828-0776
e-mail: MrGlas@redrose.net
Internet: http://
www.collectoronline.com/paper-
weight/PCA.html
*1600 member association of
paperweight collectors; antique and
modern; dealers, artists, makers of
contemporary weights.*

June Morfe
MD-DC-VA Paperweight Collectors
P.O. Box 20083
Baltimore, MD 21284-0083
phone: 410-828-0776

Barry Schultheiss
Mid-Atlantic Paperweight Collectors
P.O. Box 6259
High Point, NC 27262
phone: 910-841-6966

Bernie Simon
Ohio Paperweight Collectors
2303 Glendon Rd.
University Heights, OH 44118
phone: 216-932-1419

Joann Eck
Indiana Paperweight Collectors
135 North 9th St.
Zionsville, IN 46077-1217
phone: 317-873-2194

Wanda LeClair
Evangeline Bergstrom Paperweight
Collectors
1008 North 14th St.
Manitowoc, WI 54220
phone: 414-683-3939

Leo C. McNamee III
Paperweight Collectors Association of
Chicago
Newsletter: PCAC Newsletter
535 Delkir Court
Naperville, IL 60565-4165
phone: 630-369-2242

Leo McNamee III
Chicago Paperweight Collectors
535 Delkir Ct.
Naperville, IL 60565-4166
phone: 708-369-2242

Alvin Bates
Paperweight Collectors Association of
Texas
Newsletter: PCAT Newsletter
19302 Marlstone Ct.
Houston, TX 77094-3082
phone: 713-579-7413
e-mail: alrayb@juno.com
Internet: http://www.main.org/pcatn
*Three meetings and five or six
newsletters per year.*

Aleen Burfening
Arizona Paperweight Collectors
21405 North 142nd Drive
Sun City West, AZ 85375
phone: 605-546-4405

Janis Cadwallader
San Diego Paperweight Collectors
P.O. Box 881463
San Diego, CA 92168
phone: 619-292-5617

Lawrence H. Selman
International Paperweight Society
Newsletter: Paperweight News
761 Chestnut St.
Santa Cruz, CA 95060-3751
phone: 800-538-0766 or 408-427-1177
fax: 408-427-0111
e-mail: lselman@got.net
Internet: http://www.paperweight.com
*The purpose of the society is to
uncover knowledge about the history
and making of glass paperweights
(antique and contemporary), to bring
together collectors from around the
world, and to organize displays of
glass paperweights.*

Margaret Gunn
Northern California Paperweight
    Collectors
10110 Longview
Atwater, CA 95301
phone: 209-394-7724

Collectors

Homer G. Perkins
P.O. Box 1059
Easthampton, MA 01027-1059
phone: 413-527-2598

Andrew Dohan
49 East Lancaster Ave.
East Frazer, PA 19355-2120
phone: 610-647-3310 or 610-688-8718
fax: 610-647-3318
e-mail: Dohan@juno.com
*Collector buys antique pre-1900s
glass paperweights: French,
American, English, Bohemian,
Russian; buying one or entire
collection; surface wear & minor
chips to base not a problem; write or
call first with description.*

JoAnn Eck
135 N. Ninth St.
Zionsville, IN 46077

Tom Bradshaw
325 Carol Dr.
Ventura, CA 93003-1710
*Wants to buy antique glass paper-
weights; French, American,
Bohemian, English, and others; wants
millefiori, flower, butterflies, snakes,
etc.; also modern fine pieces by Ysart,
Kaziun, Stankard, and other makers.*

Dealers

Stanley Block
Block's Box
P.O. Box 51
Trumbull, CT 06611-0051
phone: 203-261-0057 or 203-926-8448
e-mail: BlocksChip@aol.com
Internet: http://pages.prodigy.com/
    marbles/
*Buys and sells antique French and
modern Kaziun paperweights.*

Leo Kaplan
Leo Kaplan, Ltd.
967 Madison Ave.
New York, NY 10021
phone: 212-249-6766 or 212-249-7574

George Kamm
George Kamm Paperweights
24 Townsend Ct.
Lancaster, PA 17603-6797
phone: 717-872-7858
fax: 717-872-7858
*Buys and sells antique and contempo-
rary glass paperweights; paperweight
appraisals; bi-monthly color brochure
for $5/yr.; sample upon request.*

Lawrence H. Selman
L.H. Selman, Ltd.
Newsletter: Paperweight News
761 Chestnut St.
Santa Cruz, CA 95060-3751
phone: 800-538-0766 or 408-427-1177
fax: 408-427-0111
e-mail: lselman@got.net
Internet: http://www.paperweight.com
*World's largest dealer in fine
paperweights, both antique and
contemporary; mail order company
selling directly or through paperweight auctions offered twice yearly;
call for free brochure.*

Experts

Dan McNamara
P.O. Box 163
Boston, MA 02113-0002
phone: 617-846-9465
*Buys and sells paperweights; has
identified and cataloged paperweights
for numerous museums; will identify
paperweights for others who send
photo and SASE.*

Louis O. St. Aubin, Jr.
Brookside Antiques "Art Glass Gallery"
44 North Water St.
New Bedford, MA 02740
phone: 508-993-4944
*Museum consultant, expert,
established in 1964, author of
"Pairpoint Lamps. A Collectors
Guide"; nationally known authority,
lecturer, appraiser, auction house
consultant; founder of the New
Bedford Glass Museum.*

Paul H. Dunlop
Dunlop Collection, The
P.O. Box 6269
Statesville, NC 28687
phone: 800-227-1996 or 704-871-2626
fax: 704-871-2329
*Leading paperweight dealers; buys
and sells all top quality antique and
contemporary glass paperweights,
paperweight books and related items;
author of "The Jokelson Collection of
Antique Cameo Incrustation."*

George N. Kulles
13441 Little Creek Dr.
Lockport, IL 60441-8686
phone: 708-301-0996
*Buys, appraises and repairs antique
paperweights.*

Steve Cole
Steve Cole Antiques
23897 Corte Emerado
Murrieta, CA 92562
phone: 909-600-0335
fax: 909-600-0445
e-mail: stevecol@iinet.com
Internet: http://
    www.stevecoleantiques.com
*Buy, sell, collect, trade glass
paperweights from around the world;
collections can be consigned for sale
or appraised; member of the National
Paperweight Collector's Association
and numerous local collector groups;
will answer questions.*

Lawrence H. Selman
L.H. Selman, Ltd.
761 Chestnut St.
Santa Cruz, CA 95060-3751
phone: 800-538-0766 or 408-427-1177
fax: 408-427-0111
e-mail: lselman@got.net
Internet: http://www.paperweight.com
*Buys and sells antique paperweights;
also repairs and polishes paperweights. Author of "Art of the
Paperweight."*

Man./Prod./Dist.

Joe Rice
House of Glass, Inc., The
7900 E State Road 28
Elwood, IN 46036-8449
phone: 317-552-6841
fax: 317-552-6854
*Makes paperweights all signed by
owner, Joe Rice; also makes all sorts
of other solid glass: ashtrays, pears,
ringholders, etc.*

Museums/Libraries

Museum of American Glass at Wheaton
    Village
1501 Glasstown Rd.
Millville, NJ 08332-1566
phone: 609-825-6800 or 800-998-4552
*Covers all types of American glass:
Stiegel, Amelung, flasks, pressed, art
glass, art nouveau, paperweights,
lamps & lighting, cut glass, 20th
century art glass, reproductions, pre-*

*studio movement, contemporary studio
glass, etc.*

Corning Museum of Glass, The
One Museum Way
Corning, NY 14830-2253
phone: 607-937-5371
fax: 607-937-3352
*Over 24,000 glass objects, innovative
exhibits, videos, models; glass history,
archaeology, and early manufacturing.*

Degenhart Paperweight & Glass
    Museum, Inc.
65323 Highland Hills Rd.
P.O. Box 186
Cambridge, OH 43725-0186
phone: 614-432-2626
*Over 1000 paperweights on exhibit;
video, research library, gift shop.*

Alex Vance, ExDir
Bergstrom-Mahler Museum
165 N. Park Ave.
Neenah, WI 54956
phone: 414-751-4658 or 414-751-4672
*The museum houses one of the world's
finest collections of glass paperweights.*

Periodicals

Museum of American Glass at Wheaton
    Village
Newsletter: Gatherer, The
1501 Glasstown Rd.
Millville, NJ 08332-1566
phone: 609-825-6800 or 800-998-4552
*This is a free newsletter about the
glassworks at Wheaton Village and
the paperweights currently being
made there.*

Repair Services

Edward Poore
Crystal Workshop
P.O. Box 475
Sagamore, MA 02561
phone: 508-888-1621
*Glass items made to order; also
repairs stemware, cut glass, and art
glass; repairs and recuts paperweights.*

George N. Kulles
13441 Little Creek Dr.
Lockport, IL 60441-8686
phone: 708-301-0996
*Restores and polishes damaged
paperweight surfaces; author of
"Identifying Antique Paperweights -
Millifiore and Lampwork."*

Larry Castle
Castle Fair
P.O. Box 1857
Ogden, UT 84403
phone: 801-393-8131
*Over ten years experience; all work is
hand held using water-cooled
diamond equipment to heal fractures.*

Advertising

Collectors

Bill Price
Pennsylvania Paperweight Potentate of
  Pittsburgh
P.O. Box 82501
Pittsburgh, PA 15218-0501
phone: 412-351-5297
fax: 412-271-4329
e-mail: paperwghts@aol.com
Internet: http://
  www.collectoronline.com/collect/wb-
  paperweights.html
*Wants to buy old glass advertising
paperweights featuring businesses,
World's Fair, buildings, machinery,
factories, banks, portraits of people or
anything; bottom must be milk glass
or glass or glaze-like.*

Charles Goodman
636 W. Grant Ave.
Charleston, IL 61920-3226
phone: 217-345-6771
*Wants any shape, size or form;
preferably glass paperweights with
milk glass bottoms; any theme
including railroads, steamship,
airlines, insurance, banks, most
anything.*

Glenn Fletcher
Wood Room, The
1070 State Highway 46 East
New Braunfels, TX 78130-2850
phone: 210-625-5384
*Advanced collector wants standing
promotional metal paperweights
displaying cars, trucks, buildings, RR,
ships, tools; also figural animals,
human, medical or representing
product advertising; must have
company logo, name, or trademark.*

Cast Iron

Dealers

Richard Tucker
Argyle Antiques
P.O. Box 262
Argyle, TX 76226-0262
phone: 817-464-3752
fax: 817-464-7293
e-mail: millwt@pop.intex.net
*Buys and sells cast iron advertising
paperweights; no reproductions or
repaired items.*

PAPERWEIGHTS (MODERN)

Clubs/Associations

Caithness Collectors Club
Newsletter: Caithness Report, The
Bldg. 12
141 Lanza Ave.
Garfield, NJ 07026-3530
phone: 201-340-3330 or 800-452-7987
fax: 201-340-9415
e-mail: caithness@carroll.com
Internet: http://
  www.caithnessglass.co.uk
*Focuses on paperweights; also
publishes the "Reflections" magazine.*

Paperweight Collectors Association, Inc.
Newsletter: Paperweight Collector's
  Bulletin
P.O. Box 1263
Beltsville, MD 20704
phone: 410-828-0776
e-mail: MrGlas@redrose.net
Internet: http://
  www.collectoronline.com/paper-
  weight/PCA.html
*1600 member association of
paperweight collectors; antique and
modern; dealers, artists, makers of
contemporary weights.*

Dealers

Dennis H. Gould
34 Huxley Rd.
Welling
Kent DA16 2EW, U.K.
*Specialist dealer in modern European
paperweights; interested in
exchanging modern American artists
for U.K. makers.*

George J. Grupe
Grupe Paperweight Collection, The
3 North Bishop St.
San Angelo, TX 76901-3301
phone: 915-653-0640 or 915-655-0158
*Buys and sells contemporary studio
art glass and contemporary
paperweights by noted artists.*

Eric Sinizer
Light Opera Retail Corp.
174 Grant Ave.
San Francisco, CA 94108-5405
phone: 415-956-9866
fax: 415-956-5624
*Specializes in contemporary glass
paperweights and other studio glass.*

Experts

Paul H. Dunlop
Dunlop Collection, The
P.O. Box 6269
Statesville, NC 28687
phone: 800-227-1996 or 704-871-2626
fax: 704-871-2329
*Leading paperweight dealers; buys
and sells all top quality antique and
contemporary glass paperweights,
paperweight books and related items;
author of "The Jokelson Collection of
Antique Cameo Incrustation."*

Man./Prod./Dist.

Caithness Glass Inc.
Bldg. 12
141 Lanza Ave.
Garfield, NJ 07026-3530
phone: 201-340-3330 or 800-452-7987
fax: 201-340-9415
e-mail: caithness@carroll.com
Internet: http;//
  www.caithnessglass.co.uk
*The largest producer of museum-
quality paperweights in the world;
also offers a range of new Whitefriars
designs each year.*

PASSPORTS

Collectors

Dan M. Jacobson
P.O. Box 277101
Sacramento, CA 95827-7101

PATCHES

(see also BADGES; BOY SCOUT
MEMORABILIA; FIRE FIGHTING
MEMORABILIA; LAW ENFORCE-
MENT MEMORABILIA;
MILITARIA, Insignia; GIRL SCOUT
MEMORABILIA)

Man./Prod./Dist.

Gerry White Pin, Patch & Cap Co.
10660 Saint Augustine Rd., #1514
Jacksonville, FL 32257-1061
phone: 813-371-2518
*Custom made patches, hat pins, caps,
mugs, etc.*

PATENT MODELS

Experts

Glenn McAndrews
402 E. Warren St.
Lebanon, OH 45036
phone: 513-932-5448

Museums/Libraries

Patent Model Museum
400 North 8th St.
Fort Smith, AR 72901
phone: 501-782-9014
*Collection contains over 80 miniature
models and pictures of 19th century
inventions.*

PATENTS

Misc. Services

Commissioner of Patents & Trademarks
Washington, DC 20231
phone: 703-305-8341
Send $3 for copy of a patent.

Superintendent, Government Printing
  Office
Washington, DC 20402
*Send $3.50 for "The Story of the U.S.
Patent Office", or $2 for "General
Information Concerning Patents."*

Richard Van Vleck
Greybird Publishing
P.O. Box 412
Taneytown, MD 21787
phone: 301-447-2680
e-mail: smma@fred.net
Internet: http://www.bestware.net/smma/
*Patent search and copy service for
items in your collection; a copy of any
patent from 1790 to present will be
provided, including full text and
illustrations; cost is $15 for the first
search and $9 for each additional
search.*

U.S. Patent & Trademark Office,
  Scientific Library, Foreign Patents
  Division
2021 Jefferson Davis Highway
Arlington, VA 22202
*Can obtain copies of foreign patents
for $10.*

PAWNBROKERS

Clubs/Associations

National Pawnbrokers Association
P.O. Box 420028
Dallas, TX 75342
phone: 214-745-4746 or 800-235-5400
fax: 214-745-1459

Periodicals

Brian K. Burkart, Pub.
BKB Publications Inc.
Magazine: Today's Pawnbroker
98 Greenwich Ave., #1FL
New York, NY 10011-7743
phone: 212-807-6558
fax: 212-807-1821
e-mail: bkbpub1@ix.netcom.com
*Trade news and articles, ads, refining
companies, buyers of jewelry and
coins, trade shows, etc.*

PEACE MOVEMENT ITEMS

(see also MODERNISM, 1960s
Memorabilia)

PEANUT MACHINES

(see COIN-OPERATED MACHINES,
Vending Machines)

PEANUTS

(see CHARACTER COLLECTIBLES,
Peanuts Characters; PLANTERS
PEANUTS ITEMS; TOM'S
PEANUTS)

PEARL HARBOR

(see also MILITARIA)

Collectors

Martin Jacobs
P.O. Box 22026
San Francisco, CA 94122-0026
phone: 415-661-7552
*Collector seeks WWII memorabilia
from the Homefront 1941-1945; will
purchase any size collection; wants
victory pins, Cinderella stickers and
stamps, envelope art, war propaganda, Anti-Axis art, matchcovers,
postcards, etc.*

Experts

Harvey & Sandy Dolin
Harvey Dolin & Co.
5 Beekman St.
New York, NY 10038-2206
phone: 212-267-0216
*Wants any item pertaining to Pearl
Harbor, WWI and WWII.*

PEDAL CARS

(see RIDING TOYS)

PEEP SHOWS

(see STANHOPES)

PENCIL SHARPENERS

Collectors

Craig Dinner
P.O. Box 4399
Long Island City, NY 11104-0399
phone: 718-729-3850 or 802-365-7181
*Wants pre-1920 mechanical pencil
sharpeners.*

Robert Kwalwasser
168 Camp Fatima Rd.
Renfrew, PA 16053-9104
phone: 412-789-7766
*Wants old pencil sharpeners, pocket
and desk types.*

Martha Crouse
4516 Brandon Lane
Beltsville, MD 20705-2601
phone: 301-937-2343
*Wants to buy old pencil sharpeners;
figural, celluloid, hand held; wants
one or entire collections.*

Bernice Kraker
9800 McMillan Ave.
Silver Spring, MD 20910-1149
phone: 301-589-2544
*Wants to buy old, handheld, figural
pencil sharpeners of metal, Bakelite or
celluloid.*

Jay Bolante
3058 North Honore St.
Chicago, IL 60657-2050
phone: 312-327-5091
*Collects and wants to buy mechani-
cally operated pencil sharpeners.*

Clay Tontz
4043 Nora
Covina, CA 91722
phone: 818-338-99767
*Please send SASE if requesting a
reply.*

Roger Graham
Every Era Antiques
855 57th St.
Sacramento, CA 95819-3300
phone: 916-456-1767
e-mail: roger@every-era.com
Internet: http://www.every-era.com
*Wants pre-1925 mechanical pencil
sharpeners: Little Shaver, Mills,
Stimpson, Dixon, Planetary, Perfect
Pointer, Gem, Webster, Jupiter,
Angell.*

PENCILS

(see also OFFICE EQUIPMENT;
PENCIL SHARPENERS; PENS)

Clubs/Associations

Florence Booth
American Pencil Collectors Society
Newsletter: Pencil Collector, The
R.R. North
Wilmore, KS 67155
*Members focus on the collecting of
pens & pencils: unsharpened lead
pencils with advertisements or
addresses, old mechanical pencils.*

Boris Rice
Pen Collectors of America
Newsletter: Pennant
P.O. Box 821449
Houston, TX 77282-1449
phone: 281-496-7152 or 281-496-2290
fax: 281-496-2290
e-mail: p_c_a@compuerve.com
Internet: http://
ourworld.compuserve.com/
homepages/p_c_a
*Association of fountain pen collectors;
maintains library of materials for pen
collectors; disseminates information,
holds regular meetings; promotes
collecting as a hobby and using pens.*

Collectors

Bruce Axler
Ansonia Station
P.O. Box 1288
New York, NY 10023-1288
phone: 212-362-4429
fax: 212-579-1274
*Wants pocket items, i.e. items/gadgets
designed to fit in the pocket: tools,
knives, lighters, compacts, folding
cups, items which look like a pocket
watch but are not, calculators, leather
items, matchsafes, candle safes, travel
items.*

Dealers

David Nishimura
Vintage Pens & Lighters
P.O. Box 603427
Providence, RI 02906
phone: 401-351-7607
fax: 401-351-1168
e-mail: dnishimura@aol.com
*Buys and sells all sorts of vintage
fountain pens and pencils; specializes
in European and Japanese pens,
especially those with enamel or
lacquer decoration; also offers repair
service.*

Experts

Marc L. Ames
539 Lyme Rock Rd.
Bridgewater, NJ 08807-1670
phone: 908-526-7676
fax: 908-575-0880
e-mail: magames@ix.netcom.com
*Wants to buy mechanical pencils, as
well as pre-1950 advertising pencils.*

Judith & Cliff Lawrence
1169 Overcash Dr.
Dunedin, FL 34698-5537
phone: 813-734-4742
*Buys, sells and specializes in old
fountain pens, dip pens and
mechanical pencils.*

On-Line Services

Doug Martin
Pensil Pages, The
17797 W. Toussaint N.
Graytown, OH 43432
phone: 419-862-2380
e-mail: dmartin@ealnet.com
Internet: http://www.ealnet.com
*Website contains great information of
use to pencil collectors, and can aid
collectors in contacting one another.*

Clips

Dealers

Lee Trout
17 Westdell Dr.
St. Louis, MO 63136-1936
*Wants to buy pencil clips that have
advertising on them; also wants
advertising wood pencils, but prefers
unsharpened pencils.*

PENS

(see also BLOTTERS; CALLIGRA-
PHY; GLASS, Whimsies [Pens];
INKWELLS & INKSTANDS;
OFFICE EQUIPMENT; PENCILS)

Appraisers

Joseph G. Balshone, GG, ISA
Columbus Gemological Laboratories,
Inc.
463 East Town St.
Columbus, OH 43215-4796
phone: 800-209-4367 or 614-224-2404
fax: 614-224-5630
e-mail: jbalshone@compuserve.com
*Specializing in appraising gems &
jewelry, post-1800 firearms, and
vintage and modern writing
instruments and accessories.*

Jim Gaston
Jim Gaston Vintage Fountain Pens &
Dip Pens
1777 River Road
Lakeview, AR 72642
phone: 870-431-5206 or 870-431-5204
fax: 870-431-5216
e-mail: gaston@mtnhome.com
Internet: http://
ourworld.compuserve.com/
homepages/Jim_Gaston
*Wants to buy vintage fountain pens,
dip pens; will purchase entire
collections, or appraiser single pen(s)
or collections; also repairs.*

Clubs/Associations

Boris Rice
Pen Collectors of America
Newsletter: Pennant
P.O. Box 821449
Houston, TX 77282-1449
phone: 281-496-7152 or 281-496-2290
fax: 281-496-2290
e-mail: p_c_a@compuerve.com
Internet: http://
ourworld.compuserve.com/
homepages/p_c_a
*Association of fountain pen collectors;
maintains library of materials for pen
collectors; disseminates information,
holds regular meetings; promotes
collecting as a hobby and using pens.*

Collectors

Dan McNamara
P.O. Box 163
Boston, MA 02113-0002
phone: 617-846-9465
*Buying fancy metal or overlay pens;
will help identify fountain pens for
others who send photo and SASE.*

David & Becky Beane
Beane's Antiques & Photography
58 River Road
Benton, ME 04901
phone: 207-453-6790
e-mail: dbeane@mint.net
Internet: http://www.mint.net:80/
antiques/catalog/beane.html
*Collector of quality fountain pens,
showcases, advertisements, and other
pen related items: LeBouef,
Waterman, Parker, Chilton and any
quality pen wanted.*

Jerry Jerard
402 Western Ave.
Brattleboro, VT 05301-2538
phone: 802-254-5815
Interested in buying fountain pens.

Gary Lehrer
16 Mulberry Rd.
Woodbridge, CT 06525
phone: 203-389-5295 or 800-484-1081
fax: 203-389-4515
*Wants pens of any age and condition;
single items or large collections; call
collect; write or send pens and pencils
(insured); also offers fountain pen
repair service.*

Richard Carvell
249 Sportsmans Ave.
Freeport, NY 11520-5635
phone: 516-623-1325 or 800-767-7367
*Wants old fountain pens; any large
size pen; any ornate pens; also gold
filled & silver filigree; pre-1910 pearl
overlay and solid gold; also wants to
buy pen ephemera.*

Mrs. Ky
P.O. Box J
Port Jefferson Station, NY 11776
phone: 516-584-4246
*Will buy old fountain pens, writing
implements, related ephemera, pen
advertising items (no magazine ads);
also unusual gold & silver pens.*

George J. Samuels
10122 Cape Anne Dr.
Columbia, MD 21046
phone: 410-997-4421
*Wants to buy fountain pens, regular or
cartridge; any condition.*

Howard Share
4349 La Vale Ct.
Clemmons, NC 27012-9009
phone: 910-766-6579
e-mail: denarnc@aol.com
*Wants to buy high quality fountain
pens, especially the oversized men's*

pens or the fancy pens with overlays or filigrees of gold silver, or mother-of-pearl.

Judson H. Bell
10124 Inverness Way
Port Saint Lucie, FL 34986-3210
Buys high quality fountain pens and parts, 1880-1940; prefer sterling and 14k overlays; one or entire collection; also desires pens and information about Eisenstadt Mfg. Co., St. Louis.

Stephen Berger
7759 Seminary Ridge
Columbus, OH 43235
phone: 614-885-6083 or 614-228-2727
Wants to buy pens by Parker, Shaeffer, Waterman, Conklin, Wahl-Eversharp, Chilton, Schnell.

Jim Beattie
23050 Rebecca Dr.
Elkhart, IN 46517-9173
phone: 219-875-6617
fax: 219-875-6617
e-mail: indianapen@cyberlink-inc.com
Wants quality old fountain pens or parts, 1870-1970; also does repairs.

Rich Hartzog
World Exonumia
P.O. Box 4143 BSB
Rockford, IL 61110-0643
phone: 815-226-0771
fax: 815-397-7662
Wants silver and silver overlay fountain pens.

Bob Arnell
P.O. Box 313
Grandview, MO 64030-0313
phone: 816-966-0544
Wants to buy fountain pens.

Dealers

Peter Stanton
57 Earle St.
Central Falls, RI 02863
phone: 401-725-0055
Wants to buy fountain pens, especially Waterman, Parker, Wahl Ever Sharp, Chilton, LeBoeuf, Montblanc, Triad, Conklin, Shaeffer, Carter.

David Nishimura
Vintage Pens & Lighters
P.O. Box 603427
Providence, RI 02906
phone: 401-351-7607
fax: 401-351-1168
e-mail: dnishimura@aol.com
Buys and sells all sorts of vintage fountain pens and pencils; specializes in European and Japanese pens, especially those with enamel or lacquer decoration; also offers repair service.

Charles M. Yassky
424 Madison Ave., 8th Floor
New York, NY 10017-1106
phone: 800-969-2345
fax: 212-826-6214
Active buyer of fountain pens and related advertising material; wants

fountain pens by Wahl, Waterman, Parker, Conklin, etc.

Richard Weinstein
Authorized Repair Service
30 W. 57th St.
New York, NY 10019
phone: 212-541-5618
fax: 212-586-1296
Wants to buy unusual old fountain pens in precious metal or plastic by Parker, Waterman, Wahl, Eversharp, Conklin, Chilton, Esterbrook, etc.

Frank Briola
P.O. Box 44022
Pittsburgh, PA 15205-0222
phone: 412-937-8787 or 800-372-6509
Wants to buy fountain pens.

Fahrney's Pens
8329 Old Marlboro Pike, B-13
Upper Marlboro, MD 20772
phone: 800-624-7367 or 301-568-6550
fax: 301-736-2926
Carries contemporary pen catalog; also does repairs.

Sam Fiorella
Pendemonium
15231 Larkspur Lane
Dumfries, VA 22026-1075
phone: 703-670-8549
fax: 703-670-3785
e-mail: sam@pendemonium.com
Internet: http://www.pendemonium.com
Buys and sells fountain pens, inkwells, ink bottles, pen stands, blotters, pen catalogs, magazine covers and advertisements; write for current "Writing Collectibles" catalog, it's FREE!

Judith & Cliff Lawrence
1169 Overcash Dr.
Dunedin, FL 34698-5537
phone: 813-734-4742
Issues catalog with articles on fountain pens and mechanical pencils; also pens and pencils for sale; bi-monthly; $4 for sample copy.

Vintage Fountain Pens
P.O. Box 158442
Nashville, TN 37215-8442
phone: 615-292-9790
Wants to buy old pre-1940s fountain pens; one pen or entire collections; premium paid for 14k gold, sterling silver, or oversized pens; especially wants Waterman, Parker and Conklin.

Mark Wright
P.O. Box 6007
Humble, TX 77325
phone: 800-774-8555 or 713-359-6868
Wants unusual fountain pens and related pen catalogs and pen paper ephemera.

Experts

Bernard Gagnon
29 Marguerite d'Youville
Gatineau
Quebec J8T IR8 Canada
phone: 819-568-0581
Writes column about fountain pens for "The Upper Canadian" newspaper.

Marc L. Ames
539 Lyme Rock Rd.
Bridgewater, NJ 08807-1670
phone: 908-526-7676
fax: 908-575-0880
e-mail: magames@ix.netcom.com
Wants to buy vintage fountain pens (Waterman, Parker, Shaeffer, Wahl, Eversharp, Chilton Carter, etc.); matching and non-matching pencils, as well as pre-1950 advertising pencils.

Max Davis
Davis' Vintage Collectibles
Newsletter: Journal of Vintage Pens
110 West 25th St.
Gallery 307
New York, NY 10001-7401
phone: 212-243-7090 or 212-769-9744
fax: 212-769-9199
e-mail: lrd@usa.pipeline.com
Buys and sells vintage pens; newsletter available for $12/year; also publishes a free "Journal of Vintage Nibs."

Bert Heiserman
9434 Royal Bonnet Terrace
Gaithersburg, MD 20879-2489
phone: 301-681-5893
Buys, sells, restores and specializes in old fountain pens including those made by Parker, Waterman, Shaeffer, Conklin, Swan, Wahl-Eversharp, Mont Blanc, Holland, etc.

Judith & Cliff Lawrence
1169 Overcash Dr.
Dunedin, FL 34698-5537
phone: 813-734-4742
Buys, sells and specializes in old fountain pens, dip pens and mechanical pencils.

Jack Price
Vintage Fountain Pens
P.O. Box 8212
Columbus, OH 43201-0212
phone: 614-267-8468 or 614-263-0284
fax: 614-267-8468
e-mail: jproto1@aol.com
Buys, sells, restores antique pens.

Ray & Bev Jaegers
P.O. Box 29396
Saint Louis, MO 63126-0396
e-mail: USPsiSquad@aol.com
Experts and historians.

Glen Benton Bowen
Fountain Pen Hospital - Texas
P.O. Box 6007
Kingwood, TX 77325
phone: 713-359-4363 or 713-359-8181
fax: 713-359-4468
Repairs, buys and sells; offers a consignment catalog, PENFINDER, containing the world's most valuable and rare pens; author of book about pens.

Anthony Davis
Rainbow Creations
P.O. Box 8935
Universal City, CA 91618-8935
phone: 818-762-3540
fax: 818-762-2503
e-mail: antiqphoto@earthlink.net
Specializes in the fountain pen by such makers Parker, Waterman, Shaeffer, Conklin, Wahl, and other.

Periodicals

Stuart Schneider
Hudson Valley Graphics
Newsletter: Pens
P.O. Box 64
Teaneck, NJ 07666-0064
phone: 201-261-1983
A quarterly newsletter focusing on fountain pens.

Glen Benton Bowen
World Publications
Magazine: Pen World Magazine
P.O. Box 6007
Kingwood, TX 77325
phone: 713-359-4363 or 713-359-8181
fax: 713-359-4468
Bi-monthly glossy color magazine to provide histories of pen companies and their products; full color reproductions of worlds most valuable pens.

Glen Benton Bowen
World Publications
Newsletter: Pen Finder
P.O. Box 6007
Kingwood, TX 77325
phone: 713-359-4363 or 713-359-8181
fax: 713-359-4468
A consignment, monthly glossy color catalog designed to help dealers and collectors buy and sell vintage pens.

Repair Services

Fountain Pen Hospital
Newsletter: Vintage Pen Quarterly
10 Warren St.
New York, NY 10007-2211
phone: 800-253-PENS
fax: 212-227-5916
Repairs fountain pens; also sells books, new and vintage pens, and accessories.

Thom D'Amico
P.O. Box 624
Putnam Valley, NY 10579
phone: 914-528-4350
Antique and classic writing instruments restored, repaired, replated, and recreated; special attention to nibs.

Phil D'Amico
Fine Italian Hand
154 Watson Dr.
Dallas, GA 30132
phone: 404-445-6584
fax: 404-443-9228
Antique and classic writing instruments restored, repaired,

replated, and recreated; special attention to nibs.

John Mottishaw
Classic Fountain Pens
P.O. Box 46723
Los Angeles, CA 90046
phone: 213-655-2641
fax: 213-651-0265
e-mail: 73523.3115@compuserve.com
Offers a complete fountain pen point (or nib) repair service including custom tipping, crack repair, and straightening; most other pen repairs provided as well.

Suppliers

Fr. Terence Koch
P.O. Box 128
Los Altos, CA 94023-0128
Sells pen parts, tools and repair information.

PERAMBULATORS

(see also CHILDREN'S THINGS)

Museums/Libraries

Janet L. Pallo
Victorian Perambulator Museum
26 East Cedar St.
Jefferson, OH 44047
phone: 216-576-9588
Only Victorian perambulator museum in the U.S.; over 100 examples along with related items such as sleighs, dolls, etc.

PERFORMING ARTS

(see also MAGICIANS PARAPHER-NALIA; MUSIC; NIGHTCLUB MEMORABILIA; POPULAR CULTURE; PUPPETS; SHEET MUSIC; STRIPTEASE; VAUDE-VILLE MEMORABILIA; VEN-TRILOQUIST ITEMS)

Dealers

Jonathan & Lisa Reynolds
Dramatis Personae - Booksellers
P.O. Box 1070
Sheffield, MA 01257-1070
phone: 413-229-7735
fax: 413-229-7735
e-mail: dramatisp@ad.com
Sale of antiquarian books, prints, ephemera, autographs, and manuscripts relating to theater, drama, circus, conjuring, puppetry, and popular entertainers; also select theatrical antiques; issues 4-5 catalogs per year.

Don Hoffman
P.O. Box 4231
Salinas, CA 93912-4231
phone: 408-449-7311
Wants to buy minstrel, vaudeville, ragtime items: posters, broadsides, cabinet cards, CDV's, tintypes, daguerreotypes, ambrotypes, programs, tickets, antique photos, autographs, books, booklets,

memorabilia; please describe and price.

Museums/Libraries

Consortium of Popular Culture
Collections
Popular Culture Library
Bowling Green State University
Bowling Green, OH 43403-0001
phone: 419-372-2450
fax: 419-372-7996
Consortium composed of Bowling Green State U., Kent State U., Michigan State U., and Ohio State U.; the largest academic library collections of primary research material in comic art, popular fiction, popular music, performing arts.

Gilbert & Sullivan

Collectors

David Trutt
3711 North Round Rock Dr.
Tucson, AZ 85750-2082
phone: 520-751-4215
e-mail: davettt@aol.com
Wants Gilbert & Sullivan items: books, posters, antiques, collectibles; any item relating to W.S. Gilbert, Arthur Sullivan, or their operas.

Opera Mementos

Dealers

Roger Gross
Roger Gross, Ltd.
225 East 57th St.
New York, NY 10022
phone: 212-759-2892
fax: 212-838-5425
Buys and sells signed photos of singers, instrumentalists, conductors and composers; letters, musical quotes; classical music and operatic books, memorabilia, ephemera, unsigned photos, etc.

Museums/Libraries

Nordica Homestead Museum
Holly Rd.
Farmington, ME 04938
phone: 207-778-2042

Marcella Sembrich Memorial Studio
3236 Congress St.
Fairfield, CT 06430
phone: 518-644-9839
The mailing address is as noted above. The museum is located in Bolton Landing, NY.

Theatrical Memorabilia

Collectors

D. Eliot
400 W. 43rd St. #25T
New York, NY 10036-6312
Wants theater souvenirs; pre-1920; especially commemorative items, e.g. 50th performance, 100th, etc.

Dealers

Lacy E. Long
199 Tarrytown Rd.
Manchester, NH 03103
phone: 603-622-5449
Buys, sells and trades theatrical memorabilia, holds periodic telephone auctions, sends out monthly price lists.

Chuck Haley
Sherlock's
13926 Double Girth Ct.
Matthews, NC 28105
phone: 704-843-3433 or 704-847-5480
Primarily interested in post-1940 Broadway and related items.

Museums/Libraries

Marty Jacobs
Museum of the City of New York
1220 5th Ave.
New York, NY 10029-5221
phone: 212-534-1672
fax: 212-534-5974
Access by appointment; research fee charged.

Lennis Moore
Theatre Museum of Repertoire
  Americana
1887 Threshers Rd.
Mount Pleasant, IA 52641
phone: 319-385-8937 or 319-385-9432
Largest American collection of 1850s-1950s middle plains Tent, Opera House, Repertoire Theatre and Chautauqua memorabilia, with Research Library and data base.

PERFUME LAMPS

(see also BOTTLES, Perfume & Scent)

Collectors

Sandy Katz-Leegood
P.O. Box 596553
Dallas, TX 75359-6653
phone: 214-824-7917
fax: 214-824-7917
Interested in all types of perfume lamps (similar to night lights, but has well/container to add/hold perfume; also small holes on top preventing exploding and allows perfume to escape); porcelain, glass, ceramic, French, Robj, etc.

Dealers

Tom & Linda Millman
231 S. Main St.
Bethel, OH 45106-1327
phone: 513-734-6884
fax: 513-734-6884
Wants to buy perfume lamps: Goebel, DeVilbiss, Fulper, Robj, Aladin, Aerozon, Aroma, and other foreign and domestic manufacturers.

PERIODICALS

(see the "GENERAL INTEREST PERIODICALS" Appendix as well as Periodicals listed under specific categories throughout this Directory.)

PERSONALITIES

(see also AUTOGRAPHS; FAN CLUBS; MOVIE MEMORABILIA; POLITICAL COLLECTIBLES; SPORTS COLLECTIBLES)

Wills of

Repro. Sources

Celebrity Collectibles
2303 N. 44th St., #4-175
Phoenix, AZ 85008
Sells copies of celebrity wills: Lucille Ball, Marilyn Monroe, Al Jolson, Jack Benny, the Three Stooges, Robert Reed - and 600 more.

PERSONALITIES (ARTISTS)

(see also ART; CARTOON ART, Walt Kelly; ILLUSTRATORS)

Daniel Chester French

Museums/Libraries

Chesterwood
P.O. Box 827
Stockbridge, MA 01262
phone: 413-298-3579

Edna Hibel

Clubs/Associations

Ralph Burg, Pres.
Edna Hibel Society
Magazine: Hibeletter
P.O. Box 9721
Coral Springs, FL 33075-9721
phone: 561-848-9633 or 954-731-6699
A fellowship to honor the art and achievements of internationally famous artist Edna Hibel; magazine published quarterly.

Man./Prod./Dist.

Andy Plotkin, Ph.D.
Edna Hibel Studio
Newsletter: Hibelleter
P.O. Box 9967
West Palm Beach, FL 33419-4967
phone: 407-848-9633 or 407-833-6870
fax: 407-848-9640
Publishes and distributes fine arts, collectibles, reproductions, gift items, and fashion and accessories designed by Edna Hibel, America's best loved artist.

Museums/Libraries

Andy Plotkin, Ph.D.
Edna Hibel Studio
Newsletter: Hibelleter
P.O. Box 9967
West Palm Beach, FL 33419-4967
phone: 407-848-9633 or 407-833-6870
fax: 407-848-9640
Oversees the world's oldest artist fellowship, and the world's only non-profit public museum dedicated to the art of a living American woman.

Andy Plotkin, Ph.D.
Hibel Museum of Art
Newsletter: Hibeletter
150 Royal Poinciana Plaza
Palm Beach, FL 33480
phone: 561-833-6870 or 561-848-9633
fax: 561-848-9640
e-mail: hibel@worldnet.att.net
Internet: http://www.hibel.com
*The only non-profit public museum
dedicated to the art of a living
American woman; free admission and
tours.*

Grant Wood

Collectors

Jerry A. McCoy
800 Thayer Ave.
Silver Spring, MD 20910-4504
phone: 301-565-2519
fax: 301-565-0780
*Wants anything relating to Grant
Wood: autographs, lithographs, etc.*

Saint-Gaudens

Museums/Libraries

Saint-Gaudens National Historic Site
Rte. 2 Box 73
Cornish, NH 03745
phone: 603-675-2175

Salvador Dali

Museums/Libraries

Kathleen A. White
Salvador Dali Museum
Newsletter: Dali Newsletter
1000 Third St. South
Saint Petersburg, FL 33701
phone: 813-823-3767 or 800-442-DALI
fax: 813-894-6068
*Permanent home of the world's most
comprehensive collection of Dali's
works; oil and watercolor paintings,
drawings, graphics, etc.; also a
library with over 5,000 books on Dali
and Surrealism.*

PERSONALITIES (CRIMINALS)

Al Capone

Experts

Michael Y. Graham
Chicago's Roaring 20's
33133 N Oplaine Rd.
Gurnee, IL 60031-3445
phone: 708-263-6285
*Specializes in prohibition-era (1919-
1933) gangster, speakeasy, political,
breweriana, and saloon-items;
emphasis on Chicago area.*

Billy The Kid

Periodicals

Jeff Gordon
Newsletter: Kid Newsletter, The
P.O. Box 848
New York, NY 10024-0848
*Focuses on Billy the Kid and his
compadres.*

PERSONALITIES (ENTERTAIN-ERS)

(see also RADIO SHOWS, Old Time)

Abbot & Costello

Clubs/Associations

Abbott & Costello Fan Club
Newsletter: Abbott & Costello
Quarterly, The
P.O. Box 2084
North Hollywood, CA 91610-0084
fax: 818-558-3799
e-mail: 102437.104@compuserve.com
Internet: http://www.city-net.com/
abbotandcostellofc
*Promotes the legacy of Abbott &
Costello along with selling A&C Fan
Club products and merchandise; sells
A&C products on their web site.*

Collectors

Eugene Kirschenbaum
723 E. 84th St.
Brooklyn, NY 11236

Al Jolson

Clubs/Associations

Mike Moder
International Al Jolson Society, Inc.
Magazine: Jolson Journal, The
476 Colonial Road
Roselle Park, NJ 07024
phone: 201-241-9313
*Dedicated to perpetuating the memory
"THE WORLD'S GREATEST
ENTERTAINER!" - AL JOLSON; also
publishes The Jolson News newsletter.*

British

Periodicals

Bill King
Goody Press, The
Newsletter: Anglofile
P.O. Box 33515
Decatur, GA 30033-0515
phone: 404-633-5587
fax: 404-321-3109
*Anglofile keeps tabs on British
entertainment and entertainers and
when and where they're appearing in
the U.S.*

Carpenters

Collectors

Bob Mason
381 Mayfair Drive South
Brooklyn, NY 11234
phone: 718-444-4749
*Wants Karen & Richard Carpenter
memorabilia.*

Dean Martin

Clubs/Associations

Dean Martin Association, The
P.O. Box 80
Uckfield
East Sussex TN22 1ZR, U.K.
e-mail: 106371.2556@compuserve.com
Internet: http://
ourworld.compuserve.com/
homepages/psycho/thedeanm.htm
*Promotes and publicizes the Dean
Martin legacy.*

Dean Martin Fan Center
Newsletter: Dean Martin Fan Center
Newsletter
P.O. Box 660212
Arcadia, CA 91066-0212
*Magazine-style newsletter published
quarterly: articles, news, question and
answer, auction section, editorials,
lots of photos.*

Collectors

Andrea Fuller
RD 1 Box 240
Morgantown, PA 19543
*Wants to buy photos, 45s, memora-
bilia, lobby cards, magazines, etc.*

Neil T. Daniels
P.O. Box 660203
Arcadia, CA 91066-0203
*Wants to buy anything Dino: records,
photos, programs, videos, reel-to-reel
tapes, acetates, toys, novelties, comics,
posters, oddball items, etc.*

Eddie Cantor

Clubs/Associations

Eddie Cantor Appreciation Society
Newsletter: ECAS Newsletter
P.O. Box 312
Mount Gay, WV 25637
phone: 304-752-8995
*Members receive a newsletter,
biographical information, and a
black-and-white photograph of the
1930s-1940s singer/entertainer.*

Frank Sinatra

Clubs/Associations

Sinatra Society of America
Newsletter: Sinatra Society of America
Newsletter
P.O. Box 269
Newtonville, NY 12128

Sid Mark
Sinatra Club
Newsletter: Sinarta Club Newsletter
P.O. Box 40057
Philadelphia, PA 19106-0269

International Sinatra Society
Newsletter: International Sinatra Society
Newsletter
P.O. Box 7176
Lakeland, FL 33807-7176
phone: 803-226-5610

Collectors

Bill Brooks
31 Thorns Lane
Highland, NY 12528-1213
phone: 914-691-7370

Scott Sayers
1800 Nueces
Austin, TX 78701
phone: 512-478-3483
fax: 512-473-2447
*Wants any Frank Sinatra related
collectibles including records, toys,
books, etc.; issues an auction list
quarterly.*

Dealers

Footlight Records
113 East 12th Street
New York, NY 10003
phone: 212-533-1572
fax: 212-673-1496
e-mail: footlight@aol.com
Internet: http://www.footlight.com
*Offers large selection of Sinatra
records, tapes and CDs.*

Experts

Peter Barbato
917 South Bishop St.
Chicago, IL 60607-4019
phone: 312-733-7943 or 312-746-5369
*Buys, collects, appraises Frank
Sinatra memorabilia; author of
"Sinatra: 50th Anniversary
Collector's Guide, 1935-1985"; owner
of one of the largest Sinatra
collections; collecting for over 35
years; no calls after 9 p.m. CST.*

Fred Astaire

Collectors

M. Russell
1425 4th St. SW, A206
Washington, DC 20024-2235
*Wants to buy Fred Astaire costumes,
signed letters, contracts, and other
memorabilia.*

Girl Groups

Clubs/Associations

Louis Wendruck
Girl Groups Fan Club
Newsletter: Girl Groups Gazette
P.O. Box 69A04 - Dept. Mal
West Hollywood, CA 90069-0066
phone: 213-650-5112
e-mail: airlinet@hotmail.com
Internet: http://members.tripod.com
*Fan Club for the 1960s and 1970s
female singers and singing groups of
Rock 'n Roll; sells related t-shirts,
photos, videos, records, postcards,
memorabilia.*

388

Jack Benny

Clubs/Associations

Laura Lee, Pres.
International Jack Benny Fan Club
Newsletter: Jack Benny Times, The
4759 Wilkie St.
Oakland, CA 94619-2951
phone: 510-933-3879
e-mail: jackbenny@delphi.com
Forum for acquisition and trading of memorabilia relating to Jack Benny & his associates; also JB audio tape lending library.

Johnny Mathis

Collectors

Steve Luth
1116 48th St.
Sacramento, CA 95819
Buys anything related to Johnny Mathis.

Kate Smith

Clubs/Associations

Kate Smith Foundation
P.O. Box 3575
Cranston, RI 02910

Lily Langtry

Collectors

Cummings
P.O. Box 622
Saint Helena, CA 94574-0622
Wants any Lily Langtry related memorabilia; stage posters, sheet music, newspaper and magazine articles, etc.

Marx Brothers

Clubs/Associations

Paul Wesolowski
Marx Brotherhood
Newsletter: Freedonia Gazette
335 Fieldstone Dr.
New Hope, PA 18938
phone: 215-862-9734

Collectors

Ira Dolnick
241 Golf Mill center #718
Niles, IL 60714
e-mail: ijdds@aol.com
Wants anything relating to the Marx Brothers: magazines, lobby cards, sheet music, etc.

PERSONALITIES (FAMOUS)
Charles A. Lindbergh

(see also AVIATION)

Clubs/Associations

Janet & Dick Hoerle, ExSec
C.A.L./N-X-211 Collectors Society
Newsletter: Spirit of St. Louis
727 Youn Kin Parkway, South
Columbus, OH 43207-4788
phone: 614-497-9517
Organized to perpetuate the memory of the man and the machine; interested in items concerning Charles A. Lindbergh (1902-1974.)

Collectors

Kathy Myrick
Box 54 Crowley Isl. Rd.
Corea, ME 04624

Stanley King
260 Fifth Ave.
New York, NY 10001-6408
phone: 212-447-1880
fax: 212-447-0728
A life long interest in collecting Lindbergh related material.

Lufker Airport
115 Montauk Highway
East Moriches, NY 11940
phone: 516-878-6302
Wants Lindbergh memorabilia; anything about Lindy or the Spirit of St. Louis.

Robert A. Fratkin
2322 20th St. NW
Washington, DC 20009
phone: 202-483-0274 or 800-336-0156
fax: 202-332-8538
e-mail: coxfrd@erols.com

Doug Studer
16 Orchard Terrace
Cold Spring, KY 41076
phone: 606-441-2754
Wants Lindbergh and Spirit of St. Louis items.

Janet & Dick Hoerle
727 Youn Kin Parkway, South
Columbus, OH 43207-4788
phone: 614-497-9517
Collects items related to Charles A. Lindbergh.

Lyndon Sheldon
2019 Essex
Colorado Springs, CO 80909-1423
phone: 719-597-7066
Buys, sells and trades Charles A. Lindbergh/Spirit of St. Louis memorabilia.

Dealers

Irene Brostow
92 Normandy Rd.
Colonia, NJ 07067-1010
Wants to buy anything related to Charles Lindbergh; no newspapers

Museums/Libraries

Missouri Historical Society
P.O. Box 11940
Saint Louis, MO 63112-0040
phone: 314-746-4527
fax: 314-746-4548

Dionne Quintuplets

Clubs/Associations

Fay & Jimmy Rodolfos
Dionne Quint Collectors
Newsletter: Quint News
P.O. Box 2527
Woburn, MA 01888-1027
phone: 617-933-2219
A 21-page quarterly newsletter containing articles, columns and classified ads; also reproduction alerts of newly produced items such as signs, pocket mirrors, and paper and composition dolls.

Collectors

Fay & Jimmy Rodolfos
P.O. Box 2527
Woburn, MA 01888-1027
phone: 617-933-2219
Wants Dionne quintuplet items.

Ethelyn Hulit
236 Cape Rd.
Standish, ME 04084-6232
phone: 207-642-3091
Wants to buy Dionne quintuplet items including games, china, paper, advertising, cloth, wooden, plaster items, real photos, sketches, paintings, unusual items; will reply.

Marceil Drake
RR 3
Roanoke, IN 46783-8903
phone: 219-672-2475
Wants Dionne quintuplet items: games, china, toys, paper advertising, etc.; anything related to Dionne quintuplets or Quintland.

Lois Helen Brown
708 E. Broadway
Logansport, IN 46947-3158
phone: 219-753-3323
Wants Dionne quintuplet and related items such as postcards, games, china, paper, advertising, etc.

Museums/Libraries

Dionne Quints Home & Museum, North Bay Chamber of Commerce
P.O. Box 747
North Bay
Ontario P1B 8J8 Canada
phone: 705-472-8480

William Randolph Hearst

Collectors

Robert A. LeGresley
P.O. Box 1199
Lawrence, KS 66044-8199
phone: 913-749-5458 or 913-843-0357
fax: 913-842-2203
Wants to buy original autographs, manuscripts, books and printed material on Hearst and his family.

PERSONALITIES (HISTORICAL)

(see also POLITICAL COL-LECTIBLES; WHITE HOUSE COLLECTIBLES)

Abraham Lincoln

Clubs/Associations

Jonathan H. Mann
Rail Splitter Chapter, APIC
Magazine: Rail Splitter, The
P.O. Box 275
New York, NY 10044-0205
phone: 212-980-7031
fax: 212-741-8756
Dedicated to the study and preservation of materials relating to Abraham Lincoln; assists in appraising Lincoln/Civil War and related collectibles; publishes quarterly journal on new finds and market activity.

Collectors

Donald Ackerman
P.O. Box 3487
Wallington, NJ 07057-1621
phone: 201-779-8785
Devoted collector eager to buy Lincoln memorabilia: campaign flags, ribbons, banners, posters, photographic badges, glass, china.

Cary Demont
P.O. Box 16013
Minneapolis, MN 55416-0013
phone: 612-922-1617
Wants Lincoln related items: campaign badges, tintypes, ribbons, banners, portraits, flags and the unusual; also Jeff Davis & slavery.

Dealers

Steve H. Nowlin
History Makers, Inc.
4040 E. 82nd St.
Indianapolis, IN 46250
phone: 800-424-9259 or 317-842-5828
fax: 317-842-5845
Internet: http://www.a1.com/history

Chuck Hand
310 Monterey St.
Paris, IL 61944
phone: 217-463-4555
fax: 217-463-4555
Extensive catalog of Lincoln ephemera, books, and related material issued every year.

Experts

Stuart Schneider
P.O. Box 64
Teaneck, NJ 07666-0064
phone: 201-261-1983
*Collects and authenticates Lincoln
photographs taken and printed while
Lincoln was still living (first
generation photographs); author of
"Collecting Lincoln."*

Museums/Libraries

Lincoln Homestead State Shrine
5549 Lincoln Park Rd.
Springfield, KY 40069
phone: 606-336-7461

Abraham Lincoln Birthplace National
Site
2996 Lincoln Farm Rd.
Hodgenville, KY 42748
phone: 502-358-3137

Lincoln Museum, The
1300 S. Clinton St.
Fort Wayne, IN 46801
phone: 219-455-3864

Lincoln Boyhood National Memorial
P.O. Box 1816
Lincoln City, IN 47552
phone: 812-937-4541

Lincoln Log Cabin State Historic Site
Rte. 1 Box 172A
Lerna, IL 62440
phone: 217-345-6489

Lincoln's New Salem Historic Site
Rte. 1 Box 244A
Petersburg, IL 62675
phone: 217-632-4000
*Reconstructed village where Lincoln
lived from 1831 t0 1837.*

Lincoln Home National Historical Site
426 S. 7th St.
Springfield, IL 62701
phone: 217-492-4150

Lincoln Tomb State Historic Site
Oak Ridge Cemetery
Springfield, IL 62702
phone: 217-782-2717

Christopher Columbus

Museums/Libraries

Dan & Rose Amato
Christopher Columbus Museum
239 Whitney St.
P.O. Box 151
Columbus, WI 53925-0151
phone: 414-623-1992
*Wants to buy all quality Christopher
Columbus items, old and new.*

Eleanor Roosevelt

Dealers

M. McGovern
Home Grown
1012 Manoa Rd.
Wynnewood, PA 19096
phone: 610-649-6316
fax: 610-649-2369
*Wants to buy signed Eleanor
Roosevelt documents.*

George Washington

Museums/Libraries

Mount Vernon-Ladies' Association of
the Union
Mount Vernon, VA 22121
phone: 703-780-2000

Lafayette

Collectors

Andrew B. Golbert
RR 1 Box 1820
North Ferrisburg, VT 05473-9508
phone: 802-453-2525
*Wants any Lafayette ephemera,
particularly relating to his visit to the
U.S. in 1824-25: ribbons, medals,
tokens, prints, books, etc.*

Napoleon

Appraisers

Pierre Bovis
AZ-Tex Cowboy Trading Co., The
P.O. Box 13345
Tucson, AZ 85732-3345
phone: 520-318-9512
fax: 520-318-0023
*Buy, sells, appraises cowboy
memorabilia, primitive arts, American
Indian arts, Napoleonic artifacts.*

Clubs/Associations

Robert M. Snibbe
Napoleonic Society of America
Newsletter: Member's Bulletin
1115 Ponce De Leon Blvd.
Clearwater, FL 34616-1040
phone: 813-586-1779
fax: 813-581-2578
Internet: http://www.napoleonic-
society.com
*Founded in 1983 to provide a means
of communicating and sharing views
on Napoleon as a man and as a
military genius; also memorabilia.*

Collectors

W.R. Morat
3942 Park Ave.
Memphis, TN 38111-6666
phone: 901-458-2633
*Wants Napoleon or his family &
marshals; books, pictures, statues,
paintings, plates, tables, miniatures,
letters, manuscripts, newspapers,
swords, ink wells, etc.; especially in
America after exile.*

James Hilty
Balcony Row
216 S. Broad St.
Holly, MI 48442
phone: 248-634-1400
*Wants items of Napoleonic history;
manuscripts, letters, diaries, maps,
documents, books, etc.*

Sir Winston S. Churchill

Clubs/Associations

Churchill Society, International
Newsletter: Finest Hour
1847 Stonewood Dr.
Baton Rouge, LA 70816-2861
phone: 504-752-3313
fax: 603-746-4260
*Educational/charitable assoc. devoted
to preserving the memory, thought,
writings, of Sir Winston S. Churchill
(1874-1965.)*

PERSONALITIES (INVENTORS)

Thomas Alva Edison

Collectors

John W. Hess
244 Bernaski Rd.
Amsterdam, NY 12010
phone: 518-843-6117
*Wants to buy or trade any Edison
related merchandise: inventions,
antique phonographs, cylinders,
advertising, prototypes; also original
documents, photographs, etc.*

Steven Ramm
420 Fitzwater St.
Philadelphia, PA 19147-3109
phone: 215-922-7050 or 215-545-3290
e-mail: steveramm@aol.com
*Wants items related to Thomas Alva
Edison, such as books, articles, stock
certificates, products from various
Edison companies; no magazine ads
please.*

Carolyn T. Little
725 Esla Dr.
Chula Vista, CA 91910
e-mail: ladylight@prodigy.com
*Wants miniature busts, Edison
commemoratives, Edison memorabilia, etc.*

Experts

David C. Heitz
Edison Connection, The
P.O. Box 518
New Hope, PA 18938
phone: 215-862-5717
*Wants to buy Thomas A. Edison
memorabilia: autographs, stock
certificates, company letters,
advertising, anything Edison; no
magazine ads please.*

Museums/Libraries

David C. Heitz
Edison Connection, The
P.O. Box 518
New Hope, PA 18938
phone: 215-862-5717
*Edison Museum open by appointment
only - school groups, clubs, Seniors
Groups are all welcome; lectures and
demonstrations about Edison; no
charge.*

Laurence J. Russell, Curator
Thomas Edison Birthplace Museum
P.O. Box 451
Milan, OH 44846-0451
phone: 419-499-2135
fax: 419-499-3241
e-mail: edison@accnorwalk.com
Internet: http://www.edisonbp.org
*An Edison exhibit featuring
phonographs, lamps, fans, photos, and
other items related to Thomas Edison.*

PERSONALITIES (LITERARY)

(see also LITERATURE)

Charles Dickens

Collectors

Gerald DiMinico
105 Park St.
Montclair, NJ 07042-2905
phone: 201-744-2092
*Wants Charles Dickens material;
seeking primarily prints, lithographs
or original art work pertaining to
Dickens' books.*

Edgar Allan Poe

Museums/Libraries

Edgar Allan Poe House & Museum, c/o
CHAP
417 E. Fayette St., Room 1037
Baltimore, MD 21202
phone: 410-396-4866

Edgar Rice Burroughs

(see also CHARACTER COL-
LECTIBLES, Tarzan)

Clubs/Associations

George McWhorter
Burroughs Bibliophiles
Magazine: Burroughs Bulletin
Burroughs Memorial Collection
University of Louisville
Louisville, KY 40292-0001
phone: 502-852-8729 or 502-852-6752
fax: 502-852-8734
e-mail:
gtmcwh01@ulkyvm.louisville.com
*International club interested in Edgar
Rice Burroughs; the "Gridley Wave"
newsletter is published monthly; the
"Burroughs Bulletin" is a quarterly
magazine; annual convention since
1960 with buying, selling, speakers.*

Collectors

Butch Smith
P.O. Box 390
Fort Worth, TX 76101
phone: 800-443-7381
*Wants books by Edgar Rice
Burroughs.*

Horatio Alger, Jr.

(see also BOOKS, Horatio Alger, Jr.)

Clubs/Associations

Horatio Alger Society
Newsletter: Newsboy, The
P.O. Box 70361
Richmond, VA 23255
e-mail: alger-l@listserv.wuacc.edu
Internet: http://www.wuacc.edu/sobu/
broach/algerres.html
*To further the philosophy of Horatio
Alger, Jr. and to encourage the spirit
of Strive & Succeed.*

Jack London

Museums/Libraries

Jack London State Historic Park
Museum
Newsletter: Jack London Museum
Bulletin
20 E. Spain St.
Sonoma, CA 95476
phone: 707-938-5216
*Wants Jack London books, magazines,
letters and other memorabilia;
mailing address as noted above, but
located in Glen Ellen, CA.*

Margaret Mitchell

(see also MOVIE MEMORABILIA,
Gone With The Wind)

Collectors

John Wiley, Ed.
1347 Greenmoss Dr.
Richmond, VA 23225-4112
phone: 804-330-5484
*Wants to buy early copies of Gone
With The Wind in dust jackets &
limited editions (U.S. & foreign);
original Macmillan promotional
material (catalogs, counter displays,
etc.); Margaret Mitchell items
(personal effects, business cards.)*

Mark Twain

Clubs/Associations

George Daneluck
Mark Twain Society - Jersey City State
College
2039 Kennedy Memorial Bldg.
Jersey City, NJ 07035

Dealers

Chuck Haley
Sherlock's
13926 Double Girth Ct.
Matthews, NC 28105
phone: 704-843-3433 or 704-847-5480

Museums/Libraries

Mark Twain Memorial
351 Farmington Ave.
Hartford, CT 06105
phone: 203-247-0998

Henry Sweets, Dir.
Mark Twain Home & Museum
Newsletter: Fence Painter, The
208 Hill St.
Hannibal, MO 63401
phone: 314-221-9010
*Museum operates Mark Twain's
boyhood home, J.M. Clemens Law
Office, Grant's Drug Store, and three
museum buildings; the newsletter
contains historical notes on mark
Twain and Hannibal, MO as well as
museum news.*

Randolph Caldecott

Clubs/Associations

Owen Reichert, Pres.
Randolph Caldecott Society
112 Crooked Tree Trail
Moultrie Trails, RR #4
Saint Augustine, FL 32086
Wants Charles Dickens material.

Shakespeare

Collectors

Tom
P.O. Box 288
Mount Olive, NC 28365
*Interested in items related to William
Shakespeare and/or the characters in
his plays: Staffordshire and other
figures, busts, bookends, plaques,
engravings, paintings, pictures, plates,
mugs, etc.*

Sir Arthur Conan Doyle

Collectors

Robert C. Hess
559 Potter Blvd.
Brightwaters, NY 11718-1615
phone: 516-665-8365
*Wants Sherlock Holmes/Sir Arthur
Conan Doyle items: figurines,
sculpture, statuary, dolls, original
artwork, illustrations, etc.*

Zane Grey

Clubs/Associations

Carolyn Timmerman, Sec.
Zane Grey's West Society
Newsletter: Zane Grey Review
708 Warwick Ave.
Fort Wayne, IN 46825-5653
phone: 219-484-2904
*Members are collectors of Zane Grey
books and memorabilia.*

PERSONALITIES (MILITARY)

Audie Murphy

Clubs/Associations

Shareon L. Young
Audie Murphy National Fan Club
11528 Holmes St., Apt. 1
Kansas City, MO 64131-3892

Museums/Libraries

Dr. B.D. Patterson
Confederate Research Center - Audie
Murphy Exhibit
P.O. Box 619
Hillsboro, TX 76645
phone: 817-582-2555
*Special Audie Murphy memorabilia
collection on display.*

Gen. George S. Patton

Museums/Libraries

Katie Talbot
Patton Museum of Cavalry & Armor
P.O. Box 208
Fort Knox, KY 40121-0208
phone: 502-624-3812
fax: 502-624-6968
*The "Patton Gallery" and the Emert
L. "Red" Davis Library contains Gen.
George S. Patton, Jr. artifacts and
reference materials.*

PERSONALITIES (MOVIE STARS)

(see also AUTOGRAPHS, Celebrity;
MOVIE MEMORABILIA)

Periodicals

George A. Carpinone, Ed.
Magazine: Celebrity Collector Magazine
P.O. Box 1115
Boston, MA 02117-1115
phone: 617-426-7724
fax: 617-426-7724
*Interviews with classic movie stars, TV
stars, and fan club presidents;
exploration of Hollywood memorabilia collecting and collection care;
contributions by readers; classified
ads; beautifully designed as a
collectible on glossy paper.*

Ava Gardner

Museums/Libraries

Melody Godwin
Ava Gardner Museum
Newsletter: Ava Advocate
205 S. 3rd St.
P.O. Box 1182
Smithfield, NC 27577
phone: 919-934-5830 or 919-934-0887
fax: 919-934-5830
e-mail: jmivey@ipass.net
Internet: http://www.avagardner.org/
museum
*Collection of posters, costumes,
photographs and personal items
relating to the famous Hollywood
movie star, Ava Gardner.*

Bette Davis

Collectors

James L. Harmon
P.O. Box 25
Banks, OR 97106
phone: 503-324-7041
*Want to buy Bette Davis movie
posters, lobby cards, magazines,
unusual paper items; original and
vintage material only.*

Clint Eastwood

Collectors

Fred & Jan Carlson
P.O. Box 2
Hillsboro, OR 97123-0002
phone: 503-648-8477
*Wants to buy Rawhide and Clint
Eastwood items including comics,
books, records, tapes, posters, etc.*

Errol Flynn

Clubs/Associations

Eric G. Lilley, Pres.
International Errol Flynn Society
Magazine: Sword Magazine
2 Holly Close, Crookham Park
Crookhan Common, Thatcham
Berkshire RG19 8QZ, U.K.
phone: 01635-869694
*Founded 1977, over 6000 members in
23 countries; an international club
devoted to Errol Flynn.*

Greta Garbo

Collectors

Rick Rann
P.O. Box 877
Oak Park, IL 60303-0877
phone: 708-442-7907
*Wants to buy Greta Garbo movie
posters, lobby cards, glass slides,
magazines, coming attraction flyers,
books, and pressbooks from 1920s to
1940s.*

James Dean

Clubs/Associations

Sylvia Bongiovanni
We Remember Dean International
Newsletter: We Remember Dean
International Newsletter
P.O. Box 5025
Fullerton, CA 92635-0025
*Formed in respectful memory of actor
James Dean; bi-monthly newsletter
includes Dean articles, current news,
where to buy memorabilia, etc.*

Museums/Libraries

David Loehr
James Dean Gallery, The
P.O. Box 55
Fairmount, IN 46928-0055
phone: 317-948-3326
fax: 317-948-3389
Houses the world's largest collection

of memorabilia dealing with James Dean; wants James Dean plates, posters, records, novelties, photos, autographs, etc.

James Doohan

Collectors

Jan Benham
2457 Raymond SE
Grand Rapids, MI 49507-3923
phone: 616-247-0072
e-mail: jabenham@post.grcc.cc.mi.us
Wants to buy photographs, news clippings, unique collectibles on the actor James Doohan ("Scotty" on StarTrek).

John Wayne

Collectors

Grant Underwood
3413 36th St.
Lubbock, TX 79413
phone: 806-797-6348
Wants to buy everything on the Duke except still photos.

Periodicals

Mario De Marco
Newsletter: John Wayne, The All-American Hero
152 Maple St.
West Boylston, MA 01583-1825
phone: 508-835-4085
Has a number of books on other western and serial stars; send large SASE for book list.

Tim Lilley
Newsletter: Big Trail, The
540 Stanton Ave.
Akron, OH 44301
John Wayne movie reviews, items for sale, feature articles.

Laurel & Hardy

Collectors

Gino Dercola
10134 Cape Ann Dr.
Columbia, MD 21046
phone: 301-596-6547
Wants Laurel & Hardy toys, games, novelties, dolls, comics, etc.

Jan Benham
2457 Raymond SE
Grand Rapids, MI 49507-3923
phone: 616-247-0072
e-mail: jabenham@post.grcc.cc.mi.us
Wants to buy Laurel & Hardy memorabilia such as dolls, toys, costumes, cookie jars, etc.

Marilyn Monroe

Clubs/Associations

Roman Hryniszak
All About Marilyn
Newsletter: Runnin'Wild
P.O. Box 291176
Los Angeles, CA 90029
phone: 213-469-9314
fax: 310-450-7643
An organization dedicated to Marilyn Monroe; provided fans and collectors with information about the legendary star, and a forum to contact each other; provides wonderful leads for collectors; quarterly newsletter.

Collectors

Ann Bartoli
1230 Woodridge Ct.
Princeton, IL 61356-8622
phone: 815-875-8925
Wants to buy magazines with Marilyn on the cover (American and foreign), sheet music, press books; especially wants older magazines including pre-national TV Guides; also Sunday sections newspapers like NY Daily News.

Dealers

Cindy Oakes
34025 W. 6 Mile
Livonia, MI 48152
phone: 313-591-3252
Wants dolls, jewelry, autographs, etc.

Experts

Dawn E. Reno
3280 Shingler Terrace
Deltona, FL 32738-5351
phone: 904-532-1960
fax: 904-532-1960
e-mail: DawnReno@juno.com
Author of "The Marilyn Monroe Phenomena" (Chilton, 1996).

Denis C. Jackson
P.O. Box 1958
Sequim, WA 98382-1958
phone: 360-683-2559
fax: 360-683-2559
e-mail: ticn@olypen.com
Internet: http://www.olypen.com/ticn/
Author of "The Price & Identification Guide to Marilyn Monroe" 2nd edition, 1992; lists mens' magazines, movie magazines, paper, books, etc.; send LSASE for information.

Mary Miles Minter

Experts

Ronald Krueger
P.O. Box 741
Oak Park, IL 60303-0741
phone: 708-788-8235
Always buying photos, posters, lobby cards, postcards, glass slides, theater handbills or anything related to this silent film actress; also interested in

making contact with other Minter collectors.

Shirley Temple

Collectors

Gen Jones
294 Park St.
Medford, MA 02155-2668
phone: 617-395-8598
e-mail: astevens@world.std.com
Serious collector wants anything related to Shirley Temple.

Rita Dubas
8811 Colonial Rd.
Brooklyn, NY 11209

Periodicals

Newsletter: Lollipop News
P.O. Box 6203
Oxnard, CA 93031

W.C. Fields

Clubs/Associations

Ted Wioneck, Jr.
W.C. Fields Fan Club
P.O. Box506
Stratford, NJ 08084-0506

PERSONALITIES (MUSICIANS)

(see also ROCK 'N' ROLL COL-LECTIBLES)

Beatles

Clubs/Associations

Irina Dyomkina
London Beatles Fanclub, The
Magazine: Off The Beatle Track
50a Leighton Gardens
London NW10 3PT, U.K.
phone: (181) 960 2092
e-mail: irina@lbfc.demon.co.uk
Internet: http://www.lbfc.demon.co.uk.

B. Whatmough
Working Class Hero Beatles Club
Newsletter: Working Class Hero, The
3311 Niagara St.
Pittsburgh, PA 15213-4223
Non-profit organization for and by true Beatles fans; three newsletter per year covers news, pictures and articles about the Beatles; please send SASE for information.

Beatles Connection
Newsletter: Beatles Connection
P.O. Box 1066
Pinellas Park, FL 33281

Collectors

Marc Zydiak
P.O. Box 285
Westfield, NJ 07091-0285
phone: 908-654-6505
Wants to buy rare Beatles items: Butcher Album covers, important autograph material, original photographs, etc.

Herb Van Vliet
35 Roberta Dr.
Howell, NJ 07731
phone: 908-458-3950
fax: 908-785-9585
Wants to buy KISS toys; also Beatles memorabilia: toys, records, memorabilia and rock concert ticket stubs 1955-1975.

Michael Summers
3258 Harrison St.
Paducah, KY 42001
Wants to buy Beatles memorabilia: fan club items from the 1960s, trading cards, dolls, puzzles, toys, glasses, jewelry; everything Beatles except records.

Gretchen Dziadosz
333 Grentree Lane NE
Ada, MI 49301-9796
e-mail: gretchen@aol.com
Wants original 1960s items only: games, dolls, other memorabilia; please write (include SASE if you want reply) or e-mail; please include asking price.

Jan Benham
2457 Raymond SE
Grand Rapids, MI 49507-3923
phone: 616-247-0072
e-mail: jabenham@post.grcc.cc.mi.us
Buys original Beatle memorabilia such as lunch boxes, dolls, purses, toys, yellow submarine items, ceramic tile (George), and other rare items; no records or magazines, please.

Dealers

Hein's Rare Collectibles
P.O. Box 179
Little Silver, NJ 07739-0179
phone: 908-219-1988
fax: 908-219-5940
Specializes in Beatles and Elvis Presley records and memorabilia.

Cindy Oakes
34025 W. 6 Mile
Livonia, MI 48152
phone: 313-591-3252
Wants original 1960s items only: porcelain Beatles, Remco Beatles, cloth Beatles dolls, Beatles nodders, Beatles blowup dolls, etc.

Experts

Joseph Hilton
6 Wheelwright Dr.
Durham, NH 03824-6607
phone: 603-659-3987
e-mail: JHilton@aol.com
Collecting original 1960s items only: Beatles lunch boxes, games, toys, Yellow Submarine items, promo displays, anything Beatles.

Charles F. Rosenay
P.O. Box 1008
Los Angeles, CA 90066-1088
phone: 310-391-0778
fax: 301-390-7475
e-mail: gds1964@aol.co,
Editor of Beatles Fan Club magazine; produces Beatles conventions; trades and sells memorabilia by mail; recognized expert.

Bob Gottuso
BOJO
P.O. Box 1403
Cranberry Twp., PA 16066
phone: 412-776-0621
fax: 412-776-0621
Buys, sells, trades, and collects 1960's Beatles items; send $2 for 20-page sales catalog filled with Beatles and Yellow Sub items.

Rick Rann
P.O. Box 877
Oak Park, IL 60303-0877
phone: 708-442-7907
Wants to buy toys, dolls, guitars, record player, hair spray, records, concert tickets, movie items, magazines; co-author of book on The Beatles.

Marty Eck
P.O. Box 5311
River Forest, IL 60305
phone: 309-452-9376
Toys, dolls, guitars, record player, hair spray, records, concert tickets, movie items, magazines; co-author of book on same.

Jeff Augsburger
507 Normal Ave.
Normal, IL 61761-2412
phone: 309-452-9376
fax: 309-454-2351
e-mail: Beatles@dave-world.net
Buys, collects, sells Beatles memorabilia: toys, dolls, guitars, record player, hair spray, records, concert tickets, movie items, magazines; co-author of book on same.

Museums/Libraries

Jeff Augsburger
Beatles Mobile Museum, The
507 Normal Ave.
Normal, IL 61761-2412
phone: 309-452-9376
fax: 309-454-2351
e-mail: Beatles@dave-world.net
Has the largest collection of Beatles memorabilia in the US; actively buying for the collection; will buy one item or 1,000.

Periodicals

Bill King
Goody Press, The
Magazine: Beatlefan
P.O. Box 33515
Decatur, GA 30033-0515
phone: 404-633-5587
fax: 404-321-3109
A bi-monthly magazine for Beatles fans; a news-oriented, professional publication; articles, books for sale, ads, etc.

Marsha Ewing
Magazine: Instant Karma
P.O. Box 256
Sault Ste. Marie, MI 49783
phone: 906-632-2231 or 906-635-0140
fax: 906-632-4411
News, ads, opinions.

Matt Hurwitz
Magazine: Good Day Sunshine
P.O. Box 1008
Los Angeles, CA 90066-1088
phone: 310-391-0778
fax: 301-390-7475
e-mail: gds1964@aol.co,
A leading Beatles magazine in the U.S.

Joe Pope
Magazine: Strawberry Fields Forever
P.O. Box 880981
San Diego, CA 92168
Oldest Beatles fanzine in the world.

Elvis

Auction Services

Elvis Auctions
P.O. Box 255
Port Townsend, WA 98368
phone: 360-385-1200
fax: 360-385-6572
e-mail: jpo@olympus.net
Internet: http://www.olympus.net/personal/jpo
Conducts periodic auctions of Elvis memorabilia.

Clubs/Associations

Susan Still
Elvis Forever TCB Fan Club
Newsletter: Elvis Forever TCB Fan Club Newsletter
P.O. Box 1066
Pinellas Park, FL 33281

Collectors

Burt Atwood
894 Greenway Rd.
Woodbridge, CT 06525-2413
Buyer of rare Elvis memorabilia.

B.J. Garton
401 N. 5th St.
Millville, NJ 08332
Wants ELvis memorabilia from the 1950s through 1970s; 1956 items, 45s, picture sleeves, movie, Las Vegas, sheet music, etc.

Dealers

Dwayne Spark
Nostalgia Plus
8441 Sublaines
Anjou
Quebec H1K 2C1 Canada
phone: 514-352-6892
fax: 514-352-1856
e-mail: dspark@montrealnet.ca
Buys and sells Elvis memorabilia.

Ed Wall
89 Washington St.
Gloucester, MA 01930-3526
phone: 508-281-6611
Buys, sells and trades Elvis memorabilia.

Hein's Rare Collectibles
P.O. Box 179
Little Silver, NJ 07739-0179
phone: 908-219-1988
fax: 908-219-5940
Specializes in Beatles and Elvis Presley records and memorabilia.

Peter Weldon
815 2nd Ave.
Troy, NY 12182
phone: 518-235-6795
Issues catalog containing Elvis albums, 45s, EPs, picture sleeves, colored vinyl, picture discs, magazines, books, memorabilia, etc.

Worldwide Elvis
P.O. Box 10
Brooklandville, MD 21022
A major seller and buyer of Elvis material.

Tod Hutchinson
P.O. Box 915
Griffith, IN 46319-0915
phone: 219-923-8334
fax: 219-923-8334
e-mail: Toddtcb@aol.com
Specialize in Elvis collectibles, records, movie posters, etc.

Cindy Oakes
34025 W. 6 Mile
Livonia, MI 48152
phone: 313-591-3252
Wants dolls, jewelry, autographs, etc.

Experts

Eddie Hammer
735 Roosevelt Ave.
Carteret, NJ 07008-2318
phone: 908-969-2232
fax: 908-969-2232
Authority on current releases of Elvis recordings; writes "Elvis News" column for "DISCoveries".

Jean Blankenship
P.O. Box 7274
Pasadena, TX 77508-7274
phone: 713-266-6311
Buys, sells, and specializes in Elvis records, magazines, photos, posters, books, cards, and other non-record memorabilia; since 1956; want lists

are welcome; mails new list of items for sale every other month.

Jerry Osborne
P.O. Box 255
Port Townsend, WA 98368
phone: 360-385-1200
fax: 360-385-6572
e-mail: jpo@olympus.net
Internet: http://www.olympus.net/personal/jpo
Author of "The Official Price Guide to Elvis Presley Records and Memorabilia" (House of Collectibles).

Museums/Libraries

Graceland
P.O. Box 16508
Memphis, TN 38186
phone: 800-238-2000
fax: 901-344-3119
Internet: http://www.elvis-presley.com

Billy Beeny
Elvis Is Alive Museum
P.O. Box 377
Wright City, MO 63390
phone: 314-745-3154
Cafe/arcade/museum filled with Elvis photos, memorabilia and printed material related to the controversy.

Eric Clapton

Collectors

Diane Smith
P.O. Box 262
Glenolden, PA 19036
Wants items relating to Eric Clapton (no guitars, please); wants strange or unusual items signed or unsigned; send description and photo; will return photo if SASE included.

KISS

Clubs/Associations

Gary Conn, Jr.
Kissaholics
Magazine: Kissaholics Magazine
P.O. Box 22334
Nashville, TN 37202
e-mail: gconnjr@aol.com
Internet: http://www.otaku.net/kissaholics
An internationally recognized KISS fan club and magazine geared toward the KISS fan and collector.

Collectors

Herb Van Vliet
35 Roberta Dr.
Howell, NJ 07731
phone: 908-458-3950
fax: 908-785-9585
Wants to buy KISS toys; also Beatles memorabilia: toys, records, memorabilia and rock concert ticket stubs 1955-1975.

Bob Gottuso
BOJO
P.O. Box 1403
Cranberry Twp., PA 16066
phone: 412-776-0621
fax: 412-776-0621
Buys and sells memorabilia related to KISS, the 1970s rock band: original Kiss toys, dolls, household items, etc.; send SASE for sales list.

Liberace

Collectors

N. Graf
902 Apricot
Winters, CA 95694
Wants anything Liberace: pictures, magazines, records, scrapbooks, posters, books, autographs, sheet music, etc.; send price & describe.

Museums/Libraries

Myron G. Martin, Ex. Dir.
Liberace Foundation for the Performing & Creative Arts/Liberace Museum
Newsletter: Liberace Museum Newsletter
1775 E. Tropicana
Las Vegas, NV 89119-6529
phone: 702-798-5595 or 800-626-2625
fax: 702-798-7386
Internet: http://www.liberace.org/museum.html
A non-profit foundation museum and gift shop with proceeds funding scholarships.

Merle Travis

Periodicals

Dave Stewart
Newsletter: Cannonball Rag
P.O. Box 1474
Corinth, MS 38834
phone: 601-287-4136
Dedicated to the life and music of Merle Travis.

Monkees

Clubs/Associations

Charles F. Rosenay
Liverpool Productions' Monkees Buttonmania Club
P.O. Box 1008
Los Angeles, CA 90066-1088
phone: 310-391-0778
fax: 301-390-7475
e-mail: gds1964@aol.co,
Produces Monkees conventions.

Collectors

Rick Rann
P.O. Box 877
Oak Park, IL 60303-0877
phone: 708-442-7907
Wants to buy 1960s Monkees memorabilia: toys, dolls, concert tickets, magazines, books, fan club items, etc.

Tex Ritter

Clubs/Associations

Sharon L. Sweeting
Tex Ritter Fan Club
Newsletter: Gringo, The
15326 73rd Ave. SE
Snohomish, WA 98290
12 page newsletter packed with news, reports, clippings, a trading post, discography, and more relating to Tex Ritter.

Museums/Libraries

Tommie Ritter-Gates
Ritter Museum
300 W. Panola
Carthage, TX 75633
phone: 903-693-6634
fax: 903-693-8578

PETROLIANA

(see GAS STATION COLLECTIBLES)

PEWTER

(see also REPAIR/RESTORATION/CONSERVATION, Metal Items)

Clubs/Associations

Louise Graver, Mem.
Pewter Collectors Club of America
504 W. Lafayette St.
West Chester, PA 19380-2210
Association of private collectors and interested parties; annual national as well as regional meetings; semi-annual newsletter.

Collectors

David Kilroy
154 Pleasant St.
Lexington, MA 02173-8244
phone: 617-648-4852
Wants to buy American, English, and Continental pewter pieces; editor of the Pewter Collector's Club of America Newsletter.

Bill Burkett
P.O. Box 2488
Sun City, AZ 85372-2488
phone: 602-974-4535 or 800-507-7234
fax: 602-974-4323
Collector of old American made pewter items; preferred items will contain "touch" marks including initials or a name and possibly a city name; please no new items; note that OLD items will NOT be marked "Pewter."

Experts

Robert A. Limons
RD 1 Box 162
Hellertown, PA 18055
phone: 610-838-8931
Advisor to "Warman's Antiques & Collectibles Price Guide."

Museums/Libraries

Currier Gallery of Art, The
192 Orange St.
Manchester, NH 03104
phone: 603-669-6144

Repro. Sources

Ron Kuskins
Pewter Crafters of Cape Cod
933 Rt. 6A
Yarmouth Port, MA 02675
phone: 508-362-3407
Handcrafted American pewter hollowware in traditional and contemporary designs.

James W. Wilson
Jori Handcast Pewter
12681 Metro Pkwy.
Fort Myers, FL 33912

Bill Wiebold
Pewter Reproduction Works
5950 Park Rd. #3
Madeira, OH 45243
phone: 513-831-2815
Makes replicas of pewter oil lamps, bull's-eye lamps, candlesticks, baby bottles, and funnels; complete with antique patina, nicks, dents, bends; all reproductions permanently marked as such.

PEZ

(see also CANDY CONTAINERS)

Collectors

M. Koenigsberg
700 Boulevard East #7D
Weehawken, NJ 07087
phone: 201-863-0868
Wants to buy PEZ collections.

Richard Belyski
P.O. Box 124
Sea Cliff, NY 11579-0124
phone: 516-676-1183
fax: 516-676-1183
e-mail: peznews@juno.com
Internet: http://pages.prodigy.com/PEZNEWS/pez.htm
Buys, sells, trades and collects PEZ candy containers.

Maureen Winer
5900 Brackenridge Ave.
Baltimore, MD 21212
phone: 410-435-5226
Interested in buying all PEZ containers.

Charles Beesley
P.O. Box 400
Saint Michaels, MD 21663-0400
phone: 410-745-9206
fax: 410-822-5460
Wants PEZ candy dispensers; one item or entire collection - anything PEZ.

Richard Geary
P.O. Box 622
Madison, OH 44057

Jill Cohen
P.O. Box 18139
Cleveland, OH 44118-0139
phone: 216-283-5993
e-mail: pezamania@msn.com
Organizer of the PEZ-A Mania Convention, held annually in Cleveland, OH.

deal

Michele Lorenz
5367 East Hidden Lake Dr.
East Lansing, MI 48823
phone: 517-332-3534
fax: 517-347-1522
e-mail: mgl@voyager.net
Internet: http://web2.airmail.net/pezmgl
Buys and sells PEZ candy containers.

Dealers

Mark McMahon
Cookie Jars, Etc.
110 West 25th St., 8th Floor
New York, NY 1000107401
phone: 212-633-1923
fax: 212-924-8535
e-mail: peter@peterandmark.com
Buy, sell, trade cookie jars, banks, salt & peppers and PEZ.

Graham Trievel
P.O. Box 1625
West Chester, PA 19380
phone: 610-701-9193

David A. Hull
Small Town Coins & Collectibles
7498 E. Davison Rd.
Davison, MI 48423-2014
phone: 810-658-1992
fax: 810-658-2977
e-mail: towncoin@concentric.net
Internet: http://www.concentric.net/~towncoin
Has 100s of old PEZ for sale; wants to buy singles or entire collections.

Experts

Steven L. Glew
5611 Lehman Rd.
Dewitt, MI 48820
phone: 517-669-5931
fax: 517-669-5931
Buys, sells and specializes in PEZ.

David Welch
P.O. Box 714
Murphysboro, IL 62966-0714
phone: 618-687-2282
fax: 618-684-2243
e-mail: PexDude1@aol.com
Wants anything relating to PEZ for collection and book research; paying over $3000 for certain items; author of "A Pictorial Guide to Plastic Candy Dispensers" and "Collecting PEZ."

John Devlin
"The Cool PEZ Man"
5441 Oakville Center, Ste. 119
Saint Louis, MO 63129-3554
phone: 314-416-0333
Buys, sells, collects, and trades PEZ candy containers; runs the annual

National PEZ Collectors Convention (not affiliated with the Pez Company.)

Misc. Services

Richard Geary
P.O. Box 622
Madison, OH 44057
Author of "PEZ Collectibles I" and PEZ Collectibles II"; organizes the annual PEZ-A Mania collectors' convention.

Periodicals

Richard Belyski
Newsletter: PEZ Collector's News
P.O. Box 124
Sea Cliff, NY 11579-0124
phone: 516-676-1183
fax: 516-676-1183
e-mail: peznews@juno.com
Internet: http://pages.prodigy.com/
PEZNEWS/pez.htm

PHARMACY

(see MEDICAL, DENTAL & PHARMACEUTICAL)

PHILATELICS

(see STAMP COLLECTING)

PHONOGRAPHS

(see also BOOKS, Reference [Phonographs]; HI-FI EQUIPMENT; MUSICAL INSTRUMENTS, Mechanical; RECORDS)

Book Sellers

Yesterday Once Again
P.O. Box 6773
Huntington Beach, CA 92615-6773
phone: 714-963-2474
fax: 714-963-1558
Carries a large selection of books dealing with early phonographs and related ephemera.

Clubs/Associations

Bill Pratt
Canadian Antique Phonograph Society
Journal: Antique Phonograph News
122 Major St.
Toronto
Ontario M5S 2L2 Canada
phone: 416-924-8207
e-mail: bill@rom.on.ca
Internet: http://www.rose.com/~caps
Members interested in sound recording and its history: phonographs, framophones; also related ephemera and memorabilia; journal has original articles, repair tips and how-to's, auction results, ads.

John & Linda Gramm
Hudson Valley Antique Radio & Phonograph Society
P.O. Box 1, Rt. 207
Campbell Hall, NY 10916
phone: 914-427-2602
For antique radio and phonograph collectors who want to share

information, equipment and related items with others having similar interests; monthly meetings feature educational demonstrations and mini swap meets.

Steve Dando
Buckeye Radio & Phonograph Club
Newsletter: Soundings
4572 Mark Trail
Copley, OH 44321
phone: 216-666-7222
Members exchange expertise in restoration of vintage radios and phonographs; club holds annual mall show (displaying radios and phonographs) and picnic.

Michigan Antique Phonograph Society, Inc.
Newsletter: In The Groove
60 Central St.
Battle Creek, MI 49027
A highly recommended newsletter contains articles, member ads about antique phonographs, records and music boxes; MAPS Membership & Resource Directory published every other year.

C.F. Crandell, Pres.
Vintage Radio & Phonograph Society, Inc.
Newsletter: Reproducer, The
P.O. Box 165345
Irving, TX 75016-5345
phone: 214-337-2823 or 972-315-2553
Purpose is to preserve early radios, phonographs, and related material and to conduct historical research of same; also publishes "Soundwaves" newsletter.

Karyn Sitter
California Antique Phonograph Society
P.O. Box 67
Duarte, CA 91010-0067

Collectors

Aaron Cramer
2056 E. 28th St.
Brooklyn, NY 11229
Has written columns about phonographs, or talking machines; discovered the world's oldest recording.

John W. Hess
244 Bernaski Rd.
Amsterdam, NY 12010
phone: 518-843-6117
Wants to buy Vogue picture disc records, horn phonographs, music boxes, roller organs; also wants parts, empty cabinets, horns; any condition, any material.

Alvin Heckard
RD 1 Box 88
Lewistown, PA 17044-9801
phone: 717-248-7071 or 717-248-2816
Wants wind-up type phonographs (outside horn type only, please), parts, literature and advertising.

Bernie Seinberg
714 Moredon Rd.
Meadowbrook, PA 19046-1907
phone: 215-886-6124
e-mail: phonoman-Bernie@worldnet.att.net
Wants Edison, Victor, and Columbia tabletop phonographs; also phonograph related advertising, needle tins, record dusters, puzzles, fans, pins, buttons, badges, mirrors, etc.

Steven Ramm
420 Fitzwater St.
Philadelphia, PA 19147-3109
phone: 215-922-7050 or 215-545-3290
e-mail: steveramm@aol.com
Specializes in phonographs and pre-1930 records; wants to buy sheet music, postcards, and advertising with illustrations of phonographs, records, or Thomas A. Edison; also wants cylinder rolls in playable condition.

David Giovannoni
Rockville, MD 20855-1337
phone: 301-869-1501
fax: 301-258-0420
e-mail: 71210.32@compuserve.com
Advanced collector looking for certain phonographs and records from 1890s through 1920s; call if you have 78s, cylinder records, antique phonographs, or related items for sale; if on-line, join the CompuServe Collectibles Forum!

Stuart Stein
P.O. Box 303
Frederick, MD 21705-0303
phone: 301-663-8369
fax: 301-663-8202
e-mail: steincpa@ix.netcom.com
Wants disc type wind up phonographs with horns.

Mike Ellingson
1412 2nd Ave. S.
Fargo, ND 58103-1612
phone: 701-280-1413
Has most phonographs he needs for his personal collection, but is willing to help you determine what your phonograph is worth; will try to answer any antique phonograph question 10:00 a.m. to 10:00 p.m. CST M-F.

Dealers

Bruce & Charlotte Mager
Waves
110 West 25th St., Ste. 10M
New York, NY 10001-7401
phone: 212-989-9284
fax: 201-461-7121
e-mail: c1wave@aol.com
Internet: http://www.wavesradio.com
Over 20 years experience specializing in vintage radios, phonographs, telegraphy, televisions, assorted electrical and mechanical apparatus, and related advertising memorabilia, books and pamphlets.

Allen Koenigsberg
502 E. 17th St.
Brooklyn, NY 11226-6606
phone: 718-941-6835
fax: 718-941-1408
Author of the "Patent History of the Phonograph."

Tim
Terra Firma Antiques
P.O. Box 10307
Rochester, NY 14610-0307
phone: 716-244-5546
e-mail: phonophan@aol.com
Internet: http://members.aol.com/
phonophan
Buys and sells talking machines, mechanical music, records and related books and ephemera.

Doug Negus
Phonograph Phanatic
215 Mason St.
Sutherland, IA 51058-7606
phone: 712-446-2270 or 712-446-3746
e-mail: negus@nwidt.com
Music boxes, phonographs, cylinder records, pianos, NO piano rolls, older mechanical musical instruments, pre-1930; any parts or repairables wanted.

Yesterday Once Again
P.O. Box 6773
Huntington Beach, CA 92615-6773
phone: 714-963-2474
fax: 714-963-1558
Equipped to supply almost any part necessary to restore the old handcranked phonographs; also sells accessories such as steel phonograph needles, paper record sleeves, books, instruction manual reprints, and related items.

Experts

John P. Andolina, Jr.
Early Sound Man, The
28 Glen Oaks Dr.
Rochester, NY 14624-1405
phone: 716-247-3056
Over 24 years experience in the collecting, repair, and research of crank type phonographs and related items; buys, sells, collects, repairs; also supplies original and reproduction parts and related items; Edison reproducers in stock.

Ken Danckaert
231 Kennedy Ct.
Severna Park, MD 21146-3039
phone: 410-544-0260
e-mail: ken@weasel.acs.umbc.edu
Internet: http://www.kend@lemur.org
Collects, buys, sells, appraises, and repairs music boxes, phonographs, and organettes; specialist in coin-operated phonographs; in business since 1972; an expert who gives lectures, presentations and videos.

Howard Hazelcorn
6731 Ashley Ct.
Sarasota, FL 34241-9696
phone: 941-921-1815
Collector and author of "Collectors Guide to Columbia Spring-Wound Cylinder Phonographs."

Randy & Larry Donley
Donley's Wild West Town & Museum
8512 S. Union Rd.
Union, IL 60180-9661
phone: 815-923-9000
fax: 815-923-2253
Experts in antique phonographs; buys, sells, collects and repairs.

Shawn Borri
Shawn Borri's Oldtime Talking Machine Co.
RR 1, 2600n Road
La Moille, IL 61330
phone: 815-638-2158 or 815-638-2243
Writes antique phonograph column; specializes in the repair of wind-up cylinder phonographs; also will work on early battery operated cylinder phonographs; specializes in precise adjustment of phonograph reproducers; no Dicta Phones.

Steve Oliphant
5255 Allott Ave.
Van Nuys, CA 91401-5902
phone: 310-789-2339 or 310-271-5176
fax: 310-276-5632
Adviser and dealer of old phonographs; buys entire collections or individual pieces.

Museums/Libraries

George D. Tselos, Archivist
Edison National Historic Site
Main St. at Lakeside Ave.
West Orange, NJ 07052
phone: 201-736-5050
fax: 201-736-8496
A museum with exhibits in all fields of Edison's contributions.

Johnson Victrola Museum
c/o Delaware State Visitor's Center
406 Federal St., Box 1401
Dover, DE 19903
phone: 302-739-4266
fax: 302-739-3943
Museum is a tribute to Eldridge Reeves Johnson, inventor and businessman who founded the Victor Talking Machine Company; extensive collection of talking machines, Victrolas, "Nipper", early recordings, equipment, Johnson memorabilia.

Randy & Larry Donley
Donley's Wild West Town & Museum
8512 S. Union Rd.
Union, IL 60180-9661
phone: 815-923-9000
fax: 815-923-2253
Large exhibit of Edison phonographs, cylinder and disc music machines, and other music memorabilia.

Periodicals

New Amberola Phonograph Co. The
Magazine: New Amberola Graphic, The
37 Caledonia St.
St. Johnsbury, VT 05819
A quarterly publication for collectors of early phonographs & records from the years 1895-1935; articles, book reviews, ads, auctions, etc.

James Cranshaw
Horn Speaker, The
Newspaper: Horn Speaker, The
P.O. Box 1193
Mabank, TX 75147-1193
phone: 903-848-0304
fax: 903-848-0596
e-mail: cranshaw@e-tex.com
Internet: http://home.navisoft.com/horn/ths2.htm
A newspaper for collectors and historians interested in antique radios and phonographs.

Repair Services

Talking Machine Emporium, The
42 Spring St.
Middletown, RI 02840
phone: 401-849-5360 or 401-635-2816
Antique radio and wind-up phonograph repair; also buys and sells.

Victrola
19 Cliff St.
Saint Johnsbury, VT 05819
phone: 800-239-4188
Victrola sales and repair.

Rod Lauman
Victrola Repair Service
19 Cliff St.
Saint Johnsbury, VT 05819-1002
phone: 802-748-4893 or 800-239-4188
Internet: http://www.together.net/~victrola
Repairs Victrolas and wind-up phonographs; repairs done via U.P.S.; mainsprings, parts, needles also available.

Floyd Silver
Antique Phonograph Center
P.O. Box 2574
Vincentown, NJ 08088-2574
phone: 609-859-8617
e-mail: fsilver@compuserve.com
Antique phonograph sales and service; complete restorations of Edison, Victor and Columbia phonographs.

John P. Andolina, Jr.
Early Sound Man, The
28 Glen Oaks Dr.
Rochester, NY 14624-1405
phone: 716-247-3056
Wants to buy outside horn phonographs, Edison, Victor, Columbia, others; records, brown wax cylinders, Berliner, Vogue picture discs, concert cylinders, need tins, record dusters, "Nipper"; also does repairs and adjustments.

Emerson E. Whitacre
Mechanical Music Man
7550 President Court
Dayton, OH 45414-3671
phone: 513-898-6044 or 513-898-0865
Repairs, adjusts and cleans disc music boxes, cylinder music boxes, antique phonographs, etc.

Harry Daniels
35607 Richland
Livonia, MI 48150
phone: 313-425-1168
Repairs Edison & Victor machines; also interested in buying parts and machines.

Wyatt's Musical Americana
P.O. Box 601
Lakeport, CA 95453
Carries large supply of antique phonographs parts; also specializes in the repair and restoration of all types of windup phonographs; send $4 for 64 page catalog listing over 1,500 parts.

Suppliers

J.J. Papovich
53 Magnolia Ave.
Pitman, NJ 08071
phone: 609-582-8279
Supplies parts for old phonographs.

Jim Dalton, Sr.
Dalton & Dalton
P.O. Box 487
Muncie, IN 47305-0487
phone: 317-288-9488
Has an assortment of over 2000 phonograph needles for sale; covers nearly every make and model of the past 25 years.

Nipper

Collectors

Bernie Seinberg
714 Moredon Rd.
Meadowbrook, PA 19046-1907
phone: 215-886-6124
e-mail: phonoman-Bernie@worldnet.att.net
Wants any pre-1950s items picturing the R.C.A. dog, Nipper.

Dealers

Yesterday Once Again
P.O. Box 6773
Huntington Beach, CA 92615-6773
phone: 714-963-2474
fax: 714-963-1558
Largest selection of "Nipper" available: dogs, accessories, books, and more.

PHOTOGRAPHICA

(see 3-D PHOTOGRAPHICA; CAMERAS & CAMERA EQUIPMENT; OPTICAL ITEMS; PHOTOGRAPHS; PHOTOGRAPHY; STANHOPES; STEREO VIEWERS & STEREOVIEWS)

PHOTOGRAPHS

(see also 3-D PHOTOGRAPHICA; AUDIO-VISUAL; CAMERAS & CAMERA EQUIPMENT; MOVIE MEMORABILIA; PHOTOGRAPHY; REPAIR/RESTORATION/CONSERVATION, Archival Supplies For; REPAIR/RESTORATION/CONSERVATION, Paper Items; STEREO VIEWERS & STEREOVIEWS)

Appraisers

Larry Gottheim
Fine Early Photographs
33 Orton Ave.
Binghamton, NY 13905-3409
phone: 607-797-1685
fax: 607-797-4775
Internet: http://www.be-hold.com
Specializes in appraising vintage photographs, daguerreotypes, tintypes, stereo views; entire collections as well as important single items.

Julia Nelson-Gal
826 Alvarado
San Francisco, CA 94114-3116
phone: 415-641-8004
fax: 415-641-8053
e-mail: JulesNG@aol.com
Specialist in appraisals of 19th and 20th century photographs and photographic literature; will authenticate and broker sales.

Auction Services

Daile Kaplan
Swann Galleries, Inc.
104 E. 25th St.
New York, NY 10010-2977
phone: 212-254-4710
fax: 212-979-1017
e-mail: SwannSales@aol.com
Oldest/largest U.S. auctioneer specializing in rare books, autographs & manuscripts, Judaica, photographs, and works of art on paper; auctions of photographs held three times per year.

Denise Bethel
Sotheby's
1334 York Ave.
New York, NY 10021
phone: 212-606-7370 or 212-606-7000
Internet: http://www.sothebys.com

Christie's
502 Park Ave.
New York, NY 10022
phone: 212-546-1000
fax: 212-980-8163
Internet: http://www.sirius.com/~christie/

Larry Gottheim
Fine Early Photographs
33 Orton Ave.
Binghamton, NY 13905-3409
phone: 607-797-1685
fax: 607-797-4775
Internet: http://www.be-hold.com
Conducts mail-bid auctions of vintage photographs, daguerreotypes,

*tintypes, stereo views, especially of
historic and aesthetic importance.*

Michael Griffin
4316 Hale Dr.
Lilburn, GA 30247
Does catalog auctions by mail.

Butterfield & Butterfield
220 San Bruno Ave.
San Francisco, CA 94103-5018
phone: 415-861-7500
fax: 415-553-8678

Clubs/Associations

Michael Pritchard, Editor
Photographic Collectors Club of Great
  Britain
Magazine: Photographica World
5 Station Industrial Estate
Prudhoe
Northumberland NE42 6NP U.K
phone: (+44) 0117 9831839
e-mail:
  mpritchard@cix.compulink.co.uk
Internet: http://www.nmsi.ac.uk/nmpft/
  pccgb.htm
*Club aims to promote the study and
collection of photographic equipment
and images by publications, meetings,
auctions and shows; covers cameras,
lenses, photographers, optical toys,
stereoscopes, magic lanterns, and
related areas.*

Bob Hurden
Photographic Historical Society, Inc.,
  The
Newsletter: PHS Newsletter
P.O. Box 39563
Rochester, NY 14604
Internet: http://www.rit.edu/~andpph/
  tphs.html
*Conducts a monthly meetings and a
tri-annual symposium.*

Association of International Photogra-
  phy Art Dealers
1609 Connecticut Ave. NW #200
Washington, DC 20009-1034
*Publishes the "AIPAD Membership
Directory and Illustrated Catalogue"
($25) and a 35-page brochure "On
Collecting Photographs" ($10).*

Michigan Photographic Historical
  Society
Newsletter: Photogram, The
P.O. Box 2278
Birmingham, MI 48012-2278
phone: 313-882-1113 or 810-549-6026

Chicago Photographic Collectors
  Society
Newsletter: CPCS Newsletter
P.O. Box 303
Grayslake, IL 60030
phone: 312-262-5979
*A non-profit organization in its 25th
year; over 200 U.S. and foreign
members; sponsors two trade shows a
year in the Chicago area; "CPCS
Newsletter" is published monthly;
also publishes the journal "By
Daylight".*

Collectors

George Sullivan
330 East 33rd St.
New York, NY 10016-9466
phone: 212-689-9745
*Wants to buy photographs by Mathew
Brady.*

Larry Berke
28 Marksman Ln.
Levittown, NY 11756-5110
phone: 516-796-7280
*Wants to buy photographs (da-
guerreotypes, stereoviews, tintypes,
CDVs, cards) and 19th or 20th photos
and unusual century cameras.*

Karl L. Jannen
106 Bishops Rd.
Smithtown, NY 11787-1427
phone: 516-265-3654
*Wants to buy early photographs
showing humor or suggesting an
amusing caption; nothing sensational
expected — any smile-provoker
qualifies; will pay up to $25 per; send
photocopy first, please; will reply
promptly.*

Gary Ronk
6247 Cove Rd.
Roanoke, VA 24019-1715
phone: 540-562-2368
*Wants to buy CDVs of soldiers,
animals, buildings, outdoor; tax
stamped or any unusual is preferred.*

David L. Hartline
P.O. Box 775
Columbus, OH 43085
*Wants Western photographs, Annie
Oakley, Buffalo Bill, Indian, etc.; also
images of Black soldiers, military forts
and regiments; will answer all letters.*

Betty Davis
5291 Ravenna Rd.
Newton Falls, OH 44444-9440
phone: 330-872-0318 or 330-872-0386
fax: 216-872-0386
e-mail: bdavishope@theonramp.net
*Collector wants interesting, unusual
images (cased, tin, paper, etc.) of pre-
1930 albums, horse-drawn vehicles,
soldiers, Indians, occupations, toys,
sports, motorcycles, store fronts,
cowboys, blacks, etc.; no snapshots;
send photocopy.*

Norman Kulkin
727 N. Fuller Ave.
Los Angeles, CA 90046-7504
phone: 213-653-6929
*Buy, sell, trade stereoviews,
daguerreotypes, Civil War photos,
anything in photographica 1839-1939.*

Jeff Mark
P.O. Box 5178
Santa Monica, CA 90409-5178
phone: 800-666-9553 or 310-396-9767
fax: 310-396-2666
*Wants old photographs from 1850-
1900; prefers from Old America:
cowboys, Indians, miners, slaves,
occupationals (fireman, police, etc.),*

*baseball, sports; especially wants
larger old photos.*

David Wallach
P.O. Box 150285
San Rafael, CA 94915
phone: 415-883-3242
*Wants to buy photographs, images,
antique daguerreotypes, ambrotypes,
tintypes; interested in military, Indian,
armed civilians, nudes.*

Don Callies
Mirror Images
205 N L St., Apt. 4
Aberdeen, WA 98520-6104
*Wants early daguerreotypes,
ambrotypes, melainotypes, ferrotypes,
cabinet photos of American Indians,
Civil War, Mexican War, military,
gunboats, ships, sailors, Western
Americana, gold rush, miners,
lawmen, outlaws, cowboys, etc.*

Dealers

Mack Lee
Lee Gallery
1 Mount Vernon St.
Winchester, MA 01890-2703
phone: 617-729-7445
fax: 617-729-4592
*Buys, sells, and appraises fine 19th
and 20th century photographs.*

David & Becky Beane
Beane's Antiques & Photography
58 River Road
Benton, ME 04901
phone: 207-453-6790
e-mail: dbeane@mint.net
Internet: http://www.mint.net:80/
  antiques/catalog/beane.html
*Actively buying early photography
including but not limited to
daguerreotypes, ambrotypes, tintypes,
and all related forms of
photographica.*

J. & L. Photography
P.O. Box 813
Levittown, NY 11756
phone: 516-731-7772 or 516-796-7280
*Buys, sells, and collects daguerreo-
types, stereoviews, tintypes, albums,
CDV's, cameras, equipment, etc.*

Larry Gottheim
Fine Early Photographs
33 Orton Ave.
Binghamton, NY 13905-3409
phone: 607-797-1685
fax: 607-797-4775
Internet: http://www.be-hold.com
*Buys and sells; specializes in vintage
photographs, daguerreotypes,
tintypes, stereo views, especially of
historic and aesthetic importance;
catalog is published three times a year
for $45.*

Joseph F. Loccisano
Historic Photographs & Paper
  Americana
2264 Nicholson Square Dr.
Lancaster, PA 17601-3966
phone: 717-560-7750
*Wants to buy American photographs
from 1870s to 1930s; prefers 5" x 7"
or larger; interiors or exteriors of
businesses, stores, shops, saloons,
amusement arcades, factories, etc.*

Tom Molocea
Historic Images
P.O. Box 100
North Lima, OH 44452-0100
*Buys photos of all categories and all
formats; single images to entire
collections.*

Don Hoffman
P.O. Box 4231
Salinas, CA 93912-4231
phone: 408-449-7311
*Wants old photographs, images,
prints, stereoviews, CDV's, cabinet
cards, calotypes, daguerreotypes,
ambrotypes, negatives about sports,
boxing, jazz, blues, minstrel,
vaudeville, general Americana
subjects; please describe and price.*

Jeffrey Fraenkel
Fraenkel Gallery
49 Geary St.
San Francisco, CA 94108
phone: 415-981-2661
fax: 415-981-4014
*With co-owner Frish Brandt
specializes in 19th and 20th century
photography.*

Richard C. Frey, ISA
R.T.L.H. Enterprises
1275 East Ave.
Chico, CA 95926-1020
phone: 530-343-4528 or 800-567-7854
fax: 530-343-9380
e-mail: RFREY RTLH@aol.com
*Wants to buy 19th and 20th century
photographs; prefers American
Indian, art subjects, Oriental, and
albums.*

Dave Morris
3388 Merlin Rd., Ste. 351
Grants Pass, OR 97526
phone: 541-955-8411
e-mail: smorris@cdsnet.net
*Wants to buy photographs, CDV's,
stereoviews, cabinet cards; prefer
Civil War era.*

Experts

Marv B. Chait
P.O. Box 1979
Chicago, IL 60645
phone: 312-262-5979

Anthony Davis
Rainbow Creations
P.O. Box 8935
Universal City, CA 91618-8935
phone: 818-762-3540
fax: 818-762-2503
e-mail: antiqphoto@earthlink.net
Collector/dealer wants images of all subjects particularly early flat mounts, stereo daguerreotypes, autochromes (early color photography), ambrotypes, albumen, CDVs, platinum prints; all subjects; will buy entire collections.

Julia Nelson-Gal
826 Alvarado
San Francisco, CA 94114-3116
phone: 415-641-8004
fax: 415-641-8053
e-mail: JulesNG@aol.com
Specialist in appraisals of 19th and 20th century photographs and photographic literature; will authenticate and broker sales.

Misc. Services

Mary Panzer
National Portrait Gallery
Photo Dept.
8th & F Streets N.W.
Washington, DC 20560
phone: 202-357-1356 or 202-357-1633
Internet: http://www.si.edu/
Will examine photographs brought in for inspection; make an appointment first; may be able to work from good photos of the items.

Gordon's Art Reference, Inc.
Price Guide: Gordon's International Photography Price Annual
306 West Coronado Rd.
Phoenix, AZ 85003
phone: 602-253-6948 or 800-892-4622
fax: 602-253-2104
e-mail: info@gordonart.com
Internet: http://www.gordonart.com
Database of over 5,000 entries organized by photographer and print title; includes information about negative and print dates; notes if item is signed, dated, or annotated; now on CD-ROM.

Periodicals

Journal: On Paper
39 E 78th St., #601
New York, NY 10021-0213
phone: 212-988-5959
fax: 212-988-6107
Published bi-monthly, this journal reports on the entire print and photograph market and is considered a must by print collectors and dealers; also contains scholarly articles and reviews, and auction results.

Photographic Arts Center, The
Newsletter: Photograph Collector, The
301 Hill Ave.
Langhorne, PA 19047
For photograph collectors, dealers and curators; also publishes "The

Photographic Art Market," an annual compilation of auction prices.

Photographic Arts Center, The
Directory: Photograph Collector's Resource Directory
301 Hill Ave.
Langhorne, PA 19047
The Directory lists photograph conservators, restorers, appraisers, and galleries and museums that exhibit photography

Repair Services

Laura Morrissette
Take Two Photocraft
202 Massachusetts Ave.
Arlington, MA 02174
Digitally retouches photos using computers; restore faded, torn and creased old photographs; even remove someone from a photo!

Maria Pukownik
Fine Art & Paper Conservation
1045 Orrtanna Rd.
Orrtanna, PA 17353
phone: 717-337-0668
Surface cleaning, mending tears and creases, removal/replacing of decayed backing board, B/W photographic copies of restored original.

Daniel Moyer
After Image Visual Services
121 Sweet Ave.
Moscow, ID 83843-2386
phone: 208-882-6386
fax: 208-895-3803
Uses computers to digitally restore damaged photographs.

Repro. Sources

Library of Congress, Prints & Photographs Division
10 First St. SE
Washington, DC 20540
phone: 202-707-6394 or 202-707-1771
Will duplicate photos for the public from their collection of over 10,000,000 images.

Suppliers

John A. Dunphy
University Products, Inc.
517 Main St.
P.O. Box 101
Holyoke, MA 01041-0101
phone: 413-532-3372 or 800-628-1912
fax: 800-532-9281
e-mail: jadunphy@universityproducts.com
Internet: http://www.universityproducts.com
Carries safe products for the long term storage of postcards, posters, stamps, documents, photographs, textiles, costumes; acid free archival supplies, and materials for conservation and preservation; send for free catalog.

Cases

Dealers

Gene Groves
P.O. Box 2471
Baton Rouge, LA 70821-2471
phone: 504-387-3221 or 504-927-2795
fax: 504-346-8049
Buys, sells and collects early photo cases 1840-1865; big size, mother-of-pearl, tortoise, patriotic, signed, wall frames, Union, Mascher, etc.

Celebrity

(see also MOVIE MEMORABILIA; TELEVISION SHOWS & MEMORABILIA)

Dealers

Doug Wirth
Hummerdude's
P.O. Box 4348
Dunellen, NJ 08812
phone: 908-424-9367
Buys and sells celebrity photos and autographs.

Movie Star News
134 West 18th St.
New York, NY 10011
phone: 212-620-8160
fax: 212-727-0634
Carries large variety of movie photos.

Safka & Bareis Autographs
P.O. Box 886
Flushing, NY 11375
phone: 718-263-2276
fax: 718-263-2276
e-mail: sbautog@mail.idt.net
Internet: http://www.idt.net/~sbautog/
Buys and sells signed and unsigned photographs in all categories, specializing in performing arts (film, opera, composers, musicians); free catalogs issued.

Robert M. Ready
Movie & TV Star Photos & Books
1410 Oak Tree Drive
Houston, TX 77055-4316
Sells over 2,000 B&W and color 8"x10" celebrity photographs from 1930s to present including Westerns, movie, TV stars; celebrity books are also available; catalog $5 (refundable); wholesale available to dealers.

Mike Gould
Hollywood Legends
6621A Hollywood Blvd.
Los Angeles, CA 90028
phone: 213-962-7411
fax: 213-962-6742
Specializes in signed photographs of contemporary movie stars; also autographs of television stars.

Book City Collectibles
6627 Hollywood Blvd.
Los Angeles, CA 90028-6285
phone: 213-466-0120 or 213-962-7411
fax: 213-962-6742
Sells autographed celebrity photos,

movie and TV scripts, and other Hollywood memorabilia.

S. & P. Parker's Movie Market
P.O. Box 3900
Dana Point, CA 92629-8900
phone: 714-488-8444
fax: 714-488-8445
e-mail: 103225.1310@compuserve.com
Over 20,000 celebrity photographs to choose from.

Daguerreotypes

Clubs/Associations

Daguerreian Society, The
Newsletter: Daguerreian Society Newsletter
3045 W. Liberty Ave., Ste. 7
Pittsburgh, PA 15216-2460
phone: 412-343-5525
e-mail: DagSocPgh@aol.com
Internet: http://java.austinc.edu/dag/home.html
An organization dedicated to the history, art and science of the world's first form of photography - the daguerreotype; over 850 members worldwide; also publishes an annual journal in addition to the bi-monthly newsletter.

Collectors

Paul R. Lafavore, MD
24 Drake St.
Portland, ME 04103-3816
phone: 207-797-5322
Collecting quality daguerreotype images of any subject; special interest in maker-marked Portland, Maine dags.; also seeking related Daguerreian items and ephemera.

Harold E. Boyer
2200 Clayton Rd.
Beaver Falls, PA 15010
phone: 412-843-4774
Wants to buy Daguerreian photo jewelry: daguerreotypes on all kinds of jewelry, on canes, and on other original/unusual pieces; also wants daguerreotypes in cases, especially those showing photo of jewelry.

Nancy Livingston
7618 Willow Point
Falls Church, VA 22042

Norman Kulkin
727 N. Fuller Ave.
Los Angeles, CA 90046-7504
phone: 213-653-6929
Buy, sell, trade stereoviews, daguerreotypes, Civil War photos, anything in photographica 1839-1939.

Peter E. Palmquist
1183 Union St.
Arcata, CA 95521
Editor of the Daguerreian Society's "The Daguerreian Annual."

Gary Ewer
6406 E. 18th Ave.
Spokane, WA 99212-0102
phone: 509-535-9101

Dealers

Dennis Waters
Daguerreian Forum, The
P.O. Box 1073
Exeter, NH 03833
phone: 603-772-9065
*Buys and sells daguerreotypes,
thermoplastic cases, and related
material.*

Bryan W. Ginns
2109 Cty. Rte. 21
Valatie, NY 12184-6001
phone: 518-392-5805
fax: 518-392-7925
e-mail: the3dman@aol.com
*Wants large collections of stereo
views, old cameras, daguerreotypes,
magic lanterns, optical toys; anything
relating to photographics.*

Gene Groves
P.O. Box 2471
Baton Rouge, LA 70821-2471
phone: 504-387-3221 or 504-927-2795
fax: 504-346-8049
*Buys, sells, repairs and collects
quality daguerreotypes: outdoors,
occupationals, military, blacks,
Louisiana, animals, signed, toys, large
groups, etc.*

Janos Novomeszky
8408 Kawala Dr.
Las Vegas, NV 89128-7170
*Wants to buy fine daguerreotypes and
pre-1880 photographic equipment;
single pieces or entire collections.*

Experts

Anthony Davis
Rainbow Creations
P.O. Box 8935
Universal City, CA 91618-8935
phone: 818-762-3540
fax: 818-762-2503
e-mail: antiqphoto@earthlink.net
*Collector/dealer specializing in
daguerreotypes of outdoor scenes,
military, occupationals; also hand-
tinted portraits, stereo daguerreotypes
all categories; wants single items or
entire collections; bi-monthly catalog
$40 per year.*

Repair Services

Gene Groves
P.O. Box 2471
Baton Rouge, LA 70821-2471
phone: 504-387-3221 or 504-927-2795
fax: 504-346-8049
*Professionally repairs daguerreo-
types; replaces old and damaging
glass which deteriorates with new safe
glass.*

Medical

Museums/Libraries

Michael Rhode, Archiv.
National Museum of Health & Medicine
Bldg. 54
Walter Reed Medical Center
Washington, DC 20306
phone: 202-576-2438 or 202-576-0401
fax: 202-576-2164
*Federal government museum archives
that collects photographic material
related to the history of medicine,
especially military medicine.*

Military

Misc. Services

National Archives Still Picture Branch
8601 Adelphi Rd.
College Park, MD 20740
phone: 301-713-6660
*Photos of movie stars in uniform while
serving their country can be
purchased.*

Real War Photos
P.O. Box 728
Hammond, IN 46325-0728
*Combat photographs taken by combat
photographers can be obtained;
catalogs available of Army, navy,
Marines USAF, Civil War - send $3.*

Periodicals

Magazine: Military Images
RD 1 Box 99A
Henryville, PA 18332-9726
phone: 717-629-9152
e-mail: milimage@csrlink.net
*Focuses on military images from 1839
to 1900; six issues per year; since
1979.*

PHOTOGRAPHY

(see also 3-D PHOTOGRAPHICA;
CAMERAS & CAMERA EQUIP-
MENT; PHOTOGRAPHS; STEREO
VIEWERS & STEREOVIEWS)

Clubs/Associations

Photographic Historical Society of
Canada
Magazine: Photographic Canadiana
P.O. Box 54620
Toronto
Ontario M5M 4N5 Canada
phone: 416-736-2100
fax: 416-736-5838
e-mail: phsc@onramp.ca
Internet: http://web.onramp.ca/phsc/

Thruman F. Naylor
Photographic Historical Society of New
England, Inc.
Journal: New England Journal of
Photographic History
P.O. Box 650189
West Newton, MA 02165-0189
phone: 617-731-6603 or 617-277-0207
fax: 617-277-7878
e-mail: jacknaylor@aol.com
*800 member non-profit society; 60
page journal.*

George Gilbert
American Photographic Historical
Society, Inc.
Magazine: Photographica
1150 Avenue of the Americas
New York, NY 10036
phone: 212-575-0483
e-mail: roger@unicorn-systems.com
Internet: http://www.superxpo.com/
APHS.htm
*International organization with
educational meetings six times each
year in NYC; conducts two fairs for
the selling of antique cameras,
equipment & photos; publishes
"Photographica" quarterly and a
monthly newsletter, "In Focus".*

Photographic Historical Society, Inc.,
The
Newsletter: PHS Newsletter
P.O. Box 39563
Rochester, NY 14604
Internet: http://www.rit.edu/~andpph/
tphs.html
*Conducts a monthly meetings and a
tri-annual symposium.*

Photographic Society of America
3000 United Founders Blvd., Ste. 103
Oklahoma City, OK 73112
phone: 405-843-1437
e-mail: RGorrill@compuserve.com
Internet: http://www.tiac.net/users/
bcsbob/psa/

William P. Carroll
Western Photographic Collectors
Association, Inc.
Magazine: Photographist, The
P.O. Box 4294
Whittier, CA 90607-4294
phone: 562-693-8421
fax: 562-945-6011
*Non-profit organization dedicated to
the dissemination of information on,
and to stimulate interest in, all aspects
of photographica.*

Museums/Libraries

Thruman F. Naylor
Naylor Museum of Photography
P.O. Box 23
Waltham, MA 02254
phone: 617-731-6603 or 617-277-0207
fax: 617-277-7878
e-mail: jacknaylor@aol.com
*A private museum with over 20,000
photographic items on display; by
appointment.*

International Center of Photography
1130 5th Ave.
New York, NY 10128
phone: 212-860-1777

George Eastman House
Magazine: Image
900 East Ave.
Rochester, NY 14607-2219
phone: 716-273-3361
*Devoted to the history, technology and
aesthetics of photography and motion
pictures.*

David Silver
International Photographic Historical
Association
Newsletter: INPHO News
P.O. Box 16074
San Francisco, CA 94116-0074
phone: 415-681-4356 or 415-731-5717
e-mail: silver@well.com
*Corresponding research & resource
center for those interested in studying/
collecting cameras, photographs, or
other objects pertaining to the history
of photography; free appraisals and
information services; speakers/
presentation bureau.*

Periodicals

Taylor & Francis Ltd.
Magazine: History of Photography
Rankine Road
Basingstoke
Hants RG24 8PR, U.K.
phone: +44(0) 1256 81300
fax: +44(0) 1256 479438
Internet: http://www.tandf.co.uk/JNLS/
hph.htm
*An international publication devoted
exclusively to the history and criticism
of the photograph; covers photography from the earliest times to the
present day; published quarterly.*

PIANO ROLLS

(see also MUSICAL INSTRUMENTS,
Pianos [Player])

Auction Services

Dan Wilke
QRS Music Rolls, Inc.
1026 Niagara St.
Buffalo, NY 14213-2007
phone: 716-885-0250 or 716-885-4600
fax: 716-885-7510
*Offers bi-monthly auctions by mail of
original antique 88-note and
reproducing player piano rolls; buys
collections of old rolls, but does not
accept consignments.*

Paul & Cindy Johnson
Piano Roll Center, The
26390 Big Valley Rd., NE
Poulsbo, WA 98370-9125
phone: 800-935-ROLL or 360-697-2422
fax: 360-697-2522
e-mail: pianorol@tscnet.com
*Holds periodic auctions of player
piano rolls and nickelodeon rolls;
also produces new rolls of the best in*

ragtime and jazz as well as rolls for reproducing pianos.

Collectors

Collector
P.O. Box 431875
Pontiac, MI 48343
phone: 810-751-8055
Wants to buy old piano rolls, especially Angelus Artio, also Cecillian (Connorized, Farrand, Pin Ends.)

Deno Buralli
P.O. Box 6
Spring Grove, IL 60081
Reproducing rolls and standard 88-note rolls.

Dealers

Sheet Music Center
Box 10
Old Bethpage, NY 11804
phone: 800-527-7626
e-mail: smctr@ix.netcom.com
Internet: http://
www.sheetmusiccenter.com
Buys and sells sheet music and piano rolls; FREE catalog to readers of "Maloney's Antiques & Collectibles Resource Directory."

Experts

Dan Wilke
1026 Niagara St.
Buffalo, NY 14213-2007
phone: 716-885-0250 or 716-885-4600
fax: 716-885-7510

Repro. Sources

QRS Music Rolls, Inc.
1026 Niagara St.
Buffalo, NY 14213-2007
phone: 716-885-0250 or 716-885-4600
fax: 716-885-7510
World's oldest manufacturer of player piano rolls; thousands of songs, old and new, by famous pianists of past and present.

Play-Rite Music Rolls
P.O. Box 1025
Turlock, CA 95381-1025
phone: 209-667-1996 or 800-826-5539
fax: 209-667-8241
Sells new 10 to 16 tune "O" rolls for player pianos.

PIANOS
Miniature

(see also MINIATURES; MUSICAL INSTRUMENTS, Pianos)

Clubs/Associations

Janice E. Kelsh
Miniature Piano Enthusiast Club
Newsletter: Musically Yours!
633 Pennsylvania Ave.
Hagerstown, MD 21740-3769
phone: 301-797-7675
e-mail: kelshj@nihrrlib.ncrr.nih.gov
Established in 1990 to promote the hobby of miniature piano collecting; annual convention.

Collectors

Janice E. Kelsh
633 Pennsylvania Ave.
Hagerstown, MD 21740-3769
phone: 301-797-7675
e-mail: kelshj@nihrrlib.ncrr.nih.gov
Interested in obtaining miniature pianos of all kinds; also wants old postcards depicting pianos.

PICKLE CASTORS
Collectors

Virginia Young
15463 McNeill Rd.
Sterling, NY 13156-4212
phone: 315-947-5840 or 315-947-5782
fax: 315-947-6905
Wants to buy pickle castors; frames must have a mark; especially interested in colored decorated jars or unusual castors; must be in very good condition.

PIE BIRDS

(see also KITCHEN COLLECTIBLES)

Clubs/Associations

Linda & Bobby Fields
Pie Bird Collectors Club
158 Bagsby Hill Lane
Dover, TN 37058-6248
phone: 615-232-5099
Hold annual Pie Bird Collectors convention.

Collectors

Linda & Bobby Fields
158 Bagsby Hill Lane
Dover, TN 37058-6248
phone: 615-232-5099
Buy single birds or entire collections; have a large selection of traders.

Jeannie Kolger
6906 Meade Dr.
Colleyville, TX 76034-6416
phone: 817-329-5262
Wants to buy unusual old pie birds and pie vents, particularly Disney examples, Black Mammys and/or black chefs.

Dealers

Alan Pedel
Kelly's Cottage
Guineaford
Barnstaple
Devon EX31 4EA, U.K.
phone: 011-44-1271-75166
Searches the heart of the English countryside for rare and lovely pie birds such as Black Mammies, Clowns, Wizards, Teddy Bears, Roosters, Pigs, Rabbits, Frogs, Chefs, Blue Willow and Chintz vents.

Experts

Lillian Cole
14 Harmony School Rd.
Flemington, NJ 08822-2606
phone: 908-782-3198
Interested in the older foreign and U.S. pie birds either in singles or in collections; avid collector and historian/researcher.

Periodicals

Lillian Cole
Newsletter: Pie Birds Unlimited
14 Harmony School Rd.
Flemington, NJ 08822-2606
phone: 908-782-3198
Nine issues of "Pie Birds Unlimited" (1990-1996) contained just about all that is presently known about pie birds; please SASE for information.

PIN-BACK BUTTONS

(see BUTTONS, Pin-Back)

PIN-UP ART

(see also EROTICA; PLAYBOY ITEMS)

Collectors

Louis K. Meisel
141 Prince St.
New York, NY 10012
Wants to buy pin-ups: oil paintings, pastels, watercolors, drawings.

David Kveragas
1943 Timberlane
Clarks Summit, PA 18411-9539
phone: 717-587-3429
Wants Vargas and Olivia illustrations; Vargas prior to his Playboy work, especially Shadowland mags, Ziegfeld Follies sheet music. Olivia items: catalogs, posters, greeting cards, etc.; offers made; also Rohlf Armstrong items.

Charles Martignette
P.O. Box 293
Hallandale, FL 33008
phone: 305-454-3474
Wants pin-up and glamour art; original paintings.

John Crawford
3442 Manor Hill
Cincinnati, OH 45220
phone: 513-221-6050
Wants pin-up art by Vargas, Petty, Mozert, Elugren, others.

Jerry Peters
Chestnut Hollow, Ltd.
6060 Bordman Rd.
P.O. Box 6
Almont, MI 48003
phone: 810-798-3158
Collecting pin-up photos, art and magazines; especially wants Vargas, Petty, Elvghrenn, Moran, Olivia.

Leyland & Crystal Payton
3020 S. National, #340
Springfield, MO 65804-4247
phone: 417-886-7124
fax: 417-889-3345
Wants to buy objects with women's figure, nude or pin-up; lamps, vases, novelty objects, knives, etc.; decorative or insulting; any age; photos returned.

Ed Royse
P.O. Box 33489
Fort Sill, OK 73752-1258
phone: 405-357-8000
fax: 405-875-2063
e-mail: shared@juno.com
Wants to buy Varga/Vargas pin-up art, Esquire calendars, playing cards, Esky cards, etc.

Dealers

Robert Bessette
Green Dragon Arts
P.O. Box 588
Burlington, VT 05402-0588
phone: 802-862-1930
Buys and sells pin-up art works, calendars, fantasy and pin-up postcards, men's magazines, erotic books and paper books.

Steve Colby
Off The Deep End
712 East St.
Frederick, MD 21701-5239
phone: 301-698-9006
e-mail: chilimon@offthedeepend.com
Antique to contemporary; also ephemera, 1950s home accessories, Playboy magazines, diner collectibles, pin-ups, nudes and Hula Girls (all types), used books.

Experts

Denis C. Jackson, Ed.
P.O. Box 1958
Sequim, WA 98382-1958
phone: 360-683-2559
fax: 360-683-2559
e-mail: ticn@olypen.com
Internet: http://www.olypen.com/ticn/
Author of "The Price and Identification Guide to Pin-Ups & Glamour Art", 1992; send LSASE for information; wants old prints, calendars, mutescope cards.

Periodicals

Steve Sullivan
Newsletter: Glamour Girls: Then and
Now
P.O. Box 34501
Washington, DC 20043-4501
phone: 703-641-0676
*Bi-monthly publication focusing on
pin-up art: interviews and features on
glamour girls from the 1950s to
present in movies, TV, burlesque, and
men's magazines.*

Denis C. Jackson, Ed.
Newsletter: Illustrator Collector's News,
The
P.O. Box 1958
Sequim, WA 98382-1958
phone: 360-683-2559
fax: 360-683-2559
e-mail: ticn@olypen.com
Internet: http://www.olypen.com/ticn/
*A bi-monthly publication for
collectors of magazines and other
paper illustrations; free classifieds for
subscribers; send LSASE for
information.*

PINS

(see also BADGES; BUTTONS, Pin-
Back; FAST FOOD COLLECTIBLES,
McDonald's [Pins]; OLYMPIC
GAMES COLLECTIBLES, Pins &
Buttons; SOCIAL CAUSES)

Clubs/Associations

Rowan Fay
International Pin Collectors Club
Newsletter: IPCC Newsletter
602 Chenango St.
Binghamton, NY 13901-2029
phone: 607-724-4583 or 607-723-7421
fax: 607-723-3687
*Interested in all sorts of pins:
Olympic, Coca Cola, sports, Desert
Storm, media, etc.*

Collectors

Gil & Marjorie Joanis
1329 14 St. East
Saskatoon
Saskatchewan S7H 0A6 Canada
phone: 306-665-9902
*Buys, sells, trades metal pins,
especially relating to curling (Brier,
Scotch Cup, Silver Broom), media
(CBC, SRC), figure skating (Worlds
and other major events), Olympic
Games; send photocopies;*

Fred Swindall
111 NW 2nd
Portland, OR 97209
phone: 503-224-0678 or 503-234-2454
*Wants pins, buttons, and badges:
political pins, comic pins, advertising
from tractors to cows, trucking co.
badges, McDonald's, old and new
movie promo pins, police and fire
badges, Union ribbons, tokens, old
Elks & Masonic badges, etc.*

Dealers

Bill Nelson
Newsletter: Bill Nelson Newsletter, The
P.O. Box 41630
Tucson, AZ 85717-1630
phone: 520-629-0868 or 800-368-8434
fax: 520-629-0387
*Monthly newsletter with news, tips,
and sources; for collectors of
Olympic, Sports, Disney, Coca Cola
pins; large selection in stock;
established in 1985.*

PIONEERS

(see WESTERN AMERICANA)

PIPES

(see also CANES & WALKING
STICKS; CHARACTER COL-
LECTIBLES, Sherlock Holmes;
MATCH SAFES; SMOKING
COLLECTIBLES; TOBACCO
COLLECTIBLES)

Clubs/Associations

P.C. Wiseman
Pipe Club of London, The
Journal: Journal of the Pipe Club of
London, The
40 Crescent Drive
Petts Wood, Orpington
Kent BR5 1BD, U.K.
phone: 0168 983 7761
*Premier pipe club in Great Britain;
international in scope with over 500
members in 31 countries; promotes
and protects the interests of pipe
smokers; 12 meetings a year; free 26
page bi-annual Journal to all
members.*

Sailorman Jack
New York Pipe Club
Newsletter: New York Pipe Club
Newsletter
P.O. Box 265
Gracie Station
New York, NY 10028
phone: 212-288-3832
*Club meets on the first Tuesday of
each month at 6 pm at Mary's of
Madison Restaurant, 24 East 41 St.,
between 5th Ave. and Madison Ave.*

Tom Dunn, Ed.
Universal Coterie of Pipe Smokers, The
Magazine: Pipe Smoker's Ephemeris,
The
20-37 120th St.
Flushing, NY 11356-2128
*An irregular quarterly magazine for
pipe smokers and anyone interested in
pipes, pipe smoking, or related
matters.*

Robert C. Hamlin
Pipe Collectors Club of America
Magazine: Pipe Smokers Pipeline
P.O. Box 5179
Woodbridge, VA 22194-5179
phone: 703-878-7655 or 703-878-3657
fax: 703-878-7657

Neil Murray, Sec.
International Association of Pipe
Smokers' Clubs
Newsletter: Agricultural and Mechanical
Gazette, The
47758 Hickory, Apt. 22305
Wixom, MI 48393
phone: 810-624-5124
Newsletter published 5 times a year.

Michael Reschke
Chicagoland Pipe Collectors Club
540 South Westmore
Lombard, IL 60148-3048
*A local group of pipe collectors and
smokers who gather once a month for
an informal meeting and evening of
fellowship; members have a common
interest in pipes, cigars, and
tobacciana.*

Steve Johnson
Southern California Pipe & Cigar
Smokers' Association
1532 South Bundy Dr., Apt. D
Los Angeles, CA 90025
phone: 310-820-9706

Collectors

Lee Pattison
6 Christview Dr.
Cuba, NY 14727-1202
phone: 716-968-2458
*Wants antique meerschaum pipes
carved and plain, briar pipes of more
recent manufacture brand names:
Charatan, Barling, Stanwell, Larson,
Savinelli and others; also wants to
buy tobacco jars and cigar store
items.*

Bob Spore
400 Riverside Dr.
Pasadena, MD 21122
phone: 410-437-2715
*Collector seeking pre-smoked briar
pipes; sells and appraises pipe
collections; member T.U.C.O.P.S.,
P.C.C.A.*

Lance Moore
P.O. Box 1973
Chesterfield, VA 23832-9109
*Buyer and collector of fine pipes of
quality briar and meerschaum, cigar
and cigarette holders, and antique
humidors.*

Frank P. Burla
2800 Maple Ave., Apt. 11B
Downers Grove, IL 60540-4131
phone: 630-271-1317
e-mail: FPBurla@aol.com
*Antique pipe collector wants to buy
museum-quality antique porcelains,
woods, meerschaums, clays, Orientals,
etc.; plus parts of antique pipes,
especially amber stems and metal lids.*

Gary L. Donachy
801 W. Sunset
Steeleville, IL 62288-1015
phone: 618-965-3189
*Wants to buy antique meerschaum and
high grade briar pipes; also wants*

*tobacco-related books, trade cards,
and advertising.*

Eric Fuchslocher
8050 Ventura Cyn Ave.
Panorama City, CA 91402
phone: 818-994-1492
*Wants to buy carved wood and
meerschaum pipes.*

E.S. Radcliffe
3732 Colonial Lane SE
Port Orchard, WA 98366-1846
phone: 206-876-8615
*Wants to buy cigar holders, cigarette
holders, carved and ornamental pipes,
meerschaum clay pipes.*

Dealers

Don Duco
Pikpenkabinet & Smokiana
Prinsengracht 488
1017 KH Amsterdam
The Netherlands / Pays Bas
phone: +31 20 42 11 779

Decon MacCubbin
Greybeard's of London
1625 Connectivut Ave. NW
Washington, DC 20009-1013
*Buys and sells new and antique briar
and meerschaum pipes.*

Chuck Haley
Sherlock's
13926 Double Girth Ct.
Matthews, NC 28105
phone: 704-843-3433 or 704-847-5480
*Specializing in estate pipes and
related smoking accessories.*

John B. Marrella
Investments in Time
P.O. Box 611
Birmingham, MI 48012-0611
phone: 810-644-3100
fax: 810-644-2792
*Wants to buy fine pipes, humidors,
and smoking articles.*

Experts

Benjamin Rapaport
11505 Turnbridge Ln.
Reston, VA 20194-1220
phone: 703-435-8133
*Wants antique meerschaum, opium,
porcelain, Meissen, chinoiserie,
Wedgwood, metal, cloisonne,
champleve, early wood, etc. pipes.*

James Kesterson
3881 Fulton Grove Rd.
Cincinnati, OH 45245-2504
phone: 513-752-0949
*Wants smoked or new briar pipes:
brands like Barling, Caminetto,
Charatan, Comoy, Dunhill, GBD,
Larsen, Sasieni, Savinelli, etc.*

Museums/Libraries

Don Duco
Museum of Tobacco Pipes
Prinsengracht 488
1017 KH Amsterdam
The Netherlands / Pays Bas
phone: +31 20 42 11 779

David Wright, Cur.
Museum of Tobacco Art & History
800 Harrison St.
Nashville, TN 37203-3336
phone: 615-271-2349 or 615-271-2163
fax: 615-271-2285
*Museum traces history of tobacco
from American Indians to present;
collection of pipes, Cigar Store
figures, snuff boxes, advertising, art,
etc.*

Larry Lawrence
Pipe Smoker's Hall of Fame, The
P.O. Box 219
Galveston, IN 46932
phone: 219-699-7863

Periodicals

Tom Dunn, Ed.
Universal Coterie of Pipe Smokers, The
Directory: TUCOPS Collectors
Directory
20-37 120th St.
Flushing, NY 11356-2128
*Contains a selection of the TUCOPC
members' collecting and other
interests.*

Repair Services

Carl Schmidt
22334 Hellwig Rd.
Genoa, OH 43430-9776
phone: 419-855-3361
Offers pipe making and repairs.

Clay

Clubs/Associations

S. Paul Jung
Society for Clay Pipe Research, The
Newsletter: Society for Clay Pipe
Research Newsletter
P.O. Box 817
Bel Air, MD 21014-0817
phone: 410-569-8194

Experts

S. Paul Jung
P.O. Box 817
Bel Air, MD 21014-0817
phone: 410-569-8194
*Buys and collects clay pipes;
researches the clay tobacco pipe
industry in the U.S., Canada, and
Europe; especially wants pipes
marked France or Paris, or with name
of an American city; has published a
number of books on smoking pipes.*

Hookahs

Collectors

Jason Short
114 Avondale Dr.
Smyrna, TN 37167
phone: 617-459-4029
*Wants Middle-Eastern and Indian
hookahs for smoking tobacco (not
interested in water pipes found in
"head shops.")*

Paul Goodin
3909 Beech St.
Cincinnati, OH 45227
*Wants hookahs and clay church
warden pipes.*

Bradley M. Gordon
P.O. Box 90775
San Diego, CA 92169
phone: 619-270-8052
*Wants to buy Catlinite calumets (long
pipes), hookahs, clays, corncobs,
meerschaums, cherrywoods, gourd
pipes, rosewood pipes, European
student and Delft porcelain pipes, plus
a variety of other smoking paraphernalia.*

Meerschaum

Collectors

Bernard Berlly
24 School House Ln.
Great Neck, NY 11020-1323
phone: 516-829-2777
fax: 516-829-2779
*Wants antique carved meerschaum
pipes.*

Pipe Cleaners

Collectors

Paul Scheuer
6753 Humbolt Ave.
Minneapolis, MN 55430-1533
phone: 612-561-7321
Internet: http://www.underthebridge.com
*Collects old pipe cleaner containers;
also Roll-Your-Own cigarette paper
packets and related memorabilia.*

Tampers

Collectors

Bruce D. MacPhail
64 Dogwood Rd.
Wethersfield, CT 06109
phone: 203-721-9485
*Wants to buy unusual antique and
reproduction pipe tampers.*

PIRATES

(see NAUTICAL ANTIQUES)

PISTOLS

(see FIREARMS; TOYS, Cap Guns)

PIXIES

(see ELVES)

PLANNING ITEMS

(see also ARCHITECTURE &
RELATED ITEMS; STATE
RELATED ITEMS; MAPS &
CHARTS)

Dealers

Ken Kipp, AICP
Allenwood Americana Antiques
P.O. Box 116
Allenwood, PA 17810-0116
phone: 717-538-1440
*Buys and sells city/town/regional
planning items; early to current:
plans, maps, books, memorabilia of
U.S. community planners.*

PLANTERS PEANUTS ITEMS

Clubs/Associations

Judith & Bob Walthall
Peanut Pals
Newsletter: Peanut Papers
P.O. Box 4465
Huntsville, AL 35815
phone: 205-881-9198
*Focuses on Planters Peanuts and Mr.
Peanut history and memorabilia;
national and regional conventions,
newsletter, classified ads for members
only.*

Collectors

Neil Williams
62 Prospect Hills Dr.
East Longmeadow, MA 01028-3178
*Mr. Peanut wanted; wants to buy
older, unusual Planters Peanut items.*

Joe Iozzia
P.O. Box 1005
Pomona, NJ 08240-1005
phone: 609-652-8504
Wants to buy Mr. Peanut items.

Arleane Pawlowicz
5 Edgewood Road
Goshen, NY 10924-2303
phone: 914-294-3475
fax: 914-294-3475
*Long time and avid collector of
anything relating to Planters Peanuts.*

Richard Reddock
914 Isle Ct.
Bellmore, NY 11710-1545
phone: 516-826-2032 or 800-223-PNUT
e-mail: pnutfanclb@aol.com
*Wants to buy all types of Mr. Peanut
tin displays, signs, paper items,
ceramic oil and vinegar, metal letter
openers.*

Joyce Spontak
804 Hickory Grade Rd.
Bridgeville, PA 15017
phone: 412-221-7599

Glenn Grush
5344 North Collingwood Circle
Calabasas, CA 91302-3137
phone: 818-880-6200 or 800-653-3244
fax: 818-880-6500

Dealers

Judy Posner
4195 South Tamiami Trail, Ste. 183
Venice, FL 34293-5112
phone: 941-497-7149
fax: 941-493-8085
e-mail: Judyandjef@aol.com
Internet: http://www.tias.com/stores/jpc

Experts

Marty Blank
P.O. Box 405
Flushing, NY 11365-0405
phone: 516-485-8071
e-mail: martyadver@aol.com
*Wants to buy unusual Mr. Peanut
items, especially plastic toys, counter
displays and older items; author of
"Planter's Peanut Collectibles"
(Schiffer).*

Judith & Bob Walthall
P.O. Box 4465
Huntsville, AL 35815
phone: 205-881-9198
*Serious collectors specializing in
Planter Peanut items; founded Peanut
Pals in 1978; has done extensive
research over the years; has had many
articles published.*

PLASTIC COLLECTIBLES

(see also BOXES; CELLULOID
ITEMS; CHARMS; DOLLS HOUSES
& FURNISHINGS; KITS; LUNCH
BOXES; MODELS, Cars; SOLDIERS,
Toy; TOYS; TOYS, Playsets;
TRAINS, Toy [Plasticville];
TUPPERWARE)

Dealers

Alicia & Jorge Valino
P.O. Box 1442
(11000) Montevideo
Uruguay
e-mail: vala@adinet.com.uy.
Wants to buy items made of Bakelite.

Abby Nash
Malabar Enterprises
172 Bush Lane
Ithaca, NY 14850
phone: 607-255-2905 or 607-266-0690
fax: 607-255-4179
e-mail: asn6@cornell.edu
*Buying and selling 1920-1960
Bakelite and other plastic items.*

Dee Battle
9 Orange Blossom Trail
Yalaha, FL 34797
phone: 352-324-3023
*Expert and dealer in vintage plastics:
Deco, watches, purses, radios.*

Experts

Jan Lindenberger
P.O. Box 7224
Colorado Springs, CO 80933
phone: 719-591-9558
fax: 719-591-9558
*Buys and sells plastic collectibles;
author of "Plastic Collectibles -*

Information & Price Guide" (Schiffer Pub., Ltd., 1992).

Museums/Libraries

National Plastics Center & Museum
P.O. Box 639
Leominster, MA 01453
phone: 508-537-9529

PLASTICVILLE

(see TRAINS, Toy [Plasticville])

PLATES

(see also COLLECTIBLES [MOD-ERN], Plates)

Danish

Dealers

Ed London
Parke Lloyds International, Inc.
9408 NW 70 St.
Fort Lauderdale, FL 33321-3002
phone: 954-724-4294 or 954-724-4274
Wants to buy Bing & Grondahl Christmas Plates from 1895 to 1963 and Royal Copenhagen Christmas Plates from 1908 to 1963.

PLATING

(see REPAIR/RESTORATION/ CONSERVATION, Metal Items)

PLATINUM

Scrap

Dealers

Michael A. Merrill
Michael A. Merrill, Inc.
Crestar Bank Building
2045 York Rd.
Timonium, MD 21093
phone: 410-453-9400
e-mail: merrill@home.com
Internet: http://members.home.net/ merrill/
Buying precious metals from the public, dealers since 1974; buys scrap gold, diamonds, old gold, dental gold, school rings, gold & silver numismatic coins, sterling silver (Kirk & Steiff), Franklin Mint, platinum, palladium, exotics.

PLAYBOY ITEMS

(see also EROTICA; MAGAZINES, Men's [Playboy]; PIN-UP ART)

Clubs/Associations

Tom Bonner
Playboy Collectors Association
P.O. Box 653
Phillipsburg, MO 65722-0653

Collectors

Ronnie Keshishian
P.O. Box 2654
Glendale, AZ 85311
phone: 602-435-2665
Wants Playboy memorabilia: early calendars, special editions, puzzles, hand puppets, liquor caddies, femlin statues, rabbit dolls, club items, dinner plates, candles, menus, promo items, anything Playboy except magazines.

Charlie's
P.O. Box 593
Woodland Hills, CA 91365-0593
Wants Playboy calendars, pin-ups, 50s and 60s girlie magazines.

Autographs

Collectors

David Kveragas
1943 Timberlane
Clarks Summit, PA 18411-9539
phone: 717-587-3429
Wants Playboy Playmate autographs; also autographs of other women who have appeared in the magazine. Items must be on Playboy related pages, covers, etc.; photocopies appreciated; offers made.

PLAYER PIANOS

(see MUSICAL INSTRUMENTS, Pianos [Player])

PLAYING CARDS

(see also AIRLINE MEMORABILIA, Playing Cards; BRIDGE; CARDS; GAMBLING COLLECTIBLES; PAPER COLLECTIBLES; GAMES, Cards; RAILROAD COLLECTIBLES, Playing Cards)

Clubs/Associations

Major R.T. Welsh
English Playing Card Society, The
Newsletter: English Playing Card Society Newsletter
11 Pierrepont St.
Bath
Avon BA1 1LA, U.K.
phone: 0122-5465218
For collectors, researchers, museums, archivists, manufacturers, etc. who are interested in English playing cards and card games; quarterly postal auction and sale of playing cards and card games; quarterly newsletter.

American Game Collectors Association
Newsletter: Game Times
49 Brooks Ave.
Lewiston, ME 04240-5901
phone: 215-674-1072
Internet: http://www.agca.com/~rfinn/ agca.htm
Focuses on board and card games as well as puzzles, playing cards, tops, yo-yos, and action games; also

publishes "Game Researchers' Notes" - reports on member's research.

Rhonda Hawes, Sec.
52 Plus Joker
Magazine: Clear the Decks
204 Gorham Ave.
Hamden, CT 06514-3904
phone: 203-288-6584
e-mail: robertcard@aol.com
For those interested in collecting playing cards, antique and unusual decks; magazine is published quarterly.

Barbara Lunaburg
Chicago Playing Card Collectors, Inc.
Newsletter: Bulletin
1826 Mallard Lake Dr.
Marietta, GA 30068-1644
phone: 770-992-7478
Purpose of the club is to encourage and promote the hobby of playing card collecting and to explore the history of playing cards; newsletter offers buy/sell/trade ads, articles, etc.

Barbara Clark
International Playing Card Society
Journal: IPCS Journal
3570 Delaware Common
Indianapolis, IN 46220-3787
phone: 317-251-5980
Members receive a journal six times per year, plus membership lists.

Collectors

Barbara Lunaburg
1826 Mallard Lake Dr.
Marietta, GA 30068-1644
phone: 770-992-7478
Editor of the Chicago Playing Card Collectors Club newsletter, the "Bulletin."

Robert Harrison
582 Woodlawn Ave.
Glencoe, IL 60022
phone: 708-835-0842

Bill Sachen
Waukegan Bridge Center
927 Grand Ave.
Waukegan, IL 60085
phone: 847-662-7294

Bernice De Somer
1559 West Pratt Blvd.
Chicago, IL 60626-4228
phone: 773-274-0250
Interested in playing cards, decks or single cards.

Bill Coomer
1024 South Benton
Cape Girardeau, MO 63701

Cary Basse
6927 Forbes Ave.
Van Nuys, CA 91406-4504
phone: 818-781-4856

Dealers

Glenn Currie
P.O. Box 1342
Concord, NH 03302-1342
phone: 603-228-3328
e-mail: glennkc@aol.com
Wants to buy antique or unusual decks of playing cards.

Larry Lubliner
Re-Finders
25303 Rutledge Crossing
Farmington Hills, MI 48335-1350
phone: 810-426-0066
e-mail: joker1854@aol.com
Wants to buy pre-1930 playing cards and related advertising.

Experts

David Galt
Games & Names
302 W. 78th St.
New York, NY 10024
phone: 212-769-2514
One of the premier playing card collectors in America.

Ray Hartz
120 Amberwood Ct.
Bethel Park, PA 15102-2262
e-mail: 75507.2203@compuserve.com
Will pay top dollar for old, unusual playing card and game decks, complete and in excellent condition; U.S. or foreign.

Phil Bollhagen
8222 South 51st Street
Franklin, WI 53132-9276
phone: 414-327-6220
e-mail: bollhagp@execpc.com
Has one of the largest collections of antique railroad playing card decks in the U.S.; wants to buy quality pre-1915 decks from all railroads; author of "The Great Book of Railroad Playing Cards"; railroad decks and singles.

Shami & Kathryn Maxwell
Parnell Publishing
P.O. Box 16432
Phoenix, AZ 85011-6432
phone: 602-279-2358
fax: 602-279-5754
e-mail: smaxcard@worldnet.att.net
Author of "Price Guide of Old & Unusual Playing Cards" and "Playing Cards - The Intentional Price Guide"; also recreates historical playing card decks.

Museums/Libraries

Cincinnati Art Museum
Eden Park
Cincinnati, OH 45202
phone: 513-721-5204

Margery B. Griffith, Dir.
Playing Card Museum
Park & Beech Sts.
Cincinnati, OH 45212
phone: 513-396-5700
fax: 513-396-6321
Resource for research materials

dealing with playing cards; largest playing card collection in the world.

Repro. Sources

Shami & Kathryn Maxwell
Parnell Publishing
P.O. Box 16432
Phoenix, AZ 85011-6432
phone: 602-279-2358
fax: 602-279-5754
e-mail: smaxcard@worldnet.att.net
Recreates playing cards, faro and Civil War; also makes faro equipment: casekeepers, layouts, dealing boxes.

PLUMBING

(see also ARCHITECTURAL ELEMENTS; CATALOGS; HARDWARE; OUTHOUSES)

Dealers

United House Wrecking
535 Hope St.
Stamford, CT 06906-1316
phone: 203-348-5371
fax: 203-961-9472
Internet: http://www.united-antiques.com
Sells architectural elements; stained and beveled glass, brass & copper, plumbing & lighting fixtures, Victorian gingerbread, etc.

H. Weber Wilson
Oltz-Wilson Antiques
808 51st Avenue Plz. W
Bradenton, FL 34207-2819
phone: 800-508-0022
Sells architectural antiques; garden ornaments, vintage plumbing, quality furniture, antique door hardware.

Donald Hooper
Vintage Plumbing & Bathroom Antiques
5516 Cahuenga Blvd.
North Hollywood, CA 91601-2919
phone: 818-505-9315 or 818-772-1721
fax: 818-772-4647
e-mail: Vintag@earthlink.net
Buys, sells, rents and repairs c. 1900 American bath fixtures such as unusual claw foot bathtubs, ornamental toilets, fancy pedestal sinks, rib-cage showers and more; over 20 years in business.

Museums/Libraries

American Sanitary Plumbing Museum, The
39 Piedmont St.
Worcester, MA 01610
phone: 508-754-9453
Collection includes bathtubs, sinks, toilets, plumbing books and tools.

Periodicals

Dovetale Publishers
Directory: Old-House Journal Restoration Directory
2 Main St.
Gloucester, MA 01930-5726
phone: 800-234-3797 or 508-283-3200
fax: 508-283-4629
Sourcebook listing companies large and small which manufacture and sell traditional hard-to-find items for the old house owner: sinks, siding, lumber, plumbing, stoves, etc.; also call 800-931-2931.

Bathroom Antiques

Dealers

Donald Hooper
Vintage Plumbing & Bathroom Antiques
5516 Cahuenga Blvd.
North Hollywood, CA 91601-2919
phone: 818-505-9315 or 818-772-1721
fax: 818-772-4647
e-mail: Vintag@earthlink.net
Buys, sells, rents and repairs c. 1900 American bath fixtures such as unusual claw foot bathtubs, ornamental toilets, fancy pedestal sinks, rib-cage showers and more; over 20 years in business.

PLUSH

(see STEIFF; TEDDY BEARS; TOYS, Beanie Babies; TOYS, Plush)

POCKET KNIVES

(see KNIVES, Pocket)

POCKET MIRRORS

(see also ADVERTISING COLLECTIBLES)

Collectors

Burt Purmell
P.O. Box 3016
Troy, NY 12180
phone: 518-273-2454
Wants advertising pocket mirrors.

Jerome Schaeper, Jr.
705 Philadelphia St.
Covington, KY 41011-1252
phone: 606-581-3729
Collects and appraises colorful, graphic celluloid pocket mirrors.

James E. Kattner
P.O. Box 11132
Spring, TX 77391
phone: 281-986-6916 or 281-376-4826
Wants to buy mirrors with celluloid backs that picture pretty ladies and young girls which advertise saloons and bars, or that specify a redemption value such as "12 1/2" cents or "One Drink" at a merchant's establishment.

Dealers

Dave Beck
P.O. Box 435
Mediapolis, IA 52637-0435
phone: 319-394-3943
Buys and sells advertising watch fobs, mirrors and pin-backs; send stamp for illustrated mail auction catalog.

POCKET-SIZE COLLECTIBLES

Collectors

Bruce Axler
Ansonia Station
P.O. Box 1288
New York, NY 10023-1288
phone: 212-362-4429
fax: 212-579-1274
Wants pocket items, i.e. items/gadgets designed to fit in the pocket: tools, knives, lighters, items which look like a pocket watch but are not, calculators, leather items, matchsafes, candle safes, travel items.

POGS

(see also BOTTLE CAPS, Milk; PREMIUMS; TRADING CARDS, Non-Sport)

Clubs/Associations

Worldwide Hawaiian Association of Milkcaps
P.O. Box 59256
San Jose, CA 95159-0256
phone: 408-236-3476
fax: 408-295-7507
Internet: http://www.microserve.net/vradio/sidesaddle/wham.html

Dealers

Pacific Rim Trading Caps
P.O. Box 1399
Newport Beach, CA 92663
phone: 714-434-9584
fax: 714-434-9365

Man./Prod./Dist.

Rose City Paper Box
3100 NW Industrial St.
Portland, OR 97210
phone: 503-241-6486
Printers of milk caps, "blister" card packaging; high volume.

Misc. Services

Jack L. Marcus
JM Productions
P.O. Box 2081
Sun City, CA 92586-2081
phone: 909-672-4455
Creates authentic hand drawn and numbered collectible milk caps; now over 5,000 and the numbers continue to grow; gives out one free collectible milk cap upon request.

Periodicals

Jack Mors
JM Productions
Newsletter: Radtoonz
P.O. Box 2081
Sun City, CA 92586-2081
phone: 909-672-4455
From the maker of the Juan Pollo milk cap series; a tabloid for kids; talks about milk caps and how to draw cartoons on them.

Newsletter: American Game Caps
410 W. Fletcher
Orange, CA 92665
phone: 714-921-2277
fax: 714-921-4827
A monthly newsletter.

POINTS

(see AMERICAN INDIAN; PREHISTORIC ARTIFACTS, Arrowheads & Points)

POKER CHIPS

(see GAMBLING COLLECTIBLES, Gambling Chips & Gaming Tokens)

POLICE & SHERIFF

(see LAW ENFORCEMENT MEMORABILIA, Police & Sheriff)

POLISH ITEMS

Collectors

Stephen M. Schurick
418 Read Ave.
Yonkers, NY 10707-1656
Wants Polish and Polish American ephemera including posters, books, cookbooks, photos, etc.

POLITICAL COLLECTIBLES

(see also AUTOGRAPHS; BADGES; BUTTONS, Pin-Back; CANES & WALKING STICKS; CARTOON ART; CERAMICS, Political Related; HISTORICAL AMERICANA; PERSONALITIES [HISTORICAL]; PINS; PROHIBITION ITEMS; SOCIAL CAUSES; WHITE HOUSE COLLECTIBLES)

Appraisers

U.I. "Chick" Harris
P.O. Box 20614
Saint Louis, MO 63139-0614
phone: 314-352-8623
Collects, specializes in, and appraises all types of political Americana; conducts specialized mail-auctions of political and historical Americana.

Auction Services

Rex Stark
Rex Stark Americana
P.O. Box 1029
Gardner, MA 01440
phone: 508-630-3237
Conducts mail auctions of quality

historical Americana: political, early military, advertising, sports, etc.

David Frent
Frent Auctions
P.O. Box 455
Oakhurst, NJ 07755
phone: 201-922-0768
Specializes in mail-bid auctions of political items and historical Americana.

Ted Hake
Hake's Americana & Collectibles Auction
P.O. Box 1444
York, PA 17405-1444
phone: 717-848-1333
Always purchasing items for 8 mail-bid auctions per year covering hundreds of categories including toys, character collectibles, Disney, cowboy heroes, premiums, television, politicals, pin-back buttons, advertising and more.

Robert Coup
Historicana
P.O. Box 348
Leola, PA 17540-0348
phone: 717-656-7780
Specializes in mail-bid auctions of character collectibles, Disneyana, political items & historical Americana; sample catalog $2.

Bob Slawsky
P.O. Box 864
Windermere, FL 34786-0864
phone: 407-352-7807
fax: 407-352-BIDS
e-mail: WWGD54A@prodigy.com
Buys, sells, auctions tokens, medals, badges, small advertising items, political, World's Fair, Olympic items, encased coins, etc.

Al Anderson
Anderson Auction
P.O. Box 644
Troy, OH 45373
phone: 513-339-0850
Specializes in mail-bid auctions of political items and historical Americana.

Tom Slater
Political Gallery, The
5335 N Tacoma Ave., Ste. 24
Indianapolis, IN 46220-3648
phone: 317-257-0863
fax: 317-254-9167
Specializing in mail-bid auctions of Disneyana, historical Americana, toys, political items, and other collectibles.

Kurt R. Krueger
Krueger Auctions
160 N. Washington St.
Iola, WI 54945
phone: 715-445-3845
fax: 715-445-4100

Robert M. Platt
Local, The
3810 Hyridge Dr.
Austin, TX 78759-7522
e-mail: lclare@pswtech.com
Internet: http://www.collectors.org/apic/chapters.htm
Specializing in the mail-bid auctions of pin-back political buttons of governors, congressional members, mayors, state officials, etc.

Clubs/Associations

Michael McQuillen
Indiana Political Collectors Club
Newsletter: IN A.P.I.C.
P.O. Box 11141
Indianapolis, IN 46201-0141
phone: 317-322-8518
e-mail: peter01@aa.wl.com
Internet: http://www.collectors.org/apic/chapters.htm
Club meets two times per year with annual show; send SASE to be placed on show mailing list.

Joseph D. Hayes, Sec.
American Political Items Collectors (APIC)
Newsletter: Political Bandwagon, The
P.O. Box 340339
San Antonio, TX 78234-0339
phone: 210-945-2811
fax: 210-945-8232
e-mail: apic.comments@collectors.org
Internet: http://www.collectors.org/apic/
Dedicated to the collection, study, preservation of items relating to the political campaigns of the U.S.; also publishes the "Keynoter" magazine three times a year; ask about specialty and local chapters.

Collectors

Dave Castaldi
c/o Genzyme Tissue Repair
64 Sidney St.
Cambridge, MA 02139-4170
phone: 617-494-8484
fax: 617-566-8344
e-mail: dlcjac@worldnet.att.net

Norwood H. Keeney, III
P.O. Box 1026
Georges Mills, NH 03751-1026
phone: 603-763-9157
e-mail: keeney@kear.tds.net
Wants items relating to Statesman John Hay (1838-1905), U.S. Secretary of State.

Donald Ackerman
P.O. Box 3487
Wallington, NJ 07057-1621
phone: 201-779-8785
Wants to buy presidential campaign items; wants one item or collection; 30 years in the hobby; will make an offer if requested, or will make an honest attempt to tell you what you've got.

Robert Kwalwasser
168 Camp Fatima Rd.
Renfrew, PA 16053-9104
phone: 412-789-7766
Wants political parade torches, tinder pistols.

Fred C. Noye
904 N 2nd St.
Harrisburg, PA 17102
Wants to buy political buttons and other political memorabilia.

A.E. Lear
P.O. Box 53
Pipersville, PA 18947
Wants political bandannas, flags, pennants.

Bob Cereghino
6400 Baltimore National Pike, Ste. 170A-319
Baltimore, MD 21228-3914
phone: 410-766-7593
Wants advertising, entertainment and political pin-back buttons.

Chris Hearn
125 Morven Park Rd.
Leesburg, VA 22075
phone: 703-777-7181
Wants to buy political campaign items; political buttons, banners, flags, china, posters, ribbons; especially interested in Roosevelt and Women's Suffrage; also wants Presidential White House gift items and china.

Bob Putnam
9140 Conversation Way
Springfield, VA 22153
phone: 703-644-9711
Wants to buy all presidential campaign items: buttons, banners, posters and political cartoons.

John Gingerich
P.O. Box 358
Lexington, GA 30648-0358
phone: 706-743-3420
Wants political campaign items: buttons, ribbons, badges, posters, postcards, flags, 3-D items, etc.; also wants C.C.C., Bonus Army, United Confederate Veterans, Socialist Party, etc.; want lists sent on request; SASE please.

Peggy Dillard
P.O. Box 210904
Nashville, TN 37221-0904
phone: 615-646-1605
Send SASE and photocopy of political campaign items and receive free appraisal and offer in the mail.

Don Beck
P.O. Box 15305
Fort Wayne, IN 46885-5305
phone: 219-486-3010
Lincoln to Kennedy political pins, medals, flags, banners, autographs.

David Yount
3811 Oriole Dr.
Columbus, IN 47203
phone: 812-378-2980
Wants older political buttons, badges, ribbons, flags, posters, etc.; Lincoln items a priority.

Joe Doerring
P.O. Box 94444
Des Moines, IA 50394
phone: 515-285-7702
Wants poster stamps and labels dealing with presidential campaigns, women's suffrage, labor, and prohibition.

Millie Vaccarella
1955 Hythe St.
Roseville, MN 55113
phone: 612-631-2201
Wants to buy political buttons, banners, posters, canes, and any unusual item; interested in single items or large collections.

Paul Bengston
1225 N 7th St.
Minneapolis, MN 55411
phone: 612-975-3955 or 612-287-0223
Wants pre-1964 political buttons, badges, ribbons, banners, tokens, flags, autographs, and related collectibles; send photocopy.

Cary Demont
P.O. Box 16013
Minneapolis, MN 55416-0013
phone: 612-922-1617
Wants political pre-1964 buttons, pins, flags, ribbons, banners, and the unusual; also suffrage, prohibition, slavery, and Lindbergh.

David Yates
321 West Church St.
Genoa, IL 60135
phone: 815-784-3369
Wants to buy political campaign pin-backs.

Larry Leedom
7217 Via Rio Nido
Downey, CA 90241
Wants 1840-1896 Presidential campaign ribbons, badges, pins and sulphides.

John Gearhart
3267 S.E. Hawthorne
Portland, OR 97214
phone: 503-255-8108 or 503-232-4099
Buttons, posters, ribbons, banners, etc.

Dealers

Rex Stark
Rex Stark Americana
P.O. Box 1029
Gardner, MA 01440
phone: 508-630-3237
Buys & sells political Americana; offers catalog of historical/political Americana for sale.

Paul Longo
Paul Longo Americana
P.O. Box 5510
Gloucester, MA 01930-0007
phone: 508-525-2290
Wants political pins, buttons, ribbons, banners, autographs, badges, etc.

Jon Allan
Elmer's Nostalgia, Inc.
3 Putnam St.
Sanford, ME 04073-2024
phone: 207-324-2166

Larry L. Krug
Americana Resources, Inc.
18222 Flower Hill Way, #299
Gaithersburg, MD 20879-5300
phone: 301-926-8663
fax: 301-926-7648
e-mail: ccs@collectors.org
Internet: http://www.collectors.org/ccs
Wants to buy political buttons/pins, ribbons, glassware and china/posters, autographs, and other memorabilia relating to U.S. presidents, the White House, and Camp David; has over 30 years of experience.

James M. Russell
7775 Forest Stream Club Rd.
Detour, MD 21757
phone: 410-775-2988
Buys, sells and collects any political collectibles including buttons, bandannas, textiles, pins, posters, etc.; especially interested in items relating to James G. Blaine and the election of 1884.

Tom Peeling
P.O. Box 6661
West Palm Beach, FL 33405-0661
phone: 561-585-1351
e-mail: trbuttons@aol.com
Internet: http://www.collectors.org/apic/chapters.htm
Collector and dealer of presidential/political campaign buttons, 3-D items, etc.; Theodore Roosevelt a special want.

John W. Poling
John W. Poling: Military & Political Collectibles
5998 South Ridgeview Rd.
Anderson, IN 46013-9774
phone: 765-778-2714
Mail order dealer in political collectibles; specializing in items from Alaska and Indiana; issues periodic catalog of items for sale; send $2 for latest catalog; most prices in catalog well below current retail.

Robert M. Levine
#2 Troll Court
Ballwin, MO 63011
phone: 314-394-4370
fax: 314-391-6618
Wants any political item; new or old; single or in quantity.

Ronald E. Wade
229 Cambridge
Longview, TX 75601-5102
phone: 903-236-9615
Political buttons/pins JFK and older, posters, 3-dimensional political items, e.g. clocks, glassware, bandannas, etc.; free appraisals, send photocopy with SASE.

Earl F. Dodge
P.O. Box 2635
Denver, CO 80201
phone: 303-572-0646 or 303-237-4947
15 years of buying and selling all political Americana: older items such as buttons, ferros, ribbons, etc.; specializes in Prohibition and Calvin Coolidge buy buy all types of political items; will make prompt offer if photocopies sent.

Experts

Richard Friz
P.O. Box 472
Peterborough, NH 03458
phone: 603-563-8155
Author of "The Official Price Guide to Political Memorabilia."

Tony Lee
Le Politicals
P.O. Box 134
Monmouth Junction, NJ 08852-0134
phone: 201-429-1531
Collector and dealer in all types of political campaign memorabilia, from buttons and ribbons to badges and 3-D items; also president of the big Apple Chapter of the American Political Items Collectors group.

Robert A. Fratkin
2322 20th St. NW
Washington, DC 20009
phone: 202-483-0274 or 800-336-0156
fax: 202-332-8538
e-mail: coxfrd@erols.com
Nationally recognized expert and lecturer on political collectibles; willing to give telephone assistance in identifying and valuing items; send photo and SASE or have in front of you when calling.

Howard Hazelcorn
6731 Ashley Ct.
Sarasota, FL 34241-9696
phone: 941-921-1815
Collects and specializes in political textiles and posters; especially wants buttons and 3-D items.

Michael McQuillen
P.O. Box 11141
Indianapolis, IN 46201-0141
phone: 317-322-8518
e-mail: peter01@aa.wl.com
Internet: http://www.collectors.org/apic/chapters.htm
Buys, sells, collects, appraises political collectibles; wants political items of any age: presidentials and local candidates from any state or election; writes the "Political

Parade" column for "AntiqueWeek"; send SASE for replies.

Museums/Libraries

National Museum of American History
14th & Constitution Ave. NW
Washington, DC 20560
phone: 202-357-2700
Internet: http://www.si.edu/

Periodicals

Newspaper: Political Collector, The
P.O. Box 5171
York, PA 17405-5171
phone: 717-846-0418
A monthly newspaper focusing on political collectibles.

Bob & Jeannine Coup
Newsletter: Political Bandwagon, The
P.O. Box 348
Leola, PA 17540-0348
phone: 717-656-7780
A monthly publication focusing on political collectibles; sample copy $1; contracts with American Political Items Collectors to publish for APIC membership.

Bill Clinton

Clubs/Associations

Philip J. Ross
Bill Clinton Political Items Collectors
Magazine: Arkansas Traveler, The
8226 McNeil St.
Vienna, VA 22180-6924
phone: 703-698-5883 or 703-698-0141
e-mail: politiphil@aol.com
Internet: http://www.collectors.org/apic/chapters.htm
Serves political collectors specializing in memorabilia relating to Bill Clinton campaigns, Presidential and other stages of his career; editor of "The Arkansas Traveler, writes articles about political memorabilia for other magazines.

Calvin Coolidge

Collectors

Larry L. Krug
Americana Resources, Inc.
18222 Flower Hill Way, #299
Gaithersburg, MD 20879-5300
phone: 301-926-8663
fax: 301-926-7648
e-mail: ccs@collectors.org
Internet: http://www.collectors.org/ccs
Major collector for over 25 years of Calvin Coolidge campaign memorabilia and of items relating to the Coolidge administration.

Dealers

Earl F. Dodge
P.O. Box 2635
Denver, CO 80201
phone: 303-572-0646 or 303-237-4947
15 years of buying and selling all political Americana: older items such as buttons, ferros, ribbons, etc.;

specializes in Prohibition and Calvin Coolidge buy buy all types of political items; will make prompt offer if photocopies sent.

Canadian

Dealers

Michael Rice
Michael Rice Collectibles
P.O. Box 286
Saanichton
B.C. V8M 2C5 Canada
phone: 250-652-9412
e-mail: mrice@pacificcoast.net
Particularly interested in Canadian pin-back buttons and paper election memorabilia.

Dan Quayle

Museums/Libraries

Dan Quayle Center & Museum
815 Warren St.
Huntington, IN 46750
phone: 219-356-6356

Democratic

Clubs/Associations

Doug Kelley
Democratic Political Items Collectors (DPIC)
Newsletter: Democratic Spirit
910 Sunset Rd.
Ann Arbor, MI 48103-2925
phone: 313-662-1731
Purpose is to promote beneficial collaboration among collectors of any and all types of memorabilia related to Democratic candidates and/or Democratic Party; newsletter published three times a year.

Collectors

Susan Roman
16 Littlehale Rd.
Durham, NH 03824

Dwight D. Eisenhower

Collectors

John L. Pendergrass
P.O. Box 15729
Hattiesburg, MS 39404-5729

Museums/Libraries

Dwight D. Eisenhower Library
SE 4th St.
Abilene, KS 67410
phone: 913-263-4751

Franklin D. Roosevelt

Clubs/Associations

Elizabeth Clare
Franklin D. Roosevelt Political Items
  Collectors
Newsletter: New Deal, The
3810 Hyridge Dr.
Austin, TX 78759-7522
e-mail: lclare@pswtech.com
Internet: http://www.collectors.org/apic/
  chapters.htm
  *Provides a communications network
  among FDR collectors.*

Museums/Libraries

Franklin Delano Roosevelt Library
511 Albany Rd.
Hyde Park, NY 12538
phone: 914-229-8114

George Bush

Clubs/Associations

Ronald E. Wade
Bush Political Items Collectors
Newsletter: Bush Bandwagon
229 Cambridge
Longview, TX 75601-5102
phone: 903-236-9615

Gerald R. Ford

Clubs/Associations

Chuc Coss
American Political Items Collectors
  (APIC), Gerald R. Ford Chapter
722 Fellows St.
Dixon, IL 61021
  *Dedicated to the preservation of
  political memorabilia of President
  Gerald R. Ford, the 38th President of
  the United States.*

Museums/Libraries

Gerald Ford Library & Museum
303 Pearl St. Northwest
Grand Rapids, MI 49504-5343
phone: 616-451-9263
fax: 616-451-9570

Harry S. Truman

Clubs/Associations

Jim Cassidy
American Political Items Collectors
  (APIC), Harry S. Truman Chapter
Newsletter: Buckstopper, The
6 Arthur St.
Greenwich, CT 06831-5107
  *For those interested in the Truman
  Presidency, Truman's life, and related
  memorabilia.*

Collectors

Mario Donald Thomas
860 18th Ave.
Salt Lake City, UT 84103-3719
phone: 801-532-5340 or 803-799-0030
  *Collects any items connected to
  President Harry S. Truman.*

Museums/Libraries

Clay R. Bauske, Curator
Harry S. Truman Library
Hwy. 24 & Delaware Ave.
Independence, MO 64050
phone: 816-833-1400 or 816-833-1225
fax: 816-833-4368

Herbert Hoover

Collectors

Joe Doerring
P.O. Box 94444
Des Moines, IA 50394
phone: 515-285-7702
  *Wants items from both campaigns of
  Herbert Hoover: pinback buttons,
  ribbons, paper items, novelties, etc.*

Jimmy Carter

Clubs/Associations

Roger Van Sickle
Carter Political Items Group
Newsletter: Carter Journal, The
614 PollyAnna Dr.
Delaware, OH 43015
  *Purpose is to preserve the memora-
  bilia associated with the life, political
  administrations and family members
  of our nation's 39th president, Jimmy
  Carter; quarterly newsletter.*

Museums/Libraries

Jimmy Carter Library
1 Copenhill Ave.
Atlanta, GA 30307
phone: 414-331-0296

John F. Kennedy

Clubs/Associations

Harvey Goldberg, Ed.
Kennedy Political Items Collectors
Newsletter: Hyannisporter
P.O. Box 922
Clark, NJ 07066-0922
phone: 908-382-4652
fax: 908-382-1325
e-mail: heg@worldnet.att.net
Internet: http://www.collectors.org/apic/
  chapters.htm
  *KPIC is a world-wide organization for
  collectors of Kennedy political
  campaign items; members throughout
  the U.S. and Canada and as far away
  as Australia and Europe.*

Bonnie Gardiner
Kennedy Political Items Collectors
Newsletter: Hyannisporter
1337 Olivine
Mentone, CA 92359
  *KPIC is a world-wide organization for
  collectors of Kennedy political
  campaign items; members throughout
  the U.S. and Canada and as far away
  as Australia and Europe.*

Collectors

Dave Lemon
25 Windstone Dr.
Findlay, OH 45840
  *Wants JFK related items: dolls, board
  games, Halloween bucket, PT109 kits,
  puppets, plates, busts, paperweights,
  book ends, figure dolls, thimbles,
  buttons, and badges; please send
  prices with list.*

Experts

Harvey Goldberg, Ed.
P.O. Box 922
Clark, NJ 07066-0922
phone: 908-382-4652
fax: 908-382-1325
e-mail: heg@worldnet.att.net
Internet: http://www.collectors.org/apic/
  chapters.htm
  *Author of several books about
  Kennedy-related memorabilia and a
  noted expert on Kennedy materials;
  offers evaluations and liquidations of
  political collections.*

Museums/Libraries

John F. Kennedy Library
Morrissey Blvd.
Boston, MA 02125
phone: 617-929-4523

Locals

Clubs/Associations

Bob Gillan
American Locals Political Items
  Collectors (ALPIC)
Newsletter: ALPIC Newsletter
128 N. 13th St., #704
Lincoln, NE 68508-1501
phone: 402-477-3185
e-mail: TCWM58A@prodigy.com
  *Serves political collectors of state and
  local offices including governors, U.S.
  senators and Congressmen, mayors,
  sheriffs, etc.*

Lyndon Baines Johnson

Museums/Libraries

Walt Roberts, Mngr.
Lyndon Baines Johnson Museum Store
2313 Red River Rd.
Austin, TX 78705-5702
phone: 512-476-0029
fax: 512-478-9104

Richard Nixon

Clubs/Associations

Eldon Almquist
NIXCO (Nixon Political Collectors'
  Organization)
Newsletter: NIXCO News
975 Maunawili Circle
Kailua, HI 96734-4620
phone: 808-262-9837
fax: 808-834-1046
e-mail: eldon@aloha.net
Internet: http://www.aloha.net/~eldon/
  nixco1.htm
  *For those interested in collecting
  Richard Nixon memorabilia and in
  studying the political career of our
  37th president.*

Collectors

Eldon Almquist
975 Maunawili Circle
Kailua, HI 96734-4620
phone: 808-262-9837
fax: 808-834-1046
e-mail: eldon@aloha.net
Internet: http://www.aloha.net/~eldon/
  nixco1.htm
  *Wants to buy Nixon related pin-backs,
  jewelry and novelties; send SASE and
  photocopy of your items for response
  and free appraisal or offer.*

Museums/Libraries

Sandy Quinn
Richard Nixon Library & Birthplace
18001 Yorba Linda Blvd.
Yorba Linda, CA 92686-3903
phone: 714-993-3393 or 714-993-5075
fax: 714-528-0544
e-mail: http://www.chapman.edu/nixon
  *Gift Shop and annual gifts catalog
  offers wide selection of Presidential
  and campaign memorabilia from
  contemporary administrations
  including Pres. Nixon; political
  memorabilia can be donated; library
  will buy selected items.*

Ronald Reagan

Museums/Libraries

Reagan Library
40 Presidential Dr.
Simi Valley, CA 93065
phone: 805-522-8444

Theodore Roosevelt

Clubs/Associations

Tom Peeling
Theodore Roosevelt Chapter of the
  American Political Items Collectors
  (APIC)
Newsletter: Bully Pulpit
P.O. Box 6661
West Palm Beach, FL 33405-0661
phone: 561-585-1351
e-mail: trbuttons@aol.com
Internet: http://www.collectors.org/apic/
  chapters.htm
  *For collectors and scholars of the
  Theodore Roosevelt years and the*

political memorabilia associated with it.

Dealers

Tom Peeling
P.O. Box 6661
West Palm Beach, FL 33405-0661
phone: 561-585-1351
e-mail: trbuttons@aol.com
Internet: http://www.collectors.org/apic/
chapters.htm
*Collector and dealer of presidential/
political campaign buttons, 3-D items,
etc.; Theodore Roosevelt a special
want.*

Third Party & Hopefuls

Clubs/Associations

Tom Wilson
Third Party & Hopefuls
Newsletter: Bullmoose, The
503 Kings Canyon Blvd.
Galesburg, IL 61401
*Collectors interested in the
memorabilia associated with third
party political candidates and
political hopefuls.*

Wendell L. Willkie

Clubs/Associations

Michael McQuillen
Wendell L. Willkie Political Items
Collectors
Newsletter: Willkie World
P.O. Box 11141
Indianapolis, IN 46201-0141
phone: 317-322-8518
e-mail: peter01@aa.wl.com
Internet: http://www.collectors.org/apic/
chapters.htm
*A group of collectors interested in
buttons, ribbons, paper and all items
related to Wendell Willkie's 1940
campaign; send SASE for replies.*

POLITICALLY INCORRECT COLLECTIBLES

Clubs/Associations

Leland & Crystal Payton
Politically Incorrect Collectibles
Association
Newsletter: PICA Newsletter
3020 S. National, #340
Springfield, MO 65804-4247
phone: 417-886-7124
fax: 417-889-3345
*For collectors of politically incorrect
items such as KKK, sleeping
Mexicans, items degrading to women,
blacks, etc.*

POLYNESIAN COLLECTIBLES

Dealers

M.A. Blackburn
Wholesale Rug Outlet
2448 Lincoln Highway East
Lancaster, PA 17602
phone: 800-346-7847 or 717-295-9078
fax: 717-295-3494
e-mail: wrhawaii@epix.net
Internet: http://www.scmonline.com/
blackburn
*Wants cultural art and artifacts from
all the Polynesian islands; war clubs,
items of personal adornment; also
pre-1925 Hawaiian items.*

POND BOATS

(see BOATS, Model)

POOL TABLES

(see BILLIARD RELATED ITEMS)

POP ART

(see MODERNISM)

POP CULTURE

(see MODERNISM)

POPCORN ITEMS

Collectors

Glenn Smith
3706 Westgate Rd.
Omaha, NE 68124
phone: 402-391-8876
*Wants popcorn boxes and cans: 10
and 12 oz. size cans.*

Jack Cory
7733 Spanish Bar Dr.
Las Vegas, NV 89113
phone: 702-364-1645
e-mail: kernelcory@earthlink.net
*Wants to buy popcorn memorabilia,
popcorn boxes, bags, cans, crates,
brochures, catalogs, old machines and
their parts, Cretor's steam engines
and anything related to popcorn.*

Museums/Libraries

Wyandot Popcorn Museum
Heritage Hall
169 E. Church St.
Marion, OH 43302
phone: 614-383-4031

POPULAR CULTURE

(see also ANTIQUES & COL-
LECTIBLES; CARTOON ART;
MODERNISM; SOCIAL CAUSES;
TELEVISION SHOWS & MEMORA-
BILIA; TOYS, Action Figures)

Clubs/Associations

Ephemera Society of America Inc., The
Newsletter: Ephemera News
P.O. Box 95
Cazenovia, NY 13035-0095
phone: 315-655-2810
fax: 315-655-1078
*The major organization for collectors
and dealers of paper collectibles;
focuses on the preservation and study
of ephemera (short-lived printed
matter); also publishes "The
Ephemera Journal."*

Popular Culture Association
Journal: Journal of American Culture
Popular Culture Center
Bowling Green State University
Bowling Green, OH 43403
phone: 419-372-7861
*The major center and source for the
study of popular culture (media,
music, folklore, ethnic popular
culture, cartoons, performing arts,
books, and more); maintains 200,000
volume reference library of clippings,
leaflets, pamphlets, etc.*

Museums/Libraries

Consortium of Popular Culture
Collections
Popular Culture Library
Bowling Green State University
Bowling Green, OH 43403-0001
phone: 419-372-2450
fax: 419-372-7996
*Consortium composed of Bowling
Green State U., Kent State U.,
Michigan State U., and Ohio State U.;
the largest academic library
collections of primary research
material in comic art, popular fiction,
popular music, performing arts.*

Russel B. Nye Popular Culture
Collection, Michigan State University
Libraries
Michigan State Univ. Libraries
Special Collections
East Lansing, MI 48825
phone: 517-355-3770
*Includes a popular culture vertical file
of related ephemera.*

Baby Boomer

Auction Services

Gary Kraut
Alphaville
226 W. Houston St.
New York, NY 10014-4846
phone: 212-675-6850
fax: 212-741-2609
e-mail: alphavil@mindspring.com
Internet: http://www.alphaville.com
*Along with partner Steve Karchin
conducts phone auctions of 50s and
60s toys, games, and other memorabilia.*

Dealers

Gary Kraut
Alphaville
226 W. Houston St.
New York, NY 10014-4846
phone: 212-675-6850
fax: 212-741-2609
e-mail: alphavil@mindspring.com
Internet: http://www.alphaville.com
*Along with partner Steve Karchin
buys and sells vintage 1940s, 50s, and
60s toys, games, and other memorabilia.*

Toysensations
P.O. Box 218
Woodbury, NY 11797
phone: 516-338-4929 or 516-338-2701
fax: 516-681-3612
*Specializes in selling toys from the
1940s through 1970s.*

David Hendrickson
Kitsch-n-Stuff
P.O. Box 2271
Port Angeles, WA 98362
phone: 360-457-5589
fax: 360-457-3991
*Specializes in "boomerabilia":
collectibles from the mid 1940s
through mid 1960s: kitchen items,
dinnerware, chrome and Formica
dinette sets, end tables, chairs, lamps,
radios, small appliances, etc.*

Man./Prod./Dist.

Gene Rees
Gino's Malt Shop Collection
P.O. Box 505
Bridgeville, PA 15017-0505
phone: 412-221-1495
fax: 412-221-1272
e-mail: rosginoa@bellatlantic.net
*Sells 50s and 60s malt shop furniture,
decor and accessories: booths, tables,
chairs, stools, moldings, metal trim,
lighting fixtures, quilted stainless
sheets, counter accessories, etc.*

Periodicals

John Koenig
Antique Trader Publications, Inc.
Newspaper: Toy Trader
922 Churchill St., Ste. #1
Waupaca, WI 54981
phone: 715-258-7525 or 800-768-9225
fax: 715-258-8707
e-mail: jkoenig@add-inc.com
Internet: http://www.csmonline.com
*Monthly newspaper with information
on how to buy, sell and trade all types
of toys; market trends, the latest
prices, "how-to" columns, listings of
toy clubs and upcoming toy shows and
auctions; also full of buy and sell ads.*

Magazine: Gearhead Magazine
P.O. Box 421219
San Francisco, CA 94142-1219
phone: 415-928-7154
*Marries articles about 1950s and
1960s hot rods with music.*

PORCELAIN

(see CERAMICS; DINNERWARE;
FIGURINES; OCCUPIED JAPAN;
ORIENTALIA; REPAIR/RESTORA-
TION/CONSERVATION; TABLE-
WARE)

POSTAGE STAMPS

(see POSTAL SERVICE ITEMS;
STAMP COLLECTING)

POSTAL SERVICE ITEMS

(see also POSTCARDS, Post Office
Related; STAMP COLLECTING)

Clubs/Associations

Steve Pavlina
Cheswick Historical Society
Newsletter: Stamps, Old Letters &
  History
208 Allegheny Ave.
Cheswick, PA 15024
phone: 412-274-9106
  Focuses on U.S. postal History.

Bill DiPaolo
Modern Postal History Society
Journal: Modern Postal History Journal
404 Dorado Ct.
High Point, NC 27260
  *Focuses on the collection, documenta-
  tion and study of postal history,
  practices and policies; emphasizing
  material from 1930 to date.*

Collectors

Tom Mills
30 Bay Path Rd.
Spencer, MA 01562-1602
phone: 508-885-9550
  *Wants fire alarm and police boxes
  especially ones with dates cast into
  them; seeks cast iron signs and street
  letter pickup boxes marked "U.S.
  MAIL"; best to write and send photos.*

Dr. Frank R. Scheer, Curator
Railway Mail Service Library
12 E. Rosemont Ave.
Alexandria, VA 22301-2325
phone: 703-549-4095
fax: 703-836-1955
e-mail: fscheer@email.usps.gov
  *Wants to buy obsolete official postal
  artifacts from any country: postmark-
  ing handstamps, badges, mail locks,
  street letterboxes, mail route
  schedules, postal hand guns, etc.; no
  stamps, postmarked envelopes or
  modern collectibles.*

Harold Dylhoff
23511 Paulson's Rd.
Gobles, MI 49055-9605
phone: 616-628-4051
  *Wants to buy postal history items: ship
  cancels, covers from 1946 atomic
  bomb tests Bikini Atoll "Operation
  Crossroads", any material Air Force
  509th connected with XRDs tests; send
  photocopies and LSASE for reply.*

George Cross
P.O. Box 3923
Tustin, CA 92681
  Wants to buy U.S. Post Office badges.

Dealers

Paul & Becky Huber
Fairwinds
26450 Moore Farm Lane
Onancock, VA 23417
phone: 757-787-1569
e-mail: fairwinds@esva.net
  *Dealers in naval and maritime postal
  history, postcards, historical
  documents and antiques; maintains an
  extensive stock and provides approval
  service; want lists appreciated.*

Museums/Libraries

Postal History Foundation, The
920 North First Ave.
Tucson, AZ 85719
phone: 602-623-6652
  *Houses artifacts, postmarks and
  covers dedicated to postal history.*

On-Line Services

Dr. Frank R. Scheer, Curator
Railway Mail Service Library
12 E. Rosemont Ave.
Alexandria, VA 22301-2325
phone: 703-549-4095
fax: 703-836-1955
e-mail: fscheer@email.usps.gov
  *A FREE computer web page for postal
  history researchers interested in post
  items of the USA and other countries;
  replies to requests will be down-
  loaded; upload articles to check
  technical information; send e-mail for
  current URL.*

Military

Clubs/Associations

Norman Gruenzner, Treas.
Military Postal History Society
Newsletter: MPHS Bulletin
P.O. Box 32
Schenectady, NY 77410-0032
  *Formed for the purpose of collecting
  and studying military mail of all
  periods: "Field Post" markings,
  censorship, occupation, internment,
  prisoner of war camp covers, and
  propaganda labels and leaflets;
  publishes books on the subject.*

Collectors

Harold Dylhoff
23511 Paulson's Rd.
Gobles, MI 49055-9605
phone: 616-628-4051
  *Collecting A.P.O.s (Army Post Office)
  especially from 1940s to 1950s;
  Alaska Highway construction, WWII
  Alaska Forts; also Canadian NWT
  postmarks and A.P.O.s; send
  photocopies and LSASE for reply.*

Virginia

Collectors

Lewis Leigh, Jr.
P.O. Box 4327
Leesburg, VA 20177
phone: 703-771-3081
fax: 703-771-1432
  *Wants to buy postal history items
  especially pertaining to early
  Virginia: equipment & forms, old
  letters, documents, etc.*

POSTCARDS

(see also BOOKS, Reference
[Postcards]; ILLUSTRATORS;
PAPER COLLECTIBLES)

Auction Services

Martin J. Shapiro
Postcards International
P.O. Box 5398
Hamden, CT 06518-0398
phone: 203-248-6621
fax: 203-248-6628
e-mail: postcrdint@aol.com
Internet: http://csmonline.com/
  postcardsint/
  *Buys and sells vintage picture
  postcards; offers the collector picture
  postcards or topical high quality
  postcards by auction, catalog or on
  approval; sample catalog is available
  upon request for $5.*

John H. McClintock
Virginia Mail Auction
P.O. Box 1765
Manassas, VA 22110-1765
phone: 703-368-2757
  *Conducts 4 to 5 illustrated postcard
  mail auctions per year; also promotes
  8 postcard shows per year.*

William Crawford
P.O. Box 2892
Hallandale, FL 33008
phone: 305-456-9671

M. Roger Harvey
Card Source
76 W. Dundee Rd., Ste. 405
Buffalo Grove, IL 60089-3758
phone: 874-752-08145
fax: 847-520-8145
e-mail: RHarvey@thepostcard.com
Internet: http://www.thepostcard.com
  *Deals in antique, collectible and
  modern postcards; established the
  first postcard shop on the Internet/
  world wide web; also appraises and
  auctions postcards.*

Clubs/Associations

Edith Costa
Granite State Postcard Collectors Club
P.O. Box 79
West Franklin, NH 03235
phone: 603-647-0634

Dr. James Lewis Lowe, Dir.
Deltiologists of America
Magazine: Postcard Classics
P.O. Box 8
Norwood, PA 19074
phone: 610-485-8572
  *International postcard society for
  collectors, dealers, librarians, and
  archivist.*

W. Earl Long, Pres.
Monumental Postcard Club
Newsletter: Newsheet
1010 Woodlake Dr., Apr. C
Cockeysville, MD 21030-3622
  *Non-profit organization open to the
  public; annual club-sponsored show
  in October with dealers from all over
  the world.*

John H. McClintock, Dir
Postcard History Society
Newsletter: Postcard History Society
  Bulletin
P.O. Box 1765
Manassas, VA 22110-1765
phone: 703-368-2757
  *Four quarterly newsletters, 4 to 8
  pages each, keep you informed of
  deltiological (postcard) activities and
  research.*

John H. McClintock, Sec
International Federation of Postcard
  Dealers, Inc.
Directory: Annual IFPD Directory
P.O. Box 1765
Manassas, VA 22110-1765
phone: 703-368-2757
  *The Annual IFDP Directory of nearly
  300 postcard dealers is free for $1.25
  postage.*

Laura Goldberg
Wolverine Postcard Club
23439 Davey St.
Hazel Park, MI 48030

Hal Ottaway
Wichita Postcard Club
P.O. Box 780282
Wichita, KS 67278-0282

Dalene Thomas
Denver Postcard Club
Newsletter: Denver Postcard Club News
8612 West Warren Lane
Denver, CO 80227-2352
phone: 303-986-6620
e-mail: dathomas@nyx.cs.du.edu
Internet: http://www.nyx.net/~dathomas
  *Postcard collectors meet to buy, sell,
  trade cards; programs are presented
  to educate members about postcard
  collecting.*

Edmund Fisher
Webfooters Postcard Club
2547 S.E. 174th Ave., #11
Portland, OR 97236

Collectors

Mrs. G.M. Kirchgessner
421 Washington St.
Hoboken, NJ 07030

Ben Egerton
13009 Dover Rd.
Reisterstown, MD 21136-5512
Has been collecting postcards for over 20 years.

John H. McClintock
Postcard Society, Inc.
P.O. Box 1765
Manassas, VA 22110-1765
phone: 703-368-2757
Promotes 8 postcard shows.

Gary Olsen
505 S. Royal Ave.
Front Royal, VA 22630
phone: 703-635-7157 or 703-635-7158
fax: 703-635-1818
e-mail: hpfrigko@interloc.com
Wants postcards with maps, music themes, real estate subjects and/or famous "persons" autographs.

Calvin J. Meider
P.O. Box 170
Excelsior, MN 55331-0170
phone: 612-926-2142

Jerry Abert
631 Broadway
East Alton, IL 62024
phone: 618-259-0901

George Van Trump, Jr.
6837 Murray Lane
Annandale, VA 22003

Lewis Baer
P.O. Box 621
Penngrove, CA 94951
e-mail: ursusmjr@metro.net
Writes postcard column for "Postcard Collector" magazine.

Dealers

Alicia & Jorge Valino
P.O. Box 1442
(11000) Montevideo
Uruguay
e-mail: vala@adinet.com.uy.

Siegfried Feller
Cartomania
8 Amherst Rd.
Pelham, MA 01002-9746
phone: 413-253-3115

Martin J. Shapiro
Postcards International
P.O. Box 5398
Hamden, CT 06518-0398
phone: 203-248-6621
fax: 203-248-6628
e-mail: postcrdint@aol.com
Internet: http://csmonline.com/postcardsint/
Buys and sells vintage picture postcards; offers the collector picture postcards or topical high quality postcards by auction, catalog or on approval; sample catalog is available upon request for $5.

Max Davis
Davis' Vintage Collectibles
110 West 25th St.
Gallery 307
New York, NY 10001-7401
phone: 212-243-7090 or 212-769-9744
fax: 212-769-9199
e-mail: lrd@usa.pipeline.com

Bob & Kay Schies
452 East Bissell Ave.
Oil City, PA 16301-2063
phone: 814-677-3182
Buying pre-1930 postcards, any amount.

Harry R. McKeon, Jr.
18 Rose Lane
Flourtown, PA 19031-1910
phone: 215-233-4094
Send your postcards want list for large unpicked selection also Victorian trade cards.

Jay Miller
725 S. Schell St.
Philadelphia, PA 19147

Sheldon Dobres
S. Dobres Postcards
P.O. Box 1855
Baltimore, MD 21203-1855
phone: 410-486-6569 or 800-342-5983
Postcards bought and sold; top prices paid for all U.S. and foreign postcards.

Mary L. Martin, Ltd.
P.O. Box 787
Perryville, MD 21903
phone: 410-575-7768 or 410-939-2973
fax: 410-642-2053
Specializing in state views, signed artists, sports, transportation, political, Halloween, Santas, etc.

Joseph L. Mashburn
Colonial House
P.O. Box 609 - M
Enka, NC 28728-0609
phone: 704-667-1427
fax: 704-667-1111
e-mail: jmashb@aol.com
Internet: http://www.postcard-books.com
Buys and sells antique postcards; interested mainly in artist-signed beautiful ladies, children, fantasy, animals, blacks, nudes, real photos, sports; specializing in Harrison Fisher and Philip Boileau.

Betty Powell
P.O. Box 571
Columbus, OH 43085-0571
fax: 614-885-1962
Buys and sells U.S. postcards: artist signed, holidays, topicals, views.

Jerry Garrett
Jerry's Antiques & Postcards
1807 West Madison St.
Kokomo, IN 46901-1829
phone: 765-457-5256
Wants to buy old postcards.

Abbot's Postcards
1393 S. Woodward Ave.
Birmingham, MI 48009
phone: 810-644-8565
fax: 810-644-7038

M. Roger Harvey
Card Source
76 W. Dundee Rd., Ste. 405
Buffalo Grove, IL 60089-3758
phone: 874-752-08145
fax: 847-520-8145
e-mail: RHarvey@thepostcard.com
Internet: http://www.thepostcard.com
Deals in antique, collectible and modern postcards; established the first postcard shop on the Internet/world wide web; also appraises and auctions postcards.

Trenton Boyd
P.O. Box 517
Columbia, MO 65205-0517
phone: 573-882-2461 or 573-442-5235
fax: 573-882-2950
e-mail: vetlib@showme.missouri.edu
Interested in veterinary postcards including schools and military veterinary; also wants teratology cards that show animals with birth defects (e.g. five-legged calves); Red Cross dogs, Humane Association.

Steve Schmale
Out West
2231 Creekside Rd.
Santa Rosa, CA 95405-8022
phone: 707-838-1859 or 707-575-5406
e-mail: outweststv@aol.com
Buys and sells better vintage postcards since 1976; approval service; strong in Western states views; always buying better cards and real photos; also wants railroad paper, stereoviews, photos, brochures, trade cards; member IFPD.

Tom Osjecki
Phyllis' Philatelics
P.O. Box 792
Canyonville, OR 97417
phone: 541-839-4135 or 541-839-6151
Buys, sells and specializes in postcards, paper Americana, stamps and covers; over 25,000 covers and postcards listed by state or topic.

Dave Morris
3388 Merlin Rd., Ste. 351
Grants Pass, OR 97526
phone: 541-955-8411
e-mail: smorris@cdsnet.net
Wants to buy pre-1930 U.S. postcards, especially real photo postcards; will buy collections.

Experts

Martin J. Shapiro
Postcards International
P.O. Box 5398
Hamden, CT 06518-0398
phone: 203-248-6621
fax: 203-248-6628
e-mail: postcrdint@aol.com
Internet: http://csmonline.com/postcardsint/
Buys and sells vintage picture postcards; offers the collector picture postcards or topical high quality postcards by auction, catalog or on approval; sample catalog is available upon request for $5.

Dr. James Lewis Lowe, Dir.
P.O. Box 8
Norwood, PA 19074
phone: 610-485-8572

Roy Cox
P.O. Box 3610
Hamilton, MD 21214
Author of "How to Price and Sell Old Picture Postcards," available from the author for $9.95 ppd.

V. Lee Cox
Memory Lane Postcards, Inc.
P.O. Box 66
Keymar, MD 21757
phone: 410-775-0188 or 410-775-0190

Joseph L. Mashburn
Colonial House
P.O. Box 609 - M
Enka, NC 28728-0609
phone: 704-667-1427
fax: 704-667-1111
e-mail: jmashb@aol.com
Internet: http://www.postcard-books.com
Buys and specializes in high quality postcards; author and publisher of postcard price guides "The Postcard Price Guide", "The Artist-Signed Postcard Price Guide", and "Super Rare Postcards of Harrison Fisher"; write for prices.

Susan Nicholson
Past & Present
P.O. Box 595
Lisle, IL 60532
phone: 630-964-5240
Buys and sells rare and unusual postcards, Victorian valentines, periodicals, advertising trade cards, etc.

Ada Fitzsimmons
P.O. Box 337
San Anselmo, CA 94979-0337
phone: 415-454-5552
fax: 415-454-2947
Buys, sells, appraises, lectures and write about postcards.

Museums/Libraries

Katherine Hamilton-Smith
Curt Teich Postcard Archives, Lake
 County Museum
Journal: Image File
27277 Forest Preserve Dr.
Wauconda, IL 60084-2016
phone: 847-526-8638 or 847-526-7878
fax: 847-526-1545
e-mail: teicharc@nslsilus.org
 *Archive of North American postcards
 from 1898-1978; formerly industrial
 archives of Curt Teich Printing Co.,
 Chicago; also postcard albums;
 provides full-color copies of
 postcards.*

On-Line Services

Steve Neis
Pacific Attic Online, The
10024 Burnham Dr. NW #3C
Gig Harbor, WA 98332-1879
phone: 206-851-9964 or 206-858-6721
fax: 206-858-6721
e-mail: Pstcrd@harbornet.com
Internet: http://www.web-pac.com/mall/
 pacific
 *On-line shop for vintage postcards;
 also appraises, buys, sells, auctions,
 and collects postcards.*

Periodicals

Brian & Mary Lund
Reflections of a Bygone Age
Magazine: Picture Postcard Monthly
15 Debdale Lane
Keyworth
Nottinghamshire NG12 5HT U.K
phone: 0115-9376197
 *Magazine designed for collectors of
 old picture postcards whatever your
 interest, theme or area; events, clubs,
 checklists, values, etc.; also includes a
 supplement of modern picture
 postcards from 1950; new issues,
 event, shops, values.*

Linda Kellbach
Antique Trader Publications, Inc.
Magazine: Postcard Collector
P.O. Box 1050
Dubuque, IA 52004-1050
phone: 800-334-7165 or 800-482-4155
fax: 800-531-0880
e-mail: 76143.72@compuserve.com
Internet: http://www.csmonline.com
 *The hobby's leading publication; best
 source to buy, sell, and learn about
 postcards and other paper collectibles; calendar of upcoming
 shows, postcard profiles, a collecting
 guide for moderns through the mail,
 and more.*

Linda Kellbach
Antique Trader Publications, Inc.
Directory: Postcard Collector Reference
 Annual
P.O. Box 1050
Dubuque, IA 52004-1050
phone: 800-334-7165 or 800-482-4155
fax: 800-531-0880
e-mail: 76143.72@compuserve.com
Internet: http://www.csmonline.com
 *Annual directory of postcard related
 resources - dealers, suppliers, etc.*

Coteco, Inc.
Newspaper: Barr's Post Card News
70 S. 6th St.
Lansing, IA 52151-9680
phone: 319-538-4500 or 800-397-0145
fax: 319-538-4038
Internet: http://www.tias.com/mags/barr
 *A weekly deltiology newspaper
 containing postcard events, shows,
 news, articles, club directory, current
 prices, ads, etc.*

Gloria Jackson
Gloria's Corner
Newsletter: Gloria's Corner
P.O. Box 507
Denison, TX 75021-0507
phone: 903-463-4878
fax: 903-463-4878
 *A bi-monthly newsletter about
 postcards; trades, buying, selling,
 auctions, etc.*

Repro. Sources

Evergreen Press, The
P.O. Box 5227
Walnut Creek, CA 94596-1227
 *Reproduces vintage style postcards,
 and wedding and birth certificates.*

Suppliers

NuAce Company
131 Main St.
Reading, MA 01867-3900
phone: 617-944-4960
fax: 617-944-6101
 *Display and protect your first day
 covers or postcards in NuAce 23-ring
 binders; has twenty 3-pocket pages to
 hold standard covers or postcards.*

RNProducts
39 Monmouth St.
Red Bank, NJ 07701
phone: 908-741-0626
 *Postcard albums with 4 and 6 pocket
 crystal clear vinyl pages.*

Linder Publications, Inc.
P.O. Box 5056
Syracuse, NY 13220
phone: 315-437-0463 or 800-654-0324
fax: 315-437-4832
 *Sells collector's accessories for
 stamps, coins, telephone cards,
 postcards: ring binders, blank album
 pages, UV lamps, magnifiers, stamp
 tongs, clear pocket pages, protective
 covers, coin holders, etc.*

Morgan Co., The
6301 Highbanks Rd.
Mascoutah, IL 62258
phone: 618-566-7568 or 800-422-4510
fax: 618-566-7518
 *Pocket sheets and soft sleeves for
 archival safe storage.*

Aviation Related

(see also AVIATION MEMORA-
BILIA)

Bank Related

Collectors

John & Nancy Wilson
Wilson's Syngraplics
P.O. Box 27185
Milwaukee, WI 53227-0185
phone: 414-545-8636
fax: 414-554-8894
 *Wants any pre-1934 paper money
 issued in the U.S.; also wants any pre-
 1930 postcards depicting banks.*

Baseball Related

Experts

Ron Menchine
P.O. Box 1
Long Green, MD 21092
phone: 410-592-7152
 *A leading collector of and specialist in
 baseball postcards; author of "A
 Picture History of Baseball" (Almar
 Press, 1992).*

Foreign

Dealers

Jerry Rubackin
Jerry's Cards & Collectibles
P.O. Box 1271
Framingham, MA 01701-0207
phone: 508-788-5197
fax: 508-788-5197
 *Buys early foreign postcards from
 Philippines and Hawaii: people, street
 scenes, advertising, costumes, real
 photo; no general views; need early
 atlases and Harpers Book of the
 Philippines.*

Photo (Real)

Auction Services

Bob Ward
Antique Paper Guild
P.O. Box 5742
Bellevue, WA 98006-0242
phone: 206-643-5701
fax: 206-641-4363
e-mail: rwardapg@interserv.com
Internet: http://www.web-pac.com
 *Conducts periodic auctions
 specializing in pre-1935 real photo
 postcards; six mail/phone auction
 catalogs per year for $30, 8 1/2" x
 11", profusely illustrated.*

Experts

Bob Ward
Antique Paper Guild
P.O. Box 5742
Bellevue, WA 98006-0242
phone: 206-643-5701
fax: 206-641-4363
e-mail: rwardapg@interserv.com
Internet: http://www.web-pac.com
 *Specializes in pre-1935 real photo
 postcards, stereographs and
 photographica; also conducts
 specialized auctions of same; author
 of "Investment Guide to North
 American Real Photo Postcards,"
 "Real Photo Postcards: The 'Life-
 Size' Edition.*

Photo (Real) Canadian

Dealers

Michael Rice
Michael Rice Collectibles
P.O. Box 286
Saanichton
B.C. V8M 2C5 Canada
phone: 250-652-9412
e-mail: mrice@pacificcoast.net
 *Active buyer of Canadian, U.S.,
 English, foreign pre-1930 picture
 postcards; wants used or unused;
 especially wants "real photo" views of
 Western Canadian provinces and the
 Yukon Territory; cards may be sent on
 approval; will pay postage.*

Piano Related

Collectors

Janice E. Kelsh
633 Pennsylvania Ave.
Hagerstown, MD 21740-3769
phone: 301-797-7675
e-mail: kelshj@nihrrlib.ncrr.nih.gov
 *Interested in obtaining miniature
 pianos of all kinds; also want
 postcards depicting pianos.*

Pontiacs & Olds Related

Collectors

Alfred Sherman
247 Parkview Ave. Apt. 5P
Bronxville, NY 10708
phone: 914-965-4200
 *Wants 1942, 1946, 1947, 1948
 Pontiac and Oldsmobile postcards.*

Post Office Related

Collectors

Dr. Frank R. Scheer, Curator
Railway Mail Service Library
12 E. Rosemont Ave.
Alexandria, VA 22301-2325
phone: 703-549-4095
fax: 703-836-1955
e-mail: fscheer@email.usps.gov
 *Buys post office related postcards -
 any condition, era, location or
 country. Will send free list with
 buying prices. Also wants postcards*

with views of street letterboxes, postal vehicles, post office interiors, etc.

Royalty Related

Periodicals

Lee Poleske
Newsletter: Royalty Cards
P.O. Box 871
Seward, AK 99664-0871
An informative newsletter for the collector of royalty postcards.

Sports Related

Collectors

Mike Jaime
P.O. Box 247
Stratford, CT 06497-0247
Wants sports postcards picturing boxing, baseball, football, stadiums, players, etc.; wants pre-1950 auto & horse racing postcards, pre-1950 arenas/coliseums; especially wants real photo sports postcards, jumbo-size stadium/teams photos.

States

(see also STATE RELATED COLLECTIBLES)

Collectors

Richard Pace
12556 Timber Hollow Place
Germantown, MD 20874-1561
phone: 202-708-1870 or 301-916-4913
A photographer who collects and wants to buy modern postcards depicting or related to the 50 States, the U.S. Territories, and the District of Columbia.

States (California)

Collectors

Linda Williams-White
204 1/2 Covina Ave.
Long Beach, CA 90803
phone: 310-433-7897
Wants pre-1930 California postcards from Los Angeles and Orange County towns: Long Beach (Belmont Shore, Naples, Alamitos Bay/Peninsula, downtown areas), Los Angeles, San Pedro, Seal Beach, Huntington Beach, Catalina Isl.; also San Fran.

States (Florida)

Collectors

Steve Hess
P.O. Box 3476
De Land, FL 32720-3476
phone: 904-736-1067 or 904-254-1809
Buying Florida postcards: small town, depots, blacks; anything pre-1915 Florida.

States (Maryland)

Collectors

Jerry A. McCoy
800 Thayer Ave.
Silver Spring, MD 20910-4504
phone: 301-565-2519
fax: 301-565-0780
Wants any postcards or memorabilia of Silver Spring, Maryland.

States (North Carolina)

Collectors

J. Robert Boykin, III
P.O. Box 7440
Wilson, NC 27895
phone: 919-237-1700
fax: 919-237-2314
Buying pre-1930s North Carolina postcards; no mountains; prefers early or real photo.

States (Pennsylvania)

Collectors

Richard A. Wood
P.O. Box 22165
Juneau, AK 99802-2165
phone: 907-789-8450
fax: 907-789-8450
e-mail: akrare@alaska.net
Internet: http://www.alaska.net/~akrare
Wants postcards of Penna. Pike County towns: Milford, Twin Lakes, Shohola, Parker's Glen, Walker Lake, Woodtown; also ALASKA postcards.

States (West Virginia)

Collectors

Randy Bryant
P.O. Box 62
Cannelton, WV 25036-0062
phone: 304-442-4480
Wants pre-1930 real photos and postcards of West Virginia: small towns, coal mining, lumbering, interiors, exteriors, lynchings, sports teams of WV coal towns; no scenic views (mountains, rivers, statues, etc.)

WWII Propaganda

Experts

Ron Menchine
P.O. Box 1
Long Green, MD 21092
phone: 410-592-7152
Co-author with Paul Dickson of "Send the War Home" (Shoestring Press).

POSTERS

(see also ADVERTISING COLLECTIBLES, Posters; CARTOON ART; MAGICIANS PARAPHERNALIA; MARINE CORPS ITEMS; MILITARIA, WWI [Posters]; MILITARIA, WWII [Posters]; MOVIE MEMORABILIA, Movie Posters; PAPER COLLECTIBLES; PRINTS)

Auction Services

Terry Shargel
Poster Auctions International Inc
601 West 26th St., 13th Floor
New York, NY 1001
phone: 212-787-4000
fax: 212-604-9175
Internet: http://www.posterauction.com
Conducts two poster-only auctions per year emphasizing original French advertising posters of the Belle Epoque; prices range from $1,000 to $65,000; resource for books on all aspects of poster art; catalogue available.

Swann Galleries, Inc.
104 E. 25th St.
New York, NY 10010-2977
phone: 212-254-4710
fax: 212-979-1017
e-mail: SwannSales@aol.com

R. Neil & Elaine Reynolds
Poster Mail Auction Co.
P.O. Box 133
Waterford, VA 22190-0133
phone: 540-882-3574
fax: 540-882-4765
Conducts 4 mail/telephone auctions per year of original vintage posters; 4 fully illustrated catalogs for $20.

Collectors

Dan Calandriello
53-C Beacon Village
Burlington, MA 01803-3843
phone: 617-229-9009
e-mail: dan@coe.neu.edu
Wants Disney posters, tobacco posters.

Ken Trombly
1825 K St. NW, #901
Washington, DC 20006
phone: 800-673-8158 or 202-887-5000
fax: 202-457-0343
e-mail: trombly@erols.com
Wants magic posters, Mysto Magic sets, magic books and Houdini items; also wants broadsides and old photos of magicians; will pay top dollar or will trade from his collection.

Dealers

Maurice & Laya Jakubowicz
L'affiche Francaise
Le Plateau - Bazincourt
B.P. 42
21740 Gisors, France
phone: 332-32555476
fax: 332-32271012
Buy and sell 1880-present vintage posters, mainly European, all subjects: advertising, travel, theater, sport, World War, political, etc.; catalogs sent upon request.

George Dembo
P.O. Box 657
Chatham, NJ 07928-0657
phone: 201-701-0713
fax: 201-701-0713
Wants to buy vintage posters (1860-1960) in good condition; phone or write and send photos; wants one poster or a large collection.

Susan & Mario Carrandi
Carrandi Vintage Posters
122 Monroe Ave.
Belle Mead, NJ 08502-4608
phone: 908-874-0630
fax: 908-874-4892
Buys and sells posters: French, circus, magic, Wild West, decorative.

Nancy Steinbock
Nancy Steinbock Posters & Prints
197 Holmes Dale
Albany, NY 12208-1449
phone: 800-438-1577
fax: 518-446-1649
Buys and sells posters 1880-present; subjects: war, travel, circus, literary, political, product advertising, etc.; American or foreign.

Martin Kramer
313 Arch St., Ste. 203
Philadelphia, PA 19106-1810
phone: 215-592-0103
fax: 215-592-0103
Wants to buy European and American posters; all types, including movie posters.

R. Neil & Elaine Reynolds
Fine Old Posters
1015 King St.
Alexandria, VA 22314-2922
phone: 703-684-3656
fax: 540-882-4765
Buys and sells hundreds of original vintage posters.

Pam Brin
Posters For Great Walls Gallery
8 Park Lane
Minneapolis, MN 55416-4340
phone: 612-920-3030
fax: 612-920-3031
e-mail: pambrin@msn.com
Buys and sells posters; has over 150 WWI posters; issues periodic list of items for sale.

Henry W. Taylor, Jr.
500 South Main St.
P.O. Box 2247
Ketchum, ID 83340-2247
phone: 208-726-5757
e-mail: 76234.1472@compuserve.com
Wants to buy travel posters from the Western USA (especially Sun Valley, IS or Yellowstone Park), travel posters from Bavaria (Germany) or the Austrian Tyrol, old movie posters (especially Idaho and Montana).

Roger Graham
Every Era Antiques
855 57th St.
Sacramento, CA 95819-3300
phone: 916-456-1767
e-mail: roger@every-era.com
Internet: http://www.every-era.com
Specializing in vintage posters, especially travel, entertainment, and advertising posters from 1880-1950.

Experts

Tony Fusco
Fusco & Four, Associates
One Murdock Terrace
Brighton, MA 02135-2817
phone: 617-787-2637
fax: 617-782-4430
Vintage posters 1800s to WWII plus selected modern art posters; author of "The Confident Collector Identification & Price Guide to Posters"; offers appraisal and brokerage services for vintage 1870-1940 poster collectors.

George Theofiles
Miscellaneous Man
P.O. Box 1776
New Freedom, PA 17349-0191
phone: 717-235-4766
fax: 717-235-2853
Collects, buys and sells; since 1970 offering catalogs of rare posters and early advertising and ephemera on hundreds of subjects. Descriptive flyer available.

Repair Services

Gary Goss
Funny Face Productions
320 Riverside Dr.
Northampton, MA 01060
phone: 413-586-0778
Fixes stains, missing pieces, faded areas and tears, remounts posters on Japanese paper and linen backs.

Phil Temple
Phil Temple Poster Mounting Service
P.O. Box 561
Novato, CA 94949
phone: 415-897-5130
fax: 415-897-5130
Poster mounting service since 1980; posters museum-mounted on 100% cotton acid-free panels.

Eastern European

Dealers

Judy Sullivan
Eastern European Art Company
0061 Arapahoe
Carbondale, CO 81623-8713
phone: 970-963-8789
fax: 970-963-8789
Sells rare posters, mainly from Poland and dating from 1940s of American and foreign films, sports, music, political, circus, travel, theater, and gallery shows; posters have beautiful graphics and colors.

POSTMARKS

(see STAMP COLLECTING, Postmarks)

POT LIDS

Collectors

James Hagenbuch
P.O. Box 180
East Greenville, PA 18041
phone: 215-679-5849
fax: 215-679-3068
Wants to buy American pot lids for private collection. (Pot lids are decorated lids from small ceramic containers from 1840s to 1880s; pot lids first appeared in England.)

Experts

Barbara & Sonny Jackson
2585 Kenney Dr.
San Pablo, CA 94806
Authors of "American Pot Lids."

POTTERY

(see CERAMICS; COOKIE JARS; DINNERWARE; FIGURINES; FLOWER "FROGS"; REPAIR/ RESTORATION/CONSERVATION; SALT & PEPPER SHAKERS; STEINS; TILES)

POWDER HORNS

(see also ARMS & ARMOR; FIREARMS)

Collectors

David A. Galliher
2500 W. Berwyn Rd.
Muncie, IN 47304-5113
phone: 317-289-2233 or 317-284-6668
fax: 317-289-2376
Wants very early powder horns (late 1700s to 1812), engraved and with historical significance.

Experts

William H. Guthman
Guthman Americana
P.O. Box 392
Westport, CT 06881
phone: 203-259-9763
Author of "Drums A'beating, Trumpets Sounding: Artistically Carved Powder Horns in the Provincial Manner, 1746-1781."

Jim Dresslar
Dresslar Publishing
P.O. Box 635
Bargersville, IN 46106
phone: 317-422-5147
Author of "Folk Art of Early America - The Engraved Powder Horn" (Dresslar Publishing), available from the author.

Repro. Sources

Michelle Ochonicky
Stone Hollow Scrimshaw Studio
4059 Toenges Ave.
Saint Louis, MO 63116

Japanese

Experts

Alan D. Meaux
Ronin Art Productions
P.O. Box 1271
Oak Harbor, WA 98277-1271
phone: 360-675-8429 or 360-678-8787
Wants to buy Japanese powder horns, flint strikers, matchlocks and other samurai arms and armor; also wants to buy WWII Japanese swords.

POWDER JARS

Collectors

Darryl Rehr
2591 Military Ave.
Los Angeles, CA 90064-1933
phone: 310-477-5229
fax: 310-268-8420
e-mail: dcrehr@earthlink.net
Internet: http://www.earthlink.net/ ~dcrehr/
Wants all kinds of frosted figural glass powder jars with animals or other figures on the lid; please send photo.

PRECOLUMBIAN

Auction Services

Greg Manning
Greg Manning Auctions, Inc.
775 Passaic Ave.
West Caldwell, NJ 07006
phone: 201-882-0004 or 800-221-0243
fax: 201-882-3499
Since 1905, a leading auctioneer of Americana, glass, stoneware, and antiquities.

Dealers

Norman Hurst, ISA
Hurst Gallery
53 Mount Auburn St.
Cambridge, MA 02138
phone: 617-491-6888
fax: 617-661-0439
e-mail: hurst@world.std.com
Internet: http://world/std.com/~hurst/
Buys, sells, appraises, restores African, Oceanic, Native American, PreColumbian and Asian art.

Blackwater Gallery
4753 Summer Set
Rapid City, SD 57702
phone: 605-348-8684
fax: 605-342-6249
Buys and sells Precolumbian pottery from Panama, over 1000 years old; masks, figures.

John Buxton
Shango Galleries
6717 Spring Valley
Dallas, TX 75240
phone: 972-239-4620 or 972-239-9943
fax: 972-239-9766
e-mail: jbuxton@arttrak.com
Internet: http://www.arttrak.com
Buys, sells, and appraises African, Precolumbian, Oceanic, and American Indian art.

Joel & Michael Malter
Joel L. Malter & Co., Inc.
17005 Ventura Blvd.
Encino, CA 91316-4128
phone: 818-784-7772 or 818-784-2181
fax: 818-784-4726

David Markarian
Markarian Ancient Artifacts
P.O. Box 2476
Rancho Mirage, CA 92270
phone: 760-202-5000
Buys and sells Precolumbian artifacts.

Experts

Dr. Elizabeth Benson
8314 Old Seven Locks Rd.
Bethesda, MD 20817

Museums/Libraries

Dumbarton Oaks Research Library & Collection
1703 32nd St. NW
Washington, DC 20007
phone: 202-342-3200

Dr. Ramiro Matos
National Museum of Natural History
10th St. & Constitution Ave.
Washington, DC 20560
phone: 202-357-1300
Internet: http://www.si.edu/
Distinguished Peruvian archaeologist.

PREHISTORIC ARTIFACTS

(see also AMERICAN INDIAN; ARCHAEOLOGY; FOSSILS; HERITAGE RESOURCES; MINERALS)

Auction Services

Hesse Galleries
53 Main St.
Otego, NY 13825
phone: 607-988-6322

Robert N. Converse
199 Converse St.
Plain City, OH 43064
phone: 614-873-5471

Michael Steele
5665 Oak St., Rt. 605
Westerville, OH 43081
phone: 614-984-4612

Lolli Brothers
Hwy. 63 South
Macon, MO 63552
phone: 816-385-2516

Bob Sleeper
Bob Sleeper Auction Center
90 Elm
Higginsville, MO 64037
phone: 816-587-0019

Book Sellers

Larry Garvin
Back to Earth
17 North LaSalle Dr.
Zanesville, OH 43701-6238
phone: 614-454-0874

Collectors

Scott Young
P.O. Box 8452
Port Saint Lucie, FL 34985-8452
phone: 407-878-5634
Buys, sells, trades American Indian relics, pre-historic pottery, points, tools, bone, etc.; one item or whole collection.

Lar Hothem
Hothem House
P.O. Box 458
Lancaster, OH 43130-0458
phone: 614-653-9030
Wants prehistoric American Indian artifacts, mainly from Ohio.

Robert Pick
5375 Real Del Norte
Las Cruces, NM 88001

Dealers

Kevin Cordeiro
P.O. Box 579
Somerset, MA 02726
phone: 508-675-4886

John & Allan Atkins
Pocotaug Trading Post
P.O. Box 577
South Windsor, CT 06074-0577
phone: 203-644-4476

Bruce Cantrell
1223 Blossom Lane
Kingston, TN 37763
phone: 615-376-6451

W.T. Pinkston
466 W. Office St.
Harrodsburg, KY 40330
phone: 606-734-4213

Tom Davis
Tom Davis Artifacts
P.O. Box 386-272, Airport Rd.
Stanton, KY 40380
phone: 606-663-9871

Greg Shipley
6672 Maple St., Rt. 36
Cable, OH 43009
phone: 513-652-3020

Jim Justice
Quality Indian Artifacts
246 W. Ottawa St.
Richwood, OH 43344

W.B. Baughman
Mac-O-Chee Trading Co.
301 S. Taylor St.
West Liberty, OH 43357
phone: 513-465-4001

Larry Garvin
Back to Earth
17 North LaSalle Dr.
Zanesville, OH 43701-6238
phone: 614-454-0874

Ron Helman
1993 Dingman Slage Rd.
Sidney, OH 45365
phone: 513-492-2923

Gary Mumaw
549 East Main St.
Versailles, OH 45380
phone: 513-526-5687

Larry Lentz
First Mesa
P.O. Box 1256
South Bend, IN 46624
phone: 219-232-2095

Richard B. Troyanowski
Rich Relics
P.O. Box 432
Sandia Park, NM 87047-0432
phone: 505-281-2611 or 505-281-2329
Buys/sells prehistoric/historic Indian artifacts, cowboy, militaria, old world antiquities & coins, fossils & ethnographic collectibles.

Jerry Gaither
Tamarack Trading Co.
2785 Pacific Coast Hwy., Ste 333
Torrance, CA 90505
phone: 310-832-8996
Prehistoric and historic American Indian art and artifacts; all artifacts guaranteed; return within seven days for full refund if not satisfied; photos sent on request; full mail order service.

American Indian Artifacts
P.O. Box 60
Salinas, CA 93902-0060
phone: 805-238-6129

Experts

Col. L.D. Weidner
Indian River Industries
13706 Robbins Rd.
Westerville, OH 43081
phone: 614-965-2868 or 800-444-1280
Collector, dealer, and expert paying cash for Indian relics, both historic and prehistoric; author of many books on Indian relics.

Museums/Libraries

Anne Kaupp
National Museum of Natural History, Anthropology Public Information Office
Smithsonian
NHBMRC112
Washington, DC 20560
phone: 202-357-1592
Internet: http://www.si.edu/
With questions about found artifacts first try calling your State Archaeology department or the anthropology department of a local natural history museum.

Periodicals

Magazine: Indian-Artifact Magazine
RD 1 Box 240
Turbotville, PA 17772-9599
phone: 717-437-3698
An easy reading quarterly focusing on American Indian prehistory: artifacts, tools, lifestyles, customs, archaeology, book reviews.

Repair Services

Dennis Bushley
Quality Restoration
113 Pine Forest Dr.
Selma, AL 36701
phone: 205-875-5299

Jerry Jenkins
Rte. 5 Box 472
Cynthiana, KY 41031
phone: 606-234-3350

Charles F. Wood
Prehistoric Beauty
P.O. Box 504
Wellston, OH 45692
phone: 614-384-6551

Arrowheads & Points

Collectors

Dan Stroud
P.O. Box 636
Maple
Ontario L6A 1S5 Canada

Bobby & Pat Maples
Rte. 4 Box 990
Waynesboro, TN 38485
phone: 615-722-5981

Phil Cummins
RR2 Box 505C
Augusta, KY 41002
phone: 606-756-3296

Ricky Henson
Rte. 7 Box 325
Benton, KY 42035
phone: 502-527-0841

Ray Acra
323 Thomas Lane
Harrison, OH 45030
phone: 513-367-1744
Specializes in prehistoric lithics (stone items, e.g. arrowheads, points, clubs, bowls, etc.)

Larry Dyer
11175 S. 100 W.
Columbus, IN 47201
phone: 812-342-6398

Joe Lift
3616 Platte Ct.
Lafayette, IN 47905
phone: 317-447-2307

Ralph Strope
P.O. Box 952
Pekin, IL 61554
phone: 309-347-2570

Ed Meiners
219 Westwood
East Alton, IL 62024-1642
phone: 618-259-3764
One of the largest collectors in the US.

Kenneth Hamilton
416 South Walnut
Harrison, AR 72601
phone: 501-743-2175

Dealers

Roy Mitchell
3104 Glenmere Place, S.W.
Decatur, AL 35603
phone: 205-350-3103
Wants to buy Indian relics.

Experts

Richard B. Troyanowski
Rich Relics
P.O. Box 432
Sandia Park, NM 87047-0432
phone: 505-281-2611 or 505-281-2329
Specializes in prehistoric lithics (stone items, e.g. arrowheads, points, clubs, bowls, etc.)

PREMIUMS

(see also CEREAL BOXES; CRACKER JACK COLLECTIBLES; GROCERY STORE ITEMS; FAST FOOD COLLECTIBLES; PAPER COLLECTIBLES; POGS; TELEVISION SHOWS & MEMORABILIA)

Collectors

Bob Havey
P.O. Box 183
North Sullivan, ME 04664-0183
phone: 207-422-3083
fax: 207-422-3430
Wants radio and cereal box premiums: rings, badges, decoders, etc. from Superman, Tom Mix, Buck Rogers, cowboys, etc.

Ed Pragler
P.O. Box 284
Wharton, NJ 07885-0284
phone: 201-875-8293
Wants to buy radio premiums, box top and cereal giveaways, comic character collectibles: rings, decoders, badges, paper items, manuals, maps, pinback buttons, cereal boxes, etc. from Buck Rogers, Capt. America, Flash Gordon, etc.

Dealers

Ken Mitchell
710 Conacher Dr.
Willowdale
Ontario M2M 3N6 Canada
phone: 416-222-5808
Appraises, collects, buys and sells 1890 to 1970s comic books, newspapers, comic strips, "Big Little" books, popular music/jazz books/magazines/tapes; pulp magazines, original comic art, radio and cereal premiums.

Experts

Ted Hake
Hake's Americana & Collectibles Auction
P.O. Box 1444
York, PA 17405-1444
phone: 717-848-1333
Always purchasing items for 8 mail-bid auctions per year covering hundreds of categories including toys,

*character collectibles, Disney, cowboy
heroes, premiums, television,
politicals, pin-back buttons,
advertising and more.*

Ron Donnelly
Saturday Heroes
P.O. Box 7047
Panama City, FL 32413-0047
phone: 904-234-7944
fax: 904-233-9316
Specializes in radio and TV premiums.

Periodicals

Lisa Young
Magazine: Premium Collectors
Magazine
1125 Redman Ave.
Saint Louis, MO 63138
phone: 314-355-7144
fax: 314-355-7144
e-mail: 102522.3261@compuserve.com
*Features detailed information on all
current U.S. and overseas fast food
premiums and promotions, POGS,
crew pins, glassware, paper items,
memorabilia and more.*

Cereal Box

(see also CEREAL BOXES)

Collectors

Graham Trievel
P.O. Box 4811, Rt. 113
Lionville, PA 19353
phone: 610-942-4032
*Seeking cereal boxes and cereal box
prizes from the 1960s and 1970s; will
purchase or trade for items needed.*

Roland Coover
1537 E. Strasburg Rd.
West Chester, PA 19380-6380
phone: 610-692-3112
*Wants cereal items: cereal boxes,
premiums, and store displays from the
1950s to 1980s; Cap'n Crunch, Quisp,
Quake, Freakies, Frakenberry, King
Vitamin; also wants items from kids
products such as Bosco, Fizzies,
candy, cookies, etc.*

Kevin Meisner
5400 Cheshire Meadows Way
Fairfax, VA 22032-3216
phone: 703-527-3485
e-mail: slid-erkev@aol.com
*Wants to buy Freakies stuff: cereal
boxes, prizes from Freakies cereal,
Freakies figures, Freakies boats,
Freakies rings, Goody Goody Fruit
Hat figure, and the Hamhose Good
Friends Medal, magnets, flip-n-flys,
fun dots, etc.*

David Welch
P.O. Box 714
Murphysboro, IL 62966-0714
phone: 618-687-2282
fax: 618-684-2243
e-mail: PexDude1@aol.com
*Wants giveaway or send-away items
offered through cereal boxes and
relating to TV, sports, comic, cartoon*

*or movie characters, especially super
heroes.*

Experts

Tom Tumbusch
Tomart Publications
3300 Encrete Lane
Dayton, OH 45439-1944
phone: 513-294-2250
fax: 513-294-1024
*Buys radio, cereal, comic book, etc.
premiums, i.e. rings, badges, etc.;
author of "Illustrated Radio Premium
Catalog & Price Guide."*

Paula Geister
7 Fourth St.
Battle Creek, MI 49017

Periodicals

Joel Smilgis
Magazine: Box Top Bonanza
3403 46th Ave.
Moline, IL 61265
phone: 309-797-3677
*A bi-monthly magazine focusing on
radio & TV premiums, character,
comic, western, and adventure
collectibles.*

Comics

Collectors

John S. Fawcett
P.O. Box 1156
Waldoboro, ME 04572-1156
phone: 207-832-7398
*Wants to buy comic book subscription
giveaway premiums; pictures,
membership cards, Dell Comics
premiums; especially wants Disney
Gang at Circus picture - late 1940s.*

Radio Show

(see also CHARACTER COL-
LECTIBLES; COWBOY HEROES;
RADIO SHOWS, Old Time [Straight
Arrow], SPACE COLLECTIBLES)

Collectors

Bruce Thalberg
23 Mountain View Dr.
Weston, CT 06883-1317
phone: 203-227-8175
*Wants Lone Ranger, Sky King, Space
Patrol, Tom Mix, Roy Rogers, The
Shadow, Capt. Midnight, Terry & the
Pirates, etc., especially pre-1965
rings; all novelty rings considered;
photocopy helpful; please send SASE.*

Lee Levan
1525 Dauphin Ave.
Wyomissing, PA 19610
phone: 610-666-8902
*Buys, sells and trades radio premiums
or other old-time radio related
collectibles.*

David Welch
P.O. Box 714
Murphysboro, IL 62966-0714
phone: 618-687-2282
fax: 618-684-2243
e-mail: PexDude1@aol.com
*Wants giveaway or send-away items
offered through radio programs and
comic books relating to TV, sports,
comic, cartoon or movie characters,
especially super heroes.*

Rex Miller
Rte. 1 Box 457
East Prairie, MO 63845-9761
phone: 314-649-5048
*Wants pre-1960 items such as
Superman, Green Hornet, etc; top
wants include Sherlock Holmes HFC
Map of London, George Washington
Coffee Books, The Shadow Tecto-
Light.*

Dealers

Jim Harmon
Jim Harmon, Producer
634 South Orchard Dr.
Burbank, CA 91506
phone: 818-843-5472
*Buys, sells, trades radio premiums and
tapes, comic books, and comic strips;
author of "Radio Mystery &
Adventure," "Great Radio Heroes,"
"Great Movie Serials," "The Godzilla
Book," and "Monsters of the Movies"
magazine.*

Experts

Norm Vigue
62 Bailey St.
Stoughton, MA 02072
phone: 617-344-5441
*Wants to buy rings, decoders,
manuals, badges, store displays, etc.*

Tom Tumbusch
Tomart Publications
3300 Encrete Lane
Dayton, OH 45439-1944
phone: 513-294-2250
fax: 513-294-1024
*Buys radio, cereal, comic book, etc.
premiums, i.e. rings, badges, etc.;
author of "Illustrated Radio Premium
Catalog & Price Guide."*

Periodicals

Joel Smilgis
Magazine: Box Top Bonanza
3403 46th Ave.
Moline, IL 61265
phone: 309-797-3677
*A bi-monthly magazine focusing on
radio & TV premiums, character,
comic, western, and adventure
collectibles.*

Radio Show (Jimmie Allen)

Collectors

Jack Deveny
6805 Cheyenne Trail
Edina, MN 55439-1158
phone: 612-941-2457
*Wants Jimmie Allen Flying Club
wings, I.D. bracelets, knife, whistles,
maps, blotters, membership cards,
aircraft models, etc.*

Rings

Collectors

Steve A. Geppi
Diamond Comic Distributors
1966 Greenspring Dr., Ste. 300
Lutherville Timonium, MD 21093-4161
*Wants to buy old and rare comic
rings: Spider, Howdy Doody Jack-in-
the-Box, Cisco Kid Secret Compart-
ment, Tom Mix Spinner, Radio
Orphan Annie Altascope, Superman,
Lone Ranger Meteorite, Valric the
Viking, Joe Louis, etc.*

Dealers

Robert Overstreet
Overstreet Publications Inc.
11729 Mayfair Field Dr.
Lutherville Timonium, MD 21093-7011

Bruce Mohrhard
Mo's Comics
4530 Gravois
Saint Louis, MO 63116
phone: 314-353-9500

John Snyder
Comic Book Marketplace, The
P.O. Box 1980900
Coronado, CA 92178-0900

Experts

Danny Fuchs
209-80 18th Ave., #4K
Flushing, NY 11360-1451
phone: 718-225-9030
fax: 718-225-3688
*"America's foremost Superman
Collector"; co-author of "The
Adventures of Superman Collecting."*

Tom Tumbusch
Tomart Publications
3300 Encrete Lane
Dayton, OH 45439-1944
phone: 513-294-2250
fax: 513-294-1024
*Buys radio, cereal, and comic book,
premiums, i.e. rings, badges, etc.;
author of "Illustrated Radio Premium
Catalog & Price Guide."*

PRESIDENTIAL MEMORABILIA

(see PERSONALITIES [HISTORI-
CAL]; POLITICAL COLLECTIBLES;
WHITE HOUSE MEMORABILIA)

PRESSED WOOD ITEMS

Collectors

Carole Kaifer
P.O. Box 232
Bethania, NC 27010-0232
phone: 910-924-9672
Wants to buy various pressed wood items such as brush holders, thermometers, corkscrews, small figurines, wall plaques by companies such as Syrocowood and Durawood.

PRINTING EQUIPMENT

(see also BOOK ARTS)

Collectors

Juergen Berndt
6731 Ashley Ct.
Sarasota, FL 34241-9696
phone: 941-925-0385
fax: 941-925-0487
Wants to buy early printing presses, lithographic presses, typesetting hand presses, pre-1900 books on printing technology.

David W. Peat
1225 Carroll White
Indianapolis, IN 46219-3907
phone: 317-357-6895
Wants antique printers type, catalogs of printers type (typefounders specimen books), small presses, periodicals, stock certificates, medals, and other 19th cent. printing items.

James L. Weygand
P.O. Box 215
Nappanee, IN 46550-0215
phone: 219-773-4832
Wants tabletop printing presses, catalogs, instruction booklets, literature, equipment, accessories, etc.

Paul Aken
39221 N. Lewis
Zion, IL 60099-3344
phone: 847-746-8170 or 847-731-1945
Wants printing items: presses, type, tools, books, manuals, catalogs, toys, multigraphs, litho stones, etc.

Dealers

David Schwartz
Schwartz's Antique Printing
9214 New Albion Rd.
Little Valley, NY 14755-9771
phone: 716-938-9807
Wants to buy old printers type and cuts, type specimen books, old printing equipment & supply catalogs, books about printing, certificates and badges from printers unions; anything related to letter press printing.

Periodicals

Mike & Sally Phillips
Magazine: Printer, The
337 Wilsosn St.
Findlay, OH 45840

Type Founding Items

Collectors

David W. Peat
1225 Carroll White
Indianapolis, IN 46219-3907
phone: 317-357-6895
Wants old type casting (founding) equipment: hand molds, mats (matrices) for casting antique type, Bruce type caster, catalogs.

PRINTS

(see also ART; ILLUSTRATORS; COLLECTIBLES [MODERN], Prints; ILLUSTRATORS; MAPS & CHARTS; MOTTOES [PICTURE POEMS]; PAPER COLLECTIBLES; PERSONALITIES [ARTISTS]; POSTERS; REPAIR/RESTORATION/CONSERVATION, Paper Items; WALLACE NUTTING)

Appraisers

Charles B. Goldstein, ISA CAPP
Charles Barry International
8 Hardwicke Place
Rockville, MD 20850-3010
phone: 301-340-6775
fax: 301-340-1726
Buys, sells, and appraises fine Old Master, 19th and 20th century, modern and contemporary, American and European prints; Certified Member, International Society of Appraisers; expert witness and trial consultant.

Jerry Bengis, ISA
9860 SW 122nd St.
Miami, FL 33176-4928
phone: 305-232-1143
fax: 305-251-1450
Fine art appraiser specializing in prints (especially Salvador Dali), graphics (Miro, Chagall, Picasso, Warhol), etchings, engravings, prints, bronzes.

C. Van Northrup
Geolat & Associates
14110 Dallas Pkwy., #200
Dallas, TX 75240
phone: 972-239-9314
fax: 972-239-9313

Auction Services

Louis Webre, Client Svc.
William Doyle Galleries
175 E. 87th St.
New York, NY 10128-2205
phone: 212-427-2730
fax: 212-369-0892
Internet: http://www.doylegalleries.com
Holds over 30 auctions annually of antique English, Continental and American furniture, paintings, decorations, jewelry, vintage and couture clothing, collectible toys, books and prints; specialty auctions of Majolica, Lalique and wine.

Clubs/Associations

Nancy Braun
American Historical Print Collectors Society
Magazine: Imprint
P.O. Box 201
Fairfield, CT 06430-0201
phone: 203-255-1627 or 914-795-5266
Internet: http://www.ahpcs.org
Objectives are to the foster preservation, study and exhibition of historical American prints from the 17th through the 19th century; publishes "Imprint" magazine twice and "Newsletter" four times per year; scholarly meetings.

Dan Redmon
Print Club of New York
175 Fifth Ave., Ste. 2330
New York, NY 10010
Promotes prints and print making in New York.

International Fine Print Dealers Association
485 Madison Ave., 15th Floor
New York, NY 10022
phone: 212-759-4469
fax: 212-319-7752
Membership of prestigious print dealers by election only; publishes membership directory.

Dr. Charles J. Semowich
Print Club of Albany
Newsletter: Print Club of Albany Newsletter
P.O. Box 6578
Albany, NY 12206-0578
phone: 518-432-9514
e-mail: pca@crisny.org
Internet: http://crisny.org/not-for-profit/pcaprint/index.htm
Founded in 1933 for the purpose of promoting an appreciation of fine art prints among its members and ·community; each active member receives an original print; conducts lectures and workshops; holds artists papers in its archives.

Joe Davidson
American Antique Graphics Society
5185 Windfall Rd.
Medina, OH 44256-8703
phone: 330-723-7172
Members interested in graphic arts prints: from medieval, natural history to etchings, engravings.

Collectors

Joel Goleman
607 Chilton Hills Dr.
Elkins Park, PA 19117
Collector and lecturer on prints.

T.J. Ahlberg
1000 Irvine Blvd.
Tustin, CA 92680-3527
phone: 714-730-1000 or 714-654-1331
fax: 714-730-1752
Wants any prints or posters by artists Jo Mora, Till Goodan, Maynard Dixon, Joe De Yong, Frank Meachau, Ila McAfee, A.M. Cassandra and

original prints by C.M. Russell and Frederic Remington.

Dealers

Jim Messineo
JMW Gallery
144 Lincoln St.
Boston, MA 02111-2523
phone: 617-338-9097
fax: 617-338-7636

Tony Fusco
Fusco & Four, Associates
One Murdock Terrace
Brighton, MA 02135-2817
phone: 617-787-2637
fax: 617-782-4430
Specializing in 20th century European and American works on paper, 1900-1950, especially WPA, regionalists, and urban social realists; free quarterly illustrated lists.

Ernest S. Kramer
Ernest S. Kramer Fine Arts & Prints
P.O. Box 37
Wellesley Hills, MA 02181
phone: 617-237-3635
fax: 617-235-0112
Focuses on 19th and 20th century prints; always interested in purchasing singular works or collections of prints, drawings, watercolors or oil paintings.

Reg & Sally Lombard
Lombard Antiquarian Maps & Prints
P.O. Box 281
Cape Elizabeth, ME 04107
phone: 207-799-1889
fax: 207-799-9593
e-mail: lamr@cybertours.com
Internet: http://www.cybertours.com/~lamp
Specializes in fine maps, charts, rare botanical, natural history and architectural prints.

Robert Bessette
Green Dragon Arts
P.O. Box 588
Burlington, VT 05402-0588
phone: 802-862-1930
Has over 20,000 old prints to choose from; buys and sells 18th to early 20th century lithographs, etchings, woodcuts, chromolithographs, hand colored book plates, etc.

Ellen Sragow
Sragow Gallery
73 Spring St.
New York, NY 10012-5800
phone: 212-219-1793
American prints, paintings and works on paper 1920s through 1940s.

Kenneth Newman
Old Print Shop, The
150 Lexington Ave. at 30th St.
New York, NY 10016
phone: 212-683-3950
Wants 18th-20th century American prints; Currier & Ives, Endicott Hill,

large folio American town views, marines, maps, historicals.

Sylvan Cole
Sylvan Cole Gallery
101 W. 57th St.
New York, NY 10019
phone: 212-333-7760
Specializes in buying and selling American prints from the period 1900-1970; a specialty area is James Abbott McNeil Whistler.

Donald J. Bruckner
Bardon Antiques
37 August Lane
Hicksville, NY 11801-4419
phone: 516-931-5164
Wants to buy historical 19th century American lithographs; normally has 500-600 for sale.

Dr. Charles J. Semowich
Charles Semowich Fine Arts
242 Broadway
Rensselaer, NY 12144-2705
phone: 518-449-4756
Buys and sells prints, especially American 20th century. Also sells paintings and drawings.

Christopher W. Lane
Philadelphia Print Shop, Ltd., The
8441 Germantown Ave.
Philadelphia, PA 19118
phone: 215-242-4750
fax: 215-242-6977
e-mail: PhilaPrint@PhilaPrintShop.com
Gallery of antique prints and maps with related rare books and atlases; also bookstore of reference books related to antique prints and maps; appraisals, paper conservation and restoration, museum quality framing.

W. Graham Arader III
1000 Boxwood Court
King Of Prussia, PA 19406
phone: 610-825-6570
Buys & sells Audubon and other fine prints: Indians, natural history, sporting,, Currier & Ives, etc.; also maps, paintings and books.

Debra Bartusek
Martin Lawrence Galleries
Washington Park
3222 M St. NW
Washington, DC 20007
phone: 202-965-4811
fax: 202-965-0796
Specializes in contemporary print artists with a focus on those artists which they publish.

Barbara Dawson
P&C Art
3301 M St. NW
Washington, DC 20007
phone: 202-965-4630
Specializes in contemporary print artists; also carries the "Gum Shoe" line of polychrome ceramic figurines by Marcus Pierson.

Judith Blakely
Old Print Gallery, The
1220 31st St. NW
Washington, DC 20007-3422
phone: 202-965-1818
fax: 202-965-1869
Wants antique prints: city views, historical scenes, Currier & Ives, Western, natural history, sporting, military and nautical scenes.

John Dupree
Creighton-Davis Gallery
3300 M St. NW
Washington, DC 20007-3513
phone: 202-333-3050
fax: 202-338-4470
Specializes in contemporary, old and modern print artists with national and international reputations.

Monica Burdeshaw
Print Portfolio
4701 Sangamore Rd.
Bethesda, MD 20816
phone: 301-229-5800
Buys and sells fine prints.

Richard Kornemann
Museum Shop, Ltd.
20 N. Market St.
Frederick, MD 21701
phone: 301-695-0424 or 301-871-3855
fax: 301-698-5242
Specializes in Japanese ukiyoe woodblock prints, and 1930s era by Grant Wood, Whistler, T.H. Benton, WPA artists, etc.

David Allen
David Allen Fine Art
P.O. Box 5641
Arlington, VA 22205
Dealer and expert specializing in 19th & 20th century American prints.

Robert Wieland
American Antique Prints
33 S. St. Andrews Dr.
Ormond Beach, FL 32174-3842
phone: 904-672-9972
Member, American Historical Print Collectors Society.

Susan S. Pohle, ISA
Pigeon Creek Antiques
621 N. Main
Thiensville, WI 53092-1215
phone: 414-242-2054
Sells and appraises fine art prints, period furniture, lamps, toys, dolls.

Elaine Kwan
Newsletter: Art Collectors Quarterly, The
860 Cedar Lane
Northbrook, IL 60062-3538
phone: 847-564-1660 or 847-205-1459
fax: 847-564-1660
e-mail: fineart@compuserve.com
Internet: http://ourworld.compuserve.com/homepages/FineArt
Buys and sells modern and contemporary art; resale; fine art appraiser; collections cataloging; member,

Appraisers Association of America (AAA).

Sharon M. Gergen
Nostalgia Antiques
8141 Main
Kansas City, MO 64114-2401
phone: 816-361-7539
e-mail: fcum65a@prodigy.com
Buys and sells oil paintings, prints, illustrated books, pin-ups.

Experts

William G. Hodges
Ridgefield, Inc.
12509 Patterson Ave.
Richmond, VA 23233-6414
phone: 703-768-6562
Specializes in buying and selling antique prints.

Misc. Services

Wendy Reaves, Cur.
National Portrait Gallery
Prints & Drawings
8th & F Streets N.W.
Washington, DC 20560
phone: 202-357-1356 or 202-357-1633
Internet: http://www.si.edu/
Will authenticate prints & drawings brought in for inspection; make an appointment first; may be able to work from good photographs.

Gordon's Art Reference, Inc.
Price Guide: Gordon's Print Price Annual
306 West Coronado Rd.
Phoenix, AZ 85003
phone: 602-253-6948 or 800-892-4622
fax: 602-253-2104
e-mail: info@gordonart.com
Internet: http://www.gordonart.com
Print values: 1,400 pages of facts, figures, descriptions, prices; 37,000 actual prices realized; now on CD-ROM.

Museums/Libraries

Museum of Prints & Printmaking
P.O. Box 6578
Albany, NY 12206-0578
phone: 518-432-9514
e-mail: pca@crisny.org
Internet: http://crisny.org/not-for-profit/pcaprint/index.htm
Shares space with the Print Club of Albany; open by appointment.

Periodicals

Newspaper: Journal of the Print World
1008 Winona Rd.
Meredith, NH 03253
phone: 603-279-6479
fax: 603-279-1337
A quarterly newspaper with articles, advertising and classifieds focusing on antique and contemporary prints and artists; features articles, ads, auction results, show reviews, calendar of events.

Journal: On Paper
39 E 78th St., #601
New York, NY 10021-0213
phone: 212-988-5959
fax: 212-988-6107
Published bi-monthly, this journal reports on the entire print and photograph market and is considered a must by print collectors and dealers; also contains scholarly articles and reviews, and auction results.

Denis C. Jackson, Ed.
Newsletter: Illustrator Collector's News, The
P.O. Box 1958
Sequim, WA 98382-1958
phone: 360-683-2559
fax: 360-683-2559
e-mail: ticn@olypen.com
Internet: http://www.olypen.com/ticn/
A bi-monthly publication for collectors of magazines and other paper illustrations; free classifieds for subscribers; send LSASE for information; new and old prints.

Repair Services

George J. Cohenour
4301 Beaumont Rd.
Dover, PA 17315-2405
phone: 717-292-5345
Cleans, deacidifies, repairs and restores prints: American historical, antique and decorative, handcolored lithographs, chromolithographs, etchings, engravings, watercolors, etc.

Suppliers

Cronite Co., The
P.O. Box 6330
Parsippany, NJ 07054
phone: 201-887-7900
Suppliers to engravers, etchers, and print makers for 100 years; plate printing inks and oils, steel/copper/zinc/brass plates, pantograph machines and supplies, etching acids/acid resists, photoengraving supplies, engraving tools.

Audubon

Dealers

Peter D. Cowen
225 Riverview Ave.
Waltham, MA 02154
phone: 617-899-1955
fax: 617-899-5081
Wants to buy museum-quality Audubon prints.

Bob Bascom
Bob Bascom Prints
P.O. Box 4327
Burlington, VT 05406
phone: 802-893-4082
Wants Audubon original prints; also other medium or large 19th century American prints.

Ed Kenney
Audubon Prints & Books
9720 Spring Ridge Ln.
Vienna, VA 22182-1449
phone: 703-759-5567 or 202-484-3334
Internet: http://www.infl.com/
audobonprints
*Buys & sells natural history prints
and books by John James Audubon;
also prints by Wilson, Gould, Catesby,
Bodmer, Catlin and others.*

Taylor Clark
Taylor Clark Gallery
2623 Government St.
Baton Rouge, LA 70806-5408
phone: 504-383-4929
fax: 504-383-3043
*Specializes in 18th, 19th, and 20th
century oil paintings, watercolors,
and prints, especially all editions of
Audubon prints.*

Museums/Libraries

John James Audubon State Park and
Museum
P.O. Box 576
Henderson, KY 42420
phone: 502-826-2247 or 502-827-1893
fax: 502-826-2286

Cupid

Clubs/Associations

Juanita Ingles
Cupid Collectors Club
Newsletter: Cupid Capers
2116 Lincoln St.
Cedar Falls, IA 50613-3274
phone: 319-266-9902 or 319-273-8458
fax: 319-266-9902
e-mail: ingles@cedarnet.org
Internet: http://www.pvis.com/cupids/
cupids.shtml/
*Purpose of this club is to promote the
appreciation of Cupid prints of all
types including the M.B. Parkinson
"Cupid Awake and Cupid Asleep"
print.*

Collectors

Cindy & Jerry Youngquist
P.O. Box 91
Gowrie, IA 50543

Juanita Ingles
2116 Lincoln St.
Cedar Falls, IA 50613-3274
phone: 319-266-9902 or 319-273-8458
fax: 319-266-9902
e-mail: ingles@cedarnet.org
Internet: http://www.pvis.com/cupids/
cupids.shtml/

Glen Tull
402 W. Montgomery
Creston, IA 50801
phone: 515-782-2335

Currier & Ives

Dealers

Bob Bascom
Bob Bascom Prints
P.O. Box 4327
Burlington, VT 05406
phone: 802-893-4082
*Wants Currier and Ives original
prints; also other medium or large
19th century American prints.*

Donald J. Bruckner
Bardon Antiques
37 August Lane
Hicksville, NY 11801-4419
phone: 516-931-5164
*Wants to buy historical 19th century
American lithographs; normally has
500-600 for sale; especially interested
in Currier & Ives.*

Robert Searjeant
P.O. Box 23942
Rochester, NY 14692
phone: 716-424-2489
*An avid collector and dealer in
Currier & Ives prints; has exhibited
his collection at museums and
galleries, and has written numerous
articles about Currier & Ives prints.*

George J. Cohenour
4301 Beaumont Rd.
Dover, PA 17315-2405
phone: 717-292-5345
*Buys and sells original Currier & Ives
lithographs; carries large selection
and offers a free list; also offers
cleaning and restoration service.*

Robert Wieland
American Antique Prints
33 S. St. Andrews Dr.
Ormond Beach, FL 32174-3842
phone: 904-672-9972
*A dedicated collector and dealer in
Currier & Ives prints for over 30
years; also buys & sells Kurz &
Allison, and McKenny-Hall prints;
quarterly itemized lists of prints
available.*

Experts

John & Barbara Rudisill
Rudisill's Alt Print Haus
P.O. Box 199
Worton, MD 21678-0199
phone: 410-778-9290
fax: 410-778-9310
*Buys and sells original Currier & Ives
prints; have written articles on the
history of Currier & Ives and on
identifying reproductions; send SASE
for free list.*

Museums/Libraries

Leslie Nolen
Museum of the City of New York
1220 5th Ave.
New York, NY 10029-5221
phone: 212-534-1672
fax: 212-534-5974
*Access by appointment; research fee
charged.*

Repair Services

Robert Kipp
Antique Print Restorations
16 Wedgemere Rd.
Beverly, MA 01915-1435
phone: 508-922-6852
*A noted expert and authority on
Currier & Ives prints; cleans, restores
and conserves prints for clients
throughout the U.S.; send for
brochure; author of "Currier's Price
Guide to Currier & Ives Prints."*

Dali

Appraisers

Jerry Bengis, ISA
9860 SW 122nd St.
Miami, FL 33176-4928
phone: 305-232-1143
fax: 305-251-1450
*Fine art appraiser specializing in
prints (especially Salvador Dali),
graphics (Miro, Chagall, Picasso,
Warhol), etchings, engravings, prints,
bronzes.*

Bernard Ewell, ASA
Bernard Ewell Art Appraisals
318 E. Cache La Poudre
Colorado Springs, CO 80903-2905
phone: 719-632-5035 or 800-884-3254
fax: 719-633-0959
*International expert on all Salvador
Dali artworks.*

Dealers

Janice King
Salvador Dali Gallery, The/Brana Fine
` Art Inc.
15332 Antioch St., Ste. 108
Pacific Palisades, CA 90272
phone: 310-459-8883 or 800-275-3254
fax: 310-454-2090

Experts

Albert Field
Salvador Dali Archives, The
2020 29th St.
Astoria, NY 11105
phone: 718-274-0407

Museums/Libraries

Salvador Dali Museum, The
1000 Third St. South
Saint Petersburg, FL 33701-4925
phone: 813-823-3767
e-mail: qvbg71a@prodigy.com
*Permanent home to the world's most
comprehensive collection of works
exclusively by the late SPanish
surrealist, Salvador Dali; 94 original*

oils, over 100 watercolors and
drawings, holograms, objects of art
and photographs.

French Boudoir

Dealers

Cliff Catania
David Chase Gallery
234 Griffen St.
Phoenixville, PA 19460-4419
*Wants Icart-like etchings by Ablett,
Grellet, Felix, Helleu, Milliere, Robbe,
Hardy, Meunier, etc.*

Icart

Collectors

Adrienne Leff
1550 S Dixie Hwy. #210
Miami, FL 33146-3034
phone: 305-667-4214
fax: 305-668-2592
*Buys, sell and collects original Louis
Icart etchings, oils and complete
books.*

Dr. Neil Superfon
2121 W. Indian School Rd.
Phoenix, AZ 85015
phone: 602-277-1449 or 800-258-0216
fax: 602-263-8523
Wants to buy Icart etchings.

Paul Kelly
24672 Belgreen Place
Lake Forest, CA 92630
phone: 714-770-1483
fax: 714-770-1483
*Buys, sells and collects Louis Icart
etchings, oils, and illustrated books.*

Dealers

Edward J. Meschi
129 Pinyard Rd.
Monroeville, NJ 08343-1870
phone: 609-358-7293
fax: 609-358-7293
*Buys and sells Louis Icart etchings,
illustrated books, and oil paintings.*

Cliff Catania
David Chase Gallery
234 Griffen St.
Phoenixville, PA 19460-4419
*Buys and sells original Icart etchings;
assisting major collectors. Author of
"Complete Etchings of Louis Icart"
(1990-Schiffer Pub.)*

Debra Freer
Williams & Freer Fine Art & Antiques
Newsletter: Louis Icart Collector, The
2480-4 Briarcliff Rd., #201
Briarcliff, GA 30329
phone: 404-321-6369
fax: 404-315-9569
*Buys and sells original Icart etchings,
artwork and illustrated books;
publishes quarterly newsletter "The
Louis Icart Collector" which is
available for $10/yr.*

Experts

Carole Hibel
John Hibel Antiques
185 Yerry Hill Rd.
Woodstock, NY 12498
phone: 914-679-2966 or 800-426-3357
fax: 914-679-3397
Wants to buy Louis Icart etchings and paintings.

Bill Holland
William Holland Fine Arts
1708 E. Lancaster Ave.
Paoli, PA 19301-1553
phone: 610-648-0369
fax: 610-647-4448
Buys and sells Louis Icart etchings, oils and illustrated books; co-author of "Louis Icart - The Complete Etchings"; call for details or to order.

Bruce Marine
Cherub Antiques Gallery
2918 M. St. NW
Washington, DC 20007-3713
phone: 202-337-2224
fax: 202-337-2224
Nationally known author of articles, and leading expert in original Louis Icart etchings; also wants etchings and pastels by Paul Cesar Helleu.

Leroy Neiman

Dealers

Ralph Olsen
Hammer Graphics Gallery
33 W. 57th St.
New York, NY 10019
phone: 212-644-4405

Prang-Mark

Clubs/Associations

Prang-Mark Society
Newsletter: Prang-Mark Society Newsletter
1601 Sheridan Lane
Norristown, PA 19403-3336

Vanity Fair (Spy)

Collectors

Paul Davis
308 Landsende Rd.
Devon, PA 19333
phone: 610-644-1216
Wants Vanity Fair "Spy" caricature prints.

Ken Taylor
11661 San Vicente, #211
Los Angeles, CA 90049-5110
phone: 310-442-0054
fax: 310-826-6934
e-mail: ktscicon@ix.netcom.com
Wants to buy original Vanity Fair lithographs ("Spy" prints) published in England from 1869 to 1913.

Wallace Nutting

Collectors

Bob & Pam Franscella
234 Ivanhoe Glen
Madison, WI 53711
phone: 608-274-4506

Jim & Sharon Eckert
P.O. Box 62
Anchor, IL 61720-0062
phone: 309-723-4241
e-mail: jreckert@aol.com
Wants Wallace Nutting, Bessie Pease Gutmann and Maxfield Parrish prints.

Wildlife

Museums/Libraries

American Museum of Natural History
Central Park West & 79th St.
New York, NY 10024
phone: 212-769-5000

Woodblock

Dealers

Steven Thomas
Steven Thomas, Inc.
P.O. Box 41
Woodstock, VT 05091-0041
phone: 802-457-1764 or 800-781-8028
Dealer/expert wants to buy American, European and Canadian woodblock prints from 1895-1950; color or black and white; interested in strong images by major and minor artists alike; write for free 4 page illustrated want list.

Woodblock (American)

Dealers

Peter Falk
P. Hastings Falk, Inc.
859 Boston Post Rd.
Madison, CT 06443
phone: 203-245-2246 or 203-849-1655
fax: 203-245-5116
Buys and sells color woodblock prints by American artists; 1890s to 1920s.

Woodblock (Jacoulet)

Auction Services

John H. Schofield
Eldred's
P.O. Box 796
East Dennis, MA 02641-0796
phone: 508-385-3116
fax: 508-385-7201
Internet: http://capecod.net/eldreds
Specializes in the sale of 20th century Japanese-style woodblock prints by artist Paul Jacoulet.

Woodblock (Japanese)

(see also ART, Oriental; ORIENTALIA)

Clubs/Associations

Rosemary Torre, Pres.
Ukiyo-E Society of America, Inc.
Newsletter: President's Newsletter
FDR Station
P.O. Box 665
New York, NY 10150-0665
Promotes the study/appreciation of Japanese woodblock prints through monthly meetings, seminars & exhibitions; also publishes Journal.

Collectors

Georgia Cash
10799 SW 44th St.
Miami, FL 33165
phone: 305-223-6050

Bob Vargas
P.O. Box 60611
Sunnyvale, CA 94088
phone: 415-949-3959
e-mail: bvargas@ix.netcom.com
Wants 20th century and older Japanese woodblock prints.

Dealers

G. C. Uhlenbeck
Hotei Japanese Prints
Breestraat 113a
23211 CL Leiden
The Netherlands
phone: (071) 514 35 52/512 44 59
fax: (071) 514 14 88/512 38 55
e-mail: ukiyoe@xs4all.nl
Fine Japanese prints, paintings and illustrated books by appointment.

John Clement
John Clement Fine Art
36 Oakwood Ave.
Fitchburg, MA 01420-7421
phone: 508-345-5863
Special interests include worldwide master works of art, particularly works on paper, including Japanese woodblock prints; also fine paintings.

Valerie Zakszewski
61 6th St.
Cambridge, MA 02141
phone: 800-897-2933
Specializes in works of art on paper.

Roni Neuer
Ronin Gallery
605 Madison Ave.
New York, NY 10022
Specializes in Japanese woodblock prints and publishes catalogs on specialty artists.

John Bradley
John Bradley Gallery
1020 Burlingham Rd.
Pine Bush, NY 12566
phone: 914-744-3642
Buys and sells Japanese woodblock prints.

Gilbert Luber Gallery
1220 Walnut St.
Philadelphia, PA 19107-5466
phone: 215-732-2996
fax: 215-546-2210
Specializes in Japanese woodblock prints; also carries general books on Japanese prints and art.

Elizabeth Danechild
Ukiyo-E Gallery
4736 Seventeenth St.
San Francisco, CA 94117-4329
phone: 415-731-5971
fax: 415-753-3415
Buys and sells Japanese color woodblock prints from the 18th to early 20th centuries; by appointment.

Carolyn Staley
Carolyn Staley Fine Prints
313 First Ave. South
Seattle, WA 98104-2505
phone: 206-621-1888
fax: 206-325-9047
Buys and sells fine Japanese woodblock prints, 16th - 20th century master prints, and decorative prints and maps.

Experts

Paul R. Schweitzer
Schweitzer Japanese Prints, Inc.
6313 Lenox Rd.
Bethesda, MD 20817-6023
phone: 301-229-6574
fax: 301-229-0345
Buys, sells, appraises antique Japanese woodblock prints as well as contemporary Japanese graphics including woodblocks, etchings, etc.; also sells books about Japanese culture and graphics.

Museums/Libraries

Honolulu Academy of Fine Arts
900 S. Beretania St.
Honolulu, HI 96814
phone: 808-538-3693

Yard-Long

Collectors

Al Little
151 Highway 173
Antioch, IL 60002
phone: 847-395-7752
fax: 847-395-7703
Buys and sells yard-long prints.

Sherry & Mike Miller
303 Holiday Dr. #130
Tuscola, IL 61953-2118
phone: 217-253-4991
e-mail: miller@tuscola.net
Wants to buy yard-long lithograph prints; only of lovely ladies dressed in 1900-1920s fashions; some have been trimmed to fit smaller frames; some have artist's name on front; most have advertising and small calendar on back.

Experts

Bill & June Keagy
Those Wonderful Yard-Long Prints &
More
P.O. Box 106
Bloomfield, IN 47424-0106
phone: 812-384-3471
*Co-authors with Charles and Joan
Rhoden of "Those Wonderful Yard-
Long Prints and More", and "More
Wonderful Yard-Long Prints - Book
II" (late 1995); books available from
the author; also wants to buy yard-
long prints.*

Charles & Joan Rhoden
Rhoden's Antiques
605 N. Main
Georgetown, IL 61846-1439
phone: 217-662-8046 or 217-662-8440
fax: 217-662-8223
e-mail: jmrhoden@prairienet.org
*Buys and collects yard-long prints;
co-author of "Those Wonderful Yard-
Long Prints," Books I and II which
are available from the author.*

PRISON RELATED ITEMS

(see LAW ENFORCEMENT
MEMORABILIA)

PRISONER-OF-WAR ART

Straw

Dealers

Lucille Malitz
Lucid Antiques
P.O. Box KH
Scarsdale, NY 10583
phone: 914-636-7825 or 914-636-5171

PROGRAMS

(see MOVIE MEMORABILIA;
PAPER COLLECTIBLES; SPORTS
COLLECTIBLES)

PROHIBITION ITEMS

(see also BREWERIANA; PERSON-
ALITIES [CRIMINAL]; POLITICAL
COLLECTIBLES; SALOON & BAR
COLLECTIBLES; WHISKEY
INDUSTRY ITEMS)

Clubs/Associations

Earl F. Dodge
Partisan Prohibition Historical Society
Newsletter: National Statesman, The
P.O. Box 2635
Denver, CO 80201
phone: 303-572-0646 or 303-237-4947
*Wants to buy all Prohibition related
items*

Collectors

Cary Demont
P.O. Box 16013
Minneapolis, MN 55416-0013
phone: 612-922-1617
*Wants political pre-1964 buttons,
pins, flags, ribbons, banners, and the*

*unusual; also suffrage, prohibition,
slavery, and Lindbergh.*

Experts

Michael Y. Graham
Chicago's Roaring 20's
33133 N Oplaine Rd.
Gurnee, IL 60031-3445
phone: 708-263-6285
*Specializes in prohibition-era (1919-
1933) gangster, speakeasy, political,
breweriana, saloon-items; emphasis
on Chicago area; anti-saloon league,
W.C.T.U., A.A.P.A., Treasury Dept.
Bureau of Prohibition; Hoover,
Roosevelt, Harding.*

Richard M. Bueschel
414 N. Prospect Manor Ave.
Mount Prospect, IL 60056-2046
phone: 847-253-0791
fax: 847-253-7919
e-mail: BuschlHist@aol.com
*Wants speakeasy photos, business
cards, paper ephemera, flappers, rum
running, liquor trade personalities,
etc.; send SASE if requesting a reply.*

PROMOTERS

(see ANTIQUES SHOWS PROMOT-
ERS)

PROPHYLACTICS

Tins

Collectors

Bob Weissman
P.O. Box 163
Stewartsville, NJ 08886
phone: 908-479-6494
fax: 908-479-1135
*Wants condom tins in excellent
condition.*

Dennis & George
323 Sandpiper Lane
Delray Beach, FL 33483-7135
phone: 561-243-3072
*Wants condom tins, especially Rough
Rider, 3 Pirates, Akron Tourist Tubes.*

Michael Dusek
1058 Lupin Dr. #5
Salinas, CA 93906
phone: 408-757-2526
*Wants prophylactic/condom tins:
Sphinx, Chariots, Napoleons, Carmen,
etc.; also wants related advertising.*

Vending Machines

Collectors

Mr. Condom
17964 Acorn Ano Rd.
Somerset, KY 42501
phone: 606-274-4848
*Buys/sells collectible prophylactic and
feminine hygiene vending equipment
and related items; catalog $2.*

PSYCHEDELIC ITEMS

(see SOCIAL CAUSES, Hippie Items)

PUB JUGS

(see SALOON & BAR COL-
LECTIBLES, Whiskey Pitchers)

PUPPETS

(see also PERFORMING ARTS;
VENTRILOQUIST ITEMS)

Clubs/Associations

Puppetry Guild of Greater Kansas City
Newsletter: PGGKC Newsletter
11711 Markham Rd.
Independence, MO 64052
phone: 816-252-7248
*Send SASE for price list of Hazelle
parts available.*

Gayle Schluter
Puppeteers of America, Inc.
Magazine: Puppetry Journal
#5 Cricklewood Path
Pasadena, CA 91107-1002

Collectors

Tim Isaacson
1002 Clinton
Oak Park, IL 60304-1824
phone: 708-383-5646
*Wants to buy professional ventrilo-
quist figures and wooden dummies
used by professional stage performers; please send photo.*

Andy Gross
P.O. Box 6134
Beverly Hills, CA 90212-1134
phone: 310-820-3308 or 310-285-8815
fax: 310-768-1097
e-mail: apedoll69@aol.com
*Wants ventriloquist dummies and or
any related items such as puppets,
toys, games, photos, books,
marionettes, and old pro & toy
dummies, i.e. Jerry Mahoney,
Knucklehead Smiff, Charlie
McCarthy, Mortimer Snerd, Danny
O'Day, Farfel, etc.*

Museums/Libraries

Ontario Puppetry Association Museum
171 Avondale Ave.
Willowdale
Ontario M2N 2V4 Canada
phone: 416-222-9029

Bread & Puppet Museum
Rte. 122
Glover, VT 05839
phone: 802-525-3031
*A giant collection of puppets, masks
and related graphics and paintings.*

Library & Museum of the Performing
Arts, Shelby Cullom Davis Museum
111 Amsterdam Ave.
New York, NY 10023
phone: 212-870-1613

PURSES

(see also ALLIGATOR BAGS;
BEADS; CLOTHING & ACCESSO-
RIES, Vintage; COMPACTS;
DRESSER ITEMS)

Clubs/Associations

Molly Klumpfell
California Purse Collector's Club
Newsletter: California Purse Collectors'
Club Newsletter
P.O. Box 572
Campbell, CA 95009
phone: 408-866-6250
*Members from across the US learn
how to collect antique purses, store
them, identify styles/type/quality;
historical info on pre-1940 purses;
holds meetings to swap and sell in the
San Francisco area.*

Collectors

Lydia M. Jackson-Fryer
608 Winans Way
Baltimore, MD 21229-1430
phone: 410-233-3317
*Wants to buy antique purses: mesh,
beaded, Bakelite, cloth, leather.*

Vallerie Roberts Shutterly
Victorian Touch
P.O. Box 4
Micanopy, FL 32667
phone: 352-466-4022
fax: 351-591-2872
*Wants to buy gorgeous antique purses
with jeweled frames, scenes of people,
romantic couples, landscapes, castles,
flowers, gardens, Egyptian, Persian
rug designs; one-of-a-kind beaded,
petitpoint, embroidered, or tapestry.*

Barbara Hobbs
5501 101st Ave. N
Pinellas Park, FL 33782-3311
phone: 813-541-6164
e-mail: wfhbbm@aol.com
Wants to buy beaded purses.

Purses
P.O. Box 6019
Chesterfield, MO 63006
phone: 314-227-0634
*Wants scenic and figural beaded
purses; also wants hand tooled Art
Nouveau leather bags.*

Jennifer Sykes
Jennifer Sykes Antiques
9018 Balboa Blvd. #595
Northridge, CA 91325-2610
phone: 818-993-1916
fax: 818-993-7612
e-mail: Veeda10@aol.com
*Wants purses and vanity bags: mesh,
enamel, bead, Bakelite, or celluloid;
also wants girlie items such as mugs,
ashtrays, figurines, novelties, etc.*

Betsy Stubbs
28545 Felix Valdez B-2
Temecula, CA 92590
phone: 909-694-8113
*Wants to buy hard plastic purses from
the 1950s.*

Verity
P.O. Box 2316
Newport Beach, CA 92659-1316
*Wants antique purses; beaded, mesh
or leather.*

Molly Klumpfell
Purse Snatchers
P.O. Box 572
Campbell, CA 95009
phone: 408-866-6250
Wants to buy pre-1930 antique purses in good to excellent condition; wants unusual purses such as scenic beaded, carpet bags; also buys collections; send clear photo, or zerox copies with complete description; will respond in 5 days.

Leslie Holmes
P.O. Box 596
Los Gatos, CA 95031-0596
phone: 408-354-1626
Wants to buy pre-1930s beaded purses with scenes of people and places, abstracts, Persian carpet motifs; also wants enameled mesh, bright colors, bold designs; damaged purses are OK.

Dealers

Priscilla Washed
Victorian Lady, The
102 South Main St.
P.O. Box 424
Waxhaw, NC 28173-0424
phone: 704-843-4467 or 800-786-1886
A Victorian specialty store featuring 19th century ladies decorative & fashion accessories; buys and sells purses; also sewing and needlework tools, vintage fashion, Victoriana, and combs; mail order; catalog $5.

Gail & John Dunn
P.O. Box 234
Waterville, OH 43566
phone: 419-878-9515
Buys and sells vintage purses and hatpins.

Veronica Trainer
Bayhouse
P.O. Box 40442
Bay Village, OH 44140-0442
phone: 216-871-8584
Buys and sells purses by mail order; advisor to "Schroeder's Antiques Price Guide"; specializes in beaded and enameled mesh purses; paying top dollar for scenics and purses with jeweled and ornate frames; also wants damaged purses.

Anita Davis
Baaglady
P.O. Box 7238
Little Rock, AR 72217
phone: 501-666-7631
e-mail: aadavis@baaglady.com
Internet: http://www.baaglady.com
Large selection of vintage purses and jewelry from the 1920s to 1970s; from the sublime to the ridiculous.

Experts

Irene M. Spaulding
1487 Old North Main St.
Laconia, NH 03246-2684
Specialist in antique purses and vintage clothing.

Roselyn Gerson
P.O. Box 100
Malverne, NY 11565
phone: 516-593-8746
fax: 516-593-0611
Author of "Vintage Vanity Bags & Purses."

Roseann Ettinger
Remember When
2 E. Broad St.
Hazleton, PA 18201-6530
phone: 717-454-8465 or 717-450-5542
Author of "Handbags."

Sherry & Mike Miller
303 Holiday Dr. #130
Tuscola, IL 61953-2118
phone: 217-253-4991
e-mail: miller@tuscola.net
Wants to buy painted ring mesh & enameled flat mesh purses made in the 1920s and 1930s with ornate framed and compact/mesh bag combinations, or with painted designs; must be in mint or near-mint condition; also wants ads for mesh purses.

Suzi Mounts
Perfect Purse, The
15466 Los Gatos Blvd. 109-315
Los Gatos, CA 95032
phone: 408-559-4172

Museums/Libraries

Museum of Fine Arts, Boston
465 Huntington Ave.
Boston, MA 02115-5523
phone: 617-267-9300
Internet: http://www.mfa.org/home.html
An outstanding collection of purses.

Bette Johnson
Whiting & Davis Handbag Museum
200 John Dietsch Blvd.
North Attleboro, MA 02763
phone: 508-699-7639
Vintage mesh handbags and memorabilia from the late 1800s to present; also early mesh machine on display.

Repair Services

Suzi Mounts
Suzi's Purse Restoration, The
15466 Los Gatos Blvd. 109-315
Los Gatos, CA 95032
phone: 408-559-4172
Professionally repairs pre-1940 antique purses; specializes in relining, fringing, and reframing beaded purses; can also repair metal ring mesh purses, and broken clasps; call first to discuss your needs. Send purse for exact quote.

PUZZLES

(see also GAMES; PAPER COLLECTIBLES)

Clubs/Associations

American Game Collectors Association
Newsletter: Game Times
49 Brooks Ave.
Lewiston, ME 04240-5901
phone: 215-674-1072
Internet: http://www.agca.com/~rfinn/agca.htm
Focuses on board and card games as well as puzzles, playing cards, tops, yo-yos, and action games; also publishes "Game Researchers' Notes" - reports on member's research.

Sibyl Bagai
National Puzzler's League
Newsletter: Enigma, The
P.O. Box 82289
Portland, OR 97282
The oldest puzzle organization in the U.S.; members interested in word, letter and sound games.

Collectors

David Frankel
P.O. Box 41
Kinckerbocker Station
New York, NY 10002-0041
phone: 212-473-5321
Wants old puzzles: secret opening boxes, banks, match safes, trick locks, put-together (not jigsaw), take-apart, sequential movement, impossible objects, and other mechanical puzzles.

Crosswords

Collectors

Will Shortz
55 Great Oak Lane
Pleasantville, NY 10570-2010
phone: 914-769-9128
fax: 212-727-7661
e-mail: wshortz@aol.com
Wants to buy crossword puzzles: books and magazine.

Jigsaw

Collectors

Denis Pinsonnault
Puzzles Anciens
225 Grant
Longueuil
Quebec J4H 3H8 Canada
phone: 514-679-6365
Wants pre-1950 wooden and cardboard jigsaw puzzles.

Jim Rohacs
9721 Lomond Dr.
Manassas, VA 22110-3104
phone: 703-369-5578
Wants pre-1950s puzzles.

Dealers

Robert J. Bergeron
CIA Group, The
2054 E. Balboa Dr.
Tempe, AZ 85282-4005
phone: 602-820-9902
fax: 602-941-8234
Collects, buys, sells jigsaw puzzles, specializing in Zag-Zaw wooden puzzles by Raphael Tuck, particularly the Dickens 1812-1912 series and all of Tuck's catalogs; Centenary a.k.a. Carriage Series in 2 sizes and 16 prints.

Experts

Anne D. Williams
Economics Dept.
Bates College
Lewiston, ME 04240
phone: 207-783-8732
e-mail: awilliam@bates.edu
Wants jigsaw puzzles, related ephemera, and company catalogs and information; wood, diecut, etc.; author of "Jigsaw Puzzles" (1990), "Cutting A Fine Figure" (1996), many articles about puzzles; special interest in small-scale makers.

Chris McCann
658 MacElroy Rd.
Ballston Lake, NY 12019-2202
phone: 518-877-7303
Researcher of cardboard jigsaw puzzles from 1930s to 1950s; has computer database of more than 9300 titles from 18 major collections; 7300 titles have been identified with artist name; would like to hear from other collectors.

Harry L. Rinker
Puzzle Pit, The
5093 Vera Cruz Rd.
Emmaus, PA 18049-9554
phone: 610-965-1122
fax: 610-965-1124
e-mail: rinkeron@fast.net
Wants wooden or cardboard jigsaw puzzles with advertising, mystery, personality, cartoon character, depression era, or WWII theme.

Repro. Sources

Harold Fessler
3103 34th Ave. Dr., W.
Bradenton, FL 34205-3649
phone: 813-756-9891
Custom wooden jigsaw puzzles made from your poster or print; other puzzles in stock; will reproduce "missing" pieces.

Jigsaw (Wood)

Collectors

Gordon Hayter
751 Terraine Ave.
Long Beach, CA 90804-4405
phone: 562-498-2769
Collector of adult, wood, interlocking jigsaw puzzles.

Mechanical

Collectors

Bernice Kraker
9800 McMillan Ave.
Silver Spring, MD 20910-1149
phone: 301-589-2544
Wants to buy dexterity games and puzzles.

Tom Rodgers
1466 West Wesley Rd.
Atlanta, GA 30327
phone: 404-351-7744
Wants mechanical puzzles: puzzle jugs, trick locks, puzzle trade cards, folding puzzles, paper & string puzzles, etc.; NO jigsaws, please.

Cary Basse
6927 Forbes Ave.
Van Nuys, CA 91406-4504
phone: 818-781-4856

Experts

Jerry Slocum
P.O. Box 1635
Beverly Hills, CA 90213-1635
phone: 310-273-2270
fax: 310-274-3644
Wants mechanical & dexterity puzzles, trick locks, trick matchsafes, folding puzzles, advertising string puzzles, puzzle trade cards, checkerboard puzzles, catalogs with puzzles, puzzle books.

Mechanical (Rubik's Cubes)

Collectors

Peter M. Beck
Just Puzzles
54 Richwood Place
Denville, NJ 07834
phone: 201-627-1458
Wants to buy any type of Rubik's cube memorabilia; buys and sells all forms of mechanical puzzles; send SASE for brochure.

Paper

Collectors

Will Shortz
55 Great Oak Lane
Pleasantville, NY 10570-2010
phone: 914-769-9128
fax: 212-727-7661
e-mail: wshortz@aol.com
Wants to buy paper puzzles, also puzzle books and magazines.

PYROBILIA

(see FIREWORKS MEMORABILIA)

PYROGRAPHY ITEMS

Collectors

John Lewis
912 W. 8th St.
Loveland, CO 80537-5208
phone: 970-667-2960
Wants quality "burnt wood" items such as plaques, boxes and furniture; also wants catalogs, wood burning kits, and books on pyrography.

Dealers

Linda Gibbs
10380 Miranda Ave.
Buena Park, CA 90620-4447
phone: 714-827-6488
fax: 714-840-8671
Wants wooden boxes with flower designs, beautiful ladies, etc., 1800s-1900s; please send SASE and photos.

Experts

Carole & Richard Smyth
Carole Smyth Antiques
P.O. Box 2068
Huntington, NY 11743-0861
phone: 516-673-8666
Authors of "The Burning Passion - A Study & Price Guide," now available from the authors for $22.95 ppd.

Here are some tips when contacting someone listed in this book:

When requesting information about a particular item, include a description (material, dimensions, maker's mark, model number, etc.) and a photo, sketch, or photocopy of the item in question. ■

Always ask if there are charges for samples or for the services requested. ■

When writing, please be sure to include a Large (#10 business size) Self-Addressed and Stamped Envelope (LSASE) if requesting a reply or the return of photographs. ■

Never call collect unless otherwise directed. When calling, be considerate of time zone differences and always ask if the party you are calling has time to talk. When leaving an answering machine message, always instruct the party to call you back <u>collect</u>. ■

QUILTS

(see also FEED & GRAIN BAGS;
FOLK ART; REPAIR/RESTORA-
TION/CONSERVATION, Textiles;
TEXTILES)

Appraisers

American Quilter's Society
Magazine: American Quilter
P.O. Box 3290
Paducah, KY 42001
phone: 502-442-8856
*Publishes list of certified quilt
appraisers.*

Terri Ellis
1205 Mistletoe Dr.
Fort Worth, TX 76110-1018
phone: 817-926-9424
e-mail: tquilts@cyberramp.net
*Certified quilt appraiser by the
American Quilter's Society; also buys
and sells vintage textiles.*

Deborah Roberts
1071 San Pablo
Costa Mesa, CA 92626
phone: 714-557-5258
e-mail: quiltevals@aol.com
Internet: http://quilt.com/appraiser
*Appraiser of antique hooked rugs,
quilts and quilt-related textiles;
certified by the American Quilter's
Society; written insurance, fair market
and donation appraisals; also lectures
on quilts.*

Bette G. Bell, ISA CAPP
Guildmark Appraisal Service
P.O. Box 952
Edmonds, WA 98020
phone: 425-775-5650
fax: 425-670-6957
e-mail: 102762.2240@compuserve.com
*Appraises quilts, cut glass, pottery
and a general line of antiques; also
handles estate sales throughout the
NW; Certified Member of the
International Society of Appraisers.*

Sally A. Ambrose
P.O. Box 536
11156 North Rd.
Leavenworth, WA 98826-9512
phone: 509-548-7472
fax: 509-548-0240
e-mail: 104734.701@compuserve.com
*Specializes in the appraising of
antique and contemporary American
quilted textiles, as well as contemporary wearable art. Wearable art is not
always quilted but may exhibit surface
design in a variety of art media and
embellishment.*

Clubs/Associations

National Quilting Association, Inc., The
Magazine: Quilting Quarterly
P.O. Box 393
Ellicott City, MD 21043-0393
phone: 410-461-5733
fax: 410-461-3693
Internet: http://www.his.com/~queenb/
nqa/nqa.index.html
*Purpose is to stimulate, maintain and
record interest in all matters
pertaining to the making, collecting
and preserving of quilts.*

American Quilter's Society
Magazine: American Quilter
P.O. Box 3290
Paducah, KY 42001
phone: 502-442-8856
*Members receive bi-monthly
newsletter, discount admission to
Annual National AQS Quilt Show,
discounts on quilting books, American
Quilter Magazine; also publishes list
of certified quilt appraisers.*

American Quilt Study Group
Newsletter: Blanket Statements
660 Mission Street, Ste. 400
San Francisco, CA 94105-4007
phone: 415-495-0163
fax: 415-495-3516
e-mail: aqsg@aol.com
*Goal is to develop a responsible and
accurate body of information about
quilts and their makers; membership
open to any person having an interest
in the history of quilt making; also
published the annual journal,
"Uncoverings."*

Dealers

Lawrence Miller
Marie Miller Antique Quilts
Route 30
P.O. Box 968
Dorset, VT 05251
phone: 802-867-5969
fax: 802-867-0324
e-mail: quiltslr@vermontel.com
Internet: http://www.antiquequilts.com
*Buys, sells, appraises quilts; has over
300 from 1820 to 1930s: applique,
pieced, crazy quilts, crib, doll, Amish
and Mennonite, and quilt tops; see the
on-line catalog; also sells quilt
hangers and Ensure, a quilt wash.*

Kris Driessen
Hickory Hill Antique Quilts
P.O. Box 273
Esperance, NY 12066
phone: 518-875-6299
fax: 518-875-9141
e-mail: oldquilt@albany.net
Internet: http://
www.HickoryHillQuilts.com
*Offers antique quilt tops, blocks by
catalog; also offers vintage and
reproduction fabrics, as well as
restoration supplies and Quilt
Heritage reference books.*

Bryan Kittelberger
Kittelberger Galleries
82 1/2 E. Main St.
Webster, NY 14580
phone: 716-265-1230

Stella Rubin
12300 Glen Rd.
Potomac, MD 20854-1023
phone: 301-948-4187
fax: 301-948-0460
*Buys and sells quality quilts; also
Mexican silver jewelry.*

Michael T. Meadows
Meadows House Antiques
919 Stiles St.
Baltimore, MD 21202-4426
phone: 410-837-5427

Matt Lippa
Artisans
P.O. Box 256
Mentone, AL 35984-0256
phone: 205-634-4037
fax: 205-634-4037
e-mail: artisans@folkartisans.com
Internet: http://www.folkartisans.com
*Buy and sell folk art, outsider art, fine
art; Internet WWW site offers links to
additional dealers; also offers non-
profit clubs and museums with an
outlet to post notices, press releases,
calendar items, etc. at no charge.*

Frank Gesslin
American Quilts!
P.O. Box 200
Upton, KY 42784
phone: 502-531-1619
fax: 502-531-3745
e-mail: fgeeslin@aol.com
Internet: http://
www.AmericanQuilts.com
*Over 1500 American-made quilts: new
and antique, custom-made, baby and
doll, quilt tops, applique, cutter quilts,
quilt clothing, contemporary and
traditional quilts; also repairs; buying
extraordinary quilts or tops.*

Experts

Suzy McLennan Anderson
Heritage Antiques, Inc.
65 East Main St.
Holmdel, NJ 07733-2310
phone: 908-946-8801
fax: 908-946-1036
*Authenticates, buys, sells, appraises,
lectures; author of "The Collectors
Guide to Quilts."*

Ardis & Robert James
Ardis & Robert James Quilt Collection,
The
80 Ludlow Dr.
Chappaqua, NY 10514
phone: 914-666-3774
*Buys, sells, exhibits, lends, lectures
and writes about quilts; collection
featured in several publications.*

Yvonne Khin
9459 Longs Mill Rd.
Rocky Ridge, MD 21778-8507
phone: 301-898-0091
*Author of "Collector's Dictionary of
Quilt Names and Patterns" (1980.)*

Misc. Services

Quilter's Design Studio QuiltSoft
P.O. Box 19946
San Diego, CA 92159-0946
phone: 619-583-2970
fax: 619-583-2692
e-mail: quiltsoft@aol.com
*Quilt design computer program for
Windows or for Macintosh; copy,
rotate, and flip blocks; print
templates, calculate yardage,
unlimited colors.*

Museums/Libraries

New England Quilt Museum
18 Shattuck St.
Lowell, MA 01852
phone: 508-452-4207

Shelburne Museum, Inc.
P.O. Box 10
Shelburne, VT 05482-0010
phone: 802-985-3346 or 802-985-3344
fax: 802-985-2331
*37 historic structures and exhibit
buildings; diverse collection of
American folk, fine, decorative and
utilitarian art.*

National Museum of American History,
Division of Textiles
14th & Constitution Ave. NW
Washington, DC 20560
phone: 202-357-2700
Internet: http://www.si.edu/

Yvonne Khin
Doll & Quilts Barn
9459 Longs Mill Rd.
Rocky Ridge, MD 21778-8507
phone: 301-898-0091
*Quilt museum offering quilt repairs,
enlarging, duplicating, quilting
classes, storage, and research.*

Victoria Faoro
Museum of the American Quilter's
Society
Newsletter: Friends of MAQS
Newsletter
215 Jefferson St.
P.O. Box 1540
Paducah, KY 42001-1540
phone: 502-442-8856
fax: 502-442-5448
e-mail: MAQSmus@apex.net
*World's largest quilt museum;
changing displays of new and antique
quilts; gift and book shop carries over
400 titles related to quilts and textiles.*

Quilters Hall of Fame
P.O. Box 681
Marion, IN 46952-0681
phone: 765-664-9333
fax: 765-664-9333

Periodicals

Quilt Project, The
Journal: Quilt Journal, The
635 W. Main St.
Louisville, KY 40202
phone: 502-587-6721
fax: 502-587-9411
Published twice a year, this periodical seeks to bring quilt information from other parts of the world to the American quilt community, and acts as an important reference source for American quilt information.

Newsletter: Vintage Quilt Newsletter
1305 Morphy St.
Great Bend, KS 67530-4330

Leman Publications
Magazine: Quilter's Newsletter
P.O. Box 4101
Golden, CO 80401-0101
phone: 303-420-4272 or 800-477-6089
fax: 303-420-7358
The magazine for quilt lovers; a glossy magazine published ten times per year; articles, appraisals, patterns, frames, old and new quilts, quilt history, fabric clubs, ads, calendar, techniques, supplies, shows, etc.

Leman Publications
Magazine: Quiltmaker
P.O. Box 4101
Golden, CO 80401-0101
phone: 303-420-4272 or 800-477-6089
fax: 303-420-7358
A bi-monthly magazine for today's quilters; a pattern magazine featuring original quilt art in addition to full color photographs of quilts; step-by-step instructions, yardage, and more.

Repair Services

Margaret & Audrey Ruhland Antiques
P.O. Box 245
North Gower
Ontario K0A 2T0 Canada
phone: 613-489-3298
Specializes in the repair of quilts and hooked rugs.

S. Hendrick-Wilson
370 Whitney Ave.
Trumbull, CT 06611
phone: 203-268-1321
Meticulous restoration using period textiles; estimates and references available.

Yvonne Khin
Doll & Quilts Barn
9459 Longs Mill Rd.
Rocky Ridge, MD 21778-8507
phone: 301-898-0091
Quilt museum offering quilt repairs, enlarging, duplicating, quilting classes, storage, and research.

Suppliers

Kris Driessen
Hickory Hill Antique Quilts
P.O. Box 273
Esperance, NY 12066
phone: 518-875-6299
fax: 518-875-9141
e-mail: oldquilt@albany.net
Internet: http://
www.HickoryHillQuilts.com
Offers antique quilt tops, blocks by catalog; also offers vintage and reproduction fabrics, as well as restoration supplies and Quilt Heritage reference books.

Hancock Fabrics
3841 Hinkleville Rd.
Paducah, KY 42001
phone: 800-626-2723 or 800-845-8723
fax: 502-442-3152
Quilt patterns, fabrics, supplies and more; 800-626-2723 is the order number.

Miniature

Man./Prod./Dist.

Kate Adams
Kate Adams Designs
P.O. Box 3025
Kennebunkport, ME 04046
phone: 800-553-3766 or 207-967-5077
fax: 207-967-0972
Makes miniature quilts framed as wall decorations.

RACING

(see AIRPLANES, Racing; AUTO RACING MEMORABILIA; AUTOMOBILES, Racing; MODELS, Cars [Racing]; SOAP BOX DERBY; SPORTS COLLECTIBLES, Thoroughbred Racing)

RADIO SHOWS

Old Time

(see also AUDIO-VISUAL; BROADCASTING; PERSONALITIES [ENTERTAINERS]; PREMIUMS, Radio Show; RADIOS)

Clubs/Associations

Revival of Creative Radio
P.O. Box 1585
Haverhill, MA 01831-2285

Bob Levin
Radio Collectors of America
Newsletter: RCA Newsletter
8 Ardsley Circle
Brockton, MA 02402-1422
phone: 508-588-7087
Purpose is to collect, preserve and enjoy old radio shows. Does not collect old radios, the emphasis is strictly on radio shows.

Suzanne Siegel
Manhattan Radio Club
405 E. 63rd St.
New York, NY 10021

Richard Olday
Old Time Radio Club
Newsletter: OTRC Newsletter
100 Harvey Dr.
Lancaster, NY 14086-2840
phone: 716-684-1604
A nationally oriented local chapter.

Gene Leitner
Golden Radio Buffs of Maryland, Inc.
Newsletter: On the Air
301 Jeanwood Ct.
Baltimore, MD 21222-2857
phone: 410-477-2550 or 410-477-3051
International club interested in old time radio also has an Old Time radio exhibit in the Baltimore Museum of Industry,, Baltimore, MD; lots of radios, artifacts, pictures, etc.; OTR tape lending library for members.

Jack French
Metro Washington Old Time Radio Club
Newsletter: Radio Recall
5137 Richardson Dr.
Fairfax, VA 22032-2810
phone: 703-978-1236
e-mail: OTRpiano@erols.com

Dick Baker
Goon Show Preservation Society
7004 Westmoreland Rd.
Falls Church, VA 22042-2532
phone: 703-698-8017
e-mail: dbaker@ix.netcom.com
Specializes in British comedy.

Janis DeMoss
North American Radio Archives
Newsletter: NARA News
134 Vincewood Dr.
Nicholasville, KY 40356
phone: 606-885-1031
International club dedicated to the enjoyment of classic radio shows from the 1930s to present; has a printed materials as well as over 3000 cassettes to loan out.

Robert W. Newman
Radio Listener's Lyceum
Journal: RLL on the Air
11509 Islandale Drive
Forest Park, OH 45240-2319
phone: 513-825-3662
Cassette library contains thousands of the classic old-time radio programs; publishers of "RLL on the Air", a quarterly informative journal about old-time radio and those who participated in it; please send SASE with requests.

Barry Hill
Old Time Radio Collectors Association of England (North American Division)
Rte. 1 Box 197
Belpre, OH 45714
phone: 614-423-4010
fax: 614-423-4010
Preserve English-spoken radio shows broadcast around the world and make them available for the enjoyment of the members.

Indiana Recording Club
1729 E. 77th St.
indianapolis, IN 46240

Gordon Spierling
Milwaukee Radio Enthusiasts
16670 Harmony Ct.
New Berlin, WI 53151

Nancy Warner
Illinois Old Radio Shows Society
Newsletter: Chicago Star
10 S. 540 County Line Rd.
Hinsdale, IL 60521
Over 4,000 hours of old radio shows in a lending library; also scripts, articles and comic books on radio topics.

Fred B. Korb, Jr.
Old Time Radio Collectors Traders Society
725 Cardigan Ct.
Naperville, IL 60565-1202
phone: 708-416-8968
Society members are amateur radio operators or sponsored by same; meetings held on 7.238MHZ, 7AM CST, Sundays; W9ZMR is net control. Society members trade and exchange old time radio shows on reel-to-reel tape.

Richard R. king
Radio Historical Association of Colorado
Newsletter: Return With Us Now
P.O. Box 1908
Englewood, CO 80150-1908
phone: 303-761-4139
e-mail: dick.king@worldnet.att.net
Internet: http://www.old-time.com/ffiles/rhac.zip
Club rents over 13,000 old time radio shows to members for a nominal charge.

Society To Preserve & Encourage Radio Drama, Variety & Comedy
Newsletter: Radiogram
P.O. Box 7177
Van Nuys, CA 91409-9712
phone: 310-947-9800
Local club with many national members; good lending library; newsletter published 11 times per year and is included with membership; contains news about old radio and the people who were in it - many are still active.

River City Radio Club
P.O. Box 163464
Sacramento, CA 95816-9464
Trading, collecting, selling and more; 10,000 episodes; access by personal computer with modem - call BBS at 916-451-0473 (8-n-1); on-line club services and catalogs; 24 hours; no fees; free membership.

Carolyn Kolibaba
Cinnamon Bear Brigade
10419 N.E. Knott
Portland, OR 97220

Collectors

David L. Easter
1900 Angleside Rd.
Fallston, MD 21047-1739
phone: 410-877-2949
e-mail: davie_easter@compuserve.com
*Interested in all old time radio shows,
especially in science fiction program;
American, BBC or South African.*

Herb Brandenburg
4114 Montgomery Rd.
Cincinnati, OH 45212-3612
phone: 513-841-1267

Fred B. Korb, Jr.
725 Cardigan Ct.
Naperville, IL 60565-1202
phone: 708-416-8968
*Looking for any new programs in
circulation; member of O.R.C.A.T.S;
personal library contains approximately 50,000 programs; trades
shows on a limited basis.*

Dealers

Erstwhile Radio
P.O. Box 2284
Peabody, MA 01960-7284
*Send $3 for catalog listing nearly
5,300 old time radio shows: The
Whistler, Suspense, Jack Benny,
Sherlock Holmes, The Lone Ranger,
Fiber McGee & Molly, Lux Radio
Theater, etc.; mail order only.*

Heritage Radio Classics
P.O. Box 16
Chestnut Hill, MA 02167
fax: 617-965-9984
e-mail: HERITAGE@aol.com
Internet: http://www.members.com/
HERITAGE4/index.html
*Super quality old-time radio shows
from the 1930s to 1950s on TDK
cassettes: Jack Benny, The Shadow,
The Lone Ranger, Our Miss Brooks,
The Great Gildersleeve, Lux Radio
Theatre, Suspense and 100s more;
catalog $1.50 refundable.*

Old Time Radio
#2 Heritage Farm Dr.
New Freedom, PA 17349

Can Corner, The
P.O. Box 1173 - MA
Marcus Hook, PA 19061-7173
*Jack Benny, Amos & Andy, Big Band
specials, WWII broadcasts, old
commercials for Chevrolet, Nash &
Studebaker, etc.; send for list; mail
order.*

Lawrence Rao
1009 Autumn Woods Ln. #106
Virginia Beach, VA 23454
*Sells vintage radio broadcasts on
audio-only VHS Hi-fi cassettes;
broadcasts are also available on*

*standard analog-Dolby cassettes;
Vintage Radio catalog $6 ppd.
refundable on first order.*

Charlie Garant
P.O. Box 331
Greeneville, TN 37744-0331

Bob Burchett
Hello Again, Radio
P.O. Box 6176
Cincinnati, OH 45206-0176
phone: 606-282-0333
fax: 606-282-1999
*Free catalog of Old Time radio shows
on cassette.*

Radio Vault
P.O. Box 9032
Grand Rapids, MI 49509-0032
phone: 616-531-7398
*Old radio shows on cassettes; catalog
$5.*

Experts

Jack French
5137 Richardson Dr.
Fairfax, VA 22032-2810
phone: 703-978-1236
e-mail: OTRpiano@erols.com
*Collecting, researching, and writing
about the Golden Age of radio for
over 20 years; former editor of
"NARA News", current editor of
"Radio Recall"; lecturer on old time
radio, juvenile westerns, female
detectives, soap operas, etc.*

Museums/Libraries

Arthur S. Schreiber, CEO
National Broadcasters Hall of Fame &
Museum
704 Zlotkin Circle, Apt. 4
Freehold, NJ 07728-4361
phone: 908-294-7106
fax: 908-431-2069

Museum of Broadcasting, The
25 West 52nd St.
New York, NY 10022
phone: 212-752-4690

Library of Congress, Recorded Sound
Reference Section
10 First Street, SE
Washington, DC 20540-4805
phone: 202-707-7833 or 202-426-5509
*Collection contains motion picture,
broadcasting and recorded sound
including old time radio shows.*

American Library of Radio & TV,
Thousand Oaks Library
1401 East Janss Rd.
Thousand Oaks, CA 91362

Museum of Magnetic Recording, Ampex
corporation
401 Broadway
Redwood City, CA 94063
phone: 415-367-3127

Periodicals

Jay A. Hickerson
Friends of Old-Time Radio
Newsletter: Hello Again
P.O. Box 4321
Hamden, CT 06514-0321
phone: 203-248-2887
fax: 203-281-1322
e-mail: jayhick@aol.com
*For collectors of old-time radio
shows; sponsors an annual
convention; send SASE for sample
copy of newsletter.*

Robert Brunet
Newsletter: Daily Sentinel
21 West 74th St.
New York, NY 10023-2478
phone: 212-877-2824

Royal Promotions
Magazine: Old Time Radio Digest
10280 Gunpowder Rd.
Florence, KY 41042-8253
phone: 606-282-0333 or 606-282-1999

Rob Imes
Newsletter: Tune In
1844 E. Longmeadow
Trenton, MI 48183-1776
*Forum for fans of new and old radio
plays; share ideas, express creativity
with original scripts, detailed
information about programs compiled
from research of readers; recent
issues involve The Witch's Tale and
The Shadow.*

Tom Miller
Newsletter: Old-Time Radio Gazette,
The
2004 East 6th St.
Superior, WI 54880-3632
phone: 715-398-7280
*Published six timer per year, includes
articles on radio personalities and
programs, photos, and editorials; also
each issue contains the listings of
shows to be aired on Wisconsin Public
Radio's "Old-Time Radio Drama",
Sat. 9-11 pm.*

Newsletter: Nostalgia Digest
P.O. Box 421
Morton Grove, IL 60053

Newsletter: Thrilling Days of Yesteryear
P.O. Box 36106
Denver, CO 80236
e-mail: jray71827@aol.com

Jordan Young
Moonstone Press
Directory: Nostalgia Entertainment
Sourcebook
7308-H Filmore Dr.
Buena Park, CA 90620
phone: 714-956-2246
*Complete resource guide to classic
movies, vintage radio, old time music,
and theater: programs, equipment,
where to replace and repair, where to
rent or buy old movies, theater
posters.*

Repro. Sources

Old Time Radio Co.
P.O. Box 9032
Grand Rapids, MI 49509-0032
phone: 616-531-7398

Old Time (Lum 'n' Abner)

Clubs/Associations

Tim Hollis, ExSec
National Lum 'n' Abner Society
Newsletter: Jot 'Em Down Journal, The
#81 Sharon Blvd.
Dora, AL 35062
phone: 205-648-6110
fax: 205-674-0190
e-mail: jtemple@inu.net
Internet: http://inu.net/stemple/

Museums/Libraries

Lon & Kathy Stucker
Lum 'n' Abner Museum
P.O. Box 38
Pine Ridge, AR 71966
phone: 870-326-4442
fax: 870-326-4442
e-mail: nstucker@hsnp
*On National Register of Historic
Places.*

Old Time (Straight Arrow)

Clubs/Associations

Bill Harper
POW-WOW
Newsletter: POW-WOW
P.O. Box 24751
Minneapolis, MN 55424-0751
e-mail: WaltGrogan@aol.com
Internet: http://shazam.imginc.com/fca/
*POW-WOW is the definitive source for
information on the Nabisco Straight
Arrow Promotion 1948-1954;
dedicated to the memory of the real
Straight Arrow - Howard Culver
(1919-1984) and announcer/narrator
Frank Bingham (1914-1988.)*

Old Time (Vic & Sade)

Clubs/Associations

Mrs. Barbara Schwarz
Friends of Vic & Sade
Newsletter: FVS Newsletter
7232 N. Keystone Ave.
Lincolnwood, IL 60646-2025
phone: 708-679-2706
*Devoted fans of VIC & SADE focusing
on searching for and sharing recorded
episodes as well as information on the
program and cast.*

RADIOS

(see also ART DECO; AUDIO-
VISUAL; BROADCASTING; PAPER
COLLECTIBLES, Radio Related;
PREMIUMS, Radio Shows; RADIO
SHOWS, Old Time; TELEGRAPH
ITEMS; TELEVISIONS)

Book Sellers

Joe Pfeiffer
Zapper Technologies
P.O. Box 253
Sandy, UT 84091-0253
phone: 801-571-5453
e-mail: 72622.127@compuserve.com
*Buys, sell, trade old books on early
electronics, microphones, tubes,
radio, antique electronics, telegraph;
also early manuals and catalogs.*

Clubs/Associations

Ottawa Vintage Radio Club
P.O. Box 84084
Pinecrest, Ottawa
Ontario K2C 3Z2 Canada
phone: 613-828-5152

Canadian Vintage Radio Society
Newsletter: Radio Waves
P.O. Box 43012
Edmonton
Alberta T5J 4M8 Canada

Gerald Wells
British Vintage Wireless Society,
Vintage Wireless Museum
23 Rosendale Rd.
West Dulwich
London SE21 8DS, U.K.

Richard Foster
Greater Boston Antique Radio
Collectors
12 Shawnut Ave.
Wayland, MA 01778-4812

Judy Gauthier
New England Antique Radio Club
Newsletter: Escutcheon
113 Barretts Hill Rd.
Hudson, NH 03051

Ray Lamont
Connecticut Vintage Radio Collectors
Club
Newsletter: Connecticut Wireless
Gazette
563 West Avon Rd.
Avon, CT 06001
phone: 860-675-9916
fax: 860-675-9916
*Museum, library, swap meets spring
and fall.*

Kathleen Flanagan
New Jersey Antique Radio Club
Newsletter: NJARC Newsletter
92 Joysan Terrace
Freehold, NJ 07728

Richard G. Brill
International Antique Radio Club
P.O. Box 5261
Old Bridge, NJ 08857

John & Linda Gramm
Hudson Valley Antique Radio &
Phonograph Society
Newsletter: HARPS Newsletter
P.O. Box 1, Rt. 207
Campbell Hall, NY 10916
phone: 914-427-2602
*For antique radio and phonograph
collectors who want to share*

information, equipment and related
items with others having similar
interests; monthly meetings feature
educational demonstrations and mini
swap meets.

Bob Scheps
Greater New York Vintage Wireless
Association
12 Garrity Ave.
Ronkonkoma, NY 11779-5805
phone: 516-469-1722
fax: 516-467-1741

Allen W. Tomisman
Antique Radio Club of Schenectady
33 Bailey Ave.
Latham, NY 12110
phone: 518-785-3117

Gary Parzy
Niagara Frontier Wireless Association
Newsletter: NFWA Newsletter
135 Autumnwood
Cheektowaga, NY 14227

Bruce Kelley
Antique Wireless Association
Newsletter: Old Timer's Bulletin
59 Main St.
Holcomb, NY 14469-9336
phone: 716-657-6260 or 716-657-7489
*One of the world's largest and oldest
historical radio collector organizations; purpose is to document and
preserve the history of radio,
telegraph and television artifacts.*

Richard J. Harris, Sec.
Pittsburgh Antique Radio Society
407 Woodside Road
Pittsburgh, PA 15221

Antique Radio Club of America
Magazine: Antique Radio Gazette, The
81 Steeplechaw Rd.
Devon, PA 19113
*Combined with antique wireless
association*

Mike Koste
Delaware Valley Historic Radio Club
Newsletter: DVHRC Newsletter
P.O. Box 41031
Philadelphia, PA 19127-0031
phone: 2156466488

Gerald Schneider
Radio History Society, Inc.
3101 Blueford Rd.
Kensington, MD 20895-2726
phone: 301-929-8593
*An IRS-recognized tax-exempt
nonprofit organization set up
primarily to establish a national
vintage radio and television museum
and library in the Washington DC
area.*

Jay Kiessling
Mid-Atlantic Antique Radio Club
Magazine: Radio Age
P.O. Box 67
Upperco, MD 21155
phone: 410-239-1818
*Published monthly since 1975 for
collectors interested in the history of*

radio and television; restoration,
articles by early experts; free buy and
sell ads; free sample.

Carolina Antique Radio Society
824 Fairwood Rd.
Columbia, SC 29209

Paul Currie
Florida Antique Wireless Group
Newsletter: FAWGhorn News
P.O. Box 738
Oviedo, FL 32766-0738
phone: 407-365-9305 or 407-895-0146
*A group devoted to collecting old
radios.*

Alabama Historical Radio Society
Newsletter: AHRA Newsletter
2413 Old Briar Trail
Birmingham, AL 35226
Deceased

Bill Moore
Southern Vintage Wireless Association
Newsletter: SVWA Newsletter
3049 Box Canyon Rd.
Huntsville, AL 35803-1379
phone: 205-880-1207
e-mail: Bill_Moore@mevatec.com
*Interested in antique radios; looking
for Pilor and Lagayette radios and
related advertising.*

Randy Guttery
Mississippi Historical Radio &
Broadcasting Society
Newsletter: MHRBS Newsletter
2412 C St.
Meridian, MS 39301

Steve Dando
Buckeye Radio & Phonograph Club
Newsletter: Soundings
4572 Mark Trail
Copley, OH 44321
phone: 216-666-7222
*Members exchange expertise in
restoration of vintage radios and
phonographs; club holds annual mall
show (displaying radios and
phonographs) and picnic.*

Karl Koogle
Antique Radio Collectors of Ohio
Newsletter: ARCO Newsletter
2929 Hazelwood Ave.
Dayton, OH 45419-1945
phone: 937-294-8960
*Newsletter published quarterly; holds
several meetings and swap meets each
year.*

Society for the Preservation of Antique
Radio Knowledge (SPARK)
Newsletter: SPARK Newsletter
c/o WQRP Radio
P.O. Box 482
Dayton, OH 45449

Dr. Edmund E. Taylor
Indiana Historical Radio Society
Newsletter: IHRS Bulletin
245 N. Oakland Ave.
Indianapolis, IN 46201-3360
phone: 317-638-1641
Society of antique radio collectors

who meet quarterly in Indiana;
sponsors swap-meets, auctions,
museum projects, contests.

Jim Clark
Michigan Antique Radio Club
Newsletter: Chronicle
3520 Okemos Rd., #6
Okemos, MI 48864
phone: 517-349-2249
fax: 517-349-7186
*Preserves the history and enhance the
knowledge of radio, TV and related
disciplines with special emphasis on
contributions made from the state of
Michigan.*

Dave Wiggert
Western Wisconsin Antique Radio
Collectors Club
Newsletter: Radio Recollections
1611 Redfield St.
La Crosse, WI 54601

Northland Antique Radio Club
Newsletter: NARC Newsletter
P.O. Box 18362
Minneapolis, MN 55418

Rochester Radio Theatre Guild
110 17th St. NE
Rochester, MN 55906

Jeff Aulik
Antique Radio Club of Illinois
Newsletter: ARCI Newsletter
1708 Parkview Ave.
Rockford, IL 61107
phone: 815-399-1902

Charles Haynes
Belleville Area Antique Radio Club
219 W. Spring
Marissa, IL 62257

Robert Lane, Pres.
Mid-American Antique Radio Club
Newsletter: Broadcaster, The
10332 Mowhawk Lane
Shawnee Mission, KS 66206-2525
phone: 913-648-5296
fax: 913-341-1610
e-mail: personal@shots.com
*Historical preservation and collecting
ratios with two auctions a year, April
and October.*

Steve Morton
Nebraska Antique Radio Collectors Club
Newsletter: NARCC Newsletter
905 West First
North Platte, NE 69101

Antique Radio Collectors Club of Fort
Smith, Arkansas
7917 Hermitage Dr.
Fort Smith, AR 72903

Oklahoma Vintage Radio Collectors
Newsletter: OKVRC Broadcast News
P.O. Box 332
Wheatland, OK 73097

C.F. Crandell, Pres.
Vintage Radio & Phonograph Society, Inc.
Newsletter: Reproducer, The
P.O. Box 165345
Irving, TX 75016-5345
phone: 214-337-2823 or 972-315-2553
Purpose is to preserve early radios, phonographs, and related material and to conduct historical research of same.

Houston Vintage Radio Association
Newsletter: Grid Leak, The
P.O. Box 31276
Houston, TX 77231-1276
Monthly meetings and special regional events.

Larry Weide
Colorado Radio Collectors
Newsletter: C.R.C. Flash!, The
5270 E. Nassau Cr.
Englewood, CO 80110
e-mail: terrylee@alpha.pri.k12.co.us
Holds bi-monthly meetings and swap meets; annual auction, public displays, presentations, get-togethers/ picnic.

Bill Lettow
Arizona Antique Radio Club, Inc.
Newsletter: AARC News
2025 E. LaJolla Dr.
Tempe, AZ 85282-5910
e-mail: 72310.3405@compuserve.com
Internet: http://members.gnn.com/ Dlamb62763/ARC.htm
Has swap meets in Phoenix and Tucson, regular meetings and exhibits, quarterly journal.

Bill Schultz
New Mexico Radio Collectors Club
11605 Versailles Ave.
Albuquerque, NM 87111

Clarence Hill
Southern California Antique Radio Society
Magazine: California Antique Radio Gazette
6934 Orion Ave.
Van Nuys, CA 91406

California Historical Radio Society
Journal: CHRS Journal
P.O. Box 31659
San Francisco, CA 94131-0659
phone: 415-978-9100
Members focus on vintage radios and other old electronics.

Charles Milton
Society of Wireless Pioneers Inc.
146 Coleen St.
Livermore, CA 94550

Sacramento Historical Radio Society
P.O. Box 162612
Sacramento, CA 95816

California Historical Radio Society, North Valley Chapter
Newsletter: NVC-CHRS Newsletter
P.O. Box 2443
Redding, CA 96099

Hawaii Antique Radio Club
98-1438 Koahehe St., Apt. C
Pearl City, HI 96782

Northwest Vintage Radio Society
Newsletter: NVRS Call Letter
P.O. Box 82379
Portland, OR 97282-0379
phone: 503-654-7387 or 503-281-6585

Pete Petersen
5214 120th Ave. SE
Bellevue, WA 98006
Collector of antique radios and related memorabilia.

Pete Petersen
Puget Sound Antique Radio Association
Newsletter: Horn of Plenty
P.O. Box 125
Snohomish, WA 98290-0125
phone: 425-747-1323
Internet: http://www.cyberspace.com/ ~hhagen/psara.html

Collectors

Harry Poster
Vintage TV's
P.O. Box 1883
South Hackensack, NJ 07606-0483
phone: 201-794-9606
fax: 201-794-9553
e-mail: hposter@worldnet.att.net
Buying transistor and Art Deco radios; $25-$500 early transistor radios by Sony, Mitchell, Raytheon, Toshiba, Bulova, Hoffman, etc.; $100- $10,000 for Deco or radios with chrome and black, mirrored, or colored Bakelite and Catalins.

Jim McKinnon
605 North Bridge St.
Bridgewater, NJ 08807
An avid collector specializing in early battery and AC table radios.

Radio
P.O. Box 51
Alplaus, NY 12008
phone: 518-399-0080
Wants to buy old radios made by Zenith, FADA, Emerson, Crosley, Bendix, Detrola, Grebe, Atwater Kent, and most others; early battery sets, crystal sets, cathedrals, and colorful plastics; single pieces or entire collections.

Alvin Heckard
RD 1 Box 88
Lewistown, PA 17044-9801
phone: 717-248-7071 or 717-248-2816
Wants wood table model radios, colored Bakelite and plastic radios; also any parts, tubes, literature, service manuals, advertising, etc.

Gerald Schneider
3101 Blueford Rd.
Kensington, MD 20895-2726
phone: 301-929-8593
Wants to buy vintage radios, radio equipment, parts, and related literature; specialization in radios with Oriental-style cabinets, and

radio/furniture combinations (radio lamps, bed headboards with radios, tables with radios, etc.)

Jay Kiessling
P.O. Box 67
Upperco, MD 21155
phone: 410-239-1818

Dave Walters
13805 Florida Ave.
Cresaptown, MD 21502
phone: 310-729-3133
Wants old radios and radio tubes; pre-1940.

Richard O. Gates
P.O. Box 187
Chesterfield, VA 23832-0187
phone: 804-748-0382 or 804-794-5146
fax: 804-748-6349
Wants to buy 1930s and 1940s Catalin radios with names such as FADA, Emerson, Garod, etc.; also wants Charlie McCarthy, Hopalong Cassidy, and Sparton mirrored radios.

Edward K. Bell
5311 Woodsdale Rd.
Raleigh, NC 27606-3341
phone: 919-851-1517
fax: 919-851-1517
Wants to buy old radios: pre-1925 battery sets, crystal sets, interesting plastics, cathedrals, advertising, horn speakers, old tubes, etc. Will buy entire collections.

Gary B. Schneider
9511 Sunrise Blvd. #J-23
North Royalton, OH 44133-3410
phone: 216-582-3094 or 216-251-3714
fax: 216-251-3714
e-mail: gbsptop@aol.com
Wants pre-1940 radio items: radios, tubes, parts, speakers; also technical radio magazines, catalogs, books, advertising, etc.

Steve Dando
4572 Mark Trail
Copley, OH 44321
phone: 216-666-7222

Larry Spilkin
P.O. Box 5039
Southfield, MI 48086-5039
phone: 810-642-3722
Wants Catalin & Bakelite radios especially colored, marbleized or Art Deco styles.

Doug Heimstead
1349 Hillcrest Dr.
Fridley, MN 55432
A collector with a special interest in unusual and mirror radios from both well-known and obscure manufacturers.

Dr. Barry Janov
2454 Depmster St., Ste. 416
Des Plaines, IL 60016-5320
Wants to buy early radios, microphones, speakers and related items.

William Ross
875 Gordon Terrace
Winnetka, IL 60093
phone: 708-441-6462
Organizes Radiofest, a major antique radio meet.

"Flip" Livingston
Remember When Antiques & Collectibles
P.O. Box 42224
Oklahoma City, OK 73132-3224
phone: 405-722-7034 or 405-721-1475
fax: 405-722-5754
e-mail: 76235.1441@compuserve.com
Wants to buy Zenith and Philco radios from 1936 to 1942; also wants transistor radios from the 1950s and 1960s; also tubes, speakers, radio cabinets.

Paul Thompson
315 Larkspur Dr.
Santa Maria, CA 93455-1625
phone: 805-934-2778
Wants Atwater Kent "breadboard" radios and parts for same; also early battery radios, crystal sets, parts, speakers, tubes and magazines.

Dealers

John Sakas
P.O. Box 4124
South Hackensack, NJ 07606-4124
phone: 201-794-0437
fax: 201-794-8359
e-mail: John@Radioclaze.com
Specializing in Catalin, Deco, mirror radios; also in Art Deco clocks.

Bruce & Charlotte Mager
Waves
110 West 25th St., Ste. 10M
New York, NY 10001-7401
phone: 212-989-9284
fax: 201-461-7121
e-mail: c1wave@aol.com
Internet: http://www.wavesradio.com
Over 20 years experience specializing in vintage radios, phonographs, telegraphy, televisions, assorted electrical and mechanical apparatus, and related advertising memorabilia, books and pamphlets.

Antica
P.O. Box 41
Eastchester, NY 10709-0041
phone: 914-337-7176
fax: 914-337-7176
Wants Deco radios: colorful plastic, mirrored, chrome, wood by Air King, Detrola, Emerson, FADA, Kadette, Motorola, Sparton, etc.; also wants radios from 1900s to 1920s: Marconi, Western Electric, commercial and broadcasting.

Allen W. Tomisman
33 Bailey Ave.
Latham, NY 12110
phone: 518-785-3117

Chris Savino
P.O. Box 419
Breesport, NY 14816-0419
phone: 607-739-3106
fax: 607-739-3106
*Buying plastic color radios from the
1930s to 1950s; by makers such as Air
King, Addison, Arvin, Crosley, De
Wald, Emerson, Espey, Fada, Garod,
GE, RCA, Sentinel, Sonora, Sparton,
and Stewart Warner; AM tabletop
radios only.*

Donald M. Maurer
Maurer Radio-TV Service
29 South 4th St.
York, PA 17402
phone: 717-272-2481
e-mail: dmradios@aol.com
Internet: http://members.aol.com/
dmradios/index.html
*Supplier of hard-to-find radio and TV
tubes, new old stock and in original
boxes; also buying vintage tube/
transistor radios and pre-1960 TV
Guides; send SASE for price lists and
inquiries.*

John Okolowicz
624 Cedar Hill Rd.
Ambler, PA 19002-1504
phone: 215-542-1597
e-mail: grillecloth@compuserve.com
Internet: http://ww.libertynet.org/
~grlcloth
*Buys, sells, trades pre-1950 radios
and TV's in unusual or ornate plastic
or wooden cabinets; especially those
made by Emerson, Stromberg Carlson,
or Detrola; also sells 40 types of
antique radio reproduction grille
cloth.*

Carole & Bob Lee
Lee's Antiques
8612 Wiles Court
Middletown, MD 21769
phone: 301-371-9578
*Buys, sells and repairs old electric
radios.*

Antique Radios, Inc.
P.O. Box 6352
Jackson, MI 49204-6352
phone: 517-787-2985
*Manufacturer of power supplies for
pre-1930s battery radios; complete
electrical restoration of early 20's
through 40's radios (no cabinet
work); no list of radios available;
appraisals on a fee-basis.*

John D. McKenna
Radio King, The
801-803 W Cucharras St.
Colorado Springs, CO 80905
phone: 719-630-8732
*Buys, sells, restores 1930-1950
vacuum tube radios, especially Zenith
wood radios.*

Joe Pfeiffer
Zapper Technologies
P.O. Box 253
Sandy, UT 84091-0253
phone: 801-571-5453
e-mail: 72622.127@compuserve.com
*Buy, sell, trade tube and transistor
radios, early Hi-Fi, old tubes,
microphones, HAM gear, books,
manuals, catalogs, telegraph items,
test equipment, radio ads and
collectibles, Nipper and Reddy
Kilowatt items.*

Jerry's Vintage Radio
17665 1/1 Sierra Hwy.
Canyon Country, CA 91351
*Buy, sell, trade and restore old radios;
electronic repair, wood repair and
restoration, plastic repair & paint,
tubes & parts, etc.*

Steve Oliphant
5255 Allott Ave.
Van Nuys, CA 91401-5902
phone: 310-789-2339 or 310-271-5176
fax: 310-276-5632
*Dealer in old phonographs and
radios; buys entire collections or
individual pieces.*

Experts

Marty & Sue Bunis
Radio Man, The
32 West Main St.
Bradford, NH 03221
phone: 603-938-5051
fax: 603-938-2430
*Collects and appraises old and
unusual radios, especially novelty sets
and 1950s/1960s transistors; authors
of "Collector's Guide to Antique
Radios."*

Bob Eslinger
Antique Radio Restoration & Repair
20 Gary School Rd.
Pomfret Center, CT 06259-1212
phone: 860-928-2628
fax: 860-928-2628
e-mail: oldradiodoc@aol.com
Internet: http://www.neca.com/
~radiodoc
*Professional restorations for all tube
type antique table and console radios,
communication receivers and music
amplifiers; complete overhauls;
lacquer sprayed hand rubbed and
polished cabinet refinishing; also
appraises, buys & sells.*

Gerald Schneider
3101 Blueford Rd.
Kensington, MD 20895-2726
phone: 301-929-8593
*Very active in local, national and
international radio groups; contact
point for the Radio History Society,
Inc.*

Gary B. Schneider
9511 Sunrise Blvd. #J-23
North Royalton, OH 44133-3410
phone: 216-582-3094 or 216-251-3714
fax: 216-251-3714
e-mail: gbsptop@aol.com
*Founding publisher of "Antique Radio
Classified"; author of "1988 Official
Price Guide to Antiques - Radio
Classification."*

John M. England, Jr.
P.O. Box 59136
Schaumburg, IL 60159-0136
phone: 708-823-5287
*Buys, collects, sells, appraises radios
and equipment made by Stromberg-
Carlson of Rochester, NY; also wants
to buy Stromberg-Carlson Co. radios,
Scott radios, mirrored radios, plus
related literature, magazines,
ephemera.*

David Lane
2515 W. 88th St.
Leawood, KS 66206
phone: 913-341-1610
*Co-author of "Transistor Radios - a
Collector's Encyclopedia and Price
Guide."*

Robert Lane
10332 Mowhawk Lane
Shawnee Mission, KS 66206-2525
phone: 913-648-5296
fax: 913-341-1610
e-mail: personal@shots.com
*Co-author of "Transistor Radios - a
Collector's Encyclopedia and Price
Guide."*

Mike Adams
112 Crescent Ct.
Scotts Valley, CA 95066-2815
phone: 408-924-4545
fax: 408-924-4543
e-mail: mhadams@sdsuvm1.susu.edu
*Specialty area is radio and broadcast
history; produced "Radio Collector"
series for PBS TV; writes for "Antique
Radio Classified."*

Museums/Libraries

R.W. Merriam
New England Wireless & Steam
Museum, Inc.
697 Tillinghart Rd.
East Greenwich, RI 02818
phone: 401-884-1710 or 401-885-0545
fax: 401-884-0683
Internet: http://users.ids.net/~newsm

Connecticut Vintage Radio &
Communications Museum, Inc.
1173 Main St.
East Hartford, CT 06108

Museum of Television & Radio
25 West 52nd St.
New York, NY 10019
phone: 212-621-6800
Internet: http://www.mtr.org

A.W.A. Electronic Communication
Museum
Main St.
Bloomfield, NY 14469
phone: 716-657-7489

Bruce Kelley
Antique Wireless Association's
Electronic Communication Museum
59 Main St.
Holcomb, NY 14469-9336
phone: 716-657-6260 or 716-657-7489
*Open limited hours May through
October; call or write before visiting;
please enclose SASE if requesting a
reply.*

Museum of Radio & Technology, Inc.
1640 Florence Ave.
Huntington, WV 25701
phone: 304-525-8880

Dr. Edmund E. Taylor
Ed Taylor Radio Museum
245 N. Oakland Ave.
Indianapolis, IN 46201-3360
phone: 317-638-1641
*Collection includes radio equipment,
memorabilia, electric meters, electro-
medical devices, Tesla coil, 2000 book
technical library.*

Valparaiso Technical Institute, Wilbur
H. Cummings Museum of Electronics
Hershman Hall
Valparaiso, IN 46384
phone: 219-462-2191
*Includes phonographs, early TV's,
radios, first-generation computers,
speakers, antennae, vacuum tubes,
and other electronic instruments.*

Keith R. Gill
Museum of Science & Industry
57th St. & Lake Shore Dr.
Chicago, IL 60637
phone: 312-684-1414
fax: 312-684-5580

Museum of Television & Radio
465 N. Beverly Dr.
Beverly Hills, CA 90210
phone: 310-786-1000
Internet: http://www.mtr.org

Periodicals

John V. Terrey
Magazine: Antique Radio Classified
P.O. Box 2 - V113
Carlisle, MA 01741
phone: 508-371-0512
fax: 508-371-7129
e-mail: arc@antiqueradio.com
Internet: http://www.antiqueradio.com
*Antique radio's largest monthly about
old radios, Art Deco, TV's, ham equip.
- '40s, '50s, books, telegraph, etc.;
lots of ads.*

Magazine: Gameroom Magazine
P.O. Box 41
Keyport, NJ 07735-0041
phone: 908-739-1955
fax: 908-739-2834
e-mail:
 coinop@gameroommagazine.com
 *A great source of information for the
 collector and dealer of jukeboxes,
 pinballs, Coke machines and other
 gameroom collectibles.*

James Cranshaw
Horn Speaker, The
Newspaper: Horn Speaker, The
P.O. Box 1193
Mabank, TX 75147-1193
phone: 903-848-0304
fax: 903-848-0596
e-mail: cranshaw@e-tex.com
Internet: http://home.navisoft.com/horn/
 ths2.htm
 *A newspaper for collectors and
 historians interested in antique radios
 and phonographs.*

Joe Pfeiffer
XTAL Publishing
Directory: International Dir. of Antique
 Radio Collectors
P.O. Box 253
Sandy, UT 84091-0253
phone: 801-571-5453
e-mail: 72622.127@compuserve.com
 *Lists radio collectors, dealers,
 historians, publications, stores,
 services, repairs, restorations,
 museums, clubs; free listings, display
 ads available.*

Repair Services

Talking Machine Emporium, The
42 Spring St.
Middletown, RI 02840
phone: 401-849-5360 or 401-635-2816
 *Antique radio and wind-up phono-
 graph repair; also buys and sells.*

Bob Eslinger
Antique Radio Restoration & Repair
20 Gary School Rd.
Pomfret Center, CT 06259-1212
phone: 860-928-2628
fax: 860-928-2628
e-mail: oldradiodoc@aol.com
Internet: http://www.neca.com/
 ~radiodoc
 *Professional restorations for all tube
 type antique table and console radios,
 communication receivers and music
 amplifiers; complete overhauls;
 lacquer sprayed hand rubbed and
 polished cabinet refinishing; also
 appraises, buys & sells.*

Daniel Blake
Outsider Studios
P.O. Box 63
Cedar Mountain, NC 28718-0063
phone: 704-884-2619
e-mail: pauline@citcom.net
Internet: http://members.aol.com/
 pjarna5313/index.html
 *Repair and restoration of Catalin
 radios, Plaskon.*

David B. Johnson
2336 S. Kenilworth Ave.
Berwyn, IL 60402
phone: 708-484-2743
 *Vintage TV and radio repair and
 restorations; both electronics and
 cosmetics.*

Clinton Blais
109 S Oak St.
O Fallon, IL 62269-2000
phone: 618-632-7423
 *Collects and repairs old radios;
 electronic consultant; also sells dial
 reproductions.*

David Headley
DH Distributors
P.O. Box 48623
Wichita, KS 67201-8623
phone: 316-684-0050
fax: 316-684-0050
 *Repairs and restores tube-type radios
 and audio equipment; chassis and
 cabinet restorations for tube-type
 radios; schematics.*

Suppliers

Electron Tube Enterprises
P.O. Box 8311
Essex, VT 05451
phone: 802-879-0611
fax: 802-879-7764
Internet: http://members.aol.com/
 etetubes
 *Dealers in surplus electron tubes; free
 catalog available.*

John Okolowicz
624 Cedar Hill Rd.
Ambler, PA 19002-1504
phone: 215-542-1597
e-mail: grillecloth@compuserve.com
Internet: http://ww.libertynet.org/
 ~grlcloth
 *Source for over 40 reproduction grille
 cloth patterns for antique radios from
 1920-1940.*

Old Tyme Radio Co.
2445 Lyttonsville Rd., Ste. 317
Silver Spring, MD 20910-1932
phone: 301-585-8776 or 301-587-5280
fax: 301-587-5280
 *Carries hard-to-find radio parts:
 vintage tubes, AK style battery cable,
 hook up wire, audio transformers,
 vintage headphones, etc.; also vintage
 radio repair service and vintage radio
 data packages; send 52¢ LSASE for
 20 pg. flyer.*

J.W.F. Puett
Puett Electronics
Newsletter: Antique Radio Topics
P.O. Box 28572
Dallas, TX 75228-0572
phone: 214-321-0927 or 214-327-8721
 *Mail order business in its 19th year
 servicing the antique radio collector;
 sells anything for old radios. Send for
 catalog.*

Antique Electronic Supply
6221 S. Maple Ave.
Tempe, AZ 85283-2856
phone: 602-820-5411
fax: 800-706-6789
 *Large catalog carrying tubes,
 supplies, capacitors, transformers,
 chemicals, test equipment, wire, parts,
 tools, books, old fabric lamp cords,
 etc.*

Larry Bordonaro
Old Time Replications
5744 Tobias
Van Nuys, CA 91411-3349
phone: 818-786-2500
fax: 818-909-0241
 *Supplies replacement knobs, push-
 buttons, escutcheons, plastic grills,
 handles, etc.*

Art Deco

Collectors

John M. England, Jr.
P.O. Box 59136
Schaumburg, IL 60159-0136
phone: 708-823-5287
 *Buys and sells Art Deco radios,
 clocks, machine age design.*

Dealers

Carl Ratner
550 Lamoka Ave.
Staten Island, NY 10312
e-mail: artdeco@bway.net
 *Buys, sells, trades, and restores Art
 Deco radios from the 1930s and
 1940s.*

Speakers

Experts

Floyd A. Paul
1545 Raymond Ave.
Glendale, CA 91201
 *Collects, restores and preserves radio
 horn speakers; author of "Radio Horn
 Speaker Encyclopedia"; send $14.90
 for a copy.*

Repair Services

Lakes Loudspeaker Service
4400 W. Hillsboro Blvd.
Coconut Creek, FL 33073
phone: 800-367-SPKR
 Loudspeaker rebuilding service.

Transistor

Collectors

Bob Davidson
310 Main St.
Concord, MA 01742-2319
phone: 508-369-2007
 *Wants to buy Japanese pocket
 transistor radios.*

John Treggiari
Salem, MA 01970-1225
phone: 508-744-2897
fax: 508-744-5572
e-mail: micrometer@juno.com
 *Serious collector wants to buy small
 transistor radios made in U.S.A. or in
 Japan 1950s to early 1960s; radios
 need not be working; radios molded in
 bright colors especially wanted; also
 wants catalogs and related items.*

Richard Lambert
166 East 34th St.
New York, NY 10016
phone: 212-684-6564
 *Wants to buy 1950s and 1960s
 transistor radios; Emerson, Regency,
 Zenith, Sony, etc.*

Arnold Hornstein
21 Golden Hill Ct.
Baltimore, MD 21228
 *Wants transistor radios made in
 Japan or in the U.S.*

J.L. Wilson
2007 Water Edge Dr.
Birmingham, AL 35244-1441
phone: 205-985-4254
 *Wants early, small transistor radios
 from the 1950s and early 1960s such
 as by Regency, Raytheon, Toshiba,
 Sony, Zenith, etc.*

Gary Willoughby
5930 W. Jefferson·
Los Angeles, CA 90016
phone: 310-559-0706
fax: 310-836-6518
 *Wants early pocket-sized one or two
 transistor radios; some say "Boy's
 Radio" on back.*

Darryl Rehr
Transistor Collectors
P.O. Box 641824
Los Angeles, CA 90064-6824
phone: 310-477-5229
fax: 310-268-8420
e-mail: dcrehr@earthlink.net
Internet: http://www.earthlink.net/
 ~dcrehr/trans1.html
 *Buying attractive radios 1954-1963;
 send photocopy and SASE for reply;
 no chips or cracks, please.*

Eric Wrobbel
20802 Exhibit Ct.
Woodland Hills, CA 91367-5205
phone: 818-884-2282
 *Wants shirt-pocket or coat-pocket size
 transistor radios, working or not;
 made in the U.S. or in Japan; call or
 write with radio brand name and
 model number, or send photocopy of
 front of radio; also wants toy crystal
 radios.*

Mike Kramer
P.O. Box 3257
Vallejo, CA 94590-0676
phone: 800-568-8883 or 800-446-6581
fax: 707-642-2456
 Wants to buy shirt pocket size

Japanese transistor radios; also wants Catalin table model radios.

Mike Kramer
P.O. Box 3257
Vallejo, CA 94590-0676
phone: 800-568-8883 or 800-446-6581
fax: 707-642-2456
  Wants to buy shirt pocket size Japanese transistor radios; also wants Catalin table model radios.

Mike Brooks
7335 Skyline
Oakland, CA 94611-1121
phone: 510-339-1751
e-mail: deborahwb@aol.com
  Wants to buy early American and Japanese transistor radios including boys' models, earphone only, and other miniature sets; also wants toy pocket crystal radios from the 1920s to 1960s.

Dealers

Bob Roberts
P.O. Box 152
Guilderland, NY 12084-0152
e-mail: 72376.677@compuserve.com
  Wants to buy novelty transistor radios, e.g. Atlas Battery, Brut cologne, Budweiser, Pepsi, Coke, McDonald's, etc.; also wants telephones in unusual shapes, e.g. gas pumps, food items, cartoon charac-ters, cars, movie related, TV, etc.

Chris Cuff
Forestburgh, NY 12777
  A transistor radio collector, dealer, and restorer.

Experts

Bill Burkett
P.O. Box 2488
Sun City, AZ 85372-2488
phone: 602-974-4535 or 800-507-7234
fax: 602-974-4323
  Buyer of 1950s transistor radios; especially interested in shirt-pocket or coat pocket size radios made by Mitchell, Raytheon, Regency, or Toshiba; solar-powered radios by Admiral or Hoffman and any size plastic or cabinet radio.

Periodicals

Marty & Sue Bunis
Newsletter: Transistor Network
32 West Main St.
Bradford, NH 03221
phone: 603-938-5051
fax: 603-938-2430
  A monthly newsletter featuring pictures, articles and classified ads - all exclusively about transistor radios.

Tubes For

Collectors

Electronic Communications
3630 Cavalier Dr.
Garland, TX 75042
phone: 972-272-3581
  Wants all types of radio tubes; prefer new in box, old stock tubes and new and used antique tubes.

Suppliers

David Headley
DH Distributors
P.O. Box 48623
Wichita, KS 67201-8623
phone: 316-684-0050
fax: 316-684-0050
  Buys and sells receiving, transmitting and industrial vacuum tubes.

RAILROAD COLLECTIBLES

  (see also BOOKS, Railroad; DINNERWARE, Advertising; RAILROADS; STREETCAR LINE COLLECTIBLES; TRAINS; TRANSPORTATION COL-LECTIBLES)

Clubs/Associations

Canadian Railroad Historical Associa-tion
120 Rue St. Pierre
St. Constant
Quebec J5A 2G9 Canada

Railway & Locomotive Historical Society
P.O. Box 1418
Westford, MA 01886

Joel R. Shaw
Key, Lock & Lantern, Inc.
Newsletter: Key, Lock & Lantern
31 Sandle Drive
Fairport, NY 14450
phone: 716-385-3776
  Since 1966 providing railroadiana collectors with camaraderie, education, and enjoyment; quarterly journal contains articles, information, and photos on subjects of interest to collectors of railroad artifacts.

Richard Wright
Railroadiana Collectors Association
Newsletter: Express
P.O. Box 4894
Diamond Bar, CA 91765-0894
phone: 909-681-4647 or 909-364-6620
  Over 1400 members; focuses on railroadiana; newsletter carries articles and photos; annual convention.

Collectors

Richard Schreibman
P.O. Box 121
Mountain Dale, NY 12763
phone: 914-434-6662
  Railroad timetables, annual passes, badges, depot items, calendars.

Nestle's Railroadiana
RD 2, Box 105
Greenwich, NY 12834-9425
phone: 518-692-2867
  Buys and sells all sorts of railroadiana and trolley memorabilia: timetables, guides, maps, advertising info., menus, old books and magazines, etc.

David Freeman
P.O. Box 191
Floyd, VA 24091
phone: 703-343-5358
fax: 703-343-3240
  Buys collections and accumulations of railroad passes, match books, pre-1950 timetables and playing cards, railroad sheet music.

Randy Ridgely
447 Oglethorpe Ave.
Athens, GA 30606-2236
phone: 706-549-9264
  Wants railroad china, silver, paper, etc.; also steamship and airline items.

Miles Hess
P.O. Box 942
Fitzgerald, GA 31750
  Wants to buy railroad telegraph keys, sounders, and telegraph bugs, etc.

Seth Bramson
330 N.E. 96th St.
Miami, FL 33138-2718
phone: 305-757-1016
fax: 305-895-8178
  Buys railroad and trolleyana; postage paid on approvals.

Richard Hebel
233 Dietrich Crescent Dr.
Lawrenceburg, IN 47025
phone: 317-848-2977
  Collector buying railroad items: lanterns, globes, china, silver, brass locks, etc.

Richard Wright
P.O. Box 4894
Diamond Bar, CA 91765-0894
phone: 909-681-4647 or 909-364-6620
  Wants railroad items such as china, silverware, lanterns, etc.; all inquires answered.

Dealers

Fred N. Arone
Depot Attic, The
3 Vista Place
Hartsdale, NY 10530-1202
phone: 914-693-5858
  Buys and sells pre-1960 railroadiana: paper ephemera, books, hardware, silverware and chinaware, timetables, lanterns, brass locks, posters and display advertising, calendars, passes, porcelain signs, hat badges, playing cards, etc.

L. Michael Boak
Initialed Duck Antiques & Collectibles
3812 Hamilton Ave.
Baltimore, MD 21206-3505
  Buys, sells and collects primarily B&O railroad memorabilia.

Steve Schmale
Out West
2231 Creekside Rd.
Santa Rosa, CA 95405-8022
phone: 707-838-1859 or 707-575-5406
e-mail: outweststv@aol.com
  Buys and sells better vintage postcards since 1976; approval service; strong in Western states views; always buying better cards and real photos; also wants railroad paper, stereoviews, photos, brochures, trade cards; member IFPD.

Scott Arden
Antiques & Artifacts
20457 Highway 126
Noti, OR 97461-9706
phone: 503-935-1619
  Leading RR mail order dealer for 26 years; catalog $1; buys and sells fine old transportation items, mostly non-paper; consignment.

Experts

Alan Altman
Golden Spike Enterprises Inc.
12 Southwedge
Getzville, NY 14068
phone: 716-689-9074

Richard C. Barrett
Railroad Research Publications
3400 Ridge Rd. West, Ste. 5-266
Rochester, NY 14626-3458
phone: 716-227-6903
  Publisher of books on railroad collectibles and railroad history.

Sue & Bill Knous
Railroad Memories
1903 S. Niagara St.
Denver, CO 80224
  Authors of "The Railroad Detective, a Guide to Replica & Counterfeit Railroad Collectibles."

Museums/Libraries

Ralph Justen
National Railroad Museum
Newsletter: Railines
2285 S. Broadway
Green Bay, WI 54304-7245
phone: 414-435-7623 or 414-435-7245
e-mail: staff@nationalrrmuseum.org
Internet: http://www.nationalrrmuseum.org
  One of the oldest railroad museums in the country; 75+ pieces of rolling stock; world's largest steam locomotive; seasonal train rides; well stocked gift shop.

Howard Page
Old Depot Railroad Museum, The
651 West Hwy., #12
P.O. Box 99
Dassel, MN 55325
phone: 612-275-2646
*An old Great Northern depot filled
with railroad artifacts: bells &
whistles, uniforms, signs, signals,
advertising toys & models, two
cabooses, freight car, section car,
track bicycle, pictures, calendars, etc.*

Railroad & Pioneer Museum
31st at Ave. H
P.O. Box 5126
Temple, TX 76505
phone: 817-778-6873

Periodicals

R.D. Roland
R.S. & T. Ry. Co.
Ad Paper: Main Line Journal, The
P.O. Box 121
Streamwood, IL 60107-0121
*A bi-monthly "ad" paper exclusively
for buying and selling railroad
collectibles as well as airline and
steamship memorabilia; subscribers
receive FREE ads.*

B & O Items

Collectors

Charles Boice
7003 Charles Ridge Rd.
Baltimore, MD 21204-3608
phone: 410-321-7149 or 301-897-8850
*Wants to buy Baltimore & Ohio R.R.
memorabilia and china.*

Dealers

John R. Hickman
Railroad Antiques
772 Tiffany Dr.
Gaithersburg, MD 20878-1821
phone: 301-926-5818
*Baltimore & Ohio R.R. memorabilia
and china; also other transportation
memorabilia from steamships and
airlines.*

Repro. Sources

B & O Railroad Museum
901 Pratt St.
Baltimore, MD 21223
phone: 410-237-3746
*Sells B & O railroad china and other
B & O related items.*

China

Collectors

Robert D'Achille
3972 NY Rt. 26
Whitney Point, NY 13862-2708
phone: 607-862-3914
*Wants any railroad china especially
Railroad-marked; must be in good
condition (no hairlines, cracks or
chips, etc.)*

Dealers

Alan Altman
Golden Spike Enterprises Inc.
12 Southwedge
Getzville, NY 14068
phone: 716-689-9074
*Wants to buy railroad china,
especially by Buffalo or Syracuse
China.*

Experts

Gerry & Christie Geisler
Great Delaware & New England
Antiques Trading Company
P.O. Box 1065
Chatham, NJ 07928
phone: 201-635-0756

Douglas W. McIntyre
20 Cleveland Place
Lockport, NY 14094-3104
phone: 716-433-2235
*Author of "The Official Guide to
Railroad Dining Car China."*

Museums/Libraries

B & O Railroad Museum, Chessie Shop
901 Pratt St.
Baltimore, MD 21223
phone: 410-237-3746
Shop sells B&O railroad china.

Dining Car Items

Collectors

Peter Tilp
B & T Publications
P.O. Box 580
Summit, NJ 07901-0580
*Wants railroad dining car items and
related railroad collectibles: china,
silverware, flatware, glassware,
napkins, menus, etc.*

Dealers

Charles Goodman
636 W. Grant Ave.
Charleston, IL 61920-3226
phone: 217-345-6771
*Wants railroad dining car china,
silverware, flatware, glassware,
napkins, menus, and related items;
offers catalog of items for sale.*

Hat Badges

Experts

Jim Younger
4628 Old Dragon Path
Ellicott City, MD 21042-5970
phone: 410-964-1949
e-mail: jmyr@erols.com
*Wants railroad hat badges (from all
railroads and in all occupations),
hats, uniforms, and brotherhood (RR
Unions) lapel pins.*

Paper Items

Collectors

Carl Loucks
P.O. Box 484
North Haven, CT 06473-0484
phone: 203-288-3765
fax: 203-234-2729
*Wants railroad timetables, brochures,
guides, maps, menus; also trolley, air
and bus.*

Passes

Collectors

George Johnson
P.O. Box 1449
Lexington, VA 24450-1449
phone: 703-464-4326
fax: 703-464-4326
*Wants to buy pre-1940 timetables for
railroad, trolley, airline, and bus; also
wants passes, catalogs, and postcards
of small town depots.*

Ed Lewis
P.O. Box 505
Aberdeen, NC 28315
phone: 910-692-7457
fax: 910-944-9738
*Collector wants to buy railroad
timetables and passes from small
railroads.*

Playing Cards

Experts

Phil Bollhagen
8222 South 51st Street
Franklin, WI 53132-9276
phone: 414-327-6220
e-mail: bollhagp@execpc.com
*Has one of the largest collections of
antique railroad playing card decks in
the U.S.; wants to buy quality pre-
1915 decks from all railroads; author
of "The Great Book of Railroad
Playing Cards"; railroad decks and
singles.*

Posters

Collectors

Charles G. Kratz, Jr.
17821 Golfview
Homewood, IL 60430-1210
phone: 708-799-8478 or 312-951-0336
*Wants original railroad posters
produced for American and Canadian
companies; also original railroad
paintings and any material relating to
Chicago & Eastern Illinois Railroad.*

Signal Lamps

Collectors

Jake
P.O. Box 503
Falls Church, VA 22046
*Marked railroad lanterns and marked
globes: $200 for green, amber, blue
marked RR globes.*

Experts

David Dreimiller
33200 Brainbridge Rd., Ste. #4
Solon, OH 44139
phone: 216-569-7415
*Author of "Signal Lights" which
covers railroad signal lamps and
lanterns; also buys lanterns and
manufacturer's sales literature; will
assist in lamp/lantern identification
and appraisal.*

Timetables

Collectors

Collector
4000 N. Upland
Arlington, VA 22207
*Wants to buy all pre-1910 railroad
passes and timetables.*

Ed Lewis
P.O. Box 505
Aberdeen, NC 28315
phone: 910-692-7457
fax: 910-944-9738
*Collector wants to buy railroad
timetables and passes from small
railroads.*

Uniforms

(see BUTTONS, Railroad/Transit
Uniforms)

RAILROADS

(see also BOOKS, Railroad;
RAILROAD COLLECTIBLES;
STEAM-OPERATED, Models &
Equipment; TRAINS)

Book Sellers

Harold H. Carstens
Carstens Publications
P.O. Box 700
Newton, NJ 07860-0700
phone: 201-383-3355 or 800-474-6995
fax: 201-383-4064
*Carries large line of books about
railroads.*

Clubs/Associations

New York Central System Historical
Society, Inc.
Magazine: Central Headlight
P.O. Box 58994
Philadelphia, PA 19102-8994
phone: 610-687-1207
*Publishes quarterly magazine;
information, drawings, photos
available; research sources; inquiries
welcome.*

Chesapeake & Ohio Historical Society,
Inc.
Magazine: Chesapeake & Ohio
Historical Magazine
P.O. Box 79
Clifton Forge, VA 24422
phone: 703-862-2210
*Monthly articles on history of the
C&O RR and predecessors (PM RR in*

Mich., HV RR in Ohio, etc.), as well as successor CSX Transportation.

Motor Car Collectors of America
Newsletter: Speeder
5 Bay View Hills
Wever, IA 52658
Members interested in the preservation and operation of railroad track cars, handcars, motor cars and velocipedes.

William Shapotkin, Pres
Railroad Club of America, Inc., The
Journal: Railroad Capital, The
P.O. Box 8292
Chicago, IL 60680
phone: 708-251-2262
Founded in 1934 for the purpose of coordinating interests and activities of those interested in any matter pertaining to railroads.

Collectors

Robert Gormley
334 Brownsburg Rd.
Newtown, PA 18940-9626
phone: 215-598-3520
Wants switchback and Mt. Pisqah, Mauch Chunk, PA railroad collectibles and souvenirs.

Dealers

David Thebodo
Flange R.R. Equipment Co.
P.O. Box 2019
Fairfield, IA 52556-8019
phone: 515-472-2020
Buys and sells railroad rolling stock: cabooses, Fairmont motorcars, passenger cars, box cars, bunk cars, flatcars, baggage cars, coaches, and other railroad equipment.

Experts

Joseph Gross
P.O. Box 15
Spencerport, NY 14559-0015
phone: 716-768-8918
Author of "Railroads of North America" (Gross Publications.)

Robert L. Johnson
Whistles in the Woods Museum Services
P.O. Box 309
Chickamauga, GA 30707-0309
phone: 706-375-4326
e-mail: oldgoat@voy.net
Consultants specializing in narrow-gauge, steam, industrial, logging and mining railroads; American, foreign (European, Australian); also inclines, aerial tramways, garden and large scale model railroads.

Museums/Libraries

Museum of Transportation
15 Newton St.
Brookline, MA 02146
phone: 617-522-6140

William McKelvey, Dir.
New Jersey Railroad & Transportation Museum, Inc.
103 Dogwood Lane
Berkeley Heights, NJ 07922-2327
phone: 908-464-9335

New York Museum of Transportation
P.O. Box 136
West Henrietta, NY 14586
phone: 716-533-1113

California State Railroad Museum
125 I St.
Sacramento, CA 95814

Periodicals

Harold H. Carstens
Carstens Publications
Magazine: Railfan & Railroad
P.O. Box 700
Newton, NJ 07860-0700
phone: 201-383-3355 or 800-474-6995
fax: 201-383-4064

Harold H. Carstens
Carstens Publications
: Railroad Model Craftsman
P.O. Box 700
Newton, NJ 07860-0700
phone: 201-383-3355 or 800-474-6995
fax: 201-383-4064

D.F. Barnhardt
Newsletter: Tourist Rail Newsletter
P.O. Box 1088
Mount Pleasant, NC 28124-1088
phone: 704-436-9399
Internet: http://www.denver.net/-bretzel/
Focuses on the use of old time trains in tourist locations such as parks and amusement centers.

Kalmbach Publishing Co.
Magazine: Trains
P.O. Box 1612
Waukesha, WI 53187-1612
phone: 414-796-8776 or 800-533-6644
fax: 414-796-1383
e-mail: customerservice@kalmbach.com

Flying Scotsman

Collectors

Paul R. Dowie
P.O. Box 472
Chester Springs, PA 19425-0472
phone: 610-827-7561
Collects anything related to LNR 4472 "Flying Scotsman" (both the locomotive and the train of the same name): photos (especially with second/water tender), recordings, china and flatware from the F.S. train; books, posters, models.

RANGES

(see also CAST IRON ITEMS; KITCHEN COLLECTIBLES; STOVES)

Clubs/Associations

Jackie Shedden
Old Appliance Club
Newsletter: Old Road Home, The
P.O. Box 65
Ventura, CA 93002
phone: 805-643-3532
fax: 805-643-3532
e-mail: jes@west.net
An organization for dealers, owners, restorers, users and fans of American appliances; accent is placed on mostly antique and classic ranges 1920s-1950s, Monitor-top refrigerators; builds thermostats, applies new porcelain, restores.

Dealers

Erickson's Antique Stoves, Inc.
P.O. Box 2275
At the Depot
Littleton, MA 01460
phone: 508-486-3589
Antique gas coal and wood stoves and ranges; bought, sold, restored.

Paul Schoenharl
Rectanus Stove Co.
3940 Spring Grove
Cincinnati, OH 45223-2639
phone: 513-541-0450
Buys, sells and restores antique stoves and ranges (pre 1930) with emphasis on antique gas ranges 1882-1930; also lectures and writes magazine articles about early kitchen stoves.

Macy Stern
Macy's Texas Stove Works
5515 Almeda Rd.
Houston, TX 77004-7443
phone: 713-521-0934 or 713-528-1297
fax: 713-521-0889
Buys, sells, brokers, repairs, and restores old ranges; also sells parts and publishes "Classic Ranges" newspaper.

Jack Santoro
J.E.S. Enterprises
P.O. Box 65
Ventura, CA 93002
phone: 805-643-3532
fax: 805-643-3532
e-mail: jes@west.net
Superior range restoration: mechanical systems rebuilt, genuine porcelain finishes, safety valves, Bakelite refinished, clocks & timers rebuilt, brilliant electroplating, oven controls, movie prop rentals.

Museums/Libraries

Paul Schoenharl
Cincinnati Stove Museum
3940 Spring Grove
Cincinnati, OH 45223-2639
phone: 513-541-0450
Small museum of stoves and ranges; no admission.

Periodicals

Macy Stern
Macy's Texas Stove Works
Newspaper: Classic Ranges
2617 Riverside
Houston, TX 77004-7610
phone: 713-528-2990
fax: 713-529-2122
The only newsletter for classic range owners and buyers; ranges/ovens and stoves for sale, ranges wanted to buy, parts for sale, restoration services, articles, old advertisements, etc.

Repair Services

Jack Santoro
J.E.S. Enterprises
P.O. Box 65
Ventura, CA 93002
phone: 805-643-3532
fax: 805-643-3532
e-mail: jes@west.net
Superior range restoration: mechanical systems rebuilt, genuine porcelain finishes, safety valves, Bakelite refinished, clocks & timers rebuilt, brilliant electroplating, oven controls, movie prop rentals.

RATIONING RELATED ITEMS

(see also MILITARIA, WWII Items)

Clubs/Associations

Thomas B. Smith
Society of Ration Token Collectors
Newsletter: Ration Board, The
618 Jay Drive
Gallipolis, OH 45631-1314
Society collects, trades, sells paper & token home front ration items (for food, clothing, gasoline, tires, etc.); send SASE for info.

Collectors

Lee Poleske
P.O. Box 871
Seward, AK 99664-0871
Wants OPA tokens and other WWII ration items.

Museums/Libraries

Ronald Mahoney
California State University, Madden Library
5200 N. Barton Ave.
Fresno, CA 93740
phone: 209-278-2595
Wants WWII ration items.

RAY GUNS

(see TOYS, Space & Robot [Ray Guns])

RAZORS

(see BARBER SHOP COLLECTIBLES; SHAVING COLLECTIBLES)

RECIPES

(see also FOOD COLLECTIBLES)

Periodicals

Newsletter: Recipe Express
12500 Wistful Cove
Austin, TX 78729
A quarterly newsletter: publish your recipes, read reviews of new cookbooks, meet fellow recipe nuts.

RECORD JACKETS

(see PAPER COLLECTIBLES; RECORDS)

RECORDED SOUND

(see also COMPACT DISCS; RADIO SHOWS, Old Time; RECORDS)

Clubs/Associations

Peter Shambarger, ExDir
Association for Recorded Sound Collections, Inc.
Journal: ARSC Journal
P.O. Box 543
Annapolis, MD 21404-0543
phone: 410-757-0488 or 410-956-5600
fax: 410-349-0175
e-mail: peters@umd5.umd.edu
Dedicated to the preservation and study of recordings in the fields of music and speech: Edison cylinders, rare discs, oral history, etc.; publishes the ARSC Journal twice a year and the ARSC Newsletter four times per year.

Dealers

Don Kyle
Soundtracks!
P.O. Box 107
Venice, CA 90294-0107
phone: 310-226-2883
e-mail: sndtrx@earthlink.net
Internet: http://www.batfanclub.com
Buys and sells soundtracks; original cast, children's, Disney and personality LPs; sells via mail order and at conventions; also trades and buys collections.

RECORDS

(see also BOOKS, Reference [Records]; AUDIO-VISUAL; COMPACT DISCS; DRUM & BUGLE CORPS; HI-FI EQUIPMENT; MUSIC; PHONOGRAPHS; RECORDED SOUND; ROCK 'N' ROLL COLLECTIBLES)

Appraisers

Scott Neuman
Forever Vinyl
P.O. Box 526
Lakehurst, NJ 08733
phone: 732-505-3646
fax: 732-505-5337
e-mail: sales@forevervinyl.com
Internet: http://www.forevervinyl.com
Buys, sells, trades rare and hard-to-find vinyl records and albums, 45s picture sleeves; most anything to do with music; over 500,000 items in stock; over 20 years in business; appraise for estate, insurance, etc.

Steven Smolian
Smolian Sound Preservation Studios
1 Worman's Mill Court #4
Frederick, MD 21701
phone: 301-694-5134
fax: 301-694-5179
Record collections appraised for tax donation, estate & insurance loss purposes; all formats - 78s, 45s, LPs, cylinders, radio disks, etc.; rock, classical, country, old news broadcasts; over 20 years appraising major archives.

Steve Underwood, ISA
Appraisals & Consulting by F. Steven Underwood
2516 Larwood Dr.
Charleston, WV 25302-4318
phone: 304-345-4089
Independent, professional appraisals for insurance, estate valuation, tax, legal, and other matters; Member, International Society of Appraisers.

John Vogel
Phonograph Record Appraisals & Search Service
963 Ridgemont Rd.
Charleston, WV 25314-1135
phone: 304-346-1631 or 304-345-0761
fax: 304-345-0762
Appraises single records or entire collections; also offers a finders service to locate rare items for collectors; will help locate buyers for your collections.

Auction Services

Floyd Silver
Antique Phonograph Center
P.O. Box 2574
Vincentown, NJ 08088-2574
phone: 609-859-8617
e-mail: fsilver@compuserve.com
Conducts special mail auctions of rare and unusual 78 rpm Edison diamond discs and cylinder records; $2 for catalog.

Lawrence Koons
Worldwide Record Auctions
18 Walnut, #3
Belpre, OH 45714-2429
phone: 614-423-3393 or 614-423-5478
fax: 614-423-9638
Conducts special mail auctions of records from the 1950s to 1970s; Rock 'n' Roll, blues, R&B; send $2 for catalog.

Clubs/Associations

Association of Independent Record Collectors
Newsletter: AIRC Newsletter
P.O. Box 222
Northford, CT 06472-0222
phone: 203-484-2023
e-mail: dipdadip@aol.com

Collectors

Dave A. Reiss
3920 Eve Dr.
Seaford, NY 11783-1553
phone: 516-785-8336
Collects 78 rpm's, 1900 to 1930s: popular, classical, jazz, personalities, dance records, gospel, country & western, ethnic.

Dealers

Gerald Wilson
Select Circle Records
3 Dandy Dr.
Cos Cob, CT 06807
phone: 203-661-8421
Specializes in Frank Sinatra.

Ardyth & John Stimson
What Goes Around
P.O. Box 513
Glen Ridge, NJ 07028-0513
e-mail: ajs@viconet.com
Buying and selling early jazz and rock & roll.

Rod Baum
Rare Records
1432 Queen Anne Rd.
Teaneck, NJ 07666
phone: 201-833-4883
fax: 201-833-4874

Allen Radwill
23 Hunters Lane
Vincentown, NJ 08088-2837
phone: 609-953-5473
250,000 items related to rock & roll, rhythm & blues, soul, gospel, television, movies: records, sheet music, magazines; no CDs or videos.

Princeton Record Exchange
20 S. Tulane St.
Princeton, NJ 08542
phone: 609-921-0881
Internet: http://www.prex.com
Buys and sells new and used CDs, LPs, and tapes: rock, jazz, alternative, imports, oldies, shows, new releases, soundtracks, classical, opera, etc.

Scott Neuman
Forever Vinyl
P.O. Box 526
Lakehurst, NJ 08733
phone: 732-505-3646
fax: 732-505-5337
e-mail: sales@forevervinyl.com
Internet: http://www.forevervinyl.com
Buys, sells, trades rare and hard-to-find vinyl records and albums, 45s picture sleeves; most anything to do with music; over 500,000 items in stock; over 20 years in business; appraise for estate, insurance, etc.

R. Hess
P.O. Box 963
New York, NY 10023-0963
phone: 212-579-0689
Wants 1948-1965 LP records (33 1/3 rpm): V-Discs, picture discs, Jazz, R&B, R 'n R, Blues, pop, soundtracks, Latin; also related books, photos, posters, magazines, etc.; also sells LPs, 45s, 78s, sheet music; by appointment or mail.

Debbie Sobah
Attic Records
5020 W. Grove Lane
Gibsonia, PA 15044
phone: 412-625-1116
fax: 412-625-0062
e-mail: musicman@atticrecords.com
Internet: http://www.atticrecords.com
Specializes in vinyl records; has over 10 million records of all types in stock; caters to the collector.

D & J Records
212 E. Main St.
Carnegie, PA 15106
phone: 412-279-8888
fax: 412-279-5538
Over 1 million 45s in stock; music from 1940s to 1990s.

Fred Bohn
Attic, The
513 Grant Ave.
Pittsburgh, PA 15209
phone: 412-821-8484
fax: 412-821-5179
Over 4 million records in stock; buys collections of 45s, 78s, and LPs; also phonograph records and CDs.

Jim Weaver
405 Dunbar
Pittsburgh, PA 15235-5218
Buys and sells records; has over 25,000 12" singles, promo 45's, picture sleeves, albums, rare records; has no list so send want lists.

Mike Landis
P.O. Box 544
Akron, PA 17501
phone: 888-248-2291
Buys and sells 1950s-1960s black vocal groups; call toll free!

Musical Energy
55 N. Main St.
Wilkes Barre, PA 18701
phone: 717-829-2929
e-mail: energi@epix.net
Buys and sells CDs, records, tapes, videos and books; large collection of albums and singles.

Nina's Discount Oldies
P.O. Box 77
Narberth, PA 19072
phone: 800-336-4627
Over 3 million records in stock; 12" and current hits available; mail order with music from 1950s through 1990s.

Tom Engle
P.O. Box 1802
Hyattsville, MD 20788-0802
phone: 410-750-3730
fax: 410-750-9537
e-mail: deepgroove@mindspring.com
Wants to buy jazz, classical LPs, rock 'n' roll, R&B 450s, LPs, posters, and related memorabilia.

Steven Smolian
Smolian Sound Preservation Studios
1 Worman's Mill Court #4
Frederick, MD 21701
phone: 301-694-5134
fax: 301-694-5179
Wants large LP and 78rpm collections; classical and jazz music a specialty; also appraises records for donation purposes.

Memory Lane Records
Newspaper: Record Finder
P.O. Box 1047
Glen Allen, VA 23060-1047
phone: 804-266-1154 or 804-288-4949
fax: 804-264-9660
A monthly newspaper for the record collector: articles, ads, mail-bid record auctions; also sells record collections on consignment.

Records Unlimited
2126 Wards Rd.
Lynchburg, VA 24502-5312
phone: 804-832-0729
fax: 804-239-7519
Buys and sells LPs, 45s from all periods; also new and used CDs and cassettes.

Revolution Records & CDs
1620A Alton Rd.
South Beach, FL 33139
phone: 305-673-6464
LPs, 45s, 12" singles, CDs, cassettes, box sets, videos, picture discs, sheet music, collectibles.

Bananas Records, Tapes & CDs
2226 16th Ave. N.
Saint Petersburg, FL 33713
phone: 813-327-4616 or 800-823-4113
fax: 813-343-0775
Large record and CD collector's store; over one million albums in stock; all categories.

Shelly G. Callies
4072 Scenic Rd.
Campbellsport, WI 53010
phone: 414-533-5593
Buying records, LPs, 45s, 78s, CDs; also magazines, books, and memorabilia relating to music and musicians; herself a musician collecting many kinds of recorded music, especially jazz.

Ted & Betty Salveson
Coin Machine Trader
P.O. Box 602
Huron, SD 57350-0602
phone: 605-352-3870 or 605-352-6460
fax: 605-352-7590
Specializes in old phonograph records.

John Telizyn
Sparky's Mail Order
3724 N. Page
Chicago, IL 60634
phone: 773-625-8732
Specializes in buying and selling vinyl records.

Record Ron's Good & Plenty
1129 Decatur St.
New Orleans, LA 70116
phone: 504-524-9444
Pop, jazz, R&B, soul, blues, gospel, oldies, zydeco, comedy, doo wop, Dixieland, big bands, spoken word, Broadway shows, country & western; LPs, 45s, CDs, tapes, sheet music, music memorabilia.

Nitebird Sounds
P.O. Box 643
Stuttgart, AR 72160-0643

Stan Gold
As Time Goes By
7042 Dartbrook Dr.
Dallas, TX 75240
phone: 972-239-8621 or 214-352-2765
fax: 972-239-9632
e-mail: record@unicomp.net
Internet: http://www.astimegoesby.com/atgb
Wants all formats from 78s to LPs; 1940s to 1960s jazz, rock and R&B 1950s to 1960s; also exotic/lounge, personalities, picture discs, classical, blues, folk, and related advertisements.

L.R. (Les) Docks
Shellac Shack
P.O. Box 691035
San Antonio, TX 78269-1035
phone: 210-492-6021
fax: 210-492-6489
Buying vintage popular records, especially 78's: jazz, blues, hillbilly, pop, rockabilly, etc.; wants list (a 72-page profusely illustrated booklet, including thousands of actual prices paid) for $2 (refundable.)

Randy's Record Shop
157 East 900 S.
Salt Lake City, UT 84111
phone: 801-532-4413
Thousands of LPs, CDs, 45s, cassettes and collectibles.

Vinyl Vendors
1800 S. Robertson Blvd., #279
Los Angeles, CA 90035
e-mail: paul@vinylvendors.com
Internet: http://www.vinylvendors.com
Huge selection of vinyl records.

Philip Smith
House of Records
3328 Pico Blvd.
Santa Monica, CA 90405
phone: 310-450-1222
fax: 310-450-5425
Buys, sells, trades new, used and collectible records.

American Pie Records
614 N. Milpas
Santa Barbara, CA 93103
phone: 805-965-2161
Specializing in 1960s and 1960s vinyl; no punk, heavy metal, rap, CDs or tapes - only real records.

Record Man, The
1322 El Camino Real
Redwood City, CA 94063
phone: 650-368-9065
fax: 650-368-2968
e-mail: recman@ix.netcom.com
LPs, 45s, EPs, picture discs, 78s, CDs, cassettes, reel-to-reels, videos, memorabilia, posters, books, magazines, sheet music.

Paul Aguirre
2634 Hyde St.
San Francisco, CA 94109-1221
phone: 415-775-4160
fax: 415-775-4160
e-mail: SabuSabu@sirius.com
Mail order vinyl record dealer.

Experts

Paul C. Mawhinney
Record-Rama Sound Archives
4981 McKnight Rd.
Pittsburgh, PA 15237-3407
phone: 412-367-7330 or 800-445-2357
fax: 412-367-7388
e-mail: recrama@musicmaster.com
Internet: http://www.musicmaster.com
Expert in recorded sound, albums, compact discs, 45 rpm records; search services; DJ supplies, record and disc cleaning supplies, reference material on history of recorded sound; author of "MusicMaster: The 45 RPM Record Directory."

L.R. (Les) Docks
Shellac Shack
P.O. Box 691035
San Antonio, TX 78269-1035
phone: 210-492-6021
fax: 210-492-6489
Author of "American Premium Record Guide" (Books Americana).

Jerry Osborne
Osborne Enterprises
P.O. Box 255
Port Townsend, WA 98368
phone: 360-385-1200
fax: 360-385-6572
e-mail: jpo@olympus.net
Internet: http://www.olympus.net/personal/jpo
Author of "The Official Price Guide to Records" (House of Collectibles).

On-Line Services

Edward Odel
Hot Platters
P.O. Box 4213
Thousand Oaks, CA 91359-1213
fax: 805-492-3682
e-mail: HotPlatter@aol.com
Internet: http://www.oversight.com/HotPlatters.html
On-line music store; all categories of LPs, 45s, 78s, tapes, books, magazines, CDs, posters, videos, sheet music, rock and movie memorabilia; printed catalog $20.

Periodicals

New Amberola Phonograph Co. The
Magazine: New Amberola Graphic, The
37 Caledonia St.
St. Johnsbury, VT 05819
A quarterly publication for collectors of early phonographs & records from the years 1895-1935; articles, book reviews, ads, auctions, etc.

Don Mennie, Pub.
Newspaper: Record Collectors Monthly
P.O. Box 75
Mendham, NJ 07945-0075
phone: 201-543-9520
fax: 201-543-6033
Covers collectible records primarily from 1950 to 1968; 45's, LP's, some 78's; Rock 'N' Roll, R & B, vocal groups, pop music of the era. Information about records, record companies, artists; NOT a price guide; irregularly published.

John Koenig
Antique Trader Publications, Inc.
Newsmagazine: DISCoveries Magazine
922 Churchill St., Ste. #1
Waupaca, WI 54981
phone: 715-258-7525 or 800-768-9225
fax: 715-258-8707
e-mail: jkoenig@add-inc.com
Internet: http://www.csmonline.com
The record collector's magazine; articles on artists, ads for 10s of thousands of CD's & related music memorabilia from 1930s to present; in-depth coverage of a variety of music, stars, and eras; music memorabilia wanted and for sale.

Julie A. Ulrich, PR
Krause Publications
Magazine: Goldmine
700 E. State St.
Iola, WI 54990-0001
phone: 715-445-2214
fax: 715-445-4087
e-mail: info@krause.com
Internet: http://www.krause.com
A biweekly magazine containing articles, ads about records & recording artists from 1940s to present; the record & CD marketplace.

Suppliers

Andy's Record Supplies
48 Colonial Rd.
Providence, RI 02906
phone: 401-421-9453
fax: 401-421-0841
Japanese resealable mylar sleeves, poly sleeves, CD replacement cases, cardboard jackets, mailers, blister packs, storage boxes, cassette replacement cases, white plastic divider cards, quality paper sleeves.

Bags Unlimited
7 Canal St.
Rochester, NY 14608-1910
phone: 800-767-2247 or 716-436-9006
fax: 716-328-8526
e-mail: bags@frontiernet.net
Internet: http://www.frontiernet.net/
~bags
*Sells record collector supplies: poly
and paper sleeves, mailers, filler pads,
album jackets, storage boxes, divider
cards, etc.*

Something Special Enterprises
P.O. Box 74
Allison Park, PA 15101
phone: 412-487-2626
fax: 412-487-3369
*CD jewel cases, storage boxes and
shippers; 45 rpm record sleeves, LP
albums and sleeves, white paper
sleeves, record and CD dividers; also
regular comic bags, newspaper bags,
magazine bags, baseball card holders,
sheet music bags.*

Jack Price
Cabco Products
P.O. Box 8212
Columbus, OH 43201-0212
phone: 614-267-8468 or 614-263-0284
fax: 614-267-8468
e-mail: jproto1@aol.com
*Catalog of replacement sleeves,
jackets, covers, boxes, CD supplies,
video supplies, storage boxes, frame
displays, record holders, etc.*

Big Band

Experts

L.R. (Les) Docks
Shellac Shack
P.O. Box 691035
San Antonio, TX 78269-1035
phone: 210-492-6021
fax: 210-492-6489
*Expert, dealer and avid collector of
1920s-1930s jazz and big band 78s.*

Children's

Experts

Peter Muldavin
173 W. 78th St., Apt. 5-F
New York, NY 10024-6711
phone: 212-362-9606
e-mail: metrowx@aol.com
Internet: http://members.aol.com/
kiddie785
*Expert, researcher, collector in Kiddie
Records (78s and occasionally 45s);
wants to buy any label, any year;
should be in original covers; will
make cassette recordings of hard-to-
find kiddie records; compiling
discography.*

Country & Bluegrass

Collectors

David Freeman
P.O. Box 191
Floyd, VA 24091
phone: 703-343-5358
fax: 703-343-3240
*Buys and sells 1922-1980 country &
bluegrass 78's, 45's & LP's; also
songbooks; over 25 years experience;
also specialty record auctions.*

Cylinder Records

Collectors

Steven Ramm
420 Fitzwater St.
Philadelphia, PA 19147-3109
phone: 215-922-7050 or 215-545-3290
e-mail: steveramm@aol.com
*Specializes in phonographs and pre-
1930 records; wants to buy sheet
music, postcards, and advertising with
illustrations of phonographs, records,
or Thomas A. Edison; also wants
cylinder rolls in playable condition.*

Gospel

Collectors

Arthur Crowley
207 Hamilton Rd.
Teaneck, NJ 07666-6367
phone: 201-833-0152
*Wants to buy Gospel 78s from the mid
1940s and 1950s on Chess, Downbeat,
Gotham, Nashboro, VJ, and other
labels.*

Jazz & Blues

Clubs/Associations

Vic Hall, Mem. Dir.
International Association of Jazz Record
Collectors
Journal: IAJRC Journal
15745 W. Birchwood Lane
Libertyville, IL 60048-5101
*Promotes exchange of information
and research on jazz, its musicians
and recordings.*

George Buck
Collectors Record Club
Newsletter: JazzBeat Magazine
1206 Decatur St.
New Orleans, LA 70116
phone: 504-525-1776
fax: 504-523-2629
*Catalog is dedicate to the documenta-
tion and preservation of traditional
jazz.*

Collectors

Frederick Cohen
55 Park Ave.
New York, NY 10016
*Wants Jazz records: 10" and 12" jazz
LPs (33 1/3 rpm) on labels such as
Blue Note, Prestige, Riverside, Debut,
etc., must be in excellent condition;*

*will travel for large collections; also
jazz memorabilia and books wanted.*

Dealers

R. Hess
P.O. Box 963
New York, NY 10023-0963
phone: 212-579-0689
*Wants to buy jazz and R&B records;
has been collecting for 30 years; also
wants original jazz art including sheet
music, statues, books, etc.; by
appointment or mail.*

Larry Raye
Cadence Building
Redwood, NY 13679
phone: 315-287-2852
fax: 315-287-2860
e-mail: cadence@cadencebuilding.com
Internet: http://
www.cadencebuilding.com
*Buys and sells old and new jazz and
blues LPs and CDs, books, etc.;
handles/distributes over 800 different
labels.*

Experts

L.R. (Les) Docks
Shellac Shack
P.O. Box 691035
San Antonio, TX 78269-1035
phone: 210-492-6021
fax: 210-492-6489
*Expert, dealer and avid collector of
1920s-1930s jazz and big band 78s.*

Periodicals

Larry Raye
Magazine: Cadence
Cadence Building
Redwood, NY 13679
phone: 315-287-2852
fax: 315-287-2860
e-mail: cadence@cadencebuilding.com
Internet: http://
www.cadencebuilding.com
*A monthly Jazz & Blues journal
featuring interviews, oral histories,
news and complete coverage of the
entire record scene; the most complete
coverage of jazz & blues, improvising
music in the world.*

Gene Joslin
Magazine: Joslin's Jazz Journal
P.O. Box 213
Parsons, KS 67357
phone: 316-421-0035
*JJJ is the ultimate marketplace for
original 78's, LP's, radio transcriptions, video tapes, and associated
literature and memorabilia; a
quarterly with articles, photos,
collector wants, free subscriber ads,
etc.*

Rock 'N' Roll

Collectors

Rockin' Richard
Radio Disc-Jockey
Flyer: Rockin' Richard 50's - 60's
Entertainment Guide
P.O. Box 222
Northford, CT 06472-0222
phone: 203-484-2023
e-mail: dipdadip@aol.com
*Hosts New Haven, CT's longest
running collector show on 88.7 FM
(WNHU), Tuesday 8-11 PM; reviews
recordings and products; hosts
conventions; radio show plays rare
records from the '50s & '60s; rhythm
& blues, rockabilly, rock 'n roll, etc.*

Dealers

Marc J. Cohen
P.O. Box 220153
Hollywood, FL 33022-0153
phone: 954-565-9754
*Buys and sells 1950s and early 1960s
rock and roll records: Bill Haley and
the Comets, Chuck Berry, Ricky
Nelson, Coasters, Bobby Darin, Buddy
Holly, Fats Domino, Platters, Everly
Brothers, Drifters, Elvis, Connie
Francis, etc.*

Experts

Jean Blankenship
P.O. Box 7274
Pasadena, TX 77508-7274
phone: 713-266-6311
Wants Rock 'n Roll records.

Soundtracks

Dealers

Footlight Records
113 East 12th Street
New York, NY 10003
phone: 212-533-1572
fax: 212-673-1496
e-mail: footlight@aol.com
Internet: http://www.footlight.com
*Specialty areas are cast recordings,
soundtracks and vocalists.*

Soundtrack Album Retailers
P.O. Box 487
New Holland, PA 17577
phone: 717-656-0121

Periodicals

Phil Nohl
Newsletter: Soundtrack Collector, The
5824 W. Galena
Milwaukee, WI 53208
Focuses on original soundtracks.

Lukas Kendall
Newsletter: Film Score Monthly
5967 Chula Vista Way
Los Angeles, CA 90068
phone: 213-464-7919
fax: 213-464-5916
e-mail: lukas@filmscoremonthly.com
Internet: http://
  www.filmscoremonthly.com
Focuses on original soundtracks.

Vogue Picture

Collectors

Marc Grobman
94 Paterson Rd.
Fanwood, NJ 07023

John W. Hess
244 Bernaski Rd.
Amsterdam, NY 12010
phone: 518-843-6117
*Wants to buy Vogue picture disc
records, horn phonographs, music
boxes, roller organs; also wants parts,
empty cabinets, horns; any condition,
any material.*

Paul Manganaro
P.O. Box 535
Coopersburg, PA 18036
*Wants to buy 78 rpm picture records
by Vogue, Mercury, RCA, etc.*

Michelle Pollitt
Vogue Lady, THe
P.O. Box 339
Orefield, PA 18069-0339
*Wants to buy Vogue and all types of
collectible picture records.*

Berie Seinberg
714 Moredon Rd.
Meadowbrook, PA 19046-1907
phone: 215-886-6124
e-mail: phonoman-
  Bernie@worldnet.att.net
*Wants to buy picture records, 78 rpm,
from Vogue and Victor; also any
picture records from the 1930s
through 1950s.*

John Widmar
5800 3rd Ave., Apt. 515
Kenosha, WI 53140-4237
phone: 414-654-6802

John Coates
324 Woodland Dr.
Stevens Point, WI 54481
phone: 715-341-6113
*Advanced Vogue picture record
collector.*

RED CROSS

(see also NURSES)

Collectors

Dick Lavin
2908 Cleave Dr.
Falls Church, VA 22042
phone: 703-533-8402
Wants to buy Red Cross medals,

*patches, pins, posters, tabs, and sheet
music; please send photo or call.*

Experts

Shirley Powers
7964 Sartan Way N.E.
Albuquerque, NM 87109-3128
phone: 505-821-2735
fax: 505-821-0245
e-mail: powers@crossnet.org
*Collects and documents American Red
Cross pins, posters, and uniforms;
publisher of "The Collector's Guide to
Red Cross Pins."*

RED WING POTTERY

(see CERAMICS [AMERICAN],
Stoneware [Red Wing Pottery];
CERAMICS [AMERICAN ART
POTTERY], Red Wing; CERAMICS
[AMERICAN DINNERWARE], Red
Wing)

REDDY KILOWATT

(see ADVERTISING COL-
LECTIBLES, Figures [Reddy
Kilowatt])

RELIGIOUS COLLECTIBLES

(see also ART, Asian; JUDAICA;
HYMNS; MEDALS, ORDERS &
DECORATIONS; MORMON ITEMS;
STAMP COLLECTING, Religion
Related)

Appraisers

James C. Voors
Court of King James
515 West Wayne St.
Fort Wayne, IN 46802-2123
phone: 219-426-3234
fax: 219-426-32344229940
*Specializes in ecclesiastical
furnishings, i.e. sacred vessels, church
art, vestments and other church
textiles, church furnishings, statuary,
paintings, objets d'art.*

Clubs/Associations

Emilio C. Botticelli
Foundation International for Restorers of
  Religious Medals
Newsletter: M.A.R.C., The
P.O. Box 2652
Worcester, MA 01603-2652
phone: 508-752-0612
*All types of old religious medals; club
focuses on medal history, values,
varieties, makers, rarity, countries of
origin, etc.*

Collectors

Emilio C. Botticelli
P.O. Box 2652
Worcester, MA 01603-2652
phone: 508-752-0612
*Wants to buy any and all types of old
religious medals in any metal; also
old Vatican medals.*

James D. Stambaugh
Graham Center Museum
500 East College Ave.
Wheaton, IL 60187
*Wants religious, evangelism, and
mission items; anything related to
Christianity in America.*

Greg Spiess
230 E. Washington St.
Joliet, IL 60433-1006
phone: 815-722-5639
fax: 815-722-0171
e-mail: spiessantq@aol.com
*Wants to buy church furnishings,
religious stained glass, altars, pews,
railings, confessionals, pulpits,
baptismals, lighting, architectural
renderings and blueprints, stained
glass cartoons, furnishings catalogs.*

J.A. Higgins
5017 Walnut
Kansas City, MO 64112-2758
phone: 816-931-4095
*Wants to buy Buddha and Hindu
statues.*

Ernie Reda
3997 Latimer Ave.
San Jose, CA 95130-1568
phone: 408-378-7786
*Accepting donation for the future
Museum of All Religions; has
collection of over 10,000 crosses and
thousands of religious items from all
over the world; your donated religious
items will carry your family name
forever in new museum.*

Experts

Lael Bower
507 Michigan Ave.
Grayling, MI 49738
phone: 517-348-6984 or 810-378-5785
*Wants to buy Christian and Judaic
collectibles; co-author with Penny
Forstner of "Guide to Collecting
Christian and Judaic Artifacts."*

Repair Services

Mueller Kaiser Plating Co.
5815 Hampton Ave.
Saint Louis, MO 63109
phone: 314-832-3553
*Fine metal finishing in silver, gold,
bronze, copper and brass; flatware,
tea services, antiques and church
ware including chalices, ciboria,
crosses, candelabra, sanctuary lamps,
vases, alms basins, flagons, book
stands, etc.*

Cards

Collectors

Mary Jo O'Neil
618 Riversedge Ct.
Mishawaka, IN 46544
phone: 219-259-0357
*Wants to buy Catholic holy cards,
medals, etc.*

Crosses

Collectors

Ernie Reda
3997 Latimer Ave.
San Jose, CA 95130-1568
phone: 408-378-7786
*Accepting donation for the future
Museum of All Religions; has
collection of over 10,000 crosses and
thousands of religious items from all
over the world.*

Jehovah's Witnesses

Collectors

Mike Castro
P.O. Box 2817
Providence, RI 02907
*Wants to buy Jehovah's Witness
literature, Golden Age, Watchtower,
Consolation mags, books, tracts, etc.*

Jeffrey Neumann
9960 Mt. Eaton
Wadsworth, OH 44281-9028
phone: 216-334-1784
*Wants pre-1930 literature, books,
booklets, magazines, memorabilia
relating to Pastor Russell, Watchtower, Tower Publishing, International Bible Students Association, and
Jehovah's Witnesses.*

Relics

Collectors

Collector
P.O. Box 8344
Richmond, VA 23226
Wants reliquaries and relics.

Jackie Young
P.O. Box 587
Elgin, IL 60121-0587
phone: 847-695-0108 or 847-254-8208
fax: 847-695-1679
e-mail: istamp2@msn.com
*Wants to buy reliquaries and relics of
Catholic saints; seeking relics in
mosaic crosses, small round
reliquaries, and all others; all replies
answered.*

Rosaries

Museums/Libraries

Sharon Tiffany, Ex. Dir.
Don Brown Rosary Collection,
  Skamania County Historical Society
P.O. Box 396
Stevenson, WA 98648
phone: 800-991-2338 or 509-427-8211
fax: 509-427-7429
*The Historical Society interprets the
human history surrounding and the
natural events that created Columbia
Gorge.*

Televangelism

Collectors

J.B.
P.O. Box 740877
Dallas, TX 75374-0877
Wants collectibles relating to Televangelism: mailers, videos, from Jim Bakker, Swaggart, Tilton, Popoff, etc.

REMOTE CONTROL

(see AIRPLANES, Model [Remote Control]; BOATS, Model [Remote Control]; MODELS, Cars [Remote Control])

REPAIR/RESTORATION/ CONSERVATION

(see also "REPAIR SERVICES" Appendix as well as Repair Services listed under specific categories throughout this Directory.)

Misc. Services

Andrew Gelinas
Burlesque Repair Service
18 W. 3rd. St.
Bethlehem, PA 18015-1222
phone: 610-867-3313 or 610-867-1665
fax: 610-867-4999
Sells customized computer program for household goods repair firms.

Allan Koskela
Nationwide Restoration Classes
P.O. Box 186
Webster City, IA 50595
phone: 515-832-3828 or 515-832-6623
Learn repair for invisible, ultra violet protected restorations on china, pottery, porcelain, bisque, composition, cold casts and ceramics; suitable for majolica, flow blue, Hummel, Lladro, Roseville, Weller, Hull, Royal Doulton, etc.

Allan Koskela
Nationwide Restoration Classes
P.O. Box 186
Webster City, IA 50595
phone: 515-832-3828 or 515-832-6623
Instructional videos available: "Repairing China, Pottery & Porcelain," "Airbrush Basics," "Color-Matching for the Restorer of Pottery & Porcelain," "Paintings: Cleaning & Repair," "Glass Cleaning & Repairing (Audio Tape)".

Periodicals

Joseph V. Cifala
Directory: Antique Repair Directory
P.O. Box 537
Edgewater, MD 21037
phone: 301-261-7640
Free listings for repairers of coin operated machines, porcelains, glass, furniture, etc.

Repair Services

Leon Trefler
Trefler & Sons Antique Restoring Studio, Inc.
99 Cabot St.
Needham, MA 02194-2801
phone: 617-444-2685
fax: 617-444-0659
Specializes in the repair and conservation of art objects: ceramics, prints, paintings, furniture, paper, frames, crystal, porcelain, marble, ivory, cloisonne, metals, jade, etc.

Glass Restoration by Dianne
54 Hartford Tpk.
Piccadilly Square
Vernon, CT 06066
phone: 203-647-7074
Restores crystal, china and porcelain.

Dimitri Nedelcu
Universal Fine Art Restoration
267 Derby Ave.
Orange, CT 06477-1319
phone: 203-795-8849
Repairs and restores marquetry, stone & wooden statuary, stone & wood capitals and columns, antique fireplaces, furniture, stone & wooden busts, icons, porcelain, paintings, guilding, picture frames,

Patricia Little
Restorations by Patricia
420 Centre St.
Nutley, NJ 07110
phone: 201-235-0234
Specialty in restoring plaster and religious statuary; also proficient in ceramics, china, pottery, porcelain, crystal, glass; repair of cracks, chips and replacements; Lladro, Hummel, Dept. 56, Royal Doulton, Swarovski, Armani, etc.

Ronald L. Aiello
Antique Restorations
1313 Mt. Holly Rd.
Burlington, NJ 08016-3773
phone: 609-387-2587
fax: 609-387-2587
e-mail: raiello@bellatlantic.net
Repairs and restores china, porcelain, pottery, dolls, objets d'art; specializes in professional repairs to figurines: Character and Toby Jugs, Lambeth, Burslem, Kingsware, stoneware, Flambe, etc.; 18 years full time experience.

Antiques Restoration by Julian
110 West 25th St., #208
New York, NY 10001
phone: 212-647-0305 or 201-791-7875
Gold, silver and any metal subjects; lamps and small sculptures; jewelry and costume jewelry; gold and silver plating.

Marina Pastor
Hess Restorations
200 Park Ave. South
New York, NY 10003
phone: 212-260-2255 or 212-979-1143
Since 1945 specializing in repairs and restorations of most objects of art; highly recommended by museums and leading galleries; ceramics, glass, ivory, porcelain, sculptures.

Walter C. Kahn, PE
1017 Constable Dr., S.
Mamaroneck, NY 10543-4702
phone: 914-381-3200
fax: 914-381-3200
Professional restoration of porcelain, china, glass, and pottery; also jade and ivory carvings and object d'art since 1972; life member of ASM, TMA, ASME, and SNDT.

Len Paradise, CR
Loss Recovery Systems, Inc.
10 Dwight Park Dr.
Syracuse, NY 13209-1029
phone: 315-451-9111
fax: 315-451-9222
Certified Restorer #94; repairs, cleans and restores following fire and flood loss, tree loss, smoke damage, structural collapse, etc.

Richard Michael Gramly, PhD
Great Lakes Artifact Repository
79 Perry St.
Buffalo, NY 14203-3037
phone: 716-849-0149
fax: 716-852-0093
Stores, sells, and conserves artifacts from all parts of the world in a secure, fireproof, climate-controlled working room and vault; examining room with drafting and photographic facilities; cataloguing of incoming collections, etc.

Byron Klein
A. Ludwig Klein & Son, Inc.
683 Sumneytown Pike
P.O. Box 145
Harleysville, PA 19438
phone: 215-256-9004 or 800-379-2929
fax: 215-256-9644
Specializing in the repair and restoration of all types of glass, china and porcelain as well as ivory, jade, brass, pewter.

David Sim
Nonomura Studios
3432 Connecticut Ave. NW
Washington, DC 20008
phone: 202-363-4025
Restores china, glassware, screens, scrolls, ivory, paintings, jade, lamps, furniture, etc.

Sidney Williston
Mario's Conservation Services
1738 14th St. NW
Washington, DC 20009-4309
phone: 202-234-5795
Restorers/conservators of decorative arts objects: china, glass, plaster, lacquer, metal, ivory, icons, frames, gold leaf, glass grinding and drilling.

Richard Kornemann
Museum Shop, Ltd.
20 N. Market St.
Frederick, MD 21701
phone: 301-695-0424 or 301-871-3855
fax: 301-698-5242
Highly-recommended conservator of oils, paper (etchings, lithographs, engravings, maps), icons, Oriental art, photos, 23k gold leaf, etc.

Steve Rogowsky
Frederick Refinishing Center
117 S. Bentz St.
Frederick, MD 21701
phone: 301-663-0105
Commercial and residential furniture and antiques; repairs, refinishing, restorations, touch-up; water/fire/ moving damage claim work.

Joe Howell
Pleasant Valley Restoration
1725 Reed Rd.
Knoxville, MD 21758-1118
phone: 301-432-2721
e-mail: jhowell@aol.com
Restoration, cleaning, and consultation services for china, glass, porcelain, marble, ivory, and other objets d'art; fine art and antique repair; custom color matching and air brushing.

Harold Vogel
Wood & Stone Inc.
10115 Residency Rd.
Manassas, VA 22111
phone: 703-369-1236 or 202-631-1236

Mildred R. Shepherd
Shepherd Studio
5527 Third St., South
Arlington, VA 22204-1115
phone: 703-671-1789
Offers conservation and restoration of art objects, specializing in porcelain, glass, ivory, china, stoneware, ivory, jade, pottery, etc.

Gilbert Kerry Hall
Rikki's Studio Inc.
2632 Hollywood Blvd., Ste. 301
Hollywood, FL 33020-4857
phone: 954-922-9111 or 305-624-1688
fax: 954-922-6668
Restorers and conservators of crystal, paintings, porcelains (European and Oriental), coromandel and objets d'art.

Lauraine Dunn, ISA
Lauraine Designs Inc.
68 NE 91st St.
Miami Shores, FL 33138-2808
phone: 305-758-7174 or 305-758-0126
fax: 305-756-5153
Restorers of fine arts & antiques since 1945; has an international reputation; no charge for verbal estimates.

Juergen Berndt
6731 Ashley Ct.
Sarasota, FL 34241-9696
phone: 941-925-0385
fax: 941-925-0487
Specializes in the repair and

restoration of antique mechanical devices such as typewriters, calculators, telephones, telegraphs, sewing machines, etc.; a specialty is the repair of cast iron cracks.

Sidney Kremberg
Dunhill Restorations
2309 Lee Rd.
Cleveland Heights, OH 44118
phone: 216-921-2932
Restores porcelain figurines, etc.

Douglas A. Eisele
Old World Restorations, Inc.
The Columbia/Stanley Bldg.
347 Stanley Ave.
Cincinnati, OH 45226-2100
phone: 513-321-1911
fax: 513-321-1914
Internet: http://www.restorationart.com
Fine restoration and conservation of paintings, porcelain, glass, china, art pottery, metals, crystal, frames, ivory, gold leaf, photographs, etc.; nationwide service; free estimates; call or write for more information and brochures.

Susan Johnson
Furniture Doctor, The
4465 Harbor Lane
Minneapolis, MN 55446
phone: 612-557-6519
fax: 612-557-6573
Repairs all periods of furniture, antiques and household items.

David Jasper
David Jasper's Glass Clinic
46508 267th St.
Sioux Falls, SD 57106
phone: 605-361-7524 or 800-361-7524
fax: 605-361-7216
Four generations of restorers; glass, porcelain, painting, dolls, figurines, ivory, lamps, etc.

John Edward Cunningham
Fine Art Restoration
1525 E. Berkley
Springfield, MO 65804-3203
phone: 417-889-7702
Restoration artist; porcelains, ivory, jade, gold leaf, oil paintings, and frames; registered Boehm and Royal Worcester restorer.

Eric Wrobbel
20802 Exhibit Ct.
Woodland Hills, CA 91367-5205
phone: 818-884-2282
Repair & restoration of machine-age objects; radios, toys, clocks, etc.; plastic repair, lettering, logos, fine painting & plating, mechanical and electrical repair of small items; call first before sending items.

Dr. Lawrence Vescera
Pick Up the Pieces
711 West 17th St., Unit C-12
Costa Mesa, CA 92660
phone: 714-645-9953 or 800-934-9278
fax: 714-645-8381
Repairs many types of materials including collectibles, figurines,

ceramics, marble, enamels, ivory, alabaster, antiques and paintings.

Arkady Rubenstein
Butterfield & Butterfield Restoration Department
220 San Bruno Ave.
San Francisco, CA 94103-5018
phone: 415-861-7500
fax: 415-553-8678
Services include repair, restoration and refinishing of furniture and decorative arts: marquetry & parquetry, veneer, carved wood furniture, bronzes, ceramics, porcelain.

Golberg Restoration Co.
1280 Laguna St. Apt 7L
San Francisco, CA 94115-4278
Museum quality art and antiques restoration and conservation: porcelain, ivory, pottery, paintings, stone, enamel, tapestries, cloisonne, glass, sculpture, lacquer and wood.

Suppliers

Ronald L. Aiello
Antique Restorations
1313 Mt. Holly Rd.
Burlington, NJ 08016-3773
phone: 609-387-2587
fax: 609-387-2587
e-mail: raiello@bellatlantic.net
Repair and restoration supplies available.

Restorite Systems
P.O. Box 7096
West Trenton, NJ 08628-0096
phone: 609-530-1526
Products for restoration and conservation of porcelain, pottery, and glass; sells a complete kit for repairing breaks and chips; also "How-to" videos available; send for free catalog.

Van Dykes Supply Company
P.O. Box 278
Woonsocket, SD 57385-0278
phone: 800-558-1234 or 605-796-4425
fax: 605-796-4085
Supplies for woodworkers and antique restorers: isen glass, curved & bubble glass, roll top accessories, Hoosier accessories, carvings & moldings, furniture components, over 1000 brass/glass/wooden hardware items.

Archival Supplies For

(see also ANTIQUES DEALERS & COLLECTORS, Supplies For)

Suppliers

John A. Dunphy
University Products, Inc.
517 Main St.
P.O. Box 101
Holyoke, MA 01041-0101
phone: 413-532-3372 or 800-628-1912
fax: 800-532-9281
e-mail: jadunphy@universityproducts.com
Internet: http://www.universityproducts.com
Carries safe products for the long term storage of postcards, posters, stamps, documents, photographs, textiles, costumes; acid free archival supplies, and materials for conservation and preservation; send for free catalog.

John Coutu
Rising Paper Co., Division of Fox River
P.O. Box 565
Housatonic, MA 01236-0565
phone: 413-274-3345
fax: 413-274-6684
General line of archival supplies including mat boards, framing and photographic supplies, mounting boards.

Nielsen & Bainbridge
17 S. Middlesex Ave.
Cranbury, NJ 08512
phone: 609-395-5550
General line of archival supplies including mat boards, document storage boxes, framing and photographic supplies.

TALAS
568 Broadway
New York, NY 10012-3225
phone: 212-219-0770
fax: 212-219-0735
Archival supplies for artists, restorers, collectors, bookbinders, conservators, calligraphers, museums, vintage clothing restorers, archives, libraries, etc.

Document Preservation Center
P.O. Drawer 821
Yonkers, NY 10702
phone: 914-476-8500
Sells acid-free products: boxes, paste, binders, board, folders, tapes, tissue, paper, wrapping paper, etc.

Robert H. Snyder
Cohasco, Inc. - Document Preservation Center
P.O. Box 821
Yonkers, NY 10702-0821
phone: 914-476-8500
fax: 914-476-8573
Sells acid-free products: protectors, boxes, tissues, tapes, wrapping paper, paste, board, and various types of binders.

Light Impressions Corp.
P.O. Box 940
Rochester, NY 14603-0940
phone: 800-828-6216
fax: 800-828-5539
General line of archival supplies including mat boards, document storage boxes, framing and photographic supplies.

Brodart
1609 Memorial Ave.
Williamsport, PA 17705
phone: 800-233-8959
fax: 800-283-6087
Internet: http://www.brodart.com
Offers a comprehensive catalog of library and archival products, from acid-free folders to open shelving systems.

Kathy Hullinger
Conservation Resources International
8000 H Forbes Place
Springfield, VA 22151
phone: 703-321-7730 or 800-634-6932
fax: 703-321-0629
Archival supplies for works of art on paper; document and photographic storage materials; chemicals; conservation tools; environmental monitoring supplies.

Hollinger Corporation
P.O. Box 8360
Fredericksburg, VA 22404
phone: 800-634-0491
fax: 800-947-8814
Archival supplies for works of art on paper, textiles, quilts and stamps; document and photographic storage materials.

James Saunders
E. Gerber Products
P.O. Box 906
Minden, NV 89423
phone: 702-883-4100
Restoration supplies, instructional video, for restoring paper collectibles such as magazines baseball cards, comics, original art; manufacturer of Mylar sleeves for comics artwork, posters; also carries acid free boxes.

Art

Repair Services

Canadian Conservation Institute
1030 Innes Rd.
Ottawa
Ontario K1G 0C8 Canada

Peter Kostoulakos
15 Sayles St.
Lowell, MA 01851-1625
phone: 508-453-8888
Conservation of oil paintings on canvas or solid supports; oil paintings cleaned and restored.

Henry Lie
Center for Conservation & Technical
Studies, The
Fogg Art Museum
Harvard University
Cambridge, MA 02138
phone: 617-495-2392
*Provides conservation and restoration
services for fine arts, including works
of art on paper, paintings, objects and
sculpture.*

Art Conservation Services, Inc.
30 Ipswich St., Studio 101
Boston, MA 02215
phone: 617-247-2757
*Paintings restored; treatment of
paintings on canvas, wood panel and
paper; expertly cleaned, patched and
lined.*

John Squadra
Fine Art Restoration
RFD 2 Box 1440
Brooks, ME 04921-9643
phone: 207-722-3464
fax: 207-722-3464
*Will send a written estimate from a
photo of your damaged painting; upon
approval, will UPS a wooden crate to
you for shipment; work guaranteed.*

Alyce Persky
Red Pines Farm
3513 Main St., Rt. 31
Coventry, CT 06238
phone: 203-742-0567
*Conserves and restores fine art and
frames for vendors and individuals;
also buys, sells, and appraises fine
art.*

Oscar & Debra Perez
Vigues Art Studio
54 Flanders Rd.
Woodbury, CT 06798-2103
phone: 203-263-4088
fax: 203-266-9118
*Conservation, restoration of oil
paintings (cleaning, lining, touch up
and repair), frames (gold leaf repairs,
casting of missing parts) and paper
(cleaning, repairs of prints, books,
documents); also porcelain, glass &
china repair.*

Applebaum & Himmelstein
444 Central Park West
New York, NY 10025
phone: 212-666-4630
fax: 212-316-1039
*Treats silk textiles, paintings and
objects.*

Leonard E. Sasso
23 Krystal Dr., RD 1
Somers, NY 10589
phone: 914-248-8289
*Master restorer of oil paintings &
water colors; all periods; American,
European, Old Masters; over 25 years
experience; references available.*

Sydney L. Germansky
Europa Master Gallery
16 A Lafayette Ave.
Suffern, NY 10901-5406
phone: 914-368-2707
Internet: http://members.qnn.com/europa
*Restorers of art, fine antiques, antique
jewelry, old photographs.*

Alexander Katlan
Alexander Katlan Conservation Inc.
5638 Main St.
Flushing, NY 11355-5046
phone: 718-445-7458
*Conservation of paintings and panels,
both European and American; author
of "American Artists' Materials, Vol I:
Suppliers Directory, 19th C." (Noyes
Press 1987), and "Vol. II: A Guide to
Stretchers, Panels, Millboards &
Stencil Marks."*

St. Julian Fishburne
8 Watch Hill Rd.
New Paltz, NY 12561-2705

Romayne Shay McMahon, ISA
Veronique's Antiques
124 S. Market St.
Mechanicsburg, PA 17055-6329
phone: 717-697-4924
fax: 717-697-4924

Maria Pukownik
Fine Art & Paper Conservation
1045 Orrtanna Rd.
Orrtanna, PA 17353
phone: 717-337-0668
*Cleaning, old varnish removal,
consolidation of flaking paint,
relining, structural reinforcement of
wooden panels, retouching,
revarnishing.*

American Institute for Conservation of
Historic & Artistic Works
Directory: AIC Directory
1717 K St. NW, Ste. 301
Washington, DC 20006
phone: 202-452-9545
fax: 202-452-9328
*Purpose is to advance the knowledge
and practice of the conservation of
cultural property; the AIC Directory
lists competent conservators of paper,
textiles, photographs, furniture, and
more - over 2000 members.*

Justine S. Wimsatt
Wimsatt & Associates Art Conservation
Studio, Inc.
4230 Howard Ave.
Kensington, MD 20895-2418
phone: 301-493-4250
fax: 301-493-9563
e-mail: wimsatt@nmaa.org
Internet: http://
www.artconservation.com
*For 20 years has provided profes-
sional restoration of paintings,
murals, icons, frames and related
objects.*

H.I. Gates
118 E. Church St.
Frederick, MD 21701-5404
phone: 301-663-3717
Conservator of paintings.

Robert & Marie Kuehne
9910 Green Valley Rd.
Union Bridge, MD 21791-8110
phone: 301-898-7921
*Oil painting conservation/restoration;
20 yrs. experience; please call for
expert info. & advice; FREE brochure
available on request.*

Margaret Bardwell
Bardwell Conservation, Ltd.
11373 Park Dr.
Fairfax, VA 22030
phone: 703-385-8451
*Conservation and restoration of
paintings executed on canvas, metal
or wood (including icons); also
frames and small painted furniture.*

Art Restoration
222 Skyline Dr.
Brentwood, TN 37027
phone: 615-373-4083
*Paintings professionally repaired,
cleaned and restored.*

Antique & Art Restoration By Wiebold
413 Terrace Place
Terrace Park, OH 45174
phone: 513-831-2541 or 800-321-2541
fax: 513-831-2815
Internet: http://www.weibold.com
*Expert restoration of oil paintings,
frames, mirrors, wooden artifacts,
ivory, antiquities, etc.*

Charles Wiebold, Pres.
Wiebold, Inc.
413 Terrace Place
Terrace Park, OH 45174-1164
phone: 513-831-2541 or 800-321-2541
fax: 513-831-2815
e-mail: wiebold@eos.net
Internet: http://www.wiebold.com
*Restoration of ceramics, paintings,
metal items.*

Cornelia & Marcell Illozan
Fine Arts Conservation
P.O. Box 923
Wilmette, IL 60091
phone: 847-256-8595

Robert Wiest
R.R. Donnelley & Sons Graphic
Conservation Department
350 W. 22 St.
Chicago, IL 60616
phone: 708-326-8525
fax: 708-326-8426

Cher Goodson
Art Restorations, Inc.
7803 Inwood Rd.
Dallas, TX 75209
phone: 214-350-0811
*Professional restoration of porcelains,
ceramics, crystal, paintings (cleaning,
lining, mending), frames (reconstruction, gold leaf, custom finishes), metal*

*objects, plating, marble, lacquer ware,
cloisonne, ivory, tortoise, etc.*

Ellen D. Kennedy
Kennedy & Associates Art Conservation
6211 Royalton, #D
Houston, TX 77081
phone: 713-664-0606 or 800-437-8909
*Specializes in the preservation of
paintings, murals, frames, and related
objects; over 25 years experience.*

Scott M. Haskins
Fine Art Conservation Laboratories
P.O. Box 23557
Santa Barbara, CA 93131
phone: 805-564-3438
fax: 805-568-1178
e-mail: artdoc@earthlink.net
Internet: http://home.earthlink.net/
~artdoc/
*Specializes in the preservation of
paintings, murals, works of art on
paper and period frames.*

Michael Scheglov
Michael's Art Restoration Studio
8316 Eighth N.W.
Seattle, WA 98117

Suppliers

Peter Millar
Quill, Hair & Ferrule, Ltd.
P.O. Box 23927
Columbia, SC 29224-3927
phone: 800-421-7961 or 803-788-4499
fax: 803-736-4731
*Professional restoration supplies:
Japan & oil colors, brushes, abalone
& mother-of-pearl, aluminum, copper,
composition, gold leaf, burnishing
tools, imported gold sizes, non-tarnish
iridescent & metallic pigments, etc.*

Carol Carney
Gainsborough Products Company
281 Lafayette Cir.
Lafayette, CA 94549-4316
phone: 510-283-4187 or 800-227-2186
fax: 510-283-3343
*Lining canvas and compound, repair
putty, varnish remover, manuals, etc.*

Cane & Basketry

Repair Services

Susan Dilworth
Iron Bridge Farm Antiques
2953 Appleton Rd.
Elkton, MD 21921-2176
phone: 410-398-0954

Mickey Johnson
Mickey's Chair
233 Byrnes Dr.
Waterloo, IA 50701
phone: 319-232-5934
*Restoration of cane and rush furniture
- both residential and commercial.*

Suppliers

Connecticut Cane & Reed Co.
P.O. Box 1276
Manchester, CT 06040
phone: 203-646-6586 or 800-227-8498
fax: 203-649-2221
Largest selection of materials and books; source for cane, wicker and basket supplies; all types of materials to reseat a chair.

H.H. Perkins Co.
10 South Bradley Rd.
Woodbridge, CT 06525
phone: 203-389-9501

Lilian Cummings
Canecraft
RD 1 Box 126-A (Rte 443)
Andreas, PA 18211
phone: 717-386-2441
Sells cane, reed and rushing material for seating chairs, making baskets, and repairing wicker furniture; also instruction books.

Paige W. Beasley
Carolina Caning Supply
P.O. Box 883
Smithfield, NC 27577
phone: 800-346-0142 or 414-207-0291
Chair caning and repair supplies.

Peerless Rattan & Reed
624 S Burnett Rd.
Springfield, OH 45505-2722
Source for cane, wicker, splints, fiber rush, seagrass, and basket supplies.

Barap Specialties
835 Bellows
Frankfort, MI 49635
Source for flat reed, fiber rush, decorative head nails, cane webbing and reed for reweaving chair seats, hardware, etc.

Cane & Basket Supply Co.
1283 S. Cochran Ave.
Los Angeles, CA 90019
phone: 213-939-9644
fax: 213-939-7237
Source for cane, wicker and basket supplies.

Mike Frank
Franks Cane & Rush Supply
P.O. Box 3025
Huntington Beach, CA 92605-3025
phone: 714-847-0707
fax: 714-843-5645
e-mail: gacg74b@prodigy.com
Quality supplier of unusual supplies for the craftsman; mainly wicker repair and basketry; sorry, no restoration of repairs.

Michael Frank
Frank's Cane & Rush Supply
7252 Heil Ave.
Huntington Beach, CA 92647
Carries high quality natural seat weaving supplies.

Ceramics

Misc. Services

Gerlinde Kornmesser
Porcelain Restoration Workshop
1804 1/2 Glenview Rd.
Glenview, IL 60025-2910
phone: 847-724-3059 or 847-724-1815
fax: 847-724-3060
Course instructor is Gerlinde Kornmesser, practicing restorer and Associate Member of the American Institute for Conservation of Historical and Artistic Works. She succeeds Morla Tjossem, founder and developer of the course.

Shirley Vickers
Shirley Vickers School of China Repair
P.O. Box 688
Pine, AZ 85544-0688
phone: 520-476-3703
fax: 520-476-3703
Course lasts 7 days for those wishing to go into the repair business; also suited for collectors and dealers.

Repair Services

Warner G. Friedman
P.O. Box 622
Sheffield, MA 01257
phone: 413-229-8076

Sharon Smith Abbott
Fine Wares Restoration
P.O. Box 753
Bridgton, ME 04009-0753
phone: 207-647-2093
Restores ceramics & glass for private collectors and museums; references of museum clients on request.

Oscar & Debra Perez
Vigues Art Studio
54 Flanders Rd.
Woodbury, CT 06798-2103
phone: 203-263-4088
fax: 203-266-9118
Conservation, restoration of oil paintings (cleaning, lining, touch up and repair), frames (gold leaf repairs, casting of missing parts) and paper (cleaning, repairs of prints, books, documents); also porcelain, glass & china repair.

Patricia Little
Restorations by Patricia
420 Centre St.
Nutley, NJ 07110
phone: 201-235-0234
Specialty in restoring plaster and religious statuary; also proficient in ceramics, china, pottery, porcelain, crystal, glass; repair of cracks, chips and replacements; Lladro, Hummel, Dept. 56, Royal Doulton, Swarovski, Armani, etc.

Restoration by Dudley, Inc.
47 Stanford Ave.
Elmwood Park, NJ 07407-2015
phone: 201-731-4449
fax: 201-731-1890

Ronald L. Aiello
Antique Restorations
1313 Mt. Holly Rd.
Burlington, NJ 08016-3773
phone: 609-387-2587
fax: 609-387-2587
e-mail: raiello@bellatlantic.net
Repairs and restores china, porcelain, pottery, dolls, objets d'art; specializes in professional repairs to figurines: Character and Toby Jugs, Lambeth, Burslem, Kingsware, stoneware, Flambe, etc.; 18 years full time experience.

Jonathan Mark Gershen
Jonathan Mark Gershen Porcelain, Pottery & Glass Restoration
1463 Pennington Rd.
Ewing, NJ 08618-2656
phone: 609-882-9417
Second generation restorer and long time member of the AIC; clients include museums, collectors and dealers worldwide; free brochure available upon request.

Yolando DiSalvo
Yolanda Studio
2365 Huckleberry Rd.
Lakehurst, NJ 08733-3423

Jareth Holub
Decorative Arts Restoration & Conservation
224 W. 29th St., 12th. Fl.
New York, NY 10001
phone: 212-564-8669 or 212-247-8657
fax: 212-843-3742
Specializes in the restoration & conservation of ceramics (porcelain, terra-cotta, bisque, etc.); over 20 yrs. experience; everything from pre-Columbian to Art Pottery; also marble, jade, ivory, cloisonne, tortoise shell; free estimates.

Ceramic Restorations of Westchester, Inc.
8 John Walsh Blvd.
Peekskill, NY 10566
phone: 914-734-8410
Repair and restoration service for any brand of porcelain and ceramic collectibles, antiques and art objects.

Hans J. Schindhelm
Ceramic Restorations of Westchester, Inc.
8 John Walsh Blvd., Ste. 412
Peekskill, NY 10566-5330
phone: 914-734-8410
fax: 914-734-8410
e-mail: siegmar@aol.com
Repair & restoration of ceramic/ porcelain figurines (collectibles or antique); manufactures porcelain dolls and reproductions of antiques made from ceramic and porcelain; also model and sample making for ceramic & porcelain products.

Imperial China
22 North Park Ave.
Rockville Center, NY 11590

Roger J. Krokey
Terra Nuova
38 Cedar Heights Rd.
Rhinebeck, NY 12572
phone: 914-876-3753
e-mail: RKrokey@Juno.com
Located 100 miles north of New York City; complete restoration of ceramic items.

Romayne Shay McMahon, ISA
Veronique's Antiques
124 S. Market St.
Mechanicsburg, PA 17055-6329
phone: 717-697-4924
fax: 717-697-4924

Grady Stewart
Grady Stewart Expert Porcelain Restorations
2019 Sansom St.
Philadelphia, PA 19103-4416
phone: 215-567-2888
Offering repairs for museums, dealers, collectors; highest quality repairs of fine porcelain, pottery, and stoneware.

Bill Eberhardt
Harry A. Eberhardt & Son
2010 Walnut St.
Philadelphia, PA 19103-5608
phone: 215-568-4144
America's oldest repair firm.

Sidney Williston
Mario's Conservation Services
1738 14th St. NW
Washington, DC 20009-4309
phone: 202-234-5795
Restorers/conservators of decorative arts objects: china, glass, plaster, lacquer, metal, ivory, icons, frames, gold leaf, glass grinding and drilling.

Berlkey, Inc.
2011 Hermitage Ave.
Wheaton, MD 20902
phone: 301-922-4440

Mildred R. Shepherd
Shepherd Studio
5527 Third St., South
Arlington, VA 22204-1115
phone: 703-671-1789
Offers conservation and restoration of art objects, specializing in porcelain, glass, ivory, china, stoneware, ivory, jade, pottery, etc.

Gregory A. Ehler
Antique Porcelain Restoration
4786 Lee Highway
Arlington, VA 22207
phone: 703-525-2470
Provides museum quality restoration of fine porcelain, pottery and enamels; member of Wash. D.C. Professional Restoration Associates.

McHugh's
3117 West Clay St.
Richmond, VA 23230
phone: 804-353-9596
China mending and restoration service; repairs chips, crank, and

fabricates missing pieces; Boehm restorer.

John & Donna Nichols
P.O. Box 178
Belle Haven, VA 23306
phone: 804-442-5964

Dona Danzinger
Clay Works, The
4058 S. Main St.
P.O. Box 352
Exmore, VA 23350
phone: 757-414-0567
Acquired skills working for Boehm, Goebel and the Franklin Mint; restorations of all types of fine porcelain and art pottery; specializes in Hummels; missing parts made; fully insured.

Richard Beggs
Pottery Restoration
9553 White Trail Trail
Kernersville, NC 27284-8741
phone: 910-595-2753
Specializing in invisible restoration of all types of ceramics, especially American art pottery, e.g. Rookwood, Weller, Roseville, Hull; also cookie jars and Fiestaware.

Lauraine Dunn, ISA
Lauraine Designs Inc.
68 NE 91st St.
Miami Shores, FL 33138-2808
phone: 305-758-7174 or 305-758-0126
fax: 305-756-5153
Restorers of fine arts & antiques since 1945; has an international reputation; no charge for verbal estimates.

Andrea Daley
Restorers of America
Lake Worth, FL 33460
phone: 800-260-1829
Specializes in one-on-one training apprenticeships in the field of fine porcelain restoration.

Jody Leak
Leak Enterprises
12500 SE Highway 301
Belleview, FL 34420-4410
phone: 352-245-8862
fax: 352-245-8862
e-mail: ogwen@aol.com
Specializing in the restoration of objets d'art, either antique or contemporary including Lladro, Boehm, Cybis, Hummel, Meissen, Orientalia, and all quality porcelain and ceramics.

Tice Goodson
Rte. 5, Box 985
Batesville, MS 38606
phone: 800-221-9177

Lester E. Sender
Galerie Nouvelle
23500 Mercantile Rd.
Cleveland, OH 44122-5914
phone: 216-595-0000
fax: 216-595-1111
Full cleaning and restoration of paintings, old and new; full repair

and restoration of porcelain and pottery figurines, plates, objects; member A.I.C., Washington, DC.

Antique & Art Restoration By Wiebold
413 Terrace Place
Terrace Park, OH 45174
phone: 513-831-2541 or 800-321-2541
fax: 513-831-2815
Internet: http://www.weibold.com
Restoration of all types of art pottery, fine porcelain, ceramics, glass, crystal, sculpture, antiquities, etc.

Charles Wiebold, Pres.
Wiebold, Inc.
413 Terrace Place
Terrace Park, OH 45174-1164
phone: 513-831-2541 or 800-321-2541
fax: 513-831-2815
e-mail: wiebold@eos.net
Internet: http://www.wiebold.com
Restoration of ceramics, paintings, metal items.

Anne R. Hackmann
2550 Kodiak Dr.
East Lansing, MI 48823-7208
phone: 517-351-2011
fax: 517-337-7234
Offers museum quality repair and restoration of antiques and ceramic art objects; specializing in Boehm and Stangl birds; please call or write before shipping.

Maxine's Ltd.
7144 University Ave.
Des Moines, IA 50311

Carol Coulter
Coulter's China Repair
2240 Scenic River Dr. S
Brainerd, MN 56401-8074
phone: 218-825-0283
Specializes in porcelain repair and restoration (Boehm, Lladro, Hummel, Dresden Lace); invisible repairs; mail order; free estimates.

Corey & Jo Ann Keller
Keller China Restoration
4825 Windsor Dr.
Rapid City, SD 57702-0125
phone: 605-342-6756
Professional repair of cracks, chips and missing parts on antique china, porcelain, dolls, Hummels, and antique frames; authorized restorers for the Lladro Society.

William & Michelle Marhoefer
Broken Art Restoration
1841 Weste Chicago Ave.
Chicago, IL 60622
phone: 312-226-8200

Rose Ellen Beyer
14406 No. 47th St.
Omaha, NE 68152
Provides quality repairs to ceramic items; please write before shipping pieces.

Bric-A-Brac, Inc.
8120 Nelson St.
New Orleans, LA 70118
phone: 504-861-8888

Sue Thiessen
25115 Cemetery Rd.
Middleton, ID 83644-5103
phone: 208-585-3243
Specializing in restoring model horses, Roseville, and other pottery; also collector of Hagen Renaker horse and animal figurines.

Andy Goldschmidt
Ceramicare
P.O. Box 1812
Corrales, NM 87048
phone: 505-898-2728
e-mail: agoldschmidt@waonline.com
Repairs and restores ceramic art; specializing in Native American Indian pottery - prehistoric, historic and contemporary.

Cheleen Morgan
Antiques, Etc.
1270 Autumn Wind Way
Henderson, NV 89012
phone: 702-270-9910
Specializing in museum-quality restorations of pottery, porcelain, china, ceramics and hand painted items.

House of Renew
27601 Forbes Rd., #15
Laguna Niguel, CA 92677

Mark J. Dorian
101 West Olive
Fresno, CA 93728

Michael & Donna Meyer
5229 Dent Ave.
San Jose, CA 95118
phone: 408-266-4921
fax: 408-266-5318
Figurines, statuary, ceramics, china, Oriental porcelain, marble, enamels, ivory, alabaster, etc.

Suppliers

Restorite Systems
P.O. Box 7096
West Trenton, NJ 08628-0096
phone: 609-530-1526
Products for restoration and conservation of porcelain, pottery, and glass; sells a complete kit for repairing breaks and chips; also "How-to" videos available; send for free catalog.

Allan Koskela
Restoration Services
P.O. Box 186
Webster City, IA 50595
phone: 515-832-3828 or 515-832-6623
Sells repair supplies including fillers, glazes, lacquers, resins and cleaners; no heat needed; how-to-video, "Repairing Pottery & Porcelain" recommended by Harry L. Rinker;

restoration classes 6 times a year, with glueless repairing.

Figurines

(see REPAIR/RESTORATION/ CONSERVATION; REPAIR/ RESTORATION/CONSERVATION, Ceramics)

Furniture

(see also REPAIR/RESTORATION/ CONSERVATION, Woodworking; "REPAIR SERVICES" Appendix as well as Repair Services listed under REPAIR/RESTORATION/CONSER- VATION and other specific categories throughout this Directory)

Clubs/Associations

Virginia Conservation Association
P.O. Box 4314
Richmond, VA 23220-8314

John Rybski
National Association of Furniture Repair & Refinishing Specialists
3488 Car Dr.
Commerce Township, MI 48382-1602
Membership is open to all individuals in the furniture stripping, repairing, refinishing, antique restoration and/or service field.

Periodicals

Minuteman, Inc.
Newsletter: Minuteman Crier
115 North Monroe St.
Waterloo, WI 53594-1124
phone: 800-733-1776
fax: 414-478-3966
A company-sponsored newsletter with articles about furniture restoration techniques, supplies, tools and equipment, and restoration business opportunities.

Repair Services

Alex Zhitnisky
Al's Furniture Restorers, Inc.
425 Ella T. Grasso Blvd.
New Haven, CT 06519
phone: 203-865-1885
fax: 203-562-5868
Specializes in the repair and restoration of furniture, reupholstery, brass repair, etc.; trained in Russia.

Daniel Ridgeway
Ridgeway Restorations
200 Henry St. Bldg. #30
Stamford, CT 06902-5828
phone: 203-353-0334
Consultations, antique restorations, moving damage, cabinetry, French polishing.

Dan Manning
Manning Claim Services
P.O. Box 212
Allendale, NJ 07401
phone: 201-825-8450
fax: 201-825-8301
*Specializing in cargo claims handling,
and furniture and antiques repair
services.*

Wayne R. Batten
RFD 3 #259 Jackson Rd.
Berlin, NJ 08009
phone: 609-767-5994
*High quality furniture restorations
and custom lacquering on period to
modern fine furniture.*

Jim Murphy
Jim Murphy - Furniture & Paint
19 North President Ave.
Lancaster, PA 17603
phone: 717-299-9964
*All types of paint work on reproduc-
tion or antique furniture: vinegar
painting, grain painting and
"fanciful" color work available.*

Andrew Gelinas
Burlesque Repair Service
18 W. 3rd. St.
Bethlehem, PA 18015-1222
phone: 610-867-3313 or 610-867-1665
fax: 610-867-4999
*Specializing in cargo claims handling
and repair services for moving,
insurance, retail companies; full shop
facilities; 22 years experience.*

Michael Shur
Refinishing Touch, A
604 Hillcrest Ave.
Edgemoor, DE 19809
phone: 302-762-3684
fax: 302-762-4191
*Specializing in cargo claims handling,
and furniture and antiques repair
services.*

Gene Shontere
Shontere Restoration, Inc.
P.O. Box 1805
Bowie, MD 20717-1805
phone: 301-870-3669 or 301-934-0509
fax: 301-934-0511
e-mail: shontere@erols.com
*Specializing in furniture repair and
restoration.*

Bob Neiderlander
Yesteryear Antique Farms Inc.
742 Hawkins Creamery Rd.
Laytonsville, MD 20882
phone: 301-948-3979
*Repairs and restores new and antique
furniture.*

John Pyle
Glade Valley Furniture Repair
10464 Glade Rd.
Walkersville, MD 21793-9715
phone: 301-898-3795
fax: 301-898-3795
Moving claims service.

Bill Ivey
William Ivey Fine Furniture
2710 W. Cary St.
Richmond, VA 23220
phone: 804-358-7545
*Conservation, restoration and design
of furniture.*

Thomas McGarry
Birnam Wood Joinery, The
Rte. 2 Box 397
Harpers Ferry, WV 25425-9402
phone: 304-728-0373 or 800-700-5959
*Specializes in the restoration,
refinishing, repair and recaning of
fine furniture; hand cleaning or
striping suitable to the period done
with expert care; line of handmade
Shaker-inspired American country
furniture also available.*

Dick Adams, ISA CAPP
Specialists of the South, Inc.
544 East Sixth St.
Panama City, FL 32401-3066
phone: 904-785-2577
fax: 904-872-8662
e-mail: 76652.31@compuserve.com
*Specializing in furniture restorations
& repairs, upholstery, refinishing;
designated restoration center for
northwest Florida; repairs for
individuals, and the moving and
insurance industries; also repairs
rugs, porcelain, glass, silver.*

Jack Craig
Craig's Limited Inc.
3601 N. Dixie Hwy., #16
Boca Raton, FL 33431
phone: 561-367-0096
fax: 561-368-1001
*Antique & fine furniture restoration,
stripping, refinishing, repair; over 20
years experience; licensed and
insured; free phone estimates.*

Ernest Littlejohn
Retouchables, The
9330 Grove Rd.
Cordova, TN 38018
phone: 901-383-1603
*Repair, refinish, restore furniture;
also caning; specializing in antiques.*

Jim & Helen Roose
Mt. Pleasant Restoration Shop
SR 150, Union & Market St.
P.O. Box 245
Mount Pleasant, OH 43939-0245
phone: 614-769-7565
*Furniture repair, hand stripping,
refinishing, caning, custom millwork,
furniture made to order; over 28 years
experience.*

Bob Kovach
201 W. Alyea St.
P.O. Box 522
Hebron, IN 46341-0522
phone: 219-996-2924
*Antique restorations, veneer work,
wicker repair.*

David Colglazier
Original Woodworks
360 North Main St.
Stillwater, MN 55082-5024
phone: 612-430-3622
e-mail: orgwood@iaxs.net
Internet: http://home.iaxs.net/orgwood
*A full service shop specializing in
wooden antique restorations including
furniture and architectural elements
requiring extensive restoration and
repairs, especially veneers.*

William W. Ingram
Refinishing Touch, Ltd., The
950 N. Rand Road, Unit #103
Wauconda, IL 60084-1179
phone: 847-526-3113
*A full service shop specializing in
furniture repair, hand stripping,
refinishing and antique restoration;
also caning, veneers, and custom
wood finishes.*

Dave Kummerow
Image Restoration Services Inc.
P.O. Box 8407
Bartlett, IL 60103
phone: 630-830-7965
fax: 630-830-1458
*Specializing in cargo claims handling
and repair services; wood finishes,
upholstery, fiberglass, vinyl,
porcelain, etc.; also appraises
furniture and wooden objects.*

Duane Mitch
Mercury Furniture Service
302 Sycamore St.
West Chicago, IL 60185-3150
phone: 708-293-7207
fax: 708-653-2485
Refinishing, repairs, restoration.

Ray Spencer
Spencer Corporation
23220 Maple Valley Highway SE, Unit
3B
Maple Valley, WA 98038
phone: 206-413-1660
fax: 206-413-1659
e-mail: Spencercorp@msn.com
*Specializing in cargo claims handling
and in complete repair services.*

Suppliers

David Colglazier
Restore-it Supply Co.
360 North Main St.
Stillwater, MN 55082-5024
phone: 612-430-3622
e-mail: orgwood@iaxs.net
Internet: http://home.iaxs.net/orgwood
*Brass, bronze, steel, iron hardware for
furniture, architecture, trunks, carved
wooden racetrack moldings for
drawer front, etc.; custom casting
available' also catalogs for AABCO,
Leo Hardware, Ritter & Son.*

Furniture & Upholstery

Repair Services

Linda Clark
Renaissance Furniture Repair
RD 4 Box 266-A
Wynantskill, NY 12198
phone: 518-283-5317
fax: 518-283-5380
*Specializing in cargo claims handling,
and furniture and antiques repair
services.*

Tom Kuhns
West Interior Services, Inc.
P.O. Box 540
Natrona Heights, PA 15065-0740
phone: 412-224-2215
fax: 412-226-3233
*Specializes in moving or insurance
claims; furniture repair, refinishing &
restoration, architectural refinishing;
fire, smoke, water damage.*

Timothy P. Hughes
MSS Furniture Service
211 Commerce Dr.
Montgomeryville, PA 18936-9641
phone: 800-433-1159 or 215-393-1900
fax: 800-835-0338
*Specializing in cargo claims handling,
fire and water damage repairs, and
furniture and antiques repair services.*

Charles Jourdant
Jourdant Furniture Repair
611 Alabama Ave.
North Beach, MD 20714-9602
phone: 301-855-6563 or 800-479-5427
fax: 410-257-0752
*Specializing in cargo claims handling;
furniture, upholstery and museum
quality antique restorations.*

L. Philip Oliver
Oliver's
24610 Frederick Rd.
P.O. Box 659
Clarksburg, MD 20871-0659
phone: 301-428-3336
fax: 301-428-9282
*Specializes in moving or insurance
claims; complete line of furniture
upholstery, repair, refinishing and
restoration.*

Pete Simonetti
Artisian Restoration, Inc.
P.O. Box 72035
Baltimore, MD 21237
phone: 410-682-3700
fax: 410-682-3738
*A complete furniture claims service
specializing in cargo claims and fire
water damage for insurance industry;
repairs, refinishing, antique
restoration, upholstery, touch-up,
third party services; MD's largest
furniture service.*

Joseph Miller
Joseph Miller Furniture Restoration
4811 Catharpin Rd.
Gainesville, VA 22065
phone: 703-754-7598
Refinishing, repairing, caning.

Steve Belcher
Steve's Furniture & Claims Service
3289 Greco Ct.
Woodbridge, VA 22192-1095
Specializes in moving or insurance claims; furniture repair, refinishing & restoration, nicks, scratches, splits, upholstery, silver and gold leaf, carvings, curved glass, etc.; water, moving and fire damage, etc.

Suppliers

Barbara Amster
Nineteenth Century Mercantile
No. 2 North Main St.
South Yarmouth, MA 02664
phone: 508-398-1888
Carries mohair and horsehair upholstery grade fabric in authentic c. 1800s colorways and patterns; also authentic homespun fabrics; no mail order.

Turner & Seymour
P.O. Box 358
Torrington, CT 06790
phone: 203-489-9215
Source for upholstery supplies.

John K. Burch Co.
1818 Underwood Blvd.
Delran, NJ 08075
phone: 800-257-9112
fax: 609-461-7093
Mail order source for upholstering supplies; also fabric books.

Naomi Taylor
Douglas Industries, Inc.
412 Boston Ave.
Egg Harbor City, NJ 08215
phone: 800-257-8551
Source for foam and fabrics.

Carrousel Foam
1940 S. West Blvd.
Vineland, NJ 08360
phone: 609-692-1777
Source for foam.

Jack Raskin's Upholstery Supplies
845 Timber Lane
Dresher, PA 19025-1811
phone: 800-523-3213
Mail order source for upholstering supplies.

Jack Raskin
Jack Raskin Upholstery
845 Timber Lane
Dresher, PA 19025-1811
phone: 800-523-3213
Supplier to custom upholsterers.

Minute-Man Upholstery Supply
Company of North Carolina
P.O. Box 6534
High Point, NC 27262
phone: 800-457-0029 or 910-882-4100
fax: 910-882-2300
Mail order source for upholstering supplies.

Furniture (Antique Only)

Misc. Services

Society for the Preservation of New England Antiquities, The
Conservation Center
185 Lyman St.
North Waltham, MA 02154
phone: 617-891-4882
fax: 617-893-7832
Performs wood and finish/coatings analysis; also offers conservation treatment of furniture and objects.

Repair Services

Bruce Hamilton
R. Bruce Hamilton, Furniture Restoration
P.O. Box 815
West Newbury, MA 01985
phone: 508-363-2638
fax: 508-363-2638
Antique & fine furniture restoration; French polish, cleaning and restoration of existing finishes, false graining, removal of water stains & marks, leather work, veneering, carving, etc.; 20th century lacquer finishes repaired.

John Sutton
John Sutton Antique Restorations
14 North Henry St.
Brooklyn, NY 11222
phone: 718-389-6101
Specializes in the restoration of 17th and 18th century English, French and American furniture.

Eugene E. Landon
RD 1 Box 31A
Montoursville, PA 17754
phone: 717-433-3476
Specializing in the restoration, conservation and replication of antique wooden furniture and artifacts.

Stephen Rice
Heritage Restorations
4233 Howard Ave. #F
Kensington, MD 20895-2419
phone: 301-493-4458
European trained craftsmen specializing in wooden objets d'art & antique furniture restoration; duplicating finishes, inlays, etc.

Walter Raynes
4900 Wetheredsville
Baltimore, MD 21207-6625
phone: 410-448-3515
fax: 410-448-0855
Specializes in the restoration and conservation of antique furniture only; also builds reproduction of antique furniture.

Phil Goodman
Begleiter Antique Restorations
6801 Reisterstown Rd.
Baltimore, MD 21215
phone: 410-764-7467

Robert Esterly
Robert Esterly Antiques Repairing, Refinishing, Reproductions
6675 Mt. Phillip Rd.
Frederick, MD 21702
phone: 301-694-0287 or 301-371-7430
Specializing in the repair, restoration and refinishing of antique furniture.

Bruce M. Schuettinger, ISA
Antique Restorations Ltd.
17 N. Alley
P.O. Box 244
New Market, MD 21774-0244
phone: 301-865-3009
fax: 301-865-3009
Conservators, appraisers, and consultants of wooden artifacts, specializing in the preservation of original finishes, painted or gilt decoration, and structural elements.

Phil Fogelsong
1801 Wicks Valley Dr.
Marietta, GA 30062
phone: 770-579-6520

R.B. White
White Rose Manor, Ltd.
1972 Pineview Dr.
Kent, OH 44240
phone: 216-678-7929
Antique restoration and repair; studied at Sotheby's of New York and London.

Peter Storey Pentz
P.O. Box 58408
Seattle, WA 98138
phone: 206-251-0909
fax: 206-251-0682
Specializes in the restoration of period antique wooden objects.

Gilding

(see also FRAMES)

Repair Services

Susan B. Jackson
Harvard Art
49 Littleton County Rd.
Harvard, MA 01451-1729
phone: 508-456-9050
Restoration and conservation of period frames and other gilded objects; touch-up, consolidation, gilding and toning to match the existing surface.

Romayne Shay McMahon, ISA
Veronique's Antiques
124 S. Market St.
Mechanicsburg, PA 17055-6329
phone: 717-697-4924
fax: 717-697-4924

William Adair
Gold Leaf Studios, Inc.
443 I Street NW
Washington, DC 20091
phone: 202-638-4660
fax: 202-347-4569
e-mail: bill@goldleafstudios.com
Internet: http://www.goldleafstudios.com
Gilding of anything gold leafed: frames, sculpture, sconces, etc.

Stanley Robertson
Chelsea Lane Conservation Studio
4717 S. Chelsea Ln.
Bethesda, MD 20814
phone: 301-656-9344
fax: 301-656-9344
Gilding of anything gold leafed: antique/historic mirrors, picture frames, sculpture, sconces, architectural, etc.; collection surveys for historic designations, dating styles, etc.; ornament repair, handmade special reproductions.

R. Wayne Reynolds
R. Wayne Reynolds, Inc.
3618 Falls Rd.
Baltimore, MD 21211
phone: 410-467-1800 or 410-467-1890
Specializes in the application of gold leaf; complete restoration services for gilded art objects, including furniture, frames, and mirrors.

Richard Kornemann
Museum Shop, Ltd.
20 N. Market St.
Frederick, MD 21701
phone: 301-695-0424 or 301-871-3855
fax: 301-698-5242
23k gold leafing of antiques, picture frames, signs, etc.; also complete art and frame restoration.

Ken Brown
Kenneth Brown Studio, The
2703 Stokes Ferry Rd.
Salisbury, NC 28146
phone: 704-633-0604
fax: 704-633-5664
Restoration and conservation of gilded objects: frames, mirrors, furniture, etc.; also custom made frames and reproductions.

Susan Saye, Ex. Dir.
Society of Gilders
Newsletter: Society of Gilders Newsletter
P.O. Box 920490
Norcross, GA 30092
phone: 770-452-1113
fax: 770-452-1112
Publishes a list of its members; also gives workshops and lectures on the art of gilding.

Marlene Matalon
10410 Willowisp
Houston, TX 77035
phone: 713-721-8404
fax: 713-729-5756
Conservator of gilded objects; uses these steps: 1) examination 2) written evaluation & estimate 3) technical

analysis 4) care and maintenance recommendations 5) conservation using safest techniques for the object being conserved.

Glass

(see also GLASS, Curved)

Repair Services

Edward Poore
Crystal Workshop
P.O. Box 475
Sagamore, MA 02561
phone: 508-888-1621
Glass items made to order; also repairs stemware, cut glass, and art glass.

Sharon Smith Abbott
Fine Wares Restoration
P.O. Box 753
Bridgton, ME 04009-0753
phone: 207-647-2093
Restores ceramics & glass for private collectors and museums; references of museum clients on request.

Art Cut Glass Studio
RD 1 Box 10 Fawn Drive
Matawan, NJ 07747
phone: 908-583-7648

Jonathan Mark Gershen
Jonathan Mark Gershen Porcelain,
  Pottery & Glass Restoration
1463 Pennington Rd.
Ewing, NJ 08618-2656
phone: 609-882-9417
Second generation restorer and long time member of the AIC; clients include museums, collectors and dealers worldwide; free brochure available upon request.

Flemington Cut Glass
156 Main St.
Flemington, NJ 08822
phone: 201-782-3017

Glass Restorations
1597 York Ave.
New York, NY 10028
phone: 212-517-3287

Anton Laub Glass Corp.
1873 Second Ave.
New York, NY 10029-7453
phone: 212-734-4270 or 718-430-1901
Installation, beveling and resilvering of glass and mirrors; also fabrication of reproduction antique mirrors.

Antique Workshop Inc.
150 Aerial Way
Syosset, NY 11791
phone: 516-933-6213
Repairs and restorations; chipped crystal repaired, chips removed from glass statues, cut glass, stoneware, and all glass items.

Michael Andras
P.O. Box 250
Bear Rocks, PA 15610
phone: 412-547-6419
Glass engraver and cutter.

Henry Chaudron
Chaudron Glass & Mirror Co., Inc.
1801 Lovegrove St.
Baltimore, MD 21202-2815
phone: 410-685-1568
Resilvers mirrors; also specializes in cutting, hand-beveling plate glass, and stone wheel engraving.

Mildred R. Shepherd
Shepherd Studio
5527 Third St., South
Arlington, VA 22204-1115
phone: 703-671-1789
Offers conservation and restoration of art objects, specializing in porcelain, glass, ivory, china, stoneware, ivory, jade, pottery, etc.

Jim & Sheri Van Es
222 W. Washington St.
Charles Town, WV 25414
phone: 304-725-1673 or 703-435-9045
e-mail: wdnshu@aol.com
Grinds and repairs chips on glass.

Ray Errett
Ray Errett - Glass Restoration
101 Mohican Trail
Wilmington, NC 28409-3418
phone: 910-792-1807
Restores glass figurines, sculpture crystal, cut glass, grinding, polishing.

Don & Joyce McCurley
McCurley Glass Repair
5011 Memorial Dr.
Sebring, FL 33870-1087
phone: 813-471-9814
fax: 941-471-3359
Repairs glass and crystal; chip removal, polishing, sawing, bells made from goblets; stopper specialist - carries large stock of replacement stoppers for bottles; also prism replacement.

David Jasper
David Jasper's Glass Clinic
46508 267th St.
Sioux Falls, SD 57106
phone: 605-361-7524 or 800-361-7524
fax: 605-361-7216
Four generations of restorers; glass, porcelain, painting, dolls, figurines, ivory, lamps, etc.

Josef Puehringer
Crystal Cave, The
1141 Central Ave.
Wilmette, IL 60091
phone: 708-251-1160
fax: 708-251-1172
European trained craftsmen will restore your treasures with expert care; call or write for free estimates.

Jerry Lewis
Bevel Glass Works, Inc.
900 Hacienda
Belville, TX 77418
phone: 409-865-5711
Makes replacement beveled glass and mirrors, engraved glass and mirrors, shelves with plate grooves, etc.

Mike Maher
Dr. Chips
88154 Chita Loop
Springfield, OR 97478
phone: 503-747-6532
Restoration of glass and fine crystal; also porcelain, pottery restoration; gluing, making new parts when necessary, refinishing to match original; ships nationwide.

Bill Haavisto
Blue Unicorn, The
4780 NW Maple Ave.
Redmond, OR 97756
phone: 503-923-4567
Offers traditional glass grinding services as well as a chip replacement service using a methacrylic ester resin system; also sells do-it-yourself repair kits and teaches glass repair classes in Oregon and Washington.

Suppliers

Restorite Systems
P.O. Box 7096
West Trenton, NJ 08628-0096
phone: 609-530-1526
Products for restoration and conservation of porcelain, pottery, and glass; sells a complete kit for repairing breaks and chips; also "How-to" videos available; send for free catalog.

Allan Koskela
Restoration Services
P.O. Box 186
Webster City, IA 50595
phone: 515-832-3828 or 515-832-6623
Sells glass repair materials including Diamond Hand Pads, fillers, glues and cleaners; instructional videos on Lampworking, to make glass beads, jewelry, figurines, etc.; highly recommended by many publications including Glass Art.

Ivory

Repair Services

Mildred R. Shepherd
Shepherd Studio
5527 Third St., South
Arlington, VA 22204-1115
phone: 703-671-1789
Offers conservation and restoration of art objects, specializing in porcelain, glass, ivory, china, stoneware, ivory, jade, pottery, etc.

Lamps & Lighting

Dealers

David & Phyllis Helphenstine
David's Brass Works
P.O. Box 111
Washington, KY 41096
phone: 606-759-7423
Buys, sells, repairs lamps of all sorts; custom lamp repair, rewire, polish, lacquered, complete antique lamp restoration, glass lampshades, hand painted and artist signed shades, custom shades.

Repair Services

Tom Barnard
Light Revival
Newsletter: Light Revival
35 West Elm Ave.
Quincy, MA 02170-2423
phone: 617-773-3255
Committed to the restoration of 1890-1930 period lighting; seeks out and restores quality fixtures and lamps, especially turn-of-the-century gas & electric lighting devices.

Stephen W. Conant
Conant Custom Brass
270 Pine St.
Burlington, VT 05401-4737
phone: 802-658-4482 or 800-832-4482
fax: 802-864-5914
Offers metal restoration and repair; specializes in repairing antique brass lighting fixtures.

Ray Christensen
Metzger's Lamps & Lighting
15 South Main St.
W Hartford, CT 06107
phone: 860-232-1843
fax: 860-232-5267
e-mail: rayp10@aol.com
Repairs all types of lamps and lamp shades, new and antique; family-owned since 1925; no job too large or too small.

Hugo A. Ramirez, Pres.
Hugo Ltd.
233 East 59th St.
New York, NY 10022-1425
phone: 212-750-6877 or 212-288-8444
fax: 212-750-7346
A leading authority on 19th cent. lighting; restorer and supplier to U.S. Senate, Treasury Dept., Nantucket Hist. Soc.; restores and conserves to factory original finish (no plating or polishing, all hand restoration).

David & Carol Baker
Baker's Metal & Wood Shop
11956 Augustine Herman Hwy.
P.O. Box 68
Kennedyville, MD 21645-0068
phone: 410-778-6681
fax: 410-348-5966
Polishing/lacquering/repairing gas/ electric/oil lighting; new and old parts available, prisms, shades, etc.; rewiring, gilding, leafing, antiquing in

bronze and brass; repair candlesticks; also architectural and fireplace items.

Richard Dudley
A-Bit-of-Antiquity
1412 Forest Lane
Woodbridge, VA 22191-3024
phone: 703-491-2878
e-mail: dudleyre@erols.com
Expert restoration, repair, deplating & polishing of gas and electric lamps; specializing in oil lighting; carries old parts & shades; also buys and sells old lamps and lamp parts.

Rick Charpie
Crystal Clear Chandelier Care
9602 W. 156th St.
Overland Park, KS 66221-9709
phone: 913-681-6700 or 800-373-7804
fax: 913-897-7608
Crystal & glass chandeliers a specialty: repair/cleaning/restoration, electrification of gas or candle devices, replacement of parts & prisms, buys whole or broken chandeliers and old trade catalogs, chandelier consultant, etc.

Suppliers

Crystal Mountain Prisms
P.O. Box 31
Westfield, NY 14787-0031
phone: 716-326-3676
e-mail: ameyers@epix
Sells prisms, chains, bobeches, pendants, drops, etc.; send SASE for info.

Kirk Lane Co.
2541 Pearle Buck Rd.
Bristol, PA 19007
phone: 215-785-1251
fax: 215-785-1651
Source for lamp parts including sockets, bases, harps, finials, chimneys, shades, etc.

Mike Barnes
B & P Lamp Supply, Inc.
843 Old Morrison Highway
McMinnville, TN 37110
phone: 615-473-3016
fax: 615-473-3014
Wholesale distributor of early style lamp parts including oil burners, chimneys, shades, lamp cord, and wiring devices; mail order to the trade only.

Steve Kaye
Brass Light Gallery
131 South First St.
Milwaukee, WI 53204
phone: 414-271-8300 or 800-243-9595
fax: 414-271-7755
Specializes in parts for gas wall sconces and chandeliers, and for early electric lamps; also does lamp repairs including metal work.

Marble

Repair Services

Steve Dorian
Dorian Marble & Granite
440 Broadway
Williamsburg, NY 11201
Marble repair/restoration specialist; fireplace mantels, cornices, counter tops, table tops; also reproductions of handcarved relief and full round sculpture.

Jack T. Irwin
Jack T. Irwin, Inc.
601 East Gude Dr.
Rockville, MD 20852
phone: 301-762-5800
Cuts and repairs marble tops.

Mattresses

Man./Prod./Dist.

Tucker Mattress Company
3926 Lawrenceville Hwy.
Tucker, GA 30085
phone: 770-938-1176
Manufacturer of customized mattresses for antique beds, adjustable beds, brass beds; also for boats, RV's and campers.

Scott Lipps
Sleep-Tite Mattress Company
1355 E. Second St.
Franklin, OH 45005
phone: 800-859-3703 or 513-746-2556
fax: 513-746-9101
Specializes in custom made mattresses and box springs for hard-to-fit antique beds.

Mattresses Unlimited
840 Pleasant Valley Dr.
Springboro, OH 45066
phone: 800-326-5668
Carries any size mattress for antique beds.

Metal

Suppliers

E-Z Way Chemical
P.O. Box 525
Burlington, WA 98233
Sells "Silverplater", a 99.987% real silver solution that cleans and recoats a metal surface with silver.

Metal Items

(see also FLATWARE, Sterling Silver)

Periodicals

James R. Walker, Dir.
Institute of Metal Repair, The
Newsletter: Repairing Metalware
1558 South Redwood St.
Escondido, CA 92025
phone: 619-747-5978
Promotes knowledge, skill, and understanding of the metalware repair trade; publishes repair techniques and other information, sells specialty repair tools and supplies; flatware, sculpture/statuary, duplicating parts, etc.

James R. Walker, Dir.
Institute of Metal Repair, The
Directory: IMR Sourcebook
1558 South Redwood St.
Escondido, CA 92025
phone: 619-747-5978
A source book for restoration, repair, replication and preservation of metal items; contains sources for replacement parts (original & reproduced), metal repairers/restorers, tips/techniques, schools, organizations, etc.

Repair Services

Fleming's
24 Elm Street
Cohasset, MA 02025
phone: 617-383-0684
Metal repair and restoration; replating, dent removal, breaks repaired; pewter, silver, copper, polishing, plating, repairing, lacquering.

Joseph J. Pistilli
Orum Silver Co., Inc.
51 S. Vine St.
P.O. Box 805
Meriden, CT 06450-0805
phone: 203-237-3037
fax: 203-237-3037
Repairing, restoring, replating of antique and old silver, gold, nickel; brass & copper plating; cleaning, buffing, polishing.

Sayed Antiques & Art
19 Stonehedge Lane
Madison, NJ 07940
phone: 201-301-0894
fax: 201-301-0895
Museum quality sand casting, fancy engraving and chasing, specializes in lighting and architectural fixtures, complete fixture or parts reproduced; references available.

Zophy's Fine Silver Plating
4702 Park St.
Peterboro, NY 13134
phone: 315-684-3062
Fine restoration for over 40 years of copper, brass, sterling, pewter.

Romayne Shay McMahon, ISA
Veronique's Antiques
124 S. Market St.
Mechanicsburg, PA 17055-6329
phone: 717-697-4924
fax: 717-697-4924
Fine metals refinishing: replating, cleaning, polishing, lacquering, repairing; silver, brass, copper, pewter, bronze; chandeliers, lamps, etc. rewired and restored; brass beds a specialty.

Boris Paskvan
Awesome Metal Restorations, Inc.
4233-G Howard Ave.
Kensington, MD 20895
phone: 301-897-3266
fax: 310-942-6532
European expert restores gold, gilt, bronze, silver, silver plating, icons, metal accessories, sculptures, etc. for museums, homes, insurance; repairs, solders, fabricates duplicates parts, replates, rewires, retins, polishes, lacquers.

Abercombie & Co.
9159A Brookeville Rd.
Silver Spring, MD 20910
phone: 301-585-2385
fax: 301-587-5708
Replates silverplate; repairs all sorts of metal; silver, brass, copper; also welding.

Pete Markey
Creative Metal Design
7935 Edgewood Church Rd.
Frederick, MD 21702-2713
phone: 301-473-5995
fax: 301-473-5995
Specializes in ornamental ironwork, hand forged originals; metal repairs; made the Statue of Liberty gates.

David Nelson
Jarnel Iron & Forge
221 Rowland
Hagerstown, MD 21740
phone: 301-733-0441
Recasts replacement parts in various metals; also iron work.

Alexander Bigler
Equestrian Forge
P.O. Box 1950
Leesburg, VA 22075
phone: 703-777-2110
Recasts replacement parts in various metals; also casts portrait sculptures.

Steve Kayne
Kayne & Son Custom Forged Hardware
100 Daniel Ridge Rd.
Candler, NC 28715
phone: 704-667-8868 or 704-665-1988
fax: 704-665-8303
Steel, brass, bronze reproductions of locks, pulls, hinges, thumb latches, furniture & interior/exterior hardware, fireplace tools & accessories, military accoutrements, etc.; also does repairs, restoration; $5 for two catalogs.

Alfred L. Crabtree
Brass & Silver Workshop, The
758 St. Andrew Blvd.
Charleston, SC 29407
phone: 803-571-4342
fax: 803-571-7417
Museum quality restoration and conservation of most fine metal decorative arts; emphasis on 17th, 18th and 19th century brass and silver; also purchases Southern coin silver and unusual sterling items.

Estes-Simmons Silverplating, Ltd.
1050 Northside Dr., NW
Atlanta, GA 30318
phone: 404-875-9581 or 800-645-4193
fax: 404-873-4826
e-mail: mantel@aol.com
*Repairs silver, silverplate, gold,
pewter, brass and copper; also
replates silver, gold, brass, nickel,
copper.*

Memphis Plating Works
682 Madison Ave.
Memphis, TN 38103
phone: 901-526-3051
*Gold, silver, copper, brass, nickel and
chrome plating; restoration of
chandeliers, floor lamps, brass beds,
fern tables, tea sets, trays, vanity sets,
etc.; repairs teapot feet, spouts,
missing parts, flatware, etc.*

Paul Trageser
Paul Trageser Metalsmith
10330 Howard Rd.
Harrison, OH 45030
phone: 513-367-6226
Finest quality silver repairs.

Antique & Art Restoration By Wiebold
413 Terrace Place
Terrace Park, OH 45174
phone: 513-831-2541 or 800-321-2541
fax: 513-831-2815
Internet: http://www.weibold.com
*Silver repair and replating;
restoration of bronzes, brass, copper,
pewter, lead, combs, brushes, knife
blades, mirrors, chandeliers, glass,
etc.*

Charles Wiebold, Pres.
Wiebold, Inc.
413 Terrace Place
Terrace Park, OH 45174-1164
phone: 513-831-2541 or 800-321-2541
fax: 513-831-2815
e-mail: wiebold@eos.net
Internet: http://www.wiebold.com
*Restoration of ceramics, paintings,
metal items.*

Jerry Propst
P.O. Box 45
Janesville, WI 53547-0045
phone: 608-752-2816
fax: 608-752-7691
*Repairs silver back hair brushes.
When writing, please include a LSASE
if requesting a reply.*

Roger A. Sundblom
Specialized Repair Service
1125 E. Wisconsin Ave.
Appleton, WI 54911-3905
phone: 414-993-9993
*Repairs all metal items; also designs
and fabricates replacement metal
parts; machining, welding (tig,
heliarc, oxyacetylene, silver brazing,
casting in yellow and red brass, etc.;
if it can't be repaired, will remake
from scratch!*

Oexning Silversmiths
800 N. Washington Ave., Ste. 118
Minneapolis, MN 55401
phone: 612-332-6857
*Silver replating and repair, repair and
refinishing of sterling silver, dent
removal, gold plating, pewter repair,
copper plating and repair, brass
refinishing; casts most missing parts
such as feet, pieces of ornate work or
handles.*

Glenn Taylor
Courtesy Metal Polishing
635 N. Addison Rd.
Villa Park, IL 60181
phone: 708-832-1862
*All metals polished and buffed:
motorcycle, automobile, marine parts,
antique juke boxes and slot machines.*

Mueller Kaiser Plating Co.
5815 Hampton Ave.
Saint Louis, MO 63109
phone: 314-832-3553
*Fine metal finishing in silver, gold,
bronze, copper and brass; flatware,
tea services, church ware, antiques,
and other items.*

Craig Bierman
Speed & Sport Chrome Plating
404 Broadway
Houston, TX 77012
phone: 713-921-0235
*Specializing in chrome plating of
antique jukeboxes, Coke machines,
slot machines, pedal cars, etc.*

Jay A. Watkins
Watkins & Sons
7990 Anders Circle
La Mesa, CA 91942-2303
phone: 619-441-9441
*Silversmithing and repair; silver,
brass, copper, aluminum, refinishing;
25 years experience.*

Carmelo Tringali
Colonial Silver
1219 Forest Ave.
Pacific Grove, CA 93950
phone: 408-375-0355
*Recommended for silverplating and
replating.*

Tim Maple
Omega Silver Smithing Inc.
11130 117th Pl. NE
Kirkland, WA 98033
phone: 425-822-3727
*Expert repair and restoration of fine
silver, bronze, silverplate, spelter,
brass, pewter and copper; from tea
sets to brass beds, chandeliers, new
knife blades, mirrors and combs; full
service restoration.*

Suppliers

Jax Chemical Company, Inc.
78-11 267th St.
Floral Park, NY 11004
phone: 718-347-0057
*Sells metal finishing solutions: green
patina, pewter black, black darkener,
gold finish, silver and copper plating*

solutions; also brass, copper, gold
and marble cleaners.*

Delphi Stained Glass
2116 East Michigan Ave.
Lansing, MI 48912
phone: 800-248-2048 or 517-482-2617
fax: 517-482-4028
Internet: http://www.voyager.net/
delphiglass
*Sells stained glass supplies; gives
lessons; large mail order business;
also sells chemical solutions to repair
damaged patina on brass and other
metals.*

Mirrors

Repair Services

Anton Laub Glass Corp.
1873 Second Ave.
New York, NY 10029-7453
phone: 212-734-4270 or 718-430-1901
*Installation, beveling and resilvering
of glass and mirrors; also fabrication
of reproduction antique mirrors.*

Sundial Schwartz
159 E. 118th St.
New York, NY 10035
phone: 212-289-4969 or 800-876-4776
fax: 212-996-3236
*Custom resilvering and antiquing of
mirror and glass.*

Romayne Shay McMahon, ISA
Veronique's Antiques
124 S. Market St.
Mechanicsburg, PA 17055-6329
phone: 717-697-4924
fax: 717-697-4924
Offers glass grinding and resilvering.

Henry Chaudron
Chaudron Glass & Mirror Co., Inc.
1801 Lovegrove St.
Baltimore, MD 21202-2815
phone: 410-685-1568
*Resilvers mirrors; also hand-bevels
plate glass.*

Painted Finishes

Repair Services

Ingrid Sanborn
Ingrid Sanborn & Daughter
85 Church St.
West Newbury, MA 01985-1018
phone: 508-363-2253
fax: 508-363-2049
*Specializes in paint matching,
graining, stenciling, marbleizing,
custom work.*

Ruby Newman
Roundabout Restoration Studio
P.O. Box 823
Forest Knolls, CA 94933-0823
phone: 415-488-9213
fax: 415-488-9213
*Restoration and recreating of classic
finishes; all painted surfaces
including furniture, mirror frames,
carousel carvings, etc.: trompe l'oeil,
contemporary murals, classical faux*

marbles, wood grain, gold leaf, wall
treatments.*

Paper Items

(see also PRINTS; REPAIR/
RESTORATION/CONSERVATION,
Archival Supplies For)

Repair Services

Henry Lie
Center for Conservation & Technical
Studies, The
Fogg Art Museum
Harvard University
Cambridge, MA 02138
phone: 617-495-2392
*Provides conservation and restoration
services for fine arts, including works
of art on paper, paintings, objects and
sculpture.*

Bridgitte Boyadjian
43 Fern St.
Lexington, MA 02173-6024
phone: 617-862-9395
fax: 617-862-9395
*Paper restoration and conservation;
fine prints, drawings, watercolors and
manuscripts.*

Oscar & Debra Perez
Vigues Art Studio
54 Flanders Rd.
Woodbury, CT 06798-2103
phone: 203-263-4088
fax: 203-266-9118
*Conservation, restoration of oil
paintings (cleaning, lining, touch up
and repair), frames (gold leaf repairs,
casting of missing parts) and paper
(cleaning, repairs of prints, books,
documents); also porcelain, glass &
china repair.*

Kenneth Newman
Old Print Shop, The
150 Lexington Ave. at 30th St.
New York, NY 10016
phone: 212-683-3950
*Paper conservator: preservation,
restoration, cleaning, deacidification,
encapsulation.*

George J. Cohenour
4301 Beaumont Rd.
Dover, PA 17315-2405
phone: 717-292-5345
*Cleans, deacidifies, repairs and
restores prints: American historical,
antique and decorative, handcolored
lithographs, chromolithographs,
etchings, engravings, watercolors, etc.*

Maria Pukownik
Fine Art & Paper Conservation
1045 Orrtanna Rd.
Orrtanna, PA 17353
phone: 717-337-0668
*Watercolors, charcoal and pastel,
drawings, colored engravings,
autographs, maps; cleaning, leaf
casting, tears and cracks mending,
flattening, retouching, dry mounting
removal.*

Marilyn Kemp Weidner, FAIC
612 Spruce St.
Philadelphia, PA 19106-4114
phone: 215-627-2303 or 215-627-0188
*Conservation treatment for art &
artifacts on paper, collection surveys
and care consultations; extensive
expertise and experience in the
treatment of pastels, watercolors,
drawings, maps, manuscripts, and
problems with works on paper.*

Christopher W. Lane
Philadelphia Print Shop, Ltd., The
8441 Germantown Ave.
Philadelphia, PA 19118
phone: 215-242-4750
fax: 215-242-6977
e-mail: PhilaPrint@PhilaPrintShop.com
*Gallery of antique prints and maps
with related rare books and atlases;
also bookstore of reference books
related to antique prints and maps;
appraisals, paper conservation and
restoration, museum quality framing.*

American Institute for Conservation of
Historic & Artistic Works
Directory: AIC Directory
1717 K St. NW, Ste. 301
Washington, DC 20006
phone: 202-452-9545
fax: 202-452-9328
*Purpose is to advance the knowledge
and practice of the conservation of
cultural property; the AIC Directory
lists competent conservators of paper,
textiles, photographs, furniture, and
more - over 2000 members.*

James Von Ruster
Old Print Gallery, The
1220 31st St. NW
Washington, DC 20007-3422
phone: 202-965-1818
fax: 202-965-1869
*Paper conservator: preservation,
restoration, cleaning, deacidification,
encapsulation.*

Kendra Lovette
1200 Branch Ln.
Glen Burnie, MD 21061-2922
phone: 410-764-6770
*Paper conservator and repairer;
anything on paper.*

Janice & Dennis Dobson
Dobson Studios
810 N. Daniel St.
Arlington, VA 22201
phone: 703-243-7363
*Conservator of Oriental screens,
scrolls and wood block prints; repairs
and conservation to other paper items
as well.*

Christine Smith, Pres.
Conservation of Art on Paper, Inc.
2805 Mt. Vernon Ave., Ste. B
Alexandria, VA 22301-1125
phone: 703-836-7757
*Conservation of fine art and historic
artifacts on paper and parchment;
also Japanese woodblock prints;
conservation treatments, collection*

*surveys, lectures, workshops, vault
storage.*

Paul J. Buco
Fine Arts Services, Inc.
127 N. Front St.
Wilmington, NC 28401-3904
phone: 910-251-8859
*Restoration/conservation of art on
paper: tears and paper loss repairs,
deacidification, encapsulation.*

David L. Swift
6436 Brownlee Dr.
Nashville, TN 37205
phone: 615-352-0308
*Paper conservator: preservation,
restoration, cleaning, deacidification,
encapsulation.*

John Pofelski
Resurrection Book & Paper Conservation
P.O. Box 582
330 West Georgetown St. #200A
Wood Dale, IL 60191-0582
phone: 708-616-8990

Marlene Matalon
10410 Willowisp
Houston, TX 77035
phone: 713-721-8404
fax: 713-729-5756
*Conservator of art on paper; uses
these steps: 1) examination 2) written
evaluation & estimate 3) technical
analysis 4) care and maintenance
recommendations 5) conservation
using safest techniques for the object
being conserved.*

Kelley Miles Essoe
Collector's Restoration Service
P.O. Box 110409
Big Bear Lake, CA 92315
phone: 909-866-7226
*Specializes in the restoration and
conservation of comic books, Big
Little books and movie posters;
professional, expedient, top-of-the-line
restoration at reasonable cost;
references available.*

Phil Temple
P.O. Box 561
Novato, CA 94949
phone: 415-897-5130
fax: 415-897-5130
Paper conservation (linen backing).

Suppliers

Light Impressions Corp.
P.O. Box 940
Rochester, NY 14603-0940
phone: 800-828-6216
fax: 800-828-5539
*General line of archival supplies
including mat boards, document
storage boxes, framing and
photographic supplies.*

Porcelain

(see REPAIR/RESTORATION/
CONSERVATION, Ceramics)

Reverse Painting On Glass

Repair Services

Ingrid Sanborn
Ingrid Sanborn & Daughter
85 Church St.
West Newbury, MA 01985-1018
phone: 508-363-2253
fax: 508-363-2049
*Specializes in the restoration of
reverse paintings on glass and antique
painted finishes; philosophy is to
preserve as much of the original finish
as possible and restore only those
areas that have been lost or damaged.*

Textiles

Repair Services

Textile Conservation Center, Museum of
American Textile History
491 Dutton St.
Lowell, MA 01854
phone: 508-441-0400
fax: 508-441-1412
*TCC provides evaluation, treatment
and educational services that pertain
to the conservation and preservation
of historic textiles.*

Evelyn Siefert Kennedy
Evelyn of Sewtique
391 Long Hill Rd.
P.O. Box 1293
Groton, CT 06340-1293
phone: 860-445-7320 or 860-464-2001
fax: 860-445-1448
e-mail: sewtique@aol.com
Internet: http://www.members/aol.com/
sewtique/home.htm
*Specialist in restoration, preservation
& conservation of apparel and
textiles; full service by mail/phone or
appt.; appraises textiles, laces,
tapestries, etc.; removes spots &
stains; teaches textile appraisal &
restoration workshops.*

Stephen & Carol Huber
40 Ferry Rd.
Old Saybrook, CT 06475
phone: 860-388-6809
fax: 860-388-6809
*Specializes in the repair and
conservation of antique needlework.*

Testfabrics, Inc.
P.O. Box 420
Middlesex, NJ 08846
phone: 201-469-6446
fax: 201-469-1147
Provides textile conservation services.

Applebaum & Himmelstein
444 Central Park West
New York, NY 10025
phone: 212-666-4630
fax: 212-316-1039
*Treats silk textiles, paintings and
objects.*

Patsy Orlofsky
Textile Conservation Workshop
Main St.
South Salem, NY 10590
phone: 914-736-5805
*Textile conservation lecturer and
consultant; also does conservation
and repairs of all types of textiles.*

M. Finkel & Daughter
936 Pine St.
Philadelphia, PA 19107
phone: 215-627-7797
fax: 215-627-8199
*Antique textile restoration for
collectors, museums and dealers;
specializes in mounting and repairing
of antique samplers, quilts,
needlework, hooked rugs and table
rugs.*

Thanewold Associates
P.O. Box 104
Zieglerville, PA 19492
phone: 610-287-9158
*Needlework repairs and conservation
including samplers.*

Clarissa Palmai
C. P. & Asst.
5416 Harwood Rd.
Bethesda, MD 20814
phone: 301-656-6381
*Offers textile conservation, consulta-
tion and lecturing.*

Linda Tomlin
Details in Design, A Needle Art Studio
4901 C. Helen Potts Pl.
Williamsburg, VA 23188
phone: 757-253-2483
fax: 757-253-2483
*Linens and lace restoration,
conservation; embroidered textiles;
also reproduction embroidery for
linens: Arts & Crafts, and 18th and
19th century period designs; sells
marked linen kits on Irish linen for
embroiderers.*

Mini-Magic
3910 Patricia Drive
Columbus, OH 43220
phone: 614-457-3687
fax: 614-459-2306
*Cleaning and repairing; conservation
supplies.*

Elizabeth L. Barbatelli
Linens Limited, Inc.
240 North Milwaukee St.
Milwaukee, WI 53202
phone: 414-223-1123 or 800-637-6334
fax: 414-223-1126
*Expert specializing in the repair,
restoration and cleaning of linens;
restores both new and antique linens
using old world European laundry
techniques that are superior to simple
laundering.*

Textile Conservators
215 W. Ohio St., #6
Chicago, IL 60610-4118
phone: 312-474-WARP
Antique textile gallery; offers conservation, restoration, mounting.

Alicia Repairs Textiles
New Orleans, LA 70118-3957
phone: 504-862-9956
All textile repair: clothing, costume, beaded bags, Native American, quilts, lace, embroidery, tapestry, needle-point, rugs including reweave and repiling of ORientals, Aubussons, hooked, kilim.

Bryce Reveley
Gentle Arts
936 Arabella
P.O. Box 15636
New Orleans, LA 70155
Cleaning and repairing of textiles.

Emily Sanford
Sanford Restoration Works
2102 Speyer Ln.
Redondo Beach, CA 90278
phone: 213-374-7412
Restoration of antique textiles and oriental rugs.

Suppliers

Testfabrics, Inc.
P.O. Box 420
Middlesex, NJ 08846
phone: 201-469-6446
fax: 201-469-1147
Sells delicate clamps for textile repair and restoration.

Rita Marx
Cherish
P.O. Box 941
New York, NY 10024-0941
phone: 212-724-1748
Carries Orvus soap and other conservation supplies including padded hangers, acid-free boxes and tissues, etc. for the storage, cleaning and displaying of vintage textiles and clothing.

Nancy's Notions
333 Beichl Ave.
P.O. Box 683
Beaver Dam, WI 539160683
Carries Orvus brand quilt soap.

June Roth-Splain
Lily-White Linens
1496 Rolling Acres
Argyle, TX 76226-6330
phone: 940-240-8800 or 940-565-9611
fax: 940-383-8809
Lily-White Linens is a product that can be safely used on antique linens and quilts for stain and spot removal; safe for the environment.

Wicker

Repair Services

Joan O. Silbermann
Antique Wicker Works
8002 McKenstry Dr.
Laurel, MD 20723-1152
phone: 410-792-4842
Sales, restorations, repairs.

Wicker Wizard
7455 Charlotte Pk.
Nashville, TN 37209
phone: 615-356-2935
Antique wicker restoration and repair; 13 years experience, by the piece or by the load; all expert work; no covering up.

Suppliers

Paige W. Beasley
Carolina Caning Supply
P.O. Box 883
Smithfield, NC 27577
phone: 800-346-0142 or 414-207-0291
Chair caning and repair supplies.

Woodworking

(see also HARDWARE; REPAIR/ RESTORATION/CONSERVATION, Furniture)

Suppliers

Period Furniture Hardware Co., Inc.
Charles Street Station
P.O. Box 314
Boston, MA 02114
phone: 617-227-0758
fax: 617-227-2987
Supplies fine quality reproduction hardware for furniture and the home; specializes in solid brass fittings and accessories; 120 page catalog available for $5.

Trendlines
135 American Legion Hwy.
Revere, MA 02151
phone: 800-767-9999 or 617-853-0900
fax: 617-853-0226
Mail order source for a good mix of woodworking tools.

Tremont Nail Company
P.O. Box 111
Wareham, MA 02571
phone: 508-295-0038
Carries twenty different styles of historic cut nails.

Brookstone
17 Riverside St.
Nashua, NH 03062-1373
Mail order source for hard to find tools and devices.

Barbara Horton Rockwell
Horton Brasses Inc.
P.O. Box 120
Cromwell, CT 06416
phone: 860-635-4400
fax: 860-635-6473
e-mail: barb@horton-brasses.com
Internet: http://www.horton-brasses.com
Sells authentic period reproduction hardware of the finest quality. Manufactured of solid brass or handforged black iron in CT factory.

Micro Mark
340 Snyder Ave.
Berkeley Heights, NJ 07922-1505
phone: 908-464-6764
fax: 908-665-9383
e-mail: micromark@worldnet.att.net
Mail order source for small tools only, e.g. X-Acto, knives, Dremel, airbrushes, micro-sanders, etc.; 80-pg. catalog $1.

Garrett Wade Company, Inc.
161 Ave. Of The Americas
New York, NY 10013-1299
phone: 800-221-2942 or 212-807-1155
fax: 800-566-9525
Reproduction English solid brass hardware; also 220 page catalog of the world's finest specialty woodworking tools: planes, chisels, etc.

Constantine
2050 Eastchester Rd.
Bronx, NY 10461
phone: 800-223-8087
fax: 718-792-2110
e-mail: http://www.constantines.com
A complete line of tools, hardware, finishing supplies, marquetry kits, books, moldings, parts, veneers, hardwoods, etc.

Mohawk Finishing Products
4715 State Highway 30
Amsterdam, NY 12010
phone: 800-545-0047 or 518-843-1380
fax: 518-842-3551
Major supplier of finishing tools, supplies and materials.

John M. Fisher
18th Century Hardware Co., Inc.
131 East 3rd St.
Derry, PA 15627-1607
phone: 412-694-2708
fax: 412-694-9587
Clean, polish & repair brass items; makes, sells reproduction hardware; clean and electrify brass lamps; offers catalog.

Rick Zirpoli
Hoosier Emporium, The
HC 1 Box 1826
Milanville, PA 18443
phone: 717-729-7080
Manufactures & distributes authentically reproduced "want lists" and cardboard inserts for Hoosier, Sellers, etc. style kitchen cabinets.

Ball & Ball
463 W. Lincoln Highway
Exton, PA 19341
Publishes a hardware catalog; also has a recasting service.

American Machine & Tool Company
P.O. Box 70
Oyersford, PA 19468
phone: 610-948-0400
Mail order source for hand tools and machinery.

Industrial Abrasives Co.
P.O. Box 14955
Reading, PA 19612
Carries a large line of sand paper and other abrasives.

Paxton Hardware Ltd.
P.O. Box 256
Upper Falls, MD 21156-0256
phone: 410-592-8505 or 800-241-9741
fax: 410-592-2224
Supplies brass reproduction hardware in period styles; 74 pg. catalog also contains pulls, knobs, locks, hinges, lamp parts, shades, etc.

Woodcraft
210 Wood County Industrial Park
Parkersburg, WV 26102
phone: 800-535-4482
fax: 304-428-8271
Mail order source for complete line of woodworking tools, supplies and books.

Leichtung Workshops
1125 Jay Lane
Graham, NC 27253
phone: 800-321-6840
fax: 800-545-9663
Mail order source for hand tools, supplies and small kits.

Highland Hardware
1045 N. Highland Ave., NE
Atlanta, GA 30306
phone: 800-241-6748 or 404-872-4466
fax: 404-876-1941
Internet: http://www.highland-hardware.com
Mail order source for hand tools, machinery, workbenches, books, videos, and supplies; call 888-500-4466 for free catalog.

Power Kleen Corp.
101 Bayview Blvd.
Oldsmar, FL 34677
phone: 813-854-2648 or 800-844-2648
fax: 813-854-3133
Wholesale chemicals and supplies for refinishers; paint and varnish removers, lacquer thinner, mineral spirits.

A & H Brass & Supply
126 W. Main St.
Johnson City, TN 37601
phone: 423-928-8220 or 800-638-4252
fax: 423-928-8360
Carries a wide selection of hardware, caning supplies, trunk parts, fiberboard seats, etc.

Bob Morgan Woodworking Supplies
1123 Bardstown Rd.
Louisville, KY 40204-1301
phone: 502-456-2545
Mail order source for hundreds of veneers, faces, flexibles, inlays, burls, tiger oak, etc. for restoring antique furniture; send for free catalog.

Cherry Tree Toys, Inc.
P.O. Box 369
Belmont, OH 43718
phone: 614-484-4363
Mail order source for children's toys, doll houses, whirligig kits, parts, books and supplies.

Robert Hershberger
Hershberger's Hardware
1411 Township Rd. 178
Baltic, OH 43804
phone: 330-893-2464
fax: 330-698-3200
Catalog of specialty products for antiques and woodworking such as spool cabinet decals, high chair trays, antique telephone parts, Hoosier cabinet parts, lamp parts; $4 for 64 page catalog (refundable).

Shopsmith Tool Guide
6530 Poe Ave.
Dayton, OH 45414
phone: 800-543-7586 or 800-762-7555
fax: 800-722-3965
Internet: http://www.shopsmith.com
Mail order source for hand tools and supplies. Visit local Shopsmith Store or order by phone.

Phyllis & Phil Kennedy
Phyllis Kennedy Hardware
9256 Holyoke Court
Indianapolis, IN 46268-1237
phone: 317-873-1316
fax: 317-873-8662
Hardware for antique furniture, Hoosier cabinets and trunks; manufacturer of flour bins and sifters for Hoosier cabinets.

Doug Poe
Doug Poe Antiques
4213W 500N
Huntington, IN 46750
phone: 800-348-5004
Carries antique restoration hardware: stamped-brass pulls, diecast brass knobs, casters, teardrop pulls, brass keys, cupboard latches, etc.

Woodsmith Shop
2200 Grand Ave.
Des Moines, IA 50312
phone: 800-444-7002 or 515-282-7000
fax: 515-282-6741
Internet: http://www.augusthome.com
Mail order source for woodworking tools, hardware, and project plans and supplies.

Heirloom Brass Co.
P.O. Box 146
Dundas, MN 55019
phone: 507-645-4445 or 800-533-8055
Wholesale to dealers only; Victorian, Eastlake, and turn-of-the-century

hardware; send resale number or dealer ID and $2 (refundable with first order) for catalog.*

Van Dykes Supply Company
P.O. Box 278
Woonsocket, SD 57385-0278
phone: 800-558-1234 or 605-796-4425
fax: 605-796-4085
Mail order source for refinishing supplies; large catalog of reproduction simulated and solid wood carvings, hardware, pulls, knobs, leather seats, old fashioned nails, isen glass, etc.; also issues catalog of taxidermy supplies.

Bill Becker
Craftsman Wood Service Co.
1734 W. Cortland Ct.
Addison, IL 60101
phone: 708-629-3100
fax: 708-629-8292
Supplier of hardwoods in many thicknesses from 1/64" to 4"; specialty hardware, cane and upholstery supplies, kits, plans, books and much more; free cull color catalog available.

Star Chemical Co.
360 Shore Dr.
Hinsdale, IL 60521
phone: 708-654-8650
Major supplier of finishing tools, supplies and materials.

WSI Distributors - Antique Restoration Supplies
405 N. Main St.
Saint Charles, MO 63301-2034
phone: 800-447-9974 or 314-946-5811
fax: 314-946-5832
e-mail: wsi@fastrans.net
Wholesale source for furniture & trunk hardware, cane & weaving materials, fiber chair seats, veneer, wood ornaments, Zap glues, and much more; over 1200 items for professional furniture restorers. Sorry, dealers only.

Gay Barton
Briwax Midwest, Inc.
20 Nonsuch Rd.
Lake Ozark, MO 65049-9307
phone: 573-365-4698 or 800-562-5855
Briwax is a restorative compound used mainly for restoring antique furniture and floors.

Scott's-Becher's Hardware Inc.
1411 S. 3rd St.
Ozark, MO 65721
phone: 800-247-2594 or 417-581-6525
fax: 417-485-3067
Carries hardware for antique furniture: trunk hardware, bed parts, kitchen cabinets, Hoosier, pulls, latches, hinges, locks keys.

Noel & Bernice Wise
Wise Company, The
P.O. Box 118MC
Arabi, LA 70032-0118
phone: 504-277-7551 or 504-277-7551
Sells antique reproduction hardware,

chair cane and hard-to-find items; also repairs old locks and makes new keys for old locks.*

Good Pickins'
220 Polk
Jefferson, TX 75657
phone: 903-665-3222
Mail order source for old trunk hardware, canning supplies and other hard-to-find replacement parts; send $3 for catalog; dealers include tax # for discounts.

Woodworker's Supply, Inc.
1108 North Glenn Rd.
Casper, WY 82601
phone: 800-645-9292
fax: 800-853-9663
Mail order source for hand tools, machinery, hardware, and finishes.

Woodworker's Supply, Inc.
5604 Alameda Place NE
Albuquerque, NM 87113
phone: 505-821-1511
fax: 505-821-7331
Mail order source for wood finishing tools, supplies and brass hardware.

Mother of Pearl & Sons Trading Company
P.O. Box 341133
Los Angeles, CA 90034
phone: 213-202-8959
fax: 213-202-1387
Sells traditional restoration products; call or write for catalog.

B & M Hardware Co.
4868 Carediff Bay Dr.
Oceanside, CA 92057-3413
phone: 800-783-2212
Sells brass antique reproduction hardware - Chippendale, Victorian, Mission; also glass knobs and handles, oak knobs and handles, etc.; ·send for free catalog.

Muff's Antiques
135 S. Glassell St.
Orange, CA 92866
phone: 714-997-0243
fax: 714-997-1601
Internet: http://www.tias.com/amdir/SpecTrunks.html
Mail order source for kitchen cabinet hardware (Hoosiers) including hinges, labels, canisters, castors, and rolls; also ice box parts, locks, keys (specializes in rekeying antique locks), window hardware, and much, much more; catalog $5.

Harbor Freight Tools
3491 Mission Oaks Blvd.
Camarillo, CA 93011-6010
phone: 800-423-2567
fax: 805-388-0760
Absolutely the lowest prices on quality name brand tools, equipment, machinery for both the home and professional workshop; free catalog.

Woodline the Japan Woodworker
1731 Clement Ave.
Alameda, CA 94501-1204
phone: 510-521-1810 or 800-537-7820
fax: 510-521-1864
e-mail: fdamsen@ix.netcom.com
Mail order source for highest quality woodworking tools from Japan.

American Home Supply
P.O. Box 697
Campbell, CA 95009
phone: 408-246-1962
fax: 408-248-1308
Carries the largest selection of antique reproduction hardware on the West Coast; has a 99.9% stock rate.

Anglo American Brass Company
P.O. Box 9487
San Jose, CA 95157
phone: 800-AABRASS or 408-246-0203
fax: 408-248-1308
Publishes a hardware catalog; brass hardware, household hinges, glass knobs, brass casters, nickel plate ice box hardware, wooden casters.

Ritter & Son Hardware
38001 Old Stage Rd.
P.O. Box 578
Gualala, CA 95445-9984
phone: 800-445-5044
fax: 800-445-5043
Supplier of furniture restoration hardware: carved oak gingerbread, Hoosier hardware, cast & stamped brass pulls, handles, etc.; dealers only.

Bridge City Tool Works, Inc.
1104 N.E. 28th Ave.
Portland, OR 97232
phone: 503-282-6997 or 800-253-3332
fax: 503-287-1085
Mail order source for fine woodworking hand tools.

RESTAURANT COLLECTIBLES

(see also DINERS & RELATED ITEMS; FAST FOOD COLLECTIBLES; FOOD COLLECTIBLES; MENUS)

Collectors

Glenn Grush
5344 North Collingwood Circle
Calabasas, CA 91302-3137
phone: 818-880-6200 or 800-653-3244
fax: 818-880-6500
Wants restaurant memorabilia; Bob's Big Boy, Coon Chicken Inn; nodders, ceramic display pieces, tableware with logos, etc.

Dave Lathom
P.O. Box 5053
Bellingham, WA 98227-5053
phone: 360-676-0715
Wants restaurant china from ice cream parlors, hamburger stands, frills, diners, sandwich stands, cafes.

Dealers

Steve Colby
Off The Deep End
712 East St.
Frederick, MD 21701-5239
phone: 301-698-9006
e-mail: chilimon@offthedeepend.com
*Wants to buy old restaurant and diner
items.*

Big Boy

Collectors

Steve Soelberg
29126 Laro Dr.
Agoura Hills, CA 91301-1635
phone: 818-889-9909
*Wants Big Boy collectibles such as
lamps, lunch boxes, cookie jars,
counter displays, buttons, nodders,
menus, ash trays, salt/peppers, etc.;
items must have the Big Boy logo on
them; no vinyl banks, please; the older
the better.*

Glenn Grush
5344 North Collingwood Circle
Calabasas, CA 91302-3137
phone: 818-880-6200 or 800-653-3244
fax: 818-880-6500
*A leading buyer and collector wants
Big Boy restaurant items: cups, plates,
menus, ceramic banks, lamps, figural
ashtrays, menus, salt and peppers,
display items, anything with Big Boy
logo.*

Chicken In The Rough

Collectors

Ted Hirt
4929 Butterworth Pl.
Washington, DC 20016
*Wants memorabilia and information
about "Chicken in the Rough"
restaurant chain.*

Howard Johnson's

Collectors

Jeffrey C. McCurty
P.O. Box 882
Pleasant Valley, NY 12569-0882
phone: 914-635-3566
*Wants 1930-1980 Howard Johnson's
dishes, tins, candy boxes, toys, cookie
jars.*

Sandra Obuck
517 Krause St.
Ann Arbor, MI 48103
phone: 313-996-9002
e-mail: dover@mail.ic.net
*Wants to buy Howard Johnson's
restaurant collectible items: china,
menus, paper items, anything having
to do with Howard Johnson's.*

Royal Castle

Collectors

Michael Hiscano
510 NW 86th Pl. #201
Miami, FL 33126
*Wants to buy anything from the
"Royal Castle" restaurant chain:
china, glassware, silverware, menus,
uniforms, signs, hats; must have the
name "Royal Castle" or the Crown
and the Happy Knife/Fork/Spoon.*

Sambo's

Collectors

Jeff Kline
616 Masselin Ave. #306
Los Angeles, CA 90036-3733
phone: 213-934-3117
fax: 213-934-7141
*Wants anything related to Sambo's/No
Place Like Sam's restaurants
including signage, fixtures, china,
employee items, mascots, menus, etc.*

RESTRAINT DEVICES

(see also KEYS; LOCKS; MAGI-
CIANS PARAPHERNALIA; LAW
ENFORCEMENT MEMORABILIA)

Handcuffs & Leg Shackles

Dealers

Peter D. McCahon
Handcuff Collection, The
3 Selwyn Road
New Malden
Surrey KT3 5AU, U.K.
phone: 01144 181 688 3114
fax: 01144 171 928 6770
e-mail:
    peter_mccahon@compuserve.com
Internet: http://www.u-net.com/oasis
*Collector and dealer in all forms of
handcuffs, leg irons, and manacles;
interest limited solely to antique,
police and magical related items.*

Joseph & Pamela Tanner
Wheeler-Tanner ESCAPES
3024 E. 35th Ave.
Spokane, WA 99223
phone: 509-448-8457
fax: 509-448-8457
*Specialize in handcuffs, leg shackles,
balls & chains, restraints, padlocks,
locks & locking devices of all kinds
(including railroad.)*

Experts

Michael Griffin
International Handcuff Exchange
356 W. Powell Rd.
Powell, OH 43065-9650
phone: 614-846-0585
*Buys/sells all types of handcuffs, leg
irons, locks, magicians escape items,
old or new; offers large quarterly list
of items for sale.*

REVERE GIFTWARE

Experts

Douglas M. Singleton
P.O. Box 416
Westmoreland, NY 13490-0416
phone: 315-336-7792
*Appraises and specializes in Revere
Giftware made of chrome, copper and
brass prior to 1942: cocktail shakers,
condiment sets, goblets, magazine
holders, pitchers, trays, etc.; no pots
and/or pans, please.*

REVERSE PAINTINGS ON GLASS

(see ART, Paintings (Reverse on
Glass); REPAIR/RESTORATION/
CONSERVATION, Reverse Painting
on Glass)

REVOLUTIONARY WAR ITEMS

Collectors

Larry Jarvinen
313 Condon Rd.
Manistee, MI 49660
phone: 616-723-5063
*Wants muskets, lamps, pipes, chests,
swords, polearms, tools, silverware,
compasses, bayonets, canteens, etc.*

Alex Peck
Antique Scientifica
P.O. Box 710
Charleston, IL 61920
phone: 217-348-1009
*Wants uniforms, insignia, guns,
swords, diaries, medical instruments,
hats, medals, belt plates.*

REVOLVING LAMPS

(see LAMPS & LIGHTING, Motion)

REWARDS OF MERIT

(see PAPER COLLECTIBLES;
SCHOOL RELATED MEMORA-
BILIA)

RIDING TOYS

(see also AUTOMOBILIA;
BICYCLES & RELATED MEMORA-
BILIA; GO-KARTS; SOAP BOX
DERBY)

Experts

Edmund Weinberg
Atlantic Highlands Animal Hospital
77 Memorial Parkway
Atlantic Highlands, NJ 07716-1451
phone: 908-291-4400 or 908-741-2542
*Collects and specializes in riding toys,
velocipedes, wagons, wheel toys, and
rocking horses.*

Repro. Sources

John T. Nicholas
John T. Nicholas & Son
704 N. Michigan Ave.
Howell, MI 48843

Woodshed Originals
P.O. Box 3
Itasca, IL 60143

Pedal Vehicles

Clubs/Associations

Bruce Beimers
National Pedal Vehicle Association
1720 Rupert, N.E.
Grand Rapids, MI 49505
phone: 616-361-9887
Focuses on pedal cars.

Collectors

Art Bransky
1840 Siegfriedale Rd.
Breinigsville, PA 18031-2246
phone: 610-285-6180
*Wants streamline child's wagons and
tricycles; also pre-1950 pedal cars
and any unusual riding toy.*

Frank Martin
7669 Winterberry Dr.
Youngstown, OH 44512-4723
phone: 330-758-4470
*Wants old pedal cars, pedal toys, and
any related literature.*

Nate Stoller
960 Reynolds Dr.
Ripon, CA 95366
phone: 209-956-5244 or 209-529-5300
e-mail: multimotor@aol.com
*Wants to buy or trade pre-1960 pedal
cars.*

Dealers

David A. Hull
Small Town Coins & Collectibles
7498 E. Davison Rd.
Davison, MI 48423-2014
phone: 810-658-1992
fax: 810-658-2977
e-mail: towncoin@concentric.net
Internet: http://www.concentric.net/
    ~towncoin
*Has over 100 antique (1920-1970)
pedal cars for sale; also buys pedal
cars.*

Experts

Sanford Weltman
39 Branford Rd.
Rochester, NY 14618-1707
phone: 716-442-8810 or 716-473-2498
*20 year veteran collector/buyer of
pedal vehicles and large riding toys;
buys pre-WWII pedal cars, pedal
planes, or pedal trucks; also will buy
post-WWII up to 1950s; any
condition; has parts; does not resell;
please send photos.*

Periodicals

Blue Diamond Classics
Newsletter: Peddler, The
5415 E. 65th St.
Indianapolis, IN 46220

John Rastall
Newsletter: Wheel Goods Trader, The
P.O. Box 435
Fraser, MI 48026-0435
phone: 810-949-6282
fax: 810-949-6282
Magazine for collectors pedal cars, pedal airplanes; classifieds, calendar, etc.

Repair Services

Chad Mapes
Chad Mapes Pedal Car Restoration
3216 Wayne St.
Endwell, NY 13760
phone: 607-754-7952
fax: 607-786-3549
Specializes in the restoration of pedal cars.

Ron Hanley
Mini-Motors
130 Main
Hobart, NY 13788
phone: 607-538-9926
Handcrafted "one-of-a-kind" pedal cars manufactured; can hand craft body parts and fenders for pedal cars.

Blue Diamond Classics
5415 E. 65th St.
Indianapolis, IN 46220

Portell Restorations
P.O. Box 91
Hematite, MO 63047
phone: 314-937-8192
Restorer and manufacturer of pedal cars and parts.

Suppliers

Matthew Vaznaian
Juvenile Automobiles
P.O. Box 221
Sheldonville, MA 02070
phone: 401-766-9661
Smallest pedal car parts supplier in the world: tires, wheels, hubcaps, hood ornaments, bells, bumpers, steering wheels, headlights, pods, windshields, etc.; send $5 for catalog.

Bob Ellsworth
Pedal Car Graphics
1207 Charter Oak Dr.
Taylors, SC 29687-4406
phone: 803-244-4308
Sells replacement decals for pedal cars, boats, cars and planes; large selection to choose from; send $4 for 37-page catalog and color photos.

J.D. Dorsey
Texas Pedal Car Peddler Inc.
213 Stone Drive
Fort Worth, TX 76108
phone: 817-238-8363
320 page catalog/reference book for $8.

Rocking Horses

Experts

Edmund Weinberg
Atlantic Highlands Animal Hospital
77 Memorial Parkway
Atlantic Highlands, NJ 07716-1451
phone: 908-291-4400 or 908-741-2542
Collects and specializes in riding toys, wheel toys, and rocking horses.

Patricia Mullins
P.E.I. International
6001 Johns Rd., Ste. 148
Tampa, FL 33634
phone: 813-855-4213
Author of "The Rocking Horse."

Sleds

Collectors

Joan Palicia
15 Canton Rd.
Wayne, NJ 07470
phone: 201-831-0527
Flexible Flyer memorabilia, membership cards, models, pins, advertising, sleds; anything Flexible Flyer.

Art Bransky
1840 Siegfriedale Rd.
Breinigsville, PA 18031-2246
phone: 610-285-6180
Wants streamline child's wagons and tricycles; also pre-1950 pedal cars and any unusual riding toy.

Art Bransky
1840 Siegfriedale Rd.
Breinigsville, PA 18031-2246
phone: 610-285-6180
Collects and restores children's sleds, bobsleds, and any unusual sledding related items from the past 100 years; a frequent museum exhibitor and serious collector.

Dealers

Lyle Palmiter
Canacadea Sled Shop
676 Tinker Town Rd.
Alfred Station, NY 14803
phone: 607-587-9450
Buys old sleds regardless of condition; parts accepted.

Repair Services

Art Bransky
1840 Siegfriedale Rd.
Breinigsville, PA 18031-2246
phone: 610-285-6180
Collects and restores children's sleds, bobsleds, and any unusual sledding related items from the past 100 years; a frequent museum exhibitor and serious collector.

Tricycles

Collectors

Art Bransky
1840 Siegfriedale Rd.
Breinigsville, PA 18031-2246
phone: 610-285-6180
Wants streamline child's wagons and tricycles; also pre-1950 pedal cars and any unusual riding toy.

Wagons

Collectors

Art Bransky
1840 Siegfriedale Rd.
Breinigsville, PA 18031-2246
phone: 610-285-6180
Wants streamline child's wagons and tricycles; also pre-1950 pedal cars and any unusual riding toy.

RINGS

Character/Comic

(see PREMIUMS, Rings)

RIPLEY'S BELIEVE IT OR NOT!

(see also MORBID & ODD ITEMS)

Clubs/Associations

Jan & Mick Ivanovich
Ripley's Believe It or Not! Collectors Club
Newsletter: RBION Newsletter
1433 Wyoming Ave., Apt. H
Billings, MT 59102-5351
For fans and collectors of Ripley's memorabilia; newsletter published quarterly.

Collectors

Dan Paulun
215 South Maple
West Lafayette, OH 43845-1138
phone: 614-545-9743
Wants anything Ripley: blotters, calendars, posters, museum & odditorium postcards and booklets, newspaper & magazine ads, etc.

Glen Carlisle
2163 Goshen Hill Rd. SE
New Philadelphia, OH 44663
phone: 216-339-3859
Wants "Ripley's Believe It or Not" hardback books; also memorabilia from museum, Odditorium programs, giant rings, etc.

Museums/Libraries

Ripley's Believe It Or Not! Museum
175 Jefferson St.
San Francisco, CA 94113
phone: 415-771-6188
There are 17 Ripley's Believe It Or Not! museums across the U.S. and Canada.

Church of One Tree/Robert L. Ripley Museum
492 Sonoma Ave.
Santa Rosa, CA 95401
phone: 707-524-5233
Collection is housed in the church Ripley once worshiped; contains his personal papers and related memorabilia.

RIVERBOAT COLLECTIBLES

(see STEAMBOAT COLLECTIBLES)

ROADSIDE MEMORABILIA

(see HIGHWAY COLLECTIBLES; HOTEL COLLECTIBLES; SOUVE-NIR & COMMEMORATIVE ITEMS)

ROBJ

Collectors

Charles Sorkin
19 Chatsworth Ave.
Larchmont, NY 10538-2903
phone: 914-235-4718
Wants Robj porcelains: figural bottles, inkwells, powder jars, statuettes; any piece marked "Robj"; call collect.

Jeff Leegood
DecoLectibles
P.O. Box 596553
Dallas, TX 75359-6653
phone: 214-824-7917
fax: 214-824-7917
Seeks Robj perfume lamps, incense burners, statues, powder boxes, and liquor bottles; made in porcelain, ceramic, glass during the 1920s; most marked ROBJ, Paris France; also wants other similar Art Deco perfume lamps.

Experts

Randy Monsen
Cocktails & Laughter Antiques
P.O. Box 529
Vienna, VA 22183-0529
phone: 703-938-2129

ROBOTS

(see TOYS, Space & Robot)

ROCK 'N' ROLL COLLECTIBLES

(see also AUTOGRAPHS; MAGA-ZINES, Scandal/Cult/R 'N' R; MUSIC, Rock 'N' Roll; PERSONALI-TIES [MUSICIANS]; RECORDS; SHEET MUSIC)

Dealers

Myron Ross
Heroes & Legends
P.O. Box 1038
Agoura Hills, CA 91301-1038
phone: 818-991-5979
fax: 818-222-4571
e-mail: heroesross@aol.com
Wants character memorabilia, books, comic books, Fanzines, movie

memorabilia, etc.; science fiction or fantasy, rock 'n roll, autographs.

Experts

Jean Blankenship
P.O. Box 7274
Pasadena, TX 77508-7274
phone: 713-266-6311

Greg Moore
P.O. Box 586
Aumsville, OR 97325
Author of "Here It Is! A Price Guide to Rock & Roll Collectibles"; music memorabilia from the 1950s to present including Beatles, Monkees, Elvis, KISS, California Raisins, Banana Splits, Archies, Partridge Family, and more.

ROCKETS

(see KITS; MODELS, Rockets; SCIENCE FICTION; SPACE COLLECTIBLES)

ROGERS GROUPS

Clubs/Associations

George Humphrey
Rogers Group, The
Newsletter: Newsletter of the Rogers Group
4932 Prince George Ave.
Beltsville, MD 20705-1907
phone: 301-937-7899
Focuses on the life and works of John Rogers (1829-1904), American sculptor.

Collectors

Bruce Bleier
73 Riverdale Rd.
Valley Stream, NY 11581
phone: 516-791-4353
e-mail: bellovaman@aol.com
Buys and sells John Rogers statuary.

Sangiorgi
35 Mildred Ave.
Cortland, NY 13045
phone: 607-753-6574
Wants to buy John Rogers groups; please describe and price.

Dealers

George P. Lentros
179A Main St.
Ashland, MA 01721
phone: 508-881-1160 or 508-881-1635

Carme Pederson
Carmen's Garden of Treasures
114 E. 32nd St.
New York, NY 10016-5506
phone: 212-683-9197

Experts

George Humphrey
4932 Prince George Ave.
Beltsville, MD 20705-1907
phone: 301-937-7899
Interested in the life and works of

John Rogers (1829-1904), American sculptor; wants to purchase Rogers groups for his collection.

Museums/Libraries

John Rogers Studio & Museum of the New Cannan Historical Society
13 Oenoke Ridge
New Canaan, CT 06840-4104
phone: 203-966-1776
fax: 203-972-5917
Internet: http://darien.andcnewnannan.com/nchistory

Lightner Museum
P.O. Box 334
Saint Augustine, FL 32085
phone: 904-824-2874

ROLLER COASTERS

(see also AMUSEMENT PARK ITEMS)

Clubs/Associations

Ray J. Ueberroth, Pres
American Coaster Enthusiasts, Inc.
Magazine: Rollercoaster!
P.O. Box 8226
Chicago, IL 60680
phone: 410-385-1222
fax: 410-385-1222
Promotes the preservation, appreciation and enjoyment of the roller coaster; 4700 members in 48 states and 17 countries.

Collectors

Peter Dusza
385 Reed St.
Santa Clara, CA 95050-3104
phone: 408-988-8161 or 408-723-0722
fax: 408-988-2206
e-mail: pdusza@ix.netcom.com
Wants to buy roller coaster souvenirs and memorabilia: coffee cups, drinking and shot glasses, pins, patches, post cards, posters, and buttons.

ROSE O'NEILL COLLECTIBLES

(see also DOLLS, Kewpie)

Clubs/Associations

Mary Lou Ratcliff
International Rose O'Neill Club
P.O. Box 668
Branson, MO 65616

Experts

Denis C. Jackson
P.O. Box 1958
Sequim, WA 98382-1958
phone: 360-683-2559
fax: 360-683-2559
e-mail: ticn@olypen.com
Internet: http://www.olypen.com/ticn/
Author of "The Price & Identification Guide to Rose O'Neill", 2nd edition; covering magazine covers, advertising, paper items from Puck, etc.; send LSASE for information.

ROYALTY COLLECTIBLES

(see also POSTCARDS, Royalty Related; RUSSIAN ITEMS; SOUVENIR & COMMEMORATIVE ITEMS)

Clubs/Associations

Steven N. Jackson
Commemorative Collector's Society
Lumless House, Gainsborough Road
Winthrope, New Newark
Nottingham NG24 2NR U.K.
phone: 01636-71377
Members interested in commemorative items including commemorative pieces for Royal events and personages (both U.S. and worldwide).

Collectors

Frank J. Buono
P.O. Box 1535
Binghamton, NY 13902
phone: 607-724-4444 or 800-527-8893
fax: 607-723-1656
Wants to buy royalty items: Victoria 1887, 1897 Jubilees, Edward & Alexandra 1901.

British

Collectors

Edward J. Sperling
Britannia Past
46 Beach Ave.
Kennebunk, ME 04043
phone: 207-967-5989
Buys and sells by mail order British Royalty commemoratives: china, glass, silver, paper, textile, etc.

Dealers

Anita L. Grashof
Gallerie Ani'tiques
Stage House Village
Park & Front Streets
Scotch Plains, NJ 07076
phone: 908-322-4600 or 201-377-3032
fax: 201-765-9565
Buys, sells and appraises British Royal commemoratives from Queen Victoria through Prince William.

Now & Then Antiques
401 Main St.
Laurel, MD 20707

Audrey B. Zeder
British Royalty Commemoratives
6755 Coralite St. #D
Long Beach, CA 90808-4725
phone: 562-421-0881
Buys, sells, British Royal commemorative items for all royalty events; deals in royalty ceramics, tins, textiles, ephemera and souvenirs; for sale list available for $3.

Experts

Audrey B. Zeder
British Royalty Commemoratives
6755 Coralite St. #D
Long Beach, CA 90808-4725
phone: 562-421-0881
Author of "British Royal Commemoratives."

Italian

Collectors

Mario Donald Thomas
860 18th Ave.
Salt Lake City, UT 84103-3719
phone: 801-532-5340 or 803-799-0030
Buys any items connected to the Italian royal families.

Russian

Collectors

Jason K. Phillips
130 Long Meadow Lane
State College, PA 16801
phone: 814-861-6533
e-mail: jkp107@psuvm.psu.edu
Wants to buy anything having to do with Imperial Russia; books, artifacts, etc.; also interested in items concerning Czar Nicholas II and the Russian royal family.

Experts

Timothy A. Miller
American-Russian Trade Company
P.O. Box 460574
San Antonio, TX 78246-0574
phone: 210-545-2176
fax: 210-545-2176
e-mail: artco@stic.net
Internet: http://www.stic.net/users/artco

ROYCROFT

(see ARTS & CRAFTS, Roycroft)

RUBA ROMBIC

(see GLASS, Consolidated)

RUBBER ITEMS

Collectors

Mike Woshner
2306 Spokane Ave.
Pittsburgh, PA 15210-4414
phone: 412-884-9299
e-mail: mwoshner@bellaatlantic.net
Wants gutta-percha & rubber goods of the mid-1800s; pre-1880 old rubber boots, valises, knapsacks, gun covers, cap covers, canteens, capes, life preservers; gutta-percha or hard rubber cups, inkwells, military buttons, buckles, etc.

Brunswick
P.O. Box 9729
Baltimore, MD 21286-9729
Wants rubber goods, manuals, films; hot water bottle outfits, rubber syringes, bulbs, enamel cans, etc.:

pre-1965 or foreign; also books, accessories, boxes, ads, catalogs, photos on use, etc.; also nursing, child care, sick care.

George Briese
12204 Woodlark Ct.
Manassas, VA 22111
Wants rubber hot water bottles, combination or fountain syringe outfits, douche or enema squeeze bulb syringes, folding syringes, syringe hoses and fittings related to pre-1965 health care rubber goods.

Museums/Libraries

Goodyear World of Rubber
1201 East Market St.
Akron, OH 44316
phone: 216-796-2044

Clothing

Collectors

Standish H. Smith
P.O. Box 292
Villanova, PA 19085
Wants rubber raincoats, hats, rain suits, capes; any color; or photographs of firemen, policemen, fishermen, etc. wearing same.

RUBIK'S CUBES

(see PUZZLES, Mechanical [Rubik's Cubes])

RUGS

(see also AMERICAN INDIAN, Navajo)

Man./Prod./Dist.

Dan Wax
Taylor Made Custom Rugs
121 Mansfield Circle
Lexington, SC 29073-8080
phone: 803-356-3182
fax: 803-808-6395
e-mail: dwax@netside.com
Internet: http://www.netside.com/~dwax
Specializing in handmade custom designed carved rugs; any design or idea can be reproduced into a beautiful rug for floor or wall.

Repro. Sources

David C. Kline
Family Heir-Loom Weavers
775 Meadowview Dr.
Red Lion, PA 17356-8608
phone: 717-246-2431 or 717-246-2431
fax: 717-246-2431
e-mail:
FamilyHeirloom@mindspring.com
Makers of fancy jacquard coverlets, ingrain carpets & other historic textiles; carpets in the Abe Lincoln home & various other sites.

Hooked

(see also FOLK ART; REPAIR/RESTORATION/CONSERVATION, Textiles; TEXTILES)

Appraisers

Deborah Roberts
1071 San Pablo
Costa Mesa, CA 92626
phone: 714-557-5258
e-mail: quiltevals@aol.com
Internet: http://quilt.com/appraiser
Appraiser of antique hooked rugs, quilts and quilt-related textiles; certified by the American Quilter's Society; written insurance, fair market and donation appraisals; also lectures on quilts.

Experts

Jessie A. Thurbayne
P.O. Box 2540
Westwood, MA 02090
phone: 617-769-4798
Author of "Hooked Rugs: History and the Continuing Tradition, 1991", available from the author.

Periodicals

Cathy Hart
Stackpole Publishing
Magazine: Rug Hooking
500 Vaughn St.
Harrisburg, PA 17110-2220
phone: 717-234-5091
fax: 717-234-1359
Published five times yearly; provides how-to information as well as features on outstanding or historically significant hand-hooked rugs; special annual "Celebrations" is also published by the editors of "Rug Hooking" magazine.

Repair Services

Margaret & Audrey Ruhland Antiques
P.O. Box 245
North Gower
Ontario K0A 2T0 Canada
phone: 613-489-3298
Specializes in the repair of hooked rugs and quilts.

Stephanie Harvey-Clark
Rug Lady, The
3 Melville Ave.
Halifax
Nova Scotia B3P 1C9 Canada, VT
phone: 902-479-0796
Cleaning, binding, restoration of holes, wall mounting; all work done by hand.

Linda Eliasom
RR 1 Box 715
Pawlet, VT 05761-9602
phone: 802-325-3026
Repairs hooked rugs.

Repro. Sources

Chris Bock-Howell
Highfields Sheep & Wool Farm
P.O. Box 327
Remsen, NY 13438

Ramona Cann
Cottage Rugs
460 Shiloh Dr.
Dayton, OH 45415

Peggy Teich
7846 N. Sherman Blvd.
Milwaukee, WI 53209

Suppliers

Jean L. Edmonds
Sea Holly Hooked Rug Shop
1906 North Bayview Dr.
Kill Devil Hills, NC 27948
phone: 919-441-8961 or 919-441-4104
Traditional rug hooking; sells finished pieces, patterns, wool and other supplies and equipment; also teaches classes and workshops.

Oriental

Appraisers

Alan F. Butler
P.O. Box 2818
Durham, NC 27715-2818
phone: 919-489-9342

Auction Services

Jo Kris
Skinner, Inc.
357 Main St.
Bolton, MA 01740-1104
phone: 508-779-6241 or 617-350-5400
fax: 508-779-5144
Established in 1964, Skinner Inc. is the fifth largest auction house in the US; has offices in Bolton and Boston, MA.

Grogan & Company Auctioneers
22 Harris St.
Dedham, MA 02026-1835
phone: 617-437-9550 or 617-569-1502
fax: 617-437-0513

Sotheby's
1334 York Ave.
New York, NY 10021
phone: 212-606-7370 or 212-606-7000
Internet: http://www.sothebys.com
Over 70 collecting areas are featured at Sotheby's auctions including toys, dolls, porcelain, furniture, silver, art, books; exhibitions are free and everyone is welcome; for a free copy of "Sotheby's Newsletter", call 212-606-7245.

Lynn Martin
Freeman/Fine Arts of Philadelphia
1808 Chestnut St.
Philadelphia, PA 19103
phone: 215-563-9275 or 215-563-9453
fax: 215-563-8236
America's oldest auction house: Continental, English and American furniture, paintings, silver and

decorative arts; Oriental rugs, rare books, fine jewelry, Orientalia.

Clubs/Associations

Dr. Herbert Exner
Pazyryk-Gesellschaft
Natelscheideweg 113a
D03002
Wedemark, Germany
Goal is to foster broad-based knowledge and education on Oriental rugs and textiles, with special interest on ethnological use, maintenance, preservation and restoration.

Dealers

Robert Davidson
Davidson Oriental Rugs
P.O. Box 650114
Newton, MA 02165-0114
phone: 617-630-9996 or 800-746-4320
Buys all used, old and antique Oriental rugs; all sizes and condition.

Cooper
Main Street Antiques at the Farmington Lodge
185 Main St.
Farmington, CT 06032
phone: 860-677-5423 or 860-674-1035
fax: 860-677-5423
e-mail: cyncooper@imagine.com

Solomon Bassalely
Eliko Oriental Rugs
102 Madison Ave., Fl. 4
New York, NY 10016-7417
phone: 212-725-1600 or 800-733-5456
fax: 212-725-1895
Appraises, buys, sells, and repairs Oriental rugs.

David Zahirpour
David Zahirpour Oriental Rugs
4918 Wisconsin Ave. NW
Washington, DC 20016
phone: 202-338-4141 or 202-244-1800
Specialist in Oriental rugs; cleans and repairs; hand washing, stain removal, carpet reweaving and restoration, appraisals, etc.

B. Joseph Nabatkhorian
J & J Oriental Rug Gallery
1200 King St.
Alexandria, VA 22314
phone: 703-548-0000 or 800-343-3843
Wants used oriental rugs, any size or condition.

Gerald W. Thompson
Gerald W. Thompson Oriental Rugs
P.O. Box 193
Shepherdstown, WV 25443-0193
phone: 304-876-2218
Specialist in antique and semi-antique oriental rugs with 20 years experience; also does repairs, appraisals, and lecturing; also wants to buy for his own collection.

John Lucas
Oglukian Oriental Rugs
4600 Oglukian Rd.
Charlotte, NC 28226-5124
phone: 704-366-1972
*Appraisals, cleaning, repair of
handmade rugs.*

Bob Anderson
Aaron's Oriental Rug Gallery
1217 Broadway
Fort Wayne, IN 46802-3303
phone: 219-422-5184
*Buys, sells, trades and appraises
Oriental rugs; the Midwest's finest
selection.*

Larry Bergman
Coulee Oriental Rugs
N33015 Square Bluff Road
Whitehall, WI 54773-9576
phone: 715-985-3310
*Wants to buy older hand knotted rugs,
both throw rugs and room size rugs;
especially wants rugs made before
1940.*

Farhad Radfar, ISA
MIR International Gallery, Inc.
P.O. Box 10678
Chicago, IL 60610
phone: 312-654-8510 or 773-477-2209
fax: 312-670-8182
e-mail: FRadfar@aol.com

Jimmy Vitanza
Peregrine Galleries
508 Brinkerhoff Ave.
Santa Barbara, CA 93101-3441
phone: 805-963-3134
fax: 805-963-3134

Experts

Joyce C. Ware
534B Heritage Village
Southbury, CT 06488-1535
phone: 203-264-8424
fax: 203-264-8424
e-mail: jware@mail1.nai.net
*Collector, lecturer, and author of
"The Official Identification and Price
Guide to Oriental Rugs."*

Sharon Kerwick
1715 N.E. 25th St.
Ft. Lauderdale, FL 33305-1408
phone: 305-565-9031
fax: 305-564-0648

Ellen Amirkhan
Oriental Rug Cleaning Co., Inc.
3907 Ross Ave.
Dallas, TX 75204-5248
phone: 214-821-9135
fax: 214-821-9136
*Oriental and specialty rugs custom
cleaned; rug repairing (Oriental and
specialty); Oriental rug appraising.*

Val Arbab
P.O. Box 684
La Jolla, CA 92038-0684
phone: 619-453-4686
fax: 619-457-3647
Appraises all oriental rugs and

*textiles; also buys, sells and brokers
collectible and old decorative rugs.*

Man./Prod./Dist.

Peerless Imported Rugs
3033 North Lincoln Ave.
Chicago, IL 60657
phone: 800-621-6573
fax: 773-525-4055
*Sells new oriental rugs and oriental
style rugs.*

On-Line Services

Ron O'Callaghan
Oriental Rug Review
Sinclair Hill Rd.
New Hampton, NH 03256
phone: 603-744-9191
e-mail: ronocal@1r.net
Internet: http://www.rugreview.com/
orr.htm
*Formerly a glossy magazine published
bi-monthly and focusing primarily on
old rugs; book reviews, auctions, ads,
detailed articles, etc.; now an on-line
reference source.*

Periodicals

HALI Publications, Ltd.
Magazine: HALI
Kingsgate House
Kingsgate Place
London NW6 4TA, U.K.
phone: 44 171 328 9341 or 44 171 328
1998
fax: 44 171 372 5924
e-mail: hali@centaur.co.uk
*"HALI" is the leading bi-monthly
international publication in the field
of carpet and textile art; an invaluable
encyclopedic source of information
with original research articles,
reviews of museum collections, etc.;
high color.*

Museum Books, Inc.
Magazine: Rug News
90 John St.
New York, NY 10038
phone: 212-587-1340
fax: 212-587-1344
Internet: http://www.rugnews.com
*Contains articles about the
construction and quality of new
Oriental rugs, primarily; also auction
reports, shows, buy & sell ads.*

Repair Services

Hayk Oltaci
Hayko
110 West 25th St., Ste. 705
New York, NY 10001
phone: 212-633-0700
*Restoration and conservation of
antique rugs; 20 years experience with
carpets and tapestries; at your home
or in the studio; references on request.*

Solomon Bassalely
Eliko Oriental Rugs
102 Madison Ave., Fl. 4
New York, NY 10016-7417
phone: 212-725-1600 or 800-733-5456
fax: 212-725-1895
*Appraises, buys, sells, and repairs
Oriental rugs.*

David Zahirpour
David Zahirpour Oriental Rugs
4918 Wisconsin Ave. NW
Washington, DC 20016
phone: 202-338-4141 or 202-244-1800
*Specialist in Oriental rugs; cleans and
repairs; hand washing, stain removal,
carpet reweaving and restoration,
appraisals, etc.*

Shaia Oriental Rugs
1325 Jamestown Rd.
Merrimac, VA 23185
phone: 804-220-0400
*Expert Oriental rug repairs and
restorations; reweave, reknot,
overcast, selvedge; also cleaning and
appraisals.*

Alicia Repairs Textiles
New Orleans, LA 70118-3957
phone: 504-862-9956
*All rugs including reweave/repile of
Orientals; Aubussons, hooked, kilim,
needlepoint, tapestry, embroidery,
quilts, costumes, beadwork repaired
and restored.*

Emily Sanford
Sanford Restoration Works
2102 Speyer Ln.
Redondo Beach, CA 90278
phone: 213-374-7412
*Specializing in antique village and
nomadic weavings.*

Larry Christianson
1822 MacKinnon Ave.
Cardiff By The Sea, CA 92007

RUSSEL WRIGHT

(see also CERAMICS [AMERICAN],
Russel Wright Designs)

Collectors

Dennis Boyd
P.O. Box 14642
Richmond, VA 23221-0642
phone: 804-560-0753
*Wants Russel Wright dinnerware
(American Modern, Highlight,
Iroquois, and other patterns); also
wants Russel Wright stainless
flatware, glassware, aluminum, Bauer,
etc.*

Dealers

Helene Guarnaccia
52 Coach Lane
Fairfield, CT 06430
phone: 203-374-6034

Edward E. Stump
Raccoons Tale
6 High St.
Mullica Hill, NJ 08062-9540
phone: 609-478-4488
*Wants Russel Wright items: china
dinnerware, modern, Iroquois,
sterling & highlights; also anything
unusual.*

Lee Hay
Weird & Wonderful
P.O. Box 14898
Cincinnati, OH 45250-0898
phone: 513-621-6034
fax: 513-621-6448
e-mail: heywood@sprintmail.com
*Wants to by Russel Wright dishes,
silverware, furniture; also Bauer
pottery.*

Connie Zeigler
Durwyn Smedley Antiques
853 Conner St.
Noblesville, IN 46060
phone: 317-776-0161
e-mail: smedley@iquest.net
Internet: http://www.smedley.com/
smedley
*Buys, sells, appraises all works by
Russel Wright or Mary Wright
including dinnerware, furniture,
pottery, lighting, metalwork, textiles,
glassware, books, and other related
items.*

RUSSIAN ITEMS

(see also ART, Russian; ROYALTY
COLLECTIBLES, Russian)

Collectors

Norman T. Roule
American Embassy
PSC 93 Box 5000
Apo, AE 09823-3051
*Wants Postcards on the Russian Royal
family, the Russo-Japanese War and
Russian involvement in WWI; books,
diaries, photos, postcards, etc. of the
U.S. and foreign intervention in
Russia in 1918-19; also Russian and
Baltic stamps.*

John B. Marrella
Investments in Time
P.O. Box 611
Birmingham, MI 48012-0611
phone: 810-644-3100
fax: 810-644-2792
Wants items by Faberge.

Dealers

Anita L. Grashof
Gallerie Ani'tiques
Stage House Village
Park & Front Streets
Scotch Plains, NJ 07076
phone: 908-322-4600 or 201-377-3032
fax: 201-765-9565
*Buys, sells and appraises Russian
commemoratives in brass, copper,
silver and porcelain.*

Vitaly Shukin
Russian Shop - Maison Russe
1720 Ogden Ave.
Lisle, IL 60532-1230
phone: 630-963-5160
fax: 630-963-5170
e-mail: russhop@mes.com
Internet: http://www.mcs.com/~russhop/
*Imports unusual and one-of-a-kind
Russian gifts and collectibles; experts
in identifying authentic Russian
lacquer boxes and nesting dolls;
dealer in contemporary Russian
porcelain; periodic catalogs; in
business for 20 years.*

Cynthia O'Grady
Russian Samovar
HC 63, Box 8
Pettigrew, AR 72752
phone: 501-677-2192 or 501-575-1852
*Buys and sells the finest in antique
Russian Christmas decorations and
other Russian antiques.*

Timothy A. Miller
American-Russian Trade Company
P.O. Box 460574
San Antonio, TX 78246-0574
phone: 210-545-2176
fax: 210-545-2176
e-mail: artco@stic.net
Internet: http://www.stic.net/users/artco
*Buys and sells Imperial Russian items:
enamels, metal, art; civil, military,
religious, etc.; send photo or
photocopy and price, please.*

Andre Ruzhnikov
Andre Ruzhnikov Russian Art &
Antiques
P.O. Box 1261
Palo Alto, CA 94302-1261
phone: 415-858-0469
fax: 415-858-1008
*Large inventory of Russian icons,
silver, enamels, paintings, watercolors, decorative arts and Faberge;
always interested in buying collections
of fine Russian antiques; appraisals,
consultation, and restoration services
available.*

Experts

Patricia M. Grove
PMG Antique Appraisal Research
3 Ober St.
Beverly, MA 01915-4639
phone: 508-927-2979
*Collects, researches and appraises
decorative and fine arts of the China,
Japan, India and Russia export trades,
17th through mid-19th centuries:
paintings, silver, ivory, tortoise
carvings, furniture, fans, lacquer.*

Benedict J. Hastings
2006 Columbia Rd. N.W.
Washington, DC 20009
phone: 202-483-8575
*Specializes in fine silver, Russian
decorative arts, Russian icons, 18th
and 19th century porcelain, military
medals, decorations and orders.*

James L. Jackson, ISA
Jackson's Auctioneers & Appraisers
2229 Lincoln St.
Cedar Falls, IA 50613
phone: 319-277-2256
fax: 319-277-1252
e-mail: jacksons@jacksonsauction.com
Internet: http://
www.jacksonsauction.com
*Has written and lectured widely on
Russian icons, and has traveled
extensively throughout Russia and the
former Soviet Union studying Russian
icons.*

Museums/Libraries

Hillwood, The Marjorie Merriweather
Post Collection
Journal: Hillwood Studies
4155 Linnean Ave. NW
Washington, DC 20008
phone: 202-686-8500
fax: 202-966-7846
*Most comprehensive collection of
Russian art outside the former USSR;
plus gift shop and 25 acres of
gardens, greenhouses, and auxiliary
buildings.*

Repro. Sources

Robert Whiteside
Whiteside Jewelers
7805 Inwood Rd.
Dallas, TX 75209
phone: 214-358-0089
*Specializes in recreating Faberge
style jewelry and objects of art using
original techniques including 19th
century machinery to reproduce
engine-turned enamel ware.*

Enamels

Experts

Mel & Barbara Alpern
14 Carter Rd.
West Orange, NJ 07052
phone: 201-731-9427
*Advisor to "Warman's Antiques &
Collectibles Price Guide."*

Faberge

Dealers

Philip M. Poniz
European Watch & Casemakers, Ltd.
P.O. Box 1314
Highland Park, NJ 08904-1314
phone: 908-777-0111
*Restoration of watches, clocks, and
music boxes; museum experience; can
make any part and restore any watch;
clients include Sotheby's, Cartier,
collectors in USA, Asia and Europe;
appraises, researches, restores
Faberge.*

Museums/Libraries

Forbes Magazine Collection
60 Fifth Ave.
New York, NY 10011
phone: 212-206-5548
Collection of Russian Faberge eggs.

Walters Art Gallery
600 N. Charles St.
Baltimore, MD 21201
phone: 410-547-9000

Virginia Museum of Fine Arts, Lillian
Thomas Pratt Collection
2800 Grove Ave.
Richmond, VA 23221-2466
phone: 804-367-0888
fax: 804-367-9393
*Fine arts museum covering the entire
range of history of art.*

Henry Hawley
Cleveland Museum of Art, India Early
Minshall Collection
11150 East Boulevard
Cleveland, OH 44106
phone: 216-421-7340
*The Minshall Collection consists of
approximately 50 objects and groups
of related pieces made by the firm or
Peter Karl Faberge and his
contemporaries; included is one
Imperial egg and other objects
relating to the Russian ruling family.*

Lacquer Boxes

Experts

Eric Sinizer
Light Opera Retail Corp.
174 Grant Ave.
San Francisco, CA 94108-5405
phone: 415-956-9866
fax: 415-956-5624
Appraises, buys, sells, rights catalogs.

Samovars

Collectors

Jerome M. Marks
Jerome M. Marks Agency
120 Corporate Woods, Ste. 206
Rochester, NY 14623-1455
phone: 716-475-0220
fax: 716-475-0208
*Wants to buy older Russian samovars;
also wants any samovar related
literature.*

Dealers

Mehmet Nabi Israfil
Fil Caravan Inc.
301 East 57th St.
New York, NY 10022
phone: 212-421-5972
fax: 212-421-5976
*Established in 1976, has large
selection of authentic Russian
samovars; has provided samovars to
collectors worldwide; provides
samovar restoration service as well as
a limited supply of spare parts.*

RV'S

(see TRAILERS & RV'S)

Here are some tips when contacting someone listed in this book:

When requesting information about a particular item, include a description (material, dimensions, maker's mark, model number, etc.) and a photo, sketch, or photocopy of the item in question. ■

Always ask if there are charges for samples or for the services requested. ■

When writing, please be sure to include a Large (#10 business size) Self-Addressed and Stamped Envelope (LSASE) if requesting a reply or the return of photographs. ■

Never call collect unless otherwise directed. When calling, be considerate of time zone differences and always ask if the party you are calling has time to talk. When leaving an answering machine message, always instruct the party to call you back collect. ■

SABERS

(see SWORDS)

SACKS

(see also CORN COLLECTIBLES; MILLING)

Collectors

Ross Hartsough
Sacks Appeal
98 Bryn Mawr Rd.
Winnipeg
Manitoba R3T 3P5 Canada
phone: 204-269-1022
Wants colorful flour, sugar, etc. sacks; especially with cutout patterns imprinted on the sack.

SAD IRONS

(see IRONS, Pressing)

SADDLES

(see also ANIMAL COLLECTIBLES, Horses; LEATHER; WESTERN AMERICANA)

Clubs/Associations

Saddle, Harness & Allied Trades Association
Newsletter: Harness Shop News, The
347 Elk Rd.
Sylva, NC 28779
phone: 704-586-6389
fax: 704-586-8938
Members are makers of saddles, chaps, harnesses, whips, holsters; carving & tooling, luggage repair, sewing machine maintenance.

Collectors

Bill Mackin
1137 Washington St.
Craig, CO 81625-1613
phone: 970-824-6717 or 970-824-6360
fax: 970-824-7175
e-mail: reust@nadja.com
Author of "Cowboy and Gunfighter Collectibles" with 1993-94 updated price guide; sells books for Old West collectors by mail and at shows; over 45 years collecting; wants nice gun leather and cowboy gear; appraises, consults, lectures.

Dealers

Sharon Myers
J&S Oldwestern Store, Saddle Shop and Museum
RR 1, Box 315-c-nt
Warsaw, MO 65355
phone: 816-438-2631
fax: 816-438-6517
e-mail: oldwest@iland.net
Internet: http://www. cowgirls.com/dream/oldwest
Over 200 antique saddles, hibacks, side-saddles, military, charro, etc.; Admission to museum if free; also 1300 Western collectibles for sale; 55 page catalog for $5.

Periodicals

Magazine: Harness Shop News, The
347 Elk Rd.
Sylva, NC 28779
phone: 704-586-8938
fax: 704-586-8938
Professional leather workers, saddle makers, shoe and saddle repairmen, holster manufacturers, harness makers, boot makers; ads, calendar of events.

Side

Clubs/Associations

Linda A. Bowlby, Pres.
World Side Saddle Federation, Inc.
Newsletter: Aside World
P.O. Box 1104
Bucyrus, OH 44820-1104
phone: 419-284-3176
fax: 419-284-3176
e-mail: WorldSFI@aol.com
Internet: http://members.aol.com/worldsfi/sidesadl.htm
A non-profit organization for promoting the use of the sidesaddle; provides sources of equipment and information on the use of the sidesaddle.

Collectors

Martha Coe Friddle
Hundred Oaks, Inc.
P.O. Box 886
Graham, NC 27253
phone: 818-376-8124 or 919-279-6201
fax: 919-376-8124
Dealer for new and used Western, English and period side saddles; certified instructor; saddle appraisal service available; wants to buy side saddles and related items such as books, sandwich cases, etc.

Sue Gregg
8725 N McMaken Rd.
Covington, OH 45318-9650
phone: 513-778-8765
Wants side saddles or anything relating to side saddles; saddlery catalogs, antique riding clothes and accessories, etc.

SAFARI

(see also ART, African & Tribal)

Collectors

James Podraza
RD 2 Box 626
Ruffs Dale, PA 15679
phone: 412-446-9433
Wants to buy African safari books, spears, weapons, cultural items.

SAFES

(see also ANTIQUES DEALERS & COLLECTORS, Supplies For; BANKS, Safe Shaped; LOCKS)

Clubs/Associations

Steve Millett
National Antique Safe Association
Magazine: Safe World
112 J. 1st St.
P.O. Box 218
Holly, CO 81047-0218
Source for hard-to-find information about safes.

Bob Heilemann
West Coast Lock Collectors
Newsletter: West Coast Lock Collectors Newsletter
1427 Lincoln Blvd.
Santa Monica, CA 90401-2732
phone: 310-454-7295 or 310-230-3004
Call evenings; no collect calls, please.

Collectors

Edward Stuart
P.O. Box 21114
Washington, DC 20009
phone: 202-332-6511
Wants pre-1900 safe locks, combination or key operated types; also old brass or iron safe name plates, or safe or safe lock catalogs.

Larry Egelhoff
4175 Millersville Rd.
Indianapolis, IN 46205-2966
phone: 317-846-7228
Interested in key or combination safes.

Steve Millett
112 J. 1st St.
P.O. Box 218
Holly, CO 81047-0218
Wants to buy old safe company catalogs, newspaper ads and articles; anything pre-1940 on safes.

SALMON RELATED COLLECTIBLES

Collectors

Harold Fossum
P.O. Box 210127
Auke Bay, AK 99821
phone: 907-780-4472
Wants old salmon labels from all U.S. states especially Alaska; also from Yukon, N.W. Territories; also wants related postcards, trade tokens, etc.

Dealers

Oscar Schabb
P.O. Box 1377
Brooklandville, MD 21022-1377
phone: 410-486-2436
fax: 410-486-0653
Buys, sells, trades and collects old salmon cans and related memorabilia; also wants old key wind metal tennis ball cans and horse racing glasses.

SALOON & BAR COLLECTIBLES

(see also ADVERTISING COLLECTIBLES; ALCOHOLICS ANONYMOUS ITEMS; BOTTLES; BREWERIANA; GAMBLING COLLECTIBLES; GLASSES; PROHIBITION ITEMS; WHISKEY INDUSTRY ITEMS)

Collectors

James E. Kattner
P.O. Box 11132
Spring, TX 77391
phone: 281-986-6916 or 281-376-4826
Wants to buy Texas saloon, bar and liquor advertisement items such as shot glasses, matchsafes, miniature and larger jugs, pocket mirrors with celluloid backs illustrating pretty ladies, corkscrews, old dice, tokens, coin purses.

John Goetz
P.O. Box 1570
Cedar Ridge, CA 95924
phone: 916-272-4644
Wants saloon bottles: label under glass, bottles, flasks, mugs, bottles and flasks with silver overlay, bottles with multicolored enamel pictures; also wants beer trays or signs.

Dealers

Deborah & Paul Inglis
Bootleggers Nostalgia
P.O. Box 165
South Hadley, MA 01075-0165
phone: 413-533-0419
fax: 413-533-0419
e-mail: bootleggers.nostalgia@worldnet.att.net
Buys pitchers, ashtrays, back bar statues, change receivers, and drip plates advertising Scotch whisky or other types of liquor.

Greg Spiess
Spiess Architectural Antiques
230 E. Washington St.
Joliet, IL 60433-1006
phone: 815-722-5639
fax: 815-722-0171
e-mail: spiessantq@aol.com
Buys saloon fixtures, back and front bars, liquor cabinets, saloon doors, dividers, etc.; also wants saloon catalogs and related saloon fixture advertising such as Brunswick, Passow & Sons, American, Rothschilds, Merle & Heany, etc.

Experts

Steve Visakay
Stephen Visakay Cocktail Shakers
P.O. Box 1517
West Caldwell, NJ 07007-1517
phone: 914-352-5640 or 201-575-0040
e-mail: cocktailshakers@webtv.net
Internet: http://www.martinis.com/key/
*Author of "Vintage Bar Ware,"
(Collector Books), an identification
and value guide dedicated to cocktail
shakers, stemware, ice buckets,
serving trays, recipe books, paper
collectibles, cocktail picks, swizzle
sticks, etc.*

Richard M. Bueschel
414 N. Prospect Manor Ave.
Mount Prospect, IL 60056-2046
phone: 847-253-0791
fax: 847-253-7919
e-mail: BuschlHist@aol.com
*Wants pre-prohibition speakeasy and
saloon photos, equipment, catalogs,
drink-mixer books and other
ephemera; author of book on same;
send SASE if requesting a reply.*

Roger V. Baker
Baker's Lady Luck Emporium
P.O. Box 620417
Redwood City, CA 94062-0417
phone: 369-851-7188
*Specializing in saloon collectibles:
gambling, bar bottles, shaving mugs,
razors, Bowie knives, daggers, barber
items, match safes.*

Cocktail Shakers

Dealers

Arlene Lederman
Arlene Lederman Antiques
150 Main St.
Nyack, NY 10960

Experts

Steve Visakay
Stephen Visakay Cocktail Shakers
P.O. Box 1517
West Caldwell, NJ 07007-1517
phone: 914-352-5640 or 201-575-0040
e-mail: cocktailshakers@webtv.net
Internet: http://www.martinis.com/key/
*Offers free appraisals, identification
and history of the maker of your
cocktail shaker; please enclose SASE
for reply.*

Corkstoppers

Collectors

Joe Iozzia
P.O. Box 1005
Pomona, NJ 08240-1005
phone: 609-652-8504
*Wants to buy figural wood
handcarved people, animals, elves,
pirates, monks, etc.; nutcrackers,
cigarette boxes, bookends, ashtrays,
pipe holders, figurines, bottle
stoppers, humidors and unusual
figural handcarved items.*

Philly Rains
1401 Brentwood Dr.
Harrison, AR 72601
phone: 501-743-2040
fax: 501-743-2120
*Wants to buy handcarved wooden
sculptures: corkstoppers, bar sets,
cigarette boxes, book ends, corkscrews, openers, pourers, napkin
rings, figurines, letter openers,
spoons, forks, key and spoon racks,
pipe racks, nutcrackers, etc.*

Pourers

Collectors

Perry Porter
1811 NE 80th St.
Seattle, WA 98115
phone: 206-524-4401
*Buys and trades liquor bottle pourers
(spouts) having advertising on them;
wants Jack Daniels' collector
decanters, antique whiskey jugs or
bottles; also wants interesting Wild
Turkey, Old Crow, and Beefeaters
items.*

Swizzle Sticks

Clubs/Associations

Ray P. Hoare
International Swizzle Stick Collectors
Association
Newsletter: Swizzle Stick News
P.O. Box 1117
Bellingham, WA 98227-1117
phone: 604-525-3120
e-mail: vera.hoare@mcdermid.ca
*Ray Hoare is co-founder of the
International Swizzle Stick Collectors
Association; sponsors convention
every other year.*

Collectors

Edy J. Chandler
P.O. Box 20664
Houston, TX 77225
phone: 713-781-6146

Joe Smith
4407 Seminole
Pasadena, TX 77504
*Wants to buy advertising swizzle
sticks; plastic, metal, glass, wood,
Bakelite, laminated cardboard.*

Bob Akin
7351 Picardie Lane
Las Vegas, NV 89123
phone: 702-361-0844

Georgina Ross
9525 Jellico ave.
Northridge, CA 91325
*Wants advertising swizzle sticks, old
or new; plastic, wood, metal, Bakelite,
laminated cardboard.*

Ray P. Hoare
P.O. Box 1117
Bellingham, WA 98227-1117
phone: 604-525-3120
e-mail: vera.hoare@mcdermid.ca
Ray Hoare is co-founder of the

*International Swizzle Stick Collectors
Association; sponsors convention
every other year.*

Whiskey Pitchers

Auction Services

Pete Kroll
Glasses, Mugs & Steins Auction
P.O. Box 207
Sun Prairie, WI 53590-0207
phone: 608-837-4818
fax: 608-825-4205
*Produces a semi-annual mail auction
featuring collectible advertising
glasses, mugs & steins: beer, soda,
cartoon, Disney, root beer, Budweiser,
whiskey shot glasses, whiskey
pitchers, etc.*

Clubs/Associations

Deborah & Paul Inglis
Pub Jug/Whiskey Pitcher Collectors
Newsletter: Pub Jug Trader, The
P.O. Box 165
South Hadley, MA 01075-0165
phone: 413-533-0419
fax: 413-533-0419
e-mail:
bootleggers.nostalgia@worldnet.att.net
*Bi-monthly publication dedicated to
buying, selling and trading of whiskey
pitchers/pub jugs and related items.*

Tom Duhn
Whisky Pitcher Collectors Association
of America
19341 West Tahoe Dr.
Mundelein, IL 60060-4061
phone: 847-566-9512
fax: 847-566-8303
e-mail: thdpubjug1@aol.com
*An international collector's club;
annual convention/show; members
buy, sell and trade pub jugs, liquor
advertising, water jugs, whisky
pitchers.*

Collectors

A.R. Blakeman
P.O. Box 310
Richmond
Surrey TW9 1FS, U.K.
*Wants pottery whiskey pitchers,
especially with colored tops or
colored transfer decorations; will
trade.*

Ed Miller
5636 Garden Lakes Palm
Bradenton, FL 34203-7213
phone: 941-758-5207
*Wants pub jugs, advertising, ceramic
water pitchers for personnel
collection.*

Tom Duhn
19341 West Tahoe Dr.
Mundelein, IL 60060-4061
phone: 847-566-9512
fax: 847-566-8303
e-mail: thdpubjug1@aol.com
Buys, sells and trades pub jugs, liquor

*advertising, water jugs, whisky
pitchers.*

Dealers

Deborah & Paul Inglis
Bootleggers Nostalgia
P.O. Box 165
South Hadley, MA 01075-0165
phone: 413-533-0419
fax: 413-533-0419
e-mail:
bootleggers.nostalgia@worldnet.att.net
*Buys pitchers, ashtrays, back bar
statues, change receivers, and drip
plates advertising Scotch whisky or
other types of liquor.*

SALT & PEPPER SHAKERS

Collectors

Trish Claar
2621 Manor Court
Owings, MD 20736-9145
phone: 301-855-6531
*Interested in advertising and Holiday
related salt and pepper shaker sets.*

Judy Posner
4195 South Tamiami Trail, Ste. 183
Venice, FL 34293-5112
phone: 941-497-7149
fax: 941-493-8085
e-mail: Judyandjef@aol.com
Internet: http://www.tias.com/stores/jpc
*Wants figural salt & pepper shakers:
Black Americana, Disneyana, Ceramic
Art Studio, Regal China, advertising
figurals, etc.*

Coleen Detzel
28 Lacresta Dr.
Florence, KY 41042-9663
phone: 606-282-0456
*Wants to buy novel, unique salt and
pepper shakers.*

Dealers

Vera & Steve Skorupski
P.O. Box 572
Plainville, CT 06062
phone: 230-828-4097

Helene Guarnaccia
52 Coach Lane
Fairfield, CT 06430
phone: 203-374-6034
Send requests.

Carol Silagyi
C.S. Antiques & Jewelry
P.O. Box 151
Wyckoff, NJ 07430
phone: 201-934-6528
*Wants to buy collections of salt and
pepper shakers.*

Mark McMahon
Cookie Jars, Etc.
110 West 25th St., 8th Floor
New York, NY 1000107401
phone: 212-633-1923
fax: 212-924-8535
e-mail: peter@peterandmark.com
*Buy, sell, trade cookie jars, banks, salt
& peppers and PEZ.*

Joyce & Judy
Krazy Cat Collectibles
8604 Second Ave. #235
Silver Spring, MD 20910
phone: 301-309-2513
e-mail: KrazyCatCo@aol.com
*Wants to buy salt and pepper shakers
of all kinds: animals, characters,
couples, nodders; especially wants cat
and dog s&p's.*

Lois & Ralph Behm
Lois' Collectibles of Antique Market III
413 W. Main St.
Saint Charles, IL 60174-1815
phone: 630-377-5599 or 847-831-5997
*Buys and sells salt and pepper
shakers; will buy entire collections.*

Estelle Sharp
ESCO Enterprises, Inc.
441 E. River Oaks Dr.
Baton Rouge, LA 70815-4063
phone: 504-924-5089
fax: 504-924-5089
*Buys and sells nodder salt & pepper
shakers.*

Peggy Cole
134 E. Laveta
Orange, CA 92666-1908
phone: 714-997-7379
*Wants nodder and black Americana
figural salt & pepper shakers; mini's,
Felix the Cat, Garfield.*

Experts

Larry Carey
Salt & Pepper Man, The
P.O. Box 329
Mechanicsburg, PA 17055-0329
phone: 717-766-0868
*Buys novelty salt and pepper shaker
collections; consultant to "The
Official Price Guide to Pottery and
Porcelain"; co-author of three books
on s&p's, "1001, 1002, and 1003 Salt
& Pepper Shakers."*

Mildred & Ralph Lechner
World of Salt Shakers
P.O. Box 554
Mechanicsville, VA 23111-0554
phone: 804-737-3347
*Feature writers on antique glassware
for "AntiqueWeek"; authors of "The
World of Salt Shakers," Vols. 1 & 2 ;
Victorian art and pattern glass
reproduction identification experts;
collectors of art and pattern glass salt
& pepper shakers.*

Art Glass

Clubs/Associations

Mr. & Mrs. William Avery
Antique & Art Glass Salt Shaker
Collector's Society
Newsletter: Pioneer, The
2832 Rapidan Trail
Maitland, FL 32751-5013
phone: 407-629-1168
e-mail: bill@totcon.com
*Promotes and encourages the
collection and study of salt shakers of
the Antique Victorian and Art Glass
type; quarterly newsletter.*

Collectors

Mr. & Mrs. Charles Lockwood
P.O. Box 228
Almond, NY 14804
phone: 607-276-5565
*Wants Victorian art and pattern glass
shakers and shakers containing
agitators to break up the salt; either
singles or pairs.*

Dealers

Janice C. Eldridge
64 Burt Rd.
Springfield, MA 01118
phone: 413-783-4629
*Wants to buy art glass, colored
Victorian glass salt and pepper
shakers.*

Novelty

Clubs/Associations

Lula Fuller
Novelty Salt & Pepper Shakers Club
Newsletter: Novelty Salt & Pepper
Shakers Club Newsletter
P.O. Box 3617
Lantana, FL 33465-3617
phone: 561-588-5368
fax: 561-588-5368
*Focuses on novelty salt and pepper
shakers; also anything picturing
shakers; offers "singles matching
service" for members; newsletter
published quarterly.*

Collectors

Irene Thornburg
581 Joy Rd.
Battle Creek, MI 49017-8450
phone: 616-963-7954 or 616-964-9024
*Wants to buy unusual novelty shakers
to add to collection.*

Parkcraft

Experts

Larry Carey
Salt & Pepper Man, The
P.O. Box 329
Mechanicsburg, PA 17055-0329
phone: 717-766-0868
*Buys novelty salt and pepper shaker
collections; consultant to "The
Official Price Guide to Pottery and
Porcelain"; co-author of three books*

*on s&p's, "1001, 1002, and 1003 Salt
& Pepper Shakers."*

Van Tellingen (Bendel)

Dealers

Sally Oge
2344 104th Ave.
Otsego, MI 49078
phone: 616-694-6209

SALTS

Open

Clubs/Associations

Mimi Waible
New England Society of Open Salts
Collectors
Newsletter: Salt Talk
P.O. Box 177
Sudbury, MA 01776-0177
phone: 508-443-3613
fax: 617-893-4760
*Meets semi-annually usually in N.
Reading, MA.*

Donna Wolfe
Open Salt Collectors of the Atlantic
Region
Newsletter: OSCAR Newsletter
820 Sunlight Dr.
York, PA 17402
phone: 717-755-6890
*Meets quarterly at or near members'
homes.*

Dealers

Betty Bird
Memory Lane Antiques
107 Ida St.
Mount Shasta, CA 96067-2629
phone: 916-926-4331 or 916-926-2231
*Buying fancy open salts and/or salt
spoons; prefer art glass, colored glass
and silver; any number; also
condiment sets.*

Experts

Daniel Snyder
43 Main St.
Leroy, NY 14482
phone: 716-768-6470
Specializes in master open salts.

Ed & Kay Berg
Delaware Salt Box
401 Nottingham Rd.
Newark, DE 19711-7404
phone: 302-731-5749
e-mail: edandkay@compuserve.com
*Buys, sells, and specializes in open
salts; issues lists of open salts for sale
about 4 times per year.*

Periodicals

Ed Berg
Newsletter: Salty Comments
401 Nottingham Rd.
Newark, DE 19711-7404
phone: 302-731-5749
e-mail: edandkay@compuserve.com
*The newsletter covers research on
open salt dishes.*

SALVATION ARMY ITEMS

Collectors

Nathan Johnson
P.O. Box 23526
Belleville, IL 62223-0526
phone: 618-277-9330
*Wants to buy Salvation Army/William
Booth family related items including
posters, postcards, cabinet cards,
medals, badges, magazine covers,
jewelry, FDC's, sheet music, etc.*

Museums/Libraries

George Scott Railton Salvation Army
Heritage Center
2130 Bayview Ave.
Toronto
Ontario M4N 3K6 Canada
phone: 416-481-4441

SAMPLERS

(see also FOLK ART; REPAIR/
RESTORATION/CONSERVATION,
Textiles; TEXTILES)

Collectors

Donna Litwin
P.O. Box 5865
Trenton, NJ 08638-0865
phone: 609-275-1427 or 609-275-0996
fax: 609-275-1427
e-mail: jsl58@ix.netcom.com
*Buys, sells, appraises American
samplers; please send photo and price
of items for sale; Accredited Member
of the International Society of
Appraisers.*

Denise Hamilton
899 Latta Brook Rd.
Elmira, NY 14901
phone: 607-732-2550
*Buying old samplers and other
needlework.*

Dealers

Carl McCann
Troy & Black, Inc.
P.O. Box 228
Red Creek, NY 13143-0228
phone: 315-754-8115
*Buys and sells high quality flow blue,
Staffordshire figurines, American
painted furniture, stoneware, redware,
coverlets, samplers, and other
American textiles, folk art, etc.*

Experts

Suzy McLennan Anderson
Heritage Antiques, Inc.
65 East Main St.
Holmdel, NJ 07733-2310
phone: 908-946-8801
fax: 908-946-1036
*Authenticates, buys, sells, appraises,
lectures; author of "The Collectors
Guide to Quilts."*

Museums/Libraries

Cooper-Hewitt Museum National
Museum of Design, Smithsonian
Institution
2 East 91st St.
New York, NY 10128
phone: 212-860-6868

Repro. Sources

Liz Chronister
Country Baskets & Collectables
RD 2
Dillsburg, PA 17019

Alyce Schroth
Sampler Recreations
3598 Buttonwood Dr.
Doylestown, PA 18901

SAMURAI ITEMS

(see ARMS & ARMOR, Japanese
[Swords]; ORIENTALIA, Japanese
Items)

SAND

Clubs/Associations

Karolyn B. Diefenbach, Dir
International Sand Collectors Society
Newsletter: Sand Paper, The
43 Highview Ave.
Old Greenwich, CT 06870-1703
phone: 203-637-2801 or 203-637-0093
*Serious and whimsical collections for
purposes of keepsake, analysis, bon
hommarie; collector of sand, ore, or
minerals; divisions include Beach
Sands, Microscopy, Educators.*

SANDPAPER

Museums/Libraries

Sandpaper Museum
201 Waterfront Dr.
P.O. Box 313
Two Harbors, MN 55616
phone: 218-834-4898
*Part of the Lake County Historical
Society; displays of how sandpaper is
made.*

SANTA CLAUS

(see CHRISTMAS COLLECTIBLES;
COLLECTIBLES [MODERN],
Christmas)

SCALES

(see also COIN-OPERATED ,
MACHINES; INSTRUMENTS &
DEVICES, Scientific)

Clubs/Associations

Bob Stein, Pres.
International Society of Antique Scale
Collectors
Magazine: Equilibrium
176 W. Adams St., Ste. 1706
Chicago, IL 60603-3604
phone: 312-263-7500
fax: 312-263-7748
Internet: http://
www.collectoronline.com/clubs/
ISASC/
*Club focuses on antique scales;
several hundred members worldwide;
the "Equilibrium" magazine is
published quarterly and contains
articles on scales & scale manufacturers.*

Collectors

Henri Slaets
Elf Novemberstraat 20
Mechelen B2800 Belgium
phone: (0)-54 -3635
e-mail: h.slaets@iname.com
*Collecting and trading antique and
ethnic scales and weights: old 17th,
18th, 19th century coin-weighted
boxes, apothecary scales, Chinese,
Japanese, African asahti, Burmese;
opium, drug, pearl scales;
Precolumbian bone and wood scales.*

Gerald Neufeld
50 Saratoga Dr.
Cranbury, NJ 08512-9747
phone: 212-730-0445 or 609-936-8688
*Wants to buy unusual scales; send
description and picture.*

John M. Shannon
7319 West Cedar Circle
Lakewood, CO 80226-2019
phone: 303-232-1534
e-mail: rovers@aol.com
*Wants to buy assay balances (wood
and glass encased with small pans) -
both laboratory and portable; also
wants brass scientific instruments.*

Dealers

Wynona Crossgrove
Nobody's Bizness But Our Own
P.O. Box 97
Hampton, CT 06247-0097
phone: 860-455-9447
fax: 860-455-9447
*Buys and sells antique scales, and
scientific and medical items.*

John J. Ford, Jr.
P.O. Box 10317
Phoenix, AZ 85064
phone: 602-957-6443
fax: 602-957-1861
*Collects and deals in counterfeit coin
scales and detectors.*

Repro. Sources

Sturbridge Yankee Workshop
90 Blueberry Rd.
Portland, ME 04102-1989
phone: 800-343-1144
fax: 207-774-2561

Toy

Collectors

Donald Gorlick
P.O. Box 24541
Seattle, WA 98124-0541
phone: 206-824-0508
*Wants old toy scales; small tin scales
like the old penny toys; any small toy
scale but not the pencil sharpener type
scales.*

SCHMOO MEMORABILIA

Collectors

Lee Garmon
1529 Whittier St.
Springfield, IL 62704
phone: 217-789-9574
*Al Capp designed the Schmoo (a
gourd-shaped character) in 1948;
wants Schmoo books, banks, glass
tumblers, figurines, etc.*

SCHOOL RELATED MEMORA-
BILIA

Collectors

Lee Dennis
447 Park Ave., Apt. 12
Keene, NH 03431-6506
phone: 603-358-0060
*Wants early schoolhouse memorabilia
from 1840-1880: unusual slates,
pencil boxes, lunch boxes, sheet music
depicting schoolhouses, book holders,
etc,*

Tedd Levy
P.O. Box 2217
Norwalk, CT 06850-2217
e-mail: teddlevy@aol.com
*Wants pre-1920 items related to
public schools, teaching, students,
playgrounds, school buses, etc.
including postcards, photos, journals,
documents, correspondence,
certificates and some 19th C books
(none after 1860); prompt replies.*

Diplomas

Collectors

Bob Hut
P.O. Box 1495
New York, NY 10163
phone: 800-321-7687
Wants schoolhouse diplomas.

SCIENCE FICTION

(see also ANIMATION ART;
CARTOON ART; CHARACTER
COLLECTIBLES; COMIC BOOKS;
FAN CLUBS; HORROR; MOVIE
MEMORABILIA; POPULAR
CULTURE; SPACE COL-
LECTIBLES; SUPER HEROES;
TELEVISION SHOWS & MEMORA-
BILIA; TOYS, Science Fiction;
UFO'S & UNEXPLAINED
PHENOMENA

Clubs/Associations

Dale L. Ames
Galaxy Patrol
Newsletter: Galaxy Patrol Newsletter
22 Colton St.
Worcester, MA 01610
phone: 508-755-3830
*Focuses on memorabilia relating to
radio and TV show space heroes.*

Joel Welch, Jr.
Gaylactic Network
P.O. Box 127
Brookline, MA 02146-0001
phone: 301-513-5230
*Governing organization for an
association of science fiction, fantasy
and horror groups for gay people and
their friends; several regional
chapters.*

Commander Data Fan Club
Newsletter: Commander Data Fan Club
Newsletter
2221 Wellington Pl.
Millville, NJ 08332
phone: 609-327-6991
Quarterly newsletter.

Gordy Dutt
International Figure Kit Club
Magazine: KitBuilders Magazine
P.O. Box 201
Sharon Center, OH 44274-0201
phone: 330-239-1657
fax: 330-239-2991
e-mail: Gordys_kitbuilders@juno.com
Internet: http://www.gremlins.com/
kitbuilders
*Published four times a year, this
magazine deals mostly with plastic,
vinyl, and resin figure or Sci/Fi type
model kits from the 1950s to present.*

William Center
National Fantasy Fan Federation
Newsletter: National Fantasy Fan
1920 Division St.
Murphysboro, IL 62966
e-mail: captnbilly@cup.portal.com
*National science fiction and fantasy
club.*

San Diego's Science Fiction Society
Newsletter: Interphase
P.O. Box 15373
San Diego, CA 92117-0303
phone: 619-286-0401
e-mail: actaeon@inetworl.net
Internet: http://users.aol.com/sdstar1/
Local club interested in science

fiction, fantasy, movies, gaming, costuming and conventions.

Collectors

Dale L. Ames
22 Colton St.
Worcester, MA 01610
phone: 508-755-3830
Interested in collectibles associated with science fiction TV & radio shows & recordings of the programs themselves; also sic-fi comics.

Russell K. Watkins
520 Chatham Dr.
Lakeland, FL 33803-3049
Wants books, pulps, Burroughs, Weird Tales, The Shadow, Astounding Burroughs and Fantasy Press Books.

Edy J. Chandler
P.O. Box 20664
Houston, TX 77225
phone: 713-781-6146
Wants books, fanzines, robots, character merchandise, Star Wars items, etc.

Dealers

Jon Warren
American Collectibles Exchange
P.O. Box 2512
Chattanooga, TN 37409
phone: 423-265-5515 or 800-880-4289
fax: 423-265-5506
e-mail: jonrwarren@aol.com
Specializes in Science Fiction and Fantasy items.

Steve Benz
Star Trader
9809 Hayes
Overland Park, KS 66212
phone: 913-648-5461
Buys, sells and trades science fiction collectibles from Star Trek to present.

Experts

Allen Shevy
P.O. Box 9421
Tampa, FL 33674-9421
phone: 813-933-7424
e-mail: wofshevy@gate.net
Internet: http://www.zipmail.com/wofmag
Collects, appraises and specializes in science fiction collectibles: movies, comic books, TV, music, toys, games, etc.

Museums/Libraries

MIT Science Fiction Society Library
Newsletter: Twilight Zine
MIT Student Center, Rm. W20-473
Cambridge, MA 02139
phone: 617-258-5126
e-mail: mitsfs@mit.edu
Largest publicly accessible collection of science fiction and fantasy in the world; extensive magazine collection including foreign; fanzines.

Los Angeles Science Fantasy Society Library
11513 Burbank Blvd.
North Hollywood, CA 91601-2309
phone: 818-760-9234
A club collection primarily for members' use, with 12,500 volumes and over 125 magazine titles; public use by appointment.

University of California, Dr. J. Eaton Fantasy & Science Fiction Collection
Special Collections Department
P.O. Box 5900
Riverside, CA 92517
phone: 714-787-3233 or 714-784-7324
fax: 714-787-3285
A comprehensive research resource for science fiction, fantasy and horror; tens of thousands of volumes of hardbacks and paperbacks, related boy's books, pulp magazines, comic books, video and audio library, manuscripts, etc.

Periodicals

Andrew I. Porter, Editor
Magazine: Science Fiction Chronicle
P.O. Box 022730
Brooklyn, NY 11202-2730
phone: 718-643-9011
fax: 718-522-3308
e-mail: SF_Chronicle@compuserve.com
Monthly Science Fiction, fantasy and horror newsmagazine; news stories, interviews, columns, book buyers' forthcoming guide, market reports (updated every 4 months), 500+ book and small press reviews, author sales, etc.

Roxanne Toser
Roxanne Toser Non-Sport Enterprises, Inc.
Magazine: Non-Sport Update
4019 Green St.
P.O. Box 5858
Harrisburg, PA 17110-0858
phone: 717-238-1936
fax: 717-238-3220
e-mail: nsumag@aol.com
The foremost quarterly publication for non-sport card collectors; original artwork covers, glossy paper, lots of articles by the experts, great variety of ads, separate 32-page "pop-out" price guide and free cards.

Harry Hopkins, Pub.
FANDATA Publications
Directory: FANDOM Directory
7761 Asterella Ct.
Springfield, VA 22152-3133
phone: 703-913-5575 or 888-FAN-DATA
fax: 703-913-5575
e-mail: fandata@aol.com
Internet: http://members.aol.com/fandata
Fandom Directory (R) lists over 20,000 fans, collectors, dealers, stores, clubs, and conventions worldwide: science fiction, TV shows, Star Trek, etc.; now in its 17th annual edition; your listing published free of charge upon request.

Allen Shevy
World of Fandom
Magazine: World of Fandom Magazine
P.O. Box 9421
Tampa, FL 33674-9421
phone: 813-933-7424
e-mail: wofshevy@gate.net
Internet: http://www.zipmail.com/wofmag
Covers movies, comic books, TV, music, toys, games; many exclusive interviews and stories; 108 pages, 4-color glossy covers.

Magazine: Strange New Worlds
P.O. Box 223
Tallevast, FL 34270
The science fiction collectors magazine: informative articles, columns, product alerts, and interviews.

John Koenig
Antique Trader Publications, Inc.
Newspaper: Toy Trader
922 Churchill St., Ste. #1
Waupaca, WI 54981
phone: 715-258-7525 or 800-768-9225
fax: 715-258-8707
e-mail: jkoenig@add-inc.com
Internet: http://www.csmonline.com
Monthly newspaper with information on how to buy, sell and trade all types of toys; market trends, the latest prices, "how-to" columns, listings of toy clubs and upcoming toy shows and auctions; also full of buy and sell ads.

Bjo Trimble
Magazine: Space-Time Continuum
P.O. Box 6858
Kingwood, TX 77325-6858
The major news magazine for Sci-Fi media fans; published bi-monthly; latest news on upcoming Sci-Fi and fantasy films, animation, collecting, Disney, fan clubs, Lucasfilm, space news, Spielberg; TV shows, movies, media, celebrities.

Suppliers

Thomas Walton
International Association for Direct Distribution
2319 California St.
Berkeley, CA 94703-1609
phone: 510-644-2038
International trade association of specialty distributors offering comic books, art books, graphic novels and other specialty products.

Books

Collectors

David Kveragas
1943 Timberlane
Clarks Summit, PA 18411-9539
phone: 717-587-3429
Wants to buy first edition hardcover Science Fiction books. Please state title, author, year, condition. No Book Club editions, please. Signed items of special interest; offers made.

Costuming

Clubs/Associations

Threads
Newsletter: Threads
P.O. Box 257
Brunswick W, 3055 VI Australia
International club interested in science fiction and fantasy costuming, design and hand-crafts.

International Costumer's Guild
Newsletter: Costumer's Quarterly
P.O. Box 94538
Pasadena, CA 91109
International club interested in science fiction, fantasy, comic and historical costuming.

Jana Keeler
Greater Bay Area Costumer's Guild, The
Newsletter: Costumer's Scribe, The
223 Addison St.
San Francisco, CA 94131
phone: 415-469-7602
Local chapter of the International Costumer's Guild; lots of information and networking for costume lovers in the area; includes a list of sewing circles, and costume wearing events.

Monsters

Collectors

Joe Warchol
5345 N. Canfield
Harwood Heights, IL 60656
phone: 708-843-2442 or 312-744-1628

Monsters (Japanese)

Periodicals

Daikaiju Enterprises
Newsletter: G-FAN
P.O. Box 3468
Steinbach
Manitoba ROA 2AO Canada
phone: 204-326-7754
fax: 204-326-7754
Devoted to Japanese live action Sci-Fi, with particular emphasis on Godzilla.

Journal: Kaiju Review
301 East 64th St., Ste. 5F
New York, NY 10021
The journal of Japanese monster culture.

Newsletter: Japanese Giants
5727 North Oketo
Chicago, IL 60631
Devoted exclusively to Japanese monsters.

Journal: Monster Attack Team
P.O. Box 821631
Fort Worth, TX 76182-1631
The Japanese monster superhero and fantasy fanzine.

Newsletter: Asian Trash Cinema
P.O. Box 5367
Kingwood, TX 77325
Regularly runs articles about Japanese monsters.

Newsletter: Sentai
7272 Wurzbach, Ste. 204
San Antonio, TX 78240
The journal of Asian science fiction and fantasy; regularly runs articles about Japanese monsters.

Newsletter: Cult Movies
6201 Sunset Blvd., Ste. 152
Los Angeles, CA 90028
Regularly runs articles about Japanese monsters.

Damon Foster, Ed.
Magazine: Oriental Cinema
P.O. Box 576
Fremont, CA 94537-0576
Regularly runs articles about Japanese monsters, Kung Fu films, superheroes, Japan's cartoons, Hong Kong action movies, Korean Sci-Fi, Filipino horror, Ningas, Samurai, and Chinese vampires.

Outer Space

Collectors

Donald Sheldon
P.O. Box 3313
Trenton, NJ 08619-0313
phone: 609-588-5403
Wants 1950s toys, games, puzzles, records, greeting cards, banks, puzzles, etc. that have outer space themes.

SCIENTIFIC INSTRUMENTS

(see INSTRUMENTS & DEVICES)

SCIENTIFIC TOYS

(see TOYS, Construction Sets)

SCOOTERS

(see RIDING TOYS)

SCOTTISH COLLECTIBLES

(see also ART, Scottish)

Dealers

Sir Alasdair T. Munro, BT.
Alba Antiques
P.O. Box 940
Waitsfield, VT 05673-0940
phone: 802-496-2213
Buys and sells antiques of Scottish origin or association: Mauchline ware, Tartanware, Scottish dress, dirks, powder horns, pistols, swords, Victorian Scottish silver jewelry, oil paintings, watercolors, prints, etc.

Mauchline Ware

Clubs/Associations

Barry Kottles
Mauchline Ware Collectors' Club
Journal: Journal of the Mauchline Ware Collectors Club
Unit 37, Romsey Industrial Estate
Greatbridge Rd., Romsey
Hampshire SO51 0HR, U.K.
phone: +44 (0) 1903 775120
fax: +44 (0) 1794 830284
For collectors of Mauchline Ware, a wooden ware, souvenirs and furniture from Scotland decorated with transfer prints and photographs; also tartan and fern ware.

Janet Hawkins
Mauchline Ware Collectors' Club
Journal: Journal of the Mauchline Ware Collectors Club
14 Blake Terrace, SE
Cedar Rapids, IA 52403-2830
phone: 319-362-2643
For collectors of Mauchline Ware, a wooden ware, souvenirs and furniture from Scotland decorated with transfer prints and photographs; will provide membership application for mailing to the parent club in England.

Collectors

Janet Hawkins
14 Blake Terrace, SE
Cedar Rapids, IA 52403-2830
phone: 319-362-2643

Dealers

Sir Alasdair T. Munro, BT.
Alba Antiques
P.O. Box 940
Waitsfield, VT 05673-0940
phone: 802-496-2213
Buys and sells antiques of Scottish origin or association: Mauchline ware, Tartanware, Scottish dress, dirks, powder horns, pistols, swords, Victorian Scottish silver jewelry, oil paintings, watercolors, prints, etc.

SCOUTING MEMORABILIA

(see BOY SCOUT MEMORABILIA; CAMPING EQUIPMENT; GIRL SCOUT MEMORABILIA)

SCRAP

(see GOLD, Scrap; PLATINUM, Scrap; SILVER, Scrap; GEMS & JEWELRY)

SCRAPBOOKS

(see ALBUMS; PAPER COLLECTIBLES)

SCRIMSHAW

(see also ENDANGERED SPECIES; FOLK ART; IVORY; NAUTICAL ANTIQUES; WHALING)

Dealers

Albert L. Doucette
Whale's Tale
42 North Water St.
New Bedford, MA 02740
phone: 508-997-4233
fax: 508-997-0752
Specializes in contemporary ivory carvings and scrimshaw.

Brian J. Kiracofe
Newport Scrimshander, The
14 Bowen's Wharf
Newport, RI 02840
phone: 401-849-5680 or 800-653-5234
fax: 401-849-9306
e-mail: newportscrimshaw@juno.com
Carries an extensive collection of scrimshaw items, whaler folk art c. 1870.

Museums/Libraries

Curator
Kendall Whaling Museum, The
Newsletter: KWM Newsletter
27 Everett St.
P.O. Box 297
Sharon, MA 02067-0297
phone: 617-784-5642
Internet: http://www.kwm.org
International collection of whaling artworks & artifacts specializing in paintings 1600-present, scrimshaw, tools, gear, prints, ship models, etc.; world's largest collection of scrimshaw; numerous publications; guide to fakes.

New Bedford Whaling Museum
18 Johnny Cake Hill
New Bedford, MA 02740-6317
phone: 617-997-0046
fax: 617-997-0018
A whaling and local historical museum.

Cold Spring Harbor Whaling Museum
P.O. Box 25
Cold Spring Harbor, NY 11724
phone: 516-367-3418

Lynn Cullivan
San Francisco Maritime National Historical Park
Bldg. E, Fort Mason Center
San Francisco, CA 94123
phone: 415-556-3002
fax: 415-556-1624

SCRIP

(see also LOGGING RELATED ITEMS; MINING RELATED ITEMS; STOCKS & BONDS; TOKENS)

Clubs/Associations

Bob & Sandi Underwood
National Scrip Collectors Association
Newsletter: Scrip Talk
402 Lyons Ave.
Morehead, KY 40351
e-mail: bunderwood@skn.net
Internet: http://www.miningusa.com/mh-t/nsca/nsca.htm
Promotes collecting of coal, lumber &

all mining scrip (metal & paper scrip used as a medium of wages in industries such as coal mining), merchant tokens, & mining artifacts including mining lamps.

Collectors

Tip Tippy
22 Cottonwood Ln.
Carterville, IL 62916
Interested in buying tokens, paper scrip, and stocks & bonds associated with the coal & lumber industries.

Periodicals

Walter Caldwell
Newsletter: Token Talk
P.O. Box 29
Fayetteville, WV 25840
phone: 304-574-0105
Periodical about coal, lumber & all mining scrip (metal & paper scrip used as a medium of wages in industries such as coal mining), merchant tokens, & mining artifacts including mining lamps.

Julie A. Ulrich, PR
Krause Publications
Newspaper: Bank Note Reporter
700 E. State St.
Iola, WI 54990-0001
phone: 715-445-2214
fax: 715-445-4087
e-mail: info@krause.com
Internet: http://www.krause.com
Monthly news source and marketplace for collectors of U.S. and world paper money, notes, checks and related fiscal paper.

Depression

Experts

Neil Shafer
P.O. Box 17138
Milwaukee, WI 53217
phone: 414-352-5962
e-mail: nelsshaf@aol.com
Co-author of "Standard Catalog of Depression Scrip of the United States"; the 1930s including Canada and Mexico.

SCULPTURES

(see also ART; BRONZES; FOLK ART; MEDALLIC SCULPTURE; MINIATURES, Sculptures; ROGERS GROUPS; WOOD CARVINGS)

Appraisers

Judith S. Jordan
Perrinart Associates
140 Scarborough Rd.
Briarcliff Manor, NY 10510-2006
phone: 914-762-1438 or 802-869-2784

Charles B. Goldstein, ISA CAPP
Charles Barry International
8 Hardwicke Place
Rockville, MD 20850-3010
phone: 301-340-6775
fax: 301-340-1726
*Buys, sells, and appraises 20th
century, modern and contemporary
sculpture; Certified Member,
International Society of Appraisers;
expert witness and trial consultant.*

William Lavendusky, M.S., ISA
William Lavendusky, Fine Art
3345 So. Harvard, Bldg. 100
Tulsa, OK 74135
phone: 918-747-5336
fax: 918-742-3425
*Dealer and appraiser of paintings and
sculpture; specialist in 19th century
French animal bronzes.*

Dealers

Steve Newman
112 Revonah Ave.
Stamford, CT 06905
phone: 203-327-9216
*Buys and sells bronze, marble and
wood sculpture: 19th century
American Neoclassic figures, busts
and reliefs; 19th and 20th century
animal sculptures; garden fountains
and figures.*

Robin & June Greenwald
June Greenwald Antiques, Inc.
3096 Mayfield Rd.
Cleveland, OH 44118
phone: 216-932-5535
*Buys and sells 19th and early 20th
century bronze and marble sculptures.*

Museums/Libraries

Barbara Buff
Museum of the City of New York
1220 5th Ave.
New York, NY 10029-5221
phone: 212-534-1672
fax: 212-534-5974
*Special paintings and sculpture
collections; access by appointment;
research fee charged.*

Repair Services

Dimitri Nedelcu
Universal Fine Art Restoration
267 Derby Ave.
Orange, CT 06477-1319
phone: 203-795-8849
*Museum quality restorations of
marble/stone carvings: statuary,
capitals and columns, ornamentation,
compete fireplaces, reliefs, furniture,
animals, busts; also repairs wood
carvings, antiques, paintings.*

Erte

Dealers

Gwendolyn R. Reasoner
Re Vann Galleries
1501 Boardwalk at NY Ave.
Atlantic City, NJ 08401-7012
phone: 609-345-7474 or 800-821-4278
fax: 318-762-3534
*Largest Boehm dealer in the U.S.;
specializes in the Boehm secondary
market; also Cybis, Royal Worcester,
Erte; also appraises.*

Charles Huller
Benedetti Gallery
52 Prince St.
New York, NY 10012
phone: 212-226-2238
fax: 212-431-8106
*Specializing in sculpture by Erte with
over 60 sculptures on display; also
sculptures by Felix deWeldon (creator
of Iwo Jima War Memorial and over
2000 other monuments), Robazza,
Falai, Brescianine, Li Causi; art by
Anthony Quinn.*

Outdoor

Clubs/Associations

Save Outdoor Sculpture Proj., Nat. Instit.
for the Conserv. of Cultural Property
3299 K St. NW, Ste. 602
Washington, DC 20007
phone: 800-422-4612 or 202-625-1495
fax: 202-625-1485
Internet: nttp://www.nic.org/
*Non-profit organization that works to
preserve and increase awareness
about outdoor sculpture.*

SEALS

(see also BOY SCOUT MEMORA-
BILIA, Seals; STAMP COLLECT-
ING)

Christmas & Charity

Clubs/Associations

Richard Roberts, Sec.
Christmas Seal & Charity Stamp
Society, The
Newsletter: Seal News
P.O. Box 39696
Edina, MN 55439-0696
phone: 612-721-1981
*Focuses on stamp and metered seals
such as tuberculosis, veterans,
fraternal and civic, Jewish, ethnic,
pets, wildlife, medical, Easter, etc.
seals.*

Sealing Wax

Collectors

Irwin & Eileen Prince
142 Fairway Dr.
Indianapolis, IN 46260-4218
phone: 317-255-1913 or 317-925-9200
fax: 317-923-5759
*Wants wood, sterling, bronze, agate,
glass, crystal, ivory, bone, mother-of-
pearl, etc. desk-type (non-fob type)*

*sealing wax seals; send photos and
price or call for an evaluation.*

SEASHELLS

(see also NAUTICAL ANTIQUES)

Clubs/Associations

Lynn Scheu, Editor
Conchologists of America
Journal: American Conchologist
1222 Holsworth Ln.
Louisville, KY 40222-6616
phone: 502-423-0469 or 502-458-5719
fax: 502-426-4336
e-mail: amconch@ix.netcom.com
Internet: http://www.coa.acnatsci.org/
conchnet/
*Amateurs, professionals interested in
the study, collection, conservation of
seashells; grants to deserving
malacology students & qualified
workers; annual convention with
lectures, field trips, exhibits, dealers'
bourse, auction.*

Experts

Mique & C.E. Pinkerton
Mique's Molluscs
7078 Westmoremand Dr.
Warrenton, VA 20817-4451
phone: 540-347-3839
*Collector and dealer in specimen
seashells (also includes land and
freshwater mollusks); appraisals on
collections for estate settlements; sells
collections on consignment; member
Conchologists of America and NC
Shell Club.*

Museums/Libraries

Delaware Museum of Natural History
4840 Kennett Pike
P.O. Box 3937
Wilmington, DE 19807-0937
phone: 302-658-9111 or 302-658-5004
fax: 302-658-2610
e-mail: tpearce@wittnet.com
*Has seashell research collection;
accepts donations of shells having
locality data; loans material to bona
fide researchers at research institutes.*

Rollins College, Beal-Maltbie Shell
Museum
Campus Box 2753
Winter Park, FL 32789
phone: 305-646-2364

Banka's Shell Museum
P.O. Box 1537
Conrad, MT 59425
phone: 406-278-3749

SERVICE STATION COL-
LECTIBLES

(see GAS STATION COL-
LECTIBLES)

SEWING ITEMS & GO-WITHS

(see also BUTTONS; CLOTHING &
ACCESSORIES, Vintage; TEX-
TILES)

Appraisers

Beth Szescila, ISA CAPP
9546 Enstone Circle
Spring, TX 77379-6605
phone: 281-376-4338
fax: 281-251-0608
e-mail: 76751.2141@compuserve.com
*Collects and appraises sewing items;
looking for sets of sewing tools,
preferably in their original containers; also interested in 18th and 19th
century sewing boxes in good
condition, particularly those with
sewing tools.*

Collectors

Collector
Rte. 1 Box 262
Middlebourne, WV 26149-9748
phone: 304-386-4434
fax: 304-386-4868
*Unusual sewing tools, small early
sewing machines; fancy hair
ornaments.*

Wynneth Mullins
P.O. Box 381807
Duncanville, TX 75138-1807
phone: 972-780-8278
*Wants sewing thimbles and other
sewing related tools.*

Dealers

Lillian Colern
Nimble Thimble
2117 Buffalo Rd.
Rochester, NY 14624
phone: 716-594-1237
*Buys and sells small sewing items;
thimbles, toy sewing machines, trade
cards, etc.*

Priscilla Washed
Victorian Lady, The
102 South Main St.
P.O. Box 424
Waxhaw, NC 28173-0424
phone: 704-843-4467 or 800-786-1886
*A Victorian specialty store featuring
19th century ladies decorative &
fashion accessories; buys and sells
purses; also sewing and needlework
tools, vintage fashion, Victoriana, and
combs; mail order; catalog $5.*

Barbara Cooney
Cooney's Collectibles
729 Indian Beach Circle
Sarasota, FL 34234-5740
phone: 941-355-1843
*Specializes in figural tape measures,
all types of needlework tools,
especially the unusual, chatelaines
and toy sewing machines; buy, sell
and do mail order.*

Beth Pulsipher
Prairie Home Antiques
P.O. Box 373
Schoolcraft, MI 49087-0373
phone: 616-679-2062
Internet: http://
www.macatala.demon.co.uk/
*Buys, sells and specializes in unusual
and rare needlework tools, ,thimbles,*

needle cases, lace bobbins, pincush-
ions, silk winders, sewing clamps, tape
measures, etc.; sells by mail; available
for lectures and seminars.

Diane Richardson
Gold Hatpin, The
P.O. Box 993
Oak Park, IL 60303-0993
phone: 708-848-3247 or 708-445-0610
*Wants needle cases, sterling thimbles,
scissors, unusual darning eggs,
sewing birds, thread winders, figural
tape measures, tatting shuttles, tool
sets, the unusual.*

C. Marziotto
P.O. Box 50623
Henderson, NV 89016-0623
*Buys and sells fine quality needlework
tools and related accessories; also toy
sewing machines.*

Carol Payne
Carol's Antique Gallery
14455 Big Basin Way
Saratoga, CA 95070-6008
phone: 408-867-7055
*Wants to buy sewing items especially
silver, tortoise shell, ivory, mother-of-
pearl, carved bone or woods.*

Darners

Collectors

Wayne Muller
P.O. Box 903
Pacific Palisades, CA 90272-0903
Wants to buy darners.

Experts

Wayne Muller
Darn It!
P.O. Box 903
Pacific Palisades, CA 90272-0903
*Lecturer, author of "Darn It!: The
History and Romance of Darners: A
Price Guide;" comprehensive history
of darners and darning; 370 full color
photos, descriptions, background,
prices.*

Periodicals

Linda A. Swierczewski
Newsletter: Darn Newsletter, That
461 Brown Briar Circle
Horsham, PA 19044

Machines

Clubs/Associations

Maggie Snell
International Sewing Machine Collectors
  Society
Magazine: ISMACS News
48 Nightingale House
Thomas Moore St.
London E1 9UB, U.K.
phone: 171-488-0474
*An English-based collectors club; the
world's only society for collectors of
antique sewing machines; Miss Snell
is a collector and dealer of sewing*

machines and is organizer/secretary
of the ISMCS.

Marvin Tabic
International Sewing Machine Collectors
  Society
Magazine: ISMACS News
1000E Charleston Blvd.
Las Vegas, NV 89104
*U.S. contact for the English-based
collectors club; the world's only
society for collectors of antique
sewing machines.*

Collectors

Peter Frei
P.O. Box 500
Brimfield, MA 01010-0500
phone: 800-942-8968 or 413-245-4660
Wants pre-1875 sewing machines.

Jerry Propst
P.O. Box 45
Janesville, WI 53547-0045
phone: 608-752-2816
fax: 608-752-7691
*When writing, please include a LSASE
if requesting a reply.*

Frank Smith
804 West Abram
Arlington, TX 76013
phone: 817-275-0971

Dealers

Maggie Shell
48 Nightingale House
Thomas Moore St.
London E1 9UB, U.K.
phone: 171-488-0474
*Collects, buys and sells antique
sewing machines as part of a
mechanical-antique business.*

Experts

Carter Bays
143 Spring Lake Rd.
Columbia, SC 29206-2106
phone: 800-332-2297
*One of the nation's leading sewing
machine collectors; wants only pre-
1875 machines; no oak machines; no
Wheeler & Wilson; no Wilcox &
Gibbs.*

Museums/Libraries

Frank Smith
Frank Smith's Sewing Machine Museum
804 West Abram
Arlington, TX 76013
phone: 817-275-0971

Sewing Machine Museum
3400 Park Blvd.
Oakland, CA 94610-2834
phone: 510-261-0413 or 510-527-0104

Repair Services

Cathy & Stephen Racine
Simple Machine, The
18 Masonic Home Rd. - Rt. 31
P.O. Box 234
Charlton, MA 01507-0234
phone: 508-248-6632
*Buys, sells, repairs and restores old
treadle sewing machines and antique
hand crank sewing machines; also
carries parts, belts, needles, bobbins
and manuals.*

Machines (Miniature & Toy)

Clubs/Associations

Claire Toschi
Toy Stitchers
Newsletter: Toy Stitchers Newsletter
623 Santa Florita Ave.
Millbrae, CA 94030-1203
phone: 415-589-6754
*Acts as a clearinghouse for the
exchange of factual details, tips,
advice and information on toy sewing
machines; collectors buy, sell, trade
TSM's through ads.*

Collectors

Lanelle Hodnett
2965 Avenue Z
Brooklyn, NY 11235-1658
phone: 718-891-3489
*Collects all types of miniature and toy
sewing machines, as well as any
sewing machine motifs (especially
Singer); also wants related items.*

Dana & Darlene DeMore
4645 Laurel Ridge Dr.
Harrisburg, PA 17110-3446
phone: 717-545-7320
*Wants to buy miniature and toy
sewing machines.*

Jay Bolante
3058 North Honore St.
Chicago, IL 60657-2050
phone: 312-327-5091
*Collects and wants to buy antique toy
and adult sewing machines.*

Dealers

Carole Meeker
Box 169 Kelly St.
Rhinecliff, NY 12574
phone: 914-876-7818
*Wants to buy rare and unusual small
patented mechanical antiques, early
American technology and occupational-related photography,
advertising and catalogs.*

Jude Allen
Vintage Collection
356 Main St.
Half Moon Bay, CA 94019
phone: 415-712-0366
fax: 415-654-0842
*Buys and sells linen and lace; also old
yardage, buttons, quilts, sewing
implements, sewing machines and
miniature sewing machines.*

Experts

Darryl & Roxana Matter
P.O. Box 65
Portis, KS 67474
phone: 913-346-5647
*Authors of "Collector's Guide to Toy
Sewing Machines" (Green Gate
Books.)*

Thimbles

Clubs/Associations

Barbara Acchino, Mem.
Thimble Collectors International
Newsletter: TCI Bulletin
8289 Northgate Dr.
Rome, NY 13440-1941
phone: 315-336-4072
*TCI introduces members to various
aspects of thimble collecting;
promotes research & scholarship;
quarterly newsletter and booklets on
thimbles and related needlework;
regional chapters; biennial
convention; send LSASE for
information.*

Wynneth Mullins
Thimble Guild, The
Newsletter: Thimble Guild
P.O. Box 381807
Duncanville, TX 75138-1807
phone: 972-780-8278

Collectors

Mary Innes Wagner
564 Linden St.
Rochester, NY 14620
phone: 716-271-8816
fax: 716-244-2673
*Wants to buy all types of thimbles,
especially antique, needle holders.*

Shirley Newton
656 Bermuda Run
Bermuda Run, NC 27006-9507
phone: 919-998-0828

Dealers

Melinda Hum
Thimble Talk
11828 Ranchero Bernardo Rd., Ste.
  #123-10
San Diego, CA 92128
phone: 619-487-2016
Send $1.00 for catalog.

Experts

Estelle Zalkin
7524 West Treasure Dr.
Miami, FL 33141-4118
phone: 305-864-3012
*Author of "Zalkin's Handbook of
Thimbles and Sewing Implements"
(Chilton Book Co.)*

Periodicals

Lorraine M. Crosby
Newsletter: Thimbletter
93 Walnut Hill Rd.
Newton Highlands, MA 02161-1836
phone: 617-969-9358
e-mail: jncrosby@ix.netcom.com
An informal bi-monthly newsletter, letters from subscribers, Q & A, for sale or trade, ads, new sources, misc. information.

SEX

(see BATHING BEAUTIES, Nudies & Naughties; EROTICA; PIN-UP ART; PLAYBOY ITEMS; STRIPTEASE)

SHAKER ITEMS

(see also FURNITURE [ANTIQUE])

Auction Services

David D. Newell
David D. Newell - Shaker Literature
39 Steady Lane
Ashfield, MA 01330
phone: 413-628-3240
fax: 413-628-3833
Buys, sells, appraises, auctions printed and manuscript items by/about Shakers and other like sects; also wants related photographica and ephemera; consignments available; catalog and mailing list placement $5.

Willis Henry
Willis Henry Auctions, Inc.
22 Main St.
Marshfield, MA 02059
phone: 617-834-7774
fax: 617-826-3520
Specializes in the sale of American antiques of all kinds, particularly Shaker, American Indian and early American.

Clubs/Associations

Ned Pratt
Shaker Heritage Society
Journal: Watervliet Shaker Journal, The
Shaker Meeting House
Albany-Shaker Rd.
Albany, NY 12211
phone: 518-456-7890

Fran Kramer
Rochester Shaker Study Group
17 Golf Ave.
Pittsford, NY 14534-1401
phone: 716-381-3733

Jean Middleton
NY-Penn Shaker Interest Group
RR 5 Box 2778
Nichalson, PA 18445
phone: 717-942-6908

Christine D. Ammeian
California Shaker Study Group
5353 Bardith Circle
Virginia Beach, VA 23455-3870

Sheldon Baugh
South Union Area Shaker Study Group
P.O. Box 70
South Union, KY 42283
phone: 502-726-7616

Patrick Allen
Western Shaker Study Group
7712 Eagle Creek Dr.
Dayton, OH 45459

Joan & Ivor Carter
Michigan Shaker Study Group
934 S. Brys Dr.
Grosse Pointe, MI 48236
phone: 313-885-6145

Dell & Myrna Hasse
Chicago Area Shaker Interest Group
313 E. Hazel St.
West Chicago, IL 60185
phone: 708-231-6873

Michele Ambrose
Northern California Shaker Study Group
P.O. Box 22705
Carmel, CA 93922
phone: 408-625-6554

Collectors

Steve Miller
Six Park Place
New Britain, CT 06052
phone: 860-561-3342
fax: 860-223-6316
Wants Shaker bottles, booklets, paper, etc.

Dealers

David D. Newell
David D. Newell - Shaker Literature
39 Steady Lane
Ashfield, MA 01330
phone: 413-628-3240
fax: 413-628-3833
Buys, sells, appraises printed and manuscript items by/about Shakers and other like sects; also wants related photographica and ephemera; consignments available; catalog and mailing list placement $5.

Doug Hamel
Douglas H. Hamel Antiques
56 Staniels Rd.
Chichester, NH 03234
phone: 603-798-5912
fax: 603-798-5447
e-mail: dhamel7@chi.tds.net
Buys and sells good quality Shaker items; helping to build major private and public collections for 25 years.

Richard Vandall
American Decorative Arts
RFD #1, Box 239
Canaan, NH 03741-9746
phone: 603-523-4276
fax: 603-523-4888
e-mail: amr-dec-arts@endor.com
Buying and selling Shaker goods; prompt complete service, confidential to the seller; family business, second generation; shipping service available.

Dr. M. Stephen Miller
Six Park Place
New Britain, CT 06052
phone: 203-561-3342
Buys and appraises Shaker items.

Experts

David A. Schorsch
David A. Schorsch Inc.
30 East 76th St.
New York, NY 10021
phone: 212-439-6100
fax: 212-439-6170

Gary D. Gardner
200 College St.
Hodgenville, KY 42748-1404
phone: 502-358-3222
Collector, researcher of furniture, tools, textiles, and crafts produced by Shaker communities during the 19th century; also books written/printed by Shakers, especially S. Union, Pleasant Hill.

Museums/Libraries

Hancock Shaker Village
P.O. Box 927
Pittsfield, MA 01202-0927
phone: 413-443-0188
fax: 413-447-9357
A 200-year-old Shaker site encompassing 20 restored buildings housing the largest and finest collection of Shaker furnishings & artifacts in an original Shaker site.

Erin Budis
Shaker Museum & Library, The
88 Shaker Museum Rd.
Old Chatham, NY 12136
phone: 518-794-9100
fax: 518-794-8621
The premier Shaker collection housing 24 galleries of furniture masterpieces, oval boxes, baskets, ingenious tools and machinery reflecting the "order, harmony, and utility" of Shaker design.

Shaker Village of Pleasant Hill
3500 Lexington Rd.
Harrodsburg, KY 40330
phone: 606-734-5411

Cathie Winans, Dir.
Shaker Historical Museum, The
Journal: Journal, The
16740 S. Park Blvd.
Cleveland, OH 44120-1641
phone: 216-921-1201 or 216-295-2344
e-mail: shakhist@wviz.org
Internet: http://www.cwru.edu/orgs/shakhist/shaker.htm
Collection and display of artifacts and furniture designed and used by the North Union Shaker Settlement (now known as Shaker Heights); materials about local history including early developers of Shaker Heights.

Periodicals

K.C. & Alana Parkinson
Magazine: Shakers World
P.O. Box 1276
Manchester, CT 06045
phone: 860-643-9258
e-mail: shakersworld@msn.com
A quarterly magazine focusing on the Shakers and their work products; articles, ads, Shaker news, Shaker events, study groups, auction reviews, Shaker books for sale.

Baskets

Repro. Sources

John E. McGuire
Baskets & Bears
398 S. Main St.
Geneva, NY 14456-2614
phone: 315-787-1251
e-mail: basketman@lynnet.com

Darryl & Karen Arawjo
P.O. Box 477
Bushkill, PA 18324-0477
phone: 717-588-6957
Reproduction of Nantucket, Shaker and Appalachian baskets in hand-split white oak; brochure available.

Boxes

Repro. Sources

Charles Harvey
Simple Gifts
201 C N Broadway
Berea, KY 40403

Furniture

Repro. Sources

Brian Braskie
North Woods Chair Shop
237 Old Tilton Rd.
Canterbury, NH 03224-2224
phone: 603-783-4595
fax: 603-783-3328
e-mail: 74323.546@compuserve.com

Gregory Vasileff Reproductions
797 Pomfret Rd.
Hampton, CT 06247-1217

Ian Ingersoll Cabinetmakers
Main St.
West Cornwall, CT 06796

SHAPLEIGH HARDWARE

(see DIAMOND EDGE [SHAPLEIGH HARDWARE])

SHARPENERS

(see PENCIL SHARPENERS; PENCILS)

SHAVING COLLECTIBLES

(see also BARBER SHOP COLLECTIBLES)

Experts

Phillip Krumholz
P.O. Box 4050
Peoria, IL 61607-0050
phone: 309-697-1120
*Acknowledged expert on razors;
author of "The Complete Gillette
Collectors Handbook" as well as two
other books on shaving collectibles
and Barberiana.*

Razor Sharpeners

Collectors

Jay Bolante
3058 North Honore St.
Chicago, IL 60657-2050
phone: 312-327-5091
*Collects and wants to buy mechanical
gadgets use to sharpen razor blades;
also wants wind-up or battery
operated shavers and unusual safety
razors.*

Cary Basse
6927 Forbes Ave.
Van Nuys, CA 91406-4504
phone: 818-781-4856
*Wants to buy safety razors, blade
sharpeners, blades.*

Razors

Collectors

D. Perkins
2317 N. Kessler Blvd.
Indianapolis, IN 46222
phone: 317-638-4519
*Wants early fancy or odd safety razors
in tins or sets; also fancy handled
straight razors.*

Pat Patrick
501 Crawford #302
Houston, TX 77002
phone: 713-546-3244
*Wants to buy pre-1830s razors; of
special interest are boxed sets, 7 razor
- 7 day, 4 razor - 7 day, coffin razor
boxes, shaving instruments.*

Dealers

Sigmund Wohl
Razor's Edge, The
P.O. Box 429
Bronxville, NY 10708-0429
phone: 914-476-5939
fax: 914-376-4160
e-mail: swohl@compuserve.com
*Buys and sells barber and shaving
collectibles, fancy and unusual razors,
and related advertising.*

Experts

Charles D. Stapp
7037 Haynes Rd.
Georgetown, IN 47122-8610
phone: 812-923-3483
*Free appraisals with SASE; provide
photocopy or tracing; especially
wants fancy straight razors and
complete safety razor in box.*

Hank Belasco
7939 Chastain Place
Reseda, CA 91335-2106
phone: 818-344-8790
*Wants fancy or unusual straight
razors; also wants safety razors,
sharpeners, and blank blades; sent list
and prices.*

Razors (Safety)

Clubs/Associations

William Will, Dir.
Safety Razor Collectors Guild
P.O. Box 885
Crescent City, CA 95531
*Promotes interest in collecting and
preserving safety-razors, blades and
related items; please include SASE
with inquiries.*

Collectors

Lester Dequaine
155 Brewester St.
Bridgeport, CT 06605-3149
phone: 203-335-6833
*Wants to buy early safety razors; also
wants related advertisements,
catalogs, instruction sheets,
mechanical blade sharpeners, razor
blade blanks, figural shaving mugs,
figural handle shaving brushes,
counter & window displays.*

Clay Tontz
4043 Nora
Covina, CA 91722
phone: 818-338-99767

Experts

Howard Hazelcorn
6731 Ashley Ct.
Sarasota, FL 34241-9696
phone: 941-921-1815
*Author of "Hazelcorn's Guide to
Kampfe's Star Safety Razors."*

Robert Waits
594 Endicott Dr.
Sunnyvale, CA 94087-4426
e-mail: rwaits@juno.com
*Author of "Safety Razor Reference
Guide" and "Safety Razor Reference
Guide - First Supplement"; these are
not price guides.*

Shaving Mugs

Collectors

Richard Hebel
233 Dietrich Crescent Dr.
Lawrenceburg, IN 47025
phone: 317-848-2977

SHAWLS

Kashmir (Paisley)

(see also TEXTILES)

Collectors

Stephanie M. Schnatz
17 Tallow Ct.
Baltimore, MD 21244-2516
phone: 410-944-0819
*Wants to buy paisley shawls and
scraps; please, no dry rot.*

Experts

Val Arbab
P.O. Box 684
La Jolla, CA 92038-0684
phone: 619-453-4686
fax: 619-457-3647
*Appraises all oriental rugs, Kashmir
shawls and textiles.*

SHEET MUSIC

(see also HYMNS; MOVIE
MEMORABILIA; MUSIC; PAPER
COLLECTIBLES; PERFORMING
ARTS; ROCK 'N' ROLL COL-
LECTIBLES)

Auction Services

Beverly A. Hamer
Hamer Sheet Music Sales
P.O. Box 75
East Derry, NH 03041
phone: 603-432-3528 or 207-934-1481
*Wants old collectible sheet music;
publishes a set price list and conducts
auctions of collectible sheet music;
free search service.*

Norcross
209 Township Line
Upper Darby, PA 19082
*Conducts sheet music auctions; many
old tunes in mint condition.*

Paul A. Riseman
2205 South Park Ave.
Springfield, IL 62704-4335
phone: 217-787-2634
fax: 217-787-0062
e-mail: riseman@riseman.com
*Send for free sheet music auction
catalogs in the following categories:
movie, broadway, rags, jazz, blues,
rock, Berlin, Gershwin, transportation, sports, political, etc.*

Lois Cordey
5623 N. 64th Ave.
Glendale, AZ 85301
phone: 602-931-2835
*Conducts periodic sheet music
auctions.*

Clubs/Associations

James Henderson
Sonneck Society for American Music &
Music in America
Newsletter: Sonneck Society Bulletin
P.O. Box 476
Canton, MA 02021-0476
phone: 617-828-8450
fax: 617-828-8915
e-mail: acadsvc@aol.com
*Promotes the dissemination of
accurate information on all aspects of
American music and music in
America; also publishes "American
Music", a quarterly journal
addressing music in America.*

Sam Teicher
New York Sheet Music Society
P.O. Box 354
Hewlett, NY 11557
phone: 516-295-0719
fax: 516-569-1493
e-mail: samuelt313@aol.com
*For collectors of all kinds of sheet
music with an emphasis on popular
music from 1890 to 1950.*

Lois Cordey, Ed.
Remember That Song
Newsletter: Remember That Song
5623 N. 64th Ave.
Glendale, AZ 85301
phone: 602-931-2835
*Sheet music collectors contribute
informative articles and illustrations;
illustrated newsletter covering every
aspect of old-time popular music
collecting; focuses on sheet music
from 1840 to 1940; auctions; members
get free ads.*

Mayilyn Brees, Sec.
National Sheet Music Society, Inc.
Newsletter: Song Sheet
1597 Fair Park Ave.
Los Angeles, CA 90041
*Membership includes bi-monthly
newsletter and yearly directory;
members get free 40 word listings in
each.*

City of Roses Sheet Music Collectors
Club
13447 Bush St. SE
Portland, OR 97236
*Sponsors an annual sheet music sale
and show.*

Collectors

Roger Hankins
1550 Worcester Rd., #110
Framingham, MA 01702
phone: 508-872-7173
*Wants film and show tunes by Berlin
& Wenrich.*

Stanley King
260 Fifth Ave.
New York, NY 10001-6408
phone: 212-447-1880
fax: 212-447-0728
*Wants to buy sheet music: jazz, K.K.K.
music, political music, and songsters.*

Gary Olsen
505 S. Royal Ave.
Front Royal, VA 22630
phone: 703-635-7157 or 703-635-7158
fax: 703-635-1818
e-mail: hpfrigko@interloc.com
*Wants sheet music with covers
depicting sports, WWI, or first names
in the titles.*

Margaret Horning
13447 SE Brush St.
Portland, OR 97236-3323
phone: 503-761-3817

Dealers

Beverly A. Hamer
Beverly A. Hamer Sheet Music Sales
P.O. Box 75
East Derry, NH 03041
phone: 603-432-3528 or 207-934-1481
*Wants old collectible sheet music;
publishes a set price list and conducts
auctions of collectible sheet music;
free search service.*

Wayland Bunnell
199 Tarrytown Rd.
Manchester, NH 03103-2723
phone: 603-668-5466
*Wants unpicked box lots of sheet
music, or individual pieces in any
subject category; wholesale, retail,
consignment.*

Allen Radwill
23 Hunters Lane
Vincentown, NJ 08088-2837
phone: 609-953-5473
*250,000 items related to rock & roll,
rhythm & blues, soul, gospel,
television, movies: records, sheet
music, magazines; no CDs or videos.*

R. Hess
P.O. Box 963
New York, NY 10023-0963
phone: 212-579-0689
*Wants to buy jazz and R&B records;
has been collecting for 30 years; also
wants original jazz art including sheet
music, statues, books, etc.; by
appointment or mail.*

Sheet Music Center
Box 10
Old Bethpage, NY 11804
phone: 800-527-7626
e-mail: smctr@ix.netcom.com
Internet: http://
www.sheetmusiccenter.com
*Buys and sells sheet music and piano
rolls; FREE catalog to readers of
"Maloney's Antiques & Collectibles
Resource Directory."*

Tom Morgan
110 Monte Vista Ave.
Charlottesville, VA 22903-4117
phone: 804-296-9346
e-mail: Tom@redlt.com
Internet: http://www.redlt.com/Tom
*Author of "From Cakewalk to Concert
Halls"; associate editor of the
"African American Volume of the
Dictionary of Twentieth Century
Culture"; always looking for sheet
music with photos of African
Americans.*

Roger Burgoon
107 S. Mulberry
Statesboro, GA 30458

Sandra McGovern
Global Music Enterprises
488 Archer Lane
Kissimmee, FL 34746
phone: 800-869-5251 or 407-396-4176
*Mail order business selling vintage
sheet music and movie/movie star
memorabilia; will put you on her
wants list; when requesting lists, send
LSASE for each list.*

Jeannie Peters
Mt. Washington Antiques
3742 Kellogg Ave.
c/o Ferguson Antiques Mall
Cincinnati, OH 45226-1514
phone: 513-231-6584 or 513-321-0919
*Buys, sells and specializes in sheet
music; over 200,000 available for
sale; send want list, please.*

Jim Wiemers
5312 Seiler Rd.
Dorsey, IL 62021
phone: 618-377-6379
*Hosts the annual Sheet Music Swap
Meet in mid-June in Collinsville, IL.*

Robert Johnson
Portobello Unit #126
5 Embarcadero West
Oakland, CA 94607

Jeanne Koch
Kookie Kollectorium
4312 SE Flavel St.
Portland, OR 97206-8426
Send want lists.

Experts

Radko Tichavsky
Cornalina 5349, Paseo Res. 5
Monterey
Nuevo Leon 640 00 Mexico
*Specializes in Mexican sheet music
from the 1850-1913 period.*

Sandy Marrone
113 Oakwood Dr.
Riverton, NJ 08077-2908
phone: 609-829-6104
*Sheet music collector for over 25
years; has contacts throughout the
hobby; willing to answer questions
and give advice about sheet music;
would prefer discussing by phone but
will answer mail if SASE enclosed.*

Lois Cordey
5623 N. 64th Ave.
Glendale, AZ 85301
phone: 602-931-2835
*Collects, appraises and specializes in
sheet music.*

Lynn Wenzel
29 Latham Lane
Berkeley, CA 94708-1513
phone: 510-527-0096 or 510-528-9548
fax: 510-527-0095
e-mail: 103736.2305@compuserve.com
*Co-author with Carol Binkowski of "I
Hear American Singing"; features
writer for antique and collectible*

*publications nationwide under the
syndicated name "Handed Down."*

Museums/Libraries

American Antiquarian Society
185 Salisbury St.
Worcester, MA 01609
phone: 508-755-5221

Broadcast, Music, Inc. (BMI)
320 West 57th St.
New York, NY 10019

American Society of Composers,
Authors & Publishers (ASCAP)
1 Lincoln Plaza
New York, NY 10023

Periodicals

Ed Shanaphy, Ed.
Magazine: Sheet Music Magazine
P.O. Box 58629
Boulder, CO 80321-8629
phone: 800-759-3036
*Focuses on playable sheet music;
some dealer ads for vintage sheet
music.*

Richard Zimmerman, Ed.
Maple Leaf Club
Newsletter: Rag Times, The
15522 Ricky Ct.
Grass Valley, CA 95949-6672
*A bi-monthly newsletter with
everything about ragtime - past and
present; since 1967; also sheet music
ads and articles.*

Rock 'N' Roll

Collectors

Jim Weaver
405 Dunbar
Pittsburgh, PA 15235-5218
*Wants 1950s-1960s rock 'n' roll photo
cover sheet music; send lists and
offers.*

Experts

Jean Blankenship
P.O. Box 7274
Pasadena, TX 77508-7274
phone: 713-266-6311
Interested in Rock 'n Roll sheet music.

SHEFFIELD

(see also SILVER; SILVERPLATE)

Appraisers

James C. Voors
Court of King James
515 West Wayne St.
Fort Wayne, IN 46802-2123
phone: 219-426-3234
fax: 219-426-32344229940
*Specializes in Sheffield fused plate,
first and second periods, especially
with heraldry; also in 19th century
Victorian silverplate (Elkington,
Creswick, James Dixon, etc.) and in
sterling, hallmarked, and Continental
silver.*

SHELLS

(see AMMUNITION & EXPLOSIVE
ORDNANCE, Shell Casings;
SEASHELLS; TRENCH ART)

SHIP RELATED

(see also NAUTICAL ANTIQUES;
SHIPPING; STEAMBOAT
COLLECTIBLES; TITANIC
MEMORABILIA)

Experts

Sara Conklin
239 Sierra Pt. Rd.
Brisbane, CA 94005-1664
phone: 415-467-6249
fax: 415-467-6249
e-mail: 76363.536@compuserve.com
*Managed the collections of the
National Maritime Museum in San
Francisco for ten years & is an expert
in appraising ship models, ships-in-
bottles, marine art, scrimshaw,
figureheads, paper ephemera,
instruments, whaling, diving
equipment.*

U.S.S. Constitution

Dealers

Tim O'Callaghan
P.O. Box 512
Northville, MI 48167
phone: 248-449-2652
*Wants USS Constitution "Old
Ironsides" items, especially items
made from the ship in the 1920s and
sold to raise money for restoration;
also wants postal covers from her
1931-1934 cruise around the US;
other related items considered.*

Warships

Clubs/Associations

George F. Dale, Sec.
International Naval Research Organization
Magazine: Warship International
P.O. Box 3249
1st St Station
Radford, VA 24143-3249
phone: 419-472-1331 or 703-639-2590
*Dedicated to the study of post-1860
naval vessels: histories, elements of
ballistics, design, careers, etc.;
magazine issued quarterly.*

Collectors

Stan Dickinson
307 1/2 B.E. Lake St.
Petoskey, MI 49770
phone: 616-347-1022
*Specializes in ship related items: U.S.
Navy ships, Spanish American War
era, prints.*

SHIPPING

(see also NAUTICAL ANTIQUES;
SHIP RELATED; STEAMBOAT
COLLECTIBLES)

Canadian

Dealers

Michael Rice
Michael Rice Collectibles
P.O. Box 286
Saanichton
B.C. V8M 2C5 Canada
phone: 250-652-9412
e-mail: mrice@pacificcoast.net
*Looking for paper items from
Canadian steamships and paddle
wheelers, particularly menus,
passenger lists, deck plans & similar
items; also wants any envelopes used
on board with appropriate postal
markings such as "Posted on Board",
etc.*

Chesapeake Bay Steamship

Collectors

James Tigner, Jr.
P.O. Box 700
Fairfield, PA 17320-0770
*Collector wants to buy memorabilia
relating to the Chesapeake Bay area
steamship lines: time tables,
brochures, tickets, menus, photographs, etc.*

Great Lakes Related

Dealers

Kenneth Benjamin
Island Shipyard, The
P.O. Box 599
Put In Bay, OH 43456-0599
phone: 419-285-2585
fax: 419-285-2585
*Specializes in genuine Great Lakes
nautical antiques and ship models.*

Michael Kujat
Anchor In Antiques
2122 W. U.S. 2
Saint Ignace, MI 49781-9626
phone: 906-643-8112 or 906-643-9917
fax: 906-643-9917
*Specializes in Great Lakes nautical
items.*

Experts

James A. Baumhofer
P.O. Box 65493
St. Paul, MN 55165
phone: 612-698-7151 or 612-224-3210
fax: 612-291-9179
*Great Lakes ships, books, pictures,
photos; Green's or other directories.*

SHIPS-IN-BOTTLES

(see NAUTICAL ANTIQUES, Models
[Ships-In-Bottles])

SHIRT STUDS

(see CLOTHING & ACCESSORIES,
Vintage; CUFF LINKS)

SHMOOS

Dealers

Barry Lutsky
31 Longfield Dr.
Neshanic, NJ 08853
phone: 201-369-7367
*Buys, sells, trades anything Shmoo:
figurines, salt & peppers, ash trays,
clocks, vinyl, 3D, paper, etc.*

SHOE HORNS

Dealers

Charles & Joan Rhoden
Rhoden's Antiques
605 N. Main
Georgetown, IL 61846-1439
phone: 217-662-8046 or 217-662-8440
fax: 217-662-8223
e-mail: jmrhoden@prairienet.org
Wants unusual shoe horns.

SHOESHINE STANDS

(see BARBERSHOP COL-
LECTIBLES; SHOE HORNS)

SHOULDER PATCHES

(see BADGES; MILITARIA;
PATCHES)

SHRUNKEN HEADS

(see MORBID & ODD ITEMS;
SKELETONS)

SIGNS

(see ADVERTISING COL-
LECTIBLES; BREWERIANA; GAS
STATION COLLECTIBLES;
HIGHWAY COLLECTIBLES;
LAMPS & LIGHTING, Neon;
MARINE CORPS ITEMS)

SILHOUETTES

(see also FOLK ART)

Collectors

Sheldon Lerman
7505 Osler Dr.
Baltimore, MD 21204-7736
phone: 410-321-1514 or 410-828-5310
fax: 410-825-5710

Lester E. Sender
23500 Mercantile Rd.
Cleveland, OH 44122-5914
phone: 216-595-0000
fax: 216-595-1111
*Buys and sells pre-1920 American and
Continental silhouettes.*

Experts

Alda Horner
3200 Central Ave.
Ventura, CA 93003
phone: 805-339-9343
Author, consultant, and dealer.

Museums/Libraries

Essex Institute
132 Essex St.
Salem, MA 01970
phone: 508-744-3390

National Portrait Gallery
8th & F Streets N.W.
Washington, DC 20560-0001
phone: 202-357-2866
fax: 202-786-2565
Internet: http://www.si.edu/

Repro. Sources

Susan B. Anderson
SBA Silhouettes
145 N. Laurel St.
West Hazleton, PA 18201

Ellen Mischo
Profiles
P.O. Box 412
Leesburg, VA 22075-0412
*Makes and sells authentic 18th and
19th century reproduction silhouettes.*

Glass

Experts

Shirley R. Mace
Shadow Enterprises
P.O. Box 1602
Mesilla Park, NM 88047-1602
phone: 505-524-6717
fax: 505-523-0940
e-mail: shmace@nmsu.edu
*Author of "History & Price Guide for
Glass Silhouette Pictures" (1992);
painted black on reverse of glass; sold
in dimestores from the 1920s to
1950s; often with advertising and
attached thermometers or calendars.*

SILK EMBROIDERIES

(see also STEVENGRAPHS;
TEXTILES)

SILVER

(see also BOOKS, Reference [Silver];
FLATWARE; GLASS, Silver Overlay;
GEMS & JEWELRY; REPAIR/
RESTORATION/CONSERVATION,
Metal Items; SHEFFIELD;
SILVERPLATE; SPOONS;
TABLEWARE)

Appraisers

James C. Voors
Court of King James
515 West Wayne St.
Fort Wayne, IN 46802-2123
phone: 219-426-3234
fax: 219-426-32344229940
*Specializes in Sheffield fused plate,
first and second periods, especially
with heraldry; also in 19th century
Victorian silverplate (Elkington,
Creswick, James Dixon, etc.) and in
sterling, hallmarked, and Continental
silver.*

Dewey W. Smith, ASA
Dewey W. Smith, ASA Antique
Appraisals
2000 West Littletown Blvd.
Littleton, CO 80120-2070
phone: 303-347-1797
fax: 303-347-1549

Auction Services

Stuart Slavid
Skinner, Inc.
357 Main St.
Bolton, MA 01740-1104
phone: 508-779-6241 or 617-350-5400
fax: 508-779-5144
*Established in 1964, Skinner Inc. is
the fifth largest auction house in the
US; has offices in Bolton and Boston,
MA.*

Christie's
502 Park Ave.
New York, NY 10022
phone: 212-546-1000
fax: 212-980-8163
Internet: http://www.sirius.com/
~christie/

Clubs/Associations

Society of American Silversmiths
P.O. Box 3599
Cranston, RI 02910
phone: 800-584-2352 or 401-461-3156
fax: 401-461-3196
e-mail: slvrsmth@ids.net
Internet: http://www.ids.net/~slvrsmth/
sashome.htm
*Answers questions on silversmithing
techniques, conservation and
restoration, maker's mark identification and all other silver-related
inquiries.*

International Association of Silver Art
Collectors
Newsletter: Silver Bugle, The
P.O. Box 28415
Seattle, WA 98118-8415
*Newsletter published six times per
year.*

Collectors

Bruce Johnson
P.O. Box 8773
Asheville, NC 28814-8773
phone: 704-254-1912
fax: 704-254-1912
*Wants to buy silver marked DODGE
or ASHEVILLE SILVERCRAFT.*

Dealers

Steve Duffy
Sea Eagles Sterling
20 Bridle Dr.
Winsted, CT 06098-3422
phone: 860-379-5749
fax: 860-379-5749
*Specializes in active, inactive, and
obsolete sterling silver flatware.*

John C. Foy
P.O. Box 476
Fanwood, NJ 07023-0476
phone: 908-654-3867
Buys and sells antique American coin silver, American sterling silver and souvenir spoons, and English sterling silver; also sells books on silver.

Nathan Horowicz
Nathan Horowicz Antiques
1050 2nd Ave., Gallery 82
New York, NY 10022
phone: 800-214-6320 or 212-755-6320
fax: 212-755-6438
Large assortment of flatware, tea sets, holloware; Tiffany, Georg Jensen; all American and European manufacturers.

Gary Niederkorn
Gary Niederkorn Silver
Newspaper: Silver Edition
2005 Locust St.
Philadelphia, PA 19103-5606
phone: 215-567-2606
fax: 215-567-2606
Specializes in 19th and 20th cent. silver novelties, Christmas ornaments, napkin rings, Judaica, picture frames, etc.; also Tiffany, Jensen, Mexican.

Gerald Shultz
Antique Gallery, The
8523 Germantown Ave.
Philadelphia, PA 19118-3316
phone: 215-248-1700
fax: 215-247-8411
Interested in sterling silver and Victorian silverplate (no flatware): Jensen, Tiffany, Stone, Kirk, etc.

Pikesville Jewelry & Coin Exchange
1350 Reisterstown Rd.
Baltimore, MD 21208
phone: 410-653-3430

Beverly H. Bremer
Beverly Bremer Silver Shop
3164 Peachtree Rd. NE
Atlanta, GA 30305
phone: 404-261-4009
fax: 404-261-5742
Appraises, buys, sells and matches sterling silver flatware, and new and antique sterling silver holloware & giftware; large shop; sterling silver only; want lists kept; mail order; totally computerized.

Debra Bonner
Colonial Silver Shoppe
20 Gaylan Court
Montgomery, AL 36109
phone: 800-675-4837 or 334-272-7282
Gorham, Wallace, International, Towle, Kirk-Stieff, Lunt.

Robin & June Greenwald
June Greenwald Antiques, Inc.
3096 Mayfield Rd.
Cleveland, OH 44118
phone: 216-932-5535
Buys and sells 19th and 20th century silver; offers a matching service.

John B. Marrella
Investments in Time
P.O. Box 611
Birmingham, MI 48012-0611
phone: 810-644-3100
fax: 810-644-2792
Buys and sells important silver; American, European, Chinese or Japanese.

Ted Rickard
Silver Service
Wilmette, IL 60091
phone: 708-256-5900
fax: 708-256-5952
e-mail: trick2@juno.com
Specializing in matching discontinued American and English sterling silver flatware; also locates antique sterling silver flatware.

Connie & Bill McNally
McNally Co., Inc., The
P.O. Box 1048
Rancho Santa Fe, CA 92067
phone: 619-756-1922
fax: 619-756-9928
e-mail: silver@cts.com
Buys, sells, collects and specializes in 18th and 19th century furnishings, silver and objets d'art.

Judy Brown
P.O. Box 5368
Frazier Park, CA 93222
phone: 805-242-5411
Mail order only dealer of gold and silver smalls: boxes, chatelaines, match safes, sewing items, Victorian or earlier frames and silverplate items; long time dealer.

Antique Appraisal & Estate Sale Service - K. Bailey
P.O. Box 75191
Seattle, WA 98125-5345
phone: 206-746-2777
fax: 206-365-0633
Specializes in unusual sterling 18th through 20th century silver.

Experts

V. Stephen Vaughn
c/o E.B. Horn Co.
429 Washington St.
Boston, MA 02108
phone: 617-542-3902
Specializes in 19th century American silver.

Benedict J. Hastings
2006 Columbia Rd. N.W.
Washington, DC 20009
phone: 202-483-8575
Specializes in fine silver, Russian decorative arts, Russian icons, 18th and 19th century porcelain, military medals, decorations and orders.

Gwendolyn L. Kelso
Rampant Lion, The
P.O. Box 5887
Washington, DC 20016
phone: 202-364-2431
fax: 202-364-2431
Silver expert, appraiser, dealer; also

silver reference service with extensive library; sells books about silver for appraisers, collectors, museums.

Jennifer F. Goldsborough
1688 Coventry Place
Annapolis, MD 21401
phone: 401-841-2634
American silver expert, lecturer, curator.

Suzy Van Massenhove
Fox in Flanders, A
3703 Whispering Lane
Falls Church, VA 22041
phone: 703-256-3094

Gary D. Gardner
200 College St.
Hodgenville, KY 42748-1404
phone: 502-358-3222
Expert, collector specializing in pre-1870 Southern coin grade silver crafted by silversmiths in the South; wants to purchase & research, especially KY, TN, VA, holloware and pre-1830 spoons, ledgers, receipts, inventories for study.

Rod Tinkler
Silver Vault, The
P.O. Box 421
Barrington, IL 60011-0421
phone: 847-381-3101
fax: 847-381-310i
e-mail: SilverVlt@aol.com
Buy, sell, trade, and appraises American, English and Continental silver.

Sterling Shop, The
P.O. Box 595
Silverton, OR 97381-0595
phone: 503-873-6315
Sterling and silverplate flatware matching service.

Museums/Libraries

Museum of Fine Arts, Boston
465 Huntington Ave.
Boston, MA 02115-5523
phone: 617-267-9300
Internet: http://www.mfa.org/home.html

Currier Gallery of Art, The
192 Orange St.
Manchester, NH 03104
phone: 603-669-6144

Wadsworth Atheneum
600 Main St.
Hartford, CT 06103
phone: 860-278-2670
fax: 860-527-0803
Collections include the Elizabeth B. Miles Silver Collection and the Philip H. Hammerslough Collection of American Silver.

Yale University Art Gallery
P.O. Box 2006 Yale Station
New Haven, CT 06520
phone: 203-432-0600

David Warren
Bayou Bend Collection & Gardens, The
P.O. Box 6826
Houston, TX 77265-6826
phone: 713-639-7750
fax: 713-639-7770

Periodicals

Newsletter: Silver News, The
1112 16th St. NW, Ste. 240
Washington, DC 20036
phone: 202-835-0185

Nanette Monmonier
Price Guide: Silver Update, The
P.O. Box 2157
Ellicott City, MD 21041-2157
phone: 410-750-3282
fax: 410-418-5128
Provides prices for current American and popular foreign sterling silver flatware manufacturers; published three timer each year.

Nanette Monmonier
Price Guide: Sterling Silver Hollowware Update, The
P.O. Box 2157
Ellicott City, MD 21041-2157
phone: 410-750-3282
fax: 410-418-5128
Provides illustrations and prices for current American sterling silver hollowware.

Newsletter: Silver & Gold Report
P.O. Box 109665
West Palm Beach, FL 33410
phone: 800-289-9222 or 561-627-3300
fax: 561-625-6685
e-mail: sgr@weissinc.com
Internet: http://www.wessinc.com
Financial advice newsletter in precious medals, and gold & silver bullion and coins.

Connie McNally
Silver Magazine Inc.
Magazine: Silver Magazine
P.O. Box 9690
Rancho Santa Fe, CA 92067-4690
phone: 800-756-1054 or 619-756-1054
fax: 619-756-9928
e-mail: silver@silvermag.com
Internet: http://www.silvermag.com/
Top quality bi-monthly magazine for silver collectors; English, Continental, and Colonial silver; well illustrated articles.

Repair Services

Stephen Smithers
Smithers Restorations
1057 Hawley Rd.
Ashfield, MA 01330-9626
phone: 413-625-2994
Design and making of hand hammered silver holloware and brass lighting (including chandeliers, lanterns, sconces, candlesticks); also restoration of fine early silver; demonstrations and silversmithing talks for museums and civic groups.

Jeffrey Herman
Jeffrey Herman Silver Restoration &
 Conservation
P.O. Box 3599
Cranston, RI 02910
phone: 401-461-3156 or 800-584-2352
Internet: http://www.ids.net/~slvrsmth/
 polish.htm
*Museum quality silver repair; dent
removal, repairs, cleaning, chemical
dips, silver storage and display, anti-
tarnish strips, salt shaker corrosion
repair, monogram removal, leveling a
hinged lid, etc.*

Repro. Sources

Stephen Smithers
1057 Hawley Rd.
Ashfield, MA 01330-9626
phone: 413-625-2994
*Design and making of hand hammered
silver hollowware and brass lighting
(including chandeliers, lanterns,
sconces, candlesticks); also
restoration of fine early silver;
demonstrations and silversmithing
talks for museums and civic groups.*

Suppliers

Jeffrey Herman
Herman's Best Silver Care Products
P.O. Box 3599
Cranston, RI 02910
phone: 401-461-3156 or 800-584-2352
Internet: http://www.ids.net/~slvrsmth/
 polish.htm
*Supplies and instructions for caring
for silver.*

Baltimore

Dealers

Patrick Duggan
Imperial Half Bushel
831 N. Howard St.
Baltimore, MD 21201
phone: 410-462-1192
*Specializes in Baltimore, Maryland
silver.*

Chinese

Experts

Stuart Slavid
86 Johnson Dr.
Marlborough, MA 01752-1438
phone: 508-485-5993
Interested in Chinese silver.

Georg Jensen

Matching Services

Caryl Rose Unger
Imagination Unlimited
4302 Alton Rd., Ste. 820
Miami, FL 33140-2893
phone: 305-534-2214
fax: 305-538-0914
*Specializes in Georg Jensen silver;
offers a Jensen silver matching
service; buys and sells Jensen silver:
single pieces or sets, jewelry, serving
pieces, hollowware, and other Danish*

*silver; reprints of their Jensen articles
available.*

Gorham

Man./Prod./Dist.

Gorham, Inc.
100 Lenox Dr.
Lawrenceville, NJ 08648
phone: 609-896-2800 or 800-635-3669
*Sterling and stainless steel flatware,
sterling and silverplated hollowware;
fine china, crystal stemware, giftware
and dolls; a division of Lenox Brands.*

International

Man./Prod./Dist.

International Silver Co.
175 McClellan Hwy.
Boston, MA 02128
phone: 617-561-2200

Kirk Stieff

Dealers

Michael A. Merrill
Michael A. Merrill, Inc.
Newsletter: Silver Letter, The
Crestar Bank Building
2045 York Rd.
Timonium, MD 21093
phone: 410-453-9400
e-mail: merrill@home.com
Internet: http://members.home.net/
 merrill/
*Kirk & Steiff specialists; pattern
matching, bridal registry, silver
replating, appraisals; newsletter lists
and pictures items for sale including
sterling silver and books about silver.*

Man./Prod./Dist.

Kirk Stieff Co. Outlet Store
800 Wyman Park Dr.
Baltimore, MD 21211
phone: 410-338-6080 or 800-531-7946
fax: 410-338-6097
*Sterling, silverplate, stainless steel
and pewter flatware, sterling and
silverplate hollowware; pewter,
jewelry; a division of Lenox Brands.*

Lunt

Man./Prod./Dist.

Lunt Silversmiths
298 Federal St.
Greenfield, MA 01301
phone: 413-774-2774
fax: 413-774-4393
*Sterling and plated flatware and
hollowware.*

Mexican

Collectors

Jill A. Crawford
Crawford Design
7377 Birdview Ave.
Malibu, CA 90265
phone: 310-457-8076
fax: 310-457-3453
*Interested in buying Spratling and
other Mexican silver.*

Dealers

Jimmy Vitanza
Peregrine Galleries
508 Brinkerhoff Ave.
Santa Barbara, CA 93101-3441
phone: 805-963-3134
fax: 805-963-3134

Experts

Carole A. Berk
8020 Norfolk Ave.
Bethesda, MD 20814-2504
phone: 800-382-2413
*Co-author with Penny C. Morrill of
"Mexican Silver."*

Old Newbury Crafters

Man./Prod./Dist.

Jeanne Pritchard
Old Newbury Crafters
36 Main St.
Amesbury, MA 01913-2807
phone: 508-388-0983
fax: 508-388-8430
*Sterling silver flatware and
hollowware, pewter giftware.*

Oneida

Man./Prod./Dist.

Oneida Silversmiths
Kenwood Station
Oneida, NY 13421-2829
phone: 315-361-3000
*Sterling silver, silverplate, gold
electroplate, stainless steel, flatware;
stainless and silverplate hollowware,
crystal stemware and hollowware.*

Reed & Barton

Man./Prod./Dist.

Reed & Barton
144 W. Britannia St.
Taunton, MA 02780
phone: 508-824-6611 or 800-822-1824
fax: 508-822-7269
*Produces china, crystal, silver,
silverplate, and stainless flatware,
collectible plates, bells, dolls,
ornaments and accessories.*

Scrap

Dealers

Jim Sciuto
GoldTek
P.O. Box 128
Methuen, MA 01844
phone: 508-374-2254 or 603-645-4717
fax: 508-373-1088
Internet: http://www.pm-connect.com/
 sciuto/
*Buys scrap gold and silver: class
rings, wedding bands, gold coins, gold
watches, gold plated circuit boards,
gold solder, gold wire, gold teeth;
also scrap sterling silver flatware,
coins, bars, silver flake, silver anodes,
etc.*

Greg Walsh
32 River View Lane
P.O. Box 747
Potsdam, NY 13676
phone: 315-265-9111 or 800-371-9286
fax: 315-265-9222
*Wants to buy gold and silver rings,
coins, estate jewelry, pocket watches,
diamonds, sterling silver items, scrap
gold, broken or damaged jewelry,
dental gold, etc.; 24-hour turn
around; ship on approval or call for
quote; since 1979.Dup*

Michael A. Merrill
Michael A. Merrill, Inc.
Crestar Bank Building
2045 York Rd.
Timonium, MD 21093
phone: 410-453-9400
e-mail: merrill@home.com
Internet: http://members.home.net/
 merrill/
*Buying precious metals from the
public, dealers since 1974; buys scrap
gold, diamonds, old gold, dental gold,
school rings, gold & silver numismatic
coins, sterling silver (Kirk & Steiff),
Franklin Mint, platinum, palladium,
exotics.*

Cy Phillips, Jr.
S C Coin & Stamp Co. Inc.
P.O. Drawer 661180
Arcadia, CA 91066-1180
phone: 818-445-8277 or 800-367-0779
fax: 818-445-8278
*Tokens, medals, coins, currency,
badges, expo. and fair items, scrap
gold and silver.*

Towle

Man./Prod./Dist.

Mark Roland
Towle Silversmiths
144 Addison St.
Boston, MA 02128
phone: 617-561-2200 or 617-568-1300
fax: 617-568-8134
*Sterling silver, silverplate, stainless
steel, goldplate, barware.*

Wallace

Man./Prod./Dist.

Wallace Silversmiths
175 McClellan Hwy.
Boston, MA 02128
phone: 617-561-2200
Sterling silver, silverplate, stainless steel, pewter flatware and hollow-ware.

SILVERPLATE

(see also FLATWARE; SHEFFIELD; SILVER; REPAIR/RESTORATION/ CONSERVATION, Metal Items; TABLEWARE)

Appraisers

James C. Voors
Court of King James
515 West Wayne St.
Fort Wayne, IN 46802-2123
phone: 219-426-3234
fax: 219-426-32344229940
Specializes in Sheffield fused plate, first and second periods, especially with heraldry; also in 19th century Victorian silverplate (Elkington, Creswick, James Dixon, etc.) and in sterling, hallmarked, and Continental silver.

Periodicals

Nanette Monmonier
Price Guide: Silverplated Hollowware Update, The
P.O. Box 2157
Ellicott City, MD 21041-2157
phone: 410-750-3282
fax: 410-418-5128
Provides illustrations and prices for current American silverplated hollowware manufacturers.

Connie McNally
Silver Magazine Inc.
Magazine: Silver Magazine
P.O. Box 9690
Rancho Santa Fe, CA 92067-4690
phone: 800-756-1054 or 619-756-1054
fax: 619-756-9928
e-mail: silver@silvermag.com
Internet: http://www.silvermag.com/
Top quality bi-monthly magazine for silver collectors; English, Continental, and Colonial silver; well illustrated articles.

SILVERPLATED FLATWARE

(see FLATWARE)

SILVERWARE

(see FLATWARE)

SIMMONS HARDWARE

(see KEEN KUTTER [SIMMONS HARDWARE])

SINGING BIRDS

(see MUSIC BOXES, Birds & Bird Boxes [Singing])

SKATING

(see SPORTS COLLECTIBLES, Ice Skating; SPORTS COLLECTIBLES, Roller Skating)

SKELETONS

(see also ANIMAL TROPHIES; FOSSILS; HAIR WORK; MORBID & ODD ITEMS)

Collectors

Steve DeGenaro
P.O. Box 5662
Youngstown, OH 44504-0662
phone: 216-757-7735

Dealers

Antique Workshop Inc.
150 Aerial Way
Syosset, NY 11791
phone: 516-933-6213
Wants stuffed real animals, heads, birds; also skulls and skeletons.

Bone Room, The
1569 Solano
Berkeley, CA 94707-2116
phone: 510-526-5252
Wants to buy ivory, skeletons, tusks, skulls, fossils, insect collections, shrunken heads, etc.

SLAVERY ITEMS

(see also BLACK MEMORABILIA)

Collectors

Danny Drain
Slave Mart Museum "Preserving the Past"
163-01 Foch Blvd., 7J
Jamaica, NY 11434-1701
phone: 718-341-4654 or 718-341-7916
Wants any slave related items: documents, letters, photographs, slave tokens, slave passes, slave chains and locks, collars, paintings, bills of sale, slave tags, etc.

Gene Peters
'Tiques
P.O. Box 3267
Farmingdale, NY 11735-0679
phone: 516-842-9549
Wants documents, pictures, and artifacts relating to American slavery.

James C. Allen
1178 Wildcreek Trail NE
Atlanta, GA 30324
phone: 404-321-5784
Wants memorabilia and objects from the slave era through the Civil War Movement.

Cary Demont
P.O. Box 16013
Minneapolis, MN 55416-0013
phone: 612-922-1617
Wants political pre-1964 buttons, pins, flags, ribbons, banners, and the unusual; also suffrage, prohibition, slavery, and Lindbergh.

Slave Tags

Collectors

Rich Hartzog
World Exonumia
P.O. Box 4143 BSB
Rockford, IL 61110-0643
phone: 815-226-0771
fax: 815-397-7662
Wants slave tags, and other Black tokens and medals.

SLIDE RULES

(see also CALCULATORS; COMPUTERS; INSTRUMENTS & DEVICES, Scientific)

Clubs/Associations

Wayne Lehnert
Oughtred Society
Journal: Journal of the Oughtred Society
P.O. Box 99077
Emeryville, CA 94662
phone: 510-754-9337
For people interested in the history and collection of slide rules; annual meetings feature slide rule exhibits and exchanges of information.

Collectors

W. Feely
1172 Lindsay La.
Jenkintown, PA 19046-1839
phone: 215-884-5640
fax: 215-884-8660
,Wants slide rules: linear, circular or cylindrical; also books on slide rules, pre-1945 Army Field Manuals, and K&E, Gurley, Buff, Dietzgen, or Burger catalogs.

Cal Frye
125 E. Oak St.
Kent, OH 44240-3825
phone: 330-678-7006
fax: 330-678-7006
e-mail: cj_frye@bigfoot.com
Internet: http://Phoenix.kent.edu/~cfrye
Wants oddball slide rules: circular, cylindrical, special-purpose, or big (classroom-sized); also wants pocket/ portable sundials.

Steve Leffel
Green Bay, WI 54302-3132
fax: 414-465-6505
Wants slide rules and slide rule books and literature; also interested in corresponding with anyone involved in the design, manufacturing or sales of slide rules.

Robert Otnes
2160 Middlefield Rd.
Palo Alto, CA 94301-4022
phone: 415-324-1821
A leading collector of calculating machines and slide rules.

Paul H. Hayashi, PE
18 Tarabrook Dr.
Orinda, CA 94563-3121
phone: 510-254-5074 or 510-253-1038
fax: 510-253-0592
Wants to buy old engineering instruments, slide rules, drafting sets, graphical integrators, planimeters.

Rodger Shepherd, MD
10592 Englewood Dr.
Oakland, CA 94605
phone: 510-632-1680
Treasurer of The Oughtred Society, a club for slide rule collectors.

Wayne Lehnert
P.O. Box 99077
Emeryville, CA 94662
phone: 510-754-9337
Secretary of The Oughtred Society, a club for slide rule collectors.

Osborne I. Price
8338 Colombard Ct.
San Jose, CA 95135

Robert De Cesaris
7429 Bree Ann Ct.
Citrus Heights, CA 95610-2455
phone: 916-356-5769
Actively seeking slide rules and other mechanical calculating devices: especially interested in circular slide rules, special purpose and special function rules, 20" rules, pocket watch type like Boucher, Sperry, Fowler, and others.

Dealers

Charles E. McCallum
Temple & Co.
110 Bittersweet N.E.
Ada, MI 49301
phone: 616-676-3659 or 616-776-2515
fax: 616-752-2500
Interested in slide rules, including circular and cylindrical models, as well as catalogs, and manuals/books on slide rule operations.

Experts

George Duckworth
12602 North 20 Ave.
Phoenix, AZ 85029-2610
phone: 602-582-4626
Author of "Slide Rule Collector's Guide," available from author.

SLOT CARS

(see TOYS, Cars [Racing])

SMOKEY THE BEAR ITEMS

Collectors

Pete Nowicki
1531 39th Ave.
San Francisco, CA 94122-3015
phone: 415-566-7506
Collector seeks all licensed Smokey Bear items for collection: toys, dolls, posters, etc.

SB Collector
P.O. Box 9007
Bend, OR 97708
Serious collector buying Smokey Bear items.

SMOKING COLLECTIBLES

(see also ADVERTISING COL-LECTIBLES, Trade Cards [Tobacco]; CIGAR BANDS, BOXES & LABELS; CIGARETTE COL-LECTIBLES; CIGAR STORE COLLECTIBLES; LIGHTERS; MATCHBOXES & LABELS; MATCHCOVERS; MATCH SAFES; PIPES; TOBACCO COLLECTIBLES)

Collectors

Lee Pattison
6 Christview Dr.
Cuba, NY 14727-1202
phone: 716-968-2458
Wants antique meerschaum pipes carved and plain, briar pipes of more recent manufacture brand names: Charatan, Barling, Stanwell, Larson, Savinelli and others; also wants to buy tobacco jars and cigar store items.

Les Franics
129 South Van Buren St.
Rockville, MD 20850
phone: 301-762-3003
Buys and sells tobacco cards and cigar related collectibles: silks, felts, cutters, tobacco jars, tobacco tags, books and ephemera.

D. Nordlinger Stern
385 Bayview Dr. NE
Saint Petersburg, FL 33704-2430
phone: 813-894-4000
fax: 813-894-1040
e-mail: dnordstern@aol.com
Wants tobacco memorabilia, particularly W. Duke and Duke's Mixture.

Cindy Porman
22044 Roosevelt Rd.
South Bend, IN 46614
phone: 219-291-6414
Wants Copenhagen Snuff, Weyman & Sons, Weyman Bros., Skoal Snuff, and Key Snuff tobacco items including crocks, pocket tins, store displays, metal and paper signs, and related advertising items.

Millie Vaccarella
1955 Hythe St.
Roseville, MN 55113
phone: 612-631-2201
Interested in buying old tobacco tins,

especially pocket tins in good condition.

Dealers

Charles S. Levi
19 South Wabash
Chicago, IL 60603-3182
phone: 312-372-1306
fax: 312-372-1416
Buy and sells all things related to smoking: books, pipes, gadgets, literature, etc.

Experts

Benjamin Rapaport
11505 Turnbridge Ln.
Reston, VA 20194-1220
phone: 703-435-8133
Wants antiquarian tobacciana: domestic & foreign literature, pipes & pipe smoking, snuff & its accoutre-ments, cigars & accessories, smoking technology, ephemera & lithography, pipe tampers, and tobacco jars and boxes.

Museums/Libraries

Tobacco History Corporation
2828 Duke Homestead Rd.
Durham, NC 27705-2726
phone: 919-477-5498 or 919-479-7093
fax: 919-479-7092
A non-profit support group for the Duke Homestead State Historic Site; collects materials relevant to the preservation of tobacco history: pipe, smoking, cigarette, advertising, etc.

David Wright, Cur.
Museum of Tobacco Art & History
800 Harrison St.
Nashville, TN 37203-3336
phone: 615-271-2349 or 615-271-2163
fax: 615-271-2285
Museum traces history of tobacco from American Indians to present; collection of pipes, tobacco jars, Cigar Store figures, snuff boxes, advertising, art, etc.

Art

Collectors

Dr. A. Artinian
100 Worth Ave. Ph6
Palm Beach, FL 33480
phone: 407-655-3030
Wants tobacco in art; drawings and paintings related to smoking; no prints or multiples of any sort, please.

Holders

Collectors

Jay Opperman
78 Clinton Ave.
Montclair, NJ 07042
phone: 201-509-0195
Wants to buy superb examples of exquisite antique meerschaum pipes and cigar holders.

Mark Ligett
P.O. Box 266
Harlan, KY 40831
Collects cigarette/cigar holders; would like to correspond with others who collect or use holders.

Snuff Boxes

Collectors

Eli Hecht
Mineli Assoc.
19 Evelyn Lane
Syosset, NY 11791-5806
phone: 516-921-1837
Wants to buy snuff boxes, nautical items, and inkwells.

SNACK SETS

Collectors

Delores Long
P.O. Box 158
Hallock, MN 56728
Collector of glass or ceramic snack plates with matching cups; will buy or trade for snack plates with matching cups; please send SASE with photo, photocopy plate, asking price.

Periodicals

Delores Long
Newsletter: Snack Set Searchers' Newsletter
P.O. Box 158
Hallock, MN 56728
A quarterly publication devoted to providing information and a trading medium for collectors of snack sets (also known as toast or tea sets).

SNOW BABIES

Experts

Linda L. Vines
P.O. Box 43721
Montclair, NJ 07043
phone: 973-748-4990 or 201-748-4990
Buys, sells and trades German bisque snow babies; authored "Snow Babies" in "Collectors Showcase" magazine; Snow Babies advisor to "Schroeder's"; lecturer and appraiser.

SNOWDOMES

Clubs/Associations

Nancy McMichael
Snowdome Collectors Club
Newsletter: Snow Biz Newsletter
P.O. Box 53262
Washington, DC 20009-9262
"Snow Biz" aims to enhance the knowledge, enjoyment and collections of snowdome/waterglobe enthusiasts; quarterly newsletter.

Collectors

Donna Divon
P.O. Box 756
Yonkers, NY 10704-0756
Buy, trade snowdomes: Disneyland

and Disney world scenes and figurals; unusual shapes and foreign; in plastic and glass; especially fond of older plastic location domes, Olympic and World's Fair domes; all trade and sale lists welcome.

Michael Muntner
6817 Capri Place
Bethesda, MD 20817-4209
phone: 301-365-4784 or 301-365-3727
fax: 301-365-4525
e-mail: trylon@erols.com
Wants snow domes (water globes); souvenir, advertising, and figural; will buy individual pieces or entire collections.

Lucille Miles
416 Walnut St.
San Francisco, CA 94959
phone: 707-778-8210
Buys or trades snowdomes; plastic or glass, souvenir, figural, Disney, advertising, etc.

Dealers

Helene Guarnaccia
52 Coach Lane
Fairfield, CT 06430
phone: 203-374-6034
Buys and sells snowdomes; author of "Snowdomes, A Price Guide."

Experts

Nancy McMichael
P.O. Box 53262
Washington, DC 20009-9262
"Snow Biz" aims to enhance the knowledge, enjoyment and collections of snowdome/waterglobe enthusiasts; quarterly newsletter.

Man./Prod./Dist.

Toy Krazy
P.O. Box 281
Galloway, OH 43119
Specializes in contemporary snow globes.

Sharon Jones
Global Shakeup
2265 Westwood Blvd. #618
Los Angeles, CA 90064-2016
phone: 213-259-8988
e-mail: 70431.2470@compuserve.com
Features a huge selection of American and European glass and plastic snowdomes including figurals, comic characters, locations, advertising, limited edition, science fiction, and much more; 28-page catalog $2.

Location

Experts

Chloe Ross
7553 Norton Ave. Apt. 4
Los Angeles, CA 90046-5500
phone: 213-874-3044
Seeking all plastic (NO GLASS) souvenir location or advertising snowshakers/snowdomes; any size or condition; need not have water or

snow; prefer uncracked but small leaks OK; must have inside plaque; no holidays; wants LA; all answered.

Periodicals

Chloe Ross
Newsletter: Roadside Attractions
7553 Norton Ave. Apt. 4
Los Angeles, CA 90046-5500
phone: 213-874-3044
A 2-sided, legal size format newsletter that provides hot news and tips for collectors of plastic souvenir locations snowdomes; includes a free trade/buy/sell column for all subscribers; published 5 times per year; SASE for sample.

SNOWGLOBES

(see SNOWDOMES)

SNOWMOBILES

Clubs/Associations

Antique Snowmobile Club of America
Newsletter: Iron Dog Tracks
1675-67 Golf Course Blvd.
Independence, IA 50644

Vintage Snowmobile Club of America
Newsletter: Vintage Snowmobiler, The
P.O. Box 545
Waupaca, WI 54981
e-mail: vsca@gglbbs.com
Internet: http://www.vsca.com
Caters to collectors and restorers of antique and unusual snowmobiles from the 1967-1977 era; over 700 members across the US and Canada; over 3000 snowmobiles registered in the VSCA database; regional Ride-Ins annually.

Museums/Libraries

New Hampshire Snowmobile Museum
Bear Brook State Park
Allenstown, NH 03275

Periodicals

Steve Ferguson, Ed.
National Automobile Dealers Association
Price Guide: N.A.D.A. Official Used Car Guide
P.O. Box 7800
Costa Mesa, CA 92628
phone: 800-966-6232
fax: 714-556-8715
e-mail: steve.ferguson@nadaguides.com
Internet: http://www.nadaguide.com
A series of value guides for domestic and foreign cars, trucks, vans, RV's, mobile homes, motorcycles, snowmobiles, and boats, small and large; also Heavy Duty Trucks and Aircraft Book, car clubs & organizations, museums.

SNUFF BOTTLES

(see also ORIENTALIA; SMOKING COLLECTIBLES)

Clubs/Associations

John Ford, Pres.
International Chinese Snuff Bottle Society
Journal: Chinese Snuff Bottle Journal
2601 North Charles St.
Baltimore, MD 21218-4514
phone: 410-467-9400 or 410-243-3451
Members interested in "Chinese" snuff bottles.

Collectors

Richard Sindler
859 1/2 N. Howard St.
Baltimore, MD 21201
phone: 410-728-3377
Wants to buy snuff bottles; send photo and price.

Dealers

Alan R. Glazer
36 College Ave. #B3
Somerville, MA 02144
phone: 617-776-4475
Buys, sells and specializes in Chinese and Japanese cloisonne and other enamels; wants pre-1930 (and preferably pre-1898) "smalls" such as boxes, multi-piece sets, vases, bowls; minor flaws acceptable, but no pieces with major damage.

SOAP BOX DERBY

(see also GO-KARTS)

Collectors

Carole Lundy
3 Long Lane
Hummelstown, PA 17036-9545
phone: 717-566-6016
Wants to buy Soap Box Derby memorabilia: pictures, program books, instructions, parts, trophies, etc.

SOCIAL CAUSES

(see also BLACK MEMORABILIA; IMMIGRATION; INDUSTRY RELATED ITEMS; KU KLUX KLAN COLLECTIBLES; MINING RELATED ITEMS; POLITICAL COLLECTIBLES; POLITICALLY INCORRECT COLLECTIBLES; POPULAR CULTURE; PROHIBITION ITEMS; SLAVERY ITEMS; VIETNAM)

Auction Services

Dick Oestreicher
P.O. Box 407
Dallas, NC 28034
Conducts mail/phone auctions of American social history and social movements: Blacks, Women, Ethnics, Labor, Left, Anti-War, 1960s, Social Movements.

Collectors

Dick Oestreicher
P.O. Box 407
Dallas, NC 28034
Wants items relating to history and social movements: Blacks, Women, Ethnics, Labor, Left, Anti-War, 1960s, Social Movements.

Beatnik

Collectors

Rick Synchef
16 Midway Ave.
Mill Valley, CA 94941-3439
phone: 415-381-4448
Wants 1960s "counterculture" memorabilia: hippie, political, music, drug, etc.: handbills, leaflets, books, etc.; also beatnik material.

Dealers

Skyline Books
P.O. Box T
Forest Knolls, CA 94933-0720
phone: 415-488-9491
e-mail: skylinbk@ix.netcom.com
Internet: http://www.agaa-booknet.com/usa/skyline/
Wants hippie, the Beat generation, '60s counterculture, drugs, student activism, psychedelia; books, pamphlets, posters, handbills, ephemera, etc.

Civil Rights

Collectors

Sylvia Marcotte-Cloutier
Sylvia Charles of Blythe
218 W. Hobsonway
Blythe, CA 92225-1619
phone: 619-922-3456
fax: 619-922-5651
Wants material relating to the Civil Rights movement, assassinations, radical organizations, and Vietnam from 1955 through 1970s: diaries, letters, signed books, documents, photos of sit-ins, marches, riots, demonstrations, NAACP, etc.

Hippie Items

Collectors

Rick Synchef
16 Midway Ave.
Mill Valley, CA 94941-3439
phone: 415-381-4448
Wants 1960s "counterculture" memorabilia: hippie, political, music, drug, etc.: handbills, leaflets, books, etc.; also beatnik material.

Dealers

Skyline Books
P.O. Box T
Forest Knolls, CA 94933-0720
phone: 415-488-9491
e-mail: skylinbk@ix.netcom.com
Internet: http://www.agaa-booknet.com/usa/skyline/
Wants hippie, the Beat generation, '60s counterculture, drugs, student activism, psychedelia; books, pamphlets, posters, handbills, ephemera, etc.

Labor Unions

Clubs/Associations

Michael Black
American Political Items Collectors (APIC) Labor History Chapter
Newsletter: Solidarity Forever!
P.O. Box 407
Dallas, NC 28034
Purpose is to publicize and preserve American labor history and to provide communication among collectors of labor movement memorabilia and ephemera; send SASE for more information.

Collectors

Scott Molloy
550 Usquepaugh Rd.
West Kingston, RI 02892-1924
phone: 401-782-3614
fax: 401-792-2954
Wants labor and left-wing items: badges, ribbons, pins, photos, flyers, books, pamphlets, posters, knick-knacks; wants Knights of Labor, Railroad unions, I.W.W., AFL-CIO, etc.

John Stafford
9131 College Pkwy. #13B-112
Fort Meyers, FL 33919-4827
Wants to buy Labor Union pins.

Joe Doerring
P.O. Box 94444
Des Moines, IA 50394
phone: 515-285-7702
Wants pre-1940 Industrial Workers of the World (IWW) items: pinback buttons, ribbons, paper items, etc.

Pat Kehoe
3455 S. 83rd St.
Milwaukee, WI 53219-3840
phone: 414-541-2538
Wants labor union buttons, ribbon badges, shop signs, especially 1960s and older; topics covering: 8-hour day, labor day, strikes, membership, etc.; famous labor union leaders memorabilia of Jimmy Hoffa, Eugene Debs, John L. Lewis.

Suffrage Items

Clubs/Associations

Ronnie Lapinsky
Woman Suffrage & Political Issues
  Chapter, APIC
7921 Ivymount Terrace
Potomac, MD 2085403721
  *Collectors of items relating to woman
  suffrage.*

Collectors

Andy Avery
P.O. Box 471
Jamaica, VT 05343
phone: 802-874-4207
  *Wants women's suffrage items: pins,
  ribbons, postcards, ceramics, papers,
  pennants, fans, stamps, cards, etc.*

Ken Florey
153 Haverford
Hamden, CT 06517
phone: 203-248-1233

Cary Demont
P.O. Box 16013
Minneapolis, MN 55416-0013
phone: 612-922-1617
  *Wants political pre-1964 buttons,
  pins, flags, ribbons, banners, and the
  unusual; also suffrage, prohibition,
  slavery, and Lindbergh.*

Steve Sobel
5132 Topeka Dr.
Tarzana, CA 91356-3921
phone: 818-705-4063
fax: 818-705-1123
  *Wants woman suffrage/votes for
  women materials: buttons, ribbons,
  posters, etc.*

Maya Lee
1797 N. Arrowhead Ave.
San Bernardino, CA 92405-4111
phone: 909-882-4656
  *Wants to buy Votes for Women,
  suffrage, early feminist items: flags,
  jewelry, posters, sashes, ribbons, pins,
  banners, photos, books, etc.*

John Gearhart
3267 S.E. Hawthorne
Portland, OR 97214
phone: 503-255-8108 or 503-232-4099

SODA FOUNTAIN COL-LECTIBLES

(see also MOLDS, Ice Cream; SOFT
DRINK COLLECTIBLES)

Clubs/Associations

Donald D. Snyder
Ice Screamers, The
Newsletter: Ice Screamer, The
P.O. Box 465
Warrington, PA 18976-0465
phone: 215-343-2676
e-mail: smoothsail@aol.com
  *For anyone who likes ice cream, who
  wants to learn more about the history
  of ice cream or who collects ice
  cream/soda fountain memorabilia.*

Betty Davis, Pres.
National Association of Soda Jerks
Newsletter: Fiz Biz
P.O. Box 115
Omaha, NE 68101-0115
phone: 402-341-6965 or 712-322-8685
  *Dedicated to the preservation of
  nostalgia and of the history related to
  the soda fountain and soda jerks;
  recipes, soda fountain visits, nostalgic
  remembrances, etc.*

Collectors

Beth & Mike Snyder
2415 Opal Rd.
York, PA 17404

Ed Marks
P.O. Box 5387
Lancaster, PA 17601-0387
phone: 717-569-8284
fax: 717-569-0220
  *Wants ice cream ephemera, books,
  pamphlets, dippers, scoops,
  salesman's samples, toys; anything
  relating to ice cream.*

Mary & Gus Brunner
2209 Township Rd.
Quakertown, PA 18951-3344
phone: 610-346-6650
  *Wants to buy ice cream scoops, tip
  trays, and syrup dispensers.*

William A. Shaner, Jr.
403 N. Charlotte St.
Pottstown, PA 19464-5311
phone: 610-326-0165
  *Wants ONLY Burdans Ice Cream
  items such as trays, signs, ads, and
  paper.*

Mort & Bobbe Burness
11406 Nairn Rd.
Silver Spring, MD 20902

Devall & Barbara Sollers
P.O. Box 132
Monkton, MD 21111

Ed Soost
1331 Weverton Rd.
Knoxville, MD 21758
phone: 301-694-7325
  *Wants old, odd and unusual ice cream
  scoops.*

Billy Sprague
3611 Westbrook Ave.
Nashville, TN 37205-2327
phone: 615-292-4559
e-mail: billyscoop@aol.com
  *Wants to buy unusual ice cream
  dippers.*

Rick Humphreys
214 Tuckahoe Cove
Memphis, TN 38117
phone: 901-761-9507
  *Wants to buy unusual ice cream
  dippers and syrup dispensers.*

Coleen Detzel
28 Lacresta Dr.
Florence, KY 41042-9663
phone: 606-282-0456
  Wants c.1940s soda fountain and ice

cream items: dispensers, fountains,
malt mixers, signs, neons, bars, stools,
tables, booths, etc.; also wants diner
items c. 1940s and 1950s including
furniture.

Chris Potts
8104 Fontana
Prairie Village, KS 66208
phone: 913-642-8269
  *Wants to buy unusual ice cream
  scoops.*

Danny & Denise Saleh
1520 Clubview
Tyler, TX 75701
phone: 903-595-6465
  *Wants to buy ice cream scoops
  (dippers).*

Steve Elliott
1600 Tennessee St.
Vallejo, CA 94590
phone: 707-552-8400 or 707-642-1949
fax: 707-552-0881
  Wants to buy old ice cream scoops.

Experts

Harold & Joyce Screen
2804 Munster Rd.
Baltimore, MD 21234-1131
phone: 410-661-6765
e-mail: hscreen@worldnet.att.net
  *Historian wants: "Soda Fountain"
  magazine, fountain equipment &
  industry catalogs, pre-1910 druggist
  journals, interior view photos of soda
  fountains; will try to reply to any
  queries accompanied by a SASE, but
  no free appraisals.*

Wayne Smith
P.O. Box 418
Walkersville, MD 21793-0418
  *Author of "Ice Cream Dippers," an
  illustrated history and collectors
  guide to early ice cream dippers;
  $22.45 from author; send LSASE for
  free brochure entitled "An Introduction to Collecting Ice Cream
  Dippers."*

Allan Mellis
Mr. Ice Cream
1115 W. Montana
Chicago, IL 60614-2220
phone: 773-327-9123
fax: 773-327-9456
e-mail: mellis@enteract.com
  *Wants postcards, pewter molds, ice
  cream trays, and ice cream-related
  watch fobs, magazines, valentines,
  buttons, ice cream and soda fountain
  real photo postcards, trade cards, pre-
  1920 ephemera, and supply catalogs.*

Man./Prod./Dist.

Gene Rees
Gino's Malt Shop Collection
P.O. Box 505
Bridgeville, PA 15017-0505
phone: 412-221-1495
fax: 412-221-1272
e-mail: rosginoa@bellatlantic.net
  Sells 50s and 60s malt shop furniture,

decor and accessories: booths, tables,
chairs, stools, moldings, metal trim,
lighting fixtures, quilted stainless
sheets, counter accessories, etc.

Malt Mixers

Collectors

Ken Rodoni
368 Luella Ave.
Calumet City, IL 60409
phone: 708-862-2667
fax: 708-862-9134
  *Collector wants old malt mixers by
  Hamilton Beach, Arnold, Gilchrist,
  etc.*

SODA POP

(see SOFT DRINK COLLECTIBLES)

SOFT DRINK COLLECTIBLES

(see also BOTTLES; COIN-
OPERATED MACHINES, Vending
Machines; SODA FOUNTAIN
COLLECTIBLES)

Collectors

Alex Caiola
84 Seneca
Emerson, NJ 07630-1243
phone: 201-967-9540
  Wants all types of soda bottles.

Carolyn Hammond
P.O. Box 343
Black Mountain, NC 28711-0343
phone: 704-669-6262
  *Wants to buy soft drink collectibles:
  Pepsi, Coca-Cola, Dr. Pepper, Moxie,
  and Nu-Grape; signs, posters,
  calendars, trays, etc.*

Dealers

Wayne Merritt
5 Hanson Ct.
Greenville, SC 29615-4331
phone: 803-297-3999
fax: 804-297-3999
  *Wants to buy soft drink collectibles:
  Coca-Cola, Pepsi-Cola; bottles, signs,
  calendars, paper items, colored soda
  bottles, displays, posters, etc.; please
  state price and condition in first letter.*

Lois & Ralph Behm
Lois' Collectibles of Antique Market III
413 W. Main St.
Saint Charles, IL 60174-1815
phone: 630-377-5599 or 847-831-5997
  *Buys and sells Coca-Cola and Pepsi
  collectibles.*

Experts

Craig & Donna Stifter
P.O. Box 6514
Naperville, IL 60540-6514
phone: 630-717-7949
  *Wants to buy older Coca-Cola, Pepsi-
  Cola, Dr. Pepper, Orange-Crush, Hire
  Root Beer and other brand soda
  memorabilia; writes columns for
  several antiques periodicals; also*

interested in items pertaining to country (general) stores.

Periodicals

Dan Kwate
Magazine: Club Soda
P.O. Box 489
Troy, ID 83871-0489
phone: 208-835-2306
fax: 208-835-2307
e-mail: dkwate@clubsoda.net
Internet: http://www.clubsoda.net
Articles about all types of soda collectibles: vending machines, signs, bottles, etc.; features include company histories, restoration tips, show and auction reviews, and free classified ads.

7-Up

Collectors

Brian Adamson
6732 Arlington St.
Vancouver
British Col., V5S 3N9 Canada
Wants 7-Up related collectibles: thermometers, calendars, signs, etc.; also wants Pepsi and Orange Crush items.

Gwen Daniel
18 Belleau Lake Ct.
O Fallon, MO 63366-3144
phone: 314-978-3190
e-mail: gdaniel@mail.win.org

Don Fiebiger
1970 Las Lomitas Dr.
Hacienda Heights, CA 91745-4128
phone: 562-693-6484
Serious collector buying all categories of pre-1960 7-Up memorabilia: pencils, tie bars, service pins, matchcovers, ash trays, bottles, calendars, signs, clocks, neons, "Fresh-Up" Freddie dolls, tin cars/ trucks, seltzer bottles, etc.

Applied Color Label Bottles

Clubs/Associations

Rick Sweeney
Painted Soda Bottle Collectors Association
Newsletter: Soda Net
9418 Hilmer Dr.
La Mesa, CA 91942
phone: 619-461-4354
e-mail: ACLsRus@msn.com
Internet: http://
www.collectoronline.com/PSBCA/
PSBCA.html
The only national organization for "painted" (silkscreened) soda bottle collectors.

Experts

Gary Brent Kincade
P.O. Box 7
Horner, WV 26372
phone: 304-842-3773

Thomas Marsh
914 Franklin Ave.
Youngstown, OH 44502
phone: 800-845-7930
Author of "Official Guide to Collecting Applied Color Label Soda Bottles." Applied color label (ACL) bottles (heyday was 1930s-1970s) had silkscreened labels, as opposed to a glued-on paper label or an embossed label.

Victoria Herberta
P.O. Box 8154
Houston, TX 77004-8154
phone: 713-523-0303
Buys and sells painted-labed soda bottles; over 2,000 different applied color label bottles in stock; author of "American Goes Pop."

Periodicals

Soda Mart - Can World
Newsletter: Painted-Label Soda Bottles
192 Ridgecrest Dr.
Goodlettsville, TN 37072
phone: 615-859-5236
fax: 615-859-5238
An annual periodical that focuses on soda bottles having painted, silk-screened or enameled labels.

Coca-Cola

(see also ADVERTISING COL-LECTIBLES, Tin Vienna Art Plates)

Auction Services

Allan Petretti
Nostalgia Publications
21 S. Lake Dr.
Hackensack, NJ 07601
phone: 201-488-4536
Conducts semi-annual mail-bid auctions of Coca-Cola related advertising items; catalogs are $10 for subscription.

Clubs/Associations

Alice Fisher
Cola Clan, The
2084 Continental Drive NE
Atlanta, GA 30345

Coca-Cola Collectors Club
Newsletter: Coca-Cola Collectors News
P.O. Box 49166
Atlanta, GA 30359-1166

Chris Wenzel
Florida West Coast Chapter of the Coca-Cola Collectors Club International
1007 Emerald Dr.
Brandon, FL 33511-6521
phone: 813-685-7242 or 813-875-4332
fax: 813-348-6107
Contact with questions about the club or about Coca-Cola memorabilia.

Collectors

Steve Sands
1315 Washington St.
Weymouth, MA 02189-2333
phone: 617-335-6352
fax: 617-331-2472
e-mail: cckid@tiac.net
Internet: http://www.tiac.net/users/cckid
Collects anything having to do with Coca-Cola.

Marty Weinberger
P.O. Box 50
Willow Grove, PA 19090
phone: 215-659-8434
Wants pre-1940 Coca-Cola items; calendars, trays, cut-outs, festoons, cardboards, etc.

Robb Johnson
1155 Crescent Lake Rd.
Waterford Township, MI 48327
phone: 810-673-2804

Dealers

Dwayne Spark
Nostalgia Plus
8441 Sublaines
Anjou
Quebec H1K 2C1 Canada
phone: 514-352-6892
fax: 514-352-1856
e-mail: dspark@montrealnet.ca
Buys and sells Coca-Cola memorabilia (old and new): cans, bottles, signs, Life ads, phone cards.

John Forrest
Cola Shop, The
137 Cherry St.
Black Mountain, NC 28711
phone: 704-669-4019
Buys and sells Coca-Cola memorabilia; fountain on site.

Dick & Kay Thompson
320 E. Washington St.
Pontiac, IL 61764
phone: 815-842-2586

Experts

Allan Petretti
Nostalgia Publications
21 S. Lake Dr.
Hackensack, NJ 07601
phone: 201-488-4536
Author of "Petretti's Coca-Cola Collectibles Price Guide" - 10th edition, and "Petretti's Soda-Pop Collectibles Price Guide."

Randy S. Schaeffer
611 N. 5th St.
Reading, PA 19601-2201
phone: 610-373-3333 or 610-683-4401
e-mail: schaeffe@kutztown.edu
Advanced collector seeking the old, rare and unusual in Coca-Cola collectibles; also provides expert appraisals and evaluations.

William E. Bateman
611 N. 5th St.
Reading, PA 19601-2201
phone: 610-373-3333 or 610-683-4412
e-mail: bateman@kutztown.edu
Advanced collector seeking the old, rare and unusual in Coca-Cola collectibles; also provides expert appraisals and evaluations.

Bill Ricketts
Nostalgia Store, The
P.O. Box 9605
Asheville, NC 28805-0605
phone: 704-669-2205 or 704-669-2668
fax: 704-669-2205
Buys, sells and trades Coca-Cola memorabilia: trays, signs, posters, calendars, bottles, novelty items, etc.

Richard Mix
P.O. Box 558
Marietta, GA 30061-0558
phone: 404-422-9083
fax: 404-422-5649
e-mail: mixintl@aol.com
Author of "The Mix Guide to Commemorative Coca-Cola Bottles."

Chris Wenzel
1007 Emerald Dr.
Brandon, FL 33511-6521
phone: 813-685-7242 or 813-875-4332
fax: 813-348-6107
Does Coca-Cola research for movie companies.

Thom Thompson
123 Shaw Ave.
Versailles, KY 40383-1157
phone: 606-873-8787 or 606-255-2727
fax: 606-255-2727
Serious collector and researcher of Coca-Cola collectibles since 1970; interested in buying older collectibles including posters, trays, coupons, calendars, knives, openers, fobs, etc.; especially chewing gum items; free appraisals.

Duane Bouliew
Pause That Refreshes Museum & Retail Shoppe, The
328 S. Main St.
Frankenmuth, MI 48734

Craig & Donna Stifter
P.O. Box 6514
Naperville, IL 60540-6514
phone: 630-717-7949
Wants to buy older Coca-Cola, Pepsi-Cola, Dr. Pepper, Orange-Crush, Hire Root Beer and other brand soda memorabilia; writes columns for several antiques periodicals; also interested in items pertaining to country (general) stores.

Man./Prod./Dist.

Coca-Cola Catalog Store
P.O. Box 182264
Chattanooga, TN 37422
Carries a wide assortment of current Coca-Cola material.

Museums/Libraries

Coca-Cola Company Archives
P.O. Drawer 1734
Atlanta, GA 30301
phone: 800-GET-COKE or 404-676-3491
Request information about your Coca-Cola collectibles directly from the Company; will answer questions about ingredients, recycling, products, packaging, promotions, advertising, history, and much, much more.

Philip F. Mooney, Cur.
World of Coca-Cola Pavilion, The
55 Martin Luther King Dr.
Atlanta, GA 30303-3505
phone: 404-676-5151
fax: 404-676-5432
A 45,000 square foot attraction containing high-tech, interactive exhibits and archival materials from the company's 109-yr. history.

Channing Hardy
Schmidt's Coca-Cola Memorabilia Museum
P.O. Box 647
Elizabethtown, KY 42701
phone: 502-737-4000
fax: 502-737-6665
Contains the world's largest private collection of Coca-Cola memorabilia; will buy Coke items from 1890 to 1970, especially unusual paper items, toys, cut-outs, etc.

On-Line Services

Coca-Cola Collectables
4025 Chapman
Sterling Heights, MI 48310
phone: 810-265-3075
e-mail: DaClassic1@aol.com
Internet: http://www.members.aol.com/daclassic1/home1.htm
Internet web site homepage dedicated to providing facts, information and fun for Coke fans and collectors of Coca-Cola memorabilia.

Periodicals

Magazine: Gameroom Magazine
P.O. Box 41
Keyport, NJ 07735-0041
phone: 908-739-1955
fax: 908-739-2834
e-mail: coinop@gameroommagazine.com
A great source of information for the collector and dealer of jukeboxes, pinballs, Coke machines and other gameroom collectibles.

Coca-Cola Machines

(see COIN-OPERATED MACHINES, Vending Machines; SOFT DRINK COLLECTIBLES, Soda Machines)

Dr. Pepper

Clubs/Associations

Charles Brizus
Dr. Pepper 10-2-4 Collector's Club
Newsletter: Lions Roar
3508 Mockingbird
Dallas, TX 75205-2226
phone: 214-528-2110
fax: 214-520-5795
The 10-2-4 club is a national organization of people dedicated to the study of the history and collecting of Dr. Pepper Co. memorabilia.

Collectors

Gwen Daniel
18 Belleau Lake Ct.
O Fallon, MO 63366-3144
phone: 314-978-3190
e-mail: gdaniel@mail.win.org

Ed Royse
P.O. Box 33489
Fort Sill, OK 73752-1258
phone: 405-357-8000
fax: 405-875-2063
e-mail: shared@juno.com
Wants to buy pre-1951 (script logo) Dr. Pepper signs, cardboards, clocks, trays, calendars, promotional material, etc.

Bob Thiele
620 Tinker
Pawhuska, OK 74056-4039
phone: 918-287-3845
Wants early and unusual Dr. Pepper items: celluloid, early paper, tokens, jewelry, pins, pencils, clothing, fountain pens, etc.; also items from founding co. - "Artesian Mfg. & Bottling Co." (AM&B Co.), Waco, TX or other cities.

Wilton A. Lanning, Jr.
6433 Summit Ridge
Waco, TX 76710
phone: 817-776-3130 or 817-772-2434
fax: 817-776-3153
Collector of Dr. Pepper, Circle A and Artesian Mfg. & Bottling memorabilia: bottles, signs, thermometers, advertising, etc.

Experts

Bill Ricketts
Pepper's Deli
P.O. Box 9605
Asheville, NC 28805-0605
phone: 704-669-2205 or 704-669-2668
fax: 704-669-2205
Buy/sell/trade, collects and specializes in pre-1960 Dr. Pepper advertising items; especially interested in old trays, signs, calendars; anything Dr. Pepper; will buy single items, duplicates, collections, or accumulations.

Craig & Donna Stifter
P.O. Box 6514
Naperville, IL 60540-6514
phone: 630-717-7949
Wants to buy older Coca-Cola, Pepsi-Cola, Dr. Pepper, Orange-Crush, Hire Root Beer and other brand soda memorabilia; writes columns for several antiques periodicals; also interested in items pertaining to country (general) stores.

Museums/Libraries

Dr. Pepper Company Historian/Librarian
P.O. Box 225086
Dallas, TX 75265
Request information about your collectibles directly from the Company if they are still in business.

Dr. Pepper Museum and Free Enterprise Institute
Newsletter: Bottlecaps
300 S. 5th St.
Waco, TX 76701-2115
phone: 817-757-1025 or 817-757-2433
fax: 817-757-2221
Internet: http://www.drpeppermuseum.com
The museum focuses on the soft drink industry; gift shop.

Grapette

Clubs/Associations

Van Stueart
Grapette Collectors Club
Newsletter: Grapette Collectors Club Newsletter
2240 Hwy 27 N
Nashville, AR 71852
phone: 870-845-4864
For collectors of Grapette soda collectibles.

Collectors

Van Stueart
2240 Hwy 27 N
Nashville, AR 71852
phone: 870-845-4864
Wants Grapette items: soda fountain glasses, cardboard signs, light-up clocks, tin signs, neon clocks, calendars, flange signs, porcelain signs

Dealer

Don Hunter
16502 Barcelina
Friendswood, TX 77546-3304
phone: 713-482-4098
Buys and sells Grapette items: drinking glasses, poster signs, shirt patches, shirt pins, pencils, clowns, elephants; "Grapette Price Guide" available for $29.95.

Howdy

Collectors

Don Fiebiger
1970 Las Lomitas Dr.
Hacienda Heights, CA 91745-4128
phone: 562-693-6484
Buys early Howdy soda items (note: no connection to "Howdy Doody").

Moxie

Clubs/Associations

Judy Gross
New England Moxie Congress
Newsletter: Nerve Food News
445 Wyoming Ave.
Millburn, NJ 07041-2131
e-mail: Ira_Seskin@bmugbos.org
Internet: http://xensei.com/users/iraseski/moxieNow.html
Provides a clearinghouse for all information and memorabilia relating to Moxie, supports Maine Moxie weekends, promotes the consumption of Moxie; annual meeting of NEMC 2nd weekend in July in Kennebunkport, ME at Trolley Museum.

Collectors

Jan Bacci
82 Wyman Rd.
Braintree, MA 02184-4721
phone: 617-848-1095
Advanced collector interested in rare and early Moxie items for personal collection.

Misc. Services

Frank Anicetti
Kennebec Fruit Company - The Moxie Festival
2 Main St.
Lisbon Falls, ME 04252
phone: 207-353-8173
Each year sponsors a Moxie Festival in Lisbon Falls, ME; offers contemporary Moxie collectibles.

Orange Crush

Experts

Craig & Donna Stifter
P.O. Box 6514
Naperville, IL 60540-6514
phone: 630-717-7949
Wants to buy older Coca-Cola, Pepsi-Cola, Dr. Pepper, Orange-Crush, Hire Root Beer and other brand soda memorabilia; writes columns for several antiques periodicals; also interested in items pertaining to country (general) stores.

Painted-Label Soda Bottles

(see SOFT DRINK COLLECTIBLES, Applied Color Label Bottles)

Pepsi-Cola

Clubs/Associations

Terry Lunt
Ozark Mountain Pepsi Collectors Club
9101 Columbus Ave., S
Bloomington, MN 55420

Bob Stoddard
Pepsi-Cola Collectors Club
Newsletter: Pepsi-Cola Collectors Club
Newsletter
P.O. Box 1275
Covina, CA 91722
phone: 909-593-8750

Collectors

Gwen Daniel
18 Belleau Lake Ct.
O Fallon, MO 63366-3144
phone: 314-978-3190
e-mail: gdaniel@mail.win.org

Dealers

Bill Ricketts
Nostalgia Store, The
P.O. Box 9605
Asheville, NC 28805-0605
phone: 704-669-2205 or 704-669-2668
fax: 704-669-2205
Wants to buy Pepsi-Cola items: advertising, trays, signs, posters, calendars, novelty items, bottles, etc.; please describe and price.

Experts

Bob Stoddard
P.O. Box 1275
Covina, CA 91722
phone: 909-459-3875
Author of "Introduction to Pepsi Collecting."

Museums/Libraries

Pepsi-Cola Company Archives
Anderson Hill Rd.
Purchase, NY 10577
Request information about your collectibles directly from the Company if they are still in business.

Root Beer

Collectors

Bob Averill
1942 W. Market St.
Pottsville, PA 17901-2043
phone: 800-637-6484 or 717-628-3084
Wants root beer advertising items: tin, porcelain or cardboard signs, dispensers, mugs, bottles, trade cards, postcards, or anything root beer.

Experts

Tom Morrison
2930 Squaw Valley Dr.
Colorado Springs, CO 80918-1826
phone: 719-598-1754
Interested in anything that says "Root Beer." Author of "Root Beer Advertising and Collectibles," (Schiffer Publishing, 1992) an all-color price guide

Root Beer (Hires)

Collectors

Steve Sourapas
1212 9th Ave. West #2
Seattle, WA 98119-3445
phone: 206-282-9922
Advanced collector seeks pre-1930 good to mint condition items.

Experts

Craig & Donna Stifter
P.O. Box 6514
Naperville, IL 60540-6514
phone: 630-717-7949
Wants to buy older Coca-Cola, Pepsi-Cola, Dr. Pepper, Orange-Crush, Hire Root Beer and other brand soda memorabilia; writes columns for several antiques periodicals; also interested in items pertaining to country (general) stores.

Smile

Collectors

Michael Urban
2029 N. Mitchell St.
Phoenix, AZ 85006-2126
phone: 602-252-8615
Buys early SMILE soda items.

Soda Machines

(see also COIN-OPERATED MACHINES, Vending Machines)

Collectors

Richard O. Gates
P.O. Box 187
Chesterfield, VA 23832-0187
phone: 804-748-0382 or 804-794-5146
fax: 804-748-6349
Wants coin-operated machines including Coca-Cola, Pepsi, Dr. Pepper, R.C., etc. machines, light-ups, advertising items and literature related to any of the above.

Dealers

Remember When Collectibles
6570 Memorial Dr.
Stone Mountain, GA 30083
phone: 404-879-7878
Specializing in vintage Coca-Cola machines and jukeboxes.

Bill Mock
2640 SW 29th Way
Fort Lauderdale, FL 33312
phone: 305-584-8958
Buys, sells, restores Coca-Cola vending machines.

Periodicals

Dan Kwate
Magazine: Club Soda
P.O. Box 489
Troy, ID 83871-0489
phone: 208-835-2306
fax: 208-835-2307
e-mail: dkwate@clubsoda.net
Internet: http://www.clubsoda.net
Articles about all types of soda collectibles: vending machines, signs, bottles, etc.; features include company histories, restoration tips, show and auction reviews, and free classified ads.

Repair Services

Kevin Gilreath
141 Ridgewood Terrace
Ringgold, GA 30736
phone: 706-937-5096
Collector and seller; buys, sells and restores pre-1960s soda machines (Coke, Pepsi, etc.); ground-up restorations; also gas pumps, barber chairs and old metal picnic coolers.

Hobbs Country Store
P.O. Box 158
Galveston, IN 46932
phone: 219-699-7505
Custom restorer of only Coca-Cola vending machines.

Home Arcade Corp.
1108 Front St.
Lisle, IL 60532
phone: 630-964-2555
fax: 630-964-9367
Sells restored vintage Coke machines; also juke boxes, phone booths, beer signs, tavern items, barber poles and other '50s memorabilia; send $2 for Coke Restoration Parts Catalog.

Suppliers

Fun-Tronics
P.O. Box 448
Middletown, MD 21769
Specializing in restoration supplies 'for vintage Coke machines.

Jeff Walters
Memory Lane Sodaware
P.O. Box 506
Camino, CA 95709
phone: 916-644-1924
Sells restoration parts for classic soda machines: rubber, decals, locks; $4 for catalog.

Soft Drink Cans

Clubs/Associations

Tom Kirschbaum
National Pop Can Collectors
Newsletter: Can-O-Gram
P.O. Box 7862
Rockford, IL 61125
phone: 815-227-5315
e-mail: Cokecans@aol.com
Worldwide network of collectors focusing on soda cans & bottles as well as other soda memorabilia;

articles, free ads and roster; regional trade sessions so members can meet and trade in person; club roster provided to each member.

Collectors

Rich Simmons
1211 Travis View Ct.
Gaithersburg, MD 20879
phone: 301-417-7129
fax: 301-601-9322
e-mail: Cokecans@aol.com

Museums/Libraries

Museum of Beverage Containers & Advertising, The
192 Ridgecrest Dr.
Goodlettsville, TN 37072
phone: 615-859-5236
fax: 615-859-5238
The largest collection of soda and beer cans in the world; buy, sell, trade beer & soda advertising items.

Squirt

Collectors

Jan Vonburg
3749 E. Gill Dr.
Denver, CO 80209-3510
phone: 303-777-9388
Wants Squirt picnic coolers, soda machines, clocks, decals, 6 pack holders, etc.

Vernons

Collectors

Keith Wunderlich
P.O. Box 300572
Drayton Plains, MI 48330
phone: 810-674-6311
Avid collector of Vernons soft drink items.

SOLDIERS
Toy

(see also TOYS; TOYS, Playsets)

Auction Services

Glenn Butler
Wallis & Wallis
West Street Auction Galleries
Lewes
East Sussex BN7 2NJ, U.K.
phone: 01273-480208
fax: 01273-476562
Britain's specialist auctioneers of diecast & tin plate toys & models including model soldiers.

Henry Kurtz
Henry Kurtz Ltd.
163 Amsterdam Ave., Ste. 136
New York, NY 10023
phone: 212-642-5904
fax: 212-874-6018
Specializes in the sale of jewelry, paintings, prints, silver, coins, stamps, toys (especially lead soldiers), and movie memorabilia.

Clubs/Associations

Arley Pett, Past-Pres.
North East Toy Soldier Society
Newsletter: North East Toy Soldier
  Society Newsletter
12 Beach Rd.
Gloucester, MA 09130-3214
phone: 508-283-2612
e-mail: apett92117@aol.com
  *Monthly meetings usually in the
  Boston area; sponsors two toy soldier
  sales/shows in Boston area each year.*

Miniature Figure Collectors of America
Newsletter: Guidon, The
102 St. Paul's Rd.
Ardmore, PA 19003-2811
phone: 610-649-4144
  *Interested in military history,
  miniature figures of military personnel
  in uniform, dioramic scenes, painting,
  casting, conversion of miniature
  figures.*

John Giddings
Toy Soldier Collectors of America
Newsletter: Communique
6924 Stone's Throw Cir. #8202
Saint Petersburg, FL 33710
  *An information center for all toy
  soldier collectors worldwide.*

Military Miniature Society of Illinois
Newsletter: Scabbard, The
P.O. Box 394
Skokie, IL 60077
  *Sponsors an annual exhibition on the
  3rd Saturday in October; features the
  best work from the U.S., Canada and
  Europe.*

Frank G. Frisella
American Model Soldier Society
1390 El Camino Real
San Carlos, CA 94070
phone: 415-591-8289
fax: 415-592-1203

Collectors

Bill Lango
127 74th St.
North Bergen, NJ 07047
phone: 201-861-2979
fax: 201-854-1738
  *Interested in Barclay vehicles, animals
  and soldiers from original and new
  molds.*

Lee Schaffer
504 Hillside Ave.
Rochester, NY 14610
phone: 716-244-6747
  *Wants toy soldiers, farm, zoo, civilian
  figures; especially Barclay, Manoil
  and Britains.*

Peter & Kathy Paul
1673A Town Point Rd.
Cambridge, MD 21613
phone: 410-476-4627
  *Wants old toy soldiers; lead, iron,
  composition, rubber; any quantity.*

David W. Francis
148 King St.
Wadsworth, OH 44281
phone: 330-335-3717
fax: 330-335-3617
e-mail: fphadv@bright.net
  Wants to buy toy soldiers of all types.

Dealers

John A. Rollins
Toy Soldiers
P.O. Box 486
South Wellfleet, MA 02663
phone: 508-349-1715

Arley Pett
Arley L. Pett Antiques
12 Beach Rd.
Gloucester, MA 09130-3214
phone: 508-283-2612
e-mail: apett92117@aol.com
  *Buys, sells and appraises toy soldiers
  and civilians, lead farm, zoo, circus,
  hunt, railroad figures, military
  vehicles and related items such as
  miniature gardens.*

Ron Ruddell
London Bridge Collector's Toys, Ltd.
401 Chestnut St.
Emmaus, PA 18049

Allen W. Smith
102 N. Cherry St.
Falls Church, VA 22046-3518
phone: 703-237-2164
  *Wants dimestore toy soldiers: lead,
  rubber, composition, paper; Auburn,
  Marx, Manoil, Barclay, Built-Rite,
  etc.; any number.*

Joseph Saine
Joseph Saine Toy Soldiers
P.O. Box 50506
Toledo, OH 43605-0506
phone: 419-691-0008
  *Buys and sells lead, composition, and
  plastic toy soldiers; any soldier or
  figure; issues periodic listings.*

Barry Carter
Knightstown Antiques Mall
136 W. Carey St.
Knightstown, IN 46148-1111
phone: 765-345-5665
e-mail: carter,b@suno.com
  *Buys, sells and specializes in toy
  soldiers; consultant for AntiqueWeek;
  promoter of the Indiana Toy Soldier
  Show (last Sunday in March.)*

David S. Bennett
Bennett Antiques
15800 26th Ave. N.
Minneapolis, MN 55447-1940
  *Wants American dimestore toy
  soldiers made by Barclay, Manoil,
  Gray Ives, Jones, etc.*

Bob Fisher
Old Toy Soldier Home, The
977 S. Santa Fe #11
Vista, CA 92083-6911
phone: 760-758-5481
fax: 760-758-5481
  Buys and sells toy soldiers: Britains,

*Mignot (old and new), dime store,
composition, new makers, King &
Country, Ducal, AQM, Trophy,
Imperial; has over 20,000 figures on
display.*

Experts

Chris Keller
219 Ridge Rd.
Carlisle, PA 17013-9275
phone: 717-258-3573 or 814-867-5434
e-mail: cbk108@psu.edu
  *Buying and selling antique W. Britains
  and dimestore collections; free
  appraisals; 12 years experience.*

K. Warren Mitchell
1008 Forward Pass
Pataskala, OH 43062-7505
phone: 614-927-1661
  *Buys, sells, appraises and specializes
  in all kinds of old toy soldiers
  especially Britains, "dimestore",
  Mignot, Heyde (no plastic toys,
  please.) Author of articles on toy
  soldiers.*

Periodicals

Bill Lango
Vintage Castings Inc.
Magazine: Toy Soldier Review
127 74th St.
North Bergen, NJ 07047
phone: 201-861-2979
fax: 201-854-1738
  *A worldwide quarterly magazine for
  the toy soldier enthusiast.*

Paul Stadinger
STAD'S
Magazine: Plastic Warrior
815 North 12th St.
Allentown, PA 18102
phone: 610-770-1140 or 610-433-7728
fax: 610-770-1043
  *A British bi-monthly focusing on
  leading European plastic figures,
  firms (Britains, Timpo, etc.), reviews,
  Q&A, letters, news, ads, etc.*

Linda Kellbach
Antique Trader Publications, Inc.
Newspaper: Military Trader
P.O. Box 1050
Dubuque, IA 52004-1050
phone: 800-334-7165 or 800-482-4155
fax: 800-531-0880
e-mail: 76143.72@compuserve.com
Internet: http://www.csmonline.com
  *Monthly publication focusing on
  military collectibles: articles,
  collecting, interviews with dealers,
  military toy column, book reviews,
  collectibles for sale, espionage.*

Jo & Steve Sommers
OTSN, Inc.
Magazine: Old Toy Soldier
209 North Lombard
Oak Park, IL 60302
phone: 708-383-6525
fax: 708-383-2182
Internet: http://www.pcguild.com/
  toysoldier
  A quarterly publication.

Erika Daileda
Wise Owl Worldwide Publications
Magazine: Military Modelling
4314 West 238th St. - Dept. MACR
Torrance, CA 90505-4509
phone: 310-375-6258
fax: 310-375-0548
e-mail: wiseowl@sprintmail.com
  *A monthly English publication; for
  modelers, enthusiasts and historians.*

SOUTH PACIFIC

(see ART, Oceanic; POLYNESIAN
COLLECTIBLES)

SOUVENIR & COMMEMORATIVE ITEMS

(see also CERAMICS, Souvenir &
Commemorative; DISNEY COL-
LECTIBLES, Disneyland Souvenirs;
GLASS, Souvenir & Commemorative;
HISTORICAL AMERICANA;
MILITARIA, Silk Embroideries;
ROYALTY COLLECTIBLES;
SPOONS, Souvenir; STATUE OF
LIBERTY COLL.)

Auction Services

Richard Vogel
Vogels, The
4720 SE Fort King St.
Ocala, FL 34470-1501
phone: 352-694-5776
fax: 352-694-7330
  *Bi-monthly mail order souvenir
  auctions: china, glass, spoons,
  mauchline, paper, World's Fair,
  fraternal.*

Collectors

Randy Selnick
P.O. Box 26
Merrick, NY 11566-0026
phone: 516-223-7528 or 516-868-6985
  *Wants to buy roadside memorabilia:
  mugs, ash trays, etc. from hotels,
  transportation and restaurants.*

David Ringering
Belle Ringer Antiques
1480 Tumalo Dr. SE
Salem, OR 97301
phone: 503-585-8253
  *Wants to buy Rowland & Marsellus
  rolled edge, 10" souvenir/historical
  plates; also any other c. 1890-1935
  pictorial souvenirs with scenes of
  cities, towns, etc.; also wants German
  metal tumblers with American/
  Canadian scenes.*

Periodicals

Gary Leveille
Newsletter: Antique Souvenir Collector
P.O. Box 562
Great Barrington, MA 01230-0562
phone: 413-528-5490
  *The nationwide marketplace for
  antique souvenirs of all kinds:
  souvenir china, spoons, photos, glass,
  postcards - anything souvenir.*

Buildings

Clubs/Associations

Dixie Trainer
Souvenir Building Collectors Society
Newsletter: Souvenir Building Collector
P.O. Box 70
Nellysford, VA 22958-0070
phone: 804-325-9159
*Aims to educate and entertain
collectors of miniature replicas
(primarily metal) of well-known
buildings and monuments worldwide;
newsletter published twice a year.*

Collectors

Barry D. Hoffman
393 Commonwealth Ave.
Boston, MA 02115
phone: 617-267-9000 or 617-326-3333
fax: 617-266-6666
*Wants to buy metal souvenir
buildings, all types: paperweight,
bank, inkwells, etc.; wants anything
that looks like a recognizable building
model; free appraisals.*

Bill Trainer
P.O. Box 70
Nellysford, VA 22958-0070
phone: 804-325-9159
*Wants to buy three-dimensional, metal
replicas of famous buildings and
monuments.*

Michael Hiscano
510 NW 86th Pl. #201
Miami, FL 33126
*Wants to buy souvenir miniature metal
buildings.*

Mark Dittenbir
641 S. Shore Dr.
Kalamazoo, MI 49002
phone: 616-327-4227
*Wants to buy metal replicas of
landmark skyscrapers, cathedrals,
bank buildings, etc. such as Chrysler
Building, Capitol Records Building.*

Fred Schwartz
RR 1 Box 135
Hull, IL 62343
phone: 217-432-5796 or 217-432-5502
*Wants to buy small metal buildings,
can be banks or paperweights or
anything else.*

Dave Forman
1914 11th St. #3
Santa Monica, CA 90404-4558
phone: 310-396-1272
fax: 310-392-1400
*Wants to buy potmetal souvenir
building replicas of banks, S&Ps, etc.
of famous buildings, landmarks,
monuments, etc.*

Margarete Majua
Ace Architects
332 2nd St.
Oakland, CA 94607
phone: 510-286-2290 or 510-283-3218
fax: 510-452-1175
e-mail: ace@aceland.com
Wants to buy souvenir buildings;

*found in the form of banks, souvenirs,
paperweights, inkwells, salt & pepper
shakers, World's Fair memorabilia,
pencil sharpeners, etc.*

Dealers

Bob Kneisel
1278 Mare Vista Ave.
Pasadena, CA 91104-2951
phone: 818-797-2707
*Buys and sells miniature buildings;
souvenir buildings, banks, monuments,
statues; metal and other materials.*

Man./Prod./Dist.

Dixie Trainer
Souvenir Building Network, The
P.O. Box 70
Nellysford, VA 22958-0070
phone: 804-325-9159
*Makes U.S. and foreign metal
souvenir buildings available via mail
order; also acts as middleman
between manufactures and those
wanting custom-made replicas; write
for list.*

Niagara Falls

Museums/Libraries

Niagara Falls Museum
5651 River Road
Niagara Falls
Ontario L2E 6V8 Canada
phone: 416-356-2151 or 716-285-4898

Summer Resort Items

Collectors

David W. Francis
148 King St.
Wadsworth, OH 44281
phone: 330-335-3717
fax: 330-335-3617
e-mail: fphadv@bright.net
*Wants 1880-1930 summer resort
souvenirs: Atlantic City, Coney Island,
Cedar Point, etc. - post cards,
booklets, pennants, tickets, etc.*

Tablecloths

Collectors

Chloe Ross
7553 Norton Ave. Apt. 4
Los Angeles, CA 90046-5500
phone: 213-874-3044
*Wants tablecloths with maps, graphics
or states, amusement parks, locations;
may be worn and some stains OK; no
AK or CA; especially wants east coast,
Midwest, New England or FL; buy or
trade.*

Universal Theatres

Collectors

Edwin Snyder
P.O. Box 156
Lancaster, KY 40444-0156
phone: 606-792-4816
Wants to buy penny toys, pocket

*mirrors, dexterity games, compasses,
small portrait plaques, mini books,
etc. given away to children attending
movies in the 1920s and 1930s; all
toys marked "Souvenir of Universal
Theatres - Chicago".*

SOVIET

(see RUSSIAN ITEMS)

SPACE COLLECTIBLES

(see also ASTRONOMICAL ITEMS;
AUTOGRAPHS, Astronaut; BOOKS,
Reference [Space Collectibles];
CHARACTER COLLECTIBLES;
PREMIUMS; ROCKETS; SCIENCE
FICTION; TELEVISION SHOWS &
MEMORABILIA; TOYS, Space &
Robot)

Auction Services

I. Michael Orenstein
Superior Stamp & Coin
9478 West Olympic Blvd.
Beverly Hills, CA 90212-4299
phone: 310-203-9855
fax: 310-203-0496
*Conducts specialty auctions for stamp
collections, other philatelic material,
and space memorabilia.*

Book Sellers

Lee & Peggy Price
Knollwood Books
P.O. Box 197
Oregon, WI 53575-0197
phone: 608-835-8861
fax: 608-835-8421
e-mail: books@tdsnet.com
*Issues quarterly catalogs; buys and
sells out-of-print books on astronomy,
meteorology, and space exploration;
also books about microscopes, old
scientific instruments, optics, and
related areas.*

Clubs/Associations

David Brandt
National Space Society
Magazine: Ad Astra
600 Pennsylvania Ave. SE, Ste. 201
Washington, DC 20003-4316
phone: 202-543-1900 or 800-543-1280
fax: 202-546-4189
e-mail: nsshq@nss.org
Internet: http://www.global.org/bfreed/
nss/nss-home.html
*International organization promoting
space development; 80 local and
international chapters; holds annual
Space Development Conference and
regional conferences.*

International Space Hall of Fame
The Space Center
P.O. Box 533
Alamogordo, NM 88310
phone: 505-437-2840

Collectors

Michael Mitchell
RR 1, Box 4440
Kents Hill, ME 04349
phone: 207-897-6855
*Collects space related memorabilia:
newspapers headlining space
missions, photographs, books; non-
flown items.*

Harvey & Sandy Dolin
Harvey Dolin & Co.
5 Beekman St.
New York, NY 10038-2206
phone: 212-267-0216
*Wants to buy items relating to the
space programs.*

Larry McLaughlin
17 Seventh Ave.
Smithtown, NY 11787-4508
phone: 516-265-9224
*Wants space items from Apollo,
Mercury, or Gemini; also wants NASA
logos.*

Mike Smithwick
25215 La Loma Dr.
Los Altos, CA 94022
phone: 408-244-8987

Dennis Kelly
P.O. Box 9942
Spokane, WA 99209
phone: 509-456-8488
e-mail: dennis@on-ramp.ior.com
*Wants items from space programs
Apollo, Mercury, Gemini; also
anything with NASA logo or serial
numbers, autographs, X15, X20, high
altitude equipment, helmets,
miscellaneous gear.*

Dealers

Gregg Linebaugh
AVD Services
P.O. Box 604
Glenn Dale, MD 20769
phone: 301-249-3895
*Buys and sells artifacts that have
flown in space and to the moon;
actual space craft hardware, space
suits, videos, books, patches,
medallions, flags, and other unusual
items; sponsors two Space Memorabilia shows each year.*

Ricky Lanclos
323 Ave. E
Nederland, TX 77627-2524
phone: 409-757-1829 or 409-724-1307
fax: 409-757-3350
e-mail: rlanclos@exp.net

Experts

Stuart Schneider
P.O. Box 64
Teaneck, NJ 07666-0064
phone: 201-261-1983
*Items flown in space, toys, toy ray
guns, Russian items, Sputnik, Welcome
Back astronaut buttons, coin banks,
artwork, etc.; author of "Collecting
the Space Race" (1993).*

Tom N. Tumbusch
Tomart Publications
3300 Encrete Lane
Dayton, OH 45439-1944
phone: 513-294-2250
fax: 513-294-1024
*Aliens, Flash Gordon, Empire Strikes
Back, Star Wars, Star Trek, Captain
Video; action figures, comic books,
and all related memorabilia; author of
"Space Adventure Collectibles"; only
inquiries accompanied by a SASE will
be answered.*

Museums/Libraries

Jim Johnson
c/o Alabama Space & Rocket Center
One Tranquility Base
Huntsville, AL 35805

International Space Hall of Fame, The
  Space Center
Magazine: SpaceLog
P.O. Box 533
Alamogordo, NM 88310-0533
phone: 505-437-2840 or 800-545-4021
fax: 505-437-7722
e-mail: http://abcc.nmsu.edu/~bwood/
*The ISHF is a four-story museum
which chronicles the history of man's
exploration of space; from earliest
rockets to space shuttle.*

Apollo XI Memorabilia

Collectors

Ronald Ulrich
114 East Benton
Mt. Olive, IL 62069
*Wants Apollo XI (first moon landing)
items; plates, cups, dishes, coins,
books, glasses, etc.*

SPAM

(see ADVERTISING COL-
LECTIBLES, Hormel)

SPECTACLES

(see EYE RELATED ITEMS,
Eyeglasses; OPTICAL ITEMS)

SPIES

(see CHARACTER COLLECTIBLES,
Spy Memorabilia; SPY EQUIPMENT;
TELEVISION SHOWS & MEMORA-
BILIA, Private Eye)

SPINNING WHEELS

Museums/Libraries

Museum of American Textile History
491 Dutton St.
Lowell, MA 01854
phone: 508-441-0400
fax: 508-441-1412
*Outstanding collection of textiles and
textile making machinery and
equipment; tools, machines, prints,
photographs, business records,
industry periodicals, textiles,*

swatches, sample books, trade
catalogs, etc.

Barbara Muret
Oklahoma's Yarn Spinning Museum
117 W. 7th Ave.
Stillwater, OK 74074
phone: 405-377-7195
e-mail: muret@cowboy.net
Internet: http://www.cowboy.net/~muret
*Send 52 cent LSASE for free color
photograph brochure of replicas to
help you identify your wheel and its
missing parts; or you can order
antique replicas in working order.*

Periodicals

Florence Feldman-Wood
Newsletter: Spinning Wheel Sleuth, The
P.O. Box 422
Andover, MA 01810-0008
phone: 508-475-8790
e-mail: fwood@mvlc.lib.ma.us
*A quarterly newsletter exploring all
aspects of spinning wheels; feature
articles include types of wheels,
American and European, histories of
wheels, biographies of wheel makers,
and much more; for hand spinners,
collectors, and museums.*

Repair Services

Bill Ralph
RD 1 Box 141A
Rome, PA 18837-9754
phone: 717-247-7175
e-mail: wralph@epix.net
*Restores antique wheels and looms;
over 30 years experience; over 500
spinning wheels restored; uses old-
time methods and tools.*

Mick Holloway
P.O. Box 453
Winchester, IN 47394-0453
phone: 765-584-1971
*Complete restoration of flax wheels
and wool wheels; minors' heads and
flyers repaired; distaffs turned and
dressed with flax fiber; all parts
custom fit; 22 years experience.*

Repro. Sources

Log Cabin Shop
P.O. Box 275
Lodi, OH 44254

Suppliers

Barbara Muret
Fleece & Unicorn
Seventh Avenue Center
123 West 7th Ave.
Stillwater, OK 74074-4665
phone: 405-377-7105
*Designer of yarn and fibers;
international services, exceptional
selections of doll hair and craft yarns.*

Miniature

Collectors

Lanelle Hodnett
2965 Avenue Z
Brooklyn, NY 11235-1658
phone: 718-891-3489
*Wants to buy miniature spinning
wheels and motifs.*

SPIRITUALISM

(see UFO'S & UNEXPLAINED
PHENOMENA)

SPOON WARMERS

Dealers

Vivian & James Karsnitz
1428 Jerry Lane
Manheim, PA 17545-9353
phone: 717-665-4202
Buying and selling spoon warmers.

SPOONS

(see also KITCHEN COL-
LECTIBLES; SILVER; SOUVENIR
& COMMEMORATIVE ITEMS;
SPOON WARMERS)

Clubs/Associations

Terry & Mary Haines
Silver Spoon Club of Great Britain, The
Journal: Finial, The
Glenleigh Park
St. Austell
Cornwall PL26 7JD, U.K.
phone: 01726-65269
fax: 01726-65269
*International postal club for
experienced or beginner collectors of
antique and other fine silver spoons
and associated silver cutlery;
worldwide membership; "The Finial"
contains specialist articles and
member's news and views; auctions.*

Connoisseur Spoon Collectors' Club
P.O. Box 420157
Wilmington, NC 28406

Souvenir

(see also SOUVENIR & COMMEMO-
RATIVE ITEMS)

Auction Services

Richard Vogel
Vogels, The
4720 SE Fort King St.
Ocala, FL 34470-1501
phone: 352-694-5776
fax: 352-694-7330
*Bi-monthly mail order souvenir
auctions: china, glass, spoons,
mauchline, paper, World's Fair,
fraternal.*

Clubs/Associations

Margaret Alves
Scoop Club, The
Journal: Spoony Scoop Newsletter
84 Oak Ave.
Shelton, CT 06484-3052
phone: 203-924-4768
*A club for collectors of souvenir
spoons; bi-monthly newsletter offers
research material on silver spoons,
identification, ads, values, etc.*

Erwin Goldman, PR
Northeastern Spoon Collectors Guild
Newsletter: Cauldron, The
8200 Boulevard East
North Bergen, NJ 07047-6039
phone: 201-662-1342
fax: 201-662-1342
*NSCG is dedicated to the perpetuation
of the spoon collecting hobby.*

Bill Boyd
American Spoon Collectors
Newsletter: Spooners Forum
7408 Englewood Lane
Kansas City, MO 64133-6913
phone: 816-356-7423
fax: 816-356-7423

Mary Bengston
Dallas Souvenir Spoon Collectors Club
9748 Broken Bow Rd.
Dallas, TX 75238

Diane Zinn
Southern California Souvenir Spoon
  Collectors Club
525 Cortez Rd.
Arcadia, CA 91007
phone: 818-446-1443

Bob Corson
Seattle Souvenir Spoon Collectors Club
2387 S. East Camano Dr.
Stanwood, WA 98292

Collectors

Erwin & Dorothy Goldman
8200 Boulevard East
North Bergen, NJ 07047-6039
phone: 201-662-1342
fax: 201-662-1342

W.T. Atkinson
P.O. Box 10402
Wilmington, NC 28405-3792

Chris McGlothlin
780 Rock Springs Rd.
Kingsport, TN 37664

John W. Coons
9757 S. Isabel Ct.
Littleton, CO 80126
phone: 303-791-6496
*Wants souvenir spoons: enamel bowls,
blacks, mining, hotels, libraries,
skylines, etc.*

Dealers

T.K. Treadwell
4201 Nagle Rd.
Bryan, TX 77801-3938
phone: 409-846-0209
e-mail: 71222.1571@compuserve.com

Gary Lickver
P.O. Box 1778
San Marcos, CA 92079
phone: 760-761-0868
*Wants to buy sterling silver souvenir
spoons 1890-1930; especially full
bowl enamels, American and
European.*

Experts

Bill Boyd
7408 Englewood Lane
Kansas City, MO 64133-6913
phone: 816-356-7423
fax: 816-356-7423
*Wants souvenir spoons with
embossed, enameled or engraved
handles and bowls; also World's Fair
subjects, full-figured people, etc.*

SPORTING COLLECTIBLES

(see also ANIMAL TROPHIES; ART,
Sporting; ART, Wildlife; CAMPING
EQUIPMENT; DECOYS; ENDAN-
GERED SPECIES; FIREARMS;
FISHING COLLECTIBLES;
FURNITURE [ANTIQUE], Rustic;
LICENSES, Hunting & Fishing;
TARGET SHOOTING MEMORA-
BILIA; TICKETS; TRAP SHOOT-
ING; TRAPS

Auction Services

Gerard Giguere
Giguere Auction Co.
P.O. Box 1272
Windham, ME 04062
phone: 207-892-3800
fax: 207-892-3800
*Conducts sporting auctions: fishing,
hunting, decoys, sporting art,
taxidermy.*

Ronnie Roberts, ISA
Dixie Sporting Collectibles
1206 Rama Rd.
Charlotte, NC 28211-4345
phone: 704-364-2900 or 704-364-3382
fax: 704-364-2322
e-mail: gun1898@aol.com
Internet: http://www.sportauction.com

Kurt R. Krueger
Krueger Auctions
160 N. Washington St.
Iola, WI 54945
phone: 715-445-3845
fax: 715-445-4100
*Specializing in the mail-bid auction of
hunting, fishing, shooting, and
trapping memorabilia.*

Book Sellers

David E. Foley
David E. Foley - Sporting Books
76 Bonnyview Rd.
West Hartford, CT 06107
phone: 203-561-0783
*Buys and sells fine sporting books:
angling, hunting, firearms, shooting,
archery, natural history.*

Connecticut River Bookstore
P.O. Box 461
East Haddam, CT 06423
phone: 203-873-8881
*Rare and out of print books and
ephemera on hunting, fishing, natural
history, guns.*

Judith & Jim Bowman
Judith Bowman Books
Pound Ridge Rd.
Bedford, NY 10506
phone: 914-234-7543
*Buys and sells rare and out-of-print
books and ephemera on angling,
hunting, related natural history, guns,
dogs, old tackle and gun catalogs, etc.*

Dean Dashner
Hunting Rig
349 S. Green Bay Rd.
Neenah, WI 54956
phone: 414-725-4421
e-mail: dashners@tcccom.net
Internet: http://www2.tcccom.net/
~dashners
*Buys and sells decoys, duck calls,
Ducks Unlimited Pinbacks, sporting
books, old sporting magazines.*

Wilderness Adventures
P.O. Box 627
Gallatin Gateway, MT 59730
phone: 800-925-3339 or 406-763-4900
e-mail: books@wildadv.com
Internet: http://www.wildadv.com
*World's largest selection of hunting
and fishing books for the collector and
enthusiast.*

Collectors

Bert Lindsay
315 Broad St.
Manchester, CT 06040-4036
phone: 203-649-8473
*Wants to buy sporting antiques and
artifacts from 19th to mid-20th
century; sporting event programs,
tickets, autographs, signed items,
documents, equipment, photographs,
prints, etc.*

Ron Willoughby
Rte. 171 Box 1072
Woodstock, CT 06281-2122
phone: 860-974-1226
fax: 860-974-3190
e-mail: swillo@neca.com
Internet: http://www.neca.com/~swillo
*Wants to buy shotshell boxes, gun
company posters and calendars, glass
target balls and traps, gunpowder
cans, animal traps, and related items;
a very serious buyer.*

Bob Puszcz
RFD Box 94
Great Valley, NY 14741
*Wants any item pertaining to hunting,
fishing, target shooting, gunsmithing,
etc.*

Bill Bramlett
P.O. Box 1105
Florence, SC 29503-1105
phone: 803-393-7390 or 803-665-3165
e-mail: bbramlett@pdn.net
*Wants 1890-1931 firearms-related
advertising items such as calendars,
signs and posters that advertise
firearms, shotgun shells, gunpowders;
also wants Edmund Osthaus and G.
Muss-Arnolt bird dog and duck
hunting art, prints, pictures.*

Tommie Lee Horsley
P.O. Box 728
Jackson, AL 36545
phone: 334-246-5000
e-mail: Lee@Dixienet.com
*Wants duck and turkey calls, hunting
magazines and photographs, hunting
books, Old turkey china such as plates
or platters, old hunting and gun
company advertising, WInchester
fishing items, lures, etc.*

Ron Bash
P.O. Box 888271
Grand Rapids, MI 49588-8271

Lynn Troute "Dr. Duck"
Dr. Duck
3808 Kingsley Dr.
Springfield, IL 62707-7250
phone: 217-787-3595
*Wants to buy duck stamps, duck
decoys, duck calls, licenses, wood
lures, Winchester items, Ducks
Unlimited buttons, and all hunting
and fishing artifacts.*

Bob Simmons
Rte. 1 Box 186
Richmond, MO 64085-9760
phone: 816-776-2936
fax: 816-470-5016
e-mail:
simmons_auction@raycounty.com
Internet: http://www.raycounty.com/
simmons.html
*Collects all types of sporting goods,
fishing tackle and related advertising
from SImmons Hardware Co., St.
Louis, MO; also items from
Winchester-Simmons Hardware Co.,
Diamond Edge (Shapleigh), and Keen
Kutter.*

Bill Smith, Sr.
16608 San Pedro
San Antonio, TX 78232
phone: 800-982-9507
*Wants to buy fishing and hunting
items.*

Dealers

Mary Ann Hahn
Second Hand Mary Ann's
HCR 65 Box 26
Boothbay Harbor, ME 04538-9703
phone: 207-633-2426
fax: 207-633-2426
*Buys and sells old fishing and hunting
magazines prior to 1939.*

Henry Fleckenstein
P.O. Box 577
Cambridge, MD 21613
phone: 410-221-0076
*Buys and sells, sporting collectibles:
decoys, rare books, shell boxes,
powder tins, ammo advertising,
sporting magazines and books, reels,
lures, bobbers, game calls, old
licenses, knives, fish decoys.*

Len Codella
Heritage Sporting Collectibles
2201 S. Carnegie Dr.
Inverness, FL 34450
phone: 352-637-5454
fax: 352-637-5420
*Wants to buy bamboo rods, reels,
tackle, etc.*

Tony Laws
Woods & Water, Inc.
1019 McFarland Blvd.
Northport, AL 35476
phone: 205-333-1214
fax: 205-339-9573
*Buys and sells sporting art: paintings,
prints, drawings, classic firearms,
rods & reels, sporting bronzes, wood
carvings, advertising art, catalogs,
brochures, books.*

Robert Krause
Ravenwood Gallery
38745 Butternut Ridge Rd.
Elyria, OH 44035
phone: 216-458-4929
*Wants to buy paintings, prints,
etchings, calendars, and posters
relating to hunting and fishing, birds,
dogs, guns, ammunition and power
companies; also duck and crow calls,
decoys, sporting books, bamboo fly
rods, rods, reels, etc.*

Dean Dashner
Hunting Rig
349 S. Green Bay Rd.
Neenah, WI 54956
phone: 414-725-4421
e-mail: dashners@tcccom.net
Internet: http://www2.tcccom.net/
~dashners
*Buys and sells decoys, duck calls,
Ducks Unlimited Pinbacks, sporting
books, old sporting magazines.*

Experts

Ralf Coykendall
P.O. Box 29
East Dorset, VT 05253-0029
phone: 802-362-5707
*Writes a sporting collectibles column
for "AntiqueWeek"; will answer
questions if accompanied by a SASE;
author of "Coykendall's Sporting
Collectibles Price Guide" Vol. I, II
and III.*

Vivian & James Karsnitz
Vivian Karsnitz Antiques
1428 Jerry Lane
Manheim, PA 17545-9353
phone: 717-665-4202
*Buys, sells sporting collectibles:
decoys, shotshells, 2-pc. shotshell*

boxes, prints (especially Lynn Bogue
Hunt), early sporting magazines, glass
target balls, etc.; authors of "Sporting
Collectibles" (Schiffer, 1992.)

Periodicals

Ralf Coykendall
Coykendall's Sporting Collectibles
  Newsletter

P.O. Box 29
East Dorset, VT 05253-0029
phone: 802-362-5707

Robert Woollens
R.W. Publishing
Magazine: Sporting Collector's Monthly
P.O. Box 305
Camden Wyoming, DE 19934-0305
phone: 302-678-0113
fax: 302-734-3707
  *A monthly with hundreds of buy, sell
  and trade ads; fish and waterfowl
  decoys, hunting equipment, fishing
  gear, loading tools, wildlife art,
  decorative wildlife & fish carvings,
  and related books, catalogs,
  magazines, etc.*

Julie A. Ulrich, PR
Krause Publications
Magazine: Trapper & Predator Caller,
  The
700 E. State St.
Iola, WI 54990-0001
phone: 715-445-2214
fax: 715-445-4087
e-mail: info@krause.com
Internet: http://www.krause.com
  *A monthly magazine about hunting,
  trapping and predator calling, and
  animal damage control.*

Julie A. Ulrich, PR
Krause Publications
Magazine: Turkey & Turkey Hunting
700 E. State St.
Iola, WI 54990-0001
phone: 715-445-2214
fax: 715-445-4087
e-mail: info@krause.com
Internet: http://www.krause.com
  *For serious, technical, year-round,
  gun and bow turkey hunters; features
  emphasize success and enjoyment of
  the sport; some articles on related
  collectibles.*

Archery

Clubs/Associations

Professional Bowhunters Society
P.O. Box 246
Terrell, NC 28682
phone: 704-664-2534
fax: 704-664-7471

Collectors

Lowell Hobbs
P.O. Box 226
Lynnville, IN 47619-0226
  *Wants pre-1970s bows and archery
  equipment; wood or modern recurves
  and longbows, all metal bows, books*

magazines, catalogs, old photos,
quivers, arrows, accessories.

Leslie Bolyard
787 Westbrooke Dr.
South Lyon, MI 48178-1665
phone: 810-486-3494 or 810-696-6531
  *Wants to buy archery hunting
  memorabilia including wood long
  bows, wood arrows, leather back
  quivers, folk art with animal/hunting
  theme, rustic furniture, and
  accessories.*

Periodicals

Larry Fischer
Magazine: Traditional Bowhunter
P.O. Box 15583
Boise, ID 83715-5583
phone: 208-853-0555
fax: 208-853-9925
e-mail: realbows@aol.com
Internet: http://www.tradbow.com
  *Periodically carries articles and ads
  about bowhunting and periodically
  about vintage hunting equipment.*

Game Calls

Book Sellers

Dean Dashner
Hunting Rig
349 S. Green Bay Rd.
Neenah, WI 54956
phone: 414-725-4421
e-mail: dashners@tcccom.net
Internet: http://www2.tcccom.net/
  ~dashners
  *Buys and sells decoys, duck calls,
  Ducks Unlimited Pinbacks, sporting
  books, old sporting magazines.*

Clubs/Associations

William R. Bailey, Mem.
Callmakers & Collectors Association of
  America
Newsletter: CCAA Newsletter
137 Kingswood Dr.
Clarksville, TN 37043
phone: 615-647-9092
  *Purpose is to promote interest in and
  knowledge of the history of callmaking
  in America; annual meeting, quarterly
  swap meets, trade, buy, sell.*

James C. Fitch
Call & Whistle Collectors Association
Newsletter: Whistle Notes
2839 E. 26th Place
Tulsa, OK 74114-4309
phone: 918-747-3202
e-mail: jchesterf@aol.com
  *Club for collectors of game calls,
  antique whistles, bo's 'n pipes, flutes,
  bird calls, advertising whistles, toy
  whistles, and folk art whistles.*

Collectors

Jim Fleming
518 Heather Place
Nashville, TN 37204
phone: 615-292-1463

Experts

Howard Harlan
Heavy Duty Duck Call Company
303 Murfreesboro Rd.
Nashville, TN 37210-2834
phone: 800-388-2556 or 615-832-0564
fax: 615-244-1553
  *Expert and collector wants to collect
  all types of game calls as well as
  related historical information; author
  of "Duck Calls, An Enduring
  American Folk Art," and "Turkey
  Calls, An Enduring American Folk
  Art."*

Magazines

Collectors

Hy Wood
P.O. Box 1246
Traverse City, MI 49685-1246
phone: 616-271-3898
  *Wants to buy pre-1940 sporting
  magazines such as Field & Stream,
  Outdoor Life, Sports Afield; also
  wants gun magazines and accumulations of gun and fishing tackle
  catalogs.*

Dealers

Lewis & Wilma Razek
Highwood Bookshop
P.O. Box 1246
Traverse City, MI 49684-1246
phone: 616-271-3898
  *Specializes in back issues of outdoor
  magazines on hunting, fishing, guns,
  collecting waterfowl decoys,
  collecting of old fishing tackle.*

SPORTS COLLECTIBLES

(see also ART, Sports; AUTO
RACING MEMORABILIA;
AUTOGRAPHS; CAPS; COL-
LECTIBLES [MODERN], Sports
Related; DOLLS, Bobbing Head; FAN
CLUBS; POSTCARDS; SPORTS
HISTORY; TICKETS; TRADING
CARDS, Non-Sport;
TRAPSHOOTING)

Auction Services

Leland's
36 East 22nd St., 7th Floor
New York, NY 10010
phone: 212-545-0800
fax: 212-545-0713
  Conducts specialty sports auctions.

Christie's East
219 E. 67th St.
New York, NY 10021
phone: 212-606-0400

John D. Compton
J.D. Compton Auctioneering
13833 Rockdale Rd.
Clear Spring, MD 21722
phone: 301-582-0727 or 800-662-8284
fax: 301-582-6114
  *Specializes in the sale of sports
  collectibles; call toll-free in MD 1-
  800-499-3344.*

Tom Slater
Political Gallery, The
5335 N Tacoma Ave., Ste. 24
Indianapolis, IN 46220-3648
phone: 317-257-0863
fax: 317-254-9167

Pat Quinn
Sports Collectors Store
8135 Elizabeth Ave.
Orland Park, IL 60462-1767

Superior Galleries
9478 West Olympic Blvd.
Beverly Hills, CA 90212-4299
phone: 310-203-9855
fax: 310-203-0496

Collectors

Daniel G. Miller, Sr.
P.O. Box 578
Churchville, MD 21028-0578
phone: 410-676-1813
  *Wants to buy Baltimore Oriole
  bobbin' head dolls; also other vintage
  Baltimore/Oriole memorabilia; will
  correspond with other collectors with
  same interests.*

Bob, Ken & Mike Adelson
Adelson Sports
13610 N. Scottsdale
Scottsdale, AZ 85254-4037
phone: 602-596-1913
fax: 602-596-1914
  *Wants to buy sports memorabilia:
  yearbooks, ticket stubs, pennants,
  baseball, football, hockey, basketball,
  boxing; all items from all sports.*

Goodwin Goldfaden
P.O. Box 48677
Bicentennial Station
Los Angeles, CA 90048
phone: 818-986-4914
  *Buy, sell, trade all sports related
  items: baseball, football, basketball,
  boxing, wrestling, billiards, other
  sports; books magazines, programs
  other sports collectibles from 1860 to
  present.*

John Buonaguidi
540 Reeside Ave.
Monterey, CA 93940-1828
phone: 408-655-2363
  *Wants any sports related item:
  baseball cards, World Series
  programs; autographed baseballs and
  photos, boxing posters, advertising,
  etc.; especially interested in museum-
  quality items for soon-to-open sports
  museum.*

Dealers

Paul Longo
Paul Longo Americana
P.O. Box 5510
Gloucester, MA 01930-0007
phone: 508-525-2290
  *Wants baseball and other sports
  memorabilia: sports cards, balls,
  autographs, uniforms, pennants,
  yearbooks, statues, silks, etc.*

Bob Rothschild
5 Fillmore Dr.
Clarksburg, NJ 08510
phone: 609-259-9338

Les Wolff, ISA
P.O. Box 650037
Flushing, NY 11365-0037
phone: 718-454-3956
e-mail: lwolff1823@aol.com
Buys, sells, trades sports memorabilia; specializes in all types of sports auctions fund raisers; specializing in autographs.

Ron Oser
Ron Oser Enterprises
P.O. Box 101
Huntingdon Valley, PA 19006
phone: 215-947-6575
Wants to buy distinctive sports cards and memorabilia: 1880s-1960s baseball cards, early tobacco and gum cards, display advertising pieces, autographed baseballs, written letters, game-used uniforms, balls, gloves, etc.

Richard Kohl
Strike Zone
1840 N. Federal Highway
Boynton Beach, FL 33435
phone: 800-344-9103
fax: 407-364-8765
Internet: http://www.szgallery.com
Wants to buy all types of sports memorabilia: baseball, football, basketball, and hockey cards; bats, balls, and gloves; photographs and autographs; jerseys and ball caps; letters, books and mags; Olympic memorabilia; boxing, etc.

Stephen Hansrote
Griffin Trading Company
13663 Jupiter Rd., Ste. 406
Dallas, TX 75238
phone: 214-341-0660
fax: 214-341-0660
e-mail: griffintc@aol.com
Internet: http://www.members.aol.com/griffintc/website.htm
Buying and selling 19th and 20th century American and European sports equipment, clothing and trophies.

Gary Spoerle
Milestone Collectibles
P.O. Box 607
Troutdale, OR 97060-0607
phone: 503-695-3413
fax: 503-695-5406
Wants to buy baseball, golf, fishing and other sports memorabilia.

Experts

Jerome "MiMi" Alongi
201 North Walnut St.
Du Quoin, IL 62832-1703
phone: 618-542-4133
fax: 618-542-4133
Collector and dealer specializing in the appraisal of baseball cards and sports memorabilia; writes weekly sports column "MiMi's Dugout."

Misc. Services

Steve Bass
Sports Collector's Radio Show
527 Third Ave. #294
New York, NY 10016
phone: 212-573-8100
fax: 212-573-8100
e-mail: sportradio@aol.com
Talk show on New York's WGBB (1240 AM); heard Sunday 12-1 PM and 9-10 PM; explores all aspects of sports collecting; advice and insights from well-known collectors & dealers; cards, autographs - all types of sports memorabilia.

Nationwide Publishing, Co.
P.O. Box 38
Bountiful, UT 84011
Offers listing of names, addresses and phone numbers of traders, buyers and sellers of baseball & other sports cards and memorabilia.

Museums/Libraries

New England Sports Museum
1175 Soldiers Field Rd.
Boston, MA 02134
phone: 617-787-7678

Monterey Bay Sports Museum
833 Lighthouse Ave.
Monterey, CA 93940
phone: 408-655-2363
A time capsule of sports memories: baseball, boxing, football.

Periodicals

Christine Drury
Landmark Specialty Publications, Inc.
Magazine: Tuff Stuff
P.O. Box 1637
Glen Allen, VA 23060
phone: 804-266-0140 or 800-899-8833
fax: 804-264-4205
Internet: http://www.tuffstuffonline.com
The complete monthly sports price guide publication including baseball, football, basketball, auto racing and hockey: 95% sports cards, Kenner's Starting Lineup sports figures, sports autographs.

Julie A. Ulrich, PR
Krause Publications
Newsmagazine: Sports Collectors Digest
700 E. State St.
Iola, WI 54990-0001
phone: 715-445-2214
fax: 715-445-4087
e-mail: info@krause.com
Internet: http://www.krause.com
A weekly newsmagazine for collectors of sports memorabilia; everything from baseball cards to game-worn uniforms.

Julie A. Ulrich, PR
Krause Publications
Newsletter: Trade Fax
700 E. State St.
Iola, WI 54990-0001
phone: 715-445-2214
fax: 715-445-4087
e-mail: info@krause.com
Internet: http://www.krause.com
Published each Monday and Thursday morning; contains breaking hobby news from shows, manufacturers, and other sources; $500 per year.

Beckett Publications, Inc.
Magazine: Beckett Focus on Future Stars
15850 Dallas Parkway
Dallas, TX 75248
phone: 972-991-6657
fax: 972-991-8930
Focuses on minor league and college athletes; includes Minor League baseball card price guide.

Ed Kobak
Global Sports Productions, Ltd.
Directory: Sports Address Bible, The
1223 Broadway, Ste. 102
Santa Monica, CA 90404-2707
phone: 310-454-9480
fax: 310-454-6590
A worldwide reference guide (496 pages) with over 10K listings of sports addresses, phone and fax numbers, and contact person for Leagues, teams, organizations, and publications; major, minor, semi-pro, amateur, international, college.

Baseball

Auction Services

Rob Lifson
Robert Edward Auctions
P.O. Box 1923
Hoboken, NJ 07030
phone: 201-792-9324 or 800-766-9324
Conducts specialty baseball memorabilia auctions: baseball cards, Babe Ruth & Lou Gehrig items, tobacco cards, uncut sheets, buttons, autographs, display pieces, postcards, gum cards, world series items, original artwork, documents, etc.

Clubs/Associations

Society for American Baseball Research
Journal: Baseball Research Journal
P.O. Box 93183
Cleveland, OH 44101-5183
phone: 216-575-0500
fax: 216-575-0502
e-mail: info@sabr.org
Internet: http://www.sabr.org
SABR's objectives are to facilitate and disseminate baseball research information and to establish an accurate historical account of baseball; membership is open to all who have an interest in baseball history.

Collectors

Rob Lifson
P.O. Box 1923
Hoboken, NJ 07030
phone: 201-792-9324 or 800-766-9324
Wants to buy baseball material: cards, buttons, photographs, World Series items, documents, advertising, postcards, tobacco cards, etc.

Ken Felden
2 Hemlock Lane
Marlboro, NJ 07746
phone: 908-536-5974
fax: 908-972-1976
Collector wants to buy baseball related antiques: cards (1880s-1930s), advertising, fans, pins, tins, scorecards and programs, photos, tickets (1860-1920), games, sheet music, early trophies and statuary, posters, etc.

Robert E. Schmierer
EPSCC
P.O. Box 3037
Maple Glen, PA 19002

Brian Gettings
8331 Queen Elizabeth Blvd.
Annandale, VA 22003

Bill Simmons
8955 NW 19th St.
Coral Springs, FL 33071-6109
phone: 954-340-0734
Wants to buy baseball memorabilia: anything autographed including balls, bats, and gloves; old photos, postcards, cards, programs, statues, movie stuff, pens, lighters, etc.

Dan Busby
P.O. Box 50188
Indianapolis, IN 46250
phone: 317-674-3301
fax: 317-674-3302
Wants to buy post-season baseball tickets and baseball press pins.

William Mastro
12410 Ridge Rd.
Palos Park, IL 60464
phone: 708-361-2117
Advanced collector wants baseball cards and baseball memorabilia: advertising displays, pinback buttons, player uniforms, original early photos, programs, yearbooks, bats, autographs, games, early books, sheet music, etc.

John Sullivan
3748 N. Damen
Chicago, IL 60618

Mel Bailey
5520 Intervale Dr.
Riverside, CA 92506-3612

Dealers

Jerry Smolin
P.O. Box 2234
Amherst, MA 01004
Buys and sells baseball memorabilia;

specializes in media guides and other baseball publications.

David Hall
Hall's Nostalgia
21-25 Mystic St.
P.O. Box 408
Arlington, MA 02174
phone: 800-367-4255 or 617-646-7757
Buys and sells all major sport collectibles (sport cards, publications, autographs, etc.); oldest sports store on the East Coast; opened in 1976; appraises sports memorabilia.

Jeffrey Miller
1665 Cavan Dr.
Dresher, PA 19025-1209
Buys and sells baseball memorabilia; specializes in media guides and other baseball publications.

Tom & Jill Kaczor
1550 Franklin Rd.
Langhorne, PA 19047
phone: 215-968-5776 or 215-946-6044
fax: 215-946-6056
Serious collectors who want all sorts of baseball memorabilia: early bats, gloves, photos, board games, fans, sheet music, advertising pieces with players in them, stadium artifacts, score cards, programs, signed balls, trophies, etc.

Bob McCann
108 Village Green Dr.
Gilbertsville, PA 19525
phone: 610-367-1827
Wants to buy quality Baseball memorabilia.

Joe Bosley
Old Ball Game, The
100 Old Westminster Pike
Reisterstown, MD 21156

Pat Quinn
Sports Collectors Store
8135 Elizabeth Ave.
Orland Park, IL 60462-1767

Experts

Ron Menchine
P.O. Box 1
Long Green, MD 21092
phone: 410-592-7152
Buys, sells, collects and specializes in baseball team and player memorabilia: advertising specialties (e.g. team photos by sponsors), ball park giveaways, pins, badges, programs, scorecards, postcards, team histories; no equipment.

Phil Wood
P.O. Box 204
Reisterstown, MD 21136-0204
phone: 410-833-WOOD
Editor of "Diamond Duds," a bi-monthly newsletter on game-used major league baseball uniforms; monthly memorabilia columnist in "Tuff Stuff" magazine.

Dennis Goldstein
516 Manford Rd. SW
Atlanta, GA 30310-4428
phone: 404-758-4743 or 404-763-2014
fax: 404-761-6353
Baseball historian looking for early photographs, books, programs, memorabilia.

Museums/Libraries

National Baseball Hall of Fame & Museum, Inc.
25 Main Street
Cooperstown, NY 13326
phone: 607-547-7200
fax: 607-547-2044
Internet: http://www.enews.com/ bas_hall_fame

Periodicals

Rick Toms, Editor
Baseball Cards Unlimited
Newsletter: Your Season Ticket
106 Liberty Rd.
Woodsboro, MD 21798
phone: 301-845-6076
Focuses on local MD, VA, DE, PA baseball card shows and auctions; also contains short articles, ads, tips, etc.

Chuck Hershberger
Newspaper: Old Tyme Baseball News
P.O. Box 833
Petroskey, MI 49770
phone: 616-348-3982
32+ page newspaper published bi-monthly since 1988; contains feature articles and great photos of baseball's glory years.

Julie A. Ulrich, PR
Krause Publications
Magazine: Fantasy Baseball
700 E. State St.
Iola, WI 54990-0001
phone: 715-445-2214
fax: 715-445-4087
e-mail: info@krause.com
Internet: http://www.krause.com
Complete guide to fantasy baseball league; every major league player ranked from scrub to star; hottest hobby with more than 1M players.

Frank Barning
Newspaper: Baseball Hobby News
4540 Kearny Villa Rd.
San Diego, CA 92123
phone: 619-565-2848
fax: 619-565-6608
Monthly magazine published since 1979 for collectors of sports memorabilia with an emphasis on baseball; includes price guide.

J.G. Floto, Pub.
Magazine: Diamond Angle, The
P.O. Box 409
Kaunakakai, HI 96748
phone: 808-558-8366
A journal feature articles, book reviews, trivia, lore, monthly card

columns; sells cards plus has nationwide dealer ads.

Baseball (Books)

Collectors

R. Plapinger
P.O. Box 1062
Ashland, OR 97520-0063
phone: 541-488-1220
Wants any book about baseball: non-fiction, fiction, adult, juvenile, especially turn-of-the-century; send SASE for list of most wanted.

Dealers

Andy Moursund
Georgetown Book Shop
77770 Woodmont Ave.
Bethesda, MD 20814
phone: 301-907-6923
Specializes in baseball team history books.

Paul Haas
Sports Books, Etc.
5224 Port Royal Rd.
Springfield, VA 22151-2102
phone: 703-321-8660
fax: 703-321-9743
Specializes in new sports books, especially baseball.

R. Plapinger
R. Plapinger Baseball Books
P.O. Box 1062
Ashland, OR 97520-0063
phone: 541-488-1220
Specializes in catalog sales of baseball team history books.

Baseball (Washington Senators)

Clubs/Associations

Richard Bruce
Washington Senators Baseball Association
Newsletter: Save the Senators
11417 St. Rd. 535
Orlando, FL 32836
phone: 407-239-4482
Specializes in preservation of Washington Senators baseball club memorabilia, research and preservation ti include specialty in autographs.

Collectors

Richard Bruce
11417 St. Rd. 535
Orlando, FL 32836
phone: 407-239-4482
Buys, sells, collects and specializes in memorabilia relating to the Washington Senators baseball team.

Baseball Cards

Collectors

Marc L. Ames
539 Lyme Rock Rd.
Bridgewater, NJ 08807-1670
phone: 908-526-7676
fax: 908-575-0880
e-mail: magames@ix.netcom.com
Wants to buy all pre-1965 baseball cards; also wants any autographed cards to date.

Don Poppe
229 Sixth St.
Whitehall, PA 18052

Chuck Moore
P.O. Box 280
Gladstone, OR 97027
phone: 503-654-9994
fax: 503-656-7603
Wants baseball cards, publications, memorabilia; also older football and basketball memorabilia.

Dealers

Larry Fritsch
Larry Fritsch Cards, Inc.
P.O. Box 863
Stevens Point, WI 54481
phone: 715-344-8687
Over 55 million cards in stock; buys and sells.

Pat Yeary
Pat & Larry's Baseball Cards
3708 W. Pioneer Parkway
Arlington, TX 76013-2901
phone: 817-265-0006
Buy, sell, trade baseball, football, basketball cards; specializing in sports trading cards since 1960s.

Texas Sportscard Company
2816 Center St.
Deer Park, TX 77536
phone: 713-476-9964

Man./Prod./Dist.

Fleer Corp.
1120 Route 73, Ste. 300
Mount Laurel, NJ 08054-5113
A baseball card company.

Leaf, Inc. (Donruss)
P.O. Box 2038
Memphis, TN 38101
A baseball card company.

Upper Deck Company
5909 Sea Otter Pl.
Carlsbad, CA 92008-6621
A baseball card company.

Museums/Libraries

Metropolitan Museum of Art, The
Jefferson Burdich Collection
1000 Fifth Ave.
New York, NY 10028
phone: 212-879-5500
Internet: http://www.metmuseum.org/

National Baseball Hall of Fame &
   Museum, Inc.
25 Main Street
Cooperstown, NY 13326
phone: 607-547-7200
fax: 607-547-2044
Internet: http://www.enews.com/
   bas_hall_fame

Larry Fritsch
Larry Fritsch Collection, The
P.O. Box 863
Stevens Point, WI 54481
phone: 715-344-8687

Periodicals

Newsletter: Old Judge, The
P.O. Box 137
Centerbeach, NY 11720

Julie A. Ulrich, PR
Krause Publications
Newsmagazine: Sports Collectors Digest
700 E. State St.
Iola, WI 54990-0001
phone: 715-445-2214
fax: 715-445-4087
e-mail: info@krause.com
Internet: http://www.krause.com
   *A weekly newsmagazine for collectors
   of sports memorabilia; everything
   from baseball cards to game-worn
   uniforms.*

Julie A. Ulrich, PR
Krause Publications
Magazine: Sports Cards Magazine &
   Price Guide
700 E. State St.
Iola, WI 54990-0001
phone: 715-445-2214
fax: 715-445-4087
e-mail: info@krause.com
Internet: http://www.krause.com
   *Full color monthly magazine featuring
   baseball, basketball, hockey and
   football cards from all eras; news,
   columns, feature stories, price guides;
   ads for cards and related items.*

Julie A. Ulrich, PR
Krause Publications
Newspaper: Card Trade
700 E. State St.
Iola, WI 54990-0001
phone: 715-445-2214
fax: 715-445-4087
e-mail: info@krause.com
Internet: http://www.krause.com
   *Card industry's official trade journal,
   touching on topics pertinent the sports
   hobby professional.*

Beckett Publications, Inc.
Magazine: Beckett Baseball Card
   Monthly
15850 Dallas Parkway
Dallas, TX 75248
phone: 972-991-6657
fax: 972-991-8930
   *A monthly baseball card price guide,
   articles, ads, show calendar.*

Baseball Gloves

Clubs/Associations

Joe Phillips
Glove Collector Club, The
Newsletter: Glove Collector, The
14057 Rolling Hills Lane
Dallas, TX 75240-3807
phone: 972-699-1808
fax: 972-699-9851
e-mail: glovecol@onramp.net
   *A bi-monthly newsletter containing
   buy/sell/trade ads and articles about
   old baseball gloves.*

Experts

David Bushing
217 Homewood Ave.
Libertyville, IL 60048-2123
phone: 708-816-6847
   *Author of "Vintage Baseball Glove
   Price Guide."*

Repro. Sources

Joe Phillips
14057 Rolling Hills Lane
Dallas, TX 75240-3807
phone: 972-699-1808
fax: 972-699-9851
e-mail: glovecol@onramp.net
   *Deals in re-issue USA made baseball
   gloves.*

Baseball Photos

Dealers

Mike Andersen
9-G Bond St.
Boston, MA 02118-2116
   *Buys & sells vintage baseball photos;
   wants autographed show biz photos;
   sells booklet of show biz addresses.*

Baseball Uniforms

Experts

Dick Dobbins
S.F. Giants Memorabilia
P.O. Box 193
Alamo, CA 94507-0193
phone: 510-943-7384
fax: 510-943-7104
   *Leading collector of baseball
   uniforms; focuses on Pacific Coast
   League; author of "Nuggets on the
   Diamond" (1994), the definitive book
   on baseball in the San Francisco Bay
   area, with over 30 vintage photos.*

Periodicals

Gary Hong, Pub.
Newsletter: Diamond Duds
P.O. Box 10153
Silver Spring, MD 20904
phone: 301-593-6763
   *A bi-monthly newsletter focusing on
   game-worn major league baseball
   uniforms.*

Basketball

Museums/Libraries

Naismith Memorial Basketball Hall of
   Fame
P.O. Box 179
Springfield, MA 01101-0179
phone: 413-781-6500

Basketball Cards

Periodicals

Julie A. Ulrich, PR
Krause Publications
Magazine: Sports Cards Magazine &
   Price Guide
700 E. State St.
Iola, WI 54990-0001
phone: 715-445-2214
fax: 715-445-4087
e-mail: info@krause.com
Internet: http://www.krause.com
   *Full color monthly magazine featuring
   baseball, basketball, hockey and
   football cards from all eras; news,
   columns, feature stories, price guides;
   ads for cards and related items.*

Beckett Publications, Inc.
Magazine: Beckett Basketball Card
   Magazine
15850 Dallas Parkway
Dallas, TX 75248
phone: 972-991-6657
fax: 972-991-8930
   *Articles, ads, basketball card price
   guide.*

Bowling

Collectors

Walt Sill
557 Forest Retreat Rd.
Hendersonville, TN 37075
phone: 615-824-4646 or 615-822-4217
   *Wants to buy pre-1940 bowling items:
   wooden balls and pins, photos,
   equipment, posters, trophies, clocks,
   mugs, plaques, ribbons, bags, china,
   advertising, medals, etc.*

Chuck Lande
11460 Audelia, Apt. #376
Dallas, TX 75243
phone: 817-589-3828
   *Wants bowling memorabilia of any
   kind.*

Museums/Libraries

National Bowling Hall of Fame &
   Museum
111 Stadium Plz.
Saint Louis, MO 63102
phone: 314-231-6340
   *Collection includes artifacts covering
   the history of bowling.*

Boxing

Clubs/Associations

Frederick Ryan
Boxiana & Pugilistica Collectors
International
Newsletter: BPCI Newsletter
P.O. Box 83135
Portland, OR 97203
phone: 503-286-3597 or 503-235-2279

Collectors

Lou Manfra
27 Rochelle St.
Staten Island, NY 10304
phone: 718-979-9556
   *Wants to buy boxing memorabilia:
   autographs, photos, documents,
   tickets, posters, programs, books,
   figurines.*

Ron McNair
186 Battery Ave.
Brooklyn, NY 11209
phone: 718-833-9588
   *Wants books, ring magazines,
   memorabilia, libraries, etc.*

Bob Bryla
1912 Sunset Ave.
Utica, NY 13502-5636
phone: 315-733-1846
fax: 315-733-7581
e-mail: bryfour@dreamscape.com
   *Wants items relating to boxing and
   wrestling: strength books, magazines,
   programs, dolls, games, medals,
   pennants, bottles, etc. from 1860 to
   present.*

Shawn Murphy
P.O. Box 103
Fithian, IL 61844-0103
   *Wants boxing memorabilia including
   programs, posters, tickets, books,
   souvenirs.*

Frederick Ryan
Arena Archives
P.O. Box 83135
Portland, OR 97203
phone: 503-286-3597 or 503-235-2279
   *Boxing archivist, lifelong collector;
   owner of the "Grand Ave. Gym",
   organizer of the Annual Boxing
   memorabilia show held annually in
   Portland; wants tickets, programs,
   fight films, posters, literature, awards,
   mementos.*

Lyle Whiteman
1526 Alki Ave. SW
Seattle, WA 98116
phone: 206-938-5746
   Wants to buy boxing memorabilia.

Dealers

Richard R. Regan
293 Winter St. #5
Hanover, MA 02339-2528
phone: 617-826-3537
e-mail: foregolf@tiac.net
   *Wants to buy boxing posters &
   broadsides, books, prints, cigarette
   cards, programs, autographed photos,*

early equipment; anything related to boxing.

Leonard Telesco, Jr.
In This Corner Boxing
56 Daytona Ave.
Milford, CT 06460
phone: 203-878-0774
Buys and sells boxing memorabilia, books, cards, photos, etc., especially wants heavyweight championship programs and full heavyweight tickets!

Seidman Productions, Inc.
P.O. Box 96
Clementon, NJ 08021
phone: 609-627-1356
Wants to buy boxing memorabilia: old and new programs, posters, tickets, pins, autographs, and any rare pieces or collections.

Jerome Shochet
6144 Oakland Mills Rd., CIC
Sykesville, MD 21784-6916
phone: 410-795-5879
Buys and sells boxing memorabilia of all kinds.

Bill Pollock
4267 Fox Hollow Circle
Casselberry, FL 32707-5240
phone: 407-695-9140
Wants to buy boxing posters, tickets, stubs, books, programs, autographs, pins, buttons, boxer awards, personal items of boxers such as dishes, drinking glasses from boxer-owner restaurants (i.e. Jack Dempsey's), trophies, etc.

Don Hoffman
P.O. Box 4231
Salinas, CA 93912-4231
phone: 408-449-7311
Wants to buy boxing (all fighters) autographs, posters, tickets, programs, 8mm & 16mm films, old photos, silks, broadsides, cabinet cards, books, photo buttons, lithographs, banners, equipment, Golden Gloves, pins, etc.; describe & price.

Museums/Libraries

International Boxing Hall of Fame
1 Hall of Fame Dr.
Canastota, NY 13032

Periodicals

Don Scott
Magazine: Boxing Collectors News
3316 Luallen Dr.
Carrollton, TX 75007-3916
phone: 972-492-8518
e-mail: bcn4@aol.com
Articles, addresses and ads for boxing memorabilia; nine years of monthly publishing, 16-32 pages, editor/publisher is columnist for "Ring" magazine; also offers appraisals.

Cards

(see also ADVERTISING COL-
LECTIBLES, Trading Cards; CARDS;
SPORTS COLLECTIBLES, Baseball
Cards; SPORTS COLLECTIBLES,
Basketball Cards, SPORTS
COLLECTIBLES, Football Cards,
etc.)

Auction Services

Greg Manning
Greg Manning Auctions, Inc.
775 Passaic Ave.
West Caldwell, NJ 07006
phone: 201-882-0004 or 800-221-0243
fax: 201-882-3499
Conducts four to six mail/phone bid auctions per year containing primarily sports and non-sports cards; also autographs and varied memorabilia.

Collectors

Peter Dean
2295 Benson Ave.
Santa Cruz, CA 95065-1670
phone: 408-457-4332
Wants to buy 1960s and early 1970s cards, all sports: baseball, football, basketball, hockey.

Dealers

Neil Osina
Best Variety Sports Cards & Coins
358 W. Foothill Blvd.
Glendora, CA 91740-3327
phone: 818-914-2273
fax: 818-914-6624
Wants to buy sports cards and autographed items; Life Member of all major associations; over 10 years experience.

Periodicals

Trajan Publishing Corporation
Newspaper: Canadian Sportscard
Collector
103 Lakeshore Rd., Ste. 202
St. Catharines
Ontario L2N 2T6 Canada
phone: 905-646-7744
fax: 905-646-0995
e-mail: bret@trajan.com
Internet: http://www.vaxxine.com/trajan/

Magazine: Sports Card Economizer
RFD 1 Box 350
Winthrop, ME 04364-9701
Monthly magazine with articles and ads for sports cards and sports memorabilia collectors; buy, sell, trade nationwide.

Julie A. Ulrich, PR
Krause Publications
Magazine: Sports Collectors Digest's
Price Guide Weekly
700 E. State St.
Iola, WI 54990-0001
phone: 715-445-2214
fax: 715-445-4087
e-mail: info@krause.com
Internet: http://www.krause.com
The sport card industry's first source for pricing on new card products, pricing updates, and industry trends.

Allan Kaye
Magazine: Allan Kaye's Sports Cards
News & Price Guides
10300 Watson Rd.
Saint Louis, MO 63127
phone: 314-966-2000
fax: 314-882-7564
A bi-monthly magazine focusing primarily on new sports-related trading cards; ads, card inserts, articles, card value guides; also some non-sport card ads and articles.

Crew Rowing

Collectors

Peter Falk
P. Hastings Falk, Inc.
859 Boston Post Rd.
Madison, CT 06443
phone: 203-245-2246 or 203-849-1655
fax: 203-245-5116
Wants 19th century cigarette & trade cards, posters, broadsides, stereoviews, prints, sheet music, & books on rowing.

Curling

Collectors

D.M. Sgriccia
5216 Sherry Ln.
Howell, MI 48843
Wants to buy curling stones, memorabilia, trophies, books, prints, etc.

Museums/Libraries

Turner's Curling Museum
417 Woodlawn Crescent
Weyburn
Saskatchewan S4H 0X5 Canada
phone: 306-842-3604

Equipment

Experts

David Bushing
Vintage Sports Equipment
217 Homewood Ave.
Libertyville, IL 60048-2123
phone: 708-816-6847
Wants to buy old sports equipment: bats, gloves, catchers gear, old leather football helmets, old pennants, etc.; writes a sports collectibles column for "AntiqueWeek."

Football

Dealers

Poling's Football
364 Gatewood Road, Apt. 3
Mansfield, OH 44907
Buys and sells football items, magazines, records, NCAA guides, etc.

Museums/Libraries

National Football Museum, Inc.
212 George Halas Dr. NW
Canton, OH 44708
phone: 216-456-8207

Football Cards

Periodicals

Julie A. Ulrich, PR
Krause Publications
Magazine: Sports Cards Magazine &
Price Guide
700 E. State St.
Iola, WI 54990-0001
phone: 715-445-2214
fax: 715-445-4087
e-mail: info@krause.com
Internet: http://www.krause.com
Full color monthly magazine featuring baseball, basketball, hockey and football cards from all eras; news, columns, feature stories, price guides; ads for cards and related items.

Beckett Publications, Inc.
Magazine: Beckett Football Card
Magazine
15850 Dallas Parkway
Dallas, TX 75248
phone: 972-991-6657
fax: 972-991-8930
Includes ads, show calendar, articles and football card price guide.

Golf

Auction Services

Jon Baddeley
Sotheby's
34-35 New Bond St.
London W1A 2AA, U.K.
phone: 0171-4938080 or 0171-4085205
fax: 0171-4085911
Conducts regular auctions of golfing memorabilia.

Kevin C. McGrath
Sporting Antiquities
47 Leonard Rd.
Melrose, MA 02176
phone: 617-662-6588
fax: 671-662-2643
Sells antique golf collectibles through auction and private sales; buys high quality golf paintings, prints, clubs, books, balls, etc.; subscription to well-illustrated catalogs $24/yr; also appraises golf collectibles for a fee.

Book Sellers

Rhod McEwan
Rhod McEwan Golf Books
Glengarden
Ballater
Aberdeenshr. AB35 5UB Scotland
phone: 013397-55429
fax: 013397-55995
e-mail: rhodmcewan@easynet.co-uk
Specialist full-time dealer in rare, used, and out-of-print golf books; also golf ephemera and original paintings; always looking to purchase; member Antiquarian Bookseller's Association (UK) and Golf Collector's Society.

Clubs/Associations

Tom & Karen Kuhl, Ed.
Golf Collectors Society
Journal: Bulletin, The
P.O. Box 20546
Dayton, OH 45420
phone: 937-256-2474
e-mail: KKuhl@aol.com
Internet: http://www.golfcollectors.com
An international society for the preservation of the treasures and traditions of the Royal and Ancient game; largest in the world.

Collectors

Art DiProspero
Highlands Golf
152 Bamford Ave.
Oakville, CT 06779-2149
phone: 860-274-8471
Wants wooden shaft golf clubs, early trophies, pre-1920 golf books, golf bronzes, modern "classic" clubs, golf paintings & prints, balls, golf memorabilia, early golf magazines and programs, etc.

P.M. Romano
32 Sterling Dr.
Lake Grove, NY 11755
phone: 516-585-9017
Wants golf memorabilia: programs, balls, score cards, wooden shafted clubs, post cards, photos, autographs, statues, china, trophies, ceramics.

Norman Boughton
P.O. Box 93262
Rochester, NY 14692
phone: 716-292-5550 or 716-292-0128
Wants to buy golf memorabilia including golf markers (used to mark a spot on the green), any material; especially those identifiable to a particular course or golfer.

Mark F. Emerson
4040 Poste Lane Road
Columbus, OH 43221
phone: 614-771-7272
Wants to buy old golf programs, tickets, badges, pairing sheets, passes, photos, autographs of deceased players.

D. Perkins
2317 N. Kessler Blvd.
Indianapolis, IN 46222
phone: 317-638-4519
Wants wooden shaft golf clubs, early trophies or any antique sports related item.

Frank R. Zadra
H5830 Cty. Hwy. H.
Spooner, WI 54801
phone: 715-635-2791
Wants old golf related items: unusual golf clubs, old balls, books, bronzes, quality china and ceramics, and miscellaneous related items.

Scott Sayers
1800 Nueces
Austin, TX 78701
phone: 512-478-3483
fax: 512-473-2447
Wants to buy golf related autographs and memorabilia.

Dealers

Richard R. Regan
293 Winter St. #5
Hanover, MA 02339-2528
phone: 617-826-3537
e-mail: foregolf@tiac.net
Wants to buy wood shaft clubs, books, statues, china, paintings, prints, balls, scorecards, programs, autographs, sales catalogs, trophies, miniature golf clubs & games, pinball machines, cigarette & post cards; any golf related item.

Neil Ghingold
Neil Ghingold Antiques
1230-32 Broad St.
Augusta, GA 30901-1116
phone: 706-722-3483
Wants to buy golfing collectibles.

David N. Berkowitz
P.O. Box 842
Palatine, IL 60078-0842
phone: 847-934-4108 or 847-934-4107
Buys and sells old golf items: balls, books, ceramics, tees, memorabilia, vintage golf autographs, wood shafted clubs, silver, trophies, etc.

Bob Lucas
P.O. Box 364
Geneva, IL 60134-0364
phone: 630-232-2665
fax: 630-262-1935
e-mail: antqgolf@aol.com
Old golf items, wood-shafted clubs, books, prints, china, etc.

Al Moore
Moore's of Omaha
5220 Ames
Omaha, NE 68104-2806
phone: 402-453-5230
e-mail: almor@prob.net
Wants old golf stuff: caddy badges, wood shaft clubs, etc.

Chuck Furjanic
P.O. Box 165892
Irving, TX 75016
phone: 972-594-7802
Buys and sells golf collectibles, balls, books, autographs, wood shaft clubs and other golf memorabilia; issues monthly comprehensive Golf Collectibles Catalogue; will buy large collections.

Experts

John & Morton Olman
Old Golf Shop, Ltd.
P.O. Box 220
Pleasant Plain, OH 45162
phone: 513-877-2676
fax: 513-241-7855
Authors of the "Golf Antiques & Other Treasures of the Game" (1997); to order book call warehouse at 800-433-1000.

Leo M. Kelly, Jr.
Old Chicago Golf Shop
4977 Arquilla Dr.
Richton Park, IL 60471-1643
phone: 708-747-1045
fax: 708-747-1055
e-mail: Ochicago@ix.netcom.com
Internet: http://www.webcom.com/oldgolf/wel.html
Buys and sells golf related collectibles; issues a periodic catalog, "The Hickory Club Mart", packed with golf items for sale and having 40 to 70 B/W photos of antique golf collectibles; $35 for four issues; author of golf ball book.

Kevin McCandless
P.O. Box 435
Champaign, IL 61824-0435
phone: 217-367-4466

Museums/Libraries

PGA/World Golf Hall of Fame
P.O. Box 1908
Pinehurst, NC 28374

Periodicals

Dufner
Magazine: Golfiana Magazine
222 Leverette Lane, #4
Edwardsville, IL 62025-1867
A quarterly dedicated to preserving the heritage of golf.

Golf Ball Markers

Collectors

Norman Boughton
P.O. Box 93262
Rochester, NY 14692
phone: 716-292-5550 or 716-292-0128
Wants golf markers (used to mark a spot on the green), any material; especially those identifiable to a particular course or golfer; also buys other golf memorabilia.

Golf Balls

Clubs/Associations

Sy Gersten
Logo Golf Ball Collector's Association
4552 Barclay Fairway
Lake Worth, FL 33467

Golf Clubs

Clubs/Associations

Dick Moore, Ex. Dir.
Golf Club Collectors Association, The
Newsletter: Golf Club Collectors Association Newsletter
640 E. Liberty St.
Girard, OH 44420-2308
phone: 330-545-2832
fax: 330-545-2718
e-mail: gccagolf@aol.com
For classic collectors as well as hickory collectors and collectors of other golf memorabilia; quarterly newsletter consisting of photos, articles and stories of golf collectibles, ads, news of auctions and golf trade shows.

Collectors

Dick Moore
640 E. Liberty St.
Girard, OH 44420-2308
phone: 330-545-2832
fax: 330-545-2718
e-mail: gccagolf@aol.com

Periodicals

Robin W. Berg, Pub.
Newsletter: U.S. Golf Classics & Heritage Hickories
5407 Pennock Point Rd.
Jupiter, FL 33458-3496
phone: 407-744-2553
fax: 407-744-2374
A 24-30 page "buy-sell-trade" newsletter for classic and antique golf buffs; woods, irons, putters, wedges, sets and singles, books, memorabilia.

Golf Clubs (British)

Experts

Peter Georgiady
6101 O'Briant Ct.
Greensboro, NC 27410-8606
phone: 919-665-6457
Author of "Compendium of British Club Makers," $55 ppd. and "Wood Shafter Golf Club Value Guide," $25 ppd.

Harness Racing

Museums/Libraries

Trotting Horse Museum
Newsletter: Hall of Fame Trotters News
P.O. Box 590
Goshen, NY 10924
phone: 914-294-6330

Hockey

Museums/Libraries

U.S. Hockey Hall of Fame
P.O. Box 657
Eveleth, MN 55734
phone: 218-744-5167

Periodicals

Beckett Publications, Inc.
Magazine: Beckett Hockey Monthly
15850 Dallas Parkway
Dallas, TX 75248
phone: 972-991-6657
fax: 972-991-8930
Articles, ads, show calendar and hockey card price guide.

Hockey Cards

Periodicals

Julie A. Ulrich, PR
Krause Publications
Magazine: Sports Cards Magazine & Price Guide
700 E. State St.
Iola, WI 54990-0001
phone: 715-445-2214
fax: 715-445-4087
e-mail: info@krause.com
Internet: http://www.krause.com
Full color monthly magazine featuring baseball, basketball, hockey and football cards from all eras; news, columns, feature stories, price guides; ads for cards and related items.

Ice Skating

Clubs/Associations

Professional Skaters Guild of America
Magazine: Professional Skater
P.O. Box 5904
Rochester, MN 55903
phone: 507-281-5122

Amateur Speedskating Union of the United States
Magazine: Racing Blade, The
1033 Shady Lane
Glen Ellyn, IL 60137
phone: 630-790-3230
fax: 630-790-3235
Internet: http://web.mit.edu/
  jeffrey.speedskating/asu.html

United States Figure Skating Association
Magazine: Skating
20 First St.
Colorado Springs, CO 80906
phone: 719-635-5200

Collectors

Keith Pendell
1230 N. Cypress
La Habra, CA 90631-3018
phone: 562-619-8055
fax: 562-690-6866
e-mail: kpendell@aol.com
Wants pre-1900 antique ice skates: swan's head, big turn up, brass blades; also china with skating motif, skater's lanterns, books, etc.; also wants ice show programs.

Dealers

Greg Walsh
32 River View Lane
P.O. Box 747
Potsdam, NY 13676
phone: 315-265-9111 or 800-371-9286
fax: 315-265-9222
Wants to buy antique ice skates of exceptional quality; appraises ice skates and relate material; corresponding with others.

Periodicals

H. Kermit Jackson
Group Publications, Ltd.
Magazine: American Skating World
1816 Brownsville Rd.
Pittsburgh, PA 15210-3908
phone: 412-885-7600 or 800-245-6280
fax: 412-885-7617
e-mail: editor@amsk8world.com
The only news monthly on figure skating.

Jerseys

Dealers

Grey Flannel Collectibles, Inc.
731 Middle Neck Rd.
Great Neck, NY 11024
phone: 800-242-7647
fax: 516-466-5592
Leading dealers in game-used jerseys.

Jewelry

Collectors

M. B. Spragins
501 Adams St.
Huntsville, AL 35801
phone: 800-987-7464
Wants to buy sports rings: football, baseball, basketball, hockey, college, minor league; also professional Cotton Bowl Rolexes.

Experts

Mike Safran
Collectors' Collector, The
204 South Edisto Ave.
Columbia, SC 29205
phone: 803-771-6995
e-mail: collect1@scsn.net
Internet: http://www.csmonline.com/
  collect1
Championship sports rings bought, sold, traded; from the Sugar Bowl to the Super Bowl, championship jewelry from all aspects of sports.

Lacrosse

Museums/Libraries

Steve Stenersen, Ex.Dir.
National Lacrosse Foundation & Hall of Fame, The
Magazine: Lacrosse Magazine
113 West University Parkway
Baltimore, MD 21210-3301
phone: 410-235-6882
fax: 410-366-6735
e-mail: sstenersen@lacrosse.org
Internet: http://www.lacrosse.org
Promotes and preserves the sport of lacrosse; museum includes displays and archives, and is the sport's largest resource center.

Little League

Museums/Libraries

Alan Robison
Peter J. McGovern Little League Museum
P.O. Box 3485
South Williamsport, PA 17701
phone: 717-326-3607
Focuses on Little League Baseball/ softball memorabilia; vintage baseball equipment; vintage magazine covers featuring youths and baseball.

Mountaineering

Book Sellers

Jim Havranek
Innominate Crux
58 Ramsey Ave.
Yonkers, NY 10701-5654
phone: 914-969-1554
fax: 914-969-1554
e-mail: 73362.2710@compuserve.com
Mountaineering and Alpine related material; books, equipment, ephemera, and art; also Tibet and Mountainous Regions.

Nike Sportswear

Dealers

Larry McKaugham
Heller's Far West Clothing
1000 Lenora, Ste. 116
Seattle, WA 98121
phone: 206-233-9014 or 800-328-5384
Wants old Nike sportswear.

Husky Boy Vintage
4441 S. Meridian, Ste. 471
Puyallup, WA 98373-5959
phone: 800-HUS-KYBO or 206-472-6341
Internet: http://www.huskyboy.com
Wants to buy Nike Air Jordan 1985-1991 and 1970s-1980s Nike shoes and sportswear; also buying vintage denim workwear, i.e. Levi's, Lee, etc. and vintage military flight jackets.

Polo

Collectors

Dennis Amato
5 The Crow's Nest
Port Washington, NY 11050
phone: 212-605-2959
Wants anything related to the sport of polo: books, magazines, programs, autographs, ephemera.

Rodeo

Clubs/Associations

Pro Bull Rider Fan Club
Magazine: Pro Bull Rider
6 South Tejon, Ste. 700
Colorado Springs, CO 80903
phone: 714-434-2579
fax: 719-471-4712
e-mail: fancorp@earthlink.net
Internet: http://www.pbrnow.com/
Merchandise, fashion, articles, behind the chutes, chutin' the bull, etc.

Professional Rodeo Cowboys Association
Magazine: Prorodeo Sports News
101 Pro Rodeo Dr.
Colorado Springs, CO 80919
phone: 719-548-4840
Internet: http://www.prorodeo.com/

Museums/Libraries

ProRodeo Hall of Fame & Museum of the American Cowboy
101 Pro Rodeo Dr.
Colorado Springs, CO 80919
phone: 719-528-4764 or 719-528-4761

Periodicals

Magazine: Competitor News, The
28150 N. Holiday Lane
Athol, ID 83801
phone: 208-687-0473
fax: 208-623-2683
e-mail: compnews@comtch.iea.com
Internet: http://www.iea.com/
  ~compnews/
Serving WA, OR, ID, MT, WY; keep up to date on rodeo, roping, cow horse, cutting, team penning, and barrel racing events.

Roller Skating

Clubs/Associations

Roller Skating Association
Magazine: Roller Skating Business
7301 Georgetown Rd., #123
Indianapolis, IN 46268
phone: 317-875-3390
Governing body for roller skating rinks.

Andy Seely
USA Roller Skating
Magazine: US Roller Skating
4730 South Street
P.O. Box 6579
Lincoln, NE 68506-0579
phone: 402-483-7551
fax: 402-483-1465
e-mail: Rllrsktmus@aol.com
Internet: http://usacrs.com/museum.htm
Governing body for amateur roller skating: speed skating, roller hockey, artistic skating.

Museums/Libraries

Michael Zaidman
National Museum of Roller Skating
Newsletter: Historical Roller Skating Overview
4730 South Street
P.O. Box 6579
Lincoln, NE 68506-0579
phone: 402-483-7551
fax: 402-483-1465
e-mail: Rllrsktmus@aol.com
Internet: http://usacrs.com/museum.htm
Largest collection of historical roller skates dating to 1819; roller skating history as technology, sport, recreation and personalities; sells "The Evolution of the Roller Skate: 1820 - Present" by Scott Addison Wilhite.

Schedules

Collectors

Paul Jarrell
1800 Crumbley Rd.
McDonough, GA 30253
Specializes in buying and selling baseball schedules.

Periodicals

Falk
Newsletter: Sked Notebook, The
12 Foxchase Dr.
Burlington, NJ 08016-3044
Monthly newsletter focusing on sports schedules.

Newsletter: Skedder News, The
4857 Millbrook Dr.
Dunwoody, GA 30338
Monthly newsletter focusing on baseball schedules.

Tom Wright
Newsletter: Skedhead Bulletin, The
28420 Palmer St.
Madison Heights, MI 48071-4572
Bi-monthly newsletter focusing on professional and minor sports schedules; each issue offers current skedding related news, addresses, auctions, classifieds, and a historical look at various leagues and schedules; sample $2.

Newsletter: Right on Schedule
204 N. Charro Ave.
Thousand Oaks, CA 91320
Monthly newsletter focusing on baseball schedules.

Snow Skiing

Collectors

Gary Schwartz
680 Hawthorne Dr.
Tiburon, CA 94920
phone: 415-388-6500
fax: 415-388-6575
Wants pre-1940 books, company catalogs, magazines, post cards, sheet music, posters, photographs, etc. relating to skiing.

Museums/Libraries

E. John B. Allen
New England Ski Museum
Newsletter: NESM Newsletter
P.O. Box 267
Franconia, NH 03580-0267
phone: 603-823-7177
fax: 603-823-8088
e-mail: SkiMuseum@nesm.org
Internet: http://www.nesm.org
Museum contains library research materials, photo collections, etc.; available free to members or on a fee basis to the public.

National Ski Hall of Fame & Museum
P.O. Box 191
Ishpeming, MI 49849
phone: 906-486-9281

Colorado Ski Museum - Ski Hall of Fame
15 Vail Rd.
Vail, CO 81658
phone: 303-476-1876 or 303-476-1879
Traces 100 years of Colorado's ski heritage through displays containing equipment, artifacts and photographs.

Western American Skisport Museum
P.O. Box 38
Soda Springs, CA 95728
phone: 916-426-3313
The mailing address is as noted above, but the museum is located at the Boreal Ridge Ski Area, Donner Pass, CA.

Soaring

(see also AIRPLANES, Sailplanes)

Museums/Libraries

National Soaring Museum
Harris Hill, RD 3
Elmira, NY 14903
phone: 607-734-3128

Soccer

Museums/Libraries

Albert L. Colone
National Soccer Hall of Fame, The
Newsletter: 90 Minutes
5-11 Ford Ave.
Oneonta, NY 13820
phone: 607-432-3351 or 607-432-3645
Information on soccer history, especially American; wants all forms of memorabilia relating to soccer including photographs.

Softball

Museums/Libraries

National Softball Hall of Fame
2801 NW 50th St.
Oklahoma City, OK 73100
phone: 405-424-5266

Ron Babb
Amateur Softball Association of America
Newsletter: Amateur Softball Hall of Fame Newsletter
2801 N.E. 50th St.
Oklahoma City, OK 73111
phone: 405-424-5266
fax: 405-424-3855
e-mail: info@softball.org
Internet: http://www.softball.org

Surfing

Collectors

John Casper
2605 S. Peninsula Dr.
Daytona Beach, FL 32118-5603
phone: 904-767-2075
Wants to buy 1960's and earlier surfing memorabilia including surfing magazines, books, advertising literature/items, decals, patches, films, original surf movie posters, clocks, board games, comics, trophies, 8' or longer boards, etc.

Wayne Babcock
4846 Carpenteria Ave.
Carpinteria, CA 93013-1935
phone: 805-684-8148
Collects old long surfboards, surfing trophies, magazines, photos, books, records, posters, and any pre-1968 surfing items; also wants any pre-1960s Hawaiian items.

Swimming

Museums/Libraries

Bob Duenkel
International Swimming Hall of Fame
1 Hall of Fame Dr.
Fort Lauderdale, FL 33316-1611
phone: 305-462-6536
fax: 305-525-4031
Seeks photos, memorabilia, etc. regarding the great athletes and history of the aquatic sports; swimming, diving, water polo,
synchronized swimming, water safety, pools, etc.

Table Tennis

Clubs/Associations

Gerald Gurney
Tennis Collectors Society, The
Newsletter: Tennis Tennis Collector, The
Guildhall Orchard
Great Bromley
Colchester CO7 7TU, U.K.
phone: 12016 230330

Tennis

Clubs/Associations

Gerald Gurney
Tennis Collectors Society, The
Newsletter: Tennis Collector, The
Guildhall Orchard
Great Bromley
Colchester CO7 7TU, U.K.
phone: 12016 230330

Collectors

Sheldon Katz
211 Roanoke Ave.
Riverhead, NY 11901-2778
phone: 516-369-1100

Ken Benner
217 Hewett Rd.
Wyncote, PA 19095-1203
phone: 215-885-5876
fax: 215-885-4635
Wants to buy pre-1900 unusual racquets, photos, trophies, programs, tennis ball cans (metal lids), books, prints, etc.

Donald N. Jones
24 Marvalingrove
Savannah, GA 31406-6334
phone: 912-354-2133
Wants to buy tennis items: rackets, ball cans, and tennis ephemera.

Gary Plock
408 Clinton Rd.
Lexington, KY 40502
phone: 606-266-8538
Wants to buy old tennis rackets and metal tennis cans.

Dealers

Richard R. Regan
293 Winter St. #5
Hanover, MA 02339-2528
phone: 617-826-3537
e-mail: foregolf@tiac.net
Wants to buy tennis posters & broadsides, books, prints, cigarette cards, programs, autographed photos, early equipment such as balls, ball containers and rackets; anything related to tennis.

Don Brenner
2292 Fairoaks Rd.
Decatur, GA 30333
phone: 404-315-7782
Buys and sells Tennis memorabilia;

programs, books, magazines, autographs, tickets, rackets, etc.

Experts

Jeanne Cherry
Amaryllis Press
1402 San Vicente Blvd.
Santa Monica, CA 90402
phone: 310-395-3915
fax: 310-260-9425
e-mail: jcherry@lainet.com
Internet: http://www.lainet.com/~jcherry
Collects, buys, appraises and specializes in tennis collectibles; author of "Tennis Antiques & Collectibles," covering rackets, ball cans, books, ephemera, silver and ceramics.

Museums/Libraries

Mark S. Young, II, Archivist
International Tennis Hall of Fame & Tennis Museum
194 Bellevue Ave.
Newport, RI 02840-3515
phone: 401-849-3990
fax: 401-849-8780

Tennis Rackets

Collectors

Ralph Nix
P.O. Box 655
Red Bay, AL 35582-0655
phone: 205-356-2997
Wants early lawn tennis rackets and other tennis memorabilia.

Thoroughbred Racing

Collectors

Ken Grayson
P.O. Box 24586
Lexington, KY 40524-4586
phone: 606-278-7419
fax: 606-278-4268
Wants to buy Kentucky Derby, Belmont, Preakness, and Breeder's Cup glasses, programs, etc.

Coleen Detzel
28 Lacresta Dr.
Florence, KY 41042-9663
phone: 606-282-0456
Wants thoroughbred racing items pertaining to Kentucky Derby and Jim Beam Stakes; also Latonia Race Track items: glasses, programs, photos, tickets, etc.

Gary Gatanis
3283-B Cardiff
Toledo, OH 43606-1867
phone: 419-475-3192
Wants Kentucky Derby memorabilia including programs, advertising and glasses; also Dan Patch memorabilia.

Gary Medeiros
1319 Sayre St.
San Leandro, CA 94579
phone: 510-351-6193 or 800-227-6049
e-mail: pharlap2@aol.com
Thoroughbred racing and Kentucky

Derby memorabilia: programs, books, games, glasses, photos, passes, pins, postcards; any thoroughbred related items considered.

Dealers

Dick Hering
121 Spring Chase Lane
Rocky Point, NC 28457-7807
phone: 910-602-3388
fax: 910-602-6005
e-mail: drfager132@aol.com
Internet: http://members.aol.com/drfager132/auction.htm
Buy, sell, trade horse racing (thoroughbred) memorabilia, glasses, programs, pins, advertising signs, games, books, stocks, etc.; Kentucky Derby, Preakness, Belmont, etc.

Jim Settembre
5115 Woodstone Circle E.
Lake Worth, FL 33463-5819
phone: 561-964-5434 or 561-964-8230
fax: 561-964-1143
Wants Kentucky Derby, Breeder's Cup, Preakness, and Belmont Stakes glasses and programs; also wants to buy any related horse racing items; auction service also available.

Experts

William Friedberg
462 Hillcreek Rd.
Shepherdsville, KY 40165
phone: 502-957-4039
Author of "Bill Friedberg's Pictorial Price Guide & Informative Handbook," (1996) 32 pages about Kentucky Derby glasses, plus glasses from related races; available from the author for $12.73 ppd.

Betty Hornback
Betty's Antiques
707 Sunrise Lane
Elizabethtown, KY 42701
phone: 502-765-2441 or 502-369-7279
Author of "Kentucky Derby Glass Price Guide;" specializes in Kentucky Derby glasses; sells nationwide; wants to buy pre-1974 glasses; send $2 for list of glasses for sale.

Museums/Libraries

Aiken Thoroughbred Racing Hall of Fame & Museum
P.O. Box 2213
Aiken, SC 29802
phone: 803-649-7700

Candace Perry
Kentucky Derby Museum, The
Newsletter: Inside Track
P.O. Box 3513
Louisville, KY 40201-3513
phone: 502-637-1111 or 502-637-7097
fax: 502-636-5855
Internet: http://www.derbymuseum.org
Cannot provide appraisals, but can help identify and research; located at 704 Central Ave., Louisville, KY 40208.

Track & Field

Collectors

Ed Kozloff
10144 Lincoln
Huntington Woods, MI 48070-1539
phone: 810-544-9099
fax: 810-544-4601
Wants running memorabilia: track & field, road races, Olympic material, medals, ribbons, trophies, annuals, books, magazines, etc.

Museums/Libraries

National Track & Field Hall of Fame
200 South Capitol Ave., Ste. 140
Indianapolis, IN 46206
phone: 317-638-9155

Weightlifting

Clubs/Associations

William Moore
Joe Weider Fan Club
P.O. Box 732
Tuscaloosa, AL 35402

Experts

David Chapman
656 32nd Ave. East
Seattle, WA 98112
phone: 206-329-7573
fax: 206-329-7573
Says there is more to weight training that fat Russian guys or Arnold Schwarzenegger; is interested in the early days of "physical culture" (1895-1950): wants photos, books, magazines, posters, etc.; has written extensively.

Museums/Libraries

Philip Redman
Weightlifting Hall of Fame
P.O. Box 1707
York, PA 17405-1707
phone: 717-767-6481
fax: 717-764-0044
Weightlifting, body building, power lifting history and memorabilia.

Wrestling

Collectors

Tom Burke
31 Groveland St.
Springfield, MA 01108-2920
phone: 413-733-6015
fax: 413-787-2187
Wants to buy Professional Wrestling postcards, programs, magazines, and related items from any era.

John Pantozzi
1000 Polk Ave.
Franklin Square, NY 11010-2018
fax: 516-327-8984
e-mail: mr1wrestle@aol.com
Wants to buy wrestling related toys, dolls, pennants, patches, trading cards, pins, postcards, books, posters, movie posters, board games, ring

gear, autographs, photos, scrapbooks, etc.

Bob Bryla
1912 Sunset Ave.
Utica, NY 13502-5636
phone: 315-733-1846
fax: 315-733-7581
e-mail: bryfour@dreamscape.com
Wants items relating to boxing and wrestling: strength books, magazines, programs, dolls, games, medals, pennants, bottles, etc. from 1860 to present.

Museums/Libraries

Myron Roderick
National Wrestling Hall of Fame
405 W. Hall Of Fame Ave.
Stillwater, OK 74075
phone: 405-377-5243
fax: 405-377-5244
America's shrine to the sport of amateur wrestling.

SPORTS HISTORY

Clubs/Associations

Chuck Hershberger, GM
Sports Hall of Oblivion
P.O. Box 69025
Pleasant Ridge, MI 48069-0025
phone: 248-543-9412
The Sports Hall of Oblivion is an organization dedicated to preserving the memory of defunct sports teams (HS, College, semi-pro, pro.); also covering new and weird sports.

SPRINKLERS

(see CLOTHES SPRINKLERS; WATER SPRINKLERS)

SPY EQUIPMENT

(see also CAMERAS & CAMERA EQUIPMENT, Subminiature; CHARACTER COLLECTIBLES, Spy Memorabilia; MYSTERY/DETECTIVE ITEMS; TELEVISION SHOWS & MEMORABILIA, Private Eye)

Collectors

Kenneth D. Smith
55 Howard Ave.
Staten Island, NY 10301-4404
Wants to buy cryptographic and code machines, devices, books and manuals; any era, any nation.

Keith Melton
P.O. Box 2880
Jupiter, FL 33468-2880
e-mail: 74237.202@compuserve.com
Pays top dollar for all types of old Code machines: ENIGMA's, M-209's, M-94's, M-138's, cipher disks and wheels; also devices used by OSS, SOE, KGB, MOSSAD, British intelligence, etc.

Uwe H. Breker
6731 Ashley Ct.
Sarasota, FL 34241-9696
phone: 941-925-0385
fax: 941-925-0487
*Wants secret service communication
machines and devices.*

Mike & Gladys Kessler
25749 Anchor Circle
San Juan Capistrano, CA 92675
phone: 717-661-3320
*Buys and specializes in unusual 1880-
1890s disguised or detective cameras;
also Simon Wing cameras.*

Museums/Libraries

Jack E. Ingram, Cur.
National Cryptologic Museum
DIRNSA
Attn: S542/Museum
Fort George G Meade, MD 20755
phone: 301-688-5849 or 301-688-5848
fax: 301-688-5847
*Gov't. collection open free to the
public; thousands of artifacts which
collectively serve to sustain the history
of the cryptologic profession: books,
computers, cipher devices, Enigma,
cryptanalysis, research library by
appointment.*

ST. PATRICK

(see ELVES)

Periodicals

Chuck Thompson
Newsletter: St. Patrick Notes
10802 Greencreek Dr., Ste. 703
Houston, TX 77070-5367
*Legends, facts, quotes, stories, and
other notes about St. Patrick; for fans
of the Patron Saint of Ireland and
collectors of St. Patrick memorabilia.*

STAGECOACH ITEMS

(see WESTERN AMERICANA)

STAINED GLASS

(see also ARCHITECTURAL
ELEMENTS; CRAFTS, Glass;
REPAIR/RESTORATION/CONSER-
VATION, Lamps & Lighting)

Clubs/Associations

Stained Glass Association of America
Magazine: Stained Glass
P.O. Box 22642
Kansas City, MO 64113
phone: 800-888-SGAA
fax: 816-361-9173
e-mail: sgaofa@aol.com
Internet: http://www.artglassworld.com
*Primarily a trade magazine, but also
contains articles and resources of
interest to owners of old stained glass.*

Collectors

Bob Ward
2461 E High St., #A-7
Pottstown, PA 19464-3111
phone: 610-970-6299
Wants stained glass windows.

Dealers

Jim Osella
Cannonsburg Antique Mall
145 Adams Ave.
Bridgeville, PA 15017
phone: 412-746-2451 or 412-745-1333
fax: 412-746-2451
e-mail: osella@usaor.net
*Wants to buy stained and beveled
glass windows, one or a hundred.*

Experts

H. Weber Wilson
Oltz-Wilson Antiques
808 51st Avenue Plz. W
Bradenton, FL 34207-2819
phone: 800-508-0022
*Author of books on stained glass; also
sells architectural antiques.*

Carl Heck
Carl Heck Antiques
P.O. Box 8416
Aspen, CO 81612-8416
phone: 970-925-8011
fax: 970-925-8100
*Specializes in antique stained and
beveled glass and Tiffany windows;
also leaded and reverse-painted
lamps.*

Man./Prod./Dist.

Ray Gregory
2708 Wyoming Ave.
Norfolk, VA 23513
phone: 804-855-4312
fax: 804-855-4312
*Design and create stained glass for
churches, synagogues, public
buildings, restaurants and private
homes; also repairs old stained glass
windows.*

Museums/Libraries

Corning Museum of Glass, The
One Museum Way
Corning, NY 14830-2253
phone: 607-937-5371
fax: 607-937-3352
*Over 24,000 glass objects, innovative
exhibits, videos, models; glass history,
archaeology, and early manufacturing; Robert Sowers (stained glass
artist, critic, author) collection of
archival materials pertaining to
stained glass.*

Periodicals

Magazine: Glass Patterns Quarterly
8300 Hidden Valley Rd.
P.O. Box 69
Westport, KY 40077
phone: 502-222-5631 or 800-719-0769
fax: 502-222-4527
e-mail: gpq@iglou.com
Internet: http://www.artglassworld.com/
mag/gpq/gpq.html
*Glossy quarterly magazine for the
stained glass hobbyist: stained glass
patterns, techniques, ads, etc.; also
articles about sandblasting and
etching glass, glass kiln firing, glass
painting, lamps, windows, display
cases, etc.*

Magazine: Glass Art Magazine
P.O. Box 260377
Highlands Ranch, CO 80126-0377
phone: 303-791-8998
fax: 303-791-7739
*A bi-monthly magazine which includes
glass industry news including
upcoming museum and gallery
exhibitions.*

Repair Services

AIG Stained Glass Company
414 Pine Ave.
Frederick, MD 21701-5764
phone: 301-663-1151 or 301-663-1152
*Specializing in custom stained glass
designs for doors, sidelights,
skylights, cabinets; also sandblast
carving, etching, and repairs.*

Suppliers

Hudson Glass
219 North Division St.
Peekskill, NY 10566-2716
phone: 800-431-2964 or 914-737-2124
fax: 914-737-4447
*Sells bent glass for china cabinets;
convex picture frame glass; also
carries restoration/old house glass in
stock; sells stained glass tools and
supplies (no stained glass repair);
stained glass supply catalog available
for $3.*

Rochard Blenko
Blenko Glass Company, Inc.
P.O. Box 67
Milton, WV 25541-0067
phone: 304-743-9081
fax: 304-743-0547
e-mail: warhol2@aol.com
*Supplies hand-blown "antique" glass
for stained glass windows; colored
handmade glassware, blown
tableware, tumblers and stemware,
vases, pitchers; custom mold work,
awards and barware; stained glass
studio.*

Delphi Stained Glass
2116 East Michigan Ave.
Lansing, MI 48912
phone: 800-248-2048 or 517-482-2617
fax: 517-482-4028
Internet: http://www.voyager.net/
delphiglass
*Sells stained glass supplies; gives
lessons; large mail order business;
also sells chemical solutions to repair
damaged patina on brass and other
metals.*

STAINLESS STEEL FLATWARE

(see FLATWARE)

STAMP BOXES

Collectors

Bob Morris
706 Pawnee St.
Bethlehem, PA 18015-1432
phone: 610-865-9052
*Wants to buy stamp boxes and stamp
holders; single item or collection; US
or foreign; also wants stamp scales.*

STAMP COLLECTING

(see also ADVERTISING COL-
LECTIBLES, Trading Cards;
POSTAL SERVICE ITEMS; SEALS,
Christmas & Charity; STAMP
BOXES; STAMP WETTERS;
TRADING CARDS, Non-Sport)

Auction Services

Stanley J. Richmond
Daniel F. Kelleher Company, Inc.
24 Farnsworth St., Ste. 605
Boston, MA 02210-1264
phone: 617-443-0033
fax: 617-443-0789
*U.S. and BNA stamps at auction; also
autographs and documents.*

Greg Manning
Greg Manning Auctions, Inc.
775 Passaic Ave.
West Caldwell, NJ 07006
phone: 201-882-0004 or 800-221-0243
fax: 201-882-3499
*Dealer and auctioneer in all philatelic
properties.*

Jacques C. Schiff, Jr.
Jacques C. Schiff, Jr. Inc.
195 Main St.
Ridgefield Park, NJ 07660-1620
phone: 201-641-5566
fax: 201-641-5705
*Auctioneers of worldwide stamps and
postal history; specialties include U.S.
stamps, world stamps, U.S. and world
postal history, errors and varieties;
also purchase outright and sell
consignments.*

Keith & Alison Harmer
Harmers of New York, Inc.
3 E 28th St.
New York, NY 10016-7408
phone: 212-532-3700
fax: 212-447-5625
Harmers specializes in the sale of

stamps, but also sells paper items such as autographs, manuscripts, maps, etc.

Robson Lowe
Christie's
502 Park Ave.
New York, NY 10022
phone: 212-546-1000
fax: 212-980-8163
Internet: http://www.sirius.com/
~christie/

Elizabeth C. Pope
Robert A. Siegel Auction Galleries, Inc.
65 East 55th St.
New York, NY 10022
phone: 212-753-6421
fax: 212-753-6429

Earl Apfelbaum
Earl P.L. Apfelbaum, Inc.
2006 Walnut St.
Philadelphia, PA 19103
phone: 215-567-5200
Public auctions and mail bid sales of U.S. and foreign stamps.

Charles G. Firby Auctions
6695 Highland Rd., Ste. 107
Waterford, MI 48327-5333
phone: 810-666-5333
fax: 810-666-5020

Rasdale Stamp Company
36 South Street, Stuie 1102
Chicago, IL 60603
phone: 312-263-7334
fax: 312-263-1819
Frequent public and mail auctions of U.S. and world stamps.

I. Michael Orenstein
Superior Stamp & Coin
9478 West Olympic Blvd.
Beverly Hills, CA 90212-4299
phone: 310-203-9855
fax: 310-203-0496
Conducts specialty auctions for stamp collections, other philatelic material, and space memorabilia.

Book Sellers

Empire Group, Inc.
P.O. Box 2529
West Lawn, PA 19609
phone: 215-678-5000
Publishes a yearly philatelic literature price list; many hard-to-find out-of-print books.

David G. Phillips Company, Inc.
P.O. Box 611388
Miami, FL 33161-1388
phone: 305-895-0470
Deals in U.S. covers and philatelic literature; sells the basic important references for the U.S. stamp specialist.

Leonard Hartmann
P.O. Box 36006
Louisville, KY 40233-6006
phone: 502-451-0317
fax: 502-459-8538
e-mail: pbooks@ibm.net
A "Philatelic Bibliophile"; a source for virtually all important stamp books, in or out of print.

Clubs/Associations

American Association of Philatelic Exhibitors
Journal: Philatelic Exhibitor, The
P.O. Box 432
South Orange, NJ 07079

Gus Davidson
International Stamp Club of New York
P.O. Box 321
Bowling Green Station
New York, NY 10004
Provides members opportunity to buy, sell, trade stamps.

American Stamp Dealers Association
3 School St., Ste. 205
Glen Cove, NY 11542-2548
phone: 516-759-7000
fax: 516-759-7014
e-mail: asda@inx.net
Trade association representing stamp dealers; issues free list of dealers in your area and by your special area of interest; sponsors national and regional stamp shows; offers free brochures about stamp collecting, dealing, etc.

Charles Eson
Fort Orange Stamp Club
128 Western Ave.
Altamont, NY 12009
phone: 578-861-6256
Oldest continuously meeting stamp club in the U.S.; meets 2nd and 4th Tuesday of the month from September through May in Albany, NY.

American Philatelic Society
Magazine: American Philatelist
P.O. Box 8000
State College, PA 16803-8000
phone: 814-237-3803
fax: 814-237-6128
e-mail: ambristo@stamps.org
Internet: http://www.west.net/~stamps1/
aps.html
The largest stamp collector organization in the US; provides services to 58,000 collectors in more than 100 countries; 700 local allied stamp clubs, 200 national "specialty groups", code of ethics, estate advice, expertizing.

Junior Philatelists of America
Journal: Philatelic Observer
P.O. Box 8000
State College, PA 16803-8000
phone: 814-237-3803
fax: 814-237-6128
e-mail: ambristo@stamps.org
Internet: http://www.west.net/~stamps1/
aps.html
Organization for pre-adult collectors.

David Lee
Bureau Issues Association, Inc.
Journal: Specialist, The
P.O. Box 2641
Reston, VA 20195
For collectors of U.S. stamps; publisher of reference material on U.S. stamps.

Dudley Bauerlein
CompuServe Stamp Chapter, American Philatelic Society
2117 Greenway Dr.
Winter Haven, FL 33881-1257
phone: 813-294-5279
fax: 813-299-2450
e-mail: 70661.3213@compuserve.com
Largest electronic stamp club in the world serving US and world wide collectors; 2 monthly stamp auctions; library with many files on stamp collecting; for CompuServe new member kit, dial toll free 800-848-8199 (GO COLLECT or GO STAMPS).

Janet Klug, Sec.-Treas.
American Philatelic Congress
P.O. Box 250
Pleasant Plain, OH 45162
Provides a service to philately by editing, printing, and distributing to members a quality hardbound book of original research papers annually.

Carriers & Locals Society
P.O. Box 1574
Dayton, OH 45401-1574
Members interested in collecting and study of U.S. carriers and locals: U.S. official and semi-official carrier services, 19th century local posts, independent mails, package expresses of the 19th century, fakes & forgeries.

Indiana Stamp Club
P.O. Box 40792
indianapolis, IN 46240

Jerome C. Jarnick, Sec.
British North American Philatelic Society
Journal: BNA Topics
108 Duncan Dr.
Watervliet, MI 49098-4613
phone: 248-689-1966
fax: 248-689-1966
e-mail: Jarnick@compuserve.com
Internet: http://www.compusmart.ab.ca/
stalbert/bnaps.htm
BNAPS is devoted to the study of stamps and postal history of Canada and the former colonies; also publishes the "BNA Portraits," a newsletter; annual convention.

Trans-Mississippi Philatelic Society
Journal: Trans-Mississippian, The
P.O. Box 164
Council Bluffs, IA 51502
Local chapters, annual convention, membership awards; most members are from the Midwest.

Mark D. Rogers, Mem.
U.S. Philatelic Classics Society
Journal: Chronicle, The
P.O. Box 80708
North Canton, OH 78708-0708
Focuses on stamps issued over one hundred years ago; old, rare and valuable stamps.

Israel I. Bick, Ex. Dir.
International Stamp Collectors Society
Newsletter: Interstamps
P.O. Box 854
Van Nuys, CA 91408-0854
phone: 818-997-6496
fax: 818-988-4337
e-mail: iibick@aol.com
Internet: http://www.4free.com/bick
Promoting understanding in the world through stamp collecting.

National Stamp Dealers Association
P.O. Box 7176
Redwood City, CA 94063
phone: 800-875-6633 or 415-364-6667
fax: 415-364-6972

Collectors

Marc L. Ames
539 Lyme Rock Rd.
Bridgewater, NJ 08807-1670
phone: 908-526-7676
fax: 908-575-0880
e-mail: magames@ix.netcom.com
Wants to buy essays, proofs, specimens, samples and pre-1940 issues.

Roland Roehner
North Carolina Stamp Club
P.O. Box 1674
Nags Head, NC 27959
phone: 919-441-7510

Carl Cervenka, Sec./Treas.
International Society of Worldwide Stamp Collectors
Route 1, Box 69A
Caddo Mills, TX 75135-9704
phone: 903-527-3957
Internet: http://www.philately.com/
iswsc/homepage.htm
Serves the interests of all worldwide stamp collectors.

U.S. Philatelic Classics Society, Inc.
Journal: Chronicle of the U.S. Classic Postal Issues
P.O. Box 80708
Austin, TX 78708-0708
e-mail: mdr3@swbell.net
Internet: http://www.scruz.net/~eho/
uspcs/
Members focus on U.S. stamps from the period 1851 to 1857.

Richard M. Simon
1846 27th Ave.
San Francisco, CA 94122-4212
phone: 415-566-3920
Wants to buy worldwide stamp, cover
and postcard collections; member of
the American Philatelic Society, Hong
Kong Stamp Society, and Hong Kong
Study Circle; specializing in US,
British Commonwealth, and Asia.

Dealers

Jack E. Molesworth
88 Beacon St.
Boston, MA 02108
phone: 617-523-2522
Classic U.S. stamps and covers
bought and sold.

Richard A. Champagne
P.O. Box 372
Newtonville, MA 02160
phone: 617-969-5719
Stocks U.S. classics; does important
stamp shows; an entertaining speaker
at show seminars.

Brookman Barrett & Worthen
10 Chestnut Dr.
Bedford, NH 03110
phone: 800-332-3383

Jacques C. Schiff, Jr.
Jacques C. Schiff, Jr. Inc.
195 Main St.
Ridgefield Park, NJ 07660-1620
phone: 201-641-5566
fax: 201-641-5705
Buys, sells, auctions, and appraises
U.S. and World stamps, errors and
varieties.

Downtown Stamp Company
P.O. Box 329
Whitehouse, NJ 08888-0329
phone: 908-439-3663
fax: 908-439-2414
Services want lists for U.S. and world
issues, including less expensive and
moderately priced items.

Sam Malamud
Ideal Stamp Company
460 West 34th St.
New York, NY 10001
phone: 212-629-7979
fax: 212-629-3350
Buying and selling stamps of the
world, especially U.S., British, Israel,
and United Nations.

John A. Rerecic
J.R. Stamps
838 West End Ave., 1-A
New York, NY 10025-5365
phone: 212-663-6096 or 212-807-6477
e-mail: JRerecic@aol.com
Operates a store open only on
Saturdays and Sundays from 10 a.m.
to 6 p.m. at 110 W 25th Street, Store
#609, New York, NY 10001.

Harry Hagendorf
Columbian Stamp Company, Inc.
700 White Plains Rd.
Scarsdale, NY 10583
phone: 914-725-2290
fax: 914-572-2576
Dealer in rare stamps, including the
famous 1918 inverted Jenny biplane.

Columbian Stamp Company
P.O. Box B
New Rochelle, NY 10804
phone: 914-725-2290
U.S. classics, including 19th century
multiples.

Henry Gitner Philatelists, Inc.
P.O. Box 3077
Middletown, NY 10940
phone: 800-947-8267
fax: 914-343-0068
e-mail: hgitner@aol.com
Internet: http://www.hgitner.com
Specializes in classic U.S. stamps.

Gary Posner
6340 Avenue N., Ste. 121
Brooklyn, NY 11234
phone: 718-251-1952 or 800-323-GARY
fax: 718-241-2801

Jack & Myrna Golden
Golden Philatelics
P.O. Box 484
Cedarhurst, NY 11516
phone: 516-791-1804
fax: 516-791-7846
Good stock of U.S. revenues,
including cheaper but elusive
varieties, bought and sold.

Charles Eson
128 Western Ave.
Altamont, NY 12009
phone: 578-861-6256
Specializing in U.S. coils, Revenues,
used, Canada, Mexico, and
Mediterranean countries.

Mystic Stamp Company
9700 Mill St.
Camden, NY 13316
phone: 800-835-3609
fax: 800-835-4919
Buys entire dealer stock, U.S. stamp
collections, worldwide and topical
stamp collections, rare individual
stamps both U.S. and worldwide,
mixed accumulations, U.S. and
worldwide covers.

James J. Reeves
P.O. Box 219
Huntingdon, PA 16652
phone: 800-364-2948
fax: 814-641-2600

Bob Morris
706 Pawnee St.
Bethlehem, PA 18015-1432
phone: 610-865-9052
Purchases U.S. and foreign stamps,
envelopes and philatelic literature;
will appraise in the PA, NJ, NY and
DE area; will appraise stamp

collections and cover collections in
this region.

Dale
P.O. Box 539
Emmaus, PA 18049
phone: 610-433-3303
fax: 610-965-6089

Milton & Marion Mitchell
M. Mitchell - Stamps 'N' Covers
3401 Hallaton Ct.
Silver Spring, MD 20906
phone: 301-598-7959
Purchases and appraises stamp
collections and estates.

Michael Rogers
Michael Rogers, Inc.
199 E. Welbourne Ave., Ste. 3
Winter Park, FL 32789
phone: 407-644-2290
fax: 407-645-4434
Carries full line of U.S. and foreign
stamps; good selection of stamp
collecting supplies.

Herman Herst, Jr.
P.O. Box 1583
Boca Raton, FL 33429-1583
phone: 800-321-6180 or 561-391-3223
Wants to buy old pre-1890 letters and
envelopes, with or without stamps; toll
free number to help you learn the
value of what you have; 60 years in
the business; Senior Member, ASA;
free booklet to anyone sending SASE.

Joachim Steltzer
Steltzer International
5030 Champion Blvd., Ste. G-6 #116
Boca Raton, FL 33496-2496
phone: 561-852-1435
fax: 561-451-8774
Dealer and expert in stamps.

Jim Dalton, Sr.
Dalton & Dalton
P.O. Box 487
Muncie, IN 47305-0487
phone: 317-288-9488
Stamp collections wanted, large or
small; since 1949.

Jerry & Barbara Koepp
Stamps "n' Stuff
Governor Square
2700 University, Ste. 214
West Des Moines, IA 50266-1451
phone: 800-999-5964 or 515-224-1713
fax: 515-226-1651
e-mail: bkoepp@earthlink.net

Robert M. Weisz
4562 N. Austin Ave.
Chicago, IL 60630
phone: 773-545-2929
Buys, sells, appraises stamps and
postcards.

John Rebello
Town & Country Stamps
P.O. Box 13542
North County, MO 63138
phone: 314-522-0289
Constantly buying large and small lots
of stamps; will buy just about

anything; sells mixtures and more
expensive items also.

Raymond Weill
Raymond H. Weill Company
407 Royal St.
New Orleans, LA 70130
phone: 504-581-7373
Carries a good stock of U.S. stamps.

George C. Baxley
P.O. Box 807
Alamogordo, NM 88311
phone: 505-437-8707
fax: 505-434-1571
Buying and selling worldwide stamps
and covers; specializing in Asia.

Cy Phillips, Jr.
S C Coin & Stamp Co. Inc.
P.O. Drawer 661180
Arcadia, CA 91066-1180
phone: 818-445-8277 or 800-367-0779
fax: 818-445-8278

Warren Sankey
United States Stamp Company
368 Bush St.
San Francisco, CA 94104
phone: 415-421-7398
fax: 415-421-3167
Buys and sells worldwide and U.S.
mint and used stamps; also carries
supplies.

Experts

Alfred J. Moses
P.O. Box 3547
Riverside, CA 92519
Writes stamp column for "Collectors
News"; will entertain questions if
accompanied by a self-addressed and
stamped envelope.

Misc. Services

Philatelic Foundation
501 5th Ave., Ste. 1901
New York, NY 10017-6107
phone: 212-867-3699
fax: 212-867-3984
An expertizing organization which
will verify the genuineness of a rare
stamp; write for list of fees; enclose a
SASE.

American Philatelic Society
P.O. Box 8000
State College, PA 16803-8000
phone: 814-237-3803
fax: 814-237-6128
e-mail: ambristo@stamps.org
Internet: http://www.west.net/~stamps1/
aps.html
An expertizing organization which
will verify the genuineness of a rare
stamp; write for list of fees; enclose a
SASE.

American Philatelic Expertizing Service
P.O. Box 8000
State College, PA 16803-8000
phone: 814-237-3803
fax: 814-237-6128
e-mail: ambristo@stamps.org
Internet: http://www.west.net/~stamps1/
aps.html
Run jointly by the American Philatelic Society and the American Stamp Dealers Association; offers substantial discounts on fees to members of either organization.

Citizens' Stamp Advisory Committee, c/o Stamp Development Branch
U.S. Postal Service
Washington, DC 20260
Welcomes suggestions from the private citizen for stamp ideas to honor famous (and not so famous) people, animals, historical events or sites, sports, occupations, and good causes; impressive stationery and long petitions help.

Citizens' Stamp Advisory Committee,
Stamp Information Branch, USPS
475 L'Enfant Plaza, Room 5800
Washington, DC 20260-6753
Ideas for stamp designs may be sent to the Citizens' Stamp Advisory Committee.

Museums/Libraries

Cardinal Spellman Philatelic Museum, Inc. at Regis College
235 Wellesley St.
Weston, MA 02193
phone: 617-894-6735
fax: 617-894-8056
This museum houses the personal collections of Cardinal Spellman, President Eisenhower, and Jascha Heifetz.

Collectors Club, The
Journal: Collectors Club Philatelist, The
22 East 35th St.
New York, NY 10016-3806
phone: 212-683-0559
fax: 212-481-1269
Library has over 140,000 items and is one of the largest specialized philatelic library in the world.

American Philatelic Research Library
P.O. Box 8000
State College, PA 16803-8000
phone: 814-237-3803
fax: 814-237-6128
e-mail: ambristo@stamps.org
Internet: http://www.west.net/~stamps1/
aps.html
The largest general philatelic library in the US that's open to the public.

National Postal Museum
First St. & Mass. Ave. NE
Washington, DC 20013
phone: 202-357-2700 or 202-357-2020

National Museum of American History, National Philatelic Collection
14th & Constitution Ave. NW
Washington, DC 20560
phone: 202-357-2700
Internet: http://www.si.edu/

Larry D. Sall
Wineburgh Philatelic Research Library, Univ. of TX at Dallas
P.O. Box 830643
Richardson, TX 75083-0643
phone: 972-883-2570
e-mail: sall@utdallas.edu
Contains over 5,000 stamp books, many journals, and auction catalogs.

Postal History Foundation, The
920 North First Ave.
Tucson, AZ 85719
phone: 602-623-6652
Houses artifacts, postmarks and covers dedicated to postal history.

Wells Fargo Bank History Museum, Wiltsee Memorial Collection of Western Stamps
420 Montgomery St.
San Francisco, CA 94163
phone: 415-396-2619
This collection of Western stamps, franks, and postmarks includes over 235 different express companies and such fascinating items as Pony Express stamps and early California "ghost" town cancels.

On-Line Services

Stampfinder
6175 NW 153rd St., Ste. 221
Hialeah, FL 33014
phone: 305-557-1135
fax: 309-557-1454
Internet: http://www.stampfinder.com
A multi-dealer buy site offering comparative side-by-side pricing of like items; search for stamps by topic, country or item; search for covers with full color images; download free inventory software; use the internet to buy/sell stamps.

Roger Pearce
Stamp Ink
545 N. Mountain Ave., Ste. 109
Upland, CA 91786
phone: 909-861-9547
fax: 909-860-7557
e-mail: roger@stamplink.com
Internet: http://www.stamplink.com
Jump-off platform to hottest internet stamp sites around the world.

Periodicals

Jacques Herrijgers
Newsletter: MiniPhil
1 Nachtegaallaan, B-1701
Itterbeek, Belgium
A quarterly international advertising sheet for stamp collectors only; a bilingual publication (French and English.)

Link House Publications
Magazine: Stamp Magazine
Link House, Dingwall Avenue
Croydon
Surrey CR9 2TA, U.K.
phone: 0181 686 2599
Britain's leading stamp publication; articles, G.B. covers, stamps, cancellations, postcards, auction news, stamp shows, etc.

Paul Fiocca
Trajan Publishing Corp.
Newspaper: Canadian Stamp News
103 Lakeshore Rd., Ste. 202
St. Catharines
Ontario L2N 2T6 Canada
phone: 905-646-7744
fax: 905-646-0995
e-mail: bret@trajan.com
Internet: http://www.vaxxine.com/trajan/
Insightful, up-to-date philatelic articles, world-wide new releases, reports on finds, errors and auctions.

Brookman Barrett & Worthen
Magazine: Brookman Times, The
10 Chestnut Dr.
Bedford, NH 03110
phone: 800-332-3383
Ads, articles, classifieds.

Philatelic Foundation
Newsletter: Philatelic Foundation Bulletin
501 5th Ave., Ste. 1901
New York, NY 10017-6107
phone: 212-867-3699
fax: 212-867-3984
Profiles stamp collectors and their collections.

Philatelic Communications Corp.
Newspaper: Mekeel's Weekly Stamp News
P.O. Box 5050
White Plains, NY 10602
phone: 800-635-3351
A newspaper for adult stamp collectors.

Philatelic Communications Corp.
Magazine: U.S. Stamp News Monthly Magazine
P.O. Box 5050
White Plains, NY 10602
phone: 800-635-3351

Cathi Kenyon, Pub.
H.L. Lindquist Publications
Newspaper: Stamps
85 Canisteo St.
Hornell, NY 14843-1544
phone: 607-324-2212
fax: 607-324-1753
The weekly publication of philately; features the latest in philatelic news, collections, ads, auction results, upcoming stamp shows, new stamp issues etc.

Cathi Kenyon, Pub.
H.L. Lindquist Publications
Journal: Stamp Auction News
85 Canisteo St.
Hornell, NY 14843-1544
phone: 607-324-2212
fax: 607-324-1753
A monthly market journal with recent auction prices realized; prices, ads, auction house profiles, vendor ads, etc.

Newsletter: Global Stamp News
P.O. Box 97
Sidney, OH 45365
phone: 513-492-3183
fax: 513-492-6514
Monthly newspaper with over 100 pages; articles, advertisements, etc.

Michael Laurence, Ed.
Newspaper: Linn's Stamp News
P.O. Box 29
Sidney, OH 45365-0029
phone: 937-498-0801
fax: 800-340-9501
e-mail: linns@linns.com
Internet: http://www.linns.com
World's largest stamp marketplace with up-to-the-minute hobby news, reports on topics from trends in values, special interest collections to under-collected stamps; well-respected in the hobby; indispensable for the stamp collector.

Wayne L. Youngblood
Scott Publishing Co.
Magazine: Scott's Stamp Monthly
P.O. Box 828
Sidney, OH 45365-0828
phone: 513-498-0802 or 800-5SC-OTT5
fax: 513-498-0808
Magazine features notices of new stamp issues (using copyrighted Scott Numbering system) and other articles for the collector.

Julie A. Ulrich, PR
Krause Publications
Newspaper: Stamp Collector
700 E. State St.
Iola, WI 54990-0001
phone: 715-445-2214
fax: 715-445-4087
e-mail: info@krause.com
Internet: http://www.krause.com
Covers a wide variety of U.S. as well as foreign stamp news from the world over; articles, special features, and theme issues.

Julie A. Ulrich, PR
Krause Publications
Newspaper: Stamp Wholesaler, The
700 E. State St.
Iola, WI 54990-0001
phone: 715-445-2214
fax: 715-445-4087
e-mail: info@krause.com
Internet: http://www.krause.com
World's largest stamp dealer publication; used as a "Philatelic Phonebook" by the entire industry; articles and ads are written for the dealer.

Air Mail Related

(see also AIRLINE MEMORABILIA)

Clubs/Associations

Jim Graue
American Air Mail Society
Journal: Airpost Journal, The
P.O. Box 110
Mineola, NY 11501-0110
phone: 509-924-4484 or 509-466-4602
fax: 509-466-4698
Focuses on any stamps or covers relating to air mail; areas of specialty include Crash Mail, Lindberghiana, U.S. and foreign first flights, Rocket Mail, Balloon Mail, Glider Mail, Zeppelin Mail, Amelia Earhart, Concord, etc.

Albrecht Durer

Clubs/Associations

Jack Denys
Albrecht Durer Study Unit of the American Topical Association
Newsletter: Durer Journal
3 East Cadillac Dr.
Somerville, NJ 08876
Life and works of Albrecht Durer.

American Indian

Clubs/Associations

Charles Eson
American Indian Philatelic Society of the American Topical Association
Newsletter: Council Fire
128 Western Ave.
Altamont, NY 12009
phone: 578-861-6256
Native American cultures.

Americana

Clubs/Associations

Dennis Dengel
Americana Unit of the American Topical Association
Newsletter: Americana Philatelic News
17 Peckham Rd.
Poughkeepsie, NY 12603-2018
e-mail: 70363.3621@compuserve.com
Internet: http://www.philately.com/society_news/American_unit.htm
History, culture, and industry of the U.S.

Archaeology

Clubs/Associations

Heinz Schwinge
Archaeological (Old World) Study Unit of the American Topical Association
Newsletter: Old World Archaeologist
1516 Hinman Ave., #503
Evanston, IL 60201
Archaeology of the eastern hemisphere.

Chris Moser
Archaeology (Mesoamerican) Study Unit of the American Topical Association
Newsletter: Codex Filatelica
P.O. Box 1442
Riverside, CA 92502
Pre-Columbian cultures of the Americas.

Armenia

Clubs/Associations

Armenian Philatelic Association
P.O. Box 4803
Glendale, CA 91222-0803
phone: 818-244-8139

Art

Clubs/Associations

H. Ruth Richards, Sec.
Fine & Performing Arts of the American Topical Association
: FAP Journal
10393 Derby Dr.
Laurel, MD 20723
e-mail: bersec@aol.com
Internet: http://www.philately.com/society_news/fap.htm
For collectors and those interested in fine art and the performing arts on stamps.

Astronomy

Clubs/Associations

George Young
Astronomy Unit of the American Topical Association
Newsletter: Astrofax
P.O. Box 632
Tewksbury, MA 01876
phone: 508-851-8283
e-mail: george-young@msn.com
Astronomy, astrology, zodiac.

Australia

Clubs/Associations

Stuart H. Leven
Society of Australian Specialists/Oceania
Newsletter: Transformer, The
P.O. Box 24764
San Jose, CA 95154-4764

Biblical

Clubs/Associations

Rev. Frank Pieper
Biblical Topics Study Unit of the American Topical Association
Newsletter: Biblical Philately
P.O. Box 169
Emden, IL 62635
Old and New Testaments.

Bicycle

Clubs/Associations

Bill Hofmann
Bicycle Stamp Club of the American Topical Association
Newsletter: Bicycle Stamps
610 North Pin Oak Lane
Muncie, IN 47304

Biology

Clubs/Associations

Betty Rutherford
Biology Unit of the American Topical Association
Newsletter: Biophilately
4310 Indian Creek Rd.
Marion, IA 52302
Animal and plant life, present and prehistoric.

Black Related

Clubs/Associations

Ebony Society of Philatelic Events & Reflections
P.O. Box 548
F.D.R. Station
New York, NY 10150-0548
Interested in collecting material related to all philatelic services that contribute to the long-term improvement and enhancement of black stamp collecting and black history makers, past and present.

Booklets

Clubs/Associations

Booklet Collectors Club
Newsletter: Interleaf, The
1016 E. El Camino Real, #107
Sunnyvale, CA 94087
Focuses on booklet panes (sheets) of the world.

Boy Scouting

Clubs/Associations

Carl Schauer
Scouts on Stamps Society International of the American Topical Association
Journal: SOSSI Journal
P.O. Box 526
Belen, NM 87002-0526
phone: 505-864-0098
fax: 505-865-3839

British

Clubs/Associations

Royal Philatelic Society, London
Journal: London Philatelist
41 Devonshire Place
London W1N 1PE, U.K.
phone: 0171 486 1044
fax: 0171 486 0803

Dealers

Bill Martin
William Lawrence Philatelics
P.O. Box 991756
Redding, CA 96099-1756
phone: 916-223-5448
fax: 916-223-5448
e-mail: 75247.3315@compuserve.com
Buys and sells collectible postage stamps of the British Empire.

Butterfly & Moth

Clubs/Associations

Dr. Greg Herbert
Butterfly & Moth Stamp Society of the American Topical Association
Newsletter: Swallowtail, The
3739 Spring Lake Lane
Owings Mills, MD 21117

Canadian

Clubs/Associations

Andrew D. Parr, Administrator
Royal Philatelic Society of Canada
Journal: Canadian Philatelist, The
P.O. Box 929, Station "Q"
Toronto
Ontario M4T 2P1 Canada
phone: 416-979-7474
fax: 416-979-1144
e-mail: rpsc@interlog.com
Internet: http://www.interlog.com/~rpsc
Focus in on Canadian postal history; the journal is 80 pages, 6" x 8 3/4", published bi-monthly; accepts donations of philatelic material which is appraised and tax receipts issued to owners; journal "Opusculum" published every other year.

John Peebles
Canadiana Study Unit of the American Topical Association
Newsletter: Canadian Connection, The
P.O. Box 3262
Station "A", London
Ontario N6A 4K3 Canada
History, culture, and industry of Canada.

Museums/Libraries

Canadian Postal Archives
395 Wellington St.
Ottawa
Ontario K1A 0N3 Canada
phone: 613-992-3884
fax: 613-995-6297
Part of the National Archives of Canada; houses a library of 10,000 philatelic volumes, as well as a large collection of Canadian and international stamps.

Cancels

Clubs/Associations

Art Hadley
Machine Cancel Society
Journal: Machine Cancel Forum
3407 N 925 E
Hope, IN 47246-9717
Internet: http://www.cris.com/
~Swanson/mcs.html

Captain Cook

Clubs/Associations

Brian Sanford
Captain Cook Study Unit of the
American Topical Association
Newsletter: Cook's Log
173 Minuteman Dr.
Concord, MA 01742
*Life and voyages of Captain James
Cook.*

Caribbean

Clubs/Associations

Peter Kaulback, Sec.
British Caribbean Philatelic Study Group
Journal: British Caribbean Philatelic
Journal
108 Byron Ave.
Ottawa
Ontario K1Y 3J2 Canada

Cats

Clubs/Associations

Mary Ann Brown
Cats on Stamps Unit of the American
Topical Association
Newsletter: Cat Mews
3006 Wade Rd.
Durham, NC 27705
Domestic and wild felines.

Chemistry & Physics

Clubs/Associations

Dr. Roland Hirsch
Chemistry & Physics Study Unit of the
American Topical Association
Newsletter: Philatelia Chimica et
Physica
20458 Water Point Lane
Germantown, MD 20874

Chess

Clubs/Associations

Anne Kasonic
Chess on Stamps Study Unit of the
American Topical Association
Newsletter: Chesstamp Review
7624 Country Rd., #153
Interlaken, NY 14247
Chess, other board games.

Chinese

Clubs/Associations

Paul H. Gault, Mem.
China Stamp Society, Inc., The
140 W. 18th Ave.
Columbus, OH 43210

Christmas

Clubs/Associations

Robert A. Johnson, Sec.
Christmas Philatelic Club of the
American Topical Association
Newsletter: Yule Log
5 Sanford Ave.
Baltimore, MD 21228-5004
phone: 410-778-6358
*For those interested in collecting
Christmas stamps from around the
world: seals, covers, postcards and
any related Christmas material.*

Christmas & Charity

Clubs/Associations

Richard Roberts, Sec.
Christmas Seal & Charity Stamp
Society, The
Newsletter: Seal News
P.O. Box 39696
Edina, MN 55439-0696
phone: 612-721-1981
*Focuses on stamp and metered seals
such as tuberculosis, veterans,
fraternal and civic, Jewish, ethnic,
pets, wildlife, medical, Easter, etc.
seals.*

Christopher Columbus

Clubs/Associations

David Nye
Christopher Columbus Philatelic Society
of the American Topical Association
Newsletter: Discovery
P.O. Box 1492
Frankenmuth, MI 48734
*Life and voyage of Christopher
Columbus.*

Colombia

Clubs/Associations

Colombia & Panama Philatelists
Newsletter: COPACARTA
P.O. Box 2245
El Cajon, CA 92021

Commemorative

Collectors

Kim Malcom
6410 Sierra Dr. SE
Lacey, WA 98503
phone: 206-456-8424
*Interested in U.S. commemorative
stamps.*

Computer Programs For

Man./Prod./Dist.

Ninga Software Corporation
Program: Hobbysoft Stamp Keeper
882 Pepin Cres.
Victoria
Brit. Col. V8Z 6V6 Canada
phone: 800-656-4642 or 250-881-8355
Internet: http://www.islandnet.com/
~ninga
*Relevant stamp description, year of
issue, denomination and price
information, inventory, evaluate
collections, annual market values
updates, generates reports.*

Roger S. Edelman
Program: Stamp Collector's Data Base
8505 River Rock Terrace
Bethesda, MD 20817-4321
phone: 800-321-SCDB or 301-320-2451

Changing Seasons Software, Inc.
Program: StampBase for Windows
5881 Roanoke Dr.
Madison, WI 53719
phone: 800-260-2739 or 608-273-2739
fax: 608-273-1965
*Scott Catalog Number System, yearly
catalog updates with market values,
print your want lists, design
customized inventory reports, store
and display pictures of your stamps,
and more.*

Confederate

Clubs/Associations

Richard H. Byne
Confederate Stamp Alliance
Magazine: Confederate Philatelist
7518 Buckskin Lane
San Antonio, TX 78227-2716
e-mail: rhbcsaps@flash.net
Internet: http://www.flash.net/~rhbscaps/
*Focuses on the mail and postal
systems used during the Civil War
period. The bi-monthly booklet
contains extensively researched
articles; an association (nonpolitical)
of collectors of Confederate postage
stamps and covers.*

Dealers

Jack E. Molesworth
Confederate Philately, Inc.
88 Beacon St.
Boston, MA 02108
phone: 617-523-2522
*Buys and sells; has large and
comprehensive stock of Confederate
stamps, covers, and related items.*

Brian & Maria Green
Brian Michael Green
P.O. Box 1816
Kernersville, NC 27285-1816
phone: 910-993-5100
fax: 910-993-1801
Internet: http://
ww.eastnc2.coastalnet.com/militaria/
bmginc.html
*Buy & sell Confederate States stamps,
postally used envelopes & related*
*material, military correspondences &
Generals' letters, etc.*

Costa Rica

Clubs/Associations

Society of Costa Rica Collectors, The
P.O. Box 14831
Baton Rouge, LA 70808
Internet: http://www.intersurf.com/
~hrmena

Covers

Auction Services

Richard C. Frajola
Richard C. Frajola, Inc.
P.O. Box 608
Empire, CO 80438
phone: 303-569-3241
fax: 303-569-3244
*Well-researched auction catalogs of
U.S. classic covers.*

Collectors

Lewis Leigh, Jr.
P.O. Box 4327
Leesburg, VA 20177
phone: 703-771-3081
fax: 703-771-1432
*Wants to buy items pertaining to early
Virginia postal history: old letters
with interesting content, stampless
covers, etc.*

Dealers

Bob Morris
706 Pawnee St.
Bethlehem, PA 18015-1432
phone: 610-865-9052
*Wants to purchase US and foreign
covers; anything to 1960; stampless to
WWII; large quantities wanted.*

Tom Osjecki
Phyllis' Philatelics
P.O. Box 792
Canyonville, OR 97417
phone: 541-839-4135 or 541-839-6151
*Buys, sells and specializes in
postcards, paper Americana, stamps
and covers; over 25,000 covers and
postcards listed by state or topic.*

Experts

James Kesterson
3881 Fulton Grove Rd.
Cincinnati, OH 45245-2504
phone: 513-752-0949
*Wants 19th century U.S. stamps on
envelopes (covers); also stampless
and illustrated covers; any amount.*

Periodicals

Brookman Barrett & Worthen
Magazine: Brookman's Coverline
10 Chestnut Dr.
Bedford, NH 03110
phone: 800-332-3383
*Bi-monthly magazine about covers:
U.S. first day covers, Akron and
Macon covers, Zeppelin covers, flight*

covers, WWII patriotic covers, catapult covers, Hawaii and Pacific Rim covers, etc.

Covers (First Day)

Auction Services

Michael Mellone
FDC Publishing Co.
P.O. Box 206
Stewartsville, NJ 08886-0206
phone: 908-479-4617
fax: 908-479-6158
e-mail: FDC@4-collectors.com
Conducts monthly mail auctions exclusively for First Day Covers; publishes price catalogs for first day covers.

Clubs/Associations

American First Day Cover Society
Journal: First Days
P.O. Box 65960
Tucson, AZ 85728-5960
phone: 520-321-9191
fax: 520-321-9494
e-mail: afdcs@aol.com
Internet: http://www.philately.com/
society_news/afdcs.htm
First days, annual conventions, chapters, cover exchange, auctions, cachet information, awards, foreign information, expertizing, question box, archives, translation service, sales department, slide programs, USPS liaison.

Collectors

203 Village Way
Brick, NJ 08724

Man./Prod./Dist.

Postal Commemorative Society
47 Richards Ave.
P.O. Box 57491
Norwalk, CT 06857-4910
Sells a series of new first day covers.

Covers (Naval)

Clubs/Associations

Terry Holmes, Sec.
Universal Ship Cancellation Society
Magazine: Log
10601 Lazy Day Lane
Mitchellville, MD 20721-1805
Dedicated to the collection and study of Naval and maritime Postal History; interested in covers from ships and related installations.

Dogs

Clubs/Associations

Morris Raskin
Dogs On Stamps Study Unit of the American Topical Association
Journal: DOSSU Journal
202A Newport Rd.
Cranbury, NJ 08512-3920
phone: 609-655-7411
Purpose is to further the collection

and study of philatelic postal material that pertains to dogs.

Duck/Fish & Game

(see also STAMP COLLECTING; Revenue & Tax Stamps)

Clubs/Associations

National Duck Stamp Collectors Society
Newsletter: Duck Tracks
P.O. Box 43
Harleysville, PA 19438
Promotes and encourages the collecting and study of migratory waterfowl hunting and conservation stamps: Federal/state/foreign duck stamps, first day covers, artist signed stamps, duck stamp prints.

Dealers

Sport'en Art
1015 W. Jackson
Sullivan, IL 61951
phone: 800-382-5723 or 217-728-2361

Bob Dumaine
Sam Houston Philatelics
13310 Westheimer, Ste. 150
Houston, TX 77077-3506
phone: 281-493-6386 or 800-231-5926
fax: 281-496-1445
e-mail: rwhouduck@aol.com
Handles all types of collector stamps including United States and World Wide; specialty is Duck Stamps (also known as Hunting Permit stamps); holds several auctions each year; attends nation wide stamp shows; retail store; mail order.

Michael Jaffe
P.O. Box 61484
Vancouver, WA 98666-1484
phone: 360-695-6161 or 800-782-6770
fax: 360-695-1616
Issues catalog of state and federal duck stamps, and stamps issued by Indian reservations.

Experts

Lynn Troute "Dr. Duck"
Lynn Troute Decoys
3808 Kingsley Dr.
Springfield, IL 62707-7250
phone: 217-787-3595
Buys, sells, collects, appraises and specializes in all Federal and State duck stamps available; send for free list; also buying duck stamps used, mint or on licenses, and old wooden decoys and other hunting and fishing artifacts.

David R. Torre
P.O. Box 4298
Santa Rosa, CA 95402
phone: 707-525-8785
Wants pictorial and non-pictorial waterfowl and fishing stamps; also pre-1930 pictorial hunting & fishing licenses from any state.

Misc. Services

Federal Duck Stamp Office, U.S. Fish & Wildlife Service
1849 C. St., NW, Ste. 2058
Washington, DC 20240
phone: 202-208-4354
Proceeds from the sale of Federal duck stamps go to the preservation of national wetlands.

Earth

Clubs/Associations

Fred Klein
Earth's Physical Features Study Unit of the American Topical Association
Newsletter: Nature's Wonders
515 Magdalena Ave.
Los Altos, CA 94022
Earthquakes, environment, meteorology, mountains, oceanography, rivers, volcanoes.

Errors

Clubs/Associations

Errors, Freaks & Oddities Collectors Club
Newsletter: EFO Collector
138 Lakemont Dr., East
Kingsland, GA 31548-7603

Dealers

J. Nalbandian, Inc.
P.O. Box A
Pilgrim Station
Warwick, RI 02888
Specializes in buying and selling stamp errors.

Marvin Frey
2199 Legion St.
Bellmore, NY 11710
phone: 516-826-1852
Specializes in buying and selling stamp errors.

European

Clubs/Associations

Hank Klos
Europa Study Unit of the American Topical Association
Newsletter: Europa News
4N 512 South Church Rd.
Bensenville, IL 60106
All aspects of a United Europe.

French

Clubs/Associations

Walter Parshall, Sec.
France & Colonies Philatelic Society
Journal: France & Colonies Philatelist
103 Spruce St.
Bloomfield, NJ 07003

Gay & Lesbian

Clubs/Associations

Joe Petronie
Gay & Lesbian History Stamp Club of the American Topical Association
Newsletter: Lambda Philatelic Journal
P.O. Box 575981
Dallas, TX 75251-5981

Gems & Jewelry

Clubs/Associations

George Young
Gems, Minerals, Jewelry Study Unit of the American Topical Association
Newsletter: Philagems
P.O. Box 632
Tewksbury, MA 01876
phone: 508-851-8283
e-mail: george-young@msn.com
Gems, minerals, jewelry.

German

Clubs/Associations

Christopher Deterding, Sec. Treas.
Germany Philatelic Society
Journal: German Postal Specialist
P.O. Box 779
Arnold, MD 21012
Members have an interest in stamps relating to Germany.

Burt Miller, Sec.
Germany Philatelic Society, Golden Gate Chapter
P.O. Box 911
Pacifica, CA 94044
e-mail: danziger@aol.com

Golf

Clubs/Associations

Kevin Hadlock
International Philatelic Golf Society of the American Topical Association
Newsletter: Tee Time
447 Skyline Dr.
Orange, CT 06477
Golf and golfing.

Graphics

Clubs/Associations

Dulcie Apgar
Graphics Philately Association of the American Topical Association
Newsletter: Philateli-Graphics
P.O. Box 1513
Thousand Oaks, CA 91358
History of printing.

Guatemala

Clubs/Associations

Mae Vignola, Mem.
International Society of Guatemala Collectors, Inc.
105 22nd Ave.
San Francisco, CA 94121

Hawaii

Clubs/Associations

Hawaiian Philatelic Society
P.O. Box 10115
Honolulu, HI 96816-0115
phone: 808-521-5721

Helvetic

Clubs/Associations

Mario Wiedenmeier
American Helvetic Philatelic Society
12 Lyncrest
Galveston, TX 77550

Hong Kong

Clubs/Associations

Hong Kong Stamp Society
P.O. Box 206
Glenside, PA 19038

Hungary

Clubs/Associations

Society for Hungarian Philately
P.O. Box 1162
Fairfield, CT 06432-1162

Israel

Clubs/Associations

Emil S. Dickstein, M.D.
Society of Israel Philatelists
Journal: Israel Philatelist
8358 Hitchcock Rd.
Youngstown, OH 44512

Experts

Israel I. Bick
P.O. Box 854
Van Nuys, CA 91408-0854
phone: 818-997-6496
fax: 818-988-4337
e-mail: iibick@aol.com
Internet: http://www.4free.com/bick
A leading expert in the field of Holy Land stamp collecting specializing in Israel, Judaica and related materials.

Japanese

Clubs/Associations

Kenneth Kamholz, Sec.
International Society for Japanese Philately
Journal: Japanese Philately
P.O. Box 1283
Haddonfield, NJ 08033

Dealers

Frank L. Allard, Jr.
Nippon Philatelics
P.O. Drawer 7300
Carmel, CA 93921-7300
phone: 408-625-2643 or 408-624-4617
fax: 408-624-4617
Wants anything Japanese: postcards, mail, stamps, posters, postal

stationary, First Day Covers, photos, etc.; price lists available for SASE.

Journalists/Authors

Clubs/Associations

Louis Forster
Journalists, Authors & Poets on Stamps Unit of the American Topical Association
Newsletter: JAPOS Bulletin
7561 East 24th Court
Wichita, KS 67226
Journalists, authors, poets.

Liechtenstein

Clubs/Associations

Max C. Rheinberger
Liechtenstudy USA
Newsletter: Liechtenstudy
100 Elizabeth St., #112
Duluth, MN 55803
Provides a broad range of services to Liechtenstein collectors; postal history, auctions, etc.

Lighthouses

Clubs/Associations

Dalene Thomas
Lighthouse Stamp Society of the American Topical Association
Newsletter: Philatelic Beacon, The
8612 West Warren Lane
Denver, CO 80227-2352
phone: 303-986-6620
e-mail: dathomas@nyx.cs.du.edu
Internet: http://www.nyx.net/~dathomas
Club promotes collecting stamps depicting lighthouses; bi-monthly journal discusses stamps, covers, postmarks and all philatelic items that picture lighthouses.

Lions

Clubs/Associations

Steven Walker
Lions International Stamp Club of the American Topical Association
Newsletter: Philatelion
14217 Castle Blvd.
Silver Spring, MD 20904

Maps & Charts

Clubs/Associations

Clifford Mugnier
Carto-Philatelists of the American Topical Association
Newsletter: Carto-Philatelist
Department of Civil Engineering
University of New Orleans
New Orleans, LA 70122
Maps, globes, charts.

Masks

Clubs/Associations

Carolyn Weber
Mask Study Unit of the American Topical Association
Newsletter: Mask Lore
P.O. Box 2542
Oxnard, CA 93034
Internet: http://www.philately.com/society_news/masks.htm

Masonic

Clubs/Associations

Otto Seding
Masonic Study Unit of the American Topical Association
Newsletter: Philatelic Freemason
1033 Hollytree Dr.
Cincinnati, OH 45231
Freemasonry.

Mathematics

Clubs/Associations

Estelle Buccino
Mathematical Study Unit of the American Topical Association
Newsletter: Philamath
5615 Glenwood
Bethesda, MD 20817
Computers, mathematics.

Medical

Clubs/Associations

Dr. Frederick Skvara
Medical Subjects Unit of the American Topical Association
Journal: Scalpel & Tongs
P.O. Box 6228
Bridgewater, NJ 08807
Internet: http://www.philately.com/society_news/thematic_organizations.htm
Dentistry, nursing, physicians, Red Cross, veterinary medicine.

Meter Stamps

Collectors

Jack Mayer, Treas.
Meter Stamp Society
1379 Islewood Dr.
Anacortes, WA 98221
For those interested in the segment of philately and postal history dealing with stamps produced by meters and similar equipment such as automat-stamp vending machines.

Mexico

Clubs/Associations

Kohn Kordich, Treas.
Mexico-Elmhurst Philatelic Society International
Journal: Mexicana
1014 37th St.
San Pedro, CA 90731

Mobile Post Office

Clubs/Associations

Mobile Post Office Society
P.O. Box 21
Holmdel, NJ 07733

Music Related

Clubs/Associations

Cathleen Osborne
Philatelic Music Circle of the American Topical Association
Newsletter: Baton
P.O. Box 1781
Sequim, WA 98382
Internet: http://www.philately.com/society_news/philatelic_music.htm
Music, musicians.

Napoleon

Clubs/Associations

Ken Berry
Napoleon Age Philatelist of the American Topical Association
Newsletter: Campaign
7513 Clayton Dr.
Oklahoma City, OK 73132
Life and time of Napoleon Bonaparte.

Pacific Islands

Clubs/Associations

John Ray
Pacific Islands Study Group
24 Woodvale Ave.
London SE25 4AE, U.K.

Panama Canal

Clubs/Associations

John C. Smith, Sec.
Canal Zone Study Group, The
Newsletter: Canal Zone Philatelist
408 Redwood Lane
Schaumburg, IL 60193

Dealers

C&H Stamps
P.O. Box 324
Syracuse, NY 13209-0324
Buys and sells Canal Zone stamps, used envelopes (covers) and postal memorabilia; always wants to buy; send description and price, or request an offer.

Perfins

Clubs/Associations

Sylvia Gersch, Sec.
Perfins Club
Newsletter: Perfins Bulletin
P.O. Box 13292
Scottsdale, AZ 85267-3292
Perfins are little holes in the configuration of alphabet letters which are punched into stamps as a security, anti-theft measure.

Petroleum

Clubs/Associations

Feitz Papa
Petroleum Philatelic Society International of the American Topical Association
Newsletter: PetroPhilatelist
922 Meandor Dr.
Walnut Creek, CA 94598
Oil, natural gas, petrochemical industry.

Philippines

Clubs/Associations

International Philippine Philatelic Society
P.O. Box 94
Eden, NY 14057-0094

Pitcairn Islands

Clubs/Associations

William Volk
Pitcairn Islands Study Group
2184 6th Ave.
Yuma, AZ 85364

Polar

Clubs/Associations

Richard Julian
American Society of Polar Philatelists of the American Topical Association
Newsletter: Ice Cap News
1153 Fairvgiew Dr.
York, PA 17403
Focuses on worldwide polar stamps, cancels, and covers.

Possessions of the U.S.

Clubs/Associations

United States Possessions Philatelic Society
Journal: Possessions
8100 Willow Stream Dr.
Sandy, UT 84092

Postal Stationery

Clubs/Associations

Executive Secretary
United Postal Stationery Society
Journal: Postal Stationery
P.O. Box 48
Redlands, CA 92373
For collectors of postal stationery, namely embossed stamped envelopes and government postal cards.

Postal Union

Clubs/Associations

Bob Malch
Universal Postal Union Collectors of the American Topical Association
Newsletter: Globe Union
P.O. Box 607117
Orlando, FL 32860-7117

Postmarks

Clubs/Associations

Post Mark Collectors Club
Newsletter: PMCC Bulletin
c/o Historic Lyme Village
P.O. Box 342
Bellevue, OH 44811
phone: 309-682-6774
Members have interest in postmarks and postal markings.

Collectors

Joe Bussey
3405 Canterbury Ave.
Muskogee, OK 74403

Dealers

Bob Morris
706 Pawnee St.
Bethlehem, PA 18015-1432
phone: 610-865-9052
Wants to purchase US and foreign covers; anything to 1960; stampless to WWII; large quantities wanted.

Museums/Libraries

Post Mark Museum
c/o Historic Lyme Village
P.O. Box 342
Bellevue, OH 44811
phone: 309-682-6774

Railroad

Clubs/Associations

Oliver Atchinson
Casey Jones Railroad Unit of the American Topical Association
Newsletter: Dispatcher
P.O. Box 31631
San Francisco, CA 94131
Trains, railroads, streetcars.

Rainbows

Clubs/Associations

Shirley Sutton
Rainbow Study Unit of the American Topical Association
Newsletter: Rainbow's Bend, The
P.O. Box 37
Long Pine
Alberta T0G 1M0 Canada

Religion Related

Clubs/Associations

Collectors of Religion on Stamps
Magazine: COROS Chronicle
425 North Linwood Ave., #110
Appleton, WI 54914-3476
phone: 414-734-2417
fax: 414-233-5604
COROS Chronicle is published bi-monthly.

Revenue & Tax Stamps

(see also BANK CHECKS; STAMP COLLECTING, Duck/Fish & Game)

Clubs/Associations

Scott Henault
State Revenue Society
Newsletter: State Revenue Newsletter
22 Denmark St.
Dedham, MA 02026-2407
For collectors whose prime aim is the collection, identification and cataloging of state and local revenue philately.

American Revenue Association
Newsletter: American Revenuer
511 S. First Ave.
Arcadia, CA 91006
Interested in U.S. and foreign revenue and tax stamps and stamped paper.

Collectors

Hermann Ivester
5 Leslie Circle
Little Rock, AR 72205-2529
phone: 501-225-8565 or 501-376-7788
fax: 501-376-8536
Collects all kinds of U.S. Federal, state and local revenue stamps including special tax stamps and cigar, cigarette, snuff and tobacco stamps; especially wants stamps on documents and packages.

Rotary Club

Clubs/Associations

Donald Fiery
Rotary on Stamps Unit of the American Topical Association
Newsletter: Rotary-on-Stamps
P.O. Box 333
Hanover, PA 17331
Rotary International.

Russian

Clubs/Associations

Norman Epstein
Rossica Society of Russian Philately
Newsletter: Bulletin of the RSRP
33 Crooke Ave.
Brooklyn, NY 11226
Internet: http://hercules.geology.uiuc.edu/~peterm/rossica.html

Samoa

Clubs/Associations

Dr. G.J.L. Hamilton
Fellowship of Samoa Specialists
12 Bulwer St.
Perth 6000
Western Australia

Scandinavia

Clubs/Associations

Executive Secretary
Scandinavian Collectors Club
P.O. Box 125
Newark, DE 19715-0125

Ships

Clubs/Associations

Robert Stuckert
Ships on Stamps Unit of the American Topical Association
Newsletter: Watercraft Philately
2750 Highway 21 East
Paint Lick, KY 40461
All types of watercraft.

Sir Winston S. Churchill

Clubs/Associations

Richard Langworth
Churchill Center, The
Newsletter: Finest Hour
P.O. Box 385
Contoocook, NH 03229
phone: 603-746-4433
fax: 603-746-4260
e-mail: Malakand@aol.com
Internet: http://winstonchurchill.org
Life and times of Winston Churchill; seminars, lectures, books on stamps and memorabilia.

South Africa

Clubs/Associations

Philatelic Society for Greater South Africa
7227 Sparta Rd.
Sebring, FL 33872

Souvenir Cards

Clubs/Associations

Michael Padwee
Souvenir Card Collectors Society, Metro Chapter
Newsletter: SCCS Metro Chapter Newsletter
P.O. Box 023138
Brooklyn, NY 11202-3138
phone: 718-499-4307
fax: 718-720-8897
e-mail: mwpadwee@inch.com
Members are collectors of souvenir cards in the New York, New Jersey and Connecticut area; Michael Padwee is author of "Catalog of Locally Issues USPS Souvenir Cards."

Souvenir Card Collectors Society
Journal: Souvenir Card Journal
P.O. Box 4155
Tulsa, OK 74159-0155
phone: 918-664-6724
e-mail: dmarr5569@aol.com
Souvenir cards are 8 1/2" x 11" cards with engraved reproductions of philatelic or numismatic designs from original plates.

Space

Clubs/Associations

Bernice Scholl
Space Unit of the American Topical Association
Journal: Astrophile
P.O. Box 522579
Marathon Shores, FL 33052-2579
Astronauts, astronautics.

Sports Related

Clubs/Associations

Margaret Jones
Sports Philatelists International of the
American Topical Association
Journal: Journal of Sports Philately
5310 Lindenwood Ave.
Saint Louis, MO c
*Promotes information on sports
stamps, cancels; check lists & articles
related to sports and the Olympics;
Olympics, recreation, sports.*

Stamps on Stamps

Clubs/Associations

Judy Hornaday
Stamps on Stamps/Centenary Unit of the
American Topical Association
Newsletter: SOS Journal
22446 Estallens
Mission Viejo, CA 92692
Stamps-on-stamps, stamp centenaries.

Supplies For

Suppliers

Lighthouse Publications
P.O. Box 705
Hackensack, NJ 07602-0705
phone: 201-342-1513
fax: 201-342-7142
*Carries full line of products for the
coin and stamp collector: albums,
binders, blank pages, magnifiers,
tongs, UV lamps.*

Brooklyn Gallery Coin & Stamp
8725 Fourth Ave.
P.O. Box 146
Brooklyn, NY 11209-0146
phone: 718-745-5701
fax: 718-745-2775
Send $1.50 for 104 page catalog.

Linder Publications, Inc.
P.O. Box 5056
Syracuse, NY 13220
phone: 315-437-0463 or 800-654-0324
fax: 315-437-4832
*Sells collector's accessories for
stamps, coins, telephone cards,
postcards: ring binders, blank album
pages, UV lamps, magnifiers, stamp
tongs, clear pocket pages, protective
covers, coin holders, etc.*

Global Stamp & Coin Company
460 Ridge St.
Lewiston, NY 14092
phone: 716-754-8513

Lincoln Coin & Stamp Company
33 West Tupper
Buffalo, NY 14202
phone: 716-856-1884

Subway Stamp Shop, Inc.
2121 Beale Ave.
Altoona, PA 16601
phone: 800-221-9960 or 814-946-1000
fax: 814-946-9997
e-mail: custserv@subwaystamp.com
Internet: http://www.subwaystamp.com
*Supplies for the stamp and coin
collector: albums, blank pages, cover
protectors, clear sleeves, tongs, bags,
illuminated magnifiers, SoftPRO
stamp collectors software, coin boxes,
currency holders, etc.*

Potomac Supplies
7720 Wisconsin Ave.
Bethesda, MD 20815
phone: 301-654-8828
fax: 301-942-8778

John L. Tyler
Album Publishing Co. Inc.
P.O. Box 30063
Raleigh, NC 27622
phone: 919-571-4648
fax: 919-571-4215
Supplies for the stamp collector.

Michael Rogers
Michael Rogers, Inc.
199 E. Welbourne Ave., Ste. 3
Winter Park, FL 32789
phone: 407-644-2290
fax: 407-645-4434

Stuart Morrissey
Scott Publishing Co.
P.O. Box 828
Sidney, OH 45365-0828
phone: 513-498-0802 or 800-5SC-OTT5
fax: 513-498-0808
*Publisher of catalogs, albums and
various stamp supplies.*

Warren Sankey
United States Stamp Company
368 Bush St.
San Francisco, CA 94104
phone: 415-421-7398
fax: 415-421-3167

Textiles

Clubs/Associations

Helen Cushman
Embroidery, Stitchery, Textile Unit of
the American Topical Association
Newsletter: Textgile-Rama
1001 Center St., Apt. 9H
La Jolla, CA 92037
Embroidery, stitchery, textiles.

Tonga

Clubs/Associations

Tom Jackson
Tonga & Tin Can Mail Study Circle
Newsletter: Tin Canner
121 Mullingar Ct., #1A
Schaumburg, IL 60193-3258
phone: 847-352-5842
e-mail: tjackso3@ix.netcom.com

Topical

Clubs/Associations

Douglas A. Kelsey, Ex. Dir.
American Topical Association
Magazine: Topical Time
P.O. Box 65749
Tucson, AZ 85728
phone: 520-321-9292
fax: 520-321-9494
e-mail: ATAoffice@aol.com
*Topicalists save stamps relating to a
specific topic such as birds, space,
buildings, transportation, etc.;
affiliated with many specializing study
units and clubs.*

Ukrainian

Clubs/Associations

Ukrainian Philatelic & Numismatic
Society
Newsletter: Trident Visnyk
P.O. Box 303
Southfields, NY 10975-0303

United Nations

Clubs/Associations

Blanton Clement
United Nations Philatelists of the
American Topical Association
Newsletter: Journal of United Nations
Philatelists
292 Springdale Terrace
Yardley, PA 19067
Worldwide U.N. related philately.

Windmills

Clubs/Associations

John Blocker
Windmill Study Unit of the American
Topical Association
Newsletter: Windmill Whispers
17060 Jodave St.
Hazel Crest, IL 60429
Molinology.

Wine

Clubs/Associations

James Crum
Wine on Stamps Study Unit of the
American Topical Association
Newsletter: Enophilatelica
5132 Sepulveda
San Bernardino, CA 92404-1134

Women Related

Clubs/Associations

Phebe Meek
Women on Stamps Study Unit of the
American Topical Association
Newsletter: Topical Woman
259 Middle Road
Falmouth, ME 04105

STAMP WETTERS

Collectors

Betty Franks
1831 Penthley Ave.
Akron, OH 44312-1915
phone: 330-784-2869
*Wants old and unusual china or
ceramic figural stamp wetters (stamp
lickers) with or without sponges.*

STANHOPES

(see also OPTICAL ITEMS;
PHOTOGRAPHS)

Appraisers

David L. Studebaker
10421 Delwood Dr. S.W.
Tacoma, WA 98498-4321
phone: 206-582-4878
*Specializes in classic old cameras,
colored cameras, subminiatures,
stanhopes, old images, and
photographs and daguerreotypes.*

Collectors

Sheldon Katz
211 Roanoke Ave.
Riverhead, NY 11901-2778
phone: 516-369-1100

Brenda Macomber
RD 3 Box 201-K
Delta, PA 17314-9588
phone: 717-456-6116
*Wants to buy stanhope souvenirs,
charms, unusual items; especially
seeking 1939 World's Fair and
domestic scenes.*

T.A. Coppens
6075 Pelican Bay Blvd., Apt. 305
Naples, FL 33943-8170
*Little novelty viewers with peep holes
showing scenes, Lord's Prayer, etc.;
found in letter openers, pipes,
souvenir trinkets, knives, etc.; send
description and price with SASE.*

Mike & Gladys Kessler
25749 Anchor Circle
San Juan Capistrano, CA 92675
phone: 717-661-3320

Donald Gorlick
P.O. Box 24541
Seattle, WA 98124-0541
phone: 206-824-0508
*Wants tiny viewers made of bone or
metal sometimes found in crucifixes,
pens, letter openers, needle holders,
etc.*

Dealers

Lucille Malitz
Lucid Antiques
P.O. Box KH
Scarsdale, NY 10583
phone: 914-636-7825 or 914-636-5171

STANLEY TOOLS

(see TOOLS, Stanley)

STAR TREK

(see SCIENCE FICTION; TELEVISION SHOWS & MEMORABILIA, Star Trek)

STATE RELATED COLLECTIBLES

(see also PLANNING; POSTCARDS, States; SOUVENIR & COMMEMORATIVE ITEMS)

Auction Services

Richard Vogel
Vogels, The
4720 SE Fort King St.
Ocala, FL 34470-1501
phone: 352-694-5776
fax: 352-694-7330
Bi-monthly mail order souvenir auctions: china, glass, spoons, mauchline, paper, World's Fair, fraternal.

Alaska

Collectors

Richard Reisinger
2610 Holgate St.
Tacoma, WA 98402-1204
phone: 253-272-7092
Buys, trades pre-1960 Alaska, Yukon, and N.W. Territories travel brochures, ephemera, postcards, city directories, telephone books, tourist souvenirs, china, bottles, pins, badges, posters, paintings, license plates, calendars, etc.

Kaye Dethridge
P.O. Box 438
Sitka, AK 99835
phone: 907-747-8615
Wants to buy most items from Alaska's past: tokens, Alaska-Yukon-Pacific Expo material, etc.

Dealers

Richard A. Wood
Alaskan Heritage Bookshop
P.O. Box 22165
Juneau, AK 99802-2165
phone: 907-789-8450
fax: 907-789-8450
e-mail: akrare@alaska.net
Internet: http://www.alaska.net/~akrare
Buys/sells books, maps, stereo views, prints, photos, souvenirs, Klondike, letters, paintings, ephemera, etc.; anything Alaska/Yukon/Klondike; also wants Louis Potter bronze sculptures (1904-05) of Alaska subjects.

Experts

Richard Reisinger
2610 Holgate St.
Tacoma, WA 98402-1204
phone: 253-272-7092
Buys, trades pre-1960 Alaska, Yukon, and N.W. Territories travel brochures, ephemera, postcards, city directories, telephone books, tourist souvenirs, china, bottles, pins, badges, posters, paintings, license plates, calendars, etc.

Richard A. Wood
Alaskan Heritage Bookshop
P.O. Box 22165
Juneau, AK 99802-2165
phone: 907-789-8450
fax: 907-789-8450
e-mail: akrare@alaska.net
Internet: http://www.alaska.net/~akrare
Buys/sells books, maps, stereo views, prints, photos, souvenirs, Klondike, letters, paintings, ephemera, etc.; anything Alaska/Yukon/Klondike; also wants Louis Potter bronze sculptures (1904-05) of Alaska subjects.

Arizona

Collectors

Sam Michael
P.O. Box 8025
Mesa, AZ 85214
phone: 602-962-6523
Wants to buy pre-1920 Arizona related items: calendar plates, documents, advertising, badges, pins, posters, photographs, tins, signs, broadsides, real photo postcards, tokens, etc.

California

Collectors

Gil Schmidtmann
2346 Naples Ave.
Mentone, CA 92359-9569
phone: 909-794-1211
Wants San Bernardino County, CA pre-1930 stock certificates, postcards, postmarks, merchant tokens, badges, books, calendars, checks, currency, script, documents, newspapers, photos, promotional items, souvenir slates and spoons, etc.

Colorado

Dealers

Leo Stambaugh
Powder Cache Antiques
P.O. Box 779
Georgetown, CO 80444-0779
phone: 800-651-2848 or 303-569-2109
Buy, sell, trade Colorado historical photos, paper, medals, bottles, tokens, mining artifacts, paper and lamps, etc.; also wants mining items.

Florida

Collectors

Douglas Hendriksen
P.O. Box 21153
Kennedy Space Center, FL 32815
phone: 407-452-0633
Wants to buy pre-1930 Florida items: photos, stereos, real photo and small town postcards, promotional pamphlets, paintings, souvenir china, license plates, RR and steamboat items; anything Florida.

Lee Harrison
3353 Higel Ave.
Sarasota, FL 34242
phone: 813-957-1600
Wants to buy pre-1940 Florida paper items: guides, promotional leaflets, land development, view books, railroad, hotel, tourist, steamboat, pocket or oil company maps, etc.; no postcards or prints, please.

Hawaii

Collectors

Hunter, The
149 Stackhouse St.
South Dartmouth, MA 02748
phone: 508-993-8966
Wants pre-1960 Hawaiian vintage jewelry, menus, chalk and ceramic hula dancers, palm tree items, etched glass, TV lamps, shirts, tourist items, etc.

Gene Snyder
991 McLean St.
Dunedin, FL 34699-3532
Wants Hawaiian memorabilia: ukuleles, Matson menus, nudes on black velvet, 1950s shirts.

Jim Stiso
31925 Sunset Ave.
S. Laguna, CA 92677
phone: 714-499-3667
Wants to buy Hawaiiana: vintage paintings, prints, shirts, lamps, dolls, etc.

Wayne Babcock
4846 Carpenteria Ave.
Carpinteria, CA 93013-1935
phone: 805-684-8148
Wants to buy pre-1960s Hawaiian items including cruise line menus, bamboo framed floral prints by Mundorff, Tip Freeman and others; Hula girls, Hawaiian-made ukuleles, surfing items, etc.

Rick Ralston
99-969 Iwaena St.
Aiea, HI 96701-3249
phone: 800-486-9794
fax: 808-486-1276
Wants Hawaiian prints, paintings, early wooden bowls, hula girl lamps, dolls, etc.

Evan Olins
Hula Heaven
75-5744 Alii Dr.
Kailua Kona, HI 96740
phone: 808-329-7885
Wants pre-1960s Hawaiian shirts; also wants souvenir and hula girl items.

John Honl
P.O. Box 1201
Kailua Kona, HI 96745-1201
phone: 808-325-9905
Wants pre-1960 Hawaiian items including lamps, Hula girls, postcard, menus, etc.

Makani/Bailey
RR 2 Box 144
Kula, HI 96790
Wants to buy Hawaii related items: historical, pictorial, Hawaiian Royalty, ephemera, memorabilia.

Cedric Felix
42 Market St.
Wailuku, HI 96793
phone: 808-242-9211
Wants Hawaiian artifacts, wooden carvings, dolls, drums, whaling items, documents, photo albums, hula items, maps, etc.

Bernie Berman
755 Isenberg St., 305
Honolulu, HI 96826-4505
phone: 808-941-8639
Wants pre-1920 Hawaiiana, Oceania, Asian theater countries; postcards, photographs, advertising, memorabilia, broadsides, art books, historical, collectibles, postal covers, books, ephemera, screens, scrolls, prints, documents, etc.

Anne Moore
P.O. Box 604
Bingen, WA 98605
phone: 509-493-4463
Wants all pre-1960 Hawaii memorabilia: Hula dolls, Hula lamps, ukuleles, books, menus, travel posters, paintings, prints, photos, postcards, clothing, artifacts, photos, sheet music, souvenirs, etc.

Dealers

M.A. Blackburn
Wholesale Rug Outlet
2448 Lincoln Highway East
Lancaster, PA 17602
phone: 800-346-7847 or 717-295-9078
fax: 717-295-3494
e-mail: wrhawaii@epix.net
Internet: http://www.scmonline.com/blackburn
Wants Hawaiian artifacts, calabashes, menus, souvenirs, Hula dolls, lamps, ukuleles, quilts, vintage shirts, ceramics, perfume bottles, souvenir spoons, prints, engravings, jewelry, books, ephemera, missionary, royalty, diaries, etc.

Hawaii (Hawaiian Shirts)

Dealers

Experienced Denim
P.O. Box 239
Fayetteville, AR 72702-0239
phone: 501-444-7541 or 800-336-4694
fax: 501-521-8331
e-mail: exdeni19@intellinet.com
Wants '30s-'50s Levis, denim wear of all types, any brand or condition, '40s-'50s gabardine shirts & jackets, Hawaiian and bowling shirts; also vintage fabrics, textiles, bedspreads, tablecloths with Western or Mexican theme.

David Bailey
Bailey's Antiques & Thrift
517 Kapahulu Ave.
Honolulu, HI 96815-3854
phone: 808-734-7628
Buys and appraises pre-1960 Levis, pre-1960 Aloha Shirts, and Hawaiiana; pre-1960 Aloha Shirts can be identified by double-stitched seams around the armpit and along sides.

Danny Eskenazi
Jack Hammer Ltd.
1909 First Ave.
Seattle, WA 98101-1010
phone: 800-289-5017 or 206-441-1865
fax: 206-932-1449
e-mail: k7ss@mcimail.com
Wants to buy golden age (1930-1950s) Hawaiian shirts.

Indiana

Experts

Mark Roeder
305 Akron St.
Culver, IN 46511-1805
phone: 219-842-5141
e-mail: culver4@aol.com
Wants to buy anything related to Culver, IN and the Culver Military Academy; especially postcards, books, china, photos, and items of historical interest; author of book "A History of Culver and Lake Maxinkuckee."

Kansas

Dealers

Billy & Jeane Jones
Dearing Country Antiques
3009 Independence Ave.
P.O. Box 82
Dearing, KS 67340-0082
phone: 316-948-6389
Want ceramic or glass souvenirs, plates, advertising items, calendars, vases, view cards - anything related to Dearing, Chanute, Coffeyville, Independence, Cherryvale, Iola, Fredonia, or Needesh Kansas.

Michigan

Museums/Libraries

Dennis R. Boden, Ex. Dir
Jesse Besser Museum
491 Johnson St.
Alpena, MI 49707
phone: 517-356-2202
fax: 517-356-3133
e-mail: jbmuseum@northland.lib.mi.us
Special Great Lakes collections: Native Americans, Great Lakes maps, Great Lakes (NE Michigan) photographs.

Missouri

Dealers

Trenton Boyd
P.O. Box 517
Columbia, MO 65205-0517
phone: 573-882-2461 or 573-442-5235
fax: 573-882-2950
e-mail: vetlib@showme.missouri.edu
Wants items from Missouri, except Kansas City and St. Louis.

Montana

Collectors

Tim Gordon
1750 W. Kent
Missoula, MT 59801-5508
phone: 406-728-1812
e-mail: stacey1165@aol.com
Wants any pre-1930 item marked "Montana": calendars, advertising, photos, post cards, history books, tokens, trade cards, etc.

Dealers

Idaho Street Antiques
110 East Idaho
Kalispell, MT 59911
phone: 406-755-1324
Buys and sells American Indian, National Park, and other photographic items relating to Montana.

Nevada

Collectors

Gil Schmidtmann
2346 Naples Ave.
Mentone, CA 92359-9569
phone: 909-794-1211
Wants Death Valley pre-1930 stock certificates, postcards, postmarks, merchant tokens, badges, books, calendars, checks, currency, documents, newspapers, photos, promotional items, souvenir plates and spoons, etc.

New Hampshire

Museums/Libraries

Norwood H. Keeney, III
Sunapee, New Hampshire Historical Society, Inc.
P.O. Box 501
Sunapee, NH 03782-0501
phone: 603-763-9157
e-mail: keeny@kcar.tds.net
Museum collection features steamboat and great hotel memorabilia related to Lake Sunapee: postcards, photographs, art and manufactured items related to Sunapee and the area.

New York (Brooklyn)

Collectors

Brian Merlis
68 Westminster Rd.
Lynbrook, NY 11563
phone: 516-593-4505
Wants items relating to Brooklyn and Long Island: maps, LIRR, books, medals, prints, relics, badges, souvenirs, brochures, negatives, genealogy, histories, post cards, newspapers, artwork, atlases, letterheads, etc.

North Carolina

Collectors

J. Robert Boykin, III
P.O. Box 7440
Wilson, NC 27895
phone: 919-237-1700
fax: 919-237-2314
Wants to buy any pre-1930 items from North Carolina such as billheads, letterheads, postcards, history books, advertising, tokens, art, trade cards, bottles.

Pennsylvania German Heritage

Museums/Libraries

James McMahon
Hershey Museum
170 W. Hersheypark Dr.
Hershey, PA 17033
phone: 717-534-3439
fax: 717-534-8940
Focused collection of objects detailing the town of Hershey history, regional PA German heritage, native American material culture.

Dick Rominiecki
Historical Society of Pennsylvania
Magazine: Pennsylvania Magazine of History & Biography
1300 Locust St.
Philadelphia, PA 19107
phone: 215-732-6200
e-mail: hsppr@aol.com
Internet: http://www.libertynet.org/~pahist
Largest independent center for research in Pennsylvania; over 15 million archival documents, books, maps, prints, drawings, photographs and genealogical records.

South Carolina

Dealers

Henry Barnet
516 Maverick Circle
Spartanburg, SC 29307-3707
phone: 864-579-2112
e-mail: 75347.322@compuserve.com
Buys, sells and collects original artwork done by southern artists and those from South Carolina, especially from the Piedmont area; wants prints, ephemera, books, etc.

Tennessee

Collectors

Claude Bellar
1750 Keyes Road
Greenbrier, TN 37073
phone: 615-643-0290
fax: 615-643-0290
e-mail: cbellar@aol.com
Wants Tennessee bottles, stoneware, advertising.

Paul A. Jarrett
611 West End Dr.
Waverly, TN 37185
phone: 615-296-3151
Wants to buy pre-Prohibition Tennessee jugs (miniature or full size), TN small town souvenirs, embossed druggist bottles, pre-1920 business letterhead, merchant "good for" tokens, TN business letterheads, bottles.

Peggy Dillard
P.O. Box 210904
Nashville, TN 37221-0904
phone: 615-646-1605
Wants Tennessee postcards and historical items, especially Tennessee Centennial Exposition (1897) items.

Joe Copeland
P.O. Box 4221
Oak Ridge, TN 37831-4221
phone: 423-482-4215
Wants to buy any Tennessee tokens and other memorabilia, city and county histories, pre-1950 phone books and city directories, Dun & Bradstreet directories, pins, medals, badges.

Texas

Clubs/Associations

Texas Centennial Collector
P.O. Box 8072
Longview, TX 75607
fax: 903-757-3043
e-mail: texas1936@aol.com

Collectors

James E. Kattner
P.O. Box 11132
Spring, TX 77391
phone: 281-986-6916 or 281-376-4826
Wants to buy Texas tokens from saloons, bars, military forts, post traders, lumber companies, drug stores, general stores, bakeries, etc.; also wants Texas, pocket mirrors, whiskey jugs and other Texas saloon advertisement items.

Washington DC

Collectors

Jerry A. McCoy
800 Thayer Ave.
Silver Spring, MD 20910-4504
phone: 301-565-2519
fax: 301-565-0780
Wants to buy real photo (B & W)

postcards of 19th or early 20th century Washington DC; also early DC guidebooks and souvenirs or memorabilia.

STATUE OF LIBERTY COL-LECTIBLES

(see also SOUVENIR & COMMEMO-RATIVE ITEMS)

Clubs/Associations

Iris & Mort November
Statue of Liberty Collectors' Club
Newsletter: Statue of Liberty Collectors'
  Club Newsletter
26601 Bernwood Rd.
Cleveland, OH 44122-7133
phone: 216-831-2646 or 216-831-0497
fax: 216-831-2646
e-mail: lbrtyclub@aol.com
For collectors or enthusiasts with an interest in items relating to the Statue of Liberty; dues help support the Statue of Liberty Foundation.

Collectors

Jeffrey Eger
42 Blackberry Ln.
Morristown, NJ 07960
phone: 201-455-1843
Writer/author/Statue of Liberty historian looking for unusual early items relating to the statue's history.

Iris & Mort November
26601 Bernwood Rd.
Cleveland, OH 44122-7133
phone: 216-831-2646 or 216-831-0497
fax: 216-831-2646
e-mail: lbrtyclub@aol.com
Collects items relating to the Statue of Liberty or its designer, Bartholdi.

Mike Brooks
7335 Skyline
Oakland, CA 94611-1121
phone: 510-339-1751
e-mail: deborahwb@aol.com
Buying early souvenir models, books, medals, advertising, donor certifi-cates, unveiling invitations, Bartholdi related items, etc.

Nancy Wright
3660 Thames St.
Eugene, OR 97405-1111
phone: 503-345-7194
Interested in buying earlier vintage Statue of Liberty items: posters, books, prints, jewelry, plates, etc.

Dealers

Ronald Cutadean
1235 Kennedy Ave.
Louisville, CO 80027
Buys, sells, trades Statue of Liberty items.

Experts

Harvey & Sandy Dolin
Harvey Dolin & Co.
5 Beekman St.
New York, NY 10038-2206
phone: 212-267-0216
Wants any item pertaining to the Statue of Liberty.

STEAM-OPERATED
Models & Equipment

(see also AUTOMOBILES, Steam; BOATS, Steam; ENGINES; FARM MACHINERY; HORNS & WHISTLES; INDUSTRY RELATED ITEMS; MACHINERY & EQUIP-MENT, Road Making; RAILROADS; STEAMBOAT COLLECTIBLES; TOYS, Farm; TOYS, Steam/Hot Air)

Clubs/Associations

Northwest Steam Society
Newsletter: Steam Gage
3629 NW 64th St.
Seattle, WA 98107-2667
e-mail: halathome@aol.com
Internet: http://
  www.pacific.telebyte.com/~mietner/
  steam.html
Interested in steam-operated models, equipment, and machinery; especially railroads.

Collectors

Lowell J. Wagner
Sunni-hill Farm Antiques
Waconia, MN 55387-9562
phone: 612-544-4543 or 612-442-4036
fax: 612-544-9283
Wants to buy steam engines, also toy hot air engines; wants American Weedens, Buckmans, Bing, Marklin, etc. and large German engines; also wants catalogs with steam or hot air toys shown.

D.E. Haskins
1237 Alleghany Ln.
Northbrook, IL 60062
phone: 708-498-3516
Wants old toy steam engines, parts and literature (no railroad, please).

Museums/Libraries

Hamilton Museum of Steam &
  Technology, The
900 Woodward Ave.
Hamilton
Ontario, Canada
phone: 416-549-5525
Exhibits of industrial history; children's activities.

Periodicals

Village Press
Magazine: Live Steam Magazine
P.O. Box 968
Traverse City, MI 49685
phone: 616-946-3712
fax: 616-946-3289
A magazine for the amateur machinist,

or live steam hobbyist; steam locomotives, marine vessels, tractors, stationary steam engines, etc.; full scale or models.

STEAMBOAT COLLECTIBLES

(see also BOATS; OCEAN LINER MEMORABILIA; SHIPPING; SHIP RELATED)

Clubs/Associations

Steamship Historical Society of
  America, Inc.
Magazine: Steamboat Bill
300 Ray Dr., Ste. #4
Providence, RI 02906
phone: 401-274-0805
For those interested in maritime history; publishes high quality quarterly magazine; has photo bank of thousands of negatives of powered vessels, national and regional meetings.

Tugboat Enthusiasts Society of the
  Americas
Magazine: Tug Bitts
308 Quince St.
Mount Pleasant, SC 29464-3420
phone: 803-881-1173
Published quarterly; covers steamboat & inland river history; packed with news, photos, articles on all types of tow boats, tugboats (harbor, ocean, military) and work boat salvage, restoration and history; a must for tugboat enthusiasts.

Steamboat Masters & Associations, Inc.
Journal: Egregious Steamboat Journal,
  The
P.O. Box 3046
Louisville, KY 40201-6784
phone: 502-778-6784
fax: 502-776-9006
Offers a wide variety of research and consulting services; appraises steamboat collections; sell them through a bi-monthly journal of steamboat history and technical studies; a wealth of unpublished information and photos.

Mrs. J.W. Rutter
Sons & Daughters of Pioneer Rivermen
Magazine: S & D Reflector
126 Seneca Dr.
Marietta, OH 45750
With about 1,100 members, this organization is devoted to river history; magazine published quarterly; meets annually in Marietta, OH the third weekend of September.

Collectors

Tom Cottrell
17 Mattapoisett Ave.
Swansea, MA 02777-2810
phone: 508-674-4287
Wants to buy steamboat waybills and invoices.

Experts

Jack & Sandra Custer
P.O. Box 3046
Louisville, KY 40201-3046
phone: 502-778-6784
fax: 502-776-9006
Experts, appraisers, dealers focusing on steamboats and steamboat collectibles; offers one-stop shopping for collectibles, artifacts, art prints, and resource books pertaining to steamboats.

Museums/Libraries

Steamship Historical Society Collection
  at the University of Baltimore Library
1420 Maryland Ave.
Baltimore, MD 21201
phone: 410-837-4334
A 5,000-volume library of books and 100,000 photographs in the field of powered shipping and navigation; 25,000 postcards; periodicals and shipping ephemera.

Inland Rivers Library at the Public
  Library of Cincinnati & Hamilton
  County
800 Vine St.
Cincinnati, OH 45202
phone: 513-369-6957
Specialty collections include rare book collection (history of the Ohio and Mississippi rivers and their tributaries as commercial transporta-tion routes), clipping files, illustra-tions, maps, photos, manuscripts, blueprints, broadsides.

Ohio River Museum
601 Front St.
Marietta, OH 45750
phone: 614-373-3750
Features the "W.P. Snyder, Jr." (a 1918 stern-wheeler steamboat), and collections including geological, ecological, recreational and commercial history of the Ohio River from its origin to present.

Dr. M.C. Striegel
Howard Steamboat Museum
1101 E. Market St.
Jeffersonville, IN 47130-4333
phone: 812-283-3728
Steamboat artifacts and models, photographs, half-breadth models, tools; 1894 mansion tour; Victorian furnishings; Miss Mary Starr.

Dubuque River Museum
400 E. 3rd St.
Dubuque, IA 52001
phone: 319-557-9545
Features the "William M. Black" (1934 side-wheeler river boat); also collections relating to canoes, flatboats, steamboats, steam engines.

Tracie Campbell
Mississippi River Museum
400 E 3rd St.
Dubuque, IA 52004-0266
phone: 319-557-9545
fax: 319-583-1241
Focuses on the "William M. Black" (1934 side-wheeler river boat); also collections relating to canoes, flatboats, steamboats, steam engines, and the Mississippi River.

Murphy Library at the University of Wisconsin, La Crosse
1705 State St.
La Crosse, WI 54601
phone: 608-785-8045
40,000 photographs of inland river steamboats.

Saint Louis Mercantile Library Association
510 Locust St.
Saint Louis, MO 63101
phone: 314-621-0670
Specialty collections include the National Inland Waterways Collection consisting of books, manuscripts, maps, photographs, reports and pamphlets.

Periodicals

Journal: Waterways Journal, The
319 N. 4th St.
Saint Louis, MO 63102-1907
phone: 314-241-7354
fax: 314-241-4207
Weekly newspaper reporting on current events.

STEAMSHIP MEMORABILIA

(see OCEAN LINER MEMORA-BILIA; SHIPPING; SHIP REPLATED; STEAMBOAT COLLECTIBLES)

STEIFF

(see also DOLLS; TEDDY BEARS; TOYS)

Clubs/Associations

Steiff Club USA
Magazine: Steiff Club USA Magazine
31 East 28th St., 9th Floor
New York, NY 10016
phone: 212-779-2582
fax: 212-779-2594
Plush teddy bears with trademark "button-in-ear"; a company-sponsored collectors club.

Beth B. Savino
Steiff Collectors Club
Newsletter: Collector Life
P.O. Box 798
Holland, OH 43528-0798
phone: 419-473-9801 or 800-862-8697
fax: 419-473-3947
e-mail: toystore@toynet.com
Internet: http://www.toynet.com
Focus is on collecting Steiff toys; sells exclusive Steiff Limited Edition; also buys old Steiff.

Collectors

Jeff Dykes
6 Wildwood Terrace
Glen Ridge, NJ 07028
phone: 201-748-4990 or 973-748-4990
Wants to buy any and all Steiff animals, especially teddy bears and rabbits, from 1890s to 1950s; prefer excellent condition with button and/or chest tag; send photo.

Pat Patrick
501 Crawford #302
Houston, TX 77002
phone: 713-546-3244
Wants to buy 1960s Steiff animals; no bears, please.

Dealers

Dale & Retha Tyo
Whispering Pines Antiques
280 Lawton Rd.
Hilton, NY 14468
phone: 716-637-4931

Old Friends Antiques
P.O. Box 754
Sparks, MD 21152
phone: 410-472-4632
fax: 410-472-3093
Specializing in Steiff bears and animals.

Rita Mueller
Grange Hall Antiques
1 South Alley
P.O. Box 263
New Market, MD 21774
phone: 301-865-5651
fax: 301-865-0518
e-mail: ritam@erols.com
Internet: http://www.newmarketmd.com/grange.htm
Quality Steiff animals from 1950s through 1980s; always buying one piece or entire collection: teddy bears, Schuco, Hermann, Steiff; also fine country graniteware from Germany available; mail orders and layaways.

Cheri Shivley
Cynthia's Country Store, Inc.
The Wellington Mall #15A
12794 W. Forest Hill Blvd.
West Palm Beach, FL 33414
phone: 407-793-0554
fax: 407-795-4222
e-mail: cynbears@aol.com
Internet: http://www.thecrier.com/ccs
Specializing in new, discontinued and antique Steiff, R. John Wright, and other manufacturers and artists bears.

Karen Strickland
Collector's Choice
17831 Chase St.
Northridge, CA 91325-3808
phone: 818-943-4361
fax: 818-341-9361
e-mail: drdrum@earthlink.com
Buys and sells Steiff, Schuco animals and vintage bears; four quarterly listings for $20/yr.

Experts

Beth B. Savino
Toy Store, The
P.O. Box 798
Holland, OH 43528-0798
phone: 419-473-9801 or 800-862-8697
fax: 419-473-3947
e-mail: toystore@toynet.com
Internet: http://www.toynet.com
Buys, sells and specializes in Steiff toys; sells exclusive Steiff Limited Edition; also buys old Steiff.

Man./Prod./Dist.

Steiff USA, L.P.
31 East 28th St., 9th Floor
New York, NY 10016
phone: 212-779-2582
fax: 212-779-2594
Manufacturer of collectible plush stuffed Steiff animals.

STEINS

(see also COLLECTIBLES [MOD-ERN], Steins; GLASSES, Drinking)

Appraisers

George F. Adams
Steins Unlimited
Rt. 600 Box 7-B
Pamplin, VA 23958
phone: 804-248-6114 or 800-55S-TEIN
Buys, sells, appraises and repairs (pewter) steins; Mettlach, Villeroy Boch, other German, brewery, Bud, Millers, COors, Strohs, old style, etc.

Auction Services

Gary Kirsner
Gary Kirsner Auctions
P.O. Box 8807
Coral Springs, FL 33075-8807
phone: 954-344-9856
fax: 954-344-4421
Six to seven cataloged auctions per year; steins and related items; also specialty auctions of Limited Edition and retired collectibles.

Andre Ammelounx
Stein Auction Company
P.O. Box 136
Palatine, IL 60078
Conducts live and mail bid catalog stein auctions.

Clubs/Associations

New England Steiners
65 Pierce Rd.
West Brookfield, MA 01585-3038
phone: 617-323-0018

Norman Pratore, Mem.
Stein Collectors International
Magazine: Prosit
P.O. Box 5005
Laurel, MD 20726-5005
phone: 301-498-7640
e-mail: tscheer@mcube.com
Internet: http://www.paterson.k12.nj.us/~steins/c
Dedicated to the studious appreciation of the art, culture and manufac-ture of beer steins, mugs drinking vessel and related items; has its own stein museum; books, articles and video library; over 28 chapters worldwide.

Georgia Stein Collectors
3040 Sawtooth Dr.
Alpharetta, GA 30202-5400

Jim DeMars
Sun Steiners
Newsletter: Sun Steiner News
P.O. Box 11782
Fort Lauderdale, FL 33339-1782
phone: 305-772-4490
fax: 305-772-4490
Members collect beer steins; antique, brewery, character, Mettlach, etc.

Buckeye Stein Verein
2265 Bradley Rd.
Westlake, OH 44145-1737
phone: 419-841-3195

Gateway Steiners
9843 Meadowfern Dr.
Saint Louis, MO 63126-2417
phone: 408-744-1041

Lone Star Chapter of the SCI
P.O. Box 555
Van Vleck, TX 77482-0555
phone: 713-371-2646

Collectors

Lester E. Hopper
3530 Mimosa Court
New Orleans, LA 70131-8305
phone: 504-394-3530
fax: 504-392-8937

Steve Elliott
1600 Tennessee St.
Vallejo, CA 94590
phone: 707-552-8400 or 707-642-1949
fax: 707-552-0881
Wants to buy antique beer steins.

Dealers

Heinz Roes
Heinz-N-Steins
231 Maple Ave.
Glen Burnie, MD 21061
phone: 410-760-0707
Buys and sells beer steins; military, Mettlach, character drinking vessels, cups, plaques, WWI, German, pipes, pictures, flasks, etc.; also occupa-tional shaving mugs.

George F. Adams
Steins Unlimited
Rt. 600 Box 7-B
Pamplin, VA 23958
phone: 804-248-6114 or 800-55S-TEIN
Buys, sells, appraises and repairs (pewter) steins; Mettlach, Villeroy Boch, other German, brewery, Bud, Millers, COors, Strohs, old style, etc.

Bill Cress
P.O. Box 989
Alton, IL 62002-0989
phone: 618-466-3513
Buys and sells all of the new and lots

of the old steins; quarterly lists of modern steins and mugs for sale.

Lester E. Hopper
3530 Mimosa Court
New Orleans, LA 70131-8305
phone: 504-394-3530
fax: 504-392-8937

Experts

Ron Fox
P.O. Box 2030
Brentwood, NY 11717-0997
phone: 516-231-0633
fax: 516-952-7719
Specializes in Mettlach steins.

John D. Stuart
Thirsty Knight Antiques
7-9 East Main St.
P.O. Box 48
New Market, MD 21774
phone: 301-831-9889 or 301-865-5053
Specializing in beer steins since 1972: Mettlachs, regimentals, characters, glass, porcelain, silver, pewter, faience, stoneware from 1500s to late 1800s.

Gary & Beth Kirsner
Glentiques, Ltd.
P.O. Box 8807
Coral Springs, FL 33075-8807
phone: 954-344-9856
fax: 954-344-4421
Wants quality steins: Mettlach, regimentals, character, glass, etc.; author of "The Beer Stein Book", (1990.)

Jim DeMars
P.O. Box 11782
Fort Lauderdale, FL 33339-1782
phone: 305-772-4490
fax: 305-772-4490

Les Paul
Les Paul, Steinologist
568 Country Isle #61C
Alameda, CA 94501-5614
phone: 510-523-7480
fax: 510-523-8755
Contact for free antique beer stein appraisal or information without obligation; photos are helpful, but he can usually tell you retail and a fair dealer offer over the phone; call with the stein in your hands.

Mettlach

Experts

Joe & Pat Hartzler
J & P Collectibles
P.O. Box 295
Adelphia, NJ 07710
phone: 908-364-1354
Buys, sells and specializes in Mettlach steins; willing to share information.

Regimental

Periodicals

John Harrell
Journal: Regimental Quarterly
P.O. Box 793
Frederick, MD 21705
phone: 301-694-7344
fax: 301-694-7345
Quarterly booklet focusing on Imperial German regimental steins and historical material as it relates to regimental steins.

STEREO VIEWERS & STEREOVIEWS

(see also 3-D PHOTOGRAPHICA; CAMERAS & CAMERA EQUIPMENT, Stereo Cameras; OPTICAL ITEMS; PAPER COLLECTIBLES; PHOTOGRAPHS)

Clubs/Associations

National Stereoscopic Association
Magazine: Stereo World
P.O. Box 14801
Columbus, OH 43214
phone: 614-263-4296
Internet: http://www.tisco.com/3d-web/nsa/nsa.htm
Members collect stereo views, stereoscopes, stereo cameras; View-Master reels, viewers, packets; all other 3-D collectibles; the glossy colorful magazine is published six timer per year.

Susan Pinsky
Stereo Club of Southern California
Newsletter: SCSC Newsletter
P.O. Box 2368
Culver City, CA 90231-2368
phone: 310-837-2368
fax: 310-558-1653
Internet: http://www.3d-web.com/reel/reel3d.html
A club for people interested in sharing 3-D (stereo) photography; some equipment listed in club newsletter classifieds.

Collectors

Norman Kulkin
727 N. Fuller Ave.
Los Angeles, CA 90046-7504
phone: 213-653-6929
Buy, sell, trade stereoviews, daguerreotypes, Civil War photos, anything in photographica 1839-1939.

Dealers

John Saddy
Jefferson Stereoptics
50 Foxborough Grove
London
Ontario N6K 4A8 Canada
phone: 519-641-4431
fax: 519-641-2899
e-mail: john.saddy.3d@sympatico.ca
Specializes in stereoviews; buys, sells, and operates a specialized stereoview phone and mail auction; wants boxed

sets, quality accumulations, View-Master and Tru-Vue.

Bryan W. Ginns
2109 Cty. Rte. 21
Valatie, NY 12184-6001
phone: 518-392-5805
fax: 518-392-7925
e-mail: the3dman@aol.com

Chris Perry
Doctor 3D
7470 Church St., Ste. A
Yucca Valley, CA 92284-3248
phone: 760-365-0475
fax: 760-365-0495
Can transfer stereoviews to 3D slides; also looking for views after 1900 and especially 1920 and after; no foreign travelogue of scenery; especially wants Hollywood, movie theaters, movie stars, World's Fair, magicians.

Experts

Russell Norton
Photographic Antiques
P.O. Box 1070
New Haven, CT 06504-1070
phone: 203-562-7800
Buys, sells, trades, collects, specializes in stereo views; author of "Stereoviews Illustrated Vol. 1: 50 Early American;" $20 from author; full-size illustrations, great quality duotones.

John Waldsmith
Antique Graphics
302 Granger Rd.
Medina, OH 44256-8434
phone: 216-239-1944
fax: 216-239-1944
Wants stereoscopic views, View-Master reels, photographica; conducts mail/phone auctions on regular basis; also direct sales; author of "Stereo .Views: An Illustrated History and Price Guide."

Chuck Reincke
Stereographica
2,141 Sweet Briar Rd.
Tustin, CA 92780
phone: 714-832-8563
fax: 714-832-8563
Buy, sell stereo cards, View Master, Tru-Vue and viewers; prefer higher quality and more unusual items.

Suppliers

David Starkman
Reel 3-D Enterprises, Inc.
P.O. Box 2368
Culver City, CA 90231-2368
phone: 310-837-2368
fax: 310-558-1653
Internet: http://www.3d-web.com/reel/reel3d.html
Offers a catalog with complete line of items for the modern 3-D enthusiast: books, stereo viewers, mounting supplies, etc.

Craig Daniels
StereoType
P.O. Box 1637
Florence, OR 97439-0107
phone: 541-997-8879
fax: 541-997-2686
e-mail: 104556.1656@compuserve.com
Internet: http://ourworld.compuserve.com/homepages/stereotype
Publishers, purveyors, providers of stereoscopes, views, technical services and information.

Alaska

Collectors

Richard A. Wood
P.O. Box 22165
Juneau, AK 99802-2165
phone: 907-789-8450
fax: 907-789-8450
e-mail: akrare@alaska.net
Internet: http://www.alaska.net/~akrare
Wants stereoviews of Alaska and Klondike; especially by Muybridge, Maynard, Brodeck, Haynes, etc.; also photographer L. Hensel views of PA (especially Pike County, PA) and NY.

STERLING SILVER FLATWARE

(see FLATWARE)

STEVENGRAPHS

Clubs/Associations

David L. Brown, Pres.
Stevengraph Collectors' Association
Newsletter: SCA Newsletter
2829 Arbutus Rd., #2103
Victoria
Brit. Columbia V8N 5X5 Canada
phone: 250-477-9896
Approx. 140 members worldwide; focuses on the various jacquard woven silk works (Stevengraphs) by Thomas Stevens of Coventry, England but also has articles about other weavers.

Collectors

Dr. Mark Cottrill
Good Old Days, The
The Moat House
Lymm Hall, Lymm
Chesire WA13 0AJ, U.K.
phone: 01925-754097
Specializes in Stevengraphs, silk woven bookmarks and postcards; send for sales lists.

Frank J. Buono
P.O. Box 1535
Binghamton, NY 13902
phone: 607-724-4444 or 800-527-8893
fax: 607-723-1656
Wants to buy Stevengraphs woven silk pictures and postcards.

Dealers

Wayne R. Adams
RFD 1 Box 29
Canaan, NH 03741-9712
phone: 603-523-4276
fax: 603-523-4888
e-mail: amr-dec-arts@endor.com
Buys and sells individual and complete collections of stevengraphs; looking for good quality; no bookmarks, please.

Experts

John High
415 E. 52nd St.
New York, NY 10022
phone: 212-758-1692
Advisor to "Warman's Antiques & Collectibles Price Guide."

Museums/Libraries

Nick Dodd
Herbert Art Gallery & Museum
Jordan Well
Coventry CV1 5RW, U.K.
Has the largest collection of Stevengraphs in public hands; also has a very large silk ribbon collection.

Paterson Museum
2 Market St.
Paterson, NJ 07501
phone: 201-881-3874

STICK PINS

(see CLOTHING & ACCESSORIES, Vintage; CUFF LINKS; GEMS & JEWELRY, Stick Pins)

STILLS

(see MOVIE MEMORABILIA; PHOTOGRAPHS)

STOCK TICKERS

(see also TELEGRAPH ITEMS)

Collectors

Carl Ratner
550 Lamoka Ave.
Staten Island, NY 10312
e-mail: artdeco@bway.net
Buy, sell, trade antique stock tickers; interested in all types of machines, parts and accessories, but especially seeking Edison and Western Union tickers with glass domes.

Frank Guarino
P.O. Box 89
De Bary, FL 32713

Jack Arnold
P.O. Box 2541
Reno, NV 89505-2541
phone: 702-829-8599 or 702-786-0369
fax: 702-786-5598
Wants Wall Street stock tickers (Western Union); also parts, stands, history, and repair books.

R.G. Klein
P.O. Box 24 A 06
Los Angeles, CA 90024
Please send photograph of ticker; interested in everything related to the stock market and Wall Street.

Dealers

Randy Donley
Donley's Wild West Town & Museum
8512 S. Union Rd.
Union, IL 60180-9661
phone: 815-923-9000
fax: 815-923-2253
Wants pre-1940 stock ticker tape machines made by Edison or Brunnell.

STOCKS & BONDS

(see also BANKING; CIVIL WAR ARTIFACTS, Confederate Bonds; COINS & CURRENCY, Paper Money; PAPER COLLECTIBLES; SCRIP; STOCK TICKERS)

Auction Services

R.M. Smythe & Company
26 Broadway, Ste. 271
New York, NY 10004-1701
phone: 212-943-1880 or 800-622-1880
fax: 212-908-4047
Conducts auctions of Colonial currency, Confederate currency, federal essay notes, proof vignettes, fractional and obsolete currency, stocks, bonds, coins and autographs.

Pierre Bonneau, Pres.
Stock Search International, Inc.
4761 W. Waterbuck Dr.
Tucson, AZ 85742
phone: 800-537-4523 or 520-579-5635
fax: 520-579-5639

Clubs/Associations

Bond & Share Society, c/o R.M. Smythe & Co., Inc.
Newsletter: Bond & Share Society Newsletter
26 Broadway at Bowling Green, Room 200
New York, NY 10004-1763
phone: 212-908-4110 or 212-908-4519
fax: 212-908-4600

Piere Bonneau
Old Certificates Collector's Club
Newsletter: OCCC Newsletter
4761 W. Waterbuck Dr.
Tucson, AZ 85742
phone: 800-537-4523 or 520-579-5635
fax: 520-579-5639

Collectors

Fred Herrigel
P.O. Box 599
Millburn, NJ 07041-0599
Wants to buy obsolete stock certificates and pre-1920 postcard collections.

Ray Curry
161 Bergen Ave.
Waldwick, NJ 07463-2123
Wants to buy obsolete stocks and bonds including mining, railroad, and others.

Richard Urmston
Centennial Documents
P.O. Box 5262
Clinton, NJ 08809-0262
phone: 908-703-6009
fax: 908-730-9566
e-mail: centdocs@postoffice.ptd.net
Wants stocks & bonds; send photocopy of items for sale.

Herb D. Rice
3883 Turtle Creek Blvd. #2317
Dallas, TX 75219
Wants old, obsolete stock certificates.

Mike Farmer
1406 Bigelow Ave. NW
Olympia, WA 98506-4417
phone: 360-352-7189
fax: 360-352-7189
Wants to buy pre-1930 stocks & bonds, land grants, graphic bill heads, broadsides, posters, maps, business letters, Civil War, American Indian, cancelled checks, Alaska, any old interesting paper; send copy or call; prompt reply.

Dealers

Paul Longo
Paul Longo Americana
P.O. Box 5510
Gloucester, MA 01930-0007
phone: 508-525-2290
Wants pre-1910 stocks and bonds; any amount.

George H. La Barre
La Barre Galleries
P.O. Box 746
Hollis, NH 03049
phone: 603-882-2411
Major dealer and expert in autographs, and stocks and bonds.

Scott J. Winslow
Scott J. Winslow Associates, Inc.
P.O. Box 10240
Nashua, NH 03110-0240
phone: 603-881-4071 or 800-225-6233
fax: 603-472-8773
Buys and sells stocks certificates, bonds and historical autographs; also conducts mail bid auctions of same.

Robert F. Kluge
P.O. Box 155
Roselle Park, NJ 07204
phone: 908-241-4209

R.M. Smythe & Company
26 Broadway, Ste. 271
New York, NY 10004-1701
phone: 212-943-1880 or 800-622-1880
fax: 212-908-4047

Phyllis Barrella
Buttonwood Galleries
Throggs Neck Station
P.O. Box 1006
Bronx, NY 10465-0606
phone: 718-828-0649
Specializing in high quality pre-1910 stock certificates and bonds.

D & D Scripophily International, Ltd.
P.O. Box 580063
Flushing, NY 11358
phone: 718-358-3447 or 800-941-0098
fax: 718-358-2849
Wants holed, cancelled, obsolete stock certificates.

Frank Hammelbacher
P.O. Box 660077
Flushing, NY 11366-0077
phone: 718-380-4009
fax: 718-380-9793
Deals in ephemera of all kinds, especially old stocks and bonds and Wild West posters.

Nick Johnson
1 Old Country Rd., Ste 300
Carle Place, NY 11514-1806
phone: 516-663-0606
fax: 516-663-0654
Dealer in 19th and 20th century stocks and bonds; certificate catalog is published 6 times a year for $2.35 which is refundable with first order.

Haley & Hannelore Garrison
Antique Stocks & Bonds
Drawer JH
Williamsburg, VA 23187-3632
phone: 800-451-4504 or 757-220-3838
fax: 757-220-0294
Internet: http://www.tiac.net/users/haley/index.html

David M. Beach
Paper Americana
P.O. Box 2026
Goldenrod, FL 32733-2026
phone: 407-657-7403
fax: 407-657-6382
Buys and sells antique US stocks and bonds; wants to buy stocks signed by Jay Gould, James Fisk, Jr., Comm. Vanderbilt, Daniel Drew, Jay Cooke, Cyrus Field, Hetty Green and other Robber Barons.

John Heleva
P.O. Box 375
Fair Oaks, CA 95628
phone: 916-781-2991
fax: 916-781-6564
Stocks and bonds bought and sold; mining, railroads, automotive, petroleum, utilities, banking & general issues.

Georgia Fox
Foxes' Den Antiques
P.O. Box 846
Sutter Creek, CA 95685
phone: 209-267-0774
Wants old stocks & bonds, especially relating to gold mining in California or Nevada.

Experts

Warren Anderson
America West Archives
P.O. Box 100
Cedar City, UT 84721-0100
phone: 801-586-9497 or 801-586-7323
Buys and sells issued American stocks & bonds 1840-1930; especially mining, energy, transportation; offers mail order catalog; author of "Owning Western History."

Ken Prag
Ken Prag Paper Americana
P.O. Box 14817
San Francisco, CA 94114-0817
phone: 415-586-9386
Eager to buy old stocks and bonds, quality picture postcards, western stereoviews, old timetables and brochures, etc.

Misc. Services

Warren Anderson
America West Archives
P.O. Box 100
Cedar City, UT 84721-0100
phone: 801-586-9497 or 801-586-7323
A professional stock tracer who researches stock certificates and bonds to determine whether they have value on the current stock market or to a collector of worthless securities; author of "Owning Western History."

Pierre Bonneau, Pres.
Stock Search International, Inc.
4761 W. Waterbuck Dr.
Tucson, AZ 85742
phone: 800-537-4523 or 520-579-5635
fax: 520-579-5639
Researches the background of companies no longer listed on any exchanges & help clients recover funds from what they think are worthless stocks; also ascertain the value of stocks as collectibles; research fee is $85.

Periodicals

Julie A. Ulrich, PR
Krause Publications
Newspaper: Bank Note Reporter
700 E. State St.
Iola, WI 54990-0001
phone: 715-445-2214
fax: 715-445-4087
e-mail: info@krause.com
Internet: http://www.krause.com
Monthly news source and marketplace for collectors of U.S. and world paper money, notes, checks and related fiscal paper.

Financial History

Book Sellers

R.G. Klein
Wall Street Books
P.O. Box 24 A 06
Los Angeles, CA 90024
Largest specialist dealer/collector in rare and scarce books relating to the stock market and Wall Street.

Museums/Libraries

Anne Keane
Museum of American Financial History
Magazine: Friends of Financial History
26 Broadway at Bowling Green, Room 200
New York, NY 10004-1763
phone: 212-908-4110 or 212-908-4519
fax: 212-908-4600
Dedicated to the development of the US capital markets and the people who made them famous; mission is to collect/preserve/display historical financial artifacts and to use them as an educational resource for schools & the public.

Mining Related

Dealers

Douglas McDonald
Gypsyfoot Enterprises, Inc.
P.O. Box 5833
Helena, MT 59604-5833
phone: 406-449-8076
fax: 406-443-8514
Buying all pre-1933 mining stocks; please send photocopies for offer.

Experts

Chuck Voelker
844 Fairground St.
Plymouth, MI 48170
phone: 313-451-5911
e-mail: usfmck3s@ibmmail.com
Collector and researcher of 19th and early 20th century mining stock certificates, especially Michigan related.

STOVES

(see also CAST IRON ITEMS; KITCHEN COLLECTIBLES; RANGES)

Clubs/Associations

Macy Stern
Antique Stove Association
Newsletter: Stove Parts Needed Newsletter
5515 Almeda Rd.
Houston, TX 77004-7443
phone: 713-521-0934 or 713-528-1297
fax: 713-521-0889
For those interested in antique stoves and related items; you must join to receive the benefits which are for members only.

Collectors

N.W. Neill, Jr.
Glascock Stove Co.
P.O. Box 38
Ennice, NC 28623-0038
phone: 910-657-8152
fax: 910-657-8084
Historian wants cook stoves, heaters, etc. (complete or parts) made by the Glascock Stove Co. of Greensboro, NC; models include Carolina Beauty, Victor, Charter, Giant, Carolina Hot Blast, Blue Ridge, Plymouth, etc.

Dealers

Erickson's Antique Stoves, Inc.
P.O. Box 2275
At the Depot
Littleton, MA 01460
phone: 508-486-3589
Antique gas coal and wood stoves and ranges; bought, sold, restored.

Mike Trainor
Mike's Stove Works
98 Webster St.
Haverhill, MA 01830-4123
phone: 508-373-0767
Buys, collects, sells and restores all types of coal, gas and wood stoves; old or new.

Barnstable Stove Shop
P.O. Box 472
West Barnstable, MA 02668
phone: 508-362-9913
Buys, sells and restores antique wood, coal and gas stoves; large parts inventory; 20 years in business; expert restoration work.

Macy Stern
Macy's Texas Stove Works
5515 Almeda Rd.
Houston, TX 77004-7443
phone: 713-521-0934 or 713-528-1297
fax: 713-521-0889
Buys, sells, brokers, repairs, and restores old ranges; also sells parts and publishes "Classic Ranges" newspaper.

Ron Schaffer
Classic Stoves Emporium
480 San Juan St.
P.O. Box 153
Pagosa Springs, CO 81147
phone: 303-264-2710
Buys, sells and restores antique stoves; fabricates replacement parts as needed.

Experts

Clifford Boram
417 N. Main St.
Monticello, IN 47960-1932
phone: 219-583-6465
Author of "How to Get Parts Cast for Your Antique Stove"; will answer questions, but only by phone. No mail inquiries, please; photocopies from 2000-volume archive of stove manufacturers' literature 1860-1935,

Periodicals

Macy Stern
Macy's Texas Stove Works
Newspaper: Classic Ranges
5515 Almeda Rd.
Houston, TX 77004-7443
phone: 713-521-0934 or 713-528-1297
fax: 713-521-0889
The only newsletter for classic range owners and buyers; ranges/ovens and stoves for sale, ranges wanted to buy, parts for sale, restoration services, articles, old advertisements, etc.

Art Wallace
Newsletter: Antique Stove Exchange, The
2729 SW 330th
Federal Way, WA 98023

Repair Services

Beatrice Bryant
Bryant Stove Works & Music Inc.
RR 2 Rich Rd.
P.O. Box 2048
Thorndike, ME 04986
phone: 207-568-3665
Large collection on display; also sells parts and restores antique (1780s-1940s) cook stoves, parlor stoves, and gas stoves. In addition, restores player pianos.

Tomahawk Foundry, Inc.
2337 29th St.
Rice Lake, WI 54868
phone: 715-234-4498
Makes replacement parts for cast iron stoves.

Tom Lawson
Buckeye Appliance
714 W. Fremont
Stockton, CA 95203-2702
phone: 209-464-9643
Specializes in the sales, parts and restoration of antique gas stoves; also sell kitchen collectibles, Hoosiers, 1950s chrome dinettes, and porcelain-top tables.

Tom Lawson
Buckeye Appliance
714 W. Fremont
Stockton, CA 95203-2702
phone: 209-464-9643
Specializes in the sales, parts and restoration of antique gas stoves; also sells kitchen collectibles, Hoosiers, 1950s chrome dinettes, and porcelain-top tables.

Salesman Samples & Toys

Collectors

Andrew B. Golbert
RR 1 Box 1820
North Ferrisburg, VT 05473-9508
phone: 802-453-2525
Wants to buy children's cast iron toy stoves and salesmen's sample stoves and furnaces.

Sally Swanson
3302 West 11th St.
Erie, PA 16505-3710
phone: 814-838-1866
Wants information on all cast iron toy stoves and salesman samples.

Karen Mullins
5679 Deerfield Rd.
Orlando, FL 32808-2802
phone: 407-297-9218
Wants to buy toy or salesman sample iron stoves, parts, cookware; also

wants toy catalogs that have toy stoves listed.

Judy Owen, ISA
Antique Appraisers - Grand Traverse
10332 Stoneybeach Pointe
Traverse City, MI 49686
phone: 616-946-2534
fax: 616-946-2573
Wants to buy miniature stoves.

Ralph C. Hylton
245 Hughes Ford Rd.
Sullivan, MO 63080-1924
phone: 314-468-8418
Wants to buy salesman samples and toy stoves; complete or in parts; also wants small cookware.

Marilyn Wren
P.O. Box 3025
Blaine, WA 98231-3025

Experts

Ed Hullet
5200 N. Lorraine
Hutchinson, KS 67502-2727
phone: 316-662-9381
Buys, sells, restores, and appraises exclusively salesmen's sample stoves.

STREETCAR LINE COL-LECTIBLES

(see also RAILROAD COL-LECTIBLES)

Clubs/Associations

William M. Shapotkin, Mem.
Central Electric Railfans' Association
P.O. Box 503
Chicago, IL 60690
phone: 312-346-3723
Interested in history and equipment of electric railroading: urban, rapid transit, suburban, trunk line and industrial electric railways.

Collectors

Nestle's Railroadiana
RD 2, Box 105
Greenwich, NY 12834-9425
phone: 518-692-2867
Buys and sells all sorts of railroadiana and trolley memorabilia: timetables, guides, maps, advertising info., menus, old books and magazines, etc.

Seth Bramson
330 N.E. 96th St.
Miami, FL 33138-2718
phone: 305-757-1016
fax: 305-895-8178
Buys railroad and trolleyana; postage paid on approvals.

Experts

Joseph Gross
P.O. Box 15
Spencerport, NY 14559-0015
phone: 716-768-8918
Author of "The Trolley & Interurban Directory" (Gross Publications.)

Museums/Libraries

Baltimore Streetcar Museum
P.O. Box 4881
Baltimore, MD 21211
phone: 410-547-0264

STRING HOLDERS

Collectors

Bobbie & Alan Bryson
1 St. Eleanoras Ln.
Tuckahoe, NY 10707-1307
phone: 914-779-1405
e-mail: napkindoll@aol.com

Emma Kretchek
5726 Terrace Park Dr.
Dayton, OH 45429-6048
phone: 513-434-9126

Lewis Jones
665 Wirtz Rd.
Crown Point, IN 46307
phone: 219-663-7865
Wants to buy chalk or ceramic string holders; would also like to communi- cate with other collectors.

Al Little
151 Highway 173
Antioch, IL 60002
phone: 847-395-7752
fax: 847-395-7703
Buy, sells and trades string holders; single pieces or entire collections.

Experts

Charles Reynolds
Reynolds Toys
2836 Monroe St.
Falls Church, VA 22042-2007
phone: 703-533-1322
Wants string holders made of metal, glass or wood; not interested in chalk or china types.

Repro. Sources

Bullfrog Hollow
Keeny Rd.
Old Lyme, CT 06371

STRIPTEASE

Clubs/Associations

Exotic World, The Burlesque Hall of Fame
29053 Wild Road
Helendale, CA 92342
phone: 619-243-5261

Collectors

Charles McCaughy
221 Williams St.
Bowling Green, OH 43402
phone: 419-352-7211
e-mail: cmccagh@opie.bgseu.edu
Internet: http://ernie.bgsu.edu/ ~cmccagh/
Interested in anything in paper concerning strippers and their settings: burlesque theaters, carnivals, clubs; belly dancing, carnival girl shows, shake dancing, striptease,

table dancing; photos, publications, postcards, programs.

Wayne Brown
5599 Wellman Rd.
Woodland, MI 48897
phone: 616-367-4661
Wants to buy signed or unsigned photos of strippers, photos of burlesque theaters, related lobby cards and posters, magazines and books related to striptease.

STUFFED TOYS

(see STEIFF; TEDDY BEARS; TOYS, Plush)

STUNTMEN

Clubs/Associations

John Hagner
Hollywood Stuntmen's Hall of Fame
Newsletter: Hollywood Stuntmen's Hall of Fame News
111 East 100th North
Moab, UT 84532
Non-profit organization dedicated to preserving the history and memora- bilia relating to Hollywood stuntmen. CAN't FIND ON ALTAVISTA

SUBWAY ITEMS

Museums/Libraries

New York Transit Museum
81 Willoughby St., Rm. 802
Brooklyn, NY 11201
phone: 718-243-8601 or 718-243-3060
Features displays, exhibits, archive information regarding the New York Subway System.

SUGAR PACKETS

Clubs/Associations

Mitzt Geiser
Sugar Packet Collectors Clubs International
Newsletter: Sugar Packet, The
15601 Burkhart Rd.
Orrville, OH 44667-9618
phone: 330-682-7486
Specializing in the international trading and exchange of information on sugar sacs and sugar cubes. Send SASE for information.

SUGAR SHAKERS

Collectors

Robert A. Hendel
1385 York Ave. #16B
New York, NY 10021
phone: 212-772-9070 or 212-450-4733
fax: 212-450-5521
Wants large and small collections; very interested in "diner" shakers.

SUPER BOWL RINGS

(see SPORTS COLLECTIBLES, Jewelry)

SUPER HEROES

(see also COMIC BOOKS; POPULAR CULTURE; PREMIUMS; SCIENCE FICTION; TOYS, Super Hero)

Collectors

Stephen Coovert
3039 Pimlico Lane
Corpus Christi, TX 78418-2818
phone: 512-937-3409
Wants Superman, Batman, Spiderman collectibles.

Dealers

John Kachmar
Techno-Fantasy Traders
779 Carissa Dr.
West Palm Beach, FL 33411-3412
phone: 407-798-5978
fax: 407-798-5978
e-mail: kachmar@aol.com

Periodicals

John Koenig
Antique Trader Publications, Inc.
Newspaper: Toy Trader
922 Churchill St., Ste. #1
Waupaca, WI 54981
phone: 715-258-7525 or 800-768-9225
fax: 715-258-8707
e-mail: jkoenig@add-inc.com
Internet: http://www.csmonline.com
Monthly newspaper with information on how to buy, sell and trade all types of toys; market trends, the latest prices, "how-to" columns, listings of toy clubs and upcoming toy shows and auctions; also full of buy and sell ads.

Batman

Clubs/Associations

Fred Carini
Captain Action Society of Pittsburgh
Newsletter: Capt. Action News
516 Cubbage St.
Carnegie, PA 15106
phone: 412-276-6084 or 412-276-7356
All Capt. Action club! Trading, buying, selling all Capt. Action items.

Dark Sentinel
Newsletter: Dark Sentinel Newsletter
111 Tallavana Dr.
Havana, FL 32333

Don Kyle
Batman TV Series Fan Club
Newsletter: Batman TV Series Fan Club Newsletter
P.O. Box 107
Venice, CA 90294-0107
phone: 310-226-2883
e-mail: sndtrx@earthlink.net
Internet: http://www.batfanclub.com
Newsletter published quarterly averages 20-30 pages with photos; convention and cast updates; "Bat" related merchandise; also buys and sells Batman toys, paper, film, etc.; also includes Green Hornet as it was a crossover with Batman.

Collectors

David J. Anderson
5192 Dawes Ave.
Alexandria, VA 22311
phone: 703-671-7422
fax: 703-578-1222
Aggressively seeks Batman and Superman items.

Joe Desris
Batman Addict
1202 60th St., #107
Kenosha, WI 53140
phone: 414-657-4737
fax: 414-657-4733
Batman addict; only known cure: more collectibles! Wants anything Batman related from 1930s-1990s.

Captain Midnight

Clubs/Associations

John Samorajczyk
Air Heroes Fan Club
19205 Seneca Ridge Court
Gaithersburg, MD 20879-3135
This club honors Captain Midnight.

Collectors

Bob Hritz
21 W. 262 Belden Ave.
Lombard, IL 60148
phone: 708-620-0156
Wants Captain Midnight items: Ovaltine glass jars, CM advertising, premiums, rings, pins, lobby cards, flight commander manual, etc.

Phantom

Collectors

Robert J. Griffin
P.O. Box 76
Mattawan, MI 49071
phone: 616-387-3024
Wants to buy memorabilia relating to The Phantom.

Rocketeer

Clubs/Associations

John Datz
Rocketeer Fan Club
Newsletter: Rocketeer Newsletter
10 Halick Ct.
East Brunswick, NJ 08816-1373

Superman

Collectors

David J. Anderson
5192 Dawes Ave.
Alexandria, VA 22311
phone: 703-671-7422
fax: 703-578-1222
Aggressively seeks Batman and Superman items.

Dealers

Danny Fuchs
209-80 18th Ave., #4K
Flushing, NY 11360-1451
phone: 718-225-9030
fax: 718-225-3688
Buys and sells all types of pre-1960 Superman collectibles: toys, games, figurines, puzzles, novelties, premiums, etc. rare or unusual; also buying unusual/interesting collectibles from other comic book characters.

Experts

Danny Fuchs
209-80 18th Ave., #4K
Flushing, NY 11360-1451
phone: 718-225-9030
fax: 718-225-3688
"America's foremost Superman Collector"; co-author of "The Adventures of Superman Collecting."

Periodicals

Jim Nolt
Newsletter: Adventures Continue, The
935 Fruistville Pike, #105
Lancaster, PA 17601
phone: 717-560-6380
fax: 717-560-6380
e-mail: jimnolt@redrose.net
Internet: http://geocities.com/
    Hollywood/2459
Maintains a George Reeves (Superman) homepage on the world wide web.

SUPPLIERS

(see ANTIQUES DEALERS & COLLECTORS; CLOCKS; FIREARMS; KNIVES; MODELS; REPAIR/RESTORATION/CONSERVATION; STAMP COLLECTING; TELEPHONES and other individual categories)

SURVEYING INSTRUMENTS

(see also INSTRUMENTS & DEVICES, Scientific)

Collectors

Stephen Buczko
27 Surrey Road
Salem, MA 01970
phone: 508-744-4683
Wants to buy surveying instruments.

Barry Nichols
8139 East Britton Dr.
Niagara Falls, NY 14304
Wants surveying tools: instruments, compasses, chains, etc.

Robert Miller
RD 2 Box 176
New Alexandria, PA 15670
Wants surveying instruments, catalogs, and related items.

Ron Kiser
70 Woodfin Pl. #214
Asheville, NC 28801
phone: 704-689-4845 or 704-258-1380
Wants to buy antique brass surveying instruments: transits, levels, alidades, plane tables, tripods, rods, chains, surveyor's compasses, pocket compasses, etc.

Michael S. Manier
100 E. Walnut
P.O. Box 110
Houston, MO 65483
phone: 417-967-2777 or 417-962-5221
fax: 417-967-3926
Wants to buy compasses (both brass and wooden), wire-link measuring chains, theodolites, transits, levels, octants, sextants, quadrants, solar devices, calculating devices, and drawing instruments.

Paul H. Hayashi, PE
18 Tarabrook Dr.
Orinda, CA 94563-3121
phone: 510-254-5074 or 510-253-1038
fax: 510-253-0592
Buys high precision theodolites, levels, solar compasses, mining surveying instruments, solar transits, U.S. Coast & Geodetic instruments.

D. Sanders
P.O. Box 1980
Granite Falls, WA 98252
phone: 360-691-5063
Wants old surveying instruments: transits, compasses, unusual plumb bobs.

Dealers

Al & Bobbie Roberts
Rational Past, The
221 Oceano Dr.
Los Angeles, CA 90049
phone: 310-476-6277
fax: 310-476-6278
e-mail: rational-past@mindspring.com
Organizer of West Coast Scientific & Technical Antique and Collectible Shows (Los Angeles in the winter and San Francisco are in late summer.)

Experts

Dale R. Beeks
Perceptions Scientifica
P.O. Box 117
Mount Vernon, IA 52314
phone: 800-880-5178 or 319-895-0506
Expert, appraiser, wants pre-1900 compasses, transits, unusual instruments, surveying ephemera; offers museum services.

SWANKYSWIGS

(see also GLASSES, Drinking)

Clubs/Associations

M. Fountain
Swankyswigs Unlimited
201 Alvena
Wichita, KS 67203
phone: 316-943-1925

Collectors

Gary Kane
15006 Brookpoint
Houston, TX 77062
phone: 713-488-1537
Wants to buy or trade swankyswigs with lids or labels, special issues, with advertisements.

Experts

Ian Warner
P.O. Box 93022
Brampton
Ontario LGY 4V8 Canada
phone: 905-453-9074
Specializing in Wade porcelain and swankyswigs.

M. Fountain
201 Alvena
Wichita, KS 67203
phone: 316-943-1925
Swankyswigs were decorated glasses originally filled with Kraft Cheese Spreads.

SWAROVSKI

(see COLLECTIBLES [MODERN], Crystal [Swarovski])

SWORDS

(see also ARMS & ARMOR; ARMS & ARMOR, Japanese [Swords]; CIVIL WAR ARTIFACTS; EDGED WEAPONS; MILITARIA; NAZI ITEMS)

Appraisers

Thomas Winter
817 Patton
Springfield, IL 62702-2431
phone: 217-523-8729
Collector/appraiser of swords; wants to buy quality Japanese swords & high quality or rare German and U.S. swords, daggers, fighting knives & related items; will also buy tsubas and parts for edged weapons; SASE for free evaluation.

Clubs/Associations

Leonard J. Garigliano
Association of American Sword
    Collectors, The
P.O. Box 288
Parsonsburg, MD 21849

Dealers

Ron G. Hickox
Antique Arms & Militaria
P.O. Box 360006
Tampa, FL 33673-0006
phone: 813-899-1776
fax: 813-744-5678
e-mail: rhickox@ix.netcom.com
  *American & European edged weapons
  purchased; give complete description
  and send photos when selling.*

Fred Coluzzi
Frederick's Swords
6919 Westview Dr.
Oak Forest, IL 60452-1566
phone: 708-687-3647
  *Buys and sells antique swords and
  daggers from all countries and all
  periods; issues 3 to 4 major catalogs
  per year: Japanese, US, German,
  Turkish, Moro, Indonesian,
  Philippine, Chinese.*

Museums/Libraries

Bruce M. Moseley, Cur.
Fort Ticonderoga Museum
Newsletter: Bulletin of the Fort
  Ticonderoga Museum
P.O. Box 390
Ticonderoga, NY 12883
phone: 518-585-2821
fax: 518-585-2210
  *10,000 volume research library
  specializing in 19th century military
  history and the history of the
  Champlain Valley; museum depicts
  history of the area and the campaigns
  during the 7 Year War and the
  Revolutionary War.*

Repro. Sources

Century International Arms Inc.
P.O. Box 714
Saint Albans, VT 05478
phone: 802-527-1252
fax: 802-527-0470
  *Reproduction of the finest military and
  edged weapons: US artillery saber,
  US Naval officer's sword, food officer
  sword, Souave bayonet, trooper
  sword, US Cavalry saber, Scottish
  sword, AK74 bayonet, etc.*

Nazi

Collectors

K. Wiley
719 Baldwin SE
Grand Rapids, MI 49503-4470
phone: 616-451-8410
  *Wants Japanese swords, daggers,
  sword parts. Also German 3rd Reich
  daggers, swords, bayonets.
  References available.*

Dealers

Ron G. Hickox
Antique Arms & Militaria
P.O. Box 360006
Tampa, FL 33673-0006
phone: 813-899-1776
fax: 813-744-5678
e-mail: rhickox@ix.netcom.com
  *German WWII swords and daggers
  bought, sold, traded; give description
  and send photos when selling.*

Here are some tips when contacting someone listed in this book:

When requesting information about a particular item, include a description (material, dimensions, maker's mark, model number, etc.) and a photo, sketch, or photocopy of the item in question. ■

Always ask if there are charges for samples or for the services requested. ■

When writing, please be sure to include a Large (#10 business size) Self-Addressed and Stamped Envelope (LSASE) if requesting a reply or the return of photographs. ■

Never call collect unless otherwise directed. When calling, be considerate of time zone differences and always ask if the party you are calling has time to talk. When leaving an answering machine message, always instruct the party to call you back collect. ■

TABLEWARE

(see also CERAMICS; DINNER-
WARE; FLATWARE; GLASS,
Elegant; GLASS, Crystal)

Man./Prod./Dist.

225 The International Showcase
225 Fifth Ave.
New York, NY 10010
phone: 212-685-6377 or 800-235-3512
*Showplace for purveyors specializing
in the sale of new giftware &
decorative accessories; also
tableware.*

New York Merchandise Mart
41 Madison Ave.
New York, NY 10010
phone: 212-686-1203
*Showplace for purveyors of new
tableware including gifts, glassware,
ceramicware, silverware and
decorative accessories.*

Periodicals

Magazine: China Glass & Tableware
1011 Clifton Ave.
Clifton, NJ 07013
phone: 201-779-1600
fax: 201-779-3242
*Trade magazine for new gifts,
decorative accessories, and tabletop
wares; buyer's resource directory
guide available with subscription.*

Geyer-McAllister Publications, Inc.
Magazine: Gifts & Decorative
Accessories
51 Madison Ave.
New York, NY 10010-1603
phone: 212-689-4411
fax: 212-683-7929
*Trade magazine for new gifts,
decorative accessories, collectibles,
stationery, gift baskets, and tabletop
wares; buyer's resource directory
guide available with subscription.*

Matching Services For

(see DINNERWARE; FLATWARE;
GLASS, Elegant; GLASS, Crystal)

TARGET SHOOTING MEMORA-
BILIA

(see also SPORTS COLLECTIBLES;
TARGETS, Shooting Gallery;
TRAPSHOOTING)

Collectors

David L. Hartline
P.O. Box 775
Columbus, OH 43085
Wants to buy all types of pre-1920

*shooting medals, badges and trophies
for marksmanship; will buy medals
whether complete or not; prefers items
that are engraved to winners; will
answer all letters.*

Rifle

Collectors

Allen Hallock
P.O. Box 2747
San Rafael, CA 94902-2747
phone: 415-924-1967
e-mail: arh@earthlink.net
*Wants American, German, Swiss
"Schuetzen" memorabilia circa 1865-
1915: medals, trophies, souvenirs,
targets, photographs, match
programs, posters, score books, steins,
single-shot target rifles; anything
"Schuetzen"; no military.*

Target Balls

Collectors

Art Snyder
110 White Oak Dr.
Butler, PA 16001-3446
phone: 412-287-0278
*Buys/sells/trades antique glass target
balls, ball traps or throwers, glass
house or sporting ads pertaining to
same; anything related.*

Ralph Finch
20135 Evergreen Meadows
Southfield, MI 48076-4222
phone: 248-358-4763 or 800-678-6400
fax: 313-222-2451
Wants glass target balls.

Experts

Alex Kerr
4709 Forman Ave.
N. Hollywood, CA 91602
phone: 818-762-6320

TARGETS

Shooting Gallery

(see also CAST IRON ITEMS;
TARGET SHOOTING MEMORA-
BILIA)

Experts

Richard Tucker
Argyle Antiques
P.O. Box 262
Argyle, TX 76226-0262
phone: 817-464-3752
fax: 817-464-7293
e-mail: millwt@pop.intex.net
*Buys and sells figural cast iron items
including shooting targets; no repros.
or repaired items wanted; also wants
catalogs, photographs and other
shooting gallery memorabilia*

TATTOO RELATED ITEMS

Collectors

Marvin Yagoda
28585 S. Harwich Dr.
San Francisco, CA 48018
phone: 810-851-8158
*Wants to buy tattoo related
memorabilia.*

Tim
330 Tumamoc Dr.
Lake Havasu City, AZ 86403
phone: 520-505-8327 or 520-505-8282
*Wants antique and vintage tattoo
equipment, memorabilia, posters,
signs, advertising, flash (designs).*

Museums/Libraries

Lyle Tuttle
Tattoo Art Museum, The
841 Columbus Ave.
San Francisco, CA 94133-2307
phone: 415-775-4991 or 707-462-4406
fax: 707-462-4433
*Largest collection of tattoo art and
related antiques & collectibles; buys/
sells machines, designs, artifacts,
photos, paintings, etc.*

TAXI RELATED COLLECTIBLES

Collectors

Nathan Willensky
Taxi Toys & Memorabilia
5 East 22nd St. #24C
New York, NY 10010-5329
phone: 212-982-2156
fax: 212-995-1065
*Buy and trades anything Taxi - toys
and memorabilia; Taxis only.*

Henry Winningham
3205 S. Morgan St.
Chicago, IL 60608-6609
*Wants anything pre-1950 that's
related to the Taxi industry.*

TAXIDERMY

(see ANIMAL TROPHIES)

TEA RELATED ANTIQUES

(see also CERAMICS; KITCHEN
COLLECTIBLES; ORIENTALIA,
Japanese Items; SILVER)

Dealers

Alvin & Rose Harper
Harpers Antiques & Interiors
236 Second St.
Lewes, DE 19958-1326
phone: 302-645-9750
*Buys and sells 19th and early 20th
century tea accessories such as
Staffordshire and ironstone teapots,
sterling and plate silver, salesmen
pottery samples, children's tea sets
and furniture.*

Tea Strainers

Dealers

Carol Payne
Carol's Antique Gallery
14455 Big Basin Way
Saratoga, CA 95070-6008
phone: 408-867-7055
*Wants to buy silver and silverplated
tea strainers, and other tea items such
as tea caddies, tea caddy scoops, tea
infusers, and toast racks; nothing
dented, please.*

Teapots

Collectors

Kier Linn
2591 Military Ave.
Los Angeles, CA 90064-1933
phone: 310-477-5229
fax: 310-268-8420
e-mail: dcrehr@earthlink.net
Internet: http://www.earthlink.net/
~dcrehr/

Experts

Gerard Schultz
Antique Gallery, The
8523 Germantown Ave.
Philadelphia, PA 19118
phone: 215-248-1700
fax: 215-247-8411
*Buys, sells and specializes in tea pots:
18th through 20th century - English,
American, French, Chinese; teapots
and cadagans porcelain and
creamware.*

Tina M. Carter
882 South Mollison Ave.
El Cajon, CA 92020
phone: 619-440-5043
*Author of "Teapots" - available from
the author.*

Museums/Libraries

Veilleuse-Theieres Collection
309 College Street
Trenton, TN 38382
phone: 901-855-2014
*Collection of 525 European
"Veilleuse-Theieres" (French for
"night-light teapots") sickroom and
nursery teapots used also as night
lights and for the mixture of
medications.*

Periodicals

Diana Rosen
Newsletter: Tea Talk
P.O. Box 860
Sausalito, CA 94966
phone: 415-331-1557
fax: 415-331-1557
Internet: http://www.bpe.com/drinks/tea/
teatalk.html
*A national quarterly newsletter on the
pleasures of tea as a beverage and tea
ceremonies; complete source for
places to go, articles, features and
anecdotes about TEA and TEAPOTS.*

TEDDY BEARS

(see also BOOKS, Reference [Teddy Bears]; DOLLS; STEIFF; TOYS)

Appraisers

Ann Miller, ISA
Bright-Miller Appraisals
19750 S.W. Peavine Mtn. Rd.
Mcminnville, OR 97128
phone: 503-472-1092
Appraises, collects old Teddy Bears, Raggedy Ann & Andy dolls and books; belongs to "Good Bears of the World" and "Teddy Bear Boosters"; life member of United Federation of Doll Collectors; teaches antiques at State Comm. College.

Clubs/Associations

Terri Stong
Good Bears of the World
Magazine: Bear Tracks
P.O. Box 13097
Toledo, OH 43613-0097
phone: 419-531-5365 or 419-475-3946
"Good Bears" spread love & understanding by giving away Teddy Bears to comfort every hurt, abused child or lonely, forgotten adult; quarterly newsletter.

Ann Miller
Teddy Bear Boosters Club
19750 S.W. Peavine Mtn. Rd.
Mcminnville, OR 97128
phone: 503-472-1092

Collectors

Jeff Dykes
6 Wildwood Terrace
Glen Ridge, NJ 07028
phone: 201-748-4990 or 973-748-4990
Wants to buy teddy bears made of mohair wool from 1980s to 1950s, in very good condition (send photo); also wants all Steiff animals before 1960 with button and/or chest tags.

Tom Kuster
My Old Bear
5510 Stadium Dr.
Madison, WI 53705-4642
phone: 608-238-3460
Wants early Teddy Bears, 1900 to 1960s, and related items; also Three Bears books, Raggedy Ann and Andy dolls and books, miniature Teddy Bears.

Barbara Wolters
Magazine: Teddy Tribune, The
254 W. Sidney
St. Paul, MN 55107-3494
phone: 612-291-7571
10 issues of Teddy Tribune per year; everything about teddy bears; send for free brochure.

Bill Boyd
7408 Englewood Lane
Kansas City, MO 64133-6913
phone: 816-356-7423
fax: 816-356-7423

Susan Murphy
29668 Orinda Rd.
San Juan Capistrano, CA 92675-1211
phone: 714-364-4333
Wants to buy old bears from early 1900s to 1950s.

Linda Adams
P.O. Box 1925
Seattle, WA 98111
Wants old teddy bears from 1900 to 1930s.

Dealers

Armand Thibodeau
Charmant & Big Creel Teddy Bears
RR 1, Big Creek Street
Napanee
Ontario K7R 3K6 Canada
phone: 613-354-6393 or 613-354-6393
e-mail:
charmant@limestone.kosone.com
With Donna McPherson buys and sells contemporary bears fashioned by Canadian and U.S. artists; also buys and restores old bears.

Rita Mueller
Grange Hall Antiques
1 South Alley
P.O. Box 263
New Market, MD 21774
phone: 301-865-5651
fax: 301-865-0518
e-mail: ritam@erols.com
Internet: http://www.newmarketmd.com/grange.htm
Quality Steiff animals from 1950s through 1980s; always buying one piece or entire collection: teddy bears, Schuco, Hermann, Steiff; also fine country graniteware from Germany available; mail orders and layaways.

Walter LaValley
Bachelor II Dolls & Bears
247 S. Van Dorn St.
Wheaton Plaza
Alexandria, VA 22304
phone: 703-823-BEAR
fax: 703-823-1787
Specializes in dolls and bears.

Cheri Shivley
Cynthia's Country Store, Inc.
The Wellington Mall #15A
12794 W. Forest Hill Blvd.
West Palm Beach, FL 33414
phone: 407-793-0554
fax: 407-795-4222
e-mail: cynbears@aol.com
Internet: http://www.thecrier.com/ccs
Specializing in new, discontinued and antique Steiff, R. John Wright, and other manufacturers and artists bears.

Beth B. Savino
Toy Store, The
P.O. Box 798
Holland, OH 43528-0798
phone: 419-473-9801 or 800-862-8697
fax: 419-473-3947
e-mail: toystore@toynet.com
Internet: http://www.toynet.com
Focus is on collecting Steiff toys and

teddy bears; sells exclusive Steiff Limited Edition; also buys old Steiff.

Myron Weis
Division Street Antiques
P.O. Box 374
Buffalo, MN 55313-0374
phone: 612-682-6453
Buys and sells a complete line of antiques with a specialty in Teddy Bears, Toys, and Folk Art.

World City, Inc.
6935 James Ave. South
Minneapolis, MN 55423-2147

Experts

Patricia Snyder
My Dear Dolly
P.O. Box 303
Sparta, NJ 07871-0303
phone: 201-729-8087
e-mail: dolly@intercall.com
Internet: http://www.mydeardolly.com
Wants older bears, parts, bear accessories, books, dolly-teddies; also wants Santas, bunnies, cloth Raggedy dolls.

Terry & Doris Michaud
Carrousel by Michaud
505 West Broad St.
Chesaning, MI 48616-1210
phone: 517-845-7881
Teddy bear artists, authors and lecturers; write regular column about teddy bears for "Teddy Bear & Friends" magazine.

Linda Mullins
P.O. Box 2327
Carlsbad, CA 92018
Author of "Teddy Bears Past & Present, A Collector's Identification Guide."

Man./Prod./Dist.

Bear-in-Mind, Inc.
Newsletter: Arctophile, The
53 Bradford St.
Concord, MA 01742-2901
phone: 508-369-1167
fax: 508-371-0762
A catalog company devoted to the consumer of new Teddy Bear related items; the first mail order company for Teddy Bears; started in 1977; send $1 for 40 page catalog; $5 for subscription to "The Arctophile."

Misc. Services

Monica Murray
Jenks Teddy Bear Convention
P.O. Box 728
Jenks, OK 74037
phone: 918-299-5416
Holds annual teddy bear show and sale convention in Jenks, Oklahoma.

Museums/Libraries

George B. Black, Jr.
Teddy Bear Museum of Naples
2511 Pine Ridge Rd.
Naples, FL 33942
phone: 813-598-2711
fax: 813-598-9239
Collects and displays teddy bears and related items from teddy bear artists; developing teddy bear archives from the antique to present.

Periodicals

Stephen L. Cronk, Ed.
Magazine: Teddy Bear Review
170 Fifth Ave. - 12th Floor
New York, NY 10010
phone: 212-989-8700 or 800-347-6969
fax: 212-645-8976

Hug Corp, The
Newsletter: Bear Hugs
300 East 40th St.
New York, NY 10016

Cowles Magazines, Inc.
Magazine: Teddy Bear & Friends
741 Miller Dr. SE, Ste. D2
Harrisburg, PA 20175
phone: 703-771-9400 or 800-829-3340
fax: 703-779-8345
Internet: http://www.thehistorynet.com
Magazine dedicated to teddy bears and other plush friends; editorial coverage of bears - antique to modern artists; bear manufacturers, care and repair, display ideas, buying, selling, and insuring bears, new product arrivals, etc.

Sandra Hood, Gen. Mngr.
Newspaper: Antique & Collectables
P.O. Box 13560
El Cajon, CA 92022
phone: 619-593-2925 or 619-593-2933
fax: 619-442-4043
The largest monthly newspaper in Southern California covering the antiques & collectibles industry with focus sections on Nevada and Arizona; 72+ pages; events and show section, feature articles; columns, ads.

Rose Morgan, Ed.
Penultimate Press
Newspaper: National Doll & Teddy Bear Collector
P.O. Box 4032
Portland, OR 97208-4032
fax: 503-234-6170
e-mail:
oleprospector@worldaccessnet.com
Internet: http://
www.worldaccessnet.com/~goldbug/kewpies.htm
A monthly newspaper for doll, Kewpie and teddy bear collectors, dealers and artists.

Repair Services

Sally Winey
Winey Bear Care Clinic & Adoption
Agency
P.O. Box 7
Saint Peters, PA 19470
phone: 717-774-7447 or 610-469-1020
*Specializes in repairing collector
teddy bears; also cleans stuffed
animals.*

Repro. Sources

Bullfrog Hollow
Keeny Rd.
Old Lyme, CT 06371

Stuf'd Stuff
415 W Oliver St.
Owosso, MI 48867-2251

Imriebears
1929 Lamont St.
Wausau, WI 54401

Nisbet

Clubs/Associations

Howard & Sarah Wade
Peggy Nisbet International Collectors'
Society
Newsletter: PNICS Newsletter
P.O. Box 325
Orrville, OH 44667-0325
phone: 330-682-8551
fax: 330-682-3655
e-mail: ukdolls@aol.com
*Clearinghouse for information about
Peggy Nisbet portrait and costume
dolls and Nisbet bears from Britain,
both primary and secondary markets.*

Man./Prod./Dist.

Howard & Sarah Wade
Nisbet Dolls & Bears
P.O. Box 325
Orrville, OH 44667-0325
phone: 330-682-8551
fax: 330-682-3655
e-mail: ukdolls@aol.com
*U.S. distributor for Peggy Nisbet dolls
and Nisbet bears from Britain.*

TEDDY BEARS (MODERN)

Dealers

Laura Dorrer
Lavender n' Lace
110 West 25th St.
New York, NY 10001
phone: 212-924-5230 or 516-681-4124
*Buys and sells one-of—a-kind artist
dolls, limited editions dolls and
antique dolls; also one-of-a-kind artist
bears, and vintage and collectible
bears.*

Periodicals

Rose Morgan, Ed.
Penultimate Press
Guide: 36 Ways to Sell More Bears
P.O. Box 4032
Portland, OR 97208-4032
fax: 503-234-6170
e-mail:
oleprospector@worldaccessnet.com
Internet: http://
www.worldaccessnet.com/~goldbug/
kewpies.htm
*A thoughtful, balanced annually
updated marketing guide specifically
tailored to the contemporary teddy
bear artist; how to sell, where to
market, how to track marketing
results, effective show display
techniques.*

Muffy Vanderbear

Clubs/Associations

Michelle Sterling
Muffy VanderBear Club
Newsletter: Fanfare
401 North Wabash, Ste. 500
Chicago, IL 60611-5646
phone: 312-329-0020 or 800-682-3427
fax: 312-329-1417
*Muffy VanderBear, a seven-inch,
golden pile plush stuffed dressed bear;
the club provides information,
services and limited edition bears
exclusively to Club members.*

TELECARDS

(see TELEPHONE CARDS)

TELEGRAMS

Collectors

Dr. Walter Brinker
Niedernfeld 2
42477 Radevormwald
Germany
phone: 49-219540928
fax: 49-21956517
e-mail: walter.brinker@t-online.dc
*A collector of international telegram
forms; has about 220 from 150
countries.*

TELEGRAPH ITEMS

(see also BROADCASTING;
BUMPER STICKERS, Radio Station;
ELECTRICITY RELATED ITEMS;
FIRE FIGHTING MEMORABILIA,
Fire Alarm Telegraphy; INSULA-
TORS; MAGAZINES, Radio &
Wireless; RADIOS; STOCK
TICKERS; TELEGRAMS)

Clubs/Associations

George Lingden G3ZQS
International Morse Preservation
Society, The
Newsletter: IMPS Newsletter
119 Cemetery Rd.
Darwen
Lancs BB3 2LZ, U.K.
*FISTS exists to promote amateur CW
activity; newcomers welcome; awards,
nets (including beginners' net), dial-a-
sked for beginners, straight key
activities, QSL bureau, newsletter,*

Harry Goldman
Tesla Coil Builders' Association
Newsletter: TCBA News
3 Amy Lane
Queensbury, NY 12804
phone: 518-792-1003
*TCBA is a clearinghouse on the
history of electricity, wireless,
electrotherapy, etc.; acts as
consultants for high voltage historical
equipment.*

Bruce Kelley
Antique Wireless Association
Newsletter: Old Timer's Bulletin
59 Main St.
Holcomb, NY 14469-9336
phone: 716-657-6260 or 716-657-7489
*One of the world's largest and oldest
historical radio collector organizations; purpose is to document and
preserve the history of radio,
telegraph and television artifacts.*

Collectors

Peter Thomashow
301 E 17th St., Rm 1028
New York, NY 10003-3804
phone: 718-797-1024
Wants to buy old telegraphs.

Roger W. Reinke
Brasspounder
5301 Neville Ct.
Alexandria, VA 22310-1113
phone: 703-971-4095 or 800-348-0294
*Wants telegraph instruments, stock
tickers, and related items such as call
boxes, signs, early paper; condition
not important.*

Howard Hazelcorn
6731 Ashley Ct.
Sarasota, FL 34241-9696
phone: 941-921-1815
Wants rare early items.

Dale R. Beeks
Perceptions Scientifica
P.O. Box 117
Mount Vernon, IA 52314
phone: 800-880-5178 or 319-895-0506
*Wants pre-1900 telegraph keys,
registers, and related items.*

Charles Goodman
636 W. Grant Ave.
Charleston, IL 61920-3226
phone: 217-345-6771
*Wants telegraph books, instruments,
keys, sounders, relays, resonators,
Western Union items, old stock
tickers, etc.*

Experts

Thomas B. Perera
11 Squire Hill Rd.
Caldwell, NJ 07006-4718
phone: 201-226-9185
e-mail: pererat@alpha.montclair.edu
Internet: http://www.chss.montclair.edu/
~pererat/telegraph.html
*Maintains internet telegraph and
scientific instrument museum and
collector's guide.*

Museums/Libraries

R.W. Merriam
New England Wireless & Steam
Museum, Inc.
697 Tillinghart Rd.
East Greenwich, RI 02818
phone: 401-884-1710 or 401-885-0545
fax: 401-884-0683
Internet: http://users.ids.net/~newsm

American Radio Relay League Museum
of Amateur Radio
225 Main St.
Newington, CT 06111
phone: 203-666-1541

Bruce Kelley
Antique Wireless Association's
Electronic Communication Museum
59 Main St.
Holcomb, NY 14469-9336
phone: 716-657-6260 or 716-657-7489
*Open limited hours May through
October; call or write before visiting;
please enclose SASE if requesting a
reply.*

Periodicals

John V. Terrey
Magazine: Antique Radio Classified
P.O. Box 2 - V113
Carlisle, MA 01741
phone: 508-371-0512
fax: 508-371-7129
e-mail: arc@antiqueradio.com
Internet: http://www.antiqueradio.com
*Antique radio's largest monthly about
old radios, Art Deco, TV's, ham equip.
- '40s, '50s, books, telegraph, etc.;
lots of ads.*

John McDougald
Magazine: Crown Jewels of the Wire
5N941 Ravine Dr.
Saint Charles, IL 60175-8272
phone: 630-513-1544
fax: 630-513-8278
e-mail: mcd@crownjewelsofthewire.com
Internet: http://
crownjewelsofthewire.com
*76-page monthly magazine of
insulator and telephone and telegraph
history; glass, porcelain; foreign
columns; classified ads, show dates,
etc.*

Erika Daileda
Wise Owl Worldwide Publications
Magazine: Morsum Magnificat
4314 West 238th St. - Dept. MACR
Torrance, CA 90505-4509
phone: 310-375-6258
fax: 310-375-0548
e-mail: wiseowl@sprintmail.com
A bi-monthly English publication; journal dedicated to More, past, present and future.

Telegraph Keys

Collectors

Thomas B. Perera
11 Squire Hill Rd.
Caldwell, NJ 07006-4718
phone: 201-226-9185
e-mail: pererat@alpha.montclair.edu
Internet: http://www.chss.montclair.edu/~pererat/telegraph.html
Wants to buy telegraph keys and apparatus; specializing in Civil War era, 19th century, land line, and wireless keys; has been collecting for over 40 years; has over 400 keys for trade.

Experts

Gil Schlehman
Gil Schleman Antiques
335 Indianapolis
Downers Grove, IL 60515
phone: 630-968-2320
Noted collector and author of "Telegraph Key Review" column in the "Antique Radio Classified"; largest collection of "speed keys" in the world.

TELEPHONE CARDS

(see also BANKING; CIVIL WAR ARTIFACTS, Currency; COINS & CURRENCY; CREDIT CARDS & CHARGE ITEMS; MONEYCARDS; WOODEN MONEY)

Clubs/Associations

A. Goodall
Phone Card Collectors
485a Caledonia Rd.
London N7 9RN, U.K.
A club for a special type of credit card collector focusing on phone cards.

International Telecard Association
904 Massachusetts Ave. NE
Washington, DC 20002-6228
phone: 202-544-4448
fax: 202-547-7417
Internet: http://www.telecard.org
Trade association with collectors division; offers educational material.

Collectors

Renata Lima
Cx. Postal 43533
CEP 22440-970
Rio de Janeiro BRAZIL

Dan Busby
P.O. Box 50188
Indianapolis, IN 46250
phone: 317-674-3301
fax: 317-674-3302
Wants to buy credit cards and telephone debit cards.

Dealers

Powell Associates
1270 Avenue of the Americas, Ste. 212
New York, NY 10020
phone: 800-528-8819
Large dealer in collectible telecards.

Ron Abler
5516 Maplefield Place
Alexandria, VA 22310-1891
phone: 703-971-9590 or 703-971-3524
e-mail: 73770.2110@compuserve.com
Buys and sells U.S. and worldwide phonecards, specializing in first and early edition examples of telephone company issues.

James Moran
Telequest
1566 W. Algonquin, Ste. 115
Schaumburg, IL 60195-1575
phone: 847-991-1228
fax: 847-359-4275
e-mail: telequest@juno.com
Retails and wholesales U.S. telephone cards and international cards with U.S. themes; emphasis is on world, Disney, and scarce US cards.

Steve Eyer
P.O. Box 123 -MA
Mount Zion, IL 62549-0321
phone: 217-864-4321
fax: 217-864-3021
Buys and sells collectible telephone cards.

Periodicals

International Telephone Cards
P.O. Box 777
Colchester C03 3LQ, U.K.
A large format magazine on glossy stock with superb color photos of telephone cards.

Magazine: Premier Telecard Magazine
P.O. Box 4614
San Luis Obispo, CA 93403-4614
phone: 805-547-8500
fax: 805-547-8503
Published six times per year.

TELEPHONE COMPANY ITEMS
Bell-Shaped Paperweights

Experts

Jacqueline C. Linscott
3557 Nicklaus Dr.
Titusville, FL 32780-5356
phone: 407-267-9170
Wants old, cobalt blue, bell-shaped paperweights used as giveaways by early telephone companies; author of "Blue Bell Paperweights, Telephone Pioneer Bells & Other Related Items",

1992 revised edition; $12 from the author.

TELEPHONES

(see also INSULATORS; TELE-PHONE CARDS; TELEPHONE COMPANY ITEMS)

Clubs/Associations

Deborah Jan Thomas
Mini-Phone Exchange
Newsletter: Telephonically Yours
5412 Tilden Rd.
Bladensburg, MD 20710
phone: 301-864-2482
Members interested in telephones as well as all types of items on which a telephone is depicted - postcards, ceramics, advertising, etc.; quarterly newsletter.

George W. Howard
Telephone Collectors International, Inc.
Newsletter: Singing Wires
19 North Cherry Dr.
Oswego, IL 60543
phone: 708-554-8154
For antique telephone collectors; sponsors two shows annually where old phones and related items are displayed, bought and sold; newsletter published monthly.

Ann Manning
Antique Telephone Collectors Association
Newsletter: Antique Telephone Collectors Newsletter
P.O. Box 94
Abilene, KS 67410-0094
phone: 913-263-1757
e-mail: chuck@cybercomm.net
Internet: http://www.cybercom.com/~chuck/atca.html
Dedicated to the preservation of historical telephony; membership includes monthly 8-12 page newsletter with free advertising for members, numerous ATCA-sponsored antique telephone shows each year; nearly 1000 members.

Collectors

Lydia M. Jackson-Fryer
608 Winans Way
Baltimore, MD 21229-1430
phone: 410-233-3317
Wants to buy antique telephones from the 1920s through the 1950s.

Bob Hunter
15600 Andover Lane
Wake Forest, NC 27587-9778
phone: 919-528-3469
Collecting all types of phones: antique, novelty, toy, unusual; also wants related accessories and memorabilia.

Russ Pate
235 Sandpine Rd.
Indialantic, FL 32903-2117
phone: 407-777-1759
e-mail: rpate@harris.com
Wants to buy telephones and related

items from 1876 to present; condition not important.

Paul G. Engelke
23399 Rio Del Mar Dr.
Boca Raton, FL 33486-8504
phone: 407-338-3332
Wants early wooden wall and candlestick phones, porcelain telephone signs, small coin phones, wooden coin phones, etc. but no paper.

Tom Vaughn
2016 Village Rd.
La Porte, IN 46350
phone: 219-324-3494
fax: 219-325-4511
e-mail: tjvaughn@niia.net
Wants to buy pay-station and unusual old telephones; also wants porcelain telephone and telegraph company signs.

John Huckeby
2440 W. CR 150 N
New Castle, IN 47362-9146
phone: 765-533-6369
fax: 765-533-6530
Old telephones, complete or parts.

Jon Kolger
6906 Meade Dr.
Colleyville, TX 76034-6416
phone: 817-329-5262
Always buying COLORED PLASTIC Art Deco style telephones from the 1920s through the 1950s; also seeking pre-1900 mechanical telephones that work on the "two tin cans on a string" principle; also wants telephone related paper, books, etc.

Dealers

Bruce Patterson
Phone Wizard
23 South Berlin Pike
Lovettsville, VA 20180-8502
phone: 540-822-4730
fax: 540-822-4733
e-mail: phonewizard@juno.com
Publishes a catalog ($3) providing genuine antique telephones, Art Deco telephones, and parts; offers restorations, conservation and repairs of all antique, old, and Western Electric telephones; visitors by appointment only.

Richard R. Marsh
Chicago Old Telephone Company
P.O. Box 189
Lemon Springs, NC 28355-0189
phone: 919-774-6625 or 919-775-5669
fax: 919-774-7666
Carries parts for old telephones; also repairs/restores and sells antique telephones; catalog available for free; also rents telephones to movies, TV and stage shows.

Norman Mulvey
310 Thorntree Lane
Canton, GA 30115-8196
Buys, sells and trades; wants to buy

old telephones, plus related parts and signs.

Rainbow Hirsh
20th Century Vintage Telephone Company
2780 Northbrook Place
Boulder, CO 80304-1432
phone: 303-442-3304
One of the premier restorers of vintage (1910-1937) telephones; meticulous care and attention to authenticity is given to each instrument; also sells at major antique shows throughout the US.

Jim & Shirley's Antiques
146 N. Glassell St.
Orange, CA 92866
phone: 714-639-9662 or 562-598-1914
Buys and sells antique telephones and Victrolas.

Museums/Libraries

Jefferson Telephone Museum
105 W. Harrison
Jefferson, IA 50129
phone: 515-386-2626

Illinois Bell's Oliver P. Parks Telephone Museum
529 South 7th St.
Springfield, IL 62721
A private museum based on a personal collection and including over 100 antique telephones.

Janet Groninga
Museum of Independent Telephony
412 S. Campbell
Abilene, KS 67410
phone: 913-263-2681
fax: 913-263-0380
Established to honor approximately 6000 non-Bell companies formed when patent coverage expired to meet the demands for telephone service.

Periodicals

John McDougald
Magazine: Crown Jewels of the Wire
5N941 Ravine Dr.
Saint Charles, IL 60175-8272
phone: 630-513-1544
fax: 630-513-8278
e-mail: mcd@crownjewelsofthewire.com
Internet: http://crownjewelsofthewire.com
76-page monthly magazine of insulator and telephone and telegraph history; glass, porcelain; foreign columns; classified ads, show dates, etc.

Repair Services

Richard R. Marsh
Chicago Old Telephone Company
P.O. Box 189
Lemon Springs, NC 28355-0189
phone: 919-774-6625 or 919-775-5669
fax: 919-774-7666
Sells old restored telephones to public and collectors; restores old telephones; provides old telephones to

movie companies, TV, stage shows, etc.; displays at top antique shows in major cities.

Odis W. LeVrier
House of Telephones
15 East Ave. D
San Angelo, TX 76903
phone: 915-655-4174 or 915-655-5122
fax: 915-655-4177
Repairs antique telephones and carries parts.

Repro. Sources

Don & Judy Zimmerman
Old Tyme Manufacturing Co., The
4020 49 Ave.
Innisfail
Alberta T4G 1J5 Canada
phone: 403-227-3967
fax: 403-277-6300
Experts have felt with telephones for many years; supplier of parts for Alexander G. Bell's first telephones; repairs and restores antique telephones; manufactures replica's of Alexander G. Bell's first telephones.

Suppliers

Ron & Mary Knappen
Phoneco, Inc.
19813 E. Mill Rd.
P.O. Box 70
Galesville, WI 54630-0070
phone: 608-582-4124 or 608-582-2263
fax: 608-582-4593
e-mail: phonecoinc@aol.com
Buys, sells, refurbishes any old telephone; also sells old and new parts, character phones, novelty phones; catalogs, history, price guide, diagrams and restoration help.

Art Deco

Collectors

Carl Ratner
550 Lamoka Ave.
Staten Island, NY 10312
e-mail: artdeco@bway.net
Buy, sell, trade telephones and parts; specializing in Art Deco phones of the 1920s through 1940s.

Candlestick

Experts

Howard Hazelcorn
6731 Ashley Ct.
Sarasota, FL 34241-9696
phone: 941-921-1815
Collects and specializes in candlestick phones.

Miniature

Collectors

Deborah Jan Thomas
5412 Tilden Rd.
Bladensburg, MD 20710
phone: 301-864-2482
Interested in obtaining miniature telephones of all kinds as well as old

postcards and trade cards depicting telephones.

Museums/Libraries

Deborah Jan Thomas
Miniature Telephone Museum
5412 Tilden Rd.
Bladensburg, MD 20710
phone: 301-864-2482
A private museum based on a personal collection and including over 400 miniature telephones.

Novelty

Dealers

Bob Roberts
P.O. Box 152
Guilderland, NY 12084-0152
e-mail: 72376.677@compuserve.com
Wants to buy novelty transistor radios, e.g. Atlas Battery, Brut cologne, Budweiser, Pepsi, Coke, McDonald's, etc.; also wants telephones in unusual shapes, e.g. gas pumps, food items, cartoon characters, cars, etc.

Western Electric

Dealers

Cliff Sullivan
4902 W. Monte Cristo
Glendale, AZ 85306-2638
phone: 602-978-3551
fax: 602-843-3391
e-mail: suclif@worldnet.att.net
Wants items marked "Western Electric": telephones, telegraph, sound equipment, appliances, etc.; also wants old or unusual telephones, equipment, or telephone memorabilia.

TELEVISION SHOWS & MEMO-RABILIA

(see also AUTOGRAPHS; BROAD-CASTING; CHARACTER COL-LECTIBLES; COWBOY HEROES; FAN CLUBS; GAMES, Board [TV Related]; MOVIE MEMORABILIA; PHOTOGRAPHS, Celebrity; PREMIUMS; SCIENCE FICTION; SPACE COLLECTIBLES; SUPER HEROES; TELEVISIONS; TOYS, Action Figures

Collectors

Ross Hartsough
aTaVa collectibles
98 Bryn Mawr Rd.
Winnipeg
Manitoba R3T 3P5 Canada
phone: 204-269-1022
Wants anything TV related: magazines, toys, gum cards, games, comics, TV program sound tracks, sheet music, etc.

Daniel Wachtenheim
P.O. Box 480444
Los Angeles, CA 90048
phone: 213-848-3053
e-mail: dwachte915@aol.com
Wants to buy 60s/70s TV related toys.

Scott Weiss
316 25th St.
Santa Monica, CA 90402-2522
phone: 310-395-4318
fax: 310-395-9686
Wants to buy movie and TV promotional and advertising specialty gift items such as pin-back buttons, badges (plastic, metal, cardboard, laminated), cloisonne pins, cloth usher ribbons, paperweights, tokens, snow domes, ashtrays, etc.

Dealers

Diane L. Albert
TVC Enterprise
P.O. Box 1088
Easton, MA 02334-1088
phone: 508-238-1179
28 pg. catalogs of TV, movie, rock 'n roll & other music, theater & other media-related collectibles & memorabilia for sale; send SASE.

Jon Allan
Elmer's Nostalgia, Inc.
3 Putnam St.
Sanford, ME 04073-2024
phone: 207-324-2166

Jerry Ohlinger
Jerry Ohlinger's Movie Material Store, Inc.
242 W. 14th St.
New York, NY 10011-7206
phone: 212-989-0869
fax: 212-989-1660
Buys and sells motion picture photos and posters from 1920 to present; also TV photos; research services available; free lists available; complete lists of 100,000 black & white photos or of 100,000 color photos are $4 each.

Dennis & Mary Luby
Casey's Collectible Corner
HCR 30 Box 30
No. Blenheim, NY 12131
phone: 607-588-6464
Buys and sells collectible toys: comic characters, TV shows and personalities; also space and monster toys, sports collectibles, etc.

John Kachmar
Techno-Fantasy Traders
779 Carissa Dr.
West Palm Beach, FL 33411-3412
phone: 407-798-5978
fax: 407-798-5978
e-mail: kachmar@aol.com

Scott Curtis
52 Girls Collectibles
P.O. Box 36
Morral, OH 43337

Bill & Joanne Bruegman
Toy Scouts, Inc.
137 Casterton Ave.
Akron, OH 44303-1543
phone: 330-836-0668
fax: 330-869-8668
e-mail: toyscout@newreach.net
Internet: http://www.csmonline.com/
toyscouts/

Jon & Carolyn Thurmond
Collectorholics
15006 Fuller
Grandview, MO 64030-4522
phone: 816-322-0906
e-mail: toyjet@aol.com

Eddie Brandt's Saturday Matinee
6310 Colfax Ave.
North Hollywood, CA 91602
phone: 818-506-4242
A great source for stills, posters, and lobby cards.

Jim's TV Collectibles
P.O. Box 4767
San Diego, CA 92164
Buys and sells TV collectibles of all kinds, 1950-1990, catalog $2; also sells TV Guides, 1953-1993, catalog $2; and TV photo catalog listing thousands of original TV photos, catalog $2.

J. Deson
P.O. Box 10013
Fullerton, CA 92838
Buys and sells movie and TV memorabilia by mail order; sends a list upon request; provide name of star or show you are interested in.

Experts

Diane L. Albert
TVC Enterprise
P.O. Box 1088
Easton, MA 02334-1088
phone: 508-238-1179
Consultant, freelance writer or researcher for production companies, books publishers etc. on the subject of TV nostalgia.

Ted Hake
Hake's Americana & Collectibles
Auction
P.O. Box 1444
York, PA 17405-1444
phone: 717-848-1333
Author of "Hake's Guide to TV Collectibles"; always purchasing items for mail-bid auctions of Disneyana, historical Americana, toys, premiums, political items, character and other collectibles.

David Welch
P.O. Box 714
Murphysboro, IL 62966-0714
phone: 618-687-2282
fax: 618-684-2243
e-mail: PexDude1@aol.com
Wants 1950s-1960s TV show related items such as lunch boxes, games, toys, etc.; paying $3,000+ for rare items, especially super heroes.

Museums/Libraries

Museum of Broadcasting, The
25 West 52nd St.
New York, NY 10022
phone: 212-752-4690

Arielle Greenberg
American Museum of the Moving Image
35 Avenue at 36 Street
Long Island City, NY 11106
phone: 718-784-4520 or 718-784-0077
fax: 718-784-4681
The only museum in the US devoted to the art, history, technology of film, television, video, interactive media; collection includes costumes, dolls, movie posters, magazines, TV sets, movie cameras, and other items of film & TV history.

Periodicals

George A. Carpinone, Ed.
Magazine: Celebrity Collector Magazine
P.O. Box 1115
Boston, MA 02117-1115
phone: 617-426-7724
fax: 617-426-7724
Interviews with classic movie stars, TV stars, and fan club presidents; exploration of Hollywood memorabilia collecting and collection care; contributions by readers; classified ads; beautifully designed as a collectible on glossy paper.

Diane L. Albert
TVC Enterprise
Magazine: TV Collector, The
P.O. Box 1088
Easton, MA 02334-1088
phone: 508-238-1179
In-depth articles about old TV series, behind the scenes information, etc.; also collector ads for videotapes, memorabilia, etc.

Robert Dutton
Magazine: Classic TV
P.O. Box 533468
Orlando, FL 32853-3468

Linda Kellbach
Antique Trader Publications, Inc.
Newspaper: Big Reel
P.O. Box 1050
Dubuque, IA 52004-1050
phone: 800-334-7165 or 800-482-4155
fax: 800-531-0880
e-mail: 76143.72@compuserve.com
Internet: http://www.csmonline.com
A monthly tabloid for movie and television memorabilia collectors and fans: ads, news, current & nostalgic feature articles, obits, etc.

Sharon Rhode
Viewers Voice, Inc.
Newsletter: Viewers Voice Newsletter
P.O. Box 27758
Milwaukee, WI 53227
phone: 414-541-3817
fax: 414-541-8699
A national membership organization dedicated to providing viewers with the means of communicating effectively with the TV industry.

Newsletter: Filmfax
P.O. Box 1900
Evanston, IL 60204

William J. Flechner
Magazine: Television History Magazine
700 E. Macoupin St.
Staunton, IL 62088
phone: 618-635-2712
A bi-monthly magazine devoted to TV history.

Rubber Chicken Publications
Magazine: Television Chronicles
10061 Riverside Dr., #171
North Hollywood, CA 91602
phone: 818-759-3400

Bewitched

Collectors

Carol Ann Osman
363 Mansfield Ave.
Pittsburgh, PA 15220
phone: 412-922-1865
Wants to buy anything from the TV series "Bewitched"; scripts, sheet music, games, books, toys, dolls, TV Guides, cels, drawings, etc.

Books & Magazines

Dealers

TV Archives
P.O. Box 3
Blue Point, NY 11715-0003
Wants pre-national New York City TV Guides, 1948-1953.

Charlie's Angels

Collectors

Cryan Thomas
1515 3/4 Pontius Ave.
Los Angeles, CA 90025
phone: 310-478-2719
Wants to buy "Charlie's Angels" memorabilia; also wants Farrah Fawcett items: pillows, beach towels, bean bag chairs, etc.

Jack Condon
P.O. Box 57468
Sherman Oaks, CA 91403

Dark Shadows

Clubs/Associations

Dark Shadows Festival
Newsletter: Shadow Gram
P.O. Box 92
Maplewood, NJ 07040-0092
phone: 201-762-7208
Internet: http://www.mpimedia.com/
darkshadows/dark9.html
Interested in the "Dark Shadows" TV series; holds annual convention, Dark Shadows Festival.

Louis Wendruck
Dark Shadows Fan Club, The
Magazine: Dark Shadows Announcement, The
P.O. Box 69A04 - Dept. Mal
West Hollywood, CA 90069-0066
phone: 213-650-5112
e-mail: airlinet@hotmail.com
Internet: http://members.tripod.com
Fan Club for TV's Gothic soap opera originally from the 1960s; quarterly magazine; sells T-shirts, books, videos, photos, episode guides and memorabilia.

Collectors

Steve Hall
P.O. Box 960398
Riverdale, GA 30296-0398
Wants Dark Shadows items: comics, books, models, games, cards, View-Masters, toys, misc.; anything from the TV show or movies.

Periodicals

Sue Ellen Wilson
Newsletter: Dark Shadows Collectables Classifieds
6173 Iroquois Trail
Mentor, OH 44060-2903
phone: 216-946-6348
fax: 216-951-3056
A newsletter with ads for Dark Shadows memorabilia from old and new series; published 9 times per year.

Dennis The Menace

Collectors

Pete Nowicki
1531 39th Ave.
San Francisco, CA 94122-3015
phone: 415-566-7506
Collector seeks all toys and collectibles relating to Dennis the Menace and his friends; no comics, please.

Doctor Who

Clubs/Associations

David Blaise
Friends of Doctor Who
Newsletter: Friends of Doctor Who
　Newsletter
P.O. Box 14111
Reading, PA 19612-4111
phone: 610-478-9200
fax: 610-374-5570
　*The largest active Doctor Who fan
　organization in the United States.*

St. Louis Celestial Intervention Agency
Newsletter: Time Lord Times
P.O. Box 733
Saint Louis, MO 63188
　*One of the largest strictly Doctor Who
　clubs with local meetings in North
　America; excellent source for news
　and articles.*

Periodicals

Gary Gillatt
Marvel Comics Ltd.
Magazine: Doctor Who Magazine
13/15 Arundel St.
London WC2R 3DX, U.K.
phone: 0171-2084500
fax: 0171-4972234
　*Magazine profiling actors, stories,
　behind-the-scenes news. Competitions
　and new product news.*

Dukes Of Hazzard

Clubs/Associations

Aneesh A. Sehgal
Dukes of Hazzard Fan Club
Newsletter: Dukes of Hazzard Fan Club
　Newsletter
3412 West 66th St.
Chicago, IL 60629-3406
phone: 773-476-7211
fax: 708-489-2331
　*Quarterly newsletter; also issues a fan
　club merchandise catalog.*

Experts

Aneesh A. Sehgal
3412 West 66th St.
Chicago, IL 60629-3406
phone: 773-476-7211
fax: 708-489-2331

Gilligan's Island

Clubs/Associations

Bob Rankin
Original Gilligan's Island Fan Club, The
Newsletter: Gilligan's Island News
P.O. Box 25311
Salt Lake City, UT 84125-0311
phone: 801-272-5729
　*Gilligan's is still afloat! A "cast-
　away" membership includes a "Stuck
　on Gilligan's Island" T-shirt, a
　quarterly 16-page newsletter, color
　photo of the castaways; 50 cents of
　dues goes to MAKE-A-WISH
　Foundation.*

Gunsmoke

Collectors

Hank Clark
P.O. Box 812
Waterford, CA 95386-0812
phone: 209-874-2640
　*Wants television and radio
　"Gunsmoke" items; autographs,
　photos, advertising, etc.*

Honeymooners/Jackie Gleason

Collectors

Eric Wertheimer
P.O. Box 246
Wakefield, RI 02880
　*Wants to buy Honeymooners and
　Jackie Gleason items.*

I Dream Of Jeannie

Collectors

Richard D. Barnes
1520 West 800 North
Salt Lake City, UT 84116-2019
phone: 801-521-4400
fax: 801-292-1947
　*Collector/historian wants "Jeannie"
　scripts, press photos, news articles,
　posters, books, toys, board games, etc.*

Experts

Richard D. Barnes
1520 West 800 North
Salt Lake City, UT 84116-2019
phone: 801-521-4400
fax: 801-292-1947
　*Author of I.D. of J. works including
　"Going Hollywood", a collectors
　guide to I.D. of J., Barbara Eden and
　other Hollywood collectibles; also
　"Jeannie Guide", and "Diary of a
　Genie."*

I Love Lucy

Clubs/Associations

Thomas J. Watson
We Love Lucy/The International Lucille
　Ball Fan Club
Magazine: Star Notes
P.O. Box 56234
Sherman Oaks, CA 91413-1234
phone: 818-981-0752
fax: 818-981-0757
e-mail: lucyfan@ix.netcom.com
Internet: http://www.lucyplace.com
　*Quarterly magazine focusing on
　collectibles pertaining to the "I Love
　Lucy" TV show and to Lucille Ball
　and other characters.*

Collectors

Marc Robert Colver
185 Pine St.
Allentown, PA 18102
　*Focuses on collectibles pertaining to
　the "I Love Lucy" TV show and to
　Lucille Ball and other characters.*

Dealers

Cathy's Closet
101 Greenway
Sunyvale, TX 75182
phone: 972-226-1352
　*Sells new "I Love Lucy" collectibles:
　magnets, boxer shorts, keychains,
　videos, caps, sweatshirts, earrings,
　rulers, prints, etc.*

Experts

Ric Wyman
408 S. Highland Ave.
Elderon, WI 54429-9999
phone: 715-341-6177
　*Expert within the world of Lucille Ball
　nostalgia; author of "For the Love of
　Lucy: The Complete Guide for
　Collectors and Fans" (ISBN #0-7892-
　0006-6); interested in purchasing any
　Lucile Ball or Desi Arnaz memora-
　bilia.*

Thomas J. Watson
P.O. Box 56234
Sherman Oaks, CA 91413-1234
phone: 818-981-0752
fax: 818-981-0757
e-mail: lucyfan@ix.netcom.com
Internet: http://www.lucyplace.com
　*Collects and specializes in Lucille
　Ball memorabilia.*

Laramie

Periodicals

Marcia A. Studley
Laramie Revisited
Newsletter: Laramie Revisited
2108 Lorenzo Ln.
Sacramento, CA 95864
　*The newsletter is about the Laramie
　television show and its stars; episode
　synopsis, interviews, related articles
　of the show and the Old West.*

Lassie

(see also ANIMAL COLLECTIBLES,
Dogs [Collies])

Collectors

Joan L. Neidhardt
428 Philadelphia Rd.
Joppa, MD 21085-3302
e-mail: ccolliespk@aol.com
Internet: http://www.members.aol.com/
　CColliespk
　*Wants to buy anything relating to
　Collies or to Lassie; old, new, unique;
　toys, figurines, character collectibles.*

Looney Tunes

Clubs/Associations

Looney Tunes Fan Club of America
5 Manmar Dr., Ste. 489
Plainville, MA 02762

Lost In Space

Clubs/Associations

Scott Beiner
Lost In Space Fan Club
Newsletter: Lost In Space Fan Club
　Newsletter
550 Trinity Place
Westfield, NJ 07090
phone: 908-789-7323

Flint Mitchell
Lost in Space Fannish Alliance
Newsletter: LISFAN
7331 Terri Robyn St.
Saint Louis, MO 63129
phone: 314-846-2846
e-mail: lisfan@il.net
Internet: http://www.as-inc.com/lisfan/
　lisfan.html
　Membership is free.

Collectors

Tod Evans
419 Boulevard
Westfield, NJ 07090-3227
　*Wants "Lost in Space" TV show
　items: anything including models,
　figures, games, cards, models, robots,
　etc.*

Partridge Family

Collectors

Daniel Wachtenheim
P.O. Box 480444
Los Angeles, CA 90048
phone: 213-848-3053
e-mail: dwachte915@aol.com
　*Buys, sells, trades Partridge Family
　items: bus, record cabinet, guitar,
　dolls, etc.; also wants character drum
　sets (Monkees, Kaptain Kool, etc.) and
　60s/70s TV related toys.*

Private Eye

Collectors

Gary Pimenta
64 Lakeside Dr.
Tiverton, RI 02878-3111
　*Wants to buy memorabilia related to
　television private eye shows such as
　77 Sunset Strip, Surfside 6, Hawaiian
　Eye; wants related toys, magazines,
　comic books, etc.*

Private Eye (Man From UNCLE)

Clubs/Associations

Susan Cole
U.N.C.L.E. HQ
Newsletter: HQ Newsletter
P.O. Box 8403
Rolling Meadows, IL 60008-8403
phone: 708-925-9220
　*Official fan club for the man/girl from
　U.N.C.L.E.; focuses on the "Man from
　U.N.C.L.E." reruns, the program and
　its memorabilia.*

Rin-Tin-Tin

Clubs/Associations

Rin-Tin-Tin Fan Club
Newsletter: Rinty's News
P.O. Box 1505
Rosenberg, TX 77471-1505

Sky King

Clubs/Associations

Sky King Club International
541 El Paso St.
Jacksonville, TX 75766
phone: 903-586-1355

Star Trek

Clubs/Associations

Dan McGinnis
Starfleet
Newsletter: Starfleet Communique
200 Hiawatha Blvd.
Oakland, NJ 07436-3643
International Star Trek and science fiction club with chapters in many major U.S. cities and overseas.

Russ Haslage
International Federation of Trekkers
Magazine: Voyages
P.O. Box 84
Groveport, OH 43125-0084
International club interested in Star Trek; numerous regional chapters.

Dan Madsen
Star Trek: The Official Fan Club
Magazine: Star Trek: The Official Fan Club Magazine
P.O. Box 111000
Aurora, CO 80042
phone: 303-341-1813 or 800-878-3326
Internet: http://www.sestran.com/
~accaaa/swi.html
International Star Trek club.

Dealers

Cindy Oakes
34025 W. 6 Mile
Livonia, MI 48152
phone: 313-591-3252
Wants dolls, autographs and other Star Trek memorabilia; also dolls from Star Trek The Movie & New Generation series.

Steve Benz
Star Trader
9809 Hayes
Overland Park, KS 66212
phone: 913-648-5461
Buys, sells and trades all Star Trek memorabilia from 1966 to present.

Misc. Services

Rita Cawthon-Clark
Starfleet Command
Newsletter: Starfleet Communications
P.O. Box 186037
Casselberry, FL 32718-0637
phone: 904-724-3651 or 417-781-4967
e-mail: ritaofscf@aol.com
International club interested in Star Trek, science fiction and space; several regional chapters throughout the United States, Canada, U.K., Europe, Australia, and Japan.

Star Trek Welcommittee
P.O. Box 12
Saranac, MI 48881-0012
e-mail: caryther@aol.com
International clearinghouse for Star Trek information (all generations); several departments offering help; please enclose SASE when requesting a reply.

The Addams Family

Clubs/Associations

Louis Wendruck
Munsters & the Addams Family Fan Club, The
Magazine: Munsters & the Addams Family Reunion, The
P.O. Box 69A04 - Dept. Mal
West Hollywood, CA 90069-0066
phone: 213-650-5112
e-mail: airlinet@hotmail.com
Internet: http://members.tripod.com
Fan Club for the 1960s TV shows "The Munsters" & "The Addams Family"; quarterly magazine; sells T-shirts, photos, videos, records, postcards, memorabilia.

The Fugitive

Clubs/Associations

Texas Bob Reinhardt
F.U.G.I.T.I.V.E.S., The
Newsletter: Stafford Chronicle, The
HC 001 Box 222
Canyon Lake, TX 78133-9701
phone: 210-935-4618
The Fugitives is a special interest group based upon the character of Dr. Richard Kimble as created by Roy Huggins, and brought to life by David Janssen; focus is on helping others as Dr. Kimble did; annual conventions.

Periodicals

Rusty Pollard
Newsletter: On The Run
P.O. Box 461402
Garland, TX 75046-1402
phone: 972-496-9042 or 214-922-1696
Back issues of bi-monthly newsletter (available) devoted to the 1960s TV series "The Fugitive", its star, David Janssen, and his career; each newsletter covers three episodes; subscribers get free classified ad in each issue.

The Munsters

Clubs/Associations

Louis Wendruck
Munsters & the Addams Family Fan Club, The
Magazine: Munsters & the Addams Family Reunion, The
P.O. Box 69A04 - Dept. Mal
West Hollywood, CA 90069-0066
phone: 213-650-5112
e-mail: airlinet@hotmail.com
Internet: http://members.tripod.com
Fan Club for the 1960s TV shows "The Munsters" & "The Addams Family"; quarterly magazine; sells T-shirts, photos, videos, records, postcards, memorabilia.

The Waltons

Museums/Libraries

Walton's Mountain Museum
P.O. Box 124
Schuyler, VA 22969
phone: 804-831-2000

TV Guide

Dealers

TV Guide Specialists
P.O. Box 20
Macomb, IL 61455-0020
phone: 309-833-1809
Buys and sells TV Guide and newspaper TV magazines, 1948-1997.

Twilight Zone

Clubs/Associations

Don Duecker, Jr.
Twilight Zone Fan Club
P.O. Box 3457
Syracuse, NY 13220
International club interested in Twilight Zone, Rod Serling, Outer Limits, Mission Impossible, and science fiction.

Museums/Libraries

Thomas W. Bohn
Ithaca College, School of Communications
Ithaca College
Ithaca College, NY 14850
phone: 607-274-3242
Rod Serling archives with videotapes and original scripts of most Twilight Zone episodes.

V

Clubs/Associations

Commander Diana
V Fan Club
Newsletter: Hyperlight Cable
8048 Norwich Ave.
Van Nuys, CA 91402-5616
phone: 818-901-1466
e-mail: katarra@aol.com
International club interested in the series "V"; several regional chapters located throughout the U.S.

Westerns

(see also COWBOY HEROES)

Collectors

Gary Pimenta
64 Lakeside Dr.
Tiverton, RI 02878-3111
Wants to buy pre-1970 Western television program collectibles and comic books including board games and toys based on Western TV shows.

Periodicals

Melody Rondeau
Magazine: Ghost Riders
1853 Fallbrook Ave.
San Jose, CA 95130
Each issue has over 100 pages of short story fiction based on characters in western television programs.

X-Files

Clubs/Associations

Official X-Files Fan Club
Newsletter: X-Notes
411 N. Central Ave., #300
Glendale, CA 91203
phone: 818-409-0960

Zorro

Experts

David Cook
835 Northfield Ct.
Harrisonburg, VA 22801

TELEVISIONS

(see also AUDIO-VISUAL; RADIOS; TELEVISION SHOWS & MEMORA-BILIA)

Clubs/Associations

Bruce Kelley
Antique Wireless Association
Newsletter: Old Timer's Bulletin
59 Main St.
Holcomb, NY 14469-9336
phone: 716-657-6260 or 716-657-7489
One of the world's largest and oldest historical radio collector organizations; purpose is to document and preserve the history of radio, telegraph and television artifacts.

Jay Kiessling
Mid-Atlantic Antique Radio Club
Magazine: Radio Age
P.O. Box 67
Upperco, MD 21155
phone: 410-239-1818
Published monthly since 1975 for collectors interested in the history of radio and television; restoration, articles by early experts; free buy and sell ads; free sample.

Collectors

J.E. Kendall
P.O. Box 436
Fallston, MD 21047

Tony & Lynn DeMara
40231 Day
Mt. Clemens, MI 48044

Jim & Nadiene Farago
4017 42 Ave. So.
Minneapolis, MN 55406

Doug Heimstead
1349 Hillcrest Dr.
Fridley, MN 55432

Carol Leeth
801 S. Webster #14
Anaheim, CA 92804

Dealers

Bruce & Charlotte Mager
Waves
110 West 25th St., Ste. 10M
New York, NY 10001-7401
phone: 212-989-9284
fax: 201-461-7121
e-mail: c1wave@aol.com
Internet: http://www.wavesradio.com
Over 20 years experience specializing in vintage radios, phonographs, telegraphy, televisions, assorted electrical and mechanical apparatus, and related advertising memorabilia, books and pamphlets.

John Okolowicz
624 Cedar Hill Rd.
Ambler, PA 19002-1504
phone: 215-542-1597
e-mail: grillecloth@compuserve.com
Internet: http://ww.libertynet.org/
~grlcloth
Buys, sells, trades pre-1950 radios and TV's in unusual or ornate plastic or wooden cabinets; especially those made by Emerson or Stromberg Carlson.

Ty Cutkomp
33 Oak Lane
Davenport, IA 52803
phone: 319-323-7263
Buys, sells, trades early televisions: Automatic, Atlas, Majestic, National Republic, Transvision, Silverton, Televue, Viewtone, and any 7" console TV.

Experts

Arnold Chase
9 Rushleigh Rd.
West Hartford, CT 06117
phone: 203-521-5280

Harry Poster
Vintage TV's
P.O. Box 1883
South Hackensack, NJ 07606-0483
phone: 201-794-9606
fax: 201-794-9553
e-mail: hposter@worldnet.att.net
Buying 1920s to 1950s TV's plus unusual 1960s/1970s sets; also wants

TV dealer displays, empty boxes, manufacturers' literature, old color TVs and adapters; buys complete TV shops.

Glenn F. Bubenheimer
Glenn's Vintage T.V. Service
27851 Terrence
Livonia, MI 48154-3498
phone: 313-421-5574
fax: 602-661-8304
e-mail: usfmcr9e@ibmmail.com
Has collected pre-1953 and select 1950s TVs for over ten years and has repaired them for twenty years; considers himself an expert in values, history and theory; has over 165 pieces in his collection; also repairs.

Mike Brooks
7335 Skyline
Oakland, CA 94611-1121
phone: 510-339-1751
e-mail: deborahwb@aol.com
Buying tiny screen early models, especially wants pre-WWII mechanical spinning disc sets and mirror-inlid TVs.

Museums/Libraries

Museum of Television & Radio
25 West 52nd St.
New York, NY 10019
phone: 212-621-6800
Internet: http://www.mtr.org

Bruce Kelley
Antique Wireless Association's
  Electronic Communication Museum
59 Main St.
Holcomb, NY 14469-9336
phone: 716-657-6260 or 716-657-7489
Open limited hours May through October; call or write before visiting; please enclose SASE if requesting a reply.

Larry Auman
Auman Antique Television Museum
4316 Murray Rd. N.W.
Dover, OH 44622-7758
phone: 330-343-2297 or 330-364-1058
Museum shows early days of electronic entertainment: 1940s movie theater, 1920s-1930s radios, 1930-1950 TV's, and related items.

Museum of Television & Radio
465 N. Beverly Dr.
Beverly Hills, CA 90210
phone: 310-786-1000
Internet: http://www.mtr.org

Periodicals

John V. Terrey
Magazine: Antique Radio Classified
P.O. Box 2 - V113
Carlisle, MA 01741
phone: 508-371-0512
fax: 508-371-7129
e-mail: arc@antiqueradio.com
Internet: http://www.antiqueradio.com
Antique radio's largest monthly about old radios, Art Deco, TV's, ham equip.

- '40s, '50s, books, telegraph, etc.; lots of ads.

Repair Services

David B. Johnson
2336 S. Kenilworth Ave.
Berwyn, IL 60402
phone: 708-484-2743
Vintage TV and radio repair and restorations; both electronics and cosmetics.

David B. Johnson
2336 S. Kenilworth Ave.
Berwyn, IL 60402
phone: 708-484-2743
Vintage TV and radio repairs and restorations (electronics and cosmetics).

Suppliers

Antique Electronic Supply
6221 S. Maple Ave.
Tempe, AZ 85283-2856
phone: 602-820-5411
fax: 800-706-6789
Large catalog carrying tubes, supplies, capacitors, transformers, chemicals, test equipment, wire, parts, tools, books, etc.

TEXTILES

(see also CLOTHING & ACCESSORIES, Vintage; COVERLETS; FEED & GRAIN BAGS; LOOMS; MILITARIA, Uniforms; QUILTS; REP./REST./CONSER., Textiles; RUGS; SAMPLERS; SEWING ITEMS & GO-WITHS; SHAWLS; MILITARIA, Silk Embroideries; STEVENGRAPHS; TIE-BACKS

Auction Services

Jo Kris
Skinner, Inc.
357 Main St.
Bolton, MA 01740-1104
phone: 508-779-6241 or 617-350-5400
fax: 508-779-5144
Established in 1964, Skinner Inc. is the fifth largest auction house in the US; has offices in Bolton and Boston, MA.

Clubs/Associations

Costume Society of America, The
Newsletter: Costume Society of America
Newsletter
P.O. Box 73
Earleville, MD 21919-0073
phone: 410-275-2329 or 419-372-2026
fax: 410-275-8936
e-mail:
  cunningham.190@postbox.acs.ohio-state.edu
Internet: http://www.hec.ohio-state.edu/
cts.research/dress.htm
Dedicated to advancing the global understanding of all aspects of dress and appearance; also published the journal "Dress."

Kathy Buder
Knitting Guild of America, The
Magazine: Cast On
P.O. Box 1606
Knoxville, TN 37901
phone: 615-524-2401
fax: 615-524-2401
Provides education for hand & machine knitters; "Cast On" contains articles, ads, seminars, correspondence courses, competition, etc.

Dealers

Sonnie Cucinotti
Spirits in the Attic
201 Msgr. O'Brien Hwy.
Cambridge, MA 02141
phone: 617-738-6054
Wants to buy vintage and antique textiles.

Elizabeth Bright
26 Williams Cr.
Lexington, NC 27292
phone: 910-249-2448
Old quilts, samplers, large Marseilles spreads, extra fancy white linens, unusual needlework.

Suzanne Silance
Scarlett Magnolia's Vintage Apparel, Textiles & Gifts
361 Congress Parkway
Mansfield, GA 30255
phone: 770-682-8999 or 888-999-9985
Buying and selling quality vintage apparel and textiles; selling through Buckhead Design Center, 2133 Piedmont Rd., Atlanta, GA 30324 (404-872-0751).

Barbara F. Mitchell
Barbara's Antiques
P.O. Box 9
Micanopy, FL 32667
phone: 352-466-3853 or 352-332-1175
Wants to buy "work of art" quilts in good condition; also wants handmade rugs, vintage fabrics and lace.

Diane McGee
Diane McGee Estate Clothing Company
5225 Jackson
Omaha, NE 68106-1331
phone: 402-551-0727
Mail order only; specializing in vintage linens and other textiles.

Experts

Doris May
46 Crafts Rd.
Newton, MA 02161
phone: 617-734-7131
Can help in identifying and appraising textiles.

Evelyn Siefert Kennedy
Evelyn of Sewtique
391 Long Hill Rd.
P.O. Box 1293
Groton, CT 06340-1293
phone: 860-445-7320 or 860-464-2001
fax: 860-445-1448
e-mail: sewtique@aol.com
Internet: http://www.members.aol.com/
sewtique/home.htm
Specialist in restoration, preservation & conservation of apparel and textiles; full service by mail/phone or appt.; appraises textiles, laces, tapestries, etc.; removes spots & stains; teaches textile appraisal & restoration workshops.

Ita Aber
2600 Netherland ave., Apt. 720
Bronx, NY 10463-4815
phone: 914-968-4863 or 212-877-6400
fax: 212-877-3107
Specializes in lace, linens, and needlework; also repairs; author of "The Art of Judaic Needlework."

Holly Van Sciver
130 Cascadilla Park
Ithaca, NY 14850
phone: 607-277-0498
Can help in identifying and appraising textiles.

Mary Lou Kuecker
7005 Fitzpatrick Dr.
Laurel, MD 20707
phone: 301-490-5432
Can help in identifying and appraising textiles.

Alda Horner
3200 Central Ave.
Ventura, CA 93003
phone: 805-339-9343
Author of "The Official Price Guide to Linens, Lace, and Other Fabrics."

Ruth Van Arnam
3508 Beaverton/Hillsdale Hwy.
Portland, OR 97219
phone: 503-244-3774
An expert with experience in appraising clothing, textiles, quilts and crochet.

Museums/Libraries

Museum of American Textile History
491 Dutton St.
Lowell, MA 01854
phone: 508-441-0400
fax: 508-441-1412
Outstanding collection of textiles and textile making machinery and equipment; tools, machines, prints, photographs, business records, industry periodicals, textiles, swatches, sample books, trade catalogs, etc.

Museum of Art, Rhode Island School of Design
224 Benefit St.
Providence, RI 02903-2711
phone: 401-454-6500
fax: 401-454-6556

Currier Gallery of Art, The
192 Orange St.
Manchester, NH 03104
phone: 603-669-6144

Shelburne Museum, Inc.
P.O. Box 10
Shelburne, VT 05482-0010
phone: 802-985-3346 or 802-985-3344
fax: 802-985-2331
37 historic structures and exhibit buildings; diverse collection of American folk, fine, decorative and utilitarian art.

Anne R. Fabbri, Dir.
Philadelphia College of Textiles & Science, The Goldey Paley Design Center
4200 Henry Ave.
Philadelphia, PA 19144
phone: 215-951-2860

Textile Museum, The
Newsletter: Textile Museum Bulletin, The
2320 'S' St. NW
Washington, DC 20008
phone: 202-667-0441
fax: 202-483-0994
Museum dedicated to furthering the understanding of mankind's creative achievements in the textile arts; rotating exhibits drawn largely from the museum's collections featuring works from the eastern and western hemispheres.

Colleen Callahan
Valentine Museum
1015 East Clay
Richmond, VA 23219
phone: 804-649-0711
fax: 804-643-3510
e-mail: valmus@mindspring.com
Internet: http://
www.valentinemuseum.com
Largest costume and textile collection in the South.

Josie De Falla, Dir.
Maryhill Museum of Art
35 Maryhill Museum Drive
Goldendale, WA 98620-4601
phone: 509-773-3733
fax: 509-773-6138
e-mail: MaryHill@gorge.net
Romanian folk textiles, ecclesiastical embroideries, San Blas mola's and 1946 miniature haute couture mannequins.

Periodicals

HALI Publications, Ltd.
Magazine: HALI
Kingsgate House
Kingsgate Place
London NW6 4TA, U.K.
phone: 44 171 328 9341 or 44 171 328 1998
fax: 44 171 372 5924
e-mail: hali@centaur.co.uk
"HALI" is the leading bi-monthly international publication in the field of carpet and textile art; an invaluable encyclopedic source of information with original research articles, reviews of museum collections, etc.; high color.

Repro. Sources

Gabrielle Black
Black's Handweaving Shop
497 Main St.
West Barnstable, MA 02668

Judy Robinson
Judy Robinson's Country Textiles
3350 Chickencoop Hill Rd.
Lancaster, OH 43130

Maggie Kennedy
Ozark Weaving Studio
P.O. Box 286
Canehill, AR 72717

Blankets

Experts

Barry Friedman
P.O. Box 55492
Valencia, CA 91385-0492
phone: 805-255-2365
e-mail: BaryF@fishnet.net
Buys/sells pre-1945 Indian style wool or cotton blankets by Pendleton, Beacon, Capps, Esmond, Shuler & Benninghofen, American Indian Blanket Mills, Knight, Racine, Buell, Jacobs Oregon City, Provo; plus related catalogs and ads.

Embroidery

Museums/Libraries

Cooper-Hewitt Museum National Museum of Design, Smithsonian Institution
2 East 91st St.
New York, NY 10128
phone: 212-860-6868
Can identify old lace, but are not allowed to access value.

Repro. Sources

Elizabeth Creeden
Sampler, The
84 Court St.
Plymouth, MA 02360
phone: 508-746-7077
Has knowledge of 17th, 18th and 19th C. needlework in surface embroidery, needlepoint (tent stitch) evenweave stitching and crewel; reproduction and adaptations can be drawn,

charted or designed and stitched; coat of arms, samplers, etc.

Embroidery (Stumpwork)

Clubs/Associations

Sylvia C. Fishman
Stumpwork Society
Newsletter: Stumpwork Society
55 Ferncrest Ave.
Cranston, RI 02905-3510
Interested in antique stumpwork embroidery; restoration, preservation and collection.

Fabric

Dealers

Dan
Experienced Denim
P.O. Box 239
Fayetteville, AR 72702-0239
phone: 501-444-7541 or 800-336-4694
fax: 501-521-8331
e-mail: exdeni19@intellinet.com
Wants '40s-'50s drapery (barkcloth) with tropical, mod geometrics, large flowered prints, many types of vintage fabrics; send SASE for free list of items wanted.

Folk Art

Dealers

Heritage Antiques
P.O. Box 844
Bellville, TX 77418-0844
Wants bedspreads, carpets, coverlets, clothing, needlework, quilts, hooked rugs, samplers, shawls, table linens, etc.

Lace & Linens

Clubs/Associations

International Old Lacers, Inc.
Magazine: International Old Lacers Bulletin
P.O. Box 481223
Denver, CO 80248

Dealers

Marsha Manchester
Milady's Mercantile
21 South Main St.
Middleboro, MA 02346
phone: 508-946-2121
Buys and sells linen and lace.

Shirley Frater
Arsenic & Old Lace
P.O. Box 367 Main St.
Damariscotta, ME 04543
phone: 207-563-1414
Buys and sells linen and lace.

Lydia Reed
Wyndham Needleworks
Box 65, 233 Old Colony Rd.
Eastford, CT 06242
phone: 203-974-1214
Buys and sells linen and lace.

Pahaka September
Pahaka
19 Fox Hill
Upper Saddle River, NJ 07458-1314
phone: 201-327-1464
Buys and sells quality lace, curtains, bed and table linens, fabrics, embroidery, etc.; by appointment or mail order; sorry, no catalog.

Vintage Linens
203 Camelot Dr.
Simpsonville, SC 29681-5739
phone: 864-967-1088
Wants to buy antique linens that are at least 50 years old; wants high quality linens only including pillowcases, sheets, bed covers, doilies, runners, cloths, napkins, lace curtains, etc.; linens with monograms always a plus.

Cornelia Powell
Cornelia Powell Antiques, Inc.
271 B East Paces Ferry Rd.
Atlanta, GA 30305
phone: 706-733-6073
Lace clothing, vintage and designer made from antique laces and bridal accessories.

Shirley Gruber
Elegant Eras
3800 Orion Rd.
Oakland, MI 48363-3030

Sabine Casten
Lace Collection, The
558 Monroe
River Forest, IL 60305
phone: 708-366-0756
Buys and sells linen and lace.

Dewey Cornay
214 Lafitte Ave.
Lafayette, LA 70506
phone: 318-235-5352
Buys and sells linen and lace.

Rebecca Nohe
Quartermoon Market
315 East Pikes Peak Ave.
Colorado Springs, CO 80903
phone: 719-630-8961
Buys and sells linen and lace.

Sue Morse
Emma's Trunk
1701 Orange Tree Lane
Redlands, CA 92374-2857
phone: 909-798-7865 or 909-864-8445
fax: 909-798-7386
Wants FANCY aprons, bedspreads, Christening gowns, collars, cuffs, doilies, handkerchiefs, napkins, etc.; write before sending items.

Jude Allen
Vintage Collection
356 Main St.
Half Moon Bay, CA 94019
phone: 415-712-0366
fax: 415-654-0842
Buys and sells linen and lace; also old yardage, buttons, quilts, sewing implements, sewing machines and miniature sewing machines.

Jules Kliot
Lacis
3163 Adeline St.
Berkeley, CA 94703-2401
phone: 510-843-7178
fax: 510-843-5018
Antique & historic textiles, lace from the 16th century, vintage garments and accessories; sells books and supplies for costume, lace and embroidery; also offers repairs and conservation services.

Experts

Evelyn Siefert Kennedy
Evelyn of Sewtique
391 Long Hill Rd.
P.O. Box 1293
Groton, CT 06340-1293
phone: 860-445-7320 or 860-464-2001
fax: 860-445-1448
e-mail: sewtique@aol.com
Internet: http://www.members/aol.com/sewtique/home.htm
Specialist in restoration, preservation & conservation of apparel and textiles; full service by mail/phone or appt.; appraises textiles, laces, tapestries, etc.; removes spots & stains; teaches textile appraisal & restoration workshops.

Elizabeth M. Kurella
Old Lace & Linen Merchant, The
P.O. Box 222
Plainwell, MI 49080
phone: 616-685-9792
fax: 616-685-5043
Buys, sells, and appraises lace and linens; offers many pieces of antique lace for sale; author of "The Secrets of Real Lace."

Museums/Libraries

Lace Museum, The
552 South Murphy Ave.
Sunnyvale, CA 94086
phone: 408-730-4695
Textiles, lace, linen; guild classes, teaching, museum gift shop; purpose is to keep the art of lace making alive for future generations.

Periodicals

Elizabeth M. Kurella, Pub.
Old Lace & Linen Merchant, The
Magazine: Lace Collector, The
P.O. Box 222
Plainwell, MI 49080
phone: 616-685-9792
fax: 616-685-5043
Quarterly magazine (12 pgs. illustrated); how to identify & appraise antique lace; what to use, save; market info, prices.

Elizabeth M. Kurella, Pub.
Lace Merchant, The
Newsletter: Old Lace & Linen Merchant, The
P.O. Box 222
Plainwell, MI 49080
phone: 616-685-9792
fax: 616-685-5043
Bulletin boards, classified ads, display ads to bring together buyers and sellers of antique linens, lace, pre-Edwardian clothing, and textiles.

Repair Services

Unique Art Lace Cleaners
5926 Delmar Blvd.
Saint Louis, MO 63112
phone: 314-725-2900
Cleans and repairs old textiles, linens and lace.

Needlework

Dealers

Carol Huber
40 Ferry Rd.
Old Saybrook, CT 06475
phone: 860-388-6809
fax: 860-388-6809
Buys and sells early needlework including samplers, pictures and related items.

Needlework (Judaic)

(see also JUDAICA)

Experts

Ita Aber
2600 Netherland ave., Apt. 720
Bronx, NY 10463-4815
phone: 914-968-4863 or 212-877-6400
fax: 212-877-3107
Consultations, restorations and commissions; works with architects and decorators; lecturer, historian, author of book on same.

Pillow Tops

Collectors

J.J. Murphy
920 Emerald St.
Madison, WI 53715-1614
phone: 608-257-3855
fax: 608-257-3730
Wants lithograph pillow tops: turn-of-the-century color lithographs on cloth; approximately 22 inches square; all subjects; condition important.

Tablecloths

Dealers

Paula Rubenstsein
65 Prince St.
New York, NY 10012
phone: 212-966-8954
Specializes in vintage tablecloths.

THANKSGIVING COLLECTIBLES

(see HOLIDAY COLLECTIBLES)

THEFT & FRAUD

(see ART THEFT & FRAUD)

THERMOMETERS

Clubs/Associations

Warren D. Harris
Thermometer Collectors Club of America
Newsletter: Thermometer Reference
6130 Rampart Dr.
Carmichael, CA 95608
phone: 916-966-3490 or 916-654-2097
fax: 916-966-3490

Collectors

Alan Cook
1307 Hogan Ln.
Round Rock, TX 78664
phone: 512-244-6874
Wants to buy wood, metal, and picture advertising thermometers.

Experts

Richard Porter
P.O. Box 944
Onset, MA 02558-0944
phone: 508-295-5504
"The Thermometer Man"; his large collection featured in "Ripley's Believe It or Not" and the "Guiness Computer of World Records"; curator of the world's only thermometer museum; motto: "Always open, always free, with about 3000 to see."

Warren D. Harris
6130 Rampart Dr.
Carmichael, CA 95608
phone: 916-966-3490 or 916-654-2097
fax: 916-966-3490
Wants decorative pre-1930 non advertising, non commercial, non clinical thermometers of every kind; mercury-in-the-tube type preferred; also wants thermometer related ephemera.

Museums/Libraries

Richard Porter, Curator
Porter Thermometer Museum
P.O. Box 944
Onset, MA 02558-0944
phone: 508-295-5504
World's largest private collection of thermometers from American and all over the world; representing over 100 manufacturers and featured in over 60 articles and 18 videos.

THIRD REICH

(see NAZI ITEMS)

3-D PHOTOGRAPHICA

(see Chapter "A", page 2)

TICKETS

(see also MOVIE MEMORABILIA;
MUSIC; PAPER COLLECTIBLES;
SPORTS COLLECTIBLES;
TRANSPORTATION COL-
LECTIBLES; WORLD'S FAIRS &
EXPOSITIONS)

Dealers

Jim Crump
Ticket Place Collectibles
P.O. Box 767
East Freetown, MA 02717
phone: 508-763-3502
fax: 508-763-9291
e-mail: tickets@ticketplace.com
*Specializes in unused tickets and stubs
to sporting events, special events and
concerts; wants to buy almost any
kind of ticket or ticket stub out there;
also has Elvis Presley ticket stubs for
sale.*

TIE BARS, CLIPS & TACKS

(see also CLOTHING & ACCESSO-
RIES, Vintage; CUFF LINKS; GEMS
& JEWELRY)

Collectors

Harvey Whittam
29 Shelley Close
Langley, Slough
Berkshire SL3 8JW, U.K.
*Collector of aviation and law
enforcement tie tacks from around the
world.*

Norman Landis
1315 Marbendale Ct.
Saint Louis, MO 63122

TIE-BACKS

Collectors

Sandie Bush
516 N. Brian St.
Santa Maria, CA 93454
phone: 805-925-9756
*Wants to buy glass and metal curtain
tie-back holders.*

TIFFANY ITEMS

(see also GEMS & JEWELRY;
GLASS, Art; LAMPS & LIGHTING,
Tiffany/Handel/Pairpoint; SILVER)

Dealers

Bill Holland
William Holland Fine Arts
1708 E. Lancaster Ave.
Paoli, PA 19301-1553
phone: 610-648-0369
fax: 610-647-4448
*Buys and sells Tiffany desk lamps and
desk set pieces; no reproductions
please.*

Reyne Hogan
2507 Observatory Ave.
Cincinnati, OH 45208-1212
phone: 513-321-5141 or 713-913-7289
e-mail: reyne@tias.com
Internet: http://www.tias.com/RHA
*Buys and sells Tiffany glass, lamps,
bronze, jewelry and windows; also
buys art of the same period.*

John B. Marrella
Investments in Time
P.O. Box 611
Birmingham, MI 48012-0611
phone: 810-644-3100
fax: 810-644-2792
*Wants Tiffany lamps, glass, bronze
work, drawings, etc.*

Experts

Dr. Egon Neustadt
Neustadt Museum of Tiffany Art, Inc.,
The
124 West 79th St.
New York, NY 10024
phone: 212-874-0872
*Author of "The Lamps of Tiffany", an
authoritative survey of Tiffany glass,
jewels, and lamp bases and shades.*

Sylvia Kornblum
Team Antiques
P.O. Box 1052
Great Neck, NY 11023-0052
phone: 516-487-1826
*Over 30 years experience in
cataloging and selling Louis C.
Tiffany, Tiffany Studios items by mail-
order.*

Man./Prod./Dist.

Tiffany Co.
5th Ave. at 57th St.
New York, NY 10022
phone: 212-755-8000
*Main Tiffany store; Tiffany items also
retailed through regional stores.*

Museums/Libraries

Chrysler Museum, The
Olney Rd. & Mowbray Arch
Norfolk, VA 23510
phone: 804-622-1211

TILES

(see also BOOKS, Reference [Tiles];
CERAMICS)

Clubs/Associations

Kathy Huggins, Mem.
Tiles & Architectural Ceramics Society
Magazine: Glazed Expressions
Reabrook Lodge
8 Sutton Road
Shrewsbury SY2 6DD, U.K.
*Society serves the collector, historian,
craftsman and conservator interested
in decorated ceramics relating to
buildings; also publishes biennial
journal; magazine twice a year & a
newsletter quarterly.*

Collectors

Michael Padwee
P.O. Box 023138
Brooklyn, NY 11202-3138
phone: 718-499-4307
fax: 718-720-8897
e-mail: mwpadwee@inch.com
*Tile historian who collects American
antique ceramic tiles.*

Kathy Rae
1975 Bates
Birmingham, MI 48009
phone: 810-642-1274
Wants to buy 1880s-1940s tiles.

Susan Frost
806 Rosedale Terrace
Austin, TX 78704-3159
phone: 512-447-2575 or 512-447-0407
e-mail: Reuter@io.com
*Wants to buy San Jose Pottery and
San Jose Mission Crafts tiles.*

Dealers

Sandie Fowler
Antique Articles
1 Hilltop Road
Billerica, MA 01821-2307
phone: 508-663-8083
fax: 508-663-8083
*With Wendy Harvey sells a large
variety of American and European
tiles, c. 1625-1950; sets; fireplace
surrounds, single tiles; also wants to
buy single tiles or entire lots.*

Experts

Chris Blanchett
Holly Tree House
18 Woodlands Rd, Littlehampton
West Sussex BN17 5PP, U.K.
phone: 01903 717648
fax: 01903 717648
*Collector, historian and author on
tiles and related subjects of all
periods; research/identification
undertaken; major library of tile-
related materials; large reference
collection of tiles, etc.*

Periodicals

Joseph Taylor
Tile Heritage Foundation
Newsletter: Flash Point
P.O. Box 1850
Healdsburg, CA 95448
phone: 707-431-8453
fax: 707-431-8455
*Dedicated to promote appreciation for
tiled surfaces; promotes preservation
of rare & unusual ceramics; library
on old tile; also publishes a magazine,
"Tile Heritage."*

California

Experts

Steve Soukup
California Crazed
P.O. Box 7662
Van Nuys, CA 91406-7662
phone: 818-787-5990 or 818-781-9262
*Buys and sells California pottery and
tiles: Catalina, Batchelder, Arequipa,
Calco, Malibu, Claycraft, California
Faience, S&S, D&M, CCPCO, GMB,
Tropico, Taylor, Tudor, etc.*

California (Malibu Potteries)

Museums/Libraries

Malibu Lagoon Museum
P.O. Box 291
Malibu, CA 90265-0291
phone: 310-456-8432
*Features the boldly hued tileworks of
Southern California's Malibu
Potteries (1926-1932); also tile books.*

Drain

Museums/Libraries

Mike Weaver Drain Tile Museum
P.O. Box 464
Geneva, NY 14456
phone: 315-789-3848 or 315-789-5151
*Large collection of drain tiles -
ceramic pipes used to drain excess
moisture from farm land.*

New Jersey

Experts

Helen Henderson
P.O. Box 577
Keyport, NJ 07735-0577
phone: 732-739-6799
*Wants catalogs, literature,
backstamps, maker's marks of New
Jersey decorative and architectural
tiles; collecting interests: Monmouth
and Middlesex counties manufacturers.*

Pardee

Collectors

Helen Henderson
P.O. Box 577
Keyport, NJ 07735-0577
phone: 732-739-6799
*Specializes in tiles made by the C.
Pardee Works, Matanan Tile Co.,
ATCO; conducting research on New
Jersey tile firms and seeks information
and photographs of the plant, tiles,
backstamps, advertisements, etc.*

Victorian

Experts

Pamela & Allan Luttig
Blue Boar Antiques
P.O. Box 423
Grand Ledge, MI 48837

Zsolnay

On-Line Services

Federico Santi
Zsolnay Tile Museum, The Online
152 Spring St.
Newport, RI 02840-6806
phone: 401-841-5060
fax: 401-848-0953
e-mail: zsolnay@drawrm.com
Internet: http://www.drawrm.com
*An on-line museum of Zsolnay ceramic
tiles from the 1870s through WWI;
pictures, articles and tile links;
browse to www.drawrm.com/
ztilemus.htm.*

TIN COLLECTIBLES

Containers

(see also ADVERTISING COL-
LECTIBLES; ADVERTISING
COLLECTIBLES, Tin Vienna Art
Plates; BISCUIT BARRELS/JARS/
TINS; COFFEE, Tins; FOLK ART,
Tinware; SMOKING COL-
LECTIBLES; TYPEWRITERS,
Ribbon Tins)

Clubs/Associations

Tin Container Collectors Association
Newsletter: Tin Type
P.O. Box 440101
Aurora, CO 80044
*Members collect, preserve and study
antique advertising packaging.*

Collectors

Ed Natale, Jr.
P.O. Box 222
Wyckoff, NJ 07481
phone: 201-848-8485
fax: 201-891-4252
*Wants to buy automotive related tin
container: oil, grease, bulb, fuse,
spark plug, tube patch, etc.;
motorcycle, household oil, handy oil,
gun oil, coffee, condom; also related
signage: tin, porcelain, paper; photos
helpful.*

TITANIC MEMORABILIA

(see also NAUTICAL ANTIQUES;
OCEAN LINER COLLECTIBLES)

Clubs/Associations

Edward Kamunda
Titanic Historical Society
Magazine: Titanic Commutator, The
208 Main St.
Indian Orchard, MA 01151
phone: 413-543-4770
*Focuses on all aspects of the
"Titanic", her sister ship the
"Britannic", and the White Star Line.*

Robert M. DiSogra, Pres.
Titanic International, Inc.
Magazine: Voyage
P.O. Box 7007
Freehold, NJ 07728-7007
phone: 908-462-1413 or 201-584-5930
fax: 908-462-1771
e-mail: rdisogra@compuserve.com
*Members interested in Titanic and
other ocean liner memorabilia; a
reference source for all Titanic
artifacts; a world wide society; annual
meetings; speakers available on
history of Titanic, artifact recovery,
educational display.*

Collectors

Dominic Rolla
1215 Spruce St.
Philadelphia, PA 19107
*Wants newspapers, books, sheet
music, artifacts.*

Frederick Lingenfelser
814 Byram St.
Reading, PA 19606-1446
*Buying anything related to the
Titanic: newspapers, post cards,
menus, books, photographs, letters
from survivors, paintings, artifacts,
etc.*

Experts

Edward Kamunda
208 Main St.
Indian Orchard, MA 01151
phone: 413-543-4770
*Wants newspapers, books, sheet
music, artifacts.*

Charles Ira Sachs
TransAtlantic Research
P.O. Box 8797
Studio City, CA 91618-8797
phone: 818-985-1345
fax: 818-985-1345
e-mail: transatlantic@juno.com
*Buys/sells/specializes/lectures on
ocean liner and zeppelin history &
memorabilia from the high seas (i.e.
none from coastal or river steamers)
dating from 1840 to 1960s; posters,
postcards and related material for
collectors/museums.*

TOASTERS

(see also ELECTRICITY RELATED
ITEMS)

Clubs/Associations

Electric Breakfast Club
P.O. Box 306
White Mills, PA 18473-0306

Carl Roles
Upper Crust
Newsletter: A Toast to You
P.O. Box 529
Temecula, CA 92593
phone: 909-699-5139 or 909-699-8456
fax: 909-699-8119

Collectors

William Blakeslee
116 Bethlehem Pike
P.O. Box 56
Ambler, PA 19002
phone: 215-646-6593
fax: 215-646-5459
e-mail: thugsob@aol.com
*Wants unusual electric toasters:
Mecky, Trimble, Foldex, Coleman,
Cozy, Monarch, Helion, Thoro,
Birtman, Pelouze; send photo,
markings.*

Uwe H. Breker
6731 Ashley Ct.
Sarasota, FL 34241-9696
phone: 941-925-0385
fax: 941-925-0487
*Wants to buy toasters: porcelain,
ceramic, etc.*

Richard Mathes
P.O. Box 1408
Springfield, OH 45501-1408
*Wants old fireplace, stove top and
pre-1940 electric toasters.*

Oscar P. Barkhurst
3910 Brookside Dr.
Rapid City, SD 57702-2219
phone: 605-348-1354
*Wants old, electric pre-1950 toasters;
heart shaped, perch, roaster coffee pot
combination, very old toaster ovens,
unusual, odd. Send photo and
information printed on the item.*

Joe Lukach
7111 Deframe Ct.
Arvada, CO 80004-1168
phone: 303-422-8970
*Wants unusual electric toasters 1908-
1940, good non-corroded condition;
especially ones with attached toast
racks & of porcelain.*

Dealers

Carl Roles
26245 Calle Cresta
Temecula, CA 92590
phone: 909-699-5139 or 909-699-8456
fax: 909-699-8119
*Wants to buy vintage electric toasters
and any item marked "Porcelier",
especially Porcelier toaster, waffle
irons, sandwich makers, coffee
percolators, urns.*

Experts

Helen Greguire
Helen's Antiques
103 Trimmer Rd.
Hilton, NY 14468-9305
phone: 716-392-2704

Jim A. Barker
ToasterMaster Antique Appliances
RR 5 Box 1375
Honesdale, PA 18431
phone: 717-253-1951
*Wants interesting electric toasters
1908-1940; Porcelier, GE, Toastrite,
Mecky, Pelouze; mechanical, push*

button, crank type, drop down; highest
prices paid.

Howard & Jane Hazelcorn
6731 Ashley Ct.
Sarasota, FL 34241-9696
phone: 941-921-1815
*Authors of "Price Guide to Old
Electric Toasters."*

Periodicals

Carl Roles
Newsletter: Toast To You, A
26245 Calle Cresta
Temecula, CA 92590
phone: 909-699-5139 or 909-699-8456
fax: 909-699-8119
*A bi-monthly newsletter for vintage
electric toaster collectors and dealers;
historic data, stories, old ads,
photographs and collections; for both
the advanced and beginning collector.*

TOBACCO CARDS

(see ADVERTISING COL-
LECTIBLES, Trade Cards [Tobacco];
CIGAR BANDS, BOXES &
LABELS; CIGARETTE COL-
LECTIBLES; CIGAR STORE
COLLECTIBLES; LIGHTERS;
MATCHBOXES & LABELS;
MATCHCOVERS; MATCH SAFES;
PIPES; SMOKING COLLECTIBLES)

TOBACCO COLLECTIBLES

(see also ADVERTISING COL-
LECTIBLES, Trade Cards [Tobacco];
MATCH SAFES; PAPER COL-
LECTIBLES; SMOKING COL-
LECTIBLES)

Collectors

Dan Calandriello
53-C Beacon Village
Burlington, MA 01803-3843
phone: 617-229-9009
e-mail: dan@coe.neu.edu
*Wants 1880s-1910 American tobacco
posters showing card sets; tobacco
cards; leathers from 1880s-1905.*

David & Barbara Freiberg
Cerebro
P.O. Box 327
East Prospect, PA 17317-0327
phone: 717-252-2400 or 800-69L-ABEL
fax: 717-252-3685
*Wants to buy tobacco paper items,
cigarette cards, tobacco trade cards.*

Cindy Porman
22044 Roosevelt Rd.
South Bend, IN 46614
phone: 219-291-6414
*Wants Copenhagen Snuff, Weyman &
Sons, Weyman Bros., Skoal Snuff, and
Key Snuff tobacco items including
crocks, pocket tins, store displays,
metal and paper signs, and related
advertising items.*

Chris Cooper
Rt. 2 Box 55
Pittsburg, TX 75686-9516
phone: 903-856-7286
fax: 903-856-6879
Wants tobacco tags, trade cards, tins, cigar cutters, ashtrays, billheads, caddies, labels, matchsafes, hammers, box openers, pennants, felts, key chains, bags, and most other tobacco advertising and ephemera.

Dealers

Mark Suozzi
P.O. Box 102
Ashfield, MA 01330
phone: 413-628-3241
Buys and sell tobacciana: antique tin litho and paper signs from 1850-1920, tobacco canisters, political campaign subjects, figural iron and lead cigar ad cutters and gas lighters, tobacco wood trade signs and store figures.

Lenore Monleon
33 Fifth Ave.
New York, NY 10003
phone: 212-475-7871 or 212-229-0958
Wants to buy tobacco collectibles: pocket match safes, tobacco humidors, enameled cigarette cases, etc.

Stephen C. Jones
P.O. Box 267
Homer, NY 13077-0267
phone: 607-753-8822
Wants cigar box labels, lithographers sample books of cigar box labels, cigarette cards, tobacco trade cards, tobacco business cards, tobacco store signs.

Jeff Mogilner
Racine & Laramie, Ltd.
2737 San Diego Ave.
San Diego, CA 92110-2731
phone: 619-291-7833
fax: 619-297-6653
e-mail: alexracine@aol.com
Buy, sell, collect antique tobacco pipes: meerschaum, clay, briar, porcelain, and related items.

Jars

Clubs/Associations

Charlotte Tarses
Society of Tobacco Jar Collectors
Newsletter: Tobacco Jar Newsletter
3011 Falstaff Rd. #307
Baltimore, MD 21209-2960
Purpose is to promote the collection and dissemination of information related to the manufacture, design, artistic merit, and historic, educational and cultural aspects of antique tobacco jars; annual convention.

Collectors

Sandie Goodman
3021 Courtland Blvd.
Cleveland, OH 44122-2805
phone: 216-921-0400
Focuses on collecting tobacco jars, especially figural jars.

Mail Pouch

Collectors

Mike Boggs
2075 Beaver Valley Rd.
Beaver Creek, OH 45385-9521
phone: 937-426-2171
Wants to buy anything related to Mail Pouch Tobacco - any size, any condition; also interested in any chewing tobacco items, any packs of tobacco, anything before 1965, all brands.

Tags

Clubs/Associations

Chris Cooper
Tobacco Tin Tag Collectors Club
Newsletter: Tin Tag Exchange, The
Rt. 2 Box 55
Pittsburg, TX 75686-9516
phone: 903-856-7286
fax: 903-856-6879

Collectors

John Mosely
408 Brook Dr.
Mount Airy, NC 27030-5163
Wants tin brand stamps from plug chewing tobacco; send description, condition, quantity and price.

Dealers

Lee Jacobs
P.O. Box 3098
Colorado Springs, CO 80934-3098
phone: 719-473-7101

Experts

Louis Storino
P.O. Box 189
Los Altos, CA 94023-0189
phone: 415-941-7663
fax: 415-941-8835
Collector and author of "Chewing Tobacco Tin Tags;" wants to buy tobacco tags - tin and paper used to identify brands of plug chewing tobacco; also wants related plug tobacco advertising, cards, posters, etc.

Tins

Collectors

Alex Caiola
84 Seneca
Emerson, NJ 07630-1243
phone: 201-967-9540
Wants tobacco tins.

Dealers

Richard & Ann Lehmann
Antique Station - Booth 8
194 Thomas Johnson Dr.
Frederick, MD 21702
phone: 301-253-3890
Specializes in cigar and tobacco tins.

Experts

Dick Crews
29 Cumberland St.
Boston, MA 02115-5313
phone: 617-247-1751 or 617-859-8937
Buys, collects and deals in quality tobacco tins: pockets, canisters and cigar tins.

TOBY JUGS

(see CERAMICS [ENGLISH], Royal Doulton; COLLECTIBLES [MODERN], Toby Jugs)

TOKENS

(see also BANKING; CIVIL WAR ARTIFACTS, Tokens; COINS & CURRENCY; CREDIT CARDS & CHARGE ITEMS; GAMBLING COLLECTIBLES, Poker Chips & Gaming Tokens; MEDALS, ORDERS & DECORATIONS; SCRIP)

Appraisers

Dr. Spencer Peck
P.O. Box 526
Oldwick, NJ 08858-0526
phone: 908-236-2880
One of only nine accredited appraisers of rare coins, currency, tokens and medals for IRS, estate, insurance, trust, liquidation and equitable distribution purposes in the U.S.

Auction Services

Bob Moffatt
P.O. Box 281
Auburn, MA 01501-0281
phone: 508-832-9707
fax: 508-832-2992
Conducts mail bid auctions of tokens, badges, and other historical Americana.

David M. Gale
C & D Gale
2404 Berwyn Rd.
Wilmington, DE 19810-3525
phone: 302-478-0872 or 302-478-6866
e-mail: cdgale@dol.net
Conducts mail bid auctions of medals, tokens, religious items, trade checks, miscellaneous items, Civil War tokens and other exonumia. Issues fixed-price exonumia catalogs.

Bob Slawsky
P.O. Box 864
Windermere, FL 34786-0864
phone: 407-352-7807
fax: 407-352-BIDS
e-mail: WWGD54A@prodigy.com
Buys, sells, auctions tokens, medals,

badges, small advertising items, political, World's Fair, Olympic items, encased coins, etc.

Harold Trainor
P.O. Box 13055
Fort Pierce, FL 34979
phone: 407-878-7376
fax: 407-878-3676
Conducts mail bid auctions of tokens, medals, pins, paper items, World's Fair and Exposition, beer & whiskey items, celluloid mirrors, political, fire department, Centennial items, automobilia, railroadiana, airline collectibles.

Rich Hartzog
World Exonumia
P.O. Box 4143 BSB
Rockford, IL 61110-0643
phone: 815-226-0771
fax: 815-397-7662
Wants any tokens, medals, exonumia: badges, buttons, World's Fair items, political items, banners, etc.; sample auction catalog $4.

Richard D. Mitchell
EXO Coin & Token Co.
2109 W. Britton Rd.
Oklahoma City, OK 73120-1505
phone: 405-755-7558
fax: 405-755-7595
Buys, sells merchant trade tokens, Civil War tokens; also political collectibles, World's Fair & Exposition items, rare coins, costume and estate jewelry, fine diamonds, and art glass.

Stephen P. Alpert
P.O. Box 66331
Los Angeles, CA 90066-0331
phone: 310-836-2482
fax: 310-836-5691
Conducts periodic auctions of tokens, medals, tags, credit cards, gambling chips, movie money, related coin-like items.

Clubs/Associations

Dennis P. Helmer
New Jersey Exonumia Society
Newsletter: Jerseyana
112 Carlton Ave.
Collingswood, NJ 08108-3501
Collectors of New Jersey tokens, medals, paper, etc.; annual meeting at convention; regional meetings at different coin shows.

David E. Schenkman, PR
Token & Medal Society
Journal: Token & Medal Society Journal
P.O. Box 366
Bryantown, MD 20617-0366
phone: 301-274-3441
Promotes and stimulates "exonumia", the study of non-government issue tokens and medals; an organization of collectors and researchers of tokens, medals and related items.

V. King
Indiana, Kentucky & Ohio Token &
  Medal Society
Newsletter: IKO-TAMS Newsletter
1725 North 650 West
Columbia City, IN 46725
phone: 219-327-3342
  A non-profit society for collectors of
  tokens, medals and other exonumia;
  meets four times per year; members
  have bourse tables at each meeting.

T.L. Batchelder
Michigan Token & Medal Society
Newsletter: Junk Box, The
P.O. Box 572
Comstock Park, MI 49321
  Dedicated to stimulating and
  maintaining interest in the exonumia
  of the state of Michigan.

Active Token Collectors Organization
Newsletter: ATCO Newsletter
P.O. Box 1573
Sioux Falls, SD 57101-1573
phone: 605-334-6910
  Interested in merchant trade tokens;
  each newsletter issue full of ads; trade
  tokens, medals, bank notes, etc.

Robert J. Leuver, ExDir
American Numismatic Association
Magazine: Numismatist, The
818 N. Cascade Ave.
Colorado Springs, CO 80903-3279
phone: 719-632-2646 or 800-367-9723
fax: 719-632-2646
Internet: http://www.money.org
  Worldwide assoc. of collectors of
  coins, paper money, medals and
  tokens; over 30,000 members; offers
  collector services and benefits.

Collectors

Joe Copeland
P.O. Box 4221
Oak Ridge, TN 37831-4221
phone: 423-482-4215
  Wants to buy tokens from saloons,
  CCC camps, and all southeastern US.

Jerome Schaeper, Jr.
705 Philadelphia St.
Covington, KY 41011-1252
phone: 606-581-3729
  Collects and appraises merchant
  "good for" trade tokens.

Rich Hartzog
World Exonumia
P.O. Box 4143 BSB
Rockford, IL 61110-0643
phone: 815-226-0771
fax: 815-397-7662
  Wants any tokens, medals, exonumia:
  badges, buttons, World's Fair items,
  political items, banners, etc.;
  collections and quantities wanted.

James E. Kattner
P.O. Box 11132
Spring, TX 77391
phone: 281-986-6916 or 281-376-4826
  Wants to buy tokens issued by Texas
  saloons, bars, military forts, post
  traders, lumber companies, drug

stores, barbers, general stores, and
other merchants; also tokens picturing
steer, elephants, eagles, The Alamo;
read "Good For".

Mike Farmer
1406 Bigelow Ave. NW
Olympia, WA 98506-4417
phone: 360-352-7189
fax: 360-352-7189

Dealers

Cy Phillips, Jr.
S C Coin & Stamp Co. Inc.
P.O. Drawer 661180
Arcadia, CA 91066-1180
phone: 818-445-8277 or 800-367-0779
fax: 818-445-8278
  Tokens, medals, coins, currency,
  badges, expo. and fair items, scrap
  gold and silver.

Dan M. Jacobson
P.O. Box 277101
Sacramento, CA 95827-7101
  Issues periodic lists of tokens for sale.

Experts

David E. Schenkman
P.O. Box 366
Bryantown, MD 20617-0366
phone: 301-274-3441
  Full time dealer recognized as one of
  the leading authorities in the field of
  tokens and medals; author of seven
  books, each of which is a standard
  reference; wants to buy tokens,
  medals, watch fobs, and advertising
  mirrors.

Bob Temarantz
2824 N. Bentley Ave.
Tucson, AZ 85716-5513
phone: 520-326-7014
  Buys and specializes in western state
  "saloon", military, "post trader",
  Indian trader, territorial (i.e. Tucson,
  A.T., Yakima, W.T.) tokens, "Good
  for" advertising pocket mirrors, etc.

Stephen P. Alpert
P.O. Box 66331
Los Angeles, CA 90066-0331
phone: 310-836-2482
fax: 310-836-5691
  Co-author with Lawrence E. Elman of
  "Tokens and Medals, A Guide to the
  Identification and Values of United
  States Exonumia"; dealer in all types
  of tokens, medals, tags, credit cards,
  gambling chips, movie money, related
  coin-like items.

Museums/Libraries

Robert J. Leuver, ExDir
Museum of the American Numismatic
  Association
Magazine: Numismatist, The
818 N. Cascade Ave.
Colorado Springs, CO 80903-3279
phone: 719-632-2646 or 800-367-9723
fax: 719-632-2646
Internet: http://www.money.org
  A museum collection including

400,000 items; largest numismatic
circulating library with books and A/V
material free to members.

Love

Clubs/Associations

Lloyd L. Entenmann
Love Token Society
Newsletter: Love Letter
130 Cornell Rd.
Audubon, NJ 08106-2857
phone: 609-547-2857
  For love token collectors and
  enthusiasts; newsletter published bi-
  monthly.

Experts

Lloyd L. Entenmann
130 Cornell Rd.
Audubon, NJ 08106-2857
phone: 609-547-2857
  Author of "Love Tokens as Engraved
  Coins."

Merchant

Clubs/Associations

Hal Dunn, Sec.
National Token Collector's Association
Newsletter: NTCA Newsletter
P.O. Box 5596
Elko, NV 89802
  For collectors of merchant and trade
  tokens.

Collectors

Joe Hunt
2117 Bush Dr.
Huntsville, TX 77340
  Wants all U.S. "Good For" tokens; no
  casino tokens or wood tokens.

Dealers

Jim & Rita Hinton
Collector's Choice
P.O. Box 104284
Jefferson City, MO 65110-4284
phone: 573-636-7567
  Wants merchant tokens that say
  "Good For"; prefers those listing
  town names.

Sales Tax

Clubs/Associations

American Tax Token Society
Newsletter: ATTS Newsletter
6837 Murray Lane
Annandale, VA 22003
  Interested in collecting tokens, scrip,
  punch cards, coupons, receipts, etc.
  relating to the history and collection
  of sales taxes.

Dealers

Tom Holifield
P.O. Box 533
Alderson, WV 24910-0533
phone: 304-445-7120
  Buys and sells sales tax tokens and

related materials; also wants any
tokens from the state of Mississippi.

Transportation (Fare)

Clubs/Associations

John M. Coffee, Ed.
American Vecturist Association
Newsletter: Fare Box, The
P.O. Box 1204
Boston, MA 02104-1204
phone: 617-277-8111
  Interested in collecting metal and
  plastic fare tokens.

Experts

John M. Coffee
P.O. Box 1204
Boston, MA 02104-1204
phone: 617-277-8111
  Co-author of the Atwood-Coffee
  "Catalogue of Transportation
  Tokens."

TOM'S PEANUTS

Dealers

Tina & Mark Richey
Spotted Horse Collectibles
12141 Couch Mill Rd.
Knoxville, TN 37932-1102
e-mail: shcollect@aol.com
Internet: http://members.aol.com/
  shcollect/homepage.html
  Buys and sells memorabilia related to
  Tom Houston Peanut Co., maker's of
  Tom's Toasted Peanuts; interested in
  contacting other Tom's collectors.

TOOLS

(see also ARCHITECTURE &
RELATED ITEMS;
BLACKSMITHING ITEMS;
DIAMOND EDGE; FARM
COLLECTIBLES; FIREPLACE
ITEMS; ICE INDUSTRY; HARD-
WARE; INDUSTRY RELATED
ITEMS; KEEN KUTTER; LOGGING
RELATED ITEMS; MACHINERY &
EQUIPMENT)

Auction Services

Tony Murland
Tool Shop Auctions
78 High Street
Needham Market
Suffolk IP6 8AW, U.K.
phone: 011-44-1449-722992
fax: 011-44-1449-722683
e-mail: tony@toolshop.demon.co.uk
Internet: http://
  www.toolshop.demon.co.uk
  Antique and usable tools sold mail
  order to users and collectors
  worldwide; three mixed quality tool
  auctions each year and one
  prestigious international tool auction
  every July; catalogues available.

Richard Crane
Crane Auctions
63 Poor Farm Rd.
Hillsboro, NH 03244
phone: 603-478-5723
   Specializes in the auction of antique tools.

Tom Witte
Tom Witte's Antiques
P.O. Box 399
Mattawan, MI 49071-0399
phone: 616-668-4161
fax: 616-668-5363
   Conducts on site and cataloged tool auctions in Indianapolis; also full line tool dealer.

Clubs/Associations

Peter Wood, Mem. Ch.
Tool Group of Canada
Newsletter: Tool Group of Canada
   Newsletter
7 Tottenham Rd.
Ontario MC3 2J3 Canada
phone: 416-444-4255
   Members are interested in collecting antique tools: woodworking, metalworking, leatherworking, textiles, domestic tools, hunting/ trapping, nautical, fishing, scientific, medical, railway, farm, etc.; meets five times a year.

Administrator
Tools & Trades History Society
Newsletter: Tools & Trades
60 Swanley Lane
Swanely
Kent BR8 7RG, U.K.

Elton W. Hall, Ex. Dir.
Early American Industries Association,
   The
Newsletter: Shavings, The
167 Bakersville Rd.
South Dartmouth, MA 02748
phone: 508-993-4198
Internet: http://
   ourworld.compuserve.com/
   homepages/Old_Tools/about.htm
   Interested in old tools, implements, utensils, vehicles, "Whatsits"; and to discover, identify and preserve same; also publishes the magazine "Chronicle."

Judy Hughes, Sec.
New England Tool Collectors
   Association
Newsletter: NETCA Newsletter
11 1/2 Concord Ave.
Saint Johnsbury, VT 05819
   Purpose is to promote and increase knowledge and understanding of early American trades and crafts, and of the tools with which they are associated; meeting held twice each year with swap and sale of tools.

John Whelan
Collectors of Rare & Familiar Tools
   Society (CRAFTS) of New Jersey
Newsletter: Tool Shed, The
38 Colony Ct.
New Providence, NJ 07974-2332
phone: 908-464-5424
   Members share information on tools and implements used in early trades and industries; newsletter published five times per year.

Steve Echers
Early Trades & Craft Society, The
11 Blythe Place
East Northport, NY 11731

Elliot Sayward
British-American Rhykenogical Society
60 Harvest Lane
Levittown, NY 11756

Bill Hermanek
Long Island Antique Tool Collector's
   Association
Newsletter: Workbench, The
31 Wildwood Dr.
Smithtown, NY 11787-3452
phone: 516-360-1216 or 516-265-1564
e-mail: BHermanek@aol.com
   Promotes knowledge, appreciation, collection and exchange of antique tools and machinery.

James Bovay, Sec./Treas.
Western New York Antique Tool
   Collector's Association
Newsletter: Talking Tools
104 Seldon St.
Rochester, NY 14605
e-mail: kinsey@uno.cc.geneseo.edu
Internet: http://137.238.51.88/
   WNYATCA/info.html

Robert Kaltenhauser
Three Rivers Tool Collectors
Newsletter: TRTC Newsletter
308 Ridge Lane
Saxonburg, PA 16056
phone: 412-352-1860
   Newsletter, four meetings per year, old tool sales.

J.B. Cox, Sec.
Potomac Antique Tools & Industries
   Association (PATINA)
Newsletter: Patinagram
6802 Nesbitt Pl.
Mc Lean, VA 22101-2132
phone: 703-821-2931
e-mail: jbcocox@erols.com
   Organization for men and women having an interest in the tools, crafts, techniques or manufacturing processes of the past.

Jim Hollins
Richmond Antique Tool Society
2208 Lochwood Ct.
Richmond, VA 23233
phone: 804-550-1010
e-mail: jelliott@sycomtech.com
Internet: http://www.sycomtech.com/
   oldtool.

Howie Jenner
Coastal Carolina Tool Collectors Club
545 Deer Run Rd.
New Bern, NC 28562
e-mail: cn1021@coastalnet.com

Fred Bair, Jr.
Society of Workers in Early Arts &
   Trades
: Sweat Rag, The
606 Lake Lena Blvd.
Auburndale, FL 33823-2937
phone: 941-967-3262
fax: 941-967-3262
   Members are largely those who do public demonstrations of early crafts, but membership is open to anyone; exchange knowledge of practices in crafts; promotes the finding, making and exchange of tools; annual directory.

Bill Rigler, Treas.
Midwest Tool Collectors Association
Magazine: Gristmill
Rte. 2 Box 152
Wartrace, TN 37183-9406
phone: 615-455-1935
fax: 615-455-0029
e-mail: billybob@edge.net
Internet: http://www.mtca.org
   Largest club that is dedicated to antique tool collectors.

George E. Woodard, Sec.
Ohio Tool Collectors Association
Newsletter: Ohio Tool Box
P.O. Box 261
London, OH 43140-0261
phone: 614-852-3180
   Interested in tools used for any function including construction, writing, household, etc.

Ed Pitcher
Southwest Tool Collectors Association
7032 Oak Bluff Dr.
Dallas, TX 75240

Cliff Fales, Sec.
Rocky Mountain Tool Collectors
Newsletter: Shavings, Sawdust, &
   Splinters
1435 S. Urban Way
Lakewood, CO 80228
e-mail:
   cliff.fales@postoffice.worldnet.att.net
Internet: http://www.unm.edu/~tr1005/
   index.htm
   Approximately 200 members, generally, but not limited to, the Rocky Mountain area; promotes the collection, restoration, and study of tools of bygone crafts; about 6 meetings per year in Denver area, and 6 in Albuquerque area.

Roger Phillips
Early American Industries Association -
   West
8476 West Way Dr.
La Jolla, CA 92038
phone: 619-454-5070

Bob Valich, Mem.
Preserving Arts & Skills of the Trades
   (PAST)
4329 Mayette Ave.
Santa Rosa, CA 95405
e-mail: tooltalk@expertsys.com
Internet: http://www.tooltalk.org

Jim Gillis
Pacific Northwest Tool Collectors
5022 Erskine Ave.
Seattle, WA 98136
phone: 206-937-4735
e-mail: ToolTimer@msn.com
Internet: http://www.tooltimer.com/
   PNTC.htm

Collectors

Bill Rigler
Rte. 2 Box 152
Wartrace, TN 37183-9406
phone: 615-455-1935
fax: 615-455-0029
e-mail: billybob@edge.net
Internet: http://www.mtca.org

Jay Bolante
3058 North Honore St.
Chicago, IL 60657-2050
phone: 312-327-5091
   Collects and wants to buy foot or hand-operated tools and machines.

Dr. Bill Smith
P.O. Box 19
Savoy, IL 61874

Dealers

Charles Stirling
Bristol Design
14 Perry Rd.
Bristol BS1 5BG, U.K.
phone: +44 177929 1740
e-mail: 100010.1433@compuserve.com
   Issues a catalog of tools for sale with quality color illustrations of fine English and American tools; subscription is $20 (partly refundable) for 5 issues; stocks metal planes, molding planes, plow planes, chisels, spokeshaves, etc.

Peter & Annette Habicht
Falcon-Wood Woodworking Tools
1985 S. Undermountain Rd.
Sheffield, MA 01257-9643
phone: 413-229-7745 or 800-829-7741
fax: 413-229-0144
e-mail: peterh@shaysnet.com
Internet: http://shaysnet.com/~peterh
   Buys and sells old woodworking tools; issues well-illustrated catalogs of older and more interesting tools; send $10 to be placed on the mailing list.

Ted Smith
Quality Tool Store
P.O. Box 445
Dennis Port, MA 02639
phone: 508-398-3651 or 508-398-3443
   Buys and sells tools.

Bud Steere
10 Glenwood Dr.
North Kingstown, RI 02852
*Buys and sells antique tools; be sure
to send LSASE when requesting
catalog of items for sale.*

Carole Meeker
Box 169 Kelly St.
Rhinecliff, NY 12574
phone: 914-876-7818
*Wants to buy rare and unusual small
patented mechanical antiques, early
American technology and occupational-related photography,
advertising and catalogs.*

Barb & Dan Fromer
Fromer's Antiques
P.O. Box 224
New Market, MD 21774-0224
phone: 301-831-6712
*Buys and sells antique woodworking
tools.*

Tom Witte
Tom Witte's Antiques
P.O. Box 399
Mattawan, MI 49071-0399
phone: 616-668-4161
fax: 616-668-5363
*Conducts on site and cataloged tool
auctions in Indianapolis; also full line
tool dealer.*

E.J. "Al" Renier
Renier's Antiques
P.O. Box 1323
Minnetonka, MN 55346-0323
phone: 612-937-0393
Buys and sells old woodworking tools.

John Hathaway
Hathaway's Tool Shed
731 Woodlake Dr.
Coppell, TX 75019-2849
*Publishes newsletter containing tools
for sale.*

Bob & Maxine Finch
Two Chiselers
1864 Glen Moore Dr.
Lakewood, CO 80215-3038
phone: 303-232-1932
fax: 303-232-8826
e-mail: rffinch@aol.com
*Buys, sells, collects tools; publishes
periodic catalog, 36 to 40 pages, fully
illustrated; authoring a book on the
development of braces and boring
tools.*

E.D. "Dave" Paling
Tool Guy, The
227 Ney St.
San Francisco, CA 94112-1644
phone: 415-334-7295
*Buys and sells quality used and
antique woodworking and machinists
tools*

Allan Foster
Allan Foster Antique Tools
5200 Lawton Ave.
Oakland, CA 94618

Experts

Jim Calison
Tools of Distinction
60 Reservoir Rd.
Wallkill, NY 12589
phone: 914-895-8035
*Wants Stanley tools and other old
hand woodworking tools.*

James H. Cooley
James H. Cooley Antiques
507 Joslin Hill Rd.
Frankfort, NY 13340
phone: 315-894-3483
e-mail: TizCooley@msn.com
*Buys, sells, collects, identifies,
appraises antique tools; member of
Early American Industries Association
for over 30 years; also Midwest Tool
Collectors Association.*

Ed Hobbs
4417 Inwood Rd.
Raleigh, NC 27603-3315
phone: 919-828-2754
fax: 919-828-6697
*Appraises and specializes in tools;
writes column for Antique Week;
available for speaking and demonstrations on antique tools.*

John Walter
Tool Merchant, The
208 Front St.
P.O. Box 227
Marietta, OH 45750-0227
phone: 614-373-9973
fax: 614-373-9059
e-mail: toolmerchant@sprynet.com
*Buys, sells and appraises antique and
traditional woodworking tools; author
of "Antique & Collectible Stanley
Tools" (1990, The Tool Merchants.)*

Ron Barlow
Windmill Publishing Co.
2147 Windmill View Rd.
El Cajon, CA 92020-1353
phone: 619-448-5390
*Author of "The Antique Tool
Collector's Guide to Value" (Windmill
Publishing Co.)*

Museums/Libraries

Roberto M. Rodriguez
American Precision Museum Association, Inc.
P.O. Box 679
Windsor, VT 05089
phone: 802-674-5781
fax: 802-674-2524
e-mail: 103362.1676@compuserve.com
Internet: http://
ourworld.compuserve.com/
homepages/Precision_Museum
*The museum focuses on machine tools,
early American hand tools and their
products, such as sewing machines,
typewriters and guns.*

Bucks County Historical Society
Newsletter: Penny Lots
84 S. Pine St.
Doylestown, PA 18901-4930
phone: 215-345-0210
fax: 215-230-0823
Internet: http://www.libertynet.org:80/
~bchs
*Operates three Nat. Historical
Landmarks; Mercer Museum has over
50,000 tools of Early American
trades/crafts; Spruance Library has
research material on trades & crafts;
Fonthill Museum is a concrete castle
laden with tiles & treasures.*

Hunter M. Pilkinton
World O'Tools Museum
2431 Hwy. 13 So.
Waverly, TN 37185
phone: 615-296-3218
*Always interested in old or odd
mechanical tools; also related books
and catalogs.*

Periodicals

Magazine: Fine Tool Journal, The
27 Fickett Rd.
Pownal, ME 04069
phone: 800-248-8114 or 207-688-4962
e-mail: ftjceb@aol.com
Internet: http://www.wowpages.com/ftj/
*A quarterly magazine for tool
collectors and craftsmen; features
biennial absentee tool auctions.*

Taunton Press
Magazine: Fine Woodworking
P.O. Box 5506
Newtown, CT 06470
phone: 800-283-7252 or 203-426-8171
fax: 203-426-3434
Internet: http://www.taunton.com
*Publishes a bi-monthly "How-to"
magazine written and illustrated by
master craftsmen; also publishes a
related line of books and videos; free
catalog available.*

Barry Abel, Ed.
Newsletter: Tool Ads
P.O. Box 33
Hamilton, MT 59840-0033
phone: 406-363-3805
fax: 406-363-4117
*A monthly newsletter for buyers and
sellers of all types of tools from hand
tools to machinery, parts, accessories
and related literature; contains only
ads and auction notices.*

Repro. Sources

Cracker Barrel, The
527 Narbeth Ave.
Haddonfield, NJ 08033

Zimmerman Handcrafts
254 East Main St.
Leola, PA 17540

Kevin Riddle
Mountainman Woodshop
Rte. 2
Eagle Rock, VA 24085
phone: 540-884-2197
*Traditional Appalachian Mountain
woodworking using original tools and
techniques; products include farm
tools, furniture, and toys; available
for lectures and demonstrations.*

Connie Carlton
Shaving Horse Crafts
1049 Rice Rd.
Lawrenceburg, KY 40342

Anvils

Collectors

Don Monnier
P.O. Box 772
Sidney, OH 45365
phone: 513-492-1420
*Wants to buy small, paperweight size
"anvils"; brass or iron; with
advertising; will buy one or entire
collections.*

Bruce Cynar
10023 St. Clair's Retreat
Fort Wayne, IN 46825
phone: 219-489-5004
*Wants small brass anvils with
advertising.*

Blow Torches

Clubs/Associations

Ron Carr
Blow Torch Collectors Club
Newsletter: Torch, The
3328 258th Ave. SE
Issaquah, WA 98027-9173
phone: 206-557-0634
e-mail: swcv70e@prodigy.com
*A group of blow torch collectors
dedicated to preserving the history of
blow torches and related material.*

Collectors

Samuel G. Scroggs
1073 Stonybridge Dr.
Chambersburg, PA 17201-9093
phone: 717-263-5422
*Wants pre-1900 and early 1900s brass
blow torches.*

Ron Carr
3328 258th Ave. SE
Issaquah, WA 98027-9173
phone: 206-557-0634
e-mail: swcv70e@prodigy.com
*Wants to buy brass blow torches; turn
of the century brass torches, all
models including gasoline, alcohol,
and kerosene.*

Machinist

Collectors

John Treggiari
Salem, MA 01970-1225
phone: 508-744-2897
fax: 508-744-5572
e-mail: micrometer@juno.com
Serious collector wants to buy pre-1920 measuring and layout machinist tools: micrometers, surface gages, calipers, small patented vises; speed indicators, rules, catalogs, display items, etc.; tool boxes alone are not needed.

New Jersey

Experts

Alexander Farnham
78 Tumble Falls Rd.
Stockton, NJ 08559-1309
phone: 908-996-4179
Author of "Search for Early New Jersey Toolmakers", $27.50 ppd., hardbound, "Early Tools of New Jersey and the Men Who Made THem", $22.50 ppd., hardbound, and "Tool Collectors Handbook," $3.50 ppd. softbound.

Planes

Experts

Roger K. Smith
P.O. Box 177
Athol, MA 01331-0177
phone: 508-249-5990
Buys, sells and specializes in planes; send LSASE for free catalog; author of "Patented Transitional & Metallic Planes in America" - Vols. I and II;

John Whelan
38 Colony Ct.
New Providence, NJ 07974-2332
phone: 908-464-5424
Author of "The Wooden Plane - Its History, Form and Function" (Astragal Press) and "Making Traditional Wooden Planes" (Astragal Press).

Plumb Bobs

Periodicals

Bruce Cynar
Newsletter: Plumb Line
10023 St. Clair's Retreat
Fort Wayne, IN 46825
phone: 219-489-5004
Focuses on plumb bobs, plumb lines and bobs with pulleys.

Stanley

Collectors

Bill Hermanek
31 Wildwood Dr.
Smithtown, NY 11787-3452
phone: 516-360-1216 or 516-265-1564
e-mail: BHermanek@aol.com
Wants to buy planes, levels, rulers,
braces, marking gauges, etc.; also wants tool literature, catalogs, advertising; anything Stanley.

Experts

John Walter
Tool Merchant, The
208 Front St.
P.O. Box 227
Marietta, OH 45750-0227
phone: 614-373-9973
fax: 614-373-9059
e-mail: toolmerchant@sprynet.com
Author of the illustrated "Antique & Collectible Stanley Tools: A Guide to Identification and Value" - 1997 edition (8 1/2" x 5", 885 pages), current values on 2,500 tools, over 1,500 illustrations.

A. Sellens
3120 Country Lane
Augusta, KS 67010-2369
Author of "The Stanley Plane, A History and Descriptive Inventory."

Periodicals

John Walter
Tool Merchant, The
Magazine: Stanley Tool Collector News
208 Front St.
P.O. Box 227
Marietta, OH 45750-0227
phone: 614-373-9973
fax: 614-373-9059
e-mail: toolmerchant@sprynet.com
40-page user/collector magazine; feature articles, research, 100s of select quality tools for sale, all with photos (lowest prices), user info., auction results, type studies, classified ads.

Tape Measures

Collectors

Janet Morphy
135 Wedgewood Dr.
Pittsburgh, PA 15229
phone: 412-366-6589
Wants to buy figural tape measures of metal, celluloid, porcelain.

Wes & Elaine Hart
963 Westhaven St.
Columbus, OH 43228
phone: 614-870-7141

Myron Huffman
12409 Wayne Trace
Hoagland, IN 46745
phone: 219-639-3290

Sherry L. Werdon
400 N. Washington
Lowell, MI 49331-1465
phone: 616-897-9580
Wants to buy figural tape measures.

Wrenches

Clubs/Associations

E. Eloise Alton, Ed.
Missouri Valley Wrench Club
Newsletter: Missouri Valley Wrench Club Newsletter
613 N. Long St.
Shelbyville, IL 62565-1544
phone: 217-774-5002
Club collects and studies anything having to do with wrenches; a quarterly newsletter is published with information about wrenches, manufacturers, patents, etc.

Collectors

Robert Rauhauser
RR 2 Box 766
Thomasville, PA 17364-9622
Wants wrenches with names; especially cutout (see throughs) wrenches; any farm machinery wrenches; specialty wrenches.

Shockley
1529 E. 49th St.
Tulsa, OK 74105
Wants to buy small, odd, or unusual wrenches; send picture, length, and price.

Wrenches (Adjustable)

Collectors

Charles W. Wardell
P.O. Box 195
Trinity, NC 27370-0195
phone: 910-434-1145
Wants early "monkey" wrenches of unusual design. Many 1800-1900 inventors used clever schemes to make the repair of machinery a more pleasant task. Gripping a bolt or nut securely and having a quick release mechanism were important.

TOOTH FAIRY

Experts

Dr. Rosemary Wells, Ph.D.
1129 Cherry St.
Deerfield, IL 60015
phone: 847-945-1129
fax: 847-945-1125
e-mail: stardesk@aol.com
Expert and researcher on the history and lore surrounding the Tooth Fairy; has a large collection of TF related items.

Museums/Libraries

Dr. Rosemary Wells, Ph.D.
Tooth Fairy Museum
1129 Cherry St.
Deerfield, IL 60015
phone: 847-945-1129
fax: 847-945-1125
e-mail: stardesk@aol.com

TOOTHBRUSH HOLDERS

Clubs/Associations

John & Nancy Smith
Toothbrush Holder Collectors Club
P.O. Box 371
Barnesville, MD 20838-0371
phone: 301-972-6250

Dealers

John & Nancy Smith
American Sampler
P.O. Box 371
Barnesville, MD 20838-0371
phone: 301-972-6250
Wants to buy figural toothbrush holders.

Estelle Sharp
ESCO Enterprises, Inc.
441 E. River Oaks Dr.
Baton Rouge, LA 70815-4063
phone: 504-924-5089
fax: 504-924-5089
Buys and sells toothbrush holders.

Experts

Marilyn Cooper
P.O. Box 55174
Houston, TX 77255
Author of "The Pictorial Guide to Toothbrush Holders."

TOOTHPICK HOLDERS

Clubs/Associations

Toby Shugart, Mem.
National Toothpick Holders Collectors Society
Newsletter: Toothpick Bulletin
P.O. Box 417
Safety Harbor, FL 34695-0417
phone: 813-726-9363
Internet: http://www.collectoronline.com/club-NTHCS.html
Society members interested in collecting toothpick holders of all shapes and materials; monthly newsletter, annual conventions.

Collectors

Thomas Manley
Rte. 1 Box 269
Port Trevorton, PA 17864
phone: 717-374-8031

Judy A. Knauer
1224 Spring Valley Lane
West Chester, PA 19380-5112
phone: 610-431-3477
e-mail: winkjk@voicenet.com
Collector, lecturer, and author on old glass toothpick holders; publishes "Toothpick Bulletin" monthly newsletter for and founder of National Toothpick Holder Collectors Society.

Lorraine Holt
2892 Sand Creek Highway
Adrian, MI 49221
phone: 517-265-4777

Fred Phelps
P.O. Box 217
Colesburg, IA 52035
phone: 319-856-2025

Mary Lou Trunkey
3212 Midland Ave.
White Bear Lake, MN 55110-5318

Richard & Nancy Ryan
8801 Thorndale Ct.
Fort Worth, TX 76180-1620
phone: 817-498-9046
fax: 817-788-4532

Experts

Judy Knauer
1224 Spring Valley Lane
West Chester, PA 19380-5112
phone: 610-431-3477
e-mail: winkjk@voicenet.com
Collector, lecturer, and author on old glass toothpick holders; wants to add to collection of old glass toothpick holders; buying one piece or entire collection; please describe, state condition and price.

TOURS/BUYING TRIPS

Misc. Services

Kellye French
Antique Tours of the USA
P.O. Box 361
Danville, CA 94526-0361
e-mail: PFrench@Packard.net
For over 10 years offers discounts on air, car and hotels for US antiques shows; also host specialized antique tours to unique locations.

Peter Manston
Travel Keys Tours
P.O. Box 160691
Sacramento, CA 95816-0691
phone: 916-452-5200
Buy antiques at the best fairs, flea markets, warehouses and antique centers in Europe; group tours or individual escorted travel.

TOYS

(see also BANKS; CHARACTER COLLECTIBLES; CHILDREN'S THINGS; CRACKER JACK TOYS; DISNEY COLLECTIBLES; DOLLS; GAMES; KITS; MINIATURES; MOVIE MEMORABILIA; POPULAR CULTURE; PREMIUMS; RIDING TOYS; SOLDIERS; STEIFF; SUPER HEROES; TEDDY BEARS; TRAINS; TRUCKS

Auction Services

Glenn Butler
Wallis & Wallis
West Street Auction Galleries
Lewes
East Sussex BN7 2NJ, U.K.
phone: 01273-480208
fax: 01273-476562
Britain's specialist auctioneers of diecast & tin plate toys & models including model soldiers.

Sotheby's
34-35 New Bond St.
London W1A 2AA, U.K.
phone: 0171-4938080 or 0171-4085205
fax: 0171-4085911
Conducts specialty auctions of tinplate toys, diecasts, trains, antique dolls, teddy bears, automata.

Mildred Ewing
Skinner, Inc.
357 Main St.
Bolton, MA 01740-1104
phone: 508-779-6241 or 617-350-5400
fax: 508-779-5144
Established in 1964, Skinner Inc. is the fifth largest auction house in the US; has offices in Bolton and Boston, MA.

Martin Krim
New England Auction Gallery
P.O. Box 2273
Peabody, MA 01960-7273
phone: 508-535-3140
fax: 508-535-7522
e-mail: dlkrim@star.net
Internet: http://www.old_toys.com
Conduct mail-bid auctions with full color illustrated catalogs; specializes in sales of Disney, TV and cartoon items from 1920-1970: toys, wind-ups, robots, space toys.

Withington, Inc.
RD 2 Box 440
Hillsboro, NH 03244
phone: 603-464-3232

Herb & Barb Smith
Smith House Toy Sales
26 Adlington Rd.
Eliot, ME 03903
phone: 207-439-4614
Conducts four specialty mail-bid toys and collectibles auctions each year.

Randy Inman
James D. Julia Auctioneers Inc.
Rt. 201, Skowhegan Rd.
P.O. Box 830
Fairfield, ME 04937
phone: 207-453-7125
fax: 207-453-2502
Conducts specialized auctions of toys and doll items and are one of the leaders in this field in North America.

Lloyd Ralston
Ralston Toy Auction
109 Glover Ave.
Norwalk, CT 06850
phone: 203-366-3399 or 203-255-1233
Specializes in auctioning toys, dolls, games and trains.

Bill Bertoia
Bill Bertoia Auctions
1881-G Spring Rd.
Vineland, NJ 08630
phone: 609-692-1881
fax: 609-692-8697
Specializing in the auctioning of antique toys, banks, doorstops.

Christie's East
219 E. 67th St.
New York, NY 10021
phone: 212-606-0400

Sotheby's
1334 York Ave.
New York, NY 10021
phone: 212-606-7370 or 212-606-7000
Internet: http://www.sothebys.com
Over 70 collecting areas are featured at Sotheby's auctions including toys, dolls, porcelain, furniture, silver, art, books; exhibitions are free and everyone is welcome; for a free copy of "Sotheby's Newsletter", call 212-606-7245.

Henry Kurtz
Henry Kurtz Ltd.
163 Amsterdam Ave., Ste. 136
New York, NY 10023
phone: 212-642-5904
fax: 212-874-6018
Specializes in the sale of jewelry, paintings, prints, silver, coins, stamps, toys (especially lead soldiers), and movie memorabilia.

Louis Webre, Client Svc.
William Doyle Galleries
175 E. 87th St.
New York, NY 10128-2205
phone: 212-427-2730
fax: 212-369-0892
Internet: http://www.doylegalleries.com
Holds over 30 auctions annually of antique English, Continental and American furniture, paintings, decorations, jewelry, vintage and couture clothing, collectible toys, books and prints; specialty auctions of Majolica, Lalique and wine.

Stephen Leonard
Leonard Auctions
P.O. Box 127
Albertson, NY 11507
phone: 516-742-0979

Toy Locators
5821 Diana Lane
Lake View, NY 14085
phone: 716-627-5840
Conducts monthly toy and games mail-bid auctions.

Ted Hake
Hake's Americana & Collectibles Auction
P.O. Box 1444
York, PA 17405-1444
phone: 717-848-1333
Always purchasing items for 8 mail-bid auctions per year covering hundreds of categories including toys, character collectibles, Disney, cowboy heroes, premiums, television, politicals, pin-back buttons, advertising and more.

Noel Barrett
Noel Barrett Antiques & Auctions, Ltd.
P.O. Box 1001
Carversville, PA 18913-0201
phone: 215-297-5109
fax: 215-297-0457
Specializes in the auction of toys, games, vintage advertising and country store items.

Ted Maurer
Maurer's Auctions
1003 Brookwood Dr.
Pottstown, PA 19464
phone: 610-323-1573 or 610-367-5024
Specializes in the auctioning of toys, trains and railroad related items.

Richard W. Opfer, Jr.
Richard Opfer Auctioneering, Inc.
1919 Greenspring Dr.
Lutherville Timonium, MD 21093-4113
phone: 410-252-5035
fax: 410-252-5863
Specializes in auctioning toys, dolls, games, black memorabilia, and advertising items; weekly estate auctions including antiques, fine art; monthly eclectic collector sales feature a wide variety of collectibles.

Perry R. Eichor
Eichor Associates
703 N. Almond Dr.
Simpsonville, SC 29681-3453
phone: 803-967-8770
Appraises and conducts auction sales of toys; member Antique Toy Collectors of America.

American Eagle Auction Company
6724 York Rd., SW
Pataskala, OH 43062

Lewis & Lambright, Inc.
112 N. Detroit St.
LaGrange, IN 46761
phone: 413-549-3775 or 413-549-4425
Specializes in the auctioning of trains, toys, farm toys and dolls.

James L. Jackson, ISA
Jackson's Auctioneers & Appraisers
2229 Lincoln St.
Cedar Falls, IA 50613
phone: 319-277-2256
fax: 319-277-1252
e-mail: jacksons@jacksonsauction.com
Internet: http://www.jacksonsauction.com
Conducts specialty auctions of antique toys (tin, cast iron, windup) and contemporary toys.

Korin Dunning Helsdon
Dunning's Auction Service
755 Church Rd.
Elgin, IL 60123-9302
phone: 708-741-3483 or 800-462-2444
fax: 708-741-3589
Internet: http:///www.dunnings.com

Joy Luke
Joy Luke Auction Gallery
300 E. Grove St.
Bloomington, IL 61701-5232
phone: 309-828-5533
fax: 309-829-2266
*Conducts periodic auctions
specializing in the sale of toys, banks,
trains and dolls.*

Clubs/Associations

Des Barnes
Canadian Toy Collectors Society
Newsletter: Canadian Toy Collectors'
Newsletter
67 Alpine Ave.
Hamilton
Ontario L9A 1A7 Canada
phone: 905-389-8047 or 905-388-4014
e-mail: barnesd@rogers.wave.ca
Internet: http://spartan.mowhawkc.on.ca/
audiovis/medimag/ctcs/ctcshp.htm
*Association for toy collectors
worldwide; promoters of Canada's
greatest toy collector's show & sale,
promoter of C.T.C.S. "Limited
Edition" Brooklin models; CTCS
maintains large museum collection of
early Canadian toys.*

American Game Collectors Association
Newsletter: Game Times
49 Brooks Ave.
Lewiston, ME 04240-5901
phone: 215-674-1072
Internet: http://www.agca.com/~rfinn/
agca.htm
*Focuses on board and card games as
well as puzzles, playing cards, tops,
yo-yos, and action games; also
publishes "Game Researchers' Notes"
- reports on member's research.*

Robert R. Grew
Antique Toy Collectors of America, Inc.,
The
Newsletter: Toy Chest
c/o Carter, Ledyard & Milburn
Two Wall St. - 13th Floor
New York, NY 10005
phone: 212-238-8803
fax: 212-732-3232
*An organization focusing on antique
toys and games; since membership is
by invitation only for established
collectors, there is a waiting list; bi-
monthly newsletter is available only to
members.*

Larry Orr
Heartland Toy Club
11 S. 4th St., Room 400
Pekin, IL 61554
phone: 309-477-2280

Glenda Hodson
Friends Toy Collectors Association
10227 Atkins Rd.
Bentonville, AR 72712

Carl Natter
Southern California Toy Collector's
Club
Newsletter: Southern California Toy
Collector's Club
1760 Termino, Ste. 300
Long Beach, CA 90804
phone: 310-597-4351
fax: 310-498-9513
*Members interested in all types of toys
from 19th century tin toys to G.I. Joe
and Barbie; monthly newsletter.*

Collectors

Martin Krim
P.O. Box 2273
Peabody, MA 01960-7273
phone: 508-535-3140
fax: 508-535-7522
e-mail: dlkrim@star.net
Internet: http://www.old_toys.com
*Wants wind-up and battery toys, toy
cars, robots and space toys.*

Mark Bergin
P.O. Box 3073
Peterborough, NH 03458-3073
phone: 603-924-2079
fax: 603-924-2022
*Wants old toys: tin, metal, celluloid;
wind-up toys of all kinds, battery
operated toys, friction, robots, space
toys, space guns, cars, buses, racers,
motorcycles, boats, airplanes,
character toys, etc.*

Stephen Leonard
P.O. Box 127
Albertson, NY 11507
phone: 516-742-0979
Wants antique mechanical toys, etc.

Sanford Weltman
39 Branford Rd.
Rochester, NY 14618-1707
phone: 716-442-8810 or 716-473-2498
*Buying old toys, one item or
collection.*

Larry Bruch
Larry Bruch Toys
P.O. Box 121
Mountain Top, PA 18707-0121
phone: 800-549-TOYS
*All kinds of pre-1960 toys wanted:
German, American: metal cars,
airplanes, boats; comic characters,
cast iron toys and banks, etc.; write
for free 3-page illustrated want list.*

Lee Woolf
321 Meeting House Lane
Narberth, PA 19072-2029
phone: 610-667-9378
*Wants to buy electric trains, toy trucks
and cars, lead figures and soldiers,
Daisy BB guns, model race cars.*

Ronald Wiener
Packard Bldg. - 12th Floor
111 S. 15th St.
Philadelphia, PA 19102-2625
phone: 215-977-2266
fax: 215-977-2334
e-mail: rwiener@wolfblock.com
Wants rugs, blankets, baskets.

Jim Conley
2758 Coventry Lane
Canton, OH 44708-1320
phone: 330-477-7725 or 330-499-9283
fax: 330-879-2950
*Buys and sells cars, trucks, tin wind-
ups, Buddy L, Metal Craft, Smith
Miller, Tonka, Lehmann, Bing, Ives,
Marx, etc.; also Fisher-Price, Gibbs
toys, Japanese tin cars from the '50s
and '60s; OK for sellers to call
collect.*

Jerry Peters
Chestnut Hollow, Ltd.
6060 Bordman Rd.
P.O. Box 6
Almont, MI 48003
phone: 810-798-3158
*Wants to buy robots, sci-fi related,
aviation related, cars, trucks, wind-
ups, battery operated, etc.; Rocketeer,
Star Trek, Star Wars, Buck Rogers,
King Kong, Universal movie monsters,
actual movie props, autographs.*

Dr. Greg Zemenick
Dr. "Z"
1350 Kirts, Ste. 160
Troy, MI 48084-4830
phone: 248-642-8129 or 248-244-9430
fax: 248-244-9495
e-mail: DrZzeezz@aol.com
Internet: http://www.drzzeezzi.com
*Wants to buy early American (pre-
1910) toys, banks, cigar store
collectibles, tin toys, clocks;
appraises, collects, sells, repairs.*

Lee H. Mitchell
175 E. Delaware, #8210
Chicago, IL 60611-1732
phone: 800-869-7869 or 312-337-3123
fax: 312-266-7982
*Insatiable collector eager to buy
character collectibles, battery toys,
Fisher-Price, playsuits, etc. in nicer
condition (mainly 1920-1969, no
transportation toys); buys duplicates;
welcomes hearing from dealers and
other collectors.*

Rex Miller
Rte. 1 Box 457
East Prairie, MO 63845-9761
phone: 314-649-5048
*Specializes in toys and premiums of
cartoon, comic book, movie, TV and
radio characters and personalities.*

Kenneth R. Chane
9755 Independence Ave.
Chatsworth, CA 91311-4318
phone: 818-407-0855
fax: 818-407-0850
e-mail: kschane@msn.com
Wants to buy ice cream vendors,

*baggage carts with figures, graffiti
cars, tin lithograph toys.*

Dealers

Alicia & Jorge Valino
P.O. Box 1442
(11000) Montevideo
Uruguay
e-mail: vala@adinet.com.uy.

Gary Nerman
Nerman's Books & Collectibles
721 Osborne St. South
Winnipeg
Manitoba R2K 0V7 Canada
phone: 204-475-1050 or 204-255-2196
fax: 204-947-0753
e-mail: nerman@escape.ca

Leila Dunbar
Dunbar's Gallery
76 Haven St.
Milford, MA 01757-3821
phone: 508-634-8697 or 508-634-8097
fax: 508-634-8698
*Mail order Americana - no reproduc-
tions; buys, sells and specializes in
vintage character and comic toys,
banks, advertising, automobilia, and
Halloween related items.*

George Newcomb
Plymouth Rock Toy Co.
P.O. Box 1202
Plymouth, MA 02362
phone: 508-746-2842 or 508-830-1880
fax: 508-830-0364

Robb Sequin
P.O. Box 1126
Dennis Port, MA 02639
phone: 508-760-2599
e-mail: rsequin@capecod.net
Internet: http://rsequin.com
*Wants to buy 1950s to 1970s toys and
fun stuff, battery-operated, wind-up,
character collectibles, etc.*

David Epstein
S&D Classic Toys
54 Bennington Rd.
Cranston, RI 02920
phone: 401-351-3900 or 401-943-1931

Carl Lobel
P.O. Box 74A
Warren, VT 05674
phone: 802-496-4025
*Wants to buy comic character wind-
ups, Lehman, space toys, robots/
astronauts, TPS wind-ups, 1930-1960
Japanese, plush bear wind-ups,
unusual comic character items such as
figurines, radios, clocks, and dolls.*

Lloyd Ralston
Ralston Toy Auction
109 Glover Ave.
Norwalk, CT 06850
phone: 203-366-3399 or 203-255-1233

Toyareum
1101 Asbury Ave.
Ocean City, NJ 08226
phone: 609-391-0480
A museum-like shop.

Bill Bertoia
1881-G Spring Rd.
Vineland, NJ 08630
phone: 609-692-1881
fax: 609-692-8697

Laura Dorrer
Lavender n' Lace
110 West 25th St.
New York, NY 10001
phone: 212-924-5230 or 516-681-4124
Buys and sells one-of—a-kind artist dolls, limited editions dolls and antique dolls; also one-of-a-kind artist bears, and vintage and collectible bears.

Bob Smith
Village Smith, The
62 West Ave.
Fairport, NY 14450
phone: 716-377-8394
fax: 716-377-6019
e-mail: oldtoys@frontiernet.net
Internet: http://www.frontiernet.net/~oldtoys
Avid collector and dealer of 1870-1970 toys: wind-up, automotive, European tin, pressed steel, early diecast, cast iron; promoter of Rochester Antique Toy Show; contributor to reference books on antique toys.

Jacquie Henry
Antique Treasures & Toys
2240 Academy St.
P.O. Box 17
Walworth, NY 14568-0017
phone: 315-986-1424
e-mail: JHenry5792@aol.com
Buys and sells 1860-1960 toys; cast iron, lithographed tin, wind-ups, banks, candy containers, pressed steel toys, toy soldiers, dolls, games, etc.

Chris Savino
P.O. Box 419
Breesport, NY 14816-0419
phone: 607-739-3106
fax: 607-739-3106
Wants to buy any childhood items: tin wind-ups, battery toys, cast iron toys, autos, trucks, marbles, robots; toys made in the US, Japan, Germany, France England; toys in original boxes bring more; call or write for an offer.

Bob Stevens
Keystone Toy Trader
529 N. Water St.
Masontown, PA 15461
phone: 412-583-8234
fax: 412-583-0604
Wants quality antique toys in early all categories, early comic characters, cast iron, tin, diecast Tootsie Toys.

Jim Cox
Sussex Antique Toy Shop
P.O. Box 339
Matamoras, PA 18336
phone: 717-491-2707

Vincent G. Krug
Childhood Memories, Inc.
7120 Little River Tkp.
Annandale, VA 22003
phone: 703-750-0841
Wants older tin, wood, cast iron and composition toys; especially relating to Easter, Halloween, and Christmas.

Philip Norman
Norman's Olde Store
126 W. Main
Washington, NC 27889
phone: 919-946-3448

Good Old Toys
P.O. Box 753
Edenton, NC 27932-0753
phone: 800-435-TOYS

Gordy Dutt
Gordy's
P.O. Box 201
Sharon Center, OH 44274-0201
phone: 330-239-1657
fax: 330-239-2991
e-mail: Gordys_kitbuilders@juno.com
Internet: http://www.gremlins.com/kitbuilders
Wants to buy toys from the '50s to '60s: games, gum cards, model kits, gun sets, monsters, super heroes, cereal premiums, TV-related, cartoon toys, etc.

Bill & Joanne Bruegman
Toy Scouts, Inc.
137 Casterton Ave.
Akron, OH 44303-1543
phone: 330-836-0668
fax: 330-869-8668
e-mail: toyscout@newreach.net
Internet: http://www.csmonline.com/toyscouts/
Specializes baby-boom era toys from 1950s-60s: TV, cartoon, monsters, super heroes, games, cereal premiums, model kits, etc.; anything baby-boomer era.

Ed McDandal
Ed's Toy Shop
953 East Richmond
Kokomo, IN 46901
phone: 317-459-0325
Wants to buy old toys from the 1920s to 1930s; pressed steel cars and trucks, cast iron toys, wind-ups, live steam toys.

James May
Olde Tyme Toy Shop
120 S. Main St.
Fairmount, IN 46928
phone: 317-948-3150
Focuses on toys and related pop culture collectibles such as Star Wars.

Barrett Behnke
Barrett's Toys and Collectibles
136 Chestnut
Wyandotte, MI 48192
phone: 313-282-6754 or 313-282-3072
Wants to buy Wyandotte toys and other pressed steel and tin toys.

Richard Trautwein
Toy's N Such
437 Dawson St.
Sault Sainte Marie, MI 49783-2119
phone: 906-635-0356
Wants tin and metal wind-up, battery operated, and electric toys: German, Japanese, or American.

Ed Janey
1756 65th St.
Garrison, IA 52229
phone: 319-477-8888
Always buying old toys, model kits, Western collectibles and toys, space toys, slot cars and car kits, lunch boxes, ad items, radios, Disney, soakies, etc.

Heinz Mueller
Continental Hobby House
P.O. Box 193
Sheboygan, WI 53082
phone: 414-693-3371
fax: 414-693-8211
Extensive list of toy trains (catalog $5); parts list ($5); HO train catalog ($5); wants all types of toys and trains especially European; very large inventory of all types of toys; request web page information.

Jon & Carolyn Thurmond
Collectorholics
15006 Fuller
Grandview, MO 64030-4522
phone: 816-322-0906
e-mail: toyjet@aol.com
Buys, sells, trades TV Guides, Western items, Star Trek, military toys, banks, novelty radios, radio premiums, Disney, etc.

Jim Yeager
P.O. Box 413881
Kansas City, MO 64141
phone: 816-333-2839

Bill & Pam Shepardson
Vintage Toys
201 Schiller
Hermann, MO 65041
phone: 314-486-3903
Wants to buy toys: early tin, cast iron, paper litho, character toys.

Jim & Rita Hinton
Collector's Choice
P.O. Box 104284
Jefferson City, MO 65110-4284
phone: 573-636-7567

Marjorie Jeffreys
Going to Pieces
P.O. Box 390
Cibolo, TX 78108
phone: 210-659-2458
Buys and sells old games, toys, blocks and children's dishes and children's baking items.

John D. McKenna
McKenna Bros. Wholesale
801-803 W Cucharras St.
Colorado Springs, CO 80905
phone: 719-630-8732
Buys, sells & collects pre-1960 toys in

all categories especially early American tin, cast iron automotive and horse-drawn toys.

Richard Johnson
P.O. Box 27093
Prescott Valley, AZ 86312
phone: 602-775-4714
e-mail: jfay@bslnet.com
Tin toys, robots.

Tim Hunter
1668 Golddust
Sparks, NV 89436
phone: 702-626-5029
fax: 702-626-4423
e-mail: thunter8852@aol.com

Louis Steinberg
Classic Hobbies & Toys
18928 Ventura Blvd.
Tarzana, CA 91356
phone: 818-609-7077

Anne Henderson
Anne's Dolls, Marvins Toys
13629 Victory
Van Nuys, CA 91401-1735
phone: 818-785-1177
Wants to buy Barbie and family dolls, clothes, etc.; also other dolls as well as Disney, wind-up, and battery-operated toys.

Toys 'N' Stuff
P.O. Box 2037
San Bernardino, CA 92406
phone: 909-880-8558
fax: 909-880-8096
Wants to buy Star Wars, Gremlins, Planet of the Apes, GI Joe, Nightmare, Corgi & Dinky, character toys of all kinds, all other movie and TV related toys and memorabilia.

Experts

Richard Friz
P.O. Box 472
Peterborough, NH 03458
phone: 603-563-8155
Author of "The Official Price Guide to Toys."

Gary Darrow
Darrow's Fun Antiques
1101 1st Ave.
New York, NY 10021-8737
phone: 212-838-0730
fax: 212-838-3617
Buys & sells antique games, toys, ad signs, animated art, jukeboxes, slot machines, comic watches, bicycles & memorabilia of all types.

Judith Katz-Schwartz
Twin Brooks Antiques & Collectibles
P.O. Box 6572
New York, NY 10128-0006
phone: 212-876-3512
fax: 212-876-3512
e-mail: twinb@tiac.net
Internet: http://www.tiac.net/users/twinb
Buys, sells, appraises wind-ups, character toys, board games, battery

operated, Chein, Marx, Disney, obots, Japanese celluloid, space toys, etc.

Bob Smith
Village Smith, The
62 West Ave.
Fairport, NY 14450
phone: 716-377-8394
fax: 716-377-6019
e-mail: oldtoys@frontiernet.net
Internet: http://www.frontiernet.net/
~oldtoys
Avid collector and dealer of 1870-1970 toys: wind-up, automotive, European tin, pressed steel, early diecast, cast iron; promoter of Rochester Antique Toy Show; contributor to reference books on antique toys.

Ted Hake
Hake's Americana & Collectibles
Auction
P.O. Box 1444
York, PA 17405-1444
phone: 717-848-1333
Always purchasing items for 8 mail-bid auctions per year covering hundreds of categories including toys, character collectibles, Disney, cowboy heroes, premiums, television, politicals, pin-back buttons, advertising and more.

Harry L. Rinker
Rinker Enterprises, Inc.
5093 Vera Cruz Rd.
Emmaus, PA 18049-9554
phone: 610-965-1122
fax: 610-965-1124
e-mail: rinkeron@fast.net
Researches, writes about and appraises all forms of 19th and 20th century toys, games and puzzles.

Joseph E. Freed
6209 Sandy Forks Rd.
Raleigh, NC 27624-9534
phone: 919-847-7365
fax: 919-847-3822
Buys and specializes in toys; also published books about toys.

Carol & Jerry Dinelli
Nobel House Ltd.
P.O. Box 826
Mundelein, IL 60060-0826
phone: 708-367-8588
Writes column on antique and collectible toys; has cataloged toy reproductions; send SASE with your questions.

David Welch
P.O. Box 714
Murphysboro, IL 62966-0714
phone: 618-687-2282
fax: 618-684-2243
e-mail: PexDude1@aol.com
Wants 1950s-1960s tin robots; also 1930s-1960s Disney, Popeye, Betty Boop and monster toys; $10,000+ for rare items.

Earnest & Ida Long
Long's Americana
P.O. Box 90
Mokelumne Hill, CA 95245
phone: 209-286-1348
Specializes in toys, banks, games and other children's items; publishes "Dictionary of Toys, Vol I & II" and "Penny Lane."

Museums/Libraries

Bethnel Green Museum of Childhood
Cambridge Heath Rd.
London E2 9PA, U.K.
phone: 081-980-3204
fax: 081-980-4759
National collection of dolls, toys, games, puppets, and children's costumes.

Fawcett's Toy Museum
3506 Rt. 1
Waldoboro, ME 04572
phone: 207-832-7398

Forbes Magazine Collection
60 Fifth Ave.
New York, NY 10011
phone: 212-206-5548

Sheila Clark
Museum of the City of New York
1220 5th Ave.
New York, NY 10029-5221
phone: 212-534-1672
fax: 212-534-5974
Access by appointment; research fee charged.

Strong Museum, The
1 Manhattan Square
Rochester, NY 14607
phone: 716-263-2700

Toy & Miniature Museum of Delaware
P.O. Box 4053
Wilmington, DE 19807
phone: 302-427-8697

Washington Dolls' House & Toy
Museum
5236 44th St. NW
Washington, DC 20015
phone: 202-244-0024

Lake Erie Toy Museum
P.O. Box 860
Kelleys Island, OH 43438
phone: 419-746-2451
fax: 419-281-7101
Features toys of many themes: comic strip characters, Disney, circus and amusement park, TV and cartoons, military, sports, construction, space, nursery rhyme, holiday seasons, superheroes, farm, dolls, dollhouses, boats, airplanes, etc.

Eugene Field House & Toy Museum
634 So. Broadway St.
Saint Louis, MO 63102
phone: 314-421-4689

Roger Berg
Toy & Miniature Museum of Kansas
City
5235 Oak St.
Kansas City, MO 64112-2877
phone: 816-333-2055 or 816-333-9328
fax: 816-333-2055
Museum housed in an elegant mansion features collections of miniatures, antique dolls' houses and antique toys.

Hobby City Doll & Toy Museum
1238 South Beach Blvd.
Anaheim, CA 92804
phone: 714-527-2323

Periodicals

Newspaper: Toy Collecting
200 Nuncargate Rd.
Kirby in Ashfield
Nottingham,, U.K.
A monthly newspaper.

Verlag SpielzeugAntik
Magazine: Spielzeug Antik
Ubierring 4 D-50678
Koln, Germany
Focuses on antique & collectible toys; published six times per year.

Classic Toys Ltd.
Magazine: Classic Toys
P.O. Box 47
Coventry CV5 9YY, U.K.
phone: 0120 369 1212
Bi-monthly, covers a variety of old and new toys, including die cast.

Brian Savage
Fun Publications
Newspaper: Master Collector
12513 Birchfalls Dr.
Raleigh, NC 27614-9675
phone: 800-772-6673 or 919-847-5263
e-mail: bsavage@mastercollector.com
Internet: http://
www.mastercollector.com
Ads-only newspaper; dolls (antique and modern collectible), toys, banks, models, cars, Matchbox, monsters, puzzles, political, toy trains, etc.; subscribers receive free 30 word ad each month; published monthly; reaches 20,000.

Paul Mathies
Kiddy Hawk
Magazine: Model & Toy Collector
Magazine
P.O. Box 347240
Cleveland, OH 44134-9998
phone: 216-843-9522
fax: 216-843-9523
Focuses on collectible toys, models and various other memorabilia from the '50s to the present; published quarterly; 80 pgs.

Newsletter: Johnny Lightning News
Flash
P.O. Box 3688
South Bend, IN 46619-0688
phone: 800-626-8478
For collectors of Johnny Lightning diecast collectible cars.

Teri Steele, Pub.
Magazine: YesterDaze TOYS
275 State Rd.
P.O. Box 57
Otisville, MI 48463-0057
phone: 810-631-4593
fax: 810-631-4567
The monthly meeting place for toy collectors; if children played with it, this magazine covers it; old to not-so-old toys.

Sharpe Publications
Magazine: Toy Collector Marketplace
1550 Territorial Rd.
Benton Harbor, MI 49022
Covers the entire field of toy collecting.

Tom Hammel, Ed.
Kalmbach Publishing Co.
Magazine: Collecting Toys
P.O. Box 1612
Waukesha, WI 53187-1612
phone: 414-796-8776 or 800-533-6644
fax: 414-796-1383
e-mail: customerservice@kalmbach.com
A bi-monthly magazine with articles on all aspects of the toy collecting hobby: ads, toy fair report, collections and collectors, auction reports, new diecast vehicles, and action figure reports.

John Koenig
Antique Trader Publications, Inc.
Newspaper: Toy Trader
922 Churchill St., Ste. #1
Waupaca, WI 54981
phone: 715-258-7525 or 800-768-9225
fax: 715-258-8707
e-mail: jkoenig@add-inc.com
Internet: http://www.csmonline.com
Monthly newspaper with information on how to buy, sell and trade all types of toys; market trends, the latest prices, "how-to" columns, listings of toy clubs and upcoming toy shows and auctions; also full of buy and sell ads.

Julie A. Ulrich, PR
Krause Publications
Newspaper: Toy Shop
700 E. State St.
Iola, WI 54990-0001
phone: 715-445-2214
fax: 715-445-4087
e-mail: info@krause.com
Internet: http://www.krause.com
A bi-weekly fully indexed newspaper containing classified ads for toys, tin soldiers, dolls, diecast toys, models, trains, etc.

Dale Kelley, Ed.
Magazine: Antique Toy World
P.O. Box 34509
Chicago, IL 60641
phone: 312-725-0633
fax: 312-725-3449
A monthly magazine serving toy collectors and dealers; 200 or more pages of all types of toys including antique toys, banks, cast iron toys, tin wind-ups, comic toys, pedal cars; ads, articles, etc.

Rick Polizzi
Magazine: Spin Again
4602 Morse Ave.
Sherman Oaks, CA 91423-3326
Quarterly publication on the world of toys, games, and collectibles.

Sandra Hood, Gen. Mngr.
Newspaper: Antique & Collectables
P.O. Box 13560
El Cajon, CA 92022
phone: 619-593-2925 or 619-593-2933
fax: 619-442-4043
The largest monthly newspaper in Southern California covering the antiques & collectibles industry with focus sections on Nevada and Arizona; 72+ pages; events and show section, feature articles; columns, ads.

Repair Services

Marc Olimpio
Marc Olimpio's Antique Toy Restoration Center
P.O. Box 1505
Wolfeboro, NH 03894
phone: 603-569-6739
Specializes in early handpainted German and French-American tin toys, iron and pressed steel, and cast iron.

Frank Capozzi
6 Devon Rd
Bethpage, NY 11714-1107
phone: 516-938-9765
fax: 516-938-9197
e-mail: FRCapozzi@aol.com
Repairs toys; battery operated, friction, wind-ups; all work guaranteed; send toys for free estimate; return shipping and handling your only cost if no repairs made.

Gary J. Moran
3 Finch Court
Commack, NY 11725-4901
phone: 516-864-9444
Antique toy repairs, including battery operated, friction and wind-up toys; call or write for free estimate; broken toys purchased.

Ron Hanley
Mini-Motors
130 Main
Hobart, NY 13788
phone: 607-538-9926
Repairs pedal cars and automotive toys: repair work, nickel plating,

pressed-steel vehicles such as Tonka and Buddy L.

Joe Freeman
Tin Toy Works
1313 N. 15th St.
Allentown, PA 18102-1068
phone: 610-439-8268
fax: 610-439-1288
Specializes in the repair of tin toys; tin toy autos, boats, merry-go-rounds, etc.; repairs mechanisms, makes missing parts.

Jerry Shook
6528 Cedar Brook Dr.
New Albany, OH 43054-9715
phone: 614-855-7796
fax: 614-855-7796
Makes rubber & plastic replacement parts for toys: wind-ups, robots, space toys, battery operated, etc.; also for dolls; send SASE and $2 for parts list.

Classic Tin Toy Co.
P.O. Box 193
Sheboygan, WI 53082
phone: 414-693-3371
fax: 414-693-8211
Repair and total restoration of all makes of old toys including tin, cast iron and tinplate trains; world's largest manufacturer of toy parts; catalog $10.

Suppliers

Julian Thomas
Thomas Toys
P.O. Box 405
Fenton, MI 48430
phone: 810-629-8707
Carries antique toy car replacement parts; catalog $7.

Action Figures

(see also POPULAR CULTURE, Baby Boomer; TOYS, Playsets; TELEVISION SHOWS & MEMORABILIA, Star Trek)

Clubs/Associations

Classic Action Figure Collector's Club
Magazine: CAFCC Magazine
P.O. Box 2095
Halesite, NY 11743
For collectors of Caption Action, GI Joe, Johnny West, Major Matt Mason, Marvel and DC Super Heroes, Star Trek, Star Wars, Planet of the Apes, Six Million Dollar Man, Bionic Woman, Space 1999, Ultraman, Marx, Ideal, Hasbro, Mattel, etc.

Dealers

John Marshall
P.O. Box 340
Rancocas, NJ 08073-0340
phone: 609-267-6903
Buys, sells, collects action figures.

Brian Rachfal
Craddock's Non-Sports Cards & Collectibles
P.O. Box 7772
San Jose, CA 95150-3766
phone: 408-298-9070 or 408-629-3980
Buys, sells, trades Star Wars action figures, exclusive & regional playsets (Sears, J.C. Penny's, etc.), remote control items, diecast vehicles, gum cards and related memorabilia; also wants rare Star Trek & Indiana Jones toys & figures.

Experts

John Marshall
P.O. Box 340
Rancocas, NJ 08073-0340
phone: 609-267-6903
Author of "Backyard Heroes: Action Figures of the 1970s" (Schiffer); writes articles for "Collecting Toys" magazine.

Periodicals

James Tomlinson, Ed.
Lee Publilcations
Magazine: Action Figure News & Toy Review
556 Monroe Turnpike
Monroe, CT 06468
phone: 203-452-7286
fax: 203-452-0410
AFN is a full size magazine dedicated to the collecting of action figures (plastic figures such as G.I. Joe, Captain Action, Star Wars, etc.) and toys from 1964 to present; articles, ads, shows, etc.

Tom Tumbusch
Tomart Publications
Magazine: Tomart's Action Figure Digest
3300 Encrete Lane
Dayton, OH 45439-1944
phone: 513-294-2250
fax: 513-294-1024
Devoted to action figure collectibles; published bi-monthly.

Mike Shuffield
Phase II Publishing
Magazine: G.I. Joe Patrol
P.O. Box 2362
Hot Springs National Park, AR 71914
phone: 501-525-7149
e-mail: gijp@snider.net
A bi-monthly publication that brings you up-to-date information on action figure and related collectibles from Hasbro, Marx, Mego, Kenner, Mattel and many other action figure series; identify loose accessories; ads.

Action Figures (G.I. Joe)

Clubs/Associations

Brian Savage
G.I. Joe Collectors Club
Newsletter: G.I. Joe Collectors Club Newsletter
12513 Birchfalls Dr.
Raleigh, NC 27614-9675
phone: 800-772-6673 or 919-847-5263
e-mail: bsavage@mastercollector.com
Internet: http://www.mastercollector.com
100s of members worldwide; the source for G.I. Joe information and service; monthly newsletter; send SASE for more information; membership includes subscription to "Master Collector" newspaper and 30-word ad each month.

Mrs. David S. Lane, II
G.I. Joe: Steel Brigade Club
Newsletter: Ammo Box
8362 Lomay Ave.
Westminster, CA 92683-3327
phone: 714-297-5042
International club interested in the 1982-1994 3 3/4" G.I. Joe collection; newsletter published quarterly.

Collectors

Jeff Kowalski
P.O. Box 64
Pluckemin, NJ 07978
phone: 908-526-5033
Wants G.I. Joe: dolls, clothing, accessories, vehicles.

Matthew McKeeby
149 Lake Hill Rd.
Burnt Hills, NY 12027-9573
phone: 518-384-0893
Seeking painted hair G.I. Joes, uniforms, vehicles, and accessories from 1964 to 1969; single pieces or entire collections.

Dealers

John Kachmar
Techno-Fantasy Traders
779 Carissa Dr.
West Palm Beach, FL 33411-3412
phone: 407-798-5978
fax: 407-798-5978
e-mail: kachmar@aol.com

Tina Windeler
Cotswold Collectibles, Inc.
P.O. Box 249
Clinton, WA 98236
phone: 206-579-1223
fax: 206-579-1287
e-mail: cotswold@whidbey.net
Internet: http://www.whidbey.net/~cotswold
Buys and sells 12" G.I. Joe and accessories, including replacement parts such as boots, helmets, soldier equipment, etc.; also a line of high quality custom military 12" figures, "The Elite Brigade."

Experts

Joe Bodnarchuk
G.I. Joe Nostalgia Co.
62 McKinley Ave.
Kenmore, NY 14217-2414
phone: 716-873-0264 or 800-5GI-JOES
fax: 716-873-0264
e-mail: webmaster@bodnarchuk.com
Internet: http://bodnarchuk.com/
  headquarters_quarterly/magazine.html
*G.I. Joe enthusiast and collector since
1964; pays big for mint collections of
any size; quality a must.*

James DeSimone
150 S. Glenoaks Blvd.
Burbank, CA 91510-1314
phone: 818-563-1179
*Buys, collects, appraises, and
specializes in G.I. Joe; author of "The
New Official Identification Guide to
G.I. Joe". Vols. 1, 2, 3.*

Periodicals

Joe Bodnarchuk
Newsletter: Headquarters Quarterly
62 McKinley Ave.
Kenmore, NY 14217-2414
phone: 716-873-0264 or 800-5GI-JOES
fax: 716-873-0264
e-mail: webmaster@bodnarchuk.com
Internet: http://bodnarchuk.com/
  headquarters_quarterly/magazine.html
*A quarterly publication focusing of
G.I. Joe.*

Agriculture Related

(see TOYS, Farm)

Airplane Related

(see also AIRLINE MEMORABILIA,
Models [Desk])

Clubs/Associations

G.R. Webster
International Miniature Aircraft
  Collectors Society
Newsletter: Plane News, The
P.O. Box 845
Greenwich, CT 06836-0845
phone: 203-629-5270
e-mail: grwebster@aol.com
*A quarterly magazine on aviation toys
and models (not plastic kits): diecast,
ID models, travel agency and desk
models, etc.*

Collectors

Perry R. Eichor
703 N. Almond Dr.
Simpsonville, SC 29681-3453
phone: 803-967-8770
*Wants aircraft toys and literature;
member of Antique Toy Collectors of
America.*

Dealers

Dan Wells
Dan Wells Antique Toys
7008 Main St.
Westport, KY 40077
phone: 502-225-9925
*Wants to buy all miniature/toy
aircraft, especially travel agency and
factory models.*

Experts

G.R. Webster
P.O. Box 845
Greenwich, CT 06836-0845
phone: 203-629-5270
e-mail: grwebster@aol.com
*Interested in airplane toys and
models: diecast toys, ID models, travel
agency and desk models, etc.*

Arcade

Experts

Al Aune
Mannolla Publishing
4441 Shari Ann Lane
Minneapolis, MN 55443-3461
phone: 612-560-4290 or 612-421-5151
fax: 612-421-3618
*Author of "Arcade Toys"; contains
hard-to-find information about dating
Arcade toys.*

Automotive

(see AUTOMOBILIA; TOYS, Cars)

Battery Operated

Collectors

Beau S. Cassity
Kid in Me, The
9502 Avenel Rd.
Silver Spring, MD 20903-2308
phone: 301-434-8293
*Specializes in pre and post WWII toys,
especially battery operated; wants to
buy all types of battery operated toys,
including toys for parts; wants plastic
toys and Japanese tin wind-ups.*

Stuart Stein
P.O. Box 303
Frederick, MD 21705-0303
phone: 301-663-8369
fax: 301-663-8202
e-mail: steincpa@ix.netcom.com
*Wants to buy Japanese battery toys
from the 1960s.*

Lee H. Mitchell
175 E. Delaware, #8210
Chicago, IL 60611-1732
phone: 800-869-7869 or 312-337-3123
fax: 312-266-7982
*Leading collector wants to buy/trade
mainly the less common figural
battery operated toys (but not
transportation toys); some wind-ups;
collections welcomed, as are calls
from other collectors.*

Experts

Don Hultzman
5026 Sleepy Hollow Rd.
Medina, OH 44256-8309
phone: 330-225-2668
*Buys/sells pre-1970 battery operated
and wind-up toys; wants toys in any
condition; also expert repairs -
undetectable & guaranteed.*

Repair Services

Dr. Day
Toy Doctor, The
RR 1 Box 202
Red Creek, NY 13143-9801
phone: 315-754-8846 or 315-754-6238
e-mail: TDTSNUT@aol.com
*Repairs battery operated toys; robots
and space toys a specialty; dealer
discounts; caring for all battery
operated toys; "The Toy Doctor" and
"TDTSNUT" are registered
trademarks.*

Randy King
211 Park Ave.
New Castle, IN 47362
phone: 317-529-9297

BB Guns

(see also AIRGUNS)

Clubs/Associations

Jim Buskirk
Toy Gun Collectors of America
Newsletter: Toy Gun Collectors of
  America Newsletter
3009 Oleander Ave.
San Marcos, CA 92069-6128
phone: 760-599-1054
*Focuses on pre-WWII American cap
guns and spring/air BB guns (non-
pellet guns or other high powered air
guns); newsletter published quarterly:
photos, information, articles; also free
want ads for subscribers; quarterly
newsletter.*

Collectors

Terry Burger
2323 Lincoln
Beatrice, NE 68310-3306
phone: 402-228-2797
*Wants pre-1915, preferably cast iron-
framed guns: Daisy, Atlas, Matchless,
New Rapid, etc.*

Mike Burleson
12048 CR 1168
Tyler, TX 75703
phone: 903-561-9343
*Wants old or unusual American BB
guns by Markham, King, Heilprin,
Daisy or others.*

Clay Tontz
4043 Nora
Covina, CA 91722
phone: 818-338-99767
Wants pre-1930 BB guns.

Experts

Jim Buskirk
3009 Oleander Ave.
San Marcos, CA 92069-6128
phone: 760-599-1054
*Buys, sells, collects and specializes in
BB guns and cap guns.*

Museums/Libraries

Daisy International Air Gun Museum
P.O. Box 220
Rogers, AR 72757
phone: 501-636-1200

Beanie Babies

Collectors

Bette Page
Front Parlor, The
300 Cemetery Rd.
Oakland, IL 61943
phone: 217-346-3533 or 800-346-5996
fax: 217-346-3533
e-mail: frntprlr@advant.com

Experts

Peggy Gallagher
80 Burr Ridge Parkway, STe. 123
Hinsdale, IL 60521
phone: 847-298-2001
*Author of "The Beanie Baby
Phenomenon."*

Periodicals

Newsletter: Beanie Baby Times
P.O. Box 233
Eagon, MN 55121

Bell

Collectors

Dr. Greg Zemenick
Dr. "Z"
1350 Kirts, Ste. 160
Troy, MI 48084-4830
phone: 248-642-8129 or 248-244-9430
fax: 248-244-9495
e-mail: DrZzeezz@aol.com
Internet: http://www.drzzeezzi.com
Wants bell toys.

Boats & Outboards

Collectors

Bill Hall
15 Conrad
West Hartford, CT 06107
Wants to buy toy outboard motors.

Rich Pumphrey
1001 Fairwinds Dr.
Annapolis, MD 21401
phone: 410-757-3795
*Wants toy outboard motors & boats:
late '50s to mid-60s, K+O Fleetline,
Craftmaster, Mercury, Evinrude,
Johnson, etc.*

Brent Simmons
3212 Severn Wharf Rd.
Hayes, VA 23072
phone: 804-642-2076
Wants to buy toy outboard boat motors; any condition.

Jack Browning
214 16th St. N.W.
Roanoke, VA 24017-5516
phone: 703-890-5083 or 703-982-8680
fax: 703-342-1283

Richard Gronowski
140 N. Garfield Ave.
Traverse City, MI 49686-2802
phone: 616-941-2111
Wants to buy toy metal outboard boat motors: Gale, Oliver, Johnson, Mercury, Scott, Evinrude, Wen-Mac, Sea-Fury.

Bubble Blowers

Collectors

Judith Schulz
533 Milwaukee Ave.
Burlington, WI 53105-1232
phone: 414-763-3946
Wants old bubble blowers and related packages, literature, drawings and pictures of bubble blowing; conducts the International Bubble Blowing Extravaganza Event.

Canadian

Clubs/Associations

Betty Holland
CTM Farm Toy & Collectors Club
Magazine: Canadian Toy Mania
P.O. Box 489
Rocanville
Saskatchewan S0A 3L0 Canada
phone: 306-645-4566
fax: 306-645-4566
Focuses on farm toys and dolls.

Cannons

(see also CANNONS; FIREWORKS MEMORABILIA; TOYS, Cap Guns)

Periodicals

Ray Brandes
Ray-Vin Publishing Co.
Newsletter: Toy Cannon News, The
P.O. Box 2052 - M
Norcross, GA 30071-2052
phone: 404-662-8856 or 404-476-8259
fax: 404-441-1030
Focuses on toy and small cannons: powder, cap, cartridge, gas, glass, carbide, etc.

Suppliers

Conestoga Company
P.O. Box 405
Bethlehem, PA 18016
Source for authentic Big-Bang cannons and parts.

Cap Guns

Clubs/Associations

Jim Buskirk
Toy Gun Collectors of America
Newsletter: Toy Gun Collectors of America Newsletter
3009 Oleander Ave.
San Marcos, CA 92069-6128
phone: 760-599-1054
Focuses on pre-WWII American cap guns and spring/air BB guns (non-pellet guns or other high powered air guns); newsletter published quarterly: photos, information, articles; also free want ads for subscribers; quarterly newsletter.

Collectors

George Fougere
67 East St.
North Grafton, MA 01536-1830
phone: 508-839-2701
Interested in cast iron and die cast cap pistols; no air rifles, please.

George Fougere
67 East St.
North Grafton, MA 01536-1830
phone: 508-839-2701

Ralph Perlberg
1 Strawberry hill
Andover, MA 01810

Bob Williamson
190 Washington St.
East Stroudsburg, PA 18301-2819
phone: 717-421-6957 or 717-421-8550
fax: 717-421-8605
Sells and buys rare and common cast iron cap guns, bombs, canes, cannons, BB guns (1860s to 1950s); also wants caps, boxes, catalogs, literature, etc.

Terry Burger
2323 Lincoln
Beatrice, NE 68310-3306
phone: 402-228-2797

Bill Hamburg
P.O. Box 1305
Woodland Hills, CA 91365-1305
phone: 818-346-1269
fax: 818-346-0215
Wants to buy excellent to mint-in-box only; also buys cap bun boxes.

Experts

Jim Schleyer
P.O. Box 243
Burke, VA 22015-0243
phone: 703-569-4478
Wants to buy older toy and cap pistols and holsters; will answer inquiries that are accompanied by SASE; has written extensively on the subject of toy guns; author of "Backyard Buckaroos - Collecting Western Toy Guns."

Charles W. Best
11523 Pine Valley Dr.
Franktown, CO 80116-8708
phone: 303-660-2318
Collects 19th century cap guns; author of "Cast Iron Toy Guns & Capshooters"; advanced collector interested in early toy guns.

Cars

(see also AUTOMOBILIA; MODELS, Cars; TOYS, Diecast)

Clubs/Associations

Peter H. Foss
Toy Car Collectors Club
Newsletter: Toy Car Magazine
33290 W. 14 Mile Rd. #454
West Bloomfield, MI 48322-3549
phone: 810-682-0272
fax: 810-682-5782
A club for collectors of toy cars such as Dinky, Corgi, Matchbox, Hot Wheels, Solido, Norev, Siku, Schuco, Gama, Rio, Auburn, Tootsietoy, Maisto, Ertl, banks, NASCAR, Tomica, Diapet, etc.

Antique Miniature Race Car Collectors
Newsletter: Antique Miniature Race Car Collectors Newsletter
10337 S. Cook
Oak Lawn, IL 60453-4630
phone: 708-425-4463
fax: 708-425-263
Quarterly newsletter.

Collectors

David K. Bausch
252 N. 7th St.
Allentown, PA 18102-4024
phone: 610-432-3355
fax: 610-820-9368
Major collector of automobile related material, especially automobile art.

Richard McCoy
2719 Lakeview Ave.
St. Joseph, MI 49085
Wants toy cars and boats 1900-1955; tin, pressed steel, wood.

Dealers

Trader Rick's Collectible Toy Cars
P.O. Box 161
Newark, IL 60541
phone: 815-695-9484
Wants to buy toy cars and model cars; also built or unbuilt car kits.

Experts

Steve Butler
2696 Brookmar Dr.
York, PA 17404-9489
phone: 717-792-4936
Buys, collects, appraises, specializes in automotive toys (cars and trucks) 1920-1960: iron, steel, cast metal, plastic; author & seller of "Promotionals", a '34-'83 promotional toy car and truck reference and price book; $14.65 ppd.

Clarence Young
302 Reems Creek
Weaverville, NC 28787-9792
phone: 704-645-5243
fax: 704-645-5243
Specializes in automotive promotional toys, mostly pot metal or plastic; also sells "AUTOQUOTES", a promotional toy car and truck reference and price book; $14.65 ppd.

Periodicals

Challenge Publications
Magazine: Car Toys
7950 Deering Ave.
Canoga Park, CA 91304
phone: 818-887-0550
Monthly magazine covers model cars of all types, sizes, materials, and vintage; also covers automobilia from automotive art and racing collectibles to pedal cars, porcelain signs, neon clocks, apparel, literature, gas pumps, etc.

Cars (Miniature)

Periodicals

Model Collectors Warehouse
Magazine: Model Collectors Digest
P.O. Box 8943
Waukegan, IL 60079-8943
Access to 1000s of out-of-production kits, promos & automotive toys, free ads, Model car club directory & news, swap meet calendar, etc.

Cars (Racing)

Book Sellers

Kevin Timothy
What It Is! Publishing
P.O. Box 1373
Linwood, PA 19061
phone: 302-654-3610
e-mail: Asperila@ix.netcom.com
Book publisher with a main focus on slot cars; five titles.

Clubs/Associations

Dave Cutler
H.O. Slot Racing Association
Magazine: HOSRA Magazine
3, The Strand, Starcross
Near Exeter
Devon EX6 8PP, U.K.

Bob Beers
H.O. Slot Car Collecting & Racing Club
Newsletter: HOSCCRC Newsletter
P.O. Box 255
Monroe, CT 06468-0255
phone: 203-261-3467
For the slot car collector, racer and enthusiast.

Collectors

Rod Thurgood
11 Perrins Lane
West Kempsey
New Sout Wales 2440 Australia
phone: (02) 6562 8209
fax: (02) 6562 6319
Wants 1:64 scale (HO size) model diecast, plastic, slot cars that depict the 1:1 scale Dodge Daytona, Plymouth Superbird range of vehicles.

Dave Lockwood
50 Lakeview Dr.
Norwalk, CT 06850
phone: 203-847-2815
Wants to buy electric scale racing cars by Aurora, Cox, Monogram, Revell; any scale - H.O., 1/32nd, 1/24th.

Gabriel Bogdonoff
46 Porter Rd.
Howell, NJ 07731-8614
phone: 908-363-4064
Wants toy race cars, gas powered, any condition; also wants big tin friction race cars and Smith Miller trucks in any condition.

Rick Burneson
435 1/2 South Orange St.
Orange, CA 92866-1911
phone: 714-639-4846
Internet: http://pages.prodigy.com/housa/index.htm
Collects and races H.O. scale electric slot cars.

Dealers

Robert Budano
Bud;s HO Cars Inc.
9 Barger St.
Cortlandt, NY 10566
phone: 914-526-4950
fax: 914-526-4950

John A. Clark
Slot Car Johnnie's
1195 Crestview St.
Reynoldsburg, OH 43068-1365
phone: 614-864-TJET
fax: 614-864-2800
e-mail: afx1afx@aol.com
Buys, sells, collects H.O. slot cars from the 1960s and 1970s; carries a large supply of slot cars in all scales as well as parts and accessories from used to Mint-In-Box; author of "HO Slot Car Identification and Price Guide."

Joel Vanderkork
Lots of Slots
503 Boal St.
Cincinnati, OH 45210
phone: 513-621-9353
Buys, sells, auctions, collects vintage slot cars.

Experts

John A. Clark
Slot Car Johnnie's
1195 Crestview St.
Reynoldsburg, OH 43068-1365
phone: 614-864-TJET
fax: 614-864-2800
e-mail: afx1afx@aol.com
Buys, sells, collects H.O. slot cars from the 1960s and 1970s; carries a large supply of slot cars in all scales as well as parts and accessories from used to Mint-In-Box; author of "HO Slot Car Identification and Price Guide."

On-Line Services

Joe Bodnarchuk
HO Motoring & Racing Slotcar Magazine
62 McKinley Ave.
Kenmore, NY 14217-2414
phone: 716-873-0264
fax: 716-873-0264
e-mail: webmaster@bodnarchuk.com
Internet: http://wwwbodnarchuck.com/ho_slotcar/motoring.html
The only on-line magazine devoted to the vintage slotcar collecting hobby.

Periodicals

Rod Thurgood
Newsletter: Australian Slot Car Review
11 Perrins Lane
West Kempsey
New Sout Wales 2440 Australia
phone: (02) 6562 8209
fax: (02) 6562 6319
Published four times per year and offering a comprehensive coverage of slot car racing and collecting in Australia; minimum of 36 pages; informative articles and lots of photos; free ads to subscribers; write for info.

Nick Sismey
Magazine: Derby H.O. Racing
80 Chaddesden Lane
Chaddesden
Derby DE21 6LN, U.K.
Monthly magazine.

Magazine: H.O. Cars
P.O. Box 255
Monroe, CT 06468

Art Zabrecky
Newsletter: Slot Car Trader
P.O. Box 1868
Elyria, OH 44036-1868
phone: 216-322-7415
A newsletter dedicated to the 1/64 scale H.O. slot cars; collecting and racing news, new product reviews, subscriber-submitted articles; buy-sell-trade ad section.

Joel Vanderkork
Newsletter: Lots of Slots
503 Boal St.
Cincinnati, OH 45210
phone: 513-621-9353
A professionally produced monthly magazine for vintage HO slot car collectors.

Rick Burneson
Newsletter: H.O. USA Newsletter
435 1/2 South Orange St.
Orange, CA 92866-1911
phone: 714-639-4846
Internet: http://pages.prodigy.com/housa/index.htm
For H.O. scale slot cars; free ads with membership.

Cast Iron

Clubs/Associations

Paul McGinnis
Cast Iron Toy Collectors of America
Newsletter: Iron Filings
1340 Market St.
Long Beach, CA 90805
Focuses on American cast iron toys.

Repair Services

Arnie Prince
23 Norh Houston Ln.
Lodi, CA 95240
phone: 209-334-6101
Cast iron repair and restoration, cast iron welding, fabrication, and painting; buys cast iron toys and parts.

Character

(see also CHARACTER COLLECTIBLES; DISNEY COLLECTIBLES)

Auction Services

Martin Krim
New England Auction Gallery
P.O. Box 2273
Peabody, MA 01960-7273
phone: 508-535-3140
fax: 508-535-7522
e-mail: dlkrim@star.net
Internet: http://www.old_toys.com
Conduct mail-bid auctions with full color illustrated catalogs; specializes in sales of Disney, TV and cartoon items from 1920-1970: toys, wind-ups, robots, space toys.

Collectors

Martin Krim
P.O. Box 2273
Peabody, MA 01960-7273
phone: 508-535-3140
fax: 508-535-7522
e-mail: dlkrim@star.net
Internet: http://www.old_toys.com
Wants tin & celluloid toys from Japan, Germany, etc.; character items from TV shows, westerns, stars from the 50-60s; robot & space toys; plastic wind-up toys.

Dealers

Leila Dunbar
Dunbar's Gallery
76 Haven St.
Milford, MA 01757-3821
phone: 508-634-8697 or 508-634-8097
fax: 508-634-8698
Mail order Americana - no reproductions; buys, sells and specializes in vintage character and comic toys, banks, advertising, automobilia, and Halloween related items.

Dennis & Mary Luby
Casey's Collectible Corner
HCR 30 Box 30
No. Blenheim, NY 12131
phone: 607-588-6464
Buys and sells collectible toys: comic characters, TV shows and personalities; also space and monster toys, sports collectibles, etc.

Richard Trautwein
Toy's N Such
437 Dawson St.
Sault Sainte Marie, MI 49783-2119
phone: 906-635-0356
Wants wind-up, battery, tin, pull, cast iron toys: Barney Google, Charlie Chaplin, Mickey Mouse, Donald Duck, Popeye, etc.

Character (Mickey Mouse)

Collectors

Debra Krim
P.O. Box 2273
Peabody, MA 01960-7273
phone: 508-535-3140
fax: 508-535-7522
e-mail: dlkrim@star.net
Internet: http://www.old_toys.com
Wants 1930s Mickey Mouse items: empty boxes, figurals, wind-ups, bisque figurines, games, jewelry, etc.

Comic

(see TOYS, Character)

Computer Programs For

Man./Prod./Dist.

Robert Sullenberger
Sully Enterprises
Program: Toy Collector, The
3107 Marlin Dr.
Longmont, CO 80503-7892
phone: 303-651-2074
A Windows program; generates reports based on brand name, scale size, etc.; maintains the cost and the appraisal value for each toy.

Construction Sets

Collectors

Wally Krocsko
P.O. Box 307
Atlasburg, PA 15004-0307
phone: 412-947-5671
Buys, sells, trades construction sets

(Erector, Meccano, American Model Builder); must enclose a LSASE to get a reply to buy/sell/trade inquiries; please call evenings.

George Wetzel
221 Hickory St.
Peotone, IL 60468-9108
phone: 708-747-5841
Wants Erector sets, Meccano, Anchor stone blocks, Arkirecto, any old building toys.

Arlan Coffman
1223 Wilshire Blvd., Ste. 275
Santa Monica, CA 90403
phone: 310-453-2507
Wants architectural construction toys: Erector sets, building blocks, villages, Lincoln Logs & figures, etc.

Dealers

John Maleski
Space Toys
1846 N. Melborn St.
Dearborn, MI 48128
phone: 313-277-0751

Construction Sets (Blocks)

Clubs/Associations

George Hardy
Anchor Block Foundation
Magazine: Anchor House News
1670 Hawkwood Ct.
Charlottesville, VA 22901
phone: 804-295-4863
fax: 804-295-4898
e-mail: georgeh@comet.net
Internet: http://www.comet.net/personal/georgeh
Anchor House Foundation is a club whose members have interests in and build with Anchor Blocks; quarterly newsletter.

Collectors

Paul Neuman
173 Chrystie St.
New York, NY 10021
phone: 212-861-0303 or 212-734-4274
fax: 212-780-9338
Wants to buy architectural toys, building block sets; wood, paper on wood, stone, metal, etc.

Dealers

Arley Pett
Arley L. Pett Antiques
12 Beach Rd.
Gloucester, MA 09130-3214
phone: 508-283-2612
e-mail: apett92117@aol.com
Buys, sells and collects Anchor stone blocks and puzzles.

Construction Sets (Erector)

Clubs/Associations

Bill Harrison, Founder
A.C. Gilbert Heritage Society
Newsletter: A.C. Gilbert Heritage Society Newsletter
16 Palmer St.
Medford, MA 02155
phone: 617-395-5569
e-mail: Pandyscol@aol.com
Internet: http://www.pandys.com
For A.C. Gilbert toy enthusiasts except American Flyer trains; Erector sets, Meccano a specialty; send SASE for news and information; newsletter published quarterly; over 400 members.

Frank Hare, Ed.
American Flyer Collectors Club
Magazine: Collector, The
P.O. Box 13269
Pittsburgh, PA 15243-0269
phone: 412-221-2250
fax: 412-221-8402
For collectors of A.C. Gilbert Co. American Flyer and other toy trains (all pre-1966 manufacturers); also contains information about Gilbert Erector sets.

Joel Perlin
Southern California Meccano & Erector Club
Newsletter: Southern CA Meccano & Erector Club Newsletter
1111 Acapulco St.
Oxnard, CA 93035
phone: 805-985-5498
Publishes a very good quarterly newsletter; holds regional meetings.

Collectors

Jay Smith
5 Whittier Rd.
Lexington, MA 02173
phone: 617-861-7547
e-mail: ghseditor@aol.com
Editor of The A.C. Gilbert Heritage Society Newsletter.

Larry Yesner
285 Orchid Rd.
Levittown, NY 11756
phone: 516-579-7040
Wants Erector and Mecanno sets; preferably the larger sets in mint or excellent condition.

James Mietlicki
146 Ridge Park Ave.
Cheektowaga, NY 14211
phone: 716-896-8047

Elmer Wagner
Wagner & Sons Inc.
28 E. Willow St.
Carlisle, PA 17013
phone: 717-243-3539 or 717-243-3539
Purchasing A.C. Gilbert Erector set parts, manuals, catalogs, dealer items, etc.; also purchasing construction sets by Meccano, Marklin, Ives, Bing and Metalcraft.

Dealers

Paul & Nancy Piontkowski
Pandy's Collectibles
16 Palmer St.
Medford, MA 02155
phone: 617-395-5569
e-mail: Pandyscol@aol.com
Internet: http://www.pandys.com
Buy, sell, restore Erector sets (1913-1963); also buys and sells parts, labels and manual.

Bill & Judy Harrison
16 Palmer St.
Medford, MA 02155
phone: 617-395-5569
e-mail: Pandyscol@aol.com
Internet: http://www.pandys.com
Buys, sells, trades all A.C. Gilbert toys except American Flyer trains; also restores Erector, Meccano and others; offers electroplating services.

Jay Robinson
Chicago Kid
P.O. Box 529
Deerfield, IL 60015-0529
phone: 847-940-7547 or 847-945-8691
fax: 847-945-1965
Buys construction sets; also wants electric trains of all types, toys, and robots.

Experts

Al Sternagle
RD 2 Box 400
Hollidaysburg, PA 16648-9230
phone: 814-695-7012
Sent $11.50 for "Erector Parts Illustrated," $7.50 for "Erector Advertising"; author of several articles about Erector sets; send LSASE for complete list of publications available.

Bill Bean
439 Claxton Glen Ct.
Kettering, OH 45429
phone: 937-435-6196 or 937-439-2600
e-mail: ErectrBean@aol.com
Author of "Greenberg Guide to Erector"; wants to buy Erector sets by A.C. Gilbert, Ives, and Bing; especially large sets in wood boxes and chests; also store displays and advertising pieces.

Museums/Libraries

Stephen Ebinger
Eli Whitney Museum
915 Whitney Ave.
Hamden, CT 06517
phone: 203-777-1833
fax: 203-777-1229
Dedicated to helping children learn by doing; uses Gilbert's construction and chemistry ideas in their educational program.

Repro. Sources

Tiger Enterprises
379 Summer St.
Plantsville, CT 06479
Makes reproduction A.C. Gilbert Erector parts and sets.

Suppliers

Elmer Wagner
Wagner & Sons Inc.
28 E. Willow St.
Carlisle, PA 17013
phone: 717-243-3539 or 717-243-3539
The oldest and largest stock source of original Erector parts, manuals, catalogs and sets; send SASE for catalog.

Crayola Crayons

Museums/Libraries

Crayola Hall of Fame, Binney & Smith
1100 Church Lane
P.O. Box 431
Easton, PA 18044
phone: 215-559-2632

Diecast

(see also BANKS [MODERN]; MODELS; MODELS, Cars; MODELS, Trucks & Equipment [Winross]; TOYS, Cars; TOYS, Ertl Replicas)

Appraisers

Fred J. Hill, Jr., ISA CAPP
Koty Professional Auctioneers, LLC
P.O. Box 625
Freehold, NJ 07728-0625
phone: 732-751-0504
fax: 732-751-9190
e-mail: 75754.1156@compuserve.com
Specializes in diecast models and NASCAR collectibles.

Clubs/Associations

Martin Uden
Maidenhead Static Model Club
Newsletter: Wheel Bearings
The Old Marquis, London Road
Wollaston
Northants NN9 7QP, U.K.
phone: 01256-819141
Diecast collectors club; meets 3rd Monday of month; organizes Windsor International swap meet in January, June, September; visitors to UK welcome to attend club meetings.

Diecast Exchange Club
Newsletter: Diecast Exchange Club Newsletter
P.O. Box 1066
Pinellas Park, FL 33281

Peter H. Foss
Toy Car Collectors Club
Newsletter: Toy Car Magazine
33290 W. 14 Mile Rd. #454
West Bloomfield, MI 48322-3549
phone: 810-682-0272
fax: 810-682-5782
A club for collectors of toy cars such as Dinky, Corgi, Matchbox, Hot Wheels, Solido, Norev, Siku, Schuco, Gama, Rio, Auburn, Tootsietoy, Maisto, Ertl, banks, NASCAR, Tomica, Diapet, etc.

Larry Walker
Lightning Hot Club
P.O. Box 35077
Las Vegas, NV 89133
phone: 702-363-9642

Mr. Dana Johnson
Diecast Toy Collectors Association
Newsletter: Diecast Toy Collector
P.O. Box 1824
Bend, OR 97701-1824
phone: 541-382-8410
e-mail: toynutz@teleport.com
Internet: http://www.teleport/~toynutz
Provides discounts on collector price guides, information on new products, model variations and values, resources for buying and selling, toy shows around the country; newsletter published monthly.

Dana Johnson
Diecast Toy Collectors Association
P.O. Box 1824
Bend, OR 97709-1824
e-mail: toynutz@teleport.com
Internet: http://www.teleport.com/~toynutz
For collectors of of die cast toys and model cars.

Collectors

Carl Natter
1760 Termino, Ste. 300
Long Beach, CA 90804
phone: 310-597-4351
fax: 310-498-9513
Wants to buy cast iron toys from the 1930s, Tootsie Toy and other diecast cars and trucks.

Dealers

Paul Allaire
Toy Time Specialty Die Cast Vehicles
115-125 Laurel St.
Fitchburg, MA 01420
phone: 508-827-5261

Toys for Collectors
P.O. Box 1406
North Attleboro, MA 02763
phone: 508-695-0588 or 508-695-6966
If you collect models of cars, trucks, fire trucks, construction equipment, cranes, buses, race cars, NASCARS, etc. this is the source for better quality 1/43 scale models as well as 1/50, 1/18 and 1/14 scale models.

Donald Amnott
Small Wheels of America
34 Huckleberry Lane
Southington, CT 06489
phone: 800-258-7776
fax: 860-621-8885
Diecast cars, trucks, planes and blimps by Ertl, First Gear, Spec-Cast, PEM; oil company tankers by Hess, Texaco, Servco and many others.

Apple Patch Toys
7 Hyatt Rd.
Branchville, NJ 07826-4139
phone: 201-702-0008
fax: 201-702-1699
Specializes in diecast collectibles: trucks, cycles, planes, banks; by Arch, Inc., First Gear, Scale Models, Liberty Classics, Ertl.

Mark Henderson
Specialty Diecast Co.
370 Miller Rd.
Medford, NJ 08055
phone: 609-654-8484 or 609-654-2281
fax: 609-654-2281
Sells new diecast toys: Dinky, Corgi, Matchbox, Ertl, etc.

Kid Pontiac
P.O. Box 70
Blauvelt, NY 10913

Neil H. Waldmann
Neil's Wheels, Inc.
P.O. Box 354
Old Bethpage, NY 11804-0354
phone: 516-293-9659
fax: 516-420-0483
Authorized Matchbox collectibles center; send SA2SE for list of 2000 models and brochure on Magic Box Display System.

Francis "Lash" Lerew
325 Scenic Drive
Mechanicsburg, PA 17055

Diecast Toy Exchange
P.O. Box 268
York, PA 17405
phone: 717-846-8097

Steve Mullican
325 Elm Ave.
North Wales, PA 19454
phone: 215-699-2393
Matchbox, Dinky, Corgi, early Lesney products.

Kiddie Kar Kollectibles
1161 Perry St.
Reading, PA 19604
phone: 610-375-4780

Dan Wells
Dan Wells Antique Toys
7008 Main St.
Westport, KY 40077
phone: 502-225-9925
Wants to buy Hot Wheels, Dinky, Matchbox, Johnny Lightning, Corgi, and Lesney cars; mint condition only.

Experts

Richard L. Heuser
Heuser Publishing Div. of Heuser Enterprises
508 Clapson Rd.
P.O. Box 300
West Winfield, NY 13491-0300
phone: 315-822-4804
fax: 315-822-4804
e-mail: toybanks@concentric.net
Internet: http://www.concentric.net/~toybanks
Buys, collects, appraises and specializes in modern collectible toy banks and diecast toys.

Douglas R. Kelly
17920 Ashton Club Way
Ashton, MD 20861
phone: 301-570-2206
Author of "The Die Cast Price Guide" (Antique Trader Books, 1997); Matchbox, Hot Wheels, Corgi, Tootsietoys, Winross, Schuco, Majorette, Burago, Danbury Mint, etc. from 1946 to present.

Mr. Dana Johnson
Dana Johnson Enterprises
P.O. Box 1824
Bend, OR 97701-1824
phone: 541-382-8410
e-mail: toynutz@teleport.com
Internet: http://www.teleport/~toynutz
Matchbox collector since 1961; author of "Matchbox Bluebook - A Collector's Guide to Current Prices"; "Hot Wheels Blue Book"; "Collecting Majorette Toys"; "Matchbox Toys, 1948 to 1993," available from author.

Misc. Services

Diecast Exchange, The
27 Oziers, Elsenham
Bishops Stortford
Herts. CM22 6LD, U.K.
A service to sell your surplus models directly to other collectors.

Periodicals

Raymond G. Strutt
Newspaper: Collectors Gazette
18 Calvert Close
West Park Heights, Uckfield
East Sussex TN22 2BZ, U.K.
phone: +44 (0) 1825 768776
fax: +44 (0) 1825 760600
e-mail: cliente@icn.co.uk
Internet: http://www.icn.co.uk/cg.html
Published 10 times per year for toy and model collectors worldwide; covers tinplate toys, obsolete and modern diecast cars (Corgi, Dinky, Matchbox, EFE, Lledo, Days Gone, etc.) and models, trains, airplanes, ships, dolls, etc.

Magazine: National Toy Connection
P.O. Box 651
Brigantine, NJ 08203-0615
phone: 800-704-1232
Specializes in transportation and promotional toys from the 1950s to 1980s; First Gear, Ertl, scale model

die cast replicas, Tonka, Structo, Buddy L, Migetoy, Matchbox, etc.

Richard L. Heuser
Heuser Publishing Div. of Heuser Enterprises
Price Guide: Heuser's Price Guide to Official Collectible Banks
508 Clapson Rd.
P.O. Box 300
West Winfield, NY 13491-0300
phone: 315-822-4804
fax: 315-822-4804
e-mail: toybanks@concentric.net
Internet: http://www.concentric.net/~toybanks
Quarterly price guide features Ertl, First Gear, Liberty Classics, Spec Cast, Action Racing Collectibles, Gearbox, Crown Premium/Vees Collectibles, DG Productions and others; listed by name, no., quantity, color, year made and value.

Richard L. Heuser
Heuser Publishing Div. of Heuser Enterprises
Newsletter: Heuser's Quarterly Collectible Diecast Newsletter
508 Clapson Rd.
P.O. Box 300
West Winfield, NY 13491-0300
phone: 315-822-4804
fax: 315-822-4804
e-mail: toybanks@concentric.net
Internet: http://www.concentric.net/~toybanks
Focuses on modern diecast collectible banks and custom imprinted replicas; new issues; articles of interest to collectors; listing of dealers and manufacturers; listing of upcoming toy shows.

Dan Laurence
Spec Cast
Newsletter: Spec Tacular News
P.O. Box 368
Dyersville, IA 52040
phone: 319-875-8706
fax: 319-875-8056
A quarterly focusing on farm toys and collectibles.

Jeff Atkinson
Newsletter: Traders Horn
1903 Schoettler Valley Rd.
Chesterfield, MO 63017-5203
phone: 314-532-3871
The oldest, largest bi-monthly periodical dedicated to the sales, trading of diecast toy vehicles, promotional models, model kits; obsolete, rare, current automotive & other transportation miniatures and related memorabilia; all scales.

Repro. Sources

Dan Laurence
Spec Cast
P.O. Box 368
Dyersville, IA 52040
phone: 319-875-8706
fax: 319-875-8056
Manufacturer or discast replica belt buckles, banks, tractors, trucks,

vehicle and airplane banks and non-banks, limited editions, and specialty items.

Diecast (Brooklin)

Clubs/Associations

Roger Mateo
San Francisco Bay Brooklin Club
Newsletter: SFBBC Newsletter
P.O. Box 61018
Palo Alto, CA 94306-6018
phone: 415-591-9580
fax: 415-321-5232
Newsletter published every other month; current information on Brooklin models, upcoming specials; has international club membership.

Diecast (Corgi)

Clubs/Associations

Corgie Collectors Club of the Corgi
Heritage Centre
53 York St.
Heywood, Hochdale
Lancs OL10 4NR, U.K.
phone: 01706 365812
e-mail: corgi@zen.co.uk
Internet: http://www.zen.co.uk/home/
page/corgi/#CollectorsClub

Corgi Collector Club
14 Industrial Rd.
Pequannock, NJ 07440
phone: 201-694-5006

Diecast (Hot Wheels)

Clubs/Associations

Northland Hot Wheels Club
661 Bridle Ridge Rd.
Eagan, MN 55123

Dealers

Rich Blaut
9533 W. 7 Mile Rd.
Northville, MI 48167-9106
phone: 810-347-3227
Buys, sells, trades Hotwheels by Mattel; cars, Sizzlers, Gran Toros.

Periodicals

Mike Strauss
Newsletter: Hot Wheels Newsletter
26 Madera Ave.
San Carlos, CA 94070-2937
phone: 415-591-6482
fax: 415-591-7935
e-mail: hwnwesltr@aol.com
Internet: http://www.members.aol.com/
hwnewslrt
Published bi-monthly.

Diecast (Johnny Lightning)

Clubs/Associations

Lisa Greco
Johnny Lightning Club
Newsletter: NewsFlash
P.O. Box 248
Cassopolis, MI 49031-0248
phone: 800-MANTIS-8 or 219-232-0300
Internet: http://
www.johnnylightning.com
For collectors of Johnny Lightning cars.

Dealers

Paul Allaire
Toy Time Specialty Die Cast Vehicles
115-125 Laurel St.
Fitchburg, MA 01420
phone: 508-827-5261

Diecast (Matchbox)

Clubs/Associations

Rita Schneider, Mem.
Matchbox International Collectors
Association, The
Newsletter: MICA Newsletter
P.O. Box 28072
Waterloo
Ontario N2L 6J8 Canada
phone: 519-885-0529
fax: 519-885-1902
Formed to stimulate interest among collectors of Matchbox Diecast Models and Matchbox related items as manufactured originally by Lesney Products Ltd. and later by Matchbox Toys.

Bob Fellows
American-International Matchbox
Collectors & Exchange Club
Newsletter: A.I.M. Newsletter
532 Chestnut St.
Lynn, MA 01904-2717
phone: 617-595-4135
fax: 617-595-4007
Monthly newsletter.

Charles Mack
Matchbox U.S.A.
Newsletter: Matchbox U.S.A. Newsletter
62 Saw Mill Rd.
Durham, CT 06422-2602
phone: 860-349-1655
fax: 860-349-3256
e-mail: mtchboxusa@aol.com
Conducts annual conventions and shows; newsletter published monthly.

Everett Marshall
Matchbox Collectors Club
Newsletter: Matchbox Collectors Club
Newsletter
P.O. Box 977
Newfield, NJ 08344
phone: 609-697-2800
fax: 609-697-0762
Newsletter published quarterly.

Mike Appnel
Pennsylvania Matchbox Club
11-61 Perry St.
Reading, PA 19604-2046

Collectors

Charles Mack
62 Saw Mill Rd.
Durham, CT 06422-2602
phone: 860-349-1655
fax: 860-349-3256
e-mail: mtchboxusa@aol.com

Experts

Charles Mack
62 Saw Mill Rd.
Durham, CT 06422-2602
phone: 860-349-1655
fax: 860-349-3256
e-mail: mtchboxusa@aol.com
Author of "Lesney's Matchbox Toys Regular Wheels Yrs. 1947-1969" and "Lesney's Matchbox Toys - The Superfast Years 1969-1982."

Marshall Everett
P.O. Box 977
Newfield, NJ 08344
phone: 609-697-2800
fax: 609-697-0762

Museums/Libraries

Charles Mack
Matchbox & Lesney Toy Museum
62 Saw Mill Rd.
Durham, CT 06422-2602
phone: 860-349-1655
fax: 860-349-3256
e-mail: mtchboxusa@aol.com

Marshall Everett
Matchbox Road Museum
P.O. Box 977
Newfield, NJ 08344
phone: 609-697-2800
fax: 609-697-0762

Ertl Replicas

(see also TOYS, Farm)

Clubs/Associations

Ertl Collectors Club
Newsletter: Ertl Replica, The
P.O. Box 500
Dyersville, IA 52040-0500
phone: 319-875-2000
Provides new product and historical information to collectors of Ertl replica toys.

Dealers

Clever Impressions
115 N Wernick St.
Covington, OH 45318-1741
phone: 800-762-5663
Buys and sells Ertl farm toys, die cast collectibles, NASCAR items, Ertl banks.

Clayton Sackett
2312 E. 10th
Shawnee, OK 74801
phone: 405-275-5963
Buys, sells, trades Ertl banks, specializing in oil tankers.

Man./Prod./Dist.

Ertl Inc.
P.O. Box 500
Dyersville, IA 52040-0500
phone: 319-875-2000
Manufacturer of Ertl diecast toys.

Periodicals

Mike Meyer
Newsletter: Replica Collectors Club
News
Hwys 136 & 20
Dyersville, IA 52040
phone: 319-875-2000
A bi-monthly focusing on Ertl collectibles.

Farm

(see also BOOKS, Reference [Farm Toys]; FARM COLLECTIBLES; FARM MACHINERY; TOYS, Diecast; TOYS, Ertl Replicas; TOYS, Playsets; TRACTORS)

Auction Services

Larry Martin
P.O. Box 333
Clinton, IL 61727
phone: 217-935-8211 or 217-935-3873
Monthly toy auctions of farm toys, collector trucks, industrial equipment, sport cars, wind-up toys, pedal tractors and cars, farm advertising, literature and signs.

Clubs/Associations

David Semmel
Antique Engine, Tractor & Toy Club,
Inc.
Newsletter: AETTC Newsletter
5731 Paradise Rd.
Slatington, PA 18080-4028
phone: 610-767-4768
Organized in 1986 with over 500 members; dedicated to preservation and enjoyment of old time farm engines, tractors and related toys; newsletter three times per year.

Farm Toy Collectors Club
P.O. Box 38
Boxholm, IA 50040

David Knieg
Stateline Toy Collectors Club
Newsletter: STCC Toy Collector
2920 Meadowbrook Dr. SE
Cedar Rapids, IA 52403-3046
phone: 319-362-5213

Gateway Farm Toy Club
Newsletter: Gateway Farm Toy Club
 Newsletter
P.O. Box 295
Saint Libory, IL 62282-0295
phone: 618-566-2166

Collectors

Lee Schaffer
504 Hillside Ave.
Rochester, NY 14610
phone: 716-244-6747
 *Civilian, farm and zoo figures; also
 vehicles and equipment.*

Mark S. McCracken
RD 1 Box 184
Vanderbilt, PA 15486
phone: 412-677-4650
 *Wants toy tractors, equipment, trucks,
 barns, animals, sales literature; all
 kinds in any condition.*

Jim Proctor
1395 South Concord Rd.
West Chester, PA 19382
phone: 610-399-0802

Earl Terpstra
Terpbroson
RR 4, Box 151
Washington, IN 47501-9428
phone: 812-644-7140 or 703-445-2834
 *Wants farm and construction toys and
 related memorabilia.*

Dealers

George Mayer
Garden State Farm Toy Store
416 Route 40
Elmer, NJ 08318-2536
phone: 609-358-1144
fax: 609-358-1155
 *A complete hobby and collectors
 outlet: Ertl, Spec-Cast, Scale Models,
 1st Gear, banks, farm tractors, trucks,
 planes, D.C. cars, race cars, etc.*

Bossen Implement
300 Washburn Ave., Hwy 187 S
Lamont, IA 50650-9535
phone: 319-924-2880
 *Buys, sells, and appraises farm
 implements: John Deere, Case, New
 Holland, McCormick, Cat, AGCO,
 Ford, etc.*

Warrren D. Jensen
P.O. Box 1203
Albert Lea, MN 56007
phone: 507-377-9363
fax: 507-377-9727
Internet: http://www.deskmedia.com/
 jensales/

Museums/Libraries

National Farm Toy Museum
1110 16th Ave. SE
Dyersville, IA 52040
phone: 319-875-2727
 *Large collection of cast iron toys,
 farm toys manufactured worldwide,
 first Ertl toy ever made, complete Tru-
 Scale collection, etc.*

Periodicals

Betty Holland
Magazine: Tractor Classics CTM
P.O. Box 489
Rocanville
Saskatchewan S0A 3L0 Canada
phone: 306-645-4566
fax: 306-645-4566
 *Canada's bi-monthly farm toy
 magazine: toy show reviews,
 information on new and old farm toys,
 toy shows, collector of the month
 stories, price guides, cars, comics,
 dolls, display ads, classifieds.*

Rick Larsen
Magazine: Toy Tractor Times, The
RR 3 Box 112-A
Osage, IA 50461-9635
phone: 515-732-3530
 *Features farm toys with an emphasis
 on toy tractors; articles, ads, shows,
 new releases, etc.*

Dan Laurence
Spec Cast
Newsletter: Spec Tacular News
P.O. Box 368
Dyersville, IA 52040
phone: 319-875-8706
fax: 319-875-8056
 *A quarterly focusing on farm toys and
 collectibles.*

Claire & Cathy Scheibe
Toy Farmer Ltd.
Magazine: Toy Farmer
7496 106th Ave. SE
Lamoure, ND 58458-9404
phone: 701-883-5206 or 800-533-8293
fax: 701-883-5208
e-mail: zekesez@aol.com
Internet: http://www.toytrucker.com/
 htm;/home.html
 *Toy Farmer sponsors the annual
 National Farm Toy Shoy in Dyersville,
 IA.*

Ronald Mucher
Magazine: Small Farm Today
3903 W. Ridge Trail Rd.
Clark, MO 65243-9525
phone: 314-687-3333 or 800-633-2535
fax: 314-687-3148
Internet: http://www.datasys.net/edpak/
 small.html
 *A bi-monthly magazine for the small
 farmer; sometimes contains articles
 about collectible farm toys.*

Terry & Ray Hartzell
Newsletter: Farm Toy Shopper
P.O. Box 398
Ash Grove, MO 65604
phone: 417-672-3878

Repair Services

Donald Walter
W2490 Country Highway A
Curtiss, WI 54422
phone: 715-654-5440
 *Repairs tin trucks, pedal cars and
 tractors; removes old paint, repaints,
 adds needed parts, etc.*

Suppliers

Dakotah Toys
RR 1 Box 157
Madison, SD 57042-9614
 *Catalog contains toy parts, decals,
 paints, kits, 1/64 items, books, scratch
 building materials, tools and diorama
 materials.*

Fisher-Price

Clubs/Associations

Jeanne Kennedy
Fisher-Price Collectors Club
Newsletter: Gabby-Goose, The
1442 N. Ogden
Mesa, AZ 85205
phone: 507-451-4960
fax: 507-451-3995
 *Members study, research, discusses
 and write about Fisher-Price toys;
 preserve and promote the collection of
 Fisher-Price toys and related items;
 annual convention in conjunction with
 ToyFest in August in East Aurora, NY.*

Collectors

John J. Murray
P.O. Box 29
Eden, NY 14057-0029
 *The foremost collector of older
 Fisher-Price toys; co-author with
 Bruce R. Fox of "Fisher-Price 1931-
 63"; send SASE for information on
 book.*

Lee Kauffman
324 East Lynnwood St.
Allentown, PA 18103
phone: 610-797-0179
 *Wants to buy 1930-1970 Fisher-Price
 wooden pull toys; please state
 condition and price.*

John Krupienski
5200 Hilltop Dr.
P.O. Box AA6
Brookhaven, PA 19015-1200
phone: 610-874-3003

Patricia A. Wagner
Sunni-hill Farm Antiques
Waconia, MN 55387-9562
phone: 612-544-4543 or 612-442-4036
fax: 612-544-9283
 *Wants to buy older (pre-1950s)
 Fisher-Price toys for collection.*

Sharon A. Mitchell
875 North Michigan, #3412
Chicago, IL 60611
phone: 312-787-3252 or 800-879-6948
fax: 312-266-7982
 *Dedicated collector wants to buy
 Fisher-Price, Gong-Bell, and other
 pull toys (1890-1963); also wants
 Mattel turn-toys and Plasticville; open
 to duplicates and entire collections;
 eager to hear from dealers and other
 collectors.*

Jeanne Kennedy
1442 N. Ogden
Mesa, AZ 85205
phone: 507-451-4960
fax: 507-451-3995

German & Japanese

Collectors

Martin Krim
P.O. Box 2273
Peabody, MA 01960-7273
phone: 508-535-3140
fax: 508-535-7522
e-mail: dlkrim@star.net
Internet: http://www.old_toys.com
 *Wants German and Japanese toys c.
 1900; also comic character toys,
 wind-ups, battery, etc.; celluloid, tin
 etc.*

Hess Trucks

Dealers

Mark Scherzer
54 Gates Court
Matawan, NJ 07747-9716
phone: 908-290-1407
fax: 908-290-0636
 *Specializes in Hess Trucks from 1964
 to present.*

Horse-Drawn

Experts

Leon M. Weiss
Gemini Antiques Ltd.
12 E. 76th St.
New York, NY 10021
phone: 212-734-3681

Ideal Toy Co.

Clubs/Associations

Judith Izen
Ideal Toy Co. Collector's Club
Newsletter: Ideal Toy Co. Collectors
 Club Newsletter
P.O. Box 623
Lexington, MA 02173
e-mail: jizenres@aol.com
 Send SASE for more information.

Jack-in-the-Box

Collectors

Douglas Zimmerman
4413 Longford Dr.
Sarasota, FL 34232
phone: 941-378-3266

Dealers

Bryin Dall
Pull This
P.O. Box 2124
New York, NY 10009
phone: 212-777-1868
e-mail: Sufclown@aol.com
 *Buys and sells jack-in-the-boxes and
 pull-string toys.*

Kenner

Clubs/Associations

Ed Sterling
Girder & Panel Collectors Club
Newsletter: Girder & Panel Collectors
  Club Newsletter
P.O. Box 494
Bolton, MA 01740-0494
phone: 508-779-6058 or 508-779-6058
e-mail: ed@gpcc.ultranet.com
  *Club exists to document the history
  and production of Kenner Toys Girder
  and Panel toy sets; quarterly
  newsletter; buys and sell ads; ideal
  place to purchase and restore one of
  those 1960s toy construction sets.*

Kobe

Collectors

Bob Vargas
P.O. Box 60611
Sunnyvale, CA 94088
phone: 415-949-3959
e-mail: bvargas@ix.netcom.com
  *Wants to buy Japanese Kobe toys;
  send good photo and price.*

Mattel

Collectors

Joedi Johnson
P.O. Box 565
Billings, MT 59101-0656
phone: 406-248-4875
fax: 407-248-4875
  *Buying Mattel Thingmakers, Maker
  Paks, Play Paks, store displays,
  Plastigoop, carded molds; Fright
  Factory, Creep Crawlers, etc.;
  newsletter available; also wants
  Mattel Upsy Downsy dolls, accesso-
  ries and books.*

Monsters

Collectors

Neal Austinson
P.O. Box 1691
Windsor, CA 95492-1691
phone: 707-837-9685
  *Wants movie monster toys: Franken-
  stein, Dracula, Creature From The
  Black Lagoon, etc.*

Dealers

John Skerchock
P.O. Box 733
Bellefonte, PA 16823-0733
phone: 814-353-0565
  *Specializes in monster and science
  fiction collectibles from the 1960s to
  present; writes articles for "Scary
  Monsters" magazine and related
  publications.*

Toys from the Attic
20165 N. 67th Ave., Ste 122A
Glendale, AZ 85308
phone: 602-547-2564
fax: 602-938-0925
  Always buying 1940s to present
  monster items: board games, buttons,
  rings, dolls, model kits, playsets,
  Halloween masks, soakies, magazines,
  etc.; Universal Monsters AHI and
  Remco, Hasbro monster wallets, PEZ,
  Munsters, Casper.*

Optical

(see also CAMERAS & CAMERA
EQUIPMENT; KALEIDOSCOPES;
MAGIC LANTERNS & SLIDES;
OPTICAL ITEMS; STANHOPES;
STEREO VIEWERS &
STEREOVIEWS)

Auction Services

Michael Pritchard
Christie's South Kensington, Ltd.
85 Old Brompton Rd.
London SW7 3LD, U.K.
phone: 0171 581 7611 or 0171 321 3279
fax: 0171 321 3321
e-mail:
  mpritchard@cix.compulink.co.uk
  *Specializes in the sale of optical toys
  such as persistence of vision devices,
  stereoscopes, magic lanterns/slides,
  etc.*

Collectors

Uwe H. Breker
6731 Ashley Ct.
Sarasota, FL 34241-9696
phone: 941-925-0385
fax: 941-925-0487
  *Wants to buy optical toys: magic
  lanterns, mechanical slides,
  stereoviewer, etc.*

Dealers

Bryan W. Ginns
2109 Cty. Rte. 21
Valatie, NY 12184-6001
phone: 518-392-5805
fax: 518-392-7925
e-mail: the3dman@aol.com
  *Wants large collections of stereo
  views, old cameras, daguerreotypes,
  magic lanterns, optical toys; anything
  relating to photographics.*

Schneider's
3217 Pinewyn Circle
Lancaster, PA 17601
phone: 717-285-3200
fax: 717-285-3853
  *Buys and sells optical toys: zeotropes,
  kaleidoscopes, praxinoscopes and
  theaters, magic mirrors, polyorama
  pantoptiques, artascopes, etc.*

Paper

(see also PAPER COLLECTIBLES)

Dealers

Barb & Jonathan Newman
Paper Soldier, The
8 McIntosh Lane
Clifton Park, NY 12065
phone: 518-371-9202 or 518-371-5130
  *Paper toys bought and sold. Paper
  dolls, paper soldiers, toy theaters,*
  planes, ships, paper and cardboard
  houses, etc.*

Pedal Vehicles

(see BICYCLES & RELATED
MEMORABILIA; RIDING TOYS)

Playsets

(see also SOLDIERS, Toy; TOYS,
Action Figures)

Auction Services

Peter Fritz
Toy-A-Day
P.O. Box 6026
Wolcott, CT 06716-0026
phone: 203-879-5799 or 203-879-5899
  *Conducts monthly auction of playsets,
  games, TV toys and post-WWII
  through Star Wars super heroes
  collectibles.*

Collectors

Eric J. Reinkka
P.O. Box 170-198
Ozone Park, NY 11417-0198
phone: 718-835-9764
  *Wants to buy old toy soldiers, sets,
  playsets; Marx, Sears, Wards playsets,
  1950s and 1960s model kits, battery/
  friction tinplate vehicles, G.I. Joe,
  guns, etc.; any nice military theme toy.*

Dave Gall
7180 Broadview
Parma, OH 44134
phone: 216-524-9514
  *Wants Marx playsets: Gunsmoke,
  Johnny Ringo, Ben-Hur, Blue and
  Gray; also many others such as
  westerns, military, space, etc.*

David W. Francis
148 King St.
Wadsworth, OH 44281
phone: 330-335-3717
fax: 330-335-3617
e-mail: fphadv@bright.net
  *Wants to buy zoo and farm animal
  figures.*

Thomas P. Terry
5894 Lakeview Ct. E.
Onalaska, WI 54650
phone: 608-781-1894
  *Collector wants to add to personal
  collection: complete or partial
  playsets by Marx, Ideal, Superior,
  etc.; Western Towns, Alaska, Jungle,
  Skyscrapers, Battle Action, etc.; also
  seeking boxed or bagged figure sets,
  blister cards, etc.*

Dealers

Excalibur Hobbies, Ltd.
63 Exchange St.
Malden, MA 02148
phone: 617-322-2959
fax: 617-322-7910
  *Carries large selection of playset
  figures and accessories.*

Paul Stadinger
STAD'S
815 North 12th St.
Allentown, PA 18102
phone: 610-770-1140 or 610-433-7728
fax: 610-770-1043
  *STAD'S is a leading source for plastic
  figures from U.S. makers (Marx, MPC,
  Lido, Timmee, etc.) and foreign
  (Britains, Timpo, etc.); twice monthly
  catalog subscription is $4 for six
  months.*

Stone Castle Imports
P.O. Box 141
Bardstown, KY 40004
phone: 502-897-0207

John Maleski
Space Toys
1846 N. Melborn St.
Dearborn, MI 48128
phone: 313-277-0751
  *Buys and sells post-WWII toys by
  Ideal, Marx, Superior; playsets and
  plastic figures; soldiers, farms,
  cowboys, etc.*

Terry Geppert
4532 W. 102nd St.
Minneapolis, MN 55437-2611
phone: 612-831-7454

Experts

Tim Geppert
Colorado Quality Collectibles
2818 McKeag Dr.
Fort Collins, CO 80526
phone: 303-225-9782
  *Buys, sells, collects, appraises Marx
  playsets, plastic toy soldiers and
  figures; author of "Guide for Non-
  Metallic Toy Soldiers of the U.S."*

Periodicals

Paul Stadinger
STAD'S
Magazine: Plastic Warrior
815 North 12th St.
Allentown, PA 18102
phone: 610-770-1140 or 610-433-7728
fax: 610-770-1043
  *A British bi-monthly focusing on
  leading European plastic figures,
  firms (Britains, Timpo, etc.), reviews,
  Q&A, letters, news, ads, etc.*

Paul Stadinger
STAD'S
Newsletter: Worlds of Plastic Figures
815 North 12th St.
Allentown, PA 18102
phone: 610-770-1140 or 610-433-7728
fax: 610-770-1043
  *Bi-monthly newsletter covers old and
  new plastic figures and reissues;
  product reviews, show reports, etc.*

Thomas P. Terry, Ed.
Specialty Publishing Co.
Magazine: Plastic Figure & Playset
  Collector
P.O. Box 1355
La Crosse, WI 54602-1355
phone: 608-781-1894
  The only magazines devoted to Marx
  Playsets (1950s-1970s) and related
  plastic toys and figures of the era; bi-
  monthly, 44+ pages, 8 1/2"x11" B&W
  format with articles, photos and
  factory reprints, articles, Q&A, ads,
  and more.

Playsuits

Collectors

Lee H. Mitchell
175 E. Delaware, #8210
Chicago, IL 60611-1732
phone: 800-869-7869 or 312-337-3123
fax: 312-266-7982
  Wants to buy things boys dressed up
  in, played in, sat on, rode on, etc.
  (1900-1969); examples include
  playsuits, costumes, chairs, horses,
  tents, stores, etc.; nice if, but not
  necessarily, character-related.

Plush

Collectors

Johanna & Sean Billings
111 Delps Rd.
Danielsville, PA 18038
phone: 610-760-0953 or 717-333-4561
fax: 610-760-8780
e-mail: bankie@concentric.net
Internet: http://www.facets.net/facets/
  freeserv-edu/rosebowl/
  Wants to buy furry, plush stuffed
  soccer balls; any size, any color, any
  condition; will pay a couple dollars
  for each plus shipping; also wants
  unusual stuffed objects: stuffed
  crayons, toothbrushes, guitars, etc.

Periodicals

Scott Publications
Magazine: Soft Dolls & Animals
30595 Eight Mile
Livonia, MI 48152-1761
phone: 800-458-8237 or 810-477-6650
fax: 810-477-6795
e-mail: 104137.1254@compuserve.com
  For the collector of cloth dolls and
  animals.

Pullstring

(see TOYS, Talking [Pullstring])

Push-Puppets

Collectors

Sharon A. Mitchell
875 North Michigan, #3412
Chicago, IL 60611
phone: 312-787-3252 or 800-879-6948
fax: 312-266-7982
  Collector seeks all types of push-
  puppets (push on the bottom and the

person/animal falls down or moves);
need the ones less common; wants to
hear from all fellow collectors.

PVC

(see also CHARACTER COL-
LECTIBLES; TOYS, Character)

Clubs/Associations

Colleen Lewis
PVC Collectors Club
Newsletter: PVC Collector
10120 Main St.
Clarence, NY 14031-2049
phone: 716-759-7541
fax: 716-759-7462
e-mail: pcc@toyline.com
Internet: http://www.toyline.com/pcc
  International club for PVC collectors;
  quarterly newsletter with information,
  reviews, ads, etc. about PVCs
  including the "Archives", a detailed
  listing of PVCs by series with
  pictures; special offers for club
  members.

Dealers

Colleen Lewis
Buffalo Road Hobby
10120 Main St.
Clarence, NY 14031-2049
phone: 716-759-7541
fax: 716-759-7462
e-mail: pcc@toyline.com
Internet: http://www.toyline.com/pcc
  Carries a huge selection of PVC
  cartoon figures from Animaniacs,
  Hanna Barbera, Looney Tunes, and
  Pink Panther to Little Lulu, Zorro and
  more; imported from all over the
  world; catalog $2.

Renwal

Collectors

Mary Soelberg
29126 Laro Dr.
Agoura Hills, CA 91301-1635
phone: 818-889-9909
  Advanced Renwal toy collector wants
  hard-to-find pieces, especially the
  Broom and Policeman; write with
  complete description and price; no
  broken items.

Russian

Dealers

George Francisco Paley
c/o Natural Way
Newsletter: Russian Toy Club
820-822 Massachusetts St.
P.O. Box 842
Lawrence, KS 66044-0842
phone: 913-841-0100
e-mail: natural@databank.com
  Wholesale retailer and dealer;
  periodically published a newsletter for
  collectors of Russian toys - a rapidly
  changing environment and usually a
  situation of extremely limited
  availability.

Sand

Collectors

Donald Gorlick
P.O. Box 24541
Seattle, WA 98124-0541
phone: 206-824-0508
  Wants sand toys (not very old); small
  box-like toy containing a clown or
  trapeze artist which spins when the
  box is inverted.

Experts

Carole & Richard Smyth
Carole Smyth Antiques
P.O. Box 2068
Huntington, NY 11743-0861
phone: 516-673-8666
  Authors of "Pails by Comparison," a
  study and price guide; available from
  the author for $28.50 ppd.

Schoenhut

Clubs/Associations

Pat Girbach, Sec.
Schoenhut Collectors Club
Newsletter: Schoenhut Newsletter
1003 W. Huron St.
Ann Arbor, MI 48103-4217
phone: 313-662-6676
  Quarterly newsletter includes articles,
  prices and announcements of shows
  and events of interest to Schoenhut
  collectors.

Collectors

Collector
9428 Silverside
South Lyon, MI 48178

Dealers

Judith Lile
Judith Lile Antique Toys
346 Valleybrook Dr.
Lancaster, PA 17601
phone: 717-569-8175
  Buys and sells toys, specializing in
  Schoenhut.

Harry R. McKeon, Jr.
18 Rose Lane
Flourtown, PA 19031-1910
phone: 215-233-4094
  Buys and sells Schoenhut items: dolls,
  games, circus animals, toys,
  accessories; anything Schoenhut
  except pianos.

Norman Bowers
1916 Cleveland St.
Evanston, IL 60202-1910
phone: 708-866-7165 or 708-333-7880
fax: 708-333-9561
  Buys, sells, trades, and appraises
  Schoenhut items.

Experts

E. Ackerman
P.O. Box 217
Culver City, CA 90230
  Co-author with F. Keller of "Under

The Big Top with Schoenhut's Humpty
Dumpty Circus."

Science Fiction

Dealers

John Kachmar
Techno-Fantasy Traders
779 Carissa Dr.
West Palm Beach, FL 33411-3412
phone: 407-798-5978
fax: 407-798-5978
e-mail: kachmar@aol.com

Scientific Laboratory

Collectors

Barry Lutsky
31 Longfield Dr.
Neshanic, NJ 08853
phone: 201-369-7367
  Wants toys by A.C. Gilbert,
  Chemcraft; 1915-1950; also Erector
  Sets, chemistry, electricity/radio,
  engineering, magic & tricks,
  magnetism, meteorology, mineralogy,
  optics, physics, weather, etc.

Silly Putty

Dealers

Toysensations
P.O. Box 218
Woodbury, NY 11797
phone: 516-338-4929 or 516-338-2701
fax: 516-681-3612
  Sells Silly Putty related items.

Museums/Libraries

Crayola Hall of Fame, Binney & Smith
1100 Church Lane
P.O. Box 431
Easton, PA 18044
phone: 215-559-2632
  In addition to crayons, this museum
  also honors Silly Putty.

Man./Prod./Dist.

Binney & Smith, Inc.
P.O. Box 431
Easton, PA 18044
phone: 800-272-9652
  This is the company that manufactures
  Silly Putty today.

Space & Robot

(see also SPACE COLLECTIBLES)

Auction Services

Lloyd Ralston
Ralston Toy Auction
109 Glover Ave.
Norwalk, CT 06850
phone: 203-366-3399 or 203-255-1233

Collectors

John Vahary, Jr.
41 Crosby Dr.
Battle Creek, MI 49014
phone: 616-965-0943
Wants to buy space toys including Star WArs and Star Trek.

Christmas Catalog Collector, The
175 East Delaware, #7403
Chicago, IL 60611-1731
phone: 800-879-6948 or 312-337-3123
fax: 312-266-7982
Wants to buy 1925-1970 space toys and ray guns, Buck Rogers, Captain Video, Space Patrol, etc.; also wants toy/Christmas catalogs.

Dealers

John Maleski
Space Toys
1846 N. Melborn St.
Dearborn, MI 48128
phone: 313-277-0751
Wants to buy space toy buildings, figures, premiums, 1950s TV space series' toys, Archer slot handed figures & accessories.

Space & Robot (Ray Guns)

Dealers

Gary Kraut
Alphaville
226 W. Houston St.
New York, NY 10014-4846
phone: 212-675-6850
fax: 212-741-2609
e-mail: alphavil@mindspring.com
Internet: http://www.alphaville.com
Along with partner Steve Karchin buys and sells space toys.

John Maleski
Space Toys
1846 N. Melborn St.
Dearborn, MI 48128
phone: 313-277-0751

Experts

Leslie Singer
103 W. Capitol, Ste. 1104
Little Rock, AR 72201-5727
phone: 501-375-1860
fax: 501-375-1860
e-mail: zenmotel@aol.com
Collects and specializes in pre-1960 space toys; author of "ZAP! Ray Gun Classics."

Steam/Hot Air

Collectors

Lowell J. Wagner
Sunni-hill Farm Antiques
Waconia, MN 55387-9562
phone: 612-544-4543 or 612-442-4036
fax: 612-544-9283
Wants steam toys and hot air engines; also wants steam toy catalogs, steam plants, accessories, steam autos, steam tractors, steam boats, etc.

Dealers

Diamond Enterprises & Book Publishers
P.O. Box 537
Alexandria Bay, NY 13607-0537
phone: 613-475-1771 or 800-481-1353
fax: 613-475-3748
e-mail: diamond@intranet.cq
Internet: http://www.yesteryeartoys.com
American and Canadian distributors of Mamod and Wilesco steam models; sales, parts and service.

Bruce J. Southmayd
Little Bill's Toys
9200 5th St. NE
Minneapolis, MN 55434-1107
phone: 612-786-0762
Steam toy collector and dealer.

Super Hero

(see also CHARACTER COLLECTIBLES; COMIC BOOKS; PREMIUMS; SCIENCE FICTION; TELEVISION SHOWS & MEMORABILIA)

Collectors

Dale L. Ames
22 Colton St.
Worcester, MA 01610
phone: 508-755-3830

Talking (Pullstring)

(see also DOLLS, Chatty Cathy)

Dealers

Bryin Dall
Pull This!
P.O. Box 2124
New York, NY 100090
Leading dealer in pullstring talking toys.

Repair Services

Speak-Up
25 Statler Dr.
Shirley, NY 11967
phone: 516-924-6256
Source for repairing Mattel talkers.

Kathy Lewis
Chatty Cathy's Haven
187 N. Marcello Ave.
Thousand Oaks, CA 91360
phone: 805-499-7932
Repairs, buys and sells pullstring talkers.

Teenage Mutant Ninja Turtles

Collectors

John Vahary, Jr.
41 Crosby Dr.
Battle Creek, MI 49014
phone: 616-965-0943
Wants toys that have Teenage Mutant Ninja Turtles on them.

Tin

Collectors

Jeff Dykes
6 Wildwood Terrace
Glen Ridge, NJ 07028
phone: 201-748-4990 or 973-748-4990
Wants to buy German tin "penny" toys, German windups, trains, Steiff and teddy bears, and cast iron toys.

Dealers

Harry R. McKeon, Jr.
18 Rose Lane
Flourtown, PA 19031-1910
phone: 215-233-4094
Buys and sells tin toys made by Martin, Bing, Lehmann, Gutherman, Ives. Strauss, etc.

David A. Hull
Small Town Coins & Collectibles
7498 E. Davison Rd.
Davison, MI 48423-2014
phone: 810-658-1992
fax: 810-658-2977
e-mail: towncoin@concentric.net
Internet: http://www.concentric.net/~towncoin
Dozens of original antique tin toys and Mint-In-Box for sale.

John D. McKenna
McKenna Bros. Wholesale
801-803 W Cucharras St.
Colorado Springs, CO 80905
phone: 719-630-8732
Buys, sells & collects pre-1960 toys in all categories especially early American tin, cast iron automotive and horse-drawn toys.

Experts

Jack Tempest
46 Grangethorpe Dr.
Burnage
Manchester M19 2LQ, U.K.
Author of "Collecting Tin Toys"; collectible pre-WWII tinplate toys from around the world; ($40. Bank drafts only - no checks, please.)

Tinkertoys

Museums/Libraries

Kristan McKinsey
Evanston Historical Society
225 Greenwood St.
Evanston, IL 60201-4713
phone: 708-475-3410
Tinkertoys originated in Evanston, IL; Evanston Historical Society has the largest collection of Tinkertoys and related information in the country.

Tonka

Dealers

Nancy Merrow
Champion Toys
RR1, Box 1858
Kennebunkport, ME 04046
phone: 207-985-2292
Mail order toys and automobilia.

Experts

Don DeSalle
DeSalle Promotions
Anderson, IN 46011
phone: 800-392-TOYS
Licensed by Hasbro to manufacture Tonka toys; promotes toy shows around the country; author of "Collector's Guide to Tonka Trucks 1947-1963"; always buying excellent to mint Tonka Trucks and private labeled Tonkas.

Suppliers

Thomas Toys
P.O. Box 405
Fenton, MI 48430
phone: 313-629-8707
Sells replacement parts for Tonka trucks.

Toonerville Trolley

Clubs/Associations

Asa Sparks
Toonerville Trolley Collectors
Newsletter: Toonerville Times
6045 Camelot Ct.
Montgomery, AL 36117-2555
phone: 205-270-0687
Internet: http://erols.com.diesel/toonerville

Tops & Gyroscopes

(see also TOYS, Yo-Yo's)

Collectors

Bruce R. Middleton
Top Secret
5 Lloyd Rd.
Newburgh, NY 12550-5028
phone: 914-564-2556
Buys, sells, trades tops, yo-yo's, spinners, figurals, peg tops, supported tops, diablos, gyroscopes, etc.; seeks other collectors.

Don Olney
Toycrafter, The
1237 E. Main St.
Rochester, NY 14609-6941
phone: 716-288-9000 or 800-433-TOYS
fax: 716-654-7820
e-mail: 70544.2172@compuserve.com
Buys, sells, trades new and old tops; also wants top related ads, photos, books, photos and videos of people doing tricks with tops; author of "The Little Book of Tops," and "The Tops Discovery Kit."

Experts

Judith Schulz
533 Milwaukee Ave.
Burlington, WI 53105-1232
phone: 414-763-3946
Wants to buy unusual tops, gyroscopes and yo-yo's; also wants related ads, literature, and old packages; editor of "Spin-Offs", curator of a small museum about tops, gyros, and yo-yo's; top expert of MGM's video "My Summer Story."

Museums/Libraries

Judith Schulz
Spinning Top Exploratory Museum
Journal: Spin-Offs
533 Milwaukee Ave.
Burlington, WI 53105-1232
phone: 414-763-3946
2,000 tops, gyroscopes & yo-yo's on exhibit (antique and modern); top games & experiments to try; 35 types to spin; sales of unique tops; demos, live show at museum; "Spin-offs" is a playful research publication of history, facts, etc.

Transformers

Clubs/Associations

Mark Tisdale
Transmasters
Newsletter: Matrix
P.O.Box 469
Montezuma, GA 31063
International club interested in Transformers, comics, cartoons and toys.

Collectors

Maret Webb
4118 East Vernon Ave.
Phoenix, AZ 85008-2333
phone: 602-957-0653
fax: 602-957-1631
Wants to buy Hasbro and Bandai Transformers (transformation robot toys), and related cards, books, cookie jars, games, posters, etc. - ANYTHING featuring Transformers.

Transportation

Dealers

Jim & Nancy Schaut
Aquarius Antiques
P.O. Box 10781
Glendale, AZ 85318-0781
phone: 602-878-4293
e-mail: nschaut@aztec.asu.edu
Buys and sells transportation toys and memorabilia; toys, trains; buy and sell; publishes a quarterly catalog of one-of-a-kind items for sale; authors of "AMERICAN AUTOMOBILIA."

Periodicals

Gordon Rice
Magazine: U.S. Toy Collector Magazine
P.O. Box 172
Helena, MT 59624-0172
A monthly magazine focusing on toy trucks, cars, construction toys, transportation toys, etc.; the photo-marketplace of toy vehicles for sale; also has articles on toy history; black & white and 4-color advertising available.

Trucks & Equipment

(see also GARBAGE RELATED; TOYS, Tonka)

Clubs/Associations

John Edmonds
Albany Gas Truck Collectors
76 Whitney Dr.
Valatie, NY 12184
Focuses on gas truck promos.

Miniature Truck Association
Newsletter: Miniature Truck News
3449 N. Randolph St.
Arlington, VA 22207
phone: 703-524-2061

Collectors

Larry Bruch
Larry Bruch Toys
P.O. Box 121
Mountain Top, PA 18707-0121
phone: 800-549-TOYS
Write for free 3-page illustrated want list.

N.W. Neill, Jr.
P.O. Box 38
Ennice, NC 28623-0038
phone: 910-657-8152
fax: 910-657-8084
Wants to buy Tonka, Smith-Miller, Doepke model toys, any make of toy fire trucks.

Bill Whelan
P.O. Box 617
Daly City, CA 94017-2332
phone: 415-756-1189
Wants to buy scale model tractor/trailers, 1/64th down to 1/100th and smaller, with company names, logos and advertising.

Periodicals

Claire D. Scheibe
Toy Farmer Ltd.
Magazine: Toy Trucker & Contractor
7496 106th Ave. SE
Lamoure, ND 58458-9404
phone: 701-883-5206 or 800-533-8293
fax: 701-883-5208
e-mail: zekesez@aol.com
Internet: http://www.toytrucker.com/htm;/home.html
Focuses on trucks and construction toys; sponsors an annual National Toy Truck and Construction Show in August.

Twist-Um

Collectors

Dale Abrams
960 Bryden Rd.
Columbus, OH 43205-1809
phone: 614-258-5258
fax: 614-258-6663
e-mail: 70003.2061@compuserve.com
Internet: http://ourworld.compuserve.com/homepages/da
Wants to buy Twist-Um toys - jointed figures, mostly animals, similar to Schoenhuts; made in Oakland, CA in the 1920s by the Twist-Um Toy Co.

Water Pistols

Collectors

Jean B. Hall
10 Alden Dr.
Norwood, MA 02062
phone: 617-762-3779
Wants water pistols, especially Captain Video, Jaws, Davy Crockett, Pac-Man, St. Louis Exposition 1904, etc.; also TV Sci-Fi items.

White Knob Wind-Ups

Clubs/Associations

Kim Cole
White Knob Wind-Up Collectors Club
Newsletter: WKW Newsletter
61 Garrow St.
Auburn, NY 13021-4605
phone: 315-253-9131
e-mail: wkw@ns1.relex.com
Members trade information and white-knob wind-up toys; these toys get their names from the little white ridged knob at the end of a metal rod which extends from the body and winds the motor when rotated - no "on-off" switch.

Dealers

Rene C. Anderson
Wind Me Up!
4823 Woodlawn Blvd.
Minneapolis, MN 55417-1345
phone: 612-854-0905

Richard Johnson
P.O. Box 27093
Prescott Valley, AZ 86312
phone: 602-775-4714

Lisa Gage
Great Wind-up, The
93 Pike #201
Seattle, WA 98101
phone: 206-621-9370
The Northwest's largest selection of wind-up toys - tin and other; full selection of collectibles from Paya and DBS lines of tin toys; interested in wind-up toys from all over the world.

Wooden

Collectors

Perry R. Eichor
703 N. Almond Dr.
Simpsonville, SC 29681-3453
phone: 803-967-8770
Wants to buy wooden toys made by Hustler, Rich, Ted Toy, Toy Tinkers and others.

Yo-Yo's

(see also TOYS, Tops & Gyroscopes)

Clubs/Associations

John Stangle, Pres.
American Yo-Yo Association
Newsletter: Yo-Yo Times
627 163rd St. South
Spanaway, WA 98387
phone: 707-542-YOYO
fax: 707-542-9696
e-mail: yotopia@sonic.net
Internet: http://www.ayya.pd.net
Association for yo-yo players and collectors; source for information and two publications: "AYYA News" (twice yearly) and "The Yo-Yo Times" (quarterly); Mr. Stangle is also a professional yo-yo entertainer!

Collectors

Les Gordon, II
6475 E 550 S
Whitestown, IN 46075-9696
phone: 317-769-3382
Wants old yo-yo's and related pins, patches, advertisements, trophies, strings, books, paper, memorabilia, etc.

Bob Zeuschel
1638 Highland Valley Ctr.
Chesterfield, MO 63005
phone: 314-537-3145
Wants yo-yo's by Duncan, Goody, Royal, Ja-Do, Flores, etc.

Bill Caswell
1512 Cherokee Place
Bartlesville, OK 74003
phone: 918-336-5130
e-mail: rosicas@juno.com
Wants old yo-yo's by Flores, Festival, Medalist, Cheerio, Hi-Ker, Duncan, Goody, Royal; especially wants jeweled and carved models.

Experts

Lucky Meisenheimer
7300 Sandlake Commons Blvd., Ste. 105
Orlando, FL 32819-8011
phone: 407-354-0478
e-mail: LuckyJ@msn.com
Buys old yo-yo's, singles, collections, and yo-yo memorabilia; also contest kits, store displays, patches, pins, awards, advertising, etc.

Museums/Libraries

Judith Schulz
Spinning Top Exploratory Museum
Journal: Spin-Offs
533 Milwaukee Ave.
Burlington, WI 53105-1232
phone: 414-763-3946
2,000 tops, gyroscopes & yo-yo's on exhibit (antique and modern); top games & experiments to try; 35 types to spin; sales of unique tops; demos, live show at museum; "Spin-offs" is a playful research publication of history, facts, etc.

Yozeum, The
2900 N. Country Club
Tucson, AZ 85716-1912
phone: 602-322-0100
Featuring the Duncan collection, free admission.

National Yo-Yo Museum
320 Broadway
Chico, CA 95928-5322
phone: 916-893-0545
Over 1,000 yo-yos on display; free admission.

Periodicals

Stuart F. Crump, Ed.
Creative Communications, Inc.
Newsletter: Yo-Yo Times
P.O. Box 1519 - MAC
Herndon, VA 22070-1519
phone: 703-715-6190
A quarterly publication loaded with information about current yo-yo events, leading yo-yo'ers, the latest publications and videos, and anything else related to yo-yos.

TOYS (MODERN)

Clubs/Associations

Toy Manufacturers of America, The
200 Fifth Ave.
New York, NY 10010
phone: 212-675-1141
fax: 212-633-1429
The toy, puzzle and game manufacturers' trade organization; sponsors the annual American International New York Toy Fair which is only open to the trade and to the press.

Periodicals

Magazine: Playthings
51 Madison Ave.
New York, NY 10010-1603
The unofficial trade journal for the toy industry; publishes a directory which lists manufacturers, their representatives, inventors and designers.

Newsletter: National Toy Connection
779 E. Merritt Island Cswy., Ste. 2346
Merritt Island, FL 32952
Internet: http://members.aol.com/NatlToyCon/ntc2.htm
Latest news and information; new product releases (inside information), toys of 50s through 70s, current prices, First Gear, Hess, Texaco, Ertl,

Scale Models, industry news, hard-to-find products.

TRACTORS

(see also ENGINES; FARM MACHINERY; MACHINERY & EQUIPMENT, Road Making; TOYS, Farm)

Auction Services

Iron Horse Auction Co.
519 South Hancock St.
P.O. Box 1267
Rockingham, NC 28379
phone: 919-997-2248
fax: 919-895-1530
Conducts auctions specializing in the sale of antique steam engines, tractors and farm related items.

Clubs/Associations

Charley Stark, VP
Early Day Gas Engine & Tractor Association, Inc.
Newsletter: National, The
Rte. 2 Box 167A
Republic, MO 65738
phone: 417-732-7136
e-mail: edgeta@ave.net
Internet: http://www.ave.net/~edgeta/index.html
A national organization with 90 regional "Branches" interested in early gas engines and tractors.

Experts

Dave Mowitz
1716 Locust St.
Des Moines, IA 50336
Author of "Ageless Iron, Restoring Your Legacy" and the "Ageless Iron Restoration Guide" which lists sources for parts, paint, etc.

Periodicals

Suzanne Wright
Kelsey Publishing Ltd.
Magazine: Tractor & Machinery Magazine
Kelsey House, 77 High St.
Beckenham
Kent BR3 1AN, U.K.
phone: 0181-6583531
fax: 0181-6508035
A 40-page monthly magazine dealing with all tractors and tractor-driven machinery; restorations, rallies, ploughing matches, auctions, runs and club event.

Stemgas Publishing Co.
Magazine: Gas Engine Magazine
P.O. Box 328
Lancaster, PA 17608-0328
phone: 717-392-0733
fax: 717-392-1341
Internet: http://www.sitematrix.com/stemgas/
G.E.M. is the leading magazine for antique tractor and gas engine collectors; articles, ads, auctions, models, Maytag gas engines, restoration tips, histories, auctions,

suppliers, parts, etc.; published monthly.

Newsletter: Hook, The
P.O. Box 937
Powell, OH 43065-0937
phone: 614-848-5038
Antique tractor pullers.

Magazine: Antique Power
P.O. Box 838
Yellow Springs, OH 45387
phone: 937-767-1433 or 800-767-5828
fax: 937-767-2726
e-mail: antique@antiquepower.com
Internet: http://www.antiquepower.com
Has regular columns about farm toys, tractor restoration, farm literature collecting and tractor history; free ads for subscribers.

Adept Resources
Directory: Who's Who in Antique Engines & Tractors
P.O. Box 2297
Elkhart, IN 46515
Source of people who are involved in some way with the antique engine and tractor hobby.

Dennis Polk
Dennis Polk Equipment
Magazine: Polk's
72435 SR 15
New Paris, IN 46553
phone: 219-831-3555
fax: 219-831-5717
Bi-monthly magazine covering the world of antique tractors; restoration, tractor pulls, auction results, collector stories, etc.

Barbara Schmidgall
Newsletter: Tractorcard Newsletter
1988 Willoughby Rd.
Mason, MI 48854-9491
phone: 517-676-1835 or 517-676-4030
Newsletter lists various sets of tractor cards which are available; tractor cards are trading cards with pictures of tractors on them.

John Kasmiski
Newsletter: Golden Arrow
N7209 State Hwy. 67
Mayville, WI 53050
Published quarterly; Cockshutt and Co-op.

Steve Sharp
Magazine: Tractor Magazine, The
P.O. Box 424
Rush Springs, OK 73082-0424
Bi-monthly.

Don Bennett, Ed.
Magazine: Tractor Trader Magazine, The
300 N. Elm St.
Graham, TX 76450
phone: 817-549-6611
For collectors, restorers, buyers, and sellers of antique tractors, tractor drawn equipment, toys, literature, and other related farm collectibles.

Allis-Chalmers

Periodicals

Nan Jones
Magazine: Old Allis News, The
10925 Love Rd.
Bellevue, MI 49021-9250
phone: 616-763-9770
fax: 616-763-9770
A quarterly magazine for the Allis-Chalmers collector and/or enthusiast; Allis-Chalmers related articles, photographs, histories, restoration stories, suppliers ads, shows, auctions, etc.

Case

Clubs/Associations

David Erb
J.I. Case Collectors Association
Newsletter: Old Abe's News
Rt 2 Box 242
Vinton, OH 45686
phone: 614-388-8895
Published quarterly.

Experts

Charles H. Wendel
RR 1 Box 28-A
Atkins, IA 52206
Author of "150 Years of J.I. Case."

Ferguson

Clubs/Associations

Ken Goodwin
Ferguson Club
Newsletter: Ferguson Club Journal
Denehurst, Rosehill Rd.
Stoke Heath
Market Drapton TF9 2JU, U.K.

Ford (N-Models)

Clubs/Associations

Gerard W. Rinaldi
9N-2N-8N-NAA
Magazine: 9N-2N-8N-NAA Newsletter, The
154 Blackwood Lane
Stamford, CT 06903
phone: 203-322-7283
A homespun newsletter in conversation format for enthusiasts of old Ford farm tractors and machinery; also for those with a general interest in antique farm tractors and machinery.

Fordson

Clubs/Associations

Tom Brent
Fordson Club
Newsletter: Fordson Club News
Box 150
Dewdney
B.C. V0M 1H0 Canada

Ford/Fordson Registry & Collectors
    Association
645 Loveland Miamiville Rd.
Loveland, OH 45140
phone: 513-683-4935

Fordson Tractor Club
Newsletter: FTC Newsletter
250 Robinson Rd.
Cave Junction, OR 97523-9719
phone: 503-592-3203
    *Dedicated to the restoration,
    preservation, exhibition of the
    Fordson tractor; bi-annual newsletter,
    manuals, service bulletins, etc.*

International Harvester

Periodicals

Daryl Miller
Newsletter: Red Power
P.O. Box 277
Battle Creek, IA 51006
phone: 712-365-4873
    *Bi-monthly periodical about
    International Harvester and their
    products.*

John Deere

Clubs/Associations

Dave Trumbauer
Two-Cylinder Club Worldwide
Magazine: Two-Cylinder
P.O. Box 219
Grundy Center, IA 50638-0219
phone: 319-824-5487
    *Over 20,000 members who collect
    John Deer literature and memorabilia,
    and who restore early John Deere
    tractors, engines, and implements; bi-
    monthly newsletter.*

Collectors

Jim Proctor
1395 South Concord Rd.
West Chester, PA 19382
phone: 610-399-0802
    *Wants pre-1960 John Deere 2-
    cylinder tractors; also wants tractor
    sales literature.*

Museums/Libraries

John Deere Historic Site
RR 3
Dixon, IL 61021
phone: 815-652-4551

Periodicals

Richard Hain
Magazine: Green Magazine
RR 1 Box 7
Bee, NE 68314
phone: 402-643-6269
fax: 402-643-3912
    *For collectors of John Deere tractors,
    combines, implements, etc.; articles,
    ads, how-to's, restoration hints and
    tips, parts sources, farm toy auction
    notices, etc.*

Massey-Harris

Periodicals

Keith Oltrogge
Newsletter: Wild Harvest
P.O. Box 529
Denver, IA 50622-0529
phone: 319-984-5292 or 319-984-5491
fax: 319-984-6408
    Published bi-monthly.

Minneapolis-Moline

Periodicals

Paul Lowry
Newsletter: Prairie Gold Rush
RR 1 Box 119
Francesville, IN 47946-9453

Roger Mohr
Newsletter: M-M Corresponder
3693 M Ave.
Vail, IA 51465
phone: 712-679-2491 or 712-677-2493
fax: 712-677-2491
    Published quarterly.

Oliver

Clubs/Associations

Kurt Aumann
Hart-Parr/Oliver Collectors Association
Newsletter: Hart-Parr/Oliver Collector
P.O. Box 685
Charles City, IA 50616
    *Publishes quarterly magazine as well
    as quarterly newsletter relating to all
    types of equipment built by Oliver
    Farm Equipment including brand
    names Hart-Parr, Nichols & Shepard,
    Cletrac, Farquar, Ann-Arbor,
    American Seeding & Be-Ge.*

Midwest Oliver Collectors
21576 US Hwy 52
Mount Carroll, IL 61053

Collectors

Larry D. Harsin
3426 170th St.
Estherville, IA 51334-9617
phone: 712-362-2966
    Oliver collector and restorer.

Dennis Gerszewski
RR 1 Box 44
Manvel, ND 58256
phone: 701-699-3577
    *Wants Oliver literature and almost
    anything with the Oliver name.*

Rick & Andrew Garnhart
6372 E Edwardsville Rd.
German Valley, IL 61039-9622
phone: 815-362-6531
    Buy, sell, appraise Oliver tractors.

Dealers

McMillan's Oliver Collectibles
9176 U.S. Rt. 36
Bradford, OH 45308
phone: 513-448-2216

Rumley

Periodicals

Cass Bowyer
Newsletter: Rumley Newsletter
P.O. Box 12
Moline, IL 61265
phone: 309-764-6753
    Quarterly.

TRADING CARDS

Non-Sport

(see also ADVERTISING COL-
LECTIBLES, Trade Cards; BOTTLE
CAPS, Milk; BUBBLE GUM
CARDS; BUBBLE GUM & CANDY
WRAPPERS; CARDS; COMIC
BOOKS; PAPER COLLECTIBLES;
POGS; SPORTS COLLECTIBLES)

Clubs/Associations

Ken Fox
Cartophilic Society
116 Hillview Rd.
Ensbury Park
Bournemouth BH10 5BJ, U.K.
    *Has over 50 years of service to the
    organized card collecting community.*

Christopher Benjamin
United States Cartophilic Society
Newsletter: Card Collectors Bulletin
P.O. Box 4020
Saint Augustine, FL 32085-4020
fax: 904-826-1600
    Focuses on non-sport cards.

Collectors

Dan Calandriello
53-C Beacon Village
Burlington, MA 01803-3843
phone: 617-229-9009
e-mail: dan@coe.neu.edu
    *Wants 1930s era non-sports cards:
    gum, candy, silks, Mickey Mouse,
    Indian gum, Superman, Lone Ranger,
    all war cards; also wants Northeast-
    ern University, Boston, memorabilia
    1898-1950s for upcoming 100th
    anniversary.*

Becky Loechelt
3315 E. Lavey Lane #107
Phoenix, AZ 85032
    *Wants to buy TV non-sports trading
    cards, especially "Partridge Family",
    "Waltons", etc.; also wants 1960s and
    1970s fan magazines, e.g.
    "Tigerbeat", "16", "Fave", etc.*

Walter Koenig
P.O. Box 4395
North Hollywood, CA 91617-0395
    *Wants to buy non-sports trading cards
    (gum, candy, character/comic) from
    the 1890s - 1950s.*

Dealers

Ken Mitchell
710 Conacher Dr.
Willowdale
Ontario M2M 3N6 Canada
phone: 416-222-5808
    *Wants to buy gum, candy and non-
    sports trading cards.*

Mollie & John Witney
Non Sport Network
19 Lores Plaza #160M
New Milford, CT 06776
phone: 860-355-0259
fax: 860-355-0259
e-mail: 75254.740@compuserve.com
    *Over 1700 card and set listings with
    high/low values as seen throughout
    the hobby; topical listings, artists'
    biographies, historical references;
    published quarterly.*

Gary S. Frisch
Non-Sports Cards
24 Peachtree Ct.
Monmouth Junction, NJ 08852
phone: 908-329-9203
e-mail: gfrisch@new-directions.com
    *Buys, sells, and trades non-sports
    cards: sets, singles, wrappers, and
    boxes.*

Bill Marks
Excalibur Trading
P.O. Box 14478
Philadelphia, PA 19115
phone: 215-342-6913
fax: 215-742-7056
    *Wholesaler/distributor/broker of
    sports, non-sports and adult trading
    cards.*

Jim Nicewander
Card Coach, The
P.O. Box 128
Plover, WI 54467-0128
phone: 715-341-5452
    *Wants Arm & Hammer/Church &
    Dwight trading cards, posters, and
    other related collectibles; publishes
    periodic catalog of cards and
    collectibles for sale; friendly, fast
    service since 1956.*

Bob Conway
Card Attack, The
P.O. Box 260942
Lakewood, CO 80226-0942
phone: 303-988-7106
    *Buys, sells and trades bubble gum
    cards; non-sport specialist.*

Doug Craddock
Craddock's Non-Sports Cards &
    Collectibles
P.O. Box 7772
San Jose, CA 95150-3766
phone: 408-298-9070 or 408-629-3980
    *Buys, sells and trades non-sports
    cards: 1930s - 1970s cards, singles,
    sets, wax packs, unopened boxes and
    wrappers. Main focus is 1950s-1960s.
    Finders fee paid for accumulations
    and collections purchased.*

Brian Rachfal
P.O. Box 7772
San Jose, CA 95150-3766
phone: 408-298-9070 or 408-629-3980
*Wants to buy non-sport collections
large or small.*

Experts

Mollie & John Witney
Non Sport Network
19 Lores Plaza #160M
New Milford, CT 06776
phone: 860-355-0259
fax: 860-355-0259
e-mail: 75254.740@compuserve.com
*Operates search service through many
on-line systems helping collectors
locate cards; specializes in pre-1970
cards; buys and sells throughout the
world; posts informative "press
releases" of new releases; Internet
NONSPORT@aol.com.*

John Neuner
91-50 98th St.
Jamaica, NY 11421-2732
phone: 718-849-6114
fax: 718-849-5915
*Author of "Non-Sport Wrapper
Checklist and Price Guide."*

Richard & Mark Sikes
1213 Saggus Rd.
Lincolnton, GA 30817-9667
*Authors of "Non-Sports Card Price
Guide."*

Christopher Benjamin
P.O. Box 4020
Saint Augustine, FL 32085-4020
fax: 904-826-1600
*Appraiser identifies and evaluates all
US and foreign trading cards (fee
charged), private and insurance
inquiries welcome; author of "The
Best Trading Card Guide Ever
Issued", prices, descriptions,
checklists, thousands of pictures.*

Periodicals

Magazine: NonSports Illustrated
P.O. Box 126
Lincoln, MA 01773
phone: 617-259-0258
*Monthly magazine for non-sport card
collectors; price guide information,
set descriptions, example card backs
and more.*

Ian Feller
Century Publishing Company
Magazine: Combo
5 Nassau Blvd.
Garden City, NY 11530-4111
phone: 516-292-6000
fax: 516-292-6007
e-mail: 75764.3302@compuerve.com
Internet: http://worldavenue.com/
shopping/combo
*Monthly magazine with latest news
and prices for comics, non-sports
cards, action figures, video games,
gaming and more.*

Roxanne Toser
Roxanne Toser Non-Sport Enterprises,
Inc.
Magazine: Non-Sport Update
4019 Green St.
P.O. Box 5858
Harrisburg, PA 17110-0858
phone: 717-238-1936
fax: 717-238-3220
e-mail: nsumag@aol.com
*The foremost quarterly publication for
non-sport card collectors; original
artwork covers, glossy paper, lots of
articles by the experts, great variety of
ads, separate 32-page "pop-out"
price guide and free cards.*

Christine Drury
Tuff Stuff Publications, Inc.
Magazine: Tuff Stuff's Collect
P.O. Box 1637
Glen Allen, VA 23060
phone: 804-266-0140 or 800-899-8833
fax: 804-264-4205
Internet: http://www.tuffstuffonline.com
*The complete monthly sports price
guide publication for non-sports
cards.*

Christine Drury
Landmark Specialty Publications, Inc.
Magazine: Gamer
P.O. Box 1637
Glen Allen, VA 23060
phone: 804-266-0140 or 800-899-8833
fax: 804-264-4205
Internet: http://www.tuffstuffonline.com
*Bi-monthly publication for collectors
of gamer collectible cards: Star Wars,
Killer Instinct, Mortal Kombat, Sim
City, Wing Commander, Netrunner,
Monty Python and the Holy Grail, etc.*

Barbara Schmidgall
Newsletter: Tractorcard Newsletter
1988 Willoughby Rd.
Mason, MI 48854-9491
phone: 517-676-1835 or 517-676-4030
*Newsletter lists various sets of tractor
cards which are available; tractor
cards are trading cards with pictures
of tractors on them.*

Les Davis
Non-Sport Publication
Newsletter: Wrapper, The
P.O. Box 227
Geneva, IL 60134-0227
phone: 630-443-9690
*Focuses on non-sports cards,
wrappers and related items; 8 issues
per year.*

TRAILERS & RV'S

(see also GAS STATION COL-
LECTIBLES; HIGHWAY COL-
LECTIBLES; HOTEL COL-
LECTIBLES)

Clubs/Associations

Antique Trailer Coach Club of America
7244 Mohawk Dr.
Tribes Hill, NY 12177
*For owners and admirers of 1920
through 1960s travel trailers.*

Todd & Kristin Kimmell
Classic Trailer & Motorhome Club
Magazine: Lost Highways Quarterly
P.O. Box 43737
Philadelphia, PA 19106-7737
phone: 215-925-2568
*A classic trailer and motor home club;
archives collects material relating to
trailers, motor homes and auto
camping from 1920s to 1960s.*

Recreational Vehicle Industry
Association
P.O. Box 2999
Reston, VA 22090-6003
phone: 703-620-6003
*Industry association, but helpful to
individuals.*

Tri-Rallies Van Club
P.O. Box 21
Huntingdon, TN 38344
phone: 901-986-5153
*Newsletters, rallies, trophies, fishing,
camping.*

Collectors

Todd & Kristin Kimmell
P.O. Box 43737
Philadelphia, PA 19106-7737
phone: 215-925-2568
*Wants 1920s to 1960s trailer, mobile
home and RV related material: trailer
parks, trailer travel, motor homes,
autocamping, tincan tourists, etc.;
magazines, books, pamphlets, promos,
film (16mm-8mm), photos, even old
trailers.*

Periodicals

Deals on Wheels Publications
Magazine: Truck, Race, Cycle &
Recreation
P.O. Box 205
Sioux Falls, SD 57101
phone: 605-338-7666 or 800-334-1886
fax: 605-338-5337
Internet: http://www.dealsonwheels.com
*Photo-ad magazine listing trucks, 4-
wheel drives, cycles, race equipment,
race cars, boats, recreation vehicles,
trailers, jet-skis; classifieds.*

TRAINS

(see also MODELS; RAILROADS;
RAILROAD COLLECTIBLES)

Model (O Gauge)

Collectors

Joe Weber
604 Centre St.
Ashland, PA 17921-1332
phone: 717-875-4787 or 717-875-4401
*Wants O-scale (Lionel size) toy trains,
i.e. kits assembled by the enthusiast;
made by Scalecraft, Lobaugh, Ferris,
Hines, Max Gray.*

Periodicals

Magazine: O Gauge Railroading
P.O. Box 239
Nazareth, PA 18064-0239
phone: 610-759-0406
fax: 610-759-0223
e-mail: OGaugeRwy@aol.com
Internet: http://www.members.aol.com/
OGaugeRwy/org.html
*A bi-monthly magazine exclusively for
the O Gauge collector and market.*

Model (S Gauge)

Periodicals

Donald Heimburger
Heimburger Publishing Co.
Magazine: S Gaugian
7236 West Madison Ave.
Forest Park, IL 60130-1765
phone: 708-366-1973
*The magazine focuses on S gauge
model train operation, modeling, and
collecting.*

Toy

Appraisers

Bruce C. Greenberg
7566 Main St.
Sykesville, MD 21784-5826
phone: 410-795-4749
fax: 410-549-2553
*Appraises and specializes in Lionel,
American Flyer, Marx, LGB, Marklin,
Williams, AMT, etc.; author of 22
books concerned with American toy
trains; appraiser with litigation
experience.*

Auction Services

Joe Armacost
Greenberg Auctions
7566 Main St.
Sykesville, MD 21784-5826
phone: 410-795-4749
fax: 410-549-2553
*Specialist with Linda Greenberg in toy
trains: Lionel, American Flyer, Marex,
Ives, LGB, HO, Marklin, etc.;
publishes an auction catalog and
accepts mail bids.*

Heinz Mueller
Continental Auctions
P.O. Box 193
Sheboygan, WI 53082
phone: 414-693-3371
fax: 414-693-8211
*Specializes in auctions of toy trains
and all toy-related items.*

Clubs/Associations

Louis A. Bohn, Mem. Ch.
Toy Train Collectors Society
Newsletter: Century Limited
109 Howedale Dr.
Rochester, NY 14616-1534
phone: 716-667-1548
*New York State's largest and most
active organization devoted to the
collection, preservation and operation
of the treasured electric trains of days*

gone by; runs toy train meets across NY state.

Frank Hare, Ed.
American Flyer Collectors Club
Magazine: Collector, The
P.O. Box 13269
Pittsburgh, PA 15243-0269
phone: 412-221-2250
fax: 412-221-8402
For collectors of A.C. Gilbert Co. American Flyer and other toy trains (all pre-1966 manufacturers); also contains information about Gilbert Erector sets.

Train Collectors Association
Magazine: Train Collectors Quarterly
P.O. Box 248
Strasburg, PA 17579
phone: 717-687-8976 or 717-687-8623
fax: 717-687-0742
Purpose is to bring together persons interested in collecting and operating toy trains and related items; also publishes the "National Headquarters News" newsletter.

National Model Railroad Association, Inc.
Magazine: NMRA Bulletin, The
4121 Cromwell Rd.
Chattanooga, TN 37421
phone: 615-892-2846
fax: 615-899-4869
Monthly newsletter; the NMRA's Kalmbach Memorial Library offers an extensive collection of resource material on both model and prototype railroading.

New Switzerland Model Railroad Club
Newsletter: New Switzerland Model Railroad Club Newsletter
12226 Albrecht Rd.
Alhambra, IL 62001
phone: 618-654-7127
Monthly newsletter.

Steve Shoe
Model Railroad Industry Association
Magazine: Model Railroad Industry Association Magazine
P.O. Box 28129
Denver, CO 80228
Trade association.

Toy Train Operating Society, Inc.
Magazine: TTOS Bulletin, The
25 West Walnut St., Ste. 308
Pasadena, CA 91103
phone: 818-578-0673
Formed to further the toy train hobby and to promote fellowship; members receive "The Bulletin" magazine and "Order Board" admagazine.

Collectors

Walter Makolandra
70 Cass Ave.
Woonsocket, RI 02895-4739
phone: 401-765-4756
Collector seeks Lionel, American Flyer, Marklin, Bing and other trains and related items.

Wally Krocsko
P.O. Box 307
Atlasburg, PA 15004-0307
phone: 412-947-5671
Buys, sells, trades all types of toy trains, accessories; please send LSASE with all inquiries; call evenings.

Neil K. Yerger
7 Farm Rd.
Wayne, PA 19087-3303
Wants to buy Lionel, American Flyer, Williams, K-Line, Weaver, etc. toy trains and accessories.

Tom Tomasik
2511 Pineview Dr. NE
Grand Rapids, MI 49505
phone: 616-361-9678

Edwin Wilder
1409 1st St.
Port Townsend, WA 98368-3078
Model railroad car, locomotive, structure kits - used, old. Also old locomotives and toy trains.

Dealers

Evertt A. Chapman
Dad's Trains & Granddad's Too
7 Lee Rd.
Barrington, RI 02806
phone: 401-245-0523

Bookbinder's Trains Unlimited
P.O. Box 660086
Flushing, NY 11366-0086
phone: 800-955-8729
fax: 718-657-2264
Internet: http://www.netpage1.com/bookbinderstrains/
Sells toy trains via his internet website.

Mike's Trainland, Inc.
5661 Shoulders Hill Rd.
Suffolk, VA 23435
phone: 804-484-4224
Sells vintage toy trains and scale model trains; also provides complete repair service.

Merri-Seven Trains
19155 Merriman
Livonia, MI 48152
phone: 313-474-5373
Buy, sell, trade, expert repairs, all gauges; thousands of original Lionel, American Flyer and other toy train parts in stock; large selection of post-war Lionel, Athearn and other new and used toy trains.

Dick & Shirley Durnbaugh
Trains & Things
108 South Saginaw
Holly, MI 48442
phone: 810-634-7420
Buys and sells Lionel, American Flyer, Marx, Matchbox; also operates train rooms in toy train museum.

Pat Neil
Collectible Trains & Toys
109 Medallion Center
Dallas, TX 75214
phone: 214-373-9469
fax: 214-373-1622
Buys and sells Lionel, Marklin, K-line, American Flyer, and others; also does repairs.

Experts

Richard Friz
P.O. Box 472
Peterborough, NH 03458
phone: 603-563-8155
Author of "The Official Price Guide to Toy Trains."

Ron Hollander
197 Lincoln Ave.
Newark, NJ 07104
Author of "All Aboard!" the story of the Lionel Train Company; will give free appraisal; send description, including manufacturer, type of car or engine, all numbers & lettering on any part of the car; include SASE for reply.

William M. Bean
439 Claxton Glen Ct.
Kettering, OH 45429
phone: 937-435-6196 or 937-439-2600
e-mail: ErectrBean@aol.com
Writes articles for the Train Collectors Association Quarterly.

Allan W. Miller
Antique Trader Books
P.O. Box 1050
Dubuque, IA 52004-1050
phone: 319-557-0647
e-mail: alstrains@aol.com
Editor of "O Gauge Railroading Primer"; author/contributor to "O gauge Railroader" magazine, "Vintage Rails" magazine, and Lionel Trains website; emphasis in O gauge and G gauge toy trains.

Museums/Libraries

Toy Train Museum of the Train Collectors Association
P.O. Box 248
Strasburg, PA 17579
phone: 717-687-8976 or 717-687-8623
fax: 717-687-0742
Has trains on display dating from the late 1800s to present; five operating layouts (one with hands-on buttons); gift shop and reference library also available.

Lancaster Train and Toy Museum
5661 Shoulders Hill Rd.
Suffolk, VA 23435
phone: 804-484-4224

Periodicals

Raymond G. Strutt
Newspaper: Collectors Gazette
18 Calvert Close
West Park Heights, Uckfield
East Sussex TN22 2BZ, U.K.
phone: +44 (0) 1825 768776
fax: +44 (0) 1825 760600
e-mail: cliente@icn.co.uk
Internet: http://www.icn.co.uk/cg.html
Published 10 times per year for toy and model collectors worldwide; covers tinplate toys, obsolete and modern diecast cars (Corgi, Dinky, Matchbox, EFE, Lledo, Days Gone, etc.) and models, trains, airplanes, ships, dolls, etc.

Roger Carp
Kalmbach Publishing Co.
Magazine: Classic Toy Trains
P.O. Box 1612
Waukesha, WI 53187-1612
phone: 414-796-8776 or 800-533-6644
fax: 414-796-1383
e-mail: customerservice@kalmbach.com
A bi-monthly magazine with articles on collecting, repairing, & operating Lionel, American Flyer, Marx, Ives, LGB & other toy trains; ads, toy fair reviews, layouts, museums, collectors; new and old trains.

Andy Sperandeo
Kalmbach Publishing Co.
Magazine: Model Railroader
P.O. Box 1612
Waukesha, WI 53187-1612
phone: 414-796-8776 or 800-533-6644
fax: 414-796-1383
e-mail: customerservice@kalmbach.com
A monthly magazine for the toy train collector and model railroad enthusiast; articles, ads, hardware, models, track systems, structures, layout tips, techniques, plans and projects.

Repair Services

Joe Mania
Downtown Trains
17 Douglas Rd.
Freehold, NJ 07728
phone: 908-303-8299
Repairs and restores all makes of toy trains.

Suppliers

Railroad Press Company, The
P.O. Box 2644
Novato, CA 94948
phone: 415-898-7030
fax: 415-897-2705
Toy train specialists carries books, stickers, signs, videos, whistles, stock certificates, coffee cups and much more for all Lionel, Flyer, Ives, Marx toy train fans.

Toy (American Flyer)

Dealers

Nathan Sonnheim
Private Collectors Group
Cherry Hill, NJ 08002-1562
phone: 609-667-3796
Buys Lionel and American Flyer trains; calls welcome.

Toy (Floor)

Experts

Rick Ralston
99-969 Iwaena St.
Aiea, HI 96701-3249
phone: 800-486-9794
fax: 808-486-1276
Author of "Cast Iron Floor Trains;" available from the author by calling 800-TOY-TRAIN.

Toy (Hornby)

Clubs/Associations

John Beadsmoore, Sec.
Hornby Railway Collectors' Association
Journal: Hornby Railway Collector, The
1, Park Street
Stapleford
Nottingham NG9 8EU, U.K.
phone: 0115-9497194
fax: 0115-9497194
Members also receive "The Directory of Replacement and Repair Services."

Toy (LGB)

Clubs/Associations

Dr. Mary Lentz, Sec.
LGB Model Railroad club
1854 Erin Dr.
Altoona, PA 16602-7612
A 2000+ member organization of LGB (Lehmann-Gross-Bahn) enthusiasts, mainly collectors.

Experts

Jack Barton
Buffington Publishing
1573 Landvater
Hummelstown, PA 17036
phone: 717-566-9400 or 717-566-9413
fax: 717-566-9428
e-mail: 73670.3673@compuserve.com
Internet: http://www.lgbtelegram.com
Writes "LGB Kollector" column for the "LGB Telegram" magazine; internationally known LGB collector.

Periodicals

Frances Buffington
Buffington Publishing
Magazine: LGB Telegram
1573 Landvater
Hummelstown, PA 17036
phone: 717-566-9400 or 717-566-9413
fax: 717-566-9428
e-mail: 73670.3673@compuserve.com
Internet: http://www.lgbtelegram.com
A quarterly magazine for LGB (Lehmann-Gross-Bahn) fans; features

articles on collecting as well as a column called "LGB Kollector" in every issue.

Toy (Lionel)

Clubs/Associations

Brenda Schlutow
Lionel Railroader Club
Newsletter: Inside Track
P.O. Box 748
New Baltimore, MI 48047
phone: 810-949-4100
Internet: http://www.Lionel.com
For model railroading enthusiasts; newsletter published quarterly.

Lionel Collectors Club of America
Newsletter: Lion Roars
P.O. Box 479
LaSalle, IL 61301
phone: 815-654-1705
Purpose is to promote and foster interest in Lionel electric trains.

Tom Arnold, II, VP
Lionel Operating Train Society
Magazine: Switcher
RR 2, Box 70
Teutopolis, IL 62467-9712
phone: 217-857-6314 or 217-342-2111
fax: 217-347-7343
e-mail: Trainman@effingham.net
The bi-monthly "Switcher" is loaded with layout designs, track plans, scenery construction, layout operating, maintenance, repair tips and techniques, building & rolling stock modification projects, club information & news.

Collectors

Charles Reuter
6 Joy Ave.
Mount Joy, PA 17552-1532
phone: 717-653-8505

Bob Schultz
18 Eland Ct.
Fairfield, OH 45014
phone: 513-793-9133

Robert L. Schultz
P.O. Box 62240
Cincinnati, OH 45242-0240
phone: 513-874-5583

Dealers

Nathan Sonnheim
Private Collectors Group
Cherry Hill, NJ 08002-1562
phone: 609-667-3796
Buys Lionel and American Flyer trains; calls welcome.

Gary D. Mosholder
Gary's Trains
186 Pine Springs Camp Road
Boswell, PA 15531-2421
phone: 814-629-9277
Buys and sells Lionel trains and accessories including Plasticville buildings; sends out periodical list of

items for sale; also carries parts and does repairs.

Trainmaster
Newsletter: Trainmaster
5001-B NW 34th St.
Gainesville, FL 32605
phone: 800-613-4222 or 352-373-4222
fax: 352-373-4468
Major dealer in Lionel trains; buys and sells; national market maker in secondary Lionel trains; published bi-monthly.

Experts

Ron Hollander
197 Lincoln Ave.
Newark, NJ 07104
Author of "All Aboard!" the story of the Lionel Train Company; will give free appraisal; send description, including manufacturer, type of car or engine, all numbers & lettering on any part of the car; include SASE for reply.

Tom McComas
P.O. Box 279
New Buffalo, MI 49117
Co-author with James Tuohy of "Lionel Price and Rarity Guide, Prewar O Gauge and Standard Gauge."

Periodicals

Roger P. Bryan
Lionel Collector Series Marketmaker
Price Guide: Trainmaster
3224 NW 47th Terrace
Gainesville, FL 32606-6017
phone: 904-377-7439 or 904-373-4908
fax: 904-374-6616
A quarterly publication; the number one Lionel Collector Series marketmaker/market report; geared to the advanced collector/investor.

Toy (Marklin)

(see also TOYS, Marklin)

Clubs/Associations

Marklin Club - North America
Magazine: insider
P.O. Box 51559
New Berlin, WI 53151
phone: 414-784-8854
fax: 414-784-1095
Internet: http://www.marklin.com
Dedicated to serving the interests of the Marklin enthusiast; helps enthusiasts get the most from Marklin trains and model railroading.

Marklin Digital Special Interest Group
Newsletter: Digital SIG, The
P.O. Box 51319
New Berlin, WI 53151-0319
phone: 414-784-8854
fax: 414-784-1095
Provides its members with in-depth knowledge and insight into the advanced Marklin Digital control technology.

Collectors

Ronald Wiener
Packard Bldg. - 12th Floor
111 S. 15th St.
Philadelphia, PA 19102-2625
phone: 215-977-2266
fax: 215-977-2334
e-mail: rwiener@wolfblock.com
Wants Marklin (German) metal toys and toy trains, 1895-1960 in original and excellent condition, especially pre-1942 O gauge; also other old metal toys in excellent condition.

Grant A. Krienberg
108 Brave Court
Suisun City, CA 94585-1304
phone: 707-864-1823 or 916-552-8736
fax: 707-864-9240
e-mail: grantk@castles.com
Collector seeks "O" gauge Marklin and other European trains.

Experts

Robert Monaghan
c/o Greenberg Publishing Co.
7566 Main St.
Sykesville, MD 21784
phone: 410-795-7447
Author of "Greenberg's Guide to Marklin OO/HO."

Man./Prod./Dist.

Fred Gates, Pres.
Marklin, Inc.
16988 W. Victor Rd.
P.O. Box 51319
New Berlin, WI 53151-0319
phone: 414-784-8854
fax: 414-784-1095
Marklin, Inc. is the American subsidiary of Gebr. Marklin & Cie. GmbH and is the exclusive distributor in North America for Marklin products.

Toy (Marx)

Collectors

Bill Smith
56 Locust St.
East Douglas, MA 01516-2440
phone: 508-476-2015
Wants to buy all Marx trains and related items regardless of condition; especially interested in Marx train catalogs.

Toy (Plasticville)

Dealers

Gary D. Mosholder
Gary's Trains
186 Pine Springs Camp Road
Boswell, PA 15531-2421
phone: 814-629-9277
Buys and sells Lionel trains and accessories including Plasticville buildings; sends out periodical list of items for sale; also carries parts and does repairs.

Bill Nole
319 Oak St.
Dunmore, PA 18512
phone: 717-343-2236

Dennis Teepe
6802 GLenkirk Rd.
Baltimore, MD 21239
phone: 410-832-5375
e-mail: dteepe@mail.bcpl.lib.md.us

TRAMP ART

(see also FOLK ART; HOBO
COLLECTIBLES)

Dealers

Michael T. Meadows
Meadows House Antiques
919 Stiles St.
Baltimore, MD 21202-4426
phone: 410-837-5427

Matt Lippa
Artisans
P.O. Box 256
Mentone, AL 35984-0256
phone: 205-634-4037
fax: 205-634-4037
e-mail: artisans@folkartisans.com
Internet: http://www.folkartisans.com
*Buy and sell folk art, outsider art, fine
art; Internet WWW site offers links to
additional dealers; also offers non-
profit clubs and museums with an
outlet to post notices, press releases,
calendar items, etc. at no charge.*

Anne Foster
1913 Hyde St.
San Francisco, CA 94109
phone: 415-776-8865
*Wants all kinds of tramp art including
frames, boxes, miniature pieces of
furniture, etc.*

Experts

Michael Cornish
Cigar Box Antiques
92 Florence St.
Roslindale, MA 02131-2603
phone: 617-323-6029
*Buys, sells and repairs tramp art
(layered and notched objects made
from recycled wood c. 1870-1940);
seeks unusual or furniture pieces; co-
writing a book on tramp art with
Clifford Wallach; especially wants
elaborate boxes.*

Clifford Wallach
277 W. 10th St.
New York, NY 10014-2562
phone: 212-243-1007
fax: 212-239-0747
*Co-writing a book on tramp art with
Michael Cornish; buys and sells
exceptional forms of tramp art: boxes
to furniture; special interest in signed
pieces and known makers.*

Helaine Fendelman
Helaine Fendelman & Assoc.
1248 Post Rd.
Scarsdale, NY 10583-2153
phone: 914-725-0292
fax: 914-472-2266
e-mail: HFendelman@aol.com
Writing a book on tramp art.

TRANSPORTATION COL-LECTIBLES

(see also AIRLINE MEMORABILIA;
AIRSHIPS; AUTOMOBILES;
AUTOMOBILIA; AVIATION; BUS
LINE COLLECTIBLES; BUSES;
GAS STATION COLLECTIBLES;
LUGGAGE LABELS; OCEAN
LINER COLLECTIBLES; RAIL-
ROAD COLLECTIBLES; STEAM-
BOAT COLLECTIBLES; STREET-
CAR LINE COLLECTIBLES;
TRUCKS

Clubs/Associations

Courtney Haydon
Transport Ticket Society
Journal: Transport Ticket Society
Journal
4 Gladridge Close
Earley, Reading
Berks RG6 7DL, U.K.
*Interested in the collection of tickets,
transfers, passes, tokens, and other
items issued by companies in the fare
collection process; also ticket issuing
machines.*

Collectors

Seth Bramson
330 N.E. 96th St.
Miami, FL 33138-2718
phone: 305-757-1016
fax: 305-895-8178
*Buys all U.S. RR/trolley/steamship/
airline and bus memorabilia; all
Floridiana and U.S. travel &
destination material - things put out
by boards of trade, chambers of
commerce, cities, counties, towns,
hotels, restaurants, businesses.*

Dealers

Stephen Hansrote
Griffin Trading Company
13663 Jupiter Rd., Ste. 406
Dallas, TX 75238
phone: 214-341-0660
fax: 214-341-0660
e-mail: griffintc@aol.com
Internet: http://www.members.aol.com/
griffintc/website.htm
*Buying and selling plane, train,
automobile and ship collectibles;
everything from advertising and signs
to equipment and actual parts and
supplies.*

Scott Arden
Antiques & Artifacts
20457 Highway 126
Noti, OR 97461-9706
phone: 503-935-1619
Leading RR mail order dealer for 26

*years; catalog $1; buys and sells fine
old transportation items, mostly non-
paper; consignment.*

Museums/Libraries

Charles Chiarchiaro
Owls Head Transportation Museum
Rte. 73 Box 277
Owls Head, ME 04854
phone: 207-594-4418
fax: 207-594-4410
e-mail: ohtmuseum@aol.com

Western Reserve Historical Society
10825 East Blvd.
Cleveland, OH 44106-1703
phone: 216-721-5722
fax: 216-721-0645
Internet: http://www.wrhs.org
*Oldest cultural institution in
Cleveland, with a research/
genealogical library, costume wing,
auto & aviation museum and restored
mansion under one roof; special
interest area in automobiles and
aviation.*

Pate Museum of Transportation
P.O. Box 711
Pate, TX 76101

China

Experts

Richard Luckin
621 Cascade Ct.
Golden, CO 80403-1581
phone: 303-278-8669
fax: 303-215-0095
*Collector of transportation china for
over 30 years; author of "Dining On
Rails," "Teapot Treasury", and
"Mimbres to Mimbreno"; also designs
and supplies china for private
railroad cars and for business cars for
various railroads.*

Timetables

Clubs/Associations

Norbert Shacklette, Mem.
National Association of Timetable
Collectors
Newsletter: First Edition, The
125 American Inn Rd.
Villa Ridge, MO 63089-2153
*Interested in timetables from airlines,
steamships, railroads, and bus lines.*

Collectors

George Johnson
P.O. Box 1449
Lexington, VA 24450-1449
phone: 703-464-4326
fax: 703-464-4326
*Wants to buy pre-1940 timetables;
railroad, trolley, airline or bus; any
quantity; also wants passes, catalogs,
and depot postcards.*

TRAPS

Clubs/Associations

Tom Parr
North American Trap Collectors
Association
Newsletter: TRAPS
P.O. Box 94
Galloway, OH 43119-0094
phone: 614-878-6011
*Members interested in the preserva-
tion of all trapping devices (animal,
fish, bird, insect), trap operations,
trapping literature, fur trade industry
memorabilia, sporting collectibles,
trapping magazines and paper
ephemera, etc.*

National Trappers Association
Magazine: American Trapper, The
P.O. Box 3667
Bloomington, IL 61701
phone: 309-829-2422
*Over 20,000 members; magazine
published bi-monthly.*

Collectors

Jack Lay
101 Glenview Crescent, Box 243
Princeton
Brit. Columbia VOX 1WO Canada
phone: 604-295-6010

Ron Willoughby
Rte. 171 Box 1072
Woodstock, CT 06281-2122
phone: 860-974-1226
fax: 860-974-3190
e-mail: swillo@neca.com
Internet: http://www.neca.com/~swillo
*Wants to buy oddly-shaped traps and
bear traps; also buying all trapping
paper and memorabilia as well as lure
containers, smokers, advertising
items, etc.; a very serious buyer.*

Ron B. Frodelius
P.O. Box 125
Fayetteville, NY 13066-0125
*Wants anything related to trapping;
ads, books, catalogs, magazines, hunt-
trader-trapper, fur-fish-game
magazines, mouse traps, mole traps,
rat traps; also firearms books.*

Robert Kwalwasser
168 Camp Fatima Rd.
Renfrew, PA 16053-9104
phone: 412-789-7766
*Wants old gopher, mole, mouse, fly,
minnow, and rat traps.*

Terry Swartz
RD 1 Box 197 A
Blain, PA 17006
phone: 717-536-3733

Chuck Clift
103 Duck Cove
Elmore, AL 36025
phone: 205-285-6522
*Collects animal traps - everything
from mouse to bear traps; specializes
in mouse, rat, gopher, mole, killer,*

glass minnows and glass fly traps;
odd shaped traps; traps with teeth.

Archie H. Stevens, Sr.
2196 AuSable Pt. Rd.
East Tawas, MI 48730
phone: 517-739-7006 or 602-471-7085
*Wants antique traps: bear, wolf,
handforged, Newhouse, any size.*

Sam Delavan
RR 3
Glenwood, IA 51534
phone: 717-527-9513

Terry Burger
2323 Lincoln
Beatrice, NE 68310-3306
phone: 402-228-2797

Clay Tontz
4043 Nora
Covina, CA 91722
phone: 818-338-99767
*Wants traps - from mice to moose;
only the scarce and unusual.*

Jim Gipe
21149 NE 212th Ave.
Battle Ground, WA 98604
phone: 206-687-2793

Dealers

William A. Russ
Russ Trading Post
23 William St.
Addison, NY 14801-1326
phone: 607-359-3896
*Buys and sells antique traps including
bear traps; also issues a catalog of
trapping supplies.*

Dennis Helman
6969 Wright Puthoff Rd.
Sidney, OH 45365
phone: 513-492-5769

Experts

Boyd Nedry
728 Buth Dr.
Comstock Park, MI 49321-9504
phone: 616-784-1513
*Specializes in unusual animal traps or
related items: fly, mouse, mole,
minnow, bear, rat, gopher, cockroach,
handcrafted; any material: wood,
glass, metal, etc.; any age; also books
and advertising on trapping.*

Museums/Libraries

Charles E. Hanson, Jr., Dir.
Museum of the Fur Trade
Magazine: MFT Quarterly
6321 Highway 20
Chadron, NE 69337-9501
phone: 308-432-3843
*Dedicated to the study of the American
fur trade from colonial times to the
present; furs, traps, trade guns, trade
goods, Indians; not involved with
present day trapping.*

Periodicals

Julie A. Ulrich, PR
Krause Publications
Magazine: Trapper & Predator Caller,
The
700 E. State St.
Iola, WI 54990-0001
phone: 715-445-2214
fax: 715-445-4087
e-mail: info@krause.com
Internet: http://www.krause.com
*A monthly magazine about hunting,
trapping and predator calling, and
animal damage control.*

Fly

Collectors

Ralph Finch
20135 Evergreen Meadows
Southfield, MI 48076-4222
phone: 248-358-4763 or 800-678-6400
fax: 313-222-2451
*Wants to buy fly traps in odd colors,
shapes and sizes.*

Maris Zuika
P.O. Box 175
Parchment, MI 49004
phone: 616-344-7473

Rat/Mouse/Fly

Collectors

Robert Kwalwasser
168 Camp Fatima Rd.
Renfrew, PA 16053-9104
phone: 412-789-7766
*Wants old mouse, fly, minnow, and rat
traps.*

Tom Edmonds
6306 East Pea Ridge Rd.
Huntington, WV 25705
phone: 304-697-5280
*Wants antique mousetraps; prefers
live catch or capture traps.*

TRAPSHOOTING

(see also SPORTING COL-
LECTIBLES; TARGET SHOOTING
MEMORABILIA)

Museums/Libraries

Trapshooting Hall of Fame & Museum
601 W National Rd.
Vandalia, OH 45377-1036
phone: 513-898-1945

TRAVEL COLLECTIBLES

(see HIGHWAY COLLECTIBLES;
HOTEL COLLECTIBLES; SOUVE-
NIR & COMMEMORATIVE ITEMS)

TREASURE HUNTING

(see also ARCHAEOLOGY;
BOTTLES; CIVIL WAR ARTI-
FACTS; COINS & CURRENCY;
PREHISTORIC ARTIFACTS)

Clubs/Associations

Mike Race
Federation of Metal Detector &
Archeological Clubs, Inc.
Newsletter: Quest, The
1614-O Union Valley Rd., Ste. Box 131
West Milford, NJ 07480-2222
phone: 717-355-0691
*The FMDAC is composed of over 190
clubs. Goals include the promoting
and protecting of the metal detecting
hobby.*

Wayne K. Hunt
Preservation of the Independent
Detectorist Club, The
460 W. Berwick St.
Easton, PA 18402
phone: 610-252-2988
*A club within the Federation of Metal
Detector & Archeological Clubs
primarily for individuals unable to
join a local FMDAC chapter.*

Periodicals

Newsletter: Treasure Hunter's Gazette
14 Vernon St.
Keene, NH 03431

Rosemary Anderson, MngEd
Magazine: Western & Eastern Treasures
Magazine
P.O. Box 1598
Mercer Island, WA 98040-1598
phone: 800-999-9718
*The world's treasure hunting
authority written by experts for metal
detecting enthusiasts; improve your
skills, upgrade equipment, research
treasure sites, first hand accounts of
coin, artifact, gold finds.*

TREES & SHRUBS

Clubs/Associations

International Society of Arboriculture
P.O. Box GG
Savoy, IL 61874
phone: 217-355-9411
fax: 217-355-9516
*Send for "Guide for Establishing
Values of Trees and Other Plants";
publishes catalog of arboriculture
books, gifts, study guides, plant health
manuals, brochures and videos.*

Misc. Services

Greydon Tolson
Guardian Tree Experts
12200 Nebel St.
Rockville, MD 20852
phone: 301-881-8550
Appraises trees and shrubs.

TRENCH ART

(see also AMMUNITION &
EXPLOSIVE ORDNANCE, Shell
Casings)

Collectors

C. Wolak
1703 Second Ave., Apt. 4S
New York, NY 10128
*Wants interesting and unusual pieces
of trench art.*

Ed Mickel
5011 Briargrove Ln.
Dallas, TX 75287-7408
phone: 972-407-6960
*Collector of engraved shell casings
and other items made from shell
casings or parts of shell casings,
bullets, rotating bands or shrapnel;
especially interested in WWI items.*

TRIBAL

(see AMERICAN INDIAN; ART,
African & Tribal; ART, Indonesian;
ART, Oceanic; PRECOLUMBIAN)

TRINKET BOXES

(see BOXES; FAIRINGS)

TRIVETS

(see also IRONS, Pressing)

Collectors

Carol Hansen
c/o Scientific American Magazine
415 Madison Ave., 1st Floor
New York, NY 10017
phone: 212-754-0598
e-mail: chansen@sciam.com
*Doing research for an extensive trivet
collector.*

TROLLEY LINE COLLECTIBLES

(see RAILROAD COLLECTIBLES;
STREETCAR LINE COL-
LECTIBLES)

TROLLS

(see also DOLLS; ELVES)

Collectors

Debbie Brown
541 South St. Clair St.
Painesville, OH 44077-3636
phone: 216-354-6412
*Wants trolls & related items in any
condition, any number: trolls, troll
houses, handlebar covers, charms,
outfits, animals, etc.; wants Greek
God, PAN, statues, pictures, etc.*

Cindy Meyers
8829 Fourteen Mile
Sterling Heights, MI 48312
phone: 810-268-1771
*Wants trolls and troll animals; single
piece or entire collections.*

Sally Kimmel
1471 Lark Lane
Concord, CA 94521
phone: 510-676-2857
*Troll lover wants 1960s to 1990s
trolls, any size, tailed trolls, animal
trolls (especially monkey), charms,*

pencil tops, clothes, houses, etc. - anything with trolls; any condition; one piece or entire collections.

Ellen Schmidt
P.O. Box 601292
Sacramento, CA 95860-1292
phone: 916-455-7678
fax: 916-455-7678
e-mail: 75112.1161@compuserve.com
Serious collector wants to buy 1960s trolls: animal trolls (cow, turtle, elephant, monkey, reindeer, etc.), tailed trolls, trolls in original outfits, store displays, and anything troll related.

Marci Van Ausdall
P.O. Box 946
Quincy, CA 95971
phone: 916-283-2770
e-mail: dreams@psln.com
Wants to buy pre-1960 Trolls, clothing, accessories; jewelry; unusual items.

Experts

Jeanne Niswonger
P.O. Box 338
Oakdale, CA 95361-0338
Author of "Troll Dolls."

Periodicals

Lisa Kerner
Newsletter: Troll Monthly
216 Washington St.
Canton, MA 02021
Newsletter for trollaholics; free 40-word ad for anyone with trolls for sale; also buys and sells trolls.

Ellen Schmidt
Newsletter: Troll'n
P.O. Box 601292
Sacramento, CA 95860-1292
phone: 916-455-7678
fax: 916-455-7678
e-mail: 75112.1161@compuserve.com
Newsletter for trollaholics; free 40-word ad for anyone with trolls for sale; also buys and sells trolls.

TROPHIES

(see ANIMAL TROPHIES; MORBID & ODD ITEMS; SPORTING COLLECTIBLES)

TRUCK LINE COLLECTIBLES

(see TRANSPORTATION COLLECTIBLES; TRUCKS)

TRUCKS

(see also AUTOMOBILES; AUTOMOBILIA; FIRE FIGHTING MEMORABILIA, Apparatus; MILITARIA, Vehicles; TOYS, Hess; TOYS, Transportation; TRAILERS & RV'S; TRANSPORTATION COLLECTIBLES)

Clubs/Associations

Antique Truck Club of America, Inc.
Magazine: Double Clutch
P.O. Box 291
Hershey, PA 17033-0291
phone: 717-533-9032
Focuses on antique trucks and other commercial vehicles.

Larry L. Scheef, Man. Dir.
American Truck Historical Society
Magazine: Wheels of Time
P.O. Box 531168
Birmingham, AL 35253-1168
phone: 205-870-0566
fax: 205-870-3069
Recognized by the American Trucking Association as the official archives for the trucking industry; collects & preserves the history of trucks, trucking, and its pioneers; many chapters throughout the U.S. and Canada.

Mike Anderson
Antique Aviation & Truck Society
4533 Highway 201
Ontario, OR 97914
phone: 503-889-2378

Collectors

N.W. Neill, Jr.
P.O. Box 38
Ennice, NC 28623-0038
phone: 910-657-8152
fax: 910-657-8084
Wants to buy pre-1948 Dodge trucks, literature, ads, etc.; Dodge Power Wagons 1 ton 1946-1968; anything on Dodge cab-over trucks.

Al Koenig
P.O. Box 6122
Rochester, MN 55903-6122
phone: 800-533-1702
Wants 1930s to 1950s truck drivers' cap badges; also wants any other trucking company badges, trucking company lapel pins, cloth emblems, and other trucking company memorabilia.

Museums/Libraries

Van Horn Truck Museum
15272 North St.
Mason City, IA 50401-9292
phone: 515-423-9066 or 515-423-0550
fax: 515-423-2570
Over 60 models of pre-1930 trucks; early gas engines, gas pumps, signs and mobilia, old country store items and early farm items; 1930 store front streets, circus room with large scale model circus one man spent 34 years making!

Periodicals

Magazine: This Old Truck
P.O. Box 838
Yellow Springs, OH 45387
phone: 937-767-1433 or 800-767-5828
fax: 937-767-2726
e-mail: antique@antiquepower.com
Internet: http://www.antiquepower.com
Full color magazine covering all makes of light trucks and commercial vehicles 1980 and earlier.

Deals on Wheels Publications
Magazine: Truck, Race, Cycle & Recreation
P.O. Box 205
Sioux Falls, SD 57101
phone: 605-338-7666 or 800-334-1886
fax: 605-338-5337
Internet: http://www.dealsonwheels.com
Photo-ad magazine listing trucks, 4-wheel drives, cycles, race equipment, race cars, boats, recreation vehicles, trailers, jet-skis; classifieds.

Steve Ferguson, Ed.
National Automobile Dealers Association
Price Guide: N.A.D.A. Official Used Car Guide
P.O. Box 7800
Costa Mesa, CA 92628
phone: 800-966-6232
fax: 714-556-8715
e-mail: steve.ferguson@nadaguides.com
Internet: http://www.nadaguide.com
A series of value guides for domestic and foreign cars, trucks, vans, RV's, mobile homes, motorcycles, snowmobiles, and boats, small and large; also Heavy Duty Trucks and Aircraft Book, car clubs & organizations, museums.

Chevrolet

Clubs/Associations

National Chevy/GMC Truck Association
Newsletter: Pickups 'N Panels in Print
P.O. Box 607458
Orlando, FL 32860
phone: 407-889-5387
fax: 407-886-7571
e-mail: CHECY55-72@ao.net
Internet: http://www.ao.net/CHEVY55-72
An organization by and for 1911 through 1972 Chevrolet/GMC enthusiasts; national and local shows, local clubs.

Periodicals

Dobbs Publishing Group
Magazine: Chevy Truck
3816 Industry Blvd.
Lakeland, FL 33811
phone: 941-644-0449 or 815-734-6026
e-mail: dobbs@gate.net
Internet: http://www.d-p-g.com/
Aimed at owners of Chevrolet full- and mid-size pickups and sport utility vehicles who seek to enhance performance and add individualized appearance to their truck; a bi-

monthly, manufacturer-specific truck title.

Commercial

Clubs/Associations

Light Commercial Vehicle Association
Newsletter: Classic Trucks
P.O. Box 838
Yellow Springs, OH 45387
Dedicated to the enjoyment and preservation of light truck-type vehicles of all kinds; vehicle ownership not required for membership; has regional chapters and coordinates regional meets.

Ford

Clubs/Associations

Ford Truck Club International
Route 3
Caledonia
Ontario N3W 2B9 Canada

Dennis Coning
Old Ford Truck Club
2675 Hamilton Mason Rd.
Hamilton, OH 45011-5367
phone: 513-868-3489 or 513-753-9495
e-mail: oftc@choice.net
Internet: http://www.choice.net/~oftc

TRUNKS

(see also LEATHER; LUGGAGE)

Dealers

Trunk Shop, The
23 Ceres St.
Portsmouth, NH 03801
phone: 603-431-4399
e-mail: tts@ici.net
Internet: http://www.trunk.com
Refinishes and sells antique trunks.

Antique Trunk Co.
3706 W. 169th St.
Cleveland, OH 44111
phone: 216-941-8618
Buy, sell, trade, restore, and repairs old trunks; also carries repair supplies.

Repair Services

Doris Harroff
AAA Antique Shop
953 W. Market
U.S. 6 West
Nappanee, IN 46550
phone: 219-773-4912
Buys, sells and restores trunks.

Laurie A. Root
Original Woodworks
360 North Main St.
Stillwater, MN 55082-5024
phone: 612-430-3622
e-mail: orgwood@iaxs.net
Internet: http://home.iaxs.net/orgwood
Specializing in complete antique trunk repair and restoration; will transform your trunk inside and out into a treasured family heirloom.

House of Antique Trunks
753 B Northport Dr.
P.O. Box 508
West Sacramento, CA 95691-0508
phone: 916-372-8228
*Antique trunk restoration parts &
accessories; doll trunk supplies;
chromolithographs for lids; linings,
adhesives, leather; repairs.*

Suppliers

Charlotte Ford Trunks
Newsletter: Trunk Talk
P.O. Box 536
Spearman, TX 79081
phone: 806-659-3027 or 800-553-2649
*Publishes a parts catalog for trunk
restorations; color newsletter gives
tips on cleaning, repairing and
decorating old trunks.*

Muff's Antiques
135 S. Glassell St.
Orange, CA 92866
phone: 714-997-0243
fax: 714-997-1601
Internet: http://www.tias.com/amdir/
SpecTrunks.html
*Buys, sells, trades, repairs old trunks;
also new and old repair parts, locks,
keys, supplies; catalog $5.*

TUMBLERS

(see GLASSES, Drinking)

TUPPERWARE

Museums/Libraries

Tupperware Museum, The
P.O. Box 2353
Orlando, FL 32802
phone: 305-847-3111

TURNPIKE COLLECTIBLES

(see HIGHWAY COLLECTIBLES)

TV'S

(see TELEVISION SHOWS &
MEMORABILIA; TELEVISIONS)

20th CENTURY

(see Chapter "A", page 2)

TWINS

(see BIRTH RELATED ITEMS)

TYPEWRITERS

(see also ADDING MACHINES;
ADVERTISING COLLECTIBLES,
Typewriter Related; CALCULA-
TORS; OFFICE EQUIPMENT)

Book Sellers

Barbara Lippman
1216 Garden St.
Hoboken, NJ 07030-4406
phone: 201-656-5278
e-mail: barblip@aol.com
Selling "American Typewriters: A

*Collector's Encyclopedia" by the late
Paul Lippman.*

Clubs/Associations

Darryl Rehr, Ed.
Early Typewriter Collectors Association
Magazine: ETCetera
2591 Military Ave.
Los Angeles, CA 90064-1933
phone: 310-477-5229
fax: 310-268-8420
e-mail: dcrehr@earthlink.net
Internet: http://www.earthlink.net/
~dcrehr/
*An international club for collectors of
old office equipment; provides contact
with worldwide network of over 500
members; free ads.*

Collectors

Peter Frei
P.O. Box 500
Brimfield, MA 01010-0500
phone: 800-942-8968 or 413-245-4660
*Wants old typewriters, adding
machines, sewing machines, and old
vacuum cleaners, etc.*

Anthony Casillo
325 Nassau Blvd.
Garden City, NY 11530-5313
phone: 516-489-8300 or 516-742-4919
fax: 516-489-6501
e-mail: typebar@aol.com
Internet: http://www.members.aol.com/
typebar/collectible/typewriter.htm
*Wants to buy old, unusual typewriters;
is always glad to assist anyone who
has questions about an old typewriter;
can date and evaluate.*

Frank Briola
P.O. Box 44022
Pittsburgh, PA 15205-0222
phone: 412-937-8787 or 800-372-6509
Wants early or unusual typewriters.

Howard Hazelcorn
6731 Ashley Ct.
Sarasota, FL 34241-9696
phone: 941-921-1815
*Collects and specializes in early
typewriters; wants to buy typewriters
made between 1873 and 1910.*

Jerry Propst
P.O. Box 45
Janesville, WI 53547-0045
phone: 608-752-2816
fax: 608-752-7691
*When writing, please include a LSASE
if requesting a reply.*

Mike Brooks
7335 Skyline
Oakland, CA 94611-1121
phone: 510-339-1751
e-mail: deborahwb@aol.com
*20 year collector buying early oddball
typewriters, braille writers, shorthand
machines and other 19th century
office machines; gladly provides free
appraisals by telephone; call
evenings.*

Jim Rauen
6937 Glenview Dr.
San Jose, CA 95120-5437
phone: 408-268-2943
fax: 408-268-5475
*Collects typewriters and some related
office equipment, especially pre-1900;
will buy, sell, trade, and answer
inquiries on typewriter history and
values.*

Conrad & Terry Hamil
Typewriters
615 Grandridge
Grandview, WA 98930-1542
phone: 509-882-3617
*Wants to buy typewriters, ribbon tins,
typing collectibles.*

Dealers

Graham Forsdyke
158 Hampton Rd.
Chingford
London E4 8NT, U.K.
*Buys, sells and collects mechanical
antiques, especially early typewriters.*

Sandy Sellers
P.O. Box 35
Glenburnie
Ontario K0H 1S0 Canada
phone: 613-542-5598
*Wants to buy old typewriters and
other lettering machines and related
ephemera.*

Experts

Hobart D. Van Deusen
28 The Green
Watertown, CT 06795-2118
phone: 860-945-3456
*Collects and advises on typewriter-
related items: blotters, carbon paper
boxes, erasing shields, letter heads,
rulers, letter openers, etc.*

Darryl Rehr
2591 Military Ave.
Los Angeles, CA 90064-1933
phone: 310-477-5229
fax: 310-268-8420
e-mail: dcrehr@earthlink.net
Internet: http://www.earthlink.net/
~dcrehr/
*Wants pre-1915 typewriters & related
advertising, especially typewriters w/o
keyboards; send SASE for free
information pamphlet.*

Museums/Libraries

Milwaukee Public Museum
800 W. Wells St.
Milwaukee, WI 53233
phone: 414-278-2702

Periodicals

Tom Fitzgerald
Newsletter: Typewriter Exchange, The
2125 Mount Vernon St.
Philadelphia, PA 19130
*For collectors of early office
equipment; published quarterly.*

Ribbon Tins

Collectors

Millie Vaccarella
1955 Hythe St.
Roseville, MN 55113
phone: 612-631-2201
Wants to buy or trade ribbon tins.

Darryl Rehr
2591 Military Ave.
Los Angeles, CA 90064-1933
phone: 310-477-5229
fax: 310-268-8420
e-mail: dcrehr@earthlink.net
Internet: http://www.earthlink.net/
~dcrehr/
*Wants tins of all sizes and makes,
especially those with unusual shapes
& graphics; any amount; send
description or photocopy.*

Steve Hosier
44711 N. Cedar Ave.
Lancaster, CA 93534-3210
phone: 805-946-7118
Wants typewriter ribbon tins.

Experts

Hobart D. Van Deusen
28 The Green
Watertown, CT 06795-2118
phone: 860-945-3456
*Wants typewriter ribbon tins - small
tin boxes used from 1880s to 1950
with graphic designs on them; has
duplicates to sell; will help identify;
also collects and advises on
typewriter-related items: blotters,
carbon paper boxes, etc.*

Periodicals

Hobart D. Van Deusen
Newsletter: Ribbon Tin News
28 The Green
Watertown, CT 06795-2118
phone: 860-945-3456
*Serves as a resource for collectors
looking for information, current news,
exchange of views, and social
intercourse with fellow collectors;
enhances the buying, selling, pricing,
trading of typewriter ribbon tins and
related items.*

554

Here are some tips when contacting someone listed in this book:

When requesting information about a particular item, include a description (material, dimensions, maker's mark, model number, etc.) and a photo, sketch, or photocopy of the item in question. ■

Always ask if there are charges for samples or for the services requested. ■

When writing, please be sure to include a Large (#10 business size) Self-Addressed and Stamped Envelope (LSASE) if requesting a reply or the return of photographs. ■

Never call collect unless otherwise directed. When calling, be considerate of time zone differences and always ask if the party you are calling has time to talk. When leaving an answering machine message, always instruct the party to call you back collect. ■

U.S. POSTAL SERVICE ITEMS

(see POSTAL SERVICE ITEMS; POSTCARDS, Post Office Related; STAMP COLLECTING)

UFO'S & UNEXPLAINED PHENOMENA

(see also BOOKS, Metaphysics; MAGICIANS PARAPHERNALIA; MORBID & ODD ITEMS; SCIENCE FICTION)

Collectors

Lucius Farish
2 Caney Valley Dr.
Plumerville, AR 72127-8725
phone: 501-354-2558
Wants books, booklets, periodicals, and tapes on UFO's, extraterrestrial life, Atlantis, Bigfoot, occultism, unexplained phenomena.

Museums/Libraries

International U.F.O. Museum & Research Center
40-402 N. Main
P.O. Box 2221
Roswell, NM 88202
phone: 505-625-9495
fax: 505-625-1907

UFO Enigma Museum
6108 S. Main
P.O. Box 6047
Roswell, NM 88202
phone: 505-347-2275

Periodicals

Lucius Farish
Newsletter: UFO Newsclipping Service
2 Caney Valley Dr.
Plumerville, AR 72127-8725
phone: 501-354-2558
Current press reports of UFOs/ unexplained phenomena from around the world; newsclippings compiled in 20-page monthly issues; since 1969.

UMBRELLAS

(see CANES & WALKING STICKS)

UNICORNS

Clubs/Associations

Unicorns Unanimous
248 N. Larchmont Blvd.
Los Angeles, CA 90004

VACUUM CLEANERS

Collectors

Peter Frei
P.O. Box 500
Brimfield, MA 01010-0500
phone: 800-942-8968 or 413-245-4660
Wants to buy hand powered vacuum cleaners.

Billy Lipman
7428 Park Heights Ave.
Baltimore, MD 21208
phone: 410-486-1969
Wants to buy antique vacuum cleaners: hand-pumped and hand-cranked vacuums; also VERY EARLY electric uprights and canister vacuums; also wants parts; call or send description; all calls returned.

Roger A. Proehl
205 East Joppa Rd. #1005
Baltimore, MD 21286-3221
phone: 410-296-4545
Buys, sells and trades pre-1940 vacuums; Hamilton Beach, Bee Vac, Apex, Hoover Duster; old parts needed such as bags, brushes, etc.; wants anything unusual.

Dealers

Grant Aslett
Don Aslett's Antiques
P.O. Box 39
Pocatello, ID 83204
phone: 208-232-6212
fax: 208-232-6286
Wants unique cleaning collectibles: vacuums, household items, cleaners, sweepers.

Museums/Libraries

C.A. (Stacy) Krammes, Dir.
Hoover Historical Center
Newspaper: Center News
2225 Easton St., NW
Canton, OH 44720-3339
phone: 330-499-0287 or 330-499-9200
fax: 330-499-0287
Boyhood home of W. H. Hoover; has extensive collection of antique and early electric vacuum cleaners & vacuum industry memorabilia; six herb gardens June-Sept., guided tours, extensive programming.

Christian G. Carron
Grand Rapids Public Museum
272 Pearl St. NW
Grand Rapids, MI 49504-5371
phone: 616-456-3977
fax: 616-456-3873
World's largest collection of carpet sweepers representing over 150 manufacturers worldwide; archives and advertising collection of the Bissell Carpet Sweeper Company.

Don Aslett
Don Aslett's Cleaning Museum
P.O. Box 700
Pocatello, ID 83204
phone: 800-451-2402
Wants to buy vintage vacuums,
commodes, cleaners in original packaging, ads, janitorial stuff, floor polishers, brooms, brushes, buckets, mops, posters suitable for museum.

VACUUM TUBES

(see RADIOS, Tubes for)

VALENTINES

(see also CARDS; ELVES; HOLIDAY COLLECTIBLES; PAPER COLLECTIBLES)

Auction Services

Evalene Pulati
Pulati Auctions
P.O. Box 1404
Santa Ana, CA 92702-1404
phone: 714-547-1355

Clubs/Associations

Evalene Pulati
National Valentine Collectors Association
Newsletter: National Valentine Collectors Bulletin
P.O. Box 1404
Santa Ana, CA 92702-1404
phone: 714-547-1355
The quarterly newsletter focuses on collecting valentines; identification, values, ads.

Dealers

David & Katherine Kreider
Kingsbury Antiques
P.O. Box 7957
Lancaster, PA 17604-7957
phone: 717-892-3001

Katherine Kreider
Kingsbury Antiques
P.O. Box 7957
Lancaster, PA 17604-7957
phone: 717-892-3001
One of the largest dealers of Valentines.

Experts

Evalene Pulati
P.O. Box 1404
Santa Ana, CA 92702-1404
phone: 714-547-1355
Author of "Illustrated Valentine Price Guides", updated in 1994, now available for $16.95 ppd.

VAMPIRES

(see HORROR, Dracula)

VAUDEVILLE MEMORABILIA

Collectors

Collector
6 Chancery Ln.
Chico, CA 95926
Wants original Vaudeville sheet music, posters, photos and movie memorabilia.

VENTRILOQUIST ITEMS

(see also PUPPETS; PERFORMING ARTS)

Collectors

Peter Kidd
P.O. Box 1188
Shirley, MA 01464-1188
phone: 617-894-4040
Wants ventriloquial figures; professional, full size; age and condition not critical; high level of articulation desired.

T. Keppler
145 Lake Ave.
Nesconset, NY 11767
phone: 516-361-4957
Wants ventriloquist dolls: Jerry Mahoney, Knucklehead Smiff, Moe Howard, and other uncommon vents.

M.A. Denemark
12 Harbor Circle
Cocoa Beach, FL 32931
Wants magazine ads with Edgar Bergen and Charlie McCarthy (Coke, GE, etc.), arcade cards, any ventriloquist item.

Andy Gross
P.O. Box 6134
Beverly Hills, CA 90212-1134
phone: 310-820-3308 or 310-285-8815
fax: 310-768-1097
e-mail: apedoll69@aol.com
Wants ventriloquist dummies and or any related items such as puppets, toys, games, photos, books, marionettes, and old pro & toy dummies, i.e. Jerry Mahoney, Knucklehead Smiff, Charlie McCarthy, Mortimer Snerd, Danny O'Day, Farfel, etc.

Museums/Libraries

Anne Roberts
Vent Haven Museum, The
33 West Maple Ave.
Ft. Mitchell, KY 41011-2616
phone: 606-341-0461
The museum is a collection of over 800 ventriloquist figures, pictures, playbills and memorabilia that is open to the public from May to September for guided tours by advanced appointment only.

VETERAN ITEMS

(see also BADGES; INDIAN WARS ITEMS; MEDALS, ORDERS & DECORATIONS; MILITARIA)

Civil War

Clubs/Associations

Roger L. Heiple, Sec.
Civil War Veterans Historical Association
Newsletter: Veteran, The
P.O. Box 16
South Lyon, MI 48178
For those interested in preserving the memory of Union and Confederate

veterans of the American Civil War; also memorabilia.

Collectors

Julie Brighenti
RD 2 Box 61
Belle Vernon, PA 15012-9802
phone: 412-929-7311
Wants Grand Army of the Republic items: badges, ribbons, canes, glass, gold testimonial badges, etc.; also Civil War 22nd PA items.

Rance Hulshart
4000 Old Orchard Rd.
York, PA 17402
phone: 717-755-5334
Avid collector and scholar on Civil War veterans - their history, activities, organizations and related memorabilia.

David J. Maloney
P.O. Box 2049
Frederick, MD 21702-1049
phone: 301-695-8544
fax: 301-695-6491
e-mail: dmaloney@ix.netcom.com
Internet: http://www.maloneysonline.com
Wants Union and Confederate veteran-related items: Grand Army of the Republic, United Confederate Veterans, WRC, SUV; any related item.

Peggy Dillard
P.O. Box 210904
Nashville, TN 37221-0904
phone: 615-646-1605
Wants Confederate Veterans Reunion items.

Museums/Libraries

Grand Army of the Republic Civil War Museum & Library
4278 Griscom St.
Philadelphia, PA 19124-3954
phone: 215-673-1688 or 215-289-6484
e-mail: garmuslib@aol.com
Internet: http://libertynet.org/~gencap/gar.html
Civil War Museum & Library; artifacts, personal memorabilia, paintings, G.A.R. & S.U.V.C.W. records; open first Sunday or by appt.

Paula Nelson
G.A.R. Hall & Museum
Newsletter: G.A.R. Hall & Museum Newsletter
308 North Marshall
Litchfield, MN 55355
phone: 320-693-8911
Grand Army of the Republic (GAR) Hall built in 1885 by union Veterans of the Civil War; maintained by Meeker Historical Society.

Grand Army of the Republic Memorial & Veteran's Military Museum
23 E. Downer Pl.
Aurora, IL 60505
phone: 708-897-7221

Grand Army of the Republic Memorial Museum
78 E. Washington St.
Chicago, IL 60602
phone: 312-269-2926

Mexican War

Clubs/Associations

Descendants of Mexican War Veterans
1114 Pacific
Richardson, TX 75081
A national lineage society open to men and women.

VETERINARY MEDICINE ITEMS

Auction Services

Mike Smith, D.V.M.
7431 Covington Highway
Lithonia, GA 30058-7611
phone: 770-482-5100 or 770-979-3239
fax: 770-484-1304
e-mail: petvetmike@aol.com
Conducts periodic auctions of animal and veterinary medicine collectibles.

Clubs/Associations

Mike Smith, D.V.M.
Veterinary Collectibles Roundtable
Newsletter: Veterinary Collectibles Roundtable Newsletter
7431 Covington Highway
Lithonia, GA 30058-7611
phone: 770-482-5100 or 770-979-3239
fax: 770-484-1304
e-mail: petvetmike@aol.com
Seeking collectors and consignors for newsletter and twice-yearly auctions of antique veterinary patent medicines and advertising; for collectors of animal or veterinary medicine antiques.

Collectors

Dr. Fred Cesana
49 E. Main St.
Plainville, CT 06062
phone: 203-747-2759
Wants pre-1930 veterinary advertising items, cabinets, bottles with labels, etc.

Paul Ferraglio
3332 W. Lake Rd.
Canandaigua, NY 14424-2441
phone: 716-394-7663
fax: 716-394-5424
e-mail: p4alyo@aol.com
Wants to buy veterinary medicine items: old surgical instruments, animal medicine bottles and tins, pamphlets, display cabinets, signs.

Mike Smith, D.V.M.
7431 Covington Highway
Lithonia, GA 30058-7611
phone: 770-482-5100 or 770-979-3239
fax: 770-484-1304
e-mail: petvetmike@aol.com
Wants to buy animal and veterinary medicine collectibles.

Dealers

Barbara Cole
October Farm
2609 Branch Rd.
Raleigh, NC 27610-9213
phone: 919-772-0482
fax: 919-779-6265
Buys and sells horse books and paper ephemera, especially relating to polo, carriages & driving, Morgan horses, American Saddlebred horses, and veterinary medicine; also old farm horse equipment and catalogs; mail order only.

Trenton Boyd
P.O. Box 517
Columbia, MO 65205-0517
phone: 573-882-2461 or 573-442-5235
fax: 573-882-2950
e-mail: vetlib@showme.missouri.edu
Interested in veterinary postcards including schools and military veterinary; also wants teratology cards that show animals with birth defects (e.g. five-legged calves); Red Cross dogs, Humane Association.

VIETNAM ITEMS

(see also MILITARIA; SOCIAL CAUSES, Hippie Items)

Periodicals

Cowles Magazines, Inc.
Magazine: Vietnam
741 Miller Dr. SE, Ste. D2
Harrisburg, PA 20175
phone: 703-771-9400 or 800-829-3340
fax: 703-779-8345
Internet: http://www.thehistorynet.com
Covers the controversial Vietnam War from many perspectives for both veterans of the war and students of military and political history; published bi-monthly.

Clem Kelly
Newsletter: Vietnam Insignia Collectors Newsletter
501 West 5th Ave.
Covington, LA 70433

VIEW BOOKS

(see ALBUMS; PAPER COLLECTIBLES)

VIEW-MASTERS

(see 3-D PHOTOGRAPHICA, View-Masters)

VINTAGE CLOTHING

(see CLOTHING & ACCESSORIES, Vintage)

VIOLINS

(see MUSICAL INSTRUMENTS, String [Violins])

VISUAL AIDS

(see OPTICAL ITEMS)

VOLKSWAGEN RELATED ITEMS

Collectors

Frank Konisky
RD 2 Third Ave. Extension
Rensselaer, NY 12144
phone: 518-465-0477
e-mail: pplkars@aol.com
Wants Volkswagon toys, models, etc.

Mike Wilson
23490 S.W. 82nd
Tualatin, OR 97062-9613
phone: 503-638-7074
fax: 503-638-6654
e-mail: rennopup@msn.com
Wants Volkswagen toys, memorabilia, literature, etc.

Michael Davis
East 1128 Glass
Spokane, WA 99207
Wants VW toys, games, old advertising, books, etc.

WAGONS

(see BICYCLES & RELATED MEMORABILIA; HORSE-DRAWN VEHICLES; RIDING TOYS)

WALKING STICKS

(see CANES & WALKING STICKS)

WALL POCKETS

Clubs/Associations

Janet Hausher
Wall Pocket Collectors Club
1356 Tahiti
Saint Louis, MO 63128
phone: 314-821-2745

Collectors

Bobbie & Alan Bryson
1 St. Eleanoras Ln.
Tuckahoe, NY 10707-1307
phone: 914-779-1405
e-mail: napkindoll@aol.com
Wants to buy glass wall pockets.

Experts

Pam Brin
8 Park Lane
Minneapolis, MN 55416-4340
phone: 612-920-3030
fax: 612-920-3031
e-mail: pambrin@msn.com

WALL STREET

(see STOCKS & BONDS, Financial History)

WALLACE NUTTING

(see also FURNITURE [ANTIQUE], Wallace Nutting; PRINTS, Wallace Nutting)

Auction Services

Michael Ivanovich
Ivankovich Antiques, Inc.
P.O. Box 2458
Doylestown, PA 18901-0760
phone: 215-345-6094
fax: 215-345-6692
e-mail: wnutting@comcat.com
Internet: http://www.wnutting.com
*Largest auction service for Wallace
Nutting prints, books and furniture;
conducts 3-4 auctions/yr., each with
300-500 Wallace Nutting pictures.*

Clubs/Associations

George Monro
Wallace Nutting Collectors Club
Newsletter: Wallace Nutting Collectors
Newsletter
186 Mountain Ave.
North Caldwell, NJ 07006-4006
phone: 201-226-1713
*Helps members learn more about
Wallace Nutting, the man and his
works; please include a SASE when
requesting a reply.*

Dealers

Sharon Lacasse
Sharon Lacasse Antiques
1424 Osterville - W. Barnstable Rd.
West Barnstable, MA 02668
phone: 508-428-0562
*Buying and selling pictures, books,
furniture and all memorabilia relating
to Wallace Nutting.*

Rudy Parent
P.O. Box 2362
Salem, NH 03079
phone: 603-898-7363
*Wants to buy quality prints, books,
furniture and anything with Nutting's
name on it; one piece or an entire
collection.*

Experts

Michael Ivanovich
Michael Ivankovich Antiques, Inc.
P.O. Box 2458
Doylestown, PA 18901-0760
phone: 215-345-6094
fax: 215-345-6692
e-mail: wnutting@comcat.com
Internet: http://www.wnutting.com
*Wants pictures, books, furniture;
leading collector; conducts auctions
of Wallace Nutting items; author of
books on Nutting; also pictures that
resemble Wallace Nutting works, e.g.
those by Fred Thompson, David
Davidson, Chas. Sawyer*

WALLETS

(see BUSINESS CARD HOLDERS)

WARBIRDS

(see AVIATION, Military)

WASHING MACHINES

(see also ENGINES, Gasoline;
MAYTAG)

Experts

Robert Seger
4351 Harriet Ave., S.
Minneapolis, MN 55409
phone: 612-822-3534 or 612-823-2388
e-mail: unimatic00@aol.com
*Collector of and expert in early
automatic clothes washing machines
from the mid-1940s to the early
1960s; wants to buy vintage machines,
parts and literature.*

Lee Maxwell
35901 WCR 31
Eaton, CO 80615
phone: 907-454-3856
e-mail: leemaxwell@aol.com
Internet: http://
www.max.cnr.colostate.edu
*Collector of old and unusual washing
machines, has collection of over 650
pre-1940 washing machines; please
send pictures & description; condition
is not important so long as the
machine is complete.*

WATCH FOBS

Clubs/Associations

John Carrington
Canadian Association of Watch Fob
Collectors
49 Fife St. W.
Caledonia
Ontario N3W 1J2 Canada
phone: 905-765-4836 or 905-664-4576
*Dedicated to the collection and
preservation of advertising-type watch
fobs.*

International Watch Fob Association,
Inc.
Newsletter: International Watch Fob
Association Newsletter
P.O. Box 1051
Palmetto, GA 30268-7051
phone: 770-463-1500
*Focus is on strap-type watch fobs;
members receive 2 fobs and 2
newsletter per year; membership
roster available; annual show in the
Cleveland, OH area.*

R.J. Rothlisberger
Midwest Watch Fob Collectors, Inc.
Newsletter: Watch Fob Collectors
Newsletter
11895 Highway 99
Burlington, IA 52601-8521
phone: 319-752-6749
*A group organized to preserve, collect
and educate themselves about strap
advertising watch fobs.*

Collectors

John Cline
609 N. East St.
Carlisle, PA 17013-2012
phone: 717-249-4253
Wants road or farm machinery-related
*fobs, or fobs advertising fur, traps,
powder and gun companies.*

Advertising

Dealers

Dave Beck
P.O. Box 435
Mediapolis, IA 52637-0435
phone: 319-394-3943
*Buys and sells advertising watch fobs,
mirrors and pin-backs; send stamp for
illustrated mail auction catalog.*

Machinery & Equipment

Collectors

John Leite, Jr.
44 Glenwood Rd.
Brewster, MA 02631-2202
phone: 508-385-4905
*Wants to buy watch fobs dealing with
heavy equipment and trucking.*

WATCH HOLDERS

Collectors

John Michels
1658 Hardwick Rd.
Baltimore, MD 21286-8128
phone: 410-825-3636
*Wants to buy watch holders; send
picture and price; photos will be
returned.*

WATCHES

(see also BOOKS, Reference
[Watches]; CLOCKS; GEMS &
JEWELRY; INSTRUMENTS &
DEVICES, Scientific; WATCH FOBS;
WATCH HOLDERS)

Auction Services

George Horan
Jones & Horan Auction Team
453 Mast Rd.
Goffstown, NH 03045
phone: 603-625-5314

Robert Schmidt
R.O. Schmidt Fine Arts
P.O. Box 1941
Salem, NH 03079
phone: 603-893-5915
fax: 603-893-9777
e-mail: roschmit@worldnet.att.net

Clubs/Associations

British Watch & Clock Collectors
Association
5 Cathedral Lane
Truro
Cornwall TR1 2SQ U.K.
phone: +44 01872 41953
*Geared mainly to the collector, but
also solicits membership from
restorers and repairers.*

Paul Wadsworth, Pres.
American Watchmakers Institute
64 South Ave.
P.O. Box 933
Hilton, NY 14468
*A specialty chapter within the
National Association of Watch &
Clock Collectors, Inc.*

Thomas J. Bartels, ExDir
National Association of Watch & Clock
Collectors, Inc.
Magazine: Bulletin of the NAWCC
514 Poplar St.
Columbia, PA 17512-2130
phone: 717-684-8261
fax: 717-684-0878
e-mail: patti@nawcc.org
Internet: http://www.nawcc.org
*The NAWCC is a non-profit and
scientific association founded in 1943
and now serving the horological
interests of 38,000 members
worldwide.*

American Watchmakers-Clockmakers
Institute
Magazine: Horological Times
701 Enterprise Dr.
Harrison, OH 45030-1696
e-mail: awi-info@awi-net.org
Internet: http://www.awi-net.org
*For those interested in horology as a
profession or avocation; monthly
technical magazine, technical
bulletins, training, public relations,
networking.*

Burley Bullock, Pres.
International Wrist Watch Collectors
Chapter 146
5901C Westheimer
Houston, TX 77057
*A specialty chapter within the
National Association of Watch &
Clock Collectors, Inc.; focuses on
wrist watches.*

Jon Hanson, Pres.
Early American Watch Club
P.O. Box 5499
Beverly Hills, CA 90210
phone: 310-476-2332
*A specialty chapter within the
National Association of Watch &
Clock Collectors, Inc.; focuses on
early American watches.*

Collectors

Marc L. Ames
539 Lyme Rock Rd.
Bridgewater, NJ 08807-1670
phone: 908-526-7676
fax: 908-575-0880
e-mail: magames@ix.netcom.com
*Wants to buy vintage wrist watches
especially those in working condition;
also wants current Rolex, Audemars,
IWC, Breuget, Mueller, etc.*

Secoff Watches Co.
One Welwyn Rd.
Box 2140
Great Neck, NY 11022-2140
phone: 516-482-8858
fax: 516-466-6576
Buy and sell vintage pocket wrist watches specializing in expensive antique watches and valuable clocks.

Bob Arnell
P.O. Box 313
Grandview, MO 64030-0313
phone: 816-966-0544
Wants to buy wrist and pocket watches.

Dealers

David Searles
124 Mt. Auburn St., University Place, Ste. 20
Cambridge, MA 02138
phone: 617-576-5810
fax: 617-876-8114
Wants rare pocket and wrist watches.

Robert Beaver
Classic Touch Antiques
P.O. Box 27
Newport, RI 02840-0001
phone: 401-849-1717 or 401-849-9870
Buys and sells early and complicated watches.

John & Michele
Yores & Hours
P.O. Box 1011
Peck Slip Station
New York, NY 10272
phone: 212-227-7556

Irv Temes
American International Watch Exchange
113 N. Charles St.
Baltimore, MD 21201
phone: 301-882-0580

Ed London
Parke Lloyds International, Inc.
9408 NW 70 St.
Fort Lauderdale, FL 33321-3002
phone: 954-724-4294 or 954-724-4274
Buys watches.

Timothy Haines
Got the Time?
1077 Celestial St.
Rookwood Bldg. #3, Ste. 400
Cincinnati, OH 45202-1629
phone: 513-871-0494
fax: 513-651-0860
e-mail: reyneh@aol.com
Internet: http://members.aol.com/ ReyneH
Buying men's wrist watches; vintage and new; Rolex, Patek, Universal Geneva, Breitling Chronographs, Doctors watches, etc.; please call or fax list of items for sale.

John B. Marrella
Investments in Time
P.O. Box 611
Birmingham, MI 48012-0611
phone: 810-644-3100
fax: 810-644-2792
Buys and sells any antique or modern watch.

Barbara Nyboer
Some Where in Time Antiques
3655 Quadrille
Holt, MI 48842-9723
phone: 517-699-8372 or 517-337-4988
fax: 517-694-5650
Buys and sells pocket watches, slides, chains, fobs, and any other related merchandise or ephemera; also parts, tools; member NAWCC.

Maundy International
P.O. Box 13028 - RAF
Shawnee Mission, KS 66212-3028
phone: 800-235-2866
Watches - buying Patek Philippe pocket & wrist watches and fine watches from USA & Europe; since 1976; specializes in railroad pocket watches.

Kris Meyer
Vintage Timepieces Worldwide
12900 Preston Rd., Ste. 500
N. Dallas Bank Bldg.
Dallas, TX 75230
phone: 800-833-3159 or 214-392-4281
fax: 214-392-4283
Internet: http://www.watches-meyer.com
Wants wrist watches: Rolex, Patek Philippe, Vacheron & Constain, Audemars Piguet, Cartier, Tiffany, Piaget, all high grade pocket watches; chronograph, moonphase, repeating, triple calendars, military watches, world time zone, etc.

Howard Markham
Howard Markham Professional Numismatist
5225 Canyon Crest Dr., Bldg 200, Ste. 254
Riverside, CA 92507
phone: 909-686-2122 or 800-953-3027
Buys old pocket watches, either one piece or entire collections; wants railroad watches, wrist watches, older Rolex, Patek, Vacheron, etc.; will travel to buy larger collections.

Dave Morris
3388 Merlin Rd., Ste. 351
Grants Pass, OR 97526
phone: 541-955-8411
e-mail: smorris@cdsnet.net
Wants to buy wrist and pocket watches, fobs, and any other related merchandise including parts, tools, paper ephemera.

Experts

Philip M. Poniz
European Watch & Casemakers, Ltd.
P.O. Box 1314
Highland Park, NJ 08904-1314
phone: 908-777-0111
Does history and sales research on

antique watches, clocks, musical boxes, and unusual mechanical objects of virtu.

Arthur Guy Kaplan
P.O. Box 1942
Baltimore, MD 21203
phone: 410-752-2090 or 410-664-8350
fax: 410-783-2723
Author of "The Official Price Guide to Antique Jewelry."

Joe Cohen
4250 Galt Ocean Dr., Apt. 9A
Oakland Park, FL 33308
phone: 954-561-2234
Specializing in 17th, 18th, and 19th century clocks and watches.

Cooksey Shugart
P.O. Box 3147
Cleveland, TN 37320-3147
phone: 423-479-4813
fax: 423-479-4813
Author of "The Complete Price Guide to Watches."

Misc. Services

Richard Switzer
Joseph Bulova School of Watchmaking
40-24 62nd St.
P.O. Box 465
Flushing, NY 11377
phone: 718-424-2929
The most well-known watchmaking and repair school in the US; training new students to meet the demand for people who can repair mechanical watch movements.

Museums/Libraries

Nancy Connelly
American Clock & Watch Museum
Journal: Timepiece Journal
100 Maple St.
Bristol, CT 06010-5034
phone: 203-583-6070
Preserves the history of American horology, especially Connecticut and Bristol's role; large displays of clocks & watches.

Patricia Tomes, Cur.
National Association of Watch & Clock Collectors Museum, Inc., The
514 Poplar St.
Columbia, PA 17512-2130
phone: 717-684-8261
fax: 717-684-0878
e-mail: patti@nawcc.org
Internet: http://www.nawcc.org
The Watch & Clock Museum of the NAWCC strives to illustrate the history of timekeeping from the 1600's to the present with a collection of more than 8000 horological items.

Dorothy Mastricola
Time Museum, The
7801 E. State St.
P.O. Box 5285
Rockford, IL 61125-0285
phone: 815-398-6000
fax: 815-398-4700
Has an extensive collection of time-

measuring devices from all parts of the world dating from ancient instruments to the atomic clock.

Periodicals

International Publishers Corp.
Magazine: International Wrist Watch
P.O. Box 110204
Stamford, CT 06911-0204
phone: 203-352-1817
fax: 203-352-1820
A glossy magazine full of auction reports, ads, articles about old and new wrist watches.

Magazine: Watch & Clock Review
2403 Champa St.
Denver, CO 80205-2621
phone: 303-296-1600
fax: 303-295-2159
Monthly magazine primarily for new and vintage watch and clock retailers; features articles on watches, clocks and shops; also ads for buyers, sellers, and restorers.

Repair Services

Philip M. Poniz
European Watch & Casemakers, Ltd.
P.O. Box 1314
Highland Park, NJ 08904-1314
phone: 908-777-0111
Restoration of watches, clocks, and music boxes; museum experience; can make any part and restore any watch; clients include Sotheby's, Cartier, collectors in USA, Asia and Europe; appraises, researches, lectures on watch making, fakes.

N. Kenzie Smith & Sons
3836 Jefferson Pike
Jefferson, MD 21755
phone: 301-473-4095
Repairs and restores all mechanical clocks and watches; references upon request.

Sellers Watch Repair
163 Harper Rd.
Atlanta, GA 30315
phone: 404-627-1581
e-mail: 73664.2411@compuserve.com
Expert watch repair.

Swiss Watch Services, Inc.
1402 Third Ave., Ste. 714
Seattle, WA 98101
phone: 206-622-3643
fax: 206-622-7927
Complete overhauls, makes custom dials with diamonds, names, pictures; cuts crystals; specializing in all Swiss watches including Patek Philippe, Rolex, Audemars Piguet, Cartier, Movado, Piaget, Longines, etc.

Suppliers

Rick Dunnuck, VP
S. LaRose, Inc.
3223 Yanceyville St.
P.O. Box 21208
Greensboro, NC 27420-1208
phone: 910-621-1936
fax: 910-621-0706
e-mail: slarose@worldnet.att.net
Internet: http://www.slarose.com
Supplier of clock and watch parts.

Advertising

Periodicals

Sharon Iranpour
Newsletter: Premium Watch Watch, The
24 San Rafael Dr.
Rochester, NY 14618-3702
phone: 716-381-9467 or 716-383-9248
e-mail: siranpour@aol.com
Bi-monthly newsletter: a guide to the newest advertising and logo watches; promotional, advertising and character watch news; send LSASE for sample.

Character/Comic

Collectors

Joe Ramos
2207 Manning St.
Bronx, NY 10462
phone: 212-828-1021
Wants comic & character watches from '30s-'50s; any condition; also wants original boxes, bands, parts, etc.; also expert repairs.

David Welch
P.O. Box 714
Murphysboro, IL 62966-0714
phone: 618-687-2282
fax: 618-684-2243
e-mail: PexDude1@aol.com
Wants pre-1980 watches/clocks relating to sports, TV, cartoon, comic, movie characters with original boxes ONLY; also wants empty boxes; no political, please.

Dealers

Maggie Kenyon
M. Kenyon Co.
One Christopher St. 14-G
New York, NY 10014-3581
phone: 212-675-3213
Buying, selling, collecting comic/character watches for over 30 years; included are sports, political and product promotion watches in addition to all comic watches; interested in all regardless of age; send SASE.

Experts

Norm Vigue
62 Bailey St.
Stoughton, MA 02072
phone: 617-344-5441
Want mint boxed character watches; also point-of-sale signs for same.

Howard S. Brenner
106 Woodgate Terrace
Rochester, NY 14625-1735
phone: 716-482-3641
fax: 716-288-3122
e-mail: grvd25a@prodigy.com
Specializes in mint/boxed examples of comic watches; author of "Collecting Comic Character Clock & Watches."

Man./Prod./Dist.

John J. Matteo, Jr.
Collectible Watch Co., Inc.
1100 Montrose Ave.
Charlottesville, VA 22902-6236
phone: 888-846-3101 or 804-984-5005
fax: 804-984-2777
e-mail: jdematteo@collectiblewatch.com
Internet: http://www.collectiblewatch.com
Producer of fine time pieces for the serious collector; limited edition wrist and pocket watches; new collector tips every month; sports, historical, character.

Merk Harbour
Fossil
P.O. Box 853914
Richardson, TX 75085
Manufacturer of limited edition, collectible, and antique-looking classic watches and character watches including Roy Rogers and Superman.

Periodicals

Sharon Iranpour
Newsletter: Premium Watch Watch, The
24 San Rafael Dr.
Rochester, NY 14618-3702
phone: 716-381-9467 or 716-383-9248
e-mail: siranpour@aol.com
Bi-monthly newsletter: a guide to the newest advertising and logo watches; promotional, advertising and character watch news; send LSASE for sample.

Howard S. Brenner
Newsletter: Comic Watch Times
106 Woodgate Terrace
Rochester, NY 14625-1735
phone: 716-482-3641
fax: 716-288-3122
e-mail: grvd25a@prodigy.com

Dials

Repair Services

International Dial Co., Inc.
P.O. Box 970
Wilmington, OH 45177-2226
phone: 513-382-4535

Kirk Rich Dial Corporation
404 W. 7th St., Ste. 1215
Los Angeles, CA 90014
phone: 213-626-6840

Electric (Hamilton)

Dealers

Rene Rondeau
P.O. Box 391
Corte Madera, CA 94976-0391
phone: 415-924-6534
fax: 415-924-8423
e-mail: rrondeau@prodigy.com
Internet: http://pages.prodigy.com/rondeau
Buys, sells, and repairs Hamilton electric wrist watches from the 1950s and 1960s; author of "The Watch of the Future", 2nd edition, hb, 168 pgs, 6"x9".

Swatch

Clubs/Associations

Swatch Collectors Club, The
P.O. Box 7400
Melville, NY 11747-7400
phone: 800-U4S-WATC
Internet: http://www.swatch.com
Club for collectors of any Swatch-manufactured item such as watches, bicycles, sunglasses, wall hangings, telephones, and (in the future) automobiles; also sponsors a traveling Swatch museum.

Collectors

Carl F. Pflanzer
73 Cloverhill Dr.
Flanders, NJ 07836
e-mail: carl@ewacars.com
Internet: http://www.ewacars.com
Wants Swatch watches and Swatch clothing; must be in excellent condition.

Wrist

Dealers

Paul Duggan
Horological Artifacts
P.O. Box 63
Chelmsford, MA 01824
phone: 508-256-5966
fax: 508-256-2497
International watch buyers; wants fine watches such as Rolex, Patek Philippe, Vacheron, Cartier, Tiffany, Gubelin, Jules Jurgenson, Breuget, E. Howard, American Watch Co., LeCoultre, etc.

Alan & Seth Larrabure
Arco International Ltd.
400 Madison Ave., Rm. 1708
New York, NY 10017-1909
phone: 212-486-1212
fax: 212-486-1289
International watch buyers; wants fine watches such as Rolex, Patek Philippe, Vacheron, Cartier, Tiffany, Gubelin, Breuget, LeCoultre, Movado, IWC, etc.; watches are exported; offices in Tokyo; always buying clean watches.

WATER SPRINKLERS

(see also CAST IRON ITEMS; CLOTHES SPRINKLERS; GARDEN HOSE NOZZLES; IRONS, Pressing)

Collectors

Phyllis Burt
P.O. Box 681
New Canaan, CT 06840
phone: 203-798-2763
Wants to buy ceramic laundry sprinklers.

Experts

Richard Tucker
Argyle Antiques
P.O. Box 262
Argyle, TX 76226-0262
phone: 817-464-3752
fax: 817-464-7293
e-mail: millwt@pop.intex.net
Buys and sells figural cast iron items: windmill weights, shooting targets, water sprinklers; no repros. or repaired items wanted.

WEANERS

Calf & Cow

(see also FARM COLLECTIBLES)

Collectors

Robert Rauhauser
RR 2 Box 766
Thomasville, PA 17364-9622
Wants calf and cow weaners; also hand milking machines.

Steve Deer
1503 Albin Pond
Greencastle, IN 46135
phone: 317-653-9437
Wants rare and especially homemade calf and cow weaners.

WEAPONS

(see AMERICAN INDIAN, Tomahawks; ARMS & ARMOR; CIVIL WAR ARTIFACTS; EDGED WEAPONS; FIREARMS; KNIVES; MILITARIA; POWDER HORNS; SWORDS; TARGET SHOOTING MEMORABILIA)

WEATHERVANES

(see FOLK ART; LIGHTNING PROTECTION COLLECTIBLES)

WEAVING EQUIPMENT

(see COVERLETS; SPINNING WHEELS; TEXTILES)

WEDDING COLLECTIBLES

(see BRIDAL COLLECTIBLES)

WESTERN AMERICANA

(see also AMERICAN INDIAN; ART, Western; BARBED WIRE; BOTTLES, Western Whiskey; COWBOY HEROES; ANIMAL COLLECTIBLES, Horses; LAW ENFORCEMENT MEMORABILIA, Police & Sheriff; LEATHER; OUTLAWS & LAWMEN; PAPER COLLECTIBLES, Western; SADDLES)

Appraisers

Pierre Bovis
AZ-Tex Cowboy Trading Co., The
P.O. Box 13345
Tucson, AZ 85732-3345
phone: 520-318-9512
fax: 520-318-0023
Buy, sells, appraises cowboy memorabilia, primitive arts, American Indian arts, Napoleonic artifacts.

Auction Services

Engel Auction Co.
P.O. Box 1429
Ennis, MT 59729
phone: 406-682-4499
Conducts periodic auction of gunfighter and cowboy memorabilia.

High Noon
9929 Venice Blvd.
Los Angeles, CA 90034-5111
phone: 310-202-9010
Conducts periodic auctions of authentic cowboy and gunfighter memorabilia.

Clubs/Associations

Bobby Newton
Working Cowboy, c/o Chamber of Commerce
Newspaper: Rope Burns
P.O. Box 35
Gene Autry, OK 73436
phone: 405-389-5350
Largest listing of western events: bit-spur-collectible shows & auctions, rodeos, roundups, western trade & trappings, etc.

Ranching Heritage Association
Texas Tech University
P.O. Box 4040
Lubbock, TX 79409

Alvin G. Davis
American Cowboy Culture Association
Newsletter: ACCA Newsletter
4124 62nd Dr.
Lubbock, TX 79413
phone: 806-795-2455
fax: 806-795-4749
Purpose is to promote all areas of cowboy culture; publishes newsletter, sponsors events relating to cowboys; sponsors National Cowboy Sympo-sium & Celebration - held 2nd week in September in Lubbock, TX.

National Bit, Spur & Saddle Collectors Association
Newsletter: NBSSCA Newsletter
P.O. Box 3098
Colorado Springs, CO 80934-3098
phone: 719-473-7101
Members interested in western Americana memorabilia; supports shows and auctions; Western artifacts and collectibles show and auction schedules.

Collectors

Jim Babchak
313 East 85 #4B
New York, NY 10028
phone: 212-861-1356
Wants to buy old cowboy stuff including cowboy boots, shirts, horsehair bridles, spurs, chaps, children's costumes from the 1940s and 1950s, anything Roy Rogers, Hopalong Cassidy or Gene Autry.

Lewis Leigh, Jr.
P.O. Box 4327
Leesburg, VA 20177
phone: 703-771-3081
fax: 703-771-1432
Wants papers, letters, journals, uniforms, weapons & flags of American soldiers, seamen, pioneers, adventurers: 1607-1919.

Ernest Hoodenpyle
P.O. Box 487
Walters, OK 73572
phone: 405-875-3080
Wants to buy old cowboy stuff: silver mounted spurs, horse hair bridles, rawhide items, gun belts, holsters, chaps, horn furniture, old catalogs, pre-1900 cowboy boots, etc.

Rusty Gilbert
P.O. Box 92
Adkins, TX 78101
phone: 210-649-3849
Wants highback saddles, chaps, fancy headstalls, old spurs and bits, rifle scabbards, iron stirrups, Western catalogs, cowboy items, Western style dinnerware.

George Foott
6683 S. Yukon Way
Littleton, CO 80123-3071
phone: 303-979-8688
Wants to buy early Western mining memorabilia (especially Colorado): photographs, maps, promotional pamphlets, books, mining directories, miners' candleholders; also wants Old West cattle brand books, saddle catalogs, cowboy items.

Bill Mackin
1137 Washington St.
Craig, CO 81625-1613
phone: 970-824-6717 or 970-824-6360
fax: 970-824-7175
e-mail: reust@nadja.com
Wants pre-1940s cowboy and tack items: guns, cartridge belts, chaps, law badges, neckerchiefs, brands and brand books, spurs, knives, quirts,

cowboy boots, hats, neckerchiefs, vests, cuffs, gauntlets, gun and saddle catalogs, etc.

Elizabeth Clair Flood
P.O. Box 1006
Wilson, WY 83014
Specializes in the history, fashion and gear of old time cowgirls and rodeo women.

William Manns
P.O. Box 6459
Santa Fe, NM 87502-6459
phone: 505-995-0102
fax: 505-995-0103

William Manns
Cowboy Antiques
P.O. Box 6459
Santa Fe, NM 87502-6459
phone: 505-995-0102
fax: 505-995-0103
Wants to buy cowboy related antiques: pre-1930 spurs, holsters, hats, saddles, guns, catalogs, posters, photos, chaps, wild west show items, etc.; send photos and prices; offers free identification service if LSASE is provided.

T.J. Ahlberg
1000 Irvine Blvd.
Tustin, CA 92680-3527
phone: 714-730-1000 or 714-654-1331
fax: 714-730-1752
Wants anything by Edward Bohlin (especially Ranger Buckle sets), Till Goodan; all posters and pictorial maps by Jo Mora: 101 Ranch, Wild West Show/Buffalo Bill; also cowboy and Indian bookends and books by Jo Mora.

Maria E. Raymond
Plow & Pen, Inc.
P.O. Box 251
Robbins, CA 95676-0251
phone: 916-735-6596
fax: 916-735-6112
e-mail: 73113.1362@compuserve.com
Wants items relating to the history of women in the U.S. West: 1st edition books, ephemera, photos, news articles, diaries, letters; especially interested in items relating to women of color.

Mike Farmer
1406 Bigelow Ave. NW
Olympia, WA 98506-4417
phone: 360-352-7189
fax: 360-352-7189
Wants to buy pre-1930 stocks & bonds, land grants, graphic bill heads, broadsides, posters, maps, business letters, Civil War, American Indian, cancelled checks, Alaska, any old interesting paper; send copy or call; prompt reply.

Dealers

L.R. Kauffman
Treasure Hunt
P.O. Box 3862
Woodbridge, CT 06525-0862
phone: 203-387-8759
Wants pre-1900 western ephemera, view books, promotional booklets of towns and states; documents on mining, towns, Indians, Indian language material, emigrant guides, letters, etc.

Fred Neece, Jr.
1307 Hadtner St.
Williamsport, PA 17701-3707
phone: 717-323-4679
fax: 717-323-5293
Wants to buy old Western and cowboy items: boots, books, spurs, hats, leather cuffs, fancy shirts, chaps, holsters, art, Wells Fargo, Overland, Pony Express items, 1860s-1870s saddles, rodeo posters, etc.

William Butts
Main Street Fine Books & Manuscripts
206 N. Main St.
Galena, IL 61035-2244
phone: 815-777-3749
Open shop dealing in autographs and out-of-print books in most fields; specializing in all aspects of American history; boos and autograph catalogs issued regularly; member of A.B.A.A.

Sharon Myers
J&S Oldwestern Store,Saddle Shop and Museum
RR 1, Box 315-c-nt
Warsaw, MO 65355
phone: 816-438-2631
fax: 816-438-6517
e-mail: oldwest@iland.net
Internet: http://www. cowgirls.com/ dream/oldwest
Over 200 antique saddles, hibacks, side-saddles, military, charro, etc.; Admission to museum if free; also 1300 Western collectibles for sale; 55 page catalog for $5.

Experienced Denim
P.O. Box 239
Fayetteville, AR 72702-0239
phone: 501-444-7541 or 800-336-4694
fax: 501-521-8331
e-mail: exdeni19@intellinet.com
Wants Levis, denim jackets; also fabrics, textiles, bedspreads, '40s-'50s fancy cowboy boots and belts, tablecloths with Western or Mexican theme; will consider any condition; send SASE for free list of items wanted.

Ruppert Books
5909 Darnell
Houston, TX 77074-7719
phone: 713-774-2202
fax: 713-774-2202
e-mail: bruppert@webtv.net
Wants any pre-1980 books in dust jackets about Texas and country histories.

Early West, The
P.O. Box 9292
College Station, TX 77842
phone: 800-245-5841
fax: 409-764-7758
Buys, sells, trades Western American including documents, photos, in-print and out-of-print books, paper ephemera; catalog includes items relating to lawmen, cowboys, Indians, Texans, soldiers, explorers, and mountain men.

Kurt House
Cowboy Collectibles
218 Country Wood
San Antonio, TX 78216-1607
phone: 210-490-2433
fax: 210-490-3433
Buys, sells, restores pre-1940 cowboy items: bits, spurs, guns, gunbelts, swords, badges, cattleman antiques, books, manufacturer's catalogs, photos, etc.; author of "Joe Bianchi and the Victoria Spur" (1997).

Lee Jacobs
P.O. Box 3098
Colorado Springs, CO 80934-3098
phone: 719-473-7101

Brian Lebel
Old West Antiques & Cowboy
Collectibles
1215 Sheridan Ave.
Cody, WY 82414-3629
phone: 307-587-9014
fax: 307-587-5393
Issues three catalogs per year of western Americana collectibles: saddles, chaps, spurs, bridles, etc.; also auction news, ads.

William L. King
Bozeman Trail Gallery
214 N. Main
Sheridan, WY 82801
phone: 307-672-3928 or 307-672-8318
fax: 307-672-2616
Buys, sells, appraises 19th-early 20th cent. Western art, especially by Joe DeYong, E.W. Gollings, Hans Kleiber; also wants No. Plains Indian beadwork and related items, cowboy equipment, Colt Bisley's, mod. 1885 Remington pistols.

Tyrone & Una Campbell
Una
7103 E. Main St.
Scottsdale, AZ 85251-4315
phone: 602-423-9160
Buys and sells antique American Indian weavings: Navajo, Pueblo and Hispanic weavings and folk art; specializes in appraising collections, consultations, and research of 19th & 20th C. Navajo weavings.

Old West Cowboy Store
427 E. Allen St.
Tombstone, AZ 85638
phone: 520-457-3166
Specializing in Western and cowboy memorabilia: cowboy gear, holsters, spurs, Old West star badges, old saddles, etc.

High Noon
9929 Venice Blvd.
Los Angeles, CA 90034-5111
phone: 310-202-9010
Wants to buy cowboy collectibles: bits, spurs, chaps, braided horsehair, silver saddles, saddle bags, cuffs, tack catalogs, etc.

Roger V. Baker
P.O. Box 620417
Redwood City, CA 94062-0417
phone: 369-851-7188
Buys, collects and sells Western Americana: American Indian items, cowboy paraphernalia, firearms, knives, saloon antiques, gold rush, mining and other related items.

Hank Clark
Argent Express
P.O. Box 812
Waterford, CA 95386-0812
phone: 209-874-2640
Buys/sells Western American paper, books, weapons, autographs, vintage coins, photographs, gold & silversmithing, conchos & buttons.

Douglas Vincent
Far West Antiques
P.O. Box 371
Redmond, OR 97756
phone: 541-923-1847 or 541-923-2140
fax: 541-923-3874
e-mail: dgvince@ibm.net
Internet: http://
www.farwestantiques.com
Buys, sells, trades in older Native American items and Western Americana inducing gambling collectibles; also collects native American beadwork, baskets, jewelry and Kachina dolls.

Dick Perier
Dick Perier - Books
P.O. Box 1
Vancouver, WA 98666-0001
phone: 306-696-2033
Wants to buy items relating to Alaska, Lewis & Clark, Western Americana.

Experts

Robert W.D. Ball
P.O. Box 255
Unionville, CT 06085
Author of "Cowboy Collectibles and Western Memorabilia" (Schiffer Publishing Co.), "American Shelf and Wall Clocks, A Pictorial History For Collectors", and auction catalogs for firearms and militaria auctions.

Robert Phillips
1703 North Aster Place
Broken Arrow, OK 74012
phone: 918-254-8205
fax: 918-252-9362
e-mail: rawhidebob@aol.com
Collector of cowboy memorabilia for over 30 years and has written a book

as well as many magazine articles dealing with the subject.

Bill Mackin
1137 Washington St.
Craig, CO 81625-1613
phone: 970-824-6717 or 970-824-6360
fax: 970-824-7175
e-mail: reust@nadja.com
Author of "Cowboy and Gunfighter Collectibles" with 1993-94 updated price guide; sells books for Old West collectors by mail and at shows; over 45 years collecting; wants nice gun leather and cowboy gear; appraises, consults, lectures.

Warren Anderson
America West Archives
P.O. Box 100
Cedar City, UT 84721-0100
phone: 801-586-9497 or 801-586-7323
Buys and sells paper Americana associated with the Western US: old documents, letters, photos, stocks, maps, autographs, prints, etc.; author of "Owning Western History."

Robert H. Balderson
2830 Arden Way, #110
Sacramento, CA 95825
phone: 916-484-7906
fax: 916-484-7906
Specializes and appraises firearms, Western Americana, and Native American weapons; author of "Official Price Guide to Antique and Modern Firearms."

Museums/Libraries

Robyn G. Peterson
Rockwell Museum, The
111 Cedar St.
Corning, NY 14830
phone: 607-937-5386
fax: 607-974-4536
e-mail: rmuseum@stny.1run.com
Internet: http://www.stny.1run.com/
RockwellMuseum
Largest display of American Western art in the Eastern U.S.; includes paintings, bronzes, firearms, Native American artifacts; also Frederick Carder's Steuben glass, antique toys; museum shop on premises.

Randy Donley
Donley's Wild West Town & Museum
8512 S. Union Rd.
Union, IL 60180-9661
phone: 815-923-9000
fax: 815-923-2253
Large display of all kinds of Americana, especially from the Wild West.

Pony Express Museum
P.O. Box 244
Saint Joseph, MO 64502-0274

National Cowgirl Hall of Fame &
Western Heritage Center
111 West 4th, Ste. 300
Fort Worth, TX 76102
phone: 817-336-4475

Bill Mackin
Cowboy & Gunfighter Museum, c/o
Museum of Northwest CO
590 Yampa St.
Craig, CO 81625-2612
phone: 970-824-6360
fax: 970-824-7175
e-mail: reust@nadja.com
One of the world's most extensive collections of fine antique cowboy gear, frontier guns and gun leather, spurs, badges, saddles, chaps, etc.; a public county museum in historic state armory site; free admission.

Museum of the American Cowboy
P.O. Box 7006
Sheridan, WY 82801
Devoted to the working cowboy.

Gene Autry Western Heritage Museum
Magazine: Spur
4700 Western Heritage Way
Los Angeles, CA 90027-1462
phone: 213-667-2000
fax: 213-660-5721
Collects items relating to the American West, including Western film memorabilia.

Wells Fargo History Museum
333 S. Grand Ave.
Los Angeles, CA 90071-1504
phone: 213-253-7166
Internet: http://www.wellsfargo.com

Round Up Hall of Fame & Museum
P.O. Box 609
Pendleton, OR 97801

Periodicals

Cowles Magazines, Inc.
Magazine: Wild West
741 Miller Dr. SE, Ste. D2
Harrisburg, PA 20175
phone: 703-771-9400 or 800-829-3340
fax: 703-779-8345
Internet: http://www.thehistorynet.com
A bi-monthly magazine covering America's westward expansion - major events, interesting characters, and little-known incidents, as well as Western art, artifacts, and collectibles.

Roger M. Crowley
Magazine: Westerner, The
P.O. Box 5232
Vienna, WV 26105
phone: 304-295-3143
Features stories of the Old West, Western firearms, working cattle ranches, Western towns and museums, Western artists, stuntmen, etc.

Max Harrison
Magazine: Country & Western Variety
P.O. Box 619
Hendersonville, TN 37077-0619
Published bi-monthly.

Judith Karns, Manag. Ed.
Long Publications, Inc.
Magazine: Yippy Yi Yea Magazine
8393 East Holly Rd.
Holly, MI 48442-8819
phone: 810-634-9675 or 800-437-1218
fax: 810-634-0301
The romanticism of the Old West and the style of today's western decorating is captured in the pages of Yippy Yi Yea: travel in the West; Western artists and their crafts; Western heritage and photos, etc.

Magazine: Western Horseman
P.O. Box 542
Mount Morris, IL 61054-0542
Monthly magazine focusing on western horsemanship and lifestyle.

Reid Slaughter
Magazine: Cowboys & Indians
8214 Westchester Dr., Ste. 410
Dallas, TX 75225
phone: 214-750-8222
fax: 214-750-4522
Internet: http://www.cowboysindians.com

Magazine: Southwest Art
5444 Westheimer, Ste. 1440
Houston, TX 77056
phone: 713-850-0990
fax: 713-850-1314
The best in contemporary Western, traditional, Native American and impressionist artists; published monthly.

Darrell Arnold
Magazine: Cowboy Magazine
P.O. Box 126
La Veta, CO 81055-0126
phone: 719-742-6250
Published four times per year; covers all aspects of the cowboy lifestyle; also covers Western movies and music.

WEB Publications, Inc.
Magazine: American Cowboy
P.O. Box 6630
Sheridan, WY 82801-7102
phone: 800-369-0196 or 307-672-7171
fax: 307-672-7766
Internet: http://www.cowboy.com/~cowboy/
The magazine of Western living: profiles of famous country-western singers, rodeo stars, artists, cowboys; coverage of today's western art & collectibles; auction results, history, travel, cowboy poetry, etc.; bi-monthly.

Rudy D. Gonzales, Jr.
Magazine: American Cowboy Poet
  Magazine
P.O. Box 326
Eagle, ID 83616
phone: 208-888-9838
fax: 208-887-0082
Focusing on true cowboy music and poetry; articles, poetry, events, music offered by those who live the life and not by Hollywood or Nashville

entertainers; great modern day cowboy artists featured in each issue.

William Manns
Newsletter: Cowboy Guide
P.O. Box 6459
Santa Fe, NM 87502-6459
phone: 505-995-0102
fax: 505-995-0103
Send SASE for Cowboy Guide which contains information about cowboy collectibles, upcoming cowboy auctions and shows, plus a list of dealers, museums and publications.

Cheryl Laymon
Little Oak Enterprises
Magazine: Oak Tree Express
P.O. Box 221286
Newhall, CA 91322-1286
phone: 805-255-0726
fax: 805-255-0726
Professionally designed bi-monthly magazine focusing on western films and western art.

Newspaper: Today's Old West Traveler
P.O. Box 2928
Costa Mesa, CA 92628
phone: 800-775-WEST
fax: 714-540-2476
e-mail: Olwestrvlr@aol.com
Internet: http://199.190.151.4/~WYPROD/COWBOY/OLDWEST/
Find all things Western - upcoming events nationwide, adventures, dude ranches, cattle drives, cowboy collectibles, poetry, music, historic sites, museums, living history, movies, western wear, and more.

101 Ranch

Clubs/Associations

Ruth & Jerry Murphey
101 Ranch Collectors
10701 Timbergrove Lane
Corpus Christi, TX 78410
phone: 512-241-2213
101 Ranch memorabilia collectors; for many years the 101 Ranch had a traveling wild west show; stars who worked on the ranch or appeared in the show included Buffalo Bill, Tom Mix, Will Rogers, Hoot Gibson, Buck Jones and many more.

Collectors

Ogden's
P.O. Box 248
Sudbury, MA 01776
Wants memorabilia related to the 101 Ranch.

T.J. Ahlberg
1000 Irvine Blvd.
Tustin, CA 92680-3527
phone: 714-730-1000 or 714-654-1331
fax: 714-730-1752
Wants anything by Edward Bohlin (especially Ranger Buckle sets), Till Goodan; all posters and pictorial maps by Jo Mora: 101 Ranch, Wild West Show/Buffalo Bill; also cowboy

and Indian bookends and books by Jo Mora.

Annie Oakley

(see also WESTERN AMERICANA, Buffalo Bill; WESTERN AMERICANA, Wild West Show)

Dealers

Vivian & James Karsnitz
1428 Jerry Lane
Manheim, PA 17545-9353
phone: 717-665-4202
Buys and sells anything Annie Oakley.

Bits

Collectors

Jean Gayle
Three Horses
7403 Blaine Rd.
Aberdeen, WA 98520-7409
phone: 360-533-3490
e-mail: jgayle@techline.com
Buying fancy, ornamental, military, iron horse bits; also wants to buy bridle rosettes and old tack catalogs.

Boots

Collectors

Ed Soost
1331 Weverton Rd.
Knoxville, MD 21758
phone: 301-694-7325
Wants to buy vintage Western boots.

Buffalo Bill

(see also WESTERN AMERICANA, Annie Oakley; WESTERN AMERICANA, Wild West Show)

Collectors

Ogden's
P.O. Box 248
Sudbury, MA 01776
Wants memorabilia related to Buffalo Bill and Pawnee Bill.

Michael Del Castello
23842 Cabot Blvd.
Hayward, CA 94545
phone: 510-265-3506 or 415-941-4643
Wants to buy Buffalo Bill Cody items: posters, programs, photographs and artifacts relating to Buffalo Bill, Wild West Show memorabilia, Annie Oakley, Wells Fargo.

Museums/Libraries

Buffalo Bill Museum Inc.
P.O. Box 284
LeClaire, IA 52753
phone: 319-289-5580

Buffalo Bill Historical Center
P.O. Box 1000
Cody, WY 82414-1000
phone: 307-587-4771
fax: 307-587-5714
Dedicated to the history of William F.

Cody; large collection of personal belongings, photos and documents.

Holsters

Repro. Sources

Old West Reproductions
446 Florence South Loop
Florence, MT 59833
phone: 406-273-2615
Faithful reproductions of 1849-1900 holsters, cartridge belts, saddles and more; send $3 for catalog; also seeking to buy original Western memorabilia, i.e. 1849-1900 holsters, cartridge belts, wrist cuffs, etc.

Photographs

Collectors

Tim Gordon
1750 W. Kent
Missoula, MT 59801-5508
phone: 406-728-1812
e-mail: stacey1165@aol.com
Wants early photos of the West: saloon interiors, cowboys, Indians, lawmen, hangings, etc.; also offers appraisal service.

Dealers

L.R. Kauffman
Treasure Hunt
P.O. Box 3862
Woodbridge, CT 06525-0862
phone: 203-387-8759
Wants pre-1900 western photos or stereo views of historical interest; special wants include Watkins, Jackson, Houseworth; stereos and views of towns, streets, mining, shops, etc. of 19th century Western America.

Southwest

Collectors

John W. Barry
Indian Rock Arts
P.O. Box 583
Davis, CA 95617-0583
phone: 916-758-2561
Wants traditional Pueblo paintings, prints, photos; books on Southwest Tribes and Pueblos, Southwest archaeology, exploration of Southwest, Yellowstone, Grand Canyon, Yosemite tourism, photographs, books, old tourist items.

Texas Rangers

Museums/Libraries

Texas Ranger Hall of Fame & Museum
P.O. Box 2570
Waco, TX 76702-2570
phone: 817-750-8631
fax: 817-750-8629
e-mail: bjohnson@eramp.net
Nonprofit and educational museum and Hall of Fame dedicated to the history of the Texas Rangers; artifact

collections, research library, and
audio-visual presentations.

Wells Fargo

Collectors

Bartz
25101 Cineria Way
Eltoro, CA 92630
phone: 714-768-5503
*Wants any authentic Wells Fargo
items.*

Wild West Show

(see also WESTERN AMERICANA,
Annie Oakley; WESTERN AMERI-
CANA, Buffalo Bill)

Auction Services

Kurt R. Krueger
Krueger Auctions
160 N. Washington St.
Iola, WI 54945
phone: 715-445-3845
fax: 715-445-4100
*Conducts periodic specialized
auctions of circus and Wild West
Show memorabilia.*

Collectors

William Manns
Cowboy Antiques
P.O. Box 6459
Santa Fe, NM 87502-6459
phone: 505-995-0102
fax: 505-995-0103
*Wants to buy cowboy related
antiques: pre-1930 spurs, holsters,
hats, saddles, guns, catalogs, posters,
photos, chaps, wild west show items,
etc.; send photos and prices; offers
free identification service if LSASE is
provided.*

Art Sowin
8436 Samra Dr.
Canoga Park, CA 91304
*Wants Wild West Show memorabilia:
Buffalo Bill, Annie Oakley, Wild West
Show books, advertising, photos,
programs, tickets, passes, souvenir
items, etc.*

Michael Del Castello
23842 Cabot Blvd.
Hayward, CA 94545
phone: 510-265-3506 or 415-941-4643
*Wants to buy Buffalo Bill Cody items:
posters, programs, photographs and
artifacts relating to Buffalo Bill, Wild
West Show memorabilia, Annie
Oakley, Wells Fargo.*

WESTERN ART & CRAFTS

(see also ART, Western; WESTERN
AMERICANA)

Dealers

Kline's Gallery
Alt. 40
Boonsboro, MD 21713-0041
phone: 301-432-6650
*Sells new Southwest American Indian
art and crafts: blankets, paintings,
sculpture, bronzes, jewelry, etc.*

WHALES & DOLPHINS

Collectors

Steven G. King
Whales & Friends
P.O. Box 2660
Alameda, CA 94501-0660
phone: 510-796-8500 or 800-282-8686
fax: 510-865-0851
*Wants to buy any items with images of
whales or dolphins, alive or dead:
books, photos, coins, stamps, posters,
toys, videos, models, sculptures, etc.;
when calling, ask for Steve King and
mention you're calling about whale
material.*

Flipper

Collectors

John Fredriksen
461 Loring Ave.
Salem, MA 01970
*Wants Flipper related toys, books,
cards, games.*

WHALING

(see also ENDANGERED SPECIES;
NAUTICAL ANTIQUES;
SCRIMSHAW; WHALES &
DOLPHINS)

Experts

Sara Conklin
239 Sierra Pt. Rd.
Brisbane, CA 94005-1664
phone: 415-467-6249
fax: 415-467-6249
e-mail: 76363.536@compuserve.com
*Managed the collections of the
National Maritime Museum in San
Francisco for ten years and is an
expert in appraising whaling objects
and scrimshaw.*

Museums/Libraries

Librarian
Kendall Whaling Museum, The
Newsletter: KWM Newsletter
27 Everett St.
P.O. Box 297
Sharon, MA 02067-0297
phone: 617-784-5642
Internet: http://www.kwm.org
*International collection of whaling
artworks & artifacts specializing in
paintings 1600-present, scrimshaw,
tools, gear, prints, ship models, etc.*

New Bedford Whaling Museum
18 Johnny Cake Hill
New Bedford, MA 02740-6317
phone: 617-997-0046
fax: 617-997-0018
*A whaling and local historical
museum.*

Cold Spring Harbor Whaling Museum
P.O. Box 25
Cold Spring Harbor, NY 11724
phone: 516-367-3418

Sag Harbor Whaling & Historical
Museum
P.O. Box 1327
Sag Harbor, NY 11963
phone: 516-725-0770
*Instruments, scrimshaw, ship models,
tools, artifacts.*

David Hull
National Maritime Museum Library
Bldg. E, Fort Mason Center
San Francisco, CA 94123
phone: 415-556-3002
fax: 415-556-1624
*Extensive research library open to the
public.*

Pacific Whaling Museum
Sea Life Park
Waimanalo, HI 96795
phone: 808-259-5177

WHEEL TOYS

(see BICYCLES & RELATED
MEMORABILIA; GO-KARTS;
RIDING TOYS; SOAP BOX DERBY)

WHISKEY INDUSTRY ITEMS

(see also ADVERTISING COL-
LECTIBLES; CERAMICS [EN-
GLISH], Whisky Pitchers; GLASSES;
PROHIBITION ITEMS; SALOON &
BAR COLLECTIBLES)

Museums/Libraries

Seagram Museum, The
57 Erb St.
Waterloo
Ontario N2L 6C2 Canada
phone: 519-885-1857
fax: 519-746-1673
*Provides unique and quality
educational experiences related to the
history and evolution of spirits and
wines; collects and preserves related
items: wines, spirits, drinking glasses,
bottles, prints, cork and barrel
making, etc.*

Jack Daniels

Collectors

Claude Bellar
1750 Keyes Road
Greenbrier, TN 37073
phone: 615-643-0290
fax: 615-643-0290
e-mail: cbellar@aol.com

Old Crow

Collectors

Judith & Bob Walthall
P.O. Box 4465
Huntsville, AL 35815
phone: 205-881-9198
Wants to buy Old Crow Whiskey items.

WHISTLERS

(see MUSIC BOXES, Birds & Bird
Boxes [Singing])

WHISTLES

(see HORNS & WHISTLES)

WHITE HOUSE COLLECTIBLES

(see also PERSONALITIES
[HISTORICAL]; POLITICAL
COLLECTIBLES)

Clubs/Associations

White House Historical Association
5026 Federal Office Building, No. 7
Washington, DC 20506

Dealers

H. Joseph Levine
Presidential Coin & Antique Co. Inc.
6550-I Little River Turnpike
Alexandria, VA 22312
phone: 703-354-5454
fax: 703-914-0547
e-mail: jlevine@aol.com
*Wants include Presidential jewelry,
Christmas cards, pens and White
House glass, china, and paper items;
also wants any item connected with
Presidential inaugurations such as
medals, ribbons, invitations,
programs, buttons, etc.*

China

Repro. Sources

United States Historical Society
First & Main Streets
Richmond, VA 23219
phone: 804-648-4736
fax: 804-648-0002

WICKER

(see also REPAIR/RESTORATION/
CONSERVATION, Wicker)

Dealers

Florence B. Albright
16 Main St. E, Ste. 300
Rochester, NY 14614-1803
*Wants to buy wicker furniture and
lamps.*

Michael T. Meadows
Meadows House Antiques
919 Stiles St.
Baltimore, MD 21202-4426
phone: 410-837-5427
Buys and sells ANTIQUE wicker.

Museums/Libraries

East Martello Museum
3501 South Roosevelt Blvd.
Key West, FL 33040
phone: 305-296-3913

Repro. Sources

Yesteryear Wicker
7616 Investment Ct.
Owings, MD 20736
phone: 410-257-9387
*World's only antique wicker
reproduction specialist.*

WIENER WERKSTATTE

(see MODERNISM)

WILDLIFE

(see ANIMAL TROPHIES;
SPORTING COLLECTIBLES,
Hunting & Fishing; TRAPS)

WINCHESTER COLLECTIBLES

(see also DIAMOND EDGE
[SHAPLEIGH HARDWARE];
FIREARMS, Winchester; HARD-
WARE; KEEN KUTTER [SIMMONS
HARDWARE])

Auction Services

Bob Simmons
Simmons & Company Auctioneers
Rte. 1 Box 186
Richmond, MO 64085-9760
phone: 816-776-2936
fax: 816-470-5016
e-mail:
simmons_auction@raycounty.com
Internet: http://www.raycounty.com/
simmons.html
*Conducts annual specialty auctions of
Winchester, Keen Kutter (E.C.
Simmons Hardware) and Diamond
Edge (Shapleigh Hardware)
collectibles; has a well-established
reputation for expertise and high
quality merchandise.*

Clubs/Associations

Winchester Club of America, The
3070 S. Wyandot
Englewood, CO 80110
Buys, sells, restores dolls.

Collectors

James Anderson
P.O. Box 120704
New Brighton, MN 55112
phone: 612-484-3198
*Items made by Winchester Repeating
Arms Co. (and other gun, cartridge or
powder Co's.): tools, posters, knives,
fishing items, etc.*

Museums/Libraries

Shozo Kagoshima, Dir. of Mkt.
Winchester Mystery House, Antique
  Products Museum
525 South Winchester Blvd.
San Jose, CA 95128
phone: 408-247-2000
fax: 408-247-2090
Internet: http://ca.living.net/trav/unique/
carwh.htm
*Displays cutlery, flashlights, lawn
mowers, fishing tackle, and farm tools
manufactured by the Winchester
Products company after WWI.*

Periodicals

Tom Basore
Hardware Companies Kollectors' Club
Newsletter: Winchester Keen Kutter
  Diamond Edge Chronicles
715 West 20th Ave.
Hutchinson, KS 67502
phone: 316-665-3613 or 816-776-2936
fax: 816-470-5016
e-mail: webmaster@raycounty.com
Internet: http://www.raycounty.com/
simmons.html
*A non-profit organization to serve as
an interactive information distribution
center for collectors of Keen Kutter,
Diamond Edge, Winchester Store
(non-gun), Simmons & Shapleigh and
other hardware store brands.*

WINDMILL COLLECTIBLES

Collectors

Ohio Windmill & Pump Co.
SR 534
Berlin Center, OH 44401
phone: 330-547-6300
*Interested in anything windmill:
literature, salesman samples, wooden
wheel windmills, etc.*

James Gress
13174 U.S. 127
Paulding, OH 45879
phone: 419-399-5358
*Wants to buy any kind of advertising
or literature related to American
windmills.*

Dealers

T. Lindsay Baker
Windmill Books & Sales
P.O. Box 507
Rio Vista, TX 76093-0507
*Always buying windmill trade
catalogs, brochures, price lists, parts
lists, and advertising ephemera.*

Museums/Libraries

Volendam Windmill Museum, Inc.
RD 1 Box 242
Milford, NJ 08848
phone: 201-995-4365

Windmill Collection, The
E. Star Route, box 7
Portales, NM 88130
phone: 505-356-6263

Periodicals

T. Lindsay Baker
Newsletter: Windmillers' Gazette
P.O. Box 507
Rio Vista, TX 76093-0507
*Only periodical in American devoted
exclusively to windmills and wind
power history; author of "A Field
Guide to American Windmills."*

Weights

(see also CAST IRON ITEMS)

Dealers

Doug Clemence
Treasure Chest
436 North Chicago
Salina, KS 67401-2020
phone: 913-827-9371 or 913-825-4111
*Sells, sells and trades old and
reproduction windmill weights.*

Experts

Donald E. Sites
P.O. Box 201
Grinnell, KS 67738
*Author of "Windmills and Windmill
Weights."*

Don Lawrence
P.O. Box 1141
Boise City, OK 73933
phone: 405-544-3103
*Co-author with Rick Nidey of
"Windmill Weights", available from
author for $17 ppd.*

Richard Tucker
Argyle Antiques
P.O. Box 262
Argyle, TX 76226-0262
phone: 817-464-3752
fax: 817-464-7293
e-mail: millwt@pop.intex.net
*Buys and sells figural cast iron items:
windmill weights, shooting targets,
water sprinklers; no repros. or
repaired items wanted.*

WINES & WINE RELATED ITEMS

(see also CORKSCREWS)

Appraisers

William H. Edgerton
P.O. Box 88
Darien, CT 06820-0588
phone: 203-655-0566
fax: 203-655-8066

Auction Services

Louis Webre, Client Svc.
William Doyle Galleries
175 E. 87th St.
New York, NY 10128-2205
phone: 212-427-2730
fax: 212-369-0892
Internet: http://www.doylegalleries.com
*Holds over 30 auctions annually of
antique English, Continental and
American furniture, paintings,
decorations, jewelry, vintage and
couture clothing, collectible toys,*

books and prints; specialty auctions of
Majolica, Lalique and wine.

Michael Davis
Davis & Co. Wine Auctioneers, Ltd.
1440 N Dayton St.
Chicago, IL 60622
phone: 312-587-9500
fax: 312-654-1800
Conducts six wine auctions per year.

Butterfield & Butterfield
220 San Bruno Ave.
San Francisco, CA 94103-5018
phone: 415-861-7500
fax: 415-553-8678
*Specialties include posters, toys,
decorative arts, furniture, photography, etc.; the largest full service
auction in the west.*

Collectors

Colgin-Schrader Cellars
P.O. Box 372
Calistoga, CA 94515
*Wants to buy wines and wine related
items: coasters, tastevins, decanters,
silver mounted clarets, corkscrews,
cellarettes, related paintings and
prints from all wine regions especially
CA; also wants pre 1962 vintage
wines.*

Experts

Mark Barlow
Winetiques
3107A Medlock Bridge Rd.
Norcross, GA 30071-1423
phone: 770-449-7610
fax: 770-449-1839
*Buys, sells, specializes in wine related
antiques: corkscrews, tasters, bottle
holders, old bottles, coasters,
advertising, books, art; anything
related to wine or champagne.*

Museums/Libraries

Greyton H. Taylor Wine Museum
RD 2
Hammondsport, NY 14840
phone: 607-868-4814

On-Line Services

David Harmon
Wine.com
1475 Fourth St.
Napa, CA 94559
phone: 707-257-2093
fax: 707-252-6996
e-mail: dharmon@wine.com
Internet: http://www.wine.com/
*A complete wine website for the
collector of fine and rare wines; on-
line auctions, sales and information.*

Periodicals

William H. Edgerton
Wine Price File
Book: Wine Price File
P.O. Box 88
Darien, CT 06820-0588
phone: 203-655-0566
fax: 203-655-8066
An annual publication; advice to collectors, appraisals, valuations, consulting, restaurant wine lists prepared.

WINGS

(see AIRLINE MEMORABILIA, Junior Crew Member Wings; AIRLINE MEMORABILIA, Pilots Wings; AVIATION MEMORABILIA, Military Insignia)

WIRELESS TELEGRAPHY

(see TELEGRAPH ITEMS)

WITCHES

(see also HALLOWEEN COL-LECTIBLES)

Salem

Museums/Libraries

Salem Witch Museum
19 1/2 Washington Square North
Salem, MA 01970
phone: 508-744-1692
Depicts life in 1692 and the aftermath of the Salem Witch Trials.

WIZARD OF OZ

(see also MOVIE MEMORABILIA)

Clubs/Associations

Lee Jenkins
Emerald City Club
Newsletter: Emerald City Club
  Newsletter
153 E. Main St.
New Albany, IN 47150

Peter E. Hanff, Pres.
International Wizard of Oz Club, The
Journal: Baum Bugle, The
P.O. Box 10117
Berkeley, CA 94709-5117
phone: 510-527-4222
e-mail: phanff@library.berkeley.edu
Internet: http://www.neosoft.com/~iwoc/
Promotes the study and collecting of items relating to L. Frank Baum (1856-1919), The Oz Books, toys, movies, etc.; educates its members about the writings of L. Frank Baum and other authors and illustrators who contributed to Oz books.

Collectors

Bill Stillman
981 Kings Way West
Hummelstown, PA 17036-8909
phone: 717-566-5538
fax: 717-566-7718
Long time collector wants anything

related to Wizard of Oz from 1900-1960s.

Michael Gessel
P.O. Box 748
Arlington, VA 22216-0748
phone: 703-542-0462
Wants books, posters, games, and advertising related to "The Wizard of Oz"; also wants items by W. W. Denslow.

Tod R. Machin
P.O. Box 3416
Kansas City, KS 66103
phone: 913-362-0528
Wants OZ items: old toys, books, dolls, paper and movie items dating from 1900 to 1970.

Edwin Wilder
1409 1st St.
Port Townsend, WA 98368-3078
Wants to buy Wizard of Oz books by any author; also wants related books, ephemera, and Baum non-Oz books.

Dealers

Elaine Willingham
Beyond the Rainbow Wizard of Oz
  Collectibles
P.O. Box 31672
Saint Louis, MO 63131-0672
phone: 314-799-1724
fax: 314-271-2727
Specializing in current and older MGM Wizard of OZ and Judy Garland collectibles, videos, books, jewelry.

Experts

Jay Scarfone
981 Kings Way West
Hummelstown, PA 17036-8909
phone: 717-566-5538
fax: 717-566-7718
Wants all kinds of memorabilia from the 1939 movie "The Wizard of Oz"; ads, souvenirs, posters, lobby cards, coat hangers, dolls, etc.

Periodicals

Elaine Willingham, Ed.
Newsletter: Beyond the Rainbow
  Collector's Exchange
P.O. Box 31672
Saint Louis, MO 63131-0672
phone: 314-799-1724
fax: 314-271-2727
Articles, ads.

WOOD

Clubs/Associations

Lloyd Sumner
International Wood Collectors Society
Magazine: World of Wood
5900 Chestnut Ridge Rd.
Riner, VA 24149
phone: 703-382-1974
Dedicated to the advancement of information regarding wood; members enjoy wood sample collecting, identification (dendrology) and

woodworking; trade, buy, sell and auction wood samples.

Identification

Misc. Services

Society for the Preservation of New
  England Antiquities, The
  Conservation Center
185 Lyman St.
North Waltham, MA 02154
phone: 617-891-4882
fax: 617-893-7832
Performs wood and finish/coatings analysis; also offers conservation treatment of furniture and objects.

Dr. Michael Taras
215 S. Craggmore Dr.
Salem, SC 29676-4626
phone: 864-944-0655
Send a wood sample for identification.

Forest Products Laboratory
One Clifford Pinchot Dr.
Madison, WI 53705-2398

WOOD CARVINGS

Collectors

Joe Iozzia
P.O. Box 1005
Pomona, NJ 08240-1005
phone: 609-652-8504
Wants to buy figural wood handcarved people, animals, elves, pirates, monks, etc.; nutcrackers, cigarette boxes, bookends, ashtrays, pipe holders, figurines, bottle stoppers, humidors and unusual figural handcarved items.

Philly Rains
1401 Brentwood Dr.
Harrison, AR 72601
phone: 501-743-2040
fax: 501-743-2120
Wants to buy handcarved wooden sculptures: corkstoppers, bar sets, cigarette boxes, book ends, corkscrews, openers, pourers, napkin rings, figurines, letter openers, spoons, forks, key and spoon racks, pipe racks, nutcrackers, etc.

Steve Elliott
1600 Tennessee St.
Vallejo, CA 94590
phone: 707-552-8400 or 707-642-1949
fax: 707-552-0881
Wants to buy antique Black Forest wood carvings.

Man./Prod./Dist.

Les Ramsay
Linden Tree Woodcarving Gallery
137 South Broad St.
Grove City, PA 16127-1522
phone: 412-458-5539
e-mail: lindentree@pathway.com
Internet: http://www.pathway.net/
  lindentree
Hand carved wooden figures, doors,

fireplace mantels and commissioned sculpture.

Repair Services

David Warther II
David Warther Carving Museum
2561 Crestview Dr. NW
Dover, OH 44622-7405
phone: 330-852-3455 or 330-343-1868
Restores wood and ivory carvings and turnings; specialty is in small objects in ivory: chess sets, finials, small turned items, insulators, handles, and finials of ivory or sterling hollowware.

WOODBURNING CRAFT ITEMS

(see PYROGAPHY)

WOODEN MONEY

Clubs/Associations

Robbin Quinn
International Organization of Wooden
  Money Collectors
Newsletter: Bunyan's Chips
5295 Beechwood Rd.
Ravenna, OH 44266-9119
phone: 216-296-6783
Club of over 300 focuses on woods - wooden "money" and commemoratives.

American Wooden Money Guild
Newsletter: Old Woody Views
P.O. Box 30444
Tucson, AZ 85751
phone: 602-886-0505
fax: 602-722-3607
"Lignadenarists" are interested in collecting wooden money.

Collectors

Norman Boughton
P.O. Box 93262
Rochester, NY 14692
phone: 716-292-5550 or 716-292-0128
Wants wooden money issued for celebrations, used as money or issued by restaurant chains such as McDonald's.

WORLD WAR MEMORABILIA

(see MARINE CORPS ITEMS; MILITARIA, WWI Items; MILITARIA, WWII Items; NAZI ITEMS; RATIONING RELATED ITEMS)

WORLD'S FAIRS & EXPOSITIONS

Auction Services

Janice & Richard Vogel
Vogels, The
4720 SE Fort King St.
Ocala, FL 34470-1501
phone: 352-694-5776
fax: 352-694-7330
Quarterly mail order souvenir auctions: china, glass, spoons,

mauchline, paper, World's Fair, fraternal.

Bob Slawsky
P.O. Box 864
Windermere, FL 34786-0864
phone: 407-352-7807
fax: 407-352-BIDS
e-mail: WWGD54A@prodigy.com
Buys, sells, auctions tokens, medals, badges, small advertising items, political, World's Fair, Olympic items, encased coins, etc.

Clubs/Associations

Michael R. Pender, Pres.
World's Fair Collectors Society, Inc.
Newsletter: Fair News
P.O. Box 20806
Sarasota, FL 34276-3806
phone: 941-923-2590
e-mail: wfcs@aol.com
Focuses on collecting and preserving materials pertinent to the history of World's Fairs and International expositions; bi-monthly newsletter contains articles, ads, etc.

Max Storm
1904 World's Fair Society
Newsletter: World's Fair Bulletin
529 Barcia Dr.
Saint Louis, MO 63119-1518
phone: 314-968-2810
Internet: http://www.tias.com/stores/fiar/c
Purpose is to preserve the memories and memorabilia of the 1904 St. Louis World's Fair.

Judith Rubin
World's Fair, Inc.
Journal: World's Fair
P.O. Box 339 - ABQ
Corte Madera, CA 94976-0339
phone: 415-924-6035
fax: 415-924-8245
A quarterly journal of international expositions and events; people, pageantry, planning and politics; articles, ads; free sample.

Collectors

T. Augyre
P.O. Box 1293
Bayonne, NJ 07002-6293
phone: 201-339-8375
fax: 201-339-8375
Buys 1930-40 and 1964-65 New York World's Fair, especially posters, signs; buys, sells, trades items from other Fairs.

Ken Schultz
P.O. Box M753
Hoboken, NJ 07030
phone: 201-656-0966
fax: 201-418-8640
Wants all items relating to world's fairs and expositions.

Andy Rudoff
P.O. Box 111
Oceanport, NJ 07757-0111
phone: 908-542-3712
fax: 908-542-3712
Wants early (1851-1904) World's Fair items especially 1876 Centennial and 1893 Columbian Exposition; wants all items especially china, glass, and metal souvenirs; all other early U.S. and foreign fairs also considered.

Steve Sheppard
2500 Johnson Ave.
Bronx, NY 10463
phone: 718-549-1570
Wants to buy World's Columbian Exposition items: advertising, documents, letters, diaries, photographs, and other ephemera.

Henry Heiman, III
P.O. Box 316
South Salem, NY 10590-0316
Wants 1939-1940 New York World's Fair items.

Rusty Olimpo
P.O. Box 363
Mechanicsville, PA 18934-0363
phone: 215-345-5768
e-mail: oporx@aol.com
Wants to buy anything relating to the 1939-40 New York World's Fair.

Frederick Lingenfelser
814 Byram St.
Reading, PA 19606-1446
Wants to buy World's Fair items; specializes in 1893 Columbian Exposition: photographs, post cards, art work, maps, trinkets, tickets, etc.

Paul A. Jarrett
611 West End Dr.
Waverly, TN 37185
phone: 615-296-3151
Wants to buy any type of memorabilia from the 1897 Tennessee Centennial Exposition including china, paper, glassware, badges, pins, medals, ribbons, tickets, etc.

Rick Rann
P.O. Box 877
Oak Park, IL 60303-0877
phone: 708-442-7907
Wants to buy items from the 1933-1934 Chicago Century of Progress: uniforms, toys, ride tickets, pennants, etc.

Doug Woolard
11614 Old St. Charles Rd.
Bridgeton, MO 63044-3078
phone: 314-739-4662

Max Storm
529 Barcia Dr.
Saint Louis, MO 63119-1518
phone: 314-968-2810
Internet: http://www.tias.com/stores/fiar/c
Wants any type of memorabilia from the 1904 St. Louis World's Fair: clocks, padlocks, postcards, watches, china, tickets, paper, stock certificates, etc.

Dealers

Thomas J. Diddle
Worlds Columbian Exonumist, The
802 North Rd.
Boynton Beach, FL 33435-3238
phone: 561-738-1992
fax: 561-733-4127
Buys, sells, trades all World Fair and Exposition collectibles and ephemera.

Judith Rubin
Eureka! Antiques
705 W. Washington
Evanston, IL 60202-2214
phone: 847-869-9090
Focuses on the Chicago World's Fairs and other Chicago memorabilia; a small shop - they send no lists but write detailed individual letters; SASEs get first attention.

William "Bill" Pieber
Best of Times Antiques
1010 Mallow Dr.
Ballwin, MO 63011-2365
phone: 314-227-8930
Buys and sells St. Louis World's Fair (1904) and Louisiana Purchase Exposition items; also all World's Fair items from 1915 Pan-Pacific, 1939 New York, and 1939 San Francisco.

Experts

Richard Friz
P.O. Box 472
Peterborough, NH 03458
phone: 603-563-8155
Author of "The Official Price Guide to World's Fair Memorabilia."

Harvey & Sandy Dolin
Harvey Dolin & Co.
5 Beekman St.
New York, NY 10038-2206
phone: 212-267-0216
Wants any item pertaining to the 1939 New York World's Fair and the Columbian Fair.

Judith Katz-Schwartz
Twin Brooks Antiques & Collectibles
P.O. Box 6572
New York, NY 10128-0006
phone: 212-876-3512
fax: 212-876-3512
e-mail: twinb@tiac.net
Internet: http://www.tiac.net/users/twinb
Buys, sells, appraises all categories of World's Fair memorabilia; looking for items from 1939 New York World's Fair.

Herbert Rolfes
2260 Chase Court
Mount Dora, FL 32757-6909
phone: 352-735-3947 or 352-735-3970
Co-author of "The World of Tomorrow: The 1939 New York World's Fair."

Rich Hartzog
World Exonumia
P.O. Box 4143 BSB
Rockford, IL 61110-0643
phone: 815-226-0771
fax: 815-397-7662
Pre-1940 items preferred; collections and quantities wanted.

D.D. Woollard, Jr.
11614 Old St. Charles Rd.
Bridgeton, MO 63044-3078
phone: 314-739-4662
Buy, sell, trade World Fair & Exposition memorabilia: major interest in older fairs - 1893 Chicago, 1904 St. Louis, etc.

Museums/Libraries

Buffalo & Erie County Historical Society
25 Nottingham Ct.
Buffalo, NY 14216
phone: 716-873-9644

Atwater Kent Museum - the History Museum of Philadelphia
15 S. 7th St.
Philadelphia, PA 19143
phone: 215-922-3031

Dan & Rose Amato
1893 Chicago World's Columbian Exposition Museum
239 Whitney St.
P.O. Box 151
Columbus, WI 53925-0151
phone: 414-623-1992
Focuses on the World's Columbian Exposition of 1893; over 20,000 pieces.

Keith R. Gill
Museum of Science & Industry
57th St. & Lake Shore Dr.
Chicago, IL 60637
phone: 312-684-1414
fax: 312-684-5580
Archives contains documents & photos of the 1893 Columbian Exposition and the 1933-1934 Century of Progress Exposition.

Ronald Mahoney
California State University, Madden Library
5200 N. Barton Ave.
Fresno, CA 93740
phone: 209-278-2595
World's Fairs from 1851-1940.

WRAPPERS

(see BUBBLE GUM & CANDY WRAPPERS)

WRITING INSTRUMENTS

(see CALLIGRAPHY; GLASS, Whimsies [Pens]; INKWELLS & INKSTANDS; OFFICE EQUIPMENT; PENCILS; PENS)

WWI

(see MILITARIA, WWI Items)

WWII

(see MILITARIA, WWII Items)

YACHTS

(see BOATS)

ZEPPELINS

(see AIRSHIPS)

Here are some tips when contacting someone listed in this book:

When requesting information about a particular item, include a description (material, dimensions, maker's mark, model number, etc.) and a photo, sketch, or photocopy of the item in question. ■

Always ask if there are charges for samples or for the services requested. ■

When writing, please be sure to include a Large (#10 business size) Self-Addressed and Stamped Envelope (LSASE) if requesting a reply or the return of photographs. ■

Never call collect unless otherwise directed. When calling, be considerate of time zone differences and always ask if the party you are calling has time to talk. When leaving an answering machine message, always instruct the party to call you back collect. ■

APPENDIX A

Appraisers
Listed in ZIP code order

The International Society of Appraisers is the largest nonprofit association of personal property appraisers in North America. Its Accredited and Certified members are experienced and educated appraisers who evaluate all types of personal property (including antiques & collectibles , art, gems & jewelry, and machinery & equipment) to establish accurate values for such uses as buying and selling objects, insurance coverage, damage claims, estate and gift taxes, charitable donations, bankruptcies, casualty loss, equitable distribution, and expert witness testimony.

All appraisers listed below are Accredited Members of the ISA, and many have earned the coveted CAPP (Certified Appraiser of Personal Property) designation. The ISA is the only personal property appraisal association that has always prohibited the "grandfathering" of its members. All those listed have demonstrated appraisal competency through a mandatory education/testing program and are bound to abide by a rigid Code of Ethics and Professional Conduct which embraces the highest standards of the profession. In addition, the ISA's affiliation with the University of Maryland University College insures that ISA appraiser education programs adhere to the highest standards of academia.

For additional information about the ISA or to locate a nearby appraiser, write the ISA at 16040 Christensen Rd., Suite 320, Seattle, WA 98188. You can also call 206-241-0359, fax 206-241-0436 or e-mail ISA_HQ@compuserve.com. Check out the ISA website on the Internet at http://www.isa-appraisers.org to search for an appraiser in your locale or to learn more about the ISA and its course offerings.

Please note that appraisers who specialize in a particular field of expertise may also be listed under those categories within the General Listings section of this Directory.

Karen Becker, ISA, GG
Forever Precious Fine Jewellers Inc.
730 Upper James St
Hamilton, ON   L9C 2Z9 Canada
Phone: 905-575-4415
Fax: 905-575-9920
Gemology/Gemstones, Diamonds, Gold, Jewelry

Peter S. Blundell, ISA
Birdseye Estate & Appraisals
PO Box 6
Vernon, BC   V1T 6M1 Canada
Phone: 250-542-4540
Antiques, Furniture (Oak, Victorian), Antique Kerosene Lighting & Glass, British Transfer Printed Earthen Wares

Claire P. Collins, ISA
PO Box 2754, George Town
Grand Cayman
Grand Cayman Island, BWI
Phone: 809-947-6436
Fax: 809-947-6436
Jewelry, Gemology/Gemstones, Diamonds, Pearls, Fine Art

Gary B. Coyle, ISA, MGGA
Coyle's Jewellery & Gifts, Ltd.
5876 Wyandotte St
East Windsor, ON   N8S 1M8 Canada
Phone: 519-945-1969
Fax: 519-945-5980
E-mail: gcoyle@mnsi.net
Gemology, Gemstones, Jewelry, Diamonds, Colored Stones

Charles T. Cripps, ISA CAPP
Townsend Antiques & Appraisals
15227 81 Avenue
Edmonton, AB   T5R 3P2 Canada
Phone: 403-486-5012
Fax: 403-484-2836
E-mail: 76651.340@compuserve.com
Furniture, Silver, Porcelain, Pottery, Residential Contents
CAPP In Appreciable Residential Contents

Regine David, ISA
Garry Antiques
13 Rue d'Aumale
Paris,   75009 France
Antiques, Faberge, Jewelry, Russian Art, Silver

Thomas L. G. Gibson, ISA
Gibson's Appraisers & Restoration
6319 Chebucto Rd
Halifax, NS   B3L 1K9 Canada
Phone: 902-429-3873
Antiques, Objet D'art/De Vertu, Residential Contents, Repairs, Restoration, Preservation, Consultant, Decorative Arts & Accessories,

Kathy Gowans, ISA
Serendipity Antiques
RR #2
Red Deer, AB   T4N 5E2 Canada
Phone: 403-347-7199
Fax: 403-346-2554
E-mail: kgowans@agt.net
Antiques, Collectibles

Philip Grouchy, ISA
Fitzpatrick's Auctioneering
29 Roblin Place
Torbay, NF   A1K 1A2 Canada
Phone: 709-722-5865
Fax: 709-722-9612
Residential Contents, Industrial, Vehicle, Auctioneer

Barbara B. Lines, ISA
Blades Appraisal Services, Ltd.
48 Par-la Ville Rd, Ste 810
Hamilton,   HM 11 Bermuda
Phone: 441-295-4822
Fax: 441-295-4856
Paintings (19th & 20th C.), Furniture (19th & 20th C.), Silver (English & Modern)

Kathryn C Minard, ISA
Contemporary Fine Art Services, Inc
413 Dundas St East
Toronto, ON   M5A 2A9 Canada
Phone: 416-366-9770
Fax: 416-366-8541
E-mail: 75263.2530@compuserve.com
Fine Arts, Contemporary Canadian, Historical Canadian, Canadian Craft

Ian Muncaster, ISA
Zwicker's Gallery
5415 Doyle St
Halifax, NS   B3J 1H9 Canada
Phone: 902-423-7662
Fax: 902-422-3870
Paintings, Watercolors & Drawings, (Especially Canadian); Graphics, Sculpture, Fine Art

Sheila Wills Osborne, ISA
Contemporary Fine Art Services
332 Soudan Avenue
Toronto, ON   M4S 1W7 Canada
Phone: 416-366-9770
Fax: 416-366-8541
Canadian Fine Art

Erik J. Peters, ISA
Maynards Industries Ltd.
415 W 2nd Ave
Vancouver, BC   V5Y 1E3 Canada
Phone: 604-876-6787
Fax: 604-876-2678
Canadian Historical & Modern Fine Art, Western European, British & American Fine Art

M. Lorraine Pierce-Hull, ISA
Pierce-Hull & Associates
PO Box 93
Carleton Place, ON   K7C 3P3 Canada
Phone: 613-257-2987
Fax: 613-253-0949
E-mail: lphull@magi.com
Fine Art (Contemporary Canadian & International), Sculpture (Canadian)

James Poag, ISA CAPP, GG
James O. Poag Jewelers, Ltd.
94 Frank St, Box 39
Strathroy, ON   N7G 3J1 Canada
Phone: 519-245-1040
Fax: 519-245-6073
E-mail: 76261.3242@compuserve.com
Gemology/Gemstones, Gold, Jewelry, Estates, Pearls, Insurance, Consultations
CAPP In Gemstones

Elinor A Racine, ISA
Elin Racine
175 Bessborough Dr
Toronto, ON   M4G 3J8 Canada
Phone: 416-483-8675
Fax: 416-440-2809
E-mail: 75317.2337@compuserv.com
Ceramics Experience, Appraisal Of Donations To The Permanent Collection Of Ceramics, Glass, 20th C. Studio Work

Judith Scolnik, ISA
Judith Scolnik Art Search
96 Thorncliffe Park Drive, Suite 2701
Toronto, ON   M4H 1L7 Canada
Phone: 416-421-4239
Fax: 416-423-8057
Fine Art, Candaian Art (Historical, Contemporary), American & European master graphics, Curator/Manager Art Gallery

Meyer K. Steiman, ISA CAPP
Carter's Auction Gallery
206 Princess St
Winnipeg, MB   R3B 1L4 Canada
Phone: 204-942-3397
Fax: 204-943-8960
Residential Contents, Office Furniture & Equipment, Estates, Furniture, Auction Co., Business Liquidators
CAPP In Depreciable Residential Contents

Dennis R. Storey, Jr., ISA, CAI
Forest City Auctions Inc
43 Chaucer Ct
London, ON N6K 1V1 Canada
Phone: 519-641-2844
Fax: 519-641-6143
*Residential Contents, Estates,
Machinery & Equipment (Restaurant),
Business Evaluations, Auctioneer*

Stephen P Sweeting, ISA
Appraisal Associates
80 Richmond St W, Suite 1101
Toronto, ON M5H 2A4 Canada
Phone: 416-368-4334
Fax: 416-368-6679
Fine Art, Decorative Art, Antiques

Irene Szylinger, ISA
Art Research & Appraisals, Ltd.
62 Woodlawn Ave W
Toronto, ON M4V 1G7 Canada
Phone: 416-964-6449
Fax: 416-928-2332
*Antique Furniture, Works on Paper,
Sculpture, Decorative Arts, Fine Art*

William B. Whetstone, ISA
Thompson & Whetstone, Inc.
1117 Saint Catherine St W, Ste 900
Montreal, QC H3B 1H9 Canada
Phone: 514-289-9761
Fax: 514-458-1435
E-mail: 76262.614@compuserve.com
*Jewelry (Antique & Period), Silver
(Antique), Coins (Ancient Coins, 18th
- 20th C. World Coins & Tokens),
Decorative Arts (19th - 20th C.), Fine
Arts (19th-20th C.)*

Sheila D. Wilson, ISA
Wilson & Associates
VMPO #3022
Vancouver, BC V6B 3X5 Canada
Phone: 604-685-2964
Fax: 604-685-2974
E-mail: dswilson@bc.sympatico.ca
*Antiques, Decorative Arts &
Accessories, Estates, Residential
Contents*

Edith Yeomans, ISA
Appraisal Associates
80 Richmond Street West, Suite 1101
Toronto, ON M5H 2A4 Canada
Phone: 416-368-4334
Fax: 416-368-6679
Fine Art, Antiques, Decorative Arts

Karin Ann Esposito, ISA, GG
KAE Gemological Services, Inc.
9003 Est. Hope, Lot 003
Christiansted, VI 00820
Phone: 809-778-6634
Fax: 809-778-6634
Gems, Jewelry

Walter P Petreyko, ISA
Imagine
PO Box 819
Groton, MA 01450-0819
Phone: 508-448-5044
*Antiques, Framing, Furniture &
Furnishings, Jewelry, Artwork,
Collectibles, Glass, Silver, Residential
Contents, Insurance*

Robert Loy Puterbaugh, ISA
Robert Loy Puterbaugh
159 Prospect St
Lunenburg, MA 01462
Phone: 508-342-9695
*American Art Glass, European Art
Glass, European Pottery, Slide Rules,
Art, Furniture, Textiles, Books,
Orientalia*

Frank Lenz, ISA
c/o Sudbury Arts & Antiques
730 Boston Post Rd
Sudbury, MA 01776-3368
Phone: 508-443-0994
Fax: 508-358-5085
E-mail: 73572.3614@compuserve.com
*Antiques, Art, Personal Property,
Estates, Auctioneer*

Linda Bocchino, ISA, GG CGA
Martoni Jewelers of Peabody
215 Newbury St, Ste 211
Peabody, MA 01960-2400
Phone: 508-535-5124
Fax: 508-535-1243
Gemology/Gemstones, Jewelry

Spencer Gordon, ISA
Spencer Marks
PO Box 303
E. Walpole, MA 02032-0303
Phone: 508-668-8969
E-mail: 73760.1470@compuserve.com
*Silver (American & England),
Furniture (American & England),
Fine Art, Ceramics, Glass, Decorative
Arts & Accessories, Orientalia,
Antiques*

Neili Shah, ISA, GG
DeScenza Diamonds
387 Washington St, Ste 6
Boston, MA 02108-5211
Phone: 617-542-7974
Fax: 617-426-4721
Not Appraising At This Time

Judith Dowling, ISA
Edo Gallery Of Asian Art
133 Charles St
Boston, MA 02114
Phone: 617-523-5211
Fax: 617-523-5227
*Asian Art (Japanese & Chinese),
Korean*

Peter J. Shemonsky, ISA, GG
24 Horace St
E. Boston, MA 02128-1534
Phone: 617-461-9530
Fax: 617-461-9625
*Gemology/Gemstones, Jewelry
(Antique, Estate, Arts & Crafts,
Modern)*

Norman Hurst, ISA
Hurst Gallery
53 Mount Auburn St
Cambridge, MA 02138-5053
Phone: 617-491-6888
Fax: 617-661-0439
E-mail: 76726.2761@compuserve.com
*Chinese, Japanese And Korean Art,
Graeco-Roman And Egyptian
Antiquities, African, American Indian,*

*Oceanic And Pre-Columbian Art And
Artifacts; Rare Books, Maps And
Posters.*

Martin D. Haske, ISA, GG
Adamas Gemological Lab
PO Box 470828
Brookline Village, MA 02147-0828
Phone: 617-232-5508
Fax: 617-232-5508
*Gemology/Gemstones, Diamonds,
Jewelry*

Mary Westcott, ISA
239 Common St
Belmont, MA 02178-2944
Phone: 617-484-3386
Fax: 617-484-0628
*Silver, Porcelain, Furniture,
Paintings, Glass, Residential
Contents, Victoriana, Fine Art, Objet
D'Art & De Vertu, Decorative Art &
Accessories*

Matthew Joel Fink, ISA
18 Great Marsh Rd
Centerville, MA 02632-2525
Phone: 617-552-7037
Fax: 617-332-8042
*Appreciable Residential Contents,
Porcelain, Pottery, Glass, Paper
Ephemera, Orientalia, Advertising
Items, Textiles (Fabric), Furniture
(American), Art Deco, Nouveau Art &
Accessories, Jewelry, Americana,
Glass, Clothing*

Susan Winokur, ISA
Lost Treasures Antiques
1460 Fall River Ave
Seekonk, MA 02771
Phone: 508-336-9294
Fax: 508-336-9294
*Hummels, Dept 56 Villages, Antiques,
Collectibles, Lladros*

Patricia P. Coughlin, ISA
Antique and Estate Appraisals
34 Flagg Rd
Hollis, NH 03049-6404
Phone: 603-465-3443
Fax: 603-465-3732
*Residential Contents, Antiques,
Paintings And Prints, Furniture &
Accessories (American 17th, - 20th
C.), Americana, Toys, Folk Art, Glass,
Dolls, Doll Houses & Accessories,
Ceramics, Oriental Rugs, Textiles,*

**Judith S. Fineblit Anderson, ISA
CAPP, GG CG CGA**
Bijoux ExtraOrdniaire, Ltd.
PO Box 1424
Manchester, NH 03105-1424
Phone: 603-624-8672
E-mail: judi@bijoux.mv.com
*Jewelry, Gemstones, Appraisals,
Antique And Period Jewelry,
Contemporary Jewelry, Designer
Jewelry, Diamonds, Metals*
CAPP In Gemstones

Carlton C. Ham, ISA
Carlton C. Ham Personal Property
  Appraiser
175 South Main Street
Franklin, NH 03235
Phone: 603-934-4913
Fax: 613-934-5174
*Antiques, Residential Contents,
Postwar Automobiles*

Mary H. Mussells, ISA, GG
J.M. Mussells Inc.
Middle Oxbow Rd
Hinsdale, NH 03451
Phone: 603-256-6023
Fax: 603-256-6901
*Gemology/Gemstones, Diamonds,
Pearls*

Lawrence E. Reynolds, Jr., ISA, GG
G.M. Pollack & Sons
PO Box 910
Scarborough, ME 04700-0910
Phone: 207-883-8455
Fax: 207-883-8565
E-mail: 70611.3003@compuserve.com
Diamonds

Evelyn S. Kennedy, ISA
Sewtique
391 Long Hill Rd
Box 1293
Groton, CT 06340-1293
Phone: 860-445-7320
Fax: 860-445-1448
E-mail: sewtique@aol.com
*Quilts, Tapestries, Textiles,
Needlework, Repairs, Restoration,
(Textiles Include Laces, Furs,
Leather), Costumes*

Trina McCandless, ISA, GG
McCandless Custom Jewelry
100 Starr Hill Rd
Groton, CT 06340-3333
Phone: 860-443-3039
Fax: 860-443-3039
E-mail: 76633.2762@compuserve.com
*Gemology/Gemstones, Jewelry,
Jewelry Design, Diamonds, Gold,
Pearls*

Walter Bazzini, ISA, GG
PO Box 171
Durham, CT 06422-0171
Phone: 860-349-3459
Fax: 860-349-3450
E-mail: 73300.111@compuserve.com
*Gemology/Gemstones, Jewelry,
Diamonds, Watches*

Nancy N. Richardson, ISA, CGA GG
Nancy N. Richardson, CGA
PO Box 393
Essex, CT 06426-0393
Phone: 860-767-1832
Fax: 860-767-2058
E-mail: nrichar156@aol.com
*Gemology/Gemstones, Diamonds,
Jewelry, Watches, Antique/Estate
Jewelry, Silver Flatware/Tableware*

Harry B. French, ISA, CG GG
Henry C. Reid & Son
1551 Post Rd
Fairfield, CT 06430-5910
Phone: 203-255-0447
Fax: 203-255-0448
Gems, Jewelry, Insurance Replacement, Estate Appraisal

Raymond D'Alessio, ISA
Citicorp North America
34 Fawn Brook Cir
Madison, CT 06443-2442
Phone: 914-899-7651
Machinery & Equipment, Commercial Inventories

Kathleen Connolly, ISA
Village Antique Shop
61 West Main Street
Plantsville, CT 06479
Phone: 860-628-2498
Antiques, Dolls & Toys, Pottery, Residential Contents

Paul D. Indorf, ISA, GG CGA
Peter Indorf Jewelers
1022 Chapel St
New Haven, CT 06510-2412
Phone: 203-776-4833
Fax: 203-777-8423
E-mail: pindorf@snet.net
Gemology/Gemstones, Jewelry, Diamonds, Pearls

Doreen A. Guerrera, ISA, CGA
Addessi Jewelry Stores
207 Main St
Danbury, CT 06810-6687
Phone: 203-744-2555
Fax: 203-744-2700
Gemology/Gemstones, Pearls, Jewelry

Joan Gehl, ISA
19 Spring Hill Dr
West Orange, NJ 07052-2411
Phone: 201-731-3264
Furniture, Residential Contents, Silver, Porcelain, Pottery, Ceramics, China

Elissa S. Cohen, ISA CAPP, GG
Suburban Jewelers
126 E Front St
Plainfield, NJ 07060
Phone: 908-756-1774
Fax: 908-756-6596
Gemology/Gemstones, Colored Stones, Diamonds (Loose & Mounted, Old Cut), Jewelry (Fine, Contemporary, Estate, Karat Gold), Pearls (Cultured), Figurines, (Lladro, All God's Children, Precious Moments)
CAPP In Gemstones

Patricia Sheeleigh, ISA
Patricia Sheeleigh Fine Arts
39 Old Eagle Rock Ave
Roseland, NJ 07068-1433
Phone: 201-228-4362
Fax: 201-228-4362
American Art (1810-1950), Paintings, Drawings, Watercolors, Prints, Etchings, Engravings, 19th C. European Paintings

JoAnne M. Whitteaker, ISA CAPP, GG
American Appraisal Gem Lab
23 W Westfield Ave
Roselle Park, NJ 07204-2252
Phone: 908-241-8800
Fax: 908-298-0021
Consultant, Diamonds, Gemology/Gemstones, Insurance/Damage Appraisals, Estates, Jewelry, Gold, Silver, Pearls, Watches, Jade, Damage Claims Appraisals, Art Deco, Art Nouveau
CAPP In Gemstones

Zia Ghahary, Ph.D., ISA CAPP
Zighom Int'l. Fine Arts Appraisals
240 Heather Ln
Franklin Lakes, NJ 07417-1111
Phone: 201-337-5577
Fax: 201-337-0404
Authenticate & Appraise: Paintings, (Old Masters, 19th C) Bronze & Clay Sculpture, Antiques - Pottery, Earthenware, Antique Glass, Islamic Works Of Art, Miniature Paintings, Drawings, Illuminated Miniature & Manuscripts, Oriental Rugs
CAPP In Appreciable Residential Contents

Stephen Van Cline, ISA CAPP
Van Cline & Davenport Ltd
792 Franklin Ave
Franklin Lakes, NJ 07417-1343
Phone: 201-891-4588
Paintings, Sculpture, Porcelain, Pottery, Silver, Wedgwood, Staffordshire, Expert Witness (Fine & Decorative Art, Appraisal Practice Qualifications & Reports, Blockage Rule), Fine Furniture
CAPP In Appreciable Residential Contents

William Scolnik, ISA
William L. Scolnik, Inc.
55 Long Hill Rd
Oakland, NJ 07436-2501
Phone: 201-405-0719
Clocks, Watches (Antique), Horological Books & Tools

Diane R. Patalano, ISA
Country Girls Ltd., Inc.
PO Box 144
Saddle River, NJ 07458-0144
Phone: 201-327-2499
Fax: 201-327-2094
Antiques, Furniture (19th & 20th C.), Residential Contents, Estate (Liquidations), Auctioneer, Consultants

Beth K. Meer, ISA CAPP, GG
A Meer Design
PO Box 452
Cresskill, NJ 07626-0401
Phone: 201-569-6589
Fax: 201-569-3152
Gemology/Gemstones, Jewelry
CAPP In Gemstones

Frederick J. Hill, Jr., ISA CAPP
Bob Koty Professional Auctions
PO Box 625
Freehold, NJ 07728-0625
Phone: 908-751-0504
Fax: 908-751-9190
E-mail: fhill09085@aol.com
Residential Contents, Model Cars (E.G. Match Box), Estates, Auction Co., Specializing In Estate Tax Liability Reports
CAPP In Appreciable Residential Contents

Bob Koty, ISA CAPP, CAI CAPA
Bob Koty Professional Auctioneers
PO Box 625
Freehold, NJ 07728-0625
Phone: 908-751-0504
Fax: 908-751-9190
Residential Contents, Antiques, Estates, Personal Property Consultants, Auctioneer, Specializing In Estate Tax Liability Reports
CAPP In Depreciable Residential Contents

Clara Koty, ISA CAPP
Bob Koty Professional Auctioneers
PO Box 625
Freehold, NJ 07728-0625
Phone: 908-751-0504
Fax: 908-751-9190
E-mail: 75754.1156@compuserve.com
Residential Contents, Collectibles, Hummels, Antiques, Buttons, Estates, Auction Company, Personal Property Consultants; Specializing In Estate Tax Liability Reports; CAPP in both Appreciable & Depreciable
CAPP In Appreciable Residential Contents
CAPP In Depreciable Residential Contents

Eldred A. Stenzel, ISA
The Antique Corner
10 Blue Hills Dr
Holmdel, NJ 07733-2218
Phone: 908-946-8437
Porcelain, Pottery, Ceramics, China, Furniture (American), Residential Contents

Suzy McLennan-Anderson, ISA
Heritage Antiques, Inc.
65 Main St, #529
Holmdel, NJ 07733-2310
Phone: 908-946-8801
Fax: 908-946-1036
Furniture (American), Residential Contents, Quilts, Samplers, Needlework, Silver

Victor Brown, Jr., ISA
Tri-State Auction Company
28 DeJager Dr
Augusta, NJ 07822-2111
Phone: 201-702-0800
Fax: 201-702-8666
Estates, Residential Contents, Collectibles, Machinery & Equipment, Real Estate, Auctioneer, Auction Company Appraiser, Insurance

Leon Castner, Ph.D., ISA CAPP
Castner Appraisal Service
PO Box 920
Branchville, NJ 07826-0920
Phone: 201-948-3868
Fax: 201-948-3919
Residential Contents, Americana, Estates, Auctioneer, Auction Co., Oriental Rugs, Silver, Office Equipment
CAPP In Appreciable Residential Contents

Brian Kathenes, ISA
National Appraisal Consultants
PO Box 482
Hope, NJ 07844-0482
Phone: 800-323-5996
Fax: 908-459-4899
E-mail: 76514.362@compuserve.com
Autographs, Collectibles (Baseball Cards, Sports & Space Memorabilia), Coins, Currency, Stamps, Postal History, Movie Memorabilia, Computer & Office Equipment, Documents & Manuscripts, Photography, Photographica

Benjamin A. Doerrmann, ISA
Benjamin Doerrman Auctioneers & Appraisers
131 Sherwin Rd
Sewell, NJ 08080-4431
Phone: 609-478-2389
Fax: 609-478-6606
Glass (Glassware), Furniture, Farm Machinery & Equipment, Auctioneer, Auction Company

Ronald E. Shaffer, ISA
Exemplars, Inc.
17 Pemberton Rd
Vincentown, NJ 08088-8811
Phone: 609-859-0045
Fax: 609-859-3477
Furniture (American), Antiques, Decorative Arts, Residential Contents, Estates

James Crawford, ISA
James & Jill Crawford
1017 Park Ave
Collingswood, NJ 08108-3236
Phone: 609-854-2969
Residential Contents, Antiques, Decorative Arts & Accessories, Estate Consultant

C. Frederick Horbach, Ph.D, ISA
Shibui
280 Greenville Rd
Pittsgrove, NJ 08318-3722
Phone: 609-358-3726
Fax: 609-358-3726
Orientalia, Woodblock Prints, Porcelain, Cloisonne

Jeffrey S. Litwin, MD, ISA
Litwin Antiques
PO Box 5865
Trenton, NJ 08638-0865
Phone: 609-275-1427
Fax: 609-275-1427
Chess Sets, Chess Books, Chess Related Art, Chess Ephemera, Objet

D'Art, De Vertu, Needlework, Decorative Arts & Accessories

Ralph S. Joseph, ISA CAPP, GG
Abe Sherman Fine Jewelry
151J Route 31
Flemington, NJ 08822
Phone: 908-782-1400
Fax: 908-782-3296
Gemology/Gemstones, Diamonds, Jewelry, Watches, Insurance; Appraisal Editor - National Jeweler Magazine, POLYGON Subscriber No. 2077
CAPP In Gemstones

Gregory E. Sherman, ISA, GG
Fidelity Diamond Corp.
13 Chelsea Dr
Old Bridge, NJ 08857-2619
Phone: 212-730-7830
Fax: 212-730-7453
E-mail: 105064.2243@compuserve.com
Diamonds And Diamond Jewelry, Jewelry (Period, Estate, Designer)

Richard A. Newman, ISA
Newman Fur Appraisers & Consultants Inc.
350 7th Ave
New York, NY 10001-5013
Phone: 212-564-4733
Fax: 212-564-4735
Furs (Appraiser, Consultant, All Phases Of The Fur Industry), Damage & Claim Consultants

Elisa Brisman, ISA, GG
E. Fried Diamonds
330 E 33rd St, Apt 5C
New York, NY 10016
Phone: 212-840-4358
Fax: 212-840-4113
Gemology/Gemstones, Insurance, Diamonds, Jewelry, Colored Stones (Precious-Semi), Estate Jewelry

Jerry R. Ehrenwald, ISA, GG
Int'l Gemological Institute
579 5th Ave
New York, NY 10017-1917
Phone: 212-753-7100
Fax: 212-753-7759
Gemology/Gemstones, Diamonds, Jewelry (Period & Contemporary), Pearls, Gold

Theodore M. Baer, ISA
Theodore M. Baer, Inc.
608 Fifth Ave
New York, NY 10020-2395
Phone: 212-245-6330
Fax: 212-245-6331
Gemology/Gemstone, Diamond, Pearls, Jewelry (Estate, Previously Owned)

Judy Herman Appelbaum, ISA
301 E 63rd St, Apt 2J
New York, NY 10021-7736
Phone: 212-319-3898
Fax: 212-319-3961
Dolls, Doll Houses, Miniatures, Residential Contents, Collectibles

Martin Rapaport, ISA
Rapaport Diamond Corp.
15 W 47th St
New York, NY 10036-3305
Phone: 212-354-0575
Fax: 212-840-0243
Diamonds, Jewelry, Gemology/ Gemstones; Publications: Rapaport Diamond Report

Thomas Dipasqua, ISA
401-1 Willow Rd E
Staten Island, NY 10314-1731
Phone: 718-698-0099
Porcelain, Pottery, Ceramics, Glass, Toys, Collectibles, Residential Contents

Paul Marinucci, ISA
Paul D. Marinucci & Associates
172 Pheasant Rd W
Pound Ridge, NY 10576
Phone: 914-764-4609
Fax: 914-764-4609
Paintings, Watercolors, Drawings, Prints (Limited Edition), Residential Contents, Auctioneer and Owner Of Butterscotch Auction Gallery In Bedford, NY

William J. Jenack, ISA
W.J. Jenack Estate Appraisers/ Auctioneer
18 Hambeltonian Ave
Chester, NY 10918-1023
Phone: 914-469-9095
Fax: 914-469-8445
Furniture (American & Continental), Fine Art(American & Continental), Jewelry, Books, Ephemera, Militaria, Toys, Decorative Arts & Accessories, Orientalia.

Virginia W. Baum, ISA
2 Elderfields Rd
Manhasset, NY 11030-1623
Phone: 516-627-4587
Furniture, Silver, Porcelain, Miniature Furniture, Residential Contents

Les Wolff, ISA
PO Box 650037
Flushing, NY 11365-0037
Phone: 718-454-3956
Fax: 718-454-3956
E-mail: lwolff1823@aol.com
Sports Memorabilia (Autographs, Uniforms Used By Athletes), Paintings (Sports), Lithographs (Sports) & Cards

Gail Brett Levine, ISA CAPP, GG
Auction Market Resource
PO Box 7683
Rego Park, NY 11374-7683
Phone: 718-897-7305
Fax: 718-997-9057
E-mail: 76766.614@compuserve.com;polyg
Gemology/Gemstones, Diamonds, Jewelry (Antique, Estate, Contemporary), Consulting, Publisher Of "Auction Market Resource For Gems & Jewelry", Polygon#2646
CAPP In Gemstones

Howard Rubin, ISA, GG
GemDialogue Systems, Inc.
PO Box 7683
Rego Park, NY 11374-7683
Phone: 718-997-0231
Fax: 718-997-9057
Gemology/Gemstones, Diamonds, Jewelry, Consulting, Quality Control

Ralph F. Passonno, Jr., ISA, CAI
Uncle Sam Auctions & Realty Inc.
225 Pinewoods Ave Rd
Troy, NY 12180-7246
Phone: 518-274-6464
Fax: 518-272-7189
Firearms, Oriental Rugs, Silver, Antique Furniture, Toy Trains, Pocket Knives, General Household Goods

Nehme Frangie, ISA, GG
Nehme Frangie Jewelers
125 Wolf Rd, Ste 313
Albany, NY 12205-1221
Phone: 518-438-0149
E-mail: 105042.372@compuserve.com
Gemology/Gemstones, Diamonds, Jewelry, Estates

Robert A. Doyle, ISA, CAI
Absolute Auction & Realty, Inc.
PO Box 658
Beacon, NY 12508-0658
Phone: 914-831-0200
Fax: 914-831-9671
Americana, Gambling Devices (Antique), Antiques, Collectibles, Auctioneer, Auction Co.

Susan A. Doyle, ISA
Absolute Auction & Realty, Inc.
PO Box 658
Beacon, NY 12508-0658
Phone: 914-831-0200
Fax: 914-831-9671
Antiques, Collectibles, Residential Contents, Auctioneer, Auction Co.

Bruce M. Lubman, ISA, GG
Hummingbird Jewelers
20 W Market St
Rhinebeck, NY 12572-1403
Phone: 914-876-4585
Fax: 914-876-3177
Gemology/Gemstones, Jewelry, Silver (Holloware & Flatware)

Catherine M Sankey, ISA
Catherine's Anitques
RD #4 Box 298
Auburn, NY 13021-0298
Phone: 315-685-5306
Furniture, Shaker Artifacts, Personal Property

David E. Martin, ISA, GG
Egon A. Ehrlinspiel Inc.
210 E Fayette St
Syracuse, NY 13202-1936
Phone: 315-471-8710
Fax: 315-471-3226
Gemology/Gemstones, Diamonds, Jewelry (Gold)

Carol Higgins, ISA, GG
Higgins Jewelers Inc.
440 Main St
Oneonta, NY 13820-2027
Phone: 607-433-2073
Fax: 607-433-2073
Gemology/Gemstones, Diamonds, Jewelry (Estate, Late 19th, Early 20th C., Modern)

David W. Mapes, ISA CAPP
Mapes Auctioneers-Appraisers
1729 Vestal Parkway West
Vestal, NY 13850-1156
Phone: 607-754-9193
Fax: 607-786-3549
E-mail: 76742.274@compuserve.com
Residential Contents, Furniture (American), Oriental Rugs, Decorative Arts, Collectibles, Auctioneer
CAPP In Appreciable Residential Contents

Sarah E. Blawat, ISA, GG
DBA Sarah Eve Blawat, GG
PO Box 220
Buffalo, NY 14205-0220
Phone: 716-854-6444
Jewelry (Antique, Period, Estate), Antique Diamonds, Gemstones

Elizabeth L. Smith, ISA
Elizabeth Lisy Smith Antiques & Appraisa
PO Box 347
Bergen, NY 14416-0347
Phone: 716-494-1867
Furniture (18th & 19th C. American), Decorative Arts & Accessories, (18th & 19th C. American), Antiques, Residential Contents, Estates

Michael Bruce, ISA
Bruce & Co.
52 N Main St
Fairport, NY 14450-1433
Phone: 716-388-1080
Fax: 716-388-9654
Residential Contents, Antiques, Estates, Auctioneer, Auction Co.

Duane E. Gansz, ISA, CAI-RES
Gansz Auction & Realty
14 William St
Lyons, NY 14489-1119
Phone: 315-946-9492
Antiques, Household, Farm, Commercial, Guns, Toys, Machinery & Equipment, Estate Appraiser & Auctioneer For Real & Personal Property, Auction Co.

Edythe B. Gansz, ISA
Empire Appraisal Associates
14 William St
Lyons, NY 14489-1119
Phone: 315-946-6241
Fax: 315-946-6747
Antiques (17th - 20th C.), Fine Art, Appreciable & Depreciable Residential Contents, Insurance (Coverage & Claims), Estate Auctioneer, Decorative Arts & Accessories, Liquidating Consultant, Ephemera

Ann Marszalek, ISA
211 Inspiration Point Dr
Webster, NY 14580
Phone: 716-381-7170
*Antiques, Estates, Liquidations,
Residential Contents*

**Paul R. Cassarino, ISA, GG FGA
DGA**
The Gem Lab
4098 W Henrietta Rd
Rochester, NY 14623-5222
Phone: 716-359-3900
Fax: 716-359-8932
E-mail: 102073.2774@compuserve.com
*Gemology/Gemstones, Colored
Stones, Diamonds, Jewelry (Gold)*

Pamela E. Mayo, ISA
710 Washington St
Sewickley, PA 15143-1845
Phone: 412-749-0760
Fax: 412-749-0760
*Fine Art (American 18th - Early 20th
C.), Art, Paintings, Watercolors,
Drawings, Sporting Art, Southern Art*

William M. Kline, III, ISA
Three Rivers Auction Co.
PO Box 6298
Pittsburgh, PA 15212-0298
Phone: 412-323-2647
*Furniture, Decorative Arts &
Accessories, Ceramics, Victoriana,
Antiques, Residential Contents,
Estates, Consultant, Auctioneer,
Auction Co., Americana, Arts &
Crafts, Porcelain, Folk Art*

Charles J. Behm, III, ISA
Behm's Auction Service
RD 1, Box 142
Graysville, PA 15337-9304
Phone: 412-428-3664
Fax: 412-428-4946
Auctioneer, Auction Co/Gallery

Ellen A. Roberts, ISA
120 Shady Dr
Butler, PA 16001-1420
Phone: 412-283-4441
Fax: 412-283-4441
*Glass, Orientalia, Jade, Antiques
(American, Asian), Furniture, Silver*

Frank Michael Pereny, ISA
Saisho International
401 Meadow Dr
Camp Hill, PA 17011-1228
Phone: 717-763-4729
Fax: 717-763-1875
E-mail: saisho@concentric.net
*Asian Art, Pre 1940 Native American
Art, Military Collectibles, Japanese
Swords, Fittings*

Romayne Shay McMahon, ISA
Veronique's Antiques
124 S Market St
Mechanicsburg, PA 17055-6329
Phone: 717-697-4924
Fax: 717-697-4924
*Silver, Porcelain, Furniture, Objet
D'art, De Vertu, Repairs, Restoration,
Preservation, Replating Silver, Brass,
Copper & Bronze*

Lois H. Dayett, ISA
Dayett's Clock Repair Appraisals Sales
75 Study Rd
Littlestown, PA 17340-9746
Phone: 717-359-4850
Fax: 717-359-4850
*Glass (Carnival Depression), Early
American Furniture, Hummel
Figurines, Tag Sales, Antiques,
Clocks, Watches*

John W. Rockafellow, ISA
Essential Images
382 Schottie Road
Littlestown, PA 17340-9746
Phone: 717-359-4276
*Furniture, Silver, Residential
Contents, Antiques, Porcelain,
Pottery, Ceramics, China, Textiles,
Glass, Consultant, Damage Claims,
Fine Art, Liquidator, Estates,
Orientalia*

Jane E. Chaikowsky, ISA, GG
Chaikowsky Gem & Jewelry Appraisals
1203 S 8th St
Allentown, PA 18103-4027
Phone: 610-776-2770
*Gemology/Gemstones, Diamonds,
Jewelry (Gold)*

Marguerite S. Glaser, ISA
Aston Auctioneers & Appraisers
154 Market St
Pittston, PA 18640-2532
Phone: 800-577-5508
Fax: 800-577-5508
*Residential Contents, Antiques,
Furniture, Shaving Mugs, R.S.
Prussia, Art Pottery, Porcelain
(American & European), Majolica,
Glass By C.F. Monroe & Co. (Wave
Crest, Nakara, Kelva),*

Robert C. Groves, ISA
Pig Pen Antiques
Box 618
4486 York Rd
Buckingham, PA 18912
Phone: 215-794-0957
Fax: 215-794-7899
E-mail: PPBBTBS@aol.com
*Antique Furniture, Collectibles,
English Porcelain, Auctioneer*

Walter F. Vilsmeier, ISA
Vilsmeier Auction Co. Inc.
PO Box 339
Montgomeryville, PA 18936-0339
Phone: 215-699-5833
Fax: 215-628-8010
*Machinery & Equipment (Construc-
tion Equipment, Vehicles, Line
Equipment & Industrial Supplies),
Cars, Trucks (Construction)*

Cindy Stephenson, ISA
Stephenson's Auction
1005 Industrial Hwy
Southampton, PA 18966-4066
Phone: 215-968-5962
*Residential Contents, Collectibles,
Antiques, Auctioneer, Auction Co.*

Leah Erickson, ISA
The Appraisal Network
290 Montgomery Ave
Bala Cynwyd, PA 19004-2913
Phone: 610-668-9000
Fax: 610-667-2301
*Antiques, Eskimo Art, Archeological
Art, Residential Contents, Real Estate*

Jon D. Edelman, ISA
Edelman's Coins & Stamps
301 Old York Rd
Jenkintown, PA 19046-3284
Phone: 215-572-6480
Fax: 215-572-6482
*Coins, Currency, Tokens, Stamps,
Postal History, Jewelry, Picture
Postcards, First Day Covers*

David C. Rotenberg, ISA CAPP
David Craig Jewelers, Ltd
Summer Square Shopping Center
Rt 413 332 Bypass
Langhorne, PA 19047
Phone: 215-968-8900
Fax: 215-579-2377
*Diamonds, Gemology/Gemstones,
Colored Stones, Jewelry, Pearls, All
Areas Of Gems, Jewelry And Related
Arts*
CAPP In Gemstones
CAPP In Antique & Period Jewelry

Steven E. Rosen, ISA, GG
Sydney Rosen Company
714 Sansom St
Philadelphia, PA 19106-3261
Phone: 215-922-3500
*Gemology/Gemstones, Colored
Stones, Jewelry, Diamonds*

Helene M. Huffer, ISA
Elaine Cooper & Co. Ltd.
8609 Germantown Ave
Philadelphia, PA 19118-2828
Phone: 215-248-3030
Gemology/Gemstones, Jewelry

Barry S. Slosberg, ISA
Barry S. Slosberg, Inc
2501 E Ontario St
Philadelphia, PA 19134-5327
Phone: 215-425-7030
Fax: 215-425-7039
*Antiques, Silver, Residential Contents,
Business Liquidations, Bankruptcies,
Auctioneer, Auction Co.*

William H. Bunch, ISA
Auctioneer & Appraiser
11 N Brandywine St
West Chester, PA 19380-2805
Phone: 610-696-1530
Fax: 610-701-2486
*Furniture (Antique), Glass (Cut),
Oriental Rugs, Auctioneer, Auction
Co., Silver*

Byron Grant Klein, ISA
A. Ludwig Klein & Son, Inc.
PO Box 145
Harleysville, PA 19438-0145
Phone: 215-256-9004
Fax: 215-256-9644
*Porcelain, Glass, Monuments,
Restoration & Repair*

Timothy D. Schwer, ISA
Hunyady Appraisal Service
1440 Hatfield Valley Rd
Hatfield, PA 19440-2645
Phone: 215-361-9099
Fax: 215-361-9212
*Auctioneer, Construction Equipment
& Machinery, Machinery &
Equipment, Trucks*

James R. Greenwald, ISA
Greenwald Antiques
925 Walnut St
Royersford, PA 19468-2423
Phone: 610-948-9391
Antiques

William Schuh, ISA, GG
Independent Jewelry Appraisal Co.
124 Hunter Ct
Wilmington, DE 19808-1978
Phone: 302-655-2004
Fax: 302-429-5953
*Gemology/Gemstones, Diamonds,
Jewelry, Pearls*

Paul S. Cohen, ISA, GG CGA
Continental Jewelers, Inc
2209 Silverside Rd
Wilmington, DE 19810-4501
Phone: 302-475-2000
Fax: 302-529-7688
*Gemology/Gemstones, Diamonds,
Jewelry (Gold, Platinum, Silver)*

Rochelle F. McGrory, ISA
Continental Jewelers
2209 Silverside Rd
Wilmington, DE 19810-4501
Phone: 302-798-4901
*Gemology/Gemstones, Diamonds,
Jewelry*

John Michael Overton, ISA
ESP Estate Services
3601 Connecticut Ave NW, Apt 421
Washington, DC 20008-2448
Phone: 202-244-2609
Fax: 202-244-2609
*Estate Liquidations, Residential
Contents, Estate Appraisals*

Pennye K. Jones-Napier, ISA, FGA
Jewellery Appraisal Sciences
1415 Shepherd St NW
Washington, DC 20011-5409
Phone: 202-291-5575
Fax: 202-291-5345
E-mail: pennye@ziplink.net
*Gemstones, Diamonds, Jewelry,
Antique & Contemporary Jewelry,
Consultant, Alternate Phone No. 202-
393-2747 Ext 501*

Barbara L. Spaid, ISA
Squirrel Cage
130 Chesapeake Ave
Prince Frederick, MD 20678-4473
Phone: 410-535-1158
*Furniture (Country), Residential
Contents, Tapestries, Textiles
(Linens), Needlework (Quilts)*

Helen Margaret Huber, ISA
4512 Riverdale Rd
Riverdale, MD 20737-1940
Phone: 301-229-2949
Collectibles, Glass, Residential Contents

Israel Heller, ISA
Heller Antiques Ltd.
5454 Wisconsin Ave
Chevy Chase, MD 20815-6901
Phone: 301-654-0218
Fax: 301-493-6076
Jewelry, Silver, Judaica, Diamonds, Estates

Marilyn Rudden, ISA
A.M. Sales
9900 Harrogate Rd
Bethesda, MD 20817-1543
Phone: 301-469-9437
Fax: 301-469-7833
E-mail: 76232.2466@compuserve.com
Residential Contents, Estates (Liquidation)

Jane E. Heller, ISA
6204 Leeke Forest Ct
Bethesda, MD 20817-3346
Phone: 301-493-6067
Fax: 301-493-6076
E-mail: 105460.1530@compuserve.com
Antiques, Residential Contents, Estate Liquidations

Ann D. Robertson, ISA
Ann Robertson Estate Sales
6815 Selkirk Dr
Bethesda, MD 20817-4921
Phone: 301-229-7640
Fax: 301-229-7648
E-mail: baldwin@wizard.net
Furniture, Residential Contents, Estate Liquidation

Joan Braunstein, ISA, GG FGA
J. Braunstein, Ltd.
PO Box 1474
Bethesda, MD 20827
Phone: 301-299-7270
Fax: 301-299-7270
Gemology/Gemstones, Jewelry (Antique, Modern), Diamonds, Pearls, Colored Stones

Ellen W. Shea, ISA
Antiques Critiques, Inc.
PO Box 34586
Bethesda, MD 20827-4950
Phone: 301-299-7314
Fine Art, Antiques, Decorative Arts & Accessories, Residential Contents, Prints, Drawings, Watercolors, Paintings

Carol K. Oshinsky, ISA
A Carol Oshinsky Sale
PO Box 34105
Bethesda, MD 20827-5431
Phone: 301-299-3497
Fax: 301-299-3497
Estate Liquidations, Antiques, Residential Contents, Jewelry

Barry Rogers, ISA
Barry Rogers, Appraiser
16650 Georgia Ave
Olney, MD 20832-2418
Phone: 301-570-0779
Fax: 301-570-0779
Gemology/Gemstones, Glass (Antique), Porcelain, Ceramic, Appreciable Residential Contents, Personal Property, Auctioneer, Expert Witness, Furniture, Collectibles, Silver

Barbara M. Lessig, ISA CAPP
Lessig's Pleasant Valley Antiques
21000 Georgia Ave
Brookeville, MD 20833-1138
Phone: 301-924-2293
Fax: 301-570-1625
E-mail: jlessig@lmi.org
Glass, Porcelain, Ceramics, Silver, Orientalia, Residential Contents, Furniture, Textiles, Advertising Items, Americana, Art Deco & Nouveau, Decorative Arts & Accessories, Ink Wells, Lamps & Lighting, Music Instruments, Etc.; Damage Claim
CAPP In Glass

Erik Padison, ISA
15127 Frederick Rd
Rockville, MD 20850
Phone: 301-424-0053
Japanese Swords & Fittings, Arms/Armor, Oriental Art, Russian Art

Charles B. Goldstein, ISA CAPP
Charles Barry International
8 Hardwicke Pl
Rockville, MD 20850-3010
Phone: 301-340-6775
Fax: 301-340-1726
Fine Arts: Paintings, Watercolors, Drawings; Prints, Graphics, Etchings, Engravings, Etc.; Sculpture. Assorted American & European Artists;. Expert Witness & Litigation Support Experience. Will Travel.
CAPP In Limited Edition Prints

Adrienne Moss, ISA
Moss Antiques
11510 Parkedge Dr
Rockville, MD 20852-3729
Phone: 301-770-2383
Quilts, Antique (American), Americana, Furniture & Accessories, Residential Contents

Dianne Gregg, ISA
Glassnob Antiques
10413 Gary Rd
Potomac, MD 20854-4101
Phone: 301-299-6456
Glass (European, Contemporary) Art Deco, Art Nouveau, Arts & Crafts, Russian Decorative Art

Janet Hanyak, ISA
About To Move Estate Sale
2510 Stratton Dr
Potomac, MD 20854-6231
Phone: 301-251-9899
Fax: 301-762-5252
Residential Contents, Furniture, Antiques, Estates (Liquidators)

Cynthia Monahan, ISA
Greenbrier Estate Sales
12740 Three Sisters Rd
Potomac, MD 20854-6331
Phone: 301-948-1937
Fax: 301-948-5558
Estates (Liquidation), Residential Contents, Antiques, Furniture

Susan D. Moran, ISA
Greenbrier Estate Sales
12740 Three Sisters Rd
Potomac, MD 20854-6331
Phone: 301-948-1937
Residential Contents, Antiques, Furniture, Estate (Liquidation), Personal Property

Lindsey B. Johnson, DPS, ISA
1315 Carlsbad Dr
Gaithersburg, MD 20879-3203
Phone: 301-216-0876
Prints, Painting, Collectibles, Posters, Prints, Painting,

Maria Denise Nelson, ISA, GG
Inner Circle
PO Box 2465
Kensington, MD 20891-2465
Phone: 301-530-9266
Fax: 301-530-9266
Jewelry (Fine), Gems, Diamonds, Pearls, Ivory

Martin W. Spickler, Ph.D., ISA
Tova's Treasures
909 W Nolcrest Dr
Silver Spring, MD 20903-1039
Phone: 301-593-6492
Glass, Porcelain, Silver, Orientalia, Judaica

Carol Waldman Silverman, ISA
Chelsea & Co.
2302 Musgrove Rd
Silver Spring, MD 20904-5219
Phone: 301-384-1673
Fax: 301-384-1673
E-mail: 103400.2251@compuserve.com
Furniture, Decorative Arts, Residential Contents, Antiques, Americana, Art Deco, Arts & Crafts, Collectibles, Commercial Inventories, Insurance, Damage Claims, Adjusters

Gloria Schuetze, ISA
Estate Sales By Gloria
3904 Bel Pre Rd, APT 4
Silver Spring, MD 20906-2825
Phone: 301-460-8537
Collectibles, Jewelry (Antique), Residential Contents, Liquidator, Dolls

Janice H. Hull, ISA, CAI
Appraiser - Auctioneer
526 Baltimore Blvd
Westminster, MD 21157-6102
Phone: 410-876-3694
Fax: 410-876-5694
E-mail: 104543.3322@compuserve.com
Residential Contents, Antiques, Collectibles, Estates, Auctioneer

Fred J. Winer, ISA
Appraisal Alliance Service Inc
25 W Chesapeake Ave, Ste 200
Towson, MD 21204-4820
Phone: 410-494-7000
Fax: 410-494-8832
Furniture (Antique American), Glass (American Art Nouveau), Toys (Trains), Auctioneer, Auction Co.

C. Robert Harrison, ISA
Antique Appraisal Services
817 Warwick Rd
Baltimore, MD 21229-4710
Phone: 410-242-3582
Antiques, American Furniture, Porcelain, Decorative Arts & Accessories, Insurance

Peter J. Simonetti, ISA
Artisian Restoration, Inc.
PO Box 72035
Baltimore, MD 21237
Phone: 410-682-3700
Fax: 410-682-3738
Household Contents, Porcelain, Antiques, Furniture, Objet D'Art

Joan J. Hurt, ISA
Arundel Appraisers & Estate Liquidators
9715 Philadelphia Rd
Baltimore, MD 21237-3427
Phone: 410-686-9598
Residential Contents, Furniture (18th & 19th C.), Silver, Glassware, Damage Claims, Quilts, Collectibles, Dinnerware

Joel Stuart Litzky, ISA
Walnut Leaf Enterprises, Inc.
62 Maryland Ave
Annapolis, MD 21401-1630
Phone: 410-263-4885
Antiques, Residential Contents, American Cut Glass, Porcelain (European & Oriental), Pottery, Ceramics

Mary Ellen Heibel, ISA
Personal Property Consultants
1009 Old Bay Ridge Rd
Annapolis, MD 21403-4228
Phone: 410-267-7708
Fax: 410-269-5909
E-mail: 104334.273@compuserve.com
Residential Contents, Furniture (English & American), Silver (Antique English & American), Ceramics, Glass, Decorative Arts & Accessories

Herman J. Grabenstein, ISA, GG
604 Greene St
Cumberland, MD 21502-2700
Phone: 301-759-9350
Gemology/Gemstones, Diamonds, Jewelry, Silver

John A. Woodfield, Jr., ISA
Maryland Shore Auctioneers
6612 Church Hill Rd
Chestertown, MD 21620-2388
Phone: 410-778-5777
Residential Contents, Auctioneer, Damage Claims, Consultant, Repairs & Restoration

David J. Maloney, Jr., ISA CAPP
Frederick Appraisal, Claims & Estate
  Services
PO Box 2049
Frederick, MD 21702-1049
Phone: 301-695-8544
Fax: 301-695-6491
E-mail: 71561.1706@compuserve.com
  or dmaloney@ix.netcom.com
*Antiques, Residential Contents,
Collectibles, Folk Art, Estates, Cars,
Furniture, Silver, Americana,
Insurance & Moving Damage Claims
Service; Author Of "Maloney's
Antiques & Collectibles Resource
Directory"*
**CAPP In Appreciable Residential
Contents**

John D. Compton, ISA, CAI AARE
J.D. Compton Auctioneering
13833 Rockdale Rd
Clear Spring, MD 21722-1547
Phone: 301-582-0727
Fax: 301-582-6114
*Coins, Currency (U.S. Coins),
Firearms (20th C.), Estate Liquida-
tions, Machinery & Equipment,
Antiques, Residential Contents,
Auctioneer*

Bruce M. Schuettinger, ISA
Antique Restorations, Ltd.
17 North Alley, Box 244
New Market, MD 21774-0002
Phone: 301-865-3009
Fax: 301-865-3009
*Furniture, Conservator, Consultant,
Antiques, Woodworking Tools
(Antique)*

Norma B. Blanchard, ISA
Blanchard Appraisals
1222 Aldebaran Drive
McLean, VA 22101
Phone: 703-734-1406
Fax: 703-734-1406
E-mail: 103425.2577@compuserve.com
*Antiques, Decorative Arts &
Accessories, Furniture, Fine Art,
Ceramics, Glass, Quilts, Textiles*

Mildred R. Shepherd, ISA
Shepherd Studio
5527 3rd St S
Arlington, VA 22204-1115
Phone: 703-671-1789
E-mail: 102756.2015@compuserve.com
*Repair, Restoration And Conservation
Of Porcelain, Glass, Ivory, Jade,
Pottery And Other Art And Decorative
Objects; Antiques & Collectibles*

Margaret H. Smith, ISA
M H Smith Appraisals & Estate Sales
1120 S Thomas St, Apt A
Arlington, VA 22204-3615
Phone: 703-920-7834
*Estate Liquidations, Residential
Contents, Antiques, Fine Art*

Priscilla A. Wells, ISA
Appraisal Associates
205 Yoakum Pky, Suite 314
Alexandria, VA 22304-3806
Phone: 703-370-0832
*Antiques, Residential Contents, Silver,
Decorative Arts, Furniture,
Orientalia, Art Deco, Glass,
Porcelain, Estates*

Angela Saunders, ISA, GG
Silverman Galleries, Inc.
110 N Saint Asaph St
Alexandria, VA 22314-3168
Phone: 703-836-5363
*Diamonds (Antique, Modern), Jewelry
(Antique, Modern), Antiques
(General), Culinary History, Silver*

Maurice B. Silverman, ISA
Silverman Galleries
110 N Saint Asaph St
Alexandria, VA 22314-3168
Phone: 703-836-5363
*Antiques, Jewelry (Antique, Modern),
Silver, Paintings (18th & 19th C.),
Decorative Arts & Accessories*

Marybeth Rabung, ISA
501 Chapman St
Ashland, VA 23005-1113
Phone: 804-798-7020
*Antiques (18th To Early 20th C.
American & European), Residential
Contents, Fine Art (18th - 20th C. Oil
On Canvas, Watercolor, Sculpture,
Prints), Decorative Arts & Accesso-
ries*

Barbara Walter, ISA
The Carousel Shoppe
8287 Reunion Dr
Mechanicsville, VA 23111-4539
Phone: 804-779-2452
Fax: 804-779-2452
*Glass, Costume Jewelry, Porcelain,
Residential Contents*

Christina M. Woolford, ISA, GG
C.M. Woolford
PO Box 35
Rockville, VA 23146-0035
Phone: 804-644-1941
*Gemology/Gemstones, Diamonds,
Jewelry*

Christina M. Woolford, ISA, GG
C.M. Woolford
PO Box 35
Rockville, VA 23146-0035
Phone: 804-644-1941
*Gemology/Gemstones, Diamonds,
Jewelry*

Dorothy D. Layne, ISA
Dorothy D. Layne, Auctioneer
1507 Old Williamsburg Rd
Sandston, VA 23150-1714
Phone: 804-795-7021
Fax: 804-737-4082
Antiques, Residential Contents

Owen F. Valentine, ISA
Owen F. Valentine & Co.
6417 Rigsby Road
Richmond, VA 23226
Phone: 804-282-2355
Fax: 804-288-9209
*Residential Contents, Auctioneer, 17th
& 18th C. Silver, Furniture, &
Porcelain*

Elizabeth D. Bullock, ISA
Decorative Arts Associates Inc
6432 Roselawn Rd
Richmond, VA 23226-3115
Phone: 804-285-0296
*Furniture (American), Silver,
Decorative Arts & Accessories,
Residential Contents, Household
Contents*

Christine N. Corbin, ISA
Motley's Auctions
4402 W Broad St
Richmond, VA 23230-3202
Phone: 804-355-2100
Fax: 804-355-9695
*Residential Contents, Decorative Arts
& Accessories, Antiques, Auctioneer*

Rebecca L. Holberg, ISA, GG CGA
Southeast Gemological Lab
2621 Lake Ridge Crossing
Chesapeake, VA 23323-3323
Phone: 757-487-3092
Fax: 757-547-0897
*Gemology/Gemstones, Diamonds,
Jewelry, Pearls*

Gail Wolpin, ISA
Phoebus Auction Gallery
4202 Manchester Rd
Portsmouth, VA 23703-4823
Phone: 804-484-2828
*Residential Contents, Antiques,
Auctioneer, Erotica, Black Memora-
bilia, Militaria, Art Glass, Primitives,
.Furniture, Textiles, Paintings*

Maurice H. Martin, ISA
609 Binford St
South Hill, VA 23970-1511
Phone: 804-447-5801
*Victoriana, Glass, Furniture,
Porcelain, Antiques, Residential
Contents*

Suzanne M. Sellers, ISA CAPP
Suzanne M. Sellers Appraisal Service
2609 Wycliffe Ave SW
Roanoke, VA 24014
Phone: 540-342-3771
Fax: 540-342-3771
E-mail: 104576.2113@compuserve.com
*Antiques, Residential Contents,
Household Contents, Insurance,
Liquidators, Estates*
**CAPP In Appreciable Residential
Contents**

Elizabeth N. Gladwell, ISA CAPP
Elizabeth N. Gladwell & Assoc L.L.C.
PO Box 811
Bedford, VA 24523-0811
Phone: 540-586-4567
Fax: 540-586-5175
*18th, 19th, 20th C. Decorative Arts
(American, Continental & English),
Residential Contents, Collectibles
(Including Fishing Tackle), Folk Art,
Silver, Ceramics, Antiques, Furniture*
**CAPP In Appreciable Residential
Contents**

R. Stephen Mullins, ISA
Spencer Road Antiques
2533 Kay Ln
Charleston, WV 25302-4315
Phone: 304-342-2865
Fax: 304-342-3367
*Glass (Depression Glassware),
Furniture (Period), Residential
Contents, Decorative Arts &
Accessories*

F. Steven Underwood, ISA
Appraisals & Consulting By
2516 Larwood Dr
Charleston, WV 25302-4318
Phone: 304-345-4089
E-mail: thomu@earthlink.net
*Residential Contents (19th & 20th C.
Antiques, Arts, Collectibles, &
General), Musical Instruments
(Guitars, Mandolins, Banjos, Except
Violins), Phonograph Records &
Covers, Rock N Roll Collectibles &
Memorabilia, Misc. Music Memora-
bilia*

Mary Moore Maxwell, ISA, GG
Antiquitus Jewelers
48 Washington Ave
Wheeling, WV 26003-6241
Phone: 304-242-1661
Fax: 304-242-1662
*Gemology/Gemstones, Jewelry
(Antique, Estate), Estate Liquidations,
Repairs & Restoration*

Ronald H. Young, ISA
Y.H.S., LLC., Inc.
PO Box 3353, Change
Parkersburg, WV 26103
Phone: 304-428-3494
Fax: 304-428-3291
*Heavy Equipment, Trucks, Machinery,
Personal Property, Oilfield
Equipment, Construction Equipment*

Grace Kelly, ISA
Antqiue Appraisals
239 Oakwood Drive
Winston-Salem, NC 27103
Phone: 910-725-7228
*Furniture (Antique American &
English), Decorative Arts, Residential
Contents, Antiques*

Cecil B. Price, ISA
Cecil B. Price Antiques & Appraisals
609 Wellington Rd
Winston-Salem, NC 27106-5510
Phone: 919-724-9173
E-mail: bprice@gnn.com
*Antiques, Residential Contents,
Estates (Liquidation)*

Keith J. Pierce, ISA
Pierce Auction Service & Real Estate
274 Brookwood Dr
Winston Salem, NC 27127-9121
Phone: 910-764-1964
Fax: 910-764-1807
*Residential Contents, Office
Equipment, Coins, Antiques,
Automobiles, Machinery*

Carla S. Butler, ISA
Butler & Associates
PO Box 27403
Greensboro, NC 27403-1031
Phone: 919-489-9342
Fax: 919-489-9342
*Antiques, Residential Contents,
Decorative Arts & Accessories, Silver,
Americana, Estate, Insurance,
Equitable Distribution, Personal
Property Liquidations*

Ridley Tyler Smith, ISA
Tyler-Smith Antiques
8 Leawood Ct
Greensboro, NC 27410-4217
Phone: 910-294-2771
E-mail: rtsmith@nr.infi.net
*Ceramics (18th & 19th C. American,
English, European), Furniture (18th
& 19th C. English & American),
Residential Contents, Ceramics,
Antiques, Americana*

Alan Folley Butler, ISA
Butler & Associates
PO Box 2818
Durham, NC 27715-2818
Phone: 919-489-9342
Fax: 919-489-9342
*Oriental Rugs, Residential Contents,
Antiques, Decorative Arts*

Thomas Smith, ISA
Plunder from the Past
PO Box 7981
Rocky Mount, NC 27804-0981
Phone: 919-937-6743
E-mail: asianart@interserv.com
*Antiques And Collectibles, Residential
Contents, Insurance, Books, Estates,
Auctioneer, Consultations*

J. Robert Boykin, III, ISA CAPP
Boykin Appraisals, Inc.
PO Box 7440
Wilson, NC 27895-7440
Phone: 919-237-1700
Fax: 919-237-2314
*Residential Contents, Antiques,
Decorative Arts & Accessories, Fine
Art, Ecclesiastical Art*
**CAPP In Appreciable Residential
Contents**

RoseMary Starling, ISA
Berry Appraisals, Inc.
2207 Nash St NW, Ste 7
Wilson, NC 27896-1783
Phone: 919-291-6433
Fax: 919-237-4115
E-mail: 104430.1763@compuserve.com
*Residential Contents, Estates,
Liquidators, Insurance, Damage
Claims, Antiques, Carpets/Rugs,
Furniture, Decorative Arts &
Accessories, Silver*

Fay D. Edwards, ISA
1042 N Main Hwy
Manteo, NC 27954-9666
Phone: 919-473-6971
*Etchings, Prints, Graphic Works,
Engravings, Lithographs, Animation
Art*

Melanie Smith, ISA
Seaside Art Gallery
PO Box 1
Nags Head, NC 27959-0001
Phone: 919-441-5418
Fax: 919-441-8563
E-mail: seaside@interpath.com
*Animation Art, Fine Art, Paintings,
Original Prints*

Garland D. Stewart, III, ISA, GG
Jewelry By Gail, Inc.
207 E Driftwood St
Nags Head, NC 27959-9172
Phone: 919-441-5387
Fax: 919-441-7082
E-mail: jbgjewel@interpath.com
*Gemology/Gemstones, Diamonds,
Jewelry (Estate, Contemporary)*

Tony F. Laughter, ISA, GG
Perry's At Southpark
113 Winecoff Ave NW
Concord, NC 28025
Phone: 704-364-1391
Gemology/Gemstones, Jewelry

C.D. Gallimore, ISA, CAI
AMC Appraisal Co. Inc.
PO Box 306
Concord, NC 28026-0306
Phone: 800-938-2121
Fax: 704-782-2399
E-mail: 104427.3455@compuserve.com
*Machinery & Equipment, Office
Furniture & Equipment, Bank
Equipment, Movie Studios, Props,
Antiques, Residential Contents,
Furniture, Textiles, Estates,
Auctioneer, Auction Co.*

John M. Lucas, ISA
6930 St Peter's Lane
Matthews, NC 28105
Oriental Rugs

Sue S. Whitaker, ISA, GG CMG
Gemstones
316 S Washington St
Shelby, NC 28150-5402
Phone: 704-484-0216
Fax: 704-482-2255
*Gemology/Gemstones, Jewelry, Gold,
Watches, Pearls, Diamonds*

Paul G. Hughes, ISA
Tudor House Galleries
1401 East Blvd
Charlotte, NC 28203-5817
Phone: 704-377-4748
E-mail: 75027.474@compuserve.com
*Paintings, Watercolors, Drawings,
Porcelain, Ceramic, Residential
Contents*

Ronald L. Roberts, ISA
Dixie Sporting Collectibles
1206 Rama Rd
Charlotte, NC 28211-4345
Phone: 704-364-2900
Fax: 704-364-2322
E-mail: gun1898@aol.com
*Personal Property, Antiques, Arms &
Armament, Auction Co., Duck Decoys,
Fine Art, Collectibles, Estates,
Hunting & Fishing Sports Memora-
bilia*

Caroline T. Gray, ISA
The Thistle
PO Box 220064
Charlotte, NC 28222-0064
Phone: 704-365-4539
*Furniture (18th-19th C. American And
English), Silver, Porcelain, Ceramics,
Residential Contents, Estates,
Insurance*

Louise W. Phillips, ISA CAPP
Alexander Appraisal Service
8206 1200 Providence Rd, Ste 387
Charlotte, NC 28277
Phone: 704-544-2510
Fax: 704-544-2510
*Antiques, Residential Contents,
Collectibles, Office Furniture &
Equipment, Estates, Automobiles*
**CAPP In Appreciable Residential
Contents**

Vivian Riegelman, ISA CAPP
Vivian Riegelman Appraisal Co.
8206 1200 Providence Rd, Ste 321
Charlotte, NC 28277-9705
Phone: 704-843-4033
Fax: 704-843-4033
E-mail: 104622.3172@compuserve.com
*Residential Contents (Appreciable &
Depreciable), Antiques & Collectibles
(19th & 20th C.), Furniture, Glass,
Ceramics, Silver, Victoriana, Art
Nouveau, Art Deco, Office Furniture
& Equip., Damage Claims, Divorce,
Insurance, Estates*
**CAPP In Appreciable Residential
Contents**
**CAPP In Depreciable Residential
Contents**

Jane E. Wetmore, ISA
1600 Morganton Rd, Lot H3
Pinehurst, NC 28374-6846
Phone: 910-692-8082
Fax: 910-692-3688
*Liquidations, Residential Contents,
Antiques, Decorative Arts &
Accessories, Estates*

Kathleen Di Loreto, ISA
Piccadilly
160 Hunter Trail
Southern Pines, NC 28387
Phone: 910-692-3425
Fax: 910-692-4531
*Located Near Pinehurst. Antiques,
Estates, Damage Claims, Insurance,
Liquidators, Fine Arts, China*

Bruce E. Price, ISA
Mike's Jewelers
222 Middle St
New Bern, NC 28560-2142
Phone: 919-637-9775
Jewelry, Diamonds

Louis Long, Jr., ISA
The Royal Scot, Inc.
PO Box 2107
Highlands, NC 28741-2107
Phone: 704-526-5917
*Residential Contents, Furniture
(American)*

Joette M. Humphrey, ISA, GG
Shelley's Jewelry
421 N Main St
Hendersonville, NC 28792-4903
Phone: 704-692-3615
Fax: 704-693-4305
*Jewelry, Diamonds, Pearls, Glass,
Watches*

Beverly J. Nash, ISA CAPP
Accessories & Antiques
PO Box 2537
Hendersonville, NC 28793-2537
Phone: 704-698-0020
Fax: 704-698-0020
E-mail: 76472.3251@compuserve.com
*Residential Contents (Appreciable &
Depreciable), Furniture (Antique),
Collectibles, Toys (Promotional
Cars), Furniture (1800-1940
American of Late 18th C. to Present),
Estate Liquidations; CAPP In Both
Appreciable & Depreciable Contents*
**CAPP In Appreciable Residential
Contents**
**CAPP In Depreciable Residential
Contents**

**Marylen Sue Scott-McKenzie, ISA,
GG**
MSSM Appraisals
PO Box 5010
Asheville, NC 28813-5010
Phone: 704-277-0722
Fax: 704-277-0399
*Gemology/Gemstones, Diamonds,
Jewelry (Colored Stones, Karat Gold),
Watches (Rolex), Pearls, Estates*

Howard S. Avery, ISA
Avery Gallery, Inc.
390 Roswell St
Marietta, GA 30060-8208
Phone: 770-427-2459
Fax: 770-427-2446
*Paintings, Frames, Art & Frame
Restoration, Art On Paper (Original
Prints)*

Melinda L. Wilson, ISA CAPP
Betty A. Wilson Appraisal Service
1682 Terrell Ridge Drive
Marietta, GA 30067
Phone: 770-434-0227
Fax: 770-319-9191
E-mail: 76161.565@compuserve.com
*Antiques, Art Deco, Collectible
Paperweights, Damage Claims,
Insurance, Liquidators, Estates,
Russian Art, Residential Contents,
Primitives*
**CAPP In Appreciable Residential
Contents**

Larry G. Davenport, ISA
Roswell Clock & Antique Co.
955 Canton St
Roswell, GA 30075-3612
Phone: 770-992-5232
*Antiques, Clocks (Antique), Furniture
(American & English)*

Betty A. Wilson, ISA CAPP
Betty A. Wilson Appraisal Service
3912 Lake Dr SE
Smyrna, GA 30082-3471
Phone: 770-434-0227
Fax: 770-319-9191
*Glass (Cut), Furniture (Empire,
Hepplewhite, Gothic, Early
American), Silver, Orientalia, Fine
Art, Memorabilia, Collectibles*
**CAPP In Appreciable Residential
Contents**

Nathan D. Williams, ISA
Williams Furniture Repair
4590 Lawrenceville Hwy
Tucker, GA 30084-3705
Phone: 770-498-9580
*Furniture, Repairs, Restoration,
Preservation (Furniture)*

Bronwin Clark, ISA
Collector's Choice
908 Commercial St NE
Conyers, GA 30207-4538
Phone: 770-388-9434
Fax: 770-388-7378
*Antiques & Residential Contents,
Antiques, Estates, Personal Property
Auctioneer*

David Futch, ISA
Collectors Choice
908 Commercial St Ne
Conyers, GA 30207-4538
Phone: 770-388-9434
E-mail: 71374.3212@compuserve.com
Antiques & Residential Contents

Patricia Rittenmeyer, ISA
Reminiscent Rose Antiques
1032 Wildwood Rd
Atlanta, GA 30306
Phone: 404-892-9611
E-mail: 70224.335@compuserve.com
*Furniture, Silver, Porcelain, Needle
Art Tools, Glass, Linens, Buttons*

Mark Lee Maxwell, ISA
4186 Gladney Dr
Atlanta, GA 30340-4719
Phone: 770-934-0573
*Paintings, Watercolors, Drawings,
Etchings, Frames, Furniture,
Porcelain, Pottery, Ceramics*

Debra Freer, ISA
Freer & Associates, Inc.
PO Box 98327
Atlanta, GA 30359-9045
Phone: 404-321-6369
Fax: 404-636-8531
E-mail: 76641.212@compuserve.com
*Paintings, Prints, Sculpture, 19th &
20th C. Fine & Decorative Art, Art
Deco, Pottery, Art Glass, Art
Nouveau, Arts & Crafts, Victoriana,
Lalique, Icart, Muller Frere, Tiffany,
Daum, Manuscripts - Margaret
Mitchell*

Bernard Doris, ISA, GG
Doris Diamonds, Inc.
487 Highland Ave
Augusta, GA 30909-3742
Phone: 706-733-6747
Fax: 706-731-9622
E-mail: 102573.2205@compuserve.com
*Diamonds, Silver, Gemology/
Gemstones, Gold, China*

Brian Goldman, ISA, GG
Arvin's Inc.
516 Poplar St
Macon, GA 31201-2717
Phone: 912-745-3684
Fax: 912-738-0062
Diamonds, Colored Stones

Beverly Smith Taylor, ISA
PO Box 5563
Columbus, GA 31906-0563
Phone: 706-327-3648
*Decorative Arts & Accessories,
Residential Contents, Antiques,
Estates*

Shirley Northern, ISA CAPP
Northern Associates, Inc.
PO Box 1008
Ponte Vedra Beach, FL 32004-1008
Phone: 904-285-2004
Fax: 904-285-5905
E-mail: 76162.2445@compuserve.com
*Antiques, Residential Contents,
Decorative Arts, Accessories,
Collectibles, Americana, Porcelain,
Pottery, Ceramics, Silver, Glass,
Victoriana, Damage Claims, Estates*
**CAPP In Appreciable Residential
Contents**

Patricia K. Webb, ISA
Barclay/Scott Antiques
4 Rohde Ave
St. Augustine, FL 32084-3221
Phone: 904-824-2483
Antiques, Residential Contents

Virginia S. Stratford, ISA
Stratford Appraisal Service
300 Raintree Trail
St. Augustine, FL 32086-5551
Phone: 904-797-2224
*Antiques, Collectibles, Residential
Contents*

Susan E. Fisher, ISA
Fisher & Powell
2111 River Blvd
Jacksonville, FL 32204-4413
Phone: 904-387-4800
*Decorative Arts & Accessories,
Residential Contents, Household
Goods, Damage Claims*

Caroline Cay Powell, ISA
Fisher & Powell
2111 River Blvd
Jacksonville, FL 32204-4413
Phone: 904-387-4800
Fax: 904-387-0017
*Residential Contents, Household
Goods, Decorative Arts & Accesso-
ries, Damage Claims*

Leslie Montgomery Hill, ISA
Gordon James
326 19th St
Atlantic Beach, FL 32233
Phone: 904-727-6622
Fax: 907-247-5725
Real Estate, Mortgage Industry

Joan S. Montgomery, ISA
326 19th St
Atlantic Beach, FL 32233
Real Estate

June C. Koontz, ISA
June C. Koontz Appraisals
3335 Lighthouse Point Ln
Jacksonville, FL 32250-2325
Phone: 904-223-3232
*Antiques, Residential Contents, Art,
Estates, Collectibles*

Annie L. Martin, ISA
7990 Hunters Grove Road
Jacksonville, FL 32256
Phone: 904-641-5327
Fax: 904-396-8332
Fine Art

Jeff J. Hofmeister, ISA, GG
Professional Jewelry Appraisals, Inc.
PO Box 38398
Tallahassee, FL 32315
Phone: 904-562-4253
Fax: 904-562-4253
*Gemology/Gemstones, Diamonds,
Jewelry*

Logan G. Adams, ISA CAPP
The Specialists Of The South
PO Box 87
Panama City, FL 32402-0087
Phone: 704-785-2577
Fax: 904-872-8662
E-mail: 76652.31@compuserve.com
*Residential Contents, Furniture,
Antiques, Collectibles, Ceramics,
Silver, Glass, Decorative Arts &*

*Accessories, Repairs, Restoration,
Preservation (Furniture), Estates*
**CAPP In Appreciable Residential
Contents**

Richard J. Adams, ISA CAPP
The Specialists Of The South
PO Box 87
Panama City, FL 32402-0087
Phone: 904-785-2577
Fax: 904-872-8662
*Residential Contents, Furniture,
Glass, Pottery, Office Furniture &
Equipment, Estates, Damage Claims,
Repairs, Restoration, Preservation
(Furniture), Damage Claims
Specialist, Estates, Liquidator*
**CAPP In Appreciable Residential
Contents**

Jean Mallory, ISA
Mallory's Antiques
1245 Capri Dr
Panama City, FL 32405
Phone: 904-271-5283
E-mail: 71561.1706@compuserve.com
*Antiques, Property & Casualty
Insurance*

Joy E. Bell, ISA
Bell's Estate Liquidation Service
33 Bayshore Drive
Pensacola, FL 32507-3527
Phone: 904-453-3189
Fax: 904-438-3641
*Americana, Estates, Residential
Contents, Liquidators, Antiques,
Collectibles*

Helen Brown Galloway, ISA
Helen Brown, Ltd.
107 Country Club Rd
Pensacola, FL 32507-3530
Phone: 904-456-9049
*Antiques, Fine Art, Estate Consultant,
Expert Witness, Estate Liquidation*

J. Alice McConnell, ISA
PO Box 14194
Gainesville, FL 32604-2194
Phone: 561-692-4649
E-mail: jwmcc@ix.netcom.com
*Antiques, Decorative Arts &
Accessories, Furniture, Fine Art,
Ceramics, Silver, Glass, Residential
Contents,*

Scott E. McElhiney, ISA, GG
4000 NW 51 Street, N-256
Gainesville, FL 32606-4297
Phone: 352-372-4640
E-mail: 102414.3112@compuserve.com
*Jewelry (Modern), Colored Stones,
Pearls, Gold, Diamond Valuation,
Diamond Grading, Gem Identification*

Irene Della Porta, ISA
Webs And Shadows Antiques
7218 SW 97 Lane
Gainesville, FL 32608
Phone: 352-379-1088
Fax: 352-379-1088
*Residential Contents, Antiques,
Estates*

Wayne D. Essick, ISA
310 NW 36th Ave
Gainsville, FL 32609
*Antiques, Furniture, Pottery,
Porcelain, Stamps, Coins*

Joan L. Henns, ISA
Windsor Chair Antiques
6878 S Round Lake Rd
Mt. Dora, FL 32757-9645
Phone: 904-383-7373
Household Contents

Thomas A. Kemper, ISA
KAT, Inc.
2170 State Road 434 W, Ste 388
Longwood, FL 32779-4990
Phone: 407-774-9900
Fax: 407-788-0366
*Corporate Equipment And Electron-
ics, Office Furniture & Equipment,
Scientific Equipment*

Renis S. Paton, ISA
Heritage Sales & Appraisals, Inc.
1141 Via Capri
Winter Park, FL 32789-2659
Phone: 407-628-9707
*Residential Contents, Decorative Arts
& Accessories, Estates, Antiques,
Insurance*

Beverly G. Graham, ISA
Heritage Sales & Appraisals, Inc.
1401 Grove Terrace
Winter Park, FL 32789-4030
Phone: 407-644-6742
*Residential Contents, Furniture,
Decorative Arts & Accessories,
Specializing In Estate Appraisals &
Sales*

Michael E. Leadlay, ISA
Park Place Antiques & Collectibles
50 N Grove St
Merritt Island, FL 32953
Phone: 407-454-6361
Antiques, Collectibles

Harry Stampler, ISA
Stampler Auctions
2801 Evans St
Hollywood, FL 33020-1119
Phone: 954-921-8888
Fax: 954-927-2939
*Art, Jewelry, Machinery & Equipment,
Business Liquidations*

Gilbert Hall, ISA
Hall & Hall Appraisers, Inc.
2632 Hollywood Blvd, Ste 301
Hollywood, FL 33020-4857
Phone: 954-922-9111
Fax: 954-922-6668
*Residential Furnishings, Manufac-
tured Homes, Antiques, Fine Arts,
Restaurant Equipment*

Christine Girello, ISA
Antique Appraisers Of America
1641 NW 110th Ter
Pembroke Pines, FL 33026-2722
Phone: 954-431-4150
Fax: 954-431-7399
*Residential Contents (Appreciable &
Depreciable), Furniture, Antiques,*

*Collectibles, Glass, Household
Contents, Porcelain, Oriental Art,
Estates, Decorative Arts & Accesso-
ries*

Barbara B. Fisher, ISA
Fisher Auction Co.
431 NE 1st St
Pompano Beach, FL 33060-6264
Phone: 954-942-0917
*Antiques, Fine Art, Residential
Contents, Estates, Auction Co.*

Diane P. Marvin, ISA
Diane Marvin Appraisal Svcs
4738 NW 5th Pl
Coconut Creek, FL 33063-6742
Phone: 954-968-0003
Fax: 954-968-0003
*Residential Contents, Antiques,
Collectibles, Quilts, Americana,
Dedham Pottery, Furniture, Complete
Estate Liquidations*

Jack Abrahams, ISA
Jay Sugarman Auctioneers, Inc
555 Oaks Ln, Apt 303
Pompano Beach, FL 33069-3724
Phone: 305-651-0101
Fax: 305-633-9669
*Machinery & Equipment, Office
Furniture & Equipment, Restaurant
Equipment, Cement Equipment,
Industrial Machinery Equipment*

Luis M. Garcia, ISA
Estate Sale Center, Inc.
PO Box 144812
Coral Gables, FL 33114-4812
Phone: 305-444-4931
Fax: 305-448-2197
*Residential Used Furniture, Personal
Property, Estates, Antiques*

Jay Rumbaugh, ISA
4160 Poinciana Ave
Miami, FL 33133-6331
Phone: 305-444-4931
Fax: 305-448-2197
*Residential Contents, Antiques, Fine
Art, Furniture, Silver, Decorative Arts
& Accessories, Carpets & Rugs,
Collectibles, Estates, Liquidators,*

Frederic H. Emmett, Jr., ISA
1622 Ponce de Leon Blvd
Miami, FL 33134
Phone: 305-442-8743
Fax: 305-443-3074
E-mail: modernism@gnn.com
*Art Deco, Furniture, Glass, Lighting,
Bronze, Porcelain, Prints (20th
Century), Fine Art*

Suzy Furman, ISA
Suzy Furman Fine Arts
1170 NE 97th St
Miami Shores, FL 33138-2558
Phone: 305-759-3875
Fax: 305-759-4521
*Modern And Contemporary Paintings,
Drawings, Prints, Sculpture*

Lauraine Dunn-Glispin, ISA
Lauraine Dunn & Associates, PA -
Apprais
68 NE 91st St
Miami Shores, FL 33138-2808
Phone: 305-758-7174
Fax: 305-756-5153
*Real Estate, Estates, Expert Witness,
Arbitration, Litigation Preparation,
Fine And Decorative Arts, Orientalia,
Bronzes, Porcelain, China, Pottery,
Industrial Inventory, Evaluation For
Tax Exemption, Residential Contents*

Joan Baron, ISA
Baron's Antiques
1776 Bay Dr
Miami, FL 33141-4720
Phone: 305-866-0502
*Residential Contents, Estates, Jewelry,
Antiques, Silver, Porcelain*

Sandra Steinberg, ISA, GG
Owl's Roost Antiques
900 Bay Dr, Apt 116
Miami Beach, FL 33141-5630
Phone: 305-864-5905
Fax: 305-868-4604
*Residential Contents, Antiques
(Wicker), Jewelry (Antique & Estate),
Estates*

Lorena Allen, MA, ISA
L. Allen Appraisal Studios
9720 West Bay Harbor Drive, #3
Bay Harbor Islands, FL 33154
Phone: 305-866-1023
*Fine Art (Including Prints, Paintings,
Etchings), Oriental Art, American And
European Art, English Porcelain And
Pottery (Wedgwood Jasperware)*

Jerome Bengis, ISA
Jerry Bengis, Inc.
9860 SW 122nd St
Miami, FL 33176-4928
Phone: 305-232-1143
Fax: 305-251-1450
*Collectibles, (45 Rpm Records),
Graphics (Miro Chagall, Picasso &
Warhol, Other), Etchings, Engravings,
Prints, Bronzes, Salvador Dali Prints*

Donald Kapner, ISA
United Appraisal Group
2564 NE Miami Gardens Dr
N. Miami Beach, FL 33180-2706
Phone: 305-931-5800
Fax: 305-935-0020
E-mail: 75232.2266@compuserve.com
*Residential Contents, Fine Art, Office
Furniture & Equipment, Insurance,
Estates*

Arlene Schwarz, ISA, GG
United Appraisal Group Inc
2564 NE Miami Gardens Dr
Miami, FL 33180-2706
Phone: 305-931-5800
Fax: 305-935-0020
E-mail: 75232.2266@compuserve.com
*Antiques, Jewelry (Antique, Period,
Costume), Residential Contents &
Estates*

Santo R. Blasi, ISA
Gold Coast Appraisers
18861 Biscayne Blvd
Miami, FL 33180-2839
Phone: 305-935-1471
Fax: 305-933-4146
*Jewelry, Fine Art, Porcelain, Personal
Property, Auctioneer*

J. Ellen Thompson, ISA
Heirloom Appraisals Inc.
1800 NE 114th St, Apt 809
Miami, FL 33181-3417
Phone: 305-893-1599
Fax: 305-893-7686
*Estates, Residential Contents, Silver,
Porcelain, Crystal, China, Furniture*

Edgar Kohn, ISA, GG
11910 SW 77th Ter
Miami, FL 33183-3849
Phone: 305-275-3017
Fax: 305-279-1124
*Gemology/Gemstones, Jewelry,
Watches, Coins, Currency, Pre-
Columbian Art*

Holly Nester, ISA, GG
Heather's Neste
8306 Mills Dr, Suite #251
Miami, FL 33183-4838
Phone: 305-226-6164
Fax: 305-220-7221
Gemology/Gemstones, Jewelry

Sharon M. Kerwick, ISA
Kerwick Appraisals
1713 NE 25th St
Fort Lauderdale, FL 33305-1408
Phone: 954-565-9031
Fax: 954-564-0648
E-mail: 104516.2373@compuserve.com
*Residential Contents, Oriental Rugs,
Silver (Including Georg Jensen),
Appraisal Reviews, Estates,
Insurance, Damage Claims, Lectures.*

Victoria Lee Golden, ISA
Reneaissance Appraisal Ltd.
2100 SW 52 Terrace
Plantation, FL 33317
Phone: 954-791-5330
Fax: 954-791-5330
*Fine Art, Furniture, Porcelain, Indian
Artifacts, Antiques, Jewelry, Bronzes*

Sheila M. Bemis, ISA
14250 SW 23rd St
Fort Lauderdale, FL 33325-5431
Phone: 305-424-8912
Fax: 305-564-0648
*Residential Contents, Estates,
Insurance, Antiques, Porcelain,
Pottery, Silver*

Mary Lou Nicholas, ISA
Appraiser's International Inc.
3805 S Dixie Hwy
West Palm Beach, FL 33405-2231
Phone: 407-832-0099
Fax: 407-832-4541
*Generalist, Antiques, Fine Art,
Jewelry, Coins, Stamps, Guns, Silver,
Horses, Probate, Brokerage,
Liquidation.*

Edwin L. Pry, ISA
Sun Antiques, Inc.
PO Box 3038
Boynton Beach, FL 33424-3038
Phone: 561-641-9342
*Antiques, Collectibles, Residential
Contents, Porcelain, Glass. Ceramics,
Decorative Arts & Accessories,
Estates*

**Leonid A. Livshitz-Smith, ISA, GG
CG MGA**
Mayor's Jewelers
9517 Everglades Park Ln
Boca Raton, FL 33428-2937
Phone: 305-944-0458
Fax: 305-454-5667
*Gemology/Gemstones, Diamonds,
Jewelry, Watches, Glass*

Gabrielle Siman, ISA
2889 NW 24th Terrace
Boca Raton, FL 33431-6202
Phone: 561-852-4716
Fax: 561-852-4716
E-mail: gsiman@sprintmail.com
*Fine Art, Decorative Arts, Estates,
Consultant, Art Historian/Attorney
specialized in the practice of
Intellectual Property Law*

Anthony Capodilupo, ISA
Anthony Capodilupo Fine Art
6706 Boca Pines Trail
Boca Raton, FL 33433-7714
Phone: 561-477-1210
Fax: 561-477-1237
*Fine Art (American, European, Latin
American), Consultant, Litigation
Management   Alt #:800-393-1023*

William M. Meehan, ISA
12271 Sand Wedge Dr
Boynton Beach, FL 33437-2065
Phone: 561-374-8800
Fax: 561-374-9426
E-mail: wmeehanfl@aol.com
Furniture, Antiques, Estates

Irving Pine, ISA
Irving Pine Appraisals Inc.
3505 Lowson Blvd
Delray Beach, FL 33445-5642
Phone: 407-498-5000
*Residential Contents, Jewelry
(Diamonds, Colored Stones),
Antiques, Orientalia, Carpets & Rugs*

Amy L. Walter, ISA, GG
PO Box 1513
Delray Beach, FL 33447-1513
Phone: 407-274-4941
Fax: 407-272-3722
*Gemology/Gemstones, Diamonds,
Pearls, Jewelry, Watches*

Melanie M. Hill, ISA
Appraisal & Acquisition Assoc.
315 S. County Rd
Palm Beach, FL 33480-4250
Phone: 561-655-2494
Fax: 561-655-5821
*Antiques, Residential Contents,
Decorative Arts & Accessories, Silver,
Estates*

Joel J. Cohen, ISA
Cohen Books & Collectibles
PO Box 810310
Boca Raton, FL 33481-0310
Phone: 561-487-7888
Fax: 561-487-3117
E-mail: cohendisney@prodigy.com
*Walt Disney Specialist, Expert, Buys,
Sells, Appraises Exclusively Disney;
Books, Animation Art, Ephemera,
Figurines, Autographs, Toys,
Collectibles, Disneyana*

Harold G. Flutie, ISA
Professional Appraisal Services
7932 Shelby Cir
Boca Raton, FL 33496-1324
Phone: 407-477-9989
Fax: 407-997-0559
*Antiques, Collectibles, Decorative
Arts & Accessories, Residential
Contents, Estates, Office Furniture
And Equipment, Damage Claims
Specialist*

Ruth T. Garland, ISA
1811H Chapel Tree Circle
Brandon, FL 33511
Phone: 813-685-4341
Fax: 813-685-4341
*Antiques, Residential Contents, Silver,
Orientalia, Furniture, Estate
Liquidations, Decorative Arts &
Accessories*

Ina H. Baden, ISA
Ina Baden Appraisals & Sales
1210 99th St NW
Bradenton, FL 33529-9730
Phone: 941-792-8401
Fax: 941-747-4457
*Residential Contents, Probate &
Insurance, Estate Sales, Collectibles
(Hummels, Paper Items)*

Daphne L. Rosenzweig, Ph.D., ISA
Rosenzweig Associates
PO Box 16187
Tampa, FL 33687-6187
Phone: 813-988-0880
Fax: 813-989-8091
E-mail: rosenwig@aol.com
*Oriental Fine & Decorative Art, South
& Southeast Asia, Islamic, Japanese
Prints, Minerals, Ivory, Orientalia,
Woodblock Prints, Oriental Art*

Donald A. Bartlett, ISA
Omega Automobile Appraisals
115 18th Ave SE
Saint Petersburg, FL 33705-2805
Phone: 813-894-5690
Fax: 813-894-5690
*Cars, Trucks (Antique, Classic,
Special Interest, Specializing In Rolls
Royce & Bentley), Repairs,
Restoration, Preservation (Auto
Restoration), Consultant*

Lornie Mueller, ISA, GG
Lithos Jewelry
344 Corey Ave
St. Pete Beach, FL 33706-1817
Phone: 813-367-9010
Fax: 813-367-9011
E-mail: 104534.1077@compuserve.com
*Gemology, Gemstones, Jewelry,
Diamonds, Pearls*

Rose Mueller, ISA, GG
Lithos Jewelry
344 Corey Ave
St. Pete Beach, FL 33706-1817
Phone: 813-367-9010
Fax: 813-367-9011
*Pearls, Gemology, Gemstones,
Jewelry, Diamonds*

Ruth H. Isgro, ISA CAPP
Stone Hearth Antiques
5401 US Hwy 17-92W, #105
Woodland Lakes
Haines City, FL 33844
Phone: 941-956-0409
*Furniture (18th - 20th C. - American),
Accessories, Americana, Residential
Contents, Antiques, Porcelain,
Pottery, Ceramics, China, Primitives,
Consultant*
**CAPP In Appreciable Residential
Contents**

R. N. Huff, ISA
Treasure Hunters
1502 Buckeye Rd, #1
Winter Haven, FL 33881
Phone: 941-294-1981
Fax: 941-294-1981
Estate Sales, Antiques

Jane de Lisser, ISA
Jane de Lisser Associates
1348 Alcazar Avenue
Ft. Myers, FL 33901-6617
Phone: 941-334-8199
Fax: 941-334-8799
*Silver, Fine Art, Furniture (American,
English), Decorative & Oriental Arts,
Rugs & Textiles, Residential Contents,
Brokerage Services, Estates*

Joy Kelley, ISA
Read & Kelley/ AmeriVision
PO Box 3111
North Fort Meyers, FL 33918
Phone: 941-731-2201
*Residential Contents, Estates,
Household Contents, Antiques,
Keywind Clocks, Antique & Vintage
Lighting, Billboard Structures*

Ann Barry Colgin, ISA
Fairchilds Fine Art, Inc.
17301 Frank Rd
Alva, FL 33920-3510
Phone: 941-728-2777
Fax: 941-728-3189
*Jewelry, Decorative Arts &
Accessories (19th & 20th C), Fine Art,
Residential Contents, Wine*

Carol Pier, ISA
Pier & Co.
2000 Lambience Cir, #202
Naples, FL 34108
Phone: 941-566-2828
Fax: 941-566-2866
*Residential Contents, Decorative Arts,
Collectibles, Antiques, Liquidator*

Kenneth R. McMillen, Jr., ISA
McMillen & Co.
PO Box 5111
Sarasota, FL 34277-5111
Phone: 813-366-7464
*Antiques, Fine Art, Residential
Contents, Decorative Arts &
Accessories, Estates, Insurance*

Debbie Pearl, ISA
Blough's Inc.
PO Box 624
Stuart, FL 34995-0624
Phone: 407-287-6906
*Antiques, Decorative Art, General
Household Merchandise.*

Bill Carner, ISA
Birmingham Appraisal Services
400 Lance Way
Birmingham, AL 35206-3035
Phone: 205-836-8009
Fax: 205-836-8009
E-mail: 102545.2667@compuserve.com
*Furniture, (19th & Early 20th C.), Art
Glass & Cut Glass, (19th & Early
20th C.), Pottery, Porcelain, Furniture
Restoration, Insurance Claims,
Teaching Antiques*

Lee C. Scott, ISA CAPP
Estate Services, Inc.
3716 Montrose Rd
Birmingham, AL 35213-3828
Phone: 205-870-5522
*Furniture (Antique American),
Residential Contents, Estates,
Antiques, Decorative Arts &
Accessories*
**CAPP In Appreciable Residential
Contents**

Frances C. Sommers, ISA
3844 Cromwell Dr
Birmingham, AL 35243-5513
Phone: 205-871-0433
Fax: 205-969-5888
*Silver, Furniture, Porcelain,
Collectibles, Antiques*

William C. Ornburn, ISA
Bill Ornburn Auctions
99 Gurley Drive
Decatur, AL 35603
Phone: 205-350-5305
*Antiques, Residential Contents,
Auctioneer*

Steve R. Hewitt, ISA
Investment Appraisals
319 Morning View Drive
Harvest, AL 35749-9429
Phone: 205-851-9293
*Empire, 19th C. Furniture, Coin
Silver, Transfer Ware China Sheffield
Plate, 19th C. Glass, Residential*

Contents, Furniture, Decorative Arts & Accessories

Spencer L. Glasgow, ISA
28867 Hvs Browns Ferry Rd
Madison, AL 35758
Phone: 205-232-4465
Auctioneer, Estates, Residential Contents

Jane W. Mabry, ISA CAPP
Antiques, Appraisals, Etc.
PO Box 10045
Huntsville, AL 35801-3670
Phone: 205-534-2282
E-mail: 74136.1045@compuserve.com
Furniture, Glass (Glassware), Porcelain, Pottery, Ceramics, Residential Contents, Antiques, Collectibles
CAPP In Appreciable Residential Contents

James Chapman, ISA, GG
Aries Gems
RR 1 Box 208
Fort Payne, AL 35967-9740
Phone: 205-845-5231
Gemology/Gemstones, Diamonds, Jewelry, Gold, Silver

Linda R. Pugh, ISA
Old South Antiques
121 Wildwood Drive
Cecil, AL 36013
Phone: 334-271-0727
E-mail: 107701.2605@compuserve.com
Residential Contents, Furniture, Collectibles, Pottery, Estate Sales

Connie Sue Davenport, ISA
Connie Sue's Antiques
122 Island Dr
Hendersonville, TN 37075-4507
Phone: 615-264-6307
Antiques, Estates, Residential Contents, Victoriana

Judy Stroud, ISA
Stroud & McHale Appraisals
391 Jones Mill Rd
Lavergne, TN 37086-2618
Phone: 615-459-4727
Decorative Arts & Accessories, Antiques, Collectibles, Estate Sales

Margaret Gillespie, ISA
169 S Greer St
Memphis, TN 38111-3428
Phone: 901-324-7762
Fax: 901-458-3972
Art, Antiques, Appreciable Personal Property, Decorative Arts & Accessories, Furniture, Residential Contents, Dinnerware, Silver, Estates, Alternative Phone No. 901-324-9839

Dan A. Sasser, ISA
Market Street Antiques Mall
414 N Market St
Paris, TN 38242-3405
Phone: 901-642-6996
Furniture, Antiques, Residential Contents, Collectibles, Estates

Patricia A. Witt, ISA
Way-Fil Jewelry
1123 W Main St
Tupelo, MS 38801-3453
Phone: 601-844-2427
Fax: 601-840-4791
E-mail: pattiwitt@ebicom.net
Gemology/Gemstones, Diamonds, Jewelry, Silver (Flatware), Liquidators, Antique Period Jewelry

Celia Fleishhacker, ISA
Nostalgia Alley Antiques
214 W Main St, #C
Tupelo, MS 38801-3918
Phone: 601-842-2757
Antiques, Collectibles, Residential Contents, Victoriana, Toys, Antique Dolls, Ephemera, Medical

Kenneth S. Hays, ISA
Kenneth S. Hays & Associates, Inc.
PO Box 558
Pewee Valley, KY 40056-0558
Phone: 502-499-8942
Estates, Antiques, Dolls, Doll Houses (Antique), Auctioneer

Ann G. Hays, ISA CAPP
Kenneth S. Hays & Associates, Inc.
120 S Spring St
Louisville, KY 40206-1953
Phone: 502-584-4297
Dolls, Doll Houses & Accessories, Victoriana, Auctioneer, Antiques
CAPP In Appreciable Residential Contents

Elizabeth Patterson-Coons, ISA
Elizabeth Patterson Appraisals, Ltd.
6148 Ashgrove Pike
Nicholasville, KY 40356
Phone: 606-271-2430
Fax: 606-266-9699
Antiques, Fine Art, Residential Contents, Americana, Silver

Grover V. Farr, ISA
Impressions Of Berea, Ltd.
PO Box 123
Berea, KY 40403-0123
Phone: 606-986-8177
Glass, Porcelain, Pottery, Ceramics, Jewelry (Costume)

Michael H. Thompson, ISA
Impressions Of Berea, Ltd.
PO Box 123
Berea, KY 40403-0123
Phone: 606-986-8177
Porcelain, Pottery, Ceramics, China

James S. Harris, ISA
James Harris Antiques & Appraisals
PO Box 672
Richmond, KY 40476-0672
Phone: 606-623-9100
Silver (American Coin, English), Glass (Cut), American Pottery, Art Glass, Heisey Glass, Porcelain, Ceramics, China, Residential Contents, Estates

Russell C. Pattie, ISA, GG CGA
Miller & Woodward
2238 Nicholasville Rd
Lexington, KY 40503-2418
Phone: 606-276-6100
Fax: 606-276-6112
Jewelry, Gemology/Gemstones, Diamonds

Nathaniel Ludlum, ISA
Brule Wholesale
7323 Tucker Rd
Centerburg, OH 43011
Phone: 614-436-1458
Fax: 614-436-0124
Retail Sales Of Minerals, Fossils, And Jewelry

David M. Baker, ISA, CGA
David Baker Creative Jewelers, Inc.
6672 Perimeter Loop Drive
Dublin, OH 43017
Phone: 614-764-0068
Jewelry

Joseph G. Balshone, ISA, GG
Columbus Gemological Labs
463 E Town St
Columbus, OH 43215-4757
Phone: 800-209-4367
Fax: 614-224-5630
E-mail: 76701.242@compuserve.com
Alt. Bus #:614-224-2404 Gemstones, Jewelry, Modern Firearms, Vintage Writing Instruments

Krystina M. Nielsen, ISA
Nielsen Jewelers, Inc.
753 Broadway
Lorain, OH 44052-1805
Phone: 216-244-4255
Fax: 216-244-5040
Gemology/Gemstones, Diamonds, Jewelry (Antique, Colored, Stones)

Jeanette C Bendula, ISA
30201 Royalview
Willowick, OH 44095
Phone: 216-944-4355
Fax: 216-951-7175
Antiques, Breweriana, Estates, Liquidators, Residential Contents, Silver

James I. W. Corcoran, ISA
Corcoran Fine Arts Limited, Inc.
2915 Fairfax Rd
Cleveland Heights, OH 44118-4015
Phone: 216-431-0025
Fax: 216-397-0222
Fine Art (16th-20th C. European American, Canadian Paintings, Watercolors, Drawings, Prints, And Sculpture), Insurance, Loss And Damage Claims, Expert Witness, Consultant On Sale And Deposition

Peggy L. Sebek, ISA
Century Antiques & Appraisals, Inc.
3255 Glencairn Rd
Shaker Heights, OH 44122-3407
Phone: 318-232-5100
Antiques, Residential Contents, Porcelain, Pottery, Ceramics, Jewelry (Estate), Glass

Trent Bobbitt, ISA
Sandisfield House Liquidations
18717 Winslow Rd
Shaker Heights, OH 44122-4818
Phone: 216-283-2266
Antiques, Furniture, Residential Contents, Liquidators, Estates, Decorative Arts & Accessories

Carol Pier, ISA
Pier & Co.
3250 W. Market St, Suite 307
Akron, OH 44333-3321
Phone: 330-864-8595
Fax: 330-864-8044
Residential Contents, Decorative Arts, Collectibles, Antiques, Liquidator

Judy Pier, ISA
Pier & Co.
3250 W Market St, Ste 307
Akron, OH 44333-3321
Phone: 330-864-8595
Fax: 330-864-8044
Residential Contents, Furniture, Glass, Porcelain, Pottery, Ceramics, Decorative Arts & Accessories, Collectibles

Kathleen Wieschaus, ISA CAPP
Appraisal Services
2019 Otterbin Street
Louisville, OH 44641
Phone: 330-875-1237
E-mail: 104575.1571@compuserve.com
Antiques, Decorative Art, Silver, Porcelain, Residential Contents
CAPP In Appreciable Residential Contents

Maggie M. Beckmeyer, ISA, CAI
Auctions By Maggie, Inc.
2191 Cliff Rd
North Bend, OH 45052-9781
Phone: 513-941-9519
Fax: 513-941-9519
Antiques, Residential Contents, Cars, Generalist, Estates, Real Estate

Jeanne E. Read, ISA
The Squirrel's Nest
PO Box 342
Blanchester, OH 45107-0342
Phone: 513-783-4411
Fax: 513-783-4411
E-mail: 103375.3612@compuserve.com
Glass (Pattern & Depression), Ceramics, China, Pottery

Steven S. Early, ISA
Antique Appraisals
125 Winding Brook Ln
Terrace Park, OH 45174-1035
Phone: 513-831-0072
Furniture, Glass (Victorian Art), Silver, Dolls, Doll Houses & Accessories (Antique Dolls)

Frederick W. Fehr, III, ISA, GG
The Richter & Phillips Co.
202 E 6th St
Cincinnati, OH 45202-3228
Phone: 513-241-3510
Gemology/Gemstones, Diamonds (Loose & Mounted), Jewelry (Gold, Handmade Chains)

Edward J. Keller, ISA
Antiques & Art Appraisals, Ltd.
2710 Lafeuille Circle
Cincinnati, OH 45211
Phone: 513-662-8753
*Furniture (American & English),
Brass, Copper, Decorative Arts &
Accessories, Fine Art, Silver,
Porcelain*

Dorothy Koman, ISA
DK Estates Sales
10347 Lochcrest Dr
Cincinnati, OH 45231-2737
Phone: 513-772-1247
*Antiques, Collectibles, Residential
Contents, Estates (Liquidations)*

Carrie Metz, ISA, GG
4945 Shirley Place, #2
Cincinnati, OH 45238-3504
Phone: 513-662-0049
*Gems & Jewelry, Jewelry Insurance
Appraiser*

Mary E. Mecklenborg, ISA
Special Things Antiques
5701 Cheviot Rd
Cincinnati, OH 45247-7007
Phone: 513-741-9127
*Porcelain, Pottery, Ceramics,
Antiques, Residential Contents,
Rookwood & Ohio Pottery, Post
Cards, Estates*

Jean C. Renick, ISA
Jean C. Renick
PO Box 54619
Cincinnati, OH 45254-0619
Phone: 513-232-2371
Fax: 513-232-6323
*Victorian Furniture, English Black
Lacquer, Smalls And Furniture,
Specialize In Gold Chinoiserie
Figures*

Kenneth J. Rapp, ISA, GG
Rapp Jewelers, Inc.
PO Box 222
Englewood, OH 45322-0222
Phone: 513-836-6243
*Gemology/Gemstones, Diamonds,
Jewelry*

Jane Fetters Warner, ISA
Warner's Blue Ribbon Book
7163 Frederick Garland Rd
Union, OH 45322-9621
Phone: 513-698-4508
Fax: 513-698-4508
Crystal Figurines, Swarovski

Robert Fessel, ISA, GG FGA
Fessel's Inc.
116 N Williams St
Paulding, OH 45879-1281
Phone: 419-399-3398
*Gemology/Gemstones, Diamonds,
Jewelry (Diamond, Colored Stone,
Gold And Other Precious Metal),
Silver*

Myron Noble, ISA
Myron Noble Appraisals
388 E 300 N
Anderson, IN 46012-1208
Phone: 317-642-2681
*Residential Contents, Commercial
Inventories, Machinery & Equipment
(Farm), Antiques, Estates, Real Estate*

Joyce Haverty, ISA
AA Professional Appraisals
43 Terrace Ct
Carmel, IN 46032-1544
Phone: 317-843-1885
*Art (19th & 20th Century), Antiques,
Americana, Indiana Art, Native
American, Oriental Rugs, Silver,
Residential Contents*

Margaret L. Durrer, ISA
Durrer's Antiques
112 Brierly Way
Carmel, IN 46032-1852
Phone: 317-844-8351
*Residential Contents, Silver, Glass
(Glassware), Antiques, Linens,
Needlework, Watches, Estates,
Ceramics*

David A. Budd, ISA
12210 Windsor Dr
Carmel, IN 46033-3142
Phone: 317-872-4710
Fax: 317-879-9732
*Fishing Tackle (Antique), Flow Blue
China, Furniture (Antique), Sporting
Collectibles*

Michael J. Ellis, ISA CAPP, GG
Ellis Jewelers
PO Box 208
Lebanon, IN 46052-0208
Phone: 317-482-0520
Fax: 317-482-0791
E-mail: 104561.3454@compuserve.com
*Gemology/Gemstones, Diamonds,
Jewelry, Pearls, Gold*
CAPP In Gemstones

Virginia Lucas, ISA
Trash To Treasures
5505 N Keystone Ave
Indianapolis, IN 46220-3457
Phone: 317-253-2235
Fax: 317-726-0932
E-mail: 102003.2755@compuserve.com
*Depreciable & Appreciable
Residential Contents, Antiques, Estate
& Household Liquidations, Insurance*

Carter A. Hofmeister, ISA, GG
Hofmeister Personal Jewelers
3809 E 82nd St
Indianapolis, IN 46240-4329
Phone: 317-255-9854
*Gemology/Gemstones, Diamonds,
Jewelry*

James S. Britton, ISA, GG
2265 Executive Dr
Indianapolis, IN 46241-4352
Phone: 612-290-9489
*Jewelry, Gemstones, Diamonds,
Goldsmith*

Pamela L. Hickman, ISA, GG
International Diamond & Gold
4026 E 82nd St, Ste A5
Indianapolis, IN 46250-4206
Phone: 317-578-4653
Fax: 317-578-9335
*Gemology/Gemstones, Diamonds,
Colored Stones, Rubies, Sapphires,
Emeralds, Decorative Arts &
Accessories, Insurance, Retail Jeweler*

Mary J. Khamis, ISA CAPP, GG
Khamis Fine Jewelers
9763 Fall Creek Rd
Indianapolis, IN 46256-4713
Phone: 317-841-8440
Fax: 317-841-9210
*Diamonds, Gemstones, Pearls,
Watches, Designer Jewelry, Gold,
Antique Jewelry*
CAPP In Gemstones

Dalimira A. Cmiel, ISA
Camile, Inc.
2996 N Horseshoe Bend
La Porte, IN 46350-7918
Phone: 219-326-1121
Fax: 219-326-1121
*Residential Contents, Porcelain,
Pottery, Elsie Borden Collectibles,
China, Office Furniture & Equipment*

Ronald S. Cmiel, ISA
Camile, Inc.
2996 N Horseshoe Bend
La Porte, IN 46350-7918
Phone: 219-326-1121
Fax: 219-326-1121
*Residential Contents, Porcelain,
Pottery, Ceramics, China, Repairs,
Restorations, Preservation*

Eileen R. Eichhorn, ISA, GG
Eichhorn Jewelry, Inc.
130 N 2nd St
Decatur, IN 46733-1609
Phone: 219-724-2621
Fax: 219-724-9483
*Gemology/Gemstones, Diamonds,
Jewelry, Pearls, Gold*

Sally A. Boose, ISA
Sally's Antiques
9417 Marydale Ln
Fort Wayne, IN 46804-4727
Phone: 219-432-4025
Fax: 219-459-0521
*Residential Contents, Glass,
Furniture, Porcelain, Pottery,
Ceramics, China, Repairs, Restora-
tion, Preservation, Antiques*

Carol Wamble, ISA
Antique Annie's Keeping Room
4300 Old Mill Rd
Fort Wayne, IN 46807-2550
Phone: 219-456-3150
*Antiques (19th To Present), Furniture,
Estates, Residential Contents*

Tamara J. Strickler, ISA CAPP, GG
Strickler Jewelers
140 N Dixon Rd
Kokomo, IN 46901-4100
Phone: 317-452-4075
*Gemology/Gemstones, Diamonds,
Jewelry*
CAPP In Gemstones

John F. Burger, ISA
Burger & Associates
225 Eagle Ln
New Albany, IN 47150-6129
Phone: 812-944-6796
*Bankruptcy Court Appraisals,
Auctioneer, Residential Contents,
Office Furniture & Equipment,
Antiques*

Beverly S. Reed, ISA
Whale Antiques
230 Burks Drive
Bloomington, IN 47401-8453
Phone: 812-332-2290
*Antiques, Collectibles, Residential
Contents*

Jeffery A. Vierk, ISA, GG
Vierk's Fine Jewelry
1650 Main St
Lafayette, IN 47904-2919
Phone: 317-447-0200
E-mail: 76651.2711@compuserve.com
*Gemology/Gemstones, Diamonds,
Jewelry, Gold, Coins*

Charles M. Ellias, ISA, GG
Astrein's Fine Jewelry
120 West Maple
Birmingham, MI 48009
Phone: 810-644-1651
*Jewelry, Diamonds, Pearls, Colored
Stones And Gemology, Watches,
Insurance Replacements, Appraisals*

Marie Dingley, ISA
Williams & Lipton Co.
101 Southfield Rd, Ste 302
Birmingham, MI 48009-1645
Phone: 810-646-7090
Fax: 810-646-7093
*Machinery & Equipment, Plastics
Equipment, Office Furniture &
Equipment*

Richard L. Stout, ISA
Williams & Lipton Co.
101 Southfield Rd, Ste 302
Birmingham, MI 48009-1645
Phone: 810-646-7090
Fax: 810-646-7093
*Machinery & Equipment (Metal
Working, Restaurant, Construction),
Cars & Trucks, Auctioneer*

Ruth F. Rattner, ISA
Art Advisory Services
1002 Ann St
Birmingham, MI 48009-1770
Phone: 810-258-5335
Fax: 810-540-9656
*Modern & Contemporary Paintings,
Sculpture, Prints, Decorative Arts,
Drawings, Ceramics; American Art*

Jan Chandler Durecki, ISA
Appraisal Consultants
PO Box 380227
Clinton Township, MI 48038-0062
Phone: 810-566-0353
Fax: 810-566-0353
E-mail: 75451.3253@compuserve.com
Furniture (Antiques To Contemporary) Appreciable & Depreciable Residential Contents, Golf Memorabilia, Estate Liquidations, Victoriana, Collectibles

Joseph DelGiudice, ISA
DelGiudice Antiques
515 S Lafayette Ave
Royal Oak, MI 48067-2556
Phone: 810-399-2608
Fax: 810-399-7570
Etchings (Icart), Bronzes, Jewelry (Costume, Fine), Art Deco, Art Nouveau, Antiques, Crystal, Estates, Fine Art, Silver

Jerome S. Feig, ISA
Field Art Studio
24242 Woodward Ave
Pleasant Ridge, MI 48069-1144
Phone: 810-399-9166
Fax: 810-399-7018
Fine Art, Repairs, Restorations & Preservations (Fine Art), Conservator, Picture Frames

Ann Rogers Pfrender, ISA
5764 Fox Hollow Ct
Ann Arbor, MI 48105-9510
Phone: 313-665-6058
American Art Pottery, Quilts, American Antiques, Decorative Art & Accessories, Residential Contents

Trish Davis, ISA
Red Lion Antiques
PO Box 2005
Dearborn, MI 48123
Phone: 313-274-3647
Fax: 313-278-9805
Antiques, Estates, Households, Estate Liquidators, Collectibles

Melinda Adducci, ISA, GG
Joseph DuMouchelle Fine & Estate Jewellers
199 N Main St, Ste 204
Plymouth, MI 48170-1271
Phone: 313-455-2856
Fax: 313-455-2403
Additional Bus #:313-455-4555 Gemology/Gemstones, Jewelry, Diamonds, Gold, Silver

Barbara C. Seichter, ISA
B.C. Seichter, Inc., dba Le Chatelet
5 Shadow Ln
Bloomfield Hills, MI 48302
Phone: 810-647-3660
Furniture (English, Continental), Porcelain, Pottery, Ceramics, (English, Continental, Chinese, Export)

Delores A. Nihem, ISA
5680 Hillcrest Cir E
West Bloomfield, MI 48322-1283
Phone: 810-788-0065
Department 56 Porcelain Village Pieces, Decorative Accessories For The Home, Books (Fore-Edge Painting), Antiques, Residential Contents, Personal Property

Bud Groom, ISA, CGA
521 Greenwich Lane
Grand Blanc, MI 48439
Phone: 810-694-9290
Gemology/Gemstones, Diamonds, Jewelry, Pearls

Velma J. Miller, ISA CAPP
V.J. Miller & Associates
5137 Dundas Rd
Beaverton, MI 48612-8590
Phone: 517-435-9293
Fax: 517-435-9293
Antiques, Residential Contents
CAPP In Appreciable Residential Contents

Marilyn M. Roberts, ISA
Marilyn Roberts' Antiques
8745 Central Pl
Freeland, MI 48623-9519
Phone: 517-695-6508
Antiques, Collectibles, Crystal, Furniture, Porcelain, Pottery, Primitives, Quilts, Residential Contents, Insurance

Mark E. Hazlett, ISA
Antique Appraisals & Consignments
PO Box 578
Haslett, MI 48840-0578
Phone: 517-351-2613
Antiques, Furniture, Books, Fine Art

Hans F. Fetting, ISA
Antiques, Restorations & Appraisals
3105 Mineral Springs Dr
Mount Pleasant, MI 48858-9663
Phone: 517-773-9514
Fax: 517-773-9514
E-mail: 76746.1223@compuserve.com
American Art Pottery, Glass, Collectibles, Pottery Repairs & Conservation, Metal, Ceramics, Americana

Richard A. Bloomquist, ISA
375 Turner Rd
Williamston, MI 48895-9410
Phone: 517-655-3380
Estate Sales, Furniture, Glass, Pottery, China

Martha McDonald, ISA
c/o Dunes Antiques Center, Inc.
12825 Red Arrow Hwy
Sawyer, MI 49125
Phone: 616-426-4043
Fax: 616-426-8238
E-mail: 102106.1664@compuserve.com
Furniture, Glass, Art Glass, Pottery, Household Contents, Yachts

Frank T. Wieber, ISA
Consumers Power Co.
115 W Trail St
Jackson, MI 49201-1314
Phone: 517-788-7098
Fax: 517-788-0769
Vehicles: Equipment, Trailers (Parts & Tools), Office Furniture

Timothy G. Bos, ISA
Timothy G. Bos Appraisal
4701 County Farm Rd
Jackson, MI 49201-9078
Phone: 517-784-2177
Furniture, Collectibles, Residential Contents, Depression Era Glass (Glassware), Furniture Repairs, Restoration, Preservation (Antiques), 1850's-1900's

Duane A. Leet, ISA
E'Leet Appraisals & Estate Sales
533 Colfax St
Grand Haven, MI 49417-1828
Phone: 616-842-7677
Antiques, Collectibles, Personal Property

Chad A. Van Overloop, ISA
Miedema Appraisals Inc.
PO Box 453
Grandville, MI 49418-0453
Phone: 616-538-0367
Fax: 616-538-5230
Machinery & Equipment, Auctioneer, Heavy Construction/Presses, Lathes, Industrial Equipment Sales

Scott A. Miedema, ISA
Miedema Auctioneering Appraisals Inc.
PO Box 453
Grandville, MI 49468-0453
Phone: 800-527-8243
Fax: 616-530-5230
Machinery & Equipment, Boats (Marine Equipment), Construction Equipment, Office Furniture & Equipment, Auctioneer

Leslie K. Saari, ISA
Great Lakes Appraisals
201 Iroquois Pl
Cadillac, MI 49601-9221
Phone: 616-775-6423
Laces, Needlework, Needlework Implements, Textiles, Household Contents, Residential Contents

Minnie I. Olmstead, ISA
Great Lakes Appraisals
8092 Independence Ave
Cadillac, MI 49601-9504
Phone: 616-775-5855
Residential Contents and Estate Sales

Joan F. McLain, ISA
Antique Appraisers, Grand Traverse
PO Box 416
Eastport, MI 49627-0416
Phone: 616-946-2534
Fax: 616-946-2573
Residential Contents, Liquidators, Damage Claims, Insurance, Estates

Bonnie C. Beckman, ISA
Antique Emporium
565 W Blue Star Dr
Traverse City, MI 49684-8778
Phone: 616-943-3658
Glass (Art), Lamps, Lighting Fixtures, Antiques, Collectibles, Estates, Jewelry, Liquidators, Residential Contents, Auctioneer, Consultant, Damage Claims

Susan B. Feiger, ISA
Susan Feiger Appraisal Service
2513 Nelson Rd
Traverse City, MI 49686-8557
Fax: 616-223-7387
E-mail: feiger@gtii.com
Antiques (American & General), Residential Contents, Furniture, Silver, Glass, Porcelain, Pottery, Quilts, Estate Sales, Gas Station Collectibles

Judith A. Owen, ISA
Antique Appraisers, Grand Traverse
10332 Stoneybeach Pointe
Traverse City, MI 49686-8584
Phone: 616-946-2534
Fax: 616-946-2573
Antiques, Residential Contents, Estate Sales, American Country Pottery, Silver, Breweriana

Marilynn A. Quick, ISA
Susan Feiger Appraisal Service
1036 Bayside Dr
Traverse City, MI 49686-9205
Phone: 616-946-7811
American Antiques, Collectibles, Glass (American Art Glass), Estates (Estate Sales), Residential Contents

Deborah Golden, ISA
Golden Era Sales, Inc.
3182 Twin Pine Rd
Grayling, MI 49738-7183
Phone: 517-348-2610
Residential Contents (Appreciable & Depreciable), Estates, Insurance, Liquidators

Linda Judy, ISA
Somewhere In Time Appraisals
4274 Hiawatha Trail
Petoskey, MI 49770
Phone: 616-347-9538
Fax: 616-347-9266
E-mail: judy@vixa.voyager.net
Antiques, Damage Claims, Estates, Residential Contents, Business Evaluations, Pottery, Glass

Sara Jane Harwood, ISA
Percival Galleries, Inc.
Firstar Bank Bldg
528 Walnut St
Des Moines, IA 50309-4106
Phone: 515-243-4893
Fax: 515-243-9716
Art (American & European), Paintings, Drawings, Prints (19th C.), Sculpture (19th C.), All 20th C. Art Media

Jon E. Crisman, ISA
Jackson's Auctioneer's
PO Box 585
Cedar Falls, IA 50613-0585
Phone: 319-277-2256
Fax: 319-277-1252
E-mail: jacksons@corenet.net
Residential Contents, Antique Glassware, European & Continental Pottery & Porcelain, American Art Pottery

James L. Jackson, ISA
Jackson's Auctioneers
2229 Lincoln St
Cedar Falls, IA 50613-3277
Phone: 319-277-2256
Fax: 319-277-1252
E-mail: jacksons@corenet.net
Russian Icons

Bruce C. Anderson, ISA, CGA
Thorpe & Co. Jewelers
501 4th St
Sioux City, IA 51101-1601
Phone: 712-258-7501
Fax: 712-258-8138
Gemology/Gemstones, Diamonds, Colored Stones, Jewelry, Metals (Precious)

Robert J. Biede, ISA
Antique Junction Mall
200 Timber Ln
Council Bluffs, IA 51503-1769
Phone: 712-325-1055
Fax: 712-622-9367
Antiques

Janelle V. McClain, ISA
Cornerhouse Gallery & Frame
2753 1st Ave SE
Cedar Rapids, IA 52402-4804
Phone: 319-365-4348
Fax: 319-365-1707
Fine Art (Regionalist Works)

Katherine Vandygriff, ISA CAPP, GG
Katherine's
605 Sunset Dr
Muscatine, IA 52761-2778
Phone: 319-263-6008
Fax: 319-263-1050
E-mail: 76453.1460@compuserve.com; Kat
Gemology/Gemstones, Diamonds, Jewelry, Pearls
CAPP In Gemstones

Susan S. Pohle, ISA
Accurate Appraisals
621 N Main St
Mequon, WI 53092-1215
Phone: 414-242-2054
Collectibles, Dolls, Folk Art, Miniatures, Personal Property, Residential Contents

Larry Gutbrod, ISA
10030 N Sunnycrest Dr
Mequon, WI 53092-5419
Phone: 414-873-3738
Fax: 414-873-5229
E-mail: 103062.562@compuserve.com
Residential Contents, Fine Art, Insurance, Auctioneer, Auction Co.

Kent Anderson, Ph.D., ISA
Kent Anderson Fine Art
11298 Bridget Ln
Hales Corners, WI 53130-2426
Phone: 414-425-2377
Fax: 414-425-4154
Paintings, Drawings, Prints (Original), Sculpture, Artist's Books (Livre's D'Artist), Posters

Brent Fraser, ISA
Fraser & Associates
5037 W Washington Blvd
Milwaukee, WI 53208
Phone: 414-771-2483
Residential Contents, Fine Art, Cars, Trucks, Antiques, Auctioneer

A. J. Schrager, ISA
Schrager Auction Galleries
PO Box 10390
Milwaukee, WI 53210-0390
Phone: 414-873-3738
Fax: 414-873-5229
E-mail: 103046.262@compuserve.com
Antiques, Fine Art, Residential Contents, Auctioneer, Auction Gallery, Estates Liquidator, Objet D'Art & De Vertu

John D. Schrager, ISA
Schrager Auction Galleries, LTD.
PO Box 100043
Milwaukee, WI 53210-2131
Phone: 414-873-3738
Fax: 414-731-1112
E-mail: 103046.262@compuserve.com
Auctioneer, Auction Gallery

Robert H. Laszewski, ISA
Wausau Realty & Appraisal
PO Box 3
Wausau, WI 54402-0003
Phone: 715-675-4144
Fax: 715-675-4144
Machinery & Equipment, (Forestry, Construction, Farm), Auctioneer

Harvey A. Woodward, III, ISA
Woodward Appraisal & Auction
2189 County Road Kk
Mosinee, WI 54455-9764
Phone: 715-693-2403
Estates, Farm Machinery, Guns, Residential Contents, Machinery & Equipment

Mary F. Marsden, ISA
Mary Marsden & Associates
515 Lexington Pky S, Apt 503
St. Paul, MN 55116-1742
Phone: 612-699-4740
Fax: 612-690-3191
Residential Contents, Generalist, Fair Market Valuations For Legal Purposes, Mediation Assistance

Mary Chumas Ernst, ISA
Mary's Appraisals
2016 Yorkshire Ave, Apt 106
St. Paul, MN 55116-2585
Phone: 612-698-6624
Glass, Art, Icons (Russian & Greek), Household Contents, Collectibles & Antiques

Henry G. Swiggum, ISA
Henry Swiggum Fine Art Appraisals
14246 Glencove Trl
St. Paul, MN 55124-5517
Phone: 612-891-1514
Fax: 612-891-1514
Prints (American & European), Fine Art, Paintings, Bronzes, Oriental Art, Asian (Porcelains, Bronzes, Paintings, Prints), Insurance Claims, Adjusters

Susan K. Rychlik, ISA, GG
Gemological Services
7097 Robinwood Bay
Woodbury, MN 55125-6844
Phone: 612-339-5007
Jewelry, Estate Jewelry

Dean Parker, ISA
Beep Equipment Sales
Six Mile Rd
Huson, MT 59846-9705
Phone: 406-626-5655
Machinery & Equipment (Highway, Construction Machinery, Rock Crushing, & Highway Asphalt Equipment)

Ellen M. Kornhauser, ISA, GG
I.K. Design
141 S Northwest Hwy
Barrington, IL 60010-4684
Phone: 847-381-8626
Gemology/Gemstones, Diamonds, Jewelry

Karen S. Rabe, ISA CAPP
Appraisal Specialists
PO Box 21
Lake Forest, IL 60045
Phone: 847-604-8770
Fax: 847-356-2124
E-mail: 76202.3672@compuserve.com
Antiques, Decorative Arts & Accessories, Residential Contents Including 18th & 19th C. Furniture, Ceramics, Glass, Collectibles, Sterling Silver, Metals, Damage Claims Specialist
CAPP In Appreciable Residential Contents

Sybil Tillman, ISA
Artco, Inc.
3148 RFD
Long Grove, IL 60047-9606
Phone: 847-438-8420
Fax: 847-438-6464
Art (Contemporary American - All Media), American Indian (Art & Bead Work), Decorative Arts (All Media), Fine Arts (19th & 20th C. Old Master Prints)

Beatrice Weiskopf, ISA
Weiskopf Appraisal Services, Inc.
1343 Landwehr Rd
Northbrook, IL 60062-4353
Phone: 847-509-9664
Fax: 847-509-9606
E-mail: 104345.3271@compuserve.com
Antiques, Residential Contents, Decorative Arts, Accessories, Collectibles, Americana, Porcelain, Glass, Modern Glass, Pottery, Silver, Damage Claims, Autos, Ceramics

Susan A. Larson, ISA
Susan Larson Fine Art
1150 Old Mill Dr
Palatine, IL 60067-2772
Phone: 847-359-7799
Fax: 847-359-6796
Fine Art, Etchings, Paintings & Prints (19th 20th C. American, European), Chicago Artists

Stuart M. Robertson, ISA, GG
Appraiser & Gemological Consultant
904 Country Ln
Buffalo Grove, IL 60089-1939
Phone: 847-205-9602
Fax: 847-205-9612
E-mail: 102036.275@compuserve.com
Gemology/Gemstones, Colored Stones, Contemporary Diamond Jewelry, Estate Jewelry, Pearls, Watches, Gold, Diamonds, Liquidators, Insurance

Judy F. Banasek-Bratton, ISA
Judy Bratton Appraisals
1013 Surrey Rd
Addison, IL 60101-1141
Phone: 630-628-0650
Fax: 630-628-0640
Antiques, Collectibles, Residential Contents, Post Cards, Liquidator, Estate Consultant

Elroy J. Sell, ISA, GG
The Appraisal Office Of Elroy J. Sell
679 W North Avenue, Suite #101
Elmhurst, IL 60126
Phone: 847-833-7250
Fax: 847-833-7250
Gemology/Gemstones, Diamonds, Jewelry, Watches (Pocket & Wrist)

Colin Sinclair Reed, ISA
Prairieland Estate Services
7632 Monroe St
Forest Park, IL 60130-1723
Phone: 708-771-5448
Fax: 708-383-9256
Estates (Including Liquidations)

Marcia P. Crosby, ISA
Marcia Crosby Antiques
477 Forest Ave
Glen Ellyn, IL 60137-4104
Phone: 630-858-5665
Antiques, Pottery, Ceramics, China (White Ironstone), Residential Contents (Appreciable), Decorative Arts & Accessories, Americana, Books, Maps, Prints, Collectibles, Damage Claims, Insurance, Estates, Folk Art, Furniture

Carol A. Reiman, ISA
328 S Edson Ave
Lombard, IL 60148-2414
Phone: 630-620-7555
Fax: 630-620-7585
Quilts, Textiles

Stephanie M. Dooley, ISA
SMD ARTS, INC
PO Box 598
Medinah, IL 60157-0598
Phone: 630-529-3288
Fax: 630-529-3440
Fine Art, Prints (19th & 20th C.),
Engravings, Etchings, Sculpture,
Paintings

Carolyn Gianopoulos, ISA
Carole's Coach House Antiques
6 N 680 Palomino Dr
St. Charles, IL 60175-8439
Phone: 630-584-4374
Fax: 630-584-0057
Residential Contents, Antiques,
Collectibles, Glass, Damage Claims,
Estate Sales

Maurice E. Fry, ISA
570 Arlington St
Hoffman Estates, IL 60194-1929
Phone: 708-843-1533
Fax: 708-882-8292
Founder ISA; Lifetime Member

Jane L. Baker, ISA
1431 Seward St
Evanston, IL 60202-2077
Phone: 847-864-2150
Residential Contents, Victoriana
(Furniture, Toys), Estates

Mike J. Grippo, ISA
M & M Automobile Appraisers
4349 WN Peotone Rd
Beecher, IL 60401
Phone: 708-258-6662
Fax: 708-258-9675
Cars (Collectible, Antique, Custom),
Trucks, Automotive Literature,
Automotive Related Collectibles,
Trains, Investment Counselling

James F. Sunderland, Jr., ISA CAPP,
GG
James & Sons, Ltd.
239 Gold Coast Ln
Calumet City, IL 60409-6096
Phone: 708-862-3800
Rare Coins, Diamonds, Jewelry
(Antique)
CAPP In Antique & Period Jewelry

Barbara Skeens, ISA
Keeper's Finder
2889 Hoberg Dr
Joliet, IL 60432-0717
Phone: 815-722-2345
Fax: 815-722-2333
Furs, Residential Contents (Appre-
ciable), Ceramics, Antiques,
Consultant

Harry Carpenter, ISA
Days of Yesteryear
2429 Dougall Rd
Joliet, IL 60433-1601
Phone: 815-722-8014
Antiques, Collectibles, Glass

David V. Trout, ISA
David V. Trout Appraisals
28 Monee Rd
Park Forest, IL 60466-2107
Phone: 708-748-3518
Art (19th & Early 20th C.), American
& European Paintings, Hudson River
School, Indiana Artists, Midwest &
Chicago Artists, Folk Art, Americana

Gloria Moroni, ISA CAPP
Gloria Moroni, Appraiser
21 Spinning Wheel Rd
Hinsdale, IL 60521
Phone: 630-986-1945
Fax: 630-986-1954
E-mail: 76725.746@compuserve.com
Antiques, Residential Contents, Silver,
Porcelain, Pottery, Ceramics, Antique
Furniture, Glass, Estates
CAPP In Appreciable Residential
Contents

Jane F. Washburn, ISA CAPP
Washburn & Associates
5 Morgan Ct
Burr Ridge, IL 60521-8339
Phone: 630-325-3115
Fax: 630-325-2144
E-mail: 102444.364@compuserve.com
Residential Contents, Antiques,
Decorative Arts & Accessories,
Furniture, Consultant
CAPP In Appreciable Residential
Contents

Carol J. Hutton, ISA
15 W Harris Ave
La Grange, IL 60525-2333
Phone: 708-579-5299
Fax: 708-352-2042
Antiques, Collectibles, Residential
Contents

Dinah J. Thompson, ISA
401 S Park Rd
La Grange, IL 60525-6110
Phone: 847-354-8775
Arts & Crafts, Jewelry, Metalwork,
Textiles, Pottery, Furniture,
Decorative Arts & Acccessories,
Modern Movement

Judith M. Martin, ISA CAPP
M & M Sales
1405 Culpepper Dr
Naperville, IL 60540-8310
Phone: 630-548-1436
E-mail: 76571.2141@compuserve.com
Estate Sales, Collectibles, Depre-
ciable & Appreciable Personal
Property, Office Furniture &
Equipment, Decorative Arts &
Accessories, Collectibles
CAPP In Appreciable Residential
Contents

Heidi A. Feithen, ISA CAPP, GG
Chicago Gem Evaluation Services, Inc.
5 North Wabash, Ste 1615
Chicago, IL 60602
Phone: 312-578-0440
Gemology/Gemstones, Colored
Stones, Diamonds, Ivory, Jade,
Jewelry, Pearls, Minerals
CAPP In Gemstones

Farhad Radfar, ISA
MIR International Gallery & Appraiser
Svcs.
PO Box 10678
Chicago, IL 60610
Phone: 312-670-8510
Fax: 312-670-8182
E-mail: 105405.640@compuserve.com
Porcelain (Meissen), Paintings,
Oriental Rugs, Furs

Byla Simon Kunis, ISA
Oriental Treasures
159 W Kinzie St, The Antiquarians
Building
Chicago, IL 60610-4514
Phone: 312-527-4848
Fax: 312-321-0313
Japanese & Chinese Antiques,
Porcelain, Jade, Ivory, Cloisonne

Marilyn Dresser, ISA
Dresser International
680 N Lake Shore Dr, Apt 1401
Chicago, IL 60611-4407
Phone: 312-642-4011
Fine Art, Antiques, Art & Crafts,
Glass (European & American)

Maureen F. Perou, ISA
Estate Excellence
2673 N Orchard St
Chicago, IL 60614-1548
Phone: 312-935-0715
Fax: 312-935-0715
Antiques, Furniture, Residential
Contents, Glassware, China

Donald Shannon, ISA
Graphic Appraisal Services, Inc.
9820 S Damen Ave
Chicago, IL 60643-1702
Phone: 312-233-5235
Fax: 312-233-2829
Machinery & Equipment (Graphic
Arts, Lithography), Business
Evaluations, Consultant, Liquidators,
Auctioneer

Vernon C. Thomson, Jr., ISA
PO Box 80
Vermont, IL 61484-0080
Phone: 309-784-8381
Residential Contents, Antiques,
Collectibles, Decorative Arts &
Accessories, Victoriana

Robin Yaw, ISA
The Crystal Connection
507 W Wolf Rd
Peoria, IL 61614-2054
Phone: 309-692-2221
Fax: 309-692-2221
Swarovski Crystal Figurines

Stephen C. Johnson, Ph.D., ISA
Behavorial Images Inc.
302 Leland St, Suite #101
Bloomington, IL 61701-5646
Phone: 309-829-3931
Fax: 309-829-9677
E-mail: 72230.2505@compuserve.com
Audio-Visual Recorded Media,
Literature, Equipment; Motion Picture
Film & Video Moving Image Media,
Disc & Tape Sound Recordings, Still

Photography, Negatives, Transparen-
cies, Illustration Art, Animation Cels,
Sheet Music

Marcia Lenhart, ISA
RR 2, BOX 12
Georgetown, IL 61846-9406
Phone: 217-662-8644
Fax: 217-662-6899
Antiques, Residential Contents,
Jewelry, Auction Co.

Melanie M. Hill, ISA
PO Box 235
Tuscola, IL 61953
Phone: 217-253-3150
Fax: 217-253-4356
Antiques, Residential Contents,
Decorative Arts & Accessories

Virginia Cannon, ISA CAPP
The China House
801 W Eldorado St
Decatur, IL 62522-2122
Phone: 217-428-7212
Fax: 217-422-8906
E-mail: 76573.376@compuserve.com
Residential Contents, Antiques,
Collectibles, Haviland China,
Dinnerware
CAPP In Appreciable Residential
Contents

Sally Hatcher, ISA
Hatcher Appraisals
PO Box 616
Lincoln, IL 62656-0616
Phone: 217-735-2649
Antiques, Tribal Art, Beadwork,
Beads, Buttons

Susan M. Donnelly, ISA
White Rose Antiques
221 Springcreek Drive
Springfield, IL 62702
Phone: 217-787-2721
Jewelry, Decorative Arts, Vintage
Ladies Items, Antiques

Lorraine R. O'Hern, ISA CAPP
700 East Miller St
Springfield, IL 62702
Phone: 217-523-0998
Antiques, American Furniture (18th-
20th C.), Decorative Arts &
Accessories, Residential Contents,
Estate Sales
CAPP In Appreciable Residential
Contents

Deborah Lauer-Toelle, ISA, CGA GG
Stout & Lauer Jewelers
1650 Wabash Ave
Springfield, IL 62704-5357
Phone: 217-546-4200
Fax: 217-793-8746
Gemology/Gemstones, Diamonds,
Jewelry

Marian Erb, ISA
Locust Street Gallery
PO Box 508
Centralia, IL 62801-0508
Phone: 618-533-1699
Fax: 618-533-8616
Airplanes, Antiques, Estates, Residential Contents

Michele Campbell, ISA
APEX Appraisal Services
PO Box 21713
Saint Louis, MO 63109-3441
Phone: 314-752-5039
E-mail: 75562.1536@compuserve.com
Appraisal Service, Antiques, Residential Contents, Household Contents

Carol M. Sumpter, ISA
Cardan's Doll Shop
3808 Loughborough Ave
St. Louis, MO 63116-3015
Phone: 314-351-7955
Dolls & Accessories (Antique & Collectible Dolls), Toys (Collectible)

James Roedel, ISA
1414 Frances Rd
St. Louis, MO 63122-2305
Phone: 314-821-4015
Fax: 314-821-4015
Cars (Antique, Classic, Special Interest, Reproduction, Sports, Foreign, Late Models), R.V's, Motor Home, Tucks, Trailers, Recreational Boats, Machinery & Equipment

Lee DeKriek, ISA
The Antique Merchant
102 Paula Drive
Sikeston, MO 63801
Phone: 573-472-4484
Antiques, Estate Sales, Furniture, Paper Goods, Marbles

Ted R. Young, ISA, GG
Tivol Jewels
220 Nichols Rd
Kansas City, MO 64112-1580
Phone: 816-531-5800
Diamonds, Gemology, Gemstones, Jewelry, Pearls, Watches

Ronald I. Zoglin, ISA
Brookside Antiques
6219 Oak St
Kansas City, MO 64113-2292
Phone: 816-444-4774
Woodblock Prints (Japanese), Oriental Art, Antiques, Silver, Decorative Arts & Accessories, Jewelry

John D. Conklin, ISA
2443 S Suprema Ave
Springfield, MO 65807-8130
Phone: 417-889-1782
Fax: 417-886-2934
Orientalia, Gemology/Gemstones (Jewelry), Netsuke/Inro/Ojime, Antiques, Collectibles, Fine Art, Icons, Oriental Art, Woodblock Prints, Ivory, Jade

Ann J. Steinberg, ISA, GG
PO Box 4665
Springfield, MO 65808-4665
Phone: 417-887-9062
Gemology/Gemstones, Diamonds, Jewelry, Watches, Estates, Insurance

David M. Solomons, ISA
David M. Solomons, Antiques, Art, Appraiser
PO Box 266
Baldwin City, KS 66006-0266
Phone: 913-594-4064
Residential Contents, Antiques, Collectibles, Art, Vintage Items, Broker

Susan B Reffitt-Dixon, ISA
Better Than Bass
5331 Monrovia
Shawnee, KS 66216
Phone: 913-962-9452
Collectibles, Antiques, Residential Contents

Robert K. Petro, ISA
Petro's Minitique
4400 SW Colly Creek Dr
Topeka, KS 66610-1167
Phone: 913-232-2165
Antiques, Silver, Furniture (American & English), Residential Contents, China, Collectibles

Robert L. Dunlap, II, ISA
Equity Standard
8237 E Kellogg Dr
Wichita, KS 67207-1811
Phone: 316-689-8773
Coins, U.S. Coins & Currency (But Not Limited To), Gold, Bullion (Scrap & Other Forms)

Mary R. Heim, ISA
Mary Heim Antiques/Appraisals
890 State Road 14
Lyons, KS 67554-9242
Phone: 913-841-3930
Antiques, Residential Contents

Marvin Mann, ISA
219 SW 8th St
Plainville, KS 67663-3320
Phone: 913-434-2492
Fax: 913-434-4689
Coins, Glass (Glassware), Toys, Collectibles, Antiques

Eric Bauer, ISA
Russell's Cleaning Services, Inc.
3704 Robertson
Metairie, LA 70001-5846
Phone: 504-832-1546
Fax: 504-832-9958
Cleaning & Restoration, Rugs, Oriental Rugs, Draperies

Lee Clinkscales, ISA
Appraisers of Estates & Sales of Contents
3809 East View Dr
Harvey, LA 70058
Phone: 504-340-4287
Estates, Liquidators

J. William Rosenthal, MD, ISA
New Orleans Eye Specialists
1320 Valence St
New Orleans, LA 70115-3934
Phone: 504-891-1988
Fax: 504-899-1895
Antiques (Ophthalmic & Optical), Edged Weapons, Ladies Steel Beaded Bags, Antiques

Sherry L. Kohlert, ISA
Erudite Art
605 N Alexander St
New Orleans, LA 70119-4511
Phone: 504-486-0257
Fax: 504-866-7795
Antiques, Victoriana, Clothing, Collectibles

Ward J. Stewart, ISA
Stewart's Antiques
1000 Coolidge, Change
Lafayette, LA 70503
Phone: 318-232-2957
Antiques, China, Porcelain (American & Continental), Crystal, Glass (Both Cut And Art), Furniture

Polly R. Enloe, ISA
Century Antiques & Appraisals
212 Miller St
Lafayette, LA 70503-2522
Phone: 318-234-7146
Antiques, Glass (Art), Appreciable Personal Property

Thomas H. Shelton, II, ISA, GG
1326 W Pinhook Rd, #200
Lafayette, LA 70503-2906
Phone: 318-233-2612
Gemology/Gemstones, Jewelry (Estate), Diamonds, Metals (Precious)

Kim B. Graham, ISA
Grahams Antiques
307 Cornelius Dr
Lafayette, LA 70508-6205
Phone: 318-988-5049
Fax: 318-237-8371
Antiques & Residential Contents, Antique Furniture - 18th & 19th Century American, English, French, Austrian & German

Stephen H. Martin, ISA CAPP
1455 Charmaine Ave
Baton Rouge, LA 70806-7717
Phone: 504-923-3437
Fax: 504-923-3437
E-mail: 76025.367@compuserve.com
Residential Contents, Antiques, Fine Art, Firearms, Cars, Trucks, Office Furniture & Equipment, Clocks, Auctioneer, Auction Co.
CAPP In Appreciable Residential Contents

Phillip D. Peck, ISA
Revpro Appraisal Service
4021 Indian Run Dr
Baton Rouge, LA 70816-3571
Phone: 504-755-7002
Fax: 504-755-0302
E-mail: 102432.1674@compuserve.com
Heavy Trucks & Trailers, Farm Equipment & Machinery, Industrial,
Manufacturing, Oil Field, FF&E, Restaurant Equipment, Machinery & Equipment, Industrial & Manufacturing, Drilling & Service Equipment

Jess A. Gideon, ISA, CAI
Gideon's Good Earth Real Estate Auction
130 Treasure Isle Rd
Hot Springs, AR 71913-8415
Phone: 501-767-6221
Fax: 501-767-0657
Estates, Probates, Auctioneer, Personal (Residential Contents) Selling Real Estate And Personal Property At Auction)

Shea Crain, ISA
Hertiage House Antiques
351 N Highland Ave
Fayetteville, AR 72701-4256
Phone: 501-582-5653
Fax: 501-582-5653
E-mail: 105150.2374@compuserve.com
Antiques, Collectibles, Residential Contents, Decorative Arts, Estates

Karen Hamby, ISA
Hamby's Antiques & Collectibles
3490 Remington
Springdale, AR 72764
Phone: 501-756-6650
Antiques & Residential Contents

Richard L. Watts, ISA
89er Antique Mall
810 E Warner Ave
Guthrie, OK 73044-3635
Phone: 405-282-2661
Czech Collectibles, Depression Glass, 1904 World's Fair Collectibles

Scott M. Gordon, ISA, GG FGA
Scott Gordon Jeweler
50 Penn Pl, Ste 334R
Oklahoma City, OK 73118-1841
Phone: 405-843-7856
Fax: 405-848-5921
Diamonds, Colored Stones, Contemporary & Period Jewelry From Victorian Onward

Mary Lyn Livingston, ISA CAPP
M. Livingston & Assoc. Appraisal, Claims & Estate Services
4709 NW 76th St
Oklahoma City, OK 73132-5318
Phone: 405-722-1475
Fax: 405-722-1475
E-mail: 76235.1441@compuserve.com
Residential Contents, Antiques, Collectibles, Estates, Insurance, Damage Claims, Liquidators, Furniture, American Glass, Wave Crest, Vintage Radios Alt Bus#: 405-722-7034
CAPP In Appreciable Residential Contents

John C. West, ISA
West of Boston
300 S Wyandotte Ave
Bartlesville, OK 74003-4038
Phone: 918-336-3277
E-mail: jcwest3@wow.com
Art, Antiques, Oriental Rugs

Tom E. Hill, ISA
The Woodshed
11367 E 61st St S
Broken Arrow, OK 74012-1272
Phone: 918-355-2697
*Furniture (1700's To Present),
Repairs, Restoration, Preservation
And Conservation (Furniture), Wood
Carvings, Damage Claims, Court
Testimony*

Debora Riggs Grillot, ISA
Estate & Consignment Sales &
   Appraisals
1820 E 37th St
Tulsa, OK 74105-8109
Phone: 918-743-4515
Oriental Textiles, Estate Liquidator

Janell Lyle, ISA
Lyle's Appraisals
439 S Darlington Ave
Tulsa, OK 74112-1453
Phone: 918-832-7905
Antiques, Residential Contents

Pat Anderson, ISA
Anderson Appraisal Service
6529 E Pine Pl
Tulsa, OK 74115-4608
Phone: 918-838-7779
*Residential Contents, Glass,
Collectibles, Pottery, Ceramics,
(American Art Pottery), Estate
Liquidator*

Connie J. Fletcher, ISA
6711 S Quincy Ave
Tulsa, OK 74136-3803
Phone: 918-492-1273
*Residential Contents, Antiques,
Collectibles, Estates, Liquidators*

Kay W. Barlow, ISA
Classique Glass
PO Box 52572
Tulsa, OK 74152-4964
Phone: 918-742-0862
*Antiques & Residential Contents,
American Sterling Silver, American
Tableware*

Earl H. Johnson, ISA
Classique Glass Co.
PO Box 52572
Tulsa, OK 74152-4964
Phone: 918-744-5307
*Antiques & Residential Contents, Art
Glass, American Sterling Silver,
Furniture*

Lorrie R. Semler, ISA CAPP
Semler Appraisals
2000 Via Corona
Carrollton, TX 75006-4615
Phone: 972-416-3417
Fax: 972-416-1122
E-mail: 75233.2255@compuserve.com
*RESIDENTIAL CONTENTS:
Including Furniture, Antiques, Glass,
China, Pottery, Insurance, Damage
Claims, Estate Probate, Equitable
Distribution*
**CAPP In Appreciable Residential
Contents**

Brenda Simonson-Mohle, ISA
Signet Art
2211 High Point Circle
Carrollton, TX 75007-1705
Phone: 972-306-1963
Fax: 972-306-1963
E-mail: 103752.2066@compuserve.com
*Fine Art, Paintings, Watercolors,
Drawings, Prints, Graphics, Etching,
Engravings, Sculpture, Woodblock
Prints, Contemporary American &
European Art, Folk Art, Art
Consultant Alt e-mail:
sigart7@airmail.net*

Bob Webb, ISA
Robert Webb & Associates, Inc.
2411 Glen Morris Rd
Carrollton, TX 75007-2016
Phone: 214-306-8556
Fax: 214-306-7970
*Machinery & Equipment (All, Types),
Business Evaluations-Inventory,
Construction Equipment, Real Estate*

Cynthia L. Webb, ISA
Robert Webb & Associates, Inc
2411 Glen Morris Rd
Carrollton, TX 75007-2016
Phone: 214-306-8556
Fax: 214-306-7970
Antiques

Leonard Ciesla, ISA
Price Waterhouse
3816 Townbluff Dr
Plano, TX 75023-8013
Phone: 972-867-6292
Machinery & Equipment

Marigold Lamb, ISA
Lamb Appraisals
106 Autumn Trl
Rockwall, TX 75087-8816
Phone: 972-771-9664
Fax: 972-771-9664
*Furniture (European), Decorative
Arts & Accessories (European),
Residential Contents, Antiques*

Ellen Amirkhan, ISA CAPP
Oriental Rug Cleaning Co. Inc.
3907 Ross Ave
Dallas, TX 75204-5248
Phone: 214-821-9135
Fax: 214-821-9136
Oriental Rugs
CAPP In Oriental Rugs

Avie C. Kalker, ISA
Avie C. Kalker Enterprises
5805 Birchbrook Dr
Dallas, TX 75206-4507
Phone: 214-373-7656
Fax: 214-373-7656
*Fine Art, Household Contents,
Decorative Arts & Access., Furniture,
Porcelain, Cut Glass, Art Glass,
Silver, Watches, Books, Estate
Settlement/Sales; Consultant &
Broker; Damage Claims, Dealer*

Alan Winston Smith, ISA, GG
Winston Studio & Imports
5914 Vanderbilt Ave
Dallas, TX 75206-6136
Phone: 214-357-0081
Fax: 214-821-8583
E-mail: orehouse@connect.net
*Expert Witness, Copyright, Jewelry,
NAFTA, Arts & Crafts, Faberge,
Consultant, Gemology/Gemstones,
Jewelry, Religious Items, Silver, Fine
Art 76657.11372compuserve.com*

Kathy Finch, ISA
5815 La Vista Ct
Dallas, TX 75206-7211
Phone: 214-824-4684
*Personal Property, Residential
Contents, Antiques, Decorative Arts &
Accessories, Estate Sales*

Shelley S. Stevens, ISA
SMS Fine Arts Corporation
1435 Slocum St
Dallas, TX 75207-3810
Phone: 214-748-1177
Fax: 214-748-1491
*Antiques (Fine French & Italian,
Chandeliers), Paintings, Watercolors,
Drawings (Antique European &
American, Thru 1930), Decorative
Arts & Accessories (Antique French &
Italian), Lamps, Lighting Fixtures*

James Erwin Jessup, ISA
JEJ Enterprises - The Appraisal Group
PO Box 12382
Dallas, TX 75225-0382
Phone: 214-364-1334
Fax: 214-351-0877
E-mail: 73531.3555@compuserve.com
*Antiques, Collectibles, Decorative
Arts & Accessories, Furniture, Glass,
Office FF&E, Porcelain, Pottery,
Ceramics, China, Residential
Contents, Silver, Estates, Insurance,
Litigation Support, Liquidators*

Vicki S. Harris, ISA
Gaither Harris Estate Sales
3521 Centenary Ave
Dallas, TX 75225-5014
E-mail: 103244.1313@compuserve.com
*Furniture, Residential Contents,
Antiques, Collectibles, Estates*

Barbara Gaither, ISA
Gaither Harris Estate Sale
2801 Lovers Lane
Dallas, TX 75225-7906
Phone: 214-691-0670
Fax: 214-691-6397
*Ext #11 On Fax Machine. Furniture,
Residential Contents, Antiques,
Liquidator, Estates*

Martilla Williams, ISA
Attic Galleries
9302 Canter Dr
Dallas, TX 75231-1406
Phone: 214-348-5162
*Estate Sales, Moving Sales (General
Household Goods)*

Carolyn K. Sherman, ISA, GG
Carolyn K. Sherman, Inc.
7515 Greenville Ave, Ste 903
Dallas, TX 75231-3890
Phone: 214-360-0444
Fax: 214-360-0445
E-mail: 102772.443@compuserve.com
Gemology/Gemstones, Jewelry

Martha L. Tips, ISA CAPP
For All Time Enterprises
7012 Blackwood Dr
Dallas, TX 75231-5706
Phone: 214-348-0075
Fax: 214-349-0095
E-mail: 102733.667@compuserve.com
*Antique Clocks, Estates - Clocks Only,
Clock Repair & Restoration,
Specialty Sales: Clocks*
CAPP In Clocks

Jerry Forrest, ISA CAPP, GG CGA
Jewelry Forrest, Inc.
9100 N Central Expy, Ste 185
Dallas, TX 75231-5901
Phone: 800-368-5376
Fax: 214-750-1141
E-mail: 102152.2165@compuserve.com
*Gemstones, Diamonds, Custom
Jewelry, Gold, Estates, AGS Certified
Gem Laboratory*
CAPP In Gemstones

Shane Beeson, ISA
The Christopher Company, Ltd.
6500 Cedar Springs Rd
Dallas, TX 75235-5813
Phone: 214-352-9800
Fax: 214-358-2188
*Antiques, Residential Contents,
Ceramics, Liquidators, Americana*

Karen Nelson, ISA
Art Appraisal Services Ltd
6616 Spring Valley Rd
Dallas, TX 75240-8635
Phone: 214-239-6762
Fax: 214-239-1462
E-mail: 105004.376@compuserve.com
*Art, Fine Art, Paintings, Prints,
Sculpture*

John A. Buxton, ISA
Art Trak, Inc. or Shango Galleries
6717 Spring Valley Rd
Dallas, TX 75240-8636
Phone: 214-239-4620
Fax: 214-239-9766
E-mail: 70304.257@compuserve.com
*Art (American Indian, Alaskan Indian,
Eskimo, African, Pre-Columbian,
Oceanic, Archeological)*

Shirley B. Williams, ISA
Shirley's Selections
10024 Chimney Hill Ln
Dallas, TX 75243-2906
Phone: 972-392-4733
*Estates, Residential Contents,
Liquidators, Antiques, Collectibles*

Kenna Elkins Rosen, ISA, CPA
Rosen Appraisals & Estate Sales
12225 Greenville Ave, Ste 800
Dallas, TX 75243-9338
Phone: 214-479-8811
Fax: 214-479-8809
*Residential Contents, Books
(Especially Children's), Glassware,
Tax Consulting*

Trudy Miller, ISA
Trudy Miller Antiques
4021 Morman Lane
Dallas, TX 75244-2602
Phone: 972-490-5758
Fax: 972-502-5134
*Glass (All Types - Pattern to Art),
American Silver (Sterling & Plate),
Porcelain*

Virginia Montfort, ISA
De Montfort's Fine Art
PO Box 820152
Dallas, TX 75382-0152
Phone: 214-696-2615
*Fine Art, Paintings, Watercolors,
Drawings, Prints (Limited Edition),
Objet D'Art, Porcelain, China,
Paintings, Estates, Insurance,
Damage Claims Specialist*

Guinn D. Henderson, ISA
Superior Appraisals
3602 S Cameron St
Tyler, TX 75701-9107
Phone: 512-697-0700
Fax: 903-839-4909
E-mail: ghenderson@tyler.net
*Cars, Trucks (Construction),
Machinery & Equipment (Construc-
tion, Oil Field), Oil Field (Drilling
Well Service, Pipeline Construction),
Energy Equipment*

Larry G. Lough, ISA
Appraisal Systems Inc.
PO Box 131270
Tyler, TX 75713-1270
Phone: 903-839-7029
Fax: 903-839-4909
*Oil Field, Machinery & Equipment
(Farm, Construction, Transportation,
Industrial), Boats, Yachts, Livestock,
Airplanes, Cars, Trucks, Auctioneer,
Medical Equipment, High Tech,
Computers, Restaurant & Food
Equipment, Textiles, Forestry Equ*

Dana C. Staples, ISA
Dana C. Staples
909 Hunter Dr
Palestine, TX 75801-5014
Phone: 903-723-5059
*Residential Contents, Estates,
Antiques, Furniture, Liquidators*

Stephen Neel, ISA, CGA
Neel Jewelers
PO Box 1516
Palestine, TX 75802-1516
Phone: 903-729-1750
Fax: 903-729-2193
*Gemology/Gemstones, Diamonds,
Jewelry*

Margaret Toler, ISA
Margaret Toler & Associates Appraisal
Services
PO Box 120774
Arlington, TX 76012
Phone: 817-275-0811
Fax: 817-461-3046
*Antiques, Residential Contents,
Decorative Arts, Estates*

Adelia Hale-Stanley, Ph.D., ISA
Hale-Stanley, Inc.
1800 Tennyson Dr
Arlington, TX 76013-6429
Phone: 817-265-8990
Fax: 817-265-8990
E-mail: 76331.1330@compuserve.com
*Residential Contents, Collectibles,
Glass, Porcelain, Ceramics, Office
Furniture & Equipment*

Richard I. Pongratz, ISA, GG
Gemological Services
PO Box 13130
Arlington, TX 76094
Phone: 817-457-1019
Fax: 817-457-1019
E-mail: Rpongratz@aol.com
*Gemology/Gemstones, Jewelry,
Diamonds, Colored Stones*

Charles Johnston, ISA
Classical Furniture Restoration
1601 Hurley St
Fort Worth, TX 76104
Phone: 817-923-6717
Antiques, Restoration, Furniture

Nan B. Shelton, ISA CAPP
Assets Appraisal & Sales Inc.
PO Box 121337
Fort Worth, TX 76121-1337
Phone: 817-737-0680
Fax: 817-737-8277
*Residential Contents, Antiques, Silver,
Furniture, Glass, Porcelain, Quilts,
Collectibles, Victoriana, Decorative
Arts, Estates Insurance, Damage
Claims, Liquidators*
**CAPP In Appreciable Residential
Contents**

Gail Loveman Cohen, ISA, GG
Gem Consultants
4747 S Hulen St, Ste 109
Fort Worth, TX 76132-1413
Phone: 817-346-2611
Fax: 817-370-8720
*Gemology/Gemstones, Colored
Stones, Diamonds, Pearls, Jewelry
(Contemporary, Antique, Art, Period,
Art Deco, Art Nouveau, Arts & Crafts,
Victorian, Georgian), Gold,
Insurance, Estates, Liquidation*

Stanley P. Cohen, ISA, GG
Gem Consultants
4747 S Hulen St, Ste 109
Ft. Worth, TX 76132-1413
Phone: 817-346-2611
Fax: 817-370-8720
*Gemology/Gemstones, (Colored
Stones), Pearls, Diamonds, Jewelry
(Contemporary, Antique Art, Period,
Art Deco, Art Nouveau, Arts And*

*Crafts, Victorian, Georgian)
Insurance, Estates, Liquidation*

Rick Russell, ISA
Superior Auctioneers
109 Carrizo
Bowie, TX 76230
Phone: 210-697-0777
Fax: 210-697-9744
*Construction Equipment, Trucks,
Trailers, Oil Field Equipment, Energy
Related Equipment*

Louis Edward Rork, ISA
Trappings
2503 W Ave K
San Angelo, TX 76901-3748
Phone: 915-949-7078
*Residential Contents, Furniture,
Antiques*

Virginia L. McNeely, ISA
Estate Sale Management
2923 Wroxton Rd
Houston, TX 77005-4024
Phone: 713-661-0449
Fax: 713-524-5319
E-mail: esmhoutx@aol.com
*Residential Contents, Estates,
Liquidators, Antiques, Collectibles*

Marjorie M. Jennings, ISA
Appraisals & Estate Sales
2104 Brentwood
Houston, TX 77019-3512
Phone: 713-526-5829
*Estate Sales & Appraisals, Residential
Contents, Antiques, Silver, Insurance*

Sidney Taylor McKenzie, ISA
McKenzie Galleries & Commercial
7026 Old Katy Rd, Suite 161
Houston, TX 77024-2110
Phone: 713-863-1213
Fax: 713-863-1216
*Residential Contents, Furniture,
Commercial Equipment, Estates,
Decorative Arts & Accessories*

Winston A. McKenzie, ISA
McKenzie Galleries & Commercial
7026 Old Katy Rd, Suite 161
Houston, TX 77024-2110
Phone: 713-863-1213
Fax: 713-863-1216
*Furniture, Decorative Arts &
Accessories, Residential Contents,
Furniture Repair, Restoration &
Preservation, Damage Claims,
Costumes & Textiles, Cars (Antique),
Charitable Contributions, Office
Furniture & Equip.*

Shelley Sandler, ISA, GG
Gemological Appraisers
8020 Braesmain Dr, Apt 1804
Houston, TX 77025-2825
Phone: 713-663-7610
E-mail: 105507.3147@compuserve.com
*Jewelry (Estate), Diamonds,
Gemology/Gemstones*

Lorian Welsh, ISA
Shamrock Estate Sales
3122 Fairhope St
Houston, TX 77025-3229
Phone: 713-522-5551
*Estate Sales, Residential Contents,
Antiques, Collectibles, Vintage
Clothing, Real Estate*

Rachel Pabst, ISA CAPP
Rachel Pabst Appraisal Associates
4032 Sul Ross St
Houston, TX 77027-5720
Phone: 713-626-0179
Fax: 713-877-1415
*Antiques, Residential Contents,
Americana, Estate, Furniture,
Ceramics, Silver, Glass, Victoriana*
**CAPP In Appreciable Residential
Contents**

Rose Laurette Proler, ISA, GG
Rose Proler, Inc.
5433 Westheimer, #1105
Houston, TX 77056
Phone: 713-627-3098
Fax: 713-627-0504
*Gemology/Gemstones, Jewelry,
Diamonds, Pearls*

Samuel Abraham, ISA
Abrahams Oriental Rugs
5120 Woodway Dr, Ste 6010
Houston, TX 77056-1724
Phone: 713-622-4444
*Antiques, Carpets & Rugs (Including
Oriental), Needlework, Tapestries,
Textiles, Silks, Porcelain, Pottery,
Ceramics, China, Decorative Art,
Accessories, Insurance, Investment
Counselling, Auctioneer, Auction Co.*

Diana Livingston-Erwin, ISA
Diana P. Livingston Antiques
6255 San Felipe St
Change
Houston, TX 77057-2809
Phone: 713-974-2947
*Antiques, Residential Contents,
Liquidations, Estate Sales*

Diana P. Livingston, ISA
Diana P. Livingston Antiques
6255 San Felipe St
Houston, TX 77057-2809
Phone: 713-974-2947
*Antiques, Residential Contents,
Liquidations, Estate Sales*

Sibley Kopmeier, ISA
Sibley Kopmeier Appraisal Assoc.
2407 Jamestown Mall
Houston, TX 77057-4509
Phone: 713-784-4863
Fax: 713-977-7121
*Antiques, Decorative Arts &
Accessories, Porcelain, Furniture &
Collectibles (19th & 20th C.)*

R. Rebecca Moncrief, ISA
Becky Moncrief
2007 Sea Cove Ct
Houston, TX 77058-4228
Phone: 281-333-3672
Fax: 281-333-0201
E-mail: becky@ufdc.org
Dolls, Doll Houses & Accessories (Antique, Modern), Toys, Miniatures, Antiques, Collectibles

Patricia Stone, ISA
Personal Property Appraisals
2200 S Gessner, #400
Houston, TX 77063-2009
Phone: 713-977-0116
Residential Contents, Antiques, Fine Art, Decorative Arts & Accessories, Furniture, China, Crystal, Silver, Collectibles, Dolls, Office Furniture & Equipment, Insurance, Estates

Betty W. Boyd, ISA
Boyd Appraisal Service
13 Woodlake Square, #340
Houston, TX 77063-3206
Phone: 713-827-0446
Antiques, Furniture, Silver, Glass (Art), Household Goods, Residential Contents, Divorce Cases, Furniture, Oriental Rugs

O. Craig Fashoro, ISA
African Quintessence
6134 Havendale Dr
Houston, TX 77072-1524
Phone: 713-495-9946
Fax: 713-495-9946
E-mail: 104036.2665@compuserve.com
African Antiques And Artifacts, Contemporary African Art, African Fabric And Handmade Textiles

June Adair, ISA
Adair Appraisals & Estate Sales
1311 Devon Glen Dr
Houston, TX 77077-3211
Phone: 713-861-7711
Fax: 713-496-6234
Americana, Antiques, Art Deco, Art Nouveau, Arts & Crafts, Bronzes, Carpet/Rugs, Ceramics, China, Clocks, Clothing, Collectibles,. Consultant, Crystal, Damage Claims, Decorative Art, Dinnerware, Estates, Figurines, Lamps, Insurance Claims

Judy L. Robinson, ISA
Judy Robinson Gallery, Inc.
2828 Bammel Lane, #206 & 208
Houston, TX 77098
Phone: 713-522-7509
Fax: 713-522-7498
Fine Art, Paintings, Furniture, Decorative Arts, Estates

David E. Newman, ISA
Newman & Assoc. Appraisers & Auctioneers
PO Box 42809
Houston, TX 77242-2731
Phone: 713-783-1987
Antiques, Collectibles, Residential Contents, Damage Claims, Auctioneer.

Suzanne Staley, ISA
Independent Broker & Appraiser
PO Box 1288
Houston, TX 77251-1288
Phone: 713-222-6309
Fax: 713-223-3116
E-mail: 104512.1256@compuserve.com
Fine Art, General Residential Contents, Silver, Folk Art

Brian Blackstock, ISA
Best Finishing Co., Inc.
PO Box 90213
Houston, TX 77290-0213
Phone: 713-580-8620
Fax: 713-580-2423
Residential Contents, Repairs, Restorations, Preservation (Wood)

Beth Szescila, ISA CAPP
Szescila Appraisal Services
9546 Enstone Cir
Spring, TX 77379-6605
Phone: 281-376-4338
Fax: 281-251-0608
E-mail: 76751.2141@compuserve.com
Antiques, Collectibles, Quilts & Linens, Victoriana, Needlework, Sewing Collectibles, Furniture, Boxes, Silver, Porcelain, Pottery, Ceramics, China, Glass, Residential Contents
CAPP In Appreciable Residential Contents

Penny Millican, ISA
Towne & Country Estates
5319 Holly St
Bellaire, TX 77401-4805
Phone: 713-666-0970
Fax: 713-666-2715
Western Art & Bronzes, American Indian (Art, Artifacts, Textiles), Quilts, Costume Jewelry, Carousel Animals, Estates, Personal Property, Residential Contents

Melissa Brookes, ISA, GG
D & M Diamonds
PO Box 1342
Cypress, TX 77410-1342
Identification Of Gemstones & Jewelry, Retail Replacement Value

Mike Hartman, ISA
Hendley Market
2010 Strand
Galveston, TX 77550
Phone: 409-762-2610
Fax: 409-762-9001
E-mail: hendley@phoenix.net
Antiques, Sales, Medical Antiques, Antique Books, Internet, Research

Linda H. Richard, ISA
Cajun Collection
3609 Oak Hill Dr
Bryan, TX 77802-4622
Phone: 409-846-3558
Glass, Porcelain, Pottery, Ceramics, Collectibles, Antiques

Ferol L. Rogers, ISA
Ferol L. Rogers & Co.
PO Box 33279
Kerrville, TX 78029-3279
Phone: 210-896-5959
Fax: 210-896-2879
Residential Contents, Antiques, Furniture, Ceramics, Victoriana, Primitives

Francois Duhau de Berenx, ISA
Francois De Berenx Art Advisor
115 E Wildwood Dr
San Antonio, TX 78212-1776
Phone: 210-829-4567
Fax: 210-829-4567
Antiques (French), Art (Oriental), Heraldic Works, Antique Books, Misc. Paper Items

Tara D. Kruse, ISA
Superior Auctioneers & Marketing, Inc.
11202 Disco
San Antonio, TX 78216
Phone: 210-697-0700
Fax: 210-697-9744
E-mail: http://www.saami.com
Cars & Trucks (Antique), Oil Field Equipment, Real Estate, Auctioneers, Boats And Yachts, Collectibles, Machinery & Equipment, Memorabilia

Tiffany Ann Kruse, ISA
Superior Auctioneers & Marketing
11202 Disco
San Antonio, TX 78216
Phone: 210-697-0700
Fax: 210-697-9744
E-mail: http://www.saami.com
Cars (Antique)

James Puckett, ISA
Superior Auctioneers & Marketing, Inc.
11202 Disco
San Antonio, TX 78216
Phone: 210-697-0700
Fax: 210-697-9744
E-mail: http://www.saami.com
Machinery & Equipment (Oil Field & Related Equipment), Cars (Antique), Real Estate

Rudy M. Pena, ISA, GG
Pena & Associates
7330 San Pedro Ave, Ste 544
San Antonio, TX 78216-6257
Phone: 210-349-4367
Fax: 210-366-1802
Gemology/Gemstones, Diamonds, Jewelry, Pearls, Estates (Jewelry)

Linda H. Roberts, ISA
Casagrande Appraisals
8546 Broadway, Suite 270-B
San Antonio, TX 78217-6340
Phone: 210-820-3535
Fax: 210-820-3535
E-mail: 104411.545@compuserve.com
Appreciable & Depreciable Residential Contents, Textiles

Richard Casagrande, ISA CAPP
Casagrande Appraisals
8546 Broadway St, Ste 270B
San Antonio, TX 78217-6376
Phone: 210-820-3535
Fax: 210-820-3535
E-mail: 104411.545@compuserve.com
Residential Contents, Fine Art, Decorative Arts & Accessories, Antiques, Collectibles, Furniture, Adjusters, Consultant
CAPP In Appreciable Residential Contents

Glen C. Skaggs, ISA CAPP
Classic Collections
74 Oakwell Farms Pky
San Antonio, TX 78218-1784
Phone: 210-822-5305
Glass (American Cut), Porcelain, Pottery, Ceramics, Silver, Furniture
CAPP In Appreciable Residential Contents

Larry Gumber, ISA
929 Misty Water Lane
San Antonio, TX 78258
Phone: 210-438-3597
Cars, Trucks, Construction Equipment & Machinery, Machinery & Equipment, Office Furniture & Equipment, Oil Field Equipment, Commercial Inventories

Patrick G. Perryman, ISA
Superior Auctioneers & Marketing
PO Box 786001
San Antonio, TX 78278-6001
Phone: 512-697-0700
Cars, Trucks, Trailers, Machinery & Equipment, (Construction, Oil Field, Well, Service), Auctioneer

Christopher B. Pierce, ISA
Superior Auctioneers & Marketing, Inc.
PO Box 786001
San Antonio, TX 78278-6001
Phone: 210-697-0700
Fax: 210-697-9744
Auctioneering/Sales, Oil Field Equipment, Classic Cars

Kelly D. Toney, ISA
Superior Auctioneers & Appraisals, Inc.
PO Box 792427
San Antonio, TX 78279-2427
Phone: 210-697-0700
Fax: 210-697-9744
Oil Field Equipment (Drilling & Production), Machinery & Equipment

Betty Gresham, ISA
Betty Gresham Antiques & Appraisals
10901 Leopard St
Corpus Christi, TX 78410-2609
Phone: 512-241-7062
Antiques, Porcelain, Pottery, Ceramics, China, Glass, Residential Contents, Estate (Liquidations)

Anita Eisenhauer, ISA
Anita's Antiques
11753 Up River Rd
Corpus Christi, TX 78410-3320
Phone: 512-241-7097
Fax: 512-241-7098
*Antiques, Residential Contents,
Decorative Arts & Accessories, Estate
Liquidations, Damage Claims*

Ruben Cavazos, ISA
5111 N Ware Rd
McAllen, TX 78504-5209
Phone: 210-687-5454
Fax: 210-687-5454
*Fine Arts, 18th, 19th, & 20th Century
Prints, Latin American Art (Bilin-
gual), Machinery & Equipment, Real
Estate*

Ted Brown, ISA
Austin Brown Gallery
PO Box 3324
Edinburg, TX 78540
Phone: 210-316-0090
*Antiques, Fine Art, Jewelry,
Collectibles*

Joan D. Jones, ISA
Joan Jones Appraisals
PO Box 545
In Harlingen Area
La Feria, TX 78559-0545
Phone: 210-412-1336
*Antiques, Mexican Retablos, Oriental
Rugs, Furniture, Glass, Paperweights,
Insurance, Estates, Residential
Contents*

Tom W. Carpenter, Jr., ISA
Lone Star Investments Corp.
PO Box 275
Marble Falls, TX 78654
Phone: 210-598-5971
Fax: 210-548-8180
*Machinery & Equipment, (Construc-
tion), Cars & Trucks, Airplanes*

Elisabeth W. Douglas, JD, ISA
The China Coast
11266 Taylor Draper Lane, #2024
Austin, TX 78759
Phone: 512-288-3043
*Asian Art, Oriental Art, Orientalia,
Ivory, Jade, Netsuke*

Betty A. Bray, ISA, FGA DGA
Spectrum Gems & Jewelry Appraisals
535 Apache Ln
Abilene, TX 79601-8251
Phone: 915-692-3874
Fax: 915-695-2839
Gemstones, Jewelry

Susan B. Eisen, ISA, GG
Susan Eisen Fine Jewelry
7500 N Mesa St, Ste 208
El Paso, TX 79912-3515
Phone: 915-584-0022
*Gemology/Gemstones, Jewelry
(Antique & Contemporary),
Diamonds, Watches (Contemporary &
Period)*

Charles R. Rosvall, ISA
C.W. Rosvall Auction
1238 S Broadway
Denver, CO 80210-1504
Phone: 303-722-4028
Fax: 303-777-2032
*Residential Contents, Cars, Trucks,
Coins, Currency, Auctioneer*

Mary Samora, ISA
Appriasals by Mary Samora &
Associates
541 Williams St
Denver, CO 80218-3639
Phone: 303-320-1019
*Residential Contents, Antiques,
Furniture, Estates, Collectibles,
Liquidators, Memorabilia*

Nikki C. Jersin, ISA
Nikki Jersin & Associates
2055 S Oneida St, Ste 190
Denver, CO 80224-2435
Phone: 303-758-2121
Fax: 303-758-4220
E-mail: 105517.2755@compuserve.com
*Antiques, Silver, Furniture,
Orientalia, Residential Contents*

Deborah E. Arden, ISA CAPP
Arden Van Wijk Associates, Inc.
PO Box 2515
Evergreen, CO 80437-2515
Phone: 303-567-0699
Fax: 303-567-0698
E-mail: 73573.1404@compuserve.com
*Art, Paintings, Drawings, Prints,
Sculpture, Bronzes*
CAPP In Limited Edition Prints

Harold G. Camp, ISA
Appraisal Specialties Of Colorado
PO Box 590
Fort Collins, CO 80522-0590
Phone: 970-282-9054
Fax: 970-282-8969
E-mail: 70512.217@compuserve.com
*Automobiles & Trucks 1897-1996
Recreational Vehicles, Motor homes,
Bus Conversions, Motorcycles, Boats,
Fine Art, 19th & 20th Century
Painting, Prints, Sculpture, Animation
Cels, Etc.*

Elise C. Hersey, ISA, GG
Elise C. Hersey, GG, Appraiser
PO Box 206
Niwot, CO 80544-0206
Phone: 303-581-9988
*Diamonds, Gemology/Gemstones,
Jewelry*

Debra M. Jensen, ISA
Rominger Jewelry, Inc.
PO Box 231
Sterling, CO 80751-0231
Phone: 303-522-2587
*Gemology, Gemstones, Diamonds,
Jewelry, Gold, Silver (Holloware,
Flatware)*

Christopher Jones, ISA
PO Box 50864
Colorado Springs, CO 80949-0864
Phone: 719-548-1876
*Native American Indian Jewelry,
Pottery, Kachinas Baskets &
Weavings In The Prehistoric &
Historic Periods From The Southwest-
ern United States*

Linda A. Guterman, ISA
Churchills, Ltd.
PO Box 110
Basalt, CO 81621
Phone: 970-927-3485
Fax: 970-927-9489
*Antique Furniture (American &
European), Depression Glass,
Decorative Art, Fine Art*

Barbara E. Smith, ISA
Spring Creek Appraisals
1402 25th St
PO Box 1723
Cody, WY 82414-1723
Phone: 307-587-2483
*Antiques (Glass, China), Furniture,
Residential Contents, Dinnerware,
Glass, Silver (Flatware & Holloware)*

Anne L. Shneider, ISA
2001 N 17th St
Boise, ID 83702-0802
Phone: 208-344-2618
*Antiques, Collectibles, Appreciable &
Depreciable Residential Contents,
Appraisal & Estate Services*

Jeanmarie Gorham, ISA
Waller, Gorham & Grant, Inc.
532 S Vista Ave
Boise, ID 83705
Phone: 208-381-0168
*American Art Pottery, Costume &
Sterling Silver Jewelry, Wedgwood*

Sharon Wakefield, ISA CAPP, GG
Northwest Gemological Lab
PO Box 8243
Boise, ID 83707-2243
Phone: 208-362-3938
Fax: 208-362-2889
E-mail: 70243.152@compuserve.com
*Jewelry, Gemology/Gemstones,
Diamonds*
CAPP In Gemstones

Sandra K. Bates, ISA
Professional Appraisal Services
830 Siony Lane, Apt D
Post Falls, ID 83854
Phone: 208-777-1033
Fax: 208-773-9874
E-mail: 102375.3565@compuserve.com
*Antiques, Collectibles, Residential
Contents, Estate Liquidation, Damage
Claims Specialist*

Karolyn L. Weber, ISA
Appraisal Service, Inc.
2200 N Alvarado Rd
Phoenix, AZ 85004-1414
Phone: 602-949-7798
*Art, Fine Art, Etchings, Engravings,
Prints, Residential & Office Contents,*

*Insurance, Damage Claims, Estates,
Testimony In Court (Expert Witness)*

Gail Guidry, ISA
2216 Cortez Street
Phoenix, AZ 85028-1711
Phone: 713-756-1802
*Photographs, Buttons, Czechoslova-
kian Pottery, Stamps/Postal History,
Prints*

Craig H. Jackson, ISA
Perfection Reflections
5552 E Washington
Phoenix, AZ 85034-2134
Phone: 602-941-5389
*Cars, Trucks, Preservation (Cars),
Auctioneer*

Jean K. Patten, ISA
Appraisal Service Ltd.
4222 E Agave Rd
Phoenix, AZ 85044-4618
Phone: 602-258-7267
Fax: 602-257-0710
*Antiques (English & American), Silver
(Sterling), Porcelain, Pottery, Metals*

Sindi J. Schloss, ISA, GG
Int'l Gemological Appraisal Service
2933 N. Hayden Rd
Scottsdale, AZ 85251
Phone: 602-947-5866
Fax: 602-949-1676
*Gemology/Gemstones, Colored
Stones, Jewelry (Contemporary),
Diamonds, Pearls, Beads*

Lorene A. Wilson, ISA
Appraisal Service, Inc.
6430 E Calle Redondo
Scottsdale, AZ 85251-4243
Phone: 602-970-8765
Fax: 602-949-0231
*Estates, American Indian, Residential
Contents*

Pat Sharpe, ISA
Pat Sharpe Enterprises, Inc.
5834 East Friess Drive
Scottsdale, AZ 85254
Phone: 602-953-3373
*Antiques, Fine Art, Residential
Contents, Bronzes, Damage Claims,
Estates, Silver*

Paul R. Barnes, ISA CAPP, GG CG
Barnes Gemological Resources
PO Box 31587
Mesa, AZ 85275-1587
Phone: 602-545-8585
Fax: 602-545-8585
*Gemology/Gemstones, Diamonds,
Jewelry, Gold, Watches, Pearls*
CAPP In Gemstones

Beverly A. Goss, ISA
4730 W Northern Ave, Unit 1103
Glendale, AZ 85301-8018
Phone: 602-943-3404
*Antiques, Silver, Residential Contents,
Estates*

Randy Anderson, ISA
Setterberg Anderson Jewelers
13545 W Camino Del Sol
Sun City West, AZ 85375-4416
Phone: 602-584-1546
Fax: 602-584-8896
*Jewelry, Gemology/Gemstones, Gold,
Watches, Diamonds*

Delia W. Sheldon, ISA
Green Vally Appraisal & Liquidation
PO Box 383
Green Valley, AZ 85622-0383
Phone: 602-625-4751
*Residential Contents, Collectibles,
Antiques*

Beatriz Bernal Castillo, ISA
Personal Property Appraisals
5025 E Oakmont Dr
Tucson, AZ 85718-1708
Phone: 520-577-7986
*Residential Contents, Decorative Arts,
Silver, American Furniture 1700's-
1990, Fine Arts, Art Glass, Estate
Sales*

Diana M. Warren, ISA
5555 N Via Alcalde
Tucson, AZ 85718-5107
Phone: 520-299-6645
*Residential Contents, Estates, Silver,
Decorative Arts, Antiques (South
American, Pre-Columbian), Limited
Fine Arts*

Diane V. Kruse, ISA CAPP
Art Appraisals Of Tucson
HC 1, Box 627
Tucson, AZ 85736-9712
Phone: 520-822-1842
Fax: 520-822-1842
E-mail: 74250.1555@compuserve.com
*Paintings, Sculpture, Prints,
Watercolors, Drawings*
CAPP In Paintings

James L. Lamerson, ISA, GG CGA
Lamerson's Jewelry & Lapidary Arts
105 N Cortez St
Prescott, AZ 86301-3015
Phone: 520-771-0921
*Gemology/Gemstones, Diamonds,
Jewelry, Repairs & Restoration*

Peter Eller, Ph.D., ISA
Peter Eller Gallery & Appraiser
206 Dartmouth Dr NE
Albuquerque, NM 87106-2114
Phone: 505-268-7437
*American Art, Hopi Kachinas &
Silver, Navajo Textiles & Silver, New
Mexico Paintings & Prints, SW
Artifacts [Pre-Columbian, Hispanic
(Colonial & Religious)], Pueblo
Pottery, Residential Contents, Zuni
Jewelry, Archeological Art, Insurance*

Kent W. McDonald, ISA
Appraisal & Connoisseur Assoc.
620 Sierra Dr SE
Albuquerque, NM 87108-3377
Phone: 505-265-2842
Fax: 505-265-2842
E-mail: kwmcd@indirect.com
*Paintings (Southwestern &
Contemporary), Fine Art Sculpture,
(Contemporary & Southwestern),
Drawings, Oil & Acrylic Paintings,
Residential Contents, Furniture,
Silver, Porcelain, Rugs, Fine Art,
Office Furniture & Equipment, N M
Estate Sa*

Mary E. McDonald, ISA CAPP
Appraisal & Connoisseur Assoc. (ACA)
620 Sierra Dr SE
Albuquerque, NM 87108-3377
Phone: 505-265-2842
Fax: 505-265-2842
*American Indian (Rugs, Jewelry,
Pottery), Residential Contents, Arts &
Crafts, Antiques, Fine Art, Textiles*
**CAPP In Appreciable Residential
Contents**

Claire N. Shuford, ISA CAPP, GG
7400 Montgomery Blvd NE, Ste 36
Albuquerque, NM 87109-1519
Phone: 505-884-3101
Fax: 505-883-4889
*Gemology/Gemstones, Jewelry,
Diamonds, Pearls, Gold*
CAPP In Gemstones

Eric M. Shelton, ISA, CGA
Shelton Jewelers, Ltd.
7001 Montgomery Blvd NE
Albuquerque, NM 87109-1580
Phone: 505-881-1013
Fax: 505-881-7006
*Diamonds, Gemology/Gemstones,
Gold Jewelry, Pearls*

Larry Phillips, ISA, GG
Phillips & Associates
2430 Juan Tabo Blvd NE
#275
Albuquerque, NM 87112-1818
Phone: 505-299-7999
Fax: 505-299-7999
E-mail: gemologist-appraiser.com/phill
*American Indian Jewelry, Contempo-
rary & Period Jewelry, Gemstones &
Minerals, Diamonds, Watches,*

Joan Caballero, ISA
Joan Caballero, Appraisals
PO Box 822
Santa Fe, NM 87504-0822
Phone: 505-982-8148
Fax: 505-982-7048
E-mail: 104513.1553@compuserve.com
*Art (Southwest American Indian,
Southwest Spanish Colonial), Fine Art
(Southwest Regional Paintings)*

Suzanne R. Clark, ISA
Rochelle Ltd.
PO Box 9107
Santa Fe, NM 87504-9107
Phone: 313-737-0122
Native American Art, Oriental Art

Ronald A. Urcioli, ISA CAPP, GG
The Pawn & Gunshop
1690 Duarte Dr
Henderson, NV 89014-3564
Phone: 702-435-1935
Fax: 702-564-9778
E-mail: 103625.1224@compuserve.com
*Diamonds, Gemstones, Gold And
Silver Jewelry, Alternate Phone No.
702-564-2676*
CAPP In Gemstones

Jeane Parris, ISA
Sugarplums, Etc.
2022 E Charleston Blvd
Las Vegas, NV 89104-2018
Phone: 702-385-6059
E-mail: 76462.3343@compuserve.com
*Antiques, Silver, Porcelain, Pottery,
Ceramics, China, Collectibles,
Decorative Arts & Accessories,
Perfume Bottles*

Homayoun Tony Molayem, ISA, GG
Daniel's Antiques
10750 Wilshire Blvd, #201
Los Angeles, CA 90024
Phone: 310-603-2600
Fax: 310-603-9200
E-mail: tonymolayem@msn.com
*Antiques, Jewelry, 19th Century
Porcelain, 19th Century Furniture*

Michael L. Wertz, Jr., ISA
Wertz Bros., Inc.
11879 Santa Monica Blvd
W. Los Angeles, CA 90025-2211
Phone: 310-477-4251
Estate Liquidators

Alexander Rose, ISA
Alexander Rose Appraiser and
Consultant
8300 Stewart Ave
Los Angeles, CA 90045-2749
Phone: 310-216-5735
Fax: 310-216-0435
E-mail:
arose@aol.com;105553.2667@comp
*Antiques, Residential Contents,
European And American Fine Art,
Furniture, Decorative Arts, Appraiser,
Auctioneer*

Benyamin Sassoon, ISA
Arte Galleries
8820 Beverly Blvd
Los Angeles, CA 90048-2406
Phone: 310-858-7666
Fax: 310-858-0525
*18th, 19th & Early 20th Century
Furniture; Decorative Arts*

Joan Kaufman, ISA
JK Associates, A Division of Del-
phinium
1075 Moraga Dr
Los Angeles, CA 90049-1620
Phone: 310-472-4476
Fax: 310-472-4476
*A Consortium Of Experts With
Connoisseurship In 17th, 18th, & 19th
C. American & English Furniture,
Silver, Paintings & Decorative Arts.
Identification, Authentication, Wood
Analysis*

Richard R. Silverman, ISA CAPP
838 N Doheny Dr, Apt 1102
Los Angeles, CA 90069-4851
Phone: 310-273-3838
Fax: 310-273-3843
*Prints (Japanese), Porcelain, Pottery,
Ceramics, (Japanese), Orientalia
(Indian, Nepalese, S.E. Asian Art &
Antiques,) Netsuke, Inro, Ojime*
CAPP In Netsuke

Oscar Golbert, ISA, GG
18 Karat Appraisers
139 S Beverly Dr, Ste 227
Beverly Hills, CA 90212-3028
Phone: 310-278-1022
Fax: 310-278-0803
*Gemology/Gemstones, Diamonds,
Jewelry, Pearls, Watches*

Janet F. Cobert, ISA
Janet F. Cobert Oriental Art Appraisals
PO Box 2976
Beverly Hills, CA 90213-2976
Phone: 310-470-2176
Fax: 310-470-2176
E-mail: asianart@interserv.com
*Oriental Art, Fine Art, Orientalia,
Repairs, Restoration & Preservation
(Oriental Lacquer, Ceramics),
Furniture, Conservator, Textiles,
Ceramics, Decorative Arts, Southeast
Asian Art (All Oriental), Cloisonne,
Ivory, Woodblock Prints*

**Danusia Niklewicz, ISA CAPP, GG
FGA**
Paradise & Associates
23852 Pacific Coast Hwy, Ste 549
Malibu, CA 90265-4879
Phone: 310-829-5286
Fax: 310-829-5286
E-mail: danusia@pacificnet.net
*Gemology/Gemstones (Education),
Jewelry (Fine), Diamonds, Jade, Gold,
Pearls, Consultant, Damage Claims
Specialist*
CAPP In Gemstones

Elena Alcalay, ISA, GG
Azel Gallery
916 Chautauqua Blvd
Pacific Palisades, CA 90272-3804
Phone: 310-459-6022
Fax: 310-459-0017
E-mail: 105131.2310@compuserve.com
*Jewelry, Gems, Silver, Mexican Silver,
Estates*

Pamela Leeds, ISA
Pamela Leeds Fine Art
2554 Lincoln Blvd, #770
Venice, CA 90291
Phone: 310-397-4272
Fax: 310-397-4272
*Fine Art, Photography, Collection
Management, Art Tours*

Linda Crum, ISA CAPP
Linda Crum Appraisal Service
4050 Katella Ave, Ste 111
Los Alamitos, CA 90720-3431
Phone: 310-598-7688
Fax: 310-594-9710
Estate Liquidations
**CAPP In Appreciable Residential
Contents**

Warren Finley, ISA
Finley-Gracer Jewelers
5112 E 2nd St
Long Beach, CA 90803-5322
Phone: 310-494-3949
Fax: 310-434-5699
Jewelry

William M Novotny, ISA, CGA
Novoty's Antiques & Appraisals
2591 Tenth Ave
Arcadia, CA 91006
Phone: 818-446-9663
Fax: 818-446-2503
*Antiques, Furniture, Household
Contents, Porcelain*

KerryAnn Plumer, ISA
Gems & Jewelry Appraiser
260 South Lake Avenue, Ste 104
Pasadena, CA 91101-2134
Phone: 818-574-9477
Fax: 818-447-5001
E-mail: 105403.1217@compuserve.com
*Alt E-Mail: kaplumer@aol.com
Gemology/Gemstones*

Susan Burnett, ISA
411 Gordon Ter, Apt 3
Pasadena, CA 91105-1854
Phone: 818-793-2023
*Crystal, Furniture (18th & Early 19th
C. - American, English & French),
Porcelain, Pottery, Ceramics, China*

James Haddad, ISA
Poulsen Galleries Inc
910 San Pasqual St
Pasadena, CA 91106-3309
Phone: 818-792-7410
Fax: 818-792-7247
*Art (English, French & American),
Paintings, California Plein Art Artists,
Prints (All Periods & Rare), Graphics
& Reproductions*

Neola Caveny, ISA, GG
Neola Caveny Gem & Jewelry
Appraisals
745 S Marengo Ave
Pasadena, CA 91106-3687
Phone: 818-797-1784
Fax: 818-797-1784
*Gemology/Gemstones, Diamonds,
Jewelry (Antique & Period)*

Bonnie Dunlap, ISA
Estate Sales Unlimited
3400 Country Club Dr
Glendale, CA 91208-1154
Phone: 818-957-1144
Fax: 818-957-5202
*Residential Contents, Antiques,
Estates*

Susan McCune, ISA, GG
Gemfacets, LLC
20649 Keswick St
Canoga Park, CA 91306
Phone: 818-348-6701
Fax: 818-348-6701
*Lapidary Art, Gemstones, Jewelry,
Jewelry Design, Mineral Specimens,
Leaded Glass Prisms, Glass & Acrylic
Sculpture*

Stuart Locascio, ISA, GG
The Appraisal Service
18401 Vanowen St, Ste D
Reseda, CA 91335-5300
Phone: 818-343-9016
Fax: 818-342-3865
Gemology/Gemstones, Jewelry, Gold

Ron Stark, ISA
S/R Laboratories
31200 Via Colinas, Ste 210
Westlake Village, CA 91362-3939
Phone: 818-991-9955
Fax: 818-991-5418
E-mail: 74521.1604@compuserve.com
*Animation Art, Fine Art, Collectibles,
Repairs & Restoration*

George E. Waldman, ISA
Waldman Appraisal Co.
22311 Ventura Blvd, Ste 117
Calabasas, CA 91364-1522
Phone: 818-591-8073
Fax: 818-591-2073
*Antiques (Porcelains, Silver),
Residential Contents, Real Estate,
Objet D'Art & De Vertu, Clothing,
Carpets & Rugs, Cloisonne,
Dinnerware, Estates, Fine Arts*

Jennifer Thornton-Davis, ISA, GG
In Depth Appraisals
PO Box 56591
Sherman Oaks, CA 91413-3945
Phone: 818-988-5583
Fax: 818-988-4341
*Gemology/Gemstones, Jewelry,
Watches, Consultant, Insurance*

Richard K. Houston, ISA, GG CGA
Houston Jewelers
14019 Ventura Blvd
Sherman Oaks, CA 91423-3511
Phone: 818-783-1122
Fax: 818-783-8740
*Gemology/Gemstones, Diamonds,
Jewelry*

Robert Shaw, ISA
Diamond Jewelry, Inc.
16830 Ventura Blvd, Ste 248
Encino, CA 91436-1715
Phone: 818-905-5602
Fax: 818-784-7308
E-mail: robtshaw@aol.com
*Gemology/Gemstones, Diamonds,
Jewelry, Insurance Mediation*

David B. Kushner, ISA
Tower Trading Company
1314 West Magnolia Blvd
Burbank, CA 91506
Phone: 818-848-3950
Fax: 818-449-1488
E-mail: 76352.2075@compuserve.com
*Clocks (19th & 20th C.), Bronzes,
Furniture (European, American),
Silver, Porcelain, Residential
Contents, Insurance Valuation & Loss
Reconstruction, Estates, Insurance &
Probate.*

Pamela D. Scott, ISA
Robert S. Scott Co. Appraisers
PO Box 8725
Universal City, CA 91618-8725
Phone: 818-763-6273
Fax: 818-761-1056
*Residential Contents, Fine Arts,
Antiques*

Shira J Brem, ISA
Brem's Antiques
1131 Village Dr
Chino Hills, CA 91709
Phone: 909-629-4411
*Antiques, Collectibles, Victorian Era
Furniture, Jewelry, Silverplate, &
Glass*

William L. Thompson, ISA
La Costa Appraisals
3453 Circulo Adorno
Carlsbad, CA 92009-8906
Phone: 619-633-4264
Fax: 619-636-4983
E-mail: 103156.551@compuserve.com
*Antiques, Residential Contents And
Office Furniture & Equipment*

Tayrn Wayne, ISA, GG
Tayrn's Treasures
13760 Condesa Dr
Del Mar, CA 92014
Phone: 619-481-1257
Fax: 619-481-1257
Jewelry, Gemology/Gemstones

Marcia Ann Lehr, ISA
1561 Neptune Ave
Encinitas, CA 92024
Phone: 619-436-6602
*Machinery & Equipment, Construc-
tion*

Roberta Ely, ISA
Roberta Ely Appraisal Service
175 Beechtree Dr
Encinitas, CA 92024-4031
Phone: 760-942-3480
*Antiques, Decorative Art &
Accessories, Residential Contents,
Insurance, Estates, Hypothetical
Appraisals For Loss.*

Kathleen Debolt, ISA
Debolt Fine Art
18353 Sycamore Creek Road
Escondido, CA 92025
Phone: 619-676-5913
*Fine Art, Paintings, Watercolors,
Drawings, Etchings, Prints, Art (19th
& 20th C American), Insurance*

Annette L. Jones, ISA
DM Jones & Associates
2710 Summit Drive
Escondido, CA 92025
Phone: 619-745-0949
Fax: 619-745-0629
*Fine Art, Drawings, Etchings,
Paintings, Prints, Sculpture*

Valentina Arbab, ISA CAPP
Oriental Rugs Appraiser/Broker
9705 Blackgold Rd
La Jolla, CA 92037-1114
Phone: 619-453-4686
Fax: 619-457-3647
*Oriental Rugs & Textiles (Old &
New), European-American Tapestries
(Old & New), Machine Loomed Rugs
& Textiles (Old & New)*
CAPP In Oriental Rugs

Frances G. Preisman, ISA CAPP
Fran Preisman Fine Art Appraiser
1626 Buckingham Dr
La Jolla, CA 92037-6321
Phone: 619-459-2684
Fax: 619-459-0480
*Paintings (American & European),
Sculpture, Limited Edition Prints*
CAPP In Limited Edition Prints

Daryl Schafer, ISA
1200 Harbor Dr N, Unit B
Oceanside, CA 92054-1028
Phone: 619-966-1098
Fax: 619-966-1098
*Residential Contents, Furniture,
Ceramics, Decorative Arts &
Accessories, Liquidators*

Thom Underwood, ISA, GG
San Diego Gemological Labs
3309 Juanita St
San Diego, CA 92105-3809
Phone: 619-286-6614
Fax: 619-286-7541
Diamonds, Gems, Jewelry Appraising

James W. Coote, ISA CAPP, GG FGA
James W. Coote, Gemologist
1750 Avenida Del Mundo, Apt 204
Coronado, CA 92118-3052
Phone: 619-437-6009
Fax: 619-437-1014
E-mail: 72202.3464@compuserve.com
*Gemstones/Gemology, Diamonds,
Jewelry, Antique & Period Jewelry,
Consultant*
CAPP In Gemstones

Monica Y Yeung, ISA, GG
5260 Caminito Vista Lujo, #11
San Diego, CA 92130-2857
Phone: 619-635-2868
Fax: 619-793-8787
*Fine Jewelry, Diamonds, Gemstones,
Pearls, Jade, Custom Design*

Marcia Osterkamp, ISA
Poulsen Galleries, Inc.
327 Terrace Dr
Brawley, CA 92227-3040
Phone: 619-344-4810
Fax: 619-344-4778
*19th & 20th Century Paintings
California Plein Air Artists*

Carl G. Nielsen, ISA, CGA
Nielsen's
73290 El Paseo, Ste 2
Palm Desert, CA 92260-4232
Phone: 619-346-5608
Fax: 619-568-6811
*Gemology/Gemstones, Colored,
Stones, Diamonds, Jewelry (Gold,
Antique, Platinum), Pearls*

Richard G. Guest, ISA
Guest Fine Art
PO Box 1387
Lake Elsinore, CA 92331-1387
Phone: 909-674-7185
*Fine Art, Paintings & Prints (19th &
20th C.), Appraisal & Consultation
(Painting & Prints), Also Painting
Restoration*

C. Liddell Dawson, ISA, GG
C.L. Dawson & Associates
684 Center Crest Dr
Redlands, CA 92373-7011
Phone: 909-307-0136
Fax: 909-307-0136
E-mail: cld@gte.net
*Jewelry (Insurance Replacement
Values), Gemology/Gemstones,
Rubies, Colored Stones, Silver,
Estates, Restoration*

Diane L. Bendis, ISA
Bendis Co. Auctioneers
3410 La Sierra Ave, # F 123
Riverside, CA 92503-5205
Phone: 909-354-0511
Fax: 909-780-7384
*Furniture, Decorative Arts &
Accessories, Machinery & Equipment,
Cars & Trucks, Auctioneer, Auction
Co, Vehicles*

Kathylee Cook-Roberts, ISA, GJG
The Look by Cook
2045 Teco Drive
San Jacinto, CA 92583-6004
Phone: 909-925-9548
Fax: 909-925-9548
*Jewelry, Diamonds, Colored Stones,
Gemology, Gold*

Richard Obering, ISA
Orange County Industrial Appraisers
232 Iris Ave
Corona Del Mar, CA 92625
Phone: 714-675-9411
Fax: 714-675-8984
Machinery & Equipment

Noel L. Novak-Pilch, ISA
Novak, Pilch & Associates
24982 Sausalito St
Laguna Hills, CA 92653-5626
Phone: 714-643-1745
Fax: 714-643-8997
*Decorative Arts & Accessories, Fine
Art, Residential Contents, Office
Furniture & Equipment; For
Insurance, Estates, Probate*

Mary E. Colby, ISA
Mary Colby Antiques & Appraisals
1710 Calle de Los Alamos
San Clemente, CA 92672-4305
Phone: 714-492-5233
Fax: 714-492-6695
*Furniture (Fine Antiques), Fine &
Decorative Arts, Paintings, Antiques
Accessories. "By Appointment Only"*

Maureen E. Bush, ISA
1201 Via Presa
San Clemente, CA 92672-9486
Phone: 714-498-8560
Fax: 714-498-8560
*Glass, Porcelain, Pottery, Ceramics,
China, Residential Contents*

Pearl Shiffman, ISA CAPP
Chatham Appraisal Service
PO Box 962
Tustin, CA 92681-0962
Phone: 714-832-5101
Fax: 714-544-6955
*Sterling & Silverplate (19th & 20th
C.), Furniture (19th & 20th C.),
Antiques, Decorative Arts, Residential
Contents, Office Furniture &
Equipment*
CAPP In Silver

Susan L. Narens, ISA
45 Morning Glory
Rancho St Margarita, CA 92688-1523
Phone: 714-830-6868
Fax: 714-472-9378
Quilts, Textiles

J. Dennis Mitosinka, ISA
Dennis Mitosinka's Classic Cars
619 E 4th St
Santa Ana, CA 92701-4705
Phone: 714-953-5303
Fax: 714-953-1810
*Cars (Antique, Classic, Special
Interest, Late Model Exotic Cars),
Automotive Memorabilia*

Carol L Sherwood, ISA
1217 Beachmont St
Ventura, CA 93001-4227
Phone: 805-648-5111
Fax: 805-648-7218
*Legal Experience Appraisal Personal
Property, Estates*

Susan C. Donnelly, ISA, GG
Donnelly Gemological Appraisal
355 N Lantana, Suite 300
Camarillo, CA 93012
Phone: 805-484-5515
Fax: 805-484-9460
*Consultant, Gemology/Gemstones,
Estates, Insurance*

Lynn Harding, ISA
Lynn Harding Antqiue Instruments of
the Profess. & Sciences
103 West Aliso Street
Ojai, CA 93023
Phone: 805-646-0204
Fax: 805-646-0204
*Instruments Of Professions &
Sciences (Medical, Scientific),
Collectibles, Ophthalmic/Optical
Antiques*

Leslie Vitanza, ISA
Peregrine Galleries
508 Brinkerhoff Ave
Santa Barbara, CA 93101-3441
Phone: 805-963-3134
Fax: 805-963-3134
*Silver Jewelry (Mexican, Danish),
Costume Jewelry, Vintage Clothing,
Art, Antiques*

Marlene R. Vitanza, ISA
Peregrine Galleries
1133 Coast Village Rd
Santa Barbara, CA 93108-2724
Phone: 805-647-6017
Fax: 805-565-1919
E-mail: mperegrine@aol.com
*Household Goods, Oriental Rugs,
Fine Art (Oil Paintings, Watercolors),
Silver, Jewelry, Dolls, American
Indian Artifacts, Probate, Estates*

Claudia Miller, ISA
Estate Sales Services
43465 30th St W, Apt 1
Lancaster, CA 93536-1331
Phone: 805-940-1930
Fax: 805-722-8767
*Residential Contents, Generalist,
Personal Property, Insurance Claims,
Estates Liquidators*

Dan Turrentine, ISA
La Porte's Appraisal Service
PO Box 52057
Pacific Grove, CA 93950-8479
Phone: 408-375-9565
*Furniture, Silver (English, American),
Art (California)*

Sara Conklin, ISA CAPP
Maritime Appraisals
239 Sierra Point Rd
Brisbane, CA 94005-1664
Phone: 415-467-6249
Fax: 415-467-6249
E-mail: 76363.536@compuserve.com
*Ivory (19th C. American Scrimshaw),
Nautical Items (Ship Models,
Figureheads, Navigational Instru-
ments, Nautical Tools), Alaskan
Indian/Eskimo, Scientific Instruments,
Models (Ship).*
**CAPP In Appreciable Residential
Contents**

Lucia Mathieux, ISA
20 Acorn Drive
Hillsborough, CA 94010
Phone: 415-348-7971
*French Furniture And Decorative
Arts, Fine Art, General Residential
Contents*

Patricia Darrell Knight, ISA
Patrician Antiques
197 First St
Los Altos, CA 94022-2707
Phone: 415-948-5218
*18th & 19th C. Porcelain, Pottery,
Ceramics, (English, Continental &
American), Silver (English,
Continental, American), Furniture
(English & Continental)*

Naomi B. Levinson, ISA CAPP
Bernhard Associates
576 Sand Hill Cir
Menlo Park, CA 94025-7108
Phone: 415-233-9629
Fax: 415-516-3327
E-mail: 72510.2141@compuserve.com
*Fine Art, Works Of Art On Paper,
Sculpture, Paintings, Prints,
Drawings, Photography,
Photographica*
CAPP In Paintings

David Greenaway, ISA
DGW Auctioneers
2250 Charleston Rd
Mountain View, CA 94043-1618
Phone: 415-940-1664
Fax: 415-940-1094
*Residential Contents, Antiques, Fine
Art, Decorative Art, Office Furniture
& Equipment, Auction Service*

Kathleen Greenaway, ISA
DGW Appraisal Service
2250 Charleston Rd
Mountain View, CA 94043-1618
Phone: 415-940-1542
Fax: 415-940-1094
E-mail: 103255.244@compuserve.com
*Residential Contents, Antiques, Fine
Art, Auction Services, Decorative Arts,
Office Furniture & Equipment*

Paula J. Straub, ISA CAPP, GG
Independent Gem Services
360 Esplanade, Apt 6
Pacifica, CA 94044-1880
Phone: 415-355-9017
Fax: 415-355-9017
*Jewelry (Antique & Period, Estate,
Contemporary), Gemstones
(Diamonds, Colored Stones), Pearls,
Watches, Precious Metals, Estates
(Wholesale & Retail), Consulting,
Brokering, Expert Testimony*
CAPP In Gemstones

Starla Turner, ISA, GG CG
Gemstar
228 Biar Ritz Ct
Redwood City, CA 94065
Phone: 415-349-7543
*Gemology/Gemstones, Jewelry,
Diamonds, Gold, Pearls, Lecturer*

Kathleen A. Mitchell, ISA
Old Pump Antiques
PO Box 774
San Bruno, CA 94066-0774
Phone: 415-588-4894
*Antiques, Porcelain (18th & 19th C.),
Belleek, Dresden, Meissen, Derby,
English Tea Ware, Textiles,
Residential Contents, Decorative Arts
& Accessories*

Julia K. Nelson-Gal, ISA
826 Alvarado St
San Francisco, CA 94114
Phone: 415-641-8004
Fax: 415-641-8053
*Fine-Art Photography, Photography
Books, Collectible Photography
(Historical, Decorative)*

Maurice E. Woulf, ISA CAPP, GG
Woulf & Ury Jewelers
10572 San Pablo Ave
El Cerrito, CA 94530-2893
Phone: 510-524-3600
*Gemology/Gemstones, Jewelry,
Clocks, Watches*
CAPP In Gemstones

Shirley J. Filgate, ISA
S & H Antiques
130 J St
Fremont, CA 94536-2913
Phone: 510-797-9690
*Household Contents' Generalist,
Antiques, Collectibles, Furniture,
China, Pottery, Porcelain, Glass*

Pamela M. Parker, ISA
Heart & Home
24865 Tioga Rd
Hayward, CA 94544-2014
Phone: 510-583-1722
*Damage Claims, Estates, Residential
Contents, Household Contents,
Personal Property*

Teri Tacoma, ISA, GG
30 Kings Ford Ct
Napa, CA 94558
Phone: 707-252-8131
Fax: 707-252-8577
*Gemstones & Jewelry For Insurance
Replacement, Jewelry Design &
Manufacturing*

Darla J. Crockett, ISA
Darron's
32521 Seaside Dr
Union City, CA 94587-5149
Phone: 510-487-3987
Fax: 510-487-3987
Residential Contents

Gayle M. Bennett, ISA
G.M. Bennett, Appraiser
460 El Camino Real
Vallejo, CA 94590-3420
Phone: 707-642-8404
*Glass (Art & Cut), Porcelain,
Ceramics, China, Collectibles,
Residential Contents, Estates,
Insurance*

Lilly I. Bennett, ISA
Lilly Bennett, Estate & Moving Sales
460 El Camino Real
Vallejo, CA 94590-3420
Phone: 707-642-8404
*Glass (Art & Cut), Porcelain, Pottery,
Ceramics, Dinnerware, Residential
Contents, Estates*

Barbara W. Spitzack, ISA
The Appraisal Firm of Barbara Spitzack
47 Quail Ct, Ste 101
Walnut Creek, CA 94596-5573
Phone: 510-935-5251
Fax: 510-934-0414
*Residential Contents, Antiques,
Jewelry, Coins, Stamps, Clocks,
Estates, Real Estate*

Nancy Stacy-Trahan, ISA CAPP, GG
Jewels By Stacy Appraisals
712 Bancroft Rd, #436
Walnut Creek, CA 94598-1531
Phone: 510-939-4367
Fax: 510-939-4567
*Gemology/Gemstones, Diamonds,
Jewelry*
CAPP In Gemstones

Meir Levy, ISA
Meir Levy Co. Appraiser & Auctioneer
44 Montrose Rd
Berkeley, CA 94707-2022
Phone: 510-528-7099
Fax: 510-526-1631
*Residential Contents, Machinery &
Equipment, Commercial Inventories,
Business Evaluations, Auctioneer*

Patricia Saultman, ISA
309 Willow Ave, Suite 1005
Corte Madera, CA 94925-1534
Phone: 415-788-3344
Fax: 415-945-0471
E-mail: 102202.1075@compuserve.com
*American & European Paintings &
Prints, English & French Furniture,
Fine Art, Residential Contents, Estates*

Susan Bickford, ISA, GG
Pacific Gemological Services
38 Miller Ave, # 118
Mill Valley, CA 94941-1927
Phone: 415-381-5642
*Gemology/Gemstones, Jewelry,
Diamonds, Gold, Jade, Pearls*

James M. Stephenson, ISA
Patos Enterprises
26 Eucalyptus Knoll St
Mill Valley, CA 94941-2257
Phone: 415-388-5650
*Antiques, Appreciable Residential
Contents*

Julie K. Summerville, ISA
Pacific Automobile Appraisers
PO Box 67421
Scotts Valley, CA 95067-7421
Phone: 408-335-1322
Fax: 408-335-2869
*Cars/Trucks (Antique, Muscle,
Classic, Late Model Cars, Light
Trucks), Machinery & Equipment*

Doug Neale, ISA
Neale & Sons, Inc., Appraisers
PO Box 425
Saratoga, CA 95071-0425
Phone: 408-867-3751
Fax: 408-867-3782
E-mail: kbullz@aol.com
*Antiques, Residential Contents,
Jewelry, Machinery & Equipment,
Estates*

William Hoefer, Jr., ISA, GG FGA
Hoefers' Gemological Services
5016 Alan Ave, B4
San Jose, CA 95124-5741
Phone: 408-264-0670
Fax: 408-264-0725
*Gemology/Gemstones, Jewelry,
Diamonds, Litigation Consultant,
Valuation Methodology Researcher*

Harold R. Bounds, ISA, GG
Willow Glen Custom Jewelers
1302 Lincoln Ave
San Jose, CA 95125-3015
Phone: 408-993-1313
Fax: 408-993-1379
*Gemology/Gemstone, Jewelry,
Diamonds, Estates, Insurance*

Peter Getty, ISA
Peter Getty Antiques
305 Buena Vista
Santa Rosa, CA 95404
Phone: 707-526-6737
*American Art Pottery, Furniture,
General Antiques*

Karen White, ISA
White's Cottage, Appraisals
45456 S Casper Dr
Mendocino, CA 95460-9727
Phone: 805-466-0264
*Furniture (18th C. To Present),
Antiques, Glass (Art, Victorian To
Early, 20th C.), Collectibles, Damage
Claims Specialist, Insurance*

Jeffrey Savage, ISA, GG
John Brorsen & Associates
1711 Schaeffer Rd
Sebastopol, CA 95472-5546
Phone: 707-824-1957
Fax: 707-824-1956
E-mail: 70761.1733@compuserve.com
*Residential Contents (Appreciable),
Silver, Jewelry, Decorative Arts (19th-
20th C.), Antiques, Expert Testimony,
Estate Sales, Online Database
Research.*

Nelda R. Palmer, ISA
Nelda Palmer Appraisals
PO Box 295
Cutten, CA 95534-0295
Phone: 707-443-0967
Fax: 707-443-0967
E-mail: 102774.3072@compuserve.com
*Silver, Porcelain, Pottery, Ceramics,
Crystal, Glass, Residential Contents*

Dennis West, ISA
D.B. West Auctioneers
PO Box 278
Woodland, CA 95776-0278
Phone: 916-661-0490
Fax: 916-661-2499
E-mail: dbwest@mother.com
*Specializes In All Types Of Bank-
ruptcy Property: Auctioneer/Auction
Company, Business Evaluations,
Business Liquidators, Commercial
Inventory, Oil Field & Related
Equipment, Machinery & Equipment*

Roger L. Marcus, ISA
The Unicorn Antiques
PO Box 13451
Sacramento, CA 95813-3451
Phone: 916-723-6732
*Glass (18th-20th C. American &
European, Cobalt, Venetian Glass
Beads, 19th C. Oriental), Porcelain,
(European & Oriental)*

Merilee A. Thorman, ISA
Merilee Thorman Fine Arts & Antiques
1049 11th Ave
Sacramento, CA 95818-4014
Phone: 916-448-0404
Fax: 916-448-0303
E-mail: 106254.1601@compuserve.com
*Antique Paintings, Fine Arts, Oriental
Rugs, Antiques, French Furniture &
Accessories, Estate Sales, Interior
Design*

J. Marlene White, ISA, GG FGA CGA
Grebitus & Sons
404 Spinnaker Way
Sacramento, CA 95831-3236
Phone: 916-442-9081
Fax: 916-442-7094
*Gemology/Gemstones, Jewelry,
Diamonds, Pearls*

Richard C. Frey, ISA
R T L H Enterprises
1275 East Ave
Chico, CA 95926-1020
Phone: 916-343-4528
Fax: 916-343-9380
E-mail: rfreyrtlh@aol.com
*Art (Paintings, Watercolors,
Drawings, Prints, Sculpture),
Japanese Swords, Netsuke, Inro,
Ojime, Photography (American Indian
& 20th C.), Consultant (Art, Etc.),
Residential Contents, Estate
Liquidation, Expert Witness,
Arbitrator*

Frank J. Williams, ISA
United Auction Services
PO Box 107
Crescent Mills, CA 95934-0107
Phone: 916-284-6176
*Machinery & Equipment (Rolling
Stock, Commercial, Industrial), Cars,
Trucks, Trailers, Auctioneer, Auction
Co., Office Furniture And Equipment*

Donald C. McKague, ISA
PO Box 313
Penn Valley, CA 95946-0313
Phone: 916-432-3820
*Residential Contents, Antiques,
Oriental Rugs, Silver, Furniture,
Expert Witness*

Syd Bottomley, ISA
Box 1842
Nevada City, CA 95959
Phone: 916-272-5400
Fax: 916-272-2820
American Indian Basketry, Antiques

Robert F. Trapp, ISA CAPP, GG
Robert F. Trapp Gemological Services
3219 Calistoga Dr
Chico, CA 95973-0193
Phone: 916-892-1907
*Gemology/Gemstones, Diamonds,
Jewelry, Jade, Pearls*
CAPP In Gemstones

Brenda Reichel, ISA, GG
Carats And Karats
1254 S King St
Honolulu, HI 96814-1921
Phone: 808-593-8122
Fax: 808-591-9124
E-mail: flawless@lava.net
Gemology/Gemstones, Diamonds, Jewelry, Gold, Ivory, Jade, Minerals, Pearls, Silver, Estates, Insurance, Expert Witness

Georgie O. Packwood, ISA
Plain 'n' Fancy Antiques
1413 Glenmorrie Dr
Lake Oswego, OR 97034-6328
Phone: 503-697-4493
Antiques, Collectibles (English & American), Presidential, Political, & Patriotic, Americana, Folk Art, Primitives, English Ceramics, Victoriana

Elisabeth Estes, ISA
Bullivant Houser Bailey
2722 SE Evans Ave
Troutdale, OR 97060
Phone: 503-499-4570
Fax: 503-295-0915
Estate & Moving Sales, Antiques, Collectibles, Residential Contents

Harry A. Olson, ISA
Joy's Antique Appraisals
5523 SW Menefee Dr
Portland, OR 97201-2780
Phone: 503-244-2245
Clocks (American), Paintings (American), Watercolors, Drawings

Sandra J Millius, ISA
1530 NE 48th Ave
Portland, OR 97213
Phone: 503-249-8585
Antiques, Instructor- General Survey Classes, Collecting, ID & Care, Estates, Residential Contents, Collectibles

Nancy Draper, ISA
Draper & Draper Appraisals
5403 SW Hewett Blvd
Portland, OR 97221-2237
Phone: 503-292-2485
Antiques, Fine Art, Residential Contents, Folk Art, Textiles, Estates, Decorative Arts And Accessories, Toys

Shari M. Keeler, ISA
Shari's Antiques
14914 SW 109th Ave
Portland, OR 97224-3602
Phone: 503-684-3442
Personal Property, Antiques, & Liquidation

Christine A. Zachary, ISA
Christine Zachary Appraisals & Sales
PO Box 82906
Portland, OR 97282-0906
Phone: 503-234-8143
Fax: 503-777-5813
E-mail: chris24@teleport.com
Antiques, Estate Sales, Fine Art, Residential Contents, Furniture, Decorative Arts & Accessories

Al Gilbertson, ISA, GG CGA
Gem Profiles
PO Box 191
Albany, OR 97321-0059
Phone: 503-274-2895
Fax: 505-924-9028
Gemology/Gemstones, Diamonds, Jewelry, Watches, Pearls

John Kimble, ISA
Kimble Auction & Appraisal
1192 Rio Glen Dr
Eugene, OR 97401-1871
Phone: 541-334-5130
E-mail: jkimble961@aol.com
Antiques & Residential Contents, Early American & Western; Machinery & Equipment - Farm & Ranch Equipment; Heavy Equipment; Automobiles; Farm & Ranch Real Property

Sherril A. Cavallo, ISA CAPP
The Appraisal Specialists
1269 W 10th Ave
Eugene, OR 97402-4705
Phone: 541-687-6882
Fax: 541-687-4699
E-mail: 73021.3620@compuserve.com
Antiques, Art (Fine, Decorative, & Accessories), Ceramics, Furniture (American & European), Glass, Jewelry (Antique & Collectible), Porcelain, Pottery, Residential Contents (Appreciable), Silver
CAPP In Appreciable Residential Contents

Randeen M. Cummings, ISA CAPP
Cummings & Associates
PO Box 5484
Eugene, OR 97405-0484
Phone: 503-345-5856
Fax: 503-345-8192
Residential Contents (Appreciable), Commercial Inventories (Office & Business Contents), Estates (IRS, Probate Or Disbursal),Insurance Arbitration & Equitable Distribution, Antiques, Fine Art, Jewelry (Estate)
CAPP In Appreciable Residential Contents

Robert W. Dalrymple, ISA
85488 Appletree Dr
Eugene, OR 97405-9738
Phone: 503-687-7015
Furniture (Antique), Silver, Residential Contents, Furniture Restorations

Kathleen M. Bailey, ISA CAPP
Antique Appraisal & Estate Sale Service
- The Original
12819 SE 38th St, #320
Bellevue, WA 98006
Phone: 425-746-2777
Fax: 206-365-0633
Estates, Liquidators, Insurance. Antiques, Collectibles, Americana, Art Deco/Nouveau, Ceramics, Decorative Arts, Enamels, Furniture, Glass, Ink Wells, Lamps, Objet D'Art/De Vertu, Paperweights, Porcelain, Silver, Steins, Victoriana
CAPP In Appreciable Residential Contents

Joanna S. Stearns, ISA CAPP
J. Stearns & Associates
221 Fourth Ave North
Edmonds, WA 98020
Phone: 425-672-4455
Fax: 425-672-3177
E-mail: 76333.2316@compuserve.com
Paintings, Watercolors, Drawings, Specializing In Western & Contemporary Southwestern, Prints, Bronzes & Sculpture (In Western & Contemporary, Southwestern)
CAPP In Depreciable Residential Contents

Bette G. Bell, ISA CAPP
Guildmark Appraisal & Estate Sale Service
PO Box 952
Edmonds, WA 98020-0952
Phone: 425-775-5650
Fax: 425-670-6597
E-mail: 102762.2240@compuserve.com
Antiques, Collectibles, Residential Contents, Quilts, Estates
CAPP In Appreciable Residential Contents

Christina G. Little, ISA
J. Stearns & Associates
7407 169th Pl SW
Edmonds, WA 98026-5118
Phone: 425-787-4152
Fax: 425-787-8060
Specializing In Western & Contemporary Southwestern Paintings, Watercolors, Bronzes, Prints, Sculpture

Donald L. Jensen, ISA
Cotswold Appraisal Services
7216 SoundView Dr
Edmonds, WA 98026-5566
Phone: 425-745-3941
Fax: 425-787-0548
E-mail: 76533.1531@compuserve.com
Antiques, Art Glass (American & European), 19th C. Staffordshire Pottery & Ironstone, Residential Contents, Estates, Consultant

Scott Zema, ISA CAPP
Ark Limited Appraisals
13017 101st LN NE, Apt 4
Kirkland, WA 98034-9003
Phone: 425-486-6310
Fine Arts, Antiques, Residential Contents, Paintings, Ceramics, Damage Claims
CAPP In Appreciable Residential Contents

Wayne M. Kairis, ISA
4213 221st St SW
Mountlake Terrace, WA 98043-3625
Phone: 206-440-1461
Boats, Yachts, Guns

John F Roberts, ISA
10418 SE 302nd
Auburn, WA 98092
Phone: 253-735-8641
Fax: 253-804-8655
E-mail: 105326.421@compuserve.com
Art History-First Edition Books, Depreciable & Appreciable

Residential Contents, Antiques, Estates & Household Liquidations, Insurance

Nicole Roberts, ISA
10418 SE 302
Auburn, WA 98092
Phone: 253-735-8641
Fax: 253-804-8655
E-mail: 105326.421@compuserve.com
French Antiques, Depreciable & Appreciable Residential Contents, Antiques, Estate & Household Liquidations, Insurance

Vernetta V. McCarthy, ISA, GG
1100 University Street, Apt 16J
Seattle, WA 98101
Phone: 206-749-9366
Gemstones/Gemology, Jewelry, Diamonds, Sales Represenative

Karen Lorene, ISA
Facere Jewelry Art
1420 5th Ave, Ste 108
Seattle, WA 98101-2333
Phone: 206-624-6768
Fax: 206-624-2852
Jewelry (Antique)

Donald R. Bell, ISA
Aircraft Appraisal
2312 Minor Ave E
Seattle, WA 98102-3308
Phone: 206-325-5929
Fax: 206-325-6567
Aircraft, Real Estate, Offices, Architecture

Lynn T. McAllister, Ph.D., ISA
Lynn McAllister Gallery
2309 Boylston Ave E, Lowr 33
Seattle, WA 98102-3311
Phone: 206-467-0277
Sculpture (15th-20th C.), Paintings - Watercolors - Drawings (European & American 16th Through The 20th Centuries), Glass (19th & 20th C. Art, Studio), Prints (19th & 20th C.),

Kay Frances Hurd, ISA
Hurd Antiques Appraisals & Estate Services
8554 1/2 Greenwood Ave N
Seattle, WA 98103-3416
Phone: 206-782-2405
E-mail: antiquek9@aol.com
Estate Sales Specialist & Tag Sales, Antiques, Collectibles, Household Contents, Glass (Victorian To Depression Era), Jewelry, Furniture, Porcelain, Pottery, Hummels, Smalls, Decorative Arts & Access., Silver, Expanded Res. Contents Exper

Charles G. Barker, ISA
2450 Dexter Ave N, Apt 301
Seattle, WA 98109-2246
Phone: 425-338-1607
Medical Equipment, Office Furniture & Equipment

Scott D. Singer, ISA
Singer Galleries, Ltd
411 W Galer St
Seattle, WA 98119-3335
Phone: 206-285-0394
Fax: 206-283-5264
*Art (Asian), Furniture, Porcelain,
Pottery, Ceramics, China, Glass,
Silver*

Peggy Jewell, ISA
Another Man's Treasure
11023 Bartlett Ave NE
Seattle, WA 98125
Phone: 206-362-3476
*Residential Contents, Collectibles,
Antiques, Wholesale Liquidation*

Kathleen M. Bailey, ISA CAPP
Antique Appraisal & Estate Sale
Service- The Original
PO Box 75191
Seattle, WA 98125-5345
Phone: 425-746-2777
Fax: 425-365-0633
*Estates, Liquidators, Insurance.
Antiques, Collectibles, Americana, Art
Deco/Nouveau, Ceramics, Decorative
Arts, Enamels, Furniture, Glass, Ink
Wells, Lamps, Objet D'Art/De Vertu,
Paperweights, Porcelain, Silver,
Steins, Victoriana*
**CAPP In Appreciable Residential
Contents**

Norene Ott, ISA
Antique & Collectible Dolls of Seattle
11921 26th Pl SW
Seattle, WA 98146
Phone: 206-246-2290
Fax: 206-244-8007
*Antique Dolls, Collectible Dolls, Doll
Accessories*

Christian A. Coleman, ISA CAPP
ISA Executive Director
16040 Christensen Rd, Ste 320
Seattle, WA 98188-2929
Phone: 206-241-0359
Fax: 206-241-0436
E-mail: 75304.3567@compuserve.com
**CAPP In Appreciable Residential
Contents**

Theresa K. Meurs, ISA
2515 Vining St
Bellingham, WA 98226-4231
Phone: 360-734-8087
E-mail: 104507.1474@compuserve.com
*Antiques, Collectibles, Residential
Contents, Estates, Liquidators*

Sally Ambrose, ISA CAPP
PO Box 536
11156 North Rd
Leavenworth, WA 98826-9512
Phone: 509-548-7472
Fax: 509-548-0240
E-mail: 104734.701@compuserve.com
*Needlework (Coverlets & Samplers),
Quilts (Antique, Contemporary), Art
(Wearable), Residential Contents,
Vintage Clothing*
**CAPP In Appreciable Residential
Contents**

Doris A. Dickinsen, ISA
Dickinsen Appraisal Services
6009 Douglas Dr
Yakima, WA 98908-2739
Phone: 509-966-1209
*Ice Cream Molds, Soda Fountain
Collectibles, Chocolate Candy Molds,
Tennis Collectibles, Flow Blue,
Postcards*

Marilu Ferguson, ISA
4-Wheel Country Antiques, Inc
5904 Cowiche Canyon Rd
Yakima, WA 98908-9466
Phone: 509-966-0469
*Furniture (Antique), Glass (Antique),
Residential Contents, Estates,
Damage Claims Specialist*

Molly C. Griffith, ISA
Hidden House Sterling Shop
550 Zickler Rd
Zillah, WA 98953-9223
Phone: 509-865-3353
*Silver (American Flat & Holloware -
Coin & Silverplate), Sterling
(American 19th & 20th C. - Victorian)*

Merle D. Booker, ISA, CAI
Booker Auction Company
10971 Coyan Rd
Connell, WA 99326-9713
Phone: 509-488-3011
*Farm Machinery & Equipment, Cars,
Trucks & Trailers, Airplanes,
Auctioneer, Auction Co.,
Agribusinesses*

Vincent C. Rundhaug, ISA, GG
Columbia Gem Services
8300 W Gage Blvd, #204
Kennewick, WA 99336-8104
Phone: 509-783-6363
Fax: 509-783-0211
*Gemology/Gemstones, Contemporary
Jewelry, Diamonds, Jewelry, Gold*

Randy Grudzinski, ISA
Randy Grudzinski Auctioneers Inc.
1392 W Pine St
Walla Walla, WA 99362-9496
Phone: 509-529-8099
*Farm & Construction Equipment,
General Household Contents,
Auctioneer, Auction Co.*

Here are some tips when contacting someone listed in this book:

When requesting information about a particular item, include a description (material, dimensions, maker's mark, model number, etc.) and a photo, sketch, or photocopy of the item in question.

Always ask if there are charges for samples or for the services requested.

When writing, please be sure to include a Large (#10 business size) Self-Addressed and Stamped Envelope (LSASE) if requesting a reply or the return of photographs.

Never call collect unless otherwise directed. When calling, be considerate of time zone differences and always ask if the party you are calling has time to talk. When leaving an answering machine message, always instruct the party to call you back <u>collect</u>.

APPENDIX B

Auction Services

Listed in ZIP code order

The following firms offer on-site, gallery and/or mail-phone bid auction services for all types of personal property, antiques, collectibles, and art. Those who, in addition, conduct auctions specializing in a particular field are also listed under those categories within the General Listings section of this Directory.

Michael Pritchard
Christie's South Kensington, Ltd.
85 Old Brompton Rd.
London SW7 3LD, U.K.
phone: 0171 581 7611 or 0171 321 3279
fax: 0171 321 3321
e-mail:
mpritchard@cix.compulink.co.uk
Regular sales of furniture, paintings, silver, jewelry, ceramics, textiles, books and collectibles; free verbal valuations weekdays.

Phillips Auction Gallery
101 New Bond St.
London W1Y 0AS, U.K.

Auktionshaus Michael Zeller
Bindergasse 7
8990 Lindau (Bodensee) Germany
Fine art auctioneers.

Kunsthaus Am Museum
Drusugasse 1-5
5000 Koln 1 Germany
Objects d'Art, antiques, Meissen, silver, modern glass.

Bonhams
65-69 Lots Road
London SW10 0RN, U.K.

Erik J. Peters, ISA
Maynards Auctioneers
415 West 2nd Ave.
Vancouver
Brit. Columbia V5Y 1E3 Canada
phone: 604-876-6787 or 604-531-0166
fax: 604-876-2678
e-mail: Erik@Maynards.com
Internet: http://www.maynards.com
Quarterly auctions of Canadian, American & Western European fine art, antiques, silver, jewellery, china, glass, carpets and specialty collectables; Accredited Member of International Society of Appraisers.

Waddington's
189 Queen Street, East
Toronto
Ontario M5A 1S2 Canada
phone: 416-362-1678
fax: 416-362-0905
Conducts auctions of fine and decorative arts; also Innuit and native Canadian arts.

Anthony Caropreso
Mac-Caro Antiques
P.O. Box 643
Lee, MA 01238-0643
phone: 413-243-4647
fax: 413-243-4687
Antique dealer, auction and appraisal service; estate liquidations.

Douglas P. Bilodeau
Douglas Auctioneers
Rte. 5
South Deerfield, MA 01373
phone: 413-665-3530
fax: 413-665-2877
Auction sales year-round, specializing in antiques, fine art, estates, and appraising; also conducts Auctioneering School.

Skinner, Inc.
357 Main St.
Bolton, MA 01740-1104
phone: 508-779-6241 or 617-350-5400
fax: 508-779-5144
Established in 1964, Skinner Inc. is the fifth largest auction house in the US; has offices in Bolton and Boston, MA.

Peter J. Shemonsky
Grogan & Company Auctioneers
22 Harris St.
Dedham, MA 02026-1835
phone: 617-437-9550 or 617-569-1502
fax: 617-437-0513

Willis Henry
Willis Henry Auctions, Inc.
22 Main St.
Marshfield, MA 02059
phone: 617-834-7774
fax: 617-826-3520
Specializes in the sale of American antiques of all kinds, particularly Shaker, American Indian and early American.

F.B. Hubley
364 Broadway
Cambridge, MA 02139
phone: 617-876-2030

Marc J. Matz Gallery
366-B Broadway
Cambridge, MA 02139
phone: 617-661-6200

Philip C. Shute
Shute Auction Gallery
850 W. Chestnut St.
Brockton, MA 02401
phone: 508-588-0022 or 508-588-7833
fax: 508-559-6687
Antique and custom furniture, art, silver, glass and china, collectibles, etc.

John H. Schofield
Eldred's
P.O. Box 796
East Dennis, MA 02641-0796
phone: 508-385-3116
fax: 508-385-7201
Internet: http://capecod.net/eldreds
Auctioneers and appraisers for over 45 years.

Gustave White Auctioneers
37 Bellevue
Newport, RI 02840
phone: 401-847-4250

Joseph Arman
Collector's Sales & Services
P.O. Box 39
Portsmouth, RI 02871-0039
phone: 401-841-8403
fax: 401-841-8403
Internet: http://www.oaklandpublications.com
Specialize in mail-bid auctions for historical Staffordshire, Quimper, American glass, French and American paperweights, bottles, etc.

Withington, Inc.
RD 2 Box 440
Hillsboro, NH 03244
phone: 603-464-3232

Ronald Bourgeault
Northeast Auctions
694 Lafayette Rd.
Hampton, NH 03483
phone: 603-926-9800
fax: 603-926-3545

Paul McInnis
Paul McInnis, Inc.
356 Exeter Rd.
Hampton Falls, NH 03844
phone: 603-778-8989 or 800-242-8354

Wayne Mock
Sanders & Mock Associates, Inc.
P.O. Box 37
Tamworth, NH 03886
phone: 603-323-8749 or 603-323-8784
20+ years as leading auction house in

Northern New England; antiques, fine arts, collections, paintings, rugs, vertu; on site auctions throughout New England and modern auction gallery in Chocorua, NH.

F.O. Bailey Auction Gallery
141 Middle St.
Portland, ME 04101
phone: 207-744-1479 or 207-774-1470
fax: 207-774-7914

Kaja Veilleux Antiques, Inc.
Newcastle Square
Business Rt. 1
Newcastle, ME 04553
phone: 207-563-1002
fax: 207-563-3445

James D. Julia
James D. Julia Auctioneers Inc.
Rt. 201, Skowhegan Rd.
P.O. Box 830
Fairfield, ME 04937
phone: 207-453-7125
fax: 207-453-2502

Eaton Auction Service
RR 1, Box 333
Fairlee, VT 05045
phone: 802-333-9717

Marlin G. Denlinger
P.O. Box 975
Morrisville, VT 05661-0975
phone: 802-888-2774

Linda Smith
Winter Associates, Inc.
21 Cooke St.
Plainville, CT 06062
phone: 203-793-0288
fax: 203-793-8288
Appraises and conducts estate liquidations of antiques, fine furniture, paintings, jewelry, porcelain, glass, etc.

Greg Manning
Greg Manning Auctions, Inc.
775 Passaic Ave.
West Caldwell, NJ 07006
phone: 201-882-0004 or 800-221-0243
fax: 201-882-3499
Since 1905, a leading auctioneer of Americana, glass, stoneware, and antiquities.

Berman's Auction Gallery
33 West Blackwell St.
Dover, NJ 07081
phone: 201-361-3110

Bob & Clara Koty, ISA CAPP
Koty Professional Auctioneers, LLC
P.O. Box 625
Freehold, NJ 07728-0625
phone: 732-751-0504
fax: 732-751-9190
e-mail: 75754.1156@compuserve.com
*Specializes in the auction sale of
antiques, collectibles, household
contents, estates, etc.; certified
appraisers of appreciable and
depreciable residential contents.*

Leon Castner, Pres.
Castner's
P.O. Box 920
Branchville, NJ 07826-0920
phone: 201-948-3868 or 201-383-7044
fax: 201-948-3919
*Specializing in the sale of local estate
contents including antiques and
residential contents; gallery auctions;
on site auctions; estate liquidations in
NJ, NY, and PA.*

Dawson's
128 American Rd.
Morris Plains, NJ 07950
phone: 201-984-6900
fax: 201-984-6956
e-mail: dawson1@tribeca.ios.com

Swann Galleries, Inc.
104 E. 25th St.
New York, NY 10010-2977
phone: 212-254-4710
fax: 212-979-1017
e-mail: SwannSales@aol.com
*Oldest/largest U.S. auctioneer
specializing in rare books, autographs
& manuscripts, Judaica, photographs,
and works of art on paper.*

Metropolitan Antiques
110 West 19th St.
New York, NY 10011-4103
phone: 212-463-0200
fax: 212-463-7099
*Conducts over 40 specialty antiques
shows and auctions per year:
antiquarian books, vintage fashion
and textiles, photography, Victoriana,
20th Century Design; call for
upcoming schedule.*

Christie's East
219 E. 67th St.
New York, NY 10021
phone: 212-606-0400

Sotheby's
1334 York Ave.
New York, NY 10021
phone: 212-606-7370 or 212-606-7000
Internet: http://www.sothebys.com
*Call 212-606-7000 on a touch tone
phone to access a data base to obtain
post-sale prices; have sale number
and lot number handy.*

Arlan Ettinger
Guernsey's Auction
136 East 73rd St.
New York, NY 10021-4208
phone: 212-794-2280
fax: 212-744-3638
*Auctions unique commodities and
collections, e.g. vintage automobiles,
marine art, animation cels, Soviet art,
posters, etc.*

Christie's
502 Park Ave.
New York, NY 10022
phone: 212-546-1000
fax: 212-980-8163
Internet: http://www.sirius.com/
~christie/
*Call 212-546-1199 on a touch tone
phone to access a data base to obtain
post-sale prices; have sale number
and lot number handy.*

Phillips Fine Art & Auctioneers
406 East 79th St.
New York, NY 10022
phone: 212-570-4830
fax: 212-570-2207
*Acts as a liaison with the London
home office; solicits objects for sale in
England and Europe; conducts special
appraisal days in New York.*

Louis Webre, Client Svc.
William Doyle Galleries
175 E. 87th St.
New York, NY 10128-2205
phone: 212-427-2730
fax: 212-369-0892
Internet: http://www.doylegalleries.com
*Holds over 30 auctions annually of
antique English, Continental and
American furniture, paintings,
decorations, jewelry, vintage and
couture clothing, collectible toys,
books and prints; specialty auctions of
Majolica, Lalique and wine.*

Robert H. Snyder
Cohasco, Inc.
P.O. Box 821
Yonkers, NY 10702-0821
phone: 914-476-8500
fax: 914-476-8573
*In business over 50 years, specializing
in paper collectibles, autographs,
documents, Americana, ephemera,
etc.; màil auction catalogs issued.*

Frank Porcu
Shadow Entertainment Group, Inc.
85 Hazel St.
Glen Cove, NY 11542
phone: 516-674-8122
fax: 516-674-8207
*Conducts auctions of quality
collectibles such as toys, sports
collectibles, movie memorabilia,
comics, and comic art.*

South Bay Auctions, Inc.
485 Montauk Highway
East Moriches, NY 11940
phone: 516-878-2909 or 516-878-2933
fax: 516-878-1863

Patrick T. Guariglia
Patrick Thomas & Partners
P.O. Box 119
Saugerties, NY 12477
phone: 914-247-8888
fax: 914-246-0589
*Full service auction house selling
antiques, decorative and fine arts,
estates and collectibles.*

Savoia's Auction Inc.
Rte. 23
South Cairo, NY 12482
phone: 518-622-8000
fax: 518-622-9453

Doyle Auctioneers
109 Osbornehill Rd.
Fishkill, NY 12524
phone: 914-896-9492

Iroquois Auction Gallery
P.O. Box 736
Brewerton, NY 13029
phone: 315-668-2346
*Semi-annual upscale art and antique
auctions; also regular estate art &
antique auctions; over 20 years of
service; graduate of Sotheby's Style in
Art course; always interested in
buying quality art & antiques,
paintings, art work, etc.*

David W. Mapes
Mapes Auction Gallery
1729 Vestal Pkwy. West
Vestal, NY 13850-1156
phone: 607-754-9193
fax: 607-786-3549
e-mail: 76742.274@compuserve.com
Internet: http://
www.mapesauction.baka.com
*Specializes in the sale of entire estates
including antiques, toys, pottery.*

Duane E. Gansz, CAI, ISA
Gansz Auction & Realty
14 William St.
Lyons, NY 14489
phone: 315-946-6241
fax: 315-946-6747

Samuel Cottone
Cottone
15 Genesee St.
Mount Morris, NY 14510
phone: 716-658-3119
fax: 716-658-3152

Mark Anderton
Collectors Auction Services
P.O. Box 13732
Seneca, PA 16346
phone: 814-677-6070
fax: 814-677-6166
*An absentee mail and phone bid
auction handling quality antiques and
collectibles.*

Ted Hake
Hake's Americana & Collectibles
Auction
P.O. Box 1444
York, PA 17405-1444
phone: 717-848-1333
*Always purchasing items for 8 mail-
bid auctions per year covering
hundreds of categories including toys,
character collectibles, Disney, cowboy
heroes, premiums, television,
politicals, pin-back buttons,
advertising and more.*

Conestoga Auction Company
768 Graystone Rd.
P.O. Box 1
Manheim, PA 17545
phone: 717-898-7284

Roan Bros. Auction Gallery
RR 4 Box 118
Cogan Station, PA 17728
phone: 717-494-0170 or 800-955-ROAN
fax: 717-494-1911
e-mail: roaninc@csrlink.net

Tony Macek
Aston Professional Auctioneers &
Appraisers
154 Market St.
Pittston, PA 18640
phone: 717-654-3090 or 607-785-6598

Tony Nard
Nard Auctions
U.S. Rte. 220
Milan, PA 18831
phone: 717-888-9404
fax: 717-888-7723
e-mail: tonynardAclarityconnect.com

Clinton-Ivankovich Auction Co., Inc.
P.O. Box 29
Ottsville, PA 18942
phone: 610-847-5432

Cindy Stephenson
Stephenson's Auction
1005 Industrial Blvd.
Southampton, PA 18966
phone: 215-322-6182
*Weekly general auctions of residential
contents; quarterly auctions of
antiques and decorative arts;
additional specialty auctions.*

Lynn Martin
Freeman/Fine Arts of Philadelphia
1808 Chestnut St.
Philadelphia, PA 19103
phone: 215-563-9275 or 215-563-9453
fax: 215-563-8236
*America's oldest auction house:
Continental, English and American
furniture, paintings, silver and
decorative arts; Oriental rugs, rare
books, fine jewelry, Orientalia.*

Ron & Debra Pook
Pook & Pook, Inc.
P.O. Box 268
Downingtown, PA 19335-0268
phone: 610-269-0695 or 610-269-4040
fax: 610-269-9274
*Auction management and appraisal
service; antiques appraised,
purchased and sold on consignment.*

Dana L. Pfister
Alderfer Auction Company
501 Fairground Rd.
P.O. Box 640
Hatfield, PA 19440-0640
phone: 215-368-5477
fax: 215-368-9055
e-mail: auction@alderfercompany.com
Internet: http://alderfercompany.com
A full service auction and appraisal business, specializing in Pennsylvania antiques, fine art, fire arms, Americana, and collectibles.

Luke R. Whitman
Pennypacker-Andrews
P.O. Box 588
Shillington, PA 19607
phone: 610-777-6121 or 610-777-5890
fax: 610-670-4248

Thomas M. Weschler
Weschler's
905 E St. NW
Washington, DC 20004-2006
phone: 202-628-1281 or 800-331-1430
fax: 202-628-2366
A full service auction service for art, antiques, decorative accessories, household furnishings, and commercial liquidations; also specializes in the sale of European furniture and decorative art.

C.G. Sloan & Company, Inc.
4920 Wyaconda Rd.
Rockville, MD 20852
phone: 800-649-5066 or 301-468-4911
fax: 301-468-9182

Colin Clarke
Sloan's
4920 Wyconda Rd.
Rockville, MD 20852
phone: 301-468-4911 or 800-649-5066
fax: 301-468-9182
Internet: http://www.sloansauction.com

Nancy Addison
Hantman's Auctioneers & Appraisers
P.O. Box 59366
Potomac, MD 20859-9366
phone: 301-770-3720
fax: 301-770-4135
Internet: http://www.hantmans.com

Rick Williams
Williams Auction & Appraisal Service
P.O. Box 381
Forest Hill, MD 21050
phone: 410-836-3031
fax: 410-836-1123
e-mail: Wilri@erols.com

Richard W. Opfer, Jr.
Richard Opfer Auctioneering, Inc.
1919 Greenspring Dr.
Lutherville Timonium, MD 21093-4113
phone: 410-252-5035
fax: 410-252-5863
Specializes in auctioning toys, dolls, games, black memorabilia, and advertising items; weekly estate auctions including antiques, fine art;

monthly eclectic collector sales feature a wide variety of collectibles.

DeCaro Auction Sales, Inc.
8133 Elliott Rd., Ste. 2
Easton, MD 21601-7184
phone: 410-820-4000

Tim Gordon
Gordon Auctioneers
215 E. 7th St.
Frederick, MD 21701-5223
phone: 301-663-1547

John D. Compton
J.D. Compton Auctioneering
13833 Rockdale Rd.
Clear Spring, MD 21722
phone: 301-582-0727 or 800-662-8284
fax: 301-582-6114
Call toll-free in MD 1-800-499-3344.

Laws
7209 Centreville Rd.
P.O. Box 687
Manassas Park, VA 22111
phone: 703-361-3148

Gail Wolpin, ISA
Phoebus Auction Gallery
14-16 E. Mellen St.
Hampton, VA 23663
phone: 757-722-9210
fax: 757-723-2280
e-mail: bwelch@phoebusauction.com
Internet: http://
www.phoebusauction.com
Conducts auctions of antiques, collectibles, estates, furniture, decorative and fine arts, etc.

Riverbend Auction
P.O. Box 24910
Alderson, WV 24910
phone: 304-445-2897 or 800-726-2897
e-mail: riverbend@brdv.com
Internet: http://www.auctionservice.com/riverbend/

Bob Raynor
Historical Collectible Auctions
P.O. Box 975
Burlington, NC 27215
phone: 910-570-2803
fax: 910-570-2748
e-mail: bobnews@aol.com

Gene Patrick
Gene Patrick Auction & Realty
1051 Cooley Bridge Rd.
Belton, SC 29627
phone: 803-243-2394 or 803-338-5720

Preston Evans
Opportunities Auction
5058 Kurt Lane
Conyers, GA 30208
phone: 770-483-0000

Jim Depew
Jim Depew Galleries
1860 Piedmont Rd.
Atlanta, GA 30324-4839
phone: 404-874-2286
fax: 404-874-2285
Weekly consignment and estate

auctions of antiques and traditional furniture, accessories, porcelains, silver, crystal and jewelry.

Christopher Benjamin
Great American Auction, The
P.O. Box 4020
Saint Augustine, FL 32085-4020
fax: 904-826-1600
Lists sport and non-sport trading cards, cereal box prizes and premiums, bread end labels, etc. (fee charged.)

Jack & Nancy Bomm
J & N Auctioneers
P.O. Box 656
Clarcona, FL 32710-0656
phone: 407-294-3980
fax: 407-294-7836
e-mail: rosepast@worldnet.att.net

Harry Stampler, ISA
Stampler Auctions
2801 Evans St.
Hollywood, FL 33020
phone: 800-330-BIDS or 954-921-8888
fax: 954-927-2939
Specializes in business liquidations.

Sloan's
8861 NW 18th Terrace, Ste. 100
Miami, FL 33172
phone: 305-751-4770 or 800-660-4524
fax: 305-751-9171
Internet: http://www.sloansauction.com

Jane Herz, US Rep.
Auction Team Koln
6731 Ashley Ct.
Sarasota, FL 34241-9696
phone: 941-925-0385
fax: 941-925-0487
Specializes in the sale of old office equipment, scientific instruments and devices, photographica, and old technology including toasters, typewriters, sewing machines, posters and lobby cards, tools telecommunications, etc.

Joyce Perrin
Vintage Auctions
Star Rte. Box 650
Blountsville, AL 35031
phone: 205-429-2457
fax: 205-429-2457
Holds regular bi-monthly auctions selling American & European antiques, glassware and collectibles; in-house facilities; computerized sales.

Kimball M. Sterling Inc.
125 W. Market St.
Johnson City, TN 37601
phone: 423-928-1471
fax: 423-928-8697
e-mail: kimsold@tricon.net
Internet: http://sterlingsold.com

Garth's Auction, Inc.
2690 Stratford Rd.
P.O. Box 369
Delaware, OH 43015
phone: 614-362-4771 or 614-369-508
fax: 614-363-0164
Specializing in early Americana.

DeFina Auctions
1591 State Route 45
Austinburg, OH 44010
phone: 216-275-6674
fax: 216-275-2028
Internet: http://www.csmonline.com/defina

Wolf's Auctioneers
1239 West 6th St.
Cleveland, OH 44113
phone: 216-575-9653 or 800-526-1991
fax: 216-621-8011

Maggie Beckmeyer, CAI, ISA
Auctions by Maggie
2191 Cliff Rd.
North Bend, OH 45052
phone: 513-941-9519 or 800-745-3557
fax: 513-941-9519

Lawrence Dumouchelle
Dumouchelle Art Galleries
409 East Jefferson Ave.
Detroit, MI 48226
phone: 313-963-6255 or 313-963-0248
fax: 313-963-8199
A fine arts auction house; rugs, paintings, jewelry, porcelain, silver, art glass, toys, dolls, furniture, books, sculpture, etc.

James L. Jackson, ISA
Jackson's Auctioneers & Appraisers
2229 Lincoln St.
Cedar Falls, IA 50613
phone: 319-277-2256
fax: 319-277-1252
e-mail: jacksons@jacksonsauction.com
Internet: http://www.jacksonsauction.com
Conducts auction sales of fine arts, furniture, art pottery, art glass, porcelain, toys, rugs, etc.

Milwaukee Auction Galleries
318 N. Water
Milwaukee, WI 53202
phone: 414-271-1105

Schrager Auction Galleries, Ltd.
P.O. Box 10390
2915 North Sherman Blvd.
Milwaukee, WI 53210
phone: 414-873-3738
fax: 414-873-5229

Kurt R. Krueger
Krueger Auctions
160 N. Washington St.
Iola, WI 54945
phone: 715-445-3845
fax: 715-445-4100
Specializing in the mail-bid auction of tokens, advertising, brewery items, Western Americana, postcards, World's Fair & Expo., autographs, sports, coins & currency, pinbacks,

military memorabilia, automotive, Disneyana, etc.

Dunning's Auction Service
755 Church Rd.
Elgin, IL 60123-9302
phone: 708-741-3483 or 800-462-2444
fax: 708-741-3589
Internet: http:///www.dunnings.com
Premier mid-American auction firm selling antiques, fine art, jewelry, American Indian art, and real estate.

Hanzel Galleries
1120 South Michigan Ave.
Chicago, IL 60605-2301
phone: 312-922-6234
fax: 312-922-6792

Chase Gilmore Art Galleries
724 West Washington St.
Chicago, IL 60606
phone: 312-648-1690

Leslie Hindman
Leslie Hindman Auctioneers
215 West Ohio St.
Chicago, IL 60610
phone: 312-670-0010
fax: 312-670-4248

Joy Luke
Joy Luke Auction Gallery
300 E. Grove St.
Bloomington, IL 61701-5232
phone: 309-828-5533
fax: 309-829-2266
Conducts regular auctions in fine and decorative arts.

Selkirk Galleries
7447 Forsyth Blvd.
Saint Louis, MO 63105
phone: 314-726-5515
fax: 314-726-9908

Robert Merry
Robert Merry Auction Company
5501 Milburn Rd.
Saint Louis, MO 63129
phone: 314-487-3992

Bob Simmons
Simmons & Company Auctioneers
Rte. 1 Box 186
Richmond, MO 64085-9760
phone: 816-776-2936
fax: 816-470-5016
e-mail:
simmons_auction@raycounty.com
Internet: http://www.raycounty.com/simmons.html
Conducts specialty and general line antiques and collectibles auctions.

Manion's Auction House
P.O. Box 12214
Kansas City, KS 66112-0214
phone: 913-299-6692
fax: 913-299-6792
e-mail: manions@qni.com
Internet: http://www.manions.com
A mail-bid auction company specializing in militaria from all countries, Scouting memorabilia, toys,

antique advertising, and all fine collectibles.

Woody Auction Company
P.O. Box 618
Douglass, KS 67039
phone: 316-746-2694
fax: 316-746-2145

Amanda L. Mantle
Neal Auction Co.
4038 Magazine St.
New Orleans, LA 70115
phone: 504-899-5329 or 800-467-5329
fax: 504-897-3808
Specializing in an..., s and fine art, especially Southern Art, American 19th century furniture, French furniture, and decorative objects.

New Orleans Auction Galleries, Inc.
801 Magazine St.
New Orleans, LA 70130
phone: 504-566-1849
fax: 504-566-1851

Keith Clanton
C&C The Auction Company
4801 MacKelman Dr.
Oklahoma City, OK 73135-4135
phone: 405-670-1705
Specializing in the auction sale of antiques and collectibles.

Richard Waskow
HCR 68 Box 745
Vian, OK 74962-9128
phone: 918-489-5164
Conducts specialty auctions; watches, clocks, Russian items, bronzes.

Pettigrew Auction Company
1645 South Tejon St.
Colorado Springs, CO 80906
phone: 719-633-7963
fax: 719-633-5035

Warren Anderson
America West Archives
P.O. Box 100
Cedar City, UT 84721-0100
phone: 801-586-9497 or 801-586-7323
Auction catalogs offer rare & historical documents, letters, photographs, autographs, paper Americana, maps; specializes on Western U.S., however Eastern material also accepted.

Susan Pojmonski
Star Auction, Inc.
P.O. Box 1232
Dolan Springs, AZ 86441-1232
phone: 602-767-4774 or 602-767-4107
fax: 602-767-3900

Angela Past
Butterfield & Butterfield
7601 Sunset Blvd.
Los Angeles, CA 90046-2714
phone: 213-850-7500
fax: 213-850-5843

G.E. Moore
Mail Bid Auction
P.O. Box 414
Yucca Valley, CA 92286-0414
fax: 619-365-9668
Conducts mail-bid auctions of collectibles: books, coins, medals, Disney, theater, valentines, art, railroad, medical/dental, etc.; $2 for mailing first list; Continental U.S. only.

Butterfield & Butterfield
220 San Bruno Ave.
San Francisco, CA 94103-5018
phone: 415-861-7500
fax: 415-553-8678
Specialties include posters, toys, decorative arts, furniture, photography, etc.; the largest full service auction in the west.

Here are some tips when contacting someone listed in this book:

When requesting information about a particular item, include a description (material, dimensions, maker's mark, model number, etc.) and a photo, sketch, or photocopy of the item in question. ∎

Always ask if there are charges for samples or for the services requested. ∎

When writing, please be sure to include a Large (#10 business size) Self-Addressed and Stamped Envelope (LSASE) if requesting a reply or the return of photographs. ∎

Never call collect unless otherwise directed. When calling, be considerate of time zone differences and always ask if the party you are calling has time to talk. When leaving an answering machine message, always instruct the party to call you back collect. ∎

APPENDIX C

General Interest Periodicals

Listed in alphabetical order

Each of the following general interest periodicals covers a wide range of subjects within the fields of antiques, collectibles, and art. Periodicals that focus on specific subjects are listed under those categories within the General Listings section of this Directory. Don't forget collector clubs when looking for periodicals. Most clubs publish excellent periodicals focusing on their areas of specialization.

Patricia Sproehnle
Victorian Society in America, The
19th Century Magazine
219 South 6th St.
Philadelphia, PA 19106-3719
phone: 215-627-4252 or 215-627-4253
fax: 215-627-7221
e-mail: vicsoc@libertynet.org
Internet: http://www.libertynet.org/
~vicsoc
Membership benefits include quarterly newsletter, semi-annual magazine, symposia on wide array of 19th century subjects, annual meeting; fostering appreciation in Victorian life through preservation and educational efforts; non-profit.

America's Most Wanted Collectibles
14000 Cantrell, Ste. 332
Little Rock, AR 72212-1500
phone: 501-868-7316 or 800-994-9268
fax: 501-868-8858
e-mail: amwc1@aol.com
Bi-monthly glossy cover magazine devoted entirely to specialty collector and dealer wanted-to-buy 1/8th page ads.

Donna Kaonis, Ed.
American Collector
225 Main St., Ste. 300
Northport, NY 11768-1737
phone: 516-261-8337 or 800-828-1429
fax: 516-261-8235
Internet: http://www.tias.com/mags/IC/
AntiqueDollWorld/
Glossy, color magazine on today's most popular antiques and collectibles; advertising, sports memorabilia, folk art, comics, animation, pop culture; collector profiles, shows, auctions, trends, ads, etc.; published nine times a year.

Florian McCain, Ed.
GCR Publishing Group, Inc.
American Country Collectibles
1700 Broadway
New York, NY 10019-5905
phone: 212-541-7100 or 800-955-3870
fax: 212-245-1241
Published four times a year; focuses on collecting and decorating with collectibles.

Cowles Magazines, Inc.
American History Illustrated
741 Miller Dr. SE, Ste. D2
Harrisburg, PA 20175
phone: 703-771-9400 or 800-829-3340
fax: 703-779-8345
Internet: http://www.thehistorynet.com
Feature articles on all aspects of American history; coverage of military, social, and political events and the forces that have shaped American history; published bi-monthly.

Americana Magazine Inc.
Americana Magazine
29 West 38th St.
New York, NY 10018
phone: 212-398-1550

Sandra Hood, Gen. Mngr.
Antique & Collectables
P.O. Box 13560
El Cajon, CA 92022
phone: 619-593-2925 or 619-593-2933
fax: 619-442-4043
The largest monthly newspaper in Southern California covering the antiques & collectibles industry with focus sections on Nevada and Arizona; 72+ pages; events and show section, feature articles; columns, ads.

Lonnie J. Hinton
Antique & Collectible News
P.O. Box 529
Anna, IL 62906-0529
phone: 618-833-2158 or 800-833-2699
fax: 618-833-5813
e-mail: reppert@midwest.net
A regional monthly with articles about antiques, collectors, quilts, history, crafts, craftsmen, special events, collector clubs and other topics of interest to collectors in IL, MO, KY IN MS and TN.

Antique Almanac, The
P.O. Box 1613
Bowie, TX 76230
phone: 817-872-6186
e-mail: antique@morgan.net
Internet: http://www.morgan.net/antique/
index.html
A local antiques newspaper serving the central Texas region: ads, calendar of events, columns.

Antique Collectors' Club, Ltd.
Antique Collecting Magazine
5 Church St.
Woodbridge
Suffolk 1P12 1DS, U.K.
Internet: http://www.antiquecc.com/mag/
magtoc.htm
A sophisticated English magazine of the Antique Collectors' Club, the parent organization for dozens of regional antiques clubs within the U.K.

Susan Hogan, Ed.
Farm & Dairy Publishers
**Antique Collector & Auction Guide,
The**
P.O. Box 38
Salem, OH 44460
phone: 216-337-3419 or 216-337-3164
fax: 216-337-9550
A weekly insert to "Farm and Dairy" newspaper; serving the antiques and collectibles trade; ads, auctions, articles, etc.

Publications Expediting, Inc.
**Antique Dealer & Collectors Guide,
The**
200 Meachum Ave.
Elmont, NY 11003
An English glossy international monthly magazine for dealers and collectors: articles, ads, book reviews, auction reports, etc.

Ed & Marie Welch
Antique Exchange
RFD 3 Box 1290
Winslow, ME 04901

Catherine A. Turner, Editor
Turner Publishing Co.
Antique Gazette
6949 Charlotte Pike, Ste. 106
Nashville, TN 37209-4200
phone: 615-352-0941
fax: 615-352-0941
Complete monthly antiques guide; shop/mall locator, show calendar, classifieds, articles; nationwide distribution; featuring the exclusive "Antiques Locator" - hundreds of quality antiques listed for sale with prices.

Robert Fiallo, Editor
Antique Press, The
12403 N. Florida Ave.
Tampa, FL 33612
phone: 813-935-7577
Florida's newspaper of antiques and collectibles; articles, maps, calendars, photos, book reviews, advertisements, etc. Published 18 times per year.

Bruce Causey
Antique Shoppe, The
P.O. Box 2175
Keystone Heights, FL 32656
phone: 352-475-5326 or 352-475-1679
fax: 352-475-5326
Florida's monthly antiques newspaper; interesting and entertaining articles about antiques and collectibles, historical landmarks and places of interest, including maps to Florida's best antique shops; serves FL and parts of GA.

NewsAntique Shopper, The
37600 Hills Tech Dr.
Farmington, MI 48331-5727
Monthly newsmagazine distributed in the IA, IL, SD, NE, MO, WI, MN, IN, OH and KS area; 10,000 copies per month.

Paul Fiocca
Trajan Publishing Corp.
Antique Showcase
103 Lakeshore Rd., Ste. 202
St. Catharines
Ontario L2N 2T6 Canada
phone: 905-646-7744
fax: 905-646-0995
e-mail: bret@trajan.com
Internet: http://www.vaxxine.com/trajan/
National magazine with diverse articles, show and auction reports, museum exhibits, book reviews, upcoming trends, etc.; also contains lots of display and classified ads for buyers of Canadian, US and European antiques; 9 times per year.

Linda Kellbach
Antique Trader Publications, Inc.
Antique Trader Weekly, The
P.O. Box 1050
Dubuque, IA 52004-1050
phone: 800-334-7165 or 800-482-4155
fax: 800-531-0880
e-mail: 76143.72@compuserve.com
Internet: http://www.csmonline.com
A weekly newspaper with ads, articles and news on the antiques and

collectibles hobby; buy, sell, trade smarter; over 2,000 ads in every issue; comprehensive national show and auction calendars; special feature stories.

Harold E. Johnson
Zorah Publications, Inc.
Antique Traveler, The
P.O. Box 656
Mineola, TX 75773
phone: 800-446-3588 or 903-569-2487
fax: 903-569-9080
Serving the American Southwest antiques trade; ads, dealer directory, articles, show and auction schedules nation wide.

Antiquer's Guide to the Susquehanna Region
P.O. Box 388
Sidney, NY 13838
phone: 607-563-8339

Dennis M. Sater, Ed.
Antiques & Auction News
P.O. Box 500
Mount Joy, PA 17552-0500
phone: 717-653-4300 or 800-482-2886
fax: 717-653-6165
A weekly newspaper featuring antiques, collectibles, auctions, sales, shows and exhibits.

Richard Branciforte
Antiques & Collectibles
150 Linden Ave.
P.O. Box 33
Westbury, NY 11590
phone: 516-334-9650
fax: 516-334-5740
Monthly newspaper featuring extensive area calendar, museums, art galleries, limited editions and doll sections.

Dale K. Graham, Pub.
Lightner Publishing Corp.
Antiques & Collecting Magazine
1006 S. Michigan Ave.
Chicago, IL 60605-9840
phone: 312-939-4767
fax: 312-939-0053
e-mail: lightnerpb@aol.com
Informative articles on antiques & collectors items; up-to-the-minute news in the field, auction results, ads, book reviews; published monthly; published since 1931; authoritative and informative articles on antiques and collectibles.

Antiques & Fine Art
25200 La Paz Rd., Ste. 210
Laguna Hills, CA 92653-5135
A high quality monthly magazine serving the antiques and art communities.

R. Scudder Smith
Bee Publishing Co.
Antiques & The Arts Weekly (The Newtown Bee)
5 Church Hill Rd.
P.O. Box 5503
Newtown, CT 06470-9987
phone: 203-426-3141 or 203-426-8036
fax: 203-426-1394
Leading weekly newspaper for auction advertising, show coverage, and other events in the world of antiques.

H.P. Publishing
Antiques Bulletin
2 Hampton Court Rd.
Harbourne
Birmingham B17 9AE, U.K.
phone: 441216818001
A weekly English publication.

Elaine Kruse, Pub.
Kruse-Arett Publishing
Antiques Today
977 Lehigh Circle
Carson City, NV 89705-7160
phone: 702-267-4600 or 800-267-4602
fax: 702-267-4600
e-mail: antiquestoday@powernet.net
Monthly newspaper covering all Western states with articles, news, features, calendar, classifieds, show info.

Antiques Trade Gazette
17 Whitcomb St.
London WC2H 7PL, U.K.
phone: 441719304957
fax: 441719306391
e-mail: atg@dmgexhib.co.uk
A substantial weekly newspaper with articles, calendar of shows and sales, ads, etc. focusing on the English market; call advertising agent in New York at 212-764-8555.

Monka Publishing, Inc.
Antiques West
3450 Sacramento St., Ste. 618
San Francisco, CA 94118
phone: 415-221-4645 or 207-774-8826
Upscale monthly newspaper serving the Western U.S. antiques & early fine arts markets; news and information on auctions, shows and events; substantive articles about antiques and art.

Marni Andrews, Pub./Ed.
Antiques! Communications
Antiques!
Box 1860
Suite 707, 27 Queen St. East
Toronto M5C 2M6 Canada
phone: 416-944-3880
fax: 416-944-3872
e-mail: marnia@msn.com
Glossy magazine from Canada.

Antiques-Collectibles
P.O. Box 268
Greenvale, NY 11548
phone: 516-767-0312

Tom Hoepf, Ed.
Mayhill Publications, Inc.
AntiqueWeek - Central Edition
P.O. Box 90
Knightstown, IN 46148
phone: 317-345-5133 or 800-876-5133
fax: 800-695-8153
e-mail: antiquewk@aol.com
Internet: http://www.antiqueweek.com
A leading antiques, auctions and collectors' newspaper published weekly every Monday in two regional editions, Eastern and Central.

Connie Swaim, Ed.
Mayhill Publications, Inc.
AntiqueWeek - Eastern Edition
P.O. Box 90
Knightstown, IN 46148
phone: 317-345-5133 or 800-876-5133
fax: 800-695-8153
e-mail: antiquewk@aol.com
Internet: http://www.antiqueweek.com
A leading antiques, auctions and collectors' newspaper published weekly every Monday in two regional editions, Eastern and Central.

Vallerie Allan
Apollo Magazine
P.O. Box 47
North Hollywood, CA 91603-0047
phone: 818-763-7673
fax: 818-753-9492
e-mail: apollousa@aol.com
The international magazine of art and antiques; an English monthly publication with detailed articles and glossy color photos.

Ron Smisek, Ed.
Arizona Antique News
Arizona Antique News & Southwest Antiques Journal
P.O. Box 26536
Phoenix, AZ 85068-6536
phone: 602-943-9137
A monthly publication designed for collectors and dealers; syndicated writers offer regional perspectives of the antiques hobby.

Art & Antiques
3 East 54th St.
New York, NY 10022-3108
phone: 212-752-5557 or 800-274-7594
Glossy magazine focusing on the fine and decorative arts and in antiques: colorful ads, articles, auction reports, etc.

Bob & Jeni Olsze
Auction Action News
131 East James St.
Columbus, WI 53925
phone: 414-623-3767
fax: 800-580-4568
A weekly newspaper focusing on auction ads and informative articles with lots of photos and price results for antiques and collectibles (the rare as well as those commonly found items) at auctions in the WI, MI, IL, MN and IA area.

Jack Sell
Sell Entertainment Corp.
Auction Price Check Newsletter
8728 U.S. highway 19
Port Richey, FL 34668
phone: 813-869-9114
A monthly newsletter reporting on actual hammer prices.

Brimfield Antique Guide, The
RFD 1 Box 20
Brimfield, MA 01010-9802
phone: 413-245-9329
Published 3 times per year; highlights any changes, news releases or other noteworthy information, etc. pertaining to the Brimfield Antique and Collectible shows.

Buckeye Marketeer, The
P.O. Box 954
Westerville, OH 43086
phone: 614-895-1663
A monthly newspaper focusing on antiques and collectibles shows, flea markets, auctions and festivals.

Register Newspaper, The
Cape Cod Antiques & Arts
P.O. Box 400
Yarmouth Port, MA 02675
phone: 508-362-2111
A monthly supplement to weekly newspaper "The Register"; the supplement concentrates on art & antiques in the Cape Cod area.

Phil Burrows, Pub.
Carolina Antique News
P.O. Box 241114
Charlotte, NC 28224

Trajan Publishing Corporation
Collectibles Canada
103 Lakeshore Rd., Ste. 202
St. Catharines
Ontario L2N 2T6 Canada
phone: 905-646-7744
fax: 905-646-0995
e-mail: bret@trajan.com
Internet: http://www.vaxxine.com/trajan/

Cathy Cook, Ed.
GCR Publishing Group, Inc.
Collectibles/Flea Market Finds
1700 Broadway
New York, NY 10019-5905
phone: 212-541-7100 or 800-955-3870
fax: 212-245-1241
Published four times a year; focuses on fleamarket collectibles and 20th-century collectibles that are fun, affordable, and not the standard fare of other magazines: kitchenware, toys, vintage clothing; display ideas.

Collector Magazine
436 W. Fourth St. #222 at Park Ave.
Pomona, CA 91766-1620
phone: 909-620-9014
A monthly periodical; Southern California's most popular collecting newspaper; ads, calendar of events, auctions, service directory, etc.

Linda Kunkel
Antique Trader Publications, Inc.
Collector Magazine & Price Guide
P.O. Box 1050
Dubuque, IA 52004-1050
phone: 800-334-7165 or 800-482-4155
fax: 800-531-0880
e-mail: 76143.72@compuserve.com
Internet: http://www.csmonline.com
A monthly magazine featuring stories on hot collectibles, travel log of great antiquing towns, a 25-page price guide, an in-depth look at antique collecting with advice from experts, exclusive 25-page price guide in each issue.

Collector's Digest
P.O. Box 23
Banning, CA 92220
phone: 909-849-1064

Dorothy J. Graf, Ed.
Collector's Marketplace, The
P.O. Box 25
Stewartsville, NJ 08886-0025
phone: 908-479-4614
fax: 908-479-6158
e-mail: cm@4-collectors.com
Internet: http://www.4-collectors.com
A bi-monthly publication for collectors and dealers; an international advertising publications; classifieds and display ads for buying and selling collectibles.

Lois Bowman, Ed.
Collector, The
P.O. Box 148
Heyworth, IL 61745-0158
phone: 309-473-2466 or 309-473-2940
fax: 309-473-3610
Monthly newspaper for those interested in antiques and collectibles; flea markets, shows, articles, event reviews, etc.; many ads for antiques businesses in the Illinois region; free "I Collect" and "For Sale" ads for collectors.

Statuscourt Ltd.
Collectors Guide
P.O. Box 805
Greenwich
London SE10 8TD, U.K.
A monthly English publications.

Kathy Root
CarPac Publishing Co.
Collectors Journal
1800 W. D St.
P.O. Box 601
Vinton, IA 52349-0601
phone: 319-472-4763 or 319-472-4764
fax: 319-472-3117
Weekly auction paper for collectors and antique lovers; weekly auction and flea market calendar, auction results, and articles.

Cherie Souhrada, Pub.
Collectors News Co.
Collectors News
P.O. Box 156
Grundy Center, IA 50638-0156
phone: 319-824-6981 or 800-352-8039
fax: 319-824-3414
e-mail: collectors@collectors-news.com
Internet: http://collectors-news.com
The monthly newsprint magazine for antiquers & collectors nationwide; complete show & sale calendar, articles, limited edition collectibles, expert advice, values, etc.; price guide in every issue.

Collectors' Advantage
17-10 River Rd., #4-D
Fair Lawn, NJ 07410
phone: 201-796-5552
fax: 201-796-2250
A resource journal for the collectibles enthusiast.

William Margolin
Collectors' Classified
P.O. Box 347
Holbrook, MA 02343-0347
phone: 617-961-1463
Published monthly; all collectibles - especially cards, coins, stamps, books, memorabilia; published since 1975; free subscriber ads.

Hearst Corporation, The
Colonial Homes Magazine
1790 Broadway
New York, NY 10019-1400
phone: 212-830-2919
fax: 212-586-2455
e-mail: colonialhomes@hearst.com
A bi-monthly glossy magazine that focuses on architecture, decorating, crafts, collectibles, and antiques.

Ian Feller
Century Publishing Company
Combo
5 Nassau Blvd.
Garden City, NY 11530-4111
phone: 516-292-6000
fax: 516-292-6007
e-mail: 75764.3302@compuerve.com
Internet: http://worldavenue.com/
  shopping/combo
Monthly magazine with latest news and prices for comics, non-sports cards, action figures, video games, gaming and more.

Cotton & Quail Antique Trail
205 East Washington St.
P.O. Box 326
Monticello, FL 32344-1951
phone: 800-757-7755 or 904-997-3880
fax: 904-997-3090
A monthly newspaper on antiques and collectibles; wide variety of general interest articles; covers the Southeast; 65,000 readers; distributed in over 2200 antique malls, shops and shows.

Lorraine Shea, Ed.
GCR Publishing Group, Inc.
Country Accents
1700 Broadway
New York, NY 10019-5905
phone: 212-541-7100 or 800-955-3870
fax: 212-245-1241
Published six times per year; focuses on decorating, crafts, collectibles, and antiques.

Judith Karns, Manag. Ed.
Long Publications, Inc.
Country Folk Art Magazine
8393 East Holly Rd.
Holly, MI 48442-8819
phone: 810-634-9675 or 800-437-1218
fax: 810-634-0301
Country Folk Art is the first publication to combine the catalog and magazine formats; features articles on antiques, contemporary folk artisans, travel spots, recipes, lots of ads, decorating with folk art.

Larry Erickson
Country Home
1716 Locust St.
Des Moines, IA 50309-3023
phone: 515-284-2740
fax: 515-284-2552
e-mail: lerickso@dsm.mdp.com
A monthly magazine with lots of ads and in-depth articles about antiques, collectibles, decorative accessories, reproductions, interior decorating and architecture.

Hearst Corporation
Country Living
224 West 57th St.
New York, NY 10019
phone: 800-876-8696 or 212-649-3192
A monthly magazine that focuses on decorating, crafts, collectibles, and antiques.

Cowles Magazines, Inc.
Early American Homes Magazine
741 Miller Dr. SE, Ste. D2
Harrisburg, PA 20175
phone: 703-771-9400 or 800-829-3340
fax: 703-779-8345
Internet: http://www.thehistorynet.com
All aspects of American life before 1850 and material culture, i.e. pottery, iron, textiles, furnishings, architecture, ornament, utilitarian objects in depth (formerly "Early American Life").

John & Liz Elvin
Elvin's Small Fortune
P.O. Box 229
Rexford, NY 12148-0229
phone: 518-384-1182
fax: 518-384-2027
e-mail: elvins@global2000.net
Teaches readers how to recognize and value antiques and collectibles.

Finders & Pickers Newsletter
Fort Dodge, IA 50501-0141
Monthly newsletter for finders and pickers; lists thousands of items wanted by dealers, collectors,

museums and others; timely articles, tips and resources; SASE for information; sample copy $5.

Connie Wills
Soaring Eagle Publications
Georgian Antique Digest
P.O. Box 429
Thornbury
Ontario N0H 2PO Canada
phone: 519-599-5017
fax: 519-599-5017
A quarterly magazine with informational articles on antiques to whet the appetite of the collecting public; helps them become familiar with the shops and shows around South Central Ontario, close to the Eastern Great Lakes states.

Greg Wilcox, Pub.
Great Lakes Trader
132 South Putnam
Williamston, MI 48895
phone: 517-655-5621 or 800-785-3637
fax: 517-655-5380
Michigan's prime antiques trade paper; monthly show listings, original articles on antiques and related items, monthly auction and show reviews, ads.

Hawaii Antiques
P.O. Box 853
Honolulu, HI 96808
phone: 808-591-0049

Cowles Magazines, Inc.
Historic Traveler
741 Miller Dr. SE, Ste. D2
Harrisburg, PA 20175
phone: 703-771-9400 or 800-829-3340
fax: 703-779-8345
Internet: http://www.thehistorynet.com

Barry Younce
Hobby Journal
1103 E. Applegate Ct.
Lenoir, NC 28645
A publication for hobbyists.

Hudson Valley Antiquer, The
P.O. Box 561
Rhinebeck, NY 12572-0561
phone: 914-876-8766
fax: 914-876-8768
A free newspaper published monthly; distributed at antiques businesses and other locations throughout the Hudson Valley; the only Hudson Valley antiquing paper extensively distributed in New York City; available by subscription.

J&J Publishing, Inc.
Inside Antiques
11912 Mississippi Ave. #E
Los Angeles, CA 90025
phone: 310-826-8583
A monthly magazine focusing on the Southern California market.

Jacques Herrijgers
JH All Hobbies
1 Nachtegaallaan, B-1701
Itterbeek, Belgium
A quarterly international publication for hobbyists, collectors and penpal seekers; a bilingual publication (English and French.)

Journal America
P.O. Box 459
Hewitt, NJ 07421
phone: 201-728-8355
fax: 201-728-7128
e-mail: journal@warwick.net
Internet: http://www.ajournal.com
Articles on all types of antiques and collectibles; also questions and answers.

Oxford University Press, Inc., c/o Journals Marketing Dept.
Journal of the History of Collections
2001 Evans Rd.
Cary, NC 27513
phone: 919-677-0977
fax: 919-677-1714
An international journal devoted to the study of collections from palaces and household accumulations to systematic museum collections.

Ralph & Terry Kovel
Kovels on Antiques & Collectibles
P.O. Box 22200
Beachwood, OH 44122-0200
phone: 800-571-1555 or 800-829-9158
fax: 216-752-3115
Internet: http://www.kovel.com
Focuses on antiques, decorative arts and collectibles; identification and buying tips, prices, reproduction alerts, etc.

Brant Art Publications
Magazine Antiques, The
575 Broadway
New York, NY 10012
phone: 212-941-2800 or 800-925-8059
fax: 212-941-2897
A full-color monthly magazine featuring detailed articles about art and antiques.

Sam & Sally Pennington
Maine Antique Digest, Inc.
Maine Antique Digest
911 Main St.
P.O. Box 1429
Waldoboro, ME 04572-1429
phone: 207-832-7534
fax: 207-832-7341
e-mail: mad@maine.com
Internet: http://maineantiquedigest.com
The major monthly newspaper on antiques, art and Americana.

North Shore Weeklies, Inc.
MassBay Antiques
2 Washington St.
P.O. Box 192
Ipswich, MA 01938
phone: 508-777-7070 or 508-356-5141
fax: 508-356-9188
Circulation of 20,000 plus 5000 more during big show months; shows,

auctions, people, research articles, extensive calendar section.

Brian Savage
Fun Publications
Master Collector
12513 Birchfalls Dr.
Raleigh, NC 27614-9675
phone: 800-772-6673 or 919-847-5263
e-mail: bsavage@mastercollector.com
Internet: http:// www.mastercollector.com
Ads-only newspaper; dolls (antique and modern collectible), toys, banks, models, cars, Matchbox, monsters, puzzles, political, toy trains, etc.; subscribers receive free 30 word ad each month; published monthly; reaches 20,000.

Diamandis Communications Inc.
Memories
1515 Broadway
New York, NY 10036
phone: 212-719-6000
Bi-monthly magazine featuring articles and photographs about issues, celebrities, events, etc of the last 50 years.

Metropolitan Home
P.O. Box 51892
Boulder, CO 80323-1892

Lydia A. Stainback, Ed.
MidAtlantic Antiques Magazine
P.O. Box 908
Henderson, NC 27536-0908
phone: 919-492-4001 or 800-326-3894
fax: 919-430-0125
A monthly newspaper for antiques, collectibles and the antiques trade; listing upcoming shows & auctions; display ads for shops and mail order items.

Mountain States Collector
P.O. Box 2525
Evergreen, CO 80439-2525
phone: 303-987-3994
fax: 303-674-1253
Primarily distributed through advertisers, but subscriptions are also available; focuses on the mountain states; show schedules, articles, columns, etc.

Woody Russell
NHN Publishing
National Hobby News, The
P.O. Box 612
New Philadelphia, OH 44663-0612
phone: 216-339-6338
A nation-wide quarterly publication; lots and lots of get-rich-quick and mail order ads; a few short articles of interest to the collector.

Jody Young, GM
New England Antiques Journal, The
4 Church St.
P.O. Box 120
Ware, MA 01082-0120
phone: 413-967-3505 or 800-432-3505
fax: 413-967-6009
Monthly newspaper providing the best

coverage of New England: shops listed geographically, shows, auctions and a wide range of feature material.

Charles Wibel
New Hampshire Antiques Monthly
P.O. 546
Farmington, NH 03835-0546
phone: 603-755-4568
A monthly publication.

New York Eye Publishing Co.
New York Antique Almanac
P.O. Box 2400
New York, NY 10021-0057
Antiques and collectibles trade newspaper with ads, articles, auction and show reports; nationwide coverage.

Andrew D. Wolfe, Pub.
Messenger-Wolfe Publications
New York-Pennsylvania Collector, The
P.O. Drawer C
Fishers, NY 14453
phone: 716-924-8230 or 800-836-1868
fax: 716-924-7734
e-mail: WolfePub@Frontiernet.Net
Informative articles on art, antiques & Americana; show and auction reviews; annual subject index in Jan.; calendar of events.

Harold Hanson, Ed.
Northeast Journal of Antiques & Art
P.O. Box 635
Hudson, NY 12534
phone: 518-828-1616
fax: 518-828-9437
Focuses on the New York and New England area; articles, ads, show and auction calendar.

Charles Muller
Ohio Antique Review
P.O. Box 538
Columbus, OH 43085-0538
phone: 614-885-9757 or 800-992-9757
fax: 614-885-9762
A monthly newspaper serving the dealers and collectors of Mid-America: articles, shows, auctions, ads, etc.

Don Baker, Jr.
Ohio Collectors' Magazine
P.O. Box 1522
Piqua, OH 45356
Focuses on the Ohio antique and collectibles market; published five times per year.

Bill Alexander, Ed.
Old News is Good News Antiques Gazette, The
P.O. Box 305
Hammond, LA 70403-1069
phone: 504-429-0575
fax: 504-429-0576
e-mail: gazette@i-55.com
A monthly newspaper focusing on the heritage, antiques, collectibles and attractions of the South; antiques auctions and shows, stories on

collections, shops and museums, historic attractions, etc.

Donna L. Miller
Old Stuff
P.O. Box 1084
Mcminnville, OR 97128-1084
phone: 503-434-5386 or 503-472-2139
fax: 503-472-2601
Published 6 times/year; a newspaper about the antiques, collectibles, history, and nostalgia of the Northwest U.S.; lots of ads, articles, show and auction calendar.

Tom Ratzloff
Old Times, The
P.O. Box 340
Maple Lake, MN 55350-0340
phone: 800-539-1810
fax: 320-963-6010
e-mail: oldtimes@lkdllink.net
Monthly newspaper serving antiques collectors in MN, WI, and IA.

Pat & Woody Laughnan
Plain Folks
1750 N. Farris Ave.
Fresno, CA 93704-5907
phone: 209-237-5947
fax: 209-237-5947
Monthly newspaper acts as clearinghouse for advertisers, readers and collectors of vintage music, instruments, bands, vintage music books; includes band ads, articles, announcements of concerts and festivals.

British Connection, The
Realm
P.O. Box 215
Landisburg, PA 17040-9989
A glossy magazine featuring articles about the land, history, peoples, and arts and sciences of England.

Renninger's Antique Guide
P.O. Box 495
Lafayette Hill, PA 19444-0495
phone: 610-828-4614 or 610-825-6392
fax: 610-834-1599
Newspaper covering antique shows, shops, flee markets and auctions catering primarily to the mid-Atlantic region.

Journal-Verlag Schwend GmbH
Sammler Journal
Vertriebsabteilung SJ
Postfach 10 03 04, D-74503
Schwabisch Hall, Germany
German glossy monthly auction, dealer and show ads; monthly calendar; articles about antiques and collectibles; written in German.

Der Heisse Draft Verlag
Sammler Market
Postfach 6163, D-30061
Hanover, Germany
Classified and display advertising driven newsprint monthly.

Smithsonian Institution
Smithsonian Magazine
900 Jefferson Dr. SW
Washington, DC 20560
phone: 202-786-2900
Internet: http://www.si.edu/

Sotheby's Subscriptions
Sotheby's Preview
P.O. Box 5111
Norwalk, CT 06856-9851
phone: 203-447-6843
A magazine exploring the history, forms, styles, techniques, etc. of the world of art; meet the collectors, experts & specialists.

Southern Antiques
P.O. Drawer 1107
Decatur, GA 30031-1107
phone: 404-289-0054
fax: 404-286-9727
The South's leading monthly antiques and collectibles newspaper.

Robert Stewart
Swap Meet Shopper, The
P.O. Box 35123
Panama City, FL 32412
e-mail: smshopper@aol.com
Internet: http://members.aol.com/smshopper/index.html
A classified ad paper where you can buy, sell, trade collectible items of interest: petroliana, soda items, jukeboxes, pedal cars, bicycles, pinball/arcade, advertising signs, barber shop items, etc.; 11 issues per year.

Traditional Home
Traditional Home
1716 Locust St. - 430
Des Moines, IA 50309
Colorful bi-monthly magazine emphasizing the use of antiques in today's home; also articles about reproductions, building materials, and collecting; packed with redecorating items.

David & Constance Donnelly
Treasure Chest Publishing
Treasure Chest
P.O. Box 245
North Scituate, RI 02847-0245
phone: 212-496-2234 or 800-557-9662
fax: 401-647-0051
A monthly information source & marketplace for collectors & dealers of antiques and collectibles; emphasis is on antique shop, show, auction and classified ads; distributed in the NY, NJ, PA, CT, MA, and RI area.

GEMI Verlags GmbH
Trodler & Sammeln
Pfaffenhofener Strasse 3, D-85293
Reichertshafen, Germany
Glossy monthly magazine focusing exclusively on the antiques market.

Kathy Greer, Ed.
Unravel the Gavel
9 Hurricane Rd. #1
Belmont, NH 03220-5603
phone: 603-524-4281
fax: 603-528-3565
e-mail: Gavel96@aol.com
Internet: http://www.the-forum.com/gavel
Focusing on the northern New England area: covers auctions, antiques and collectibles in NH, VT, ME, MA, plus upstate NY.

Bill Dobson
Upper Canadian, The
P.O. Box 653
Smiths Falls
Ontario K7A 5B8 Canada
phone: 613-283-1168
fax: 613-283-1345
e-mail: uppercanadian@recorder.ca
A bi-monthly Canadian newspaper with auction and show coverage, educational content, photo-ads, show and auction calendar, restoration section, and price guides; presents current trends in the Canadian antiques and collectibles business.

Hearst Corporation
Victoria
224 West 57th St.
New York, NY 10019
phone: 800-876-8696 or 212-649-3192
Glossy monthly magazine; home decorating, recipes, gardening, architecture, country living; some articles about antiques & collectibles.

Florian McCain, Ed.
GCR Publishing Group, Inc.
Victorian Decorating & Lifestyle
1700 Broadway
New York, NY 10019-5905
phone: 212-541-7100 or 800-955-3870
fax: 212-245-1241
A glossy bi-monthly magazine that focuses on decorating, crafts, collectibles, antiques, Victorian people and costumes.

Victorian Homes
Victorian Homes
P.O. Box 61
Millers Falls, MA 01349
phone: 413-659-3785
fax: 413-659-3113
Glossy magazine with information sources for locating special items for restoring and decorating Victorian homes.

Vintage Collector, The
P.O. Box 764
Hotchkiss, CO 81419-0764
phone: 970-872-2226
Western Colorado's information source for collectors.

Angelia Jordan
Vintage Times, The
5692 Zebulon Rd., #368
Macon, GA 31202
phone: 912-757-4755 or 800-560-4887
fax: 912-474-4092
e-mail: antiques@mylink.net
A monthly newspaper focusing on the antiques & collectibles trade of the Southeast U.S.; articles, columns, ads, shop directories and maps, some modern collectibles; free calendar listings for auctions, shows and fairs.

Julie A. Ulrich, PR
Krause Publications
NewsWarman's Today's Collector
700 E. State St.
Iola, WI 54990-0001
phone: 715-445-2214
fax: 715-445-4087
e-mail: info@krause.com
Internet: http://www.krause.com
Monthly magazine with the latest news and market reports for dozens of areas of collector interest; classified ads, nationwide auction results, updated auction & collectibles show calendar in every issue.

Jay Telfer
Wayback Times, The
RR #1, Rednersville Rd.
Belleville
Ontario K8N 4Z1 Canada
phone: 613-966-8749
fax: 613-966-8747
e-mail: waybackt@intranet.on.ca
Covering the Ontario area antique stores and B&Bs.

Rosalie Dannenbaum, Pub.
West Coast Peddler
P.O. Box 5134
Whittier, CA 90607
phone: 310-698-1718
fax: 310-698-1500
Oldest monthly newspaper about antiques, the arts, and collectibles serving the Pacific States, California, Oregon, and Washington.

Western CT/Western MA Antiquer, The
P.O. Box 561
Rhinebeck, NY 12572-0561
phone: 914-876-8766
fax: 914-876-8768
A free newspaper published monthly; distributed at antiques businesses and other locations throughout Western CT and MA; available by subscription.

RoseAnn L. Donahoo
Wonderful Things
P.O. Box 2288
Winter Park, FL 32790
phone: 406-332-0954
Published monthly; for collectors, hobbyists, & people who enjoy interesting, wholesome lifestyles & events; all fields of collectibles and hobbies; emphasis on reader

participation and sharing; letters and commentary welcome.

Yankee, Inc.
Yankee Magazine
P.O. Box 37017
Boone, IA 50037-0017
phone: 800-288-4284
Internet: http://www.newengland.com/store/store.YKsub.html

Michael Jacobi
Yesteryear
P.O. Box 2
Princeton, WI 54968
phone: 920-787-4808
fax: 920-787-7381
A monthly newspaper featuring articles and ads about antiques & collectibles; shop directory, extensive calendar of events covering flea markets, antique shows, etc.; covering the North Central states.

When requesting information about a particular item, include a description (material, dimensions, maker's mark, model number, etc.) and a photo, sketch, or photocopy of the item in question. ■

Always ask if there are charges for samples or for the services requested. ■

When writing, please be sure to include a Large (#10 business size) Self-Addressed and Stamped Envelope (LSASE) if requesting a reply or the return of photographs. ■

Never call collect unless otherwise directed. When calling, be considerate of time zone differences and always ask if the party you are calling has time to talk. When leaving an answering machine message, always instruct the party to call you back collect. ■

APPENDIX D

Repair Services
Listed in ZIP code order

The firms listed below are professionals specializing in the repair and refinishing of damaged household goods. They are members of the *Claims Prevention & Procedure Council*, the only nonprofit association that is exclusively dedicated to claims prevention and claims handling in the moving and storage industry. The CPPC studies the reasons for loss and damage and researches methods to reduce these problems. The CPPC also addresses ways to properly handle claims once they do occur. Membership in the CPPC consists of the major van lines and carriers, local movers and warehousemen,

shippers, insurance firms, adjustors, appraisers, repair services, transit attorneys, government facilities and others. For more information contact the CPPC at P.O. Box 1367, Englewood, FL 34295-1367 or call 941-473-CPPC or (fax 941-473-2775). Refer also to the REPAIR/RESTORATOIN/CONSERVATION section of this directory's General Listings as well as to the *Repair Services* listed under specific categories for additional repairers, restorers, and conservators.

Ray Blais
The Finishing Touch
795 Westhampton Rd.
Northampton MA 01060
phone: (413) 586-5562

Carl Bryant
Furniture Medic
22 Porter Rd.
Littleton MA 01460
phone: (508) 486-9554
fax: (508) 486-9554

Gerald Brodeur, Jr.
Furniture Plus
312 N. Main St.
N. Uxbridge MA 01538
phone: (508) 278-7910
fax: (508) 278-4249

Joseph Branzetti
J.O.B. Finishing
3 Dundee Park Dr., #10
Andover MA 01810
phone: (508) 470-1800
fax: (508) 470-0015

Bill Stack
Salem Village Furn. Repair
11 Elmwood St.
Amesbury MA 01913
phone: (508) 388-0420
fax: (508) 388-6255

Eric Miklas
Fantastic Finishes
5 Old Wharf Rd.
West Newbury MA 01985
phone: (508) 363-2985
fax: (508) 363-5340

Robert Judd
Judd, Robert Refinishing
234 York Street
Canton MA 02021
phone: (617) 828-6629
fax: (617) 821-2699

Jon White
Classic Furniture Services
25 Kenwood Circle, Unit 1
Franklin MA 02038
phone: (508) 528-6747
fax: (508) 520-0408

Walter & Carol Anderson
The Leather Solution
P.O. Box 966
Mansfield MA 02048
phone: (508) 339-5293
fax: (508) 261-9398

Leon Trefler
Trefler & Sons Antique Rest.
99 Cabot St.
Needham MA 02194
phone: (617) 444-2685

Ed Or Larry Mathews
Bird's "Chem-Clean" Furn
Rest.
402 Gifford Street
Falmouth MA 02540
phone: (508) 548-5370
fax: (508) 540-2859

Patrick Mahoney
Furniture Medic
4 Mullen Way
Falmouth MA 02540
phone: (508) 457-5200

Joseph Sabatino
People In The Woods
178 East Main Rd.
Middletown RI 02842
phone: (401) 846-3335
fax: (401) 846-3378

Edward And Ida Trenn
Furniture Medic
1 Marla Court
Warwick RI 02886
phone: (401) 739-9336

Paul Ziarnowski
Furniture Medic
3 Chappelll Dr.
Milford NH 03055-3206
phone: (603) 672-9400
fax: (603) 672-2620

Jim Jordan
Jordan Furniture Repair
214 County Road
Bedford NH 03110
phone: (603) 669-7118
fax: (603) 645-6226

Charles P. Matteson
Furniture Medic
P.O. Box 231
Stratford NH 03884-0231
phone: (603) 664-5305
fax: (603) 664-6971

Larry Clements
Furniture Medic
8 Gloucester Hill Rd.
New Gloucester ME 04260
phone: (207) 926-3563
fax: (207) 926-3797

Trevett Hooper
Furniture Medic
Rr#1, Box 283
Orrington ME 04474
phone: (207) 989-0366
fax: (207) 989-0366

George Parker
Interstate Furniture Repair
Rf D2 Box 2136
Farmington ME 04938
phone: (207) 778-6678
fax: (207) 778-2945

Jonathan Schechtman
Meeting House Furn. Restor.
11 Waterman Hill
Quechee VT 05059
phone: (802) 295-1309
fax: (802) 296-5911

David Kent
Kent's Furniture Service
P.O. Box 8001
Essex VT 05451
phone: (802) 878-9955
fax: (802) 878-0225

Brad Witham
Country Village Antique Rest.
652 Williston Rd.
Williston VT 05495
phone: (802) 878-8269
fax: (802) 872-8046

Greg Fowler
Furniture Medic
P.O. Box 5
Waterbury VT 05676
phone: (800) 458-1984
fax: (802) 244-1944

Jim Jarvis
Furniture Medic
P.O. Box 248
Barton VT 05822-0248
phone: (802) 525-1100
fax: (802) 525-1100

Stanley Mylek
Furniture Medic
23 Griswold Dr.
Windsor CT 06095
phone: (860) 688-1568
fax: (860) 688-1568

Tom Selmecki
Woodshed, The
20 Parkview Dr.
Niantic CT 06357
phone: (860) 739-6802
fax: (860) 739-7199

Terrence Flynn
Furniture Medic
561 Old Colchester Rd.
Uncasville CT 06382
phone: (203) 848-2972

Kenneth J. Shackford
Furniture Medic
19 Lasky Rd.
Beacon Falls CT 06403
phone: (203) 723-0679
fax: (203) 723-1263

Vladimir Zhitnitsky
Alladin's Touch
10 Roger St.
Cheshire CT 06410
phone: (203) 271-1709
fax: (203) 271-1910

Andrew Daly
The Leather Solution
231 Sterling St.
Fairfield CT 06430
phone: (203) 330-9050
fax: (203) 330-9050

Michael Pellegrino
Custom Furniture Refinishing
107 Richards Dr.
Monroe CT 06468
phone: (203) 268-0478
fax: (203) 261-7449

Dimitri & Georgiana Nedelcu
Universal Restoration
267 Derby Ave.
Orange CT 06477
phone: (203) 795-8849
fax: (203) 795-8849

Alex Zhitnitsky
Al's Furniture Restorers, Inc.
425 Ella T. Grasso Boulevard
New Haven CT 06519
phone: (203) 865-1885
fax: (203) 562-5868

Marty Horowitz
Connecticut Claims Svc. Inc.
78 Anthony Ct.
Bethany CT 06524
phone: (203) 393-2711
fax: (203) 393-0489

James Letis
Final Touch
34 Ranch Rd.
Woodbridge CT 06525
phone: (203) 389-5485
fax: (203) 389-5553

Carl A. Colagrossi
C. Colagrossi Furn. R & R
P.O. Box 376
Waterbury CT 06720
phone: (203) 757-0793
fax: (203) 757-5773

Stephen S. Minsk
L & S Furniture Service
P.O. Box 57
Cedar Grove NJ 07009
phone: (201) 228-5833
fax: (201) 228-3566

Fernando Gonzales
The Leather Solution
179 Berger St.
Wood-Ridge NJ 07075
phone: (201) 438-1237
fax: (201) 438-1432

Daniel Manning
Manning Claim Services
P.O. Box 212
Allendale NJ 07401
phone: (201) 825-8450
fax: (201) 825-8301

Scott Perry
AE Nationwide Mechanical
Rep
184 Franklin Turnpike
Mahwah NJ 07430
phone: (800) 631-7174
fax: (201) 529-8143

Bob Preis
Preis Carpentry/Formica Work
24 Davidson Ave.
Ramsey NJ 07446
phone: (201) 825-6958
fax: (201) 825-7514

James Walsh
Household Movers Services
P.O. Box 19
Ridgewood NJ 07451
phone: (800) 526-0887
fax: (800) 555-4675

Duncan Peterson
Furniture Medic
879 West Park Ave., #226
Ocean NJ 07712
phone: (908) 542-7283
fax: (908) 542-2251

Kendall Frantz
Furniture Medic
46 Prospect Circle
Atlantic Highlands NJ 07716
phone: (908) 872-2626
fax: (908) 872-2626

Dave Lindeblad
Atlantic Restoration Co.
62 W. Blackwell St.
Dover NJ 07801
phone: (800) 729-1433
fax: (201) 989-9232

Charles Martens
Furniture Medic
8 Adams Dr.
Denville NJ 07834
phone: (201) 625-3775
fax: (201) 625-3775

Victor Franco,Jr.
Franco Furniture Repair Svc.
999 Willow Grove St., 8-A
Hackettstown NJ 07840
phone: (908) 813-0941
fax: (908) 852-1311

Terry Howard
Philadelphia Furn. Rep. Svc.
1802 Winding Way
Clementon NJ 08021
phone: (800) 318-1859
fax: (609) 772-2161

Bob Wieckowski
Furniture Medic
16 Fox Hill Rd.
Edison NJ 08820
phone: (908) 549-1736
fax: (908) 549-1736

Mordechai Shlomo
Fine Art Wood Repair Corp.
500 C Grand St.
New York NY 10002
phone: (212) 260-8219
fax: (212) 260-3692

Peter Lightstone
P. Lightstone & Son
2211 Broadway
New York NY 10024
phone: (212) 799-4330
fax: (212) 580-0900

Beverly D'onofrio
Renaissance Restoration
Main P.O. Box 562
Purchase NY 10577
phone: (914) 667-9866
fax: (914) 699-7174

Steve Amato
Amato's Furniture Repair
847 Wilmot Rd.
Scarsdale NY 10583
phone: (914) 723-6477
fax: (914) 723-6450

Robert Cinquemani
Sebastian Restorations
118 New Hyde Park Rd.
Franklin Square NY 11010
phone: (516) 354-6051
fax: (516) 354-0589

John E. Malnosky
New Masters Restoration, Inc.
243-28 132nd Rd.
Queens NY 11422
phone: (718) 525-1100

John Rosini
Rosini Furniture Service
232 Herricks Road
Mineola NY 11501
phone: (516) 739-6900
fax: (516) 739-6999

Robert Kugelmass
Robert Kugelmass Tran Clm
Svc
979 Van Buren St.
Baldwin NY 11510
phone: (516) 379-2982
fax: (516) 379-2982

R. J. Daly
The Leather Solution, Inc.
18 Johnson Place
Baldwin NY 11510
phone: (800) 468-5852
fax: (516) 223-3748

Carmine Auriemma
A & M Restoration
19 Broadoak Lane
Dix Hills NY 11746-5901
phone: (516) 351-6171
fax: (516) 351-4978

Jeff Ritzmann
J & J Woodworking & Furn.
Svc.
21 Dunn Ct.
Sayville NY 11782
phone: (516) 563-4450
fax: (516) 244-2925

Ronald Ricca
Furniture Medic
1140 Mill Lane
Peconic NY 11958
phone: (516) 765-5410

W. Jay Thomas
Furniture Medic
129 Shawn Dr.
Gloversville NY 12078
phone: (518) 456-5838
fax: (518) 456-5838

Michael Derocha
Atlantic Restoration Svc.
P.O. Box 102
Pleasant Valley NY 12569
phone: (914) 471-2293
fax: (914) 452-3606

Steve Fisch
Finisher's Touch
10 W. Main St.
Wappingers Falls NY 12590
phone: (914) 298-8882
fax: (914) 298-8945

Sylvia & James Sheehan
J & S Invisible Repairs
29 Elm Street
Glens Falls NY 12801
phone: (518) 798-6445
fax: (518) 745-5934

Joseph Pryor
Furniture Medic
1447 State Road 31
Bridgeport NY 13030
phone: (315) 424-0909
fax: (315) 424-0909

Carol A. Citra
Mario Citra Furniture Service
328 N. Beech St.
Syracuse NY 13203
phone: (315) 472-4988
fax: (315) 424-0050

Len Paradise
Loss Recovery Systems
10 Dwight Park Dr.
Syracure NY 13209
phone: (315) 451-9111
fax: (315) 451-9222

Donald P. Levesque
Wood Finishers New York
108 Baum Ave.
N. Syracuse NY 13212-2320
phone: (315) 452-3375
fax: (315) 458-4457

Richard Toombs
Furniture Medic
135 Edgehill Rd.
Syracuse NY 13224
phone: (315) 445-1100
fax: (315) 445-1206

Marge Vanslyke
Furniture Refinishing
905 Highland Ave.
Rome NY 13440
phone: (315) 339-2226
fax: (315) 334-9568

Jim Sullivan
Furniture Repair Service
Rd #1 Box 64b
Bainbridge NY 13733
phone: (607) 639-1326
fax: (607) 639-1686

Paul Atkinson
Atkinson, Paul
15 Wellington
Kenmore (Buffalo) NY 14223
phone: (716) 832-6267
fax: (716) 832-6267

Tom/Katie
A Special Touch
235 Humphrey Rd.
Scottsville NY 14546
phone: (716) 889-9045
fax: (716) 889-2319

Hackim Hosein
The Leather Solution
8 Robert Quigley Dr.
Scottsville NY 14546
phone: (716) 889-7916
fax: (716) 889-7916

Thomas A. Kuhns,Jr.
West Interior Services
P.O. Box 540
Natrona Heights PA 15065
phone: (412) 224-2215
fax: (412) 226-3233

Bill Blair
The Leather Solution
121 Watt Lane
Pittsburgh PA 15221
phone: (412) 247-9480
fax: (412) 247-9481

David Cappalonga
Furniture Medic
Rd #2, Box 291e
Connellsville PA 15425
phone: (412) 626-1799
fax: (412) 626-1881

Dennis Foster
Furniture Medic
Rd 2, Box 61
Indiana PA 15701
phone: (412) 465-8660
fax: (412) 465-8667

Gregory A. Budd
Furniture Medic
3304 Holland St.
Erie PA 16504
phone: (814) 451-0217
fax: (814) 451-0217

Jimmie Goodwin
Furniture Medic
Rd #1, Box 107a, Chestnut St.
Spring Mills PA 16875
phone: (814) 364-2727

Gary Kopperman
Restoration Clinic
5222 E. Trindle Rd.
Mechanicsburg PA 17055
phone: (717) 691-8881
fax: (717) 691-8880

John Repp, Jr.
New Life Service Co.
37 South Constitution Ave.
New Freedom PA 17349
phone: (717) 235-7490
fax: (717) 235-7490

Tim Burns
Mobile Furniture/Uphol Rep.
11 Oak Lane
Stevens PA 17578-9706
phone: (717) 336-3399
fax: (717) 336-3339

Pat Wucher
Furniture Medic
105 Winding Hill Rd.
Lancaster PA 17601
phone: (717) 898-6822
fax: (717) 898-6824

Andrew W. Gelinas
Burlesque Repair Service
18 W. 3rd St.
Bethlehem PA 18015
phone: (610) 867-3313
fax: (610) 867-4999

Joe Bergen
Accurate Furniture Service
85 Bristol Rd.
Chalfont PA 18914
phone: (215) 822-8600
fax: (215) 822-8232

Timothy P. Hughes
Movers Specialty Service Inc
211 Commerce Dr.
Montgomeryville PA 18936
phone: (800) 433-1159
fax: (800) 835-0338

Greg Chassin
Showcase Movers' Services
P.O. Box 855
Richboro PA 18954
phone: (215) 357-3316
fax: (215) 357-5465

Frank Kiska
Furniture Restorations - Plus
1621 Norristown Rd.
Maple Glen PA 19002
phone: (215) 533-5621
fax: (215) 533-5622

Chris Pritchard
The Leather Solution
P.O. Box 211
Willow Grove PA 19090
phone: (215) 657-7811
fax: (215) 659-0709

David Leininger
D & S Restoration Svcs. (Fm)
2128 Sanger St.
Philadelphia PA 19124
phone: (215) 537-1112
fax: (215) 537-1555

Arthur Faber
Furniture Medic
707 West Dekalb Pike, #200
King Of Prussia PA 19406
phone: (610) 265-2622
fax: (610) 265-2642

Byron Klein
A. L. Klein & Son, Inc.
P.O. Box 145
Harleysville PA 19438
phone: (215) 256-9004
fax: (215) 256-9644

John Cooper
Heritage Furniture Systems
521 Grove Ave., #105
Reading PA 19540-1313
phone: (800) 889-6498
fax: (800) 889-0112

Jospeh H. Kaiser
Able Furniture Re. Warr. Co.
25 Shull Dr.
Newark DE 19711
phone: (302) 737-7729
fax: (302) 455-0745

Jeffrey D. Stanley
Jeffrey D. Stanley Furn Rest
50 Germay Dr., Unit 3-C
Wilmington DE 19804
phone: (302) 656-4461
fax: (302) 656-8864

Michael Shur
A Refinishing Touch
604 Hillcrest Avenue
Wilmington DE 19809
phone: (302) 762-3684
fax: (302) 762-4191

Robert Glausser
Furniture Medic
11898 Falling Creek Dr.
Manassas VA 20112
phone: (800) 372-5821
fax: (703) 791-8485

Maudud Alam
Alam Furniture & Claim Svc.
134-Lakeland Dr.
Sterling VA 20164
phone: (703) 450-4222
fax: (703) 444-9564

W. Michael Hartsky
AAA Professional Claim Svcs
12860 Parapet Way
Herndon VA 20171-1725
phone: (703) 758-7442
fax: (703) 758-7443

Frances Schoenbauer
Schoenbauer, RJ, Furn Rep Svc
1008 Ivy Lane
Waldorf MD 20602
phone: (301) 843-0579
fax: (301) 645-9454

Glenn Chaplin
G.A.C. Restorations
P.O. Box 342
Waldorf MD 20604
phone: (800) 282-4814
fax: (800) 282-4828

Bill Schoenbauer
Schoenbauer Furniture Service
30507 Potomac Way
Charlotte Hall MD 20622
phone: (301) 870-7391
fax: (301) 884-3672

Larry Manoly
Manoly Furniture Service, Inc.
8981 Hillary Ct.
La Plata MD 20646
phone: (301) 843-5955
fax: (301) 932-1030

Charles & Isabelle Jourdant
Jourdant, Charles Furn. Rep.
611 Alabama Ave.
North Beach MD 20714-9602
phone: (800) 479-5427
fax: (410) 257-0752

Gene Shontere
Shontere Restoration, Inc.
P.O. Box 1805
Mitchellville MD 20717
phone: (800) 937-3786
fax: (301) 934-0511

Carol Manoly
Manoly Furniture Repair Svc.
11605 Candor Dr.
Mitchellville MD 20721
phone: (301) 805-4221
fax: (301) 464-2034

Mike O'dea
Furniture Medic
14672-J Southlawn Lane
Rockville MD 20850
phone: (301) 315-9600
fax: (301) 315-9602

L. Philip Oliver
L.P. Oliver & Sons Inc.
Po Box 659/24610 Frederick
Rd
Clarksburg MD 20871-0659
phone: (800) 752-2168
fax: (301) 428-9282

David R. Harrison
Antique Art & Furniture Co.
17214 Birdsong Lane
Gaithersburg MD 20878
phone: (301) 258-9317
fax: (301) 208-1287

Bob Maclellan
Strip Joint Etc., Inc, The
514 Pulaski Hwy.
Joppa MD 21085
phone: (410) 679-0795
fax: (410) 679-0812

Pete Simonetti
Artisian Restoration
P.O. Box 72035
Baltimore MD 21237
phone: (410) 682-3700
fax: (410) 682-3738

Thomas Schoenbauer
T. Schoenbauer Restorations
29 Francis St.
Annapolis MD 21401
phone: (410) 268-8315
fax: (410) 268-1649

John C. Pyle
Glade Valley Furn. Repair
10464 Glade Road
Walkersville MD 21793
phone: (301) 898-3795

Lewis Brumberg, Jr.
Furniture Medic
P.O. Box 2218, Mbs
Ocean City MD 21842-8218
phone: (302) 436-5077
fax: (302) 436-8215

Paul Hirmer
Paul's Furniture Repair
16020 Fleetwood Dr.
Catlett VA 22019
phone: (703) 594-3268
fax: (703) 594-3601

Albert Ibrahim
Albert Ibrahim Furn. Repair
6050 Rockton Ct.
Centerville VA 22020
phone: (703) 968-3386
fax: (703) 803-0620

Reece Conner, Jr.
Servicemaster of Arl'ton Etc.
14325-D Willard Rd.
Chantilly VA 22021
phone: (703) 527-5900
fax: (703) 968-0568

Gene Shontere
Shontere Restoration, Inc.
P.O. Box 1018
Springfield VA 22151
phone: (800) 937-3786
fax: (301) 934-0511

Joseph Skinner
Furniture Medic
7911 Larrick Court
Springfield VA 22153
phone: (703) 451-8035
fax: (703) 913-3225

Bill Kola
Transportation Related Svcs.
P.O. Box 188
Woodbridge VA 22194
phone: (703) 491-0285

David Sisson
Metal Magic
6647 S. Kings Hwy.
Alexandria VA 22306
phone: (703) 660-9180
fax: (703) 660-9181

Orrin Tyler
Five Star Restorations
3807 Timber Ridge Rd.
Midlothian VA 23112
phone: (804) 744-7103
fax: (804) 744-7164

Ernie & Doyle Miller
Classic Touch Furn. Rep. Svc.
P.O. Box 11163
Richmond VA 23230
phone: (804) 358-0010
fax: (804) 359-0084

Harold Smith
Smith Furniture Svc., Inc
3618 Tidewater Drive
Norfolk VA 23509
phone: (804) 623-0022
fax: (804) 623-0672

Mark Weathersby
Craftsmanship By Weathersby
9521 Shore Drive
Norfolk VA 23518
phone: (804) 362-8412
fax: (804) 362-9013

Lowell A. Galumbeck
Furniture By Lowell
605-N Industrial Park Drive
Newport News VA 23602
phone: (757) 874-7977
fax: (757) 898-9815

Susan Price
Furniture Medic
4 Quail Place
Newport News VA 23608-
1820
phone: (757) 874-2858
fax: (757) 874-9445

Tommy Nelson, Jr.
Pro-Finish
1006 East Third St.
Farmville VA 23901
phone: (804) 392-5761
fax: (800) 435-0776

Troy Y. Miller
Furniture Medic
P.O. Box 11541
Roanoke VA 24022
phone: (703) 366-2175

Joe Mcgowen
Renovators Workshop
5815 Kanawha Trail
Covington VA 24426
phone: (540) 559-4818
fax: (540) 559-4014

Stephan R. Phelps
P & P Transit Claims
P.O. Box 4196
Lynchburg VA 24502
phone: (804) 385-6367
fax: (804) 385-0618

Larry Somerville
Woodco Furniture Restoration
Rt. 11, Box 539-E
Parkersburg WV 26101
phone: (304) 489-1418
fax: (304) 489-3284

Rick Davis
Carolina Furniture Specialist
111-A Griffith Plaza Drive
Winston-Salem NC 27103
phone: (910) 760-9999
fax: (910) 760-4045

Larry Tysinger
Lt Transit Claims Svc., Inc.
1438 E. Dixie Dr., Ste. 135
Asheboro NC 27203
phone: (910) 629-8451
fax: (910) 629-1761

Jerry Mcentire
J & M Furniture Repair
708 Carr St.
High Point NC 27262
phone: (910) 454-6101
fax: (910) 454-1636

Bill Brown
Wood-Pro
2005 Kildare Woods Drive
Greensboro NC 27407
phone: (910) 889-8287
fax: (910) 889-8287

Mike Pennington
Day-Mar Furniture Repair
600 Stage Coach Trail
Greensboro NC 27409
phone: (910) 632-9000
fax: (910) 632-9903

Indrek Lepson
Reflections In Wood
P.O. Box 1088
Wake Forest NC 27588
phone: (919) 556-8810

Bill Johnson
Bishop Furniture & Upholst.
1128 N. Blount St.
Raleigh NC 27604
phone: (919) 829-1200
fax: (919) 829-1305

Jeff & Beverly Bartholomew
Furniture Medic
4509 Connell Drive
Raleigh NC 27612
phone: (919) 510-8787
fax: (919) 510-8787

Mark Stocking
Furniture Medic
3504 Old Chapel Hill Rd.
Durham NC 27707
phone: (919) 493-4963
fax: (919) 493-4963

Gary Geldmacher
Beach Vinyl & Leather Repair
P.O. Box 2022
Kill Devil Hills NC 27948
phone: (919) 480-3798

Dennis W. Bell
The Finishing Touch
1033 West Gaston Avenue
Gastonia NC 28052
phone: (704) 868-8538
fax: (704) 868-8543

Dan Jones
Claim Services
1324 Princeton Ave.
Gastonia NC 28054
phone: (704) 866-8817
fax: (704) 866-8860

Hugh Weiss
Studio Shop
307 N. Caswell Rd.
Charlotte NC 28204
phone: (704) 375-9121

Michael Walter
American Woodworking
Spl'ists
2217 Chesterfield Ave.
Charlotte NC 28205-6015
phone: (704) 372-1006
fax: (704) 372-5736

Scott Benner
Furniture Medic
2313 Linda Lou Court
Charlotte NC 28213
phone: (704) 593-0575

Mike Moody
T.R.S. Claim Service
P.O. Box 18706
Charlotte NC 28218
phone: (919) 687-5112
fax: (704) 882-8618

Tommy Morales
T.R.S. Claim Service Co.
P.O. Box 18703
Charlotte NC 28218
phone: (704) 882-1117
fax: (704) 882-8618

Greg Clark
Furniture Medic
9210 Hemingford Ct.
Charlotte NC 28277
phone: (704) 332-2898
fax: (704) 332-2899

Bud Steere
Furniture Medic
P.O. Box 197
Fayetteville NC 28302-0197
phone: (910) 484-4055
fax: (910) 484-5991

John Humphreys
Furniture Medic
825-C Merrimon Ave., #146
Asheville NC 28804
phone: (704) 255-8022
fax: (704) 255-8022

Steven T. Brantley
Colonial Woodworks Inc.
1709 Laurel St.
Columbia SC 29201
phone: (803) 254-7519
fax: (803) 765-2643

Rob Beard
Furniture Medic
1375 Emerald Forest Pkway
Charleston SC 29414
phone: (803) 763-9968
fax: (803) 769-0257

Dave Mcbee
The Finishing Touch/Carolinas
334 E. Poplar Branch Dr.
Moncks SC 29461
phone: (803) 761-5513
fax: (803) 761-6612

Robert Wilkins
Furniture Medic
5765 Rosewood Dr.
Myrtle Beach SC 29575
phone: (803) 293-6462
fax: (803) 293-6461

Larry Tysinger
Lt Transit Claims Svc., Inc.
640 F. Leigh Plaza, Hwy 17 S.
Surfside Beach SC 29575
phone: (803) 238-5922
fax: (803) 238-9095

E. Porter Huskey
Furniture Medic
503 Poinsett Hwy
Greenville SC 29609
phone: (864) 242-0997
fax: (864) 242-6161

Teresa Davis
Furniture Clinic of GA, Inc.
P.O. Box 14801
Greenville SC 29610
phone: (864) 306-9600
fax: (864) 306-9690

Max Falls
Furniture Clinic of GA, Inc.
2057 Collins Blvd.
Austell GA 30001
phone: (770) 941-4607
fax: (770) 941-9416

Al Lopez
Furniture Medic
485 Pensdale Rd.
Decatur GA 30030
phone: (404) 370-1119
fax: (404) 370-1208

Jack Williams
Jack Williams Mover's Clm
   Svc.
2447 Kingsley Dr.
Marietta GA 30062
phone: (770) 977-1679
fax: (770) 973-6089

John Majewski
Furniture Medic
6541 Walden Pond Rd.
Stone Mountain GA 30087
phone: (770) 498-9040
fax: (770) 469-0064

Malcolm T. Yarbrough
Yarbrough Furn. Rest., Inc.
2713 Old Burnt Hickory Rd.
Dallas GA 30132-2953
phone: (770) 975-3666
fax: (770) 975-0478

Rick Mckelvey
Furniture Medic
9684 Wood Rd.
Douglasville GA 30134
phone: (770) 920-1016
fax: (770) 920-1016

Pat Weichold
3r Artisans
4790 Coppedge Trail
Duluth GA 30136
phone: (404) 476-5152
fax: (404) 446-0296

Steven W. James
Furniture Medic
P.O. Box 656
Kennsaw GA 30144
phone: (770) 917-0802
fax: (770) 917-0802

Bill Smith
Service Solutions Associates
5879-D New Peachtree Rd.
Doraville GA 30340
phone: (404) 986-9676
fax: (404) 986-9677

Steve Bentz
Bentz & Weathersby Furn. Rep.
3691 Toxaway Court
Atlanta GA 30341
phone: (770) 491-0387
fax: (770) 414-9372

Bill See
Lt Transit Claims Svc. South
3363 W. Hospital Ave. - E
Chamblee GA 30341
phone: (770) 455-6640
fax: (770) 455-6110

Terry Bell
The Finishing Touch (GA/TN)
351 Cops Rd.
Blue Ridge GA 30513
phone: (706) 632-3464
fax: (706) 632-3464

Mike Self
Furniture Medic of N.A.
Rt. 9, Box 1450
Dahlonega GA 30533
phone: (770) 849-9512
fax: (770) 849-9512

Mickey Stephenson
Furniture Medic
P.O. Box 82152
Athens GA 30608-2152
phone: (706) 546-1140
fax: (706) 546-1438

Jerry Weber
Furniture Medic
20 Parkview Circle
Ringgold GA 30736-9735
phone: (706) 861-9521
fax: (706) 861-9521

Bruce Smith
Furniture Doctor, Inc.
3345 Peach Orchard Rd.
Augusta GA 30906
phone: (404) 793-0716

F. Michael Johnston
F. Michael Johnston Co.
P.O. Box 2697
Orange Park FL 32067
phone: (904) 908-0305
fax: (904) 908-0309

Al Oliver
Furniture Care Service
P.O. Box 1535
Orange Park FL 32067-1535
phone: (904) 272-5020
fax: (904) 272-2900

Glenn Camp
Central Florida Furniture Svc.
P.O. Box 283
Sparr FL 32192
phone: (352) 351-4944
fax: (352) 351-8841

Donald Rose
Movers Claim Svc., Inc.
4194 St. Augustine Rd.
Jacksonville FL 32207
phone: (904) 396-4636
fax: (904) 396-1667

Todd Harrell
Furniture Medic
2012-G North Point Blvd.
Tallahassee FL 32308
phone: (904) 385-1377
fax: (904) 422-3525

Logan Adams
Specialists of the South, Inc.
544 E. 6th St.
Panama City FL 32401
phone: (904) 785-2577
fax: (904) 872-8662

Jack Tanner
Tanner's Repair & Caning
102 E. 4th St.
Panama City FL 32401
phone: (904) 763-5603

W. Edward Williamson
Furniture Medic
3411 Edinborough Ct.
Pensacola FL 32514
phone: (904) 494-6627
fax: (904) 484-3521

Marion Sack
Master Furniture Service
P.O. Box 1421
Apopka FL 32704
phone: (407) 884-9090
fax: (407) 884-9270

David Schoenbauer
Schoenbauer's Restorations
Po Box 161876
Altamonte Springs FL 32716
phone: (407) 886-9206
fax: (407) 886-1291

Walt Abbe
Movers Claim Svc., Inc.
621 E. Horatio Ave.
Maitland FL 32751
phone: (407) 539-2050
fax: (407) 539-2582

Mitch Treider
Complete Furniture/Interiors
3005 Rosemarie Dr.
Titusville FL 32796
phone: (407) 269-1141
fax: (407) 383-0432

Branch Manager
Disar Furniture Service, Inc.
326 N. Magnolia Ave.
Orlando FL 32801
phone: (407) 849-4111
fax: (305) 556-0700

John Demola
Total Leather Care F. Rep/Cln
7425 Tufts Ct.
Orlando FL 32807-6426
phone: (407) 678-8778
fax: (407) 679-1277

Genevieve Blurton
Furniture Medic
5501 Valley Oak Rd.
Orlando FL 32808
phone: (407) 299-5080
fax: (407) 884-4434

Darrell Phillips
Furniture Medic
3956 Town Center Blvd., #138
Orlando FL 32837
phone: (407) 857-3803
fax: (407) 826-4712

Mark Shaffer
Crown Furniture Service
P.O. Box 561451
Orlando FL 32856
phone: (800) 551-0001
fax: (407) 380-2661

Eric A. Verzi
Merchants Services Co.
P.O. Box 780511
Orlando FL 32878-0511
phone: (407) 380-2836
fax: (407) 380-3915

Kim Allen Nielsen
Furniture Medic
1498 Riviera Dr., N.E.
Palm Bay FL 32905
phone: (407) 728-1630
fax: (407) 727-0234

Branch Manager
Disar Furniture Service, Inc.
P.O. Box 060177
Palm Bay FL 32906-0177
phone: (407) 727-7782
fax: (305) 556-0700

Lawrence M. Dowling
Dowling's Claim Service
1040 Lassen Ave. N.W.
Palm Bay FL 32907
phone: (407) 768-8661
fax: (407) 728-9044

Larry Parks
Transit Claim Repair
1622 91st Ct.
Vero Beach FL 32966
phone: (407) 569-3304
fax: (407) 569-0480

Gary Sarduy
Disar Furniture Service, Inc.
P.O. Box 4573
Hialeah FL 33014
phone: (305) 558-5141
fax: (305) 556-0700

Diane Zawislak
Furniture Medic
12359 S.W. 249 Street
Miami FL 33032
phone: (305) 258-0680

James West
American Refinishing/Clm Svc
5431 Nw 15th St., #4
Margate FL 33063
phone: (954) 970-0022
fax: (954) 970-1445

Barry Toder
Personal Touch Claim Svc.
6975 Nw 11th St.
Margate FL 33063
phone: (305) 973-4314
fax: (305) 973-4339

Allyn Schmidt
Woodcraft Custom Design
4100 N. Powerline Rd., I-5
Pompano Beach FL 33073
phone: (954) 971-2320
fax: (954) 971-6657

John R. Petersen
Petersen Restorations, Inc.
7345 S.W. 45 Street
Miami FL 33155
phone: (305) 261-6988
fax: (305) 261-9233

David Glassberg
The Shop Furniture Repair Svc
6278 N. Federal Hwy., #308
Ft. Lauderdale FL 33308
phone: (954) 969-2996
fax: (954) 969-2997

Ray Stone
Restoration Specialists/ Nc
P.O. Box 9683
Ft. Lauderdale FL 33310-9683
phone: (954) 430-9942
fax: (954) 450-9949

Ken May
Furniture Medic
2121 S.W. 52nd Terrace
Plantation FL 33317
phone: (305) 583-8133
fax: (305) 583-9524

Carl Germana
Palm Beach Claim Service
P.O. Box 17663
West Palm Beach FL 33416
phone: (407) 471-5009
fax: (407) 471-4268

Mary P. Talbutt
The Shop Furniture Repair Svc
23296 Country Club Dr. West
Boca Raton FL 33428
phone: (561) 483-0447
fax: (954) 969-2997

Richard Raines
Furniture Medic
21346 St. Andrews
Boca Raton FL 33433
phone: (407) 451-0505
fax: (305) 981-9663

Andrea Daley
Restorers of America
810 Lake Ave.
Lake Worth FL 33460
phone: (407) 533-3888
fax: (407) 533-0520

William F. Schalck
Schalck Services, Inc.
P.O. Box 915
Lutz (Tampa) FL 33548
phone: (813) 920-8085
fax: (813) 920-9373

James Jarrell
Unique Finishing Services
P.O. Box 2098
Valrico FL 33595-2098
phone: (813) 685-1626
fax: (813) 654-3217

Branch Manager
Disar Furniture Service, Inc.
1221 N. Florida Ave., Ste. B
Tampa FL 33602
phone: (813) 229-5448
fax: (305) 556-0700

John J. Ogden
Furniture Medic
913 East Skagway Ave.
Tampa FL 33604
phone: (813) 930-6701
fax: (813) 915-8763

Stephen Seaton
Artisan Furniture Repair Svc.
4001 Lynwood Ave.
Tampa FL 33611
phone: (813) 839-8996
fax: (813) 839-8996

Fred Blaylock
Fred's Furniture Repair
4436 Leila Ave.
Tampa FL 33616
phone: (813) 835-4420
fax: (813) 835-4421

Leon Davis
Southern Transit Repair. Inc.
5008 Linebaugh Ave., Suite 51
Tampa FL 33624
phone: (813) 968-7440
fax: (813) 968-5144

Chris Scirica
Caribe Interiors, Inc.
1444 - 19 St. North
St. Petersburg FL 33713
phone: (813) 896-5948

Branch Manager
Disar Furniture Service, Inc.
4458 Cleveland Ave.
Ft. Myers FL 33901
phone: (941) 275-1632
fax: (305) 556-0700

Charles Loomis
Furniture Medic
2170 Gulfview Rd.
Punta Gorda FL 33950
phone: (941) 505-0560
fax: (941) 639-5417

Gino Germana
Gino Germana & Son
2200 Kings Hwy., Bldg 3-L, #67
Pt. Charlotte FL 33980
phone: (941) 629-8122
fax: (941) 624-2883

Kevin Blizman
Carrier Consultants
1939 Racimo Dr.
Sarasota FL 34240
phone: (941) 377-2243
fax: (941) 377-2164

Jack Florian
Dependable Furniture Service
1550 66th Ave. Dr. E.
Sarasota FL 34243
phone: (941) 751-2391
fax: (941) 751-9986

Mark Shaffer
Coast To Coast Svc.
P.O. Box 2411
Inverness FL 34450-2411
phone: (904) 726-5589
fax: (904) 726-6733

Jeremy Lowe
Furniture Medic
12011 Lacey Dr.
New Port Richey FL 34654
phone: (813) 857-9663
fax: (813) 857-0579

Andy Dearth
Furniture Medic By Dearth
33514 E. Picciola Dr.
Fruitland Park FL 34731
phone: (352) 728-6262
fax: (352) 728-6262

Lori Donnelly
Furniture Clinic
2497 S.W. Warwick
Port St. Lucie FL 34984-5021
phone: (407) 879-1155
fax: (407) 878-9471

Sammie Muns
Muns Furniture Repair
5986 Miles Spring Rd.
Pinson AL 35126
phone: (205) 681-2116
fax: (205) 681-2116

David S. Harrell
Harrell Repair and Inspection
1074 Deaver-Walker Rd.
Trafford(B'ham) AL 35172
phone: (205) 681-2422
fax: (800) 681-3343

Don Douglas
Alabama Inspection/Repair Svc
P.O. Box 320092
Birmingham AL 35232
phone: (205) 595-6707
fax: (205) 592-7744

Steve Balkenbush
Old Style Furniture
2381 Us Hwy 231
Wetumpka AL 36092-4581
phone: (334) 567-4304
fax: (334) 567-4304

Oasbin Hicks
Furniture Medic
4100 S. Oates, #503-D
Dothan AL 36301
phone: (334) 794-0044
fax: (334) 671-4775

Roddy Martin
H.R. Martin Companies, Inc.
P.O. Box 1245
Fairhope AL 36533
phone: (334) 928-4581
fax: (800) 951-4256

Jane Schatzman
F.A.S.T.
1540 Deerwood Dr. West
Mobile AL 36618
phone: (334) 343-4325
fax: (334) 344-7067

Doug Hillis
Furniture Medic
3917 E. Medford Dr.
Mobile AL 36693
phone: (334) 660-8010

Sydney Charnley
Fixit Services
106 Couples Ct.
Murfreesboro TN 37128
phone: (615) 849-8895
fax: (615) 849-8895

Judd Sulcer
Project America Claims Svc
1784 W Northfield Blvd #277
Murfreesboro TN 37129
phone: (615) 895-6000
fax: (615) 895-0180

Ronald K. Schneider, Sr.
Furniture Restoration
4951 Sherman Oak Rd.
Nashville TN 37211
phone: (615) 833-4979
fax: (615) 833-5012

Robert Moore
Reynolds Restoration
5543 Edmondson Pike #142
Nashville TN 37211
phone: (615) 254-0271
fax: (615) 254-0271

Keith Smith
Transit Claims Service
P.O. Box 292181
Nashville TN 37229
phone: (615) 952-9904
fax: (615) 952-9901

Hank Wolfe
The Furniture Finisher
2720 St. Lawrence Rd.
Chattanooga TN 37421
phone: (423) 892-7788
fax: (423) 499-5580

Marion Walker
Walkers Furniture Refinishing
7160 Lee Hyw
Chattanooga TN 37421
phone: (423) 899-3913
fax: (423) 894-6668

Chuck Veach
Chuck's Repair Service
P.O. Box 483
Stanton TN 38069
phone: (901) 548-2626
fax: (901) 548-2627

Donald & Carlene Clay
Clay Uphost. & Refinish. Co.
2608 Poplar Ave
Memphis TN 38112
phone: (901) 454-7147
fax: (901) 454-7150

Todd Vieyra
Furniture Medic
860 Ridge Lake Blvd
Memphis TN 38120
phone: (800) 408-7378
fax: (901) 820-8660

Blake Soule
Blake Soule Furn. Rest., Inc.
2099 Thomas Rd., #12
Memphis TN 38134
phone: (901) 377-3646
fax: (901) 377-3615

Mike Schwie
Southern Furniture Svcs., Inc.
2108 Kimbrough Woods Place
Memphis TN 38139
phone: (901) 753-1314
fax: (901) 751-9652

Steve Walls
Furniture Medic
Route 1, Box 10-Ab
Mendenhall MS 39114
phone: (601) 977-9256

Dennis & Cindy Frazier
Frazier Claim Service
P.O. Box 7326
Jackson MS 39282-7326
phone: (601) 371-9826
fax: (601) 372-0332

Corky Morse
Bluegrass Claims Service
100 Taylor Blvd.
Vine Grove KY 40175
phone: (502) 877-6643
fax: (502) 877-6668

Gary Brown
Creative Constructions
930 Baxter Ave.
Louisville KY 40204
phone: (502) 583-2732

Steven Weber
Excel Shop, Inc.
112 Bauer Ave.
Louisville KY 40207
phone: (502) 895-7374
fax: (502) 895-7374

Dave Hoskins
Hoskins Furniture Service
3809 Broadland Trail
Louisville KY 40241
phone: (502) 361-7146
fax: (502) 361-7146

David Haughey
Action Furniture Repair
220c Normandy Court
Nicholasville KY 40356
phone: (606) 885-1290
fax: (606) 885-1377

Steve Elias
Furniture Medic
158 Rue Thierry
Paducah KY 42001
phone: (502) 554-0099
fax: (502) 554-0099

David Howard
Dave's Restoration
5215 S. Wilson Rd.
Elizabethtown KY 42701
phone: (502) 737-8203
fax: (502) 737-2215

Wm. A. Wilson
Wilson Furn. Svc.
669 Powhatan
Columbus OH 43204
phone: (614) 279-1572

Earl Muenze
Furniture Fix, The
4930 Brittany Ct. E.
Columbus IN 43229
phone: (614) 848-8776

John A. Johnson
Columbus In-Home Furn. Svc.
4555 Groves Rd., #25
Columbus OH 43232
phone: (614) 863-5247
fax: (614) 863-6362

Hope Ann Ingalls
Furniture Medic
P.O. Box 101
Sparta OH 43350
phone: (800) 984-8561
fax: (614) 397-2382

William L. Sudderberg
Styl-Rite Lampshade, Inc.
4125 Monroe St.
Toledo OH 43606
phone: (419) 474-5781

Fred Rickard
Fred Rickard Furniture Svcs.
P.O. Box 118055
Toledo OH 43611
phone: (419) 729-2559
fax: (419) 726-5959

Jim Nesmith
American Wood Technology
1172 Hidden Ridge
Toledo OH 43615
phone: (419) 868-3030
fax: (419) 868-6418

William Hush
Furniture Medic
4312 Holland-Sylvania Rd.
Toledo OH 43623
phone: (419) 882-6680
fax: (419) 882-6680

Wilfred Born
W.A. Born Furn Rest/Trnst
Clms
3467 Tree Lane
Cleveland OH 44070-1682
phone: (216) 779-5563
fax: (216) 779-5564

James Grimes
Pro Touch Up
33974 Beachpark
Eastlake OH 44095
phone: (216) 951-5874
fax: (216) 953-1249

Jeff Jewitt
J.B. Jewitt Co., Inc.
11929 Abbey Rd., Unit G
North Royalton OH 44133
phone: (216) 582-8929
fax: (216) 582-8506

David Sells
The Leather Solution
2977 Barber Rd., G-9
Norton OH 44203
phone: (330) 848-3313
fax: (330) 848-3326

Jim Anderson
Jim Anderson Furn. Touch Up
5163 Oakcrest Dr.
Youngstown OH 44515
phone: (330) 792-4786
fax: (330) 792-8412

Jim Justice
The "Finishing" Line
1432 Tumbleweed St., N.E.
Uniontown OH 44685
phone: (330) 877-1516
fax: (330) 877-1777

Heath Hostetler
Furniture Medic
5917 Secreast Rd.
Wooster OH 44691
phone: (330) 263-4447

Patrick C. Blank
Furniture Medic
3607 Ridgeton Rd.
Bucyrus OH 44820
phone: (419) 562-9944

C. David Dunn
Dunn's Furniture Service
4421 New Haven Rd.
Tiro OH 44887
phone: (419) 562-5456
fax: (419) 562-9300

Bill Ruble
Artistic Furn. Restoration
5179 Layhigh Rd.
Hamilton OH 45013
phone: (513) 738-4818
fax: (513) 738-2499

Kelly Mccann
Furniture Medic
125 Deerview Ct.
Harrison OH 45030
phone: (513) 367-4490
fax: (513) 367-5290

Ken Larbes
Professional Furniture Svc.
95 West Main St.
Amelia OH 45102
phone: (513) 753-5578
fax: (513) 752-3006

Doug Eisele
Old World Restorations, Inc.
347 Stanley Ave.
Cincinnati OH 45226-2100
phone: (513) 321-1911
fax: (513) 321-1914

Brian Aycock
Pete's Furniture Repair
9155 N. Dixie Dr.
Dayton OH 45414
phone: (937) 454-1801
fax: (937) 454-1802

Paul Serbu
AAA Furniture Refinishing
3132 S. Smithville Rd.
Dayton OH 45420
phone: (513) 293-2735
fax: (513) 252-6700

James T. Stone
Stone's Fine Wood Service
5036 Croftshire Drive
Kettering OH 45440
phone: (513) 434-4208
fax: (513) 434-0091

Jon Helm
Action Furniture Repair
1118 S. Sherman Dr.
Indianapolis IN 46203-2205
phone: (317) 357-2095
fax: (317) 357-2959

Ron & Al Sanders
Shambles Furn. Restor., The
7183 W. Us 40
Cumberland IN 46229
phone: (317) 894-7075
fax: (317) 894-8645

Thomas J. Keevin
Furniture Medic
2040 Marlinspike Ct.
Crown Point IN 46307
phone: (219) 988-4330
fax: (219) 988-4331

Steve Jedrysek
The Wooden Noga
1111 Washington St.
La Porte IN 46350
phone: (800) 995-0578
fax: (219) 325-8004

Jerry W. Heeter
Heeter Furniture Repair
1545 W. Lusher
Elkhart IN 46517
phone: (219) 293-8708
fax: (219) 522-6337

Kelly Kohne
Kelly's Furn. Service, Inc
P.O. Box 48
Wolcottville IN 46795-0048
phone: (800) 868-4873
fax: (219) 854-3730

Tim Crum
Furniture Medic
7506 West Jefferson Blvd.
Ft. Wayne IN 46804
phone: (219) 436-8663

Karen Cook
Furniture Medic
500 Wayne Ave.
Crawfordsville IN 47933
phone: (317) 272-7947
fax: (317) 272-7947

Gayle Roudabush
Furniture Medic By RGW
42285 E. Edward
Clinton Township MI 48038
phone: (810) 412-3330
fax: (810) 412-3331

Art Dart
Dart's Finishing
6981 Deerhurst Dr.
Westland MI 48185
phone: (313) 981-9404
fax: (313) 981-9405

Bill Witkowski
Michigan Antique Preservation
2034 Eureka Rd.
Wyandotte MI 48192
phone: (313) 283-5700
fax: (313) 283-4312

Domenica Raschella
Raschella's Custom Service
1450 Grayton Rd.
Grosse Pointe Park MI 48230
phone: (313) 882-5436
fax: (313) 882-0874

Al Sunshine
Furniture Care Specialists
42495 Park Ridge
Novi MI 48375-2660
phone: (810) 348-9090

Daniel J. Martin
Martin Furniture Refinishers
239 E. Walled Lake Dr.
Walled Lake MI 48390
phone: (810) 624-3080
fax: (810) 471-7062

Anita P. Devriendt
B & L Antiqurie Inc.
6217 S. Lakeshore Rd Pobox
453
Lexington MI 48450-0453
phone: (800) 840-1110
fax: (810) 359-7498

Gerald A. Hensler
Hensler Furn. Refinishing Inc.
3100 Christy Way
Saginaw MI 48603-2225
phone: (517) 792-1311
fax: (517) 249-5291

Dick Spadafore
S & R Refinishing
1440 N. Iva Road
Hemlock MI 48626
phone: (517) 642-9143
fax: (517) 642-9145

John Decarli
Furniture Medic
175 Gale Rd.
Mason MI 48854
phone: (800) 656-2507
fax: (517) 628-2056

Benno Trenkle
Benno's Woodworking
1852 S. Burdick
Kalamazoo MI 49001
phone: (616) 342-9079
fax: (616) 342-6221

Duane E. Smith, Jr.
West Michigan Furn. Repair
5457 Meredith, Apt. D
Kalamazoo MI 49002
phone: (616) 323-0163
fax: (616) 323-0163

Michael John Anderson
The Furniture Masters
801 Woodmere
Traverse City MI 49684
phone: (616) 941-4369
fax: (616) 941-0641

John Mahler
Specialty Enterprises
650 N.E. 47th Place
Des Moines IA 50313
phone: (515) 244-4494
fax: (515) 280-3784

Larry Raschella
Raschella's Custom Service
16620 Rosewood Ct.
Brookfield WI 53005
phone: (414) 785-6626
fax: (414) 785-1950

Carl W. Holzbauer
Holzbauer & Sons (Repair)
W160n9636 Colonial Dr.
Germantown WI 53022
phone: (414) 253-9789
fax: (414) 253-4644

Robert Harrold
Furniture Medic
5090 Brown St.
Oconomowoc WI 53066
phone: (414) 567-0722
fax: (414) 567-0722

Bruce Gee
Heartland Furniture
1923 Hawkinson Road
Oregon WI 53575
phone: (608) 873-1810
fax: (608) 873-1810

Roger Sundblom
Specialized Repair Service
1125 E. Wisconsin Ave.
Appleton WI 54911
phone: (414) 993-9993

Daniel Klein
Woodcraft Furniture Service
P.O. Box 294
Appleton WI 54912-0294
phone: (414) 757-5300
fax: (414) 757-5300

Brad Jelle
Furniture Caretakers
2045 63rd St. E.
Inver Grove Heights MN
55077
phone: (612) 552-8302
fax: (612) 552-8304

John Ackerman
Ackerman's Furniture Svc.
1110 E. Hwy 13
Burnsville MN 55337
phone: (612) 890-2284
fax: (612) 890-2296

Susan Johnson Hoffman
Furniture Doctor, The
4465 Harbor Lane
Minneapolis MN 55446
phone: (612) 557-6519
fax: (612) 557-6573

Jack Vaupel
Furniture Medic
1432e. Third St.
Sioux Falls SD 57103
phone: (605) 338-4100
fax: (605) 338-4890

C. Dale Apeland
Serendipity Masters
2535 Glen Lake Rd.
Eureka MT 59917
phone: (406) 889-3656
fax: (406) 889-3903

Scott & Jan Kuba
Craft Antique Repair
204 North Old Rand Road
Lake Zurich IL 60047
phone: (847) 438-3392
fax: (847) 438-2329

Pete Barbacovi
Furniture Medic
520 N. Seymour Ave.
Mundelein IL 60060
phone: (847) 367-9663
fax: (847) 566-0516

Bruce Hanson
Hanson Furniture Service
P.O. Box 245
Woodstock IL 60098
phone: (815) 728-8809
fax: (815) 728-1617

Robert Kurz
B & B Custom Care
815 Faith Lane
Bartlett IL 60103
phone: (708) 837-8507

David Kummerow
Image Restoration Services
P.O. Box 8516
Bartlett IL 60103
phone: (708) 830-7965
fax: (708) 830-1458

Todd Anderson
Ackerman's Refinishing/Uphol
1525 E. Burgundy Pkway
Streamwood IL 60107
phone: (630) 736-8880
fax: (630) 736-8883

Brian K. Healy
Double Eagle W'working/F
Med.
156-A East Lake St.
Bloomingdale IL 60108
phone: (708) 539-2440
fax: (708) 539-2641

Deloris & Larry Gilmer
D & L Furniture Service Co.
P.O. Box 232
Elmhurst IL 60126
phone: (708) 279-7242
fax: (708) 279-8925

Steve Kaniewski
Great Frame Up Systems, The
9335 Belmont Ave.
Franklin Park IL 60131
phone: (708) 671-2530
fax: (708) 671-2580

Duane Mitch
Mercury Furniture Service
302 Sycamore
West Chicago IL 60185
phone: (630) 293-7207
fax: (630) 293-7207

John Hozian
Associates Claim Service Inc.
722 W. Lunt Ave.
Schaumburg IL 60193
phone: (847) 985-1726
fax: (847) 985-8372

Raymond T. Smith
Furniture Medic
16127 Beth Ct.
Oak Forest IL 60452
phone: (708) 535-0889
fax: (708) 535-0889

Michael J. Morris
Furniture Medic
210 E. Kendall Rd.
Yorkville IL 60560
phone: (630) 553-1813
fax: (630) 553-1832

Robert E. Dudle
Furn. Patching & Touch-Up
Svc
1907 W. Waveland
Chicago IL 60613
phone: (312) 525-3549
fax: (312) 525-3535

Bob Shannon, Jr.
Affordable Art Galley
7745 S. Halsted St.
Chicago IL 60620
phone: (312) 874-1295
fax: (312) 238-9208

Bob Shannon
Bobcat Wood Refinishing
7745 S. Halsted
Chicago IL 60620
phone: (312) 238-2054

Robert Loncarevic
The Leather Solution
6108 1/2 W. Irving Park Rd.
Chicago IL 60634
phone: (312) 685-2162
fax: (312) 685-2268

Julia Ruder
Ruder Antique Furn. Conserv.
1771 W. Sunnyside Ave.
Chicago IL 60640
phone: (312) 878-8692

James Murphy
Superior Custom Rpr. Svc. Inc.
4444 W. Chicago Ave.
Chicago IL 60651
phone: (312) 862-8000
fax: (312) 862-8017

William Parsons, III
Furniture Medic
4428 N. Ottawa
Norridge IL 60656
phone: (708) 452-7020
fax: (708) 452-1598

Robert Loncarevic
The Leather Solution
4434 N. Oak Park
Harwood Heights IL 60656
phone: (708) 867-4955
fax: (708) 867-4966

David Mcnulty
Weber Furniture Service, Inc.
5915 N. Ravenswood Ave.
Chicago IL 60660
phone: (312) 275-9061
fax: (312) 275-1943

Dieter Off
Furniture Medic
8212 Oleander
Niles IL 60714
phone: (847) 967-1187
fax: (847) 967-1193

Donald Kistner
Kistner's Full Clms Svc. Inc.
520 20th St.
Rock Island IL 61201
phone: (309) 786-5868
fax: (309) 794-0559

Randy Cone
Cone Furniture Service
P.O. Box 5474
Morton IL 61550
phone: (309) 263-2502
fax: (309) 263-7128

Charles Eppel
Furniture Medic
5917 N. Rosemead
Peoria IL 61614
phone: (309) 692-3525
fax: (309) 692-4946

Wayne Warner
Warner's Art Rest/Obj of Art
Rr16, Box 557
Bloomington IL 61704
phone: (309) 828-0994
fax: (309) 829-8785

Robert L. Wills
R.L. Wills Claim Service
R.R. 2, Box 157
Heyworth IL 61745
phone: (309) 473-3330
fax: (309) 473-3304

Tom Horton
Horton's Furniture Center
534 Wood Thrush, "A"
Troy IL 62294
phone: (888) 937-3848
fax: (888) 475-4469

Tom Medley
Art Wood Furniture Service
P.O. Box 1343
Ballwin MO 63011
phone: (314) 256-7758
fax: (314) 256-7758

Bob & Tom Stanze
Furniture Medic
16048 Meadow Oak Dr.
Chesterfield MO 63017
phone: (314) 532-0232
fax: (314) 532-0232

Robert Brannon, Jr.
Furniture Doctor, The
5591 Ruth Dr.
House Springs MO 63051
phone: (314) 942-2909
fax: (314) 942-4528

Bob Soell
House Doctor, The
9311 Sappington
St. Louis MO 63126
phone: (314) 842-6444
fax: (314) 843-6101

Craig Dodge
Craig Dodge Restorations
12828 Sunset Glen
St. Louis MO 63127
phone: (314) 843-1931
fax: (314) 843-5644

Norm Shoults
Workbench Refinishing
9435 Workbench
Sunset Hills MO 63127
phone: (314) 843-4224
fax: (314) 843-4664

Stuart A. Klearman
Furniture Medic
48 Kimberly Ln.
St. Peters MO 63376
phone: (314) 970-7915
fax: (314) 970-7915

Timothy M. Finn
Renaissance Svcs Woodworks
738 N. 7 Hwy., #1
Blue Springs MO 64014
phone: (816) 229-6400
fax: (816) 229-1396

Tim and Pam Finn
Arrowhead Claim Service
702a Blue Ridge Extension
Grandview MO 64030
phone: (816) 765-9770
fax: (816) 765-1640

Norman S. Witmer
Abbot's Furn. Refin. & Uphol
5900 Red Bridge Rd.
Kansas City MO 64137
phone: (816) 765-8838
fax: (816) 765-6377

Deborah L. Brunner
Ms. Fix-It
3501 E. New Haven Rd., #128
Columbia MO 65201
phone: (573) 817-2477
fax: (573) 817-2478

Hughey Bellue
Bellue's Repair
Rt. 3, Box 3326
Seymour MO 65746
phone: (417) 767-2440
fax: (417) 738-4310

John L. Patton
Furniture Medic
13502 W. 115th St.
Olathe KS 66062
phone: (913) 451-5955
fax: (913) 451-0369

Rick Schlitzer
Furniture Caretakers
P. O. Box 44
Stilwell KS 66085
phone: (913) 685-4908
fax: (913) 685-4909

Larry Kistner
Kistner's Services
16113 Riggs Rd.
Stilwell KS 66085
phone: (913) 685-3264
fax: (913) 685-3442

J. Timothy Wilson
The Wood Works, Inc.
7710 W 63rd St/Shwnee Ms
Pkwy
Overland Park KS 66202
phone: (913) 362-2432
fax: (913) 362-0588

Bobby W. Seigler
Seigler Woodwrkng Specl'ties
2624 S. Oliver #107
Wichita KS 67210
phone: (316) 686-0783
fax: (316) 686-4538

Don Sindelar
Don's Refinishing & Furn. Rep.
3719 "Q" Street
Omaha NE 68107
phone: (402) 731-3222
fax: (402) 731-6431

Elliott Wimberly
Furniture Medic
3217 25th St.
Metairie LA 70002
phone: (504) 455-3229
fax: (504) 831-2271

Shad Weathersby
Weathersby Furn. Rep.
P.O. Box 8486
New Orleans LA 70182
phone: (504) 945-7566
fax: (504) 947-8972

Mike Dorsett
Woodpecker Furn. Rest. Cntr.
216 E. Texas Ave.
Rayne LA 70578
phone: (318) 334-4005
fax: (318) 334-5434

Dick Sager
Furniture Medic
12521 Country Ridge Ave.
Baton Rouge LA 70816
phone: (504) 753-6193
fax: (504) 753-6194

Harry Marshall
Furniture Medic
183 Rye Dr.
Cabot AR 72023
phone: (501) 374-3600
fax: (501) 843-5236

Evia Breshears
Mr. Honey Do, Inc.
6 Laura Lane
Conway AR 72032
phone: (501) 327-1217
fax: (501) 513-1217

Hal Resnikoff
Village Woodsmith, The
1 Combonne Court
Little Rock AR 72211
phone: (501) 228-0580
fax: (501) 221-1904

Stephen Davis
Davis Furniture Restor., Inc.
P.O. Box 1961
Fayetteville AR 72702-1961
phone: (501) 521-5976
fax: (501) 443-7106

Glenn Foster
Furniture Medic
2551 Houston St.
Fayetteville AR 72703
phone: (501) 587-9493

Richard Estes
Furniture Medic
8071 N. Classen, "A"
Oklahoma City OK 73114
phone: (405) 848-7863
fax: (405) 848-9602

Larry & Donna Marks
Heartland Full Claims Svc.
5420 Nw 65th St.
Oklahoma City OK 73132
phone: (405) 728-1937
fax: (405) 728-2939

Tom Hill
Woodshed, The
11367 E. 61 St South
Broken Arrow OK 74012
phone: (918) 258-8553
fax: (918) 250-5169

Michael Mcgehee
Furniture Medic
9818 S. Maybelle Ave.
Jenks OK 74037
phone: (918) 299-6300
fax: (918) 298-1542

Denny And Suzanne Harris
Classic Refinishing, Inc.
2241 Valley Mill
Carrollton TX 75006
phone: (972) 418-6218
fax: (972) 416-5306

Mike Mcdaniel
M2 Construction
P.O. Box 294641
Lewisville TX 75029
phone: (214) 355-0308
fax: (214) 355-0308

Jeff Henderson
Signature Claim Service, Inc.
P.O. Box 295270
Lewisville TX 75029
phone: (972) 724-0470
fax: (972) 355-1263

David Rackley
D & D Restorations
412 Elwood St., #101-A
Irving TX 75061
phone: (214) 579-9822

Steve Hart
Dallas Central Services
2701 W. 15th St., #536
Plano TX 75075
phone: (972) 527-8071
fax: (972) 527-9234

Steve Griffith
Furniture Medic/Grtr Dallas
2809 Bedfordshire Ln
Plano TX 75075-2207
phone: (214) 578-8683
fax: (214) 424-5823

John Campbell
Camco Furniture Repair
P.O. Box 707
Lancaster TX 75146
phone: (972) 227-4162
fax: (972) 227-4155

Paul Auld
Furniture Medic
1504 Culberson Dr.
Mesquite TX 75150
phone: (214) 682-5402
fax: (214) 682-5403

Ellen Amirkhan
Oriental Rug Cleaning Co.
3907 Ross Ave.
Dallas TX 75204
phone: (214) 821-9135
fax: (214) 821-9136

Rudy T. Tovar
Tovar Furniture Studio
6506 Walnut Hill Lane
Dallas TX 75230
phone: (214) 243-3460
fax: (214) 691-4623

Keith Elliott
Elliott's Furniture Repair
5711 Sadler Circle
Dallas TX 75235
phone: (214) 358-3538
fax: (214) 352-5132

Steve Long
Antique World Furniture Svc.
2774 Matt Dr.
Longview TX 75605
phone: (903) 757-6792
fax: (903) 757-6201

Cyndi Smith
Smith's Antiques/Refinishing
3650 Garner Blvd.
Arlington TX 76013
phone: (817) 265-7048
fax: (817) 265-7819

Roger Ballou
Furniture Medic
6009 Saddle Ridge Rd.
Arlington TX 76016
phone: (817) 496-9977
fax: (817) 492-9598

Ray Daughhetee
Craftsmen Furn. Restoration
3800 Horizon Dr.
Bedford TX 76021
phone: (817) 858-9034
fax: (817) 283-5943

Sammi Buehner
Sammi's Specialty Services
P.O. Box 922
Midlothian TX 76065
phone: (972) 923-3233
fax: (972) 923-3233

Andy Chapman
Accent Furniture Repair
P.O. Box 543
Burleson TX 76097
phone: (817) 572-0274

Kelvin Robertson
Furniture Medic
P.O. Box 1084
Grapevine TX 76099
phone: (817) 498-7900

Stanley W. Kowalczyk
S.W.K. Furniture Restoration
2208 Tierney Rd.
Fort Worth TX 76112
phone: (817) 496-0136
fax: (817) 496-4232

Joe Gilley
Furniture Medic
5504 Dublin Ln.
N. Richland Hills TX 76180
phone: (817) 581-0352
fax: (817) 581-0352

Larry W. Shumake
Shumake & Associates/Rest
Svc
P.O. Box 8703
Waco TX 76714
phone: (817) 776-7216
fax: (817) 772-8005

Paul Arena
Furniture Medic
8345 West Little York #3
Houston TX 77040
phone: (713) 939-0007
fax: (713) 462-2887

M.J. Kucera
Key Restoration Services
20819 Essman #16
Houston TX 77073
phone: (281) 443-6688
fax: (281) 443-6789

Cecil Nidever
The Leather Solution
9220 Summerbell
Houston TX 77074
phone: (713) 776-2090
fax: (713) 776-1222

Bruce Eden
The Touch-Up Men
P.O. Box 711353
Houston TX 77271-1353
phone: (713) 774-5642
fax: (713) 774-1212

Brian Blackstock
Best Finishing Co. Inc.
P.O. Box 90213
Houston TX 77290
phone: (713) 580-8620
fax: (713) 580-2423

Zoe Higgins
Wakewood Furniture Shop
2038 Little Cedar
Kingwood TX 77339
phone: (281) 358-7154
fax: (281) 358-1714

Paul M. Raybern
Positive Micro Results
P.O. Box 58
Barker TX 77413-0058
phone: (713) 647-0146
fax: (713) 647-0145

Dick Rain
Deliverance Movers Service
P.O. Box 1982
Sugarland TX 77478
phone: (713) 955-6822
fax: (713) 342-4613

Allison Sims
Windmill Country Store/
Wdwrks
11027 Wetmore Rd.
San Antonio TX 78216
phone: (210) 494-6678
fax: (210) 402-0692

Al Clauss
Furniture Medic
6907 Timberhill
San Antonio TX 78238
phone: (210) 509-3727
fax: (210) 509-3727

Leo T. Edralin
Furniture Caretakers
120 Commercial Parkway
Austin TX 78613
phone: (512) 258-9984
fax: (512) 258-9985

Rex Darley
Furniture Medic
2302 El Sol
Cedar Park TX 78613
phone: (512) 918-9875
fax: (512) 918-9875

Len Leslie
Furniture Medic
1905 Brookfield Cove
Cedar Park TX 78613
phone: (512) 918-9875
fax: (512) 918-9875

Jim Neuberger
Neuberger Furniture Service
8908 Tweed Berwick Dr.
Austin TX 78750
phone: (512) 258-9916
fax: (512) 219-0301

Frank And Rosemary Bergen
Bix Refinishing & Upholstery
816 W. Yager Lane
Austin TX 78753
phone: (512) 837-1677
fax: (512) 837-1678

Garry Baccus
Furniture Medic
872 N. Us Hwy 385
Levelland TX 79336
phone: (806) 799-8551
fax: (806) 894-1924

Mitch Anthony
Furniture Medic
1306 Pueblo Rd.
Midland TX 79705-9036
phone: (915) 570-8773
fax: (915) 570-8773

Brooks Smith
Master Craft
1300 S. Co. Rd. 1110
Midland TX 79706
phone: (915) 682-8250
fax: (915) 682-5840

Sandy Gieseking
Grace Furniture Repair
4552 Bob'o'link Rd.
El Paso TX 79922
phone: (915) 585-1626
fax: (915) 585-3409

Jim Ackerman
Ackerman & Sons Furn.
Wkshop
2400 W. Belleview Ave.
Littleton CO 80120
phone: (303) 798-3220
fax: (303) 798-9888

Vern Sybesma
Queen City Furniture Repair
7447 S. Dowining Cir. W.
Littleton CO 80122
phone: (303) 794-3346
fax: (303) 794-1740

Dale Slaughter
Colorado D&S Enterprises, Inc.
12483 Meade Way
Littleton CO 80125
phone: (303) 791-1616
fax: (303) 791-1620

S. Brian Mcfadden
Leather Tech Plus
P.O. Box 4103
Highlands Ranch CO 80126
phone: (303) 688-1199
fax: (303) 932-0019

Rene Wahl
Rene Wahl Furniture Repair
3085 Hamal Circle
Monument CO 80132
phone: (719) 488-8894
fax: (719) 488-8851

Steven Goll
Furniture Medic
1390 Forest St.
Denver CO 80209
phone: (303) 377-3659
fax: (303) 377-3659

Jeffrey S. Messer
Furniture Medic
4954 E. 41st Ave.
Denver CO 80216
phone: (303) 321-6554
fax: (303) 321-6558

Tom Langston
Transportation Related Svcs.
4720 Ivy St.
Denver CO 80216
phone: (303) 321-8858

L.R.(Randy) Lanier
Lanier's Refinishing
9760b E. Alameda
Denver CO 80231
phone: (303) 363-7788
fax: (303) 343-6933

David Weatherford
Woodtech Services
P.O. Box 4627
Breckenridge CO 80424
phone: (970) 453-2355
fax: (970) 453-6088

Bob Brooks
Brooks Furniture Service
7 Via Sierra Grande
Manitou Springs CO 80829
phone: (719) 685-5094
fax: (719) 685-9412

Robert Hill
Furniture Medic
4784 Sagebrush
Cheyenne WY 82009
phone: (307) 638-7991
fax: (307) 637-4203

Janet Wonacutt
Artcraft Refinishing
4655 Macarthur
Boise ID 83705
phone: (208) 342-4144
fax: (208) 336-2155

Paul Malinauskas
Furniture Doctors, The
2750 W. Prairie Ave.
Coeur D'alene ID 83814
phone: (208) 772-6431
fax: (208) 772-4772

Curt Mcarthur
Transportation Related Svcs.
P.O. Box 540230
North Salt Lake UT 84054
phone: (801) 296-7463

Duane Thornton
Call's Furniture Repair
P.O. Box 294
Pleasant Grove UT 84062
phone: (801) 785-1329
fax: (801) 785-1717

Ken Gallacher
Specialized Repair Co.
12101 S. 1390 W.
Riverton UT 84065
phone: (801) 254-2777
fax: (801) 254-3513

Donald A. Lopeman
Lopeman Furniture Services
940 W. Hatcher Rd.
Phoenix AZ 85021-3139
phone: (602) 943-2189
fax: (602) 943-3698

Jim Whitten
Customer Claim Service
2105 E. Lone Cactus Drive
Phoenix AZ 85024
phone: (602) 971-4019
fax: (602) 569-1791

John Lindley
Central Claim Service
20817 N. 21st Ave., #13
Phoenix AZ 85027
phone: (602) 780-1286
fax: (602) 780-0620

Dave Wooden
Furniture Medic
4222 S. 37th St.
Phoenix AZ 85040
phone: (602) 470-0834
fax: (602) 470-0844

Thomas Gowan
Furniture Medic
2556 S. Santa Barbara
Mesa AZ 85202
phone: (602) 777-1933
fax: (602) 967-4168

Wade Denson
Artistic Finisher's East
2350 E. Javelina
Mesa AZ 85204
phone: (602) 892-6348
fax: (602) 892-3010

Richard L. & Peggy J. Bennet
Lost Art Finishing
3025 E. Dolphin Ave.
Mesa AZ 85204
phone: (602) 833-7038
fax: (602) 833-8293

Peter Clark
Furniture Medic
1227 S. Brentwood
Chandler AZ 85248
phone: (602) 821-0815
fax: (602) 821-0815

Rick Freeman
F.A.S.T. Services
903 S. Rural Rd., #101-332
Tempe AZ 85281
phone: (602) 610-8815
fax: (602) 890-8230

Tim Martell
Professional Furniture Svc Inc
5762 W. Shaw Butte
Glendale AZ 85304
phone: (602) 272-1001
fax: (602) 878-9285

Stephen Call
Quality Furniture Repair
P.O. Box 1103
Buckeye AZ 85326
phone: (602) 702-7702
fax: (602) 702-7702

Denny Kuller
Denny Kuller Piano Polish/Dtl
C/O Synnott/27226 N 147th Av
Sun City West AZ 85375
phone: (800) 684-1202

Jim Bullen
Furniture Medic
P.O. Box 2136
Edgewood NM 87015
phone: (505) 286-1890
fax: (505) 281-0142

Andy Vanetsky
Bizzy Furn. Repair
12154 San Rafael, Ne
Albuquerque NM 87122
phone: (505) 856-1070
fax: (505) 856-1071

Tony Blanco
Furniture Medic
229 Tonalea Ave.
Henderson NV 89015
phone: (702) 564-6780
fax: (702) 564-6780

Brian Meaton
Furniture Medic
850 S. Boulder Hwy., #220
Henderson NV 89015
phone: (702) 564-0786
fax: (702) 558-2205

Barbara Charlton
Barbara Charlton Furn. Repair
4205 Linniki St.
N. Las Vegas NV 89030
phone: (702) 648-1995
fax: (702) 646-1849

Andy Daniels
Tink's Decorative Art Studio
1536 "D" Street
Sparks NV 89431
phone: (702) 359-0852

Frances Perez
Vinyl Repair Co.
1811 Tamarind Ave., #202
Hollywood CA 90028
phone: (213) 871-0329

Maxine Woody
Apex Furniture Restoration
15500 S. Main St.
Gardena CA 90248
phone: (310) 217-8771
fax: (310) 538-4513

Owner
Furniture Medic South Bay
25202 Crenshaw Blvd., #102
Torrance CA 90505
phone: (310) 326-4247
fax: (310) 326-7168

Ty Drake
Drake Enterprises
P.O. Box 21290
Long Beach CA 90801-4290
phone: (310) 424-5403
fax: (310) 424-6403

Michael Trlica
T & T Claims & Restor. Svc
1947 S. Myrtle Ave.
Monrovia CA 91016
phone: (818) 357-3617
fax: (818) 357-5376

Gary Novotny
Novotny's Contracting/Refin.
1106 1/2 W. Glenoaks Blvd.
Glendale CA 91202
phone: (818) 500-8577
fax: (818) 243-5313

Albert D. Luongo
Al. D. Luongo Furn Rep/Refin
22819 Trigger St.
Chatsworth CA 91311
phone: (818) 882-2273
fax: (818) 882-0148

Richard Rosenberger
Horton's Furniture Center Inc
26792 Oak Ave.
Santa Clarita CA 91351
phone: (800) 948-9340
fax: (805) 252-9635

Walter Greenes
Southern Calif. Craftsmen
4321 Matilija Ave., #13
Sherman Oaks CA 91423
phone: (818) 907-7544
fax: (818) 907-7544

Daniel Sadeh
Home Design
5018 Denny Ave., Unit #2
Toluca Lake CA 91601
phone: (818) 766-6911
fax: (818) 766-6911

Neil Matheis
Matheis, Neil & Associates
7966 Surrey Lane
Alta Loma CA 91701
phone: (909) 989-3725
fax: (909) 941-1586

Jerry Trlica
Trlica and Associates
2117 Foothill Blvd., #107
Laverne CA 91750
phone: (909) 593-4737
fax: (909) 593-4737

Gary & Betsy Carney
Furniture Medic
71 Corte Maria Ave.
Chula Vista CA 91910
phone: (619) 426-1952
fax: (619) 426-1945

Shawn Dolan
Furniture Medic
2018 Via Alexandra
Escondido CA 92026
phone: (619) 741-9258
fax: (619) 735-6407

Mike Turner
The Leather Solution
12570 Lemon Crest Dr.
Lakeside CA 92040
phone: (619) 561-6221
fax: (619) 443-7902

Nancy Craychee
Dr. Spot Carpet Care
4089 Oceanside Blvd., "A"
Oceanside CA 92056
phone: (619) 726-6232

Craig Montgomery
Priority Repair Service
705 Sea Cliff Way
Oceanside CA 92056
phone: (619) 967-9301
fax: (619) 967-9301

Dwight Greene
Moving Damage Repair
P.O. Box 1027
Poway CA 92074-1027
phone: (619) 486-4230
fax: (619) 486-0783

Jim Carrico
Jim Carrico Furniture Repair
2003 Bayview Hgts Dr, #107
San Diego CA 92105
phone: (619) 262-7032
fax: (619) 263-9116

William West
West Wood Work
40321 Avenida Cerrovista
Cherry Valley CA 92223
phone: (909) 845-8658
fax: (909) 845-6598

Terry Hansen
Terry's Furniture Repair
P.O. Box 2636
Palm Desert CA 92261
phone: (800) 965-3210
fax: (800) 726-4210

Lawrence Vescera, Ph.D.
Pick Up The Pieces
711 W. 17th St., C-12
Costa Mesa CA 92627
phone: (714) 645-9955
fax: (714) 645-8381

Mark Hedges
Furniture Artists, The
22600 Lambert #G 1403
Lake Forest CA 92630
phone: (714) 770-8369
fax: (714) 770-0409

Michael T. Stout
Stout's Finishing
27758 Santa Margarita
Pkw#114
Mission Viejo CA 92691
phone: (714) 837-1364
fax: (714) 830-3926

Jim Price
Price's Finishing
23052-H Alicia Parkway #305
Mission Viejo CA 92692
phone: (714) 858-1961
fax: (714) 858-0811

Steven Perry
Furniture Medic
1257 Olenia Circle
Tulare CA 93274
phone: (209) 684-9040
fax: (209) 684-9041

Chuck Blackmon
Furniture Medic
3412 Stine Rd., #121
Bakersfield CA 93309-6341
phone: (805) 397-5198
fax: (805) 397-5198

Ron & Joan Rogers
Ron Rogers Claim Service
10240 Atascadero Ave.
Atascadero CA 93422
phone: (805) 461-5292
fax: (805) 461-9106

Bob Yeager
Furniture Medic
5790 E. Shields, #103
Fresno CA 93727
phone: (209) 346-1800
fax: (209) 346-0905

Al & Mary Ann Zajec
Bay Area Restoration
417 Casa Del Mar Drive
Half Moon Bay CA 94019
phone: (415) 728-1662
fax: (415) 728-1663

John Sappingfield
Furniture Medic
2699 Spring St.
Redwood City CA 94063
phone: (415) 299-9080
fax: (415) 299-9086

Chris Gilbert
Furniture Medic
1000 Atlantic Ave., #114
Alameda CA 94105
phone: (510) 749-9052
fax: (510) 268-3751

Richard Roder
Roder, Richard Co.
2161 Turk Blvd., #7
San Francisco CA 94115
phone: (415) 922-9541

Bill & Shirley James
J & J Finishers/Shirley's Cs
771 Hampton Rd.
Hayward CA 94541
phone: (510) 276-0336
fax: (510) 317-0233

Yvonne Gillian
The Leather Solution
27343 Industrial Blvd., "E"
Hayward CA 94545
phone: (510) 786-6059
fax: (510) 785-9078

William Lakman
Furniture Medic
34121 Langhorn Ct.
Fremont CA 94555
phone: (510) 742-1944
fax: (510) 742-1944

Ron Bepler
Bepler, Ron Furniture Service
606 43rd St.
Richmond CA 94805
phone: (510) 652-8841
fax: (510) 652-9275

Linda Sugar
Linda Sugar Furniture Service
471 Ethel Ave.
Mill Valley CA 94941
phone: (415) 388-2579
fax: (415) 388-5082

Jim & Janice Jacobson
Trans Bay Furniture Repair
121 Santa Maria Drive
Novato CA 94947
phone: (415) 892-4525
fax: (415) 897-1740

Larry Fisher
Fisher's Unique Restoration
520 Mcglincey Ln., #13
Campbell CA 95008
phone: (408) 377-3499
fax: (408) 377-2997

George Barnes
Furniture Medic
1585 N. 4th St., #J
San Jose CA 95112
phone: (408) 452-7779
fax: (408) 441-9112

Kimberly Nelson
Furniture Medic
5951 Burchell Ave.
San Jose CA 95120
phone: (408) 268-1191
fax: (408) 268-7336

Dennis R. Dunne
Dunne's Finishing Service
2179 Stone Ave., Ste. #20
San Jose CA 95125
phone: (408) 293-9895
fax: (408) 293-1074

Terry Jiminez
Universal Furniture Services
96 Rosebay Ct.
San Jose CA 95127
phone: (408) 937-1626
fax: (408) 937-1626

Rita Hilinski
Zeiger, Ed Furniture Svc.
P.O. Box 447
Clements CA 95227
phone: (209) 368-0640
fax: (209) 368-2729

James T. Morrow
Furniture Medic
P.O. Box 690726
Stockton CA 95269-0726
phone: (209) 931-8440
fax: (209) 931-6100

Pete Creamer
Furniture Medic
400 S. Jensen Rd.
Gustine CA 95322
phone: (209) 854-6944
fax: (209) 854-6944

Robin Cowden
Furniture Medic
216 Fitch St.
Healdsburg CA 95448
phone: (707) 431-2424
fax: (707) 433-5601

Michael Matthew
Freedom Services
Box 4581
Auburn CA 95603
phone: (916) 367-4128
fax: (916) 367-4128

Tony Martin
Martin's Classic Rest. Svcs.
221 Sterling Oak Dr.
Galt CA 95632
phone: (209) 745-6989
fax: (209) 745-6999

Raul Guzman
Raul Guzman Furniture Repair
1310 Large Oak Dr.
Placerville CA 95667
phone: (916) 642-2477
fax: (916) 642-2745

Walt Knighton
A-Masters Touch
1866 Southwood Dr.
Vacaville CA 95687
phone: (707) 449-3662
fax: (707) 449-3662

Robert And Gary Churchwell
Furniture Medic
P.O. Box 588
Applegate CA 95703
phone: (916) 878-2117
fax: (916) 878-8384

Carole/Mel Stanley
Carmel Restoration Svcs.
5037 C College Oak Dr.
Sacramento CA 95841
phone: (916) 338-0404
fax: (916) 338-0126

Robin Cady
Cady Co., The
1732 N.W. 25th Ave.
Portland OR 97210
phone: (503) 227-2851
fax: (503) 227-2049

Glenn Sjodin
Coatings & Claims Inc.
P.O. Box 14714
Portland OR 97214
phone: (503) 786-1318
fax: (503) 786-1317

Gordon Fiddes
Image Restoration
10454 Sw Kent St.
Portland OR 97224
phone: (503) 639-4333
fax: (503) 423-7148

Allen Darrow
Oregon Furniture & Claim Svc
P.O. Box 253
Independence OR 97351-0253
phone: (503) 838-4117
fax: (503) 838-3802

Don Frosland
Furniture Clinic, The
2210 Hwy 99 North
Eugene OR 97402
phone: (541) 689-0262
fax: (541) 689-7292

David Wagar
Oregon Restoration Co., The
P.O. Box 26314
Eugene OR 97402
phone: (541) 689-7338
fax: (541) 689-7338

James Church
Out of Sight
5015 Dark Hollow Rd.
Medford OR 97501
phone: (541) 734-3747

John Yakel
Furniture Doctor
112 Nw 3rd St.
Merlin OR 97532
phone: (541) 479-4850
fax: (541) 479-4850

Norma Jean Van Pay
Furniture Medic
P.O. Box 1676
Bellevue WA 98009
phone: (206) 451-1306
fax: (206) 451-7402

Ray Spencer
Spencer Corp.
23220 Maple Vly Hwy, Se, #3b
Maple Valley WA 98038
phone: (206) 413-1660
fax: (206) 413-1659

George Lanphear
Furniture Medic
310 74th St. Sw
Everett WA 98203
phone: (206) 347-7270
fax: (206) 710-4055

Richard Conley
Artisan Furniture Service
3214 114th St., N.W.
Gig Harbor WA 98332
phone: (206) 857-7584
fax: (206) 851-7389

Ron Lawrence
Town & Country Furniture Svc
6817 So. D St.
Tacoma WA 98408
phone: (206) 472-2705
fax: (206) 472-2021

H. A. Mansfield
Reliable Furniture Svc
P.O. Box 152, Fern Hill Sta.
Tacoma WA 98412
phone: (206) 588-6668
fax: (206) 588-0082

Terry Stratton
The Leather Solution
2749 Summerhill Ct., Sw
Olympia WA 98512-7405
phone: (360) 357-7366
fax: (360) 943-0618

Terry Shanahan
Shanahan & Sons Furniture
S. 2206 Inland Empire Way
Spokane WA 99204-4536
phone: (509) 624-7851
fax: (509) 747-2434

Max & Delsa Pospical
Delmax Furn. Rep. & Uphol.
706 Symons
Richland WA 99352
phone: (509) 946-7571
fax: (509) 946-2238

Lynn Knapp
Knapp Furniture Restoration
1219 W. Pine
Walla Walla WA 99362
phone: (509) 529-7495
fax: (509) 529-7496

Jerome Bridges
Amicus Corp./Furniture Medic
5639 Silverado Way
Anchorage AK 99518
phone: (907) 562-8585
fax: (907) 562-8586

Lyle & Barb Stricker
Artistic Furn Touchup/Rep Svc
Rr #1, Group Box 103
Havelock, Ontario CANADA
K0L 1Z0
phone: (705) 778-3203
fax: (705) 778-3203

Gordon Greig
Furniture Medic
468 Adelaide Ave. E.
Oshawa, Ont CANADA L1G
2A3
phone: (905) 723-2399
fax: (905) 723-3910

Llewellyn & Sean Rowlands
Furniture Medic
1913 The Chase
Mississauga, Ont. CANADA
L5M 3A2
phone: (905) 607-4894
fax: (905) 607-0694

David Messenger
Furniture Medic of Canada
6540 Tomken Rd.
Mississauga, Ont CANADA
L5T 2E9
phone: (905) 670-0000
fax: (905) 670-0077

Robert Field
Furniture Medic
7-981 Wellington Rd. S., #401
London, Ont. CAN N6E 3A9
phone: (519) 878-3177
fax: (519) 633-9110

Garry Hoffman
Furniture Medic
4047 Aspen Dr. East
Edmonton, Alberta CANADA
T6J 2A7
phone: (403) 944-2669
fax: (403) 435-4348

Basil Pappas
The Craftsman's Touch
18-3871 North Fraser Way
Burnaby, B.C. CANADA V5J
5G6
phone: (604) 437-3383
fax: (604) 437-3313

X-Y-Z

Would you like to be included in the next edition of
Maloney's Antiques & Collectibles Resource Directory?

If you are a dealer, collector or expert, or if you offer specific services to the antiques and collectibles trade, please consider completing and submitting the form on the following page so that you too can be included in the next edition of this Directory. Specialty clubs, periodicals, and museums are especially encouraged to become listed. By the way, listings are **free** of charge.

Here is some information you should keep in mind when checking over your listings. Because of the overwhelming response, we must limit the number of listings for Collectors and Dealers to five per person. **If you are not the current official point-of-contact for your club/ association or periodical, please forward these forms to the appropriate person or office.**

1. Specialty Area: This is the category under which your entry will be listed. Tell us your areas of interest and we'll see that you are placed under the proper heading(s). Remember, Dealers and Collectors are limited to five (5) listings per person.

2. Entry Type: Include the type of listing. Choices include appraiser, auction service, book seller, club/association, collector, dealer, expert, matching service, museum/library, periodical, vendor/supplier, repair/restoration/conservation service, reproductions source, manufacturer/producer/distributor, exchange service (for Limited Edition collectibles), or other (explain). While most entry types are self-explanatory, please note the following definitions as used in this Resource Directory:

> **"Collectors"** buy or trade primarily for their own enjoyment, with any profit motive being secondary.
> **"Dealers"** buy, sell, or trade. They may also be "collectors", but "dealers" anticipate making a profit.
> **"Experts"** (while they may also be a "collector" and/or "dealer") are considered to be expert because they have lectured or written extensively on the subject, have authored books or articles, have curated exhibits or managed collections, have dealt extensively in the subject, appraise within a specialized field, have conducted lengthy studies on the subject, or otherwise have such a degree of experience that they are recognized within the trade as having an uncommonly high degree of knowledge about the subject.
> **"Book Sellers"** are retailers/distributors/publishers of collector books written about antiques, collectibles, or art.
> **"Exchange Services"** match buyers and sellers of, primarily, limited edition collectibles.
> **"On-line Services"** are providers of services or products to the trade which can only be found on the Internet.

3. Point-of-Contact: Please provide your full name or the name of your company's or club's designated point-of-contact. Museums and auctions houses, please provide the names of your curators or specialty department heads, respectively, for each specialty area listed.

4. Business Name: List the exact name of your business, club/association, museum, publishing house, etc.

5. Address: Provide your mailing address. If you use a Post Office Box, you may also list a street address (for UPS) if you like. For publishers of periodicals, please provide the mailing address for your <u>editorial or publisher's office</u>, not the address to your subscription service.

6. Phone and Fax Numbers: People would often prefer to call you rather than write to you, so please list up to two phone numbers and one fax number. For periodicals, please provide phone/fax numbers to your editorial or publisher's office as well as your 800 subscription service number, if any.

7. E-mail and Internet: We now list Internet e-mail addresses and Internet websites. If you have an e-mail address enter its Internet form. If you have a site on the Web, enter its URL. Please be exact and complete when listing your e-mail and website addresses. And remember to PRINT CLEARLY so we don't make a mistake entering your information.

8. Periodical: If the listing is for a periodical **or** for a club that publishes a periodical, please list your periodical's exact name, its format (newspaper, newsletter, magazine, journal, directory, price guide, etc.), and its frequency of publication.

9. Comment: *This is a most important field to fill out.* It gives the reader a flavor of your wants, what service you provide, what your club is all about, or what your periodical covers. Please provide a couple of concise sentences (up to 240 characters in length) to let the reader know more about yourself and/or the products or services you provide or seek. Include key words associated with your specialty area for more accurate computer searches.

<u>Read this if you publish Books or Periodicals:</u>
Maloney's Antiques & Collectibles Resource Directory is published every other year, but **Collector's Information Clearinghouse** answers written and telephone inquiries between editions regarding information that is maintained in our database. We also provide answers to questions from callers made during radio talk shows or received on CompuServe or at our Internet website for *Maloney's On-line Resource Directory*. In addition, we review any book or video received that is about antiques, collectibles, and related subjects such as auctions, antique repairs, etc. To insure that our files are maintained between editions and that accurate information is being disseminated, it is important that we receive copies of your publications such as catalogs, videos, newsletters, newspapers, magazines, flyers, brochures, etc. **To be eligible for preferred referral status, please place CIC on your *permanent* mailing list for complimentary copies of your books, videos and periodicals.** Send them to **CIC**, P.O. Box 2049, Frederick, MD 21702-1049.

Maloney's Antiques & Collectibles Resource Directory
Listing Application and Change Form
This application form is also available ONLINE at our web site http://www.maloneysonline.com
(Save and use this form for future additions or changes to your listings.)

1. List your SPECIALTY AREA (Please limit listings to five per Dealer or Collector). Make copies of this form if you have specialties in more than one area.

_____

2. Check the ENTRY TYPE(S) that applies to this listing. More than one selection is OK:

_____ Appraiser	_____ Dealer	_____ Vendor/Supplier
_____ Auction Service	_____ Expert	_____ Repair/Restoration/Conservator Service
_____ Book Seller	_____ Matching Service	_____ Reproductions Source
_____ Club/Association	_____ Museum/Library	_____ Manufacturer, Producer or Distributor
_____ Collector	_____ Periodical	_____ Exchange Service (for Limited Edition collectibles)
_____ Internet Web Site only	Other (specify): _____	

3. POINT-OF-CONTACT. Your name as you want it listed:_____

4. BUSINESS NAME of your company, club, association, publishing house, museum, etc.:_____
_____

5. ADDRESS (Note: for periodicals, include your **Editorial** or **Publisher's** address (not your subscription service) and your toll-free subscription telephone number, if any):

    Address: _____

                _____

    City: _____ State (or Province): _____ Zip (or Postal Code): _____

    Country (if other than USA): _____

6. TELEPHONE #1: (   )_____ TELEPHONE #2: (   )_____ FAX: (   )_____

7.   a. Internet e-mail address:_____
    b. Internet website address (URL): _____

8. PERIODICALS (magazines, newsletters, newspapers, etc.) that you publish. **To insure continued accuracy of your listing and to be eligible for preferred referral status, please make certain that complimentary subscriptions to your periodical are sent to CIC, Attn: File Editor, P.O. Box 2049, Frederick, MD 21702-1049 for review.**

    Periodical : _____

        Format (newsletter, magazine, journal, newspaper, etc.):_____

        Frequency of publication: _____

9. COMMENT LINE: (Describe your club, association, periodical, or service. For the collector or dealer, describe your wants. If you are an author, please list your most recent books dealing with this specialty area. Also, please attach catalogs, brochures, flyers, business cards, etc. that relate to this listing. 240 character limit.)

_____

_____

_____

☐ CHECK HERE to receive FREE information about how you can advertise your products and services on the Internet in **Maloney's Online Resource Directory**. No computer needed!

The above information gives an accurate and realistic description of my business or areas of interest. I understand that this information is for distribution in electronic and written form including publication in *Maloney's Antiques & Collectibles Resource Directory* published by Antique Trader Publications.

Date _____ Signature _____ Title_____
Please complete and mail or fax to: Collector's Information Clearinghouse, P.O. Box 2049, Frederick, MD 21702-1049
phone: (301) 695-8544, fax: (301) 695-6491, e-mail: dmaloney@ix.netcom.com

U.S. PATENT NUMBER/DATE REFERENCE TABLE

compliments of
David J. Maloney, Jr., ISA CAPP

author of the
"Maloney's Antiques & Collectibles Resource Directory"

YEAR	PATENT #	YEAR	PATENT #
		1875	158,350
1836	1	1876	171,641
1837	110	1877	185,813
1838	546	1878	198,733
1839	1,061	1879	211,078
1840	1,465	1880	223,211
1841	1,923	1881	236,137
1842	2,413	1882	251,685
1843	2,901	1883	269,820
1844	3,395	1884	291,016
1845	3,873	1885	310,163
1846	4,348	1886	333,494
1847	4,914	1887	355,291
1848	5,409	1888	375,720
1849	5,993	1889	395,305
1850	6,981	1890	418,665
1851	7,865	1891	443,987
1852	8,622	1892	466,315
1853	9,512	1893	488,976
1854	10,358	1894	511,744
1855	12,117	1895	531,619
1856	14,009	1896	552,502
1857	16,324	1897	574,369
1858	19,010	1898	596,467
1859	22,477	1899	616,871
1860	26,642	1900	640,167
1861	31,005	1901	664,827
1862	34,045	1902	690,385
1863	37,266	1903	717,521
1864	41,047	1904	748,567
1865	45,685	1905	778,834
1866	51,784	1906	808,618
1867	60,658	1907	839,799
1868	72,959	1908	875,679
1869	85,503	1909	908,436
1870	98,460	1910	945,010
1871	110,617	1911	980,178
1872	122,304	1912	1,013,095
1873	134,504	1913	1,049,326
1874	146,120	1914	1,083,267

To determine the approximate age of your patented item, find the patent number nearest to yours and note the date

Cut-out and laminate back-to-back!

YEAR	PATENT #	YEAR	PATENT #
1915	1,123,212	1955	2,698,434
1916	1,166,419	1956	2,728,913
1917	1,210,389	1957	2,775,762
1918	1,251,458	1958	2,818,567
1919	1,290,027	1959	2,866,973
1920	1,326,899	1960	2,919,443
1921	1,364,063	1961	2,966,681
1922	1,401,948	1962	3,015,103
1923	1,440,362	1963	3,070,801
1924	1,478,996	1964	3,116,487
1925	1,521,590	1965	3,163,865
1926	1,568,040	1966	3,226,729
1927	1,612,700	1967	3,295,143
1928	1,654,521	1968	3,360,800
1929	1,696,897	1969	3,419,907
1930	1,742,181	1970	3,487,470
1931	1,787,424	1971	3,551,909
1932	1,839,190	1972	3,631,539
1933	1,892,663	1973	3,707,729
1934	1,941,449	1974	3,781,914
1935	1,985,878	1975	3,858,241
1936	2,026,516	1976	3,930,271
1937	2,066,309	1977	4,000,520
1938	2,104,004	1978	4,065,812
1939	2,142,080	1979	4,131,952
1940	2,185,170	1980	4,180,867
1941	2,227,418	1981	4,242,757
1942	2,268,540	1982	4,308,622
1943	2,307,007	1983	4,366,579
1944	2,338,081	1984	4,423,523
1945	2,366,154	1985	4,490,885
1946	2,391,856	1986	4,562,596
1947	2,413,675	1987	4,633,526
1948	2,433,824	1988	4,716,594
1949	2,457,797	1989	4,794,652
1950	2,492,944	1990	4,890,335
1951	2,536,016	1991	4,980,927
1952	2,580,379	1992	5,077,836
1953	2,624,046	1993	5,175,886
1954	2,664,562	1994	5,274,846
		1995	5,377,359
		1996	5,450,670